UNIVERSITY CASEBOOK SERIES®

THE LAW OF EMPLOYMENT DISCRIMINATION

CASES AND MATERIALS

TWELFTH EDITION

JOEL WM. FRIEDMAN

Jack M. Gordon Professor of Procedural Law & Jurisdiction
Tulane Law School

FOUNDATION
PRESS

University Casebook Series is a trademark registered in the U.S. Patent and Trademark Office.

© 1983, 1987, 1993, 1997, 2001 FOUNDATION PRESS
© 2007, 2009, 2011 THOMSON REUTERS/FOUNDATION PRESS
© 2013 LEG, Inc. d/b/a West Academic Publishing
© 2015, 2017 LEG, Inc. d/b/a West Academic
© 2019 LEG, Inc. d/b/a West Academic
    444 Cedar Street, Suite 700
    St. Paul, MN 55101
    1-877-888-1330

Printed in the United States of America

ISBN: 978-1-68467-245-5

TO MY WIFE AND CHILDREN: VIVIANE, ALEXA, CHLOE & MAX ("THE MAN")

JWF

PREFACE TO THE TWELFTH EDITION

This TWELFTH edition of the casebook integrates all significant developments that have occurred since publication of the preceding edition, while maintaining my commitment to keeping the book a manageable size. Finally, as I have done in the last seven editions, this book has been produced in camera-ready form, which permitted me to incorporate all relevant Supreme Court and important lower court decisions through the end of the 2019 term. I believe that these changes have significantly improved the book as a teaching tool and I hope that you agree.

J.W.F.

New Orleans, LA.
August 2019

ACKNOWLEDGMENTS

I wish to thank the following authors and copyright holders for permitting the inclusion of portions of their publications in this book.

Fisher, Franklin M., "Multiple Regression in Legal Proceedings," Columbia Law Review, Vol. 80, pp. 702, 705-06 (1980). Reprinted with permission of the Columbia Law Review.

Kanowitz, Leo, "Sex Based Discrimination in American Law III," Hastings Law Review, Vol.20, pp. 305, 310-313 (1968); reprinted at L. KANOWITZ, WOMEN AND THE LAW: THE UNFINISHED REVOLUTION 103-105 (1969). Reprinted by permission of the publisher.

Reiss, Michael, "Requiem for an 'Independent Remedy': The Civil Rights Acts of 1866 and 1871 As Remedies for Employment Discrimination," Southern California Law Review, Vol. 50, pp. 961, 971-974 (1977). Reprinted with permission of the Southern California Law Review.

Most importantly, as always, I want to thank my wife Viviane, and our children Alexa, Chloe, and Max ("The Man") for their constant inspiration and support.

SUMMARY OF CONTENTS

TABLE OF CONTENTS

**PART III.   OTHER ANTI-DISCRIMINATION
                   LEGISLATION**

**CHAPTER 11.   The Statutory Response to Disability-
Based Discrimination**................................... 953

TABLE OF CASES

Principal cases are in italic type. Non-principal cases are in roman type. References are to pages.

UNIVERSITY CASEBOOK SERIES®

THE LAW OF EMPLOYMENT DISCRIMINATION

CASES AND MATERIALS

TWELFTH EDITION

PART I

EMPLOYMENT DISCRIMINATION LAW BEFORE THE MODERN ERA

The common law described the relation between employer and employee as "employment-at-will." The employer was free to refuse to hire (and free to discharge) an employee for any reason or, indeed, no reason. Likewise an employee was free to leave his employment at any time for any reason. With modifications in some states, the employment-at-will doctrine continues as the basic default rule regarding employment in this country. The employer and employee are free, either on an individual or collective basis, to contract for terms and conditions of employment, thus limiting the freedom of management and labor for fixed periods of time. Such contracts are generally enforceable in our courts as are other kinds of private agreements and, at least with individual contracts, are governed by general contract law. A separate set of rules, largely derived from federal legislation such as the National Labor Relations Act and the Railway Labor Act, governs the interpretation and enforcement of collective bargaining agreements between employers and unions. The relationship between management and organized labor is covered in the basic Labor Law course offered in most law schools.

Beginning in the late nineteenth century and continuing in the twentieth century, the federal and state governments to a limited extent have sought to regulate the employment relationship through statutes intended to alleviate the plight of workers unable to protect themselves from exploitation in the workplace. In the Fair Labor Standards Act (FLSA), for example, Congress has created a statutory floor (the minimum wage) to the compensation that may be paid certain classes of wage earners and has prohibited altogether the employment of children in industry. The Occupational Safety and Health Act (OSHA) and similar state legislation require employers to provide safe working conditions, and the Employment Retirement Income Security Act (ERISA) provides protection for pension plans and related benefits.

The subject of this casebook is another type of legal restraint placed on employers and unions: the prohibitions of actions based on human characteristics having, at least in the abstract, no relation to job performance or ability. Most of the protected characteristics are immutable (race, gender, national origin), but some are matters of choice (religion) and some change over time (age, disability). As so defined, the law of employment discrimination is of recent origin. The bulk of the material contained in this book relates to legislative and judicial developments occurring after July 1965, the effective date of Title VII of the 1964 Civil Rights Act. There were, however, some legal restrictions on discrimination against minorities before the modern civil rights statutes.

SECTION A. THE CONSTITUTION

Section 1 of the Fourteenth Amendment to the United States Constitution provides in part that:

> No State shall make or enforce any law which shall abridge the privileges or immunities of citizens of the United States; nor shall any State deprive any person of life, liberty, or property, without due process of law; nor deny to any person within its jurisdiction the equal protection of the laws.

Kerr v. Enoch Pratt Free Library of Baltimore City

United States Court of Appeals, Fourth Circuit, 1945.
149 F.2d 212, cert. denied, 326 U.S. 721, 66 S.Ct. 26, 90 L.Ed. 427 (1945).

SOPER, Circuit Judge.

This suit is brought by Louise Kerr, a young Negress, who complains that she has been refused admission to a library training class conducted by The Enoch Pratt Free Library of Baltimore City to prepare persons for staff positions in the Central Library and its branches. It is charged that the Library is performing a governmental function and that she was rejected in conformity with the uniform policy of the library corporation to exclude all persons of the colored race from the training school, and that by this action the State of Maryland deprives her of the equal protection of the laws in violation of §1 of the Fourteenth Amendment of the Constitution of the United States and of the Civil Rights Act codified in 8 U.S.C.A. §41. She asks for damages, as provided in that act, 8 U.S.C.A. §43, for a permanent injunction prohibiting the refusal of her application, and for a declaratory judgment to establish her right to have her application considered without discrimination because of her race and color. Her father joins in the suit as a taxpayer, and asks that, if it be held that the library corporation is a private body not bound by the constitutional restraint upon state action, the Mayor and City Council of Baltimore be enjoined from making contributions to the support of the Library from the municipal funds on the ground that such contributions are ultra vires and in violation of the Fourteenth Amendment since they constitute a taking of his property without due process of law.

The defendants in the suit are the library corporation, nine citizens of Baltimore who constitute its board of trustees, the librarian and the Mayor and City Council of Baltimore. The defendants first named defend on two grounds: (1) That the plaintiff was not excluded from the Training School solely because of her race and color; and (2) that the Library is a private corporation, controlled and managed by the board of trustees, and does not perform any public function as a representative of the state. The municipality joins in the second defense and also denies that its appropriations to the Library are ultra vires or constitute a taking of property without due process of law. The District Judge sustained all of the defenses and dismissed the suit.

In our view it is necessary to consider only the first two defenses which raise the vital issues in the case. It is not denied that the applicant is well qualified to enter the training school. She is a native and resident of Baltimore City, twenty-seven years of age, of good character and reputation, and in good health. She is a graduate with high averages from the public high schools of Baltimore, from a public teachers' training school in Baltimore, has taken courses for three summers at the University of Pennsylvania, and has taught in the elementary public schools of the City. We must therefore consider whether in fact she was excluded from the training school because of her race, and if so, whether this action was contrary to the provisions of the federal constitution and laws.

There can be no doubt that the applicant was excluded from the school because of her race. The training course was established by the Library in 1928, primarily to prepare persons for the position of library assistant on the Library staff. There is no other training school for librarians in the state supported by public funds. Applicants are required to take a competitive entrance examination which, in view of the large number of applications for each class, is limited to fifteen or twenty persons who are selected by the director of the Library and his assistants as best qualified to function well in the work in view of their initiative, personality, enthusiasm and serious purpose. Members of the class are paid $50 monthly during training, since the practical work which they perform is equivalent to part time employment. In return for the training given, the applicant is expected to work on the staff one year after graduation, provided a position is offered. All competent graduates have been in fact appointed to the staff as library assistants, and during the past two or three years there have been more vacancies than graduates.

During the existence of the school, more than two hundred applications have been received from Negroes. All of them have been rejected. On June 14, 1933, the trustees of the Library formally resolved to make no change in the policy, then existing, not to employ Negro assistants on the Library service staff "in view of the public criticism which would arise and the effect upon the morale of the staff and the public." This practice was followed until 1942 when the trustees engaged two Negroes, who had not attended the Training School, as technical assistants for service in a branch of the Library which is patronized chiefly by Negroes. There are in all seventy senior and eighty junior library assistants employed at the Central Building and the twenty-six branches. There is no segregation of the races in any of them and white and colored patrons are served alike without discrimination. The population of Baltimore City is approximately eighty per cent white and twenty per cent colored.

Notwithstanding the appointment of two colored assistants in one branch of the Library, the board of trustees continued to exclude Negroes from the Training School for the reasons set forth in the following resolution passed by it on September 17, 1942:

"Resolved that it is unnecessary and unpracticable to admit colored persons to the Training Class of The Enoch Pratt Free Library. The trustees being advised that there are colored persons now available with adequate training for library employment have given the librarian authority to employ such personnel where vacancies occur in a branch or branches with an established record of preponderant colored use."

It was in accordance with this policy that the application made by the plaintiff on April 23, 1943, was denied.

The view that the action of the Board in excluding her was not based solely on her race or color rests on the contention that as the only positions as librarian assistants, which are open to Negroes, were filled at the time of her application, and as a number of adequately trained colored persons in the community were then available for appointment, should a vacancy occur, it would have been a waste of her time and a useless expense to the Library to admit her. The resolution of September 17, 1942, and the testimony given on the part of the defendants indicate that these were in fact the reasons which led to the plaintiff's rejection, and that the trustees were not moved by personal hostility or prejudice against the Negro race but by the belief that white library assistants can render more acceptable and more efficient service to the public where the majority of the patrons are white. The District Judge so found and we accept his finding. But it is nevertheless true that the applicant's race was the only ground for the action upon her application. She was refused consideration because the Training School is closed to Negroes, and it is closed to Negroes because, in the judgment of the Board, their race unfits them to serve in predominantly white neighborhoods. We must therefore determine whether, in view of the prohibition of the Fourteenth Amendment, the Board is occupying tenable ground in excluding Negroes from the Training School and from positions on the Library's staff.

The District Judge found that the Board of Trustees controls and manages the affairs of the Library as a private corporation and does not act in a public capacity as a representative of the state. Hence he held that the Board is not subject to the restraints of the Fourteenth Amendment which are imposed only upon state action that abridges the privileges or immunities of citizens of the United States or denies to any person the equal protection of the laws. His opinion reviews at length the corporate history of the institution and applies the rule, enunciated in state and federal courts, that to make a corporation a public one its managers must not only be appointed by public authority, but subject to its control.

* * *

[The Court reviews the history of the Baltimore Library. It was founded in 1882 through the philanthropy of Enoch Pratt who gave the city a building and a fund of $833,000. Pratt's gift was conditioned on the city's agreement to provide a perpetual annuity of $50,000 for maintenance of the library and the creation of four branches. In addition, the city was required to allow control of the library to be exercised by a self-perpetuating private board of trustees the initial members of which were named by Pratt. In 1907 Andrew Carnegie gave the city $500,000 for the erection of 20 additional branches on the condition that the city provide the land and an annual sum of not less than 10 percent of the cost of the buildings for maintenance. By 1927 the central library had outgrown its quarters and a new building was constructed with funds from a $3,000,000 city bond issue authorized by the state legislature. Over the years the city gradually increased its appropriations to the library and by the time of the suit those expenditures far exceeded the city's financial obligations under the gifts from Pratt and Carnegie.]

                                    * * *

From this recital certain conclusions may be safely drawn. First. The purpose which inspired the founder to make the gift and led the state to accept it, was to establish an institution to promote and diffuse knowledge and education amongst all the people.

Second. The donor could have formed a private corporation under the general permissive statutes of Maryland with power both to own the property and to manage the business of the Library independent of the state. He chose instead to seek the aid of the state to found a public institution to be owned and supported by the city but to be operated by a self perpetuating board of trustees to safeguard it from political manipulation; and this was accomplished by special act of the legislature with the result that the powers and obligations of the city and the trustees were not conferred by Mr. Pratt but by the state at the very inception of the enterprise. They were in truth created by the state in accordance with a plan which was in quite general operation in the Southern and Eastern parts of the United States at the time.[*]

Third, during the sixty years that have passed since the Library was established, the city's interests have been greatly extended and increased, as the donor doubtless foresaw would be the case, until the existence and maintenance of the central library and its twenty-six branches as now conducted are completely dependent upon the city's voluntary appropriations. So great have become the demands upon the city that it now requires the budget of the Library to be submitted to the municipal budget authorities for approval and in this way the city exercises a control over the activities of the institution.

We are told that all of these weighty facts go for naught and that the Library is entirely bereft of governmental status because the executive control is vested in a self perpetuating board first named by Enoch Pratt. The District Court held that Pratt created in effect two separate trusts, one in the physical property, of which the city is the trustee, and the other a trust for management, committed to the board of trustees,

---

[*]We learn from Joeckel, The Government of the American Public Library, University of Chicago Press, 1935, that the oldest form of free public library existent today is that having a corporate existence. Accurate description of the libraries comprising this group is impossible because of the many variations of legal detail but the essential distinction between these and other public libraries lies in the fact that control and sometimes ownership is vested wholly or in part in a corporation, association or similar organization which is not part of the municipal or other government. Frequently there is some form of contractual relationship between the corporation and the city. But regardless of legal organization, these libraries all render service freely to all citizens on precisely the same terms as public libraries under direct municipal control. No less than 56 or 17% of all the public libraries in American cities having a population in excess of 30,000 fall into this category. Geographically these libraries are confined to the East and especially to the South where more than one-third of the cities in the 30,000 or over population group are served by libraries of this type. The Enoch Pratt Free Library belongs to this group.

and that the purpose and effect of the act of the legislature "was merely to ratify and approve the agreement between Mr. Pratt and the city, and to give the necessary authority of the state to the city to carry out the agreement"; and that the practical economic control of the Library by the city, by virtue of its large voluntary contributions, is immaterial, because "the problem must be resolved on the basis of the legal right to control and not possible practical control through withholding appropriations."

We do not agree with this analysis of the situation * * *. It is our view that although Pratt furnished the inspiration and the funds initially, the authority of the state was invoked to create the institution and to vest the power of ownership in one instrumentality and the power of management in another, with the injunction upon the former to see to it that the latter faithfully performed its trust. We know of no reason why the state cannot create separate agencies to carry on its work in this manner, and when it does so, they become subject to the constitutional restraints imposed upon the state itself.

* * *

[I]t is our duty in this case in passing upon the nature of the library corporation and its relationship to the state not to be guided by the technical rules of the law of principal and agent, but to apply the test laid down in Nixon v. Condon, 286 U.S. 73, 52 S.Ct. 484, 76 L.Ed.2d 984, 88 A.L.R. 458. There the Supreme Court held that an executive committee of a political party, which had been authorized by a Texas statute to determine the qualification of the members of the party, was not acting merely for the political organization for which it spoke but was acting as a representative of the state when it excluded Negroes from participation in a primary election. In declaring that this action was subject to the condemnation of the Fourteenth Amendment the court said (286 U.S. at pages 88, 89, 52 S.Ct. at page 487, 76 L.Ed. 984, 88 A.L.R. 458):

> " * * * The pith of the matter is simply this, that, when those agencies are invested with an authority independent of the will of the association in whose name they undertake to speak, they become to that extent the organs of the state itself, the repositories of official power. They are then the governmental instruments whereby parties are organized and regulated to the end that government itself may be established or continued. What they do in that relation, they must do in submission to the mandates of equality and liberty that bind officials everywhere. They are not acting in matters of merely private concern like the directors or agents of business corporations. They are acting in matters of high public interest, matters intimately connected with the capacity of government to exercise its functions unbrokenly and smoothly. Whether in given circumstances parties or their committees are agencies of government within the Fourteenth or the Fifteenth Amendment is a question which this court will determine for itself. It is not concluded upon such an inquiry by decisions rendered elsewhere. The test is not whether the members of the executive committee are the representatives of the state in the strict sense in which an agent is the representative of his principal. The test is whether they are to be classified as representatives of the state to such an extent and in such a sense that the great restraints of the Constitution set limits to their action."

For further application of this principle, see Smith v. Allwright, 321 U.S. 649, 64 S.Ct. 757, 88 L.Ed. 987.

We have no difficulty in concluding that in the same sense the Library is an instrumentality of the State of Maryland. Even if we should lay aside the approval and authority given by the state to the library at its very beginning we should find in the present relationship between them so great a degree of control over the activities and existence of the Library on the part of the state that it would be unrealistic to speak of it as a corporation entirely devoid of governmental character. It would be conceded that if the state legislature should now set up and maintain a public library and should entrust its operation to a self perpetuating board of trustees and authorize it to exclude Negroes from its benefits, the act would be unconstitutional. How then can the well known policy of the Library, so long continued and now formally expressed in the resolution of the Board, be justified as solely the act of a private organization when the state, through the municipality, continues to supply it with the means of existence.

The plaintiff has been denied a right to which she was entitled and the judgment must be reversed and the case remanded for further proceedings.

Reversed and remanded.

NOTES AND PROBLEMS FOR DISCUSSION

1. What is "the spirit of the constitutional prohibition against race discrimination" referred to by the Fourth Circuit? *See* Strauder v. West Virginia, 100 U.S. (10 Otto) 303, 25 L.Ed. 664 (1880) (equal protection clause provides "positive immunity" from racial discrimination incorporated in state law). In the Supreme Court's lexicon, racial classifications are subject to "strict scrutiny," meaning that they will be upheld only if justified by "compelling necessity." Under "strict scrutiny," explicit racial classifications have almost always been struck down as a violation of equal protection. Thus in Professor Gunther's memorable formulation, strict scrutiny is "strict" in theory and "fatal" in fact. Gerald Gunther, *The Supreme Court, 1971 Term – Foreword: In Search of Evolving Doctrine on a Changing Court: A Model for a Newer Equal Protectio*n, 86 Harv. L.Rev. 1, 8 (1972).

If the Baltimore library had a policy of admitting only men to the training program, would Kerr have had a claim under the Fourteenth Amendment? In REED v. REED, 404 U.S. 71, 92 S.Ct. 251, 30 L.Ed.2d 225 (1971), the Supreme Court held that a state probate law that gave an absolute preference for men over women for appointment as estate administrators violated the equal protection clause of the Fourteenth Amendment. The Supreme Court has not, however, applied the same constitutional test to distinctions drawn on the basis of gender as it has to state action on the basis of race. For a discussion of the level of judicial scrutiny applied to state action based on gender as contrasted with state action based on race, see Personnel Administrator of Massachusetts v. Feeney, *infra,* Chapter 8B.

2. In *Kerr*, the defendant conceded a racially discriminatory employment policy while apparently denying that plaintiff was refused admission to the training program because of that policy. But if the library had no formalized rule excluding blacks from the program, what kind of evidence would Kerr have had to present to prove that she was denied admission because of her race? Would the fact that, during the training school's existence, all 200 applications by blacks had been rejected be sufficient for a finder of fact to conclude that Kerr had been denied admission because of her race? Would such evidence establish as a matter of law that Kerr was the victim of discrimination? *See* Chapter 2B, *infra*.

Does the Fourth Circuit's reversal and remand for further proceedings mean that Kerr should be placed in the training program? What if all the positions in the program have been filled? If Kerr has an absolute constitutional right not to be discriminated against because of her race, what is the appropriate measure of relief? See, Chapter 7, *infra*.

3. The Civil Rights Act, 8 U.S.C. §41, referred to by the Fourth Circuit in *Kerr*, was the predecessor to the current 42 U.S.C. §1983. That Act, passed in 1871, provides a federal cause of action for any person whose constitutional or federal statutory rights have been violated by any person acting "under color of any statute, ordinance, regulation, custom or usage, of any State or Territory . . .." Section 1983 thus creates no substantive rights but does furnish a federal cause of action against public officials and institutions for the violation of rights insured by the constitution or by federal statutes.

The Fourteenth Amendment applies on its face only to states, but has been consistently interpreted, as in *Kerr*, to apply to any non-federal public body. Thus, the employment practices of cities, and other political subdivisions, as well as of agencies of the state itself, constitute state action for purposes of Fourteenth Amendment coverage. The "state action" requirement of the Fourteenth Amendment and the "under color of law" requirement of §1983 are technically separate areas of inquiry. *See* Lugar v. Edmondson Oil Co., Inc., 457 U.S. 922, 935 n.18, 102 S.Ct. 2744, 2752 n.18, 73 L.Ed.2d 482 (1982) ("under color of state law" means that the individual has acted with knowledge of and pursuant to law, but such conduct will not necessarily constitute state action). In practice the two requirements are frequently treated as being one and the same. *See* United States v. Price, 383 U.S. 787, 794 n.7, 86 S.Ct. 1152, 1156 n.7, 16 L.Ed.2d 267, 272 n.7 (1966) ("'under color' of law consistently treated as same thing as 'state action' required under 14th Amendment"). Section 1983 remains the basic vehicle for challenging constitutional violations by state and local officials and governments. Its application in the employment discrimination context is discussed in Chapter 8B, *infra*.

4. In *Kerr,* the Court of Appeals devotes almost its entire opinion to the question of whether the actions of the library board of trustees constitute state action. Because of the myriad ways in which the public and private sectors of society interact, a persistent problem has been determining what constitutes sufficient state involvement to render an activity that of the state for purposes of the Fourteenth Amendment. In BURTON v. WILMINGTON PARKING AUTH., 365 U.S. 715, 81 S.Ct. 856, 6 L.Ed.2d 45 (1961), the Court found state action in the racially discriminatory operation of a privately owned restaurant that leased space from a publicly owned parking garage, because the state had "so far insinuated itself into a position of interdependence with the restaurant that it must be recognized as a joint participant in the challenged activity." 365 U.S. at 725, 81 S.Ct. at 861. But *Burton* has been read narrowly. In MOOSE LODGE NO. 107 v. IRVIS, 407 U.S. 163, 92 S.Ct. 1965, 32 L.Ed.2d 627 (1972), for example, the Court held that state licensing of a private club did not constitute sufficient state action to make racial discrimination by the club violative of the Fourteenth Amendment. The Court noted that the state licensing did not "foster or encourage" discrimination and distinguished *Burton* on the ground that the Moose Lodge was not located on public property and did not have the sort of "symbiotic relationship" with the state enjoyed by the restaurant. 407 U.S. at 175, 92 S.Ct. at 1972. And though the Court has declared that a sufficiently close nexus between the government and the challenged conduct such that the conduct "may be fairly treated as that of the state itself" will constitute state action, it also has stated that extensive state regulation of a private entity will not necessarily transform that entity into a state actor. Jackson v. Metro. Edison Co., 419 U.S. 345, 351, 95 S.Ct. 449, 42 L.Ed.2d 477 (1974). Alternatively, the Court also has proclaimed that although "the mere acquiescence of a state official in the actions of a private party is not sufficient" to establish state action, the willful participation of a private entity with the state or its agents will be enough. Flagg Bros. v. Brooks, 436 U.S. 149, 164, 98 S.Ct. 2777, 56 L.Ed. 2d 185 (1978). The Court also has looked closely at the degree of control the state exercises over the challenged decisions of private actors in determining whether or not the state action threshold has been met. *See* Blum v. Yaretsky, 457 U.S. 991, 1004, 102 S.Ct. 2777, 2785, 73 L.Ed.2d 534 (1982) (to establish state action the plaintiff must prove that the state "has exercised coercive power or has provided such significant encouragement, either overt or covert, that the choice must be in law deemed that of the State."). At the same time, however, dependency on public funding has been deemed not enough to make the state responsible for the actions of an otherwise private entity. *See* Rendell-Baker v. Kohn, 457 U.S. 830, 102 S.Ct. 2764, 73 L.Ed.2d 418 (1982) (school's discharge of teacher was not state action although 90% to 99% of school's funding came from public sources); Blum v. Yaretsky, *supra* (nursing home's discharge of patients not state action even though state subsidized operating costs and paid Medicaid for more than 90% of its patients).

In light of the Supreme Court decisions noted above, would *Kerr* be decided the same way today? *Consider* Gilliard v. N. Y. Pub. Library Sys., 597 F.Supp. 1069, 1074-75 (S.D.N.Y. 1984) (discharged employee's §1983 suit against publicly funded library dismissed for lack of state action because of lack of control of city over personnel matters).

SECTION B. FEDERAL CIVIL RIGHTS LEGISLATION AND EXECUTIVE ACTION

Following the Civil War, Congress passed a series of statutes designed to implement the commands of the Thirteenth, Fourteenth, and Fifteenth Amendments by protecting the civil rights of former slaves. These Reconstruction Era civil rights statutes were not, however, sympathetically received by the Supreme Court. In 1873 in THE SLAUGHTER-HOUSE CASES, 83 U.S. (16 Wall.) 36, 21 L.Ed. 394 (1873), the Court upheld the validity of a Louisiana law that created a monopoly for a private slaughterhouse. A majority of the Court held that the law did not abridge the privileges and immunities of Louisiana citizens under the Fourteenth Amendment because such privileges and immunities encompassed only those rights which grew directly out of the relationship between the citizen and the national government, such as the right to sue in federal court, and did not include fundamental individual rights which arose only from state citizenship. The decision, though not directly involving the civil rights statutes, nonetheless affected them, because the Court construed the constitutional basis for much of the civil rights legislation in the narrowest possible way. The Slaughter-House Cases were followed shortly by UNITED STATES v. CRUIKSHANK, 92 U.S. (2 Otto) 542, 23 L.Ed. 588 (1876), where the Court held that an indictment under a section of the post-war statutes, which charged that defendants conspired to prevent black citizens from assembling, was defective because of the failure to allege that the right to assemble grew out of the black citizens' relation to the federal government. Applying the *Slaughter-House* doctrine to a statute, the Court held that the right to assemble peacefully was not an attribute of national citizenship unless the assemblage was for the purpose of petitioning the federal government. But even more significantly, the Court also announced that the first section of the Fourteenth Amendment consisted only of restrictions on the states and did not "add anything to the rights which one citizen has under the constitution against another." It followed that legislation founded on the Fourteenth Amendment could not reach private action. The combination of the narrow construction of the privileges and immunities clause in The Slaughter-House Cases and the elimination of private action from the reach of the Fourteenth Amendment in *Cruikshank* foreshadowed the effective negation of all the Reconstruction civil rights statutes.[a]

One of the series of legislative efforts which could have become a vehicle for protecting the employment rights of blacks was the Civil Rights Act of 1866, which provided that all citizens, without regard to color, were entitled in every state to the same rights to contract, sue, give evidence, and to take, hold and convey property, and to the equal benefits of all laws for the security of persons and property as was enjoyed by white citizens. In 1903, a federal grand jury in Arkansas indicted a number of individuals for conspiring to violate the rights of black citizens protected by the 1866 Act. The indictment stated that a lumber mill in White Hall, Arkansas, had employed eight black citizens as "laborers and workmen," such employment "being a right similar to that enjoyed in said state by the white citizens thereof." The indictment further alleged that:

> defendants being then and there armed with deadly weapons, threatening and intimidating the said workmen there employed, with the purpose of compelling them, by violence and threats and otherwise, to remove from said place of business, to stop said work, and to cease the enjoyment of said right and privilege, and by then and there willfully, deliberately, and unlawfully compelling [the employees] to quit said work and abandon said place and cease the free enjoyment of all advantages under said contracts, the same being so done by said defendants and each of them for the purpose of driving [the employees] from said place of business and from their labor because they were colored men and citizens of African descent . . .

A demurrer to the indictment on the ground that the offense created by the Civil Rights Act was not within the jurisdiction of the federal courts was overruled and the

---

[a]A good account of the post-war civil rights legislation and of its judicial destruction is contained in Eugene Gressman, *The Unhappy History of Civil Rights Legislation*, 50 MICH. L. REV. 1323 (1952).

respondents were convicted. On appeal, the Supreme Court reversed. Hodges v. United States, 203 U.S. 1, 27 S.Ct. 6, 51 L.Ed. 65 (1906). The Court held that since the attempt to protect the employment rights of the black workers was directed against private action, the Fourteenth Amendment provided no basis for the prosecution. The Thirteenth Amendment, which outlawed slavery, was equally inapplicable because interference with an employee's right to contract was not the equivalent of forcing him into slavery or involuntary servitude. Concluding that neither the federal constitution nor the laws passed pursuant thereto secured "'to a citizen of the United States the right to work at a given occupation or particular calling free from injury, oppression, or interference by individual citizens,'" the court held that "the United States court had no jurisdiction of the wrongs charged in the indictment." The section of the 1866 Act at issue in *Hodges* has survived as 42 U.S.C. §1981.[b] Small wonder, however, that it and other of the post-war statutes remained deadletters during the first two thirds of this century. A modern resurrection of the 1866 Act is described in Chapter 8A, *infra*.

After the practical nullification of the civil rights statutes by the Court, federal efforts to eliminate employment discrimination in the first half of this century were half-hearted at best. Religious discrimination in federal employment was prohibited by a civil service rule as early as 1883 (U.S. Civil Service Commission, Rule VIII, 1883), but not until 1940 was discrimination on the basis of race against federal employees and applicants for employment specifically barred.

In 1941 President Roosevelt issued Executive Order 8802, 6 Fed. Reg. 3109 (1941), which "reaffirmed" the policy of the United States against "discrimination in the employment of workers in defense industries or government because of race, creed, color, or national origin."[c] The order established the Committee on Fair Employment Practice, which could "receive and investigate complaints of discrimination" and "take appropriate steps to redress grievances which it finds to be valid." Those "appropriate steps" were not spelled out in subsequent Executive Orders, however, and the Committee was never given direct means of enforcing any directives it might issue. Twenty years later, President Kennedy issued Executive Order No. 10925, 26 Fed. Reg. 1,977 (1961), which created the President's Committee on Equal Employment Opportunity, an agency charged with the responsibility of effectuating equal employment opportunity in government employment and in private

---

[b]It is unclear why the Court in *Hodges* did not declare the 1866 Act unconstitutional as an unlawful assumption of state powers in violation of the Tenth Amendment, as it did with other civil rights legislation in The Civil Rights Cases, 109 U.S. 3, 3 S.Ct. 18, 27 L.Ed. 835 (1883). Justice Harlan in his dissent in *Hodges* commented that "if [the majority opinion] scope and effect are not wholly misapprehended by me, the court does adjudge that Congress cannot make it an offense against the United States for individuals to combine or conspire to prevent, even by force, citizens of African descent, solely because of their race, from earning a living." 203 U.S. at 8, 27 S.Ct. at 16.

[c]President Roosevelt was embarrassed into acting by the threat of a mass demonstration in Washington organized by A. Philip Randolph, President of the Brotherhood of Sleeping Car Porters, to protest racial discrimination by defense contractors. The march was scheduled for July 1, 1941. The administration, fearing international repercussions from such a demonstration, sought to dissuade Randolph, but he and other black leaders refused to cancel the march without a public commitment from the President to use his powers to obtain equal employment opportunity. Finally, on June 25th, the President promulgated Executive Order 8802.

employment on government contracts. Executive Order 10925 was a dramatic break with the past. For while certain order had imposed on government contractors an obligation not to discriminate on the basis of race, creed, color, or national origin, the Kennedy order required contractors to take affirmative action to make the policy effective and gave the Committee some enforcement powers. The Committee was authorized to: (a) publish the names of noncomplying contractors and unions; (b) recommend suits by the Department of Justice to compel compliance with contractual obligations not to discriminate; (c) recommend criminal actions against employers supplying false compliance reports; (d) terminate the contract of a noncomplying employer; and (e) forbid contracting agencies to enter into contracts with contractors guilty of discrimination. The work of the Committee and its successor agency, the Office of Federal Contract Compliance Programs, will be examined in Part V, *infra*.

The executive orders had minimal impact on discriminatory practices in private industry because enforcement was inadequate and many employers had no direct dealings with the federal government. Commission findings did, however, contribute to political pressure for broad federal fair employment legislation.

SECTION C. FEDERAL LABOR STATUTES

In response to disruptive strikes and labor-related violence during the 1930's, Congress enacted a series of statutes, the effect of which was to nationalize the regulation of relations between organized labor and industry. Two statutes, the National Labor Relations Act, 29 U.S.C. §151, et seq. (1935) and the Railway Labor Act, 45 U.S.C. §151, et seq. (1934), provided legal protection for union organizing and established a federally monitored system for workplace elections to determine whether a union should be established as the officially recognized ("certified") bargaining agent for employees in the bargaining unit. A union elected as a certified bargaining agent is entitled to recognition by the employer and the right to engage in collective bargaining regarding terms and conditions of employment for those in the bargaining unit. Most importantly, the certified bargaining agent has the exclusive right to bargain for employees in the unit without regard to whether such employees are union members or in agreement with the terms established by a collective bargaining agreement.

Unions, whether national or local, are unincorporated private associations not bound by the strictures of the Fourteenth Amendment. During the first three quarters of the twentieth century, unions, like the industries in which they operated, were frequently racially segregated and/or actively engaged in racial discrimination. Neither the National Labor Relations Act nor the Railway Labor Act explicitly prohibited racial or other forms of discrimination by either employers or unions. The statutes did invest unions which attained certified bargaining agent status with power and authority which they plainly lacked absent the federal legislation. The anomaly of a private association using powers conferred on it by federal law to discriminate on the basis of race led to the Court-created "fair representation" doctrine.

In STEELE v. LOUISVILLE & NASHVILLE R.R. CO., 323 U.S. 192, 65 S.Ct. 226, 89 L.Ed. 173 (1944), the Brotherhood of Locomotive Firemen and Enginemen, which admitted only whites to membership, had under the RLA become the exclusive bargaining representative for the craft of firemen employed by the railroad. Black firemen, a significant minority of the craft, were thus bound by the collective bargaining agreements negotiated by the railroad and the Brotherhood. Through a series of amendments negotiated with the railroad, the Brotherhood sought to restrict the seniority rights of black firemen in favor of whites and to eliminate black firemen from the most desirable job assignments. Black firemen sued the Brotherhood in state court for an injunction against enforcement of the discriminatory agreements. The state court dismissed the suit on the ground that the RLA conferred on the union "plenary authority to treat with the Railroad and enter into contracts fixing rates of pay and working conditions for the craft as a whole without any legal obligation to protect the rights of minorities from discrimination or unfair treatment, however gross." The Supreme Court granted certiorari and reversed.

> We think that the Railway Labor Act imposes upon the statutory representative of a craft at least as exacting a duty to protect equally the interests of the members of the craft as the Constitution imposes upon a legislature to give equal protection to the interests of those for whom it legislates. Congress has seen fit to clothe the bargaining representative with powers comparable to those possessed by a legislative body both to create and restrict the rights of those whom it represents, but it has also imposed on the representative a corresponding duty. We hold that the language of the Act to which we have referred, read in the light of the purposes of the Act, expresses the aim of Congress to impose on the bargaining representative of a craft or class of employees the duty to exercise fairly the power conferred upon it in behalf of all those for whom it acts, without hostile discrimination against them.

323 U.S. at 202-03, 65 S.Ct. at 232.

The *Steele* majority cautioned that it was not denying to the union "the right to determine eligibility to its membership" nor barring it from making contracts which might impact adversely on some of the members of the craft. Such differential impact was, however, to be based on legitimate factors such as seniority, skill, and type of work performed. Discrimination based on "race alone" was "irrelevant and invidious" and outside of the authority of the bargaining representative. The Court's opinion was based on an interpretation of congressional intent. Justice Murphy, concurring, scolded the Court for not squarely facing the "grave constitutional issue."

> The constitutional problem inherent in this instance is clear. Congress, through the Railway Labor Act, has conferred upon the union selected by a majority of a craft or class of railway workers the power to represent the entire craft or class in all collective bargaining matters. While such a union is essentially a private organization, its power to represent and bind all members of a class or craft is derived solely from Congress. The Act contains no language which directs the manner in which the bargaining representative shall perform its duties. But it cannot be assumed that Congress meant to authorize the representative to act so as to ignore rights guaranteed by the Constitution. Otherwise the Act would bear the stigma of unconstitutionality under the Fifth Amendment in this respect. For that reason I am willing to read the statute as not permitting or allowing any action by the bargaining representative in the exercise

of its delegated powers which would in effect violate the constitutional rights of individuals.

323 U.S. at 208, 65 S.Ct. at 235.

Steele was followed by BROTHERHOOD OF R.R. TRAINMEN v. HOWARD, 343 U.S. 768, 72 S.Ct. 1022, 96 L.Ed. 1283 (1952), where black train porters complained that the all-white Brotherhood of Railroad Trainmen representing the craft of brakemen had entered into an agreement with the employer, the effect of which was to abolish the job of train porter and assign all porter functions to brakemen. The case differed from *Steele* in that the plaintiffs were not members of the bargaining unit represented by the defendant union, but were members of a different craft and were represented by a union of their own choosing. The question thus posed was whether the defendant union owed any duty under the Railway Labor Act not to discriminate against black employees which it did not represent as bargaining agent. In a brief opinion the majority, relying on *Steele*, concluded that "[t]he Federal Act thus prohibits bargaining agents it authorizes from using their position and power to destroy colored workers' jobs in order to bestow them on white workers." 343 U.S. at 774, 72 S.Ct. at 1025. In dissent, Justice Minton, joined by Chief Justice Reed, argued that:

> The majority reaches out to invalidate the contract, not because the train porters are brakemen entitled to fair representation by the Brotherhood, but because they are Negroes who were discriminated against by the carrier at the behest of the Brotherhood. I do not understand that private parties such as the carrier and the Brotherhood may not discriminate on the ground of race. Neither a state government nor the Federal Government may do so, but I know of no applicable federal law which says that private parties may not. That is the whole problem underlying the proposed Federal Fair Employment Practices Code. Of course, this Court by sheer power can say this case is Steele, or even lay down a code of fair employment practices. But sheer power is not a substitute for legality.

343 U.S. at 777-78, 72 S.Ct. at 1027.

In CONLEY v. GIBSON, 355 U.S. 41, 78 S.Ct. 99, 2 L.Ed.2d 80 (1957), the *Steele* doctrine of fair representation was extended to apply to a union's failure to protect black employees in the bargaining unit from unilateral action by the employer. In that case the railroad eliminated forty-five jobs held by blacks in violation of a contract with the Brotherhood of Railway Clerks, whose all-white local accepted the employer's excuses and refused to process grievances filed by the displaced employees. Because the district court dismissed the case on jurisdictional grounds, the Supreme Court could hold no more than that the complaint stated a cause of action under the Railway Labor Act. 355 U.S. at 45, 78 S.Ct. at 101. Thus the question of exactly what relief black employees were entitled to against union or employer under the Act remained unanswered. See Neil M. Herring, *The "Fair Representation" Doctrine: An Effective Weapon Against Union Racial Discrimination?*, 24 MD. L. REV. 113 (1964).

The development of the fair representation doctrine occurred chiefly in litigation under the Railway Labor Act arising in the southern railroad industry. In the 1950's the fair representation doctrine was applied to unions certified under the National Labor Relations Act, and in HUMPHREY v. MOORE, 375 U.S. 335, 84 S.Ct. 363, 11 L.Ed.2d 370 (1964), the Supreme Court explicitly stated that a union operating under the NLRA has the same "responsibility and duty of fair representation" as that imposed on unions by the RLA. Shortly thereafter, in METAL WORKER'S UNION (HUGHES TOOL CO.), 147 N.L.R.B. 1573 (1964), the National Labor Relations Board held that a union's breach of its duty to fairly represent black workers constituted a violation of the NLRA and warranted rescission of the union's certification as exclusive bargaining agent.

While the *Steele* doctrine provided a limited remedy for discrimination by a union that caused (or possibly allowed) an employer operating under a collective bargaining agreement to discriminate, it provided no recourse against an employer who discriminated without union involvement or against a union for discrimination in its membership policies. For the vast majority of American workers, those employed in non-union shops, the doctrine was of no benefit.

SECTION D. STATE LAW

Commencing in the 1940's, a number of states enacted fair employment practice statutes to combat discrimination in employment. As of 1963, twenty-two states barred in one form or another racial discrimination in private employment.[d] These statutes took one of two forms: (1) those which expressed a public policy against discrimination in employment, but contained no remedial provisions; and (2) those which defined prohibited employment practices and provided an enforcement mechanism.[e] A series of statutes[f] enacted by the state of New York typified the second type of act: the New York laws, variously applicable to employers, employment agencies, and labor organizations, defined unlawful discrimination to include the refusal of an employer to hire or to discharge from employment because of an individual's race, color, or creed. Discrimination with regard to "compensation or terms of employment" also was prohibited, and labor unions were forbidden from discriminating against their members or employers because of race, creed, or color. The New York laws provided for enforcement by a State Commission for Human Rights. Upon the filing of a complaint of discrimination, the Commission was authorized to investigate, conduct hearings, issue judicially enforceable cease and desist orders, and take other affirmative action.[g] Violators of the acts were subject to criminal prosecution as well as civil liability. An individual discriminated against by a labor union enjoyed a private right of action for damages, but when a labor

---

[d]Duane Lockard, TOWARD EQUAL OPPORTUNITY: A STUDY OF STATE AND LOCAL ANTI-DISCRIMINATION LAWS 24 (1968).

[e]For a comprehensive survey of state legislation as of 1949, see Note, *Fair Employment Practices — A Comparison of State Legislation and Proposed Bills*, 24 N.Y.U.L.Q. REV. 398 (1949).

[f]See, e.g., N.Y. Civil Rights Law, ch. 6, §§40–43; N.Y. Executive Law, ch. 18, §§290–301; N.Y. Labor Laws, ch. 31, §220–e; N.Y. Penal Law, ch. 40, §§700–701, 514.

[g]Under N.Y. Executive Law, ch. 18, §§295–297, the Commission was authorized to issue cease and desist orders upon a finding that a violation was occurring; to order reinstatement, back pay, restoration of or admission to union membership; and to order payment of compensatory damages.

organization was not implicated, the individual's exclusive remedy was before the Commission.[h]

In RAILWAY MAIL ASS'N v. CORSI, 326 U.S. 88, 65 S.Ct. 1483, 89 L.Ed. 2072 (1945), an association of postal workers which limited its membership to "Caucasians and native American Indians" charged that the New York statute prohibiting discriminatory exclusion from membership violated due process by denying to the group the right to select its own membership. Citing Tunstall v. Brotherhood of Locomotive Firemen & Engineers, a companion case to Steele v. Louisville & Nashville R.R., the Supreme Court declared there was "no constitutional basis for the contention that a state cannot protect workers from exclusion solely on the basis of race, color or creed by an organization . . ." Significantly, the Court did not refer to *The Slaughter-House Cases* or the other judicial nullifications of federal civil rights legislation. The implication of *Railway Mail Association* and *The Slaughter-House Cases* — that states could prohibit private discrimination but that Congress was constitutionally barred from such action — was, at the very least, anomalous.

Twenty years after *Railway Mail Association,* the modern era of employment discrimination law began with the enactment of Title VII of the Civil Rights Act of 1964. Congress had not, however, forgotten the fate of the Reconstruction era civil rights statutes, and the constitutional underpinning of Title VII was not the Thirteenth or Fourteenth Amendments but that great font of federal power — the commerce clause of Article I, Section 8.

---

[h]For an analysis and criticism of the New York State Commission for Human Rights see Herbert Hill, *Twenty Years of State Fair Employment Practice Commissions: A Critical Analysis With Recommendations*, 14 BUFFALO L.REV. 22, 52 (1965).

PART II

TITLE VII OF THE CIVIL RIGHTS ACT OF 1964

CHAPTER 1

An Overview of the Substantive Provisions

None of the various federal statutes designed to promote the goal of equal employment opportunity has been the basis of more litigation, nor the subject of more intense and wide-ranging judicial and academic scrutiny, than Title VII of the Civil Rights Act of 1964[a], as amended by the Equal Employment Opportunity Act of 1972[b], the Pregnancy Discrimination Act of 1978[c], the Civil Rights Act of 1991[d], and the Lily Ledbetter Fair Pay Act of 2009[e]. The explosion of litigation that followed the enactment of Title VII can be traced, at least in part, to the expansive language Congress used to define the classes of persons and employment-related decisions subject to the Act's substantive proscriptions. In fact, on several occasions when the Supreme Court interpreted this statute in a manner that perceptibly constricted the scope of its substantive and procedural provisions, Congress amended the law to expand its applicability. The passage of the 1991 Civil Rights Act amendments to Title VII, for example, was a direct reaction to several opinions in which the Supreme

---

[a]The 1964 Civil Rights Act, Pub.L. 88-352; 78 Stat. 241; 42 U.S.C. §§1971, 1975a-d, 2000a et seq., is an omnibus civil rights statute designed to prohibit discrimination in, inter alia, public accommodations and facilities, participation in federally assisted programs, and education, as well as in employment.
[b]Pub.L. 92-261, 86 Stat. 103, 42 U.S.C. §2000e et seq.
[c]Pub.L. 95-555, 92 Stat. 2076, 42 U.S.C. §2000e(k).
[d]Pub.L. 102-166, 105 Stat. 1071, 42 U.S.C. §1981a et seq.
[e] Pub.L. 111-2, 29 U.S.C. §621 et seq.

Court either restricted the remedies available under the statute or made it more difficult for plaintiffs to establish liability.

Title VII prohibits employers, unions and employment agencies from discriminating with respect to a broadly defined class of employment-related decisions on the basis of five specifically enumerated classifications—race, color, religion, national origin and sex. It also created the Equal Employment Opportunity Commission (EEOC), a five member, presidentially-appointed agency, to administer and interpret its provisions. The following selection of cases and note materials addresses a range of issues relating to the coverage of this statute.

SECTION A. COVERED ENTITIES

Read Sections 701(a)-(i), 703(a)-(c), and 717(a) of Title VII.[e]

1. EMPLOYERS

Title VII prohibits three types of employment-related institutions — employers, employment agencies, and unions — from engaging in discriminatory employment practices. Section 701(b) defines "employer" as [1] a "person," [2] "engaged in an industry affecting commerce," [3] who has at least fifteen employees for twenty weeks during the current or preceding calendar year. The broadly worded definitions in §701 of "person" and "industry affecting commerce" clearly reflect Congress' desire to maximize the scope of Title VII's jurisdiction since they result in the inclusion of virtually all organizational structures used to further business purposes within the statutory definition of "employer." Consequently, the only significant limitation on the definition of this term is the requirement that an "employer" have fifteen "employees" within the prescribed time period. Moreover, while the Act originally required a covered employer to have twenty-five employees, the reduction of this requirement to fifteen employees effected by the 1972 Amendments is further evidence of the legislature's desire to expand the reach of Title VII. Several interpretative questions, nevertheless, have arisen in connection with this minimum employee requirement.

Equal Employment Opportunity Commission v. Rinella & Rinella

United States District Court, Northern District of Illinois, 1975.
401 F.Supp. 175.

---

[e]All references to Title VII will be made to the Act's original section numbers rather than to the parallel U.S. Code citations.

WILL, District Judge.

* * * Arlene Nagy was employed by the defendants as a legal secretary from January 1971 to March 1973, when she resigned and from October 1973, when she was rehired, to July 10, 1974 when she was discharged. From March of 1974, she was also a member of Women Employed, an Illinois not-for-profit corporation whose purpose is to oppose discrimination based on sex and otherwise to work to improve the employment status and working conditions of women in Chicago, Illinois.

Between March 1973 and July 30, 1974, Ms. Nagy engaged in various activities in opposition to what she alleges to be unlawful employment practices by Rinella & Rinella, which discriminated against women. These activities included joining Women Employed, soliciting other women employees of Rinella & Rinella to join Women Employed, attending meetings and participating in the activities of Women Employed, and publicly alleging that Rinella & Rinella discriminated on the basis of sex in its health insurance benefits. On July 30, 1974, Samuel A. Rinella, the owner of the law firm, discharged Ms. Nagy because of her participation in these activities.

* * *

The defendants have filed motions to dismiss both lawsuits raising numerous alleged jurisdictional and procedural deficiencies. Specifically, their totally non-frivolous claims include:

1. The court is without subject matter jurisdiction in that:

    a. The defendant does not qualify as an employer engaged in an industry affecting interstate commerce.

    b. The defendant has not continuously employed fifteen (15) or more persons. * * *

For the reasons set forth hereinafter, we find none of defendants' arguments offered in support of their motions to be meritorious and, accordingly, their motions to dismiss will be denied.

I. SUBJECT MATTER JURISDICTION

The plaintiffs allege that the defendant law firm is an employer within the meaning of Section 701(b) of Title VII, and is, therefore, subject to the proscriptions of the Civil Rights Act of 1964. The term "employer" is defined by the Act as:

* * * a person engaged in an industry affecting commerce who has fifteen or more employees for each working day in each of twenty or more calendar weeks in the current or preceding calendar year, and any agent of such person * * *.

Title VII goes on to define an "employee" in almost unrestricted terms:

The term "employee" means an individual employed by an employer * * *.

The defendants admit that they employed at least eleven employees during the relevant period consisting of secretaries and other clerical personnel and law clerks. Ms. Nagy's status as an employee is contested by the defendants; however, it would appear that she constituted a twelfth employee. The firm also included a group of lawyers which ranged from six to eight during the period under investigation. It is the defendants' contention that, due to the nature of these attorneys' status, they were independent contractors and not employees of the firm. As such, defendants contend, their numbers may not be applied toward reaching the required fifteen employees, and, accordingly, the firm is beyond the purview of Title VII.

The defendants argue that a primary consideration in determining whether an individual is an employee is whether the employer had the power to direct, control and supervise the employee in the performance of his work. The defendants contend that the element of control is not present here. They stress that the lawyers associated with the firm divide fees on the basis of productivity pursuant to a pre-arranged agreement providing for periodic salary draws, that the attorneys have no fixed office hours, set their own vacation schedules, and fix the fees in those cases for which they have responsibility. They further claim that the lawyer to whom a case is assigned is solely responsible for working on that case and does not receive instructions or guidance.

While the defendants' representations would indicate that, as professionals, the attorneys associated with Rinella & Rinella are subject to minimal direct supervision, the conclusion that the defendants would have us accept — that professional employment situations are not covered by Title VII — clearly is not the case. That sections 701, 703 and 704(a) of Title VII were intended to reach "professionals" is borne out by the legislative history of the 1972 amendments to Title VII.

* * *

The courts also have found little distinction between professional and nonprofessional job situations, concluding that, since the primary objective of Title VII is the elimination of the major social ills of job discrimination, discriminatory practices in professional fields are not immune from attack.

Accordingly, we do not find that the greater independence and authority generally afforded attorneys associated with smaller law firms precludes their being employees of the firm. Rather, the court must examine the totality of the firm's arrangements to determine whether an employer-employee relationship in fact exists. In the instant case, the evidence overwhelmingly supports a finding that the attorneys associated with Samuel Rinella in Rinella & Rinella are employees.

Samuel Rinella admits to being the sole owner of the firm of Rinella & Rinella. All of the other attorneys are associated with him in the practice of law. Samuel Rinella hires each of his associates and he has the authority to fire them. Samuel Rinella maintains that the reason that he has associates is to accommodate the amount of business he attracts and so he can have control over the cases.

Samuel Rinella refers significant numbers of his cases to his associates. * * * Associates' cases which are not referred directly from Samuel Rinella are also apparently considered firm work as most of the associates deposit the fees from their own cases in the firm bank account * * *.

Samuel Rinella also exerts considerable control over the compensation paid to those associated with his firm. While the attorneys' compensation, regular or bi-weekly salary draws out of the firm account with quarterly adjustments, is the result of negotiation and mutual agreement between Samuel Rinella and the individual attorney, no one disputes that Samuel Rinella has the final say with respect to the sums involved. The lawyers' compensation strongly resembles a salary in that it is regular and in round numbers, and there is no indication that an attorney has ever returned money to the firm following a quarterly adjustment or paid any interest. These factors controvert the defendants' suggestion that the draws are merely loans to independent contractors based upon expected earnings. Samuel Rinella also determines and pays the salaries of all secretarial and clerical employees.

* * *

Finally, all outward appearances to the public indicate that the attorneys are employed by the firm. The list of names on the law office's outer door, as well as the letterhead on the firm's stationery and billhead, suggest that the attorneys are working for the firm. The firm's stationery and billhead are apparently used by the associates on their own cases as well as those referred to them by Samuel Rinella. The firm's listings in various legal directories also suggest that the associates are employees. Since the firm is not a partnership, and the associates are not listed as "of counsel," it is only reasonable to conclude that they are employed by the firm.

Based upon all of these considerations, it is inconceivable that the associates of Rinella & Rinella could be considered anything but employees of the firm. Added to the secretarial and other clerical employees whom defendants concede to be employees within the meaning of Title VII, the law firm does employ more than the requisite fifteen employees, and therefore comes within its coverage.

The defendants contend that they are not engaged in an industry affecting interstate commerce due to the local nature of their business which involves predominately divorce litigation. Few cases have dealt with whether the practice of law affects commerce. * * *

* * * [I]n keeping with the general principle that remedial legislation such as Title VII should be liberally construed for jurisdictional purposes, we find that the dynamics inherent in a general law practice necessarily affects interstate commerce. * * *

The incidents of interstate commerce are * * * apparent in the instant case * * *. Notwithstanding the defendants' divorce orientation, they admit that their practice encompasses other types of business, i.e., corporate, probate and real estate. They further admit that various attorneys travel out of state on firm business. Samuel Rinella, for instance, traveled to London, England and to Arizona, and Richard Rinella traveled to Washington, D.C. The firm's long distance phone bill in calendar year 1974 was $1,277.01; its out-of-state travel expenses amounted to approximately $2,000 for the same year. The firm also purchased both office intercommunication equipment from an out-of-state company for $8,400, and law and reference books from out-of-state publishers billed at approximately $2,500. These various factors establish that Rinella & Rinella indeed affects interstate commerce and, accordingly, is subject to the proscriptions of Title VII.

* * *

In summary, defendants' motion to dismiss for lack of jurisdiction * * * [is] denied. * * *

NOTES AND PROBLEMS FOR DISCUSSION

1. (a) Would the result in the principal case have been different if all the attorneys in the defendant law firm had been partners? Most circuit courts have adopted an ad hoc balancing test rather than a bright line standard to determine whether a partner meets the statutory definition of "employee". Under this formulation, rather than relying on the label that the employer affixes to the challenged position, the courts look at the totality of circumstances — no one of which is determinative — to resolve the issue. What factors should be considered in making this assessment? *See, e.g.,* Burke v. Friedman, 556 F.2d 867 (7th Cir. 1977); Wheeler v. Hurdman, 825 F.2d 257 (10th Cir.), cert. denied, 484 U.S. 986, 108 S.Ct. 503, 98 L.Ed.2d 501 (1987). But for a suggestion that treating partners as "employees" is consistent with the purposes of Title VII, see Note, *Applicability of Federal Antidiscrimination Legislation to the Selection of a Law Partner*, 76 MICH.L.REV. 282 (1977).

(b) Suppose a law firm is organized as a professional corporation rather than as a partnership. If some of the attorneys are shareholders and directors, should they be considered "employees" or "employers" for the purpose of meeting the fifteen employee jurisdictional requirement? In CLACKAMAS GASTROENTEROLOGY ASSOCIATES v. WELLS, 538 U.S. 440, 123 S.Ct. 1673, 155 L.Ed.2d 615 (2003), the Supreme Court resolved a conflict among the circuits on this precise question in the context of a professional medical corporation. In an ADA case brought by a discharged bookkeeper, the trial court had granted summary judgment in favor of the defendant. Applying the prevailing "economic realities" test of the meaning of "employee," the district judge concluded that the entity's four physician-shareholders were more analogous to partners in a partnership than to shareholders in a traditional corporation. Accordingly, it concluded that the four doctors-shareholders were not employees for the purpose of meeting the ADA's fifteen employee requirement. Noting that the "economic realities" test had not been uniformly adopted by the federal appellate courts, the Ninth Circuit reversed, concluding that the choice of the corporate form of doing business precluded any examination designed to determine whether that entity actually operated like a partnership. The Ninth Circuit refused to permit the defendant to reap the taxation and civil liability advantages accruing to the corporate form and then also to seek shelter in the partnership model for purposes of statutory coverage under the ADA.

The Supreme Court rejected the approaches taken by both lower courts. Focusing, as the trial judge did, on whether a shareholder-director is the functional equivalent of a "partner", the Court explained, ignored the reality that the concept of partnership had expanded to include members who might qualify as "employees" in those settings where control is concentrated in a small group of managing partners. And the Ninth Circuit's approach, which paid particular attention to the broad purposes of the ADA, the Supreme Court observed, ignored the precept that congressional silence as to the meaning of a statutory term should be construed to reflect an expectation that the courts will look to the common law to fill the gap, at least where the undefined term has a settled meaning at common law. Consequently, the Supreme Court adopted a common law test for determining who qualified as an "employee" under the ADA — the conventional master-servant relationship as understood by common-law agency doctrine. (In a footnote, the Court noted that this same term is found in the ADEA and Title VII, suggesting that it will employ the same interpretive rule in cases arising under those statutes.) And the touchstone of that standard, the Court added, is the element of the master's control over the servant. To further flush out the "control" standard, the Court adopted the following six factors set forth in the EEOC Guidelines as relevant criteria for determining whether a shareholder-director is a statutory employee: (1) whether the organization can hire or fire or set the rules of work of the individual; (2) the extent, if any, to which the organization supervises the individual's work; (3) whether the individual reports to someone higher in the organization; (4) the extent, if any, to which the individual can influence the organization; (5) the existence, or not, of a written document expressing the parties intention to treat the individual as an employee; and (6) whether the individual shares in the profits, losses and liabilities of the organization. The Court added that neither the possession of a particular title nor the existence of an employee agreement should necessarily be dispositive of the characterization of an individual as an owner or employee. The Court then remanded the case for application of the newly articulated standard.

(c) Is the question of whether or not an employer satisfies the fifteen employee requirement a jurisdictional or merit-based question? This distinction is important because although subject matter jurisdictional objections are never waiveable, non-jurisdictional objections can be waived by the defendant's failure to timely assert them. In ARBAUGH v. Y&H CORP, 546 U.S. 500, 126 S.Ct. 1235, 163 L.Ed.2d 1097 (2006), the Supreme Court unanimously determined that the fifteen employee requirement was not jurisdictional. The Court pointed to the fact that rather than locating this requirement in §706(f)(3), the provision conferring jurisdiction over all Title VII actions to the federal district courts, Congress chose to place the numerosity requirement in a definitional provision that made no reference to jurisdiction. It also noted that where Congress had intended to impose limitations on the federal courts' subject matter jurisdiction in other substantive statutes, it expressly had done so. In light of these factors, the Court erected a bright line rule that threshold restrictions or limitations on a statute's applicability will be deemed nonjurisdictional in nature absent a clear expression by Congress to the contrary. Applying this new interpretative canon, the Court concluded that Congress' failure to expressly delineate this minimum employee size requirement as jurisdictional compelled the courts to construe the restriction as nonjurisdictional. The Court ended by inviting Congress to amend the statute if it desired to ensure that the numerosity requirement be treated as jurisdictional. Consequently, the Court ruled, since the defendant had not raised the minimum employee requirement issue until its motion to dismiss the case filed after the jury had rendered a verdict in favor of the plaintiff, the objection had been waived and the trial court should not have dismissed the case for lack of subject matter jurisdiction.

Subsequently, in a case involving a limitations period rather than a numerosity requirement, HAMER v. NEIGHBORHOOD HOUSING SERVICES of CHICAGO, 583 U.S. ___, 138 S.Ct. 13, 199 L.Ed.2d 249 (2017), the Supreme Court unanimously held that when a time limit (in that case, the period within which an appellant was entitled to file a notice of appeal from a district court judgment) is created by *statute*, that filing deadline would be regarded as jurisdictional. However, it added, when the limit was prescribed in a court-made rule (in that case, Federal Rule of Appellate Procedure 4(a)(5)(C)), it was deemed to be a mandatory (but non-jurisdictional) claim-processing rule, thereby subject to waiver if not timely filed.

2. (a) Jane Baker claims that she was refused a position as night manager by Pine Valley Motor Lodge on the basis of her sex. Pine Valley is a small, local business with only ten (10) employees. It is a wholly owned subsidiary, however, of Great American Hotel & Motel, Inc., a corporation with over one thousand employees. After Baker filed a Title VII action against Pine Valley, the defendant moved to dismiss the case on the ground that it was not an employer within the meaning of the statute. How should the court rule on this motion? *Compare* Nesbit v. Gears Unlimited, Inc., 347 F.3d 72 (3d Cir. 2003), *with* Armbruster v. Quinn, 711 F.2d 1332 (6th Cir. 1983).

(b) Suppose that the Apex Hotel chain purchased Pine Valley two months after Jane filed her Title VII action. If Jane amended her complaint could she state a cognizable claim against Apex? *See* In Re National Airlines, Inc., 700 F.2d 695 (11th Cir. 1983).

3. Under §701(b), an employer is subject to the terms of Title VII if it has fifteen or more employees "for each working day" in twenty or more calendar weeks in a particular year. In order to "count," is it sufficient that an individual is on the payroll, or must she either be working on that day or at least be entitled to compensation regardless of whether or not she reports for work, such as when she is on paid sick leave, vacation, or other form of paid leave? In WALTERS v. METROPOLITAN EDUCATIONAL ENTERPRISES, INC., 519 U.S. 202, 117 S.Ct. 660, 136 L.Ed.2d 644 (1997), the Supreme Court unanimously adopted the "payroll" method for determining whether an employer satisfied the fifteen employee requirement. The Court ruled that an employer "has" an employee whenever there is an employment relationship between the employer and the employee, regardless of whether the individual actually works or is compensated on any specific day during the period of that relationship. And, the Court continued, the existence of that relationship "is most readily demonstrated by the individual's appearance on the employer's payroll." It was simply too unwieldy, in the Court's view, to require a plaintiff to determine which of the employer's workers were in attendance or on some form of paid leave. Hence, the use of a bright line test. "[A]ll one needs to know," the Court declared, "is whether the employee started or ended employment during that year and, if so, when. He is counted as an employee for each working day after arrival and before departure."

(a) The Court's ruling in *Walters* presumably means that all part-time workers also must be counted towards the jurisdictional requirement. Does the Court's rejection of the suggestion that an individual must be compensated on each working day to satisfy the statutory test also mean, however, that unpaid volunteers similarly qualify as statutory employees? *See* Pietras v. Bd. of Fire Commissioners of the Farmingville Fire District, 180 F.3d 468 (2d Cir. 1999) (the definition of "employee" turns on an *ad hoc* assessment of whether or not this individual received "direct or indirect remuneration" from the alleged employer; although this plaintiff was unsalaried, she was deemed an employee because she was entitled to numerous benefits under state law, including a retirement pension, life insurance, death benefits, disability insurance and some medical benefits); and Marie v. Am. Red Cross, 771 F.3d 344 (6th Cir. 2014) (lack of remuneration is only one of many nondispositive factors to be considered including employer's degree of control over manner in which work is accomplished, source of the tools, skill required, location of the work, duration of the relationship between the parties, extent of individual's discretion over when and how long to work; method pf payment; and tax treatment of the hired party). Note however, that whether or not an individual is an "employee" relates directly only to the numerosity definition of "employer" and not to whether the "individual" is covered by the anti-discrimination provisions of Title VII.

(b) Can the discharged employee of a McDonald's franchise bring a Title VII claim against McDonald's as well as against the owner/operator of the franchise? *See* Evans v. McDonald's Corp., 936 F.2d 1087 (10th Cir. 1991).

4. Section 701(b) includes "agents" within the class of covered employers. This raises two interesting issues.

(a) To what extent can an employing entity with fewer than the minimum required employee complement be considered the "agent" of a larger entity that does satisfy the quantitative standard? *See* Owens v. Rush, 636 F.2d 283 (10th Cir. 1980) (claim against County Sheriff, whose office employed fewer than 15 persons, is cognizable under Title VII as Sheriff is under contract of, and is therefore an agent of County).

(b) Can a supervisory employee or other "agent" be deemed a statutory "employer" for liability purposes such that this supervisor or agent may be held personally liable in his or her individual capacity? In MILLER v. MAXWELL'S INTERNATIONAL, 991 F.2d 583 (9th Cir. 1993), cert. denied, 510 U.S. 1109, 114 S.Ct. 1049, 127 L.Ed.2d 372 (1994), the Ninth Circuit rejected this suggestion, declaring that the "obvious purpose" of the agent provision was to codify the imposition of respondeat superior liability upon the company and not to subject individual employees to personal liability. The court also reasoned that since the exemption of employers with fewer than fifteen employees from Title VII coverage reflected Congress' desire to shield small employers with limited resources from financial liability, it was inconceivable that this same Congress intended to subject individual supervisory workers to liability.

2. EMPLOYMENT AGENCIES

Greenfield v. Field Enterprises, Inc.

United States District Court, Northern District of Illinois, 1972.
4 FEP Cases 548.

McGARR, District Judge.

The plaintiffs describe themselves as six " * * * female members of the employment market in the Chicago area * * * over twenty-one years of age." The defendants are corporations in the business of publishing newspapers and particularly newspapers containing classified advertisement sections in the Chicago area. The complaint alleges that these classified advertisement sections contain help-wanted listings under separate male and female headings without reference to whether sex is a bona fide occupational qualification reasonably necessary to the normal operation of the advertiser's business or enterprise. It is contended that this practice is a violation of Title VII of the Civil Rights Act of 1964 and particularly Section 703(b):

> It shall be an unlawful employment practice for an employment agency to fail or refuse to refer for employment, or otherwise to discriminate against, any individual because of his race, color, religion, sex, or national origin, or to classify or refer for employment any individual on the basis of his race, color, religion, sex, or national origin.

The definition of the phrase "employment agency" used in this section is found elsewhere in the same statute. Paragraph (c) reads in pertinent part as follows:

The term "employment agency" means any person regularly undertaking with or without compensation to procure employees for an employer or to procure for employees opportunities to work for an employer and includes an agent of such person. * * *

Plaintiffs allege that the publication of said listings causes them irreparable injury by depriving them of equal access to employment where sex is not a bona fide occupational qualification. * * * The complaint seeks a preliminary and permanent injunction against the defendants, prohibiting the listing of jobs under male and female headings where sex is not a bona fide occupational qualification.

Defendants have filed motions * * * based on the contention that the complaint fails to state a cause of action cognizable before this court. * * *

* * *

The paramount issue in the adjudication of the motions * * * [is] whether the language of the statute controlling here, in its reference to employment agencies, was intended to apply, and does apply, to newspapers publishing classified ads. * * *

At the outset, we must examine Section 703(b), and consider it together with the definition of the term employment agency in Section 701(c). Those sections, together with such light as the legislative history may throw upon them, control this court's decision on these motions. * * *

* * *

In examining Section 701(c) of the Act, which defines employment agency, we note that it begins with the phrase "any person." Corporations are included in the meaning of the word person. The section goes on, " * * * regularly undertaking with or without compensation to procure employees for an employer or to procure for employees opportunities to work for an employer * * *." This definition clearly describes the activities of an employment agency in the traditional and generally accepted sense of that term, that is, any agency in the business of finding jobs for its worker clientele and finding workers for its employer clientele. Nothing in the statute or legislative history suggests a broader or different meaning. Only the most forced and tortured construction of those words could bring within that definition a newspaper publishing corporation which, as part of its publishing activities, accepts and lists classified ads for compensation.

The final relevant phrase of the definition of the term employment agency, after defining this phrase in the words set forth above, concludes by saying, " * * * and includes an agent of such person. * * * " Plaintiffs' brief makes the point that if the newspapers in their classified ad activities are not employment agencies, that they certainly are the agents of employment agencies, and thus come within the statutory definition. * * * The definition of employment agency refers to a person regularly undertaking to procure employees for an employer or to procure opportunities to work for employees. Persons are defined by the statute as individuals, unions, partnerships, associations, corporations, legal representatives, mutual companies, joint stock companies, trusts, unincorporated associations, trustees, etc. This variety of legal entities having been included in the definition of persons, it made clear and obvious sense for the statutory draftsmen to inject into the description of activities by such persons constituting them as employment agencies in the traditional and recognized sense, the notion that entities in the business world act through and are responsible for the actions of their agents. Therefore, the meaning of the phrase, " * * * includes an agent of such person * * * " must necessarily mean an agent of such person engaged in the same activity as brings the person within the definition of the term employment agency. This, again, is the regular undertaking of procuring employees for an employer client or employers for employee clients. While the publishing of classified advertising may further the business of employment agencies, it does not constitute the business of employment agencies. The assistance that the newspapers may or may not furnish to their customers in the course of servicing their advertising requirements as set forth on page four of plaintiffs' memorandum may indeed constitute the newspaper defendants a link in the job procurement chain, may indeed make them indispensable to the successful operation of employment agencies. But these activities do not make them employment agencies themselves. * * * In addition, * * * the legislative history of the section under consideration is consistent with this interpretation, and while not controlling as a matter of statutory construction, lends support to the conclusions here reached. * * *

* * *

The plaintiffs' brief contains much material suggesting the impropriety and undesirability of the separate classification by sex of help-wanted and employment opportunity ads. Much of this material is persuasive. It is the business and jurisdiction of this court to decide only the applicability of the statute upon which the cause of action here under consideration is predicated. That statute has been determined to be non-applicable and for this reason this court has no jurisdiction. It seems appropriate to suggest, however, to the defendant, however gratuitously, that the position of the plaintiffs is an idea whose time has come and that serious consideration be given to a revision of the classification practices in employment advertising without reference to and free from the compulsion of the jurisdiction of the court.

The several motions of the defendants to strike and dismiss and for judgment on the pleadings are hereby granted.

NOTES AND PROBLEMS FOR DISCUSSION

1. Would a contrary result in *Greenfield* have created a constitutional problem? In PITTSBURGH PRESS CO. v. PITTSBURGH COMMISSION ON HUMAN RELATIONS, 413 U.S. 376, 93 S.Ct. 2553, 37 L.Ed.2d 669 (1973), the Supreme Court upheld a state court order forbidding newspapers from publishing "help-wanted" advertisements in sex-designated columns except for jobs exempt from the provisions of a city antidiscrimination ordinance. The Court rejected the newspaper's claim that the court order infringed upon its constitutional right to free speech, ruling that the First Amendment does not protect commercial advertising. Three years later, however, in VIRGINIA STATE PHARMACY BOARD v. VIRGINIA CITIZENS CONSUMER COUNCIL, INC., 425 U.S. 748, 96 S.Ct. 1817, 48 L.Ed.2d 346 (1976), the Court indicated that its prior ruling in *Pittsburgh Press* was limited by the fact that the restriction on publication in that case applied only to otherwise illegal (sex discriminatory) commercial speech. The Court then struck down a Virginia statute that declared it unprofessional conduct for a licensed pharmacist to advertise prescription drug prices and specifically stated that commercial speech is entitled to some measure of First Amendment protection.

2.   In addition to the "regularly undertaking" requirement discussed in *Greenfield*, §701(c) demands that an employment agency procure "employees" for an "employer."

(a) Does Title VII apply, for example, to transactions between a statutory employment agency and a client with fewer than fifteen employees? *See* Shrock v. Altru Nurses Registry, 810 F.2d 658 (7th Cir. 1987) (an agency that refers nurses to private patients or to doctors acting on behalf of their patients does not procure employees for an "employer").

(b) Section 701(c) imposes no size limitation on covered employment agencies. Note, however, that an employment agency also may qualify as an employer under §701(b) vis-à-vis its own staff and thus be subject to the provisions of §703(a) as well as §703(b), if it meets the employee numerosity requirement of §703(a).

3.   (a) Is a law school placement office a statutory employment agency? If so, must it ensure that all prospective employers using its facilities or services employ non-discriminatory recruitment and hiring practices? *See* Kaplowitz v. University of Chicago, 387 F.Supp. 42 (N.D.Ill.1974).

(b) What about a State Board of Bar Examiners? *See* Tyler v. Vickery, 517 F.2d 1089 (5th Cir. 1975), cert. denied, 426 U.S. 940, 96 S.Ct. 2660, 49 L.Ed.2d 393 (1976).

3. LABOR ORGANIZATIONS

Sections 701(d) and (e) define "labor organization" in such general terms that there are few reported cases dealing with the application of Title VII to unions. A statutory union must either (a) operate a hiring hall that procures employees for a statutory employer, or (b) have fifteen members and either (1) be a certified or otherwise recognized bargaining representative of employees of a statutory employer, or (2) be affiliated with a body that represents or is actively seeking to represent employees of a statutory employer. The statute, therefore, covers international, national, and state as well as local bodies. It also applies to agents of covered unions.

Local No. 293 of IATSE v. Local No. 293-A of IATSE

United States Court of Appeals, Fifth Circuit, 1976.
526 F.2d 316.

BELL, Circuit Judge.

This is an appeal from the grant of a partial summary judgment ordering the merger of two segregated local unions. The district court held the maintenance of segregated locals to be violative of Title VII of the Civil Rights Act of 1964. The court also denied a motion to dismiss for lack of jurisdiction. Finding the latter ruling erroneous, we reverse.

Appellee Local 293 is a predominantly white union with over 90 members. Local 293-A is a predominantly black union having fewer than 10 members, two of whom are white. Both unions operate in the same geographical area of New Orleans and have existed as separate locals for many years. Each local is affiliated with the International Alliance of Theatrical Employees and Moving Picture Operators of the United States and Canada (IATSE).

Local 293 and its members brought this action claiming that the failure and refusal of Local 293-A to merge has denied Local 293 the opportunity to enter into collective-bargaining agreements with many employers and has denied many employees the right to be represented by any labor organization. This was caused by both unions seeking contracts with the same employer. Plaintiffs also alleged in conclusionary terms, that Local 293-A discriminated against them on the grounds of race and color. Both injunctive relief and damages were sought. Without an evidentiary hearing and on a bare record, the district court ordered the merger of the two unions but reserved ruling on the damage claim until a trial on the merits.

* * *

At the outset it is observed that Local 293 makes no claim that Local 293-A "maintains or operates a hiring hall or hiring office." Absent such an allegation, Local 293 must show that the membership of Local 293-A satisfies the minimum membership requirement of the Act.

Appellant contended in its motion to dismiss for lack of jurisdiction that it had fewer than 15 members and thus was not subject to the Act. Indeed, plaintiffs alleged that appellant-defendant had fewer than ten members. The district court denied the motion without explanation.

A review of the legislative history of 42 U.S.C.A. §2000e(e) leads this court to the conclusion that Congress intended to exempt small local labor organizations of the type here at issue. The jurisdictional requirements of 42 U.S.C.A. §2000e(e) were copied nearly verbatim from the Labor-Management Reporting and Disclosure Act of 1959. There was, however, one notable change. The 1959 Act contained no requirement that a labor organization be of a certain size in order to be regulated. In originally limiting Title VII's coverage to 100-member labor organizations (since reduced to 15 members) we must assume that Congress intended to restrict its regulation short of the power invested in it by the Commerce Clause.

Local 293 asserts, however, that the Act applies to Local 293-A because of the affiliation with the International, IATSE. It is claimed that IATSE exercises "sufficient control" over the membership and transfer policies of the local to allow the aggregation of membership numbers in reaching the jurisdictional minimum. * * *

This approach of aggregating International and Local memberships may be likened to the "substantial identity" theory advanced in United States v. Jacksonville Terminal Co., M.D.Fla., 1972, 351 F.Supp. 452. In that case private plaintiffs brought an action against several international unions and their locals, some of whom had fewer than 25 members. The district court found jurisdiction over the locals because there existed,

> " * * * such a substantial identity between the members of defendant unions in the employ of the Terminal and the various and respective national and international labor organizations of which they are members [as to be] indistinguishable for the purposes of 42 U.S.C. §2000e(d), (e) and (h)."

We note that the instant case involves only one defendant local. The International, IATSE, was not joined as a party defendant as was the case in *Jacksonville Terminal*. Without deciding the propriety of the "substantial identity" or "substantial control" test, we hold that no such theory of jurisdiction may be advanced absent joinder of the International as a party defendant. Once this is done, there must be some showing to support the claim of substantial identity.

We conclude that the district court erred in denying the motion to dismiss for lack of jurisdiction.

Reversed and remanded for further proceedings not inconsistent herewith.

NOTES AND PROBLEMS FOR DISCUSSION

1. (a) Why was the plaintiff's failure to join the International Union fatal to the court's exercise of jurisdiction? The court states that Congress intended to exclude small local unions from the compass of Title VII, but suggests nevertheless that where there is a substantial identity of members between two locals (as in the cited case of *Jacksonville Terminal*), or where the International exercises substantial control over the activities of the local, jurisdiction may attach. Is the court saying that in the presence of such a connection, the otherwise exempt local will be viewed as satisfying the jurisdictional minimum member requirement and thus be subject to liability under the Act, or that where such a close connection exists, the International (or other related local union) should be liable for the acts of the local? This distinction will be significant, for example, when it comes to collecting on the judgment since the International typically will have deeper pockets than any of its affiliated local unions. If the court in the principal case was not considering imposing liability on the International, why did it insist that the International be joined as a party defendant? There would seem to be little if any reason to require the joinder of the International if the court intended to limit liability to the originally named local.

(b) Should an International be held liable for the discriminatory practices of its affiliated local? In BERGER v. IRON WORKERS REINFORCED RODMEN LOCAL 201, 843 F.2d 1395 (D.C. Cir. 1988), cert. denied, 490 U.S. 1105, 109 S.Ct. 3155, 104 L.Ed.2d 1018 (1989), the court noted that §301 of the Labor Management Relations Act (LMRA) sets forth a common law agency test to govern the liability of Internationals for their affiliated locals' collective bargaining agreement violations. It extended this standard to Title VII cases, rejecting the plaintiff's claim that liability under civil rights statutes should be more expansive. In the absence of any statutory language, the court could not discern any Congressional intent to hold international unions under any special standard of liability for the failings of their locals with regard to civil rights. Accordingly, it held that an International could be held vicariously liable only for the discriminatory practices of a local union with which it enjoyed an agency relationship. It added, however, that there might be circumstances in which a union's failure to act in opposition to the discriminatory practices of an entity with which it did not have an agency relationship might be an independent basis for liability under Title VII.

2. Charles Embry claims that he was denied membership by the Independent Drugstore Workers Union # 2 solely on the basis of his race. The Union has 50 members, consisting of all ten of the employees of each of the five independent drugstores with whom it engages in collective bargaining. How should the trial court rule on the defendant Union's motion to dismiss Embry's Title VII suit for lack of jurisdiction or failure to state a cause of action? *See* Renfro v. Office and Professional Employee's International Union, Local 277, 545 F.2d 509 (5th Cir. 1977); EEOC

Policy Statement No. 915.030 (July 11, 1988) (as long as a labor organization deals with at least one statutory employer, it is covered by Title VII with respect to all of its activities, including those involving employers with fewer than the statutory minimum number of employees).

3. (a) Sally Jones is employed as an administrative assistant by a local union. The union is the exclusive bargaining representative for hundreds of hotel and motel employees and has a staff of ten full time employees. Sally claims that the union has refused to promote her because of her sex. Can she state a cause of action under Title VII?

(b) Would your answer to the prior hypothetical change if the local union's activities were governed by a board of directors made up of fifty members, all of whom were full time employees of the hotels and restaurants organized by this union and all of whom were paid on a per diem basis by the union for the days they conduct union business? *See* Chavero v. Local 241, 787 F.2d 1154 (7th Cir. 1986). *See also* §§703(a)(1), (c)(1).

4. Are public sector unions within the reach of Title VII? *See* EEOC v. California Teachers' Association, 534 F.Supp. 209 (N.D.Cal.1982).

5. Should the successorship issue discussed in connection with employers be applied to unions? In EEOC v. LOCAL 638, 700 F.Supp. 739 (S.D.N.Y.1988), the court held that the defendant local union was subject to the terms of a federal district court's order requiring another local to stop discriminating where the two locals had been merged by order of the International union. The court reasoned that the successorship doctrine previously applied to employers in the NLRA and Title VII contexts was equally applicable to unions in the Title VII context. It stated that the defendant local's duty to comply with the judicial order survived the merger because the local named in that judicial order ceased to have any independent existence after the merger and because the defendant local inherited all the assets, operations, records and collective bargaining responsibilities of the merged local. The trial court also relied on the fact that the defendant local had notice of the judicial order and the other local's obligations under it. To not hold the defendant to the terms of the order, the trial judge indicated, would nullify the federal court's order and encourage future "mergers" in an attempt to evade judicial orders and judgments.

4. "INDIVIDUALS" VS. "EMPLOYEES"

Alexander v. Rush North Shore Medical Center

United States Court of Appeals, Seventh Circuit, 1996.
101 F.3d 487, cert. denied, 522 U.S. 811, 118 S.Ct. 54, 139 L.Ed.2d 19 (1997).

KANNE, Circuit Judge.

This appeal invites us to reconsider our divided decision in Doe v. St. Joseph's Hosp. of Fort Wayne, 788 F.2d 411 (7th Cir.1986), concerning whether a self-employed physician with staff privileges at a hospital may bring a Title VII action alleging that the hospital's revocation of his privileges constituted unlawful discrimination. Finding Doe's holding — that a physician may bring such an action even absent proof of an employment relationship with either the hospital or his patients — to be irreconcilable with our later decisions in Knight v. United Farm Bureau Mut. Ins. Co., 950 F.2d 377 (7th Cir.1991), and Ost v. West Suburban Travelers Limousine, Inc., 88 F.3d 435 (7th Cir.1996), we overrule *Doe* and affirm the district court's judgment in favor of the hospital.

I. HISTORY

The plaintiff in this case is an Egyptian-born Muslim and a physician. He became affiliated with and was granted staff privileges as an anesthesiologist at Skokie Valley Hospital in 1974. Two years later Mohammed Faoud Abdallah changed his name to Mark Alexander in what he testifies was an attempt to gain greater acceptance among the patients and staff at the hospital. In 1987, Skokie Valley Hospital merged with Rush-Presbyterian Hospital, and from then on it became known as Rush North Shore Medical Center (Rush North Shore).

After the merger, Dr. Alexander continued to have staff privileges as an anesthesiologist at Rush North Shore. As a condition of his privileges, Dr. Alexander was required to spend a specified amount of time per week "on call" to the hospital's emergency room. Rush North Shore's on call policy, adopted in November 1985, requires a physician on call to be reachable by pager or by phone, to call the hospital within twenty minutes of being paged, to remain within forty-five minutes potential travel time to the hospital, and to come to the hospital if requested to do so by the emergency room physician on duty.

* * * [A] patient who had suffered a head injury rendering her comatose was brought into the Rush North Shore emergency room. * * * Dr. Patricia Bitter, the emergency room physician on duty, attempted several intubations * * * but her attempts were unsuccessful. Dr. Bitter paged two on-call surgeons who could perform a tracheotomy (a surgical procedure for creating an airway through the throat). While awaiting the surgeons' responses, Dr. Bitter phoned Dr. Alexander for help.

Dr. Bitter claims that she asked Dr. Alexander to come in and assist with intubating the emergency room patient, but that he refused to report to the hospital. Dr. Alexander, on the other hand, maintains that Dr. Bitter never actually requested his presence. He contends that after Dr. Bitter called him and explained the situation, he informed her that in light of the bleeding and swelling in the patient's throat caused by her failed intubation attempts, any further efforts to intubate could prove fatal. Dr. Alexander states that he told Dr. Bitter that the patient was in need of a tracheotomy, a procedure that, as an anesthesiologist, he was not qualified to perform. He claims that he told Dr. Bitter he would remain available to come into the hospital if his particular skills were needed, but that she left him waiting on hold and never asked him to come in.

* * *

The next day, Dr. Bitter filed a complaint concerning the incident. * * * After consideration and deliberation by several panels of the hospital's hierarchical internal review structure, the board of trustees informed Dr. Alexander by letter that his staff privileges had been revoked for violation of the hospital's on-call policy.

Dr. Alexander filed a charge with the Illinois Department of Human Rights and with the Equal Employment Opportunity Commission, alleging that Rush North Shore had revoked his staff privileges not because he had violated the hospital's on-call policy, but because of his religion and national origin. Both the IDHR and the EEOC investigated and dismissed Dr. Alexander's charge, finding no evidence of discrimination.

Thereafter he filed suit in the Northern District of Illinois, claiming that Rush North Shore's revocation of his privileges constituted unlawful discrimination in violation of Title VII. After discovery, Rush North Shore moved for summary judgment on * * * [the ground] that Dr. Alexander was precluded from bringing a Title VII action against the hospital because the undisputed facts in the record demonstrated that he was an independent contractor, rather than an employee of the hospital * * * .

* * *

In ruling on the motion for summary judgment, the district court held first that, under Doe v. St. Joseph's Hospital, it was unnecessary for Dr. Alexander to demonstrate an employment relationship with the hospital in order to maintain a Title VII action; the district court found it sufficient for Dr. Alexander to have alleged that the hospital discriminatorily interfered with the business relationships he had with his present or potential patients. * * *

* * *

II. ANALYSIS

In deciding this appeal, we need turn no further than to the district court's ruling on Rush North Shore's motion for summary judgment, citing Doe v. St. Joseph's Hospital, that Dr. Alexander could maintain a Title VII action against Rush North Shore even absent a demonstration of an employment relationship between himself and the hospital. * * *

In *Doe*, St. Joseph's Hospital revoked a physician's staff privileges as a disciplinary measure after the hospital's internal review board ruled against her in proceedings concerning a complaint filed by another physician. After the appropriate administrative filings proved unsuccessful, Doe (the aggrieved physician) filed an action in district court alleging, among other things, that the hospital's revocation of her privileges constituted unlawful racial discrimination in violation of Title VII. The district court, however, dismissed Doe's suit at the pleading stage because she did not contend that she was an employee of the hospital.

On appeal, in a divided decision, we held that the dismissal was unwarranted because it was unnecessary for Doe to allege an employment relationship with the hospital in order to maintain a discrimination suit against it. Title VII provides, in part, that it is unlawful for an employer:

> to fail or refuse to hire or to discharge any individual, or otherwise to discriminate against any individual with respect to his compensation, terms, conditions, or privileges of employment, because of such individual's race, color, religion, sex, or national origin.

The *Doe* majority opined that because this section expressly applies to "any individual" rather than to "any employee," interpretively restricting the Act's protection to only former, present, and potential employees would be inconsistent with our charge to construe Title VII "liberally so as to further the goals and purposes of eliminating discrimination in employment." Given that the Act outlaws employer discrimination against "any individual" with respect to his "privileges of employment," the *Doe* majority held that Doe needed only to show that the hospital met the statutory definition of an "employer" and that it interfered with her present or future employment opportunities on the basis of her membership in a protected class.

The partial dissent argued that it was impossible for the hospital to have interfered with Doe's employment opportunities because, under the common law meaning of "employee," Doe was not employed by her patients any more than she was employed by the hospital. The partial dissent maintained that Doe was instead an independent contractor and, thus, that she was precluded from bringing her suit against the hospital because she did not fall under Title VII's protection. To this, the majority responded that perhaps the common law employee/independent contractor dichotomy was inappropriate as applied to antidiscrimination legislation. The majority concluded that dismissal of Doe's claim was inappropriate even though she could not demonstrate an employer-employee relationship with either her patients or the hospital, so long as she could show that the hospital interfered in some way with her economic possibilities.

Doe's conceptual underpinnings, however, can no longer hold fast after our more recent decisions in Knight v. United Farm Bureau Mut. Ins. Co., and Ost v. West Suburban Travelers Limousine, Inc. The *Knight* case concerned an insurance agent who brought a Title VII sex discrimination action against the insurance company with which she was affiliated. Similarly, *Ost* involved an airport limousine driver who brought a Title VII sex discrimination claim against her dispatching company after the company terminated its business relationship with her. In deciding both *Knight* and *Ost*, we looked — contrary to *Doe's* assertion that the common law employee/independent contractor framework is inapplicable to a Title VII action — to whether under a test of common law agency principles the plaintiff was an employee of the defendant or an independent contractor. We then affirmed the district court judgments against the plaintiffs in both cases, announcing the rule — contrary to *Doe's* holding that a doctor can maintain a Title VII action even if he is an employee of neither the hospital nor his own patients — that a plaintiff "must prove the existence of an employment relationship in order to maintain a Title VII action against [the defendant]," and that "[i]ndependent contractors are not protected by Title VII." *Knight*, 950 F.2d at 380; Ost, 88 F.3d at 440. It was insufficient that United Farm Bureau Mutual Insurance Co. interfered with Knight's present and potential business opportunities with her clients, or that West Suburban Travelers Limousine, Inc., interfered with Ost's economic possibilities with her customers. The simple fact that the plaintiffs were not employees, that they could not demonstrate the existence of an employment relationship, rendered them without the ambit of Title VII protection and precluded them from bringing discrimination actions alleging violations of the Act.

Application of this rule in *Doe* — where the plaintiff conceded that she was not an employee of the hospital and, thus, was an independent contractor — would have effected precisely the opposite result from that reached in *Doe's* majority opinion.

On the other hand, it could be argued that a physician who enjoys hospital staff privileges does, under certain factual situations, share an indirect employer-employee relationship with the hospital sufficient to invoke Title VII protection. Dr. Alexander attempted just this at summary judgment by arguing that on the basis of the undisputed facts, he was an employee of Rush North Shore as a matter of law.

Dr. Alexander's claim, however, is untenable in light of our employee/independent contractor analysis in *Ost*. There, we applied a common law test, which involves the application of the general principles of agency to the facts in order to determine whether Ost, a limousine driver, was an employee of the dispatching company or an independent contractor. *Ost*, 88 F.3d at 437-38. The test requires us to focus on five factors:

> the extent of the employer's control and supervision over the worker, including directions on scheduling and performance of work, (2) the kind of occupation and nature of skill required, including whether skills are obtained in the workplace, (3) responsibility for the costs of operation, such as equipment, supplies, fees, licenses, workplace, and maintenance of operations, (4) method and form of payment and benefits, and (5) length of job commitment and/or expectations.

"Of [the] several factors to be considered, the employer's right to control is the most important when determining whether an individual is an employee or an independent contractor." *Ost*, 88 F.3d at 438. Thus, "[i]f an employer has the right to control and direct the work of an individual, not only as to the result to be achieved, but also as to the details by which that result is achieved, an employer/employee relationship is likely to exist." Id. at 439.

Looking to these five criteria, paying special attention to potential employer control over the manner in which work is accomplished, one finds that the business relationship between Dr. Alexander and Rush North Shore is strikingly similar to that shared by Ost and West Suburban Travelers Limousine. In *Ost*, West Suburban drivers were skilled in more mundane ways, but they owned their own limousines; they were responsible for paying their own insurance premiums, license fees, and employment taxes; they collected their own fees directly from customers and never received paychecks from West Suburban; they were able to work on those days that they preferred; they could choose the routes by which they would reach desired destinations; and they were allowed to work for other dispatching services if they wished to do so. From this, we determined that "[e]ach of these facts indicates that the manner in which the drivers performed their services for West Suburban was primarily within their own control."

Similarly, Dr. Alexander did not supply his own equipment or assistants, but he did possess significant specialized skills; he listed his employer on income tax returns as Central Anesthesiologists, Ltd., his personal wholly owned professional corporation that was responsible for paying his malpractice insurance premiums, employment benefits, and income and social security taxes; he was responsible for billing his patients and he collected his fees directly from them; he never received any compensation, paid vacation, private office space, or any other paid benefits from Rush North Shore; he had the authority to exercise his own independent discretion concerning the care he delivered to his patients based on his professional judgment as to what was in their best interests; he was not required to admit his patients to Rush North Shore; and he was free to associate himself with other hospitals if he wished to do so. As in Ost, it seems clear that the manner in which Dr. Alexander rendered services to his patients was primarily within his sole control.

Dr. Alexander argues that he was, in fact, an employee of Rush North Shore because he was required to spend a specified amount of time per week "on call" and because, by virtue of the nature of being an anesthesiologist, most of his operating room patients were assigned to him on a daily basis by the anesthesiology section head. Yet, Ost submitted similar evidence, noting that West Suburban determined its drivers' starting times, required them to call in when they signed off duty, assigned the drivers' morning passengers, required that the drivers' vehicles be made available during certain times, set the rates the drivers charged, and determined which drivers would receive which customers. We held there that "[t]hese constraints do not, however, establish an employer-employee relationship because the details concerning performance of the work remained essentially within the control of the driver." The same is true of this case, and we must find that on the basis of the undisputed facts in the record, Dr. Alexander is an independent contractor as a matter of law.[2] Given that *Doe's* holding is inconsistent with *Knight* and *Ost*, Dr. Alexander's status as an independent contractor precludes him from bringing a Title VII action against the hospital, and thus the entry of summary judgment against Dr. Alexander would have been appropriate. The ultimate disposition at trial provided a correct result and the judgment of the district court in favor of Rush North Shore is AFFIRMED.

NOTES AND PROBLEMS FOR DISCUSSION

1.   (a) Why would Congress have used the term "any individual" in Section 703(a)(1) if what it meant was "employee," a term used repeatedly in other sections of the statute? The *Doe* panel concluded that Congress intended to prohibit employers from exerting any power they might have to foreclose, on discriminatory grounds, any individual's access to employment-like opportunities. Given the remedial purposes of Title VII, isn't *Doe's* explanation for the use of "any individual" both reasonable and consistent with the basic purpose of the Act?

   (b) With respect to the limiting language in footnote 2 of the principal case, did the court intend to restrict the impact of its decision to cases involving physicians with hospital staff privileges, or did it intend to reverse *Doe* in all cases where the plaintiff is determined to be an independent contractor and not an employee of any employer? If the latter, is the court suggesting that the "interfere with employment opportunities" test in *Doe* might still apply to other situations?

---

[2]We come to the conclusion that Dr. Alexander is an independent contractor because he is also not an employee of his patients, just as an insurance agent or a limousine driver is not an employee of her customers. It is important to note that our ruling today is limited to overturning *Doe's* holding that a physician may bring a Title VII action against a hospital even though he is an independent contractor and not an employee. We have no occasion to go further and determine if a Title VII plaintiff must always demonstrate that he is an employee of the defendant employer. Thus, we continue to leave open the question that went unanswered in *Shrock*, i.e., whether an employee of employer X may bring a Title VII action against employer Y when Y is not his employer, but merely someone whose discriminatory conduct interferes with his employment with employer X.

SECTION B. COVERED EMPLOYMENT DECISIONS

Sections 703(a) - (c) set forth the substantive limitations placed by Title VII on employers, employment agencies, and labor organizations. Once again, Congress' use of broad language in these provisions reflected its desire to bring almost all employment-related decisions made by these three entities within the scope of the statute's proscriptions. The following case illustrates the breadth of the antidiscrimination mandate.

Hishon v. King & Spalding

Supreme Court of the United States, 1984.
467 U.S. 69, 104 S.Ct. 2229, 81 L.Ed.2d 59.

CHIEF JUSTICE BURGER delivered the opinion of the Court.

We granted certiorari to determine whether the District Court properly dismissed a Title VII complaint alleging that a law partnership discriminated against petitioner, a woman lawyer employed as an associate, when it failed to invite her to become a partner.

I

A

In 1972 petitioner Elizabeth Anderson Hishon accepted a position as an associate with respondent, a large Atlanta law firm established as a general partnership. When this suit was filed in 1980, the firm had more than 50 partners and employed approximately 50 attorneys as associates. Up to that time, no woman had ever served as a partner at the firm.

Petitioner alleges that the prospect of partnership was an important factor in her initial decision to accept employment with respondent. She alleges that respondent used the possibility of ultimate partnership as a recruiting device to induce petitioner and other young lawyers to become associates at the firm. According to the complaint, respondent represented that advancement to partnership after five or six years was "a matter of course" for associates "who receive[d] satisfactory evaluations" and that associates were promoted to partnership "on a fair and equal basis." Petitioner alleges that she relied on these representations when she accepted employment with respondent. The complaint further alleges that respondent's promise to consider her on a "fair and equal basis" created a binding employment contract.

In May 1978 the partnership considered and rejected Hishon for admission to the partnership; one year later, the partners again declined to invite her to become a partner.[1] Once an associate is passed over for partnership at respondent's firm, the

---

[1]The parties dispute whether the partnership actually reconsidered the 1978 decision at the 1979 meeting. Respondent claims it voted not to reconsider the question and that Hishon therefore

associate is notified to begin seeking employment elsewhere. Petitioner's employment as an associate terminated on December 31, 1979.

B

Hishon filed a charge with the Equal Employment Opportunity Commission on November 19, 1979, claiming that respondent had discriminated against her on the basis of her sex in violation of Title VII of the Civil Rights Act of 1964. Ten days later the Commission issued a notice of right to sue, and on February 27, 1980, Hishon brought this action in the United States District Court for the Northern District of Georgia. She sought declaratory and injunctive relief, back pay, and compensatory damages in lieu of reinstatement and promotion to partnership. This, of course, negates any claim for specific performance of the contract alleged.

The District Court dismissed the complaint on the ground that Title VII was inapplicable to the selection of partners by a partnership.[2] A divided panel of the United States Court of Appeals for the Eleventh Circuit affirmed. We granted certiorari and we reverse.

II

At this stage of the litigation, we must accept petitioner's allegations as true. * * * The issue before us is whether petitioner's allegations state a claim under Title VII * * *.

A

Petitioner alleges that respondent is an "employer" to whom Title VII is addressed. She then asserts that consideration for partnership was one of the "terms, conditions, or privileges of employment" as an associate with respondent.[4] If this is correct, respondent could not base an adverse partnership decision on "race, color, religion, sex, or national origin."

Once a contractual relationship of employment is established, the provisions of Title VII attach and govern certain aspects of that relationship.[5] In the context of Title

---

was required to file her claim with the Equal Employment Opportunity Commission within 180 days of the May 1978 meeting, not the meeting one year later, see 42 U.S.C. §2000e-5(e). The District Court's disposition of the case made it unnecessary to decide that question, and we do not reach it.

[2]The District Court dismissed under Fed. Rule Civ.Proc. 12(b)(1) on the ground that it lacked subject-matter jurisdiction over petitioner's claim. Although limited discovery previously had taken place concerning the manner in which respondent was organized, the court did not find any "jurisdictional facts" in dispute. Its reasoning makes clear that it dismissed petitioner's complaint on the ground that her allegations did not state a claim cognizable under Title VII. Our disposition makes it unnecessary to consider the wisdom of the District Court's invocation of Rule 12(b)(1), as opposed to Rule 12(b)(6).

[4]Petitioner has raised other theories of Title VII liability which, in light of our disposition, need not be addressed.

[5]Title VII also may be relevant in the absence of an existing employment relationship, as when an employer *refuses* to hire someone. However, discrimination in that circumstance does not

VII, the contract of employment may be written or oral, formal or informal; an informal contract of employment may arise by the simple act of handing a job applicant a shovel and providing a workplace. The contractual relationship of employment triggers the provision of Title VII governing "terms, conditions, or privileges of employment." Title VII in turn forbids discrimination on the basis of "race, color, religion, sex, or national origin."

Because the underlying employment relationship is contractual, it follows that the "terms, conditions, or privileges of employment" clearly include benefits that are part of an employment contract. Here, petitioner in essence alleges that respondent made a contract to consider her for partnership.[6] Indeed, this promise was allegedly a key contractual provision which induced her to accept employment. If the evidence at trial establishes that the parties contracted to have petitioner considered for partnership, that promise clearly was a term, condition, or privilege of her employment. Title VII would then bind respondents to consider petitioner for partnership as the statute provides, i.e., without regard to petitioner's sex. The contract she alleges would lead to the same result.

Petitioner's claim that a contract was made, however, is not the only allegation that would qualify respondent's consideration of petitioner for partnership as a term, condition, or privilege of employment. An employer may provide its employees with many benefits that it is under no obligation to furnish by any express or implied contract. Such a benefit, though not a contractual right of employment, may qualify as a "privileg[e]" of employment under Title VII. A benefit that is part and parcel of the employment relationship may not be doled out in a discriminatory fashion, even if the employer would be free under the employment contract simply not to provide the benefit at all. Those benefits that comprise the incidents of employment, or that form an aspect of the relationship between the employer and employees, may not be afforded in a manner contrary to Title VII.

Several allegations in petitioner's complaint would support the conclusion that the opportunity to become a partner was part and parcel of an associate's status as an employee at respondent's firm, independent of any allegation that such an opportunity was included in associates' employment contracts. Petitioner alleges that respondent's associates could regularly expect to be considered for partnership at the end of their "apprenticeships," and it appears that lawyers outside the firm were not routinely so considered.[9] Thus, the benefit of partnership consideration was allegedly linked

---

concern the "terms, conditions, or privileges of employment," which is the focus of the present case.

[6]Petitioner not only alleges that respondent promised to consider her for partnership, but also that it promised to consider her on a "fair and equal basis." This latter promise is not necessary to petitioner's Title VII claim. Even if the employment contract did not afford a basis for an implied condition that the ultimate decision would be fairly made on the merits, Title VII itself would impose such a requirement. If the promised consideration for partnership is a term, condition, or privilege of employment, then the partnership decision must be without regard to "race, color, religion, sex, or national origin."

directly with an associate's status as an employee, and this linkage was far more than coincidental: petitioner alleges that respondent explicitly used the prospect of ultimate partnership to induce young lawyers to join the firm. Indeed, the importance of the partnership decision to a lawyer's status as an associate is underscored by the allegation that associates' employment is terminated if they are not elected to become partners. These allegations, if proved at trial, would suffice to show that partnership consideration was a term, condition, or privilege of an associate's employment at respondent's firm, and accordingly that partnership consideration must be without regard to sex.

B

Respondent contends that advancement to partnership may never qualify as a term, condition, or privilege of employment for purposes of Title VII. First, respondent asserts that elevation to partnership entails a change in status from an "employee" to an "employer." However, even if respondent is correct that a partnership invitation is not itself an offer of employment, Title VII would nonetheless apply and preclude discrimination on the basis of sex. The benefit a plaintiff is denied need not be employment to fall within Title VII's protection; it need only be a term, condition, or privilege of employment. It is also of no consequence that employment as an associate necessarily ends when an associate becomes a partner. A benefit need not accrue before a person's employment is completed to be a term, condition, or privilege of that employment relationship. Pension benefits, for example, qualify as terms, conditions, or privileges of employment even though they are received only after employment terminates. Accordingly, nothing in the change in status that advancement to partnership might entail means that partnership consideration falls outside the terms of the statute. Second, respondent argues that Title VII categorically exempts partnership decisions from scrutiny. However, respondent points to nothing in the statute or the legislative history that would support such a per se exemption.[10] When Congress wanted to grant an employer complete immunity, it expressly did so.[11]

---

[10]The only legislative history respondent offers to support its position is Senator Cotton's defense of an unsuccessful amendment to limit Title VII to businesses with 100 or more employees. In this connection the Senator stated: "[W]hen a small businessman who employs 30 or 25 or 26 persons selects an employee, he comes very close to selecting a partner; and when a businessman selects a partner, he comes dangerously close to the situation he faces when he selects a wife." 110 Cong.Rec. 13,085 (1964); accord 118 Cong.Rec. 1524, 2391 (1972).

Because Senator Cotton's amendment failed, it is unclear to what extent Congress shared his concerns about selecting partners. In any event, his views hardly conflict with our narrow holding today: that in appropriate circumstances partnership consideration may qualify as a term, condition, or privilege of a person's employment with an employer large enough to be covered by Title VII.

[11]For example, Congress expressly exempted Indian tribes and certain agencies of the District of Columbia, 42 U.S.C. §2000e(b)(1), small businesses and bona fide private membership clubs, §2000e(b)(2), and certain employees of religious organizations, §2000e-1. * * *

Third, respondent argues that application of Title VII in this case would infringe constitutional rights of expression or association. Although we have recognized that the activities of lawyers may make a "distinctive contribution * * * to the ideas and beliefs of our society," NAACP v. Button, 371 U.S. 415, 431, 83 S.Ct. 328, 337, 9 L.Ed.2d 405 (1963), respondent has not shown how its ability to fulfill such a function would be inhibited by a requirement that it consider petitioner for partnership on her merits. Moreover, as we have held in another context, "[i]nvidious private discrimination may be characterized as a form of exercising freedom of association protected by the First Amendment, but it has never been accorded affirmative constitutional protections." Norwood v. Harrison, 413 U.S. 455, 470, 93 S.Ct. 2804, 2813, 37 L.Ed.2d 723 (1973). There is no constitutional right, for example, to discriminate in the selection of who may attend a private school or join a labor union. Runyon v. McCrary, 427 U.S. 160, 96 S.Ct. 2586, 49 L.Ed.2d 415 (1976); Railway Mail Association v. Corsi, 326 U.S. 88, 93-94, 65 S.Ct. 1483, 1487-1488, 89 L.Ed. 2072 (1945).

III

We conclude that petitioner's complaint states a claim cognizable under Title VII. Petitioner therefore is entitled to her day in court to prove her allegations. The judgment of the Court of Appeals is reversed, and the case is remanded for further proceedings consistent with this opinion.

It is so ordered.

JUSTICE POWELL, concurring.

I join the Court's opinion holding that petitioner's complaint alleges a violation of Title VII and that the motion to dismiss should not have been granted. Petitioner's complaint avers that the law firm violated its promise that she would be considered for partnership on a "fair and equal basis" within the time span that associates generally are so considered. Petitioner is entitled to the opportunity to prove these averments.

I write to make clear my understanding that the Court's opinion should not be read as extending Title VII to the management of a law firm by its partners. The reasoning of the Court's opinion does not require that the relationship among partners be characterized as an "employment" relationship to which Title VII would apply. The relationship among law partners differs markedly from that between employer and employee — including that between the partnership and its associates.[2] The judgmental and sensitive decisions that must be made among the partners embrace a wide range of subjects.[3] The essence of the law partnership is the common conduct of

---

[2]Of course, an employer may not evade the strictures of Title VII simply by labeling its employees as "partners." Law partnerships usually have many of the characteristics that I describe generally here.

[3]These decisions concern such matters as participation in profits and other types of compensation; work assignments; approval of commitments in bar association, civic or political activities; questions of billing; acceptance of new clients; questions of conflicts of interest;

a shared enterprise. The relationship among law partners contemplates that decisions important to the partnership normally will be made by common agreement or consent among the partners.

Respondent contends that for these reasons application of Title VII to the decision whether to admit petitioner to the firm implicates the constitutional right to association. But here it is alleged that respondent as an employer is obligated by contract to consider petitioner for partnership on equal terms without regard to sex. I agree that enforcement of this obligation, voluntarily assumed, would impair no right of association.[4]

* * *

NOTES AND PROBLEMS FOR DISCUSSION

1. In LUCIDO v. CRAVATH, SWAINE & MOORE, 425 F.Supp. 123 (S.D.N.Y.1977), the trial judge refused to recognize "any First Amendment privacy or associational rights for a commercial, profit-making business organization" such as a law firm. Moreover, the court added, even if such a constitutional guarantee existed, the application of Title VII to the partnership selection process did not violate that right since it did not prevent the partners from associating for political, social, and economic goals. Does the right to freedom of association extend beyond a group's exercise of protected First Amendment rights of speech and petition? In HEART OF ATLANTA MOTEL, INC. v. UNITED STATES, 379 U.S. 241, 85 S.Ct. 348, 13 L.Ed.2d 258 (1964), the Supreme Court declared that Title II of the 1964 Civil Rights Act, which prohibits discrimination or segregation on the basis of race, color, religion or national origin by certain places of public accommodation, did not infringe upon constitutional guarantees of personal liberty or due process. A town zoning ordinance

---

retirement programs; and expansion policies. Such decisions may affect each partner of the firm. Divisions of partnership profits, unlike shareholders' rights to dividends, involve judgments as to each partner's contribution to the reputation and success of the firm. This is true whether the partner's participation in profits is measured in terms of points or percentages, combinations of salaries and points, salaries and bonuses, and possibly in other ways.

[4]The Court's opinion properly reminds us that "invidious private discrimination * * * has never been afforded affirmative constitutional protections." This is not to say, however, that enforcement of laws that ban discrimination will always be without cost to other values, including constitutional rights. Such laws may impede the exercise of personal judgment in choosing one's associates or colleagues. Impediments to the exercise of one's right to choose one's associates can violate the right of association protected by the First and Fourteenth Amendments. Cf. NAACP v. Button, 371 U.S. 415, 83 S.Ct. 328, 9 L.Ed.2d 405 (1963); NAACP v. Alabama, 357 U.S. 449, 78 S.Ct. 1163, 2 L.Ed.2d 1488 (1958).

With respect to laws that prevent discrimination, much depends upon the standards by which the courts examine private decisions that are an exercise of the right of association. For example, the courts of appeals generally have acknowledged that respect for academic freedom requires some deference to the judgment of schools and universities as to the qualifications of professors, particularly those considered for tenured positions. The present case, before us on a motion to dismiss for lack of subject matter jurisdiction, does not present such an issue.

restricting land use to one-family dwellings was challenged in VILLAGE OF BELLE TERRE v. BORAAS, 416 U.S. 1, 94 S.Ct. 1536, 39 L.Ed.2d 797 (1974). The ordinance's definition of "family" precluded occupancy of a single dwelling by more than two unrelated persons but permitted occupancy by an unlimited number of persons related by blood, marriage and adoption. Plaintiffs, six unrelated college students seeking to reside in a single home, claimed that the ordinance infringed upon their constitutional rights of privacy and association. The Supreme Court summarily rejected this contention. Subsequently, however, in MOORE v. CITY OF EAST CLEVELAND, 431 U.S. 494, 97 S.Ct. 1932, 52 L.Ed.2d 531 (1977) the Court ruled that a housing ordinance permitting only certain categories of related persons to live together constituted an intrusive regulation of family life and therefore infringed upon the freedom of personal choice in marriage and family matters protected by the Constitution. Nevertheless, the Court added, the statute could survive constitutional attack if it served an important governmental interest.

Should the rights of associational privacy extend beyond marriage and family life matters to commercial relationships, and, if so, should this right overwhelm the government interest in eradicating employment discrimination embodied in Title VII? The Supreme Court took another shot at examining the constitutional status of private discrimination in another case decided during the same term as *Hishon*. In ROBERTS v. UNITED STATES JAYCEES, 468 U.S. 609, 104 S.Ct. 3244, 82 L.Ed.2d 462 (1984), the Court upheld the constitutionality of the application of a state public accommodations law to the Junior Chamber of Commerce (Jaycees), an organization which barred women from full membership. The Jaycees argued that their right to discriminate in membership policies was constitutionally protected. Justice Brennan, writing for the majority, distinguished between two types of associational freedoms. In one line of decisions, he explained, the Court had recognized that choices to enter into and maintain certain "intimate human relationships" such as the marriage, childbirth, the raising and education of children and cohabitation with relatives receive protection from undue state interference as a fundamental element of personal liberty under the due process clause of the Fourteenth Amendment. In another line of cases, Brennan continued, the right to associate with others in pursuit of shared social, economic and political goals was held to be implicit in the right to engage in activities protected by the First Amendment. In the instant case, he concluded that the Jaycees were not an "intimate association, and that admission of women to membership would not infringe on the organization's ability to engage in protected speech. These factors, coupled with the state's strong interest in eliminating gender discrimination, led the Court to uphold the constitutionality of the state statute. Do the opinions in *Roberts* and *Hishon* suggest that any type of employer might enjoy a constitutionally protected right to discriminate in hiring?

2. In his concurring opinion in *Hishon*, Justice Powell attempted to limit the scope of the majority opinion by suggesting that Title VII would not apply to the business relationship among partners. His opinion implies that although the plaintiff Hishon was protected as a statutory "employee" while she was an associate (and therefore was entitled to nondiscriminatory treatment of the partnership decision — a privilege of employment), if she were to become a partner, Title VII would not apply to the manner in which the partnership treated her, since her status would change from "employee" to "employer."

(a) Does this mean, for example, that the level of her participation in profits could be set lower than that awarded to a similarly situated male partner? If so, does she really enjoy an equal right to partnership consideration?

(b) Would it make a difference if the profit participation differential were instituted one minute or one month or one decade after the partnership decision? On the other hand, should there be some limit to governmental intrusion into the partnership relationship?

(c) Would the result in *Hishon* have changed if the plaintiff had been an associate in a different law firm, seeking a lateral move to the partnership level?

3.   Peroni Macaroni Co. restricts the sale of its corporate stock to persons of Italian ancestry. Would the lawfulness under Title VII of such a policy depend upon whether the company also limited stock purchases to employees? *See* Bonilla v. Oakland Scavenger Co., 697 F.2d 1297 (9th Cir. 1982), cert. denied, 467 U.S. 1251, 104 S.Ct. 3533, 82 L.Ed.2d 838 (1984), on remand sub nom., Martinez v. Oakland Scavenger Co., 680 F.Supp. 1377 (N.D.Ca.1987).

SECTION C. PROSCRIBED BASES OF CLASSIFICATION

Since Title VII prohibits discrimination by employers, unions and employment agencies against "any individual," the protections afforded by the statute extend to all persons.[a] This does not mean, however, that all forms of discrimination are prohibited by this enactment.   Title VII prohibits covered employment institutions from discriminating with respect to covered employment decisions on the basis of only five classifications—race, color, religion, sex and national origin. Thus, for example, while an alien, blind person or minor can assert a claim under Title VII alleging discrimination on the basis of national origin, race, or sex, the statute does not support a claim of discrimination on the basis of alienage, handicap, or age. Specific problems associated with each of the protected classifications are examined *infra* at Chapter 3.

SECTION D. EXEMPTIONS

Read §§701(b)(1), (2); 702; 703(e)(2), (f), (i).

The broad coverage of Title VII is subject to a few statutorily created exemptions. Indian tribes and bona fide private membership clubs are immune from Title VII liability. Businesses located on or near Indian reservations are permitted to give preferential treatment to Indians living on or near a reservation. Discrimination also is permitted against members of the Communist Party or Communist-front organizations

---

[a]Two relatively minor exceptions to this rule are found at §§702 and 703(f). *See infra*, at Section D of this Chapter.

and against alien employees of American businesses located abroad or where enforcement of Title VII on behalf of American citizen employees of American employers employed outside of the United States would cause that employer to violate the domestic law in the country in which it is located. State and federal statutes creating preferences for veterans enjoy a similar exemption from the provisions of Title VII. The most controversial of these exemptions, however, is the immunity accorded religious institutions under §702.

Equal Employment Opportunity Commission v. Mississippi College

United States Court of Appeals, Fifth Circuit, 1980.
626 F.2d 477, cert. denied, 453 U.S. 912, 101 S.Ct. 3143, 69 L.Ed.2d 994 (1981).

CHARLES CLARK, Circuit Judge.

The Equal Employment Opportunity Commission (EEOC) appeals the district court's denial of its petition seeking enforcement of a subpoena issued in connection with its investigation of a charge of discrimination filed against Mississippi College (College). At issue is a significant interplay between the effective enforcement of Title VII and the religious protections of the first amendment. We vacate the judgment appealed from and remand the action to the district court.

I. FACTS

A. *The College*

Mississippi College is a four-year coeducational liberal arts institution located in Clinton, Mississippi. The College is owned and operated by the Mississippi Baptist Convention (Convention), an organization composed of Southern Baptist churches in Mississippi.

The Convention conceives of education as an integral part of its Christian mission. It acquired the College in 1850 and has operated it to the present day to fulfill that mission by providing educational enrichment in a Christian atmosphere. As part of its policy, Mississippi College seeks to assure that faculty and administrative officers are committed to the principle that "the best preparation for life is a program of cultural and human studies permeated by the Christian ideal, as evidenced by the tenets, practices and customs of the Mississippi Baptist Convention and in keeping with the principles and scriptures of the Bible." In accordance with this purpose, the College has a written policy of preferring active members of Baptist churches in hiring. The evidence the College presented to the district court indicates that approximately ninety-five percent of the college's full-time faculty members are Baptists. The evidence also shows that eighty-eight percent of the College's students are Baptists. The undergraduate curriculum for all students, regardless of major, includes two courses in which the Bible is studied, and all students are required to attend chapel meetings held twice weekly. The College's facilities include prayer rooms available for use by the students and the College employs a full-time director of Christian activities. Because no woman has been ordained as a minister in a Southern Baptist church in Mississippi, the College hires only males to teach courses concerning the Bible.

B. *The Charging Party*

Dr. Patricia Summers, the charging party, obtained part-time employment with the College as an assistant professor in the psychology department for the 1975-76 school year. While employed by the College, Summers learned of a vacancy in the full-time faculty of the department of educational psychology created by the departure of Raymond Case, an experimental psychologist. She expressed her desire both orally and in writing to be considered for the position, but she was not interviewed by College officials. Instead, the College hired William Bailey to fill the vacant position. When Summers inquired why she had not been considered for the vacancy, the Vice President of Academic Affairs informed her that the College sought someone with a background in experimental psychology.

In May 1976, Summers filed a charge of discrimination with the EEOC, alleging that Mississippi College had discriminated against her on the basis of sex in hiring someone to fill the vacant full-time position in the psychology department. She later amended her charge to include the additional allegations that the College discriminated against women as a class with respect to job classifications, promotions, recruitment, and pay and that it discriminated on the basis of race in recruiting and hiring.

The evidence before the district court demonstrates that Summers had received a doctoral degree in education from the University of Virginia with a major in counseling and had engaged in post-doctoral studies at Harvard University and other nationally recognized schools. In an affidavit filed with the court, Summers averred that she previously had taught experimental psychology. The President of Mississippi College, Dr. Lewis Nobles, stated both in an affidavit filed with the EEOC and in his testimony before the district court that the College sought to fill the vacancy with an experimental psychologist, that Bailey had been trained in this field, and that Summers' experience was in clinical psychology. Nobles also stated that an additional factor in the College's selection of Bailey was that he was a Baptist, while Summers was not. Although Summers had been baptized in the Baptist faith while a child, she joined the Presbyterian church, the faith of her husband, when she married in 1970.

Although the College did not hire Summers to fill the vacant full-time position, it did offer to renew her part-time contract for the 1976-77 school year at an increased salary. In offering to renew her contract the College did not indicate that it had any objections to her religious views.

C. *The Subpoena Enforcement Proceedings*

The College refused to comply voluntarily with the EEOC's request for information that the Commission considered necessary to investigate Summers' charge. * * * The College responded to the subpoena by filing a petition with the EEOC seeking revocation of the subpoena. The EEOC denied the College's petition. The College still declined to comply with the subpoena and the EEOC brought this action in the district court seeking enforcement of the subpoena under §710 of Title

VII.[4] After a hearing on the merits, the district court denied enforcement of the petition.

* * *

On this appeal the EEOC contends that the district court erred in denying its petition for enforcement. First, it asserts that Summers, although white, can assert a charge of race discrimination against the College because she has standing to assert discrimination that affects her "working environment." Second, it argues that §702 does not exempt race or sex discrimination by a religious education institution from the scope of Title VII. Third, it maintains that its investigation of the College's hiring practices violates neither the establishment clause nor the free exercise clause of the first amendment.

II. SUMMERS' STANDING TO ASSERT A CHARGE OF RACIAL DISCRIMINATION

* * *

A. *Can a Person Charge Discrimination Against a Group of Which he is not a Member?*

* * *

We conclude that §706 of Title VII permits Summers to file a charge asserting that Mississippi College discriminates against blacks on the basis of race in recruitment and hiring.[8] Our decision today does not allow Summers to assert the rights of others. We hold no more than that, provided she meets the standing requirements imposed by Article III, Summers may charge a violation of her own personal right to work in an environment unaffected by racial discrimination.

* * *

III. SECTION 702 OF TITLE VII

Section 702 of Title VII exempts from the application of Title VII religious educational institutions "with respect to the employment of individuals of a particular religion to perform work connected with the carrying on by such * * * educational institution * * * of its activities."

---

[4]Section 710 of Title VII grants to the EEOC, for the purposes of any hearing or investigation it conducts, the same investigatory powers exercised by the National Labor Relations Board under 29 U.S.C. §161. Thus §710 empowers the district court within whose jurisdiction either the EEOC is conducting its inquiry or the person resides against whom enforcement of the subpoena is sought to order any person who refuses to obey a subpoena issued by the EEOC to appear before the EEOC, to produce evidence if so ordered, or to give testimony concerning the matter under investigation. Any failure to obey is punishable as a contempt of court.

[8]We decide only the issue before us of whether a white employee can charge her employer with discriminating against blacks in violation of Title VII. We expressly pretermit the question of whether any form of discrimination other than racial discrimination can be charged by a person who is not a member of the group against whom the discrimination is directed. We likewise pretermit and intimate no opinion concerning Summers' adequacy as a class representative for any blacks against whom the College may have discriminated.

The EEOC contends that §702 only exempts from the coverage of Title VII discrimination based upon religion, not discrimination predicated upon race, color, sex, or national origin. It argues that the College's mere assertion that it declined to hire Summers because of her religion should not prevent it from investigating to determine if the College used Summers' religion as a pretext for some other form of discrimination. The College asserts that its hiring decision falls squarely within the statutory exemption created by §702.

This court previously rejected the argument that the exemption provided by §702 applies to all of the actions of a religious organization taken with respect to an employee whose work was connected with its "religious activities." *See* McClure v. Salvation Army, 460 F.2d 553 (5ᵗʰ Cir.), cert. denied, 409 U.S. 896, 93 S.Ct. 132, 34 L.Ed.2d 153 (1972). In McClure we restricted the application of that exemption to a religious organization's discrimination in employment against an individual on the basis of religion, stating:

> The language and the legislative history of §702 compel the conclusion that Congress did not intend that a religious organization be exempted from liability for discriminating against its employees on the basis of race, color, sex or national origin with respect to their compensation, terms, conditions or privileges of employment.

The College argues first that once it showed (1) an established policy of preferring Baptists in its hiring decisions, (2) that the individual hired for the position was Baptist, and (3) that the charging party was not a Baptist, §702 prevented the EEOC from investigating further the charge of discrimination. *McClure* did not address the EEOC's authority to investigate an individual charge of race or sex discrimination asserted against a religious institution that presents evidence showing that it made the challenged employment decision on the basis of an individual's religion. We conclude that if a religious institution of the kind described in §702 presents convincing evidence that the challenged employment practice resulted from discrimination on the basis of religion, §702 deprives the EEOC of jurisdiction to investigate further to determine whether the religious discrimination was a pretext for some other form of discrimination. This interpretation of §702 is required to avoid the conflicts that would result between the rights guaranteed by the religion clauses of the first amendment and the EEOC's exercise of jurisdiction over religious educational institutions.

The College argues second, and more broadly, that the employment relationship between a religious educational institution and its faculty is exempt from Title VII. It relies on *McClure's* holding that the relationship between a church and its ministers was not intended by Congress to be covered by Title VII. The College's reliance on *McClure* as support for this argument is misplaced.

In *McClure* this court expressly restricted its decision to the context of the church-minister relationship. We concluded that matters touching the relationship between a church and its ministers, including the selection of a minister, determination of salary, and assignment of duties and location, are "matters of church administration and government and thus, purely of ecclesiastical cognizance." The facts distinguish this case from *McClure*. The College is not a church. The College's faculty and staff do not function as ministers. The faculty members are not intermediaries between a church and its congregation. They neither attend to the religious needs of the faithful nor instruct students in the whole of religious doctrine. That faculty members are expected to serve as exemplars of practicing Christians does not serve to make the terms and conditions of their employment matters of church administration and thus purely of ecclesiastical concern. The employment relationship between Mississippi College and its faculty and staff is one intended by Congress to be regulated by Title VII.

Because the College is not a church and its faculty members are not ministers, *McClure's* construction of Title VII does not bar the EEOC in the instant case from investigating Summers' allegations that the college engages in class discrimination against women and blacks.[10] However, as pointed out above, §702 may bar investigation of her individual claim. The district court did not make clear whether the individual employment decision complained of by Summers was based on the applicant's religion. Thus, we cannot determine whether the exemption of §702 applies. If the district court determines on remand that the College applied its policy of preferring Baptists over non-Baptists in granting the faculty position to Bailey rather than Summers, then §702 exempts that decision from the application of Title VII and would preclude any investigation by the EEOC to determine whether the College used the preference policy as a guise to hide some other form of discrimination. On the other hand, should the evidence disclose only that the College's preference policy could have been applied, but in fact it was not considered by the College in determining which applicant to hire, §702 does not bar the EEOC's investigation of Summers' individual sex discrimination claim.

IV. FIRST AMENDMENT QUESTIONS

The EEOC contends that the district court erred in concluding that application of Title VII to a religious educational institution would foster the excessive government entanglement with religion prohibited by the establishment clause and would impermissibly burden the institution's practice of its religious beliefs in violation of the free exercise clause.

---

[10]The College has asserted both before this court and before the district court that its desire to employ Southern Baptists whenever possible to facilitate the carrying out of its religious mission has resulted in its adoption of several recruiting and employment practices that tend to have a disparate impact upon women and blacks. The College contends, for example, that it recruits faculty members through the Association of Baptist Colleges, the member colleges of which have predominantly white student bodies. To the extent that this employment practice is based upon religious discrimination, §702 exempts it from the application of Title VII. However, any choice by the College to recruit only among Baptist colleges that are predominantly white as opposed to all Baptist colleges is not protected by §702 and could be investigated by the EEOC. Also, §702 does not prevent the EEOC from investigating whether the College discriminates against any blacks who may apply from the schools at which it does recruit. The determination of which of the College's employment practices are based upon religious discrimination and therefore exempt under §702 can best be made by the district court on remand. On remand the College should be granted a further opportunity to present evidence demonstrating which parts of the information sought concern practices based upon religious discrimination.

A. *Establishment Clause*

The establishment clause of the first amendment prohibits Congress from enacting any law "respecting an establishment of religion." In determining whether a congressional enactment violates the establishment clause, the Supreme Court has examined three principal criteria: (1) whether the statute has a secular legislative purpose, (2) whether the principal or primary effect of the statute is neither to advance nor to inhibit religion, and (3) whether the statute fosters "an excessive government entanglement with religion." Lemon v. Kurtzman, 403 U.S. 602, 612-13, 91 S.Ct. 2105, 2111, 29 L.Ed.2d 745, 752 (1971). The College does not contend that Title VII has no secular legislative purpose or that it inhibits or advances religion as its primary effect. We therefore focus our inquiry upon the third criteria: whether the statute fosters an excessive entanglement with religion.

In *Lemon* the Court evaluated three factors in determining whether government entanglement with religion is excessive:

the character and purposes of the institutions that are benefited, the nature of the aid that the State provides, and the resulting relationship between the government and the religious authority.

Although the Supreme Court generally has construed the establishment clause in the context of governmental action that benefited a religious activity, it is now clear that the establishment clause is implicated by a statute that potentially burdens religious activities. The three-prong test employed in *Lemon* to determine whether government entanglement is excessive applies with equal force to such cases.

The evidence presented to the district court makes it readily apparent that the character and purposes of the College are pervasively sectarian. The purpose of the College is to provide a college education in an atmosphere saturated with Christian ideals. The College is formally affiliated with the Mississippi Baptist Convention. Indeed, the College exists primarily to serve the evangelical mission of the Convention. The Convention selects the Board of Trustees that exercises effective control over the College.

The nature of the burden that might be imposed upon the College by the application of Title VII to it is largely hypothetical at this stage of the proceedings. The information requested by the EEOC's subpoena does not clearly implicate any religious practices of the College. The College's primary concern is that the EEOC's investigation will not cease should it comply with the subpoena, but instead will intrude further into its operations. The College worries that the EEOC will seek to require it to alter the employment practices by which it seeks to ensure that its faculty members are suitable examples of the Christian ideal advocated by the Southern Baptist faith. These hypothetical concerns are of limited validity. As noted previously, the exemption granted to religious institutions by §702 of Title VII must be construed broadly to exclude from the scope of the act any employment decision made by a religious institution on the basis of religious discrimination. This construction of

§702 largely allays the College's primary concern that it will be unable to continue its policy of preferring Baptists in hiring. The only practice brought to the attention of the district court that is clearly predicated upon religious beliefs that might not be protected by the exemption of §702 is the College's policy of hiring only men to teach courses in religion.[12] The bare potential that Title VII would affect this practice does not warrant precluding the application of Title VII to the College. Before the EEOC could require the College to alter that practice, the College would have an opportunity to litigate in a federal forum whether §702 exempts or the first amendment protects that particular practice. We thus determine that, in the factual context before us, the application of Title VII to the College could have only a minimal impact upon the College's religion based practices.

The relationship between the federal government and the College that results from the application of Title VII does have limits both in scope and effect. It is true that the subpoena issued to the College by the EEOC presages a wide ranging investigation into many aspects of the College's hiring practices. Furthermore, should the EEOC conclude that cause exists to believe that the College discriminates on the basis of sex or race, the College in all likelihood would be subjected to a court action if it did not voluntarily agree to alter its actions. The College would, however, be entitled to a de novo determination of whether its practices violate Title VII. In that action the College could reassert the protection of the first amendment prior to being ordered to amend its practices. If the challenged employment practices survived the scrutiny of the district court, the EEOC could not attack again those particular practices absent some change in circumstances.

Although the College is a pervasively sectarian institution, the minimal burden imposed upon its religious practices by the application of Title VII and the limited nature of the resulting relationship between the federal government and the College cause us to find that application of the statute would not foster excessive government entanglement with religion. Employment practices based upon religious discrimination are exempt under §702 from the coverage of Title VII and the College could not be required to alter any of its other employment practices until it exercised its opportunity to justify those practices on first amendment grounds before a federal district court. Because no religious tenets advocated by the College or the Mississippi Baptist Convention involve discrimination on the basis of race or sex, an investigation by the EEOC will only minimally intrude upon any of the College's or Convention's religious beliefs. No ongoing interference with the College's religious practices will result from an EEOC investigation of the charge filed by Summers. Therefore, we conclude that imposing the requirements of Title VII upon the College does not violate the establishment clause of the first amendment.

---

[12]In his testimony before the district court Dr. Nobles explained that the practice of not hiring women to teach religion courses was based upon Bible scriptures indicating that pastors and deacons should be men. He testified that to his knowledge no member church of the Mississippi Baptist Convention had an ordained woman preacher.

B. *The Free Exercise Clause*

The free exercise clause of the first amendment proscribes any congressional legislation "prohibiting the free exercise" of religion.

In determining whether a statutory enactment violates the free exercise of a sincerely held religious belief, the Supreme Court has examined (1) the magnitude of the statute's impact upon the exercise of the religious belief, (2) the existence of a compelling state interest justifying the burden imposed upon the exercise of the religious belief, and (3) the extent to which recognition of an exemption from the statute would impede the objectives sought to be advanced by the state.

As discussed previously, the impact of Title VII upon the exercise of the religious belief is limited in scope and degree. Section 702 excludes from the scope of Title VII those employment practices of the College that discriminate on the basis of religion. We acknowledge that, except for those practices that fall outside of Title VII, the impact of Title VII on the College could be profound. To the extent that the College's practices foster sexual or racial discrimination, the EEOC, if unable to persuade the College to alter them voluntarily, could seek a court order compelling their modification, imposing injunctive restraints upon the College's freedom to make employment decisions, and awarding monetary relief to those persons aggrieved by the prohibited acts. However, the relevant inquiry is not the impact of the statute upon the institution, but the impact of the statute upon the institution's exercise of its sincerely held religious beliefs. The fact that those of the College's employment practices subject to Title VII do not embody religious beliefs or practices protects the College from any real threat of undermining its religious purpose of fulfilling the evangelical role of the Mississippi Baptist Convention, and allows us to conclude that the impact of Title VII on the free exercise of religious beliefs is minimal.

Second, the government has a compelling interest in eradicating discrimination in all forms. Congress manifested that interest in the enactment of Title VII and the other sections of the Civil Rights Act of 1964. The proscription upon racial discrimination in particular is mandated not only by congressional enactments but also by the thirteenth amendment. We conclude that the government's compelling interest in eradicating discrimination is sufficient to justify the minimal burden imposed upon the College's free exercise of religious beliefs that results from the application of Title VII.

Moreover, we conclude that creating an exemption from the statutory enactment greater than that provided by §702 would seriously undermine the means chosen by Congress to combat discrimination and is not constitutionally required. Although the number of religious educational institutions is minute in comparison to the number of employers subject to Title VII, their effect upon society at large is great because of the role they play in educating society's young. If the environment in which such institutions seek to achieve their religious and educational goals reflects unlawful discrimination, those discriminatory attitudes will be perpetuated with an influential segment of society, the detrimental effect of which cannot be estimated. Because the burden placed upon the free exercise of religion by the application of Title VII to religious educational institutions is slight, because society's interest in eradicating discrimination is compelling, and because the creation of an exemption greater than that provided by §702 would seriously undermine Congress' attempts to eliminate discrimination, we conclude the application of Title VII to educational institutions such as Mississippi College does not violate the free exercise clause of the first amendment.

* * * We vacate the district court's findings of fact, its conclusions of law, and its initial opinion and remand for further proceedings consistent with this opinion. We specifically note that on remand the district court * * * should allow the parties to present further evidence demonstrating which employment practices of Mississippi College are exempt from the coverage of Title VII under §702 as construed by this opinion. We leave for resolution by the district court on remand the question of what portions of the EEOC's subpoena should be enforced.

Vacated and Remanded.

NOTES AND PROBLEMS FOR DISCUSSION

1. As originally enacted in 1964, §702 permitted religious discrimination by religious institutions only with respect to the employment of individuals connected with the institution's *religious* activities. The 1972 amendments broadened this exemption to permit religious discrimination against individuals connected with the secular as well as religious activities of religious organizations. Moreover, note that §702's exemption applies to any "religious corporation, association or society". Does this mean that the exemption extends to organizations other than houses of worship? In SPENCER v. WORLD VISION, INC., 633 F.3d 723 (9th Cir.) (en banc), cert. denied, 132 S.Ct. 96, 181 L.Ed.2d 25 (2011), the Ninth Circuit rejected the plaintiffs' claim that the exemption was limited to houses of worship. It ruled that an entity is entitled to the exemption if it (1) is organized for a religious purpose; (2) carries out that religious purpose; (3) holds itself out to the public as an entity dedicated to carrying out that religious purpose; and (4) does not engage primarily or substantially in commercial transactions beyond nominal amounts. Applying that standard to the instant case, the court ruled that the defendant, "a Christian humanitarian organization dedicated to working with families, and their communities worldwide to reach their full potential by tackling the causes of poverty and injustice" was entitled to the statutory exemption and affirmed the trial court's grant of summary judgment to the defense.

(a) By permitting a religious organization to limit employment to members of its sect in a restaurant it owns, does §702 violate the First Amendment's Establishment Clause? *See* King's Garden, Inc. v. Federal Communications Commission, 498 F.2d 51 (D.C. Cir. 1974), cert. denied, 419 U.S. 996, 95 S.Ct. 309, 42 L.Ed.2d 269 (1974).

Would it make a difference if the church's secular undertaking constituted a nonprofit activity? In CORPORATION OF PRESIDING BISHOP OF THE CHURCH OF JESUS CHRIST OF LATTER-DAY SAINTS v. AMOS, 483 U.S. 327, 107 S.Ct. 2862, 97 L.Ed.2d 273 (1987), the members of the Supreme Court unanimously agreed that the application of §702 to a religious institution's nonprofit activities did not violate the establishment clause of the First Amendment. The plaintiff had been discharged from his position as building engineer of a nonprofit gymnasium facility run by a religious entity associated with the Mormon Church. The discharge was predicated on the employee's failure to qualify for a certificate attesting to his membership in the Church. In response to his Title VII claim that this discharge constituted unlawful religious discrimination, the defendant asserted a §702 exemption from religious discrimination liability. (The trial court had found that the plaintiff's duties involved solely nonreligious activity.) In his majority opinion, Justice White stated that §702 served the secular purpose of minimizing governmental interference with the decision-making processes of religious institutions. He added that its application to nonprofit activities of such religious institutions did not have the primary effect of advancing religion since it merely permitted, but did not require, the church to engage in this type of secular endeavor. Thus, White reasoned, any advancement of religion that would be occasioned by the use of the gymnasium would be attributed to (i.e., accomplished by) the activities of the church and not the government.

In a concurring opinion joined by Justice Marshall, Justice Brennan stated that a reasonable accommodation to a religion's need to exercise its religious beliefs, as well as its need to define and maintain its religious character, was satisfied by permitting religious institutions to discriminate on the basis of religion, but only with respect to religious activities. Yet the application of this principle, he added, would require *ad hoc* determinations of the religious or secular character of each challenged activity. These determinations, in turn, could result in government entanglement in religious affairs and, he added, might chill religious activity — at least with respect to those activities whose religious or secular classification by a court cannot be predicted by the church. Thus, Brennan concluded, the requirement of a case-by-case analysis for all activities was constitutionally unacceptable. Nevertheless, Brennan added, as the risk of chilling religious organizations was most likely to arise with respect to such institutions' nonprofit activities (since nonprofit activities are more likely than commercial activities to be seen as infused with some religious purpose), it was reasonable to avoid this chilling effect by automatically categorizing all nonprofit activities as religious in nature and thus constitutionally subject to the §702 exemption. Therefore, since the instant activity was indisputably a not-for-profit endeavor, he concluded that an individual determination of its religious character was not required and thus agreed with the majority's conclusion that §702 could be constitutionally applied in this case. On the other hand, Justice Brennan left little doubt that he would have required an *ad hoc* assessment of the religious character of the enterprise had it not been a nonprofit affair. Is it really very helpful to characterize activities as religious depending on whether or not they are viewed as nonprofit? Consider that, at least for tax purposes, an activity or organization is determined to be nonprofit on the basis of the nature and purpose of its activities and not according to the financial bottom line.

Justices Blackmun and O'Connor also filed separate concurring opinions, underscoring that the constitutionality of the application of §702 to for-profit activities remained unanswered by the majority's opinion. Justice O'Connor added that the majority had applied the wrong analysis in determining whether the application of §702 to nonprofit activities violated the establishment clause. Specifically, she stated, the majority's distinction between state action that permits religious groups to advance their religious beliefs and state action that directly promotes religion served "to obscure far more than to enlighten" since almost any government benefit to religion could be characterized simply as conduct that allows the religion to advance its own belief and thereby escape establishment clause scrutiny. She preferred to recognize that any government action immunizing religious organizations from a generally applicable statutory obligation has the effect of advancing religion. For her, the real question was whether the government's action was intended to and had the effect of conveying an endorsement of religion. With respect, then, to non-profit activities, Justice O'Connor concluded, the fact that such activities are likely to be involved with the institution's religious mission should persuade an objective observer that §702 was intended to serve as an accommodation of the exercise of religious beliefs (by lifting from religious organizations the burden of demonstrating that each nonprofit activity is religious in nature) and not as an endorsement of religion. In ALLEGHENY COUNTY v. ACLU, GREATER PITTSBURGH CHAPTER, 492 U.S. 573, 109 S.Ct. 3086, 106 L.Ed.2d 472 (1989), a case involving the display of a crèche and menorah on public property, a majority of the Court, in a series of opinions, ultimately adopted the "endorsement" test propounded by Justice O'Connor in her concurrence in *Amos*. For an interesting discussion of the constitutional implications of §702's application to "nonreligious" activities see Duane E. Okamoto, *Religious Discrimination and The Title VII Exemption For Religious Organizations: A Basic Values Analysis For the Proper Allocation of Conflicting Right*s, 60 S.CAL.L.REV. 1375 (1987).

(b) Since §702 does not exempt religious organizations from the duty not to discriminate on the basis of race, color, national origin, or sex, does this level of state regulation of their employment practices constitute an impermissible entanglement with religion violative of the religion clauses of the First Amendment? The principal case examined two related aspects of this problem: (1) whether there are circumstances under which Title VII was not intended to restrict the employment relationship between the parties; and (2) in those circumstances where Title VII was designed to apply to religious institutions, does such regulation exceed the limitations on government conduct imposed by the religion clauses of the First Amendment?

For four decades, the circuit courts uniformly read into Title VII a "ministerial exception" that totally exempted all decisions made by a "church" that concerned the employment of a "minister" from challenge under Title VII. Although the circuits could not agree on whether this exemption was mandated by either the Free Exercise or Establishment Clause of the First Amendment, or both, they did recognize that any application of Title VII to decisions concerning the employment relationship between a "church" and its "ministers" would violate either or both of the Religion Clauses. (See, e.g., *McClure* v. *Salvation Army*, a Fifth Circuit case cited in *Mississippi College*.). And though there was rarely litigation on whether a particular defendant constituted a "church" within the meaning of this exemption, there was a significant divergence between the circuits in determining when a particular individual was a "minister" for purposes of insulating the church employer's decision from Title VII scrutiny.

The Supreme Court addressed the scope and nature of the ministerial exemption, albeit in a case brought under the Americans with Disabilities Act (ADA), in HOSANNA-TABOR EVANGELICAL LUTHERAN CHURCH AND SCHOOL v. E.E.O.C., 565 U.S. 171, 132 S.Ct. 694, 181 L.Ed.2d 650 (2012). The defendant was an elementary school that was owned and operated by a Lutheran Church and that offered a "Christ-centered education". The school employed both lay and "called" teachers. "Called" teachers were individuals deemed to have been called for this vocation by God. In order to receive a "call" from the congregation, an individual had to complete a program of theological study at a Lutheran college or university, pass an oral examination, and obtain the endorsement of the local Synod district. Once "called", a teacher received the title "Minister of Religion, Commissioned". "Called" and lay teachers taught the same secular and religious courses, but the school employed lay teachers only when called teachers were unavailable. Cheryl Perich initially was employed as a lay teacher, but subsequently was asked to become a called teacher, accepted the call, and received designation as a commissioned minister. After developing narcolepsy, Perich was put on disability leave; but when she informed the school that she was able to return to work the following month, the school told her that she had been replaced by a lay teacher and offered to let her resign as a called teacher in exchange for payment of some of her health insurance premiums. Perich refused that offer and subsequently informed the school's principal that she intended to assert her legal rights. Thereafter, the congregation voted to rescind the plaintiff's call and she was terminated on the ground that her threat to take legal action damaged her working relationship with the church and violated the Church's belief that Christians should resolve their disputes internally.

Perich filed an EEOC charge alleging that she had been terminated in violation of the ADA. The EEOC brought suit on her behalf under the anti-retaliation provision of the ADA, alleging that she had been terminated in retaliation for threatening to file an ADA suit. The trial court granted summary judgment to the defense, concluding that the suit was barred by the ministerial exception. But the Sixth Circuit vacated that ruling on the ground that Perich did not qualify as a minister since her duties as a called teacher were identical to the duties performed by lay teachers.

The Supreme Court unanimously reversed the Sixth Circuit and reinstated the trial court's grant of summary judgment. The unanimous Court expressly recognized the existence of the ministerial exception, stating that it was mandated by both Religion Clauses of the First Amendment in order to prevent the government from interfering with the employment relationship between a religious institution and its ministers. Although the instant suit was brought under the ADA, the Court announced in broad terms that *any* employment discrimination statute would be unconstitutional to the extent it attempted to regulate in any way a "church's" employment relationship with any of its "ministers". And although all the Justices joined in the unanimous opinion authored by Chief Justice Roberts, there were concurring opinions written by Justices Thomas and Alito (who was joined by Justice Kagan) that sought to offer a different approach towards determining when a particular individual qualified as a "minister" where the defendant sought to invoke this blanket exemption from statutory coverage.

In his opinion for the Court, the Chief Justice stated that the Court was "reluctant * * * to adopt a rigid formula for deciding when an employee qualifies as a minister." It was sufficient, he continued, to conclude that this employee fell within the ministerial exception. That determination, in turn, was based on the Court's assessment of several factors: (1) the Church held Perich out as a minister by giving her the title "Minister of Religion, Commissioned"; (2) she was tasked with performing her job "according to the Word of God" and the standards of the Lutheran Church as draws from sacred scriptures; (3) Perich was granted the title of Minister by the congregation only after a significant degree of religious training followed by a formal commissioning process culminating in election by the congregation; (4) Perich had held herself out as a minister by claiming a special housing allowance on her tax return that was available only to employees who earn compensation in the exercise of the ministry; and (5) Perich's job duties included conveying the Church's message and carrying out its religion mission of transmitting the faith to the next generation in that she taught religion classes, led the students in daily prayers, and occasionally led chapel services. Based on all of these factors, and in the face of finding that Perich's religious duties consumed only 45 minutes of each workday and that the rest of her day was devoted to teaching secular subjects, the Court concluded that Perich was a "minister" covered by the exemption. Though none of these factors was individually dispositive, each one was relevant to making the ministerial determination. Moreover, the Court rejected the Sixth Circuit's conclusion that the fact that these same functions were performed by lay teachers automatically precluded Perich from being designated a minister. Similarly, it rejected the EEOC's claim that the ministerial exception should be restricted to individuals who perform exclusively religious functions, noting that most, if not all, clergy perform a mix of duties, including secular ones. The Court also noted that its ruling applied only to suits brought under employment discrimination statutes. It left for another day the question of whether a ministerial exception should be recognized in common law employment-related breach of contract or tort actions by employees against religious institutions. Finally, it added, by way of footnote, that the ministerial exception was a waivable affirmative defense and not a (nonwaivable) jurisdictional bar to suit.

In a concurring opinion, Justice Thomas took a narrower view of the Court's proper role in the ministerial designation process. In order to give full effect to the Religion Clauses, he maintained, the courts should defer to the religions organization's good faith determination of who qualifies as its minister. If the courts could second-guess a religious entity's determination of who was one of its ministers, he maintained, that organization's constitutional right to choose its own ministers without governmental interference would be hollow. Moreover, he added, the determination of who is a minister was itself a religious question which needed to be within the sole province of the religious institution. Since, in his view, the defendant sincerely considered Perich to be a minister, that was enough for him to invoke the ministerial exception.

Justice Alito, joined by Justice Kagan, offered a third approach. Their primary concern was based on the use of the word "minister" to define those employees subject to the exemption since that precise designation, although used by many Protestant denominations to refer to members of their clergy, was not employed by other religious groups such as Catholics, Jews, Muslims, Hindus, or Buddhists. Additionally, they were concerned that the term might encompass a requirement of ordination, a concept or practice that was not a prerequisite to being a member of the clergy of many religions. So they proposed that the courts undertake a functional, rather than titular analysis of the employee in question to determine whether or not that person was subject to the exemption. For Justices Alito and Kagan, in order to maintain the constitutionally-mandated autonomy of religious institutions, the key question was whether the individuals performed important functions in worship services and in the performance of religious ceremonies and rituals and whether they were entrusted with teaching the tenets of the faith to the next generation. Neither a ministerial title nor ordination, while relevant to making that determination, they declared, was either necessary or sufficient to resolution of the functional analysis.

Based on this approach, these two Justices agreed that Perich was an employee as to whom the exemption applied.

Applying the teachings of *Hosanna-Tabor*, the Fifth Circuit, in CANNATA v. CATHOLIC DIOCESE OF AUSTIN, 700 F.3d 169 (5th Cir. 2012), abandoned its tripartite test for determining when an employee qualified as a "minister" within the meaning of the exception. That standard had required the court to consider (1) whether employment decisions concerning the position in question were made largely on religious criteria; (2) whether the plaintiff was authorized to perform religious ceremonies; and, most importantly, (3) whether the plaintiff engaged in ecclesiastical or religious activities, including whether the plaintiff attended to the religious needs of the faithful. The appellate panel concluded that *Hosanna-Tabor* mandated a more fact-intensive, totality-of-the-circumstances inquiry and rejected the type of rigid formula represented by its extant three-part standard. The plaintiff, Music Director for a Catholic Church, played piano at Mass, kept the Church's books, ran the sound system, and performed custodial work. Although the court found that none of these duties were religious in nature, it read *Hosanna-Tabor* to hold that the performance of secular duties should not be overemphasized in assessing the applicability of the ministerial exception. The court emphasized that the defendant church had offered evidence of the important role that music played in the celebration of the Mass and that all musicians therefore assisted the parish pastor in carrying out the church's religious mission. Because the plaintiff planned and coordinated the church's music program, which fostered the active participation of the congregation in singing, the court found that he played an integral part of the Mass and that by playing the piano during services, he furthered the church's religious mission and helped convey its message to the congregants. Moreover, the court explained, the fact that the plaintiff was neither ordained nor possessed any formal training in Catholic doctrine was not fatal to the defendant's assertion of the exception.

From time to time, there is an issue as to whether the defendant is eligible for the ministerial exception. In SHALIEHSHABOU v. HEBREW HOME OF GREATER WASHINGTON, INC., 363 F.3d 299 (4th Cir.2004), the plaintiff, a "masgiach", a person trained and hired to ensure that an entity's food services are prepared in accordance with Jewish religious dietary laws, brought an action under the Fair Labor Standards Act against his employer, a Jewish nursing home. The FLSA has been construed to be subject to a ministerial exception coextensive with the exemption recognized under Title VII. When the plaintiff alleged that his employer had failed to pay him his statutorily entitled overtime pay, the defendant alleged that it was a religious entity and that the plaintiff, as a minister, fell within the ministerial exception. Relying on Title VII jurisprudence, the Fourth Circuit upheld the trial judge's grant of summary judgment in favor of the defendant. It held that "religions institutions" include religiously affiliated entities that provide secular functions so long as they are imbued with a substantial religious character. The nursing home, the court concluded, had such a religious character since it was religiously affiliated, its By-Laws defined it as a religious corporation, and its mission was to provide elder care to Jewish elderly in accordance with Jewish law. (In this pre-*Hosanna-Tabor* case, the court also concluded that the masgiach was a minister for purposes of applying the ministerial exception. Applying a "primary duties" test that looks to whether or not the function of the position are important to the spiritual and pastoral mission rather than on whether the holder of the position is formally ordained, the court found that the masgiach's primary duties were ministerial in nature. Even though his duties did not involve religious worship, the court emphasized that the masgiach supervised a vitally important religious ritual and occupied a position that was central to the spiritual and pastoral mission of Judaism.). This same analysis was applied post-*Hosanna-Tabor* by the Sixth Circuit in holding that a nationwide Christian evangelical college campus organization that served students and faculty for the purpose of advancing the understanding and practice of Christianity was eligible for the ministerial exception. In CONLON v. INTERVARSITY CHRISTIAN FELLOWSHIP/USA, 777 F.3d 829 (6th Cir. 2015), the appellate panel held that the constitutionally mandated ministerial exception was not limited to houses of worship of any particular denomination such as churches and synagogues. Rather, it continued, the exception extended to multidenominational or nondenominational "religiously affiliated entities" (regardless of whether they were or were not operated by a traditional religious organization) whose mission included teaching and ministry.

The Second Circuit went one step further. In PENN v. NEW YORK METHODIST HOSPITAL, 884 F.3d 416 (2d Cir. 2018), cert. denied, 139 S.Ct. 424, 202 L.Ed.2d 317 (2018), the plaintiff was denied a promotion and later terminated from his position as a "Duty Chaplain" with the hospital's Department of Pastoral Care. Although the defendant was founded by the Methodist Church and retained its religious affiliation for many years, it ultimately abandoned this relationship by changing its Articles of Incorporation and Bylaws. But while operating its medical facility on a secular basis, it also operated a Department of Pastor Care which offered religious services to individuals of all religions. The parties did not dispute the designation of the plaintiff as a "minister" within the meaning of the exception. The issue was whether this otherwise secular hospital qualified for the exception in connection with the employment decisions concerning a chaplain in its pastoral care department. The majority of the Second Circuit panel agreed with the defendant that it was subject to the ministerial exception with respect to its employment decisions concerning the plaintiff. Since this department provided only religious services to the hospital's patients and staff, the fact that these services were not limited to the tenets or practices of a particular religion did not, in the majority's view, detract from the conclusion that its services were religious in nature. The majority noted, however, that its ruling was limited to the facts of this case and did not address whether the exception would apply generally to an otherwise secular hospital with respect to its chaplaincies. The dissenting judge was unwilling to carve out a department-specific basis of eligibility for the ministerial exception. In his view, the facts that the pastoral care department was not an independent entity separate from the hospital and that the plaintiff was terminated by the hospital's secular general administration and not by the director of the pastoral care department compelled the conclusion that the department was not entitled to separate analysis as to whether it was a religious institution.

Can a religiously affiliated entity waive the ministerial exception by, for example, adopting a policy of nondiscrimination on religious grounds? In *Conlon, supra*, the Sixth Circuit construed *Hosanna-Tabor* to mean that the constitutionally mandated ministerial exception can never be waived.

Particularly nuanced variations on the interplay between the constitutionally-based "ministerial exception" and the application of Title VII to religious organizations when the statutory exception of §702 is inapplicable, i.e., in cases alleging discrimination on grounds other than religion, appear when the plaintiff asserts a claim of sexual harassment against a religious institution. This issue is discussed in Note 11 following *Burlington* in Chapter 2B4, *infra*.

2. If an admittedly religious organization represented in all of its publications that it was an equal opportunity employer, could an individual denied a position on the basis of her religion nevertheless state a claim under Title VII on the theory that the defendant had waived its Title VII immunity? *See* Hall v. Baptist Memorial Health Care Corp., 215 F.3d 618 (6th Cir. 2000) (the exemption reflected Congress' decision that religions organizations enjoy a constitutional right to be free from governmental intervention into religion-based decision-making and, therefore, this protection cannot be waived).

3. Section 702 states that Title VII shall not apply to religious institutions with respect to the employment of "individuals of a particular religion." Suppose a Catholic school hires a Protestant lay teacher, but subsequently refuses to renew her contract when it discovers that she has remarried. It claims that this decision was not based on the plaintiff's affiliation with the Protestant Church, but because she engaged in conduct (remarriage) that is inconsistent with the Catholic Church's religious precepts. Can she state a claim of religious discrimination? *See* Little v. Wuerl, 929 F.2d 944 (3d Cir. 1991) (the statutory grant of permission to employ persons "of a particular religion" includes permission to employ only those individuals whose beliefs and conduct are consistent with the employer's religious precepts; a contrary decision would raise sensitive First Amendment free exercise and establishment clause concerns).

4. Prior to the enactment of the 1991 Civil Rights Act, §702 provided, *inter alia*, that Title VII did not apply to "the employment of aliens outside any State." It was unclear from this language, however, whether Congress meant to exclude both aliens and U.S. citizens employed abroad by an American corporation from the protections of the statute. Lurking in the background of this interpretive question was the traditional rule of statutory construction that federal legislation, unless a contrary intent appears, is intended to apply solely within the territorial limits of the U.S. Section 109(a) of the 1991 Civil Rights Act amended Title VII's definition of "employee" to include U.S. "citizens" employed in a foreign country. The statute did not change the existing jurisprudence holding that Title VII does not apply to aliens employed outside of the U.S. And since the 1991 amendment extended Title VII's extraterritorial effect only to "citizens", the court in SHEKOYAN v. SIBLEY INTERNATIONAL, 409 F.3d 414 (D.C.Cir.2005), cert. denied, 546 U.S. 1173, 126 S.Ct. 1337, 164 L.Ed.2d 53 (2006), ruled that in light of the general presumption against extraterritoriality, the statute did not apply to permanent resident aliens employed abroad.

At the same time, however, §109(b) of the 1991 Act limited the breadth of this change by adding new subsection "(b)" to §702 of Title VII and providing therein that Title VII does not apply to an employee in a foreign workplace if compliance with the requirements of Title VII would result in a violation of domestic law. Section 702(b) also extends the application of Title VII to foreign incorporated businesses that are controlled by U.S. companies and provides that the employment practices of such entities are presumed to be engaged in by the American parent. And it sets forth four factors to be used in determining the existence of the requisite control, all of which relate to centrality of control over operations, management, labor relations and ownership. Presumably, then, §702(b) was intended to make the American parent company liable for the acts of its foreign subsidiary. But it is not clear from the statutory language whether the American employee can also state a claim against the American-controlled foreign company. Is it significant, in resolving this ambiguity, that the definition of "employer" in §701(b) of Title VII is not expressly limited to American companies? On the other hand, beyond the obvious difficulty of obtaining personal jurisdiction over a foreign company in a U.S. court, any attempt at extraterritorial enforcement of the statute over a foreign company is complicated by the absence in the Act of either any venue provision for foreign employers or any provision for extraterritorial EEOC subpoena power.

Suppose, however, that an employment contract between the employer and employee expressly states that it is to be governed exclusively by "applicable United States law". Further suppose that the employee is a non-U.S. citizen employed abroad by a U.S. corporation. Can she state a Title VII claim against the employer? In RABÉ v. UNITED AIR LINES, INC., 636 F.3d 866 (7th Cir. 2011), the Seventh Circuit held that such contractual language had the effect of applying the substantive provisions of U.S. employment discrimination laws to a termination claim as a matter of contract law. An employer, the court ruled, can *contractually* agree to extend *statutory* legal protections to an employee who would not otherwise be covered by that statute. Moreover, applying the teachings of the Supreme Court's ruling in *Arbaugh*, the court concluded that the domestic-work requirement of Title VII and the ADEA should be treated the same as the minimum employee requirement, i.e., that challenges based on failure to meet that requirement are non-jurisdictional in nature and are properly made as motion to dismiss for failure to state a claim upon which relief can be granted under F.R.Civ.P. 12(b)(6) and not as motions to dismiss for lack of subject matter jurisdiction under Rule 12(b)(1).

CHAPTER 2

Defining and Proving Discrimination

SECTION A. INTRODUCTION

As the materials in the preceding chapter indicate, Title VII's definitional and substantive provisions place a wide range of institutions and employment practices within the reach of the statute's anti-discrimination principle. Yet while the word "discriminate" is contained within the definition of each group of proscribed policies, Congress, at least initially, provided no definition of this critical term. After the statute was enacted, no one doubted that an employer's refusal, for example, to hire a qualified applicant solely because of skin color or sex or place of birth was now prohibited. But in the absence of an overt, unambiguous policy of exclusion, many important interpretive questions remained unanswered. They included the following: (1) in the absence of an employer's formal policy of excluding a protected class, what kind of proof must the plaintiff muster to establish unlawful discrimination?; (2) if the employer was motivated by both unlawful bias *and* by a legitimate factor, such as the applicant's relative qualifications, has a violation the Title VII occurred?; (3) can unlawful discrimination occur in the absence of a loss of pay or job status or other tangible employment benefit?; (4) does an employer violate the Act when it implements a policy, such as a minimum height and weight requirement or passage of a standardized test, that disproportionately affects one gender or racial group but is not intended to discriminate?; and (5) does an employer whose current hiring or promotion practices are affected by the lingering effects of discrimination that occurred prior to the effective date of Title VII thereby violate Title VII?

The absence of a statutory definition of discrimination left the courts with the task of formulating a workable concept of unlawful discrimination. For a quarter of a century, the Supreme Court and the lower federal courts struggled with the task of formulating and refining a framework for analyzing discrimination claims. The courts' construction of Title VII was generally accepted by Congress until 1991 when, in response to a series of Supreme Court opinions which altered previously established patterns of proof and defense, Congress enacted the Civil Rights Act of 1991. That act modified in some respects the courts' decisions regarding the meaning of unlawful discrimination. The material in this chapter explores the issues generated by Congress and by the Supreme Court's attempts to explore and explain the dimensions of unlawful employment discrimination.

SECTION B. INTENTIONAL DISCRIMINATION AGAINST THE INDIVIDUAL: DISPARATE TREATMENT

1. THE CONCEPTUAL FRAMEWORK

The most easily recognized form of discrimination occurs when an employer, union, or employment agency intentionally treats people differently because of their race, color, religion, sex, or national origin. In a series of cases spanning more than twenty years, the Supreme Court sought to establish an evidentiary scheme to guide the parties in prosecuting and defending, and the lower courts in analyzing, what the Court termed "disparate treatment" claims, i.e., those containing allegations of intentional discrimination.

Texas Department of Community Affairs v. Burdine

Supreme Court of the United States, 1981.
450 U.S. 248, 101 S.Ct. 1089, 67 L.Ed.2d 207.

JUSTICE POWELL delivered the opinion of the Court.

This case requires us to address again the nature of the evidentiary burden placed upon the defendant in an employment discrimination suit brought under Title VII of the Civil Rights Act of 1964. The narrow question presented is whether, after the plaintiff has proved a prima facie case of discriminatory treatment, the burden shifts to the defendant to persuade the court by a preponderance of the evidence that legitimate, nondiscriminatory reasons for the challenged employment action existed.

I

[Respondent was employed as an accounting clerk in a division of the Petitioner Department that was funded completely by the federal government. To retain this funding, the Petitioner was forced to reduce its staff, which it accomplished by firing Respondent and two other employees, while retaining one male employee. B.R. Fuller, the Department's Executive Director, testified that this decision was based upon a nondiscriminatory evaluation of the relative qualifications of his staff members, and that the three terminated individuals did not work well together. Before her termination, Respondent had been denied a promotion to a supervisory position. She brought the instant action alleging that the failure to promote and subsequent decision to terminate her were the result of sex discrimination in violation of Title VII. The District Court, after a bench trial, ruled in favor of the defendant, finding no evidence to support plaintiff's claim that either decision had been based on gender discrimination.]

The Court of Appeals for the Fifth Circuit reversed in part. The court * * * affirmed the District Court's finding that respondent was not discriminated against when she was not promoted. The Court of Appeals, however, reversed the District Court's finding that Fuller's testimony sufficiently had rebutted respondent's prima facie case of gender discrimination in the decision to terminate her employment at

PSC. The court reaffirmed its previously announced views that the defendant in a Title VII case bears the burden of proving by a preponderance of the evidence the existence of legitimate nondiscriminatory reasons for the employment action and that the defendant also must prove by objective evidence that those hired or promoted were better qualified than the plaintiff. The court found that Fuller's testimony did not carry either of these evidentiary burdens. It, therefore, reversed the judgment of the District Court and remanded the case for computation of backpay. Because the decision of the Court of Appeals as to the burden of proof borne by the defendant conflicts with interpretations of our precedents adopted by other courts of appeals, we granted certiorari. We now vacate the Fifth Circuit's decision and remand for application of the correct standard.

II

In McDonnell Douglas Corp. v. Green, we set forth the basic allocation of burdens and order of presentation of proof in a Title VII case alleging discriminatory treatment. First, the plaintiff has the burden of proving by the preponderance of the evidence a prima facie case of discrimination. Second, if the plaintiff succeeds in proving the prima facie case, the burden shifts to the defendant "to articulate some legitimate, nondiscriminatory reason for the employee's rejection." Third, should the defendant carry this burden, the plaintiff must then have an opportunity to prove by a preponderance of the evidence that the legitimate reasons offered by the defendant were not its true reasons, but were a pretext for discrimination.

The nature of the burden that shifts to the defendant should be understood in light of the plaintiff's ultimate and intermediate burdens. The ultimate burden of persuading the trier of fact that the defendant intentionally discriminated against the plaintiff remains at all times with the plaintiff. See Board of Trustees of Keene State College v. Sweeney. *See generally*, 9 Wigmore, Evidence §2489 (3d ed. 1940) (the burden of persuasion "never shifts"). The *McDonnell Douglas* division of intermediate evidentiary burdens serves to bring the litigants and the court expeditiously and fairly to this ultimate question.

The burden of establishing a prima facie case of disparate treatment is not onerous. The plaintiff must prove by a preponderance of the evidence that she applied for an available position, for which she was qualified, but was rejected under circumstances which give rise to an inference of unlawful discrimination.[6] The prima facie case serves an important function in the litigation: it eliminates the most common nondiscriminatory reasons for the plaintiff's rejection. * * * Establishment of the prima facie case in effect creates a presumption that the employer unlawfully discriminated against the employee. If the trier of fact believes the plaintiff's

---

[6]In the instant case, it is not seriously contested that respondent has proved a prima facie case. She showed that she was a qualified woman who sought an available position, but the position was left open for several months before she finally was rejected in favor of a male who had been under her supervision.

evidence, and if the employer is silent in the face of the presumption, the court must enter judgment for the plaintiff because no issue of fact remains in the case.[7]

The burden that shifts to the defendant, therefore, is to rebut the presumption of discrimination by producing evidence that the plaintiff was rejected, or someone else was preferred, for a legitimate, nondiscriminatory reason. The defendant need not persuade the court that it was actually motivated by the proffered reasons. It is sufficient if the defendant's evidence raises a genuine issue of fact as to whether it discriminated against the plaintiff.[8] To accomplish this, the defendant must clearly set forth, through the introduction of admissible evidence, the reasons for the plaintiff's rejection.[9] The explanation provided must be legally sufficient to justify a judgment for the defendant. If the defendant carries this burden of production, the presumption raised by the prima facie case is rebutted,[10] and the factual inquiry proceeds to a new level of specificity. Placing this burden of production on the defendant thus serves simultaneously to meet the plaintiff's prima facie case by presenting a legitimate reason for the action and to frame the factual issue with sufficient clarity so that the plaintiff will have a full and fair opportunity to demonstrate pretext. The sufficiency of the defendant's evidence should be evaluated by the extent to which it fulfills these functions.

The plaintiff retains the burden of persuasion. She now must have the opportunity to demonstrate that the proffered reason was not the true reason for the employment decision. This burden now merges with the ultimate burden of persuading the court that she has been the victim of intentional discrimination. She may succeed in this either directly by persuading the court that a discriminatory reason more likely

---

[7]The phrase "prima facie case" may denote not only the establishment of a legally mandatory, rebuttable presumption, but also may be used by courts to describe the plaintiff's burden of producing enough evidence to permit the trier of fact to infer the fact at issue. 9 Wigmore, Evidence §2494 (3d ed. 1940). *McDonnell Douglas* should have made it apparent that in the Title VII context we use "prima facie case" in the former sense.

[8]This evidentiary relationship between the presumption created by a prima facie case and the consequential burden of production placed on the defendant is a traditional feature of the common law. "The word 'presumption' properly used refers only to a device for allocating the production burden." F. James & G. Hazard, Civil Procedure §7.9, at 255 (2d ed.1977) (footnote omitted). See Fed.Rule Evid. 301. Usually, assessing the burden of production helps the judge determine whether the litigants have created an issue of fact to be decided by the jury. In a Title VII case, the allocation of burdens and the creation of a presumption by the establishment of a prima facie case is intended progressively to sharpen the inquiry into the elusive factual question of intentional discrimination.

[9]An articulation not admitted into evidence will not suffice. Thus, the defendant cannot meet its burden merely through an answer to the complaint or by argument of counsel.

[10]In saying that the presumption drops from the case, we do not imply that the trier of fact no longer may consider evidence previously introduced by the plaintiff to establish a prima facie case. A satisfactory explanation by the defendant destroys the legally mandatory inference of discrimination arising from the plaintiff's initial evidence. Nonetheless, this evidence and inferences properly drawn therefrom may be considered by the trier of fact on the issue of whether the defendant's explanation is pretextual. Indeed, there may be some cases where the plaintiff's initial evidence, combined with effective cross-examination of the defendant, will suffice to discredit the defendant's explanation.

motivated the employer or indirectly by showing that the employer's proffered explanation is unworthy of credence.

III

In reversing the judgment of the District Court that the discharge of respondent from PSC was unrelated to her sex, the Court of Appeals adhered to two rules it had developed to elaborate the defendant's burden of proof. First, the defendant must prove by a preponderance of the evidence that legitimate, nondiscriminatory reasons for the discharge existed. Second, to satisfy this burden, the defendant "must prove that those he hired * * * were somehow *better* qualified than was plaintiff; in other words, comparative evidence is needed."

A

The Court of Appeals has misconstrued the nature of the burden that *McDonnell Douglas* and its progeny place on the defendant. We stated in *Sweeney* that "the employer's burden is satisfied if he simply 'explains what he has done' or 'produc[es] evidence of legitimate nondiscriminatory reasons.' ' It is plain that the Court of Appeals required much more: it placed on the defendant the burden of persuading the court that it had convincing, objective reasons for preferring the chosen applicant above the plaintiff.

The Court of Appeals distinguished *Sweeney* on the ground that the case held only that the defendant did not have the burden of proving the absence of discriminatory intent. But this distinction slights the rationale of *Sweeney* and of our other cases. We have stated consistently that the employee's prima facie case of discrimination will be rebutted if the employer articulates lawful reasons for the action; that is, to satisfy this intermediate burden, the employer need only produce admissible evidence which would allow the trier of fact rationally to conclude that the employment decision had not been motivated by discriminatory animus. The Court of Appeals would require the defendant to introduce evidence which, in the absence of any evidence of pretext, would persuade the trier of fact that the employment action was lawful. This exceeds what properly can be demanded to satisfy a burden of production.

The court placed the burden of persuasion on the defendant apparently because it feared that "[i]f an employer need only *articulate* — not prove — a legitimate, nondiscriminatory reason for his action, he may compose fictitious, but legitimate, reasons for his actions." We do not believe, however, that limiting the defendant's evidentiary obligation to a burden of production will unduly hinder the plaintiff. First, as noted above, the defendant's explanation of its legitimate reasons must be clear and reasonably specific. This obligation arises both from the necessity of rebutting the inference of discrimination arising from the prima facie case and from the requirement that the plaintiff be afforded "a full and fair opportunity" to demonstrate pretext. Second, although the defendant does not bear a formal burden of persuasion, the defendant nevertheless retains an incentive to persuade the trier of fact that the employment decision was lawful. Thus, the defendant normally will attempt to prove the factual basis for its explanation. Third, the liberal discovery rules applicable to any civil suit in federal court are supplemented in a Title VII suit by the plaintiff's access to the Equal Employment Opportunity Commission's investigatory files concerning her complaint. Given these factors, we are unpersuaded that the plaintiff will find it particularly difficult to prove that a proffered explanation lacking a factual basis is a pretext. We remain confident that the *McDonnell Douglas* framework permits the plaintiff meriting relief to demonstrate intentional discrimination.

B

The Court of Appeals also erred in requiring the defendant to prove by objective evidence that the person hired or promoted was more qualified than the plaintiff. *McDonnell Douglas* teaches that it is the plaintiff's task to demonstrate that similarly situated employees were not treated equally. The Court of Appeals' rule would require the employer to show that the plaintiff's objective qualifications were inferior to those of the person selected. If it cannot, a court would, in effect, conclude that it has discriminated.

* * *

The views of the Court of Appeals can be read, we think, as requiring the employer to hire the minority or female applicant whenever that person's objective qualifications were equal to those of a white male applicant. But Title VII does not obligate an employer to accord this preference. Rather, the employer has discretion to choose among equally qualified candidates, provided the decision is not based upon unlawful criteria. The fact that a court may think that the employer misjudged the qualifications of the applicants does not in itself expose him to Title VII liability, although this may be probative of whether the employer's reasons are pretexts for discrimination.

IV

In summary, the Court of Appeals erred by requiring the defendant to prove by a preponderance of the evidence the existence of nondiscriminatory reasons for terminating the respondent and that the person retained in her stead had superior objective qualifications for the position. When the plaintiff has proved a prima facie case of discrimination, the defendant bears only the burden of explaining clearly the nondiscriminatory reasons for its actions. The judgment of the Court of Appeals is vacated and the case is remanded for further proceedings consistent with this opinion.

It is so ordered.

NOTES AND PROBLEMS FOR DISCUSSION

1. The elements of the prima facie case described in *McDonnell Douglas* and *Burdine* create a low threshold of proof for plaintiffs. As the Court announced, a plaintiff need only persuade the fact-finder that the plaintiff is a (1) member of a protected class, (2) who applied for and was denied an available position, (3) for which he or she was qualified, (4) under circumstances which give rise to an inference of unlawful discrimination. Although plaintiffs typically have no difficulty establishing elements 1 and 2, elements 3 and 4 do pose a variety of proof problems.

(a) With respect to whether the plaintiff is "qualified" for the position sought, what happens when the qualifications for the job are subjective ("team players," "leadership potential," etc.)? In recognition of the opportunity for subjective factors to mask discrimination, the courts generally require the plaintiff only to show she satisfies the objective criteria for the job in order to establish a prima facie case. The defendant, if it chooses, can articulate the subjective factor(s) in explanation for its action. *See, e.g.*, Medina v. Ramsey Steel, 238 F.3d 674 (5th Cir. 2001). But suppose a female plaintiff acknowledges that although she did not meet the objective qualifications for promotion to a new position, neither did the chosen male candidate. Is her failure to meet the objective qualifications fatal to establishing a prima facie case? *See* Scheidemantle v. Slippery Rock University State System of Higher Education, 470 F.3d 535 (3d Cir. 2006) (trial court erred in granting summary judgment to defendant on ground that the plaintiff had failed to establish a prima facie case; the employer's departure from its posted objective qualification meant that it had established a different qualification by which the plaintiff, like the successful candidate, had to be judged without reference to her sex).

The circuits are split on the question of whether a discharged plaintiff has to establish that she was performing satisfactorily or that she merely satisfied the job's basic eligibility requirements in order to meet the "qualifications" hurdle. *Compare* Coco v. Elmwood Care, Inc., 128 F.3d 1177 (7th Cir.1997) (in an ADEA case, a discharged plaintiff must establish that she was performing up to the employer's "legitimate expectations" to meet the qualifications component of the prima facie case) *with* Arnold v. Nursing and Rehabilitation Center At Good Shepherd, LLC., 471 F.3d 843 (8th Cir.2006) (a licensed practical nurse is qualified by dint of having served as a licensed practical nurse for nearly a year before her discharge and does not have to establish that she was performing her job satisfactorily). But regardless of whether or not the courts require evidence related to job performance and irrespective of whether they couch this requirement, where imposed, in terms of proving that the plaintiff met the employer's "legitimate expectations" or was "performing satisfactorily", the plaintiff is not required to anticipate and/or disprove the employer's explanation for its decision in order to meet its prima facie burden. In other words, when determining whether the plaintiff has made a prima facie showing that compels the employer to come forward with evidence of a legitimate explanation to avoid judgment as a matter of law against it, the court will examine only the plaintiff's evidence independent of anything the employer offers by way of denying the adequacy of the plaintiff's performance. The comparative assessment of the evidence tendered by both parties occurs at the final stage of the analysis, i.e., when the court is determining the ultimate question of discrimination. *See* Cline v. Catholic Diocese of Toledo, 206 F.3d 651, 660-61 (6th Cir. 1999) (to require the plaintiff to disprove the employer's reasons at the prima facie stage is to improperly conflate the distinct stages of the *McDonnell Douglas* inquiry); Slattery v. Swiss Reinsurance America Corp., 248 F.3d 87 (2d Cir. 2001) (a plaintiff must only show he possesses the basic skills necessary for performance of the job and not that he actually satisfies the employer).

Alternatively, where the employer has not published the qualifications for a position, the plaintiff cannot be required to present evidence of actual job qualifications as part of her prima facie case. *See* Shannon v. Ford Motor Co., 72 F.3d. 678, 682 (8th Cir. 1996). But even where the employer has established objective qualifications for a position, an applicant who does not satisfy the qualifications may still be able to make out a prima facie case if it can be proved that the employer did not apply these qualifications to all applicants. *See* Johnson v. Louisiana, 351 F.3d 616, 624 (5th Cir. 2003) ("Allowing an employer to point to objective requirements in arguing that a plaintiff is unqualified, even though the requirements were not applied to other employees, would subvert the intent of Title VII and *McDonnell Douglas*.").

(b) The fourth component of the *McDonnell Douglas* test generally has been ignored by the courts. For the most part, they view this component as redundant of the other elements, i.e., if a qualified person is denied an available employment opportunity, the courts typically find, if they mention it at all, that the circumstances give rise to an inference of unlawful discrimination. Nevertheless, on rare occasion, a court will determine that facts sufficient to satisfy the first three elements of the *McDonnell Douglas* standard do not suggest that the defendant's action was the product of unlawful discrimination. For example, in COLLINS v. NEW YORK CITY TRANSIT AUTHORITY, 305 F.3d 113 (2d Cir. 2002), an African-American plaintiff initially challenged his discharge by filing a grievance that was resolved by an arbitrator who rejected the plaintiff's claim of discrimination and upheld the discharge. On the basis of that finding by a fully independent and unbiased decisionmaker, the court concluded that the plaintiff had not sustained the normally "minimal" burden of establishing a prima facie case because these circumstances did not support an inference of discrimination.

But where the courts take an independent look at the fourth element of the *McDonnell Douglas* test, must the plaintiff prove that the employer chose a person of a different race, color, religion, national origin, or sex for the position in question? Most courts agree that a plaintiff need not prove she was replaced or passed over in favor of someone from outside her class in order to establish a prima facie case. *See, e.g.,* Kendrick v. Penske Transportation Service, 220 F.3d 1220, 1229 (10th Cir. 2000) (comparison to a person outside of protected class is unnecessary to create inference of discrimination). But the Sixth Circuit has ruled that the plaintiff can establish the fourth element *either* by evidence that a similarly situated individual was treated differently or simply that the plaintiff was replaced by a person outside the protected class. In that latter situation, the court declared, the plaintiff need not also offer evidence that she was as qualified as that favorably treated individual. Vincent v. Brewer Co., 514 F.3d 489 (6th Cir. 2007).

What about a person who was terminated pursuant to a reduction-in-force and, therefore, was not replaced? Although the courts typically require evidence beyond the fact of the plaintiff's termination, there is no consensus on precisely what other information would establish the existence of circumstances leading to an inference of discrimination. *Compare* Currier v. United Techs. Corp., 393 F.3d 246, 254 (1st Cir. 2004) (fourth element in ADEA prima facie case satisfied by proof that employer retained younger workers in the same position that the plaintiff had occupied) *with* Sullivan v. Liberty Mut. Ins. Co., 444 Mass. 34, 44, 825 N.E.2d 522, 534 (2005) (plaintiff in a reduction-in-force case "may satisfy the fourth element of her prima facie case by producing some evidence that her layoff occurred in circumstances that would raise a reasonable inference of unlawful discrimination.").

The Court also cautioned in *McDonnell Douglas* that the "facts necessarily will vary in Title VII cases, and the specification . . . of the prima facie proof required from [the plaintiff] is not necessarily applicable in every respect to differing factual situations." 411 U.S. at 802 n.13, 93 S.Ct at 1824 n.13. To what extent, if at all, should application of the standard formula be adjusted in cases of so-called "reverse discrimination" brought by white male plaintiffs? Some courts have held that plaintiffs who are members of a historically favored group are not entitled to the presumption of discrimination that flows from satisfying the *McDonnell Douglas* standard unless they demonstrate the existence of "background circumstances that support an inference that the defendant is one of those unusual employers who discriminates against the majority." Taken v. Oklahoma Corp. Comm'n, 125 F.3d 1366, 1369 (10th Cir. 1997). In PHELAN v. CITY of CHICAGO, 347 F.3d 679 (7th Cir. 2003), cert. denied, 541 U.S. 989, 124 S.Ct. 2034, 158 L.Ed.2d 493 (2004), for example, a white city employee who was discharged for alleged poor work habits argued that the "background circumstances" requirement in reverse discrimination cases was unfair to non-minority plaintiffs because such claimants had to prove more facts than minority claimants to establish a prima facie case. The Court of Appeals declared that this proof differential was justified because discrimination against white men was a less common phenomenon than discrimination against minorities. *But see* Iadimarco v. Runyon, 190 F.3d 151, 161 (3d Cir. 1999) ("[A]ll that should be required to establish a prima facie case in the context of 'reverse discrimination' is for the plaintiff to present sufficient evidence to allow a fact finder to conclude that the employer is treating some people less favorably than others based upon a trait that is protected under Title VII.").

In addition to offering evidence that goes to the defendant's motivation, a plaintiff alleging intentional discrimination must also establish that she was the victim of an adverse employment action. This issue comes up with regularity in cases of alleged retaliation brought under §704(a). But it also can arise in a garden variety §703(a) claim. For example, suppose a terminated employee claims that her discharge was the product of sex discrimination. But also suppose that the employer subsequently reinstated her with back pay from the date of her termination. Does the employer's action negate the employee's right to pursue her Title VII claim? Obviously, termination is a classic adverse employment action. But if it is followed by full reinstatement with back pay, does that take the employer's conduct out of the adverse employment action category and immunize the employer from Title VII liability? *See* Phelan v. Cook County, 463 F.3d 773 (7th Cir.2006) (termination followed by reinstatement with back pay is still an adverse employment action since plaintiff could recover compensatory and punitive damages, interest on back pay and attorney fees in successful Title VII action; additionally, statutory goal of deterring discrimination is not furthered by permitting employer to escape liability by merely reinstating aggrieved employee when it determines that costs of reinstatement are lower than its exposure in Title VII action).

Or suppose an employee unsuccessfully applies for a transfer but subsequently is given the position when it becomes vacant. Does the fact that the worker initially sought out the position preclude the court from finding that the subsequent involuntary assignment to that position is an adverse employment action? In DELEON v. KALAMAZOO COUNTY ROAD COMMISSION, 739 F.3d 914 (6th Cir. 2014), cert. denied, 135 S.Ct. 783, 190 L.Ed.2d 887 (2015), the trial judge granted summary judgment in favor of the employer on a plaintiff's claim that his involuntary transfer to a position involving hazardous working conditions did not constitute an adverse employment action because the plaintiff previously had applied for, and been denied, that position. The Sixth Circuit reversed and remanded for trial on the ground that transfer to a previously-sought position *could* constitute an adverse employment action where it either constituted a constructive discharge or where it involved a quantitative or qualitative change in the terms and conditions of employment such that it would be viewed as objectively intolerable to a reasonable person in the plaintiff's position. Since the plaintiff originally sought the transfer with the expectation of a substantial salary increase, and the involuntary transfer did not include any salary adjustment, the divided panel concluded that the trial court had erred in ruling that the plaintiff had not established an adverse employment action as a matter of law and remanded for further proceedings.

For a fascinating exploration of the factual and legal context in which the Supreme Court issued its seminal opinion in *McDonnell Douglas*, with emphasis on the captivating story of the plaintiff, Percy Green, see David Benjamin Oppenheimer, *The Story of Green v. McDonnell Douglas*, EMPLOYMENT DISCRIMINATION STORIES 13 (Joel Wm. Friedman, ed. 2006).

2. The *McDonnell Douglas/Burdine* prima facie case is an evidentiary standard, not a special pleading requirement. In SWIERKIEWICZ v. SOREMA N.A., 534 U.S. 506, 122 S.Ct. 992, 152 L.Ed.2d 1 (2002), the district court had dismissed the plaintiff's complaint and the court of appeals had affirmed because the plaintiff failed to allege facts sufficient to support a prima facie case. The Supreme Court reversed on the ground that the prima facie case operated as a flexible evidentiary standard and not as a rigid pleading rule. The heightened pleading standard imposed by the lower courts, the Supreme Court continued, was inconsistent with Rule 8 of the Federal Rules of Civil Procedure which requires only a "short and plain statement of the claim showing that the pleader is entitled to relief." Rule 8 could be satisfied, it declared, simply by conclusory pleadings of ultimate facts. Since the plaintiff had alleged that he was terminated because of his national origin and age, the employer had been accorded fair notice of the plaintiff's claims and, therefore, the plaintiff's allegations were sufficient to survive a motion to dismiss for failure to state a claim. But in BELL ATLANTIC CORP. v. TWOMBLY, 550 U.S. 544, 125 S.Ct. 1955, 167 L.Ed.2d 929 (2007), the Supreme Court appeared to backtrack on its adherence to the notice pleading foundations of Rule 8 when it held that to defeat a motion to dismiss for failure to state a claim, the complaint in an antitrust conspiracy case must contain more than a mere allegation of parallel business conduct and a conspiracy. The allegations should "plausibly suggest" that the pleader is entitled to relief; i.e., the pleader must allege facts that would "raise a reasonable expectation that discovery will reveal evidence" of a conspiracy. However, only two weeks after issuing its ruling in *Bell Atlantic*, the Court seemingly shifted course back towards a more liberal interpretation of the pleading requirements of Rule 8. In ERICKSON v. PARDUS, 551 U.S. 89, 127 S.Ct. 2197, 167 L.Ed.2d 1081 (2007) (per curiam), the Court concluded that the largely conclusory allegations of an inmate's complaint challenging cruel and unusual prison conditions of his imprisonment satisfied Rule 8's short, plain statement requirement, *Bell Atlantic* notwithstanding. In his civil rights action under 42 U.S.C. §1983, the plaintiff alleged that the prison officials had been indifferent to his medical condition (Hepatitis C) in violation of the Eighth Amendment's prohibition on cruel and unusual punishment. The prisoner's complaint alleged that the termination of his medical treatment "endanger[ed] his life," that he was "still in need of treatment for the disease," and that the defendants "refused to provide treatment." These allegations, the Court determined, were sufficient to satisfy Rule 8(a). The Court declared that allegations of "specific facts are not necessary; the statements necessarily give the defendant fair notice of what the claim in and the grounds on which it rests."

It reversed the court of appeals, which had concluded that the plaintiff's allegations were "too conclusory to establish that plaintiff had suffered a cognizable 'independent harm' as a result of his removal from the Hepatitis C treatment program." As, perhaps, a basis for distinguishing the result in the instant case from *Bell Atlantic*, the Court also emphasized that:

> The Court of Appeals' departure from the liberal pleading standards set forth by Rule 8(a)(2) is even more pronounced in this particular case because petitioner has been proceeding, from the litigation's outset, without counsel. A document filed pro se is to be liberally construed, . . . and a pro se complaint, however inartfully pleaded, must be held to a less stringent standards than formal pleadings drafted by lawyers[.] Cf. Fed. Rule Civ. Proc. 8(f) ("All pleadings shall be so construed as to do substantial justice").

But the suggestion that the *Erickson* Court intended to limit the impact of its prior ruling in *Bell Atlantic* seemingly was contradicted by the Court's ruling two years thereafter in ASHCROFT v. IQBAL, 556 U.S. 662, 129 S.Ct. 1937, 173 L.Ed.2d 868 (2009). There, in a suit filed by a Muslim Pakistani against a group of current and former federal government officials alleging that he had been confined under harsh conditions on the basis of his race, religion, or national origin in violation of the First and Fifth Amendments to the U.S. Constitution, two defendants — the then-Attorney General and the then-Director of the FBI, brought a Rule 12(b)(6) motion to dismiss the claims against them based on allegations that they knew and approved of the imposition of harsh conditions of confinement because of the plaintiff's race, religion, and/or national origin. Without a single reference to *Erickson*, the Court rejected the plaintiff's argument that its ruling in *Bell Atlantic* was intended to be limited to antitrust and/or conspiracy claims. It declared that the decision in *Bell Atlantic* was based on the Court's interpretation of Rule 8 of the Federal Rules of Civil Procedure and, therefore, that the pleading standard set forth in that case applied to all civil actions, including discrimination suits. Applying that standard to the instant case, the Court ruled that since, under governing jurisprudence, these defendants could not be held liable for the unconstitutional conduct of their subordinates under a *respondeat superior* theory, the plaintiff's complaint had to plead facts sufficient to establish that these two defendants, through their own actions, had adopted and implemented the challenged detention policies for the purpose of discriminating on the bases alleged. To survive a motion to dismiss, the Court declared, the complaint must contain sufficient factual matter to state a claim that is, in the words of *Bell Atlantic*, "plausible on its face". And the determination of whether a complaint has facial plausibility is a "context-specific task that requires the reviewing court to draw on its judicial experience and common sense." While requiring less than a "probability" requirement, the Court stated that it would be insufficient to allege facts that permit the court to infer no more than the mere possibility of misconduct.

In EEOC v. CONCENTRA HEALTH SERVICES, INC., 496 F.3d 773 (7th Cir. 2007), the Seventh Circuit affirmed the dismissal with prejudice of the plaintiff EEOC's amended complaint in a §704(a) retaliation case. The court declared that a retaliation plaintiff must provide some specific description of the protected conduct that prompted the alleged retaliatory response. Merely alleging that the retaliation victim had engaged in protected opposition conduct did not provide sufficient specificity to provide the notice required by Rule 8(a)(2). Similarly, in GILBERT v. COUNTRY MUSIC ASSOCIATION, INC., 432 Fed.Appx. 516 (6th Cir. 2011), the

Sixth Circuit held that the assertion only that an avowedly gay Title VII plaintiff was subjected to adverse action because he did not conform to male stereotypes "will not do" to defeat a motion to dismiss. *See also* Fowler v. UPMC Shadyside, 578 F.3d 203 (3d Cir. 2009) (applying *Iqbal* pleading standard to disability discrimination case filed under Rehabilitation Act).   Finally, in SURTAIN v. HAMLIN TERRACE FOUNDATION, 789 F.3d 1239 (11th Cir. 2015), the Eleventh Circuit reiterated its view that a Title VII plaintiff does not need to allege facts sufficient to make out a prima facie case; it is sufficient for the plaintiff to "provide enough factual matter (taken as true) to suggest intentional race discrimination."

3.   The *McDonnell Douglas* prima facie case formulation invariably applies to cases where the plaintiff can only offer circumstantial evidence of the defendant's motivation.   Direct evidence, as contrasted with circumstantial evidence, refers to evidence that, if believed, requires no inferential leap to find the fact that the evidence is offered to prove.   Where direct evidence of bias is available, it typically is deemed sufficient *per se* to establish a prima facie case without resort to the *McDonnell Douglas* formulaic analysis. *See e.g.*, Wright v. Southland Corp., 187 F.3d 1287, 1293 (11th Cir. 1999)

But what constitutes direct evidence sufficient to generate a prima facie case is sometimes unclear or disputed.   For example, if the evidence takes the form of an overtly racist or sexist comment, does it matter whether or not that statement was made by the formal decisionmaker or is it sufficient that it was uttered by a subordinate or other individual whose statement influenced the ultimate decision?   And regardless of who makes the statement, must it refer specifically to the plaintiff or are generalized statements of racial or other bias sufficient?   Some courts have limited direct evidence to statements of bias by decisionmakers that explicitly refer to the allegedly discriminatory decision.   In TAYLOR v. VIRGINIA UNION UNIVERSITY, 193 F.3d 219, 232 (4th Cir. 1999) (en banc*)*, cert. denied, 528 U.S. 1189, 120 S.Ct. 1243, 146 L.Ed.2d 101 (2000), a plaintiff alleged that she had been denied the opportunity to attend a police training school because she was a woman.   The Court of Appeals affirmed summary judgment for the defendant despite testimony that the Police Chief, who decided who would attend the school, said, "I'm never going to send a female to the Police Academy."   According to the Court, the statement did not bear directly on the decision not to send this plaintiff to the training school. *See also* Gorance v. Eagle Food Centers, Inc., 242 F.3d 759, 762 (7th Cir. 2001) ("Bigotry, per se is not actionable.   It is actionable only if it results in injury to a plaintiff; there must be a real link between the bigotry and an adverse employment action.").

What if the direct evidence consists of the decisionmaker's inaction in response to biased statements by a third party?   Some courts have been willing to infer bias from a decisionmaker's inaction in the face of a biased statement by a non-decisionmaker. *See* McDevitt v. Bill Good Builders, Inc., 175 N.J. 519, 531, 816 A.2d 164, 170 (2003) (head nod by employer's president when his secretary stated that plaintiff was discharged because he was "too old" may qualify as direct evidence of unlawful motivation).   This same issue often arises at the final or "pretext" stage of the *McDonnell Douglas* analysis. See Note 5(c), *infra*.

4.   In *Burdine*, the Court stated that the nondiscriminatory explanation offered by the defendants must be "legally sufficient."   Does this mean something other than "nondiscriminatory"?   For example, what if the justification is silly or unethical? *See*

Nix v. WLCY Radio/Rahall Communications, 738 F.2d 1181, 1187 (11th Cir. 1984) ("employer may fire an employee for a good reason, a bad reason, a reason based on erroneous facts, or for no reason at all, as long as its action is not for a discriminatory reason."). The *Burdine* Court also stated that the employer's explanation must be "clear and reasonably specific." This affords the plaintiff some protection against reasons so nebulous or vague as to make disproving them impossible. *See* Robbins v. White-Wilson Medical Clinic, Inc., 660 F.2d 1064, 1067 (5th Cir. 1981) (employer's rejection of applicant because of her "yucky" attitude legally insufficient when viewed in context of evidence in plaintiff's prima facie case). But neither the "legally sufficient" nor "clear and specific" requirement precludes reliance on subjective evaluations of performance or qualifications merely because such assessments can be vehicles for discrimination.

> Subjective interviews could be smokescreens for bias, but in professions such as social work (or law, medicine, architecture, and many others) they are also necessary; no formulary of approved answers can replace a nuanced evaluation of candidates. Nor does federal law require private employers to behave as if they were running bureaucracies, and to prefer paper-heavy evaluations over contextual assessments by knowledgeable reviewers, or to exalt an assessment of past conduct over a prediction of future performance. Unless the evidence demonstrates that an open-ended process was used to evade statutory anti-discriminatory rules, subjectivity cannot be condemned.

Scott v. Parkview Memorial Hospital, 175 F.3d 523, 525 (7th Cir. 1999). Nevertheless, some courts have required the employer to show more than a seat-of-the-pants assessment. In CHAPMAN v. AI TRANSPORT, 229 F.3d 1012, 1034 (11th Cir. 2000) (en banc*),* the court explained:

> A subjective reason is a legally sufficient, legitimate nondiscriminatory reason if the [employer] articulates a clear and reasonably specific factual basis upon which it based its subjective opinion. . . . [I]t might not be sufficient for a defendant employer to say it did not hire the plaintiff applicant simply because "I did not like his appearance" with no further explanation. However, if the defendant employer said, "I did not like his appearance because his hair was uncombed and he had dandruff all over his shoulders" . . . the defendant would have articulated a "clear and reasonably specific" basis for its subjective opinion — the applicant's bad (in the employer's view) appearance. That subjective reason would therefore be a legally sufficient reason for not hiring the plaintiff applicant.

5. As noted in *Burdine,* the plaintiff's burden of establishing a prima facie case is "not onerous." Nor is the burden on the employer great: it is the rare employer who loses a disparate treatment claim on the ground that his articulated reasons for the challenged decision are not legally sufficient. Thus, most disparate treatment cases are resolved at the third, or pretext, stage. The Court stated in *McDonnell Douglas,* and reaffirmed in *Burdine,* that if the defendant rebuts the plaintiff's prima facie case, the plaintiff still can prevail if she can prove that the defendant's "stated reason for [plaintiff's] rejection was in fact pretext." As used in *McDonnell Douglas* and *Burdine,* "pretext" is a false explanation put forward to cover up unlawful discrimination.

(a) Although the courts have held that a plaintiff cannot prove that an employer's stated reasons are pretextual *merely* by showing that the employer was mistaken or relied on incorrect information, s*ee* Pollard v. Rea Magnet Wire Co., 824 F.2d 557 (7th Cir.), cert. denied, 484 U.S. 977, 108 S.Ct. 488, 98 L.Ed.2d 486 (1987) ("A reason honestly described but poorly founded is not a pretext, as that term is used in the law of discrimination."), some of the circuits have recognized some flexibility in this principle through their application of a "honest belief" rule. In the Seventh Circuit, for example, a plaintiff cannot establish pretext "so long as the employer honestly believed in the proffered reason," even if it is shown to be "mistaken, foolish, trivial, or baseless." *See* Kariotis v. Navistar Int'l Trans. Corp., 131 F.3d 672, 676 (7th Cir. 1997). On the other hand, the Sixth Circuit has rejected that approach on the ground that it credits the employer's belief without requiring that the belief be reasonably based on particularized facts, rather than on ignorance or mythology. Accordingly, under its "modified honest belief" doctrine, the Sixth Circuit requires that if, and only if, the plaintiff has come forward with evidence that the defendant's proffered reason appears "mistaken, foolish, trivial, or baseless", the defendant shoulders the burden of coming forward with evidence of specific facts in its possession at the time the decision was made that would reasonably justify its belief in the proffered reason. If the plaintiff meets its burden and the defendant is silent, the case goes to trial. On the other hand, if the defendant can meet this burden of production, the court can still grant summary judgment in its favor. *See* Clay v. United Parcel Service, Inc., 501 F.3d 695 (6th Cir. 2007).

(b) A common method of demonstrating pretext is by proof (usually acquired in discovery) that "similarly situated" employees, to whom the articulated reason could or should have been applied, have in fact been treated more favorably than the plaintiff. But the courts differ on how closely the circumstances of the plaintiff must match those of a comparable employee in order to qualify as "similarly situated". *Compare* Perez v. Texas Dept. of Criminal Justice, 395 F.3d 206, 213 (5th Cir. 2004) ("the jury must find the employees' circumstances to have been nearly identical in order to find them similarly situated.") *with* Ezell v. Potter, 400 F.3d 1041, 1050 (7th Cir. 2005) ("the other employees must engage in similar – not identical – conduct to qualify as similarly situated.").

Alternatively, plaintiffs sometimes seek to rely on "me too" evidence — evidence that other "similarly situated" employees also were subjected to discriminatory conduct. In such cases, the lower courts have struggled with the question of whether the evidence is relevant to the plaintiff's claim and, if so, whether its probative value is exceeded by the prejudicial impact on the defendant. Defendants claim that juries will be distracted by evidence of conduct directed towards other employees, that the cumulative effect of all this "extraneous" information will prejudice their client in the jury's eyes, and that the introduction of this evidence will compel the defendant to defend itself against discrimination claims not asserted in the complaint. In SPRINT/UNITED MANAGEMENT CO. v. MENDELSOHN, 552 U.S. 379, 128 S.Ct. 1140, 170 L.Ed.2d 1 (2008), the plaintiff was terminated during a company-wide reduction in force and alleged that she had been selected for discharge on the basis of her age (51) in violation of the ADEA. As evidence of the employer's allegedly discriminatory animus towards older workers, the plaintiff sought to introduce evidence from former Sprint employees who alleged similar discrimination during the same reduction in force. The defendant moved *in limine* to exclude the evidence as irrelevant under Federal Rule of Evidence 401 or as unduly prejudicial under Rule 403. The trial judge granted the motion by minute order, stating that the plaintiff could only offer evidence of discrimination against "similarly situated" employees and defined "similarly situated employees" as employees who had been supervised by the plaintiff's supervisor and who had been terminated in close temporal proximity to the plaintiff's termination. The case went to a jury which returned a verdict in favor of the defendant. On appeal, the Tenth Circuit construed the district court's ruling to apply a *per se* rule that evidence from employees with other supervisors was irrelevant to prove discrimination, concluded that the trial judge had abused its discretion in excluding the evidence, and therefore reversed and remanded for new trial. In the appellate court's judgment, the evidence was probative of the employer's discriminatory animus towards older workers and its admission was not unduly prejudicial under Rule 403.

The Supreme Court unanimously reversed the Tenth Circuit, concluding that the appellate court had erred in determining that the trial court had adopted a *per se* rule of exclusion. In the Supreme Court's judgment, the record was sufficiently ambiguous to prevent the appellate court from concluding that the trial judge had applied a *per se* rule excluding this form of "me too" evidence. Moreover, the Court continued, the Tenth Circuit also erred in undertaking its own balancing of the probative value and prejudicial impact of the evidence under Rule 403 since that assessment should have been left for the trial judge on remand. The Court further declared, however, that "had the District Court applied a per se rule excluding the evidence," the Tenth Circuit would have been correct in concluding that this constituted an abuse of discretion. Relevance and prejudice determinations under Rules 401 and 403, the Court explained, "are generally not amendable to broad *per se* rules." Whether "me too" evidence of discriminatory conduct by other supervisors is or is not relevant, and, if so, whether its probative value is exceeded by its prejudicial impact, the Court advised, is a fact-intensive, context-specific matter for ad hoc assessment in each individual ADEA case. Thus, the Court stated, albeit in *dictum*, "me too" evidence of conduct by other supervisors is neither *per se* admissible nor *per se* inadmissible. The Court ordered the case remanded to the trial court for a clarification of the basis of its evidentiary rulings in light of these instructions.

(c) Evidence showing that an employer hired or promoted a less qualified applicant over the plaintiff may be probative of whether the employer's proffered reason was pretextual. *See, e.g.,* Taylor v. Runyon, 175 F.3d 861 (11th Cir. 1999). Most circuit courts, however, reasoned that the plaintiff cannot prove pretext simply by introducing evidence of her relatively superior qualifications. Rather, they required a demonstration that the plaintiff was *substantially* better qualified. Many, though not all, circuits vividly described their approach to evidence of comparative qualifications as requiring evidence of a disparity "so apparent as virtually to jump off the page and slap you in the face." *Compare, e.g.,* Deines v. Texas Dep't of Protective and Regulatory Services, 164 F.3d 277, 279 (5th Cir.1999) (upholding jury instruction that "disparities in qualifications are not enough in and of themselves to demonstrate discriminatory intent unless those disparities are so apparent as virtually to jump off the page and slap you in the face.") *with* Raad v. Fairbanks North Star Borough School Dist., 91 FEP Cases 785, 791 (9th Cir. 2003) (plaintiff's superior qualifications to person selected is enough to prove pretext; this circuit has "never followed the Fifth Circuit in holding that disparity in candidates' qualifications 'must be so apparent as to jump off the page and slap us in the face to support a finding of pretext.'"). But in ASH v. TYSON FOODS, INC., 546 U.S. 454, 126 S. Ct. 1195, 163 L.Ed.2d 1053, 163 L.Ed.2d 1053 (2006), the Supreme Court sought to resolve this conflict. In a short *per curiam* opinion, the Court sharply disparaged and summarily dispatched the "jump and slap" standard. "The visual image of words jumping off the page to slap you (presumably a court) in the face," the Court announced, "is unhelpful and imprecise as an elaboration of the standard for inferring pretext from superior qualifications." Resisting the temptation to offer a more precise standard to govern pretext claims based on superior qualifications, the Court simply stated that "some formulation other than the test the Court of Appeals articulated in this case would better ensure that trial courts reach consistent results." 126 S.Ct. at 1198. The Court did, however, cite by way of contrast the standard used by the Eleventh Circuit in another case. There, the court had stated that qualification disparities "must be of such weight and significance that no reasonable person, in the exercise of impartial judgment, could have chosen the candidate selected over the plaintiff for the job in question." On remand, the Eleventh Circuit applied that standard and found that the plaintiff's evidence failed to meet it. Ash v. Tyson Foods, Inc., 190 Fed Appx. 924 (11th Cir. 2006).

Direct evidence in the form of discriminatory statements made by a decisionmaker also can be used by a plaintiff to establish the pretextual nature of the defendant's proffered nondiscriminatory justification. *See, e.g.,* Back v. Hastings on Hudson Union Free School Dist., 365 F.3d 107 (2d Cir. 2004). But biased comments, even by supervisors, that are unconnected with the employment decision in question are frequently described as "stray remarks" — admissible but not alone enough to raise a triable issue on pretext. *See* Indurante v. Local 705, Int'l. Bhd. of Teamsters, 160 F.3d 364, 367 (7th Cir. 1998) (comments by union officials demonstrated hostility toward individuals of Italian heritage but were not made concerning the plaintiff or his termination and were made more than a year prior to the discharge: the expressions of bias constituted evidence of pretext but could not alone demonstrate pretext).

(d) An affirmative action plan normally calls for the employer at some level to take into account race or sex in making employment decisions — exactly the kind of conduct that is generally barred by Title VII and state anti-discrimination laws. The complex history of affirmative action and its uneasy relation with Title VII and the equal protection clause of the Fourteenth Amendment is explored in Part IV, *infra*. At this stage it is enough to say that the Supreme Court has not absolutely barred affirmative action by either private or public employers. Affirmative action may be legally justified as a cure for the effects of past discrimination or other compelling reasons. Normally if an employer acts pursuant to an affirmative action plan and is challenged by a person claiming to be disadvantaged on account of race or sex, the question is whether the plan and its application is justified as either a response to past discrimination or by some other employer-specific reason. *See* Cotter v. City of Boston, 323 F.3d 160 (1st Cir.), cert. denied, 540 U.S. 825, 124 S.Ct. 179, 157 L.Ed.2d 47 (2003). If, however, the employer *denies* acting pursuant to an affirmative action plan, the plan itself constitutes direct evidence of discrimination where the plaintiff establishes that the challenged decision resulted from implementation of the plan. In such instances, this direct evidence of discrimination relieves the plaintiff of proving the case under the *McDonnell Douglas* framework. See Frank v. Xerox Corp., 347 F.3d 130 (5th Cir. 2003).

(e) Disparate treatment cases typically involve questions of intent and credibility, issues not generally appropriate for resolution by motion for summary judgment which, per Federal Rule of Civil Procedure 56, requires the moving party to establish that there is no genuine issue as to any material fact and that the moving party is entitled to a judgment as a matter of law. Nevertheless, many such cases are resolved by summary judgment where the employer presents evidence of a legitimate reason for its action and the plaintiff is unable to convince the court that there is a genuine issue as to the employer's motivation. *See, e.g.*, Adams v. Wal-Mart Stores, Inc., 324 F.3d 935, 940 (7th Cir. 2003) (where the defendant maintained that the plaintiff was discharged for stealing from a co-worker, summary judgment was affirmed because the plaintiff had failed to produce evidence that the decisionmaker did not genuinely believe that the plaintiff had stolen the co-worker's money).

6. In *McDonnell Douglas* the Court noted that "statistics as to [defendant's] employment policy and practice may be helpful" in determining whether its explanation is pretextual particularly where "the racial composition of defendant's labor force is itself reflective of restrictive or exclusionary practices." 411 U.S. at 805, 933 S.Ct. at 1826, 36 L.Ed.2d at 679. The Court cautioned, however that "such general determinations, while helpful, may not be in and of themselves controlling as to an individualized hiring decision." *Id.*, at n.19.

In INTERNATIONAL BROTHERHOOD OF TEAMSTERS v. UNITED STATES, 431 U.S. 324, 339 n.20, 97 S.Ct. 1843, 1857 n.20, 52 L.Ed.2d 396, 418 n.20 (1977), a case involving a claim of class-based disparate treatment, the Court offered a probability-based explanation of the probative value of statistics in disparate treatment cases. "Statistics showing racial or ethnic imbalance are probative . . . only because such imbalance is often a telltale sign of purposeful discrimination; absent explanation, it is ordinarily to be expected that nondiscriminatory hiring practices will in time result in a workforce more or less representative of the racial and ethnic composition of the population in the community from which employees are hired." Simply put, the Court's theory can be reduced to two propositions. First, where there is an otherwise unexplained departure from the expected results of the rules of probability, it is reasonable for a fact-finder to conclude that this general pattern was the product of discrimination. Second, proof of this general pattern tends also to establish that the defendant's decision in the individual case was the consequence of discrimination. But precisely because the probative force of the nexus between a general pattern and an individual decision is not likely to be very strong, few, if any, individual disparate treatment cases are proved by such evidence alone. Thus, even when it is available, statistical evidence usually is tendered as a supplement to other evidence. *See, e.g.*, Smith v. Horner, 839 F.2d 1530 (11th Cir. 1988). In KADAS v. MCI SYSTEMHOUSE CORP., 255 F.3d 359 (7th Cir. 2001), Judge Posner speculated on whether statistical evidence alone could substitute for a prima facie case and thus shift to the employer the burden of production.

> Although it is unlikely that a pure correlation, say between age and terminations, would be enough to establish a prima facie case of intentional discrimination, it would be precipitate to hold that it could never do so. If 100 employees in a department of 1,000 employees were riffed and every one of the 100 was 40 years

old or older and everyone of the 900 retained was under 40, that would, we should think, be enough evidence of age discrimination (the probability of its occurring by chance being inconceivably minute) to place on the employer a burden of explaining, which is all that making out a prima facie case means.

255 F.3d at 363. In many disparate treatment cases, however, no statistical pattern may exist, or, because the work force is so small or the job qualifications so unique, statistically significant data may be unavailable. By way of comparison, statistical evidence plays a crucial, albeit different, role in both class-based claims of intentional discrimination and allegations of nonintentional, i.e., impact-based, discrimination. A more detailed analysis of statistical methodology in employment discrimination litigation will be found in Sections C and D of this chapter.

7. When *McDonnell Douglas* and *Burdine* were decided, the remedies available in Title VII cases (including back pay) were treated as equitable relief and thus jury trials were unavailable. Not until the passage of the Civil Rights Act of 1991 did Congress amend Title VII to allow for legal damages and to provide for jury trials. See *infra* Chapter 7A(3). Clearly, in a jury trial of a disparate treatment case tried under the *McDonnell Douglas/Burdine* framework, the jury must decide the ultimate question of whether the employer's action was the result of unlawful motivation. But what, if anything, should the jury be told about the plaintiff's obligation to establish a prima facie case and the shifting of the burden of production to the employer? Whether the plaintiff has established a prima facie case and whether the employer has satisfied its burden by presenting a sufficiently specific non-discriminatory explanation are matters for the judge to sort out via motions for summary judgment or judgment as a matter of law. Most courts have held that juries should not be instructed on the *McDonnell Douglas/Burdine* burden-shifting framework. *See, e.g.*, Gordon v. New York City Bd. of Education, 232 F.3d 111, 118 (2d Cir. 2000) ("The jury . . . does not need to be lectured on the concepts that guide a judge in determining whether a case should go to the jury."). That said, jury verdicts have not been reversed solely because the trial judge issued a *McDonnell Douglas* instruction. *See* Sanders v. New York City Human Resources Admin., 361 F.3d 749, 758-59 (2d Cir. 2004) (jury instruction on *McDonnell Douglas* burden-shifting scheme was harmless error). In fact, one court has maintained that, "even if the giving of the *McDonnell Douglas* test is not required, it is often beneficial in assisting a jury's comprehension of the issues it has been asked to resolve." Brown v. Packaging Corp. of America, 338 F.3d 586, 598 (6th Cir. 2003).

8. In words that would come back to haunt it on more than one occasion, the *Burdine* Court declared that the plaintiff could establish that the employer's explanation was a pretext for discrimination "either directly by persuading the court that a discriminatory reason more likely motivated the employer or indirectly by showing that the employer's proffered explanation is unworthy of credence." Notwithstanding the seeming clarity of the Court's declaration that a plaintiff could establish pretext, and thus win the case, indirectly simply by meeting the minimal requirement for establishing a prima facie case and proving that the employer's reason was false, this language left lingering doubt in the minds of many lower courts about precisely what could or should be the impact of taking this "indirect" evidentiary route. Some courts construed the language to mean that such a showing by the plaintiff should result in the issuance of judgment as a matter of law in its favor. Others, however, reasoned that such a showing by the plaintiff merely entitled the plaintiff to defeat a defense motion for judgment as a matter of law and submit its case to the jury. Yet a third group insisted that the plaintiff needed to offer additional evidence of the pretextual nature of the defendant's explanation simply to avoid judgment as a matter of law.

The Supreme Court did little to clarify its intentions in its next disparate treatment case, UNITED STATES POSTAL SERVICE Bd. OF GOVERNORS v. AIKENS, 460 U.S. 711, 103 S.Ct. 1478, 75 L.Ed.2d 403 (1983). In *Aikens*, the Court emphasized that once the prima facie case was rebutted, the factual inquiry for the court was whether the defendant intentionally discriminated against the plaintiff, but the Court repeated its language from *Burdine* suggesting that there were two alternate routes by which the plaintiff could satisfy her burden. Rather unhelpfully the Court added, "the district court must decide which party's explanation of the employer's motivation it believes." In a concurring opinion, Justice Blackmun stressed that while "the ultimate determination of factual liability in discrimination cases should be no different from that in other types of civil suits, . . . the McDonnell Douglas framework requires that a plaintiff prevail when at the third stage of a Title VII trial he demonstrates that the legitimate, nondiscriminatory reason given by the employer is in fact not the true reason for the employment decision." Following *Aikens* the circuit courts remained divided on the question of whether a plaintiff could prevail at the "third stage" of a disparate treatment case by proof that the employer's reason was false without also establishing affirmatively that an unlawful motivation lay behind the employer's action. A decade after its decision in *Aikens*, the Supreme Court revisited the issue of the plaintiff's burden.

St. Mary's Honor Center v. Hicks

Supreme Court of the United States, 1993.
509 U.S. 502, 113 S.Ct. 2742; 125 L.Ed. 2d 407.

JUSTICE SCALIA delivered the opinion of the Court.

We granted certiorari to determine whether, in a suit against an employer alleging intentional racial discrimination in violation of §703(a)(1) of Title VII of the Civil Rights Act of 1964, the trier of fact's rejection of the employer's asserted reasons for its actions mandates a finding for the plaintiff.

I

Petitioner St. Mary's Honor Center (St. Mary's) is a halfway house operated by the Missouri Department of Corrections and Human Resources (MDCHR). Respondent Melvin Hicks, a black man, was hired as a correctional officer at St. Mary's in August 1978 and was promoted to shift commander, one of six supervisory positions, in February 1980.

In 1983 MDCHR conducted an investigation of the administration of St. Mary's, which resulted in extensive supervisory changes in January 1984. Respondent retained his position, but John Powell became the new chief of custody (respondent's immediate supervisor) and petitioner Steve Long the new superintendent. Prior to these personnel changes respondent had enjoyed a satisfactory employment record, but soon thereafter became the subject of repeated, and increasingly severe, disciplinary actions. He was suspended for five days for violations of institutional rules by his subordinates on March 3, 1984. He received a letter of reprimand for alleged failure to conduct an adequate investigation of a brawl between inmates that occurred during his shift on March 21. He was later demoted from shift commander to correctional officer for his failure to ensure that his subordinates entered their use of a St. Mary's vehicle into the official log book on March 19, 1984. Finally, on June 7, 1984, he was discharged for threatening Powell during an exchange of heated words on April 19.

Respondent brought this suit * * * alleging that petitioner St. Mary's violated §703(a)(1) of Title VII * * * by demoting and then discharging him because of his race. After a full bench trial, the District Court found for petitioners. The Eighth Circuit reversed and remanded and we granted certiorari.

II

* * *

With the goal of "progressively . . . sharpening the inquiry into the elusive factual question of intentional discrimination," *Texas Department of Community Affairs v. Burdine*, our opinion in *McDonnell Douglas Corp. v. Green*, established an allocation of the burden of production and an order for the presentation of proof in Title VII discriminatory-treatment cases. The plaintiff in such a case, we said, must first establish, by a preponderance of the evidence, a "*prima facie*" case of racial discrimination. Petitioners do not challenge the District Court's finding that respondent satisfied the minimal requirements of such a *prima facie* case by proving (1) that he is black, (2) that he was qualified for the position of shift commander, (3) that he was demoted from that position and ultimately discharged, and (4) that the position remained open and was ultimately filled by a white man.

Under the *McDonnell Douglas* scheme, "establishment of the *prima facie* case in effect creates a presumption that the employer unlawfully discriminated against the employee." *Burdine*. To establish a "presumption" is to say that a finding of the predicate fact (here, the prima facie case) produces "a required conclusion in the absence of explanation" (here, the finding of unlawful discrimination). Thus, the *McDonnell Douglas* presumption places upon the defendant the burden of producing an explanation to rebut the *prima facie* case — i.e., the burden of "producing evidence" that the adverse employment actions were taken "for a legitimate, nondiscriminatory reason." *Burdine*. The defendant must clearly set forth, through the introduction of admissible evidence, reasons for its actions which, *if believed by the trier of fact*, would support a finding that unlawful discrimination was not the cause of the employment action. It is important to note, however, that although the *McDonnell Douglas* presumption shifts the burden of production to the defendant, "the ultimate burden of persuading the trier of fact that the defendant intentionally discriminated against the plaintiff remains at all times with the plaintiff." * * *

Respondent does not challenge the District Court's finding that petitioners sustained their burden of production by introducing evidence of two legitimate, nondiscriminatory reasons for their actions: the severity and the accumulation of rules violations committed by respondent. Our cases make clear that at that point the shifted burden of production became irrelevant: "If the defendant carries this burden of production, the presumption raised by the *prima facie* case is rebutted" and "drops from the case." *Burdine*. The plaintiff then has "the full and fair opportunity to demonstrate," through presentation of his own case and through cross-examination of the defendant's witnesses, "that the proffered reason was not the true reason for the employment decision," Id., and that race was. He retains that "ultimate burden of persuading the [trier of fact] that [he] has been the victim of intentional discrimination."

The District Court, acting as trier of fact in this bench trial, found that the reasons petitioners gave were not the real reasons for respondent's demotion and discharge. It found that respondent was the only supervisor disciplined for violations committed by his subordinates; that similar and even more serious violations committed by respondent's coworkers were either disregarded or treated more leniently; and that Powell manufactured the final verbal confrontation in order to provoke respondent into threatening him. It nonetheless held that respondent had failed to carry his ultimate burden of proving that *his race* was the determining factor in petitioners' decision first to demote and then to dismiss him.[2] In short, the District Court concluded that "although [respondent] has proven the existence of a crusade to terminate him, he has not proven that the crusade was racially rather than personally motivated."

The Court of Appeals set this determination aside on the ground that "[o]nce [respondent] proved all of [petitioners'] proffered reasons for the adverse employment actions to be pretextual, [respondent] was entitled to judgment as a matter of law." 970 F.2d at 492. The Court of Appeals reasoned:

> Because all of defendants' proffered reasons were discredited, defendants were in a position of having offered no legitimate reason for their actions. In other words, defendants were in no better position than if they had remained silent, offering no rebuttal to an established inference that they had unlawfully discriminated against plaintiff on the basis of his race. *Ibid.*

That is not so. By producing *evidence* (whether ultimately persuasive or not) of nondiscriminatory reasons, petitioners sustained their burden of production, and thus placed themselves in a "better position than if they had remained silent."

In the nature of things, the determination that a defendant has met its burden of production (and has thus rebutted any legal presumption of intentional discrimination) can involve no credibility assessment. For the burden-of-production determination necessarily precedes the credibility-assessment stage. At the close of the defendant's case, the court is asked to decide whether an issue of fact remains for the trier of fact to determine. None does if, on the evidence presented, (1) any rational person would have to find the existence of facts constituting a *prima facie* case, and (2) the defendant has failed to meet its burden of production — i.e., has failed to introduce evidence which, *taken as true*, would *permit* the conclusion that there was a nondiscriminatory reason for the adverse action. In that event, the court must award judgment to the plaintiff as a matter of law under Federal Rule of Civil Procedure 50(a)(1) (in the case of jury trials) or Federal Rule of Civil 52(c) (in the case of bench trials). If the defendant has failed to sustain its burden but reasonable minds *could*

---

[2]Various considerations led it to this conclusion, including the fact that two blacks sat on the disciplinary review board that recommended disciplining respondent, that respondent's black subordinates who actually committed the violations were not disciplined, and that "the number of black employees at St. Mary's remained constant." 756 F. Supp. 1244, 1252 (ED Mo. 1991).

differ as to whether a preponderance of the evidence establishes the facts of a *prima facie* case, then a question of fact *does* remain, which the trier of fact will be called upon to answer.[3]

If, on the other hand, the defendant has succeeded in carrying its burden of production, the *McDonnell Douglas* framework — with its presumptions and burdens — is no longer relevant. To resurrect it later, after the trier of fact has determined that what was "produced" to meet the burden of production is not credible, flies in the face of our holding in *Burdine* that to rebut the presumption "[t]he defendant need not persuade the court that it was actually motivated by the proffered reasons." The presumption, having fulfilled its role of forcing the defendant to come forward with some response, simply drops out of the picture. The defendant's "production" (whatever its persuasive effect) having been made, the trier of fact proceeds to decide the ultimate question: whether plaintiff has proven "that the defendant intentionally discriminated against [him]" because of his race. The factfinder's disbelief of the reasons put forward by the defendant (particularly if disbelief is accompanied by a suspicion of mendacity) may, together with the elements of the *prima facie* case, suffice to show intentional discrimination. Thus, rejection of the defendant's proffered reasons, will *permit* the trier of fact to infer the ultimate fact of intentional discrimination,[4] and the Court of Appeals was correct when it noted that, upon such rejection, "[n]o additional proof of discrimination is *required*." But the Court of Appeals' holding that rejection of the defendant's proffered reasons *compels* judgment for the plaintiff disregards the fundamental principle of Rule 301 that a presumption does not shift the burden of proof, and ignores our repeated admonition that the Title

---

[3]If the finder of fact answers affirmatively — if it finds that the prima facie case *is* supported by a preponderance of the evidence — it *must* find the existence of the presumed fact of unlawful discrimination and *must*, therefore, render a verdict for the plaintiff. See Texas Dept. of Community Affairs v. Burdine, *supra.* Thus, the *effect* of failing to produce evidence to rebut the McDonnell Douglas Corp. v. Green presumption is not felt until the prima facie case has been *established*, either as a matter of law (because the plaintiff's facts are uncontested) or by the factfinder's determination that the plaintiff's facts are supported by a preponderance of the evidence. It is thus technically accurate to describe the sequence as we did in *Burdine*:

"First, the plaintiff has the burden of proving by the preponderance of the evidence a prima facie case of discrimination. Second, if the plaintiff succeeds in proving the prima facie case, the burden shifts to the defendant to articulate some legitimate, nondiscriminatory reason for the employee's rejection."

As a practical matter, however, and in the real-life sequence of a trial, the defendant *feels* the "burden" not when the plaintiff's prima facie case is *proved*, but as soon as evidence of it is *introduced*. The defendant then knows that its failure to introduce evidence of a nondiscriminatory reason will cause judgment to go against it *unless* the plaintiff's prima facie case is held to be inadequate in law or fails to convince the factfinder. It is this practical coercion which causes the *McDonnell Douglas* presumption to function as a means of "arranging the presentation of evidence," Watson v. Fort Worth Bank & Trust, 487 U.S. 977, 986, 101 L. Ed. 2d 827, 108 S. Ct. 2777 (1988).

[4]Contrary to the dissent's confusion-producing analysis, there is nothing whatever inconsistent between this statement and our later statements that (1) the plaintiff must show "*both* that the reason was false, *and* that discrimination was the real reason," and (2) "it is not enough . . . to *dis*believe the employer." Even though (as we say here) rejection of the defendant's proffered reasons is enough at law to *sustain* a finding of discrimination, *there must be a finding of discrimination.*

VII plaintiff at all times bears the "ultimate burden of persuasion." See, e.g., *Aikens*, *supra*.

III

Only one unfamiliar with our case-law will be upset by the dissent's alarm that we are today setting aside "settled precedent," "two decades of stable law in this Court," "a framework carefully crafted in precedents as old as 20 years," which "Congress is [aware]" of and has implicitly approved. Panic will certainly not break out among the courts of appeals, whose divergent views concerning the nature of the supposedly "stable law in this Court" are precisely what prompted us to take this case — a divergence in which the dissent's version of "settled precedent" cannot remotely be considered the "prevailing view." * * * We mean to answer the dissent's accusations in detail, by examining our cases, but at the outset it is worth noting the utter implausibility that we would ever have held what the dissent says we held.

* * *

Here (in the context of the now-permissible jury trials for Title VII causes of action) is what the dissent asserts we have held to be a proper assessment of liability for violation of this law: Assume that 40% of a business' work force are members of a particular minority group, a group which comprises only 10% of the relevant labor market. An applicant, who is a member of that group, applies for an opening for which he is minimally qualified, but is rejected by a hiring officer of that *same minority group*, and the search to fill the opening continues. The rejected applicant files suit for racial discrimination under Title VII, and before the suit comes to trial, the supervisor who conducted the company's hiring is fired. Under *McDonnell Douglas*, the plaintiff has a *prima facie* case, and under the dissent's interpretation of our law not only must the company come forward with some explanation for the refusal to hire (which it will have to try to confirm out of the mouth of its now antagonistic former employee), but the jury must be instructed that, if they find that explanation to be *incorrect*, they must assess damages against the company, *whether or not they believe the company was guilty of racial discrimination*. The disproportionate minority makeup of the company's work force and the fact that its hiring officer was of the same minority group as the plaintiff will be irrelevant, because the plaintiff's case can be proved "indirectly by showing that the employer's proffered explanation is unworthy of credence."[5] Surely nothing short of inescapable prior *holdings* (the dissent does not pretend there are any) should make one assume that this is the law we have created.

---

[5]The dissent has no response to this (not at all unrealistic) hypothetical, except to assert that *surely* the employer must have "personnel records" to which it can resort to demonstrate the reason for the failure to hire. The notion that every reasonable employer keeps "personnel records" on people who never became personnel, showing *why* they did not become personnel (*i.e.*, in what respects all other people who were hired were better) seems to us highly fanciful — or for the sake of American business we hope it is. But more fundamentally, the dissent's response misses the point. Even if such "personnel records" *do* exist, it is a mockery of justice to say that if the jury believes the reason they set forth is probably *not* the "true" one, all the other utterly compelling evidence that discrimination was not the reason will then be excluded from the jury's consideration.

We have no authority to impose liability upon an employer for alleged discriminatory employment practices unless an appropriate factfinder determines, according to proper procedures, *that the employer has unlawfully discriminated.* We may, according to traditional practice, establish certain modes and orders of proof, including an initial rebuttable presumption of the sort we described earlier in this opinion, which we believe *McDonnell Douglas* represents. But nothing in law would permit us to substitute for the required finding that the employer's action was the product of unlawful discrimination, the much different (and much lesser) finding that the employer's explanation of its action was not believable. The dissent's position amounts to precisely this, *unless* what is required to establish the *McDonnell Douglas* prima facie case is a degree of proof so high that it would, in absence of rebuttal, require a directed verdict for the plaintiff (for in that case proving the employer's rebuttal noncredible would leave the plaintiff's directed-verdict case in place, and compel a judgment in his favor). Quite obviously, however, what is required to establish the *McDonnell Douglas* prima facie case is infinitely less than what a directed verdict demands. The dissent is thus left with a position that has no support in the statute, no support in the reason of the matter, no support in any holding of this Court (that is not even contended), and support, if at all, only in the dicta of this Court's opinions. It is to those that we now turn — begrudgingly, since we think it generally undesirable, where holdings of the Court are not at issue, to dissect the sentences of the United States Reports as though they were the United States Code.

The principal case on which the dissent relies is *Burdine.* While there are some statements in that opinion that could be read to support the dissent's position, all but one of them bear a meaning consistent with our interpretation, and the one exception is simply incompatible with other language in the case. *Burdine* describes the situation that obtains after the employer has met its burden of adducing a nondiscriminatory reason as follows: "Third, should the defendant carry this burden, the plaintiff must then have an opportunity to prove by a preponderance of the evidence that the legitimate reasons offered by the defendant were not its true reasons, but were a pretext for discrimination." The dissent takes this to mean that if the plaintiff proves the asserted reason to be *false,* the plaintiff wins. But a reason cannot be proved to be "a pretext for *discrimination*" unless it is shown *both* that the reason was false, *and* that discrimination was the real reason. *Burdine's* later allusions to proving or demonstrating simply "pretext," are reasonably understood to refer to the previously described pretext, *i.e.,* "pretext for discrimination."

Burdine also says that when the employer has met its burden of production "the factual inquiry proceeds to a new level of specificity." The dissent takes this to mean that the factual inquiry reduces to whether the employer's asserted reason is true or false — if false, the defendant loses. But the "new level of specificity" may also (as we believe) refer to the fact that the inquiry now turns from the few generalized factors that establish a *prima facie* case to the specific proofs and rebuttals of discriminatory motivation the parties have introduced.

In the next sentence, *Burdine* says that "[p]lacing this burden of production on the defendant thus serves . . . to frame the factual issue with sufficient clarity so that the plaintiff will have a full and fair opportunity to demonstrate pretext." The dissent thinks this means that the only factual issue remaining in the case is whether the employer's reason is false. But since in our view "pretext" means "pretext for discrimination," we think the sentence must be understood as addressing the form rather than the substance of the defendant's production burden: The requirement that the employer "clearly set forth" its reasons, gives the plaintiff a "full and fair" rebuttal opportunity.

A few sentences later, *Burdine* says: "[The plaintiff] now must have the opportunity to demonstrate that the proffered reason was not the true reason for the employment decision. This burden now merges with the ultimate burden of persuading the court that she has been the victim of intentional discrimination." The dissent takes this "merger" to mean that "the ultimate burden of persuading the court that she has been the victim of intentional discrimination" is *replaced* by the mere burden of "demonstrating that the proffered reason was not the true reason for the employment decision." But that would be a merger in which the little fish swallows the big one. Surely a more reasonable reading is that proving the employer's reason false becomes part of (and often considerably assists) the greater enterprise of proving that the real reason was intentional discrimination.

Finally, in the next sentence *Burdine* says: "[The plaintiff] may succeed in this [*i.e.*, in persuading the court that she has been the victim of intentional discrimination] either directly by persuading the court that a discriminatory reason more likely motivated the employer or indirectly by showing that the employer's proffered explanation is unworthy of credence." We must agree with the dissent on this one: The words bear no other meaning but that the falsity of the employer's explanation is *alone enough* to compel judgment for the plaintiff. The problem is, that that dictum contradicts or renders inexplicable numerous other statements, both in *Burdine* itself and in our later case-law — commencing with the very citation of authority *Burdine* uses to support the proposition. *McDonnell Douglas* does not say, at the cited pages or elsewhere, that all the plaintiff need do is disprove the employer's asserted reason. In fact, it says just the opposite: "[O]n the retrial respondent must be given a full and fair opportunity to demonstrate by competent evidence that the presumptively valid reasons for his rejection *were in fact a cover-up for a racially discriminatory decision*." "We . . . insist that respondent under §703(a)(1) must be given a full and fair opportunity to demonstrate by competent evidence *that whatever the stated reasons for his rejection, the decision was in reality racially premised*." The statement in question also contradicts *Burdine's* repeated assurance (indeed, its holding) regarding the burden of persuasion: "The ultimate burden of persuading the trier of fact that the defendant intentionally discriminated against the plaintiff remains at all times with the plaintiff." "The plaintiff retains the burden of persuasion." And lastly, the statement renders inexplicable *Burdine's* explicit reliance, in describing the shifting burdens of *McDonnell Douglas*, upon authorities setting forth the classic law of presumptions we have described earlier. In light of these inconsistencies, we think that the dictum at issue here must be regarded as an inadvertence, to the extent that it describes disproof of the defendant's reason as a totally independent, rather than an auxiliary, means of proving unlawful intent.

In sum, our interpretation of *Burdine* creates difficulty with one sentence; the dissent's interpretation causes many portions of the opinion to be incomprehensible or deceptive. But whatever doubt *Burdine* might have created was eliminated by *Aikens*. There we said, in language that cannot reasonably be mistaken, that "the ultimate question [is] discrimination *vel non*." Once the defendant "responds to the plaintiff's proof by offering evidence of the reason for the plaintiff's rejection, the factfinder must then decide" *not* (as the dissent would have it) whether that evidence is credible, but "whether the rejection was discriminatory within the meaning of Title VII." At that stage, we said, "[t]he District Court was . . . in a position to decide the ultimate factual issue in the case," which is "whether the defendant intentionally discriminated against the plaintiff." The *McDonnell Douglas* methodology was "'never intended to be rigid, mechanized, or ritualistic.'" Rather, once the defendant has responded to the plaintiff's *prima facie* case, "the district court has before it all the evidence it needs to decide" *not* (as the dissent would have it) whether defendant's response is credible, but "whether the defendant intentionally discriminated against the plaintiff." "On the state of the record at the close of the evidence, the District Court in this case should have proceeded to this specific question directly, just as district courts decide disputed questions of fact in other civil litigation." *In confirmation of this* (rather than in contradiction of it), the Court then quotes the problematic passage from *Burdine*, which says that the plaintiff may carry her burden either directly "'or indirectly by showing that the employer's proffered explanation is unworthy of credence.'" It then characterizes that passage as follows: "In short, the district court must decide which party's explanation of the employer's motivation it believes." It is not enough, in other words, to *dis*believe the employer; the factfinder must *believe* the plaintiff's explanation of intentional discrimination. It is noteworthy that Justice Blackmun, although joining the Court's opinion in *Aikens*, wrote a separate concurrence for the sole purpose of saying that he understood the Court's opinion to be saying what the dissent today asserts. That concurrence was joined only by Justice Brennan. Justice Marshall would have none of that, but simply refused to join the Court's opinion, concurring without opinion in the judgment. We think there is little doubt what *Aikens* meant.

IV

We turn, finally, to the dire practical consequences that the respondents and the dissent claim our decision today will produce. What appears to trouble the dissent more than anything is that, in its view, our rule is adopted "for the benefit of employers who have been found to have given false evidence in a court of law," whom we "favo[r]" by "exempting them from responsibility for lies." As we shall explain, our rule in no way gives special favor to those employers whose evidence is disbelieved. But initially we must point out that there is no justification for assuming (as the dissent repeatedly does) that those employers whose evidence is disbelieved are perjurers and liars. * * * Even if these were typically cases in which an individual defendant's sworn assertion regarding a physical occurrence was pitted against an individual plaintiff's sworn assertion regarding the same physical occurrence, surely it would be imprudent to call the party whose assertion is (by a mere preponderance of the evidence) disbelieved, a perjurer and a liar. And in these Title VII cases, the defendant is ordinarily *not* an individual but a company, which must rely upon the statement of an employee — often a relatively low-level employee — as to the central fact; and that central fact is not a physical occurrence, but rather that employee's state of mind. To say that the company which in good faith introduces such testimony, or even the testifying employee himself, becomes a liar and a perjurer when the testimony is not believed, is nothing short of absurd.

Undoubtedly some employers (or at least their employees) will be lying. But even if we could readily identify these perjurers, what an extraordinary notion, that we "exempt them from responsibility for their lies" unless we enter Title VII judgments for the plaintiffs! Title VII is not a cause of action for perjury; we have other civil and criminal remedies for that. The dissent's notion of judgment-for-lying is seen to be not even a fair and even-handed punishment for vice, when one realizes how strangely selective it is: the employer is free to lie to its heart's content about whether the plaintiff ever applied for a job, about how long he worked, how much he made — indeed, about anything and everything *except* the reason for the adverse employment action. And the plaintiff is permitted to lie about absolutely *everything* without losing a verdict he otherwise deserves. This is not a major, or even a sensible, blow against fibbery.

The respondent's argument based upon the employer's supposed lying is a more modest one: "A defendant which unsuccessfully offers a 'phony reason' logically cannot be in a better legal position [i.e., the position of having overcome the presumption from the plaintiff's *prima facie* case] than a defendant who remains silent, and offers no reasons at all for its conduct." But there is no anomaly in that, once one recognizes that the *McDonnell Douglas* presumption is a *procedural* device, designed only to establish an order of proof and production. The books are full of procedural rules that place the perjurer (initially, at least) in a better position than the truthful litigant who makes no response at all. A defendant who fails to answer a complaint will, on motion, suffer a default judgment that a deceitful response could have avoided. Fed. Rule Civ. Proc. 55(a). A defendant whose answer fails to contest critical averments in the complaint will, on motion, suffer a judgment on the pleadings that untruthful denials could have avoided. Rule 12(c). And a defendant who fails to submit affidavits creating a genuine issue of fact in response to a motion for summary judgment will suffer a dismissal that false affidavits could have avoided. Rule 56(e). In all of those cases, as under the *McDonnell Douglas* framework, perjury may purchase the defendant a chance at the factfinder — though there, as here, it also carries substantial risks, see Rules 11 and 56(g); 18 U.S.C. §1621.

The dissent repeatedly raises a procedural objection that is impressive only to one who mistakes the basic nature of the *McDonnell Douglas* procedure. It asserts that "the Court now holds that the further enquiry [i.e., the inquiry that follows the employer's response to the prima facie case] is wide open, not limited at all by the scope of the employer's proffered explanation." The plaintiff cannot be expected to refute "reasons not articulated by the employer, but discerned in the record by the factfinder." He should not "be saddled with the tremendous disadvantage of having to confront, not the defined task of proving the employer's stated reasons to be false, but the amorphous requirement of disproving all possible nondiscriminatory reasons that a factfinder might find lurking in the record." "Under the scheme announced today, any conceivable explanation for the employer's actions that might be suggested by the evidence, however unrelated to the employer's articulated reasons, must be addressed by [the plaintiff]." These statements imply that the employer's "proffered explanation," his "stated reasons," his "articulated reasons," somehow exist *apart from the record* — in some pleading, or perhaps in some formal, nontestimonial statement made on behalf of the defendant to the factfinder. * * * Of course it does not work like that. The reasons the defendant sets forth are set forth "through the introduction of admissible evidence." *Burdine*. In other words, the defendant's "articulated reasons" *themselves* are to be found "lurking in the record." It thus makes no sense to contemplate "the employer who is caught in a lie, but succeeds in *injecting* into the trial an *unarticulated* reason for its actions." There is a "lurking-in-the-record" problem, but it exists not for us but for the dissent. *If*, after the employer has met its preliminary burden, the plaintiff need not prove discrimination (and therefore need not disprove all other reasons suggested, no matter how vaguely, in the record) there must be some device for determining which particular portions of the record represent "articulated reasons" set forth with sufficient clarity to satisfy *McDonnell Douglas* — since it is only *that* evidence which the plaintiff must refute. But of course our *McDonnell Douglas* framework makes no provision for such a determination, which would have to be made not at the close of the trial but *in medias res*, since otherwise the plaintiff would not know what evidence to offer. It makes no sense.

Respondent contends that "[t]he litigation decision of the employer to place in controversy only . . . particular explanations eliminates from further consideration the alternative explanations that the employer chose not to advance." The employer should bear, he contends, "the responsibility for its choices and the risk that plaintiff will disprove any pretextual reasons *and therefore prevail*." It is the "therefore" that is problematic. Title VII does not award damages against employers who cannot prove a nondiscriminatory reason for adverse employment action, but only against employers who are proven to have taken adverse employment action by reason of (in the context of the present case) race. That the employer's proffered reason is unpersuasive, or even obviously contrived, does not necessarily establish that the plaintiff's proffered reason of race is correct. That remains a question for the factfinder to answer, subject, of course, to appellate review — which should be conducted on remand in this case under the "clearly erroneous" standard of Federal Rule of Civil Procedure 52(a), see, e.g., *Anderson v. Bessemer City*, 470 U.S. 564, 573-576, 84 L. Ed. 2d 518, 105 S. Ct. 1504 (1985).

Finally, respondent argues that it "would be particularly ill-advised" for us to come forth with the holding we pronounce today "just as Congress has provided a right to jury trials in Title VII" cases. See §102 of the Civil Rights Act of 1991. (providing jury trial right in certain Title VII suits). We think quite the opposite is true. Clarity regarding the requisite elements of proof becomes all the more important when a jury must be instructed concerning them, and when detailed factual findings by the trial court will not be available upon review.

* * *

We reaffirm today what we said in *Aikens*:

[T]he question facing triers of fact in discrimination cases is both sensitive and difficult. The prohibitions against discrimination contained in the Civil Rights Act of 1964 reflect an important national policy. There will seldom be 'eyewitness' testimony as to the employer's mental processes. But none of this means that trial courts or reviewing courts should treat discrimination differently from other ultimate questions of fact. Nor should they make their inquiry even more difficult by applying legal rules which were devised to govern 'the basic allocation of burdens and order of presentation of proof,' in deciding this ultimate question.

The judgment of the Court of Appeals is reversed, and the case is remanded for further proceedings consistent with this opinion.

It is so ordered.

JUSTICE SOUTER, with whom JUSTICE WHITE, JUSTICE BLACKMUN, and JUSTICE STEVENS join, dissenting.

Twenty years ago, in *McDonnell Douglas Corp. v. Green*, this Court unanimously prescribed a "sensible, orderly way to evaluate the evidence" in a Title VII disparate-treatment case, giving both plaintiff and defendant fair opportunities to litigate "in light of common experience as it bears on the critical question of discrimination." *Furnco Construction Corp. v. Waters.* We have repeatedly reaffirmed and refined the *McDonnell Douglas* framework, most notably in *Texas Department of Community Affairs v. Burdine*, another unanimous opinion. But today, after two decades of stable law in this Court and only relatively recent disruption in some of the Circuits, the Court abandons this practical framework together with its central purpose, which is "to sharpen the inquiry into the elusive factual question of intentional discrimination." *Burdine.*. Ignoring language to the contrary in both *McDonnell Douglas* and *Burdine*, the Court holds that, once a Title VII plaintiff succeeds in showing at trial that the defendant has come forward with pretextual reasons for its actions in response to a prima facie showing of discrimination, the factfinder still may proceed to roam the record, searching for some nondiscriminatory explanation that the defendant has not raised and that the plaintiff has had no fair opportunity to disprove. Because the majority departs from settled precedent in substituting a scheme of proof for disparate-treatment actions that promises to be unfair and unworkable, I respectfully dissent.

* * *

At the outset, under the *McDonnell Douglas* framework, a plaintiff alleging disparate treatment in the workplace in violation of Title VII must provide the basis for an inference of discrimination. In this case, as all agree, Melvin Hicks met this initial burden by proving by a preponderance of the evidence that he was black and therefore a member of a protected class; he was qualified to be a shift commander; he was demoted and then terminated; and his position remained available and was later filled by a qualified applicant.[1] Hicks thus proved what we have called a "*prima facie* case" of discrimination, and it is important to note that in this context a prima facie case is indeed a proven case. Although, in other contexts, a *prima facie* case only requires production of enough evidence to raise an issue for the trier of fact, here it means that the plaintiff has actually established the elements of the *prima facie* case to the satisfaction of the factfinder by a preponderance of the evidence. By doing so, Hicks "eliminate[d] the most common nondiscriminatory reasons" for demotion and firing: that he was unqualified for the position or that the position was no longer available. Given our assumption that "people do not act in a totally arbitrary manner, without any underlying reasons, especially in a business setting," we have explained that a *prima*

---

[1]The majority, following the courts below, mentions that Hicks's position was filled by a white male. This Court has not directly addressed the question whether the personal characteristics of someone chosen to replace a Title VII plaintiff are material, and that issue is not before us today.

facie case implies discrimination "because we presume [the employer's] acts, if otherwise unexplained, are more likely than not based on the consideration of impermissible factors." *Furnco*.

Under *McDonnell Douglas* and *Burdine*, however, proof of a *prima facie* case not only raises an inference of discrimination; in the absence of further evidence, it also creates a mandatory presumption in favor of the plaintiff. Although the employer bears no trial burden at all until the plaintiff proves his *prima facie* case, once the plaintiff does so the employer must either respond or lose. As we made clear in *Burdine*, "If the employer is silent in the face of the presumption, the court *must* enter judgment for the plaintiff." (in these circumstances, the factfinder "*must* find the existence of the presumed fact of unlawful discrimination and *must*, therefore, render a verdict for the plaintiff") (emphasis in original). Thus, if the employer remains silent because it acted for a reason it is too embarrassed to reveal, or for a reason it fails to discover, the plaintiff is entitled to judgment under *Burdine*.

Obviously, it would be unfair to bar an employer from coming forward at this stage with a nondiscriminatory explanation for its actions, since the lack of an open position and the plaintiff's lack of qualifications do not exhaust the set of nondiscriminatory reasons that might explain an adverse personnel decision. If the trier of fact could not consider other explanations, employers' autonomy would be curtailed far beyond what is needed to rectify the discrimination identified by Congress. On the other hand, it would be equally unfair and utterly impractical to saddle the victims of discrimination with the burden of either producing direct evidence of discriminatory intent or eliminating the entire universe of possible nondiscriminatory reasons for a personnel decision. The Court in *McDonnell Douglas* reconciled these competing interests in a very sensible way by requiring the employer to "articulate," through the introduction of admissible evidence, one or more "legitimate, nondiscriminatory reason[s]" for its actions. Proof of a *prima facie* case thus serves as a catalyst obligating the employer to step forward with an explanation for its actions. St. Mary's, in this case, used this opportunity to provide two reasons for its treatment of Hicks: the severity and accumulation of rule infractions he had allegedly committed.

The Court emphasizes that the employer's obligation at this stage is only a burden of production, and that, if the employer meets the burden, the presumption entitling the plaintiff to judgment "drops from the case." This much is certainly true,[2] but the obligation also serves an important function neglected by the majority, in requiring the employer "to frame the factual issue with sufficient clarity so that the plaintiff will have a full and fair opportunity to demonstrate pretext." The employer, in other words, has a "burden of production" that gives it the right to choose the scope of the factual issues to be resolved by the factfinder. But investing the employer with this

---

[2]The majority contends that it would "fl[y] in the face of our holding in *Burdine*" to "resurrect" this mandatory presumption at a later stage, in cases where the plaintiff proves that the employer's proffered reasons are pretextual. Hicks does not argue to the contrary. The question presented in this case is not whether the mandatory presumption is resurrected (everyone agrees that it is not), but whether the factual enquiry is narrowed by the *McDonnell Douglas* framework to the question of pretext.

choice has no point unless the scope it chooses binds the employer as well as the plaintiff. Nor does it make sense to tell the employer, as this Court has done, that its explanation of legitimate reasons "must be clear and reasonably specific," if the factfinder can rely on a reason not clearly articulated, or on one not articulated at all, to rule in favor of the employer.[3] ("An articulation not admitted into evidence will not suffice").

Once the employer chooses the battleground in this manner, "the factual inquiry proceeds to a new level of specificity." During this final, more specific enquiry, the employer has no burden to prove that its proffered reasons are true; rather, the plaintiff must prove by a preponderance of the evidence that the proffered reasons are pretextual. *McDonnell Douglas* makes it clear that if the plaintiff fails to show "pretext," the challenged employment action "must stand." If, on the other hand, the plaintiff carries his burden of showing "pretext," the court "must order a prompt and appropriate remedy."[5] Or, as we said in *Burdine*: "[The plaintiff] now must have the opportunity to demonstrate that the proffered reason was not the true reason for the employment decision. This burden now merges with the ultimate burden of persuading the court that [the plaintiff] has been the victim of intentional discrimination."[6] *Burdine* drives home the point that the case has proceeded to "a new level of specificity" by explaining that the plaintiff can meet his burden of persuasion

---

[3]The majority is simply wrong when it suggests that my reading of *McDonnell Douglas* and *Burdine* proceeds on the assumption that the employer's reasons must be stated "apart from the record." As I mentioned above, and I repeat here, such reasons must be set forth "through the introduction of admissible evidence." See *Burdine*, 450 U.S. at 255. Such reasons cannot simply be found "lurking in the record," as the Court suggests, for *Burdine* requires the employer to articulate its reasons through testimony or other admissible evidence that is "clear and reasonably specific." Accordingly, the plaintiff need not worry about waiting for the court to identify the employer's reasons at the end of trial, or in this case six months after trial, because *McDonnell Douglas* and *Burdine* require the employer to articulate its reasons clearly during trial. No one, for example, had any trouble in this case identifying the two reasons for Hicks's dismissal that St. Mary's articulated during trial.

[5]The Court makes a halfhearted attempt to rewrite these passages from *McDonnell Douglas*, arguing that "pretext for discrimination" should appear where "pretext" actually does. I seriously doubt that such a change in diction would have altered the meaning of these crucial passages in the manner the majority suggests, but even on the majority's assumption that there is a crucial difference, it must believe that the *McDonnell Douglas* Court was rather sloppy in summarizing its own opinion. Earlier in the *McDonnell Douglas* opinion, the Court does state that an employer may not use a plaintiff's conduct "as a pretext for . . . discrimination." But in the next sentence, when the *McDonnell Douglas* Court's focus shifts from what the employer may not do to what the plaintiff must show, the Court states that the plaintiff must "be afforded a fair opportunity to show that [the employer's] stated reason for [the plaintiff's] rejection was in fact pretext," plain and simple. To the extent choosing between "pretext" and "pretext for discrimination" is important, the *McDonnell Douglas* Court's diction appears to be consistent, not sloppy. *Burdine*, of course, nails down the point that the plaintiff satisfies his burden simply by proving that the employer's explanation does not deserve credence.

[6]The majority puts forward what it calls "a more reasonable reading" of this passage, but its chosen interpretation of the "merger" that occurs is flatly contradicted by the very next sentence in *Burdine*, which indicates, as the majority subsequently admits, that the burden of persuasion is limited to the question of pretext. It seems to me "more reasonable" to interpret the "merger" language in harmony with, rather than in contradiction to, its immediate context in *Burdine*.

in either of two ways: "either directly by persuading the court that a discriminatory reason more likely motivated the employer or indirectly by showing that the employer's proffered explanation is unworthy of credence."[7]   That the plaintiff can succeed simply by showing that "the employer's proffered explanation is unworthy of credence" indicates that the case has been narrowed to the question whether the employer's proffered reasons are pretextual.[8] Thus, because Hicks carried his burden of persuasion by showing that St. Mary's proffered reasons were "unworthy of credence," the Court of Appeals properly concluded that he was entitled to judgment.[9]

The Court today decides to abandon the settled law that sets out this structure for trying disparate-treatment Title VII cases, only to adopt a scheme that will be unfair to plaintiffs, unworkable in practice, and inexplicable in forgiving employers who present false evidence in court. Under the majority's scheme, once the employer succeeds in meeting its burden of production, "the *McDonnell Douglas* framework . . . is no longer relevant."   Whereas we said in *Burdine* that if the employer carries its burden of production, "the factual inquiry proceeds to a new level of specificity," the Court now holds that the further enquiry is wide open, not limited at all by the scope of the

---

[7]The majority's effort to rewrite *Burdine* centers on repudiating this passage, which has provided specific, concrete guidance to courts and Title VII litigants for more than a decade, and on replacing "pretext" wherever it appears with "pretext for discrimination," as defined by the majority. These two efforts are intertwined, for *Burdine* tells us specifically how a plaintiff can prove either "pretext" or "pretext for discrimination": "*either* directly by persuading the court that a discriminatory reason more likely motivated the employer *or* indirectly by showing that the employer's proffered explanation is unworthy of credence." The majority's chosen method of proving "pretext for discrimination" changes *Burdine*'s "either . . . or" into a "both . . . and": "[A] reason cannot be proved to be 'a pretext for discrimination' unless it is shown both that the reason was false, and that discrimination was the real reason." The majority thus takes a shorthand phrase from *Burdine* ("pretext for discrimination"), discovers requirements in the phrase that are directly at odds with the specific requirements actually set out in *Burdine*, and then rewrites *Burdine* in light of this "discovery." No one "familiar with our case-law," will be persuaded by this strategy.

[8]That the sole, and therefore determinative, issue left at this stage is pretext is further indicated by our discussion in *McDonnell Douglas* of the various types of evidence "that may be relevant to any showing of pretext," by our decision to reverse in *Furnco* because the Court of Appeals "did not conclude that the [challenged] practices were a pretext for discrimination," and by our reminder in *Burdine* that even after the employer meets the plaintiff's prima facie case, the "evidence previously introduced by the plaintiff to establish a prima facie case" and the "inferences properly drawn therefrom may be considered by the trier of fact on the issue of whether the [employer's] explanation is pretextual."

[9]The foregoing analysis of burdens describes who wins on various combinations of evidence and proof. It may or may not also describe the actual sequence of events at trial. In a bench trial, for example, the parties may be limited in their presentation of evidence until the court has decided whether the plaintiff has made his prima facie showing. But the court also may allow in all the evidence at once. In such a situation, under our decision in *Aikens*, the defendant will have to choose whether it wishes simply to attack the prima facie case or whether it wants to present nondiscriminatory reasons for its actions. If the defendant chooses the former approach, the factfinder will decide at the end of the trial whether the plaintiff has proven his prima facie case. If the defendant takes the latter approach, the only question for the factfinder will be the issue of pretext. Aikens.

employer's proffered explanation.[10] Despite the Court's assiduous effort to reinterpret our precedents, it remains clear that today's decision stems from a flat misreading of *Burdine* and ignores the central purpose of the *McDonnell Douglas* framework, which is "progressively to sharpen the inquiry into the elusive factual question of intentional discrimination." We have repeatedly identified the compelling reason for limiting the factual issues in the final stage of a *McDonnell Douglas* case as "the requirement that the plaintiff be afforded a full and fair opportunity to demonstrate pretext." The majority fails to explain how the plaintiff, under its scheme, will ever have a "full and fair opportunity" to demonstrate that reasons not articulated by the employer, but discerned in the record by the factfinder, are also unworthy of credence. The Court thus transforms the employer's burden of production from a device used to provide notice and promote fairness into a misleading and potentially useless ritual.

The majority's scheme greatly disfavors Title VII plaintiffs without the good luck to have direct evidence of discriminatory intent. The Court repeats the truism that the plaintiff has the "ultimate burden" of proving discrimination, without ever facing the practical question of how the plaintiff without such direct evidence can meet this burden. *Burdine* provides the answer, telling us that such a plaintiff may succeed in meeting his ultimate burden of proving discrimination "indirectly by showing that the employer's proffered explanation is unworthy of credence." The possibility of some practical procedure for addressing what *Burdine* calls indirect proof is crucial to the success of most Title VII claims, for the simple reason that employers who discriminate are not likely to announce their discriminatory motive. And yet, under the majority's scheme, a victim of discrimination lacking direct evidence will now be saddled with the tremendous disadvantage of having to confront, not the defined task of proving the employer's stated reasons to be false, but the amorphous requirement of disproving *all* possible nondiscriminatory reasons that a factfinder might find lurking in the record. In the Court's own words, the plaintiff must "disprove *all* other reasons suggested, no matter how vaguely, in the record."

While the Court appears to acknowledge that a plaintiff will have the task of disproving even vaguely suggested reasons, and while it recognizes the need for "[c]larity regarding the requisite elements of proof," it nonetheless gives conflicting signals about the scope of its holding in this case. In one passage, the Court states that although proof of the falsity of the employer's proffered reasons does not "compe[l] judgment for the plaintiff," such evidence, without more, "will permit the trier of fact to infer the ultimate fact of intentional discrimination." The same view is implicit in the Court's decision to remand this case, keeping Hicks's chance of winning a judgment alive although he has done no more (in addition to proving his *prima facie* case) than show that the reasons proffered by St. Mary's are unworthy of credence. But other language in the Court's opinion supports a more extreme conclusion, that proof of the falsity of the employer's articulated reasons will not even be sufficient to sustain judgment for the plaintiff. For example, the Court twice states that the plaintiff must show "*both* that the reason was false, *and* that discrimination was the real

---

[10]Under the Court's unlikely interpretation of the "new level of specificity" called for by *Burdine* (and repeated in *Aikens*), the issues facing the plaintiff and the court can be discovered anywhere in the evidence the parties have introduced concerning discriminatory motivation.

reason." In addition, in summing up its reading of our earlier cases, the Court states that "[i]t is not enough . . . to disbelieve the employer." This "pretext-plus" approach would turn *Burdine* on its head, and it would result in summary judgment for the employer in the many cases where the plaintiff has no evidence beyond that required to prove a prima facie case and to show that the employer's articulated reasons are unworthy of credence.

The Court fails to explain, moreover, under either interpretation of its holding, why proof that the employer's articulated reasons are "unpersuasive, or even obviously contrived," falls short. Under *McDonnell Douglas* and *Burdine*, there would be no reason in this situation to question discriminatory intent. The plaintiff has raised an inference of discrimination (though no longer a presumption) through proof of his *prima facie* case, and as we noted in *Burdine*, this circumstantial proof of discrimination can also be used by the plaintiff to show pretext. Such proof is merely strengthened by showing, through use of further evidence, that the employer's articulated reasons are false, since "common experience" tells us that it is "more likely than not" that the employer who lies is simply trying to cover up the illegality alleged by the plaintiff. *Furnco.* Unless *McDonnell Douglas's* command to structure and limit the case as the employer chooses is to be rendered meaningless, we should not look beyond the employer's lie by assuming the possible existence of other reasons the employer might have proffered without lying. By telling the factfinder to keep digging in cases where the plaintiff's proof of pretext turns on showing the employer's reasons to be unworthy of credence, the majority rejects the very point of the *McDonnell Douglas* rule requiring the scope of the factual enquiry to be limited, albeit in a manner chosen by the employer. What is more, the Court is throwing out the rule for the benefit of employers who have been found to have given false evidence in a court of law. There is simply no justification for favoring these employers by exempting them from responsibility for lies. It may indeed be true that such employers have nondiscriminatory reasons for their actions, but ones so shameful that they wish to conceal them. One can understand human frailty and the natural desire to conceal it, however, without finding in it a justification to dispense with an orderly procedure for getting at "the elusive factual question of intentional discrimination."

With no justification in the employer's favor, the consequences to actual and potential Title VII litigants stand out sharply. To the extent that workers like Melvin Hicks decide not to sue, given the uncertainties they would face under the majority's scheme, the legislative purpose in adopting Title VII will be frustrated. To the extent such workers nevertheless decide to press forward, the result will likely be wasted time, effort, and money for all concerned. Under the scheme announced today, any conceivable explanation for the employer's actions that might be suggested by the evidence, however unrelated to the employer's articulated reasons, must be addressed by a plaintiff who does not wish to risk losing. Since the Court does not say whether a trial court may limit the introduction of evidence at trial to what is relevant to the employer's articulated reasons, and since the employer can win on the possibility of an unstated reason, the scope of admissible evidence at trial presumably includes any evidence potentially relevant to "the ultimate question" of discrimination, unlimited by the employer's stated reasons. If so, Title VII trials promise to be tedious affairs. But even if, on the contrary, relevant evidence is still somehow to be limited by reference to the employer's reasons, however "vaguely" articulated, the careful plaintiff will have to anticipate all the side issues that might arise even in a more limited evidentiary presentation. Thus, in either case, pretrial discovery will become more extensive and wide-ranging (if the plaintiff can afford it), for a much wider set of facts could prove to be both relevant and important at trial. The majority's scheme, therefore, will promote longer trials and more pre-trial discovery, threatening increased expense and delay in Title VII litigation for both plaintiffs and defendants, and increased burdens on the judiciary.

In addition to its unfairness and impracticality, the Court's new scheme, on its own terms, produces some remarkable results. Contrary to the assumption underlying the *McDonnell Douglas* framework, that employers will have "*some* reason" for their hiring and firing decisions, the majority assumes that some employers will be unable to discover the reasons for their own personnel actions. Under the majority's scheme, however, such employers, when faced with proof of a prima facie case of discrimination, still must carry the burden of producing evidence that a challenged employment action was taken for a nondiscriminatory reason. Thus, if an employer claims it cannot produce any evidence of a nondiscriminatory reason for a personnel decision,[12] and the trier of fact concludes that the plaintiff has proven his prima facie case, the court must enter judgment for the plaintiff. The majority's scheme therefore leads to the perverse result that employers who fail to discover nondiscriminatory reasons for their own decisions to hire and fire employees not only will benefit from lying,[13] but must lie, to defend successfully against a disparate-treatment action. By

---

[12]The Court is unrealistically concerned about the rare case in which an employer cannot easily turn to one of its employees for an explanation of a personnel decision. Most companies, of course, keep personnel records, and such records generally are admissible under Rule 803(6) of the Federal Rules of Evidence. Even those employers who do not keep records of their decisions will have other means of discovering the likely reasons for a personnel action by, for example, interviewing co-workers, examining employment records, and identifying standard personnel policies. The majority's scheme rewards employers who decide, in this atypical situation, to invent rather than to investigate.

This concern drives the majority to point to the hypothetical case, of the employer with a disproportionately high percentage of minority workers who would nonetheless lose a Title VII racial discrimination case by giving an untrue reason for a challenged personnel action. What the majority does not tell us, however, is why such an employer must rely solely on an "antagonistic former employee," rather than on its own personnel records, among other things, to establish the credible, nondiscriminatory reason it almost certainly must have had, given the facts assumed. The majority claims it would be a "mockery of justice" to allow recovery against an employer who presents "compelling evidence" of nondiscrimination simply because the jury believes a reason given in a personnel record "is probably not the 'true' one." But prior to drawing such a conclusion, the jury would consider all of the "compelling evidence" as at least circumstantial evidence for the truth of the nondiscriminatory explanation, because the employer would be able to argue that it would not lie to avoid a discrimination charge when its general behavior had been so demonstrably meritorious. If the jury still found that the plaintiff had carried his burden to show untruth, the untruth must have been a real whopper, or else the "compelling evidence" must not have been very compelling. In either event, justice need not worry too much about mockery.

[13]As the majority readily admits, its scheme places any employer who lies in a better position than the employer who says nothing. Under *McDonnell Douglas* and *Burdine*, an employer caught in a lie will lose on the merits, subjecting himself to liability not only for damages, but also for the prevailing plaintiff's attorney's fees, including, presumably, fees for the extra time

offering false evidence of a nondiscriminatory reason, such an employer can rebut the presumption raised by the plaintiff's prima facie case, and then hope that the factfinder will conclude that the employer may have acted for a reason unknown rather than for a discriminatory reason. I know of no other scheme for structuring a legal action that, on its own terms, requires a party to lie in order to prevail.

Finally, the Court's opinion destroys a framework carefully crafted in precedents as old as 20 years, which the Court attempts to deflect, but not to confront. The majority first contends that the opinions creating and refining the *McDonnell Douglas* framework consist primarily of dicta, whose bearing on the issue we consider today presumably can be ignored. But this readiness to disclaim the Court's considered pronouncements devalues them. Cases, such as *McDonnell Douglas*, that set forth an order of proof necessarily go beyond the minimum necessary to settle the narrow dispute presented, but evidentiary frameworks set up in this manner are not for that reason subject to summary dismissal in later cases as products of mere dicta. Courts and litigants rely on this Court to structure lawsuits based on federal statutes in an orderly and sensible manner, and we should not casually abandon the structures adopted.

Because the Court thus naturally declines to rely entirely on dismissing our prior directives as dicta, it turns to the task of interpreting our prior cases in this area, in particular *Burdine*. While acknowledging that statements from these earlier cases may be read, and in one instance must be read, to limit the final enquiry in a disparate-treatment case to the question of pretext, the Court declares my reading of those cases to be "utter[ly] implausib[le]," imputing views to earlier Courts that would be "beneath contempt." The unlikely reading is, however, shared by the Solicitor General and the Equal Employment Opportunity Commission, which is charged with implementing and enforcing Title VII and related statutes, see Brief for United States et al. as *Amici Curiae* 1-2, not to mention the Court of Appeals in this case and, even by the Court's count, more than half of the Courts of Appeals to have discussed the question (some, albeit, in dicta). The company should not be cause for surprise. For reasons explained above, *McDonnell Douglas* and *Burdine* provide a clear answer to the question before us, and it would behoove the majority to explain its decision to depart from those cases.

The Court's final attempt to neutralize the force of our precedents comes in its claim that *Aikens* settled the question presented today. This attempt to rest on *Aikens* runs into the immediate difficulty, however, that *Aikens* repeats what we said earlier in *Burdine*: the plaintiff may succeed in meeting his ultimate burden of persuasion "'either directly by persuading the court that a discriminatory reason more likely motivated the employer or indirectly by showing that the employer's proffered explanation is unworthy of credence.'" *Aikens*. Although the *Aikens* Court quoted this statement approvingly, the majority here projects its view that the latter part of the statement is "problematic," arguing that the next sentence in *Aikens* takes care of the "problem." The next sentence, however, only creates more problems for the majority,

---

spent to show pretext. Under the majority's scheme, the employer who is caught in a lie, but succeeds in injecting into the trial an unarticulated reason for its actions, will win its case and walk away rewarded for its falsehoods.

as it directs the District Court to "decide *which* party's explanation of the employer's motivation it believes." By requiring the factfinder to choose between the employer's explanation and the plaintiff's claim of discrimination (shown either directly or indirectly), *Aikens* flatly bars the Court's conclusion here that the factfinder can choose a third explanation, never offered by the employer, in ruling against the plaintiff. Because *Aikens* will not bear the reading the majority seeks to place upon it, there is no hope of projecting into the past the abandonment of precedent that occurs today.

I cannot join the majority in turning our back on these earlier decisions. "Considerations of *stare decisis* have special force in the area of statutory interpretation, for here, unlike in the context of constitutional interpretation, the legislative power is implicated, and Congress remains free to alter what we have done." *Patterson v. McLean Credit Union,* 491 U.S. 164, 172-173, 105 L. Ed. 2d 132, 109 S. Ct. 2363 (1989). It is not as though Congress is unaware of our decisions concerning Title VII, and recent experience indicates that Congress is ready to act if we adopt interpretations of this statutory scheme it finds to be mistaken. See Civil Rights Act of 1991. Congress has taken no action to indicate that we were mistaken in *McDonnell Douglas* and *Burdine.*

* * *

The enhancement of a Title VII plaintiff's burden wrought by the Court's opinion is exemplified in this case. Melvin Hicks was denied any opportunity, much less a full and fair one, to demonstrate that the supposedly nondiscriminatory explanation for his demotion and termination, the personal animosity of his immediate supervisor, was unworthy of credence. In fact, the District Court did not find that personal animosity (which it failed to recognize might be racially motivated) was the true reason for the actions St. Mary's took; it adduced this reason simply as a possibility in explaining that Hicks had failed to prove "that the crusade [to terminate him] was racially rather than personally motivated." 756 F. Supp. 1244, 1252 (ED Mo. 1991). It is hardly surprising that Hicks failed to prove anything about this supposed personal crusade, since St. Mary's never articulated such an explanation for Hicks's discharge, and since the person who allegedly conducted this crusade denied at trial any personal difficulties between himself and Hicks. While the majority may well be troubled about the unfair treatment of Hicks in this instance and thus remands for review of whether the District Court's factual conclusions were clearly erroneous, the majority provides Hicks with no opportunity to produce evidence showing that the District Court's hypothesized explanation, first articulated six months after trial, is unworthy of credence. Whether Melvin Hicks wins or loses on remand, many plaintiffs in a like position will surely lose under the scheme adopted by the Court today, unless they possess both prescience and resources beyond what this Court has previously required Title VII litigants to employ.

Because I see no reason why Title VII interpretation should be driven by concern for employers who are too ashamed to be honest in court, at the expense of victims of discrimination who do not happen to have direct evidence of discriminatory intent, I respectfully dissent.

NOTES AND PROBLEMS FOR DISCUSSION

1. Notwithstanding Justice Scalia's incredulity concerning the reasoning of both the Eighth Circuit and Justice Souter's dissent, prior to *Hicks*, the circuits were evenly divided on the legal effect of a finding of pretext. And, as Justice Souter reminds us, the EEOC and the Justice Department argued in *Hicks* that the Eighth Circuit's holding was correct. Was this divergence of views about the meaning of *McDonnell Douglas, Burdine,* and *Aikens* the result of sloppy draftsmanship by the Court in its prior opinions (as implied by Justice Scalia) or of a fundamental division on the Court over the legal significance of the presumption created by the establishment of a prima facie case? Is the interpretive problem inherent in an evidentiary scheme that creates a presumption of unlawful discrimination on the basis of a prima facie case, the bare elements of which often will not convince a rational trier of fact of discrimination? *See* Deborah Malamud, *The Last Minuet: Disparate Treatment After Hicks,* 93 MICH. L.REV. 2229 (1995) (arguing that in the aftermath of *Hicks* the *McDonnell Douglas-Burdine* proof structure should be abandoned).

2. Arguing that disbelief of the employer's reason for an employment action is different from a finding of unlawful motivation, Justice Scalia poses a hypothetical concerning an employer with a majority-black work force that would still lose a disparate treatment case if a black applicant for employment convinced a jury that the employer's reason for the refusal to hire him was incorrect. According to Justice Scalia, the hypothetical demonstrates the illogic of the dissent's reading of *Burdine* and *Aikens*. How does the dissent respond to the hypothetical? How likely is it that a jury actually would be instructed as Justice Scalia suggests — i.e., that it must assess the employer's articulated reasons independently from other evidence in the case bearing on the employer's unlawful motivation? Would a sounder approach to the enforcement of Title VII be the development of a special rule for the rare case in which an employer is unable to explain its actions, while retaining as a general rule the two-route approach to proof of pretext for cases in which the employer does provide an explanation?

Hicks has generated its share of academic controversy. *Compare* Mark S. Brodin, *The Demise of Circumstantial Proof in Employment Discrimination Litigation: St. Mary's Honor Center v. Hicks, Pretext, and the "Personality" Excuse,* 18 BERKLEY J. EMP. & LAB. L. 183, 209-10 (1997) (by permitting the fact-finder to reject both the employer's defense and the plaintiff's proof of motive and to substitute an entirely different scenario, the Court in *Hicks* not only abandoned the *McDonnell Douglas Burdine* framework, but "two of the most basic tenets of American procedure as well — first, that the court is a passive tribunal, not an active player in the construction of arguments and theories, and second, that cases are to be decided solely on the basis of the evidence presented, not the conjecture of the fact-finder.") *with* JuLyn M. McCarty & Michael J. Levy, *Focusing Title VII: The Supreme Court Continues the Battle Against Intentional Discrimination in St. Mary's Honor Center v. Hicks,* 14 HOFSTRA LAB. L.J. 177, 226 (1996) (arguing that *Hicks* follows precedent and that "[b]y permitting, but not compelling, the factfinder to conclude the existence of intentional discrimination from proof of a prima facie case and falsity, the Court furthers the purposes of Title VII: to eradicate discrimination wherever there is an *actual* finding of intentional discrimination.")

3. In ASH v. TYSON FOODS, INC., 546 U.S. 454, 126 S. Ct. 1195, 163 L.Ed.2d 1053 (2006), the Supreme Court offered additional guidance on the quantum or type of evidence necessary to defeat a motion for judgment as a matter of law with respect to the issue of pretext. Plaintiff offered evidence that the defendant's plant manager referred to each of the two African-American plaintiffs who were denied promotions as "boy". After the jury issued a verdict in favor of the plaintiffs, the trial judge granted the defendant's renewed motion for judgment as a matter of law. The Eleventh Circuit panel affirmed the grant of the motion with respect to the claim asserted by one of the two plaintiffs. It based this ruling on the ground that evidence of the reference to the plaintiff as "boy" was insufficient as a matter of law to establish discriminatory intent. The Supreme Court, in a *per curiam* opinion, ruled that the appellate court had erred in declaring that the presence of a modifier such as "white" or "black" in front of "boy" was necessary, as a matter of law, to render the use of that term sufficient evidence of discriminatory bias to support a jury finding of discrimination. "Although it is true the disputed word will not always be evidence of racial animus," the Court explained, "it does not follow that the term, standing alone is always benign. The speaker's meaning may depend on various factors including context, inflection, tone of voice, local custom, and historical usage." Additionally, as discussed in Note 5(c) following *Burdine, supra*, the Court rejected the "jump off the page and slap in the face" standard that several appellate courts had applied to cases where the plaintiff offered comparative qualifications evidence to establish pretext.

On remand, a chastened Eleventh Circuit nevertheless reinstated its previous determinations that there was nothing in the record to support an inference of racial animus in the use of "boy". In an unpublished opinion, the court characterized the usage of that word in the instant case as "conversational" and "non-racial in context". Moreover, even if the words were construed as racial, the court found that they were not more than "ambiguous stray remarks" and, therefore, insufficient circumstantial evidence from which a reasonable jury could find that the denial of promotion was racially biased. The court emphasized that the absence of a modifier to "boy" was not, on remand, essential to the its finding that the word was not used racially and was not evidence of racial bias. 190 Fed.Appx. 924 (11th Cir. 2006).

4. Justice Souter's principal argument in dissent in *Hicks* is that plaintiffs in disparate treatment cases will be required under the majority's reading of *McDonnell Douglas*, *Burdine,* and *Aikens* to disprove not only the reasons articulated by the employer, but also any and all other nondiscriminatory explanations "lurking in the record," a difficult if not impossible task in many circumstances. How does Justice Scalia respond to this argument?

In FOSTER v. DALTON, 71 F.3d 52 (1st Cir.1995), for example, an African-American woman alleged that she had been denied a position at a naval hospital because of her race. After a bench trial, the court ruled in favor of the defendant. Although the district judge found that the plaintiff had established a prima facie case, it ruled that the defense had established a nondiscriminatory explanation, i.e., that it had pre-selected a friend of the appointing officer. The appellate court refused to disturb this finding, determining that reliance on cronyism was a plausible, nondiscriminatory explanation for the employer's decision. The First Circuit added that even though the trial judge disbelieved the defendant's only articulated nondiscriminatory explanation — that the chosen candidate was the most qualified aspirant — and even though the defendant's witnesses expressly had denied the existence of favoritism, the trial court properly could conclude that cronyism, and not race, had motivated the employer's decision. As a practical matter, how could the plaintiff have anticipated that cronyism would emerge as a reason that had to be rebutted? In a bench trial, as in *Foster*, the trial judge conceivably could have informed the parties during the case that he had identified from the evidence a possible reason for the employer's conduct, other than that claimed by the employer, for whatever guidance that might have provided the litigants. But would such guidance from the court be possible in a case tried to a jury?

5. *Hicks* made clear that a trier of fact *may* base a finding of discrimination on the plaintiff's presentation of a prima facie case plus a finding that the employer's explanation is untrue, but is not compelled to do so. *Foster* illustrates that a district court's ultimate finding that discrimination did not occur, despite its disbelief of the employer's explanation, can be set aside only if clearly erroneous. But does a prima facie case plus evidence that the employer's articulated reason for the decision is false always entitle the plaintiff to a trial on the ultimate issue of discrimination? This issue arises when courts consider a defendant's motion for judgment as a matter of law. In the wake of *Hicks*, the question of whether anything in addition to evidence establishing a prima facie case and evidence discrediting the defendant's proffered explanation is necessary to withstand a defense motion for judgment as a matter of law and allow the trier of fact to resolve the ultimate question of discrimination divided the federal appellate courts. Seven years after deciding *Hicks*, the Supreme Court took another run at the problem in the case below.

Reeves v. Sanderson Plumbing Products, Inc.

Supreme Court of the United States, 2000.
530 U.S. 133, 120 S.Ct. 2097, 147 L.Ed.2d 105.

Justice O'Connor delivered the opinion of the Court.

This case concerns the kind and amount of evidence necessary to sustain a jury's verdict that an employer unlawfully discriminated on the basis of age. Specifically, we must resolve whether a defendant is entitled to judgment as a matter of law when the plaintiff's case consists exclusively of a prima facie case of discrimination and sufficient evidence for the trier of fact to disbelieve the defendant's legitimate, nondiscriminatory explanation for its action. We must also decide whether the employer was entitled to judgment as a matter of law under the particular circumstances presented here.

I

In October 1995, petitioner Roger Reeves was 57 years old and had spent 40 years in the employ of respondent, Sanderson Plumbing Products, Inc., a manufacturer of toilet seats and covers. Petitioner worked in a department known as the "Hinge Room," where he supervised the "regular line." Joe Oswalt, in his mid-thirties, supervised the Hinge Room's "special line," and Russell Caldwell, the manager of the Hinge Room and age 45, supervised both petitioner and Oswalt. Petitioner's responsibilities included recording the attendance and hours of those under his supervision, and reviewing a weekly report that listed the hours worked by each employee.

In the summer of 1995, Caldwell informed Powe Chesnut, the director of manufacturing and the husband of company president Sandra Sanderson, that "production was down" in the Hinge Room because employees were often absent and were "coming in late and leaving early." Because the monthly attendance reports did not indicate a problem, Chesnut ordered an audit of the Hinge Room's timesheets for July, August, and September of that year. According to Chesnut's testimony, that investigation revealed "numerous timekeeping errors and misrepresentations on the part of Caldwell, Reeves, and Oswalt." Following the audit, Chesnut, along with Dana Jester, vice president of human resources, and Tom Whitaker, vice president of operations, recommended to company president Sanderson that petitioner and Caldwell be fired. In October 1995, Sanderson followed the recommendation and discharged both petitioner and Caldwell.

In June 1996, petitioner filed suit in the United States District Court for the Northern District of Mississippi, contending that he had been fired because of his age in violation of the Age Discrimination in Employment Act of 1967 (ADEA). At trial, respondent contended that it had fired petitioner due to his failure to maintain accurate attendance records, while petitioner attempted to demonstrate that respondent's explanation was pretext for age discrimination. Petitioner introduced evidence that he had accurately recorded the attendance and hours of the employees under his supervision, and that Chesnut, whom Oswalt described as wielding "absolute power" within the company, had demonstrated age-based animus in his dealings with petitioner.

During the trial, the District Court twice denied oral motions by respondent for judgment as a matter of law under Rule 50 of the Federal Rules of Civil Procedure, and the case went to the jury. The court instructed the jury that "if the plaintiff fails to prove age was a determinative or motivating factor in the decision to terminate him, then your verdict shall be for the defendant." So charged, the jury returned a verdict in favor of petitioner, awarding him $35,000 in compensatory damages, and found that respondent's age discrimination had been "willful". The District Court accordingly entered judgment for petitioner in the amount of $70,000, which included $35,000 in liquidated damages based on the jury's finding of willfulness. Respondent then renewed its motion for judgment as a matter of law and alternatively moved for a new trial, while petitioner moved for front pay. The District Court denied respondent's motions and granted petitioner's, awarding him $28,490.80 in front pay for two years' lost income.

The Court of Appeals for the Fifth Circuit reversed, holding that petitioner had not introduced sufficient evidence to sustain the jury's finding of unlawful discrimination. After noting respondent's proffered justification for petitioner's discharge, the court acknowledged that petitioner "very well may" have offered sufficient evidence for "a reasonable jury [to] have found that [respondent's] explanation for its employment decision was pretextual." The court explained, however, that this was "not dispositive" of the ultimate issue — namely, "whether Reeves presented sufficient evidence that his age motivated [respondent's] employment decision." Addressing this question, the court weighed petitioner's additional evidence of discrimination against other circumstances surrounding his discharge. Specifically, the court noted that

Chesnut's age-based comments "were not made in the direct context of Reeves's termination"; there was no allegation that the two other individuals who had recommended that petitioner be fired (Jester and Whitaker) were motivated by age; two of the decisionmakers involved in petitioner's discharge (Jester and Sanderson) were over the age of 50; all three of the Hinge Room supervisors were accused of inaccurate recordkeeping; and several of respondent's management positions were filled by persons over age 50 when petitioner was fired. On this basis, the court concluded that petitioner had not introduced sufficient evidence for a rational jury to conclude that he had been discharged because of his age.

We granted certiorari, to resolve a conflict among the Courts of Appeals as to whether a plaintiff's prima facie case of discrimination (as defined in *McDonnell Douglas Corp. v. Green),* combined with sufficient evidence for a reasonable factfinder to reject the employer's nondiscriminatory explanation for its decision, is adequate to sustain a finding of liability for intentional discrimination.

II

Under the ADEA, * * * [w]hen a plaintiff alleges disparate treatment, "liability depends on whether the protected trait (under the ADEA, age) actually motivated the employer's decision." Hazen Paper Co. v. Biggins. That is, the plaintiff's age must have "actually played a role in [the employer's decisionmaking] process and had a determinative influence on the outcome." This Court has not squarely addressed whether the McDonnell Douglas framework, developed to assess claims brought under § 703(a)(1) of Title VII of the Civil Rights Act of 1964 also applies to ADEA actions. Because the parties do not dispute the issue, we shall assume, arguendo, that the McDonnell Douglas framework is fully applicable here.

McDonnell Douglas and subsequent decisions have "established an allocation of the burden of production and an order for the presentation of proof in . . . discriminatory-treatment cases." St. Mary's Honor Center v. Hicks. First, the plaintiff must establish a prima facie case of discrimination. It is undisputed that petitioner satisfied this burden here: (i) at the time he was fired, he was a member of the class protected by the ADEA ("individuals who are at least 40 years of age," he was otherwise qualified for the position of Hinge Room supervisor, (iii) he was discharged by respondent, and (iv) respondent successively hired three persons in their thirties to fill petitioner's position. The burden therefore shifted to respondent to "produce evidence that the plaintiff was rejected, or someone else was preferred, for a legitimate, nondiscriminatory reason." Burdine. This burden is one of production, not persuasion; it "can involve no credibility assessment." St. Mary's. Respondent met this burden by offering admissible evidence sufficient for the trier of fact to conclude that petitioner was fired because of his failure to maintain accurate attendance records. Accordingly, "the McDonnell Douglas framework — with its presumptions and burdens" — disappeared, and the sole remaining issue was "discrimination vel non." Postal Service Bd. of Governors v. Aikens.

Although intermediate evidentiary burdens shift back and forth under this framework, "the ultimate burden of persuading the trier of fact that the defendant intentionally discriminated against the plaintiff remains at all times with the plaintiff." Burdine. And in attempting to satisfy this burden, the plaintiff — once the employer produces sufficient evidence to support a nondiscriminatory explanation for its decision — must be afforded the "opportunity to prove by a preponderance of the evidence that the legitimate reasons offered by the defendant were not its true reasons, but were a pretext for discrimination." Ibid.   That is, the plaintiff may attempt to establish that he was the victim of intentional discrimination "by showing that the employer's proffered explanation is unworthy of credence."   Burdine.   Moreover, although the presumption of discrimination "drops out of the picture" once the defendant meets its burden of production, the trier of fact may still consider the evidence establishing the plaintiff's prima facie case "and inferences properly drawn therefrom . . . on the issue of whether the defendant's explanation is pretextual," Burdine.

In this case, the evidence supporting respondent's explanation for petitioner's discharge consisted primarily of testimony by Chesnut and Sanderson and documentation of petitioner's alleged "shoddy record keeping."   Chesnut testified that a 1993 audit of Hinge Room operations revealed "a very lax assembly line" where employees were not adhering to general work rules.   As a result of that audit, petitioner was placed on 90 days' probation for unsatisfactory performance.   In 1995, Chesnut ordered another investigation of the Hinge Room, which, according to his testimony, revealed that petitioner was not correctly recording the absences and hours of employees.   Respondent introduced summaries of that investigation documenting several attendance violations by 12 employees under petitioner's supervision, and noting that each should have been disciplined in some manner.   Chesnut testified that this failure to discipline absent and late employees is "extremely important when you are dealing with a union" because uneven enforcement across departments would keep the company "in grievance and arbitration cases, which are costly, all the time."   He and Sanderson also stated that petitioner's errors, by failing to adjust for hours not worked, cost the company overpaid wages.   Sanderson testified that she accepted the recommendation to discharge petitioner because he had "intentionally falsified company pay records."

Petitioner, however, made a substantial showing that respondent's explanation was false.   First, petitioner offered evidence that he had properly maintained the attendance records.   Most of the timekeeping errors cited by respondent involved employees who were not marked late but who were recorded as having arrived at the plant at 7 a.m. for the 7 a.m. shift.   Respondent contended that employees arriving at 7 a.m. could not have been at their workstations by 7 a.m., and therefore must have been late.   But both petitioner and Oswalt testified that the company's automated timeclock often failed to scan employees' timecards, so that the timesheets would not record any time of arrival.   On these occasions, petitioner and Oswalt would visually check the workstations and record whether the employees were present at the start of the shift.   They stated that if an employee arrived promptly but the timesheet contained no time of arrival, they would reconcile the two by marking "7 a.m." as the employee's arrival time, even if the employee actually arrived at the plant earlier.   On cross-examination, Chesnut acknowledged that the timeclock sometimes malfunctioned, and that if "people were there at their work stations" at the start of the shift, the supervisor "would write in seven o'clock."   Petitioner also testified that when employees arrived before or stayed after their shifts, he would assign them additional work so they would not be overpaid.

Petitioner similarly cast doubt on whether he was responsible for any failure to discipline late and absent employees. Petitioner testified that his job only included reviewing the daily and weekly attendance reports, and that disciplinary writeups were based on the monthly reports, which were reviewed by Caldwell. Sanderson admitted that Caldwell, and not petitioner, was responsible for citing employees for violations of the company's attendance policy. Further, Chesnut conceded that there had never been a union grievance or employee complaint arising from petitioner's recordkeeping, and that the company had never calculated the amount of overpayments allegedly attributable to petitioner's errors. Petitioner also testified that, on the day he was fired, Chesnut said that his discharge was due to his failure to report as absent one employee, Gina Mae Coley, on two days in September 1995. But petitioner explained that he had spent those days in the hospital, and that Caldwell was therefore responsible for any overpayment of Coley. Finally, petitioner stated that on previous occasions that employees were paid for hours they had not worked, the company had simply adjusted those employees' next paychecks to correct the errors.

Based on this evidence, the Court of Appeals concluded that petitioner "very well may be correct" that "a reasonable jury could have found that [respondent's] explanation for its employment decision was pretextual." Nonetheless, the court held that this showing, standing alone, was insufficient to sustain the jury's finding of liability: "We must, as an essential final step, determine whether Reeves presented sufficient evidence that his age motivated [respondent's] employment decision." And in making this determination, the Court of Appeals ignored the evidence supporting petitioner's prima facie case and challenging respondent's explanation for its decision. The court confined its review of evidence favoring petitioner to that evidence showing that Chesnut had directed derogatory, age-based comments at petitioner, and that Chesnut had singled out petitioner for harsher treatment than younger employees. It is therefore apparent that the court believed that only this additional evidence of discrimination was relevant to whether the jury's verdict should stand. That is, the Court of Appeals proceeded from the assumption that a prima facie case of discrimination, combined with sufficient evidence for the trier of fact to disbelieve the defendant's legitimate, nondiscriminatory reason for its decision, is insufficient as a matter of law to sustain a jury's finding of intentional discrimination.

In so reasoning, the Court of Appeals misconceived the evidentiary burden borne by plaintiffs who attempt to prove intentional discrimination through indirect evidence. This much is evident from our decision in St. Mary's. There we held that the factfinder's rejection of the employer's legitimate, nondiscriminatory reason for its action does not compel judgment for the plaintiff. The ultimate question is whether the employer intentionally discriminated, and proof that "the employer's proffered reason is unpersuasive, or even obviously contrived, does not necessarily establish that the plaintiff's proffered reason . . . is correct." In other words, "it is not enough . . . to disbelieve the employer; the factfinder must believe the plaintiff's explanation of intentional discrimination."

In reaching this conclusion, however, we reasoned that it is permissible for the trier of fact to infer the ultimate fact of discrimination from the falsity of the employer's explanation. Specifically, we stated:

"The factfinder's disbelief of the reasons put forward by the defendant (particularly if disbelief is accompanied by a suspicion of mendacity) may, together with the elements of the prima facie case, suffice to show intentional discrimination. Thus, rejection of the defendant's proffered reasons will permit the trier of fact to infer the ultimate fact of intentional discrimination."

Proof that the defendant's explanation is unworthy of credence is simply one form of circumstantial evidence that is probative of intentional discrimination, and it may be quite persuasive. In appropriate circumstances, the trier of fact can reasonably infer from the falsity of the explanation that the employer is dissembling to cover up a discriminatory purpose. Such an inference is consistent with the general principle of evidence law that the factfinder is entitled to consider a party's dishonesty about a material fact as affirmative evidence of guilt. Moreover, once the employer's justification has been eliminated, discrimination may well be the most likely alternative explanation, especially since the employer is in the best position to put forth the actual reason for its decision. Thus, a plaintiff's prima facie case, combined with sufficient evidence to find that the employer's asserted justification is false, may permit the trier of fact to conclude that the employer unlawfully discriminated.

This is not to say that such a showing by the plaintiff will always be adequate to sustain a jury's finding of liability. Certainly there will be instances where, although the plaintiff has established a prima facie case and set forth sufficient evidence to reject the defendant's explanation, no rational factfinder could conclude that the action was discriminatory. For instance, an employer would be entitled to judgment as a matter of law if the record conclusively revealed some other, nondiscriminatory reason for the employer's decision, or if the plaintiff created only a weak issue of fact as to whether the employer's reason was untrue and there was abundant and uncontroverted independent evidence that no discrimination had occurred. To hold otherwise would be effectively to insulate an entire category of employment discrimination cases from review under Rule 50, and we have reiterated that trial courts should not "treat discrimination differently from other ultimate questions of fact." St. Mary's.

Whether judgment as a matter of law is appropriate in any particular case will depend on a number of factors. Those include the strength of the plaintiff's prima facie case, the probative value of the proof that the employer's explanation is false, and any other evidence that supports the employer's case and that properly may be considered on a motion for judgment as a matter of law. For purposes of this case, we need not — and could not — resolve all of the circumstances in which such factors would entitle an employer to judgment as a matter of law. It suffices to say that, because a prima facie case and sufficient evidence to reject the employer's explanation may permit a finding of liability, the Court of Appeals erred in proceeding from the premise that a plaintiff must always introduce additional, independent evidence of discrimination.

III

A

The remaining question is whether, despite the Court of Appeals' misconception of petitioner's evidentiary burden, respondent was nonetheless entitled to judgment as a matter of law. Under Rule 50, a court should render judgment as a matter of law when "a party has been fully heard on an issue and there is no legally sufficient evidentiary basis for a reasonable jury to find for that party on that issue."

* * *

* * * [I]n entertaining a motion for judgment as a matter of law, the court should review all of the evidence in the record.

In doing so, however, the court must draw all reasonable inferences in favor of the nonmoving party, and it may not make credibility determinations or weigh the evidence. "Credibility determinations, the weighing of the evidence, and the drawing of legitimate inferences from the facts are jury functions, not those of a judge." Anderson v. Liberty Lobby, Inc., 477 U.S. 242, 255 (1986). Thus, although the court should review the record as a whole, it must disregard all evidence favorable to the moving party that the jury is not required to believe. That is, the court should give credence to the evidence favoring the nonmovant as well as that "evidence supporting the moving party that is uncontradicted and unimpeached, at least to the extent that that evidence comes from disinterested witnesses." Id.

B

Applying this standard here, it is apparent that respondent was not entitled to judgment as a matter of law. In this case, in addition to establishing a prima facie case of discrimination and creating a jury issue as to the falsity of the employer's explanation, petitioner introduced additional evidence that Chesnut was motivated by age-based animus and was principally responsible for petitioner's firing. Petitioner testified that Chesnut had told him that he "was so old [he] must have come over on the Mayflower" and, on one occasion when petitioner was having difficulty starting a machine, that he "was too damn old to do [his] job." According to petitioner, Chesnut would regularly "cuss at me and shake his finger in my face." Oswalt, roughly 24 years younger than petitioner, corroborated that there was an "obvious difference" in how Chesnut treated them. He stated that, although he and Chesnut "had [their] differences," "it was nothing compared to the way [Chesnut] treated Roger." Oswalt explained that Chesnut "tolerated quite a bit" from him even though he "defied" Chesnut "quite often," but that Chesnut treated petitioner "in a manner, as you would . . . treat . . . a child when . . . you're angry with [him]." Petitioner also demonstrated that, according to company records, he and Oswalt had nearly identical rates of productivity in 1993. Yet respondent conducted an efficiency study of only the regular line, supervised by petitioner, and placed only petitioner on probation. Chesnut conducted that efficiency study and, after having testified to the contrary on direct examination, acknowledged on cross-examination that he had recommended that petitioner be placed on probation following the study.

Further, petitioner introduced evidence that Chesnut was the actual decisionmaker behind his firing. Chesnut was married to Sanderson, who made the formal decision to discharge petitioner. Although Sanderson testified that she fired petitioner because he had "intentionally falsified company pay records," respondent only introduced evidence concerning the inaccuracy of the records, not their falsification. A 1994 letter authored by Chesnut indicated that he berated other company directors, who were supposedly his co-equals, about how to do their jobs. Moreover, Oswalt testified that all of respondent's employees feared Chesnut, and that Chesnut had exercised "absolute power" within the company for "as long as [he] can remember."

In holding that the record contained insufficient evidence to sustain the jury's verdict, the Court of Appeals misapplied the standard of review dictated by Rule 50. Again, the court disregarded critical evidence favorable to petitioner — namely, the evidence supporting petitioner's prima facie case and undermining respondent's nondiscriminatory explanation. The court also failed to draw all reasonable inferences in favor of petitioner. For instance, while acknowledging "the potentially damning nature" of Chesnut's age-related comments, the court discounted them on the ground that they "were not made in the direct context of Reeves's termination." And the court discredited petitioner's evidence that Chesnut was the actual decisionmaker by giving weight to the fact that there was "no evidence to suggest that any of the other decisionmakers were motivated by age." Moreover, the other evidence on which the court relied — that Caldwell and Oswalt were also cited for poor recordkeeping, and that respondent employed many managers over age 50 — although relevant, is certainly not dispositive. See Furnco, 438 U.S., at 580 (evidence that employer's work force was racially balanced, while "not wholly irrelevant," was not "sufficient to conclusively demonstrate that [the employer's] actions were not discriminatorily motivated"). In concluding that these circumstances so overwhelmed the evidence favoring petitioner that no rational trier of fact could have found that petitioner was fired because of his age, the Court of Appeals impermissibly substituted its judgment concerning the weight of the evidence for the jury's.

The ultimate question in every employment discrimination case involving a claim of disparate treatment is whether the plaintiff was the victim of intentional discrimination. Given the evidence in the record supporting petitioner, we see no reason to subject the parties to an additional round of litigation before the Court of Appeals rather than to resolve the matter here. The District Court plainly informed the jury that petitioner was required to show "by a preponderance of the evidence that his age was a determining and motivating factor in the decision of [respondent] to terminate him." The court instructed the jury that, to show that respondent's explanation was a pretext for discrimination, petitioner had to demonstrate that the stated reasons were not the real reasons for petitioner's discharge; and that age discrimination was the real reason for [petitioner's] discharge. Given that petitioner established a prima facie case of discrimination, introduced enough evidence for the jury to reject respondent's explanation, and produced additional evidence of age-based animus, there was sufficient evidence for the jury to find that respondent had intentionally discriminated. The District Court was therefore correct to submit the case to the jury, and the Court of Appeals erred in overturning its verdict.

For these reasons, the judgment of the Court of Appeals is reversed.

It is so ordered.

JUSTICE GINSBURG, concurring.

The Court today holds that an employment discrimination plaintiff may survive judgment as a matter of law by submitting two categories of evidence: first, evidence establishing a "prima facie case," as that term is used in McDonnell Douglas Corp. v. Green; and second, evidence from which a rational factfinder could conclude that the employer's proffered explanation for its actions was false. Because the Court of Appeals in this case plainly, and erroneously, required the plaintiff to offer some evidence beyond those two categories, no broader holding is necessary to support reversal.

I write separately to note that it may be incumbent on the Court, in an appropriate case, to define more precisely the circumstances in which plaintiffs will be required to submit evidence beyond these two categories in order to survive a motion for judgment as a matter of law. I anticipate that such circumstances will be uncommon. As the Court notes, it is a principle of evidence law that the jury is entitled to treat a party's dishonesty about a material fact as evidence of culpability. Under this commonsense principle, evidence suggesting that a defendant accused of illegal discrimination has chosen to give a false explanation for its actions gives rise to a rational inference that the defendant could be masking its actual, illegal motivation. Whether the defendant was in fact motivated by discrimination is of course for the finder of fact to decide; that is the lesson of *St. Mary's Honor Center v. Hicks*. But the inference remains — unless it is conclusively demonstrated, by evidence the district court is required to credit on a motion for judgment as a matter of law, that discrimination could not have been the defendant's true motivation. If such conclusive demonstrations are (as I suspect) atypical, it follows that the ultimate question of liability ordinarily should not be taken from the jury once the plaintiff has introduced the two categories of evidence described above. Because the Court's opinion leaves room for such further elaboration in an appropriate case, I join it in full.

NOTES AND PROBLEMS FOR DISCUSSION

1. Does Justice O'Connor's opinion for the unanimous Court in *Reeves* simplify or add a new later of uncertainty to the handling of defense motions for judgment as a matter of law? The opinion declares that even where the plaintiff has established a prima facie case and introduced evidence contradicting the validity of the defendant's proffered nondiscriminatory explanation, the defense can still prevail on its motion if the record "conclusively revealed some other nondiscriminatory reason," or if the plaintiff's evidence of pretext was "weak" and "there was abundant and uncontroverted independent evidence that no discrimination had occurred." How is a trial court to determine whether the plaintiff has generated only a "weak" issue of fact concerning the defendant's tendered explanation? Isn't that the concern that prompted Justice Ginsburg to write a concurring opinion? Is this "weak" issue of fact standard consistent with the language in Federal Rule of Civil Procedure 56 that requires the movants on a summary judgment motion to establish the absence of a "genuine" issue of fact?

As Justice Ginsburg suggested, even post-*Reeves*, defense judgments as a matter of law should be relatively rare in cases where the plaintiff presents substantial evidence that the employer's reasons are false. If, however, the plaintiff concedes that the employer's professed nondiscriminatory explanation is a pretext for some other, but nevertheless lawful motive, summary judgment may be appropriate. In NEAL v. ROCHE, 349 F.3d 1246 (10th Cir. 2003), the plaintiff testified that she thought the real reason for the employer's promotion of a less qualified white employee was to rescue the white employee from layoff. Seizing on that concession, the district court granted summary judgment to the defendant and the court of appeals affirmed. "[T]he employer's decision to save a white employee from an impending layoff by giving that employee preference over an African-American employee who did not face a layoff, does not give rise to an inference of discrimination." *Id.* at 1252. The court stressed that the plaintiff did not argue that the employer would not have rescued a black employee's job had it been in jeopardy.

2. Surprisingly, the circuits are divided over whether a jury must be given a *Hicks/Reeves* pretext instruction. The Second, Third, Fifth, and Tenth Circuits mandate such an instruction. See e.g., Smith v. Borough of Wilkinsburg, 147 F.3d 272, 280 (3d Cir. 1998) ("the jurors must be instructed that they are entitled to infer, but need not, that the plaintiff's ultimate burden of demonstrating intentional discrimination by a preponderance of the evidence can be met if they find that the facts needed to make up the prima facie case have been established and they disbelieve the employer's explanation for its decision."). However, the First, Seventh and Eighth Circuits have either expressed doubts as to whether *Reeves* mandates the giving of a pretext instruction or have concluded that it does not require such an instruction.

> [A] judge need not deliver instructions describing all valid legal principles. Especially not when the principle in question describes a permissible, but not an obligatory, inference. Many an inference is permissible. Rather than describing each, the judge may and usually should leave the subject to the argument of counsel.

Gehring v. Case Corp., 43 F.3d 340, 343 (7th Cir. 1994), cert. denied, 515 U.S. 1159, 115 S.Ct. 2612, 132 L.Ed.2d 855 (1995). See generally, Conroy v. Abraham Chevrolet-Tampa, Inc., 375 F.3d 1228 (11th Cir. 2004), cert. denied, 125 S.Ct. 811, 160 L.Ed.2d 598 (2004) Without such an instruction, isn't a jury likely to make the same error that the Fifth Circuit did in *Reeves*, i.e., concluding that the plaintiff cannot prevail without affirmative evidence that an unlawful factor motivated the employer? In any event, where an instruction is given, *Reeves* certainly makes the wording critical.

2. PROOF OF CAUSATION

Price Waterhouse v. Hopkins

Supreme Court of the United States, 1989.
490 U.S. 228, 109 S.Ct. 1775, 104 L.Ed.2d 268.

JUSTICE BRENNAN announced the judgment of the Court and delivered an opinion, in which JUSTICE MARSHALL, JUSTICE BLACKMUN, and JUSTICE STEVENS join.

Ann Hopkins was a senior manager in an office of Price Waterhouse when she was proposed for partnership in 1982. She was neither offered nor denied admission to the partnership; instead, her candidacy was held for reconsideration the following year. When the partners in her office later refused to repropose her for partnership, she sued Price Waterhouse under Title VII, charging that the firm had discriminated against her on the basis of sex in its decisions regarding partnership. Judge Gesell in the District Court for the District of Columbia ruled in her favor on the question of liability, and the Court of Appeals for the District of Columbia Circuit affirmed. We granted certiorari to resolve a conflict among the Courts of Appeals concerning the respective burdens of proof of a defendant and plaintiff in a suit under Title VII when it has been shown that an employment decision resulted from a mixture of legitimate and illegitimate motives.

I

At Price Waterhouse, a nationwide professional accounting partnership, a senior manager becomes a candidate for partnership when the partners in her local office submit her name as a candidate. All of the other partners in the firm are then invited to submit written comments on each candidate — either on a "long" or a "short" form, depending on the partner's degree of exposure to the candidate. Not every partner in the firm submits comments on every candidate. After reviewing the comments and interviewing the partners who submitted them, the firm's Admissions Committee makes a recommendation to the Policy Board. This recommendation will be either that the firm accept the candidate for partnership, put her application on "hold," or deny her the promotion outright. The Policy Board then decides whether to submit the candidate's name to the entire partnership for a vote, to "hold" her candidacy, or to reject her. The recommendation of the Admissions Committee, and the decision of the Policy Board, are not controlled by fixed guidelines: a certain number of positive comments from partners will not guarantee a candidate's admission to the partnership, nor will a specific quantity of negative comments necessarily defeat her application. Price Waterhouse places no limit on the number of persons whom it will admit to the partnership in any given year.

Ann Hopkins had worked at Price Waterhouse's Office of Government Services in Washington, D.C., for five years when the partners in that office proposed her as a candidate for partnership. Of the 662 partners at the firm at that time, 7 were women. Of the 88 persons proposed for partnership that year, only 1 — Hopkins — was a woman. Forty-seven of these candidates were admitted to the partnership, 21 were rejected, and 20 — including Hopkins — were "held" for reconsideration the following year.[1] Thirteen of the 32 partners who had submitted comments on Hopkins supported her bid for partnership. Three partners recommended that her candidacy be placed on hold, eight stated that they did not have an informed opinion about her, and eight recommended that she be denied partnership.

In a jointly prepared statement supporting her candidacy, the partners in Hopkins' office showcased her successful 2-year effort to secure a $25 million contract with the Department of State, labeling it "an outstanding performance" and one that Hopkins carried out "virtually at the partner level." Despite Price Waterhouse's attempt at trial to minimize her contribution to this project, Judge Gesell specifically found that Hopkins had "played a key role in Price Waterhouse's successful effort to win a multi-

---

[1]Before the time for reconsideration came, two of the partners in Hopkins' office withdrew their support for her, and the office informed her that she would not be reconsidered for partnership. Hopkins then resigned. Price Waterhouse does not challenge the Court of Appeals' conclusion that the refusal to repropose her for partnership amounted to a constructive discharge. That court remanded the case to the District Court for further proceedings to determine appropriate relief, and those proceedings have been stayed pending our decision. We are concerned today only with Price Waterhouse's decision to place Hopkins' candidacy on hold. Decisions pertaining to advancement to partnership are, of course, subject to challenge under Title VII. Hishon v. King & Spalding.

million dollar contract with the Department of State." Indeed, he went on, "[n]one of the other partnership candidates at Price Waterhouse that year had a comparable record in terms of successfully securing major contracts for the partnership."

The partners in Hopkins' office praised her character as well as her accomplishments, describing her in their joint statement as "an outstanding professional" who had a "deft touch," a "strong character, independence and integrity." Clients appear to have agreed with these assessments. At trial, one official from the State Department described her as "extremely competent, intelligent," "strong and forthright, very productive, energetic and creative." Another high-ranking official praised Hopkins' decisiveness, broadmindedness, and "intellectual clarity"; she was, in his words, "a stimulating conversationalist." Evaluations such as these led Judge Gesell to conclude that Hopkins "had no difficulty dealing with clients and her clients appear to have been very pleased with her work" and that she "was generally viewed as a highly competent project leader who worked long hours, pushed vigorously to meet deadlines and demanded much from the multidisciplinary staffs with which she worked."

On too many occasions, however, Hopkins' aggressiveness apparently spilled over into abrasiveness. Staff members seem to have borne the brunt of Hopkins' brusqueness. Long before her bid for partnership, partners evaluating her work had counseled her to improve her relations with staff members. Although later evaluations indicate an improvement, Hopkins' perceived shortcomings in this important area eventually doomed her bid for partnership. Virtually all of the partners' negative remarks about Hopkins — even those of partners supporting her — had to do with her "interpersonal skills." Both "[s]upporters and opponents of her candidacy," stressed Judge Gesell, "indicated that she was sometimes overly aggressive, unduly harsh, difficult to work with and impatient with staff."

There were clear signs, though, that some of the partners reacted negatively to Hopkins' personality because she was a woman. One partner described her as "macho"; another suggested that she "overcompensated for being a woman"; a third advised her to take "a course at charm school." Several partners criticized her use of profanity; in response, one partner suggested that those partners objected to her swearing only "because it['.]s a lady using foul language." Another supporter explained that Hopkins "ha[d] matured from a tough-talking somewhat masculine hard-nosed mgr to an authoritative, formidable, but much more appealing lady ptr candidate." But it was the man who, as Judge Gesell found, bore responsibility for explaining to Hopkins the reasons for the Policy Board's decision to place her candidacy on hold who delivered the *coup de grace*: in order to improve her chances for partnership, Thomas Beyer advised, Hopkins should "walk more femininely, talk more femininely, dress more femininely, wear make-up, have her hair styled, and wear jewelry."

Dr. Susan Fiske, a social psychologist and Associate Professor of Psychology at Carnegie-Mellon University, testified at trial that the partnership selection process at Price Waterhouse was likely influenced by sex stereotyping. Her testimony focused not only on the overtly sex-based comments of partners but also on gender-neutral remarks, made by partners who knew Hopkins only slightly, that were intensely critical of her. One partner, for example, baldly stated that Hopkins was "universally disliked" by staff, and another described her as "consistently annoying and irritating";

yet these were people who had had very little contact with Hopkins. According to Fiske, Hopkins' uniqueness (as the only woman in the pool of candidates) and the subjectivity of the evaluations made it likely that sharply critical remarks such as these were the product of sex stereotyping — although Fiske admitted that she could not say with certainty whether any particular comment was the result of stereotyping. Fiske based her opinion on a review of the submitted comments, explaining that it was commonly accepted practice for social psychologists to reach this kind of conclusion without having met any of the people involved in the decisionmaking process.

In previous years, other female candidates for partnership also had been evaluated in sex-based terms. As a general matter, Judge Gesell concluded, "[c]andidates were viewed favorably if partners believed they maintained their femin[in]ity while becoming effective professional managers"; in this environment, "[t]o be identified as a 'women's lib[b]er' was regarded as [a] negative comment." In fact, the judge found that in previous years "[o]ne partner repeatedly commented that he could not consider any woman seriously as a partnership candidate and believed that women were not even capable of functioning as senior managers — yet the firm took no action to discourage his comments and recorded his vote in the overall summary of the evaluations."

Judge Gesell found that Price Waterhouse legitimately emphasized interpersonal skills in its partnership decisions, and also found that the firm had not fabricated its complaints about Hopkins' interpersonal skills as a pretext for discrimination. Moreover, he concluded, the firm did not give decisive emphasis to such traits only because Hopkins was a woman; although there were male candidates who lacked these skills but who were admitted to partnership, the judge found that these candidates possessed other, positive traits that Hopkins lacked.

The judge went on to decide, however, that some of the partners' remarks about Hopkins stemmed from an impermissibly cabined view of the proper behavior of women, and that Price Waterhouse had done nothing to disavow reliance on such comments. He held that Price Waterhouse had unlawfully discriminated against Hopkins on the basis of sex by consciously giving credence and effect to partners' comments that resulted from sex stereotyping. Noting that Price Waterhouse could avoid equitable relief by proving by clear and convincing evidence that it would have placed Hopkins' candidacy on hold even absent this discrimination, the judge decided that the firm had not carried this heavy burden.

The Court of Appeals affirmed the District court's ultimate conclusion, but departed from its analysis in one particular: it held that even if a plaintiff proves that discrimination played a role in an employment decision, the defendant will not be found liable if it proves, by clear and convincing evidence, that it would have made the same decision in the absence of discrimination. Under this approach, an employer is not deemed to have violated Title VII if it proves that it would have made the same decision in the absence of an impermissible motive, whereas under the District Court's approach, the employer's proof in that respect only avoids equitable relief. We decide today that the Court of Appeals had the better approach, but that both courts erred in requiring the employer to make its proof by clear and convincing evidence.

II

The specification of the standard of causation under Title VII is a decision about the kind of conduct that violates that statute. According to Price Waterhouse, an employer violates Title VII only if it gives decisive consideration to an employee's gender, race, national origin, or religion in making a decision that affects that employee. On Price Waterhouse's theory, even if a plaintiff shows that her gender played a part in an employment decision, it is still her burden to show that the decision would have been different if the employer had not discriminated. In Hopkins' view, on the other hand, an employer violates the statute whenever it allows one of these attributes to play any part in an employment decision. Once a plaintiff shows that this occurred, according to Hopkins, the employer's proof that it would have made the same decision in the absence of discrimination can serve to limit equitable relief but not to avoid a finding of liability.[2] We conclude that, as often happens, the truth lies somewhere in-between.

A

In passing Title VII, Congress made the simple but momentous announcement that sex, race, religion, and national origin are not relevant to the selection, evaluation, or compensation of employees.[3] Yet, the statute does not purport to limit the other qualities and characteristics that employers *may* take into account in making employment decisions. The converse, therefore, of "for cause" legislation,[4] Title VII eliminates certain bases for distinguishing among employees while otherwise

---

[2]This question has, to say the least, left the Circuits in disarray. The Third, Fourth, Fifth, and Seventh Circuits require a plaintiff challenging an adverse employment decision to show that, but for her gender (or race or religion or national origin), the decision would have been in her favor. The First, Second, Sixth, and Eleventh Circuits, on the other hand, hold that once the plaintiff has shown that a discriminatory motive was a "substantial" or "motivating" factor in an employment decision, the employer may avoid a finding of liability only by proving that it would have made the same decision even in the absence of discrimination. These courts have either specified that the employer must prove its case by a preponderance of the evidence or have not mentioned the proper standard of proof. The Court of Appeals for the D.C. Circuit, as shown in this case, follows the same rule except that it requires that the employer's proof be clear and convincing rather than merely preponderant. The Court of Appeals for the Ninth Circuit also requires clear and convincing proof, but it goes further by holding that a Title VII violation is made out as soon as the plaintiff shows that an impermissible motivation played a part in an employment decision — at which point the employer may avoid reinstatement and an award of backpay by proving that it would have made the same decision in the absence of the unlawful motive. Last, the Court of Appeals for the Eighth Circuit draws the same distinction as the Ninth between the liability and remedial phases of Title VII litigation, but requires only a preponderance of the evidence from the employer.

[3]We disregard, for purposes of this discussion, the special context of affirmative action.

[4]Congress specifically declined to require that an employment decision have been "for cause" in order to escape an affirmative penalty (such as reinstatement or backpay) from a court. As introduced in the House, the bill that became Title VII forbade such affirmative relief if an "individual was * * * refused employment or advancement, or was suspended or discharged *for cause*." H.R. 7152, 88th Cong., 1st Sess. 77 (1963) (emphasis added). The phrase "for cause" eventually was deleted in favor of the phrase "for any reason other than" one of the enumerated characteristics. See 110 Cong.Rec. 2567-2571 (1964). Representative Celler explained that this substitution "specif[ied] cause"; in his view, a court "cannot find any violation of the act which is based on facts other * * * than discrimination on the grounds of race, color, religion, or national origin." Id., at 2567.

preserving employers' freedom of choice. This balance between employee rights and employer prerogatives turns out to be decisive in the case before us.

Congress' intent to forbid employers to take gender into account in making employment decisions appears on the face of the statute. In now-familiar language, the statute forbids an employer to "fail or refuse to hire or to discharge any individual, or otherwise to discriminate with respect to his compensation, terms, conditions, or privileges of employment," or to "limit, segregate, or classify his employees or applicants for employment in any way which would deprive or tend to deprive any individual of employment opportunities or otherwise adversely affect his status as an employee, *because of* such individual's * * * sex." (emphasis added).[5] We take these words to mean that gender must be irrelevant to employment decisions. To construe the words "because of" as colloquial shorthand for "but-for causation," as does Price Waterhouse, is to misunderstand them.[6]

But-for causation is a hypothetical construct. In determining whether a particular factor was a but-for cause of a given event, we begin by assuming that that factor was present at the time of the event, and then ask whether, even if that factor had been absent, the event nevertheless would have transpired in the same way. The present, active tense of the operative verbs of §703(a)(1) ("to fail or refuse"), in contrast, turns our attention to the actual moment of the event in question, the adverse employment decision. The critical inquiry, the one commanded by the words of §703(a)(1), is whether gender was a factor in the employment decision *at the moment it was made.* Moreover, since we know that the words "because of" do not mean "*solely* because of,"[7] we also know that Title VII meant to condemn even those decisions based on a mixture of legitimate and illegitimate considerations. When, therefore, an employer considers both gender and legitimate factors at the time of making a decision, that decision was "because of" sex and the other, legitimate considerations — even if we may say later, in the context of litigation, that the decision would have been the same if gender had not been taken into account.

To attribute this meaning to the words "because of" does not, as the dissent asserts, divest them of causal significance. A simple example illustrates the point. Suppose two physical forces act upon and move an object, and suppose that either

---

[5]In this Court, Hopkins for the first time argues that Price Waterhouse violated §703(a)(2) when it subjected her to a biased decisionmaking process that "tended to deprive" a woman of partnership on the basis of her sex. Since Hopkins did not make this argument below, we do not address it.

[6]We made passing reference to a similar question in McDonald v. Santa Fe Trail Transportation Co., where we stated that when a Title VII plaintiff seeks to show that an employer's explanation for a challenged employment decision is pretextual, "no more is required to be shown than that race was a 'but for' cause." This passage, however, does not suggest that the plaintiff *must* show but-for cause; it indicates only that if she does so, she prevails. More important, *McDonald* dealt with the question whether the employer's stated reason for its decision was *the* reason for its action; unlike the case before us today, therefore, *McDonald* did not involve mixed motives. This difference is decisive in distinguishing this case from those involving "pretext."

[7]Congress specifically rejected an amendment that would have placed the word "solely" in front of the words "because of." 110 Cong.Rec. 2728, 13837 (1964).

force acting alone would have moved the object. As the dissent would have it, *neither* physical force was a "cause" of the motion unless we can show that but for one or both of them, the object would not have moved; to use the dissent's terminology, both forces were simply "in the air" unless we can identify at least one of them as a but-for cause of the object's movement. Events that are causally overdetermined, in other words, may not have any "cause" at all. This cannot be so.

We need not leave our common sense at the doorstep when we interpret a statute. It is difficult for us to imagine that, in the simple words "because of," Congress meant to obligate a plaintiff to identify the precise causal role played by legitimate and illegitimate motivations in the employment decision she challenges. We conclude, instead, that Congress meant to obligate her to prove that the employer relied upon sex-based considerations in coming to its decision.

Our interpretation of the words "because of" also is supported by the fact that Title VII does identify one circumstance in which an employer may take gender into account in making an employment decision, namely, when gender is "bona fide occupational qualification reasonably necessary to the normal operation of th[e] particular business or enterprise." The only plausible inference to draw from this provision is that, in all other circumstances, a person's gender may not be considered in making decisions that affect her. Indeed, Title VII even forbids employers to make gender an indirect stumbling block to employment opportunities. An employer may not, we have held, condition employment opportunities on the satisfaction of facially neutral tests or qualifications that have a disproportionate, adverse impact on members of protected groups when those tests or qualifications are not required for performance of the job.

To say that an employer may not take gender into account is not, however, the end of the matter, for that describes only one aspect of Title VII. The other important aspect of the statute is its preservation of an employer's remaining freedom of choice. We conclude that the preservation of this freedom means that an employer shall not be liable if it can prove that, even if it had not taken gender into account, it would have come to the same decision regarding a particular person. The statute's maintenance of employer prerogatives is evident from the statute itself and from its history, both in Congress and in this Court.

To begin with, the existence of the BFOQ exception shows Congress' unwillingness to require employers to change the very nature of their operations in response to the statute. And our emphasis on "business necessity" in disparate-impact cases, see *Watson* and *Griggs*, and on "legitimate, nondiscriminatory reason[s]" in disparate-treatment cases, results from our awareness of Title VII's balance between employee rights and employer prerogatives. In *McDonnell Douglas*, we described as follows Title VII's goal to eradicate discrimination while preserving workplace efficiency: "The broad, overriding interest, shared by employer, employee, and consumer, is efficient and trustworthy workmanship assured through fair and racially neutral employment and personnel decisions. In the implementation of such decisions, it is abundantly clear that Title VII tolerates no racial discrimination, subtle or otherwise."

When an employer ignored the attributes enumerated in the statute, Congress hoped, it naturally would focus on the qualifications of the applicant or employee. The intent to drive employers to focus on qualifications rather than on race, religion, sex, or national origin is the theme of a good deal of the statute's legislative history. An interpretive memorandum entered into the Congressional Record by Senators Case and Clark, comanagers of the bill in the Senate, is representative of this general theme.[8] According to their memorandum, Title VII "expressly protects the employer's right to insist that any prospective applicant, Negro or white, must meet the applicable job qualifications. Indeed, the very purpose of title VII is to promote hiring on the basis of job qualifications, rather than on the basis of race or color."[9] The memorandum went on: "To discriminate is to make a distinction, to make a difference in treatment or favor, and those distinctions or differences in treatment or favor which are prohibited by section 704 are those which are based on any five of the forbidden criteria: race, color, religion, sex, and national origin. Any other criterion or qualification for employment is not affected by this title." 110 Cong.Rec. 7213 (1964).

Many other legislators made statements to a similar effect; we see no need to set out each remark in full here. The central point is this: while an employer may not take gender into account in making an employment decision (except in those very narrow circumstances in which gender is a BFOQ), it is free to decide against a woman for other reasons. We think these principles require that, once a plaintiff in a Title VII case shows that gender played a motivating part in an employment decision, the defendant may avoid a finding of liability[10] only by proving that it would have made

---

[8]We have in the past acknowledged the authoritativeness of this interpretive memorandum, written by the two bipartisan "captains" of Title VII. See, e.g., Firefighters v. Stotts, 467 U.S. 561, 581, n. 14, 104 S.Ct. 2576, 2589, n. 14, 81 L.Ed.2d 483 (1984).

[9]Many of the legislators' statements, such as the memorandum quoted in text, focused specifically on race rather than on gender or religion or national origin. We do not, however, limit their statements to the context of race, but instead we take them as general statements on the meaning of Title VII. The somewhat bizarre path by which "sex" came to be included as a forbidden criterion for employment — it was included in an attempt to *defeat* the bill, see C. & B. Whalen, The Longest Debate: A Legislative History of the 1964 Civil Rights Act 115-117 (1985) — does not persuade us that the legislators' statements pertaining to race are irrelevant to cases alleging gender discrimination. The amendment that added "sex" as one of the forbidden criteria for employment was passed, of course, and the statute on its face treats each of the enumerated categories exactly the same.

By the same token, our specific references to gender throughout this opinion, and the principles we announce, apply with equal force to discrimination based on race, religion, or national origin.

[10]Hopkins argues that once she made this showing, she was entitled to a finding that Price Waterhouse had discriminated against her on the basis of sex; as a consequence, she says, the partnership's proof could only limit the relief she received. She relies on Title VII's §706(g), which permits a court to award affirmative relief when it finds that an employer "has intentionally engaged in or is intentionally engaging in an unlawful employment practice," and yet forbids a court to order reinstatement of, or backpay to, "an individual * * * if such individual was refused * * * employment or advancement or was suspended or discharged *for any reason other than* discrimination on account of race, color, religion, sex, or national origin." 42 U.S.C. §2000-5(g) (emphasis added). We do not take this provision to mean that a court inevitably can find a violation of the statute without having considered whether the employment decision would have been the same absent the impermissible motive. That would be to interpret §706(g) — a provision defining *remedies* — to influence the substantive commands of the statute. We think that this provision merely limits courts' authority to award affirmative relief in

the same decision even if it had not allowed gender to play such a role. This balance of burdens is the direct result of Title VII's balance of rights.

Our holding casts no shadow on *Burdine*, in which we decided that, even after a plaintiff has made out a prima facie case of discrimination under Title VII, the burden of persuasion does not shift to the employer to show that its stated legitimate reason for the employment decision was the true reason. We stress, first, that neither court below shifted the burden of persuasion to Price Waterhouse on this question, and in fact, the District Court found that Hopkins had not shown that the firm's stated reason for its decision was pretextual. Moreover, since we hold that the plaintiff retains the burden of persuasion on the issue whether gender played a part in the employment decision, the situation before us is not the one of "shifting burdens" that we addressed in *Burdine*. Instead, the employer's burden is most appropriately deemed an affirmative defense: the plaintiff must persuade the factfinder on one point, and then the employer, if it wishes to prevail, must persuade it on another. See NLRB v. Transportation Management Corp., 462 U.S. 393, 400, 103 S.Ct. 2469, 2473, 76 L.Ed.2d 667 (1983).[11]

Price Waterhouse's claim that the employer does not bear any burden of proof (if it bears one at all) until the plaintiff has shown substantial evidence that Price Waterhouse's explanation for failing to promote Hopkins was not the "true reason" for

---

those circumstances in which a violation of the statute is not dependent upon the effect of the employer's discriminatory practices on a particular employee, as in pattern-or-practice suits and class actions. "The crucial difference between an individual's claim of discrimination and a class action alleging a general pattern or practice of discrimination is manifest. The inquiry regarding an individual's claim is the reason for a particular employment decision, while 'at the liability stage of a pattern-or-practice trial the focus often will not be on individual hiring decisions, but on a pattern of discriminatory decisionmaking.'" Cooper v. Federal Reserve Bank of Richmond.

Without explicitly mentioning this portion of §706(g), we have in the past held that Title VII does not authorize affirmative relief for individuals as to whom, the employer shows, the existence of systemic discrimination had no effect. See Franks v. Bowman Transportation Co.; Teamsters v. United States; East Texas Motor Freight System, Inc. v. Rodriguez. These decisions suggest that the proper focus of §706(g) is on claims of systemic discrimination, not on charges of individual discrimination. Cf. NLRB v. Transportation Management Corp. (upholding the National Labor Relations Board's identical interpretation of §10(c) of the National Labor Relations Act, 29 U.S.C. §160(c), which contains language almost identical to §706(g)).

[11]Given that both the plaintiff and defendant bear a burden of proof in cases such as this one, it is surprising that the dissent insists that our approach requires the employer to bear "the ultimate burden of proof." It is, moreover, perfectly consistent to say both that gender was a factor in a particular decision when it was made and that, when the situation is viewed hypothetically and after the fact, the same decision would have been made even in the absence of discrimination. Thus, we do not see the "internal inconsistency" in our opinion that the dissent perceives. Finally, where liability is imposed because an employer is unable to prove that it would have made the same decision even if it had not discriminated, this is not an imposition of liability "where sex made no difference to the outcome." In our adversary system, where a party has the burden of proving a particular assertion and where that party is unable to meet its burden, we assume that that assertion is inaccurate. Thus, where an employer is unable to prove its claim that it would have made the same decision in the absence of discrimination, we are entitled to conclude that gender did make a difference to the outcome.

its action merely restates its argument that the plaintiff in a mixed-motives case must squeeze her proof into *Burdine's* framework. Where a decision was the product of a mixture of legitimate and illegitimate motives, however, it simply makes no sense to ask whether the legitimate reason was "the 'true reason'" for the decision — which is the question asked by *Burdine*. See *Transportation Management*, *supra*, at 400, n. 5.[12] Oblivious to this last point, the dissent would insist that *Burdine's* framework perform work that it was never intended to perform. It would require a plaintiff who challenges an adverse employment decision in which both legitimate and illegitimate considerations played a part to pretend that the decision, in fact, stemmed from a single source—for the premise of *Burdine* is that *either* a legitimate or an illegitimate set of considerations led to the challenged decision. To say that *Burdine's* evidentiary scheme will not help us decide a case admittedly involving both kinds of considerations is not to cast aspersions on the utility of that scheme in the circumstances for which it was designed.

* * *

C

In saying that gender played a motivating part in an employment decision, we mean that, if we asked the employer at the moment of the decision what its reasons were and if we received a truthful response, one of those reasons would be that the applicant or employee was a woman.[13] In the specific context of sex stereotyping, an employer who acts on the basis of a belief that a woman cannot be aggressive, or that she must not be, has acted on the basis of gender.

Although the parties do not overtly dispute this last proposition, the placement by Price Waterhouse of "sex stereotyping" in quotation marks throughout its brief seems to us an insinuation either that such stereotyping was not present in this case or that it

---

[12]Nothing in this opinion should be taken to suggest that a case must be correctly labeled as either a "pretext" case or a "mixed motives" case from the beginning in the District Court; indeed, we expect that plaintiffs often will allege, in the alternative, that their cases are both. Discovery often will be necessary before the plaintiff can know whether both legitimate and illegitimate considerations played a part in the decision against her. At some point in the proceedings, of course, the District Court must decide whether a particular case involves mixed motives. If the plaintiff fails to satisfy the factfinder that it is more likely than not that a forbidden characteristic played a part in the employment decision, then she may prevail only if she proves, following *Burdine,* that the employer's stated reason for its decision is pretextual. The dissent need not worry that this evidentiary scheme, if used during a jury trial, will be so impossibly confused and complex as it imagines. Juries long have decided cases in which defendants raise affirmative defenses. The dissent fails, moreover, to explain why the evidentiary scheme that we endorsed over ten years ago in *Mt. Healthy* has not proved unworkable in that context but would be hopelessly complicated in a case brought under federal antidiscrimination statutes.

[13]After comparing this description of the plaintiff's proof to that offered by the concurring opinion, we do not understand why the concurrence suggests that they are meaningfully different from each other. Nor do we see how the inquiry that we have described is "hypothetical". It seeks to determine the content of the entire set of reasons for a decision, rather than shaving off one reason in an attempt to determine what the decision would have been in the absence of that consideration. The inquiry that we describe thus strikes us as a distinctly non-hypothetical one.

lacks legal relevance. We reject both possibilities. As to the existence of sex stereotyping in this case, we are not inclined to quarrel with the District Court's conclusion that a number of the partners' comments showed sex stereotyping at work. As for the legal relevance of sex stereotyping, we are beyond the day when an employer could evaluate employees by assuming or insisting that they matched the stereotype associated with their group, for "[i]n forbidding employers to discriminate against individuals because of their sex, Congress intended to strike at the entire spectrum of disparate treatment of men and women resulting from sex stereotypes." Los Angeles Dept. of Water & Power v. Manhart, 435 U.S. 702, 707, n. 13, 98 S.Ct. 1370, 1375, n. 13, 55 L.Ed.2d 657 (1978). An employer who objects to aggressiveness in women but whose positions require this trait places women in an intolerable and impermissible Catch-22: out of a job if they behave aggressively and out of a job if they don't. Title VII lifts women out of this bind.

Remarks at work that are based on sex stereotypes do not inevitably prove that gender played a part in a particular employment decision. The plaintiff must show that the employer actually relied on her gender in making its decision. In making this showing, stereotyped remarks can certainly be *evidence* that gender played a part. In any event, the stereotyping in this case did not simply consist of stray remarks. On the contrary, Hopkins proved that Price Waterhouse invited partners to submit comments; that some of the comments stemmed from sex stereotypes; that an important part of the Policy Board's decision on Hopkins was an assessment of the submitted comments; and that Price Waterhouse in no way disclaimed reliance on the sex-linked evaluations. This is not, as Price Waterhouse suggests, "discrimination in the air"; rather, it is, as Hopkins puts it, "discrimination brought to ground and visited upon" an employee. By focusing on Hopkins' specific proof, however, we do not suggest a limitation on the possible ways of proving that stereotyping played a motivating role in an employment decision, and we refrain from deciding here which specific facts, "standing alone," would or would not establish a plaintiff's case, since such a decision is unnecessary in this case.

As to the employer's proof, in most cases, the employer should be able to present some objective evidence as to its probable decision in the absence of an impermissible motive.[14] Moreover, proving "that the same decision would have been justified * * * is not the same as proving that the same decision would have been made." Givhan v. Western Consolidated School District, 439 U.S. 410, 416, 99 S.Ct. 693, 697 (1979). An employer may not, in other words, prevail in a mixed-motives case by offering a legitimate and sufficient reason for its decision if that reason did not motivate it at the time of the decision. Finally, an employer may not meet its burden in such a case by merely showing that at the time of the decision it was motivated only in part by a legitimate reason. The very premise of a mixed-motives case is that a legitimate reason was present, and indeed, in this case, Price Waterhouse already has made this showing by convincing Judge Gesell that Hopkins' interpersonal problems were a

---

[14]Justice White's suggestion that the employer's own testimony as to the probable decision in the absence of discrimination is due special credence where the court has, contrary to the employer's testimony, found that an illegitimate factor played a part in the decision, is baffling.

legitimate concern. The employer instead must show that its legitimate reason, standing alone, would have induced it to make the same decision.

III

The courts below held that an employer who has allowed a discriminatory impulse to play a motivating part in an employment decision must prove by clear and convincing evidence that it would have made the same decision in the absence of discrimination. We are persuaded that the better rule is that the employer must make this showing by a preponderance of the evidence.

* * *

Significantly, the cases from this Court that most resemble this one, *Mt. Healthy and Transportation Management,* did not require clear and convincing proof. We are not inclined to say that the public policy against firing employees because they spoke out on issues of public concern or because they affiliated with a union is less important than the policy against discharging employees on the basis of their gender. Each of these policies is vitally important, and each is adequately served by requiring proof by a preponderance of the evidence.

Although Price Waterhouse does not concretely tell us how its proof was preponderant even if it was not clear and convincing, this general claim is implicit in its request for the less stringent standard. Since the lower courts required Price Waterhouse to make its proof by clear and convincing evidence, they did not determine whether Price Waterhouse had proved by a *preponderance of the evidence* that it would have placed Hopkins' candidacy on hold even if it had not permitted sex-linked evaluations to play a part in the decision-making process. Thus, we shall remand this case so that that determination can be made.

IV

The District Court found that sex stereotyping "was permitted to play a part" in the evaluation of Hopkins as a candidate for partnership. Price Waterhouse disputes both that stereotyping occurred and that it played any part in the decision to place Hopkins' candidacy on hold. In the firm's view, in other words, the District Court's factual conclusions are clearly erroneous. We do not agree.

In finding that some of the partners' comments reflected sex stereotyping, the District Court relied in part on Dr. Fiske's expert testimony. Without directly impugning Dr. Fiske's credentials or qualifications, Price Waterhouse insinuates that a social psychologist is unable to identify sex stereotyping in evaluations without investigating whether those evaluations have a basis in reality. This argument comes too late. At trial, counsel for Price Waterhouse twice assured the court that he did not question Dr. Fiske's expertise and failed to challenge the legitimacy of her discipline. Without contradiction from Price Waterhouse, Fiske testified that she discerned sex stereotyping in the partners' evaluations of Hopkins and she further explained that it was part of her business to identify stereotyping in written documents. We are not inclined to accept petitioner's belated and unsubstantiated characterization of Dr. Fiske's testimony as "gossamer evidence" based only on "intuitive hunches" and of her detection of sex stereotyping as "intuitively divined." Nor are we disposed to adopt the dissent's dismissive attitude toward Dr. Fiske's field of study and toward her own professional integrity.

Indeed, we are tempted to say that Dr. Fiske's expert testimony was merely icing on Hopkins' cake. It takes no special training to discern sex stereotyping in a description of an aggressive female employee as requiring "a course at charm school." Nor, turning to Thomas Beyer's memorable advice to Hopkins, does it require expertise in psychology to know that, if an employee's flawed "interpersonal skills" can be corrected by a soft-hued suit or a new shade of lipstick, perhaps it is the employee's sex and not her interpersonal skills that has drawn the criticism.[15]

Price Waterhouse also charges that Hopkins produced no evidence that sex stereotyping played a role in the decision to place her candidacy on hold. As we have stressed, however, Hopkins showed that the partnership solicited evaluations from all of the firm's partners; that it generally relied very heavily on such evaluations in making its decision; that some of the partners' comments were the product of stereotyping; and that the firm in no way disclaimed reliance on those particular comments, either in Hopkins' case or in the past. Certainly a plausible — and, one might say, inevitable — conclusion to draw from this set of circumstances is that the Policy Board in making its decision did in fact take into account all of the partners' comments, including the comments that were motivated by stereotypical notions about women's proper deportment.[16]

Price Waterhouse concedes that the proof in *Transportation Management, supra,* adequately showed that the employer there had relied on an impermissible motivation in firing the plaintiff. But the only evidence in that case that a discriminatory motive contributed to the plaintiff's discharge was that the employer harbored a grudge toward the plaintiff on account of his union activity; there was, contrary to Price Waterhouse's suggestion, no direct evidence that that grudge had played a role in the decision, and in fact, the employer had given other reasons in explaining the plaintiff's discharge. If the partnership considers that proof sufficient, we do not know why it takes such vehement issue with Hopkins' proof.

Nor is the finding that sex stereotyping played a part in the Policy Board's decision undermined by the fact that many of the suspect comments were made by supporters rather than detractors of Hopkins. A negative comment, even when made in the context of a generally favorable review, nevertheless may influence the decisionmaker to think less highly of the candidate; the Policy Board, in fact, did not simply tally the "yes's" and "no's" regarding a candidate, but carefully reviewed the content of the submitted comments. The additional suggestion that the comments were

---

[15]We reject the claim, advanced by Price Waterhouse here and by the dissenting judge below, that the District Court clearly erred in finding that Beyer was "responsible for telling [Hopkins] what problems the Policy Board had identified with her candidacy." This conclusion was reasonable in light of the testimony at trial of a member of both the Policy Board and the Admissions Committee, who stated that he had "no doubt" that Beyer would discuss with Hopkins the reasons for placing her candidacy on hold and that Beyer "knew exactly where the problems were" regarding Hopkins.

[16]We do not understand the dissenters' dissatisfaction with the District Judge's statements regarding the failure of Price Waterhouse to "sensitize" partners to the dangers of sexism. Made in the context of determining that Price Waterhouse had not disclaimed reliance on sex-based evaluations, and following the judge's description of the firm's history of condoning such evaluations, the judge's remarks seem to us justified.

made by "persons outside the decisionmaking chain" * * * — and therefore could not have harmed Hopkins — simply ignores the critical role that partners' comments played in the Policy Board's partnership decisions.

Price Waterhouse appears to think that we cannot affirm the factual findings of the trial court without deciding that, instead of being overbearing and aggressive and curt, Hopkins is in fact kind and considerate and patient. If this is indeed its impression, petitioner misunderstands the theory on which Hopkins prevailed. The District Judge acknowledged that Hopkins' conduct justified complaints about her behavior as a senior manager. But he also concluded that the reactions of at least some of the partners were reactions to her as a *woman* manager. Where an evaluation is based on a subjective assessment of a person's strengths and weaknesses, it is simply not true that each evaluator will focus on, or even mention, the same weaknesses. Thus, even if we knew that Hopkins had "personality problems," this would not tell us that the partners who cast their evaluations of Hopkins in sex-based terms would have criticized her as sharply (or criticized her at all) if she had been a man. It is not our job to review the evidence and decide that the negative reactions to Hopkins were based on reality; our perception of Hopkins' character is irrelevant. We sit not to determine whether Ms. Hopkins is nice, but to decide whether the partners reacted negatively to her personality because she is a woman.

V

We hold that when a plaintiff in a Title VII case proves that her gender played a motivating part in an employment decision, the defendant may avoid a finding of liability only by proving by a preponderance of the evidence that it would have made the same decision even if it had not taken the plaintiff's gender into account. Because the courts below erred by deciding that the defendant must make this proof by clear and convincing evidence, we reverse the Court of Appeals' judgment against Price Waterhouse on liability and remand the case to that court for further proceedings.

It is so ordered.

JUSTICE WHITE, concurring in the judgment.

* * *

Because the Court of Appeals required Price Waterhouse to prove by clear and convincing evidence that it would have reached the same employment decision in the absence of the improper motive, rather than merely requiring proof by a preponderance of the evidence as in *Mt. Healthy*, I concur in the judgment reversing this case in part and remanding. With respect to the employer's burden, however, the plurality seems to require, at least in most cases, that the employer submit objective evidence that the same result would have occurred absent the unlawful motivation. In my view, however, there is no special requirement that the employer carry its burden by objective evidence. In a mixed motive case, where the legitimate motive found would have been ample grounds for the action taken, and the employer credibly testifies that the action would have been taken for the legitimate reasons alone, this should be ample proof. This would even more plainly be the case where the employer denies any illegitimate motive in the first place but the court finds that illegitimate, as well as legitimate, factors motivated the adverse action.[*]

JUSTICE O'CONNOR, concurring in the judgment.

I agree with the plurality that on the facts presented in this case, the burden of persuasion should shift to the employer to demonstrate by a preponderance of the evidence that it would have reached the same decision concerning Ann Hopkins' candidacy absent consideration of her gender. I further agree that this burden shift is properly part of the liability phase of the litigation. I thus concur in the judgment of the Court. My disagreement stems from the plurality's conclusions concerning the substantive requirement of causation under the statute and its broad statements regarding the applicability of the allocation of the burden of proof applied in this case. The evidentiary rule the Court adopts today should be viewed as a supplement to the careful framework established by our unanimous decisions in McDonnell Douglas Corp. v. Green, and Texas Dept. of Community Affairs v. Burdine, for use in cases such as this one where the employer has created uncertainty as to causation by knowingly giving substantial weight to an impermissible criterion. I write separately to explain why I believe such a departure from the *McDonnell Douglas* standard is justified in the circumstances presented by this and like cases, and to express my views as to when and how the strong medicine of requiring the employer to bear the burden of persuasion on the issue of causation should be administered.

I

* * *

Like the common law of torts, the statutory employment "tort" created by Title VII has two basic purposes. The first is to deter conduct which has been identified as contrary to public policy and harmful to society as a whole. As we have noted in the past, the award of backpay to a Title VII plaintiff provides "the spur or catalyst which causes employers and unions to self-examine and to self-evaluate their employment practices and to endeavor to eliminate, so far as possible, the last vestiges" of discrimination in employment. Albemarle Paper Co. v. Moody, 422 U.S. 405, 417-418, 95 S.Ct. 2362, 2371-2372, 45 L.Ed.2d 280 (1975). The second goal of Title VII is "to make persons whole for injuries suffered on account of unlawful employment discrimination." Id., at 418, 95 S.Ct., at 2372.

Both these goals are reflected in the elements of a disparate treatment action. There is no doubt that Congress considered reliance on gender or race in making employment decisions an evil in itself. As Senator Clark put it, "[t]he bill simply eliminates consideration of color [or other forbidden criteria] from the decision to hire or promote." 110 Cong.Rec. 7218 (1964). Reliance on such factors is exactly what the threat of Title VII liability was meant to deter. While the main concern of the statute was with employment opportunity, Congress was certainly not blind to the stigmatic harm which comes from being evaluated by a process which treats one as an inferior by reason of one's race or sex. This Court's decisions under the Equal

---

[*]I agree with the plurality that if the employer carries this burden, there has been no violation of Title VII.

Protection Clause have long recognized that whatever the final outcome of a decisional process, the inclusion of race or sex as a consideration within it harms both society and the individual. At the same time, Congress clearly conditioned legal liability on a determination that the consideration of an illegitimate factor caused a tangible employment injury of some kind.

Where an individual disparate treatment plaintiff has shown by a preponderance of the evidence that an illegitimate criterion was a *substantial* factor in an adverse employment decision, the deterrent purpose of the statute has clearly been triggered. More importantly, as an evidentiary matter, a reasonable factfinder could conclude that absent further explanation, the employer's discriminatory motivation "caused" the employment decision. The employer has not yet been shown to be a violator, but neither is it entitled to the same presumption of good faith concerning its employment decisions which is accorded employers facing only circumstantial evidence of discrimination. Both the policies behind the statute, and the evidentiary principles developed in the analogous area of causation in the law of torts, suggest that at this point the employer may be required to convince the factfinder that, despite the smoke, there is no fire.

We have given recognition to these principles in our cases which have discussed the "remedial phase" of class action disparate treatment cases. Once the class has established that discrimination against a protected group was essentially the employer's "standard practice," there has been harm to the group and injunctive relief is appropriate. But as to the individual members of the class, the liability phase of the litigation is not complete. See Dillon v. Coles, 746 F.2d 998, 1004 (CA3 1984) ("It is misleading to speak of the additional proof required by an individual class member for relief as being a part of the damage phase, that evidence is actually an element of the liability portion of the case") (footnote omitted). Because the class has already demonstrated that, as a rule, illegitimate factors were considered in the employer's decisions, the burden shifts to the employer "to demonstrate that the individual applicant was denied an employment opportunity for legitimate reasons." Teamsters v. United States, 431 U.S. 324, 362, 97 S.Ct. 1843, 1868, 52 L.Ed.2d 396 (1977).

The individual members of a class action treatment case stand in much the same position as Ann Hopkins here. There has been a strong showing that the employer has done exactly what Title VII forbids, but the connection between the employer's illegitimate motivation and any injury to the individual plaintiff is unclear. At this point calling upon the employer to show that despite consideration of illegitimate factors the individual plaintiff would not have been hired or promoted in any event hardly seems "unfair" or contrary to the substantive command of the statute. In fact, an individual plaintiff who has shown that an illegitimate factor played a substantial role in the decision in her case has proved *more* than the class member in a *Teamsters* type action. The latter receives the benefit of a burden shift to the defendant based on the *likelihood* that an illegitimate criterion was a factor in the individual employment decision.

* * *

II

The dissent's summary of our individual disparate treatment cases to date is fair and accurate, and amply demonstrates that the rule we adopt today is a at least a change in direction from some of our prior precedents. We have indeed emphasized in the past that in an individual disparate treatment action the plaintiff bears the burden of persuasion throughout the litigation. Nor have we confined the word "pretext" to the narrow definition which the plurality attempts to pin on it today. *McDonnell Douglas* and *Burdine* clearly contemplated that a disparate treatment plaintiff could show that the employer's proffered explanation for an event was not "the true reason" either because it *never* motivated the employer in its employment decisions or because it did not do so in a particular case. *McDonnell Douglas* and *Burdine* assumed that the plaintiff would bear the burden of persuasion as to both these attacks, and we clearly depart from that framework today. Such a departure requires justification, and its outlines should be carefully drawn.

First, *McDonnell Douglas* itself dealt with a situation where the plaintiff presented no direct evidence that the employer had relied on a forbidden factor under Title VII in making an employment decision. The prima facie case established there was not difficult to prove, and was based only on the statistical probability that when a number of potential causes for an employment decision are eliminated an inference arises that an illegitimate factor was in fact the motivation behind the decision. In the face of this inferential proof, the employer's burden was deemed to be only one of production; the employer must articulate a legitimate reason for the adverse employment action. The plaintiff must then be given an "opportunity to demonstrate by competent evidence that the presumptively valid reasons for his rejection were in fact a coverup for a racially discriminatory decision." *McDonnell Douglas*. Our decision in *Burdine* also involved the "narrow question" whether, after a plaintiff had carried the "not onerous" burden of establishing the prima facie case under *McDonnell Douglas*, the burden of persuasion should be shifted to the employer to prove that a legitimate reason for the adverse employment action existed. As the discussion of *Teamsters* and *Arlington Heights* indicates, I do not think that the employer is entitled to the same presumption of good faith where there is direct evidence that it has placed substantial reliance on factors whose consideration is forbidden by Title VII.

The only individual treatment case cited by the dissent which involved the kind of direct evidence of discriminatory animus with which we are confronted here is United States Postal Service Bd. of Governors v. Aikens. The question presented to the Court in that case involved only a challenge to the elements of the prima facie case under *McDonnell Douglas* and *Burdine*, and the question we confront today was neither briefed nor argued to the Court. As should be apparent, the entire purpose of the *McDonnell Douglas* prima facie case is to compensate for the fact that direct evidence of intentional discrimination is hard to come by. That the employer's burden in rebutting such an inferential case of discrimination is only one of production does not mean that the scales should be weighted in the same manner where there is direct evidence of intentional discrimination. Indeed, in one Age Discrimination in Employment Act case, the Court seemed to indicate that "the *McDonnell Douglas* test is inapplicable where the plaintiff presents direct evidence of discrimination." Trans World Airlines, Inc. v. Thurston, 469 U.S. 111, 121, 105 S.Ct. 613, 621-622, 83 L.Ed.2d 523 (1985).

Second, the facts of this case, and a growing number like it decided by the Courts of Appeals, convince me that the evidentiary standard I propose is necessary to make real the promise of *McDonnell Douglas* that "[i]n the implementation of [employment] decisions, it is abundantly clear that Title VII tolerates no * * * discrimination, subtle or otherwise." In this case, the District Court found that a number of the evaluations of Ann Hopkins submitted by partners in the firm overtly referred to her failure to conform to certain gender stereotypes as a factor militating against her election to the partnership. The District Court further found that these evaluations were given "great weight" by the decisionmakers at Price Waterhouse. In addition, the District Court found that the partner responsible for informing Hopkins of the factors which caused her candidacy to be placed on hold, indicated that her "professional" problems would be solved if she would "walk more femininely, talk more femininely, wear make-up, have her hair styled, and wear jewelry." As the Court of Appeals characterized it, Ann Hopkins proved that Price Waterhouse "permitt[ed] stereotypical attitudes towards women to play a significant, though unquantifiable, role in its decision not to invite her to become a partner."

At this point Ann Hopkins had taken her proof as far as it could go. She had proved discriminatory input into the decisional process, and had proved that participants in the process considered her failure to conform to the stereotypes credited by a number of the decisionmakers had been a substantial factor in the decision. It is as if Ann Hopkins were sitting in the hall outside the room where partnership decisions were being made. As the partners filed in to consider her candidacy, she heard several of them make sexist remarks in discussing her suitability for partnership. As the decisionmakers exited the room, she was *told* by one of those privy to the decisionmaking process that her gender was a major reason for the rejection of her partnership bid. If, as we noted in *Teamsters*, "[p]resumptions shifting the burden of proof are often created to reflect judicial evaluations of probabilities and to conform with a party's superior access to the proof," one would be hard pressed to think of a situation where it would be more appropriate to require the defendant to show that its decision would have been justified by wholly legitimate concerns.

Moreover, there is mounting evidence in the decisions of the lower courts that respondent here is not alone in her inability to pinpoint discrimination as the precise cause of her injury, despite having shown that it played a significant role in the decisional process. Many of these courts, which deal with the evidentiary issues in Title VII cases on a regular basis, have concluded that placing the risk of nonpersuasion on the defendant in a situation where uncertainty as to causation has been created by its consideration of an illegitimate criterion makes sense as a rule of evidence and furthers the substantive command of Title VII. See, e.g., Bell v. Birmingham Linen Service, 715 F.2d 1552, 1556 (CA11 1983) (Tjoflat, J.) ("It would be illogical, indeed ironic, to hold a Title VII plaintiff presenting direct evidence of a defendant's intent to discriminate to a more stringent burden of proof, or to allow a defendant to meet that direct proof by merely articulating, but not proving, legitimate, nondiscriminatory reasons for its action"). Particularly in the context of the professional world, where decisions are often made by collegial bodies on the basis of largely subjective criteria, requiring the plaintiff to prove that *any* one factor was the definitive cause of the decisionmakers' action may be tantamount to declaring Title VII inapplicable to such decisions. See, e.g., Fields v. Clark University, 817 F.2d 931, 935-937 (CA1 1987) (where plaintiff produced "strong evidence" that sexist attitudes infected faculty tenure decision burden properly shifted to defendant to show that it would have reached the same decision absent discrimination).

Finally, I am convinced that a rule shifting the burden to the defendant where the plaintiff has shown that an illegitimate criterion was a "substantial factor" in the employment decision will not conflict with other congressional policies embodied in Title VII. Title VII expressly provides that an employer need not give preferential treatment to employees or applicants of any race, color, religion, sex, or national origin in order to maintain a work force in balance with the general population. The interpretive memorandum, whose authoritative force is noted by the plurality, specifically provides: "There is no requirement in title VII that an employer maintain a racial balance in his work force. On the contrary, any deliberate attempt to maintain a racial balance, whatever such a balance may be, would involve a violation of title VII because maintaining such a balance would require an employer to hire or refuse to hire on the basis of race." 110 Cong.Rec. 7213 (1964).

* * *

While the danger of forcing employers to engage in unwarranted preferential treatment is thus less dramatic in this setting * * *, it is far from wholly illusory. Based on its misreading of the words "because of" in the statute, the plurality appears to conclude that if a decisional process is "tainted" by awareness of sex or race in any way, the employer has violated the statute, and Title VII thus *commands* that the burden shift to the employer to justify its decision. The plurality thus effectively reads the causation requirement out of the statute, and then replaces it with an "affirmative defense."

In my view, in order to justify shifting the burden on the issue of causation to the defendant, a disparate treatment plaintiff must show by direct evidence that an illegitimate criterion was a substantial factor in the decision. As the Court of Appeals noted below, "[w]hile most circuits have not confronted the question squarely, the consensus among those that have is that once a Title VII plaintiff has demonstrated by direct evidence that discriminatory animus played a significant or substantial role in the employment decision, the burden shifts to the employer to show that the decision would have been the same absent discrimination." Requiring that the plaintiff demonstrate that an illegitimate factor played a substantial role in the employment decision identifies those employment situations where the deterrent purpose of Title VII is most clearly implicated. As an evidentiary matter, where a plaintiff has made this type of strong showing of illicit motivation, the factfinder is entitled to presume that the employer's discriminatory animus made a difference to the outcome, absent proof to the contrary from the employer. Where a disparate treatment plaintiff has made such a showing, the burden then rests with the employer to convince the trier of fact that it is more likely than not that the decision would have been the same absent consideration of the illegitimate factor. The employer need not isolate the sole cause for the decision, rather it must demonstrate that with the illegitimate factor removed from the calculus, sufficient business reasons would have induced it to take the same employment action. This evidentiary scheme essentially requires the employer to place the employee in the same position he or she would have occupied absent discrimination. Cf. Mt. Healthy Board of Education v. Doyle. If the employer fails to carry this burden, the factfinder is justified in concluding that the decision was made "because of" consideration of the illegitimate factor and the substantive standard for liability under the statute is satisfied.

Thus, stray remarks in the workplace, while perhaps probative of sexual harassment, see Meritor Savings Bank v. Vinson, cannot justify requiring the employer to prove that its hiring or promotion decisions were based on legitimate criteria. Nor can statements by nondecisionmakers, or statements by decisionmakers unrelated to the decisional process itself suffice to satisfy the plaintiff's burden in this regard. In addition, in my view testimony such as Dr. Fiske's in this case, standing alone, would not justify shifting the burden of persuasion to the employer. Race and gender always "play a role" in an employment decision in the benign sense that these are human characteristics of which decisionmakers are aware and may comment on in a perfectly neutral and nondiscriminatory fashion. For example, in the context of this case, a mere reference to "a lady candidate" might show that gender "played a role" in the decision, but by no means could support a rational factfinder's inference that the decision was made "because of" sex. What is required is what Ann Hopkins showed here: direct evidence that decisionmakers placed substantial negative reliance on an illegitimate criterion in reaching their decision.

It should be obvious that the threshold standard I would adopt for shifting the burden of persuasion to the defendant differs substantially from that proposed by the plurality, the plurality's suggestion to the contrary notwithstanding. The plurality proceeds from the premise that the words "because of" in the statute do not embody any causal requirement at all. Under my approach, the plaintiff must produce evidence sufficient to show that an illegitimate criterion was a substantial factor in the particular employment decision such that a reasonable factfinder could draw an inference that the decision was made "because of" the plaintiff's protected status. Only then would the burden of proof shift to the defendant to prove that the decision would have been justified by other, wholly legitimate considerations.

In sum, because of the concerns outlined above, and because I believe that the deterrent purpose of Title VII is disserved by a rule which places the burden of proof on plaintiffs on the issue of causation in all circumstances, I would retain but supplement the framework we established in *McDonnell Douglas* and subsequent cases. The structure of the presentation of evidence in an individual treatment case should conform to the general outlines we established in *McDonnell Douglas* and *Burdine*. First, the plaintiff must establish the *McDonnell Douglas* prima facie case by showing membership in a protected group, qualification for the job, rejection for the position, and that after rejection the employer continued to seek applicants of complainant's general qualifications. The plaintiff should also present any direct evidence of discriminatory animus in the decisional process. The defendant should then present its case, including its evidence as to legitimate, nondiscriminatory reasons for the employment decision. As the dissent notes, under this framework, the employer "has every incentive to convince the trier of fact that the decision was lawful." Once all the evidence has been received, the court should determine whether the *McDonnell Douglas* or *Price Waterhouse* framework properly applies to the evidence before it. If the plaintiff has failed to satisfy the *Price Waterhouse* threshold, the case should be decided under the principles enunciated in *McDonnell Douglas* and *Burdine*, with the plaintiff bearing the burden of persuasion on the ultimate issue whether the employment action was taken because of discrimination. In my view, such a system is both fair and workable and it calibrates the evidentiary requirements demanded of the parties to the goals behind the statute itself.

I agree with the dissent, that the evidentiary framework I propose should be available to all disparate treatment plaintiffs where an illegitimate consideration played a substantial role in an adverse employment decision. The Court's allocation of the burden of proof in Johnson v. Transportation Agency, 480 U.S. 616, 626-627, 107 S.Ct. 1442, 1449, 94 L.Ed.2d 615 (1987), rested squarely on "the analytical framework set forth in *McDonnell Douglas*," which we alter today. It would be odd to say the least if the evidentiary rules applicable to Title VII actions were themselves dependent on the gender or the skin color of the litigants.

In this case, I agree with the plurality that petitioner should be called upon to show that the outcome would have been the same if respondent's professional merit had been its only concern. On remand, the District Court should determine whether Price Waterhouse has shown by a preponderance of the evidence that if gender had not been part of the process, its employment decision concerning Ann Hopkins would nonetheless have been the same.

JUSTICE KENNEDY, with whom THE CHIEF JUSTICE and JUSTICE SCALIA join, dissenting.

Today the Court manipulates existing and complex rules for employment discrimination cases in a way certain to result in confusion. Continued adherence to the evidentiary scheme established in *McDonnell Douglas* and *Burdine* is a wiser course than creation of more disarray in an area of the law already difficult for the bench and bar, and so I must dissent.

Before turning to my reasons for disagreement with the Court's disposition of the case, it is important to review the actual holding of today's decision. I read the opinions as establishing that in a limited number of cases Title VII plaintiffs, by presenting direct and substantial evidence of discriminatory animus, may shift the burden of persuasion to the defendant to show that an adverse employment decision would have been supported by legitimate reasons. The shift in the burden of persuasion occurs only where a plaintiff proves by direct evidence that an unlawful motive was a substantial factor actually relied upon in making the decision. As the opinions make plain, the evidentiary scheme created today is not for every case in which a plaintiff produces evidence of stray remarks in the workplace.

Where the plaintiff makes the requisite showing, the burden that shifts to the employer is to show that legitimate employment considerations would have justified the decision without reference to any impermissible motive. The employer's proof on the point is to be presented and reviewed just as with any other evidentiary question: the Court does not accept the plurality's suggestion that an employer's evidence need be "objective" or otherwise out of the ordinary.

In sum, the Court alters the evidentiary framework of *McDonnell Douglas* and *Burdine* for a closely defined set of cases. Although Justice O'Connor advances some thoughtful arguments for this change, I remain convinced that it is unnecessary and unwise. More troubling is the plurality's rationale for today's decision, which includes a number of unfortunate pronouncements on both causation and methods of proof in employment discrimination cases. To demonstrate the defects in the plurality's reasoning, it is necessary to discuss first, the standard of causation in Title VII cases, and second, the burden of proof.

I

The plurality describes this as a case about the standard of *causation* under Title VII, but I respectfully suggest that the description is misleading. Much of the plurality's rhetoric is spent denouncing a "but-for" standard of causation. The theory of Title VII liability the plurality adopts, however, essentially incorporates the but-for standard. The importance of today's decision is not the standard of causation it employs, but its shift to the defendant of the burden of proof. The plurality's causation analysis is misdirected, for it is clear that, whoever bears the burden of proof on the issue, Title VII liability requires a finding of but-for causation.

* * *

By any normal understanding, the phrase "because of" conveys the idea that the motive in question made a difference to the outcome. We use the words this way in everyday speech. And assuming, as the plurality does, that we ought to consider the interpretive memorandum prepared by the statute's drafters, we find that this is what the words meant to them as well. "To discriminate is to make a distinction, to make a difference in treatment or favor." 110 Cong.Rec. 7213 (1964). Congress could not have chosen a clearer way to indicate that proof of liability under Title VII requires a showing that race, color, religion, sex, or national origin caused the decision at issue.

* * *

What we term "but-for" cause is the least rigorous standard that is consistent with the approach to causation our precedents describe. If a motive is not a but-for cause of an event, then by definition it did not make a difference to the outcome. The event would have occurred just the same without it. Common law approaches to causation often require proof of but-for cause as a starting point toward proof of legal cause. The law may require more than but-for cause, for instance proximate cause, before imposing liability. Any standard less than but-for, however, simply represents a decision to impose liability without causation. As Dean Prosser puts it, "[a]n act or omission is not regarded as a cause of an event if the particular event would have occurred without it." W. Keeton, D. Dobbs, R. Keeton, & D. Owen, Prosser and Keeton on Law of Torts 265 (5th ed. 1984).

One of the principal reasons the plurality decision may sow confusion is that it claims Title VII liability is unrelated to but-for causation, yet it adopts a but-for standard once it has placed the burden of proof as to causation upon the employer. This approach conflates the question whether causation must be shown with the question of how it is to be shown. Because the plurality's theory of Title VII causation is ultimately consistent with a but-for standard, it might be said that my disagreement with the plurality's comments on but-for cause is simply academic. * * *

* * *

* * * Labels aside, the import of today's decision is not that Title VII liability can arise without but-for causation, but that in certain cases it is not the plaintiff who must prove the presence of causation, but the defendant who must prove its absence.

II

We established the order of proof for individual Title VII disparate treatment cases in *McDonnell Douglas*, and reaffirmed this allocation in *Burdine*. Under *Burdine*, once the plaintiff presents a prima facie case, an inference of discrimination arises. The employer must rebut the inference by articulating a legitimate nondiscriminatory reason for its action. The final burden of persuasion, however, belongs to the plaintiff. *Burdine* makes clear that the "ultimate burden of persuading the trier of fact that the defendant intentionally discriminated against the plaintiff remains at all times with the plaintiff."[3] I would adhere to this established evidentiary framework, which provides the appropriate standard for this and other individual disparate treatment cases. Today's creation of a new set of rules for "mixed-motive" cases is not mandated by the statute itself. The Court's attempt at refinement provides limited practical benefits at the cost of confusion and complexity, with the attendant risk that the trier of fact will misapprehend the controlling legal principles and reach an incorrect decision.

In view of the plurality's treatment of *Burdine* and our other disparate treatment cases, it is important first to state why those cases are dispositive here. The plurality tries to reconcile its approach with *Burdine* by announcing that it applies only to a "pretext" case, which it defines as a case in which the plaintiff attempts to prove that the employer's proffered explanation is itself false. This ignores the language of *Burdine*, which states that a plaintiff may succeed in meeting her ultimate burden of persuasion "*either* directly by persuading the court that a discriminatory reason more likely motivated the employer or indirectly by showing that the employer's proffered explanation is unworthy of credence." Under the first of these two alternative methods, a plaintiff meets her burden if she can "persuade the court that the employment decision more likely than not was motivated by a discriminatory reason." USPS Board of Governors v. Aikens, 460 U.S. 711, 717-718, 103 S.Ct. 1478, 1483, 75 L.Ed.2d 403 (1983) (Blackmun, J., concurring). The plurality makes no attempt to address this aspect of our cases.

Our opinions make plain that *Burdine* applies to all individual disparate treatment cases, whether the plaintiff offers direct proof that discrimination motivated the employer's actions or chooses the indirect method of showing that the employer's proffered justification is false, that is to say, a pretext. See *Aikens*, ("As in any lawsuit, the plaintiff may prove his case by direct or circumstantial evidence"). The plurality is mistaken in suggesting that the plaintiff in a so-called "mixed motives" case will be disadvantaged by having to "squeeze her proof into *Burdine's* framework." As we acknowledged in *McDonnell Douglas*, "[t]he facts necessarily will vary in Title VII cases," and the specification of the prima facie case set forth there "is not necessarily applicable in every respect to differing factual situations." The framework was "never intended to be rigid, mechanized, or ritualistic." *Aikens*. *Burdine* compels the employer to come forward with its explanation of the decision and permits the plaintiff to offer evidence under either of the logical methods for proof of discrimination. This is hardly a framework that confines the plaintiff; still less is it a justification for saying

---

[3]The interpretive memorandum on which the plurality relies makes plain that "the plaintiff, as in any civil case, would have the burden of proving that discrimination had occurred." 110 Cong.Rec. 7214 (1964). Coupled with its earlier definition of discrimination, the memorandum tells us that the plaintiff bears the burden of showing that an impermissible motive "made a difference" in the treatment of the plaintiff. This is none other than the traditional requirement that the plaintiff show but-for cause.

that the ultimate burden of proof must be on the employer in a mixed motives case. *Burdine* provides an orderly and adequate way to place both inferential and direct proof before the factfinder for a determination whether intentional discrimination has caused the employment decision. Regardless of the character of the evidence presented, we have consistently held that the ultimate burden "remains at all times with the plaintiff." *Burdine.*

Aikens illustrates the point. There, the evidence showed that the plaintiff, a black man, was far more qualified than any of the white applicants promoted ahead of him. More important, the testimony showed that "the person responsible for the promotion decisions at issue had made numerous derogatory comments about blacks in general and Aikens in particular." Yet the Court in *Aikens* reiterated that the case was to be tried under the proof scheme of *Burdine.* Justice Brennan and Justice Blackmun concurred to stress that the plaintiff could prevail under the *Burdine* scheme in either of two ways, one of which was directly to persuade the court that the employment decision was motivated by discrimination. *Aikens* leaves no doubt that the so-called "pretext" framework of *Burdine* has been considered to provide a flexible means of addressing all individual disparate treatment claims.

* * *

In contrast to the plurality, Justice O'Connor acknowledges that the approach adopted today is a "departure from the *McDonnell Douglas* standard." Although her reasons for supporting this departure are not without force, they are not dispositive. As Justice O'Connor states, the most that can be said with respect to the Title VII itself is that "nothing in the language, history, or purpose of Title VII *prohibits* adoption" of the new approach. Justice O'Connor also relies on analogies from the common law of torts, other types of Title VII litigation, and our equal protection cases. These analogies demonstrate that shifts in the burden of proof are not unprecedented in the law of torts or employment discrimination. Nonetheless, I believe continued adherence to the *Burdine* framework is more consistent with the statutory mandate. Congress' manifest concern with preventing imposition of liability in cases where discriminatory animus did not actually cause an adverse action suggests to me that an affirmative showing of causation should be required. And the most relevant portion of the legislative history supports just this view. The limited benefits that are likely to be produced by today's innovation come at the sacrifice of clarity and practical application.

The potential benefits of the new approach, in my view, are overstated. First, the Court makes clear that the *Price Waterhouse* scheme is applicable only in those cases where the plaintiff has produced direct and substantial proof that an impermissible motive was relied upon in making the decision at issue. The burden shift properly will be found to apply in only a limited number of employment discrimination cases. The application of the new scheme, furthermore, will make a difference only in a smaller subset of cases. The practical importance of the burden of proof is the "risk of nonpersuasion," and the new system will make a difference only where the evidence is so evenly balanced that the factfinder cannot say that either side's explanation of the case is "more likely" true. This category will not include cases in which the allocation of the burden of proof will be dispositive because of a complete lack of evidence on the causation issue, cf. Summers v. Tice, 33 Cal.2d 80, 199 P.2d 1 (1948) (allocation of burden dispositive because no evidence of which of two negligently fired shots hit plaintiff).   Rather, *Price Waterhouse* will apply only to cases in which there is substantial evidence of reliance on an impermissible motive, as well as evidence from the employer that legitimate reasons supported its action.

Although the *Price Waterhouse* system is not for every case, almost every plaintiff is certain to ask for a *Price Waterhouse* instruction, perhaps on the basis of "stray remarks" or other evidence of discriminatory animus. Trial and appellate courts will therefore be saddled with the task of developing standards for determining when to apply the burden shift.   One of their new tasks will be the generation of a jurisprudence of the meaning of "substantial factor." Courts will also be required to make the often subtle and difficult distinction between "direct" and "indirect" or "circumstantial" evidence. Lower courts long have had difficulty applying *McDonnell Douglas* and *Burdine*.   Addition of a second burden-shifting mechanism, the application of which itself depends on assessment of credibility and a determination whether evidence is sufficiently direct and substantial, is not likely to lend clarity to the process. * * *

* * *

I do not believe the minor refinement in Title VII procedures accomplished by today's holding can justify the difficulties that will accompany it.   Rather, I "remain confident that the *McDonnell Douglas* framework permits the plaintiff meriting relief to demonstrate intentional discrimination." Although the employer does not bear the burden of persuasion under *Burdine*, it must offer clear and reasonably specific reasons for the contested decision, and has every incentive to persuade the trier of fact that the decision was lawful. Further, the suggestion that the employer should bear the burden of persuasion due to superior access to evidence has little force in the Title VII context, where the liberal discovery rules available to all litigants are supplemented by EEOC investigatory files.   In sum, the *Burdine* framework provides a "sensible, orderly way to evaluate the evidence in light of common experience as it bears on the critical question of discrimination," *Aikens*, and it should continue to govern the order of proof in Title VII disparate treatment cases.[4]

III

The ultimate question in every individual disparate treatment case is whether discrimination caused the particular decision at issue.   Some of the plurality's comments with respect to the District Court's findings in this case, however, are

---

[4]The plurality states that it disregards the special context of affirmative action. It is not clear that this is possible. Some courts have held that in a suit challenging an affirmative action plan, the question of the plan's validity need not be reached unless the plaintiff shows that the plan was a but-for cause of the adverse decision. See McQuillen v. Wisconsin Education Association Council, 830 F.2d 659, 665 (CA7 1987), cert. denied, 485 U.S. 914, 108 S.Ct. 1068, 99 L.Ed.2d 248 (1988). Presumably it will be easier for a plaintiff to show that consideration of race or sex pursuant to an affirmative action plan was a substantial factor in a decision, and the court will need to move on to the question of a plan's validity. Moreover, if the structure of the burdens of proof in Title VII suits is to be consistent, as might be expected given the identical statutory language involved, today's decision suggests that plaintiffs should no longer bear the burden of showing that affirmative action plans are illegal. See Johnson v. Transportation Agency, 480 U.S. 616, 626-627, 107 S.Ct. 1442, 1449, 94 L.Ed.2d 615 (1987).

potentially misleading. As the plurality notes, the District Court based its liability determination on expert evidence that some evaluations of respondent Hopkins were based on unconscious sex stereotypes,[5] and on the fact that Price Waterhouse failed to disclaim reliance on these comments when it conducted the partnership review. The District Court also based liability on Price Waterhouse's failure to "make partners sensitive to the dangers [of stereotyping], to discourage comments tainted by sexism, or to investigate comments to determine whether they were influenced by stereotypes."

Although the District Court's version of Title VII liability is improper under any of today's opinions, I think it important to stress that Title VII creates no independent cause of action for sex stereotyping. Evidence of use by decision-makers of sex stereotypes is, of course, quite relevant to the question of discriminatory intent. The ultimate question, however, is whether discrimination caused the plaintiff's harm. Our cases do not support the suggestion that failure to "disclaim reliance" on stereotypical comments itself violates Title VII. Neither do they support creation of a "duty to sensitize." As the dissenting judge in the Court of Appeals observed, acceptance of such theories would turn Title VII "from a prohibition of discriminatory conduct into an engine for rooting out sexist thoughts." 825 F.2d 458, 477 (1987) (Williams, J., dissenting).

Employment discrimination claims require factfinders to make difficult and sensitive decisions. Sometimes this may mean that no finding of discrimination is justified even though a qualified employee is passed over by a less than admirable employer. In other cases, Title VII's protections properly extend to plaintiffs who are by no means model employees. As Justice Brennan notes, courts do not sit to determine whether litigants are nice. In this case, Hopkins plainly presented a strong case both of her own professional qualifications and of the presence of discrimination in Price Waterhouse's partnership process. Had the District Court found on this record that sex discrimination caused the adverse decision, I doubt it would have been reversible error. That decision was for the finder of fact, however, and the District Court made plain that sex discrimination was not a but-for cause of the decision to place Hopkin's partnership candidacy on hold. Attempts to evade tough decisions by erecting novel theories of liability or multitiered systems of shifting burdens are misguided.

---

[5]The plaintiff who engages the services of Dr. Susan Fiske should have no trouble showing that sex discrimination played a part in any decision. Price Waterhouse chose not to object to Fiske's testimony, and at this late stage we are constrained to accept it, but I think the plurality's enthusiasm for Fiske's conclusions unwarranted. Fiske purported to discern stereotyping in comments that were gender neutral — e.g., "overbearing and abrasive" — without any knowledge of the comments' basis in reality and without having met the speaker or subject. "To an expert of Dr. Fiske's qualifications, it seems plain that no woman could *be* overbearing, arrogant, or abrasive: any observations to that effect would necessarily be discounted as the product of stereotyping. If analysis like this is to prevail in federal courts, no employer can base any adverse action as to a woman on such attributes." 825 F.2d 458, 477 (1987) (Williams, J., dissenting). Today's opinions cannot be read as requiring factfinders to credit testimony based on this type of analysis.

IV

The language of Title VII and our well-considered precedents require this plaintiff to establish that the decision to place her candidacy on hold was made "because of" sex. Here the District Court found that the "comments of the individual partners and the expert evidence of Dr. Fiske do not prove an intentional discriminatory motive or purpose," and that "[b]ecause plaintiff has considerable problems dealing with staff and peers, the Court cannot say that she would have been elected to partnership if the Policy Board's decision had not been tainted by sexually based evaluations." Hopkins thus failed to meet the requisite standard of proof after a full trial. I would remand the case for entry of judgment in favor of Price Waterhouse.

CAUSATION AND THE CIVIL RIGHTS ACT OF 1991

One issue in *Price Waterhouse* on which all the Justices agreed was the relationship between the causation determination and liability under Title VII. If the fact finder determined that the employer would have made the same decision absent discriminatory motivation, there was no Title VII liability. In the fall of 1991, Congress enacted the Civil Rights Act of 1991, Pub.L. 102-166, 105 Stat. 1071 (1991), which was intended to reverse, in part, *Price Waterhouse*. Section 107 of the 1991 Act added the following subsection to §703 of Title VII:

> (m) Except as otherwise provided in this title, an unlawful employment practice is established when the complaining party demonstrates that race, color, religion, sex, or national origin was a motivating factor for any employment practice, even though other factors also motivated the practice.

The 1991 Act thus defines an unlawful employment practice to include any employment practice which proceeds, at least in part, from an unlawful motivation. But at the same time that the 1991 Act expanded the scope of Title VII liability, it also restricted the *kind* of relief available in mixed-motive cases. Section 706(g) of Title VII generally provides for a wide range of remedies against an employer guilty of unlawful employment practices, including reinstatement, back pay, and compensatory and punitive damages. *See* Chapter 7, Remedies, *infra*. Section 107 of the 1991 Act added the following subparagraph to §706(g)(2):

> (B) On a claim in which an individual proves a violation under section 703(m) and a respondent demonstrates that the respondent would have taken the same action in the absence of the impermissible motivating factor, the court —
>
> (i) may grant declaratory relief, injunctive relief (except as provided in clause (ii)), and attorney's fees and costs demonstrated to be directly attributable only to the pursuit of a claim under section 703(m); and
>
> (ii) shall not award damages or issue an order requiring any admission, reinstatement, hiring, promotion, or payment, described in subparagraph 706(A).

Thus, while legislatively reversing the liability/causation holding of *Price Waterhouse*, Congress adopted the affirmative defense and the defendant's burden of proof on causation established by the Court in that case. The plaintiff who proves that the challenged employment decision was at least in part motivated by unlawful bias has established a violation §703 and will be entitled at least to some relief. In the face of such a finding, the employer who establishes that it would have made the same decision absent unlawful motivation escapes the most concrete kinds of remedies. After passage of the 1991 Act, the circuits were divided over whether "direct evidence" was required to trigger mixed-motive analysis. The Supreme Court resolved that question in the following case.

Desert Palace, Inc. v. Costa

Supreme Court of the United States, 2003.

539 U.S. 90, 123 S.Ct. 2148, 156 L.Ed. 2d 84.

JUSTICE THOMAS delivered the opinion of the Court.

The question before us in this case is whether a plaintiff must present direct evidence of discrimination in order to obtain a mixed-motive instruction under Title VII as amended by the Civil Rights Act of 1991. We hold that direct evidence is not required.

I

A.

Since 1964, Title VII has made it an "unlawful employment practice for an employer . . . to discriminate against any individual . . ., because of such individual's race, color, religion, sex, or national origin." In *Price Waterhouse v. Hopkins*, the Court considered whether an employment decision is made "because of" sex in a "mixed-motive" case, i.e., where both legitimate and illegitimate reasons motivated the decision. The Court concluded that, under §703(a)(1), an employer could "avoid a finding of liability . . . by proving that it would have made the same decision even if it had not allowed gender to play such a role." The Court was divided, however, over the predicate question of when the burden of proof may be shifted to an employer to prove the affirmative defense.

Justice Brennan, writing for a plurality of four Justices, would have held that "when a plaintiff . . . proves that her gender played a *motivating* part in an employment decision, the defendant may avoid a finding of liability only by proving by a preponderance of the evidence that it would have made the same decision even if it had not taken the plaintiff's gender into account." The plurality did not, however, "suggest a limitation on the possible ways of proving that [gender] stereotyping played a motivating role in an employment decision."

Justice White and Justice O'Connor both concurred in the judgment. Justice White would have held that the case was governed by Mt. Healthy City Bd. of Ed. v. Doyle and would have shifted the burden to the employer only when a plaintiff "showed that the unlawful motive was a *substantial* factor in the adverse employment action." Justice O'Connor, like Justice White, would have required the plaintiff to show that an illegitimate consideration was a "substantial factor" in the employment decision. But, under Justice O'Connor's view, "the burden on the issue of causation" would shift to the employer only where "a disparate treatment plaintiff [could] show by *direct evidence* that an illegitimate criterion was a substantial factor in the decision." (emphasis added).

Two years after *Price Waterhouse*, Congress passed the 1991 Act "in large part [as] a response to a series of decisions of this Court interpreting the Civil Rights Acts of 1866 and 1964." Landgraf v. USI Film Products, 511 U.S. 244, 250, 128 L. Ed. 2d 229, 114 S. Ct. 1483 (1994). In particular, §107 of the 1991 Act, which is at issue in this case, "responded" to *Price Waterhouse* by "setting forth standards applicable in 'mixed motive' cases" in two new statutory provisions.[1] The first establishes [in §703(m)] an alternative for proving that an "unlawful employment practice" has occurred:

> Except as otherwise provided in this subchapter, an unlawful employment practice is established when the complaining party demonstrates that race, color, religion, sex, or national origin was a motivating factor for any employment practice, even though other factors also motivated the practice.

The second provides that, with respect to "'a claim in which an individual proves a violation under section 703(m),'" the employer has a limited affirmative defense that does not absolve it of liability, but restricts the remedies available to a plaintiff. The available remedies include only declaratory relief, certain types of injunctive relief, and attorney's fees and costs. In order to avail itself of the affirmative defense, the employer must "demonstrate that [it] would have taken the same action in the absence of the impermissible motivating factor."

Since the passage of the 1991 Act, the Courts of Appeals have divided over whether a plaintiff must prove by direct evidence that an impermissible consideration was a "motivating factor" in an adverse employment action. Relying primarily on Justice O'Connor's concurrence in *Price Waterhouse*, a number of courts have held that direct evidence is required to establish liability under §703(m). In the decision below, however, the Ninth Circuit concluded otherwise.

B.

Petitioner Desert Palace, Inc., dba Caesar's Palace Hotel & Casino of Las Vegas, Nevada, employed respondent Catharina Costa as a warehouse worker and heavy equipment operator. Respondent was the only woman in this job and in her local Teamsters bargaining unit.

Respondent experienced a number of problems with management and her co-workers that led to an escalating series of disciplinary sanctions, including informal rebukes, a denial of privileges, and suspension. Petitioner finally terminated respondent after she was involved in a physical altercation in a warehouse elevator with fellow Teamsters member Herbert Gerber. Petitioner disciplined both employees because the facts surrounding the incident were in dispute, but Gerber, who had a clean disciplinary record, received only a 5-day suspension.

Respondent subsequently filed this lawsuit against petitioner in the United States District Court for the District of Nevada, asserting claims of sex discrimination and sexual harassment under Title VII. The District Court dismissed the sexual harassment claim, but allowed the claim for sex discrimination to go to the jury. At trial, respondent presented evidence that (1) she was singled out for "intense 'stalking'" by one of her supervisors, (2) she received harsher discipline than men for the same conduct, (3) she was treated less favorably than men in the assignment of overtime,

---

[1] This case does not require us to decide when, if ever, §107 applies outside of the mixed-motive context.

and (4) supervisors repeatedly "stacked" her disciplinary record and "frequently used or tolerated" sex-based slurs against her.

Based on this evidence, the District Court denied petitioner's motion for judgment as a matter of law, and submitted the case to the jury with instructions, two of which are relevant here. First, without objection from petitioner, the District Court instructed the jury that "'the plaintiff has the burden of proving . . . by a preponderance of the evidence" that she "suffered adverse work conditions" and that her sex "was a motivating factor in any such work conditions imposed upon her.'"

Second, the District Court gave the jury the following mixed-motive instruction:

> You have heard evidence that the defendant's treatment of the plaintiff was motivated by the plaintiff's sex and also by other lawful reasons. If you find that the plaintiff's sex was a motivating factor in the defendant's treatment of the plaintiff, the plaintiff is entitled to your verdict, even if you find that the defendant's conduct was also motivated by a lawful reason.

> However, if you find that the defendant's treatment of the plaintiff was motivated by both gender and lawful reasons, you must decide whether the plaintiff is entitled to damages. The plaintiff is entitled to damages unless the defendant proves by a preponderance of the evidence that the defendant would have treated plaintiff similarly even if the plaintiff's gender had played no role in the employment decision.

Petitioner unsuccessfully objected to this instruction, claiming that respondent had failed to adduce "direct evidence" that sex was a motivating factor in her dismissal or in any of the other adverse employment actions taken against her. The jury rendered a verdict for respondent, awarding backpay, compensatory damages, and punitive damages. The District Court denied petitioner's renewed motion for judgment as a matter of law.

The Court of Appeals initially vacated and remanded, holding that the District Court had erred in giving the mixed-motive instruction because respondent had failed to present "substantial evidence of conduct or statements by the employer directly reflecting discriminatory animus." In addition, the panel concluded that petitioner was entitled to judgment as a matter of law on the termination claim because the evidence was insufficient to prove that respondent was "terminated because she was a woman."

The Court of Appeals reinstated the District Court's judgment after rehearing the case en banc. The en banc court saw no need to decide whether Justice O'Connor's concurrence in *Price Waterhouse* controlled because it concluded that Justice O'Connor's references to "direct evidence" had been "wholly abrogated" by the 1991 Act. And, turning "to the language" of §703(m), the court observed that the statute "imposes no special [evidentiary] requirement and does not reference 'direct evidence.'" Accordingly, the court concluded that a "plaintiff . . . may establish a violation through a preponderance of evidence (whether direct or circumstantial) that a protected characteristic played 'a motivating factor.'" Based on that standard, the Court of Appeals held that respondent's evidence was sufficient to warrant a mixed-motive instruction and that a reasonable jury could have found that respondent's sex was a "motivating factor in her treatment." Four judges of the en banc panel dissented, relying in large part on "the reasoning of the prior opinion of the three-judge panel."

We granted certiorari.

II

This case provides us with the first opportunity to consider the effects of the 1991 Act on jury instructions in mixed-motive cases. Specifically, we must decide whether a plaintiff must present direct evidence of discrimination in order to obtain a mixed-motive instruction under §703(m). Petitioner's argument on this point proceeds in three steps: (1) Justice O'Connor's opinion is the holding of *Price Waterhouse;* (2) Justice O'Connor's *Price Waterhouse* opinion requires direct evidence of discrimination before a mixed-motive instruction can be given; and (3) the 1991 Act does nothing to abrogate that holding. Like the Court of Appeals, we see no need to address which of the opinions in *Price Waterhouse* is controlling: the third step of petitioner's argument is flawed, primarily because it is inconsistent with the text of §703(m).

Our precedents make clear that the starting point for our analysis is the statutory text. See *Connecticut Nat. Bank v. Germain*, 503 U.S. 249, 253-254, 117 L. Ed. 2d 391, 112 S. Ct. 1146 (1992). And where, as here, the words of the statute are unambiguous, the "judicial inquiry is complete." Id. at 254. Section 703(m) unambiguously states that a plaintiff need only "demonstrate" that an employer used a forbidden consideration with respect to "any employment practice." On its face, the statute does not mention, much less require, that a plaintiff make a heightened showing through direct evidence. Indeed, petitioner concedes as much.

Moreover, Congress explicitly defined the term "demonstrates" in the 1991 Act, leaving little doubt that no special evidentiary showing is required. Title VII defines the term "'demonstrates'" as to "meet the burdens of production and persuasion." §701(m). If Congress intended the term "demonstrates" to require that the "burdens of production and persuasion" be met by direct evidence or some other heightened showing, it could have made that intent clear by including language to that effect in §701(m). Its failure to do so is significant, for Congress has been unequivocal when imposing heightened proof requirements in other circumstances * * *. See, e.g., 8 U.S.C. §1158(a)(2)(B) (stating that an asylum application may not be filed unless an alien "demonstrates by clear and convincing evidence" that the application was filed within one year of the alien's arrival in the United States); 42 U.S.C. §5851(b)(3)(D) (providing that "relief may not be ordered" against an employer in retaliation cases involving whistleblowers under the Atomic Energy Act where the employer is able to "*demonstrate by clear and convincing evidence* that it would have taken the same unfavorable personnel action in the absence of such behavior" (emphasis added)); cf. *Price Waterhouse* (plurality opinion) ("Only rarely have we required clear and convincing proof where the action defended against seeks only conventional relief").

In addition, Title VII's silence with respect to the type of evidence required in mixed-motive cases also suggests that we should not depart from the "conventional rule of civil litigation [that] generally applies in Title VII cases." That rule requires a plaintiff to prove his case "by a preponderance of the evidence," using "direct or circumstantial evidence," *Postal Service Bd. of Governors v. Aikens*, 460 U.S. 711, 714, n. 3, 75 L. Ed. 2d 403, 103 S. Ct. 1478 (1983). We have often acknowledged the utility of circumstantial evidence in discrimination cases. For instance, in *Reeves v. Sanderson*, we recognized that evidence that a defendant's explanation for an employment practice is "unworthy of credence" is "one form of *circumstantial evidence* that is probative of intentional discrimination." (emphasis added). The reason for treating circumstantial and direct evidence alike is both clear and deep-rooted: "Circumstantial evidence is not only sufficient, but may also be more certain, satisfying and persuasive than direct evidence." Rogers v. Missouri Pacific R. Co., 352 U.S. 500, 508, n. 17, 1 L. Ed. 2d 493, 77 S. Ct. 443 (1957).

The adequacy of circumstantial evidence also extends beyond civil cases; we have never questioned the sufficiency of circumstantial evidence in support of a criminal conviction, even though proof beyond a reasonable doubt is required. See *Holland v. United States*, 348 U.S. 121, 140, 99 L. Ed. 150, 75 S. Ct. 127 (1954) (observing that, in criminal cases, circumstantial evidence is "intrinsically no different from testimonial evidence"). And juries are routinely instructed that "the law makes no distinction between the weight or value to be given to either direct or circumstantial evidence." 1A K. O'Malley, J. Grenig, & W. Lee, Federal Jury Practice and Instructions, Criminal §12.04 (5th ed. 2000). It is not surprising, therefore, that neither petitioner nor its amici curiae can point to any other circumstance in which we have restricted a litigant to the presentation of direct evidence absent some affirmative directive in a statute.

Finally, the use of the term "demonstrates" in other provisions of Title VII tends to show further that §703(m) does not incorporate a direct evidence requirement. For instance, §706(g)(2)(B) requires an employer to "demonstrate that [it] would have taken the same action in the absence of the impermissible motivating factor" in order to take advantage of the partial affirmative defense. Due to the similarity in structure between that provision and §703(m), it would be logical to assume that the term "demonstrates" would carry the same meaning with respect to both provisions. But when pressed at oral argument about whether direct evidence is required before the partial affirmative defense can be invoked, petitioner did not "agree that . . . the defendant or the employer has any heightened standard" to satisfy. Absent some congressional indication to the contrary, we decline to give the same term in the same Act a different meaning depending on whether the rights of the plaintiff or the defendant are at issue. See *Commissioner v. Lundy*, 516 U.S. 235, 250, 133 L. Ed. 2d 611, 116 S. Ct. 647 (1996) ("The interrelationship and close proximity of these provisions of the statute presents a classic case for application of the normal rule of statutory construction that identical words used in different parts of the same act are intended to have the same meaning.").

For the reasons stated above, we agree with the Court of Appeals that no heightened showing is required under §703(m).

In order to obtain an instruction under §703(m), a plaintiff need only present sufficient evidence for a reasonable jury to conclude, by a preponderance of the evidence, that "race, color, religion, sex, or national origin was a motivating factor for any employment practice." Because direct evidence of discrimination is not required in mixed-motive cases, the Court of Appeals correctly concluded that the District Court did not abuse its discretion in giving a mixed-motive instruction to the jury. Accordingly, the judgment of the Court of Appeals is affirmed.

It is so ordered.

Justice O'Connor, concurring.

I join the Court's opinion. In my view, prior to the Civil Rights Act of 1991, the evidentiary rule we developed to shift the burden of persuasion in mixed-motive cases was appropriately applied only where a disparate treatment plaintiff "demonstrated by direct evidence that an illegitimate factor played a substantial role" in an adverse employment decision. *Price Waterhouse v. Hopkins*, (O'CONNOR, J., concurring in judgment). This showing triggered "the deterrent purpose of the statute" and permitted a reasonable factfinder to conclude that "absent further explanation, the employer's discriminatory motivation 'caused' the employment decision."

As the Court's opinion explains, in the Civil Rights Act of 1991, Congress codified a new evidentiary rule for mixed-motive cases arising under Title VII. I therefore agree with the Court that the District Court did not abuse its discretion in giving a mixed-motive instruction to the jury.

NOTES AND PROBLEMS FOR DISCUSSION

1. As the discussion in the principal case demonstrates, the passage of the 1991 Civil Rights Act codified the mixed-motive theory of discrimination, thereby ending the controversy over the precedential impact of the mixed motive component of the decision in *Price Waterhouse*. But, until the Court's ruling in *Desert Palace*, the circuit courts disagreed on whether this method of proving intentional discrimination was available when plaintiffs could not offer *direct* evidence of a discriminatory motive. At that time, in the absence of direct evidence, the plaintiff was not entitled to a mixed-motive instruction. *Desert Palace* has put an end to that approach, at least at the trial stage. Consequently, whether the trial court chooses to invoke and apply the *McDonnell Douglas/Burdine* or *Price Waterhouse as modified by the 1991 Civil Rights Act* analytical framework depends entirely on whether the claim is perceived as asserting a single or mixed set of motivations. Yet won't many, if not most disparate treatment cases that make it past summary judgment involve evidence of both legitimate and unlawful motives? After all, once the defense denies the existence of discrimination by offering a nondiscriminatory explanation, doesn't that mean that there are now multiple motivations at issue? And if that is the case, then won't the *typical* disparate treatment case always call for a mixed-motive instruction? One district judge has worried that, "[i]f *Desert Palace* means what this court otherwise reads it to mean, it is not clear what case would *not* be governed by [§107]." Dunbar v. Pepsi-Cola Gen. Bottlers of Iowa, Inc., 285 F.Supp.2d 1180, 1196 n.1 (N.D. Iowa 2003). *See* Rowland v. American General Finance, 340 F.3d 187, 193 (4th Cir. 2003) (refusal to give mixed-motive instruction was reversible error because without that instruction the plaintiff had almost no chance of prevailing and, had the instruction been given, it is possible that the jury would have found sex to be a motivating factor in the employer's decision not to promote the plaintiff).

2. The question whether *Desert Palace* fundamentally changed the *McDonnell Douglas/Burdine* framework at the *summary judgment* stage has divided the circuits into multiple analytical camps. The Eighth Circuit has concluded that the traditional *McDonnell Douglas/Burdine* burden-shifting approach applies unchanged by *Desert Palace* to summary judgment analysis of mixed motive cases. *See e.g.*, Griffith v. City of Des Moines, 387 F.3d 733 (8th Cir. 2004). While the Second, Third, Fifth and Tenth Circuits has ruled that *Desert Palace* mandates a modification in the standard *McDonnell Douglas/Burden* pretext formulation in handling summary judgment motions. Under this view, after the plaintiff has established a prima facie case and the defendant has come forward with evidence of a non-discriminatory reason for its decision, the plaintiff must then come forward with sufficient evidence to create a genuine issue of material fact either (1) that the defendant's reason is not true and is a pretext for unlawful discrimination (the pretext alternative), or (2) that the defendant's reason, while true, is only one of the reasons for its conduct and another motivating factor is unlawful bias (the mixed-motive alternative). Under the second of these alternatives, the plaintiff could survive summary judgment even where she is unable to demonstrate a genuine issue as to the truthfulness of the employer's reasons. *See, e.g.,* Rachid v. Jack In The Box, Inc., 376 F.3d 305 (5th Cir. 2004). The First, Fourth, Seventh, Ninth, and D.C. Circuits split the difference between these two approaches; they permit the plaintiff in a mixed motive case to defeat a motion for summary judgment by proceeding under the traditional *McDonnell Douglas/Burdine* formulation or by presenting direct or circumstantial evidence that produces a genuine issue of fact on whether a forbidden factor was a motivating factor for the challenged decision. *See e.g.,* Diamond v. Colonial Life & Accident Ins. Co., 416 F.3d 310 (4th Cir. 2005); Fogg v. Gonzales, 492 F.3d 447 (D.C.Cir. 2007); McGinset v. GTE Serv. Corp., 360 F.3d 1103 (9th Cir. 2004). Finally, the Sixth and Eleventh Circuits have taken the position that the *McDonnell Douglas/Burdine* burden-shifting framework does not apply at all to summary judgment analysis of mixed-motive claims, ruling that a plaintiff can defeat a summary judgment motion by producing evidence that would permit a reasonable jury to conclude that a forbidden classification was a motivating factor for the employer's adverse employment action. This burden, they explain, should preclude sending the case to the jury only where the record is devoid of evidence that could reasonably be construed to support the plaintiff's claim. These courts reason that in a mixed motive case, the plaintiff does not have to discredit the defendant's asserted nondiscriminatory justification because it isn't required to eliminate all of the defendant's legitimate motivations; it only needs to establish that an illegitimate discriminatory animus was one motivating factor for the decision. Quinn v. Thomas County School District, 814 F.3d 1227 (11th Cir. 2016); White v. Baxter Healthcare Corp., 533 F.3d 381 (6th Cir. 2008), cert. denied, 556 U.S. 1235, 129 S.Ct. 2380, 173 L.Ed. 2d 1293 (2009).

Which side has the better argument? Under the Fifth Circuit's approach, a plaintiff is not entitled to a mixed motive instruction unless she has established a prima facie case. So, for example, if a plaintiff cannot demonstrate that she was qualified for the job, but also has evidence that her sex played a role in the decision not to hire her, she presumably is not entitled to invoke the mixed motive analysis and will lose at the summary judgment stage even though she could demonstrate that sex was a motivating factor for the employer's decision. Is this consistent with *Costa* & §703(m)? *See* Wright v. Murray Guard, Inc., 455 F.3d 702, 716 (6th Cir. 2006) (Moore, J., concurring). On the other hand, does the Eighth Circuit really mean that a plaintiff with evidence of an unlawful motivation will still suffer summary judgment unless she can cast doubt with *other evidence* on the legitimacy of the employer's explanation? Or does that court merely mean that evidence of an unlawful motive will necessarily put in doubt the employer's explanation? Commentators have weighed in on both sides of the issue. *Compare* Jeffrey A. Van Detta, *"Le Roi Est Mort; Vive Le Roi!": An Essay on the Quiet Demise of McDonnell Douglas and the Transformation of Every Title VII Case after Desert Palace, Inc. v. Costa into a "Mixed Motives" Case, 52*

DRAKE L.REV. 71 (2003), *with* Matthew R. Scott & Russell D. Chapman, *Much Ado About Nothing — Why Desert Palace Neither Murdered McDonnell Douglas Nor Transformed All Employment Discrimination Cases to Mixed-Motive*, 36 ST. MARY'S L.J. 395, 397 (2005).

3.   Section 107 of the 1991 Act makes no mention of either retaliation or §704 of Title VII. Does this mean that this statutorily revised mixed-motive analysis applies only to §703 cases and that *Price Waterhouse* continues to apply to Title VII retaliation cases?   In GROSS v. FBL FINANCIAL SERVICES, INC., 557 U.S. 167, 129 S.Ct. 2343, 174 L.Ed.2d 119 (2009), the Supreme Court relied, in substantial part, on this aspect of the statutory text in ruling that that mixed motive analysis was completely unavailable in ADEA cases. Thereafter, relying on this same analysis, the Court, by a 5-4 margin, in UNIVERSITY OF TEXAS SOUTHWESTERN MEDICAL CENTER v. NASSAR, 570 U.S. 338, 133 S.Ct. 2517, 186 L.Ed.2d 503 (2013), ruled that §704(a) retaliation claims also were not susceptible to mixed motive analysis. For more on this see Chapter 2, §B6, at Note 4 after *Burlington Northern, infra.*

4.   Both *Price Waterhouse* and *Desert Palace* address the problem of determining liability when the challenged employment decision was motivated by both lawful and unlawful reasons. In the typical case, the evidence will show that a supervisory employee with decision-making authority either was or was not unlawfully motivated. Yet many corporate employers are complex organizations with supervisory employees with different levels of responsibility having input in employment decisions. *Reeves* was an easy case because the record showed that although the decisionmaker did not have the formal authority to discharge, he enjoyed actual authority within the corporation: he was married to the company president and exercised "absolute power" within the company. But what if that is not the case and the actual decisionmaker is merely influenced by a biased subordinate? Should an employer be liable under Title VII where its institutional decision was the product of information initially supplied by an employee acting on an unlawful bias, but where the actual decision-maker acted without any discriminatory intent? Would it matter whether the biased employee enjoyed supervisory status?

Most of the circuit courts that have considered the question have imposed some form of employer liability predicated upon the bias of a mid or low level supervisor who lacked actual decision-making authority. They alternatively rely on either a "cat's paw"[a] or "rubber stamp"[b] explanation. But the circuits could not agree on the precise

---

[a]The term "cat's paw" is derived from the following one of Aesop's fables: "A cat and a monkey were sitting one day in the chimney corner watching some chestnuts which their master had laid down to roast in the ashes. The chestnuts had begun to burst with the heat, and the monkey said to the cat, 'It is plain that your paws were made especially for pulling out those chestnuts. Do you reach forth and draw them out. Your paws are, indeed, exactly like our master's hands.' The cat was greatly flattered by this speech, and reached forward for the tempting chestnuts, but scarcely had he touched the hot ashes than he drew back with a cry, for he had burnt his paw; but he tried again, and managed to pull one chestnut out; then he pulled another, and a third, though each time he singed the hair on his paws. When he could pull no more out he turned about and found that the monkey had taken the time to crack the chestnuts and eat them." http://fairytales4u.com/fable/fable2.htm. Dictionaries define "cat's paw" as the use of someone to do one's own bidding. The term is used in employment discrimination cases

set of circumstances under which they would attach the subordinate's bias to the actual decision maker. In STAUB v. PROCTOR HOSPITAL, 562 U.S. 411, 131 S.Ct. 1186, 179 L.Ed.2d 144 (2011), however, the Supreme Court addressed this question, albeit in a non-Title VII case. *Staub* was a case brought by a military reservist alleging a discriminatory discharge by the defendant hospital because of his military status in violation of the Uniformed Services Employment and Reemployment Rights Act, a statute that the Court acknowledged was "very similar to Title VII". The Supreme Court rejected the defense contention that the fact of an independent investigation by the actual decision-maker immunized the employer from liability for the discriminatorily motivated actions of the plaintiff's supervisors. Instead, the Court ruled that as long as the plaintiff could establish that his supervisors acted with discriminatory animus (here, in issuing a disciplinary warning) *and* that they committed that act with the intention of causing the plaintiff's discharge *and* that their action (writing the report) was in fact *a* cause of the termination (by showing that this information was considered by the actual decision-maker without any determination of whether the adverse action was independently justified), the employer will be liable despite the fact that the actual decision-maker conducted an independent investigation.

The *Staub* Court's analysis has been applied to Title VII cases. For example, in LOBATO v. NEW MEXICO ENVIRONMENT DEPARTMENT, 733 F.3d 1283 (10th Cir. 2013), a terminated Latino employee of Mexican ancestry claimed that the manager who fired him had relied on racially biased reports from the plaintiff's immediate supervisor. The plaintiff admitted that the company had conducted an independent investigation into the plaintiff's conduct before discharging him. Affirming the trial judge's granting of summary judgment to the defendant, the Tenth Circuit rejected the plaintiff's claim that *Staub* required a finding of employer liability if a biased supervisor's animus led in any way to an adverse employment decision, even if the employer had conducted its own independent investigation. Rather, it construed *Staub* to mean that as long as the employer independently verifies the facts contained in the subordinate's report based on its own independent non-biased investigation, there is no liability, even if the biased subordinate's report first alerted the employer to alleged misconduct by the plaintiff.

In VASQUEZ v. EMPRESS AMBULANCE SERV., INC., 835 F.3d 267 (2d Cir. 2016), the Second Circuit added another wrinkle to the *Staub* analysis. It ruled that where an employer was itself negligent in allowing a low-level employee's false and intentionally biased information to materially affect an adverse decision, that employer's negligence was a sufficient basis for the imposition of Title VII liability. In such a case, the court explained, the plaintiff would have to prove (1) that the low-level employee's information was not only false but also the product of an unlawful (e.g., race, sex, or retaliatory) intent; and (2) that the employer negligently relied on that information, i.e., that it knew or should have known of that animus but nevertheless allowed it to play a meaningful role in the adverse decision. Whether the

---

in circumstances where the decision maker is manipulated by a biased subordinate to make a discriminatory employment decision.
bThe "rubber stamp" doctrine applies to situations where the decision maker perfunctorily approves an action recommended by a biased subordinate.

information provided by the employee was false, the court explained, was not the issue; an employer will not be held liable merely because it relied on information that was false. Nor would it be liable if it non-negligently and in good faith relied on a false and intentionally biased report. The plaintiff must prove *both* that the employee's information was both false and discriminatorily motivated *and* that the employer negligently credited it by not engaging in due diligence in determining its falsity and bias.

But in MARSHALL v. THE RAWLINGS CO., LLC, 854 F.3d 368 (6th Cir. 2017), the Sixth Circuit noted that as long as the biased non-decision maker intentionally manipulated (provided biased information to the decision maker for the purpose of influencing the decision maker's action) the ultimate decision maker, the latter's honest or sincere belief in the accuracy of the supervisor's report would not shield the employer from liability.

5. *Price Waterhouse* and §107 of the 1991 Act address the problem of the employer whose action is motivated by both unlawful and lawful factors. A different but related problem is posed by the employer that discovers, after the decision in question, that it had a legitimate basis for action against the employee in addition to its articulated reasons. That problem is discussed in the following case.

McKennon v. Nashville Banner Publishing Co.

Supreme Court of the United States, 1995.
513 U.S. 352, 115 S. Ct. 879; 130 L. Ed. 2d 852.

JUSTICE KENNEDY delivered the opinion of the Court.

The question before us is whether an employee discharged in violation of the Age Discrimination in Employment Act of 1967 is barred from all relief when, after her discharge, the employer discovers evidence of wrongdoing that, in any event, would have led to the employee's termination on lawful and legitimate grounds.

I

For some 30 years, petitioner Christine McKennon worked for respondent Nashville Banner Publishing Company. She was discharged, the Banner claimed, as part of a work force reduction plan necessitated by cost considerations. McKennon, who was 62 years old when she lost her job, thought another reason explained her dismissal: her age. She filed suit in the United States District Court for the Middle District of Tennessee, alleging that her discharge violated the Age Discrimination in Employment Act of 1967 (ADEA). The ADEA makes it unlawful for any employer:

"to discharge any individual or otherwise discriminate against any individual with respect to his compensation, terms, conditions, or privileges of employment, because of such individual's age."

McKennon sought a variety of legal and equitable remedies available under the ADEA, including backpay.

In preparation of the case, the Banner took McKennon's deposition. She testified that, during her final year of employment, she had copied several confidential documents bearing upon the company's financial condition. She had access to these records as secretary to the Banner's comptroller. McKennon took the copies home and showed them to her husband. Her motivation, she averred, was an apprehension she was about to be fired because of her age. When she became concerned about her job, she removed and copied the documents for "insurance" and "protection." A few days after these deposition disclosures, the Banner sent McKennon a letter declaring that removal and copying of the records was in violation of her job responsibilities and advising her (again) that she was terminated. The Banner's letter also recited that had it known of McKennon's misconduct it would have discharged her at once for that reason.

For purposes of summary judgment, the Banner conceded its discrimination against McKennon. The District Court granted summary judgment for the Banner, holding that McKennon's misconduct was grounds for her termination and that neither backpay nor any other remedy was available to her under the ADEA. The United States Court of Appeals for the Sixth Circuit affirmed on the same rationale. We granted, certiorari to resolve conflicting views among the Courts of Appeals on the question whether all relief must be denied when an employee has been discharged in violation of the ADEA and the employer later discovers some wrongful conduct that would have led to discharge if it had been discovered earlier. * * * We now reverse.

II

We shall assume, as summary judgment procedures require us to assume, that the sole reason for McKennon's initial discharge was her age, a discharge violative of the ADEA. Our further premise is that the misconduct revealed by the deposition was so grave that McKennon's immediate discharge would have followed its disclosure in any event. The District Court and the Court of Appeals found no basis for contesting that proposition, and for purposes of our review we need not question it here. We do question the legal conclusion reached by those courts that after-acquired evidence of wrongdoing which would have resulted in discharge bars employees from any relief under the ADEA. That ruling is incorrect.

The Court of Appeals considered McKennon's misconduct, in effect, to be supervening grounds for termination. That may be so, but it does not follow, as the Court of Appeals said in citing one of its own earlier cases, that the misconduct renders it "irrelevant whether or not [McKennon] was discriminated against." We conclude that a violation of the ADEA cannot be so altogether disregarded.

The ADEA, enacted in 1967 as part of an ongoing congressional effort to eradicate discrimination in the workplace, reflects a societal condemnation of invidious bias in employment decisions. The ADEA is but part of a wider statutory scheme to protect employees in the workplace nationwide. See Title VII; the Americans with Disabilities Act of 1990; the National Labor Relations Act; the Equal Pay Act of 1963. The ADEA incorporates some features of both Title VII and the Fair Labor Standards Act, which has led us to describe it as "something of a hybrid." *Lorillard v. Pons*, 434 U.S. 575, 578, 55 L. Ed. 2d 40, 98 S. Ct. 866 (1978). * * *

The ADEA and Title VII share common substantive features and also a common purpose: "the elimination of discrimination in the workplace." *Oscar Mayer & Co. v. Evans*, 441 U.S. 750, 756, 60 L. Ed. 2d 609, 99 S. Ct. 2066 (1979). Congress designed the remedial measures in these statutes to serve as a "spur or catalyst" to cause employers "to self-examine and to self-evaluate their employment practices and to endeavor to eliminate, so far as possible, the last vestiges" of discrimination. *Albemarle Paper Co. v. Moody,* 422 U.S. 405, 417-418, 45 L. Ed. 2d 280, 95 S. Ct. 2362 (1975). Deterrence is one object of these statutes. Compensation for injuries caused by the prohibited discrimination is another. The ADEA, in keeping with these purposes, contains a vital element found in both Title VII and the Fair Labor Standards Act: it grants an injured employee a right of action to obtain the authorized relief. The private litigant who seeks redress for his or her injuries vindicates both the deterrence and the compensation objectives of the ADEA. It would not accord with this scheme if after-acquired evidence of wrongdoing that would have resulted in termination operates, in every instance, to bar all relief for an earlier violation of the Act.

The objectives of the ADEA are furthered when even a single employee establishes that an employer has discriminated against him or her. The disclosure through litigation of incidents or practices which violate national policies respecting nondiscrimination in the work force is itself important, for the occurrence of violations may disclose patterns of noncompliance resulting from a misappreciation of the Act's operation or entrenched resistance to its commands, either of which can be of industry-wide significance. The efficacy of its enforcement mechanisms becomes one measure of the success of the Act.

The Court of Appeals in this case relied upon two of its earlier decisions, *Johnson v. Honeywell Information Systems, Inc.,* 955 F.2d 409 (CA6 1992); *Milligan-Jensen v. Michigan Technological Univ.,* 975 F.2d 302 (CA6 1992), and the opinion of the Court of Appeals for the Tenth Circuit in *Summers v. State Farm Mutual Automobile Ins. Co.,* 864 F.2d 700 (1988). Consulting those authorities, it declared that it had "firmly endorsed the principle that after-acquired evidence is a complete bar to any recovery by the former employee where the employer can show it would have fired the employee on the basis of the evidence." Summers, in turn, relied upon our decision in *Mt. Healthy City Bd. of Ed. v. Doyle*, 429 U.S. 274, 50 L. Ed. 2d 471, 97 S. Ct. 568 (1977), but that decision is inapplicable here.

In *Mt. Healthy* we addressed a mixed-motives case, in which two motives were said to be operative in the employer's decision to fire an employee. One was lawful, the other (an alleged constitutional violation) unlawful. We held that if the lawful reason alone would have sufficed to justify the firing, the employee could not prevail in a suit against the employer. The case was controlled by the difficulty, and what we thought was the lack of necessity, of disentangling the proper motive from the improper one where both played a part in the termination and the former motive would suffice to sustain the employer's action.

That is not the problem confronted here. As we have said, the case comes to us on the express assumption that an unlawful motive was the sole basis for the firing. McKennon's misconduct was not discovered until after she had been fired. The employer could not have been motivated by knowledge it did not have and it cannot now claim that the employee was fired for the nondiscriminatory reason. Mixed motive cases are inapposite here, except to the important extent they underscore the necessity of determining the employer's motives in ordering the discharge, an essential element in determining whether the employer violated the federal antidiscrimination law. See *Price Waterhouse* (plurality opinion) (employer's legitimate reason for discharge in mixed-motive case will not suffice "if that reason did not motivate it at the time of the decision"). As we have observed, "proving that the same decision would have been justified . . . is not the same as proving that the same decision would have been made." Id.

Our inquiry is not at an end, however, for even though the employer has violated the Act, we must consider how the after-acquired evidence of the employee's wrongdoing bears on the specific remedy to be ordered. Equity's maxim that a suitor who engaged in his own reprehensible conduct in the course of the transaction at issue must be denied equitable relief because of unclean hands, a rule which in conventional formulation operated *in limine* to bar the suitor from invoking the aid of the equity court, has not been applied where Congress authorizes broad equitable relief to serve important national policies. We have rejected the unclean hands defense "where a private suit serves important public purposes." *Perma Life Mufflers, Inc. v. International Parts Corp.,* 392 U.S. 134, 138, 20 L. Ed. 2d 982, 88 S. Ct. 1981 (1968) (Sherman and Clayton Antitrust Acts). That does not mean, however, the employee's own misconduct is irrelevant to all the remedies otherwise available under the statute. The statute controlling this case provides [in §7(b)] that "the court shall have jurisdiction to grant such legal or equitable relief as may be appropriate to effectuate the purposes of this chapter, including without limitation judgments compelling employment, reinstatement or promotion, or enforcing the liability for [amounts owing to a person as a result of a violation of this chapter]." In giving effect to the ADEA, we must recognize the duality between the legitimate interests of the employer and the important claims of the employee who invokes the national employment policy mandated by the Act. The employee's wrongdoing must be taken into account, we conclude, lest the employer's legitimate concerns be ignored. The ADEA, like Title VII, is not a general regulation of the workplace but a law which prohibits discrimination. The statute does not constrain employers from exercising significant other prerogatives and discretions in the course of the hiring, promoting, and discharging of their employees. See *Price Waterhouse* ("Title VII eliminates certain bases for distinguishing among employees while otherwise preserving employers' freedom of choice"). In determining appropriate remedial action, the employee's wrongdoing becomes relevant not to punish the employee, or out of concern "for the relative moral worth of the parties," *Perma Mufflers,* but to take due account of the lawful prerogatives of the employer in the usual course of its business and the corresponding equities that it has arising from the employee's wrongdoing.

The proper boundaries of remedial relief in the general class of cases where, after termination, it is discovered that the employee has engaged in wrongdoing must be addressed by the judicial system in the ordinary course of further decisions, for the factual permutations and the equitable considerations they raise will vary from case to case. We do conclude that here, and as a general rule in cases of this type, neither reinstatement nor front pay is an appropriate remedy. It would be both inequitable and pointless to order the reinstatement of someone the employer would have terminated, and will terminate, in any event and upon lawful grounds.

The proper measure of backpay presents a more difficult problem. Resolution of this question must give proper recognition to the fact that an ADEA violation has occurred which must be deterred and compensated without undue infringement upon the employer's rights and prerogatives. The object of compensation is to restore the employee to the position he or she would have been in absent the discrimination, but that principle is difficult to apply with precision where there is after-acquired evidence of wrongdoing that would have led to termination on legitimate grounds had the employer known about it. Once an employer learns about employee wrongdoing that would lead to a legitimate discharge, we cannot require the employer to ignore the information, even if it is acquired during the course of discovery in a suit against the employer and even if the information might have gone undiscovered absent the suit. The beginning point in the trial court's formulation of a remedy should be calculation of backpay from the date of the unlawful discharge to the date the new information was discovered. In determining the appropriate order for relief, the court can consider taking into further account extraordinary equitable circumstances that affect the legitimate interests of either party. An absolute rule barring any recovery of backpay, however, would undermine the ADEA's objective of forcing employers to consider and examine their motivations, and of penalizing them for employment decisions that spring from age discrimination.

Where an employer seeks to rely upon after-acquired evidence of wrongdoing, it must first establish that the wrongdoing was of such severity that the employee in fact would have been terminated on those grounds alone if the employer had known of it at the time of the discharge. The concern that employers might as a routine matter undertake extensive discovery into an employee's background or performance on the job to resist claims under the Act is not an insubstantial one, but we think the authority of the courts to award attorney's fees, mandated under the statute, and in appropriate cases to invoke the provisions of Rule 11 of the Federal Rules of Civil Procedure will deter most abuses.

The judgment is reversed, and the case is remanded to the Court of Appeals for the Sixth Circuit for further proceedings consistent with this opinion.

It is so ordered.

NOTES AND PROBLEMS FOR DISCUSSION

1. In *McKennon,* the Court emphasized that an employer cannot make any use of after-acquired evidence unless it can "establish that the wrongdoing was of such severity that the employee in fact would have been terminated on those grounds alone if the employer had known of it at the time of the discharge." The lower courts have taken this to mean that the defendant shoulders both the burden of production and persuasion on this factual matter. And some circuits have construed this to require, absent exceptional circumstances, that the employer establish that it took action against the plaintiff as soon as it discovered the misconduct, Russell v. Microdyne Corp., 65 F.3d 1229, 1240 (4th Cir. 1995), or that it would have taken action had it known of the employee's misconduct. *See* Sagendorf-Teal v. Rensselaer County, N.Y., 100 F.3d 270, 275 (2d Cir. 1996).

Without proof that the employer has discharged employees in the past for comparable misconduct, how can an employer "establish" that it would have terminated the plaintiff for the subsequently discovered misconduct? An EEOC guideline promulgated after *McKennon* states that if no comparable past incidents are discovered, other criteria may be used in ascertaining whether the misconduct would have prompted the employer to take the adverse action, including whether (1) the misconduct was criminal in nature; (2) the employee's behavior compromised the integrity of the employer's business (divulgence of trade secrets, security, or confidential information); (3) the nature of the conduct was such that the adverse action appears reasonable and justified. EEOC Enforcement Guidance 4-5 (12/14/1995).

2. *McKennon* involved after-acquired evidence of *on-the-job* misconduct. Does the decision necessarily resolve the questions raised by after-acquired evidence of *pre-employment* conduct, such as "resume fraud," which would have precluded employment from the outset? In WALLACE v. DUNN CONSTRUCTION CO., 62 F.3d 374 (11th Cir. 1995) (en banc), the employer argued that *McKennon* was not applicable because anyone who secured a job by misrepresentation had no employee status and no standing to sue for alleged employment-related wrongs. Reasoning that the same policy concerns of deterrence and compensation on which the Supreme Court relied in *McKennon* existed in "resume fraud" cases, the *en banc* court held that the *McKennon* rule was equally applicable "to cases in which the after-acquired evidence concerns the employee's misrepresentations in a job application or resume, as well as cases in which the after-acquired evidence relates to employee wrongdoing during employment." Other courts have held that, except in refusal to hire cases, the appropriate inquiry is whether the employee would have been fired on discovery of misconduct, not whether he would have been hired. *See* Shattuck v. Kinetic Concepts, Inc., 49 F.3d 1106, 1109 (5th Cir. 1995) ("Merely asking whether the employee would have been hired fails to recognize that an employer may retain an individual who has performed successfully, despite lack of formal qualification.").

Should *McKennon* have any bearing on evidence of *post-employment* conduct, referred to variously as "after after-acquired evidence" and "after-acquired motive" cases? In CARR v. WOODBURY COUNTY JUVENILE DETENTION CENTER, 905 F.Supp. 619 (N.D. Iowa 1995), aff'd per curiam, 97 F.3d 1456 (8th Cir. 1996), the plaintiff alleged that she was constructively discharged as a result of a racially and sexually hostile work environment. During discovery, the employer obtained evidence that the plaintiff had used marijuana after she had ended her employment with it and maintained that it should be allowed to use such evidence at trial because of its policy prohibiting the use of controlled substances. The trial court concluded that *McKennon* was not applicable.

> In an after-acquired evidence case, the employer plainly lacked the legitimate basis for its decision the after-acquired evidence provides at the time the decision was made, because, obviously, the employer did not have knowledge of the legitimating, "constructive" reason at the time it made the employment decision. Equity may require that some effect be given to the employee's wrongdoing during employment, even if it was not known to the employer. However, when the after-acquired evidence involves misconduct that occurred only after employment terminated, that misconduct is even more distant from the employer's decision-making process, because the misconduct is not temporally related to the decision as well as unknown to the employer. Thus, such "after after-acquired evidence" is even less relevant to the defense of a discrimination claim.

905 F.Supp. at 628. Accordingly, the district court ruled that the evidence of plaintiff's drug use was not admissible at trial. This is the prevailing rule. But it is one thing to say that evidence of post-employment misconduct is inadmissible at trial, particularly if the matter is to go to a jury. It is quite another thing to say, as *Carr* suggests, that such evidence is irrelevant for all purposes. Couldn't a former

employee's post-employment conduct have a bearing on whether reinstatement was an appropriate remedy? What if the plaintiff in *Carr* had committed a violent crime? In SELLERS v. MINETA, 358 F.3d 1058 (8th Cir. 2004), a jury found the plaintiff had been sexually harassed and discharged from her job as an air traffic controller in violation of Title VII. The plaintiff sought equitable relief in the form of reinstatement or front pay from the court. The district judge denied reinstatement because of the level of animosity between the parties which the judge determined would make a working relationship between them impossible. In lieu of reinstatement the court awarded more than $600,000 in front pay. (Remedies, including front pay are discussed in Chapter 7, *infra*.) While the request for injunctive relief was pending, the defendant learned that the plaintiff had been discharged from her subsequent job at a bank for processing an unauthorized loan application for her spouse's ex-wife. On appeal, the defendant argued that any front pay award was improper because the plaintiff's post-termination conduct had rendered her unsuitable for reinstatement and thus for front pay. The court of appeals agreed.

> The availability of front pay as a remedy * * * presupposes that reinstatement is impractical or impossible due to circumstances not attributable to the plaintiff. It would be inequitable for a plaintiff to avail herself of the disfavored remedy and exceptional remedy of front pay where her own misconduct precludes her from availing herself of the favored and more traditional remedy of reinstatement. As such, we hold that a plaintiff's post-termination conduct is relevant in determining whether front pay is available, and if so, in determining the extent of the award.

358 F.3d at 1064. The court noted, however, that under *McKennon*, the burden is on the employer to establish that the employee's wrongdoing would preclude reinstatement. Because the district court had denied reinstatement solely because of the acrimonious relationship of the parties and had made no finding that the defendant's policies would in fact preclude reemployment of the plaintiff, the case was remanded for a determination of whether Sellers was in fact "unsuitable for reinstatement solely because of her post-termination conduct."

3.   The general rule of *McKennon* is that when an employee is shown to have committed an act that would have resulted in termination had the employer learned of the misconduct during employment, "neither reinstatement nor front pay is an appropriate remedy." In such a case, back pay should be calculated "from the date of the unlawful discharge to the date the new information was discovered," with the court "taking into further account extraordinary equitable circumstances that affect the legitimate interests of either party." The Court also suggested that efforts by employers to uncover employee transgressions which might provide an excuse for an unlawful discharge might constitute an "abuse" meriting sanctions under FRCP Rule 11. But how should these considerations be applied when the employer believes a discharge is legitimate and nevertheless goes looking for evidence of a former employee's transgressions as a means of limiting any liability that is assessed? In an Enforcement Guideline, the EEOC has indicated that any purposeful attempt to obtain derogatory information about a charging party should be presumed to be retaliatory. The agency concludes that if such an investigation bears fruit (revealing grounds for discharge), reinstatement would not be appropriate under *McKennon*, but a retaliatory investigation is the kind of "extraordinary equitable circumstance" that would warrant extending back pay to the date the complaint was resolved. "An employer who chooses to wage a retaliatory investigation must lose the advantage of equities that would, absent the retaliation, favor that employer, especially since retaliation is an independent violation of the federal employment discrimination laws." Enforcement Guidance at 7 (12/14/1995). Should such a rule be adopted by courts? If after-acquired evidence has a legitimate role to play in employment discrimination cases, does it make sense to penalize employers who go looking for it after they have been sued?

In RIVERA v. NIBCO, INC., 364 F.3d 1057 (9th Cir. 2004), cert. denied, 544 U.S. 905, 125 S.Ct. 1603, 161 L.Ed.2d 279 (2005) the plaintiffs, 23 Hispanic and Asian immigrants, were discharged after performing poorly on English proficiency tests. They filed suit alleging national origin discrimination in violation of Title VII. The employer sought to discover the immigration status of the plaintiffs. The plaintiffs resisted discovery and obtained a protective order from the district court on the ground that such discovery would unnecessarily chill the legitimate claims of undocumented workers. The employers took an interlocutory appeal arguing that it was entitled to such discovery under the "after-acquired evidence" doctrine because undocumented aliens would not be entitled to reinstatement or back pay. Noting that the defendant had already stipulated that the plaintiffs were members of a protected class — and that *McKennon* had authorized federal courts to invoke the Federal Rules of Civil Procedure to prevent employers from engaging in wholesale searches for evidence that might serve to limit damages for their wrongful conduct — the Ninth Circuit affirmed.

> * * * Regrettably, many employers turn a blind eye to immigration status during the hiring process; their aim is to assemble a workforce that is both cheap to employ and that minimizes their risk of being reported for violations of statutory rights. Therefore, employers have a perverse incentive to ignore immigration laws at the time of hiring but insist upon their enforcement when their employees complain. We have placed the burden of proof squarely on employers who seek to assert an after-acquired evidence defense. Thus, in the immigration context, the employer must prove that it would actually have fired the employees had it known that they were undocumented. It does not appear that there is any evidence in the record, at this stage of the litigation, that would tend to satisfy NIBCO's burden that it would have done so. In this circumstance, a district court may well be reluctant to order discovery that would inquire into the immigrant's status, given the harm that such investigations cause.

364 F.3d at 1072. The Ninth Circuit denied rehearing and rehearing en banc. Four judges dissented from the en banc denial. They argued that "the panel's decision impedes the ascertainment of the truth in advance of trial, thereby profoundly subverting the purposes of liberal discovery in civil cases. The decision also frustrates the purposes of national Immigration policy: to limit employment benefits to American citizens and foreign persons authorized to work in this country." Rivera v. NIBCO, Inc., 384 F.3d 822, 823 (9th Cir. 2004) (Bea, J. dissenting from denial of rehearing en banc).

FINDINGS OF FACT AND APPELLATE REVIEW

Rule 52(a) of the Federal Rules of Civil Procedure requires the district judge, in actions tried without a jury, to make separate findings of fact and conclusions of law in support of a judgment. The Rule further provides that "[f]indings of fact, whether based on oral or documentary evidence, shall not be set aside unless clearly erroneous, and due regard shall be given to the opportunity of the trial court to judge of the credibility of the witnesses." The Supreme Court has held that a finding is "clearly erroneous" when "although there is evidence to support it, the reviewing court on the entire evidence is left with the definite and firm conviction that a mistake has been committed." United States v. United States Gypsum Co., 333 U.S. 364, 395, 68 S.Ct. 525, 542, 92 L.Ed. 746, 766 (1948). Inherent in the clearly erroneous standard is the rule that a court of appeal does not try issues of fact *de novo* and does not set aside district court findings merely because, on the record before it, the appellate court would have reached a different conclusion.

In PULLMAN-STANDARD v. SWINT, 456 U.S. 273, 102 S.Ct. 1781, 72 L.Ed.2d 66 (1982), the Court held the question of unlawful intent in a Title VII case to be a pure question of fact, subject to Rule 52's clearly erroneous standard of review. The Court reexamined the application of Rule 52 to findings of fact in employment discrimination cases in ANDERSON v. CITY OF BESSEMER, 470 U.S. 564, 105 S.Ct. 1504, 84 L.Ed.2d 518 (1985). In *Anderson*, the district court found that the plaintiff had been denied employment because of her sex and that the employer's explanation for preferring a male applicant was pretextual. Critical to the district court's determination was its findings that the plaintiff was better qualified for the position than the successful male applicant and that the plaintiff, but not any of the male applicants, was seriously questioned concerning her spouse's feelings about her working. The Fourth Circuit reversed on the ground that the district court's subsidiary factual findings were clearly erroneous. The Supreme Court granted reversed the appellate court and reinstated the trial court's judgment.

As to the relative qualifications of the two candidates for the position, the Supreme Court noted that the district court's finding was based on essentially undisputed documentary evidence regarding the respective backgrounds of the applicants and the duties of the position in question. The Court of Appeals, reading the same record, differed with the district court as to the most important duties of the job in question and concluded that the male applicant was better qualified. The Supreme Court held that the Court of Appeals had overstepped its authority under Rule 52.

> Based on our own reading of the record, we cannot say that either interpretation of the facts is illogical or implausible. Each has support in inferences that may be drawn from the facts in the record; and if either interpretation had been drawn by a district court on the record before us, we would not be inclined to find it clearly erroneous. The question we must answer, however, is not whether the Fourth Circuit's interpretation of the facts was clearly erroneous, but whether the District Court's finding was clearly erroneous. The District Court determined that petitioner was better qualified, and, as we have stated above, such a finding is entitled to deference notwithstanding that it is not based on credibility determinations. When the record is examined in light of the appropriately deferential standard, it is apparent that it contains nothing that mandates a finding that the District Court's conclusion was clearly erroneous.

470 U.S. at 577, 105 S.Ct. at 1513.

There was conflicting testimony, however, with respect to the issue of whether male candidates were or were not seriously questioned about the feelings of their wives toward the job in question. Nevertheless, the Supreme Court held that the Court of Appeals had failed to give due regard to the ability of the district judge to resolve conflicts in the oral testimony of witnesses and to make credibility determinations. Since the testimony of the witnesses that the trial judge chose to believe was not "implausible on its face" and was not "contradicted by any reliable extrinsic evidence," the Supreme Court ruled that the district judge's decision to credit the witnesses was not clearly erroneous.

As a consequence of amendments contained in the 1991 Civil Rights Act, not only are compensatory and punitive damages available under Title VII in connection with claims of intentional discrimination, but either party can demand a jury trial where damages are claimed by the plaintiff. If anything, appellate courts give even greater deference to findings of fact by juries than by judges. The Seventh Amendment to the U.S. Constitution provides in part: "No fact tried to a jury, shall be otherwise reexamined in any Court of the United States, than according to the rules of the common law." As illustrated in *Reeves*, the courts have developed a "reasonableness" test for review of jury verdicts. The evidence must be considered in the light most favorable to the party who obtained the verdict, the winning party is entitled to all reasonable inferences from the evidence, and a verdict will not be set aside unless on the record before the appellate court reasonable minds could not have reached the verdict rendered.

The practical effect of these standards of appellate review is to place a heavy burden on a party who would challenge a district court's fact finding, regardless of whether the fact finder is a judge or jury. *See, e.g.*, Benzies v. Illinois Department of Mental Health, 810 F.2d 146, 148 (7th Cir.), cert. denied, 483 U.S. 1006, 107 S.Ct. 3231, 97 L.Ed.2d 737 (1987) ("findings, even on the ultimate issue, are all but conclusive"). *See generally* Charles R. Calleros, *Title VII and Rule 52(c): Standards of Appellate Review in Disparate Treatment Cases — Limiting the Reach of Pullman-Standard v. Swint*, 58 TUL.L.REV. 403 (1983).

3. THE DEFENDANT'S CASE

As in any civil case, a defendant can respond to a plaintiff's allegations and proof in two ways. It can attempt to deny or rebut the elements of the plaintiff's claim and/or assert an affirmative defense. The plaintiff, of course, retains the burden of persuasion as to each and every element of the prima facie showing. Consequently, where the defendant seeks to deny or rebut the plaintiff's claim, it shoulders only the burden of producing evidence. In the rare case where the plaintiff fails to muster sufficient proof to establish a prima facie case, the appropriate defense response is a motion for summary judgment or, if the case has gone to trial, for judgment as a matter of law under Rule 50(a) of the Federal Rules of Civil Procedure. But where the plaintiff is able to establish a prima facie case under the *McDonnell Douglas/Burdine* formula, the defendant is placed in the position of having, at a minimum, to rebut the presumption of discrimination generated by that prima facie case in order to avoid judgment as a matter of law. To meet that burden, the defendant must come forward with admissible evidence showing a legitimate, nondiscriminatory reason for the challenged employment decision. And though the employer does not have the burden of persuading the factfinder that its challenged decision was motivated by the tendered nondiscriminatory explanation, the employer typically will not rest solely on a mere "articulation" of a nondiscriminatory reason. Rather, it will put on as much evidence as it can produce in an effort to persuade the factfinder that it did not discriminate. The trier of fact (judge or jury) must then decide the ultimate issue — whether a determinative cause of the challenged decision was unlawful bias. And as to that, the plaintiff retains the burden of persuasion. Moreover, pursuant to the Court's post-*Burdine* refinement/modification of the *McDonnell Douglas formulation* offered in *Hicks* and *Reeves*, that determination may be influenced, but will not necessarily be controlled, by a rejection of the employer's articulated reason for its action.

In some cases, however, the defendant does more than simply deny the plaintiff's allegation of discrimination. We have seen already how Congress through the 1991 Civil Rights Act refined the Supreme Court's approach to "mixed motive" cases by creating an affirmative defense for employers in suits where the plaintiff established, per §703(m), that a forbidden factor played a determinative role in the challenged decision. Under §706(g)(2)(B), the defendant can limit the remedies recoverable by a plaintiff by persuading the factfinder that it would have reached the same decision in the absence of a discriminatory motivation. And in §703(e), Congress created another affirmative defense, one that goes directly to liability and not just to remedies. This provision shields the employer from liability even though the plaintiff has established that he was the victim of certain kinds of proscribed discrimination. The expanse of this bona fide occupational qualification (BFOQ) defense is discussed below.

International Union, United Automobile, and Agricultural Implement Workers of America, UAW v. Johnson Controls, Inc.

Supreme Court of the United States, 1991.
499 U.S. 187, 111 S.Ct. 1196, 113 L.Ed.2d 158.

JUSTICE BLACKMUN delivered the opinion of the Court.

In this case we are concerned with an employer's gender-based fetal-protection policy. May an employer exclude a fertile female employee from certain jobs because of its concern for the health of the fetus the woman might conceive?

I

Respondent Johnson Controls, Inc. manufactures batteries. In the manufacturing process, the element lead is a primary ingredient. Occupational exposure to lead entails health risks, including the risk of harm to any fetus carried by a female employee.

Before the Civil Rights Act of 1964 became law, Johnson Controls did not employ any woman in a battery-manufacturing job. In June 1977, however, it announced its first official policy concerning its employment of women in lead-exposure work:

"Protection of the health of the unborn child is the immediate and direct responsibility of the prospective parents. While the medical profession and the company can support them in the exercise of this responsibility, it cannot assume it for them without simultaneously infringing their rights as persons.

". . . . Since not all women who can become mothers wish to become mothers (or will become mothers), it would appear to be illegal discrimination to treat all who are capable of pregnancy as though they will become pregnant."

Consistent with that view, Johnson Controls "stopped short of excluding women capable of bearing children from lead exposure," but emphasized that a woman who expected to have a child should not choose a job in which she would have such exposure. The company also required a woman who wished to be considered for employment to sign a statement that she had been advised of the risk of having a child while she was exposed to lead. The statement informed the woman that although there was evidence "that women exposed to lead have a higher rate of abortion," this evidence was "not as clear . . . as the relationship between cigarette smoking and cancer," but that it was, "medically speaking, just good sense not to run that risk if you want children and do not want to expose the unborn child to risk, however small. . . ."

Five years later, in 1982, Johnson Controls shifted from a policy of warning to a policy of exclusion. Between 1979 and 1983, eight employees became pregnant while maintaining blood lead levels in excess of 30 micrograms per deciliter. This appeared to be the critical level noted by the Occupational Health and Safety Administration (OSHA) for a worker who was planning to have a family. The company responded by announcing a broad exclusion of women from jobs that exposed them to lead:

"* * * It is [Johnson Controls'] policy that women who are pregnant or who are capable of bearing children will not be placed into jobs involving lead exposure or which could expose them to lead through the exercise of job bidding, bumping, transfer or promotion rights."

The policy defined "women . . . capable of bearing children" as "all women except those whose inability to bear children is medically documented." It further stated that an unacceptable work station was one where, "over the past year," an employee had recorded a blood lead level of more than 30 micrograms per deciliter or the work site had yielded an air sample containing a lead level in excess of 30 micrograms per cubic meter.

II

In April 1984, petitioners filed * * * a class action challenging Johnson Controls' fetal-protection policy as sex discrimination that violated Title VII. Among the individual plaintiffs were petitioners Mary Craig, who had chosen to be sterilized in order to avoid losing her job, Elsie Nason, a 50-year-old divorcee, who had suffered a loss in compensation when she was transferred out of a job where she was exposed to lead, and Donald Penney, who had been denied a request for a leave of absence for the purpose of lowering his lead level because he intended to become a father.

The District Court granted summary judgment for defendant-respondent Johnson Controls. Applying a three-part business necessity defense derived from fetal-protection cases in the Courts of Appeals for the Fourth and Eleventh Circuits, the District Court concluded that while "there is a disagreement among the experts regarding the effect of lead on the fetus," the hazard to the fetus through exposure to lead was established by "a considerable body of opinion"; that although "expert opinion has been provided which holds that lead also affects the reproductive abilities of men and women . . . [and] that these effects are as great as the effects of exposure of the fetus . . . a great body of experts are of the opinion that the fetus is more vulnerable to levels of lead that would not affect adults"; and that petitioners had "failed to establish that there is an acceptable alternative policy which would protect the fetus." The court stated that, in view of this disposition of the business necessity defense, it did not "have to undertake a bona fide occupational qualification's (BFOQ) analysis."

The Court of Appeals for the Seventh Circuit, sitting en banc, affirmed the summary judgment by a 7-to-4 vote. The majority held that the proper standard for evaluating the fetal-protection policy was the defense of business necessity; that Johnson Controls was entitled to summary judgment under that defense; and that even if the proper standard was a BFOQ, Johnson Controls still was entitled to summary judgment.

The Court of Appeals first reviewed fetal-protection opinions from the Eleventh and Fourth Circuits. Those opinions established the three-step business necessity inquiry: whether there is a substantial health risk to the fetus; whether transmission of the hazard to the fetus occurs only through women; and whether there is a less discriminatory alternative equally capable of preventing the health hazard to the fetus. The Court of Appeals agreed with the Eleventh and Fourth Circuits that "the components of the business necessity defense the courts of appeals and the EEOC have utilized in fetal protection cases balance the interests of the employer, the employee and the unborn child in a manner consistent with Title VII." * * *

* * *

* * * We granted certiorari to resolve the obvious conflict between the * * * Circuits on this issue, and to address the important and difficult question whether an employer, seeking to protect potential fetuses, may discriminate against women just because of their ability to become pregnant.

III

The bias in Johnson Controls' policy is obvious. Fertile men, but not fertile women, are given a choice as to whether they wish to risk their reproductive health for a particular job. Section 703(a) of the Civil Rights Act of 1964 prohibits sex-based classifications in terms and conditions of employment, in hiring and discharging decisions, and in other employment decisions that adversely affect an employee's status. Respondent's fetal-protection policy explicitly discriminates against women on the basis of their sex. The policy excludes women with childbearing capacity from lead-exposed jobs and so creates a facial classification based on gender. Respondent assumes as much in its brief before this Court.

Nevertheless, the Court of Appeals assumed, as did the two appellate courts who already had confronted the issue, that sex-specific fetal-protection policies do not involve facial discrimination. These courts analyzed the policies as though they were facially neutral, and had only a discriminatory effect upon the employment opportunities of women. * * * The court assumed that because the asserted reason for the sex-based exclusion (protecting women's unconceived offspring) was ostensibly benign, the policy was not sex-based discrimination. That assumption, however, was incorrect.

First, Johnson Controls' policy classifies on the basis of gender and childbearing capacity, rather than fertility alone. Respondent does not seek to protect the unconceived children of all its employees. Despite evidence in the record about the debilitating effect of lead exposure on the male reproductive system, Johnson Controls is concerned only with the harms that may befall the unborn offspring of its female employees. * * * Johnson Controls' policy is facially discriminatory because it requires only a female employee to produce proof that she is not capable of reproducing.

Our conclusion is bolstered by the Pregnancy Discrimination Act of 1978 (PDA), in which Congress explicitly provided that, for purposes of Title VII, discrimination "on the basis of sex" includes discrimination "because of or on the basis of pregnancy, childbirth, or related medical conditions."[3] "The Pregnancy Discrimination Act has now made clear that, for all Title VII purposes, discrimination based on a woman's pregnancy is, on its face, discrimination because of her sex." Newport News Shipbuilding & Dry Dock Co. v. EEOC, 462 U.S. 669, 684, 103 S.Ct. 2622, 2631, 77 L.Ed.2d 89 (1983). In its use of the words "capable of bearing children" in the 1982 policy statement as the criterion for exclusion, Johnson Controls explicitly classifies on the basis of potential for pregnancy. Under the PDA, such a classification must be regarded, for Title VII purposes, in the same light as explicit sex discrimination. Respondent has chosen to treat all its female employees as potentially pregnant; that choice evinces discrimination on the basis of sex.

We concluded above that Johnson Controls' policy is not neutral because it does not apply to the reproductive capacity of the company's male employees in the same way as it applies to that of the females. Moreover, the absence of a malevolent motive does not convert a facially discriminatory policy into a neutral policy with a discriminatory effect. Whether an employment practice involves disparate treatment through explicit facial discrimination does not depend on why the employer discriminates but rather on the explicit terms of the discrimination. * * * The beneficence of an employer's purpose does not undermine the conclusion that an explicit gender-based policy is sex discrimination under §703(a) and thus may be defended only as a BFOQ.

* * *

IV

Under §703(e)(1) of Title VII, an employer may discriminate on the basis of "religion, sex, or national origin in those certain instances where religion, sex, or national origin is a bona fide occupational qualification reasonably necessary to the normal operation of that particular business or enterprise." We therefore turn to the question whether Johnson Controls' fetal-protection policy is one of those "certain instances" that come within the BFOQ exception.

---

[3]The Act added subsection (k) to §701 of the Civil Rights Act of 1964 and reads in pertinent part:

"The terms 'because of sex' or 'on the basis of sex' [in Title VII] include, but are not limited to, because of or on the basis of pregnancy, childbirth, or related medical conditions; and women affected by pregnancy, childbirth, or related medical conditions shall be treated the same for all employment-related purposes . * * * as other persons not so affected but similar in their ability or inability to work. * * *"

The BFOQ defense is written narrowly, and this Court has read it narrowly. See, e.g., Dothard v. Rawlinson, 433 U.S. 321, 332-337, 97 S.Ct. 2720, 2728-2731, 53 L.Ed.2d 786 (1977); Trans World Airlines, Inc. v. Thurston, 469 U.S. 111, 122-125, 105 S.Ct. 613, 622-624, 83 L.Ed.2d 523 (1985). We have read the BFOQ language of §4(f) of the Age Discrimination in Employment Act of 1967 (ADEA), 29 U.S.C. §623(f)(1), which tracks the BFOQ provision in Title VII, just as narrowly. See Western Air Lines, Inc. v. Criswell, 472 U.S. 400, 105 S.Ct. 2743, 86 L.Ed.2d 321 (1985). Our emphasis on the restrictive scope of the BFOQ defense is grounded on both the language and the legislative history of §703.

The wording of the BFOQ defense contains several terms of restriction that indicate that the exception reaches only special situations. The statute thus limits the situations in which discrimination is permissible to "certain instances" where sex discrimination is "reasonably necessary" to the "normal operation" of the "particular" business. Each one of these terms — certain, normal, particular — prevents the use of general subjective standards and favors an objective, verifiable requirement. But the most telling term is "occupational"; this indicates that these objective, verifiable requirements must concern job-related skills and aptitudes.

Justice White defines "occupational" as meaning related to a job. According to him, any discriminatory requirement imposed by an employer is "job-related" simply because the employer has chosen to make the requirement a condition of employment. In effect, he argues that sterility may be an occupational qualification for women because Johnson Controls has chosen to require it. This reading of "occupational" renders the word mere surplusage. "Qualification" by itself would encompass an employer's idiosyncratic requirements. By modifying "qualification" with "occupational," Congress narrowed the term to qualifications that affect an employee's ability to do the job.

Johnson Controls argues that its fetal-protection policy falls within the so-called safety exception to the BFOQ. Our cases have stressed that discrimination on the basis of sex because of safety concerns is allowed only in narrow circumstances. In Dothard v. Rawlinson, this Court indicated that danger to a woman herself does not justify discrimination. We there allowed the employer to hire only male guards in contact areas of maximum-security male penitentiaries only because more was at stake than the "individual woman's decision to weigh and accept the risks of employment." We found sex to be a BFOQ inasmuch as the employment of a female guard would create real risks of safety to others if violence broke out because the guard was a woman. Sex discrimination was tolerated because sex was related to the guard's ability to do the job — maintaining prison security. We also required in *Dothard* a high correlation between sex and ability to perform job functions and refused to allow employers to use sex as a proxy for strength although it might be a fairly accurate one.

Similarly, some courts have approved airlines' layoffs of pregnant flight attendants at different points during the first five months of pregnancy on the ground that the employer's policy was necessary to ensure the safety of passengers. See Harris v. Pan American World Airways, Inc., 649 F.2d 670 (CA9 1980); Burwell v. Eastern Air Lines, Inc., 633 F.2d 361 (CA4 1980), cert. denied, 450 U.S. 965, 101 S.Ct. 1480, 67 L.Ed.2d 613 (1981). In two of these cases, the courts pointedly indicated that fetal, as opposed to passenger, safety was best left to the mother. .

We considered safety to third parties in Western Airlines, Inc. v. Criswell, in the context of the ADEA. We focused upon "the nature of the flight engineer's tasks," and the "actual capabilities of persons over age 60" in relation to those tasks. Our safety concerns were not independent of the individual's ability to perform the assigned tasks, but rather involved the possibility that, because of age-connected debility, a flight engineer might not properly assist the pilot, and might thereby cause a safety emergency. Furthermore, although we considered the safety of third parties in *Dothard* and *Criswell*, those third parties were indispensable to the particular business at issue. In *Dothard*, the third parties were the inmates; in Criswell, the third parties were the passengers on the plane. We stressed that in order to qualify as a BFOQ, a job qualification must relate to the "essence," *Dothard* or to the "central mission of the employer's business," *Criswell*.

Justice White ignores the "essence of the business" test and so concludes that "the safety to fetuses in carrying out the duties of battery manufacturing is as much a legitimate concern as is safety to third parties in guarding prisons (*Dothard*) or flying airplanes (*Criswell*)." By limiting its discussion to cost and safety concerns and rejecting the "essence of the business" test that our case law has established, he seeks to expand what is now the narrow BFOQ defense. Third-party safety considerations properly entered into the BFOQ analysis in *Dothard* and *Criswell* because they went to the core of the employee's job performance. Moreover, that performance involved the central purpose of the enterprise. *Dothard* ("The essence of a correctional counselor's job is to maintain prison security"); *Criswell* (the central mission of the airline's business was the safe transportation of its passengers). Justice White attempts to transform this case into one of customer safety. The unconceived fetuses of Johnson Controls' female employees, however, are neither customers nor third parties whose safety is essential to the business of battery manufacturing. No one can disregard the possibility of injury to future children; the BFOQ, however, is not so broad that it transforms this deep social concern into an essential aspect of battery making.

Our case law, therefore, makes clear that the safety exception is limited to instances in which sex or pregnancy actually interferes with the employee's ability to perform the job. This approach is consistent with the language of the BFOQ provision itself, for it suggests that permissible distinctions based on sex must relate to ability to perform the duties of the job. Johnson Controls suggests, however, that we expand the exception to allow fetal-protection policies that mandate particular standards for pregnant or fertile women. We decline to do so. Such an expansion contradicts not only the language of the BFOQ and the narrowness of its exception but the plain language and history of the Pregnancy Discrimination Act.

The PDA's amendment to Title VII contains a BFOQ standard of its own: unless pregnant employees differ from others "in their ability or inability to work," they must be "treated the same" as other employees "for all employment-related purposes." This language clearly sets forth Congress' remedy for discrimination on the basis of pregnancy and potential pregnancy. Women who are either pregnant or potentially pregnant must be treated like others "similar in their ability . . . to work." In other words, women as capable of doing their jobs as their male counterparts may not be forced to choose between having a child and having a job.

Justice White asserts that the PDA did not alter the BFOQ defense. He arrives at this conclusion by ignoring the second clause of the Act which states that "women affected by pregnancy, childbirth, or related medical conditions shall be treated the same for all employment-related purposes . . . as other persons not so affected but similar in their ability or inability to work." Until this day, every Member of this Court had acknowledged that "the second clause [of the PDA] could not be clearer: it mandates that pregnant employees 'shall be treated the same for all employment-related purposes' as nonpregnant employees similarly situated with respect to their ability or inability to work." California Federal S. & L. Assn. v. Guerra, 479 U.S. 272, 297, 107 S.Ct. 683, 698, 93 L.Ed.2d 613 (1987) (White, J., dissenting). Justice White now seeks to read the second clause out of the Act.

* * *

We conclude that the language of both the BFOQ provision and the PDA which amended it, as well as the legislative history and the case law, prohibit an employer from discriminating against a woman because of her capacity to become pregnant unless her reproductive potential prevents her from performing the duties of her job. We reiterate our holdings in *Criswell* and *Dothard* that an employer must direct its concerns about a woman's ability to perform her job safely and efficiently to those aspects of the woman's job-related activities that fall within the "essence" of the particular business.[4]

V

We have no difficulty concluding that Johnson Controls cannot establish a BFOQ. Fertile women, as far as appears in the record, participate in the manufacture of batteries as efficiently as anyone else. Johnson Controls' professed moral and ethical concerns about the welfare of the next generation do not suffice to establish a BFOQ of female sterility. Decisions about the welfare of future children must be left to the parents who conceive, bear, support, and raise them rather than to the employers who hire those parents. Congress has mandated this choice through Title VII, as amended by the Pregnancy Discrimination Act. Johnson Controls has attempted to exclude women because of their reproductive capacity. Title VII and the PDA simply do not allow a woman's dismissal because of her failure to submit to sterilization.

Nor can concerns about the welfare of the next generation be considered a part of the "essence" of Johnson Controls' business. Judge Easterbrook in this case pertinently observed: "It is word play to say that 'the job' at Johnson [Controls] is to make batteries without risk to fetuses in the same way 'the job' at Western Air Lines is to fly planes without crashing."

Johnson Controls argues that it must exclude all fertile women because it is impossible to tell which women will become pregnant while working with lead. This

---

[4]Justice White predicts that our reaffirmation of the narrowness of the BFOQ defense will preclude considerations of privacy as a basis for sex-based discrimination. We have never addressed privacy-based sex discrimination and shall not do so here because the sex-based discrimination at issue today does not involve the privacy interests of Johnson Controls' customers. Nothing in our discussion of the "essence of the business test," however, suggests that sex could not constitute a BFOQ when privacy interests are implicated. See, e.g., Backus v. Baptist Medical Center, 510 F.Supp. 1191 (E.D.Ark.1981), vacated as moot, 671 F.2d 1100 (CA8 1982) (essence of obstetrics nurse's business is to provide sensitive care for patient's intimate and private concerns).

argument is somewhat academic in light of our conclusion that the company may not exclude fertile women at all; it perhaps is worth noting, however, that Johnson Controls has shown no "factual basis for believing that all or substantially all women would be unable to perform safely and efficiently the duties of the job involved." Weeks v. Southern Bell Tel. & Tel. Co., 408 F.2d 228, 235 (CA5 1969). Even on this sparse record, it is apparent that Johnson Controls is concerned about only a small minority of women. Of the eight pregnancies reported among the female employees, it has not been shown that any of the babies have birth defects or other abnormalities. The record does not reveal the birth rate for Johnson Controls' female workers but national statistics show that approximately nine percent of all fertile women become pregnant each year. The birthrate drops to two percent for blue collar workers over age 30. Johnson Controls' fear of prenatal injury, no matter how sincere, does not begin to show that substantially all of its fertile women employees are incapable of doing their jobs.

VI

A word about tort liability and the increased cost of fertile women in the workplace is perhaps necessary. One of the dissenting judges in this case expressed concern about an employer's tort liability and concluded that liability for a potential injury to a fetus is a social cost that Title VII does not require a company to ignore. It is correct to say that Title VII does not prevent the employer from having a conscience. The statute, however, does prevent sex-specific fetal-protection policies. These two aspects of Title VII do not conflict.

More than 40 States currently recognize a right to recover for a prenatal injury based either on negligence or on wrongful death. According to Johnson Controls, however, the company complies with the lead standard developed by OSHA and warns its female employees about the damaging effects of lead. It is worth noting that OSHA gave the problem of lead lengthy consideration and concluded that "there is no basis whatsoever for the claim that women of childbearing age should be excluded from the workplace in order to protect the fetus or the course of pregnancy." 43 Fed. Reg. 52952, 52966 (1978). Instead, OSHA established a series of mandatory protections which, taken together, "should effectively minimize any risk to the fetus and newborn child." Id., at 52966. Without negligence, it would be difficult for a court to find liability on the part of the employer. If, under general tort principles, Title VII bans sex-specific fetal-protection policies, the employer fully informs the woman of the risk, and the employer has not acted negligently, the basis for holding an employer liable seems remote at best.

Although the issue is not before us, Justice White observes that "it is far from clear that compliance with Title VII will preempt state tort liability." The cases relied upon by him to support its prediction, however, are inapposite. For example, in California Federal S. & L. Assn. v. Guerra, we considered a California statute that expanded upon the requirements of the PDA and concluded that the statute was not pre-empted by Title VII because it was not inconsistent with the purposes of the federal statute and did not require an act that was unlawful under Title VII. Here, in contrast, the tort liability that Justice White fears will punish employers for complying with Title VII's clear command. When it is impossible for an employer to comply with both state and federal requirements, this Court has ruled that federal law preempts that of the States. See, e.g., Florida Lime & Avocado Growers, Inc. v. Paul, 373 U.S. 132, 142-143, 83 S.Ct. 1210, 1217-1218, 10 L.Ed.2d 248 (1963).

* * *

If state tort law furthers discrimination in the workplace and prevents employers from hiring women who are capable of manufacturing the product as efficiently as men, then it will impede the accomplishment of Congress' goals in enacting Title VII. Because Johnson Controls has not argued that it faces any costs from tort liability, not to mention crippling ones, the pre-emption question is not before us. We therefore say no more than that the concurrence's speculation appears unfounded as well as premature.

The tort-liability argument reduces to two equally unpersuasive propositions. First, Johnson Controls attempts to solve the problem of reproductive health hazards by resorting to an exclusionary policy. Title VII plainly forbids illegal sex discrimination as a method of diverting attention from an employer's obligation to police the workplace. Second, the specter of an award of damages reflects a fear that hiring fertile women will cost more. The extra cost of employing members of one sex, however, does not provide an affirmative Title VII defense for a discriminatory refusal to hire members of that gender. Indeed, in passing the PDA, Congress considered at length the considerable cost of providing equal treatment of pregnancy and related conditions, but made the "decision to forbid special treatment of pregnancy despite the social costs associated therewith." Arizona Governing Committee v. Norris, 463 U.S. 1073, 1084, n. 14, 103 S.Ct. 3492, 3499, n.14, 77 L.Ed.2d 1236 (1983) (opinion of Marshall, J.). See Price Waterhouse v. Hopkins, 490 U.S. 228, 109 S.Ct. 1775, 104 L.Ed.2d 268 (1988).

We, of course, are not presented with, nor do we decide, a case in which costs would be so prohibitive as to threaten the survival of the employer's business. We merely reiterate our prior holdings that the incremental cost of hiring women cannot justify discriminating against them.

VII

Our holding today that Title VII, as so amended, forbids sex-specific fetal-protection policies is neither remarkable nor unprecedented. Concern for a woman's existing or potential offspring historically has been the excuse for denying women equal employment opportunities. See, e.g., Muller v. Oregon, 208 U.S. 412, 28 S.Ct. 324, 52 L.Ed. 551 (1908). Congress in the PDA prohibited discrimination on the basis of a woman's ability to become pregnant. We do no more than hold that the Pregnancy Discrimination Act means what it says.

It is no more appropriate for the courts than it is for individual employers to decide whether a woman's reproductive role is more important to herself and her family than her economic role. Congress has left this choice to the woman as hers to make.

The judgment of the Court of Appeals is reversed and the case is remanded for further proceedings consistent with this opinion.

It is so ordered.

JUSTICE WHITE, with whom THE CHIEF JUSTICE and JUSTICE KENNEDY join, concurring in part and concurring in the judgment.

The Court properly holds that Johnson Controls' fetal protection policy overtly discriminates against women, and thus is prohibited by Title VII unless it falls within the bona fide occupational qualification (BFOQ) exception. The Court erroneously holds, however, that the BFOQ defense is so narrow that it could never justify a sex-specific fetal protection policy. I nevertheless concur in the judgment of reversal because on the record before us summary judgment in favor of Johnson Controls was improperly entered by the District Court and affirmed by the Court of Appeals.

I

In evaluating the scope of the BFOQ defense, the proper starting point is the language of the statute. Title VII forbids discrimination on the basis of sex, except "in those certain instances where . . . sex . . . is a bona fide occupational qualification reasonably necessary to the normal operation of that particular business or enterprise." For the fetal protection policy involved in this case to be a BFOQ, therefore, the policy must be "reasonably necessary" to the "normal operation" of making batteries, which is Johnson Controls' "particular business." Although that is a difficult standard to satisfy, nothing in the statute's language indicates that it could never support a sex-specific fetal protection policy.[1]

On the contrary, a fetal protection policy would be justified under the terms of the statute if, for example, an employer could show that exclusion of women from certain jobs was reasonably necessary to avoid substantial tort liability. Common sense tells us that it is part of the normal operation of business concerns to avoid causing injury to third parties, as well as to employees, if for no other reason than to avoid tort liability and its substantial costs. This possibility of tort liability is not hypothetical; every State currently allows children born alive to recover in tort for prenatal injuries caused by third parties, see W. Keeton, D. Dobbs, R. Keeton, & D. Owen, Prosser and Keeton on Law of Torts §55 p. 368 (5th ed. 1984), and an increasing number of courts have recognized a right to recover even for prenatal injuries caused by torts committed prior to conception, see 3 F. Harper, F. James, & O. Gray, Law of Torts §18.3, pp. 677-678, n. 15 (2d ed. 1986).

The Court dismisses the possibility of tort liability by no more than speculating that if "Title VII bans sex-specific fetal-protection policies, the employer fully informs the woman of the risk, and the employer has not acted negligently, the basis for holding an employer liable seems remote at best." Such speculation will be small comfort to employers. First, it is far from clear that compliance with Title VII will

---

[1]The Court's heavy reliance on the word "occupational" in the BFOQ statute is unpersuasive. Any requirement for employment can be said to be an occupational qualification, since "occupational" merely means related to a job. See Webster's Third New International Dictionary 1560 (1976). Thus, Johnson Controls' requirement that employees engaged in battery manufacturing be either male or non-fertile clearly is an "occupational qualification." The issue, of course, is whether that qualification is "reasonably necessary to the normal operation" of Johnson Controls' business. It is telling that the Court offers no case support, either from this Court or the lower Federal Courts, for its interpretation of the word "occupational."

pre-empt state tort liability, and the Court offers no support for that proposition. Second, although warnings may preclude claims by injured employees, they will not preclude claims by injured children because the general rule is that parents cannot waive causes of action on behalf of their children, and the parents' negligence will not be imputed to the children. Finally, although state tort liability for prenatal injuries generally requires negligence, it will be difficult for employers to determine in advance what will constitute negligence. Compliance with OSHA standards, for example, has been held not to be a defense to state tort or criminal liability. See National Solid Wastes Management Assn. v. Killian, 918 F.2d 671, 680, n. 9 (CA7 1990). Moreover, it is possible that employers will be held strictly liable, if, for example, their manufacturing process is considered "abnormally dangerous." See Restatement (Second) of Torts §869, comment b (1979).

Relying on Los Angeles Dept. of Water and Power v. Manhart, the Court contends that tort liability cannot justify a fetal protection policy because the extra costs of hiring women is not a defense under Title VII. This contention misrepresents our decision in *Manhart*. There, we held that a requirement that female employees contribute more than male employees to a pension fund, in order to reflect the greater longevity of women, constituted discrimination against women under Title VII because it treated them as a class rather than as individuals. We did not in that case address in any detail the nature of the BFOQ defense, and we certainly did not hold that cost was irrelevant to the BFOQ analysis. Rather, we merely stated in a footnote that "there has been no showing that sex distinctions are reasonably necessary to the normal operation of the Department's retirement plan." We further noted that although Title VII does not contain a "cost-justification defense comparable to the affirmative defense available in a price discrimination suit," "no defense based on the total cost of employing men and women was attempted in this case."

Prior decisions construing the BFOQ defense confirm that the defense is broad enough to include considerations of cost and safety of the sort that could form the basis for an employer's adoption of a fetal protection policy. In Dothard v. Rawlinson, the Court held that being male was a BFOQ for "contact" guard positions in Alabama's maximum-security male penitentiaries. The Court first took note of the actual conditions of the prison environment: "In a prison system where violence is the order of the day, where inmate access to guards is facilitated by dormitory living arrangements, where every institution is understaffed, and where a substantial portion of the inmate population is composed of sex offenders mixed at random with other prisoners, there are few visible deterrents to inmate assaults on women custodians." The Court also stressed that "more [was] at stake" than a risk to individual female employees: "The likelihood that inmates would assault a woman because she was a woman would pose a real threat not only to the victim of the assault but also to the basic control of the penitentiary and protection of its inmates and the other security personnel." Under those circumstances, the Court observed that "it would be an oversimplification to characterize [the exclusion of women] as an exercise in 'romantic paternalism.' Cf. Frontiero v. Richardson, 411 U.S. 677, 684 (93 S.Ct. 1764, 1769, 36 L.Ed.2d 583)."

We revisited the BFOQ defense in Western Air Lines, Inc. v. Criswell, this time in the context of the Age Discrimination in Employment Act of 1967 (ADEA). There, we endorsed the two-part inquiry for evaluating a BFOQ defense used by the Fifth

Circuit Court of Appeals in Usery v. Tamiami Trail Tours, Inc., 531 F.2d 224 (1976). First, the job qualification must not be "so peripheral to the central mission of the employer's business" that no discrimination could be "'reasonably necessary to the normal operation of the particular business.'" Although safety is not such a peripheral concern[4] the inquiry "'adjusts to the safety factor — the greater the safety factor, measured by the likelihood of harm and the probable severity of that harm in case of an accident, the more stringent may be the job qualifications,'" (quoting *Tamiami*). Second, the employer must show either that all or substantially all persons excluded "'would be unable to perform safely and efficiently the duties of the job involved,'" or that it is " 'impossible or highly impractical'" to deal with them on an individual basis (quoting *Tamiami*). We further observed that this inquiry properly takes into account an employer's interest in safety — "when an employer establishes that a job qualification has been carefully formulated to respond to documented concerns for public safety, it will not be overly burdensome to persuade a trier of fact that the qualification is 'reasonably necessary' to safe operation of the business."

Dothard and *Criswell* make clear that avoidance of substantial safety risks to third parties is inherently part of both an employee's ability to perform a job and an employer's "normal operation" of its business. Indeed, in both cases, the Court approved the statement in Weeks v. Southern Bell Telephone & Telegraph Co., 408 F.2d 228 (CA5 1969), that an employer could establish a BFOQ defense by showing that "all or substantially all women would be unable to perform safely and efficiently the duties of the job involved." The Court's statement in this case that "the safety exception is limited to instances in which sex or pregnancy actually interferes with the employee's ability to perform the job," therefore adds no support to its conclusion that a fetal protection policy could never be justified as a BFOQ. On the facts of this case, for example, protecting fetal safety while carrying out the duties of battery manufacturing is as much a legitimate concern as is safety to third parties in guarding prisons (*Dothard*) or flying airplanes (*Criswell*).[5]

Dothard and *Criswell* also confirm that costs are relevant in determining whether a discriminatory policy is reasonably necessary for the normal operation of a business. In *Dothard*, the safety problem that justified exclusion of women from the prison

---

[4]An example of a "peripheral" job qualification was in Diaz v. Pan American World Airways, Inc., 442 F.2d 385(CA5), cert. denied, 404 U.S. 950, 92 S.Ct. 275, 30 L.Ed.2d 267 (1971). There, the Fifth Circuit held that being female was not a BFOQ for the job of flight attendant, despite a determination by the trial court that women were better able than men to perform the "non-mechanical" functions of the job, such as attending to the passengers' psychological needs. The court concluded that such non-mechanical functions were merely "tangential" to the normal operation of the airline's business, noting that "no one has suggested that having male stewards will so seriously affect the operation of an airline as to jeopardize or even minimize its ability to provide safe transportation from one place to another."

[5]I do not, as the Court asserts, reject the "essence of the business" test. Rather, I merely reaffirm the obvious — that safety to third parties is part of the "essence" of most if not all businesses. Of course, the BFOQ inquiry "'adjusts to the safety factor.'" *Criswell* (quoting *Tamiami*). As a result, more stringent occupational qualifications may be justified for jobs involving higher safety risks, such as flying airplanes. But a recognition that the importance of safety varies among businesses does not mean that safety is completely irrelevant to the essence of a job such as battery manufacturing.

guard positions was largely a result of inadequate staff and facilities. If the cost of employing women could not be considered, the employer there should have been required to hire more staff and restructure the prison environment rather than exclude women. Similarly, in *Criswell* the airline could have been required to hire more pilots and install expensive monitoring devices rather than discriminate against older employees. The BFOQ statute, however, reflects "Congress' unwillingness to require employers to change the very nature of their operations." Price Waterhouse v. Hopkins (plurality opinion).

The PDA, contrary to the Court's assertion, did not restrict the scope of the BFOQ defense. The PDA was only an amendment to the "Definitions" section of Title VII, and did not purport to eliminate or alter the BFOQ defense. Rather, it merely clarified Title VII to make it clear that pregnancy and related conditions are included within Title VII's antidiscrimination provisions. As we have already recognized, "the purpose of the PDA was simply to make the treatment of pregnancy consistent with general Title VII principles." Arizona Governing Committee for Tax Deferred Annuity and Deferred Compensation Plans v. Norris.

* * *

In enacting the BFOQ standard, "Congress did not ignore the public interest in safety." *Criswell.* The Court's narrow interpretation of the BFOQ defense in this case, however, means that an employer cannot exclude even pregnant women from an environment highly toxic to their fetuses. It is foolish to think that Congress intended such a result, and neither the language of the BFOQ exception nor our cases requires it.[8]

* * *

[Despite his disagreement with the majority, Justice White concluded that, on the state of the record, summary judgment was not appropriate because of disputes over material issues of fact.]

JUSTICE SCALIA, concurring in the judgment.

I generally agree with the Court's analysis, but have some reservations, several of which bear mention.

---

[8]The Court's cramped reading of the BFOQ defense is also belied by the legislative history of Title VII, in which three examples of permissible sex discrimination were mentioned — a female nurse hired to care for an elderly woman, an all-male professional baseball team, and a masseur. See 110 Cong. Rec. 2718 (1964) (Rep. Goodell); id., at 7212-7213 (interpretive memorandum introduced by Sens. Clark and Case); id., at 2720 (Rep. Multer). In none of those situations would gender "actually interfere with the employee's ability to perform the job," as required today by the Court.

The Court's interpretation of the BFOQ standard also would seem to preclude considerations of privacy as a basis for sex-based discrimination, since those considerations do not relate directly to an employee's physical ability to perform the duties of the job. The lower federal courts, however, have consistently recognized that privacy interests may justify sex-based requirements for certain jobs. See, e.g., Fesel v. Masonic Home of Delaware, Inc., 447 F.Supp. 1346 (Del.1978), aff'd, 591 F.2d 1334 (CA3 1979) (nurse's aide in retirement home).

First, I think it irrelevant that there was "evidence in the record about the debilitating effect of lead exposure on the male reproductive system." Even without such evidence, treating women differently "on the basis of pregnancy" constitutes discrimination "on the basis of sex," because Congress has unequivocally said so. Pregnancy Discrimination Act of 1978.

Second, the Court points out that "Johnson Controls has shown no factual basis for believing that all or substantially all women would be unable to perform safely . . . the duties of the job involved." In my view, this is not only "somewhat academic in light of our conclusion that the company may not exclude fertile women at all"; it is entirely irrelevant. By reason of the Pregnancy Discrimination Act, it would not matter if all pregnant women placed their children at risk in taking these jobs, just as it does not matter if no men do so. As Judge Easterbrook put it in his dissent below, "Title VII gives parents the power to make occupational decisions affecting their families. A legislative forum is available to those who believe that such decisions should be made elsewhere."

Third, I am willing to assume, as the Court intimates, that any action required by Title VII cannot give rise to liability under state tort law. That assumption, however, does not answer the question whether an action is required by Title VII (including the BFOQ provision) even if it is subject to liability under state tort law. It is perfectly reasonable to believe that Title VII has accommodated state tort law through the BFOQ exception. However, all that need be said in the present case is that Johnson has not demonstrated a substantial risk of tort liability — which is alone enough to defeat a tort-based assertion of the BFOQ exception.

Last, the Court goes far afield, it seems to me, in suggesting that increased cost alone — short of "costs . . . so prohibitive as to threaten survival of the employer's business,"—cannot support a BFOQ defense. I agree with Justice White's concurrence that nothing in our prior cases suggests this, and in my view it is wrong. I think, for example, that a shipping company may refuse to hire pregnant women as crew members on long voyages because the on-board facilities for foreseeable emergencies, though quite feasible, would be inordinately expensive. In the present case, however, Johnson has not asserted a cost-based BFOQ.

I concur in the judgment of the Court.

NOTES AND PROBLEMS FOR DISCUSSION

1. Despite *Johnson Controls,* confusion can still arise regarding whether an employment policy is "facially neutral" and thus whether disparate impact or disparate treatment analysis is applicable. In RAYTHEON CO. v. HERNANDEZ, 540 U.S. 44, 124 S.Ct. 513, 157 L. Ed. 2d 357 (2003), the plaintiff was terminated because he was found to be under the influence of drugs and alcohol at work. After he was rehabilitated and had been clean and sober for two years, the plaintiff reapplied for employment at the company. He was refused employment and subsequently sued under the Americans With Disabilities Act (ADA) alleging that he was denied employment, not because of any current impairment, but because of his history of drug and alcohol addiction, which under the ADA rendered him "disabled." Although there was evidence that the company had denied him employment because of his prior drug and alcohol use, the company claimed that the reason for discharge was a company policy of not rehiring employees who had been terminated for workplace misconduct regardless of the nature of such misconduct. In response to the defendant's motion for summary judgment, the plaintiff maintained that a genuine issue of fact existed regarding the company's motivation. Additionally, however, and for the first time in this litigation, the plaintiff argued in the alternative that even if the company had applied a neutral no-rehire policy, this violated the ADA because such a policy would have a disparate exclusionary impact on the statutorily protected class of recovering addicts. The district court granted the motion for summary judgment on the disparate treatment claim and refused to consider the disparate impact claim because it had not been pled or raised in a timely manner. On appeal, the Ninth Circuit reversed the trial court. The appellate court agreed that the disparate impact claim was not before it, but nevertheless ruled that the no-hire rule was unlawful "as applied to former drug addicts whose only work-related offense was testing positive because of their addiction." The court concluded that the application of the no-hire rule was not a legitimate nondiscriminatory reason for rejecting the plaintiff. The Supreme Court unanimously reversed.

> [W]hile ostensibly evaluating whether [the defendant] had proffered a legitimate, non discriminatory reason for failing to rehire respondent sufficient to rebut respondent's prima facie showing of disparate treatment, the Court of Appeals held that a neutral no-rehire policy could never suffice in a case where the employee was terminated for illegal drug use, because such a policy has a disparate impact on recovering drug addicts. In so holding, the Court of Appeals erred by conflating the analytical framework for disparate-impact and disparate-treatment claims. Had the Court of Appeals correctly applied the disparate-treatment framework, it would have been obliged to conclude that a neutral no-rehire policy is, by definition, a legitimate, nondiscriminatory reason under the ADA. And thus the only remaining question would be whether respondent could produce sufficient evidence from which a jury could conclude that "petitioner's stated reason for respondent's rejection was in fact pretext." (*citing McDonnell Douglas*).

540 U.S. at 51, 124 S.Ct. at 518-19. On remand the Ninth Circuit reconsidered and again reversed. Hernandez v. Hughes Missile Systems Co., 362 F.3d 564, 568 (9th Cir. 2004) ("we conclude that there is a genuine issue of material fact as to whether Raytheon failed to re-hire Hernandez because of his 'status as an alcoholic,' rather than in reliance on a uniform no re-hire policy.").

2. The message of *Johnson Controls* — that to qualify as a BFOQ, a discriminatory job criterion must "affect an employee's ability to do the job" and "must relate to the 'essence' or to the 'central mission of the employer's business'" — is unlikely to resolve a central difficulty with the application of the BFOQ defense: who gets to decide what is the employer's "central mission"? In EEOC v. KAMEHAMEHA SCHOOLS, 990 F.2d 458 (9th Cir.), cert. denied, 510 U.S. 963, 114 S.Ct. 439, 126 L.Ed.2d 372 (1993), private schools created by a will which required that the schools' teachers be Protestant argued that adherence to the Protestant faith was a BFOQ for teachers because the central mission of the schools was to provide native Hawaiians with an education from the Protestant point of view. The Ninth Circuit reversed the trial court's ruling in favor of the defendant. Although, the appellate court stated, the schools had "embraced a broad mandate" to help native Hawaiians participate in contemporary society by providing education in a range of secular subjects, "[t]he requirement of Protestant affiliation in a teacher's past is largely irrelevant to this mission." On the other hand, in PIME v. LOYOLA UNIVERSITY of CHICAGO, 803 F.2d 351 (7th Cir. 1986), the Seventh Circuit had ruled that because of the University's long Jesuit tradition and largely Catholic student body, it was entitled to reserve four faculty positions in the Philosophy Department for Jesuits. In *Kamehameha Schools,* the Ninth Circuit suggested that *Pime* was no longer good law in light of *Johnson Controls.* Is that right? *See generally* Joanne C. Brant, *Our Shield Belongs to the Lord": Religious Employers and the Right to Discriminate,* 21 HASTINGS CONST. L.Q. 275 (1994). What if an employer desires that its employees fit a particular "role model"? Can such a rule constitute a BFOQ? In CHAMBERS v. OMAHA GIRLS CLUB, INC., 834 F.2d 697 (8th Cir. 1987), the plaintiff, a single woman, was discharged when she became pregnant because she violated the employer's "negative role model" rule which barred "single parent pregnancies" by employees. The court upheld the rule as a BFOQ.

3. How does the Court resolve the question of whether a BFOQ defense can be founded on the cost to the employer of hiring in a non-discriminatory manner? The majority suggests that it might allow such a defense if the costs to the employer "would be so prohibitive as to threaten the survival of the employer's business." The four concurring Justices apparently would not place that severe a restriction on a cost-based BFOQ. Can or should an employer be able to successfully invoke the BFOQ exception by arguing that its commercial success was the result of employing only women in customer-contact jobs? Consider the following case.

Wilson v. Southwest Airlines Co.

United States District Court, Northern District of Texas, 1981.
517 F.Supp. 292.

PATRICK E. HIGGINBOTHAM, District Judge.

This case presents the important question whether femininity, or more accurately female sex appeal, is a bona fide occupational qualification ("BFOQ") for the jobs of flight attendant and ticket agent with Southwest Airlines. Plaintiff Gregory Wilson and the class of over 100 male job applicants he represents have challenged Southwest's open refusal to hire males as a violation of Title VII. * * *

At the phase one trial on liability, Southwest conceded that its refusal to hire males was intentional. * * * Southwest contends, however, that the BFOQ exception to Title VII's ban on sex discrimination justifies its hiring only females for the public contact positions of flight attendant and ticket agent. The BFOQ window through which Southwest attempts to fly permits sex discrimination in situations where the employer can prove that sex is a "bona fide occupational qualification reasonably necessary to the normal operation of that particular business or enterprise." Southwest reasons it may discriminate against males because its attractive female flight attendants and ticket agents personify the airline's sexy image and fulfill its public promise to take passengers skyward with "love." Defendant claims maintenance of its females-only hiring policy is crucial to the airline's continued financial success.

Since it has been admitted that Southwest discriminates on the basis of sex, the only issue to decide is whether Southwest has proved that being female is a BFOQ reasonably necessary to the normal operation of its particular business. As the application of §703(e) depends, in large part, upon an analysis of the employer's "particular" business, it is necessary to set forth the factual background of this controversy as a predicate to consideration of Southwest's BFOQ defense. The facts are undisputed.

Factual Background

Defendant Southwest Airlines is a scheduled air carrier engaged in the transportation of passengers. Southwest's inaugural flight was June 18, 1971. It presently serves major cities in Texas, Oklahoma, Louisiana and New Mexico.

Southwest was incorporated in March of 1967 and filed its initial application with the Texas Aeronautics Commission ("TAC") in November of 1967 to serve the intrastate markets of Dallas, Houston and San Antonio. Southwest's proposed entry as an intrastate commuter carrier sparked a hostile reaction from the incumbent air carriers serving the Texas market. The airline's application to the TAC was bitterly contested and the original TAC decision to permit Defendant to begin serving Dallas, Houston and San Antonio was litigated for over four years through a succession of state and federal courts. The legal controversy was not resolved until December of 1970, when the U.S. Supreme Court denied the incumbent air carriers' petition for a writ of certiorari. According to Southwest's Chairman Herbert Kelleher, the airline in the interim had lost a commitment from a major insurance company to purchase $3 million of preferred stock; had lost a commitment for the sale of aircraft necessary to commence operations; had lost $2 million in subscriptions for stock by individual investors; and had spent over $530,000 in legal fees litigating the issue of its right to commence operations, all as a result of the defensive tactics of Southwest's competitors. In December of 1970, Southwest had $143 in the bank and was over $100,000 in debt, though no aircraft had ever left the ground.

Barely intact, Southwest, in early 1971, called upon a Dallas advertising agency, the Bloom Agency, to develop a winning marketing strategy. Planning to initiate service quickly, Southwest needed instant recognition and a "catchy" image to distinguish it from its competitors.

The Bloom Agency evaluated both the images of the incumbent competitor airlines as well as the characteristics of passengers to be served by a commuter airline. Bloom determined that the other carriers serving the Texas market tended to project an image of conservatism. The agency also determined that the relatively short haul commuter market which Southwest hoped to serve was comprised of predominantly male businessmen. Based on these factors, Bloom suggested that Southwest break away from the conservative image of other airlines and project to the traveling public an airline personification of feminine youth and vitality. A specific female personality description was recommended and adopted by Southwest for its corporate image:

> This lady is young and vital * * * she is charming and goes through life with great flair and exuberance * * * you notice first her exciting smile, friendly air, her wit* * * yet she is quite efficient and approaches all her tasks with care and attention. * * *

From the personality description suggested by The Bloom Agency, Southwest developed its now famous "Love" personality. Southwest projects an image of feminine spirit, fun and sex appeal. Its ads promise to provide "tender loving care" to its predominantly male, business passengers.[3] The first advertisements run by the airline featured the slogan, "AT LAST THERE IS SOMEBODY ELSE UP THERE WHO LOVES YOU." Variations on this theme have continued through newspaper, billboard, magazine and television advertisements during the past ten years.[4] Bloom's "Love" campaign was given a boost in 1974-1975 when the last of Southwest's competitors moved its operations to the new Dallas/Fort Worth Regional Airport, leaving Southwest as the only heavy carrier flying out of Dallas' convenient and fortuitously named, Love Field.

Over the years, Southwest gained national and international attention as the "love airline." Southwest Airlines' stock is traded on the New York Stock Exchange under the ticker symbol "LUV." During 1977 when Southwest opened five additional markets in Texas, the love theme was expanded to "WE'RE SPREADING LOVE ALL OVER TEXAS."

As an integral part of its youthful, feminine image, Southwest has employed only females in the high customer contact positions of ticket agent and flight attendant. From the start, Southwest's attractive personnel, dressed in high boots and hot-pants, generated public interest and "free ink." Their sex appeal has been used to attract male customers to the airline. Southwest's flight attendants, and to a lesser degree its ticket agents, have been featured in newspaper, magazine, billboard and television advertisements during the past ten years. Some attendants assist in promotional events for other businesses and civic organizations. Southwest flight attendants and ticket agents are featured in the company's in-flight magazine and have received notice in numerous other national and international publications.[5] The airline also encourages its attendants to entertain the passengers and maintain an atmosphere of informality and "fun" during flights. According to Southwest, its female flight attendants have come to "personify" Southwest's public image.

Southwest has enjoyed enormous success in recent years.[6] This is in no small part due to its marketing image. Though Southwest now enjoys a distinct advantage by operating its commuter flights out of "convenient" Love and Hobby Fields, the airline

---

[3]According to an October, 1979 on-board marketing survey commissioned before this lawsuit was filed, 69.01% of the respondents were male, while 58.41% of all respondents listed their occupation as either professional/technical, manager/administrator, or sales. Only 49.75% of the passengers surveyed, however, gave "business" as the reason for their trip.

[4]Unabashed allusions to love and sex pervade all aspects of Southwest's public image. Its T.V. commercials feature attractive attendants in fitted outfits, catering to male passengers while an alluring feminine voice promises inflight love. On board, attendants in hot-pants (skirts are now optional) serve "love bites" (toasted almonds) and "love potions" (cocktails). Even Southwest's ticketing system features a "quickie machine" to provide "instant gratification."

[5]For example, in 1974 a Southwest Airlines' flight attendant was featured on the cover of *Esquire* magazine as being "the best in America."

[6]From 1979 to 1980, the company's earnings rose from $17 million to 28 million when most other airlines suffered heavy losses. As a percentage of revenues, Southwest's return is considered to be one of the highest in the industry.

achieved a commanding position in the regional commuter market while flying "wing tip to wing tip" with national carriers who utilized the same airport, fares, schedules, and aircraft. The evidence was undisputed that Southwest's unique, feminized image played and continues to play an important role in the airline's success.[7]

Less certain, however, is Southwest's assertion that its females-only hiring policy is necessary for the continued success of its image and its business. Based on two onboard surveys, one conducted in October, 1979, before this suit was filed, and another in August, 1980, when the suit was pending,[8] Southwest contends its attractive flight attendants are the "largest single component" of its success. In the 1979 survey, however, of the attributes considered most important by passengers, the category "courteous and attentive hostesses" ranked fifth in importance behind (1) on time departures, (2) frequently scheduled departures, (3) friendly and helpful reservations and ground personnel, and (4) convenient departure times,[9] Apparently, one of the remaining eight alternative categories, "attractive hostesses," was not selected with sufficient frequency to warrant being included in the reported survey results.

* * *

In evaluating Southwest's BFOQ defense, therefore, the Court proceeds on the basis that "love," while important, is not everything in the relationship between Defendant and its passengers. Still, it is proper to infer from the airline's competitive successes that Southwest's overall "love image" has enhanced its ability to attract passengers. To the extent the airline has successfully feminized its image and made attractive females an integral part of its public face, it also follows that femininity and sex appeal are qualities related to successful job performance by Southwest's flight attendants and ticket agents. The strength of this relationship has not been proved. It

---

[7]Even Plaintiff Wilson in his original charge filed with the Equal Employment Opportunity Commission stated:

The airline [Southwest] does not hire male flight attendants and has built its business by attracting businessmen and employing attractive female flight attendants.

[8]The results of a briefer third survey conducted on March 10-11, 1981 at the request of Southwest's trial counsel cannot be considered. Conducted expressly to "determine" passenger preference for females in anticipation of trial, the survey showed bias and lacked statistical reliability for many reasons. Among other problems, the survey suffered from non-random sampling [passengers were sampled only at Love (Dallas) and Hobby (Houston) Fields, during the prime hours for business transportation (6:15-11:00 A.M.) and a disproportionately high (80%) number of males were included], and from a loaded setting [Southwest employed Kelly Temporary Services (59 of 60 interviewers were female) to conduct face-to-face interviews (the interviewers asked questions and recorded the responses) who identified themselves as agents of Southwest]. The survey also asked "loaded" and "double" questions, Question 10, for example, stated; "Southwest feels its 'Love Image' as featured by its attractive female flight attendants and ticket agents is one of the reasons people prefer to use Southwest over other airlines. If you could fly on another airline for the same price, out of the same airport, would you be as likely to use the services of Southwest, if Southwest changed this image — that is, would you be as likely to fly Southwest if they substituted males for some of the female flight attendants and ticket agents?" Given these deficiencies, and the failure to perform any test for statistical reliability, the survey conclusion that hiring males would have a negative impact on Southwest's business cannot be given weight.

[9]Of the attributes reported, "delivering checked baggage promptly" ranked sixth in importance while "lower fares" ranked seventh.

is with this factual orientation that the Court turns to examine Southwest's BFOQ defense.

* * *

[Judge Higginbotham's discussion of the legislative history and case law development of the BFOQ exception is omitted. Relying on Weeks v. Southern Bell Telephone & Telegraph Co., 408 F.2d 228 (5th Cir.1969) and Diaz v. Pan American World Airways, Inc., 442 F.2d 385 (5th Cir.1971), cert. denied, 404 U.S. 950, 92 S.Ct. 275, 30 L.Ed.2d 267 (1971), Judge Higginbotham reasoned that application of the BFOQ exception to Title VII's prohibitions requires a two-part test: (1) does the particular job under consideration require that the worker be of one sex only; and, if so, (2) is that requirement reasonably necessary to the "essence" of the employer's business.]

Application of the Bona Fide Occupational Qualification to Southwest Airlines

Applying the first level test for a BFOQ, with its legal gloss, to Southwest's particular operations results in the conclusion that being female is not a qualification required to perform successfully the jobs of flight attendant and ticket agent with Southwest. Like any other airline, Southwest's primary function is to transport passengers safely and quickly from one point to another.[25] To do this, Southwest employs ticket agents whose primary job duties are to ticket passengers and check baggage, and flight attendants, whose primary duties are to assist passengers during boarding and deboarding, to instruct passengers in the location and use of aircraft safety equipment, and to serve passengers cocktails and snacks during the airline's short commuter flights. Mechanical, non-sex-linked duties dominate both these occupations. Indeed, on Southwest's short-haul commuter flights there is time for little else. That Southwest's female personnel may perform their mechanical duties "with love" does not change the result. "Love" is the manner of job performance, not the job performed.

While possession of female allure and sex appeal have been made qualifications for Southwest's contact personnel by virtue of the "love" campaign, the functions served by employee sexuality in Southwest's operations are not dominant ones. According to Southwest, female sex appeal serves two purposes: (1) attracting and entertaining male passengers and (2) fulfilling customer expectations for female service engendered by Southwest's advertising which features female personnel. As in *Diaz*, these non-mechanical, sex-linked job functions are only "tangential" to the essence of the occupations and business involved. Southwest is not a business where vicarious sex entertainment is the primary service provided. Accordingly, the ability of the airline to perform its primary business function, the transportation of passengers, would not be jeopardized by hiring males.

---

[25]Southwest's argument that its primary function is "to make a profit," not to transport passengers, must be rejected. Without doubt the goal of every business is to make a profit. For purposes of BFOQ analysis, however, the business "essence" inquiry focuses on the particular service provided and the job tasks and functions involved, not the business goal. If an employer could justify employment discrimination merely on the grounds that it is necessary to make a profit, Title VII would be nullified in short order.

Southwest does not face the situation anticipated in *Diaz*[26] and encountered in [Fernandez v. Wynn Oil Co., 20 FEP Cases 1162 (C.D.Cal.1979)] where an established customer preference for one sex is so strong that the business would be undermined if employees of the opposite sex were hired. Southwest's claim that its customers prefer females rests primarily upon inferences drawn from the airline's success after adopting its female personality. But according to Southwest's own surveys, that success is attributable to many factors. There is no competent proof that Southwest's popularity derives directly from its females-only policy to the exclusion of other factors like dissatisfaction with rival airlines and Southwest's use of convenient Love and Hobby Fields. Nor is there competent proof that the customer preference for females is so strong that Defendant's male passengers would cease doing business with Southwest as was the case in *Fernandez*. In short, Southwest has failed in its proof to satisfy *Diaz's* business necessity requirement, without which customer preference may not give rise to a BFOQ for sex.

Southwest contends, nevertheless, that its females-only policy is reasonably necessary to the continued success of its "love" marketing campaign. Airline management testified that Southwest's customers will be disappointed if they find male employees after seeing only female personnel advertised. As a matter of law, this argument fails to support a BFOQ for sex. The court in Diaz emphasized that its test was one of business *necessity*, not business *convenience*. In Weeks v. Southern Bell Telephone and Telegraph Co., the Fifth Circuit expressly disapproved of the broad construction of the BFOQ exception in Bowe v. Colgate Palmolive Co., 272 F.Supp. 332, 362 (S.D.Ind.1967), aff'd in part and rev'd in part 416 F.2d 711 (7th Cir.1969) which would have permitted sex discrimination where sex was "rationally related to an end which [the employer] has a right to achieve — production, profit, or business reputation."

It is also relevant that Southwest's female image was adopted at its discretion, to promote a business unrelated to sex. Contrary to the unyielding South American preference for males encountered by the Defendant company in *Fernandez*, Southwest exploited, indeed nurtured, the very customer preference for females it now cites to justify discriminating against males. Moreover, the fact that a vibrant marketing campaign was necessary to distinguish Southwest in its early years does not lead to the conclusion that sex discrimination was then, or is now, a business *necessity*. Southwest's claim that its female image will be tarnished by hiring males is, in any case, speculative at best.

The few cases on point support the conclusion that sex does not become a BFOQ merely because an employer chooses to exploit female sexuality as a marketing tool, or to better insure profitability. In Guardian Capital Corp. v. New York State Division of Human Rights, 46 App.Div.2d 832, 360 N.Y.S.2d 937 (1974), *app. dismissed* 48 A.D.2d 753, 368 N.Y.S.2d 594 (1975) for example, the court prohibited an employer from firing male waiters to hire sexually attractive waitresses in an attempt to change

---

[26]To reiterate, the Fifth Circuit in *Diaz*, *supra*, 442 F.2d at 389, announced that " * * * customer preference may be taken into account only when it is based on the company's inability to perform the primary function or service it offers."

the appeal of the business and boost sales. Similarly, in University Parking, Inc. v. Hotel and Restaurant Employees & Bartenders' Int'l Un., 71-2 Lab.Arb.Awards 5360 (1971) (Peck, Arb.), the arbitrator denied an employer's right to replace three waitresses with waiters in order to "upgrade" his business and respond to customer desires for "classier" French service. Merely because Southwest's female image was established in "good faith"[28] and has become its trademark does not distinguish Defendant's conduct from the discriminatory business decisions disapproved of in these cases.

Neither, in the final analysis, does Southwest's "battle-for-inches" with its competitors rise to the level of business *necessity*. *Diaz's* necessity test focuses on the company's ability "to perform the primary function or service it offers," not its ability to compete. As one court has noted in the context of racial discrimination, "[t]he expense involved in changing from a discriminatory system * * * [fails to constitute] a business necessity that would justify the continuation of * * * discrimination." Bush v. Lone Star Steel Co., 373 F.Supp. 526, 533 (E.D.Tex.1974). Similarly, a potential loss of profits or possible loss of competitive advantage following a shift to non-discriminatory hiring does not establish business necessity under *Diaz*. To hold otherwise would permit employers within the same industry to establish different hiring standards based on the financial condition of their respective businesses. A rule prohibiting only financially successful enterprises from discriminating under Title VII, while allowing their less successful competitors to ignore the law, has no merit.

Southwest, however, has failed to establish by competent proof that revenue loss would result directly from hiring males. Analogous to the holding in Guardian Capital Corp. v. New York State Division of Human Rights, an employer's mere "beforehand belief" that sex discrimination is a financial imperative, alone, does not establish a BFOQ for sex.

Conclusion

In rejecting Southwest's BFOQ defense, this court follows Justice Marshall's admonition that the BFOQ exception should not be permitted to "swallow the rule." See Phillips v. Martin Marietta Corp., 400 U.S. 542, 545, 91 S.Ct. 496, 498, 27 L.Ed.2d 613 (1971) (Marshall, J. concurring). Southwest's position knows no principled limit. Recognition of a sex BFOQ for Southwest's public contact personnel based on the airline's "love" campaign opens the door for other employers freely to discriminate by tacking on sex or sex appeal as a qualification for any public contact position where customers preferred employees of a particular sex.[29] In order not to undermine Congress' purpose to prevent employers from "refusing to hire an individual based on stereotyped characterizations of the sexes," see Phillips v. Martin Marietta Corp., a BFOQ for sex must be denied where sex is merely useful for

---

[28]Under Title VII, it is immaterial that Southwest's feminized marketing strategy was conceived and implemented in "good faith," not in a desire to discriminate against males. Even in cases of unintentional discrimination, the absence of bad motive or intent does not redeem employment practices with forbidden discriminatory consequences. See Griggs v. Duke Power Co., 401 U.S. 424, 432, 91 S.Ct. 849, 854, 28 L.Ed.2d 158 (1971).

[29]See Note: "Developments in the Law — Employment Discrimination and Title VII of the Civil Rights Act of 1964," 84 Harv.L.Rev. 1109, 1185 (1971).

attracting customers of the opposite sex, but where hiring both sexes will not alter or undermine the essential function of the employer's business. Rejecting a wider BFOQ for sex does not eliminate the commercial exploitation of sex appeal. It only requires, consistent with the purposes of Title VII, that employers exploit the attractiveness and allure of a sexually integrated workforce. Neither Southwest, nor the traveling public, will suffer from such a rule. More to the point, it is my judgment that this is what Congress intended.

One final observation is called for. This case has serious underpinnings, but it also has disquieting strains. These strains, and they were only that, warn that in our quest for non-racist, non-sexist goals, the demand for equal rights can be pushed to silly extremes. The rule of law in this country is so firmly embedded in our ethical regimen that little can stand up to its force — except literalistic insistence upon one's rights. And such inability to absorb the minor indignities suffered daily by us all without running to court may stop it dead in its tracks. We do not have such a case here — only warning signs rumbling from the facts.

WILSON V. SOUTHWEST AIRLINES: A REPRISE

Fifteen years after the decision in *Southwest Airlines*, the BFOQ argument made by the airline was resurrected by the Hooters restaurant chain in response to claims of sex discrimination in the employment of food servers. Hooters' risqué ambiance has been based on its scantily clad waitresses known as "Hooters Girls."* In 1991, an EEOC Commissioner charged that the restaurant chain's policy of refusing to hire men to serve tables violated Title VII. Efforts to conciliate the claim failed, at least in part because of Hooters' refusal of the agency's demand that it hire men to work alongside Hooters Girls. A company spokesman explained, "The [EEOC] is asking us to destroy the essence of our concept. . . . A lot of places serve good burgers. The Hooters Girls, with their charm and All-American sex appeal, are what our customers come for." N.Y. TIMES, Nov. 16, 1995, at A20, col.5. While the EEOC's investigation was pending, an attorney for Hooters' argued that her client's BFOQ defense was sound because food was "secondary" to the business' main commodity, "the sexiness of the Hooters' Girls." The analogy to *Southwest Airlines* was rejected.

> And don't tell me about flight attendants unless you are prepared to argue that sexiness is just as important as a safe and timely arrival to your next business trip. Hooters can argue that its patrons care as much—or more—about being in the presence of the Hooters girls as they do about the burgers and beer.

Patricia A. Casey, *Does Refusing to Hire Men as Food Servers Violate the Civil Rights Act: No: A Business Has a Right to Choose its Own Character*, 82 ABA J. 41 (1996).

Apparently in response to Hooters' aggressive public relations campaign (featuring pictures of a burly, mustachioed man wearing a blond wig and Hooters' uniform, holding a plate of chicken wings and exclaiming: "Come on, Washington.

---

*The scheduling of a business meeting at a Hooters restaurant was described by one court as "grossly unprofessional" but not sufficient to establish that the company was generally biased against female employees. Ray v. Tandem Computers, Inc., 63 F.3d 429, 434 (5th Cir. 1995).

Get a grip.") and complaints from congressmen who questioned the agency's use of its resources in the matter, the EEOC dropped its investigation. Hooters subsequently settled a class action filed by males who were denied employment. The settlement reportedly allows Hooters to continue hiring an exclusively female staff as food servers but requires the company to fill other positions such as bartenders and hosts without regard to gender. The settlement has hardly resolved the dispute over the legitimacy of basing employment decisions on sexual stereotypes and/or appearance. In answering that question, consider whether customer or co-worker preferences for Caucasians or males would or should be regarded as a "legitimate" ground for an employer's preference for individuals that fit within either of these categories.

Should a restaurant, but not an airline, be allowed to make vicarious sex the "essence of its business" and thus qualify for a BFOQ? If the answer is "yes," does that not open the door to the same kind of marketing strategy by other kinds of businesses such as car washes and clothing stores? If the answer is "no," where exactly is the BFOQ line to be drawn between Hooters and a striptease parlor that serves food and drink? Should Title VII be construed as a legislative bar to businesses providing sexual titillation? Is the Hooters case an illustration of the kind of "literalistic insistence upon rights" that Judge Higginbotham warned in *Southwest Airlines* could undermine our rule of law?

NOTES AND PROBLEMS FOR DISCUSSION

1. As in *Southwest Airlines*, efforts to justify discriminatory hiring practices on the basis of customer preferences have met with little success. In *Fernandez*, the case distinguished by Judge Higginbotham in *Southwest Airlines*, the district court ruled that being a male was a BFOQ for the job of international marketing director for a company that did extensive foreign business because the position involved attracting and transacting business with Latin American and Southeast Asian customers who were not comfortable doing business with women. The court found that hiring a female "would have totally subverted any business [the defendant] hoped to accomplish in those areas of the world." Two months after the release of the ruling in *Southwest Airlines,* the Ninth Circuit reversed the trial court's ruling in *Fernandez*. The appellate court held that foreign prejudice against women in business cannot justify non-enforcement of Title VII in this country. Fernandez v. Wynn Oil Co., 653 F.2d 1273 (9th Cir. 1981). *See also* Abrams v. Baylor College of Medicine, 581 F.Supp. 1570 (S.D.Tex. 1984), aff'd in part, 805 F.2d 528 (5th Cir. 1986) ("patronizing, paternalistic 'concerns'" of a medical school for the safety of Jewish staff members, did not justify, either under the BFOQ or business necessity rationales, its policy of excluding such employees from a program in Saudi Arabia). The EEOC has ruled that an employer who refuses to hire women for work in a foreign country because that country prohibits commingling of the sexes will have its proffered reason for rejecting an applicant viewed as pretextual unless it has "current, authoritative, and factual basis for its belief." For more on this question, see Cass Sunstein, *Three Civil Rights Fallacies*, 79 CAL. L. REV. 751, 760 (1991) (noting that economically "rational" discrimination tends to reinforce ordinary prejudice).

A minor, but certainly note-worthy, exception to the general rule that a BFOQ cannot be based in the discriminatory preference of customers was established in

KERN v. DYNALECTRON CORP., 577 F. Supp. 1196 (N.D.Tex. 1983), aff'd, 746 F.2d 810 (5th Cir. 1984). There, the court ruled that an employer's requirement that helicopter pilots hired to fly into Mecca be of the Moslem faith (adopted to comply with Saudi Arabian law which prohibits entry of non-Moslems into Mecca) is a BFOQ, exempt from the religious discrimination provisions of Title VII. The district courts' opinion also deserves at least Honorable Mention in the category of judicial understatement.

> The Defendants' burden of producing a legitimate reason for the existing discrimination is properly sustained through the application of the B.F.O.Q. exception to Kern's case. * * * [T]his Court holds that Dynalectron has proven a factual basis for believing that *all* non-Moslems would be unable to perform this job safely. Specifically, non-Moslems flying into Mecca are, if caught, beheaded. * * * [T]he essence of Dynalectron's business is to provide helicopter pilots. * * * Thus, the essence of Dynalectron's business would be undermined by the beheading of all the non-Moslem pilots based in Jeddah.

577 F.Supp. at 1200.

2. As noted in *Johnson Controls* and *Southwest Airlines,* the BFOQ exception has been successfully utilized in only three contexts:

(a) Authenticity

The EEOC Guidelines provide that "[w]here it is necessary for the purpose of authenticity or genuineness, the Commission will consider sex to be a bona fide occupational qualification, e.g. an actor or actress." 29 C.F.R. §1604.2. One court has suggested that the "authenticity" rule would justify a BFOQ for Chinese nationality where necessary to maintain the authentic atmosphere of an ethnic Chinese restaurant. Utility Workers v. Southern California Edison Co., 320 F.Supp. 1262 (C.D.Cal. 1970).

(b) Privacy

Employers have met with more success in basing a BFOQ on customer desires where those desires are related to personal privacy and modesty. In FESEL v. MASONIC HOME of DELAWARE, INC., 447 F.Supp. 1346 (D.Del. 1978), aff'd, 91 F.2d 1334 (3d Cir. 1979), numerous residents of a nursing home stated that they would leave if it abandoned its policy of hiring only female nurses. The court held that the home had sustained its burden of proving that the essence of its business would be undermined by employing members of the male sex:

> While these attitudes may be characterized as "customer preference," this is, nevertheless, not the kind of case governed by the regulatory provision that customer preference alone cannot justify a job qualification based upon sex. Here personal privacy interests are implicated which are protected by law and which have to be recognized by the employer in running its business.

447 F.Supp. at 1352. *See also* Healey v. Southwood Psychiatric Hospital, 78 F.3d 128, 133 (3d Cir. 1996) (policy of requiring at least one staff member of each sex to be available to patients at all times is necessary to provide therapeutic care that was the "essence" of the hospital's business); Jones v. Hinds General Hospital, 666 F.Supp. 933 (S.D.Miss. 1987) (to preserve privacy, defendant allowed to restrict catheterization of male patients to male nurses).

(c) Safety

In DOTHARD v. RAWLINSON, 433 U.S. 321, 97 S.Ct. 2720, 53 L.Ed.2d 786 (1977), while striking down Alabama's height and weight requirements for prison personnel, the Supreme Court upheld a regulation explicitly barring the employment of females in "contact positions" in male penitentiaries as a BFOQ. Citing the "rampant violence" and "jungle atmosphere" in the state's prisons, the Court stated that:

> The essence of a correctional counselor's job is to maintain prison security. A woman's relative ability to maintain order in a male maximum-security unclassified penitentiary of the type Alabama now runs could be directly reduced by her womanhood. * * *

> * * * The likelihood that inmates would assault a woman because she was a woman would pose a real threat not only to the victim of the assault but also to the basic control of the penitentiary and protection of its inmates and the other security personnel. The employee's very womanhood would then directly undermine her capacity to provide the security that is the essence of a correctional counselor's responsibility.

433 U.S. at 335, 336, 97 S.Ct. at 2729, 2730. Since *Dothard*, efforts to designate positions in prisons as male or female-only on "personal privacy" or safety grounds have met with mixed results. *Compare* Robino v. Iranon, 145 F.3d 1109, 1111 (9th Cir. 1998) (affirming summary judgment for employer on basis that designation of six guard positions out of 41 on a single shift as female-only positions was a BFOQ justified by privacy concerns), *with, e.g.*, Hardin v. Stynchcomb, 691 F.2d 1364, 1374 (11th Cir. 1982) (inmate privacy no justification for refusal to hire female jail guards).

In TORRES v. WISCONSIN DEPT. of HEALTH and SOCIAL SERVICES, 859 F.2d 1523 (7th Cir. 1988) (*en banc*), cert. denied, 489 U.S. 1017, 109 S.Ct. 1133, 103 L.Ed.2d 194 (1989), prison officials justified the restriction of certain guard positions in a women's prison to females on the rehabilitative needs of inmates, many of whom had were victims of abuse by males. The district court determined that defendants had offered no more than a theory of rehabilitation and that, without empirical evidence, such a theory could not support a BFOQ. A divided court of appeals reversed. Emphasizing the necessity of innovation in correctional policy, the court held that defendants had been required to meet an "unrealistic, and therefore unfair, burden" when they were required to produce objective evidence supporting the validity of the rehabilitative theory.

3. Concerns for authenticity, privacy and safety may not exhaust the reasons that an employer may prefer employees of a particular gender, ethnic background, or religion. If an airline cannot justify hiring only female flight attendants as necessary to its image, can it at least demand that its female attendants be conventionally attractive — i.e., slender? In FRANK v. UNITED AIRLINES, 216 F.3d 845 (9th Cir. 2000), cert. denied, 532 U.S. 914, 121 S.Ct. 1247, 149 L.Ed.2d 154 (2001), the airline required female flight attendants to adhere to weight maximums corresponding to medium body frames while the weight maximums for male flight attendants were based on large body frames. The effect of the policy was that female flight attendants were required to weigh 14 to 25 pounds less than male colleagues of the same height and age. Citing the "unequal burden" imposed by the weight restrictions, the court concluded that the case was "analytically indistinguishable" from *Johnson Controls* and held that United had failed to show the facially discriminatory weight requirements were a BFOQ.

* * * United made no showing that having disproportionately thinner female than male flight attendants bears a relation to flight attendants' ability to greet passengers, push carts, move luggage, and, perhaps most importantly, provide physical assistance in emergencies. * * * Far from being reasonably necessary to the "normal operation" of United's business, the evidence suggests that, if anything, United's discriminatory weight requirements may have inhibited the job performance of female flight attendants.

216 F.3d at 855. What is the difference between sex-specific weight requirements and sex-differentiated grooming requirements, for example, hair length restrictions, that have generally been upheld as outside the purview of Title VII? *See* Chapter 3(D) *infra.*

4.   Section 703(e) does not mention race as a possible BFOQ, and it is generally thought that the omission was not a legislative oversight. *See, e.g.,* Swint v. Pullman-Standard, 624 F.2d 525, 535 (5th Cir. 1980), overruled on other grounds, 456 U.S. 273, 102 S.Ct. 1781, 72 L.Ed.2d 66 (1982) (omission of race as BFOQ by Congress was deliberate and intentional). It is, for example, permissible under Title VII to take race into account in order to remedy past discrimination. *See, e.g.,* United Steelworkers of America v. Weber, 443 U.S. 193, 99 S.Ct. 2521, 61 L.Ed.2d 480 (1979). On the other hand, job assignments based on the racial stereotype that co-employees work better or that customers respond better to employees of their race are *per se* violations of Title VII. *See* Ferrill v. The Parker Group, Inc., 168 F.3d 468, 477 (11th Cir. 1999) (telemarketing firm discriminated on the basis of race when it placed black and white workers in separate rooms under separate supervisors for purpose of making race-matched telephone calls according to "black" and "white" scripts); Knight v. Nassau County Bd. of Civil Service, 649 F.2d 157, 162 (2d Cir.), cert. denied, 454 U.S. 818, 102 S.Ct. 97, 70 L.Ed.2d 87 (1981) (assignment of black employee because of his race to minority recruitment was violation of Title VII despite employer's laudable goal of attracting more minority employees).

But isn't taking race into account simply common sense, if not absolutely necessary, in some contexts? If a motion picture about Thurgood Marshall is being cast, must the director consider white actors for the part? Or if the FBI is infiltrating the Aryan Nation, can it not make undercover assignments on the basis of race? Senator Case, a sponsor of Title VII, suggested that a director casting for the role of a black person could specify that he wished to hire an actor "with the physical appearance of a Negro." 110 Cong. Rec. 7213, 7217 (1964). *See also* Miller v. Texas State Bd. of Barber Examiners, *supra*, 615 F.2d 650, 654 (5th Cir. 1980) (suggesting in *dicta* that a "business necessity defense may be appropriate in the selection of actors to play certain roles); Baker v. City of St. Petersburg, 400 F.2d 294, 301 n.10 (5th Cir. 1968) (suggesting that race could be considered for "the undercover infiltration of an all-Negro criminal organization or plain-clothes work in an area where a white man could not pass without notice.").

4. HARASSMENT

Section 703(a) prohibits employers from discriminating on the basis of the five proscribed classifications with respect to "terms, conditions, or privileges of employment." From its beginning in cases alleging verbal and other forms of harassment directed against individuals because of their race or ethnicity, the overwhelming focus of litigation challenging alleged workplace harassment has shifted to the arena of sex-based conduct. In recent years, the Supreme Court has devoted a significant amount of its attention to the separate, but frequently interlaced questions of (1) what constitutes actionable harassment, and (2) under what circumstances an employer should be held responsible for acts of harassment undertaken by either its supervisory or nonsupervisory personnel. In the following case, the Court grappled with the question of whether sex-based harassment that does not result in any economic injury to the victim constitutes actionable discrimination under Title VII and, if so, how such claims are proven and defended.

Meritor Savings Bank, FSB v. Vinson

Supreme Court of the United States, 1986.
477 U.S. 57, 106 S.Ct. 2399, 91 L.Ed.2d 49.

MR. JUSTICE REHNQUIST delivered the opinion of the Court.

This case presents important questions concerning claims of workplace "sexual harassment" brought under Title VII.

I

* * *

Respondent brought this action against Taylor and the bank, claiming that during her four years at the bank she had "constantly been subjected to sexual harassment" by Taylor [her supervisor, a bank Vice-President and branch manager] in violation of Title VII. She sought injunctive relief, compensatory and punitive damages against Taylor and the bank, and attorney's fees.

At the * * * bench trial, the parties presented conflicting testimony about Taylor's behavior during respondent's employment. Respondent testified that * * * he invited her out to dinner and, during the course of the meal, suggested that they go to a motel to have sexual relations. At first she refused, but out of what she described as fear of losing her job she eventually agreed. According to respondent, Taylor thereafter made repeated demands upon her for sexual favors, usually at the branch, both during and after business hours; she estimated that over the next several years she had intercourse with him some 40 or 50 times. In addition, respondent testified that Taylor fondled her in front of other employees, followed her into the women's restroom when she went there alone, exposed himself to her, and even forcibly raped her on several occasions. These activities ceased after 1977, respondent stated, when she started going with a steady boyfriend.

* * * [R]espondent testified that because she was afraid of Taylor she never reported his harassment to any of his supervisors and never attempted to use the bank's complaint procedure.

Taylor denied respondent's allegations of sexual activity, testifying that he never fondled her, never made suggestive remarks to her, never engaged in sexual intercourse with her and never asked her to do so. He contended instead that respondent made her accusations in response to a business-related dispute. The bank also denied respondent's allegations and asserted that any sexual harassment by Taylor was unknown to the bank and engaged in without its consent or approval.

The District Court denied relief * * *. It found * * * that

"If [respondent] and Taylor did engage in an intimate or sexual relationship during the time of [respondent's] employment with [the bank], that relationship was a voluntary one having nothing to do with her continued employment at [the bank] or her advancement or promotions at that institution."

The court ultimately found that respondent "was not the victim of sexual harassment and was not the victim of sexual discrimination" while employed at the bank.

Although it concluded that respondent had not proved a violation of Title VII, the District Court nevertheless went on to address the bank's liability. After noting the bank's express policy against discrimination, and finding that neither respondent nor any other employee had ever lodged a complaint about sexual harassment by Taylor, the court ultimately concluded that "the bank was without notice and cannot be held liable for the alleged actions of Taylor."

The Court of Appeals for the District of Columbia Circuit reversed. * * * [T]]he court stated that a violation of Title VII may be predicated on either of two types of sexual harassment: harassment that involves the conditioning of concrete employment benefits on sexual favors, and harassment that, while not affecting economic benefits, creates a hostile or offensive working environment. * * * Believing that "Vinson's grievance was clearly of the [hostile environment] type," and that the District Court had not considered whether a violation of this type had occurred, the court concluded that a remand was necessary.

The court further concluded that the District Court's finding that any sexual relationship between respondent and Taylor "was a voluntary one" did not obviate the need for a remand. * * * [T]he Court of Appeals held that if the evidence otherwise showed that "Taylor made Vinson's toleration of sexual harassment a condition of her employment," her voluntariness "had no materiality whatsoever." The court then surmised that the District Court's finding of voluntariness might have been based on "the voluminous testimony regarding respondent's dress and personal fantasies," testimony that the Court of Appeals believed "had no place in this litigation."

As to the bank's liability, the Court of Appeals held that an employer is absolutely liable for sexual harassment practiced by supervisory personnel, whether or not the employer knew or should have known about the misconduct. The court relied chiefly on Title VII's definition of "employer" to include "any agent of such a person," as well as on the EEOC guidelines. The court held that a supervisor is an "agent" of his employer for Title VII purposes, even if he lacks authority to hire, fire, or promote, since "the mere existence — or even the appearance — of a significant degree of influence in vital job decisions gives any supervisor the opportunity to impose on employees."

In accordance with the foregoing, the Court of Appeals reversed the judgment of the District Court and remanded the case for further proceedings. A subsequent suggestion for rehearing *en banc* was denied, with three judges dissenting. We granted certiorari, and now affirm but for different reasons.

II

* * * The prohibition against discrimination based on sex was added to Title VII at the last minute on the floor of the House of Representatives. The principal argument in opposition to the amendment was that "sex discrimination" was sufficiently different from other types of discrimination that it ought to receive separate legislative treatment. This argument was defeated, the bill quickly passed as amended, and we are left with little legislative history to guide us in interpreting the Act's prohibition against discrimination based on "sex."

Respondent argues, and the Court of Appeals held, that unwelcome sexual advances that create an offensive or hostile working environment violate Title VII. Without question, when a supervisor sexually harasses a subordinate because of the subordinate's sex, that supervisor "discriminate[s]" on the basis of sex. Petitioner apparently does not challenge this proposition. It contends instead that in prohibiting discrimination with respect to "compensation, terms, conditions, or privileges" of employment, Congress was concerned with what petitioner describes as "tangible loss" of "an economic character," not "purely psychological aspects of the workplace environment." In support of this claim petitioner observes that in both the legislative history of Title VII and this Court's Title VII decisions, the focus has been on tangible, economic barriers erected by discrimination.

We reject petitioner's view. First, the language of Title VII is not limited to "economic" or "tangible" discrimination. The phrase "terms, conditions, or privileges of employment" evinces a congressional intent to strike at the entire spectrum of disparate treatment of men and women in employment. Petitioner has pointed to nothing in the Act to suggest that Congress contemplated the limitation urged here.

Second, in 1980 the EEOC issued guidelines specifying that "sexual harassment," as there defined, is a form of sex discrimination prohibited by Title VII. As an administrative interpretation of the Act by the enforcing agency, these guidelines, while not controlling upon the courts by reason of their authority, do constitute a body of experience and informed judgment to which courts and litigants may properly resort for guidance. The EEOC guidelines fully support the view that harassment leading to noneconomic injury can violate Title VII.

In defining "sexual harassment," the guidelines first describe the kinds of workplace conduct that may be actionable under Title VII. These include "[u]nwelcome sexual advances, requests for sexual favors, and other verbal or physical conduct of a sexual nature." Relevant to the charges at issue in this case, the guidelines provide that such sexual misconduct constitutes prohibited "sexual harassment," whether or not it is directly linked to the grant or denial of an economic *quid pro quo*, where "such conduct has the purpose or effect of unreasonably interfering with an individual's work performance or creating an intimidating, hostile, or offensive working environment."

In concluding that so-called "hostile environment" (i.e., non *quid pro quo*) harassment violates Title VII, the EEOC drew upon a substantial body of judicial decisions and EEOC precedent holding that Title VII affords employees the right to work in an environment free from discriminatory intimidation, ridicule, and insult. * * * Courts applied this principle to harassment based on race, religion, and national origin. Nothing in Title VII suggests that a hostile environment based on discriminatory sexual harassment should not be likewise prohibited. The guidelines thus appropriately drew from, and were fully consistent with, the existing caselaw.

Since the guidelines were issued, courts have uniformly held, and we agree, that a plaintiff may establish a violation of Title VII by proving that discrimination based on sex has created a hostile or abusive work environment. * * *

Of course, * * * not all workplace conduct that may be described as "harassment" affects a "term, condition, or privilege" of employment within the meaning of Title VII. For sexual harassment to be actionable, it must be sufficiently severe or pervasive to alter the conditions of the victim's employment and create an abusive working environment. Respondent's allegations in this case — which include not only pervasive harassment but also criminal conduct of the most serious nature — are plainly sufficient to state a claim for "hostile environment" sexual harassment.

The question remains, however, whether the District Court's ultimate finding that respondent "was not the victim of sexual harassment," effectively disposed of respondent's claim. The Court of Appeals recognized, we think correctly, that this ultimate finding was likely based on one or both of two erroneous views of the law. First, the District Court apparently believed that a claim for sexual harassment will not lie absent an economic effect on the complainant's employment. Since it appears that the District Court made its findings without ever considering the "hostile environment" theory of sexual harassment, the Court of Appeals' decision to remand was correct.

Second, the District Court's conclusion that no actionable harassment occurred might have rested on its earlier "finding" that "[i]f [respondent] and Taylor did engage in an intimate or sexual relationship * * *, that relationship was a voluntary one." But the fact that sex-related conduct was "voluntary," in the sense that the complainant was not forced to participate against her will, is not a defense to a sexual harassment suit brought under Title VII. The gravamen of any sexual harassment claim is that the alleged sexual advances were unwelcome. While the question whether particular conduct was indeed unwelcome presents difficult problems of proof and turns largely on credibility determinations committed to the trier of fact, the District Court in this case erroneously focused on the "voluntariness" of respondent's participation in the claimed sexual episodes. The correct inquiry is whether respondent by her conduct indicated that the alleged sexual advances were unwelcome, not whether her actual participation in sexual intercourse was voluntary.

Petitioner contends that even if this case must be remanded to the District Court, the Court of Appeals erred in one of the terms of its remand. Specifically, the Court of Appeals stated that testimony about respondent's "dress and personal fantasies," which the District Court apparently admitted into evidence, had no place in this litigation. The apparent ground for this conclusion was that respondent's voluntariness *vel non* in submitting to Taylor's advances was immaterial to her sexual harassment claim. While "voluntariness" in the sense of consent is not a defense to such a claim, it does not follow that a complainant's sexually provocative speech or dress is irrelevant as a matter of law in determining whether he or she found particular sexual advances unwelcome. To the contrary, such evidence is obviously relevant. The EEOC guidelines emphasize that the trier of fact must determine the existence of sexual harassment in light of "the record as a whole" and "the totality of circumstances, such as the nature of the sexual advances and the context in which the alleged incidents occurred." Respondent's claim that any marginal relevance of the evidence in question was outweighed by the potential for unfair prejudice is the sort of argument properly addressed to the District Court. In this case the District Court concluded that the evidence should be admitted, and the Court of Appeals' contrary conclusion was based upon the erroneous, categorical view that testimony about provocative dress and publicly expressed sexual fantasies "had no place in this litigation." While the District Court must carefully weigh the applicable considerations in deciding whether to admit evidence of this kind, there is no per se rule against its admissibility.

III

Although the District Court concluded that respondent had not proved a violation of Title VII, it nevertheless went on to consider the question of the bank's liability. Finding that "the bank was without notice" of Taylor's alleged conduct, and that notice to Taylor was not the equivalent of notice to the bank, the court concluded that the bank therefore could not be held liable for Taylor's alleged actions. The Court of Appeals took the opposite view, holding that an employer is strictly liable for a hostile environment created by a supervisor's sexual advances, even though the employer neither knew nor reasonably could have known of the alleged misconduct. The court held that a supervisor, whether or not he possesses the authority to hire, fire, or promote, is necessarily an "agent" of his employer for all Title VII purposes, since "even the appearance" of such authority may enable him to impose himself on his subordinates.

* * *

[The] debate over the appropriate standard for employer liability has a rather abstract quality about it given the state of the record in this case. We do not know at this stage whether Taylor made any sexual advances toward respondent at all, let alone whether those advances were unwelcome, whether they were sufficiently pervasive to constitute a condition of employment, or whether they were so pervasive and so long continuing that the employer must have become conscious of them.

We therefore decline the parties' invitation to issue a definitive rule on employer liability, but we do agree with the EEOC that Congress wanted courts to look to agency principles for guidance in this area. While such common-law principles may not be transferable in all their particulars to Title VII, Congress' decision to define "employer" to include any "agent" of an employer, surely evinces an intent to place some limits on the acts of employees for which employers under Title VII are to be held responsible. For this reason, we hold that the Court of Appeals erred in concluding that employers are always automatically liable for sexual harassment by their supervisors. For the same reason, absence of notice to an employer does not necessarily insulate that employer from liability.

Finally, we reject petitioner's view that the mere existence of a grievance procedure and a policy against discrimination, coupled with respondent's failure to invoke that procedure, must insulate petitioner from liability. While those facts are plainly relevant, the situation before us demonstrates why they are not necessarily dispositive. Petitioner's general nondiscrimination policy did not address sexual harassment in particular, and thus did not alert employees to their employer's interest in correcting that form of discrimination. Moreover, the bank's grievance procedure apparently required an employee to complain first to her supervisor, in this case

Taylor. Since Taylor was the alleged perpetrator, it is not altogether surprising that respondent failed to invoke the procedure and report her grievance to him. Petitioner's contention that respondent's failure should insulate it from liability might be substantially stronger if its procedures were better calculated to encourage victims of harassment to come forward.

IV

In sum, we hold that a claim of "hostile environment" sex discrimination is actionable under Title VII, that the District Court's findings were insufficient to dispose of respondent's hostile environment claim, and that the District Court did not err in admitting testimony about respondent's sexually provocative speech and dress. As to employer liability, we conclude that the Court of Appeals was wrong to entirely disregard agency principles and impose absolute liability on employers for the acts of their supervisors, regardless of the circumstances of a particular case.

Accordingly, the judgment of the Court of Appeals reversing the judgment of the District Court is affirmed, and the case is remanded for further proceedings consistent with this opinion.

It is so ordered.

[The concurring opinion of Justice Stevens has been omitted.]

JUSTICE MARSHALL, with whom JUSTICE BRENNAN, JUSTICE BLACKMUN, and JUSTICE STEVENS join, concurring in the judgment.

I fully agree with the Court's conclusion that workplace sexual harassment is illegal, and violates Title VII. Part III of the Court's opinion, however, leaves open the circumstances in which an employer is responsible under Title VII for such conduct. Because I believe that question to be properly before us, I write separately.

* * *

An employer can act only through individual supervisors and employees; discrimination is rarely carried out pursuant to a formal vote of a corporation's board of directors. Although an employer may sometimes adopt company-wide discriminatory policies violative of Title VII, acts that may constitute Title VII violations are generally effected through the actions of individuals, and often an individual may take such a step even in defiance of company policy. Nonetheless, Title VII remedies, such as reinstatement and backpay, generally run against the employer as an entity. The question thus arises as to the circumstances under which an employer will be held liable under Title VII for the acts of its employees.

The answer supplied by general Title VII law, like that supplied by federal labor law, is that the act of a supervisory employee or agent is imputed to the employer. Thus, for example, when a supervisor discriminatorily fires or refuses to promote a black employee, that act is, without more, considered the act of the employer. The courts do not stop to consider whether the employer otherwise had "notice" of the action, or even whether the supervisor had actual authority to act as he did. Following that approach, every Court of Appeals that has considered the issue has held that sexual harassment by supervisory personnel is automatically imputed to the employer when the harassment results in tangible job detriment to the subordinate employee.

The brief filed by the Solicitor General on behalf of the EEOC in this case suggests that a different rule should apply when a supervisor's harassment "merely" results in a discriminatory work environment. The Solicitor General concedes that sexual harassment that affects tangible job benefits is an exercise of authority delegated to the supervisor by the employer, and thus gives rise to employer liability. But * * * he argues that the case of a supervisor merely creating a discriminatory work environment is different because the supervisor "is not exercising, or threatening to exercise, actual or apparent authority to make personnel decisions affecting the victim." In the latter situation, he concludes, some further notice requirement should therefore be necessary.

The Solicitor General's position is untenable. A supervisor's responsibilities do not begin and end with the power to hire, fire, and discipline employees, or with the power to recommend such actions. Rather, a supervisor is charged with the day-to-day supervision of the work environment and with ensuring a safe, productive, workplace. There is no reason why abuse of the latter authority should have different consequences than abuse of the former. In both cases it is the authority vested in the supervisor by the employer that enables him to commit the wrong: it is precisely because the supervisor is understood to be clothed with the employer's authority that he is able to impose unwelcome sexual conduct on subordinates. There is therefore no justification for a special rule, to be applied only in "hostile environment" cases, that sexual harassment does not create employer liability until the employee suffering the discrimination notifies other supervisors. No such requirement appears in the statute, and no such requirement can coherently be drawn from the law of agency.

* * *

* * * I would apply in this case the same rules we apply in all other Title VII cases, and hold that sexual harassment by a supervisor of an employee under his supervision, leading to a discriminatory work environment, should be imputed to the employer for Title VII purposes regardless of whether the employee gave "notice" of the offense.

NOTES AND PROBLEMS FOR DISCUSSION

1.   Pursuant to the ruling in *Meritor*, in order to establish the existence of actionable sex-based harassment, plaintiffs with hostile environment-styled claims must prove that the challenged conduct (a) was severe or pervasive; (b) created a hostile or abusive working environment; (c) was unwelcome; and (d) was based on the plaintiff's sex. It then became the task of the lower courts to flesh out each of these criteria.

(a) Severe or Pervasive: The determination of what constitutes "severe or pervasive conduct" is based on an examination of the totality of circumstances. In assessing the totality of circumstances, courts typically focus on some or all of four factors: (1) the level of offensiveness of the unwelcome acts or words; (2) the frequency or pervasiveness of the offensive encounters; (3) the total length of time over which the encounters occurred; and (4) the context in which the harassing conduct occurred. In VANCE v. SOUTHERN BELL TEL. & TEL. CO., 863 F.2d 1503 (11th Cir. 1989), the trial court had granted the defendant's renewed motion for judgment as a matter of law on the ground that a noose hung over an African-American employee's desk on two different occasions was not enough, as a matter of law, to establish that the alleged racial harassment was a persistent, pervasive practice. The Eleventh Circuit ruled that the determination of whether the defendant's conduct was sufficiently "severe and pervasive" did not turn solely on the number of incidents alleged by the plaintiff, but was to be based on a consideration of all of the circumstances, including the number and severity of individual incidents of harassment.

Should evidence of prior acts of racial, ethnic or gender-based harassment committed by either the alleged perpetrator in the instant case or by others in the company's employ be admissible in a sexual harassment case? Federal Rule of Evidence 404 precludes evidence of a person's character or prior acts to prove action in conformity therewith, but permits the introduction of these forms of evidence if they are offered to prove motive or intent. In HEYNE v. CARUSO, 69 F.3d 1475 (9th Cir. 1995), the Ninth Circuit reversed the trial court's exclusion of evidence of other female employees who were allegedly sexually harassed by the company owner. The appellate court held that although Rule 404 precluded admission of this evidence for purpose of establishing the employer's past bad acts, it was admissible to prove the defendant's motive in discharging the plaintiff since sexual harassment of other workers was probative of the employer's general attitude of disrespect towards, and sexual objectification of, his female employees. Any danger that the jury would improperly use such evidence to influence its decision on whether the employer sexually had propositioned the employee, the court reasoned, could be avoided by a limiting instruction.

(b) Hostile/Abusive Environment: Post-*Meritor*, the lower courts have struggled mightily with this element of a hostile environment claim. Initially, the cases required evidence of psychological damage, but over time most of the circuit courts, with the notable exception of the Sixth Circuit, did not cling to this requirement, stating that the plaintiff did not have to experience anxiety or other psychological distress requiring psychiatric assistance as a precondition to obtaining judicial relief. There also was some disagreement between the circuits on the appropriate method of assessing the impact of the alleged harassment. Specifically, the courts could not agree on whether the impact of the harassment should be gauged objectively or subjectively, i.e., by its affect on either the plaintiff or some variation of the classical "reasonable person" standard bearer that is the hallmark of tort litigation.

Both of these issues came to a head in HARRIS v. FORKLIFT SYSTEMS, INC., 510 U.S. 17, 114 S.Ct. 367, 126 L.Ed.2d 295 (1993). There, a female manager of an equipment rental company alleged that the company president frequently insulted her, subjected her to unwanted sexual innuendoes and made lewd references to her attire. After a trial before a Magistrate Judge, the District Judge adopted the Magistrate Judge's report and recommendations, which included findings that although some of the company president's remarks "offended plaintiff and would offend the reasonable woman," they were not "so severe as to be expected to seriously affect plaintiff's psychological well-being." The trial court's decision to dismiss the plaintiff's complaint for failing to establish damage to her psychological well being was summarily affirmed by the Sixth Circuit following established circuit precedent. The Supreme Court agreed to hear the case because of a circuit split on the issue of whether a harassment plaintiff was required to establish the presence of psychological damages issue.   Justice O'Connor, writing for a unanimous Court, offered this explanation for its decision to reverse the lower courts:

> * * * As we made clear in *Meritor*, [§703(a)] is not limited to "economic" or "tangible" discrimination.   The phrase "terms, conditions, or privileges of employment" evinces a congressional intent "to strike at the entire spectrum of disparate treatment of men and women" in employment, which includes requiring people to work in a discriminatorily hostile or abusive environment.   When the workplace is permeated with discriminatory intimidation, ridicule, and insult, that is sufficiently severe or pervasive to alter the conditions of the victim's employment and create an abusive working environment, Title VII is violated.

> This standard, which we reaffirm today, takes a middle path between making actionable any conduct that is merely offensive and requiring the conduct to cause a tangible psychological injury.   As we pointed out in *Meritor*, "mere utterance of an *** epithet which engenders offensive feelings in a employee," does not sufficiently affect the conditions of employment to implicate Title VII.   Conduct that is not severe or pervasive enough to create an objectively hostile or abusive work environment — an environment that a reasonable person would find hostile or abusive — is beyond Title VII's purview.   Likewise, if the victim does not subjectively perceive the environment to be abusive, the conduct has not actually altered the conditions of the victim's employment, and there is no Title VII violation.

> But Title VII comes into play before the harassing conduct leads to a nervous breakdown.   A discriminatorily abusive work environment, even one that does not seriously affect employees' psychological well-being, can and often will detract from employees' job performance, discourage employees from remaining on the job, or keep them from advancing in their careers.   Moreover, even without regard to these tangible effects, the very fact that the discriminatory conduct was so severe or pervasive that it created a work environment abusive to employees because of their race, gender, religion, or national origin offends Title VII's broad rule of workplace equality.   The appalling conduct alleged in *Meritor*, and the reference in that case to environments "so heavily polluted with discrimination as to destroy completely the emotional and psychological stability of minority group workers," merely present some especially egregious examples of harassment. They do not mark the boundary of what is actionable.

> We therefore believe the District Court erred in relying on whether the conduct "seriously affected plaintiff's psychological well-being" or led her to "suffer injury."   Such an inquiry may needlessly focus the factfinder's attention on concrete psychological harm, an element Title VII does not require.   Certainly Title VII bars conduct that would seriously affect a reasonable person's psychological well-being, but the statute is not limited to such conduct.   So long as the environment would reasonably be perceived, and is perceived, as hostile or abusive, there is no need for it also to be psychologically injurious.

> This is not, and by its nature cannot be, a mathematically precise test.   We need not answer today all the potential questions it raises * * *.   But we can say that whether an environment is "hostile" or "abusive" can be determined only by looking at all the circumstances.   These may include the frequency of the

discriminatory conduct; its severity; whether it is physically threatening or humiliating, or a mere offensive utterance; and whether it unreasonably interferes with an employee's work performance.   The effect on the employee's psychological well-being is, of course, relevant to determining whether the plaintiff actually found the environment abusive. But while psychological harm, like any other relevant factor, may be taken into account, no single factor is required.

Forklift, while conceding that a requirement that the conduct seriously affect psychological well-being is unfounded, argues that the District Court nonetheless correctly applied the *Meritor* standard. We disagree. Though the District Court did conclude that the work environment was not "intimidating or abusive to [Harris]," it did so only after finding that the conduct was not "so severe as to be expected to seriously affect plaintiff's psychological well-being," and that Harris was not "subjectively so offended that she suffered injury." The District Court's application of these incorrect standards may well have influenced its ultimate conclusion, especially given that the court found this to be a "close case."

We therefore reverse the judgment of the Court of Appeals, and remand the case for further proceedings consistent with this opinion.

510 U.S. at 21-23, 114 S.Ct. at 370-71.

Beyond stating that evidence of psychological injury is not required, what guidance did the Court offer in *Harris* as to the type of evidence that would establish the existence of a hostile or abusive working environment? Although she joined in the Court's opinion in *Harris*, Justice Ginsburg issued a brief concurring opinion in which she suggested that in making this evaluation:

> "* * * the adjudicator's inquiry should center, dominantly, on whether the discriminatory conduct has unreasonably interfered with the plaintiff's work performance. To show such interference, the plaintiff need not prove that his or her tangible productivity has declined as a result of the harassment. It suffices to prove that a reasonable person subjected to the discriminatory conduct would find, as the plaintiff did, that the harassment so altered working conditions as to make it more difficult to do the job."

510 U.S. at 25, 114 S.Ct. at 372. On the other hand, Justice O'Connor indicated that the court must look at the totality of circumstances, only *one* of which is whether the supervisor's conduct interfered with the plaintiff's work performance. Can either or both of these opinions be construed to suggest that the plaintiff does not have to establish that her work productivity suffered as a result of the allegedly harassing conduct as long as she can show that the challenged conduct made it more difficult to do her job? *Compare* Deangelis v. El Paso Mun. Police Officers Ass'n, 51 F.3d 591, 593 (5th Cir. 1995) (a plaintiff in a hostile environment case must establish that "extremely insensitive conduct" created an environment in which working conditions had "palpably deteriorated" as any lesser standard that would make actionable conduct that "sporadically wounds or offends but does not hinder a female employee's performance," and would not serve the goal of equality but, rather, would only "insulate women from everyday insults as if they remained models of Victorian reticence.") *with* Davis v. USPS, 142 F.3d 1334 (10th Cir. 1998) (trial court erred in determining that since the plaintiff remained on the job after filing her complaint and

continued thereafter to enjoy and succeed in her employment, no rational jury could find that she subjectively suffered from a hostile work environment; it was error to conclude that a plaintiff who otherwise enjoys her work, is successful, and hopes to continue in that position cannot perceive the work environment to be abusive as a matter of law; issuance of defense judgment as a matter of law reversed and case remanded for trial).

Is the existence of a hostile or abuse environment measured according to an objective and/or subjective standard? And to the extent that an objective standard is employed, should that be measured by the impact on a reasonable "person," "woman," "victim," or "person of the plaintiff's classification"? Pre-*Harris*, some lower courts had adopted a reasonable woman (or victim), as opposed to reasonable person, version of the objective standard. Although the *Harris* Court did not expressly discuss this issue, and made no mention of the circuit split on the question, Justice O'Connor's opinion does contain two references to the "reasonable person." Do these references reflect the Court's determination that the "reasonable woman" or "reasonable victim" criterion should not be utilized?

The Ninth Circuit, which had adopted a "reasonable woman" standard in pre-*Harris* hostile environment cases, subsequently ruled that *Harris* did not prevent a trial court from instructing the jurors to determine whether the workplace was objectively hostile "from the perspective of a reasonable person with the same fundamental characteristics." Fuller v. City of Oakland, 47 F.3d 1522 (9th Cir. 1995). The Ninth Circuit continued to apply a "reasonable woman" standard because, in its judgment, a sex-blind reasonable person standard tended to be male-biased and to systematically ignore the experiences of women. Since men are rarely the victims of sexual assault, the Ninth Circuit has explained, they are inclined to view sexual conduct in a vacuum "without a full appreciation of the social setting or the underlying threat of violence that a woman may perceive" and relying on their perspective "would run the risk of reinforcing the prevailing level of discrimination" and allow harassers to "continue to harass merely because a particular discriminatory practice was common." Ellison v. Brady, 924 F.2d 872, 878-79 (9th Cir. 1991). On the other hand, the Second Circuit expressly rejected the "reasonable African-American" or "reasonable woman" standard in favor of an approach that focuses on the reaction of a "reasonable person who is the target of racially or ethnically oriented remarks." Richardson v. N.Y. State. Dep't of Corr. Ser., 180 F.3d 426 (2d Cir. 1999). The court explained that this standard had the virtue of precluding the trier or fact from determining whether a particular racial, gender, or ethnic group was more or less thin-skinned than others.

Is there a meaningful distinction between these standards and, if so, how is the availability of a jury in harassment cases likely to affect the implementation of the articulated standard? It has been suggested that the utilization of a "reasonable woman" or "reasonable African-American" (in racial harassment cases) rests on the erroneous assumption that each of these classifications is monolithic and that neither criteria accurately reflects the diversity of experiences, attitudes and perceptions that exists among members of these groups. *See, e.g.*, Kathryn Abrams, *Social Construction, Roving Biologism, And Reasonable Women: A Response to Professor Epstein*, 41 DEPAUL L.REV. 1021 (1992). On the other hand, isn't the "reasonable individual" standard, when applied to any group, subject to this same criticism? *See*

Toni Lester, *The Reasonable Woman Test in Sexual Harassment Law — Will It Really Make a Difference?*, 26 IND.L.R. 227 (1993).

(c) Unwelcomed: With respect to whether or not the alleged harassing conduct was "unwelcome", the *Meritor* Court stated that evidence of the alleged victim's "sexually provocative speech or dress" might be relevant. Does this suggest that the defendant can offer evidence of the plaintiff's frequently use of foul language to show that she welcomed obscene remarks generally? In SWENTEK v. USAIR, INC., 830 F.2d 552 (4th Cir. 1987), the appellate court concluded that the trial judge had misconstrued the meaning of unwelcome sexual harassment by ruling that the plaintiff's use of foul language indicated that she was the kind of person who could not be offended by such comments and thus welcomed them generally. Rather, it concluded, the appropriate question was whether the plaintiff had welcomed the particular conduct in question from the alleged harasser.

Suppose a female employee appeared in nude photos in a lewd magazine. Would such action (occurring outside of work hours) on the plaintiff's part defeat her claim that the on-the-job sexual harassment was unwelcome? *See* Burns v. McGregor Elect. Indus., 989 F.2d 959,963 (8th Cir. 1993) (trial court erred in concluding that anyone who would appear nude in a national magazine could not be offended by behavior that occurred on the jobsite; the plaintiff's choice to pose for a nude magazine outside work hours is not material to the issue of whether plaintiff found her employer's work-related conduct offensive).

In Note 1(a), *supra*, we examined the admissibility of the alleged harasser's prior bad acts in a sexual harassment suit. But in response to the plaintiff's claim that the challenged conduct was unwelcome, can the defendant offer evidence of her prior sexual history with either the alleged harasser or other individuals? As part of the Violent Crime Control and Law Enforcement Act of 1994, Pub.L. 103-322, 108 Stat. 1919, Congress amended Federal Rule of Evidence 412. The amended rule makes inadmissible in any civil or criminal proceeding "involving alleged sexual misconduct" the following types of evidence: (1) evidence offered to prove that any alleged victim engaged in other sexual behavior; and (2) evidence offered to prove any alleged victim's sexual predisposition. One exception, however, is provided for civil cases:

> evidence offered to prove the sexual behavior predisposition of any alleged victim is admissible if it is otherwise admissible under these rules and its probative value substantially outweighs the danger of harm to any victim and of unfair prejudice to any party.

The Advisory Committee Notes to the revised rule make clear that it is intended to apply broadly to "any civil case in which a person claims to be the victim of sexual misconduct, such as actions for sexual battery or sexual harassment." 154 F.R.D. 526, 529. Under what circumstances might the probative value of a plaintiff's prior sexual behavior "substantially outweigh" the danger of harm and unfair prejudice to the plaintiff, and could sexually provocative speech or dress ever meet this standard? According to the Advisory Committee Notes, the rule was intended to preclude admission of evidence "relating to the alleged victim's mode of dress, speech, or lifestyle," as well as evidence that "does not directly refer to sexual activities or thoughts, but that the proponent believes may have a sexual connotation for the factfinder." *See* Sheffield v. Hilltop Sand & Gravel Co., 895 F.Supp. 105 (E.D. Va. 1995) (although Rule 412 prevented the employer from offering evidence of the plaintiff's participation in sexually explicit discussions with co-workers, the employer could introduce evidence that the plaintiff had engaged in sexually explicit discussions with the alleged harasser since this testimony was relevant to the question of whether the plaintiff welcomed his attentions).

What if the alleged harassment took the form of consensual sexual intercourse with a minor? Although not forcible rape, consensual sex with a minor constitutes the felony of statutory rape under state law. How should the court deal with the defense claim that the plaintiff's active participation in consensual sex made the harassment welcomed? In DOE v. OBERWEIS DAIRY, 456 F.3d 704 (7th Cir.2006), the court observed that since the age of consent fixed by state law reflects a legislative judgment about the maturity of individuals below that age on matters concerning sexual intercourse, to avoid *ad hoc* determinations of maturity and the capacity to welcome the sexual advances of an older person in Title VII cases, the federal courts should defer to that legislative judgment and the age of consent in the state in which the plaintiff is employed should be the rule of decision in Title VII cases. The court took pains to note, however, that it did not mean to suggest that the plaintiff's conduct in cases involving statutory rape should be ignored. The Seventh Circuit declared that the plaintiff's active and voluntary participation in the sexual conduct could be used to reduce the defendant's damages by allowing the fact finder to assess the extent of the damages that could fairly be traced to the harasser's conduct.

From whose perspective should the (un)welcomeness inquiry be evaluated, i.e., should the factfinder seek to determine whether this plaintiff actually welcomed the conduct or whether the defendant believed (reasonably and/or actually) that the plaintiff did not welcome this conduct? If the reason for making the inquiry into welcomeness is to limit recovery to cases where the plaintiff suffered actual harm, then there is good reason for relying on the plaintiff's subjective perspective. On the other hand, if the purpose of this inquiry is to ensure that recovery is provided only when the defendant has acted badly, i.e., when it had notice that such conduct was unwelcome, then the defendant's state of mind should prevail. For an interesting discussion of this issue see Henry L. Chambers, Jr., *(Un)Welcome Conduct and the Sexually Hostile Environment*, 53 ALAB.L.REV. 733 (2002).

(d) Based on Plaintiff's Sex: The issues surrounding whether or not harassment is based on sex are examined in Chapter 3D2, *infra*.

2.   Claims of sexual harassment are not limited to charges that the allegedly harassing conduct contained sexual references or overtones. As long as the conduct occurs because of the plaintiff's gender, any harassment, including the actual or threatened use of physical force, regardless of whether it was taken with sexual overtones, can constitute prohibited sexual harassment. See e.g., E.E.O.C. v. Costco Wholesale Corp., 903 F.3d 618 (7th Cir. 2019).

3.   Under Title VII, a plaintiff can seek compensatory and punitive damages with respect to claims of intentional (although not impact-based) discrimination.

(a) While nearly all sexual harassment claims fall within the intentional discrimination category, if the defendant asserts that the challenged conduct or statements, though admittedly unwelcome by and distasteful to the plaintiff, were "well intentioned" does this also constitute intentional discrimination?

(b) What type of conduct would subject the defendant to an award of punitive damages in light of the language in 42 U.S.C. §1981A(b)(1) permitting an award of punitive damages against a private employer when the plaintiff demonstrates that the defendant acted either with "malice" or with "reckless indifference to the federally protected rights" of the plaintiff? In DELPH v. DR. PEPPER BOTTLING CO. OF PARAGOULD, INC., 130 F.3d 349 (8th Cir. 1997), the appellate court affirmed the trial court's award of $50,000 in punitive damages where the plaintiff's supervisors had subjected the plaintiff to a "steady barrage of name-calling" by repeatedly referring to him, in the presence of co-employees, as "nigger," "black boy," "token black boy," and "my little black boy." Even though the supervisors had not received any training on workplace discrimination, the court concluded that no one could refer to an African-American employee in this fashion without knowing that such language would offend a reasonable person in the plaintiff's position. Accordingly, it found that the supervisors were indifferent to the plaintiff's right to be free from workplace harassment, that their conduct was reckless, and that their action could be imputed to the defendant employer.

4. Can a female employee who was not subjected personally to any harassing conduct file a claim charging that the defendant's conduct towards other female employees nevertheless created a hostile working environment for her and others who found such conduct repugnant and offensive? The Seventh Circuit refers to these as cases involving the "target area" form of harassment, i.e., where the plaintiff is not the direct target of the offending conduct, but is a member of the group that is being vilified. *See* Yuknis v. First Student, Inc., 481 F.3d 552 (7th Cir. 2007) (affirming grant of summary judgment to defendant because the alleged comments made outside of the plaintiff's presence could not be construed as either being intended to or having the effect of causing distress or offense to women *qua* women); Chambers v. American Trans Air, Inc., 17 F.3d 998 (7th Cir. 1994) (a female employee who claims that the company president referred to other female employees in sexist, vulgar and patently offensive terms could state a claim of hostile environment harassment). In LEIBOVITZ v. N.Y.C. TRANSIT AUTHORITY, 252 F.3d 179 (2d Cir.2001), the court overturned a jury verdict in favor of a female worker who claimed that she had suffered emotional trauma because her working environment had been rendered hostile and abusive as the result of hearing hearsay reports that female workers in another department were subjected to sexual harassment out of her presence by a supervisor who did not supervise the plaintiff. After ruling that the plaintiff had standing to file suit since she alleged that *she* had suffered emotional damage because discrimination against members of a class of which she was a member created an abusive working environment for *her*, the court nevertheless found that she did not prove that she actually suffered harassment in subjective or objective terms as the result of receiving hearsay reports of harassment of other women out of her presence.

Suppose, instead, that the plaintiff was a male employee who alleged that his working environment had been rendered hostile by a supervisor's use of offensive language directed at, as well as offensive touchings of, female employees. Should he be able to state a claim?

In these "bystander" or "target zone" cases, should it matter whether the actual subject of that challenged conduct welcomed it? This latter scenario is especially likely to occur in the situation where a supervisor grants a tangible benefit to an employee on the basis of a consensual sexual relationship. Suppose, for example, that two female employees applied for the same promotion and the supervisor chose the one with whom he was having a consensual sexual relationship. Assuming that the promotion was granted solely on the basis of the consensual relationship, could the unsuccessful applicant successfully file a claim of sexual harassment? *See* Taken v. Okla. Corp. Comm'n, 125 F.3d 1366, 1370 (10th Cir. 1997) ("preferential treatment [promotion] on the basis of a consensual romantic relationship between a supervisor and an employee is not gender-based discrimination" because it is "based on a voluntary romantic affiliation, and not on any gender differences"). Would your answer to this problem change if the rejected candidate had been a man? *See* Miller v. Aluminum Co. of America, 679 F.Supp. 495 (W.D. Pa. 1988) (no gender-based discrimination in case of favoritism by male supervisor towards his female subordinate s ince both male and female employees share the disadvantage of not holding this special place in the affections of the supervisor). Note also that if favoritism on the basis of a consensual romantic relationship does not constitute unlawful sex-based discrimination, then an employee who is retaliated against for complaining informally about a supervisor's decision to promote a paramour employee will not be able to state a retaliation claim under §704 because that informal complaint will not constitute protected opposition "to an employment practice made unlawful by Title VII". *See* Anderson v. Oklahoma State University Bd. Of Regents, 342 Fed.Appx. 365 (10th Cir. 2009).

Suppose that one of the parties to a previously consensual romantic/intimate relationship alleges that the former paramour, either a co-employee or supervisor, subjected him or her to harassment. Can the plaintiff successfully state a claim under Title VII or does this fail to meet the requirement of being discrimination on the basis of the plaintiff's sex? *Compare* Succar v. Dade County School Board, 229 F.3d 1343 (11th Cir. 2000) (male teacher who alleged hostile environment discrimination by co-employee with whom he had a consensual prior sexual relationship cannot state claim under Title VII because harassment was not motivated by the plaintiff's sex but by the harasser's contempt for the plaintiff following their failed relationship; the plaintiff's gender was "merely coincidental" to action taken out of personal animosity), *with* Forrest v. Brinker Int'l Payroll Co., LP, 511 F.3d 225 (1st Cir. 2007) (female employee can state Title VII harassment claim based on behavior of co-employee with whom she had a prior consensual intimate relationship; "[i]n cases involving a prior failed relationship between an accused harasser and alleged victim, reasoning that the harassment could not have been motivated by the victim's sex because it was instead motivated by a romantic relationship gone sour establishes a false dichotomy. Presumably the prior relationship would never have occurred if the victim were not a member of the sex preferred by the harasser, and thus the victim's sex is inextricably linked to the harasser's decision to harass."). *See also* Lipphardt v. Durango Steakhouse of Brandon, Inc., 267 F.3d 1183 (11th Cir. 2001) (suggesting that this circuit's prior ruling in *Succar* was limited by the fact that the alleged harassment was not sexual in nature; "while a prior intimate relationship is an important factor to consider [in determining whether the conduct was based on the plaintiff's sex], it is not determinative of a sexual harassment claim" and that where the harassment is sexual in nature, a jury can infer that the harasser's decision to harass was motivated by the victim's sex).

5.   Section 717, the provision of Title VII that sets forth the substantive rights of federal employees, states that "[a]ll personnel actions affecting [federal] employees * * * shall be made free from any discrimination based on race, color, religion, sex, or national origin." Section 703(a), on the other hand, makes it an unlawful employment practice to discriminate against any individual "with respect to his compensation, terms, condition, or privileges of employment." Does this difference in terminology suggest that federal employees do not enjoy the same level of protection from sexual harassment that is available to nonfederal employees? *See* Jordan v. Clark, 847 F.2d 1368 (9th Cir. 1988) (Title VII protects government employees from sexual harassment to the same degree private employees are protected.).

6.   In many sexual harassment cases, the courts are called upon to determine the extent, if any, to which a wide variety of speech either contributed to or created *per se* an unlawfully hostile environment.

(a) Does the restriction of offensive, vulgar, sexist, or racist statements under Title VII violate the free speech provision of the First Amendment? *See* Jenson v. Eveleth Taconite Co., 824 F. Supp. 847, 884 n.89 (D. Minn. 1993) ("Title VII prohibits behavior that creates a work environment which is hostile to a protected group. In contrast to the larger social context, therefore, expression in the workplace that is offensive to and has a psychological impact on a member of a protected group may be prohibited. Title VII may legitimately proscribe conduct, including undirected expressions of gender intolerance, which create an offensive working environment. That expression is 'swept up' in this proscription does not violate First Amendment principles."). Cf. R.A.V. v. City of St. Paul, 505 U.S. 377, 112 S.Ct. 2538, 2546, 120 L.Ed.2d 305 (1992) (a municipal ordinance criminalizing hate speech that aroused anger or resentment on the basis of race, color, creed, religion or gender is facially invalid under the First Amendment because by proscribing only that speech which communicated messages with respect to the five proscribed areas, the ordinance was not content neutral; but suggesting that interpreting Title VII to prohibit the use of sexually derogatory "fighting words" might survive constitutional scrutiny).

(b) If a public employer bans the viewing of sexually-oriented magazines containing pictures of nude females from the workplace in order to avoid the creation of a hostile environment, has it violated the First Amendment rights of those employees that wish to read these magazines during their non-working time? In JOHNSON v. COUNTY OF LOS ANGELES, 865 F. Supp. 1430 (C.D. Cal. 1994), the Los Angeles Fire Department's policy prohibiting sexually oriented magazines, particularly those containing nude pictures, in all work locations, including dormitories, rest rooms and lockers, was challenged under the First Amendment as it applied to the private possession, reading and consensual sharing of Playboy in the firehouse. In this unique working environment, where employees work, eat and sleep in the same location, the court concluded that the policy banned the reading of Playboy at times when firefighters' behavior was not otherwise restricted and that it permitted no opportunity for the plaintiff to quietly and privately read his copy of Playboy while he was off duty. Thus, while several female firefighters complained that the shared viewing of these magazines created a hostile environment for them, the court determined that the Department's policy unreasonably interfered with the plaintiff's First Amendment rights as was, therefore, invalid as applied to his quiet reading and possession of the magazine. For some interesting discussions of the problems raised in this area, see Cynthia Estlund, *Freedom of Expression in the Workplace and the Problem of Discriminatory Harassment*, 75 U. TEX. L. REV. 687 (1997); Charles Calleros, *Title VII and the First Amendment: Content-Neutral Regulation, Disparate Impact, and the 'Reasonable Person'*, 58 OHIO ST. L.J. 1217 (1997); and Eugene Volokh, *What Speech Does "Hostile Work Environment" Harassment Law Restrict?*, 85 GEO. L.J. 627 (1997).

7. An issue left unresolved by the Court in both *Meritor* and *Harris* is the extent to which an "employer" will be held liable for acts of harassment committed by its supervisory and nonsupervisory employees. While the *Meritor* Court "decline[d] the parties' invitation to issue a definitive rule on employer liability," it did offer a set of general guidelines for future cases. On the one hand, the Supreme Court reversed the circuit court's ruling that employers are always liable for acts of harassment by supervisory personnel. It also stated, however, that a lack of employer notice would not "necessarily insulate that employer from liability." Since the statutory definition of "employer" includes any "agent" of the employer, the Court reasoned, the appropriate approach was to "look to agency principles for guidance in this area."

It then fell to the lower courts to implement this general instruction and to develop a method for handling the wide variety of harassment cases that followed *Meritor* and *Harris*. Over the five years following the *Harris* ruling, the federal courts adopted a variety of standards of employer liability ranging from strict liability to negligence. The Supreme Court attempted to bring a measure of uniformity to this matter when it decided a pair of companion cases, including the following:

Burlington Industries, Inc. v. Ellerth

Supreme Court of the United States, 1998.

524 U.S. 742, 118 S.Ct. 2257, 141 L.Ed. 633.

MR. JUSTICE KENNEDY delivered the opinion of the Court.

We decide whether, under Title VII of the Civil Rights Act of 1964, an employee who refuses the unwelcome and threatening sexual advances of a supervisor, yet suffers no adverse, tangible job consequences, can recover against the employer without showing the employer is negligent or otherwise at fault for the supervisor's actions.

I

* * * The employee * * * Kimberly Ellerth * * * worked as a salesperson in one of Burlington's divisions in Chicago, Illinois. During her employment, she alleges, she was subjected to constant sexual harassment by her supervisor, one Ted Slowik.

In the hierarchy of Burlington's management structure, Slowik was a mid-level manager. Burlington has eight divisions, employing more than 22,000 people in some 50 plants around the United States. Slowik was a vice president in one of five business units within one of the divisions. He had authority to make hiring and promotion decisions subject to the approval of his supervisor, who signed the paperwork.

According to Slowik's supervisor, his position was not considered an upper-level management position, and he was not amongst the decision-making or policy-making hierarchy. Slowik was not Ellerth's immediate supervisor. Ellerth worked in a two-person office in Chicago, and she answered to her office colleague, who in turn answered to Slowik in New York.

Against a background of repeated boorish and offensive remarks and gestures which Slowik allegedly made, Ellerth places particular emphasis on three alleged incidents where Slowik's comments could be construed as threats to deny her tangible job benefits. In the summer of 1993, while on a business trip, Slowik invited Ellerth to the hotel lounge, an invitation Ellerth felt compelled to accept because Slowik was her boss. When Ellerth gave no encouragement to remarks Slowik made about her breasts, he told her to "loosen up" and warned, "[y]ou know, Kim, I could make your life very hard or very easy at Burlington."

In March 1994, when Ellerth was being considered for a promotion, Slowik expressed reservations during the promotion interview because she was not "loose enough." The comment was followed by his reaching over and rubbing her knee. Ellerth did receive the promotion; but when Slowik called to announce it, he told Ellerth, "you're gonna be out there with men who work in factories, and they certainly like women with pretty butts/legs."

In May 1994, Ellerth called Slowik, asking permission to insert a customer's logo into a fabric sample. Slowik responded, "I don't have time for you right now, Kim — unless you want to tell me what you're wearing." Ellerth told Slowik she had to go and ended the call. A day or two later, Ellerth called Slowik to ask permission again. This time he denied her request, but added something along the lines of, "are you wearing shorter skirts yet, Kim, because it would make your job a whole heck of a lot easier."

A short time later, Ellerth's immediate supervisor cautioned her about returning telephone calls to customers in a prompt fashion. In response, Ellerth quit. She faxed a letter giving reasons unrelated to the alleged sexual harassment we have described. About three weeks later, however, she sent a letter explaining she quit because of Slowik's behavior.

During her tenure at Burlington, Ellerth did not inform anyone in authority about Slowik's conduct, despite knowing Burlington had a policy against sexual harassment. In fact, she chose not to inform her immediate supervisor (not Slowik) because "it would be his duty as my supervisor to report any incidents of sexual harassment." On one occasion, she told Slowik a comment he made was inappropriate.

In October 1994, * * * Ellerth filed suit in the United States District Court for the Northern District of Illinois, alleging Burlington engaged in sexual harassment and forced her constructive discharge, in violation of Title VII. The District Court granted summary judgment to Burlington. The Court found Slowik's behavior, as described by Ellerth, severe and pervasive enough to create a hostile work environment, but found Burlington neither knew nor should have known about the conduct. There was no triable issue of fact on the latter point, and the Court noted Ellerth had not used Burlington's internal complaint procedures. Although Ellerth's claim was framed as a hostile work environment complaint, the District Court observed there was a *quid pro quo* "component" to the hostile environment. Proceeding from the premise that an employer faces vicarious liability for *quid pro quo* harassment, the District Court thought it necessary to apply a negligence standard because the *quid pro quo* merely contributed to the hostile work environment. The District Court also dismissed Ellerth's constructive discharge claim.

The Court of Appeals en banc reversed in a decision which produced eight separate opinions and no consensus for a controlling rationale. The judges were able to agree on the problem they confronted: Vicarious liability, not failure to comply with a duty of care, was the essence of Ellerth's case against Burlington on appeal. The judges seemed to agree Ellerth could recover if Slowik's unfulfilled threats to deny her tangible job benefits was sufficient to impose vicarious liability on Burlington. With the exception of Judges Coffey and Easterbrook, the judges also agreed Ellerth's claim could be categorized as one of *quid pro quo* harassment, even though she had received the promotion and had suffered no other tangible retaliation.

The consensus disintegrated on the standard for an employer's liability for such a claim. Six judges * * * agreed the proper standard was vicarious liability, and so Ellerth could recover even though Burlington was not negligent. They had different reasons for the conclusion. * * *

* * *

Chief Judge Posner, joined by Judge Manion, disagreed. He asserted Ellerth could not recover against Burlington despite having stated a *quid pro quo* claim. According to Chief Judge Posner, an employer is subject to vicarious liability for "act[s] that significantly alter the terms or conditions of employment," or "company act[s]." In the emergent terminology, an unfulfilled *quid pro quo* is a mere threat to do a company act rather than the act itself, and in these circumstances, an employer can be found liable for its negligence only. Chief Judge Posner also found Ellerth failed to create a triable issue of fact as to Burlington's negligence.

* * *

The disagreement revealed in the careful opinions of the judges of the Court of Appeals reflects the fact that Congress has left it to the courts to determine controlling agency law principles in a new and difficult area of federal law. We granted certiorari to assist in defining the relevant standards of employer liability.

II

At the outset, we assume * * * a trier of fact could find in Slowik's remarks numerous threats to retaliate against Ellerth if she denied some sexual liberties. The threats, however, were not carried out or fulfilled. Cases based on threats which are carried out are referred to often as *quid pro quo* cases, as distinct from bothersome attentions or sexual remarks that are sufficiently severe or pervasive to create a hostile work environment. The terms *quid pro quo* and hostile work environment are helpful, perhaps, in making a rough demarcation between cases in which threats are carried out and those where they are not or are absent altogether, but beyond this are of limited utility.

* * *

"*Quid pro quo*" and "hostile work environment" do not appear in the statutory text. The terms appeared first in the academic literature, found their way into decisions of the Courts of Appeals, and were mentioned in this Court's decision in *Meritor*.

In *Meritor*, the terms served a specific and limited purpose. There we considered whether the conduct in question constituted discrimination in the terms or conditions of employment in violation of Title VII. We assumed, and with adequate reason, that if an employer demanded sexual favors from an employee in return for a job benefit, discrimination with respect to terms or conditions of employment was explicit. Less obvious was whether an employer's sexually demeaning behavior altered terms or conditions of employment in violation of Title VII. We distinguished between *quid pro quo* claims and hostile environment claims, and said both were cognizable under Title VII, though the latter requires harassment that is severe or pervasive. The principal significance of the distinction is to instruct that Title VII is violated by either explicit or constructive alterations in the terms or conditions of employment and to explain the latter must be severe or pervasive. The distinction was not discussed for its bearing upon an employer's liability for an employee's discrimination. On this question Meritor held, with no further specifics, that agency principles controlled.

Nevertheless, as use of the terms grew in the wake of *Meritor*, they acquired their own significance. The standard of employer responsibility turned on which type of harassment occurred. If the plaintiff established a *quid pro quo* claim, the Courts of Appeals held, the employer was subject to vicarious liability. The rule encouraged Title VII plaintiffs to state their claims as *quid pro quo* claims, which in turn put expansive pressure on the definition. The equivalence of the *quid pro quo* label and vicarious liability is illustrated by this case. The question presented on certiorari is whether Ellerth can state a claim of *quid pro quo* harassment, but the issue of real concern to the parties is whether Burlington has vicarious liability for Slowik's alleged misconduct, rather than liability limited to its own negligence. * * *

We do not suggest the terms *quid pro quo* and hostile work environment are irrelevant to Title VII litigation. To the extent they illustrate the distinction between cases involving a threat which is carried out and offensive conduct in general, the terms are relevant when there is a threshold question whether a plaintiff can prove discrimination in violation of Title VII. When a plaintiff proves that a tangible employment action resulted from a refusal to submit to a supervisor's sexual demands, he or she establishes that the employment decision itself constitutes a change in the terms and conditions of employment that is actionable under Title VII. For any sexual harassment preceding the employment decision to be actionable, however, the conduct must be severe or pervasive. Because Ellerth's claim involves only unfulfilled threats, it should be categorized as a hostile work environment claim that requires a showing of severe or pervasive conduct. For purposes of this case, we accept the District Court's finding that the alleged conduct was severe or pervasive. The case before us involves numerous alleged threats, and we express no opinion as to whether a single unfulfilled threat is sufficient to constitute discrimination in the terms or conditions of employment.

When we assume discrimination can be proved, however, the factors we discuss below, and not the categories *quid pro quo* and hostile work environment, will be controlling on the issue of vicarious liability. That is the question we must resolve.

III

We must decide, then, whether an employer has vicarious liability when a supervisor creates a hostile work environment by making explicit threats to alter a subordinate's terms or conditions of employment, based on sex, but does not fulfill the threat. We turn to principles of agency law, for the term "employer" is defined under Title VII to include "agents." In express terms, Congress has directed federal courts to interpret Title VII based on agency principles. Given such an explicit instruction, we conclude a uniform and predictable standard must be established as a matter of federal law. We rely on the general common law of agency, rather than on the law of any particular State, to give meaning to these terms. The resulting federal rule, based on a body of case law developed over time, is statutory interpretation pursuant to congressional direction. This is not federal common law in the strictest sense, i.e., a rule of decision that amounts, not simply to an interpretation of a federal statute, but, rather, to the judicial "creation" of a special federal rule of decision. State court decisions, applying state employment discrimination law, may be instructive in applying general agency principles, but, it is interesting to note, in many cases their determinations of employer liability under state law rely in large part on federal court decisions under Title VII.

As *Meritor* acknowledged, the Restatement (Second) of Agency (1957) (hereinafter Restatement), is a useful beginning point for a discussion of general agency principles. Since our decision in Meritor, federal courts have explored agency principles, and we find useful instruction in their decisions, noting that common-law principles may not be transferable in all their particulars to Title VII. * * *

A

Section 219(1) of the Restatement sets out a central principle of agency law:

> "A master is subject to liability for the torts of his servants committed while acting in the scope of their employment."

An employer may be liable for both negligent and intentional torts committed by an employee within the scope of his or her employment. Sexual harassment under Title VII presupposes intentional conduct. * * * The Restatement defines conduct, including an intentional tort, to be within the scope of employment when "actuated, at least in part, by a purpose to serve the [employer]," even if it is forbidden by the employer. * * *

As Courts of Appeals have recognized, a supervisor acting out of gender-based animus or a desire to fulfill sexual urges may not be actuated by a purpose to serve the employer. The harassing supervisor often acts for personal motives, motives unrelated and even antithetical to the objectives of the employer. There are instances, of course, where a supervisor engages in unlawful discrimination with the purpose, mistaken or otherwise, to serve the employer.

* * *

The general rule is that sexual harassment by a supervisor is not conduct within the scope of employment.

B

Scope of employment does not define the only basis for employer liability under agency principles. In limited circumstances, agency principles impose liability on employers even where employees commit torts outside the scope of employment. The principles are set forth in the much-cited § 219(2) of the Restatement:

> "(2) A master is not subject to liability for the torts of his servants acting outside the scope of their employment, unless:

"(a) the master intended the conduct or the consequences, or

"(b) the master was negligent or reckless, or

"(c) the conduct violated a non-delegable duty of the master, or

"(d) the servant purported to act or to speak on behalf of the principal and there was reliance upon apparent authority, or he was aided in accomplishing the tort by the existence of the agency relation."

See also § 219, Comment e (Section 219(2) "enumerates the situations in which a master may be liable for torts of servants acting solely for their own purposes and hence not in the scope of employment").

Subsection (a) addresses direct liability, where the employer acts with tortious intent, and indirect liability, where the agent's high rank in the company makes him or her the employer's alter ego. None of the parties contend Slowik's rank imputes liability under this principle. There is no contention, furthermore, that a nondelegable duty is involved. So, for our purposes here, subsections (a) and (c) can be put aside.

Subsections (b) and (d) are possible grounds for imposing employer liability on account of a supervisor's acts and must be considered. Under subsection (b), an employer is liable when the tort is attributable to the employer's own negligence. Thus, although a supervisor's sexual harassment is outside the scope of employment because the conduct was for personal motives, an employer can be liable, nonetheless, where its own negligence is a cause of the harassment. An employer is negligent with respect to sexual harassment if it knew or should have known about the conduct and failed to stop it. Negligence sets a minimum standard for employer liability under Title VII; but Ellerth seeks to invoke the more stringent standard of vicarious liability.

Subsection 219(2)(d) concerns vicarious liability for intentional torts committed by an employee when the employee uses apparent authority (the apparent authority standard), or when the employee "was aided in accomplishing the tort by the existence of the agency relation" (the aided in the agency relation standard). As other federal decisions have done in discussing vicarious liability for supervisor harassment, we begin with §219(2)(d).

C

As a general rule, apparent authority is relevant where the agent purports to exercise a power that he or she does not have, as distinct from where the agent threatens to misuse actual power. In the usual case, a supervisor's harassment involves misuse of actual power, not the false impression of its existence. Apparent authority analysis therefore is inappropriate in this context. If, in the unusual case, it is alleged there is a false impression that the actor was a supervisor, when he in fact was not, the victim's mistaken conclusion must be a reasonable one. When a party seeks to impose vicarious liability based on an agent's misuse of delegated authority, the Restatement's aided in the agency relation rule, rather than the apparent authority rule, appears to be the appropriate form of analysis.

D

We turn to the aided in the agency relation standard. In a sense, most workplace tortfeasors are aided in accomplishing their tortious objective by the existence of the agency relation: Proximity and regular contact may afford a captive pool of potential victims. Were this to satisfy the aided in the agency relation standard, an employer would be subject to vicarious liability not only for all supervisor harassment, but also for all co-worker harassment, a result enforced by neither the EEOC nor any court of appeals to have considered the issue. The aided in the agency relation standard, therefore, requires the existence of something more than the employment relation itself.

At the outset, we can identify a class of cases where, beyond question, more than the mere existence of the employment relation aids in commission of the harassment: when a supervisor takes a tangible employment action against the subordinate. Every Federal Court of Appeals to have considered the question has found vicarious liability when a discriminatory act results in a tangible employment action. * * * Although few courts have elaborated how agency principles support this rule, we think it reflects a correct application of the aided in the agency relation standard.

In the context of this case, a tangible employment action would have taken the form of a denial of a raise or a promotion. The concept of a tangible employment action appears in numerous cases in the Courts of Appeals discussing claims involving race, age, and national origin discrimination, as well as sex discrimination. Without endorsing the specific results of those decisions, we think it prudent to import the concept of a tangible employment action for resolution of the vicarious liability issue we consider here. A tangible employment action constitutes a significant change in employment status, such as hiring, firing, failing to promote, reassignment with significantly different responsibilities, or a decision causing a significant change in benefits.

When a supervisor makes a tangible employment decision, there is assurance the injury could not have been inflicted absent the agency relation. A tangible employment action in most cases inflicts direct economic harm. As a general proposition, only a supervisor, or other person acting with the authority of the company, can cause this sort of injury. A co-worker can break a co-worker's arm as easily as a supervisor, and anyone who has regular contact with an employee can inflict psychological injuries by his or her offensive conduct. But one co-worker (absent some elaborate scheme) cannot dock another's pay, nor can one co-worker demote another. Tangible employment actions fall within the special province of the supervisor. The supervisor has been empowered by the company as a distinct class of agent to make economic decisions affecting other employees under his or her control.

Tangible employment actions are the means by which the supervisor brings the official power of the enterprise to bear on subordinates. A tangible employment decision requires an official act of the enterprise, a company act. The decision in most cases is documented in official company records, and may be subject to review by higher level supervisors. The supervisor often must obtain the imprimatur of the enterprise and use its internal processes.

For these reasons, a tangible employment action taken by the supervisor becomes for Title VII purposes the act of the employer. Whatever the exact contours of the aided in the agency relation standard, its requirements will always be met when a supervisor takes a tangible employment action against a subordinate. In that instance, it would be implausible to interpret agency principles to allow an employer to escape liability, as Meritor itself appeared to acknowledge.

Whether the agency relation aids in commission of supervisor harassment which does not culminate in a tangible employment action is less obvious. Application of the standard is made difficult by its malleable terminology, which can be read to either expand or limit liability in the context of supervisor harassment. On the one hand, a supervisor's power and authority invests his or her harassing conduct with a particular threatening character, and in this sense, a supervisor always is aided by the agency relation. On the other hand, there are acts of harassment a supervisor might commit which might be the same acts a co-employee would commit, and there may be some circumstances where the supervisor's status makes little difference.

It is this tension which, we think, has caused so much confusion among the Courts of Appeals which have sought to apply the aided in the agency relation standard to Title VII cases. The aided in the agency relation standard, however, is a developing feature of agency law, and we hesitate to render a definitive explanation of our understanding of the standard in an area where other important considerations must affect our judgment. In particular, we are bound by our holding in *Meritor* that agency principles constrain the imposition of vicarious liability in cases of supervisory harassment. Congress has not altered *Meritor*'s rule even though it has made significant amendments to Title VII in the interim.

Although *Meritor* suggested the limitation on employer liability stemmed from agency principles, the Court acknowledged other considerations might be relevant as well. For example, Title VII is designed to encourage the creation of antiharassment policies and effective grievance mechanisms. Were employer liability to depend in part on an employer's effort to create such procedures, it would effect Congress' intention to promote conciliation rather than litigation in the Title VII context, and the EEOC's policy of encouraging the development of grievance procedures. To the extent limiting employer liability could encourage employees to report harassing conduct before it becomes severe or pervasive, it would also serve Title VII's deterrent purpose. As we have observed, Title VII borrows from tort law the avoidable consequences doctrine, and the considerations which animate that doctrine would also support the limitation of employer liability in certain circumstances.

In order to accommodate the agency principles of vicarious liability for harm caused by misuse of supervisory authority, as well as Title VII's equally basic policies of encouraging forethought by employers and saving action by objecting employees, we adopt the following holding in this case and in Faragher v. Boca Raton, also decided today. An employer is subject to vicarious liability to a victimized employee for an actionable hostile environment created by a supervisor with immediate (or successively higher) authority over the employee. When no tangible employment action is taken, a defending employer may raise an affirmative defense to liability or damages, subject to proof by a preponderance of the evidence. The defense comprises two necessary elements: (a) that the employer exercised reasonable care to prevent and correct promptly any sexually harassing behavior, and (b) that the plaintiff employee unreasonably failed to take advantage of any preventive or corrective opportunities provided by the employer or to avoid harm otherwise. While proof that an employer had promulgated an anti-harassment policy with complaint procedure is not necessary in every instance as a matter of law, the need for a stated policy suitable to the employment circumstances may appropriately be addressed in any case when litigating the first element of the defense. And while proof that an employee failed to fulfill the corresponding obligation of reasonable care to avoid harm is not limited to showing any unreasonable failure to use any complaint procedure provided by the employer, a demonstration of such failure will normally suffice to satisfy the employer's burden under the second element of the defense. No affirmative defense is available, however, when the supervisor's harassment culminates in a tangible employment action, such as discharge, demotion, or undesirable reassignment.

IV

Relying on existing case law which held out the promise of vicarious liability for all *quid pro quo* claims, Ellerth focused all her attention in the Court of Appeals on proving her claim fit within that category. Given our explanation that the labels *quid pro quo* and hostile work environment are not controlling for purposes of establishing employer liability, Ellerth should have an adequate opportunity to prove she has a claim for which Burlington is liable.

Although Ellerth has not alleged she suffered a tangible employment action at the hands of Slowik, which would deprive Burlington of the availability of the affirmative defense, this is not dispositive. In light of our decision, Burlington is still subject to vicarious liability for Slowik's activity, but Burlington should have an opportunity to assert and prove the affirmative defense to liability.

For these reasons, we will affirm the judgment of the Court of Appeals, reversing the grant of summary judgment against Ellerth. On remand, the District Court will have the opportunity to decide whether it would be appropriate to allow Ellerth to amend her pleading or supplement her discovery. * * *

[Justice Ginsburg's concurring judgment is omitted.]

MR. JUSTICE THOMAS, with whom Justice Scalia joins, dissenting.

The Court today manufactures a rule that employers are vicariously liable if supervisors create a sexually hostile work environment, subject to an affirmative defense that the Court barely attempts to define. This rule applies even if the employer has a policy against sexual harassment, the employee knows about that policy, and the employee never informs anyone in a position of authority about the supervisor's conduct. As a result, employer liability under Title VII is judged by different standards depending upon whether a sexually or racially hostile work environment is alleged. The standard of employer liability should be the same in both instances: An employer should be liable if, and only if, the plaintiff proves that the employer was negligent in permitting the supervisor's conduct to occur.

I

* * *

In race discrimination cases, employer liability has turned on whether the plaintiff has alleged an adverse employment consequence, such as firing or demotion, or a hostile work environment. If a supervisor takes an adverse employment action because of race, causing the employee a tangible job detriment, the employer is vicariously liable for resulting damages. This is because such actions are company acts that can be performed only by the exercise of specific authority granted by the employer, and thus the supervisor acts as the employer. If, on the other hand, the employee alleges a racially hostile work environment, the employer is liable only for negligence: that is, only if the employer knew, or in the exercise of reasonable care should have known, about the harassment and failed to take remedial action. Liability has thus been imposed only if the employer is blameworthy in some way.

This distinction applies with equal force in cases of sexual harassment. When a supervisor inflicts an adverse employment consequence upon an employee who has rebuffed his advances, the supervisor exercises the specific authority granted to him by his company. His acts, therefore, are the company's acts and are properly chargeable to it.

If a supervisor creates a hostile work environment, however, he does not act for the employer. As the Court concedes, a supervisor's creation of a hostile work environment is neither within the scope of his employment, nor part of his apparent authority. Indeed, a hostile work environment is antithetical to the interest of the employer. In such circumstances, an employer should be liable only if it has been negligent. That is, liability should attach only if the employer either knew, or in the exercise of reasonable care should have known, about the hostile work environment and failed to take remedial action.

* * *

Under a negligence standard, Burlington cannot be held liable for Slowick's conduct. Although respondent alleged a hostile work environment, she never contended that Burlington had been negligent in permitting the harassment to occur, and there is no question that Burlington acted reasonably under the circumstances. The company had a policy against sexual harassment, and respondent admitted that she was aware of the policy but nonetheless failed to tell anyone with authority over Slowick about his behavior. Burlington therefore cannot be charged with knowledge of Slowick's alleged harassment or with a failure to exercise reasonable care in not knowing about it.

II

Rejecting a negligence standard, the Court instead imposes a rule of vicarious employer liability, subject to a vague affirmative defense, for the acts of supervisors who wield no delegated authority in creating a hostile work environment. This rule is a whole-cloth creation that draws no support from the legal principles on which the Court claims it is based. Compounding its error, the Court fails to explain how employers can rely upon the affirmative defense, thus ensuring a continuing reign of confusion in this important area of the law.

In justifying its holding, the Court refers to our comment in *Meritor* that the lower courts should look to "agency principles" for guidance in determining the scope of employer liability. The Court then interprets the term "agency principles" to mean the Restatement (Second) of Agency. The Court finds two portions of the Restatement to be relevant: § 219(2)(b), which provides that a master is liable for his servant's torts if the master is reckless or negligent, and §219(2)(d), which states that a master is liable for his servant's torts when the servant is "aided in accomplishing the tort by the existence of the agency relation." The Court appears to reason that a supervisor is "aided . . . by . . . the agency relation" in creating a hostile work environment because the supervisor's "power and authority invests his or her harassing conduct with a particular threatening character."

Section 219(2)(d) of the Restatement provides no basis whatsoever for imposing vicarious liability for a supervisor's creation of a hostile work environment. Contrary to the Court's suggestions, the principle embodied in § 219(2)(d) has nothing to do with a servant's "power and authority," nor with whether his actions appear "threatening." Rather, as demonstrated by the Restatement's illustrations, liability under § 219(2)(d) depends upon the plaintiff's belief that the agent acted in the ordinary course of business or within the scope of his apparent authority. In this day and age, no sexually harassed employee can reasonably believe that a harassing supervisor is conducting the official business of the company or acting on its behalf. Indeed, the Court admits as much in demonstrating why sexual harassment is not committed within the scope of a supervisor's employment and is not part of his apparent authority.

Thus although the Court implies that it has found guidance in both precedent and statute — its holding is a product of willful policymaking, pure and simple. The only agency principle that justifies imposing employer liability in this context is the principle that a master will be liable for a servant's torts if the master was negligent or reckless in permitting them to occur; and as noted, under a negligence standard, Burlington cannot be held liable.

The Court's decision is also in considerable tension with our holding in *Meritor* that employers are not strictly liable for a supervisor's sexual harassment. Although the Court recognizes an affirmative defense — based solely on its divination of Title VII's *gestalt* — it provides shockingly little guidance about how employers can actually avoid vicarious liability. Instead, it issues only Delphic pronouncements and leaves the dirty work to the lower courts. * * * What [this] mean[s] for district courts ruling on motions for summary judgment — the critical question for employers now subject to the vicarious liability rule — remains a mystery. Moreover, employers will be liable notwithstanding the affirmative defense, even though they acted reasonably, so long as the plaintiff in question fulfilled her duty of reasonable care to avoid harm. In practice, therefore, employer liability very well may be the rule. But as the Court acknowledges, this is the one result that it is clear Congress did not intend.

The Court's holding does guarantee one result: There will be more and more litigation to clarify applicable legal rules in an area in which both practitioners and the courts have long been begging for guidance. It thus truly boggles the mind that the Court can claim that its holding will effect "Congress' intention to promote conciliation rather than litigation in the Title VII context." All in all, today's decision is an ironic result for a case that generated eight separate opinions in the Court of Appeals on a fundamental question, and in which we granted certiorari "to assist in defining the relevant standards of employer liability."

* * * I would restore parallel treatment of employer liability for racial and sexual harassment and hold an employer liable for a hostile work environment only if the employer is truly at fault. I therefore respectfully dissent.

NOTES AND PROBLEMS FOR DISCUSSION

1. To learn more about the story behind the Court's ruling in *Burlington*, see Michael C. Harper & Joan Flynn, *The Story of Burlington Industries v. Ellerth and Faragher v.*

City of Boca Raton: Federal Common Lawmaking for the Modern Age, EMPLOYMENT DISCRIMINATION STORIES 225 (Joel Wm. Friedman, ed. 2006).

2. The Supreme Court reiterated its new policy concerning employer vicarious liability for acts of supervisorial harassment (*Burlington* did not address the standard for imposing vicarious liability upon employers for acts of harassment by co-workers) in FARAGHER v. CITY OF BOCA RATON, 524 U.S. 775, 118 S.Ct. 2275, 141 L.Ed.2d 662 (1998), decided the same day as *Burlington*. There, the defendant City had adopted a sexual harassment policy, but had not disseminated its policy among the members of the department whose supervisors were charged by the plaintiff with creating a hostile environment. The Court ruled that by failing to disseminate its policy to these supervisors, the City had not exercised reasonable care to prevent the supervisors' harassing conduct as a matter of law. Consequently, since the City could not establish this prong of its affirmative defense, the Court reinstated the district court's judgment holding the City liable for the harassment suffered by the plaintiff.

Nevertheless, the mere fact that an employer's anti-harassment policy was adequately disseminated amongst its employees and supervisors will not be sufficient, standing alone, to establish the "defendant's non-negligence" strand of the affirmative defense available in cases of supervisorial harassment not involving a tangible employment practice. The disseminated policy must also be shown to be valid and effective. *See* Watson v. Blue Circle Inc., 324 F.3d 1252 (11th Cir.2003). And in EEOC v. V&J FOODS, INC., 507 F.3d 575 (7th Cir. 2007), the court ruled that although "an employer is not required to tailor its complaint procedure to the competence of each individual employee," where the defendant fast food restaurant operator's business plan called for the hiring of teenagers, the company was obligated "to suit its procedures to the understanding of the average teenager." It also stated that an anti-harassment policy that does not guarantee that a harassing supervisor can be bypassed in the complaint process is unreasonable as a matter of law.

3. Although the Supreme Court in *Burlington* went to great pains to downplay the importance of the *quid pro quo* and hostile environment categories in assessing employer liability, how different is this new "uniform and predictable" national formulation of the governing agency standard?

(a) The Court in *Burlington* announced that in cases of retaliation by a supervisor involving a "tangible employment action", the employer will be strictly liable. Some courts have gone one step further and held that the perpetrator must not only be a supervisor but must be the plaintiff's supervisor, i.e., must have the authority to directly affect the terms and conditions of the plaintiff's employment. *See, e.g.*, Rhodes v. Ill. Dep't of Transp., 359 F.3d 498 (7th Cir.2004).

The Court noted that the *quid pro* quo/hostile environment analytical categories were "helpful, perhaps, in making a rough demarcation between cases in which threats are carried out and those where they are not or are absent altogether but beyond this are of limited utility." But is there any difference between the antecedent *quid pro quo* analysis and this newly articulated tangible employment action criterion? After all, isn't the answer to the sole question raised in the petition for a writ of *certiorari* — whether a plaintiff alleging an unfulfilled threat of retaliation could state a claim of *quid pro quo* harassment — the same under either standard?

Where the supervisor occupies a sufficiently elevated position in the management hierarchy that he or she is deemed the proxy of the company, these courts have applied the absolute liability standard and barred the defendant from invoking the *Burlington* affirmative defense. *See, e.g.*, Townsend v. Benjamin Enterprises, Inc., 679 F.3d 41 (2d Cir. 2012); Ackel v. National Communications, Inc., 339 F.3d 376 (5th Cir.2003).

(b) Where the supervisory harassment does *not* produce a tangible job detriment, however, *Burlington* did produce a significant change in the standard used to impose employer liability. Previously, the plaintiff had to establish the employer's negligence by proving that it knew or should have known about the harassment and failed to take prompt remedial action. Under *Burlington*, the employer is now held strictly liable, subject, however, to an affirmative defense as to which it must establish that it was non-negligent, i.e., that it "exercised reasonable care to prevent and correct promptly any sexually harassing behavior" *and* that the plaintiff was negligent (she "unreasonably failed to take advantage of any preventive or corrective opportunities provided by the employer or to avoid harm otherwise").

4. The majority in *Burlington* defined a "tangible employment action" as "a significant change in employment status, such as hiring, firing, failing to promote, reassignment with significantly different responsibilities, or a decision causing a significant change in benefits." Since the presence of a tangible employment action is now the focal point for determining whether or not a defendant can invoke the affirmative defense in cases involving supervisorial harassment, the lower courts have been flooded with cases that turn on the meaning of this term.

(a) Judy Allen alleged that she was assigned extra work, given inappropriate work assignments, and denied the opportunity to attend a professional conference as a result of her rejection of her supervisor's sexual advances. Will the employer be absolutely liable or can it assert a *Burlington* affirmative defense? *Compare* Reinhold v. Commonwealth of Virginia, 151 F.3d 172 (4th Cir. 1998) (these consequences did not amount to a tangible employment practice because they were not akin to a demotion or a reassignment entailing significantly different job responsibilities), *with* Durham Life Insurance Co. v. Evans, 166 F.3d 139 (3d Cir. 1999) (the firing of the plaintiff's secretary, the loss of the plaintiff's private office, and the removal of certain files from her office each constituted a tangible employment action because the use of a secretary and a private office were specific, negotiated conditions of the plaintiff's employment contract with the defendant firm, and were essential to sustain her successful job performance; the disappearance of the plaintiff's files substantially decreased her earning potential and caused significant disruption in her working conditions).

(b) Suppose a plaintiff either (1) submits to her supervisor's sexual demands in order to avoid a threatened discharge, or (2) calls the supervisor's bluff by refusing to accede to his demands, whereupon he fails to carry out his threat. Has a tangible employment action occurred in either or both of these situations? In JIN v. METROPOLITAN LIFE INSURANCE CO., 295 F.3d 335 (2d Cir.2002), the Second Circuit recognized a clear distinction. In *Jin*, the plaintiff appealed the trial court's refusal to include in its jury instructions, among the list of tangible employment actions, the supervisor's explicit conditioning the retention of her job upon submission to his sexual demands. The jury found that the plaintiff had been subjected to proscribed sexual harassment, but that this harassment did not result in a tangible employment action. This meant that the defendant could assert the affirmative defense. Since the jury also found that the defendant had established both portions of its affirmative defense, it rendered a verdict for the defendant. The appellate court vacated the judgment entered upon the verdict, ruling that the trial court had erred in defining tangible employment action too narrowly in its jury instructions. The Second Circuit concluded that if a supervisor makes an employment-related decision based on the subordinate's submission to the supervisor's sexual demands, that decision constitutes a tangible employment action. Consequently, the court ruled, the trial court's refusal to instruct the jury that submission to a supervisor's threat conditioning continued employment on meeting his sexual demands qualified as an adverse employment action constituted prejudicial error and the plaintiff was entitled to a new trial. The Second Circuit distinguished the instant situation from *Burlington,* where the plaintiff had been able to resist the supervisor's demands (i.e., there was no submission) and the threat was *not* carried out. Because that scenario involved neither a submission nor an decision that affected the plaintiff's terms and conditions of employment, the Second Circuit reasoned, the plaintiff could not establish the presence of a tangible employment action. .

(c) Does a constructive discharge constitute a tangible employment action? Under well established labor law principles, if an employee can establish that her working conditions have been rendered so intolerable that a reasonable person in her position would feel compelled to resign, the employee's decision is treated, for remedial purposes, like an actual discharge and not a voluntary resignation. Does this mean that a constructive discharge resulting from supervisorial harassment constitutes a "tangible employment action" in terms of determining the availability of the *Burlington* affirmative defense?

The Supreme Court answered this question in PENNSYLVANIA STATE POLICE v. SUDERS, 542 U.S. 129, 124 S.Ct. 2342, 159 L.Ed.2d 204 (2004). The plaintiff, a police communications operator with the literary name of Nancy Drew Suders, alleged that several of her supervisors had subjected her to a barrage of harassing comments and actions. She reached out to the department's EEOC officer for assistance, but after telling the officer that she was being harassed, the plaintiff never followed up by filing a formal complaint. Neither did the EEOC officer make any effort to pursue the matter, other than to advise the plaintiff to file a complaint. Two days after this conversation, however, Suders' supervisors arrested her for theft, after which she resigned from the police force. She subsequently filed a VII action against the state police department, alleging, *inter alia*, that she had been the victim of sexual harassment that resulted in a constructive discharge. Although the trial court acknowledged that the plaintiff had introduced evidence from which a jury could find that the supervisors had created a hostile work environment, it granted the defendant's motion for summary judgment on the ground that a constructive discharge did not constitute a tangible employment practice and, therefore, that the employer could, and did, establish both elements of the *Burlington* affirmative defense. The Third Circuit overturned the dismissal of the plaintiff's claim, ruling that a constructive discharge was the functional equivalent of an actual discharge and, therefore, constituted a tangible employment practice as a matter of law. This, in turn, meant that the defendant could not invoke the *Burlington* affirmative defense. But since there were material issues of fact concerning whether or not the plaintiff had been constructively discharged, the appellate court ordered the case remanded for trial.

In an 8-1 opinion authored by Justice Ginsburg, the Supreme Court rejected the Third Circuit's ruling that a constructive discharge, if established, constituted a tangible employment practice as a matter of law. After acknowledging that the doctrine of constructive discharge, formulated in cases arising under the National Labor Relations Act, was also applicable to Title VII claims, and that "a constructive discharge is functionally the same as an actual termination in damages-enhancing respects," the majority ruled that proof of a constructive discharge was not independently determinative of whether or not the plaintiff's harassment had resulted in a tangible employment practice.

The fact that the plaintiff had been constructively discharged, the Court explained, while relevant to the type of damages available if she prevailed, was not germane to determining whether or not the alleged harassment had resulted in a tangible employment practice. The Court, instead, narrowly defined "tangible employment practice" to include only an "official act" of the employer. Consequently, since, by definition, the employer in a constructive discharge case did not affirmatively terminate the plaintiff's employment, the fact of her harassment did not transform her resignation into an official act by the enterprise. Rather, the Court reasoned, the proper focus of attention was the harassing conduct that gave rise to the constructive discharge. Only if the plaintiff could establish that the constructive discharge was precipitated by some other tangible employment action attributable to a supervisor, such as a demeaning demotion, reduction in salary, or transfer to a significantly inferior position, would the defendant be precluded from asserting the affirmative defense. "Absent such an official act," the Court reasoned, "the extent to which the supervisor's misconduct has been aided by the agency relation * * * is less certain. That uncertainty * * * justifies affording the employer the chance to establish, through the * * * affirmative defense, that it should not be held vicariously liable." The Court also noted that the fact that constructive discharge was not included in *Burlington*'s list of examples of tangible employment actions was "conspicuous" and "telling". Having determined that the Third Circuit had erred in concluding that the affirmative defense should never be available to the employer in constructive discharge cases, the Court remanded the case for determination of whether or not the constructive discharge was the product of some other tangible employment action.

5.   In order to establish the first of the two components of the affirmative defense erected in *Burlington*, an employer must prove that it acted reasonably to both prevent and correct harassing behavior.

(a)   What does an employer have to do to satisfy the "prevention" component of this first portion of the affirmative defense? Is it sufficient for the employer to establish that it has an anti-harassment policy or must it do more such as ensure that a written copy of the policy is distributed to each employee? What about requiring managers and/or others to undergo sexual harassment training? See DeBord v. Mercy Health System of Kansas, Inc., 737 F.3d 642 (10th Cir. 2013), cert. denied, 134 S.Ct. 2664, 189 L.Ed.1d 210 (2014) (an employer has acted reasonably as a matter of law to prevent harassment if it adopted a valid sexual harassment policy and distributed the policy to employees, even if it did not provide sexual harassment training to managers or to anyone else).

(b) In determining whether an employer has fulfilled its duty to promptly "correct" any harassing behavior, the courts typically look to see whether the defendant's response was "reasonably calculated to end the harassment," with the level of response assessed proportionately to the seriousness of the offense and with an eye towards whether it was likely to stop the harassment by the person who engaged in it. This usually means that a simple request to refrain from further harassing conduct will not be viewed as a sufficient response. A few circuit courts, however, also consider whether the remedial action is likely to dissuade other potential harassers from engaging in such conduct. See, e.g., Mockler v. Multnomah County, 140 F.3d 808 (9th Cir. 1998).

But suppose an employee who believes that she was the victim of supervisory harassment that did not involve a tangible employment action files a harassment claim but, to avoid being subjected to rumors and furtive glances, asks the person charged with processing these claims to keep the matter entirely confidential and to refrain from taking action for a prescribed period of time, what are the consequences to the company if it chooses to honor this request? In TORRES v. PISANO, 116 F.3d 625 (2d Cir. 1997), cert. denied, 522 U.S. 997, 118 S.Ct. 563, 139 L.Ed.2d 404 (1997), the court concluded that whether the company will be found to have fulfilled its duty to prevent and correct harassment by honoring such a request would depend upon the circumstances. Noting that "there is certainly a point at which harassment becomes so severe that a reasonable employer simply cannot stand by, even if requested to do so by a terrified employee," the court concluded that the instant case did not fall into that category since there was no evidence or allegation that any serious physical or psychological harm resulted from the employer's failure to take immediate action. Moreover, the court explained, it was not prepared to presume that every victim of harassment is unable to know what is best for him or herself and is incapable of making a reasonable decision to delay pursuing a harassment claim. Finally, the court added, although an employer would not be entitled to abide by one employee's request for confidentiality and/or delay in a case in light of its duty to its other employees where the supervisor charged with harassment was also allegedly victimizing other employees, that was not the situation in the instant case.

6. With respect to the second element of the *Burlington* affirmative defense — the plaintiff's *unreasonable* failure "to take advantage of any preventive or corrective opportunities provided by the employer or to avoid harm" — the *Burlington* Court noted that a demonstration of the plaintiff's failure to use the company's complaint procedure "will normally suffice to satisfy the employer's burden". But what about an unreasonable delay in taking advantage of the employer's anti-harassment policy? In TAYLOR v. SOLIS, 571 F.3d 1313 (D.C. Cir. 2009), a divided panel held that a plaintiff who did not report the alleged harassment for five or six months but, instead, only posted a copy of the company's anti-harassment policy on her office door, had not acted reasonably and, therefore, upheld a grant of summary judgment to the employer based on its successful assertion of the *Burlington* affirmative defense.

Under what circumstances might proof of the plaintiff's failure to utilize the extant complaint procedure not satisfy the defendant's burden as a matter of law? *See* Leopold v. Baccarat, Inc., 239 F.3d 243 (2d Cir. 2001) (the affirmative defense does not survive where the plaintiff can prove that she had a credible fear that her complaint would not be taken seriously or that she would suffer some adverse action as a result of filing a complaint as long as that showing is based on more than the employee's subjective belief; objective evidence must be produced showing that the employer has previously ignored or resisted similar complaints or has taken adverse actions against complainants in response to such complaints); Monteagudo v. AEELA, 554 F.3d 164 (1st Cir. 2009) (although there is no bright line rule as to when failure to report is reasonable, "more than ordinary fear or embarrassment is needed"; fact that complaint recipient was friendly and went out drinking with alleged harasser and that the plaintiff was substantially younger than alleged harasser was a sufficient basis for jury to conclude that failure to report was reasonable). Moreover, note that this second half of the affirmative defense consists of two clauses: (1) "the plaintiff employee unreasonably failed to take advantage of any preventive or corrective opportunities provided by the employer" and (2) "to avoid harm otherwise". Does a focus solely on the plaintiff's failure to timely invoke the extant anti-harassment policy suggest that the courts are disregarding the "avoid harm otherwise" component of the plaintiff's obligation? For a suggestion that most courts either conflate these two components into one (the "failure to take advantage" option) or simply disregard the "avoid harm otherwise" language and an exploration of other ways of giving meaning to this term, see Margaret E. Johnson, *"Avoiding Harm Otherwise": Reframing Women Employees' Responses to the Harms of Sexual Harassment*, 80 TEMP.L.REV. 743 (2007).

In GORZYNSKI v. JETBLUE AIRWAYS CORP., 596 F.3d 93 (2d Cir. 2010), the district court had granted summary judgment to the defense based on the *Burlington* affirmative defense. The trial judge had concluded that the plaintiff's decision to complain about an allegedly hostile work environment only to her supervisor, who was both the alleged harasser and one of the persons listed in the company's written sexual harassment policy as a proper recipient of complaints, and to not pursue alternative options listed in that policy, was unreasonable as a matter of law. The Second Circuit reversed, concluding that it was error to interpret *Burlington* to mean that a plaintiff "must go from manager to manager until they find someone who will address their complaints." Rather, the court concluded, the determination of whether a plaintiff acted reasonably was an issue of fact that must be resolved on an ad hoc basis. It suggested that where there are other channels that are adequately indicated and accessible and open, it could be deemed unreasonable for the victim of harassment to complain only to the harasser. On the other hand, it noted, where the evidence suggest that alternative recipients have proven unreceptive to receiving complaints, the trier of fact could determine that complaining only to the alleged harasser was reasonable. Since, in the instant case, there was evidence that an alternative recipient had proven unreceptive to receiving complaints, the Second Circuit ruled that the plaintiff had established a fact question as to whether she had acted reasonably in complaining only to her harasser. Consequently, it reversed the grant of summary judgment and remanded for further proceedings.

Suppose that a company's anti-harassment policy, with which the plaintiff is fully aware, provided a list of supervisors to whom employees could report instances of alleged harassment, one of which was the supervisor of the plaintiff's immediate supervisor's. Further assume that the plaintiff informed this person that her supervisor had harassed her. Instead of investigating, that second level supervisor began harassing the plaintiff. The plaintiff filed no further claims against her immediate supervisor and no claim whatsoever against the second level supervisor. The company acknowledges that the plaintiff has established a claim of hostile environment harassment, but asserts its affirmative defense. The plaintiff alleges that the second level supervisor has an informal policy, known to all employees, that no one is to "go over his head" with any complaint. Should the defendant prevail on its affirmative defense? *See* Wyatt v. Hunt Plywood Co., 297 F.3d 405 (5th Cir.2002) (the plaintiff's alleged concern over the supervisor's informal policy of not permitting subordinates to go over his head did not excuse her failure to disclose harassment to a higher authority listed on the company's anti-harassment policy as an authorized recipient of harassment claims).

7.   Since the alleged harassers in both *Burlington* and *Faragher* were supervisors, neither of these rulings had any impact on the pre-existing jurisprudence that had developed post-*Meritor* concerning co-employee harassment. By definition, co-employee harassment can only take the form of hostile environment harassment since co-employees are not in a position to subject other co-workers to any form of retribution that would rise to the level of a tangible employment practice. In such cases, the plaintiff must establish the employer's negligence in order to subject it to liability for the harassing conduct of its nonsupervisory personnel. Specifically, the plaintiff must prove that the defendant had actual or constructive knowledge of the harassment and failed to take prompt and appropriate corrective action. Thus, while employer liability in supervisorial cases is based on (strict) vicarious liability, employer liability for co-employee harassment is based on proof of the employer's primary negligence in failing to take prompt remedial action to acts of harassment that are or should have been known to it. This analytical distinction led the Ninth Circuit, in SWINTON v. POTOMAC CORP., 270 F.3d 794 (9th Cir.2001, cert. denied, 535 U.S. 1018, 122 S.Ct. 1609, 152 L.Ed.2d 623 (2002), to conclude that the *Burlington* affirmative defense was available only in cases based on vicarious liability, i.e., cases involving supervisorial harassment. Where, on the other hand, the alleged harasser is a co-worker, and, therefore, employer liability is based on the employer's, rather than the individual harasser's negligence, the affirmative defense is unavailable. But, as the court acknowledged, whether or not the employer took appropriate remedial action is relevant in both situations. In cases of supervisorial harassment, it is part of the defendant's burden of establishing an affirmative defense and in cases of co-employee harassment it is part of the plaintiff's burden of proving negligence.

Although the Supreme Court has not weighed in directly on the standard governing employer liability in co-employee harassment cases, it has endorsed the uniform position taken by the circuit courts. In VANCE v. BALL STATE UNIVERSITY, 133 S.Ct. 2434, 186 L.Ed.2d 565 (2013), the Supreme Court addressed the other question left unanswered in *Burlington* and *Faragher*, i.e., who qualifies as a "supervisor" when determining employer liability in a sexual harassment case. In *Vance*, the Court explained that the standard for determining employer liability depends upon whether the alleged harasser was a "supervisor" or a "co-employee" since, it noted, where the harasser is only a co-employee, the employer will be liable only if the plaintiff proves that the employer was negligent in controlling working conditions. Since, by definition, a co-employee, unlike a supervisor, has not been delegated authority over another co-employee by the employer, the plaintiff must prove that the employer was negligent in order to subject the employer to liability for the acts of its harassing employees. This, in turn, requires the plaintiff to establish that the employer (1) knew or should have known of the harassing conduct; and (2) failed to take prompt and appropriate remedial action. The first of these two elements – constructive notice -- can be established by proof that the plaintiff provided management level personnel with information sufficient to raise a probability of the existence of harassment in the mind of a reasonable employer. *See e.g.*, Huston v. Proctor & Gamble, 568 F.3d 100 (3d Cir. 2009). Obviously, therefore, it is advantageous to the plaintiff for the alleged perpetrator to be classified as a supervisor so the plaintiff can take advantage of the strict liability standard governing such cases.

Consequently, it is critical to resolution of the employer liability issue in a sexual harassment claim to determine whether or not the alleged harasser was a "supervisor". In *Vance*, a 5-4 decision, the majority ruled that an employee is a "supervisor" for these purposes only when he or she was empowered by the employer to take tangible employment actions against the alleged victim. In so ruling, the Court expressly rejected what it termed the "nebulous" standard employed by the EEOC and some federal circuits which tied supervisory status simply to the ability to exercise significant direction over another worker's daily work. Although the majority acknowledged that "supervisor" has varying meanings both in colloquial usage and in the law, it criticized the EEOC's "open ended" standard as making supervisory status determinations dependent upon a highly case-specific evaluation of numerous factors rather than the more "easily workable" tangible employment-based standard that it chose to adopt. Under its chosen definition, the majority insisted, supervisory status typically could and would be resolved as a matter of law prior to trial, thereby simplifying the task of the jury at trial. Moreover, in response to the dissenters' claim that an employee possessing the power to direct another worker's tasks was capable of creating a hostile working environment, the majority noted that the same could be said of co-workers. Finally, the majority emphasized that its ruling did not leave workers unprotected against harassment by co-workers who possess the authority to create a hostile environment by assigning them unpleasant tasks. It simply requires such plaintiffs to prove employer negligence in order to recover under Title VII.

As the preceding paragraphs demonstrate, whether or not the alleged harassing employee was a "supervisor" dramatically affects the allocation of proof in a case not involving a tangible employment practice. In MACK v. OTIS ELEVATOR CO., 326 F.3d 116 (2d Cir.2003), the Second Circuit offered an expansive definition of "supervisor" in a sexual harassment case that did not involve a tangible employment practice. It rejected the approach taken by the trial court, which had been to focus on whether or not the alleged harasser had been delegated authority by the employer to make tangible employment practice decisions respecting the alleged victim, i.e., discharge, promotion, etc. The appellate court concluded that the trial court should have assessed whether the employer had given the supervisor authority that materially augmented his ability to create a hostile work environment for the alleged victim. The Second Circuit concluded that the alleged harasser met this standard because he controlled the plaintiff's work assignments and, as the senior employee on a work site remotely located from other work sites, there was no one superior to him whose continuing presence might have acted as a check on his misbehavior.

8. Since "employer" is defined in Title VII to include any "agent", can a supervisory employee or other "agent" be deemed the plaintiff's employer and, therefore, be sued and held liable in his or her individual capacity? In MILLER v. MAXWELL'S INTERNATIONAL, 991 F.2d 583 (9th Cir. 1993), a case reflective of the consensus view of the federal appellate courts, the Ninth Circuit rejected this suggestion, declaring that the "obvious purpose" of the agent provision was to codify the concept of *respondeat superior* liability vis-à-vis the company and not to subject individual employees to personal liability. The court also noted that the exemption of employers with less than fifteen employees from the coverage of Title VII reflected Congress' desire to shield small employers with limited resources from financial liability. It was inconceivable to the Ninth Circuit panel that this same Congress could desire to protect small entities and not individual workers. Thus, it concluded, civil liability under either Title VII or the ADEA was limited to employers and did not extend to individual agents of that employer who committed violations.

9. Can an employee state an actionable claim of harassment when she alleges that a non-employee committed the harassment in or out of the workplace? The courts have generally adopted the approach codified in the EEOC Guidelines, which state that an employer "may also be responsible for the acts of non-employees, with respect to sexual harassment of employees in the workplace, where the employer (or its agents or supervisory employees) knows or should have known of the conduct and fails to take immediate and appropriate corrective action. 29 C.F.R. §16011(e) (1985). In DUNN v. WASHINGTON COUNTY HOSPITAL, 429 F.3d 689 (7th Cir.2005), for example, a hospital nurse brought a Title VII claim against her employing hospital claiming that she had been subjected to sexual harassment by an independent contractor doctor. The trial judge granted summary judgment in favor of the defendant, ruling that the employer could not be held vicariously liable for the acts of those not under its control. A split Seventh Circuit reversed, holding that vicarious liability doctrine was irrelevant to the case since, under *Burlington*, employer liability in a case not involving supervisorial harassment was direct rather than derivative. Consequently, the majority declared, "it makes no difference whether the person whose acts are complained of is an employee, an independent contractor, or for that matter a customer. Ability to 'control' the actor plays no role." 429 F.3d at 691. The court concluded that when a supervisor is not the perpetrator, the employer is responsible for every discriminatory term or condition of employment that the employer fails to take reasonable care to prevent or redress, and the plaintiff bears the burden of showing that the employer knew or should have known of the discriminatory conduct and thereafter did not act reasonably to equalize working conditions. *See also* Lockard v. Pizza Hut, Inc., 162 F.3d 1062 (10th Cir. 1998) (an employer is liable for the harassing conduct of its customers under the same negligence theory applied to harassment by co-employees).

This third party harassment doctrine also has been extended to sexual harassment claims brought by prison employees against the prison employer based on its failure to remedy sexually harassing conduct by inmates. Additionally, these courts have ruled that just as in cases where the harasser is a co-employee (i.e., not a supervisor), the plaintiff must prove that the employer negligently failed to take corrective action of harassment by the non-employee (e.g., customer or prison inmate) that it knew or should have known about and that the *Burlington* affirmative defense is unavailable. *See e.g.*, Beckford v. Department of Corrections, 605 F.3d 951 (11th Cir. 2010).

Must the harassment actually have taken place within the physical confines of the workplace to constitute actionable harassment? Would your answer to that question depend upon whether the harassment was undertaken by a supervisor or a co-employee? In FERRIS v. DELTA AIR LINES, INC., 277 F.3d 128 (2d Cir.2001), cert. denied, 537 U.S. 824, 123 S.Ct. 110, 154 L.Ed.2d 34 (2002), a female flight attendant was raped by another member of her flight crew during a brief layover between flights in Italy in a hotel room booked and paid for by the airline. The trial court granted the defense motion for summary judgment on the ground that the attack in the male flight attendant's hotel room could not be found as a matter of law to have occurred in a work environment. The Second Circuit disagreed, reasoning that a layover in a hotel room booked and paid for by the employer could reasonably be found to have been a part of the plaintiff's work environment. The court, in a footnote, mentioned that although a few cases had held that cognizable sexual harassment could occur outside of the workplace, it distinguished each of these cases on the ground that they involved supervisorial harassment. The clear implication of the opinion is that since the plaintiff needed to prove that the airline knew or should have known of the harassment in order to hold it liable for this act of nonsupervisory harassment, the plaintiff had to establish that the inappropriate conduct occurred within the work environment, i.e., an environment under the company's control. Recognize, however, that this is a separate question from whether the off-workplace conduct was severe or pervasive enough to create a hostile environment.

10. Under 42 U.S.C. §1981A(a), a Title VII plaintiff can recover compensatory and punitive damages in cases of intentional discrimination when he or she "cannot recover under §1981." Since §1981 has been interpreted to be inapplicable to claims of sex-based discrimination, this requirement poses no difficulty for the claimant in a sexual harassment claim. But what about the plaintiff who asserts a claim of racial harassment? Presumably, since race-based discrimination is cognizable under §1981, the harassment plaintiff could file a claim under that statute. Is the plaintiff's refusal or failure to file a §1981 claim enough to satisfy the statutory requirement or is the "cannot recover" language of the 1991 Act intended merely to prevent double recovery and not to require an election of remedies? *See* Bradshaw v. Univ. of Maine System, 870 F.Supp. 406 (D. Me. 1994) (the purpose of the 1991 amendment was to prevent double recovery; the fact that the plaintiff could have plead a claim under §1981 "is no reason to bar his claim for damages" under §1981).

11. You will recall that §702 of Title VII immunizes religious institutions against claims of religious discrimination. Moreover, the statute's otherwise applicable prohibitions against discrimination on the bases of race, color, national origin, and sex are subject to the constitutionally based "ministerial exemption." Under this doctrine, to protect the relationship between a religious institution and its clergy from impermissible governmental interference, the First Amendment religion clauses have been construed to prohibit the application of Title VII to any decision by a religious institution that either concerns the selection of its religious functionaries (regardless of its motivation) or whose justification implicates religious doctrine. Suppose, then, a minister brings a Title VII claim against her church, seeking damages in connection with her claim that her supervisor subjected her to sexual harassment and that the church did nothing to respond to her complaints. Since this is not a claim of religious discrimination, the §702 exemption clearly is inapposite. But can the Church convince the court to dismiss the plaintiff's claim on the ground that it falls within the ministerial exemption?

In ELVIG v. CALVIN PRESBYTERIAN CHURCH, 375 F.3d 951 (9th Cir.2004), an ordained Associate Pastor alleged that she had been subjected to acts of sexual harassment by her supervisor, the Pastor of the defendant church. She also alleged that after she made a formal complaint to the church, the Pastor and the church engaged in a series of retaliatory actions consisting of relieving her of certain duties, suspending her, terminating her, and prohibiting her from circulating a resume to other Presbyterian churches to seek alternative employment. Her Title VII claim sought damages against the church for both the acts of harassment and retaliation.

With respect to her attempt to hold the church liable for the sexual harassment, the court explained that the ministerial exception prohibited it from examining any decision involving the selection of a minister, regardless of the reason behind that decision, in evaluating the merits of her harassment claim. Accordingly, because each of the four alleged tangible employment actions (relieving of duties, suspension, termination and prohibition of resume circulation) involved the selection of a minister, the court ruled that it could not consider any of these actions in assessing whether she had been the victim of unlawful harassment. However, the court added, since the alleged acts of harassment amounting to a hostile environment, i.e., the Pastor's conduct and not the church's response thereto, did not involve these four tangible employment actions, and since the Church did not assert that his allegedly harassing conduct was justified by religious doctrine, the ministerial exception did not preclude the plaintiff from stating a claim of hostile environment harassment against the church. Accordingly, it concluded, the plaintiff could prevail if she could satisfy the routine elements of a sexual harassment claim and if the defendant could not sustain both elements of the *Burlington* affirmative defense applicable to claims of supervisorial harassment not resulting in a tangible employment practice.

With respect to the retaliation claim, the split panel similarly ruled that the plaintiff could not rely on the four alleged acts of retaliation to sustain her claim since each of these adverse employment actions involved the choosing of a minister and thus fell within the ministerial exception. However, it added, the ministerial exception would not preclude the plaintiff from asserting a retaliation claim based on an adverse employment action that did not involve either the choosing of a minister or conduct justified on the basis of religious doctrine. Since the Church had not asserted that the Pastor's alleged acts of harassment were justified by religious doctrine, if the plaintiff's retaliation claim was limited to a charge that the retaliation took the form of the Pastor's sexual harassment that created only a hostile environment unaccompanied by a tangible employment action, her claim could proceed.

Alternatively, suppose a female employee of an indisputably religious institution claims that she has been subjected to harassment because of her religion. Can she state a claim under Title VII or does §702(e) immunize the defendant from a religiously-based harassment claim? In KENNEDY v. ST. JOSEPH's MINISTRIES, INC., 657 F.3d 189 (4th Cir. 2011), the plaintiff, a member of the Church of the Brethren, was employed as a nurse's assistant by a nursing home that was owned and operated by an order within the Roman Catholic Church. The plaintiff wore modest garb as a matter of religious principle. She was terminated after she refused to adhere to a supervisor's request to change her attire based on complaints from residents and their family members who reported that the plaintiff's attire made them feel uncomfortable. In response, she filed suit under Title VII, asserting claims of religious harassment and retaliatory harassment on the basis of religion. The trial court denied the defense motion to dismiss, finding that the harassment and retaliation claims were not barred by the §702(e) exemption. Noting that the exemption states that the antidiscrimination provision (§703(a)) shall not apply with respect to the "employment" of individuals because of religion, the Fourth Circuit concluded that the §702(e) exemption was intended by Congress to apply to all employment-related claims, including harassment and retaliation. The appellate panel rejected the defense claim that the exemption was limited to hiring and firing decisions. Since the harassment and retaliation all arose from the plaintiff's "employment", the court reasoned, the exemption applied as long as these decision were alleged to have been based on the plaintiff's religion. Accordingly, it reversed the trial court's order and directed it to enter judgment in favor of the defendant.

12. The standard of employer liability under Title VII for individual acts of harassment has been extended to harassment claims arising under other federal statutes as well. For example, the employee protection provisions of the Energy Reorganization Act of 1974, 42 U.S.C. §5851 (1994) ("ERA") prohibit employers from discriminating against employees in retaliation for engaging in protected whistle-blowing activity. The statute expressly requires a claimant to show establish that he suffered an adverse employment action as a result of his whistle-blowing activity. Nevertheless, in WILLIAMS v. ADMINISTRATIVE REVIEW BOARD, 376 F.3d 471 (5th Cir.2004), the Fifth Circuit held not only that the statute recognized a claim for hostile environment discrimination (i.e., harassment not resulting in a tangible employment practice), but that the *Burlington* standard for employer liability was similarly applicable to claims brought under the ERA.

5. DISCRIMINATION BY UNIONS

Disparate treatment claims may also be raised against unions. Section 703(c) sets forth three classes of prohibited union employment practices. The first two categories deal predominantly with actions taken by the union directly against either its members or membership applicants. Subsection (1), for example, makes it an lawful employment practice for a union "otherwise to discriminate against any individual" on the basis of the five proscribed classifications. Subsection (3), however, prohibits a union from doing anything to "cause or attempt to cause an employer" to violate the statute. These two provisions raise the interesting question of the extent of a union's duty to oppose employer discriminatory conduct. For example, does a union's acquiescence to, as opposed to participation in or instigation of, employer misconduct subject the union to liability? The Supreme Court had an opportunity to examine this problem in the following case.

Goodman v. Lukens Steel Company

Supreme Court of the United States, 1987.

482 U.S. 656, 107 S.Ct. 2617, 96 L.Ed.2d 572.

JUSTICE WHITE delivered the opinion of the Court.

In 1973, individual employees of Lukens Steel Company (Lukens) brought this suit on behalf of themselves and others, asserting racial discrimination claims under Title VII * * * against their employer and their collective-bargaining agents, the United Steelworkers of America and two of its local unions (Unions). After a bench trial, the District Court * * * concluded that the Unions were * * * guilty of discriminatory practices, specifically in failing to challenge discriminatory discharges of probationary employees, failing and refusing to assert instances of racial discrimination as grievances, and in tolerating and tacitly encouraging racial harassment. The District Court entered * * * injunctive orders against * * * the Unions, reserving damages issues for further proceedings. * * * [T]he Unions appealed, challenging the District Court's liability conclusions * * *.

The Court of Appeals * * * affirmed the liability judgment against the Unions. * * * The Unions' petition * * * claimed error in finding them liable under Title VII * * *.

* * *

II

* * *

The Unions contend that the judgment against them rests on the erroneous legal premise that Title VII * * * [is] violated if a Union passively sits by and does not affirmatively oppose the employer's racially discriminatory employment practices. It is true that the District Court declared that mere Union passivity in the face of employer discrimination renders the Union liable under Title VII * * *.[10] We need not discuss this rather abstract observation, for the court went on to say that the evidence proves "far more" than mere passivity.[11] As found by the court, the facts were that since 1965, the collective-bargaining contract contained an express clause binding both the employer and the Unions not to discriminate on racial grounds; that the employer

---

[10] * * * [T]his statement must have been addressed to disparate impact, for discriminatory motive is required in disparate treatment Title VII cases * * *. *See* Teamsters v. United States.

[11] The District Court commented that there was substantial evidence, related to events occurring prior to the statute of limitations period, which "casts serious doubt on the unions' total commitment to racial equality." The District Court noted that it was the company, not the Unions, which pressed for a nondiscrimination clause in the collective-bargaining agreement. The District Court found that the Unions never took any action over the segregated locker facilities at Lukens and did not complain over other discriminatory practices by the company. The District Court found that when one employee approached the president of one of the local unions to complain about the segregated locker facilities in 1962, the president dissuaded him from complaining to the appropriate state agency. The District Court, however, found "inconclusive" the evidence offered in support of the employees' claim that the Unions discriminated against blacks in their overall handling of grievances under the collective-bargaining agreement.

was discriminating against blacks in discharging probationary employees, which the Unions were aware of but refused to do anything about by way of filing proffered grievances or otherwise; that the Unions had ignored grievances based on instances of harassment which were indisputably racial in nature; and that the Unions had regularly refused to include assertions of racial discrimination in grievances that also asserted other contract violations.[12]

In affirming the District Court's findings against the Unions, the Court of Appeals also appeared to hold that the Unions had an affirmative duty to combat employer discrimination in the workplace. But it, too, held that the case against the Unions was much stronger than one of mere acquiescence in that the Unions deliberately chose not to assert claims of racial discrimination by the employer. It was the Court of Appeals' view that these intentional and knowing refusals discriminated against the victims who were entitled to have their grievances heard.

* * *

The Unions insist that it was error to hold them liable for not including racial discrimination claims in grievances claiming other violations of the contract. The Unions followed this practice, it was urged, because these grievances could be resolved without making racial allegations and because the employer would "get its back up" if racial bias was charged, thereby making it much more difficult to prevail. The trial judge, although initially impressed by this seemingly neutral reason for failing to press race discrimination claims, ultimately found the explanation "unacceptable" because the Unions also ignored grievances which involved racial harassment violating the contract covenant against racial discrimination but which did not also violate another provision. The judge also noted that the Unions had refused to complain about racially based terminations of probationary employees, even though the express undertaking not to discriminate protected this group of employees, as well as others, and even though, as the District Court found, the Unions knew that blacks were being discharged at a disproportionately higher rate than whites. In the judgment of the District Court, the virtual failure by the Unions to file any race-bias grievances until after this lawsuit started, knowing that the employer was practicing what the contract prevented, rendered the Unions' explanation for their conduct unconvincing.

As we understand it, there was no suggestion below that the Unions held any racial animus against or denigrated blacks generally. Rather, it was held that a collective bargaining agent could not, without violating Title VII, * * * follow a policy of refusing to file grievable racial discrimination claims however strong they might be and however sure the agent was that the employer was discriminating against blacks. The Unions, in effect, categorized racial grievances as unworthy of pursuit and, while pursuing thousands of other legitimate grievances, ignored racial discrimination claims on behalf of blacks, knowing that the employer was discriminating in violation of the contract. Such conduct, the courts below concluded, intentionally discriminated against blacks seeking a remedy for disparate treatment based on their race and

---

[12]The District Court also found that although the Unions had objected to the company's use of certain tests, they had never done so on racial grounds, even though they "were certainly chargeable with knowledge that many of the tests" had a racially disparate impact.

violated * * * Title VII * * *. As the District Court said, "A union which intentionally avoids asserting discrimination claims, either so as not to antagonize the employer and thus improve its chances of success on other issues, or in deference to the perceived desires of its white membership, is liable under * * * Title [VII] * * *, regardless of whether, as a subjective matter, its leaders were favorably disposed toward minorities."

The courts below, in our view, properly construed and applied Title VII * * *. Those provisions do not permit a union to refuse to file any and all grievances presented by a black person on the ground that the employer looks with disfavor on and resents such grievances. It is no less violative of * * * [this law] for a union to pursue a policy of rejecting disparate treatment grievances presented by blacks solely because the claims assert racial bias and would be very troublesome to process.

* * * [T]he judgment of the Court of Appeals is affirmed.

It is so ordered.

[Justice Brennan's opinion concurring with the majority's ruling that the Union violated Title VII is omitted.]

JUSTICE POWELL, with whom JUSTICE SCALIA joins, and with whom JUSTICE O'CONNOR joins as to Parts I through IV, concurring in part and dissenting in part.

* * * I dissent, however, from Part II of the Court's opinion, that affirms the judgment against the Unions for violating * * * Title VII * * *. The ambiguous findings of the District Court, accepted by the Court of Appeals for the Third Circuit, do not provide adequate support for the Court's conclusion that the Unions engaged in intentional discrimination against black members. Neither of the courts below specifically found that the Unions were motivated by racial animus, or that they are liable to black members under the alternate Title VII theory of disparate impact. Accordingly, I would remand to permit the District Court to clarify its findings of fact and to make additional findings if necessary.

I

Close examination of the findings of the District Court is essential to a proper understanding of this case. * * * The plaintiffs' allegations were directed primarily at the Unions' handling of grievances on behalf of black members. The District Court found that "[t]he steady increase in grievance filings each year has not produced a corresponding increase in the capacity of the grievance-processing system to handle complaints." Consequently, the court found, the Unions gave priority to "[s]erious grievances" — that is, "those involving more than a four-day suspension, and those involving discharges." In an effort to reduce the backlog of grievances, the Unions disposed of many less serious grievances by simply withdrawing them and reserving the right to seek relief in a later grievance proceeding. The District Court found "no hard evidence to support an inference that these inadequacies disadvantage blacks to a greater extent than whites." The incomplete evidence in the record suggests that the percentage of grievances filed on behalf of black employees was proportional to the number of blacks in the work force. Of the relatively few grievances that proceeded all the way to arbitration, the District Court found that the number asserted on behalf of black members was proportional to the number of blacks in the work force.

Moreover, black members had a slightly higher rate of success in arbitration than white members. In sum, the District Court found that "plaintiffs' generalized evidence concerning perceptions about racial inequities in the handling of grievances does not, without more, establish a prima facie case * * *."

The District Court concluded, however, that the plaintiffs were "on firmer ground" in challenging the Unions' "repeated failures, during the limitations period, to include racial discrimination as a basis for grievances or other complaints against the company." * * * The court found the Unions' explanation for this reluctance facially reasonable. The Unions observed that employees were more likely to obtain relief if a grievance based on racial discrimination was framed as a violation of another provision of the collective-bargaining agreement that did not require proof of racial animus. * * * The court nevertheless rejected the Unions' explanation, for two reasons. First, the court found that the Unions "virtually ignored" the "numerous instances of harassment, which were indisputably racial in nature, but which did not otherwise plainly violate a provision of the collective bargaining agreement." Second, the court concluded that "vigorous pursuit of claims of racial discrimination would have focused attention upon racial issues and compelled some change in racial attitudes," and that the Unions' "unwillingness to assert racial discrimination claims as such rendered the non-discrimination clause in the collective bargaining agreement a dead letter."

* * *

The Court of Appeals accepted each of the District Court's findings of fact and affirmed the judgment against the Unions. The appellate court concluded that the Unions' "deliberate choice not to process grievances" violated Title VII "because it discriminated against the victims who were entitled to representation." * * *

II

A

* * * [A] valid claim under Title VII must be grounded on proof of disparate treatment or disparate impact. A disparate treatment claim * * * requires proof of a discriminatory purpose. Of course, "discriminatory purpose" implies more than intent as volition or intent as awareness of consequences. It implies that the challenged action was taken at least in part "because of," not merely "in spite of," its adverse effects upon an identifiable group. The Court concedes that "there was no suggestion below that the Unions held any racial animus against or denigrated blacks generally." It nevertheless concludes that the Unions violated Title VII * * * because they "refuse[d] to file any and all grievances presented by a black person on the ground that the employer looks with disfavor on and resents such grievances," and "pursue[d] a policy of rejecting disparate treatment grievances presented by blacks solely because the claims assert racial bias and would be very troublesome to process." In my view, this description of the Union's conduct, and thus the Court's legal conclusion, simply does not fit the facts found by the District Court.

The Unions offered a nondiscriminatory reason for their practice of withdrawing grievances that did not involve a discharge or lengthy suspension. According to the Unions, this policy, that is racially neutral on its face, was motivated by the Unions' nondiscriminatory interest in using the inadequate grievance system to assist members who faced the most serious economic harm. The District Court made no finding that the Unions' explanation was a pretext for racial discrimination. * * * Similarly, the Unions' stated purpose for processing racial grievances on nonracial grounds — to obtain the swiftest and most complete relief possible for the claimant, was not racially invidious. The Unions opposed the use of tests that had a disparate impact on black members, although not on that ground. Their explanation was that more complete relief could be obtained by challenging the tests on nonracial grounds. The District Court made no finding that the Unions' decision to base their opposition on nonracial grounds was motivated by racial animus.[c] Absent a finding that the Unions intended to discriminate against black members, the conclusion that the Unions are liable under * * * the disparate treatment theory of Title VII is unjustified.

B

Although the District Court stated that the plaintiffs raised both disparate treatment and disparate impact claims, it did not make specific findings nor did it conclude that the plaintiffs are entitled to recover under a disparate impact theory. Indeed, the limited amount of statistical evidence discussed by the District Court indicates that the Unions' grievance procedures did not have a disparate impact on black members. Moreover, neither the District Court nor the Court of Appeals considered the validity of potential defenses to disparate impact claims. For example, before the court properly could have held the Unions liable on a disparate impact theory, the court should have considered whether the Unions' practices were justified by the doctrine of business — or union — necessity. See Griggs v. Duke Power Co. The court also should have considered arguments that some of the challenged practices, such as the Unions' refusal to pursue grievances of probationary employees, were justifiable as part of a bona fide seniority system.[d] Because this Court is reluctant to consider alternative theories of liability not expressly passed upon by the lower

---

[c]Of course, an inference of discriminatory intent may arise from evidence of objective factors, including the inevitable or foreseeable consequences of the challenged policy or practice. But when the impact is essentially an unavoidable consequence of a policy that has in itself always been deemed to be legitimate, the inference simply fails to ripen into proof.

The District Court did not expressly rely on any inference of racial animus drawn from the consequences of the Unions' grievance policies. Indeed, it appears that the District Court imposed liability for intentional discrimination without finding that the Unions acted, or failed to act, with the purpose of harming black members. The District Court's primary justification for imposing liability was that "mere union passivity in the face of employer-discrimination renders the unions liable under Title VII * * *." It then stated:

"Moreover, the evidence in this case proves far more than mere passivity on the part of the unions. The distinction to be observed is between a union which, through lethargy or inefficiency simply fails to perceive problems or is inattentive to their possible solution (in which case, at least arguably, the union's inaction has no connection with race) and a union which, aware of racial discrimination against some of its members, fails to protect their interests."

Far from inferring racial animus from the foreseeable consequences of the Unions' inaction, the District Court merely stated its view that union passivity — whether deliberate or inadvertent — is a basis for liability without regard to the Unions' purpose or intent.

[d]Although these defenses do not appear to have been raised by the Unions in courts below, this is not surprising in view of the fact that the plaintiffs did not present evidence or legal arguments to support a disparate impact theory.

courts, I would remand to the District Court to permit it to consider whether the Unions are liable under a disparate impact theory.

III

The Court does not reach the question whether a union may be held liable under Title VII for "mere passivity" in the face of discrimination by the employer, because it agrees with the courts below that the record shows more than mere passivity on the part of the Unions. I disagree with that conclusion, and so must consider whether the judgment can be affirmed on the ground that Title VII imposes an affirmative duty on unions to combat discrimination by the employer.

* * * Section 703(c) * * * does not suggest that the union has a duty to take affirmative steps to remedy employer discrimination. Section 703(c)(1) makes it unlawful for a union "to exclude or to expel from its membership, or otherwise to discriminate against, any individual because of his race, color, religion, sex, or national origin." This subsection parallels §703(a)(1), that applies to employers. This parallelism, and the reference to union membership, indicate that §703(c)(1) prohibits direct discrimination by a union against its members; it does not impose upon a union an obligation to remedy discrimination by the employer. Moreover, §703(c)(3) specifically addresses the union's interaction with the employer, by outlawing efforts by the union "to cause or attempt to cause an employer to discriminate against an individual in violation of this section." If Congress had intended to impose on unions a duty to challenge discrimination by the employer, it hardly could have chosen language more ill-suited to its purpose. * * * [T]he language of §703(c)(3) is taken *in haec verba* from §8(b)(2) of the National Labor Relations Act (NLRA). That provision of the NLRA has been held not to impose liability for passive acquiescence in wrongdoing by the employer. Indeed, well before the enactment of Title VII, the Court held that even encouraging or inducing employer discrimination is not sufficient to incur liability under §8(b)(2).

In the absence of a clear statement of legislative intent, the Court has been reluctant to read Title VII to disrupt the basic policies of the labor laws. Unquestionably an affirmative duty to oppose employer discrimination could work such a disruption. A union, unlike an employer, is a democratically controlled institution directed by the will of its constituents, subject to the duty of fair representation. Like other representative entities, unions must balance the competing claims of its constituents. A union must make difficult choices among goals such as eliminating racial discrimination in the workplace, removing health and safety hazards, providing better insurance and pension benefits, and increasing wages. * * * For these reasons unions are afforded broad discretion in the handling of grievances. Union members' suits against their unions may deplete union treasuries, and may induce unions to process frivolous claims and resist fair settlement offers. The employee is not without a remedy, because union members may file Title VII actions directly against their employers. I therefore would hold that Title VII imposes on unions no affirmative duty to remedy discrimination by the employer.

* * *

JUSTICE O'CONNOR, concurring in the judgment in No. 85-1626 and dissenting in No. 85-2010.

　　　* * * I join * * * Justice Powell's opinion * * *.

NOTES AND PROBLEMS FOR DISCUSSION

1. What is the bone of contention between the majority and dissenters in the principal case?

2. The collective bargaining agreement in *Goodman* contained an anti-discrimination clause. In the absence of such a clause, how should the courts deal with a Title VII claim against a union challenging the lawfulness of an allegedly discriminatory provision in a collective bargaining agreement? Several circuit courts have held, in general terms, that in negotiating a collective agreement, a union has an affirmative duty to bargain to try to eliminate discriminatory contractual provisions. In JACKSON v. SEABOARD COAST LINE RAILROAD CO., 678 F.2d 992 (11th Cir. 1982), for example, the court found the union in violation of Title VII primarily on the ground that it was a party to a collective agreement containing racially discriminatory terms. On the other hand, in TERRELL v. UNITED STATES PIPE & FOUNDRY CO., 644 F.2d 1112 (5th Cir. 1981), vacated and remanded for reconsideration on other grounds, 456 U.S. 968, 102 S.Ct. 2229, 72 L.Ed.2d 841 (1982), the Fifth Circuit examined the bargaining history that preceded the agreement to determine whether the union had taken every reasonable step to bring the contract's employment policies into compliance with the law. And in BURWELL v. EASTERN AIR LINES, INC., 633 F.2d 361 (4th Cir. 1980), the Fourth Circuit took the *Terrell* analysis one step further, holding that even where the union had not taken every such reasonable step, it could still avoid liability by establishing that it merely had acquiesced in a practice or provision that was imposed by the company and which it had no realistic power to stop. Applying the *Burwell* standard, the court in MARTINEZ v. OAKLAND SCAVENGER CO., 680 F.Supp. 1377, 1398-99 (N.D. Cal. 1987), held that where the union succeeded in narrowing the scope of a discriminatory provision (but not in removing it entirely from the contract), the union was not liable for this discriminatory practice. This court also ruled that where the bargaining history revealed that the union had sought to eliminate another discriminatory provision in the contract, but that the employer consistently had rejected its proposals, the union had made a bona fide attempt to eliminate the discriminatory practice and, therefore, was not liable under Title VII.

3. The labor law doctrine of a union's duty of fair representation has some application in the Title VII context. The duty of fair representation was read into §9 of the National Labor Relations Act as a corollary to the status enjoyed by unions under that provision as exclusive bargaining representative of all members of the bargaining unit. *See* Vaca v. Sipes, 386 U.S. 171, 87 S.Ct. 903, 17 L.Ed.2d 842 (1967). The duty requires the union to fairly and impartially represent all members of the bargaining unit and prohibits conduct found to be arbitrary, discriminatory, or in bad faith. Where the union's conduct is shown to be based on the individual member's race, religion, color, sex or national origin, such a breach of the duty of fair representation subjects the union to liability under Title VII.

4. Is a union subject to an affirmative statutory duty to prevent proscribed discrimination in the workplace? For example, can African-American workers state a Title VII claim against their union for failing to take any action after being informed of acts of racial harassment in the workplace? *See* EEOC v. Pipefitters Association Local Union 597, 334 F.3d 656 (7th Cir.2003) (union does not have an affirmative duty to prevent harassment or other form of unlawful discrimination in the workplace because the employer controls the workplace and, therefore, is in a better position than the union to prevent or eliminate harassment).

6. RETALIATION

The preceding subsections in this chapter have examined the way in which the courts have interpreted the broad language setting forth Title VII's general proscription against intentional discrimination in employment. The statute, however, also prohibits another, more specifically described form of job bias. Section 704(a) states:

> "It shall be an unlawful employment practice for an employer to discriminate against any of his employees or applicants for employment, for an employment agency, or joint labor-management committee controlling apprenticeship or other training * * * to discriminate against any individual, or for a labor organization to discriminate against any member thereof or applicant for membership, because he has opposed any practice made an unlawful employment practice by this title, or because he has made a charge, testified, assisted, or participated in any manner in an investigation, proceeding or hearing under this title."

Payne v. McLemore's Wholesale & Retail Stores

United States Court of Appeals, Fifth Circuit, 1981.
654 F.2d 1130, cert. denied, 455 U.S. 1000, 102 S.Ct. 1630, 71 L.Ed.2d 866 (1982).

Sam D. Johnson, Circuit Judge:

This is a Title VII action alleging that in early 1971, defendant McLemore's Wholesale & Retail Stores, Inc. failed to rehire plaintiff Charles Payne because of his participation in activities protected by §704(a) of the Civil Rights Act of 1964. The district court concluded that plaintiff successfully carried his ultimate burden of proving discrimination. The district court found that plaintiff established a prima facie case of discrimination under §704(a) by showing that the employer's failure to rehire plaintiff was caused by plaintiff's participation in boycott and picketing activities in opposition to an unlawful employment practice of the defendant. In addition, the district court found that plaintiff proved that the employer's proffered explanation for its failure to rehire the plaintiff — that plaintiff failed to reapply for a job with the employer — was merely pretextual. Because the finding of retaliatory discrimination is supported by requisite subsidiary facts, we affirm the district court judgment for the plaintiff.

* * *

* * * Plaintiff originally worked in McLemore's fertilizer plant. The operation of the plant was seasonal in nature since the demand for fertilizer was dependent upon the farmers' planting seasons. During the first two years of plaintiff's employment with defendant, he was laid off for three months each year during the seasonal decline in work. In later years, during the off-season plaintiff was not laid off, but was instead shifted to positions in other parts of the defendant's operations. * * *

In November 1970, plaintiff was once again laid off due to the seasonal business decline. Two other black employees and two white employees were laid off at the same time. About a month later, plaintiff became involved in the formation and organization of the Franklin Parish Improvement Organization, a non-profit civil rights organization. * * * The organization was interested in improving social conditions of blacks in Franklin Parish, and it focused especially on the need to get blacks hired in retail stores in money-handling and supervisory positions in order to improve the treatment that blacks received while shopping in stores. Shortly after its formation, the members of the organization decided to boycott several retail businesses, including those of defendant * * *. Plaintiff organized and implemented the boycott and was actively involved in picketing McLemore's * * *. Defendant knew of plaintiff's involvement in the boycott and picketing. Moreover, the boycott and picketing were effective and defendant's business suffered as a result.

In previous years when he had been laid off, plaintiff had always gone back to work for defendant when the work picked back up. In the year of the boycott, however, he was not recalled or rehired.[3] * * *

* * * [P]laintiff filed this action in federal district court alleging that defendant's failure to rehire plaintiff was a result of plaintiff's race and his civil rights activity. In its answer, McLemore's denied that it had committed any discriminatory actions, and asserted that the reason the plaintiff was not rehired was because he failed to reapply for a position with McLemore's after he was laid off. The district court held that plaintiff did reapply for his job, but that he was not rehired because of his participation in boycotting and picketing activities. The court further found that participation in the boycott and picketing was protected activity under §704(a) of Title VII; in other words, the district court concluded that the boycott and picketing were in opposition to an unlawful employment practice of the defendant. The court awarded plaintiff back pay, costs, and attorney's fees * * *.

The opposition clause of §704(a) of Title VII provides protection against retaliation for employees who oppose unlawful employment practices committed by an employer. (§704(a) also contains a participation clause that protects employees against retaliation for their participation in the procedures established by Title VII to enforce its provisions. The participation clause is not involved in this lawsuit.). * * *

In this case, plaintiff contends that he was not rehired in retaliation for his boycott and picketing activities which were, according to plaintiff, in opposition to unlawful

---

[3]Of the four other employees who were laid off at the same time as plaintiff, only one was rehired — a black employee who was not involved in the boycott or picketing by the Franklin Parish Improvement Organization. Both plaintiff and Russell Brass (the other black employee who was laid off and not rehired) were involved in the boycott and picketing. According to defendant, the employee who was rehired was the only one of the five employees who were laid off that reapplied for a job.

employment practices committed by McLemore's. Plaintiff asserted that the unlawful employment practices his boycott and picketing activities were intended to protest were McLemore's discrimination against blacks in hiring and promotion — specifically, McLemore's failure to employ blacks in money-handling, clerking, or supervisory positions. In demonstrating his contentions at trial, plaintiff had the initial burden of establishing a prima facie case of discrimination. McDonnell Douglas Corp. v. Green. The burden then shifted to the defendant to articulate a legitimate, nondiscriminatory reason for the failure to rehire the plaintiff. Finally, if the defendant carried his burden, the plaintiff was entitled to an opportunity to show that the defendant's stated reason for its failure to rehire plaintiff was in fact pretextual.

"To establish a prima facie case under [§704(a)] the plaintiff must establish (1) statutorily protected expression, (2) an adverse employment action, and (3) a causal link between the protected expression and the adverse action." Smalley v. City of Eatonville, 640 F.2d 765, 769 (5ᵗʰ Cir.1981). The first element of the prima facie case — statutorily protected expression — requires conduct by the plaintiff that is in opposition to an unlawful employment practice of the defendant. Thus, for the plaintiff to prove that he engaged in statutorily protected expression, he must show that the boycott and picketing activity in which he participated was in opposition to conduct by McLemore's that was made unlawful by Title VII. According to the plaintiff, the purpose of the boycott and picketing was to oppose McLemore's discrimination against blacks in hiring and promotion. * * * [T]here is substantial evidence to support the district court finding that the purpose of the boycott and picketing was to oppose defendant's discrimination against blacks in certain employment opportunities[7]—an unlawful employment practice under §703(a)(1).

Defendant argues, however, that plaintiff failed to establish his prima facie case because he failed to prove that defendant had committed any unlawful employment practices. Plaintiff responds that he was not required to prove the actual existence of those unlawful employment practices; instead, he asserts that it was sufficient to establish a prima facie case if he had a *reasonable belief* that defendant had engaged in the unlawful employment practices. We agree with plaintiff and conclude that it was not fatal to plaintiff's §704(a) case that he failed to prove, under the *McDonnell Douglas* criteria for proving an unlawful employment practice under §703(a)(1), that McLemore's discriminated against blacks in retail store employment opportunities.

The Ninth Circuit was apparently the first appellate court to decide whether the opposition clause of §704(a) required proof of actual discrimination. Sias v. City

---

[7]Defendant claims that plaintiff did not engage in the boycott and picketing to oppose unlawful employment practices of McLemore's. Instead, it is McLemore's contention that the boycott and picketing were conducted to publicize the issues of integration of public facilities and common courtesy to blacks. To support this allegation, defendant points to the incident that initiated the formation of the Franklin Parish Improvement Organization — two black children being turned away from the town's segregated public swimming pool. * * * Although the Improvement Organization was, in part, occasioned by the position of blacks in Winnsboro in general, and although the boycott and picketing may have been to some extent a protest of this position, the district court's conclusion that the boycott and picketing activity was in opposition to unlawful employment practices of McLemore's is supported by substantial evidence.

Demonstration Agency, 588 F.2d 692 (9th Cir.1978). In *Sias*, the * * * City did not deny that plaintiff was discharged for writing a letter of grievance to the Regional Administrator of the Department of Housing and Urban Development (HUD). Rather, it contend[ed] that, inasmuch as the trial court made no finding of actual discrimination, it could not be held to have violated §704(a). The Ninth Circuit concluded that "[s]uch a narrow interpretation * * * would not only chill the legitimate assertion of employee rights under Title VII but would tend to force employees to file formal charges rather than seek conciliation or informal adjustment of grievances." The *Sias* court quoted extensively from Hearth v. Metropolitan Transit Commission, 436 F.Supp. 685 (D.Minn.1977), which went on to state:

> But this Court believes that appropriate informal opposition to perceived discrimination must not be chilled by the fear of retaliatory action in the event the alleged wrongdoing does not exist. It should not be necessary for an employee to resort immediately to the EEOC or similar State agencies in order to bring complaints of discrimination to the attention of the employer with some measure of protection. The resolution of such charges without governmental prodding should be encouraged.
>
> * * *

Id., at 688-69. * * *

The Fifth Circuit has not heretofore directly addressed the issue whether proof of an actual unlawful employment practice is necessary under the opposition clause, or whether an employee is protected from retaliation under the opposition clause if the employee reasonably believes that the employer is engaged in unlawful employment practices. To the extent that earlier Fifth Circuit cases provide guidance to this Court, however, they indicate that the reasonable belief test of the * * * Ninth Circuit comports with the decisions of this Circuit and the policies underlying Title VII. In Pettway v. American Cast Iron Pipe Co., 411 F.2d 998 (5th Cir.1969), this Court held that an employee was protected by the participation clause of §704(a) from discharge in retaliation for filing a charge with the EEOC, regardless of the truth or falsity of the contents of the charge. The Court stated that:

> There can be no doubt about the purpose of §704(a). In unmistakable language it is to protect the employee who utilizes the tools provided by Congress to protect his rights. The Act will be frustrated if the employer may unilaterally determine the truth or falsity of charges and take independent action.

Id. at 1004-05. Thus, the Court held that where the communication with the EEOC satisfied the requirements of a "charge," the charging party could not be discharged for the writing and the court could not "either sustain any employer disciplinary action or deny relief because of the presence of * * * malicious material."[9]

---

[9]Although this Court considers the reasoning of the *Pettway* decision to support the reasonable belief test in opposition clause cases, at least one district court has viewed the *Pettway* case quite differently. The district court in EEOC v. C & D Sportswear Corp., 398 F.Supp. 300 (M.D.Ga.1975), held that "baseless accusations" were protected "only as a means of protecting access to the Commission." Thus, that court concluded that the result in *Pettway* was limited to

The Ninth Circuit recognized that the "considerations controlling the interpretation of the opposition clause are not entirely the same as those applying to the participation clause," and that the opposition clause "serves a more limited purpose" than does the participation clause. However, interpreting the opposition clause to require proof of an actual unlawful employment practice would "chill the legitimate assertion of employee rights under Title VII," just as surely as would interpreting the participation clause to require a truthful charge. On the other hand, interpreting the opposition clause to protect an employee who reasonably believes that discrimination exists "is consistent with a liberal construction of Title VII to implement the Congressional purpose of eliminating discrimination in employment."

* * *

To effectuate the policies of Title VII and to avoid the chilling effect that would otherwise arise, we are compelled to conclude that a plaintiff can establish a prima facie case of retaliatory discharge under the opposition clause of §704(a) if he shows that he had a reasonable belief that the employer was engaged in unlawful employment practices.[11] While the district court made no explicit finding that plaintiff's opposition

---

actions under the participation clause, and did not apply to actions under the opposition clause. The *C & D Sportswear* court held:

> Accordingly, the only reasonable interpretation to be placed on §704(a) is that where accusations are made in the context of charges before the EEOC, the truth or falsity of that accusation is a matter to be determined by the EEOC, and thereafter by the courts. However, where accusations are made outside the procedures set forth by Congress that accusation is made at the accuser's peril. In order to be protected, it must be established that the accusation is well-founded. If it is, there is, in fact, an unlawful employment practice and he has the right, protected by §704(a), to oppose it. However, where there is no underlying unlawful employment practice the employee has no right to make that accusation in derogation of the procedures provided by statute.

Id. at 306. We find the reasoning of the *C & D Sportswear* district court unpersuasive and the result unjustifiably restrictive. In *C & D Sportswear*, an employee called the president of the company a racist and was discharged for making that accusation. The district court reasoned that

> access to the EEOC must be protected. On the other hand, accusations of racism ought not to be made lightly. Unfounded accusations might well incite racism where none had previously existed. Were employees free to make unfounded accusations of racism against their employers and fellow employees, racial discord, disruption, and disharmony would likely ensue. This would be wholly contrary to Congress' intention that race be removed, as far as possible, as an issue in employment.

Id. at 305-06. While unfounded, inflammatory accusations of racism might, on balance, be found to provide the employer with a legitimate, nondiscriminatory reason for discharging an employee, this would neither require nor suggest that all unfounded accusations should be totally unprotected by the opposition clause of §704(a). It is as important to protect an employee's right to oppose perceived discrimination by appropriate, informal means as it is to protect his right of access to the EEOC. An employee who engages in opposition activity should not be required to act at his own peril if it turns out that no unlawful employment practice actually exists, as long as the employee holds a reasonable belief that the unlawful employment practices do exist.

[11]The First Circuit has adopted a somewhat different test than * * the Ninth * * *. The First Circuit has not explicitly decided whether a §704(a) plaintiff must demonstrate that he harbored a "reasonable belief" of discriminatory employer behavior or whether the plaintiff must show that he harbored a "conscientiously held belief" of such misconduct. Monteiro v. Poole Silver

was based upon a reasonable belief that McLemore's hiring and promotional policies violated Title VII, such a finding is implicit and is sufficiently supported by evidence in the record. Thus, plaintiff established that he reasonably believed that defendant McLemore's discriminated against blacks in employment opportunities. Moreover, plaintiff showed that his boycott and picketing activities were in opposition to this unlawful employment practice. Defendant's failure to rehire the plaintiff was undoubtedly an adverse employment action. Finally, there was evidence to support an inference that defendant's failure to rehire plaintiff was causally related to plaintiff's boycott and picketing activities.[13] Thus, plaintiff successfully established a prima facie case, thereby raising an inference of unlawful discrimination under §704(a). The burden then shifted to the defendant to rebut the presumption of discrimination by producing evidence of a legitimate, nondiscriminatory reason for its failure to rehire plaintiff.

Defendant McLemore's steadfastly maintained at trial that the *only* reason plaintiff was not rehired was because he failed to reapply for a position with defendant. This comprised the full and complete extent of the rebuttal evidence presented by the agents of the defendant in an effort to articulate a legitimate, nondiscriminatory reason for the failure to rehire the plaintiff. * * *

* * * This reason — the failure to reapply — would, if believed, be legally sufficient to justify a judgment for the defendant. Thus, the defendant carried its rebuttal burden at trial.

After the defendant has an opportunity to rebut plaintiff's prima facie case, the plaintiff has a corresponding opportunity to show that the defendant's proffered explanation was in fact pretextual. Here, plaintiff presented substantial evidence that he did reapply for a job with McLemore's. The trial court found "as a fact that Mr. Payne did reapply for his position with the defendant corporation." There is, therefore, substantial evidence in the record to support the district court's conclusion that the defendant's explanation for its failure to rehire the plaintiff was merely pretextual. The district court further found that members of McLemore's knew of plaintiff's participation in the boycott and picketing, and that there was a causal relationship between defendant's failure to rehire plaintiff and plaintiff's participation in the protest

---

Co., 615 F.2d 4 (1st Cir.1980). The *Monteiro* court found that "[u]nder either standard — the employer's conduct being non-discriminatory in fact — the plaintiff must show that his so-called opposition was in response to some *honestly held*, if mistaken, feeling that discriminatory practices existed." Thus, according to that court, if a reasonable person might have believed that the employer was engaged in unlawful employment practices, but the plaintiff actually did not in good faith hold such a belief, then the plaintiff's opposition conduct is unprotected. We need not decide here whether it is necessary to adopt a good faith requirement in addition to the reasonable belief requirement since, in the case before this Court, the plaintiff believed — reasonably and in good faith — that McLemore's was engaged in unlawful employment practices, and plaintiff's opposition conduct was in response to this belief.

[13]An inference that defendant's failure to rehire the plaintiff was caused by plaintiff's participation in the boycott and picketing activity was proper in view of the existence of evidence that the employer was aware of the plaintiff's activities and that, within a relatively short time after those activities took place, the adverse employment consequence occurred. The defendant was then entitled to an opportunity to introduce evidence to rebut this inference.

activity. There is also substantial evidence in the record to support the district court's conclusion in this regard. Thus, on the facts and arguments presented to the trial court, that court correctly held that the defendant's failure to rehire the plaintiff violated §704(a); that is, that the defendant's stated reason for not rehiring the plaintiff (the plaintiff's failure to reapply for a job) was merely pretextual and that the defendant's actual reason for not rehiring the plaintiff was the plaintiff's participation in activities in opposition to unlawful employment practices of the defendant.

Now on appeal, for the first time, defendant contends that even if plaintiff's activity was in opposition to unlawful employment practices of defendant, plaintiff's actions were not protected by §704(a) because the form of plaintiff's opposition was not covered by the statute. It is well-established that not all activity in opposition to unlawful employment practices is protected by §704(a). Certain conduct — for example, illegal acts of opposition or unreasonably hostile or aggressive conduct — may provide a legitimate, independent, and nondiscriminatory basis for an employee's discharge. "There may arise instances where the employee's conduct in protest of an unlawful employment practice so interferes with the performance of his job that it renders him ineffective in the position for which he was employed. In such a case, his conduct, or form of opposition, is not covered by §704(a)." Rosser v. Laborers' International Union, Local 438, 616 F.2d 221, 223 (5th Cir.1980), cert. denied, 449 U.S. 886, 101 S.Ct. 241, 66 L.Ed.2d 112. In order to determine when such a situation exists, the court must engage in a balancing test: The courts have required that the employee conduct be reasonable in light of the circumstances, and have held that the employer's right to run his business must be balanced against the rights of the employee to express his grievances and promote his own welfare.

It appears that a number of cases have assumed that it is part of defendant's rebuttal burden to show that the form of plaintiff's opposition was unprotected by the statute. If the defendant took an adverse employment action against the plaintiff because of opposition conduct by the plaintiff that was outside the protection of the statute, then the defendant may have had a legitimate, nondiscriminatory reason to justify its actions. Thus, in the case before this Court, if the form of plaintiff's activities placed them outside the protection of §704(a), then the defendant may have had a legitimate, nondiscriminatory reason for its failure to rehire the plaintiff. However, if the form of plaintiff's activities was the nondiscriminatory reason for the defendant's failure to rehire the plaintiff, it was the defendant's responsibility to introduce evidence to that effect at trial. * * *

* * *

It therefore becomes apparent that in the instant case, after plaintiff established his prima facie case, it was the responsibility of the defendant to show that the form of plaintiff's activities placed them outside the protection of §704(a) and provided defendant with a legitimate reason for its failure to rehire the plaintiff. If the defendant intended to rely upon this contention, it was the defendant's responsibility to raise the issue at trial. Here, the defendant failed to offer any evidence at trial that its legitimate and nondiscriminatory reason for not rehiring the plaintiff was that plaintiff had engaged in hostile, unprotected activity that was detrimental to the employer's interests.[14] With respect to the defendant's burden of rebutting plaintiff's prima facie case, the *Burdine* Court stated that: "An articulation not admitted into evidence will not suffice. Thus, the defendant cannot meet its burden merely through an answer to the complaint or by argument of counsel." If the defendant cannot meet its rebuttal burden by answer to the complaint or by argument of counsel at trial, the defendant undoubtedly cannot meet its rebuttal burden solely by argument of counsel for the first time on appeal. It is not permissible for this Court to relate the defendant's arguments on appeal back to the time of trial in order to determine whether defendant met its rebuttal burden at trial. Since the defendant failed to present any evidence at trial that the egregious and disruptive form of plaintiff's opposition constituted the legitimate reason for defendant's failure to rehire plaintiff, the defendant surely did not carry its rebuttal burden on this issue at trial.

* * *

[The court then refused to make its own determination as to whether the form of the plaintiff's activities provided the defendant with a legitimate, nondiscriminatory reason for not rehiring the plaintiff.]

* * * Since plaintiff made out his prima facie case of discrimination under §704(a), and since the only explanation offered by the defendant for its failure to rehire plaintiff was correctly determined to be pretextual, the judgment of the district court for plaintiff is

Affirmed.

COLEMAN, Circuit Judge, dissenting.

* * *

The statute speaks in terms of practices — not what someone "reasonably believes" to have been a practice when, in fact, the practice did not exist. I cannot believe that Congress intended (since it did not say so) to penalize employers for what an employee or applicant "believes" when, in fact, the employer is innocent. To hold otherwise is to deprive employers of their property rights in violation of the due process clause.

Finally, I dissent because, as the majority concedes, the District Court made no finding [the majority adds the word "explicit"] that the plaintiff's opposition was based upon "reasonable belief." In proceeding to make its own, inferential, findings of fact the majority cites not a single specific fact that would support a finding of reasonable belief. * * *

* * *

I respectfully dissent.

---

[14]* * * The only contention made by the defendant that the conduct of the plaintiff was not protected by §704(a) was that the boycott and picketing were not in opposition to an unlawful employment practice of the defendant and so did not satisfy the requirements of §704(a). * * * While defendant did allege that plaintiff's activity was not in opposition to an unlawful employment practice of McLemore's, defendant did *not* assert that the form of plaintiff's activity was outside the scope of §704(a)

NOTES AND PROBLEMS FOR DISCUSSION

1. As *Payne* indicates, §704(a) offers protection from retaliation directed at two types of conduct: "participation" in the formal Title VII enforcement process and informal "opposition" to what the actor reasonably perceives to be a proscribed employment practice. Most of the cases arising under §704(a) raise one or more of the following four interpretative questions: (a) whether the plaintiff's conduct constitutes either participation or opposition; (b) what happens if the plaintiff's participation or opposition is premised on a factually or legally erroneous belief that the employer is engaged in unlawful conduct; (c) whether the nature or form of the plaintiff's conduct can remove it from the protection of the statute; and (d) whether the defendant's response constitutes retaliation. In many cases, including *Payne*, there also is a factual dispute as to the causal connection between the plaintiff's conduct and the defendant's response.

In light of all of the above-mentioned issues, consider the following:

(a) Jane Leston, an electrical engineer with Chicago Industries, Inc., was denied a promotion to department supervisor in favor of her colleague, Bill Thomas. Shortly thereafter, Ms. Leston filed a sex discrimination charge under Illinois law with the appropriate Illinois administrative agency. When the company learned of Leston's charge, it asked Mr. Thomas to sign an affidavit prepared by the company to aid in its defense. Thomas refused and was demoted one week later.

1. Can Thomas state a claim under §704(a)? *See* Smith v. Columbus Metropolitan Housing Authority, 443 F.Supp. 61 (S.D. Ohio 1977).

2. Would your answer change if Leston's charge alleged that she had been denied the promotion because of her age? See Rodriguez-Vives v. Puerto Rico Firefighters Corps of Puerto Rico, 743 F.3d 278 (1st Cir. 2014) (although plaintiff's underlying claim asserted a violation of §1983 and not Title VII, she can state a retaliation claim under §704(a) of Title VII because her initial claim constitutes "opposition" to conduct the plaintiff reasonably believed violates Title VII).

3. If the company terminated Leston after she filed a charge that she had been denied the promotion because of her age, could she challenge the discharge under §704(a)? *See* Learned v. City of Bellevue, 860 F.2d 928 (9th Cir. 1988).

4. Suppose that during the company's internal investigation of Leston's sex discrimination allegation, Thomas told an investigator that Leston's supervisor told admitted that Leston was denied the promotion because of her sex. Suppose also that Thomas was discharged immediately upon giving that information to the supervisor. Could Thomas state a retaliation claim under Title VII?

5. Suppose that after filing her sex discrimination charge, Ms. Leston resigned her position with Chicago Industries and subsequently applied for a consultant position with Illinois Electric Co. She is informed by Illinois Electric that they will not hire her as a consultant because she had filed a discrimination charge against Chicago Industries. Can she state a §704(a) claim against Illinois Electric? See Alam v. Miller Brewing Co., 709 F.3d 662 (7th Cir. 2013) (as §704(a) prohibits an "employer" from retaliating against any "employee" or "applicant for employment", it does not apply to retaliation against a prospective independent contractor).

Whether or not an employee's involvement in an employer's internal investigation constitutes protected activity under §704(a) was addressed, in part, by the Supreme Court in CRAWFORD v. METROPOLITAN GOVERNMENT OF NASHVILLE AND DAVIDSON COUNTY, TENNESSEE, 555 U.S. 271, 129 S.Ct. 846, 172 L.Ed.2d 650 (2009). There, as part of an employer-initiated investigation into rumors of sexual harassment by a supervisor, the plaintiff responded to questions from an investigator by describing several instances of sexually harassing behavior. The employer ultimately took no action against the alleged harasser but did terminate the plaintiff and two other accusers. The employer maintained that the plaintiff had been discharged for embezzlement. Subsequently, the plaintiff filed a retaliation charge with the EEOC, followed by the instant suit. The Sixth Circuit affirmed the trial court's granting of summary judgment in favor of the defendant, finding that the plaintiff's conduct did not constitute either opposition or participation activity within the meaning of §704(a). According to the circuit court, the plaintiff had not engaged in protected "opposition" because it read that clause to require "active, consistent" opposition activity. And this standard was not met, the Sixth Circuit explained, because the plaintiff had not instigated or initiated the employer's investigation and had not taken further action after responding to the employer's questions. The court also ruled that the plaintiff had not engaged in protected "participation" conduct. Since the employer's internal investigation in which the plaintiff had been involved had not been conducted pursuant to a pending EEOC charge, the Sixth Circuit held, the plaintiff's conduct did not amount to participation in an "investigation under this subchapter" as required by §704(a).

The Supreme Court unanimously reversed the Sixth Circuit's ruling. Since the meaning of "opposition" was left undefined by Title VII, the Court looked to its "ordinary meaning" as reflected in dictionaries. And these definitions, it declared, did not require either that the plaintiff's activity be repetitive or consistent or that the plaintiff have instigated or initiated the investigation into the alleged discriminatory conduct. Rather, it endorsed the position set forth in the relevant EEOC guideline that "[w]hen an employee communicates to her employer a belief that the employer has engaged in * * * a form of employment discrimination, that communication virtually always constitutes the employee's opposition to the activity." And though the Court acknowledged that an exception to the rule could exist in the rare "eccentric" case where such a communication was made in a context indicating that the speaker did not find the conduct personally offensive, the instant case did not fit into that category. The Court rejected the employer's contention that requiring "active" and "consistent" opposition was necessary to avoid placing employers in the position of being encouraged to decline to ask employees questions about alleged discrimination for fear of being hit with a retaliation charge if the responding employee subsequently was the victim of some adverse employment decision. To the contrary, the Court responded, employers were incentivized to ferret out discriminatory activity by the availability of the *Burlington/Faragher* affirmative defense to imputed liability in cases not involving a tangible employment practice. Consequently, the Court ruled, this plaintiff had engaged in protected "opposition" activity. Having so ruled, the Court then declared that it would not review the Sixth Circuit's reading of the scope of the participation clause. *See* Clover v. Total System Services, Inc., 176 F.3d 1346 (11th Cir. 1999). Relying on *Crawford*, the First Circuit has held that an employee's conduct need not be verbal in order to constitute opposition. In COLLAZO v. BRISTOL-MYERS SQUIBB MFG., 617 F.3d 39 (1st Cir. 2010), the court ruled that an employee need not verbally communicate his opposition to an unlawful employment practice to engage in protected opposition activity. In the instant case, the court found that the plaintiff's counseling of a co-employee about that co-employee's potential harassment claim, arranging a meeting for that co-employee with the employer's Human Resources official, accompanying the co-employee to that meeting, and interceding on her behalf with the alleged harasser constituted protected opposition conduct.

The Fair Labor Standards Act of 1938, 29 U.S.C. §201 et seq., which addresses, *inter alia*, minimum wage, overtime, and sex-based equal pay, also contains an antiretaliation provision that is worded a bit differently from §704(a) of Title VII. It protects any employee who has "filed a complaint" or instituted a proceeding under the Act. In KASTEN v. SAINT-GOBAIN PERFORMANCE PLASTICS CORP., 563 U.S. 1, 131 S.Ct. 1325, 179 L.Ed.2d 379 (2011), the Supreme Court, by as 6-2 margin (Justice Kagan did not participate), ruled that a worker who allegedly was disciplined and later discharged in retaliation for *orally* complaining to company official about a practice that he believed was in violation of that statute, could state a retaliation claim because he did "file" a complaint. The Seventh Circuit had affirmed the trial court's grant of summary judgment to the defendant on the ground that the FLSA antiretaliation provision did *not* protect *non-written* complaints. The Supreme Court reversed, concluding that while the meaning of "file", in isolation, could be open to competing interpretations, considerations of purpose and context led it to conclude that the only permissible interpretation was to construe this text to apply to both oral and written complaints. Noting that both state and federal agencies permit complaints to be filed orally, the Court concluded that the text, taken alone, did not provide a dispositive answer to the interpretive question. On the other hand, the Court reasoned, limiting the scope of the antiretaliation provision to the filing of written complaints would impede the statutory enforcement scheme which relies, in part, on workers complaining to their employers about alleged statutory violations. But to ensure that employers are given fair notice of complaints, the Court ruled that a complaint will be deemed "filed" for retaliation purposes only if it is sufficiently detailed and clear that a reasonable, objective person would have understood the employee to have put the employer on notice that the employee is asserting statutory rights under the FLSA. And this standard can be met by oral, as well as written complaints. The Court remanded with instructions to apply this standard to the instant plaintiff's oral complaints.

(b) Liza Darling is an accountant employed by Professionals For You (PFY). PFY contracts to provide lawyers, accountants, and other professionals for its customers. Liza was assigned by PFY to provide accounting services to Highland Express, Inc. While working at Highland's office, Liza was subjected to a barrage of sexually abusive comments and conduct. She filed a charge of sex discrimination with the EEOC, naming Highland as her employer. Highland complained about this to PFY which then fired Liza solely because she had complained about Highland's allegedly discriminatory practices. After invoking her administrative remedies, Liza filed suit under Title VII. How should the court rule on PFY's motion to dismiss the suit for failure to state a claim upon which relief can be granted? *See* Flowers v. Columbia College Chicago, 397 F.3d 532 (7th Cir.2005) (an individual who alleges retaliation by her employer is protected under the participation clause of §704(a) even when her participation consisted of filing a charge against an entity who is not her employer).

(c) Karlen Construction, Inc. was awarded a contract by the federal government to help build a post office. The contract contained an affirmative action plan requiring Karlen to employ a specified percentage of minority workers. In the middle of construction, the company concluded that it could not afford to retain all four of the electricians it had hired for the post office project. To maintain compliance with the affirmative action plan, Karlen chose to lay off its three white electricians and retain its one black electrician. One of the laid off electricians, Fred Hill, circulated a letter around the site charging Karlen with racial discrimination in connection with the lay off of electricians. One month later, when its economic condition improved, Karlen rehired all of the laid off electricians, except for Hill. Hill subsequently filed a Title VII action alleging that Karlen's refusal to rehire him violated §704(a). The trial court ruled in favor of the defendant, holding that the company's original decision to lay off the three white electricians and retain the black electrician did not violate Title VII and, therefore, that Hill's conduct after being laid off was not protected by §704. How should the appellate court rule on Hill's appeal? *See* Sisco v. J. S. Alberici Construction Co., Inc., 655 F.2d 146 (8th Cir. 1981), cert. denied, 455 U.S. 976, 102 S.Ct. 1485, 71 L.Ed.2d 688 (1982).

What if Hill had been denied a promotion and then filed a Title VII suit against the company. Thereafter, while continuing to work for Karlen, Hill mentioned to one of the company's customers that he felt that he had been discriminated against by Karlen and that he was suing them to challenge that conduct. The customer reports this back to the company and they discharge Hill. Can he state a claim under §704(a)? In FOX v. EAGLE DISTRIBUTING CO., 510 F.3d 587 (6th Cir. 2007), the circuit court affirmed the trial court's grant of summary judgment to the defendant in a case like this. Applying Title VII jurisprudence in a retaliation case brought under the Age Discrimination in Employment Act, the court ruled that because the plaintiff had made only a general reference to being discriminated against, i.e., he had offered no evidence that his complaints to the customer contained any specific reference to discrimination on the basis of a statutorily proscribed classification (in that case, age), even though the lawsuit to which he referred did allege discrimination on the basis of age, the non-specific complaint to a customer did not constitute a protected act of opposition to an unlawful employment practice.

Suppose that Karlen Construction issued a new employee handbook that included an arbitration provision mandating that all claims of discrimination (whether contractual or statutory) by Karlen employees be resolved through arbitration. The company required all of its employees to agree to the arbitration provision as a condition of continued employment. When Fred Hill, and other Karlen employees, refused to agree to the new arbitration policy, they were terminated. They brought a claim under §704 alleging that they were discharged for opposing what they reasonably believed was an unlawful employment policy — requiring them to arbitrate statutory discrimination claims. How should the court rule? Is it relevant to your analysis that the U.S. Supreme Court, and every federal circuit court, has upheld the enforceability of compulsory arbitration agreements that cover Title VII disputes? *See* Chapter 4A5, *infra*; Weeks v. Harden Mfg. Corp., 291 F.3d 1307 (11th Cir. 2002).

Manny Relstaff filed a retaliation claim asserting that he was discharged after he terminated a theretofore consensual sexual relationship with his supervisor. How should the court rule on the defendant's motion to dismiss for failure to state a claim? *Compare* LeMaire v. La. Dep't of Transp., 480 F.3d 383 (5th Cir. 2007) (the plaintiff's one-time rejection of sexual advances by a supervisor does *not* constitute protected opposition conduct) *with* Ogden v. Wax Works, Inc., 214 F.3d 999 (8th Cir. 2008) (a plaintiff's request that a supervisor stop harassing her is a form of protected opposition conduct) and Tate v. Executive Management Services, Inc., 546 F.3d 528 (7th Cir. 2008), cert. denied, 129 S.Ct. 1379 (2009) (assuming that there might be circumstances in which an employee who rejects a supervisor's sexual advances has engaged in protected opposition conduct, this plaintiff did not show that he reasonably believed in good faith that he was opposing an unlawful employment practice when he terminated his sexual relationship with his supervisor as the facts establish that he did it only to protect his marriage). Note that there is also an issue here of whether the discharge constituted proscribed sexual harassment in violation of §703(a). See Note 4 following *Meritor* in §B4 of this Chapter, *supra*.

(d) Richard Kane, the Equal Opportunity Director of Williams Steelworks, Inc. (W.S.I.), a company with many government contracts, was required to design the company's affirmative action programs and to monitor their effectiveness. But over time, Kane concluded that the company demonstrated a lack of commitment to its equal opportunity obligation by continually ignoring his reports that detailed management's failure to accomplish the reforms outlined in the affirmative action programs. This ultimately caused Kane to file a complaint against W.S.I. with the federal agency authorized to monitor the antidiscrimination policies of government contractors. When W.S.I. was notified by the agency that such a charge had been filed, the company president asked Kane if Kane knew the identity of the charging party. Kane denied knowledge of this fact and continued to conceal his role as the charging party while actively cooperating with the federal agency's investigation of his charge. During this period Kane also organized a clandestine meeting of minority employees to solicit complaints of discrimination. After W.S.I. learned of the true nature of Kane's various activities, he was fired.

1. Can Kane state a retaliation claim against W.S.I.? *See* Jennings v. Tinley Park Community Consol. School Dist. No. 146, 796 F.2d 962 (7th Cir. 1986), cert. denied, 481 U.S. 1017, 107 S.Ct. 1895, 95 L.Ed.2d 502 (1987); Holden v. Owens-Illinois, Inc., 793 F.2d 745 (6th Cir. 1986).

2. What if Kane had filed a charge against W.S.I. with the EEOC prior to his discharge? *See* Gonzalez v. Bolger, 486 F.Supp. 595 (D.D.C.1980), affirmed, 656 F.2d 899 (D.C.Cir. 1981).

3. Suppose that, instead of firing Kane, the company transferred him to an undesirable position. When notified of the transfer, Kane refused to report to the new job and went home. Two days later he was fired for insubordination. Has the company violated §704(a)? *See* Hazel v. Postmaster General, 7 F.3d 1 (1st Cir. 1993).

4. If Kane had been the General Counsel for W.S.I. instead of the firm's equal opportunity director, could the company seek to get his §704 claim dismissed on the ground that Kane's action would compel the disclosure of confidential information protected by the attorney-client privilege? And would pursuing this claim violate

Kane's ethical obligation of confidentiality owed to his now-ex client?   In KACHMAR v. SUNGARD DATA SYSTEMS, INC., 109 F.3d 173 (3d Cir. 1997), the Third Circuit reversed the trial court's dismissal of a Title VII retaliation claim brought by the defendant's former in-house counsel.   The court based its ruling on its determinations that (1) state ethical rules permit exceptions to nondisclosure obligation when disclosure is necessary to establish a claim in a controversy between the lawyer and the client, (2) other means such as protective orders and in camera proceedings exist to prevent unwarranted disclosure of otherwise confidential information, and (3) it was questionable whether much of the information observed by the plaintiff would actually implicate the privilege.   However, in DOUGLAS v. DYNMcDERMOTT PETROLEUM OPERATIONS COMPANY, 144 F.3d 364 (5th Cir. 1998), cert. denied, 525 U.S. 1068, 119 S.Ct. 798, 142 L.Ed.2d 660 (1999), the Fifth Circuit ruled that where an in-house counsel "opposes" the perceived discriminatory practices of her employer by disclosing information in violation of her ethical obligations of confidentiality and loyalty, this opposition conduct is unprotected as a matter of law. In *Douglas*, the plaintiff in-house counsel had responded to an unfavorable performance rating by sending copies of her response letter to an outside entity and had included within that letter information that she had obtained from confidential company personnel records.   The Fifth Circuit concluded that her employer/client's right to ethical representation and her profession's interest in assuring the ethical conduct of its members trumped the plaintiff's Title VII right to oppose her employer/client's allegedly discriminatory practices by disclosing confidential information in violation of her ethical obligations.

5.   Suppose that a class action had been filed against Williams Steamworks on behalf of all of its female employees alleging a series of decisions that discriminated against them on the basis of their sex. During the course of discovery, the plaintiffs' lawyers asked all their clients to provide any documents that might be helpful in pursuit of their claims. Jean Starfish, an employee with access to confidential client records, sent some of these documents to the class action lawyers even though she did not believe they related directly or indirectly to the sex discrimination claims. When the plaintiffs' attorneys responded to a defense request for the production of documents, the company received copies of these confidential documents. When the company discovered that Jean was the source of the documents, she was terminated. Did Jean engage in conduct protected under §704(a)?   In NISWANDER v. CINCINNATI INSURANCE CO., 529 F.3d 714 (6th Cir. 2008), where the plaintiff filed a retaliation suit after being discharged for transmitting admittedly confidential company records to the attorneys handling a previously filed equal pay-based class action, the court ruled that the plaintiff's delivery of confidential documents, in violation of the company's privacy policy and employee handbook, that were not relevant, directly or indirectly, to the attorneys handling a class action suit of which the plaintiff was a member, did not constitute a protected act of participation. Although an individual's delivery of *relevant* documents during discovery to her lawyer would have fallen within the protective ambit of §704(a)'s participation clause, the court concluded that knowingly providing irrelevant confidential information did not constitute a protected act of participation. Noting that opposition conduct is only protected when it is deemed to be reasonable, the court agreed with the other circuits that had considered this question and applied a multifactor balancing test to determine

the reasonableness of transmitting confidential company documents. These included the manner by whether the plaintiff came upon the documents innocently or as the result of a premeditated search for confidential documentation; to whom the documents were transmitted; the contents of the documents; and the plaintiff's ability to preserve that evidence in a manner that did not violate the company's privacy policy.

Similarly, in BENES v. A.B. DATA, LTD., 724 F.3d 752 (7th Cir. 2013), the Seventh Circuit upheld the lower court's grant of summary judgment to the employer in a retaliation claim brought by a plaintiff who had been discharged after he stormed into the room occupied by his employer's representative at an EEOC mediation conference concerning the antecedent sex discrimination charge he had filed against his employer with the EEOC and shouted "you can take your proposal and shove it up your a**". The Seventh Circuit agreed that such misconduct during a mediation was unprotected by §704(a) because (1) it sabotaged the mediation and therefore subverted the goals of the antiretaliation provision; and (2) §704(a) only proscribes those employer responses that would dissuade a reasonable worker from engaging in protected activity and the prospect of being terminated for such egregious conduct would not discourage a reasonable worker from pursuing an EEOC charge.

(e) Irish Pleshette filed a series of sex discrimination charges with the EEOC against her employer, Heavenly Foods, Inc., over a two year period. The EEOC found that there was no reasonable cause to believe discrimination had occurred in any of these instances and dismissed all of the charges. Some months later, Iris was discharged. Thereafter, to aid her effort to obtain a new job with Consolidated Containers, Ms. Pleshette asked Al Newman, President of Heavenly, for a letter of recommendation. He refused this request, but sent a letter to the Personnel Director of Consolidated stating that Ms. Pleshette had filed a series of sex discrimination charges against his company with the EEOC and that all of these charges had been dismissed. Ms. Pleshette subsequently filed an action against Heavenly Foods alleging that Newman's refusal to provide a letter of recommendation, and his sending of the unsolicited letter to Consolidated Containers violated §704(a).

1.   Section 704(a) prohibits retaliation against any "employee or applicant" for employment. Is it fatal to Iris' case that she filed her §704 claim against Heavenly Foods after she had been discharged or that the event that gave rise to her claim (the letter) occurred after the termination of her employment relationship with the defendant? In ROBINSON v. SHELL OIL CO., 519 U.S. 337, 117 S.Ct. 843, 136 L.Ed.2d 808 (1997), the Court resolved a conflict among the circuit courts on the question of whether a former employee could state a claim under §704(a). Writing for a unanimous court, Justice Thomas rejected the suggestion that the absence of any reference to "former employees" in §704(a) reflected Congress's intention to include only present employees within the protection of the anti-retaliation provision. After all, he pointed out, §704(a) did not explicitly refer to "current" employees. And the fact that other statutes were more specific in the language used to describe the protected class was also unpersuasive, he maintained, since it suggested no more than use of the unqualified term "employees" could, but did not have to, refer only to incumbent employees. Justice Thomas then pointed to several other provisions in Title VII, including the remedial provisions of §706(b) where "employee" had to be construed to include former employees. All of these considerations led the Court to

conclude that "employee" had no single, consistent meaning throughout the statute and that its interpretation had to be resolved on a section-by-section basis in order to arrive at a proper contextual understanding of Congressional intent. In the context of §704(a), the Court adopted the EEOC's position that restricting the application of the anti-retaliation provision to current employees would be inconsistent with the provision's primary purpose of maintaining unfettered access to statutory remedial mechanisms. The Court agreed with the EEOC that precluding former employees from stating a claim against post-employment retaliation would undermine the effectiveness of the statue by allowing the threat of such post-employment retaliation to deter victims of discrimination from filing official complaints with the EEOC. Justice Thomas also reasoned that since §704(a) prohibits retaliation for filing a Title VII charge, the statute had to be read to extend to former employees in order to provide victims of retaliatory discharge with a cause of action. Do you agree? In *Robinson*, the act of retaliation — sending an unfavorable letter of recommendation to a potential employer after the plaintiff had been discharged — occurred after the plaintiff's employment relationship had been terminated. In a retaliatory discharge case, the allegedly retaliatory act — the discharge — obviously occurs during the employment relationship. Isn't, therefore, the real issue in *Robinson* whether a former employee can state a claim under §704(a) for an act of post-employment termination rather than simply whether any retaliation claim can be filed after the plaintiff's employment relationship has expired?

2. Would it make a difference to the disposition of Iris's retaliation claim if the Newman letter had been solicited by the prospective employer?

3. Would Ms. Pleshette have a claim against the prospective employer, Consolidated, if she did not obtain a position with them? If so, would she have to prove that she would have been hired had Heavenly not sent the letter, or is it enough that she prove that she was eliminated from consideration because of the information in the letter? *See* Ruggles v. California Polytechnic State University, 797 F.2d 782 (9th Cir. 1986). And is it relevant that the alleged retaliation by Consolidated was taken in response to protected conduct directed against Heavenly? *See* McMenemy v. City of Rochester, 241 F.3d 279 (2d Cir. 2001).

4. Could Iris state a §704(a) claim if, instead of being discharged by Heavenly, she had received unfavorable performance evaluations after all of her EEOC charges had been dismissed. *See* Smart v. Ball State Univ., 89 F.3d 437 (7th Cir. 1996) (issuance of undeservedly negative performance evaluations, without more, does not constitute an actionable "adverse action").

5. Assume that as a standard part of its hiring policy, Consolidated had requested a letter of recommendation about Ms. Pleshette from Heavenly. And suppose that the folks at Heavenly sent in a strongly negative reference. But also suppose that it is undisputed that Consolidated would not have hired Ms. Pleshette even in the absence of this negative recommendation. Would this latter fact be fatal to Iris's §704(a) claim against Heavenly? *See* Hashimoto v. Dalton, 118 F.3d 671 (9th Cir. 1997), cert. denied, 523 U.S. 1122, 118 S.Ct. 1803, 140 L.Ed.2d 943 (1998).

(f) Melody Ponny filed a Title VII claim alleging that her employer's promotion policies discriminated on the basis of sex and obtained a judgment ordering the defendant to promote her. After complying with the court's order, the employer issued a press release stating that it had been compelled by court order to promote Ms. Ponny even though she was unqualified.

> 1.   Can Ponny state a claim under §704(a)? *See* Jordan v. Wilson, 851 F.2d 1290 (11th Cir. 1988).

> 2.   After Ponny filed her retaliation claim, the owner of the company instructed all of Ponny's co-workers to ignore her, to spy on her, and to refuse to have anything to do with her. Does she have a viable retaliation claim under §704(a)? *See* Munday v. Waste Management of North America, Inc., 126 F.3d 239 (4th Cir. 1997) (instructing co-workers to ignore and spy on employee who engaged in protected activity does not constitute an adverse employment action and, therefore, employer did not engage in unlawful retaliation).

In setting forth the elements of a retaliation claim, the Fifth Circuit in *Payne* stated that the plaintiff must establish that he suffered "an adverse employment action" as a result of having engaged in statutorily protected activity. And though all the circuits agree that the plaintiff must establish that he or she suffered a meaningfully adverse action, is it obvious that the consequences must be employment-related? And regardless of whether the adverse action must be employment-related or not, how adverse must it be? Does any petty slight or minor annoyance meet the statutory requirement where the plaintiff can establish that the employer's reaction was causally linked to his protected activity? For years, the circuit courts were split on both of these questions. The Supreme Court resolved the conflict on both of these issues in the following case:

Burlington Northern & Santa Fe Railway Co. v. White

Supreme Court of the United States, 2006.

548 U.S. 53, 126 S.Ct. 2405, 165 L.Ed.2d 345.

JUSTICE BREYER delivered the opinion of the Court.

Title VII of the Civil Rights Act of 1964 forbids employment discrimination against "any individual" based on that individual's "race, color, religion, sex, or national origin." §703(a). A separate section of the Act-its anti-retaliation provision-forbids an employer from "discriminat[ing] against" an employee or job applicant because that individual "opposed any practice" made unlawful by Title VII or "made a charge, testified, assisted, or participated in" a Title VII proceeding or investigation. §704(a).

The Courts of Appeals have come to different conclusions about the scope of the Act's anti-retaliation provision, particularly the reach of its phrase "discriminate against." Does that provision confine actionable retaliation to activity that affects the terms and conditions of employment? And how harmful must the adverse actions be to fall within its scope?

We conclude that the anti-retaliation provision does not confine the actions and harms it forbids to those that are related to employment or occur at the workplace. We also conclude that the provision covers those (and only those) employer actions that would have been materially adverse to a reasonable employee or job applicant. In the present context that means that the employer's actions must be harmful to the point that they could well dissuade a reasonable worker from making or supporting a charge of discrimination.

I

A

This case arises out of actions that supervisors at petitioner Burlington Northern & Santa Fe Railway Company took against respondent Sheila White, the only woman working in the Maintenance of Way department at Burlington's Tennessee Yard. In June 1997, Burlington's roadmaster, Marvin Brown, interviewed White and expressed interest in her previous experience operating forklifts. Burlington hired White as a "track laborer," a job that involves removing and replacing track components, transporting track material, cutting brush, and clearing litter and cargo spillage from the right-of-way. Soon after White arrived on the job, a co-worker who had previously operated the forklift chose to assume other responsibilities. Brown immediately assigned White to operate the forklift. While she also performed some of the other track laborer tasks, operating the forklift was White's primary responsibility.

In September 1997, White complained to Burlington officials that her immediate supervisor, Bill Joiner, had repeatedly told her that women should not be working in the Maintenance of Way department. Joiner, White said, had also made insulting and inappropriate remarks to her in front of her male colleagues. After an internal investigation, Burlington suspended Joiner for 10 days and ordered him to attend a sexual-harassment training session.

On September 26, Brown told White about Joiner's discipline. At the same time, he told White that he was removing her from forklift duty and assigning her to perform only standard track laborer tasks. Brown explained that the reassignment reflected co-worker's complaints that, in fairness, a "more senior man" should have the "less arduous and cleaner job" of forklift operator.

On October 10, White filed a complaint with the Equal Employment Opportunity Commission. She claimed that the reassignment of her duties amounted to unlawful gender-based discrimination and retaliation for her having earlier complained about Joiner. In early December, White filed a second retaliation charge with the Commission, claiming that Brown had placed her under surveillance and was monitoring her daily activities. That charge was mailed to Brown on December 8.

A few days later, White and her immediate supervisor, Percy Sharkey, disagreed about which truck should transport White from one location to another. The specific facts of the disagreement are in dispute, but the upshot is that Sharkey told Brown later that afternoon that White had been insubordinate. Brown immediately suspended White without pay. White invoked internal grievance procedures. Those procedures led Burlington to conclude that White had not been insubordinate. Burlington reinstated White to her position and awarded her backpay for the 37 days she was suspended. White filed an additional retaliation charge with the EEOC based on the suspension.

B

After exhausting administrative remedies, White filed this Title VII action against Burlington in federal court. As relevant here, she claimed that Burlington's actions — (1) changing her job responsibilities, and (2) suspending her for 37 days without pay

— amounted to unlawful retaliation in violation of §704(a). A jury found in White's favor on both of these claims. It awarded her $43,500 in compensatory damages, including $3,250 in medical expenses. The District Court denied Burlington's post-trial motion for judgment as a matter of law.

Initially, a divided Sixth Circuit panel reversed the judgment and found in Burlington's favor on the retaliation claims. The full Court of Appeals vacated the panel's decision, however, and heard the matter en banc. The court then affirmed the District Court's judgment in White's favor on both retaliation claims. While all members of the en banc court voted to uphold the District Court's judgment, they differed as to the proper standard to apply.

II

Title VII's anti-retaliation provision forbids employer actions that "discriminate against" an employee (or job applicant) because he has "opposed" a practice that Title VII forbids or has "made a charge, testified, assisted, or participated in" a Title VII "investigation, proceeding, or hearing." No one doubts that the term "discriminate against" refers to distinctions or differences in treatment that injure protected individuals. But different Circuits have come to different conclusions about whether the challenged action has to be employment or workplace related and about how harmful that action must be to constitute retaliation.

Some Circuits have insisted upon a close relationship between the retaliatory action and employment. The Sixth Circuit majority in this case, for example, said that a plaintiff must show an "adverse employment action," which it defined as a "materially adverse change in the terms and conditions" of employment. The Sixth Circuit has thus joined those Courts of Appeals that apply the same standard for retaliation that they apply to a substantive discrimination offense, holding that the challenged action must result in an adverse effect on the 'terms, conditions, or benefits' of employment." The Fifth and the Eighth Circuits have adopted a more restrictive approach. They employ an "ultimate employment decision" standard, which limits actionable retaliatory conduct to acts such as hiring, granting leave, discharging, promoting, and compensating.

Other Circuits have not so limited the scope of the provision. The Seventh and the District of Columbia Circuits have said that the plaintiff must show that the "employer's challenged action would have been material to a reasonable employee," which in contexts like the present one means that it would likely have "dissuaded a reasonable worker from making or supporting a charge of discrimination." And the Ninth Circuit, following EEOC guidance, has said that the plaintiff must simply establish "adverse treatment that is based on a retaliatory motive and is reasonably likely to deter the charging party or others from engaging in protected activity." The concurring judges below would have applied this last mentioned standard.

We granted certiorari to resolve this disagreement. To do so requires us to decide whether Title VII's anti-retaliation provision forbids only those employer actions and resulting harms that are related to employment or the workplace. And we must characterize how harmful an act of retaliatory discrimination must be in order to fall within the provision's scope.

A

Petitioner and the Solicitor General both argue that the Sixth Circuit is correct to require a link between the challenged retaliatory action and the terms, conditions, or status of employment. They note that Title VII's substantive anti-discrimination provision protects an individual only from employment-related discrimination. They add that the anti-retaliation provision should be read *in pari materia* with the anti-discrimination provision. And they conclude that the employer actions prohibited by the anti-retaliation provision should similarly be limited to conduct that affects the employee's compensation, terms, conditions, or privileges of employment.

We cannot agree. The language of the substantive provision differs from that of the anti-retaliation provision in important ways. Section 703(a) sets forth Title VII's core anti-discrimination provision in the following terms:

"It shall be an unlawful employment practice for an employer-

"(1) *to fail or refuse to hire or to discharge* any individual, or otherwise to discriminate against any individual *with respect to his compensation, terms, conditions, or privileges of employment*, because of such individual's race, color, religion, sex, or national origin; or

"(2) to limit, segregate, or classify his employees or applicants for employment in any way which would deprive or tend to deprive any individual of employment opportunities or otherwise adversely affect his status as an employee, because of such individual's race, color, religion, sex, or national origin." §703(a) (emphasis added).

Section 704(a) sets forth Title VII's anti-retaliation provision in the following terms:

"It shall be an unlawful employment practice for an employer *to discriminate against* any of his employees or applicants for employment ... because he has opposed any practice made an unlawful employment practice by this subchapter, or because he has made a charge, testified, assisted, or participated in any manner in an investigation, proceeding, or hearing under this subchapter." §704(a) (emphasis added).

The underscored words in the substantive provision — "hire," "discharge," "compensation, terms, conditions, or privileges of employment," "employment opportunities," and "status as an employee" — explicitly limit the scope of that provision to actions that affect employment or alter the conditions of the workplace. No such limiting words appear in the anti-retaliation provision. Given these linguistic differences, the question here is not whether identical or similar words should be read in pari materia to mean the same thing. Rather, the question is whether Congress intended its different words to make a legal difference. We normally presume that, where words differ as they differ here, "Congress acts intentionally and purposely in the disparate inclusion or exclusion." Russello v. United States, 464 U.S. 16, 23, 104 S.Ct. 296, 78 L.Ed.2d 17 (1983).

There is strong reason to believe that Congress intended the differences that its language suggests, for the two provisions differ not only in language but in purpose as well. The anti-discrimination provision seeks a workplace where individuals are not discriminated against because of their racial, ethnic, religious, or gender-based status. The anti-retaliation provision seeks to secure that primary objective by preventing an employer from interfering (through retaliation) with an employee's efforts to secure or advance enforcement of the Act's basic guarantees. The substantive provision seeks to prevent injury to individuals based on who they are, i.e., their status. The anti-retaliation provision seeks to prevent harm to individuals based on what they do, i.e., their conduct.

To secure the first objective, Congress did not need to prohibit anything other than employment-related discrimination. The substantive provision's basic objective of "equality of employment opportunities" and the elimination of practices that tend to bring about stratified job environments would be achieved were all employment-related discrimination miraculously eliminated.

But one cannot secure the second objective by focusing only upon employer actions and harm that concern employment and the workplace. Were all such actions and harms eliminated, the anti-retaliation provision's objective would *not* be achieved. An employer can effectively retaliate against an employee by taking actions not directly related to his employment or by causing him harm outside the workplace. See, e.g., Rochon v. Gonzales, 438 F.3d 1211 (D.C.Cir.2006) (FBI retaliation against employee "took the form of the FBI's refusal, contrary to policy, to investigate death threats a federal prisoner made against [the agent] and his wife"). A provision limited to employment-related actions would not deter the many forms that effective retaliation can take. Hence, such a limited construction would fail to fully achieve the anti-retaliation provision's "primary purpose," namely, "[m]aintaining unfettered access to statutory remedial mechanisms." Robinson v. Shell Oil Co., 519 U.S. 337, 346, 117 S.Ct. 843, 136 L.Ed.2d 808 (1997).

Thus, purpose reinforces what language already indicates, namely, that the anti-retaliation provision, unlike the substantive provision, is not limited to discriminatory actions that affect the terms and conditions of employment. Cf. Wachovia Bank, N.A. v. Schmidt, 546 U.S. 303, 126 S.Ct. 941, 952, 163 L.Ed.2d 797 (2006) (rejecting statutory construction that would "trea[t] venue and subject-matter jurisdiction prescriptions as *in pari materia*" because doing so would "overloo[k] the discrete offices of those concepts").

Our precedent does not compel a contrary conclusion. Indeed, we have found no case in this Court that offers petitioner or the United States significant support. Burlington Industries, Inc. v. Ellerth, 524 U.S. 742, 118 S.Ct. 2257, 141 L.Ed.2d 633 (1998), as petitioner notes, speaks of a Title VII requirement that violations involve "tangible employment action" such as "hiring, firing, failing to promote, reassignment with significantly different responsibilities, or a decision causing a significant change in benefits." But *Ellerth* does so only to "identify a class of [hostile work environment] cases" in which an employer should be held vicariously liable (without an affirmative defense) for the acts of supervisors. *Ellerth* did not discuss the scope of the general anti-discrimination provision. And *Ellerth* did not mention Title VII's anti-retaliation provision at all. At most, *Ellerth* sets forth a standard that petitioner and the Solicitor General believe the anti-retaliation provision ought to contain. But it does not compel acceptance of their view.

Nor can we find significant support for their view in the EEOC's interpretations of the provision. We concede that the EEOC stated in its 1991 and 1988 Compliance Manuals that the anti-retaliation provision is limited to "adverse employment-related action." But in those same manuals the EEOC lists the "[e]ssential [e]lements" of a retaliation claim along with language suggesting a broader interpretation.

Moreover, both before and after publication of the 1991 and 1988 manuals, the EEOC similarly expressed a broad interpretation of the anti-retaliation provision. See 2 EEOC Compliance Manual §8, p. 8-13 (1998) (hereinafter EEOC 1998 Manual), available at http:// www.eeoc.gov/policy/docs/ retal.html (as visited June 20, 2006, and available in Clerk of Court's case file) (§704(a) "prohibit[s] any adverse treatment that is based on a retaliatory motive and is reasonably likely to deter the charging party or others from engaging in protected activity"). And the EEOC 1998 Manual, which offers the Commission's only direct statement on the question of whether the anti-retaliation provision is limited to the same employment-related activity covered by the anti-discrimination provision, answers that question in the negative-directly contrary to petitioner's reading of the Act.

Finally, we do not accept the petitioner's and Solicitor General's view that it is "anomalous" to read the statute to provide broader protection for victims of retaliation than for those whom Title VII primarily seeks to protect, namely, victims of race-based, ethnic-based, religion-based, or gender-based discrimination. Congress has provided similar kinds of protection from retaliation in comparable statutes without any judicial suggestion that those provisions are limited to the conduct prohibited by the primary substantive provisions. The National Labor Relations Act, to which this Court has drawn analogies in other Title VII contexts, provides an illustrative example. Compare 29 U.S.C. §158(a)(3) (substantive provision prohibiting employer "discrimination in regard to ... any term or condition of employment to encourage or discourage membership in any labor organization") with §158(a)(4) (retaliation provision making it unlawful for an employer to "discharge or otherwise discriminate against an employee because he has filed charges or given testimony under this subchapter").

In any event, as we have explained, differences in the purpose of the two provisions remove any perceived "anomaly," for they justify this difference of interpretation. Title VII depends for its enforcement upon the cooperation of employees who are willing to file complaints and act as witnesses. Interpreting the anti-retaliation provision to provide broad protection from retaliation helps assure the cooperation upon which accomplishment of the Act's primary objective depends.

For these reasons, we conclude that Title VII's substantive provision and its anti-retaliation provision are not coterminous. The scope of the anti-retaliation provision extends beyond workplace-related or employment-related retaliatory acts and harm. We therefore reject the standards applied in the Courts of Appeals that have treated the anti-retaliation provision as forbidding the same conduct prohibited by the anti-discrimination provision and that have limited actionable retaliation to so-called "ultimate employment decisions."

B

The anti-retaliation provision protects an individual not from all retaliation, but from retaliation that produces an injury or harm. As we have explained, the Courts of Appeals have used differing language to describe the level of seriousness to which this harm must rise before it becomes actionable retaliation. We agree with the formulation set forth by the Seventh and the District of Columbia Circuits. In our view, a plaintiff must show that a reasonable employee would have found the challenged action materially adverse, which in this context means it well might have dissuaded a reasonable worker from making or supporting a charge of discrimination.

We speak of *material* adversity because we believe it is important to separate significant from trivial harms. Title VII, we have said, does not set forth "a general civility code for the American workplace." Oncale v. Sundowner Offshore Services, Inc., 523 U.S. 75, 80, 118 S.Ct. 998, 140 L.Ed.2d 201 (1998). An employee's decision to report discriminatory behavior cannot immunize that employee from those petty slights or minor annoyances that often take place at work and that all employees experience. The anti-retaliation provision seeks to prevent employer interference with "unfettered access" to Title VII's remedial mechanisms. Robinson, 519 U.S., at 346, 117 S.Ct. 843. It does so by prohibiting employer actions that are likely "to deter victims of discrimination from complaining to the EEOC," the courts, and their employers. Ibid. And normally petty slights, minor annoyances, and simple lack of good manners will not create such deterrence. See 2 EEOC 1998 Manual §8, p. 8-13.

We refer to reactions of a reasonable employee because we believe that the provision's standard for judging harm must be objective. An objective standard is judicially administrable. It avoids the uncertainties and unfair discrepancies that can plague a judicial effort to determine a plaintiff's unusual subjective feelings. We have emphasized the need for objective standards in other Title VII contexts, and those same concerns animate our decision here. See, e.g., Pennsylvania State Police v. Suders, 542 U.S. 129, 124 S.Ct. 2342, 159 L.Ed.2d 204 (2004) (constructive discharge doctrine); Harris v. Forklift Systems, Inc., 510 U.S. 17, 114 S.Ct. 367, 126 L.Ed.2d 295 (1993) (hostile work environment doctrine).

We phrase the standard in general terms because the significance of any given act of retaliation will often depend upon the particular circumstances. Context matters. "The real social impact of workplace behavior often depends on a constellation of surrounding circumstances, expectations, and relationships which are not fully captured by a simple recitation of the words used or the physical acts performed." *Oncale, supra,* at 81-82, 118 S.Ct. 998. A schedule change in an employee's work schedule may make little difference to many workers, but may matter enormously to a young mother with school age children. A supervisor's refusal to invite an employee to lunch is normally trivial, a nonactionable petty slight. But to retaliate by excluding an employee from a weekly training lunch that contributes significantly to the employee's professional advancement might well deter a reasonable employee from complaining about discrimination. See 2 EEOC 1998 Manual §8, p. 8-14. Hence, a legal standard that speaks in general terms rather than specific prohibited acts is preferable, for an act that would be immaterial in some situations is material in others.

Finally, we note that contrary to the claim of the concurrence, this standard does not require a reviewing court or jury to consider "the nature of the discrimination that led to the filing of the charge." (ALITO, J., concurring in judgment). Rather, the standard is tied to the challenged retaliatory act, not the underlying conduct that forms the basis of the Title VII complaint. By focusing on the materiality of the challenged action and the perspective of a reasonable person in the plaintiff's position, we believe this standard will screen out trivial conduct while effectively capturing those acts that are likely to dissuade employees from complaining or assisting in complaints about discrimination.

III

Applying this standard to the facts of this case, we believe that there was a sufficient evidentiary basis to support the jury's verdict on White's retaliation claim. The jury found that two of Burlington's actions amounted to retaliation: the reassignment of White from forklift duty to standard track laborer tasks and the 37-day suspension without pay.

Burlington does not question the jury's determination that the motivation for these acts was retaliatory. But it does question the statutory significance of the harm these acts caused. The District Court instructed the jury to determine whether respondent "suffered a materially adverse change in the terms or conditions of her employment," and the Sixth Circuit upheld the jury's finding based on that same stringent interpretation of the anti-retaliation provision (the interpretation that limits §704 to the same employment-related conduct forbidden by § 703). Our holding today makes clear that the jury was not required to find that the challenged actions were related to the terms or conditions of employment. And insofar as the jury also found that the actions were "materially adverse," its findings are adequately supported.

First, Burlington argues that a reassignment of duties cannot constitute retaliatory discrimination where, as here, both the former and present duties fall within the same job description. We do not see why that is so. Almost every job category involves some responsibilities and duties that are less desirable than others. Common sense suggests that one good way to discourage an employee such as White from bringing discrimination charges would be to insist that she spend more time performing the more arduous duties and less time performing those that are easier or more agreeable. * * *

To be sure, reassignment of job duties is not automatically actionable. Whether a particular reassignment is materially adverse depends upon the circumstances of the particular case, and should be judged from the perspective of a reasonable person in the plaintiff's position, considering all the circumstances. But here, the jury had before it considerable evidence that the track labor duties were "by all accounts more arduous and dirtier"; that the "forklift operator position required more qualifications, which is an indication of prestige"; and that "the forklift operator position was objectively considered a better job and the male employees resented White for occupying it." Based on this record, a jury could reasonably conclude that the reassignment of responsibilities would have been materially adverse to a reasonable employee.

Second, Burlington argues that the 37-day suspension without pay lacked statutory significance because Burlington ultimately reinstated White with backpay. Burlington says that it defies reason to believe that Congress would have considered a rescinded investigatory suspension with full back pay to be unlawful, particularly because Title VII, throughout much of its history, provided no relief in an equitable action for victims in White's position.

We do not find Burlington's last mentioned reference to the nature of Title VII's remedies convincing. After all, throughout its history, Title VII has provided for injunctions to bar like discrimination in the future, an important form of relief. And we have no reason to believe that a court could not have issued an injunction where an employer suspended an employee for retaliatory purposes, even if that employer later provided backpay. In any event, Congress amended Title VII in 1991 to permit victims of intentional discrimination to recover compensatory (as White received here) and punitive damages, concluding that the additional remedies were necessary help make victims whole. We would undermine the significance of that congressional judgment were we to conclude that employers could avoid liability in these circumstances.

Neither do we find convincing any claim of insufficient evidence. White did receive backpay. But White and her family had to live for 37 days without income. They did not know during that time whether or when White could return to work. Many reasonable employees would find a month without a paycheck to be a serious hardship. And White described to the jury the physical and emotional hardship that 37 days of having "no income, no money" in fact caused. A reasonable employee facing the choice between retaining her job (and paycheck) and filing a discrimination complaint might well choose the former. That is to say, an indefinite suspension without pay could well act as a deterrent, even if the suspended employee eventually received backpay. Thus, the jury's conclusion that the 37-day suspension without pay was materially adverse was a reasonable one.

IV

For these reasons, the judgment of the Court of Appeals is affirmed.

Justice Alito, concurring in the judgment.

I concur in the judgment, but I disagree with the majority's interpretation of the antiretaliation provision of Title VII. The majority's interpretation has no basis in the statutory language and will, I fear, lead to practical problems.

I

Two provisions of Title VII are important here. Section 703(a) prohibits a broad range of discriminatory employment practices. Among other things, §703(a) makes it unlawful for an employer "to discriminate against any individual with respect to his compensation, terms, conditions, or privileges of employment, because of such individual's race, color, religion, sex, or national origin." * * *

A complementary and closely related provision, §704(a), makes it unlawful to "discriminate against" an employee for retaliatory purposes. * * *

In this case, we must ascertain the meaning of the term "discriminate" in §704(a). Two possible interpretations are suggested by the language of §§703(a) and 704(a).

The first is the interpretation that immediately springs to mind if §704(a) is read by itself — i.e., that the term "discriminate" in §704(a) means what the term literally means, to treat differently. Respondent staunchly defends this interpretation, which the majority does not embrace, but this interpretation presents problems that are at least sufficient to raise doubts about its correctness. Respondent's interpretation makes §703(a) narrower in scope than §704(a) and thus implies that the persons whom Title VII is principally designed to protect — victims of discrimination based on race, color, sex, national origin, or religion — receive less protection than victims of retaliation. In addition, respondent's interpretation "makes a federal case" out of any small difference in the way an employee who has engaged in protected conduct is treated. On respondent's view, a retaliation claim must go to the jury if the employee creates a genuine issue on such questions as whether the employee was given any more or less work than others, was subjected to any more or less supervision, or was treated in a somewhat less friendly manner because of his protected activity. There is reason to doubt that Congress meant to burden the federal courts with claims involving relatively trivial differences in treatment. See Oncale v. Sundowner Offshore Services, Inc., 523 U.S. 75, 81, 118 S.Ct. 998, 140 L.Ed.2d 201 (1998); Faragher v. Boca Raton, 524 U.S. 775, 786-788, 118 S.Ct. 2275, 141 L.Ed.2d 662 (1998).

The other plausible interpretation, and the one I favor, reads §§703(a) and 704(a) together. Under this reading, "discriminat[ion]" under §704(a) means the discriminatory acts reached by §703(a) — chiefly, discrimination "with respect to ... compensation, terms, conditions, or privileges of employment." This is not, admittedly, the most straightforward reading of the bare language of §704(a), but it is a reasonable reading that harmonizes §§703(a) and 704(a). It also provides an objective standard that permits insignificant claims to be weeded out at the summary judgment stage, while providing ample protection for employees who are subjected to real retaliation.

The Courts of Appeals that have interpreted § 704(a) in this way state that it requires a materially adverse employment action. In Burlington Industries, Inc. v. Ellerth, 524 U.S. 742, 761-762, 118 S.Ct. 2257, 141 L.Ed.2d 633 (1998), we "import[ed]" this test for use in a different context — to define the term "tangible employment action," a concept we used to limit an employer's liability for harassment carried out by its supervisors. We explained that "[a] tangible employment action constitutes a significant change in employment status, such as hiring, firing, failing to promote, reassignment with significantly different responsibilities, or a decision causing a significant change in benefits."

II

The majority does not adopt either of the two interpretations noted above. In Part II-A of its opinion, the majority criticizes the interpretation that harmonizes §§703(a) and 704(a) as not sufficiently faithful to the language of §704(a). Although we found the materially adverse employment action test worthy of "import[ation]" in *Ellerth*, the majority now argues that this test is too narrow because it permits employers to take retaliatory measures outside the workplace. But the majority's concern is misplaced.

First, an employer who wishes to retaliate against an employee for engaging in protected conduct is much more likely to do so on the job. There are far more opportunities for retaliation in that setting, and many forms of retaliation off the job constitute crimes and are therefore especially risky.

Second, the materially adverse employment action test is not limited to on-the-job retaliation, as *Rochon*, one of the cases cited by the majority, illustrates. There, a Federal Bureau of Investigation agent claimed that the Bureau had retaliated against him by failing to provide the off-duty security that would otherwise have been furnished. But, for an FBI agent whose life may be threatened during off-duty hours, providing security easily qualifies as a term, condition, or privilege of employment. Certainly, if the FBI had a policy of denying protection to agents of a particular race, such discrimination would be actionable under §703(a).

But in Part II-B, rather than adopting the more literal interpretation based on the language of §704(a) alone, the majority instead puts that language aside and adopts a third interpretation — one that has no grounding in the statutory language. According to the majority, §704(a) does not reach all retaliatory differences in treatment but only those retaliatory acts that "well might have dissuaded a reasonable worker from making or supporting a charge of discrimination."

I see no sound basis for this test. The language of §704(a), which employs the unadorned term "discriminate," does not support this test. The unstated premise of the majority's reasoning seems to be that §704(a)'s only purpose is to prevent employers from taking those actions that are likely to stop employees from complaining about discrimination, but this unstated premise is unfounded. While surely *one of the purposes* of §704(a) is to prevent employers from engaging in retaliatory measures that dissuade employees from engaging in protected conduct, there is no reason to suppose that this is §704(a)'s only purpose. Indeed, the majority itself identifies another purpose of the antiretaliation provision: "to prevent harm to individuals" who assert their rights. Under the majority's test, however, employer conduct that causes harm to an employee is permitted so long as the employer conduct is not so severe as to dissuade a reasonable employee from making or supporting a charge of discrimination.

III

The practical consequences of the test that the majority adopts strongly suggest that this test is not what Congress intended.

First, the majority's test leads logically to perverse results. Under the majority's test, §704(a) reaches retaliation that well might dissuade an employee from making or supporting "a charge of discrimination." I take it that the phrase "a charge of discrimination" means the particular charge that the employee in question filed,[e] and if that is the proper interpretation, the nature of the discrimination that led to the filing of the charge must be taken into account in applying §704(a). Specifically, the majority's interpretation logically implies that the degree of protection afforded to a victim of retaliation is inversely proportional to the severity of the original act of discrimination that prompted the retaliation. A reasonable employee who is subjected to the most severe discrimination will not easily be dissuaded from filing a charge by the threat of retaliation; the costs of filing the charge, including possible retaliation, will have to be great to outweigh the benefits, such as preventing the continuation of the discrimination in the future and obtaining damages and other relief for past discrimination. Because the possibility of relatively severe retaliation will not easily dissuade this employee, the employer will be able to engage in relatively severe retaliation without incurring liability under §704(a). On the other hand, an employee who is subjected to a much milder form of discrimination will be much more easily dissuaded. For this employee, the costs of complaining, including possible retaliation,

---

[e]The alternative interpretation — that "a charge" does not mean the specific charge filed by the employee but an average or generic charge-would be unworkable. Without gauging the severity of the initial alleged discrimination, a jury cannot possibly compare the costs and benefits of filing a charge and, thus, cannot possibly decide whether the employer's alleged retaliatory conduct is severe enough to dissuade the filing of a charge. A jury will have no way of assessing the severity of the average alleged act of discrimination that leads to the filing of a charge, and, therefore, if "a charge" means an average or generic charge, the majority's test will leave juries hopelessly at sea.

will not have to be great to outweigh the lesser benefits that might be obtained by filing a charge. These topsy-turvy results make no sense.

Second, the majority's conception of a reasonable worker is unclear. Although the majority first states that its test is whether a "reasonable worker" might well be dissuaded, it later suggests that at least some individual characteristics of the actual retaliation victim must be taken into account. The majority comments that "the significance of any given act of retaliation will often depend upon the particular circumstances," and provides the following illustration: "A schedule change in an employee's work schedule may make little difference to many workers, but may matter enormously to a young mother with school age children."

This illustration suggests that the majority's test is not whether an act of retaliation well might dissuade the average reasonable worker, putting aside all individual characteristics, but, rather, whether the act well might dissuade a reasonable worker who shares at least some individual characteristics with the actual victim. The majority's illustration introduces three individual characteristics: age, gender, and family responsibilities. How many more individual characteristics a court or jury may or must consider is unclear.

Finally, the majority's interpretation contains a loose and unfamiliar causation standard. As noted, the majority's test asks whether an employer's retaliatory act "*well might have dissuaded* a reasonable worker from making or supporting a charge of discrimination." (emphasis added). Especially in an area of the law in which standards of causation are already complex, the introduction of this new and unclear standard is unwelcome.

For these reasons, I would not adopt the majority's test but would hold that §704(a) reaches only those discriminatory practices covered by §703(a).

IV

Applying this interpretation, I would affirm the decision of the Court of Appeals. The actions taken against respondent-her assignment to new and substantially less desirable duties and her suspension without pay-fall within the definition of an "adverse employment action."

With respect to respondent's reassignment, *Ellerth* specifically identified a "reassignment with significantly different responsibilities" as a "tangible employment action." 524 U.S., at 761, 118 S.Ct. 2257. Here, as the Court of Appeals stated, "[i]n essence, ... the reassignment was a demotion." The "new position was by all accounts more arduous and "dirtier", and petitioner's sole stated rationale for the reassignment was that respondent's prior duties were better suited for someone with greater seniority. This was virtually an admission that respondent was demoted when those responsibilities were taken away from her.

I would hold that respondent's suspension without pay likewise satisfied the materially adverse employment action test. Accordingly, although I would hold that a plaintiff asserting a §704(a) retaliation claim must show the same type of materially adverse employment action that is required for a §703(a) discrimination claim, I would hold that petitioner met that standard in this case, and I, therefore, concur in the judgment.

NOTES AND PROBLEMS FOR DISCUSSION

1. *Burlington Northern* raised two important issues: (1) how harmful the allegedly retaliatory response must be to be actionable; and (2) whether that response must affect the terms and conditions of the plaintiff's employment.

(a) With respect to the first of these issues, the majority sought to resolve the circuit conflict with an objective standard designed to promote §704(a)'s primary objective — to prevent conduct that "well might have" discouraged a reasonable employee from engaging in protected activity. To accomplish this, the majority concluded that the test should be whether the response was (1) materially adverse (2) to a reasonable employee. The majority indicated that the "materiality" standard was designed to exclude responses that are no more than "petty slights or minor annoyances" that result in "trivial" harm. And the objective standard, the majority explained, served to avoid the uncertainties associated with inquiry into any particular plaintiff's subjective feelings. (Note that in support of this argument, the majority cites its decision in *Harris* as evidence of the importance of an objective standard. But you will recall that in *Harris,* the Court ruled that in determining whether a supervisor's conduct created a hostile or abusive environment, the plaintiff must establish that the environment was hostile or abusive under *both* an objective and subjective test.).

In his concurring opinion, Justice Alito faults the majority for confecting both an unduly harsh and "unclear" standard. He suggests that attempting to determine whether a retaliatory act "might well have" dissuaded a reasonable employee from engaging in protected conduct will create the uncertainties that the majority sought to avoid by erecting an objective standard. He also charges that the majority's objectively-determined materiality standard will lead to "perverse results" since it ignores situations where the plaintiff, or a reasonable employee, would suffer real harm but in light of the seriousness of the alleged retaliation would not have been discouraged from filing a charge to challenge that employer action. Finally, he asserts that in applying this "objective" standard, the majority instructed the lower courts to evaluate the impact in light of the "particular circumstances" of the instant case. This, he maintains, necessarily incorporates some consideration of the individual plaintiff's circumstances or characteristics, an inquiry whose limits, he urges, are undefined. Who has the better of these arguments?

Applying the majority's objective standard, the Tenth Circuit held that rude and disrespectful conduct by co-employees and/or the transmission of derogatory emails would not deter a reasonable employee from filing and supporting a charge. It also held that the fact that the alleged retaliatory conduct did not, in fact, deter the plaintiff from filing a charge, while not fatal to the plaintiff's case, was relevant to a determination of its impact on a reasonable employee. *See* Somoza v. University of Denver, 513 F.3d 1206 (10th Cir. 2008). On the other hand, the Seventh Circuit has ruled that listing the plaintiff by name and reporting that she had filed an EEOC charge against the defendant employer in its publicly available (and statutorily mandated) annual SEC filings consisted an "adverse action" under the *Burlington Northern* "might well dissuade" standard. Greengrass v. International Monetary Systems, 776 F.3d 481 (7th Cir. 2015).

At least one circuit that previously adhered to the "ultimate employment practice" definition of adverse impact has continued to apply that standard in Title VII discrimination claims brought under §703(a), reading *Burlington Northern* as limited solely to the meaning of adverse action for retaliation claims brought under §704(a). *See e.g.*, McCoy v. City of Shreveport, 492 F.3d 551 (5th Cir. 2007) (per curiam).

(b) The Court also chose to resolve the issue of whether the retaliatory response must be limited to conduct that affects the plaintiff's terms and conditions of employment to be actionable. Since this plaintiff alleged that she had been reassigned to a less desirable job and suspended for 37 days before being reinstated with back pay, is there any doubt that this employer's response affected her terms and conditions of employment? If not, why did the Court nevertheless reach out to answer the question of whether §704(a) extended to an employer's non-employment related responses?

In addressing this question, the majority focused on the differences in statutory text and purpose between §§703(a) and 704(a) as the basis for concluding that the anti-retaliation provision extends to acts of retaliation that do not affect the plaintiff's terms and conditions of employment. And though Justice Alito admits that this is the more "straightforward" reading of the text, he nevertheless argues that to harmonize the meaning of these two provisions, the meaning of "discriminate" in §704(a) should be read to incorporate the employment-related elements of that term expressly contained in §703(a). Who has the better of that argument?

2. As the opinion in *Payne* reflects, individuals who engage in acts of "participation" are accorded a wider berth in terms of protection against retaliation than those who engage in acts of "opposition". However, one circuit court has decided to reject the notion that acts of participation are entitled to absolute immunity from employment-related retaliation. In MATTSON v. CATERPILLAR, INC., 359 F.3d 885 (7th Cir.2004), the court rejected the *dicta* in *Pettway* concerning this heightened level of protection to participants and concluded that providing individuals who engage in acts of participation with absolute immunity from employment-based retaliation was inconsistent with the objectives of Title VII. Any employee who, in bad faith, files an unreasonable and baseless charge with the EEOC or state enforcement agency, the court held, should not receive Title VII protection. Title VII, the court reasoned, was designed to protect the rights of workers who assert a good faith protest against action they reasonably believe constitutes unlawful discrimination. It was not, the court continued, intended to arm employees with a tactical weapon under which they can make baseless claims merely to advance their own retaliatory motives. To rule otherwise, the court maintained, would encourage an individual who maliciously files an utterly baseless internal complaint to follow up with an equally meritless complaint with a governmental agency in order to wrap himself in the cloak of participation immunity. Accordingly, the court concluded, the same threshold standard, i.e., the underlying claim must not be utterly baseless, should apply to both opposition and participation clause cases. And since the court found that the plaintiff's initial sexual harassment complaint was unreasonable, non-meritorious, and motivated by bad faith, it held that the plaintiff was not protected by the participation clause of §704 and affirmed the trial judge's grant of summary judgment to the defendant. *See also* Hatmaker v. Memorial Medical Center, 619 F.3d 741 (7th Cir. 2010), cert. denied, 562 U.S. 1270, 131 S.Ct. 1603, 179L.Ed.2d 500 (2011) (another Seventh Circuit panel ruling that, at a minimum, an employee should not enjoy participation immunity for gratuitously malicious and baseless statements contained in an EEOC charge that are not suggestive of any form of unlawful discrimination).

Assuming, however, that an employer does not want to run the risk of §704 liability, does it have any other recourse against a spiteful employee? For example:

(a) If an employer believes that it has been the victim of a false and maliciously filed Title VII claim, can it bring a defamation action against the disgruntled employee or would the filing of such an action constitute prohibited retaliation?

(b) Alternatively, what if the defamation suit was filed in response to a letter sent by the employee to a local newspaper charging that the employer was a racist?

A somewhat more novel remedy was sought and secured by the defendants in BECKER v. SHERWIN WILLIAMS, 717 F.Supp. 288 (D.N.J.1989). There, the trial court found that the plaintiff had filed 321 groundless charges of discrimination against the defendant over the preceding eight or nine years in an effort to extort a settlement and that the vast majority of these charges had been dismissed by the EEOC upon a finding of no reasonable cause to believe that discrimination had occurred. (The court noted that processing these claims had cost the EEOC approximately $250,000.) To prevent "further abuse of the federal court system" by the plaintiff, the court granted the defendants' request for an order permanently enjoining the plaintiff from submitting further employment applications with the defendant employer, from filing age discrimination complaints against that employer with any governmental agency or tribunal without the court's permission, from filing any new employment discrimination charge with any office of the defendant EEOC or state or local fair employment practice agency without a supporting affidavit containing specific information regarding the facts supporting a charge of discrimination, and from filing any lawsuit against the EEOC in any federal or state court without a supporting affidavit and without notifying that court of this permanent injunction.

3. When Title VII was amended in 1972, a new provision, §717, was enacted to extend the statutory guarantee of equal employment opportunity to federal employees. Does the absence in §717 of any language pertaining to retaliation suggest that federal employees are not protected against retaliation? *See* Brazoria County, Texas v. E.E.O.C., 391 F.3d 685 (5th Cir.2004) (although §717 does not expressly prohibit retaliation, the language stating that "all personnel actions" shall be made free from "any discrimination" based on race, etc., reflects a clear legislative intention to bar the federal government from engaging all forms of discrimination, including those identified in both §§703 and 704; and since the GERA extended the protections of §717 to the class of federal employees previously exempted from protection under §717, these federal employees also can state a claim of retaliation under the GERA).

Suppose that a public school teacher is represented by a labor union and that after she was discharged by the school district, the teacher complained to her union representative that she was fired because of her race. She asked the union to pursue a grievance on her behalf, but the union refused to go forward with the grievance. The teacher believes that the union based that decision on the fact that she previously had filed racial discrimination charges against the union with the EEOC. Can she state a claim of retaliation against the union under §704(a)? *See* Green v. American Federation of Teachers, 740 F.3d 1104 (7th Cir. 2014) (§704(a) extends to claims of retaliation by a union; allegation that the union failed to process a grievance because of prior EEOC filings against the union by the plaintiff states a claim of participation-based retaliation; the fact that this public employee union did not have a duty of fair representation under the National Labor Relations Act because the NLRA does not apply to state or local government employees is not fatal to her claim; a retaliation plaintiff does not have to allege that the adverse action violated some statutory or contractual duty found outside of Title VII).

4.   Suppose the employer in a retaliation case asserts that the plaintiff was discharged because she was constantly late for work and that she would have been discharged for that reason alone, without regard to her participation in protected §704(a) activity. Do the mixed motive provisions of §§703(m) and 706(g)(2)(B) (enacted as part of the 1991 Civil Rights Act to partially reverse the Supreme Court's mixed motives ruling in *Price Waterhouse*) apply to retaliation claims or does the fact that §§703(m) and 706(g)(2)(B) refer to claims asserted under §703, but not §704, reflect Congress' intention *not* to extend them to retaliation claims? And does the Supreme Court's ruling in *Gross v. FBL Financial Services, Inc.*, 557 U.S. 167, 129 S.Ct. 2343, 174 L.Ed.2d 119 (2009), see Chapter 10 B. *infra*, that mixed motive analysis is never available under the ADEA because, in large part, the 1991 provision codifying mixed motive analysis amended only Title VII and not the ADEA, shed any light on this question? Pre-*Gross*, all of the circuit courts that had ruled on the issue agreed that the absence of any explicit reference to either §704 or retaliation claims in the amended provisions reflected Congress' intention for the amendment *not* to apply to retaliation claims. However, they also held that the *Price Waterhouse* Court's pre-existing version of mixed motive claim could be invoked in retaliation cases. The Supreme Court resolved the matter in UNIVERSITY OF TEXAS SOUTHWESTERN MEDICAL CENTER v. NASSAR, 570 U.S. 338, 133 S.Ct. 2517, 186 L.Ed.2d 503 (2013). In *Nassar*, another 5-4 decision, the Court ruled that §704(a) retaliation cases were not susceptible to mixed motive analysis. In other words, a Title VII plaintiff claiming retaliation under §704(a), unlike a Title VII plaintiff alleging a claim of status-based discrimination under §703(a), has to meet a "but-for" causation standard. In reaching this decision, the Court majority employed the same analysis it had relied on four years earlier in *Gross*. Once again, the majority reasoned that since the plaintiff's portion of mixed motive analysis originally enunciated by the Supreme Court in *Price Waterhouse*, had been codified in §703 (specifically, §703(m)), but not in §704, by the 1991 Civil Rights Act, this reflected the legislature's deliberate intention to limit the availability of the mixed motive causation standard to claims brought under §703. Moreover, the majority pointed to the fact that the text of mixed motive provision in §703(m) refers only to status-based unlawful employment practices and does not mention retaliation. Accordingly, the Court ruled that retaliation claims brought under §704(a) of Title VII, like claims of age discrimination filed under the ADEA, are subject only to a but-for causation standard. However, post-*Nassar*, the circuit courts have been unable to agree on whether the "but-for" causation requirement attaches at the prima facie stage or only after the defendant has come forward with a non-retaliatory explanation and the plaintiff seeks to carry its ultimate burden of persuasion by proving pretext. In other words, did the Court in *Nassar* intend to preclude any application of the *McDonnell Douglas/Burdine* proof framework to retaliation cases? *Compare* Carvalho-Grevious v. Delaware State

University, 851 F.3d 249 (3d Cir. 2017)(*McDonnell Douglas* still applies in retaliation cases; the plaintiff only needs to proffer evidence sufficient to prove that retaliation was "the likely reason" for the adverse action, not the but-for reason, in order to withstand a motion to dismiss) with E.E.O.C. v. Ford Motor Co., 782 F.3d 753 (6th Cir. 2015)(a §704(a) plaintiff must prove but-for causation as part of the prima facie case).

5. With respect to the issue of causation, how much significance should be accorded the temporal proximity between the date the defendant learns of the plaintiff's protected activity and the adverse action? In MICKEY v. ZEIDLER TOOL & DIE CO., 516 F.3d 516 (6th Cir. 2008), the defendant terminated the plaintiff immediately upon receiving notice of the filing of his EEOC charge. The trial judge ruled that the plaintiff had failed to establish a prima facie claim of retaliation because he had offered no other evidence of a causal connection other than the fact of the timing of the discharge. The Sixth Circuit panel reversed, noting that though the law was "unsettled" on whether temporal proximity alone could establish a causal connection, the prevailing view, which it adopted, was that where an adverse employment action occurs "very close in time" after the employer learns of the protected activity, such temporal proximity is significant enough *per se* to establish the causation element of the prima facie case of retaliation. But where "some time" elapsed between these two events, the court continued, the employee must offer additional evidence to establish causality.

6. In most retaliation cases, the adverse response to the plaintiff's protected activity is taken by a supervisor or some other management official. In establishing that the defendant employer knew that the plaintiff had engaged in protected activity, does the plaintiff have to establish that the specific company official who took the adverse action possessed that knowledge? See Zann Kwan v. Andalex Group LLC, 737 F.3d 834 (2d Cir. 2013)(plaintiff satisfied the knowledge requirement by establishing that she had complained to one corporate officer about being a victim of sex discrimination and then was terminated by a different corporate officer; nothing more is necessary than "general corporate knowledge" that the plaintiff has engaged in protected activity).

Suppose, on the other hand, that the adverse response to the plaintiff's protected activity was taken by a co-employee. Would or should that affect the §704(a) analysis? Pre-*Burlington Northern*, the circuit courts disagreed on this question. Although the majority took the position that §704(a) extended to co-worker retaliation claims, a few circuits rejected that position on the ground that this sort of response did not constitute an "adverse action". How should this issue be handled in light of the rulings in *Burlington Northern* (1) that §704(a) is not limited to instances of retaliation that solely affect terms or conditions of employment; and (2) that the adverse action need not be an ultimate employment action but rather a response that likely would have dissuaded a reasonable employee from engaging in protected activity? And if co-worker retaliation claims should be recognized, what should the plaintiff be required to prove to establish employer liability? *Compare* Hawkins v. Anheuser-Busch, Inc., 517 F.3d 321 (6th Cir. 2008) (a plaintiff must establish that (1) the co-worker's retaliatory conduct was sufficient severe to dissuade a reasonable worker from engaging in protected conduct; (2) supervisors or other management officials knew or should have known of the retaliatory behavior; and (3) supervisors or other management officials either condoned, tolerated or encouraged the co-worker's actions, or responded to the plaintiff's complaints so inadequately that the response manifested indifference or unreasonableness under the circumstances, *with* Carpenter v. Con-Way Cent. Express, Inc., 481 F.3d 611 (8ᵗʰ Cir. 2007) (the plaintiff must demonstrate that the employer's failure to take sufficient remedial action in response to co-worker retaliation was motivated by the fact that the plaintiff engaged in protected activity).

7.   Lou Bernstein and his daughter, Judy, worked for Martinez Paper Co. After the company denied Judy's application for a promotion, she filed a charge with the EEOC alleging that the denial of the promotion was based exclusively on her sex. Shortly after receiving notice of this charge, the company discharged her father. Can Lou state a cause of action under §704? Does the standard adopted by the majority in *Burlington Northern* shed light on this problem? The Supreme Court resolved a circuit conflict on this issue in the following case.

Thompson v. North American Stainless, LP.

Supreme Court of the United States, 2011.
562 U.S. 170, 131 S.Ct. 863, 178 L.Ed.2d 694.

JUSTICE SCALIA delivered the opinion of the Court, in which all other Members joined, except JUSTICE KAGAN., who took no part in the consideration or decision of the case. GINSBURG, J., filed a concurring opinion, in which BREYER, J., joined.

Until 2003, both petitioner Eric Thompson and his fiancée, Miriam Regalado, were employees of respondent North American Stainless (NAS). In February 2003, the Equal Employment Opportunity Commission (EEOC) notified NAS that Regalado had filed a charge alleging sex discrimination. Three weeks later, NAS fired Thompson.

Thompson then filed a charge with the EEOC. After conciliation efforts proved unsuccessful, he sued NAS in the United States District Court for the Eastern District of Kentucky under Title VII, claiming that NAS had fired him in order to retaliate against Regalado for filing her charge with the EEOC. The District Court granted summary judgment to NAS, concluding that Title VII "does not permit third party retaliation claims." After a panel of the Sixth Circuit reversed the District Court, the Sixth Circuit granted rehearing en banc and affirmed by a 10-to-6 vote. The court reasoned that because Thompson did not "engag [e] in any statutorily protected activity, either on his own behalf or on behalf of Miriam Regalado," he "is not included in the class of persons for whom Congress created a retaliation cause of action."

We granted certiorari.

I

Title VII provides that "[i]t shall be an unlawful employment practice for an employer to discriminate against any of his employees ... because he has made a charge" under Title VII. §704(a). The statute permits "a person claiming to be aggrieved" to file a charge with the EEOC alleging that the employer committed an unlawful employment practice, and, if the EEOC declines to sue the employer, it permits a civil action to "be brought ... by the person claiming to be aggrieved ... by the alleged unlawful employment practice." §706(b), (f)(1).

It is undisputed that Regalado's filing of a charge with the EEOC was protected conduct under Title VII. In the procedural posture of this case, we are also required to assume that NAS fired Thompson in order to retaliate against Regalado for filing a charge of discrimination. This case therefore presents two questions: First, did NAS's firing of Thompson constitute unlawful retaliation? And second, if it did, does Title VII grant Thompson a cause of action?

II

With regard to the first question, we have little difficulty concluding that if the facts alleged by Thompson are true, then NAS's firing of Thompson violated Title VII. In *Burlington N. & S.F.R. Co. v. White,* we held that Title VII's antiretaliation provision must be construed to cover a broad range of employer conduct. We reached that conclusion by contrasting the text of Title VII's antiretaliation provision with its substantive antidiscrimination provision. Title VII prohibits discrimination on the basis of race, color, religion, sex, and national origin "with respect to ... compensation, terms, conditions, or privileges of employment," and discriminatory practices that would "deprive any individual of employment opportunities or otherwise adversely affect his status as an employee." §703(a). In contrast, Title VII's antiretaliation provision prohibits an employer from "discriminat[ing] against any of his employees' " for engaging in protected conduct, without specifying the employer acts that are prohibited. §704(a). Based on this textual distinction and our understanding of the antiretaliation provision's purpose, we held that "the antiretaliation provision, unlike the substantive provision, is not limited to discriminatory actions that affect the terms and conditions of employment." Rather, Title VII's antiretaliation provision prohibits any employer action that "well might have dissuaded a reasonable worker from making or supporting a charge of discrimination."

We think it obvious that a reasonable worker might be dissuaded from engaging in protected activity if she knew that her fiancé would be fired. Indeed, NAS does not dispute that Thompson's firing meets the standard set forth in *Burlington*. NAS raises the concern, however, that prohibiting reprisals against third parties will lead to difficult line-drawing problems concerning the types of relationships entitled to protection. Perhaps retaliating against an employee by firing his fiancée would dissuade the employee from engaging in protected activity, but what about firing an employee's girlfriend, close friend, or trusted co-worker? Applying the *Burlington* standard to third-party reprisals, NAS argues, will place the employer at risk any time it fires any employee who happens to have a connection to a different employee who filed a charge with the EEOC.

Although we acknowledge the force of this point, we do not think it justifies a categorical rule that third-party reprisals do not violate Title VII. As explained above, we adopted a broad standard in *Burlington* because Title VII's antiretaliation provision is worded broadly. We think there is no textual basis for making an exception to it for third-party reprisals, and a preference for clear rules cannot justify departing from statutory text.

We must also decline to identify a fixed class of relationships for which third-party reprisals are unlawful. We expect that firing a close family member will almost always meet the *Burlington* standard, and inflicting a milder reprisal on a mere acquaintance will almost never do so, but beyond that we are reluctant to generalize. As we explained in *Burlington,* "the significance of any given act of retaliation will often depend upon the particular circumstances." Given the broad statutory text and the variety of workplace contexts in which retaliation may occur, Title VII's antiretaliation provision is simply not reducible to a comprehensive set of clear rules. We emphasize, however, that "the provision's standard for judging harm must be objective," so as to "avoi[d] the uncertainties and unfair discrepancies that can plague a judicial effort to determine a plaintiff's unusual subjective feelings." *Id.*

III

The more difficult question in this case is whether Thompson may sue NAS for its alleged violation of Title VII. The statute provides that "a civil action may be brought ... by the person claiming to be aggrieved." §706(f)(1). The Sixth Circuit concluded that this provision was merely a reiteration of the requirement that the plaintiff have Article III standing. We do not understand how that can be. The provision unquestionably permits a person "claiming to be aggrieved" to bring "a civil action." It is arguable that the aggrievement referred to is nothing more than the minimal Article III standing, which consists of injury in fact caused by the defendant and remediable by the court. But Thompson's claim undoubtedly meets those requirements, so if that is indeed all that aggrievement consists of, he may sue.

We have suggested in dictum that the Title VII aggrievement requirement conferred a right to sue on all who satisfied Article III standing. *Trafficante v. Metropolitan Life Ins. Co.,* 409 U.S. 205, 93 S.Ct. 364, 34 L.Ed.2d 415 (1972), involved the "person aggrieved" provision of Title VIII (the Fair Housing Act) rather than Title VII. In deciding the case, however, we relied upon, and cited with approval, a Third Circuit opinion involving Title VII, which, we said, "concluded that the words used showed a congressional intention to define standing as broadly as is permitted by Article III of the Constitution." We think that dictum regarding Title VII was too expansive. Indeed, the *Trafficante* opinion did not adhere to it in expressing its Title VIII holding that residents of an apartment complex could sue the owner for his racial discrimination against prospective tenants. The opinion said that the "person aggrieved" of Title VIII was coextensive with Article III *"insofar as tenants of the same housing unit that is charged with discrimination are concerned."* (emphasis added). Later opinions, we must acknowledge, reiterate that the term "aggrieved" in Title VIII reaches as far as Article III permits, see *Bennett v. Spear,* 520 U.S. 154, 165-166, 117 S.Ct. 1154, 137 L.Ed.2d 281 (1997); *Gladstone, Realtors v. Village of Bellwood,* 441 U.S. 91, 109, 99 S.Ct. 1601, 60 L.Ed.2d 66 (1979), though the holdings of those cases are compatible with the "zone of interests" limitation that we discuss below. In any event, it is Title VII rather than Title VIII that is before us here, and as to that we are surely not bound by the *Trafficante* dictum.

We now find that this dictum was ill-considered, and we decline to follow it. If any person injured in the Article III sense by a Title VII violation could sue, absurd consequences would follow. For example, a shareholder would be able to sue a company for firing a valuable employee for racially discriminatory reasons, so long as he could show that the value of his stock decreased as a consequence. At oral argument Thompson acknowledged that such a suit would not lie. We agree, and therefore conclude that the term "aggrieved" must be construed more narrowly than the outer boundaries of Article III.

At the other extreme from the position that "person aggrieved" means anyone with Article III standing, NAS argues that it is a term of art that refers only to the employee who engaged in the protected activity. We know of no other context in which the words carry this artificially narrow meaning, and if that is what Congress intended it would more naturally have said "person claiming to have been discriminated against" rather than "person claiming to be aggrieved." We see no basis in text or prior practice for limiting the latter phrase to the person who was the subject of unlawful retaliation. Moreover, such a reading contradicts the very holding of *Trafficante,* which was that residents of an apartment complex were "person[s] aggrieved" by discrimination against prospective tenants. We see no reason why the same phrase in Title VII should be given a narrower meaning.

In our view there is a common usage of the term "person aggrieved" that avoids the extremity of equating it with Article III and yet is fully consistent with our application of the term in *Trafficante.* The Administrative Procedure Act, 5 U.S.C. § 551 *et seq.*, authorizes suit to challenge a federal agency by any "person ... adversely affected or aggrieved ... within the meaning of a relevant statute." § 702. We have held that this language establishes a regime under which a plaintiff may not sue unless he "falls within the 'zone of interests' sought to be protected by the statutory provision whose violation forms the legal basis for his complaint." *Lujan v. National Wildlife Federation,* 497 U.S. 871, 883, 110 S.Ct. 3177, 111 L.Ed.2d 695 (1990). We have described the "zone of interests" test as denying a right of review "if the plaintiff's interests are so marginally related to or inconsistent with the purposes implicit in the statute that it cannot reasonably be assumed that Congress intended to permit the suit." *Clarke v. Securities Industry Assn.,* 479 U.S. 388, 399-400, 107 S.Ct. 750, 93 L.Ed.2d 757 (1987). We hold that the term "aggrieved" in Title VII incorporates this test, enabling suit by any plaintiff with an interest "arguably [sought] to be protected by the statutes," *National Credit Union Admin. v. First Nat. Bank & Trust Co.,* 522 U.S. 479, 495, 118 S.Ct. 927, 140 L.Ed.2d 1 (1998) (internal quotation marks omitted), while excluding plaintiffs who might technically be injured in an Article III sense but whose interests are unrelated to the statutory prohibitions in Title VII.

Applying that test here, we conclude that Thompson falls within the zone of interests protected by Title VII. Thompson was an employee of NAS, and the purpose of Title VII is to protect employees from their employers' unlawful actions. Moreover, accepting the facts as alleged, Thompson is not an accidental victim of the retaliation-collateral damage, so to speak, of the employer's unlawful act. To the contrary, injuring him was the employer's intended means of harming Regalado. Hurting him was the unlawful act by which the employer punished her. In those circumstances, we think Thompson well within the zone of interests sought to be protected by Title VII. He is a person aggrieved with standing to sue.

The judgment of the Sixth Circuit is reversed, and the case is remanded for further proceedings consistent with this opinion.

It is so ordered.

JUSTICE KAGAN took no part in the consideration or decision of this case.

JUSTICE GINSBURG, with whom JUSTICE BREYER joins, concurring.

I join the Court's opinion, and add a fortifying observation: Today's decision accords with the longstanding views of the Equal Employment Opportunity

Commission (EEOC), the federal agency that administers Title VII. In its Compliance Manual, the EEOC counsels that Title VII "prohibit[s] retaliation against someone so closely related to or associated with the person exercising his or her statutory rights that it would discourage or prevent the person from pursuing those rights." Such retaliation "can be challenged," the Manual affirms, "by both the individual who engaged in protected activity and the relative, where both are employees. The EEOC's statements in the Manual merit deference under *Skidmore v. Swift & Co.,* 323 U.S. 134, 65 S.Ct. 161, 89 L.Ed. 124 (1944). The EEOC's interpretation of Title VII, I further note, is consistent with interpretations of analogous statutes by other federal agencies. See, *e.g., NLRB v. Advertisers Mfg. Co.,* 823 F.2d 1086, 1088-1089 (C.A.7 1987) (adopting NLRB's position that retaliation against a relative violates the National Labor Relations Act); *Tasty Baking Co. v. NLRB,* 254 F.3d 114, 127-128 (C.A.D.C.2001) (same).

NOTES AND PROBLEMS FOR DISCUSSION

1. Do you agree with the Supreme Court's unanimous decision that third party retaliation claims are cognizable under Title VII? The obvious difficulty with this ruling, which the Court acknowledged, is the slippery slope problem. Are you satisfied with the Court's response that it was unnecessary and even inappropriate to identify a fixed class of relationships that would meet the *Burlington* chilling effect standard? And when the Court suggests that the standard for assessing the extent of the harm caused to that third party must be "objective" to avoid the inconsistent judgments that would result if the courts attempted to assess each plaintiff's subjective feelings, what meaningful direction does that provide to the lower courts tasked with applying this standard? For a pre-*Thompson* in-depth analysis of third-party retaliation claims, see Alex B. Long, *The Troublemaker's Friend: Retaliation Against Third Parties and the Right of Association in the Workplace,* 59 FLA. L. REV. 931 (2007).

2. Who was the *Thompson* Court protecting – the plaintiff husband or his fiancée? Suppose, for example, that we change one fact in the principal case. Imagine that the plaintiff Eric's fiancée, Miriam, had worked for a company other than Stainless and that she had filed a sex discrimination charge against *her* employer, Apex Construction. Suppose also that it turned out that the supervisor that she had charged with engaging in the sex discrimination had an uncle who worked for Stainless. When Miriam's supervisor told his uncle that Miriam had filed a charge naming him as the perpetrator, that uncle convinced Eric's supervisor to fire Eric. Eric then filed a §704(a) claim against Stainless. Same result? In UNDERWOOD v. DEP'T OF FINANCIAL SERVICES STATE OF FLORIDA, 518 Fed.Appx. 637 (11th Cir. 2013)(unpublished), the Eleventh Circuit upheld the trial court's issuance of summary judgment in favor of the defendant. Rejecting the plaintiff's contention that his claim fell squarely within the ruling in *Thompson,* the Eleventh Circuit panel, in an unpublished opinion, ruled that the plaintiff could not state a claim under §704(a) because the defendant employer did not retaliate against the person who engaged in the protected conduct. After finding that the employer who had been the subject of the underlying charge was a separate employer from the defendant named in the plaintiff's §704(a) charge (the two employers were separate agencies of the State of Florida), the court construed the *Thompson* Court's reliance on *Burlington Northern* as requiring it to assess the impact of the retaliatory act on the person who filed the underlying charge. In the instant case, the court explained, the §704(a) plaintiff claimed that *his* employer had retaliated against *him*, and not against his wife (who had filed the underlying sex discrimination charge and who worked for a separate state agency). As far as the Eleventh Circuit was concerned, "the retaliatory action must be against an employee who engaged in protected conduct." And since the defendant was not the employer of the person who had engaged in 704(a)-protected activity, the appellate panel concluded, this employer could not said to have retaliated against *her*. The fact that it retaliated against someone else, the court reasoned, did not meet the *Burlington Northern* standard. Having determined that the plaintiff's claim did not fall within the scope of §704(a), the panel declared that it was unnecessary to consider the standing question of whether the plaintiff fell the zone of interests protected by Title VII.

SECTION C. NONINTENTIONAL DISCRIMINATION

As originally enacted, §703 of Title VII did not define "discrimination." Consequently, until the statute was amended in 1991, the courts had to resolve whether this statute barred the use of facially neutral practices which disproportionately affected members of a statutorily protected classification.

1. THE CONCEPTUAL FRAMEWORK

Griggs v. Duke Power Co.

Supreme Court of the United States, 1971.
401 U.S. 424, 91 S.Ct. 849, 28 L.Ed.2d 158.

MR. CHIEF JUSTICE BURGER delivered the opinion of the Court.

We granted the writ in this case to resolve the question whether an employer is prohibited by the Civil Rights Act of 1964, Title VII, from requiring a high school education or passing of a standardized general intelligence test as a condition of employment in or transfer to jobs when (a) neither standard is shown to be significantly related to successful job performance, (b) both requirements operate to disqualify Negroes at a substantially higher rate than white applicants, and (c) the jobs in question formerly had been filled only by white employees as part of a longstanding practice of giving preference to whites.

* * * [T]his proceeding was brought by a group of incumbent Negro employees against Duke Power Company. All the petitioners are employed at the Company's Dan River Steam Station, a power generating facility located at Draper, North Carolina. At the time this action was instituted, the Company had 95 employees at the Dan River Station, 14 of whom were Negroes; 13 of these are petitioners here.

The District Court found that prior to July 2, 1965, the effective date of the Civil Rights Act of 1964, the Company openly discriminated on the basis of race in the hiring and assigning of employees at its Dan River plant. The plant was organized into five operating departments: (1) Labor, (2) Coal Handling, (3) Operations, (4)

Maintenance, and (5) Laboratory and Test. Negroes were employed only in the Labor Department where the highest paying jobs paid less than the lowest paying jobs in the other four "operating" departments in which only whites were employed. Promotions were normally made within each department on the basis of job seniority. Transferees into a department usually began in the lowest position.

In 1955 the Company instituted a policy of requiring a high school education for initial assignment to any department except Labor, and for transfer from the Coal Handling to any "inside" department (Operations, Maintenance, or Laboratory). When the Company abandoned its policy of restricting Negroes to the Labor Department in 1965, completion of high school also was made a prerequisite to transfer from Labor to any other department. From the time the high school requirement was instituted to the time of trial, however, white employees hired before the time of the high school education requirement continued to perform satisfactorily and achieve promotions in the "operating" departments. * * *

The Company added a further requirement for new employees on July 2, 1965, the date on which Title VII became effective. To qualify for placement in any but the Labor Department it became necessary to register satisfactory scores on two professionally prepared aptitude tests, as well as to have a high school education. Completion of high school alone continued to render employees eligible for transfer to the four desirable departments from which Negroes had been excluded if the incumbent had been employed prior to the time of the new requirement. In September 1965 the Company began to permit incumbent employees who lacked a high school education to qualify for transfer from Labor or Coal Handling to an "inside" job by passing two tests—the Wonderlic Personnel Test, which purports to measure general intelligence, and the Bennett Mechanical Comprehension Test. Neither was directed or intended to measure the ability to learn to perform a particular job or category of jobs. The requisite scores used for both initial hiring and transfer approximated the national median for high school graduates.[3]

The District Court had found that while the Company previously followed a policy of overt racial discrimination in a period prior to the Act, such conduct had ceased. The District Court also concluded that Title VII was intended to be prospective only and, consequently, the impact of prior inequities was beyond the reach of corrective action authorized by the Act.

The Court of Appeals was confronted with a question of first impression, as are we, concerning the meaning of Title VII. After careful analysis a majority of that court concluded that a subjective test of the employer's intent should govern, particularly in a close case, and that in this case there was no showing of a discriminatory purpose in the adoption of the diploma and test requirements. On this basis, the Court of Appeals concluded there was no violation of the Act.

* * * In so doing, the Court of Appeals rejected the claim that because these two requirements operated to render ineligible a markedly disproportionate number of

---

[3]The test standards are thus more stringent than the high school requirement, since they would screen out approximately half of all high school graduates.

Negroes, they were unlawful under Title VII unless shown to be job related. We granted the writ on these claims.

The objective of Congress in the enactment of Title VII * * * was to achieve equality of employment opportunities and remove barriers that have operated in the past to favor an identifiable group of white employees over other employees. Under the Act, practices, procedures, or tests neutral on their face, and even neutral in terms of intent, cannot be maintained if they operate to "freeze" the status quo of prior discriminatory employment practices.

The Court of Appeals' opinion, and the partial dissent, agreed that, on the record in the present case, "whites register far better on the Company's alternative requirements" than Negroes.[6] This consequence would appear to be directly traceable to race. Basic intelligence must have the means of articulation to manifest itself fairly in a testing process. Because they are Negroes, petitioners have long received inferior education in segregated schools * * *. Congress did not intend by Title VII, however, to guarantee a job to every person regardless of qualifications. In short, the Act does not command that any person be hired simply because he was formerly the subject of discrimination, or because he is a member of a minority group. Discriminatory preference for any group, minority or majority, is precisely and only what Congress has proscribed. What is required by Congress is the removal of artificial, arbitrary, and unnecessary barriers to employment when the barriers operate invidiously to discriminate on the basis of racial or other impermissible classification.

* * * The Act proscribes not only overt discrimination but also practices that are fair in form, but discriminatory in operation. The touchstone is business necessity. If an employment practice which operates to exclude Negroes cannot be shown to be related to job performance, the practice is prohibited.

On the record before us, neither the high school completion requirement nor the general intelligence test is shown to bear a demonstrable relationship to successful performance of the jobs for which it was used. Both were adopted, as the Court of Appeals noted, without meaningful study of their relationship to job-performance ability. Rather, a vice president of the Company testified, the requirements were instituted on the Company's judgment that they generally would improve the overall quality of the work force.

The evidence, however, shows that employees who have not completed high school or taken the tests have continued to perform satisfactorily and make progress in departments for which the high school and test criteria are now used.[7] The promotion record of present employees who would not be able to meet the new criteria thus

---

[6]In North Carolina, 1960 census statistics show that, while 34% of white males had completed high school, only 12% of Negro males had done so.

Similarly, with respect to standardized tests, the EEOC in one case found that use of a battery of tests, including the Wonderlic and Bennett tests used by the Company in the instant case, resulted in 58% of whites passing the tests, as compared with only 6% of the blacks.

[7]For example, between July 2, 1965, and November 14, 1966, the percentage of white employees who were promoted but who were not high school graduates was nearly identical to the percentage of nongraduates in the entire white work force.

suggests the possibility that the requirements may not be needed even for the limited purpose of preserving the avowed policy of advancement within the Company. * * *

The Court of Appeals held that the Company had adopted the diploma and test requirements without any "intention to discriminate against Negro employees." We do not suggest that either the District Court or the Court of Appeals erred in examining the employer's intent; but good intent or absence of discriminatory intent does not redeem employment procedures or testing mechanisms that operate as "built-in headwinds" for minority groups and are unrelated to measuring job capability.

The Company's lack of discriminatory intent is suggested by special efforts to help the undereducated employees through Company financing of two-thirds the cost of tuition for high school training. But Congress directed the thrust of the Act to the consequences of employment practices, not simply the motivation. More than that, Congress has placed on the employer the burden of showing that any given requirement must have a manifest relationship to the employment in question.

* * *

The Company contends that its general intelligence tests are specifically permitted by §703(h) of the Act.[8] That section authorizes the use of "any professionally developed ability test" that is not "designed, intended or used to discriminate because of race * * *." (Emphasis added.)

The Equal Employment Opportunity Commission, having enforcement responsibility, has issued guidelines interpreting §703(h) to permit only the use of job-related tests.[9] The administrative interpretation of the Act by the enforcing agency is entitled to great deference. Since the Act and its legislative history support the Commission's construction, this affords good reason to treat the guidelines as expressing the will of Congress.

* * *

Nothing in the Act precludes the use of testing or measuring procedures; obviously they are useful. What Congress has forbidden is giving these devices and mechanisms controlling force unless they are demonstrably a reasonable measure of job performance. Congress has not commanded that the less qualified be preferred over the better qualified simply because of minority origins. Far from disparaging job

---

[8]Section 703(h) applies only to tests. It has no applicability to the high school diploma requirement.

[9]EEOC Guidelines on Employment Testing Procedures, issued August 24, 1966, provide:

"The Commission accordingly interprets 'professionally developed ability test' to mean a test which fairly measures the knowledge or skills required by the particular job or class of jobs which the applicant seeks, or which fairly affords the employer a chance to measure the applicant's ability to perform a particular job or class of jobs. The fact that a test was prepared by an individual or organization claiming expertise in test preparation does not, without more, justify its use within the meaning of Title VII."

The EEOC position has been elaborated in the new Guidelines on Employees Selection Procedures, 29 CFR §1607, 35 Fed.Reg. 12333 (Aug. 1, 1970). These guidelines demand that employers using tests have available "data demonstrating that the test is predictive of or significantly correlated with important elements of work behavior which comprise or are relevant to the job or jobs for which candidates are being evaluated."

qualifications as such, Congress has made such qualifications the controlling factor, so that race, religion, nationality, and sex become irrelevant. What Congress has commanded is that any tests used must measure the person for the job and not the person in the abstract.

The judgment of the Court of Appeals is, as to that portion of the judgment appealed from, reversed.

MR. JUSTICE BRENNAN took no part in the consideration or decision of this case.

NOTES AND PROBLEMS FOR DISCUSSION

1. How does the concept of discrimination recognized by the Court in *Griggs* differ from the one examined in *Burdine*? *Griggs* provoked considerable academic debate over the statutory authority and policy rationale for the disparate impact theory. *Compare* Michael E. Gold, *Griggs' Folly: An Essay on the Theory, Problems, and Origins of the Adverse Impact Definition of Employment Discrimination and a Recommendation for Reform*, 7 IND.REL.L.J. 429 (1985), *with* George Rutherglen, *Disparate Impact Under Title VII: An Objective Theory of Discrimination*, 73 Va.L.Rev. 1297 (1987). *See also* Alfred Blumrosen, *Strangers in Paradise: Griggs v. Duke Power Co. and the Concept of Employment Discrimination*, 71 MICH.L.REV. 59 (1972).

2. The Age Discrimination in Employment Act (ADEA) was enacted in 1967. *Griggs* was decided in 1971 and did not refer to the ADEA. For almost 30 years after *Griggs*, the Supreme Court did not speak to the question of whether ADEA violations could be established through disparate impact. To resolve a split in the circuits, the Court finally resolved the controversy in SMITH v. CITY OF JACKSON, 544 U.S. 228, 125 S.Ct. 1536, 161 L.Ed.2d 410 (2005). There, in a plurality decision, the Court declared that disparate impact analysis does apply to ADEA claims. The four justice plurality based its decision on Congress' use of identical language in §703 of Title VII and the corresponding substantive provisions of the ADEA, on the ADEA's legislative history, and on the consistent interpretation of the ADEA as authorizing relief on a disparate impact theory by the EEOC and the Department of Labor. But the plurality also held that critical differences between Title VII and the ADEA meant that the scope of disparate impact liability under the ADEA was significantly narrower than under Title VII. Those limitations will be discussed *infra*, at Chapter 2(C)(3). Without objecting to the plurality's statutory construction, Justice Scalia concurred solely on the ground that the Court should defer to the reasonable views of the EEOC. Justice O'Connor, joined by two other justices, maintained that neither the language nor the legislative history of the ADEA supported application of disparate impact analysis. To the contrary, she reasoned, it supported the opposite conclusion. The ruling in *Smith* also is discussed in more detail in Chapter 10B, *infra*.

3. Post-*Griggs*, disproportionate impact analysis was applied to a wide variety of objective employment standards including minimum height and weight requirements, Dothard v. Rawlinson, 433 U.S. 321, 97 S.Ct. 2720, 53 L.Ed.2d 786 (1977) (sex discrimination); prior experience requirements, Chrisner v. Complete Auto Transit, Inc., 645 F.2d 1251 (6th Cir. 1981) (sex discrimination); arrest record history, Gregory v. Litton Systems, Inc., 316 F.Supp. 401 (C.D. Cal. 1970), affirmed as modified, 472

F.2d 631 (9th Cir. 1972) (racial discrimination); garnishment experience, Johnson v. Pike Corp. of America, 332 F.Supp. 490 (C.D. Cal. 1971) (racial discrimination); and parentage of illegitimate children, Davis v. America Nat'l Bank of Texas, 12 FEP Cases 1052 (N.D. Tex. 1971) (sex and race discrimination).).

In NEW YORK CITY TRANSIT AUTHORITY v. BEAZER, 440 U.S. 568, 99 S.Ct. 1355, 59 L.Ed.2d 587 (1979), the plaintiffs claimed that the Transit Authority's blanket exclusion from employment of all persons receiving methadone treatment for drug addiction disproportionately impacted blacks and Hispanics. The Supreme Court held that the plaintiffs had failed to establish that the percentage of blacks and Hispanics in the class of methadone users was significantly greater than the percentage of those minorities in the general population of the city and had thus failed to prove a prima facie case of disparate impact. But even if this statistical showing had sufficed, the Court concluded, the defendant had established that its narcotics rule as applied to methadone users was job-related because of public safety concerns.

To the extent that disproportionate impact analysis is applied to a standard, such as height and weight, that itself is not a function of prior societal or other discrimination, is this consistent with the Court's foundational statement in *Griggs* that Title VII cannot tolerate the use of barriers to employment opportunity "if they operate to 'freeze' the status quo of prior discriminatory employment practices?" Since Title VII does not bar discrimination on the basis of, *inter alia*, height, weight, or prior garnishment history, can it be said that reliance on these factors freezes the effect of preexisting discriminatory practices? For an in-depth accounting of the factual and legal background of the Court's ruling in *Griggs*, see Samuel Estreicher, *The Story of Griggs v. Duke Power Co.*, EMPLOYMENT DISCRIMINATION STORIES 153 (Friedman, ed. 2006).

DISPARATE IMPACT AND THE CIVIL RIGHTS ACT OF 1991

The *Griggs* Court stated that the employer's burden in a disparate impact case was one "of showing that [the] requirement must have a manifest relationship to the employment in question." In subsequent rulings, the Court reaffirmed that job-relatedness/business necessity was an affirmative defense as to which the defendant bore the burden of persuasion. *See* Albemarle Paper Co. v. Moody, 422 U.S. 405, 425, 95 S.Ct. 2362, 45 L.Ed.2d 280 (1975) (employer must "meet the burden of proving that its tests are 'job related'"); Dothard v. Rawlinson, 433 U.S. 321, 329, 97 S.Ct. 2720, 2727, 53 L.Ed.2d 786 (1977) (employer must "prov[e] that the challenged requirements are job related"). And so for seventeen years following *Griggs*, the lower federal courts uniformly adopted that evidentiary framework. But in WARDS COVE PACKING CO. v. ATONIO, 490 U.S. 642, 109 S.Ct. 2115, 104 L.Ed.2d 733 (1989), a five member majority held that the Court's prior rulings on the allocation of burdens in disproportionate impact cases had been misinterpreted.

In [the defendant's case] the employer carries the burden of producing evidence of business justification for his employment practice. The burden of persuasion, however, remains with the disparate-impact plaintiff. To the extent that the Ninth Circuit * * * [suggested] that the persuasion burden should shift to the petitioners once the respondents established a prima facie case of disparate impact — its decisions were erroneous. * * * We acknowledge that some of our earlier decisions can be read as suggesting otherwise. But to the extent that those cases speak of an employer's "burden of proof" with respect to a legitimate business justification defense, they should have been understood to mean an employer's production — but not persuasion — burden. The persuasion burden here must remain with the plaintiff, for it is he who must prove that it was "because of such individual's race, color," etc., that he was denied a desired employment opportunity.

490 U.S. at 659-60, 109 S.Ct. at 2126, 104 L.Ed.2d at 753. In a dissent, Justice Stevens accused the majority of "perfunctorily reject[ing] a longstanding rule of law" and of "turning a blind eye to the meaning and purposes of Title VII." 490 U.S. at 663, 109 S.Ct. at 2128, 104 L.Ed.2d at 755 (Stevens, J., dissenting). The majority opinion in *Wards Cove* was viewed widely as having altered *Griggs* and substantially undermined disparate impact analysis. *See, e.g.*, Alfred W. Blumrosen, *Society in Transition II: Price Waterhouse and the Individual Employment Discrimination Case*, 42 RUTGERS L. REV. 1023, 1025 (1990) (*Wards Cove* "severely restricted the 'disparate impact' principle of *Griggs*").

Wards Cove was a focal point of the proposed Civil Rights Act of 1990, which was designed to reverse it and four other 1989 Supreme Court rulings in employment discrimination cases, including *Price Waterhouse*. Although the bill Act passed both houses of Congress, it was vetoed by President George H.W. Bush. The Senate's vote to override the veto fell one vote short. In the fall of 1991, Congress tried again. Although the Civil Rights Act of 1991, Pub.L. 102-166, 105 Stat. 1071 (1991), was targeted at the same five Supreme Court decisions and contained language very similar to the 1990 Act, President Bush signed the 1991 version, which was the product of a compromise between the Administration and Senate sponsors of the Act.

Among the stated purposes of the 1991 Act was "to codify the concepts of 'business necessity' and 'job related' enunciated by the Supreme Court in *Griggs* and in other Supreme Court decisions prior to Wards Cove Packing Co. v. Atonio . . . ." Congress legislatively overruled the Court's re-interpretation of its own court-made doctrine by expressly codifying a definition of disproportionate impact. Section 105 of the 1991 Act amended §703 of Title VII by adding the following new subsection:

(k)(1)(A)   An unlawful employment practice based on disparate impact is established under this Title only if —

(i) a complaining party demonstrates that a respondent uses a particular employment practice that causes a disparate impact on the basis of race, color, religion, sex, or national origin and the respondent fails to demonstrate that the challenged practice is job related for the position in question and consistent with business necessity; or

(ii) the complaining party makes the demonstration described in subparagraph (C) with respect to an alternative employment practice and the respondent refuses to adopt such alternative employment practice.

(B)(i)   With respect to demonstrating that a particular employment practice causes a disparate impact as described in subparagraph (A)(i), the complaining party shall demonstrate that each particular challenged employment practice causes a disparate impact, except that if the complaining party can demonstrate to the court that the elements of a respondent's decisionmaking process are not capable of separation for analysis, the decisionmaking process may be analyzed as one employment practice.

(ii) If the respondent demonstrates that a specific employment practice does not cause the disparate impact, the respondent shall not be required to demonstrate that such practice is required by business necessity.

(C) The demonstration referred to by subparagraph (A)(ii) shall be in accordance with the law as it existed on June 4, 1989 [the day before *Wards Cove* was decided], with respect to the concept of "alternate employment practice."

The term "demonstrates" is defined in §104 of the Act as "meets the burdens of production and persuasion."

The 1990 Civil Rights Act that was vetoed by the President was accompanied by a full legislative history consisting of committee reports and Senate and House debate, much of which was directed at *Wards Cove*. The 1991 Act was not preceded by legislative hearings or much debate and the Administration feared that the legislative history of the 1990 Act might be used by courts in interpreting the 1991 Act. Thus, as part of the compromise that led to its enactment, the 1991 Act contains an unusual statutory designation of legislative history in §105(b):

No statements other than the interpretive memorandum appearing at Vol. 137 Congressional Record S 15276 (daily ed. Oct. 25, 1991) shall be considered legislative history of, or relied upon in any way as legislative history in construing or applying, any provision of this Act that relates to Wards Cove—Business necessity/cumulation/alternative business practice.

The interpretive memorandum referenced in this paragraph states as follows:

INTERPRETIVE MEMORANDUM

The final compromise on S. 1745 agreed to by several Senate sponsors, including Senators DANFORTH, KENNEDY, and DOLE, and the Administration states that with respect to Wards Cove-Business necessity/cumulation/alternative business practice—the exclusive legislative history is as follows:

The terms "business necessity" and "job related" are intended to reflect the concepts enunciated by the Supreme Court in Griggs v. Duke Power Co., 401 U.S. 424 (1971), and in other Supreme Court decisions prior to Wards Cove Packing Co. v. Atonio, 490 U.S. 642 (1989).

When a decision-making process includes particular, functionally-integrated practices which are components of the same criterion, standard, method of administration, or test, such as the height and weight requirements designed to measure strength in Dothard v. Rawlinson, 433 U.S. 321 (1977), the particular, functionally-integrated practices may be analyzed as one employment practice.

The 1991 Act has been construed to reflect Congress' intention to return disproportionate impact doctrine to its pre-*Wards Cove* status. *See* Note, *The Civil Rights Act of 1991; The Business Necessity Standard*, 106 HARV.L.REV. 896, 900 (1993) ("On the issue of business necessity, the Act merely returns the courts to where they were just prior to *Wards Cove*, and appears to provide little guidance as to what direction they should take from there. The courts are saddled, instead, with a rich but uncertain legislative history arising from two years of complicated political maneuvering."); Rosemary Alito, *Disparate Impact Discrimination Under the 1991 Civil Rights Act*, 45 RUTGERS L.REV. 1011 (1993).

One question raised by the 1991 Act which has yet to be answered is how to determine when multiple components of a selection process are "capable of separation for analysis" within the meaning of §703(k)(1)(B). The reference in the Interpretive Memorandum to *Dothard v. Rawlinson* is puzzling. Did the memorandum's authors mean that the impact of height and weight requirements could not, as a practical matter, be separated for statistical analysis? Or did they mean that, since the height and weight requirements in that case were used as a proxy for physical strength, they should be analyzed as one component? *See* Stout v. Potter, 276 F.3d 1118, 1124 (9ᵗʰ Cir. 2002) (suggesting that overall decision-making process for promotions should not be treated as one employment practice for disparate impact analysis because the process included several distinct elements and plaintiffs made no effort to isolate the various elements).

If a plaintiff establishes a prima face case of impact-based discrimination, and the defendant establishes that the challenged practice is "job related for the position in question and consistent with business necessity", then, per §703(k)(1)(A)(ii), the plaintiff can still prevail if it demonstrates that the defendant "refuses to adopt" an alternative employment practice that produces less disparate impact while serving the employer's legitimate needs. To meet this burden, must the plaintiff prove that the company knew of the existence of a less discriminatory alternative practice and affirmatively chose not to adopt it? If so, wouldn't that interject into *impact* analysis, an element of *intentional* discrimination? And if that is so, does that mean that *scienter* is, or at least should not be an element of this rebuttal phase of a plaintiff's case and that it should be sufficient for the plaintiff to demonstrate that the less discriminatory alternative was available and discoverable with the use of due diligence? *See* Jones v. City of Boston, 845 F.3d 28 (1ˢᵗ Cir. 2016)(the plaintiff must establish that it proposed the less discriminatory alternative to the defendant and gave the employer an opportunity to adopt it).

2. THE PLAINTIFF'S CASE

Griggs involved an employer's reliance upon an objective qualification for hiring or transfer: a passing score on the test. If the candidate failed the test, he or she was disqualified from further consideration. But many hiring and promotion decisions are based on multiple considerations with no single factor being determinative. For example, a promotion decision might be influenced by the cumulative assessment of the candidates' relative seniority, job record, educational background, and performance on a test. To what extent does *Griggs* apply to such a multi-factor decision? Can a plaintiff demonstrate disproportionate impact with proof that a class of applicants simply faired worse than the majority at the end of the process without proving which particular factors caused that statistical discrepancy? Also left unresolved by *Griggs* and the text of the 1991 Act is the issue of determining where in the process one gauges the level of impact. For example, what happens if an employer seeks to avoid the disproportionate exclusionary impact of a particular screening device by selecting a larger percentage of those whose class was most disadvantaged by that selection criterion. Should the court judge measure the level of impact at the point when a particular selection criterion disqualifies candidates, or at the "bottom line" when hiring or promotion actually takes place? The Supreme Court addressed these and other questions associated with impact claims in the following cases.

Connecticut v. Teal

Supreme Court of the United States, 1982.
457 U.S. 440, 102 S.Ct. 2525, 73 L.Ed.2d 130.

JUSTICE BRENNAN delivered the opinion of the Court.

We consider here whether an employer sued for violation of Title VII may assert a "bottom line" theory of defense. Under that theory, as asserted in this case, an employer's acts of racial discrimination in promotions — effected by an examination having disparate impact — would not render the employer liable for the racial discrimination suffered by employees barred from promotion if the "bottom line" result of the promotional process was an appropriate racial balance. We hold that the "bottom line" does not preclude respondent-employees from establishing a prima facie case, nor does it provide petitioner-employer with a defense to such a case.

I

Four of the respondents, Winnie Teal, Rose Walker, Edith Latney, and Grace Clark, are black employees of the Department of Income Maintenance of the State of Connecticut. Each was promoted provisionally to the position of Welfare Eligibility Supervisor and served in that capacity for almost two years. To attain permanent status as supervisors, however, respondents had to participate in a selection process that required, as the first step, a passing score on a written examination. This written test was administered on December 2, 1978, to 329 candidates. Of these candidates, 48 identified themselves as black and 259 identified themselves as white. The results of the examination were announced in March 1979. With the passing score set at 65,[3] 54.17% of the identified black candidates passed. This was approximately 68 percent of the passing rate for the identified white candidates.[4] The four respondents were

---

[3]The mean score on the examination was 70.4 percent. However, because the black candidates had a mean score 6.7 percentage points lower than the white candidates, the passing score was set at 65, apparently in an attempt to lessen the disparate impact of the examination.

[4]The following table shows the passing rates of various candidate groups:

Candidate Group	Number	No. Receiving Passing Score	Passing Rate (%)
Black	48	26	54.17
Hispanic	4	3	75.00
Indian	3	2	66.67
White	259	206	79.54
Unid.	15	9	60.00
Total	329	246	74.77

Petitioners do not contest the District Court's implicit finding that the examination itself resulted in disparate impact under the "eighty percent rule" of the Uniform Guidelines on Employee

among the blacks who failed the examination, and they were thus excluded from further consideration for permanent supervisory positions. In April 1979, respondents instituted this action in the United States District Court for the District of Connecticut against petitioners, the State of Connecticut, two state agencies, and two state officials. Respondents alleged, *inter alia*, that petitioners violated Title VII by imposing, as an absolute condition for consideration for promotion, that applicants pass a written test that excluded blacks in disproportionate numbers and that was not job related.

More than a year after this action was instituted, and approximately one month before trial, petitioners made promotions from the eligibility list generated by the written examination. In choosing persons from that list, petitioners considered past work performance, recommendations of the candidates' supervisors and, to a lesser extent, seniority. Petitioners then applied what the Court of Appeals characterized as an affirmative action program in order to ensure a significant number of minority supervisors. Forty-six persons were promoted to permanent supervisory positions, 11 of whom were black and 35 of whom were white. The overall result of the selection process was that, of the 48 identified black candidates who participated in the selection process, 22.9 percent were promoted and of the 259 identified white candidates, 13.5 percent were promoted. It is this "bottom-line" result, more favorable to blacks than to whites, that petitioners urge should be adjudged to be a complete defense to respondents' suit.

After trial, the District Court entered judgment for petitioners. The court treated respondents' claim as one of disparate impact under Griggs, Albemarle Paper Co. v. Moody, and Dothard v. Rawlinson. However, the court found that, although the comparative passing rates for the examination indicated a prima facie case of adverse impact upon minorities, the result of the entire hiring process reflected no such adverse impact. Holding that these "bottom line" percentages precluded the finding of a Title VII violation, the court held that the employer was not required to demonstrate that the promotional examination was job related. The United States Court of Appeals for the Second Circuit reversed, holding that the District Court erred in ruling that the results of the written examination alone were insufficient to support a prima facie case of disparate impact in violation of Title VII. The Court of Appeals stated that where "an identifiable pass-fail barrier denies an employment opportunity to a disproportionately large number of minorities and prevents them from proceeding to the next step in the selection process," that barrier must be shown to be job related. We granted certiorari, and now affirm.

II

A

We must first decide whether an examination that bars a disparate number of black employees from consideration for promotion, and that has not been shown to be

---

Selection Procedures adopted by the Equal Employment Opportunity Commission. Those guidelines provide that a selection rate that "is less than [80 percent] of the rate for the group with the highest rate will generally be regarded . . . as evidence of adverse impact." 29 CFR §1607.4D (1981).

job related, presents a claim cognizable under Title VII. Section 703(a)(2) of Title VII provides in pertinent part:

It shall be an unlawful employment practice for an employer —

* * *

(2) to limit, segregate, or classify his employees or applicants for employment in any way which would deprive or tend to deprive any individual of employment opportunities or otherwise adversely affect his status as an employee, because of such individual's race, color, religion, sex, or national origin.

Respondents base their claim on our construction of this provision in *Griggs.*

* * *

Griggs and its progeny have established a three-part analysis of disparate impact claims. To establish a prima facie case of discrimination, a plaintiff must show that the facially neutral employment practice had a significantly discriminatory impact. If that showing is made, the employer must then demonstrate that "any given requirement [has] a manifest relationship to the employment in question," in order to avoid a finding of discrimination. *Griggs.* Even in such a case, however, the plaintiff may prevail, if he shows that employer was using the practice as a mere pretext for discrimination.[7]

* * *

Petitioners' examination, which barred promotion and had a discriminatory impact on black employees, clearly falls within the literal language of §703(a)(2), as interpreted by *Griggs.*[8] The statute speaks, not in terms of jobs and promotions, but in terms of *limitations* and *classifications* that would deprive any individual of employment *opportunities.*[9] A disparate impact claim reflects the language of §703(a)(2) and Congress' basic objectives in enacting that statute: "to achieve equality of employment *opportunities* and remove barriers that have operated in the

---

[7]Petitioners apparently argue both that the nondiscriminatory "bottom line" precluded respondents from establishing a prima facie case and, in the alternative, that it provided a defense.

[8]The legislative history of the 1972 amendments to Title VII is relevant to this case because those amendments extended the protection of the Act to respondents here by deleting exemptions for state and municipal employers. That history demonstrates that Congress recognized and endorsed the disparate impact analysis employed by the Court in *Griggs.* Both the House and Senate reports cited *Griggs* with approval, the Senate Report noting that:
"Employment discrimination as viewed today is a * * * complex and pervasive phenomenon. Experts familiar with the subject now generally describe the problem in terms of 'systems' and 'effects' rather than simply intentional wrongs." In addition, the Section-by-Section Analyses of the 1972 amendments submitted to both houses explicitly stated that in any area not addressed by the amendments, present case law — which as Congress had already recognized included our then recent decision in *Griggs* — was intended to continue to govern.

[9]In contrast, the language of §703(a)(1), if it were the only protection given to employees and applicants under Title VII, might support petitioners' exclusive focus on the overall result. That subsection makes it an unlawful employment practice "to fail or refuse to hire or to discharge any individual, or otherwise to discriminate against any individual with respect to his compensation, terms, conditions or privileges of employment, because of such individual's race, color, religion, sex, or national origin."

past to favor an identifiable group of white employees over other employees." When an employer uses a nonjob-related barrier in order to deny a minority or woman applicant employment or promotion, and that barrier has a significant adverse effect on minorities or women, then the applicant has been deprived of an employment *opportunity* "because of * * * race, color, religion, sex, or national origin." In other words, §703(a)(2) prohibits discriminatory "artificial, arbitrary, and unnecessary barriers to employment," that "limit * * * or classify * * * applicants for employment * * * in any way which would deprive or tend to deprive any individual of employment *opportunities*."

Relying on §703(a)(2), *Griggs* explicitly focused on employment "practices, procedures, or tests," that deny equal employment "opportunity." We concluded that Title VII prohibits "procedures or testing mechanisms that operate as 'built-in headwinds' for minority groups." We found that Congress' primary purpose was the prophylactic one of achieving equality of employment "opportunities" and removing "barriers" to such equality. The examination given to respondents in this case surely constituted such a practice and created such a barrier.

Our conclusion that §703(a)(2) encompasses respondents' claim is reinforced by the terms of Congress' 1972 extension of the protections of Title VII to state and municipal employees. See n. 8, *supra*. Although Congress did not explicitly consider the viability of the defense offered by the state employer in this case, the 1972 amendments to Title VII do reflect Congress' intent to provide state and municipal employees with the protection that Title VII, as interpreted by *Griggs*, had provided to employees in the private sector: equality of *opportunity* and the elimination of discriminatory *barriers* to professional development. The committee reports and the floor debates stressed the need for equality of opportunity for minority applicants seeking to obtain governmental positions. Congress voiced its concern about the wide-spread use by state and local governmental agencies of "invalid selection techniques" that had a discriminatory impact.

The decisions of this Court following *Griggs* also support respondents' claim. In considering claims of disparate impact under §703(a)(2) this Court has consistently focused on employment and promotion requirements that create a discriminatory bar to *opportunities*. This Court has never read §703(a)(2) as requiring the focus to be placed instead on the overall number of minority or female applicants actually hired or promoted. Thus Dothard v. Rawlinson found that minimum statutory height and weight requirements for correctional counselors were the sort of arbitrary barrier to equal employment opportunity for women forbidden by Title VII. Although we noted in passing that women constituted 36.89 percent of the labor force and only 12.9 percent of correctional counselor positions, our focus was not on this "bottom line." We focused instead on the disparate effect that the minimum height and weight standards had on applicants: classifying far more women than men as ineligible for employment. Similarly, in Albemarle Paper Co. v. Moody, the action was remanded to allow the employer to attempt to show that the tests that he had given to his employees for promotion were job related. We did not suggest that by promoting a sufficient number of the black employees who passed the examination, the employer could avoid this burden. See also New York Transit Authority v. Beazer, 440 U.S. 568, 584, 99 S.Ct. 1355, 1365, 59 L.Ed.2d 587 (1979) ("A prima facie violation of the Act may be established by statistical evidence showing that an employment *practice* has the effect of denying members of one race equal access to employment *opportunities*.") (emphasis added).

In short, the District Court's dismissal of respondents' claim cannot be supported on the basis that respondents failed to establish a prima facie case of employment discrimination under the terms of §703(a)(2). The suggestion that disparate impact should be measured only at the bottom line ignores the fact that Title VII guarantees these individual respondents the *opportunity* to compete equally with white workers on the basis of job-related criteria. Title VII strives to achieve equality of opportunity by rooting out "artificial, arbitrary and unnecessary" employer-created barriers to professional development that have a discriminatory impact upon individuals. Therefore, respondents' rights under §703(a)(2) have been violated, unless petitioners can demonstrate that the examination given was not an artificial, arbitrary, or unnecessary barrier, because it measured skills related to effective performance in the role of Welfare Eligibility Supervisor.

B

The United States, in its brief as *amicus curiae*, apparently recognizes that respondents' claim in this case falls within the affirmative commands of Title VII. But it seeks to support the District Court's judgment in this case by relying on the defenses provided to the employer in §703(h).[11] Section 703(h) provides in pertinent part:

"Notwithstanding any other provision of this title, it shall not be an unlawful employment practice for an employer * * * to give and to act upon the results of any professionally developed ability test provided that such test, its administration or action upon the results is not designed, intended or used to discriminate because of race, color, religion, sex or national origin."

The Government argues that the test administered by the petitioners was not "used to discriminate" because it did not actually deprive disproportionate numbers of blacks of promotions. But the Government's reliance on §703(h) as offering the employer some special haven for discriminatory tests is misplaced. We considered the relevance of this provision in *Griggs*. After examining the legislative history of §703(h), we concluded that Congress, in adding §703(h), intended only to make clear that tests that were *job related* would be permissible despite their disparate impact. As the Court recently confirmed, §703(h), which was introduced as an amendment to Title VII on the Senate floor, "did not alter the meaning of Title VII, but 'merely clarifie[d] its present intent and effect.'" American Tobacco v. Patterson, 456 U.S. 63, 73, n. 11, 102 S.Ct. 1534, 1539, n. 11, 71 L.Ed.2d 748 (1982), quoting 110 Cong.Rec. 12723 (remarks of Sen. Humphrey). A nonjob-related test that has a disparate racial impact, and is used to "limit" or "classify" employees, is "used to discriminate" within the meaning of Title VII, whether or not it was "designed or intended" to have this effect and despite an employer's efforts to compensate for its discriminatory effect. See *Griggs*.

---

[11]The Government's brief is submitted by the Department of Justice, which shares responsibility for federal enforcement of Title VII with the Equal Employment Opportunity Commission (EEOC). The EEOC declined to join this brief.

In sum, respondents' claim of disparate impact from the examination, a pass-fail barrier to employment opportunity, states a prima facie case of employment discrimination under §703(a)(2), despite their employer's nondiscriminatory "bottom line," and that "bottom line" is no defense to this prima facie case under §703(h).

III

Having determined that respondents' claim comes within the terms of Title VII, we must address the suggestion of petitioners and some *amici curiae* that we recognize an exception, either in the nature of an additional burden on plaintiffs seeking to establish a prima facie case or in the nature of an affirmative defense, for cases in which an employer has compensated for a discriminatory pass-fail barrier by hiring or promoting a sufficient number of black employees to reach a nondiscriminatory "bottom line." We reject this suggestion, which is in essence nothing more than a request that we redefine the protections guaranteed by Title VII.[12]

Section 703(a)(2) prohibits practices that would deprive or tend to deprive *"any individual* of employment opportunities." The principal focus of the statute is the protection of the individual employee, rather than the protection of the minority group as a whole. Indeed, the entire statute and its legislative history are replete with references to protection for the individual employee. See, e.g., §§703(a)(1), (b), (c), 704(a). * * *

In suggesting that the "bottom line" may be a defense to a claim of discrimination against an individual employee, petitioners and *amici* appear to confuse unlawful discrimination with discriminatory intent. The Court has stated that a nondiscriminatory "bottom line" and an employer's good faith efforts to achieve a nondiscriminatory work force, might in some cases assist an employer in rebutting the inference that particular action had been intentionally discriminatory: "Proof that [a] work force was racially balanced or that it contained a disproportionately high

---

[12]Petitioners suggest that we should defer to the EEOC Guidelines in this regard. But there is nothing in the Guidelines to which we might defer that would aid petitioners in this case. The most support petitioners could conceivably muster from the Uniform Guidelines on Employee Selection Procedures (now issued jointly by the EEOC, the Civil Service Commission, the Department of Labor, and the Department of Justice), is *neutrality* on the question whether a discriminatory barrier that does not result in a discriminatory overall result constitutes a violation of Title VII. Section 1607.4C of the Guidelines, relied upon by petitioners, states that as a matter of *"administrative and prosecutorial discretion, in the usual case,"* the agencies will not take enforcement action based upon the disparate impact of any component of a selection process if the total selection process results in no adverse impact. (Emphasis added.) The agencies made clear that the "guidelines do not address the underlying question of law," and that an individual "who is denied the job because of a particular component in a procedure which otherwise meets the 'bottom line' standard * * * retains the right to proceed through the appropriate agencies, and into Federal court." In addition, in a publication entitled, "Adoption of Questions and Answers to Clarify and Provide a Common Interpretation of the Uniform Guidelines on Employee Selection Procedures," the agencies stated:
"Since the [bottom line] concept is not a rule of law, it does not affect the discharge by the EEOC of its statutory responsibilities to investigate charges of discrimination, render an administrative finding on its investigation, and engage in voluntary conciliation efforts. Similarly, with respect to the other issuing agencies, the bottom line concept applies not to the processing of individual charges, but to the initiation of enforcement action."

percentage of minority employees is not wholly irrelevant on the issue of intent when that issue is yet to be decided." Furnco Construction Corp. v. Waters, 438 U.S. 567, 580, 98 S.Ct. 2943, 2951, 57 L.Ed.2d 957 (1978). See also Teamsters v. United States, 431 U.S. 324, 340, n. 20, 97 S.Ct. 1843, 1856-1857, n. 20, 52 L.Ed.2d 396 (1977). But resolution of the factual question of intent is not what is at issue in this case. Rather, petitioners seek simply to justify discrimination against respondents, on the basis of their favorable treatment of other members of respondents' racial group. Under Title VII, "A racially balanced work force cannot immunize an employer from liability for specific acts of discrimination." Furnco.

> "It is clear beyond cavil that the obligation imposed by Title VII is to provide an equal opportunity for each applicant regardless of race, without regard to whether members of the applicant's race are already proportionately represented in the work force." Ibid. (emphasis in original).

It is clear that Congress never intended to give an employer license to discriminate against some employees on the basis of race or sex merely because he favorably treats other members of the employees' group. We recognized in Los Angeles Dept. of Water & Power v. Manhart, 435 U.S. 702, 98 S.Ct. 1370, 55 L.Ed.2d 657 (1978), that fairness to the class of women employees as a whole could not justify unfairness to the individual female employee because the "statute's focus on the individual is unambiguous." Similarly, in Phillips v. Martin Marietta Corp., 400 U.S. 542, 91 S.Ct. 496, 27 L.Ed.2d 613 (1971) (per curiam), we recognized that a rule barring employment of all married women with preschool children, if not a bona fide occupational qualification under §703(e), violated Title VII, even though female applicants without preschool children were hired in sufficient numbers that they constituted 75 to 80 percent of the persons employed in the position plaintiff sought.

Petitioners point out that *Furnco, Manhart,* and *Phillips* involved facially discriminatory policies, while the claim in the instant case is one of discrimination from a facially neutral policy. The fact remains, however, that irrespective of the form taken by the discriminatory practice, an employer's treatment of other members of the plaintiffs' group can be "of little comfort to the victims of * * * discrimination." Teamsters. Title VII does not permit the victim of a facially discriminatory policy to be told that he has not been wronged because other persons of his or her race or sex were hired. That answer is no more satisfactory when it is given to victims of a policy that is facially neutral but practically discriminatory. Every *individual* employee is protected against both discriminatory treatment and against "practices that are fair in form, but discriminatory in operation." Griggs. Requirements and tests that have a discriminatory impact are merely some of the more subtle, but also the more pervasive, of the "practices and devices which have fostered racially stratified job environments to the disadvantage of minority citizens." McDonnell Douglas.

IV

In sum, petitioners' nondiscriminatory "bottom line" is no answer, under the terms of Title VII, to respondents' prima facie claim of employment discrimination. Accordingly, the judgment of the Court of Appeals for the Second Circuit is affirmed, and this case is remanded to the District Court for further proceedings consistent with this opinion.

It is so ordered.

JUSTICE POWELL, with whom THE CHIEF JUSTICE, JUSTICE REHNQUIST, and JUSTICE O'CONNOR join, dissenting.

In past decisions, this Court has been sensitive to the critical difference between cases proving discrimination under Title VII by a showing of disparate treatment or discriminatory intent and those proving such discrimination by a showing of disparate impact. Because today's decision blurs that distinction and results in a holding inconsistent with the very nature of disparate-impact claims, I dissent.

I

Section 703(a)(2), provides that it is an unlawful employment practice for an employer to

> "limit, segregate or classify his employees or applicants for employment in any way which would deprive or tend to deprive any individual of employment opportunities or otherwise adversely affect his status as an employee, because of such individual's race, color, religion, sex, or national origin."

Although this language suggests that discrimination occurs only on an individual basis, in *Griggs* the Court held that discriminatory intent on the part of the employer against an individual need not be shown when "employment procedures or testing mechanisms * * * operate as 'built-in headwinds' for minority groups and are unrelated to measuring job capability." Thus, the Court held that the "disparate impact" of an employer's practices on a racial group can violate §703(a)(2) of Title VII. In *Griggs* and each subsequent disparate-impact case, however, the Court has considered, not whether the claimant as an individual had been classified in a manner impermissible under §703(a)(2), but whether an employer's procedures have had an adverse impact on the protected *group* to which the individual belongs.

Thus, while disparate-*treatment* cases focus on the way in which an individual has been treated, disparate-*impact* cases are concerned with the protected group. * * *

In keeping with this distinction, our disparate impact cases consistently have considered whether the result of an employer's *total selection process* had an adverse impact upon the protected group.[2] If this case were decided by reference to the total process — as our cases suggest that it should be — the result would be clear. Here 22.9% of the blacks who entered the selection process were ultimately promoted, compared with only 13.5% of the whites. To say that this selection process had an unfavorable "disparate impact" on blacks is to ignore reality.

The Court, disregarding the distinction drawn by our cases, repeatedly asserts that Title VII was designed to protect individual, not group, rights. It emphasizes that some individual blacks were eliminated by the disparate impact of the preliminary test. But this argument confuses the aim of Title VII with the legal theories through which its aims were intended to be vindicated. It is true that the aim of Title VII is to protect

---

[2]See Dothard (statutory height and weight requirements operated as a bar to *employment* of disproportionate number of women); Albemarle (seniority system allegedly locked blacks into lower paying jobs; applicants to skilled lines of progression were required to pass two tests); Griggs (tests were an absolute bar to transfers or hiring; the Court observed that all Congress requires is "the removal of artificial, arbitrary, and unnecessary barriers to *employment* * * *.") (emphasis added).

individuals, not groups. But in advancing this commendable objective, Title VII jurisprudence has recognized two distinct methods of proof. In one set of cases — those involving direct proof of discriminatory intent — the plaintiff seeks to establish direct, intentional discrimination against him. In that type case, the individual is at the forefront throughout the entire presentation of evidence. In disparate impact cases, by contrast, the plaintiff seeks to carry his burden of proof by way of *inference* — by showing that an employer's selection process results in the rejection of a disproportionate number of members of a protected group to which he belongs. From such a showing a fair inference then may be drawn that the rejected applicant, as a member of that disproportionately excluded group, was himself a victim of that process's " 'built-in head winds.'" *Griggs.* But this method of proof — which actually *defines* disparate impact theory under Title VII — invites the plaintiff to prove discrimination by reference to the group rather than to the allegedly affected individual.[3] There can be no violation of Title VII on the basis of disparate impact in the absence of disparate impact on a *group.*

In this case the plaintiff seeks to benefit from a conflation of "discriminatory treatment" and "disparate impact" theories. But he cannot have it both ways. Having undertaken to prove discrimination by reference to one set of group figures (used at a preliminary point in the selection process), the plaintiff then claims that *non* discrimination cannot be proved by viewing the impact of the entire process on the group as a whole. The fallacy of this reasoning — accepted by the Court — is transparent. It is to confuse the individualistic *aim* of Title VII with the methods of proof by which Title VII rights may be vindicated. The respondent, as an individual, is entitled to the full personal protection of Title VII. But, having undertaken to prove a violation of his rights by reference to group figures, respondent cannot deny petitioner the opportunity to rebut his evidence by introducing figures of the same kind. Having pleaded a disparate impact case, the plaintiff cannot deny the defendant the opportunity to show that there was no disparate impact. * * *

Where, under a facially neutral employment process, there has been no adverse effect on the group — and certainly there has been none here—Title VII has not been infringed.

II

The Court's position is no stronger in case authority than it is in logic. None of the cases relied upon by the Court controls the outcome of this case.[5] Indeed, the

---

[3]Initially, the plaintiff bears the burden of establishing a prima facie case that Title VII has been infringed. See Burdine. In a disparate-impact case, this burden is met by showing that an employer's selection process results in the rejection of a disproportionate number of members of a protected group. See Teamsters. Regardless of whether the plaintiff's prima facie case must itself focus on the defendant's overall selection process or whether it is sufficient that the plaintiff establish that at least one pass-fail barrier has resulted in disparate impact, the employer's presentation of evidence showing that its overall selection procedure does not operate in a discriminatory fashion certainly dispels any inference of discrimination. In such instances, at the close of the evidence, the plaintiff has failed to show disparate impact by a preponderance of the evidence.

[5]The Court concentrates on cases of questionable relevance. Most of the lower courts that have squarely considered the question have concluded that there can be no violation of Title VII on a

disparate-impact cases do not even support the propositions for which they are cited. For example, the Court cites Dothard * * * and observes that "[a]lthough we noted in passing that women constituted 36.89 percent of the labor force and only 12.9 percent of correctional counselors, our focus was not on this bottom line. We focused instead on the disparate effect that the minimum height and weight standards had on applicants; classifying far more women than men as ineligible for employment." In *Dothard*, however, the Court was not considering a case in which there was any difference between the discriminatory effect of the employment standard and the number of minority members actually hired. The *Dothard* Court itself stated that

> "to establish a prima facie case of discrimination, a plaintiff need only show that the facially neutral standards in question *select* applicants *for hire* in a discriminatory pattern. Once it is shown that *the employment standards* are discriminatory in effect, the employer must meet 'the burden of showing that any given requirement [has] * * * a manifest relationship to the employment in question.'" (emphasis added).

The *Dothard* Court did not decide today's case. It addressed only a case in which the challenged standards had a discriminatory impact at the bottom line — the hiring decision. And the *Dothard* Court's "focus," referred to by the Court, is of no help in deciding the instant case.[6]

The Court concedes that the other major cases on which it relies, *Furnco*, and Phillips v. Martin Marietta Corp., "involved facially discriminatory policies, while the claim in the instant case is one of discrimination from a facially neutral policy." The Court nevertheless applies the principles derived from those cases to the case at bar. It does so by reiterating the view that Title VII protects *individuals*, not *groups*, and therefore that the manner in which an employer has treated other members of a group cannot defeat the claim of an individual who has suffered as a result of even a facially neutral policy. As appealing as this sounds, it confuses the distinction — uniformly recognized until today — between disparate *impact* and disparate *treatment*. Our

---

disparate-impact basis when there is no disparate impact at the *bottom line.* See, e.g., EEOC v. Greyhound Lines, 635 F.2d 188 (CA3 1980); EEOC v. Navajo Refining Co., 593 F.2d 988 (CA10 1979); Friend v. Leidinger, 588 F.2d 61, 66 (CA4 1978); Rule v. Ironworkers Local 396, 568 F.2d 558 (CA8 1977); Smith v. Troyan, 520 F.2d 492, 497-498 (CA6 1975), cert. denied, 426 U.S. 934, 96 S.Ct. 2646, 49 L.Ed.2d 385 (1976).

[6]The Court cites language from two other disparate-impact cases. The Court notes that in Albemarle Paper Co. v. Moody, the Court "remanded to allow the employer to attempt to show that the tests * * * given * * * for promotion were job related." But the fact that the Court did so without suggesting "that by promoting a sufficient number of black employees who passed the examination, the employer could avoid this hurdle," can hardly be precedent for the negative of that proposition when the issue was neither presented in the facts of the case nor addressed by the Court.

Similarly, New York Transit Authority v. Beazer, provides little support despite the language quoted by the Court. * * * In *Beazer,* the Court ruled that the statistical evidence actually presented was insufficient to establish a prima facie case of discrimination, and in doing so it indicated that it would have found statistical evidence of the number of applicants *and* employees in a methadone program quite probative. *Beazer* therefore does not justify the Court's speculation that the number of blacks and Hispanics actually employed were irrelevant to whether a case of disparate impact had been established under Title VII.

cases, cited above, have made clear that discriminatory-impact claims cannot be based on how an individual is treated in isolation from the treatment of other members of the group. Such claims necessarily are based on whether the group fares less well than other groups under a policy, practice, or test. Indeed, if only one minority member has taken a test, a disparate-impact claim cannot be made, regardless of whether the test is an initial step in the selection process or one of several factors considered by the employer in making an employment decision.

III

Today's decision takes a long and unhappy step in the direction of confusion. Title VII does not require that employers adopt merit hiring or the procedures most likely to permit the greatest number of minority members to be considered for or to qualify for jobs and promotions. See *Burdine*; *Furnco*. Employers need not develop tests that accurately reflect the skills of every individual candidate; there are few if any tests that do so. Yet the Court seems unaware of this practical reality, and perhaps oblivious to the likely consequences of its decision. By its holding today, the Court may force employers either to eliminate tests or rely on expensive, job-related, testing procedures, the validity of which may or may not be sustained if challenged. For state and local governmental employers with limited funds, the practical effect of today's decision may well be the adoption of simple quota hiring.[8] This arbitrary method of employment is itself unfair to individual applicants, whether or not they are members of minority groups. And it is not likely to produce a competent workforce. Moreover, the Court's decision actually may result in employers employing *fewer* minority members. As Judge Newman noted in Brown v. New Haven Civil Service Comm'n, 474 F.Supp. 1256, 1263 (D.Conn.1979):

> "[A]s private parties are permitted under Title VII itself to adopt voluntary affirmative action plans, * * * Title VII should not be construed to prohibit a municipality's using a hiring process that results in a percentage of minority policemen approximating their percentage of the local population, instead of relying on the expectation that a validated job-related testing procedure will produce an equivalent result, yet with the risk that it might lead to substantially less hiring." (citations omitted).

Finding today's decision unfortunate in both its analytical approach and its likely consequences, I dissent.

---

[8]Another possibility is that employers may integrate consideration of test results into one overall hiring decision based on that "factor" *and* additional factors. Such a process would not, even under the Court's reasoning, result in a finding of discrimination on the basis of disparate impact unless the actual hiring decisions had a disparate impact on the minority group. But if employers integrate test results into a single-step decision, they will be free to select *only* the number of minority candidates proportional to their representation in the workforce. If petitioner had used this approach, it would have been able to hire substantially fewer blacks without liability on the basis of disparate impact. The Court hardly could have intended to encourage this.

NOTES AND PROBLEMS FOR DISCUSSION

1. Do you agree with the dissent that there was no adverse effect on the group in this case? To what "group" is Justice Powell referring? Is it the same "group" being referred to by the majority? Is Justice Powell correct in assuming that a balanced bottom line dispels the inference of discrimination created by the plaintiff's prima facie showing? For a thorough discussion of *Teal* and its impact on the group interest concept that originated in *Griggs* see Alfred W. Blumrosen, *The Group Interest Concept, Employment Discrimination, and Legislative Intent: The Fallacy of Connecticut v. Teal*, 20 HARV. J. LEG. 99 (1983).

2. In *Teal*, a prima facie case of disparate impact was established by comparing the pass rates on the Welfare Supervisor test of the African-American and white applicants for the Supervisor position. In promotion and hiring cases, the racial composition of the group actually hired or promoted is typically compared with the composition of those who *applied* for hiring or promotion in order to determine whether a test or other procedure has a disparate impact. *See* Paige v. California, 291 F.3d 1141, 1145 (9th Cir. 2002), cert. denied, 123 S.Ct. 1256, 154 L.Ed.2d 1021 (2003) ("In evaluating the impact of a particular process, we must compare the group that 'enters' the process with the group that emerges from it. * * * Ordinarily, we would compare the racial composition of officers who are appointed to the supervisory positions as a result of the challenged examination with the racial composition of the officers who applied for promotion to those positions."). If the composition of the applicant group is unavailable, can the composition of another group be used for comparison?

In MALAVE v. POTTER, 320 F.3d 321 (2d Cir. 2003) the plaintiff, a Hispanic Postal Service employee in Connecticut claimed that the Service had discriminated throughout its system against Hispanics in regard to promotions. In support of his disparate impact claim he compared the ethnic composition of the Postal Service's Connecticut workforce with the composition of upper management in the state and submitted an expert report which concluded that Hispanics were substantially underrepresented in management positions and that this under representation was likely caused by discrimination. The district court granted the Postmaster's motion for summary judgment on the ground that plaintiff had failed to make out a prima facie case of disproportionate impact. The court reasoned that because the plaintiff's expert provided no data on how many Hispanics had applied for promotions, the disparity noted by the expert "may well have been attributed to the lack of qualified Hispanic candidates applying for positions rather than the challenged promotional practices." The Second Circuit reversed. While recognizing that the appropriate comparison is "customarily between the composition of candidates seeking to be promoted and the composition of those actually promoted," the court noted that neither the Supreme Court nor the Second Circuit had excluded the possibility of other comparisons, such as the population of those eligible for promotion, where the data on actual applicants is unavailable. . The parties conceded that the number of Hispanics who had applied for promotion during the relevant time period was not available. The court concluded that it was error "for the district court to reject out of hand Malave's statistical analysis simply because it failed to conform to the preferred methodology * * * given the Supreme Court's express endorsement * * * of alternative methodologies if the preferred statistics are 'difficult' or 'impossible' to obtain." 320 F.3d at 326 The case was remanded for the district court to determine "the most appropriate labor pool * * * and whether the expert's method utilized the best and most appropriate available labor pool information." 320 F.3d at 327.

What subset of the Postal Service's Connecticut workforce might be an appropriate substitute for actual applicants for promotion? Could the Postal Service's overall workforce in the state ever be the appropriate comparison pool for determining disparate impact in promotions? What assumptions would one have to make about the qualifications and desire of the general workforce for promotions in order to make the comparison work? The question of the appropriate comparison labor pools is explored in EEOC v. Joe's Stone Crab, Inc., *infra.*

3.   Does a job requirement that disproportionately affects males violate Title VII if males constitute the majority of the work force? In LIVINGSTON v. ROADWAY EXPRESS, INC., 802 F.2d 1250 (10th Cir. 1986), a 6'7" white male was rejected for employment as a truck driver pursuant to the defendant company's 6'4" maximum height limitation. The Tenth Circuit affirmed the trial court's dismissal of the complaint, concluding that evidence of impact alone did not suffice to create a presumption of discrimination when the plaintiff is a member of a historically favored group. Rather, it held, where a member of a favored group alleges impact discrimination, the plaintiff "must show background circumstances supporting the inference that a facially neutral policy with a disparate impact is in fact a vehicle for unlawful discrimination." Since the plaintiff did not establish that the disproportionate impact of the height limitation was reflected in the actual work force nor offer any other "background facts supporting the inference that Roadway Express is one of those unusual employers that discriminate against the majority * * * the only reasonable inference to be drawn from our common experience is that a maximum height restriction does not limit a male job applicant because of his sex but because of his height, a form of discrimination not prohibited by Title VII." 802 F.2d at 1252, 1253. The court also stated that *Teal* did not apply to cases where the plaintiff is a member of a favored group. Do you agree with this characterization of *Teal?* Does *Teal* apply to a height and weight requirement when the employment in question is restricted to females under the BFOQ exception? *See* Costa v. Markey, 706 F.2d 1 (1st Cir. 1982), cert. denied, 464 U.S. 1017, 104 S.Ct. 547, 78 L.Ed.2d 722 (1983).

4.   The impact of certain criteria (height and weight requirements, criminal conviction) can be determined from available demographic data. In *Griggs,* for example, census data showed the disparate racial impact of the high school diploma requirement on black males in North Carolina. But a test like that involved in *Teal,* administered by an individual employer, will only be taken by those seeking the job in question. The select group taking the test may not be representative of the population as a whole. How is the disproportionate impact of such a test on a whole class of people to be determined? As noted in *Teal* (footnote 4), federal agencies have adopted a set of uniform testing guidelines to provide standards for ruling on the legality of selection procedures used by private and public employers subject to these agencies' rules. Section 4D, or the "four-fifths rule," provides that a passing rate for members of a protected group of less than 80% of the passing rate for the highest scoring group generally will create a prima facie case of disproportionate impact. The rule was proposed only as a general guideline, and the agencies retained discretion to make adjustments in individual cases. *See* 29 C.F.R. §1607.4(D). For a thorough discussion, see Elaine W. Shoben, *Differential Pass — Fail Rates in Employment*

Testing: Statistical Proof Under Title VII, 91 HARV. L. REV. 793 (1978). Many courts have utilized the rule as a means of determining disparate impact. In WATSON v. FORT WORTH BANK & TRUST, 487 U.S. 977, 995 n.3, 108 S.Ct. 2777, 2789 n.3, 101 L.Ed.2d 827 (1988), the Supreme Court, while endorsing a "case-by-case" approach to statistical proof, noted that the Uniform Guidelines had provided a useful rule of thumb for the courts.

Proof of disparate impact under the "four-fifths" or "80%" rule requires a statistically significant showing of impact. For a showing to be statistically significant the challenged test or employment practice must have been applied to a large enough group of employees or applicants, including minorities, to produce statistically meaningful results. For example, if only five employees (four male and one female) have taken a test, the fact that three males have made passing scores and one male and one female have failed tells us nothing statistically significant about the impact of the test on females because not enough employees have been tested. How small can the sample be and still yield statistically significant results? The answer to that question depends in part on the nature of the statistical test used (some tests are designed for small samples), and statisticians often will disagree on the minimum number necessary. *Compare* Fudge v. City of Providence Fire Dep't, 766 F.2d 650, 658-59 & n.10 (1ˢᵗ Cir. 1985) (holding that sample of 24 people is too small to support an inference of disparate impact based purely on a statistical analysis) *with* Pietras v. Bd. of Fire Comm'rs of Farmingville Fire Dist., 180 F.3d 468, 472 (2d Cir. 1999) (sample of 66 male and 7 female test takers sufficient to establish disproportionate impact).

5. For more than twenty-five years after *Griggs*, the Supreme Court did not speak to the question of whether impact analysis was applicable to other than objective employment selection criteria. In neither *Griggs* nor *Teal*, for example, did the Court differentiate between objective and subjective practices and procedures. Nor did it examine whether impact theory was limited to single factor employment criteria as opposed to multi-component selection devices that generate an adverse impact. As a result, there was a significant amount of litigation raising the question of whether impact analysis was properly applied to subjective criteria and/or to a multi-component selection process. In WATSON v. FORT WORTH BANK & TRUST, 487 U.S. 977, 108 S.Ct. 2777, 101 L.Ed.2d 827 (1988), the Court unanimously ruled that subjective employment criteria could be subject to a disproportionate impact claim. To have done otherwise, the Court reasoned, would have encouraged employers to replace objective with subjective criteria having precisely the same exclusionary effect, and "disparate impact analyses might effectively be abolished." With respect to multi-factor decisions, the 1991 Act amendments to Title VII specified that the plaintiff's burden is to demonstrate "that each particular challenged employment practice causes a disparate impact, except that if the complaining party can demonstrate to the court that the elements of a respondent's decisionmaking process are not capable of separation for analysis, the decisionmaking process may be analyzed as one employment practice." §703(k)(1)(B)(i). The following case illustrates the difficulty of applying disparate impact analysis to multi-factor selection procedures that involve subjective evaluations.

Equal Employment Opportunity Commission v. Joe's Stone Crab, Inc.

United States Court of Appeals, Eleventh Circuit, 2000.
220 F.3d 1263.

MARCUS, Circuit Judge:

This is the paradigmatic "hard" case, and we have labored for many months to reach the right result. On appeal, Defendant, Joe's Stone Crab, Inc. ("Joe's"), challenges the district court's entry of judgment in favor of Plaintiff, the Equal Employment Opportunity Commission (the "EEOC"), on its gender-based disparate impact claims under Title VII. Joe's is a landmark Miami Beach seafood restaurant which from 1986 to 1990 hired 108 male food servers and zero female food servers. After the EEOC filed its discrimination charge in June 1991, Joe's hired 88 food servers from 1991 to 1995, nineteen, or roughly 21.7%, of whom were female. The district court concluded that while Joe's was not liable for intentional discrimination, it was liable for disparate impact discrimination based on these statistical disparities. After thorough review, we vacate the district court judgment, and remand for reconsideration of the EEOC's intentional discrimination claim consistent with this opinion.

In our view, the facts of this case render a disparate impact finding inappropriate. A disparate impact claim requires the identification of a specific, facially-neutral, employment practice causally responsible for an identified statistical disparity. On this record, the district court has identified no *facially-neutral* practice responsible for the gender disparity in Joe's food server population and we can find none. However, some of the district court's subsidiary findings suggest that there may have been *facially-discriminatory* practices of Joe's that were responsible for the identified hiring disparity, although the district court expressly rejected the EEOC's intentional discrimination claim in summary fashion.

I.

The facts of this case are reasonably straightforward and are fully outlined by the district court. 969 F. Supp. 727 (S.D.Fla.1997). Joe's Stone Crab, Inc. is a fourth-generation, family-owned seafood restaurant and Miami Beach landmark. During the stone crab season, which lasts from October to May, the restaurant is extremely busy — serving up to 1450 patrons each weeknight and up to 1800 patrons each weekend night. Today, the restaurant employs between 230 and 260 employees; of those, approximately 70 are food servers. Throughout its history, Joe's has experienced extremely low food server turnover — a result of Joe's family ethos, generous salary and benefits package, and its seven-month employment season. From 1950 onward, however, the food servers have been almost exclusively male.

* * *

On June 8, 1993, the EEOC filed a complaint in the Southern District of Florida alleging that Joe's violated Title VII through both intentional disparate treatment discrimination as well as unintentional disparate impact discrimination. The gravamen of the complaint centered around the EEOC's findings with respect to Joe's hiring and recruiting practices for food servers. * * *

To hire new food servers, Joe's conducts a "roll call" every year on the second Tuesday in October. Although Joe's rarely advertises, significantly, the district court found that the roll call is "widely known throughout the local food server community," and typically attracts over 100 applicants for only a limited number of slots. At a typical roll call, each applicant completes a written application and an individual interview. Selected applicants then enter a three-day training program where they shadow experienced servers. Upon successful completion of the program, they then become permanent hires.

Until the EEOC's charge, roll call interviews and hiring selections were handled exclusively by the daytime maitre d' with occasional interview assistance from other staff members. Hiring decisions were made by the daytime maitre d' on the basis of four subjective factors (appearance, articulation, attitude, and experience) and without upper management supervision or the benefit of instructive written or verbal policies. After the EEOC's discrimination charge in 1991, Joe's changed its roll call format somewhat. All applicant interviews were conducted by three members of Joe's management. In addition, each applicant was required to take and pass a "tray test," which involved the lifting and carrying of a loaded serving tray, or else be automatically disqualified from a food server position. The district court found the tray test to be a "legitimate indicator of an individual's ability to perform an essential component of a food server's job at Joe's," and that "women have the physical strength to carry serving trays."

In addition to its description of Joe's hiring process, the district court also made several subsidiary findings relating to the historical operation of the roll call system. The district court observed that while "women have predominated as owner/managers," "most of Joe's female employees have worked in positions traditionally viewed as 'women's jobs,' e.g., as cashiers or laundry workers. Food servers generally have been male." Although Joe's hired female food servers during World War II, most of these positions "reverted to men at the conclusion of the war."

In explaining this historical dearth of female food servers, the district court found that Joe's maintained an "Old World" European tradition, in which the highest level of food service is performed by men, in order to create an ambience of "fine dining" for its customers. The district court elaborated:

> The evidence presented at trial does not establish that Joe's management had an express policy of excluding women from food server positions. To the contrary, the evidence portrays owner/managers who have been courageous in opposing overt discrimination. For example, Joe's was picketed for two years when the owners insisted on hiring African-American employees who had been excluded from union membership because of race. What the evidence in this case does prove is that Joe's management acquiesced in and gave silent approbation to the notion that male food servers were preferable to female food servers.

The district court added that "Joe's [had] sought to emulate Old World traditions by creating an ambience in which tuxedo-clad men served its distinctive menu."

With this historical background in place, the district court then focused on Joe's female hiring statistics for the relevant pre- and post-charge periods. For the pre-charge period of 1986-1990, the number of female food server applicants at Joe's annual hiring roll calls was minuscule. While there is little available evidence as to the actual numbers of female applicants at these roll calls (because Joe's historically did not retain any employment data from its roll calls), the district court determined, and both parties agreed, that during this period, no more than two or three women per year (or, at most, 3% of the overall applicant class) actually attended the roll calls. In that same period, 108 new male food servers were hired while zero women were hired. During the post-charge period (from 1991 to 1995), many more women (in all, 22% of the actual applicant pool) applied for food server positions. Of Joe's 88 new food server hires during this period, 19 were women. These post-charge figures translate into a female hiring percentage of 21.7% — a percentage almost exactly proportional to the percentage of females in the actual applicant pool. Joe's female applicant flow data for the post-charge period breaks down the following way:

Season	Women applicants	Women hired
1991-92	15.1%	20.0%
1992-93	21.9%	22.7%
1993-94	23.0%	10.5%
1994-95	26.8%	35.3%
Oct.-Dec.1995	23.3%	20.0%
Average	22.02%	21.7%

However, in making its findings, the district court found this actual applicant flow data "unreliable because it is skewed." Relying on hearsay trial testimony from local female food servers, the district court found that Joe's public reputation for not hiring women encouraged women to self-select out of the hiring process — thereby skewing the actual applicant flow. * * * Although the district court noted that female food server applications to Joe's dramatically increased as a result of publicity about the EEOC charge, it still found Joe's post-charge applicant pool data (depicting a female applicant pool of 22%) unreliable after comparing it with hiring rates, between 30% and 40% female, for other area seafood restaurants.

Having found the actual applicant pool data wholly unreliable, the district court discarded it and then set about selecting alternative non-applicant labor market data. The EEOC's expert witness, a labor economist, suggested a qualified female labor pool of 44.1% based on 1990 census data for female food servers living and/or working in the Miami Beach area (a labor pool which included cocktail and buffet servers). Not surprisingly, the district court rejected this figure in part because there was no demonstration that this female labor pool necessarily was qualified to work at Joe's. Instead, the district court "refined" the relevant labor pool to include all female servers who lived or worked on Miami Beach and earned between $25,000 and $50,000 — thereby "using past earning capacity as a proxy for experience, and by extension, experience as a proxy for qualification." Solely based on this alternative methodology, the district court was able to find "that at all relevant times, 31.9% of the available labor pool has been female."

With these findings in place, the district court then drew two pertinent conclusions of law. First, the district court summarily rejected the EEOC's disparate treatment claims without analysis, stating only that "the court finds that the EEOC has not met its burden of proof under disparate treatment analysis." * * * Second, however, the district court determined that Joe's was liable for disparate impact discrimination.[7] Specifically, the district court found that "the challenged employment practice in this case . . . , [Joe's] undirected and undisciplined delegation of hiring authority to subordinate staff," was responsible for the statistical disparity between the 31.9% female "available" labor pool and Joe's female hiring rates in the pre-charge (0%) and post-charge (21.7%) periods. The district court then entered a partial judgment of liability in favor of the EEOC.

On April 15, 1998, a bench trial was held on the remedies portion. The EEOC presented five female plaintiffs who unsuccessfully applied for food server positions at Joe's in the 1990's. They testified that they would have applied to Joe's at an earlier juncture but for the fact that they knew applying was futile based on Joe's male-only reputation. The district court awarded four of them backpay relief plus prejudgment interest. The district court also ordered extensive injunctive relief through the year 2001 that required Joe's to adopt a statement of non-discrimination in the hiring of food servers, comply with the district court's monitoring of Joe's future hiring and recruiting practices (including its public advertising of hiring roll-calls), allow the supervision of each roll-call by a court-appointed monitor, permit the introduction of a standardized tray test at the roll-call, and provide mandatory training sessions with an industrial psychologist for all of Joe's hiring decisionmakers.

                                        II.

The first and central issue in this appeal is whether the district court erred in finding that the EEOC had established disparate impact discrimination. We review the district court's conclusions of law de novo, and its factual findings for clear error. In this case, where the bulk of the evidence came in the form of conflicting witness testimony, we allot even greater deference to the factfinder who is in a better position to assess the credibility of the witnesses.

That said, we have struggled on appeal to find the proper resolution of this case. As we explain in detail, we believe that the district court's factual findings simply do not support a legal conclusion that Joe's is liable for disparate impact discrimination. Based on the district court's findings, no specific facially-neutral employment practice of Joe's can be causally connected to the statistical disparity between the percentage of women in the qualified labor pool and the percentage of women hired as food servers by Joe's.

A. Disparate Impact
                                      * * *

The disparate impact framework under Title VII by now is well-settled. * * * As correctly identified by the district court, a plaintiff in a sex discrimination suit must

---

[7]Although not originally included in the amended complaint, at the conclusion of the trial, the EEOC moved to amend its complaint to include an allegation that the subjective interviewing process had an adverse effect on women. The district court granted the motion and denied Joe's corresponding motion to strike this claim. Joe's has not specifically challenged these rulings on appeal.

establish three elements: first, that there is a significant statistical disparity between the proportion of women in the available labor pool and the proportion of women hired; second, that there is a specific, facially-neutral, employment practice which is the alleged cause of the disparity; and finally, and most critically in this case, that a causal nexus exists between the specific employment practice identified and the statistical disparity shown.

* * *

As for the first prong of the analysis, it is critical to observe that no statistically-significant disparity exists between the percentage of women who actually applied to Joe's and the percentage of women who were hired as servers by Joe's. The record indicates that for the pre-charge period (October 1986 to June 1991) very few female food servers applied to Joe's, "perhaps 3% of [all] applicants," out of an actual applicant pool of between 80 and 120 people a year. In this five-year time period, 108 male food servers were hired and no women were hired. Despite the fact that no women were hired during this period, Joe's pre-charge hiring rate demonstrated no significant statistical disparity because so few women actually applied for food server positions.[11] For the post-charge period (July 1991 to December 1995), the district court found that, on average, 22.02% of Joe's food server applicants were women and that Joe's hired roughly 21.7% women for these positions. Both parties admit (as they must) that, based on this record, there is no statistically-significant hiring disparity when the actual number of female applicants is compared to the actual number of female hires for either period.[12] In other words, Joe's hiring system did not produce a significant statistical disparity between the actual percentage of women who applied to Joe's for server positions and the percentage of women actually hired for these positions.

This insight is important for disparate impact analysis because the mere fact that Joe's hired no women in the pre-charge period is not, alone, sufficient to impose upon Joe's Title VII liability. To hold otherwise would be to impose liability upon Joe's based on "bottom line" reasoning which the Supreme Court has expressly forbade. In Watson, the Supreme Court made clear that Title VII liability could not be based solely on "bottom line" statistical imbalances in an employer's workforce. See Watson, 487 U.S. at 992, 108 S. Ct. 2777 (explaining that it is "unrealistic to suppose

---

[11]While it is true that during this period Joe's hired 108 men and zero women, this zero hiring percentage is deceptive. So few women applied to Joe's during this time period (perhaps one to three a year or, at most, fifteen in total as compared to 80 to 120 men or, at most, 600 men in total) that Joe's zero hiring rate is not significantly deviant from what Joe's female hiring rate ought to be according to laws of random probability (around 1.5% at best). "The mere absence of minority employees in [particular] positions does not suffice to prove a prima facie case of discrimination." Carter v. Ball, 33 F.3d 450, 456 (4th Cir.1994).

[12]While we adopt a flexible approach for determining whether a particular statistical deviation is "significant" for disparate impact analysis in light of all the facts and circumstances, on appeal the EEOC concedes that there is no legally significant statistical disparity in either relevant time period when actual applicant flow data is used. Both parties' statistical experts agreed that women needed to comprise five percent of the actual applicant class (they comprised between one and three percent) to have generated a significant disparate impact in Joe's pre-charge actual hiring pool.

that employers can eliminate, or discover and explain, the myriad of innocent causes that may lead to statistical imbalances in the composition of their workforces"). * * *

This disdain for "bottom line" reasoning reflects the belief that holding employers liable for statistical imbalances per se is inconsistent with Title VII's plain language and statutory purpose. Section 703(j) of Title VII, in fact, explicitly rejects the notion that employers must adopt numerical hiring quotas or "grant preferential treatment . . . on account of an imbalance which may exist with respect to the total number or percentage of persons . . . in comparison with the total number or percentage . . . in any community." Based on this statutory language, the Supreme Court has interpreted this provision of Title VII to mean that employers possess no affirmative duty to redress workforce imbalances not attributable to their own corporate conduct. Indeed, if employers could be held liable for an unlawful disparate impact on account of statistical workforce imbalances per se, then they would be forced to use numerical quotas and other forms of preferential treatment in their hiring and promotion policies, in express contravention of Title VII, in order to insulate themselves from the potential legal liability that would arise if their workforce demographics did not closely mirror the demographics of their surrounding community or local competitors. As a result, a plaintiff must do more than simply identify a workforce imbalance to establish a prima facie disparate impact case; it must causally connect a facially-neutral employment practice to the identified disparity.

In this case, the district court could create a statistically-significant disparity only by first throwing out the actual applicant data as a point of comparison and instead comparing the percentage of women hired for server positions at Joe's with the percentage of women in the "qualified" labor pool. The district court recognized that the number of women who actually applied for server positions at Joe's was disproportionately low when compared with the number of women in the Miami Beach area who were seemingly qualified for such positions. There was, in fact, a significant statistical disparity between the percentage of female applicants to Joe's during the pre- and post-charge periods and the percentage of female applicants to comparable area restaurants. Joe's female applicant percentage of 3% and 22.02% for the pre-and post-charge periods respectively varied sharply from the female applicant percentage of area restaurants which ranged from 29.5% to 42.1%. As a result of these findings, the district court found the actual applicant flow data to be "unreliable because it is skewed." It concluded that the data was skewed because of the pronounced self-selection of women out of Joe's hiring process. The district court then expressly rejected the actual applicant flow data in favor of an alternative labor pool consisting of those local food servers who were theoretically "available" and "qualified" to work at Joe's.[13] After hearing testimony from the expert witnesses of

---

[13]On appeal, Joe's challenges the district court's use of this alternative labor data as clear error. Joe's contends that the district court improperly relied on hearsay reputation evidence in finding the actual applicant flow data unreliable. Joe's also argues that the district court erred in using "refined" census data to define the relevant labor market for Miami Beach food servers qualified to work at Joe's. The district court narrowed the labor pool to those Miami Beach food servers who made between $25,000 and $50,000 — a salary range comparable to what Joe's food servers earn. Joe's claims that the district court's methodology of using income as a proxy for

both parties, the district court arrived at an "eligible" labor pool, based on 1990 census data refined for qualification/experience on the basis of past earning capacity, which was 31.9% female. The district court then used this alternative labor data and compared it to Joe's actual hire statistics. By comparing Joe's pre-charge female hiring percentage (0%) with the percentage of women in the qualified labor market (31.9%), the district court created a legally-cognizable statistical disparity.[14]

Assuming this substitution of data was appropriate, in order to establish disparate impact discrimination, the EEOC still was required to show a causal link between some *facially-neutral* employment practice of Joe's and the statistical disparity.[15] In other words, the EEOC was required to prove that at least one facially neutral employment practice proximately caused the disparity. This finding is essential to avoid the potential conflation of disparate treatment and disparate impact claims. As we have noted, the central difference between disparate treatment and disparate impact claims is that disparate treatment requires a showing of discriminatory intent and disparate impact does not. See *In re Employment*, 198 F.3d at 1310 n. 8. In fact, the

---

job qualifications in no way assures that the labor pool actually consists only of those food servers who have the special food-serving skills requisite to work at Joe's. In the disparate impact context, we have explained that the "definition of a qualified applicant pool will shift with the nature of the job or job benefit, and the nature of the challenged employment practice at issue." In re Employment, 198 F.3d at 1312. We also have observed that "'when special qualifications are required to fill particular jobs,'" the use of certain statistics such as general population figures "becomes troublesome." Id. at 1313 (quoting Hazelwood School Dist. v. United States, 433 U.S. 299 at 308 n.13, 97 S. Ct. 2736, 53 L. Ed. 2d 768); see also Alexander v. Fulton County, Ga., 207 F.3d 1303, 1327-28 (11th Cir.2000) (noting that class-based disparate treatment statistics showing that a given minority is underrepresented in the work force by comparison with the general population is generally useful only for claims involving jobs with low skill levels where the applicant pool can be considered roughly coextensive with the general population). We have had no prior occasion to determine specifically whether salary is an adequate proxy for food server job qualifications at a fine dining establishment. Because we conclude infra that the district court erred in finding that the EEOC established disparate impact discrimination, even if we accept the alternative labor pool data, we need not address whether the alternative labor pool selected by the district court was comprised of "qualified" potential applicants.

[14]When this same 31.9% figure was applied to Joe's post-charge hiring statistics, a slight disparity, bordering on the significant, was found. The statistical variation was between 1.96 to 2.07 under "standard deviation" analysis. However, no particular numerical deviation is required to establish a prima facie case; instead courts employ a case-by-case approach dependent on the particularized case facts. See Watson. In addition, our caselaw has recognized that post-charge hiring behavior is less probative than pre-charge conduct because a business may be improving its hiring practices to avoid liability or large damages in their pending discrimination case. See James v. Stockham Valves & Fittings Co., 559 F.2d 310, 325 n. 18 (5th Cir.1977).

[15]In addition, because of the district court's own causation reasoning we must focus our inquiry on the alleged causes of the gender disparity in both Joe's applicant and hire pool. According to the district court, both disparities necessarily share the same cause since it was the disparity in Joe's applicant pool which directly led to the disparity in Joe's hire pool. Under the district court's factual findings, Joe's public reputation as a sex discriminator caused (1) a gender disparity in Joe's applicant pool which, in turn, created (2) a gender disparity in Joe's hire pool because there were so few women who actually applied to Joe's as a food server. Therefore, in order to understand the causes of Joe's hiring pool disparity, it is essential to determine the causes of Joe's applicant pool disparity.

judicial doctrine of disparate impact was created in *Griggs* specifically to redress *facially-neutral* policies or practices which visited disproportionate effects on groups protected by Title VII. * * *

* * *

The central problem in this case, however, is that the district court has identified no *facially-neutral* employment practice responsible for the gender disparity in Joe's food server population, and we can find none. The EEOC and the district court have identified, at most, two neutral employment practices on which to ground a disparate impact analysis: first, Joe's word of mouth recruiting, and second, Joe's "undirected and undisciplined delegation of hiring authority to subordinate staff," resulting in its subjective "roll call" hiring process. Disparate impact analysis fails in this case because neither neutral practice can be causally connected to the gender disparity.

First, there is no evidence that Joe's word of mouth recruiting method caused any disparity between the percentage of women in the qualified labor pool and the percentage of women actually hired by Joe's as servers. Notably, this is not a case where Joe's formal recruiting practices or its informal word-of-mouth recruiting network kept women from learning about available jobs at Joe's. Rather, the district court specifically found quite the opposite, namely that local female food servers knew about the availability of positions at Joe's and the logistical details of Joe's hiring roll calls. Indeed, it observed that although the hiring roll calls were "rarely advertised," they were "widely known [about] throughout the local food server community." No woman testified that she failed to apply for a position at Joe's because she was unaware of Joe's roll call method for filling openings. Plainly, the disparity between the percentage of women in the qualified labor pool and the percentage of women actually hired as servers by Joe's cannot be causally linked to Joe's word-of-mouth recruiting process because this practice in no way prevented women from applying to or being hired by Joe's.

Nor is there any evidence that Joe's facially-neutral, albeit undisciplined and subjective, hiring practices caused the disparity the district court found between the percentage of women in the qualified labor pool and the percentage of women actually hired as servers by Joe's. There is no evidence that Joe's subjective hiring criteria either caused women not to apply to Joe's or caused those who applied not to be hired. Joe's hiring roll call decisions were made through a subjective hiring process in which Joe's hiring maitre d' relied on short applicant interviews to assess an applicant's qualification based on a range of subjective factors, including "appearance, attitude, articulation, and experience." No witnesses testified and no evidence was presented into the record indicating that any women failed to apply to Joe's because its hiring criteria included specific judgments about an applicant's appearance, attitude, articulation, or experience. Nor was any evidence presented showing that women who did apply for server positions at Joe's were disadvantaged by these specific hiring criteria. Indeed, as we have stated previously, there is in fact no disparity between the percentage of women who actually applied to Joe's for server positions and the percentage of women hired. Plainly, therefore, the subjective hiring criteria did not harm women once they entered the application process.[16]

The district court, recognizing that it could not causally connect Joe's neutral, albeit subjective, recruiting and hiring practices with the disparity between the percentage of women in the qualified labor pool and the percentage of women actually hired as servers by Joe's, identified Joe's reputation as a discriminator against women as the causal agent for the disparity. For the district court, Joe's reputation for not hiring female food servers acted as the essential bridge connecting the neutral practices to the statistical disparity. In other words, according to the district court's own reasoning, it was not Joe's neutral recruiting or hiring practices that caused the disparity, but rather Joe's reputation as a discriminator against women. Because of Joe's reputation for discriminating, the district court essentially found, women did not apply to Joe's and therefore were not hired as servers.

We conclude that the district court's use of reputation was, on the face of this record, both problematic and inadequate for several independent reasons. First, reputation itself is neither a specific act or a practice. It is far more amorphous. * * * Reputation is the community "picture" of an individual or corporate entity formed over a number of years. Reputation has never been used, as far as we can tell, as a facially-neutral employment act or practice for disparate impact purposes. In the *intentional* discrimination context, some cases have considered reputation evidence for the limited purpose of defining the parameters of Title VII remedial relief where *intentional* discrimination either has been conceded or proven and there is evidence that an employer's discriminatory practices prevented qualified applicants from applying for new jobs. *See Morrow v. Crisler*, 491 F.2d 1053, 1055-57 (5th Cir.1974) (en banc) (instructing district court on remand to consider the role of Mississippi Highway Patrol Department's entrenched reputation for race discrimination — a reputation based on their historical practice of intentional race discrimination — in discouraging black applicants when shaping remedial recruiting policies for the Department). We have been pointed to *no* case, however, and can find none that has treated an employer's reputation as a discriminator as itself an act or practice for the purposes of establishing a prima facie case under a theory of disparate impact. Indeed, no case has ever used reputation as a bridge connecting a neutral hiring practice to a statistical disparity in order to establish disparate impact liability where the neutral employment practices alone did not cause the disparity.

In addition, even if reputation could somehow be used in theory as a causal bridge, in this case there is no logical or factual connection between any facially-neutral component of Joe's employment practices and Joe's reputation as a discriminator. Nothing in this record indicates that Joe's recruitment by "word-of-mouth" rather than through other recruiting mechanisms such as print or television

---

[16]This case differs significantly from the paradigmatic disparate impact case in which the plaintiffs show direct causation between an *objective* hiring requirement and the statistical disparity at issue. In *Griggs,* for example, the plaintiffs showed that the objective and facially neutral requirements of possessing a high school diploma and passing a general intelligence test in order to be hired or transferred to the company's more desirable departments had a disproportionate effect on white and black applicants.

advertising contributed in any way to Joe's reputation for discrimination. Nor is there any evidence that the use of appearance, articulation, attitude, and experience as hiring criteria contributed to Joe's reputation for discrimination. Indeed, there is no suggestion from either party that these hiring criteria are themselves somehow illegitimate or discriminatory.[17] Instead, the suggestion from the EEOC is that these criteria are simply a cover or a smokescreen and do not reflect the real bases for Joe's hiring decisions. Rather than hiring on the bases of appearance, articulation, attitude and experience, the EEOC contends, Joe's really hired servers on the basis of sex and it is this discriminatory hiring, rather than the use of subjective hiring criteria, that arguably led to Joe's reputation as a discriminator. But, where Joe's neutral hiring and recruiting practices did not cause its reputation, we think it is wholly inappropriate to use reputation as the causal bridge connecting neutral practices to a statistical disparity for the purposes of establishing Joe's disparate impact liability. *See Lewis v. Tobacco Workers' Int'l Union*, 577 F.2d 1135, 1143 (4th Cir.1978) (holding that an employer cannot be found liable under Title VII simply because potential minority applicants subjectively believe the company will not hire them because of their race where this belief is not attributable to the employer's conduct).

* * *

While a company may be held liable for a discriminatory reputation if there is evidence it caused or perpetuated that reputation through some *intentional* affirmative act, we know of no federal circuit that has found an employer liable under Title VII on the basis of a reputation for discrimination it did not cause. Nor are we prepared to impose on an employer an affirmative duty under Title VII to ameliorate a public reputation not attributable to its own employment conduct. In fact, we are unaware of any case that requires a Title VII employer to affirmatively dispel a negative public image not of its own making or else be subject to a finding of Title VII discrimination.

That said, the record extant and some of the district court's findings of fact can be read to support the alternate conclusion that Joe's management intentionally excluded women from food serving positions in order to provide its customers with an "Old World," fine-dining ambience. Thus, for example, the district court found that "Joe's management acquiesced in and gave silent approbation to the notion that male food servers were preferable to female food servers." At another point in its findings, the district court observed that "Joe's sought to emulate Old World traditions by creating an ambience in which tuxedo-clad men served its distinctive menu." Moreover, the district court apparently also credited the testimony of one of Joe's former hiring maitre d', Roy Garrett, who explained that Joe's was "a male server type of job" by tradition. As a result, the district court said that "women have systematically been excluded from the most lucrative entry level position, that of server." Finally, the district court found that this historical practice of hiring only men was responsible for Joe's "male-only" reputation. The district court held that "Joe's reputation in the community, which reflected the restaurant's historical hiring practice, led potential

---

[17]We have made clear that employment decisions may legitimately be based on subjective criteria as long as the criteria are capable of objective evaluation and are stated with a sufficient degree of particularity. See Conner v. Fort Gordon Bus Co., 761 F.2d 1495, 1500 (11th Cir.1985).

female applicants not to apply for server positions. Joe's reputation, therefore, was largely responsible for the gender skew in the pool of applicants at the annual roll call."

But, these factual findings do not mesh easily with a disparate impact theory because they suggest that Joe's hiring system was not in practice *facially-neutral*, but rather was *facially-discriminatory* on the basis of gender. They suggest the conclusion that in fact Joe's had a desired preference for male servers and that this preference influenced the hiring decisions of Joe's decisionmakers resulting in the deliberate and systematic exclusion of women as food servers. If this were true, Joe's could be found liable for intentional discrimination in violation of Title VII. We emphasize that this is not a case like *Griggs*, where there was a pronounced history of intentional discrimination followed by a facially-neutral employment practice which perpetuates the effects of an employer's previous discrimination. The district court's findings and the record evidence indicate that Joe's hiring methodology and practices have remained relatively constant throughout the relevant time periods. Therefore, if Joe's was guilty of intentionally discriminating against women in hiring servers, it would be liable for intentional discrimination throughout the entire pre-charge period since there is absolutely no evidence that Joe's adopted new facially-neutral hiring requirements until, at best, the post-charge period when it implemented an objective tray test and started to use a three-person interview panel.

Having said all this, we reiterate that nothing in this record supports a disparate impact theory of liability. Rather, much of the district court's findings (as well as the credited record evidence), may be read to support the conclusion that Joe's employment practices in hiring servers were really permeated with an unlawful intention to discriminate. None of the district court's findings support the conclusion that a *facially-neutral* practice or policy of Joe's caused its reputation, and there is not a scintilla of evidence in the record to support this notion. In short, under the district court's findings, it is not the formal mechanics of Joe's roll-call system or the criteria embedded in its subjective hiring practices, nor its formal delegation of hiring authority to its maitre d's which kept women from applying to and being hired by Joe's during the pre- and post-charge periods.

At bottom then, this case really centers around the theory that women refrained from making the "futile gesture," of applying to Joe's when they knew that Joe's only hired men as food servers. If Joe's reputation came from anything causally attributable to the restaurant, it emanated from Joe's own purportedly discriminatory hiring practices, *not* from the specific facially neutral practices identified by the district court. While we agree that in some situations evidence of prior historical discrimination may provide relevant background to a contemporary disparate impact challenge, the facts of this case may be read to suggest something quite different; i.e. that Joe's hiring decisionmakers systematically excluded female applicants from consideration, that over time this male-only preference became common knowledge, and that eventually most potential, qualified, female applicants self-selected out of Joe's hiring process precisely because of its reputation for intentional sex discrimination. Indeed, the subsidiary factual findings in this case could be read in simple syllogistic form: first, "Old World" fine-dining meant hiring only tuxedo-clad male servers; second, Joe's sought to emulate "Old World" fine-dining; and finally, Joe's therefore only hired male servers. If this is what the district court meant to find, it is indicative of something quite different from the theory of disparate impact. But we cannot affirm a disparate impact judgment where the case centers entirely around allegations and evidence of intentional discrimination. The record does not support it, and to do so would unwisely conflate the distinct theories of disparate impact and disparate treatment.

* * *

[The Court's review of the law of class-wide intentional ("pattern and practice") discrimination is omitted. The Court concluded that the district court's conclusion that the EEOC had not met its burden of proving intentional discrimination "may have been based on an erroneous view" of the case law.]

III.

Accordingly, we vacate the district court's judgment of liability as to the EEOC's disparate impact claims, and we remand to the district court so that it may reconsider its factual findings and conclusions of law on the EEOC's intentional discrimination claims in light of this opinion. Because of our holding, we have no occasion to reach the various issues raised on appeal regarding the propriety of the remedies awarded by the district court.

VACATED AND REMANDED.

HULL, Circuit Judge, specially concurring in part and dissenting in part:

* * * The trial evidence amply supports all of the district court's factual findings, and the majority does not contend otherwise. Thus, I concur in the majority opinion to this extent.

I also agree with the majority that disparate *impact* liability requires a showing that facially-neutral employment practices caused the lack of female food servers at Joe's. I disagree, however, with the majority's conclusion that the district court "identified no *facially-neutral* practice responsible for the gender disparity in Joe's food server population and we can find none." I disagree because the district court (1) did single out certain employment practices that are facially neutral and (2) did not err in finding that these practices caused the gender disparity in Joe's food servers. In my view, the district court's finding of disparate *impact* liability should be affirmed in full.

* * *

* * * The majority opinion only assumes that the district court properly found that the EEOC demonstrated that the required gender disparity between the available labor pool and Joe's actual hires. In my view, however, the EEOC clearly proved that the available qualified labor pool of food servers was 31.9% female.[3] Thus, the

---

[3][T]he district court did not err in finding the available qualified labor pool was 31.9% female, and not the 0 to 3% or 21.9% actual applicants as claimed by Joe's. The district court's findings were amply supported by evidence (a) that 30 to 40% of the food servers at nearby Miami restaurants were female, (b) that the 1990 census data showed the available qualified labor pool of servers being 44.1% female, and (c) the testimony of Dr. McClave, Joe's own expert, who had refined this 44.1% to 31.9% to reflect only experienced food servers in the higher income brackets of Joe's food servers. Finally, the waiter or server work force in Dade County, Florida,

proven statistical disparity — between 31.9% and 0% in the pre-charge period and 31.9% and 21.7% in the post-charge period — is legally significant.[4]

Because the evidence overwhelmingly showed a legally significant gender disparity in Joe's food servers, the majority opinion necessarily focuses on the second and third prongs of a prima facie disparate impact case — whether the EEOC and the district court identified *facially-neutral* employment practices as *causing* this gender disparity. The majority concludes they did not. I conclude they did.

The main facially-neutral employment practice identified by the district court was management's lack of any hiring guidelines and policies and the resultant "undirected and undisciplined delegation of hiring authority to subordinate staff."[5] Within the ambit of "undirected and undisciplined delegation of hiring authority to subordinate staff," the district court included these facially-neutral practices: (1) management's lack of any written or even oral guidelines for its staff to follow in hiring; (2) the staff's use of mainly a subjective interview process and "subjective intuition" for hiring its servers; (3) management's sitting in on the roll call process but providing no input; and (4) lack of any managerial oversight and lack of any standardization, as exemplified by management's failure to raise a question when the subordinate staff filled 108 consecutive vacancies with only male servers. The majority states that "the subjective hiring criteria did not harm women once they entered the application process." I disagree because the record evidence supports the district court's findings that it did. Many qualified women attended Joe's roll calls and were interviewed, but were not hired.

The district court emphasized that the subjective criteria that Joe's hiring staff used, and the majority focuses on — appearance, attitude, articulation, and experience — were not defined in any way or standardized between interviewers. For example, the district court found that the criteria of experience was not defined by management and varied among staff interviewers based upon their subjective beliefs about what constituted experience. The district court also found that some of Joe's hiring staff believed that prior single service experience — as opposed to team service experience — is required; others did not. As a result, the district court found that some female candidates with decades of experience were rejected by Joe's staff, while other males without any experience were hired. Likewise, the district court found that Joe's hiring staff differed as to what restaurants are "similar" to Joe's for purposes of experience.

---

was 69.6% female. Thus, this 31.9% figure was substantially less and a conservative percentage given the overall evidence.

[4]The statistical disparity between 0% and 31.9% is stark. And, even when this 31.9% figure is compared to the 21.7% hiring statistics in the post-charge period, the "standard deviation" is between 1.96 and 2.07, which is a legally significant disparity under the case law. See Watson.

[5]Joe's did not have any objective guidelines for hiring food servers but utilized only subjective hiring practices. Thus, the EEOC claimed that Joe's subjective hiring practices had a disparate impact on women. The Supreme Court has expressly held that disparate impact analysis may be applied to subjective hiring practices. See Wards Cove Packing Co. v. Atonio, 490 U.S. 642, 648, 109 S. Ct. 2115, 2120, 104 L. Ed. 2d 733 (1989) (citing Watson). The Supreme Court has stated that the delegation of hiring decisions can constitute an employment practice under disparate impact theory. See Watson.

The district court also observed that after the EEOC's charge, Joe's management directed the daytime maitre d' to interview with another maitre d' and subsequently used a panel of three interviewers, later changed to include a woman. The district court found, however, that "while management's introduction of a panel system for interviewing may dilute the subjective views of any one evaluator, it does not overcome management's failure to develop uniform, gender-neutral guidelines to ensure that all interviewers interpret criteria in the same manner and apply them consistently." The district court summarized Joe's hiring decisions as being left to each interviewer's "own subjective intuition" and the interviewers' judgment being "informed largely by their own experience in the restaurant's atmosphere of all-male service."

Another major employment practice at Joe's, which the district court identified as causing the gender disparity, was Joe's use of only a "word-of-mouth" roll call system for recruiting new servers. The district court pointed out that year after year only a few women came to the roll call due to Joe's well-known historical practice of hiring, and using, only tuxedo-clad men as servers. The district court emphasized that Joe's did not advertise in the newspaper or elsewhere that it was an equal opportunity employer or that Joe's hired both men and women as servers. Instead, Joe's continued recruiting through only the "word-of-mouth" roll call on the first Tuesday in October — just as it had done for decades.

The majority stresses that the particular date of the roll call was widely known in the Miami Beach community, and that no woman testified that she failed to apply because she was unaware of the roll call. However, the district court found that Joe's historical practice of hiring only men as servers was also well known in that community and caused women servers to self-select out and not come to Joe's roll call. Joe's own conduct caused the dearth of women applicants. The district court, in effect, found women refrained from making the futile gesture of attending the roll call when they knew Joe's hired only men as servers.

Although the undisciplined delegation of hiring, subjective interview process, and the use of a roll call are facially-neutral employment practices, the district court also referenced "Joe's history of being an all-male server establishment." Excluding women as servers — even if to create a fine dining ambience of tuxedo-clad men — is a facially-discriminatory practice, as the majority notes. However, Joe's past discriminatory hiring is part of the factual background against which the district court analyzed whether the above facially-neutral practices caused the gender disparity to continue. The district court's order raised the precise question of whether "Joe's undirected and undisciplined delegation of hiring authority caused the disparity between the number of women hired as servers and the number of women available, or are forces outside the hiring process — such as a deteriorating neighborhood, low turnover, or the heavy lifting required of servers — to blame?"[8]

---

[8]Joe's contends that the fact that during the 1980s, South Beach Miami was a high-crime area explains the low pre-charge applicant numbers. In addition, Joe's asserts that the area began to be revitalized at almost the same time as the EEOC commenced its investigation, thus accounting for the increase in female applicants during the post-charge period. Joe's also

In short, the district court considered the above facially-neutral employment practices, not in a vacuum, but in the context of Joe's historical discriminatory practice of excluding women as food servers. The district court properly considered Joe's historical discriminatory practices, and the "males-only" reputation Joe's created for itself, as relevant background evidence in examining whether Joe's facially-neutral employment practices *caused and continued* the gender disparity in Joe's food servers. In doing so, the district court did not err because it is well settled that past discrimination is admissible to demonstrate that facially-neutral employment practices continue to perpetuate the effects of past discrimination.

* * *

Additionally, the district court correctly found that Joe's facially-neutral recruiting and hiring practices did not address the entrenched "male-only" hiring and "male-only" reputation Joe's created for itself and thereby further caused the gender disparity to continue. The district court found that, at a minimum, Joe's needed to advertise that it now hired both men and women as servers. Instead, Joe's continued reliance on the facially-neutral, "word-of-mouth" roll call caused the gender disparity in its applicant pool and, in turn, its hires, to continue. Furthermore, as to the women who did apply, the district court found that "without additional guidance and structuring by management, there is no assurance that female applicants who [do] attend roll call will be treated even-handedly."

The district court's findings are akin to those in *Griggs* and other cases in which neutral employment practices have been found to perpetuate historical discrimination. In situations where a protected group has been historically and systematically frozen out of certain employment positions, a purely subjective recruiting and hiring system can act to perpetuate that problem.

* * * Joe's had a historical practice of excluding a protected group. Nor was any direction given to Joe's hiring staff or potential applicants that an effort was being made to change its longstanding historical practice of excluding women as food servers. Indeed, just the opposite occurred. Joe's hired 108 male servers between 1986 and 1990 but no women, without management voicing an objection to its staff. Further, the hiring staff continued to use only the "word-of-mouth" roll call for recruiting without objection, and was given little to no guidance in terms of how to assess even those female applicants who did apply. As a result, Joe's staff admittedly relied upon vague "gut feelings." The staff themselves testified that they viewed Joe's as a place for male servers.[11] Without guidance from their superiors, this stereotype undoubtedly guided their "gut" feelings as to whom to hire.

---

presented evidence that its server's job involves carrying extremely heavy trays and a "frantic" pace. Joe's evidence was countered at trial, however, by the facts (1) that many of Joe's other staff members were female, (2) that there was security at Joe's, and (3) that Southpointe Seafood, directly across the street, had a wait staff that was 25% female. Further, the increase in female applicants at Joe's after 1991 did not correspond to any change in the strenuous nature of the server position.

[11]Maitre d' Garrett testified that Joe's always had qualified women but hired male food servers because it was traditionally a male-server establishment. Similarly, Anthony Arneson, the maitre d' in charge of hiring beginning in 1987, testified that gender was never mentioned by Joe's

Because Joe's delegated authority over both recruiting and hiring to staff who admittedly felt that the restaurant was a male-server type of establishment and had historically known it to be so, Joe's staff was content to hire only men and to use a "word-of-mouth" roll call system which recruited mostly men. Further, the interviewers' admitted bias for male servers went unchecked by guidance from management. Given the historical context, the district court did not err in finding that management's continued lack of any guidance to its hiring staff, the staff's continued use of only the "word-of-mouth" roll call, and the use of a subjective interview process caused the gender disparity to continue in both the attendance at the roll call, from which Joe's hired exclusively, and in the actual hires.

Thus, I conclude that the district court's findings — that Joe's specific facially-neutral recruiting and hiring practices caused the gender disparity in its serving staff — are not clearly erroneous.

* * *

[Judge Hull's alternative argument that the liability judgment should be affirmed on disparate treatment analysis is omitted.]

For all of these reasons, I would affirm the district court's liability decision in this case.

NOTES AND PROBLEMS FOR DISCUSSION

1. In *Wards Cove,* the Supreme Court held that in a hiring/promotion case, a comparison between the racial composition of the pool of qualified persons in the labor market and the racial composition of the population holding the at-issue jobs "generally forms the proper basis for the initial inquiry in a disparate impact case." 490 U.S. at 650, 109 S.Ct. at 2121. Isn't that exactly what the district court did in *Joe's Stone Crab*? Before the EEOC filed its charge, Joe's hiring statistics were stark: 108 men and no women. Why then, according to the majority, did the EEOC fail to establish a prima facie case of disparate impact? Why was the comparison of the gender composition of the applicant pool with the gender composition of those hired (generally referred to as "applicant flow" statistics) important to the majority?

What exactly does it mean to ask whether a facially neutral practice has *caused* an impact on a protected class? In STOUT v. POTTER, 276 F.3d 1118 (9th Cir. 2002), female applicants for a managerial position in the U.S. Postal Service claimed that the screening process by which candidates were selected for interviews had a disparate impact on female applicants. The selection process involved two stages. A panel initially screened all applicants on the strength of their supervisor evaluations and applications. The most qualified applicants were passed on as potential interviewees to a separate selection committee that made the final hiring decisions. Of 38 applicants, six were women. Two of the fifteen applicants selected for interviews were women and one of those women was ultimately promoted along with four men. The district court granted summary judgment to the defendants and the court of appeals

managers or employees because of a "perception that people didn't even think about" — "that many fine dining establishments throughout the world have an all male staff."

affirmed on the ground that the plaintiffs had not demonstrated a statistically significant impact on women since the selection rate for interviews for female applicants was 81% that of male applicants. But the court also found that the plaintiffs had failed to demonstrate a causal link between any screening process and the claimed gender disparity. Comparing these plaintiffs' proof to the evidence offered in *Griggs* linking the defendant's workforce racial imbalance and the challenged employment practices, the court compared stated:

> In this case, by contrast, the [plaintiffs] * * * fail to demonstrate how the screening process excludes female applicants due to gender. The elements of the screening process are facially gender neutral. An applicant is measured by performance on the validated competencies in the application and strength of supervisor evaluations. There is no evidence that women perform worse than men on the competencies or that women receive poorer supervisor evaluations. Unlike in Griggs, where it was shown that the lower scores of black candidates were a factor in employment decisions that caused fewer black employees to be promoted, the postal inspectors here fail to show that women are measured lower than men on the neutral criteria involved in the screening decision. There is no evidence demonstrating that the neutral practices or criteria in the screening process "operate as built-in headwinds" for female applicants.

276 F.2d at 1125. The screening panel apparently engaged in a subjective selection process in comparing candidates who had been evaluated by different supervisors and who had different work histories. If female candidates had been screened out of the final stage of the selection process at a significantly higher rate than men, is the Ninth Circuit saying that plaintiffs would have still failed to establish a prima facie case because of an inability to show how the practice excluded women?

2. The EEOC's original complaint in the principal case asserted only a claim of intentional discrimination against Joe's. But the trial court allowed the agency to amend its complaint during trial to include an allegation of disproportionate impact. Because the nature of the theory on which plaintiff elects to proceed will affect the nature of the defenses the defendant may raise, courts have generally held that the plaintiff must plead disparate impact or at least alert the defendant to the claim before trial. *See* Coleman v. Quaker Oats Co., 232 F.3d 1271, 1294 (9th Cir. 2000) (plaintiffs who pleaded disparate treatment claims but who sought to pursue claims of disparate impact were required either to (1) plead disparate impact theory in their complaint or (2) make known during discovery their intention to pursue recovery on disparate impact theory).

3. THE DEFENSES

As in any civil case, a defendant in a Title VII case can either deny the existence of a prima facie case and/or assert an affirmative defense. In impact cases, as in *Joe's Stone Crab*, the defendant can attempt to deny the plaintiff's prima facie claim by attacking the accuracy and/or relevance of the plaintiff's statistical data. Once the court has determined that the plaintiff has established the existence of a disproportionate impact on a protected class, as the Court declared in *Griggs*, and later amplified in *Albemarle Paper*, "[t]he touchstone is business necessity. If an employment practice which operates to exclude [a protected class] cannot be shown to be related to job performance, the practice is prohibited." The defendant's affirmative defense to an impact-based claim is discussed in the following case:

(a) Job Relatedness & Business Necessity

Fitzpatrick v. City of Atlanta

United States Court of Appeals, Eleventh Circuit, 1993.
2 F.3d 1112.

ANDERSON, Circuit Judge:

This suit was brought against the City of Atlanta by several African-American firefighters employed by the Atlanta Department of Public Safety, Bureau of Fire Services who suffer from a medical condition on account of which they cannot shave their faces. Plaintiffs challenge a fire department regulation that requires all firefighters to be clean-shaven. They allege * * * that this "no-beard" rule has a discriminatory disparate impact on African-Americans in violation of Title VII of the 1964 Civil Rights Act * * *. The City defends the policy, contending that the respirator masks used by firefighters cannot safely be worn by bearded men. The district court granted summary judgment for the City and the firefighters have appealed. For the reasons set forth below, we affirm the judgment of the district court.

I.   FACTS AND PROCEDURAL HISTORY

In order to breathe in smoke-filled environments, firefighters must wear respirators, otherwise known as positive pressure self-contained breathing apparatuses ("SCBA's"). For the SCBA mask to operate properly and safely, its edges must be able to seal securely to the wearer's face. The parties do not dispute that a wearer's long facial hair can interfere with the forming of a proper seal. In an attempt to address the hazard posed by such hair, the City Fire Department until 1982 enforced a policy requiring all male firefighters to be completely clean-shaven.

The twelve plaintiff-appellant firefighters in this case are all African-American men who suffer from pseudofolliculitis barbae ("PFB"), a bacterial disorder which causes men's faces to become infected if they shave them. It is generally recognized that PFB disproportionately afflicts African-American men. At least one of the appellants, firefighter Darryl Levette, has been fighting with the City over its no-beard policy for more than ten years. Levette first challenged the requirement in 1982. In response to his complaints, the City modified its policy in order to accommodate firefighters with PFB.

Under the modified policy, firefighters with PFB were permitted to participate in a program known as the "shaving clinic." Shaving clinic participants were allowed to wear very short "shadow" beards, which were not to exceed length limits specified by a dermatologist employed by the City. To enforce these limits, the Fire Department subjected the participating firefighters to a series of periodic beard inspections. It was believed that so long as the shadow beards were kept very short, the SCBA masks would still be able to seal sufficiently well to enable the firefighters to use them safely.

In 1988, * * * the Fire Department decided that shadow beards would no longer be permitted, on the grounds that even shadow beards may interfere with the safe use of SCBA's.

On November 4, 1988, the Department of Public Safety * * * direct[ed] the Fire Department to resume enforcement of * * * the no-beard rule. Under the new policy, firefighters who cannot be clean-shaven must be removed from firefighting duty. Such persons may be transferred to non-firefighting positions within the Department, if suitable openings are available. They may also apply for other available positions with the City but are accorded no special priority and must compete on an equal basis with other eligible candidates. Under the new policy such persons are granted the right to be temporarily reassigned from firefighting duties for a one-time period of ninety days. Male firefighters who cannot shave and for whom non-firefighting positions are not available within the Department are terminated, once they have exhausted their ninety days of temporary reassignment.

Firefighter Hutchinson challenged the new policy by filing a charge with the U.S. Equal Employment Opportunity Commission * * *. * * * [T]he EEOC certified the charge as a "class" charge on behalf of all city firefighters adversely affected by the policy change. The appellant firefighters initiated this suit * * *. The district court issued and then extended a restraining order prohibiting the City from changing the terms or conditions of the plaintiff firefighters' employment during the pendency of the litigation before the district court. The City has kept the appellant firefighters on the payroll and has permitted them to continue reporting for work at their regular fire stations, but it has required them to perform various janitorial duties instead of their regular jobs.

The City answered the complaint and moved for summary judgment. The district court referred that motion to a magistrate judge and * * * adopted the magistrate's recommendation that the motion be granted. This appeal followed.

* * *

IV. DISCUSSION OF ISSUES ON APPEAL

* * * As explained below, we affirm the judgment of the district court * * *.

A.   Title VII Disparate Impact Claim

1.   Elements of Claim

* * * In order to establish Title VII liability under [the] effects-based definition of discrimination, a plaintiff must first demonstrate that a challenged employment action or practice has a disproportionate adverse impact on a category of persons protected by the statute. Once such a prima facie case has been made out, the defendant must show that the challenged action is demonstrably necessary to meeting a goal of a sort that, as a matter of law, qualifies as an important business goal for Title VII purposes.

* * *

The Supreme Court held in *Wards Cove Packing Co. v. Atonio* that the defendant's burden on the "business necessity" defense is only one of production; under *Wards Cove* the burden of persuasion remains at all times with the plaintiff. Congress, however, statutorily reversed this ruling in the Civil Rights Act of 1991, which amended Title VII to provide that, once a plaintiff makes out a prima facie case, the full burden of proof shifts to the defendant who must demonstrate business necessity in order to avoid liability.[5] In this case the district court entered summary judgment * * * one day before the President signed the 1991 Civil Rights Act into law. We shall assume *arguendo* that the burden allocation set out in the new statute applies retroactively to this case, for we conclude that defendant is entitled to summary judgment even under the 1991 Civil Rights Act standard — that is, the standard most favorable for plaintiffs

Upon a showing of "business necessity," the challenged action or practice is deemed justifiable, its regrettable discriminatory effects notwithstanding. However, even after such a showing, the plaintiff may still overcome a proffered business necessity defense by demonstrating that there exist alternative policies with lesser discriminatory effects that would be comparably as effective at serving the employer's identified business needs. Upon such a showing, Title VII liability is established.

2. Grounds for Summary Judgment Urged by the City

The City moved for summary judgment on the Title VII disparate impact claim, contending that it was entitled to prevail for two separate reasons. First, the City argued that the firefighters had failed to adduce statistics of the sort required under Title VII doctrine to show that PFB indeed afflicts African-Americans disproportionately and that, consequently, the firefighters had failed to show that the no-beard rule disproportionately excludes African-American men from firefighting jobs. Thus, the City claimed that the firefighters had failed even to create a genuine issue as to whether — let alone to prove as a fact that — the rule has a disparate racial impact. If it were in fact true that the firefighters lacked the evidence necessary to prove at trial that there is a disproportionate incidence of PFB among blacks, then the City would indeed be entitled to summary judgment, for where a Title VII disparate impact plaintiff fails to make out a prima facie case, the defendant is entitled to prevail.

Second, the City proffered an affirmative "business necessity" defense, asserting that the ban on shadow beards is necessary to meeting the goal of ensuring worker safety. Contending that ensuring worker safety constitutes an important business goal for Title VII purposes, and that there was no genuine issue that the no-beard rule was necessary to meeting that goal, the City maintained that it was therefore entitled to summary judgment.

3. Propriety of Summary Judgment

The district court granted summary judgment in favor of the City on the ground that there was an absence of evidence showing that the no-beard rule has a disparate impact. We, however, find it unnecessary to address that issue on appeal. Exercising

---

[5]Prior to 1989, the "business necessity" showing was an affirmative defense for which the defendant bore the burden of proof and risk of nonpersuasion. Griggs. In 1989, the Supreme Court in Wards Cove changed the law, holding that the defendant bore only the burden of coming forward with an alleged business-related justification for the challenged practice which the plaintiff would then have to disprove in order to prevail. The Court also broadened the scope of the necessity defense by holding that practices causing a disparate impact were permissible, even if they could not be shown to be absolutely necessary, so long as they "served, in a significant way, the legitimate employment goals of the employer." These changes were statutorily reversed by the Civil Rights Act of 1991 (codified at §703(k)(1)(A)).

our discretion to affirm grants of summary judgment on any adequate alternative ground fairly presented in the record, we uphold the court's order regarding the firefighters' Title VII disparate impact claim on the ground that appellants have failed to create a genuine issue as to the City's contention that the ban on shadow beards is necessitated by safety concerns.

In ruling on this ground, we assume *arguendo* that the firefighters have adequately alleged a prima facie case of disparate impact. Where a Title VII disparate impact challenge is mounted against a practice or action which admittedly causes a disparate impact, the defendant is entitled to prevail if (1) the defendant shows that the practice or action is necessary to meeting a goal that, as a matter of law, qualifies as an important business goal for Title VII purposes, and (2) the plaintiff fails to show the availability of less discriminatory alternative practice or action that would provide a comparably effective means of meeting that goal. Thus, in order for such a defendant to be entitled to summary judgment, the following must be true: (1) there must be no genuine issue that the practice or action is required to meet a goal that, as a matter of law, qualifies as an important business goal under Title VII; and (2) there must be no genuine issue with respect to the existence of a comparably effective less discriminatory alternative.

a. Business Necessity Defense

The City defends its decision to ban shadow beards on the ground that the prohibition is required to protect the firefighters from health and safety risks. If true, these safety claims would afford the City an affirmative defense, for protecting employees from workplace hazards is a goal that, as a matter of law, has been found to qualify as an important business goal for Title VII purposes. *Dothard v. Rawlinson.*[6] Measures demonstrably necessary to meeting the goal of ensuring worker safety are therefore deemed to be "required by business necessity" under Title VII.

Whether the no-beard rule is demonstrably necessary to meeting the acknowledged business goal of worker safety is a factual issue on which, for the purposes of this case, we have assumed that the City, the movant, would bear the burden of proof at trial. Thus, our analysis of whether there exists a genuine issue as to this material fact begins with an examination of whether the City has carried the initial burden imposed on parties moving for judgment on issues on which they would bear the burden of proof at trial. The City has supported its safety allegations with

---

[6]Though recognizing that measures necessary to protect employees or third parties from documented health or safety hazards are "required by business necessity," courts have stressed that merely asserting a safety rationale does not suffice to prove the defense. An employer's subjective belief that a practice is necessary, without any supporting evidence, is plainly insufficient to justify a discriminatory practice. In order to establish a safety-based business necessity defense, employers have been required to present convincing expert testimony demonstrating that a challenged practice is in fact required to protect employees or third parties from documented hazards. See Burwell v. Eastern Air Lines, Inc., 633 F.2d 361, 365-66 (4th Cir.1980) (plurality opinion), cert. denied, 450 U.S. 965, 101 S. Ct. 1480, 67 L. Ed. 2d 613 (1981). The sources of proof invoked by the City in this case to prove its safety defense meet this evidentiary standard.

evidence in the form of an affidavit from an expert in the field of occupational safety and health and with a citation to a U.S. Occupational Safety and Health Administration regulation concerning use of respirators by persons with facial hair.

The City's expert, Kevin Downes, swore that, "Based upon my research and experience in training on the proper use of SCBA's, it is my opinion that the SCBA should not be worn with any amount of facial hair that contacts the sealing surface of the face piece." In the affidavit Downes detailed particular safety risks that he maintained were posed by use of SCBA's by men with facial hair. Such use would be dangerous, asserted Downes, because facial hair is likely to interfere with the forming of a proper seal between the SCBA mask and the wearer's face. An imperfect seal may permit air from the outside environment to leak into the mask — when this occurs the wearer is said to have "overbreathed" — thereby risking exposing the wearer to contaminants.

* * * Downes noted that three national organizations that set occupational safety and health standards — the American National Standards Institute, the National Institute for Occupational Safety and Health, and OSHA — all recommend that SCBA's should not be worn with facial hair which contacts the sealing surface of the face piece. * * * {T]he City * * * also * * * cited directly to the OSHA respirator standard. The OSHA regulation provides: "Respirators shall not be worn when conditions prevent a good face seal. Such conditions may be a growth of beard. . . ."

We hold that this evidence that safety concerns necessitate the ban on shadow beards is credible evidence that would entitle the City to a directed verdict if not controverted at trial. The City has thus carried its movant's initial summary judgment burden on the business necessity issue.

At this point, responsibility devolves upon the firefighters to come forward with evidence that, when considered together with the City's evidence, is sufficient to create a genuine issue as to the reality of the City's safety claims. The only real evidence invoked by the firefighters to counter the City's claims is the fact that for the six years between 1982 and 1988 the City permitted firefighters with PFB to wear their SCBA's over shadow beards. The firefighters argue that the fact that the shadow beard program was tested over this period, apparently without mishap or reported problems obtaining adequate seals, creates at least a genuine issue that shadow beards may in fact be safe. We disagree. The firefighters have not adduced evidence showing how carefully the firefighters' seals were monitored over this period, or whether examinations were made that would have uncovered any resulting safety or health problems. The mere absence of unfortunate incidents is not sufficient to establish the safety of shadow beards; otherwise, safety measures could be instituted only once accidents had occurred rather than in order to avert accidents. Although the six-year history is not irrelevant to the question of whether it is unsafe to wear SCBA's over shadow beards, we hold that when considered in the context of the totality of the evidence, it would not be sufficient to prevent the City from obtaining a directed verdict at trial.

In reaching this conclusion we are swayed particularly by the recommendations of the occupational safety and health standards organizations. Although public employers such as the City are not required by law to comply with OSHA standards, such standards certainly provide a trustworthy bench mark for assessing safety-based business necessity claims. It is true that the OSHA and ANSI standards speak in somewhat general terms about "facial hair" and "growths of beard" and do not specifically address the case of very short shadow beards; however, the NIOSH standard provides that "even a few days growth of stubble should not be permitted." At least in the absence of any evidence showing that safety experts view shadow beards as a special case, we hold that the only reasonable inference supported by the OSHA, ANSI, and NIOSH standards is that shadow beards are encompassed by the prohibitions.

This is not to say that allegations that a challenged practice is required for safety are by any means unassailable. Expert testimony or results from adequately conducted field tests tending to show that shadow beards do not prevent SCBA's from sealing to the face would be sufficient to create a genuine issue as to the reality of the City's safety claims. However, the firefighters have come forward with no such evidence. We thus hold that the firefighters have failed to carry their non-movant's summary judgment rebuttal burden and that, therefore, there was in the record before the district court at the time of the summary judgment motion no evidence creating a genuine issue as to whether safety requires the ban on shadow beards.

b. Less Discriminatory Alternative Issue

As stated above, in order for the City to be entitled to summary judgment on the disparate impact claim, there must also be no genuine issue of fact with respect to whether a less discriminatory comparably effective alternative to the no-beard rule is available. The existence of a less discriminatory alternative is an issue on which the firefighters, the non-movants, would bear the burden of proof at trial. Thus, our analysis of whether there exists a genuine issue as to this material fact begins with an examination of whether the City has carried the movant's initial burden applicable for issues on which the movant would not bear the burden of proof at trial.

In such circumstances, the movant may carry the initial burden by adducing evidence affirmatively negating the material fact at issue, or else by showing an absence of evidence on the part of the non-movant to prove the fact at trial. As discussed above, the City has cited the OSHA, ANSI, and NIOSH safety standards which advise that safety requires that SCBA-wearers be clean-shaven. We believe that this evidence affirmatively demonstrates, not only that being clean-shaven is a business necessity for firefighters, but also that any proposed less discriminatory alternatives to the no-beard rule that would not require firefighters to be clean-shaven would not be adequately safe. Thus the evidence is sufficient to satisfy the City's initial burden as the summary judgment movant on the less discriminatory alternative issue.

Responsibility then devolves upon the firefighters to adduce evidence creating a genuine issue as to the availability of a comparably safe, less discriminatory alternative. The firefighters have proposed two possible alternatives to the City's rule requiring firefighters to be clean-shaven. The first is simply reinstitution of the shadow beard shaving clinic. However, in order for the shadow beard program to constitute a legitimate less discriminatory alternative, shadow beards must adequately serve the Fire Department's acknowledged business need, namely, safety. As we have explained above in addressing the City's business necessity defense, the firefighters have failed to create a genuine issue that shadow beards are safe. Thus, for the same reason, they have also failed to create a genuine issue that the shaving clinic would be a comparably effective alternative to the shadow beard ban.

The second possible alternative suggested by the firefighters is shaving only the portion of the face where the SCBA seal would come into contact with the skin. However, in the two sentences of their summary judgment papers in which they propose this alternative, the firefighters cite no evidence to show that partial shaving would be a viable and safe alternative. Moreover, as a matter of common knowledge, it is apparent that partial shaving would pose the same PFB problems as full-face shaving, and thus it is doubtful that the firefighters could have adduced evidence that partial shaving constitutes a viable less discriminatory alternative. Thus, the firefighters have failed to carry their summary judgment rebuttal burden of creating a genuine issue as to the viability of either of the two less discriminatory alternatives they propose. Having concluded (1) that the City has carried its initial summary judgment burdens on the business necessity and less discriminatory alternative issues, and (2) that the firefighters have failed to carry their summary judgment rebuttal burdens on either of these two points, we affirm the grant of summary judgment on the Title VII disparate impact claim.

* * *

V.   CONCLUSION

For the foregoing reasons, we affirm the ruling of the district court granting summary judgment for the City on each of the firefighters' claims.

AFFIRMED.

NOTES AND PROBLEMS FOR DISCUSSION

1.   In light of the fact that for six years the city allowed firemen with PFB to wear SCBA's over shadow beards without incident, how could the court find there was no genuine issue as to whether the no-beard rule was a business necessity? Under the Eleventh Circuit's analysis, would any work rule that contributed, even marginally, to worker safety be justified as "consistent with business necessity"? By way of comparison, consider the ruling of the Eighth Circuit in BRADLEY v. PIZZACO OF NEB., INC., 7 F.3d 795 (8th Cir. 1993). There, the plaintiff, who suffered from PFB, challenged a nation-wide no-beard policy established by his employer's franchiser, Domino's Pizza. In this post-1991 Act case, the court concluded that the defendants must show a "manifest relationship to the employment in question," a "compelling need" to maintain the practice, and the non-existence of a less discriminatory alternative. The court found unpersuasive the defense evidence of business justification, which consisted of management's opinion that "the better our people look, the better our sales will be," and of a customer survey purporting to show that twenty percent of those surveyed would "react negatively to a delivery man wearing a beard." The court rejected the testimony of Domino's witness as "speculative and conclusory", declaring that "[a]n employer cannot rely on purely conclusory testimony by company personnel to prove that a [challenged practice] is job-related and required by business necessity." 7 F.3d at 798. Nor did the customer survey suffice.

Even if the survey results indicated significant customer apprehension regarding beards, which they do not, the results would not constitute evidence of sufficient business justification for Domino's strict no-beard policy. Although this circuit had not directly addressed customer preference as a business justification for policies having a disparate impact on a protected class, cases from other circuits have not looked favorably on this kind of evidence. . . . The existence of a beard on the face of a pizza delivery man does not affect in any manner Domino's ability to make or deliver pizzas to their customers. Customer preference, which is at best weakly shown by Domino's survey, is clearly not a colorable business justification defense in this case. Significantly, the survey makes no showing that customers would order less pizza in the absence of a strictly enforced no-beard rule.

7 F.3d at 799. Is the difference between *Fitzpatrick* and *Bradley* merely that the no-beard rule as applied to firefighters had a safety rationale while Domino's rule was driven by solely by economic concerns? The circuit courts have not agreed on a precise definition of "business necessity." *Compare* United States v. Bethlehem Steel Corp., 446 F.2d 652, 662 (2d Cir. 1971) ("Necessity connotes an irresistible demand. . . . [A practice] must not only directly foster safety and efficiency of a plant, but also be essential to those goals."), *with* Nolting v. Yellow Freight System, Inc., 799 F.2d 1192, 1198-99 (8th Cir. 1986) (showing employee evaluation system "significantly served" interest in production quantity established business necessity).

2. As the court suggested in *Joe's Stone Cr*ab, the employer's burden of proving business necessity may be greater where it is shown that the challenged practice perpetuates the effects of prior intentional discrimination. In WALKER v. JEFFERSON COUNTY HOME, 726 F.2d 1554 (11th Cir. 1984), the Court of Appeals noted that a nursing home's requirement of prior supervisory experience as a prerequisite for promotion to a supervisory position, though neutral on its face, produced a disproportionate exclusionary impact upon African-American employees as a consequence of past discrimination in job assignments to supervisory positions. Under those circumstances, the court held, the employer should have a "heavy burden" of proving business necessity. The defendant failed to satisfy the burden because it did not prove either that the job of supervisor was highly skilled or that the economic and human risks associated with hiring an unqualified applicant were great.

An employer's reliance on an employment criteria as a business necessity may backfire and result in a finding of intentional discrimination if the criteria has not, in fact, been uniformly applied by the employer. In KILGO v. BOWMAN TRANSP. CO., 789 F.2d 859 (11th Cir. 1986), a trucking company argued that its requirement of a one-year over-the-road experience for new drivers was necessary for safety. The court of appeals concluded that even if the requirement was a business necessity and there was no less discriminatory alternative, since the company had hired over 60 men who did not satisfy the prior experience requirement the trial court's determination that the requirement was a pretext for intentional discrimination was not erroneous.

Zamlen v. City Of Cleveland

United States Court of Appeals, Sixth Circuit, 1990.
906 F.2d 209.

NORRIS, Circuit Judge.

Plaintiffs appeal from an order of the district court entering judgment for defendants in this class action lawsuit alleging * * * municipal conduct causing a prohibited disparate impact under Title VII. The suit, which was brought on behalf of entry-level female firefighters in the City of Cleveland, challenged the rank-order written and physical capabilities selection examination established by the city as perpetuating the exclusion of women from firefighting positions. The district court * * * at the close of all the evidence, found for defendants on the Title VII claim.

* * *

I. BACKGROUND

Much has been written about historical discrimination based upon race, sex, and national origin in public service occupations such as law enforcement and firefighting. In order to address the problem, many municipalities have employed rank-order written and physical abilities tests which ostensibly allow employers to select candidates who possess the highest degree of skills required to perform the job.[2] Although these tests have been designed to eliminate discriminatory hiring practices, some have been shown to have a disparate impact on women and, for that reason, are challenged.

Two claims are usually advanced in support of the argument that rank-order physical tests unfairly discriminate against women. First, it is said that these tests measure attributes in which men traditionally excel, such as speed and strength (anaerobic traits), while ignoring those in which women traditionally are said to excel, such as stamina and endurance (aerobic traits). Second, it is claimed that the tested attributes are not necessarily related to the skills which the specific job requires. The examination at issue was challenged for precisely these reasons.

As of 1977, the city had never hired any woman firefighters. In that year, it hired Dr. Norman Henderson, a tenured professor of psychology at Oberlin College who had significant experience developing tests for various municipalities throughout the country, to design, administer and score an entry-level firefighter examination. Dr. Henderson was again hired to develop and administer an entry-level exam in 1980.

No women were hired after the 1977 and 1980 examinations were scored and the applicants ranked. Out of 911 applicants who took both the written and physical portions of the examination in 1980, 18 were female. Only one female, or 5.6% of the women who took the exam, scored high enough to be placed on the eligibility list.

---

[2]In jurisdictions employing rank-order testing, candidates are graded on their test performance and an eligibility list is compiled in which scores are ranked from high to low. In contrast, tests administered on a pass/fail basis allow employers to select candidates from a pool of qualified applicants. Applicants may be chosen from the pool randomly or in accordance with an affirmative action policy.

With a ranking of 634, however, she was too far down the list to be hired. In contrast, 787 male applicants, or 88.2%, were placed on the eligibility list.

In 1983, Dr. Henderson was once again hired by the city to design and administer an exam for firefighters. In light of the female applicants' poor performance on the 1977 and 1980 examinations, and in order to minimize any disparate impact which his previous examinations may inadvertently have had on female applicants, Dr. Henderson prepared a new job analysis. The purpose of this new job analysis was to:

(1) establish a list of tasks required of entry-level firefighters;

(2) determine the frequency with which each task is performed and its importance to acceptable job performance;

(3) group tasks into broad job dimensions;

(4) assess the knowledge, skills and abilities required for learning and adequately performing critical and highly important job tasks;

(5) determine overall knowledge, skills and abilities required for entry-level firefighters with respect to the above tasks; and

(6) identify and define abilities and skills to be tested based upon the above data.

He then compiled an initial tasks list based upon a 1974 survey of 271 Cleveland firefighters. In the survey, fire-fighters rated 95 firefighting tasks in terms of frequency and importance. This initial list was then reviewed in conjunction with the Ohio Trade and Industrial Education Fire Service Training Manual and tasks lists from other cities. Dr. Henderson then produced a revised list consisting of 150 tasks and submitted this list to Chief William E. Lee, Director of the Cleveland Fire Training Academy. Chief Lee pared this list down to a final checklist of 135 tasks. Dr. Henderson also prepared a list of 12 intellectual and perceptual abilities relevant to effective firefighting.

Based upon this initial research, Dr. Henderson developed final written and physical components of the examination. The written component was designed to test reading comprehension, the ability to follow directions, mathematical skills, and other forms of cognitive reasoning. The physical component consisted of three events:

Event 1: Overhead Lift — using a 33 lb. barbell, candidates must lift the barbell overhead repeatedly for one minute or up to a maximum of 35 lifts.

Event 2: Fire Scene Set Up and Tower Climb—while wearing a custom-tailored self-contained breathing apparatus, candidates must drag two lengths of standard 2 ½" hose 180 feet (90 feet one way, drop coupling, run to the other end of the hose, pick up and return 90 feet, drop coupling in designated area), run 75 feet to pumper, remove a one-person ladder (approximately 35 lbs.) from the side of the pumper, carry the ladder into the fire tower, place it against the back rail of the first landing and continue up the inside stairwell to the fifth floor where a monitor observes the candidates' arrival. Then, candidates return to the first landing, retrieve the ladder and place it on the pumper.

Event 3: Dummy Drag — still wearing their self-contained breathing apparatus, candidates must drag a 100 lb. bag 70 feet (40 of which includes low headroom), turn and, still dragging the bag, return to the starting point.

After the test was developed, but before it was administered, the city embarked on a program to recruit and train female firefighters. As part of its recruitment program, the city provided potential female recruits with a free twelve-week training program. This program, which included a two and one-half hour physical and cognitive portion, began on February 14, 1983. The written portion of the training program was based primarily upon the 1982 edition of the ARCO Civil Service Test training manual. The physical portion, which was based primarily on the content of previous examinations, included training in such activities as dummy lift and carry, dummy drag, hose drag, tower run, fence climb, ladder lift, balance beam walk, and hose coupling. The program did not include training in the use of barbells, nor did the director of the program recommend to any of the women that she work with barbells prior to the examination.

One week before the actual physical examination, the city notified all applicants of the content of the examination, including the barbell event. The training program obtained a set of barbells which was made available to the applicants.

On April 30, 1983, the city administered the written portion of the test and, on May 7 and 13, the physical portion of the test. There were 3,612 applicants initially, but only 2,212 took the written part and 1,233 the physical part. Each portion of the examination was worth a raw score of 50 points with a maxim achievable score of 100. The raw scores on the written portion were adjusted by capping the scores from different sections, by awarding five extra points to qualifying veterans, by awarding ten extra points to city residents, and by adding up to six points to the scores of minority candidates. The minority adjustment was undertaken as a means of complying with a consent decree entered against the city in a suit by minority candidates alleging bias in hiring. Only those applicants with an adjusted score of at least 35 were eligible to take the physical portion of the exam.

Of the 285 females who took the written portion, 122 passed; of the 1,927 males who took the written examination, 1,206 passed. After taking the physical portion of the examination, 29 females scored high enough on both portions of the exam to be placed on the eligibility list while 1,069 males were placed on the list. However, the woman with the highest score still only ranked 334 on the eligibility list — too low to be hired. The class of 35 firefighters, therefore, contained no women.

On June 14, 1983, plaintiffs filed this class action. The principal defense was that the selection procedure was job-related and properly validated. * * *

* * *

V. ADEQUACY OF VALIDATION PROCEDURES AND FAILURE TO MEASURE AEROBIC CAPACITY

* * *

The Equal Employment Opportunity Commission has developed guidelines to assist employers to comply with requirements of Federal law prohibiting employment practices which discriminate on grounds of race, color, religion, sex and national origin and to provide a framework for determining the proper use of tests and other selection procedures. Under the guidelines, employers may use three types of studies to validate an employee selection procedure: content, construct, or criterion-related validity studies. The particular device that is chosen depends upon the nature of the job, the way in which the test will be interpreted, and the type of data that is available.

A content validity study is appropriate when test items directly measure abilities that are prerequisites to entry-level job performance (for example, a shorthand test for a secretarial position). Content validity studies must include a thorough job analysis identifying the most important knowledge, skills, and abilities necessary to successful job performance. An employer who seeks to validate a physical examination on the basis of a content validity study must therefore focus on the job's actual physical requirements. In addition, an employer must avoid testing for those skills that can readily be learned on the job.[6]

A construct validity study tests for abstract qualities that are difficult to test but that are, nonetheless, important characteristics for proper job performance. Such studies are appropriate where the necessary qualities, such as creativity, cannot be measured directly. Construct validity studies are usually not appropriate for validating physical exams because these qualities are readily observable and quantifiable.

Finally, a criterion-related study, which also makes use of empirical data, indirectly tests for those skills necessary for successful job performance. According to the guidelines, a criterion-related study "should consist of empirical data demonstrating that the selection procedure is predictive of or significantly correlated with important elements of job performance." 29 C.F.R. § 1607.5(B).

The district court found that the 1983 examination was properly validated according to content, construct, and criterion validation principles. Nonetheless, plaintiffs attack the district court's finding on the ground that the test that Dr. Henderson developed was not properly validated and, in addition, did not test for all of the attributes he identified in his job analysis as important to an effective firefighter. Although Dr. Henderson recognized that successful firefighters must possess a high level of aerobic capacity and aerobic fitness, as well as muscle strength, muscular endurance, flexibility, coordination, muscle balance, and speed, the physical portion of the 1983 examination measured anaerobic — maximal speed and strength — but not aerobic — stamina or paced performance — traits.

We first note that there was substantial evidence before the district court supporting the conclusion that the examination was properly validated. Each event in the physical examination was designed to test a representative firefighting task. The barbell lift was designed to simulate the use of a pike pole to tear out ceilings. The fire scene set-up and tower climb event was intended to duplicate critical firefighting tasks performed where speed is the most critical factor, such as setting up ladders and climbing stairs. The dummy drag simulated the rescue of a disabled person under circumstances where heat and smoke make it difficult to stand upright. Although plaintiffs attack the content validity of these events as only superficially replicating an actual sequence of job tasks, an expert testified that these events did, in fact, simulate actual firefighting tasks. Plaintiffs may find fault with the way in which the district

---

[6] 29 C.F.R. §§1607.5(F) states:
Caution against selection on basis of knowledge, skills, or ability learned in brief orientation period. In general, users should avoid making employment decisions on the basis of measures of knowledge, skills, or abilities which are normally learned in a brief orientation period, and which have an adverse impact.

court came to certain conclusions but there is an insufficient basis for us to conclude that these conclusions are clearly erroneous.

Similarly, plaintiffs argue that there was insufficient evidence supporting the district court's conclusion that the examination was construct and criterion valid. However, plaintiffs ignore the substantial evidence before the district court, including Dr. Henderson's technical report correlating higher test scores with higher supervisor ratings as well as Dr. Henderson's further analyses, supporting the conclusion that the examination was construct and criterion valid.

Plaintiffs' most forceful argument is that the 1983 examination failed to measure attributes which are concededly important to effective firefighting, attributes in which it is often argued that women traditionally excel, such as stamina and endurance. By failing to test for these aerobic qualities, plaintiffs argue, Dr. Henderson devised an examination hopelessly biased in favor of male applicants who will almost always score higher than female applicants on tests which solely measure anaerobic qualities such as strength and speed.

A similar case was decided recently in the Second Circuit. In *Berkman v. City of New York*, 812 F.2d 52 (2d Cir.1987), plaintiffs argued that a firefighter exam used by the City of New York to select entry-level firefighters should be invalidated because it failed to measure aerobic capacity and placed undue emphasis on anaerobic performance. Recognizing that aerobic attributes are an important component of effective firefighting, the court nonetheless held that the city's failure to include events that test for such qualities did not invalidate the examination. While the court implied that an examination that included events which tested an applicant's aerobic energy system would be preferable, "[it] does not follow, however, that a physical test of the ability to perform simulated job tasks of firefighters, without a specific measurement of stamina, lacks validity to a degree that renders it vulnerable to a Title VII challenge." 812 F.2d at 59.

While aerobic ability enables firefighters to sustain a consistent level of energy over a long period of time, speed and strength are critical at the initial stages of a fire where matters of life and death are most acute. A firefighter who tires may be replaced by a fresh recruit but, as the *Berkman* court recognized, "if the first firefighters on the scene are deficient in the speed and strength necessary to handle their tasks, those in need of immediate rescue will not be comforted by the fact that those first on the scene might be able to sustain their modest energy levels for a prolonged period of time." 812 F.2d at 60. Here, the district court concluded that anaerobic qualities are more important. Certainly, we are unable to say a fire department is not entitled to select firefighters whose abilities enable them to act more effectively in the first moments of a fire. Accordingly, although a simulated firefighting examination that does not test for stamina in addition to anaerobic capacity may be a less effective barometer of firefighting abilities than one that does include an aerobic component, the deficiencies of this examination are not of the magnitude to render it defective, and vulnerable to a Title VII challenge.

VI. LESS RESTRICTIVE ALTERNATIVE

Finally, plaintiffs contend that a different scoring system — one which would eliminate the addition of variable numbers of minority points, the use of the capping system and the addition of veterans' points — would have raised the rank-order of women on the eligibility list and, thus, constitutes a less restrictive alternative. * * *

The district court concluded that plaintiffs failed to demonstrate a less restrictive alternative, a conclusion with which we agree. Although the use of a different scoring system might raise the rank-order of women on the eligibility list, given the fact that the woman with the highest test score still only ranked 334 on the eligibility list, and that the city only hired approximately forty firefighters each year, it is doubtful that any alternative scoring system would have had less of a disparate impact on women. The evidence suggests that, at best, an alternative scoring system would result in female applicants ranking higher on the eligibility list, but still too low to actually be hired. Since rescoring the examination is unlikely to result in higher numbers of successful female applicants, it is an insufficient reason to invalidate an otherwise lawful examination.

VII. CONCLUSION

Because the examination did parallel the actual tasks which firefighters perform on the job, and the city did demonstrate a direct correlation between higher test scores and better job performance, the examination withstands plaintiffs' challenge. Accordingly, the judgment of the district court is affirmed.

NOTES AND PROBLEMS FOR DISCUSSION

1. The court in *Zamlen* briefly describes the three methods of test validation incorporated in the EEOC Guidelines.

Criterion-related Validation. In UNITED STATES v. GA. POWER CO., 474 F.2d 906, 912 (5th Cir. 1973), the Fifth Circuit described this validation strategy:

> The most accurate way to validate an employment test is to administer the test to be validated to all applicants but proceed to select new employees without regard for their test achievement, and then, after an appropriate period of work experience, compare job performance with test scores. . . . An alternative is "concurrent validation," a process in which a representative sample of current employees is rated, then tested, and their scores are compared to their job ratings.

The EEOC's Uniform Guidelines describe a criterion-related study as consisting of "empirical data demonstrating that the selection procedure is predictive of or significantly correlated with important elements of job performance." 29 C.F.R. §1607.5B. Of the three methods of validation, criterion-related validation is the only one which correlates test results with actual work performance and is thus considered preferable to methods based on less direct evidence. *See* Bridgeport Guardians, Inc. v. Members of Bridgeport Civil Service Comm'n, 482 F.2d 1333, 1337 (2d Cir. 1973), cert. denied, 421 U.S. 991, 95 S.Ct. 1997, 44 L.Ed.2d 481 (1975).

Efforts at concurrent validation have frequently been rejected because the data produced by the studies has not shown that the test was valid for the purpose for which it was used. In ALBEMARLE PAPER CO. v. MOODY, 422 U.S. 405, 95 S.Ct. 2362, 45 L.Ed.2d 280 (1975), the Supreme Court's pre-eminent statement on the employer's burden of proving the job-relatedness of a disproportionate impact-generating device, the defendant attempted to validate a general ability test by giving that test to selected groups of current employees and then comparing their scores with supervisors' subjective evaluations of their work. The Supreme Court rejected this attempt at validation because the standard by which supervisors ranked employees "was extremely vague and open to divergent interpretations" and because "[t]he fact that the best of . . . employees working near the top of a line of progression score well on a test does not necessarily mean that that test, or some particular cutoff score on that test, is a permissible measure of the minimal qualifications of new workers entering lower level jobs." 422 U.S. at 432, 95 S.Ct. at 2379.

Content Validation: Unlike criterion validation, content validation does not require a correlation between success on the test and success in the job. Content validation must, however, be based on a job analysis "of the important work behavior(s) required for successful performance and their relative importance and, if the behavior results in work product(s), an analysis of the work product(s)." 29 C.F.R. §1607.14C(2). The prevailing judicial view is that for a test to have content validity, it must measure "with proper relevant emphasis all or . . . most of the essential areas of knowledge and the traits needed for proper job performance." *See e.g.,* Bridgeport Guardians, Inc. v. Members of Bridgeport Civil Service Comm'n, 354 F.Supp. 778, 792 (D. Conn.), affirmed in pertinent part, reversed in part, 482 F.2d 1333 (2d Cir.1973), cert. denied, 421 U.S. 991, 95 S.Ct. 1997, 44 L.Ed.2d 481 (1975).

Construct Validation: Construct validation is the least understood and least utilized of the three validation methods. Creativity, assertiveness or the ability to "get along" with others are the kinds of qualities which an employer might wish to assess in an applicant, but which are not susceptible to criterion or content validation studies. The EEOC Uniform Guidelines outline the following procedure for construct validation: (1) a job analysis which identifies work behavior(s) required for successful job performance; (2) an identification of the construct(s) believed to underlie success in the critical job behavior(s); and (3) a selection procedure which measures the important construct(s). 29 C.F.R. §1607.14D(2).

The trial court in *Zamlen* found that the firefighter examination was validated under *all three* validation theories. Could that possibly be the case? Upon what kind of validation did the Court of Appeals rely?

2. Do the rulings in *Zamlen* and *Berkman* mean that an employer is free to emphasize certain factors which favor male applicants in the selection procedure and de-emphasize those equally job-related factors which favor female applicants without regard to how relatively important the factors are in performing the job? *Compare* Brunet v. City of Columbus, 642 F.Supp. 1214 (S.D. Ohio 1986), appeal dismissed, 826 F.2d 1062 (6th Cir. 1987), cert. denied, 485 U.S. 1034, 108 S.Ct. 1593, 99 L.Ed.2d 908 (1988) (physical test for firefighter was not properly validated because it placed undue emphasis on speed of limb movement and dynamic flexibility and underemphasized endurance), *with* Cleghorn v. Herrington, 813 F.2d 992 (9th Cir. 1987) (physical ability test used to screen applicants for job of guarding nuclear facilities was properly validated even though test emphasized emergency duties rather than daily routine work which was largest component of job).

3. The plaintiffs' class in *Zamlen* was affected by the firefighters' test in two ways: (1) the content of the test resulted in a much smaller percentage of female than of male applicants attaining a passing score, and (2) the use of test scores to rank applicants meant that, of those women who passed the test, most were ranked at the bottom of the list of acceptable candidates. The EEOC Uniform Guidelines provide that rank-ordering should be used only if it can be shown that "a higher score . . . is likely to result in better job performance." 29 C.F.R. §1607.14(C)(9).

In contrast to the ruling in *Zamlen*, the Third Circuit rejected the defendant's attempt to validate a physical fitness test in LANNING v. SOUTHEASTERN PENNSYLVANIA TRANSIT AUTHORITY, 181 F.3d 478 (3d Cir. 1999), cert. denied, 120 S.Ct. 970, 145 L.Ed.2d 840 (2000). There, unsuccessful female applicants for a transit police force claimed that the first component of a physical fitness test which required applicants to run 1.5 miles within twelve minutes violated Title VII. The test was designed for the defendant by an expert physiologist who studied the work done by transit police and recommended the 1.5 mile run as an accurate measure of the aerobic capacity necessary to perform the job. During a three-year period an average of only 12% of women applicants passed the run test in comparison to the almost 60% of male applicants who passed. The defendant conceded that transit officers were not required to actually run 1.5 miles in the course of their duties and there was no proof that the cutoff reflected the *minimum* aerobic capacity necessary for successful performance of the job. Nevertheless, the district court found that the 1.5 mile run was a valid test for the position and that the twelve minute cutoff was "readily justifiable" under the business necessity test. The Court of Appeals reversed, concluding that the district judge had applied the wrong standard for business necessity. The validation studies of the defense experts upon which the district court had relied showed that the higher an officer's aerobic capacity, the better she could perform the job, but this showing, characterized by the Court as "more is better," had no bearing on the validity of the twelve-minute cutoff for the run. "[T]he business necessity standard . . . demand[s] that a discriminatory cutoff score be shown to measure the minimum qualifications necessary for the successful performance of the job in question in order to survive a disparate impact challenge." 181 F.3d at 490.

On remand, the trial court concluded that the defendant had established that its requirement that candidates for transit police officer run 1.5 miles in at least twelve minutes measured the minimum aerobic capacity necessary to perform successfully the job of transit officer and thus was justified by business necessity. The plaintiffs appealed again, but this time the circuit affirmed. 308 F.3d 286 (3d Cir. 2002) (*Lanning II*). The district court had relied on several studies conducted by the defendant's experts which showed that individuals who passed the run test had a substantially higher success rate on the performance of a number of "job standards" and concluded that a low rate of success on such standards was unacceptable for employees regularly called upon to apprehend criminals and protect the public. The court of appeals panel majority upheld the lower court's findings as not clearly erroneous. While admitting that the record showed that some people who could not pass the run test could nevertheless satisfactorily perform the job, the court rejected the argument that such evidence showed that the run test did not establish the "minimum qualification necessary" for the job. "It is perfectly reasonable * * * to demand a chance of success that is better than 5% to 20%. * * * SEPTA transit police officers and the public they serve should not be required to engage in high-stakes gambling when it comes to public safety and law enforcement." 308 F.3d at 292. Does this ruling mean that, at least in public safety positions, a theoretical correlation between a test cutoff and successful job performance is sufficient for business necessity even if there is no empirical demonstration of a correlation?

Public employers seem to have more difficulty defending pass/fail or cut-off scores on *written* tests. In ISABEL v. CITY OF MEMPHIS, 404 F.3d 404 (6th Cir. 2005), African-American police officers challenged a written test administered as part of the promotion process from the rank of Sergeant to Lieutenant. The process consisted of the written test, a practical exercise test, performance evaluations, and consideration of seniority. The written test was administered first and a passing score was required to remain in the promotion process. The cutoff score originally was set at 70, but after it was discovered that use of that score would create a disproportionate impact the cutoff was lowered to 66. Under that cutoff, the pass rate for African-American candidates was 83% of the pass rate of white candidates, thus satisfying the EEOC's 4/5ths measure of disproportionate impact. But as there was still a statistically significant difference between the pass rates of blacks and whites, the trial judge found that both use of the test and the cutoff score violated Title VII because the City had failed to establish business necessity. The Sixth Circuit affirmed. The court noted that "[t]o validate a cutoff score, the inference must be drawn that the cutoff score measures minimum qualifications." 404 F.3d at 413. But the evidence showed that the cutoff score adopted by the City was adopted solely because it was believed it would insulate the process from an impact-based challenge. Moreover, other evidence showed a lack of correlation between test scores of those passing and overall qualifications. For example, a non-minority candidate who barely passed the written test ended up with the second highest total score in the pool of candidates. Is there any principled reason for more rigorous analysis of written tests than of physical tests?

4. If minorities or women are disproportionately excluded by an employment criterion, one way to increase their number in the work force without abandoning the selection device is to set lower pass rates or cut off points for minorities and/or women. Such practices, referred to as race or sex "norming," are explicitly prohibited by §703(l), which makes it an unlawful employment practice " to adjust the scores of, use different cutoff scores for, or otherwise alter the results of, employment related tests on the basis of race, color, religion, sex, or national origin." In light of the general antidiscrimination mandate contained in §703(a), why did Congress think 703(l) was necessary?

Another method of reducing the impact of employment tests on minorities is "banding." In OFFICERS FOR JUSTICE v. CIVIL SERVICE COMM'N OF SAN FRANCISCO, 979 F.2d 721 (9th Cir. 1992), cert. denied, 507 U.S. 1004, 113 S.Ct. 1645, 123 L.Ed.2d 267 (1993), a police officers' union appealed from the district court's approval of the city's "banding" of scores for promotional examinations. The city had proposed to treat test scores that fell within a statistically derived "band" as substantially equivalent for purpose of measuring knowledge, skills, and abilities in order to promote a higher percentage of minority officers to higher positions than would have been promoted under a strict rank order system. For those candidates in the same band, the city proposed considering secondary criteria, not measured by the examination, including race, sex, professional conduct, education, and experience. The Ninth Circuit explained the theory of banding as follows:

> Banding is premised on the belief that minor differences in test scores do not reliably predict differences in job performance. It also recognizes that an

individual is unlikely to achieve an identical score on consecutive administrations of the same examination. Because some measurement error is inevitable, strict rank order promotions will not necessarily reflect the correct comparative abilities of the candidates. The smaller the difference between observed scores, the more likely it is a result of measurement error, and not a variance in job-related skills and abilities.

979 F.2d at 723. In CHICAGO FIREFIGHTERS LOCAL 2 v. CITY OF CHICAGO, 249 F.3d 649 (7th Cir.2001), after describing banding as "a universal and normally unquestioned method of simplifying scoring by eliminating meaningless gradations," the Seventh Circuit held that the practice was not proscribed "race norming" within the meaning of §703(l). Thus, where rank order hiring or promotions on the basis of test scores results in disparate impact which cannot be justified by business necessity, use of statistically appropriate bands may allow the employer to avoid liability while still using the test scores to assist in evaluation of candidates.

5. As codified at §703(k)(1)(A)(ii), if an employment practice is shown to generate a disproportionate impact and the employer proves that the practice is "job related" and "consistent with business necessity," the plaintiff nonetheless can prevail by proving that the employer has refused to implement an alternative practice which satisfies the employer's legitimate interests and has a lesser impact on the protected class. As *Fitzpatrick* and *Zamlen* illustrate, it is exceedingly difficult for plaintiffs to satisfy this burden, and cases where plaintiffs have successfully asserted this less-discriminatory alternative argument are rare. This lack of success is due, in large part, to the expense of devising and testing an alternative practice. And where the employer chooses instead simply to modify its incumbent impact-generating device, the burden of proof may be formidable. In ALLEN v. CITY OF CHICAGO, 351 F.3d 306 (7th Cir. 2003), the City's multi-step process governing promotion to the rank of sergeant consisted of a qualifying examination, a written assessment exercise, and a merit selection component. To qualify for promotion all candidates had to pass the qualifying examination. Thereafter, 70% of the promotions to sergeant were made on the basis of rank-order scores on the assessment exercise. The remaining 30% of the promotions were made on merit selection, a process in which a panel of high-ranking officials evaluated the performance of a select group of officers nominated for merit promotion by their commanders. Rank-order promotion based on the written assessment exercise was shown to have a disproportionate impact on minority candidates; the success rate for black officers was 34.7% of the success rate of white candidates and the success rate for Latino officers was 31.6% of the white rate. But since the plaintiffs conceded that the written assessment exercise was job related, the sole remaining issue was whether there was an equally valid, less discriminatory alternative. The plaintiffs proposed that the percentage of promotions based on merit selection be substantially increased because the evidence showed that the success rate for whites and minority officers on the merit selection component was virtually identical. The court rejected this argument, finding that evidence that the city had reserved 30% of its promotions for merit-based consideration and that even more officers could be nominated for merit-based promotion was not enough to sustain the plaintiff's burden of demonstrating that increased merit selection would satisfy the employer's legitimate interests.

Because increasing the percentage of merit-based promotions actually creates a different merit selection procedure with increased potential for evaluation error, the officers must separately show the substantially equivalent validity of increased merit promotions. The officers do not attempt to do so.

* * *

Without any evidence that the officers' alternative of increasing merit promotions would lead to a workforce substantially equally qualified, we cannot accept the officers' alternative as substantially equally valid.

351 F.3d at 313-14. Has not the court imposed an impossible burden on plaintiffs? After all, unless the City was willing to try increased merit promotions, how could the plaintiffs produce the kind of evidence that the court required?

(b) Bona Fide Seniority Systems

International Brotherhood of Teamsters v. United States

Supreme Court of the United States, 1977.
431 U.S. 324, 97 S.Ct. 1843, 52 L.Ed.2d 396.

MR. JUSTICE STEWART delivered the opinion of the Court.

This litigation brings here several important questions under Title VII. The issues grow out of alleged unlawful employment practices engaged in by an employer and a union. The employer is a common carrier of motor freight with nationwide operations, and the union represents a large group of its employees. The District Court and the Court of Appeals held that the employer had violated Title VII by engaging in a pattern and practice of employment discrimination against Negroes and Spanish-surnamed Americans, and that the union had violated the Act by agreeing with the employer to create and maintain a seniority system that perpetuated the effects of past racial and ethnic discrimination. In addition to the basic questions presented by these two rulings, other subsidiary issues must be resolved if violations of Title VII occurred — issues concerning the nature of the relief to which aggrieved individuals may be entitled.

I

The United States brought an action in a Tennessee federal court against the petitioner T.I.M.E.-D.C., Inc. pursuant to §707(a).[1] The complaint charged that the company had followed discriminatory hiring, assignment, and promotion policies

---

[1] * * * Section 707 was amended by §5 of the Equal Employment Opportunity Act of 1972 to give the Equal Employment Opportunity Commission, rather than the Attorney General, the authority to bring "pattern or practice" suits under that section against private-sector employers. In 1974, an order was entered in this action substituting the EEOC for the United States but retaining the United States as a party for purposes of jurisdiction, appealability, and related matters.

against Negroes at its terminal in Nashville, Tenn.[2] The Government brought a second action against the company almost three years later in a Federal District Court in Texas, charging a pattern and practice of employment discrimination against Negroes and Spanish-surnamed persons throughout the company's transportation system. The petitioner International Brotherhood of Teamsters was joined as a defendant in that suit. The two actions were consolidated for trial in the Northern District of Texas.

The central claim in both lawsuits was that the company had engaged in a pattern or practice of discriminating against minorities in hiring so-called line drivers. Those Negroes and Spanish-surnamed persons who had been hired, the Government alleged, were given lower paying, less desirable jobs as servicemen or local city drivers, and were thereafter discriminated against with respect to promotions and transfers.[3] In this connection the complaint also challenged the seniority system established by the collective-bargaining agreements between the employer and the union. The Government sought a general injunctive remedy and specific "make whole" relief for all individual discriminatees, which would allow them an opportunity to transfer to line-driver jobs with full company seniority for all purposes.

The cases went to trial and the District Court found that the Government had shown "by a preponderance of the evidence that T.I.M.E.-D.C. and its predecessor companies were engaged in a plan and practice of discrimination in violation of Title VII * * *." The court further found that the seniority system contained in the collective-bargaining contracts between the company and the union violated Title VII because it "operate[d] to impede the free transfer of minority groups into and within the company." Both the company and the union were enjoined from committing further violations of Title VII.

* * *

The Court of Appeals for the Fifth Circuit agreed with the basic conclusions of the District Court: that the company had engaged in a pattern or practice of employment discrimination and that the seniority system in the collective-bargaining agreements violated Title VII as applied to victims of prior discrimination. * * *

* * *

II

In this Court the company and the union contend that their conduct did not violate Title VII in any respect, asserting first that the evidence introduced at trial was insufficient to show that the company engaged in a "pattern or practice" of

---

[2]The named defendant in this suit was T.I.M.E. Freight, Inc., a predecessor of T.I.M.E.-D.C., Inc. T.I.M.E.-D.C., Inc., is a nationwide system produced by 10 mergers over a 17-year period. It currently has 51 terminals and operates in 26 States and three Canadian Provinces.

[3]*Line drivers*, also known as over-the-road drivers, engage in long-distance hauling between company terminals. They compose a separate bargaining unit at the company. Other distinct bargaining units include *servicemen*, who service trucks, unhook tractors and trailers, and perform similar tasks; and *city operations*, composed of dockmen, hostlers, and city drivers who pick up and deliver freight within the immediate area of a particular terminal. All of these employees were represented by the petitioner union.

employment discrimination. The union further contends that the seniority system contained in the collective-bargaining agreements in no way violated Title VII.

* * *

B

The District Court and the Court of Appeals also found that the seniority system contained in the collective-bargaining agreements between the company and the union operated to violate Title VII of the Act.

For purposes of calculating benefits, such as vacations, pensions, and other fringe benefits, an employee's seniority under this system runs from the date he joins the company, and takes into account his total service in all jobs and bargaining units. For competitive purposes, however, such as determining the order in which employees may bid for particular jobs, are laid off, or are recalled from layoff, it is bargaining-unit seniority that controls. Thus, a line driver's seniority, for purposes of bidding for particular runs[25] and protection against layoff, takes into account only the length of time he has been a line driver at a particular terminal.[26] The practical effect is that a city driver or serviceman who transfers to a line-driver job must forfeit all the competitive seniority he has accumulated in his previous bargaining unit and start at the bottom of the line drivers' "board."

The vice of this arrangement, as found by the District Court and the Court of Appeals, was that it "locked" minority workers into inferior jobs and perpetuated prior discrimination by discouraging transfers to jobs as line drivers. While the disincentive applied to all workers, including whites, it was Negroes and Spanish-surnamed persons who, those courts found, suffered the most because many of them had been denied the equal opportunity to become line drivers when they were initially hired, whereas whites either had not sought or were refused line-driver positions for reasons unrelated to their race or national origin.

The linchpin of the theory embraced by the District Court and the Court of Appeals was that a discriminatee who must forfeit his competitive seniority in order finally to obtain a line-driver job will never be able to "catch up" to the seniority level of his contemporary who was not subject to discrimination.[27] Accordingly, this continued, built-in disadvantage to the prior discriminatee who transfers to a line-driver job was held to constitute a continuing violation of Title VII, for which both the

---

[25]Certain long-distance runs, for a variety of reasons, are more desirable than others. The best runs are chosen by the line drivers at the top of the "board" — a list of drivers arranged in order of their bargaining-unit seniority.

[26]Both bargaining-unit seniority and company seniority rights are generally limited to service at one particular terminal, except as modified by the Southern Conference Area Over-the-Road Supplemental Agreement. See n. 10, *supra*.

[27]An example would be a Negro who was qualified to be a line driver in 1958 but who, because of his race, was assigned instead a job as a city driver, and is allowed to become a line driver only in 1971. Because he loses his competitive seniority when he transfers jobs, he is forever junior to white line drivers hired between 1958 and 1970. The whites, rather than the Negro, will henceforth enjoy the preferable runs and the greater protection against layoff. Although the original discrimination occurred in 1958 — before the effective date of Title VII — the seniority system operates to carry the effects of the earlier discrimination into the present.

employer and the union who jointly created and maintain the seniority system were liable.

The union, while acknowledging that the seniority system may in some sense perpetuate the effects of prior discrimination, asserts that the system is immunized from a finding of illegality by reason of §703(h), which provides in part:

> "Notwithstanding any other provision of this subchapter, it shall not be an unlawful employment practice for an employer to apply different standards of compensation, or different terms, conditions, or privileges of employment pursuant to a bona fide seniority * * * system, * * * provided that such differences are not the result of an intention to discriminate because of race * * * or national origin * * *."

It argues that the seniority system in this case is "bona fide" within the meaning of §703(h) when judged in light of its history, intent, application, and all of the circumstances under which it was created and is maintained. More specifically, the union claims that the central purpose of §703(h) is to ensure that mere perpetuation of *pre-Act* discrimination is not unlawful under Title VII. And, whether or not §703(h) immunizes the perpetuation of *post-Act* discrimination, the union claims that the seniority system in this litigation has no such effect. Its position * * * is that the seniority system presents no hurdle to *post-Act* discriminatees who seek retroactive seniority to the date they would have become line drivers but for the company's discrimination. Indeed, the union asserts that under its collective-bargaining agreements the union will itself take up the cause of the post-Act victim and attempt, through grievance procedures, to gain for him full "make whole" relief, including appropriate seniority.

The Government responds that a seniority system that perpetuates the effects of prior discrimination — pre-Act or post-Act — can never be "bona fide" under §703(h); at a minimum Title VII prohibits those applications of a seniority system that perpetuate the effects on incumbent employees of prior discriminatory job assignments.

The issues thus joined are open ones in this Court.[28] We considered §703(h) in Franks v. Bowman Transportation Co., 424 U.S. 747, 96 S.Ct. 1251, 47 L.Ed.2d 444, but there decided only that §703(h) does not bar the award of retroactive seniority to job applicants who seek relief from an employer's post-Act hiring discrimination. We stated that "the thrust of [§703(h)] is directed toward defining what is and what is not an illegal discriminatory practice in instances in which the post-Act operation of a

---

[28]Concededly, the view that §703(h) does not immunize seniority systems that perpetuate the effects of prior discrimination has much support. It was apparently first adopted in Quarles v. Philip Morris, Inc., 279 F.Supp. 505 (E.D.Va.). The court there held that "a departmental seniority system *that has it genesis in racial discrimination* is not a *bona fide* seniority system." The *Quarles* view has since enjoyed wholesale adoption in the Courts of Appeals. Insofar as the result in *Quarles* and in the cases that followed it depended upon findings that the seniority systems were themselves "racially discriminatory" or had their "genesis in racial discrimination," the decisions can be viewed as resting upon the proposition that a seniority system that perpetuates the effects of pre-Act discrimination cannot be bona fide if an intent to discriminate entered into its very adoption.

seniority system is challenged as perpetuating the effects of discrimination occurring prior to the effective date of the Act." Beyond noting the general purpose of the statute, however, we did not undertake the task of statutory construction required in this litigation.

(1)

Because the company discriminated both before and after the enactment of Title VII, the seniority system is said to have operated to perpetuate the effects of both pre- and post-Act discrimination. Post-Act discriminatees, however, may obtain full "make whole" relief, including retroactive seniority under Franks v. Bowman, without attacking the legality of the seniority system as applied to them. *Franks* made clear and the union acknowledges that retroactive seniority may be awarded as relief from an employer's discriminatory hiring and assignment policies even if the seniority system agreement itself makes no provision for such relief.[29] Here the Government has proved that the company engaged in a post-Act pattern of discriminatory hiring, assignment, transfer, and promotion policies. Any Negro or Spanish-surnamed American injured by those policies may receive all appropriate relief as a direct remedy for this discrimination.[30]

(2)

What remains for review is the judgment that the seniority system unlawfully perpetuated the effects of pre-Act discrimination. We must decide, in short, whether §703(h) validates otherwise bona fide seniority systems that afford no constructive seniority to victims discriminated against prior to the effective date of Title VII, and it is to that issue that we now turn.

The primary purpose of Title VII was "to assure equality of employment opportunities and to eliminate those discriminatory practices and devices which have fostered racially stratified job environments to the disadvantage of minority citizens."

---

[29]Article 38 of the National Master Freight Agreement between The Company and the union in effect as of the date of the systemwide lawsuit provided:

"The Employer and the Union agree not to discriminate against any individual with respect to his hiring, compensation, terms or conditions of employment because of such individual's race, color, religion, sex, or national origin, nor will they limit, segregate or classify employees in any way to deprive any individual employee of employment opportunities because of his race, color, religion, sex, or national origin."

Any discrimination by the company would apparently be a "grievable" breach of this provision of the contract.

[30]The legality of the seniority system insofar as it perpetuates post-Act discrimination nonetheless remains at issue in this case, in light of the injunction entered against the union. Our decision today in United Air Lines, Inc. v. Evans, 431 U.S. 553, 97 S.Ct. 1885, 52 L.Ed.2d 571, is largely dispositive of this issue. *Evans* holds that the operation of a seniority system is not unlawful under Title VII even though it perpetuates post-Act discrimination that has not been the subject of a timely charge by the discriminatee. Here, of course, the Government has sued to remedy the post-Act discrimination directly, and there is no claim that any relief would be time barred. But this is simply an additional reason not to hold the seniority system unlawful, since such a holding would in no way enlarge the relief to be awarded. Section 703(h) on its face immunizes all bona fide seniority systems, and does not distinguish between the perpetuation of pre- and post-Act discrimination.

McDonnell Douglas Corp. v. Green.[31]   To achieve this purpose, Congress "proscribe[d] not only overt discrimination but also practices that are fair in form, but discriminatory in operation." Id.. Thus, the Court has repeatedly held that a prima facie Title VII violation may be established by policies or practices that are neutral on their face and in intent but that nonetheless discriminate in effect against a particular group.

One kind of practice "fair in form, but discriminatory in operation" is that which perpetuates the effects of prior discrimination. As the Court held in *Griggs*: "Under the Act, practices, procedures, or tests neutral on their face, and even neutral in terms of intent, cannot be maintained if they operate to 'freeze' the status quo of prior discriminatory employment practices."

Were it not for §703(h), the seniority system in this case would seem to fall under the *Griggs* rationale. The heart of the system is its allocation of the choicest jobs, the greatest protection against layoffs, and other advantages to those employees who have been line drivers for the longest time. Where, because of the employer's prior intentional discrimination, the line drivers with the longest tenure are without exception white, the advantages of the seniority system flow disproportionately to them and away from Negro and Spanish-surnamed employees who might by now have enjoyed those advantages had not the employer discriminated before the passage of the Act. This disproportionate distribution of advantages does in a very real sense "operate to 'freeze' the status quo of prior discriminatory employment practices." But both the literal terms of §703(h) and the legislative history of Title VII demonstrate that Congress considered this very effect of many seniority systems and extended a measure of immunity to them.

Throughout the initial consideration of HR 7152, later enacted as the Civil Rights Act of 1964, critics of the bill charged that it would destroy existing seniority rights. The consistent response of Title VII's congressional proponents and of the Justice Department was that seniority rights would not be affected, even where the employer had discriminated prior to the Act. An interpretative memorandum placed in the Congressional Record by Senators Clark and Case stated:

"Title VII would have no effect on established seniority rights. Its effect is prospective and not retrospective. Thus, for example, *if a business has been discriminating in the past and as a result has an all-white working force, when the title comes into effect the employer's obligation would be simply to fill future vacancies on a non-discriminatory basis.* He would not be obliged — or indeed, permitted — to fire whites in order to hire Negroes, or to prefer Negroes for future vacancies, or, once Negroes are hired, to give them special seniority rights at the

---

[31]We also noted in *McDonnell Douglas*:
"There are societal as well as personal interests on both sides of this [employer-employee] equation. The broad, overriding interest, shared by employer, employee, and consumer, is efficient and trustworthy workmanship assured through fair and racially neutral employment and personnel decisions. In the implementation of such decisions, it is abundantly clear that Title VII tolerates no racial discrimination, subtle or otherwise." 411 U.S. at 801, 93 S.Ct., at 1823.

expense of the white workers hired earlier." 110 Cong.Rec. 7213 (1964) (emphasis added).[35]

A Justice Department statement concerning Title VII, placed in the Congressional Record by Senator Clark, voiced the same conclusion:

"Title VII would have no effect on seniority rights existing at the time it takes effect. If, for example, a collective bargaining contract provides that in the event of layoffs, those who were hired last must be laid off first, such a provision would not be affected in the least by Title VII. *This would be true even in the case where owing to discrimination prior to the effective date of the title, white workers had more seniority than Negroes.*" (emphasis added).[36]

While these statements were made before §703(h) was added to Title VII, they are authoritative indicators of that section's purpose. Section 703(h) was enacted as part of the Mansfield-Dirksen compromise substitute bill that cleared the way for the passage of Title VII.[37] The drafters of the compromise bill stated that one of its principal goals was to resolve the ambiguities in the House-passed version of HR 7152. As the debates indicate, one of those ambiguities concerned Title VII's impact on existing collectively bargained seniority rights. It is apparent that §703(h) was drafted with an eye toward meeting the earlier criticism on this issue with an explicit provision embodying the understanding and assurances of the Act's proponents: namely, that Title VII would not outlaw such differences in treatment among employees as flowed from a bona fide seniority system that allowed for full exercise of seniority accumulated before the effective date of the Act. It is inconceivable that §703(h), as part of a compromise bill, was intended to vitiate the earlier representations of the Act's supporters by increasing Title VII's impact on seniority systems. The statement of Senator Humphrey, noted in *Franks*, confirms that the addition of §703(h) "merely clarifies [Title VII's] present intent and effect."

In sum, the unmistakable purpose of §703(h) was to make clear that the routine application of a bona fide seniority system would not be unlawful under Title VII. As the legislative history shows, this was the intended result even where the employer's pre-Act discrimination resulted in whites having greater existing seniority rights than Negroes. Although a seniority system inevitably tends to perpetuate the effects of pre-

---

[35]Senators Clark and Case were the "bipartisan captains" responsible for Title VII during the Senate debate. Bipartisan captains were selected for each title of the Civil Rights Act by the leading proponents of the Act in both parties. They were responsible for explaining their title in detail, defending it, and leading discussion on it.

[36]* * * Senator Clark also introduced a set of answers to questions propounded by Senator Dirksen, which included the following exchange:

"Question. Would the same situation prevail in respect to promotions, when that management function is governed by a labor contract calling for promotions on the basis of seniority? What of dismissals? Normally, labor contracts call for 'last hired, first fired.' If the last hired are Negroes, is the employer discriminating if his contract requires they be first fired and the remaining employees are white?

"Answer. Seniority rights are in no way affected by the bill. If under a 'last hired, first fired' agreement a Negro happens to be the 'last hired,' he can still be 'first fired' as long as it is done because of his status as 'last hired' and not because of his race."

[37]See Franks v. Bowman, at 761.

Act discrimination in such cases, the congressional judgment was that Title VII should not outlaw the use of existing seniority lists and thereby destroy or water down the vested seniority rights of employees simply because their employer had engaged in discrimination prior to the passage of the Act.

To be sure, §703(h) does not immunize all seniority systems. It refers only to "bona fide" systems, and a proviso requires that any differences in treatment not be "the result of an intention to discriminate because of race * * * or national origin * * *." But our reading of the legislative history compels us to reject the Government's broad argument that no seniority system that tends to perpetuate pre-Act discrimination can be "bona fide." To accept the argument would require us to hold that a seniority system becomes illegal simply because it allows the full exercise of the pre-Act seniority rights of employees of a company that discriminated before Title VII was enacted. It would place an affirmative obligation on the parties to the seniority agreement to subordinate those rights in favor of the claims of pre-Act discriminatees without seniority. The consequence would be a perversion of the congressional purpose. We cannot accept the invitation to disembowel §703(h) by reading the words "bona fide" as the Government would have us do.[38] Accordingly, we hold that an otherwise neutral, legitimate seniority system does not become unlawful under Title VII simply because it may perpetuate pre-Act discrimination. Congress did not intend to make it illegal for employees with vested seniority rights to continue to exercise those rights, even at the expenses of pre-Act discriminatees.[39]

That conclusion is inescapable even in a case, such as this one, where the pre-Act discriminatees are incumbent employees who accumulated seniority in other bargaining units. Although there seems to be no explicit reference in the legislative history to pre-Act discriminatees already employed in less desirable jobs, there can be no rational basis for distinguishing their claims from those of persons initially denied any job but hired later with less seniority than they might have had in the absence of

---

[38]For the same reason, we reject the contention that the proviso in §703(h), which bars differences in treatment resulting from "an intention to discriminate," applies to any application of a seniority system that may perpetuate past discrimination. In this regard the language of the Justice Department memorandum introduced at the legislative hearings, is especially pertinent: "It is perfectly clear that when a worker is laid off or denied a chance for promotion because under established seniority rules he is 'low man on the totem pole' he is not being discriminated against because of his race. * * * Any differences in treatment based on established seniority rights would not be based on race and would not be forbidden by the title.".

[39]The legislative history of the 1972 amendments to Title VII, summarized and discussed in Franks in no way points to a different result. As the discussion in Franks indicates, that history is itself susceptible of different readings. The few broad references to perpetuation of pre-Act discrimination or "de facto segregated job ladders," did not address the specific issue presented by this case. And the assumption of the authors of the Conference Report that "the present case law as developed by the courts would continue to govern the applicability and construction of Title VII," of course does not foreclose our consideration of that issue. More importantly, the section of Title VII that we construe here, §703(h), was enacted in 1964, not 1972. The views of members of a later Congress, concerning different sections of Title VII, enacted after this litigation was commenced, are entitled to little if any weight. It is the intent of the Congress that enacted §703(h) in 1964, unmistakable in this case, that controls.

pre-Act discrimination.[40] We rejected any such distinction in *Franks*, finding that it had "no support anywhere in Title VII or its legislative history." As discussed above, Congress in 1964 made clear that a seniority system is not unlawful because it honors employees' existing rights, even where the employer has engaged in pre-Act discriminatory hiring or promotion practices. It would be as contrary to that mandate to forbid the exercise of seniority rights with respect to discriminatees who held inferior jobs as with respect to later hired minority employees who previously were denied any job. If anything, the latter group is the more disadvantaged. As in *Franks*, " 'it would indeed be surprising if Congress gave a remedy for the one [group] which it denied for the other."[41]

(3)

The seniority system in this litigation is entirely bona fide. It applies equally to all races and ethnic groups. To the extent that it "locks" employees into non-linedriver jobs, it does so for all. The city drivers and servicemen who are discouraged from transferring to linedriver jobs are not all Negroes or Spanish-surnamed Americans; to the contrary, the overwhelming majority are white. The placing of line drivers in a separate bargaining unit from other employees is rational, in accord with the industry practice, and consistent with National Labor Relations Board precedents. It is conceded that the seniority system did not have its genesis in racial discrimination, and that it was negotiated and has been maintained free from any illegal purpose. In these circumstances, the single fact that the system extends no retroactive seniority to pre-Act discriminatees does not make it unlawful.

Because the seniority system was protected by §703(h), the union's conduct in agreeing to and maintaining the system did not violate Title VII. On remand, the District Court's injunction against the union must be vacated.[43]

[The Court's discussion of the relief to be afforded victims of post-Act discrimination and the concurring and dissenting opinions of Justices Marshall and Brennan are omitted.]

---

[40]That Title VII did not proscribe the denial of fictional seniority to *pre-Act* discriminatees who got no job was recognized even in Quarles v. Philip Morris, Inc., 279 F.Supp. 505 (E.D.Va.), and its progeny. Quarles stressed the fact that the references in the legislative history were to employment seniority rather than departmental seniority. In Local 189, United Papermakers & Paperworkers v. United States, 416 F.2d 980(CA5), another leading case in this area, the court observed: "No doubt, Congress, to prevent 'reverse discrimination' meant to protect certain seniority rights that could not have existed but for previous racial discrimination. For example a Negro who had been rejected by an employer on racial grounds before passage of the Act could not, after being hired, claim to outrank whites who had been hired before him but after his original rejection, even though the Negro might have had senior status but for the past discrimination."

[41]In addition, there is no reason to suppose that Congress intended in 1964 to extend less protection to legitimate departmental seniority systems than to plant-wide seniority systems. Then, as now, seniority was measured in a number of ways, including length of time with the employer, in a particular plant, in a department, in a job, or in a line of progression. The legislative history contains no suggestion that any one system was preferred.

[43]The union will properly remain in this litigation as a defendant so that full relief may be awarded the victims of the employer's post-Act discrimination. Fed. Rule Civ. Proc. 19(a).

NOTES AND PROBLEMS FOR DISCUSSION

1.   The seniority provisions questioned in *Teamsters* were created before the effective date of Title VII. In AMERICAN TOBACCO Co. v. PATTERSON, 456 U.S. 63, 102 S.Ct. 1534, 71 L.Ed.2d 748 (1982), the Court held that §703(h) is not limited to seniority systems predating passage of Title VII. But if a seniority system was created after 1965, should a court be able to infer discriminatory intent from evidence of the system's disproportionate impact on a protected class and its toleration by the employer and/or union? In PULLMAN-STANDARD v. SWINT, 456 U.S. 273, 102 S.Ct. 1781, 72 L.Ed.2d 66 (1982), the Court said no.

> Differentials among employees that result from a seniority system are not unlawful employment practices unless the product of an intent to discriminate. It would make no sense, therefore, to say that the intent to discriminate required by §703(h) may be presumed from such an impact. As §703(h) was construed in *Teamsters*, there must be a finding of actual intent to discriminate on racial grounds on the part of those who negotiated or maintained the system.

456 U.S. at 289, 102 S.Ct. at 1790.

2.   Although the Supreme Court has not addressed directly the question of what proof is required to demonstrate that a seniority system is not bona fide, in *Teamsters* it did identify four factors relevant to that inquiry: (1) whether the seniority system operates to discourage all employees equally from transferring between seniority units; (2) whether the seniority units are in the same or separate bargaining units (if the latter, whether that structure is rational and in conformance with industry practice); (3) whether the seniority system had its genesis in racial discrimination; and (4) whether the system was negotiated and has been maintained free from any illegal purpose. Most post-*Teamsters* decisions have adopted the four-factor inquiry. *See, e.g.*, James v. Stockham Valves & Fittings Co., 559 F.2d 310, 351-52 (5th Cir. 1977), cert. denied, 434 U.S. 1034, 98 S.Ct. 767, 54 L.Ed.2d 781 (1978). Should proof that a union favored non-transferable departmental seniority as a means of maintaining its all-white status preclude a finding that the system was bona fide? In LARKIN v. PULLMAN-STANDARD DIV, 854 F.2d 1549 (11th Cir. 1988), vacated on other grounds, 493 U.S. 929, 110 S.Ct. 316, 107 L.Ed.2d 307 (1989), the court held that the union's racist motivation could not be imputed to the employer without independent evidence of the employer's intent. Not only was there no evidence that the employer had acted with discriminatory intent in negotiating and maintaining non-transferable seniority, but there was evidence that the employer would have preferred no seniority rules at all. The company had accepted the seniority system as "a compromise negotiated and maintained without discriminatory intent." But if the union wanted the seniority system to maintain segregation and the company had no business purpose in maintaining the system, how can it be said that the "genesis" of the system was not racial discrimination? *See* Harvey v. United Transp. Union, 878 F.2d 1235, 1238 (10th Cir. 1989), cert. denied, 493 U.S. 1074, 110 S.Ct. 1121, 107 L.Ed.2d 1028 (1990) (district court clearly erred in finding that seniority system did not have its genesis in racial discrimination where it ignored its own prior finding that seniority system was created when segregation was standard operating procedure).

3.   Title VII does not define the term "seniority system," and no comprehensive definition of the term appears in the legislative history of §703(h). In CALIFORNIA

BREWERS ASS'N v. BRYANT, 444 U.S. 598, 100 S.Ct. 814, 63 L.Ed.2d 55 (1980), the plaintiff complained that certain provisions of a collective bargaining agreement covering employees in the brewery industry had operated to preclude him and other African-American employees from achieving job security through attainment of "permanent" employee status. The provisions in question accorded greater job protection and benefits to "permanent" than to "temporary" employees and provided that a temporary worker had to be employed for at least 45 weeks in a single calendar year before becoming permanent. The plaintiff claimed that although he had been employed for many years in the industry, the 45-week rule had prevented him from becoming a permanent employee. The Ninth Circuit held that the 45-week requirement was not a seniority system within the meaning of §703(h) and could thus be attacked directly on a disparate impact theory. The Supreme Court disagreed.

> A "seniority system" is a scheme that alone or in tandem with non-"seniority" criteria, allots to employees ever improving employment rights and benefits as their relative lengths of pertinent employment increase. Unlike other methods of allocating employment benefits and opportunities, such as subjective evaluations or educational requirements, the principal feature of any and every "seniority system" is that preferential treatment is dispensed on the basis of some measure of time served in employment.

444 U.S. at 819, 100 S.Ct. at 605-06. The Court reasoned that every seniority system has to contain "ancillary rules" for determining when seniority begins to accrue, what kind of employment will count toward seniority accrual, and how seniority may be forfeited. "Rules that serve these necessary purposes do not fall outside §703(h) simply because they do not, in and of themselves, operate on the basis of some factor involving the passage of time." Using that yardstick, the Court concluded that "[t]he 45-week rule does not depart significantly from commonly accepted concepts of seniority." Is a rule under which employees hired on the same day are ranked in seniority according to their scores on pre-employment tests a "seniority system" within the meaning of §703(h)? *See* United States v. City of Cincinnati, 771 F.2d 161 (6th Cir. 1985). Does a pay schedule that automatically increases each employee's pay annually without reference to the employee's actual length of service constitute a "seniority system"? *See* Mitchell v. Jefferson County Bd. of Educ., 936 F.2d 539 (11th Cir. 1991). What about a contract provision requiring the employer to prefer active "surplus" employees for new positions over laid-off employees? *See* Altman v. AT & T Technologies, Inc., 870 F.2d 386 (7th Cir. 1989).

4. The Court in *California Brewers Ass'n* noted that on remand the plaintiff could still show that the 45-week rule was not a "bona fide" seniority system under §703(h). Assume that the plaintiff is unable to prove that the rule was created or maintained for a discriminatory purpose, but does prove that it was used in a discriminatory fashion against him — i.e., that he was intentionally laid off because of his race to prevent him from obtaining permanent status. To what relief would he be entitled? *See* Franks v. Bowman Transp. Co., 424 U.S. 747, 96 S.Ct. 1251, 47 L.Ed.2d 444 (1976). The relief available to successful Title VII plaintiffs is discussed in Chapter 7, *infra*.

SECTION D. INTENTIONAL DISCRIMINATION AGAINST A CLASS: PATTERN OR PRACTICE LITIGATION

Hazelwood School District v. United States

Supreme Court of the United States, 1977.

433 U.S. 299, 97 S.Ct. 2736, 53 L.Ed.2d 768.

MR. JUSTICE STEWART delivered the opinion of the Court.

The petitioner Hazelwood School District covers 78 square miles in the northern part of St. Louis County, Mo. In 1973 the Attorney General brought this lawsuit against Hazelwood and various of its officials, alleging that they were engaged in a "pattern or practice" of employment discrimination in violation of Title VII. The complaint asked for an injunction requiring Hazelwood to cease its discriminatory practices, to take affirmative steps to obtain qualified Negro faculty members, and to offer employment and give backpay to victims of past illegal discrimination.

Hazelwood was formed from 13 rural school districts between 1949 and 1951 by a process of annexation. By the 1967-1968 school year, 17,550 students were enrolled in the district, of whom only 59 were Negro; the number of Negro pupils increased to 576 of 25,166 in 1972-1973, a total of just over 2%.

From the beginning, Hazelwood followed relatively unstructured procedures in hiring its teachers. Every person requesting an application for a teaching position was sent one, and completed applications were submitted to a central personnel office, where they were kept on file.[2] During the early 1960's the personnel office notified all applicants whenever a teaching position became available, but as the number of applications on file increased in the late 1960's and early 1970's, this practice was no longer considered feasible. The personnel office thus began the practice of selecting anywhere from 3 to 10 applicants for interviews at the school where the vacancy existed.   The personnel office did not substantively screen the applicants in determining which of them to send for interviews, other than to ascertain that each applicant, if selected, would be eligible for state certification by the time he began the job. Generally, those who had most recently submitted applications were most likely to be chosen for interviews.[3]

Interviews were conducted by a department chairman, program coordinator, or the principal at the school where the teaching vacancy existed. Although those conducting the interviews did fill out forms rating the applicants in a number of respects, it is undisputed that each school principal possessed virtually unlimited discretion in hiring teachers for his school. The only general guidance given to the principals was to hire the "most competent" person available, and such intangibles as "personality, disposition, appearance, poise, voice, articulation, and ability to deal with people"

---

[2]Before 1954 Hazelwood's application forms required designation of race, and those forms were in use as late as the 1962-1963 school year.

[3]Applicants with student or substitute teaching experience at Hazelwood were given preference if their performance had been satisfactory.

counted heavily. The principal's choice was routinely honored by Hazelwood's Superintendent and the Board of Education.

In the early 1960's Hazelwood found it necessary to recruit new teachers, and for that purpose members of its staff visited a number of colleges and universities in Missouri and bordering States. All the institutions visited were predominantly white, and Hazelwood did not seriously recruit at either of the two predominantly Negro four-year colleges in Missouri.[4] As a buyer's market began to develop for public school teachers, Hazelwood curtailed its recruiting efforts. For the 1971-1972 school year, 3,127 persons applied for only 234 teaching vacancies; for the 1972-1973 school year, there were 2,373 applications for 282 vacancies. A number of the applicants who were not hired were Negroes.[5]

Hazelwood hired its first Negro teacher in 1969. The number of Negro faculty members gradually increased in successive years: six of 957 in the 1970 school year; 16 of 1,107 by the end of the 1972 school year; 22 of 1,231 in the 1973 school year. By comparison, according to 1970 census figures, of more than 19,000 teachers employed in that year in the St. Louis area, 15.4% were Negro. That percentage figure included the St. Louis City School District, which in recent years has followed a policy of attempting to maintain a 50% Negro teaching staff. Apart from that school district, 5.7% of the teachers in the county were Negro in 1970.

Drawing upon these historic facts, the Government mounted its "pattern or practice" attack in the District Court upon four different fronts. It adduced evidence of (1) a history of alleged racially discriminatory practices, (2) statistical disparities in hiring, (3) the standardless and largely subjective hiring procedures, and (4) specific instances of alleged discrimination against 55 unsuccessful Negro applicants for teaching jobs. Hazelwood offered virtually no additional evidence in response, relying instead on evidence introduced by the Government, perceived deficiencies in the Government's case, and its own officially promulgated policy "to hire all teachers on the basis of training, preparation and recommendations, regardless of race, color or creed."

The District Court ruled that the Government had failed to establish a pattern or practice of discrimination. The court was unpersuaded by the alleged history of discrimination, noting that no dual school system had ever existed in Hazelwood. The statistics showing that relatively small numbers of Negroes were employed as teachers were found nonprobative, on the ground that the percentage of Negro pupils in Hazelwood was similarly small. The court found nothing illegal or suspect in the teacher-hiring procedures that Hazelwood had followed. Finally, the court reviewed the evidence in the 55 cases of alleged individual discrimination, and after stating that the burden of proving intentional discrimination was on the Government, it found that this burden had not been sustained in a single instance. Hence, the court entered judgment for the defendants.

---

[4]One of those two schools was never visited even though it was located in nearby St. Louis. The second was briefly visited on one occasion, but no potential applicant was interviewed.

[5]The parties disagree whether it is possible to determine from the present record exactly how many of the job applicants in each of the school years were Negroes.

The * * * Eighth Circuit reversed. After suggesting that the District Court had assigned inadequate weight to evidence of discriminatory conduct on the part of Hazelwood before the effective date of Title VII,[7] the Court of Appeals rejected the trial court's analysis of the statistical data as resting on an irrelevant comparison of Negro teachers to Negro pupils in Hazelwood. The proper comparison, in the appellate court's view, was one between Negro teachers in Hazelwood and Negro teachers in the relevant labor market area. Selecting St. Louis County and St. Louis City as the relevant area,[8] the Court of Appeals compared the 1970 census figures, showing that 15.4% of teachers in that area were Negro, to the racial composition of Hazelwood's teaching staff. In the 1972-1973 and 1973-1974 school years, only 1.4% and 1.8%, respectively, of Hazelwood's teachers were Negroes. This statistical disparity, particularly when viewed against the background of the teacher hiring procedures that Hazelwood had followed, was held to constitute a prima facie case of a pattern or practice of racial discrimination.

In addition, the Court of Appeals reasoned that the trial court had erred in failing to measure the 55 instances in which Negro applicants were denied jobs against the four-part standard for establishing a prima facie case of individual discrimination set out in this Court's opinion in McDonnell Douglas Corp. v. Green. Applying that standard, the appellate court found 16 cases of individual discrimination, which "buttressed" the statistical proof. Because Hazelwood had not rebutted the Government's prima facie case of a pattern or practice of racial discrimination, the Court of Appeals directed judgment for the Government and prescribed the remedial order to be entered.[11]

* * *

The petitioners primarily attack the judgment of the Court of Appeals for its reliance on "undifferentiated work force statistics to find an unrebutted prima facie case of employment discrimination."[12] The question they raise, in short, is whether a

---

[7] * * * The evidence of pre-Act discrimination relied upon by the Court of Appeals included the failure to hire any Negro teachers until 1969, the failure to recruit at predominantly Negro colleges in Missouri, and somewhat inconclusive evidence that Hazelwood was responsible for a 1962 Mississippi newspaper advertisement for teacher applicants that specified "white only."

[8] The city of St. Louis is surrounded by, but not included in, St. Louis County.

[11] The District Court was directed to order that the petitioners cease from discriminating on the basis of race or color in the hiring of teachers, promulgate accurate job descriptions and hiring criteria, recruit Negro and white applicants on an equal basis, give preference in filling vacancies to the 16 discriminatorily rejected applicants, make appropriate backpay awards, and submit periodic reports to the Government on its progress in hiring qualified Negro teachers. Id., at 819-820.

[12] * * * [T]he * * * petition for certiorari and brief on the merits did raise a second question: "Whether Congress has authority under Section 5 of the Fourteenth Amendment to prohibit by Title VII employment practices of an agency of a state government in the absence of proof that the agency purposefully discriminated against applicants on the basis of race." That issue, however, is not presented by the facts in this case. The Government's opening statement in the trial court explained that its evidence was designed to show that the scarcity of Negro teachers at Hazelwood "is the result of purpose" and is attributable to "deliberately continued employment policies." Thus here, the Government's theory of discrimination was simply that the employer,

basic component in the Court of Appeals' finding of a pattern or practice of discrimination — the comparatively small percentage of Negro employees on Hazelwood's teaching staff — was lacking in probative force.

This Court's recent consideration in International Brotherhood of Teamsters v. United States, of the role of statistics in pattern-or-practice suits under Title VII provides substantial guidance in evaluating the arguments advanced by the petitioners. In that case we stated that it is the Government's burden to "establish by a preponderance of the evidence that racial discrimination was the [employer's] standard operating procedure — the regular rather than the unusual practice." We also noted that statistics can be an important source of proof in employment discrimination cases, since

> "absent explanation, it is ordinarily to be expected that nondiscriminatory hiring practices will in time result in a work force more or less representative of the racial and ethnic composition of the population in the community from which employees are hired. Evidence of long-lasting and gross disparity between the composition of a work force and that of the general population thus may be significant even though §703(j) makes clear that Title VII imposes no requirement that a work force mirror the general population."

431 U.S. at 340 n.20. Where gross statistical disparities can be shown, they alone may in a proper case constitute prima facie proof of a pattern of practice of discrimination. *Teamsters.*

There can be no doubt, in light of the *Teamsters* case, that the District Court's comparison of Hazelwood's teacher work force to its student population fundamentally misconceived the role of statistics in employment discrimination cases. The Court of Appeals was correct in the view that a proper comparison was between the racial composition of Hazelwood's teaching staff and the racial composition of the qualified public school teacher population in the relevant labor market.[13] The percentage of Negroes on Hazelwood's teaching staff in 1972-1973 was 1.4%, and in

---

in violation of §703(a), regularly and purposefully treated Negroes less favorably than white persons.

[13]In *Teamsters*, the comparison between the percentage of Negroes on the employer's work force and the percentage in the general areawide population was highly probative, because the job skill there involved — the ability to drive a truck — is one that many persons possess or can fairly readily acquire. When special qualifications are required to fill particular jobs, comparisons to the general population (rather than to the smaller group of individuals who possess the necessary qualifications) may have little probative value. The comparative statistics introduced by the Government in the District Court, however, were properly limited to public school teachers, and therefore this is not a case like Mayor v. Educational Equality League, 415 U.S. 605, 94 S.Ct. 1323, 39 L.Ed.2d 630, in which the racial-composition comparisons failed to take into account special qualifications for the position in question.

Although the petitioners concede as a general matter the probative force of the comparative work-force statistics, they object to the Court of Appeals' heavy reliance on these data on the ground that applicant-flow data, showing the actual percentage of white and Negro applicants for teaching positions at Hazelwood, would be firmer proof. As we have noted, see n.5, *supra*, there was not clear evidence of such statistics. We leave it to the District Court on remand to determine whether competent proof of those data can be adduced. If so, it would, of course, be very relevant. Cf. Dothard v. Rawlinson, 433 U.S. 321 (1977).

1973-1974 it was 1.8%. By contrast, the percentage of qualified Negro teachers in the area was, according to the 1970 census, at least 5.7%.[14] Although these differences were on their face substantial, the Court of Appeals erred in substituting its judgment for that of the District Court and holding that the Government had conclusively proved its "pattern or practice" lawsuit.

The Court of Appeals totally disregarded the possibility that this prima facie statistical proof in the record might at the trial court level be rebutted by statistics dealing with Hazelwood's hiring after it became subject to Title VII. Racial discrimination by public employers was not made illegal under Title VII until March 24, 1972. A public employer who from that date forward made all its employment decisions in a wholly nondiscriminatory way would not violate Title VII even if it had formerly maintained an all-white work force by purposefully excluding Negroes.[15] For this reason, the Court cautioned in the *Teamsters* opinion that once a prima facie case has been established by statistical work-force disparities, the employer must be given an opportunity to show that "the claimed discriminatory pattern is a product of pre-Act hiring rather than unlawful post-Act discrimination."

The record in this case showed that for the 1972-1973 school year, Hazelwood hired 282 new teachers, 10 of whom (3.5%) were Negroes; for the following school year it hired 123 new teachers, 5 of whom (4.1%) were Negroes. Over the two-year period, Negroes constituted a total of 15 of the 405 new teachers hired (3.7%). Although the Court of Appeals briefly mentioned these data in reciting the facts, it wholly ignored them in discussing whether the Government had shown a pattern or practice of discrimination. And it gave no consideration at all to the possibility that

---

[14]As is discussed below, the Government contends that a comparative figure of 15.4%, rather than 5.7%, is the appropriate one. But even assuming arguendo that the 5.7% figure urged by the petitioners is correct, the disparity between that figure and the percentage of Negroes on Hazelwood's teaching staff would be more than fourfold for the 1972-1973 school year, and threefold for the 1973-1974 school year. A precise method of measuring the significance of such statistical disparities was explained in Castaneda v. Partida, 430 U.S. 482, 496-497, n.17, 97 S.Ct. 1272, 1281, n.17, 51 L.Ed.2d 498, n.17. It involves calculation of the "standard deviation" as a measure of predicted fluctuations from the expected value of a sample. Using the 5.7% figure as the basis for calculating the expected value, the expected number of Negroes on the Hazelwood teaching staff would be roughly 63 in 1972-1973 and 70 in 1973-1974. The observed number in those years was 16 and 22, respectively. The difference between the observed and expected values was more than six standard deviations in 1972-1973 and more than five standard deviations in 1973-1974. The Court in *Castaneda* noted that "[a]s a general rule for such large samples, if the difference between the expected value and the observed number is greater than two or three standard deviations," then the hypothesis that teachers were hired without regard to race would be suspect.

[15]This is not to say that evidence of pre-Act discrimination can never have any probative force. Proof that an employer engaged in racial discrimination prior to the effective date of Title VII might in some circumstances support the inference that such discrimination continued, particularly where relevant aspects of the decisionmaking process had undergone little change. Cf. Fed.Rule Evid. 406; Arlington Heights v. Metropolitan Housing Development Corp., 429 U.S. 252, 267, 97 S.Ct. 555, 564, 50 L.Ed.2d 450; 1 J. Wigmore, Evidence §92, 2 id., §§302-305, 371, 375 (3d ed. 1940). And, of course, a public employer even before the extension of Title VII in 1972 was subject to the command of the Fourteenth Amendment not to engage in purposeful racial discrimination.

post-Act data as to the number of Negroes hired compared to the total number of Negro applicants might tell a totally different story.

What the hiring figures prove obviously depends upon the figures to which they are compared. The Court of Appeals accepted the Government's argument that the relevant comparison was to the labor market area of St. Louis County and the city of St. Louis, in which, according to the 1970 census, 15.4% of all teachers were Negro. The propriety of that comparison was vigorously disputed by the petitioners, who urged that because the city of St. Louis has made special attempts to maintain a 50% Negro teaching staff, inclusion of that school district in the relevant market area distorts the comparison. Were that argument accepted, the percentage of Negro teachers in the relevant labor market area (St. Louis County alone) as shown in the 1970 census would be 5.7% rather than 15.4%.

The difference between these figures may well be important; the disparity between 3.7% (the percentage of Negro teachers hired by Hazelwood in 1972-1973 and 1973-1974) and 5.7% may be sufficiently small to weaken the Government's other proof, while the disparity between 3.7% and 15.4% may be sufficiently large to reinforce it.[17] In determining which of the two figures — or, very possibly, what intermediate figure — provides the most accurate basis for comparison to the hiring figures at Hazelwood, it will be necessary to evaluate such considerations as (i) whether the racially based hiring policies of the St. Louis City School District were in effect as far back as 1970, the year in which the census figures were taken;[18] (ii) to what extent those policies have changed the racial composition of that district's teaching staff from what it would otherwise have been; (iii) to what extent St. Louis'

---

[17]Indeed, under the statistical methodology explained in Castaneda v. Partida, involving the calculation of the standard deviation as a measure of predicted fluctuations, the difference between using 15.4% and 5.7% as the areawide figure would be significant. If the 15.4% figure is taken as the basis for comparison, the expected number of Negro teachers hired by Hazelwood in 1972-1973 would be 43 (rather than the actual figure of 10) of a total of 282, a difference of more than five standard deviations; the expected number in 1973-1974 would be 19 (rather than the actual figure 5) of a total of 123, a difference of more than three standard deviations. For the two years combined, the difference between the observed number of 15 Negro teachers hired (of a total of 405) would vary from the expected number of 62 by more than six standard deviations. Because a fluctuation of more than two or three standard deviations would undercut the hypothesis that decisions were being made randomly with respect to race, each of these statistical comparisons would reinforce rather than rebut the Government's other proof. If, however, the 5.7% areawide figure is used, the expected number of Negro teachers hired in 1972-1973 would be roughly 16, less than two standard deviations from the observed number of 10; for 1973-1974, the expected value would be roughly seven, less than one standard deviation from the observed value of 5; and for the two years combined, the expected value of 23 would be less than two standard deviations from the observed total of 15. A more precise method of analyzing these statistics confirms the results of the standard deviation analysis. See F. Mosteller, R. Rourke, & G. Thomas, Probability with Statistical Applications 494 (2d ed. 1970).

These observations are not intended to suggest that precise calculations of statistical significance are necessary in employing statistical proof, but merely to highlight the importance of the choice of the relevant labor market area.

[18]In 1970 Negroes constituted only 42% of the faculty in St. Louis city schools, which could indicate either that the city's policy was not yet in effect or simply that its goal had not yet been achieved.

recruitment policies have diverted to the city, teachers who might otherwise have applied to Hazelwood;[19] (iv) to what extent Negro teachers employed by the city would prefer employment in other districts such as Hazelwood; and (v) what the experience in other school districts in St. Louis County indicates about the validity of excluding the City School District from the relevant labor market.

It is thus clear that a determination of the appropriate comparative figures in this case will depend upon further evaluation by the trial court. * * * Only the trial court is in a position to make the appropriate determination after further findings. And only after such a determination is made can a foundation be established for deciding whether or not Hazelwood engaged in a pattern or practice of racial discrimination in its employment practices in violation of the law.[20]

We hold, therefore, that the Court of Appeals erred in disregarding the post-Act hiring statistics in the record, and that it should have remanded the case to the District Court for further findings as to the relevant labor market area and for an ultimate determination whether Hazelwood engaged in a pattern or practice of employment discrimination after March 24, 1972.[21] Accordingly, the judgment is vacated, and the case is remanded to the District Court for further proceedings consistent with this opinion.

It is so ordered.

[The concurring opinion of Justice Brennan and dissenting opinion of Justice Stevens are omitted].

NOTES AND PROBLEMS FOR DISCUSSION

1. In COOPER v. FED. RESERVE BANK, 467 U.S. 867, 104 S.Ct. 2794, 81 L.Ed.2d 718 (1984), the Court characterized the difference between an individual's claim of discrimination and a class action alleging a general pattern or practice of discrimination as "manifest." Quoting its ruling in *Teamsters*, the Court observed that "[t]he inquiry regarding an individual's claim is the reason for a particular employment decision, while 'at the liability stage of a pattern-or-practice trial the focus often will not be on individual hiring decisions, but on a pattern of discriminatory decisionmaking.'"

Evidence of class-wide discrimination is relevant in an individual case, but such evidence, even if very probative of class discrimination, does not alone establish that

---

[19]The petitioners observe, for example, that Harris Teachers College in St. Louis, whose 1973 graduating class was 60% Negro, is operated by the city. It is the petitioners' contention that the city's public elementary and secondary schools occupy an advantageous position in the recruitment of Harris graduates.

[20]Because the District Court focused on a comparison between the percentage of Negro teachers and Negro pupils in *Hazelwood*, it did not undertake an evaluation of the relevant labor market, and its casual dictum that the inclusion of the city of St. Louis "distorted" the labor market statistics was not based upon valid criteria.

[21]It will also be open to the District Court on remand to determine whether sufficiently reliable applicant-flow data are available to permit consideration of the petitioners' argument that those data may undercut a statistical analysis dependent upon hirings alone.

the individual plaintiff was a victim of such discrimination. *See, e.g.*, Bell v. EPA, 232 F.3d 546, 553 (7th Cir. 2000) (evidence of systemic disparate treatment is probative on issue of pretext even where it is insufficient to support a claim of pattern and practice discrimination: though statistical evidence may have been too broad with respect to the relevant labor market to support a finding of pattern and practice, it should have been admitted as circumstantial evidence of pretext).

Pattern and practice cases typically are filed by the government or litigated as class actions. *See* Chapter 6, *infra.* Can an individual plaintiff who has not filed a class action establish pattern and practice liability? Reasoning that an individual plaintiff should not be able to establish employer liability without showing that he was the victim of intentional discrimination, the Fourth and Sixth Circuits have ruled that the pattern-or-practice method of proving discrimination is not available an individual claiming intentional discrimination, who must proceed under the *McDonnell Douglas-Burdine* formula. *See* Lowery v. Circuit City Stores, Inc., 158 F.3d 742, 761 (4th Cir. 1998); Bacon v. Honda of America Mfg., Inc., 370 F.3d 565 (6th Cir. 2004), cert. denied, 543 U.S. 1151, 125 S.Ct. 1334, 161 L.Ed.2d 115 (2005). Does anything said in *Teamsters* or *Hazelwood* dictate this result? *Lowery* is discussed in Chapter 6, *infra.*

The plaintiffs' *statistical* evidence in a pattern and practice case may be the same as the proof offered in a case tried under the disproportionate impact theory. Compare, for example, the government's statistical proof in *Hazelwood* with that tendered by the EEOC in *Joe's Stone Crab*. However, the function of the statistical proof in these two types of cases will differ. In a disproportionate impact case, the statistical evidence is direct proof that the challenged practice or policy disproportionately affects the plaintiffs' class. In a pattern and practice case, by contrast, the statistical proof constitutes circumstantial evidence of intentional discrimination against a class of applicants or employees. Recall that in *Joe's Stone Crab* the EEOC tried the case on both pattern and practice and disparate impact theories and that the Court of Appeals strongly suggested that the agency's proof demonstrated a pattern and practice (though not a disparate impact) violation. Does this difference in function in the two types of cases mean that a different kind or quality of statistical evidence should be required to establish a prima facie case in cases tried under the different theories? Several courts have suggested that, in pattern and practice cases, the trier of fact may demand proof by the plaintiff of a larger statistical deviation from what would have been expected absent discrimination than would satisfy the plaintiff's burden of proof in a disproportionate impact case. *See e.g.*, Rivera v. City of Wichita Falls, 665 F.2d 531, 535 n.5 (5th Cir. 1982) ("gross disparity" between minority percentage of employer's work force and minority percentage of relevant labor market required for prima facie case of intentional discrimination while only a "marked disproportion" required for disparate impact); Falcon v. Gen. Tel. Co., 815 F.2d 317, 322 (5th Cir. 1987) (disparities between Mexican-Americans in the available population and the percentage of Mexican-Americans in the employer's work force were not egregious enough to support an inference of intentional discrimination). What could be the rationale of such decisions?

2. *Hazelwood* and *Joe's Stone Crab* illustrate a common use of statistical comparisons in pattern and practice and disproportionate impact cases. To prove that a practice or policy is discriminatory in design or effect, the composition of the employer's work force is compared to the composition of an outside "population."

The difference between the work force composition and the composition of the population is used to prove the discriminatory effect in a disproportionate impact case and as circumstantial evidence of discriminatory intent in a disparate treatment case. The assumption underlying the evidentiary use of such comparisons is that, absent discrimination (effect or intent), the composition of the work force should reflect that of the outside population. Sometimes, as in *Hazelwood,* the composition of one of the relevant populations (the applicant pool) is unknown and the courts must assume that the composition of larger populations, such as the area work force, is sufficiently similar to the relevant pool for the proper inferences to be drawn. The relevance and probative value of this type of statistical evidence thus turns on the validity of the assumption about the outside population. The critical question is whether the proper outside population has been used for comparison with the work force statistics. What assumptions were drawn in *Hazelwood* about the population of teachers in the St. Louis area? Were all African-American teachers in the St. Louis area available for employment in Hazelwood? Were all teachers in the area equally qualified? What assumptions were made in *Joe's Stone Crab* about the gender composition of persons available for employment as waiters/waitresses?

Hazelwood and *Joe's Stone Crab* also demonstrate the importance of "controlling" labor market statistics to provide a relevant population to compare with the employer's work force. The Supreme Court in *Wards Cove* described as "nonsensical" comparisons to a baseline pool that is not adequately tailored to reflect only those potential applicants who are actually qualified and available for the job at issue. 490 U.S. at 651. Typically, gross labor market statistics must be adjusted for both requisite skills and geographic scope.

(a) Requisite Skill

In JOHNSON v. TRANSP. AGENCY, 480 U.S. 616, 107 S.Ct. 1442, 94 L.Ed.2d 615 (1987), the Court explained that an affirmative action plan that favored minorities could be justified only by proof of past discrimination and that such discrimination could not be inferred from a simple comparison of minorities already hired with those in the general population. The Court stated that:

> [a] comparison of the percentage of minorities or women in the employer's work force with the percentage in the area labor market or general population is appropriate in analyzing jobs that require no special expertise, or training programs designed to provide expertise. When a job requires special training, however, the comparison should be with those in the labor force who possess the relevant qualifications.

480 U.S. at 632. *See also* Peightal v. Metro. Dade County, 26 F.3d 1545, 1554 (11th Cir. 1994) ("For positions requiring minimal training or for certain entry level positions, statistical comparison to the racial composition of the relevant population suffices, whereas positions requiring special skills necessitate a determination of the number of minorities qualified to undertake the particular task.").

(b) Geographic Area

The geographic area used to define the statistical pool may also significantly affect its composition. In *Hazelwood,* the Court of Appeals ruled that the relevant labor market included the entire Metropolitan Statistical Area of St. Louis as calculated by the Census Bureau. The Supreme Court remanded for a determination by the district court of whether the appropriate labor market for the school district included the city of St. Louis or, as contended by the school board, should be limited to the suburban area surrounding the city. What should the district court consider in making this determination? In his dissent, Justice Stevens noted that the record of the case showed that one third of the teachers hired by the school district in 1972-73 lived in the city of St. Louis at the time of initial employment. Should not that fact alone demonstrate that the city was properly included in the relevant labor market? In MARKEY v. TENNECO OIL CO., 707 F.2d 172, 173-74 (5th Cir. 1983), where the employer drew its work force from a four-county area, the court calculated the racial composition of the relevant labor market by weighing the black population of each county according to percentage of actual applicants from that county).

In *Joe's Stone Crab* the district court determined that females made up 32% of the labor pool of local food servers available and qualified to work at Joe's. How was that labor pool defined? How did the court adjust labor statistics to arrive at a population "qualified" to work at Joe's?

3. In *Hazelwood*, the Court, while not rejecting the government's general population statistics, concluded that the case should be remanded to allow the defendants to introduce applicant flow statistics which "might tell a totally different story." In what sense might applicant flow statistics tell a "different story" in *Hazelwood*? In MISTER v. ILL. CEN. GULF R.R. CO., 832 F.2d 1427, 1436 (7th Cir. 1987), cert. denied, 485 U.S. 1035, 108 S.Ct. 1597, 99 L.Ed.2d 911 (1988), the Court of Appeals explained that, as a general matter, applicant flow statistics were to be preferred over general population comparisons because applicant statistics have a more direct relation to the actual hiring process. He cautioned, however, that applicant flow could be affected by known discriminatory policies of the employer:

> [d]iscrimination affects the applicant pool in a way that makes the discrimination harder to detect. The discriminating employer induces qualified blacks not to apply, and these non-applicants — victims of discrimination as much as the non-hired applicants — will make the employer's hiring look "better" than it is. An applicant pool analysis is biased against finding discrimination, if potential applicants know or suspect that the employer is discriminating. If a study based on applicants nonetheless implies discrimination, this is potent evidence.

832 F.2d at 1436. Remember that the district court in *Joe's Stone Crab* considered the applicant flow data unreliable because Joe's public reputation for not hiring women had discouraged female applicants. That finding and other anecdotal evidence in the case led the Court of Appeals to conclude that the EEOC had established the existence of a pattern and practice of discrimination, but had not proven disproportionate impact.

4. As used in *Hazelwood*, the standard deviation is a way to calculate the likelihood that chance is responsible for the difference between a predicted result and an actual result. "Statisticians tend to discard chance as an explanation for a result when deviations from the expected value approach two standard deviations." Payne v. Travenol Laboratories, Inc., 673 F.2d 798, 821 n.32 (5th Cir.), cert. denied, 459 U.S. 1038, 103 S.Ct. 451, 74 L.Ed.2d 605 (1982). Statistical significance also exists where it can be demonstrated that the probability of the discrepancy occurring by chance is no more than one in twenty. This is referred to as significant at the .05 level of significance.

For large samples, the test of two or three standard deviations was found by the Supreme Court to constitute sufficient proof of intentional discrimination in *Hazelwood,* and in Castaneda v. Partida, 430 U.S. 482, 496-97 n.17, 97 S.Ct. 1272, 1281 n.17, 51 L.Ed.2d 498 (1977). Two to three standard deviations "is essentially equivalent to a rule requiring significance at a level in the range below 0.05 or 0.01." Craik v. Minn. State Univ. Bd., 731 F.2d 465, 476 n.13 (8th Cir. 1984). Despite *Hazelwood* and numerous lower court decisions holding that a discrepancy of two standard deviations or more is highly probative of discriminatory intent, the courts have refrained from declaring that a specified level of statistical significance will, as a matter of law, give rise to a rebuttable presumption of discrimination. For example, in WATSON v. FORT WORTH BANK & TRUST, 487 U.S. 977, 994, 108 S.Ct. 2777, 2789, 101 L.Ed.2d 827 (1988), the Supreme Court stated that "we have not suggested that any particular number of 'standard deviations' can determine whether a plaintiff has made out a prima facie case." For a fascinating accounting of the story behind the Supreme Court's ruling in *Hazelwood*, see Stewart J. Schwab & Steven L. Willborn, *The Story of Hazelwood: Employment Discrimination by the Numbers*, EMPLOYMENT DISCRIMINATION STORIES 37 (Friedman, ed. 2006).

EEOC v. Olson's Dairy Queens, Inc.

United States Court of Appeals for the Fifth Circuit, 1993.
989 F.2d 165.

PER CURIAM:

The Equal Employment Opportunity Commission (EEOC) appeals the district court's judgment that Olson's Dairy Queens, Inc. (Olson's) had not committed unlawful employment discrimination and awarding Olson's attorney's fees. We reverse and render as to Olson's liability and remand for determination of damages.

I. BACKGROUND

[The EEOC claimed that Olson's, which operated nine ice cream shops in metropolitan Houston, was discriminating against black applicants for employment because of their race. The district court concluded that the Commission had failed to establish a *prima facie* case of intentional discrimination and, even if its evidence did raise and inference of discrimination, Olson's had provided a non-discriminatory explanation for its hiring practices.]

Our departure from the district court's recitation, and ultimately its opinion, is based largely upon the testimony of the EEOC's expert witness, Dr. Mahlon Straszheim, and Olson's expert witness, Dr. Ira Chorush.

A. DR. STRASZHEIM'S STUDY.

Dr. Straszheim analyzed the extent to which Olson's actual hiring patterns produced a different black-nonblack employee mix than would be expected if Olson's hiring policies were entirely race-neutral. He did so by two distinct means.

1. External Availability Analysis.

The first approach, which was the focus of the district court's opinion, was to compare Olson's hiring history with the percentage of black food preparation and service workers in the relevant labor market from which Olson's draws its work force. Dr. Straszheim, relying on years of experience in labor, transportation, and urban economic analysis, determined that the relevant labor market was the metropolitan Houston area — more specifically, the Houston Standard Metropolitan Statistical Area, or "SMSA," as defined by the United State Bureau of the Census.

Using detailed census data for the Houston SMSA, Dr. Straszheim determined that blacks comprise roughly 25.2% of the food preparation and service workers in the Houston SMSA. By comparison, only 8.1% of employees of known race hired by Olson's between 1978 and 1987 were black.

Dr. Straszheim refined the Houston SMSA figures to account for travel time to and from Olson's locations and the average travel times for black food preparation and service workers reported in the census data. He also distinguished between the Spring Branch (6 locations), Bellaire (2 locations), and Katy (1 location) labor markets. Based upon the demographics of each of these distinct markets and the relevant travel times, Dr. Straszheim concluded that blacks comprised 19.8% of the relevant labor pool for Olson's Spring Branch and Bellaire locations, and 8.1% for the Katy store. By comparison, blacks comprised 6.5% of hires of known race at Olson's six Spring Branch stores, 12.3% of hires of known race at Olson's two Bellaire-area stores, and 9.4% of hires of known race at Olson's Katy location.

Employing standard statistical techniques, Dr. Straszheim concluded that there was less than one chance in 100,000 (.00001) that Olson's observed hiring patterns in the Spring Branch stores could have resulted from truly race-neutral hiring practices, and less than three chances in one thousand (.0026) that Olson's observed hiring patterns in the Bellaire stores could have resulted from truly race-neutral hiring practices. Dr. Straszheim found no statistically significant difference between the number of blacks hired in the Katy store and the number which would be expected based upon black representation in the relevant labor market.

2. Applicant Flow Analysis.

As a separate and distinct means of assessing the race-neutrality of Olson's hiring practices, Dr. Straszheim compared the percentage of blacks among Olson's applicants of known race to the percentage of blacks among Olson's hired employees of known race. The results of this analysis were completely disregarded by the district court's opinion and largely ignored by Olson's own expert, as well as by Olson's counsel in his argument to this court.

Between 1984 and 1987, the period for which rejected applications were available, blacks constituted 29.6% of the roughly 1,800 applicants of known race. In the Spring Branch market, 30.1% of the applicants of known race for the relevant period were black; 39.5% in the Bellaire market; and 27.6% in the Katy market. By comparison, roughly 13.2% of the persons of known race hired by Olson's Spring Branch stores during the same time period were black, while blacks constituted 27.3% and 11.1% of the hires of known race for Olson's Bellaire and Katy locations, respectively, for the same period.

In light of the racial mix of actual applications made to each of the stores, Dr. Straszheim concluded that the likelihood that Olson's observed hiring patterns resulted from truly race-neutral hiring practices was less than one chance in ten thousand (.0001) for the Spring Branch stores, less than seven chances in one thousand (.0070) for the Bellaire stores, and less than two chances in one thousand (.0020) in the Katy store.

B. DR. CHORUSH'S STUDY

Dr. Chorush testified that he had requested data from Olson's Spring Branch stores for April 1990. He found that, of the 60 employees working at the six Spring Branch locations in April 1990, more than one-half lived within one mile of the store at which they worked, and more than 80 percent lived within three miles. He testified that many of Olson's Spring Branch-area employees were high school students and that many were employed part time. Dr. Chorush did not quarrel with Dr. Straszheim's depiction of Olson's Spring Branch-area employees as predominantly nonblack. Based upon his observations, Dr. Chorush concluded that "most persons willing to accept positions at Olson's are young, seeking part-time employment and residing within a very short distance of the restaurant."

II. DISCUSSION

A. EEOC'S COMPLAINT.

To prevail on its claim of disparate treatment, the EEOC must establish by a preponderance of the evidence that a pattern of intentional discrimination existed in Olson's hiring of black applicants. That is, the EEOC must show that racially discriminatory hiring was Olson's regular, rather than unusual, practice. *Teamsters.* If the EEOC establishes a prima facie violation, it is incumbent upon Olson's to articulate a legitimate, nondiscriminatory reason for its hiring patterns. If Olson's articulates an acceptable rationale, the EEOC bears the burden of showing that Olson's explanation is a pretext for unlawful discrimination. *Teamsters.*

1. Prima Facie Violation.

The EEOC may establish a prima facie violation of Title VII through statistical evidence, evidence of Olson's treatment of individual job applicants and employees, or both. *See* Hazelwood. EEOC presented both statistical and anecdotal evidence. While we do not dispute the district court's assessment of the anecdotal testimony of rejected applicants Kathy Richie, Angela Burks, Ruby Cantu, Lillie Lewis, and Jessica J. Jones, we hold that the district court erred both in its assessment of the statistical evidence offered by the EEOC and in its conclusion that the EEOC failed to establish a prima facie violation of Title VII.

The district court correctly observes that "the usefulness of statistical data in assessing discriminatory practices depends . . . on the validity of the basic reference population as the pole star being compared to the work force of the employer," and that, "in a disparate treatment case, the statistical evidence must be 'finely tuned' to compare the employer's relevant workforce with the qualified populations in the relevant labor market." However, we disagree with the district court's conclusion that the EEOC's statistical evidence fails to raise a claim of intentional discrimination. First, Dr. Straszheim's "external availability" methodology is sufficiently similar to that approved by the court in *United States v. Pasadena Indep. Sch. Dist.,* 43 Fair Emp. Prac. Cas. (BNA) 1319, 1987 WL 9919 (S.D. Tex. Apr. 18, 1987) to beg the question why the court found it so lacking here.

Second, the travel times which the district court found "simply untenable," were confirmed by the census data, which was, in turn, legitimized by the actual applications received by Olson's. We do not understand how the district court can completely discount the possibility that prospective employees will travel further than a few blocks to work at Olson's when it was presented with evidence of hundreds of applications from job seekers not residing in the immediate vicinity of an Olson's location.

Third, Dr. Chorush's analysis, which the district court found "persuasive," is fundamentally unsound. Dr. Chorush's analysis considers only a portion of Olson's work force at only one point in time, presuming that what was true for the Spring Branch stores in April 1990 must be true for all Olson's locations over the entire period under dispute. Dr. Chorush begins with the presumption that one can describe Olson's labor market by describing Olson's work force; thus, he concludes, since most of Olson's Spring Branch employees are white teenagers living a short distance from the store, then white teenagers living a short distance from the store constitute Olson's available labor force. This is wholly at odds with the fundamental premise of employment discrimination law. In order to test for discriminatory hiring, we evaluate an employer's work force in terms of the available labor pool, not the other way around. The fact that Olson's April 1990 Spring Branch work force was predominantly white teenagers living close to the store does not mean that there were not qualified applicants who were not white teenagers living close to the store.

Finally, the district court's assessment of the EEOC's statistical evidence completely disregards the "applicant flow" analysis conducted by Dr. Straszheim. Dr. Chorush "opined" that Olson's could "expect" to draw its work force from a given area. By contrast, Dr. Straszheim analyzed the actual applications. The district court found, based upon Dr. Chorush's testimony, that "applicants for employment [at Olson's] are therefore likely to be substantially different from those actually holding employment in the food preparation and service classification [of the Census]." However, Olson's own applications indicate that blacks not living within the immediate vicinity of Olson's locations comprise a higher percentage of applicants than was suggested by Dr. Straszheim's census-based analysis.

Guided by this circuit's previous admonition that the "most direct route to proof of racial discrimination in hiring is proof of disparity between the percentage of blacks among those applying for a particular position and the percentage of blacks among those hired," *Hester v. Southern Ry.*, 497 F.2d 1374, 1379 (5th Cir.1974), we conclude that the district court clearly erred when it held, without fully considering the "applicant flow" analysis offered by the EEOC's expert, that the EEOC had failed to provide ample statistical evidence to establish a prima facie violation of Title VII.[1] To the contrary, we find the record replete with evidence to establish such a violation.

2. Olson's Rationale.

The district court summarily accepted, without description or explanation, Olson's articulated nondiscriminatory reasons for its hiring and found that the EEOC failed to show that those articulated reasons were a pretext disguising discrimination. We

---

[1]We also express concern for the short shrift which the district court gave the EEOC's "external availability" analysis, especially when we consider the dearth of countervailing evidence offered by Olson's expert.

disagree with the district court's assessment of Olson's proffered explanation. The record clearly demonstrates that any explanation which the district court may have perceived to be facially nondiscriminatory is, in fact, mere pretext.

Discarding Mr. Watson's statement that Olson's customers prefer to be served by persons of their own "culture," the only other "reasons" which may be gleaned from Olson's case are (1) the proximity of an applicant's residence to the restaurant, and (2) the racial make-up of the Spring Branch school district. While the former might conceivably satisfy the McDonnell Douglas-Teamsters test if there was a showing that proximity to the restaurant was either a critical factor or even a stated criteria in Olson's hiring guidelines, that showing was not made or even attempted. This leaves only the intimation that people from nearby were hired because only people from nearby would apply. However, we know that is not true, based upon Dr. Straszheim's review of Olson's applications. As for the second explanation, the racial make-up of the Spring Branch school district explaining the racial make-up of the employees, aside from ignoring conditions at the Bellaire and Katy stores and in their surrounding neighborhoods, presumes that Olson's potential work force is composed of area high school students. However, while it may be true that Olson's employees are predominantly area high school students, the applications make it clear that Olson's available labor force includes many persons who are not area high school students.

* * *

III. CONCLUSION

We REVERSE and RENDER judgment in favor of the EEOC on the question of Olson's liability. We return this matter to the district court in order to proceed to the damages stage of this employment discrimination class action.

NOTES AND PROBLEMS FOR DISCUSSION

1. In *Hazelwood*, the Court suggested that applicant flow statistics "might tell an entirely different story" than the "story" told by comparing the racial compositions of the relevant labor market and the employer's work force. Did the applicant flow statistics in *Olson's Dairy Queen* tell a "different story"?

2. What method did Dr. Straszheim use for determining the labor market for Olson's various locations? In some cases where the composition of the work force is so obviously out of kilter with that of the relevant population, fine-tuned statistical analyses will be unnecessary. For example, in EEOC v. O&G SPRING & WIRE FORMS SPECIALTY CO., 38 F.3d 872 (7th Cir. 1994), cert. denied, 115 S.Ct. 1270, 131 L.Ed.2d 148 (1995) the employer had hired 87 employees between 1979 and 1985, none of whom were African-Americans. Under even the most conservative definition, African-Americans comprised 22.5% of the labor market. The statistical probability using standard deviation analysis of zero black hires during the relevant period was "infinitesimal." Relying on *Teamsters*, the Court of Appeals concluded that "[t]he company's inability to rebut the inference of discrimination comes not from a measure of statistics but from the inexorable zero." How, then, could the trial court *not* have found pattern and practice discrimination in *Joe's Stone Crab*?

3. The use of binomial distribution analysis, as in, for example, *Hazelwood* and *Olson's Dairy Queen*, is appropriate when the employment practice in question, such as hiring or promotion, has only two possible outcomes. But some pattern and practice cases involve employment decisions with many possible outcomes. The prime example of such a decision is the setting of wages. For an employer operating without a collective bargaining agreement, there could be as many different salaries as there are employees. As compensation decisions typically are influenced by multiple factors, an issue arises as to whether an unlawful motivation was one of those factors. In such instances, a different kind of statistical analysis, referred to as multiple regression, must be used to isolate and measure the effect of the various factors on the decision in question. The function of multiple regression analysis has been described as follows:

> [O]ne might describe multiple regression as a method used to extract a systematic signal from the noise prescribed by data. There are two primary problems involved in extracting such a signal. First, it is typically the case that the factor whose influence one wishes to test or measure is not the only major factor affecting the dependent variable. * * * Second, even if one can somehow account for the effects of the other important systematic factors, there typically remain chance components.

* * *

> In multiple regression one first specifies the major variables that are believed to influence the dependent variable. * * * There inevitably remain minor influences, each one perhaps small, but creating in combination a non-negligible effect. These minor influences are treated by placing them in what is called a random disturbance term and assuming that their joint effect is not systematically related to the effects of the major variables being investigated — in other words by treating their effects as due to chance. Obviously, it is very desirable to have the random part of the relationships small, particularly relative to the systematic part. Indeed, the size of the random part provides an indication of how correctly one has judged what the systematic part is. Multiple regression thus provides a means not only for extracting the systematic effects from the data but also for assessing how well one has succeeded in doing so in the presence of the remaining random effects.

> The relationship between the dependent variable and the independent variable of interest is then estimated by extracting the effects of the other major variables (the systematic part). When this has been done, one has the best available substitute for controlled experimentation. The results of multiple regressions can be read as showing the effects of each variable on the dependent variable, holding the others constant. Moreover, those results allow one to make statements about the probability that the effect described has merely been observed as a result of chance fluctuation.

Franklin M. Fisher, *Multiple Regression in Legal Proceedings*, 80 COLUM. L. REV. 702, 705-06 (1980). See also Michael O. Finkelstein, *The Judicial Reception of Multiple Regression Studies in Race and Sex Discrimination Cases*, 80 COLUM. L. REV. 737 (1980).

In BAZEMORE v. FRIDAY, 478 U.S. 385, 106 S.Ct. 3000, 92 L.Ed.2d 315 (1986), a pattern and practice suit alleging racial discrimination against African-American state agricultural agents, the plaintiffs relied in large part on regression analyses to demonstrate that black agents were paid less than similarly situated whites. The defendants asserted that the salaries of agricultural agents were determined by four factors: education, tenure, job title, and performance. The plaintiffs' regression analyses used four independent variables — race, education, tenure, and job title. Both the district court and the Court of Appeals rejected the regression analyses as evidence of discrimination because they did not include all measurable variables that could have an effect on salary level. The Supreme Court concluded that this assessment of the evidentiary value of the regression analyses was incorrect.

> While the omission of variables from a regression analysis may render the analysis less probative than it otherwise might be, it can hardly be said, absent some other infirmity, that an analysis which accounts for the major factors must be considered unacceptable as evidence of discrimination. Normally, failure to include variables will affect the analysis' probativeness, not its admissibility.

> Importantly, it is clear that a regression analysis that includes less than "all measurable variables" may serve to prove a plaintiff's case. A plaintiff in a Title VII suit need not prove discrimination with scientific certainty; rather, his or her burden is to prove discrimination by a preponderance of the evidence.

478 U.S. at 400. The post-*Bazemore* use of regression analysis is discussed in the following case.

Ottaviani v. University of New York at New Paltz

United States Court of Appeals, Second Circuit, 1989.
875 F.2d 365, cert. denied, 493 U.S. 1021, 110 S.Ct. 721, 107 L.Ed.2d 740 (1990).

PIERCE, Circuit Judge.

This is an appeal from a judgment * * * in which the court found in favor of defendants on all of the Title VII claims asserted by individual faculty members and a class of similarly situated plaintiffs, following a lengthy bench trial. * * * Appellants * * * principally attack the district court's treatment of the evidence presented in support of their Title VII claims. For the reasons that follow, we affirm.

BACKGROUND

This complicated Title VII suit was commenced by and on behalf of full-time, academic rank female faculty members at the State University of New York at New Paltz who were employed in the University's Division of Liberal Arts and Sciences at any time between academic years 1973 and 1984. The plaintiffs alleged that between 1973 and 1984, the University discriminated against female members of its faculty on the basis of gender in three separate categories: (1) placement in initial faculty rank at the University, (2) promotion into higher rank, and (3) salary. * * *

During the trial, the district court basically considered two types of evidence — objective statistical evidence and extensive "anecdotal" evidence. The statistical evidence presented by both sides consisted primarily of data produced by means of various "multiple regression analyses." Depending upon the party presenting the statistical evidence, the data was intended to either demonstrate or rebut the plaintiffs' claim of a pattern of ongoing discrimination against women within the University in all three of the contested categories.

A. *The Statistical Evidence*

Multiple regression analysis is a statistical tool commonly used by social scientists to determine the influence that various independent, predetermined factors (so-called "independent variables") have on an observed phenomenon (the so-called "dependent variable"). In disparate treatment cases involving claims of gender discrimination, plaintiffs typically use multiple regression analysis to isolate the influence of gender on employment decisions relating to a particular job or job benefit, such as salary.

The first step in such a regression analysis is to specify all of the possible "legitimate" (i.e. nondiscriminatory) factors that are likely to significantly affect the dependent variable and which could account for disparities in the treatment of male and female employees. By identifying those legitimate criteria that affect the decision making process, individual plaintiffs can make predictions about what job or job benefits similarly situated employees should ideally receive, and then can measure the difference between the predicted treatment and the actual treatment of those employees. If there is a disparity between the predicted and actual outcomes for female employees, plaintiffs in a disparate treatment case can argue that the net "residual" difference represents the unlawful effect of discriminatory animus on the allocation of jobs or job benefits.[2]

In this case, the parties' statistical experts each determined what factors they thought were relevant to the setting of salaries and rank at the University, and used those factors as independent variables in their multiple regression analyses. By accounting for all of the "legitimate" factors that could affect salary and rank in general, the plaintiffs hoped to prove that there was a net "residual" difference or disparity between the predicted and actual salaries and rank of female faculty members that could only be attributed to ongoing gender discrimination within the University. Conversely, the defendants sought to attribute observed disparities in the pay and rank of male versus female faculty members to "legitimate" factors such as unequal job qualifications.

1. Plaintiffs' Proof of Salary Discrimination

a. Plaintiffs' Main Salary Study

The plaintiffs' main salary study was contained in Trial Exhibit 882 and purported to demonstrate the difference in salaries between male and female faculty members at New Paltz. According to the plaintiffs' statistical expert, Dr. Mary Gray, women actually earned from $1,036 to $2,277 less than their predicted salaries in each year of the class period. The defendants challenged these findings on several grounds, but principally attacked the plaintiffs' study for its failure to include certain independent variables which the defendants claimed were influential in the setting of faculty salaries at the University.

---

[2]Another way in which statisticians can measure the influence of gender on a particular employment decision is by using gender as one of the independent variables in a regression analysis. For each independent variable in a multiple regression analysis, the statistician calculates a coefficient, which is a measure of the effect that the variable has on the dependent variable being examined. If the regression coefficient for gender is sufficiently large, then it is probative of the impact that gender has on the employment decision at issue.

The plaintiffs' main salary study incorporated the following independent variables: (1) number of years of full-time teaching experience prior to hire at New Paltz; (2) number of years' teaching experience in academic rank at New Paltz; (3) possession of a doctorate degree; (4) number of years since obtaining the doctorate degree; (5) number of publications; (6) other experience prior to hire at New Paltz; and (7) years of full-time high school teaching experience. The plaintiffs' statistical expert, however, did not include academic rank variables in her main salary study such as prior rank, current rank, and years in current rank. Although Dr. Gray conceded that these three factors may influence salary decisions, she maintained that academic rank itself was subject to discrimination at New Paltz, and that the use of rank variables would therefore be inappropriate.

In connection with this assertion, the plaintiffs attempted to demonstrate that female faculty members were placed in lower academic ranks at New Paltz than their male counterparts, and promoted more slowly into higher academic ranks than their male counterparts, solely because of their gender.[3] The defendants' statistical expert, Dr. Judith Stoikov, responded by attempting to prove that rank at New Paltz was not discriminatory. After considering all the evidence as to rank, the district court rejected plaintiffs' proof as "unpersuasive," and concluded that plaintiffs had "failed to prove that rank at New Paltz was discriminatory."

The district court's rejection of plaintiffs' claims as to discrimination in rank at New Paltz had two important consequences for the plaintiffs' case. First, the court's ruling eliminated two of the contested categories of discrimination at New Paltz, and left the salary discrimination claim as plaintiffs' only remaining Title VII claim. Second, and equally important from the plaintiffs' perspective, the court's ruling "validated" academic rank as one of the legitimate factors to consider in accounting for salary disparities between male and female faculty members. Since the court considered the academic rank of faculty members to be a legitimate influencing factor on faculty salaries at New Paltz, and since the plaintiffs' main salary study failed to include academic rank variables, the court found the plaintiffs' principal study to be fundamentally flawed and less probative of discrimination than it otherwise might have been.

b. Plaintiffs' Other Salary Studies

Apart from their main salary study, the plaintiffs had also performed salary regressions which did include rank variables. Since these other studies did include what the court considered to be most of the relevant legitimate factors which could influence salary at New Paltz, the court accordingly looked primarily to these studies to determine whether the plaintiffs had made out a prima facie case of gender discrimination.

After considering and weighing all the evidence presented, the district court reached certain conclusions with respect to both the plaintiffs' and the defendants' statistical evidence. While the district judge found some of the plaintiffs' statistical

---

[3]There are four types of "academic rank" at New Paltz (1) professor, (2) associate professor, (3) assistant professor, and (4) instructor. Faculty members in one of these academic ranks either hold tenure or are on a "tenure track."

evidence "persuasive," she thought that it was insufficient to establish a prima facie case of gender discrimination. On the other hand, the district judge did not believe that defendants' statistical evidence was sufficient to rebut the plaintiffs' discrimination claims altogether. Since the judge found the statistical evidence to be inconclusive one way or the other, she ruled that whether or not the plaintiffs could prevail on their discrimination claims would depend upon whether the totality of the evidence adduced at trial supported a finding of discrimination. Accordingly, the district judge next considered whether the extensive anecdotal evidence proffered by plaintiffs supported their claims of discrimination.

B. *The Anecdotal Evidence*

The anecdotal evidence at trial consisted of various narrative descriptions of events at the University which the plaintiffs contended illustrated or proved that the University had discriminated against its female faculty members. Specifically, the plaintiff class members sought to establish that: (1) the University did not have a viable affirmative action program; (2) New Paltz's methods for identifying and correcting existing salary inequities from 1973 to 1984 were either flawed or non-existent; (3) the University either retrenched or eliminated faculty positions to the detriment of its female faculty members; and (4) the University demonstrated a disdain for women's issues through its handling of the Women's Studies Program at New Paltz. Eleven witnesses also testified about individual instances of alleged salary discrimination at New Paltz, which the plaintiffs contended were illustrative of the administration's policies toward women as a whole.

On rebuttal, the defendants sought to negate the plaintiffs' claims through the specific testimony of University administrators and faculty members, and other types of anecdotal evidence. The defendants contended that such evidence demonstrated that there were nondiscriminatory reasons for all of the actions taken by the University during the period in question which negatively affected its female faculty members, and that none of the employment practices at issue were motivated by discriminatory animus.

After reviewing the anecdotal evidence, the district judge held that the plaintiffs had not proven their Title VII claims against the University. Although she found that the anecdotal evidence supported an inference of prima facie discrimination in a few of the individual class members' cases, in each of those cases she either accepted the defendants' explanations for the pay disparities, or found that the isolated incidents of discrimination were insufficient to support the class' claim of a pattern or practice of gender discrimination. Accordingly, the district court entered judgment in favor of defendants on all of the Title VII claims.

On appeal, the appellants contend that the district court erred in its treatment and analysis of the evidence in several key respects, and that as a result, the court's finding of no discrimination was erroneous. First, appellants challenge the district court's determination that the statistical evidence was inconclusive. Appellants contend that the statistical evidence adduced at trial was more than sufficient to establish a prima facie case of gender discrimination as a matter of law. Moreover, they also contend that the district judge's decision to allow allegedly "tainted" variables such as "rank" to be used in the multiple regression analyses minimized the overall impact of defendants' alleged discriminatory treatment of female faculty members, and resulted in weaker statistical proof. Appellants also take issue with the district court's rejection of the proffered anecdotal evidence of discrimination. Finally, appellants contend that the district court erroneously excluded or ignored evidence of pre-Title VII discrimination, in contravention of the Supreme Court's decision in Bazemore v. Friday.

For the reasons that follow, we hold that Judge Kram did not clearly err in finding in favor of the defendants, and we affirm the decision of the district court.

DISCUSSION

* * *

A. *Significance of Plaintiffs' Statistical Evidence*

At trial, the plaintiffs herein contended that the statistical evidence alone was sufficient to establish a prima facie case of discrimination. According to plaintiffs, female faculty members were clearly treated less favorably than their male counterparts, and that unfavorable, disparate treatment was due solely to gender bias. The district court, however, found that the plaintiffs' statistical evidence was not "statistically significant" enough to establish a prima facie case of discrimination. For the reasons that follow, we conclude that the district court did not clearly err in ruling that the plaintiffs' proffered statistical evidence was not dispositive of their Title VII claims.

* * * [P]laintiffs in a disparate treatment case frequently rely on statistical evidence to establish that there is a disparity between the predicted and actual treatment of employees who are members of a disadvantaged group, and to argue that such disparities exist because of an unlawful bias directed against those employees. Not all disparities, however, are probative of discrimination. Before a deviation from a predicted outcome can be considered probative, the deviation must be "statistically significant."

Statistical significance is a measure of the probability that a disparity is simply due to chance, rather than any other identifiable factor. Because random deviations from the norm can always occur, statisticians do not consider slight disparities between predicted and actual results to be statistically significant. As the disparity between predicted and actual results becomes greater, however, it becomes less likely that the deviation is a random fluctuation. When the probability that a disparity is due to chance sinks to a certain threshold level, statisticians can then infer from the statistical evidence, albeit indirectly, that the deviation is attributable to some other cause unrelated to mere chance.

One unit of measurement used to express the probability that an observed result is merely a random deviation from a predicted result is the "standard deviation." * * * Generally, the fewer the number of standard deviations that separate an observed from a predicted result, the more likely it is that any observed disparity between predicted and actual results is not really a "disparity" at all but rather a random fluctuation. Conversely, the greater the number of standard deviations, the less likely it is that chance is the cause of any difference between the expected and observed results. A finding of two standard deviations corresponds approximately to a one in twenty, or five percent, chance that a disparity is merely a random deviation from the norm, and most social scientists accept two standard deviations as a threshold level of "statistical significance." When the results of a statistical analysis yield levels of statistical significance at or below the 0.05 level, chance explanations for a disparity become suspect, and most statisticians will begin to question the assumptions underlying their predictions.

Cognizant of the important role that statistics play in disparate treatment cases, the Supreme Court has held that "[where] gross statistical disparities can be shown, they alone may in a proper case constitute prima facie proof of a pattern or practice of discrimination." Hazelwood. The threshold question in disparate treatment cases, then, is at what point is the disparity in selection rates sufficiently large, or the probability that chance was the cause sufficiently low, for the numbers alone to establish a legitimate inference of discrimination? In answer to this question, most courts follow the conventions of social science which set 0.05 as the level of significance below which chance explanations become suspect. The existence of a 0.05 level of statistical significance indicates that it is fairly unlikely that an observed disparity is due to chance, and it can provide indirect support for the proposition that disparate results are intentional rather than random.[6] By no means, however, is a five percent probability of chance (or approximately two standard deviations) considered an exact legal threshold.

In the present case, the three salary studies which the district court considered most probative of a pattern or practice of discrimination produced a range of standard deviations between approximately one and five, and of the total thirty-three standard deviation measures cited, twenty-four exceeded two standard deviations.[7] Significantly, however, nine of the measures cited fell below two standard deviations. Also, the negative residuals associated with being female were not significant in every year of the liability period.

Given the range of standard deviations associated with their salary regressions, the plaintiffs contended that the statistical evidence clearly gave rise to a presumption of discrimination. * * * [H]owever, although the district judge found the studies to be "persuasive," she nevertheless held that these levels of "statistical significance" alone were "not sufficiently high to support a prima facie claim of salary discrimination."

On appeal, appellants argue *inter alia* that, as a matter of law, a finding of two standard deviations should be equated with a prima facie case of discrimination. According to appellants, the district court therefore erred in finding that they had not met their burden of establishing a prima facie case. * * * While appellants' argument that a finding of two standard deviations should be equated with a prima facie case of discrimination under Title VII is not without initial appeal, we are constrained to reject such a formal "litmus" test for assessing the legitimacy of Title VII claims.

---

[6] * * * [H]owever, that no matter how great the number of standard deviations is, statistical tests can never entirely rule out the possibility that chance caused the disparity.

[7] As discussed *supra*, two standard deviations corresponds roughly to a 1 in 20 chance that the outcome is a random fluctuation. Three standard deviations corresponds to approximately a 1 in 384 chance of randomness. Finally, a range of four to five standard deviations corresponds to a probability range of 1 chance in 15,786 to 1 chance in 1,742,160. M. Abramowia & I. Steigan, Handbook of Mathematical Functions, National Bureau of Standards, U.S. Government Printing Office, Applied Mathematics Series No. 55 (1966) (Tables 26.1, 26.2).

It is certainly true that a finding of two to three standard deviations can be highly probative of discriminatory treatment. As tempting as it might be to announce a black letter rule of law, however, recent Supreme Court pronouncements instruct that there simply is no minimum threshold level of statistical significance which mandates a finding that Title VII plaintiffs have made out a prima facie case. See, e.g., Watson v. Fort Worth Bank & Trust ("We have emphasized the useful role that statistical methods can have in Title VII cases, but we have not suggested that any particular number of 'standard deviations' can determine whether a plaintiff has made out a prima facie case in the complex area of employment discrimination."). Accordingly, in accordance with Supreme Court pronouncements, we must reject appellants' suggestion that this court announce a rule of law with respect to what level of statistical significance automatically gives rise to a rebuttable presumption of discrimination.

* * *

The net import of Judge Kram's rulings regarding the significance of plaintiffs' statistical evidence is that she found the evidence to be "persuasive" but not dispositive. Contrary to appellants' assertions, it is clear from the district judge's rulings that she did not simply ignore the statistical evidence of discrimination presented by plaintiffs. The court found this evidence sufficient to cause her to deny the defendants' motion to dismiss at the end of plaintiffs' case, and to accept rebuttal evidence from the defendants. On rebuttal, however, the defendants were able to successfully undermine the plaintiffs' case by attacking the validity of the plaintiffs' statistical evidence, and by introducing statistical evidence of their own to negate the inference of discrimination that had been raised.

Specifically, the defendants criticized the plaintiffs' most probative studies for excluding one factor which they claimed exerted a highly significant positive influence on current salary, namely, whether a faculty member had held a prior, full-time administrative position at SUNY New Paltz before returning to full-time teaching. The defendants also criticized these studies because the salary regressions were "fitted" only to male faculty members, i.e., they used independent variables that were derived only from the male population. The district court noted in its opinion that a "males only regression" based exclusively on values existing only in the male population might have tended to overestimate the predicted salaries of certain female faculty members, because it might not have taken into account legitimate factors existing solely in the female population which could have affected the rate of pay for women teachers at the University. If the predicted salary for a female faculty member was overestimated, this type of regression arguably would have overestimated the discrepancies between male and female salaries at the University. Finally, the defendants criticized these studies because they inappropriately aggregated Instructors and Assistant Professors into a single "rank." The defendants pointed out at trial that when the two ranks were combined into a single rank, the predicted salary of a female Instructor would essentially be based on the higher salary of an Assistant Professor, and hence the net residual difference between the predicted and actual salary of a female Instructor would be overstated. Apart from these criticisms of plaintiffs' statistical evidence, the defendants also offered persuasive anecdotal evidence to negate the plaintiffs' claims of discriminatory animus. After considering all of the evidence presented, both statistical and anecdotal, the district court simply found that plaintiffs had failed to preponderate on their claims.

Recent Supreme Court precedent has made it clear that this court can reverse such a factual determination only if it is clearly erroneous in light of all the evidence in the record or if it rests on legal error. Bazemore. Especially in cases where statistical evidence is involved, great deference is due the district court's determination of whether the resultant numbers are sufficiently probative of the ultimate fact in issue. As the Supreme Court cautioned in the *Teamsters* case, "statistics are not irrefutable; they come in infinite variety and, like any other kind of evidence, they may be rebutted. In short, their usefulness depends on all of the surrounding facts and circumstances." The district judge herein gave due consideration to all of the evidence presented, and after reviewing the record, we do not perceive a convincing basis for finding her interpretation of that evidence to be clearly erroneous. Accordingly, we affirm her rulings with respect to the statistical evidence presented.

B. *Use of Rank Variables*

In conjunction with their attack on the district court's assessment of the sufficiency of plaintiffs' statistical evidence, appellants also challenge the district court's determination that "rank" was an appropriate factor to consider in assessing pay disparities between male and female faculty members. According to appellants, if the court had rejected the rank variables and considered only those salary studies which excluded rank, then the number of standard deviations associated with their findings of discrimination would have been much greater, and their statistical proof would have been even more probative.

Although we recognize that the use of rank variables in testing for salary discrimination against women faculty members is not universally accepted, see Finkelstein, The Judicial Reception of Multiple Regression Studies in Race and Sex Discrimination Cases, 80 Colum.L.Rev. 737, 741-42 (1980), in Sobel v. Yeshiva University, this court specifically upheld the use of rank variables in a multiple regression analysis, stating that rank could be used as a legitimate factor in explaining pay disparities so long as rank itself was clearly not tainted by discrimination. As the plaintiffs' statistical expert, Dr. Mary Gray, explained in her own report: "In a bias-free system, one could use rank as a measure of productivity since the review process for promotion or hire should evaluate teaching, scholarship and service." (Emphasis added). The question to be resolved, then, in cases involving the use of academic rank factors, is whether rank is tainted by discrimination at the particular institution charged with violating Title VII. Although appellants reiterate on appeal their claim that rank at New Paltz was tainted, it is clear that the district judge accepted and considered evidence from the parties on both sides of this issue, and that she rejected the plaintiffs' contentions on this point.

At trial, the plaintiffs failed to adduce any significant statistical evidence of discrimination as to rank. As the district court stated in its opinion, the plaintiffs' studies of rank, rank at hire, and waiting time for promotion "were mere compilations of data" which neither accounted for important factors relevant to assignment of rank and promotion, "nor demonstrated that observed differences were statistically significant." The defendants, on the other hand, offered persuasive objective evidence to demonstrate that there was no discrimination in either placement into initial rank or promotion at New Paltz between 1973 and 1984, and the district court chose to credit the defendants' evidence. Upon review of the record, we cannot state that the court's rulings in this regard were clearly erroneous. Accordingly, the district court's decision to focus primarily on those studies which included rank as an essential independent variable was not improper, and appellants' contentions to the contrary must be rejected.

C. *Anecdotal Evidence*

Appellants also contend on appeal that the district court did not give sufficient weight to the anecdotal evidence adduced at trial, and that the court should have rejected the explanations proffered by University administrators to explain pay and rank inequities as "pretextual." Our review of the anecdotal evidence, however, is limited to ascertaining whether the district judge committed clear error in making her findings. See Anderson v. City of Bessemer, 470 U.S. 564, 573, 105 S.Ct. 1504, 1511, 84 L.Ed.2d 518 (1985); Pullman-Standard v. Swint, 456 U.S. 273, 287, 102 S.Ct. 1781, 1789, 72 L.Ed.2d 66 (1982). It is not the function of this court to reweigh the evidence anew, particularly when findings by a district court are based on in-court credibility determinations. Rather, under the clearly erroneous standard, we may only reject findings by the trial court when we are left with the "definite and firm conviction that a mistake has been committed." United States v. United States Gypsum Co., 333 U.S. 364, 395, 68 S.Ct. 525, 542, 92 L.Ed.2d 746 (1948).

In this case, the district court found that the defendants had successfully rebutted the plaintiffs' anecdotal proof, and that, in any event, the anecdotal evidence on its face was too limited to prove class-wide discrimination. After reviewing the entire record, we do not think that the court's decision to credit the testimony of the defendants rather than that of the plaintiffs was clearly erroneous. Since the district court's account of the evidence is plausible in light of the record viewed in its entirety, we may not overturn the findings of the court even if we might have weighed the evidence differently, had we been sitting as the trier of fact. Accordingly, we affirm the findings of the district court with respect to the anecdotal evidence presented.

D. *Bazemore Claim*

In Bazemore, the Supreme Court held that employers have an obligation to eradicate employment discrimination that began prior to the effective date of Title VII * * * if the discrimination continues into the post-[Act] liability period. The Supreme Court also stated that statistical evidence of pre-Act discrimination can be probative of ongoing, post-Act discrimination.

On appeal, appellants contend that the district court erroneously excluded evidence of pre-Act discrimination in violation of the Supreme Court's dictates in *Bazemore*. In particular, appellants claim that the district judge improperly excluded Exhibit 990, which purported to document statistically significant evidence of discrimination as to initial faculty rank. This claim is without merit, however. At trial, the defendants objected to the admission of Exhibit 990 not because it was offered to prove pre-Act discrimination, but because it was unreliable and incomplete. While the weakness of statistical evidence should not ordinarily preclude its admission, see *Bazemore*, 478 U.S. at 400, the Supreme Court has recognized that some statistical evidence may be so unreliable as to be irrelevant, see id. at 400 n. 10. Apparently the district judge herein thought that to be the case with respect to this particular exhibit, because she sustained the defendants' objection to its admission on the grounds that it was irrelevant and unduly confusing. Upon review of the record, we do not find the district court's decision to exclude the study to be clearly erroneous, and therefore we affirm the evidentiary ruling.

Moreover, we note that appellant's reliance on this court's decision in Sobel v. Yeshiva University as support for their more generalized, *Bazemore*-type claims is misplaced. In *Sobel*, the plaintiffs introduced evidence specifically designed to prove that women were discriminated against prior to the effective date of Title VII, and argued that "Yeshiva had a legal obligation to equalize women's salaries immediately upon application of Title VII to universities." In the present case, even though the Supreme Court handed down its decision in *Bazemore* the same month that plaintiffs' trial was commenced, the plaintiffs did not introduce any statistical evidence of substance to prove that there was discrimination at New Paltz prior to the effective date of Title VII. Instead, nearly all of the plaintiffs' studies focused on the class liability period, which covered the years 1973 to 1984. This is in marked contrast to *Sobel* and *Bazemore*, wherein the plaintiffs offered direct, independent proof of pre-Act discrimination. Accordingly, we find appellants' arguments on this point generally to be without merit.

CONCLUSION

In sum, the burden of persuasion was on the plaintiffs to prove by a preponderance of the evidence that there was a pattern or practice of discrimination at SUNY New Paltz, and they failed to meet that burden. We have considered all of the arguments presented on appeal, and find them to be without merit. For the reasons stated above, the judgment of the district court is affirmed.

NOTES AND PROBLEMS FOR DISCUSSION

1. If faculty rank was a factor used by SUNY in the setting of wages, how could plaintiffs argue that rank should not be included as an independent variable in the regression analysis? What did the plaintiffs in *Ottaviani* believe were the "major variables" affecting faculty salaries? In contrast to the ruling in *Ottaviani*, the Ninth Circuit in EEOC v. GEN. TEL. CO. of NORTHWEST, INC., 885 F.2d 575, 582 (9th Cir. 1989), cert. denied, 498 U.S. 950, 111 S.Ct. 370, 112 L.Ed.2d 332 (1990), ruled that the failure of the plaintiff's regression analysis to account for gender-based differences in career interests between men and women was not fatal to establishing a prima facie case; it merely rendered the analysis less precise.

Bazemore and *Ottaviani* demonstrate that: (1) it is next to impossible to account in the analysis for all factors which may play a role in the disputed decision process and, (2) some factors will be extremely difficult to quantify for purposes of analysis. The courts continue to grapple with the weight to be accorded regression analyses and the question of which party shoulders the burden concerning the significance of variables not accounted for in analyses. *See e.g.*, Smith v. Va. Commonwealth Univ., 84 F.3d 672, 676 (4th Cir. 1996) (*en banc*) ("*Bazemore* and common sense require that any multiple regression analysis used to determine pay disparity must include all the major factors on which pay is determined. The very factors (performance, productivity, and merit) that VCU admittedly considered in determining prior pay increases were left out of the study"); *and* Bickerstaff v. Vassar Coll., 196 F.3d 435 (2d Cir. 1999) (the failure to account for two of the three factors that college used in setting salaries made the plaintiff's regression analysis "so incomplete as to be irrelevant").

Job performance is a factor commonly used in setting salaries and making promotions, but it is a factor that in many settings is notoriously difficult to quantify for purposes of a statistical study. In a regression analysis designed to determine the effect of sex on salaries, is it appropriate to assume that men and women are equally productive? In *Smith v. Va. Commonwealth, supra,* the Fourth Circuit rejected a regression analysis which incorporated the assumption that productivity was not dependent on sex. A dissenting judge took his colleagues to task for misunderstanding the role of the statistical analysis.

> At the heart of this case is the plaintiffs' argument that VCU's regression analysis was flawed because it assumed that male and female faculty members are on the average equally productive. Because the plurality and concurring opinions all criticize VCU's Study for not taking into account performance factors, the only conclusion I can draw is that they accept (at least tacitly) the male plaintiffs' argument that a salary equity study cannot assume that men and women on the average are equally productive. I, however, cannot accept the plaintiffs' argument, and I believe that it was completely proper for VCU to assume, when conducting its Study, that men and women are on the average equally productive.

> Specifically, the plurality and concurring opinions fail to realize that performance factors are important in determining pay at VCU because they measure qualitative differences in productivity between particular individuals. They are not intended to measure differences in productivity between general groupings of individuals, such as between men and women or between blacks and whites. Thus, while performance factors can measure the differences in the productivity between a particular female faculty member and a particular male counterpart, performance factors cannot (and do not) provide a guide for measuring differences between the productivity of men and women on the average. That is simply not their function.

84 F.3d at 690 (Michael, J, dissenting). But if the question is whether sex of employees is affecting salaries and the employer says that it bases salary at least in part on performance, how can performance be ignored in the analysis? Why was work performance not included in the salary study in *Ottaviani*?

In MORGAN v. UNITED PARCEL SERVICE, 380 F.3d 459 (8th Cir. 2004), a class of African-American store managers claimed systemic racial discrimination in pay and promotional opportunities. Their experts performed regression analyses and found statistically significant pay disparities between black and white managers but did not take into account prior salary and performance, factors which UPS claimed were involved in setting salaries. While recognizing that under *Bazemore,* the plaintiffs' statistical evidence was admissible, the court of appeals held it was insufficient to preclude summary judgment for the defendant.

> Statistical evidence like that adduced here, at best, can only show a correlation between race and the dependent variable that gives rise to a further inference of pattern-or-practice discrimination in a proper case. Here the flaws are too many and the probative value too slight for Plaintiffs' regressions to carry the day by a preponderance of the evidence in the context of this case. It would be manifestly

unreasonable to infer from Plaintiffs' regression analyses that UPS set center managers' base pay lower for blacks as a matter of practice all across the country during the period in question. Accordingly, summary judgment was appropriate.

380 F.3d at 472. The plaintiffs presented no anecdotal evidence of discrimination and that, in turn, reinforced "doubt arising from the questions about the validity of the statistical evidence." Id. at 471.

2. Most pattern and practice cases are proved by a combination of statistical evidence and "anecdotal" testimony of the named plaintiffs or class members about specific instances of discrimination. But the courts have demonstrated a marked reluctance to find intentional discrimination solely on the basis of statistical evidence. *See, e.g.*, EEOC v. Sears, Roebuck & Co., 839 F.2d 302, 310-12 (7th Cir. 1988) (noting that one of the basic problems with the plaintiff's case was the failure to bring forward any supporting testimony by individual victims of discrimination).

3. Are some forms of discrimination, by their very nature, not susceptible to pattern or practice litigation? In EEOC v. MITSUBISHI MOTOR MFG. OF AMERICA, INC., 990 F.Supp. 1059 (C.D. Ill. 1998), the agency filed a pattern or practice case of sexual harassment. The EEOC's theory was that Mitsubishi created and maintained a sexually hostile and abusive work environment in one of its assembly plants by refusing to take notice of, investigate, and/or discipline male employees who sexually harassed female employees. Mitsubishi moved for summary judgment, arguing that, since proof of sexual harassment included a subjective component (unwelcomeness), unlawful sexual harassment could only be proved one employee at a time. The district court denied the motion and allowed the action to proceed. The court held that the EEOC could establish a pattern or practice of sexual harassment based solely on proof that as a regular practice the employer tolerated *objectively* offensive conduct toward female employees.

> In a pattern or practice case brought by the EEOC for injunctive relief, it is really not necessary or appropriate to consider the subjective issues of individuals. If a company engages in a pattern or practice which is proved by an objective test, and the company is negligent in preventing it, then the EEOC can and should be able to obtain injunctive relief, regardless of whether some of the individuals may have no subjective objection to the harassing conduct (i.e., the conduct may be welcome to some). The [Supreme Court decisions defining sexual harassment] do not address these issues, and this court believes that the teachings of [those cases] are not intended to apply lockstep in a case such as this one. The law, therefore, must be that at the pattern and practice phase, subjective proofs are not necessary and should not be considered to find a pattern or practice of sexual harassment.

990 F.Supp. at 1073. The district court went on to hold that the individual victims of that harassment would only be awarded damages after demonstrating that they had been subject to harassing conduct and that it the conduct was subjectively unwelcome. Mitsubishi ultimately settled with the EEOC for $34 million. Barnaby Feder, *$34 Million Settles Suit for Women at Auto Plant*, N.Y. TIMES, June 12, 1998 at 12,A. The relief aspects of the decision are discussed in Chapter 7D, *infra*.

CHAPTER 3

The Prohibited Classifications: Special Problems

As noted in Chapter 1, Title VII was intended to proscribe a wide range of discriminatory employment practices. Congress intentionally drafted the provisions that define the covered employment institutions and decisions in broad and general terms. Nevertheless, Title VII, in one important respect, is a statute of limited application. It prohibits discrimination on the basis of five specifically enumerated classifications — race, color, sex, religion and national origin. Consequently, the courts have ruled, allegations of bias based on any other classification do not state a claim under this statute. On the other hand, however, keep in mind that the availability of disproportionate impact-based claims serves to expand the universe of practices perceived as discriminating on the basis of the enumerated categories. The materials in this chapter are designed to examine several problems unique to each of the five statutory classifications.

SECTION A. RELIGION AND THE DUTY TO ACCOMMODATE

Section 701(j) of Title VII defines religion as including "all aspects of religious observance and practice, as well as belief * * *." While the statute does not set out the limits of these general terms, the federal courts have uniformly adopted the interpretation given to the religious exemption provision of the selective service statutes by the Supreme Court in two conscientious objector cases, Welsh v. United States, 398 U.S. 333, 90 S.Ct. 1792, 26 L.Ed.2d 308 (1970); and United States v. Seeger, 380 U.S. 163, 85 S.Ct. 850, 13 L.Ed.2d 733 (1965). Accordingly, a plaintiff need only prove (1) that his belief is "religious" in his own scheme of things[a]; and (2) that it is sincerely held.

---

[a] In *Welsh*, this was held to include moral or ethical beliefs which occupy the role of religion in an individual's life. Political or social ideologies, on the other hand, have been held to fall outside the limits of Title VII protected religious belief. See Bellamy v. Mason's Stores, Inc., 368 F.Supp. 1025 (W.D.Va. 1973), affirmed on other grounds, 508 F.2d 504 (4th Cir. 1974) (racist and anti-Semitic philosophy espoused by Ku Klux Klan does not constitute religion). Atheism, however, does fit within the statutory definition of religion. Young v. Southwestern Savings & Loan Ass'n, 509 F.2d 140 (5th Cir. 1975). One circuit has construed *Seeger* and

This definition of religion, which was added to the Act by the 1972 amendments, contains one clause that has been the subject of most of the controversy and litigation in the area of religious discrimination in employment.

Trans World Airlines, Inc. v. Hardison

Supreme Court of the United States, 1977.
432 U.S. 63, 97 S.Ct. 2264, 53 L.Ed.2d 113.

MR. JUSTICE WHITE delivered the opinion of the Court.

Section 703(a)(1) makes it an unlawful employment practice for an employer to discriminate against an employee or a prospective employee on the basis of his or her religion. At the time of the events involved here, a guideline of the Equal Employment Opportunity Commission required, as the Act itself now does, that an employer, short of "undue hardship," make "reasonable accommodations" to the religious needs of its employees. The issue in this case is the extent of the employer's obligation under Title VII to accommodate an employee whose religious beliefs prohibit him from working on Saturdays.

I

Petitioner Trans World Airlines operates a large maintenance and overhaul base in Kansas City, Mo. On June 5, 1967, respondent Larry G. Hardison was hired by TWA to work as a clerk in the Stores Department at its Kansas City base. Because of its essential role in the Kansas City operation, the Stores Department must operate 24 hours per day, 365 days per year, and whenever an employee's job in that department is not filled, an employee must be shifted from another department, or a supervisor must cover the job, even if the work in other areas may suffer.

Hardison, like other employees at the Kansas City base, was subject to a seniority system contained in a collective-bargaining agreement that TWA maintains with petitioner International Association of Machinists and Aerospace Workers. The seniority system is implemented by the union steward through a system of bidding by employees for particular shift assignments as they become available. The most senior employees have first choice for job and shift assignments, and the most junior employees are required to work when the union steward is unable to find enough people willing to work at a particular time or in a particular job to fill TWA's needs.

In the spring of 1968 Hardison began to study the religion known as the Worldwide Church of God. One of the tenets of that religion is that one must observe

---

Welsh to mean that a belief system is "religious" if it (1) addresses fundamental and ultimate questions having to do with deep and imponderable matters; (2) is comprehensive in nature; and (3) is manifested in formal and external signs such as formal services, ceremonial functions, the existence of clergy, observation of holidays, and other manifestations associated with the traditional religions. Fallon v. Mercy Catholic Medical Center, 877 F.3d 487 (3d Cir. 2017) (an employee who was terminated for refusing to be inoculated against the flu because he believed the vaccine did more harm than good did not have a "religious" basis for refusing because this belief was medical, was not p[art of a comprehensive belief system, and was not manifested by external signs).

the Sabbath by refraining from performing any work from sunset on Friday until sunset on Saturday. The religion also proscribes work on certain specified religious holidays.

When Hardison informed Everett Kussman, the manager of the Stores Department, of his religious conviction regarding observance of the Sabbath, Kussman agreed that the union steward should seek a job swap for Hardison or a change of days off; that Hardison would have his religious holidays off whenever possible if Hardison agreed to work the traditional holidays when asked; and that Kussman would try to find Hardison another job that would be more compatible with his religious beliefs. The problem was temporarily solved when Hardison transferred to the 11 p. m.–7 a. m. shift. Working this shift permitted Hardison to observe his Sabbath.

The problem soon reappeared when Hardison bid for and received a transfer from Building 1, where he had been employed, to Building 2, where he would work the day shift. The two buildings had entirely separate seniority lists; and while in Building 1 Hardison had sufficient seniority to observe the Sabbath regularly, he was second from the bottom on the Building 2 seniority list.

In Building 2 Hardison was asked to work Saturdays when a fellow employee went on vacation. TWA agreed to permit the union to seek a change of work assignments for Hardison, but the union was not willing to violate the seniority provisions set out in the collective-bargaining contract, and Hardison had insufficient seniority to bid for a shift having Saturdays off.

A proposal that Hardison work only four days a week was rejected by the company. Hardison's job was essential, and on weekends he was the only available person on his shift to perform it. To leave the position empty would have impaired supply shop functions, which were critical to airline operations; to fill Hardison's position with a supervisor or an employee from another area would simply have undermanned another operation; and to employ someone not regularly assigned to work Saturdays would have required TWA to pay premium wages.

When an accommodation was not reached, Hardison refused to report for work on Saturdays. A transfer to the twilight shift proved unavailing since that schedule still required Hardison to work past sundown on Fridays. After a hearing, Hardison was discharged on grounds of insubordination for refusing to work during his designated shift.

Hardison, having first invoked the administrative remedy provided by Title VII, brought this action for injunctive relief in the United States District Court * * *, claiming that his discharge by TWA constituted religious discrimination in violation of Title VII. * * * Hardison's claim of religious discrimination rested on 1967 EEOC guidelines requiring employers "to make reasonable accommodations to the religious needs of employees" whenever such accommodation would not work an "undue hardship," and on similar language adopted by Congress in the 1972 amendments to Title VII.

After a bench trial, the District Court ruled in favor of the defendants. * * * [T]he District Court rejected at the outset TWA's contention that requiring it in any way to accommodate the religious needs of its employees would constitute an unconstitutional establishment of religion. As the District Court construed the Act, however, TWA had satisfied its "reasonable accommodations" obligation, and any further accommodation would have worked an undue hardship on the company.

The Court of Appeals for the Eighth Circuit reversed the judgment for TWA. It agreed with the District Court's constitutional ruling, but held that TWA had not satisfied its duty to accommodate. * * *

In * * * [its] petition for certiorari TWA * * * contended that adequate steps had been taken to accommodate Hardison's religious observances and that to construe the statute to require further efforts at accommodation would create an establishment of religion contrary to the First Amendment of the Constitution. TWA also contended that the Court of Appeals improperly ignored the District Court's findings of fact.

* * * Because we agree with petitioner that * * * [its] conduct was not a violation of Title VII, we need not reach the other questions presented.

II

The Court of Appeals found that TWA had committed an unlawful employment practice under §703(a)(1) of the Act * * *. The emphasis of both the language and the legislative history of the statute is on eliminating discrimination in employment; similarly situated employees are not to be treated differently solely because they differ with respect to race, color, religion, sex, or national origin. This is true regardless of whether the discrimination is directed against majorities or minorities.

The prohibition against religious discrimination soon raised the question of whether it was impermissible under §703(a)(1) to discharge or refuse to hire a person who for religious reasons refused to work during the employer's normal workweek. In 1966 an EEOC guideline dealing with this problem declared that an employer had an obligation under the statute "to accommodate to the reasonable religious needs of employees * * * where such accommodation can be made without serious inconvenience to the conduct of the business."

In 1967 the EEOC amended its guidelines to require employers "to make reasonable accommodations to the religious needs of employees and prospective employees where such accommodations can be made without undue hardship on the conduct of the employer's business." The EEOC did not suggest what sort of accommodations are "reasonable" or when hardship to an employer becomes "undue."

This question — the extent of the required accommodation — remain[s] unsettled. * * *

In part "to resolve [this question] by legislation" * * *, Congress included the following definition of religion in its 1972 amendments to Title VII:

> "The term 'religion' includes all aspects of religious observance and practice, as well as belief, unless an employer demonstrates that he is unable to reasonably accommodate to an employee's or prospective employee's religious observance or practice without undue hardship on the conduct of the employer's business." §701(j).

The intent and effect of this definition was to make it an unlawful employment practice under §703(a)(1) for an employer not to make reasonable accommodations, short of undue hardship, for the religious practices of his employees and prospective employees. But like the EEOC guidelines, the statute provides no guidance for determining the degree of accommodation that is required of an employer. The brief legislative history of §701(j) is likewise of little assistance in this regard.[9] * * *

* * * With this in mind, we turn to a consideration of whether TWA has met its obligation under Title VII to accommodate the religious observances of its employees.

III

The Court of Appeals held that TWA had not made reasonable efforts to accommodate Hardison's religious needs under the 1967 EEOC guidelines in effect at the time the relevant events occurred.[11] In its view, TWA had rejected three reasonable alternatives, any one of which would have satisfied its obligation without undue hardship. First, within the framework of the seniority system, TWA could have permitted Hardison to work a four-day week, utilizing in his place a supervisor or another worker on duty elsewhere. That this would have caused other shop functions to suffer was insufficient to amount to undue hardship in the opinion of the Court of Appeals. Second—according to the Court of Appeals, also within the bounds of the collective-bargaining contract—the company could have filled Hardison's Saturday shift from other available personnel competent to do the job, of which the court said there were at least 200. That this would have involved premium overtime pay was not deemed an undue hardship. Third, TWA could have arranged a "swap between Hardison and another employee either for another shift or for the Sabbath days." In response to the assertion that this would have involved a breach of the seniority provisions of the contract, the court noted that it had not been settled in the courts whether the required statutory accommodation to religious needs stopped short of transgressing seniority rules, but found it unnecessary to decide the issue because, as the Court of Appeals saw the record, TWA had not sought, and the union had therefore not declined to entertain, a possible variance from the seniority provisions of the collective-bargaining agreement. The company had simply left the entire matter to the union steward who the Court of Appeals said "likewise did nothing."

We disagree with the Court of Appeals in all relevant respects. It is our view that TWA made reasonable efforts to accommodate and that each of the Court of Appeals' suggested alternatives would have been an undue hardship within the meaning of the statute as construed by the EEOC guidelines.

A

It might be inferred from the Court of Appeals' opinion and from the brief of the EEOC in this Court that TWA's efforts to accommodate were no more than negligible.

---

[9]* * * The legislative history of the measure consists chiefly of a brief floor debate in the Senate, contained in less than two pages of the Congressional Record and consisting principally of the views of the proponent of the measure, Senator Jennings Randolph.

[11]Ordinarily, an EEOC guideline is not entitled to great weight where, as here, it varies from prior EEOC policy and no new legislative history has been introduced in support of the change. But where Congress has not just kept its silence by refusing to overturn the administrative construction, but has ratified it with positive legislation, the guideline is entitled to some deference, at least sufficient in this case to warrant our accepting the guideline as a defensible construction of the pre-1972 statute, *i.e.*, as imposing on TWA the duty of "reasonable accommodation" in the absence of "undue hardship." We thus need not consider whether §701(j) must be applied retroactively to the facts of this litigation.

The findings of the District Court, supported by the record, are to the contrary. In summarizing its more detailed findings, the District Court observed:

> "TWA established as a matter of fact that it did take appropriate action to accommodate as required by Title VII. It held several meetings with plaintiff at which it attempted to find a solution to plaintiff's problems. It did accommodate plaintiff's observance of his special religious holidays. It authorized the union steward to search for someone who would swap shifts, which apparently was normal procedure."

It is also true that TWA itself attempted without success to find Hardison another job. The District Court's view was that TWA had done all that could reasonably be expected within the bounds of the seniority system.

The Court of Appeals observed, however, that the possibility of a variance from the seniority system was never really posed to the union. This is contrary to the District Court's findings and to the record. The District Court found that when TWA first learned of Hardison's religious observances in April 1968, it agreed to permit the union's steward to seek a swap of shifts or days off but that "the steward reported that he was unable to work out scheduling changes and that he understood that no one was willing to swap days with plaintiff." Later, in March 1969, at a meeting held just two days before Hardison first failed to report for his Saturday shift, TWA again "offered to accommodate plaintiff's religious observance by agreeing to any trade of shifts or change of sections that plaintiff and the union could work out. * * * Any shift or change was impossible within the seniority framework and the union was not willing to violate the seniority provision set out in the contract to make a shift or change." * * *

* * *

B

We are also convinced, contrary to the Court of Appeals, that TWA itself cannot be faulted for having failed to work out a shift or job swap for Hardison. Both the union and TWA had agreed to the seniority system; the union was unwilling to entertain a variance over the objections of men senior to Hardison; and for TWA to have arranged unilaterally for a swap would have amounted to a breach of the collective-bargaining agreement.

(1)

Hardison and the EEOC insist that the statutory obligation to accommodate religious needs takes precedence over both the collective-bargaining contract and the seniority rights of TWA's other employees. We agree that neither a collective-bargaining contract nor a seniority system may be employed to violate the statute, but we do not believe that the duty to accommodate requires TWA to take steps inconsistent with the otherwise valid agreement. Collective bargaining, aimed at effecting workable and enforceable agreements between management and labor, lies at the core of our national labor policy, and seniority provisions are universally included in these contracts. Without a clear and express indication from Congress, we cannot agree with Hardison and the EEOC that an agreed-upon seniority system must give way when necessary to accommodate religious observances. * * *

* * *

Had TWA * * * circumvented the seniority system by relieving Hardison of Saturday work and ordering a senior employee to replace him, it would have denied the latter his shift preference so that Hardison could be given his. The senior employee would also have been deprived of his contractual rights under the collective-bargaining agreement.

It was essential to TWA's business to require Saturday and Sunday work from at least a few employees even though most employees preferred those days off. Allocating the burdens of weekend work was a matter for collective bargaining. In considering criteria to govern this allocation, TWA and the union had two alternatives: adopt a neutral system, such as seniority, a lottery, or rotating shifts; or allocate days off in accordance with the religious needs of its employees. TWA would have had to adopt the latter in order to assure Hardison and others like him of getting the days off necessary for strict observance of their religion, but it could have done so only at the expense of others who had strong, but perhaps nonreligious, reasons for not working on weekends. There were no volunteers to relieve Hardison on Saturdays, and to give Hardison Saturdays off, TWA would have had to deprive another employee of his shift preference at least in part because he did not adhere to a religion that observed the Saturday Sabbath.

Title VII does not contemplate such unequal treatment. The repeated, unequivocal emphasis of both the language and the legislative history of Title VII is on eliminating discrimination in employment, and such discrimination is proscribed when it is directed against majorities as well as minorities. * * * It would be anomalous to conclude that by "reasonable accommodation" Congress meant that an employer must deny the shift and job preference of some employees, as well as deprive them of their contractual rights, in order to accommodate or prefer the religious needs of others, and we conclude that Title VII does not require an employer to go that far.

(2)

Our conclusion is supported by the fact that seniority systems are afforded special treatment under Title VII itself. Section 703(h) provides in pertinent part:

"Notwithstanding any other provision of this subchapter, it shall not be an unlawful employment practice for an employer to apply different standards of compensation, or different terms, conditions, or privileges of employment pursuant to a bona fide seniority or merit system * * * provided that such differences are not the result of an intention to discriminate because of race, color, religion, sex, or national origin * * *."

"[T]he unmistakable purpose of §703(h) was to make clear that the routine application of a bona fide seniority system would not be unlawful under Title VII." International Brotherhood of Teamsters v. United States, 431 U.S. 324, 352, 97 S.Ct. 1843, 1863, 52 L.Ed.2d 396 (1977). * * * [A]bsent a discriminatory purpose, the operation of a seniority system cannot be an unlawful employment practice even if the system has some discriminatory consequences.

There has been no suggestion of discriminatory intent in this case. * * * The Court of Appeals' conclusion that TWA was not limited by the terms of its seniority system was in substance nothing more than a ruling that operation of the seniority system was itself an unlawful employment practice even though no discriminatory purpose had been shown. That ruling is plainly inconsistent with the dictates of §703(h), both on its face and as interpreted in the recent decisions of this Court.[13]

As we have said, TWA was not required by Title VII to carve out a special exception to its seniority system in order to help Hardison to meet his religious obligations.[14]

C

The Court of Appeals also suggested that TWA could have permitted Hardison to work a four-day week if necessary in order to avoid working on his Sabbath. Recognizing that this might have left TWA short-handed on the one shift each week that Hardison did not work, the court still concluded that TWA would suffer no undue hardship if it were required to replace Hardison either with supervisory personnel or with qualified personnel from other departments. Alternatively, the Court of Appeals suggested that TWA could have replaced Hardison on his Saturday shift with other available employees through the payment of premium wages. Both of these alternatives would involve costs to TWA, either in the form of lost efficiency in other jobs or higher wages.

---

[13]Franks v. Bowman Transportation Co. is not to the contrary. In *Franks* we held that "once an illegal discriminatory practice occurring after the effective date of the Act is proved," §703(h) does not bar an award of retroactive seniority status to victims of that discriminatory practice. Here the suggested exception to the TWA–IAM seniority system would not be remedial; the operation of the seniority system itself is said to violate Title VII. In such circumstances, §703(h) unequivocally mandates that there is no statutory violation in the absence of a showing of discriminatory purpose. See United Air Lines, Inc. v. Evans, 431 U.S. 553, 97 S.Ct. 1885, 52 L.Ed.2d 571 (1977).

[14]Despite its hyperbole and rhetoric, the dissent appears to agree with — at least it stops short of challenging — the fundamental proposition that Title VII does not require an employer and a union who have agreed on a seniority system to deprive senior employees of their seniority rights in order to accommodate a junior employee's religious practices. This is the principal issue on which TWA and the union came to this Court. The dissent is thus reduced to (1) asserting that the statute requires TWA to accommodate Hardison even though substantial expenditures are required to do so; and (2) advancing its own view of the record to show that TWA could have done more than it did to accommodate Hardison without violating the seniority system or incurring substantial additional costs. We reject the former assertion as an erroneous construction of the statute. As for the latter, we prefer the findings of the District Judge who heard the evidence. Thus, the dissent suggests that through further efforts TWA or the union might have arranged a temporary or permanent job swap within the seniority system, despite the District Court's express finding, supported by the record, that "[t]he seniority provisions * * * precluded the possibility of plaintiff's changing his shift." Similarly, the dissent offers two alternatives — sending Hardison back to Building 1 or allowing him to work extra days without overtime pay — that it says could have been pursued by TWA or the union, even though neither of the courts below even hinted that these suggested alternatives would have been feasible under the circumstances. Furthermore, Buildings 1 and 2 had separate seniority lists, and insofar as the record shows, a return to Building 1 would not have solved Hardison's problems. Hardison himself testified that he "gave up" his Building 1 seniority when he came to Building 2, and that the union would not accept his early return to Building 1 in part "because the problem of seniority came up again." We accept the District Court's findings that TWA had done all that it could do to accommodate Hardison's religious beliefs without either incurring substantial costs or violating the seniority rights of other employees.

To require TWA to bear more than a *de minimis* cost in order to give Hardison Saturdays off is an undue hardship.[15] Like abandonment of the seniority system, to require TWA to bear additional costs when no such costs are incurred to give other employees the days off that they want would involve unequal treatment of employees on the basis of their religion. By suggesting that TWA should incur certain costs in order to give Hardison Saturdays off the Court of Appeals would in effect require TWA to finance an additional Saturday off and then to choose the employee who will enjoy it on the basis of his religious beliefs. While incurring extra costs to secure a replacement for Hardison might remove the necessity of compelling another employee to work involuntarily in Hardison's place, it would not change the fact that the privilege of having Saturdays off would be allocated according to religious beliefs.

As we have seen, the paramount concern of Congress in enacting Title VII was the elimination of discrimination in employment. In the absence of clear statutory language or legislative history to the contrary, we will not readily construe the statute to require an employer to discriminate against some employees in order to enable others to observe their Sabbath.

Reversed.

MR. JUSTICE MARSHALL, with whom MR. JUSTICE BRENNAN joins, dissenting.

* * *

Today's decision deals a fatal blow to all efforts under Title VII to accommodate work requirements to religious practices. The Court holds, in essence, that although the EEOC regulations and the Act state that an employer must make reasonable adjustments in his work demands to take account of religious observances, the regulation and Act do not really mean what they say. An employer, the Court concludes, need not grant even the most minor special privilege to religious observers to enable them to follow their faith. As a question of social policy, this result is deeply troubling, for a society that truly values religious pluralism cannot compel adherents of minority religions to make the cruel choice of surrendering their religion or their job. And as a matter of law today's result is intolerable, for the Court adopts the very position that Congress expressly rejected in 1972, as if we were free to disregard congressional choices that a majority of this Court thinks unwise. I therefore dissent.

I

With respect to each of the proposed accommodations to respondent Hardison's religious observances that the Court discusses, it ultimately notes that the accommodation would have required "unequal treatment," in favor of the religious observer. That is quite true. But if an accommodation can be rejected simply because it involves preferential treatment, then the regulation and the statute, while brimming with "sound and fury," ultimately "signif[y] nothing."

---

[15]The dissent argues that "the costs to TWA of either paying overtime or not replacing respondent would [not] have been more than *de minimis*." This ignores, however, the express finding of the District Court that "[b]oth of these solutions would have created an undue burden on the conduct of TWA's business," and it fails to take account of the likelihood that a company as large as TWA may have many employees whose religious observances, like Hardison's, prohibit them from working on Saturdays or Sundays.

The accommodation issue by definition arises only when a neutral rule of general applicability conflicts with the religious practices of a particular employee. * * * What all * * * [the accommodation] cases have in common is an employee who could comply with the rule only by violating what the employee views as a religious commandment. In each instance, the question is whether the employee is to be exempt from the rule's demands. To do so will always result in a privilege being "allocated according to religious beliefs," unless the employer gratuitously decides to repeal the rule in toto. What the statute says, in plain words, is that such allocations are required unless "undue hardship" would result.

* * *

II

Once it is determined that the duty to accommodate sometimes requires that an employee be exempted from an otherwise valid work requirement, the only remaining question is whether this is such a case: Did TWA prove that it exhausted all reasonable accommodations, and that the only remaining alternatives would have caused undue hardship on TWA's business? To pose the question is to answer it, for all that the District Court found TWA had done to accommodate respondent's Sabbath observance was that it "held several meetings with [respondent] * * * [and] authorized the union steward to search for someone who would swap shifts." To conclude that TWA, one of the largest air carriers in the Nation, would have suffered undue hardship had it done anything more defies both reason and common sense.

The Court implicitly assumes that the only means of accommodation open to TWA were to compel an unwilling employee to replace Hardison; to pay premium wages to a voluntary substitute; or to employ one less person during respondent's Sabbath shift.[5] Based on this assumption, the Court seemingly finds that each alternative would have involved undue hardship not only because Hardison would have been given a special privilege, but also because either another employee would have been deprived of rights under the collective-bargaining agreement, or because "more than a *de minimis* cost," would have been imposed on TWA. But the Court's myopic view of the available options is not supported by either the District Court's findings or the evidence adduced at trial. Thus, the Court's conclusion cannot withstand analysis, even assuming that its rejection of the alternatives it does discuss is justifiable.[6]

---

[5]It is true that these are the only options the Court of Appeals discussed. But that court found that TWA could have adopted these options without undue hardship; once that conclusion is rejected it is incumbent on this Court to decide whether any other alternatives were available that would not have involved such hardship.

[6]I entertain grave doubts on both factual and legal grounds about the validity of the Court's rejection of the options it considers. As a matter of fact, I do not believe the record supports the Court's suggestion that the costs to TWA of either paying overtime or not replacing respondent would have been more than *de minimis*. While the District Court did state, as the Court notes, that both alternatives "would have created an undue burden on the conduct of TWA's business," the court did not explain its understanding of the phrase "undue burden," and may have believed that such a burden exists whenever any cost is incurred by the employer, no matter how slight. Thus the District Court's assertion falls far short of a factual "finding" that the costs of these accommodations would be more than *de minimis*. Moreover, the record is devoid of any

To begin with, the record simply does not support the Court's assertion, made without accompanying citations, that "[t]here were no volunteers to relieve Hardison on Saturdays." Everett Kussman, the manager of the department in which respondent worked, testified that he had made no effort to find volunteers, and the union stipulated that its steward had not done so either.[8] * * * Thus, respondent's religious observance might have been accommodated by a simple trade of days or shifts without necessarily depriving any employee of his or her contractual rights[10] and without imposing significant costs on TWA. Of course, it is also possible that no trade — or none consistent with the seniority system — could have been arranged. But the burden under the EEOC regulation is on TWA to establish that a reasonable accommodation was not possible. Because it failed either to explore the possibility of a voluntary trade or to assure that its delegate, the union steward, did so, TWA was unable to meet its burden.

---

evidence documenting the extent of the "efficiency loss" TWA would have incurred had it used a supervisor or an already scheduled employee to do respondent's work, and while the stipulations make clear what overtime would have cost, the price is far from staggering: $150 for three months, at which time respondent would have been eligible to transfer back to his previous department. The Court's suggestion that the cost of accommodation must be evaluated in light of the "likelihood that * * * TWA may have many employees whose religious observances * * * prohibit them from working on Saturdays or Sundays," is not only contrary to the record, which indicates that only one other case involving a conflict between work schedules and Sabbath observance had arisen at TWA since 1945, but also irrelevant, since the real question is not whether such employees exist but whether they could be accommodated without significant expense. Indeed, to the extent that TWA employed Sunday as well as Saturday Sabbatarians, the likelihood of accommodation being costly would diminish, since trades would be more feasible.

As a matter of law, I seriously question whether simple English usage permits "undue hardship" to be interpreted to mean "more than *de minimis* cost," especially when the examples the guidelines give of possible undue hardship is the absence of a qualified substitute. I therefore believe that in the appropriate case we would be compelled to confront the constitutionality of requiring employers to bear more than *de minimis* costs. The issue need not be faced here, however, since an almost cost-free accommodation was possible.

[8]The Court relies, on the District Court's conclusory assertion that "[a]ny shift or change was impossible within the seniority framework." But the District Court also found that "TWA did not take part in the search for employees willing to swap shifts * * * and it was admitted at trial that the Union made no real effort." Thus, the District Court's statement concerning the impact of "the seniority framework" lends no support to the Court's assertion that there were no volunteers. See also n. 10, *infra*.

[10]If, as appears likely, no one senior to the substitute employee desired respondent's Sabbath assignment or his Thursday–Monday shift, then the substitute could have transferred to respondent's position without depriving anyone of his or her seniority expectations. Similarly, if, as also appears probable, no one senior to respondent desired the substitute's spot, respondent could have assumed it. Such a trade would not have deprived any employee of seniority expectations. The trade apparently still would have violated the collective-bargaining agreement, however, since the agreement authorized transfers only to vacant jobs. This is undoubtedly what the District Court meant when it found that "the seniority framework" precluded shift changes. Indeed, the first time in the District Court's opinion that such a finding appears, it is preceded by the finding that "there were no jobs open for bid."

Even if a trade could not have been arranged without disrupting seniority expectations TWA could have requested the Union Relief Committee to approve an exemption. The record reveals that the Committee's function was to ameliorate the rigidity of the system, and that on at least one occasion it had approved a permanent transfer apparently outside the seniority system.

Nor was a voluntary trade the only option open to TWA that the Court ignores; to the contrary, at least two other options are apparent from the record. First, TWA could have paid overtime to a voluntary replacement for respondent — assuming that someone would have been willing to work Saturdays for premium pay — and passed on the cost to respondent. In fact, one accommodation Hardison suggested would have done just that by requiring Hardison to work overtime when needed at regular pay. Under this plan, the total overtime cost to the employer — and the total number of overtime hours available for other employees — would not have reflected Hardison's Sabbath absences. Alternatively, TWA could have transferred respondent back to his previous department where he had accumulated substantial seniority, as respondent also suggested.[11] Admittedly, both options would have violated the collective-bargaining agreement; the former because the agreement required that employees working over 40 hours per week receive premium pay, and the latter because the agreement prohibited employees from transferring departments more than once every six months. But neither accommodation would have deprived any other employee of rights under the contract or violated the seniority system in any way.[12] Plainly an employer cannot avoid his duty to accommodate by signing a contract that precludes all reasonable accommodations; even the Court appears to concede as much. Thus I do not believe it can be even seriously argued that TWA would have suffered "undue hardship" to its business had it required respondent to pay the extra costs of his replacement, or had it transferred respondent to his former department.

What makes today's decision most tragic, however, is not that respondent Hardison has been needlessly deprived of his livelihood simply because he chose to follow the dictates of his conscience. Nor is the tragedy exhausted by the impact it will have on thousands of Americans like Hardison who could be forced to live on welfare as the price they must pay for worshipping their God.[14] The ultimate tragedy is that despite Congress' best efforts, one of this Nation's pillars of strength — our hospitality to religious diversity — has been seriously eroded. All Americans will be a little poorer until today's decision is erased.

I respectfully dissent.

---

[11] The Court states, that because of TWA's departmental seniority system, such a transfer "would not have solved Hardison's problems." But respondent testified without contradiction that had he returned to his previous department he would have regained his seniority in that department, and thereby could have avoided work on his Sabbath. According to respondent, the only objection that was raised to this solution was that it violated the rule prohibiting transfers twice within six months.

[12] The accommodations would have disadvantaged respondent to some extent, but since he suggested both options I do not consider whether an employer would satisfy his duty to accommodate by offering these choices to an unwilling employee.

[14] Ironically, the fiscal costs to society of today's decision may exceed the costs that would accrue if employers were required to make all accommodations without regard to hardship, since it is clear that persons on welfare cannot be denied benefits because they refuse to take jobs that would prevent them from observing religious holy days.

NOTES AND PROBLEMS FOR DISCUSSION

1. Do you agree with dissenting Justice Marshall's contention that the majority in *Hardison* effectively nullified the statutory duty to accommodate through its interpretation of "undue hardship?" Can you conceive of an accommodation that would not impose an undue hardship under a literal reading of the Court's tripartite formulation of that term? If not, can the Court's restrictive interpretation of §701(j) perhaps be explained as a method of avoiding the constitutional issue that would arise when a defendant is ordered to make some accommodation?

2. The courts uniformly have adopted the following allocation of the burden of proof in religious discrimination cases:

> "In order to establish a prima facie case of religious discrimination under [§§703(a) and 701(j)], a plaintiff must plead and prove that (1) he had a bona fide belief that compliance with an employment requirement is contrary to his religious faith; (2) he informed his employer about the conflict; and (3) he was discharged because of his refusal to comply with the employment requirement."

Brown v. General Motors Corp., 601 F.2d 956, 959 (8th Cir.1979).

With respect to the second element of the plaintiff's prima facie case, must the plaintiff affirmatively inform the employer of a religious mandate that requires an accommodation or is it sufficient if the employer has indirect notice of the need for an accommodation? In EEOC v. ABERCROMBIE & FITCH STORES, INC., 575 U.S. ___, 135 S.Ct. 2028, 192 L.Ed.2d 35 (2015), the EEOC filed suit under Title VII on behalf of a Muslim woman, Ms. Elauf, who had been denied employment by the defendant because the headscarf that she wore in compliance with her religion's requirements conflicted with the company's "Look Policy". This policy prohibited employees from wearing "caps" (a term undefined by the policy) as not in compliance with Abercrombie's desired image. Elauf was wearing a headscarf during her job interview. The interviewer gave her a qualified rating, but informed her supervisor that Elauf had worn a headscarf. The interviewer consulted with the district manager and told the district manager that she believed that Elauf wore the headscarf because of her faith. Nevertheless, the interviewer was directed by the district manager not to hire Elauf. The Tenth Circuit reversed the trial court's grant of summary judgment to the EEOC and directed the trial court to enter summary judgment in favor of the company. The circuit panel concluded that an employer cannot be liable for failure to accommodate an applicant's religious practices unless the applicant provides the company with *actual* knowledge of the need for an accommodation.

The Supreme Court, by a vote of 7-1-1, reversed and remanded, ruling that an applicant asserting a claim of religious discrimination under Title VII only needs to establish that the need for an accommodation was a motivating factor in the employer's decision not to hire her. The Court explained that the only issue in the case was one of causation. Since the definition of proscribed religious discrimination includes a failure to make a reasonable accommodation short of an undue hardship, the Court reasoned, failing to hire an individual "because of" her religious practice is synonymous with refusing to accommodate that person's religious practice. And per §703(m)'s mixed motive provision, it was sufficient to establish that the need for accommodation was *a* motivating factor, rather than the but for cause of the decision. The majority also noted that unlike the ADA, which imposes a duty to accommodate only to "the known physical or mental limitations" of an applicant, §703(a)(1) contains no scienter requirement. Finally, the court distinguished between the relevance of knowledge and motive in any Title VII intentional discrimination claim. The essence of any intentional (as opposed to impact) discrimination claim, the Court stated, is the allegation that the employer took an action to avoid the duty to accommodate. The mere fact that the employer *knew* of the applicant's need for an accommodation would not suffice where the plaintiff could not establish that the adverse action was *motivated* by the desire to avoid accommodation. But, conversely, if the employer acts for the purpose of avoiding an accommodation, the Court held, it can violate Title VII even if it has only an unsubstantiated suspicion that an accommodation would be needed. Accordingly, as long as the plaintiff can prove that his or her religious practice was factored into the decision-making process, the plaintiff can establish a prima facie case.

Once the plaintiff has established a prima facie case,

> "[t]he burden [is] thereafter upon [the defendants] to prove that they made good faith efforts to accommodate [the plaintiff's] religious beliefs and, if these efforts were unsuccessful, to demonstrate that they were unable reasonably to accommodate his beliefs without undue hardship."

Anderson v. General Dynamics Convair Aerospace Div., 589 F.2d 397, 401 (9th Cir.1978).

The third element of the prima facie case typically is restated to require that the plaintiff establish that he or she was discharged or otherwise disciplined for failing to comply with the conflicting employment requirement. If an employer who previously voluntarily accommodated the employee's religious practices terminates that accommodation, has the plaintiff established the third element of the prima facie showing of a religious accommodation claim? *See* Tepper v. Potter, 505 F.3d 508 (6th Cir. 2007) (termination of work assignment accommodation that permitted the plaintiff not to work on the Sabbath or on Jewish holidays does not constitute a discharge or discipline and so the plaintiff has not established this element of a religious accommodation claim).

3. (a) Does the employee's conduct have to be *required* by her religious beliefs, or is it enough to establish either that the conduct is permitted or motivated by religious belief, or that the employee sincerely, though erroneously, believes it to be a religious obligation? In FRAZEE v. ILLINOIS DEPARTMENT OF EMPLOYMENT SECURITY, 489 U.S. 829, 109 S.Ct. 1514, 103 L.Ed.2d 914 (1989), the Supreme Court held that an individual's sincerely held religious belief was protected by the free exercise clause of the First Amendment even though the plaintiff did not claim to be a member of any particular religious sect or church. The Court also noted that the belief would have been protected even if it had not been a clear commandment of a religious sect, as long as the plaintiff had a sincere belief that his religion required him to take or not take particular action, such as, in this case, working on Sunday. The EEOC final Guidelines on Discrimination Because of Religion, issued in October 1980, provide: that "the fact that no religious group espouses such beliefs or the fact that the religious group to which the individual professes to belong may not accept such belief will not determine whether the belief is a religious belief of the employee or prospective employee." 29 C.F.R. §1605.1.

(b) On occasion, the courts are faced with the thorny problem of determining whether or not the plaintiff's alleged religious belief is sufficiently "bona fide" to fit within the statutory definition. For example, suppose an employer has a strict policy precluding workers from taking paid or unpaid leave during its peak selling period. Further assume that in the middle of this sales period, an employee informed her supervisor that she received "a call from God" telling her to make a religious pilgrimage to her religion's holiest site. The employee has requested a grant of vacation time during the first week of December, which the employer refused, even after the employee explained that she was compelled by her religion to make this trip. When the supervisor denied the request, the employee disregarded this decision and went on the trip. Upon her return, she learned that she had been discharged for violation of the company's leave policy. Can she state a claim of religious discrimination based on the defendant's alleged failure to reasonably accommodate her religious beliefs? *See* Tiano v. Dillard Department Stores, Inc., 139 F.3d 679 (9th Cir.1998) (a devout Catholic who was denied a vacation request to make a ten day pilgrimage to Medjugorje did not establish a prima facie case of religious discrimination because she failed to prove that she had a bona fide religious belief to make the pilgrimage at that particular time. While she had a bona fide religious belief that she needed to go on a pilgrimage to that site, there was insufficient evidence upon which to conclude that her belief included a temporal mandate.)

4. Does the §702 exemption accorded religious institutions from the general ban on religious discrimination mean that these institutions also are not subject to the §701(j) duty to accommodate? See Larsen v. Kirkham, 499 F.Supp. 960 (D. Utah 1980), affirmed without opinion, 35 FEP 1799 (10th Cir.1982), cert. denied, 464 U.S. 849, 104 S.Ct. 157, 78 L.Ed.2d 144 (1983).

5. If the employee and the company each propose a reasonable accommodation, does Title VII require the employer to accept the employee's proposal where it does not impose an undue hardship? In ANSONIA BOARD OF EDUCATION v. PHILBROOK, 479 U.S. 60, 107 S.Ct. 367, 93 L.Ed.2d 305 (1986), the Supreme Court ruled that §701(j) only requires the employer to make *a* reasonable accommodation, not the most reasonable accommodation or the employee's preferred or desired accommodation. *Any* reasonable accommodation satisfies the statutory obligation; the employer does not have to show that the employee's proposed accommodation(s) would result in an undue hardship. Justice Marshall, concurring and dissenting in part, suggested that an employer should not be required to adopt the employee's proposed accommodation only when its proposal fully resolved the conflict between the worker's employment and religious obligations. Since this employee was required to accept a loss of compensation in order to honor his religious obligations, Marshall concluded that the employer's accommodation did not fully resolve the conflict and, therefore, that the company was obliged to consider the employee's reasonable proposals. Does the Court's ruling in *Ansonia* that any accommodation that eliminates the religious conflict entirely is reasonable as a matter of law mean that any accommodation that does *not* eliminate the religious conflict entirely is unreasonable as a matter of law? *See* Sturgill v. United Parcel Service, Inc., 512 F.3d 1024 (8th Cir. 2008) (district court erred in instructing the jury that a reasonable accommodation must eliminate the religious conflict entirely; there may be situations where a partial elimination of the conflict is a reasonable accommodation and this is a fact-intensive assessment that is to be made by the jury in light of, *inter alia*, the strength and nature of the employee's religious conviction, the terms of an applicable collective bargaining agreement, and the contractual rights and workplace attitudes of co-workers).

6. (a) Does the statute mandate that the employer make at least some attempt to accommodate? *Compare* United States v. City of Albuquerque, 545 F.2d 110, 113 (10th Cir.1976), cert. denied, 433 U.S. 909, 97 S.Ct. 2974, 53 L.Ed.2d 1092 (1977) (an employer must first show some attempt at accommodation and then establish that additional accommodation would impose an undue hardship) *with* United States v. Board of Educ. for School Dist. of Philadelphia, 911 F.2d 882 (3d Cir.1990) (an employer can claim undue hardship without showing any effort to accommodate where it can present evidence, beyond relying on mere speculation, that any reasonable accommodation would impose an undue hardship).

(b) Is the "undue hardship" standard met when the only possible accommodation would require the employer to violate state law? In UNITED STATES v. BOARD OF EDUC. FOR THE SCHOOL DIST. OF PHILADELPHIA, 911 F.2d 882 (3d Cir.1990), a devout Muslim schoolteacher's religiously held conviction required that she cover her entire body except for her face and hands. As a result, she wore a head scarf while teaching in order to cover her head and neck. When she reported to duty as a substitute teacher at another school, the principal informed her that, pursuant to state law, she could not teach in her religious clothing because a state statute prohibited a teacher in any public school from wearing any dress or insignia indicating the fact that such teacher is a member or adherent of any religious order or denomination. The statute added that any public school director who failed to comply with its provisions was subject to criminal sanction. The teacher was given a chance to go home and change; she refused to do so and was not allowed to teach. The school conceded that it had not proffered any accommodation, but claimed that the accommodation sought by the teacher could not be accomplished without undue hardship. The court stated that whatever the precise meaning of "undue hardship" in terms of non-economic burdens, forcing the school district to sacrifice the compelling state interest codified in the state statute would clearly constitute an undue hardship. Similarly, the appellate courts uniformly have held that Title VII does not require an employer to make an accommodation to an employee's religious beliefs that would require it to violate federal law. *See* Yeager v. FirstEnergy Generation Corporation, 777 F.3d 362 (6th Cir, 2015).

Is it sufficient to say that, as a public entity, this school district shared in the state interest underlying the statute? On the other hand, would it be reasonable to require the school to violate a law whose constitutionality has been upheld? With reference to this last issue, the Third Circuit did state that exposing the Board and its administrators to a substantial risk of criminal prosecution, fines, and other penalties would have imposed an undue hardship on the School Board. The court reasoned that if violating the seniority provision of a collective bargaining agreement is an undue hardship, so is requiring a school board to violate an apparently valid criminal statute. Furthermore, the court added, since the statute was designed to prevent the appearance of sectarianism in the administration of public schools, this state law was not inconsistent with the objectives of, and therefore not in violation of the terms of Title VII.

The Supreme Court consistently has held that the Eleventh Amendment right to sovereign immunity does not protect states from suit filed by the federal government in federal court. Suppose, however, that the action against the Philadelphia Board of Education had been brought directly by the schoolteacher rather than by the federal government. Assuming that the school board could be deemed a unit of state government and, therefore, as the State of Pennsylvania, could the defendant successfully assert an Eleventh Amendment claim of sovereign immunity from suit in federal court or does §701(j) represent a constitutionally permissible abrogation by Congress of the states sovereign immunity from suit in federal court? Applying the two-part "congruence and proportionality" standard articulated by the Supreme Court in cases involving federal statutory provisions prohibiting age, disability, and sex discrimination (see Chapter 10, §A, *infra*), the court in ENDRES v. INDIANA STATE POLICE, 334 F.3d 618 (7th Cir.2003) held that §701(j) was not enacted pursuant to Congress' authority under §5 of the Fourteenth Amendment, and, therefore, did not constitutionally abrogate the state's right to sovereign immunity from suit in federal court. While the court concluded that limits built into §701(j) satisfied the proportionality element of the constitutional standard, the absence of any legislative record or other extrinsic evidence of a pattern of prior state employment practices that discriminated on the basis of religion failed the congruence requirement. Accordingly, it ruled that suits by state employees seeking accommodation under §701(j) were relegated to state court.

7. (a) Has the employer met its accommodation obligation by permitting a Sabbatarian employee to locate a co-worker who would voluntarily swap shifts with her when her religious beliefs not only preclude working on the Sabbath day but forbid her from asking anyone to work in her place? Has the employer satisfied its accommodation obligation by consenting to shift swaps arranged by the employee whose religious beliefs preclude him from working on the Sabbath? *See* Smith v. Pyro Mining Co., 827 F.2d 1081 (6th Cir.1987).

(b) If it is a reasonable accommodation for the employer to attempt to find a voluntary swap for the plaintiff, but the employer can't find a volunteer, does the statute also require the company to force a reluctant employee to swap shifts with the plaintiff? *See* Eversley v. MBank Dallas, 843 F.2d 172 (5th Cir.1988).

8. Wessjak Manufacturing Company, a corporation owned by Mark Wessman and Julie Jackson, produces plastic doughnuts. As part of their religious commitment, Wessman and Jackson include a Gospel tract in every box of plastic doughnuts and require all employees to attend weekly devotional services that are held during working hours. Michael Collins, a baker and avowed atheist, was discharged after announcing that he would not attend the services.

(a) Can Collins state a claim of religious discrimination? *Compare* Reed v. Great Lakes Companies, Inc., 330 F.3d 931 (7th Cir.2003) (hotel employee who was fired for leaving meeting with Gideon representatives when they began to pray after delivering free Bibles did not establish a prima facie case of religious discrimination because there was no indication that he was fired because of his religious beliefs, identity or observance or aversion to religion since there was no evidence that the employer knew of the plaintiff's religious affiliations or lack thereof) *with* Noyes v. Kelly Services, 488 F.3d 1163 (9th Cir. 2007) (fact that the plaintiff does not share the employer's religious beliefs is sufficient to state prima facie claim of "reverse religious discrimination" even when the plaintiff does not claim that she adheres to a particular religion or set of beliefs).

(b) If so, can the company assert either that to accommodate Collins' atheistic beliefs would impose a spiritual cost on it that would constitute an undue hardship, or that it is covered by the §702 exemption for religious corporations? *See* Reed v. Great Lakes Companies, Inc., 330 F.3d 931 (7th Cir.2003) (right to accommodation does not extend to unqualified right to disobey orders that worker deems inconsistent with his religious beliefs; employee has not given fair warning to his employer of the need for accommodation when he refuses to indicate which specific job duties interfere with his religious or which duties he wants waived or adjusted); EEOC v. Townley Engineering & Mfg. Co., 859 F.2d 610 (9th Cir.1988), cert. denied, 489 U.S. 1077, 109 S.Ct. 1527, 103 L.Ed.2d 832 (1989). For a discussion of the right of secular employees of religiously oriented employers, see Thomas D. Brierton, *An Unjustified Hostility Toward Religion in the Workplace*, 34 CATH.LAW. 289 (1991); Steven D. Jamar, *Accommodating Religion at Work: A Principled Approach to Title VII and Religious Freedom*, 40 N.Y.L.SCH.L.REV. 719 (1996); and Laura S. Underkuffler, *Discrimination on the Basis of Religion: An Examination of Attempted Value Neutrality in Employment*, 30 WM. & MARY L. REV. 581 (1989).

9. A police officer is assigned the job of providing security at a state-licensed gambling casino. The officer's sincerely held religious beliefs forbid him from gambling or from helping others to do so. When he asked for a different assignment, the request was denied. He then refused to report for duty and was discharged for insubordination. Has the police department violated §701(j)? See Endres v. Indiana State Police, 349 F.3d 922 (7th Cir.2003) (requesting a paramilitary law enforcement agency to accommodate the varying religiously-based demands of a heterogeneous police force, even if without undue hardship, would be per se unreasonable; police officers are expected to enforce all laws without regard to their own religious beliefs).

10. An employee complains to her supervisor that the co-employee working in the adjacent cubicle posts religious sayings in that cubicle which disturbs and distracts her. Can she state a claim of religious harassment under Title VII? In POWELL v. YELLOW BOOK USA, 445 F.3d 1074 (8th Cir.2006), the court granted summary judgment to the defendant on the ground that "an employer has no legal obligation to suppress any and all religious expression merely because it annoys a single employee." The plaintiff's religious harassment claim failed, the court explained, because it did not constitute severe or pervasive harassment that altered the plaintiff's terms or conditions of employment.

Tooley v. Martin-Marietta Corp.

United States Court of Appeals, Ninth Circuit, 1981.
648 F.2d 1239, cert. denied, 454 U.S. 1098, 102 S.Ct. 671, 70 L.Ed.2d 639.

FARRIS, Circuit Judge.

* * *

In 1976, the Martin–Marietta Corporation and Steelworkers Local 8141 executed a collective bargaining agreement containing a "union shop" clause, under which the company was obligated to discharge all employees who failed to join the union. Plaintiffs Tooley, Bakke, and Helt are Seventh Day Adventists who, under the tenets of their faith, are prohibited from becoming members in or paying a service fee to a union. Plaintiffs informed the company and the union of this proscription, and offered to pay an amount equal to union dues to a mutually acceptable charity. The union refused.

After exhausting their administrative remedies, plaintiffs instituted this action, alleging that the union's and the company's refusal to honor the requested accommodation constituted religious discrimination under Title VII of the Civil Rights Act of 1964. In particular, the plaintiffs argued that both the union and the company were required under section 701(j) of the Act to make good faith efforts to institute their requested exemption unless it would result in undue hardship to either the Steelworkers or the company. The Steelworkers contended that the "substituted charity" accommodation was unreasonable, that its implementation would cause the union undue hardship, and that by authorizing such an accommodation, section 701(j) violated the Establishment Clause. The district court enjoined the union and the company from attempting to discharge the plaintiffs for failing to pay union dues so long as they make equivalent contributions to a mutually acceptable charity.

[The appellate court upheld as not clearly erroneous the trial judge's findings that the plaintiff's proposed accommodation was reasonable and did not impose an undue hardship upon the defendants. Consequently, the court was then obliged to consider the constitutional question left unanswered by the Supreme Court in *Hardison*.]

* * *

III. THE CONSTITUTIONALITY OF SECTION 701(j) OF TITLE VII

The Steelworkers argue that section 701(j) as applied here violates the Establishment Clause.[8] The district court held that section 701(j) withstood constitutional attack under the three-pronged test enunciated in Committee for Public Education & Religious Liberty v. Nyquist, 413 U.S. 756, 93 S.Ct. 2955, 39 L.Ed.2d 948 (1973).

The Establishment Clause ensures government neutrality in matters of religion. But government neutrality "is not so narrow a channel that the slightest deviation from an absolutely straight course leads to condemnation." Sherbert v. Verner, 374 U.S. 398, 422, 83 S.Ct. 1790, 1803, 10 L.Ed.2d 965 (1963) (Harlan, J., dissenting). Courts have defined the government's obligation as one of "benevolent neutrality." Walz v. Tax Commission, 397 U.S. 664, 669, 90 S.Ct. 1409, 1411, 25 L.Ed.2d 697 (1970). While the government must avoid "partiality to any one group," Zorach v. Clauson, 343 U.S. 306, 313, 72 S.Ct. 679, 683, 96 L.Ed. 954 (1952), it may deviate from

---

[8]The plaintiffs contend that the constitutional validity of §701(j) as applied here has been determined conclusively by the Supreme Court's dismissal of the appeal in Rankins v. Comm'n on Professional Competence, 24 Cal.3d 167, 593 P.2d 852, 154 Cal.Rptr. 907, appeal dismissed, 444 U.S. 986, 100 S.Ct. 515, 62 L.Ed.2d 416 (1979). There, the California state constitutional employment discrimination provision, construed to require the same accommodations as those required by Title VII's §701(j), was held not to offend the Establishment Clause in requiring a school district to accommodate a teacher who refused to work on religious holidays. The dismissal of the appeal in *Rankins* binds this court only on the precise issues presented and necessarily decided. Because this case and *Rankins* involve entirely different kinds of religious accommodations, the constitutional dimension of each is necessarily different.

absolute rigidity to accommodate the religious practices of each group.

Government can accommodate the beliefs and practices of members of minority religions without contravening the prohibitions of the Establishment Clause. Cf. Wisconsin v. Yoder, 406 U.S. 205, 92 S.Ct. 1526, 32 L.Ed.2d 15 (1972) (exempting Amish children from state compulsory education laws); Sherbert v. Verner, 374 U.S. 398, 83 S.Ct. 1790, 10 L.Ed.2d 965 (1963) (exempting Seventh–Day Adventists from state unemployment compensation requirements). Government may legitimately enforce accommodations of religious beliefs when the accommodation reflects the "obligation of neutrality in the face of religious differences," and does not constitute "sponsorship, financial support, [or] active involvement of the sovereign in religious activities" with which the Establishment Clause is mainly concerned.

Like the accommodations allowed in Sherbert v. Verner and Wisconsin v. Yoder, the substituted charity accommodation satisfies these requirements. By exempting the plaintiffs from union membership or the payment of mandatory union dues, the accommodation places the plaintiffs on an equal footing with other employees whose religious convictions find no impediment in the workplace. To this extent, the accommodation reflects governmental neutrality in the face of religious differences. Further, the substituted charity accommodation does not involve government "sponsorship" or "financial support" of the Seventh–Day Adventist religion: the accommodation requires that the plaintiffs suffer the same economic loss as their co-workers who are not similarly restricted in paying union dues or in obtaining union membership. The accommodation demands neither direct nor indirect financial support of the plaintiffs' religion by the government, and cannot be reasonably construed as actively advancing or assisting their religion.

This same conclusion is compelled under the test enunciated in Committee for Public Education & Religious Liberty v. Nyquist. The Nyquist test, typically applied to state legislation, requires that for section 701(j) to be consistent with the demands of the Establishment Clause, it must (1) reflect a clearly secular purpose, (2) have a primary effect that neither inhibits nor advances religion, and (3) avoid excessive government entanglement with religion.

1. Legislative Purpose

The primary motivation for the enactment of section 701(j) was to resolve many of the issues left open by prior "Sabbatarian" cases, where employees refused to work on their Sabbath and requested that their employers accommodate them. Hardison. The Steelworkers contend that because section 701(j) was intended to secure special treatment for Sabbatarians and other religious proponents, the legislation has an improper sectarian purpose.

Although section 701(j)'s enactment may have resolved certain problems confronting sectarians, this alone is insufficient to establish that the legislation lacks a clearly secular purpose. Section 701(j) was intended to promote Title VII's broader policy of prohibiting discrimination in employment. The bill's sponsor in the Senate, recognizing the problems confronting Sabbatarians in particular, stated that the legislation was intended to "assure that freedom from religious discrimination in the employment of workers is for all time guaranteed in law." Section 701(j) functions to "secure equal economic opportunity to members of minority religions." It therefore has a legitimate secular purpose.

2. Primary Effect

The Steelworkers contend that the substituted charity accommodation has the primary effect of advancing the plaintiffs' religion by conferring various alleged economic benefits. It is argued that as a consequence of the accommodation, the plaintiffs have a greater choice than their co-workers in determining how their money is spent, and are more easily able to make charitable contributions.

We reject this argument. It confuses ancillary or incidental benefits with primary benefits to those accommodated. It could be argued, for example, that the exemption allowed the Amish children in Wisconsin v. Yoder permitted the children to contribute additional economic benefit to their families, and that the exemption allowed in Sherbert v. Verner permitted the Seventh–Day Adventist to exercise a greater choice in determining which day of the week was to be free of employment responsibilities.

The substituted charity accommodation allows the plaintiffs to work without violating their religious beliefs, at a cost equivalent to that paid by their co-workers without similar beliefs. It neither increases nor decreases the advantages of membership in the Seventh–Day Adventist faith in a manner so substantial and direct that it "advances" or "inhibits" the plaintiffs' religion.

The Steelworkers also contend that the accommodation violates the Establishment Clause because it will ultimately result in either the union curtailing necessary services, or forcing the accommodation cost on other employees. In either case, the Steelworkers argue that the plaintiffs receive the benefit of their religious beliefs at the expense of their co-workers. As a result, it is urged that the accommodation impermissibly places the burdens of accommodation on unaccommodated private parties.

A religious accommodation does not violate the Establishment Clause merely because it can be construed in some abstract way as placing an inappreciable but inevitable burden on those not accommodated. Exemption of conscientious objectors from military conscription has been upheld despite the effect of requiring nonobjectors to serve in their stead. Sectarian institutions are exempt from the payment of property taxes, even though the effect may be to increase marginally the property taxes paid by unaccommodated private citizens. Sunday closing laws have been upheld even though their effect may be to burden those who sincerely observe another Sabbath.

The substituted charity does not have a primary effect which either advances or inhibits the plaintiffs' religion.

3. Government Entanglement

Nor do we find that the accommodation here requires that the government become impermissibly entangled with the accommodation's administration. The Establishment Clause prohibits only excessive government entanglement. The implementation of the substituted charity accommodation requires a minimal amount of supervision and administrative cost. Once the sincerity of a religious objector's belief is established, the only administrative burden involves the employee and the union agreeing on a mutually acceptable charity. The Steelworkers have not demonstrated that the burden of administering this accommodation involves sufficiently significant amounts of time or money or that the government involvement is sufficiently "comprehensive, discriminating, and continuing" to draw into question the validity of the accommodation.

Affirmed.

NOTES AND PROBLEMS FOR DISCUSSION

1. This edited version of *Tooley* does not include that portion of the court's opinion dealing with the statutory objection to discharges undertaken pursuant to union security clauses. Typically, as in the principal case, the employee is willing to contribute an amount equal to the union dues to a non-sectarian, non-union charity chosen by the union and the employer.

(a) Does the union have a §701(j) duty to accommodate the employee's religious beliefs? Several federal circuit courts have concluded that the presence of the word "employer" in §701(j) notwithstanding, unions are under a statutory duty to accommodate. *See, e.g.*, Nottelson v. Smith Steel Workers, 643 F.2d 445 (7th Cir.), cert. denied, 454 U.S. 1046, 102 S.Ct. 587, 70 L.Ed.2d 488 (1981).

(b) Would requiring the Union to make this suggested accommodation impose an undue hardship upon either it or the employer? In nearly all cases, the courts have held that neither the loss of an employee's union dues nor the grumblings of other employees not offered such a choice constituted undue hardship to the union or employer as a matter of law. While the courts recognize that the loss of dues generated by a large number of requests for substitute payments could result in undue hardship as a matter of fact, they also have concluded that undue hardship can be established only by offering evidence of actual, as opposed to anticipated multiple requests for substitute payments. Accordingly, the union's and employer's blanket refusal to permit substitute payments and their failure to prove that this accommodation would result in undue hardship as a matter of fact, typically result in judgment for the plaintiff.

(c) How do the rulings discussed in "(a)" and "(b)"comport with *Hardison*? For example, do they require the union to bear more than a *de minimis* cost? Alternatively, if the accommodations required in these cases compel both the union and employer to violate the contractual union security clause is this permissible under *Hardison*? Finally, can't it also be said that the unionized worker in *Tooley* was accorded differential treatment because of his religion in violation of *Hardison*?

2. (a) The constitutionality of §701(j) under the First Amendment has been upheld by every circuit court that has considered the question. But consider the concerns raised by dissenting Judge Celebrezze in CUMMINS v. PARKER SEAL CO., 516 F.2d 544 (6th Cir.1975):

* * *

* * * Section 701(j) defines religion so as to require that persons receive preferential treatment because of their religion. This contradicts the secular purpose behind the original Title VII. Rather than "putting teeth" into the Act, it mandates religious discrimination, thus departing from the Act's basic purpose.

* * *

The absence of a religious accommodation rule * * * would not amount to punishment. It would simply be a "hands-off" attitude on government's part, allowing employers and employees to settle their own differences. The rule grants benefits to religious practitioners because of their religion. The * * * rationale the majority advances, therefore, amounts to an assertion that it is a valid secular purpose to grant preferences to persons whose religious practices do not fit prevailing patterns. * * *

It is, of course, fundamental that the First Amendment protects the free exercise of all religions, whatever the number of their practitioners. * * * Thus, Government may not penalize persons on the basis of their religion.

* * *

The fact that Government may not penalize particular religions does not mean that Congress may favor particular religions. On the contrary, it means that Congress may not. The argument that aid to religious institutions is justified under a broad reading of the Free Exercise Clause has been raised on behalf of aid to parochial schools and other benefits to religious groups. The argument has appeared in dissenting opinions, and Supreme Court majorities have consistently rejected it. * * * T he Free Exercise Clause provides a shield against government interference with religion, but it does not offer a sword to cut through the strictures of the Establishment Clause. * * * There is no valid secular legislative purpose behind the rule. Its purpose is to protect and advance particular religions.

* * *

Not only does the religious accommodation rule lack a secular purpose. It lacks "a primary effect that neither advances nor inhibits religion." It is, in other words, neither "even-handed in operation" nor "neutral in primary impact." The religious accommodation rule violates these principles in two respects.

First, the religious accommodation requirement discriminates between religion and non-religion. Only those with "religious practices" may benefit from the rule. Others are forced to submit to uniform work rules and to bear the burdens imposed by their employers' accommodation to religious practitioners. Thus, the rule discriminates against those with no religion, although the freedom not to believe is within the First Amendment's protection.

Second, it discriminates among religions. Only those which require their followers to manifest their belief in acts requiring modification of an employer's work rules benefit, while other employees are inconvenienced by the employer's accommodation. By singling out particular sects for government protection, the Federal Government has forfeited the pretense that the rule is merely part of the general ban on religious discrimination. * * *

* * *

Because the religious accommodation rule violates the First Amendment under the first two tests of *Nyquist*, it is unnecessary to consider whether it also fosters "excessive entanglement" of Church and State. It is fair to note, however, that the 1972 amendment is worded far more broadly than Regulation 1605.1. The 1972 amendment extends to "all aspects of religious observance and practice, as well as belief." * * * Disposition of complaints under the amendment will require inquiry into the sincerity with which beliefs are held and force consideration of the validity of the religious nature of claims, procedures which are not favored and may themselves be improper because they put courts in review of religious matters.

* * *

Is Judge Celebrezze correct in suggesting that §701(j) creates a conflict between the Free Exercise and Establishment Clauses of the First Amendment? *See* Anderson v. General Dynamics Convair Aerospace Div., 489 F.Supp. 782, 790 (S.D.Cal.1980), reversed on other grounds, 648 F.2d 1247 (9th Cir.1981).

(b) Although the Supreme Court has not ruled definitively on the constitutionality of §701(j), in ESTATE OF THORNTON v. CALDOR, INC., 472 U.S. 703, 105 S.Ct. 2914, 86 L.Ed.2d 557 (1985), it held that a Connecticut statute that prohibited an employer from requiring an employee to work on the day of the week observed as his or her Sabbath and that provided that refusal to work on the Sabbath could not constitute grounds for dismissal, violated the Establishment Clause of the First Amendment. By providing Sabbath observers with the unqualified right not to work on whatever day they designated as their Sabbath, regardless of the burden or inconvenience imposed thereby on the employer or other workers, the statute was held to have the primary effect of impermissibly advancing a particular religious practice. In a concurring opinion, Justice O'Connor stated that the Connecticut statute unconstitutionally conveyed a message of endorsement of the Sabbath observance by granting, only to Sabbath observers, the benefit of selecting the day of the week in which to refrain from labor. She added that she did not read the majority's opinion as suggesting that §701(j) was similarly invalid since that provision promoted the valid secular purpose of assuring equal employment opportunity and required reasonable rather than absolute accommodation. She also distinguished §701(j) from the Connecticut statute on the ground that the former extended protection to all religious observance while the latter mandated accommodation only to Sabbath observance. Several circuit courts, relying, in part, on Justice O'Connor's reasoning, have concluded that *Tooley* survives *Caldor*. *See, e.g.*, International Ass'n of Machinists & Aerospace Workers, Lodge 751 v. Boeing Co., 833 F.2d 165 (9th Cir.1987); Protos v. Volkswagen of America, Inc., 797 F.2d 129 (3d Cir.1986), cert. denied, 479 U.S. 972, 107 S.Ct. 474, 93 L.Ed.2d 418 (1986).

SECTION B. NATIONAL ORIGIN

Espinoza v. Farah Manufacturing Co.

Supreme Court of the United States, 1973.
414 U.S. 86, 94 S.Ct. 334, 38 L.Ed.2d 287.

MR. JUSTICE MARSHALL delivered the opinion of the Court.

This case involves interpretation of the phrase "national origin" in Tit. VII of the Civil Rights Act of 1964. Petitioner Cecilia Espinoza is a lawfully admitted resident alien who was born in and remains a citizen of Mexico. She resides in San Antonio, Texas, with her husband, Rudolfo Espinoza, a United States citizen. In July 1969, Mrs. Espinoza sought employment as a seamstress at the San Antonio division of respondent Farah Manufacturing Co. Her employment application was rejected on the basis of a longstanding company policy against the employment of aliens. After exhausting their administrative remedies with the Equal Employment Opportunity Commission, petitioners commenced this suit in the District Court alleging that respondent had discriminated against Mrs. Espinoza because of her "national origin" in violation of §703 of Tit. VII. The District Court granted petitioners' motion for summary judgment, holding that a refusal to hire because of lack of citizenship constitutes discrimination on the basis of "national origin." The Court of Appeals reversed, concluding that the statutory phrase "national origin" did not embrace citizenship. We granted the writ to resolve this question of statutory construction and now affirm.

* * * Certainly the plain language of the statute supports the result reached by the Court of Appeals. The term "national origin" on its face refers to the country where a person was born, or, more broadly, the country from which his or her ancestors came.

The statute's legislative history, though quite meager in this respect, fully supports this construction. The only direct definition given the phrase "national origin" is the following remark made on the floor of the House of Representatives by Congressman Roosevelt, Chairman of the House Subcommittee which reported the bill: "It means the country from which you or your forebears came. * * * You may come from Poland, Czechoslovakia, England, France, or any other country." 110 Cong. Rec. 2549 (1964). We also note that an earlier version of §703 had referred to discrimination because of "race, color, religion, national origin, or ancestry." The deletion of the word "ancestry" from the final version was not intended as a material change, see H.R.Rep.No. 914, 88th Cong., 1st Sess., 87 (1963), suggesting that the terms "national origin" and "ancestry" were considered synonymous.

There are other compelling reasons to believe that Congress did not intend the term "national origin" to embrace citizenship requirements. Since 1914, the Federal Government itself, through Civil Service Commission regulations, has engaged in what amounts to discrimination against aliens by denying them the right to enter competitive examination for federal employment. But it has never been suggested that the citizenship requirement for federal employment constitutes discrimination because of national origin, even though since 1943, various Executive Orders have expressly prohibited discrimination on the basis of national origin in Federal Government employment.

Moreover, §701(b) of Tit. VII, in language closely paralleling §703, makes it "the policy of the United States to insure equal employment opportunities for Federal employees without discrimination because of * * * national origin * * *." The legislative history of that section reveals no mention of any intent on Congress' part to reverse the longstanding practice of requiring federal employees to be United States citizens. To the contrary, there is every indication that no such reversal was intended. Congress itself has on several occasions since 1964 enacted statutes barring aliens from federal employment. The Treasury, Postal Service, and General Government Appropriation Act, 1973, for example, provides that "no part of any appropriation contained in this or any other Act shall be used to pay the compensation of any officer or employee of the Government of the United States * * * unless such person (1) is a citizen of the United States * * *."[3]

---

[3]Petitioners argue that it is unreasonable to attribute any great significance to these provisions in determining congressional intent because the barrier to employment of noncitizens has been

To interpret the term "national origin" to embrace citizenship requirements would require us to conclude that Congress itself has repeatedly flouted its own declaration of policy. This Court cannot lightly find such a breach of faith. So far as federal employment is concerned, we think it plain that Congress has assumed that the ban on national-origin discrimination in §701(b) did not affect the historical practice of requiring citizenship as a condition of employment. And there is no reason to believe Congress intended the term "national origin" in §703 to have any broader scope.

Petitioners have suggested that the statutes and regulations discriminating against noncitizens in federal employment are unconstitutional under the Due Process Clause of the Fifth Amendment. We need not address that question here, for the issue presented in this case is not whether Congress has the power to discriminate against aliens in federal employment, but rather, whether Congress intended to prohibit such discrimination in private employment. Suffice it to say that we cannot conclude Congress would at once continue the practice of requiring citizenship as a condition of federal employment and, at the same time, prevent private employers from doing likewise. Interpreting §703 as petitioners suggest would achieve the rather bizarre result of preventing Farah from insisting on United States citizenship as a condition of employment while the very agency charged with enforcement of Tit. VII would itself be required by Congress to place such a condition on its own personnel.

The District Court drew primary support for its holding from an interpretative guideline issued by the Equal Employment Opportunity Commission which provides:

> "Because discrimination on the basis of citizenship has the effect of discriminating on the basis of national origin, a lawfully immigrated alien who is domiciled or residing in this country may not be discriminated against on the basis of his citizenship * * *." 29 CFR §1606.1(d) (1972).

Like the Court of Appeals, we have no occasion here to question the general validity of this guideline insofar as it can be read as an expression of the Commission's belief that there may be many situations where discrimination on the basis of citizenship would have the effect of discriminating on the basis of national origin. In some instances, for example, a citizenship requirement might be but one part of a wider scheme of unlawful national-origin discrimination. In other cases, an employer might use a citizenship test as a pretext to disguise what is in fact national-origin discrimination. Certainly Tit. VII prohibits discrimination on the basis of citizenship whenever it has the purpose or effect of discriminating on the basis of national origin. "The Act proscribes not only overt discrimination but also practices that are fair in form, but discriminatory in operation." Griggs.

It is equally clear, however, that these principles lend no support to petitioners in this case. There is no indication in the record that Farah's policy against employment of aliens had the purpose or effect of discriminating against persons of Mexican national origin.[5] It is conceded that Farah accepts employees of Mexican origin,

---

tucked away in appropriations bills rather than expressed in a more affirmative fashion. We disagree. Indeed, the fact that Congress has occasionally enacted exceptions to the general barrier indicates to us that Congress was well aware of what it was doing.

[5]There is no suggestion, for example, that the company refused to hire aliens of Mexican or Spanish-speaking background while hiring those of other national origins. * * * While the

provided the individual concerned has become an American citizen. Indeed, the District Court found that persons of Mexican ancestry make up more than 96% of the employees at the company's San Antonio division, and 97% of those doing the work for which Mrs. Espinoza applied. While statistics such as these do not automatically shield an employer from a charge of unlawful discrimination, the plain fact of the matter is that Farah does not discriminate against persons of Mexican national origin with respect to employment in the job Mrs. Espinoza sought. She was denied employment, not because of the country of her origin, but because she had not yet achieved United States citizenship. In fact, the record shows that the worker hired in place of Mrs. Espinoza was a citizen with a Spanish surname.

The Commission's guideline may have significance for a wide range of situations, but not for a case such as this where its very premise—that discrimination on the basis of citizenship has the effect of discrimination on the basis of national origin—is not borne out.[6] It is also significant to note that the Commission itself once held a different view as to the meaning of the phrase "national origin." When first confronted with the question, the Commission, through its General Counsel, said: "'National origin' refers to the country from which the individual or his forebears came * * *, not to whether or not he is a United States citizen * * *." EEOC General Counsel's Opinion Letter, 1 CCH Employment Prac. Guide ¶ 1220.20 (1967). The Commission's more recent interpretation of the statute in the guideline relied on by the District Court is no doubt entitled to great deference, but that deference must have limits where, as here, application of the guideline would be inconsistent with an obvious congressional intent not to reach the employment practice in question. Courts need not defer to an administrative construction of a statute where there are "compelling indications that it is wrong."

Finally, petitioners seek to draw support from the fact that Tit. VII protects all individuals from unlawful discrimination, whether or not they are citizens of the United States. We agree that aliens are protected from discrimination under the Act. That result may be derived not only from the use of the term "any individual" in §703, but also as a negative inference from the exemption in §702, which provides that Tit. VII "shall not apply to an employer with respect to the employment of aliens outside any State * * *." Title VII was clearly intended to apply with respect to the employment of aliens inside any State.

The question posed in the present case, however, is not whether aliens are protected from illegal discrimination under the Act, but what kinds of discrimination the Act makes illegal. Certainly it would be unlawful for an employer to discriminate against aliens because of race, color, religion, sex, or national origin—for example, by

---

company asks job applicants whether they are United States citizens, it makes no inquiry as to their national origin.

[6] It is suggested that a refusal to hire an alien always disadvantages that person because of the country of his birth. A person born in the United States, the argument goes, automatically obtains citizenship at birth, while those born elsewhere can acquire citizenship only through a long and sometimes difficult process. The answer to this argument is that it is not the employer who places the burdens of naturalization on those born outside the country, but Congress itself, through laws enacted pursuant to its constitutional power "[t]o establish an uniform Rule of Naturalization." U.S.Const., Art. 1, §8, cl. 4. * * *

hiring aliens of Anglo–Saxon background but refusing to hire those of Mexican or Spanish ancestry. Aliens are protected from illegal discrimination under the Act, but nothing in the Act makes it illegal to discriminate on the basis of citizenship or alienage.

We agree with the Court of Appeals that neither the language of the Act, nor its history, nor the specific facts of this case indicate that respondent has engaged in unlawful discrimination because of national origin.

Affirmed.

MR. JUSTICE DOUGLAS, dissenting.

* * *

Alienage results from one condition only: being born outside the United States. Those born within the country are citizens from birth. It could not be more clear that Farah's policy of excluding aliens is de facto a policy of preferring those who were born in this country. Therefore the construction placed upon the "national origin" provision is inconsistent with the construction this Court has placed upon the same Act's protections for persons denied employment on account of race or sex.

* * *

These petitioners against whom discrimination is charged are Chicanos. But whether brown, yellow, black, or white, the thrust of the Act is clear: alienage is no barrier to employment here. *Griggs*, as I understood it until today, extends its protective principles to all, not to blacks alone. Our cases on sex discrimination under the Act yield the same result as *Griggs*.

The construction placed upon the statute in the majority opinion is an extraordinary departure from prior cases, and it is opposed by the Equal Employment Opportunity Commission, the agency provided by law with the responsibility of enforcing the Act's protections. The Commission takes the only permissible position: that discrimination on the basis of alienage always has the effect of discrimination on the basis of national origin. Refusing to hire an individual because he is an alien "is discrimination based on birth outside the United States and is thus discrimination based on national origin in violation of Title VII." The Commission's interpretation of the statute is entitled to great weight.

* * *

NOTES AND PROBLEMS FOR DISCUSSION

1. While foreign citizens are not protected by Title VII against private sector alienage bars, similarly restrictive employment practices used by a public employer can be challenged under the equal protection guarantees of the Fifth or Fourteenth Amendments to the U.S. Constitution. The Supreme Court has invalidated statutes that prevented aliens from entering a state's classified civil service, Sugarman v. Dougall, 413 U.S. 634, 93 S.Ct. 2842, 37 L.Ed.2d 853 (1973), practicing law, Application of Griffiths, 413 U.S. 717, 93 S.Ct. 2851, 37 L.Ed.2d 910 (1973) and working as an engineer, Examining Board of Engineers v. Flores de Otero, 426 U.S. 572, 96 S.Ct. 2264, 49 L.Ed.2d 65 (1976). But it also has upheld a state statute that excluded aliens from serving as "peace officers," Cabell v. Chavez–Salido, 454 U.S.

432, 102 S.Ct. 735, 70 L.Ed.2d 677 (1982), another that prohibited aliens who did not manifest an intention to apply for U.S. citizenship from working as elementary and secondary school teachers, Ambach v. Norwick, 441 U.S. 68, 99 S.Ct. 1589, 60 L.Ed.2d 49 (1979), and a third that precluded aliens from working for a state police force, Foley v. Connelie, 435 U.S. 291, 98 S.Ct. 1067, 55 L.Ed.2d 287 (1978). These latter decisions indicate, at least with respect to "political function" positions, i.e., those "intimately related to the process of democratic self-government," Bernal v. Fainter, 467 U.S. 216, 104 S.Ct. 2312, 81 L.Ed.2d 175 (1984), that the Supreme Court will apply a less demanding standard than the strict scrutiny traditionally accorded alienage classifications.

2. Congress enacted the Immigration Reform and Control Act of 1986, 8 U.S.C. §1324a (1986) (IRCA), as amended by the Immigration Act of 1990, P.L. 101–649, 104 Stat. 5053,5056 (1990), and the Omnibus Consolidated Appropriations Act of 1996, P.L. 104-208 (1996) to deal with some of the problems posed by the employment of illegal aliens in the United States. This statute forbids the hiring, recruitment, or fee-based referral for employment of any person known to be an undocumented alien (one without documentation of permission either to work or to reside permanently in the U.S.). It imposes civil and criminal sanctions for the violation of these provisions and requires employers, unions, and employment agencies to take steps (by requiring the presentation of prescribed documents such as a driver's license or alien documentation) to verify that individuals seeking employment or job referral or recruitment are lawfully eligible for employment. In addition, as a result of the 1996 amendments to the IRCA, an employer's request for more or different documents than are required to confirm an employee's employment eligibility will violate the statutory ban on discrimination only if that request was made for a discriminatory purpose or with the intention to discriminate. Separate provisions apply to seasonal agricultural workers.

At the same time that the IRCA prohibits the employment of undocumented alien workers, it provides a level of protection to documented alien workers that is unavailable under Title VII. It prohibits employers with more than three employees from discriminating on the basis of citizenship status with respect to all but undocumented aliens and except, in the case of public employers, where the discrimination is permitted or required by statute, regulation, or executive order. However, the Act does permit an employer to discriminate against a lawful alien when that alien is competing for a job with an "equally qualified" American citizen or national. The 1990 amendments also added a provision comparable to §704(a) of Title VII that prohibits an employer from intimidating or retaliating against anyone who seeks relief under the IRCA or who participates in any proceeding, hearing, or investigation related to that statute. Finally, an alien who prevails on a claim under the IRCA is entitled to attorney's fees, but only upon a showing that the losing party's argument was "without reasonable foundation in law and fact."

Since Title VII extends its protections to "individuals", how, if at all, does the provision of the IRCA prohibiting the employment of undocumented workers affect the right of undocumented aliens to bring suit under Title VII for discrimination on the basis of any of its five protected classifications? In EGBUNA v. TIME-LIFE LIBRARIES, INC., 153 F.3d 184 (4th Cir. 1998), a Nigerian national's valid student work visa expired shortly after he was hired by the defendant. The employer was unaware of the explanation and continued to employ the plaintiff until he resigned to return to Nigeria. But when the plaintiff changed his mind and applied for reemployment, his request was denied. He brought a retaliation claim under §704(a), alleging that the company failed to reemploy him because he had corroborated the sexual harassment charges brought by another employee against a supervisor. The trial court granted the defense motion for summary judgment on the ground that as an undocumented alien, the plaintiff was ineligible to work in the U.S. when he applied for re-employment. This opinion was reversed by a Fourth Circuit panel but when the circuit voted to hear the case *en banc*, a majority voted to reverse the panel and to reinstate the trial court's judgment. The *en banc* majority ruled that since the IRCA statutorily disqualifies all undocumented workers from employment within the U.S. as a matter of law, such individuals cannot state a claim under Title VII.

3. (a) Does an employer's rule prohibiting employees from speaking Spanish on the job unless they are communicating with Spanish-speaking customers constitute national origin discrimination? *Compare* Maldonado v. City of Altus, 433 F.3d 1294 (10th Cir.2006) *with* Garcia v. Spun Steak Co., 998 F.2d 1480 (9th Cir.1993), cert. denied, 512 U.S. 128, 114 S.Ct. 2726, 129 L.Ed.2d 849 (1994) *and* Garcia v. Gloor, 618 F.2d 264 (5th Cir.1980), cert. denied, 449 U.S. 1113, 101 S.Ct. 923, 66 L.Ed.2d 842 (1981).

(b) If an employer denies a job or promotion to an individual because of his or her foreign accent, can this employee state a prima facie case claim of national origin discrimination? In FRAGANTE v. CITY AND COUNTY OF HONOLULU, 888 F.2d 591 (9th Cir.1989), cert. denied, 494 U.S. 1081, 110 S.Ct. 1811, 108 L.Ed.2d 942 (1990), the plaintiff was denied a position that, among other things, required him to provide information to the public over the telephone, on the basis of evaluations by two interviewers who reported that they had difficulty understanding him and that his "heavy Filipino accent" would interfere with the performance of certain important aspects of the job. Applicants who were found to be superior in their verbal communication ability were selected for the two available positions. The trial court dismissed the complaint on the ground that the plaintiff's rejection was based on his inability to communicate effectively with the public and not because of his national origin. The Ninth Circuit affirmed, agreeing that the defendant was motivated exclusively by its reasonable business interest in hiring someone who could communicate effectively with the public. Consequently, the appellate panel reasoned, regardless of whether the plaintiff had established a prima facie case, the defendant had convinced the court that the decision was motivated by a legitimate, nondiscriminatory interest. The court emphasized that the plaintiff had not been denied employment simply because the employer did not like foreign accents or because the employer was afraid that its customers would not like foreign accents. The court, however, expressly refused to rule on whether the plaintiff's lack of qualifications prevented him from satisfying the *Burdine* elements of a prima facie case. Instead, it held that the defendant had established a nondiscriminatory, non-pretextual explanation for its conduct. *But see* Carino v. University of Oklahoma Board of Regents, 750 F.2d 815 (10th Cir.1984).

In revised guidelines on national origin discrimination issued on December 2, 2002, the EEOC defined national origin discrimination to include adverse action based on an individual's or his or her ancestor's place of origin *or* "because an individual has the physical, cultural, or linguistic characteristics of a national origin group. 29 C.F.R. §1606.1. Consistent with this definition, the EEOC also has declared that because linguistic characteristics such as accent and English language proficiency are a component of national origin, employment decisions based on these factors are permissible only when they materially interfere with an individual's ability to perform his or her specific job duties safely or efficiently such as when an employee seeks to communicate with customers, co-workers, or supervisors who only speak English. On the other hand, an English-only rule shown to have been adopted with the intent to discriminate on the basis of national origin, such as when a policy prohibits some but not all of the foreign languages spoken in a workplace, would be unlawful. II EEOC Compliance Manual §623. *See* Mark L. Adams, *Fear of Foreigners: Nativism and Workplace Language Restrictions*, 74 OR.L.REV. 849 (1995), Michael F. Patterson, *English-Only Rules in the Workplace*, 27 ARIZ.ST.L.J. 277 (1995).

4. The Court in *Espinoza* defined national origin as "the country where a person was born, or, more broadly, the country from which his or her ancestors came." Did the Court intend to limit the concept of "national" origin to politically recognized nations? What if one's ancestors came from a country or nation that no longer politically exists? Or what if the plaintiff is harassed by negative comments about a national origin that he does not actually possess?

(a) For example, can a plaintiff state a claim of national origin discrimination where he alleges that he was discriminated against because he is Serbian even though Serbia no longer existed as a nation at the time the claim was filed? *See* Pejic v. Hughes Helicopters, Inc., 840 F.2d 667 (9th Cir.1988).

(b) What about a plaintiff who alleges that she was discriminated against because she is a member of the Roma people (aka Gypsy)? Would it matter whether or not the plaintiff's complaint referred to any particular country or region as the place of her ancestors' origin? *See* Janko v. Illinois State Toll Highway Authority, 704 F.Supp. 1531 (N.D.Ill.1989) (denying motion to dismiss complaint on ground that dictionary refers to Gypsies as an ethnic group from Mediterranean area and, therefore, that Gypsy constitutes a national origin within meaning of statute).

(c) Suppose a Native American who is a member of the Hopi tribe is not hired because the employer will only hire members of the Navajo tribe. Can he state a claim of national origin discrimination? *See* Dawavendewa v. Salt River Project, 154 F.3d 1117 (9th Cir.1998) (discrimination based on tribal affiliation constitutes "national origin" discrimination because the different tribes were at one time considered to be nations by the United States and, to a certain extent, still are. Moreover, even if the various tribes never enjoyed formal "nation" status, discrimination on the basis of one's ancestor's place of origin is sufficient to state a national origin-based claim under Title VII).

(d) If the plaintiff alleges that he was discriminated against because he is a "Latino", without reference to the country of origin of himself or his forebears, can he state a claim of national origin discrimination under Title VII? In SALAS v. WISCONSIN DEPARTMENT OF CORRECTIONS, 493 F.3d 913 (7th Cir. 2007), the court ruled that since "Hispanics" qualify as a "national origin group" within the meaning of the EEOC Guidelines mentioned in Note 3(b), *supra,* a Title VII plaintiff alleging that he is Hispanic sufficiently identifies his national origin to state a claim under Title VII and defeat a defense motion for summary judgment.

(e) If a person of Indian ancestry is believed by his co-workers to be an Arab and is subjected to hostile remarks degrading his perceived Arab ancestry, can he state a claim of national origin discrimination even though he is not an Arab? *See* EEOC v. WC&M Enterprises, Inc., 496 F.3d 393 (5th Cir. 2007) (based on the EEOC guideline's definition of national origin discrimination [discussed in Note 3(b), *supra*], Indian plaintiff can state a claim because it is sufficient to show that he was treated differently because of his foreign accent, appearance, or physical characteristics; Title VII does not require that the discrimination be based on the victim's actual national origin).

5. Can the owner of an Italian restaurant refuse to hire a non-Italian chef? What about a server?

6. How does a plaintiff in a national origin discrimination case establish that she is a member of a particular ethnic group? Is it sufficient, for example, for her to rely on evidence of her subjective feelings about her own ethnicity, or must she proffer evidence relating to her physical appearance, speech or mannerisms in order to demonstrate her objective appearance to others? *See* Bennun v. Rutgers State University, 941 F.2d 154 (3d Cir.1991), cert. denied, 502 U.S. 1066, 112 S.Ct. 956, 117 L.Ed.2d 124 (1992).

SECTION C.   RACE AND COLOR

McDonald v. Santa Fe Trail Transportation Co.

Supreme Court of the United States, 1976.
427 U.S. 273, 96 S.Ct. 2574, 49 L.Ed.2d 493.

MR. JUSTICE MARSHALL delivered the opinion of the Court.

Petitioners, L. N. McDonald and Raymond L. Laird, brought this action * * * seeking relief against Santa Fe Trail Transportation Co. (Santa Fe) and International Brotherhood of Teamsters Local 988 (Local 988), which represented Santa Fe's Houston employees, for alleged violations of * * * Title VII in connection with their discharge from Santa Fe's employment. The District Court dismissed the complaint on the pleadings. The Court of Appeals for the Fifth Circuit affirmed. In determining whether the decisions of these courts were correct, we must decide * * * whether a complaint alleging that white employees charged with misappropriating property from their employer were dismissed from employment, while a black employee similarly charged was not dismissed, states a claim under Title VII. * * *

Because the District Court dismissed this case on the pleadings, we take as true the material facts alleged in petitioners' complaint. On September 26, 1970, petitioners, both white, and Charles Jackson, a Negro employee of Santa Fe, were jointly and severally charged with misappropriating 60 one-gallon cans of antifreeze which was part of a shipment Santa Fe was carrying for one of its customers. Six days later, petitioners were fired by Santa Fe, while Jackson was retained. * * *

* * *

Title VII prohibits the discharge of "any individual" because of "such individual's race," §703(a)(1). Its terms are not limited to discrimination against members of any particular race. Thus, although we were not there confronted with racial discrimination against whites, we described the Act in Griggs v. Duke Power Co., as prohibiting "[d]iscriminatory preference for any [racial] group, minority or majority". Similarly the EEOC, whose interpretations are entitled to great deference, has consistently interpreted Title VII to proscribe racial discrimination in private employment against whites on the same terms as racial discrimination against nonwhites, holding that to proceed otherwise would

> "constitute a derogation of the Commission's Congressional mandate to eliminate all practices which operate to disadvantage the employment opportunities of any group protected by Title VII, including Caucasians." EEOC Decision No. 74–31, 7 FEP 1326, 1328, CCH EEOC Decisions ¶ 6404, p. 4084 (1973).

This conclusion is in accord with uncontradicted legislative history to the effect that Title VII was intended to "cover white men and white women and all Americans," 110 Cong. Rec. 2578 (1964) (remarks of Rep. Celler), and create an "obligation not to discriminate against whites," id., at 7218 (memorandum of Sen. Clark). We therefore hold today that Title VII prohibits racial discrimination against the white petitioners in this case upon the same standards as would be applicable were they Negroes and Jackson white.

* * *

NOTES AND PROBLEMS FOR DISCUSSION

1. The absence of a statutory definition of "race" notwithstanding, few definitional problems have arisen in connection with this term. Since the statute also protects individuals from discrimination on the basis of color, national origin and religion, choosing the specific classification into which any particular claim fits usually is not a controversial issue. There are, however, two exceptions to this general rule. The bona fide occupational qualification defense provided in §703(e) cannot be used to justify a classification based on race. Thus, characterizing a claim as alleging national origin, as opposed to race discrimination, can be critical where the defendant wants to take advantage of this defense. Secondly, affirmative action policies often define the class included within their provisions by racial membership. In light of the inapplicability of the BFOQ defense to race or color claims, would a movie producer violate Title VII by insisting on a dark-complexioned black actor to play the lead role in "The Idi Amin Story?"

2. According to EEOC reports, 374 color-based discrimination charges were filed with the agency in 1992 compared with 1241 such charges in 2006. Most color discrimination cases consist of a claim by a dark-skinned person that he was denied a position given to a light-skinned member of his or another race (or vice versa) with similar qualifications. *See* Walker v. Internal Revenue Service, 713 F.Supp. 403 (N.D.Ga.1989) (light-skinned black employee can state claim under Title VII on ground that dark-skinned black supervisor discharged her on the basis of her skin color).

3. Plaintiff, a white woman, was discharged from her job because she was involved in a social relationship with a black man. The defendant admits that it has a policy prohibiting employees, upon penalty of discharge, from engaging in inter-racial relationships, but insists that it applies this policy uniformly to all employees, regardless of their race. Can the plaintiff state a claim under Title VII? *See* Holcomb v. Iona College, 521 F.3d 130 (2d Cir. 2008) (where an adverse action is taken pursuant to an employer's disapproval of interracial association, the employee suffers discrimination because of that employee's *own* race). *Accord,* Deffenbaugh-Williams v. Wal-Mart Stores, Inc., 156 F.3d 581 (5th Cir.1998); Parr v. Woodmen of the World Life Ins. Co., 791 F.2d 888 (11th Cir. 1986).

4. In MORTON v. MANCARI, 417 U.S. 535, 94 S.Ct. 2474, 41 L.Ed.2d 290 (1974), the Supreme Court rejected a claim that a 1934 federal statute granting qualified American Indians an employment preference in the Bureau of Indian Affairs was inconsistent with, and thus superseded by the anti-racial discrimination provisions of Title VII. In reaching this result, the Court noted that Title VII itself specifically exempts Indian tribes from its provisions and permits private businesses located on or near Indian reservations to give preferential treatment to Indians living on or near reservations. In DAWAVENDEWA v. SALT RIVER PROJECT, 154 F.3d 1117 (9th Cir.1998), the Ninth Circuit, however, narrowly read the Title VII preference not to permit a business located on a reservation to give a preference to a member of one Indian tribe over a member of a different tribe. The Court interpreted the preference provision of §703(i) to permit according a preference to a Native American over a non-Native American, but not to give a preference on the basis of tribal affiliation. And in EEOC v. PEABODY WESTERN COAL CO., 773 F.3d 977 (9th Cir. 2014), the Ninth Circuit ruled that a lease requiring a coal company to give hiring preferences to Native Americans who were members of the Navajo tribe was not prohibited by Title VII. The court construed the use of a tribal preference not as a classification based on national origin but as a political classification designed to fulfill the federal government's trust obligations to this tribe. Accordingly, it ruled that Title VII was inapplicable to the lease's hiring preference.

SECTION D. SEX

Leo Kanowitz, *Sex–Based Discrimination in American Law III: Title VII of the 1964 Civil Rights Act and the Equal Pay Act of 1963*

20 HASTINGS L.Rev. 305, 310-12 (1968).

* * *

Any consideration of the sex provisions of Title VII of the 1964 Civil Rights Act requires a preliminary glance at what can only be described as their peculiar legislative history. In the light of its tremendous potential for profoundly affecting the daily lives of so many Americans — both men and women — Title VII's prohibition against sex-discrimination in employment had a rather inauspicious birth.

This is not to say that some species of federal legislation outlawing sex-based discrimination in employment might not have emerged eventually from a Congress in which male representatives out-numbered female representatives overwhelmingly.

Agitation for such a law, after all, had been going on for many years. * * * But the prospects for the passage of legislation prohibiting sex discrimination in hiring and promotional practices in employment were exceedingly dim in 1964. Had the sex provisions of Title VII been presented then as a separate bill, rather than being coupled as they were in an effusion of Congressional gimmickry with legislation aimed at curbing racial and ethnic discrimination, their defeat in 1964 would have been virtually assured. We have no less an authority for this conclusion than Oregon's Representative Edith Green, whose strong advocacy of equal legal treatment for American women lends great force to her appraisal. In her view, stated in Congress, the legislation against sex discrimination in employment, "considered by itself, and * * * brought to the floor with no hearings and no testimony * * * would not [have] receive[d] one hundred votes."

In fact, it was not until the last day of the bill's consideration in Chairman Howard Smith's House Rules committee, where it had gone after a favorable report from the Judiciary Committee, that there first appeared a motion to add "sex" discrimination to the other types of employment discrimination that the original bill sought to curb. That motion was defeated in Committee by a vote of 8–7. But after almost two weeks of passionate floor debate in the House and just one day before the act was passed, Representative Smith, a principal opponent of the original bill, offered an amendment to include sex as a prohibited basis for employment discrimination. Under that amendment, the previously proposed sanctions against employers, unions, hiring agencies, or their agents, for discrimination in hiring or promotional practices against actual or prospective employees on the basis of race, creed, or national origin, were, with some exceptions, also to apply to discrimination based upon the "sex" of the job applicant or employee. Offering his amendment, Representative Smith remarked: "Now I am very serious * * * I do not think it can do any harm to this legislation; maybe it will do some good."

Despite Congressman Smith's protestations of seriousness, there was substantial cause to doubt his motives. For four months Congress had been locked in debate over the passage of the Civil Rights Act of 1964. Most southern Representatives and a few of their northern allies had been making every effort to block its passage. In the context of that debate and of the prevailing Congressional sentiment when the amendment was offered, it is abundantly clear that a principal motive in introducing it was to prevent passage of the basic legislation being considered by Congress, rather than solicitude for women's employment rights.

It is not surprising, therefore, that Representative Green, expressing her hope that "the day will come when discrimination will be ended against women," also registered her opposition to the proposed amendment, stating that it "will clutter up the bill and it may later — very well — be used to help destroy this section of the bill by some of the very people who today support it."

Despite these misgivings, and despite the apparent objectives of its sponsors to block passage of the entire Act, the legislation that finally emerged contained Representative Smith's amendment intact. As a result of this stroke of misfired political tactics, our federal positive law now includes a provision that had been desired for many years by those who were concerned with the economic, social and political status of American women, but which had been delayed because of the feeling that the time had not ripened for such legislation, and had been specifically opposed in this instance partly because of a belief that "discrimination based on sex involves problems sufficiently different from discrimination based on * * * other factors * * * to make separate treatment preferable."

What significance should be drawn from this peculiar legislative history of Title VII's prohibition against sex discrimination? It would be a most serious error to attribute to Congress as a corporate unit the apparently cynical motives of the amendment's sponsor. Though most members of Congress were intent on prohibiting employment discrimination based on race, religion and national origin, they did vote to do the same with respect to sex discrimination once the matter, regardless of its sponsor's apparent intentions, was brought to them for a vote. And when Congress adopts any legislation, especially a law with such important ramifications, one must infer a Congressional intention that such legislation be effective to carry out its underlying social policy—which in this case is to eradicate every instance of sex-based employment discrimination that is not founded upon a bona fide occupational qualification.

* * *

1. "SEX–PLUS" DISCRIMINATION AND PREGNANCY

After the enactment of Title VII, the federal courts treated sex discrimination claims just like claims alleging discrimination on the basis of the four other classifications. The disparate treatment and disproportionate impact theories, which originated in race cases, were easily adapted to allegations of sex bias. In DOTHARD v. RAWLINSON, 433 U.S. 321, 97 S.Ct. 2720, 53 L.Ed.2d 786 (1977), for example, the Supreme Court invalidated a minimum height and weight requirement for jobs with the Alabama Board of Corrections because of its disproportionate exclusionary impact on women. There was, however, one development in the treatment of Title VII claims that was peculiar to sex-based charges. Employers with a significant proportion of female employees implemented policies that restricted employment opportunities to specific classes of women. For example, some companies refused to employ married or pregnant women, women over a certain age, or women with pre-school-age children. The employers contended that the presence of women on their payrolls negated claims that they discriminated on the basis of sex. Opponents of these policies, on the other hand, argued that the restrictions did violate Title VII since they applied only to female employees. Thus, the courts were faced with determining whether an employment policy that does not discriminate solely on the basis of sex, but on the basis of sex plus some other, facially neutral qualification, is violative of Title VII.

Phillips v. Martin Marietta Corp.

Supreme Court of the United States, 1971.
400 U.S. 542, 91 S.Ct. 496, 27 L.Ed.2d 613.

PER CURIAM.

Petitioner Mrs. Ida Phillips commenced an action in the United States District Court for the Middle District of Florida under Title VII alleging that she had been denied employment because of her sex. The District Court granted summary judgment for Martin Marietta Corp. on the basis of the following showing: (1) in 1966 Martin informed Mrs. Phillips that it was not accepting job applications from women with pre-school-age children; (2) as of the time of the motion for summary judgment, Martin employed men with pre-school-age children; (3) at the time Mrs. Phillips applied, 70–75% of the applicants for the position she sought were women; 75–80% of those hired for the position, assembly trainee, were women, hence no question of bias against women as such was presented.

The Court of Appeals for the Fifth Circuit affirmed, and denied a rehearing *en banc*. We granted certiorari.

Section 703(a) requires that persons of like qualifications be given employment opportunities irrespective of their sex. The Court of Appeals therefore erred in reading this section as permitting one hiring policy for women and another for men — each having pre-school-age children. The existence of such conflicting family obligations, if demonstrably more relevant to job performance for a woman than for a man, could arguably be a basis for distinction under §703(e) of the Act. But that is a matter of evidence tending to show that the condition in question "is a bona fide occupational qualification reasonably necessary to the normal operation of that particular business or enterprise." The record before us, however, is not adequate for resolution of these important issues. Summary judgment was therefore improper and we remand for fuller development of the record and for further consideration.

Vacated and remanded.

MR. JUSTICE MARSHALL, concurring.

While I agree that this case must be remanded for a full development of the facts, I cannot agree with the Court's indication that a "bona fide occupational qualification reasonably necessary to the normal operation of" Martin Marietta's business could be established by a showing that some women, even the vast majority, with pre-school-age children have family responsibilities that interfere with job performance and that men do not usually have such responsibilities. Certainly, an employer can require that all of his employees, both men and women, meet minimum performance standards, and he can try to insure compliance by requiring parents, both mothers and fathers, to provide for the care of their children so that job performance is not interfered with.

But the Court suggests that it would not require such uniform standards. I fear that in this case, where the issue is not squarely before us, the Court has fallen into the trap of assuming that the Act permits ancient canards about the proper role of women to be a basis for discrimination. Congress, however, sought just the opposite result.

By adding the prohibition against job discrimination based on sex to the 1964 Civil Rights Act Congress intended to prevent employers from refusing "to hire an individual based on stereotyped characterizations of the sexes." Equal Employment Opportunity Commission, Guidelines on Discrimination Because of Sex, 29 CFR §1604.1(a)(1)(ii). Even characterizations of the proper domestic roles of the sexes were not to serve as predicates for restricting employment opportunity. The exception for a "bona fide occupational qualification" was not intended to swallow the rule.

That exception has been construed by the Equal Employment Opportunity Commission, whose regulations are entitled to great deference, to be applicable only to job situations that require specific physical characteristics necessarily possessed by only one sex. Thus the exception would apply where necessary "for the purpose of authenticity or genuineness" in the employment of actors or actresses, fashion models, and the like. If the exception is to be limited as Congress intended, the Commission has given it the only possible construction.

When performance characteristics of an individual are involved, even when parental roles are concerned, employment opportunity may be limited only by employment criteria that are neutral as to the sex of the applicant.

NOTES AND PROBLEMS FOR DISCUSSION

1. Although the Supreme Court did not employ "sex-plus" terminology in *Phillips*, this case, the first Title VII sex discrimination suit decided by the Court, clearly fits within that framework. Into which of the two previously discussed proof schemes — disparate treatment or disproportionate impact — does this type of claim fall?

2. What is your reaction to the majority's suggestion that sex might be a BFOQ? Justice Marshall contends that even if the premise upon which the application of that defense is predicated — that the responsibility for pre-school-age children more frequently falls on mothers than fathers — is statistically correct, Congress did not intend to sanction employment practices based on stereotyped characterizations of sex roles. Do you agree?

3. An employer decides to shut down one of its three plants because the employees of that plant were almost exclusively women. Can the few male employees who lost their jobs as a result of the sex-based shutdown state a claim of sex discrimination under Title VII? *See* Allen v. American Home Foods, Inc., 644 F.Supp. 1553 (N.D.Ind.1986) ("[The] 'person aggrieved' [language of Title VII] confers standing to all persons injured by an unlawful employment practice. These male plaintiffs allege such an injury, and thus have standing. * * * These males suffered the same injury as did the females that lost their jobs; the injuries of the males and females were occasioned by the same corporate decision; and if, as the plaintiffs allege, considerations of sex motivated the corporate decision to close the * * * plant, the corporate decision that injured the male plaintiffs constituted an unlawful employment practice under Title VII.").

Willingham v. Macon Telegraph Publishing Co.

United States Court of Appeals, Fifth Circuit, 1975.
507 F.2d 1084.

SIMPSON, Circuit Judge.

Alan Willingham, plaintiff-appellant, applied for employment with defendant-appellee Macon Telegraph Publishing Co., Macon, Georgia as a display or copy layout artist on July 28, 1970. Macon Telegraph refused to hire Willingham. The suit below alleged that the sole basis for refusal to hire was objection to the length of his hair. On July 30, 1970, he filed a complaint with the Equal Employment Opportunity Commission, asserting discrimination by Macon in its hiring policy based on sex * * *.

The E.E.O.C. investigated the alleged discrimination and eventually advised Willingham that there was reasonable cause to believe that Macon Telegraph had violated the * * * Civil Rights Act of 1964, and that he was entitled to file suit. On December 17, 1971, Willingham filed suit, alleging inter alia that Macon Telegraph's hiring policy unlawfully discriminated on the basis of sex. On April 17, 1972, the district court granted summary judgment in favor of defendant Macon Telegraph, finding no unlawful discrimination. Upon Willingham's appeal from the district court decision a panel of this circuit reversed, finding the presence of a prima facie case of sexual discrimination and directing remand for an evidentiary hearing. Upon *en banc* consideration we vacate the remand order of the original panel and affirm the district court.

THE FACTS
* * *

* * *   Macon Telegraph's management believed that the entire business community it served — and depended upon for business success — associated long hair on men with the counter-culture types who gained extensive unfavorable national and local exposure at the time of [a local music] * * * festival. Therefore the newspaper's employee grooming code, which required employees (male and female) who came into contact with the public to be neatly dressed and groomed in accordance with the standards customarily accepted in the business community, was interpreted to exclude the employing of men (but not women) with long hair. Willingham's longer than acceptable shoulder length hair was thus the grooming code violation upon which Macon Telegraph based its denial of employment.

* * * Willingham's argument is that Macon Telegraph discriminates amongst employees based upon their sex, in that female employees can wear their hair any length they choose, while males must limit theirs to the length deemed acceptable by Macon Telegraph. He asserts therefore that he was denied employment because of his sex: were he a girl with identical length hair and comparable job qualifications, he (she) would have been employed. A majority of the original panel which heard the case agreed, and remanded the cause to the district court for a finding of whether or not the discrimination might not be lawful under the "bona fide occupational qualification" (B.F.O.Q.) statutory exception to Sec. 703. Since we agree with the district court that Macon Telegraph's dress and grooming policy does not unlawfully

discriminate on the basis of sex, the applicability of the B.F.O.Q. exception will not be considered in this opinion.

THE NATURE OF SEXUAL DISCRIMINATION

The unlawfulness vel non of employer practices with respect to the hiring and treatment of employees in the private sector, as contemplated by Sec. 703 and applied to the facts of this case, can be determined by way of a three step analysis: (1) has there been some form of discrimination, i.e., different treatment of similarly situated individuals; (2) was the discrimination based on sex; and (3) if there has been sexual discrimination, is it within the purview of the bona fide occupational qualification (BFOQ) exception and thus lawful? We conclude that the undisputed discrimination practiced by Macon Telegraph is based not upon sex, but rather upon grooming standards, and thus outside the proscription of Sec. 703. This determination pretermits any discussion of whether, if sexual discrimination were involved, it would be within the BFOQ exception.

Although our judicial inquiry necessarily focuses upon the proper statutory construction to be accorded Sec. 703, it is helpful first to define narrowly the precise issue to be considered. * * * [W]e are not concerned with discrimination based upon sex alone. That situation obtains when an employer refuses to hire, promote, or raise the wages of an individual solely because of sex, as, for instance, if Macon Telegraph had refused to hire any women for the job of copy layout artist because of their sex.

Willingham relies on a more subtle form of discrimination, one which courts and commentators have often characterized as "sex plus." In general, this involves the classification of employees on the basis of sex plus one other ostensibly neutral characteristic. The practical effect of interpreting Sec. 703 to include this type of discrimination is to impose an equal protection gloss upon the statute, i.e. similarly situated individuals of either sex cannot be discriminated against vis a vis members of their own sex unless the same distinction is made with respect to those of the opposite sex. Such an interpretation may be necessary in order to counter some rather imaginative efforts by employers to circumvent Sec. 703.

Inclusion of "sex plus" discrimination within the proscription of Sec. 703 has legitimate legislative and judicial underpinning. An amendment which would have added the word "solely" to the bill, modifying "sex," was defeated on the floor in the House of Representatives. Presumably, Congress foresaw the debilitating effect such a limitation might have upon the sex discrimination amendment. Further, the Supreme Court, in Phillips v. Martin Marietta Corp., found expressly that "sex plus" discrimination violates the Civil Rights Act. In a short per curiam decision, the Supreme Court held that if the legislative purpose of giving persons of like qualifications equal employment opportunity irrespective of sex were to be effected, employers could not have one hiring policy for men and another for women. Thus "sex plus" discrimination against being a woman plus having pre-school age children, was under the facts of that case just as unlawful as would have been discrimination based solely upon sex.

In this analytical context, then, the single issue in this case is precisely drawn: Does a particular grooming regulation applicable to men only constitute "sex plus" discrimination within the meaning of Sec. 703, as construed by the Supreme Court?

Willingham and numerous amici curiae have advanced several arguments supporting an affirmative answer to the question. We proceed to consider these arguments.

The primary premise of Willingham's position is that "sex plus" must be read to intend to include "sex plus any sexual stereotype" and thus, since short hair is stereotypically male, requiring it of all male applicants violates Sec. 703. While the Supreme Court did not explicate the breadth of its rationale in *Phillips*, it seems likely that Mr. Justice Marshall at least might agree with Willingham. In his special concurrence he noted that any hiring distinction based upon stereotyped characterizations of the sexes violates the Act, and went on to say that such discrimination could never be a BFOQ exception, an issue expressly left open in the majority's per curiam opinion.

Willingham finds further comfort in Sprogis v. United Air Lines, Inc., 7 Cir.1971, 444 F.2d 1194. Plaintiff there was a female stewardess who challenged an airline rule that stewardesses were not allowed to marry, but with no such provision for male stewards or other employees. The *Sprogis* court found the rule to be an unlawful form of "sex plus" discrimination, relying in part on *Phillips*. * * * [I]t is possible that the court felt that all sexual stereotypes violate Sec. 703. Several district courts apparently agree with this construction, at least insofar as personal dress and appearance codes are concerned. See Aros v. McDonnell Douglas Corp., C.D.Cal.1972, 348 F.Supp. 661 (dress and grooming code constitutes sexual discrimination when applied differently to males and females); Donohue v. Shoe Corp. of America, C.D.Cal.1972, 337 F.Supp. 1357 (rule requiring short hair on men, but not on women, is prima facie violation of Sec. 703); Roberts v. General Mills, Inc., N.D.Ohio 1971, 337 F.Supp. 1055 (rule allowing female employees to wear hairnets, but requiring men to wear hats — and therefore keep their hair short — violates Sec. 703).

Finally, the E.E.O.C. by administrative decision, regulation, and on amicus brief here, fully supports Willingham's position. In its administrative decisions, the Commission has uniformly held that dress and grooming codes that distinguish between sexes are within Sec. 703, and can only be justified if proven to be a BFOQ. * * *

SEXUAL STEREOTYPES AND LEGISLATIVE INTENT

The beginning (and often the ending) point of statutory interpretation is an exploration of the legislative history of the Act in question. We must decide, if we can there find any basis for decision, whether Congress intended to include all sexual distinctions in its prohibition of discrimination (based solely on sex or on "sex plus"), or whether a line can legitimately be drawn beyond which employer conduct is no longer within reach of the statute.

We discover, as have other courts earlier considering the problem before us, that the meager legislative history regarding the addition of "sex" in Sec. 703(a) provides slim guidance for divining Congressional intent. * * * And while it is argued that a lack of change in this section in the 1972 amendments to the Act evidences Congressional agreement with the position of the E.E.O.C., it may be argued with equal force that the law was insufficiently developed at the time the amendments were considered to support any change. We find the legislative history inconclusive at best and draw but one conclusion, and that by way of negative inference. Without more extensive consideration, Congress in all probability did not intend for its proscription of sexual discrimination to have significant and sweeping implications. We should not therefore extend the coverage of the Act to situations of questionable application without some stronger Congressional mandate.

We perceive the intent of Congress to have been the guarantee of equal job opportunity for males and females. Providing such opportunity is where the emphasis rightly lies. This is to say that the Act should reach any device or policy of an employer that serves to deny acquisition and retention of a job or promotion in a job to an individual because the individual is either male or female. * * *

Juxtaposing our view of the Congressional purpose with the statutory interpretations advanced by the parties to this action elucidates our reasons for adopting the more narrow construction. Equal employment opportunity may be secured only when employers are barred from discriminating against employees on the basis of immutable characteristics, such as race and national origin. Similarly, an employer cannot have one hiring policy for men and another for women if the distinction is based on some fundamental right. But a hiring policy that distinguishes on some other ground, such as grooming codes or length of hair, is related more closely to the employer's choice of how to run his business than to equality of employment opportunity. In *Phillips, supra*, the Supreme Court condemned a hiring distinction based on having pre-school age children, an existing condition not subject to change. In Sprogis v. United Air Lines, *supra*, the Seventh Circuit reached a similar result with respect to marital status. We have no difficulty with the result reached in those cases; but nevertheless perceive that a line must be drawn between distinctions grounded on such fundamental rights as the right to have children or to marry and those interfering with the manner in which an employer exercises his judgment as to the way to operate a business. Hair length is not immutable and in the situation of employer vis a vis employee enjoys no constitutional protection. If the employee objects to the grooming code he has the right to reject it by looking elsewhere for employment, or alternatively he may choose to subordinate his preference by accepting the code along with the job.

* * *

We adopt the view, therefore, that distinctions in employment practices between men and women on the basis of something other than immutable or protected characteristics do not inhibit employment opportunity in violation of Sec. 703(a). Congress sought only to give all persons equal access to the job market, not to limit an employer's right to exercise his informed judgment as to how best to run his shop.

* * *

CONCLUSION

Nothing that we say should be construed as disparagement of what many feel to be a highly laudable goal—maximizing individual freedom by eliminating sexual stereotypes. We hold simply that such an objective may not be read into the Civil Rights Act of 1964 without further Congressional action. Private employers are prohibited from using different hiring policies for men and women only when the distinctions used relate to immutable characteristics or legally protected rights. While of course not impervious to judicial scrutiny, even those distinctions do not violate Sec. 703(a) if they are applied to both sexes.

Affirmed.

NOTES AND PROBLEMS FOR DISCUSSION

1. (a) As the court in *Willingham* noted, sex-plus theory has been used to strike down no-marriage rules applied only to female employees. Other courts have similarly invalidated policies that discriminate against unwed mothers, Dolter v. Wahlert High School, 483 F.Supp. 266 (N.D.Iowa 1980); female homosexuals, Valdes v. Lumbermen's Mutual Casualty Co., 507 F.Supp. 10 (S.D.Fla.1980); black women, Jefferies v. Harris County Community Action Association, 615 F.2d 1025 (5th Cir.1980); and women who did not use their husband's surname on personnel forms, Allen v. Lovejoy, 553 F.2d 522 (6th Cir.1977). Although the "plus" factor was applied in each of the aforementioned cases only to disqualify women, under *Phillips* that would not insulate the defendants from Title VII liability.

(b) Could an African-American plaintiff state a claim of race-plus discrimination if her employer prohibited all employees from wearing beads in their hair? What if, instead, the employer prohibited all employees from sporting a "natural" hairstyle? *See* Carswell v. Peachford Hospital, 1981 WL 224 (N.D.Ga.1981) (employer did not discriminate on the basis of race because it did not prohibit the wearing of an "afro" hairstyle or even braids; it simply prohibited the wearing of beads in the hair); Rogers v. American Airlines, Inc., 527 F.Supp. 229 (S.D.N.Y.1981) (airline that dismissed a black woman for violating its grooming policy by wearing cornrows did not violate Title VII, although court notes that the case might have come out differently if the airline had prohibited employees from wearing "afros" which would discriminate on the basis of a "natural" hairstyle and, therefore, involve a classification predicated upon an immutable characteristic).

2. In Section A of this Chapter, *infra*, we discussed the employer's statutory duty to make a reasonable accommodation to an employee's religious beliefs or practices. To what extent might this obligation constrict an employer's ability to impose dress or grooming standards? For example, suppose that an employee with extensive facial piercings is terminated for refusing to comply with the company's dress code that prohibits the wearing of all facial jewelry other than earrings. She insists that her conduct is part of her religious practices. Would the employer be obligated to exempt her from the no-facial-jewelry policy?

In CLOUTIER v. COSTCO WHOLESALE CORP., 390 F.3d 126 (1st Cir.2004), the plaintiff alleged that she was a member of the 1000 member Church of Body Modification, that her eyebrow piercing was part of her religion, and that her religious mandate to be a confident role model required her to display all of her facial piercings at all times. Consequently, she maintained, the only reasonable accommodation would be exemption from the no-facial-jewelry policy. The First Circuit upheld the trial court's grant of summary judgment in favor of the defendant, ruling that requiring the company to exempt the plaintiff from its grooming code would impose an undue hardship upon it. The company, the court reasoned, had a legitimate interest in presenting a workforce to its customers that was reasonably professional in appearance, particularly with respect to workers, like the plaintiff, who regularly interacted with customers. The First Circuit accepted the company's contention that permitting the plaintiff to continue to wear facial jewelry (other than earrings) would adversely affect its public image by detracting from the professional image it sought to cultivate and promote.

Several other appellate courts have adopted the limitation imposed on sex-plus theory by the Fifth Circuit in *Willingham* — that Title VII only prohibits policies which discriminate on the basis of "plus" characteristics that are either immutable or involve fundamental rights — to uphold sex-differentiated grooming and dress codes. *See, e.g.*, Jefferies v. Harris County Community Action Association, 615 F.2d 1025 (5th Cir.1980); Allen v. Lovejoy, 553 F.2d 522 (6th Cir.1977). The Ninth Circuit initially adhered to the immutable characteristics rationale, but subsequently supplemented it with an "undue burden" test. Under this standard, the fact that a grooming and/or appearance standard is sex-specific is not sufficient *per se* to establish a prima facie claim of sex-based discrimination; the plaintiff also must demonstrate that application of that standard imposes an undue burden on members of one sex. In JESPERSON v. HARRAH'S OPERATING COMPANY, INC., 444 F.3d 1104 (9th Cir.2006)(*en banc*), for example, the defendant's grooming and appearance code imposed both a unisex uniform requirement and some sex-differentiated appearance requirements related to nails, hair, and makeup. Specifically, female beverage servers and bartenders were required to wear makeup while their male counterparts were prohibited from so doing. The defendant required male bartenders to have short-cut hair but imposed no hair length requirement upon its female bartenders. Finally, females, but not males, were permitted to wear colored nail polish. The plaintiff, a female bartender, claimed that wearing makeup not only made her feel sick, degraded, exposed, and violated, but interfered with her ability to do her job effectively because it detracted from her credibility and conflicted with her self-image. When she refused to comply with the makeup requirement, the plaintiff was effectively terminated.

The trial court granted summary judgment for the defendant on the ground that the policy did not discriminate on the basis of sex because it did not differentiate on the basis of immutable sex-linked characteristics. It also held that the policy did not discriminate on the basis of sex because it imposed equal burdens on members of both sexes, i.e., while women were required to wear makeup, men were required to have their hair cut to a length above the collar. On appeal, the Ninth Circuit panel applied the undue burden test and determined that the plaintiff had not established that the employer's policy imposed a greater burden on women than on men. The plaintiff/appellant had argued that the makeup requirement imposed a heavier burden on females because of the cost of purchasing makeup and the expenditure of time required to apply it. But the appellate panel ruled that since the plaintiff had offered no evidence to support that claim, she had failed even to raise a triable issue of fact as to whether the makeup requirement imposed unequal burdens on male and female employees. Accordingly, it affirmed the grant of summary judgment in favor of the defendant.

This ruling was upheld by the entire court in its *en banc* opinion. It agreed that the mere fact of the presence of sex-differentiated requirements did not *per se* establish a prima facie claim of sex-based discrimination. It demanded evidence that the policy imposed an undue burden on members of one sex. It then noted that the only evidence tendered by the plaintiff was (1) her deposition testimony that she found the makeup requirement offensive and that it interfered with her ability to perform her job, and (2) customer feedback and employer evaluation forms that attested to her outstanding performance. That showing, the *en banc* majority ruled, was insufficient to establish a genuine issue of fact concerning the existence of an unequal burden upon women. To demonstrate unequal burden, the court continued, required the presentation of evidence that the policy would impose an undue burden on the class of women as a whole. And as to this, the *en banc* court rejected the plaintiff's request that it take judicial notice of the fact that it cost more money and took more time for a woman to comply with the makeup requirement than it took for a man to comply with the short hair mandate.

Do decisions adopting and extending the *Willingham* analysis permit the use of employment policies that perpetuate sexual stereotypes in violation of the spirit, if not the letter, of the Court's ruling in *Price Waterho*use? In *Jespersen*, the *en banc* court ruled that *Price Waterhouse*'s sex-stereotyping doctrine was available for grooming/appearance code cases when either (1) there was evidence that the plaintiff had been subjected to sexual harassment for failure to conform; or (2) the policy was intended to compel women to comply with sex-stereotyped standards of behavior or appearance or to objectify them as sex objects. And the motivation analysis must reflect the fact that the sex-differentiated components of the grooming code constituted but a "small part" of an overall grooming and appearance policy that "applies largely the same requirements to both men and women". See Devon Carbado, Mitu Gulati & Gowri Ramachandran, *The Story of Jesperson v. Harrah's: Makeup and Women at Work*, EMPLOYMENT DISCRIMINATION STORIES 105 (Friedman, ed. 2006); Joel Wm. Friedman, *Gender Nonconformity and the Unfulfilled Promise of Price Waterhouse v. Hopkins*, 14 DUKE J. GEND.L. & POL. 205 (2007).

3. Is "sex-plus" analysis applicable to decisions that discriminate on the basis of pregnancy, a factor that can be possessed only by members of one gender? In GENERAL ELECTRIC CO. v. GILBERT, 429 U.S. 125, 97 S.Ct. 401, 50 L.Ed.2d 343 (1976), the plaintiffs claimed that the company's non-occupational disability plan violated Title VII because it did not provide payment for any absence due to pregnancy. They contended that the employer's failure to include pregnancy-related disabilities on the same terms and conditions as other non-occupational disabilities constituted sex-based discrimination. The Supreme Court rejected this claim, holding that the exclusion of pregnancy from an otherwise nearly comprehensive disability plan was neither gender-based discrimination nor a pretext for such discrimination, but simply an economically motivated decision to remove one expensive risk from the list of compensable disabilities. In addition, the Court ruled, by failing to prove that the benefit package was worth more to men than to women, either financially or in terms of aggregate risk protection, the plaintiffs had not demonstrated that the pregnancy-related exclusion had a *Griggs*-like disproportionate discriminatory effect on women.

The Court soon thereafter had another opportunity to examine a pregnancy-based employment policy and used it to limit the impact of *Gilbert*. In NASHVILLE GAS CO. v. SATTY, 434 U.S. 136, 98 S.Ct. 347, 54 L.Ed.2d 356 (1977), company policy required pregnant employees to take a formal leave of absence without pay and to forfeit their accumulated job seniority upon returning to work after childbirth. Employees disabled by non-occupational sickness or injury, however, were entitled to sick pay and retention of accumulated seniority. The Court concluded that the sick leave policy was indistinguishable from General Electric's denial of disability benefits to pregnant employees. Accordingly, the Court ruled, *Gilbert* controlled and this portion of the case was remanded to allow the trial court to determine whether the sick leave plan was a pretext for sex discrimination. It was the Court's treatment of the seniority provision, however, that generated the most controversy. The Court held that while the company's practice of denying accumulated seniority to employees returning from pregnancy leave was neutral on its face, it nevertheless had a discriminatory effect upon women and thus violated Title VII. In reaching this conclusion, the *Satty* Court distinguished *Gilbert* in the following manner:

> "In *Gilbert*, there was no showing that General Electric's policy of compensating for all non-job-related disabilities except pregnancy favored men over women. No evidence was produced to suggest that men received more benefits from General Electric's disability insurance fund than did women; both men and women were subject generally to the disabilities covered and presumably drew similar amounts from the insurance fund. We therefore upheld the plan under Title VII. * * *
>
> Here, by comparison, petitioner has not merely refused to extend to women a benefit that men cannot and do not receive, but has imposed on women a substantial burden that men need not suffer. The distinction between benefits and burdens is more than one of semantics. We held in *Gilbert* that §703(a)(1) did not require that greater economic benefits be paid to one sex or the other "because of their differing roles in 'the scheme of human existence,' " 429 U.S., at 139 n. 17. But that holding does not allow us to read §703(a)(2) to permit an employer to burden female employees in such a way as to deprive them of employment opportunities because of their different role."

434 U.S. at 141-142

Thereafter, in attempting to reconcile the Supreme Court's decisions in *Gilbert* and *Satty*, the lower courts felt compelled to undertake an elusive benefit/burden analysis to determine which decision controlled the case at bar. Congress responded to the controversy and confusion surrounding these two decisions by passing the Pregnancy Discrimination Act of 1978. This amendment to Title VII added a new provision — 701(k) — designed specifically to reverse these two rulings by declaring (1) that all pregnancy-based distinctions constitute discrimination on the basis of sex; and (2) that pregnancy must be treated like other temporary disabilities for all employment-related purposes. How far Congress intended for this amendment to go towards undoing the result and/or reasoning in *Gilbert* is the subject of the following case.

Read §701(k) of Title VII.

Newport News Shipbuilding & Dry Dock Co. v. EEOC

Supreme Court of the United States, 1983.
462 U.S. 669, 103 S.Ct. 2622, 77 L.Ed.2d 89.

MR. JUSTICE STEVENS delivered the opinion of the Court.

In 1978 Congress decided to overrule our decision in General Electric Co. v. Gilbert by amending Title VII "to prohibit sex discrimination on the basis of pregnancy." On the effective date of the act, petitioner amended its health insurance plan to provide its female employees with hospitalization benefits for pregnancy-related conditions to the same extent as for other medical conditions. The plan continued, however, to provide less favorable pregnancy benefits for spouses of male employees. The question presented is whether the amended plan complies with the amended statute.

Petitioner's plan provides hospitalization and medical-surgical coverage for a defined category of employees and a defined category of dependents. Dependents covered by the plan include employees' spouses * * *. Prior to April 29, 1979, the scope of the plan's coverage for eligible dependents was identical to its coverage for employees. All covered males, whether employees or dependents, were treated alike for purposes of hospitalization coverage. All covered females, whether employees or dependents, also were treated alike. Moreover, with one relevant exception, the coverage for males and females was identical. The exception was a limitation on hospital coverage for pregnancy that did not apply to any other hospital confinement.

After the plan was amended in 1979, it provided the same hospitalization coverage for male and female employees themselves for all medical conditions, but it differentiated between female employees and spouses of male employees in its provision of pregnancy-related benefits.[7] In a booklet describing the plan, petitioner explained the amendment that gave rise to this litigation in this way:

"B. Effective April 29, 1979, maternity benefits for female employees will be paid the same as any other hospital confinement as described in question 16. This applies only to deliveries beginning on April 29, 1979 and thereafter."

"C. Maternity benefits for the wife of a male employee will continue to be paid as described in part 'A' of this question."

In turn, Part A stated, "The Basic Plan pays up to $500 of the hospital charges and 100% of reasonable and customary for delivery and anesthesiologist charges." As the Court of Appeals observed, "To the extent that the hospital charges in connection with an uncomplicated delivery may exceed $500, therefore, a male employee receives less complete coverage of spousal disabilities than does a female employee."

After the passage of the Pregnancy Discrimination Act, and before the amendment to petitioner's plan became effective, the Equal Opportunity Employment Commission issued "interpretive guidelines" in the form of questions and answers. Two of those questions, numbers 21 and 22, made it clear that the EEOC would consider petitioner's amended plan unlawful. Number 21 read as follows:

"21. Q. Must an employer provide health insurance coverage for the medical expenses of pregnancy-related conditions of the spouses of male employees? Of the dependents of all employees?

A. Where an employer provides no coverage for dependents, the employer is not required to institute such coverage. However, if an employer's insurance program covers the medical expenses of spouses of female employees, then it must equally cover the medical expenses of spouses of male employees, including those arising from pregnancy-related conditions.

---

[7]Thus, as the EEOC found after its investigation, "the record reveals that the present disparate impact on male employees had its genesis in the gender-based distinction accorded to female employees in the past."

But the insurance does not have to cover the pregnancy-related conditions of non-spouse dependents as long as it excludes the pregnancy-related conditions of such non-spouse dependents of male and female employees equally."[9]

On September 20, 1979, one of petitioner's male employees filed a charge with the EEOC alleging that petitioner had unlawfully refused to provide full insurance coverage for his wife's hospitalization caused by pregnancy; a month later the United Steelworkers filed a similar charge on behalf of other individuals. Petitioner then commenced an action in the United States District Court for the Eastern District of Virginia, challenging the Commission's guidelines and seeking both declaratory and injunctive relief. The complaint named the EEOC, the male employee, and the United Steelworkers of America as defendants. Later the EEOC filed a civil action against petitioner alleging discrimination on the basis of sex against male employees in the company's provision of hospitalization benefits. Concluding that the benefits of the new Act extended only to female employees, and not to spouses of male employees, the District Court held that petitioner's plan was lawful and enjoined enforcement of the EEOC guidelines relating to pregnancy benefits for employees' spouses. It also dismissed the EEOC's complaint. The two cases were consolidated on appeal.

A divided panel of the United States Court of Appeals for the Fourth Circuit reversed, reasoning that since "the company's health insurance plan contains a distinction based on pregnancy that results in less complete medical coverage for male employees with spouses than for female employees with spouses, it is impermissible under the statute." * * * [W]e granted certiorari.

Ultimately the question we must decide is whether petitioner has discriminated against its male employees with respect to their compensation, terms, conditions, or privileges of employment because of their sex within the meaning of §703(a)(1). Although the Pregnancy Discrimination Act has clarified the meaning of certain terms in this section, neither that Act nor the underlying statute contains a definition of the word "discriminate." In order to decide whether petitioner's plan discriminates against male employees because of their sex, we must therefore go beyond the bare statutory language. Accordingly, we shall consider whether Congress, by enacting the Pregnancy Discrimination Act, not only overturned the specific holding in General Electric v. Gilbert, but also rejected the test of discrimination employed by the Court in that case. We believe it did. Under the proper test petitioner's plan is unlawful,

---

[9]Question 22 is equally clear. It reads:

"22. Q. Must an employer provide the same level of health insurance coverage for the pregnancy-related medical conditions of the spouses of male employees as it provides for its female employees?"

"A. No. It is not necessary to provide the same level of coverage for the pregnancy-related medical conditions of spouses of male employees as for female employees. However, where the employer provides coverage for the medical conditions of the spouses of its employees, then the level of coverage for pregnancy-related medical conditions of the spouses of male employees must be the same as the level of coverage for all other medical conditions of the spouses of female employees. For example, if the employer covers employees for 100 percent of reasonable and customary expenses sustained for a medical condition, but only covers dependent spouses for 50 percent of reasonable and customary expenses for their medical conditions, the pregnancy-related expenses of the male employee's spouse must be covered at the 50 percent level."

because the protection it affords to married male employees is less comprehensive than the protection it affords to married female employees.

I

At issue in General Electric v. Gilbert was the legality of a disability plan that provided the company's employees with weekly compensation during periods of disability resulting from nonoccupational causes. Because the plan excluded disabilities arising from pregnancy, the District Court and the Court of Appeals concluded that it discriminated against female employees because of their sex. This Court reversed.

After noting that Title VII does not define the term "discrimination," the Court applied an analysis derived from cases construing the Equal Protection Clause of the Fourteenth Amendment to the Constitution. The *Gilbert* opinion quoted at length from a footnote in Geduldig v. Aiello, 417 U.S. 484, 94 S.Ct. 2485, 41 L.Ed.2d 256 (1974), a case which had upheld the constitutionality of excluding pregnancy coverage under California's disability insurance plan. "Since it is a finding of sex-based discrimination that must trigger, in a case such as this, the finding of an unlawful employment practice under §703(a)(1)," the Court added, "*Geduldig* is precisely in point in its holding that an exclusion of pregnancy from a disability-benefits plan providing general coverage is not a gender-based discrimination at all."

The dissenters in *Gilbert* took issue with the majority's assumption "that the Fourteenth Amendment standard of discrimination is coterminous with that applicable to Title VII."[13] As a matter of statutory interpretation, the dissenters rejected the Court's holding that the plan's exclusion of disabilities caused by pregnancy did not constitute discrimination based on sex. As Justice Brennan explained, it was facially discriminatory for the company to devise "a policy that, but for pregnancy, offers protection for all risks, even those that are 'unique to' men or heavily male dominated." It was inaccurate to describe the program as dividing potential recipients into two groups, pregnant women and nonpregnant persons, because insurance programs "deal with future risks rather than historic facts." Rather, the appropriate classification was "between persons who face a risk of pregnancy and those who do not." The company's plan, which was intended to provide employees with protection against the risk of uncompensated unemployment caused by physical disability, discriminated on the basis of sex by giving men protection for all categories of risk but giving women only partial protection. Thus, the dissenters asserted that the statute had been violated because conditions of employment for females were less favorable than for similarly situated males.

When Congress amended Title VII in 1978, it unambiguously expressed its disapproval of both the holding and the reasoning of the Court in the *Gilbert* decision. It incorporated a new subsection in the "definitions" applicable "[f]or the purposes of

---

[13]As the text of the *Geduldig* opinion makes clear, in evaluating the constitutionality of California's insurance program, the Court focused on the "non-invidious" character of the State's legitimate fiscal interest in excluding pregnancy coverage. This justification was not relevant to the statutory issue presented in *Gilbert*. See n. 25, *infra*.

this subchapter." The first clause of the Act states, quite simply: "The terms 'because of sex' or 'on the basis of sex' include, but are not limited to, because of or on the basis of pregnancy, childbirth, or related medical conditions."[14] The House Report stated, "It is the Committee's view that the dissenting Justices correctly interpreted the Act." Similarly, the Senate Report quoted passages from the two dissenting opinions, stating that they "correctly express both the principle and the meaning of title VII." Proponents of the bill repeatedly emphasized that the Supreme Court had erroneously interpreted Congressional intent and that amending legislation was necessary to reestablish the principles of Title VII law as they had been understood prior to the *Gilbert* decision. Many of them expressly agreed with the views of the dissenting Justices.

As petitioner argues, congressional discussion focused on the needs of female members of the work force rather than spouses of male employees. This does not create a "negative inference" limiting the scope of the act to the specific problem that motivated its enactment. Congress apparently assumed that existing plans that included benefits for dependents typically provided no less pregnancy-related coverage for the wives of male employees than they did for female employees. When the question of differential coverage for dependents was addressed in the Senate Report, the Committee indicated that it should be resolved "on the basis of existing title VII principles." The legislative context makes it clear that Congress was not thereby referring to the view of Title VII reflected in this Court's *Gilbert* opinion. Proponents of the legislation stressed throughout the debates that Congress had always intended to protect all individuals from sex discrimination in employment — including but not limited to pregnant women workers.[21] Against this background we review the terms of the amended statute to decide whether petitioner has unlawfully discriminated against its male employees.

II

Section 703(a) makes it an unlawful employment practice for an employer to "discriminate against any individual with respect to his compensation, terms, conditions, or privileges of employment, because of such individual's race, color, religion, sex, or national origin * * *." Health insurance and other fringe benefits are "compensation, terms, conditions, or privileges of employment." Male as well as

---

[14]The meaning of the first clause is not limited by the specific language in the second clause, which explains the application of the general principle to women employees.

[21]See, e.g., 123 Cong.Rec. 7539 (1977) (remarks of Sen. Williams) ("the Court has ignored the congressional intent in enacting title VII of the Civil Rights Act—that intent was to protect all individuals from unjust employment discrimination, including pregnant workers"). In light of statements such as these, it would be anomalous to hold that Congress provided that an employee's pregnancy is sex-based, while a spouse's pregnancy is gender-neutral.

During the course of the Senate debate on the Pregnancy Discrimination Act, Senator Bayh and Senator Cranston both expressed the belief that the new act would prohibit the exclusion of pregnancy coverage for spouses if spouses were otherwise fully covered by an insurance plan. Because our holding relies on the 1978 legislation only to the extent that it unequivocally rejected the *Gilbert* decision, and ultimately we rely on our understanding of general Title VII principles, we attach no more significance to these two statements than to the many other comments by both Senators and Congressmen disapproving the Court's reasoning and conclusion in *Gilbert*.

female employees are protected against discrimination. Thus, if a private employer were to provide complete health insurance coverage for the dependents of its female employees, and no coverage at all for the dependents of its male employees, it would violate Title VII. The same result would be reached even if the magnitude of the discrimination were smaller. For example, a plan that provided complete hospitalization coverage for the spouses of female employees but did not cover spouses of male employees when they had broken bones would violate Title VII by discriminating against male employees.

Petitioner's practice is just as unlawful. Its plan provides limited pregnancy-related benefits for employees' wives, and affords more extensive coverage for employees' spouses for all other medical conditions requiring hospitalization. Thus the husbands of female employees receive a specified level of hospitalization coverage for all conditions; the wives of male employees receive such coverage except for pregnancy-related conditions. Although *Gilbert* concluded that an otherwise inclusive plan that singled out pregnancy-related benefits for exclusion was nondiscriminatory on its face, because only women can become pregnant, Congress has unequivocally rejected that reasoning. The 1978 Act makes clear that it is discriminatory to treat pregnancy-related conditions less favorably than other medical conditions. Thus petitioner's plan unlawfully gives married male employees a benefit package for their dependents that is less inclusive than the dependency coverage provided to married female employees.

There is no merit to petitioner's argument that the prohibitions of Title VII do not extend to discrimination against pregnant spouses because the statute applies only to discrimination in employment. A two-step analysis demonstrates the fallacy in this contention. The Pregnancy Discrimination Act has now made clear that, for all Title VII purposes, discrimination based on a woman's pregnancy is, on its face, discrimination because of her sex. And since the sex of the spouse is always the opposite of the sex of the employee, it follows inexorably that discrimination against female spouses in the provision of fringe benefits is also discrimination against male employees.[25] By making clear that an employer could not discriminate on the basis of an employee's pregnancy, Congress did not erase the original prohibition against discrimination on the basis of an employee's sex.

In short, Congress' rejection of the premises of General Electric v. Gilbert forecloses any claim that an insurance program excluding pregnancy coverage for female beneficiaries and providing complete coverage to similarly situated male beneficiaries does not discriminate on the basis of sex. Petitioner's plan is the mirror

---

[25]See n. 22, *supra*. This reasoning does not require that a medical insurance plan treat the pregnancies of employees' wives the same as the pregnancies of female employees. For example, as the EEOC recognizes, see n. 9, *supra* (Question 22), an employer might provide full coverage for employees and no coverage at all for dependents. Similarly, a disability plan covering employees' children may exclude or limit maternity benefits. Although the distinction between pregnancy and other conditions is, according to the 1978 Act, discrimination "on the basis of sex," the exclusion affects male and female *employees* equally since both may have pregnant dependent daughters. The EEOC's guidelines permit differential treatment of the pregnancies of dependents who are not spouses.

image of the plan at issue in *Gilbert*. The pregnancy limitation in this case violates Title VII by discriminating against male employees.[26]

The judgment of the Court of Appeals is affirmed.

JUSTICE REHNQUIST, with whom JUSTICE POWELL joins, dissenting.

In General Electric Co. v. Gilbert, we held that an exclusion of pregnancy from a disability-benefits plan is not discrimination "because of [an] individual's * * * sex" within the meaning of Title VII. In our view, therefore, Title VII was not violated by an employer's disability plan that provided all employees with non-occupational sickness and accident benefits, but excluded from the plan's coverage disabilities arising from pregnancy. Under our decision in *Gilbert*, petitioner's otherwise inclusive benefits plan that excludes pregnancy benefits for a male employee's spouse clearly would not violate Title VII. For a different result to obtain, *Gilbert* would have to be judicially overruled by this Court or Congress would have to legislatively overrule our decision in its entirety by amending Title VII.

Today, the Court purports to find the latter by relying on the Pregnancy Discrimination Act of 1978, a statute that plainly speaks only of female employees affected by pregnancy and says nothing about spouses of male employees. Congress, of course, was free to legislatively overrule *Gilbert* in whole or in part, and there is no question but what the Pregnancy Discrimination Act manifests congressional dissatisfaction with the result we reached in *Gilbert*. But I think the Court reads far more into the Pregnancy Discrimination Act than Congress put there, and that therefore it is the Court, and not Congress, which is now overruling *Gilbert*.

In a case presenting a relatively simple question of statutory construction, the Court pays virtually no attention to the language of the Pregnancy Discrimination Act or the legislative history pertaining to that language. * * *

The Court recognizes that this provision is merely definitional and that "[u]ltimately the question we must decide is whether petitioner has discriminated against its male employees * * * because of their sex within the meaning of §703(a)(1)" of Title VII. * * * It is undisputed that in §703(a)(1) the word "individual" refers to an employee or applicant for employment. As modified by the first clause of the definitional provision of the Pregnancy Discrimination Act, the proscription in §703(a)(1) is for discrimination "against any individual * * * *because of such individual's * * * pregnancy,* childbirth, or related medical conditions." This can only be read as referring to the pregnancy of an *employee*.

---

[26]Because the 1978 Act expressly states that exclusion of pregnancy coverage is gender-based discrimination on its face, it eliminates any need to consider the average monetary value of the plan's coverage to male and female employees.

The cost of providing complete health insurance coverage for the dependents of male employees, including pregnant wives, might exceed the cost of providing such coverage for the dependents of female employees. But although that type of cost differential may properly be analyzed in passing on the constitutionality of a State's health insurance plan, see Geduldig v. Aiello, *supra*, no such justification is recognized under Title VII once discrimination has been shown. *Manhart* ("It shall not be a defense under Title VII to a charge of sex discrimination in benefits that the cost of such benefits is greater with respect to one sex than the other.").

That this result was not inadvertent on the part of Congress is made very evident by the second clause of the Act, language that the Court essentially ignores in its opinion. When Congress in this clause further explained the proscription it was creating by saying that "women affected by pregnancy * * * shall be treated the same * * * as other persons not so affected but similar in their ability or inability to work " it could only have been referring to female employees.

The Court concedes that this is a correct reading of the second clause. Ante, at n. 14. Then in an apparent effort to escape the impact of this provision, the Court asserts that "[t]he meaning of the first clause is not limited by the specific language in the second clause." Ante, at n. 14. I do not disagree. But this conclusion does not help the Court, for as explained above, when the definitional provision of the first clause is inserted in §703(a)(1), it says the very same thing: the proscription added to Title VII applies only to female employees.

The plain language of the Pregnancy Discrimination Act leaves little room for the Court's conclusion that the Act was intended to extend beyond female employees. The Court concedes that "congressional discussion focused on the needs of female members of the work force rather than spouses of male employees." In fact, the singular focus of discussion on the problems of the pregnant worker is striking.

When introducing the Senate Report on the bill that later became the Pregnancy Discrimination Act, its principal sponsor, Senator Williams, explained:

"Because of the Supreme Court's decision in the *Gilbert* case, this legislation is necessary to provide fundamental protection against sex discrimination for our Nation's 42 million working women. This protection will go a long way toward insuring that American women are permitted to assume their rightful place in our Nation's economy."

"In addition to providing protection to working women with regard to fringe benefit programs, such as health and disability insurance programs, this legislation will prohibit other employment policies which adversely affect *pregnant workers*." (emphasis added).

* * * [T]he Congressional Record is overflowing with similar statements by individual members of Congress expressing their intention to insure with the Pregnancy Discrimination Act that working women are not treated differently because of pregnancy. Consistent with these views, all three committee reports on the bills that led to the Pregnancy Discrimination Act expressly state that the Act would require employers to treat pregnant employees the same as "other employees."

The Court tries to avoid the impact of this legislative history by saying that it "does not create a 'negative inference' limiting the scope of the act to the specific problem that motivated its enactment." This reasoning might have some force if the legislative history was silent on an arguably related issue. But the legislative history is not silent. The Senate Report provides:

"* * * Presumably because plans which provide comprehensive medical coverage for spouses of women employees but not spouses of male employees are rare, we are not aware of any Title VII litigation concerning such plans. It is certainly not this committee's desire to encourage the institution of such plans. If such plans should be instituted in the future, the question would remain whether, under Title

VII, the affected employees were discriminated against on the basis of their sex as regards the extent of coverage for their dependents."

This plainly disclaims any intention to deal with the issue presented in this case. Where Congress says that it would not want "to encourage" plans such as petitioner's, it cannot plausibly be argued that Congress has intended "to prohibit" such plans. * * *

It seems to me that analysis of this case should end here. Under our decision in General Electric Co. v. Gilbert petitioner's exclusion of pregnancy benefits for male employee's spouses would not offend Title VII. Nothing in the Pregnancy Discrimination Act was intended to reach beyond female employees. Thus, *Gilbert* controls and requires that we reverse the Court of Appeals. But it is here, at what should be the stopping place, that the Court begins. * * *

The crux of the Court's reasoning is that even though the Pregnancy Discrimination Act redefines the phrases "because of sex" and "on the basis of sex" only to include discrimination against female employees affected by pregnancy, Congress also expressed its view that in *Gilbert* "the Supreme Court * * * erroneously interpreted Congressional intent." Somehow the Court then concludes that this renders all of *Gilbert* obsolete.

In support of its argument, the Court points to a few passages in congressional reports and several statements by various members of the 95th Congress to the effect that the Court in *Gilbert* had, when it construed Title VII, misperceived the intent of the 88th Congress. The Court also points out that "[m]any of [the members of 95th Congress] expressly agreed with the views of the dissenting Justices." Certainly various members of Congress said as much. But the fact remains that Congress as a body has not expressed these sweeping views in the Pregnancy Discrimination Act.

Under our decision in General Electric Co. v. Gilbert, petitioner's exclusion of pregnancy benefits for male employee's spouses would not violate Title VII. Since nothing in the Pregnancy Discrimination Act even arguably reaches beyond female employees affected by pregnancy, *Gilbert* requires that we reverse the Court of Appeals. Because the Court concludes otherwise, I dissent.

NOTES AND PROBLEMS FOR DISCUSSION

1. (a) The majority and the dissenters in *Newport News* acknowledged the need to construe the second clause of §701(k). The majority appears to conclude that since spousal health care benefits, like other fringe benefits, are terms and conditions of employment, they are provided for "employment related purposes" and thus must cover pregnancy to the same extent as other medical conditions. But this analysis is not furthered by the text in footnote 14, much to the dissenters' delight. Yet how convincing is the dissent's legislative history-based argument that since the amendment was aimed predominantly at protecting *female* employees from discrimination, it should not be interpreted to prevent discrimination against *male* employees with respect to *their* fringe benefits? Not surprisingly, the three dissenting Justices in *Gilbert* were part of the majority in *Newport* News. A fourth majority member, Justice O'Connor, had not been a member of Court when it decided *Gilbert*.

But the seven member majority in *Newport News* also included Chief Justice Burger and Justices White and Blackmun, all of whom had been in the majority in *Gilbert*.

(b) The passage of the PDA forced employers now to treat pregnancy like all other covered conditions. But does the statute's mandate to terminate pregnancy distinctions apply to an employer's pension plan that limited years-of-service credit for individuals who took pregnancy leave *prior* to the enactment of the PDA while giving full credit for disability leave for all other conditions taken during that same period? In AT&T CORP. v. HULTEEN, 556 U.S. 701, 129 S.Ct. 1962, 173 L.Ed.2d 898 (2009), the Court acknowledged that adopting a service credit rule unfavorable to those taking pregnancy leave *after* the enactment would violate Title VII. But, the majority continued, because seniority systems are afforded special consideration under §703(h) of Title VII, and, therefore, maintaining their stability is a valued statutory objective, a seniority system "does not necessarily" violate the statute when it gives *current* effect (through lower pension payments) to rules that operated *before* the enactment of the PDA. The Court construed §703(h) to permit benefit differentials produced by a bona fide seniority-based pension plan unless they were the result of an intention to discriminate. It rejected the plaintiffs' argument that the enactment of the PDA was intended to exclude pregnancy-based distinctions in seniority-based fringe benefit plans from the application of §703(h). As long as the seniority system was not formulated for the purpose of discriminating, the Court added, the mere fact that it operated to disadvantage employees on the basis of pregnancy was not unlawful. To the contrary, the Court explained, the language of §703(h) reflected Congress' desire to protect seniority systems from attack unless they were created for a discriminatory purpose. And at the time the employer's calculation–of-service credit rule was created, an accrual rule limiting seniority credit for time taken for pregnancy leave did not constitute, per *General Electric*, unlawful sex-based discrimination. Thus, since the employer's differential accrual rule contained a permissible pregnancy-based distinction when it was created, it could not have been formulated with an intention to discriminate. Moreover, the Court emphasized, to read the PDA as applying retroactively to recharacterize such a pregnancy-differentiated plan as having been unlawful when created "is not a serious possibility." Statutes are presumed to apply non-retroactively in order to conform to expectations and to avoid potential unfairness, absent a clear demonstration of legislative intent to the contrary. In the absence of such intent, as here, the Court reasoned, the PDA would apply prospectively, i.e., to leave taken after this statute's effective date. Accordingly, the employer's method of calculating years of service for pension purposes as to pre-PDA pregnancy leave was protected by §703(h) because it was the product of a bona fide system.

2. (a) Suppose an employer had no paid sick leave policy, but permitted all employees to take up to two weeks unpaid sick leave before discharging them. Further assume that the employer uniformly discharged any employee who exceeded the two-week limit. If the employer denied a pregnant female employee's request for additional unpaid leave for pregnancy and maternity purposes and discharged her after the expiration of the two-week period, can she state a claim of sex discrimination? Is *Griggs* applicable here? In STOUT v. BAXTER HEALTHCARE CORP., 282 F.3d 856 (5th Cir.2002), an employer's attendance policy mandated the discharge of any probationary employee who missed more than three days during the probationary period. The plaintiff was discharged after missing two weeks as the result of a miscarriage. The appellate court affirmed the trial court's grant of summary judgment on the plaintiff's disproportionate impact claim of pregnancy-based discrimination. The Fifth Circuit held that regardless of whether the policy created a disproportionate impact on pregnant employees, since the PDA did not require preferential treatment of pregnant employees, and, in fact, mandated that pregnant employees be treated the same for all employment related purposes as non-pregnant employees, the statute could not be construed to require an employer to treat pregnancy-related absences more leniently than other absences. To do so, the court explained, would impermissibly transform the PDA into a guarantee of medical leave for pregnant employees.

The California legislature adopted the contrary view when it enacted a statute that required employers subject to the provisions of Title VII to provide every female employee with up to four months unpaid pregnancy disability leave and the right to return to her job or, if it was unavailable, to a substantially similar position. In CALIFORNIA FEDERAL SAVINGS AND LOAN ASS'N v. GUERRA, 479 U.S. 272, 107 S.Ct. 683, 93 L.Ed.2d 613 (1987), the Supreme Court took up the question of whether this "preferential" treatment of pregnant employees collided with the clause in §701(k) stating that "women affected by pregnancy, childbirth, or related medical conditions shall be treated the same for all employment-related purposes". In *Guerra*, the defendant's unpaid disability leave policy expressly reserved the right to terminate any returning employee for whom a similar position was not available. The company filed an action seeking a declaration that the California statute was inconsistent with and pre-empted by Title VII and an injunction against enforcement of the state law. The district court ruled that the preferential-to-pregnancy provisions of the state law were pre-empted by Title VII and thus were inoperative under the Supremacy Clause of the U.S. Constitution. The Ninth Circuit reversed on the ground that a state law guaranteeing women employees a certain amount of pregnancy disability leave not only was not inconsistent with Title VII, but was in furtherance of the federal policy of ensuring equal employment opportunity to women.

A majority of six members of the Supreme Court, in three separate opinions, agreed to affirm the judgment of the court of appeals. The opinion of the Court, written by Justice Marshall and joined in by Justices Brennan, Blackmun and O'Connor, noted that §708 of Title VII provided that Title VII only pre-empted a state law "which purports to require or permit the doing of any act which would be an unlawful employment practice under this title" and that §1104 of Title XI, applicable to all titles of the 1964 Civil Rights Act, stated that state laws were pre-empted by the 1964 Act when a state law "is inconsistent with any of the purposes of this Act or any provision thereof." Accordingly, the plurality reasoned, state laws could provide more extensive protections than Title VII offered as long as these extra protections did not conflict with either the terms or policies of the federal law. The plurality explained that in deciding in *Newport News* that Congress, through the enactment of the PDA, had intended to overturn both the Court's judgment and analysis in *Gilbert*, the Court had not held that Congress also had intended to prohibit employers from affording preferential treatment to pregnant workers. Rather, the *Guerra* plurality concluded, the legislative history of the PDA indicated that this enactment was intended to guarantee to women the right to fully participate in the workforce without being forced to sacrifice their participation in family life. Thus, since Title VII did not preclude this form of preferential treatment of pregnancy, the state law could not be pre-empted under either §§708 or 1104. Title VII merely created a minimum level of protections for pregnant workers that could be augmented by state legislation. Moreover, by limiting the right to disability leave and reinstatement to the period of physical disability occasioned by pregnancy, the state law did not erect or reflect a stereotypical view of pregnancy that would be inconsistent with, and thus pre-empted by Title VII. Finally, the plurality added, since the state law did not prevent employers from according identical disability leave and reinstatement rights to non-pregnant employees, the statute did not mandate that pregnant workers be treated more generously than non-pregnant workers. Thus, compliance with the federal and state statutes was not a physical impossibility.

Justice Stevens agreed with the plurality's view that the California statute did not conflict with the purposes of the PDA, but wrote separately to state his view that preferential treatment of pregnant workers was only permitted by the PDA when that preference was designed to achieve equality of employment opportunities. Justice Scalia also agreed with the result reached by the plurality, but based his decision solely on the ground that the state law did not purport to require or permit any act that would be an unlawful employment practice under any conceivable interpretation of the PDA. Justice White, joined by the Chief Justice and Justice Powell, stated that the "shall be treated the same" clause of the PDA codified a federal mandate of neutrality that precluded enforcement of a state statute requiring employers to provide disability benefits to pregnant workers that they didn't have to give to non-pregnant employees.

Did the Supreme Court adequately resolve the statutory dilemma? For thoughtful insights into the "special treatment/equal treatment" debate, see Herma H. Kay, *Equality and Difference: The Case of Pregnancy,* 1 BERKELEY WOMEN'S L.J. 1 (1985); Lucinda M. Finley, *Transcending Equality Theory: A Way Out Of The Maternity And The Workplace Debate,* 86 COL.L.REV. 1118 (1986); Joan C. Williams, *Dissolving The Sameness/Difference Debate: A Postmodern Path Beyond Essentialism in Feminist and Critical Race Theory,* 1991 DUKE L.J. 296 (1991).

Would the result in *Guerra* have been different if the policy had been implemented on a voluntary basis by a private employer rather than instituted pursuant to state law? *See* Harness v. Hartz Mountain Corp., 877 F.2d 1307 (6th Cir.1989), cert. denied, 493 U.S. 1024, 110 S.Ct. 728, 107 L.Ed.2d 747 (1990).

(b) Does the ruling in *Guerra* that the PDA was not intended to prohibit employers from affording preferential treatment to pregnant workers also mean that pregnant employees must be provided every employment benefit that is accorded to any other category of employee? In answering that question, the courts again were faced with addressing the meaning of the second clause of §701(k) mandating that employers treat pregnant workers "the same for all employment-related purposes * * * as other persons not so affected but *similar in their ability or inability to work'* (emphasis added).

This issue came to a head in YOUNG v. UNITED PARCEL SERVICE, INC., 575 U.S. ___, 135 S.Ct. 1338 (2015). UPS required all drivers to manipulate packages weighing up to 70 pounds and to assist in moving packages weighing up to 150 pounds. Additionally, its governing collective bargaining agreement provided for temporary alternate work for workers who were unable to perform normal work assignments because of an on-the-job injury. Pursuant to that obligation, the company offered light duty work to employees who were either (1) injured on the job, or (2) suffering from any permanent impairment cognizable under the Americans with Disabilities Act (ADA). But it did not extend this option for reassignment to light duty work to any female worker whose limitation arose solely as a result of her pregnancy. The plaintiff Young, an early morning "air driver", was required to pick up packages that had arrived by air carrier the previous night, load them on her van, and deliver them. After she became pregnant, the plaintiff requested and received a leave of absence. But when Young was ready to return to work, she gave her supervisor a note from her doctor stating that Young should not lift more than twenty pounds for the first twenty weeks of her pregnancy, and then not more than ten pounds thereafter. The company told Young that it would not permit her to return to work with any such restriction, even though she told them that her job rarely required her to lift more than twenty pounds, that other employees had agreed to help her, and that she was willing to shift to a job involving light work. The company also decided that she was not eligible for light duty reassignment because her limitation was not the result of an on-the-job injury or a disability subject to the duty to accommodate under the ADA and that the light duty offer was not available to individuals whose limitation was caused by pregnancy. Accordingly, since the plaintiff was not prepared to return to work and be subject to the normal lifting requirement, she was not permitted to return. She filed suit alleging discrimination on the bases of sex, pregnancy, and disability.

The trial court granted summary judgment in favor of the defendant as to all of Young's claims. It dismissed the ADA claim on the ground that the plaintiff was not disabled within the meaning of the statute, including rejecting the plaintiff's claim that she had been regarded as being disabled. But the preeminent issue in the case was whether the defendant's light duty policy limiting that option to injured and disabled workers, but not pregnant workers, violated the PDA. The trial court ruled that the fact that the light duty option was not extended to pregnant workers did *not* constitute discrimination on the basis of pregnancy. The Fourth Circuit agreed, holding that the restriction on the availability of the light duty option to injured and disabled workers was pregnancy-blind. It rejected the plaintiff's argument that the PDA imposed on employers the obligation to accord pregnant workers "most favored nation" status vis-à-vis all other employees, i.e., a requirement that any benefit or accommodation made available to any group of workers also had to be provided to pregnant workers. The statutory requirement that pregnant workers be treated the same for all employment-related purposes as non-pregnant workers only meant, according to the Fourth Circuit, that pregnant workers must be treated the same as the entire universe of male and female nonpregnant workers. To do otherwise, the court explained, would provide pregnant workers with a right to accommodations not encompassed by the PDA. For example, accepting the plaintiff's argument, the court reasoned, would require a pregnant worker to be offered light work that would not be offered to a nonpregnant worker whose limitation was caused by an off-the-job, non-ADA injury. Thus, it concluded, where an employer treats pregnant and nonpregnant workers alike, the employer has fulfilled its obligations under the PDA.

In July, 2014, two weeks after the Supreme Court granted certiorari in *Young*, the EEOC amended its Enforcement Guidance on the Pregnancy Discrimination Act. This new guideline provided, *inter alia*, that "a pregnant worker with a work restriction who challenges a denial of light duty should be able to establish a prima facie case of discrimination . . . by identifying any other employee who is similar in his or her ability or inability to work and who was treated more favorably, including employees injured on the job and/or covered by the ADA."

Moreover, in this section of the Guidance, the EEOC specifically rejected the reasoning, which was central to the ruling of the Fourth Circuit, that "the PDA does not require an employer to provide light duty for a pregnant worker if the employer has a policy or practice limiting light duty to workers injured on the job and/or to employees with disabilities under the ADA."

By a vote of 5-1-3, the Supreme Court reversed the Fourth Circuit, holding that the plaintiff had established a genuine issue of fact with respect to the existence of the elements of the prima facie case. Accordingly, it remanded for further proceedings. In so ruling, the majority explained that the fact that the employer's accommodation policy did not expressly exclude pregnant workers or include all but pregnant workers only meant that the plaintiff could not establish a prima facie case of intentional discrimination by direct evidence. However, the majority insisted, the plaintiff could rely on the circumstantial evidence-based formula set forth in *McDonnell Douglas* and its progeny. And that framework, in a failure-to-accommodate-to-pregnancy context, meant that the plaintiff had to establish that (1) she was pregnant when; (2) she sought accommodation; (3) she was not accommodated; and (4) the employer did accommodate others who were similar in their ability or inability to work.

This then required the Court to explain what a plaintiff had to show to prove that those who were accommodated were "similar in ability or inability to work" to pregnant workers. The majority, agreeing with the Fourth Circuit, rejected the plaintiff's proposed interpretation – that the PDA granted pregnant workers a "most-favored-nation" status, i.e., requiring that any accommodation made to any individual also had to be made available to all pregnant employees. It also declined to defer to the EEOC's July, 2014 revised Guideline, noting that this guideline had been issued after *certiorari* had been granted and that this Guideline took a position on an issue about which previously guidelines had been silent and did so without any explanation. At the same time, the Court also held that the plaintiff did not have to prove that the accommodated employees were identical in all respects (other than the fact of pregnancy) to pregnant-employees. And while it did not precisely indicate what would typically suffice to meet the "similarity" standard, the Court held that this plaintiff had offered evidence that established a genuine issue of fact as to whether the defendant had provided more favorable treatment to some employees whose situation "cannot reasonably be distinguished" from hers.

The Court also offered further insight into the application of the other components of the *McDonnel Douglas* standard to pregnancy-based failure to accommodate claims. Once a plaintiff has established a prima facie and the defendant has offered evidence of a nondiscriminatory explanation for its decision (and a claim that it is more expensive or less convenient to extend the accommodation to pregnant employees is not, the Court declared, such a legitimate, nondiscriminatory reason), the plaintiff has to establish that this explanation is a pretext for pregnancy-based discrimination. And pretext, in this context, can be established by proving that the employer's policies *impose a significant burden on pregnant workers* and that the defendant's nondiscriminatory reasons are not sufficiently strong to justify that burden. Furthermore, the plaintiff can establish a genuine issue of fact (and thereby defeat a motion for judgment as a matter of law and get to the jury on this issue) on the existence of a "significant burden" by offering evidence that the employer accommodated a large percentage (but not all) of its nonpregnant workers while not accommodating a large percentage of pregnant workers. Applying this analysis to the instant case, the majority concluded that the fact that the defendant had three separate accommodation policies for three classes of non-pregnant employees created an issue of fact as to the existence of a significant burden on pregnant employees.

The Court noted that the plaintiff Young had *not* asserted a disparate impact-based claim of discrimination. Consequently, the entire opinion focused solely and expressly on the framework for proving intentional discrimination. Yet what do you make of the Court's holding that the plaintiff could establish pretext by showing that the employer's policy *significantly burdened* pregnant workers? Isn't that another way of saying that it had a disproportionately adverse effect on pregnant workers? If so, does this opinion suggest that the Court is beginning to conflate these two previously alternative methods of proving discrimination?

In one of the first post-*Young* appellate court decisions, the Second Circuit addressed an employer's accommodation policy that was similar to the one examined in *Young*. In LEGG v. ULSTER COUNTY, 820 F.3d 67 (2d Cir. 2016), the defendant had a light duty policy that applied only to employees who were injured on the job. When the plaintiff became pregnant and asked for reassignment to light duty work pursuant to that policy, the employer declined, as it said it would do for any pregnant employee. At the end of the plaintiff's case-in-chief at trial, the trial court granted a defense motion for judgment as a matter of law on the ground that the policy was facially neutral since it denied light duty accommodation to any employee whose request was based on anything other than an on-the-job injury. The Second Circuit reversed, ruling that a reasonable jury could find that the plaintiff had offered sufficient circumstantial evidence to support a claim of intentional discrimination. Specifically, it held that since the employer's light duty policy excluded 100% of all pregnant workers, but that a large percentage of non-pregnant workers were, at least, eligible for this accommodation, a reasonable jury could conclude that the policy imposed a significant burden of pregnant employees. And the court also held that a reasonable jury could have found that the defendant's purported nondiscriminatory justification – that its accommodation policy was limited to persons injured on the job because state workers' compensation law required payment for persons injured on the job but not to employees who became unable to work for other reasons – was a pretext for intentional discrimination. While it acknowledged that reliance on the state workers' compensation law was a nondiscriminatory explanation, the court determined that a reasonable jury could have found from the evidence that the employer actually was motivated by the desire to avoid the extra costs associated with providing this benefit to pregnant workers. Therefore, it held, a reasonable jury could have found that the defendant's explanation was an insufficient reason for denying accommodation to pregnant employees. Accordingly, the appellate court ruled that it was error to issue judgment as a matter of law to the defense and ordered the case remanded for a new trial so the issues could be resolved by a jury.

(c) University Hospital's written policy on the treatment of AIDS patients clearly states that although all nurses are required to take "Universal Precautions" provided by the Center for Disease Control, any nurse who refuses to treat any patient to whom he or she has been assigned is subject to termination. When Nurse Carol Hathaway was assigned a patient diagnosed as HIV positive, she refused to treat him on the ground that she was pregnant. In addition, Hathaway informed her supervisor that she had gestational diabetes (a diabetic condition that occurs only when a woman is pregnant) and that because of this condition, she had a weakened immune system and was particularly susceptible to transmission of infectious diseases such as the opportunistic infections commonly present in AIDS patients. The supervisor informed Hathaway of the hospital's policy and when Hathaway refused either to treat the patient or to resign, she was terminated.   Hathaway filed a Title VII claim, alleging that she was discriminated against on the basis of her pregnancy.   Can she state a disparate treatment or disproportionate impact claim? *See* Armstrong v. Flowers Hospital, Inc., 33 F.3d 1308 (11th Cir.1994).

3.   Suppose an employer permits employees, at the company's sole discretion, to take unpaid personal leaves of absence. Further assume that Suzie Cones requested such leave based on her inability to wean her six-week-old infant from breast-feeding, that the company denied the request and that she was discharged when she refused to report for work. Was the denial of her request for personal leave proscribed sex discrimination under Title VII? *See* Wallace v. Pyro Mining Co., 789 F.Supp. 867 (W.D. Ky. 1990), aff'd without opinion, 951 F.2d 351 (6th Cir.1991).

4.   (a) Is infertility a pregnancy or childbirth-related medical condition such that the exclusion of coverage for infertility treatments by a company's health insurance plan violates the PDA? In KRAUEL v. IOWA METHODIST MEDICAL CENTER, 95 F.3d 674 (8th Cir.1996), the circuit court agreed with the trial judge that both pregnancy and childbirth are conditions that occur after conception and that infertility is not a sex-based condition since it can afflict both men and women. Consequently, it held that infertility was not intended by Congress to fall within the protective ambit of the PDA.   The circuit court also rejected the plaintiff's claim that since women undergo a majority of the fertility treatment and, consequently, bear most of the treatment expenses, an infertility-based exclusion created a disproportionate impact upon women. In the instant case, the courts noted, the employer provided medical coverage for employee spouses and the plaintiff offered no evidence that female employees were affected more adversely that the female spouses of male employees. Consequently, it reasoned, since the infertility exclusion would produce the same medical and financial impact upon female employees and male employees with dependent coverage for their female spouses, the plaintiffs had not established a prima facie case of impact discrimination and affirmed the grant of summary judgment in favor of the defendant. *But see* Hall v. Nalco Company, 534 F.3d 644 (7th Cir. 2008) (terminating an employee for taking time off to undergo in vitro fertilization is a sex-specific action because it discriminates on the basis of the sex-specific characteristic of childrearing capacity and as to a surgical procedure performed only on women). Doesn't this suggest that if an employer excludes coverage for IVF (or any other female-specific) infertility treatment but extends coverage to male-specific fertility treatments, it would be in violation? Whether an infertile individual can state a claim under the Americans With Disabilities Act is examined *infra*, at Chapter 11, Sec. A.

(b) Can a female employee discharged for having an abortion state a claim under Title VII? *See* Turic v. Holland Hospitality, Inc., 85 F.3d 1211 (6ᵗʰ Cir.1996) (yes; an abortion is "a related medical condition" within the meaning of the PDA where the plaintiff was discharged for having had an abortion, for intending to have an abortion, or for announcing that she was considering having an abortion.); Doe v. C.A.R.S. Protection Plus, Inc., 527 F.3d 358 (3d Cir. 2008) (Id., relying on *Turic*). What about a woman who was terminated from her job because she was lactating? In EEOC v. HOUSTON FUNDING II, LTD., 717 F.3d 425 (5ᵗʰ Cir. 2013), the Fifth circuit held that discharging an employee because she was lactating constituted sex-based discrimination because (1) it imposes upon women a burden that male employees could not suffer; and (2) lactation is a physiological result of being pregnant and therefore is a "related medical condition" of pregnancy for purposes of the PDA). But having said that, suppose a female employee asks the employer to provide a private room where she can breastfeed or asks for a rest period during which she can repair to a restroom to breastfeed. Would the employer's refusal to accommodate her request constitute discrimination on the basis of sex within the meaning of the PDA? In HICKS v. CITY OF TUSCALOOSA, 870 F.3d 1253 (11ᵗʰ Cir. 2017), the Eleventh Circuit, noting the Fifth circuit's ruling in *Houston Funding* with approval, nevertheless held that there was a distinction between discrimination on the basis of sex, which is prohibited, and sex-based accommodation, which is not required by Title VII. As support for that ruling the Eleventh Circuit noted the Supreme Court's rejection of the "most favored nation" status claim that the pregnant workers had asserted in *Young v. v.UPS*. (*See* Note 2(b), *supra*.). Accordingly, it held that the employer was not obligated to provide any such accommodation under the PDA.

(c) Margo Jones, a nurse at County Hospital, resigned her position as a result of complications from her pregnancy. Two years later, she applied for a part-time position with the hospital. During the pre-employment interview, Margo was asked whether she planned to have more children. According to Margo, the interviewer then told her that she would not be rehired because of the complications in scheduling caused by the many absences that had occurred during her past pregnancy. Margo filed a sex discrimination charge under Title VII, relying on §701(k). The defense responded with a motion to dismiss for failure to state a claim upon which relief can be granted on the ground that the plaintiff was not pregnant at the time she was denied re-employment. How should the court rule on this motion? In KOCAK v. COMMUNITY HEALTH PARTNERS, 400 F.3d 466 (6ᵗʰ Cir.2005), on these exact facts, the Sixth Circuit ruled that the plaintiff could state a claim. Relying on its prior ruling in *Turic, supra*, the court reasoned that since an employer violates the PDA if it terminates an employee because of her potential to have an abortion, an applicant cannot be refused employment on the basis of her potential pregnancy. However, because the plaintiff had not raised a genuine issue of fact with respect to whether the defendant's tendered nondiscriminatory explanation was a pretext, the Sixth Circuit affirmed the trial court's grant of summary judgment in favor of the defendant.

(d) Mark Shipke and Louise Frame were co-employees who were both terminated when their employer discovered that Louise had become pregnant by Mark. Mark filed a Title VII claim alleging that the employer's action violated the Pregnancy Discrimination Amendment. How should the trial court ruled on the defense motion for summary judgment? In GRIFFIN v. SISTERS OF SAINT FRANCIS, INC., 489

F.3d 838 (7th Cir. 2007), the court affirmed the trial court's grant of summary judgment in such a case, rejecting the male plaintiff's claim that he had been discriminated against because of his lover's pregnancy. The court explained that §701(k) made discrimination on the basis of pregnancy a form of sex-based discrimination. Consequently, in order for a man to state a claim related to pregnancy, the man would have to allege that he had suffered an adverse action because of *his* sex, as the male plaintiffs did in *Newport News Shipping* when they alleged that the defendant's benefit plan provided greater benefits to female employees. Since the plaintiff Griffin had not alleged that he was fired because of his sex, he could not state a claim under Title VII. Section 701(k)'s ban on pregnancy discrimination, the court concluded, covered only discrimination because of sex and not because of sexual activity or reproductive capacity

5.   Does an employer who provides only female employees with the option of taking a one year unpaid leave of absence for childrearing violate Title VII or does this constitute permissible preferential treatment pursuant to the *Guerra* Court's interpretation of the PDA? In SCHAFER v. BOARD OF PUBLIC EDUCATION OF SCHOOL DISTRICT OF PITTSBURGH, 903 F.2d 243 (3d Cir.1990), the court struck down as violative of Title VII a collective bargaining provision that granted only female teachers the right to a one year unpaid leave of absence for childrearing if taken immediately after childbirth. The court distinguished this plan from the statutory scheme in *Guerra* on the ground that the *Guerra* plurality limited its holding to a preference that was specifically limited to the period of actual physical disability. The contractual provision in *Schafer*, however, did not require that the female be disabled in order to obtain the unpaid leave. Therefore, the court reasoned, the leave was not related to conditions of pregnancy as required by the PDA.

6.   Note that a defendant will be exempted from the statutory prohibition against pregnancy classifications in cases where it can successfully invoke either the business necessity or BFOQ defense. *Compare* Harriss v. Pan American World Airways, Inc., 649 F.2d 670 (9th Cir.1980) (policy requiring flight attendants to take maternity leave immediately upon discovery of pregnancy justified under BFOQ defense) *with* Burwell v. Eastern Air Lines, Inc., 633 F.2d 361 (4th Cir.1980), cert. denied, 450 U.S. 965, 101 S.Ct. 1480, 67 L.Ed.2d 613 (1981) (business necessity defense justifies mandatory maternity leave only from the commencement of the 28th week of pregnancy.).

7.   Pregnancy and maternity policies used by public employers have been challenged under the Equal Protection and Due Process Clauses of the Constitution as well as under Title VII. In GEDULDIG v. AIELLO, 417 U.S. 484, 94 S.Ct. 2485, 41 L.Ed.2d 256 (1974), the Supreme Court rejected an equal protection attack upon an employee-funded California disability insurance system that specifically excluded pregnancy from its list of compensable disabilities. The Court held that the State's determination not to provide a totally comprehensive insurance program did not amount to invidious sex-based discrimination under the Equal Protection Clause. Since the plan provided equivalent aggregate risk protection to both sexes, the exclusion of pregnancy, though admittedly affecting only women, was not a sex-based classification for constitutional purposes. This reasoning later served as the foundation for the Court's Title VII ruling in *Gilbert*.

The constitutionality of mandatory maternity leave for public school teachers was addressed in CLEVELAND BOARD OF EDUCATION v. LAFLEUR, 414 U.S. 632, 94 S.Ct. 791, 39 L.Ed.2d 52 (1974). There, the Court struck down the petitioner's policy requiring every pregnant teacher to take unpaid maternity leave at the end of the fourth month of pregnancy as violative of the Due Process Clause of the Fourteenth Amendment. This inflexible cutoff date, the Court reasoned, contained an irrebutable presumption — that all pregnant teachers become physically incapable of teaching at the same designated moment — and applied it even in the face of undisputed contrary medical evidence as to an individual teacher. The Court concluded that the Due Process Clause could not tolerate an irrebutable presumption that was not necessarily or universally true when the School Board had a reasonable alternative method of making individualized determinations as to physical competence. The Court applied this same analysis in also invalidating the Board's policy permitting teachers to return from maternity leave no sooner than the beginning of the regular semester following the date the teacher's child attained the age of three months. However, the Court's subsequent ruling in WEINBERGER v. SALFI, 422 U.S. 749, 95 S.Ct. 2457, 45 L.Ed.2d 522 (1975), in which it rejected a due process challenge to a Social Security Act provision that awarded benefits to a deceased wage earner's surviving widow and stepchildren only if they had been related to the deceased for at least nine months prior to his death, indicates that the Court subsequently abandoned the irrebutable presumption doctrine. See generally Jonathon B. Chase, *The Premature Demise of Irrebutable Presumptions*, 47 U.Colo.L.Rev. 653 (1976).

THE FAMILY AND MEDICAL LEAVE ACT

The Family and Medical Leave Act of 1993, 29 U.S.C. §2601 et seq. (1993), requires employers with 50 or more employees to provide eligible employees with up to 12 weeks of unpaid leave in a 12-month period in order to provide infant care or to provide care for a child, spouse or parent with a "serious health condition." The statute defines a "serious health condition" as a condition that involves either inpatient care in a hospital or residential medical care facility, or continuing treatment by a health care provider. The legislative history also provides a non-exhaustive list of qualifying conditions, including heart attacks, back conditions requiring extensive therapy, strokes and pneumonia. Interpretive regulations issued by the Department of Labor define "serious health condition" to include a period of incapacity that requires a child's absence from school for more than three days and that involves receiving either inpatient care or continuing treatment by a medical care provider. In CALDWELL v. HOLLAND OF TEXAS, 208 F.3d 671 (8th Cir.2000), the court was presented with a claim by a single mother who was fired for absence caused by the illness of her three year old child. The court indicated that since most three year old children do not attend school, the administrative regulations were an insufficient guide to determining whether or not the child was incapacitated for the purpose of resolving whether that child had a serious health condition. The court concluded that a fact finder must determine whether the child's illness demonstrably affected his normal activity by looking, for example, at whether he participated in his daily routines or was particularly difficult to care for during the relevant period.

With respect to the parent's right to leave to care for a sick child, the statute distinguishes between children under and over the age of eighteen. The statute limits the right to leave to care for a child eighteen years of age or older to situations where that individual is "incapable of self-care because of a mental or physical disability." 29 U.S.C. §2611(12). Elsewhere in the statute, Congress delegated the task of defining "disability" to the Secretary of Labor who issued a regulation defining it as an "impairment that substantially limits one or more of the major life activities of an individual." 29 C.F.R. §825.113(c)(2). This language tracks the definition of "disability" contained in the Americans With Disabilities Act (ADA). Not surprisingly, instead of providing a separate definition of these terms, the Labor Department regulations incorporate the meaning of "impairment," "substantially limits" and "major life activity" contained in EEOC regulations issued pursuant to the ADA. These EEOC regulations, in turn, provide that among the factors to be considered in determining whether an impairment substantially limits a major life activity is the duration of the impairment and the actual or anticipated permanent or long-term impact resulting from that impairment. In NAVARRO v. PFIZER CORP., 261 F.3d 90 (1st Cir. 2001), the plaintiff was denied unpaid leave to care for her pregnant adult daughter whose high blood pressure precluded the daughter from caring for her other children. The trial court granted summary judgment for the defendant, ruling and ruled that since the plaintiff's daughter's condition was a temporary and non-chronic condition of short duration, it did not amount to a disability under the EEOC's interpretative guidelines. The First Circuit reversed, concluding that since, *inter alia*, the FMLA provides a lesser level of employment benefits than the ADA (temporary leave versus the right to potentially lifelong accommodation), Congress could not have intended to require FMLA litigants to make the same showing of durational incapacity as ADA litigants. Consequently, it was error for the trial court to defer to the ADA guidelines and to require the plaintiff to show that her daughter's impairment was long-lasting. Instead, the court concluded, it was sufficient for the impairment to be of "modest" duration to be regarded as "substantially limiting" for FMLA purposes.

In addition to providing leave to care for a child, spouse or parent, the FMLA provides employees with the right to take unpaid leave when it is needed for that employee's own illness. Eligible employees must have been employed by this employer for at least one year and have worked at least 1250 hours during the year period immediately preceding the time the leave is taken. The law encompasses public and private sector employees, with special provisions for elementary and secondary schoolteachers. A statutory employer, however, is granted the option of requiring an eligible employee to exhaust his accrued paid leave before requesting unpaid family leave. The employer also can require employees to provide medical certification where serious illness is the basis for the leave request, to give the employer thirty days' advance notice, where practicable, and to inform the employer on a regular basis as to the employee's condition and intention to return to work. The employer cannot withdraw group health insurance during the employee's absence and the employee is entitled to return to the previous or equivalent position with no loss of benefits when she returns. While the Act requires an employee to provide the employer with notice of the need for FMLA leave as soon as practicable, the employee does not have to expressly assert rights under the FMLA or even mention the FMLA in the notification; the notice must only state that leave is required.

If an employer questions the accuracy or soundness of the medical certification provided by the employee in support of a leave request, the FMLA states that the employer "may" require, at its own expense, that the employee obtain a second opinion. It further provides that if the first and second judgments differ, the employer "may" require, at its expense, that the employee obtain a third opinion. If an employer denies a leave request on the ground that it does not believe that the certification tendered by the employee established the existence of a "serious medical condition", without demanding either a second or third opinion, does its failure to invoke the statutory second opinion procedures establish the existence of a "serious medical condition" as a matter of law? In RHOADS v. FDIC, 257 F.3d 373 (4th Cir.2001), cert. denied, 535 U.S. 933, 122 S.Ct. 1309, 152 L.Ed.2d 219 (2002), the court held that the plain language of the statute, i.e., its use of the permissive "may" to define the employer's response, provided the employer who questions the validity of certification with the *option* of seeking a second and third opinion, without being required to do so. This language, the court reasoned, did not suggest that the employer's failure to follow these procedures would foreclose it from challenging whether the employee suffered from a qualifying condition. The court noted, however, the possible pitfall that could befall an employer who does not pursue a second opinion. Where, for example, the employer does not obtain contemporaneous medical information to contradict the employee's medical certification, contrary documentation obtained by the employer long after it denies the leave request might not be viewed as sufficient to generate a genuine issue of material fact for the jury as to the nonexistence of the qualifying condition.

When the plaintiff seeks to invoke the protections of the FMLA for absence occasioned by her own medical condition, Labor Department regulations provide that the employee must be "incapacitated" for more than three days in order to claim a serious health condition. If the employee's absence is caused not by one discrete illness, but a series of conditions that, individually, do not rise to the level of a "serious medical condition", can this series of illnesses, taken together, satisfy the statutory requirement? *See* Price v. City Of Fort Wayne, 117 F.3d 1022 (7th Cir.1997) (multiple diagnoses can cumulatively give rise to a "serious health condition").

In comparison to the language found in Title VII, the FMLA defines "employer" to include, *inter alia*, "any person who acts, directly or indirectly, in the interest of an employer to any of the employees of such employer * * *." Does this suggest that an individual employee could be sued under the FMLA? In FREEMON v. FOLEY, 911 F.Supp. 326 (N.D.Ill.1995), the court noted that the FMLA language tracked the definition of "employer" contained in the Fair Labor Standards Act (FLSA). Accordingly, it ruled, it was appropriate to look to FLSA, rather than to Title VII, jurisprudence to resolve this question. The court then pointed to Fourth Circuit cases holding that an individual could be suable as an "employer" under the FLSA where the individual employee possessed supervisory authority over the complaining employee and was responsible in whole or part for the alleged violation. In the instant case, the court ruled, although the plaintiff's supervisors did not possess unilateral authority to deny the plaintiff's request for leave or to terminate her, they did control "in whole or in part" her ability to take a leave of absence and return to her position. Accordingly, the court denied the defendants' motion for summary judgment. On the other hand, in MITCHELL v. CHAPMAN, 343 F.3d 811 (6th Cir.2003), the Sixth Circuit concluded that because the definition of "employer" in the FLSA incorporated the individual liability provision and "public agency" provision within a single clause, while these two provisions were disaggregated into separate subsections of the FMLA, the FMLA should be construed not to extend individual liability to supervisors employed by public agencies.

Suppose an employee voluntarily resigns and subsequently seeks reemployment with her former employer. If the employer refuses to rehire that individual solely because of excessive absences taken as FMLA leave during her previous period of employment, can the employee state a retaliation claim under the FMLA? The FMLA prohibits an employer from interfering with an "employee's" attempt to exercise her right to leave under that statute. But does the private right of action granted to "employees" extend to former employees? In SMITH v. BELLSOUTH TELECOMMUNICATIONS, INC., 273 F.3d 1303 (11th Cir.2001), the trial court had granted summary judgment to the defendant on the ground that the statutory right of action was available only to individuals who suffered adverse action during their period of employment. The Eleventh Circuit reversed, holding that although the statutory definition of "employee" was ambiguous, the Department of Labor regulation that construed the FMLA to prohibit an employer from taking FMLA leave into account in hiring decisions was reasonable and, therefore, was entitled to deference by the court. The narrow interpretation of "employee" applied by the district court, the circuit court explained, would embolden employers to retaliate against individuals who previously (in their employ or in the employ of others) had exercised their statutory right to leave and this, in turn, would chill the exercise of FMLA guaranteed rights and thereby frustrate the purposes of the Act. Consequently, the court ruled that a former employee who alleges that his former employer refused to rehire her because of her past use of FMLA leave qualifies as an "employee" under the Act.

Can a husband whose wife filed an FMLA action against their joint employer state a claim of retaliation under the FMLA when he allegedly was retaliated against in response to his wife's filing? *See* Elsensohn v. St. Tammany Parish Sheriff's Office, 530 F.3d 368 (5th Cir. 2008) (declining to extend FMLA's anti-retaliation provision to such a derivative claim).

Section 107, the enforcement provision of the FMLA, does not mention whether an individual bringing a civil action to enforce the statute is entitled to a jury trial. Nevertheless, the language of §107 is nearly identical to that found in the Fair Labor Standards Act. Although the FLSA also does not expressly discuss the right to a jury trial, the Supreme Court in LORILLARD v. PONS, 434 U.S. 575, 98 S.Ct. 866, 55 L.Ed.2d 40 (1978), ruled that the Seventh Amendment right to jury trial applies to the civil enforcement provisions of that statute. In FRIZZELL v. SOUTHWEST MOTOR FREIGHT, 154 F.3d 641 (6th Cir.1998), the Sixth Circuit ruled that the structure of the FMLA remedial provision that distinguishes between equitable relief and damages evinced Congress' intention to make juries available to plaintiffs seeking damages and that the reference in the FMLA's legislative history to the FLSA similarly revealed a legislative design to include a right to jury under the FMLA.

Section 107 also expressly creates a private right of action to seek both equitable and money damages against any public or private employer in federal or state court.

Does the unambiguous provision of a right of action against a State employer in federal court constitute a constitutionally valid abrogation of the states' Eleventh Amendment right of sovereign immunity? In NEVADA DEPARTMENT OF HUMAN RESOURCES v. HIBBS, 538 U.S. 721, 123 S.Ct. 1972, 155 L.Ed.2d 953 (2003), the Supreme Court resolved a conflict among the circuits by upholding the constitutionality of this portion of the Act as it applied to the provision requiring unpaid leave to take care of a family member with a serious health condition. Applying the bipartite standard it had previously announced in cases assessing the constitutionality of analogous provisions in the ADEA and ADA, see *infra,* at Chapters 10 §A and 11 §A7, the Court held that this enactment (1) contained a legislative record revealing a pattern of state unconstitutional gender-based conduct, and (2) exhibited congruence and proportionality between the injury to be prevented or remedied and the means adopted to that end.

The majority reported that the legislative record of the FMLA was replete with references to the persistence of unconstitutional gender-based discrimination by the States with respect to the administration of leave benefits and concluded that this statute was designed to eliminate this documented reliance on stereotyped views of the roles of male and female employees. The majority distinguished its ruling in the instant case from its contrary conclusion with respect to Congress' attempted abrogation of sovereign immunity in the ADEA and the ADA on the ground that the age and disability-based distinctions addressed in those enactments are not subject to the heightened review standard applicable to gender-based classifications. Consequently, the burden of establishing that Congress had identified a pattern of state constitutional violations in the age and disability context was greater than in the instant case where the underlying statute seeks to combat gender discrimination.

The Court also determined that the substantive provisions of the FMLA were congruent and proportional to the targeted violation. In comparison to the provisions of the ADA and ADEA that governed every aspect of a state employer's operations, by limiting the scope of the FMLA to the administration of leave benefits, Congress had narrowly targeted its remedy to the precise interface of work and family where sex-based overgeneralizations have been and remain most prevalent. The Court additionally pointed to other limitations in the scope of the FMLA (e.g., its mandate for only unpaid leave, its application only to employees with at least one year seniority, and its exclusion of high-ranking or sensitive positions, elected officials, and appointed policymakers) as further justification for this conclusion.

Prior to the Supreme Court's ruling in *Hibbs,* the Second Circuit had struck down the FMLA's creation of a right of action for damages against state employers in federal court on the ground that by providing both male and female employees with an equal right to obtain leave to deal with their *own* serious medical conditions, the FMLA did not fall within Congress' enforcement authority under §5 of the Fourteenth Amendment because this gender-neutral remedy was not congruent or proportional to the harm — sex-based discrimination — targeted by the Fourteenth Amendment. Hale v. Mann, 219 F.3d 61 (2d Cir.2000). The Supreme Court did not address this issue in *Hibbs.* However, the majority in *Hibbs* did state that the creation of an across-the-board benefit for male and female employees was essential to attacking the state-sanctioned stereotype that only women were responsible for family care-giving and thereby ensuring that family-care leave would no longer be stigmatized as an inordinate drain on the workplace created primarily by female employees. It also made certain that employers could not evade their leave obligations by only hiring men. Post-*Hibbs*, however, the Tenth Circuit distinguished the self-care provision of leave in the FMLA from its grant of leave to care for family members. In BROCKMAN v. WYOMING DEPARTMENT OF FAMILY SERVICES, 342 F.3d 1159 (10th Cir.2003), cert. denied, 540 U.S. 1219, 124 S.Ct. 1509, 158 L.Ed.2d 155 (2004), the court ruled that since the legislative history did not tie the FMLA's personal medical leave provision to the prevention of gender-based discrimination by state employers, Congress did not effect a valid abrogation of state sovereign immunity from suits for money damages for claimed violation of the self-care medical leave provision of the FMLA.

The Supreme Court subsequently agreed that the self-care provision was distinguishable and separable from the family care provision and struck down the provision providing state employees with a right of action for damages for violations of the self-care provision. In COLEMAN v. COURT OF APPEALS OF MARYLAND, 566 U.S. 30, 132 S.Ct. 1327, 182 L.Ed.2d 296 (2012), a male employee of the Maryland Court of Appeals who requested sick leave was informed that he had to either resign or be terminated. He brought suit for damages alleging a violation of the self-care provision of the FMLA. A five member majority of the Court agreed that the FMLA's self-care provision did not validly abrogate the State's immunity from suit for damages in federal court and struck it down. A four member plurality, in an opinion by Justice Kennedy, held that this provision failed to meet the "congruent and proportionality" test the Court previously had confected to determine whether Congress's abrogation of the States' sovereign immunity was justified as an exercise of its enforcement authority under §5 of the Fourteenth Amendment. Applying that standard, the plurality determined that unlike the family-care provision of the FMLA, the self-care provision was not passed in response to a well-documented pattern of state constitutional violations accompanied by a remedy drawn in narrow terms to address or prevent those violations. The plurality explained that the evidence did not suggest that States either had facially discriminatory self-care leave policies or that they administered neutral self-care leave policies in a discriminatory way or pursuant to any sex-stereotyped attitudes. Accordingly, the plurality reasoned, the provision of a right of action for damages was not congruent or proportional to any identified constitutional violations. The plurality also rejected the argument that the self-care provision was such a necessary adjunct to the family-care provision that it should fall within the holding in *Hibbs*. Finally, the plurality noted that even if the evidence demonstrated that women were more likely to need self-care time because they are more likely to be single parents and thus need the unpaid leave to retain their jobs, evidence of disparate impact was insufficient by itself to establish a constitutional violation. Thus, they concluded, the provision was not directed at a pattern of constitutional violations. Justice Scalia provided the fifth vote to strike down this portion of the FMLA. But he emphasized that he was not relying on the congruence and proportionality test. To the contrary, he reiterated his belief that this "flabby" test "makes no sense". Instead, he adhered to his view that the proper approach towards determining whether or not an attempted abrogation of the States' sovereign immunity fell within Congress' authority under §5 of the Fourteenth Amendment was to ask simply whether the conduct that it forbad violated the Fourteenth Amendment. Since it was manifest to him that failing to grant state employees leave for the purpose of self-care did not violate the Fourteenth Amendment, the remedies provision had to fall. The four dissenters, in an opinion by Justice Ginsburg, agreed with the plurality that Congress attempted abrogation of immunity had to be subjected to the congruence and proportionality; they simply came to the opposite conclusion on the application of that standard. This quartet concluded that the self-care provision did enforce the right to be free from sex-based discrimination. They pointed to both statutory text and legislative history to support their conclusion that the entirety of the FMLA was directed at sex-based discrimination. Specifically, they maintained that the self-care provision was designed to guarantee that pregnant women would not lose their jobs after they gave birth. Consequently, they concluded that the self-care provision was a valid exercise of congressional power under §5 of the Fourteenth Amendment.

When an employee does file a claim under the FMLA, is the trial court supposed to apply the *Burdine* tripartite proof formula developed for Title VII actions? In DIAZ v. FORT WAYNE FOUNDRY CORP., 131 F.3d 711 (7th Cir.1997), the court noted that claims under the FMLA, unlike those brought under Title VII, do not depend upon a finding of discrimination but, rather, upon a finding that an eligible employee has been denied benefits. Thus, the court reasoned, an FMLA plaintiff need not show that other employees were treated less favorably. The question under the FMLA is not how the employer treats others, but whether the plaintiff was accorded the benefits to which she was entitled. Accordingly, it ruled, the trial court had erred in extending the *Burdine* proof formulation to the plaintiff's FMLA claim.

The FMLA also directs the Department of Labor to issue regulations "necessary to carry out" the act. One of the administrative regulations issued by the Secretary of Labor provided that if an employee takes medical leave and the employer does not expressly designate the leave as FMLA leave, that leave does not count against the employee's FMLA entitlement of twelve weeks unpaid leave. In RAGSDALE v. WOLVERINE WORLD WIDE, INC., 535 U.S. 81, 122 S.Ct. 1155, 152 L.Ed.2d 167 (2002), an employee who had been granted thirty weeks of leave when cancer prevented her from working alleged that her employer violated the FMLA when it denied her request for additional leave. She claimed that since the company did not express notify her that her thirty-week absence would count against her FMLA entitlement, she was still entitled, per Labor Department regulation, to another twelve weeks of FMLA-mandated unpaid leave. By a 5-4 vote, the Court affirmed the lower courts' grant of summary judgment to the defendant. The majority ruled that the regulation was contrary to the Act and, therefore, beyond the Secretary of Labor's statutorily designated authority to promulgate regulations "necessary to carry out" the Act. Accordingly, the Court ruled that the plaintiff was not entitled to additional leave. Since the regulation imposed the penalty of requiring the employer to provide the additional leave without regard to whether the failure to give such notice actually impaired the plaintiff's ability to exercise FMLA rights, or otherwise actually prejudiced the employee, the Court found that the regulation imposed a "categorical penalty" that was incompatible with a statutory remedial scheme that conditioned relief upon a demonstration of consequential harm

Finally, as the FMLA expressly provides that its 12-week unpaid leave requirement does not supersede any State or local statute offering a more generous level of benefits, many states have enacted a more wide-ranging level of benefits than is mandated by the FMLA.

2. SEXUAL HARASSMENT

In Chapter 2, we explored in some detail the unique evidentiary scheme that has been developed for cases alleging sexual harassment, both with respect to what constitutes actionable harassment and the standards for employer liability for acts of harassment undertaken by its employees. Despite the creation of this specially tailored proof formula, harassment cases share one common feature with all claims of sex-based discrimination and, for that matter, with all claims asserted under this statute. Title VII only prohibits discrimination "because of such individual's race, color, religion, sex, or national origin." A crucial element of *any* Title VII claim, including allegations of sexual harassment, is proof that the challenged action was taken because of the plaintiff's membership in one of the five statutorily protected classifications. Thus, as the Supreme Court noted in *Meritor* and *Harris*, the plaintiff in every sexual harassment case must prove that the harassment was gender-based. It is not sufficient for the plaintiff to prove that she was subjected to severe or pervasive conduct that made her working environment intolerable. Title VII is not a general workplace civility code; a harassment plaintiff must prove that this conduct occurred because of her sex.

One area in which this question has been particularly problematic involves what has become known as "same-sex" sexual harassment. As we explain in Section D 4 of this Chapter, *infra*, Title VII has been construed not to prohibit discrimination on the basis of sexual orientation. If a male employee alleges that he was subjected to sexual harassment by a male supervisors or co-employee, does the fact that sexual orientation-based discrimination is not forbidden by Title VII necessarily preclude him from stating a sexual harassment claim under that statute? Should the answer to that question depend upon whether or not the perpetrator was homosexual?

For several years, the circuit courts were in disarray on these issues. Some held that "same-sex" sexual harassment claims were never cognizable under Title VII because the statute does not prohibit discrimination on the basis of sexual orientation. Others disagreed, focusing on whether or not the harassment was predicated upon the victim's sex. For this latter group, if the alleged perpetrator was gay, they were prepared to presume that the harassment was the result of sexual attraction and, therefore, that it was sex-based.

Earlier in the term in which it subsequently issued its ruling in *Burlington* and *Faragher*, the Supreme Court directly addressed the problem that had divided and frequently confounded the appellate courts.

Oncale v. Sundowner Offshore Services, Inc.

Supreme Court of the United States, 1998.
523 U.S. 75, 118 S.Ct. 998, 140 L.Ed.2d 201.

Justice Scalia delivered the opinion of the Court.

This case presents the question whether workplace harassment can violate Title VII's prohibition against "discriminat[ion] ... because of ... sex," when the harasser and the harassed employee are of the same sex.

I

* * * In late October 1991, Oncale was working for respondent Sundowner Offshore Services, Inc., on a Chevron U.S.A., Inc., oil platform in the Gulf of Mexico. He was employed as a roustabout on an eight-man crew which included respondents John Lyons, Danny Pippen, and Brandon Johnson. Lyons, the crane operator, and Pippen, the driller, had supervisory authority. On several occasions, Oncale was forcibly subjected to sex-related, humiliating actions against him by Lyons, Pippen, and Johnson in the presence of the rest of the crew. Pippen and Lyons also physically assaulted Oncale in a sexual manner, and Lyons threatened him with rape.

Oncale's complaints to supervisory personnel produced no remedial action; in fact, the company's Safety Compliance Clerk, Valent Hohen, told Oncale that Lyons and Pippen "picked [on] him all the time too," and called him a name suggesting homosexuality. Oncale eventually quit — asking that his pink slip reflect that he "voluntarily left due to sexual harassment and verbal abuse." When asked at his deposition why he left Sundowner, Oncale stated: "I felt that if I didn't leave my job, that I would be raped or forced to have sex."

Oncale filed a complaint against Sundowner in the United States District Court for the Eastern District of Louisiana, alleging that he was discriminated against in his employment because of his sex. * * * [T]he District Court held that "Mr. Oncale, a male, has no cause of action under Title VII for harassment by male co-workers." * * * [T]he Fifth Circuit * * * affirmed. We granted certiorari.

II

Title VII * * * provides, in relevant part, that "[i]t shall be an unlawful employment practice for an employer ... to discriminate against any individual with respect to his compensation, terms, conditions, or privileges of employment, because of such individual's race, color, religion, sex, or national origin." We have held that this not only covers "terms" and "conditions" in the narrow contractual sense, but "evinces a congressional intent to strike at the entire spectrum of disparate treatment of men and women in employment." Meritor Savings Bank v. Vinson.

Title VII's prohibition of discrimination "because of ... sex" protects men as well as women, Newport News Shipbuilding & Dry Dock Co. v. EEOC, and in the related context of racial discrimination in the workplace we have rejected any conclusive presumption that an employer will not discriminate against members of his own race. * * * If our precedents leave any doubt on the question, we hold today that nothing in Title VII necessarily bars a claim of discrimination "because of ... sex" merely because the plaintiff and the defendant (or the person charged with acting on behalf of the defendant) are of the same sex.

Courts have had little trouble with that principle in cases * * * where an employee claims to have been passed over for a job or promotion. But when the issue arises in the context of a "hostile environment" sexual harassment claim, the state and federal courts have taken a bewildering variety of stances. Some, like the Fifth Circuit in this case, have held that same-sex sexual harassment claims are never cognizable under Title VII. Other decisions say that such claims are actionable only if the plaintiff can prove that the harasser is homosexual (and thus presumably motivated by sexual desire). Still others suggest that workplace harassment that is sexual in content is always actionable, regardless of the harasser's sex, sexual orientation, or motivations.

We see no justification in the statutory language or our precedents for a categorical rule excluding same-sex harassment claims from the coverage of Title VII. As some courts have observed, male-on-male sexual harassment in the workplace was assuredly not the principal evil Congress was concerned with when it enacted Title VII. But statutory prohibitions often go beyond the principal evil to cover reasonably comparable evils, and it is ultimately the provisions of our laws rather than the principal concerns of our legislators by which we are governed. Title VII prohibits discrimination "because of" sex in the "terms" or "conditions" of employment. Our holding that this includes sexual harassment must extend to sexual harassment of any kind that meets the statutory requirements.

Respondents * * * contend that recognizing liability for same-sex harassment will transform Title VII into a general civility code for the American workplace. But that risk is no greater for same-sex than for opposite-sex harassment, and is adequately met by careful attention to the requirements of the statute. Title VII does not prohibit all verbal or physical harassment in the workplace; it is directed only at "*discriminat [ion] ... because of ... sex.*" We have never held that workplace harassment, even harassment between men and women, is automatically discrimination because of sex merely because the words used have sexual content or connotations. "The critical issue, Title VII's text indicates, is whether members of one sex are exposed to disadvantageous terms or conditions of employment to which members of the other sex are not exposed." Harris v. Forklift Systems, Inc. (GINSBURG, J., concurring).

Courts and juries have found the inference of discrimination easy to draw in most male-female sexual harassment situations, because the challenged conduct typically involves explicit or implicit proposals of sexual activity; it is reasonable to assume those proposals would not have been made to someone of the same sex. The same chain of inference would be available to a plaintiff alleging same-sex harassment, if there were credible evidence that the harasser was homosexual. But harassing conduct need not be motivated by sexual desire to support an inference of discrimination on the basis of sex. A trier of fact might reasonably find such discrimination, for example, if a female victim is harassed in such sex-specific and derogatory terms by another woman as to make it clear that the harasser is motivated by general hostility to the presence of women in the workplace. A same-sex harassment plaintiff may also, of course, offer direct comparative evidence about how the alleged harasser treated members of both sexes in a mixed-sex workplace. Whatever evidentiary route the plaintiff chooses to follow, he or she must always prove that the conduct at issue was not merely tinged with offensive sexual connotations, but actually constituted "*discrimina[tion] ... because of ... sex.*"

And there is another requirement that prevents Title VII from expanding into a general civility code: As we emphasized in *Meritor* and *Harris*, the statute does not reach genuine but innocuous differences in the ways men and women routinely interact with members of the same sex and of the opposite sex. The prohibition of harassment on the basis of sex requires neither asexuality nor androgyny in the workplace; it forbids only behavior so objectively offensive as to alter the "conditions" of the victim's employment. * * * We have always regarded that requirement as crucial, and as sufficient to ensure that courts and juries do not mistake ordinary socializing in the workplace — such as male-on-male horseplay or intersexual flirtation — for discriminatory "conditions of employment."

We have emphasized, moreover, that the objective severity of harassment should be judged from the perspective of a reasonable person in the plaintiff's position, considering "all the circumstances." *Harris.* In same-sex (as in all) harassment cases, that inquiry requires careful consideration of the social context in which particular behavior occurs and is experienced by its target. A professional football player's working environment is not severely or pervasively abusive, for example, if the coach smacks him on the buttocks as he heads onto the field — even if the same behavior would reasonably be experienced as abusive by the coach's secretary (male or female) back at the office. The real social impact of workplace behavior often depends on a constellation of surrounding circumstances, expectations, and relationships which are not fully captured by a simple recitation of the words used or the physical acts performed. Common sense, and an appropriate sensitivity to social context, will enable courts and juries to distinguish between simple teasing or roughhousing among members of the same sex, and conduct which a reasonable person in the plaintiff's position would find severely hostile or abusive.

III

Because we conclude that sex discrimination consisting of same-sex sexual harassment is actionable under Title VII, the judgment of the Court of Appeals for the Fifth Circuit is reversed, and the case is remanded for further proceedings consistent with this opinion.

[JUSTICE THOMAS' concurring opinion is omitted].

NOTES AND PROBLEMS FOR DISCUSSION

1. Reversing the Fifth Circuit's categorical rule excluding same-sex harassment claims from the coverage of Title VII, the Supreme Court in *Oncale* stressed that the courts below should have focused on the essential issue of whether or not the harassment was based on the victim's sex, i.e., whether members of one sex class were exposed to conduct altering the terms and conditions of employment to which members of the other sex were not exposed. Having said that, the Court admitted that determining whether or not the harassment was sex-based often requires the fact finder to draw inferences from circumstantial conduct. The Court noted that in the paradigmatic scenario of a heterosexual male perpetrator and a female victim, "it is reasonable to assume those proposals would not have been made to someone of the same sex." And this same inference, the Court suggested, would be equally reasonable in a same-sex case where the alleged perpetrator was homosexual. But the Court also went out of its way to indicate that sexual attraction need not be the only basis for sexual harassment. It recognized that a heterosexual perpetrator could be motivated by general hostility to members of his or her own gender class and, therefore, be guilty of an unlawful act of sexual harassment against a member of his or her gender group. Finally, the Court added that a plaintiff could establish sex-based causation by offering comparative evidence about how members of the other sex were treated by the alleged harasser. Although the Court remanded the case, the parties settled the matter before any further proceedings were undertaken.

In its first post-*Oncale* case addressing the question of the type of evidence that would suffice to establish sex-based causation in a "same sex" harassment case, the Fifth Circuit (which had been reversed unanimously in *Oncale*) in LA DAY v. CATALYST TECHNOLOGY, INC., 302 F.3d 474 (5th Cir. 2002), stated that the plaintiff could establish that the harassment was based on sexual attraction (as opposed to general gender hostility) by either offering evidence that the alleged harasser intended to have some kind of sexual contact with the plaintiff rather than merely to humiliate him for reasons unrelated to sexual interest, or by proving that the alleged harasser made same sex sexual advances to others, particularly to other employees. But in a subsequent unpublished case, another Fifth Circuit panel construed *Oncale* to mean that the only two possible situations in which a same-sex harassment case could fall within Title VII was where the harasser was motivated either by sexual desire or group animus. In LOVE v. MOTIVA ENTERPRISES LLC, 349 Fed. Appx. 900 (5th Cir. 2009) (unpublished), a divided panel upheld the trial court's grant of summary judgment to the defense. The majority reasoned that the offensive and inappropriate touching, comments, gestures, and proposals made by a female co-employee could not be found to be based on sexual desire because (1) the fact that they were made in conjunction with derisive remarks by the harasser against the plaintiff demonstrated that the harasser's allegedly harassing conduct had not been motivated by amorous desire; and because (1) the female plaintiff had not established that the female harasser was gay. Dissenting Judge Dennis maintained that the sexual desire and group animus scenarios were meant by the *Oncale* Court to be merely illustrative and not exhaustive examples of how the plaintiff could establish causation in a same-sex harassment case. The fact that the harasser's conduct and remarks were "all aimed at [the plaintiff] as a woman", Dennis concluded, demonstrated, *per se*, that the plaintiff had been abused "because of sex".

The Ninth Circuit has adopted a broader reading of *Oncale*. In RENE v. MGM GRAND HOTEL, 305 F.3d 1061 (9th Cir.2002) (*en banc*), an openly gay butler brought a Title VII action against his employer alleging that he had been subjected to repeated, hostile and unwelcomed acts of a sexual nature by his male supervisor and male co-workers because of his sexual orientation. The trial court granted the defendant's motion for summary judgment on the ground that Title VII did not prohibit discrimination based on sexual orientation. After a split circuit court panel upheld the trial court's decision, the court agreed to hear the case *en banc*.

By a vote of 7 to 4, the *en banc* court overturned the rulings below and held that the plaintiff had stated a cognizable claim under Title VII. A four-member plurality declared that with respect to the issue of causation, it was sufficient for the plaintiff to have alleged that he had been subjected to unwelcomed physical conduct of a sexual nature. Consequently, the plurality reasoned, the fact that the harasser might have been motivated by hostility to the victim's sexual orientation was not fatal to his cause of action. Moreover, the plurality stated that the plaintiff did not have to prove that he was treated worse than members of the opposite sex. Rather, it was enough that the plaintiff show that he suffered discrimination "in comparison to other men." Two other members of the majority based their decision to reverse on the ground that the plaintiff had state a claim of actionable gender stereotyping harassment. They stated that in *Oncale,* the Court had ruled that the *Price Waterhouse* gender stereotyping doctrine was applicable to a case involving alleged same-sex gender stereotyping.

The four dissenters insisted that the plaintiff had failed to allege that the admittedly severe and pervasive physical acts of a sexual nature were undertaken "because of" his gender. The mere fact that the alleged harassment consisted of physical acts of a sexual nature, they declared, did not establish the gender-based causation required by Title VII. They also reasoned that since the plaintiff never had asserted a claim of sexual stereotyping, and because there was virtually no evidentiary basis upon which such a claim could have been made, the two judges who based their decision on that theory had merely manufactured a claim that was never advanced by the plaintiff or supported by the evidence. Who has the better of the argument? For suggestions that harassment cases should be subjected to the same analysis as other forms of gender-based conduct, see Vicki Schultz, *Reconceptualizing Sexual Harassment,* 107 YALE L.J. 1683 (1998); Steven L. Willborn, *Taking Discrimination Seriously: Oncale and The Fate of Exceptionalism in Sexual Harassment Law,* 7 WM. & MARY BILL RTS. J. 677 (1999).

In DICK v. PHONE DIRECTORIES COMPANY, INC., 397 F.3d 1256 (10th Cir.2005), a female employee who had been subjected to a verbal barrage and collection of unwanted physical touchings in her intimate areas by a female supervisor and female co-workers brought a sexual harassment claim under Title VII. The trial court granted a defense motion for summary judgment on the ground that the plaintiff had not been discriminated against because of her sex. Construing *Oncale,* the Tenth Circuit reversed the trial court. It held that where the plaintiff alleges that the harassment was motivated by sexual desire (rather than hostility to the gender class) per *Oncale,* the plaintiff in a case where the victim and harassers were of the same sex did not have to establish that the harassers were gay. Although it recognized that most other circuit courts, including the Fifth Circuit in *La Day, supra,* required the same-sex-based-on-sexual-desire harassment plaintiff to establish both that the motivation was sexual desire and that the perpetrator was a homosexual, this court found that the latter requirement was not necessary in every same-sex harassment case. It was sufficient, the court concluded, to establish that the perpetrators were motivated by sexual desire. The court based this interpretation on the notion that an alleged harasser may consider herself to be a "heterosexual" but nonetheless propose or desire sexual activity with another woman in a harassing manner. Presumably, although the court did not say so, to be true to the requirement that the harassment occur "because of sex," i.e., that it would not have occurred if the plaintiff had been a man, the court meant "in a harassing manner" to mean that the plaintiff would have to show that these harassers would not have had sexual desire for a male employee. How exactly the plaintiff would do that without showing that the perpetrators were gay is unclear.

In addition to establishing causation by showing either sexual desire or gender-based hostility, the Court in *Oncale* also mentioned that the plaintiff could establish that the harassment was sex-based by offering comparative evidence about how members of the other sex were treated by the alleged harasser. This showing, of course, is only available in a mixed sex working environment. In SMITH v. ROCK-TENN SERVICES, INC., 813 F.3d 298 (6th Cir. 2016), the circuit ruled that a workplace that was composed 70% of males and 30% of women, was *not* gender-*segregated* and, therefore, that there was sufficient evidence for the jury to infer causation, from the facts showing that the male harasser had engaged in unwelcomed touchings only with other male employees.

2.   Does the Supreme Court's statement in *Price Waterhouse* that action taken against a plaintiff for failure to conform to gendered stereotypes can constitute sex-based discrimination suggest that a gay male victim of sexual harassment could successfully argue that he was subjected to gender-based discrimination because in the eyes of his harassers he did not live up to the stereotypical male "macho" image? In EEOC v. BOH BROTHERS CONSTRUCTION CO., 731 F.3d 444 (5th Cir. 2013)(*en banc*), the *en banc* Court expressly rejected the defendant's assertion that the evidentiary paths set forth in *Oncale* were the exclusive methods of proving sex-based causation in a same-sex harassment claim. Instead, it ruled that these evidentiary routes were illustrative and not exhaustive and agreed with the plaintiff that the sex-stereotyping doctrine recognized by the Supreme Court in *Price Waterhouse* was applicable in the same-sex harassment context. Accordingly, it ruled that a plaintiff in a same-sex harassment case can prove that the sexual harassment was conducted because of the victim's sex by relying on gender-stereotyping evidence that the plaintiff was harassed because he did not conform to the harasser's stereotyped view of appropriate gendered conduct. But in HAMM v. WEYAUWEGA MILK PRODUCTS, INC., 332 F.3d 1058 (7th Cir. 2003), the Seventh Circuit concluded that the instant harassment was motivated by the perpetrators' speculation about the plaintiff's gay sexual orientation rather than, as in *Boh Brothers*, by a belief that the plaintiff did not fit the sexual stereotype of male behavior. For a critique of this attempt at distinguishing sex-based from sexual orientation-based conduct, see Joel Wm. Friedman, *Gender Nonconformity and the Unfulfilled Promise of Price Waterhouse v. Hopkins*, 14 DUKE J. GEND.L. & POL. 205 (2007). *See generally* Sassaman v. Gamache, 566 F.3d 307 (2d Cir. 2009) (trial court erred in granting defense motion for summary judgment on ground that the plaintiff had not established a prima facie case of discrimination; after female co-employee had complained that the plaintiff had sexually harassed her, their common supervisor's statement during conversation in which he pressured the plaintiff to resign that the supervisor believed that men have a propensity to commit sexual harassment was a sufficient basis for a reasonable jury to infer the existence of discrimination based on sex stereotyping).

3.   Should the ruling in *Oncale* extend to the situation where an African-American plaintiff brings a Title VII claim of racial harassment based on an allegation that his African-American supervisor subjected him to the repeated use of racial epithets? *See* Ross v. Douglas County, 234 F.3d 391 (8th Cir.2000)(African-American supervisor's repeated use of such racial epithets as "nigger" and "black boy" constituted verbal racial harassment cognizable under Title VII; *Oncale* means that as a matter of law a black male could discriminate against another black male because of the latter's race).

4. Can a bisexual supervisor commit unlawful sexual harassment? *Compare* Holman v. Indiana, 211 F.3d 399 (7th Cir. 2000), cert. denied, 531 U.S. 880, 121 S.Ct. 191, 148 L.Ed.2d 132 (2000) ("equal opportunity harasser" did not engage in sex-based discrimination since male and female employees were not subjected to disparate treatment) *with* Steiner v. Showboat Operating Co., 25 F.3d 1459 (9th Cir.1994) (although supervisor was abusive to male and female subordinates, the abuse of women was different because his sexual epithets and offensive references to women's bodies and sexual conduct demonstrated that it was based on their sex; moreover, using sexual epithets equal in intensity and in an equally degrading manner against male employees would not cure the conduct towards women). For a further discussion of the "equal opportunity harasser" issue, see Christine A. Littleton, *Feminist Jurisprudence: The Difference Method Makes*, 41 STAN.L.REV. 751 (1989).

Suppose that instead of the situation where one supervisor harassed both male and female employees, a husband and wife who were employed by the same company allege that they each were victims of a sexually hostile environment as a result of the conduct of different employees. Could each of them state a claim of sexual harassment under Title VII? In VENEZIA v. GOTTLIEB MEMORIAL HOSP. INC., 421 F.3d 468 (7th Cir.2005), the husband/employee reported that pictures of nude men were left on his bulletin board and that coworkers crassly inquired about his sexual activity with his wife. The wife/employee claimed that she was also the victim of a hostile environment, including the display of a nude photo with her name in the caption. Both employees reported these incidents to the defendant's Human Resources Department but the hospital took no corrective action in either case. The trial court granted the defense motion to dismiss on the ground that a married couple could not establish that the same employer harassed and discriminated against both of them on the basis of their sex since the conduct was directed at both a man and a woman. The Seventh Circuit reversed, distinguished this case from one in which the same supervisor was alleged to have harassed a man and a woman. To treat that situation the same as one where a man and woman were harassed by different individuals would, in the court's view, improperly extend the "equal opportunity harasser" concept from the individual harasser to the overall entity. The court was unwilling to do that. Since the plaintiffs reported to different supervisors and had alleged different acts of harassment by different supervisors and co-workers, the court ruled that they each had stated a claim and reversed the trial court's dismissal of their complaint.

5. Can a female or male employee who is offended by the presence in the workplace of pornographic materials, of either a homosexual or heterosexual nature, state a hostile environment-styled claim of sexual harassment even though that material is observable by both male and female employees? In FOX v. SIERRA DEVELOPMENT CO., 876 F.Supp. 1169 (D.Nev.1995), a group of male employees alleged that their supervisors' distribution and discussion of depictions of male homosexual acts subjected them to a hostile working environment in violation of Title VII. The trial court found that writing, drawing, and explicitly discussing homosexual sex acts created a working environment that a reasonable person could find to be hostile. Reasonable persons, the court stated, could find that a working environment that was saturated with sexual references, whether homosexual or heterosexual in orientation, was abusive, hostile, or offensive. Nevertheless, the court granted the defendant's motion to dismiss for failure to state a claim because the plaintiffs had not alleged facts from which one could find that the working environment was hostile on a gender discriminatory basis. A workplace saturated with sexual references, the court reasoned, is potentially abusive or hostile to men and women in equal measure. The complaint did not allege facts from which reasonable men could conclude that they were being intimidated or ridiculed because they were men. And these plaintiffs did not allege that they felt offended because they were men. They perceived the atmosphere to be hostile either because they were offended by depictions and discussions of homosexual sex acts, or because they were heterosexual or homophobic. As to the first, there was nothing in the complaint to suggest to the court that men would be more offended by such material than women and so the offensiveness, if felt, was not gender-based. And with respect to the alternative explanation, the court added, such discrimination is not prohibited by Title VII. Finally, the court suggested that cases involving sexually explicit heterosexual conduct could be distinguished from the instant case. Heterosexual materials, in the court's view, could be said to create a hostile environment on a gender discriminatory basis. The public display of heterosexual sex acts, the court reasoned, could be said to be more hurtful to women than to men since such materials are part of a larger environment of hostility directed at women. Women historically have been subjugated and subjected to rape and sexual assault and are commonly depicted in pornography in images of objectification and coercion. Pictures and discussions of homosexual conduct, on the other hand, the court stated, do not inherently intimidate or insult men since there is no historical tradition from which the court could conclude that such materials include scenes of objectification of and violence directed towards men.

The Second Circuit offered a somewhat different approach to this question in PETROSINO v. BELL ATLANTIC, 385 F.3d 210 (2d Cir.2004). There, the trial court had granted summary judgment in favor of the defendant on the theory that since both men and women were exposed to the same sexually offensive remarks and graffiti and because this conduct was not directed specifically at the female plaintiff, no reasonable jury could find that this conduct subjected the plaintiff to a hostile work environment based on her sex. The appellate court rejected this reasoning, declaring that even though the comments and graphics that permeated the working environment may have sexually ridiculed both men and women, the insults were directed at specific male employees, not men as a group. Conversely, however, the depiction of women in these remarks and graphics was uniformly sexually demeaning to women as a group. Consequently, it ruled, a jury could reasonably find this conduct more demeaning of women than men and, therefore, that it created a hostile environment based on the plaintiff's sex. Accordingly, it reversed the grant of summary judgment and remanded for trial. *See also* Reeves v. C.H. Robinson Worldwide, Inc., 594 F.3d 798 (11th Cir. 2010)(*en banc*) (reversing grant of summary judgment to defendant on ground that evidence of severe or pervasive instances of sex-specific profanity and conduct is sufficient to support a jury finding of intentional sex-based discrimination in a hostile environment claim even when that conduct was not directed specifically at the plaintiff because a reasonable jury could determine that such language and conduct is degrading to women as a group); Gallagher v. C.H. Robinson Worldwide, Inc., 567 F.3d 263 (6th Cir. 2009) (adopting analysis in *Reeves* and also ruling that the natural effect of exposure to sex-specific profanity is degradation and embarrassment irrespective of the harasser's motivation and, therefore, the trial court "focused too narrowly on the motivation for the harassers' offensive conduct rather than on the effects of the conduct on the victim-recipient" in determining whether the plaintiff had established that the harassing conduct that had been directed at her and other such conduct that had been common and indiscriminate but which, because of the office configuration, she had no means of escaping, had occurred "because of" her sex).

To meet the causation requirement, does the plaintiff in a harassment case have to prove that the perpetrator intended to harass women, or men, because of their sex? In EEOC v. NATIONAL EDUCATION ASSOCIATION, 422 F.3d 840 (9th Cir.2005), three female employees of a labor union charged that the defendant union had created a sexually hostile working environment. They reported multiple incidents in which the union's executive director, without provocation, shouted at female employees in a loud, vulgar, and hostile manner and engaged in physically threatening behavior including lunging at them, grabbing their shoulders, and pumping his fist in their direction. The trial court granted summary judgment in favor of the defendant on the ground that no reasonable jury could find that the alleged harassment was "because of sex". The Ninth Circuit reversed, ruling that the plaintiffs did not have to prove that the harasser had a specific intent to discriminate against women. Rather, it reasoned, it was sufficient to focus on the consequences or effects of the conduct, rather than its motivation, in assessing the existence of a hostile working environment. The court explained that regardless of the motive, the ultimate question was whether the alleged harasser's behavior affected women more adversely than it affected men. Moreover, it reasoned, "evidence of differences in subjective effects (along with, of course, evidence of differences in objective quality and quantity) is relevant to determining whether or not men and women were treated differently, even where the conduct is not facially sex – or gender – specific." And because the record established the presence of an issue of fact as to both the objective differences in treatment of men and women and differences in the subjective effects upon men and women, the case was not appropriate for summary judgment.

3. SEX-LINKED FACTORS

City of Los Angeles, Department of Water & Power v. Manhart

Supreme Court of the United States, 1978.
435 U.S. 702, 98 S.Ct. 1370, 55 L.Ed.2d 657.

MR. JUSTICE STEVENS delivered the opinion of the Court.

As a class, women live longer than men. For this reason, the Los Angeles Department of Water and Power required its female employees to make larger contributions to its pension fund than its male employees. We granted certiorari to decide whether this practice discriminated against individual female employees because of their sex in violation of §703(a)(1) * * *.

For many years the Department has administered retirement, disability, and death-benefit programs for its employees. Upon retirement each employee is eligible for a monthly retirement benefit computed as a fraction of his or her salary multiplied by years of service. The monthly benefits for men and women of the same age, seniority, and salary are equal. Benefits are funded entirely by contributions from the employees and the Department, augmented by the income earned on those contributions. No private insurance company is involved in the administration or payment of benefits.

Based on a study of mortality tables and its own experience, the Department determined that its 2,000 female employees, on the average, will live a few years longer than its 10,000 male employees. The cost of a pension for the average retired female is greater than for the average male retiree because more monthly payments must be made to the average woman. The Department therefore required female employees to make monthly contributions to the fund which were 14.84% higher than the contributions required of comparable male employees. Because employee contributions were withheld from paychecks, a female employee took home less pay than a male employee earning the same salary.

* * * In 1973, respondents brought this suit in the United States District Court for the Central District of California on behalf of a class of women employed or formerly employed by the Department. They prayed for an injunction and restitution of excess contributions.

While this action was pending, the California Legislature enacted a law prohibiting certain municipal agencies from requiring female employees to make higher pension fund contributions than males. The Department therefore amended its plan, effective January 1, 1975. The current plan draws no distinction, either in contributions or in benefits, on the basis of sex. On a motion for summary judgment, the District Court held that the contribution differential violated §703(a)(1) and ordered a refund of all excess contributions made before the amendment of the plan. The United States Court of Appeals for the Ninth Circuit affirmed.

The Department and various amici curiae contend that: (1) the differential in take-home pay between men and women was not discrimination within the meaning of §703(a)(1) because it was offset by a difference in the value of the pension benefits provided to the two classes of employees; (2) the differential was based on a factor "other than sex" within the meaning of the Equal Pay Act of 1963 and was therefore protected by the so-called Bennett Amendment; (3) the rationale of General Electric Co. v. Gilbert, requires reversal; and (4) in any event, the retroactive monetary recovery is unjustified. We consider these contentions in turn.

There are both real and fictional differences between women and men. It is true that the average man is taller than the average woman; it is not true that the average woman driver is more accident prone than the average man. Before the Civil Rights Act of 1964 was enacted, an employer could fashion his personnel policies on the basis of assumptions about the differences between men and women, whether or not the assumptions were valid.

It is now well recognized that employment decisions cannot be predicated on mere "stereotyped" impressions about the characteristics of males or females. Myths and purely habitual assumptions about a woman's inability to perform certain kinds of work are no longer acceptable reasons for refusing to employ qualified individuals, or for paying them less. This case does not, however, involve a fictional difference between men and women. It involves a generalization that the parties accept as unquestionably true: Women, as a class, do live longer than men. The Department treated its women employees differently from its men employees because the two classes are in fact different. It is equally true, however, that all individuals in the respective classes do not share the characteristic that differentiates the average class representatives. Many women do not live as long as the average man and many men outlive the average woman. The question, therefore, is whether the existence or nonexistence of "discrimination" is to be determined by comparison of class characteristics or individual characteristics. A "stereotyped" answer to that question may not be the same as the answer that the language and purpose of the statute command.

The statute makes it unlawful "to discriminate against any individual with respect to his compensation, terms, conditions, or privileges of employment, because of such individual's race, color, religion, sex, or national origin." The statute's focus on the individual is unambiguous. It precludes treatment of individuals as simply components of a racial, religious, sexual, or national class. If height is required for a job, a tall woman may not be refused employment merely because, on the average, women are too short. Even a true generalization about the class is an insufficient reason for disqualifying an individual to whom the generalization does not apply.

That proposition is of critical importance in this case because there is no assurance that any individual woman working for the Department will actually fit the generalization on which the Department's policy is based. Many of those individuals will not live as long as the average man. While they were working, those individuals received smaller paychecks because of their sex, but they will receive no compensating advantage when they retire.

It is true, of course, that while contributions are being collected from the employees, the Department cannot know which individuals will predecease the average woman. Therefore, unless women as a class are assessed an extra charge, they will be subsidized, to some extent, by the class of male employees.[14] It follows, according to the Department, that fairness to its class of male employees justifies the extra assessment against all of its female employees.

But the question of fairness to various classes affected by the statute is essentially a matter of policy for the legislature to address. Congress has decided that classifications based on sex, like those based on national origin or race, are unlawful. Actuarial studies could unquestionably identify differences in life expectancy based on race or national origin, as well as sex.[15] But a statute that was designed to make race irrelevant in the employment market could not reasonably be construed to permit a take-home-pay differential based on a racial classification.

Even if the statutory language were less clear, the basic policy of the statute requires that we focus on fairness to individuals rather than fairness to classes. Practices that classify employees in terms of religion, race, or sex tend to preserve

---

[14]The size of the subsidy involved in this case is open to doubt, because the Department's plan provides for survivors' benefits. Since female spouses of male employees are likely to have greater life expectancies than the male spouses of female employees, whatever benefits men lose in "primary" coverage for themselves, they may regain in "secondary" coverage for their wives.
[15]For example, the life expectancy of a white baby in 1973 was 72.2 years; a nonwhite baby could expect to live 65.9 years, a difference of 6.3 years.

traditional assumptions about groups rather than thoughtful scrutiny of individuals. The generalization involved in this case illustrates the point. Separate mortality tables are easily interpreted as reflecting innate differences between the sexes; but a significant part of the longevity differential may be explained by the social fact that men are heavier smokers than women.

Finally, there is no reason to believe that Congress intended a special definition of discrimination in the context of employee group insurance coverage. It is true that insurance is concerned with events that are individually unpredictable, but that is characteristic of many employment decisions. Individual risks, like individual performance, may not be predicted by resort to classifications proscribed by Title VII. Indeed, the fact that this case involves a group insurance program highlights a basic flaw in the Department's fairness argument. For when insurance risks are grouped, the better risks always subsidize the poorer risks. Healthy persons subsidize medical benefits for the less healthy; unmarried workers subsidize the pensions of married workers; persons who eat, drink, or smoke to excess may subsidize pension benefits for persons whose habits are more temperate. Treating different classes of risks as though they were the same for purposes of group insurance is a common practice that has never been considered inherently unfair. To insure the flabby and the fit as though they were equivalent risks may be more common than treating men and women alike;[19] but nothing more than habit makes one "subsidy" seem less fair than the other.

An employment practice that requires 2,000 individuals to contribute more money into a fund than 10,000 other employees simply because each of them is a woman, rather than a man, is in direct conflict with both the language and the policy of the Act. Such a practice does not pass the simple test of whether the evidence shows "treatment of a person in a manner which but for that person's sex would be different." It constitutes discrimination and is unlawful unless exempted by the Equal Pay Act of 1963 or some other affirmative justification.

Shortly before the enactment of Title VII in 1964, Senator Bennett proposed an amendment providing that a compensation differential based on sex would not be unlawful if it was authorized by the Equal Pay Act, which had been passed a year earlier. The Equal Pay Act requires employers to pay members of both sexes the same wages for equivalent work, except when the differential is pursuant to one of four specified exceptions. The Department contends that the fourth exception applies here. That exception authorizes a "differential based on any other factor other than sex."

The Department argues that the different contributions exacted from men and women were based on the factor of longevity rather than sex. It is plain, however, that any individual's life expectancy is based on a number of factors, of which sex is only one. The record contains no evidence that any factor other than the employee's sex was taken into account in calculating the 14.84% differential between the respective contributions by men and women. * * *

---

[19]The record indicates, however, that the Department has funded its death-benefit plan by equal contributions from male and female employees. A death benefit — unlike a pension benefit — has less value for persons with longer life expectancies. Under the Department's concept of fairness, then, this neutral funding of death benefits is unfair to women as a class.

* * *

The Department argues that reversal is required by General Electric Co. v. Gilbert. We are satisfied, however, that neither the holding nor the reasoning of Gilbert is controlling.

In *Gilbert* the Court held that the exclusion of pregnancy from an employer's disability benefit plan did not constitute sex discrimination within the meaning of Title VII. * * * The two groups of potential recipients which that case concerned were pregnant women and nonpregnant persons. "While the first group is exclusively female, the second includes members of both sexes." Gilbert. In contrast, each of the two groups of employees involved in this case is composed entirely and exclusively of members of the same sex. On its face, this plan discriminates on the basis of sex whereas the General Electric plan discriminated on the basis of a special physical disability.

In *Gilbert* the Court did note that the plan as actually administered had provided more favorable benefits to women as a class than to men as a class. This evidence supported the conclusion that not only had plaintiffs failed to establish a prima facie case by proving that the plan was discriminatory on its face, but they had also failed to prove any discriminatory effect.

In this case, however, the Department argues that the absence of a discriminatory effect on women as a class justifies an employment practice which, on its face, discriminated against individual employees because of their sex. But even if the Department's actuarial evidence is sufficient to prevent plaintiffs from establishing a prima facie case on the theory that the effect of the practice on women as a class was discriminatory, that evidence does not defeat the claim that the practice, on its face, discriminated against every individual woman employed by the Department.[30]

In essence, the Department is arguing that the prima facie showing of discrimination based on evidence of different contributions for the respective sexes is rebutted by its demonstration that there is a like difference in the cost of providing benefits for the respective classes. That argument might prevail if Title VII contained a cost-justification defense comparable to the affirmative defense available in a price discrimination suit. But neither Congress nor the courts have recognized such a defense under Title VII.

Although we conclude that the Department's practice violated Title VII, we do not suggest that the statute was intended to revolutionize the insurance and pension industries. All that is at issue today is a requirement that men and women make

---

[30] Some *amici* suggest that the Department's discrimination is justified by business necessity. They argue that, if no gender distinction is drawn, many male employees will withdraw from the plan, or even the Department, because they can get a better pension plan in the private market. But the Department has long required equal contributions to its death-benefit plan, and since 1975 it has required equal contributions to its pension plan. Yet the Department points to no "adverse selection" by the affected employees, presumably because an employee who wants to leave the plan must also leave his job, and few workers will quit because one of their fringe benefits could theoretically be obtained at a marginally lower price on the open market. In short, there has been no showing that sex distinctions are reasonably necessary to the normal operation of the Department's retirement plan.

unequal contributions to an employer-operated pension fund. Nothing in our holding implies that it would be unlawful for an employer to set aside equal retirement contributions for each employee and let each retiree purchase the largest benefit which his or her accumulated contributions could command in the open market.[33] Nor does it call into question the insurance industry practice of considering the composition of an employer's work force in determining the probable cost of a retirement or death benefit plan. Finally, we recognize that in a case of this kind it may be necessary to take special care in fashioning appropriate relief.

* * *

There can be no doubt that the prohibition against sex-differentiated employee contributions represents a marked departure from past practice. Although Title VII was enacted in 1964, this is apparently the first litigation challenging contribution differences based on valid actuarial tables. Retroactive liability could be devastating for a pension fund. The harm would fall in large part on innocent third parties. If, as the courts below apparently contemplated, the plaintiffs' contributions are recovered from the pension fund, the administrators of the fund will be forced to meet unchanged obligations with diminished assets. If the reserve proves inadequate, either the expectations of all retired employees will be disappointed or current employees will be forced to pay not only for their own future security but also for the unanticipated reduction in the contributions of past employees.

Without qualifying the force of the * * * presumption in favor of retroactive relief, we conclude that it was error to grant such relief in this case. Accordingly, although we agree with the Court of Appeals' analysis of the statute, we vacate its judgment and remand the case for further proceedings consistent with this opinion.

It is so ordered.

MR. JUSTICE BRENNAN took no part in the consideration or decision of this case.

[Justice Blackmun's concurring opinion, Chief Justice Burger's dissenting opinion, and Justice Marshall's concurring opinion are omitted.]

NOTES AND PROBLEMS FOR DISCUSSION

1. In ARIZONA GOVERNING COMMITTEE v. NORRIS, 463 U.S. 1073, 103 S.Ct. 3492, 77 L.Ed.2d 1236 (1983), the Court extended its ruling in *Manhart* to a deferred compensation plan that provided employees of the State of Arizona with the option of postponing the receipt of a portion of their wages until retirement by selecting among various plans offered by several companies chosen by the State to participate in its plan. The employees were not required to participate in the plan but

---

[33]Title VII and the Equal Pay Act primarily govern relations between employees and their employer, not between employees and third parties. We do not suggest, of course, that an employer can avoid his responsibilities by delegating discriminatory programs to corporate shells. Title VII applies to "any agent" of a covered employer, and the Equal Pay Act applies to "any person acting directly or indirectly in the interest of an employer in relation to an employee." * * *

participation was limited to a choice of one of the companies selected by the State; an employee could not invest its deferred compensation in any other way. The State was responsible for withholding the appropriate sum from a participating employee's wages, but did not contribute any money to supplement the employee's contribution. All of the companies selected by the State used sex-based mortality tables to calculate the monthly payments received by employees who chose to participate in a monthly annuity program. (The companies also offered a single lump-sum payment upon retirement option and an option making periodic payments of a fixed sum over a fixed time period.) Sex, however, was the only factor used to determine the longevity of individuals of the same age; other factors correlating with longevity such as smoking or alcohol consumption, weight, or medical history were not considered. The Court held that the use of sex-based actuarial tables was "no more permissible at the pay-out stage of a retirement plan than at the pay-in stage." In so holding, it rejected the State's contention that the plan did not violate Title VII because a man and woman who deferred the same amount of wages would receive, upon retirement, annuity policies having approximately the same present actuarial value, since the lower value of each monthly payment received by a woman was offset by the likelihood that she would receive more payments. The defect in this argument, the Court declared, was that the plan calculated longevity solely on the basis of gender, a practice prohibited in *Manhart*. In addition, the Court noted that, as in *Manhart*, if a female employee wished to receive the same monthly benefits paid to a similarly situated man, she would have to make greater monthly contributions than that male employee.

The fact that participation in the plan was voluntary was irrelevant, the Court reasoned, since Title VII prohibits discrimination concerning all terms and conditions of employment and the option of participating in a deferred compensation plan constitutes a condition of employment. Similarly irrelevant was the fact that the plan provided other nondiscriminatory options such as the lump-sum and fixed-sum-over-fixed-period alternatives. Offering nondiscriminatory benefits, the Court declared, did not excuse the provision of another benefit on a discriminatory basis. Finally, to avoid a potentially devastating financial impact on pension funds, a majority of the Court concluded that this case should fall outside the presumption in favor of awarding retroactive relief announced by the Court in Albemarle Paper Co. v. Moody, *see* Chapter 7, §A1, *infra*. Accordingly, it required employers to calculate benefits without regard to the sex of the employee only as to benefits derived from contributions collected after the effective date of the trial court's judgment. Benefits derived from contributions made prior to that date, a majority ruled, could be calculated as provided by the existing terms of the Arizona plan.

2. In FLORIDA v. LONG, 487 U.S. 223, 108 S.Ct. 2354, 101 L.Ed.2d 206 (1988), the Court rejected the Eleventh Circuit's conclusion that the ruling in *Manhart* put employers on notice that benefits must be calculated in a nondiscriminatory manner. Rather, the Court concluded, this issue was not resolved until its subsequent decision in *Norris*. Accordingly, it held that employees who retired before the effective date of *Norris* were not entitled to benefit readjustment.

3. Will forbidding the use of sex-based mortality tables increase the cost of employing female workers? If so, can it be argued that the decision in *Manhart* will have an adverse effect on the employment of women? For an interesting and insightful debate over the meaning and impact of *Manhart*, see George J. Benston, *The*

Economics of Gender Discrimination in Employee Fringe Benefits: Manhart Revisited, 49 U.CHI.L.REV. 489 (1982); Lea Brilmayer, Richard W. Hekeler, Douglas Laycock & Teresa A. Sullivan, *Sex Discrimination in Employer–Sponsored Insurance Plans: A Legal and Demographic Analysis,* 47 U.CHI.L.REV. 505 (1980).

4. SEXUAL ORIENTATION DISCRIMINATION

Hively v. Ivy Tech Community College, South Bend

United States Court of Appeals, Seventh Circuit, 2016.
830 F.3d 698.

ROVNER, Circuit Judge.

Once again this court is asked to consider whether Title VII of the Civil Rights Act of 1964 protects employees from or offers redress for discrimination based on sexual orientation. This time, however, we do so in the shadow of a criticism from the Equal Employment Opportunity Commission (EEOC) that this court and others have continued to reflexively declare that sexual orientation is not cognizable under Title VII without due analysis or consideration of intervening case law. The EEOC's criticism has created a groundswell of questions about the rationale for denying sexual orientation claims while allowing nearly indistinguishable gender non-conformity claims, which courts have long recognized as a form of sex-based discrimination under Title VII. After a careful analysis of our precedent, however, this court must conclude that Kimberly Hively has failed to state a claim under Title VII for sex discrimination; her claim is solely for sexual orientation discrimination which is beyond the scope of the statute. Consequently, we affirm the decision of the district court.

I.

Hively began teaching as a part-time adjunct professor at Ivy Tech Community College in 2000. On December 13, 2013, she filed a bare bones pro se charge with the Equal Employment Opportunity Commission (EEOC) claiming that she had been "discriminated against on the basis of sexual orientation" as she had been blocked from fulltime employment without just cause in violation of Title VII. After exhausting the procedural requirements in the EEOC, she filed a complaint, again pro se, in the district court alleging that although she had the necessary qualifications for full-time employment and had never received a negative evaluation, the college refused even to interview her for any of the six full-time positions for which she applied between 2009 and 2014, and her part-time employment contract was not renewed in July 2014. In short, she alleged that she had been denied full time employment and promotions "based on sexual orientation" in violation of Title VII.

The college's defense in both the district court and on appeal is simply that Title VII does not apply to claims of sexual orientation discrimination and therefore Hively has made a claim for which there is no legal remedy. The district court agreed and granted Ivy Tech's motion to dismiss.

II.

A.

This panel could make short shrift of its task and affirm the district court opinion by referencing two cases (released two months apart), in which this court held that Title VII offers no protection from nor remedies for sexual orientation discrimination. *Hamner v. St. Vincent Hosp. & Health Care Ctr., Inc.*, 224 F.3d 701 (7th Cir. 2000); *Spearman v. Ford Motor Co.*, 231 F.3d 1080 (7th Cir. 2000). Title VII makes it "unlawful employment practice for an employer to fail or refuse to hire or to discharge any individual, or otherwise to discriminate against any individual ... because of such individual's race, color, religion, sex, or national origin." This circuit, however, in both *Hamner* and *Spearman*, made clear that "harassment based solely upon a person's sexual preference or orientation (and not on one's sex) is not an unlawful employment practice under Title VII." Both *Hamner* and *Spearman* relied upon our 1984 holding in *Ulane v. Eastern Airlines, Inc.*, 742 F.2d 1081 (7th Cir. 1984) in which this court, while considering the Title VII claim of a transsexual airline pilot, stated in dicta that "homosexuals and transvestites do not enjoy Title VII protection." In *Ulane*, we came to this conclusion by considering the ordinary meaning of the word "sex" in Title VII, as enacted by Congress, and by determining that "[t]he phrase in Title VII prohibiting discrimination based on sex, in its plain meaning, implies that it is unlawful to discriminate against women because they are women and against men because they are men." We also considered the legislative history of Title VII, explaining that it was primarily meant to remedy racial discrimination, with sex discrimination thrown in at the final hour in an attempt to thwart adoption of the Civil Rights Act as a whole. Therefore, we concluded, "Congress had a narrow view of sex in mind when it passed the Civil Rights Act." In a later case describing *Ulane*, we said that at the time of *Ulane* "we were confident that Congress had nothing more than the traditional notion of 'sex' in mind when it voted to outlaw sex discrimination, and that discrimination on the basis of sexual orientation and transsexualism, for example, did not fall within the purview of Title VII." *Doe by Doe v. City of Belleville, Ill.*, 119 F.3d 563 (7th Cir. 1997) (citing *Ulane*), *abrogated by Oncale v. Sundowner Offshore Servs., Inc.*, 523 U.S. 75, 118 S.Ct. 998, 140 L.Ed.2d 201 (1998).

Since *Hamner* and *Spearman*, our circuit has, without exception, relied on those precedents to hold that the Title VII prohibition on discrimination based on "sex" extends only to discrimination based on a person's gender, and not that aimed at a person's sexual orientation.

The district court, relying on *Hamner* and two district court cases, thus dismissed Hively's complaint with prejudice.

* * *. Our precedent has been unequivocal in holding that Title VII does not redress sexual orientation discrimination. That holding is in line with all other circuit courts to have decided or opined about the matter. *But see Rene v. MGM Grand Hotel, Inc.*, 305 F.3d 1061 (9th Cir. 2002) (gay male employee taunted and harassed by coworkers for having feminine traits successfully pleaded claim of sex harassment under Title VII).

Our holdings and those of other courts reflect the fact that despite multiple efforts, Congress has repeatedly rejected legislation that would have extended Title VII to cover sexual orientation. Moreover, Congress has not acted to amend Title VII even in the face of an abundance of judicial opinions recognizing an emerging consensus that sexual orientation in the workplace can no longer be tolerated. In short, Congress' failure to act to amend Title VII to include sexual orientation is not from want of knowledge of the problem. And as a result, our understanding in *Ulane* that Congress intended a very narrow reading of the term "sex" when it passed Title VII of the Civil Rights Act, so far, appears to be correct.

To overcome a motion to dismiss, Hively's complaint must contain sufficient factual matter, accepted as true, to "state a claim to relief that is plausible on its face." *Ashcroft v. Iqbal*, 556 U.S. 662, 129 S.Ct. 1937, 173 L.Ed.2d 868 (2009). In this case, Hively fails to thwart the motion to dismiss for the simple reason that this circuit has undeniably declared that claims for sexual orientation are not cognizable under Title VII. Nor are they, without more, cognizable as claims for sex discrimination under the same statute.

B.

We could end the discussion there, but we would be remiss not to consider the EEOC's recent decision in which it concluded that "sexual orientation is inherently a 'sex-based consideration,' and an allegation of discrimination based on sexual orientation is necessarily an allegation of sex discrimination under Title VII." *Baldwin v. Foxx*, EEOC Appeal No. 0120133080, 2015 WL 4397641 (July 16, 2015). The EEOC, the body charged with enforcing Title VII, came to this conclusion for three primary reasons. First, it concluded that "sexual orientation discrimination is sex discrimination because it necessarily entails treating an employee less favorably because of the employee's sex." (proffering the example of a woman who is suspended for placing a photo of her female spouse on her desk, and a man who faces no consequences for the same act). Second, it explained that "sexual orientation discrimination is also sex discrimination because it is associational discrimination on the basis of sex," in which an employer discriminates against lesbian, gay, or bisexual employees based on who they date or marry. Finally, the EEOC described sexual orientation discrimination as a form of discrimination based on gender stereotypes in which employees are harassed or punished for failing to live up to societal norms about appropriate masculine and feminine behaviors, mannerisms, and appearances. In coming to these conclusions, the EEOC noted critically that "courts have attempted to distinguish discrimination based on sexual orientation from discrimination based on sex, even while noting that the borders between the two classes are ... imprecise." The EEOC rejected the argument that the plain language of Title VII, along with Congressional inaction, mandated a conclusion that Title VII does not prohibit such discrimination. Instead, the EEOC noted that even the Supreme Court, when applying Title VII's prohibition on "sex" discrimination to same-sex sexual harassment, stated that "statutory prohibitions often go beyond the principal evil to cover reasonably comparable evils, and it is ultimately the provisions of our laws rather than the principal concerns of our legislators by which we are governed." *Oncale*.

This July 2015 EEOC decision is significant in several ways. It marks the first time that the EEOC has issued a ruling stating that claims for sexual orientation discrimination are indeed cognizable under Title VII as a form of sex discrimination. Although the holding in *Baldwin* applies only to federal government employees, its reasoning would be applicable in private employment contexts too. And although the rulings of the EEOC are not binding on this court, they are entitled to some level of deference. Based on our holding today, which is counter to the EEOC's holding in *Baldwin*, we need not delve into a discussion of the level of deference we owe to the EEOC's rulings. Whatever deference we might owe to the EEOC's adjudications, we conclude for the reasons that follow, that Title VII, as it stands, does not reach discrimination based on sexual orientation. Although we affirm our prior precedents on this point, we do so acknowledging that other federal courts are taking heed of the reasoning behind the EEOC decision in *Baldwin*. As we will discuss further below, the district courts, which are the front line experimenters in the laboratories of difficult legal questions, are beginning to question the doctrinaire distinction between gender non-conformity discrimination and sexual orientation discrimination and coming up short on rational answers.

In the process of concluding, after thorough analysis, that allegations of discrimination on the basis of sexual orientation necessarily state a claim of discrimination on the basis of sex, the EEOC criticized courts — and pointed particularly to this circuit — that "simply cite earlier and dated decisions without any additional analysis" even in light of the relevant intervening Supreme Court law. We take to heart the EEOC's criticism of our circuit's lack of recent analysis on the issue. Moreover, recent legal developments and changing workplace norms require a fresh look at the issue of sexual orientation discrimination under Title VII. We begin, therefore, with that intervening Supreme Court case — *Price Waterhouse v. Hopkins*, 490 U.S. 228, 109 S.Ct. 1775, 104 L.Ed.2d 268 (1989) — and discuss its implication for distinguishing between gender non-conformity claims, which are cognizable under Title VII, and sexual orientation claims, which are not.

C.

As far back as 1989, the Supreme Court declared that Title VII protects employees who fail to comply with typical gender stereotypes. *Price Waterhouse*. In *Price Waterhouse*, when Ann Hopkins failed to make partner in the defendant accounting firm, the partners conducting her review advised her that her chances could be improved the next time around if she would, among other gender-based suggestions, "walk more femininely, talk more femininely, dress more femininely, wear make-up, have her hair styled, and wear jewelry." The Supreme Court declared that this type of gender stereotyping constituted discrimination on the basis of sex in violation of Title VII, stating,

> [a]s for the legal relevance of sex stereotyping, we are beyond the day when an employer could evaluate employees by assuming or insisting that they matched the stereotype associated with their group, for in forbidding employers to discriminate against individuals because of their sex, Congress intended to strike at the entire spectrum of disparate treatment of men and women resulting from sex stereotypes.

The holding in *Price Waterhouse* has allowed many employees to marshal successfully the power of Title VII to state a claim for sex discrimination when they have been discriminated against for failing to live up to various gender norms. *See, e.g.*, *City of Belleville* (finding that a worker who wore an earring and was habitually called "fag" or "queer" made a sufficient allegation of gender-based discrimination to defeat a motion for summary judgment);[3] *Bellaver v. Quanex Corp.*, 200 F.3d 4852 (7th Cir. 2000) ("the evidence suggests the employer here may have relied on impermissible stereotypes of how women should behave" by criticizing plaintiff's deficient interpersonal skills while tolerating the same deficiencies in male employees.).

As a result of *Price Waterhouse*, a line of cases emerged in which courts began to recognize claims from gay, lesbian, bisexual, and transgender employees who framed their Title VII sex discrimination claims in terms of discrimination based on gender non-conformity (which we also refer to, interchangeably, as sex stereotype discrimination) and not sexual orientation. But these claims tended to be successful only if those employees could carefully cull out the gender non-conformity discrimination from the sexual orientation discrimination. *See Hamm v. Weyauwega Milk Products, Inc.*, 332 F.3d 1058 (7th Cir. 2003) (upholding the grant of summary judgment in the employer's favor because the plaintiff "himself characterizes the harassment of his peers in terms of ... his sexual orientation and does not link their comments to his sex."). When trying to separate the discrimination based on sexual orientation from that based on sex stereotyping, however, courts soon learned that the distinction was elusive. *Prowel v. Wise Bus. Forms, Inc.*, 579 F.3d 285 (3d Cir. 2009) ("the line between sexual orientation discrimination and discrimination 'because of sex' can be difficult to draw."); *Dawson v. Bumble & Bumble*, 398 F.3d 211 (2d Cir. 2005) ("it is often difficult to discern when [the plaintiff] is alleging that the various adverse employment actions allegedly visited upon her by [her employer] were motivated by animus toward her gender, her appearance, her sexual orientation, or some combination of these" because "the borders [between these classes] are so imprecise."); *Hamm* ("We recognize that distinguishing between failure to adhere to sex stereotypes (a sexual stereotyping claim permissible under Title VII) and discrimination based on sexual orientation (a claim not covered by Title VII) may be difficult. This is especially true in cases in which a perception of homosexuality itself may result from an impression of nonconformance with sexual stereotypes."); *Id.* at 1067 (Posner, J., concurring) ("Hostility to effeminate men and to homosexual men, or to masculine women and to lesbians, will often be indistinguishable as a practical matter.").

And so for the last quarter century since *Price Waterhouse*, courts have been haphazardly, and with limited success, trying to figure out how to draw the line between gender norm discrimination, which can form the basis of a legal claim under *Price Waterhouse's* interpretation of Title VII, and sexual orientation discrimination, which is not cognizable under Title VII. * * * As we will describe below, courts have gone about this task in different ways — either by disallowing any claims where sexual orientation and gender non-conformity are intertwined, (and, for some courts, by not allowing claims from lesbian, gay, or bisexual employees at all), or by trying to

---

[3]The Supreme Court's decision in *Oncale* nominally abrogated the decision in *City of Belleville*, but nothing in the Supreme Court's decision in *Oncale* called into question this circuit's holding regarding gender stereotypes and application of the *Price Waterhouse* holding. See Bibby, 260 F.3d at 263 n.5 ("Absent an explicit statement from the Supreme Court that it is turning its back on *Price Waterhouse*, there is no reason to believe that the remand in *City of Belleville* was intended to call its gender stereotypes holding into question.").

tease apart the two claims and focusing only on the gender stereotype allegations. In both methods, the opinions tend to turn circles around themselves because, in fact, it is exceptionally difficult to distinguish between these two types of claims. Discrimination against gay, lesbian, and bisexual employees comes about because their behavior is seen as failing to comply with the quintessential gender stereotype about what men and women ought to do — for example, that men should have romantic and sexual relationships only with women, and women should have romantic and sexual relationships only with men. In this way, almost all discrimination on the basis of sexual orientation can be traced back to some form of discrimination on the basis of gender nonconformity. Gay men face discrimination if they fail to meet expected gender norms by dressing in a manner considered too effeminate for men, by displaying stereotypical feminine mannerisms and behaviors, by having stereotypically feminine interests, or failing to meet the stereotypes of the rough and tumble man. Co-workers and employers discriminate against lesbian women for displaying the parallel stereotypical male characteristics. But even if those employees display no physical or cosmetic signs of their sexual orientation, lesbian women and gay men nevertheless fail to conform to gender norm expectations in their attractions to partners of the same sex. Lesbian women and gay men upend our gender paradigms by their very status — causing us to question and casting into doubt antiquated and anachronistic ideas about what roles men and women should play in their relationships. Who is dominant and who is submissive? Who is charged with earning a living and who makes a home? Who is a father and who a mother? In this way the roots of sexual orientation discrimination and gender discrimination wrap around each other inextricably. In response to the new EEOC decision, one court has bluntly declared that the lines are not merely blurry, but are, in fact, un-definable. *See Videckis v. Pepperdine Univ.*, No. CV1500298, 150 F.Supp.3d 1151,1159 (C.D. Cal. 2015) ("Simply put, the line between sex discrimination and sexual orientation discrimination is 'difficult to draw' because that line does not exist, save as a lingering and faulty judicial construct.") Whether the line is nonexistent or merely exceedingly difficult to find, it is certainly true that the attempt to draw and observe a line between the two types of discrimination results in a jumble of inconsistent precedents.

For example, some courts attempting to differentiate between actions which constitute discrimination on the basis of sexual orientation and those which constitute discrimination on the basis of gender non-conformity essentially throw out the baby with the bathwater. For those courts, if the lines between the two are not easily discernible, the right answer is to forego any effort to tease apart the two claims and simply dismiss the claim under the premise that "a gender stereotyping claim should not be used to bootstrap protection for sexual orientation into Title VII." *See, e.g., Dawson.* In *Dawson*, a lesbian hair salon assistant alleged that she was discriminated against because she did not conform to feminine stereotypes and because she was gay. The court expressed concern that the plaintiff had "significantly conflated her claims," and because the court could not discern whether the allegedly discriminatory acts were motivated by animus toward her gender or her sexual orientation, it deemed the acts beyond the scope of Title VII and upheld the motion for summary judgment in the salon's favor. Several other courts likewise have thrown up their hands at the muddled lines between sexual orientation and gender non-conformity claims and simply have disallowed what they deem to be "bootstrapping" of sexual orientation claims onto gender stereotyping claims. For example, in *Vickers v. Fairfield Med. Ctr.,* 453 F.3d 757 (6th Cir. 2006), the Sixth Circuit upheld the dismissal of a gender nonconformity claim brought by an employee whose co-workers perceived him to be gay, because recognition of that claim

> would have the effect of de facto amending Title VII to encompass sexual orientation as a prohibited basis for discrimination. In all likelihood, any discrimination based on sexual orientation would be actionable under a sex stereotyping theory if this claim is allowed to stand, as all homosexuals, by definition, fail to conform to traditional gender norms in their sexual practices.

See also, Simonton v. Runyon, 232 F.3d 33 (2d Cir. 2000) (noting that the *Price Waterhouse* theory could not allow plaintiffs to "bootstrap protection for sexual orientation into Title VII because not all homosexual men are stereotypically feminine, and not all heterosexual men are stereotypically masculine."); *Spearman* (ignoring the plaintiff's claim that he was discriminated against because his co-workers perceived him to be too feminine to fit into the male image of the company, and finding instead that the discriminatory comments were directed solely at the plaintiff's sexual orientation).

This line of cases, in which the gender non-conformity claim cannot be tainted with any hint of a claim that the employer also engaged in sexual orientation discrimination, leads to some odd results. As the concurrence in this circuit's decision in *Hamm* pointed out, "the absurd conclusion follows that the law protects effeminate men from employment discrimination, but only if they are (or are believed to be) heterosexuals." *Hamm* (Posner, J. concurring). And the concurrence was not merely crying wolf. At least one district court has taken the anti-bootstrapping pronouncements in *Dawson* and *Simonton, supra* and declared that when determining whether a claim for gender nonconformity can stand, "the critical fact under the circumstances is the actual sexual orientation of the harassed person. If the harassment consists of homophobic slurs directed at a homosexual, then a gender-stereotyping claim by that individual is improper bootstrapping. If, on the other hand, the harassment consists of homophobic slurs directed at a *heterosexual*, then a gender-stereotyping claim by that individual is possible." *Estate of D.B. by Briggs v. Thousand Islands Cent. Sch. Dist.,* 2016 WL 945350 (N.D.N.Y. 2016).[4] In this circuit, however, we have made it clear that "Title VII protects persons, not classes" and that anyone can pursue a claim under Title VII no matter what her gender or sexual orientation or that of her harasser. *City of Belleville* ("[w]e have never made the viability of sexual harassment claims dependent upon the sexual orientation of the harasser, and we are convinced that it would be both unwise and improper to begin doing so."); *see also Prowel* ("This does not mean, however, that a homosexual individual is barred from bringing a *sex discrimination* claim under Title VII, which plainly prohibits discrimination 'because of sex.' "). Our intuition was confirmed by

---

[4]The plaintiff in *Estate of D.B.* brought a claim under Title IX of the Education Amendments of 1972, but "because a Title IX sex discrimination claim is treated in much the same way as a Title VII sex discrimination claim, Title VII jurisprudence therefore applies." Estate of D.B.

the Supreme Court in *Oncale*, which held that same-sex sexual harassment does not depend on the sexual orientation of the harasser. *Oncale* ("harassing conduct need not be motivated by sexual desire to support an inference of discrimination on the basis of sex.") It is hard to reconcile the holding in *Oncale* with a legal theory that only non-gay plaintiffs can have a viable claim for gender non-conformity discrimination under Title VII. And in this circuit, at least, it is clear that "we do not focus on the sexuality of the plaintiff in determining whether a Title VII violation has occurred." *Hamm.*

Other courts address the problem of the ill-defined lines between sexual orientation and gender non-conformity claims by carefully trying to tease the two apart and looking only at those portions of the claim that appear to address cognizable gender non-conformity discrimination.[5] *See, e.g. EEOC v. Boh Bros. Const. Co., L.L.C.,* 731 F.3d 444 (5th Cir. 2013) (sustaining a jury verdict finding sex discrimination by emphasizing the very specific testimony isolating gender-based discrimination from sexual orientation). But because of the indeterminate boundaries, one is left to wonder whether the court has, in fact successfully separated the two claims. For example, in *Prowel*, a factory worker who described himself both as gay and effeminate succeeded in defeating summary judgment by proffering just enough evidence of harassment based on gender stereotypes, as opposed to that based on sexual orientation, to satisfy the court that the claim might succeed. Notably, Prowel succeeded because he convinced the court that he displayed stereotypically feminine characteristics by testifying that he had a high voice, did not curse, was well-groomed, neat, filed his nails, crossed his legs, talked about art and interior design, and pushed the buttons on his factory equipment "with pizzazz." The Third Circuit concluded that a jury could find that "Prowel was harassed because he did not conform to [his employer's] vision of how a man should look, speak, and act — rather than harassment based solely on his sexual orientation." But it is not at all clear that the court successfully segregated characteristics based on sexual orientation from those based on gender, or if such a task is even possible. Having a high voice and an interest in grooming, art, interior design and civil language, are not merely attributes associated with women, but also attributes stereotypically associated with gay men. So for purposes of Title VII, should a court deem that pushing a factory button "with pizzazz" is a trait associated with gay men or straight women? It is difficult to know. We can assume that the vast majority of the stereotypes of gay men have come about particularly because they are associated with feminine attributes. The attempts to identify behaviors that are uniquely attributable to gay men and lesbians often lead to strange discussions of sexual orientation stereotypes. For example, one district court

---

[5]Some of these courts go half a step further and articulate that the sexual orientation claim has no effect whatsoever on the gender non-conformity claim. *See Rene* ("an employee's sexual orientation is irrelevant for purposes of Title VII. It neither provides nor precludes a cause of action for sexual harassment."); *Centola v. Potter,* 183 F.Supp. 2d 403 (D.Mass. 2002) ("Centola does not need to allege that he suffered discrimination on the basis of his sex alone or that sexual orientation played no part in his treatment ... if Centola can demonstrate that he was discriminated against 'because of ... sex' as a result of sex stereotyping, the fact that he was also discriminated against on the basis of his sexual orientation has no legal significance under Title VII.").

concluded that mimicking a gay co-worker with a lisp and "flamboyant" voice is discrimination based solely on sexual orientation and not gender. *Anderson v. Napolitano*, 2010 WL 431898 (S.D. Fla. Feb. 8, 2010). "[T]he logical conclusion is that his coworkers were lisping because of the stereotype that gay men speak with a lisp. Lisping is not a stereotype associated with women. Thus, again, the coworkers' actions were not "because of sex," but because of Anderson's sexual orientation"

Nevertheless, although disentangling gender discrimination from sexual orientation discrimination may be difficult, we cannot conclude that it is impossible. There may indeed be some aspects of a worker's sexual orientation that create a target for discrimination apart from any issues related to gender. Harassment may be based on prejudicial or stereotypical ideas about particular aspects of the gay and lesbian "lifestyle," including ideas about promiscuity, religious beliefs, spending habits, child-rearing, sexual practices, or politics. Although it seems likely that most of the causes of discrimination based on sexual orientation ultimately stem from employers' and co-workers' discomfort with a lesbian woman's or a gay man's failure to abide by gender norms, we cannot say that it must be so in all cases. Therefore we cannot conclude that the two must necessarily be coextensive unless or until either the legislature or the Supreme Court says it is so.

Because we recognize that Title VII in its current iteration does not recognize any claims for sexual orientation discrimination, this court must continue to extricate the gender nonconformity claims from the sexual orientation claims. We recognize that doing so creates an uncomfortable result in which the more visibly and stereotypically gay or lesbian a plaintiff is in mannerisms, appearance, and behavior, and the more the plaintiff exhibits those behaviors and mannerisms at work, the more likely a court is to recognize a claim of gender non-conformity which will be cognizable under Title VII as sex discrimination. *See, e.g., Rene* (gay male employee taunted and harassed by co-workers for having feminine traits successfully pleaded claim of sex discrimination under Title VII); *Nichols v. Azteca Rest. Enter., Inc.*, 256 F.3d 864 (9th Cir. 2001) (noting that the abuse directed at plaintiff reflected a belief that he did not act as a man should act—he had feminine mannerisms, did not have sex with a female friend, and did not otherwise conform to gender-based stereotypes — and thus the discrimination was closely linked to gender and therefore actionable under Title VII); *Reed v. S. Bend Nights, Inc.*, 128 F.Supp.3d 996 (E.D. Mich. 2015) (lesbian employee "put forth sufficient evidence in support of her allegation that she was discriminated against because she did not conform to traditional gender stereotypes in terms of her appearance, behavior, or mannerisms at work," where her supervisor testified that she "dressed more like a male" and her " 'demeanor' was a 'little more mannish.' "); *Koren v. Ohio Bell Tel. Co.*, 894 F.Supp.2d 1032 (N.D. Ohio 2012) (gay man alleged sufficient facts to support a claim of sex discrimination based on his failure to comply with gender norms where he changed his last name to his husband's and his employer refused to call him by his new name); *Centola* (concluding that plaintiff's coworkers must have surmised that the plaintiff was gay because they found him to be effeminate); *Heller v. Columbia Edgewater Country Club*, 195 F.Supp.2d 1212 (D. Or. 2002) (holding that a jury could find that the employer repeatedly harassed, and ultimately discharged, the plaintiff because she did not conform to the employer's stereotype of how a woman ought to behave, both because she dated other women and because she wore male-styled clothing).

Plaintiffs who do not look, act, or appear to be gender non-conforming but are merely known to be or perceived to be gay or lesbian do not fare as well in the federal courts. In a Sixth Circuit case, for example, the plaintiff, who was not openly gay and, in fact, even in the lawsuit "declined to reveal whether or not he [was], in fact, homosexual" could not defeat a motion to dismiss his Title VII claim because

> the gender non-conforming behavior which Vickers claims supports his theory of sex stereotyping is not behavior observed at work or affecting his job performance. Vickers has made no argument that his appearance or mannerisms on the job were perceived as gender nonconforming in some way and provided the basis for the harassment he experienced. Rather, the harassment of which Vickers complains is more properly viewed as harassment based on Vickers' perceived homosexuality, rather than based on gender non-conformity.

Vickers.

Likewise, in the Third Circuit granted summary judgment against the plaintiff where he "did not claim that he was harassed because he failed to comply with societal stereotypes of how men ought to appear or behave or that as a man he was treated differently than female co-workers. His claim was, pure and simple, that he was discriminated against because of his sexual orientation." *Id. See also Hamm* (Hamm's claim could not survive a motion for summary judgment where his claim was based on speculation by co-workers that he was gay rather than any specifically alleged gender non-conforming attributes); *Hamner* (upholding judgment as a matter of law for the employer where the plaintiff's discrimination claim was based only on the fact that his employer knew his status as a gay man and "absolutely could not handle that"); *Johnson v. Hondo, Inc.*, 125 F.3d 408 (7th Cir. 1997) (concluding that a slew of gay epithets could not sustain a claim of gender discrimination where there was no evidence that the plaintiff failed to conform to male stereotypes); *Simonton* (holding that a plaintiff could not defeat a motion to dismiss based on a gender non-conformity claim under Title VII where he never set forth any claim that he "behaved in a stereotypically feminine manner."); *Pambianchi v. Arkansas Tech Univ.*, 95 F.Supp.3d 1101 (E.D. Ark. 2015) ("Sexual orientation alone cannot be the alleged gender nonconforming behavior that gives rise to an actionable Title VII claim under a sex-stereotyping theory."). *But see Boutillier v. Hartford Pub. Sch.*, 2014 WL 4794527 (D. Ct. 2014) (allowing claim of lesbian teacher to go forward where the only evidence of gender non-conformity was the fact that she was openly married to a woman because "[c]onstrued most broadly, she has set forth a plausible claim she was discriminated against based on her nonconforming gender behavior."); *Terveer v. Billington*, 34 F.Supp.3d 100 (D.D.C. 2014) (the plaintiff defeated the summary judgment motion by alleging that the defendant denied him promotions and created a hostile work environment because of the plaintiff's failure to conform to male sex stereotypes solely because of his status as a gay man.); *Centola* ("Conceivably, a plaintiff who is perceived by his harassers as stereotypically masculine in every way except for his actual or perceived sexual orientation could maintain a Title VII cause of action alleging sexual harassment because of his sex due to his failure to conform with sexual stereotypes about what 'real' men do or don't do.")

In sum, the distinction between gender non-conformity claims and sexual orientation claims has created an odd state of affairs in the law in which Title VII protects gay, lesbian, and bisexual people, but frequently only to the extent that those plaintiffs meet society's stereotypical norms about how gay men or lesbian women look or act — i.e. that gay men tend to behave in effeminate ways and lesbian women have masculine mannerisms. By contrast, lesbian, gay or bisexual people who otherwise conform to gender stereotyped norms in dress and mannerisms mostly lose their claims for sex discrimination under Title VII, although why this should be true is not entirely clear. It is true that "not all homosexual men are stereotypically feminine and not all heterosexual men are stereotypically masculine" as the Second Circuit explained while defending the exclusion of sexual orientation protection under Title VII. *Simonton*. But it is also true, as we pointed out above, that all gay, lesbian and bisexual persons fail to comply with the sine qua non of gender stereotypes — that all men should form intimate relationships only with women, and all women should form intimate relationships only with men.

Because courts have long held that Title VII will not support a claim for sexual orientation discrimination *per se*, many courts have been attempting to dress sexual orientation discrimination claims in the garb of gender nonconformity case law, with the unsatisfactory results seen in the confused hodge-podge of cases we detail above. This has led some courts toward a more blunt recognition of the difficulty of extricating sexual orientation claims from gender non-conformity claims. Thus the *Videckis* court's observation, which noted that "[s]imply put, the line between sex discrimination and sexual orientation discrimination is 'difficult to draw' because that line does not exist, save as a lingering and faulty judicial construct." This court long ago noted the difficulty and began to grapple with it in a case involving same-sex sexual harassment:

> There is, of course, a considerable overlap in the origins of sex discrimination and homophobia, and so it is not surprising that sexist and homophobic epithets often go hand in hand. Indeed, a homophobic epithet like "fag," for example, may be as much of a disparagement of a man's perceived effeminate qualities as it is of his perceived sexual orientation. Observations in this vein have led a number of scholars to conclude that anti-gay bias should, in fact, be understood as a form of sex discrimination.

City of Belleville. We had no need to decide the matter directly in that case because we were satisfied that there was adequate proof that the harassment recounted by the plaintiff was animated by his failure to conform to stereotypic gender norms. ("One may reasonably infer from the evidence before us that [the plaintiff] was harassed 'because of' his gender. If that cannot be inferred from the sexual character of the harassment itself, it can be inferred from the harassers' evident belief that in wearing an earring, [the plaintiff] did not conform to male standards."). Nevertheless, by noting the overlay between anti-gay bias and sex discrimination we seemed to have anticipated the EEOC's path in *Baldwin*.

Likewise, the Sixth Circuit was on to something when it said, "In all likelihood, any discrimination based on sexual orientation would be actionable under a sex stereotyping theory if this claim is allowed to stand, as all homosexuals, by definition, fail to conform to traditional gender norms in their sexual practices." *Vickers*. The *Vickers* court thought the solution to the inability to segregate sexual orientation from gender non-conformity claims was to deny all gender non-conformity claims where there was also a claim of sexual orientation discrimination. But the other approach could be to recognize the fact that sexual orientation discrimination is, in fact, discrimination based on the gender stereotype that men should have sex only with women and women should have sex only with men. "Conceivably, a plaintiff who is perceived by his harassers as stereotypically masculine in every way except for his actual or perceived sexual orientation could maintain a Title VII cause of action alleging sexual harassment because of his sex due to his failure to conform with sexual stereotypes about what 'real' men do or don't do." *Centola*. As the next paragraph explains, with increasing frequency, the lower courts are beginning to see the false distinction and are turning to this latter approach.

The idea that the line between gender non-conformity and sexual orientation claims is arbitrary and unhelpful has been smoldering for some time, but the EEOC's decision in *Baldwin* threw fuel on the flames. Since the EEOC released its decision in *Baldwin*, stating that "allegations of discrimination on the basis of sexual orientation necessarily state a claim of discrimination on the basis of sex," more and more district court judges have begun to scratch their heads and wonder whether the distinction between the two claims does indeed make any sense. For example, a district court in the Southern District of New York, noting the holding of *Baldwin*, the changing legal landscape, and the arbitrariness of distinguishing between gender based discrimination and sexual orientation discrimination, stated:

> The lesson imparted by the body of Title VII litigation concerning sexual orientation discrimination and sexual stereotyping seems to be that no coherent line can be drawn between these two sorts of claims. Yet the prevailing law in this Circuit—and, indeed, every Circuit to consider the question—is that such a line must be drawn. *Simonton* is still good law, and, as such, this Court is bound by its dictates.

Christiansen v. Omnicom Grp., Inc. 2016 U.S.Dist. LEXIS 29972 (S.D.N.Y. 2016) ("Title VII does not proscribe discrimination because of sexual orientation). And as we just noted above, the Eastern District of Virginia has concluded that

> the distinction [between sexual orientation discrimination and gender discrimination] is illusory and artificial, and that sexual orientation discrimination is not a category distinct from sex or gender discrimination. Thus, claims of discrimination based on sexual orientation are covered by Title VII and Title IX, but not as a category of independent claims separate from sex and gender stereotype. Rather, claims of sexual orientation discrimination are gender stereotype or sex discrimination claims.

Videckis. Likewise, several other district courts have indicated their agreement with the EEOC's decision in *Baldwin,* or, at least recognized that the blurring line between gender and sexual orientation claims might require courts to reconsider the long line of precedent distinguishing them. *Isaacs v. Felder Servs., LLC*, 143 F.Supp.3d 1190 (M.D. Ala. 2015) ("This court agrees instead with the view of the Equal Employment Opportunity Commission that claims of sexual orientation-based discrimination are cognizable under Title VII."); *Koke v. Baumgardner*, 2016 WL 93094 (S.D.N.Y. 2016) ("Given the door left ajar by *Simonton* for claims based on 'failure to conform to sex stereotypes,' the EEOC's recent holding that Title VII prohibits discrimination on the basis of sexual orientation, and the lack of a Supreme Court ruling on whether Title VII applies to such claims, I cannot conclude, at least at this stage, that plaintiff's Title VII claim is 'wholly insubstantial and frivolous.' ").

In short, the district courts — the laboratories on which the Supreme Court relies to work through cutting-edge legal problems — are beginning to ask whether the sexual orientation-denying emperor of Title VII has no clothes.

While this eddy of statutory Title VII sexual orientation decisions has been turning in the lower federal courts, the Supreme Court has been expounding upon the rights of lesbian, gay, and bisexual persons in a constitutional context. Of course, these constitutional cases have no direct bearing on the outcome of litigation under Title VII of the Civil Rights Act, but they do inform the legal landscape that courts face as they interpret "because of sex" in Title VII. In 1996 in *Romer v. Evans*, 517 U.S. 620, 116 S.Ct. 1620, 134 L.Ed.2d 855 (1996), for example, the Court invalidated, under the Equal Protection Clause, an amendment to Colorado's Constitution that sought to foreclose any branch or political subdivision of the State from protecting persons against discrimination based on sexual orientation. Next, in *Lawrence v. Texas*, the Court determined that individuals' rights to liberty under the Due Process Clause gives them the full right to engage in private consensual sexual conduct without intervention of the government. Then, in 2013, the Supreme Court struck down the Defense of Marriage Act (DOMA), finding that it violated the equal protection guarantee of the Fifth Amendment. *United States v. Windsor*, 133 S.Ct. 2675, 186 L.Ed.2d 808 (2013). And finally, two years later, the Supreme Court ruled that under both the Due Process and Equal Protection Clauses of the Fourteenth Amendment, same-sex couples had the right to marry in every state of the Union. *Obergefell v. Hodges*, 135 S.Ct. 2584, 192 L.Ed.2d 609 (2015). We emphasize yet again that none of these cases directly impacts the statutory interpretations of Title VII. The Supreme Court neither created Title VII nor was required to address any issues regarding employment discrimination in considering the issues it chose to address. The role of the Supreme Court is to interpret the laws passed by Congress. And, in fact, in *Obergefell*, one amicus brief urged the Court to view the same sex marriage debate through the lens of gender discrimination arguing that the state's permission to marry depends on the gender of the participants. In oral arguments Chief Justice John Roberts delved into this realm of questioning wondering whether "if Sue loves Joe and Tom loves Joe, Sue can marry him and Tom can't. And the difference is based upon their different sex. Why isn't that a straightforward question of sexual discrimination?" But despite having considered this option, the Court rejected it for a holding based in the Fourteenth Amendment. The Court did not address the issue of gender nor of workplace discrimination.

The cases as they stand do, however, create a paradoxical legal landscape in which a person can be married on Saturday and then fired on Monday for just that act. For although federal law now guarantees anyone the right to marry another person of the same gender, Title VII, to the extent it does not reach sexual orientation discrimination, also allows employers to fire that employee for doing so. From an employee's perspective, the right to marriage might not feel like a real right if she can be fired for exercising it. Many citizens would be surprised to learn that under federal law any private employer can summon an employee into his office and state, "You are a hard-working employee and have added much value to my company, but I am firing you because you are gay." And the employee would have no recourse whatsoever — unless she happens to live in a state or locality with an anti-discrimination statute that includes sexual orientation. More than half of the United States, however, do not have such state protections: Alabama, Alaska, Arkansas, Arizona, Florida, Georgia, Idaho, Indiana, Kansas, Kentucky, Louisiana, Michigan, Mississippi, Missouri, Montana, Nebraska, North Carolina, North Dakota, Ohio, Oklahoma, Pennsylvania, South Carolina, South Dakota, Tennessee, Texas, Virginia, West Virginia, and Wyoming.[6] Moreover, the truth of this scenario would also apply to perceived sexual orientation. And so, for example, an employer who merely has a hunch that an employee is gay can terminate that employee for being gay whether or not she actually is. And even if the employer is wrong about the sexual orientation of the non-gay employee, the employee has no recourse under Title VII as the discharge still would be based on sexual orientation.

In one sense, the paradox is not our concern. Our task is to interpret Title VII as drafted by Congress, and as we concluded in *Ulane*, Title VII prohibits discrimination only on the basis of gender. If we, and every other circuit to have considered it are wrong about the interpretation of the boundaries of gender discrimination under the "sex" prong of Title VII, perhaps it is time for the Supreme Court to step in and tell us so.

As things stand now, however, our understanding of Title VII leaves us with a somewhat odd body of case law that protects a lesbian who faces discrimination because she fails to meet some superficial gender norms — wearing pants instead of dresses, having short hair, not wearing makeup — but not a lesbian who meets cosmetic gender norms, but violates the most essential of gender stereotypes by marrying another woman. We are left with a body of law that values the wearing of pants and earrings over marriage. It seems likely that neither the proponents nor the opponents of protecting employees from sexual orientation discrimination would be satisfied with a body of case law that protects "flamboyant" gay men and "butch" lesbians but not the lesbian or gay employee who act and appear straight. This type of gerrymandering to exclude some forms of gender-norm discrimination but not others leads to unsatisfying results.

D.

In addition to the inconsistent application of Title VII to gender non-conformity, these sexual orientation cases highlight another inconsistency in courts' applications of Title VII to sex as opposed to race. As the EEOC noted in *Baldwin*, when applying Title VII's prohibition of race discrimination, courts and the Commission have

---

[6]States with laws that prohibit sexual orientation discrimination in employment: California, Colorado, Connecticut, Delaware, Hawaii, Illinois, Iowa, Maine, Maryland, Massachusetts, Minnesota, Nevada, New Hampshire, New Jersey, New Mexico, New York, Oregon, Rhode Island, Utah, Vermont, Washington, and Wisconsin. The following states have sexual orientation discrimination protections for government employees only, but not private employees: Alaska, Arizona, Indiana, Kentucky, Louisiana, Michigan, Missouri, Montana, North Carolina, Ohio, Pennsylvania, and Virginia.

consistently concluded that the statute prohibits discrimination based on an employee's association with a person of another race, such as an interracial marriage or friendship. But although it has long been clear that Title VII protects white workers who are discriminated against because they have close associations with African-American partners and vice versa, it has not protected women employees who are discriminated against because of their intimate associations with other women, and men with men.

Since the earliest days of Title VII, the EEOC has taken the position that Title VII, in proscribing race-based discrimination, includes a prohibition on discrimination toward employees because of their interracial associations. *See, e.g., Equal Employment Opportunity Comm'n*, EEOC Dec. No. 76-23 (1975) (Title VII claim properly alleged where job applicant not hired due to his white sister's domestic partnership with an African American). The courts that have considered this question agree: Title VII protects employees in interracial relationships. That is to say, courts have concluded that if a white employee is fired because she is dating or married to an African-American man, this constitutes discrimination on the basis of race. Had she been in a relationship with a white man, she would not have faced the same consequences. The rationale is that "where an employee is subjected to adverse action because an employer disapproves of interracial association, the employee suffers discrimination because of the employee's own race." *Holcomb v. Iona Coll.*, 521 F.3d 130 (2d Cir. 2008) (plaintiff claiming that he suffered an adverse employment action because of his interracial marriage has alleged discrimination as a result of his membership in a protected class under Title VII); *See also Floyd v. Amite Cty. Sch. Dist.*, 581 F.3d 244 (5th Cir. 2009) (collecting cases); *Stacks v. Sw. Bell Yellow Pages, Inc.*, 27 F.3d 1316 (8th Cir. 1994) (agreeing with district court that claim for discrimination based on interracial relationships was cognizable under Title VII, but finding that plaintiff failed to present sufficient evidence to support the claim); *Parr v. Woodmen of the World Life Ins. Co.*, 791 F.2d 888 (11th Cir. 1986) (white man married to African-American woman can state a claim for failure to hire under Title VII); *Whitney v. Greater N.Y. Corp. of Seventh–Day Adventists*, 401 F.Supp. 1363 (S.D.N.Y.1975) (white woman alleged viable claim of discrimination based on casual social relationship with African-American man); *Gresham v. Waffle House, Inc.*, 586 F.Supp. 1442 (N.D. Ga. 1984) (holding that plaintiff has stated a claim under Title VII by alleging that she was discharged by her employer because of her interracial marriage to a black man).

The relationship in play need not be a marriage to be protected. A number of courts have found that Title VII protects those who have been discriminated against based on interracial friendships and other associations. *See, e.g., Blanks v. Lockheed Martin Corp.*, 568 F.Supp.2d 740 (S.D. Miss. 2007) (compiling cases in which courts have found viable claims under Title VII where plaintiffs alleged discrimination based on workplace or other associations with members of racial and national origin minority groups); *see also McGinest v. GTE Serv. Corp.*, 360 F.3d 1103 (9th Cir. 2004) (noting that a white employee who was also targeted for discrimination was not a good comparator to plaintiff as he was targeted because of his close associations with black friends and co-workers); *Johnson v. Univ. of Cincinnati*, 215 F.3d 561 (6th Cir. 2000) (advocacy on behalf of women and minorities); *Tetro v. Elliott Popham Pontiac, Oldsmobile, Buick, & GMC Trucks, Inc.*, 173 F.3d 988 (6th Cir. 1999) ("A white employee who is discharged because his child is biracial is discriminated against on the basis of his race, even though the root animus for the discrimination is a prejudice against the biracial child").

It is also well established that, unlike equal protection claims that apply differing levels of scrutiny depending on the nature of the class, the classifications within Title VII — race, color, religion, sex, or national origin — must all be treated equally. "The statute on its face treats each of the enumerated categories exactly the same." *Price Waterhouse. See also Nat'l R.R. Passenger Corp. v. Morgan*, 536 U.S. 101, 122 S.Ct. 2061, 153 L.Ed.2d 106 (2002) ("Hostile work environment claims based on racial harassment are reviewed under the same standard as those based on sexual harassment."). Consequently, if Title VII protects from discrimination a white woman who is fired for romantically associating with an African-American man, then logically it should also protect a woman who has been discriminated against because she is associating romantically with another woman, if the same discrimination would not have occurred were she sexually or romantically involved with a man. It is true that Hively has not made the express claim that she was discriminated against based on her relationship with a woman, but that is, after all, the very essence of sexual orientation discrimination. It is discrimination based on the nature of an associational relationship — in this case, one based on gender.

E.

A court would not necessarily need to expand the definition of "sex discrimination" beyond the narrow understanding of "sex" we adopted in *Ulane,* to conclude that lesbian, gay, and bisexual employees who are terminated for their sexual conduct or their perceived sexual conduct have been discriminated against on the basis of sex. Yet, by failing to conform with both superficial and quintessential gender norms, gay, lesbian, and bisexual employees could be seen as facing discrimination comparable to that which Ann Hopkins faced when her supervisors insisted that she live up to the feminine stereotype the supervisors associated with women. "Congress intended to strike at the *entire* spectrum of disparate treatment of men and women resulting from sex stereotypes." *Price Waterhouse* (emphasis ours). There is no reason to believe that the disparate treatment caused when employees do not live up to the stereotype of how "real" men and women act in their sexual lives should be excluded. As the Supreme Court stated in *Oncale*, "Statutory prohibitions often go beyond the principal evil to cover reasonably comparable evils, and it is ultimately the provisions of our laws rather than the principal concerns of our legislators by which we are governed."

Curiously, however, despite *Price Waterhouse* and *Oncale*, the Supreme Court has opted not to weigh in on the question of whether Title VII's prohibition on sex-based discrimination would extend to protect against sexual orientation discrimination. Even in the watershed case of *Obergefell*, when the Court declared that "laws excluding same-sex couples from the marriage right impose stigma and injury of the kind prohibited by our basic charter," it made no mention of the stigma and injury that comes from excluding lesbian, gay, and bisexual persons from the workforce or subjecting them to un-remediable harassment and discrimination. Perhaps the majority's statement in *Obergefell* that "[i]t demeans gays and lesbians for the State to lock them out of a central institution of the Nation's society" could be read as a forecast that the Supreme Court might someday say the same thing about locking gay men and lesbians out of the workforce — another "central institution of the Nation's society." But, as we noted earlier, in the same-sex marriage case, the Court was presented with the opportunity to consider the question as one of sex discrimination but declined to do so and thus far has declined to take any opportunity to weigh in on the question of sexual orientation discrimination under Title VII.

In addition to the Supreme Court's silence, Congress has time and time again said "no," to every attempt to add sexual orientation to the list of categories protected from discrimination by Title VII.

This circuit has not remained silent on the matter, but rather, as we have described above, our own precedent holds that Title VII provides no protection from nor redress for discrimination on the basis of sexual orientation. We require a compelling reason to overturn circuit precedent. Ordinarily this requires a decision of the Supreme Court or a change in legislation. But it is also true that precedent can be overturned when "the rule has proven to be intolerable simply in defying practical workability ... whether related principles of law have so far developed as to have left the old rule no more than a remnant of abandoned doctrine ... or whether facts have so changed, or come to be seen so differently, as to have robbed the old rule of significant application or justification." *Planned Parenthood of Se. Pa. v. Casey*, 505 U.S. 833, 112 S.Ct. 2791, 120 L.Ed.2d 674 (1992). It may be that the rationale appellate courts, including this one, have used to distinguish between gender non-conformity discrimination claims and sexual orientation discrimination claims will not hold up under future rigorous analysis. It seems illogical to entertain gender non-conformity claims under Title VII where the non-conformity involves style of dress or manner of speaking, but not when the gender non-conformity involves the sine qua non of gender stereotypes — with whom a person engages in sexual relationships. And we can see no rational reason to entertain sex discrimination claims for those who defy gender norms by looking or acting stereotypically gay or lesbian (even if they are not), but not for those who are openly gay but otherwise comply with gender norms. We allow two women or two men to marry, but allow employers to terminate them for doing so. Perchance, in time, these inconsistencies will come to be seen as defying practical workability and will lead us to reconsider our precedent.

Perhaps the writing is on the wall. It seems unlikely that our society can continue to condone a legal structure in which employees can be fired, harassed, demeaned, singled out for undesirable tasks, paid lower wages, demoted, passed over for promotions, and otherwise discriminated against solely based on who they date, love, or marry. The agency tasked with enforcing Title VII does not condone it; many of the federal courts to consider the matter have stated that they do not condone it; and this court undoubtedly does not condone it (*see Ulane*). But writing on the wall is not enough. Until the writing comes in the form of a Supreme Court opinion or new legislation, we must adhere to the writing of our prior precedent, and therefore, the decision of the district court is AFFIRMED.

NOTES AND PROBLEMS FOR DISCUSSION

1. Although this panel opinion was reversed by the *en banc* court, see *infra*, it valuably describes the extant "hodge-podge" of district and appellate court jurisprudence in sexual orientation-related cases that the product of the Supreme Court's recognition of stereotyped-based claims of sex discrimination in *Price*

Waterhouse. Prior to *Price Waterhouse*, the courts uniformly dismissed all Title VII claims alleging discrimination on the basis of sexual orientation as not within the literal meaning of "sex" and as supported by Congress' consistent refusal to amend the statute to add sexual orientation as a protected classification.   But after *Price Waterhouse*, as this opinion recounts, the lower courts were prepared to recognize Title VII claims brought by gay or lesbian plaintiffs as long as they were properly plead. Any claim expressly alleging sexual orientation discrimination was dismissed; but a complaint alleging sex-based discrimination founded on an allegation that the plaintiff had been denied an employment opportunity for failure to adhere to a sex-based stereotype *could* survive a motion to dismiss for failure to state a cognizable claim.   Over time, however, the courts began to chafe under this formalistic distinction. They found it increasingly difficult to distinguish between discrimination targeted at someone because of his or her sexual orientation status and discrimination based on gender nonconformity.   As a result, the lower courts took different approaches towards explaining "how to draw the line" between sex-stereotype (gender-norm) discrimination and sexual orientation discrimination.   Some decided there was no point in attempting to "tease the two apart" and decried any use of sex-stereotype analysis in this context as an unacceptable attempt to "bootstrap" protection for sexual orientation into Title VII.   Others were willing to thread this analytical needle by focusing on the nature of the gender-stereotype that was being applied to the plaintiff.   If the plaintiff could establish that the employer relied on the plaintiff's display of overt mannerisms, appearances, behaviors, or other characteristics that did not conform to gender-based stereotypes, the courts would recognize these claims. *See e.g.,* Evans v. Georgia Regional Hospital, 850 F.3d 1248 (11th Cir. 2017), cert. denied, 138 S.Ct. 557, 199 L.Ed.2 446 (2017).   On the other hand, if the gay or lesbian plaintiff did conform to traditional gender stereotyped behavior (other than choice of sexual partner), the gender conformity claim would not survive. *See e.g.,* Christiansen v. Omnicom Group, Inc., 852 F.3d 195 (2d Cir. 2017) ("being gay, lesbian, or bisexual, standing alone, does not constitute nonconformity with a gender stereotype that can give rise to a cognizable gender stereotyping claim."). A third group of courts took the position, ultimately adopted by the EEOC, that any manifestation of sexual orientation-based discrimination was, by definition, a form of gender nonconformity discrimination since all gay and lesbian individuals failed to comply with the "sine qua non of gender stereotypes – that all men should form intimate relationships only with women, and all women should form intimate relationships only with men."

Recall that in Section C of this chapter, *supra,* we examined the issue of whether an employer who discriminates against individuals involved in inter-racial social relationships engages in proscribed racial discrimination.   As the citations contained therein reflect, the few circuits that addressed this issue have concluded that this type of "associational" discrimination is race-based.   The panel opinion in *Hively* rejected this analysis. But a majority of the full court disagreed with the panel's view and this was one of two grounds upon which the Seventh Circuit *en banc* reversed the panel opinion. 853 F.3d 339 (2017) (*en banc*). Although it acknowledged that the original panel properly felt bound to apply extant circuit precedent, the *en banc* majority declared that it was free to change that circuit policy.   And so it did, and on two grounds.   First, it explained that to determine whether a sexual orientation-based policy was a subset of prohibited sex discrimination, the proper analysis was to simply change the sex of the plaintiff to determine if that would have changed the employer's decision.   And clearly if the female plaintiff had been a man, and all other circumstances remained unchanged, i.e., the plaintiff was involved with a female, the employer would not have been denied a contract renewal.   The majority expressly rejected the dissenting judges' position that the proper comparator was a male employee who, like the plaintiff, was engaged in a homosexual relationship.   The majority also concluded that any attempt to divine Congressional intent on the basis of its history of unsuccessful efforts at amending Title VII to include sexual orientation-based discrimination was pointless.   The majority determined that it was "simply too difficult to draw a reliable inference from these truncated legislative initiatives".   Secondly, relying on those cases in which other circuit had ruled that a policy that discriminated against individuals who engaged in interracial relationships constituted discrimination on the basis of the plaintiff's race, the majority agreed with the "associational theory" that the original panel had rejected.   It held that any discrimination on the basis of a protected characteristic of one with whom the plaintiff associates constitutes discrimination against the plaintiff based on the plaintiff's status.

In a concurring opinion, Judge Posner declined to rely on either of the grounds asserted by the *en banc* majority.   He acknowledged that the Congress that enacted the 1964 Act certainly did not envision, and could not have imagined, that prohibited "sex" discrimination included discrimination on the basis of sexual orientation.   Nevertheless, he explained, the concept of sex discrimination has significantly broadened in the public discourse.   In his view, it was within the purview of judges who, he acknowledged, are not members of Congress, to interpret a statute in a manner "to avoid statutory obsolescence and concomitantly to avoid placing the entire burden of updating old statutes on the legislative branch."

The Second Circuit subsequently endorsed and expanded upon the *en banc* Seventh Circuit's reasoning and conclusion in an *en banc* opinion of its own.   In ZARDA v. ALTITUDE EPRESS, INC., 883 F.3d 100 (2d Cir. 2018) (*en banc*), a case that spawned eight separate opinions, including four concurring opinions and three dissenting opinions, a five member plurality of the twelve member *en banc* court concluded that discrimination on the basis of sexual orientation did constitute a form of sex-based discrimination.   Its broadly worded opinion offered four justifications for this ruling: (1) that sex is necessarily a factor in sexual orientation since one cannot fully define an individual's sexual orientation without accounting for that individual's (and its partner's) sex; (2) that sexual orientation discrimination is "almost invariably" rooted in gender stereotypes because it is predicated on assumptions about how persons of a certain sex should or can behave; (3) that since sexual orientation discrimination is motivated primarily by the employer's opposition to romantic association between particular sexes it is a form of sex-based associational discrimination; and (4) in determining whether or not a decision is based on sex, the proper comparison is not whether both men and women are subjected to the same stereotype or associational ban, but rather on whether a particular individual was subjected to a gendered stereotype or associational ban. The court also rejected as "unpersuasive" the assertion that Congress' failure to amend Title VII to expressly apply to sexual orientation discrimination reflected congressional adoption or even acquiescence to the prevailing judicial view that sexual orientation was not a form of sex-based discrimination under Title VII.   The plurality disclaimed any insight into congressional intent and concluded, therefore, that it could not choose among the various inferences that could be drawn from legislative inaction. Two concurring members limited their decision to the conclusion that sexual orientation constituted sex-based associational discrimination. The two other concurring members simply held that sexual orientation constituted sex-based discrimination without further amplification. Three judges dissented. The Supreme Court granted certiorari on April 22, 2019. 139 S.Ct. 1599 (2019).

2. Public sector employment policies that discriminate on the basis of sexual orientation are subject also to constitutional scrutiny. Such practices have been challenged under (a) the First Amendment, (b) the penumbral right of privacy, and (c) the equal protection guarantees of the Fifth and Fourteenth Amendments.

(a) First Amendment challenges to anti-gay policies have focused on the infringement of the individual's rights of freedom of expression and association and have met with mixed results. For example, in NATIONAL GAY TASK FORCE v. BOARD OF EDUC. OF OKLAHOMA CITY, 729 F.2d 1270 (10th Cir.1984), aff'd in a per curiam opinion by an equally divided Supreme Court. 470 U.S. 903, 105 S.Ct. 1858, 84 L.Ed.2d 776 (1985). a state statute that permitted teachers to be discharged or not hired for advocating, encouraging, or promoting homosexual activity was struck down as violative of the free speech provision of the First Amendment. (That same court noted, however, that the constitutional right of privacy would not prevent the discharge of teachers for engaging in homosexual conduct.).

Should the First Amendment analysis change when the sanctioned speech consists of a declaration of the speaker's homosexual status as opposed to statements about homosexuality in general? Most of these cases were brought by members of the armed forces challenging regulations that mandated discharge and prevented reenlistment for any individual who admitted his or her homosexual status. The circuit courts consistently upheld the constitutionality of these regulations. For example, in BEN–SHALOM v. MARSH, 881 F.2d 454 (7th Cir.1989), cert. denied, 494 U.S. 1004, 110 S.Ct. 1296, 108 L.Ed.2d 473 (1990), the Seventh Circuit reasoned that since an admission of homosexuality "implies, at the very least, a desire to commit homosexual acts," the Army could reasonably conclude that an admitted homosexual would have a desire and propensity to commit homosexual acts. And since none of the parties disputed the constitutionality of denying reenlistment for engaging in homosexual conduct, the court deemed the regulations operated as a restriction on conduct and not on protected First Amendment speech. This regulation imposed, in the court's view, at most, an incidental limitation on her protected First Amendment freedom of speech since it did not prevent the plaintiff from making declarations about homosexuality in general or about the Army's policy towards homosexuality. The court also concluded that the Army had a legitimate interest in excluding individuals who had acknowledged their propensity to commit proscribed conduct. It deferred to the Army's judgment that accepting acknowledged homosexuals into the armed forces might imperil morale, discipline, and the effectiveness of the fighting forces.

After extensive negotiation with the Clinton Administration, Congress enacted its version of a "don't ask, don't tell" (DADT) policy. Section 571 of the National Defense Authorization Act for Fiscal Year 1994, 10 U.S.C. §654 amended the armed forces regulations to provide that an individual subject to separation from the service for making a statement of homosexual status could avoid separation if s/he demonstrated that s/he did not engage in, attempt to engage in or have a propensity or intent to engage in homosexual acts. Subsequently, the Secretary of Defense issued an implementing memorandum which declared that while "statements that reflect an intent or propensity to engage" in homosexual acts would still be a basis for separation, no applicant would be affirmatively asked about his or her sexual orientation. The constitutionality of this policy under the First Amendment has been affirmed on the same grounds used to uphold the original armed forces regulations. In these cases the courts emphasized that the opportunity for the aggrieved to avoid separation by showing that s/he did not engage in or intend to engage in homosexual acts established that the declaration of status did not create an irrebutable presumption of engaging in homosexual conduct and, therefore, that the policy was aimed at conduct and not at speech. *See* Able v. U.S. 155 F.3d 628 (2d Cir.1998); Thomasson v. Perry, 80 F.3d 915 (4th Cir.1996) (*en banc*), cert. denied, 519 U.S. 948, 117 S.Ct. 358 136 L.Ed 2d 250 (1996). And in COOK v. GATES, 528 F.3d 42 (1st Cir. 2008), the First Circuit ruled that the First Amendment did not bar the military from using a member's declaration of homosexual status as evidence of a violation of the Act and as a basis for separation from military service. On December 22, 2010, President Barak Obama signed the Don't Ask, Don't Tell Repeal Act of 2010, 10 U.S.C. §654 (2010), which repealed the armed forces' policy at such time as the President, the Secretary of Defense, and the Chairman of the Joint Chiefs of Staff certify that repeal will not harm military readiness, followed by a 60-day waiting period. Those certifications have been made and the policy was terminated on September 20, 2011.

(b) Constitutional challenges to public sector policies prohibiting homosexual conduct based on the right to privacy have been even less successful than those alleging a violation of the First Amendment. In BOWERS v. HARDWICK, 478 U.S. 186, 106 S.Ct. 2841, 92 L.Ed.2d 140 (1986), the Supreme Court denied relief in a suit for declaratory judgment challenging the constitutionality of a Georgia statute that criminalized sodomy as applied to consensual homosexual sodomy between adults in the respondent's home. A five-member majority declared that none of the Court's prior constitutional right of privacy rulings recognized a right to be free from state proscription of all kinds of private sexual conduct between consenting adults. More specifically, it concluded that there was no substantive fundamental right under the Due Process Clause to engage in consensual homosexual sodomy. Since state law historically had proscribed homosexual consensual sodomy, the Court reasoned, the freedom to engage in this conduct could not be said to be either a fundamental liberty that was deeply rooted in the Nation's history and tradition, or a right whose sacrifice would threaten the continued existence of liberty or justice. In addition, the fact that the statute proscribed activity undertaken in the privacy of the respondent's home was not of constitutional significance.

But in LAWRENCE v. TEXAS, 539 U.S. 558, 123 S.Ct. 2472, 156 L.Ed.2d 508 (2003), a five member majority voted to overrule *Bowers* in all of its aspects. Unlike the Georgia statute in *Bowers*, the Texas criminal statute challenged in *Lawrence* proscribed only acts of sodomy engaged in by participants of the same sex. Nevertheless, instead of relying on that distinction and deciding the case on equal protection grounds, the opinion authored by Justice Kennedy took *Bowers* on directly. The *Lawrence* majority rejected the historical grounds relied upon by the majority in *Bower*s and held, instead, that the liberty interest protected by the Due Process Clause of the Fourteenth Amendment extended to all intimate sexual conduct between consenting adults in the privacy of their home, regardless of whether it is engaged in by persons of the same or opposite sex. While carefully noting that its ruling did not extend formal recognition to any relationship that homosexual persons seek to enter, the Court declared that the State "cannot demean their existence or control their destiny by making their private sexual conduct a crime." Justice O'Connor, in a concurring opinion, voted to overturn the Texas statute, but only on equal protection grounds.

In WITT v. DEPARTMENT OF AIR FORCE, 527 F.3d 806 (9th Cir. 2008), the Ninth Circuit read *Lawrence* to apply "something more than" traditional rational basis review" to a constitutional challenge to governmental action regulating adult consensual sexual acts. But after concluding that *Lawrence* did not precisely define the level of review, the court looked for guidance to Sell v. United States, 539 U.S. 166 (2003), where the Supreme Court had applied a heightened level of scrutiny to a substantive due process challenge to a governmental policy which forcibly administered anti-psychotic drugs to a mentally ill defendant to render that defendant competent to stand trial. The Ninth Circuit construed *Sell* to mean that when the government attempts to intrude upon the personal and private lives of gay individuals, the government must (1) advance an *important* governmental interest that (2) must *significantly* further that interest in a manner that is (3) *necessary* to further that interest, i.e., that a less intrusive means would be unlikely to achieve substantially that interest. Additionally, the court ruled that in a substantive due process challenge to the military's DADT policy, this heightened level of scrutiny must be applied to the facts of the specific case and not to the general terms of the policy on its face. Applying that standard to the Air Force's application of DADT against this plaintiff, the court found that although the government advanced an important interest in management of the military (including maintaining "unit cohesion"), the record was unclear as to whether discharging the plaintiff would advance that interest or whether a less intrusive response would not achieve substantially that interest. Accordingly, it remanded the case for further development of the record.

On the other hand, in COOK v. GATES, 528 F.3d 42 (1st Cir. 2008), while the First Circuit, citing *Witt* with approval, also construed *Lawrence* and *Sell* to require the invocation of intermediate scrutiny to a due process challenge to the military's DADT policy, the court split company with the Ninth Circuit on the application of that standard to the DADT policy. The First Circuit rejected the plaintiffs' *facial* challenge to the policy on the ground that *Lawrence* limited its identification of a protected liberty interest to adult consensual intimacy within the confines of one's home and private life. Since the DADT policy mandated separation for other types of sexual activity, including public homosexual acts and these forms of conduct were excluded from the liberty interest recognized by *Lawrence*, the Act could constitutionally operate under those set of circumstances, and, therefore, the plaintiffs' facial challenge to the DADT policy failed. Moreover, in light of the longstanding policy of judicial deference to legislative choices made in the area of military affairs, the court also rejected the plaintiffs' *as-applied* due process challenge to the DADT policy. Examining the circumstances surrounding the enactment of the DADT statute, the court concluded that Congress had passed the act in order to preserve unit cohesion of the troops and that the court's deferential posture required it to take this interest at face value and, accordingly, reject the plaintiffs' as-applied challenge.

(c) Discrimination on the basis of sexual orientation in the public sector also has been challenged as violative of the equal protection guarantees of the Fifth and Fourteenth Amendments. The circuit courts uniformly have rejected the claim that gays are a suspect classification. Instead, they have concluded that homosexual classifications should be subjected to rational basis scrutiny because (1) the ruling in *Bowers* that the Constitution does not afford a privacy right to engage in homosexual conduct foreclosed any argument that homosexuals should be viewed as a suspect classification because it would be anomalous, on its face, to declare status defined by conduct that states may constitutionally criminalize as deserving of strict scrutiny; and (2) members of suspect classes exhibit immutable characteristics whereas homosexuality is primarily behavioral in nature. *See, e.g.*, Padula v. Webster, 822 F.2d 97 (D.C.Cir.1987); Woodward v. United States, 871 F.2d 1068 (Fed.Cir.1989); High Tech Gays v. Defense Industrial Security Clearance Office, 895 F.2d 563 (9th Cir.1990). The courts then invariably find that the homosexual classification is rationally related to the government's interests in maintaining credibility in the eyes of the public, avoiding the employment of individuals who might be targets of blackmail threatening the exposure of their sexual orientation (even as applied to publicly acknowledged homosexuals), and preventing the conversion of heterosexuals to a homosexual lifestyle. Should these decisions be reconsidered in light of the Supreme Court's wholesale overruling of *Bowers* in *Lawrence?* In WITT v. DEPARTMENT OF AIR FORCE, 527 F.3d 806 (9th Cir. 2008) and COOK v. GATES, 528 F.3d 42 (1st Cir. 2008), the Ninth and First Circuits, respectively, rejected the plaintiff's argument that the ruling in *Lawrence* required courts to apply a heightened standard of scrutiny in equal protection challenges to the armed forces' DADT policy on the ground that *Lawrence* declined to address the equal protection clause.

Attempts to limit the holding in cases such as *Padula*, *Woodward*, and *High Tech Gays*, by suggesting that classifications based upon homosexual status should be subjected to a higher degree of scrutiny than classifications based on homosexual conduct also have not prevailed. Adopting the same rationale articulated in *Ben-Shalom*, the courts conclude that the government (typically the military) is entitled to classify those who demonstrate the intent to engage in proscribable conduct with those who actually engage in the forbidden conduct. They also reason that statements of status could rationally be used as a proxy for proof of intent to engage in forbidden conduct. *See, e.g.*, Steffan v. Perry, 41 F.3d 677 (D.C.Cir.1994).

In ROMER v. EVANS, 517 U.S. 620, 116 S.Ct. 1620, 134 L.Ed. 2d 855 (1996), however, the Supreme Court struck down a provision of Colorado's Constitution that prohibited all legislative, executive, or judicial action by any state or local government agent designed to protect homosexuals from discrimination on the basis of "homosexual, lesbian or bisexual orientation, conduct, practices or relationships." The majority concluded that the amendment failed to survive rational basis scrutiny because it lacked a rational relationship to any legitimate state interest. In its judgment, "the amendment seems inexplicable by anything but animus toward the class that it affects." Nevertheless, since this statute failed to pass muster under this most lenient of constitutional standards, the Court studiously avoided expressly ruling on whether homosexuals constituted a suspect or quasi-suspect class.

(d) There is also an important constitutional issue on the flip side of this equation. Suppose a state law *prohibits* discrimination on the basis of sexual orientation and that a family owned company is charged with violating that statute by not hiring a gay man because, in the sincerely held religious views of the owners, conforming to the statutory requirement would force them to violate their religious beliefs concerning sexual orientation and/or gay marriage. This important question of the intersection between antidiscrimination policy and the constitutional right to freely exercise one's religious beliefs is not unique to the sexual orientation context. It has been raised, and rejected, as a defense to decisions to refuse to adhere to the policy against racial or other forms of proscribed discrimination. See e.g., Hurley v. Irish-American Gay, Lesbian and Bisexual Group of Boston, Inc., 515 U.S. 557, 115 S.Ct. 2338, 132 L.Ed.2d 487 (1995); Newman v. Piggy Park Enterprises, Inc., 390 U.S. 400, 88 S.Ct. 964, 19 L.Ed.2d 1263 (1968) (per curiam). The Supreme Court was confronted with this problem in a non-employment case but declined to address the general issue. Instead, in MASTERPIECE CAKESHOP, LTD v. COLORADO CIVIL RIGHTS COMMISSION, 584 U.S. ___, 138 S.Ct. 1719, 201 L.Ed.2d 35 (2018), the Supreme Court ruled that the state entities that had found a baker in violation of state antidiscrimination law that prohibited businesses from refusing to provide services to individuals on the basis of, *inter alia*, sexual orientation, violated the State's First Amendment duty to assess the baker's religiously-predicated defense in a non-hostile manner. The 7-2 majority stated that the baker's claim that he had to use his artistic skills to make an expressive statement endorsing gay marriage "has a significant First Amendment speech component" and the state agency's handling of the complaint against the baker did not accord the baker the neutral and respectful consideration of his freedom of speech and freedom of religious claims that is mandated by the First Amendment. It relied on statements made by some of the state Civil Rights Commission members to the effect that religious beliefs must bend to the dictates of antidiscrimination law as manifesting a hostile reception to the baker's religious beliefs. By implicitly, if not explicitly, questioning whether the baker's conscience-based objection was legitimate, the majority declared, the state government was "neither tolerant nor respectful of" the baker's religious beliefs and, therefore, did not consider his defense with the neutrality required by the Free Exercise Clause of the First Amendment. Thus, it was the process used by the Commission in this particular instance, and not the actual decision, that, in the majority's determination, ran afoul of the First Amendment. Accordingly, the majority expressly declined to rule on "other cases like this in other circumstances"

3. In light of the approach taken by the Seventh and Second Circuits in *Hively* and *Zarada* (Note 1, *infra*) regarding the applicability of gender nonconformity claims to suits by gay or lesbian plaintiffs, how should the courts treat Title VII claims of discrimination brought by other members of the LBGT community?

In SMITH v. CITY OF SALEM, OHIO, 378 F.3d 566 (6th Cir.2004), the Sixth Circuit relied on *Price Waterhouse* as the basis for ruling that a biologically male transsexual diagnosed with Gender Identity Disorder who alleged that he was discriminated against because of his display of non-masculine behavior stated a cognizable claim of sex discrimination under Title VII. The court ruled that the male plaintiff's gender non-conforming *appearance and behavior* fit within the *Price Waterhouse* paradigm of unlawful sex stereotyping. It also noted that the fact that the cause of the non-conforming behavior was the plaintiff's status as a transsexual was not fatal to his claim. Another panel of that circuit subsequently went one step further in the following case:

Equal Employment Opportunity Commission v. R.G. & G.R. Harris Funeral Homes, Inc.

United States Court of Appeals, Sixth Circuit, 2018.
884 F.3d 560

MOORE, Circuit Judge.

Aimee Stephens (formerly known as Anthony Stephens) was born biologically male.[1] While living and presenting as a man, she worked as a funeral director at R.G. & G.R. Harris Funeral Homes, Inc. ("the Funeral Home"), a closely held for-profit corporation that operates three funeral homes in Michigan. Stephens was terminated from the Funeral Home by its owner and operator, Thomas Rost, shortly after Stephens informed Rost that she intended to transition from male to female and would represent herself and dress as a woman while at work. Stephens filed a complaint with the Equal Employment Opportunity Commission ("EEOC"), which investigated Stephens's allegations that she had been terminated as a result of unlawful sex discrimination. During the course of its investigation, the EEOC learned that the Funeral Home provided its male public-facing employees with clothing that complied with the company's dress code while female public-facing employees received no such allowance. The EEOC subsequently brought suit against the Funeral Home in which the EEOC charged the Funeral Home with violating Title VII of the Civil Rights Act of 1964 ("Title VII") by (1) terminating Stephens's employment on the basis of her transgender or transitioning status and her refusal to conform to sex-based stereotypes; and (2) administering a discriminatory-clothing-allowance policy.

The parties submitted dueling motions for summary judgment. The EEOC argued that it was entitled to judgment as a matter of law on both of its claims. For its part, the Funeral Home argued that it did not violate Title VII by requiring Stephens to comply with a sex-specific dress code that it asserts equally burdens male and female employees, and, in the alternative, that Title VII should not be enforced against the Funeral Home because requiring the Funeral Home to employ Stephens while she dresses and represents herself as a woman would constitute an unjustified substantial burden upon Rost's (and thereby the Funeral Home's) sincerely held religious beliefs, in violation of the Religious Freedom Restoration Act ("RFRA"). As to the EEOC's discriminatory-clothing-allowance claim, the Funeral Home argued that Sixth Circuit case law precludes the EEOC from bringing this claim in a complaint that arose out of Stephens's original charge of discrimination because the Funeral Home could not reasonably expect a clothing-allowance claim to emerge from an investigation into Stephens's termination.

---

[1] We refer to Stephens using female pronouns, in accordance with the preference she has expressed through her briefing to this court

The district court granted summary judgment in favor of the Funeral Home on both claims. For the reasons set forth below, we hold that (1) the Funeral Home engaged in unlawful discrimination against Stephens on the basis of her sex; (2) the Funeral Home has not established that applying Title VII's proscriptions against sex discrimination to the Funeral Home would substantially burden Rost's religious exercise, and therefore the Funeral Home is not entitled to a defense under RFRA; (3) even if Rost's religious exercise were substantially burdened, the EEOC has established that enforcing Title VII is the least restrictive means of furthering the government's compelling interest in eradicating workplace discrimination against Stephens; and (4) the EEOC may bring a discriminatory-clothing-allowance claim in this case because such an investigation into the Funeral Home's clothing-allowance policy was reasonably expected to grow out of the original charge of sex discrimination that Stephens submitted to the EEOC. Accordingly, we REVERSE the district court's grant of summary judgment on both the unlawful-termination and discriminatory-clothing-allowance claims, GRANT summary judgment to the EEOC on its unlawful-termination claim, and REMAND the case to the district court for further proceedings consistent with this opinion.

I. BACKGROUND

Aimee Stephens, a transgender woman who was "assigned male at birth," joined the Funeral Home as an apprentice on October 1, 2007 and served as a Funeral Director/Embalmer at the Funeral Home from April 2008 until August 2013. During the course of her employment at the Funeral Home, Stephens presented as a man and used her then-legal name, William Anthony Beasley Stephens.

The Funeral Home is a closely held for-profit corporation. Thomas Rost ("Rost"), who has been a Christian for over sixty-five years, owns 95.4% of the company and operates its three funeral home locations. Rost proclaims "that God has called him to serve grieving people" and "that his purpose in life is to minister to the grieving." To that end, the Funeral Home's website contains a mission statement that states that the Funeral Home's "highest priority is to honor God in all that we do as a company and as individuals" and includes a verse of scripture on the bottom of the mission statement webpage. The Funeral Home itself, however, is not affiliated with a church; it does not claim to have a religious purpose in its articles of incorporation; it is open every day, including Christian holidays; and it serves clients of all faiths. Although the Funeral Home places the Bible, "Daily Bread" devotionals, and "Jesus Cards" in public places within the funeral homes, the Funeral Home does not decorate its rooms with visible religious figures to avoid offending people of different religions. Rost hires employees belonging to any faith or no faith to work at the Funeral Home, and he does not endorse or consider himself to endorse his employees' beliefs or non-employment-related activities.

The Funeral Home requires its public-facing male employees to wear suits and ties and its public-facing female employees to wear skirts and business jackets. The Funeral Home provides all male employees who interact with clients, including funeral directors, with free suits and ties, and the Funeral Home replaces suits as needed. All told, the Funeral Home spends approximately $470 per full-time employee per year and $235 per part-time employee per year on clothing for male employees.

Until October 2014 — after the EEOC filed this suit — the Funeral Home did not provide its female employees with any sort of clothing or clothing allowance. Beginning in October 2014, the Funeral Home began providing its public-facing female employees with an annual clothing stipend ranging from $75 for part-time employees to $150 for full-time employees. Rost contends that the Funeral Home would provide suits to all funeral directors, regardless of their sex, id., but it has not employed a female funeral director since Rost's grandmother ceased working for the organization around According to Rost, the Funeral Home has received only one application from a woman for a funeral director position in the thirty-five years that Rost has operated the Funeral Home, and the female applicant was deemed not qualified.

On July 31, 2013, Stephens provided Rost with a letter stating that she has struggled with "a gender identity disorder" her "entire life," and informing Rost that she has "decided to become the person that [her] mind already is." The letter stated that Stephens "intend[ed] to have sex reassignment surgery," and explained that "[t]he first step [she] must take is to live and work full-time as a woman for one year." To that end, Stephens stated that she would return from her vacation on August 26, 2013, "as [her] true self, Amiee [sic] Australia Stephens, in appropriate business attire." After presenting the letter to Rost, Stephens postponed her vacation and continued to work for the next two weeks. Then, just before Stephens left for her intended vacation, Rost fired her. Rost said, "this is not going to work out," and offered Stephens a severance agreement if she "agreed not to say anything or do anything." Stephens refused. Rost testified that he fired Stephens because "he was no longer going to represent himself as a man. He wanted to dress as a woman."

Rost avers that he "sincerely believe[s] that the Bible teaches that a person's sex is an immutable God-given gift," and that he would be "violating God's commands if [he] were to permit one of [the Funeral Home's] funeral directors to deny their sex while acting as a representative of [the] organization" or if he were to "permit one of [the Funeral Home's] male funeral directors to wear the uniform for female funeral directors while at work. In particular, Rost believes that authorizing or paying for a male funeral director to wear the uniform for female funeral directors would render him complicit "in supporting the idea that sex is a changeable social construct rather than an immutable God-given gift."

After her employment was terminated, Stephens filed a sex-discrimination charge with the EEOC, alleging that "[t]he only explanation" she received from "management" for her termination was that "the public would [not] be accepting of [her] transition." She further noted that throughout her entire employment at the Funeral Home, there were no other female Funeral Director/Embalmers. During the course of investigating Stephens's allegations, the EEOC learned from another employee that the Funeral Home did not provide its public-facing female employees with suits or a clothing stipend.

The EEOC issued a letter of determination on June 5, 2014, in which the EEOC stated that there was reasonable cause to believe that the Funeral Home discharged Stephens due to her sex and gender identity, female, in violation of Title VII and discriminated against its female employees by providing male employees with a clothing benefit which was denied to females, in violation of Title VII. The EEOC and the Funeral Home were unable to resolve this dispute through an informal conciliation process, and the EEOC filed a complaint against the Funeral Home in the district court on September 25, 2014.

The Funeral Home moved to dismiss the EEOC's action for failure to state a claim. The district court denied the Funeral Home's motion, but it narrowed the basis upon which the EEOC could pursue its unlawful-termination claim. In particular, the district court agreed with the Funeral Home that transgender status is not a protected trait under Title VII, and therefore held that the EEOC could not sue for alleged discrimination against Stephens based solely on her transgender and/or transitioning status. Nevertheless, the district court determined that the EEOC had adequately stated a claim for discrimination against Stephens based on the claim that she was fired because of her failure to conform to the Funeral Home's "sex- or gender-based preferences, expectations, or stereotypes."

The parties then cross-moved for summary judgment. With regard to the Funeral Home's decision to terminate Stephens's employment, the district court determined that there was direct evidence to support a claim of employment discrimination against Stephens on the basis of her sex, in violation of Title VII. However, the court nevertheless found in the Funeral Home's favor because it concluded that the Religious Freedom Restoration Act ("RFRA") precludes the EEOC from enforcing Title VII against the Funeral Home, as doing so would substantially burden Rost and the Funeral Home's religious exercise and the EEOC had failed to demonstrate that enforcing Title VII was the least restrictive way to achieve its presumably compelling interest "in ensuring that Stephens is not subject to gender stereotypes in the workplace in terms of required clothing at the Funeral home." Based on its narrow conception of the EEOC's compelling interest in bringing the claim, the district court concluded that the EEOC could have achieved its goals by proposing that the Funeral Home impose a gender-neutral dress code. The EEOC's failure to consider such an accommodation was, according to the district court, fatal to its case. Separately, the district court held that it lacked jurisdiction to consider the EEOC's discriminatory-clothing-allowance claim because, under longstanding Sixth Circuit precedent, the EEOC may pursue in a Title VII lawsuit only claims that are reasonably expected to grow out of the complaining party's — in this case, Stephens's — original charge. The district court entered final judgment on all counts in the Funeral Home's favor * * * and the EEOC filed a timely notice of appeal shortly thereafter.

Stephens moved to intervene in this appeal * * *. We determined that Stephens's request was timely * * *. We further determined that Stephens's intervention would not prejudice the Funeral Home because Stephens stated in her briefing that she did not intend to raise new issues.

II. DISCUSSION

* * *

B. Unlawful Termination Claim

Here, the district court correctly determined that Stephens was fired because of her failure to conform to sex stereotypes, in violation of Title VII. The district court erred, however, in finding that Stephens could not alternatively pursue a claim that she was discriminated against on the basis of her transgender and transitioning status. Discrimination on the basis of transgender and transitioning status is necessarily discrimination on the basis of sex, and thus the EEOC should have had the opportunity to prove that the Funeral Home violated Title VII by firing Stephens because she is transgender and transitioning from male to female.

1. Discrimination on the Basis of Sex Stereotypes

In *Price Waterhouse v. Hopkins*, a plurality of the Supreme Court explained that Title VII's proscription of discrimination "'because of ... sex' ... mean[s] that gender must be irrelevant to employment decisions." In enacting Title VII, the plurality reasoned, "Congress intended to strike at the entire spectrum of disparate treatment of men and women resulting from sex stereotypes." The *Price Waterhouse* plurality, along with two concurring Justices, therefore determined that a female employee who faced an adverse employment decision because she failed to "walk ... femininely, talk ... femininely, dress ... femininely, wear make-up, have her hair styled, [or] wear jewelry," could properly state a claim for sex discrimination under Title VII — even though she was not discriminated against for being a woman per se, but instead for failing to be womanly enough.

Based on *Price Waterhouse*, we determined that "discrimination based on a failure to conform to stereotypical gender norms" was no less prohibited under Title VII than discrimination based on "the biological differences between men and women." Smith v. City of Salem, 378 F.3d 566, 573 (6th Cir. 2004). And we found no "reason to exclude Title VII coverage for non sex-stereotypical behavior simply because the person is a transsexual." Thus, in *Smith*, we held that a transgender plaintiff (born male) who suffered adverse employment consequences after "he began to express a more feminine appearance and manner on a regular basis" could file an employment discrimination suit under Title VII, because such "discrimination would not [have] occur[red] but for the victim's sex." As we reasoned in *Smith*, Title VII proscribes discrimination both against women who "do not wear dresses or makeup" and men who do. Under any circumstances, sex stereotyping based on a person's gender non-conforming behavior is impermissible discrimination.

Here, Rost's decision to fire Stephens because Stephens was "no longer going to represent himself as a man" and "wanted to dress as a woman," falls squarely within the ambit of sex-based discrimination that *Price Waterhouse* and *Smith* forbid. For its part, the Funeral Home has failed to establish a non-discriminatory basis for Stephens's termination, and Rost admitted that he did not fire Stephens for any performance-related issues. We therefore agree with the district court that the Funeral Home discriminated against Stephens on the basis of her sex, in violation of Title VII.

The Funeral Home nevertheless argues that it has not violated Title VII because sex stereotyping is barred only when the employer's reliance on stereotypes results in disparate treatment of employees because they are either male or female. According to the Funeral Home, an employer does not engage in impermissible sex stereotyping when it requires its employees to conform to a sex-specific dress code — as it purportedly did here by requiring Stephens to abide by the dress code designated for the Funeral Home's male employees — because such a policy impose[s] equal burdens on men and women, and thus does not single out an employee for disparate treatment based on that employee's sex. In support of its position, the Funeral Home relies principally on Jespersen v. Harrah's Operating Co., 444 F.3d 1104 (9th Cir. 2006) (*en banc*) and Barker v. Taft Broadcasting Co., 549 F.2d 400 (6th Cir. 1977). *Jespersen* (holding that the plaintiff failed to demonstrate how a grooming code that required women to wear makeup and banned men from wearing makeup was a violation of Title VII because the plaintiff failed to produce evidence showing that this sex-specific makeup policy was "more burdensome for women than for men") held that a sex-specific grooming code that imposed different but equally burdensome requirements on male and female employees would not violate Title VII. *Barker* (holding that a grooming code that established different hair-length limits for male and female employees did not violate Title VII because failure to comply with the code resulted in the same consequences for men and women), for its part, held that a sex-specific grooming code that was enforced equally as to male and female employees would not violate Title VII. For three reasons, the Funeral Home's reliance on these cases is misplaced.

First, the central issue in *Jespersen* and *Barker* — whether certain sex-specific appearance requirements violate Title VII — is not before this court. We are not considering, in this case, whether the Funeral Home violated Title VII by requiring men to wear pant suits and women to wear skirt suits. Our question is instead whether the Funeral Home could legally terminate Stephens, notwithstanding that she fully intended to comply with the company's sex-specific dress code, simply because she refused to conform to the Funeral Home's notion of her sex. When the Funeral Home's actions are viewed in the proper context, no reasonable jury could believe that Stephens was not targeted for disparate treatment and that no sex stereotype factored into the Funeral Home's employment decision.

Second, even if we would permit certain sex-specific dress codes in a case where the issue was properly raised, we would not rely on either *Jespersen* or *Barker* to do so. *Barker* was decided before *Price Waterhouse*, and it in no way anticipated the Court's recognition that Title VII "strike[s] at the entire spectrum of disparate treatment of men and women resulting from sex stereotypes." *Price Waterhouse*. Rather, according to *Barker*, "[w]hen Congress makes it unlawful for an employer to 'discriminate ... on the basis of ... sex ...', without further explanation of its meaning, we should not readily infer that it meant something different than what the concept of discrimination has traditionally meant." Of course, this is precisely the sentiment that *Price Waterhouse* "eviscerated" when it recognized that "Title VII's reference to 'sex' encompasses both the biological differences between men and women, and gender discrimination, that is, discrimination based on a failure to conform to stereotypical gender norms." Indeed, *Barker's* incompatibility with *Price Waterhouse* may explain why this court has not cited *Barker* since *Price Waterhouse* was decided.

As for *Jespersen*, that Ninth Circuit case is irreconcilable with our decision in *Smith*. Critical to *Jespersen's* holding was the notion that the employer's grooming standards, which required all female bartenders to wear makeup (and prohibited males from doing so), did not on their face violate Title VII because they did not require the plaintiff to conform to a stereotypical image that would objectively impede her ability to perform her job. We reached the exact opposite conclusion in *Smith*, as we explained that requiring women to wear makeup does, in fact, constitute improper sex stereotyping. And more broadly, our decision in *Smith* forecloses the *Jespersen* court's suggestion that sex stereotyping is permissible so long as the required conformity does not impede an employee's ability to perform her job, as the *Smith* plaintiff did not and was not required to allege that being expected to adopt a more masculine appearance and manner interfered with his job performance. *Jespersen's* incompatibility with *Smith* may explain why it has never been endorsed (or even cited) by this circuit—and why it should not be followed now.

Finally, the Funeral Home misreads binding precedent when it suggests that sex stereotyping violates Title VII only when the employer's sex stereotyping resulted in disparate treatment of men and women. This interpretation of Title VII cannot be squared with our holding in *Smith*. There, we did not ask whether transgender persons transitioning from male to female were treated differently than transgender persons transitioning from female to male. Rather, we considered whether a transgender person was being discriminated against based on "his failure to conform to sex stereotypes concerning how a man should look and behave." *Smith*. It is apparent from both *Price Waterhouse* and *Smith* that an employer engages in unlawful discrimination even if it expects both biologically male and female employees to conform to certain notions of how each should behave. See Zarda v. Altitude Express, Inc., 2018 WL 1040820 (2d Cir. Feb. 26, 2018) (*en banc*) (plurality) ("[T]he employer in *Price Waterhouse* could not have defended itself by claiming that it fired a gender-nonconforming man as well as a gender-non-conforming woman any more than it could persuasively argue that two wrongs make a right.").

In short, the Funeral Home's sex-specific dress code does not preclude liability under Title VII. Even if the Funeral Home's dress code does not itself violate Title VII — an issue that is not before this court — the Funeral Home may not rely on its policy to combat the charge that it engaged in improper sex stereotyping when it fired Stephens for wishing to appear or behave in a manner that contradicts the Funeral Home's perception of how she should appear or behave based on her sex. Because the EEOC has presented unrefuted evidence that unlawful sex stereotyping was at least a motivating factor in the Funeral Home's actions, and because we reject the Funeral Home's affirmative defenses, we GRANT summary judgment to the EEOC on its sex discrimination claim.

2. Discrimination on the Basis of Transgender/Transitioning Status

We also hold that discrimination on the basis of transgender and transitioning status violates Title VII. The district court rejected this theory of liability at the motion-to-dismiss stage, holding that transgender or transsexual status is currently not a protected class under Title VII. The EEOC and Stephens argue that the district court's determination was erroneous because Title VII protects against sex stereotyping and transgender discrimination is based on the non-conformance of an individual's gender identity and appearance with sex-based norms or expectations; therefore, discrimination because of an individual's transgender status is always based on gender-stereotypes: the stereotype that individuals will conform their appearance and behavior — whether their dress, the name they use, or other ways they present themselves — to the sex assigned them at birth. The Funeral Home, in turn, argues that Title VII does not prohibit discrimination based on a person's transgender or transitioning status because "sex," for the purposes of Title VII, refers to a binary characteristic for which there are only two classifications, male and female, and which classification arises in a person based on their chromosomally driven physiology and reproductive function. According to the Funeral Home, transgender status refers to a person's self-assigned gender identity rather than a person's sex, and therefore such a status is not protected under Title VII.

For two reasons, the EEOC and Stephens have the better argument. First, it is analytically impossible to fire an employee based on that employee's status as a transgender person without being motivated, at least in part, by the employee's sex. The Seventh Circuit's method of "isolat[ing] the significance of the plaintiff's sex to the employer's decision" to determine whether Title VII has been triggered illustrates this point. See Hively v. Ivy Tech Cmty. Coll. of Ind., 853 F.3d 339, 345 (7th Cir. 2017). In *Hively*, the Seventh Circuit determined that Title VII prohibits discrimination on the basis of sexual orientation — a different question than the issue before this court — by asking whether the plaintiff, a self-described lesbian, would have been fired if she had been a man married to a woman (or living with a woman, or dating a woman) and everything else had stayed the same. If the answer to that question is no, then the plaintiff has stated a "paradigmatic sex discrimination" claim. *Hively*. Here, we ask whether Stephens would have been fired if Stephens had been a woman who sought to comply with the women's dress code. The answer quite obviously is no. This, in and of itself, confirms that Stephens's sex impermissibly affected Rost's decision to fire Stephens.

The court's analysis in Schroer v. Billington, 577 F.Supp.2d 293 (D.D.C. 2008), provides another useful way of framing the inquiry. There, the court noted that an employer who fires an employee because the employee converted from Christianity to Judaism has discriminated against the employee "because of religion," regardless of whether the employer feels any animus against either Christianity or Judaism, because "discrimination because of religion easily encompasses discrimination because of a change of religion." By the same token, discrimination "because of sex" inherently includes discrimination against employees because of a change in their sex. See id. at 307–08.[4] Here, there is evidence that Rost at least partially based his employment decision on Stephens's desire to change her sex: Rost justified firing Stephens by explaining that Rost "sincerely believes that the Bible teaches that a person's sex (whether male or female) is an immutable God-given gift and that it is wrong for a

---

[4]Moreover, discrimination because of a person's transgender, intersex, or sexually indeterminate status is no less actionable than discrimination because of a person's identification with two religions, an unorthodox religion, or no religion at all. And "religious identity" can be just as fluid, variable, and difficult to define as "gender identity"; after all, both have "a deeply personal, internal genesis that lacks a fixed external referent." Sue Landsittel, Strange Bedfellows? Sex, Religion, and Transgender Identity Under Title VII, 104 NW. U. L. REV. 1147, 1172 (2010) (advocating for "[t]he application of tests for religious identity to the problem of gender identity [because it] produces a more realistic, and therefore more appropriate, authentication framework than the current reliance on medical diagnoses and conformity with the gender binary").

person to deny his or her God-given sex, " and "the Bible teaches that it is wrong for a biological male to deny his sex by dressing as a woman."[5] As amici point out in their briefing, such statements demonstrate that Ms. Stephens's sex necessarily factored into the decision to fire her.

The Funeral Home argues that *Schroer's* analogy is structurally flawed because, unlike religion, a person's sex cannot be changed; it is, instead, a biologically immutable trait. We need not decide that issue; even if true, the Funeral Home's point is immaterial. As noted above, the Supreme Court made clear in *Price Waterhouse* that Title VII requires "gender [to] be irrelevant to employment decisions." Gender (or sex) is not being treated as "irrelevant to employment decisions" if an employee's attempt or desire to change his or her sex leads to an adverse employment decision.

Second, discrimination against transgender persons necessarily implicates Title VII's proscriptions against sex stereotyping. As we recognized in *Smith*, a transgender person is someone who fails to act and/or identify with his or her gender" — i.e., someone who is inherently "gender non-conforming. Thus, an employer cannot discriminate on the basis of transgender status without imposing its stereotypical notions of how sexual organs and gender identity ought to align. There is no way to disaggregate discrimination on the basis of transgender status from discrimination on the basis of gender non-conformity, and we see no reason to try.

We did not expressly hold in *Smith* that discrimination on the basis of transgender status is unlawful, though the opinion has been read to say as much — both by this circuit and others. In * * * Dodds v. United States Department of Education, 845 F.3d 217 (6th Cir. 2016), we refused to stay a preliminary injunction ordering the school district to treat an eleven-year old transgender girl as a female and permit her to use the girls' restroom because, among other things, the school district failed to show that it would likely succeed on the merits. In so holding, we cited *Smith* as evidence that this circuit's "settled law" prohibits "[s]ex stereotyping based on a person's gender non-conforming behavior," and then pointed to out-of-circuit cases for the propositions that a person is defined as transgender precisely because of the perception that his or her behavior transgresses gender stereotypes * * *.[6] Such references support what we now directly hold: Title VII protects transgender persons because of their transgender or transitioning status, because transgender or transitioning status constitutes an

---

[5]On the other hand, there is also evidence that Stephens was fired only because of her nonconforming appearance and behavior at work, and not because of her transgender identity. At his deposition, when asked whether "the reason you fired [Stephens], was it because [Stephens] claimed that he was really a woman; is that why you fired [Stephens] or was it because he claimed – or that he would no longer dress as a man," Rost answered: "That he would no longer dress as a man," and when asked, "if Stephens had told you that he believed that he was a woman, but would only present as a woman outside of work, would you have terminated him," Rost answered: "No.").

[6]We acknowledge that Barnes v. City of Cincinnati, 401 F.3d 729 (6th Cir. 2005), read *Smith* as focusing on "look and behav[ior]." ("By alleging that his failure to conform to sex stereotypes concerning how a man should look and behave was the driving force behind defendant's actions, Smith stated a claim for relief pursuant to Title VII's prohibition of sex discrimination."). That is not surprising, however, given that only "look and behavior," not status, were at issue in *Barnes*.

inherently gender non-conforming trait.

The Funeral Home raises several arguments against this interpretation of Title VII, none of which we find persuasive. First, the Funeral Home contends that the Congress enacting Title VII understood "sex" to refer only to a person's physiology and reproductive role, and not a person's self-assigned gender identity. But the drafters' failure to anticipate that Title VII would cover transgender status is of little interpretive value, because "statutory prohibitions often go beyond the principal evil to cover reasonably comparable evils, and it is ultimately the provisions of our laws rather than the principal concerns of our legislators by which we are governed." Oncale v. Sundowner Offshore Servs., Inc., 523 U.S. 75 (1998); see also *Zarda* (rejecting the argument that Title VII was not originally intended to protect employees against discrimination on the basis of sexual orientation, in part because the same argument "could also be said of multiple forms of discrimination that are [now] indisputably prohibited by Title VII ... [but] were initially believed to fall outside the scope of Title VII's prohibition," such as "sexual harassment and hostile work environment claims"). And in any event, *Smith* and *Price Waterhouse* preclude an interpretation of Title VII that reads "sex" to mean only individuals' chromosomally driven physiology and reproductive function. Indeed, we criticized the district court in *Smith* for relying on a series of pre-*Price Waterhouse* cases from other federal appellate courts holding that transsexuals, as a class, are not entitled to Title VII protection because Congress "had a narrow view of sex in mind" and "never considered nor intended that Title VII apply to anything other than the traditional concept of sex." According to *Smith*, such a limited view of Title VII's protections had been "eviscerated by *Price Waterhouse*." The Funeral Home's attempt to resurrect the reasoning of these earlier cases thus runs directly counter to *Smith's* holding.

In a related argument, the Funeral Home notes that both biologically male and biologically female persons may consider themselves transgender, such that transgender status is not unique to one biological sex. It is true, of course, that an individual's biological sex does not dictate her transgender status; the two traits are not coterminous. But a trait need not be exclusive to one sex to nevertheless be a function of sex. As the Second Circuit explained in *Zarda*,

Title VII does not ask whether a particular sex is discriminated against; it asks whether a particular "individual" is discriminated against "because of such individual's ... sex." Taking individuals as the unit of analysis, the question is not whether discrimination is borne only by men or only by women or even by both men and women; instead, the question is whether an individual is discriminated against because of his or her sex.

Because an employer cannot discriminate against an employee for being transgender without considering that employee's biological sex, discrimination on the basis of transgender status necessarily entails discrimination on the basis of sex — no matter what sex the employee was born or wishes to be. By the same token, an employer need not discriminate based on a trait common to all men or women to violate Title VII. After all, a subset of both women and men decline to wear dresses or makeup, but discrimination against any woman on this basis would constitute sex discrimination under *Price Waterhouse*. See *Hively*.

Nor can much be gleaned from the fact that later statutes, such as the Violence Against Women Act, expressly prohibit discrimination on the basis of "gender identity," while Title VII does not, because "Congress may certainly choose to use both a belt and suspenders to achieve its objectives." *Hively*. We have, in fact, already read Title VII to provide redundant statutory protections in a different context. In In re Rodriguez, 487 F.3d 1001 (6th Cir. 2007), for instance, we recognized that claims alleging discrimination on the basis of ethnicity may fall within Title VII's prohibition on discrimination on the basis of national origin, even though at least one other federal statute treats "national origin" and "ethnicity" as separate traits. Moreover, Congress's failure to modify Title VII to include expressly gender identity lacks persuasive significance because several equally tenable inferences may be drawn from such inaction, including the inference that the existing legislation already incorporated the offered change. In short, nothing precludes discrimination based on transgender status from being viewed both as discrimination based on "gender identity" for certain statutes and, for the purposes of Title VII, discrimination on the basis of sex.

The Funeral Home places great emphasis on the fact that our published decision in *Smith* superseded an earlier decision that stated explicitly, as opposed to obliquely, that a plaintiff who "alleges discrimination based solely on his identification as a transsexual ... has alleged a claim of sex stereotyping pursuant to Title VII." Smith v. City of Salem, 369 F.3d 912, 922 (6th Cir.), opinion amended and superseded, 378 F.3d 566 (6th Cir. 2004). But such an amendment does not mean, as the Funeral Home contends, that the now-binding *Smith* opinion "directly rejected" the notion that Title VII prohibits discrimination on the basis of transgender status. The elimination of the language, which was not necessary to the decision, simply means that *Smith* did not expressly recognize Title VII protections for transgender persons based on identity. But *Smith's* reasoning still leads us to the same conclusion.

We are also unpersuaded that our decision in Vickers v. Fairfield Medical Center, 453 F.3d 757 (6th Cir. 2006), precludes the holding we issue today. We held in *Vickers* that a plaintiff cannot pursue a claim for impermissible sex stereotyping on the ground that his perceived sexual orientation fails to conform to gender norms unless he alleges that he was discriminated against for failing to "conform to traditional gender stereotypes in any observable way at work." *Vickers* thus rejected the notion that "the act of identification with a particular group, in itself, is sufficiently gender non-conforming such that an employee who so identifies would, by this very identification, engage in conduct that would enable him to assert a successful sex stereotyping claim." The *Vickers* court reasoned that recognizing such a claim would impermissibly "bootstrap protection for sexual orientation into Title VII." Id. (quoting Dawson v. Bumble & Bumble, 398 F.3d 211, 218 (2d Cir. 2005)). The Funeral Home insists that, under Vickers, Stephens's sex-stereotyping claim survives only to the extent that it concerns her appearance or mannerisms on the job, but not as it pertains to her underlying status as a transgender person.

The Funeral Home is wrong. First, *Vickers* does not control this case because *Vickers* concerned a different legal question. As the EEOC and amici Equality Ohio note, *Vickers* addressed only whether Title VII forbids sexual orientation discrimination, not discrimination against a transgender individual. While it is indisputable that a panel of this Court cannot overrule the decision of another panel when the prior decision constitutes controlling authority, one case is not controlling authority over another if the two address substantially different legal issues. After all, we do not overrule a case by distinguishing it.

Second, we are not bound by *Vickers* to the extent that it contravenes *Smith*. When a later decision of this court conflicts with one of our prior published decisions, we are still bound by the holding of the earlier case. As noted above, *Vickers* indicated that a sex-stereotyping claim is viable under Title VII only if a plaintiff alleges that he was discriminated against for failing to conform to traditional gender stereotypes in any observable way at work. The *Vickers* court's new "observable-at-work" requirement is at odds with the holding in *Smith*, which did not limit sex-stereotyping claims to traits that are observable in the workplace. The "observable-at-work" requirement also contravenes our reasoning in Barnes v. City of Cincinnati, 401 F.3d 729 (6th Cir. 2005) — a binding decision that predated *Vickers* by more than a year — in which we held that a reasonable jury could conclude that a transgender plaintiff was discriminated against on the basis of his sex when, among other factors, his "ambiguous sexuality and his practice of dressing as a woman outside of work were well-known within the [workplace]."[7] From *Smith* and *Barnes*, it is clear that a plaintiff may state a claim under Title VII for discrimination based on gender nonconformance that is expressed outside of work. The *Vickers* court's efforts to develop a narrower rule are therefore not binding in this circuit.

Therefore, for the reasons set forth above, we hold that the EEOC could pursue a claim under Title VII on the ground that the Funeral Home discriminated against Stephens on the basis of her transgender status and transitioning identity. The EEOC should have had the opportunity, either through a motion for summary judgment or at trial, to establish that the Funeral Home violated Title VII's prohibition on discrimination on the basis of sex by firing Stephens because she was transgender and transitioning from male to female.

3. Defenses to Title VII Liability

Having determined that the Funeral Home violated Title VII's prohibition on sex discrimination, we must now consider whether any defenses preclude enforcement of Title VII in this case. As noted above, the district court held that the EEOC's enforcement efforts must give way to the Religious Freedom Restoration Act

---

[7]Oddly, the *Vickers* court appears to have recognized that its new "observable-at-work" requirement cannot be squared with earlier precedent. Immediately after announcing this new requirement, the *Vickers* court cited *Smith* for the proposition that "a plaintiff hoping to succeed on a claim of sex stereotyping [must] show that he fails to act and/or identify with his or her gender" — a proposition that is necessarily broader than the narrow rule *Vickers* sought to announce. The *Vickers* court also seemingly recognized *Barnes* as binding authority, but portrayed the decision as "affirming [the] district court's denial of defendant's motion for summary judgment as a matter of law on discrimination claim where pre-operative male-to-female transsexual was demoted based on his ambiguous sexuality and his practice of dressing as a woman' and his co-workers' assertions that he was 'not sufficiently masculine." This summary is accurate as far as it goes, but it entirely omits the discussion in *Barnes* of discrimination against the plaintiff based on his practice of dressing as a woman outside of work.

("RFRA"), which prohibits the government from enforcing a religiously neutral law against an individual if that law substantially burdens the individual's religious exercise and is not the least restrictive way to further a compelling government interest. The EEOC seeks reversal of this decision; the Funeral Home urges affirmance. In addition, certain amici ask us to affirm the district court's grant of summary judgment on different grounds — namely that Stephens falls within the "ministerial exception" to Title VII and is therefore not protected under the Act.

We hold that the Funeral Home does not qualify for the ministerial exception to Title VII; the Funeral Home's religious exercise would not be substantially burdened by continuing to employ Stephens without discriminating against her on the basis of sex stereotypes; the EEOC has established that it has a compelling interest in ensuring the Funeral Home complies with Title VII; and enforcement of Title VII is necessarily the least restrictive way to achieve that compelling interest. We therefore REVERSE the district court's grant of summary judgment in the Funeral Home's favor and GRANT summary judgment to the EEOC on the unlawful-termination claim.

* * *

C. Clothing-Benefit Discrimination Claim

The district court erred in granting summary judgment in favor of the Funeral Home on the EEOC's discriminatory clothing-allowance claim. We long ago held that the scope of the complaint the EEOC may file in federal court in its efforts to enforce Title VII is limited to the scope of the EEOC investigation reasonably expected to grow out of the charge of discrimination.

* * *

* * * [T]he EEOC may sue for matters beyond those raised directly in the EEOC's administrative charge for two reasons. First, limiting the EEOC complaint to the precise grounds listed in the charge of discrimination would undercut Title VII's effective functioning because laypersons who are unfamiliar with the niceties of pleading and are acting without the assistance of counsel submit the original charge. Second, an initial charge of discrimination does not trigger a lawsuit; it instead triggers an EEOC investigation. The matter evolves into a lawsuit only if the EEOC is unable to obtain voluntary compliance with the law. Thus it is obvious that the civil action is much more intimately related to the EEOC investigation than to the words of the charge which originally triggered the investigation.

At the same time, however, * * * allowing the EEOC to sue for matters beyond those reasonably expected to arise from the original charge would undermine Title VII's enforcement process. In particular, * * * an original charge provide[s] an employer with notice of the allegation, an opportunity to participate in a complete investigation of such allegation, and an opportunity to participate in meaningful conciliation discussions should reasonable cause be found following the EEOC investigation. We believe that the full investigatory process would be short-circuited, and the conciliation process thereby threatened, if the EEOC did not file a separate charge and undertake a separate investigation when facts are learned suggesting an employer may have engaged in "discrimination of a type other than that raised by the individual party's charge and unrelated to the individual party.

* * * Stephens would have been directly affected by the Funeral Home's allegedly discriminatory clothing-allowance policy had she not been terminated, as the Funeral Home's current practice indicates that she would have received either no clothing allowance or a less valuable clothing allowance once she began working at the Funeral Home as a woman. And * * * the EEOC's investigation into the Funeral Home's discriminatory clothing-allowance policy concerns precisely the same type of discrimination — discrimination on the basis of sex — that Stephens raised in her initial charge.

[W]e have developed a broad conception of the sorts of claims that can be reasonably expected to grow out of the initial charge of discrimination. * * * EEOC charges must be liberally construed to determine whether there was information given in the charge that reasonably should have prompted an EEOC investigation of a separate type of discrimination. Here, Stephens alleged that she was fired after she shared her intention to present and dress as a woman because the Funeral Home management told her that it did not believe the public would be accepting of her transition from male to female. It was reasonable to expect, in light of this allegation, that the EEOC would investigate the Funeral Home's employee-appearance requirements and expectations, would learn about the Funeral Home's sex-specific dress code, and would thereby uncover the Funeral Home's seemingly discriminatory clothing-allowance policy. * * * Stephens's claim that she was fired because of her planned change in appearance and presentation contains an implicit allegation that the Funeral Home requires its male and female employees to look a particular way, and this fact could (and did) reasonably prompt the EEOC to investigate whether these appearance requirements imposed unequal burdens — in this case, fiscal burdens — on its male and female employees.

We therefore REVERSE the district court's grant of summary judgment to the Funeral Home on the EEOC's discriminatory-clothing-allowance claim and REMAND with instructions to consider the merits of the EEOC's claim.

III. CONCLUSION

Discrimination against employees, either because of their failure to conform to sex stereotypes or their transgender and transitioning status, is illegal under Title VII. The unrefuted facts show that the Funeral Home fired Stephens because she refused to abide by her employer's stereotypical conception of her sex, and therefore the EEOC is entitled to summary judgment as to its unlawful-termination claim. RFRA provides the Funeral Home with no relief because continuing to employ Stephens would not, as a matter of law, substantially burden Rost's religious exercise, and even if it did, the EEOC has shown that enforcing Title VII here is the least restrictive means of furthering its compelling interest in combating and eradicating sex discrimination. We therefore REVERSE the district court's grant of summary judgment in favor of the Funeral Home and GRANT summary judgment to the EEOC on its unlawful-termination claim. We also REVERSE the district court's grant of summary judgment on the EEOC's discriminatory-clothing-allowance claim, as the district court erred in failing to consider the EEOC's claim on the merits. We REMAND this case to the district court for further proceedings consistent with this opinion.

NOTES AND PROBLEMS FOR DISCUSSION

1.   Note that in the principal case, the Sixth Circuit went one step beyond its prior ruling in *Smith*; declaring, for the first time, that discrimination on the basis of transgender and/or transitioning *status*, as well as discrimination based on an individual's appearance or gender representation, inherently involves the use of a sex-based stereotype and, therefore, per *Price Waterhouse*, is a proscribed form of sex-based discrimination. Do you agree with the comparator reasoning employed by both the Sixth Circuit in *Harris Funeral Home*, and the Second Circuit in *Zarda,* (see Note 1(c) after *Hively*, *infra*), i.e., that the fact that the employer discriminates against both female and male individuals with transgender or transitioning status, is not fatal to a claim of sex-based discrimination? *See also* Etsitty v. Utah Transit Authority, 502 F.3d 1215 (10th Cir. 2007) (assuming *arguendo* that *Price Waterhouse* sex-stereotyping doctrine extends to claims by transsexuals, the defendant's explanation that it fired the transsexual plaintiff because of its fear of liability occasioned by the plaintiff's use of female public restrooms while wearing the employer's identifiable uniform when she still possessed male genitalia constituted a legitimate nondiscriminatory reason and the plaintiff failed to raise a genuine issue of fact as to whether that explanation was pretextual). *But see generally*, Wittmer v. Phillips 66 Co., 915 F.3d 328 (5th Cur. 2019)(affirming trial court's grant of summary judgment to defendant on narrow evidentiary grounds – that the plaintiff failed to establish a prima facie claim because the employee did not offer evidence that non-transgendered individuals were treated better than her and also did not present a general issue of fact that the defendant's non-discriminatory explanation was pretextual – while noting that binding circuit precedent holds that Title VII does not apply to claims of sexual orientation or transgender-based discrimination).

Do you agree with the *Harris* court's conclusion that discrimination based on either one's gender representation/appearance or an individual's transgender or transitioning status inherently involves reliance upon a sex-based stereotype? And what about the Sixth Circuit's rejection of the Ninth Circuit's determination in *Jesperson* (see Note 2 after *Willingham*, *supra*) that requiring male and female workers to adhere to a sex-specific dress code does not constitute unlawful sex stereotyping?

Both the Second Circuit in *Zarda* and the Sixth Circuit in *Harris Funeral* declared that Congress' repeated failure to amend Title VII to expressly extend its antidiscrimination mandate to decisions based on sexual orientation, transgender and transitioning status and other forms of gender identity "lacks persuasive significance" as to the meaning of the statutory "because of sex" language. Both courts insisted that there were "several equally tenable inference" to be drawn from such inaction, including the inference that the extant language supported the inclusion of these classifications within the compass of §703(a). The Supreme Court granted certiorari in both cases on April 22, 2019. 139 S.Ct. 1599 (2019).

2. In May 1998, President Clinton signed Executive Order 13087, which amended Executive Order 11478 to proscribe sexual orientation discrimination within the federal civilian workforce. This amended Order, however, only states administration policy and does not create any enforcement mechanism. Additionally, a large number of cities and counties enacted laws that prohibit sexual preference discrimination and more than twenty states (e.g., Illinois, New Jersey, Hawaii, Massachusetts, Wisconsin,

Vermont, Minnesota, California, Nevada, New Hampshire, New York, Rhode Island and Connecticut) and the District of Columbia have passed legislation that protects gays and lesbians from employment discrimination in the public and private sectors. Some states (Louisiana, Maryland, Michigan, New Mexico, Ohio, Pennsylvania, and Washington) prohibit sexual orientation discrimination solely in the public sector. At least one plaintiff has successfully challenged an anti-homosexual policy under state common law. See Collins v. Shell Oil Co., Triton Biosciences, Inc., 56 FEP Cases 440 (Cal.Sup.1991) (trial court awarded over $5 million in punitive and compensatory damages to executive who was fired for private homosexual conduct occurring away from his place of employment; complaint included fraud, contract and intentional infliction of emotional distress claims).

New Jersey's public accommodations law prohibits discrimination on the basis of, *inter alia*, sexual orientation in places of public accommodations. When an avowedly gay male was expelled from his position as assistant scoutmaster in a local Boy Scouts troop after the organization learned of his prominent role in a gay rights organization, he brought suit alleging that the Scouts had violated the state public accommodations law by expelling him solely on the basis of his sexual orientation. The Boy Scouts insisted (1) that it was not a public accommodation within the meaning of the state law; and (2) that application of that statute would violate its First Amendment right of expressive association. The New Jersey Supreme Court held that the Scouts organization was a place of public accommodation subject to the state law. With respect to the First Amendment issue, the state Supreme Court ruled that although the Boy Scouts expressed a belief in moral values, including the view that homosexuality was immoral, the organization had not established that its members shared the goal of associating in order to preserve that moral view. Consequently, it held that the plaintiff's membership in the Scouts did not violate the organization's constitutional right of expressive association and that his presence would not significantly affect its ability to carry out its varied objectives. The U.S. Supreme Court granted review solely on the issue whether the application of New Jersey's public accommodations statute to the Scouts violated the First Amendment.

In BOY SCOUTS OF AMERICA v. DALE, 530 U.S. 649, 120 S.Ct. 2446, 147 L.Ed.2d 554 (2000), the Supreme Court, by a 5-4 vote, reversed the constitutional ruling by the New Jersey Supreme Court. It found that the Scouts did enjoy a constitutionally protected right of expressive association because its general mission was to associate for the purpose of having its adult leaders transmit a system of values, including the value that homosexuality is immoral, to its youth members. Moreover, it deferred to the Scouts' determination that the forced inclusion of the plaintiff as an assistant scoutmaster would significantly impair its ability to advocate this point of view by, at a minimum, sending a message to its membership and to the outside world that it accepted homosexual conduct as a legitimate form of behavior. It also summarily rejected the claim that New Jersey's interest in eliminating discrimination in places of public accommodation justified this intrusion on the group's freedom of expressive association. Although this case did not involve the application of Title VII or, for that matter, any other statute dealing expressly with employment discrimination, the relationship between the Scouts and a scoutmaster bears many of the attributes of an employment relationship. Does the *Dale* Court's expansive recognition of this nonprofit organization's constitutional right to expressive association suggest that the First Amendment could be construed to bar the enforcement of an overtly employment-related statute to some other organization, including a commercial one, which was created to promote some expressive agenda?

5.   Federal employees receive health benefits pursuant to the terms of the Federal Employee Health Benefits Act (FEHBA), 5 U.S.C. §§8901-8914. This statute permits federal employees to elect either individual or family coverage and includes a "spouse of an employee" as a family member. The federal Defense of Marriage Act (DOMA), 1 U.S.C. §7, provides that in determining the meaning of any federal statute, the word marriage "means only a legal union between one man and one woman" and the word spouse "refers only to a person of the opposite sex who is a husband or a wife." Does DOMA, then, operate as a limitation on the right of those same-sex spouses of federal employees who were married in states that recognize same-sex marriages to obtain health benefits under FEHBA? In IN RE LEVENSON, 560 F.3d 1145 (9th Cir. 2009), the court ruled that although the FEHBA provisions defining family members to include spouses must be interpreted, pursuant to DOMA, to include only opposite-sex spouses, interpreting the FEHBA to deny a federal employee's request that his same-sex spouse receive federal benefits violated the Due Process Clause of the Fifth Amendment. Without ruling on whether this classification should be subject to heightened scrutiny, the court concluded that it did not even survive rational basis scrutiny. The court declared that the policy could not be justified as an expression of the government's disapproval of homosexuality, preference for heterosexuality, or desire to discourage gay marriage. It also found no rational relationship between the sex of an employee's spouse and the government's desire to limit its employee health insurance outlays since, the court explained, the government could save far more money using other measures, such as by eliminating coverage for all spouses. *But see* In the Matter of Golinski, 587 F.3d 901 (9th Cir. 2009) (construing FEHBA, notwithstanding DOMA, to permit the coverage of same-sex spouses).

5. "PROTECTIVE" STATE LABOR LEGISLATION

Rosenfeld v. Southern Pacific Co.

United States Court of Appeals, Ninth Circuit, 1971.
444 F.2d 1219.

HAMLEY, Circuit Judge.

Leah Rosenfeld brought this action against Southern Pacific Company pursuant to section 706(f) of Title VII * * *. Plaintiff, an employee of the company, alleged that in filling the position of agent-telegrapher at Thermal, California, in March, 1966, Southern Pacific discriminated against her solely because of her sex, by assigning the position to a junior male employee.

* * *

On the merits, Southern Pacific argues that it is the company's policy to exclude women, generically, from certain positions. The company restricts these job opportunities to men for two basic reasons: (1) the arduous nature of the work-related activity renders women physically unsuited for the jobs; (2) appointing a woman to the position would result in a violation of California labor laws and regulations which limit hours of work for women and restrict the weight they are permitted to lift. Positions such as that of agent-telegrapher at Thermal fall within the ambit of this policy. The company concludes that effectuation of this policy is not proscribed by Title VII * * * due to the exception created by the Act for those situations where sex is a "bona fide occupational qualification."

While the agent-telegrapher position at Thermal is no longer in existence, the work requirements which that position entailed are illustrative of the kind of positions which are denied to female employees under the company's labor policy described above. During the harvesting season, the position may require work in excess of ten hours a day and eighty hours a week.[6] The position requires the heavy physical effort involved in climbing over and around boxcars to adjust their vents, collapse their bunkers and close and seal their doors. In addition, the employee must lift various objects weighing more than twenty-five pounds and, in some instances, more than fifty pounds.

The critical question presented by this argument is whether, consistent with Title VII * * *, the company may apply such a labor policy. * * *

* * *

* * * [T]he company points out that, apart from its intrinsic merit, its policy is compelled by California labor laws. One of the reasons Mrs. Rosenfeld was refused assignment to the Thermal position, and would presumably be refused assignment to like positions, is that she could not perform the tasks of such a position without placing the company in violation of California laws. Not only would the repeated lifting of weights in excess of twenty-five pounds violate the state's Industrial Welfare Order No. 9-63, but for her to lift more than fifty pounds as required by the job would violate section 1251 of the California Labor Code. Likewise, the peak-season days of over ten hours would violate section 1350 of the California Labor Code.

It would appear that these state law limitations upon female labor run contrary to the general objectives of Title VII of the Civil Rights Act of 1964 * * * and are therefore, by virtue of the Supremacy Clause, supplanted by Title VII. However, appellants * * * rely on section 703(e) and argue that since positions such as the Thermal agent-telegrapher required weight-lifting and maximum hours in excess of those permitted under the California statutes, being a man was indeed a bona fide occupational qualification. This argument assumes that Congress, having established by Title VII the policy that individuals must be judged as individuals, and not on the basis of characteristics generally attributed to racial, religious, or sex groups, was willing for this policy to be thwarted by state legislation to the contrary.

* * *

* * * [S]ection 708 of the Act * * * provides that nothing in Title VII shall be deemed to exempt or relieve any person from any liability, duty, penalty, or

---

[6]It was, indeed, this opportunity to earn overtime pay that made this position attractive to plaintiff.

punishment provided by any present or future state law " * * * other than any such law which purports to require or permit the doing of any act which would be an unlawful employment practice under this title." This section was designed to preserve the effectiveness of state antidiscrimination laws.[7]

* * *

Under the principles set forth above, we conclude that Southern Pacific's employment policy is not excusable under * * * the state statutes. * * *

In the district court one of the company's defenses was that of good faith reliance upon the [EEOC] Guidelines then in effect. This defense was relevant to plaintiff's prayer for damages. While the district court did not award damages, it did find that the company did not rely on any written interpretation or opinion of the Commission, and concluded that the company "discriminated" against plaintiff solely because of her sex by refusing to assign her to the Thermal position.

In our opinion the finding on the question of reliance is unnecessary to the disposition of the cause and, in any event, should not have been entered without according Southern Pacific an evidentiary hearing. Moreover, in view of the California statutes referred to above, the conclusion that the company engaged in "discrimination" in refusing to assign plaintiff to the Thermal position carries with it no invidious connotation. Prior to a judicial determination such as evidenced by this opinion, an employer can hardly be faulted for following the explicit provisions of applicable state law.

* * *

Affirmed.

[CHIEF JUDGE CHAMBERS' dissenting opinion is omitted.]

NOTES AND PROBLEMS FOR DISCUSSION

1.   State "protective" labor statutes have been uniformly invalidated under the Supremacy Clause of the U.S. Constitution on the ground that enforcement of the state mandate violates Title VII's ban on sex discrimination. Accordingly, the courts have struck down state laws imposing special requirements on women with respect to required rest periods, Ridinger v. General Motors Corp., 325 F.Supp. 1089 (S.D.Ohio 1971), reversed on other grounds, 474 F.2d 949 (6th Cir.1972); seating arrangements, Manning v. General Motors Corp., 3 FEP Cases 968 (N.D.Ohio 1971), affirmed, 466 F.2d 812 (6th Cir.1972), cert. denied, 410 U.S. 946, 93 S.Ct. 1366, 35 L.Ed.2d 613 (1973); and exclusion from certain occupations, Sail'er Inn, Inc. v. Kirby, 5 Cal.3d 1, 95 Cal.Rptr. 329, 485 P.2d 529 (1971).

2.   In *Rosenfeld*, the court held that an employer should be insulated from back pay liability by its good faith reliance on extent state labor legislation. The principal case is reflective of the prevailing jurisprudence that denies back pay if the employer demonstrates good faith reliance on state protective legislation so as to avoid

---

[7]The legislative history is replete with statements making it clear that Congress was specifically aware that Title VII would undercut many state labor laws.

compelling employers to subject themselves to possible state prosecution in order to comply with Title VII. *See* Williams v. General Foods Corp., 492 F.2d 399 (7th Cir.1974).

(a) Do you agree that it is preferable to impose the cost of discrimination on innocent employees rather than on the innocent employer? Does this ruling create any disincentive on employees to challenge other potentially discriminatory state laws?

(b) Should a different result obtain if a similar or identical statute from another state had been judicially invalidated before the employer's conduct occurred? *See* Alaniz v. California Processors, Inc., 785 F.2d 1412 (9th Cir.1986) (employer liable for back pay from date it became aware of suspension of agency order restricting women from heavy lifting).

3. Once a court determines that a state protective labor statute conflicts with Title VII, what action should it take with respect to that enactment? Ordinarily, a court can achieve sexual parity in one of two alternative ways. It can invalidate the law entirely or it can take the benefit or restriction originally applicable only to women and extend it to all employees. The latter option, however, is not realistically available in the context of exclusionary statutes — i.e., statutes that exclude women from certain occupations, from lifting objects over a specified weight, or from working more than a certain number of hours or days. In HAYS v. POTLATCH FORESTS, INC., 465 F.2d 1081 (8th Cir.1972), the court held that any conflict between Title VII and an Arkansas statute requiring employers to pay only women employees premium pay for time worked in excess of eight hours per day could be avoided by requiring employers to pay premium compensation to all employees after eight hours of daily work. The EEOC Guidelines go beyond *Hays* by requiring that the "benefits" of all sex-oriented State protective statutes be extended to both sexes. However, for all but minimum wage and premium pay statutes, the Guidelines recognize a business necessity defense to the extension requirement. See 29 C.F.R. §1604.2(b)(3), (4) (1972). Do you agree with this result? It has been suggested that extension of benefits (a) results in governmental imposition of terms and conditions of employment that should be left to private negotiation absent a clear declaration of legislative intent to intervene in this area, see Burns v. Rohr Corp., 346 F.Supp. 994 (S.D.Cal.1972) (refusing to order extension of California regulation requiring employers to give ten minute rest breaks every four hours to female employees), and (b) generates federalism problems when a federal court extends the meaning of state legislation, see Homemakers, Inc. v. Division of Industrial Welfare, 509 F.2d 20 (9th Cir.1974), cert. denied, 423 U.S. 1063, 96 S.Ct. 803, 46 L.Ed.2d 655 (1976) (refusing to extend California statute requiring payment of premium pay to covered women employees).

CHAPTER 4

Procedural Requirements for Private Sector Employees

Section 705 of Title VII created the Equal Employment Opportunity Commission as the agency responsible for enforcement of the Act. Congress did not, however, give the EEOC the kind of cease and desist powers enjoyed by some government agencies such as the National Labor Relations Board. Under §706, the EEOC must accept and investigate complaints of discrimination filed by individuals or by EEOC Commissioners. If the commission finds "reasonable cause to believe the charge is true," it must "endeavor to eliminate any such alleged unlawful employment practice by informal methods of conference, conciliation and persuasion." Although Title VII vested the EEOC with substantial discretion over how to fulfill this statutory obligation to conciliate, the Supreme Court has ruled that the courts have the power to review, to a limited degree, whether or not the Commission has complied with this duty. In MACH MINING, LLC v. E.E.O.C.,[a] a unanimous Supreme Court ruled that the duty to conciliate includes, at a minimum, the obligation to (1) communicate the nature of the plaintiff's claim to the defendant; and (2) engage the employer in either written or oral discussion in order to give the defendant an opportunity to remedy the allegedly discriminatory practice through voluntary compliance. But in reviewing whether or not the Commission has met that standard, courts are to impose a limited scope of review. The role of the courts is limited to verifying the Commission's claim that it actually tried to conciliate. To that end, a sworn affidavit from the agency stating that it performed these tasks will usually suffice. But if the employer provides credible evidence that the agency did not provide the requisite information about the charge or did not attempt to engage in a discussion about conciliating the claim, the court must conduct sufficient factfinding to resolve that factual question. Beyond that, however, the choice of the methods by which it chooses to conciliate, or the extent of that effort, is left solely to the discretion of the agency.

The EEOC also has the authority to file suit in cases where cause has been found and conciliation has been unsuccessful. Realizing that the EEOC would not be able to resolve all complaints filed with it under the act, Congress also provided in §§706(e) and (f) for a private right of action by persons claiming unlawful discrimination.

Private actions filed under Title VII, the Age Discrimination in Employment Act (ADEA), and the Americans With Disabilities Act (ADA) constitute a significant

---

[a]135 S.Ct. 1645, 191 L.Ed.2d 607 (2015).

portion of the work of the federal courts. In the decade before 1990 new filings of employment discrimination cases ranged from 8,000 to 9,000 cases annually. The passage of the ADA in 1990 and of the Civil Rights Act of 1991, which provided for compensatory and punitive damages and jury trials in Title VII cases alleging intentional discrimination, created new incentives for private claims and resulted in an three-fold increase in filings during the 1990s. By 1997 the annual filings of employment discrimination cases in the federal district courts exceeded 24,000. As of 1999 new filings had leveled off at around 22,000 new cases annually. Employment discrimination cases now account for just under 10% of all civil filings in federal courts. See Bureau of Justice Statistics, CIVIL RIGHTS COMPLAINTS IN U.S. DISTRICT COURTS, 1990-98 (Jan. 2000).

Title VII, the ADEA, and the ADA require, however, that persons filing their own suits under these statutes first file timely charges of discrimination with the EEOC and observe other technical requirements as prerequisites to litigation. The procedural requirements of Title VII for private litigants and the EEOC are discussed in this chapter.

SECTION A. SUITS BY INDIVIDUALS

1. THE "TIMELINESS" REQUIREMENTS OF TITLE VII

Allen v. Avon Products, Inc.

United States District Court for the Southern District of New York, 1988.
55 FEP Cases 1662.

SHIRLEY WOHL KRAM, District Judge.

The above-captioned action is presently before this Court upon the motion of defendant Avon for summary judgment with respect to plaintiff Lorraine Allen's federal employment discrimination claim and pendent state law slander claim, pursuant to Rule 56 of the Federal Rules of Civil Procedure. Avon moves to dismiss the pendent claim, pursuant to Rules 12(b)(1) and (6) of the Federal Rules of Civil Procedure. In addition, Avon moves to dismiss the action in its entirety, pursuant to 28 U.S.C. §1915(d). For the reasons stated below, Avon's motion to dismiss and for summary judgment with respect to the federal claim is denied. With respect to the pendent claim, Avon's motion to dismiss is granted and the Court will thus not reach Avon's motion for summary judgment.

UNDISPUTED FACTS

Avon employed Allen as an art director in its sales promotion department from July, 1968, until her discharge on or about January 28, 1972. On August 29, 1972, Allen filed a sex discrimination charge ("first charge") against Avon with the Equal Employment Opportunity Commission. The EEOC forwarded the first charge to the New York State Division of Human Rights. The NYSDHR acknowledged receipt of

Allen's papers from the EEOC on August 31, 1972. On February 14, 1973, Allen filed a second sex discrimination charge ("second charge") against Avon with the EEOC.

On or about June 1, 1974, the EEOC filed an action against Avon in this Court, alleging gender and racial discrimination. The EEOC forwarded Allen's charges to its litigation center in the interest of including them in negotiations between the EEOC and Avon. Although the EEOC litigation was settled on June 21, 1977, the parties were unable to enter into a consent decree covering the issues raised in Allen's charges. Allen rejected numerous offers from the EEOC for a statutory notice of a right to sue Avon in federal court, and requested that the EEOC continue conciliation efforts. On July 1, 1981, over Allen's objection, the EEOC issued Allen a right to sue notice and dismissed her charges, finding that there was no reasonable cause to believe that discrimination had occurred.

On September 29, 1981, Allen, proceeding pro se, submitted a complaint and an application for leave to proceed forma pauperis * * *. In a letter dated September 30, 1981, the pro se clerk requested that Allen submit a supplemental affidavit clarifying her pauperis application. On or about October 5, 1981, Allen complied with this request. On November 9, 1981, this Court granted leave to proceed in forma pauperis and her complaint was docketed. On December 1981, Allen, proceeding pro se, filed an amended complaint. On March 11, 1983, she filed an order to show cause seeking leave to amend the amended complaint. Her application was granted and on April 8, 1983, a second amended complaint was filed. Allen alleges that Avon engaged in unlawful employment practices in violation of §706 and slander in violation of state tort law. Allen subsequently retained an attorney who filed a notice of appearance in this case on December 3, 1987.

DISCUSSION

Avon moves for summary judgment with respect to the federal employment discrimination claim on the grounds that: Allen failed to file a timely charge with the NYSDHR as required under 42 U.S.C. §706(c); Allen failed to commence this action within the 90-day right to sue period as required under 42 U.S.C. §706(f); and laches. Avon moves to dismiss the complaint on the ground that Allen submitted a false affidavit of poverty, in violation of 28 U.S.C. §1915(d). * * *

Filing of Charge with NYSDHR

Avon alleges that Allen failed to file a timely charge with the NYSDHR. Section 706(e) requires that all claims for employment discrimination be filed with the EEOC within 180 days from the date the alleged unlawful employment discrimination occurred. An exception to this requirement allows local agencies in states which have them, known as deferral states, the opportunity to review discrimination claims and act on them before the EEOC proceeds. In such cases the statute requires that the claimant file with the EEOC within a total of 300 days, or within 30 days after receiving notice that the state agency has terminated proceedings, whichever is earlier.

A separate section provides that a claimant may not file a complaint with the EEOC in deferral states until 60 days after the proceedings have been commenced by the appropriate state agency unless that state has terminated its proceedings in less than the allotted 60 days. §706(c). If a claim is filed first with the EEOC, the EEOC will defer it to the state agency for action for a period of 60 days. §706(d).

The Supreme Court has interpreted these rules to require that a claimant in deferral states has 240 days within which to file with the state agency in order to preserve federal jurisdiction. Mohasco Corporation v. Silver, 447 U.S. 807, 815, n. 16, 100 S.Ct. 2486, 2491, n. 16, 65 L.Ed.2d 532 (1980). A complaint cannot be filed with the EEOC until after the state agency has had the statutorily prescribed 60-day deferral period. When a charge is filed with the EEOC prior to exhaustion of state remedies, state proceedings may be initiated by the EEOC acting on behalf of the complainant rather than by the complainant herself. Love v. Pullman Co., 404 U.S. 522, 525, 92 S.Ct. 616, 618, 30 L.Ed.2d 679 (1972). "Upon termination of the state proceedings or expiration of the 60-day deferral period, whichever comes first, the EEOC automatically assumes concurrent jurisdiction of the complaint." New York Gaslight Club, Inc. v. Carey, 447 U.S. 54, 64, 100 S.Ct. 2024, 2031, 64 L.Ed.2d 723 (1980), (citing Love v. Pullman Co., *supra*, 404 U.S. at 526, 92 S.Ct. at 618).

In the instant case, Allen was discharged from her employment on or about January 28, 1972. She filed her first charge with the EEOC on August 29, 1972, 215 days later. The EEOC, acting on behalf of Allen, forwarded this charge to the NYSDHR. Love v. Pullman Co. In a letter dated August 31, 1972, the NYSDHR verified having received Allen's papers from the EEOC. Accordingly, the Court finds that proceedings were initiated with the NYSDHR within the requisite 240 day period. Mohasco v. Silver.

Filing of the Case at Bar

Avon alleges that Allen failed to commence this action within the 90-day right to sue period as required under §706(f). Section 706(f)(1) provides in relevant part that:

> If a charge filed with the [EEOC] * * * is dismissed by the [EEOC] or if within one hundred and eighty days from the filing of such charge * * * [the EEOC], has not filed a civil action * * *, or the [EEOC] has not entered into a conciliation agreement to which the person aggrieved is a party, the [EEOC] * * * shall so notify the person aggrieved and within ninety days after * * * [receipt] of such notice a civil action may be brought against respondent named in the charge * * *.

In the case at bar, the EEOC issued Allen her Notice of Right to Sue on July 1, 1981. On September 29, 1981, Allen proceeding pro se submitted her original complaint and an application for leave to proceed in forma pauperis to the Pro Se Office of this Court. In a letter dated September 30, 1981, the pro se clerk requested that Allen submit a supplemental affidavit clarifying her in forma pauperis application. On or about October 5, 1981, Allen complied with this request. On November 9, 1981, this Court granted leave to proceed in forma pauperis and docketed her complaint. Although Allen's original complaint and the Order granting leave to proceed in forma pauperis were not docketed with the Clerk of the Court until November 9, 1981, the delay between Allen's application and that date resulted from delays brought about by requests from the Court, and not from any lack of diligence by the plaintiff. Therefore, this Court holds that Allen's filing of the suit occurred when she submitted her complaint to the pro se Office on September 30, 1981 and that her action was commenced within the 90-day period pursuant to §706(f)(1).

Laches

Citing the fact that more than nine years passed between the time Allen filed her initial charge of discrimination with the EEOC and the time she finally filed suit in this

Court, Avon moves for summary judgment based on laches. In order for an action to be barred under the equitable theory of laches, defendant must establish (1) that the plaintiff's delay in bringing the lawsuit was unreasonable and inexcusable, and (2) that this delay resulted in material prejudice to the defendant's case.

The facts * * * indicate that proceedings were initiated with the appropriate administrative agencies within the requisite time period. As this Court stated in Cosgrove v. Sears Roebuck and Co., No. 81 Civ. 3482(CSH) (S.D.N.Y. May 26, 1982) (available October 11, 1987, on LEXIS, Genfed library, Dist file), "a disgruntled employee should be commended rather than criticized for attempting to stay out of court by allowing the administrative agency charged with enforcement of Title VII to attempt to settle amicably her suit * * *." Allen brought suit within the time allotted after receiving a Notice of Right to Sue from the EEOC. She was not required to litigate prior to the termination of the EEOC's investigation and attempts at conciliation. The Court finds that Allen's delay in filing this action was neither unreasonable nor inexcusable, and thus will not reach the issue of prejudice to Avon. Accordingly, Avon's motion for summary judgment with respect to the federal claim is denied.

NOTES AND PROBLEMS FOR DISCUSSION

1 In MOHASCO CORP. v. SILVER, 447 U.S. 807, 100 S.Ct. 2486, 65 L.Ed.2d 532 (1980), the Supreme Court stated that the longer filing time in a deferral state was intended only to prevent forfeiture of the charging party's federal rights while the state agency processed the charge. The Court noted that the statutory plan was not designed to give the worker in a deferral State the option of choosing between his state remedy and his federal remedy, nor to allow additional time in which to obtain state relief.

State fair employment laws typically provide for limitation periods of less than 300 days for filing charges with the appropriate state agencies. Should a timely filing of one's state law charge with the state agency be prerequisite to eligibility for the 300-day period for filing with the EEOC? In EEOC v. COMMERCIAL OFFICE PRODUCTS CO., 486 U.S. 107, 108 S.Ct. 1666, 100 L.Ed.2d 96 (1988), the Supreme Court held that the 300-day filing period in deferral states should apply irrespective of whether the claimant's state law charge was filed within the state limitations period. A majority of the Court reasoned that a contrary result would confuse lay persons attempting to file charges and would require the EEOC to undertake ad hoc determinations of whether state limitation periods were jurisdictional and of whether the periods were equitably tolled under state law; determinations that "the EEOC has neither the time nor the expertise to make . . . under the varying laws of the many deferral States." 486 U.S. at 122, 108 S.Ct. at 1675. When a timely charge is filed with a state agency there is no requirement that administrative remedies provided by state law be exhausted before filing with the EEOC. Title VII merely requires that the state remedy be invoked, not exhausted. *See* Zugay v. Progressive Care SC, 180 F.3d 901, 903 (7th Cir. 1999).

2. As was the case in *Allen*, charging parties in deferral states frequently file their charges with the EEOC without proceeding initially with a state law claim before the state agency. Although the EEOC cannot begin its investigation of such a complaint, it will not dismiss that claim as premature. As the court explained in *Allen,* the

Supreme Court in LOVE v. PULLMAN, 404 U.S. 522, 92 S.Ct. 616, 30 L.Ed.2d 679 (1972) approved the EEOC's "deferral" procedure, now incorporated in 29 C.F.R. §1601.13. Where a plaintiff begins the process by filing a charge with the EEOC, the Commission refers that charge to the appropriate state or local agency on behalf of the grievant and defers its own action until the period of reference to the agency expires.

This "deferral" procedure, however, has been superceded in many states by "work sharing" agreements under which each agency designates the other as its agent for purpose of receiving charges. A charge that is received by one agency (federal or state) is deemed received by the other at that moment for purposes of determining the timeliness of the charge. Moreover, under most of these work sharing agreements, the state agency can waive completely the right to process a charge referred to it by the EEOC, thus allowing the federal agency to process the charge without waiting the 60 days prescribed by §706(c). The validity of these agreements was upheld by the Supreme Court in *Commercial Office Products*. There, the claimant filed her charge of sex discrimination with the EEOC on the 289th day after discharge and the EEOC referred the charge to the state agency. The state agency returned the charge to the EEOC, indicating that it was waiving its right to process the charge, and the EEOC began the investigation that resulted in the suit. The Court held that §706(c)'s requirement that the state agency "terminate" its proceedings included an agency's decision not to proceed for some interval of time even if the agency retained authority to activate its investigatory mechanisms in the future. The Court reasoned that the two goals underlying the deferral provisions of the statute — deference to the states and efficient processing of claims — supported its conclusion that waiver by the state agency of the 60 day deferral period was sufficient to "terminate" the state agency's proceeding.

Some worksharing agreements provide that the state agency's waiver of the right to process a charge is self executing, so that the filing of a charge with the EEOC simultaneously initiates and terminates state proceedings. Relying on *Commercial Office Products,* the courts generally have upheld such agreements. *See, e.g.*, Puryear v. County of Roanoke, 214 F.3d 514 (4th Cir. 2000). Are self-executing worksharing agreements consistent with the Court's statement in *Mohasco v. Silver* that the "statutory plan was not designed to give the worker in a deferral state the option of choosing between his state and federal remedy"? *See* Hong v. Children's Mem. Hosp., 936 F.2d 967, 970 (7th Cir. 1991) (characterizing a work sharing agreement as an "administrative shell game"). But not every state deferral agency maintains a work sharing agreement with the EEOC. In such jurisdictions, timely filing with the state agency will not preserve the federal claim absent a timely filing with the EEOC, subject to the tolling exceptions discussed in the following Note.

3. (a) In ZIPES v. TRANS WORLD AIRLINES, INC., 455 U.S. 385, 102 S.Ct. 1127, 71 L.Ed.2d 234 (1982), the Supreme Court held that filing a timely charge of discrimination with the EEOC is not a jurisdictional prerequisite to suit in federal court, but a requirement that, like a statute of limitations, is subject to waiver, estoppel, and equitable tolling. The lower courts have recognized a number of equitable considerations that will interrupt or delay the period for filing the charge with EEOC. They include:

Filing with the Wrong Agency: A timely filing of a complaint of discrimination with the wrong state or federal agency will generally toll the limitations period. *See, e.g.*, Husch v. Szabo Food Serv. Co., 851 F.2d 999 (7th Cir. 1988) (mistakenly filing charge in state where employer was headquartered rather than in state where discrimination occurred, tolled filing period); Morgan v. Washington Mfg. Co., 660 F.2d 710 (6th Cir. 1981) (letter to White House forwarded to Department of Labor which forwarded it to EEOC after 180 day period had run should toll the limitations period because the Labor Department has jurisdiction in some fields of employment discrimination and the instant complaint was forwarded to the EEOC shortly after the limitations period has expired). *But see* Smith v. General Scanning, Inc., 832 F.2d 96 (7th Cir. 1987) (filing charge in state with no connection to alleged discrimination will not toll running of filing period).

Mistaken or Misleading Information From Agency: Where the EEOC or a state agency misleads the charging party regarding the applicable time limits, equitable considerations support tolling of the filing period. In SCHLUETER v. ANHEUSER-BUSCH, INC., 132 F.3d 455 (8th Cir. 1998), EEOC employees within the filing period instructed the plaintiff to fill out an "intake form" which they mistakenly believed would either qualify as a charge or would toll the filing period so that a verified charge would relate back to its filing. The plaintiff filed her formal charge after the filing period expired, and the district court granted summary judgment. The Eighth Circuit reversed on the ground that the plaintiff should not be burdened by the agency's mistake.

Misconduct of Defendant: Misrepresentation, concealment, intimidation, or other actions by the employer which it knew or reasonably should have known would cause a delay in filing the EEOC charge will toll the 180-day period. *See, e.g.*, Clark v. Resistoflex Co., 854 F.2d 762 (5th Cir. 1988) (an employer's warning that severance benefits could end if the terminated employee took any action prejudicial to the employer may estop the employer from raising untimeliness of charge as defense; reasonable trier of fact could conclude that the employer worded severance agreement so as to deter the employee from asserting his rights under ADEA). *But see* Speer v. Rand McNally & Co., 123 F.3d 658 (7th Cir. 1997) (an employer's statement to an employee who complained of sexual harassment that the employer would investigate her charge internally and that if she filed charge with the EEOC "it might take two or three years and nothing would be resolved" did not toll the limitations period where there was no evidence that the employer intended to deceive or prevent the employee from pursuing her claim).

Should an employer's threat to retaliate against an employee for going outside the company's management with a complaint of discrimination constitute grounds for equitable tolling of the time for filing a charge? In BECKEL v. WAL-MART ASSOCIATES, INC., 301 F.3d 621 (7th Cir. 2002) the plaintiff filed a charge alleging sexual harassment more than 300 days after the claim accrued, but argued that her supervisor's threat at the time of the harassment to retaliate against her if she took legal action should estop the company from pleading that her EEOC charge was untimely. The Seventh Circuit affirmed dismissal of the plaintiff's suit on the ground that there was insufficient evidence that such a threat had actually been made. But the court went further to opine that even if the threat had been made, that conduct would not justify tolling the filing period.

Rather than deterring a reasonable person from suing, it would increase her incentive to sue by giving her a second claim, in this case a claim for retaliation on top of her original claim of sexual harassment. To allow the use of retaliation as a basis for extending the statute of limitations would not only distort the doctrine of equitable estoppel but circumvent the limitations that Title VII imposes on suits for retaliation, including the statute of limitations, which the plaintiff's argument implies never runs on such a suit.

301 F.3d at 624. Do you agree? Might not an employee who did not appreciate the legal significance of such a retaliatory threat and wished to retain her job be dissuaded from filing an EEOC charge? If so, is the result in this case consistent with the remedial purposes of Title VII?

What other circumstances might reasonably operate to toll the filing period? What about a charging party's mental illness? No court has held that mental illness automatically justifies tolling, but some courts have recognized that incapacity may do so in specific cases. *Compare* Miller v. Runyon, 77 F.3d 189, 191 (7th Cir.), cert. denied, 519 U.S. 937, 117 S.Ct. 316, 136 L.Ed.2d 231 (1996) (applying "traditional rule that mental illness tolls a statute of limitations only if the illness in fact prevents the sufferer from understanding his legal rights and acting upon them.") *with* Hood v. Sears Roebuck, 168 F.3d 231, 233 (5th Cir. 1999) (fact that the plaintiff hired an attorney during the filing period "indicates that her mental state did not prevent her from pursuing her legal rights under Title VII during filing period"). How about the mental incapacity of the charging party's attorney? *See* Cantrell v. Knoxville Cmty. Dev. Corp., 60 F.3d 1177 (6th Cir. 1995) (an attorney's incapacity, as well as an attorney's abandonment of the charging party, could result in tolling but only if the employee presents evidence that he was entitled to such relief).

(b) Suppose that the Title VII plaintiff filed a timely EEOC charge alleging race and national origin discrimination and subsequently timely filed a civil action after receiving a notice of right to sue. But suppose that this complaint also included a claim of religious discriminaton. Assume further that the trial judge granted summary judgment to the defense on all claims but that the appellate court reversed the grant of summary judgment as to the claim of religious discrimination, remanding that claim for trial. Finally, assume that thereafter, the defense filed a motion to dismiss the religious discrimination claim on the ground that it had not been included in the EEOC charge and, accordingly, that the plaintiff had failed to properly invoke her administrative remedies prior to suit. How should the court rule on that motion? This raises the question of whether this type of filing error is a jurisdictional or non-jurisdictional defect. Recall that in *Arbaugh v. Y & H* (see *supra,* at Note 1(c) following EEOC v. Rinella & Rinella in Chapter 1, Section A), the Court previously ruled that the fifteen employee requirement was *not* jurisdictional, and in *Zipes, supra,* that the limitations period for filing an EEOC charge similarly was a non-jurisdictional defect. The Court unanimously reached the same conclusion with respect to the filing requirements for EEOC claims governing relationship between the content of the EEOC charge and suit (see *infra,* at Chapter 4, Section A(4)) in FORT BEND COUNTY v. DAVIS, 587 U.S. ___, 139 S.Ct. 1843 (2019). There, based on the above facts, the Court unanimously held that while proper charge-filing was "mandatory" – in the sense that the plaintiff's failure to follow this requirement could be the basis of a *timely* challenge – it was a waiveable, non-jurisdictional prerequisite, i.e., this defect could not be asserted at any time in the proceedings.

4.   Section 706(b) states that charges of discrimination "shall be in writing under oath or affirmation and shall contain such information and be in such form as the Commission requires." Section 706(e) provides that "a charge . . . shall be filed within 180 [or in some cases, 300] days after the alleged unlawful employment practice occurred." Nowhere in the statute, however, is "charge" defined. Yet although the EEOC supplies formal charge forms which may be filled out at an agency office, it is, nevertheless, common for complainants to send unverified letters alleging discrimination to the agency. And when agency employees are not available for interviews, it is not unusual for claimants to fill out unverified "intake questionnaires" at EEOC offices. In FEDERAL EXPRESS CORP. v. HOLOWECKI, 552 U.S. 389, 128 S.Ct. 1147, 170 L.Ed.2d 10 (2008), the Supreme Court sought to resolve a circuit conflict concerning the meaning of the word "charge" in the context of an ADEA suit that had been preceded by the plaintiff's filing only an intake questionnaire accompanied by a signed affidavit describing the alleged discriminatory practices in greater detail. The Court, in a 7-2 opinion, concluded that the EEOC's guidelines, as well as the agency's interpretations of those guidelines and of the relevant provisions of the ADEA were reasonable and entitled to deference. Accordingly, the Court adopted the EEOC's position that a filing is deemed a charge where — in addition to an allegation of age discrimination and the name of the charged party — "the document reasonably can be construed to request agency action and appropriate relief on the employee's part." Interestingly, the majority opened its opinion with a "cautionary preface" that workers and their counsel "must be careful not to apply rules applicable under one [antidiscrimination] statute to a different statute without careful and critical examination * * * even if the EEOC forms and the same definition of charge apply in more than one type of discrimination case." Consequently, the applicability of this definition of "charge" in the Title VII context remains unresolved.

In HOLENDER v. MUTUAL INDUSTRIES NORTH INC., 527 F.3d 352 (3d Cir. 2008), the Third Circuit extended the definition of "charge" that had been set forth in *Holowecki* to an age discrimination case where the plaintiff was represented by counsel at the time that the document in question was filed with the EEOC. Here, the plaintiff had filed EEOC Form 5, which is entitled "Charge of Discrimination" in which he checked the box indicating "age" discrimination, along with an affidavit setting forth the particulars of the alleged discrimination. But on Form 5 the plaintiff did not check the box next to the statement that "I want this charge filed with both the EEOC and the State or local Agency...." Two months after receiving these documents, the EEOC sent a letter to the plaintiff's counsel indicating that before the agency would docket the matter as a "charge" and begin its investigatory process, it needed additional information and requested the attorney to return a completed questionnaire within 33 days. The plaintiff did not do so but, instead, filed suit. The suit was filed 60 days after the filing of the original document with the EEOC and so the question presented in the defense motion to dismiss was whether or not this constituted a "charge". Applying the objective standard (whether an objective observer would construe the filing to request the agency to activate its machinery) set forth in *Holowecki*, the Third Circuit concluded that these documents constituted a "charge". After all, Form 5 was denominated "Charge of Discrimination" and the attached affidavit referred to the "instant charge filed on behalf of all persons similarly situated." This was enough for the court to conclude that the document made it clear to the EEOC that the plaintiff wished to begin the process of seeking ADEA relief. It rejected the defendant's contention that a counseled filing should meet a higher standard than set forth in *Holowecki* since that case involved a *pro se* filing. The court acknowledged that while the *Holowecki* Court adopted a flexible standard "at least in part" to protect alleged victims of age discrimination who proceed *pro se*, there was nothing in the opinion to indicate that an entirely different analysis applied to counseled submissions to the EEOC. "There is no need to require that counseled submissions to the EEOC," the court explained, "contain some magic combination of words explicitly seeking agency action. A charge, submitted by counsel or not, may imply such a request."

An EEOC regulation provides that a charge can be subsequently amended or that defects, "including failure to verify the charge," can be cured by subsequent filings and that such amendments "relate back to the date the charge was first received." 29 C.F.R. §1601.12(b). The circuits were split on the validity of this "relating back" regulation until the Supreme Court stepped in. In EDELMAN v. LYNCHBURG COLLEGE, 535 U.S. 928, 122 S.Ct. 1145, 152 L.Ed.2d 188 (2002), the plaintiff, who had been denied tenure, faxed an unverified letter alleging sex discrimination to an EEOC field office. The fax was received by the agency 161 days after the denial of tenure. But a verified charge was not filed until 313 days after the denial. The district court dismissed the plaintiff's action on the ground that the unverified letter was not a "charge" within the meaning of Title VII and that there was no timely filing to which the verification could relate back. The Fourth Circuit affirmed but on the ground that the relation back regulation was invalid. The Supreme Court reversed the appellate court. In its view, the EEOC regulation constituted an "unassailable" interpretation of §706.

> Construing §706 to permit the relation back of an oath omitted from an original filing ensures that the lay complainant, who may not know enough to verify on filing, will not risk forfeiting his right inadvertently. At the same time, the Commission looks out for the employer's interest by refusing to call for any response to an otherwise sufficient complaint until the verification has been supplied.

535 U.S. at 115. However, because the EEOC had failed to give the defendant college notice of the plaintiff's original letter within 10 days of its receipt as required by the statute, the Court remanded the case for determination of whether the letter was a "charge" (to which the subsequently verified form could relate back) because neither the plaintiff nor the agency treated it as such. On remand, the Fourth Circuot reasoned that since the problem was not a deficiency in the charge but a failure of the EEOC to fulfill its statutory responsibility, the plaintiff's original letter did constitute a "charge" to which the subsequently verified form could relate back. 300 F.3d 400 (4th Cir. 2002). *But see* Zerilli-Edelglass v. New York City Transit Auth., 333 F.3d 74 (2d Cir. 2003) (an unsworn letter of inquiry filed with the EEOC within the limitations period did not constitute a "charge" because it was not treated by the claimant as one and was not incorporated by reference into the verified charge filed outside of the limitations period).

5. The period for filing the EEOC charge is not tolled by the pursuit of a remedy, separate and apart from Title VII, such as a grievance procedure contained in a collective bargaining agreement. Since contractual rights are totally separate from and independent of the employee's rights under Title VII, the Court held in INTERNATIONAL UNION OF ELECTRICAL, RADIO AND MACHINE WORKERS, LOCAL 790 v. ROBBINS & MYERS, INC., 429 U.S. 229, 97 S.Ct. 441, 50 L.Ed.2d 427 (1976) that pursuit of relief through a grievance procedure does not interrupt the period for filing an EEOC charge. The Court rejected arguments that equitable tolling principles should be applied because the employee was not seeking to assert his statutory (Title VII) claim in the grievance proceeding. Presumably, the Court felt the employee could not be misled under these circumstances as to the legal effect of filing the grievance. The filing of an EEOC charge does not ordinarily toll the running of any statute of limitations applicable to a claim filed under another federal or state law.

6. Just as equitable estoppel may extend a filing period, so the doctrine of laches may be used to contract it. *See* Teamsters & Employers Welfare Trust v. Gorman Bros. Ready Mix, 283 F.3d 877 (7th Cir. 2002). Laches cuts off the right to sue when the plaintiff unreasonably has delayed filing suit and the defendant is harmed by that delay. Recall that in *Allen*, the trial court concluded that the plaintiff's decision to wait nine years for the EEOC to conclude its administrative process prior to instituting suit was neither "unreasonable nor inexcusable." But sitting back while the EEOC languishes has not always been a successful strategy. In CLEVELAND NEWSPAPER GUILD, LOCAL 1 v. PLAIN DEALER PUBLISHING CO., 839 F.2d 1147 (6th Cir.) (*en banc*), cert. denied, 488 U.S. 899, 109 S.Ct. 245, 102 L.Ed.2d 234 (1988), a union had filed a charge in 1972 that the newspaper discriminated against women in a variety of terms and conditions of employment. Although the employer was informed of the filing of the charge in a timely manner, it did not receive a copy of the charge for four years, at which point the EEOC began its investigation. Thereafter, the employer refused to cooperate in the agency's investigation on the ground that its ability to respond to the charges had been impaired by this lengthy delay. Nothing further happened until 1979, when the union wrote the EEOC concerning the status of the charge. In 1980, the EEOC made a reasonable cause determination and commenced conciliation efforts. These efforts proved to be fruitless and it issued a right-to-sue letter in 1982, whereupon the union filed suit. The trial court granted the defense motion for summary judgment on the ground that the union had not sufficiently explained its ten year delay in filing suit and that the employer had been prejudiced by virtue of the resultant unavailability of some witnesses, the erosion of memory of others, and the destruction of documents. The Sixth Circuit agreed. Rejecting the union's claim that it was entitled to wait out the EEOC process and that, even if laches could be invoked, it had not inexcusably delayed the proceedings, the court declared that the mere fact that the EEOC contributed to the delay did not immunize the plaintiff from application of the doctrine of laches if its own delay or inaction prejudiced the defendant. Plaintiffs cannot, the court announced, always wait indefinitely for the termination of the EEOC's proceedings. Since the union had "sophisticated knowledge and responsibility in equal employment matters," it could not reasonably account for its continued inaction during the extended period that the charge was pending. For example, the union knew that it could have requested a right to sue letter at any time during the ensuing decade. Nor did the union justify its limited contact with the EEOC during the entire period. Consequently, the court upheld the trial judge's invocation of laches. *See also* Garrett v. General Motors

Corp., 844 F.2d 559 (8th Cir.), cert. denied, 488 U.S. 908, 109 S.Ct. 259, 102 L.Ed.2d 248 (1988) (passage of 15 years between filing of EEOC charge and institution of suit constituted inexcusable delay for purpose of laches defense where plaintiff's contacts with EEOC were minimal until he learned of successful litigation against company by other employees).

Baldwin County Welcome Center v. Brown

Supreme Court of the United States, 1984.
466 U.S. 147, 104 S.Ct. 1723, 80 L.Ed.2d 196.

PER CURIAM

On November 6, 1979, respondent Celinda Brown filed a complaint with the Equal Employment Opportunity Commission alleging discriminatory treatment by her former employer, petitioner Baldwin County Welcome Center. A notice of right to sue was issued to her on January 27, 1981. It stated that if Brown chose to commence a civil action "such suit must be filed in the appropriate United States District Court within ninety days of [her] receipt of this Notice."[1] Later, Brown mailed the notice to the United States District Court, where it was received on March 17, 1981.[2] In addition, she requested appointment of counsel.

On April 15, 1981, a United States Magistrate entered an order requiring that Brown make application for court-appointed counsel using the District Court's motion form and supporting questionnaire. The Magistrate's order to Brown reminded her of the necessity of filing a complaint within 90 days of the issuance of the right-to-sue letter. The questionnaire was not returned until May 6, 1981, the 96th day after receipt of the letter. The next day, the Magistrate denied Brown's motion for appointment of counsel because she had not timely complied with his orders, but he referred to the District Judge the question whether the filing of the right-to-sue letter with the court constituted commencement of an action within the meaning of Rule 3 of the Federal Rules of Civil Procedure. On June 9, 1981, the 130th day after receipt of the right-to-sue letter, Brown filed an "amended complaint," which was served on June 18.

On December 24, 1981, the District Court held that Brown had forfeited her right to pursue her claim under Title VII because of her failure to file a complaint meeting the requirements of Rule 8 of the Federal Rules of Civil Procedure within 90 days of her receipt of the right-to-sue letter. It noted that the right-to-sue letter did not qualify as a complaint under Rule 8 because there was no statement in the letter of the factual basis for the claim of discrimination, which is required by the Rule.

The Court of Appeals for the Eleventh Circuit reversed, holding that the filing of a right-to-sue letter "tolls" the time period provided by Title VII. Although conceding that its interpretation was "generous," the court stated that "[t]he remedial nature of the

---

[1] The presumed date of receipt of the notice was January 30, 1981. Fed. Rule Civ. Proc. 6(e).
[2] Brown mailed the letter to the United States District Court for the Middle District of Alabama. The case was transferred to the Southern District of Alabama, however, because the events giving rise to the charge had occurred there.

statute requires such an interpretation." The court then stated that the filing of the right-to-sue letter "satisfied the ninety day statutory limitation."

The Welcome Center petitioned for a writ of certiorari from this Court. We grant the petition and reverse the judgment of the Court of Appeals.

The section of Title VII at issue here states that within 90 days after the issuance of a right-to-sue letter "a civil action may be brought against the respondent named in the charge." §706(f)(1). Rule 3 of the Federal Rules of Civil Procedure states that "[a] civil action is commenced by filing a complaint with the court." A complaint must contain, inter alia, "a short and plain statement of the claim showing that the pleader is entitled to relief." Fed. Rule Civ. Proc. 8(a)(2). The District Court held that the right-to-sue letter did not satisfy that standard. The Court of Appeals did not expressly disagree, but nevertheless stated that the 90-day statutory period for invoking the court's jurisdiction was satisfied, apparently concluding that the policies behind Title VII mandate a different definition of when an action is "commenced."[3] However, it identified no basis in the statute or its legislative history, cited no decision of this Court, and suggested no persuasive justification for its view that the Federal Rules of Civil Procedure were to have a different meaning in, or were not to apply to, Title VII litigation. Because we also can find no satisfactory basis for giving Title VII actions a special status under the Rules of Civil Procedure, we must disagree with the conclusion of the Court of Appeals.[4]

With respect to its apparent alternative holding that the statutory period for invoking the court's jurisdiction is "tolled" by the filing of the right-to-sue letter, the

---

[3]Neither the parties nor the courts below addressed the application of Rule 15(c) to the "amended complaint" filed on June 9. That Rule provides that amendment of a pleading "relates back" to the date of the original pleading. We do not believe that Rule 15(c) is applicable to this situation. The rationale of Rule 15(c) is that a party who has been notified of litigation concerning a particular occurrence has been given all the notice that statutes of limitations were intended to provide. Although the Federal Rules of Civil Procedure do not require a claimant to set forth an intricately detailed description of the asserted basis for relief, they do require that the pleadings "give the defendant fair notice of what the plaintiff's claim is and the grounds upon which it rests." Conley v. Gibson, 355 U.S. 41, 47, 78 S.Ct. 99, 102, 2 L.Ed.2d 80 (1957). Because the initial "pleading" did not contain such notice, it was not an original pleading that could be rehabilitated by invoking Rule 15(c).

[4]Justice Stevens makes much of a letter dated March 21, 1981, sent by Brown to the District Court in which she describes the basis of her claim. Suffice it to say that no one but the dissent has relied upon this letter to sustain Brown's position. There is nothing in the record to suggest that the letter was considered by the District Court or the Court of Appeals, and Brown does not rely upon it before this Court as a basis for affirming the judgment. The issue before the Court of Appeals and before this Court is whether the filing of a right-to-sue letter with the District Court constituted the commencement of an action. The Court of Appeals held that it did and based its judgment on that ground. We reverse that judgment. Even if respondent had relied on the letter in this Court, we would not be required to assess its significance without having the views of the lower courts in the first instance.

Justice Stevens also suggests that we should be more solicitous of the pleadings of the pro se litigant. It is noteworthy, however, that Brown was represented by counsel at the time of the dismissal by the District Court, before the Court of Appeals, and before this Court. Neither Brown nor her counsel ever requested that the letter in the record be construed as a complaint.

Court of Appeals cited no principle of equity to support its conclusion.[5] Brown does little better, relying only on her asserted "diligent efforts." Nor do we find anything in the record to call for the application of the doctrine of equitable tolling.

The right-to-sue letter itself stated that Brown had the right to sue within 90 days. Also, the District Court informed Brown that "to be safe, you should file the petition on or before the ninetieth day after the day of the letter from the EEOC informing you of your right to sue." Finally, the order of April 15 from the Magistrate again reminded Brown of the 90-day limitation.

This is not a case in which at claimant has received inadequate notice, or where a motion for appointment of counsel is pending and equity would justify tolling the statutory period until the motion is acted upon, or where the court has led the plaintiff to believe that she had done everything required of her. Nor is this a case where affirmative misconduct on the part of a defendant lulled the plaintiff into inaction. The simple fact is that Brown was told three times what she must do to preserve her claim, and she did not do it. One who fails to act diligently cannot invoke equitable principles to excuse that lack of diligence.

Brown also contends that the doctrine of equitable tolling should apply because the Welcome Center has not demonstrated that it was prejudiced by her failure to comply with the Rules.[6] This argument is unavailing. Although absence of prejudice is a factor to be considered in determining whether the doctrine of equitable tolling should apply once a factor that might justify such tolling is identified, it is not an independent basis for invoking the doctrine and sanctioning deviations from established procedures.

Procedural requirements established by Congress for gaining access to the federal courts are not to be disregarded by courts out of a vague sympathy for particular litigants. As we stated in Mohasco Corp. v. Silver, 447 U.S. 807, 826, 100 S.Ct. 2486, 2497, 65 L.Ed.2d 532 (1980), "in the long run, experience teaches that strict adherence to the procedural requirements specified by the legislature is the best guarantee of evenhanded administration of the law."

The petition for certiorari is granted, respondent's motion to proceed in forma pauperis is granted, and the judgment of the Court of Appeals is reversed.

It is so ordered.

[The dissenting opinion of Justices Stevens, Brennan and Marshall is omitted. The dissenters argued that: (1) the plaintiff's letter which accompanied the right-to-sue

---

[5]It is not clear from the opinion of the Court of Appeals for how long the statute is tolled. Presumably, under its view, the plaintiff has a "reasonable time" in which to file a complaint that satisfies the requirements of Rule 8. See Huston v. General Motors Corp., 477 F.2d 1003 (CA8 1973). In this case, it was another 84 days until such a complaint was filed.

[6]Brown also contends that application of the doctrine of equitable tolling is mandated by our decision in Zipes v. Trans World Airlines, Inc. In Zipes, we held that the requirement of a timely filing of a charge of discrimination with the EEOC under §706(e) is not a jurisdictional prerequisite to a suit in district court and that it is subject to waiver and equitable tolling. Brown's argument is without merit, for we did not in Zipes declare that the requirement need not ever be satisfied; we merely stated that it was subject to waiver and tolling. There was neither waiver nor tolling in this case.

notice constituted a "short and plain statement of the claim" in compliance with Rule 8 of the Federal Rules of Civil Procedure; and (2) in light of the remedial scheme of Title VII, filing the right to sue letter and exercising reasonable diligence in the trial court to obtain counsel and file a formal complaint should toll the statute of limitations.]

NOTES AND PROBLEMS FOR DISCUSSION

1. In light of Title VII's remedial purposes and the fact that plaintiffs frequently must initiate proceedings without assistance of counsel, do you agree that lack of prejudice to the defendant should not be an "independent basis" for equitable tolling? The factors that will justify equitable tolling remain somewhat in doubt. In IRWIN v. VETERANS ADMINISTRATION, 498 U.S. 89, 111 S.Ct. 453, 112 L.Ed.2d 435 (1990), a right to sue notice was delivered to the office of the charging party's attorney, who was out of the country. The lawyer did not learn of the notice until he returned and the complaint was not filed until the statuory period had run. Affirming dismissal of the case, the Court noted that "the principles of equitable tolling . . . do not extend to what is at best a garden variety claim of excusable neglect." 498 U.S. at 96. Despite *Baldwin County*, courts have been more generous in the application of equitable tolling principles when the charging party has acted without an attorney. In BROWN v. J.I. CASE CO., 756 F.2d 48 (7th Cir. 1985), for example, the Court of Appeals held that a good faith request for appointment of counsel made within the 90-day period tolled the running of the time for filing suit until disposition of the motion. *Baldwin County* was distinguished on the ground that the plaintiff had "engaged in inequitable conduct" by not returning the magistrate's questionnaire until after the period had expired. *See also* Judkins v. Beech Aircraft Corp., 745 F.2d 1330 (11th Cir. 1984) (the filing of the plaintiff's right-to-sue notice with a copy of his EEOC charge, the latter of which explained the factual basis for the discrimination claim in considerable detail, met F.R.C.v.P 8(a)(2)'s requirements for a complaint). And some courts have ruled that it is appropriate to invoke equitable estoppel where the charging party's attorney's misconduct was so egregious that the plaintiff "was abandoned by his attorney." *See e.g.*, Gordon v. England, 354 Fed.Appx. 975 (6th Cir. 2009) (unpublished).

Just as the courts have invoked tolling with respect to the filing requirement for an EEOC charge, they have recognized a variety of equitable grounds for tolling the 90-day period for filing suit. *See, e.g.*, Browning v. AT&T Paradyne, 120 F.3d 222 (11th Cir. 1997) (90-day period tolled because of agency's failure to advise plaintiff of the deadline for filing); Brown v. Parkchester South Condominiums, 287 F.3d 58 (2d Cir. 2002) (tolling of 90-day period may be appropriate where the plaintiff's failure to comply is attributable to mental illness).

2. If nothing else, *Baldwin County* highlights the importance to the claimant of obtaining legal assistance before the expiration of the filing period. Section 706(f)(1) authorizes the district court to appoint counsel "upon application by the complainant and in such circumstances as the court may deem just." Congress, however, has not created a fund (as it has for the Criminal Justice Act) from which appointed counsel can be compensated. Thus, appointed counsel will be paid for their services only if the plaintiff is a prevailing party, and counsel will probably have to bear the costs of the litigation pending its outcome. *See* Chapter 7C, *infra.* Under these circumstances, the lower courts have been reluctant to force private attorneys to take on employment discrimination cases; in practice, "appointments" under Title VII are more like referrals to counsel who may accept or reject the cases. But locating a lawyer venturesome enough to take on a hard-to-prove case on a wholly contingent basis can prove difficult. In BRADSHAW v. UNITED STATES DISTRICT COURT FOR SOUTHERN DISTRICT OF CALIFORNIA, 742 F.2d 515 (9th Cir. 1984), the district court strove unsuccessfully for over thirteen months to find an attorney who would agree to represent the plaintiff. Only after twenty lawyers had turned the case down, did the court direct the plaintiff to proceed pro se. On the plaintiff's petition for a writ of mandamus to compel the district court to appoint counsel, the Ninth Circuit held that district courts may resort to coercive appointments of counsel under Title VII but that the lower court had not abused its discretion in light of this plaintiff's litigious history and the court's diligent search for counsel.

Additionally, the statutory right to request court-appointed counsel has been construed not to include either a right to appointed counsel or the right to effective assistance of counsel. As is the rule in all civil suits other than immigration cases, a client's recourse for alleged ineffective assistance of counsel is a separate action for legal malpractice and not appeal or retrial. Nelson v. The Boeing Co., 446 F.3d 1118 (10th Cir. 2006).

3. Section 706(f)(1) provides that a Title VII claimant must file a civil action ninety days "after the *giving*" (emphasis added) of notice by the EEOC of the right to sue. At the same time, the corresponding EEOC regulation provides that the right to sue letter must state that the aggrieved can bring suit within 90 days from "receipt" of its authorization. 29 C.F.R. §1601.28(e)(1). The courts agree that the start of this ninety-day limitations period is measured from the date on which the right-to-sue notice arrives at the claimant's address of record, as opposed to the date on which the notice is issued by the EEOC. And when the date of actual receipt is known, the courts deem the claimant to have received notice on that date, irrespective of whether or not the claimant actually saw the right-to-sue letter. However, where the date of (as opposed to the fact of) actual receipt is unknown, the courts have disagreed on how to affix the date of receipt. In *Baldwin*, the Supreme Court presumed, without discussion, that the right-to-sue letter was received by the claimant three days after its issuance date. Post-*Baldwin*, most, but not all, circuits have adhered to that three-day rule. In PAYAN v. MANAGEMENT SERVICES LIMITED PARTNERSHIP, 495 F.3d 1119 (9th Cir. 2007), for example, the Ninth Circuit adopted the majority rule, holding that it would invoke a rebuttable presumption that the claimant received the letter three days after its issuance date. In doing so, the court noted that this three day presumption was consistent with the well-known and reasonable three-day rule set forth in Fed. Rule of Civ. Proc. 6(e) governing the affixing of the date of receipt of service. The court added, however, that it would apply this three-day rule only in cases where the facts established (1) the date on which the EEOC had issued the letter; (2) that the EEOC had mailed the letter to the claimant's address of record; and (3) that the claimant had actually received the notice letter at that address. It also advised that the presumption could be rebutted by evidence suggesting that receipt had been delayed beyond the presumed period such as testimony that the notice was mailed later than its typewritten date or that it took longer than three days to reach the claimant; although it warned that a general claim that mail is sometimes delayed would not suffice. A minority of courts, on the other hand, construing the language in *Baldwin* as setting only a minimum allowance for mailing time, alternatively have adopted or suggested the use of a five-day rule. *See e.g.*, Banks v. Rockwell Int'l N. Am. Aircraft Operations, 855 F.2d 324 (6th Cir. 1988). Finally, although all of the other circuits agree that the plaintiff bears the burden of establishing that suit was timely filed. *See, e.g.*, Green v. Union Foundry Co., 281 F.3d 1229 (11th Cir.), cert. denied, 123 S.Ct. 422, 154 L.Ed.2d 302 (2002), the Ninth Circuit in held in *Payan* that the defendant shoulders the burden of persuasion regarding the affirmative defense of expiration of the limitations period.

When there is a dispute as to whether the EEOC right-to-sue letter was ever received at all, as opposed to when it was received, the courts apply the "mailbox presumption" that is generally available in civil litigation. "[P]roof that a letter properly directed was placed in a post office creates a [rebuttable] presumption that it reached its destination in usual time and was actually received by the person to whom it was addressed." Hagner v. U.S., 285 U.S. 427,430, 52 S.Ct. 417,419, 76 L.Ed. 861 (1932). And the party seeking to invoke the presumption can establish mailing by direct or circumstantial evidence, including a sworn statement of mailing or customary mailing practices used in the sender's business. *See e.g.*, Duron v. Albertson's LLC, 560 F.3d 288 (5th Cir. 2009).

4. Notice that in *Allen,* the plaintiff filed her charge with the EEOC in 1972 and was not issued the right to sue notice until 1981. Section 706(f)(1) unambiguously requires the EEOC to issue notice of right to sue to the charging party not later than 180 days after the charge is filed. The purpose of the 180-day period is to protect the charging party from extended administrative proceedings and bureaucratic backlog. But given the EEOC's workload and resources, it is the rare case in which the agency can start, much less complete, an investigation during the 180-day period. In ZAMBUTO v. AT&T, 544 F.2d 1333 (5th Cir. 1977), the Court of Appeals relied on the fact of the EEOC's insurmountable workload in ruling that the Commission was not required to issue an *unsolicited* right-to-sue notice at the end of the 180-day period. This construction of the statute was given apparent approval by the Supreme Court in OCCIDENTAL LIFE INS. CO. v. EEOC, 432 U.S. 355, 97 S.Ct. 2447, 53 L.Ed.2d 402 (1977), where the Court stated that "[a]n aggrieved person unwilling to await the conclusion of extended EEOC proceedings may institute a private lawsuit 180 days after a charge has been filed." 432 U.S. at 366. Accordingly, the EEOC is not precluded from continuing its investigatory and/or conciliatory efforts at the conclusion of the 180-day period. And the aggrieved is not mandated to request a right to sue letter at the close of that period. Thus, it is possible that a grievant will choose to wait and allow the EEOC to continue its efforts beyond the 180-day window from the time of filing the EEOC charge. In such a case, as long as the aggrieved does not request a right to sue letter, is there a time limit within which the EEOC *must* send out that right to sue authorization? The statute does not expressly provide any such limitation period and the courts have not read one into the statute, except as subject to a laches defense. This question is important because it can affect the commencement of the 90 day period for filing suit. Specifically, does the 90 day period for filing suit begin to run only when the aggrieved has *received* the right to sue authorization or does it begin to run on the day in which the aggrieved was *eligible to receive* the right to sue letter, i.e., 180 days after the EEOC filing? See Scott v. Gino Morena Enters., LLC, 888 F.3d 1101 (9th Cir. 2018)(trial court erred in concluding that the 90 day clock to file Title VII claim began when the plaintiff became eligible to receive a right to sue notice rather than when she actually received that notice from the EEOC).

Should the charging party's refusal to cooperate with the EEOC's investigation of her charge bar her from bringing a Title VII suit? *Compare* Shikles v. Sprint/United Mgmt. Co., 426 F.3d 1304 (10th Cir. 2005) (the plaintiff's failure to cooperate in good faith with EEOC investigation of age discrimination charge is a bar to suit under the ADEA) *with* Doe v. Oberweis Dairy, 456 F.3d 704 (7th Cir.2006) (expressly repudiating the 10th Circuit's "gloss" as unsupported by the text of either the ADEA or Title VII, creating the potential for protracted litigation over the meaning of "good faith" cooperation, and unnecessary in the nonexistence of any evidence that absence of cooperation requirement would discourage claimants from cooperating with agency and diminish the Commission's ability to resolve disputes at administrative stage). If the charging party's refusal to cooperate with the EEOC's investigation can justify dismissal of her subsequent suit, what effect should her rejection of a conciliation offer that arguably contains full relief have? *Compare* Long v. Ringling Bros. Barnum & Bailey Combined Shows, Inc., 9 F.3d 340 (4th Cir. 1993) (an aborted conciliation agreement cannot bar resort to the courts), *with* Wrenn v. Sec'y, Dep't of Veterans Affairs, 918 F.2d 1073, 1078-79 (2d Cir. 1990), cert. denied, 499 U.S. 977, 111 S.Ct. 1625, 113 L.Ed.2d 721 (1991) ("claimant who is offered full relief in the administrative process must either accept the relief offered or abandon claim": "litigation is not a sport in which the hunter may release a trapped quarry for the thrill of further chase.").

In light of the Supreme Court's ruling in *Zipes* that timely filing with the EEOC is a nonjurisdictional requirement subject to waiver, estoppel, and equitable tolling, the lower courts have agreed that the requirement of obtaining a right-to-sue letter prior to filing suit is similarly nonjurisdictional. And in SURRELL v. CALIFORNIA WATER SERVICE CO., 518 F.3d 1097 (9th Cir. 2008), the Ninth Circuit adopted the position taken by several other circuits that where the plaintiff was entitled to receive a right-to-sue letter, whether or not the plaintiff actually obtained it prior to filing suit is immaterial. The court ruled that as long as the plaintiff meets the ninety day filing limit, the absence of a right-to-sue letter will not bar suit as long as the plaintiff had obtained a right-to-sue letter from the appropriate state agency where a worksharing agreement existed between the EEOC and that state agency.

5. EEOC Regulations permit issuance of a right-to-sue notice, on request of the charging party, *before* the expiration of the 180-day period "provided, that the District Director . . .has determined that it is probable that the Commission will be unable to complete its administrative processing of the charge within 180 days . . . ." 29 C.F.R. §1601.28(a)(2). The circuit courts are divided over the agency's authority to promulgate the rule. In MARTINI v. FED. NAT'L MTG. ASS'N., 178 F.3d 1336 (D.C. Cir. 1999), cert. dismissed, 528 U.S. 1147, 120 S.Ct. 1155, 145 L.Ed.2d 1065 (2000), the D.C. Circuit held that an early right-to-sue notice was beyond the statutory authority of the agency because such a notice terminated the mandatory investigation and processing of the charge. The court believed that enforcement of the 180-day period would produce greater compliance with the mandatory duties Congress assigned to the EEOC. Other courts, however, have upheld the regulation. *See*

Walker v. United Parcel Serv., Inc., 240 F.3d 1268, 1277 (10th Cir. 2001) ("*Martini*'s holding that aggrieved individuals must sit on their charges until 180 days has passed, even when the EEOC knows full well that it cannot complete its processing in that time, strikes us as not only imprudent as a practical matter but also as an overly strict and technical reading of a statute susceptible to more than one reasonable interpretation.").

2. RES JUDICATA, COLLATERAL ESTOPPEL, AND THE IMPACT OF STATE PROCEEDINGS ON TITLE VII LITIGATION

Section 706 makes resort to state administrative remedies, in a state with a deferral agency, a prerequisite to litigation under Title VII. Many state laws provide for judicial review of state agency findings. It is important to understand that resort to the state courts to obtain a remedy under state law may affect the claimant's right to litigate his federal statutory claim in court. In KREMER v. CHEMICAL CONSTRUCTION CORP., 456 U.S. 461, 102 S.Ct. 1883, 72 L.Ed.2d 262 (1982), the claimant unsuccessfully sought review of the state agency's decision in state court. Subsequently, the EEOC issued a no-cause determination and a right-to-sue notice, whereupon Kremer filed a timely Title VII action in federal district court. The Supreme Court, in a 5-4 decision, upheld the lower courts' decision to dismiss the complaint on preclusion grounds. While conceding that initial resort to state *administrative* remedies cannot deprive a charging party of a trial *de novo* on the Title VII claim, the majority found nothing in the legislative history of Title VII to suggest that Congress thought it either necessary or desirable to provide an absolute right to relitigate an issue in federal court that had been resolved by a state court. Since, the Court continued, there was not a clear and manifest legislative purpose behind Title VII to deny preclusive effect to state court judgments on discrimination claims, it would apply traditional rules of preclusion. And where the claimant obtains judicial review of the state law claim, the Court continued, the extent to which that judicial decision precludes litigation of the federal claim is governed by the terms of the federal Full Faith & Credit Act, 28 U.S.C. §1738. This statute instructs federal courts to give the same preclusive effect to state court judgments that a court of the judgment-rendering state would give per that state's principles of preclusion. This, in turn, means that to determine whether a state court's decision on the state law antidiscrimination claim will have any preclusive effect on a federal court's disposition of the Title VII claim, the federal court conduct a two-prong inquiry: (1) would the state court judgment be given preclusive effect if the Title VII claim had been filed in state court; and (2) did the party against whom preclusion is asserted have a full and fair opportunity in the state court proceeding to litigate the claims raised in the federal complaint.

Justice Blackmun, joined by Justices Brennan and Marshall in dissent, argued that Congress intended for Title VII claimants to be able to pursue their Title VII claims *de novo* in federal court despite the conclusion of state proceedings, including judicial review of an agency's decision. The majority's ruling, Justice Blackmun warned, provided a clear message to potential Title VII litigants:

> The lesson of the Court's ruling is: *An unsuccessful state discrimination complainant should not seek state judicial review.* If a discrimination complainant

pursues state judicial review and loses — a likely result given the deferential standard of review in state court — he forfeits his right to seek redress in a federal court. If, however, he simply bypasses the state courts, he can proceed to the EEOC and ultimately to federal court. Instead of a deferential review of an agency record, he will receive in federal court a de novo hearing accompanied by procedural aids such as broad discovery rules and the ability to subpoena witnesses. Thus, paradoxically, the Court effectively has eliminated state reviewing courts from the fight against discrimination in an entire class of cases. Consequently, the state courts will not have the chance to correct state agency errors when the agencies rule against discrimination victims, and the quality of decisionmaking can only deteriorate. It is a perverse sort of comity that eliminates the reviewing function of state courts in the name of giving their decisions due respect.

456 U.S. at 504-05. Justice Blackmun's assumption that charging parties can "simply bypass" state court review at the end of the state administrative process is not necessarily correct. Courts have uniformly construed *Kremer* as applicable regardless of which party initiates the appeal to the state court. Thus, if the plaintiff prevails before the state agency and is *forced* into state court by the employer's appeal, the court's reversal of the agency's ruling will bar the federal Title VII action. *See* Gonsalves v. Alpine Country Club, 727 F.2d 27 (1st Cir. 1984). The "lesson" of *Kremer* may be that in a deferral state where judicial review of the agency process is possible, the claimant must abandon the agency proceedings *before* an appealable decision in order to guarantee his right to a federal forum.

On the other hand, suppose a particular remedy that would be recoverable under Title VII, such as compensatory or punitive damages, is not awardable under the applicable state antidiscrimination statute. Can a plaintiff who prevailed both before the state administrative agency and on the defendant's appeal to the state courts nevertheless file a separate action under Title VII to recover damages that were unavailable in the state proceedings? The federal circuit courts are split on this question. Some courts have construed *Kremer* to preclude *any* subsequent federal action after a state administrative agency's decision has been reviewed by a state court. *See, e.g.*, Chris v. Tenet, 221 F.3d 648 (4th Cir.2000), cert. denied, 531 U.S. 1191, 121 S.Ct. 1189, 149 L.Ed.2d 105 (2001). Others, however, have recognized an exception to the *Kremer* doctrine where the federal action is limited to seeking a remedy that was unrecoverable under state law on the ground that Title VII remedies are designed to be supplemental to state remedies, at least where the plaintiff prevailed before the state agency and state courts. In these circumstances, the federal court's *de novo* consideration is limited to the remedial issue and, per *Kremer*, the federal court must give full faith and credit to the state court's determination of liability. *See, e.g.*, Nestor v. Pratt & Whitney, 466 F.3d 65 (2d Cir.2006).

Under *Kremer* and the Full Faith and Credit Act, the preclusive effect of a state court judgment in a federal proceeding turns on the effect the judgment would be given in the courts of that state. Under the law of some states, decisions of administrative tribunals that have accorded litigants the procedural safeguards available in court are given the same preclusive effect as decisions of the courts of those states. Although not required by §1738, would common law rules of preclusion require a federal court to give preclusive effect to such an administrative ruling? In

UNIV. OF TENN. v. ELLIOTT, 478 U.S. 788, 106 S.Ct. 3220, 92 L.Ed.2d 635 (1986), the Supreme Court held that Congress did not intend for unreviewed state administrative decisions to have preclusive effect on Title VII claims, regardless of the nature of the state administrative procedures. *See* McInnes v. California, 943 F.2d 1088 (9th Cir. 1991) (the clear teaching of *Elliott* is that unreviewed administrative determinations lack preclusive effect in a subsequent Title VII action regardless of any preclusive effect state law might accord to them).

3. THE DATE OF DISCRIMINATION: WHEN DOES THE PERIOD FOR FILING THE CHARGE BEGIN TO RUN?

Delaware State College v. Ricks

Supreme Court of the United States, 1980.

449 U.S. 250, 101 S.Ct. 498, 66 L.Ed.2d 431.

JUSTICE POWELL delivered the opinion of the Court.

The question in this case is whether respondent, a college professor, timely complained under the civil rights laws that he had been denied academic tenure because of his national origin.

I

Columbus Ricks is a black Liberian. In 1970, Ricks joined the faculty at Delaware State College, a state institution attended predominantly by blacks. In February 1973, the Faculty Committee on Promotions and Tenure recommended that Ricks not receive a tenured position in the education department. The tenure committee, however, agreed to reconsider its decision the following year. Upon reconsideration, in February 1974, the committee adhered to its earlier recommendation. The following month, the Faculty Senate voted to support the tenure committee's negative recommendation. On March 13, 1974, the College Board of Trustees formally voted to deny tenure to Ricks.

Dissatisfied with the decision, Ricks immediately filed a grievance with the Board's Educational Policy Committee (the grievance committee), which in May 1974 held a hearing and took the matter under submission. During the pendency of the grievance, the College administration continued to plan for Ricks' eventual termination. Like many colleges and universities, Delaware State has a policy of not discharging immediately a junior faculty member who does not receive tenure. Rather, such a person is offered a "terminal" contract to teach one additional year. When that contract expires, the employment relationship ends. Adhering to this policy, the Trustees on June 26, 1974 told Ricks that he would be offered a one-year "terminal" contract that would expire June 30, 1975.[2] Ricks signed the contract

---

[2]The June 26 letter stated: * * *

without objection or reservation on September 4, 1974. Shortly thereafter, on September 12, 1974, the Board of Trustees notified Ricks that it had denied his grievance.

Ricks attempted to file an employment discrimination charge with the Equal Employment Opportunity Commission on April 4, 1975. Under Title VII, however, state fair employment practices agencies have primary jurisdiction over employment discrimination complaints. See §706(c). The EEOC therefore referred Ricks' charge to the appropriate Delaware agency. On April 28, 1975, the state agency waived its jurisdiction, and the EEOC accepted Ricks' complaint for filing. More than two years later, the EEOC issued a "right to sue" letter.

Ricks filed this lawsuit in the District Court on September 9, 1977. The complaint alleged, *inter alia,* that the College had discriminated against him on the basis of his national origin in violation of Title VII * * *. The District Court sustained the College's motion to dismiss [the claim]* * * as untimely. It concluded that the only unlawful employment practice alleged was the College's decision to deny Ricks' tenure, and that the limitations periods * * * had commenced to run by June 26, 1974, when the President of the Board of Trustees officially notified Ricks that he would be offered a one-year "terminal" contract. See n.2, *supra.* The Title VII claim was not timely because Ricks had not filed his charge with the EEOC within 180 days after that date. * * *

The Court of Appeals for the Third Circuit reversed. It agreed with the District Court that Ricks' essential allegation was that he had been denied tenure illegally. According to the Court of Appeals, however, the Title VII filing requirement * * * did not commence to run until Ricks' "terminal" contract expired on June 30, 1975. * * *

The Court of Appeals believed that the initial decision to terminate an employee sometimes might be reversed. The aggrieved employee therefore should not be expected to resort to litigation until termination actually has occurred. Prior resort to judicial or administrative remedies would be "likely to have the negative side effect of reducing that employee's effectiveness during the balance of his or her term. Working relationships will be injured, if not sundered, and the litigation process will divert attention from the proper fulfillment of job responsibilities." Finally, the Court of Appeals thought that a rule focusing on the last day of employment would provide a "bright line guide both for the courts and for the victims of discrimination." It

---

"On March 13, 1974, the Board of Trustees of Delaware State College officially endorsed the recommendations of the Faculty Senate at its March 11, 1974 meeting, at which time the Faculty Senate recommended that the Board not grant you tenure.

As we are both aware, the Educational Policy Committee of the Board of Trustees has heard your grievance and it is now in the process of coming to a decision. * * * In order to comply with the 1971 Trustee Policy Manual and AAUP requirements with regard to the amount of time needed in proper notification of non-reappointment for non-tenured faculty members, the Board has no choice but to follow actions according to its official position prior to the grievance process, and thus, notify you of its intent not to renew your contract at the end of the 1974-75 school year.

* * * Should the Educational Policy Committee decide to recommend that you be granted tenure, and should the Board of Trustees concur with their recommendation, then of course, it will supersede any previous action taken by the Board." * * *

therefore reversed and remanded the case to the District Court for trial on the merits of Ricks' discrimination claims. We granted certiorari.

For the reasons that follow, we think that the Court of Appeals erred in holding that the filing limitations periods did not commence to run until June 30, 1975. We agree instead with the District Court that * * * the Title VII [claim was] untimely. Accordingly, we reverse.

II

Title VII requires aggrieved persons to file a complaint with the EEOC within one hundred and eighty days after the alleged unlawful employment practice occurred. §706(e).[7] * * * The limitations period, while guaranteeing the protection of the civil rights laws to those who promptly assert their rights, also protect employers from the burden of defending claims arising from employment decisions that are long past.

Determining the timeliness of Ricks' EEOC complaint, and this ensuing lawsuit, requires us to identify precisely the "unlawful employment practice" of which he complains. Ricks now insists that discrimination not only motivated the College in denying him tenure, but also in terminating his employment on June 30, 1975. In effect, he is claiming a "continuing violation" of the civil rights laws with the result that the limitations periods did not commence to run until his one-year "terminal" contract expired. This argument cannot be squared with the allegations of the complaint. Mere continuity of employment, without more, is insufficient to prolong the life of a cause of action for employment discrimination. If Ricks intended to complain of a discriminatory discharge, he should have identified the alleged discriminatory acts that continued until, or occurred at the time of, the actual termination of his employment. But the complaint alleges no such facts.[8]

Indeed, the contrary is true. It appears that termination of employment at Delaware State is a delayed, but inevitable, consequence of the denial of tenure. In order for the limitations periods to commence with the date of discharge, Ricks would have had to allege and prove that the manner in which his employment was terminated differed discriminatorily from the manner in which the College terminated other professors who also had been denied tenure. But no suggestion has been made that Ricks was treated differently from other unsuccessful tenure aspirants. Rather, in accord with the College's practice, Ricks was offered a one-year "terminal" contract, with explicit notice that his employment would end upon its expiration.

In sum, the only alleged discrimination occurred — and the filing limitations periods therefore commenced — at the time the tenure decision was made and communicated to Ricks.[9] That is so even though one of the *effects* of the denial of

---

[7] Under certain circumstances, the filing period is extended to 300 days. §706(e).

[8] Sixteen paragraphs in the complaint describe in detail the sequence of events surrounding the tenure denial. Only one paragraph even mentions Ricks' eventual departure from Delaware State, and nothing in that paragraph alleges any fact suggesting discrimination in the termination of Ricks' employment. * * *

[9] Complaints that employment termination resulted from discrimination can present widely varying circumstances. * * * The application of the general principles discussed herein necessarily must be made on a case-by-case basis.

tenure — the eventual loss of a teaching position — did not occur until later. The Court of Appeals for the Ninth Circuit correctly held, in a similar tenure case, that "[t]he proper focus is upon the time of the *discriminatory acts*, not upon the time at which the *consequences* of the acts became most painful." Abramson v. University of Hawaii, 594 F.2d 202, 209 (1979) (emphasis added). It is simply insufficient for Ricks to allege that his termination "gives present effect to the past illegal act and therefore perpetuates the consequences of forbidden discrimination." United Air Lines v. Evans, 431 U.S. 553, 557, 97 S.Ct. 1885, 1888, 52 L.Ed.2d. 571 (1977). The emphasis is not upon the effects of earlier employment decisions; rather, it "is [upon] whether any present *violation* exists." 431 U.S. at 558.

III

We conclude for the foregoing reasons that the limitations periods commenced to run when the tenure decision was made and Ricks was notified. The remaining inquiry is the identification of this date.

A

Three dates have been advanced and argued by the parties. As indicated above, Ricks contended for June 30, 1975, the final date of his "terminal" contract, relying on a continuing violation theory. This contention fails, as we have shown, because of the absence of any allegations of facts to support it. The Court of Appeals * * * found that the only alleged discriminatory act was the denial of tenure, but nevertheless adopted the "final date of employment" rule primarily for policy reasons. Although this view has the virtue of simplicity, the discussion in Part II of this opinion demonstrates its fallacy as a rule of general application. Congress has decided that time limitations periods commence with the date of the "alleged unlawful employment practice." See §706(e). Where, as here, the only challenged employment practice occurs before the termination date, the limitations periods necessarily commence to run before that date. It should not be forgotten that time-limitations provisions themselves promoted important interests; "the period allowed for instituting suit inevitably reflects a value judgment concerning the point at which the interests in favor of protecting valid claims are outweighed by the interests in prohibiting the prosecution of stale ones." Johnson v. Railway Express Agency, Inc., 421 U.S. 454, 463-464, 95 S.Ct. 11716, 1721-1722, 44 L.Ed.2d 295 (1975).[12]

B

The EEOC, in its *amicus* brief, contends in the alternative for a different date. It was not until September 12, 1974, that the Board notified Ricks that his grievance had been denied. The EEOC therefore asserts that, for purposes of computing limitations periods, this was the date of the unfavorable tenure decision.[13] Two possible lines of

---

[12]It is conceivable that the Court of Appeals' "final day of employment" rule might discourage colleges even from offering a "grace period," such as Delaware State's practice of one-year "terminal" contracts, during which the junior faculty member not offered tenure may seek a teaching position elsewhere.

[13]If September 12 were the critical date, * * * the Title VII claim * * * would be timely if Ricks is entitled to 300 days, rather than 180 days, in which to file with the EEOC. In its brief before this Court, the EEOC as *amicus curiae* noted that Delaware is a state with its own fair employment practices agency. According to the EEOC, therefore, Ricks was entitled to 300

reasoning underlie this argument. First, it could be contended that the Trustees' initial decision was only an expression of intent that did not become final until the grievance was denied. In support of this argument, the EEOC notes that the June 26 letter explicitly held out to Ricks the possibility that he would receive tenure if the Board sustained his grievance. See n.2, *supra*. Second, even if the Board's first decision expressed its official position, it could be argued that the pendency of the grievance should toll the running of the limitations periods.

We do not find either argument to be persuasive. As to the former, we think that the Board of Trustees had made clear well before September 12 that it had formally rejected Ricks' tenure bid. The June 26 letter itself characterized that as the Board's "official position." It is apparent, of course, that the Board in the June 26 letter indicated a willingness to change its prior decision if Ricks' grievance were found to be meritorious. But entertaining a grievance complaining of the tenure decision does not suggest that the earlier decision was in any respect tentative. The grievance procedure, by its nature, is a *remedy* for a prior decision, not an opportunity to *influence* that decision before it is made.

As to the latter argument, we already have held that the pendency of a grievance, or some other method of collateral review of an employment decision, does not toll the running of the limitations periods. International Union of Electrical Workers v. Robbins & Myers, Inc., 429 U.S. 229, 97 S.Ct. 441, 50 L.Ed.2d 427 (1976). The existence of careful procedures to assure fairness in the tenure decision should not obscure the principle that limitations periods normally commence when the employer's decision is made.[15]

C

The District Court rejected both the June 30, 1975 date and the September 12, 1974 date, and concluded that the limitations periods had commenced to run by June 26, 1974, when the President of the Board notified Ricks that he would be offered a "terminal" contract for the 1974-1975 school year. We cannot say that this decision was erroneous. By June 26, the tenure committee had twice recommended that Ricks not receive tenure; the Faculty Senate had voted to support the tenure committee's recommendation; and the Board of Trustees formally had voted to deny Ricks tenure.[16]

---

days to file his complaint. See n.7, *supra*. Because we hold that the time limitations periods commenced to run no later than June 26, 1974, we need not decide whether Ricks was entitled to 300 days to file under Title VII. Counting from the June 26 date, Ricks' filing with the EEOC was not timely even with the benefit of the 300-day period.

[15]We do not suggest that aspirants for academic tenure should ignore available opportunities to request reconsideration. Mere requests to reconsider, however, cannot extend the limitations periods applicable to the civil rights laws.

[16]We recognize, of course, that the limitations periods should not commence to run so soon that it becomes difficult for a layman to invoke the protection of the civil rights statutes. But, for the reasons we have stated, there can be no claim here that Ricks was not abundantly forewarned. In NLRB v. Yeshiva University, 444 U.S. 672, 674, 100 S.Ct. 856, at 859, 63 L.Ed.2d 115 (1980), we noted that university boards of trustees customarily rely on the professional expertise of the tenured faculty, particularly with respect to decisions about hiring, tenure, termination, and promotion. Thus, the action of the Board of Trustees on March 13, 1974, affirming the faculty recommendation, was entirely predictable. The Board's letter of June 26, 1974 simply

In light of this unbroken array of negative decisions, the District Court was justified in concluding that the College had established its official position — and made that position apparent to Ricks — no later than June 26, 1974.[17]

We therefore reverse the decision of the Court of Appeals and remand to that Court so that it may reinstate the District Court's order dismissing the complaint.

Reversed.

Justice Stewart, with whom Justice Brennan and Justice Marshall join, dissenting.

I agree * * * that the unlawful employment practice * * * was a discriminatory denial of tenure, not a discriminatory termination of employment. Nevertheless, I believe that a fair reading of the complaint reveals a plausible allegation that the College actually denied Ricks' tenure on September 12, 1974, the date on which the Board finally confirmed its decision to accept the faculty's recommendation that he not be given tenure.

Therefore, unlike the Court, I think Ricks should be allowed to prove to the District Court that the allegedly unlawful denial of tenure occurred on that date.[1] As noted by the Court, if Ricks succeeds in this proof, * * * the timeliness of his Title VII claim would then depend on whether his filing of a complaint with the Delaware Department of Labor entitled him to file his EEOC charge within 300 days of the discriminatory act, rather than within the 180 days limitation that the Court of Appeals and the District Court assumed to be applicable.[2]

A brief examination of the June 26, 1974 letter * * * provides a reasonable basis for the allegation that the College did not effectively deny Ricks' tenure until September 12. The letter informed Ricks of the Board's "intent not to renew" his contract at the end of the 1974-1975 academic year. * * * The Board expressly stated * * * that a decision of the Board's Educational Policy Committee favorable to Ricks would "of course * * * supersede any previous action taken by the Board."

---

repeated to Ricks the Board's official position and acknowledged the pendency of the grievance through which Ricks hopes to persuade the Board to change that position.

[17]We need not decide whether the District Court correctly focused on the June 26 date, rather than the date the Board communicated to Ricks its unfavorable tenure decision made at the March 13, 1974 meeting. As we have stated, see n.13, *supra*, * * * the Title VII [claim was] not timely filed even counting from the June 26 date.

[1]The Court treats the District Court's determination of June 26, 1974, as the date of tenure denial as a factual finding which is not clearly erroneous. But it must be stressed that the District Court dismissed Ricks' claims on the pleadings, and so never made factual determinations on this or any other issue.

[2]Title VII would allow Ricks 300 days if he had "initially instituted" proceedings with a local or state agency with authority to grant him relief. §706(b). To benefit from this provision, however, Ricks would arguably have had to make a timely filing with the state agency. Delaware law requires that a charge of discrimination be filed with the Department of Labor within 90 days after the allegedly discriminatory practice occurred or within 120 days after the practice is discovered, whichever date is later. Neither the District Court nor the Court of Appeals considered the timliness Ricks' filing with the state agency, nor the significance of the state agency's action in waiving jurisdiction over Ricks' charge, and so these questions would be appropriately addressed on remand.

Thus, the Board itself may have regarded its earlier actions as tentative or preliminary, pending a thorough review triggered by the respondent's request to the Committee. The Court acknowledges that this letter expresses the Board's willingness to change its earlier view on Ricks' tenure, but considers the grievance procedure under which the decision might have been changed to be a remedy for an earlier tenure decision and not a part of the overall process of making the initial tenure decision. Ricks, however, may be able to prove to the District Court that at his College, the original Board response to the faculty's recommendation was not a virtually final action subject to reopening only in the most extreme cases, but a preliminary decision to shift the burden from the College to the tenure candidate, and to advance the tenure question to the Board's grievance committee as the next conventional stage in the process.

Whether this is an accurate view of the tenure process at Delaware State College is, of course, a factual question we cannot resolve here. But Ricks lost his case in the trial court on a motion to dismiss. I think that motion was wrongly granted, and that Ricks was entitled to a hearing and a determination of this factual issue.

I would, therefore, vacate the judgment of the Court of Appeals and remand the case to the District Court so that it can make this determination and then, if necessary, resolve whether Title VII allowed Ricks 300 days from the denial of tenure to file his charge with the Commission.

JUSTICE STEVENS, dissenting.

The custom widely followed by colleges and universities of offering a one-year terminal contract immediately after making an adverse tenure decision is, in my judgment, analogous to the custom in many other personnel relationships of giving an employee two weeks advance notice of discharge. My evaluation of this case can perhaps best be explained by that analogy.

Three different reference points could arguably determine when a cause of action for a discriminatory discharge accrues: (1) when the employer decides to terminate the relationship; (2) when notice of termination is given to the employee; and (3) when the discharge becomes effective. The most sensible rule would provide that the date of discharge establishes the time when a cause of action accrues and the statute of limitations begins to run. Prior to that date, the allegedly wrongful act is subject to change; more importantly, the effective discharge date is the date which can normally be identified with the least difficulty or dispute.

I would apply the same reasoning here in identifying the date on which respondent's allegedly discriminatory discharge became actionable. Thus under my analysis the statute of limitations began to run on June 30, 1975, the termination date of respondent's one year contract. In reaching that conclusion, I do not characterize the college's discharge decision as a "continuing violation"; nor do I suggest that a teacher who is denied tenure and who remains in a school's employ for an indefinite period could file a timely complaint based on the tenure decision when he or she is ultimately discharged. Rather, I regard a case such as this one, in which a college denies tenure and offers a terminal one year contract as part of the adverse tenure decision, as a discharge case. The decision to deny tenure in this situation is in all respects comparable to another employer's decision to discharge an employee and, in due course, to give the employee notice of the effective date of that discharge. Both the interest in harmonious working relations during the terminal period of the employment relationship,[2] and the interest in certainty that is so important in litigation of this kind,[3] support this result.

For these reasons, I would affirm the judgment of the Court of Appeals.

NOTES AND PROBLEMS FOR DISCUSSION

1. (a) Is a denial of tenure fundamentally different from a notice of discharge? Should the period for filing in the latter case run from the date the employee learns of his discharge or from his last day of work? In CHARDON v. FERNANDEZ, 454 U.S. 6, 102 S.Ct. 28, 70 L.Ed.2d 6 (1981), a case filed under 42 U.S.C. §1983, the Supreme Court, relying on *Ricks,* concluded that in a discharge case, the "unlawful employment practice" (from which date the limitation period runs) occurs when the decision to terminate is made and communicated to the employee, not the date that actual termination occurs.

(b) If the employee's discharge results from a prior discriminatory act, such as a biased performance evaluation, should the filing period run from the date of the evaluation or the date of the discharge? In THOMAS v. EASTMAN KODAK CO., 183 F.3d 38 (1st Cir. 1999), cert. denied, 528 U.S. 1161, 120 S.Ct. 1174, 145 L.Ed.2d 1082 (2000), the plaintiff was laid off several years after receiving unfavorable performance evaluations which she claimed were the result of racial bias. The plaintiff's EEOC charge was filed after her discharge. The First Circuit decided that the limitations period should begin running when the implications of the evaluation had crystallized and some tangible effects of the discrimination had become apparent to the plaintiff. Applying that standard to the instant facts, the court ruled:

> that the performance appraisals Thomas received in 1990, 1991, and 1992 did not trigger the statute of limitations in §706(e)(1) at the time they were presented to Thomas because they did not initially have any crystallized implications or apparent tangible effects. The notice of the layoff is the date on which the limitations period began to run because Thomas' low appraisal scores first resulted in concrete injury in 1993 when they led to her layoff.

183 F.3d at 55.

---

[2]This interest has special force in the college setting. Because the employee must file a charge with the EEOC within 180 days after the occurrence, the Court's analysis will necessitate the filing of a charge while the teacher is still employed. The filing of such a charge may prejudice any pending reconsideration of the tenure decision and also may impair the teacher's performance of his or her regular duties. Neither of these adverse consequences would be present in a discharge following a relatively short notice such as two weeks.

[3]The interest in certainty lies not only in choosing the most easily identifiable date, but also in avoiding the involvement of the EEOC until the school's decision to deny tenure is final. The American Association of University Professors, as *amicus curiae* here, has indicated that under the "prevailing academic employment practices" of American higher education, * * * initial tenure determinations are often reconsidered, and the reconsideration process may take the better part of the terminal contract year.

2. Most lower courts have found implicit in *Ricks* the common law "discovery rule" under which the limitation period begins to run when the employee discovers or by exercise of reasonable diligence could have discovered the discriminatory act. Should the limitation period begin to run when the employee knows, or should know, of the discriminatory act or when she realizes (or should realize) the discriminatory animus underlying the act? The circuit courts have construed *Ricks* to mean that the plaintiff's claim accrues, and thus the limitations period begins to run, at the time of awareness of the adverse employment action and *not* when the plaintiff knows or should have known of the employer's discriminatory intention. *See e.g.*, Lukovsky v. City and County of San Francisco, 535 F.3d 1034 (9th Cir. 2008), cert. denied, 129 S.Ct. 1997 (2009) (citing other concurring circuit court opinions).

3. When should the filing period begin to run in cases where the plaintiff alleges that the discrimination occurred as a consequence of either the application of an ongoing policy or a series of adverse actions? Read the following case:

United Air Lines, Inc. v. Evans

Supreme Court of the United States, 1977.
431 U.S. 553, 97 S.Ct. 1885, 52 L.Ed.2d 571.

MR. JUSTICE STEVENS delivered the opinion of the Court.

Respondent was employed by United Air Lines as a flight attendant from November 1966 to February 1968. She was rehired in February 1972. Assuming, as she alleges, that her separation from employment in 1968 violated Title VII, the question now presented is whether the employer is committing a second violation of Title VII by refusing to credit her with seniority for any period prior to February 1972.

* * *

During respondent's initial period of employment, United maintained a policy of refusing to allow its female flight attendants to be married. When she married in 1968, she was therefore forced to resign. Although it was subsequently decided that such a resignation violated Title VII, Sprogis v. United Air Lines, 444 F.2d 1194 (CA7 1971), cert. denied, 404 U.S. 991, 92 S.Ct. 536, 30 L.Ed.2d 543, respondent was not a party to that case and did not initiate any proceedings of her own in 1968 by filing a charge with the EEOC within 90 days of her separation.[3] A claim based on that discriminatory act is therefore barred.

In November 1968, United entered into a new collective-bargaining agreement which ended the pre-existing "no marriage" rule and provided for the reinstatement of certain flight attendants who had been terminated pursuant to that rule. Respondent was not covered by that agreement. On several occasions she unsuccessfully sought reinstatement; on February 16, 1972, she was hired as a new employee. Although her personnel file carried the same number as it did in 1968, for seniority purposes she has

---

[3] * * * The 1972 amendments to Title VII * * * enlarge[d] the limitations period to 180 days.

been treated as though she had no prior service with United.[5] She has not alleged that any other rehired employees were given credit for prior service with United, or that United's administration of the seniority system has violated the collective-bargaining agreement covering her employment.

Informal requests to credit her with pre-1972 seniority having been denied, respondent commenced this action.[7] The District Court dismissed the complaint, holding that the failure to file a charge within 90 days of her separation in 1968 caused respondent's claim to be time barred and foreclosed any relief under Title VII.[8]

A divided panel of the Court of Appeals initially affirmed; then, after our decision in Franks v. Bowman Transportation Co., 424 U.S. 747, 96 S.Ct. 1251, 47 L.Ed.2d 444, the panel granted respondent's petition for rehearing and unanimously reversed. We granted certiorari and now hold that the complaint was properly dismissed.

Respondent recognizes that it is now too late to obtain relief based on an unlawful employment practice which occurred in 1968. She contends, however, that United is guilty of a present, continuing violation of Title VII and therefore that her claim is timely.[9] She * * * [alleges that] the seniority system gives present effect to the past illegal act and therefore perpetuates the consequences of forbidden discrimination. * * *

* * *

Respondent is correct in pointing out that the seniority system gives present effect to a past act of discrimination. But United was entitled to treat that past act as lawful

---

[5]Respondent is carried on two seniority rolls. Her "company" or "system" seniority dates from the day she was rehired, February 16, 1972. Her "stewardess" or "pay" seniority dates from the day she completed her flight attendant training, March 16, 1972. One or both types of seniority determine a flight attendant's wages; the duration and timing of vacations; rights to retention in the event of layoffs and rights to re-employment thereafter; and rights to preferential selection of flight assignments.

[7]The relief requested in respondent's complaint included an award of seniority to the starting date of her initial employment with United and backpay "lost as a result of the discriminatory employment practices of [United]." In her brief in this Court, respondent states that she seeks backpay only since her date of rehiring, February 16, 1972, which would consist of the increment in pay and benefits attributable to her lower seniority since that time. .

[8]The District Court recited that the motion was filed pursuant to Fed. Rule Civ. Proc. 12(b)(1) and dismissed the complaint on the ground that it had no jurisdiction of a time-barred claim. The District Court also held, however, that the complaint did not allege any continuing violation. For that reason, the complaint was ripe for dismissal under Rule 12(b)(6). The District Court stated:

* * * "Plaintiff, however, has not been suffering from any 'continuing' violation. She is seeking to have this court merely reinstate her November, 1966 seniority date which was lost solely by reason of her February, 1968 resignation. The fact that that resignation was the result of an unlawful employment practice is irrelevant for purposes of these proceedings because plaintiff lost her opportunity to redress that grievance when she failed to file a charge within ninety days of February, 1968. United's subsequent employment of plaintiff in 1972 cannot operate to resuscitate such a time-barred claim."

[9]Respondent cannot rely for jurisdiction on the single act of failing to assign her seniority credit for her prior service at the time she was rehired, for she filed her discrimination charge with the Equal Employment Opportunity Commission on February 21, 1973, more than one year after she was rehired on February 16, 1972. The applicable time limit in February 1972, was 90 days; effective March 24, 1972, this time was extended to 180 days.

after respondent failed to file a charge of discrimination within the 90 days then allowed by §706(d). A discriminatory act which is not made the basis for a timely charge is the legal equivalent of a discriminatory act which occurred before the statute was passed. It may constitute relevant background evidence in a proceeding in which the status of a current practice is at issue, but separately considered, it is merely an unfortunate event in history which has no present legal consequences.

Respondent emphasizes the fact that she has alleged a continuing violation. United's seniority system does indeed have a continuing impact on her pay and fringe benefits. But the emphasis should not be placed on mere continuity; the critical question is whether any present violation exists. She has not alleged that the system discriminates against former female employees or that it treats former employees who were discharged for a discriminatory reason any differently from former employees who resigned or were discharged for a non-discriminatory reason. In short, the system is neutral in its operation.

Our decision in Franks v. Bowman Transportation Co. does not control this case. In *Franks* we held that retroactive seniority was an appropriate remedy to be awarded under §706(g) after an illegal discriminatory act or practice had been proved. When that case reached this Court, the issues relating to the timeliness of the charge and the violation of Title VII had already been decided; we dealt only with a question of remedy. In contrast, in the case now before us we do not reach any remedy issue because respondent did not file a timely charge based on her 1968 separation and she has not alleged facts establishing a violation since she was rehired in 1972.[13]

The difference between a remedy issue and a violation issue is highlighted by the analysis of §703(h) of Title VII in *Franks*. As we held in that case, by its terms that section does not bar the award of retroactive seniority after a violation has been proved. Rather, §703(h) "delineates which employment practices are illegal and thereby prohibited and which are not," 424 U.S., at 758, 96 S.Ct., at 1261.

That section expressly provides that it shall not be an unlawful employment practice to apply different terms of employment pursuant to a bona fide seniority system, provided that any disparity is not the result of intentional discrimination. Since respondent does not attack the bona fides of United's seniority system, and since she makes no charge that the system is intentionally designed to discriminate because of race, color, religion, sex, or national origin, §703(h) provides an additional ground for rejecting her claim.

The Court of Appeals read §703(h) as intended to bar an attack on a seniority system based on the consequences of discriminatory acts which occurred prior to the effective date of Title VII in 1965, but having no application to such attacks based on acts occurring after 1965. This reading of §703(h) is too narrow. The statute does not foreclose attacks on the current operation of seniority systems which are subject to challenge as discriminatory. But such a challenge to a neutral system may not be

---

[13]At the time she was rehired in 1972, respondent had no greater right to a job than any other applicant for employment with United. Since she was in fact treated like any other applicant when she was rehired, the employer did not violate Title VII in 1972. And if the employer did not violate Title VII in 1972 by refusing to credit respondent with back seniority, its continued adherence to that policy cannot be illegal.

predicated on the mere fact that a past event which has no present legal significance has affected the calculation of seniority credit, even if the past event might at one time have justified a valid claim against the employer. A contrary view would substitute a claim for seniority credit for almost every claim which is barred by limitations. Such a result would contravene the mandate of §703(h).

The judgment of the Court of Appeals is reversed.

MR. JUSTICE MARSHALL, with whom MR. JUSTICE BRENNAN joins, dissenting.

But for her sex, respondent Carolyn Evans presently would enjoy all of the seniority rights that she seeks through this litigation. Petitioner United Air Lines has denied her those rights pursuant to a policy that perpetuates past discrimination by awarding the choicest jobs to those possessing a credential married women were unlawfully prevented from acquiring: continuous tenure with United. While the complaint respondent filed in the District Court was perhaps inartfully drawn,[1] it adequately draws into question this policy of United's.

For the reasons stated in the Court's opinion and in my separate opinion in Teamsters v. United States, I think it indisputable that, absent §703(h), the seniority system at issue here would constitute an "unlawful employment practice" under Title VII. And for the reasons developed at length in my separate opinion in *Teamsters,* I believe §703(h) does not immunize seniority systems that perpetuate post-Act discrimination.

The only remaining question is whether Ms. Evans' complaint is barred by the applicable statute of limitations, §706(e). Her cause of action accrued, if at all, at the time her seniority was recomputed after she was rehired. Although she apparently failed to file a charge with the EEOC within 180 days after her seniority was determined, Title VII recognizes that certain violations, once commenced, are continuing in nature. In these instances, discriminatees can file charges at any time up to 180 days after the violation ceases. (They can, however, receive backpay only for the two years preceding the filing of charges with the Equal Employment Opportunity Commission. §706(g)). In the instant case, the violation — treating respondent as a new employee even though she was wrongfully forced to resign — is continuing to this day. Respondent's charge therefore was not time barred, and the Court of Appeals judgment reinstating her complaint should be affirmed.[2]

---

[1]Although the District Court dismissed respondent's complaint for lack of jurisdiction pursuant to Fed. Rule Civ. Proc. 12(b)(1), the basis for its ruling was that the complaint was time barred. Thus, the dismissal closely resembles a dismissal for failure to state a claim upon which relief can be granted, and the only issue before us is whether it appears beyond doubt that the plaintiff can prove no set of facts in support of her claim which would entitle her to relief.

[2]It is, of course, true that to establish her entitlement to relief, respondent will have to prove that she was unlawfully forced to resign more than 180 days prior to filing her charge with the EEOC. But if that is sufficient to defeat her claim, then discriminatees will never be able to challenge "practices, procedures, or tests * * * [which] operate to 'freeze' the status quo of prior discriminatory employment practices," Griggs v. Duke Power Co., even though *Griggs* holds that such practices are impermissible, and the legislative history of the Equal Employment Opportunity Act of 1972 indicates that Congress agrees, see Teamsters (Marshall, J., concurring in part and dissenting in part). The consequence of Ms. Evans' failure to file charges after she

NOTES AND PROBLEMS FOR DISCUSSION

1. As discussed in Chapter 2, Section C, *supra*, seniority systems that are not "bona fide" within the meaning of §703(h), such as a seniority system that is designed to disadvantage a protected class, violate Title VII. Is the *application* of a discriminatory seniority system, which may occur years after the seniority provisions are incorporated in a collective bargaining agreement, a violation of the Act, or, as in *Evans*, the unfortunate consequence of prior unchallenged discrimination? Section 706(e) of Title VII directly answers this question:

> (2) For purposes of this section, an unlawful employment practice occurs, with respect to a seniority system that has been adopted for an intentionally discriminatory purpose in violation of this title (whether or not that discriminatory purpose is apparent on the face of the seniority provision), when the seniority system is adopted, when an individual becomes subject to the seniority system, or when a person aggrieved is injured by the application of the seniority system or provision of the system.

Section 703(e) was added by the 1991 amendments well after the decision in *Evans*. Does this legislative development change the result in *Evans*?

2. Should the rationale of *Evans* — that the continuing effects of past discriminatory acts do not constitute current violations of Title VII — be applied to paysetting decisions? Should, for example, a sex-based discriminatory pay decision be viewed as a "discrete act" which would start the period for filing a charge, or can a plaintiff successfully argue that this decision produced continuing effects that would extend the EEOC charging period? In BAZEMORE v. FRIDAY, 478 U.S. 385, 106 S.Ct. 3000, 92 L.Ed.2d 315 (1986), a state agricultural extension service had been organized, prior to the enactment of Title VII, in two racially segregated branches. Employees in the black division of the service had been paid significantly lower wages than their white counterparts. After the enactment of Title VII, the two branches were merged, but the disparities in salaries continued, primarily as a consequence of the historic pattern of separate pay scales. The appellate court affirmed the district court's dismissal of the black employees' Title VII claims on the ground that the defendants were not obligated to eliminate salary disparities that originated prior to 1972, the date on which Title VII was made applicable to state agencies. The Supreme Court reversed, ruling that the fact that the discriminatory salary decisions were made pre-Act did not excuse perpetuating the discrimination after Title VII was in force. "Each week's paycheck that delivers less to black than to a similarly situated white is a wrong actionable under Title VII," the Court declared, "regardless of the fact that the pattern was begun prior to the effective date of Title VII." 478 U.S. at 395-96. The Court reasoned that "[t]o hold otherwise would have the effect of exempting from liability those employers who were historically the greatest offenders of the rights of blacks." *Ibid.* Since the Court made no reference to either *Evans* or the continuing violation doctrine, this decision caused the circuit courts to split on whether the continuing violation doctrine applied to wage claims.

---

was discharged is that she has lost her right to backpay; not her right to challenge present wrongs.

The controversy was resolved when the Supreme Court extended its ruling in *Evans* to wage discrimination claims in LEDBETTER v. GOODYEAR TIRE & RUBBER CO., INC., 550 U.S. 618, 127 S.Ct. 2162, 167 L.Ed.2d 982 (2007). There, the plaintiff had filed a questionnaire with the EEOC in March 1998 alleging acts of sex discrimination. Although she subsequently filed a formal charge in July of that year, the parties and the Court assumed that the EEOC charging period dated from the date of the filing of the questionnaire and not the formal charge. The trial judge let her Title VII claim go to trial and the jury rendered a verdict in the plaintiff's favor even though the alleged discriminatory supervisorial evaluations and pay decisions occurred outside the EEOC charging period. The Eleventh Circuit reversed on the ground that a Title VII pay discrimination claim could not be based on any paysetting decision that occurred outside the EEOC charging period, even if the effect of those decisions continued to be felt through the receipt of paychecks that occurred during the charging period. A 5-4 Court upheld the Eleventh Circuit's decision. The Court declared that the plaintiff's argument that subsequent salary payments "carried forward" the effects of antecedent, uncharged discriminatory paysetting decisions was "foreclosed" by its ruling in *Evans*. Each paysetting decision was a discrete act, one of which needed to occur within the charging period. "A new violation does not occur, and a new charging period does not commence, upon the occurrence of subsequent non-discriminatory acts that entail adverse effects resulting from the past discrimination." The Court narrowly construed *Bazemore* to mean that an employer triggers a new charging period only when it issues paychecks pursuant to a facially discriminatory pay structure because that involves freestanding acts of discrimination and not the carrying forward of a past act of discrimination. But since the plaintiff had not offered evidence that the employer had either adopted its performance-based compensation scheme with discriminatory intent, or subsequently had applied this system to the plaintiff within the charging period with any discriminatory animus, *Bazemore* was inapplicable.

Congress rejected this interpretation of the Act by passing a statute designed expressly to reverse the ruling in *Ledbetter*. The Lilly Ledbetter Fair Pay Act of 2009, Pub. L. No. 111-2, §3, 123 Stat. 5, 5-6 (2009), 42 U.S.C. §2000e-5(e)(3)(A), the first bill signed into law by President Obama, amends Title VII, the ADEA, the ADA and the Rehabilitation Act "to clarify that a discriminatory compensation decision or other practice that is unlawful under such Acts occurs each time compensation is paid pursuant to the discriminatory compensation decision or other practice". Under this statute, an unlawful employment practice occurs, with respect to compensation claims, when the discriminatory compensation decision is initially adopted, when an individual initially becomes subject to the discriminatory compensation decision, or when an individual is affected by the application of the discriminatory compensation decision "including each time wages, benefits, or other compensation is paid". The fact that this statute amended the ADEA, ADA, Rehabilitation Act, and Title VII, means that Congress expanded the meaning of when an act of discrimination occurs not only in cases, such as *Ledbetter*, that involved claims of sex-based wage discrimination, but also in cases alleging race, color, religion, national origin, age, and disability-based discrimination affecting compensation. However, it limits backpay recovery to no more than two years prior to the date the charge was filed. And the statute also expressly applies to all claims pending as of the day prior to the Court's ruling in *Ledbetter.*

The Fair Pay Act amended Title VII by inserting new §706(e)(3)(A), which states that with respect to an unlawful employment practice concerning "discrimination in compensation", one looks to the date of adoption or application (including each paycheck) of "a discrminatory compensation decision *or other practice*". (emphasis added). Does this suggest that the revised charging period effected by the Fair Play Act would apply to non-compensation decisions, such as those dealing with promotion, which have a direct impact on compensation? *See* Schuler v. PriceWaterhouseCoopers, LLP, 595 F.3d 370 (D.C.Cir. 2010) (failing to promote an employee to a more remunerative position [a partnership decision in the instant case] is not a "compensation decision or other practice" within the meaning of the Fair Pay Act). *Accord,* Noel v. Boeing Co., 622 F.3d 266 (3d Cir. 2010) (citing *Schuler* and noting that unlike discrete compensation decisions, failure to promote decisions are readily appatent and easily discoverable before the expiration of the filing period). For a discussion of why the statute should be interpreted in an expansive manner to include such decisions, see Charles A. Sullivan, *Raising the Dead? The Lilly Ledbetter Fair Pay Act,* 84 TUL. L.REV. 499 (2010).

3.   How should the following situations be resolved?

(a)   Should a change in a pension plan that results in a reduction in the plaintiff's pension payments be treated as a wage claim or as a discrete act occurring at the time the change in the plan is announced? *See, e.g.*, Campbell v. BankBoston, N.A., 327 F.3d 1 (1st Cir. 2003) (the change in the pension plan that occurred long before any charge was filed was a discrete act that triggered the filing period even though the company's final rejection of the plaintiff's request to correct the plan occurred within 300 days of the filing of the charge)

(b)   Suppose an employer required all applicants for promotion to receive above a certain cut-off score on a written examination to be eligible for promotion and that the test's results have a disproportionate discriminatory impact upon African-American applicants. Finally, assume that the employer created the test and the cut-off score on January 1, 2009, but that it made several rounds of promotion decisions pursuant to that cut-off score policy in the period from March 1, 2010 through June 30, 2010. The plaintiff, an African-American applicant who scored below the cut-off score on June 1, 2010 was not eligible for the round of promotions granted on June 30, 2010. He filed an EEOC charge on August 1, 2010 on behalf of all African-American applicants who were denied promotion on that day. His charge alleges that the company's use of the cut-off score produced a discriminatory impact on African-Americans in violation of Title VII. The company maintains that the charge should be dismissed as untimely filed since the alleged unlawful employment practice was its decision to adopt a cut-off score back in January of 2009. The plaintiffs maintain that the company's continued use of the cut-off policy constituted a separate violation on each occasion in which promotion decisions were made. Who is correct? In LEWIS v. CITY OF CHICAGO, 560 U.S. 205, 130 S.Ct. 2191, 178 L.Ed.2d 967 (2010), a unanimous Supreme Court ruled that where the plaintiff brings a disparate impact claim, the discriminatory event for determining the relevant charging period includes any "use" of an employment practice that produces a disparate impact upon a protected class. The Court relied on the language of §703(k)(1)(A), which codified impact analysis into Title VII as part of the 1991 Civil Rights Act amendments to Title VII. This subsection provides that a plaintiff states a cognizable claim if it demonstrates that a defendant "uses a particular employment practice that causes a disparate impact". Consequently, the Court ruled, although the decision to create a cut-off score might also constitute a freestanding unlawful employment practice (which would have to be timely challenged), the use of that practice each time the company decided to hire workers constituted a separate violation. The Court distinguished this ruling from its prior decisions in cases such as *Evans* and *Ledbetter* in which it had held that present effects of prior decisions cannot lead to Title VII liability. Those cases, the Court explained, all involved allegations of intentional discrimination and, accordingly, those plaintiffs were required to establish that a separate act of intentional discrimination had occurred within the limitations period. But as the instant case involved only an allegation of impact-based discrimination, the Court concluded, the reasoning in those disparate treatment cases had no application. Finally, although the Court acknowledged that its ruling would produce the puzzling result that employers could face impact suit liability for practices they had used regularly, without challenge, for years, a contrary reading would permit a company to use a practice with disparate impact indefinitely with impunity. In the end, the Court insisted that its role was limited to interpreting the extant text and that any fixes were up to Congress to confect.

Ledbetter, Evans, and *Ricks* involve employment decisions that were the products of antecedent, unchallenged actions — supervisorial recommendations and pay decisions in *Ledbetter,* a tenure denial in *Ricks*, and the discharge in *Evans.* But some violations of Title VII result not from the implementation of an explicit policy, but from an accumulation of individual incidents. What if the last occurrence that the plaintiff complains of is within the limitations period, but considered in isolation, is not a violation of the Act? What if the last occurrence is within the limitation period but the employee seeks relief for related discriminatory actions outside of the limitation period? Consider the following case.

National Railroad Passenger Corp. v. Morgan

Supreme Court of the United States, 2002.
536 U.S. 101, 122 S.Ct. 2061, 153 l.Ed.2d 106.

THOMAS, J., delivered the opinion of the Court, in which STEVENS, SOUTER, GINSBURG, and BREYER, JJ., joined, and in which REHNQUIST, C. J., and O'CONNOR, SCALIA, AND KENNEDY, JJ., joined as to Part II-A. O'CONNOR, J., filed an opinion concurring in part and dissenting in part, in which REHNQUIST, C. J., joined, in which SCALIA and KENNEDY, JJ., joined as to all but Part I, and in which BREYER, J., joined as to Part I.

JUSTICE THOMAS delivered the opinion of the Court.

Respondent Abner Morgan, Jr., sued petitioner National Railroad Passenger Corporation (Amtrak) under Title VII, alleging that he had been subjected to discrete discriminatory and retaliatory acts and had experienced a racially hostile work environment throughout his employment. Section 706(e)(1) requires that a Title VII plaintiff file a charge with the Equal Employment Opportunity Commission either 180 or 300 days "after the alleged unlawful employment practice occurred." We consider whether, and under what circumstances, a Title VII plaintiff may file suit on events that fall outside this statutory time period.

The * * * Ninth Circuit held that a plaintiff may sue on claims that would ordinarily be time barred so long as they either are "sufficiently related" to incidents that fall within the statutory period or are part of a systematic policy or practice of discrimination that took place, at least in part, within the limitations period. We reverse in part and affirm in part. We hold that the statute precludes recovery for discrete acts of discrimination or retaliation that occur outside the statutory time period. We also hold that consideration of the entire scope of a hostile work environment claim, including behavior alleged outside the statutory time period, is permissible for the purposes of assessing liability, so long as any act contributing to that hostile environment takes place within the statutory time period. The application of equitable doctrines, however, may either limit or toll the time period within which an employee must file a charge.

I

On February 27, 1995, Abner J. Morgan, Jr., a black male, filed a charge of discrimination and retaliation against Amtrak with the EEOC and cross-filed with the California Department of Fair Employment and Housing. Morgan alleged that during the time period that he worked for Amtrak he was consistently harassed and disciplined more harshly than other employees on account of his race.[2] The EEOC issued a "Notice of Right to Sue" on July 3, 1996, and Morgan filed this lawsuit on October 2, 1996. While some of the allegedly discriminatory acts about which Morgan complained occurred within 300 days of the time that he filed his charge with the EEOC, many took place prior to that time period. Amtrak filed a motion, arguing, among other things, that it was entitled to summary judgment on all incidents that occurred more than 300 days before the filing of Morgans EEOC charge. The District Court granted summary judgment in part to Amtrak, holding that the company could not be liable for conduct occurring before May 3, 1994, because that conduct fell outside of the 300-day filing period. The court employed a test established by the * * * Seventh Circuit in Galloway v. General Motors Service Parts Operations, 78 F.3d 1164 (1996): A "plaintiff may not base [the] suit on conduct that occurred outside the statute of limitations unless it would have been unreasonable to expect the plaintiff to sue before the statute ran on that conduct, as in a case in which the conduct could constitute, or be recognized, as actionable harassment only in the light of events that occurred later, within the period of the statute of limitations." The District Court held that "[b]ecause Morgan believed that he was being discriminated against at the time that all of these acts occurred, it would not be unreasonable to expect that Morgan

---

[2]Such discrimination, he alleges, began when the company hired him in August 1990 as an electrician helper, rather than as an electrician. Subsequent alleged racially motivated discriminatory acts included a termination for refusing to follow orders, Amtrak's refusal to allow him to participate in an apprenticeship program, numerous "written counselings" for absenteeism, as well as the use of racial epithets against him by his managers.

should have filed an EEOC charge on these acts before the limitations period on these claims ran."[3]

Morgan appealed. The * * * Ninth Circuit reversed, relying on its previous articulation of the continuing violation doctrine, which allows courts to consider conduct that would ordinarily be time barred "as long as the untimely incidents represent an ongoing unlawful employment practice." Contrary to both the Seventh Circuit's test, used by the District Court, and a similar test employed by the Fifth Circuit,[4] the Ninth Circuit held that its precedent "precludes such a notice limitation on the continuing violation doctrine."

In the Ninth Circuit's view, a plaintiff can establish a continuing violation that allows recovery for claims filed outside of the statutory period in one of two ways. First, a plaintiff may show a series of related acts one or more of which are within the limitations period. Such a "serial violation" is established if the evidence indicates that the alleged acts of discrimination occurring prior to the limitations period are sufficiently related to those occurring within the limitations period. The alleged incidents, however, cannot be isolated, sporadic, or discrete. Second, a plaintiff may establish a continuing violation if he shows "a systematic policy or practice of discrimination that operated, in part, within the limitations period; a systemic violation."

To survive summary judgment under this test, Morgan had to "raise a genuine issue of disputed fact as to 1) the existence of a continuing violation, be it serial or systemic," and 2) the continuation of the violation into the limitations period. Because Morgan alleged three types of Title VII claims, namely, discrimination, hostile environment, and retaliation, the Court of Appeals considered the allegations with respect to each category of claim separately and found that the pre-limitations conduct was sufficiently related to the post-limitations conduct to invoke the continuing violation doctrine for all three. Therefore, in light of the relatedness of the incidents, the Court of Appeals found that Morgan had sufficiently presented a genuine issue of disputed fact as to whether a continuing violation existed. Because the District Court should have allowed events occurring in the pre-limitations period to be presented to the jury not merely as background information, but also for purposes of liability, the Court of Appeals reversed and remanded for a new trial.

We granted certiorari, and now reverse in part and affirm in part.

II

The Courts of Appeals have taken various approaches to the question whether acts that fall outside of the statutory time period for filing charges set forth in §706(e) are actionable under Title VII. While the lower courts have offered reasonable, albeit

---

[3]The District Court denied summary judgment to Amtrak with respect to those claims it held were timely filed. The remaining claims then proceeded to trial, where the jury returned a verdict in favor of Amtrak.

[4]The Fifth Circuit employs a multifactor test, which, among other things, takes into account: (1) whether the alleged acts involve the same type of discrimination; (2) whether the incidents are recurring or independent and isolated events; and (3) whether the earlier acts have sufficient permanency to trigger the employee's awareness of and duty to challenge the alleged violation. See *Berry v. Board of Supervisors,* 715 F.2d 971, 981 (1983).

divergent solutions, none are compelled by the text of the statute. In the context of a request to alter the timely filing requirements of Title VII, this Court has stated that "strict adherence to the procedural requirements specified by the legislature is the best guarantee of evenhanded administration of the law." *Mohasco Corp. v. Silver,* 447 U.S. 807, 826, 100 S.Ct. 2486, 65 L.Ed.2d 532 (1980). In *Mohasco,* the Court rejected arguments that strict adherence to a similar statutory time restriction[5] for filing a charge was "unfair" or that "a less literal reading of the Act would adequately effectuate the policy of deferring to state agencies." Instead, the Court noted that "[b]y choosing what are obviously quite short deadlines, Congress clearly intended to encourage the prompt processing of all charges of employment discrimination." Similarly here, our most salient source for guidance is the statutory text.

Section 706(e)(1) is a charge filing provision that "specifies with precision" the prerequisites that a plaintiff must satisfy before filing suit. *Alexander v. Gardner-Denver Co.,* 415 U.S. 36, 47, 94 S.Ct. 1011, 39 L.Ed.2d 147 (1974). An individual must file a charge within the statutory time period and serve notice upon the person against whom the charge is made. In a State that has an entity with the authority to grant or seek relief with respect to the alleged unlawful practice, an employee who initially files a grievance with that agency must file the charge with the EEOC within 300 days of the employment practice; in all other States, the charge must be filed within 180 days. A claim is time barred if it is not filed within these time limits.

For our purposes, the critical sentence of the charge filing provision is: "A charge under this section *shall be filed* within one hundred and eighty days *after the alleged unlawful employment practice occurred.*" (emphasis added). The operative terms are "shall," "after . . . occurred," and "unlawful employment practice." "[S]hall" makes the act of filing a charge within the specified time period mandatory." [O]ccurred" means that the practice took place or happened in the past.[6] The requirement, therefore, that the charge be filed "after" the practice "occurred" tells us that a litigant has up to 180 or 300 days *after* the unlawful practice happened to file a charge with the EEOC.

The critical questions, then, are: What constitutes an "unlawful employment practice" and when has that practice "occurred"? Our task is to answer these questions for both discrete discriminatory acts and hostile work environment claims. The answer varies with the practice.

A

---

[5]The Court there considered both the 300-day time limit of §706(e) and the requirement of §706(c) that, in the case of an unlawful employment practice that occurs in a State that prohibits such practices, no charge may be filed with the EEOC before the expiration of 60 days after proceedings have been commenced in the appropriate state agency unless such proceedings have been earlier terminated.

[6]In the absence of an indication to the contrary, words in a statute are assumed to bear their ordinary, contemporary, common meaning. Webster's Third New International Dictionary 1561 (1993) defines "occur" as "[t]o present itself: come to pass: take place: HAPPEN." See also Black's Law Dictionary 1080 (6th ed. 1990) (defining "[o]ccur" as "[t]o happen; . . . to take place; to arise").

We take the easier question first. A discrete retaliatory or discriminatory act "occurred" on the day that it "happened." A party, therefore, must file a charge within either 180 or 300 days of the date of the act or lose the ability to recover for it.

Morgan argues that the statute does not require the filing of a charge within 180 or 300 days of each discrete act, but that the language requires the filing of a charge within the specified number of days after an "unlawful employment *practice*." "Practice," Morgan contends, connotes an ongoing violation that can endure or recur over a period of time. In Morgan's view, the term "practice" therefore provides a statutory basis for the Ninth Circuit's continuing violation doctrine.[7] This argument is unavailing, however, given that §703 explains in great detail the sorts of actions that qualify as unlawful employment practices and includes among such practices numerous discrete acts. See e.g., §703(a) ("It shall be an unlawful employment practice for an employer — (1) to fail or refuse to hire or to discharge any individual, or otherwise to discriminate against any individual with respect to his compensation, terms, conditions, or privileges of employment, because of such individual's race, color, religion, sex, or national origin . . ."). There is simply no indication that the term "practice" converts related discrete acts into a single unlawful practice for the purposes of timely filing. Cf. §707(a) (providing that the Attorney General may bring a civil action in "pattern or practice" cases).

We have repeatedly interpreted the term "practice" to apply to a discrete act or single "occurrence," even when it has a connection to other acts. For example, in Electrical Workers v. Robbins & Myers, Inc., 429 U.S. 229, 234, 97 S.Ct. 441, 50 L.Ed.2d 427 (1976), an employee asserted that his complaint was timely filed because the date "the alleged unlawful employment practice occurred" was the date after the conclusion of a grievance arbitration procedure, rather than the earlier date of his discharge. The discharge, he contended, was "tentative" and "nonfinal" until the grievance and arbitration procedure ended. Not so, the Court concluded, because the discriminatory act occurred on the date of discharge, the date that the parties understood the termination to be final. Similarly, in *Bazemore v. Friday*, 478 U.S. 385, 106 S.Ct. 3000, 92 L.Ed.2d 315 (1986) (per curiam), a pattern-or-practice case, when considering a discriminatory salary structure, the Court noted that although the salary discrimination began prior to the date that the act was actionable under Title VII, "[e]ach week's paycheck that deliver[ed] less to a black than to a similarly situated white is a wrong actionable under Title VII."

This Court has also held that discrete acts that fall within the statutory time period do not make timely acts that fall outside the time period. In *United Air Lines, Inc. v. Evans*, 431 U.S. 553, 97 S.Ct. 1885, 52 L.Ed.2d 571 (1977), United forced Evans to

---

[7]Morgan also argues that the EEOC's discussion of continuing violations in its Compliance Manual, which provides that certain serial violations and systemic violations constitute continuing violations that allow relief for untimely events, as well as the positions the EEOC has taken in prior briefs, warrant deference under Chevron U.S.A. Inc. v. Natural Resources Defense Council, Inc., 467 U.S. 837 (1984). But we have held that the EEOC's interpretive guidelines do not receive Chevron deference. See EEOC v. Arabian American Oil Co., 499 U.S. 244, 257 (1991). Such interpretations are "entitled to respect" under our decision in Skidmore v. Swift & Co., 323 U.S. 134, 140 (1944), but only to the extent that those interpretations have the "power to persuade." Christensen v. Harris County, 529 U.S. 576, 587 (2000).

resign after she married because of its policy against married female flight attendants. Although Evans failed to file a timely charge following her initial separation, she nonetheless claimed that United was guilty of a present, continuing violation of Title VII because its seniority system failed to give her credit for her prior service once she was re-hired. The Court disagreed, concluding that "United was entitled to treat [Evans' resignation] as lawful after [she] failed to file a charge of discrimination within the" charge filing period then allowed by the statute. At the same time, however, the Court noted that "[i]t may constitute relevant background evidence in a proceeding in which the status of a current practice is at issue." The emphasis, however, "should not be placed on mere continuity" but on "whether any present *violation* exist[ed]." (emphasis in original).

In *Delaware State College v. Ricks*, 449 U.S. 250, 101 S.Ct. 498, 66 L.Ed.2d 431 (1980), the Court evaluated the timeliness of an EEOC complaint filed by a professor who argued that he had been denied academic tenure because of his national origin. Following the decision to deny tenure, the employer offered him a terminal" contract to teach an additional year. Claiming, in effect, a "continuing violation," the professor argued that the time period did not begin to run until his actual termination. The Court rejected this argument: "Mere continuity of employment, without more, is insufficient to prolong the life of a cause of action for employment discrimination." In order for the time period to commence with the discharge, "he should have identified the alleged discriminatory acts that continued until, or occurred at the time of, the actual termination of his employment." He could not use a termination that fell within the limitations period to pull in the time-barred discriminatory act. Nor could a time-barred act justify filing a charge concerning a termination that was not independently discriminatory.

We derive several principles from these cases. First, discrete discriminatory acts are not actionable if time barred, even when they are related to acts alleged in timely filed charges. Each discrete discriminatory act starts a new clock for filing charges alleging that act. The charge, therefore, must be filed within the 180- or 300-day time period after the discrete discriminatory act occurred. The existence of past acts and the employee's prior knowledge of their occurrence, however, does not bar employees from filing charges about related discrete acts so long as the acts are independently discriminatory and charges addressing those acts are themselves timely filed. Nor does the statute bar an employee from using the prior acts as background evidence in support of a timely claim.

As we have held, however, this time period for filing a charge is subject to equitable doctrines such as tolling or estoppel. See *Zipes v. Trans World Airlines*, Inc., 455 U.S. 385, 393, 102 S.Ct. 1127, 71 L.Ed.2d 234 (1982) ("We hold that filing a timely charge of discrimination with the EEOC is not a jurisdictional prerequisite to suit in federal court, but a requirement that, like a statute of limitations, is subject to waiver, estoppel, and equitable tolling"). Courts may evaluate whether it would be proper to apply such doctrines, although they are to be applied sparingly. See *Baldwin County Welcome Center v. Brown*, 466 U.S. 147, 152, 104 S.Ct. 1723, 80 L.Ed.2d 196 (1984) (per curiam) ("Procedural requirements established by Congress for gaining access to the federal courts are not to be disregarded by courts out of a vague sympathy for particular litigants").

The Court of Appeals applied the continuing violations doctrine to what it termed "serial violations," holding that so long as one act falls within the charge filing period, discriminatory and retaliatory acts that are plausibly or sufficiently related to that act may also be considered for the purposes of liability. With respect to this holding, therefore, we reverse.

Discrete acts such as termination, failure to promote, denial of transfer, or refusal to hire are easy to identify. Each incident of discrimination and each retaliatory adverse employment decision constitutes a separate actionable "unlawful employment practice." Morgan can only file a charge to cover discrete acts that "occurred" within the appropriate time period.[8] While Morgan alleged that he suffered from numerous discriminatory and retaliatory acts from the date that he was hired through March 3, 1995, the date that he was fired, only incidents that took place within the timely filing period are actionable. Because Morgan first filed his charge with an appropriate state agency, only those acts that occurred 300 days before February 27, 1995, the day that Morgan filed his charge, are actionable. During that time period, Morgan contends that he was wrongfully suspended and charged with a violation of Amtrak's "Rule L" for insubordination while failing to complete work assigned to him, denied training, and falsely accused of threatening a manager.[9] All prior discrete discriminatory acts are untimely filed and no longer actionable.[10]

B

Hostile environment claims are different in kind from discrete acts. Their very nature involves repeated conduct. The "unlawful employment practice" therefore cannot be said to occur on any particular day. It occurs over a series of days or perhaps years and, in direct contrast to discrete acts, a single act of harassment may not be actionable on its own. Such claims are based on the cumulative affect of individual acts.

* * *

In determining whether an actionable hostile work environment claim exists, we look to all the circumstances including the frequency of the discriminatory conduct; its severity; whether it is physically threatening or humiliating, or a mere offensive

---

[8]Because the Court of Appeals held that the "discrete acts" were actionable as part of a continuing violation, there was no need for it to further contemplate when the time period began to run for each act. The District Court noted that "Morgan believed that he was being discriminated against at the time that all of these acts occurred." There may be circumstances where it will be difficult to determine when the time period should begin to run. One issue that may arise in such circumstances is whether the time begins to run when the injury occurs as opposed to when the injury reasonably should have been discovered. But this case presents no occasion to resolve that issue.

[9]The final alleged discriminatory act, he contends, led to his termination on March 3, 1995. Morgan alleges that after the manager reported that Morgan had threatened him, he was ordered into a supervisor's office. Then, after he asked for union representation or the presence of a co-worker as a witness, the supervisor denied both, ordered everyone out of the office, and yelled at Morgan to get his "black ass" into the office. Morgan refused and went home. He was subsequently suspended and charged with violations of two company rules and, following an investigatory hearing, terminated.

[10]We have no occasion here to consider the timely filing question with respect to "pattern-or-practice" claims brought by private litigants as none are at issue here.

utterance; and whether it unreasonably interferes with an employee's work performance. To assess whether a court may, for the purposes of determining liability, review all such conduct, including those acts that occur outside the filing period, we again look to the statute. It provides that a charge must be filed within 180 or 300 days "after the alleged unlawful employment practice occurred." A hostile work environment claim is comprised of a series of separate acts that collectively constitute one "unlawful employment practice." §706(e)(1). The timely filing provision only requires that a Title VII plaintiff file a charge within a certain number of days after the unlawful practice happened. It does not matter, for purposes of the statute, that some of the component acts of the hostile work environment fall outside the statutory time period. Provided that an act contributing to the claim occurs within the filing period, the entire time period of the hostile environment may be considered by a court for the purposes of determining liability.[11]

That act need not, however, be the last act. As long as the employer has engaged in enough activity to make out an actionable hostile environment claim, an unlawful employment practice has "occurred," even if it is still occurring. Subsequent events, however, may still be part of the one hostile work environment claim and a charge may be filed at a later date and still encompass the whole.

It is precisely because the entire hostile work environment encompasses a single unlawful employment practice that we do not hold, as have some of the Circuits, that the plaintiff may not base a suit on individual acts that occurred outside the statute of limitations unless it would have been unreasonable to expect the plaintiff to sue before the statute ran on such conduct. The statute does not separate individual acts that are part of the hostile environment claim from the whole for the purposes of timely filing and liability. And the statute does not contain a requirement that the employee file a charge prior to 180 or 300 days "after" the single unlawful practice "occurred." Given, therefore, that the incidents comprising a hostile work environment are part of one unlawful employment practice, the employer may be liable for all acts that are part of this single claim. In order for the charge to be timely, the employee need only file a charge within 180 or 300 days of any act that is part of the hostile work environment.

The following scenarios illustrate our point: (1) Acts on days 1-400 create a hostile work environment. The employee files the charge on day 401. Can the employee recover for that part of the hostile work environment that occurred in the first 100 days? (2) Acts contribute to a hostile environment on days 1-100 and on day 401, but there are no acts between days 101-400. Can the act occurring on day 401 pull the other acts in for the purposes of liability? In truth, all other things being equal, there is little difference between the two scenarios as a hostile environment constitutes one "unlawful employment practice" and it does not matter whether nothing occurred within the intervening 301 days so long as each act is part of the whole. Nor, if

---

[11]Amtrak argues that recovery for conduct taking place outside the time period for filing a timely charge should be available only in hostile environment cases where the plaintiff reasonably did not know such conduct was discriminatory or where the discriminatory nature of such conduct is recognized as discriminatory only in light of later events. The * * * Seventh Circuit adopted this approach in *Galloway*. Although we reject the test proposed by petitioner, other avenues of relief are available to employers.

sufficient activity occurred by day 100 to make out a claim, does it matter that the employee knows on that day that an actionable claim happened; on day 401 all incidents are still part of the same claim. On the other hand, if an act on day 401 had no relation to the acts between days 1-100, or for some other reason, such as certain intervening action by the employer, was no longer part of the same hostile environment claim, then the employee can not recover for the previous acts, at least not by reference to the day 401 act.

Our conclusion with respect to the incidents that may be considered for the purposes of liability is reinforced by the fact that the statute in no way bars a plaintiff from recovering damages for that portion of the hostile environment that falls outside the period for filing a timely charge. Morgan correctly notes that the timeliness requirement does not dictate the amount of recoverable damages. It is but one in a series of provisions requiring that the parties take action within specified time periods, see, e.g., §§706(b), (c), (d), none of which function as specific limitations on damages.

Explicit limitations on damages are found elsewhere in the statute. Section 1981a(b)(3), for example, details specific limitations on compensatory and punitive damages. Likewise, §706(g)(1) allows for recovery of backpay liability for up to two years prior to the filing of the charge. If Congress intended to limit liability to conduct occurring in the period within which the party must file the charge, it seems unlikely that Congress would have allowed recovery for two years of backpay. And the fact that Congress expressly limited the amount of recoverable damages elsewhere to a particular time period indicates that the timely filing provision was not meant to serve as a specific limitation either on damages or the conduct that may be considered for the purposes of one actionable hostile work environment claim.

It also makes little sense to limit the assessment of liability in a hostile work environment claim to the conduct that falls within the 180- or 300-day period given that this time period varies based on whether the violation occurs in a state or political subdivision that has an agency with authority to grant or seek relief. It is important to remember that the statute requires that a Title VII plaintiff must wait 60 days after proceedings have commenced under state or local law to file a charge with the EEOC, unless such proceedings have earlier terminated. In such circumstances, however, the charge must still be filed within 300 days of the occurrence. See *Mohasco*. The extended time period for parties who first file such charges in a State or locality ensures that employees are neither time barred from later filing their charges with the EEOC nor dissuaded from first filing with a state agency. The history identifies only one reason for treating workers in deferral States differently from workers in other States: to give state agencies an opportunity to redress the evil at which the federal legislation was aimed, and to avoid federal intervention unless its need was demonstrated. Surely, therefore, we cannot import such a limiting principle into the provision where its effect would be to make the reviewable time period for liability dependent upon whether an employee lives in a State that has its own remedial scheme.[12]

---

[12]The same concern is not implicated with discrete acts given that, unlike hostile work environment claims, liability there does not depend upon proof of repeated conduct extending over a period of time.

Simply put, §706(e)(1) is a provision specifying when a charge is timely filed and only has the consequence of limiting liability because filing a timely charge is a prerequisite to having an actionable claim. A court's task is to determine whether the acts about which an employee complains are part of the same actionable hostile work environment practice, and if so, whether any act falls within the statutory time period.

With respect to Morgan's hostile environment claim, the Court of Appeals concluded that "the pre- and post-limitations period incidents involve[d] the same type of employment actions, occurred relatively frequently, and were perpetrated by the same managers." To support his claims of a hostile environment, Morgan presented evidence from a number of other employees that managers made racial jokes, performed racially derogatory acts, made negative comments regarding the capacity of blacks to be supervisors, and used various racial epithets. Although many of the acts upon which his claim depends occurred outside the 300 day filing period, we cannot say that they are not part of the same actionable hostile environment claim.[13] On this point, we affirm.

C

Our holding does not leave employers defenseless against employees who bring hostile work environment claims that extend over long periods of time. Employers have recourse when a plaintiff unreasonably delays filing a charge. As noted in *Zipes,* the filing period is not a jurisdictional prerequisite to filing a Title VII suit. Rather, it is a requirement subject to waiver, estoppel, and equitable tolling "when equity so requires." These equitable doctrines allow us to honor Title VII's remedial purpose "without negating the particular purpose of the filing requirement, to give prompt notice to the employer." *Ibid.*

This Court previously noted that despite the procedural protections of the statute "a defendant in a Title VII enforcement action might still be significantly handicapped in making his defense because of an inordinate EEOC delay in filing the action after exhausting its conciliation efforts." *Occidental Life Ins. Co. of Cal. v. EEOC*, 432 U.S. 355, 373, 97 S.Ct. 2447, 53 L.Ed.2d 402 (1977). The same is true when the delay is caused by the employee, rather than by the EEOC. In such cases, the federal courts have the discretionary power "to locate a just result in light of the circumstances peculiar to the case." *Albemarle Paper Co. v. Moody*, 422 U.S. 405, 424-425, 95 S.Ct. 2362, 45 L.Ed.2d 280 (1975).

In addition to other equitable defenses, therefore, an employer may raise a laches defense, which bars a plaintiff from maintaining a suit if he unreasonably delays in filing a suit and as a result harms the defendant. This defense requires proof of (1) lack of diligence by the party against whom the defense is asserted, and (2) prejudice to the party asserting the defense. We do not address questions here such as how and how much prejudice must be shown or what consequences follow if laches is established.[14] We observe only that employers may raise various defenses in the face of unreasonable and prejudicial delay.

---

[13]We make no judgment, however, on the merits of Morgan's claim.

[14]Nor do we have occasion to consider whether the laches defense may be asserted against the EEOC, even though traditionally the doctrine may not be applied against the sovereign. We

III

We conclude that a Title VII plaintiff raising claims of discrete discriminatory or retaliatory acts must file his charge within the appropriate time period — 180 or 300 days — set forth in §706(e)(1). A charge alleging a hostile work environment claim, however, will not be time barred so long as all acts which constitute the claim are part of the same unlawful employment practice and at least one act falls within the time period. Neither holding, however, precludes a court from applying equitable doctrines that may toll or limit the time period.

For the foregoing reasons, the Court of Appeals' judgment is affirmed in part and reversed in part, and the case is remanded for further proceedings consistent with this opinion.

JUSTICE O'CONNOR, with whom THE CHIEF JUSTICE joins, with whom JUSTICE SCALIA and JUSTICE KENNEDY join as to all but Part I, and with whom JUSTICE BREYER joins as to Part I, concurring in part and dissenting in part.

I join Part IIA of the Court's opinion because I agree that Title VII suits based on discrete discriminatory acts are time barred when the plaintiff fails to file a charge with the Equal Employment Opportunity Commission within the 180- or 300-day time period designated in the statute. I dissent from the remainder of the Court's opinion, however, because I believe a similar restriction applies to all types of Title VII suits, including those based on aclaim that a plaintiff has been subjected to a hostile work environment.

I

The Court today holds that, for discrete discriminatory acts, §706(e)(1) serves as a form of statute of limitations, barring recovery for actions that take place outside the charge-filing period. The Court acknowledges, however, that this limitation period may be adjusted by equitable doctrines. Like the Court, I see no need to resolve fully the application of the discovery rule to claims based on discrete discriminatory acts. I believe, however, that some version of the discovery rule applies to discrete-act claims. In my view, therefore, the charge-filing period precludes recovery based on discrete actions that occurred more than 180 or 300 days after the employee had, or should have had, notice of the discriminatory act.

II

Unlike the Court, I would hold that §706(e)(1) serves as a limitations period for all actions brought under Title VII, including those alleging discrimination by being subjected to a hostile working environment. Section 706(e)(1) * * * draws no distinction between claims based on discrete acts and claims based on hostile work environments. If a plaintiff fails to file a charge within that time period, liability may not be assessed, and damages must not be awarded, for that part of the hostile environment that occurred outside the charge-filing period.

---

note, however, that in Occidental there seemed to be general agreement that courts can provide relief to defendants against inordinate delay by the EEOC.

The Court's conclusion to the contrary is based on a characterization of hostile environment discrimination as composing a single claim based on conduct potentially spanning several years. I agree with this characterization. I disagree, however, with the Court's conclusion that, because of the cumulative nature of the violation, if any conduct forming part of the violation occurs within the charge-filing period, liability can be proved and damages can be collected for the entire hostile environment. Although a hostile environment claim is, by its nature, a general atmosphere of discrimination not completely reducible to particular discriminatory acts, each day the worker is exposed to the hostile environment may still be treated as a separate "occurrence" and claims based on some of those occurrences forfeited. In other words, a hostile environment is a form of discrimination that occurs every day; some of those daily occurrences may be time barred, while others are not.

The Court's treatment of hostile environment claims as constituting a single occurrence leads to results that contradict the policies behind §706(e)(1). Consider an employee who has been subjected to a hostile work environment for 10 years. Under the Court's approach, such an employee may, subject only to the uncertain restrictions of equity, sleep on his or her rights for a decade, bringing suit only in year 11 based in part on actions for which a charge could, and should, have been filed many years previously in accordance with the statutory mandate. §706(e)(1). Allowing suits based on such remote actions raises all of the problems that statutes of limitations and other similar time limitations are designed to address:

> "[P]romot[ing] justice by preventing surprises through the revival of claims that have been allowed to slumber until evidence has been lost, memories have faded, and witnesses have disappeared. The theory is that even if one has a just claim it is unjust not to put the adversary on notice to defend within the period of limitation and that the right to be free of stale claims in time comes to prevail over the right to prosecute them." *Railroad Telegraphers v. Railway Express Agency, Inc.*, 321 U.S. 342, 348-349, 64 S.Ct. 582, 88 L.Ed.2d 788 (1944)

Although the statute's 2-year limitation on backpay partially addresses these concerns, under the Court's view, liability may still be assessed and other sorts of damages (such as damages for pain and suffering) awarded based on long-past occurrences. An employer asked to defend such stale actions, when a suit challenging them could have been brought in a much more timely manner, may rightly complain of precisely this sort of unjust treatment.

The Court is correct that nothing in §706(e)(1) can be read as imposing a cap on damages. But reading §706(e)(1) to require that a plaintiff bring an EEOC charge within 180 or 300 days of the time individual incidents comprising a hostile work environment occur or lose the ability to bring suit based on those incidents is not equivalent to transforming it into a damages cap. The limitation is one on *liability*. The restriction on damages for occurrences too far in the past follows only as an obvious consequence.

Nor, as the Court claims, would reading §706(e)(1) as limiting hostile environment claims conflict with Title VII's allowance of backpay liability for a period of up to two years prior to a charge's filing. Because of the potential adjustments to the charge-filing period based on equitable doctrines, two years of backpay will sometimes be available even under my view. For example, two years of backpay may be available where an employee failed to file a timely charge with the EEOC because his employer deceived him in order to conceal the existence of a discrimination claim.

The Court also argues that it makes "little sense" to base relief on the charge-filing period, since that period varies depending on whether the State or political subdivision where the violation occurs has designated an agency to deal with such claims. The Court concludes that "[s]urely . . . we cannot import such a limiting principle . . . where its effect would be to make the reviewable time period for liability dependent upon whether an employee lives in a State that has its own remedial scheme." But this is precisely the principle the Court has adopted for discrete discriminatory acts — depending on where a plaintiff lives, the time period changes as to which discrete discriminatory actions may be reviewed. The justification for the variation is the same for discrete discriminatory acts as it is for claims based on hostile work environments. The longer time period is intended to give States and other political subdivisions time to review claims themselves, if they have a mechanism for doing so. The same rationale applies to review of the daily occurrences that make up a part of a hostile environment claim.

* * *

I would, therefore, reverse the judgment of the Court of Appeals in its entirety.

NOTES AND PROBLEMS FOR DISCUSSION

1. The continuing violation doctrine addresses three different, though related, questions: (1) Was the EEOC charge timely? (2) Can liability be based on events that occurred outside of the limitation period? (3) How far back in the past may the plaintiff go in seeking relief for unlawful conduct? In *Morgan*, the Court concluded that in the context of hostile environment claims, the continuing violation doctrine enables the plaintiff to both establish liability and obtain relief for discriminatory acts that occurred well outside of the EEOC charging period. The charge is timely with respect to the entire course of hostile environment so long as one incident of harassment occurred within the filing period. Unlike cases involving a "discrete violation," a hostile work environment, according to the Court, is the consequence of a succession of harassing acts, each of which might not be actionable on its own.

In *Ledbetter*, a 5-4 Supreme Court rejected the plaintiff's request to treat wage discrimination claims like hostile environment allegations. Wage discrimination cases, the majority reasoned, involve only a series of actionable wrongs and so a timely charge must be filed with respect to each discrete paysetting decision. The four dissenters, on the other hand, would have extended *Morgan* to pay discrimination claims. Given the secrecy in most workplaces about salaries, they reasoned, many employees initially would have no idea that they had received a lower raise than others; the discriminatory motivation might not be ascertainable for years. As previously mentioned, however, Congress reversed the Court's ruling in *Ledbetter* by passing the Fair Pay Act, which amended Title VII, the ADEA, the ADA and the Rehabilitation Act to clarify that an unlawful employment practice occurs, with respect to compensation claims, when the discriminatory compensation decision is initially adopted, when an individual initially becomes subject to the discriminatory compensation decision, or when an individual is affected by the application of the discriminatory compensation decision "including each time wages, benefits, or other compensation is paid".

The Court's rejection in *Morgan* and *Ledbetter* of the "serial violation" version of the continuing violation doctrine places, hoever, left unanswered whether that doctrine applies to "pattern or practice" claims alleging systemic discrimination when manifestations of that pattern extend beyond the filing period of the class representative's charge. The impact of *Morgan* on this question is discussed in Chapter 6, *infra.*

2.   The fact that discrete acts of discrimination outside of the limitations period are not independently actionable does not mean that *evidence* of such actions is inadmissible. As the Court noted in *Morgan*, such prior acts may be offered "as background evidence in support of a timely claim." In LYONS v. ENGLAND, 307 F.3d 1092 (9th Cir. 2002), civilian Navy employees alleged that the Navy had denied them favorable work assignments and job promotions because of their race over a period of several consecutive years . The plaintiffs failed to complain to the Navy's EEO counselor (the equivalent for federal employees of filing an EEOC charge) until the filing period for most of the allegedly discriminatory actions had expired. After determining, per *Morgan*, that the pre-limitation claims were not continuing violations, and thus were time-barred, the court ruled that cumulative evidence of these time barred claims was relevant and admissible on the question of whether the actionable denials of promotions were race-based. Does this mean that all prior acts of discrimination, no matter how far outside of the applicable limitations period, can be used as evidence? Given the broad definition of "relevance," what evidence of past discrimination would not be admissible?

3.   As noted previously, the Supreme Court in *Zipes* treated the requirement of a timely filed EEOC charge as functionally equivalent to a statute of limitations. A claim that the charge was not timely filed is, therefore, an affirmative defense as to which the employer bears the burden of persuasion. Prior to *Morgan*, the continuing violation doctrine was commonly treated as an equitable exception to the timely filing requirement, which meant that the burden of proving its applicability fell on the plaintiff seeking to invoke the exception. *See, e.g.*, Klein v. McGowan, 198 F.3d 705, 709 (8th Cir. 1999). *Morgan* does not address this frequently crucial burden of proof issue. In WILSON v. BRINKER INTERNATIONAL., INC., 382 F.3d 765 (8th Cir. 2004), the plaintiff alleged that a fellow employee had subjected her to a sexually hostile work environment. Although most of the incidents constituting the hostile environment had occurred outside of the filing period, the plaintiff claimed that at least one incident had occurred within 300 days of her EEOC charge, a charge that the defendant disputed. Over the plaintiff's objection, the trial judge submitted the timeliness issue to the jury with an instruction that the plaintiff bore the burden of proving that at least one incident occurred within the statutory period. The jury returned a verdict in favor of the plaintiff. But in response to a special interrogatory asking whether "any act of harassment" occurred within the filing period, the jury responded "no." The trial judge, concluding that the plaintiff's claim was time barred, entered judgment as a matter of law for the defendant. On appeal, the plaintiff argued that whether the action was time-barred was an ordinary affirmative defense as to which the defendant bore the burden of persuasion. The Eighth Circuit disagreed, ruling that even if the question was unresolved by *Morgan*, the trial judge had followed existing circuit precedent.

4. THE RELATION BETWEEN THE SUBSTANCE OF THE EEOC CHARGE AND SUIT

Clark v. Kraft Foods, Inc.

United States Court of Appeals, Fifth Circuit, 1994.
18 F.3d 1278.

POLITZ, Chief Judge.

Vonda Sue Brehm Clark appeals an adverse summary judgment in her Title VII sex-discrimination suit against Kraft General Foods. We vacate and remand.

Background

Clark was fired in December 1988 after being employed as a line technician by Kraft for several years. Shortly thereafter she filed a charge of discrimination with the Equal Employment Opportunity Commission, the primary thrust of which was an allegation of sexual harassment and retaliation for grievances she filed in response to that harassment. In 1991 Clark filed the instant action, claiming that she was pressured to take a lower paying position and was ultimately fired because of her gender. The sexual harassment claim, the dominant theme in her EEOC complaint, was not advanced, apparently because it was time-barred.

Kraft moved for summary judgment asserting that Clark had not raised her disparate treatment claim before the EEOC and, therefore, had not exhausted administrative remedies. The magistrate judge accepted Kraft's challenge and recommended that summary judgment be granted because the "disparate treatment claim * * * was not presented to the EEOC, nor was it within the scope of the EEOC investigation of plaintiff's charge." That recommendation was adopted without comment by the district court. Clark timely appealed.

Analysis

Clark maintains that she properly raised the disparate treatment issue before the EEOC. Kraft counters that although Clark's EEOC complaint included claims of sexual harassment and retaliation for that harassment, it did not include a separate allegation of disparate treatment on the basis of gender. We review the district court's grant of summary judgment de novo.

As a jurisdictional predicate Clark had to exhaust EEOC remedies for the sex-based discrimination advanced in this action.[4] * * * [O]ur sole inquiry is whether the disparate treatment claim pursued in the present litigation was advanced before the EEOC. We decide that question in the affirmative because the EEOC investigation of

---

[4]We note, however, that this proposition does not preclude Clark from offering more than one basis of discrimination in a single EEOC claim, or from relying on a single set of facts in support of more than one basis.

that claim was a reasonable consequence of Clark's EEOC complaint and supporting documentation.

We look first to Clark's original "Charge of Discrimination." This document sets forth several claims, the most important of which are: "1. I was harassed because of my sex, female. 2. I was sexually harassed." Viewed in isolation the first complaint reasonably could be read as either an allegation of sexual harassment or as a claim that she had been persecuted in her job because of her gender. These points, however, were presented in tandem. Were we to read Clark's first claim as simply alleging sexual harassment, we would render her second claim redundant. Long established principles of interpretation and Clark's pro se status at the time of her EEOC complaint[7] militate against such a construction of her filing.

We conclude that Clark's statements to the EEOC presented a sufficient predicate upon which one reasonably would expect the agency to investigate a disparate treatment claim. Her EEOC affidavit explained that females on her line "were forced to bust off their job and take lower bracket pay jobs." Her EEOC Discharge Questionnaire expanded on this point, noting that "due to the cut in Matinence [sic] Dept. they wanted the women off the line operators jobs to place the xtra [sic] men."[8] These statements at least raise inferences supporting Clark's claim of gender-based harassment. Her allegation that women on her line were removed to lower paying jobs to make room for men should have given the EEOC investigators reasonable cause to examine whether she was pressured to do the same or whether her ultimate firing resulted from systematic replacement of any female in her position.

Despite its present position on appeal, at the time of Clark's EEOC complaint Kraft apparently considered Clark to be claiming disparate treatment on the basis of gender. In answer to the EEOC's request for information Kraft denied the existence of any "evidence that female employees are more frequently terminated or otherwise more harshly treated in the disciplinary process." Kraft concluded its response by noting that Clark's termination "had nothing to do with her sex." If Clark had presented no colorable allegation of disparate treatment that reaction would have been a non sequitur.

Albeit mindful that the actual scope of an EEOC investigation does not determine whether a claim is exhausted, we are also mindful that investigation of a particular claim creates a strong inference that such a claim was presented. In the instant case the EEOC investigated Clark's gender-based disparate treatment claim. Its determination expressly mentions a gender-based harassment claim which it treats as distinct from claims of sexual harassment or retaliation for reporting such harassment. The first half of the EEOC report deals exclusively with Clark's "sexual harassment allegation." The determination then separately addresses "the Charging Party's allegation that she was harassed because of her sex, and in retaliation for complaining about sexual harassment." EEOC inquiries discussed thereunder include the question whether males and other females in Clark's position received comparable work

---

[7]Fellows, 701 F.2d at 451 ("liberal construction [is] accorded EEOC charges, especially those by unlawyered complainants").

[8]Kraft suggests that Clark, having refused to "bust off" her job, cannot claim this episode as discrimination. This argument ignores the fact that she was fired shortly after her refusal.

assignments and duties. These questions, like Kraft's representation that males and females are treated equally, manifestly are consistent with an EEOC inquiry into a gender-based disparate treatment claim. The EEOC determination concluded that "the investigation discovered no evidence that Charging Party was asked to resign and was subsequently discharged because of her sex, female, or because she complained of sexual harassment."

It is apparent that sexual harassment and retaliation for reporting sexual harassment were Clark's principal allegations at the administrative stage. It is also apparent in the statements of Clark, Kraft, and the EEOC that Clark raised a gender-based disparate treatment claim sufficient to prompt an EEOC investigation. Suggesting no particular resolution on the merits, we conclude that administrative remedies for the instant complaint of gender-based disparate treatment were exhausted and that Clark's claim is properly before the district court.

The district court's judgment in favor of Kraft is therefore VACATED and the cause is REMANDED for further proceedings consistent herewith.

NOTES AND PROBLEMS FOR DISCUSSION

1. Prior to issuing its ruling in *Clark,* the Fifth Circuit had decided SANCHEZ v. STANDARD BRANDS, INC., 431 F.2d 455 (5th Cir. 1970), where it had offered this explanation for its decision to tie the permissible scope of a Title suit to the scope of the EEOC's investigation rather than to the precise terminology in the EEOC charge:

> [T]he civil action is much more intimately related to the EEOC investigation than to the words of the charge which originally triggered the investigation. Within this statutory scheme, it is only logical to limit the permissible scope of the civil action to the scope of the EEOC investigation which can reasonably be expected to grow out of the charge of discrimination.

431 F.2d at 466. Although the precise wording of the standard varies among the circuits, the essence of the *Sanchez* "scope of investigation" doctrine has been adopted by the overwhelming majority of appellate courts. *See, e.g.*, Stuart v. General Motors Corp., 217 F.3d 621, 631 (8th Cir. 2000) ("the breadth of the civil suit is . . . as broad as the scope of any investigation that reasonably could have been expected to result from the initial charge of discrimination"). Nevertheless, the circuits have diverged in the manner in which they apply the *Sanchez* standard. While they all require a demonstration of some kind of relationship between the allegations in the charge and those set forth in the complaint, the courts differ on how they treat situations where the plaintiff relates different or new incidents of discrimination or ane entirely new theory in the complaint. *See, e.g.*, Ang v. Procter & Gamble Co., 932 F.2d 540 (6th Cir. 1991) (an EEOC charge limited to national origin discrimination could not encompass a claim of race discrimination); Pacheco v. Mineta, 448 F.3d 783 (5th Cir.2006) (EEOC charge alleging claim of intentional discrimination on the basis of national origin did not encompass a suit setting forth a disproportionate impact-based claim of national origin discrimination; a charge alleging intentional discrimination could not reasonably be expected to trigger an investigation into impact-based discrimination). *But see* Reiter v. Center Consol. Sch. Dist., 618 F.Supp. 1458 (D. Co. 1985) (the plaintiff's failure to allege national origin discrimination in her EEOC charge was irrelevant since the state FEP agency determined that she had been the victim of discrimination

because of her connection with Hispanic community and had notified the employer of that finding).

Contrary to the suggestion in *Clark,* many courts have held that harassment is sufficiently distinct from other forms of discrimination that it must be explicitly alleged in the EEOC charge in order to be claimed in the law suit. *See, e.g.,* Park v. Howard Univ., 71 F.3d 904, 907-08 (D.C. Cir. 1995), cert. denied, 519 U.S. 811, 117 S.Ct. 57, 136 L.Ed.2d 20 (1996) (EEOC charge alleging national origin discrimination in filling promotions did not express or even hint at national origin hostile work environment claim). But in GREEN v. ELIXIR INDUSTRIES, INC., 407 F.3d 1163, 1168 (11th Cir. 2005), after granting summary judgment to the defendant on the plaintiff's racial harassment claim because the EEOC charge alleged only a discriminatory discharge, the trial judge permitted the admission at trial of evidence relating to the racial harassment. Confronted with a substantial record regarding the nature of the harassment, the Eleventh Circuit reversed the grant of summary judgment on the harassment claim, finding that the facts involving the harassment and termination claims were "inextricably intertwined" and that the employer had or should have had ample notice of the racially hostile working conditions at its plant. The court also emphasized the unfairness of penalizing a lay person for his inability to parse legal claims in an EEOC charge. No lay plaintiff, the court reasoned, should be expected to understand "the distinctive legal nuances between claims that constitute hostile work environment discrimination and those instead which constitute wrongful termination based on race."

2. Suppose a plaintiff files an EEOC charge alleging discriminatory denial of a promotion. Within days of the filing of that charge, the plaintiff is discharged. After receiving his right-to-sue letter on the promotion claim, the plaintiff files suit alleging both a promotion claim under §703(a) and a claim of retaliation under §704(a). Is the plaintiff's failure to have filed an amended or separate EEOC charge claiming retaliation fatal to his inclusion of the retaliation count in his lawsuit? The circuit courts are split on the question. Some conclude that the *Sanchez* "reasonable scope of the EEOC investigation" standard is met where the plaintiff alleges that he was retaliated against for filing that EEOC charge. These courts do not require the plaintiff to file a separate EEOC charge of retaliation in order to assert the retaliation claim in the subsequent lawsuit. They reason that to require a plaintiff to file a second charge would add a technical barrier to the plaintiff's enforcement of her rights and would reward the employer for the very conduct made unlawful by §704. *See, e.g.,* Clockedile v. N. H. Dept. of Corr., 245 F.3d 1 (1st Cir. 2001). This rule has even been applied to cases where the alleged retaliation occurred after the final disposition of the underlying charge. *See* Jones v. Calvert Group, Ltd., 551 F.3d 297 (4th Cir. 2009). On the other hand, some circuits have ruled that, as a matter of law, a retaliation claim is not sufficiently related to the underlying charge to avoid the necessity for a separate EEOC filing. This argument is based, at least in part, on an application of the Supreme Court's ruling in *National R.R. v. Morgan* that an "unlawful employment practice" for the purposes of triggering the EEOC filing period consists of a discrete act of discrimination. These courts reason that the requirement of a separate filing for each discrete act of discrimination applies to incidents that occurred both before (*Morgan* context) and after (retaliation context) the filing of the EEOC charge. *See, e.g.,* Richter v. Advance Auto Parts Inc., 686 F.3d 847 (8th Cir. 2012)

What if, however, the aggrieved had filed an EEOC charge alleging retaliation for filing a prior charge and that alleged retaliation was alleged to consist of denying the plaintiff a promotion and giving her a negative performance evaluation? Subsequently, the plaintiff was terminated. When she thereafter filed suit challenging the retaliatory termination, the defense sought a dismissal on the ground that the suit challenging retaliatory termination did not arise out of the EEOC retaliation charge (because it referred only to the promotion denial and negative performance review). How should the court rule? *See* Jones v. Calvert Group, Ltd., 551 F.3d 297 (4th Cir. 2009) (the alleged retaliatory termination was a predictable culmination and continuation of the retaliatory treatment alleged in the EEOC charge and therefore the termination claim was reasonably related to the retaliation charge).

3. The courts' emphasis on the kind of administrative investigation that reasonably could grow out of a charge is somewhat ironic because only a relatively small percentage of all charges are administratively resolved by the agency, and very few other charges receive anything like an effective investigation. In light of this observation, what sense does it make to dismiss a claim, which very likely would not have been investigated in any event, because a hypothetical agency investigation of the plaintiff's charge might not have included the claim? The Ninth Circuit has responded to this concern. In FREEMAN v. OAKLAND UNIFIED SCH.DIST., 291 F.3d 632 (9th Cir. 2002), it ruled that the trial court coule exercise jurisdiction over all allegations in a Title VII suit that either fell within the scope of the EEOC's *actual* investigation or any investigation that *could reasonably be expected* to grow out of the charge. Some commentators have argued that the EEOC and its cumbersome complaint process should be abandoned or, at a minimum, that the agency's procedures be radically revamped. See Michael Selmi, *The Value of the EEOC: Reexamining the Agency's Role in Employment Discrimination Law*, 57 OHIO ST. L.J. 1 (1996) (arguing that EEOC's enforcement efforts are not worth the costs of the agency); Maurice E.R. Munroe, *The EEOC: Pattern and Practice Imperfect*, 13 YALE L. & POL'Y REV. 219 (1995) (arguing that EEOC should be relieved of obligation to process individual charges so that it can focus efforts on systemic discrimination).

Calloway v. Partners National Health Plans

United States Court of Appeals, Eleventh Circuit, 1993.
986 F.2d 446.

JOHNSON, Senior Circuit Judge.

This appeal presents the question of whether a Title VII claim for wage discrimination is a single or continuing violation. The district court found that Felisha Calloway's claim of wage discrimination was a single violation which occurred the day she was hired, and entered final judgment in favor of her employer, Partners National Health Plans. We reverse.

I. STATEMENT OF FACTS

A. *Factual background*

In June 1987, Jeffrey Winokur, Partners' Marketing Director, offered Calloway the position of Marketing Secretary/Secretary I, at the rate of $ 14,996 annually.

Before accepting the offer, Calloway attempted to negotiate a higher salary, but Winokur told her that he was unable to offer more money. Calloway accepted the offer, replacing Kim Martin, a white female who had been hired nine months earlier at the rate of $ 16,000 per year.

Over the next two years, Calloway unsuccessfully applied for several positions of increased responsibility. In November 1989, Calloway resigned. To replace her, Winokur hired Kim Brasher, a white female. Although Brasher had neither a college degree nor any prior experience working with health maintenance organizations, Winokur offered Brasher a salary greater than Calloway was making when she left.

From June 1987, when Calloway was hired, until February 1988, Partners employed only two black individuals — Calloway and Ivory Steward. In February 1988, Winokur fired Steward. Steward filed a charge with the Equal Employment Opportunity Commission on February 19, 1988, alleging that "similarly situated Caucasians and males have been treated more favorably than I, with regard to wages, discharge and in their terms and conditions of employment." In 1989, after receiving her notice of a right to sue, Steward filed suit against Partners in district court.

B. *Procedural background*

Shortly after resigning from Partners, Calloway filed a timely motion to intervene in Steward's suit, alleging that she relied on Steward's EEOC charge. The district court denied Calloway's motion to intervene, citing the dissimilar nature of Calloway's claims and the advanced stage of Steward's suit. Instead, the district court treated Calloway's motion to intervene as the filing of a separate lawsuit.

After a two-day bench trial before the same judge who denied Calloway's motion to intervene, the district court found that Calloway's claim was "very similar" to Steward's charge, thereby permitting Steward's charge to support Calloway's claim. The court proceeded to find that Calloway had proven that her initial wage rate was discriminatory. Nevertheless, the court held that Calloway's wage discrimination claim was time barred, reasoning that the wage discrimination was the product of a single discrete act which occurred on the day Calloway began her employment with Partners, two months outside of the time-frame supported by the Steward charge.

On appeal, Calloway argues that the district court's finding that Partners' discriminatory wage payments were the product of a discrete act is clearly erroneous. In response, Partners argues that even if the discriminatory wage payments constitute a continuing violation, the district court's judgment denying Calloway relief should be affirmed * * * [because] the district court erred in permitting Calloway to rely on Steward's charge. * * *

II. DISCUSSION

A. *Continuing violation*

As a prerequisite to bringing suit under Title VII, a charge must be filed with the EEOC within 180 days of the date of the act giving rise to the charge. Because Calloway brought her claim under Steward's EEOC charge, Calloway's claim is timely only if the alleged wage discrimination occurred after August 18, 1987, 180 days prior to the date Steward filed her EEOC charge. The district court termed Steward's claim as one for discrimination in initial wage rate, and held that her claim was time barred because it was the product of a single discrete act that occurred on the day Calloway was hired, two months outside of the relevant 180-day period.

Whether a discriminatory act constitutes a continuing violation of Title VII or a past violation with a present effect is a finding of fact which we review under the clearly erroneous standard.

In determining whether a discriminatory employment practice constitutes a continuing violation, this Circuit distinguishes between the present consequence of a one time violation, which does not extend the limitations period, and the continuation of the violation into the present, which does. Although the district court found that Calloway had established her Title VII claim for wage discrimination, the district court found that the wage discrimination was not continuing, but was the present consequence of a discriminatory act which occurred the day Calloway was hired. This finding was clear error. Partners discriminated against Calloway not only on the day that it offered her less than her white predecessor, but also on every day of her employment. See Bazemore v. Friday, 478 U.S. 385, 395, 106 S. Ct. 3000, 3006, 92 L. Ed. 2d 315 (1986) ("Each week's paycheck that delivers less to a black than to a similarly situated white is a wrong actionable under Title VII * * *").

* * *

B. *Single-filing rule*

Partners argues that even if its discriminatory wage payments to Calloway constituted a continuing violation of Title VII, the district court's decision denying Calloway relief should be affirmed because Calloway should not have been allowed to proceed on Steward's EEOC charge.

The timely filing of an EEOC charge is a prerequisite to a Title VII suit. However, in certain instances we have permitted a plaintiff who has not filed an EEOC charge to rely on another plaintiff's charge, provided two essential requirements are met: (1) the charge being relied upon must be timely and not otherwise defective; and (2) the individual claims of the filing and non-filing plaintiffs must have arisen out of similar discriminatory treatment in the same time frame. Partners does not dispute that Calloway satisfied both of these requirements.[2] Rather, Partners argues that Calloway may not rely on Steward's charge because she is not part of the same lawsuit as Steward.

---

[2] Our review of the record, however, reveals that the district court made somewhat contradictory findings as to the similarity of Calloway's and Steward's claims. This case began after the district court denied Calloway's motion for intervention in the Steward case, citing the imminence of the Steward action as well as "the dissimilar nature of her claims." In its final order, the district court apparently changed its mind, finding that Steward's charge was "very similar to plaintiff's claims."

Although we are unable to reconcile the two findings, we note reconciliation is not required. First, in making its determination that Steward's charge was similar enough to support Calloway's claim, the district court was not bound by the law of the case to follow its prior ruling, because the prior ruling concerned an entirely separate issue. Second, the district court's denial of Calloway's motion to intervene is not before us. The only question possibly before us is whether the district court's finding in this case that Calloway's claim was "very similar" to Steward's claim was clearly erroneous. We do not find clear error in the district court's determination.

Whether a plaintiff may invoke the single-filing rule to rely on an EEOC charge filed by another plaintiff in another lawsuit is a question of first impression in this Circuit. We first invoked the "single-filing rule" in the context of a class action to permit unnamed plaintiffs to rely on the EEOC charge filed by the named plaintiff. Oatis v. Crown Zellerbach Corp., 398 F.2d 496 (5th Cir.1968). We then extended the single-filing rule to permit intervenors who had not filed EEOC charges to rely on the charge of one of the original plaintiffs. Wheeler v. American Home Products Corp., 582 F.2d 891 (5th Cir.1977). Finally, we permitted plaintiffs in multiple-plaintiff, non-class action lawsuits to rely on the charge filed by one of their co-plaintiffs. Crawford v. United States Steel Corp., 660 F.2d 663 (5th Cir.Unit B 1981).

Each of these applications of the single-filing rule has been grounded in the purpose of the EEOC charge requirement that the settlement of grievances be first attempted through the office of the EEOC. By requiring that the relied upon charge be otherwise valid, and that the individual claims of the filing and non-filing plaintiff arise out of similar discriminatory treatment in the same time frame, we have ensured that no plaintiff be permitted to bring suit until the EEOC has been given the opportunity to address the grievance. Indeed, we have rebuffed attempts to invoke the single-filing rule where the relied upon charge is invalid, or where the claimed discriminatory treatment is not similar or does not arise out of the same time frame. E.g., Hill v. MARTA, 841 F.2d 1533 (11th Cir.1988) (charge for discriminatory hiring policy would not support claims for discriminatory hiring arising before adoption of policy).

Accordingly, we hold that a plaintiff, such as Calloway, who unsuccessfully moves to intervene in the lawsuit of a plaintiff who has filed an EEOC charge may invoke the single filing rule, provided (1) the relied upon charge is not invalid, and (2) the individual claims of the filing and non-filing plaintiff arise out of similar discriminatory treatment in the same time frame. Such a rule comports with the purpose of the EEOC charge requirement by ensuring that the settlement of grievances will be attempted first through the EEOC. Moreover, there is no reason to distinguish between a plaintiff who successfully intervenes and one who does not. As we stated in Wheeler, *supra*, when we extended the single filing rule from class actions to successful intervenors, "it would frustrate the Congressional purpose expressed in Title VII if there were a rule which produced different results for discriminatory practices in situations governed by the same policy."

* * *

III. CONCLUSION

For the foregoing reasons, we REVERSE the district court's judgment finding that Calloway's wage discrimination claim was a discrete act, and REMAND for further proceedings in conformity with this opinion.

Reversed and remanded.

NOTES AND PROBLEMS FOR DISCUSSION

1. Calloway was allowed to piggyback on Steward's EEOC charge because Calloway *could* have filed a timely charge concerning the same kind of discrimination during the 180-day period prior to Steward's charge. Thus, Calloway's independent filing of a charge would not have provided any opportunity for conciliation by the EEOC or notice to the employer that was not already produced by Steward's charge. But where an employer persists in the same kind of discriminatory conduct over time, should it be necessary that the non-charging party *could* have filed a timely charge? In EEOC v. WILSON METAL CASKET CO., 24 F.3d 836, 840 (6th Cir. 1994), the same company official was found to have harassed two female employees on separate occasions. The first employee was fired in 1984 and filed an EEOC charge. The second employee was harassed for three months in 1987 but did not file a charge. The court concluded that the employer had engaged in a common practice of sexual harassment" which had continued for three years. Accordingly, it concluded that the second employee's claim had arisen during the same time period as that of the first employee and thus came within the single filing rule. *But see* Walker v. Mountain States Tel. & Tel. Co., 112 F.R.D. 44, 47 (N.D. Cal. 1991) ("The latest date on which potential plaintiffs may claim discrimination occurred is also circumscribed by [the representative] charge. * * * The EEOC could not have been expected to perform its conciliatory function for alleged acts of discrimination which could have occurred long after the charge was filed and of which no notice was given."). What if the charge sequence in *Wilson Metal Casket* was reversed and the second employee, but not the first, had filed the EEOC charge? *See* Bolden v. PRC Inc., 43 F.3d 545 (10th Cir. 1994), cert. denied, 516 U.S. 826, 116 S.Ct. 92, 133 L.Ed.2d 48 (1995) (the plaintiff could not invoke the single filing rule to complain of denial of a promotion which occurred more than 300 days prior to filing of the EEOC charge).

2.   The court in *Calloway* makes no reference to what happened to Steward's suit. To what extent should application of the single filing rule depend on the ultimate validity of the claim made by the charging party? In THOMURE v. PHILLIPS FURNITURE CO., 30 F.3d 1020 (8th Cir.1994), cert. denied, 513 U.S. 1191, 115 S.Ct. 1255, 131 L.Ed.2d 135 (1995), the employer reduced the wages of several of its employees. Thomure brought suit under the ADEA suit after filing an EEOC charge alleging age discrimination. He was joined in the suit by a fellow employee, Williams, who had not filed an EEOC charge but who complained of the same kind of discrimination. The district court concluded that Williams had failed to satisfy the filing prerequisites for an ADEA suit and granted summary judgment to the employer on Williams' claim. The jury found for Thomure. On appeal, the Eighth Circuit reversed the jury award, finding that Thomure's evidence was insufficient to support a finding of age discrimination as a matter of law. The appellate court then turned to Williams' claim that he should have been allowed to take advantage of the single filing rule.

> [I]n the absence of a properly filed discrimination charge, a party cannot be permitted to proceed with his discrimination lawsuit if he is attempting to piggyback on another's meritless charge (a charge Williams claims has essentially the same factual basis as his own) in order to exhaust his administrative remedies and satisfy the statutory prerequisite.

30 F.3d at 1027.

If the point, or at least one of the objectives of the single filing rule is to ensure that no Title VII complaint should be litigated unless the EEOC has had an opportunity to resolve that claim or a separate, substantially similar claim, should it matter whether the charging party actually filed suit? *See* Bettcher v. Brown Schs., Inc., 262 F.3d 492,

495 (5th Cir. 2001) ("In the absence of a lawsuit — properly supported by an EEOC charge — that a non-charging individual can join, a would-be plaintiff cannot invoke the piggyback rationale of the single filing rule because, indeed, there is no civil action upon which to piggyback"). Should a plaintiff who has filed an EEOC charge but failed to file a timely law suit after receiving a right-to-sue notice be allowed to piggyback on timely suits by fellow workers? *See* Mooney v. Aramco Servs. Co., 54 F.3d 1207 (5th Cir. 1995) (employees who have received right-to-sue letters may not enjoy benefit of "piggy-backing").

3.   Application of the single filing rule is not uniform among the circuits. Some courts have held that the single filing rule can be invoked only when the EEOC charge alleges that multiple employees were subjected to discrimination. In TOLLIVER v. XEROX CORP., 918 F.2d 1052 (2d Cir. 1990), cert. denied, 499 U.S. 983, 111 S.Ct. 1641, 113 L.Ed.2d 736 (1991) the Second Circuit summarized three versions of the single filing rule.

> Courts have used different tests, either alone or in combination, for determining whether an administrative charge suffices to permit piggybacking by a subsequent plaintiff. The broadest test requires only that the claims of the administrative claimant and the subsequent plaintiff arise out of the same circumstances and occur within the same general time frame. * * * A somewhat narrower test requires that the administrative claim give notice that the discrimination is "class-wide," i.e., that it alleges discrimination against a class of which the subsequent plaintiff is a member. A still narrower test requires that the administrative claim not only allege discrimination against a class but also allege that the claimant purports to represent the class or others similarly situated.

918 F.2d at 1057-58. The court in *Tolliver* distinguished between application of the single filing rule in work units of "modest size" where "mere similarity of the grievances within the same general time frame" suffices to put the employer on notice, and in large units where "lack of conciliation of one individual grievance does not necessarily mean that conciliation efforts would be unavailing if the EEOC and the employer were alerted to the broad scope of the claim." In the latter case "there must be some indication that the grievance affects a group of individuals defined broadly enough to include those who seek to piggyback on the claim." 918 F.2d at 1058.

The Third Circuit has rejected the single filing rule altogether except as applied to class actions.

> [O]utside the context of a representative or class action, an individual plaintiff must file a timely administrative charge. * * * [F]iling a charge with allegations broad enough to support a subsequent class action lawsuit [does not] alleviate the burden of filing the class action itself, with the attendant requirement of class certification. * * * [I]f plaintiffs choose to bring suit individually, they must first satisfy the prerequisite of filing a timely EEOC charge.

Communication Workers of Am.., Local 1033 v. N. J. Dept. Of Personnel, 282 F.3d 213, 218 (3d Cir. 2002). The Seventh Circuit has limited the doctrine to cases where the intervenor complains of exactly the same unlawful practice that was the subject of a timely charge on the basis of the following rationale:

> Unless the single-filing doctrine is limited to cases in which the claims arise from the same facts rather than merely from facts that resemble each other or are

causally linked to each other, courts will perforce be excusing the filing of a timely charge in *every* case in which an employee alleges retaliation for supporting another employee's charge. Such a rule would undermine the EEOC's conciliation procedure for no good reason.

Horton v. Jackson County Bd. Of County Comm'rs., 343 F.3d 897, 900-01 (7th Cir. 2003). Other courts have groped for a compromise between the "broad test" described in *Tolliver* and the Third Circuit's ultra-narrow approach to the single filing rule. *See* Greene v. City of Boston, 204 F. Supp. 2d 239 (D. Mass. 2002) (predicting that the First Circuit would not endorse the Third Circuit's rigid approach but would require that an allegation of class discrimination be apparent on the face of the charge in order for individuals to invoke the single filing rule).

5. The Effect of Compulsory Arbitration Agreements

Compulsory arbitration is a common feature of dispute resolution in mucj of the organized workplace and in the commercial world. By agreeing to arbitrate, a party waives the right to submit a claim to litigation. An arbitration agreement is enforceable in the same manner as any other contract and is grounds for dismissal or stay of a legal action. The Federal Arbitration Act (FAA),[a] enacted in 1925, was intended to reverse a tradition of hostility to arbitration agreements that American courts had inherited from their English forbearers and to place arbitration agreements upon the same footing as other contracts. The FAA's coverage provision, §2, provides that written arbitration agreements "in any maritime transaction or a contract evidencing a transaction involving commerce . . . shall be valid, irrevocable, and enforceable, save upon such grounds as exist at law or in equity for the revocation of any contract." But §1 provides the Act shall not apply "to contracts of employment of seamen, railroad employees, or any other class of workers engaged in foreign or interstate commerce."

As initially enacted, Title VII said nothing about arbitration. Section 118 of the Civil Rights Act of 1991 provides that "[w]here appropriate and to the extent authorized by law, the use of alternative means of dispute resolution, including * * * arbitration, is encouraged to resolve disputes arising under the Acts or provisions of Federal law amended by this Act." Should an employee covered by a compulsory arbitration agreement be forced to submit a statutory discrimination claim, such as one under Title VII, to arbitration, thus foregoing judicial resolution of the claim?[b] The Supreme Court's initial answer to that question was "no." In ALEXANDER v. GARDNER-DENVER CO., 415 U.S. 36, 94 S.Ct. 1011, 39 L.Ed.2d 147 (1974), the Court ruled that a discharged employee whose grievance had been submitted to

---

[a]9 U.S.C. §§1-14, 201-08 (1982).

[b]In McDonald v. City of West Branch, 466 U.S. 284, 104 S.Ct. 1799, 80 L.Ed.2d 302 (1984), the Court held that an arbitration was not a "judicial proceeding" within the meaning of 28 U.S.C. §1738, and thus an arbitration award could have no *preclusive* effect on subsequent federal litigation involving the issue subject to arbitration. *McDonald* did not address the question of whether a compulsory arbitration agreement could be enforced so as to deny an employee a judicial forum for resolution of the claim.

arbitration pursuant to the terms of a collective bargaining agreement was not foreclosed from bringing a Title VII action based on the conduct that was the subject of that grievance. The court noted that the employee's contractual rights under the collective bargaining agreement were distinct from his statutory Title VII rights and that the arbitrator's role was to "effectuate the intent of the parties [as expressed in the collective bargaining agreement]," not to enforce public laws. The Court also stressed that "federal courts have been assigned plenary powers to secure compliance with Title VII" and that "[t]here is no suggestion in the statutory scheme that a prior arbitral decision either forecloses an individual's right to sue or divests federal courts of jurisdiction." Most circuit courts construed *Gardner-Denver* to mean that employees could not be compelled through employment contracts to submit statutory discrimination claims to binding arbitration and thereby forfeit their statutory right to a judicial forum.

Subsequently, in GILMER v. INTERSTATE/JOHNSON LANE CORP., 500 U.S. 20, 111 S.Ct. 1647, 114 L.Ed.2d 26 (1991), the Supreme Court held that a claim under the Age Discrimination in Employment Act was subject to compulsory arbitration pursuant to terms of a contract entered into at the time of employment. The plaintiff in *Gilmer* was required as part of his employment as a broker to register with several stock exchanges. A rule of one of the exchanges required the arbitration of any controversy between the employee and his employer arising out of termination of employment. After his discharge, the plaintiff filed an ADEA charge with the EEOC and subsequently brought suit against his former employer. The employer, relying on the arbitration agreement and upon the FAA, moved to compel arbitration of the ADEA claim. The district court denied the motion on the ground that Congress had intended in the ADEA to protect claimants from the waiver of a judicial forum. The Supreme Court disagreed.

The Supreme Court declared that the FAA was applicable to statutory discrimination claims and that the plaintiff had failed to demonstrate that Congress intended to preclude arbitration of claims made under the ADEA. Nothing in the text or legislative history of the ADEA precluded arbitration, and arbitration was not inherently inconsistent with the ADEA's statutory framework and objectives. "[B]y agreeing to arbitrate a statutory claim, [an employee] does not forgo the substantive rights afforded by the statute; [he] only submits to their resolution in an arbitral, rather than a judicial, forum." 500 U.S. at 26. The Court emphasized that "so long as the prospective litigant effectively may vindicate his statutory cause of action in the arbitral forum, the statute will continue to serve both its remedial and deterrent function." 500 U.S. at 28. *Gardner-Denver* was distinguished on several grounds. First, the arbitration agreement in that case was intended to cover only contractual, and not statutory, claims. Second, in *Gardner-Denver* the plaintiffs were represented in the arbitration by their unions. "An important concern therefore was the tension between collective representation and individual statutory rights, a concern not applicable [in *Gilmer*]." Finally, *Gardner-Denver* was not decided under the FAA, a statute designed to encourage federal enforcement of arbitration agreements. For an interesting, behind-the-scenes account of the story behind the Court's ruling in *Gilmer*, see Charles A. Sullivan, *The Story of Gilmer v. Interstate/Johnson Lane Corp: Gilmering Antidiscrimination Law*, EMPLOYMENT DISCRIMINATION STORIES 305 (Friedman, ed. 2006).

The meaning of the FAA's exemption in §1 of "contracts of employment of seamen, railroad employees, or any other class of workers engaged in foreign or interstate commerce" was not decided in *Gilmer* because the arbitration clause was in the registration agreement with the stock exchange, not the plaintiff's contract with the employer. An expansive reading of the "engaged in . . . interstate commerce" language of §1 would have made the FAA inapplicable to most employment contracts and rendered *Gilmer* of little importance. In CIRCUIT CITY STORES v. ADAMS, 532 U. S. 105, 121 S.Ct. 1302, 149 L.Ed.2d 234 (2001), the Court construed the provision narrowly and held in another 5-4 decision that §1 exempts from the FAA only contracts of employment of transportation workers.

For nearly two decades after the Court issued its ruling in *Gilmer,* the lower courts struggled to address the tensions between the Court's rulings in *Gardner-Denver* and *Gilmer.* In WRIGHT v. UNIVERSAL MARINE SERVICE CORP., 525 U.S. 70, 119 S.Ct. 391, 142 L.Ed.2d 361 (1998), the Court, after emphasizing that the intention of the parties to extend the arbitration promise to statutory (as opposed to contractual) claims, thereby waiving the opportunity of a judicial forum, would have to be "clear and unmistakable" offered this assessment of the impact of *Gilmer* upon *Gardner-Denver*:

> [W]hether or not *Gardner-Denver*'s seemingly absolute prohibition of union waiver of employees' federal forum rights survives *Gilmer, Gardner-Denver* at least stands for the proposition that the right to a federal judicial forum is of sufficient importance to be protected against less-than-explicit union waiver in a CBA. The CBA [collective bargaining agreement] in this case does not meet that standard. Its arbitration clause is very general, providing for arbitration of "[m]atters under dispute," which could be understood to mean matters in dispute under the contract. * * * The Fourth Circuit relied upon the fact that the equivalently broad arbitration clause in *Gilmer* — applying to "any dispute, claim or controversy" — was held to embrace federal statutory claims. But *Gilmer* involved an individual's waiver of his own rights, rather than a union's waiver of the rights of represented employees — and hence the "clear and unmistakable" standard was not applicable.

119 S.Ct. at 396-97.

The matter eventually was addressed head-on by the Court in 14 PENN PLAZA LLC v. PYETT, 556 U.S. 247, 129 S.Ct. 1456 (2009), where the Court distinguished the two lines of cases and ruled that the enforceability rule set forth in *Gilmer* should be as applicable to collectively bargained arbitration agreements as those found in non-collectively bargained contracts. In 14 *Penn Plaza*, a collectively bargained agreement between the Service Employees International Union (SEIU) and a multiemployer bargaining association for the New York City real estate industry required all union members to submit all of their employment discrimination claims, both statutory and contractual in origin, to binding arbitration if they were not resolved through the earlier stages of the contract's grievance and dispute resolution procedure. The plaintiffs, a group of night watchmen, were reassigned to jobs as night porters at a lower salary when the defendant, an operator of an office building that had contracted with the watchmen's employer, signed a new deal with another company to provide security services. The Union that represented the plaintiffs filed grievances challenging the reassignments alleging, *inter alia*, that the plaintiffs had been reassigned because of their age. When the Union did not obtain relief through the grievance process, it requested arbitration. After the hearing, the Union withdrew its age discrimination claim but pursued other contractually based allegations, all of which ultimately were denied by the arbitrator. After the Union had withdrawn its discrimination claims, but while arbitration of the remaining allegations was still pending, the plaintiffs filed an EEOC charge alleging a violation of the ADEA. The EEOC dismissed the charge based on a lack of reasonable cause. The plaintiffs then filed suit alleging age discrimination in violation of the ADEA and state and local laws. The employer filed a motion to compel arbitration of these claims under the Federal Arbitration Act. The trial court denied the motion on the ground that even an unmistakable collectively bargained waiver of the right to litigate statutory claims of discrimination was unenforceable. The Second Circuit affirmed, relying on the Supreme Court's ruling in *Gardner-Denver* as authority for the proposition that a collective bargaining agreement could not waive a worker's right to a judicial forum for federal statutory claims. It reconciled *Gardner-Denver* with *Gilmer,* in which the Court had enforced an individually negotiated arbitration agreement covering federal statutory age discrimination claims, by limiting *Gilmer* to the non-collectively bargained arbitration agreement context.

By a 5-4 vote, the Supreme Court reversed, holding that enforcement of all terms of collectively bargained agreements, including arbitration clauses that cover federal statutory claims, was a central component of federal labor law policy as codified in the National Labor Relations Act, and, therefore, unless the ADEA itself removed age discrimination claims from the arbitral realm, federal labor policy mandated the enforcement of collectively bargained arbitration promises. The Court found no expression in the ADEA of any intention to preclude enforcement of arbitration agreements. It turned to *Gilmer* and declared that all of the reasons set forth therein to support the enforcement of an arbitration promise contained in a non-collectively bargained agreement should apply equally to a collectively bargained agreement. Per its ruling in *Wright*, as long as the agreement to arbitrate statutory disputes was "explicitly stated" in the collective agreement, that promise should be enforced. Agreeing to arbitrate statutory disputes, the majority reasoned, did not constitute a waiver of the "substantive right" guaranteed by the ADEA. The substantive right is the right to be free from discrimination; not a guarantee that the right will be construed or enforced by a judicial officer as opposed to an arbitrator. The Court also noted that this result was fully consistent with §118 of the 1991 Civil Rights Act, as that provision expressed Congress' support for alternative means of dispute resolution including arbitration. The Court also emphasized that *Gardner-Denver* and its progeny did not preclude the extension of *Gilmer* to collectively bargained arbitration agreements. Noting that none of the *Gardner-Denver* cases involved arbitration clauses that applied to statutory claims, the Court stressed that these cases dealt only with the limited issue of whether arbitration of contractual claims precluded subsequent judicial resolution of statutory claims and not the enforceability of an arbitration agreement that expressly covered statutory claims. Thus, since its ruling in this case did not contradict *Gardner-Denver*, the majority explained, there was no *stare decisis* barrier to the decision to enforce the instant arbitration agreement. Finally, to the extent that *Gardner-Denver* contained dicta that criticized the use of arbitration to resolve statutory claims, that statement was based on (1) an erroneous assumption that an agreement to arbitrate a statutory discrimination claim was tantamount to a waiver of the substantive statutory right to be free from discrimination; and (2) the misconceived notion that arbitral tribunals are not competent or otherwise suited to resolve statutory discrimination claims. Moreover, with respect to the *Gardner-Denver* Court's expression of concern over the possibility that the union, which controls the processing of a grievance through arbitration, might have an institutional interest that conflicted with the interest of the aggrieved individual, the majority declared that until Congress amends the ADEA to address such a conflict of interest concern, it was inappropriate for the judiciary to rely on such a concern to trump the federal pro-arbitration policy. Moreover, the Court noted that a union is subject to suit under the NLRA for failure to live up to its duty of fair representation when it discriminates against a member.

Suppose a collective bargaining agreement contains a clause providing that the employer "acknowledges its obligation to maintain policies prohibiting all forms of discrimination in accordance with all applicable state and federal laws." The agreement also contains an arbitration clause covering "all disputes arising under the terms of this agreement." An employee files a grievance claiming that she was denied a promotion because of her national origin. The arbitrator rules in favor of the company. Can the employee then file suit under Title VII challenging the allegedly discriminatory denial of promotion or has she waived her right to judicial enforcement of statutory claims of discrimination? In MATHEWS v. DENVER NEWSPAPER AGENCY, 2011 WL 892752 (10th Cir. 2011), the Tenth Circuit ruled in favor of the employee in such a situation, holding that the fact that the contract referred to statutory rights and, therefore, that the contractual duty of nondiscrimination was coterminous with the statutory obligation was "of no moment" in determining whether the arbitration clause covered statutory claims. The court based its ruling on two factors: (1) there was no express language in the arbitration provision referring to statutory claims; and (2) the dispute submitted to the arbitrator did not contain any assertion of a statutory claim and the arbitral decision made no mention of statutory claims.

The fact that the Supreme Court has now declared that all arbitration greements that expressly and unmistakably extend to statutory claims are enforceable did not end judicial scrutiny of these agreements. The fact that arbitration clauses are presumptively enforceable does not mean that they will be enforced in every case. The FAA provides that arbitration agreements are enforceable "save upon such grounds as exist at law or in equity for the revocation of any contract," 9 U.S.C. §2, and courts have been more than willing to void arbitration clauses on a variety of grounds.

Lack of Consideration. Whether an employee has entered into an enforceable contract to arbitrate is determined under state contract law. In GIBSON v. NEIGHBORHOOD HEALTH CLINICS, INC., 121 F.3d 1126, 1130 (7th Cir. 1997), the court of appeals held that an arbitration clause which was no more than an employee's unilateral promise to submit her claim to arbitration and which was not supported by any consideration or bargained-for detriment to the employer was not enforceable under Indiana law. The plaintiff's employment was not consideration for the agreement because, at the time the agreement was signed, the plaintiff was already employed and the employer did not promise to continue her employment but in fact reserved the right to terminate her at any time, with or without notice and with or without cause. *See also* Floss v. Ryan's Family Steak Houses, Inc., 211 F.3d 306 (6th

Cir. 2000), cert. denied, 531 U.S. 1072, 121 S.Ct. 763, 148 L.Ed.2d 664 (2001) (consideration deemed illusory under state law because the employer retained complete discretion over arbitration rules, including an unlimited right to modify procedures); Walker v. Ryan's Family Steak Houses, Inc., 400 F.3d 370, 378 (6th Cir. 2005) (no consideration because the employer was not obliged to submit its employment disputes to arbitration).

Knowing Waiver of Judicial Forum. The circuits are divided over whether the employer must demonstrate that the employee knowingly agreed to arbitrate the dispute in question. *Compare* Prudential Ins. Co. v. Lai, 42 F.3d 1299 (9th Cir. 1994), cert. denied, 516 U.S. 812, 116 S.Ct. 61, 133 L.Ed.2d 24 (1995) (arbitration agreement not enforced because the employees did not knowingly contract to forgo their statutory remedies in favor of arbitration), *with* Haskins v. Prudential Ins. Co., 230 F.3d 231 (6th Cir. 2000), cert. denied, 531 U.S. 1113, 121 S.Ct. 859, 148 L.Ed.2d 773 (2001) (criticizing the ruling in *Lai* for holding that a party to a contract is not chargeable with knowledge of its terms and holding that absent a showing of fraud, duress, mistake, or some other ground on which a contract can be voided, a court must enforce a contractual agreement to arbitrate).

Can an applicant for a minimum wage job who has little formal education be expected to understand the meaning of a complex, multi-page arbitration agreement? *See* Penn v. Ryan's Family Steak Houses, Inc., 269 F.3d 753, 761 (7th Cir. 2001) (expressing doubt whether an applicant for a waiter's position in a chain restaurant could have "knowingly and voluntarily" signed a complex legal agreement and suggesting that if the applicant had questioned the agreement's meaning and complexities, it is doubtful that he would have been hired) (Wood, J., concurring). On the other hand if arbitration clauses in individual employment contracts are to be enforceable in practice, and not just in theory, what steps can an employer *practicably* be required to take in order to ensure "knowing" waiver by the employee? Courts naturally have been more inclined to strike down arbitration agreements forced on unsophisticated wage earners than when such agreements are signed by educated professionals. *Compare* Alexander v. Anthony Int'l., 341 F.3d 256 (3d Cir. 2003) (equipment operators with grade school educations and narrow options for other employment could not be forced to arbitrate their termination where the corporation clearly possessed more bargaining power and required the plaintiffs to agree to a mandatory arbitration agreement as condition of employment without any ability to negotiate), *with* Gold v. Deutsche Aktiengesellschaft, 365 F.3d 144 (2d Cir.), cert. denied, 543 U.S. 874, 125 S.Ct. 87, 160 L.Ed.2d 124 (2004) (enforcing an arbitration clause where the plaintiff held an MBA from a "top-tier school" and did not claim that he could not read or otherwise understand the form; mere inequality in bargaining power is not alone sufficient to hold clause unenforceable).

Unconscionability. An agreement to arbitrate, like other contractual provisions, may be unenforceable because it is unconscionable. As with consideration, unconscionability is a matter of state law. Although state standards differ, unconscionability generally requires that the contract be both procedurally and substantively unfair. Procedural unfairness is commonly established by the unequal bargaining positions of the parties accompanied by one-sided control of the arbitration process. *See, e.g.*, McMullen v. Meijer, Inc., 355 F.3d 485 (6th Cir. 2003). Substantive unconscionability usually results from terms of the agreement that are unequal and oppressive. *See* Hooters of Am., Inc. v. Phillips, 173 F.3d 933, 938 (4th Cir. 1999) (arbitration rules imposed by employer were "so one-sided that their only possible purpose is to undermine the neutrality of the proceeding"). Some state courts have held that substantive unconscionability alone renders an arbitration clause unenforceable. *See, e.g.*, Adler v. Fred Lind Manor, 103 P.3d 773, 782 (Wash. 2004) ("[I]ndividual contractual provisions may be so one-sided and harsh as to render them substantively unconscionable despite the fact that the circumstances surrounding the parties' agreement to the contract do not support a finding of procedural unconsionability.").

The Ninth Circuit has been particularly hostile to arbitration clauses in employment contracts. In CIRCUIT CITY STORES, INC. v. ADAMS, 279 F.3d 889 (9th Cir.), cert. denied, 535 U.S. 1112, 122 S.Ct. 2329, 153 L.Ed.2d 160 (2002), on remand from the Supreme Court's ruling that arbitration agreements in individual employment contracts were enforceable under the FAA, the circuit court refused to enforce the arbitration clause on grounds of unconscionability. The contract was procedurally unfair because it was drafted by the employer and was offered to the job applicant on a take-it-or-leave-it basis, i.e., the employee had the option of accepting it or not being employed. The court also found that the agreement was substantively unfair because although the employee was required to arbitrate any and all employment disputes, the employer was not required to arbitrate any claims it had against the employee. "This unjustified one-sidedness deprives the arbitration agreement of the modicum of bilaterality that the California Supreme Court requires for contracts to be enforceable under California law." 279 F.3d at 894. But in CIRCUIT CITY STORES, INC. v. AHMED, 283 F.3d 1198 (9th Cir. 2002), the same court held that a substantively similar arbitration clause was enforceable because the provision allowed employees to opt out ("a meaningful choice not to participate") of the arbitration agreement. "In *Adams,* we found that the agreement was procedurally unconscionable because it was a contract of adhesion. By contrast, this case lacks the necessary element of procedural unconscionability." 283 F.3d at 1199. Then, in INGLE v. CIRCUIT CITY STORES, INC., 328 F.3d 1165 (9th Cir. 2003), the court went so far as to create a presumption of unconscionability to account for the "gross one-sided" nature of arbitration agreements. The presumption can be rebutted by showing, as the employer did in *Ahmed*, that the agreement to arbitrate maintained a "modicum of bilaterality." Does this all mean that, at least in the Ninth Circuit, "take-it-or-leave-it" arbitration clauses in employment contracts will not be enforceable as a practical matter because of the lack of "bilaterality," i.e., an escape clause allowing the employee to opt out of arbitration? See Circuit City Stores v. Mantor, 335 F.3d 1101 (9th Cir. 2003) (arbitration clause unenforced because the plaintiff had "no meaningful choice or legitimate opportunity to negotiate or reject the terms of the arbitration agreement).

Outside of the Ninth Circuits, most of the appellate courts take the position that an arbitration clause is not unenforceable solely because it is a standardized form offered on a take-it-or-leave-it basis. *See* Cooper v. MRM Inv. Co., 367 F.3d 493 (6th Cir. 2004) (agreement presented on standardized form with no ability to negotiate terms, contract is enforceable unless it also is substantively unconscionable).

Who determines whether or not an arbitration agreement is unconscionable? A court or the arbitrator named in the agreement? In RENT-A-CENTER, WEST, INC.

v. JACKSON, 559 U.S. 662, 130 S.Ct. 2772, 177 L.Ed.2d 403 (2010), the Supreme Court, by a 5-4 vote, held that when a party challenges the enforceability of an arbitration agreement that represents the entirety of the agreement between the parties, the threshold issue of unconscionability is to be resolved by the arbitrator when that agreement expressly and unambiguously delegates exclusive authority over that issue to the arbitrator. Previously, in Prima Paint Corp. v. Flood & Conklin Mfg. Co., 388 U.S. 395, 87 S.Ct. 1801, 18 L.Ed.2d 1270 (1967), the Court had construed §2 of the Federal Arbitration Act (providing for the enforcement of written arbitration agreements subject to challenge under grounds recognized at law or in equity) to mean that a challenge to a contract as a whole, as opposed to a specific challenge to the arbitration provision within that contract, was to be resolved by the arbitrator and not a court. Extending that analysis to the instant case, the majority in *Rent-A-Car* reasoned that the entire contract before it was the arbitration agreement and that the employee had not specifically and independently challenged the unconscionability of the particular provision within that contract as a whole that delegated authority over unconscionability determinations to the arbitrator. Accordingly, it upheld the trial judge's decision to dismiss the employee's §1981 suit and to compel arbitration on the ground that because the plaintiff former employee had challenged the validity of the contract as a whole, the unconscionability determination was for the arbitrator, and not a court, to decide. The four dissenters rejected the majority's extension of *Prima Paint* to the instant facts. In their view, *Prima Paint* "akin to a pleading standard, whereby a party seeking to challenge the validity of an arbitration agreement must expressly say so in order to get his dispute into court." They read *Prima Paint* to mean that the threshold question of enforceability can go to the arbitrator only when the challenge relates to the validity of the substantive contract "within which an arbitration clause is nested." On the other hand, where a party challenges the validity of the arbitration agreement, which is severable from the substantive terms, that issue is a matter for a court to resolve. The presence of the provision delegating unconscionability determinations to the arbitrator was "beside the point", the dissenters declared, because the essence of the former employee's claim was that he never consented to arbitrate in the first place because that agreement was procedurally and substantively unconscionable. And so, they concluded, the decision over whether the arbitration promise was enforceable had to be resolved by a court. Finally, the dissenters found *Prima Paint* to be inapposite to the case at bar because, in their view, the determination of whether the arbitration agreement was unconscionable was severable from the merits of the underlying employment discrimination dispute.

Payment of Fees and Costs of Arbitration. A plaintiff who files suit under a federal employment discrimination statute (and most equivalent state statutes) will not have to pay the costs of litigation (other than minimal filing fees), will not, unless the action is baseless, have to pay the attorney fees of the employer, and, if she prevails, will be entitled to recover reasonable attorney fees and costs from the employer. In GREEN TREE FINANCIAL CORP.-ALA. v. RANDOLPH, 531 U.S. 79, 121 S.Ct. 513, 148 L.Ed.2d 373 (2000), a Truth In Lending Act case, the Supreme Court acknowledged that "the existence of large arbitration costs could preclude a litigant * * * from effectively vindicating her federal statutory rights in the arbitral forum." 531 U.S. at 90. The loan agreement contained an arbitration clause that was silent on the issue of who was responsible for paying the costs of arbitration. The Court held that the party resisting arbitration had the burden of demonstrating the likelihood of incurring costs that would be prohibitively expensive. The courts are divided on the effect of *Green Tree* in employment cases where the obligation on the employee to share the cost of arbitration is spelled out in the agreement. *Compare* Musnick v. King Motor Co., 325 F.3d 1255, 1259 (11th Cir. 2003) ("After *Green Tree,* an arbitration agreement is not unenforceable merely because it may involve some fee-shifting. The party seeking to avoid arbitration under any agreement has the burden of establishing that enforcement of the agreement would preclude him from effectively vindicating his federal statutory right in the arbitral forum.), *with* Circuit City Stores, Inc. v. Adams, 279 F.3d 889 (9th Cir. 2002), cert. denied, 535 U.S. 1112, 122 S.Ct. 2329, 153 L.Ed.2d 160 (2002) (mere presence of fee-shifting provision invalidates agreement). The Sixth Circuit has predicted that courts "will find, in many cases, that high level management employees and others with substantial means can afford the costs of arbitration, thus making cost-splitting provisions in such cases enforceable" but that "this standard will render cost-splitting provisions unenforceable for many, if not most cases." Morrison v. Circuit City Stores, Inc., 317 F.3d 646, 665 (6th Cir. 2003) (en banc).

In *Gilmer,* the Supreme Court stated that by agreeing to arbitrate a statutory claim, an employee was not foregoing the substantive rights afforded by the statute but was only submitting resolution to a different forum. But one of the basic concepts of binding arbitration is that the arbitrator will decide the case and that the arbitrator's decision — both as to facts and law — will be final.

Although the generally accepted rule was that arbitral awards could be set aside upon a determination that the arbitrator acted in "manifest disregard" of the applicable law, the circuit courts applied differing levels of deference to arbitration awards. The Supreme Court addressed this issue in a non-employment case involving arbitration of a lease dispute. In HALL STREET ASSOCIATES, L.L.C. v. MATTEL, INC., 552 U.S. 576, 128 S.Ct. 1396, 170 L.Ed. 2d 254 (2008), Hall Street sued Mattel in federal district court for wrongful termination and for indemnification of costs incurred for environmental violations as provided under the lease. After a court trial in which the defendant won on the termination issue, the parties agreed to submit the indemnification issue to arbitration. The arbitration agreement, approved by the trial judge, expressly provided that the court could vacate or modify any award where the arbitrator's legal conclusions were erroneous. The arbitrator ruled in favor of Mattel, finding that the particular state statute that Hall Street alleged that Mattel had violated did not come within the scope of the lease's indemnification clause. The trial judge refused to enforce that award and remanded for further consideration by the arbitrator, invoking the standard of review for legal error set forth in the arbitration agreement. On remand, the arbitrator followed the trial judge's ruling that the state law was applicable under the lease agreement and ruled in favor of Hall Street. On cross-motions for modification, the trial judge applied the contractually stipulated standard of review for legal error and upheld the award. The Ninth Circuit reversed, holding that the contractual judicial review provision was unenforceable and that the exclusively applicable bases for vacating or modifying arbitration awards were those contained in the Federal Arbitration Act (FAA). It therefore ordered that the arbitration award reinstated.

The Supreme Court noted that Section 10 of the Act sets forth four criteria for vacating awards: (1) corruption, fraud, or undue means in the procurement of the award; (2) evident partiality or corruption by the arbitrator(s); (3) misconduct by the arbitrator that prejudiced the rights of any party; or (4) action in excess of the arbitrator's delegated powers, and that none of these factors expressly referred to legal error or "manifest disregard of the law".   The Court noted (without expressly disapproving) that some circuits had reasoned that "manifest disregard" referred either to the §10 grounds collectively or that it was "shorthand" for the arbitrator misconduct or acting in excess of powers factors.   It rejected the claim that the arbitration agreement's allowance for review for legal error should be enforced.   Although it recognized that the FAA enforces many aspects of arbitration agreements, the statutory provision concerning judicial review under both sections 10 and 11 were intended to be exclusive and to preempt contractual attempts to expand the grounds for judicial review.   To permit review of arbitration awards on these more expansive grounds would be inconsistent with the federal policy of encouraging arbitration as an expedited and efficient method of dispute resolution.   The Court added, however, that judicial enforcement of arbitration awards was not limited to the expedited proceedings available under the FAA.   Parties wanting review of arbitration awards "may contemplate enforcement under state statutory or common law, for example, where judicial review of different scope is arguable."   But because the instant arbitration agreement was confected during the pendency of litigation for the purpose of deviating from standard trial procedure, it was unclear to the Court whether this arbitration agreement, which had been approved by the trial judge, should be treated as an exercise of that court's case management authority under Federal Rule of Civil Procedure 16.   Thus, it was uncertain whether or not the provisions of the FAA were applicable.   Accordingly, the Court remanded the case to the Ninth Circuit for consideration of that issue.

Post-*Hall Street Associates*, however, some circuit courts continue to recognize the availability of the "manifest disregard of the law" basis for vacating or modifying arbitration awards.   *See e.g.*, Comedy Club Inc. v. Improv West Assocs., 553 F.3d 1277 (9th Cir. 2009) (manifest disregard is a shorthand for arbitrator conduct in excess of delegated powers).   Others, however, read *Hall Street Associates* as declaring that manifest disregard of the law no longer is a basis for vacating or modifying arbitration awards under the FAA.   *See e.g.*, Citigroup Global Markets, Inc. v. Bacon, 562 F.3d 349 (5th Cir. 2009).

But suppose that the grievant prevailed before the arbitrator on the merits and instead of seeking to vacate the award, seeks only to modify it by asking the court to increase the size of the arbitrator's award.   Does this affect the judicial role on appeal and what, if any, impact does the Court's ruling in *Hall Street Associates* play? Section 11 of the FAA sets forth three bases for modifications: (1) an "evident material miscalculation of figures" (generally interpreted as limited to computational errors in determining the amount of an award), (2) an award based upon a matter not submitted to the arbitrator; and (3) an imperfection in the award that amounts to "a matter of form not affecting the merits of the controversy."   In GRAIN v. TRINITY HEALTH, MERCY HEALTH SERVICES, INC., 551 F.3d 374 (6th Cir. 2008), the Sixth Circuit noted that the *Hall Street Associates* Court "suggested" that "manifest disregard" might be shorthand for some of the statutorily enumerated bases for judicial review.   Nevertheless, it ultimately rejected the application of the manifest disregard standard to the instant case, ruling that even pre-*Hall Street* Associates, this circuit had never applied the manifest disregard standard to a request for modification, as opposed to vacatur, of an arbitration award. .

Since arbitrators are perceived as generally not well equipped to decide public law issues, most commentators have been highly critical of *Gilmer* and its progeny. *See, e.g.*, Jean R. Sternlight, *Panacea or Corporate Tool?: Debunking the Supreme Court's Preference for Binding Arbitration*, 74 WASH. U. L.Q. 637 (1996) (arguing that to protect individual self-determination and promote fairness, arbitration should be preferred over litigation only when contracting parties have reasonably equivalent bargaining power and knowingly and voluntarily agree to arbitration); Robert Gorman, *The Gilmer Decision and the Private Arbitration of Public Law Disputes*, 1995 U. ILL. L. REV. 635, 678 ("Given the very different purposes, sources, and dynamics of grievance arbitration under collective agreements, that model cannot be imposed unquestioningly upon the post-Gilmer world of public-law arbitration.").

Ironically, the arbitration agreement that generated the litigation in *Gilmer* has been abandoned. In January 1999, the National Association of Securities Dealers eliminated mandatory arbitration of statutory employment discrimination claims from its brokerage agreement. The revised NASD policy allows a broker to choose between signing the broker's registration form (Form U-4) or reserving the right to file suit in court.

Finally, where a large number of claimants are employed by a company whose employment contracts contain a mandatory arbitration clause, they sometimes prefer to pursue arbitration on a class-wide basis. For years, the lower courts were in disarray on the question of whether the FAA permitted the arbitration of class wide claims. In STOLT-NIELSEN S.A. v. ANIMALFEEDS INT'L CORP., 559 U. S. 662, 130 S.Ct. 1758, 176 L.Ed.2d 605 (2010), the Supreme Court, by a 5-3 margin, ruled that where the arbitration agreement was absolutely silent on the question of whether it permitted class arbitration, *and* where the parties agreed that they had never reached any sort of agreement on the availability of class wide arbitration, an arbitrator was not empowered to construe the agreement to permit class arbitration. Since, the Court explained, arbitration is a private dispute resolution mechanism that is purely consensual in nature, the parties could not be compelled to engage in class wide arbitration in the absence of any evidence, express or implied, of an intention to permit the arbitration of class claims. Yet although the Court imposed an anti-class arbitration presumption, it noted that it was not necessary for the agreement to contain an express statement agreeing to class arbitration in order to rebut that presumption. The Court acknowledged that the agreement could contain an implicit agreement to authorize class arbitration. However, that implicit agreement could not be inferred *solely* from the fact of the parties' agreement to arbitrate. But this left open the question of whether, when the issue is in dispute, the availability of class-wide arbitration is a decision for the arbitrator or a court. The circuits agree that it is a decision only for the court, at least absent clear and unmistakeable language in the arbirtration clause to the contrary. They have determined that the availability of class arbitration, like contract formation, is a "gateway" issue that a court must decide, unless the contractual language unambiguously reserves that issue of arbitrability to the arbitrator. *See* 20/20 Communications, Inc. v. Crawford, 2019 WL 3281412 (5th Cir. 2019).

Eventually, the courts had to confront the other side of this question, i.e., whether employers and their employees should be permitted to agree to limit the arbitration of statutory disputes to individual claims or whether workers had a right to assert class-based claims in arbitration. The Supreme Court resolved a circuit split on this issue in EPIC SYSTEMS CORP. v. LEWIS, 584 U.S. ___, 138 S.Ct. 1612, 200 L.Ed.2d 889 (2018). In a 5-4 ruling, the majority held that the language in the Federal Arbitration Act directing the courts to "rigorously" enforce arbitration agreements "according to their terms" was neither impliedly nor expressly overridden by §7 of the National Labor Relations Act, which gives workers the right to engage in "concerted activity" for their "mutual aid or protection". In a case involving a claim by an accountant that his employer had violated the terms of the FLSA by not paying him and similarly situated accountants overtime pay, the Ninth Circuit had ruled that the agreement between the company and its employees requiring individualized arbitration proceedings violated §7 of the NLRA by prohibiting these workers from engaging in the "concerted activity' of pursuing claims in arbitration on a class-wide basis. The Supreme Court majority disagreed, ruling that §7 did not extend to collective action outside of the workplace when workers sought to resolve workplace disputes in a judicial or arbitral forum. It emphasized the consensual nature of arbitration proceedings and the Court's longstanding policy encouraging the enforcement of these consensual agreements as well as the FAA's provision directing courts to enforce such agreements "according to their terms. The majority also rejected the dissent's declaration that the FAA's "savings clause" – which recognized defenses to enforcement of arbitration agreements – extended to a claim of illegality under the NLRA.

SECTION B. SUITS BY THE EEOC

Equal Employment Opportunity Commission v. Sherwood Medical Industries, Inc.

United States District Court, Middle District of Florida, 1978.
452 F.Supp. 678.

GEORGE C. YOUNG, Chief Judge.

This is a Title VII enforcement action brought by the Equal Employment Opportunity Commission against Sherwood Medical Industries, Inc., alleging that Sherwood engaged in discriminatory employment practices with respect to race and male gender. Now before the Court is Sherwood's Motion to Strike and/or for Dismissal for Failure to State a Claim and/or for Summary Judgment, which puts in issue the permissible scope of the Commission's judicial complaint in this cause. The decisive question raised is whether the EEOC is now foreclosed from prosecuting its claim of male sex discrimination because it neither included this claim in its reasonable cause determination nor afforded Sherwood an opportunity to conciliate the matter prior to filing suit.

I. BACKGROUND

This Title VII case was set in motion on July 16, 1973 when Larry C. Dilligard, a black male, filed a charge with the EEOC, complaining that he had been denied employment by defendant Sherwood solely because of his race. The details of his charge of discrimination, assumed to be true for the purpose of this motion, are as follows: Dilligard entered the personnel office of Sherwood's Deland facility on the morning of July 9, 1973 and requested an application for employment. He informed a Caucasian female employee that he was seeking a clerical position and that he had a college degree in business. Dilligard was told that there were no vacancies in the clerical area and that there was no need to fill out an application because "we only accumulate a lot of applications and eventually throw them in the garbage can". Dilligard responded that he wished to complete an application in any event so that he could have one on file if a vacancy did occur. The employee refused to give him an application. Dilligard observed at the time a number of white job applicants waiting in a nearby reception center for interviews.

The EEOC responded to Dilligard's charge by sending Sherwood the statutory notice of charge and initiating a broad scale investigation into Sherwood's employment practices. In the course of its investigation the Commission compiled statistical data on the race and sex composition of Sherwood's clerical work force.

On February 18, 1975 the Commission issued a formal "reasonable cause determination" finding reasonable cause to believe that Sherwood failed to hire charging party because of his race. Despite the fact that the investigation clearly encompassed male gender discrimination, the determination made no finding on that issue and it invited conciliation only on Dilligard's narrow charge of race discrimination. Indeed, there were merely two references to male gender employment practices in the entire three page document:

> "The Commission also notes that all of respondent's clericals are female except one.

> The foregoing statistics coupled with the fact that there were clerical vacancies after July 9, 1973, is sufficient to establish that exclusion of blacks, and particularly black males, has occurred."

Apparently at no point during the conciliation negotiations that followed the Commission's determination did male gender employment discrimination emerge as a subject of concern. The conciliation agreement ultimately proposed by the Commission (and rejected by Sherwood) was completely silent on that issue; the agreement focused exclusively on Dilligard's charge of race discrimination. And from all that appears in the record it was not until the judicial complaint in this cause was filed that Sherwood first learned of the Commission's claim that it had discriminated against males.

Sherwood now argues that the Commission's failure to put it on notice of the sex discrimination claim and to afford it an opportunity to conciliate the matter bars the Commission from pressing that claim in this action. In substance, Sherwood's contention is that the Commission has filed to satisfy all of the statutory pre-requisites to its power to sue under Title VII, hence this Court lacks subject matter jurisdiction over the sex discrimination claim. The Commission's response is that it has satisfied the minimum conditions on its power to bring a Title VII enforcement action. It takes issue with the contention that the reasonable cause determination did not sufficiently apprise Sherwood of its claim of male gender discrimination. And it maintains that it can assert its sex discrimination claim even if that issue were never made an explicit subject of conciliation. Moreover, the Commission argues, the scope of matters sought to be conciliated is not a proper subject of judicial scrutiny and hence the Court should not even inquire into whether the sex claim was a subject of attempted conciliation.

II. THE SCOPE OF THE CHARGE AND THE INVESTIGATION

It is now well settled that the allowable scope of a civil enforcement action by the Commission is not fixed strictly by the allegations of the charging party's charge of discrimination. Rather, as the Fifth Circuit held in the often-cited decision of Sanchez v. Standard Brands, Inc., the scope of the civil action is to be determined by the "scope of the EEOC investigation which can reasonably be expected to grow out of the charge of discrimination."[1] The charge should be viewed merely as the starting point for a reasonable investigation, not as a common-law pleading which narrowly circumscribes the Commission's freedom of action in carrying out its statutory duties. If the Commission uncovers during a reasonable investigation facts which support a charge of some form of discrimination other than that alleged in the original charge, it is free to develop these facts and, if necessary, to require the respondent to account for them.
* * *

In the present case the Commission's investigation clearly exceeded the scope of the charging party's charge of discrimination. For Dilligard's charge dealt solely with race and the Commission, in the course of its investigation of that charge, compiled statistical data on sex as well. But Sherwood does not say that the broader focus of the investigation was in any way improper or abusive in relation to the charge filed; indeed it appears to concede the reasonableness of the investigation. So there is no real question here about the scope of the judicial complaint per se. If the Commission complied with the statutory pre-requisites to bringing suit, it was free to assert its sex claim against Sherwood because that claim arose out of a reasonable investigation of the original charge of discrimination. The scope of the complaint is in issue here only because it is contended that with respect to the sex discrimination claim the Commission has failed to comply with two statutory conditions on its power to sue: a reasonable cause determination and an effort to conciliate.

III. THE REASONABLE CAUSE DETERMINATION

Under §706(b), after the Commission investigates a charge of discrimination, it should "so far as practical not later than 120 days from the filing of the charge" make a determination on whether it believes the charge is true. This reasonable cause determination is a very crucial step in the administrative process. For it marks the conclusion of the Commission's investigation into a respondent's employment practices and it represents the Commission's formal opinion about what its investigation revealed. The determination may even bring the administrative process to an end with respect to many charges; if a "no cause" determination is made the

---

[1]The post-*Sanchez* decisions have applied slightly different tests to determine whether the Commission's judicial complaint was unreasonably broad in light of the charge of discrimination. It is doubtful that there is any meaningful distinction between the tests employed. The inquiry in every case is essentially whether the additional charge of employment discrimination could reasonably have grown out of an investigation into the original charge.

charge of discrimination will be dismissed and the complaining party left to his private remedies in court. And where a "cause" determination is reached, the Commission, by law, must undertake an attempt to conciliate the dispute. In that event, the reasonable cause determination is intended to serve both as a formal means of placing the respondent on notice of the particular employment practice which the Commission views as violative of Title VII and as a framework for the conciliation efforts to follow.

Because of the importance of the reasonable cause determination, as a means of finally drawing the investigation to a close, as an embodiment of the Commission's legal conclusions from the evidence, as a means of notice to the respondent and as a device to frame the issues for conciliation, it seems evident that any and all of a respondents' employment practices viewed by the Commission as probably discriminatory, must be explicitly included in the determination. That is, the Commission must make an express finding in the determination concerning each employment practice which it concludes to be violative of Title VII. The Courts which have addressed themselves to this question have so concluded.

The reasonable cause determination at issue here falls far short of making any such finding on the sex discrimination claim now asserted against Sherwood. Indeed, the closest scrutiny of the determination could not have effectively placed Sherwood on notice that sex discrimination was a matter in issue. The only material reference to sex in the entire determination was the comment that statistical analysis indicated that there were clerical vacancies after July 9, 1973 sufficient to establish that "the exclusion of blacks, and particularly black males, has occurred." This comment was manifestly insufficient to afford Sherwood notice of the sex discrimination claim. If anything, the inference that should be drawn from the statement is that there was no discrimination against white males. Race discrimination was all that Sherwood could reasonably have viewed as being in dispute.

IV. THE FAILURE TO CONCILIATE

Conciliation is the final step in an EEOC administrative proceeding and a condition precedent to the Commission's power to sue. The language of the statute admits of no exception. If the Commission finds reasonable cause it "shall endeavor to eliminate any such unlawful employment practice by informal methods of conference, conciliation and persuasion," and only when conciliation "acceptable to the Commission" fails may it bring a civil action against the respondent. §706(b). The Courts have interpreted the statute to mean precisely what it says and it is thus now well established that failure to conciliate is fatal to a Title VII action brought by the Commission;[2] the suit or claim must be dismissed as premature.

The record in this case, as counsel for the Commission concedes, establishes that conciliation on the sex discrimination claim was never offered and never attempted. The only subject of conciliation efforts was Dilligard's race discrimination charge; when the negotiations on that charge failed, the Commission filed suit without ever attempting to settle the sex discrimination claim. It would thus seem to follow that the

---

[2]By contrast, conciliation by the Commission is not a condition precedent to the institution of a private action for relief under Title VII by an individual plaintiff.

sex discrimination aspects of the Commission's claim against Sherwood would have to be stricken from this case. But the Commission argues that it would be error to do so because the Commission need conciliate only the original charge of discrimination, not the additional discrimination claims which come to life during an investigation of the original charge. That is, as the Commission views it, its duty is to conciliate the charging party's charge only and if it is unable to reach a conciliation agreement on that charge it is under no obligation to seek settlement with respect to additional discriminatory employment practices developed during the investigation of the original charge. Under this theory only Dilligard's charge was required to be conciliated.

This contention, if accepted, would run contrary to Congressional intent and could well have the affect of rendering the conciliation requirement an empty formality. The mandate that conciliation be attempted is unique to Title VII and it clearly reflects a strong Congressional desire for out-of-court settlement of Title VII violations. The legislative history of the 1972 amendments confirms that Congress viewed judicial relief as a recourse of last resort, sought only after a settlement has been attempted and failed.[3] Conciliation is clearly the heart of the Title VII administrative process. In light of the clear Congressional preference for conciliation it would be anomalous to conclude that the Commission is under no obligation to conciliate a claim of discrimination simply because it originated during the course of its investigation rather than from an aggrieved person's charge.

Certainly one can find no support for the Commission's position in the decisions dealing with the scope of the judicial complaint. To the contrary, every decision recognizing a right in the Commission to expand its investigation — and ultimately its judicial complaint — beyond the scope of the charging party's charge, has presupposed that the additional employment practices complained of were included in the conciliation attempt along with the original charge. In EEOC v. Raymond Metal Prod. Co., 385 F.Supp. 907, 915 (D.Md.1974) for instance, the Court concluded:

> " * * * the judicial complaint in an EEOC civil action may properly embrace, in addition to those allegations contained in the initial charge, any allegations of other discriminatory employment practices for which there has been *an investigation, a determination of reasonable cause and a genuine attempt at conciliation.*" (emphasis supplied)

* * * Like language can be found in a long line of decisions concerning the scope of the Commission's judicial complaint. These decisions recognize a right in the

---

[3]A reference to the legislative history of the Act * * * is particularly instructive:

> " * * * Senator Dominick, the principle architect of the 1972 amendment that empowered the Commission to bring suit in its own name, stated that '[M]y amendment would take over at the level where conciliations fail' 118 Cong.Rec.S. 170 (Jan. 20, 1972). 'What the amendment does * * * is * * * provide for trial in the U.S. District Courts whenever the EEOC has investigated a charge, found reasonable cause to believe that an unlawful employment practice has occurred, and is *unable* to obtain voluntary compliance.' 118 Cong.Rec.S. 221 (Jan. 21, 1972). Similarly, the Senior House Conferee on the 1972 amendment ventured the opinion that '*[O]nly if conciliation proves to be impossible* do we expect the Commission to bring action in federal district court to seek enforcement.' Cong.Rec.H. 1861 (Mar. 18, 1972) (remarks of Congressman Perkins, introduced in the Conference Report on House Resolution 1746)." (emphasis supplied).

Commission to pursue its investigation beyond the bounds of the original charge of discrimination. But in so doing they do not vest the Commission with the authority to pick and choose the matters to be conciliated.

The only construction of the statute which is at all in harmony with the Congressional desire for conciliation is that the Commission's authority to sue is conditioned upon full compliance with the administrative process — investigation, determination, and conciliation — with respect to each discriminatory practice alleged. Congress, committed as it was to voluntary compliance, could not have intended that the Commission could attempt conciliation on one set of issues and, having failed, litigate a different set. Once having determined that a respondent has violated Title VII the Commission must make a genuine effort to conciliate with respect to each and every employment practice complained of. In this way, the respondent is afforded a fair opportunity to weigh all the factors which must be taken into account in deciding whether to settle a dispute out of court, even if the charge of discrimination in dispute arose from the Commission's own investigation rather than the charging party's charge. And if litigation then results, all parties are assured that they have had a fair opportunity to settle every matter in dispute. The Congressional mandate that litigation be a matter of last resort will have been observed.

It is contended, however, that this Court lacks jurisdiction to inquire into the degree of the Commission's compliance with the conciliation requirements of Title VII, hence Sherwood's complaint that it was afforded no opportunity to conciliate the sex discrimination claim may not be heard. Essentially, the Commission takes the position that the scope of the matters sought to be conciliated is not a proper subject of judicial scrutiny; the Courts inquiry into its jurisdiction must cease upon proof that conciliation was attempted on at least some matters in dispute. This contention is without merit. The Court recognizes that the conciliation requirement of the statute is phrased in terms of conciliation "acceptable to the Commission"; and thus district courts are not empowered to second guess the Commission with respect to particular settlement negotiations. But the question in this case is not whether the Commission properly exercised its discretion during settlement negotiations, but whether it afforded the respondent Sherwood the opportunity to conciliate at all with respect to one of the claims asserted in its judicial complaint. It is frivolous to contend that the court lacks jurisdiction to decide this question. If the Commission is to seek relief in federal court it must be prepared to show that it has satisfied the jurisdictional prerequisites — including submitting the matters in issue to conciliation. It has not done so here and it therefore follows that suit on the sex discrimination claim was premature. This is a matter of subject matter jurisdiction, not of Commission discretion.

V. CONCLUSION

* * * The Commission must substantially satisfy the requirements of each step in this process — investigation, determination and conciliation — before it can progress to the next. In the present case the Commission has bypassed two of the most essential — determination and conciliation. These defects may not be overlooked, and the sex discrimination claim must therefore be stricken. A separate order dismissing the Commission's sex discrimination claim will be entered. The race discrimination claim, of course, will remain pending and the issue for trial will be whether during the relevant period Sherwood discriminated against employees or prospective employees on the basis of race.

Johnson v. Nekoosa-Edwards Paper Co.

United States Court of Appeals, Eighth Circuit, 1977.
558 F.2d 841, cert. denied, 434 U.S. 920, 98 S.Ct. 394, 54 L.Ed.2d 276.

HEANEY, Circuit Judge.

This action was filed by Linda Johnson and the United Paperworkers International Union against Nekoosa Papers, Inc., alleging the existence of sex discrimination in its employment practices at Nekoosa's Ashdown, Arkansas, facilities. The named plaintiffs sought to represent a class including all past and present female employees and all female job applicants who were denied employment opportunities because of their sex. The Equal Employment Opportunity Commission was allowed to intervene. The District Court initially certified the class to include only present employees but later decertified the class entirely and ruled that "the EEOC may not expand the scope of this action beyond that which the Plaintiffs are permitted to pursue."[1] The District Court's decision to * * * to limit the scope of the EEOC's intervention is challenged in this consolidated appeal.

Prior to bringing this action, Johnson and the Union had filed a charge with the EEOC alleging that "[f]emale employees have been denied job opportunities, wages and fringe benefits because of their sex, including but not limited to the treatment of maternity conditions by the employer."[3] After an investigation, the EEOC found reasonable cause to believe that Nekoosa discriminated against women in violation of Title VII with respect to maternity benefits, job opportunities and wages. The EEOC issued its determination of probable cause on June 19, 1974, and indicated that an EEOC representative would be in contact with each party in the near future to begin conciliation. In early August, 1974, the attorney for Nekoosa contacted the EEOC by letter and telephone seeking to expedite the conciliation process. The EEOC did not respond to Nekoosa's overtures. The EEOC issued a right-to-sue letter to Johnson and the Union at their request on August 19, 1974. This action was filed on September 9, 1974.

* * *

II.

We next consider whether the District Court properly held that the EEOC may not expand the scope of the action beyond that of the charge filed by the plaintiffs with the EEOC. The District Court certified the following questions to this Court pursuant to 28 U.S.C. §1292(b).

1. Whether the commission's suit in intervention properly enlarges the scope of the private plaintiffs' suit so as to include all forms of discrimination described in the Commission's Determination of Plaintiffs' underlying charges.

---

[1]Thus, the EEOC would not be able to raise the claims of those who were denied job opportunities because of their sex and to challenge the virtual exclusion of females from production jobs.
[3]The charge was filed with the EEOC on November 29, 1973, by Johnson and the Union acting through their attorney.

2.   Whether the Court properly held that "the EEOC may not expand the scope of this action beyond that which the Plaintiffs are permitted to pursue" in view of the fact that the EEOC had not prior to the filing of its Motion to Intervene endeavored "to eliminate any such alleged, unlawful employment practice by informal methods of conference, conciliation, and persuasion" as required by §706(b) of Title VII and that the EEOC had not as required by its rules, 29 CFR §1601-23 (1974), notified the Defendant in writing "that such efforts have been unsuccessful and will not be resumed except on the Respondent's written request within the time specified in such notice."

3.   Whether the Court abused its discretion in permitting the EEOC to intervene in this action in view of the fact that the EEOC had not, prior to the filing of its Motion for Intervention, endeavored to eliminate any alleged unlawful employment practice by informal methods of conference, conciliation and persuasion as required by §706(b) of Title VII and that the EEOC had not, as required by its own rules, 29 CFR §1601-23 (1974), notified the Defendant, in writing "that such efforts have been unsuccessful and will not be resumed except on the Respondent's written request with the time specified in such notice."

In order to resolve these questions relating to the permissible scope of the EEOC's suit in intervention, we are faced with the task of reconciling our holding in Equal Employment Op. Comm'n v. Missouri Pacific R. Co., 493 F.2d 71 (8th Cir.1974), with the EEOC's general obligation to conciliate.

In *Missouri Pacific*, this Circuit held "that, once the charging party has filed suit pursuant to a 'right to sue' notice the Commission is relegated to its right of permissive intervention." The Court relied upon the express statutory scheme,[7] §706(f)(1), and the legislative history of the 1972 amendments to Title VII[8] in reaching its conclusion that duplicitous suits were barred by the statute.[9]

A problem arises, however, because different issues may be raised by the private suit and the suit filed by the EEOC even though the same charge originally filed with the EEOC serves as the basis for both suits. In this case, in its suit in intervention, the EEOC seeks to raise the claims of unsuccessful job applicants and to challenge the

---

[7]The scheme of the statute itself * * * negates the Commission's double-barreled approach. Once either the Commission or the charging party has filed suit, §706(f)(1) speaks only in terms of intervention — the absolute right of the charging party to intervene if the Commission elects to file suit within 180 days; the permissive right of intervention on the part of the Commission in the private action. The statute cannot be read to warrant duplicitous lawsuits when both actions find their genesis in one unlawful employment practice charge. .

[8]H.R.Rep.No.92-238, 92d Cong., 2d Sess., 1972 U.S. Code Cong. & Admin. News p. 2148.

[9]Other Circuits, have however, developed different approaches to the problem of duplicitous suits. The Fifth and Sixth Circuits, allow the EEOC to file suit if the EEOC suit would be broader in scope than the private action, even if a private suit based upon the same EEOC charge has already been filed. This approach was rejected by the Tenth Circuit because it was unable to find any statutory basis for defining the EEOC's right to sue in terms of the scope of its suit.
    The Third Circuit reads the statute and the legislative history differently and places no limitation on the right of the EEOC to bring suit after a private action has been filed. Any problem with duplicitous suits is to be resolved under Fed.R.Civ.P. 42(a) which provides for the consolidation of actions involving common questions of law and fact.
    We adhere to our decision in *Missouri Pacific*, for the reasons stated in that opinion.

apparent exclusion of females from production jobs.[10] Thus, the scope of the EEOC suit is broader than that of the private suit which the District Court has limited to those issues raised by the charge filed with the EEOC which only alleged discrimination against present female employees.[11] The Court in *Missouri Pacific* recognized that the scope of the EEOC suit might be broader than that of the private suit when it stated that it was "fully confident that [the District Court] * * * will permit intervention and enlargement of the scope of the action by the Commission if necessary to the rendering of full and complete justice." My concurring opinion went one step further and would have required the District Court to broaden the scope of the suit to include those issues raised by the EEOC because the EEOC is charged with the responsibility of eliminating discriminatory employment practices and, thus, must be allowed to bring the broader issues before the court. Indeed, it would be anomalous if we did not allow the EEOC's suit in intervention to broaden the issues beyond those raised by the charge filed with the EEOC since the EEOC is not so restricted if it brings a direct suit. See E.E.O.C. v. General Elec. Co., 532 F.2d 359 (4th Cir.1976). We cannot, however, simply order that the EEOC be permitted to broaden the scope of its suit in intervention because we must also consider the obligation of the EEOC to attempt conciliation.

Because of the enormous backlog of cases pending before the EEOC, a private party will usually be able to bring an action before the EEOC has attempted conciliation and completed the administrative process.[12] When this occurs, as it did

---

[10]The EEOC investigation revealed that only 4.5% of Nekoosa's employees were female even though the community work force was 22.4% female. Moreover, 78.5% of the female Nekoosa employees occupied clerical positions.

[11]We emphasize that we are without jurisdiction to review this aspect of the District Court's order. We note, however, that it has been held that a private suit is not necessarily restricted to the scope of the charge filed with the EEOC and may extend to those issues revealed by a reasonable investigation by the EEOC. See Jenkins v. Blue Cross Mutual Hospital Ins., Inc., 522 F.2d 1235, 1241 (7th Cir.1975) (en banc); Sanchez v. Standard Brands, Inc., 431 F.2d 455, 466 (5th Cir.1970).

[12]A charging party cannot bring a private action unless permission is received from the EEOC. However, the EEOC is required to issue a right-to-sue letter if it either dismisses a charge or does not bring suit within 180 days of the date the charge was filed. The charging party then has 90 days in which to initiate his own court action. §706(f)(1). It is, thus, possible for a charging party to bring suit within a short period of time after the charge has been filed.

While the EEOC can bring an action within 30 days after the charge has been filed, it can only do so if it finds reasonable cause to believe the charge to be true and if conciliation has failed. Since it has often taken the EEOC two to three years to attempt conciliation, U.S. Comm'n on Civil Rights, The Federal Civil Rights Enforcement Effort — 1974, 529 (1975), the EEOC will usually be unable to bring its own action before a private action has been filed. The EEOC's delay in processing cases is reflected by its backlog of cases. As of June 30, 1975, over 126,000 cases were pending before the EEOC. As the following table indicates, some of the pending charges date back to 1968.

Fiscal Year in Which Charge was Filed	Number of Open Charges
1968	2,213
1969	3,260
1970	4,245
1971	5,917
1972	8,114

here, the EEOC is precluded from bringing a direct action and is relegated to its right of permissive intervention. If conciliation was required prior to intervention, the EEOC's motion to intervene might not be considered timely under Fed.R.Civ.P. 24 because the process of conciliation is often time-consuming. While conciliation is mandatory prior to direct suit by the EEOC, §706(f)(1); it is not mandatory under the statutory scheme prior to intervention by the EEOC.[13] 42 U.S.C. §706(f)(1). Thus, the EEOC cannot be precluded from intervention because it failed to conciliate.

Conciliation is nonetheless an integral part of Title VII, and is desirable for a variety of policy reasons including giving the defendant notice and an opportunity to respond to any additional claims revealed by the EEOC investigation and in order to avoid expensive and time-consuming court actions.[14] Because we believe strongly in the value of conciliation, we hold that while the EEOC is not barred from intervention by its failure to attempt to conciliate, it is under a continuing obligation to attempt to conciliate even after it has intervened in the action. To this end, we order the District Court to stay the action for sixty days and to require the EEOC to make a prompt offer to conciliate. If the offer is accepted by Nekoosa and if thereafter EEOC fulfills its obligation to conciliate in good faith and if no settlement is forthcoming by the end of the sixty-day period, the District Court is directed to then enter an order permitting the EEOC to expand its intervention in accordance with its petition. If Nekoosa refuses to conciliate, then the District Court's order permitting the EEOC to expand the scope of its intervention shall be issued forthwith.

We believe such a stay is not so long as to unduly prejudice the individual claimants. We realize that requiring the EEOC to expedite its conciliation process after intervention might be difficult for them because of their backlog of cases. We feel, however, it is the best balance between the right of the EEOC to intervene, the obligation of the EEOC to attempt conciliation and the right of the individual claimants to proceed with their action.

1973	18,550
1974	30,812
1975	46,919
Unspecified	6,310
	———
TOTAL	126,340

Report to the Congress by the Comptroller General of the United States, The Equal Employment Opportunity Commission Has Made Limited Progress in Eliminating Employment Discrimination 9 (September 28, 1976).

[13]The EEOC has been permitted to intervene in three District Court cases even though it had not attempted to conciliate. Willis v. Allied Maintenance Corp., 13 FEP Cases 767 (S.D.N.Y. 1976); NOW v. Minnesota Mining & Mfg., 11 FEP Cases 720 (D.Minn.1975); Jones v. Holy Cross Hospital Silver Springs, Inc., 64 F.R.D. 586 (D.MD.1974). In each case, the EEOC was not permitted to expand the scope of the action because it had not attempted to conciliate. Because we are ordering a stay to permit conciliation, the EEOC will be permitted to expand the scope of its action here.

[14]We are aware that the conciliation process has to date been relatively unsuccessful. See Peck, The Equal Employment Opportunity Commission: Developments in the Administrative Process 1965, 1975, 51 Wash. L. Rev. 831, 852-853 (1976); Report to Congress by the Comptroller General of the United States, *supra* at 7-37. Action by the legislative and executive branches of the federal government is apparently necessary to make the process a more effective one.

Accordingly, we reverse and remand this action to the District Court for action consistent with this opinion.

NOTES AND PROBLEMS FOR DISCUSSION

1. Section 706(f)(1) permits the EEOC, once conciliation has failed, to sue a non-governmental defendant and authorizes private parties to intervene as a matter of right in EEOC suits. The same section permits an aggrieved private party, after receiving a right-to-sue notice, to bring an independent suit and provides that the court may, as in *Johnson*, permit the EEOC to intervene in such private actions. The Act contains no other qualification of the agency's general authority to bring suit. In *Johnson*, however, the Court stated that when a private party has instituted suit, "the EEOC is precluded from bringing a direct action and is relegated to its right of permissive intervention." On this issue the circuits are divided. Several courts have interpreted the legislative history to mean that §706(f)(1) was intended to prohibit the EEOC from filing an independent suit once a private suit arising from the same charge has been filed. *See, e.g.,* EEOC v. Duval Corp., 528 F.2d 945 (10th Cir. 1976). Other courts have read the same legislative history and reached the opposite conclusion. *See, e.g.,* EEOC v. Kimberly-Clark Corp., 511 F.2d 1352, 1363 (6th Cir.), cert. denied, 423 U.S. 994, 96 S.Ct. 420, 46 L.Ed.2d 368 (1975) ("The Congressional intent that duplicitous proceedings be avoided does not mean, however, that the EEOC should be limited to permissive intervention in a private suit when its investigation on the one charge has disclosed a number of violations which require judicial attention.").

Unlike Title VII, the ADEA provides that "the right of any person to bring [an ADEA suit] shall terminate upon the commencement of an action by the Equal Employment Opportunity Commission to enforce the right of such employee under [the ADEA]." 29 U.S.C. §626(c)(1). Courts have construed that language as placing the EEOC in privity with the individual for whom it seeks relief and have held that the EEOC is barred from seeking victim-specific relief where the employee would be barred. In EEOC v. HARRIS CHERNIN, INC., 10 F.3d 1286 (7th Cir. 1993), the court held that the EEOC could not seek back pay, liquidated damages, and reinstatement for an employee whose own suit had been dismissed as time-barred. As the employee's representative, the EEOC was barred by res judicata from seeking relief on his behalf. Nevertheless, the court also stated that "[t]here is no privity such that res judicata as to the employee's claim for individual relief would bar the EEOC from bringing an action seeking an injunction to prevent future violations." 10 F.3d at 1291. *See also* EEOC v. Huttig Sash & Door Co., 511 F.2d 453 (5th Cir. 1975) (although termination of the charging party's suit does not bar the EEOC from suing to end discriminatory practices that were identified in its investigation, it does bar the agency from seeking relief for the charging party). The Seventh Circuit has extended *Harris Chernin* to cases where the employee has not filed a timely charge and could thus not file a viable suit himself. *See* EEOC v. North Gibson Sch. Corp., 266 F.3d 607 (7th Cir. 2001).

2. Under *14 Penn Plaza*, discussed in Section A.5, *supra*, mandatory arbitration clauses in individual and collectively bargained employment contracts which bar *litigation* of employment disputes, including statutory discrimination claims, are presumptively enforceable under the Federal Arbitration Act. But the existence of such an enforceable arbitration clause does not bar an employee from filing an *administrative* charge with the EEOC. Can the EEOC sue on the basis of a charge filed by an employee who is contractually bound to arbitrate a discrimination claim? If so, what kind of relief can the EEOC seek for the employee? In EEOC v. WAFFLE HOUSE, INC., 534 U.S. 279, 122 S.Ct. 754, 151 L.Ed.2d 755 (2002), a former employee who had signed an arbitration clause as a condition of employment filed a charge with the EEOC alleging that he was discharged in violation of the ADA. After an investigation and unsuccessful attempt at conciliation, the agency filed an enforcement action in which it requested that the employee be reinstated, awarded back pay, and compensatory and punitive damages. The employee did not intervene and was not a party to the litigation. Waffle House moved to stay the EEOC's suit and to compel arbitration. The district court denied the motion. The Fourth Circuit concluded that the EEOC was not a party to the arbitration agreement and was thus not bound by it. But it also ruled that the agency was precluded from seeking victim-specific relief because the competing goals of the ADA and the FAA required giving some effect to the arbitration contract. The Supreme Court reversed the circuit court's ruling, emphasizing the independent statutory authority of the EEOC to sue to enforce the statute.

> The compromise solution reached by the Court of Appeals turns what is effectively a forum selection clause into a waiver of a nonparty's statutory remedies. But if the federal policy favoring arbitration trumps the plain language of Title VII and the contract, the EEOC should be barred from pursuing any claim outside the arbitral forum. If not, then the statutory language is clear; the EEOC has the authority to pursue victim-specific relief regardless of the forum that the employer and the employee have chosen to resolve their disputes. Rather than attempt to split the difference, we are persuaded that, pursuant to Title VII and the ADA, whenever the EEOC chooses from among the many charges filed each year to bring an enforcement action in a particular case, the agency may be seeking to vindicate a public interest, not simply provide make-whole relief for the employee, even when it pursues entirely victim-specific relief. To hold otherwise would undermine the detailed enforcement scheme created by Congress simply to give greater effect to an agreement between private parties that does not even contemplate the EEOC's statutory function.

534 U.S. at 295-296.

Arguing that the majority opinion reduced the arbitration agreement "to all but a nullity," Justice Thomas dissented on behalf of two other justices. He reasoned that the statute gives the EEOC only the right to seek "appropriate relief" and that when the EEOC seeks specific relief for a charging party, it is inappropriate to award more relief than the individual could obtain for himself. The difference between the majority and dissent boils down to differing interpretations of what the EEOC accomplishes or seeks to accomplish when it seeks victim-specific relief as opposed to broad class-based injunctive relief. Is the EEOC merely vindicating the charging party's rights, or, by seeking such relief accomplishing broader functions of deterrence?

What is the impact of the ruling in *Waffle House* on the individual employee's right to intervene in the EEOC suit? Can she intervene in the EEOC suit and assert a cross claim against the employer or must she pursue her claim through arbitration? In EEOC v. WOODMEN OF THE WORLD LIFE INS. SOCIETY, 479 F.3d 561 (8th Cir. 2007), the Eighth Circuit directed the trial court to issue an order compelling arbittation, staying the individual employee's cross-claim filed in the EEOC enforcement action, but not staying the EEOC's enforcement action itself. The court rejected the employee's argument that requiring her to arbitrate her individual employment discrimination claim would interfere with the agency's ability to pursue its enforcement action. It reasoned that the employee id not lose her substantive rights under Title VII once the EEOC filed an enforcement action. Consequently, it ruled, the cross-claim that she attempted to bring as an intervenor in the EEOC's enforcement action had to be decided in the arbitral forum.

Does the majority's rationale in *Waffle House* mean that the EEOC should be allowed to seek victim-specific relief without regard to whether the charging party would be barred from obtaining such suit in an individual suit under the Act? For example, what if the charge was untimely? In EEOC v. SIDLEY AUSTIN LLP, 437 F.3d 695 (7th Cir.2006), cert. denied, 549 U.S. 815, 127 S.Ct. 76, 166 L.Ed.2d 27 (2006), the EEOC had filed an ADEA claim against the defendant law firm seeking damages for thirty-two partners who had been retired involuntarily on the basis of their age. In connection with the defendant's motion for partial summary judgment, the trial court ruled that the EEOC could obtain monetary relief on behalf of the individual partners even though they had failed to file timely EEOC charges challenging their involuntarily retirement. The Seventh Circuit upheld the trial court, construing *Waffle House* to be predicated on the notion that the agency's enforcement authority was not derivative of the individuals for whom it was seeking relief. Consequently, it ruled, the agency was not bound by the failure of the individual partners to exhaust their administrative remedies. Furthermore, the court declared, since the EEOC was not required to exhaust administrative remedies pursuant to its own statutory authority to bring suit, it had no duty to exhaust in this case.

3. Although the EEOC's investigation of a charge, and thus the claims it may raise in a subsequent suit, may be considerably broader that the substance of the charge, claims which the EEOC has not attempted to conciliate with the defendant will be stricken from the suit. *See* EEOC v. Allegheny Airlines, 436 F.Supp. 1300, 1305 (W.D.Pa. 1977). But what kind of effort by the Commission to arrange conciliation is necessary? To what extent should the court delve into the conciliation process to determine whether an appropriate effort was made? *See, e.g.*, EEOC v. Klingler Elec. Corp., 636 F.2d 104 (5th Cir. 1981). Would a court's review of the actual offers and counter offers of the parties during the conciliation process to determine the EEOC's good faith be fair to the parties? To satisfy its statutory obligation the EEOC must (1) outline to the employer the reasonable cause for its belief that Title VII has been violated; (2) offer an opportunity for voluntary compliance; and (3) respond in a reasonable and flexible manner to the reasonable proposals of the employer. "[A]n 'all or nothing' approach on the part of a government agency, one of whose most essential functions is to attempt conciliation with the private party will not do." EEOC v. Asplundh Tree Expert Co., 340 F.3d 1256, 1261 (11th Cir. 2003) (awarding costs and attorney fees to the employer as sanction for the EEOC's bad faith refusal to engage in discussion of proposed conciliation agreement). *See* EEOC v. Norvell & Wallace, Inc., 2003 WL 21183037 (M.D. Tenn. 2003) (letter from agency inviting employer to engage in conciliation and stating what steps would be necessary to reach agreement fulfills EEOC's obligation to attempt conciliation; motion to stay proceedings denied).

4. Title VII imposes strict limits on the time within which private parties may file charges with the EEOC, but it does not contain an express limitation on the time within which the Commission may bring suit. A Commission suit may be barred by the doctrine of laches when it has been inexcusably delayed and the defendant has been materially prejudiced by the delay. Occidental Life Ins. Co. v. EEOC, 432 U.S. 355, 373, 97 S.Ct. 2447, 2457, 53 L.Ed.2d 402, 415 (1977). Laches is only available as a defense where both unreasonable delay and substantial or material prejudice to the defendant have occurred. The EEOC's workload has been rejected as an excuse for delay. *See* EEOC v. Liberty Loan Corp., 584 F.2d 853 (8th Cir. 1978). The burden of proving prejudice is on the defendant and is normally established by demonstrating the unavailability of witnesses, changed personnel, or loss of pertinent records. *See* EEOC v. Alioto Fish Co., Ltd., 623 F.2d 86 (9th Cir. 1980).

5. To enable the EEOC to investigate charges, §709(a) of Title VII provides the agency with a broad right of access to "any evidence of any person being investigated * * * that relates to unlawful employment practices covered by [the Act] and is relevant to the charge under investigation." If an employer refuses to voluntarily provide information, the Commission is authorized to issue subpoenas and to seek judicial enforcement of subpoenas. In a subpoena enforcement proceeding, the court's duty is to "satisfy itself that the charge is valid and that the material requested is 'relevant' to the charge * * * and more generally to assess any contentions by the employer that the demand for information is too indefinite or has been made for an illegitimate purpose." EEOC v. Shell Oil Co., 466 U.S. 54, 72 n.26, 104 S.Ct. 1621, 1633 n.26, 80 L.Ed.2d 41, 59 n.26 (1984). In UNIV. of PENN. v. EEOC, 493 U.S. 182, 110 S.Ct. 577, 107 L.Ed.2d 571 (1990), the Commission, during its investigation of a charge against a university arising from the denial of tenure for a faculty member, subpoenaed confidential peer review materials. The University resisted the subpoena on privacy, academic freedom and First Amendment grounds. The Court unanimously rejected those arguments.

> Acceptance of [the University's] claim would also lead to a wave of similar privilege claims by other employers who play significant roles in furthering speech and learning in society. What of writers, publishers, musicians, lawyers? It surely is not unreasonable to believe, for example, that confidential peer reviews play an important part in partnership determinations at some law firms. We perceive no limiting principle in petitioner's argument. Accordingly, we stand behind the breakwater Congress has established: unless specifically provided otherwise in the statute, the EEOC may obtain "relevant" evidence. Congress has made the choice. If it dislikes the result, it may of course revise the statute.

493 U.S. at 194, 110 S.Ct. at 585.

Pursuant to the teachings of *Shell Oil*, the lower courts generally have ruled that the scope of the EEOC's investigation and thus, the breadth of the subpoena it can issue, are limited by the type of discrimination alleged in the underlying charge. In EEOC v. SOUTHERN FARM BUREAU CASUALTY INS. CO., 271 F.3d 209 (5th Cir. 2001), during the course of the investigation of a racial discrimination charge, the EEOC discovered possible sex discrimination and issued a subpoena calling for information regarding the sex of employees. The employer refused to comply and the EEOC filed suit to enforce the subpoena. The district court refused enforcement and the court of appeals affirmed on the ground that the data sought was irrelevant to the charge that the EEOC had authority to investigate. The Fifth Circuit noted that upon discovering evidence of sex discrimination, the agency could have filed a commissioner's charge "thereby freeing the EEOC to demand information relevant to Southern Farm's employment of women." 271 F.3d at 211. Commissioner charges are discussed in Note 6 below. Courts are reluctant however to allow employers to contest subpoenas on grounds that the underlying claim is without merit. In EEOC v. SIDLEY AUSTIN BROWN & WOOD, 315 F.3d 696 (7th Cir. 2002), the EEOC issued subpoenas during its investigation of a claim that a law firm violated the ADEA when it demoted 32 partners to counsel status during a restructuring. The law firm objected to the subpoenas on the ground that the partners were not employees and thus were not covered by the ADEA. The agency claimed that it needed documents regarding profit distribution to all partners to determine whether the 32 claimants were "partners in name only." The Court of Appeals agreed. "The commission is entitled to the information that it thinks it needs in order to be able to formulate its theory of coverage before the court is asked to choose between the commission's theory and that of the subpoenaed firm." 315 F.3d at 700.

6. Section 706(b) of Title VII provides for the initiation of proceedings by an aggrieved person or by "a member of the Commission." The statutory requirements for and procedures applicable to private charges and "Commissioner charges" are the same. Courts have tended, however, to require a good deal more specificity of Commissioner-filed charges than of charges filed by private individuals. Disputes over the validity of Commissioner charges frequently arise during efforts by the Commission to enforce subpoenas issued in the course of investigations. In EEOC v. SHELL OIL CO., 466 U.S. 54, 104 S.Ct. 1621, 80 L.Ed.2d 41 (1984), the Commissioner's charge alleged that the company had engaged in a generic variety of unlawful practices from the effective date of Title VII to the present. The Court of Appeals blocked enforcement of the EEOC's broad-ranging subpoena on the ground that the agency had failed to comply with §706(b) because the charge had not included sufficient factual and statistical information or alleged victims of the discrimination, nor did it inform the company of the approximate dates of the unlawful practices. The Supreme Court agreed that a charge and notice meeting the requirements of §706 are jurisdictional prerequisites to judicial enforcement of an agency subpoena, but held that in this case the requirements had been met. The Court concluded that the Eighth Circuit's holding would, in effect, have obliged the Commissioner to substantiate his allegations before the EEOC could investigate, thus impairing the agency's enforcement powers. The purpose of the notice requirement in §706(b), the Court explained, is to give an employer fair notice of the existence and nature of the allegations against it, not to impose a substantive constraint on the EEOC's investigative authority. The statute requires that a Commissioner charging a pattern or practice of discrimination should, to the extent practicable, identify (1) the groups of persons that he has reason to believe have been discriminated against; (2) the categories of employment positions from which they have been excluded; (3) the methods by which the discrimination may have been effected; and (4) the time period during which he suspects the discrimination occurred.

In a case filed under §706(a) where the EEOC acts on the basis of an individual charge, the agency may not obtain relief for individuals whose claims are time-barred.

But where the suit is based on a Commissioner charge and the allegation is one of systemic discrimination, what is the limitation period for relief? *See* EEOC v. Mitsubishi Motor Mfg. of Am., 990 F.Supp. 1059, 1086-87 (C.D. Ill. 1998) ("Once the EEOC establishes that a pattern or practice exists, * * * this evidence will determine when the provable pattern or practice began. Any individual claims that fall within that period will be allowed to proceed to the individual relief stage.") The subject of class-wide relief is discussed in Chapter 7 D, *infra*.

Adams v. Proctor & Gamble Manufacturing Co.

United States Court of Appeals, Fourth Circuit, 1983.
697 F.2d 582, cert. denied, 465 U.S. 1041, 104 S.Ct. 1318, 79 L.Ed.2d 714 (1984).

Per Curiam.

This case, concerning the preclusive effect upon charging parties of a consent decree in an action brought against an employer by the EEOC, was first heard by a panel of this court. A majority of the panel held there was no preclusive effect, while Senior Judge Haynsworth dissented. Thereafter, an order was entered granting rehearing *en banc*.

The question turns upon a proper interpretation of §706(f)(1) of Title VII, 42 U.S.C.A. §706(f)(1), which, insofar as pertinent, provides:

(f)(1) If within thirty days after a charge is filed with the Commission * * *, the Commission has been unable to secure from the respondent a conciliation agreement acceptable to the Commission, the Commission may bring a civil action against any respondent not a government, governmental agency, or political subdivision named in the charge * * *. The person or persons aggrieved shall have the right to intervene in a civil action brought by the Commission * * *. If a charge filed with the Commission pursuant to subsection (b) of this section is dismissed by the Commission, or if within one hundred and eighty days from the filing of such charge * * *, the Commission has not filed a civil action under this section * * *, or the Commission has not entered into a conciliation agreement to which the person aggrieved is a party, the Commission * * * shall so notify the person aggrieved and within ninety days after the giving of such notice a civil action may be brought against the respondent named in the charge (A) by the person claiming to be aggrieved * * *.

In 1976 the EEOC brought an action against Proctor & Gamble alleging employment discrimination. Some two dozen Proctor & Gamble employees had filed charges with the EEOC, but none of them chose to intervene in the EEOC action, though each had an unqualified right to do so under §706(f)(1). Negotiations between the employer and the EEOC resulted in a settlement of the action by consent decree. Thereafter, the EEOC issued right-to-sue letters to those charging parties who rejected awards under the decree. When sixteen of those Proctor & Gamble workers with right-to-sue letters sued individually, the district court granted the company's motion to dismiss on the ground that the letters were invalid.

* * * [W]e hold the district court's dismissal was appropriate. We read §706(f)(1) in these circumstances to preclude suits by individuals who are charging

parties, but who have not intervened in the pending EEOC action in their behalf, once the EEOC action has been concluded by a consent decree.

Under §706(f)(1) right-to-sue letters may be issued by the Commission to charging parties under several different circumstances, but there is no provision for the issuance of such a letter under any circumstance after the EEOC has filed an action on behalf of the charging parties. * * * [T]here must be an exception if the EEOC's action is concluded on technical grounds without a judgment on the merits. In every sense, however, this consent decree was a judgment on the merits, and it awarded benefits which were then available to the charging parties.

The statutory scheme is fair and reasonable. A charging party has an unqualified right to intervene in the EEOC's action. If he wishes to participate in settlement negotiations or to have the right to reject any settlement agreement negotiated by the EEOC, he may fully protect himself by intervening. If he does not intervene, it is not unfair to him to conclude that he placed the conduct of the litigation entirely upon the EEOC and expressed a conclusive willingness to be bound by the outcome, whether or not the outcome was negotiated.

General Telephone Co. of the Northwest, Inc. v. EEOC, 446 U.S. 318, 100 S.Ct. 1698, 64 L.Ed.2d 319 (1980), is not to the contrary. In that case the employer had sought a ruling that the EEOC could not obtain broad class relief without compliance with Federal Rule of Civil Procedure 23. There were only four charging parties in that case, but there were allegations of pervasive discrimination affecting a great many persons. In those circumstances, if the EEOC were required to comply with rule 23, the efficacy of the EEOC's §706(f)(1) remedy would be substantially impaired. Thus, the Supreme Court observed that it was "unconvinced that it would be consistent with the remedial purpose of the statutes to bind all 'class' members * * * by the relief obtained under an EEOC judgment or settlement against the employer." Id. at 333, 100 S.Ct. at 1707-08.

The question before the Supreme Court in *General Telephone* was exclusively related to the effect of a possible judgment upon persons who were not charging parties and who had no right of intervention. The Court's dicta must be read as referable to them and entirely inapplicable to the question of the preclusive effect of a judgment upon charging parties who had not exercised their right of intervention.

* * *

There has been some expression of concern among our dissenting brothers that a charging party may not recognize any reason to intervene in an EEOC action before an undesirable consent decree has been entered, by which time the right to intervene will have been lost. We appreciate their concern, but it cannot change the plain meaning of §706(f)(1). Moreover, one who wishes to participate in tactical decisions which may substantially affect the outcome of the litigation or in settlement negotiations has reason for early intervention. In this, as in many other situations, one who invokes administrative and judicial machinery in his behalf should have a continuing interest or participation in it. If he does not intervene and leaves it to the EEOC to do whatever seems best to the EEOC for him, he should not be heard to complain of the consequences of his own indifference.

The judgment of the district court is affirmed.

[The concurring opinion of Judge Widener is omitted]

PHILLIPS, Circuit Judge, dissenting:

I respectfully dissent for the reasons expressed in the superseded panel opinion, which held that plaintiffs' individual rights of action were not terminated by the institution of an EEOC action nor precluded by the entry in that action of a consent judgment to which they were not parties and whose terms they had affirmatively rejected. I continue to believe (as presumably does the EEOC, the federal agency charged with enforcing the statutory scheme in issue) that under the circumstances the EEOC was entitled under §706(f)(1) to issue to these plaintiffs the right-to-sue letters upon which this action was brought and that the underlying rights of action are subsisting ones.

With all deference, nothing said in the per curiam opinion of the en banc court dissuades me from the interpretation given the controlling statutory provision by the original panel decision. As the majority opinion notes, those of us in dissent are particularly concerned that the contrary interpretation now reached imposes an utterly unrealistic burden upon Title VII charging parties. Under that interpretation, charging parties are required at their peril, and unaided by the principals, to follow the course of agency-employer conciliation or "settlement" efforts closely enough to protect their individual interests by formal intervention if, following institution of an agency action, those negotiations seem headed toward an unfavorable settlement.

There is nothing in the relevant statutory framework that lays upon the EEOC or the employer any obligation to keep charging parties advised of the details of those negotiations; of whether any "settlement" is imminent; of whether any settlement under consideration is to be expressed in a conciliation agreement or in a consent judgment; of the details or even the substance of a "settlement" that has been informally reached and remains only to be formalized by either means; of whether and when an agency action is to be commenced; of the fact that one has been commenced; or of anything else about the course of agency-employer dealings. The formal agency documents on file and a part of the record in this case contain no information along these lines of which charging parties might be held to have constructive notice. On oral argument we were given to understand by counsel for the EEOC, appearing as amicus, that the agency does not consider itself under any obligation and does not routinely keep all charging parties even generally apprised of the course of its conciliation-"settlement" negotiations. Certainly there is no suggestion that in this case — where presumably the normal course of proceedings was followed — these charging party-plaintiffs were ever sufficiently advised along these lines to make an informed decision that they must formally intervene — with the attendant expense — in order to protect their interests against an imminent consent judgment that did not satisfactorily protect them.

* * *

If to all this it be rejoined that it is not our function to re-write statutes to cure perceived difficulties but simply to apply them according to their plain import, my response remains as it was in the panel majority opinion: that the dispositive statutory provision here is sufficiently ambiguous to require judicial interpretation drawing on the traditional aids. Among those traditional aids — in addition to * * * legislative history * * * — is that ancient and honorable canon of construction that when a literal interpretation ("conciliation" means only "conciliation") would lead to mischievous consequences, legislative intent is properly sought at deeper levels of purpose. I continue to believe that in *General Telephone*, the Supreme Court, by the clearest possible implication, and perhaps drawing *sub silentio* upon that canon, has already rejected the narrowly literal interpretation of §706(f)(1) for which Proctor & Gamble has contended and which the en banc majority now adopts. The *General Telephone* Court's careful discussion of the practical means by which employers entering into Title VII consent judgments with the EEOC may protect themselves against the private claims of employees — including charging parties — who may later reject the agency-employer settlement, is sensible only if it assumes that such judgments are not legally binding on those employees and that the employees' private rights of action are not terminated by mere institution of agency actions under §706.

I am authorized to say that Chief Judge Winter and Judge Sprouse join in this opinion.

NOTES AND PROBLEMS FOR DISCUSSION

1. The Fourth Circuit's construction of §706(f)(1) in *Adams* has been rejected by one circuit. In RIDDLE v. CERRO WIRE & CABLE GROUP, INC., 902 F.2d 918 (11th Cir. 1990), the EEOC instituted an action based on Riddle's charge and sought specific relief for her. Riddle did not intervene. The EEOC and the employer settled the case, but Riddle was not happy with the terms of the agreement, refused to sign it, and requested a right-to-sue notice. Riddle's suit was dismissed by the district court on the ground that under §706(f)(1), her right to commence a private action was cut off by the EEOC's filing suit on her behalf. Her only option according to the district court was to have intervened in the agency's action. The Eleventh Circuit reversed. That court held that Riddle's suit was not barred by either the terms of the statute or the doctrine of res judicata. The Court of Appeals interpreted §706(f)(1) as precluding the issuance of a right to sue notice only if (1) the EEOC filed suit within 180 days of the charge or (2) if the EEOC had entered into a conciliation agreement with the employer and the charging party. In *Riddle*, the EEOC had not filed suit within 180 days of the charge, and there was no conciliation agreement. Nor was Riddle bound by the consent decree negotiated by the EEOC because she had not been a party to the proceeding, she had refused to accept the benefits of the settlement, and her interests and those of the EEOC were so different that the agency could not be treated as her representative for preclusion purposes.

2. What steps might a district court take to protect the rights of employees affected by resolution of an EEOC suit? For example, can the district court reject a settlement between the employer and the EEOC on the ground that it is not fair to employees who would be bound by a consent decree? *See* EEOC v. Pan American World Airways, Inc., 622 F.Supp. 633 (N.D. Cal. 1985), appeal dismissed, 796 F.2d 314 (9th Cir. 1986), cert. denied, 479 U.S. 1030, 107 S.Ct. 874, 93 L.Ed.2d 829 (1987).

3. The rulings in both *Adams* and *Riddle* examine the effect of an EEOC-filed suit on a subsequent individual action. Circuits differ on whether an individual action precludes an EEOC action based on the same charge. In a circuit that allows the EEOC to file suit under these circumstances, what effect will resolution of the private suit have on the agency-filed case? In EEOC v. UNITED STATES STEEL CORP., 921 F.2d 489 (3d Cir. 1990), the agency sought to obtain individual relief under the ADEA for a group of former employees that included individuals who had been unsuccessful in their private actions against the employer. The Court of Appeals held that individuals who had fully litigated their own claims under the ADEA were precluded by claim preclusion principles from obtaining individual relief in a subsequent EEOC action based on the same claims.

> By claiming or accepting individual relief won by the EEOC, the individuals would necessarily concede that the EEOC was their representative and that they were embraced by the EEOC's judgment. For those individuals who had previously brought their own suits against USX and lost on the merits, this concession would be fatal. Having had their day in court, these individuals could not relitigate the same claim through a representative any more than they could relitigate the same claim on their own behalf.

921 F.2d at 496. *But see* EEOC v. Pemco Aeroplex, Inc., 383 F.3d 1280 (11th Cir. 2004), cert. denied, 546 U.S. 811, 126 S.Ct. 42, 163 L.Ed.2d 44 (2005) (reversing trial court's dismissal, on claim preclusion grounds, of EEOC suit alleging racially hostile work environment and seeking injunctive and monetary relief for individual victims after jury issued verdict against individual plaintiffs who had not serttled their hostile environment claims; EEOC was not a party to the private action and judgment in that action could not preclude the agency since the private litigants were not "virtual representatives" of the EEOC and it would be "anomalous" to bar the EEOC from acting on behalf of those employees who were not parties to the previous action); *and* EEOC v. Jefferson Dental Clinics, Pa., 478 F.3d 690 (5th Cir. 2007) (where the EEOC filed Title VII suit seeking both monetary and equitable relief based on allegations of sexual harassment by individuals who previously had filed an EEOC charge and suffered adverse judgment after trial in state court on state law tort claims, the EEOC claim seeking make-whole relief is precluded but its claim for injunctive relief is not subject to issue preclusion as the agency in this context serves a public interest independent of the right of the charging parties).

CHAPTER 5

Procedural Requirements for Public Sector Employees

SECTION A. FEDERAL GOVERNMENT EMPLOYEES

Read §717 of Title VII.

Title VII, as originally enacted, did not prohibit discrimination by public employers. As part of the Equal Employment Opportunity Act of 1972, however, Congress expanded the coverage of Title VII to include many federal, and most state and local government employees. State and local governments were brought under the statute's jurisdiction through a broadened definition of "person" in §701(a). A new provision — §717 — was added to bring many, but not all federal employees within the compass of the Act. Coverage was limited by the express terms of §717(a) to employees or applicants for employment in (1) executive agencies, and (2) those units of the legislative and judicial branches having positions in the competitive service. It was not until 1991, when Congress passed the Civil Rights Act of 1991 and the Government Employee Rights Act (GERA), that jurisdiction under Title VII was broadened to include a wider range of federal employees.

As part of the 1991 Civil Rights Act amendments to Title VII, Congress extended the applicability of the substantive (though not remedial or procedural) terms of Title VII to employees of the U.S. House of Representatives, agencies of the legislative branch and instrumentalities of the House including the Capitol Architect, the Congressional Budget Office, the Government Printing Office, the Office of Technology Assessment and the U.S. Botanic Garden. Similarly, the GERA extended the substantive provisions of Title VII to all employment-related decisions affecting Senate employees (defined as incumbent and former employees as well as applicants for employment) and presidential appointees (a term defined to include employees of all units of the executive branch, including the Executive Office, but excluding appointees whose appointments are made with the advice and consent of the Senate as well as members of the uniformed services). On the remedial/enforcement side, as a result of the 1991 Civil Rights Act, enforcement of the substantive rights of House employees is governed exclusively by the terms of the House Fair Employment Practices Resolution adopted in 1988. Additionally, enforcement authority of rights provided by both Title VII and the GERA has been assigned exclusively to the chief official of each Congressional instrumentality.

Neither the 1991 Act nor the GERA, however, provided Congressional employees with the right to a *judicial* trial of discrimination claims. This situation was remedied by the Congressional Accountability Act of 1995, a statute designed to extend the application of eleven labor and antidiscrimination statutes (including Title VII, the ADEA, the Rehabilitation Act, the ADA and the Family and Medical Leave Act) to the legislative branch. This statute established an Office of Compliance to oversee *administrative* enforcement of all employment claims of Congressional employees covered under the 1991 Civil Rights Act and the GERA. The Office consists of a five member Board of Directors appointed jointly by the Congressional leadership and a professional staff. Pursuant to the statute and its implementing regulations, to initiate proceedings, a congressional employee must seek counseling from the Office within 180 days of the alleged violation. Such counseling can last up to 30 days, although the employee may withdraw at any time. If the employee is not satisfied with the results of counseling, he or she must file a request for mediation within 15 days after the termination of counseling. Mediation may last for up to 30 days, although this length can be extended upon the agreement of the parties, at the discretion of the Office. If mediation is not successful at resolving the situation, the employee can either have an administrative hearing or file a claim in the federal district court in either the district where the employee works or in the District for the District of Columbia. In either case, the employee must wait for 30 days after the completion of mediation before filing a formal complaint and must do so no later than 90 days after the termination of mediation. If the employee chooses the administrative route, the Office's Executive Director appoints an independent hearing officer. Parties unsatisfied with the hearing officer's decision can file a petition for review by the Office Board of Directors within 30 days after the hearing officer's decision is rendered. The Board can overrule, modify, remand or affirm the hearing officer's ruling. Judicial review of the decision of the Office of Compliance Board lies with the Federal Circuit Court of Appeals. The Board also has the authority to ask the Office's General Counsel to petition the Federal Circuit for enforcement of an administrative decision or order. If the employee files a court action, the employee has the right to ask for a jury trial and the defendant will be the employing office where the alleged violation occurred.

Non-Congressional federal employees who fall within the protection of §717 of Title VII are authorized to file discrimination claims with the EEOC. Pursuant to the EEOC's procedural regulations, 29 C.F.R. §1613 (1979), the aggrieved first must seek review of the challenged action within his or her own agency by consulting with that agency's Equal Employment Opportunity Counselor within 45 days of the "matter alleged to be discriminatory." So, for example, in a standard discharge case, the 45-day limit begins to run from the date of the discharge. But the circuit courts had not agreed on the appropriate timing period for cases alleging *constructive* discharge. While a majority of the circuits agreed that the period began to run only on the date of the *plaintiff's* resignation, at least three circuits adhered to a "last discriminatory act" rule, whereby the 45-day period was deemed to commence on the date of the *defendant's* last discriminatory act leading to the resignation. The Supreme Court resolved this conflict in favor of the majority approach. In GREEN v. BRENNAN, ___ U.S. ___, 136 S.Ct. 1769, 195 L.Ed.2d 44 (2016), the Supreme Court, by an 8-1 majority, concluded that the "matter alleged to be discriminatory" in a constructive discharge case was the date of the plaintiff's resignation since that resignation was an element of the substantive claim of constructive discharge. Although this case dealt expressly with the limitations period for actions filed by *federal* employees alleging constructive discharge, the Court noted that the EEOC's 45 day filing period, applicable to federal employees only, was analogous to the statutorily created 180 or 300 days period for filing EEOC charges by nonfederal employees and that even though the source of these filing periods and their precise language were different, the EEOC treated both federal and private-sector employee limitations periods as identical in operation. Does this suggest that the period for filing EEOC charges in constructive discharge case asserted by nonfederal employees will be subject to this same standard?

If the employee is not satisfied with the Counselor's informal resolution of the matter, s/he can file a formal complaint with the official designated by the agency to receive such complaints. After an investigation and opportunity for a hearing, the agency EEO official renders a decision that is appealable to the agency head. An aggrieved that is not satisfied with the agency's final decision can either seek immediate judicial review of that decision or appeal to the EEOC.[a] If the aggrieved decides to seek administrative, rather than judicial review of an adverse decision by the agency head, the EEOC, in contrast to its limited role with respect to private sector discrimination claims, is empowered under §717(b) to issue "appropriate remedies, including reinstatement or hiring of employees with or without backpay."

---

[a]There is a special process for situations where a federal employee asserts a claim of discrimination in connection with certain specified serious types of employment decisions (removal, suspension for more than fourteen days, and reduction in grade or pay, or a furlough). This sort of discrimination claim is referred to as a "mixed case". Pursuant to the Civil Service Reform Act of 1978, 5 U.S.C. §1101 et seq., a federal employee with such a claim can initiate the process by either filing a discrimination claim with the Merits Systems Protection Board (MSPB) or by filing a discrimination claim with the agency itself. If the employee chooses to first file a claim with the employing agency and the agency decides against the employee on the merits of the claim, the employee then has two alternative ways to seek review. It can seek further administrative review by appealing the decision to the MPSB. Alternatively, the employee can bypass further administrative review by bringing suit against the agency in federal district court. If the claim is decided against the employee on the merits by the MPSB, either because the employee filed initially with the MPSB or because it appealed an adverse decision by the employing agency to the MPSB, the employee then has two alternative opportunities for further review. It can seek additional administrative review by appealing that decision to the EEOC or it can seek judicial review by filing suit in federal district court. If the employee chooses the EEOC route and the EEOC disagrees with the MPSB's decision, the EEOC must refer the case back to the Board for reconsideration. If the Board refuses to adopt the Commission's decision, and reaffirms its original ruling, it must certify the matter to a special three member panel consisting of a member of the Board, a member of the Commission and a presidentially appointed neutral. This panel then renders the final administrative decision in the case. The aggrieved subsequently can seek judicial review by filing suit in federal court. Similarly, where the MSPB dismisses an appeal of a mixed case solely on procedural grounds, and does not address the merits of the movant's discrimination claim, the employee seeking judicial review must file suit in federal district court. Kloeckner v. Solis, 133 S.Ct. 596 (2012). The Civil Service Reform Act also sets forth a separate series of limitations periods governing the filing of suit with respect to these limited types of personnel actions. Specifically, an aggrieved can file a civil action in federal district court after:

(a) the 120th day following the filing of a complaint with the employer agency where that complaint is appealable to the MSPB and there is no final decision by the agency and the aggrieved has not filed an appeal with the MSPB; or

(b) the 120th day after the filing of an appeal with the MSPB and there is no judicially reviewable action by the MSPB; or

(c) the 180th day after the filing of a petition with the EEOC and there is no final action by the EEOC.

The fact that the EEOC has statutorily-vested remedial authority raised an interesting question in light of the fact that Title VII also provides federal employees with the right to seek compensatory damages in cases in which either party has the right to demand a jury trial (i.e., cases alleging intentional discrimination). Since juries are not a part of an EEOC proceeding, and since Title VII provides only for awarding compensatory damages in an "action" brought under the statute, did Congress mean to arm the Commission with this remedial authority or merely to direct employees with damage claims to the courts? In WEST v. GIBSON, 527 U.S. 212, 119 S.Ct. 1906, 144 L.Ed.22d 196 (1999), by a 5-4 margin, the Court concluded that the EEOC could issue compensatory damage awards against federal agencies. The Court construed the language in §717(b) providing the EEOC with authority to issue "appropriate remedies" to include any relief authorized under Title VII, including relief that was unavailable when §717(b) was enacted. The Court also reasoned that authorizing the EEOC to issue compensatory damage awards was consistent with the legislative purpose of creating a dispute resolution system for federal employees that requires exhaustion of the administrative process. To deny the EEOC this remedial authority, the majority stated, would undermine this remedial scheme since it would force complainants seeking compensatory relief to file court actions instead of resolving the matter through the faster, and cheaper administrative mechanism. As to the unavailability of a jury in EEOC proceedings, the majority concluded that Congress meant only to guarantee either party a jury trial when seeking compensatory damages in a court of law. Similarly, the use of the word "action" did not, in the majority's judgment, reflect a legislative intent to deprive the EEOC of the authority to award compensatory relief. Finally, the Court rejected the notion that Congress intended for its indisputable waiver of sovereign immunity against compensatory damages awards to be limited to judicial awards.

The limitations period for filing discrimination claims is codified in EEOC regulations. Once an aggrieved files a charge with his or her employing agency, that agency must complete its investigation within 180 days, unless the parties agree to an extension of up to 90 additional days. The agency also is required to issue a notice after 180 days providing the grievant with the right to request a hearing before an EEOC administrative judge. Additionally, if the aggrieved chooses to bypass the EEOC, both §717 and the EEOC regulations authorize him or her to file a civil action in federal district court:

(a) Within ninety days of receipt[b] of notice of final action taken by the employer agency on a complaint; or

---

[b]As you recall from the discussion in Chapter 4, *supra*, of IRWIN v. VETERANS ADMINISTRATION, the statutory requirement of "receipt" does not require personal receipt by the claimant. It is satisfied when notice of final action is received by the office of the aggrieved's attorney. The *Irwin* Court added, however, that the thirty day limitations rule contained within §717 was subject to equitable estoppel even though it operated as a waiver of the government's sovereign immunity. The Court characterized its prior cases dealing with the effect of limitations periods in suits against the government as inconsistent and decided against continuing to resolve each case on an *ad hoc* basis. So, to promote predictability, the Court concluded that it was more appropriate to adopt a general policy that the same rebuttable presumption of equitable tolling presently applicable to suits against private defendants should also extend to suits against the United States.

(b) After one hundred eighty days from the filing of a complaint with the employer agency if there has been no decision.

But if the employee chooses to appeal the agency's action to the EEOC before bringing suit, the court action must be filed

(a) Within ninety days after receipt of notice of final action taken by the EEOC on the complaint; or

(b) After one hundred eighty days from the date of filing an appeal with the EEOC if there has been no EEOC decision. 29 C.F.R. §1613.281.

Section 717(c) requires that the named defendant in a suit brought by a federal employee be the head of the agency or department employing that worker rather than the agency or department. A conflict has arisen as to the appropriate consequence to a plaintiff who erroneously names the agency as the defendant and who fails to correct this error within the applicable filing period. Some courts have held that the filing period is a statute of limitations, rather than a jurisdictional prerequisite and, therefore, that it can be equitably tolled in cases, for example, where the plaintiff was not represented by counsel. These courts have permitted the plaintiff to amend his or her complaint to name the correct defendant after the expiration of the filing period. *See, e.g.,* Warren v. Department of Army, 867 F.2d 1156 (8th Cir.1989). Other courts, however, have ruled that failure to name the proper defendant within the filing period results in a dismissal of the complaint, even where the plaintiff had no attorney at the time the defective complaint was filed. While these courts recognize that the Supreme Court in *Zipes* held that the filing period governing the filing of EEOC complaints is not jurisdictional for private sector workers, and that the circuit courts have extended this ruling to cover the period for filing suit by private sector employees, they appear to distinguish the claims of federal employees on the ground that the federal filing period is premised on a waiver of sovereign immunity and that such waivers should be narrowly construed. *See, e.g.,* Lubniewski v. Lehman, 891 F.2d 216 (9th Cir.1989).

NOTES AND PROBLEMS FOR DISCUSSION

1. Acts of employment discrimination by the federal government also can violate the equal protection and due process guarantees of the Fifth Amendment as well as Executive Order 11478. Additionally, a federal employee might wish to challenge job discrimination under the 1866 or 1871 Civil Rights Acts and the Equal Pay Act. In BROWN v. G.S.A., 425 U.S. 820, 96 S.Ct. 1961, 48 L.Ed.2d 402 (1976), however, the Supreme Court held that Congress intended Title VII to be the exclusive and pre-emptive administrative and judicial remedy for employment discrimination claims by federal workers. Should Title VII preempt state as well as federal statutory remedies, particularly if the state statute provides relief that is unavailable under Title VII or proscribes conduct that is not forbidden by Title VII? *Compare* Pfau v. Reed, 125 F.3d 927 (5th Cir. 1997) (when a federal employee relies on "the same facts" to establish a Title VII and non-Title VII claim, the non-Title VII claim is preempted, regardless of whether the elements that the plaintiff must establish to state a claim under the two statutes are different from one another), *with* Langster v. Schweiker, 565 F.Supp. 407 (N.D.Ill.1983) (Title VII does not preempt other relief for conduct beyond the scope of Title VII).

2.   (a) In light of the extensive administrative procedures made available to federal employees, to what extent should a federal judge be obliged to defer to the agency determinations in adjudicating a federal employee's Title VII claim? In CHANDLER v. ROUDEBUSH, 425 U.S. 840, 96 S.Ct. 1949, 48 L.Ed.2d 416 (1976), the Court concluded that federal employees enjoyed the same right to a judicial trial *de novo* of Title VII claims as private sector or state government employees. Central to this holding was the Court's determination that in enacting the 1972 amendment to extend Title VII to public employees, Congress intended to give federal employees the same measure of rights enjoyed by private employees. Yet in *Brown* (decided on the same day as *Chandler*), the Court stated that Title VII is a federal employee's exclusive federal cause of action whereas private sector employees are not similarly restricted. It has been suggested that *Brown* 's divergence from the *Chandler* parity principle can be explained as a desire to compel federal employees to utilize the more elaborate administrative procedure provided to them in Title VII actions than is available to nonfederal workers. But doesn't the ruling in *Chandler* according federal courts the right to completely disregard agency findings of fact and law in suits brought by federal employees cut against that argument?

(b)   Should the *de novo* review rule of *Chandler* also apply to an action brought in federal court to *enforce* an EEOC that was favorable to the claimant? In MOORE v. DEVINE, 780 F.2d 1559 (11th Cir. 1986), the court held that a final EEOC order *favorable* to a federal employee is binding on that employee's agency and is subject to an enforcement order by the district court without *de novo* review if the agency fails to comply with the EEOC order. The court distinguished *Chandler*, stating that *Chandler* was limited to cases where the federal employee had *lost* before the EEOC. But where the plaintiff wins, the court reasoned, the statute indicated that federal employees are to be treated differently than private or state employees since it provides the EEOC with the authority to issue remedial orders upon a finding of discrimination by the federal government. See also 29 C.F.R. §1614.504(a) (EEOC Guidelines) ("A final decision that has not been the subject of an appeal or civil action [by the complainant] shall be binding on the agency.")

If a plaintiff seeks judicial review only of an agency's remedial order, can it limit the court's inquiry solely to the remedial issue? In SCOTT v. JOHANNS, 409 F.3d 466 (D.C.Cir. 2005), cert. denied, 546 U.S. 1089, 126 S.Ct. 1121, 163 L.Ed.2d 853 (2006), the court answered this question in the negative. It construed the language in §706(g) (which governs federal employee actions per the terms of §716(c)) stating that "*if the court finds* that the respondent has intentionally engaged in * * * an unlawful employment practice" it may order various remedies, to mean that in a federal employee Title VII case, any remedial order must rest on a *judicial* finding of liability. The court added that nothing in the statutory language suggested that such findings are unnecessary in cases where a final administrative disposition already had found discrimination and awarded relief. Consequently, the court ruled, where the aggrieved seeks judicial review of a final agency determination, the federal court is to try *de novo* both liability and remedy.

3.   Who should bear the burden of establishing exhaustion of administrative remedies? Is it significant that since a federal employee must first seek redress within her or his own agency, the defendant would have custody of the relevant records? *See* Brown v. Marsh, 777 F.2d 8 (D.C. Cir. 1985).

SECTION B. STATE AND LOCAL GOVERNMENT EMPLOYEES

The Equal Employment Opportunity Act of 1972 extended the coverage of Title VII to state and local government employees. In Fitzpatrick v. Bitzer,[a] moreover, the Supreme Court ruled that the Eleventh Amendment did not preclude the granting of monetary damages against a state or local government defendant for back pay and attorney's fees in an action brought under that statute. Although the Supreme Court has indicated that the proof standards applicable to private Title VII claims also should govern claims against state and local governments,[b] there is one procedural difference between the enforcement of private and nonfederal public discrimination claims. Section 706(f)(1) authorizes the Attorney General, rather than the EEOC, to file a civil action against a nonfederal public employer.

NOTES AND PROBLEMS FOR DISCUSSION

1. Should the exclusivity doctrine announced in *Brown* apply to state and local government employee claims under §1983? Although the Supreme Court has not addressed this question, the circuit courts overwhelmingly have adopted the position that Title VII does not preempt an action brought under §1983 based on a violation of rights that are independent of Title VII, as, for example, those guaranteed by the Fourteenth Amendment. *See, e.g.*, Jackson v. City of Atlanta, 73 F.3d 60 (5th Cir. 1996), cert. denied, 519 U.S. 818, 117 S.Ct. 70, 136 L.Ed.2d 30 (1996). *See also* Stephen J. Shapiro, *Section 1983 Claims To Redress Discrimination In Public Employment: Are They Preempted by Title VII*? 35 AMER. U. L.REV. 93 (1985).

2. Should the fact that Title VII plaintiffs alleging intentional discrimination, just like §1983 claimants, now can obtain compensatory and punitive damages and a jury trial affect the disposition of the preemption question? *Compare* Marrero-Rivera v. Dep't of Justice of Commonwealth of Puerto Rico, 800 F. Supp. 1024 (D.P.R. 1992), aff'd, 36 F.3d 1089 (1st. Cir. 1994) (Congress did not intend to endow Title VII plaintiffs with all the remedies previously available only under §1983 and, at the same time, intend to preserve a cause of action that allows plaintiffs to bypass the Title VII administrative mechanism; fact that §1983 claim can be based on an underlying constitutional violation is an "abstract notion" that does not affect resolution of this case when plaintiff's §1983 claim was based on a violation of Title VII rights), *with* Beardsley v. Webb, 30 F.3d 524 (4th Cir. 1994) (damages and jury trial provisions were not intended to make Title VII the exclusive remedy for employment discrimination claims by public sector employees).

3. The 1991 Government Employee Rights Act (GERA), wiped out the pre-existing exemption from Title VII applicable to a state elected official's personal staff members, policymaking assistants, and immediate advisers. In STATE OF ALASKA

---

[a]427 U.S. 445, 96 S.Ct. 2666, 49 L.Ed.2d 614 (1976).
[b]See Dothard v. Rawlinson, 433 U.S. 321, 331 n.14, 97 S.Ct. 2720, 2728 n.14, 53 L.Ed.2d 786, 799 n.14 (1977) (" * * * Congress expressly indicated that the same Title VII principles be applied to governmental and private employers alike.").

v. EEOC, 564 F.3d 1062 (9th Cir. 2009)(en banc), the Ninth Circuit, en banc, overruled a panel opinion which had ruled that since Congress did not make any findings as to state practices of discrimination against these sorts of state employees, its abrogation of the States' Eleventh Amendment sovereign immunity did not meet the Supreme Court's previously articulated standards and, therefore, was unconstitutional.   A majority of the full court rejected that argument, ruling that the state could not assert sovereign immunity as a defense since Congress' intention to abrogate that immunity was "unequivocal and textual".   It was unnecessary, the court declared, for the statute to contain the magic words "this act abrogates state sovereign immunity."   And to the second question of whether Congress had the authority to abrogate state sovereign immunity, the court answered that it was sufficient that the statute provided a remedy for unconstitutional conduct.   Since the GERA expressly provided a cause of action for damages against states for unconstitutional conduct, the court concluded, it was unnecessary to determine whether the GERA was valid prophylactic legislation.

CHAPTER 6

Class Actions

SECTION A. INTRODUCTION

Rule 23 of the Federal Rules of Civil Procedure provides in part:

(a) **Prerequisites to a Class Action**. One or more members of a class may sue or be sued as representative parties on behalf of all only if (1) the class is so numerous that joinder of all members is impracticable, (2) there are questions of law or fact common to the class, (3) the claims or defenses of the representative parties are typical of the claims or defenses of the class, and (4) the representative parties will fairly and adequately protect the interests of the class.

(b) **Class Actions Maintainable**. An action may be maintained as a class action if the prerequisites of subdivision (a) are satisfied, and in addition:

(1) The prosecution of separate actions by or against individual members of the class would create a risk of

(A) inconsistent or varying adjudications with respect to individual members of the class which would establish incompatible standards of conduct for the party opposing the class, or

(B) adjudications with respect to individual members of the class which would as a practical matter be dispositive of the interests of the other members not parties to the adjudications or substantially impair or impede their ability to protect their interests; or

(2) the party opposing the class has acted or refused to act on grounds generally applicable to the class, thereby making appropriate final injunctive relief or corresponding declaratory relief with respect to the class as a whole; or

(3) the court finds that the questions of law or fact common to the members of the class predominate over any questions affecting only individual members, and that a class action is superior to other available methods for the fair and efficient adjudication of the controversy. The matters pertinent to the findings include: (A) the interest of members of the class in individually controlling the prosecution or defense of separate actions; (B) the extent and nature of any litigation concerning the controversy already commenced by or against members of the class; (C) the desirability or undesirability of concentrating the litigation of the claims in the particular forum; (D) the difficulties likely to be encountered in the management of a class action.

(c) **Determining by Order Whether to Certify a Class Action; Appointing a Class Counsel; Notice and Membership in Class; Judgment; Multiple Classes and Subclasses.**

(1) (A) When a person sues or is sued as a representative of a class, the court must, at an early practicable time, determine by order whether to certify the action as a class action.

(B) An order certifying a class must define the class and the class claims, issues, or defenses, and must appoint class counsel under Rule 23(g).

(2) (A) For any class certified under Rule 23(b)(1) or (2), the court may direct appropriate notice to the class.

(B) For any class certified under Rule 23(b)(3), the court must direct to class members the best notice practicable under the circumstances, including individual notice to all members who can be identified through reasonable effort. The notice must concisely and clearly state in plain easily understood language:

- the nature of the action,

- the definition of the class certified,

- the class claims, issues or defenses,

- that a class member may enter an appearance through counsel if the member so desires,

- that the court will exclude from the class any member who requests exclusion, stating when and how members may elect to be excluded, and

- the binding effect of a class judgment on class members under Rule 23(c)(3).

(3) The judgment in a class action maintained as a class action under subdivision (b)(1) or (b)(2), whether or not favorable to the class, shall include and describe those whom the court finds to be members of the class. The judgment in an action maintained as a class action under subdivision (b)(3), whether or not favorable to the class, shall include and specify or describe those to whom the notice provided in subdivision (c)(2) was directed, and who have not requested exclusion, and whom the court finds to be members of the class.

(4) Then appropriate (A) an action may be brought or maintained as a class action with respect to particular issues, or (B) a class may be divided into subclasses and each subclass treated as a class, and the provisions of this rule shall then be construed and applied accordingly.

* * *

(e) **Settlement, Voluntary Dismissal, or Compromise**.

(1) (A) The court must approve any settlement, voluntary dismissal, or compromise of the claims, issues or defenses of a certified class.

(B) The court must direct notice in a reasonable manner to all class members who would be bound by a proposed settlement, voluntary dismissal, or compromise.

(C) The court may approve a settlement, voluntary dismissal, or compromise that would bind class members only after a hearing and on finding that the settlement, voluntary dismissal, or compromise is fair, reasonable, and adequate.

(2) The parties seeking approval of a settlement, voluntary dismissal or compromise under Rule 23(e)(1) must file a statement identifying any agreement made in connection with the proposed settlement, voluntary dismissal or compromise.

(3) In an action previously certified as a class action under Rule 23(b)(3), the court may refuse to approve a settlement unless it affords a new opportunity to request exclusion to individual class members who had an earlier opportunity to request exclusion but did not do so.

(4) (A) Any class member may object to a proposed settlement, voluntary dismissal or compromise that requires court approval under Rule 23(e)(1)(A).

(B) An objection made under Rule 23(e)(4)(A) may be withdrawn only with the court's approval.

* * *

(g) **Class Counsel**.

(1) Appointing Class Counsel.

(A) Unless a statute provides otherwise, a court that certifies a class must appoint class counsel.

(B) An attorney appointed to serve as class counsel must fairly and adequately represent the interests of the class.

(C) In appointing class counsel, the court

(i) must consider:

- the work counsel has done in identifying or investigating potential claims in the action,

- counsel's experience in handling class actions, other complex litigation, and claims of the type asserted in the action,

- counsel's knowledge of the applicable law, and

- the resources counsel will commit to representing the class;

(ii) may consider any other matter pertinent to counsel's ability to fairly and adequately represent the interests of the class;

(iii) may direct potential class counsel to provide information on any subject pertinent to the appointment and to propose terms for attorney fees and nontaxable costs; and

(iv) may make further orders in connection with the appointment.

(2) Appointment Procedure.

(A) The court may designate interim counsel to act on behalf of the putative class before determining whether to certify the action as a class action.

(B) When there is one applicant for appointment as class counsel, the court may appoint that applicant only if the applicant is adequate under Rule 23(g)(1)(B) and (C). If more than one adequate applicant seeks appointment as class counsel, the court must appoint the applicant best able to represent the interests of the class.

(C) The order appointing class counsel may include provisions about award of attorney fees or nontaxable costs under Rule 23(h).

* * *

The class action did not originate with the adoption of the Federal Rules, but was "an invention of equity to enable it to proceed to a decree in suits where the number of those interested in the subject of the litigation is so great that their joinder as parties in conformity to the usual rules of procedure is impracticable." Hansberry v. Lee, 311 U.S. 32, 41, 61 S.Ct. 115, 118, 85 L.Ed. 22 (1940). Following the Supreme Court's landmark ruling in Brown v. Bd. of Educ., 347 U.S. 483, 74 S.Ct. 686, 98 L.Ed. 873 (1954), the civil rights class action became a frequently used device for attacking racial discrimination in education, voting rights, and housing. Typical of these cases were school desegregation suits where relief could not be granted to an individual plaintiff without, in effect, affording the same relief (i.e., desegregated schools) to a class, whether the suit was denominated a "class" action or not.

In 1966, Rule 23 was revised in part by the addition of section (b)(2), which was created specifically to facilitate civil rights actions "where a party is charged with discriminating unlawfully against a class, usually one whose members are incapable of specific enumeration." 1966 Advisory Committee's Note, 39 F.R.D. 98, 102. Not surprisingly, suits in which class-wide relief was automatic if the plaintiff prevailed did not encourage close attention to the requirements of Rule 23.

The 1966 revision of Rule 23 followed closely the enactment of Title VII. That statute brought with it a complex type of class action in which different kinds of discriminatory conduct were attacked in one proceeding. Early employment discrimination class actions frequently attacked a whole range of employment practices (hiring, promotion, job assignment, pay scales, working conditions, etc.) and were referred to as "across the board" cases. The justification for allowing such cases to proceed as class actions was that a common discriminatory policy formed the basis for all the employer's actions.

A typical example of an "across the board" type of case was JOHNSON v. GEORGIA HIGHWAY EXPRESS, INC., 417 F.2d 1122 (5th Cir. 1969). In *Johnson* a discharged African-American employee sought to represent a class composed of "all other similarly situated Negroes seeking equal employment opportunities." Johnson alleged that his former employer had discriminated on the basis of race in virtually all aspects of its operation, including hiring, discharge, promotion, and maintenance of segregated facilities. The district court restricted the class to black employees who had been discharged. The Fifth Circuit reversed on the ground that the alleged underlying policy of racial discrimination was sufficiently common to, and typical of, the claims of all class members to permit joinder of all the claims. The decision made plain that the factual and legal differences between the named plaintiff's claim arising from his discharge and the claims made on behalf of the non-discharged class members would not render the plaintiff an inadequate representative. *See also* George M. Strickler,

Protecting the Class: The Search for the Adequate Representative in Class Action Litigation, 34 DePaul L. Rev. 73, 110-124 (1984).

The free-wheeling approach to class certification in Title VII cases ended with the Supreme Court's decision in EAST TEXAS MOTOR FREIGHT SYSTEM INC. v. RODRIGUEZ, 431 U.S. 395, 97 S.Ct. 1891, 52 L.Ed.2d 453 (1977), a case filed against the employer by three Latino truck drivers. The plaintiffs had been denied transfer to over-the-road or "line" driver positions and alleged that the employer's no transfer policy and collective bargaining agreements with the Teamsters Union effectively locked them and other minorities into lower paying "local" driver positions, thus perpetuating the effects of discrimination in initial job assignment. The plaintiffs proposed in their complaint to represent a class composed of all Latino and African-American local drivers as well as all minority applicants for line driver jobs, but failed to move for class certification and confined their evidence at trial to their individual claims. The district court found against the plaintiffs on the merits and dismissed the class claims. The Court of Appeals reversed, holding that the district court should have certified the class sua sponte and should have found class-wide liability on the basis of statistical proof introduced in support of the plaintiffs' individual claims. The Supreme Court unanimously reversed on the ground that the named plaintiffs were not proper class representatives because they were not members of the class.

> [T]he trial proceedings made clear that [the plaintiffs] were not members of the class of discriminatees they purported to represent. As this Court has repeatedly held, a class representative must be part of the class and "possess the same interest and suffer the same injury" as the class members. The District Court found upon abundant evidence that these plaintiffs lacked the qualifications to be hired as line drivers. Thus, they could have suffered no injury as a result of the alleged discriminatory practices, and they were, therefore, simply not eligible to represent a class of persons who did allegedly suffer injury. Furthermore, each named plaintiff stipulated that he had not been discriminated against with respect to his initial hire. In the light of that stipulation they were hardly in a position to mount a class-wide attack on the no-transfer rule and seniority system on the ground that these practices perpetuated past discrimination and locked minorities into less desirable jobs to which they had been discriminatorily assigned.

431 U.S. at 403-04. A number of lower courts confined *East Texas Motor Freight* to its peculiar facts (the combination of a loss on the merits with the failure of the plaintiffs to move for class certification or to put on class-wide proof) and held that across-the-board class actions survived. *See, e.g.*, Payne v. Travenol Laboratories, Inc., 565 F.2d 895 (5th Cir.), cert. denied, 439 U.S. 835, 99 S.Ct. 118, 58 L.Ed.2d 131 (1978) (claim challenging the defendant's college degree requirement sustained though the plaintiff was not a degree candidate). The Supreme Court rejected that narrow interpretation of *East Texas Motor Freight* in the following case.

SECTION B. THE SCOPE OF THE CLASS AND THE PROPER CLASS REPRESENTATIVE

General Telephone Co. of Southwest v. Falcon

Supreme Court of the United States, 1982.
457 U.S. 147, 102 S.Ct. 2364, 72 L.Ed.2d 740.

JUSTICE STEVENS delivered the opinion of the Court.

The question presented is whether respondent Falcon, who complained that petitioner did not promote him because he is a Mexican-American, was properly permitted to maintain a class action on behalf of Mexican-American applicants for employment whom petitioner did not hire.

I

In 1969 petitioner initiated a special recruitment and training program for minorities. Through that program, respondent Falcon was hired in July 1969 as a groundman, and within a year he was twice promoted, first to lineman and then to lineman-in-charge. He subsequently refused a promotion to installer-repairman. In October 1972 he applied for the job of field inspector; his application was denied even though the promotion was granted several white employees with less seniority.

Falcon thereupon filed a charge with the Equal Employment Opportunity Commission stating his belief that he had been passed over for promotion because of his national origin and that petitioner's promotion policy operated against Mexican-Americans as a class. In due course he received a right to sue letter from the Commission and, in April 1975, he commenced this action under Title VII in the United States District Court for the Northern District of Texas. His complaint alleged that petitioner maintained "a policy, practice, custom, or usage of: (a) discriminating against [Mexican-Americans] because of national origin and with respect to compensation, terms, conditions, and privileges of employment, and (b) * * * subjecting [Mexican-Americans] to continuous employment discrimination."[1] Respondent claimed that as a result of this policy whites with less qualification and experience and lower evaluation scores than respondent had been promoted more rapidly. The complaint contained no factual allegations concerning petitioner's hiring practices.

Respondent brought the action "on his own behalf and on behalf of other persons similarly situated, pursuant to Rule 23(b)(2) of the Federal Rules of Civil Procedure." The class identified in the complaint was "composed of Mexican-American persons who are employed, or who might be employed, by GENERAL TELEPHONE

---

[1] In paragraph VI of the complaint, respondent alleged:
"The Defendant has established an employment, transfer, promotional, and seniority system, the design, intent, and purpose of which is to continue and preserve, and which has the effect of continuing and preserving, the Defendant's policy, practice, custom and usage of limiting the employment, transfer, and promotional opportunities of Mexican-American employees of the company because of national origin."

COMPANY at its place of business located in Irving, Texas, who have been and who continue to be or might be adversely affected by the practices complained of herein."[3]

After responding to petitioner's written interrogatories,[4] respondent filed a memorandum in favor of certification of "the class of all hourly Mexican American employees who have been employed, are employed, or may in the future be employed and all those Mexican Americans who have applied or would have applied for employment had the Defendant not practiced racial discrimination in its employment practices." His position was supported by the ruling of the United States Court of Appeals for the Fifth Circuit in Johnson v. Georgia Highway Express, Inc., 417 F.2d 1122 (1969), that any victim of racial discrimination in employment may maintain an "across the board" attack on all unequal employment practices alleged to have been committed by the employer pursuant to a policy of racial discrimination. Without conducting an evidentiary hearing, the District Court certified a class including Mexican-American employees and Mexican-American applicants for employment who had not been hired.

Following trial of the liability issues, the District Court entered separate findings of fact and conclusions of law with respect first to respondent and then to the class. The District Court found that petitioner had not discriminated against respondent in hiring, but that it did discriminate against him in its promotion practices. The court reached converse conclusions about the class, finding no discrimination in promotion practices, but concluding that petitioner had discriminated against Mexican-Americans at its Irving facility in its hiring practices.[6]

After various post-trial proceedings, the District Court ordered petitioner to furnish respondent with a list of all Mexican-Americans who had applied for employment at the Irving facility during the period between January 1, 1973, and October 18, 1976. Respondent was then ordered to give notice to those persons advising them that they might be entitled to some form of recovery. Evidence was taken concerning the applicants who responded to the notice and backpay was

---

[3]The paragraph of the complaint in which respondent alleged conformance with the requirements of Rule 23 continued:

"There are common questions of law and fact affecting the rights of the members of this class who are, and who continue to be, limited, classified, and discriminated against in ways which deprive and/or tend to deprive them of equal employment opportunities and which otherwise adversely affect their status as employees because of national origin. These persons are so numerous that joinder of all members is impracticable. A common relief is sought. The interests of said class are adequately represented by Plaintiff. Defendant has acted or refused to act on grounds generally applicable to the Plaintiff."

[4]Petitioner's Interrogatory No. 8 stated:

"Identify the common questions of law and fact which affect the rights of the members of the purported class."

Respondent answered that interrogatory as follows:

"The facts which affect the rights of the members of the class are the facts of their employment, the ways in which evaluations are made, the subjective rather than objective manner in which recommendations for raises and transfers and promotions are handled, and all of the facts surrounding the employment of Mexican-American persons by General Telephone Company. The questions of law specified in Interrogatory No. 8 call for a conclusion on the part of the Plaintiff."

[6]The District Court ordered petitioner to accelerate its affirmative action plan by taking specified steps to more actively recruit and promote Mexican-Americans at its Irving facility.

ultimately awarded to 13 persons, in addition to respondent Falcon. The total recovery by respondent and the entire class amounted to $67,925.49, plus costs and interest.[7]

Both parties appealed. The Court of Appeals rejected respondent's contention that the class should have encompassed all of petitioner's operations in Texas, New Mexico, Oklahoma, and Arkansas.[8] On the other hand, the court also rejected petitioner's argument that the class had been defined too broadly. For, under the Fifth Circuit's across-the-board rule, it is permissible for an employee complaining of one employment practice to represent another complaining of another practice, if the plaintiff and the members of the class suffer from essentially the same injury. "In this case, all of the claims are based on discrimination because of national origin."[9] The court relied on Payne v. Travenol Laboratories, Inc., 565 F.2d 895 (1978), cert. denied, 439 U.S. 835, 99 S.Ct. 118, 58 L.Ed.2d 131, in which the Fifth Circuit stated:

> Plaintiffs' action is an "across the board" attack on unequal employment practices alleged to have been committed by Travenol pursuant to a policy of racial discrimination. As parties who have allegedly been aggrieved by some of these discriminatory practices, plaintiffs have demonstrated a sufficient nexus to enable them to represent other class members suffering from different practices motivated by the same policies.

On the merits, the Court of Appeals upheld respondent's claim of disparate treatment in promotion,[10] but held that the District Court's findings relating to

---

[7]Respondent's individual recovery amounted to $1,040.33. A large share of the class award, $28,827.50, represented attorneys' fees. Most of the remainder resulted from petitioner's practice of keeping all applications active for only 90 days; the District Court found that most of the applications had been properly rejected at the time they were considered, but that petitioner could not justify the refusal to extend employment to disappointed applicants after an interval of 90 days.

[8]The Court of Appeals held that the District Court had not abused its discretion since each of petitioner's divisions conducted its own hiring and since management of the broader class would be much more difficult.

[9]The court continued:

"While similarities of sex, race or national origin claims are not dispositive in favor of finding that the prerequisites of Rule 23 have been met, they are an extremely important factor in the determination, that can outweigh the fact that the members of the plaintiff class may be complaining about somewhat different specific discriminatory practices. In addition here, the plaintiff showed more than an alliance based simply on the same type of discriminatory claim. He also showed a similarity of interests based on job location, job function and other considerations."

The court did not explain how job location, job function, and the unidentified other considerations were relevant to the Rule 23(a) determination.

[10]The District Court found that petitioner's proffered reasons for promoting the whites, rather than respondent, were insufficient and subjective. The Court of Appeals held that respondent had made out a prima facie case under the test set forth in McDonnell Douglas Corp. v. Green, 411 U.S. 792, 802, 93 S.Ct. 1817, 1824, 36 L.Ed.2d 668, and that the District Court's conclusion that petitioner had not rebutted that prima facie case was not clearly erroneous. In so holding, the Court of Appeals relied on its earlier opinion in Burdine v. Texas Department of Community Affairs. Our opinion in *Burdine* had not yet been announced.

The Court of Appeals disposed of a number of other contentions raised by both parties, and reserved others pending the further proceedings before the District Court on remand. Among the latter issues was petitioner's objection to the District Court's theory for computing the class backpay awards. See n. 7, *supra*.

disparate impact in hiring were insufficient to support recovery on behalf of the class.[11] After this Court decided Texas Department of Community Affairs v. Burdine, 450 U.S. 248, 101 S.Ct. 1089, 67 L.Ed.2d 207, we vacated the judgment of the Court of Appeals and directed further consideration in the light of that opinion. The Fifth Circuit thereupon vacated the portion of its opinion addressing respondent's promotion claim but reinstated the portions of its opinion approving the District Court's class certification. With the merits of both respondent's promotion claim and the class hiring claims remaining open for reconsideration in the District Court on remand, we granted certiorari to decide whether the class action was properly maintained on behalf of both employees who were denied promotion and applicants who were denied employment.

II

* * *

Title VII authorizes the Equal Employment Opportunity Commission to sue in its own name to secure relief for individuals aggrieved by discriminatory practices forbidden by the Act. See §706(f)(1). In exercising this enforcement power, the Commission may seek relief for groups of employees or applicants for employment without complying with the strictures of Rule 23. General Telephone Co. v. EEOC, 446 U.S. 318, 100 S.Ct. 1698, 64 L.Ed.2d 319. Title VII, however, contains no special authorization for class suits maintained by private parties. An individual litigant seeking to maintain a class action under Title VII must meet "the prerequisites of numerosity, commonality, typicality, and adequacy of representation" specified in Rule 23(a). Id., at 330. These requirements effectively "limit the class claims to those fairly encompassed by the named plaintiff's claims." Ibid.

We have repeatedly held that "a class representative must be part of the class and 'possess the same interest and suffer the same injury' as the class members." East Texas Motor Freight System, Inc. v. Rodriguez. In *East Texas Motor Freight*, a Title VII action brought by three Mexican-American city drivers, the Fifth Circuit certified a class consisting of the trucking company's black and Mexican-American city drivers allegedly denied on racial or ethnic grounds transfers to more desirable line-driver jobs. We held that the Court of Appeals had "plainly erred in declaring a class action." 431 U.S., at 403. Because at the time the class was certified it was clear that the named plaintiffs were not qualified for line-driver positions, "they could have suffered no injury as a result of the allegedly discriminatory practices, and they were, therefore, simply not eligible to represent a class of persons who did allegedly suffer injury." Id.

Our holding in *East Texas Motor Freight* was limited; we noted that "a different case would be presented if the District Court had certified a class and only later had it appeared that the named plaintiffs were not class members or were otherwise inappropriate class representatives." Id., at 406, n. 12. We also recognized the theory

---

[11]The District Court's finding was based on statistical evidence comparing the number of Mexican-Americans in the company's employ, and the number hired in 1972 and 1973, with the percentage of Mexican-Americans in the Dallas-Fort Worth labor force. Since recovery had been allowed for the years 1973 through 1976 based on statistical evidence pertaining to only a portion of that period, and since petitioner's evidence concerning the entire period suggested that there was no disparate impact, the Court of Appeals ordered further proceedings on the class hiring claims.

behind the Fifth Circuit's across-the-board rule, noting our awareness "that suits alleging racial or ethnic discrimination are often by their very nature class suits, involving classwide wrongs," and that "[c]ommon questions of law or fact are typically present." Id., at 405. In the same breath, however, we reiterated that "careful attention to the requirements of Fed. Rule Civ. Proc. 23 remains nonetheless indispensable" and that the "mere fact that a complaint alleges racial or ethnic discrimination does not in itself ensure that the party who has brought the lawsuit will be an adequate representative of those who may have been the real victims of that discrimination." Id., at 405-406.

We cannot disagree with the proposition underlying the across-the-board rule — that racial discrimination is by definition class discrimination. But the allegation that such discrimination has occurred neither determines whether a class action may be maintained in accordance with Rule 23 nor defines the class that may be certified. Conceptually, there is a wide gap between (a) an individual's claim that he has been denied a promotion on discriminatory grounds, and his otherwise unsupported allegation that the company has a policy of discrimination, and (b) the existence of a class of persons who have suffered the same injury as that individual, such that the individual's claim and the class claims will share common questions of law or fact and that the individual's claim will be typical of the class claims.[13] For respondent to bridge that gap, he must prove much more than the validity of his own claim. Even though evidence that he was passed over for promotion when several less deserving whites were advanced may support the conclusion that respondent was denied the promotion because of his national origin, such evidence would not necessarily justify the additional inferences (1) that this discriminatory treatment is typical of petitioner's promotion practices, (2) that petitioner's promotion practices are motivated by a policy of ethnic discrimination that pervades petitioner's Irving division, or (3) that this policy of ethnic discrimination is reflected in petitioner's other employment practices, such as hiring, in the same way it is manifested in the promotion practices. These additional inferences demonstrate the tenuous character of any presumption that the class claims are "fairly encompassed" within respondent's claim.

Respondent's complaint provided an insufficient basis for concluding that the adjudication of his claim of discrimination in promotion would require the decision of any common question concerning the failure of petitioner to hire more Mexican-

---

[13]The commonality and typicality requirements of Rule 23(a) tend to merge. Both serve as guideposts for determining whether under the particular circumstances maintenance of a class action is economical and whether the named plaintiff's claim and the class claims are so interrelated that the interests of the class members will be fairly and adequately protected in their absence. Those requirements therefore also tend to merge with the adequacy-of-representation requirement, although the latter requirement also raises concerns about the competency of class counsel and conflicts of interest. In this case, we need not address petitioner's argument that there is a conflict of interest between respondent and the class of rejected applicants because an enlargement of the pool of Mexican-American employees will decrease respondent's chances for promotion. See General Telephone Co. v. EEOC, 446 U.S. 318, 331, 100 S.Ct. 1698, 1706-1707, 64 L.Ed.2d 319 ("In employment discrimination litigation, conflicts might arise, for example, between employees and applicants who were denied employment and who will, if granted relief, compete with employees for fringe benefits or seniority. Under Rule 23, the same plaintiff could not represent these classes."); see also East Texas Motor Freight System, Inc. v. Rodriguez, 431 U.S. 395, 404-405, 97 S.Ct. 1891, 1897-1898, 52 L.Ed.2d 453.

Americans. Without any specific presentation identifying the questions of law or fact that were common to the claims of respondent and of the members of the class he sought to represent,[14] it was error for the District Court to presume that respondent's claim was typical of other claims against petitioner by Mexican-American employees and applicants. If one allegation of specific discriminatory treatment were sufficient to support an across-the-board attack, every Title VII case would be a potential company-wide class action. We find nothing in the statute to indicate that Congress intended to authorize such a wholesale expansion of class-action litigation.[15]

The trial of this class action followed a predictable course. Instead of raising common questions of law or fact, respondent's evidentiary approaches to the individual and class claims were entirely different. He attempted to sustain his individual claim by proving intentional discrimination. He tried to prove the class claims through statistical evidence of disparate impact. Ironically, the District Court rejected the class claim of promotion discrimination, which conceptually might have borne a closer typicality and commonality relationship with respondent's individual claim, but sustained the class claim of hiring discrimination. As the District Court's bifurcated findings on liability demonstrate, the individual and class claims might as well have been tried separately. It is clear that the maintenance of respondent's action as a class action did not advance "the efficiency and economy of litigation which is a principal purpose of the procedure." American Pipe & Construction Co. v. Utah, 414 U.S. 538, 553, 94 S.Ct. 756, 766, 38 L.Ed.2d 713.

We do not, of course, judge the propriety of a class certification by hindsight. The District Court's error in this case, and the error inherent in the across-the-board rule, is the failure to evaluate carefully the legitimacy of the named plaintiff's plea that he is a proper class representative under Rule 23(a). As we noted in Coopers & Lybrand v. Livesay, 437 U.S. 463, 98 S.Ct. 2454, 57 L.Ed.2d 351, "the class determination generally involves considerations that are enmeshed in the factual and legal issues comprising the plaintiff's cause of action." Sometimes the issues are plain enough from the pleadings to determine whether the interests of the absent parties are fairly encompassed within the named plaintiff's claim, and sometimes it may be necessary for the court to probe behind the pleadings before coming to rest on the certification question. Even after a certification order is entered, the judge remains free to modify it in the light of subsequent developments in the litigation.[16] For such an order,

---

[14]See n. 4, *supra.*

[15]If petitioner used a biased testing procedure to evaluate both applicants for employment and incumbent employees, a class action on behalf of every applicant or employee who might have been prejudiced by the test clearly would satisfy the commonality and typicality requirements of Rule 23(a). Significant proof that an employer operated under a general policy of discrimination conceivably could justify a class of both applicants and employees if the discrimination manifested itself in hiring and promotion practices in the same general fashion, such as through entirely subjective decisionmaking processes. In this regard it is noteworthy that Title VII prohibits discriminatory employment *practices*, not an abstract policy of discrimination. The mere fact that an aggrieved private plaintiff is a member of an identifiable class of persons of the same race or national origin is insufficient to establish his standing to litigate on their behalf all possible claims of discrimination against a common employer.

[16]"As soon as practicable after the commencement of an action brought as a class action, the court shall determine by order whether it is to be so maintained. An order under this subdivision

particularly during the period before any notice is sent to members of the class, "is inherently tentative." 437 U.S., at 469, n. 11. This flexibility enhances the usefulness of the class-action device; actual, not presumed, conformance with Rule 23(a) remains, however, indispensable.

III

The need to carefully apply the requirements of Rule 23(a) to Title VII class actions was noticed by a member of the Fifth Circuit panel that announced the across-the-board rule. In a specially concurring opinion in Johnson v. Georgia Highway Express, Inc., Judge Godbold emphasized the need for "more precise pleadings," for "without reasonable specificity the court cannot define the class, cannot determine whether the representation is adequate, and the employer does not know how to defend." He termed as "most significant" the potential unfairness to the class members bound by the judgment if the framing of the class is overbroad. And he pointed out the error of the "tacit assumption" underlying the across-the-board rule that "all will be well for surely the plaintiff will win and manna will fall on all members of the class." With the same concerns in mind, we reiterate today that a Title VII class action, like any other class action, may only be certified if the trial court is satisfied, after a rigorous analysis, that the prerequisites of Rule 23(a) have been satisfied.

The judgment of the Court of Appeals affirming the certification order is reversed and the case is remanded for further proceedings consistent with this opinion.

CHIEF JUSTICE BURGER, concurring in part and dissenting in part.

I agree with the Court's decision insofar as it states the general principles which apply in determining whether a class should be certified in this case under Rule 23. However, in my view it is not necessary to remand for further proceedings since it is entirely clear on this record that no class should have been certified in this case. I would simply reverse the Court of Appeals with instructions to dismiss the class claim.

As the Court notes, the purpose of Rule 23 is to promote judicial economy by allowing for litigation of common questions of law and fact at one time. We have stressed that strict attention to the requirements of Rule 23 is indispensable in employment discrimination cases. *East Texas Motor Freight System.* This means that class claims are limited to those "fairly encompassed by the named plaintiff's claims." General Telephone Co. v. EEOC, 446 U.S. 318, 330, 100 S.Ct. 1698, 1706, 64 L.Ed.2d 319 (1980).

Respondent claims that he was not promoted to a job as field inspector because he is a Mexican-American. To be successful in his claim, which he advances under the "disparate treatment" theory, he must convince a court that those who were promoted were promoted not because they were better qualified than he was, but, instead, that he was not promoted for discriminatory reasons. The success of this claim depends on evaluation of the comparative qualifications of the applicants for promotion to field inspector and on analysis of the credibility of the reasons for the promotion decisions provided by those who made the decisions. Respondent's class claim on behalf of

---

may be conditional, and may be altered or amended before the decision on the merits." Fed. Rule Civ. Proc. 23(c)(1).

unsuccessful applicants for jobs with petitioner, in contrast, is advanced under the "adverse impact" theory. Its success depends on an analysis of statistics concerning petitioner's hiring patterns.[*]

The record in this case clearly shows that there are no common questions of law or fact between respondent's claim and the class claim; the only commonality is that respondent is a Mexican-American and he seeks to represent a class of Mexican-Americans. We have repeatedly held that the bare fact that a plaintiff alleges racial or ethnic discrimination is not enough to justify class certification. *East Texas Motor Freight.* Accordingly, the class should not have been certified.

Moreover, while a judge's decision to certify a class is not normally to be evaluated by hindsight, since the judge cannot know what the evidence will show, there is no reason for us at this stage of these lengthy judicial proceedings not to proceed in light of the evidence actually presented. The Court properly concludes that the Court of Appeals and the District Court failed to consider the requirements of Rule 23. In determining whether to reverse and remand or to simply reverse, we can and should look at the evidence. The record shows that there is no support for the class claim. Respondent's own statistics show that 7.7% of those hired by petitioner between 1972 and 1976 were Mexican-American while the relevant labor force was 5.2% Mexican-American. Petitioner's unchallenged evidence shows that it hired Mexican-Americans in numbers greater than their percentage of the labor force even though Mexican-Americans applied for jobs with petitioner in numbers smaller than their percentage of the labor force. This negates any claim of Falcon as a class representative.

Like so many Title VII cases, this case has already gone on for years, draining judicial resources as well as resources of the litigants. Rather than promoting judicial economy, the "across-the-board" class action has promoted multiplication of claims and endless litigation. Since it is clear that the class claim brought on behalf of unsuccessful applicants for jobs with petitioner cannot succeed, I would simply reverse and remand with instructions to dismiss the class claim.

NOTES AND PROBLEMS FOR DISCUSSION

1. What precisely is the holding of *Falcon*? Is it that a named plaintiff may represent a class composed only of those persons who have been affected by a discriminatory policy in exactly the same manner as the plaintiff? Or does the decision merely stand for the proposition that the district court may not assume a sufficient nexus between the individual and class claims absent a factual showing of a link between the two? The Court in *Falcon* stated that proof sufficient to establish Falcon's individual claim would not necessarily support a finding of class discrimination. Presumably, in a case where proof of the individual claim would support an inference of class discrimination, the commonality and typicality requirements of Rule 23(a) would be satisfied. Thus, if

---

[*]There is no allegation that those who made the hiring decisions are the same persons who determined who was promoted to field inspector. Thus there is no claim that the same person or persons who made the challenged decisions were motivated by prejudice against Mexican-Americans, and that this prejudice manifested itself in both the hiring decisions and the decisions not to promote respondent.

a company's policy was to refuse employment to pregnant women, a female employee discharged because of pregnancy would be allowed under *Falcon* to represent a class composed of discharged employees and persons refused employment because of that policy. *See* Hartman v. Duffey, 19 F.3d 1459 (D.C. Cir. 1994), cert. denied, 520 U.S. 1240, 117 S.Ct. 1844, 137 L.Ed.2d 1048 (1997). But, conversely, if proof of class-wide discrimination is sufficiently relevant to the plaintiff's individual claim to be admissible in support of that claim, would the commonality and typicality requirements be satisfied?

2. The Court's statement in *Falcon* that the propriety of class actions should not be determined "by hindsight" presumably means that the success (or lack thereof) at trial of plaintiff's individual claim should have no bearing on the class claim. If, however, the named plaintiff's claim is dismissed prior to trial, can he be an adequate representative of a class? *Compare* Sample v. Aldi, Inc., 61 F.3d 544 (7th Cir. 1995) (grant of summary judgment on plaintiff's individual claim meant he could not represent the class), *with* Hartman v. Duffey, 19 F.3d 1459, 1471 (D.C. Cir. 1994), cert. denied, 520 U.S. 1240, 117 S.Ct. 1844, 137 L.Ed.2d 1048 (1997) ("*East Texas Motor Freight* only held that certification was unwarranted when at the time of certification it was abundantly clear that plaintiffs were not members of the class.").

Unlike the plaintiffs in *East Texas Motor Freight,* the plaintiff in *Falcon* actively sought to represent a class even larger than that certified by the district court, and at trial put on substantial proof to support the class claims. Assuming that Falcon was an "adequate" representative of the class in the sense that he had both the desire and the means to vigorously pursue the class claims, does the ruling in *Falcon* further the goals of Title VII? Falcon obtained relief for a class of applicants and was found to be an inadequate representative, not because of any actual failure to prosecute the class claims, but because of the lack of typicality. Why should the members of the class be deprived of relief? For a discussion of the different meanings of "adequacy" see George M. Strickler, *Protecting the Class: The Search for the Adequate Representative in Class Action Litigation*, 34 DEPAUL L. REV. 73 (1984).

3. *Falcon* has not resulted in the complete demise of the broad-based class action. Relying on footnote 15 of the Court's opinion, a number of lower courts have certified or refused to decertify classes composed of persons whose relation to the defendant differ distinctly from that of the named plaintiff on the ground that the various discriminatory practices were infected by the same "subjective decision making processes." For example, in CARIDAD v. METRO-NORTH COMMUTER R.R., 191 F.3d 283 (2d Cir. 1999), cert. denied, 529 U.S. 1107, 120 S. Ct. 1959, 146 L.Ed.2d 791 (2000), the plaintiffs alleged that the company delegated to department supervisors substantial discretionary authority to make final decisions about discipline and promotion and that this authority was exercised in a racially discriminatory manner and produced a disproportionate impact on African-American employees. They sought to represent a class composed of current and former African-American employees in all departments. In support of class certification, the plaintiffs presented an expert's statistical analysis that showed that being black rendered employees three and a half times more likely to be disciplined than if they were white and reduced by 33% their likelihood of promotion. The expert testified that the probability of such discrepancies occurring by chance was less than one in 10,000. The district court denied class certification on the ground that the plaintiffs had failed to establish both commonality and typicality.

On the question of commonality, the trial judge found that the broad delegation of authority was not itself a discriminatory policy, and the uncoordinated individual decisions made by many supervisors meant that the claims of named plaintiffs could not be typical of the claims of class members "in the absence of any proof that [the delegation] opens the door to generalized discrimination." The plaintiffs' statistics could not show generalized discrimination because the studies did not take account of the fact that different jobs had materially different individual rates of discipline and promotion associated with them. The Second Circuit reversed. Noting that the Supreme Court in *Falcon* had stated that under certain circumstances disparate treatment cases challenging subjective decision-making processes could be certified as class actions and that disparate impact analysis could be applied to subjective as well as objective employment practices, the Court explained:

> Where the decision-making process is difficult to review because of the role of subjective assessment, significant statistical disparities are relevant to determining whether the challenged employment practice has a class-wide impact. Regardless of their ultimate persuasiveness on the issue of liability, the statistical report and anecdotal evidence submitted by the Class Plaintiffs are sufficient to demonstrate common questions of fact regarding the discriminatory implementation and effects of Metro-North's company-wide policies regarding promotion and discipline.

191 F.3d at 292. The Court went on to caution that the railroad's critique of the plaintiffs' statistical evidence could mean that plaintiffs would fail on the merits. At the class certification stage, however, "statistical dueling" and the weighing of the parties' evidence was not appropriate.

Regarding typicality, the Court noted that for the named plaintiffs who alleged they were not promoted and/or were disciplined more severely as a result of racial discrimination, "the question of whether Metro-North's policy of delegating discretion to department supervisors to make subjective decisions * * * is administered in a racially discriminatory manner or has a disparate impact on African-American workers is crucial to their claims, as well as to those of the proposed class." *Id.* at 293.

Representational adequacy problems under *Falcon* may be cured by allowing intervention of additional named plaintiffs as subclass representatives. *See* Hill v. W. Elec. Co., 672 F.2d 381 (4th Cir.), cert. denied, 459 U.S. 981, 103 S.Ct. 318, 74 L.Ed.2d 294 (1982) and Robert P. Monyak, Note, *Reinstating Vacated Findings in Employment Discrimination Class Actions: Reconciling General Telephone Co. v. Falcon with Hill v. Western Electric Co.*, 1983 DUKE L.J. 821 (1983).

In ANDERSON v. WESTINGHOUSE SAVANNAH RIVER CO., 406 F.3d 248 (4th Cir. 2005), cert. denied, 546 U.S. 1214, 126 S.Ct. 1431, 164 L.Ed.2d 133 (2006), the district court granted summary judgment on the named plaintiff's claims and denied class certification. The Fourth Circuit affirmed the dismissal of the plaintiff's individual claims and concluded that because her claims were without merit she could not adequately represent a class. But the court also stated that evidence in the record indicated the possible existence of class claims of discrimination in promotional opportunities and remanded to the district court for determination of whether another class member could step in to represent the class.

> While we express no opinion on whether or not the class action may fail for want of commonality or typicality, we remand to the district court the question of whether or not a class action should be permitted to proceed with respect to the [promotional claims].   Upon remand, if a proper plaintiff or plaintiffs with grievances similar to those of Miss Anderson with respect to that discrete portion of the [promotion procedure] presents himself to prosecute, himself, as a class representative, the district court should then decide whether a class action is maintainable and whether the then named plaintiff should represent the class.

406 F.3d at 275. Should a defendant be allowed to moot out a putative class action by making a pre-certification offer of judgment under Rule 68 of the Federal Rules that will provide the only individual relief available to the named plaintiff? *See* Weiss v. Regal Collections, 385 F.3d 337 (3d Cir. 2004) (allowing defendants to "pick off" a representative plaintiff with a swift offer of judgment could frustrate the goal of enabling plaintiffs to aggregate small claims).

4.   It may be difficult at the certification stage to determine the *practical* adequacy of the named plaintiff and his attorney to represent the interests of the class. The district court should decertify the class if the attorney proves unable to properly protect class interests. *See* Jordan v. County of L. A., 669 F.2d 1311, 1323 n.13 (9th Cir.) (adequacy of class counsel may be reviewed continually throughout pendency of action), vacated for further consideration in light of *Falcon*, 459 U.S. 810, 103 S.Ct. 35, 74 L.Ed.2d 48 (1982); Colby v. J.C. Penney Co., 128 F.R.D. 247, 250 (N.D. Ill. 1989), affirmed, 926 F.2d 645 (7th Cir. 1991) (ineffectiveness of counsel in conducting discovery and responding to motion for summary judgment warrants decertification of class). Even after a trial on the merits, the court may decertify the class, thus relieving it of the preclusive effects of an adverse judgment, if class counsel has proved incompetent. *See* Johnson v. Shreveport Garment Co., 422 F.Supp. 526, 533 (W.D. La. 1976), affirmed, 577 F.2d 1132 (5th Cir. 1978).

In CULVER v. CITY OF MILWAUKEE, 277 F.3d 908 (7th Cir. 2002), a class of unsuccessful applicants for the city police force was originally certified but later decertified because the class was too heterogeneous and class counsel had refused to cooperate in dividing the class into subdivisions. The court of appeals affirmed on the ground that by breaching his fiduciary duties to the class the lawyer had demonstrated she was not an adequate representative of the interests of the class. The court also offered this description of the role of class counsel.

> For purposes of determining whether the class representative is an adequate representative of the members of the class, the performance of the class lawyer is inseparable from that of the class representative. This is so because even when the class representative has some stake * * * it is usually very small in relation to the stakes of the class as a whole, magnifying the role of the class lawyer and making him (or in this case her) realistically a principal. Indeed *the* principal. Realistically, functionally, practically, she is the class representative, not he. "Experience teaches that it is counsel for the class representative and not the named parties, who direct and manage these actions. Every experienced federal judge knows that any statements to the contrary is [sic] sheer sophistry."

277 F.3d at 913. To what extent, if at all, is this view of the role of class counsel inconsistent with Rule 23(g)?

5.   In WAL-MART STORES, INC. v. DUKES, 564 U.S. 338, 131 S.Ct. 2541, 180 L.Ed.2d 374 (2011), about one and one half million present and former female employees joined in a class action alleging that Wal-Mart, in its 3400 stores in 41 regions in the United States, systemically discriminated against women in pay and promotion decisions, for which they sought back pay, punitive damages, injunctive and declaratory relief, but not compensatory damages. Regarding the commonality requirement, Wal-Mart argued that its decisions on pay and promotion were decentralized with individual store and regional managers accorded substantial discretion to operate under broad general guidelines issued by the home office. According to Wal-Mart, the differences between management practices in different stores precluded any finding of commonality respecting pay or promotions. It also argued that the six named plaintiffs were not typical of the broad diverse class because all but one were hourly employees and none had worked in upper levels of in-store management and thus could not represent women in management positions.

The district court granted class certification under Rule 23(b)(2) on the equal pay claim, on the promotional claim for injunctive relief, and on the back pay claim for denial of promotional opportunities for those promotions where applicant flow data was available. The trial judge concluded that the commonality requirement was satisfied by the fact that the subjective decision-making occurred in the context of strong central control of all aspects of corporate management

The Supreme Court, by a 5-4 margin, reversed this portion of the lower courts' rulings. The majority emphasized that the commonality requirement was more than a pleading requirement; it was the trial court's job to determine whether the plaintiffs had proven that all of the members' claims involved a common contention whose resolution would resolve an issue central to the validity of all claims. In a Title VII case, the Court explained, this requirement would not be met by claiming simply that all members had a claim under Title VII or that all had a disparate impact claim under that statute. Moreover, the Court expressly acknowledged that the requisite commonality analysis could often overlap with the plaintiffs' merits contention and added, in a footnote, that any suggestion to the contrary in *Eisen* was both dictum in that case and bad law. Applying this test to the instant case, the Court concluded that the essence of the plaintiffs' claim – the existence of a decentralized decision-making process that allowed individual store managers to make discretionary decisions – was by nature the antithesis of a claim that the defendant used a common evaluation process that was infected with discriminatory bias or resulted in discriminatory results. Nor had the plaintiffs established the existence of a common method of exercising discretion by the managers at its various stores. Thus, the Court determined, the plaintiffs had not offered any significant proof that Wal-Mart employed a general policy of discriminating at its stores throughout the country. Moreover, the Court declared, evidence of a discriminatory "bottom line" at a regional or national level did not establish the existence of a common pattern of discriminatory decisions at individual stores throughout the country. All of these considerations led the five member majority to conclude that not only did common issues not predominate, but that the plaintiffs had not established the existence of even one single common question.

The four dissenters, who ultimate agreed that the trial court had erred in certifying the class under Rule 23(b)(2), disagreed with that portion of Justice Scalia's opinion for the Court that set forth the standard for determining commonality in a (b)(2) class action. The dissenters believed that the majority had incorrectly applied the sort of commonality analysis that was appropriate for certification of a (b)(3) class action in a case seeking certification under (b)(2). In their opinion, the plaintiffs had established the existence of a common question sufficient to meet the standards of Rule 23(b)(2). They ultimately agreed, however, with the decision to reverse the lower courts' certification of the class under (b)(2) on the ground that the presence of individualized claims for monetary relief that were not merely incidental to the sought-after injunctive or declaratory relief precluded (b)(2) certification.

SECTION C.   THE SIZE OF THE CLASS

A prerequisite for a class action under Rule 23(a)(1) is that the class be "so numerous that joinder of all members is impracticable." No precise standard has been established that demarcate the number of persons necessary to satisfy the numerosity requirement: the determination will be made on the facts of each case. "Practicability of joinder depends on the size of the class, ease of identifying its members and determining their addresses, facility of making service on them if joined and their geographic dispersion." Garcia v. Gloor, 618 F.2d 264 (5th Cir. 1980), cert. denied, 449 U.S. 1113, 101 S.Ct. 923, 66 L.Ed.2d 842 (1981) (proposed class of 31 persons whose identity and addresses were readily ascertainable and who lived in same area rejected on ground that joinder was practicable). The courts are divided on the issue of whether the remedial purposes of Title VII should influence the numerosity determination. *Compare Garcia* ("Whether a class should be certified depends entirely on whether the proposal satisfies the requirements" of Rule 23), *with* Gay v. Waiters' & Dairy Lunchmen's Union, Local 30, 549 F.2d 1330, 1334 (9th Cir.1977) (reversing the district court's denial of class certification on numerosity grounds and declaring that the court "must consider the broad remedial purposes of Title VII and must liberally interpret and apply Rule 23 so as not to undermine the purpose and effectiveness of Title VII in eradicating class-based discrimination."). A number of courts have recognized that the fear that putative class members would file individual actions is a relevant factor in determining the practicability of joinder and justifies the certification of relatively small classes. *See, e.g.*, Slanina v. William Penn Parking Corp., 106 F.R.D. 419 (W.D. Pa. 1984) (class of 25 employees sufficiently large because of fear of reprisals if forced to sue individually)

Although Rule 23(a) does not explicitly limit the *maximum* size of a class, the representational adequacy requirement, as a practical matter, may place limits on certification. The larger and more widespread the class, the more costly and time-consuming will be its representation. Certification may be denied if the court determines the plaintiff lacks the resources to adequately represent the class. Eisen v. Carlisle & Jacquelin, 417 U.S. 156, 94 S.Ct. 2140, 40 L.Ed.2d 732 (1974). In assessing manageability, a court will consider the financial resources of the plaintiff, her attorney's ability to pursue extensive and costly discovery, the geographic dispersion of class members, problems of communication, and the reconciling of adverse interests. When an extremely large class is proposed, courts may permit discovery, prior to certification, of plaintiff and his counsel as to their ability to manage the class. *See* Guse v. J.C. Penney Co., 409 F.Supp. 28 (E.D. Wis. 1976), reversed on other grounds, 562 F.2d 6 (7th Cir. 1977).

In WAL-MART STORES, INC. v. DUKES, 564 U.S. 338, 131 S.Ct. 2541, 180 L.Ed.2d 374 (2011), the trial court had certified a class consisting of as many as 1.5 million female current and former employees. One of many arguments made by Wal-Mart in opposition to certification was that a case of this size would be completely unmanageable in both the liability and remedial stages. Wal-Mart maintained, for example, that determining liability for the alleged pattern and practice of discrimination would be unmanageable because it enjoyed a constitutional due process right to put on evidence from 3,244 individual stores to rebut claims that it discriminated against class members employed at each store. Noting that evidence introduced at the liability stage should focus on matters relevant to the class as a whole, the court rejected the unmanageability argument.

> Wal-Mart of course can defend against Plaintiffs' claim of a nationwide pattern and practice by arguing that its more decentralized store sub-unit by store sub-unit statistical analysis refutes the existence of any company-wide policy of discrimination. It also can introduce evidence to rebut any evidence Plaintiffs present of centralized, nationwide policies regarding Defendant's corporate culture, personnel policies or gender stereotyping. It is not, however, entitled to circumvent or defeat the class nature of the proceeding by litigating whether every individual store discriminated against individual class members.

222 F.R.D. at 174. Wal-Mart also contended that in the remedial stage, Title VII required individualized determinations of back pay and injunctive relief and that such individualized hearings rendered the class action unmanageable. The plaintiffs asserted, on the other hand, that both back pay and injunctive relief could be determined by adopting formulas which could be applied to all class members without necessitating individual hearings. The trial judge agreed with the plaintiffs, finding that Title VII did not mandate the holding of individualized hearings. And in response to Wal-Mart's claim that a punitive damages award in the absence of individualized hearings would violate its constitutional right to due process because it might result in the awarding of damages to non-victims, the trial court imposed conditions to prevent unjust enrichment by non-injured plaintiffs. Its order specified that any punitive damages award would be based solely on evidence of conduct that was directed towards the class, limited recovery of punitive damages to class members who recovered an award of lost pay, and required that allocations of punitive damages to individual members be in reasonable proportion to individual lost pay awards.

The Ninth Circuit affirmed all of these determinations, finding that the trial judge had not abused its discretion in arriving at these conclusions and had imposed safeguards that adequately protected the defendant's due process rights. And though the court ruled that putative class members who no longer were Wal-Mart employees when the plaintiffs filed the complaint lacked standing to pursue injunctive or declaratory relief, those putative members who remained employed by Wal-Mart as of the date of filing had standing to see such relief and, therefore, injunctive and declaratory relief continued to predominate over monetary relief for purposes of certifying the class under Rule 23(b)(2). Accordingly, the appellate court remanded for a determination of the appropriate scope of the class. This ruling was affirmed by a 6-5 vote of the Ninth Circuit *en banc*, except that except that the court remanded the claims for punitive damages with instructions to the district court to determine whether the class should be certified under Rule 12(b)(2) or (b). The *en banc* opinion also remanded to the trial court the claims of putative class members who no longer worked for Wal-Mart when the complaint was filed for the purpose of determining whether to certify an additional class or classes under Rule 23(b)(3). But all of these rulings became moot when the Supreme Court ruled that the trial judge had erroneously certified the class under (b)(2) because the claims did not meet that Rule's commonality requirement and because claims for monetary relief were not recoverable in a (b)(2) class action, at least where the request for monetary relief was not incidental to the requests for injunctive and declaratory relief.

Section D. The Class Action and the Prerequisites to Title VII Litigation

Oatis v. Crown Zellerbach Corp.

United States Court of Appeals, Fifth Circuit, 1968.
398 F.2d 496.

Griffin B. Bell, Circuit Judge.

This appeal presents the issue whether membership in a class action brought under §706(e) is restricted to individuals who have filed charges with the Equal Employment Opportunity Commission. The District Court answered in the affirmative. Being of the view that the class was unduly restricted, we reverse.

The suit giving rise to this issue was instituted on March 1, 1967 by four Negro employees (Hill, Oatis, Johnson and Young) of Crown Zellerbach Corporation. The suit was filed against the company and the two local unions representing employees at the Bogalusa, Louisiana plant of the company. Each plaintiff sued on behalf of himself and all present and prospective Negro employees of the plant, as a class, seeking injunctive relief against unfair employment practices as defined by Title VII.

Prior to this action Hill filed a formal charge against the defendants with the Equal Employment Opportunity Commission in the manner provided for under §706(a) of the Act. The Commission informed Hill by letter that it had been unable to obtain voluntary compliance from appellees within the 60 days required by the Act. The suit was commenced two weeks later.

Crown and the unions filed motions to dismiss. They contended that an action under Title VII cannot be brought on behalf of a class, and that in any event plaintiffs Oatis, Johnson and Young could not join in the action as co-plaintiffs inasmuch as they had not filed a charge with the EEOC. The Attorney General, representing the EEOC, was permitted to intervene. See §706(e).

The District Court ruled that the action could be maintained as a class action, but that the class was limited to those Negro employees who had filed charges with EEOC pursuant to §706(a). Oatis, Johnson and Young had not filed such a charge and the motions to dismiss were granted as to them. It is from this dismissal that they appeal.[1]

Under the enforcement provisions of Title VII an aggrieved person is required to file a written charge with the EEOC. §706(a), *supra*. Assuming the EEOC finds reasonable cause to believe the charge is true, informal efforts to settle with the employer or union are to be made through conference, conciliation, and persuasion. The filing of such a charge is a condition precedent to seeking judicial relief. See §706(e). It is thus clear that there is great emphasis in Title VII on private settlement and the elimination of unfair practices without litigation.

The plaintiffs-appellants maintain that a class action will lie if at least one aggrieved person has filed a charge with the EEOC. Defendants, on the other hand, assert that the administrative, private remedy intent and purposes of the statute will be circumvented and avoided if only one person may follow the administrative route dictate of the Act and then sue on behalf of the other employees. This, they urge, would result in the courts displacing the EEOC role in fostering the purposes of the Act. Defendants also argue that the Act provides for protection of the rights of a class in that §707(a) envisions a suit by the Attorney General when he finds that a pattern or practice of discrimination exists. This provision, they say, militates against the position of plaintiffs.

The arguments of defendants are not persuasive for several reasons. A similar argument regarding a suit by the Attorney General was rejected by this court in a case brought under Title II of the Civil Rights Act of 1964. Lance v. Plummer, 5th Cir., 1965, 353 F.2d 585. We again reject it. The Act permits private suits and in nowise precludes the class action device.

Moreover, it does not appear that to allow a class action, within proper confines, would in any way frustrate the purpose of the Act that the settlement of grievances be first attempted through the office of the EEOC. It would be wasteful, if not vain, for numerous employees, all with the same grievance, to have to process many identical complaints with the EEOC. If it is impossible to reach a settlement with one discriminatee, what reason would there be to assume the next one would be successful. The better approach would appear to be that once an aggrieved person raises a particular issue with the EEOC which he has standing to raise, he may bring an action for himself and the class of persons similarly situated and we proceed to an examination of this view.

Plaintiff Hill raised several claims in the charge which he filed with the EEOC. One of these was that he was being discriminated against by the use of segregated locker rooms. Under the District Court's ruling Hill might bring suit and be placed in the white locker room. Other Negroes would have to wait until they could process their charges through EEOC before they could obtain the same relief from the same employer. We do not believe that Congress intended such a result from the application of Title VII. The class should not be so narrowly restricted. This conclusion is in line with several District Court decisions.

---

[1] The express determination and direction required by Rule 54(b) F.R.Civ.P., in connection with the entry of judgment has been made and appeal is proper although the case is still pending as to Hill's complaint.

The Supreme Court recently made an apt comment on the nature of suits brought under the Civil Rights Act of 1964. See Newman v. Piggie Park Enterprises, 1968, 390 U.S. 400, 88 S.Ct. 964, 19 L.Ed.2d 1263, where the court stated:

"A Title II suit is thus private in form only. When a plaintiff brings an action under that Title, he cannot recover damages. If he obtains an injunction, he does so not for himself alone, but also as a 'private attorney general', vindicating a policy that Congress considered of the highest priority."

Clearly the same logic applies to Title VII of the Act. Racial discrimination is by definition class discrimination, and to require a multiplicity of separate, identical charges before the EEOC, filed against the same employer, as a prerequisite to relief through resort to the court would tend to frustrate our system of justice and order.

We thus hold that a class action is permissible under Title VII within the following limits. First, the class action must, as it does here, meet the requirements of Rule 23(a) and (b)(2). Next, the issues that may be raised by plaintiff in such a class action are those issues that he has standing to raise (i.e., the issues as to which he is aggrieved, see §706(a)), and that he has raised in the charge filed with the EEOC pursuant to §706(a). Here then the issues that may be considered in the suit are those properly asserted by Hill in the EEOC charge and as are reasserted in the complaint.

Additionally, it is not necessary that members of the class bring a charge with the EEOC as a prerequisite to joining as co-plaintiffs in the litigation. It is sufficient that they are in a class and assert the same or some of the issues. This emphasizes the reason for Oatis, Johnson and Young to appear as co-plaintiffs. They were each employed in a separate department of the plant. They were representative of their respective departments, as Hill was of his, in the class action. They, as co-plaintiffs, must proceed however, within the periphery of the issues which Hill could assert. Under Rule 23(a) they would be representatives of the class consisting of the Negro employees in their departments so as to fairly and adequately protect their interests. This follows from the fact that due to the inapplicability of some of the issues to all members of the class, the proceeding might be facilitated by the use of subclasses. In such event one or more of the co-plaintiffs might represent a subclass. It was error, therefore, to dismiss appellants. They should have been permitted to remain in the case as plaintiffs but with their participation limited to the issues asserted by Hill.

Reversed and remanded for further proceedings not inconsistent herewith.

Griffin v. Dugger

United States Court of Appeals, Eleventh Circuit, 1987.
823 F.2d 1476, cert. denied, 486 U.S. 1005, 108 S.Ct. 1729, 100 L.Ed.2d 193 (1988).

TJOFLAT, Circuit Judge.

I.

In April 1971, Peners L. Griffin became the first black Road Prison Officer at the Tallahassee Road Prison, operated by the Florida Department of Corrections (FDOC or Department). Beginning in 1973, Griffin frequently sought promotion to higher-grade correctional officer positions, as well as various other positions. On each occasion, the FDOC turned him down.

In December 1974, Griffin's supervisor fired him for disciplinary reasons. The next day, the Regional Superintendent reinstated Griffin because the supervisor had not followed proper termination procedures. In early 1975, the FDOC again terminated Griffin's employment, without notice, for disciplinary reasons. He appealed the termination to the State of Florida Career Service Commission. The Commission found no just cause for Griffin's discharge and ordered the FDOC to reinstate him with back pay. The Florida District Court of Appeal affirmed the Commission's decision, and the FDOC reinstated Griffin to his position.

Soon after his reinstatement, Griffin filed a complaint with the FDOC's Equal Employment Opportunity Program Office, charging that his two dismissals were racially discriminatory. An investigator in that office wrote Griffin a month later and informed him of his conclusion that racial discrimination had not been a factor in the dismissals. Within a day or two of having received that letter, Griffin filed a complaint with the Equal Employment Opportunity Commission, detailing the events leading up to his allegedly discriminatory discharges. A notation at the beginning of Griffin's complaint, probably made by an EEOC counselor, describes Griffin's allegations of racial discrimination as also encompassing "[s]incerity of recruiting, hiring, and promoting of minority groups within the Florida's Division of Adult Corrections. Specific attention within the Community Service Program."

Griffin asked the EEOC for a right-to-sue letter and received one in July 1979. On October 15, 1979, Griffin brought this action in the district court against Louis L. Wainwright, as Secretary of the FDOC, the FDOC, and the State of Florida. Griffin alleged that the FDOC had denied him several promotions because of his race. He also alleged that the FDOC impermissibly considered race in all of its promotion decisions, as well as in its hiring and job assignment decisions. In hiring correctional officers, according to Griffin, the Department used written entry-level examinations having a detrimental impact upon blacks.[1]

Griffin sued "individually and on behalf of all others similarly situated," pursuant to Rule 23(b)(2) of the Federal Rules of Civil Procedure, seeking declaratory and injunctive relief and money damages under Title VII * * *. The class identified in his complaint was composed "of all past, present and potential black American citizens and residents who have been, are or may be employees of the Defendants or applicants for employment."

On June 17, 1980, Griffin obtained leave of court to amend his complaint to add Henry L. Dejerinett as a party-plaintiff and class representative. Dejerinett, who is black, had applied for an FDOC clerical position but was not hired.[5] On March 10, 1981, based on a stipulation between the parties and without a hearing, the district court preliminarily certified the case as a class action with Griffin and Dejerinett

---

[1]The district court found the following facts concerning the FDOC's written entry-level examination: "Every person seeking a position as a correctional officer is required to take a written examination. The Department of Administration developed the Correctional Officer I entry level test which consists of seventy-five questions. An applicant must receive a score of at least thirty-eight for employment consideration."

[5]Dejerinett subsequently filed a timely charge of racial discrimination against the FDOC with the Florida Commission on Human Relations, a deferral agency for the EEOC. He requested and received a right-to-sue letter from the EEOC in April 1980.

representing the class of "all past, present, and potential black employees of the State of Florida Department of Corrections."

On June 25, 1982, the defendants filed a "Notice Regarding the Adequacy of the Preliminary Class Certified," which called to the court's attention a Supreme Court decision rendered eleven days previously. That decision, General Tel. Co. v. Falcon, 457 U.S. 147, 102 S.Ct. 2364, 72 L.Ed.2d 740 (1982), announced the appropriate standards courts should apply when determining class action certifications in the context of a Title VII suit, reversing a former Fifth Circuit decision permitting "across-the-board" class actions that had been binding precedent in the new Eleventh Circuit. On July 8, 1982, the defendants moved the court, in light of *Falcon*, to vacate its order certifying the class.

To avoid the risk that the district court might vacate its order certifying the class, Griffin and Dejerinett took steps to obtain an additional named plaintiff to represent those in the class who had applied for the position of correctional officer, failed the written entry-level examination, and not been hired. Accordingly, on July 8, 1982, Alvin Smith, joined by Griffin and Dejerinett, moved the court to intervene as an additional named plaintiff and class representative. In 1980 and 1981, Smith, who is black, applied for the same entry-level position that Griffin held. The FDOC did not hire Smith, because he did not have a high school diploma or a general equivalency diploma (GED), a prerequisite for employment as a correctional officer. Smith later obtained a GED, but when he reapplied with the FDOC in July 1981, he failed the written entry-level correctional officer examination and was again denied the job.[8]

On July 28, 1982, the district court denied the defendants' motion to decertify the class and permitted Smith to intervene because

> Smith, [as] an unsuccessful applicant, certainly has an interest in this suit which seeks to challenge defendants' employment practices, including hiring. Unless he is permitted to intervene, his interest may not be adequately represented by the named parties. Mr. Smith eases this court's concern that the class claim against the [FDOC]'s objective criteria was not fairly and adequately protected by the named plaintiffs. Alvin Smith is a proper representative for potential black employees.

As to the defendants' contention that Smith could not be a class representative because he had not timely filed an EEOC complaint, the district court found that the charges of discrimination Griffin had filed with the EEOC included "the hiring claim in addition to promotion, job classification, discipline, and termination claims." The court thus reasoned that the Fifth Circuit's single-filing rule excused Smith from having failed to exhaust his administrative remedies. See Oatis v. Crown Zellerbach Corp., 398 F.2d 496, 498 (5th Cir.1968) ("[O]nce an aggrieved person raises a particular issue with the EEOC which he has standing to raise, he may bring an action for himself and the class of persons similarly situated * * *.").

On July 30, 1982, the district court entered partial summary judgment for the plaintiffs, including Griffin and Dejerinett, on the liability issue as to the written entry-level examination. The court found that the FDOC examination "has a disparate impact upon class members which has not been justified by business necessity." The

---

[8]Smith never filed a timely charge of racial discrimination with the EEOC.

plaintiffs had sought summary judgment on two other issues — the class hiring and promotion claims — but the court denied summary judgment on those issues because they presented material issues of fact.

A trial was held * * *. The court entered judgment on August 25, 1983, disposing of the following issues in favor of the defendants: whether the FDOC's policies and practices discriminated against past, present, and potential black employees; whether the FDOC's employment practices as to Peners L. Griffin were racially discriminatory; and whether the FDOC's hiring practices as to Henry L. Dejerinett were racially discriminatory. The court entered judgment for the plaintiffs on the liability issue concerning the correctional officer examination, on which it had previously granted summary judgment for the plaintiffs. The issue of relief for the class of black persons who took and failed the correctional officer written examination is still pending. The parties agreed that notice should be given to the affected members of the class and to seek interlocutory appeal of the district court's decision permitting Griffin, Dejerinett, and Smith to serve as named plaintiffs for a class that included applicants with testing claims. We granted this appeal pursuant to 28 U.S.C. §1292(b). Because we conclude that the district court incorrectly applied the dictates of *Falcon*, we vacate the district court's order certifying the class.

II.

As with any private class action, the legitimacy of a private Title VII suit brought on behalf of a class depends upon the satisfaction of two distinct prerequisites. First, there must be an individual plaintiff with a cognizable claim, that is, an individual who has constitutional standing to raise the claim (or claims) and who has satisfied the procedural requirements of Title VII.[12] Second, the requirements of Rule 23 of the Federal Rules of Civil Procedure must be fulfilled; in other words, the individual plaintiff must be qualified to represent the members of the class in accordance with the four prerequisites of Rule 23(a), and the action must be one of the three types Rule 23(b) identifies. We emphasize that any analysis of class certification must begin with the issue of standing and the procedural requirements of Title VII. Thus, the threshold question is whether the named plaintiffs have individual standing, in the constitutional sense, to raise certain issues. Only after the court determines the issues for which the named plaintiffs have standing should it address the question whether the named plaintiffs have representative capacity, as defined by Rule 23(a), to assert the rights of others.

* * *

[The Court held that since he had suffered no injury as a result of the FDOC's use of the written entry-level examination, plaintiff Griffin had no constitutional standing under Article III to assert the testing claim on behalf of himself or others. The Court further held that because the FDOC's decision-making process for promotions was subjective, though its hiring process was objective, the case did not come within the "same general fashion" classification of related forms of discrimination mentioned in

---

[12]This circuit has held that the conditions precedent to filing a Title VII suit are not jurisdictional, but rather are akin to a statute of limitations. A plaintiff's failure to satisfy the conditions precedent does not, standing alone, deprive federal district courts of subject matter jurisdiction. Nevertheless, a plaintiff must generally allege in his complaint that "all conditions precedent to the institution of the lawsuit have been fulfilled." Fed.R.Civ.P. 9(c)).

footnote 15 of *Falcon*. Thus Griffin, who could assert discipline and promotion claims under Title VII, did not have representative capacity, within the meaning of Rule 23(a), to assert testing claims on behalf of others. The Court then proceeded to examine whether the joinder of Dejerinett and Smith as plaintiff-intervenors affected the class certification question.]

III.

A.

Eight months after filing his complaint in district court, Griffin sought leave to amend his complaint to add Henry L. Dejerinett as a party-plaintiff and as a class representative. In November 1978, Dejerinett applied for an FDOC clerical position, entitled "Property Manager III." Dejerinett was not required, as part of the application process, to produce an educational degree or to take the written entry-level examination required of correctional officer applicants. He was required, however, to have an interview. Dejerinett was not hired; instead, the FDOC hired a white male. A month later, Dejerinett filed a charge of racial discrimination against the FDOC with the Florida Commission on Human Relations, a deferral agency for the EEOC. He requested and received a right-to-sue letter from the EEOC in April 1980. The district court, with no written analysis of standing or Rule 23, granted Griffin leave to amend his complaint and add Dejerinett as a named plaintiff.

Dejerinett had standing to assert a subjective hiring claim. He applied for a clerical position, requiring no correctional officer examination or educational degrees, and was not hired. Because Dejerinett never took the correctional officer examination, and never applied for that position, he suffered no injury as a result of that test. He thus lacked constitutional standing to assert a testing or a hiring claim arising out of the FDOC's correctional officer application process.

Accordingly, we hold that the district court erred when it permitted Dejerinett to raise the testing claim on behalf of himself and on behalf of others. We hold in the alternative that even if Dejerinett somehow had constitutional standing to assert the testing claim, he did not, in light of *Falcon*, have representative capacity to assert the testing claim on behalf of those who took the FDOC's written entry-level examination, failed it, and were not hired. In other words, Dejerinett did not meet the prerequisites of Rule 23(a).

The district court, in effect, presumed the similarity of hiring claims of those denied clerical positions to hiring claims of those denied correctional officer positions. In our view, applicants who were subjectively denied clerical positions cannot sufficiently identify with other applicants who failed an objective written examination and, on that basis, were not hired for the higher-ranking position of correctional officer. See Walker v. Jim Dandy Co., 747 F.2d 1360, 1364 (11th Cir.1984) ("The [district] court [correctly] reasoned that because [the plaintiffs] were applicants for supervisory positions, they did not sufficiently identify with other applicants for lower level labor jobs or employees complaining of disparate job assignments or pay."). The district court abused its discretion when, in light of *Falcon*, it continued to permit Dejerinett to represent those members of the class who took and failed the written entry-level correctional officer examination.

B.

Intervenor Alvin Smith twice applied for the entry-level correctional officer position held by Griffin. Smith was first denied the job because he did not have a high school diploma or a general equivalency diploma (GED), both requirements for the job. Later he obtained a GED, but he then failed the written correctional officer examination. Consequently, he was denied the position a second time.

Smith had constitutional standing to assert a testing claim under Title VII. He could, and did, allege injury as a result of the FDOC's testing requirement: he took and failed the written examination required of entry-level correctional officers. Although Smith may very well have had representative capacity, under Rule 23(a), to assert testing claims on behalf of other black applicants who failed the same test and were consequently not hired, we need not address that point. Smith did not file a timely charge of racial discrimination with the EEOC, a precondition to a Title VII suit. Furthermore, as we discuss below, Smith could not avail himself of the single-filing rule. For these reasons, we hold that the district court erred when it allowed Smith to intervene as a class representative.

In Oatis v. Crown Zellerbach Corp., our predecessor circuit[1] held that it is not necessary for each person with the same grievance to file an EEOC charge as a prerequisite to class membership. Nor is it necessary that an intervenor bring a charge with the EEOC as a prerequisite to serving as a class representative. Id. As long as at least one named plaintiff timely filed an EEOC charge, the precondition to a Title VII action is met for all other named plaintiffs and class members. Id.[36]

This rule, which has become known as the "single-filing rule," contains two essential requirements: First, at least one plaintiff must have timely filed an EEOC complaint that is not otherwise defective. Second, the individual claims of the filing and non-filing plaintiffs must have arisen out of similar discriminatory treatment in the same time frame. In the case before us, the first requirement was met: Griffin, one of the named plaintiffs, timely filed an adequate EEOC complaint, as far as it detailed his promotion and discipline claims. The second requirement, however, was not satisfied. Smith, a non-filing plaintiff, had an objective testing claim while Griffin, on the other hand, had subjective promotion and discipline claims.

We hold that Griffin and Smith were not sufficiently similarly situated. That is, employee Griffin's claims and applicant Smith's claims did not arise out of similar discriminatory treatment. Griffin alleged that the FDOC's subjective promotion and discipline practices were illegally discriminatory. Smith alleged that the FDOC's objective correctional officer examination illegally discriminated against black applicants. The FDOC's promotion and discipline practices were not manifested in similar fashion to its hiring and testing practices. See Ezell v. Mobile Housing Bd.,

---

[1] [In 1980, Congress passed and President Carter signed the Fifth Circuit Court of Appeals Reorganization Act, which split the Fifth Circuit into two separate circuit courts. Texas, Louisiana and Mississippi were designated to comprise the new Fifth Circuit, while Alabama, Georgia, and Florida constituted the new Eleventh Circuit. — ed.]

[36]The *Oatis* reasoning was extended to intervention in non-class suits in Wheeler v. American Home Prods. Corp., 582 F.2d 891, 897-98 (5th Cir.1977) (similarly situated a who had not filed EEOC charges nevertheless could assert back pay claims if one or more of original plaintiffs had filed timely charges). The *Oatis* rationale was further extended in Crawford v. United States Steel Corp., 660 F.2d 663, 665-66 (5th Cir.Unit B Nov. 1981), which held that every original plaintiff in a multi-plaintiff, non-class action suit need not file charges with the EEOC.

709 F.2d 1376, 1381 (11th Cir.1983) (non-filing incumbent plaintiff's discriminatory examination claim was not sufficiently similar to filing plaintiffs' discriminatory discharge and broad-based, ongoing campaign of discrimination claims to invoke single-filing rule to excuse filing requirement). Although both employment practices could have been racially discriminatory, that alone is not enough to implicate the second requirement of the single-filing rule. Otherwise, "intervention [could] bootstrap the court's jurisdiction to encompass claims regarding practices broader than the * * * claims properly assertable by the named plaintiffs." Vuyanich v. Republic Nat'l Bank, 723 F.2d 1195, 1201 (5th Cir.) (former employees who sought to intervene in class action but who did not file timely charges with EEOC could only proceed within periphery of issues that named plaintiffs could assert), cert. denied, 469 U.S. 1073, 105 S.Ct. 567, 83 L.Ed.2d 507 (1984).

We also note that merely because a notation at the beginning of Griffin's EEOC complaint stated that Griffin's charge also encompassed "[s]incerity of recruiting, hiring, and promoting of minority groups within the Florida's Division of Adult Corrections," Smith's status as a class representative was not saved. As the pleadings make clear, Griffin never had constitutional standing to raise a testing or a hiring claim, a fundamental requirement underlying the single-filing rule: "once an aggrieved person raises a particular issue with the EEOC which he has standing to raise, he may bring an action for himself and the class of persons similarly situated." *Oatis*.[37] Smith cannot point to Griffin's EEOC charge, which arguably contained a testing claim brought on behalf of others, to excuse his failure to have filed his own testing charge with the EEOC when Griffin did not have standing to raise the testing issue. We cannot permit the single-filing rule to be used to circumvent the constitutional requirement of standing.

IV.

In sum, based on standing principles and on the dictates of *Falcon*, we hold that the district court erred when it certified the class with the named plaintiffs as representatives. None of the named plaintiffs — Griffin, Dejerinett, or Smith — should have been allowed to represent the class of black correctional officer applicants with testing claims. The district court's order certifying the class is therefore

Vacated.

HATCHETT, Circuit Judge, dissenting:

I dissent. The majority holds that Smith did not meet the second element of the single-filing rule. That rule [requires that] the individual *claims* of the filing and non-filing plaintiffs must have arisen out of similar discriminatory treatment in the same time frame. One of Griffin's claims in his EEOC complaint was that the FDOC discriminated against black job applicants. Non-filing intervenor Smith's claim arose "out of similar discriminatory treatment," because he alleges that the FDOC

---

[37] By "standing," the *Oatis* court meant "the issues as to which [the employee] is aggrieved," *Oatis* (citing Title VII's enforcement provision that requires the EEOC to investigate the charges of a person claiming to be aggrieved, §706(a)). By "standing," the *Oatis* court also meant, even if implicitly, personal injury, that is, constitutional standing. See Vuyanich v. Republic Nat'l Bank, 723 F.2d 1195, 1200-01 (5th Cir.) (interpreting *Oatis'* single-filing rule as implicating constitutional standing), cert. denied, 469 U.S. 1073, 105 S.Ct. 567, 83 L.Ed.2d 507 (1984).

discriminated against him and other applicants through administration of a test with a discriminatory impact on blacks. The majority ignores the fact that Griffin raised the claim of discrimination against black applicants in his EEOC complaint.

The majority erroneously assumes that if Griffin lacks standing to raise the hiring claim in federal court, then his raising of that claim before the EEOC is somehow ineffective for purposes of the single filing rule. The majority's reasoning is based upon its failure to differentiate between the policy underlying the standing requirement in federal court and the policy underlying the single filing rule in an EEOC action. The policy underlying the standing requirement is to ensure that a party litigating an issue has a concrete stake in the outcome of the case, and is therefore motivated to vigorously litigate the issues. The policy underlying the EEOC filing requirement is to ensure "that the settlement of grievances be first attempted through the office of the EEOC * * *." *Oatis*. The purpose underlying the EEOC filing requirement is therefore to promote the resolution of Title VII claims out of court. The EEOC proceeding is not designed as a way-station on the road to the federal courthouse.

By asserting a hiring grievance in his EEOC complaint, Griffin ensured that the settlement of hiring grievances would be first attempted through the office of the EEOC. The fact that Griffin may not have had standing in federal district court to raise the hiring issue is irrelevant to the fact that his EEOC complaint gave the EEOC an opportunity to settle the hiring grievance before that grievance was sued upon in federal district court. Since Smith's claim in federal district court of discriminatory hiring practices is identical to the claim of discriminatory hiring practices asserted in Griffin's complaint before the EEOC, invoking the single filing rule will not frustrate the purpose of the EEOC filing requirement: to give the EEOC a chance to resolve Title VII claims before they go to court. The fact that Griffin may not have had standing to raise the hiring claim in court is irrelevant to the issue of whether the EEOC has had a chance to resolve that claim before it is taken to court, whether by Griffin, Smith, or anyone else.

In short, the majority has grafted the constitutional standing requirement for parties litigating in federal district court onto the filing requirements for persons alleging Title VII claims before the EEOC. Such a requirement does not, and never has, existed. The majority, however, misinterprets Fifth Circuit dicta to reach just that conclusion. That dicta says, "Once an aggrieved person raises a particular issue with the EEOC which he has standing to raise, he may bring an action for himself and the class of persons similarly situated." *Oatis*. The majority fails to mention that the sole issue in the *Oatis* case was whether a Title VII class action could include in the class persons who had not previously filed charges with the EEOC. The court held that the class could include such persons. The *Oatis* court gave its reasoning for this holding in the sentence immediately preceding the language relied upon by the majority in this case. That sentence states, "If it is impossible to reach a settlement with one discriminatee, what reason would there be to assume the next one would be successful." *Oatis*. In short, the court in *Oatis* was not faced with the question of whether an EEOC complainant could effectively file claims with the EEOC even though the complainant would not have standing to assert the claim in federal district court. The majority's application of constitutional standing requirements to the EEOC complainant puts the EEOC in the nonsensical position of having to anticipate how the federal district court will rule on the complainant's standing to litigate various claims if the EEOC does not resolve them. Such a rule will result in the EEOC narrowing its resolution of claims to those which it anticipates the complainant will have standing to sue upon in federal district court, regardless of the apparent existence of the alleged discrimination with respect to other employees or job applicants. Such a situation would hardly further the purpose of the EEOC filing requirement: to resolve Title VII claims out of court.

Section 705(b) * * * requires the Commission to investigate all charges which a person "claims" to be aggrieved of. In no way does the provision suggest that the Commission is limited to the investigation of claims which the complainant will have standing to bring in a federal court. Any suggestion in *Oatis* of such a requirement is dicta that is in conflict with the intent of the statute that the EEOC resolve "claimed" discrimination out of court. Smith should therefore be allowed to proceed in federal district court as a class representative for the class of applicants who failed the objective test.

NOTES AND PROBLEMS FOR DISCUSSION

1. In *Oatis*, the court held that the class action "must proceed * * * within the periphery of the issues which Hill could assert." As discussed in Chapter 4, Section A.4, *supra*, the claims in a Title VII action are limited to some degree by the allegations in the EEOC charge filed pursuant to §706(a). The civil action is generally limited to the "scope of the EEOC investigation which [could] reasonably be expected to grow out of the charge of discrimination." Sanchez v. Standard Brands, Inc., 431 F.2d 455, 466 (5th Cir. 1970). While most circuits adhere to the *Sanchez* test for determining the proper scope of class allegations in a Title VII action, there is substantial divergence among them as to the application of that standard. In FELLOWS v. UNIVERSAL RESTS., INC., 701 F.2d 447 (5th Cir. 1983), cert. denied, 464 U.S. 828, 104 S.Ct. 102, 78 L.Ed.2d 106 (1983), for example, the court held that neither a class allegation in the EEOC charge nor a class investigation by the EEOC was a prerequisite to a class suit. All that was required was that the substance of the charge afford "a reasonable expectation that the EEOC's investigation could encompass not only Universal's alleged discrimination against Ms. Fellows but also that against all female applicants and employees." 701 F.2d at 451. But in EVANS v. UNITED STATES PIPE & FOUNDRY CO., 696 F.2d 925 (11th Cir. 1983), on the other hand, the district court dismissed class allegations of discrimination in initial job assignments, promotions, layoffs, discipline, and termination on behalf of all of the defendant's African-American employees because the plaintiff's EEOC charge had alleged only racial discrimination in the areas of promotion and job assignment and because the EEOC investigation had been limited to those matters. The Eleventh Circuit, while recognizing contrary authority, affirmed.

> The record reveals that the substantive inquiry by the Commission was limited to defendant's claims of discrimination in promotion and harassment. Appellant's concept of widespread discrimination rooted in the subjective decisionmaking of the white supervisory staff was not a part of the investigation by the Commission.

696 F.2d at 929. Does the majority's opinion in *Griffin* rest merely on the fact that Dugger's EEOC charge was not broad enough to encompass the claims made by Smith? Some courts have held that the single filing rule is applicable only where the

EEOC charge alleges class-wide discrimination. *See* Tolliver v. Xerox Corp., 918 F.2d 1052 (2d Cir. 1990), cert. denied, 499 U.S. 983, 111 S.Ct. 1641, 113 L.Ed.2d 736 (1991) (requiring that the charge not only allege discrimination against a class but also that the claimant purports to represent the class or others similarly situated.). Given the purpose of the filing requirements in §706 (opportunity for conciliation and notice to employer), is there any purpose to be served by requiring that the class representative have filed a class claim with the EEOC?

After the Eleventh Circuit issued its ruling in *Griffin*, five members of the former plaintiff class who had failed the correctional officer examination moved to intervene individually and as class representatives of the vacated testing class and requested recertification of that class. The would-be intervenors relied on an EEOC charge filed by one of their number in March, 1986, while the appeal in *Griffin* was pending. The trial court denied the motion to intervene, denied the motion to recertify, and granted summary judgment to the defendant on the testing issue on the ground that no plaintiff or movant had filed a timely EEOC charge regarding testing and thus stood in no better position that Alvin Smith did in *Griffin*. On appeal, the Eleventh Circuit affirmed the denial of intervention and the trial court's refusal to recertify the class, but held that the would-be intervenors should be allowed to proceed on their individual claims. Griffin v. Singletary, 17 F.3d 356 (11th Cir. 1994), cert. denied, 513 U. S. 1077, 115 S.Ct. 723, 130 L.Ed.2d 628 (1995).

2. For the single filing rule to work, the class representative must have filed a timely EEOC charge. *See* City of Hialeah v. Rojas, 311 F.3d 1096 (11th Cir. 2002) (a plaintiff whose EEOC charge was untimely had no standing to bring a class action on behalf of similarly situated employees). Nor can a person who has not filed a charge use the single filing rule to become the representative of a class that could not have been represented by the filing party. *See* Hines v. Widnall, 334 F.3d 1253, 1258 (11th Cir. 2003) (an unsuccessful applicant for employment who failed to file an EEOC charge may not represent a class of applicants in a case filed by an employee who did file a timely charge because discrimination towards employees and applicants is not similar treatment for purposes of single filing rule).

Under the single-filing rule, the class may include only those persons who had viable claims at the time the class representative on whom they depend filed a charge with the EEOC. For example, in a Title VII class action on behalf of persons unlawfully denied employment, the named plaintiff necessarily would have filed an EEOC charge within 180 days (in a non-deferral state) of the defendant's rejection of his application. Thus, only those persons who were denied employment within 180 days prior to the date on which the named plaintiff filed his EEOC charge (i.e., those persons who could have filed an EEOC charge at the same time the plaintiff did) may be included in the class. McDonald v. United Air Lines, Inc., 587 F.2d 357, 361 n.10 (7th Cir. 1978), cert. denied, 442 U.S. 934, 99 S.Ct. 2869, 61 L.Ed.2d 303 (1979). For those persons rejected by the employer more than 180 days prior to the date on which the named plaintiff filed his charge, their rights to either file their own suit or to participate in a class action under Title VII ended 180 days after they were turned down for employment.

3. In *National R.R. Passenger Corp.*, discussed in Chapter 4, Section A.3, *supra,* the Supreme Court held that the continuing violation doctrine allows plaintiffs who are claiming unlawful harassment to seek relief for actions outside of the filing period so long as one act contributing to the harassment occurred within the filing period. The Court ruled however that "discrete acts" of discrimination, even if related to one another (so-called "serial violations"), do not constitute a continuing violation. Presumably this means that in a class action alleging class-wide discrete act discrimination, the class can consist only of those individuals who were victims of discrimination within the filing period covered by named plaintiff's EEOC charge. Thus, under *Morgan,* the continuing violation doctrine cannot be used to expand the class in most Title VII class actions. In footnote 9 of its opinion, however, the *Morgan* Court explicitly refrained from deciding how the continuing violation doctrine applies to claims of class-wide, systemic discrimination. ("We have no occasion here to consider the timely filing question with respect to 'pattern-or-practice' claims brought by private litigants as none are at issue here."). Should systemic discrimination which consists of a pattern of discrete acts, a "glass ceiling" for female employees for example, be treated in a class action the same as such claims are in individual disparate treatment actions, i.e. subject to the timely filing requirement and not entitled to continuing violation status? Or, because of the insidious nature of systemic discrimination and in light of the purpose of the single-filing rule, should a putative class member, whose own individual claim would be time-barred, be allowed to shoehorn into the class under the continuing violation doctrine? In a pre-*Morgan* decision, the Eleventh Circuit expressed a negative view of such an extension. Hipp v. Liberty National Life Co., 252 F.3d 1208, 1221 (11th Cir. 2001), cert. denied, 534 U.S. 1127, 122 S.Ct. 1064, 151 L.Ed.2d 968 (2002) ("no authority * * * for allowing one plaintiff to revive a stale claim simply because the allegedly discriminatory policy still exists and is being enforced against others.").

Crown, Cork & Seal Co., Inc. v. Parker

Supreme Court of the United States, 1983.
462 U.S. 345, 103 S.Ct. 2392, 76 L.Ed.2d 628.

Justice Blackmun delivered the opinion of the Court.

The question that confronts us in this case is whether the filing of a class action tolls the applicable statute of limitations, and thus permits all members of the putative class to file individual actions in the event that class certification is denied, provided, of course, that those actions are instituted within the time that remains on the limitations period.

I

Respondent Theodore Parker, a Negro male, was discharged from his employment with petitioner Crown, Cork & Seal Company, Inc., in July 1977. In October of that year, he filed a charge with the Equal Employment Opportunity Commission alleging that he had been harassed and then discharged on account of his race. On November 9, 1978, the EEOC issued a Determination Letter finding no reasonable cause to believe respondent's discrimination charge was true, and, pursuant to §706(f) of the Civil Rights Act of 1964(Act), sent respondent a Notice of Right to Sue.

Two months earlier, while respondent's charge was pending before the EEOC, two other Negro males formerly employed by petitioner filed a class action in the

United States District Court for the District of Maryland. Pendleton v. Crown, Cork & Seal Co. The complaint in that action alleged that petitioner had discriminated against its Negro employees with respect to hiring, discharges, job assignments, promotions, disciplinary actions, and other terms and conditions of employment, in violation of Title VII of the Act. The named plaintiffs purported to represent a class of "black persons who have been, continue to be and who in the future will be denied equal employment opportunities by defendant on the grounds of race or color." It is undisputed that respondent was a member of the asserted class.

In May 1979, the named plaintiffs in Pendleton moved for class certification. Nearly a year and a half later, on September 4, 1980, the District Court denied the motion. The court ruled that the named plaintiffs' claims were not typical of those of the class, that the named plaintiffs would not be adequate representatives, and that the class was not so numerous as to make joinder impracticable. Thereafter, Pendleton proceeded as an individual action on behalf of its named plaintiffs.[1]

On October 27, 1980, within 90 days after the denial of class certification but almost two years after receiving his Notice of Right to Sue, respondent filed the present Title VII action in the United States District Court for the District of Maryland, alleging that his discharge was racially motivated. Respondent moved to consolidate his action with the pending Pendleton case, but petitioner opposed the motion on the ground that the two cases were at substantially different stages of preparation. The motion to consolidate was denied. The District Court then granted summary judgment for petitioner, ruling that respondent had failed to file his action within 90 days of receiving his Notice of Right to Sue, as required by the Act's §706(f)(1).

The United States Court of Appeals for the Fourth Circuit reversed. Relying on American Pipe & Constr. Co. v. Utah, 414 U.S. 538, 94 S.Ct. 756, 38 L.Ed.2d 713 (1974), the Court of Appeals held that the filing of the Pendleton class action had tolled Title VII's statute of limitations for all members of the putative class. Because the Pendleton suit was instituted before respondent received his Notice, and because respondent had filed his action within 90 days after the denial of class certification, the Court of Appeals concluded that it was timely.

Two other Courts of Appeals have held that the tolling rule of *American Pipe* applies only to putative class members who seek to intervene after denial of class certification, and not to those who, like respondent, file individual actions.[2] We granted certiorari to resolve the conflict.

II

A

American Pipe was a federal antitrust suit brought by the State of Utah on behalf of itself and a class of other public bodies and agencies. The suit was filed with only 11 days left to run on the applicable statute of limitations. The District Court eventually ruled that the suit could not proceed as a class action, and eight days after

---

[1]The named plaintiffs in *Pendleton* later settled their claims, and their action was dismissed with prejudice. Respondent Parker * * * then intervened in that lawsuit for the limited purpose of appealing the denial of class certification. He failed, however, to take a timely appeal.

[2]See Pavlak v. Church, 681 F.2d 617 (CA9 1982), cert. pending, No. 82-650; Stull v. Bayard, 561 F.2d 429, 433 (CA2 1977), cert. denied, 434 U.S. 1035, 98 S.Ct. 769, 54 L.Ed.2d 783 (1978); Arneil v. Ramsey, 550 F.2d 774, 783 (CA2 1977).

this ruling a number of putative class members moved to intervene. This Court ruled that the motions to intervene were not time-barred. The Court reasoned that unless the filing of a class action tolled the statute of limitations, potential class members would be induced to file motions to intervene or to join in order to protect themselves against the possibility that certification would be denied. The principal purposes of the class action procedure — promotion of efficiency and economy of litigation — would thereby be frustrated. To protect the policies behind the class action procedure, the Court held that "the commencement of a class action suspends the applicable statute of limitations as to all asserted members of the class who would have been parties had the suit been permitted to continue as a class action."

Petitioner asserts that the rule of *American Pipe* was limited to intervenors, and does not toll the statute of limitations for class members who file actions of their own.[3] Petitioner relies on the Court's statement in *American Pipe* that "the commencement of the original class suit tolls the running of the statute for all purported members of the class *who make timely motions to intervene* after the court has found the suit inappropriate for class action status." While *American Pipe* concerned only intervenors, we conclude that the holding of that case is not to be read so narrowly. The filing of a class action tolls the statute of limitations "as to all asserted members of the class," not just as to intervenors.

The *American Pipe* Court recognized that unless the statute of limitations was tolled by the filing of the class action, class members would not be able to rely on the existence of the suit to protect their rights. Only by intervening or taking other action prior to the running of the statute of limitations would they be able to ensure that their rights would not be lost in the event that class certification was denied. Much the same inefficiencies would ensue if *American Pipe's* tolling rule were limited to permitting putative class members to intervene after the denial of class certification. There are many reasons why a class member, after the denial of class certification, might prefer to bring an individual suit rather than intervene. The forum in which the class action is pending might be an inconvenient one, for example, or the class member might not wish to share control over the litigation with other plaintiffs once the economies of a class action were no longer available. Moreover, permission to intervene might be refused for reasons wholly unrelated to the merits of the claims.[4] A putative class member who fears that class certification may be denied would have every incentive to file a separate action prior to the expiration of his own period of limitations. The result would be a needless multiplicity of actions — precisely the

---

[3]Petitioner also argues that *American Pipe* does not apply in Title VII actions, because the time limit contained in §706(f)(1) is jurisdictional and may not be tolled. This argument is foreclosed by the Court's decisions in Zipes v. Trans World Airlines, Inc., 455 U.S. 385, 398, 102 S.Ct. 1127, 1135, 71 L.Ed.2d 234 (1982), and Mohasco Corp. v. Silver, 447 U.S. 807, 811, 100 S.Ct. 2486, 2489 and n. 9, 65 L.Ed.2d 532 (1980).

[4]Putative class members frequently are not entitled to intervene as of right under Fed. Rule Civ. Proc. 24(a), and permissive intervention under Fed. Rule Civ. Proc. 24(b) may be denied in the discretion of the District Court. American Pipe. In exercising its discretion the District Court considers "whether the intervention will unduly delay or prejudice the adjudication of the rights of the original parties," Fed. Rule Civ. Proc. 24(b), and a court could conclude that undue delay or prejudice would result if many class members were brought in as plaintiffs upon the denial of class certification. Thus, permissive intervention well may be an uncertain prospect for members of a proposed class.

situation that Federal Rule 23 and the tolling rule of *American Pipe* were designed to avoid.

B

Failure to apply *American Pipe* to class members filing separate actions also would be inconsistent with the Court's reliance on *American Pipe* in Eisen v. Carlisle & Jacquelin, 417 U.S. 156, 94 S.Ct. 2140, 40 L.Ed.2d 732 (1974). In *Eisen*, the Court held that Rule 23(c)(2) required individual notice to absent class members, so that each class member could decide whether to "opt out" of the class and thereby preserve his right to pursue his own lawsuit. The named plaintiff in *Eisen* argued that such notice would be fruitless because the statute of limitations had long since run on the claims of absent class members. This argument, said the Court, was "disposed of by our recent decision in *American Pipe* * * * which established that commencement of a class action tolls the applicable statute of limitations as to all members of the class."

If *American Pipe's* tolling rule applies only to intervenors, this reference to *American Pipe* is misplaced and makes no sense. *Eisen's* notice requirement was intended to inform the class member that he could "preserve his opportunity to press his claim *separately*" by opting out of the class. But a class member would be unable to "press his claim separately" if the limitations period had expired while the class action was pending. The *Eisen* Court recognized this difficulty, but concluded that the right to opt out and press a separate claim remained meaningful because the filing of the class action tolled the statute of limitations under the rule of *American Pipe*. If *American Pipe* were limited to intervenors, it would not serve the purpose assigned to it by *Eisen*; no class member would opt out simply to intervene. Thus, the *Eisen* Court necessarily read *American Pipe* as we read it today, to apply to class members who choose to file separate suits.[5]

C

The Court noted in *American Pipe* that a tolling rule for class actions is not inconsistent with the purposes served by statutes of limitations. Limitations periods are intended to put defendants on notice of adverse claims and to prevent plaintiffs from sleeping on their rights, but these ends are met when a class action is commenced. Class members who do not file suit while the class action is pending cannot be accused of sleeping on their rights; Rule 23 both permits and encourages class members to rely on the named plaintiffs to press their claims. And a class

---

[5]Several members of the Court have indicated that *American Pipe's* tolling rule can apply to class members who file individual suits, as well as to those who seek to intervene. See Johnson v. Railway Express Agency, Inc., 421 U.S. 454, 474-475, 95 S.Ct. 1716, 1727, 44 L.Ed.2d 295 (1975) (Marshall, J., joined by Douglas and Brennan, JJ., concurring in part and dissenting in part) ("In *American Pipe* we held that initiation of a timely class action tolled the running of the limitation period as to individual members of the class, enabling them to institute separate actions after the District Court found class action an inappropriate mechanism for the litigation"); United Airlines, Inc. v. McDonald, 432 U.S. 385, 402, 97 S.Ct. 2464, 2474, 53 L.Ed.2d 423 (1977) (Powell, J., joined by The Chief Justice and White, J., dissenting) ("Under *American Pipe*, the filing of a class action complaint tolls the statute of limitations until the District Court makes a decision regarding class status. If class status is denied, * * * the statute of limitations begins to run again as to class members excluded from the class. In order to protect their rights, such individuals must seek to intervene in the individual action (or possibly file an action of their own) before the time remaining in the limitations period expires").

complaint "notifies the defendants not only of the substantive claims being brought against them, but also of the number and generic identities of the potential plaintiffs who may participate in the judgment." The defendant will be aware of the need to preserve evidence and witnesses respecting the claims of all the members of the class. Tolling the statute of limitations thus creates no potential for unfair surprise, regardless of the method class members choose to enforce their rights upon denial of class certification.

Restricting the rule of *American Pipe* to intervenors might reduce the number of individual lawsuits filed against a particular defendant but, as discussed above, this decrease in litigation would be counterbalanced by an increase in protective filings in all class actions. Moreover, although a defendant may prefer not to defend against multiple actions in multiple forums once a class has been decertified, this is not an interest that statutes of limitations are designed to protect. Other avenues exist by which the burdens of multiple lawsuits may be avoided; the defendant may seek consolidation in appropriate cases, see Fed. Rule Civ. Proc. 42(a); 28 U.S.C. §1404 (change of venue), and multidistrict proceedings may be available if suits have been brought in different jurisdictions, see 28 U.S.C. §1407.[6]

III

We conclude, as did the Court in *American Pipe*, that "the commencement of a class action suspends the applicable statute of limitations as to all asserted members of the class who would have been parties had the suit been permitted to continue as a class action." Once the statute of limitations has been tolled, it remains tolled for all members of the putative class until class certification is denied. At that point, class members may choose to file their own suits or to intervene as plaintiffs in the pending action.

In this case, respondent clearly would have been a party in *Pendleton* if that suit had been permitted to continue as a class action. The filing of the *Pendleton* action thus tolled the statute of limitations for respondent and other members of the *Pendleton* class. Since respondent did not receive his Notice of Right to Sue until after the *Pendleton* action was filed, he retained a full 90 days in which to bring suit after class certification was denied. Respondent's suit was thus timely filed.

The judgment of the Court of Appeals is affirmed.

JUSTICE POWELL, with whom JUSTICE REHNQUIST and JUSTICE O'CONNOR join, concurring.

I join the Court's opinion. It seems important to reiterate the view expressed by Justice Blackmun in *American Pipe*. He wrote that our decision "must not be regarded as encouragement to lawyers in a case of this kind to frame their pleadings as a class action, intentionally, to attract and save members of the purported class who have slept on their rights." The tolling rule of *American Pipe* is a generous one, inviting abuse. It preserves for class members a range of options pending a decision on class certification. The rule should not be read, however, as leaving a plaintiff free to raise different or peripheral claims following denial of class status.

---

[6]Petitioner's complaints about the burden of defending multiple suits ring particularly hollow in this case, since petitioner opposed respondent's efforts to consolidate his action with Pendleton.

In *American Pipe* we noted that a class suit "notifies the defendants not only of the substantive claims being brought against them, but also of the number and generic identities of the potential plaintiffs who participate in the judgment. Within the period set by the statute of limitations, the defendants have the essential information necessary to determine both the subject matter and size of the prospective litigation." When thus notified, the defendant normally is not prejudiced by tolling of the statute of limitations. It is important to make certain, however, that *American Pipe* is not abused by the assertion of claims that differ from those raised in the original class suit. As Justice Blackmun noted, a district court should deny intervention under Rule 24(b) to "preserve a defendant whole against prejudice arising from claims for which he has received no prior notice." Similarly, when a plaintiff invokes *American Pipe* in support of a separate lawsuit, the district court should take care to ensure that the suit raises claims that "concern the same evidence, memories, and witnesses as the subject matter of the original class suit," so that "the defendant will not be prejudiced." Claims as to which the defendant was not fairly placed on notice by the class suit are not protected under *American Pipe* and are barred by the statute of limitations.

In this case, it is undisputed that the *Pendleton* class suit notified petitioner of respondent's claims. The statute of limitations therefore was tolled under *American Pipe* as to those claims.

NOTES AND PROBLEMS FOR DISCUSSION

1. What if Parker had received his right-to-sue letter before the class action had been filed? Would the 90-day period have been merely suspended during the pendency of the action, or would the period have begun to run anew when class certification was denied? In CHARDON v. FUMERO SOTO, 462 U.S. 650, 103 S.Ct. 2611, 77 L.Ed.2d 74 (1983), a suit filed under 42 U.S.C. §1983, the Court held that where federal law is silent, state law must be looked to for both the applicable statute of limitations and to determine the tolling effect of a class action unless they are "inconsistent with the Constitution and laws of the United States." Under Puerto Rican law applicable in *Chardon*, the statute of limitations began to run anew when tolling ceased. Title VII, unlike §1983, provides the applicable limitations period, but does not provide for the "tolling effect" of a class action. Does *Chardon* mean that in Title VII case, the tolling effect of a class action is to be determined by reference to state law? Under *Crown, Cork & Seal,* if class certification is denied, should the limitation period for filing an individual case be tolled until completion of an appeal from the denial of certification? Apparently the answer to that question is "no." *See* Armstrong v. Martin Marietta Corp., 138 F.3d 1374, 1385 (11th Cir. 1998) (*en banc*), cert. denied, 525 U.S. 1019, 119 S.Ct. 545, 142 L.Ed.2d 453 (2000) ("[n]o reasonable person would rely on the hope that either the district court or this court might someday determine that the suit should have proceeded as a class action.").

2. For the tolling doctrine to apply, how similar must the claims raised in the original class action be to those in the subsequent suit? In DAVIS v. BETHLEHEM STEEL CORP., 769 F.2d 210 (4th Cir.), cert. denied, 474 U.S. 1021, 106 S.Ct. 573, 88 L.Ed.2d 557 (1985), the Fourth Circuit held that a class action filed in 1971 containing a "laundry list" of pattern and practice allegations was not specific enough to put the defendants on notice of the discriminatory acts alleged in a 1982 complaint, thus precluding the application of *Crown, Cork & Seal.* Should the rule that the statute of limitations is tolled for all class members until class certification is denied or until they opt out of the class be limited to those members who can prove reliance on the pendency of the class action? *See* Tosti v. City of L.A., 754 F.2d 1485 (9th Cir. 1985).

3. Under *Crown, Cork & Seal,* the filing of a class action tolls the statutes of limitation for individual actions by putative class members. But does the pendency of a class action also toll the limitation period for the filing of other class actions by putative class members? After the Eleventh Circuit issued its ruling in Griffin v. Dugger, *supra,* several unsuccessful applicants for correctional officer positions who had failed the written test moved to intervene and to recertify the class of those applicants who had failed the test. The movants relied on a charges filed while the case had been pending before the Eleventh Circuit. In GRIFFIN v. SINGLETARY, 17 F.3d 356, 359 (11th Cir. 1994), cert. denied, 513 U.S. 1077, 115 S.Ct. 723, 130 L.Ed.2d 628 (1995), the Eleventh Circuit ruled that the pendency of the previously filed class action in Griffin v. Dugger did not toll the limitations period for additional class actions by putative members of the originally asserted class. "The plaintiffs may not piggyback one class action onto another," the court explained, "and thereby engage in endless rounds of litigation in the district court and in this Court over the adequacy of successive named plaintiffs to serve as class representatives." But the appellate court also recognized that the piggyback rule for individual claims was different from that for class actions.

> The district court reasoned that there is an exception to the tolling rule announced in *American Pipe* and *Crown, Cork & Seal* when the class action relied upon was decertified on grounds that no class representative had standing to bring the claim asserted in the individual suits. We disagree. Insofar as the individual claims are concerned, putative class members should be entitled to rely on a class action as long as it is pending. That reliance is particularly justified in this case, in which the district court certified a plaintiff class.

17 F.3d at 360. It concluded that there was no difference, for tolling purposes, between an administrative limitations period (the timely filing rule for EEOC charges) and a statute of limitations like that involved in *Crown, Cork & Seal.* The court thus held that the charge-filing period for individuals who were members of the class in Griffin v. Dugger was tolled during the pendency of the testing class in that case — from the time the lawsuit was filed until the Eleventh Circuit's ruling.

SECTION E. THE PRECLUSIVE EFFECT OF THE CLASS ACTION JUDGMENT ON THE CLAIMS OF INDIVIDUAL CLASS MEMBERS

In JOHNSON v. GEORGIA HIGHWAY EXPRESS, INC., 417 F.2d 1122 (5th Cir. 1969), a case discussed in the introduction to this chapter, concurring Judge Godbold cautioned that:

> The broad brush approach of some of the Title VII cases is in sharp contrast to the diligence with which in other areas we carefully protect those whose rights may be affected by litigation * * *. But when the problem is multiplied

> many-fold [by a class action], counsel, and at times the courts, are moving
> blithely ahead tacitly assuming all will be well for surely the plaintiff will win
> and manna will fall on all members of the class. It is not quite that easy.

417 F.2d at 1127 (Godbold, J., concurring). As a general rule, a judgment entered in a
properly certified class action binds, under preclusion principles, all class members on
the issues decided in the case. Thus, a class member who will benefit by a finding of
class-wide discrimination will also be bound by a decision adverse to the class in the
same way as if he had been a named plaintiff.

But a finding that class-wide discrimination did not occur, does not always mean
that the employer has not discriminated against one or more individuals who are class
members. In COOPER v. FEDERAL RESERVE BANK OF RICHMOND, 467 U.S.
867, 104 S.Ct. 2794, 81 L.Ed.2d 718 (1984), a properly certified (b)(2) action on
behalf of former and current employees of the bank, the plaintiffs tried but failed to
prove a pattern and practice of racial discrimination in promotions. Thereafter, several
class members filed separate actions, each alleging that he had been denied promotions
because of race. The Bank moved to dismiss the individual complaints on the ground
that each of the plaintiffs had been a member of the class certified in the prior action
and that they were bound by the determination in that case that no class-wide
discrimination had occurred. The Fourth Circuit ruled that the judgment in the class
action precluded the individual class members from maintaining their claims. Holding
that the Court of Appeals had erred in the preclusive effect accorded the class action
judgment, the Supreme Court reversed.

> That judgment (1) bars the class members from bringing another class action
> against the Bank alleging a pattern or practice of discrimination for the relevant
> time period and (2) precludes the class members in any other litigation with the
> Bank from relitigating the question whether the Bank engaged in a pattern and
> practice of discrimination against black employees during the relevant time
> period. The judgment is not, however, dispositive of the individual claims the * *
> * petitioners have alleged in their separate action. Assuming they establish a
> prima facie case of discrimination under *McDonnell Douglas*, the Bank will be
> required to articulate a legitimate reason for each of the challenged decisions, and
> if it meets that burden, the ultimate questions regarding motivation in their
> individual cases will be resolved by the District Court.

467 U.S. at 880. To rule otherwise the Court stated "would be tantamount to requiring
that every member of the class be permitted to intervene [in the class action] to litigate
the merits of his individual claim" and would defeat the purpose of the class device as
a procedure for the efficient adjudication of common questions of law or fact. *Ibid.*

If a class member is allowed to opt out of the class and the court subsequently
finds class-wide discrimination, of what use is that determination to the claimant in his
individual case? *Cf.* Parklane Hosiery Co. v. Shore, 439 U.S. 322, 99 S.Ct. 645, 58
L.Ed.2d 552 (1979) (approving use of offensive non-mutual issue preclusion under
certain circumstances).

An agreement settling a class action, which has been judicially approved under
Rule 23(e), ordinarily will bar a class member who is dissatisfied with the settlement
from pursuing an individual claim encompassed within the class claims that were
settled. *See* Huguley v. GMC, 52 F.3d 1364 (6thCir. 1995) (the court has the power

under the "relitigation exception" to the Anti Injunction Act, 28 U.S.C. §2283, to enjoin state court litigation on issues covered by consent decree). But which individual claims will be encompassed within the previous class settlement will not always be easy to determine. For example, in KING v. SOUTH CENTRAL BELL TELEPHONE AND TELEGRAPH CO., 790 F.2d 524 (6th Cir. 1986), under the defendant's policy, persons taking maternity leave, unlike individuals who took leave resulting from other temporary disabilities, did not continue to acquire seniority while on leave and were not assured of being returned to their prior positions. After returning from maternity leave and being assigned to a lower paying job, King filed an EEOC charge. While the charge was pending, King received notice of the settlement of a class action that had been filed on behalf of female employees who had taken maternity leave and had been denied reinstatement or had been delayed in returning to work. King responded to the notice by filing a claim for backpay for an eight day delay between her request to return to work from leave and her actual return. She included with the claim a statement that the settlement did not satisfy her claim for lost wages resulting from her being placed in a lower job and an assertion that she did not wish to waive her claim by participating in the settlement. King subsequently filed her own lawsuit. The district court granted summary judgment to the employer on claim preclusion grounds. Despite the fact that the settlement notice was ambiguous as to the scope of claims to which the settlement applied, the Sixth Circuit affirmed. "Even if it can be argued that the notice was somewhat ambiguous, King could not opt out because the action (23(b)(2)) did not include that privilege. The most she could do was object to the decree and she did." 790 F.2d at 530. What, if anything, could King have done to protect her ability to litigate her individual claim?

Should a class member who has opposed the terms of a class settlement be allowed to appeal *on behalf of the class* from the district court's approval of the settlement? *See* Cotton v. United States Pipe & Foundry Co., 856 F.2d 158 (11th Cir. 1988) (in the absence of a new class certification, individuals who are dissatisfied with a consent decree have no standing to appeal on behalf of the class).

SECTION F. CERTIFICATION UNDER RULE 23(B)(2) AND 23(B)(3): NOTICE TO THE CLASS AND THE RIGHT TO OPT OUT

Jefferson et al. v. Ingersoll International, Inc.

United States Court of Appeals, Seventh Circuit, 1999.
195 F.3d 894.

EASTERBROOK, Circuit Judge.

Plaintiffs contend in this suit under Title VII that Ingersoll International and affiliated companies discriminated on account of race in considering applications for employment. It is a pattern-or-practice suit, and like most similar claims of persistent discrimination affecting large numbers of persons was filed as a class action. The district court certified a class limited to persons who actually applied for employment but were turned down; the court rejected plaintiffs' effort to include in the class persons discouraged from applying. It also declined to certify classes of employees who were not promoted, or whose compensation allegedly was depressed because of their race; these groups of employees were not sufficiently numerous to justify class handling, the court explained. The opinion is a careful and measured treatment of the class-certification issue. But one part of the disposition is problematic and is the focus of defendants' petition for leave to take an interlocutory appeal under Fed. R. Civ. P. 23(f).

Plaintiffs seek an injunction that would require Ingersoll to change its hiring practices. That relief, if granted, would affect applicants as a group, and plaintiffs therefore sought certification under Rule 23(b)(2), which applies when "the party opposing the class has acted or refused to act on grounds generally applicable to the class, thereby making appropriate final injunctive relief or corresponding declaratory relief with respect to the class as a whole". For many years Rule 23(b)(2) was the normal basis of certification in Title VII pattern-or-practice cases. When this tradition took hold, however, Title VII allowed only equitable relief and therefore nicely fit the language of Rule 23(b)(2). True enough, class members could receive money, because back pay is a form of equitable relief, but this relief was treated as incidental to the injunction — and, because it was deemed equitable, neither side had a right to jury trial, so that handling the suit as a consolidated proceeding in equity did not threaten anyone's rights.

After the Civil Rights Act of 1991, however, prevailing plaintiffs in a Title VII suit are entitled not only to equitable relief but also to compensatory and punitive damages. Either side may demand a jury trial if the plaintiff seeks damages. Because the representative plaintiffs seek both compensatory and punitive damages, Ingersoll contended that any class should be certified under Rule 23(b)(3) rather than Rule 23(b)(2). If the action proceeds under Rule 23(b)(3), then each member of the class must receive notice and an opportunity to opt out and litigate (or not) on his own behalf. See Rule 23(c)(2). If it proceeds under Rule 23(b)(2), by contrast, then no notice will be given, and no one will be allowed to opt out. Because of this difference, Rule 23(b)(2) gives the class representatives and their lawyers a much freer hand than does Rule 23(b)(3). Although class members who want control of their own litigation are vitally concerned about the choice, so too are defendants — for the final resolution of a suit that proceeds to judgment (or settlement) under Rule 23(b)(2) may be collaterally attacked by class members who contend that they should have been notified and allowed to proceed independently. Defendants who want the outcome of a damages action (no matter which side wins) to be conclusive favor Rule 23(b)(3), because it alone insulates the disposition from collateral attack by dissatisfied class members.

In the district court the parties joined issue on the question when, if at all, a suit may proceed under Rule 23(b)(2) if the plaintiffs seek not only equitable relief but also substantial money damages. All the district judge said on this subject, however, is that Rule 23(b)(2) is well suited to pattern-or-practice suits, which no one doubts. The judge wrapped up: "Because the court has determined that the hiring class is properly certified under Rule 23(b)(2), it need not address the applicability of subsection (b)(3)." It is this decision that Ingersoll wants us to review by interlocutory appeal under Rule 23(f). This issue fits the third category of appropriate [interlocutory] appeals * * * — situations in which the legal question is important, unresolved, and has managed to escape resolution by appeals from final judgments. Both sides cite a welter of district court decisions (many in this circuit) addressing the subject, but none has reached this court since the Civil Rights Act of 1991, and only one has reached another court of appeals. See Allison v. Citgo Petroleum Corp., 151 F.3d 402 (5th Cir. 1998). Thus we grant the petition for leave to appeal. Moreover, because the petition and the response lay out the legal arguments, further briefing is unnecessary. We have seen enough to know that the district court must confront rather than dodge the fundamental legal question.

Earlier this year the Supreme Court stressed that proper interpretation of Rule 23, principles of sound judicial management, and constitutional considerations (due process and jury trial), all lead to the conclusion that in actions for money damages class members are entitled to personal notice and an opportunity to opt out. Ortiz v. Fibreboard Corp., 527 U.S. 815, 144 L. Ed. 2d 715, 119 S. Ct. 2295, 2314-15 (1999). This entitlement may be overcome only when individual suits would confound the interest of other plaintiffs — when, for example, there is a limited fund that must be distributed ratably, the domain of Rule 23(b)(1), or when an injunction affects everyone alike, the domain of Rule 23(b)(2). *Ortiz* disapproved a creative use of Rule 23(b)(1) that employed the "limited fund" rationale to eliminate notice and opt-out rights; the Court's analysis applies equally when a request for an injunction is being used to override the rights of class members to notice and an opportunity to control their own litigation.

Rule 23(b)(2) authorizes a no-notice and no-opt-out class for "final injunctive relief or corresponding declaratory relief [that operates] with respect to the class as a whole". In such a situation class certification protects the missing class members by obliging the representatives (and their counsel) to act as fiduciaries of the other affected persons. Money damages under § 1981a(b) are neither injunctive nor declaratory, and they do not affect a class as a whole. It is possible for one applicant for employment to recover substantial damages while another recovers nothing (for example, because the second person would have been rejected under nondiscriminatory conditions, or found a better job elsewhere). Class members sensibly may decide that direct rather than vicarious representation is preferable, and they may reject the aid of self-appointed fiduciaries. Rule 23(c)(2) gives them that right.

It is an open question in this circuit — and in the Supreme Court, whether Rule 23(b)(2) ever may be used to certify a no-notice, no-opt-out class when compensatory or punitive damages are in issue. Rule 23(b)(2) is designed for all-or-none cases in which "final relief of an injunctive nature or of a corresponding declaratory nature, settling the legality of the behavior with respect to the class as a whole, is appropriate." Advisory Committee's Note explaining Rule 23(b)(2). Rule 23(b) begins by saying that an action "may" be maintained as a class action when the prerequisites of subdivision (a) and a part of subdivision (b) have been satisfied; it does not say that the class must be certified under the first matching subsection. A court should endeavor to select the most appropriate subsection, not just the first linguistically applicable one in the list. When substantial damages have been sought, the most appropriate approach is that of Rule 23(b)(3), because it allows notice and an opportunity to opt out.

Divided certification also is worth consideration. It is possible to certify the injunctive aspects of the suit under Rule 23(b)(2) and the damages aspects under Rule

23(b)(3), achieving both consistent treatment of class-wide equitable relief and an opportunity for each affected person to exercise control over the damages aspects. Beacon Theatres, Inc. v. Westover, 359 U.S. 500, 3 L. Ed. 2d 988, 79 S. Ct. 948 (1959), and Dairy Queen, Inc. v. Wood, 369 U.S. 469, 8 L. Ed. 2d 44, 82 S. Ct. 894 (1962), would require the district judge to try the damages claims first, to preserve the right to jury trial, a step that would complicate the management of separate classes — and mean, as a practical matter, that the damages claims and the Rule 23(b)(3) class would dominate the litigation — but the damages-first principle holds even when there is a single class under a single subdivision of Rule 23. That the seventh amendment gives damages the dominant role just strengthens the conclusion that Rule 23(b)(3) must be employed. Instead of divided certification — perhaps equivalently to it — the judge could treat a Rule 23(b)(2) class as if it were under Rule 23(b)(3), giving notice and an opportunity to opt out on the authority of Rule 23(d)(2).

If Rule 23(b)(2) ever may be used when the plaintiff class demands compensatory or punitive damages, that step would be permissible only when monetary relief is incidental to the equitable remedy — so tangential that the principle of Beacon Theatres and Dairy Queen does not apply, and that the due process clause does not require notice. On this subject we agree with the fifth circuit's principal holding in Allison, 151 F.3d at 411-16. As the Advisory Committee put it: "The subdivision does not extend to cases in which the appropriate final relief relates exclusively or predominantly to money damages." Since 1966, when the Advisory Committee penned this Note, the Supreme Court regularly has emphasized the importance of allowing affected persons to opt out of representative suits, see *Ortiz*, as have we, see Tice v. American Airlines, Inc., 162 F.3d 966, 972-73 (7th Cir. 1998). Changes made by the Civil Rights Act of 1991 raise the monetary stakes in suits of this sort, and thus tilt the balance toward certification under Rule 23(b)(3).

* * *

The district court must squarely face and resolve the question whether the money damages sought by the plaintiff class are more than incidental to the equitable relief in view. If the answer is yes, then the district court should either certify the class under Rule 23(b)(3) for all purposes or bifurcate the proceedings — certifying a Rule 23(b)(2) class for equitable relief and a Rule 23(b)(3) class for damages (assuming that certification under Rule 23(b)(3) otherwise is sound, a question we do not broach). If, however, the district judge believes that the damages sought here are merely incidental to the equitable relief, then the judge must face and resolve the question that we have elided: whether certification of a class under Rule 23(b)(2) ever is proper when the class seeks money damages (as opposed to equitable monetary relief such as back pay). The district judge may consider following still a third course on remand: modifying or vacating the class certification now that the Equal Employment Opportunity Commission has appeared as plaintiffs' champion.

Shortly after Ingersoll filed its petition for leave to appeal, the EEOC asked the district court for permission to intervene as an additional plaintiff. General Telephone Co. v. EEOC, 446 U.S. 318, 64 L. Ed. 2d 319, 100 S. Ct. 1698 (1980), holds that, as the plaintiff in a pattern-or-practice suit under § 706(f)(1), the EEOC may seek classwide relief without regard to the standards of Rule 23, for the EEOC does not act on behalf of private parties and a suit under § 706(f)(1) is not a class action. The private plaintiffs contend that the EEOC's intervention moots the dispute about the use of Rule 23(b)(2). No, it does not make the subject moot, for the EEOC may not seek (or the district judge may not award) the same relief that the private plaintiffs want in their class action. The EEOC could dismiss its action or settle with Ingersoll on terms that leave the private plaintiffs dissatisfied. Section 706(g) permits the court to award equitable relief (including back pay) in an action prosecuted by the EEOC, but this subsection, which was not amended as part of the 1991 Act, does not mention compensatory or punitive damages. Although § 1981a(d)(1) defines the EEOC as a "complaining party" for purposes of damages under § 1981a(a), this is conditioned on inability to recover under 42 U.S.C. § 1981, and many of the class members advance § 1981 claims. Thus the Commission may or may not be able to obtain on behalf of the class the full extent of monetary relief, and it may not attempt to secure all legally available relief. Disappointed job applicants may find that their own suit remains useful. Whether to maintain parallel litigation is their choice: the Court concluded in *General Telephone* that "where the EEOC has prevailed in its action, the court may reasonably require any individual who claims under its judgment to relinquish his right to bring a separate private action." 446 U.S. at 333. The Court did not hold that an action by the EEOC supersedes pending private litigation or disables victims of discrimination from preferring relief under §1981a(b) to whatever relief the Commission secures. The agency's claim is both logically and legally distinct from the private suit. Cf. EEOC v. G-K-G, Inc., 39 F.3d 740 (7th Cir. 1994) (if the EEOC files suit while private litigation is under way, the district judge may elect to give the private plaintiff the lead role and relegate the EEOC to the status of litigating amicus); Colby v. J.C. Penney Co., 811 F.2d 1119 (7th Cir. 1987) (a private plaintiff may prevail even when the EEOC loses its parallel action).

What is more, the fact that the EEOC chose to intervene in an ongoing case — which assuredly is a class action — may affect the application of *General Telephone*. Compare Horn v. Eltra Corp., 686 F.2d 439, 441 n.1 (6th Cir. 1982) (holding that the approach of *General Telephone* is limited to cases in which the EEOC initiates the suit on its own behalf), with Harris v. Amoco Production Co., 768 F.2d 669 (5th Cir. 1985), and United Telecommunications, Inc. v. Saffels, 741 F.2d 312 (10th Cir. 1984) (disagreeing with Horn). We do not choose sides; it is enough to say that the existence of this conflict is yet another reason why the EEOC's filing does not cast Rule 23 out of the picture. Nonetheless, if the plaintiffs continue to believe that the EEOC's appearance makes the class allegations of their complaint irrelevant, then they are free to withdraw the request to represent a class, subject to the court's approval under Rule 23(e), or the district judge may adjust his class certification in light of the EEOC's position to reflect the likelihood that the private action is now effectively limited to the pursuit of compensatory and punitive damages. The district court's order concerning class certification is vacated, and the case is remanded for further proceedings consistent with this opinion.

NOTES AND COMMENTS FOR DISCUSSION

1. Judge Easterbrook left open the possibility in *Ingersoll* that a (b)(2) class might be certified where damages are "merely incidental to the equitable relief." In ALLISON v. CITGO PETROLEUM CORP., 151 F.3d 402 (5th Cir. 1998), the decision upon which the court in *Ingersoll* relied upon in part, the Fifth Circuit provided the following definition of "incidental damages."

> By incidental, we mean damages that flow directly from liability to the class *as a whole* on the claims forming the basis of the injunctive or declaratory relief. Ideally, incidental damages should be only those to which class members automatically would be entitled once liability to the class (or subclass) as a whole is established. That is, the recovery of incidental damages should typically be concomitant with, not merely consequential to, the injunctive or declaratory relief. Moreover, such damages should at least be capable of computation by means of objective standards and not dependent in any significant way on the intangible, subjective differences of each class member's circumstances. Incidental damages should not require additional hearings to resolve the disparate merits of each individual's case; it should neither introduce new and substantial legal or factual issues, nor entail complex individualized determinations.

151 F.3d at 415. The Supreme Court has held that in civil rights cases compensatory damages cannot be assumed on proof that there has been a violation of law but must be proved as in ordinary tort cases. *See* Carey v. Piphus, 435 U.S. 247, 98 S.Ct. 1042, 55 L.Ed.2d 252 (1978) ("although mental and emotional distress caused by the denial of procedural due process itself is compensable under §1983, we hold that neither the likelihood of such injury nor the difficulty of proving it is so great as to justify awarding compensatory damages without proof that such injury actually was caused."). As a practical matter, *Carey* means that in a Title VII case, damages cannot be computed without reference to the circumstances of individual class members. As Judge Easterbrook concedes in *Ingersoll*, back pay, a traditional Title VII remedy, also must be computed on an individual basis; class-wide discrimination will have affected employees to different degrees depending on their work history, seniority, etc. Back pay always has been classified as equitable relief, and there is a long history of certifying (b)(2) classes where back pay was a major component of the requested relief. Do putative class members have less need for notice and the right to opt out when back pay is at issue as opposed to compensatory damages? Are you satisfied that there is enough difference between back pay and damages to justify the radically different treatment of class actions based on that distinction?

The Second Circuit has rejected the bright-line incidental damage approach to (b)(2) certification used in *Allison* and *Ingersoll*. In ROBINSON v. METRO-NORTH COMMUTER R.R. CO., 267 F.3d 147 (2d Cir. 2001), cert. denied, 535 U.S. 951, 122 S.Ct. 1349, 152 L.Ed.2d 251 (2002), the plaintiffs asserted both pattern-and-practice and disparate impact claims on behalf of an estimated class of some 1300 African-American railroad employees. They sought injunctive relief and back pay for the class and compensatory damages for individual class members who were the victims of intentional discrimination. Relying on the incidental damage standard of *Allison*, the district court denied class certification under (b)(2). The court of appeals reversed.

> [W]e hold that when presented with a motion for (b)(2) class certification of a claim seeking both injunctive and non-incidental monetary damages, a district court must consider the evidence presented at a class certification hearing and the arguments of counsel," and then assess whether (b)(2) certification is appropriate in light of "the relative importance of the remedies sought, given all of the facts and circumstances of the case. The district court may allow (b)(2) certification if

it finds in its informed, sound judicial discretion that (1) the positive weight or value to the plaintiffs of the injunctive or declaratory relief sought is predominant even though compensatory or punitive damages are also claimed, and (2) class treatment would be efficient and manageable, thereby achieving an appreciable measure of judicial economy.

267 F.3d at 164. The court considered its ad hoc approach preferable to *Allison*'s bright-line incidental damage rule because it was more consistent with the discretion district judges are accorded under Rule 23 to determine whether the prerequisites for certification have been satisfied. The court also recognized the "due process risk" for those class members with significant, non-incidental damage claims posed by (b)(2) certification which does not expressly afford for notice and the right to opt out. "But any due process risk posed by (b)(2) class certification of a claim for non-incidental damages can be eliminated by the district court simply affording notice and opt out rights to absent class members for those portions of the proceedings where the presumption of class cohesion falters — i.e., the damages phase of the proceedings." Id. at 166. Is the due process problem as easily solvable as the Second Circuit makes it sound? What if a jury trial is demanded for the non-incidental damage claims? Would not the individual damage claims have to be tried first to insure compliance with the Seventh Amendment? If so, what issues would be left to be tried in the class action phase?

2. In *Ingersoll*, the court stated that the options available to the district court on remand included (b)(3) certification of the class and certification of a (b)(2) class for equitable relief and a (b)(3) class for damages. But it did not explain how the trial of a (b)(3) class would be conducted. Could a single jury decide class liability for damages, leaving decisions on individual computations to separate proceedings with separate juries, or would one jury have to resolve all damage claims? In *Allison*, the Fifth Circuit reasoned that a (b)(3) class would not be appropriate because of the lack of common issues.

> The plaintiffs' claims for compensatory and punitive damages must therefore focus almost entirely on facts and issues specific to individuals rather than the class as a whole: what kind of discrimination was each plaintiff subjected to; how did it affect each plaintiff emotionally and physically, at work and at home; what medical treatment did each plaintiff receive and at what expense; and so on and so on. Under such circumstances, an action conducted nominally as a class action would "degenerate in practice into multiple lawsuits separately tried."

151 F.3d. at 419.

The court in *Allison* also rejected certification of a (b)(2) class for purposes of injunctive and declaratory relief. The class claims could not be tried before related damage claims without infringing on the Seventh Amendment rights of the class members, and any effort to try class claims after jury trials on the damages would be barred by claim and issue preclusion principles. Thus, the Fifth Circuit concluded, the plaintiffs' damage claims involved too many individual issues to allow (b)(3) certification, but too many issues common with the injunctive claims to allow class certification under (b)(2) for the injunctive aspects of the case. In enacting the damage provisions of the 1991 Civil Rights Act, could Congress have intended to preclude class action treatment of damage claims? The dissent in *Allison* maintained that

> [b]y adopting an absolute rule against compensatory or punitive damages claims in (b)(2) class actions, the majority ignores the intent of the drafters of Rule 23 that class actions against discriminatory employment practices would be maintained under (b)(2). The majority's rule, contrary to the intent of the drafters and Congress, threatens a drastic curtailment of the use of (b)(2) class actions in the enforcement of Title VII and other civil rights acts.

151 F.3d at 431. (Dennis, J., dissenting).

Allison has been virtually eclipsed in the Seventh Circuit. In ALLEN v. INTERNATIONAL TRUCK & ENGINE CORP., 358 F.3d 469 (7th Cir. 2004), twenty-seven current and former employees sued for systemic racial harassment. The plaintiffs sought to certify, under Rule 23(b)(2), a class composed of all African-American employees during the relevant time period for injunctive relief only, and to pursue their damage claims individually. The district court, citing the same concerns voiced by the Fifth Circuit in *Allison,* denied class certification. Writing for the appellate court, Judge Easterbrook had an opportunity to put into practice the suggestions he had tendered in *Ingersoll.*

> Certifying a class for injunctive purposes, while handling damages claims individually, does not transgress the seventh amendment. Just as in a single-person (or 27-person) suit, a jury will resolve common factual disputes, and its resolution will control when the judge takes up the request for an injunction. International Truck will enjoy its jury-trial right either way; and once one jury (in individual or class litigation) has resolved a factual dispute, principles of issue preclusion can bind the defendant to that outcome in future litigation consistently with the seventh amendment. * * * The other 323 employees' right to jury trial can be protected in either or both of two ways: By offering them the opportunity to opt out, or by denying them (in any later damage proceedings) both the benefits and the detriments of issue and claim preclusion. * * * Thus a class proceeding for equitable relief vindicates the seventh amendment as fully as do individual trials, is no more complex than individual trials, yet produces benefits compared with the one-person-at-a-time paradigm. The district court erred in concluding that seventh amendment concerns foreclose certification of a class under Rule 23(b)(2).

358 F.3d at 471-72. Judge Easterbrook went on to suggest that on remand

> it would be prudent for the district court to reconsider whether at least some of the issues bearing on damages — such as the existence of plant-wide racial animosity which collectively "constitutes one unlawful employment practice," *Morgan* — could be treated on a class basis (with opt-out rights under Rule 23(b)(3) or a hybrid Rule 23(b)(2) certification) even if some other issues, such as assessment of damages for each worker, must be handled individually."

Id. at 472. *Compare* Cooper v. Southern Co., 390 F.3d 695, 722 (11th Cir. 2004) (questioning whether the plaintiffs adequately would represent the interests of the class by foregoing class certification on damages: "[E]ven assuming that the district court could conduct an initial bench trial on the merits of the equitable claims, and that the court actually found in favor of the plaintiffs, it would still be necessary for a single jury to hear and rule on more than 2000 individual claims for compensatory damages.").

Following *Ingersoll*, another trial court in Chicago has certified a 23(b)(2) class for purposes of injunctive relief *and punitive damages.* In PALMER v. COMBINED INSURANCE. CO. OF AMERICA, 217 F.R.D. 430 (N.D. Ill. 2003), the court explained that because punitive damages could be awarded to the entire class without any individualized determination, the award could be considered "incidental" to the injunctive relief.

> Because the focus of punitive damages is on the defendant's conduct, not the class members, it is possible to fashion a punitive damage award that would punish Combined for past wrongdoing, if such wrongdoing was proved, and not require individualized inquiry. The other purpose of this punitive damages award would be to deter future wrongdoing, which may also have the effect of encouraging compliance with any awarded injunctive relief by insuring that Combined understands the adverse monetary consequences of disobeying the injunction. This purpose could also be served without having to assess each class member's circumstances.

217 F.R.D. at 440. The court suggested that a lump sum punitive damage award could be distributed to the class pro rata or allocated according to some formula not requiring individual analysis of each class member's circumstances. While conceding that class certification for monetary relief should be rare, the court concluded that the public interest was served by such a certification in the context of this case.

> It is possible for an employer, especially one of this size, to commit systemic discrimination against a class of protected individuals. However varied such individual harms may be, if they are all caused by the same pattern or practice, the wrongdoer should not be able to avoid class liability simply because the class cannot be certified for compensatory damages. * * * If a class is willing to sacrifice compensatory relief in their class action to meet Rule 23 requirements, thus evincing a paramount desire to stop systemic discrimination and prevent future harm, they should be allowed to proceed. The difficulties often encountered in certifying a Title VII class for compensatory damages should not preclude a class of plaintiffs from seeking alternative ways to serve the public interest by ending widespread discrimination (assuming such discrimination can be proved, which has not yet been determined in this case). Taking the size of this defendant and the nature of Ms. Palmer's allegations into account, a class action appears to be the better way to effectively eradicate the alleged discrimination taking place on an institutional scale.

217 F.R.D. at 441.

In WAL-MART STORES, INC. v. DUKES, 564 U.S. 338, 131 S.Ct. 2541, 180 L.Ed.2d 374 (2011), the plaintiffs sought injunctive relief, back pay, and punitive damages in a class action sought to be certified under Rule 23(b)(2). Wal-Mart argued, however, that the claim for punitive damages was incompatible with (b)(2) certification because such relief would not be incidental to, but would overwhelm, the claim for injunctive relief. Rejecting that argument, the trial court concluded that punitive damages were secondary to plaintiffs' primary goal of achieving "long-term relief in the form of fundamental changes to the manner in which Wal-Mart makes its pay and promotions decisions nationwide." The Ninth Circuit affirmed, but also stated that although putative class members who no longer were Wal-Mart employees when the plaintiffs filed the complaint lacked standing to pursue injunctive or declaratory relief, those putative members who remained employed by Wal-Mart as of that date had standing to see such relief and, therefore, injunctive and declaratory relief continued to predominate over monetary relief for (b)(2) purposes. If these current employees prevailed on the merits, the court explained, injunctive or declaratory relief preventing Wal-Mart from continuing to engage in unlawful sex-based discrimination would be "appropriate" within the meaning of Rule 23(b)(2). Accordingly, the appellate court remanded for a determination of the appropriate scope of the class. The Ninth Circuit panel's judgment was affirmed by a 6-5 voter of the Ninth Circuit *en banc*, except that the court remanded the claims for punitive damages with instructions to the district court to determine whether the class should be certified under Rule 12(b)(2) or (b). The *en banc* opinion also remanded to the trial court the claims of putative class members who no longer worked for Wal-Mart when the complaint was filed for the purpose of determining whether to certify an additional class or classes under Rule 23(b)(3). However, the Supreme Court unanimously reversed the rulings below and held that the action could not be certified under Rule 23(b)(2) because claims for monetary relief precluded certification under (b)(2) at least, as in the instant case, where the claims for monetary relief were not incidental to the requests for injunctive and declaratory relief.

3.   Class actions under the Age Discrimination in Employment Act and the Equal Pay Act are governed not by Rule 23, but by §16(b) of the Fair Labor Standards Act (FLSA), 29 U.S.C. §216(b), which provides that persons may bring suit on behalf of themselves and "other employees similarly situated." That statute expressly requires, however, that to be included in the class, employees must opt into the suit by filing a written notice with the court. In a Rule 23 class action, each person falling within the class definition is considered to be a class member and is bound by the judgment, favorable or unfavorable, unless he has opted out. By contrast, a putative plaintiff must affirmatively *opt into* a §16(b) action by filing a written consent with the court in order to be considered a class member and thus bound by the outcome of the action. *See* LaChapelle v. Owens-Illinois, Inc., 513 F.2d 286 (5th Cir. 1975) (recognizing "fundamental" difference between Rule 23 class actions and §16(b) class actions). In HOFFMAN-LA ROCHE, INC. v. SPERLING, 493 U.S. 165, 110 S. Ct. 482, 107 L.Ed.2d 480 (1989), the Supreme Court held that a district court has inherent authority to direct and supervise the sending of notice to potential plaintiffs in order to facilitate their opting into the action. At the request of the plaintiffs, the district court directed the employer to produce the names and addresses of all employees who had been discharged in a reduction in force that the plaintiffs challenged as discriminatory and authorized the plaintiffs to send a court-approved notice to all employees who had not previously filed consent forms. The Supreme Court noted that the benefits of collective action (both to age discrimination claimants and the courts) "depend on employees receiving accurate and timely notice concerning the pendency of the collective action, so that they may make informed decisions about whether or not to participate." 493 U.S. at 170. Once such an action has been filed, "the court has a managerial responsibility to oversee the joinder of additional parties to assure that the task is accomplished in an efficient and proper way." 493 U.S. at 170-71.

Compensatory and liquidated damages are available in ADEA actions and thus jury trials of such claims are common. See Chapter 10, The Age Discrimination in

Employment Act, *infra*. Is there any fundamental difference between a damage claim under the ADEA and a damage claim under Title VII? If, as suggested by the majority in *Hoffman-La Roche,* damage claims and ADEA class actions are not mutually exclusive, should not the same rule apply to Title VII cases?

4.   An order certifying or refusing to certify a class is not a final judgment and would not normally be appealable under 28 U.S.C §1291 until a judgment granting or denying relief was entered. As noted by the court in *Ingersoll*, however, Rule 23(f) explicitly provides for interlocutory appeals from orders "granting or denying class certification * * * if application is made to the court of appeals within 10 days of entry of the order." The Supreme Court has indicated that a denial of class certification can be appealed by putative class members who intervene for that purpose. *See* United Airlines, Inc. v. McDonald, 432 U.S. 385, 97 S. Ct. 2464, 53 L.Ed.2d 423 (1977).

Section G. Class Actions and the EEOC

Section 706(c) of Title VII authorizes the EEOC, acting on the basis of a charge filed by an individual or by an EEOC Commissioner, to bring a civil action against the employer seeking all relief authorized by the Act. See Chapter 4, *supra*. In GENERAL TELEPHONE CO. OF THE NORTHWEST, INC. v. EEOC, 446 U.S. 318, 100 S.Ct. 1698, 64 L.Ed.2d 319 (1980), the Supreme Court held that the EEOC may seek class-wide relief without being certified as a class representative and without complying with the requirements of Rule 23(a) and (b). The Court concluded that to force compliance by the EEOC with Rule 23 requirements would be contrary to the purpose of §706, under which the Commission was to act not merely as a representative of private interests, but to vindicate public policy. Moreover, some actions authorized by §706 would be foreclosed by requiring EEOC compliance with Rule 23 requirements, such as numerosity or typicality. The Court also noted that it would not be consistent with the remedial purpose of Title VII to bind all "class" members with discrimination grievances against an employer by the relief obtained by an EEOC judgment or settlement against the employer, especially in view of the possible differences between the public and private interests involved. As noted in *Ingersoll,* the agency is not obligated to seek all the relief to which a complaining party might be entitled and may settle a case without the consent of the charging party.

CHAPTER 7

Remedies

SECTION A. MONETARY RELIEF

1. BACK PAY

Albemarle Paper Co. v. Moody

Supreme Court of the United States, 1975.
422 U.S. 405, 95 S.Ct. 2362, 45 L.Ed.2d 280.

MR. JUSTICE STEWART delivered the opinion of the Court.

These consolidated cases raise two important questions under Title VII: First: When employees or applicants for employment have lost the opportunity to earn wages because an employer has engaged in an unlawful discriminatory employment practice, what standards should a federal district court follow in deciding whether to award or deny backpay? * * *

I

The respondents — plaintiffs in the District Court — are a certified class of present and former Negro employees at a paper mill in Roanoke Rapids, N.C.; the petitioners — defendants in the District Court — are the plant's owner, the Albemarle Paper Co., and the plant employees' labor union, Halifax Local No. 425. In August 1966, after filing a complaint with the Equal Employment Opportunity Commission and receiving notice of their right to sue, the respondents brought a class action in the * * * Eastern District of North Carolina, asking permanent injunctive relief against "any policy, practice, custom or usage" at the plant that violated Title VII. The respondents assured the court that the suit involved no claim for any monetary awards on a class basis, but in June 1970, after several years of discovery, the respondents moved to add a class demand for backpay. The court ruled that this issue would be considered at trial.

At the trial * * * the major issues were the plant's seniority system, its program of employment testing, and the question of backpay. In its opinion of November 9, 1971, the court found that the petitioners had "strictly segregated" the plant's departmental "lines of progression" prior to January 1, 1964, reserving the higher paying and more skilled lines for whites. The "racial identifiability" of whole lines of progression persisted until 1968, when the lines were reorganized under a new collective-bargaining agreement. The court found, however, that this reorganization left Negro employees "'locked' in the lower paying job classifications." The formerly "Negro" lines of progression had been merely tacked on to the bottom of the formerly "white" lines, and promotions, demotions, and layoffs continued to be governed — where skills were "relatively equal" — by a system of "job seniority." Because of the plant's previous history of overt segregation, only whites had seniority in the higher job categories. Accordingly, the court ordered the petitioners to implement a system of "plantwide" seniority.

The court refused, however, to award backpay to the plaintiff class for losses suffered under the "job seniority" program.[3] The court explained:

"In the instant case there was no evidence of bad faith non-compliance with the Act. It appears that the company as early as 1964 began active recruitment of blacks for its Maintenance Apprentice Program. Certain lines of progression were merged on its own initiative, and as judicial decisions expanded the then existing interpretations of the Act, the defendants took steps to correct the abuses without delay. . . .

"In addition, an award of back pay is an equitable remedy. . . . The plaintiffs' claim for back pay was filed nearly five years after the institution of this action. It was not prayed for in the pleadings. Although neither party can be charged with deliberate dilatory tactics in bringing this cause to trial, it is apparent that the defendants would be substantially prejudiced by the granting of such affirmative relief. The defendants might have chosen to exercise unusual zeal in having this court determine their rights at an earlier date had they known that back pay would be at issue."

* * *

II

Whether a particular member of the plaintiff class should have been awarded any backpay and, if so, how much, are questions not involved in this review. The equities of individual cases were never reached. Though at least some of the members of the plaintiff class obviously suffered a loss of wage opportunities on account of Albemarle's unlawfully discriminatory system of job seniority, the District Court decided that no backpay should be awarded to anyone in the class. The court declined to make such an award on two stated grounds: the lack of "evidence of bad faith non-compliance with the Act," and the fact that "the defendants would be substantially prejudiced" by an award of backpay that was demanded contrary to an earlier representation and late in the progress of the litigation. Relying directly on Newman v. Piggie Park Enterprises, 390 U.S. 400, 88 S.Ct. 964, 19 L.Ed.2d 1263 (1968), the Court of Appeals reversed, holding that backpay could be denied only in "special circumstances." The petitioners argue that the Court of Appeals was in error — that a district court has virtually unfettered discretion to award or deny backpay, and that there was no abuse of that discretion here.[8]

---

[3]Under Title VII backpay liability exists only for practices occurring after the effective date of the Act, July 2, 1965, and accrues only from a date two years prior to the filing of a charge with the EEOC. See §706 (g). Thus no award was possible with regard to the plant's pre-1964 policy of "strict segregation."

[8]The petitioners also contend that no backpay can be awarded to those unnamed parties in the plaintiff class who have not themselves filed charges with the EEOC. We reject this contention.

Piggie Park Enterprises is not directly in point. The Court held there that attorneys' fees should "ordinarily" be awarded — i.e., in all but "special circumstances" — to plaintiffs successful in obtaining injunctions against discrimination in public accommodations, under Title II of the Civil Rights Act of 1964. While the Act appears to leave Title II fee awards to the district court's discretion, 42 U.S.C. §2000a-3(b), the court determined that the great public interest in having injunctive actions brought could be vindicated only if successful plaintiffs, acting as "private attorneys general," were awarded attorneys' fees in all but very unusual circumstances. There is, of course, an equally strong public interest in having injunctive actions brought under Title VII, to eradicate discriminatory employment practices. But this interest can be vindicated by applying the *Piggie Park* standard to the attorneys' fees provision of Title VII, §706(k), see Northcross v. Memphis Board of Education, 412 U.S. 427, 428, 93 S.Ct. 2201, 2202, 37 L.Ed.2d 48 (1973). For guidance as to the granting and denial of backpay, one must, therefore, look elsewhere.

The petitioners contend that the statutory scheme provides no guidance, beyond indicating that backpay awards are within the district court's discretion. We disagree. It is true that backpay is not an automatic or mandatory remedy; like all other remedies under the Act, it is one which the courts "may" invoke. The scheme implicitly recognizes that there may be cases calling for one remedy but not another, and — owing to the structure of the federal judiciary — these choices are, of course, left in the first instance to the district courts. However, such discretionary choices are not left to a court's "inclination, but to its judgment; and its judgment is to be guided by sound legal principles." United States v. Burr, 25 F.Cas. No. 14,692d, pp. 30, 35 (CC Va.1807) (Marshall, C. J.). The power to award backpay was bestowed by Congress, as part of a complex legislative design directed at a historic evil of national proportions. A court must exercise this power "in light of the large objectives of the Act," Hecht Co. v. Bowles, 321 U.S. 321, 331, 64 S.Ct. 587, 592, 88 L.Ed. 754 (1944). That the court's discretion is equitable in nature, hardly means that it is unfettered by meaningful standards or shielded from thorough appellate review. In Mitchell v. Robert DeMario Jewelry, 361 U.S. 288, 292, 80 S.Ct. 332, 335, 4 L.Ed.2d 323 (1960), this Court held, in the face of a silent statute, that district courts enjoyed the "historic power of equity" to award lost wages to workmen unlawfully discriminated against under §17 of the Fair Labor Standards Act of 1938. The Court simultaneously noted

---

The Courts of Appeals that have confronted the issue are unanimous in recognizing that backpay may be awarded on a class basis under Title VII without exhaustion of administrative procedures by the unnamed class members. The Congress plainly ratified this construction of the Act in the course of enacting the Equal Employment Opportunity Act of 1972, Pub.L. 92-261, 86 Stat. 103. The House of Representatives passed a bill, H.R. 1746, 92d Cong., 1st Sess., that would have barred, in §3(e), an award of backpay to any individual who "neither filed a charge [with the EEOC] nor was named in a charge or amendment thereto." But the Senate Committee on Labor and Public Welfare recommended, instead, the re-enactment of the backpay provision without such a limitation, and cited with approval several cases holding that backpay was awardable to class members who had not personally filed, nor been named in, charges to the EEOC, S.Rep. No. 92-415, p. 27 (1971). The Senate passed a bill without the House's limitation, and the Conference Committee adopted the Senate position. A Section-by-Section Analysis of the Conference Committee's resolution notes that "[a] provision limiting class actions was contained in the House bill and specifically rejected by the Conference Committee." The Conference Committee bill was accepted by both Chambers.

that "the statutory purposes [leave] little room for the exercise of discretion not to order reimbursement." 361 U.S., at 296, 80 S.Ct. at 337.

It is true that "[e]quity eschews mechanical rules . . . [and] depends on flexibility." Holmberg v. Armbrecht, 327 U.S. 392, 396, 66 S.Ct. 582, 584, 90 L.Ed. 743 (1946). But when Congress invokes the Chancellor's conscience to further transcendent legislative purposes, what is required is the principled application of standards consistent with those purposes and not "equity [which] varies like the Chancellor's foot."[10] Important national goals would be frustrated by a regime of discretion that "produce[d] different results for breaches of duty in situations that cannot be differentiated in policy." Moragne v. States Marine Lines, 398 U.S. 375, 405, 90 S.Ct. 1772, 1790, 26 L.Ed.2d 339 (1970).

The District Court's decision must therefore be measured against the purposes which inform Title VII. As the Court observed in Griggs v. Duke Power Co., the primary objective was a prophylactic one:

> "It was to achieve equality of employment opportunities and remove barriers that have operated in the past to favor an identifiable group of white employees over other employees."

Backpay has an obvious connection with this purpose. If employers faced only the prospect of an injunctive order, they would have little incentive to shun practices of dubious legality. It is the reasonably certain prospect of a backpay award that "provide[s] the spur or catalyst which causes employers and unions to self-examine and to self-evaluate their employment practices and to endeavor to eliminate, so far as possible, the last vestiges of an unfortunate and ignominious page in this country's history." United States v. N. L. Industries, Inc., 8 Cir., 479 F.2d at 354, 379 (CA8 1973).

It is also the purpose of Title VII to make persons whole for injuries suffered on account of unlawful employment discrimination. This is shown by the very fact that Congress took care to arm the courts with full equitable powers. For it is the historic purpose of equity to "secur[e] complete justice," Brown v. Swann, 10 Pet. 497, 503, 9 L.Ed. 508 (1836). "[W]here federally protected rights have been invaded, it has been the rule from the beginning that courts will be alert to adjust their remedies so as to grant the necessary relief." Bell v. Hood, 327 U.S. 678, 684, 66 S.Ct. 773, 777, 90 L.Ed. 939 (1946). Title VII deals with legal injuries of an economic character occasioned by racial or other antiminority discrimination. The terms "complete justice" and "necessary relief" have acquired a clear meaning in such circumstances. Where racial discrimination is concerned, "the [district] court has not merely the power but the duty to render a decree which will so far as possible eliminate the discriminatory effects of the past as well as bar like discrimination in the future." Louisiana v. United States, 380 U.S. 145, 154, 85 S.Ct. 817, 822, 13 L.Ed.2d 709 (1965). And where a legal injury is of an economic character,

> "[t]he general rule is, that when a wrong has been done, and the law gives a remedy, the compensation shall be equal to the injury. The latter is the standard by which the former is to be measured. The injured party is to be placed, as near

---

[10]Eldon, L. C., in Gee v. Pritchard, 2 Swans. * 403, * 414, 36 Eng.Rep. 670, 674 (1818).

as may be, in the situation he would have occupied if the wrong had not been committed." Wicker v. Hoppock, 6 Wall. 94, 99, 18 L.Ed. 752 (1867).

The "make whole" purpose of Title VII is made evident by the legislative history. The backpay provision was expressly modeled on the backpay provision of the National Labor Relations Act.[11] Under that Act, "[m]aking the workers whole for losses suffered on account of an unfair labor practice is part of the vindication of the public policy which the Board enforces." Phelps Dodge Corp. v. NLRB, 313 U.S. 177, 197, 61 S.Ct. 845, 854, 85 L.Ed. 1271 (1941). We may assume that Congress was aware that the Board, since its inception, has awarded backpay as a matter of course — not randomly or in the exercise of a standardless discretion, and not merely where employer violations are peculiarly deliberate, egregious, or inexcusable.[12] Furthermore, in passing the Equal Employment Opportunity Act of 1972, Congress considered several bills to limit the judicial power to award backpay. These limiting efforts were rejected, and the backpay provision was re-enacted substantially in its original form.[13] A Section-by-Section Analysis introduced by Senator Williams to accompany the Conference Committee Report on the 1972 Act strongly reaffirmed the "make whole" purpose of Title VII:

---

[11]Section 10(c) of the NLRA provides that when the Labor Board has found that a person has committed an "unfair labor practice," the Board "shall issue" an order "requiring such person to cease and desist from such unfair labor practice, and to take such affirmative action including reinstatement of employees with or without back pay, as will effectuate the policies of this subchapter." The backpay provision of Title VII provides that when the court has found "an unlawful employment practice," it "may enjoin" the practice "and order such affirmative action as may be appropriate, which may include, but is not limited to, reinstatement or hiring of employees, with or without back pay * * *." §706(g). The framers of Title VII stated that they were using the NLRA provision as a model. 110 Cong.Rec. 6549 (1964) (remarks of Sen. Humphrey); id., at 7214 (interpretative memorandum by Sens. Clark and Case). In early versions of the Title VII provision on remedies, it was stated that a court "may" issue injunctions, but "shall" order appropriate affirmative action. This anomaly was removed by Substitute Amendment No. 656. The framers regarded this as merely a "minor language change." (remarks of Sen. Humphrey). We can find here no intent to back away from the NLRA model or to denigrate in any way the status of backpay relief.

[12]"The finding of an unfair labor practice and discriminatory discharge is presumptive proof that some back pay is owed by the employer," NLRB v. Mastro Plastics Corp., 354 F.2d 170, 178 (CA2 1965). While the backpay decision rests in the NLRB's discretion, and not with the courts, NLRB v. J. H. Rutter-Rex Mfg. Co., 396 U.S. 258, 263, 90 S.Ct. 417, 420, 24 L.Ed.2d 405 (1969), the Board has from its inception pursued "a practically uniform policy with respect to these orders requiring affirmative action." NLRB, First Annual Report 124 (1936).

"[I] all but a few cases involving discriminatory discharges, discriminatory refusals to employ or reinstate, or discriminatory demotions in violation of section 8(3), the Board has ordered the employer to offer reinstatement to the employee discriminated against and to make whole such employee for any loss of pay that he has suffered by reason of the discrimination." NLRB Annual Report, Second p. 148 (1937).

[13]As to the unsuccessful effort to restrict class actions for backpay, see n. 8, *supra.* In addition, the Senate rejected an amendment which would have required a jury trial in Title VII cases involving backpay, 118 Cong.Rec. 4917, 4919-4920 (1972) (remarks of Sens. Ervin and Javits), and rejected a provision that would have limited backpay liability to a date two years prior to filing a complaint in court. Compare H.R. 1746, which passed the House, with the successful Conference Committee bill, analyzed at 118 Cong.Rec. 7168 (1972), which adopted a substantially more liberal limitation, i.e., a date two years prior to filing a charge with the EEOC. See §706(g).

"The provisions of this subsection are intended to give the courts wide discretion exercising their equitable powers to fashion the most complete relief possible. In dealing with the present section 706(g) the courts have stressed that the scope of relief under that section of the Act is intended to make the victims of unlawful discrimination whole, and that the attainment of this objective rests not only upon the elimination of the particular unlawful employment practice complained of, but also requires that persons aggrieved by the consequences and effects of the unlawful employment practice be, so far as possible, restored to a position where they would have been were it not for the unlawful discrimination." 118 Cong.Rec. 7168 (1972).

As this makes clear, Congress' purpose in vesting a variety of "discretionary" powers in the courts was not to limit appellate review of trial courts, or to invite inconsistency and caprice, but rather to make possible the "fashion[ing][of] the most complete relief possible."

It follows that, given a finding of unlawful discrimination, backpay should be denied only for reasons which, if applied generally, would not frustrate the central statutory purposes of eradicating discrimination throughout the economy and making persons whole for injuries suffered through past discrimination.[14] The courts of appeals must maintain a consistent and principled application of the backpay provision, consonant with the twin statutory objectives, while at the same time recognizing that the trial court will often have the keener appreciation of those facts and circumstances peculiar to particular cases.

The District Court's stated grounds for denying backpay in this case must be tested against these standards. The first ground was that Albemarle's breach of Title VII had not been in "bad faith."[15] This is not a sufficient reason for denying backpay. Where an employer has shown bad faith — by maintaining a practice which he knew to be illegal or of highly questionable legality — he can make no claims whatsoever on the Chancellor's conscience. But, under Title VII, the mere absence of bad faith simply opens the door to equity; it does not depress the scales in the employer's favor. If backpay were awardable only upon a showing of bad faith, the remedy would become a punishment for moral turpitude, rather than a compensation for workers' injuries. This would read the "make whole" purpose right out of Title VII, for a worker's injury is no less real simply because his employer did not inflict it in "bad faith."[16] Title VII is not concerned with the employer's "good intent or absence of discriminatory intent" for "Congress directed the thrust of the Act to the consequences of employment practices, not simply the motivation." Griggs v. Duke Power Co., 401

---

[14]It is necessary, therefore, that if a district court does decline to award backpay, it carefully articulate its reasons.

[15]The District Court thought that the breach of Title VII had not been in "bad faith" because judicial decisions had only recently focused directly on the discriminatory impact of seniority systems. The court also noted that Albemarle had taken some steps to recruit black workers into one of its departments and to eliminate strict segregation through the 1968 departmental merger.

[16]The backpay remedy of the NLRA on which the Title VII remedy was modeled, see n. 11, *supra*, is fully available even where the "unfair labor practice" was committed in good faith. See, e.g., NLRB v. J. H. Rutter-Rex Mfg. Co., 396 U.S., at 265, 90 S.Ct. 417, 421, 24 L.Ed.2d 405.

U.S., at 432, 91 S.Ct., at 854.[17] To condition the awarding of backpay on a showing of "bad faith" would be to open an enormous chasm between injunctive and backpay relief under Title VII. There is nothing on the face of the statute or in its legislative history that justifies the creation of drastic and categorical distinctions between those two remedies.[18]

The District Court also grounded its denial of backpay on the fact that the respondents initially disclaimed any interest in backpay, first asserting their claim five years after the complaint was filed. The court concluded that the petitioners had been "prejudiced" by this conduct. The Court of Appeals reversed on the ground that the broad aims of Title VII require that the issue of back pay be fully developed and determined even though it was not raised until the post-trial stage of litigation.

It is true that Title VII contains no legal bar to raising backpay claims after the complaint for injunctive relief has been filed, or indeed after a trial on that complaint has been had. Furthermore, Fed. Rule Civ. Proc. 54(c) directs that

> "every final judgment shall grant the relief to which the party in whose favor it is rendered is entitled, even if the party has not demanded such relief in his pleadings."

But a party may not be "entitled" to relief if its conduct of the cause has improperly and substantially prejudiced the other party. The respondents here were not merely tardy, but also inconsistent, in demanding backpay. To deny backpay because a particular cause has been prosecuted in an eccentric fashion, prejudicial to the other party, does not offend the broad purposes of Title VII. This is not to say, however, that the District Court's ruling was necessarily correct. Whether the petitioners were in fact prejudiced, and whether the respondents' trial conduct was excusable, are questions that will be open to review by the Court of Appeals, if the District Court, on remand, decides again to decline to make any award of backpay.[20] But the standard of review will be the familiar one of whether the District Court was "clearly erroneous" in its factual findings and whether it "abused" its traditional discretion to locate "a just result" in light of the circumstances peculiar to the case, Langnes v. Green, 282 U.S. 531, 541, 51 S.Ct. 243, 247, 75 L.Ed. 520 (1931). On these issues of procedural regularity and prejudice, the "broad aims of Title VII" provide no ready solution.

Judgment vacated and case remanded.

---

[17]Title VII itself recognizes a complete, but very narrow, immunity for employer conduct shown to have been undertaken "in good faith, in conformity with, and in reliance on any written interpretation or opinion of the [Equal Employment Opportunity] Commission." §713(b). It is not for the courts to upset this legislative choice to recognize only a narrowly defined "good faith" defense.

[18] We note that some courts have denied backpay, and limited their judgments to declaratory relief, in cases where the employer discriminated on sexual grounds in reliance on state "female protective" statutes that were inconsistent with Title VII. There is no occasion in this case to decide whether these decisions were correct. As to the effect of Title VII on state statutes inconsistent with it, see §708.

[20]The District Court's stated grounds for denying backpay were, apparently, cumulative rather than independent. The District Court may, of course, reconsider its backpay determination in light of our ruling on the "good faith" question.

[The concurring opinion of Justices Marshall and Rehnquist and the concurring and dissenting opinion of Chief Justice Burger are omitted.]

NOTES AND PROBLEMS FOR DISCUSSION

1. Under the *Albemarle* standard, does the district court have any actual discretion over whether or not to award back pay in a case where the plaintiff has proved a violation of Title VII? In ARIZONA GOVERNING COMMITTEE v. NORRIS, 463 U.S. 1073, 103 S.Ct. 3492, 77 L.Ed.2d 1236 (1983), the Court held that a state retirement plan that paid lower benefits to women than to men, solely because of their longer life expectancy, violated Title VII. The Court limited retroactive application of the decision on the grounds that prior to its decision, the employer could have reasonably assumed that the plan was lawful, and that full retroactive application would have a devastating effect on the employer and the pension plan.

The only special circumstance that courts typically recognize as relieving an employer that has been found to have violated Title VII of back pay liability is where good faith compliance with a state law has caused the violation. *See, e.g.,* Le Beau v. Libbey-Owens-Ford Co., 727 F.2d 141 (7th Cir. 1984) (it is within a district court's discretion to deny back pay where the employer complied with state law restricting overtime work of women). Can such decisions be reconciled with *Albemarle's* holding that the employer's "good faith" is not a special circumstance justifying a denial of back pay?

But another potential basis for denying back pay could be the situation where issuing such an award would conflict with an overriding national policy. In HOFFMAN PLASTIC COMPOUNDS v. NLRB, 535 U.S. 137, 122 S.Ct. 1275, 152 L.Ed.2d 271 (2002), an action brought under the National Labor Relations Act, the Court reversed the National Labor Relations Board's award of back pay to an unauthorized alien who had obtained employment by use of false documentation. Awarding back pay under these circumstances, the Court reasoned was inconsistent with the policies underlying the Immigration Reform and Control Act of 1986, policies the NLRB had no authority to enforce or to administer. But inlight of differences between the remedial schemes of the National Labor Relations Act and Title VII, the Ninth Circuit has suggested, without directly holding, that *Hoffman* will not apply to Title VII actions. *See* Rivera v. NIBCO, Inc., 364 F.3d 1057, 1069 (9th Cir. 2004), cert. denied, 125 S.Ct. 1603 (2005) ("[T]he overriding national policy against discrimination would seem likely to outweigh any bar against payment of back wages to unlawful immigrants in Title VII cases. Thus, we seriously doubt that *Hoffman* applies in such actions."). The Eleventh Circuit, however, in BURNES v. PEMCO AEROPLEX, INC., 291 F.3d 1282 (11th Cir. 2002), ruled that an employee who concealed his pending employment discrimination suit from a bankruptcy court was judicially estopped from seeking monetary relief against the employer in the discrimination suit. The court reasoned that the plaintiff's actions were "calculated to make a mockery of the judicial system" and that the employer was entitled to judicial estoppel which "protects the integrity of the judicial system" even though it was not prejudiced by plaintiff's failure to disclose his discrimination suit in the bankruptcy case. The court limited its ruling to the claims for monetary relief and allowed the plaintiff to proceed with claims for injunctive relief.

2.   Theoretically, in order to "make whole" an employee for lost wages, the back pay period would have to begin with the first act of discrimination that resulted in lost pay, regardless of how far in the past that incident occurred. A continuing pay violation, for example, may have begun decades before the employee initiated a Title VII claim by filing an EEOC charge. Section 706(g), however, provides in part that "[b]ack pay liability shall not accrue from a date more than two years prior to the filing of a charge with the [EEOC]." The back pay period thus cannot begin earlier than two years prior to the EEOC charge on which the suit is based. This two-year accrual rule, in combination with the continuing violation theory, can make an enormous difference in the calculation of back pay. For example, in PALMER v. KELLY, 17 F.3d 1490 (D.C. Cir. 1994), the plaintiff, believing he had been denied a promotion, retired nine days later and filed an EEOC charge. After the court determined that the plaintiff was the victim of racial discrimination, the employer argued that, at most, the plaintiff was entitled to back pay for the nine days that he worked after the denial of the promotion. Because the court determined that the promotion denial was part of a continuing violation involving the racially discriminatory denials of promotions, the plaintiff was awarded back pay for the two year-period prior to his EEOC charge.

The back pay period typically will extend to the date of final judgment. *See, e.g.,* EEOC v. Monarch Mach. Tool Co., 737 F.2d 1444 (6th Cir. 1980). But in McKENNON v. NASHVILLE BANNER PUB. CO., 513 U.S. 352, 115 S.Ct. 879, 130 L.Ed.2d 852 (1995), the Supreme Court held that "after acquired" evidence of an employee's malfeasance, while not relieving the employer of liability for a violation of the statute, could justify terminating the back pay period as of the date of discovery of the misconduct.

3.   Although *Albermarle* establishes a strong presumption that back pay should be awarded, it is the plaintiff's burden to prove both that the discrimination caused loss of wages and the amount of that loss. *See* Goff v. USA Truck, Inc., 929 F.2d 429, 430 (8th Cir. 1991) (the trial judge did not abuse its discretion in denying back pay to a successful Title VII plaintiff who presented no evidence of lost wages). The plaintiff's burden of proof and the calculation of backpay are addressed in the following materials.

Ford Motor Co. v. Equal Employment Opportunity Commission

Supreme Court of the United States, 1982.
458 U.S. 219, 102 S.Ct. 3057, 73 L.Ed.2d 721.

JUSTICE O'CONNOR delivered the opinion of the Court.

This case presents the question whether an employer charged with discrimination in hiring can toll the continuing accrual of backpay liability under §706(g) of Title VII, simply by unconditionally offering the claimant the job previously denied, or whether the employer also must offer seniority retroactive to the date of the alleged discrimination.[1]

The question has considerable practical significance because of the lengthy delays that too often attend Title VII litigation.[2] The extended time it frequently takes to obtain satisfaction in the courts may force a discrimination claimant to suffer through years of underemployment or unemployment before being awarded the job the claimant deserves. Court delays, of course, affect all litigants. But for the victim of job discrimination, delay is especially unfortunate. The claimant cannot afford to stand aside while the wheels of justice grind slowly toward the ultimate resolution of the lawsuit. The claimant needs work that will feed a family and restore self-respect. A job is needed — now. In this case, therefore, we must determine how best to fashion the remedies available under Title VII to fulfill this basic need.

I

A

In June and July 1971, Judy Gaddis, Rebecca Starr, and Zettie Smith applied at a Ford Motor Co. parts warehouse located in Charlotte, N. C., for jobs as "picker-packers," "picking" ordered parts from storage, and "packing" them for shipment. At the time, no woman had ever worked in that capacity at the Ford warehouse. All three women were qualified for the positions: Gaddis and Starr recently had been laid off from equivalent jobs at a nearby General Motors (GM) warehouse, and Smith had comparable prior experience. Smith applied before any of the openings were filled, and Gaddis and Starr applied while at least two positions remained available. Ford, however, filled the three vacant positions with men, and Gaddis filed a charge with the federal Equal Employment Opportunity Commission, claiming that Ford had discriminated against her because of her sex.[4]

In January 1973, GM recalled Gaddis and Starr to their former positions at its warehouse. The following July, while they were still working at GM, a single vacancy opened up at Ford. Ford offered the job to Gaddis, without seniority retroactive to her 1971 application. Ford's offer, however, did not require Gaddis to abandon or

---

[1]The dissent asserts that by so "fram[ing] the question presented" we have "simply and completely misstate[d] the issue." Apparently, neither party agrees with the dissent. The petitioner summarizes the question presented as "whether back pay due an employment discrimination claimant continues to accrue after the claimant has rejected an unconditional job offer that does not include retroactive seniority or back pay." Brief for Petitioner i. The respondent sums up the question presented as "[w]hether an employer who unlawfully refused to hire job applicants because they were women can terminate its liability for back pay by subsequently offering the applicants positions without seniority at a time when they had obtained, and accumulated seniority in, other jobs." Brief for Respondent i.

To buttress the assertion that the Court has addressed a question not presented, the dissent claims that we have "misrea[d]" the Court of Appeals' decision, "transform[ing] a narrow Court of Appeals ruling into a broad one, just so [we could] reverse and install a broad new rule of [our] own choosing," rather than attempt, as best we are able, to decide the particular case actually before us. Because we believe we have correctly and fairly framed the question, we decline the opportunity to address further this *ad hominem* argument.

[2]The discriminatory refusals to hire involved in this case occurred 11 years ago.

[4]After Gaddis had filed her complaint, she and Starr continued to seek work at the Ford warehouse. In November 1972, Ford hired them and four other workers for six weeks to fill temporary jobs at the warehouse.

compromise her Title VII claim against Ford. Gaddis did not accept the job, in part because she did not want to be the only woman working at the warehouse, and in part because she did not want to lose the seniority she had earned at GM. Ford then made the same unconditional offer to Starr, who declined for the same reasons. Gaddis and Starr continued to work at the GM warehouse, but in 1974 the warehouse was closed and they were laid off. They then unsuccessfully sought new employment until September 1975, when they entered a Government training program for the unemployed.

Smith applied again for work at Ford in 1973, but was never hired. She worked elsewhere, though at lower wages than she would have earned at Ford, during much of the time between 1971 and the District Court's decision in 1977.

In contrast to Gaddis', Starr's, and Smith's difficulties, at least two of the three men hired by Ford in 1971 were still working at the warehouse at the time of the trial in 1977.

B

In July 1975, the EEOC sued Ford in the United States District Court for the Western District of North Carolina, alleging that Ford had violated Title VII by refusing to hire women at the Charlotte warehouse. The Commission sought injunctive relief and backpay for the victims.

After trial, the District Court found that Ford had discriminated against the three women on the basis of their sex and awarded them backpay in an amount equal to "the difference between the amount they would have earned had they been hired in August 1971, and the amounts actually earned or reasonably earnable by them" between that date and the date of the court's order. The District Court rejected Ford's contention that Gaddis and Starr were not entitled to backpay accruing after the dates on which they declined Ford's offer of employment.

The * * * Fourth Circuit affirmed the District Court's finding of unlawful discrimination, as well as the court's award to Gaddis and Starr of backpay that had accrued after July 1973, when the women rejected Ford's unconditional job offer. The court suggested that, had Ford promised retroactive seniority with its job offer, the offer would have cut off Ford's backpay liability. The court concluded, however, that without the promise of retroactive seniority, Ford's 1973 offer was "incomplete and unacceptable."

Ford then petitioned this Court for a writ of certiorari, contending, inter alia, that its unconditional job offer to Gaddis and Starr should have cut off the further accrual of backpay liability. We granted the writ.

II

* * *

In this case, Ford and the EEOC offer competing standards to govern backpay liability. Ford argues that if an employer unconditionally offers a claimant the job for which he previously applied, the claimant's rejection of that offer should toll the continuing accrual of backpay liability.[9] The EEOC, on the other hand, defends the

---

[9]It should be clear that the contested backpay in this suit stems from the period following Ford's offer, and during which Gaddis and Starr were unemployed, i.e., after the GM warehouse closed.

lower court's rule,[10] contending that backpay liability should be tolled only by the rejection of an offer that includes seniority retroactive to the date on which the alleged discrimination occurred. Our task is to determine which of these standards better coincides with the "large objectives" of Title VII.

III

The "primary objective" of Title VII is to bring employment discrimination to an end, *Albemarle Paper*, by achieving equality of employment opportunities and removing barriers that have operated in the past to favor an identifiable group * * * over other employees. "[T]he preferred means for achieving" this goal is through "[c]ooperation and voluntary compliance." Alexander v. Gardner-Denver Co., 415 U.S. 36, 44, 94 S.Ct. 1011, 1017, 39 L.Ed.2d 147 (1974).

To accomplish this objective, the legal rules fashioned to implement Title VII should be designed, consistent with other Title VII policies, to encourage Title VII defendants promptly to make curative, unconditional job offers to Title VII claimants, thereby bringing defendants into "voluntary compliance" and ending discrimination far more quickly than could litigation proceeding at its often ponderous pace. Delays in litigation unfortunately are now commonplace, forcing the victims of discrimination to suffer years of underemployment or unemployment before they can obtain a court order awarding them the jobs unlawfully denied them. In a better world, perhaps, law suits brought under Title VII would speed to judgment so quickly that the effects of legal rules on the behavior of the parties during the pendency of litigation would not be as important a consideration. We do not now live in such a world, however, as this case illustrates.

The rule tolling the further accrual of backpay liability if the defendant offers the claimant the job originally sought well serves the objective of ending discrimination through voluntary compliance, for it gives an employer a strong incentive to hire the Title VII claimant. While the claimant may be no more attractive than the other job applicants, a job offer to the claimant will free the employer of the threat of liability for further backpay damages. Since paying backpay damages is like paying an extra worker who never came to work, Ford's proposed rule gives the Title VII claimant a decided edge over other competitors for the job he seeks.

The rule adopted by the court below, on the other hand, fails to provide the same incentive, because it makes hiring the Title VII claimant more costly than hiring one of the other applicants for the same job. To give the claimant retroactive seniority before an adjudication of liability, the employer must be willing to pay the additional costs of the fringe benefits that come with the seniority that newly hired workers usually do not

---

Our decision today does not affect their right to claim backpay for the period before they rejected Ford's offers.

[10]For reasons of its own, the dissenting opinion reads the decision below narrowly and takes us to task for discerning the outlines of a "general rule" in the opinion of the Court of Appeals. In this regard, we note that already at least one district court evidently not only has read the opinion below as prescribing a general rule, but in addition has interpreted that rule more broadly than we do. See Saunders v. Hercules, Inc., 510 F.Supp. 1137, 1142 (W.D. Virginia 1981) ("in view of the recent Fourth Circuit Court of Appeals decision in Equal Employment Opportunity Commission v. Ford Motor Company, 645 F.2d 183 (4th Cir.1981) * * * [i]t is clear * * * that a person who has been discriminated against does not have to accept an offer of reemployment where back pay has not been offered").

receive. More important, the employer must also be prepared to cope with the deterioration in morale, labor unrest, and reduced productivity that may be engendered by inserting the claimant into the seniority ladder over the heads of the incumbents who have earned their places through their work on the job. In many cases, moreover, disruption of the existing seniority system will violate a collective bargaining agreement, with all that such a violation entails for the employer's labor relations.[11] Under the rule adopted by the court below, the employer must be willing to accept all these additional costs if he hopes to toll his backpay liability by offering the job to the claimant. As a result, the employer will be less, rather than more, likely to hire the claimant.

In sum, the Court of Appeals' rule provides no incentive to employers to hire Title VII claimants. The rule advocated by Ford, by contrast, powerfully motivates employers to put Title VII claimants to work, thus ending ongoing discrimination as promptly as possible.[12]

IV

Title VII's primary goal, of course, is to end discrimination; the victims of job discrimination want jobs, not lawsuits.[13] But when unlawful discrimination does occur, Title VII's secondary, fallback purpose is to compensate the victims for their injuries. To this end, §706(g) aims "to make the victims of unlawful discrimination whole" by restoring them, "so far as possible . . . to a position where they would have been were it not for the unlawful discrimination." *Albemarle Paper*. We now turn to consider whether the rule urged by Ford not only better serves the goal of ending discrimination, but also properly compensates injured Title VII claimants.

A

If Gaddis and Starr had rejected an unconditional offer from Ford before they were recalled to their jobs at GM, tolling Ford's backpay liability from the time of Ford's offer plainly would be consistent with providing Gaddis and Starr full compensation for their injuries. An unemployed or underemployed claimant, like all other Title VII claimants, is subject to the statutory duty to minimize damages set out

---

[11]See American Tobacco Co. v. Patterson, 456 U.S. 63, 76, 102 S.Ct. 1534, 1541, 71 L.Ed.2d 748 (1982) ("Seniority provisions are of 'overriding importance' in collective bargaining, * * * and they are universally included in these contracts.").

[12]In his dissent, Justice Blackmun suggests that it is we who speak from the "comfor[t]" of the "sidelines," somewhere outside "the real world" of sex discrimination. For all the dissent's rhetoric, however, nowhere does the dissent seriously challenge our conclusion that the rule we adopt will powerfully motivate employers to offer Title VII claimants the jobs they have been denied. But Rebecca Starr's trial testimony eloquently explains what claimants need: "I was just wanting that job so bad because you can't, a woman, when you've got three children, I needed the money, and I was wanting the job so bad." Thus, it is the rule applied by the court below which manifests a "studied indifference to the real-life concerns" of the victims of sex discrimination.

[13]See 118 Cong.Rec. 7569 (remarks of Rep. Dent during debate on 1972 amendments to Title VII) ("Most people just want to work. That is all. They want an opportunity to work. We are trying to see that all of us, no matter of what race, sex, or religious or ethnic background, will have an equal opportunity in employment").

in §706(g).[14] This duty, rooted in an ancient principle of law,[15] requires the claimant to use reasonable diligence in finding other suitable employment. Although the unemployed or underemployed claimant need not go into another line of work, accept a demotion, or take a demeaning position,[16] he forfeits his right to backpay if he refuses a job substantially equivalent to the one he was denied. Consequently, an employer charged with unlawful discrimination often can toll the accrual of backpay liability by unconditionally offering the claimant the job he sought, and thereby providing him with an opportunity to minimize damages.[18]

An employer's unconditional offer of the job originally sought to an unemployed or underemployed claimant, moreover, need not be supplemented by an offer of retroactive seniority to be effective, lest a defendant's offer be irrationally disfavored relative to other employers' offers of substantially similar jobs. The claimant, after all, plainly would be required to minimize his damages by accepting another employer's offer even though it failed to grant the benefits of seniority not yet earned.[19] Of

---

[14]The provision expressly states that "[i]nterim earnings or amounts earnable with reasonable diligence by the person or persons discriminated against shall operate to reduce the back pay otherwise allowable."

Claimants often take other lesser or dissimilar work during the pendency of their claims, even though doing so is not mandated by the statutory requirement that a claimant minimize damages or forfeit his right to compensation. See, e.g., Merriweather v. Hercules, Inc., 631 F.2d 1161 (CA5 1980) (voluntary minimization of damages in dissimilar work).

[15]See generally, e.g., C. McCormick, Handbook on the Law of Damages 127-158 (1935). McCormick summarizes "the general rule" as follows: "Where one person has committed a tort, breach of contract, or other legal wrong against another, it is incumbent upon the latter to use such means as are reasonable under the circumstances to avoid or minimize the damages. The person wronged cannot recover for any item of damage which could thus have been avoided."

In connection with the remedial provisions of the NLRA, we said: "Making the workers whole for losses suffered on account of an unfair labor practice is part of the vindication of the public policy which the Board enforces. Since only actual losses should be made good, it seems fair that deductions should be made not only for actual earnings by the worker but also for losses which he willfully incurred." Phelps Dodge Corp. v. NLRB, 313 U.S. 177, 197-198, 61 S.Ct. 845, 853-854, 85 L.Ed. 1271 (1941).

[16]See, e.g., NLRB v. The Madison Courier, Inc., 153 U.S.App.D.C. 232, 245-246, 472 F.2d 1307, 1320-1321 (1972) (employee need not "seek employment which is not consonant with his particular skills, background, and experience" or "which involves conditions that are substantially more onerous than his previous position").

Some lower courts have indicated, however, that after an extended period of time searching for work without success, a claimant must consider taking a lower-paying position. See, e.g., NLRB v. The Madison Courier, Inc., *supra*, at 245-246, 472 F.2d, at 1320-1321; NLRB v. Southern Silk Mills, Inc., 242 F.2d 697, 700(CA6), cert. denied, 355 U.S. 821, 78 S.Ct. 28, 2 L.Ed.2d 37 (1957). If the claimant decides to go into a dissimilar line of work, or to accept a demotion, his earnings must be deducted from any eventual backpay award. See §706(g); Merriweather v. Hercules, Inc., 631 F.2d 1161, 1168 (CA5 1980); Taylor v. Philips Industries, Inc., 593 F.2d 783, 787 (CA7 1979) (per curiam).

[18]The claimant's obligation to minimize damages in order to retain his right to compensation does not require him to settle his claim against the employer, in whole or in part. Thus, an applicant or discharged employee is not required to accept a job offered by the employer on the condition that his claims against the employer be compromised. See, e.g., NLRB v. St. Marys Sewer Pipe Co., 146 F.2d 995, 996 (CA3 1945).

[19]For the same reasons, a defendant's job offer is effective to force minimization of damages by an unemployed or underemployed claimant even without a supplemental offer of backpay, since the claimant would be required to accept another employer's offer of a substantially similar job without a large front-end, lump-sum bonus. See, e.g., NLRB v. Midwest Hanger Co., 550 F.2d

course, if the claimant fulfills the requirement that he minimize damages by accepting the defendant's unconditional offer, he remains entitled to full compensation if he wins his case.[20] A court may grant him backpay accrued prior to the effective date of the offer, retroactive seniority, and compensation for any losses suffered as a result of his lesser seniority before the court's judgment.

In short, the unemployed or underemployed claimant's statutory obligation to minimize damages requires him to accept an unconditional offer of the job originally sought, even without retroactive seniority. Acceptance of the offer preserves, rather than jeopardizes, the claimant's right to be made whole; in the case of an un- or underemployed claimant, Ford's suggested rule merely embodies the existing requirement of §706(g) that the claimant minimize damages, without affecting his right to compensation.

B

Ford's proposed rule also is consistent with the policy of full compensation when the claimant has had the good fortune to find a more attractive job than the defendant's, because the availability of the better job terminates the ongoing ill effects of the defendant's refusal to hire the claimant. For example, if Gaddis and Starr considered their jobs at GM to be so far superior to the jobs originally offered by Ford that, even if Ford had hired them at the outset, they would have left Ford's employ to take the new work, continuing to hold Ford responsible for backpay after Gaddis and Starr lost their GM jobs would be to require, in effect, that Ford insure them against the risks of unemployment in a new and independent undertaking. Such a rule would not merely restore Gaddis and Starr to the "position where they would have been were it not for the unlawful discrimination," Albemarle Paper Co. v. Moody; it would catapult them into a better position than they would have enjoyed in the absence of discrimination.

Likewise, even if Gaddis and Starr considered their GM jobs only somewhat better or even substantially equivalent to the positions they would have held at Ford had Ford hired them initially,[24] their rejection of Ford's unconditional offer could be taken to mean that they believed that the lingering ill effects of Ford's prior refusal to hire them had been extinguished by later developments. If, for example, they thought that the Ford and GM jobs were identical in every respect, offering identical pay, identical conditions of employment, and identical risks of layoff, Gaddis and Starr would have been utterly indifferent as to which job they had — Ford's or GM's.

1101, 1103(CA8) ("It is clear that had the Company's offer of reinstatement been conditioned solely on its refusal to give back pay, as the Company strenuously argues, then the offer of reinstatement would not have been invalidated"), cert. denied, 434 U.S. 830, 98 S.Ct. 112, 54 L.Ed.2d 90 (1977).

[20]In tailoring a Title VII remedy a court "has not merely the power but the duty to render a decree which will so far as possible eliminate the discriminatory effects of the past as well as bar like discrimination in the future." Albemarle Paper Co.

[24]It is possible that they did so value the GM jobs, since they applied at Ford only after being laid off at GM, and since after being recalled to the GM jobs they rejected Ford's offer. Therefore, contrary to the dissent's erroneous suggestion, the possibility that Gaddis and Starr considered their GM jobs superior to the positions they would have had at Ford had Ford hired them at the outset is not merely a "hypothetical case." We cannot infer that they so valued their GM jobs, however, solely from their rejection of Ford's offer.

Assuming that they could work at only one job at a time, the ongoing economic ill effects caused by Ford's prior refusal to hire them would have ceased when they found the identical jobs at GM, and they would have had no reason to accept Ford's offers. As in the case of a claimant who lands a better job, therefore, requiring a defendant to provide what amounts to a form of unemployment insurance to claimants, after they have found identical jobs and refused the defendant's unconditional job offer, would be, absent special circumstances, to grant them something more than compensation for their injuries.

In both of these situations, the claimant has the power to accept the defendant's offer and abandon the superior or substantially equivalent replacement job. As in the case of an unemployed or underemployed claimant, under the rule advocated by Ford acceptance of the defendant's unconditional offer would preserve fully the ultimately victorious claimant's right to full redress for the effects of discrimination. The claimant who chooses not to follow this path does so, then, not because it provides inadequate compensation, but because the value of the replacement job outweighs the value of the defendant's job supplemented by the prospect of full court-ordered compensation. In other words, the victim of discrimination who finds a better or substantially equivalent job no longer suffers ongoing injury stemming from the unlawful discrimination.

C

Thus, the rule advocated by Ford rests comfortably both on the statutory requirement that a Title VII claimant must minimize damages and on the fact that a claimant is no longer incurring additional injury if he has been able to find other suitable work that, all things considered, is at least as attractive as the defendant's. For this reason, in almost all circumstances the rule is fully consistent with Title VII's object of making injured claimants whole.

The sole question that can be raised regarding whether the rule adequately compensates claimants arises in that narrow category of cases in which the claimant believes his replacement job to be superior to the defendant's job without seniority, but inferior to the defendant's job with the benefits of seniority. In the present case, for example, it is possible that Gaddis and Starr considered their GM jobs more attractive than the jobs offered by Ford, but less satisfactory than the positions they would have held at Ford if Ford had hired them initially. If so, they were confronted with two options. They could have accepted Ford's unconditional offer, preserving their right to full compensation if they prevailed on their Title VII claims, but forfeiting their favorable positions at GM. Alternatively, they could have kept their jobs at GM, retaining the possibility of continued employment there, but, under the operation of the rule advocated here by Ford, losing the right to claim further backpay from Ford after the date of Ford's offer. The court below concluded that under these circumstances Ford's rule would present Gaddis and Starr with an "intolerable choice," depriving them of the opportunity to receive full compensation.

We agree that Gaddis and Starr had to choose between two alternatives. We do not agree, however, that their opportunity to choose deprived them of compensation. After all, they had the option of accepting Ford's unconditional offer and retaining the right to seek full compensation at trial, which would comport fully with Title VII's goal of making discrimination victims whole. Under the rule advocated by Ford, if

Gaddis and Starr chose the option of remaining at their GM jobs rather than accept Ford's offer, it was because they thought that the GM jobs, plus their claims to backpay accrued prior to Ford's offer, were more valuable to them than the jobs they originally sought from Ford, plus the right to seek full compensation from the court.[26] It is hard to see how Gaddis and Starr could have been deprived of adequate compensation because they chose to venture upon a path that seemed to them more attractive than the Ford job plus the right to seek full compensation in court.

If the choice presented to Gaddis and Starr was difficult, it was only because it required them to assess their likelihood of prevailing at trial. But surely it cannot be contended for this reason alone that they were deprived of their right to adequate compensation. It is a fact of life that litigation is risky and that a plaintiff with a claim to compensation for his losses must consider the possibility that the claim might be lost at trial, either wrongly, because of litigation error, or rightly, because the defendant was innocent. Ford's rule merely requires the Title VII claimant to decide whether to take the job offered by the defendant, retaining his rights to an award by the court of backpay accrued prior to the effective date of the offer, and any court-ordered retroactive seniority plus compensation for any losses suffered as a result of his lesser seniority before the court's judgment, or, instead, whether to accept a more attractive job from another employer and the limitation of the claim for backpay to the damages that have already accrued. The rule urged by the EEOC and adopted by the court below, by contrast, would have the perverse result of requiring the employer in effect to insure the claimant against the risk that the employer might win at trial.

Therefore, we conclude that, when a claimant rejects the offer of the job he originally sought, as supplemented by a right to full court-ordered compensation, his choice can be taken as establishing that he considers the ongoing injury he has suffered at the hands of the defendant to have been ended by the availability of better opportunities elsewhere. For this reason, we find that, absent special circumstances,[27]

---

[26]Employees value a job for many reasons besides the rate of pay, including, for example, the presence of other workers of the employee's own sex, the availability of recreational facilities at the worksite, staggered work hours, better health benefits, longer vacations, and so forth. What makes one job better than another varies from one employee to another.

Gaddis and Starr presumably rejected Ford's offer because they thought their jobs at GM were worth more to them than full compensation (Ford's offer plus a court award) discounted by the risks of litigation. In essence, the position adopted by the court below and advocated here by the EEOC turns on the fact that we cannot be sure that, had Gaddis and Starr known they were going to win their lawsuit, they still would have rejected Ford's offer. Had they known they were going to win, of course, they would have rejected the Ford job only if they valued the GM jobs more than they valued the combination of Ford's job plus the value of court-ordered compensation *un* discounted by the risks of litigation. To agree with the EEOC is, in effect, to contend that a claimant is not made whole for purposes of Title VII unless he decided to stay at a replacement job that was worth to him more than the sum of (1) the defendant's job, (2) the right to seek full court-ordered compensation, and, in addition, (3) a sum analogous to insurance against the risk of loss at trial. We discern, however, no reason for concluding that Title VII requires the defendant to insure the claimant against the possibility that the defendant might prevail in the lawsuit.

[27]If, for example, the claimant has been forced to move a great distance to find a replacement job, a rejection of the employer's offer might reflect the costs of relocation more than a judgment that the replacement job was superior, all things considered, to the defendant's job. In exceptional circumstances, the trial court, in the exercise of its sound discretion, could give

the simple rule that the ongoing accrual of backpay liability is tolled when a Title VII claimant rejects the job he originally sought comports with Title VII's policy of making discrimination victims whole.

V

Although Title VII remedies depend primarily upon the objectives discussed above, the statute also permits us to consider the rights of "innocent third parties." *City of Los Angeles Department of Water & Power v. Manhart,* 435 U.S. 702, 723, 98 S.Ct. 1370, 1383, 55 L.Ed.2d 657 (1978). The lower court's rule places a particularly onerous burden on the innocent employees of an employer charged with discrimination. Under the court's rule, an employer may cap backpay liability only by forcing his incumbent employees to yield seniority to a person who has not proven, and may never prove, unlawful discrimination. As we have acknowledged on numerous occasions, seniority plays a central role in allocating benefits and burdens among employees.[28] In light of the "overriding importance" of these rights, *American Tobacco Co. v. Patterson,* 456 U.S. 63, 76, 102 S.Ct. 1534, 1541, 71 L.Ed.2d 748 (1982) (quoting *Humphrey v. Moore,* 375 U.S. 335, 346, 84 S.Ct. 363, 370, 11 L.Ed.2d 370 (1964)), we should be wary of any rule that encourages job offers that compel innocent workers to sacrifice their seniority to a person who has only claimed, but not yet proven, unlawful discrimination.

The sacrifice demanded by the lower court's rule, moreover, leaves the displaced workers without any remedy against claimants who fail to establish their claims. If, for example, layoffs occur while the Title VII suit is pending, an employer may have to furlough an innocent worker indefinitely while retaining a claimant who was given retroactive seniority. If the claimant subsequently fails to prove unlawful discrimination, the worker unfairly relegated to the unemployment lines has no redress for the wrong done him. We do not believe that "'the large objectives'" of Title VII, *Albemarle Paper Co.,* require innocent employees to carry such a heavy burden.[29]

---

weight to such factors when deciding whether backpay damages accrued after the rejection of an employer's offer should be awarded to the claimant.

The dissent attempts to characterize "the loss of accumulated seniority at [a] replacement jo[b]" as such a cost of relocation. By so doing, the dissent simply confuses the costs of changing from one job to another — whatever the respective advantages and disadvantages of the two jobs might be — with the differences between the two jobs.

[28]Seniority may govern, "not only promotion and layoff, but also transfer, demotion, rest days, shift assignments, prerogative in scheduling vacation, order of layoff, possibilities of lateral transfer to avoid layoff, 'bumping' possibilities in the face of layoff, order of recall, training opportunities, working conditions, length of layoff endured without reducing seniority, length of layoff recall rights will withstand, overtime opportunities, parking privileges, and even a preferred place in the punch-out line." *Franks v. Bowman Transportation Co.,* 424 U.S., at 766-767, 96 S.Ct., at 1265 (1976).

[29] In addition to the rights of innocent employees, the rule urged by the EEOC and adopted by the court below burdens innocent employers. An innocent employer — or one who believes himself innocent — has the right to challenge in court claims he considers weak or baseless. The approach endorsed by the lower court undermines this right by requiring the employer, if he wishes to offer some relief to the claimant and toll the mounting backpay bill, to surrender his defense to the charge that the claimant is entitled to retroactive seniority. If the employer offers the claimant retroactive seniority as well as a job, and then prevails at trial, he will have no recourse against the claimant for the costs of the retroactive seniority that the claimant erroneously received. The rule urged by Ford permits the parties to stem the ongoing effects of

VI

In conclusion, we find that the rule adopted by the court below disserves Title VII's primary goal of getting the victims of employment discrimination into the jobs they deserve as quickly as possible. The rule, moreover, threatens the interests of other, innocent employees by disrupting the established seniority hierarchy, with the attendant risk that an innocent employee will be unfairly laid off or disadvantaged because a Title VII claimant unfairly has been granted seniority.

On the other hand, the rule that a Title VII claimant's rejection of a defendant's job offer normally ends the defendant's ongoing responsibility for backpay suffers neither of these disadvantages, while nevertheless adequately satisfying Title VII's compensation goals. Most important, it also serves as a potent force on behalf of Title VII's objective of bringing discrimination to an end more quickly than is often possible through litigation. For these reasons we hold that, absent special circumstances, the rejection of an employer's unconditional job offer ends the accrual of potential backpay liability. We reverse the judgment of the Court of Appeals and remand for proceedings consistent with this opinion.

JUSTICE BLACKMUN, with whom JUSTICE BRENNAN and JUSTICE MARSHALL join, dissenting.

After finding that petitioner Ford Motor Company had discriminated unlawfully against Judy Gaddis and Rebecca Starr because of their sex, the Court of Appeals affirmed the District Court's backpay award to the two women "as a proper exercise of discretion founded on not clearly erroneous factual determinations." The Court today reverses this unremarkable holding with a wide-ranging advisory ruling stretching far beyond the confines of this case. The Court's rule provides employers who have engaged in unlawful hiring practices with a unilateral device to cut off their backpay liability to the victims of their past discrimination.

To justify its new rule, the Court mischaracterizes the holding of the Court of Appeals, undertakes an intricate economic analysis of hypothetical situations not presented here, and invokes the rights of "innocent third parties" who are not before the Court. By so doing, the Court not only supplants traditional district court discretion to mold equitable relief, but also ensures that Judy Gaddis and Rebecca Starr — the only Title VII claimants whose rights are at issue in this lawsuit — will not be made whole for injury they indisputably have suffered. I find the Court's ruling both unnecessary and unfair. I dissent.

I

* * *

B

* * *

---

the alleged discrimination without compelling either claimant or employer to compromise his claims or surrender his defenses. Cf. *Moro Motors Ltd.*, 216 N.L.R.B. 192, 193 (1975) ("were [an employer] required to offer to an employee, allegedly discharged for discriminatory reasons, reinstatement *with accrued back pay*, the [employer's] right to litigate the issue of whether the discharge was unlawful would for all practical purposes be nullified").

The Court of Appeals rested its narrow ruling on two key facts: that "Gaddis and Starr could accept [Ford's] offer only by *forfeiting the seniority* they had accumulated at General Motors and *without a compensating offer of seniority at Ford* to alleviate the effects of the discrimination against them in 1971." (Emphasis added.) The court expressed no view as to whether Ford's backpay liability would have been tolled if Gaddis and Starr could have accepted Ford's job offer without forfeiting seniority accumulated elsewhere. Nor did the Court of Appeals decide whether the women would have been obliged to accept Ford's offer had it encompassed some compensating offer of seniority, short of full retroactive seniority.

Contrary to this Court's suggestion today, the Court of Appeals announced no general rule that an employer's "backpay liability should be tolled only by the rejection of an offer that includes seniority retroactive to the date on which the alleged discrimination occurred." The Court of Appeals merely refused to announce a broad new rule, urged by Ford, requiring victims of Title VII discrimination to "accept job offers which include a loss of seniority in order to preserve their back pay rights." Such an inflexible approach, the court decided, would frustrate Title VII's central purposes by permitting employers to present discriminatees with an "intolerable choice."[7]

<h2 style="text-align:center">II</h2>

The Court today accepts Ford's invitation, wisely declined by the Court of Appeals, and adopts its broad new rule governing awards of backpay relief in Title VII cases: henceforth, "absent special circumstances, the rejection of an employer's unconditional job offer ends the accrual of potential backpay liability."[8] This ruling is disturbing in four respects.

First: The Court's new rule is flatly inconsistent with *Albemarle*'s unambiguous directive "that, given a finding of unlawful discrimination, backpay should be denied only for reasons which, if applied generally, would not frustrate the central statutory purposes of eradicating discrimination throughout the economy and making persons whole for injuries suffered through past discrimination." Applied generally, the Court's rule interferes with both objectives.

The Court's approach authorizes employers to make "cheap offers" to the victims of their past discrimination. Employers may now terminate their backpay liability unilaterally by extending to their discrimination victims offers they cannot reasonably accept. Once an employer has refused to hire a job applicant, and that applicant has mitigated damages by obtaining and accumulating seniority in another job, the employer may offer the applicant the same job that she was denied unlawfully several

---

[7]"[I]f Gaddis and Starr rejected Ford's offer and stayed at General Motors, they would forego their rights to further back pay benefits. On the other hand, if they accepted the job offered by Ford, which they had not held for the previous two years because of Ford's discriminatory hiring policy, they would lose their seniority rights at General Motors." 645 F.2d, at 192.

[8]The Court's explanation for its misreading of the Court of Appeals' decision is that the United States District Court for the Western District of Virginia has interpreted that decision as stating a somewhat different proposition. But if one District Court in the Fourth Circuit has misconstrued the Fourth Circuit's opinion, surely that is a matter properly to be corrected by the United States Court of Appeals for the Fourth Circuit. This Court is not entitled to transform a narrow Court of Appeals ruling into a broad one, just so that it may reverse and install a broad new rule of its own choosing.

years earlier. In this very case, for example, Ford offered Gaddis and Starr jobs only after they had obtained employment elsewhere and only because they had filed charges with the EEOC. If, as here, the applicant declines the offer to preserve existing job security, the employer has successfully cut off all future backpay liability to that applicant. By insulating a discriminating employer from proper liability for his discriminatory acts, the Court's rule reduces his "incentive to shun practices of dubious legality," and hinders the eradication of discrimination.

The Court's rule also violates Title VII's second objective — making victims of discrimination whole. Again, the rule's anomalies are well-illustrated by the facts of this case. Had petitioner not discriminated against Gaddis and Starr, both would have begun to work at Ford in August 1971. By July 1973, both would have accumulated nearly two years of seniority. Because of Ford's discrimination, however, each experienced long periods of unemployment and temporary employment before obtaining jobs elsewhere.[9] The District Court therefore determined that only full backpay awards, mitigated by wages earned or reasonably earnable elsewhere, would make Gaddis and Starr whole.

This Court now truncates those awards simply because Gaddis and Starr refused to accept Ford's offers of beginning employment in 1973. Yet even if Gaddis and Starr had accepted those offers, they would not have been made whole. Deprived of two years of seniority, Gaddis and Starr would have enjoyed lesser health, life, and unemployment insurance benefits, lower wages, less eligibility for promotion and transfer, and greater vulnerability to layoffs than persons hired after they were unlawfully refused employment. Even if Gaddis and Starr had continued to litigate the question of their retroactive seniority after accepting Ford's offer, they still would have spent many years at Ford "subordinate to persons who, but for the illegal discrimination, would have been[,] in respect to entitlement to [competitive seniority] benefits[,][their] inferiors." *Franks v. Bowman Transportation Co.*

The Court claims that its new rule "powerfully motivates employers to put Title VII claimants to work, thus ending ongoing discrimination as promptly as possible." In fact, the discrimination is not ended, because a discrimination victim who accepts a "cheap offer" will be obliged to work at a seniority disadvantage, and therefore will suffer ongoing effects from the employer's discriminatory act. The Court also alleges that its rule promotes "cooperation and voluntary compliance" with Title VII by giving both employers and claimants incentives to make and accept "unconditional" job offers. If the Court's rule furthers this end, however, it does so only by weakening the bargaining position of a claimant vis-a-vis the employer. Discrimination victims will be forced to accept otherwise unacceptable offers, because they will know that rejection of those offers truncates their backpay recovery. A rule that shields discriminating employers from liability for their past discrimination and coerces bona fide Title VII claimants to accept incomplete job offers is fundamentally incompatible with the purposes of Title VII.

---

[9]Gaddis, for example, sought employment in South Carolina, at various parts places, independent part places, car dealers, such as Chrysler-Plymouth, the Ford place which was Lewis Ford at that time, all the car dealers, * * * some of the hosiery mills, * * * [and] Radiator Specialty Company before obtaining her job at General Motors.

Second: The Court's rule unjustifiably limits a district court's discretion to make individual discrimination victims whole through awards of backpay. The Court suggests that, "absent special circumstances," a district court abuses its discretion per se if it fails to terminate an employer's backpay liability at the point where that employer has extended an unconditional job offer to a discrimination claimant. Yet "[i]n Albemarle Paper the Court read Title VII as creating a presumption in favor of backpay." Franks v. Bowman Transportation Co., 424 U.S., at 786, 96 S.Ct., at 1275 (Powell, J., concurring in part and dissenting in part) (emphasis added).[10] *Franks* supplied "emphatic confirmation that federal courts are empowered to fashion such relief as the *particular circumstances of a case may require* to effect restitution, making whole insofar as possible the victims of * * * discrimination in hiring." Id. at, 764, 96 S.Ct., at 1264 (opinion of the Court) (emphasis added).

The Court recognizes that its new rule interferes with district court discretion to make complete backpay awards in individual cases. Thus, the Court expressly preserves the principle of appellate deference to the "sound discretion" of the trial court in "exceptional circumstances." Yet, curiously, the Court offers no explanation why the facts of this very case fail to satisfy its own "exceptional circumstances" test.[11] Given the Court's concession that district courts must retain their discretion to make bona fide Title VII claimants whole in some cases, I see no advantage in prescribing a blanket rule that displaces that discretion in other cases where complete relief is equally justified.

Third: I am disturbed by the Court's efforts to justify its rule by relying on situations not presented by this case. For example, the Court partially rests its rule on an "unemployed or underemployed claimant's statutory obligation to minimize damages" by accepting an unconditional job offer without seniority. Because Gaddis and Starr were fully employed when Ford finally offered them jobs, however, neither the District Court nor the Court of Appeals exempted unemployed or underemployed victims of discrimination from accepting offers like Ford's.[12] Similarly, the Court analyzes the hypothetical case of a Title VII claimant who "has had the good fortune to

---

[10]The Court cites language from *Albemarle* suggesting that a district court's discretion is not limitless. But the Court conspicuously omits *Albemarle*'s clear statement that if Congress intended to limit the equitable discretion of district courts in any way, it did so only by leaving "little room for the exercise of discretion *not* to order reimbursement." Albemarle Paper Co. v. Moody, 422 U.S., at 417 (emphasis added).

[11]The Court suggests, for example, that if a hypothetical Title VII "claimant has been forced to move a great distance to find a replacement job, a rejection of the employer's offer might reflect the costs of relocation more than a judgment that the replacement job was superior, all things considered, to the defendant's job." For Gaddis and Starr, however, the loss of their accumulated seniority at their replacement jobs certainly reflected "costs of relocation" at least as substantial as high moving expenses.

I expect that federal courts will find no meaningful distinction between a worker's refusal to accept a job offer because he believes that acceptance would force him to incur costs, and a similar refusal based on the worker's judgment that changing jobs would prove costly. In either case, for purposes of awarding Title VII relief, the reasonableness of the worker's refusal should be left to the trial court's discretion.

[12]The purpose of §706(g)'s "mitigation of damages" requirement is to encourage claimants to work while their Title VII claims are being adjudicated. The Court cannot deny that Gaddis and Starr fully mitigated damages by seeking and obtaining other employment while litigating their claims against Ford.

find a more attractive job than the defendant's." But, as the Court later recognizes, there is no assurance that the present case fits this category either. After speculating at length about how Gaddis and Starr may have valued the relative worth of their Ford and General Motors jobs, the Court finally acknowledges that on this paper record, "[w]e cannot infer" how much Gaddis and Starr "valued their GM jobs . . . solely from their rejection of Ford's offer."

Equally unconvincing is the Court's repeated invocation of, and preoccupation with, "the rights of 'innocent third parties,'" and the "disruption of the existing seniority system[s]," that would result from adoption of the Court of Appeals' "rule." The Court nowhere demonstrates how petitioner's labor relations would have suffered had Ford extended offers of retroactive seniority to Gaddis and Starr. The details of Ford's collective-bargaining agreement were not litigated in either the District Court or the Court of Appeals. Thus, those courts never passed on petitioner's obligation to offer retroactive seniority to Gaddis and Starr if such an offer would have disrupted its labor relations or existing seniority systems.[13] Nor did the Court of Appeals decide, as a general matter, whether or not offers of retroactive seniority to discrimination claimants adversely affect the rights of incumbent employees.[14] The Court cannot justify reversal in the case at hand by vague reference to classes of claimants and third parties who are not before the Court. To the extent that it seeks to do so, its intricate argument is both irrelevant and advisory.

Fourth and finally: I am struck by the contrast between the Court's concern for parties who are not here and its studied indifference to the real-life concerns of the parties whose interests are directly affected. When the Court finally confronts the choice that actually faced Gaddis and Starr, it blithely suggests that "[a]fter all, they had the option of accepting Ford's unconditional offer and retaining the right to seek full compensation at trial" in the form of retroactive seniority. Yet the Court earlier acknowledges that "[d]elays in litigation unfortunately are now commonplace, forcing

---

[13]The Court of Appeals did not foreclose the possibility that Ford could have terminated its backpay liability to Gaddis and Starr by offering them employment plus an award of *provisional* seniority, defeasible in the event that they lost their continuing lawsuit for backpay. Nor did the Court of Appeals deny that offering a job without seniority might terminate Ford's backpay liability, should any provision of Ford's collective-bargaining agreement preclude it from making offers of retroactive seniority. Had petitioner pointed to such a collective-bargaining agreement provision, or proved that its incumbent employees actually had objected to offers of retroactive seniority to Title VII claimants, the Court of Appeals would have considered those factors in determining whether the District Court abused its discretion in shaping Gaddis' and Starr's relief.

[14]In any event, the Court's claim that offers of retroactive seniority would injure the rights of incumbent employees is vastly overstated. If any employer sued by a Title VII claimant could toll the accrual of backpay liability by making a unilateral offer that included some form of retroactive seniority, he still would have every incentive to make such an offer as soon as possible after the discriminatory act. The amount of retroactive seniority offered would necessarily be small, and the seniority rights of relatively few incumbent employees would be affected.

Under the Court's approach, in contrast, employers will no longer have any incentive to offer retroactive seniority. Any awards of retroactive seniority to bona fide Title VII claimants will thus be court-ordered, and will be entered only after "the lengthy delays that too often attend Title VII litigation." By delaying awards of retroactive seniority until final judgment in a significant number of cases, the Court's approach ensures that the seniority rights of comparatively greater numbers of incumbent employees will be affected adversely.

the victims of discrimination to suffer years of underemployment or unemployment before they can obtain a court order awarding them the jobs unlawfully denied them."

"If the choice presented to Gaddis and Starr was difficult," the Court continues, "it was only because it required them to assess their likelihood of prevailing at trial." Without consulting the record, the Court then states:

> "Gaddis and Starr presumably rejected Ford's offer because they thought their jobs at GM were worth more to them than full compensation (Ford's offer plus a court award) discounted by the risks of litigation.... Had they known they were going to win [their lawsuit], of course, they would have rejected the Ford job only if they valued the GM jobs more than they valued the combination of Ford's job plus the value of court-ordered compensation un discounted by the risks of litigation."

This is a comfortable rationale stated from the sidelines. Unfortunately, the abstract and technical concerns that govern the Court's calculations bear little resemblance to those that actually motivated Judy Gaddis and Rebecca Starr. When asked on cross-examination why she had turned down Ford's 1973 offer, Gaddis testified: "I had seniority [at General Motors] and I knew that I wasn't in danger of any layoff, where if I had accepted the job at Ford I might have worked a week or two weeks and been laid off because I would have been low seniority." Similarly, Starr testified on cross-examination: "I had seniority at General Motors. I had about fifteen people working under me. I could go to work at Ford and work a week and I knew that they could lay me off."

To a person living in the real world, the value of job security today far outstrips the value of full court-ordered compensation many years in the future. The Court's elaborate speculation about the concerns that "presumably" motivated Gaddis and Starr nowhere recognizes what a Ford job without seniority actually meant to Gaddis and Starr — a job from which they could be laid off at any moment. Unlike the Court, Gaddis and Starr recognized that if they traded their jobs with seniority for jobs without seniority, they could quickly become unemployed again, long before they had the chance to vindicate their rights at trial.

To people like Gaddis and Starr, the knowledge that they might someday establish their Title VII claims on the merits provides little solace for their immediate and pressing personal needs. Starr's trial testimony reveals just how much job security meant to her:

> "It was just a couple of days after I had [started working] there [at a temporary job] and this is, I was just wanting that job so bad because you can't, a woman, when you've got three children, I needed the money, and I was wanting the job so bad. I worked so hard. I'll never forget one day when [the unit supervisor] came to me. I'll never forget that, and he said, I had just been there a few days, I'll have to let you go.... It broke my heart because I knew I had worked so hard."[15]

---

[15] Without embarrassment, the Court cites Rebecca Starr's testimony to support its argument that the Court of Appeals' "rule," and not its own new rule, is indifferent to the real-life concerns of victims of sex discrimination. Under the Court of Appeals' "rule," however, Rebecca Starr was awarded full backpay as compensation for Ford's sex discrimination. Under this Court's rule, a large portion of Starr's compensation will simply be cut off. By claiming

I agree with the Court that "the victims of job discrimination want jobs, not lawsuits." When Ford made its 1973 offers to Gaddis and Starr, however, they had jobs, in which they had accumulated seniority despite Ford's discrimination. I therefore cannot accept the Court's conclusion that these women should have traded those jobs for uncertain employment in which back seniority could be won only by lawsuit. Nor can I justify penalizing Gaddis and Starr because they "discounted" the ultimate likelihood of obtaining court-ordered retroactive seniority at a different rate than the Court does today.

After hearing all the witnesses and appraising all the evidence, the District Court exercised its equitable discretion to shape complete backpay relief for Gaddis and Starr. In light of all the circumstances, the District Court refused to penalize Gaddis and Starr for declining Ford's 1973 job offer. Applying the correct standard of review over Title VII remedies, the Court of Appeals concluded that the District Court had exercised its remedial discretion properly. Sitting at this remove, I cannot say that Gaddis and Starr acted unreasonably. I would affirm the judgment of the Court of Appeals and thereby, for these two victims of discrimination, fulfill, and not defeat, the promise of Title VII.

NOTES AND PROBLEMS FOR DISCUSSION

1. In *Ford Motor Co.*, both the majority and the dissent rely on the Court's decision in *Albemarle*. Which opinion is most consistent with the "make whole" philosophy of *Albemarle*? The majority reasons that an employer may choose not to gamble on the outcome of future litigation and, therefore, decide to limit his potential liability for back pay by offering the claimant a position equivalent to that for which she originally applied. The plaintiff, who has obtained other employment, must give up her current job (and any seniority rights which have accrued) in order to preserve her right to 'full" back pay and retroactive seniority if she prevails at trial. But the question of what constitutes full relief will arise only after the employer has been found guilty of discrimination. Why then should it be the innocent employee who is forced to gamble? Is the majority's opinion based on the assumption that the relief afforded to Gaddis and Starr by the courts below made them more than whole? And should its reasoning also apply to a discriminatorily discharged employee offered reinstatement without accumulated back pay and seniority?

2. Failure to mitigate is in the nature of an affirmative defense: the employer has the burden of production and persuasion on the issue. *See, e.g.*, Booker v. Taylor Milk Co., 64 F.3d 860, 864 (3d Cir. 1995) ("To meet its burden, an employer must demonstrate that (1) substantially equivalent work was available, and (2) the Title VII claimant did not exercise reasonable diligence to obtain the employment."). The burden cannot be satisfied merely by discrediting the plaintiff's testimony concerning mitigation. *See, e.g.*, Floca v. Homcare Health Services, Inc., 845 F.2d 108 (5th Cir. 1988). If the plaintiff's efforts to find work are shown to be insufficient, must the employer, in order to take advantage of the failure-to-mitigate defense, also prove that there were substantially equivalent jobs available? *Compare* Sellers v. Delgado Cmty.

---

that the Court of Appeals was somehow *more* indifferent to Starr's real-life concerns, the Court only confirms how far removed from the real world it is.

Coll., 839 F.2d 1132, 1139 (5th Cir. 1988) ("If an employer proves that an employee has not made reasonable efforts to obtain work, the employer does not have to establish the availability of substantially comparable work."), *with* Quint v. A.E. Stanley Mfg. Co., 172 F.3d 1 (1st Cir. 1999) (as long as the claimant has made some effort to secure other employment, the burden of proving failure to mitigate rests on the employer). Several courts have held that once the employee acquires a comparable position, the duty to mitigate includes reasonable diligence in holding onto the job. *See* Brady v. Thurston Motor Lines, Inc., 753 F.2d 1269 (4th Cir. 1985) (duty to mitigate includes reasonable and good faith efforts to maintain a job once accepted.")

3. (a) For mitigation purposes, "substantially equivalent employment" means a job with essentially the same promotional opportunities, compensation, job responsibilities, working conditions, and status. As the Court observed in *Ford Motor Co.*, there is no obligation to seek out work in another community, or to accept a position inferior in terms of pay, status, or conditions to the position the plaintiff was denied. An employee who has been terminated will be fortunate immediately to find equivalent employment and may have to take a lesser job to make ends meet. Should accepting work which is not substantially equivalent affect the plaintiff's obligation to mitigate? In BOEHMS v. CROWELL, 139 F.3d 452 (5th Cir. 1998), cert. denied, 525 U.S. 1102, 119 S.Ct. 866, 142 L.Ed.2d 768 (1999), the plaintiff was denied a promotion, and his job subsequently was eliminated. He opted to go into a transition program that allowed him to remain employed for another six months. While in the transition program, Boehms was offered several jobs that paid the same salary as, but were inferior in terms of responsibility and authority to, his former position. When Boehms won his age discrimination case, the employer argued that under the "reasonable efforts" standard, he was obligated to accept any position better than the temporary position in the transition program, and that when he turned down such offers, he had forfeited his right to back pay. The Court of Appeals would not have it.

> We are unimpressed with this argument, as it would lead to the untenable result that a claimant in Boehms' position must accept almost any position that becomes available while participating in a temporary employee assistance program — provided it qualifies, as it likely will, as an improvement over his position therein. * * * [O]ur focus in a mitigation analysis — and the base from which all comparisons about whether "reasonable efforts" to obtain comparable work are made — must be the employment position with respect to which the discrimination occurred.

139 F.3d at 460.

The kind of effort that will constitute "reasonable diligence" to obtain "substantially equivalent" employment depends on the circumstances in which the plaintiff finds herself, and there are substantial differences from court to court in the implementation of that standard. *See, e.g.*, Nord v. United States Steel Co., 758 F.2d 1462 (11th Cir. 1985) (2 1/2 years spent helping her husband establish a business was not unreasonable in light of the plaintiff's inability to find comparable work); Orzel v. Wauwatosa Fire Dept., 697 F.2d 743, 757 (7th Cir.), cert. denied, 464 U.S. 992, 104 S.Ct. 484, 78 L.Ed.2d 680 (1983) (one temporary job, one application for work, and registration with state job service, while "less than vigorous," did not constitute a failure to mitigate); Smith v. American Services Co., 796 F.2d 1430 (11th Cir. 1986) (the claimant's decision to attend school full-time was not a failure to mitigate since she made reasonable efforts to get work before beginning school).

(b) The *Ford Motor Co.* Court held that offer of a position substantially equivalent to the one plaintiff was denied will toll the accrual of back pay. Are there circumstances which would allow a plaintiff to refuse such an offer without forfeiting back pay? *See, e.g.*, Smith v. World Ins. Co., 38 F.3d 1456, 1464 (8th Cir. 1994) (the jury reasonably could conclude that the plaintiff had acted reasonably in rejecting an offer of reinstatement where the offer included no assurances that bad treatment which the plaintiff had suffered would not reoccur; "we believe the burden is correctly placed upon the employer to prove that it made an offer of reinstatement and that the plaintiff's rejection of it was objectively unreasonable.").

Does an employee who voluntarily quits her job after a discriminatory incident automatically forfeit back pay? Should that depend on what kind of earnings plaintiff has during the back pay period? In DENNIS v. COLUMBIA COLLETON MEDICAL CENTER, INC., 290 F.3d 639 (4th Cir. 2002), the plaintiff was denied a promotion and resigned on the spot. At trial, she introduced evidence that she had earned more salary over the three years between leaving the hospital and trial than she would have made if she had stayed in her job after being denied the promotion; though not as much as she would have earned had she been promoted. The appellate court rejected the employer's argument that the plaintiff had forfeited back pay by quitting. "[T]he Fourth Circuit does not apply the 'constructive discharge rule' denying [back] pay to persons who leave an employer who has committed intentional discrimination unless it is under conditions of a constructive discharge. * * * [W]e simply apply the general statutory duty * * * to mitigate the employer damages." 290 F.3d at 651.

4. Section 706(g) provides that "[i]nterim earnings or amounts earnable with reasonable diligence by the person or persons discriminated against shall operate to reduce the back pay otherwise allowable." Despite this language, and the limited nature of the Supreme Court's holding in *Ford Motor Co.*, some courts hold that a failure to mitigate will terminate rather than reduce back pay. *See, e.g.*, Sellers v. Delgado Cmty. Coll., 902 F.2d 1189, 1195-96 (5th Cir.), cert. denied, 498 U.S. 987, 111 S.Ct. 525, 112 L.Ed.2d 536 (1990) (the plaintiff's failure to mitigate in the year following her discharge cut off all back pay even though she subsequently made diligent, though unsuccessful, efforts to find work). On the other hand, in HOPKINS v. PRICE WATERHOUSE, 920 F.2d 967 (D.C Cir. 1990), the district court, on remand from the Supreme Court, found that the plaintiff's maximum earning potential following her constructive discharge was $100,000 per year. After her constructive discharge, the plaintiff had set up her own business, but earned less than what she would have made had she sought work with an established accounting firm. Rather than cutting off all back pay, the district court reduced her back pay award by the amount she could have earned. In affirming, the Court of Appeals distinguished the forfeiture cases on the ground that all of them involved situations where the plaintiffs had failed to seek jobs that would have compensated them completely for their losses.

What should the effect on back pay be if, after obtaining comparable employment, the victim of discrimination by employer A loses his job with employer B as a result of his own misconduct? In JOHNSON v. SPENCER PRESS OF MAINE, INC., 364 F.3d 368 (1st Cir. 2004), Johnson was forced to resign his employment because of severe harassment. Several days later, he obtained comparable employment with another employer, a job he held for seven months before he was discharged for misconduct. After that discharge, Johnson did not seek other employment and was classified as disabled by the Veterans' Administration. A jury awarded him compensatory and punitive damages and the court awarded back pay calculated as Johnson's wage loss between his termination by the defendant and the date when his second employer discharged him. The district court held that Johnson had ceased mitigating his damages as of the date he was discharged by the second employer, and, therefore, was not entitled to back pay or front pay after the date of that termination. The First Circuit affirmed, but expressly rejected the district court's reasoning.

> We hold that back pay is not permanently terminated when an employee is fired for misconduct or voluntarily quits interim employment. This view comports with the purpose of the back pay remedy as articulated in *Albermarle*. *Albermarle* taught that back pay is a presumptive entitlement of a victim of discrimination and that the discriminating employer is responsible for all wage losses that result from its unlawful discrimination, at least until the time of judgment. Had there been no discrimination at employer A, the employee would never have come to work (or have been fired) from employer B. The discriminating employer (employer A) should not benefit from the windfall of not paying the salary differential when the employee is re-employed by employer C. Further, the use of per se rules is contrary to the general principle that the necessary balancing of the equities requires a case-by-case approach.

364 F.3d at 382-83. Nevertheless, the court of appeals affirmed on the ground that the plaintiff had failed to mitigate after he lost his job with the second employer and had not established that his inability to mitigate (the disability) was caused by the defendant's harassment. The court held that employee misconduct that results in the loss of comparable employment suspends, rather than tolls, back pay. The court insisted that its rule comports with *Albermarle*. But is it consistent with *Ford Motor Co.*? How are Gaddis and Starr to be distinguished from Johnson? Why shouldn't their back pay period resume after they were laid off by General Motors? Assume that Johnson had begun looking for another job diligently after his discharge, but had been unable to find employment as of the date of trial. Under the First Circuit's rule in *Johnson*, how should his back pay be calculated? *Compare* Brady v. Thurston Motor Lines, Inc., 753 F.2d 1269 (4th Cir. 1985) (back pay should equal zero during periods of unemployment following justified discharge), *with* NLRB v. Hopcroft Art & Stained Glass Works, Inc., 692 F.2d 63, 65 (8th Cir. 1982) ("[T]he amount the employee would have earned had he not quit is to be offset for the remainder of the backpay period").

5. If a back pay award must be reduced by "interim earnings," why should such an award not be reduced by a substitute for earnings, i.e., unemployment compensation? If a claimant is awarded what he would have earned had he been employed, and that amount is not reduced by unemployment compensation received, hasn't he been made more than whole? Under the "collateral source rule", a tortfeasor generally may not set up in mitigation of damages indemnity the plaintiff has received from a collateral source, such as insurance or workmen's compensation benefits, even where the employer has contributed to the benefit fund. Pursuant to the "collateral source rule", most appellate courts hold that it is error as a matter of law to deduct benefits such as unemployment compensation or social security payments from back pay awards in discrimination cases. *See, e.g.*, EEOC v. Ford Motor Co., 645 F.2d 183 (4th Cir. 1981) (back pay award not reduced by unemployment benefits as doing so would make it less costly to wrongfully terminate employee and thus dilute the prophylactic purposes of a back pay award), rev'd and remanded on other grounds, 458 U.S. 219, 102 S.Ct. 3057, 73 L.Ed.2d 721 (1982). A minority of circuit courts, however, consider it within the trial judge's discretion to deduct unemployment compensation from a back pay award. *See* Cooper v. Asplundh Tree Expert Co., 836 F.2d 1544 (10th Cir. 1988).

Is an employer-funded pension fund a "collateral source"? *Compare* Doyne v. Union Elec. Co., 953 F.2d 447 (8th Cir. 1992) (pension benefits were earned by the employee and are thus a collateral source not to be deducted from back pay), *with* Guthrie v. J.C. Penney Co., 803 F.2d 202 (5th Cir. 1986) (payments from the employer's retirement fund are not "collateral" in nature and thus should reduce back pay). Post-termination benefits, such as severance pay, which plaintiff would not have received had he remained employed, will be deducted in the calculation of back pay. *See e.g.*, Brunnemann v. Terra Int'l Inc., 975 F.2d 175 (5th Cir. 1992).

6. In order to "make whole" the economic loss suffered by the victim of discrimination, all fringe benefits which would have been enjoyed, but for the discrimination, should be included in the back pay award. *See, e.g.*, Crabtree v. Baptist Hosp. of Gadsden, Inc., 749 F.2d 1501 (11th Cir. 1985) (executive retirement benefits); Scarfo v. Cabletron Systems, Inc., 54 F.3d 931 (1st Cir. 1995) (value of stock options); Love v. Pullman Co., 569 F.2d 1074 (10th Cir. 1978) (insurance premiums, estimated tips, and sick and vacation pay). If overtime work is at the option of the employee, how should the lost opportunity for such work be compensated in the back pay award? *See* Bruno v. Western Elec. Co., 829 F.2d 957 (10th Cir. 1987) (if the plaintiff was required to work uncompensated overtime as a result of his discriminatory transfer, back pay should include compensation at the overtime rate).

A victim of discrimination is hardly "made whole" by the award of the amount she should have earned years after she should have earned it. Courts have addressed this problem by awarding prejudgment interest on the back pay award. *See, e.g.*, Pettway v. Am. Cast Iron Pipe Co., 494 F.2d 211, 263 (5th Cir. 1974), cert. denied, 439 U.S. 1115, 99 S.Ct. 1020, 59 L.Ed.2d 74 (1979). The award of interest is in the discretion of the trial court, but some courts suggest that the discretion to deny interest is, like the discretion to deny back pay, limited. *See, e.g.*, Barbour v. Merrill, 48 F.3d 1270, 1279 (D.C Cir. 1995), cert. dismissed, 516 U.S. 1155, 116 S.Ct. 1037, 134 L.Ed.2d 113 (1996) ("presumption runs strongly in favor of imposing prejudgment interest," and court may refuse "only when it provides a justification that reasonably supports this departure."). There is no consensus, however, on the manner of calculation or rate of interest to be used in that calculation. *See, e.g.*, EEOC v. Guardian Pools, Inc., 828 F.2d 1507 (11th Cir. 1987) (IRS prime rates for back pay period); Gelof v. Papineau, 829 F.2d 452, 456 (3d Cir. 1987) (prejudgment interest at 17% based on the rate of interest allowed on judgments under state law); United States v. City of Warren, 138 F.3d 1083, 1096 (6th Cir. 1998) (rejecting use of Consumer Price Index: "merely adjusting the dollars the plaintiff would have earned to compensate for diminished earning power because of inflation does not compensate for the lost use of the money in the intervening time.").

7. Back pay usually is calculated by creating a "hypothetical work history" for the plaintiff based on the employment history of the person or persons who actually held the position which was unlawfully denied the plaintiff. A plaintiff's interim earnings are subtracted from these hypothetical earnings to arrive at the amount of back pay. There is no way, of course, particularly in a hiring case, to say with certainty that the plaintiff's work history, absent discrimination, would have resembled the hypothetical work history. The burden of persuasion on back pay calculation is, however, different than that regarding liability. The plaintiff's burden is to produce evidence sufficient to allow the court reasonably to estimate the wages lost as a result of the discrimination. The burden of persuasion then shifts to the defendant to rebut the evidence establishing the hypothetical work history or to demonstrate the plaintiff's failure to mitigate. *See, e.g.*, Horn v. Duke Homes, 755 F.2d 599 (7th Cir. 1985). Because of the speculative nature of the enterprise, the calculation cannot be precise, but unrealistic exactitude is not required in this context and ambiguities in what an employee would have earned but for the discrimination are resolved against the discriminating employer. Stewart v. Gen. Motors Corp., 542 F.2d 445 (7th Cir. 1976), cert. denied, 433 U.S. 919, 97 S.Ct. 2995, 53 L.Ed.2d 1105 (1977). *See also* Grimes v. Athens Newspaper, Inc., 604 F.Supp. 1166 (M.D. Ga. 1985) (because of the impossibility of creating hypothetical work histories for female editors, back pay calculated by comparing actual earnings to "highest male salary being paid for the job").

Some courts have been unwilling to assume that, absent discrimination, claimants would have enjoyed maximum success in their work. For example, in EEOC v. MIKE SMITH PONTIAC GMC, INC., 896 F.2d 524 (11th Cir. 1990), the employer refused to hire a woman as a car salesperson. The EEOC requested back pay for the full forty-seven months tht elapsed between the refusal to hire and the date the dealership was sold, even though it was conceded that the charging party would have been terminated. Based on evidence that no salesperson was employed for as long as forty-seven months and that the tenure of most salespersons was less than eighteen months, the district court limited the back pay period to the average length of employment of all salespersons. With respect to the back pay period, the Court of Appeals affirmed.

> [T]he EEOC simply provided no factual basis, besides mere speculation, for concluding that [the charging party] would have remained employed for the entire forty-seven month period. We find that the district court properly exercised its discretion when it opted to use averages in computing the back pay period.

896 F.2d at 530. Uncertainty regarding the employee's hypothetical work history also can result from lack of evidence regarding how well the employee would have performed, absent discrimination, in the job to which she was entitled. Consider the following case.

Griffin v. Michigan Department Of Corrections

United States Court of Appeals for the Sixth Circuit, 1993.
5 F.3d 186.

BOGGS, Circuit Judge.

This case involves the question of what monetary compensation and compensatory promotions are required to place a female employee of the Michigan

Department of Corrections, who has been discriminated against, in the same position as if she had not been discriminated against. Constance Anderson is a female employee who was unquestionably discriminated against in prison employment, at least through 1982. After that time, discrimination in the areas under consideration apparently ceased, but Anderson had suffered harm in her career. By a 1988 order, not appealed on this issue by the defendants, the district court ordered that she be compensated and promoted as though she had followed the career track of a male prison employee, Gerald Hofbauer, "to the present time." Pursuant to that order, a hearing was held in November 1990 to calculate the job classification that Anderson would currently hold had she not been the victim of gender discrimination. Based on that hearing, the special master recommended that Anderson be promoted to Deputy Prison Warden XII. There are eleven level XII positions in the Department of Corrections, of which only two are Deputy Prison Warden positions. In March 1991, the district court adopted the special master's recommendation, requiring that, based on Hofbauer's actual employment progression, Anderson be promoted to the Deputy Prison Warden XII position. That order was appealed and is the subject of the case before us.

Michigan now attacks any compensation to Anderson that is based on promotions Hofbauer received after his first post-1982 promotion, to Administrative Manager VIII. * * *

I

* * *

We are thus required to consider plaintiff's contention, supported by the most recent order of the district court, that she is to be compensated based on an assumed career path linked inextricably to that of Warden Hofbauer, however high that may go, until the state complies and promotes and pays her accordingly. The state's position, on the other hand, is that all the actions of the district court should be reversed back to Hofbauer's first promotion after 1982 to Administrative Manager VII, and that Anderson should be required to prove specifically that she would have received each promotion beyond that point.

II

The purpose of front pay in a Title VII case is to put an injured party in the same position the party would have occupied in the absence of the discrimination, neither more nor less. As in all exercises predicting the future, considerable difficulties are involved. In particular, such an exercise involves an attempt to determine the degree to which a plaintiff possesses qualities that would make plaintiff successful in attaining career advancement. For advancements that come simply with longevity, courts have uniformly assumed that such advancement would occur, in the absence of specific disqualifying information.

On the other hand, courts will not automatically assume that a person discriminated against possesses characteristics so sterling as to receive every advancement not made illegal or logically impossible under the employer's rules.

Few cases involving front pay drag on a long as this one has, and thus the time, complexity, and number of speculative decision points are rarely as great as they are in this case. Even so, we believe that we can discern the outline of a proper conceptual framework for cases such as this one.

In advancement through bureaucratic structures, such as the military, state and federal governments, and large private organizations, promotions generally involve very widely differing criteria. For example, some promotions, such as from Second Lieutenant to First Lieutenant in the Army, or from GS 11 to GS 12 in federal government professional grades, generally require little more than longevity and satisfactory performance. The proportion of workers in the lower grade who advance to the higher grade upon the satisfactory completion of a certain time of service is very high, approaching 100%. On the other hand, certain promotions are the result of extraordinary success, such as achieving a level of tenure, or avoiding an "up and out" removal, that clearly does not occur with all, or even most, of the candidates. Such promotions include those from Colonel to Brigadier General in the military, from GS 15 to supergrade or Senior Executive Service in the federal government, from assistant to associate professor (achieving tenure) in prestigious universities, or from associate to partner in major law firms.

In an ideal situation, where the data is available and the parties cooperative, a court could determine what would be the progression of an average worker with the basic qualifications possessed by the injured party. The burden of proof would then be on the defendant to prove that the plaintiff would have performed more poorly than the average and the burden of proof would be on the plaintiff to show that she would have performed better than that average. Here, however, the court simply selected, albeit from between two persons presented by the competing parties, a "comparable male," Gerald Hofbauer, and attached Ms. Anderson's wagon to his star. As it has turned out, that has been quite favorable to Ms. Anderson. However, it might not have turned out as well. Hofbauer could have left the state, been killed in an accident, acquired a drug habit, or simply not performed very well. Under those circumstances, it would surely have been inequitable to say that she could advance no further than Hofbauer had in fact advanced before those events.

The "comparable male" approach is, in truth, simply an analogue for the "average worker" method outlined above, in those circumstances where a cohort of workers tend to advance together. If most workers advance, then simply choosing one and tracking his advancement is likely to serve as a good approximation of the truth.

However, picking one worker and tracking his advancement, when advancement is the result of the difficult traversing of the shoals and channels, pools and narrows, of a bureaucracy is a highly suspect enterprise, *if other methods are available.*

* * *

[The Court concluded that the district court's 1988 order, even though it left the calculation of back pay for further proceedings, was a final, appealable decision. That decision became the law of the case and by failing to appeal at that time, the Department of Corrections had forfeited its right to complain later about the basics of the decision.]

V

* * *

Had Michigan properly appealed the 1988 order, the shortcomings set forth above would require us to reverse the determination that plaintiff is entitled to receive the fruits of all that Hofbauer accomplished. In the usual case, the district court should determine whether the promotions Hofbauer received were promotions that would have accrued to an average member of the cohort of workers of the class he occupied at that time. If they would not have accrued to an average member, the burden would then be on plaintiff to demonstrate to the court, by a preponderance of the evidence, that in the absence of illicit discrimination, she would have attained additional advancement. If Michigan wished to argue that plaintiff was not as good as average, it would have that burden. However, the procedural posture of this case pretermits that inquiry, and we thus AFFIRM the judgment of the district court.

NOTES AND PROBLEMS FOR DISCUSSION

1. The court in *Griffin* was concerned with uncertainty as to the career path the plaintiff would have followed had she not been denied the promotion. There may be uncertainty, particularly in competitive hiring or promotion cases, as to whether the victim of discrimination would have gotten the job. In a mixed-motive case, the employer can escape back pay liability (though not all relief) by proving that the same decision would have been made absent discrimination. What if the court is convinced only that the plaintiff had been deprived of a chance at the job, but is unable to say that the plaintiff would or would not have been successful if hired? In DOLL v. BROWN, 75 F.3d 1200 (7th Cir. 1996), the district court found that the plaintiff had been the victim of discrimination because of a handicap that the employer refused to accommodate. Back pay was based on the salary of the foreman's position that the plaintiff had been denied. The appellate court expressed puzzlement over why the trial judge had not granted plaintiff the promotion itself and speculated that the district judge might have been "splitting the difference" in recognition that it was "far from certain that Doll would have been given the foreman's job" in light of the superior qualifications of the employee who was promoted. 75 F.3d at 1205. In remanding the case for additional findings, the Seventh Circuit argued for the application of a "lost-chance" calculation similar to that used in medical malpractice cases.

> [The lost-chance theory] strikes us as peculiarly appropriate in employment cases involving competitive promotion. In such a case the plaintiff's chances are inherently uncertain because of the competitive setting. Suppose there were five applicants for one job, the employer discriminated against four, all four were equally well qualified, and the fifth got the job. Would all four of the discriminated-against applicants be entitled to back pay, one to the job, and the other three to front pay? Obviously not; yet without the lost-chance concept which could grant reinstatement to none of the four and 25 percent front pay to each of them, the employer would get off scot-free. This case is less extreme, yet not so much as to make the traditional dichotomous treatment appropriate. If the issue is posed in either-or terms — either Doll would have gotten the foreman's job or he would not have — then in all likelihood Doll loses, because the case for promoting Stein was very strong. If the issue is posed in lost-chance terms — Doll had a chance, though maybe not a very good one, to get the foreman's job, and the government deprived him of that chance and by doing so injured him — then Doll's prospects in litigation are much brighter. If plaintiffs are risk averse, moreover, they will, within limits, prefer a bigger chance of a smaller recovery to a smaller chance of a larger recovery.

The difference between employment discrimination and medical and other forms of personal-injury tort is that the relevant probabilities may be more difficult to compute in the employment setting. It would be hard to pick a number that would reliably estimate the probability of Doll's receiving the promotion but for discrimination. Would it be 5 percent? 10 percent? 40 percent? Who knows? Yet no less uncertainty attends the efforts of triers of fact to fix the percentage of a plaintiff's negligence in a tort case governed as most tort cases are today, by the rule of comparative negligence. If the uncertainty is bearable there, why not in an employment discrimination case?

75 F.3d at 1206-07. But if the plaintiff's chances of securing the promotion were remote, doesn't that mean that a trier of fact should find, under the preponderance of evidence standard, that he would not have been awarded the job? Is compensation for the "lost chance" at a job back pay or legal damages? With *Doll* compare TAXMAN v. BD. of ED. of PISCATAWAY, 91 F.3d 1547 (3d Cir. 1996) (en banc). There, budget problems required the school board to lay off a single high school teacher. The two candidates for the layoff, one black and one white, were of equal seniority and qualifications. Pursuant to an affirmative action plan which allowed race to be considered in such decisions, the board laid off the white teacher, who filed suit under Title VII. Both the district court and the Third Circuit concluded that the affirmative action plan was unlawful. Because the plaintiff and the black teacher who was retained were equal in qualifications and seniority, there was no better than a 50% chance (a coin toss would have been used) that, absent the affirmative action plan, the white teacher would have been retained. Nevertheless, the district court awarded the plaintiff 100% of the back pay claim, and the Court of Appeals affirmed. Relying on *Price Waterhouse*, the court reasoned that the school board could not avoid paying full back pay unless it could prove that Taxman would have lost the coin toss. Given the purposes of Title VII, which approach, *Doll* or *Taxman*, is sounder?

In BISHOP v. GAINER, 272 F.3d 1009 (7th Cir. 2001), cert. denied, 535 U.S. 1055, 122 S.Ct. 1912, 152 L.Ed.2d 822 (2002), the trial court accepted the Seventh Circuit's invitation in *Doll* and applied the "lost chance" theory to a back pay calculation in a case where three candidates for a single promotion had been denied consideration because of their race. Based on their relative placements on the promotion list, the district court calculated each plaintiff's odds of obtaining the promotion absent discrimination and awarded back pay for the position in question accordingly. On appeal, the plaintiffs argued that because the employer had failed to prove which of them would have received the promotion, each of them was entitled to a full award. Rejecting the plaintiffs' argument as "obviously wrong," the court of appeals affirmed the trial court's ruling.

The [lost-chance] approach obviously involves more art than science. But as we said in *Doll*, that is true in all comparative negligence calculations as well. It strikes us that in this particular situation, it was the likeliest way to arrive at a just result.

272 F.3d at 1016-17.

BIONDO v. CITY OF CHICAGO, 382 F.3d 680 (7th Cir. 2004), cert. denied, 543 U.S. 1152, 125 S.Ct. 1336, 161 L.Ed.2d 115 (2005) arose from the city's use in 1986 of a written test for promotion of firefighters to the rank of Lieutenant. Fearful that promoting in rank order from the test scores would have an disparate impact on minority candidates, the city created racially segregated lists and then made promotions from each list in exactly the same percentage as that racial group had taken the test: 29% of the test takers were minorities, so 29% of the promotions were made from the minority list. This process meant that the promotion of some white candidates was delayed and others were not promoted at all even though minority candidates with lower scores became lieutenants. Nineteen white firefighters filed suit. By the time the case reached trial, most of the plaintiffs had achieved the rank of Lieutenant and three had gone on to Captain. On the merits, the district court found that the use of the segregated lists was unlawful and that the test was a valid means of assessing skills necessary to the rank of Lieutenant. At the remedy phase, two juries were asked to determine for each plaintiff (1) the likelihood that, but for the discrimination, he would have been promoted to Captain and then to the next rank of Battalion Chief; and (2) when each such promotion would have been obtained. Based on the juries' findings, the trial judge then ordered the City to make retroactive the positions of those plaintiffs who had achieved one or more of the promotions and granted front pay to those who the jury found would have been promoted further. On appeal, the Seventh Circuit affirmed the judgment on the merits, but reversed and remanded for a new trial on relief. The problem, the court explained, was that:

> [T]he juries' estimates do not reflect a plausible appreciation of the lost chances: the juries concluded that every one of the plaintiffs who had not yet achieved a captaincy was *certain* to have done so — even though four plaintiffs had been unsuccessful in post-1986 attempts to become lieutenants and 9 of the 15 plaintiffs who reached lieutenant had tried and failed to achieve higher ranks. * * * Even in a world of grade inflation, where teachers living far from Lake Wobegon think nothing of rating all students as "above average," it is hard to swallow a conclusion that *all* candidates held back from promotion to lieutenant in 1986 were sure to become captains.

382 F.3d at 688-89. The court then concluded that for the plaintiffs who had become lieutenants before trial, the most favorable estimate of their chances of attaining the rank of Captain was the average chance that a candidate who had been promoted to Lieutenant as a result of the 1986 exam had of making Captain; and that chance was 33%.

> Accordingly, on remand each of the 13 [those who had become lieutenants but had not made Captain] is entitled to all of the benefits he would have received from a timely promotion to lieutenant, plus 33% of the benefits available from promotion to captain. And as about 41% of captains eventually become battalion chiefs, the award for the 10 plaintiffs who the jury thought likely to achieve that goal could include about 14% of the benefits of that position (a 33% chance of becoming a captain times the 41% chance that a captain eventually will advance again).

Id. at 690.

2. The calculation of back pay also is problematic where multiple claimants for a limited number of positions are shown to have been the victims of discrimination. In DOUGHERTY v. BARRY, 869 F.2d 605, 615 (D.C. Cir. 1989), where the employer discriminated against eight applicants for two positions, the Court of Appeals reversed an award of full back pay to all eight employees. The court ruled that if the district court had been able to determine with certainty which of the two plaintiffs would have received the promotions, the proper course would have been to award those two firefighters full relief and the others none. But since such a determination could not be made, the monetary value of the two promotions, the court concluded, had to be0 divided among the plaintiffs pro rata. In *Doll*, the Seventh Circuit rejected out of hand the possibility that in a multiple claimant case each of the claimants could be awarded full relief. Should the burden of uncertainty fall upon the plaintiffs? Why shouldn't an employer that has been found to have acted unlawfully be required to pay full back pay to all claimants unless *it* can persuade the court which claimant would have received the position(s) in the absence of discrimination? Is it not the employer's unlawful conduct that has created the uncertainty?

2. FRONT PAY

Section 706(g), as originally enacted, provided for injunctive relief including, but not limited to, "reinstatement or hiring of employees, with or without back pay." Back pay ordinarily is defined as lost wages up to the date the discrimination has ceased or the date of judgment. Sometimes the effect of discrimination will extend beyond the date of judgment; as, for example, when the plaintiff cannot be put in his rightful place without dislodging an incumbent employee or when reinstatement is not viable because of substantial hostility between the parties. Where reinstatement is not a viable option, courts have recognized that an award of "front pay" as a substitute for reinstatement is a necessary part of the "make whole" relief mandated by §706(g) as interpreted in *Albemarle*.

As a substitute for reinstatement, front pay is designed to compensate the victim of discrimination who cannot be placed in the position to which she is entitled. But front pay is appropriate only where reinstatement is impractical on account of circumstances not attributable to the plaintiff; where it is the plaintiff's own misconduct that makes reinstatement impossible, front pay is inappropriate. *See, e.g.*, Sellers v. Mineta, 358 F.3d 1058 (8th Cir. 2004) (post-termination misconduct that would prevent reinstatement also limits front pay as it would be inequitable for a plaintiff receive front pay where her own misconduct precludes her from relying on the more traditional remedy of reinstatement."). Some states treat front pay as an independent component of damages and not as a substitute for reinstatement. *See, e.g.*, Ray v. Miller Meester Advertising, 684 N.W.2d 404 (Minn. 2004) (under the Minnesota Human Rights Act, front pay is a distinct measure of damages that may be awarded in combination with reinstatement).

Like back pay, front pay is generally considered equitable relief, and thus, in a jury trial, both the liability for front pay and quantum will be decided by the judge. *See, e.g.*, Newhouse v. McCormick & Co., Inc., 110 F.3d 635 (8th Cir. 1997). The calculation of front pay is necessarily more speculative than that of back pay, and courts exercise more discretion than with the determination of back pay. The longer a proposed front pay period, the more speculative an award becomes and the less likely a plaintiff will be able to establish that her current circumstances are representative of her job prospects in the future. *See, e.g.*, Peyton v. DiMario, 287 F.3d 1121 (D.C. Cir. 2002) (award of 26 years of front pay vacated as unduly speculative). Ordinarily, front pay should consist of the employee's predicted salary for the years in question, including expected raises, with each year's sum discounted to present value through the use of an appropriate discount rate, which must also take into account the rate of inflation. *See, e.g.*, Suggs v. ServiceMaster Ed. Food Mgmt., 72 F.3d 1228 (6th Cir. 1996). The mitigation requirement codified in §706(g) is applicable to determinations of front pay as well as to back pay.

3. DAMAGES

The Seventh Amendment "preserves" the right to trial by jury in "suits at common law, where the value in controversy * * * exceeds twenty dollars." The amendment long has been interpreted as guaranteeing the right to jury trial, not just in actions recognized at common law in 1791 when the Bill of Rights was adopted, but in all "suits in which legal rights [are] to be ascertained and determined, in contradistinction to those where equitable rights alone [are] recognized, and equitable remedies [are] administered." Parsons v. Bedford, Breedlove & Robeson, 28 U.S. (3 Pet.) 433, 447, 7 L.Ed. 732 (1830). Where legal damages (compensatory or punitive) are claimed, either party is entitled to a jury trial on liability and quantum. *See* Hetzel v. Prince William County, 523 U.S. 208, 118 S.Ct. 1210, 140 L.Ed.2d 336 (1998).

As the Supreme Court explained in *Albemarle*, the remedies outlined in §706(g) of Title VII, including back pay, have been characterized by the courts as equitable relief. Although the Court never directly addressed the question whether a jury trial was available in a Title VII action, the circuit courts universally held that where Title VII provided the only cause of action, in light of its limitation to equitable relief, neither party was entitled to a trial by jury. However, Title VII is not the exclusive federal statutory remedy for all employment discriminatin claims, claims under other statutes did offer the opportunity for the recovery of legal damages. For example, state and local government workers with equal protection-based claims under 42 U.S.C. §1983, private and public sector workers with race-based claims against private employers under 42 U.S.C. §1981[2] could obtain both compensatory and punitive damages. Where claims under these statutes were joined with Title VII claims, the parties were entitled to a jury trial on all issues of fact common to both claims. While bound by the jury's findings of fact in such cases, the trial judge determined whether equitable relief, including back pay, should be awarded. *See* Jefferson v. Ingersoll Int'l, *supra*, Chapter 6, Section D.

The anomaly of allowing full legal relief in some types of employment cases but not others as well as the inadequacy of an award of back pay in some employment contexts, particularly hostile environment-based harassment claims, led Congress to include in the Civil Rights Act of 1991 a damage remedy for Title VII actions. Section 102 of the Act, codified at 42 U.S.C. §1981a, provides in part that:

(a) RIGHT OF RECOVERY

(1) CIVIL RIGHTS.— In an action brought by a complaining party under section 706 or 717 of the Civil Rights Act of 1964 against a respondent who engaged in unlawful intentional discrimination (not an employment practice

---

[2]See Chapter 8, Section A, *infra*.

that is unlawful because of its disparate impact) prohibited under section 703, 704, or 717 of the Act and provided that the complaining party cannot recover under * * * 42 U.S.C. Sec. 1981, the complaining party may recover compensatory and punitive damages as allowed in subsection (b), in addition to any relief authorized by section 706(g) of the Civil Rights Act of 1964, from respondent.

* * *

(b) COMPENSATORY AND PUNITIVE DAMAGES.

(1) DETERMINATION OF PUNITIVE DAMAGES — A complaining party may recover punitive damages under this section against a respondent (other than a government, government agency or political subdivision) if the complaining party demonstrates that the respondent engaged in a discriminatory practice or discriminatory practices with malice or with reckless indifference to the federally protected rights of an aggrieved individual.

(2) EXCLUSIONS FROM COMPENSATORY DAMAGES —

Compensatory damages awarded under this section shall not include backpay, interest on backpay, or any other type of relief authorized under section 706(g) of the Civil Rights Act of 1964.

(3) LIMITATIONS — The sum of the amount of compensatory damages awarded under this section for future pecuniary losses, emotional pain, suffering, inconvenience, mental anguish, loss of enjoyment of life, and other nonpecuniary losses, and the amount of punitive damages awarded under this section, shall not exceed, for each complaining party —

> [the Act also places the following maximum limitations on damage awards depending on the size of the employer: more than 14 and fewer than 101 employees: $50,000; more than 100 and fewer than 201 employees: $100,000; more than 200 and fewer than 501 employees: $200,000; more than 500 employees: $300,000]

* * *

(c) JURY TRIAL.—If a complaining party seeks compensatory or punitive damages under this section —

(1) any party may demand a trial by jury; and

(2) the court shall not inform the jury of the limitations described in subsection (b)(3).

Thus, in addition to the equitable relief, including back pay, available under §706(g), the 1991 Act provides for legal damages and jury trials in all Title VII actions involving allegations of intentional discrimination. Such legal relief is not available, however, in connection with disproportionate impact claims. The application of the damage provisions is explored in the following material.

(a) COMPENSATORY DAMAGES

In CAREY v. PIPHUS, 435 U.S. 247, 98 S.Ct. 1042, 55 L.Ed.2d 252 (1978), the Court held that compensatory damages such as emotional harm caused by the deprivation of constitutional rights may be awarded only when claimants submit proof of actual injury. Injury cannot be presumed, and the plaintiff must offer testimony and/or other evidence to show the nature and extent of the emotional harm caused by the violation. The Court stated:

> We use the term "distress" to include mental suffering or emotional anguish. Although essentially subjective, genuine injury in this respect may be evidenced by one's conduct and observed by others. Juries must be guided by appropriate instructions, and an award of damages must be supported by competent evidence concerning the injury.

435 U.S. at 264, n.20. Although *Carey* was a suit filed under 42 U.S.C. §1983 and involved a claimed violation of procedural due process, the courts have extended the holding of the case to apply to damage claims brought under Title VII and other civil rights statutes. *See, e.g.*, Patterson v. P.H.P. Healthcare Corp., 90 F.3d 927 (5th Cir. 1996), cert. denied, 519 U.S. 1091, 117 S.Ct. 767, 136 L.Ed.2d 713 (1997) ("we read *Carey* to require a plaintiff to present the same level of competent evidence under a Title VII emotional distress claim as is required to sustain a finding for emotional distress under §§1981 and 1983."). The EEOC has explained its position on the availability of recovery for intangible injury as follows:

> Damages are available for the intangible injuries of emotional harm such as emotional pain, suffering, inconvenience, mental anguish, and loss of enjoyment of life. Other nonpecuniary losses could include injury to professional standing, injury to character and reputation, injury to credit standing, loss of health, and any other nonpecuniary losses that are incurred as a result of the discriminatory conduct. Nonpecuniary losses for emotional harm are more difficult to prove than pecuniary losses. Emotional harm will not be presumed simply because the complaining party is a victim of discrimination. The existence, nature, and severity of emotional harm must be proved. Emotional harm may manifest itself, for example, as sleeplessness, anxiety, stress, depression, marital strain, humiliation, emotional distress, loss of self esteem, excessive fatigue, or a nervous breakdown. Physical manifestations of emotional harm may consist of ulcers, gastrointestinal disorders, hair loss, or headaches. * * * The Commission will typically require medical evidence of emotional harm to seek damages for such harm in conciliation negotiations.

EEOC Policy Guidance No. 915.002 §II(A)(2), at 10-12.

The courts are substantially divided over whether a plaintiff's testimony alone is sufficient to support anything more than a nominal damage award for emotional harm. *Compare* Fitzgerald v. Mountain States Tel. & Tel. Co., 68 F.3d 1257 (10th Cir. 1995) (remanding an emotional damage award of $250,000 as clearly excessive when the award was based solely on the testimony of the plaintiff without any testimony from physicians or psychologists and the plaintiffs continued to work in their chosen fields), *with* Smith v. Norwest Fin. Acceptance, Inc., 129 F.3d 1408 (10th Cir. 1998) (affirming $200,000 compensatory damage award based solely on testimony of plaintiff concerning humiliation, stress, and sleeplessness; corroborating testimony from physician or psychologist not required in every case).

As is the case in general personal injury litigation, juries, even within the same jurisdiction, often award vastly different damages for emotional suffering in discrimination cases. The factors that influence such awards are infinite and inherently difficult to quantify. When damage awards are appealed as excessive, courts differ on the importance of awards in similar cases. In PEYTON v. DIMARIO, 287 F.3d 1121 (D.C. Cir. 2002), the court upheld a $300,000 award against a government agency, rejecting the defendant's argument that the damage award was excessive because it substantially exceeded awards in similar cases. The court pointed to the unique circumstances of each case and concerns for inflation adjustment in affirming the jury award. "[T]he proper approach is to determine whether the judgment awarded * * * is supported by the evidence, and does not shock the conscience, or is not inordinately large so as to be obviously unreasonable." 287 F.3d at 1127. The Fifth Circuit uses a "maximum recovery rule" which requires a remittitur to the maximum amount that a jury could have awarded based on previous awards in similar cases supplemented by a "multiplier" or percentage enhancement. In SALINAS v. O'NEILL, 286 F.3d 827 (5th Cir. 2002), for example, the court ordered a remittitur of a $300,000 award to $150,000 on the ground that awards in three other employment discrimination cases in that circuit had been in the $100,000 range. "In practice, our evaluation of what a jury could have awarded is tied to awards in cases with similar injuries." 286 F.3d at 831.

(b) The Title VII Damage Caps

The 1991 amendments to Title VII limit the quantum of compensatory and punitive damages that may be awarded according to the size of the employer. This cap applies to the sum of compensatory and punitive damages that a single plaintiff can obtain against a single defendant. See e.g., Hogan v. Bangor & Aroostook R.R. Co., 61 F.3d 1034 (1st Cir. 1995) (cap applies to the sum of compensatory and punitive damages, not on each type of award). For the largest category of employers (over 500 employees), damages are capped at $300,000; for the smallest category (fewer than 101 employees) the cap is $50,000. The damage caps did not, of course, result from any congressional findings regarding the amount of harm that employers of different sizes may do, but are part of the political compromise required for passage of the amendments. The limits apply only to the aggregate of all the Title VII claims of an individual plaintiff. See, e.g., Baty v. Willamette Indus., 172 F.3d 1232, 1246 (10th Cir. 1999) (the remedial provision refers to "an action," which means a lawsuit, not the separate legal claims that may be included in the suit; consequently, the caps apply to each party in an action, not to each claim). If, however, there are other claims in a case, not subject to the caps, a court can allocate a general jury award in excess of the caps to the non-capped claims. See e.g., Martini v. Fed. Nat'l Mortgage Ass'n, 178 F.3d 1336, 1349-50 (D.C. Cir. 1999), cert. denied, 528 U.S. 1147, 120 S.Ct. 1155, 145 L.Ed.2d 1065 (2000) (punitive damages exceeding statutory cap should be reallocated to plaintiff's claim under D.C. Human Rights Act: "Were we not to treat damages under federal and local law as fungible where the standards of liability are the same, we would effectively limit the local jurisdiction's prerogative to provide greater remedies for employment discrimination than those Congress has afforded under Title VII.").

The cap provision ties the award limit to the number of employees in the "current or preceding" calendar year. In a case of first impression, the Eighth Circuit has construed that text to refer to the year in which the alleged discrimination occurred and not the year in which the verdict was awarded. Hernandez-Miranda v. Empresas Diaz Masso Inc., 651 F.3d 157 (1st Cir. 2011). But since the cap categories refer only to the number of employees, should the cap apply and, if so, under what circumstances, when the plaintiff seeks damages against a defendant union with more than 15 members? In DOWD v. UNITED STEELWORKERS, LOCAL 286, 253 F.3d 1093 (8th Cir. 2001), the plaintiffs obtained judgments against their local union for its participation in creating a racially hostile work environment. The union claimed that it was immune from a damage award because it employed only 4 workers and the lowest cap category under the Act refers to employers with between 14 and 101 employees. The court rejected that argument, ruling that when a union is sued in its capacity as a union rather than as an employer, its potential liability for purposes of the damage cap should be measured by the number of its members. Adopting the union's position, the court reasoned, would create the "anomalous result" of having a labor union liable under Title VII but exempt from any compensatory damages liability. Because the damage award of $20,000 fell within the lowest category of damages, the court was not required to decide which damage cap would apply to the union which had 1400 members.

If a jury awards damages in excess of the applicable cap, the court must reduce the award. See, e.g., EEOC v. AIC Sec. Investigations, Ltd., 55 F.3d 1276 (7th Cir. 1995) (punitive damages award of $500,000 reduced to $150,000 to fit statutory limit of $200,000 in case where jury also awarded $50,000 in compensatory damages). Jury verdicts that are within the statutory caps may nevertheless be reduced as excessive if not supported by sufficient evidence. But they are split on the question of whether the maximum available award under the cap should be reserved for the most egregious cases. Compare Hennessy v. Penril Datacomm Networks, Inc., 69 F.3d 1344, 1355-56 (7th Cir. 1995) (reducing a jury award of $100,000, the statutory cap available against this employer on ground that the "maximum permissible award should be reserved for egregious cases.), with Peyton v. Dimario, 287 F.3d 1121, 1127 (D.C. Cir. 2002), (affirming the trial court's decision to reduce the jury's $482,000 to $300,000 to comply with the cap and rejecting defense request for a further reduction on the ground that the case was not so egregious as to justify the maximum award, finding "no authority for the proposition that cases involving some perceived or even evident degree of injury less than the most egregious must inherently be awarded some figure lower than the cap").

The Act expressly prohibits the court from advising the jury of the limitation on damages, and a violation of this provision can lead to a retrial on the damages issue. See, e.g., Saski v. Class, 92 F.3d 232 (4th Cir. 1996) (new trial on damages ordered because the plaintiff's attorney advised the jury of damage caps during closing argument).

The Act explicitly excludes back pay from the definition of compensatory damages. Since back pay awards are not capped, it is critical how any monetary award is characterized. For example, should the value of lost stock options be treated as lost wages or as an element of damages? *See* Greene v. Safeway Stores, Inc., 210 F.3d 1237 (10th Cir. 2000) (stock options treated as part of the plaintiff's compensation package).

The statute defines damages to include compensation for "future pecuniary losses." Should that include front pay? In POLLARD v. E. I. DU PONT DE NEMOURS & CO., 532 U.S. 843, 121 S.Ct. 1946, 150 L.Ed.2d 62 (2001), the Supreme Court reasoned that since front pay was a remedy authorized sub silento by §706(g), it should be treated like back pay and, therefore, be excluded from the meaning of compensatory damages. This, in turn, meant that it fell outside of the statutory cap on the recovery of the sum of compensatory and punitive damages. This also means that front pay issues, such as the employer's liability for front pay and the amount to be awarded, fall to the court, and not the jury, to decide.

Congress was concerned with the possibility of double recovery of damages under Title VII and §1981 and provided in §102 of the 1991 Act that legal damages are available under Title VII only to a complaining party who "cannot recover under" 42 U.S.C. §1981. The Senate sponsors of the Act stated that "[t]he complaining party need not prove that he or she does not have a cause of action under section 1981 in order to recover damages in the section 1981A action." 137 Cong.Rec. S 15484 (daily ed., Oct. 30, 1991). *See, e.g.*, Bradshaw v. University of Maine System, 870 F.Supp. 406, 408 (D.Maine 1994); West v. The Boeing Co., 851 F.Supp. 395, 398 (D.Kan. 1994) (sole purpose of "cannot recover" limitation is the avoidance of duplicate recoveries: plaintiff, who could have filed §1981 claim but who has chosen not to, may recover damages under 1991 Act.) The Act's sponsors went on to say that a complaining party could recover both 1981 damages and damages under Title VII where there are "demonstrably different harms under each of the statutes." Id. In theory, such a showing could be made, for example, where the plaintiff proves she was subject to both gender discrimination (unlawful under Title VII) and racial discrimination (unlawful under §1981). In practice, how would a court distinguish between harm caused by different biases? The applicability of §1981 and the other Reconstruction Era civil rights statutes in employment discrimination litigation is discussed in Chapter 8, *infra*.

(c) PUNITIVE DAMAGES

Kolstad v. American Dental Association

Supreme Court of the United States, 1999.
527 U.S. 526, 119 S.Ct. 2118, 144 L.Ed.2d 494.

O'CONNOR, J., delivered the opinion of the Court, Part I of which was unanimous, Part II-A of which was joined by STEVENS, SCALIA, KENNEDY, SOUTER, GINSBURG, AND BREYER, J.J., and Part II-B of which was joined by REHNQUIST, C.J., and SCALIA, KENNEDY, and THOMAS, J.J. REHNQUIST, C.J., filed an opinion concurring in part and dissenting in part, in which THOMAS, J., joined. STEVENS, J. filed an opinion concurring in part and dissenting in part, in which SOUTER, GINSBURG, and BREYER, J.J., joined.

JUSTICE O'CONNOR delivered the opinion of the Court.

Under the terms of the Civil Rights Act of 1991, punitive damages are available in claims under Title VII of the Civil Rights Act of 1964 and the Americans with Disabilities Act of 1990. Punitive damages are limited, however, to cases in which the employer has engaged in intentional discrimination and has done so "with malice or with reckless indifference to the federally protected rights of an aggrieved individual." 42 U.S.C. §1981a(b)(1). We here consider the circumstances under which punitive damages may be awarded in an action under Title VII.

I

A

In September 1992, Jack O'Donnell announced that he would be retiring as the Director of Legislation and Legislative Policy and Director of the Council on Government Affairs and Federal Dental Services for respondent, American Dental Association (respondent or Association). Petitioner, Carole Kolstad, was employed with O'Donnell in respondent's Washington, D. C., office, where she was serving as respondent's Director of Federal Agency Relations. When she learned of O'Donnell's retirement, she expressed an interest in filling his position. Also interested in replacing O'Donnell was Tom Spangler, another employee in respondent's Washington office. At this time, Spangler was serving as the Association's Legislative Counsel, a position that involved him in respondent's legislative lobbying efforts. Both petitioner and Spangler had worked directly with O'Donnell, and both had received "distinguished" performance ratings by the acting head of the Washington office, Leonard Wheat.

Both petitioner and Spangler formally applied for O'Donnell's position, and Wheat requested that Dr. William Allen, then serving as respondent's Executive Director in the Association's Chicago office, make the ultimate promotion decision. After interviewing both petitioner and Spangler, Wheat recommended that Allen select Spangler for O'Donnell's post. Allen notified petitioner in December 1992 that he had, in fact, selected Spangler to serve as O'Donnell's replacement. Petitioner's challenge to this employment decision forms the basis of the instant action.

B

After first exhausting her avenues for relief before the Equal Employment Opportunity Commission, petitioner filed suit against the Association in Federal District Court, alleging that respondent's decision to promote Spangler was an act of employment discrimination proscribed under Title VII. In petitioner's view, the entire selection process was a sham. Counsel for petitioner urged the jury to conclude that Allen's stated reasons for selecting Spangler were pretext for gender discrimination and that Spangler had been chosen for the position before the formal selection process began. Among the evidence offered in support of this view, there was testimony to the effect that Allen modified the description of O'Donnell's post to track aspects of the job description used to hire Spangler. In petitioner's view, this "preselection" procedure suggested an intent by the Association to discriminate on the basis of sex. Petitioner also introduced testimony at trial that Wheat told sexually offensive jokes and that he had referred to certain prominent professional women in derogatory terms. Moreover, Wheat allegedly refused to meet with petitioner for several weeks regarding her interest in O'Donnell's position. Petitioner testified, in fact, that she had historically experienced difficulty gaining access to meet with Wheat. Allen, for his part, testified that he conducted informal meetings regarding O'Donnell's position with both petitioner and Spangler, although petitioner stated that Allen did not discuss the position with her.

The District Court denied petitioner's request for a jury instruction on punitive damages. The jury concluded that respondent had discriminated against petitioner on the basis of sex and awarded her backpay totaling $52,718. Although the District Court subsequently denied respondent's motion for judgment as a matter of law on the issue of liability, the court made clear that it had not been persuaded that respondent had selected Spangler over petitioner on the basis of sex, and the court denied petitioner's requests for reinstatement and for attorney's fees.

* * *

[The D.C. Circuit reversed the trial judge, reasoning that "because the state of mind necessary to trigger liability for the wrong is at least as culpable as that required to make punitive damages applicable," the fact that the jury could reasonably have found intentional discrimination meant that the jury should have been permitted to consider punitive damages. The circuit then agreed to hear the case en banc.]

* * * In a divided opinion, the court affirmed the decision of the District Court. The en banc majority concluded that, "before the question of punitive damages can go to the jury, the evidence of the defendant's culpability must exceed what is needed to show intentional discrimination." Based on the 1991 Act's structure and legislative history, the court determined, specifically, that a defendant must be shown to have engaged in some "egregious" misconduct before the jury is permitted to consider a request for punitive damages. Although the court declined to set out the "egregiousness" requirement in any detail, it concluded that petitioner failed to make the requisite showing in the instant case. * * * [The five dissenters] agreed generally with the panel majority.

We granted certiorari to resolve a conflict among the Federal Courts of Appeals concerning the circumstances under which a jury may consider a request for punitive damages under § 1981a(b)(1).

II

A

* * *

The very structure of § 1981a suggests a congressional intent to authorize punitive awards in only a subset of cases involving intentional discrimination. Section 1981a(a)(1) limits compensatory and punitive awards to instances of intentional discrimination, while §1981a(b)(1) requires plaintiffs to make an additional "demonstration" of their eligibility for punitive damages. Congress plainly sought to impose two standards of liability — one for establishing a right to compensatory damages and another, higher standard that a plaintiff must satisfy to qualify for a punitive award.

The Court of Appeals sought to give life to this two-tiered structure by limiting punitive awards to cases involving intentional discrimination of an "egregious" nature. We credit the en banc majority's effort to effectuate congressional intent, but, in the end, we reject its conclusion that eligibility for punitive damages can only be described in terms of an employer's "egregious" misconduct. The terms "malice" and "reckless" ultimately focus on the actor's state of mind. While egregious misconduct is evidence of the requisite mental state, § 1981a does not limit plaintiffs to this form of evidence, and the section does not require a showing of egregious or outrageous discrimination independent of the employer's state of mind. Nor does the statute's structure imply an independent role for "egregiousness" in the face of congressional silence. On the contrary, the view that §1981a provides for punitive awards based solely on an employer's state of mind is consistent with the 1991 Act's distinction between equitable and compensatory relief. Intent determines which remedies are open to a plaintiff here as well; compensatory awards are available only where the employer has engaged in "*intentional* discrimination." §1981a(a)(1) (emphasis added).

Moreover, § 1981a's focus on the employer's state of mind gives some effect to Congress' apparent intent to narrow the class of cases for which punitive awards are available to a subset of those involving intentional discrimination. The employer must act with "malice or with reckless indifference *to the [plaintiff's] federally protected rights*." §1981a(b)(1) (emphasis added). The terms "malice" or "reckless indifference" pertain to the employer's knowledge that it may be acting in violation of federal law, not its awareness that it is engaging in discrimination.

* * *

* * * Applying this standard in the context of § 1981a, an employer must at least discriminate in the face of a perceived risk that its actions will violate federal law to be liable in punitive damages.

There will be circumstances where intentional discrimination does not give rise to punitive damages liability under this standard. In some instances, the employer may simply be unaware of the relevant federal prohibition. There will be cases, moreover, in which the employer discriminates with the distinct belief that its discrimination is lawful. The underlying theory of discrimination may be novel or otherwise poorly recognized, or an employer may reasonably believe that its discrimination satisfies a bona fide occupational qualification defense or other statutory exception to liability. * * *

* * *

Egregious misconduct is often associated with the award of punitive damages, but the reprehensible character of the conduct is not generally considered apart from the requisite state of mind. Conduct warranting punitive awards has been characterized as "egregious," for example, because of the defendant's mental state. See Restatement (Second) of Torts § 908(2) (1979) ("Punitive damages may be awarded for conduct that is outrageous, because of the defendant's evil motive or his reckless indifference to the rights of others"). That conduct committed with the specified mental state may be characterized as egregious, however, is not to say that employers must engage in conduct with some independent, "egregious" quality before being subject to a punitive award.

* * *

B

The inquiry does not end with a showing of the requisite malice or reckless indifference on the part of certain individuals, however. The plaintiff must impute liability for punitive damages to respondent. * * *

* * *

The common law has long recognized that agency principles limit vicarious liability for punitive awards. See, e.g., G. Field, Law of Damages §§ 85-87 (1876). This is a principle, moreover, that this Court historically has endorsed. See, e.g., Lake Shore & Michigan Southern R. Co. v. Prentice, 147 U.S. 101, 114-115, 37 L. Ed. 97, 13 S. Ct. 261 (1893); The Amiable Nancy, 3. Wheat. 546, 558-559 (1818).

We have observed that, "in express terms, Congress has directed federal courts to interpret Title VII based on agency principles." Burlington Industries, Inc. v. Ellerth, 524 U.S. 742, 754, 141 L. Ed. 2d 633, 118 S. Ct. 2257 (1998); see also Meritor Savings Bank, FSB v. Vinson, 477 U.S. 57, 72, 91 L. Ed. 2d 49, 106 S. Ct. 2399 (1986) (noting that, in interpreting Title VII, "Congress wanted courts to look to agency principles for guidance"). Observing the limits on liability that these principles impose is especially important when interpreting the 1991 Act. In promulgating the Act, Congress conspicuously left intact the "limits of employer liability" established in *Meritor*. Faragher v. Boca Raton, 524 U.S. 775, 804, n. 4, 141 L. Ed. 2d 662, 118 S. Ct. 2275 (1998); see also Burlington Industries, Inc., 524 U.S. at 763-764 ("We are bound by our holding in Meritor that agency principles constrain the imposition of vicarious liability in cases of supervisory harassment").

The common law as codified in the Restatement (Second) of Agency (1957), provides a useful starting point for defining this general common law. See Burlington Industries. The Restatement of Agency places strict limits on the extent to which an agent's misconduct may be imputed to the principal for purposes of awarding punitive damages:

Punitive damages can properly be awarded against a master or other principal because of an act by an agent if, but only if:

    (a) the principal authorized the doing and the manner of the act, or

    (b) the agent was unfit and the principal was reckless in employing him, or

    (c) the agent was employed in a managerial capacity and was acting in the scope of employment, or

(d) the principal or a managerial agent of the principal ratified or approved the act.

Restatement (Second) of Agency, supra, § 217 C. See also Restatement (Second) of Torts § 909 (same).

The Restatement, for example, provides that the principal may be liable for punitive damages if it authorizes or ratifies the agent's tortious act, or if it acts recklessly in employing the malfeasing agent. The Restatement also contemplates liability for punitive awards where an employee serving in a "managerial capacity" committed the wrong while "acting in the scope of employment." Restatement (Second) of Agency, supra, § 217 C; see also Restatement (Second) of Torts, supra, § 909 (same). Unfortunately, no good definition of what constitutes a "managerial capacity" has been found," 2 J. Ghiardi & J. Kircher, Punitive Damages: Law and Practice § 24.05, at 14, and determining whether an employee meets this description requires a fact-intensive inquiry, id. § 24.05; 1 L. Schlueter & K. Redden, Punitive Damages, § 4.4(B)(2)(a), p. 182 (3d ed. 1995). "In making this determination, the court should review the type of authority that the employer has given to the employee, the amount of discretion that the employee has in what is done and how it is accomplished." Id. § 4.4(B)(2)(a), at 181. Suffice it to say here that the examples provided in the Restatement of Torts suggest that an employee must be "important," but perhaps need not be the employer's "top management, officers, or directors," to be acting "in a managerial capacity." Ibid.; see also 2 Ghiardi, supra, § 24.05, at 14; Restatement (Second) of Torts, § 909, at 468, Comment b and Illus. 3.

Additional questions arise from the meaning of the "scope of employment" requirement. The Restatement of Agency provides that even intentional torts are within the scope of an agent's employment if the conduct is "the kind [the employee] is employed to perform," "occurs substantially within the authorized time and space limits," and "is actuated, at least in part, by a purpose to serve the" employer. Restatement (Second) of Agency, supra, § 228(1), at 504. According to the Restatement, so long as these rules are satisfied, an employee may be said to act within the scope of employment even if the employee engages in acts "specifically forbidden" by the employer and uses "forbidden means of accomplishing results." Id. § 230, at 511, Comment b. On this view, even an employer who makes every effort to comply with Title VII would be held liable for the discriminatory acts of agents acting in a "managerial capacity."

Holding employers liable for punitive damages when they engage in good faith efforts to comply with Title VII, however, is in some tension with the very principles underlying common law limitations on vicarious liability for punitive damages — that it is "improper ordinarily to award punitive damages against one who himself is personally innocent and therefore liable only vicariously." Restatement (Second) of Torts, supra, § 909, at 468, Comment b. Where an employer has undertaken such good faith efforts at Title VII compliance, it demonstrates that it never acted in reckless disregard of federally protected rights.

Applying the Restatement of Agency's "scope of employment" rule in the Title VII punitive damages context, moreover, would reduce the incentive for employers to implement antidiscrimination programs. In fact, such a rule would likely exacerbate concerns among employers that §1981a's "malice" and "reckless indifference" standard penalizes those employers who educate themselves and their employees on Title VII's prohibitions. Dissuading employers from implementing programs or policies to prevent discrimination in the workplace is directly contrary to the purposes underlying Title VII. The statute's "primary objective" is "a prophylactic one," Albemarle Paper Co. v. Moody, 422 U.S. 405, 417, 45 L. Ed. 2d 280, 95 S. Ct. 2362 (1975); it aims, chiefly, "not to provide redress but to avoid harm." Faragher. With regard to sexual harassment, "for example, Title VII is designed to encourage the creation of antiharassment policies and effective grievance mechanisms." Burlington Industries. The purposes underlying Title VII are similarly advanced where employers are encouraged to adopt antidiscrimination policies and to educate their personnel on Title VII's prohibitions.

In light of the perverse incentives that the Restatement's "scope of employment" rules create, we are compelled to modify these principles to avoid undermining the objectives underlying Title VII. See generally Faragher (noting that Court must "adapt agency concepts to the practical objectives of Title VII"). Recognizing Title VII as an effort to promote prevention as well as remediation, and observing the very principles underlying the Restatements' strict limits on vicarious liability for punitive damages, we agree that, in the punitive damages context, an employer may not be vicariously liable for the discriminatory employment decisions of managerial agents where these decisions are contrary to the employer's good-faith efforts to comply with Title VII.). As the [en banc] dissent recognized, "giving punitive damages protection to employers who make good-faith efforts to prevent discrimination in the workplace accomplishes" Title VII's objective of "motivating employers to detect and deter Title VII violations."

We have concluded that an employer's conduct need not be independently "egregious" to satisfy §1981a's requirements for a punitive damages award, although evidence of egregious misconduct may be used to meet the plaintiff 's burden of proof. We leave for remand the question whether petitioner can identify facts sufficient to support an inference that the requisite mental state can be imputed to respondent. The parties have not yet had an opportunity to marshal the record evidence in support of their views on the application of agency principles in the instant case, and the en banc majority had no reason to resolve the issue because it concluded that petitioner had failed to demonstrate the requisite "egregious" misconduct. Although trial testimony established that Allen made the ultimate decision to promote Spangler while serving as petitioner's interim executive director, respondent's highest position, it remains to be seen whether petitioner can make a sufficient showing that Allen acted with malice or reckless indifference to petitioner's Title VII rights. Even if it could be established that Wheat effectively selected O'Donnell's replacement, moreover, several questions would remain, e.g., whether Wheat was serving in a "managerial capacity" and whether he behaved with malice or reckless indifference to petitioner's rights. It may also be necessary to determine whether the Association had been making good faith efforts to enforce an antidiscrimination policy. We leave these issues for resolution on remand.

For the foregoing reasons, the decision of the Court of Appeals is vacated, and the case is remanded for proceedings consistent with this opinion.

[The separate opinions of Chief Justice Rehnquist and Justices Thomas, Stevens, Souter, Ginsberg and Breyer are omitted. Justices Rehnquist and Thomas dissented from Part IIA of the majority opinion on the ground that "the two-tiered scheme of Title VII monetary liability implies that there is an egregiousness requirement that reserves punitive damages only for the worst cases of intentional discrimination" but concurred with the majority's discussion of vicarious liability in Part IIB.]

Justice STEVENS, with whom Justice SOUTER, Justice GINSBURG, and Justice BREYER join, concurring in part and dissenting in part.

* * *

* * * It is enough to say that Congress provided in the 1991 Act its own punitive damages standard that focuses solely on willful mental state, and it did not suggest that there is any class of willful violations that are exempt from exposure to punitive damages. Nor did it indicate that there is any point on the spectrum of deliberate or recklessly indifferent conduct that qualifies as "egregious." * * *

* * *

The absence of briefing or meaningful argument by the parties makes this Court's gratuitous decision to volunteer an opinion on this nonissue particularly ill advised. It is not this Court's practice to consider arguments - specifically, alternative defenses of the judgment under review -that were not presented in the brief in opposition to the petition for certiorari. * * *

* * *

[Justice Stevens felt that there was ample evidence in the record to support an award of punitive damages under the willful or reckless standard and accordingly dissented from the majority's refusal to remand for a trial on punitive damages.]

NOTES AND PROBLEMS FOR DISCUSSION

1. Does focusing the inquiry on the employer's state of mind mean that virtually every disparate treatment case with enough evidence to go to a jury will qualify for a punitive damage instruction? Speaking for the Court, Justice O'Connor stated that Congress intended to limit punitive damage awards to a "subset" of disparate treatment cases, but won't that "subset" include most such cases? Can there really be very many employers who, thirty-five years after the enactment of Title VII, will be "unaware of the relevant federal prohibition" or will discriminate in the belief that their conduct is lawful? Other than a good faith yet mistaken BFOQ defense, can you think of a case of intentional discrimination that would not merit consideration for punitive damages? In FERRILL v. THE PARKER GROUP, INC., 168 F.3d 468 (11th Cir. 1999), a telephone marketing firm made race-based job assignments to facilitate race-matched "get-out-the-vote" solicitations. African-American voters were called by black employees using a "black" script, while white voters were called by whites using a "white" script. The court held that although the discriminatory job assignments violated Title VII, the employer was not motivated by "racial animus" and thus acted without the requisite malice or reckless disregard of the plaintiff's federal rights to warrant an award of punitive damages. But won't the vast majority of disparate treatment cases involve unlawful "animus"? In *Kolstad*, the jury found that Allen and Wheat had denied the promotion to Ms. Kolstad because of her sex. Yet Justice O'Connor announced for the Court that on remand "it remains to be seen whether petitioner can make a sufficient showing that Allan [and/or Wheat] acted with malice or reckless indifference to petitioner's Title VII rights." What exactly does that mean? Is Justice O'Connor suggesting that Ms. Kolstad will need to present additional evidence to qualify for punitive damages?

Following *Kolstad*, most courts have found the presence of "malice" and/or "reckless indifference" in cases where managers responsible for setting or enforcing policy in the area of discrimination have either been responsible for discrimination or have been aware of it and have taken no corrective action. *See, e.g.*, Deters v. Equifax Credit Info. Services, Inc., 202 F.3d 1262, 1269 (10th Cir. 2000) (allowing punitive damages award because a reasonable jury could reasonably have concluded that the copany acated with malice or reckless indifference based on evidence from which it could have inferred not only that management did not respond to the plaintiff's complaints, but also minimized and disregarded them to protect the revenue producers in the operation).

Is constructive knowledge of unlawful discrimination sufficient to impose liability for punitive damages on a corporate employer? In OCHELTREE v. SCOLLON PRODUCTIONS, INC., 335 F.3d 325 (4th Cir. 2003) (*en banc*), cert. denied, 540 U.S. 1177, 124 S.Ct. 1411, 158 L.Ed.2d 77 (2004), the Fourth Circuit upheld a jury verdict for the plaintiff in a hostile environment sexual harassment case. Noting that the employer's sexual harassment policy did not require its supervisors to report employee complaints and that the plaintiff repeatedly had been rebuffed in her attempts to report the harassment to upper management, the court reasoned that the jury could have concluded that the company had constructive knowledge of the harassment and therefore was responsible for the plaintiff's compensatory damages on a negligence theory. But the same evidence was not sufficient to support the jury's punitive damagesaward.

> * * * To be liable in punitive damages, "an employer must at least discriminate in the face of a perceived risk that its actions will violate federal law" [quoting *Kolstad*]. There is not much to be said here. We have combed the record, and we find no evidence that would allow a jury to find that Scollon Productions knew, either directly or by imputation, that it might have been acting in violation of Ocheltree's "federally protected rights." As a result, the award of punitive damages must be set aside.

335 F.3d at 336. The record showed that Ms. Ocheltree repeatedly had tried to complain to the president and the senior vice president of the company, the only persons with formal management authority. Their offices were adjacent to the production area where all the harassment occurred. How can it be said that management officials who have turned a blind eye to complaints of unlawful conduct should not have known *of the risk* that they were acting in violation of federal law? Are not management's actions in *Ocheltree* exactly the kind of conduct that ought to result in punitive damages?

2.   As discussed in Chapter 2, Sec. B, *supra*, the Supreme Court ruled in *Burlington Industries* and *Faragher* that an employer in sexual harassment cases is vicariously liable for harassment by a supervisor that resulted in "a tangible employment action." In so doing, the *Faragher* Court noted that "there is nothing remarkable in the fact that claims against employers for discriminatory employment actions with tangible results, like hiring, firing, promotion, compensation, and work assignment, have resulted in employer liability once the discrimination was shown." *Kolstad* certainly seems to mean that the employer may not be liable for punitive damages for all discrimination by supervisory employees; the supervisor must have acted in a "managerial capacity." In *Kolstad*, Allen was the executive director of the association, and Wheat was the acting head of its Washington office. How could they not have been acting in a "managerial capacity"? *See* Deffenbaugh-Williams v. Wal-Mart Stores, Inc., 188 F.3d 278 (5th Cir. 1999) (a district manager who terminated the plaintiff because of an interracial relationship was in charge of jewelry departments in six stores and thus was high enough in the corporate hierarchy to qualify as a "managerial agent.").

3.   *Kolstad* also provides that an employer will not be liable for the discriminatory employment decisions of management-level employees where their acts are contrary to good faith efforts on the part of the employer to comply with Title VII. Despite Justice O'Connor's cautionary language for the Court in *Kolstad*, employers have had little success with this "good faith effort" defense. In LOWERY v. CIRCUIT CITY STORES, INC., 206 F.3d 431 (4th Cir. 2000), cert. denied, 531 U.S. 822, 121 S.Ct. 66, 148 L.Ed.2d 31 (2000), for example, the Fourth Circuit held that evidence that top corporate executives were racially biased and had ignored internal reports of discrimination would allow reasonable jury to infer that formal corporate anti-discrimination policy was a sham. *See also* Ogden v. Wax Works, Inc., 214 F.3d 999 (8th Cir. 2000) (mere existence of anti-sexual harassment policy and policy encouraging employees with complaints to contact the home office did not suffice, as a matter of law to satisfy good faith defense). Successful invocation of a "good faith effort" defense seems to depend largely on the court's assessment of the seriousness of employer's anti-discrimination efforts. *Compare* Swinton v. Potomac Corp., 270 F.3d 794, 810 (9th Cir. 2001), cert. denied, 535 U.S. 1018, 122 S.Ct. 1609, 152 L.Ed.2d 623 (2002) (inaction of the employee designated to receive complaints of discrimination is properly imputable to employer; adoption of an anti-harassment policies is insufficient, the employer also must implement them), *with* Hatley v. Hilton Hotels Corp., 308 F.3d 473 (5th Cir. 2002) (even though a manager acted in reckless indifference to rights of employees in ignoring complaints of sexual harassment, the employer can establish a "good faith effort" defense by showing that it had a well-publicized policy against sexual harassment, gave training on the subject to new employees, and established a grievance procedure for such complaints).

Failing to respond promptly and appropriately to complaints of sexual harassment, the same kind of failure that will expose the employer to liability under *Burlington Industries* and *Farragher* for co-employee harassment, also will expose the employer to punitive damages under *Kolstad*. *See, e.g.*, Blackmon v. Pinkerton Sec. & Investigative Serv., 182 F.3d 629 (8th Cir. 1999) (half-hearted responses to appellant's serious complaints of sexual harassment is not sufficient to overturn the jury's determination that the employer's actions warranted punitive damages). Should the employer's failure to make good faith efforts to avoid discrimination render it automatically liable for punitive damages? *Compare* Madison v. IBP, Inc., 257 F.3d 780 (8th Cir. 2001), vacated on other grounds, 536 U.S. 919, 122 S.Ct. 2583, 153 L.Ed.2d 773 (2002) (submission of punitive damages issue to the jury is appropriate where company's anti-discrimination policy and procedures were not followed by managers), *with* Hatley v. Hilton Hotels Corp., 308 F.3d 473 (5th Cir. 2002) (where the reponsible official did not take reasonable measures to correct or prevent harassment, the employer nevertheless may still escape punitive damages by demonstrating that it has a well-publicized policy against harassment, has provided training on the subject, and has a grievance mechanism for harassment complaints). Which of these rulings is more consistent with *Kolstad's* holding that the employer should be responsible for punitive damages where a manager has engaged in intentional discrimination? What if an employer takes steps to clean up its act *after* a charge of discrimination is filed? Is evidence of the employer's belated efforts admissible regarding the amount of punitive damages? In *Swinton, supra,* the Ninth Circuit, while holding that the district court had not abused its discretion in excluding evidence of the institution of an anti-harassment training program after the plaintiff had sued, ruled that district courts have discretion to admit evidence of remedial actions taken in response to post-complaint discovery of discrimination where offered to mitigate damages. Employers should be encouraged, the court explained, to take remedial measures and must be given the opportunity at the district court's discretion to present evidence of such measures, even if taken after a complaint was filed.

4. Should the award of punitive damages be contingent on an award of compensatory damages or back pay? *Compare* Cush-Crawford v. Adchem Corp., 271 F.3d 352 (2d Cir. 2001) (to the extent that requiring actual damages reflects apprehension about limitless damage awards where no concrete harm has occurred, that concern was eliminated by the statutory cap on damages; court expresses concern over "unseemliness" of denying punitive damages merely because "good fortune" or "unusual strength or resilience" on the part of the plaintiff meant that no harm was actually suffered), *with* Kerr-Segas v. Am. Airlines, 69 F.3d 1205 (1st Cir. 1995) (Title VII plaintiff must establish liability for compensatory or nominal damages to be eligible for punitive damages).

5. To what extent, if at all, should the amount of the punitive damage award in a Title VII case be influenced by the applicable statutory cap? In HENNESSY v. PENRIL DATACOMM NETWORKS, INC., 69 F.3d 1344 (7th Cir. 1995), the Seventh Circuit suggested a rule of proportionality:

> In fashioning new remedies under Title VII, Congress determined that a company the size of Penril, with more than 100 but less than 201 employees, should have to pay no more, in total compensatory (with back pay excluded) and punitive damages, than $100,000. It would seem logical, therefore, that the maximum permissible award against a company of Penril's size should be reserved for egregious cases. * * *

> In our case, the jury as we have seen, denied compensatory damages — pain and suffering, emotional distress, and that sort of thing — to Hennessy. The question then becomes whether 100 percent of the available damages to Hennessy in this case can be soaked up by a punitive damage award. We don't believe that it can. Although we believe, as we have noted, that the jury could have awarded punitive damages in this case, we do not think that the case is so egregious that an

award at 100 percent of what can legally be awarded against a company of Penril's size is appropriate.

69 F.3d at 1355-56. *But see* Luciano v. Olsten Corp., 110 F.3d 210, 221 (2d Cir. 1997) (the cap is not an endpoint of a scale according to which judges might recalibrate jury awards; "Only where an award would shock the judicial conscience and constitute a denial of justice * * * and thereby deny due process, should the court reduce an award of punitive damages below the appropriate cap.") The purpose of the statutory caps presumably is to shield employers from economically crippling awards. In light of that purpose, does the proportionality rule articulated in *Hennessy* make sense? The jury in a Title VII case cannot be informed of the caps. Doesn't that fact suggest that the determination of the amount of punitive damages was to be left to the jury uninfluenced by the caps?

6.   The Supreme Court has struggled for more than a decade with the constitutional limits on punitive damage awards. In PACIFIC MUTUAL LIFE INSURANCE CO. v. HASLIP, 499 U.S. 1, 111 S.Ct. 1032, 113 L.Ed.2d 1 (1991), while affirming a state court award of punitive damages far surpassing the compensatory damages and more than 200 times the plaintiff's actual out-of-pocket loss, the Court observed that "unlimited jury discretion * * * in the fixing of punitive damages may invite extreme results that jar one's constitutional sensibilities." In BMW OF NORTH AMERICA, INC. v. GORE, 517 U.S. 559, 116 S.Ct. 1589, 134 L.Ed.2d 809 (1996), for the first time, the Court invalidated a state court punitive damage assessment on constitutional grounds. The Due Process Clause, it held, bans the imposition of grossly excessive or arbitrary punishments on a tortfeasor. In *Gore*, an Alabama jury had awarded $4000 in compensatory damages and $4 million in punitive damages to the purchaser of a new car who, contrary to the dictates of state law, had not been informed that his vehicle had been repainted at the dealership. The Alabama Supreme Court had reduced the punitive award to $2 million, but the U.S. Supreme Court held that the punitive damage award was still "grossly excessive" and thus violated due process. In reviewing punitive damage awards, *Gore* instructed the courts to consider three factors: (1) the reprehensibility of the defendant's misconduct; (2) the disparity between the actual or potential harm suffered by plaintiff and the punitive award; and (3) the difference between the punitive damages awarded and the civil or criminal sanctions that could be imposed for comparable conduct.

The Court revisited this issue in STATE FARM MUTUAL INSURANCE CO. v. CAMPBELL, 538 U.S. 408, 123 S.Ct. 1513, 155 L.Ed.2d 585 (2003), a case where the plaintiff's automobile liability insurer unreasonably refused to settle a claim, thereby exposing the insured to a damage award far in excess of the policy limits. Although State Farm eventually paid the entire judgment, including the amounts in excess of the policy limits, the insured filed suit alleging bad faith, fraud, and intentional infliction of emotional distress. A Utah jury awarded the plaintiffs $2.6 million in compensatory damages and $145 million in punitive damages, which the trial court reduced to $1 million and $25 million, respectively. The Utah Supreme Court reinstated the $145 million punitive damages award. Applying the three guideposts from *Gore*, the U.S Supreme Court concluded that the punitive damage award was "neither reasonable nor proportionate to the wrong committed" and thus "was an irrational and arbitrary deprivation of the property of the defendant." While acknowledging that the defendant's handling of its insured's claim "merits no praise" and, indeed, justified an award of punitive damages, the Court concluded that "a more modest punishment for this reprehensible conduct could have satisfied the State's legitimate objectives [deterrence and punishment] and the Utah courts should have gone no further." With respect to the relationship between compensatory and punitive damages, the Court again declined "to impose a bright-line ratio which a punitive damages award cannot exceed," but cautioned that "in practice few awards exceeding a single-digit ratio between punitive and compensatory damages, to a significant degree, will satisfy due process." How reprehensible the defendant's conduct will be deemed to be invariably is in the eye of the beholder (i.e., the jury), but an objective comparison of compensatory and punitive damages is readily determinable and thus easy to apply. Despite the Court's protestations in this case regarding "bright lines," it obviously comes very close to establishing one. The Court advised that "[s]ingle-digit multipliers are more likely to comport with due process, while still achieving the State's goals of deterrence and retribution, than awards with ratios in the range of 500 to 1, or in this case, of 145 to 1."

Because of the damage caps on compensatory and punitive damages applicable to claims brought under both Title VII and the ADA and the limits on treble damages incorporated in the ADEA, it is unlikely that employment discrimination actions filed under these statutes will result in the kind of breathtaking discrepancies between compensatory damages (including back pay) and punitive damages that have attracted the Supreme Court's ire. *See* Lampley v. Onyx Acceptance Corp., 340 F.3d 478 (7th Cir. 2003), cert. denied, 540 U.S. 1182, 124 S.Ct. 1421, 158 L.Ed.2d 85 (2004) (court normally will not disturb award of punitive damages at or near statutory cap). Large punitive damage awards are nonetheless possible where state law-based causes of action are joined with federal statutory claims. For example, in DAKA, INC. v. McCRAE, 839 A.2d 682 (D.C. Ct. App. 2003), a sexual harassment case filed under the District of Columbia Human Rights Act, a jury awarded less than $200,000 in compensatory damages, but $4.8 million in punitive damages. In setting aside the punitive damage award the court explained that: "The 26:1 ratio here exceeds a 'single-digit' ratio 'significantly'; and it is far beyond both the 4:1 ratio the Court had said in [BMW v. Gore] 'might be close to the line of constitutional impropriety' and the traditional statutory double, treble, or quadruple damages which the Court found 'instructive' as a measure in *State Farm*." As noted in Notes 4 and 5, *supra*, a number of federal courts have upheld awards of punitive damages in employment cases in the absence of compensatory damages.

Do *Gore* and *Campbell* mean that a court that has submitted the punitive damage issue to the jury under *Kolstad* must undertake an examination of any award for a due process violation? In ROSS v. KANSAS CITY POWER & LIGHT CO., 293 F.3d 1041 (8th Cir. 2002), the court of appeals reduced a $750,000 award to $60,000 because of the discrepancy between compensatory and punitive damages.

   * * * KCPLC's reprehensibility, while enough for liability, was not enough for a punitive damages award which totaled a ratio 125:1 over the compensatory award. * * * While the courts should not employ a mechanical mathematical approach in determining the reasonableness of punitive damages awards, we note that the district court's formula still results in a 20:1 ratio with the compensatory damages award. From our de novo review of the record, this is still too high for the conduct which occurred in this case. Thus, while we agree with the district

court that a $750,000 award violated due process, we further reduce the punitive damages award from $120,000 to $60,000, resulting in a 10:1 ratio.

293 F.3d at 1049. What if the punitive damage award is within the statutory cap, but nevertheless exceeds compensatory damage by more than the 10:1 ratio? In LUST v. SEALY, INC., 383 F.3d 580 (7th Cir. 2004), the court ruled that an award within the cap is per se constitutional.

> * * * When Congress sets a limit, and a low one, on the total amount of damages that may be awarded, the ratio of punitive to compensatory damages in a particular award ceases to be an issue of constitutional dignity. * * *

> The purpose of placing a constitutional ceiling on punitive damages is to protect defendants against outlandish awards, awards that are not only irrational in themselves because so out of whack with any plausible conception of the social function of punitive damages but potentially catastrophic for the defendants subjected to them and, in prospect a means of coercing settlement. That purpose falls out of the picture when the legislature has placed a tight cap on the total, including punitive, damages and the courts honor the cap.

383 F.3d at 590-91.

4. THE TAX CONSEQUENCES OF MONETARY RELIEF

The Internal Revenue Code defines gross income as "all income from whatever source derived." 26 U.S.C. §61(a). Section 104(a) of the Code formerly provided that gross income did not include amounts received "on account of personal injuries or sickness." 26 U.S.C. §104(a). The Code did not define "personal injury," which led to substantial confusion concerning the tax consequences of monetary awards in employment discrimination cases. Prior to the 1991 Act, the Supreme Court held in UNITED STATES v. BURKE, 504 U.S. 229, 112 S.Ct. 1867, 119 L.Ed.2d 34 (1992), that the amount received in settlement of a Title VII suit was to be considered a recovery for lost wages and not recompense "for any of the other traditional harms associated with personal injury, such as pain and suffering, emotional distress, harm to reputation, or other consequential damages." Such relief was not "on account" of a personal injury within the meaning of §104(a) and was thus included in gross income tax purposes.

When compensatory damages for employment discrimination claims became available, it generally was assumed that such awards would be treated the same as recoveries in tort cases for pain and suffering, i.e., not included in gross income for tax purposes. Congress thought differently and amended §104(a) of the Internal Revenue Code to provide that gross income does not include "(2) the amount of any damages (other than punitive damages) received (whether by suit or agreement and whether as lump sums or as periodic payments) on account of personal physical injuries or physical sickness." Section 104(a) also espressly excludes "emotional distress" from the meaning of "physical" injury or sickness. The legislative history of the amendments makes clear Congress' intent to treat all damages from employment discrimination claims as taxable income, except in the rare case where a physical injury is involved. Litigants may not avoid §104(a) by a settlement which characterizes amounts paid to the plaintiff as "on account of" physical injuries unless such characterization is supported by the underlying claim. Vincent v. C.I.R., 2005 WL 1022953 (T.C. 2005).

Backpay or front pay awards are certainly taxable income, but are they "wages" subject to employer witholding? That seems to depend on the nature of the employment relationship that led to the lawsuit. The Internal Revenue Code provides that "every employer making payments of wages shall deduct and withhold upon such wages a tax determined in accordance with tables or computational procedures prescribed by the Secretary." 26 U.S.C. §3402(a)(1). The Code defines "wages" broadly as "all remuneration for employment" unless specifically exempted. 26 U.S.C. §3121(a). In NEWHOUSE v. McCORMICK & CO., INC., 157 F.3d 582 (8th Cir. 1998), a plaintiff who had been denied employment because of his age was awarded back pay and front pay in his ADEA suit. Following entry of final judgment, McCormick tendered the plaintiff a check representing the back pay and front pay awards less amounts withheld to satisfy payroll withholding requirements for state and federal taxes. The plaintiff refused the tender and the employer moved under Rule 65(b)(5) of the Federal Rules of Civil Procedure for relief from judgment on grounds that it had tendered full payment. The district court denied the motion, McCormick appealed, and the Eighth Circuit concluded that in the absence of a current or previous employment relationship, an award of back pay or front pay simply did not constitute "wages" subject to payroll taxes within the meaning of the IRS Code.

> In our view, Newhouse's back pay award does not represent wages in the context presented here because Newhouse was not an employee for withholding purposes within the meaning of the Tax Code at the time of the discrimination resulting in the judgment, and the judgment did not arise out of any previous employment relationship. While the definitions of wages and employment are to be broadly construed, we hesitate to stretch them to cover a situation that never involved either wages or employment. Any such redefinition of those terms is a job for the Congress, not the federal courts. The Tax Code requires withholding for wages arising out of an employment relationship, not for a judgment representing wages upon loss of a prospective employment relationship.

157 F.3d at 587. When an award of back or front pay is subject to withholding taxes, that money must be taxed at the rate then applicable, not the rate applicable at the time the wages should have been paid. United States v. Cleveland Indian Baseball Co., 532 U.S. 200, 121 S.Ct. 1433, 149 L.Ed.2d 401 (2001).

The payment of a lump-sum award representing years of lost wages in addition to compensatory damages may throw the plaintiff into a higher tax bracket than he would have been in absent discrimination. This will result in a larger share of the award going to the government than would have been the case absent the discrimination. Is such a tax penalty consistent with the "make whole" philosophy of the Act? The Tenth Circuit has upheld a "tax component" of the back pay award to compensate plaintiffs for their additional tax liability as a result of receiving over seventeen years of back pay in one lump sum. Sears v. Atchison, Topeka & Santa Fe Ry., Co., 749 F.2d 1451, 1456 (10th Cir. 1984), cert. denied, 471 U.S. 1099, 105 S.Ct. 2322, 85 L.Ed.2d 840 (1985). Several state courts have held that prevailing plaintiffs in employment discrimination actions are entitled to compensation for the negative tax consequences of lump-sum awards. *See, e.g,* Ferrante v. Sciaretta, 839 A.2d 993 (N.J. Super. Ct. Law Div. 2003) (state law discrimination claim only); Blaney v.

International Ass'n Machinists and Aerospace Workers, 151 Wn.2d 203, 87 P.3d 757 (2004) (state law and Title VII claims).

Plaintiffs in employment discrimination cases often retain counsel with contingent fee agreements under which the attorney is contractually entitled to a percentage of the award. Such agreements have become much more common after passage of the 1991 Civil Rights Act now that compensatory and punitive damages are available in intentional discrimination cases. The Internal Revenue Service takes the position that a contingent fee contract is an assignment of income to a creditor and is thus included in gross income. Under this view, a successful plaintiff must pay income taxes on the entire award of damages, including that portion which must be paid to the attorney. The attorney, of course, also is taxed on his income from contingent fee contracts. The Supreme Court has agreed with the IRS. In COMMISSIONER v. BANKS, 543 U.S. 426, 125 S.Ct. 826, 160 L.Ed.2d 859 (2005), the Court agreed with the Service that a contingent fee agreement is an anticipatory assignment of a portion of the client's income and thus is taxable to the client. "The attorney is an agent who is duty bound to act only in the interests of the principal, and so it is appropriate to treat the full amount of the recovery as income to the principal." The Court further stated that fees paid to an attorney "may be deductible, but absent some other provision of law it is not excludable from the principal's gross income." While *Banks* was pending, Congress enacted the American Jobs Creation Act of 2004, Pub. L. No. 108-357, 118 Stat. 1418, which includes a provision amending Section 62 of the IRS code (defining "adjusted gross income") to allow a taxpayer to deduct from gross income "attorney fees and court costs paid by, or on behalf of, the taxpayer in connection with any action involving a claim of unlawful discrimination." The Act defines "unlawful discrimination" to include all federal, state and local employment discrimination laws. 118 Stat. 1546-47. The taxpayers in *Banks* could not benefit from the statute because it was not retroactive. The Court therein noted that "[h]ad the Act been in force for the transactions now under review, these cases likely would not have arisen."

Title VII, the ADEA, the ADA and most state anti-discrimination statutes contain fee shifting provisions authorizing courts to award reasonable attorney fees to prevailing counsel. See Chapter 7, Section C, *infra*. Awards under fee-shifting provisions are separate from monetary awards to plaintiffs and plaintiffs have little, if any, control over the amounts awarded counsel. The *Banks* Court emphasized that the only arrangements before it were contingent fee agreements and that it was not addressing the tax consequences, if any, of awards made under fee-shifting statutes. Both the Ninth Circuit and the Tax Court, however, have held that fees awarded to attorneys under fee shifting statutes are included in the client's gross income. See Sinyard v. Comm'r, 268 F.3d 756 (9th Cir. 2001), cert. denied, 536 U.S. 904, 122 S.Ct. 2357, 153 L.Ed.2d 179 (2002); Vincent v. C.I.R., 2005 WL 1022953 (T.C. 2005).

SECTION B. INJUNCTIVE RELIEF

1. "RIGHTFUL PLACE" RELIEF

Franks v. Bowman Transportation Co., Inc.

Supreme Court of the United States, 1976.
424 U.S. 747, 96 S.Ct. 1251, 47 L.Ed.2d 444.

MR. JUSTICE BRENNAN delivered the opinion of the Court.

This case presents the question whether identifiable applicants who were denied employment because of race after the effective date and in violation of Title VII may be awarded seniority status retroactive to the dates of their employment applications.

Petitioner Franks brought this class action in the United States District Court for the Northern District of Georgia against his former employer, respondent Bowman Transportation Co., and his unions, the International Union of District 50, Allied and Technical Workers of the United States and Canada, and its local, No. 13600, alleging various racially discriminatory employment practices in violation of Title VII. Petitioner Lee intervened on behalf of himself and others similarly situated alleging racially discriminatory hiring and discharge policies limited to Bowman's employment of over-the-road (OTR) truck drivers. Following trial, the District Court found that Bowman had engaged in a pattern of racial discrimination in various company policies, including the hiring, transfer, and discharge of employees, and found further that the discriminatory practices were perpetrated in Bowman's collective-bargaining agreement with the unions. The District Court certified the action as a proper class action under Fed.R.Civ.P. 23(b)(2), and of import to the issues before this Court, found that petitioner Lee represented all black applicants who sought to be hired or to transfer to OTR driving positions prior to January 1, 1972. In its final order and decree, the District Court subdivided the class represented by petitioner Lee into a class of black nonemployee applicants for OTR positions prior to January 1, 1972 (class 3), and a class of black employees who applied for transfer to OTR positions prior to the same date (class 4).

In its final judgment entered July 14, 1972, the District Court permanently enjoined the respondents from perpetuating the discriminatory practices found to exist, and, in regard to the black applicants for OTR positions, ordered Bowman to notify the members of both subclasses within 30 days of their right to priority consideration for such jobs. The District Court declined, however, to grant to the unnamed members of classes 3 and 4 any other specific relief sought, which included an award of backpay and seniority status retroactive to the date of individual application for an OTR position.

On petitioners' appeal to the Court of Appeals for the Fifth Circuit, raising for the most part claimed inadequacy of the relief ordered respecting unnamed members of the various subclasses involved, the Court of Appeals affirmed in part, reversed in part, and vacated in part. The Court of Appeals held that the District Court had exercised its discretion under an erroneous view of law insofar as it failed to award backpay to the unnamed class members of both classes 3 and 4, and vacated the judgment in that respect. The judgment was reversed insofar as it failed to award any seniority remedy to the members of class 4 who after the judgment of the District Court sought and obtained priority consideration for transfer to OTR positions.[3] As respects unnamed members of class 3 — nonemployee black applicants who applied for and were denied OTR positions prior to January 1, 1972 — the Court of Appeals affirmed the District Court's denial of any form of seniority relief. Only this last aspect of the Court of Appeals' judgment is before us for review under our grant of the petition for certiorari.

I

[The named plaintiffs included only one representative of class 3 (Lee). After being discriminatorily refused employment, Lee was hired by Bowman, but then was discharged before trial for cause. The district court awarded him back pay for the intervening period of discrimination. The defendant's argument that the class claim for seniority relief was moot, because the sole class representative's claim had become moot, was rejected by the Supreme Court.]

* * *

The unnamed members of the class are entitled to the relief already afforded Lee, hiring and back pay, and thus to that extent have such a personal stake in the outcome of the controversy whether they are also entitled to seniority relief as to assure that concrete adverseness which sharpens the presentation of issues upon which the court so largely depends for illumination of difficult questions. Given a properly certified class action, * * * mootness turns on whether, in the specific circumstances of the given case at the time it is before this Court, an adversary relationship sufficient to fulfill this function exists." * * *

* * *

[The Court also held that §703(h) of Title VII, which recognizes the legality of bona fide seniority and merit systems, does not bar seniority relief to persons who were not seeking modification or elimination of the existing seniority system, but only an award of the seniority status they would have individually enjoyed under the present system but for the illegal discriminatory refusal to hire.]

* * *

II

In affirming the District Court's denial of seniority relief to the class 3 group of discriminatees, the Court of Appeals held that the relief was barred by §703(h) of Title VII. We disagree. Section 703(h) provides in pertinent part:

> "Notwithstanding any other provision of this title, it shall not be an unlawful employment practice for an employer to apply different standards of compensation, or different terms, conditions, or privileges of employment pursuant to a bona fide seniority or merit system * * * provided that such

---

[3]In conjunction with its directions to the District Court regarding seniority relief for the members of other subclasses not involved in the issues presently confronting this Court, the Court of Appeals directed that class 4 members who transferred to OTR positions under the District Court's decree should be allowed to carry over all accumulated company seniority for all purposes in the OTR department.

differences are not the result of an intention to discriminate because of race, color, religion, sex, or national origin * * *.'"

The Court of Appeals reasoned that a discriminatory refusal to hire "does not affect the bona fides of the seniority system. Thus, the differences in the benefits and conditions of employment which a seniority system accords to older and newer employees is protected [by §703(h)] as 'not an unlawful employment practice.'" Significantly, neither Bowman nor the unions undertake to defend the Court of Appeals' judgment on that ground. It is clearly erroneous.

The black applicants for OTR positions composing class 3 are limited to those whose applications were put in evidence at the trial.[10] The underlying legal wrong affecting them is not the alleged operation of a racially discriminatory seniority system but of a racially discriminatory hiring system. Petitioners do not ask for modification or elimination of the existing seniority system, but only an award of the seniority status they would have individually enjoyed under the present system but for the illegal discriminatory refusal to hire. It is this context that must shape our determination as to the meaning and effect of §703(h).

* * *

We * * * hold that the Court of Appeals erred in concluding that, as a matter of law, §703(h) barred the award of seniority relief to the unnamed class 3 members.

III

There remains the question whether an award of seniority relief is appropriate under the remedial provisions of Title VII, specifically, §706(g).

* * *

Seniority standing in employment with respondent Bowman, computed from the departmental date of hire, determines the order of layoff and recall of employees. Further, job assignments for OTR drivers are posted for competitive bidding and seniority is used to determine the highest bidder. As OTR drivers are paid on a per-mile basis, earnings are therefore to some extent a function of seniority. Additionally, seniority computed from the company date of hire determines the length of an employee's vacation and pension benefits. Obviously merely to require Bowman to hire the class 3 victim of discrimination falls far short of a "make whole" remedy.[27] A concomitant award of the seniority credit he presumptively would have earned but for

---

[10]By its terms, the judgment of the District Court runs to all black applicants for OTR positions prior to January 1, 1972, and is not qualified by a limitation that the discriminatory refusal to hire must have taken place after the effective date of the Act. However, only post-Act victims of racial discrimination are members of class 3. Title VII's prohibition on racial discrimination in hiring became effective on July 2, 1965, one year after the date of its enactment. Petitioners sought relief in this case for identifiable applicants for OTR positions "whose applications were put in evidence at the trial." There were 206 unhired black applicants prior to January 1, 1972, whose written applications are summarized in the record and none of the applications relates to years prior to 1970.

[27]Further, at least in regard to "benefit"-type seniority such as length of vacation leave and pension benefits in the instant case, any general bar to the award of retroactive seniority for victims of illegal hiring discrimination serves to undermine the mutually reinforcing effect of the dual purposes of Title VII; it reduces the restitution required of an employer at such time as he is called upon to account for his discriminatory actions perpetrated in violation of the law. See Albemarle Paper Co. v. Moody, 422 U.S. 405, 417-418 (1975).

the wrongful treatment would also seem necessary in the absence of justification for denying that relief. Without an award of seniority dating from the time when he was discriminatorily refused employment, an individual who applies for and obtains employment as an OTR driver pursuant to the District Court's order will never obtain his rightful place in the hierarchy of seniority according to which these various employment benefits are distributed. He will perpetually remain subordinate to persons who, but for the illegal discrimination, would have been in respect to entitlement to these benefits his inferiors.[28]

The Court of Appeals apparently followed this reasoning in holding that the District Court erred in not granting seniority relief to class 4 Bowman employees who were discriminatorily refused transfer to OTR positions. Yet the class 3 discriminatees in the absence of a comparable seniority award would also remain subordinated in the seniority system to the class 4 discriminatees. The distinction plainly finds no support anywhere in Title VII or its legislative history. Settled law dealing with the related "twin" areas of discriminatory hiring and discharges violative of the National Labor Relations Act provides a persuasive analogy. "[I]t would indeed be surprising if Congress gave a remedy for the one which it denied for the other." Phelps Dodge Corp. v. NLRB, 313 U.S. 177, 187, 61 S.Ct. 845, 849, 85 L.Ed. 1271, 1279 (1941). For courts to differentiate without justification between the classes of discriminatees "would be a differentiation not only without substance but in defiance of that against which the prohibition of discrimination is directed." Id., at 188.

Similarly, decisions construing the remedial section of the National Labor Relations Act, §10(c) — the model for §706(g), *Albemarle Paper*,[29] — make clear that remedies constituting authorized "affirmative action" include an award of seniority status, for the thrust of "affirmative action" redressing the wrong incurred by an unfair labor practice is to make "the employees whole, and thus restor[e] the economic status quo that would have obtained but for the company's wrongful [act]." NLRB v. Rutter-Rex Mfg. Co., 396 U.S. 258, 263, 90 S.Ct. 417, 420, 24 L.Ed.2d 405, 411 (1969). The task of the NLRB in applying §10(c) is "to take measures designed to recreate the conditions and relationships that would have been had there been no unfair labor practice." Carpenters v. NLRB, 365 U.S. 651, 657, 81 S.Ct. 875, 879, 6 L.Ed.2d 1, 5 (1961) (Harlan, J., concurring). And the NLRB has often required that the hiring of employees who have been discriminatorily refused employment be accompanied by an

---

[28]Accordingly, it is clear that the seniority remedy which petitioners seek does not concern only the "make-whole" purposes of Title VII. The dissent errs in treating the issue of seniority relief as implicating only the "make whole" objective of Title VII and in stating that "Title VII's 'primary objective' of eradicating discrimination is not served at all * * *." Nothing could be further from reality — the issue of seniority relief cuts to the very heart of Title VII's primary objective of eradicating present and future discrimination in a way that backpay, for example, can never do.

[29]To the extent that there is a difference in the wording of the respective provisions, §706(g) grants, if anything, broader discretionary powers than those granted the National Labor Relations Board. Section 10(c) of the NLRA authorizes "such affirmative action including reinstatement of employees with or without back pay, as will effectuate the policies of this subchapter," whereas §706(g) * * * authorizes "such affirmative action as may be appropriate, which may include, *but is not limited to,* reinstatement *or hiring* of employees, with or without back pay * * *, *or any other equitable relief as the court deems appropriate.*" 42 U.S.C. §2000e-5(g) (1970 ed., Supp. IV) (emphasis added).

award of seniority equivalent to that which they would have enjoyed but for the illegal conduct. See, e.g., In re Phelps Dodge Corp., 19 N.L.R.B. 547, 600, and n. 39, 603-604 (1940), modified on other grounds, 313 U.S. 177, 61 S.Ct. 845, 85 L.Ed. 1271 (1941) (ordering persons discriminatorily refused employment hired "without prejudice to their seniority or other rights and privileges"); In re Nevada Consolidated Copper Corp., 26 N.L.R.B. 1182, 1235 (1940), enforced, 316 U.S. 105, 62 S.Ct. 960, 86 L.Ed. 1305 (1942) (ordering persons discriminatorily refused employment hired with "any seniority or other rights and privileges they would have acquired, had the respondent not unlawfully discriminated against them"). Plainly the "affirmative action" injunction of §706(g) has no lesser reach in the district courts. "Where racial discrimination is concerned, 'the [district] court has not merely the power but the duty to render a decree which will so far as possible eliminate the discriminatory effects of the past as well as bar like discrimination in the future.'" *Albemarle Paper.*

IV

We are not to be understood as holding that an award of seniority status is requisite in all circumstances. The fashioning of appropriate remedies invokes the sound equitable discretion of the district courts. Respondent Bowman attempts to justify the District Court's denial of seniority relief for petitioners as an exercise of equitable discretion, but the record is its own refutation of the argument.

Albemarle Paper made clear that discretion imports not the court's "inclination, but * * * its judgment; and its judgment is to be guided by sound legal principles." Discretion is vested not for purposes of "limit[ing] appellate review of trial courts, or * * * invit[ing] inconsis-tency and caprice," but rather to allow the most complete achievement of the objectives of Title VII that is attainable under the facts and circumstances of the specific case. Accordingly, the District Court's denial of any form of seniority remedy must be reviewed in terms of its effect on the attainment of the Act's objectives under the circumstances presented by this record. No less than with the denial of the remedy of backpay, the denial of seniority relief to victims of illegal racial discrimination in hiring is permissible "only for reasons which, if applied generally, would not frustrate the central statutory purposes of eradicating discrimination throughout the economy and making persons whole for injuries suffered through past discrimination." Ibid.

The District Court stated two reasons for its denial of seniority relief for the unnamed class members.[30] The first was that those individuals had not filed administrative charges under the provisions of Title VII with the Equal Employment Opportunity Commission and therefore class relief of this sort was not appropriate. We rejected this justification for denial of class-based relief in the context of backpay awards in *Albemarle Paper*, and for the same reasons reject it here. This justification for denying class-based relief in Title VII suits has been unanimously rejected by the courts of appeals, and Congress ratified that construction by the 1972 amendments.

---

[30]Since the Court of Appeals concluded that an award of retroactive seniority to the unnamed members of class 3 was barred by §703(h), a conclusion which we today reject, the court did not address specifically the District Court's stated reasons for refusing the relief. The Court of Appeals also stated, however, that the District Court did not abuse its discretion in refusing such relief, and we may therefore appropriately review the validity of the District Court's reasons.

The second reason stated by the District Court was that such claims "presuppose a vacancy, qualification, and performance by every member. There is no evidence on which to base these multiple conclusions." The Court of Appeals rejected this reason insofar as it was the basis of the District Court's denial of backpay, and of its denial of retroactive seniority relief to the unnamed members of class 4. We hold that it is also an improper reason for denying seniority relief to the unnamed members of class 3.

We read the District Court's reference to the lack of evidence regarding a "vacancy, qualification, and performance" for every individual member of the class as an expression of concern that some of the unnamed class members (unhired black applicants whose employment applications were summarized in the record) may not in fact have been actual victims of racial discrimination. That factor will become material however only when those persons reapply for OTR positions pursuant to the hiring relief ordered by the District Court. Generalizations concerning such individually applicable evidence cannot serve as a justification for the denial of relief to the entire class. Rather, at such time as individual class members seek positions as OTR drivers, positions for which they are presumptively entitled to priority hiring consideration under the District Court's order,[31] evidence that particular individuals were not in fact victims of racial discrimination will be material. But petitioners here have carried their burden of demonstrating the existence of a discriminatory hiring pattern and practice by the respondents and, therefore, the burden will be upon respondents to prove that individuals who reapply were not in fact victims of previous hiring discrimination. Only if this burden is met may retroactive seniority — if otherwise determined to be an appropriate form of relief under the circumstances of the particular case — be denied individual class members.

Respondent Bowman raises an alternative theory of justification. Bowman argues that an award of retroactive seniority to the class of discriminatees will conflict with the economic interests of other Bowman employees. Accordingly, it is argued, the District Court acted within its discretion in denying this form of relief as an attempt to accommodate the competing interests of the various groups of employees.[33]

We reject this argument for two reasons. First, the District Court made no mention of such considerations in its order denying the seniority relief. As we noted in *Albemarle Paper*, if the district court declines, due to the peculiar circumstances of the particular case, to award relief generally appropriate under Title VII, "[i]t is necessary . . . that . . . it carefully articulate its reasons" for so doing. Second, and more fundamentally, it is apparent that denial of seniority relief to identifiable victims of racial discrimination on the sole ground that such relief diminishes the expectations of other, arguably innocent, employees would if applied generally frustrate the central

---

[31] The District Court order is silent as to whether applicants for OTR positions who were previously discriminatorily refused employment must be presently qualified for those positions in order to be eligible for priority hiring under that order. The Court of Appeals, however, made it plain that they must be. We agree.

[33] Even by its terms, this argument could apply only to the award of retroactive seniority for purposes of "competitive status" benefits. It has no application to a retroactive award for purposes of "benefit" seniority — extent of vacation leave and pension benefits. Indeed, the decision concerning the propriety of this latter type of seniority relief is analogous, if not identical, to the decision concerning an award of backpay to an individual discriminatee hired pursuant to an order redressing previous employment discrimination.

"make whole" objective of Title VII. These conflicting interests of other employees will, of course, always be present in instances where some scarce employment benefit is distributed among employees on the basis of their status in the seniority hierarchy. But, as we have said, there is nothing in the language of Title VII, or in its legislative history, to show that Congress intended generally to bar this form of relief to victims of illegal discrimination, and the experience under its remedial model in the National Labor Relations Act points to the contrary.[34] Accordingly, we find untenable the conclusion that this form of relief may be denied merely because the interests of other employees may thereby be affected. "If relief under Title VII can be denied merely because the majority group of employees, who have not suffered discrimination, will be unhappy about it, there will be little hope of correcting the wrongs to which the Act is directed." United States v. Bethlehem Steel Corp., 446 F.2d 652, 663 (C.A. 2 1971).

With reference to the problems of fairness or equity respecting the conflicting interests of the various groups of employees, the relief which petitioners seek is only seniority status retroactive to the date of individual application, rather than some form of arguably more complete relief.[36] No claim is asserted that nondiscriminatee

---

[34]With all respect, the dissent does not adequately treat with and fails to distinguish the standard practice of the National Labor Relations Board granting retroactive seniority relief under the National Labor Relations Act to persons discriminatorily discharged or refused employment in violation of the Act. The Court in Phelps Dodge Corp. v. NLRB, 313 U.S. 177, 196, 61 S.Ct. 845, 853, 85 L.Ed. 1271, 1284 (1941), of course, made reference to "restricted judicial review" as that case arose in the context of review of the policy determinations of an independent administrative agency, which are traditionally accorded a wide-ranging discretion under accepted principles of judicial review. "Because the relation of remedy to policy is peculiarly a matter for administrative competence, courts must not enter the allowable area of the Board's discretion." Id., at 194.. As we made clear in *Albemarle Paper*, however, the pertinent point is that in utilizing the NLRA as the remedial model for Title VII, reference must be made to actual operation and experience as it has evolved in administrating the Act. E.g., "We may assume that Congress was aware that the Board, since its inception, has awarded backpay as a matter of course." 422 U.S., at 419-420. "[T]he Board has from its inception pursued a practically uniform policy with respect to these orders requiring affirmative action." Id., at 2373 n. 12. The dissent has cited no case, and our research discloses none, wherein the Board has ordered hiring relief and yet withheld the remedy of retroactive seniority status. Indeed, the Court of Appeals for the First Circuit has noted that a Board order requiring hiring relief "without prejudice to * * * seniority and other rights and privileges" is "language * * * in the standard form which has long been in use by the Board." NLRB v. Draper Corp., 159 F.2d 294, 296-297, and n. 1 (1947). The Board routinely awards both back pay and retroactive seniority in hiring discrimination cases. See Edwards & Zaretsky, Preferential Remedies for Employment Discrimination, 74 Mich.L.Rev. 1, 45 n. 224 (1975) (a "common remedy"). This also is a "presumption" in favor of this form of seniority relief. If victims of racial discrimination are under Title VII to be treated differently and awarded less protection than victims of unfair labor practice discrimination under the NLRA, some persuasive justification for such disparate treatment should appear. That no justification exists doubtless explains the position of every union participant in the proceedings before the Court in the instant case arguing for the conclusion we have reached.

[36]Another countervailing factor in assessing the expected impact on the interests of other employees actually occasioned by an award of the seniority relief sought is that it is not probable in instances of class-based relief that all of the victims of the past racial discrimination in hiring will actually apply for and obtain the prerequisite hiring relief. Indeed, in the instant case, there appear in the record the rejected applications of 166 black applicants who claimed at the time of application to have had the necessary job qualifications. However, the Court was informed at oral argument that only a small number of those individuals have to this date actually been hired

employees holding OTR positions they would not have obtained but for the illegal discrimination should be deprived of the seniority status they have earned. It is therefore clear that even if the seniority relief petitioners seek is awarded, most if not all discriminatees who actually obtain OTR jobs under the court order will not truly be restored to the actual seniority that would have existed in the absence of the illegal discrimination. Rather, most discriminatees even under an award of retroactive seniority status will still remain subordinated in the hierarchy to a position inferior to that of a greater total number of employees than would have been the case in the absence of discrimination. Therefore, the relief which petitioners seek, while a more complete form of relief than that which the District Court accorded, in no sense constitutes "complete relief."[37] Rather, the burden of the past discrimination in hiring is with respect to competitive status benefits divided among discriminatee and nondiscriminatee employees under the form of relief sought. The dissent criticizes the Court's result as not sufficiently cognizant that it will "directly implicate the rights and expectations of perfectly innocent employees." We are of the view, however, that the result which we reach today — which, standing alone,[38] establishes that a sharing of the burden of the past discrimination is presumptively necessary — is entirely consistent with any fair characterization of equity jurisdiction, particularly when considered in light of our traditional view that "[a]ttainment of a great national policy . . . must not be confined within narrow canons for equitable relief deemed suitable by chancellors in ordinary private controversies." Phelps Dodge Corp. v. NLRB, 313 U.S., at 188.

Certainly there is no argument that the award of retroactive seniority to the victims of hiring discrimination in any way deprives other employees of indefeasibly vested rights conferred by the employment contract. This Court has long held that employee expectations arising from a seniority system agreement may be modified by statutes furthering a strong public policy interest.[40] Tilton v. Missouri Pacific R. Co., 376 U.S. 169, 84 S.Ct. 595, 11 L.Ed.2d 590 (1964) (construing §§9(c)(1) and (c)(2) of the Universal Military Training and Service Act, which provided that a re-employed returning veteran should enjoy the seniority status he would have acquired but for his

---

pursuant to the District Court's order ("five, six, seven, something in that order"), although ongoing litigation may ultimately determine more who desire the hiring relief and are eligible for it.

[37]In no way can the remedy established as presumptively necessary be characterized as "total restitution," or as deriving from an "absolutist conception of 'make whole'" relief.

[38]In arguing that an award of the seniority relief established as presumptively necessary does nothing to place the burden of the past discrimination on the wrongdoer in most cases — the employer — the dissent of necessity addresses issues not presently before the Court. Further remedial action by the district courts, having the effect of shifting to the employer the burden of the past discrimination in respect of competitive-status benefits, raises such issues as the possibility of an injunctive "hold harmless" remedy respecting all affected employees in a layoff situation, the possibility of an award of monetary damages (sometimes designated "front pay") in favor of each employee and discriminatee otherwise bearing some of the burden of the past discrimination, and the propriety of such further remedial action in instances wherein the union has been adjudged a participant in the illegal conduct. Such issues are not presented by the record before us, and we intimate no view regarding them.

[40]"[C]laims under Title VII involve the vindication of a major public interest * * *." Section-by-Section Analysis of H.R. 1746, accompanying the Equal Employment Opportunity Act of 1972 — Conference Report, 118 Cong.Rec. 7166, 7168 (1972).

absence in military service); Fishgold v. Sullivan Drydock & Repair Corp., 328 U.S. 275, 66 S.Ct. 1105, 90 L.Ed. 1230 (1946) (construing the comparable provision of the Selective Training and Service Act of 1940). The Court has also held that a collective-bargaining agreement may go further, enhancing the seniority status of certain employees for purposes of furthering public policy interests beyond what is required by statute, even though this will to some extent be detrimental to the expectations acquired by other employees under the previous seniority agreement. Ford Motor Co. v. Huffman, 345 U.S. 330, 73 S.Ct. 681, 97 L.Ed. 1048 (1953). And the ability of the union and employer voluntarily to modify the seniority system to the end of ameliorating the effects of past racial discrimination, a national policy objective of the "highest priority," is certainly no less than in other areas of public policy interests. Pellicer v. Brotherhood of Ry. & S.S. Clerks, 217 F.2d 205 (C.A.5 1954), cert. denied, 349 U.S. 912, 75 S.Ct. 601, 99 L.Ed. 1246 (1955).

V

In holding that class-based seniority relief for identifiable victims of illegal hiring discrimination is a form of relief generally appropriate under §706(g), we do not in any way modify our previously expressed view that the statutory scheme of Title VII "implicitly recognizes that there may be cases calling for one remedy but not another, and — owing to the structure of the federal judiciary—these choices are, of course, left in the first instance to the district courts." *Albemarle Paper*. Circumstances peculiar to the individual case may, of course, justify the modification or withholding of seniority relief for reasons that would not if applied generally undermine the purposes of Title VII.[41] In the instant case it appears that all new hirees establish seniority only upon completion of a 45-day probationary period, although upon completion seniority is retroactive to the date of hire. Certainly any seniority relief ultimately awarded by the District Court could properly be cognizant of this fact. Amici and the respondent union point out that there may be circumstances where an award of full seniority should be deferred until completion of a training or apprenticeship program, or other preliminaries required of all new hirees.[42] We do not undertake to delineate all such possible circumstances here. Any enumeration must await particular cases and be determined in light of the trial courts' "keener appreciation" of peculiar facts and circumstances. *Albemarle Paper*.

Accordingly, the judgment of the Court of Appeals affirming the District Court's denial of seniority relief to class 3 is reversed, and the case is remanded to the District Court for further proceedings consistent with this opinion.

Reversed and remanded.

---

[41]Accordingly, to no "significant extent" do we "[strip] the district courts of [their] equity powers." Rather our holding is that in exercising their equitable powers, district courts should take as their starting point the presumption in favor of rightful-place seniority relief, and proceed with further legal analysis from that point; and that such relief may not be denied on the abstract basis of adverse impact upon interests of other employees but rather only on the basis of unusual adverse impact arising from facts and circumstances that would not be generally found in Title VII cases. To hold otherwise would be to shield "inconsisten[t] and capri[cious]" denial of such relief from "thorough appellate review." *Albemarle Paper*.

[42]Brief for United States et al. as *Amici Curiae* 26; Brief for Respondent United Steelworkers of America, AFL-CIO, and for American Federation of Labor and Congress of Industrial Organizations as *Amicus Curiae* 28 n. 32.

MR. JUSTICE STEVENS took no part in the consideration or decision of this case.

MR. CHIEF JUSTICE BURGER, concurring in part and dissenting in part.

I agree generally with Mr. Justice POWELL, but I would stress that although retroactive benefit-type seniority relief may sometimes be appropriate and equitable, competitive-type seniority relief at the expense of wholly innocent employees can rarely, if ever, be equitable if that term retains traditional meaning. More equitable would be a monetary award to the person suffering the discrimination. An award such as "front pay" could replace the need for competitive-type seniority relief. Such monetary relief would serve the dual purpose of deterring wrongdoing by the employer or union — or both — as well as protecting the rights of innocent employees. In every respect an innocent employee is comparable to a "holder-in-due-course" of negotiable paper or a bona fide purchaser of property without notice of any defect in the seller's title. In this setting I cannot join in judicial approval of "robbing Peter to pay Paul."

I would stress that the Court today does not foreclose claims of employees who might be injured by this holding from securing equitable relief on their own behalf.

MR. JUSTICE POWELL, with whom MR. JUSTICE REHNQUIST joins, concurring and dissenting in part.

* * *

Although I am in accord with much of the Court's discussion in Parts III and IV, I cannot accept as correct its basic interpretation of §706(g) as virtually requiring a district court, in determining appropriate equitable relief in a case of this kind, to ignore entirely the equities that may exist in favor of innocent employees. Its holding recognizes no meaningful distinction, in terms of the equitable relief to be granted, between "benefit"-type seniority and "competitive"-type seniority.[1] The Court reaches this result by taking an absolutist view of the "make whole" objective of Title VII, while rendering largely meaningless the discretionary authority vested in district courts by §706(g) to weigh the equities of the situation. Accordingly, I dissent from Parts III and IV.

* * *

III

A

In *Albemarle Paper* the Court read Title VII as creating a presumption in favor of backpay. Rather than limiting the power of district courts to do equity, the presumption insures that complete equity normally will be accomplished. Backpay

---

[1]My terminology conforms to that of the Court. "Benefit"-type seniority refers to the use of a worker's earned seniority credits in computing his level of economic "fringe benefits." Examples of such benefits are pensions, paid vacation time, and unemployment insurance. "Competitive"-type seniority refers to the use of those same earned credits in determining his right, relative to other workers, to job-related "rights" that cannot be supplied equally to any two employees. Examples can range from the worker's right to keep his job while someone else is laid off, to his right to a place in the punch-out line ahead of another employee at the end of a workday.

forces the employer[4] to account for economic benefits that he wrongfully has denied the victim of discrimination. The statutory purposes and equitable principles converge, for requiring payment of wrongfully withheld wages deters further wrongdoing at the same time that their restitution to the victim helps make him whole.

Similarly, to the extent that the Court today finds a like presumption in favor of granting benefit-type seniority, it is recognizing that normally this relief also will be equitable. As the Court notes, this type of seniority, which determines pension rights, length of vacations, size of insurance coverage and unemployment benefits, and the like, is analogous to backpay in that its retroactive grant serves "the mutually reinforcing effect of the dual purposes of Title VII," *ante*, at n.27. Benefit-type seniority, like backpay, serves to work complete equity by penalizing the wrongdoer economically at the same time that it tends to make whole the one who was wronged.

But the Court fails to recognize that a retroactive grant of competitive-type seniority invokes wholly different considerations. This is the type of seniority that determines an employee's preferential rights to various economic advantages at the expense of other employees. These normally include the order of layoff and recall of employees, job and trip assignments, and consideration for promotion.

It is true, of course, that the retroactive grant of competitive-type seniority does go a step further in "making whole" the discrimination victim, and therefore arguably furthers one of the objectives of Title VII. But apart from extending the make-whole concept to its outer limits, there is no similarity between this drastic relief and the granting of backpay and benefit-type seniority. First, a retroactive grant of competitive-type seniority usually does not directly affect the employer at all. It causes only a rearrangement of employees along the seniority ladder without any resulting increase in cost.[5] Thus, Title VII's "primary objective" of eradicating discrimination is not served at all,[6] for the employer is not deterred from the practice.

---

[4]In an appropriate case, of course, Title VII remedies may be ordered against a wrongdoing union as well as the employer.

[5]This certainly would be true in this case, as conceded by counsel for Bowman at oral argument. There the following exchange took place:

"QUESTION: How is Bowman injured by this action?

"MR. PATE [Counsel for Bowman]: By seniority? By the grant of this remedy?

"QUESTION: Either way.

"MR. PATE: It is not injured either way and the company, apart from the general interest of all of us in the importance of the question, has no specific tangible interest in it in this case as to whether seniority is granted to this group or not. That is correct. In a supplemental memorandum filed after oral argument, petitioners referred to this statement by Bowman's counsel and suggested that he apparently was referring to the competitive aspects of seniority, such as which employees were to get the best job assignments, since Bowman certainly *would* be economically disadvantaged by the benefit-type seniority, such as seniority-related increases in backpay. I agree that in the context Bowman's counsel spoke, he was referring to the company's lack of a tangible interest, in whether or not competitive-type seniority was granted.

[6]The Court in *Albemarle* noted that this primary objective had been recognized in Griggs v. Duke Power Co., 401 U.S. 424, 91 S.Ct. 849, 28 L.Ed.2d 158 (1971). In *Griggs*, the Court found this objective to be "plain from the language of the statute." In creating a presumption in favor of a retroactive grant of competitive-type seniority the Court thus exalts the make-whole purpose, not only above fundamental principles of equity, but also above the primary objective of the statute recently found to be plain on its face.

The second, and in my view controlling, distinction between these types of relief is the impact on other workers. As noted above, the granting of backpay and of benefit-type seniority furthers the prophylactic and make-whole objectives of the statute without penalizing other workers. But competitive seniority benefits, as the term implies, directly implicate the rights and expectations of perfectly innocent employees.[7] The economic benefits awarded discrimination victims would be derived not at the expense of the employer but at the expense of other workers. Putting it differently, those disadvantaged — sometimes to the extent of losing their jobs entirely — are not the wrongdoers who have no claim to the Chancellor's conscience, but rather are innocent third parties.

* * * Congress in §706(g) expressly referred to "appropriate" affirmative action and "other equitable relief as the court deems appropriate." And the 1972 Section-by-Section Analysis still recognized that the touchstone of any relief is equity. Congress could not have been more explicit in leaving the relief to the equitable discretion of the court, to be determined in light of all relevant facts and circumstances. Congress did underscore "backpay" by specific reference in §706(g), but no mention is made of the granting of other benefits upon ordering reinstatement or hiring. The entire question of retroactive seniority was thus deliberately left to the discretion of the district court, a discretion to be exercised in accordance with equitable principles. * * *

The decision whether to grant competitive-type seniority relief therefore requires a district court to consider and weigh competing equities. In any proper exercise of the balancing process, a court must consider both the claims of the discrimination victims and the claims of incumbent employees who, if competitive seniority rights are awarded retroactively to others, will lose economic advantages earned through satisfactory and often long service.[8] If, as the Court today holds, the district court may not weigh these equities much of the language of §706(g) is rendered meaningless. We cannot assume that Congress intended either that the statutory language be ignored

---

[7]Some commentators have suggested that the expectations of incumbents somehow may be illegitimate because they result from past discrimination against others. Cooper & Sobol, Seniority and Testing under Fair Employment Laws: A General Approach to Objective Criteria of Hiring and Promotion, 82 Harv.L.Rev. 1598, 1605-1606 (1969). Such reasoning is badly flawed. Absent some showing of collusion, the incumbent employee was not a party to the discrimination by the employer. Acceptance of the job when offered hardly makes one an accessory to a discriminatory failure to hire someone else. Moreover, the incumbent's expectancy does not result from discrimination against others, but is based on his own efforts and satisfactory performance.

[8]The Court argues that a retroactive grant of competitive-type seniority always is equitable because it "divides the burden" of past discrimination between incumbents and victims. Aside from its opacity, this argument is flawed by what seems to be a misperception of the nature of Title VII relief. Specific relief necessarily focuses upon the individual victim, not upon some "class" of victims. A grant of full retroactive seniority to an individual victim of Bowman's discriminatory hiring practices will place that person exactly where he would have been had he been hired when he first applied. The question for a district court should be whether it is equitable to place that individual in that position despite the impact upon all incumbents hired after the date of his unsuccessful application. Any additional effect upon the entire work force — incumbents and the newly enfranchised victims alike — of similar relief to still *earlier* victims of the discrimination, raises distinctly different issues from the equity, vis-a-vis incumbents, of granting retroactive seniority to each victim.

or that the earned benefits of incumbent employees be wiped out by a presumption created by this Court.[9]

IV

In expressing the foregoing views, I suggest neither that Congress intended to bar a retroactive grant of competitive-type seniority in all cases,[13] nor that district courts should indulge a presumption against such relief.[14] My point instead is that we are dealing with a congressional mandate to district courts to determine and apply equitable remedies. Traditionally this is a balancing process left, within appropriate constitutional or statutory limits, to the sound discretion of the trial court. At this time it is necessary only to avoid imposing, from the level of this Court, arbitrary limitations on the exercise of this traditional discretion specifically explicated in §706(g). There will be cases where, under all of the circumstances, the economic penalties that would be imposed on innocent incumbent employees will outweigh the claims of discrimination victims to be made entirely whole even at the expense of others. Similarly, there will be cases where the balance properly is struck the other way.

* * *

In attempted justification of its disregard of the explicit equitable mandate of §706(g) the Court today relies almost exclusively on the practice of the National Labor

---

[9]Indeed, the 1972 amendment process which produced the Section-by-Section Analysis containing the statement of the Act's "make whole" purpose, also resulted in an addition to §706(g) itself clearly showing congressional recognition that total restitution to victims of discrimination is not a feasible goal. As originally enacted, §706(g) contained simply an authorization to district courts to order reinstatement with or without backpay, with no limitation on how much backpay the courts could order. In 1972, however, the Congress added a limitation restricting the courts to an award to a date two years prior to the filing of a charge with EEOC. While it is true that Congress at the same time rejected an even more restrictive limitation, see *Albemarle Paper*, its adoption of any limitation at all suggests an awareness that the desire to "make whole" must yield at some point to other considerations.

[13]Nor is it suggested that incumbents have "indefeasibly vested rights" to their seniority status that invariably would foreclose retroactive seniority. But the cases cited by the Court for that proposition do not hold, or by analogy imply, that district courts operating under §706(g) lack equitable discretion to take into account the rights of incumbents. In Tilton v. Missouri Pacific R. Co., 376 U.S. 169, 84 S.Ct. 595, 11 L.Ed.2d 590 (1964), and Fishgold v. Sullivan Corp., 328 U.S. 275, 66 S.Ct. 1105, 90 L.Ed. 1230 (1946), the Court only confirmed an express congressional determination, presumably made after weighing all relevant considerations, that for reasons of public policy veterans should receive seniority credit for their time in military service. In Ford Motor Co. v. Huffman, 345 U.S. 330, 73 S.Ct. 681, 97 L.Ed. 1048 (1953), the Court affirmed the authority of a collective-bargaining agent, presumably after weighing the relative equities, see id., at 337-339, to advantage certain employees more than others. All I contend is that under §706(g) a district court, like Congress in *Tilton* and *Fishgold*, and the bargaining agent in *Huffman*, also must be free to weigh the equities.

[14]The Court suggests I am arguing that retroactive competitive-type seniority should be "less available" as relief than backpay. This is not my position. All relief not specifically prohibited by the Act is equally "available" to the district courts. My point is that equitable considerations can make competitive-type seniority relief less "appropriate" in a particular situation than backpay or other relief. Again, the plain language of §706(g) compels careful determination of the "appropriateness" of each "available" remedy in a specific case, and does not permit the inflexible approach taken by the Court.

Relations Board under §10(c) of the National Labor Relations Act.[18] It is true that in the two instances cited by the Court, and in the few others cited in the briefs of the parties, the Board has ordered reinstatement of victims of discrimination "without prejudice to their seniority or other rights and privileges." But the alleged precedents are doubly unconvincing. First, in none of the cases is there a discussion of equities either by the Board or the enforcing court. That the Board has granted seniority relief in several cases may indicate nothing more than the fact that in the usual case no one speaks for the individual incumbents. * * *

I also suggest, with all respect, that the Court's appeal to Board practice wholly misconceives the lesson to be drawn from it. In the seminal case recognizing the Board's power to order reinstatement for discriminatory refusals to hire, this Court in a reasoned opinion by Mr. Justice Frankfurter was careful to emphasize that the decision on the type and extent of relief rested in the Board's discretion, subject to limited review only by the courts.

> "But in the nature of things Congress could not catalogue all the devices and stratagems for circumventing the policies of the Act. Nor could it define the whole gamut of remedies to effectuate these policies in an infinite variety of specific situations. Congress met these difficulties by leaving the adaptation of means to end to the empiric process of administration. The exercise of the process was committed to the Board, subject to limited judicial review. * * *

* * *

> " * * * All these and other factors outside our domain of experience may come into play. Their relevance is for the Board, not for us. In the exercise of its informed discretion the Board may find that effectuation of the Act's policies may or may not require reinstatement. We have no warrant for speculating on matters of fact the determination of which Congress has entrusted to the Board. All we are entitled to ask is that the statute speak through the Board where the statute does not speak for itself." Phelps Dodge Corp. v. NLRB, 313 U.S. 177, 194-196, 61 S.Ct. 845, 852-853, 85 L.Ed. 1271, 1283-1284 (1941) (emphasis added).

---

[18]By gathering bits and pieces of the legislative history of the 1972 amendments, the Court attempts to patch together an argument that full retroactive seniority is a remedy equally "available" as backpay. There are two short responses. First, as emphasized elsewhere, *supra*, n. 14, no one contends that such relief is less *available*, but only that it may be less *equitable* in some situations. Second, insofar as the Court intends the legislative history to suggest some presumption in favor of this relief, it is irrefutably blocked by the plain language of §706(g) calling for the exercise of *equitable* discretion in the fashioning of *appropriate* relief. There are other responses. As to the committee citations of lower court decisions and the Conference Report Analysis reference to "present case law," it need only be noted that as of the 1972 amendments no appellate court had considered a case involving retroactive seniority relief to victims of discriminatory hiring practices. Moreover, the cases were cited only in the context of a general discussion of the complexities of employment discrimination, never for their adoption of a "rightful place" theory of relief. And by the terms of the Conference Report Analysis itself, the existing case law could not take precedence over the explicit language of §706(g), added by the amendments, that told courts to exercise *equitable* discretion in granting *appropriate* relief.
    Moreover, I find no basis for the Court's statement that the Committee Reports indicated "rightful place" to be the objective of Title VII relief. In fact, in both instances cited by the Court the term was used in the context of a general comment that minorities were still "far from reaching their rightful place in society." S.Rep.No.92-416, p. 6 (1971). There was no reference to the scope of relief under §706(g), or indeed even to Title VII remedies at all.

The fallacy of the Court's reliance upon Board practice is apparent: the district courts under Title VII stand in the place of the Board under the NLRA. Congress entrusted to their discretion the appropriate remedies for violations of the Act, just as it previously had entrusted discretion to the Board. The Court today denies that discretion to the district courts, when 35 years ago it was quite careful to leave discretion where Congress had entrusted it. It may be that the district courts, after weighing the competing equities, would order full retroactive seniority in most cases. But they should do so only after determining in each instance that it is appropriate, and not because this Court has taken from them the power — granted by Congress — to weigh the equities.

In summary, the decision today denying district courts the power to balance equities cannot be reconciled with the explicit mandate of §706(g) to determine "appropriate" relief through the exercise of "equitable powers." Accordingly, I would remand this case to the District Court with instructions to investigate and weigh competing equities before deciding upon the appropriateness of retroactive competitive-type seniority with respect to individual claimants.[20]

NOTES AND PROBLEMS FOR DISCUSSION

1. (a) Post-*Franks*, the lower courts have treated retroactive seniority, like back pay, as a remedy to be denied the victim of discrimination only for the most compelling reasons. In EEOC v. M.D. PNEUMATICS, INC., 779 F.2d 21 (8th Cir. 1985), the district court denied retroactive seniority to women who had been refused employment with the defendant because the employer "had gone the extra mile in remedying its past discrimination" and because there was no evidence "from which a reasonable determination could be made as to a date on which a class member might have been hired absent the sex discrimination which was then practiced by the defendant." The Court of Appeals reversed, concluding that the employer's remedial efforts, "although commendable, are not the kind of compelling reasons which justify the denial of retroactive seniority." With respect to computation of seniority dates, the court noted that all the district court needed was the womens' dates of application and the dates on which men subsequently were hired. That data was either in the record of the case or could be obtained from the parties. With retroactive seniority, as with back pay, "unrealistic exactitude" is not required. *See also* Sands v. Runyon, 28 F.3d 1323, 1329 (2d Cir. 1994) ("retroactive seniority is ordinarily considered to be a relatively

---

[20]This is not to suggest that district courts should be left to exercise a standardless, unreviewable discretion. But in the area of competitive-type seniority, unlike backpay and benefit-type seniority, the twin purposes of Title VII do not provide the standards. District courts must be guided in each instance by the mandate of §706(g). They should, of course, record the considerations upon which they rely in granting or refusing relief, so that appellate review could be informed and precedents established in the area.

In this case, for example, factors that could be considered on remand and that could weigh in favor of full retroactive seniority, include Bowman's high employee turnover rate and the asserted fact that few victims of Bowman's discrimination have indicated a desire to be hired. Other factors, not fully developed in the record, also could require consideration in determining the balance of the equities. I would imply no opinion on the merits and would remand for full consideration in light of the views herein expressed.

fundamental form of relief where a plaintiff was subject to unlawful discrimination in the hiring process.").

(b) In *Franks*, the Court held that retroactive seniority may not be denied merely because of an adverse impact on the interests of other employees, but in a footnote qualified that rule by saying that in exercising its equitable discretion, a court could deny such relief "on the basis of unusual adverse impact that would not be generally found in Title VII cases." In ROMASANTA v. UNITED AIR LINES, INC., 717 F.2d 1140 (7th Cir. 1983), cert. denied, 466 U.S. 944, 104 S.Ct. 1928, 80 L.Ed.2d 474 (1984), the Seventh Circuit relied on that footnote to deny immediate reinstatement, with full competitive seniority, to a class of 1,400 former airline stewardesses who had been terminated pursuant to an unlawful no-marriage rule. The plaintiffs had argued that upon being reinstated, each class member should have received the full seniority she would have enjoyed had she never been terminated. The appellate court concluded that, though such an award of retroactive seniority would appear to be necessary to make the discriminatees whole, to award more competitive seniority than the time actually worked before termination would have an unusual adverse impact on incumbents, resulting in furloughs, possible discharges, involuntary transfers, and curtailment of job opportunities for recently hired minorities. In balancing the interests of all affected parties, the court approved competitive seniority for time actually worked, but awarded noncompetitive seniority (used for pay and fringe benefit purposes) to cover the time from date of hire for each class member who was reinstated.

2. In *International Brotherhood Of Teamsters* and *American Tobacco Co.*, discussed in Chapter 2, Section C, *supra*, the Supreme Court held that under §703(h) of Title VII, a "bona fide" seniority system (one not designed or maintained for a discriminatory purpose) was not illegal simply because it perpetuated the effects of past discrimination. In both of these cases, the discrimination which was perpetuated by the seniority systems either had occurred before the enactment of Title VII or had not been the subject of a timely EEOC charge. The Court's determination that such seniority systems did not themselves violate the Act in no way affected the holding in *Franks* that where discrimination in hiring or job assignment over which the court has jurisdiction is established, retroactive seniority is a proper remedy to make the victim of the discrimination whole. The Court in *Teamsters* was careful to distinguish between pre-Act discrimination, which was not illegal and for which the courts could not provide a remedy, and post-Act discrimination. Post-Act discriminatees, the Court emphasized, could obtain full "make whole" relief, including retroactive seniority, without attacking the seniority system as applied to them.

Assume that Craig Mesa, an African-American, was hired in 1980 and assigned to a maintenance job. Two white job applicants were hired the follwoing day and were given machine operator positions to which only whites were assigned. All three of these employees possessed identical qualifications at the time they were hired. Under the employer's seniority system, competitive seniority is acquired only in the particular job, and an employee who transfers from one job to another loses all seniority amassed in the old position. In 1982 and again in 1985, Craig attempted to transfer into a machine operator position, but was denied the transfer because of his race. After his 1985 rejection, Craig filed an EEOC charge and subsequently a lawsuit under Title VII. If the court finds that he was discriminated against in 1980, 1982, and 1985, to what seniority relief is Craig entitled?

3. Tenure in educational institutions and partnership in large law and accounting firms are, at least in part, the product of seniority. Because factors other than seniority influence decisions to award tenure and partnership, the courts are particularly leery about granting requests for court-awarded tenure. As the First Circuit explained:

> * * * Neither the district court nor this court is empowered to sit as a super tenure board. I believe that courts must be extremely wary of intruding into the world of university tenure decisions. These decisions necessarily hinge on subjective judgments regarding the applicant's academic excellence, teaching ability, creativity, contributions to the university community, rapport with students and colleagues, and other factors that are not susceptible of quantitative measurement. Absent discrimination, a university must be given a free hand in making such tenure decisions. Where, as here, the university's judgment is supportable and the evidence of discrimination negligible, a federal court should not substitute its judgment for that of the university.

Kumar v. Bd. of Trustees, Univ. of Mass., 774 F.2d 1, 12 (1st Cir. 1985) (Campbell, J., concurring), cert. denied, 475 U.S. 1097, 106 S.Ct. 1496, 89 L.Ed.2d 896 (1986). In another tenure case, the First Circuit rejected a university's argument that the trial court's award of tenure infringed its First Amendment right to determine for itself who may teach. "[T]o deny tenure because of the intrusiveness of the remedy and because of the University's interest in making its own tenure decisions," the court reasoned, "would frustrate Title VII's purpose of 'aking persons whole for injuries suffered through past discrimination." Brown v. Trustees of Boston Univ., 891 F.2d 337, 360 (1st Cir. 1989), cert. denied, 446 U.S. 937, 110 S.Ct. 3217, 110 L.Ed.2d 664 (1990).

On remand from the Supreme Court's decision in *Price Waterhouse*, the district court directed that Ms. Hopkins be made a partner retroactive to 1983. Price Waterhouse appealed on the ground that an injunction requiring that a plaintiff be made a partner was beyond the equitable powers of the court under Title VII because, once made a partner, the plaintiff would be outside the protection of the Act. The Court of Appeals rejected this argument on the ground that it "would directly subvert what Congress intended in the 1972 amendments if we were to hold that partnership could not be awarded to a person who was denied it because of unlawful discrimination," and affirmed the district court's injunction as well as the award of $371,000 in back pay. Hopkins v. Price Waterhouse, 920 F.2d 967, 977 (D.C.Cir. 1990). The Court took pains, however, to delineate the reach of its decision.

> It is, of course, true, as Justice Powell noted in his concurrence to Hishon, that a partnership relationship is "markedly" different from the relationship of an employer and employee. But this consideration is not controlling in this case. The instant case involves only an employee's elevation to partnership; it does not involve Ms. Hopkin's retention of partnership or the regulation of the relationship among partners at Price Waterhouse. Thus, we are not confronted by the concerns expressed in Justice Powell's concurring opinion. Justice Powell emphasized that the Court in Hishon did not reach the question whether Title VII protects employees after they become partners: nor do we reach that question in this case.

920 F.2d at 979. Courts have ordered law firms found to have unlawfully denied partnership to admit plaintiffs to full partnership. *See* Ezold v. Wolf, Block, Schorr & Solis-Cohen, 56 FEP Cases 580 (E.D. Pa. 1991), reversed on other grounds, 983 F.2d 509 (3d Cir.), cert. denied, 510 U.S. 826, 114 S.Ct. 88, 126 L.Ed.2d 56 (1993); Masterson v. LaBrum & Doak, 846 F.Supp. 1224 (E.D. Pa. 1993).

4. The seniority systems of many industrial employers are organized in "lines of progression." In such systems, employees can use their competitive seniority to bid on jobs in a line of progression only in the order in which the jobs are ranked in the line; the employee must start at the bottom or "entry level" position and then can only use his seniority to bid on the next job up in the progression. The common rationale for such systems is that the employee needs to know the lower jobs in the progression before he can competently perform the higher positions. Sometimes progression line seniority is linked with the provision that an employee acquires competitive seniority only in a line of progression and relinquishes his seniority when he transfers to a new line of progression.

Line of progression seniority complicates the job of "making whole" the victim of discrimination. For example, an employee may have been excluded from a progression line because of race or sex. The court can, of course, order that the employee be placed in the seniority line from which he has been discriminatorily excluded, but if the progression line seniority system is not itself illegal (i.e., it is "bona fide" under *Teamsters*), how is he to be made whole for his earlier exclusion from the line? But for the discrimination the employee would be at a position in the line well above the entry-level job, which will typically be the lowest paying and most arduous job in the line. This kind of problem is addressed in the following case.

Locke v. Kansas City Power & Light Co.

United States Court of Appeals, Eighth Circuit, 1981.
660 F.2d 359.

McMILLIAN, Circuit Judge.

Kansas City Power & Light Co. (KCP&L) appeals from a judgment entered in the District Court for the Western District of Missouri finding that KCP&L unlawfully discriminated against appellee Julius B. Locke on the basis of his race. The district court found that KCP&L had denied appellee employment in violation of Title VII and awarded appellee backpay, reinstatement and attorney's fees.

For reversal appellant argues that the district court erred in (1) requiring appellant to show by a "preponderance of evidence" a legitimate, nondiscriminatory reason for refusing Locke's bid for employment; (2) finding the reason given by KCP&L for refusing Locke's bid to be a pretext; (3) ordering appellee reinstated to a higher position than that for which he had applied, with backpay computed, in part, at a rate commensurate with that higher position; and (4) eliminating the probationary period applied to all other employees.

For the reasons discussed below, we affirm in part and reverse in part and remand the case to the district court for further consideration of the remedy issue.

I.   *Background*

On November 3, 1976, KCP&L hired Locke, a black male, as a "Temporary Plant Helper" at KCP&L's Hawthorn generating facility to work for a period of sixty days. Locke worked the full sixty-day term which ended on December 30, 1976. Shortly thereafter, on January 26, 1977, KCP&L rehired Locke, again as a "Temporary Plant Helper," this time for a period of ninety days. Locke completed this term of employment on April 27, 1977.

Temporary employees are hired by KCP&L for a specified period of time at the end of which the company automatically lays off the temporary employee unless he or she is transferred to a permanent position. (By contrast, in a permanent position at KCP&L after a probationary period the employee attains full permanent status, under which the employee automatically stays on unless appropriate steps are taken to end employment.)[2] While employed as a temporary plant helper at KCP&L, Locke applied to fill openings in three permanent job positions — one in November, 1976, for a janitor, and two in March, 1977, for plant helpers. Each time KCP&L returned the application to Locke, indicating that it would not be considered because a company policy prohibited accepting applications from temporary employees until the end of their temporary stints. Concerning the November, 1976, application, the company explained it had been filed after the closing date on the job announcement for accepting applications and that Locke was not eligible to apply until his temporary job ended. Concerning the March, 1977, applications, KCP&L explained only that Locke was not eligible to apply until his temporary job ended.[3] The company personnel department returned each application to Locke with an explanatory note dated the same day the application was submitted.

KCP&L continued to seek applicants for the available positions and ultimately filled them. Acting contrary to company policy as it was represented to Locke, KCP&L hired three white male temporary employees for the permanent positions which Locke also had sought. The applications of these temporary employees were considered even before their projects had been substantially completed.

Locke's second period of temporary employment ended April 27, 1977, and he was not rehired by the company. On May 9, 1977, Locke filed a charge of discrimination with the Equal Employment Opportunity Commission, alleging generally that the company had discriminated against him on the basis of race and specifically that a "probationary period" was used as a pretext to discharge him. The

---

[2]As KCP&L describes its policy, its plant supervisors may hire temporary employees only in an emergency or nonrecurring situation and must obtain authorization from the company which permits hiring of only a limited number of temporaries. The district court was not convinced, however, that this policy was actually followed, because the record suggested that at least in some instances KCP&L hired temporary plant helpers to do essentially the same job as permanent plant helpers on a regular basis. In addition to the groups of temporary plant helpers (including Locke) hired in late 1976 and 1977, a third group was hired later in 1977 in what appeared to be an ongoing process despite absence of any evidence in the record of a year-long emergency under the company's stated policy.

[3]There is some indication that Locke made these latter two applications after the closing date listed on the job announcement. The district court, however, found specifically that KCP&L continued to accept applications after Locke was turned down, and KCP&L does not challenge that finding on appeal. Indeed, KCP&L does not assign any error to the district court's finding that Locke established a *prima facie* case of racial discrimination under the analysis of *McDonnell Douglas*.

EEOC processed this charge and found no reasonable cause to believe that Locke's allegations were true and on June 7, 1978, notified Locke of his right to sue. Locke commenced this proceeding on August 29, 1978, complaining that KCP&L had discriminatorily failed to hire him into a permanent position and discharged him from temporary employment on the basis of race, all in violation of Title VII * * *.[4]

At trial it was stipulated that KCP&L had hired into the permanent plant helper positions in question three white males who had, like Locke, been temporary employees at the time of their applications and, like Locke, had not yet completed their temporary stints. KCP&L did not, however, attempt to justify its failure to hire Locke on the basis of the supposed policy against accepting applications from temporary workers before their jobs ended.[5] Instead, the company offered a new justification that it had actually given consideration to appellant's application and decided to reject him because of poor work performance. In particular KCP&L relied upon testimony by Glendon Paul Curry, the maintenance supervisor at the plant where Locke worked, that Curry had decided not to accept Locke's bid on the permanent plant helper jobs because of Locke's poor performance as a temporary employee. Curry testified that he had reports from foremen that Locke had been away from his work station, had argued with them, and had refused work assignments from more senior employees authorized by the foremen to direct him. The company also presented testimony of foremen and workers as direct evidence of Locke's poor performance.

The district court, however, determined this explanation was a pretext for a number of reasons which the court specified in an oral decision delivered from the bench.[6] The company had obtained written reports from foremen on Locke's supposedly poor performance after Locke's employment ended; the timing, of course, casts some doubt on whether those reports were actually considered in deciding not to give a permanent position to Locke. Moreover, KCP&L witnesses could not name any

---

[4]KCP&L does not assert that the allegations in the complaint were not "like or related" to the substance of the EEOC charge. The EEOC determination of the charge is not in the record before us.

[5]It was stipulated that

> During the periods of [Locke's] employment, [KCP&L] maintained the following bidding procedure on permanent positions:
>
> (a)   Initially, regular bids will be considered.
>
> (b)   After regular employee bids are accepted or rejected, consideration may then be given to probationary employee bidders.
>
> (c)   Probationary employees are hired without time limitation and after six months of satisfactory service become employees.
>
> (d)   For the purposes of bidding, temporary employees are also probationary except that they are hired for a specific period of time only.
>
> (e)   The Company may elect to defer consideration of any bid submitted by a temporary employee until the project upon [which] they are working has been completed or nearly completed.
>
> (f)   The plant superintendent or his representative makes the decision regarding acceptance or rejection of bids.

[6]Although the district court issued a document identified as written findings of fact and conclusions of law which had been approved as to form by counsel for both sides, the document does not fully reflect the substance of the factual findings and legal reasoning relied on by the court in announcing from the bench its decision on liability. In evaluating the district court's decision we consider both the document and the transcript of [the trial judge's] remarks which do not contradict the document but supplement it.

other employee who had been the subject of such post-termination reports. Locke's supposedly poor performance had not been grounds for failing to rehire him for a second period of temporary employment or for dismissing him. In the district court's view Locke's supposed absence from his work station and failure to follow orders from senior nonsupervisory workers would not be unusual in a job like plant helper where new workers were shuffled between various tasks, some requiring movement around various areas of the plant. It was not clear from the record which KCP&L official was responsible for the decisions about Locke's future employment or what standards or considerations were normally applied in making the decision.[7] Finally, KCP&L's proffered justification for the failure to hire Locke was entirely different from what Locke was told when his application was returned to him.

The district court concluded that Locke had established a prima facie case of racial discrimination under the test of *McDonnell Douglas* and that the reasons proffered by KCP&L for denying him a permanent position were pretextual. In its memorandum the court specified also that the "claim that [Locke] was less than a perfect employee fails to rebut [Locke's] prima facie case as it isn't necessary for [Locke] to show perfect performance or even average performance," and that KCP&L's "claim that [Locke] was not entitled to further employment because of an alleged failure to get along with his co-workers fails to rebut [Locke's] prima facie case as [Locke] is not required to have a pleasing personality in order to be entitled to further employment." The district court also concluded that KCP&L had "failed to show by a preponderance of the evidence that [the] failure to accept plaintiff's bid for regular employment was for a legitimate nondiscriminatory reason."

Accordingly, the district court found that KCP&L had violated Title VII by denying Locke a permanent plant helper position as of April, 1977, because of his race. In fashioning a remedy the court sought to put Locke in the position he would have occupied but for the discrimination against him. As the white temporary employees hired in place of Locke had all been promoted from plant helper to relief man positions at KCP&L, the district court ruled that Locke also was entitled to a relief man position. The court also held that Locke would not be required to undergo the normal six-month probationary period for new permanent employees. Finally, the court awarded backpay from April 27, 1977, the date KCP&L filled the permanent plant helper position sought by Locke. Backpay was computed at the rate for a plant helper until January 18, 1978 (the date found by the court to be the "average date" for promotion to relief man of the three white plant helpers hired in April, 1977, ahead of Locke), and after January 18, 1978, at the rate for a relief man.[8]

---

[7]For example, although KCP&L stipulated the decision would be made by the plant supervisor or his representative, KCP&L at trial took the position that the decision was delegated by the plant supervisor to the supervisor of maintenance in the plant. The district court remarked on the absence of any evidence that the plant manager made even a cursory review of a decision that was apparently his responsibility or that there were any standards at all to guide the decision. Although the court considered this as background evidence, it clearly did not hold the subjectiveness or vagueness of the decision making process *per se* improper, but rather went on to consider the ultimate question of whether race was a factor in this particular case.

[8]The award was increased by adding prejudgment interest and decreased by subtracting interim earnings of Locke.

[The court upheld the district court's finding that the plaintiff had been denied permanent employment because of his race and that the reasons put forward by the employer for its decisions were pretextual.]

* * *

III. *Remedy*

    A. *Instatement as Permanent Plant Helper and Backpay at Plant Helper Rates*

* * * [T]he district court found that absent discrimination Locke would have been hired as a plant helper on April 27, 1977 and continued in that position until January 20, 1978. The court awarded backpay at the plant helper rate until January 20, 1978; afterward it awarded backpay at the higher relief man rate. Including interest, a deduction for Locke's interim earnings, and probable overtime, the backpay award was $6,131.63 for 1977. During 1978 the award was zero because Locke's interim earnings fully offset his lost backpay even at the higher relief man rate. For 1979, the award was $7,359.14 and for 1980 up to the date of the district court's judgment the award was $2,060.80, all calculated at the relief man rate. In addition, the court ordered Locke instated as a relief man on a theory that Locke would have been promoted by that time in the absence of discrimination. The court further ordered that Locke should not have to undergo a six-month probationary period provided in KCP&L's contract with the union representing plant employees, because Locke would have served his probationary period long ago in the absence of discrimination.

On appeal KCP&L challenges certain aspects of this remedy, including the backpay award at the relief man rate, the instatement of Locke as a relief man, and the cancellation of the probationary period. KCP&L does not argue that backpay at the plant helper rate or instatement as a plant helper was improper as a remedy for the discrimination found by the district court and KCP&L did not appeal these matters. KCP&L's brief nevertheless seeks reversal of the entire judgment on grounds that, even if the district court was correct in finding discrimination, the remedy was an abuse of discretion. We take this to apply only to those parts of the remedy KCP&L objects to, and note that neither instatement of Locke as a plant helper nor backpay at the plant helper rate have been appealed. In view of our affirmance of the district court's finding of discrimination, no challenge remains to the portions of the judgment ordering Locke instated as a plant helper and $6,131.63 in backpay at the plant helper rate for 1977, and those parts of the judgment stand. However, as discussed below, the record before us is not adequate to support the other portions of the judgment. Therefore, we vacate and remand these questions for further consideration in light of this opinion.

    B. *Standard of Review*

Preliminarily we note that we review the district court's remedial order only to correct abuse of discretion. That discretion is not unbounded but must be exercised consistently with the strong remedial aims of Title VII.

One of the central purposes of Title VII is "to make persons whole for injuries suffered on account of unlawful employment discrimination." *Albemarle Paper Company v. Moody.* "To effectuate this 'make whole' objective, Congress [has] vested broad equitable discretion in the federal courts to 'order such affirmative action as may be appropriate, which may include, but is not limited to, reinstatement . . . with or without back pay . . ., or any other equitable relief as the court deems appropriate.'" *Franks v. Bowman.*

Harper v. General Grocers Co., supra, 590 F.2d at 716. Under this standard none of the remedial measures ordered by the district court *per se* went beyond the broad equitable powers specifically granted in §706(g) of Title VII. The problem is that there are insufficient findings in the record for us to evaluate the soundness of the district court's exercise of discretion and we therefore vacate parts of the judgment and remand for further findings and reconsideration.

C. *The Probationary Period*

The district court obviously had some basis for concern on this record that requiring Locke to go through a six-month probationary period, presumably giving him something less than the protection of a "just cause" clause in a typical collective bargaining agreement, would provide a ready pretext for further discrimination. There of course may well be valid nondiscriminatory reasons for requiring a probationary period. The probationary period has not been used to discriminate against Locke, however, and eliminating it may therefore be at odds with the equitable principle that the scope of the remedy should be tailored to the scope of the violation.

If the probationary period is a uniform requirement imposed by KCP&L on new employees for valid business purposes, we think Locke would be in the same position as other employees if he too was subject to it. If the probationary period in fact was not imposed uniformly, the district court may have been justified in exempting Locke from it in order to put him in the position he would have held but for the discrimination against him. We cannot tell what the outcome should be on this record, and the district court has not made adequate subsidiary findings to support this remedial measure.

Rather than make the substantial inquiry that may be required to resolve a matter of only peripheral importance in this case, we suggest that it may be more appropriate for the district court simply to require Locke to serve the six-month probationary period and retain jurisdiction over the case during that time. Such a resolution would provide opportunity for close scrutiny of any employment decision which Locke may claim to have a discriminatory taint, while allowing KCP&L to use the probationary period for valid business objectives. Of course any action disfavoring Locke would have to be viewed in the context of the finding of discrimination already made in this case.[11]

D. *Promotion to Relief Man*

The district court apparently considered Locke qualified for a relief man job and thought Locke would have been promoted to relief man but for the discrimination against him. We cannot tell whether the court was of the view that the relief man job required essentially the same qualifications as the plant helper job or that Locke had

---

[11]In this light, if the district court allows the probationary period and retains jurisdiction, further proceedings will not be on a clean slate and KCP&L should be required to carry the burden of persuasion that any dismissal of Locke is based entirely on legitimate, nondiscriminatory factors. Compare *International Bhd. of Teamsters* (after finding of discrimination against class the burden may be on the employer to demonstrate legitimate reasons for denying employment opportunity to a member of the class) with *Burdine* (plaintiff's burden of persuasion as to existence of discriminatory disparate treatment).

any additional qualifications required for the relief man job or for some other reason. In any event the findings concerning Locke's qualifications and KCP&L's promotion practices are inadequate for us to evaluate the promotion of Locke to relief man as a remedial measure.

A court can in appropriate circumstances order a promotion as make whole relief for a victim of discrimination, but cannot under Title VII properly order the promotion of an employee to a position for which he or she is not qualified. Our research has not, however, discovered any cases precisely similar to this one, where a court has ordered a Title VII plaintiff who has suffered discrimination in the hiring process instated to a higher position than entry level.

There is some support for the district court's action in a series of cases providing for "job-skipping" where an employer has discriminatorily excluded some employees from whole lines of progression within the employer's work force. E.g., Watkins v. Scott Paper Co., 530 F.2d 1159 (5th Cir.), cert. denied, 429 U.S. 861, 97 S.Ct. 163, 50 L.Ed.2d 139 (1976); Rogers v. International Paper Co., 510 F.2d 1340, 1354 (8th Cir.), vacated on other grounds, 423 U.S. 809, 96 S.Ct. 19, 46 L.Ed.2d 29 (1975). Such "job-skipping" cases have involved lines of progression between lower and higher level jobs in a plant, where a certain amount of time in a lower level job is generally required before moving up to the next higher job. Victims of discriminatory exclusion from the whole line of progression, especially those who have worked in other jobs within a facility, may be left without any real remedy if, for example, they must take a reduction in pay to transfer into the line of progression at entry level. Courts have in this context carefully scrutinized the lower level jobs prerequisite for advancement within lines of progression and have allowed job-skipping to make whole victims of discrimination where it has specifically been found that the lower level jobs prerequisite is not justified by business necessity. But job-skipping is only appropriate where the beneficiary has demonstrated the skills or other qualifications legitimately required or the higher level job and the promotion is in a line of progression where a promotion is normally forthcoming after some interval of time in the lower level job.

Under the job-skipping cases the district court has discretion to order Locke instated as a relief man only if it makes the following findings: (1) that Locke had the particular skills or other job-related qualifications required by KCP&L for a relief man, (2) that the relief man position was in a line of progression upward from the plant helper position, that is, a plant helper would normally be promoted to relief man after some interval of acceptable performance as a plant helper, and (3) that the prerequisite service as a plant helper is not itself justified by business necessity aside from the skills or other qualifications to perform the relief man job. Moreover, in exercising its discretion we think the court should consider the possibility for making Locke whole economically by other means such as retroactive seniority, see *Franks v. Bowman*, or front pay discussed below.

In any event, KCP&L does not appear to contend that Locke is not entitled to instatement as a plant helper on the basis of the district court's discrimination finding that we have affirmed above and to nondiscriminatory consideration for promotion in the future. Therefore, regardless of the decision on the relief man issue, Locke is in this posture of the case entitled to no less than instatement in a plant helper position.

E. *Backpay*

In view of our treatment of the promotion issue, the backpay award must be amended. If the district court finds that Locke is entitled under the above standards to a relief man position, Locke would be entitled to backpay at the relief man rate from the date his entitlement began, as under the present order. Otherwise, the backpay award must be recomputed at the lower plant helper rate for the year 1979 and any subsequent period of backpay award.

For the reasons stated above, the judgment of the district court is affirmed in part, vacated in part and remanded to the district court.

NOTES AND PROBLEMS FOR DISCUSSION

1. The Eighth Circuit instructed the district court on remand in *Locke* to make certain findings with respect to Locke's qualifications for the relief man position and the functional relation of that job to the position of plant helper. Who should have the burden of proof on these issues? *See* Ingram v. Mo. Pacific R. Co., 897 F.2d 1450 (8th Cir. 1990) (retroactive promotion available to successful plaintiff unless the employer shows by a preponderance of the evidence that the employee would not have been promoted in the absence of discrimination). Of course, reinstatement will not be ordered unless, absent discrimination, the plaintiff would have been employed by the defendant at the time of trial. *See, e.g.,* Easley v. Anheuser-Busch, Inc., 758 F.2d 251 (8th Cir. 1985) (plaintiffs are not entitled to reinstatement because the positions for which they had applied had been eliminated in a reduction of force before trial).

2. If the claimant lacks the qualifications to move directly into a non-entry-level job, he may be delayed in attaining his "rightful place" in the employment hierarchy. To financially compensate for this delay, monetary remedies have been developed.

Red Circling. In plants with functionally related lines of progression, the minority/female employee, formerly excluded from bidding into a desirable department because of race or sex, may not be able to go directly into the job in that department to which he would have progressed absent discrimination (see the discussion of job-skipping in *Locke*), but may be required to start at the entry level job for that line, notwithstanding the award of retroactive seniority. But the employee may be dissuaded from seeking his rightful place, because the entry-level job may pay less than the dead-end position the employee now holds at the top of his formerly segregated line of progression. In such situations, the employer generally is required to "red circle" the employee's current wage rate, i.e., to allow the employee to carry it with him until he attains a job in the progression with a higher wage rate. *See, e.g.,* Grann v. City of Madison, 738 F.2d 786, 790 (7th Cir.), cert. denied, 469 U.S. 918, 105 S.Ct. 296, 83 L.Ed.2d 231 (1984). Red circling can be combined with the job-skipping remedy described in *Locke*.

Front Pay. The Eighth Circuit's opinion in *Locke* suggests that front pay might be an alternative to placing the plaintiff directly into the relief man job. (Compare Chief Justice Burger's separate opinion in *Franks*, suggesting front pay as an alternative to retroactive seniority). Front pay has become virtually mandatory in cases when the "rightful place" position pays a higher wage rate than the claimant's current salary and, for whatever reason, the employee cannot immediately attain his "rightful place."

> * * * Some employees who have been victims of discrimination will be unable to move immediately into jobs to which their seniority and ability entitle them. The back pay award should be fashioned to compensate them until they can obtain a job commensurate with their status. * * * [B]ack pay * * * until the date of judgment * * * should be supplemented by an award equal to the estimated present value of lost earnings that are reasonably likely to occur between the date of judgment and the time when the employee can assume his new position. Alternatively, the court may exercise continuing jurisdiction over the case and make periodic back pay awards until the workers are promoted to the jobs their seniority and qualifications merit.

Patterson v. American Tobacco Co., 535 F.2d 257, 269 (4th Cir.), cert. denied, 429 U.S. 920, 97 S.Ct. 314, 50 L.Ed.2d 286 (1976). *See* Gregg N. Grimsley, Note, *Front Pay — Prophylactic Relief Under Title VII of the Civil Rights Act of 1964*, 29 VAND. L. REV. 211 (1976).

Since front pay does not put the victim of discrimination in her rightful place, it should be awarded only where reinstatement is not feasible. *See, e.g.*, Schwartz v. Gregori, 45 F.3d 1017 (6th Cir.), cert. denied, 516 U.S. 819, 116 S.Ct. 77, 133 L.Ed.2d 36 (1995). As a substitute for reinstatement, front pay is designed to compensate a victim of discrimination for the time it will take him to attain comparable employment. So to be entitled to front pay, a plaintiff must show that he would be available for comparable work. In SHICK v. ILLINOIS DEP'T OF HUMAN SERVICES, 307 F.3d 605 (7th Cir. 2002), a jury found that discrimination directed at the plaintiff had adversely affected his mental state and had caused him to commit an armed robbery for which he was convicted and sentenced to prison. Upon a jury verdict in favor of the plaintiff, the trial judge awarded front pay in the amount of $303,830 which covered the time that the plaintiff would spend in prison. The Seventh Circuit reversed.

> Shick could not have spent any more time with his employer due to his conviction, and obviously there is no chance that Shick would find any work, much less comparable work, once he was incarcerated. Thus, a front pay award encompassing prison time would be inappropriate, as returning to his job would have been impossible for reasons apart from the strained relationship that existed with his employer.

307 F.3d at 614.

Some courts have held that hostility between the parties is another ground for substituting front pay for reinstatement. *See, e.g.*, Brooks v. Woodline Motor Freight, Inc., 852 F.2d 1061 (8th Cir. 1988) (award of front pay in lieu of reinstatement is supported by evidence that nature of the defendant's business requires a high degree of mutual trust and employer's president testified that he wanted to choke the plaintiff). Of course, such concerns are not present in every employment setting. On remand from the Supreme Court's decision in *Price Waterhouse*, the district court was faced with the question of whether it should force Price Waterhouse to make Ann Hopkins a partner. The district judge noted that while "extreme workplace hostility and disruption may influence a court to deny reinstatement," this was not such a case. Price Waterhouse had over 900 partners spread among 90 offices, and only a few of them had ever met Ms. Hopkins. The trial judge thus concluded that "Price

Waterhouse lacks the intimacy and interdependence of smaller partnerships, so concerns about freedom of association have little force." The judge also offered additional reasons for his determination that front pay was not a viable remedy:

> Since Ms. Hopkins' claim that partnership was always her objective cannot be tested, the alternative of front pay for the rest of Ms. Hopkins' business life does not appear to make her whole and, in any event, might well provide a wholly unwarranted windfall. The Court cannot determine whether she will be a successful, inadequate or superior partner. Nor can it determine how factors affecting her health, availability or the firm's own fortunes will impinge on her earnings. In addition, the Court is skeptical as to whether monetary relief alone provides a sufficient deterrent against future discrimination for a group of highly-paid partners. Given these considerations, equity favors the course that will most vindicate the purpose of the sex discrimination statute, consistent with established national policy.

737 F.Supp. 1202, 1210 (D.D.C. 1990). The court's decision to order the firm to make Ms. Hopkins a partner was affirmed on appeal. 920 F.2d 967 (D.C. Cir. 1990). But this type of hostility cannot me established merely by the fact that the employer and/or co-workers testified at trial. There must be evidence in the record to support a finding of the kind of extraordinary antagonism that is necessary before reinstatement can be denied. *See* Che v. Mass. Bay Transp. Auth., 342 F.3d 31 (1st Cir. 2003) (antagonisms resulting from testimony of co-workers at trial are routine and therefore insufficient without more to tip scales against reinstatement).

3. Assuming that Mr. Locke was qualified for the relief man position and that service as plant helper is not a legitimate prerequisite to the relief man job, could the court displace a white employee from that position in order to put Locke in his "rightful place?" Reconciling the right of the victim of discrimination to be "made whole" with the interests of the incumbent employee has proved difficult for the courts. The legislative history of Title VII indicates that the Act's sponsors did not intend that employees hired before the effective date of the Act be bumped by those making claims under the Act. 110 Cong. Rec. 6992 (1964) (interpretive memorandum of Senators Clark and Case). Title VII's operation was to intended be prospective rather than retrospective. But employees hired after the Act's passage, such as the white temporary worker employed instead of Locke as plant helper, frequently are the beneficiaries of unlawful discrimination against minority and female workers. In footnote 35 of its opinion in *Franks*, the Court stressed that "make whole" relief cannot "be denied merely because the majority group of employees, who have not suffered discrimination, will be unhappy about it" and that "adjustment of the rights of white employees" may be necessary "to shape remedies that will most effectively protect and redress the rights of the Negro victims of discrimination." Are the equitable considerations surrounding the "bumping" of an employee from his job different from those surrounding deprivation of the employee's earned place on a seniority roster? *Compare* Spanguolo v. Whirlpool Corp., 717 F.2d 114 (4th Cir. 1983) (a district court's equitable discretion does not extend to ordering displacement of an "innocent" incumbent employee), *with* Doll v. Brown, 75 F.3d 1200, 1205 (7th Cir. 1996) (criticizing the ruling in *Spangulo* and concluding that "[n]o one has a right to occupy a position that he obtained as a result of unlawful discrimination, even if he himself was not complicit in the discrimination."). *See also* Fuhr v. School District of

City of Hazel Park, 364 F.3d 753 (6th Cir. 2004) (district judge had not abused his authority in ordering the instatement of plaintiff as the boy's varsity basketball coach even though the order required the bumping of the male coach who had been hired for the position; denying the plaintiff an equitable remedy would perpetuate the effects of the discrimination that he suffered).

In his concurring opinion in City Of Richmond v. J.A. Croson Co., discussed in Part IV, *infra*, Justice Scalia commented:

> * * * [O]f course, a State may "undo the effects of past discrimination" in the sense of giving the identified victim of state discrimination that which it wrongfully denied him — for example, giving to a previously rejected black applicant the job that, by reason of discrimination, had been awarded to a white applicant, even if this means terminating the latter's employment. In such a context, the white job-holder is not being selected for disadvantageous treatment because of his race, but because he was wrongfully awarded a job to which another is entitled.

488 U.S. at 526, 109 S.Ct. at 738 (Scalia, J., concurring). Do you agree? Is an incumbent employee who might be "bumped" as the result of a Title VII action a necessary party to the proceeding? Consider Federal Rule of Civil Procedure 19 and Martin v. Wilks, discussed, *infra*, at Section D.

4. In a hiring or promotion case, a plaintiff who establishes that he was unlawfully denied the position ordinarily will be entitled to an injunction placing him in that position, or, where an "innocent" incumbent would be affected, at least to a preference for the next vacancy. But what if discrimination is established and there was more than one minority applicant for the position? Are both entitled to injunctive relief? In MILTON v. WEINBERGER, 696 F.2d 94 (D.C. Cir. 1982), the Court noted that

> * * * [I]f two employees are denied the same promotion for concededly discriminatory reasons, the employer may nonetheless establish that one of the claimants is not entitled to a promotion * * * by offering clear and convincing evidence that there was only one job opening and that the other applicant was more qualified. Since only one of the two victims of discrimination would have been promoted 'but for' the discrimination, the other would not be entitled to an award of the job notwithstanding the unlawful reason for the denial.

696 F.2d at 99. The circuit court offered no explanation of what the outcome should be if the employer failed to meet its burden. Could the employer ever be ordered to hire both applicants if only one vacancy was originally available? *See* Isabel v. City of Memphis, 404 F.3d 404 (6th Cir. 2005) (in absence of evidence of which plaintiffs who were barred from promotion process by discriminatory written examination would have received promotion in non-discriminatory process, all are entitled to promotion). Alternatively, if, as the court in *Milton* assumed, both applicants are "victims of discrimination," would it be fair to at least award the less qualified of two applicants a hiring or promotion preference for a future vacancy? *See* Dougherty v. Barry, 869 F.2d 605 (D.C. Cir. 1989) (multiple claimants to single position must split back pay award). Is the winner-take-all approach to injunctive relief suggested in *Milton* required by the Supreme Court's decision in *Price Waterhouse*?

2. CONSTRUCTIVE DISCHARGE

In Section 1, we examined issues relating to reinstatement and other "rightful place" forms of injunctive relief. But prerequisite to the issuance of any form of equitable relief is a finding that the employer's unlawful conduct caused the denial of employment. This causal relationship between the employer's unlawful conduct and the employee's termination, however, is not always clear. Consider the following case.

Derr v. Gulf Oil Corporation

United States Court of Appeals, Tenth Circuit, 1986.
796 F.2d 340.

McKAY, Circuit Judge.

Gail Derr filed an action against her employer, Gulf Oil Corporation, alleging, among other claims, that Gulf discriminated against her because of her sex in violation of Title VII. The trial court found that Gulf discriminated against Ms. Derr when it demoted her from an associate lease analyst position to an accounting clerk position. The court entered a judgment against Gulf from which the company appeals.

Gulf hired Ms. Derr as a clerk floater in the accounting department of Gulf Mineral Resources Company (GMRC), a division of Gulf Oil Corporation. Ms. Derr was later promoted to associate lease analyst in GMRC's lease records unit where she worked with three male lease analysts. Subsequently, as GMRC's business declined, Mr. Dale Lyon, GMRC's assistant comptroller, removed Ms. Derr from the lease records unit and assigned her to the accounting clerk position. Dissatisfied with her demotion, Ms. Derr resigned.

Gulf first contends that the trial court's finding that Gulf discriminated against Ms. Derr when it transferred her to the accounting clerk position is clearly erroneous. We conclude there is ample evidence from which the trial court could conclude that Ms. Derr's sex was a determinative factor in Gulf's decision to demote her. As an associate lease analyst, Ms. Derr was in a career ladder position, a few months away from becoming a lease analyst. She was doing better than satisfactory work and was being groomed by her supervisor to become a lease analyst. Gulf knew that an opening for Ms. Derr's promotion to lease analyst would occur very soon because two lease analysts were nearing retirement age, and one of them had indicated that he wanted to take advantage of Gulf's early retirement program. In deciding to demote Ms. Derr, Mr. Lyon did not consult Ms. Derr's immediate supervisor even though Mr. Lyon knew little about the duties and workload of the lease records unit. Instead he consulted only Mr. A.C. Weiler, the manager of accounting. The evidence shows that Mr. Weiler was biased against Ms. Derr because of her sex. For example, Mr. Weiler scolded Ms. Derr for attempting to achieve her career goals while having two small children at home. He also commented repeatedly that problems arise if a woman gets too much education. Additionally he was antagonistic toward Ms. Derr after she was demoted and refused to acknowledge her presence.

The evidence also shows that Mr. Lyon chose Ms. Derr for demotion without considering any other Gulf employee for the accounting clerk position. At least one other Gulf employee was not only interested in the accounting clerk job but, unlike Ms. Derr, was also trained for the job. Also, unlike Ms. Derr, the other employee was not very busy with her work at Gulf.

Finally, the following juggling of employees occurred all within a few months: Ms. Derr replaced a Mr. Whittaker, at a lower salary; Mr. Whittaker was transferred into a Mr. Villamor's department; and Mr. Villamor was transferred into the lease records unit, the unit from which Ms. Derr had been removed. Although varying inferences may be drawn from this evidence, the record clearly supports the judgment.

Gulf next contends the trial court erred when it ordered Gulf to reinstate Ms. Derr and awarded her back pay of $7,980 plus interest. These remedies, Gulf argues, are not available to Ms. Derr because she was not constructively discharged. Gulf's contentions require us to examine the basis for the trial court's award to Ms. Derr and the law of constructive discharge.

Ms. Derr resigned from Gulf on November 30, 1982. Apparently, the demotion to accounting clerk would not have made a difference in her salary until March 1, 1983, at which time, absent the discriminatory demotion, she would have been promoted to lease analyst. Thus, the trial court calculated damages for the period from March 1, 1983, to February 1, 1985, the date reinstatement was to take effect. The court determined that Ms. Derr's damages were the difference between what she would have earned as a lease analyst and what she would have earned had she remained in the accounting clerk position. Thus, all of the damages awarded relate to the period of time after Ms. Derr resigned but before she was to be reinstated.

We agree with Gulf that the remedies of back pay and reinstatement are not available to Ms. Derr unless she was constructively discharged. In Muller v. United States Steel Corp., 509 F.2d 923 (10th Cir.), cert. denied, 423 U.S. 825, 96 S.Ct. 39, 46 L.Ed.2d 41 (1975), we reversed the trial court's holding that an employee had been constructively discharged and then examined the effect of our conclusion on the trial court's damage award. We stated:

Unless [the employee] was constructively discharged, he would not be entitled to back pay, interest and retirement from the date of [his resignation]. His damage would be measured by the difference between actual pay and the amount he would have made [had he not been discriminated against] until he quit. . . .

Id. at 930. Our conclusion in Muller is in harmony with the law in other jurisdictions. See, e.g., Satterwhite v. Smith, 744 F.2d 1380, 1381 n. 1 (9th Cir.1984) ("an employee who quits cannot secure back pay unless his employer constructively discharged him."); Bourque v. Powell Electrical Manufacturing Co., 617 F.2d 61, 66 & n. 8 (5th Cir.1980); Harrington v. Vandalia-Butler Board of Education, 585 F.2d 192, 197 (6th Cir.1978), cert. denied, 441 U.S. 932, 99 S.Ct. 2053, 60 L.Ed.2d 660 (1979). We agree with the Fifth Circuit's statement in *Bourque* that "society and the policies underlying Title VII will be best served if, wherever possible, unlawful discrimination is attacked within the context of existing employment relationships." 617 F.2d at 66.

Applying this rationale to the present case, we conclude that unless Ms. Derr was constructively discharged, she is entitled to only the difference in pay between what she earned as an accounting clerk and what she would have earned as an associate lease analyst until she resigned. That difference is, according to the record, zero.[2]

In addition, Ms. Derr is not entitled to reinstatement if she was not constructively discharged. In response to Gulf's contention that Ms. Derr was not entitled to back pay and reinstatement because she was not constructively discharged, the trial court stated:

> [W]here the court has found discrimination in demoting her, changing her to another job, and the court has allowed a setoff or a deduction on what she would have made had she stayed with the company, even though she was not constructively fired, even though she was not forced out, she had other alternatives. She could have stayed. Nevertheless, it was certainly not unreasonable that being denied this job that she had held for a long period of time in anticipation of promotion and reduced back to an accounting clerk — *it was not unreasonable that she quit her job.*

Record, vol. 11, at 1247-48 (emphasis added). The trial court's findings that Ms. Derr was not constructively discharged and that she acted reasonably in resigning are inconsistent when viewed in light of the proper test for determining when an employee is constructively discharged, which we enunciate below.

The constructive discharge doctrine has been applied to Title VII cases by every circuit court of appeals but one. There is, however, a divergence of opinion among the circuits as to the findings necessary to apply the doctrine. While some courts require the employee to prove the employer's specific intent to force him to leave, Bristow v. Daily Press, Inc., 770 F.2d 1251, 1255 (4th Cir.1985), others have adopted a less stringent objective standard requiring the employee to prove that the employer has made working conditions so difficult that a reasonable person in the employee's shoes would feel forced to resign. Goss v. Exxon Office Systems Co., 747 F.2d 885, 887-88 (3d Cir.1984). In Satterwhite v. Smith, 744 F.2d 1380, 1383 n. 4 (9th Cir.1984), the court noted that "[t]he state of the law in the Tenth Circuit on this subject is confusing. . . . [L]anguage in the cases purports to embrace the reasonable employee standard as well as the employer's subjective-intent standard."

It is true that the Tenth Circuit's position on this issue has been less than clear. But in Irving v. Dubuque Packing Co., 689 F.2d 170 (10th Cir.1982), our most recent pronouncement in this area, we intended to clarify our position by adopting the standard set out in *Bourque. Irving* cites *Bourque* with approval and concludes:

> A finding of constructive discharge depends upon whether a reasonable [person] would view the working conditions as intolerable, not upon the subjective view of the employee-claimant.[3]

---

[2]Ms. Derr's counsel apparently agrees that Ms. Derr is not entitled to "back pay" absent constructive discharge. He argued to the trial court that, even if Ms. Derr prevailed on her discrimination claim, a finding that she was not constructively discharged "foreclosed her from any monetary recovery at all."

[3]*Bourque* has become the leading case on the subject of constructive discharge under Title VII. In *Bourque,* the court ruled that, in order to find constructive discharge, "the trier of fact must be satisfied that the . . . working conditions would have been so difficult or unpleasant that a reasonable person in the employee's shoes would have felt compelled to resign."

689 F.2d at 172. While some language in Muller v. United States Steel Corp., 509 F.2d 923, 929 (10th Cir.), cert. denied, 423 U.S. 825, 96 S.Ct. 39, 46 L.Ed.2d 41 (1975), and *Irving* suggests that our focus may once have been on the explicit subjective intent of the employer to force the employee to leave, our conclusion and discussions in *Irving* indicate that we have been struggling with the problem of what the employee must prove.

The examples of the quality and quantity of proof given in *Irving* demonstrate that typically proof of any element in these cases is circumstantial. What *Bourque* has done for the problem of proof is to cut through the details and difficulty of analyzing the employer's state of mind and focus on an objective standard. Thus, proof of constructive discharge "depends upon whether a reasonable [person] would view the working conditions as intolerable." *Irving*. This shift in emphasis is consistent with the District of Columbia Circuit's observation that "[t]o the extent that [the employer] denies a conscious design to force [the employee] to resign, we note that an employer's subjective intent is irrelevant; *[the employer] must be held to have intended those consequences it could reasonably have foreseen.*" Clark v. Marsh, 665 F.2d 1168, 1175 n. 8 (D.C. Cir.1981) (emphasis added).

We trust that our unqualified adoption of this objective standard will clarify any ambiguity which may have remained in our cases to this point. We also believe the standard will simplify the task of the finder of fact in determining not only whether the employer discriminated against the employee but also whether the manner of discrimination rendered work conditions intolerable. In brief, this standard addresses the concerns expressed in both our Muller and Irving cases. Our position, then, is that the question on which constructive discharge cases turn is simply whether the employer by its illegal discriminatory acts has made working conditions so difficult that a reasonable person in the employee's position would feel compelled to resign. In light of our clarification of the standard for finding a constructive discharge, we remand to the trial court to determine whether Ms. Derr was constructively discharged.

* * *

NOTES AND PROBLEMS FOR DISCUSSION

1. Is the Court's "objective" test for constructive discharge fair to the victim of discrimination who is more emotionally vulnerable or sensitive than the hypothetical "reasonable" person? A standard principle of tort law is that the wrongdoer "takes his victim as he finds him" and cannot complain if his actions cause more harm to his victim than the tortfeasor would have expected. Why should this same principle not apply to the constructive discharge analysis?

Although most circuit courts adopted this "objective" test for constructive discharge, a few of them required, in addition to proof of objectively intolerable conditions, that, "the actions complained of were intended by the employer as an effort to force the employee to quit." Martin v. Cavalier Hotel Corp., 48 F.3d 1343, 1354 (4th Cir. 1995). The conflict was resolved when, in PENNSYLVANIA STATE POLICE v. SUDERS, 542 U.S. 129, 124 S.Ct. 2342, 159 L.Ed.2d 204 (2004), the Supreme Court adopted the objective standard. The Court noted that the constructive discharge concept was well established in litigation under the National Labor Relations

Act when Title VII was enacted and that the doctrine had been recognized in employment discrimination cases in many circuits.

"Under the constructive discharge doctrine, an employee's reasonable decision to resign because of unendurable working conditions is assimilated to a formal discharge for remedial purposes. The inquiry is objective: Did working conditions become so intolerable that a reasonable person in the employee's position would have felt compelled to resign?"

542 U.S. at 141; 124 S.Ct. at 2351.

In *Bourque*, the Fifth Circuit opinion described in *Derr* as "the leading case on the subject of constructive discharge, the court stated that one rationale for the constructive discharge doctrine is that "society and the policies underlying Title VII will be best served if, wherever possible, unlawful discrimination is attacked within the context of existing employment relationships." But does this rationale make sense where the victim of discrimination has no opportunity, within the employment relationship, to overcome discrimination? Is any interest served by making an employee stay on the job while she sues her employer? *See* Martini v. The Boeing Co., 137 Wash.2d 357, 376, 971 P.2d 45, 55 (Wash. 1999) (affirming an award of back pay and front pay in a state statutory claim despite a jury finding that a constructive discharge had not occurred on the ground that "allowing the possibility of damages for back pay where an employer has violated the law * * * provides an incentive for employers to work with employees in the workplace to eradicate discrimination"); Mark S. Kende, *Deconstructing Constructive Discharge: The Misapplication of Constructive Discharge Standards in Employment Discrimination Remedies*, 71 NOTRE DAME L. REV. 39 (1995) (arguing that use of constructive discharge doctrine as limit on relief is inconsistent with Title VII's purposes because it forces victims to continue to endure discrimination).

Should an employee who transfers to a lesser position in order to avoid intolerable working conditions obtain the benefit of a "constructive demotion" rule? *See* Fenney v. Dakota, Minnesota & Eastern R.R. Co., 327 F.3d 707, 717 (8th Cir. 2003) ("to survive summary judgment on the issue of constructive demotion, Fenney must show both that he found the environment to be abusive and that an objective person in his position would have felt that he had to demote himself because of his discriminatory work conditions").

2.   What kind of conduct renders continued employment "intolerable" to the "reasonable" employee? What about a demotion and reduction in pay? *See* Grube v. Lau Industries, 257 F.3d 723 (7th Cir. 2001) (mere transfer from one shift to another, unaccompanied by any significant change in job responsibilities, pay, or benefits isn't a constructive discharge); Brown v. Kinney Shoe Corp., 237 F.3d 556, 566 (5th Cir.), cert. denied, 534 U.S. 817, 122 S.Ct. 45, 151 L.Ed.2d 17 (2001) ("Discrimination alone, without aggravating factors, is insufficient for a claim of constructive discharge, as is a discriminatory failure to promote."). What about overzealous supervision of an employee's work? *See* Clowes v. Allegheny Valley Hosp., 991 F.2d 1159, 1162 (3d Cir. 1993), cert. denied, 510 U.S. 964, 114 S.Ct. 441, 126 L.Ed.2d 374 (1993) ("While we do not hold that an employer's imposition of unreasonably exacting standards of job performance may never amount to a constructive discharge, we are convinced that a constructive discharge claim based solely on evidence of close supervision of job performance must be critically examined so that the ADEA is not improperly used as a means of thwarting an employer's nondiscriminatory efforts to insist on high standards."). Or a supervisor's racial slurs? *See* Delph v. Dr. Pepper Bottling Co. of Paragould, Inc., 130 F.3d 349 (8th Cir. 1998) (affirming finding that the plaintiff's resignation was a constructive discharge because repeated references by supervisor in presence of other workers to "my token black boy" directed at African-American employee constituted sufficiently severe and pervasive pattern of racial harassment that it was reasonable to foresee that an employee subjected to it would resign). The "cold shoulder" treatment from management and other employees? *See* Moore v. KUKA Welding Systems, 171 F.3d 1073 (6th Cir. 1999) (affirming jury finding of constructive discharge but describing as a "close question" whether management-promoted isolation and lack of communication was sufficient to support that finding). Finally, can a supervisor's announced decision to recommend termination of an employee by a decision-maker constitute a constructive discharge? *See* Cigan v. Chippewa Falls School Dist., 388 F.3d 331 (7th Cir. 2004) (rejecting the plaintiff's argument that working conditions are irrelevant when the prospect of discharge lurks in the background and finding no constructive discharge where the plaintiff did not contend that her working conditions were unmanageable and that she was not given tasks demeaning to her education and accomplishments prior to the employer's announced intention not to renew her contract).

3. Who should bear the burden of persuasion on the constructive discharge issue? Since the question of whether a constructive discharge has occurred will not arise until there has been a determination that the employer unlawfully discriminated against the plaintiff, does it make sense to place the burden of persuasion on the victim of discrimination? *See* Garner v. Wal-Mart Stores, Inc., 807 F.2d 1536 (11th Cir. 1987) (plaintiff bears the burden of persuasion on the issue of constructive discharge).

4. Most courts agree with *Derr* that a victim of discrimination who leaves her employment as a result of the discrimination must show either an actual or constructive discharge in order to qualify for reinstatement or back pay. Is that bright-line rule justified by the requirement that plaintiffs mitigate their damages or by some concept that voluntary resignation constitutes a waiver of equitable remedies? Does the bright-line rule make sense in a case where, after a voluntary resignation, the employee *has* properly mitigated? In DENNIS v. COLUMBIA COLLETON MEDICAL CENTER, INC., 290 F.3d 639 (4th Cir. 2002), the plaintiff was denied a promotion and promptly quit her job. After the jury found that Dennis had been denied the promotion because of her gender, the court awarded back pay and other relief. On appeal, the employer maintained that by quitting, Dennis had forfeited any claim to back pay. Noting that the Fourth Circuit does not apply the constructive discharge rule denying back pay to persons who leave an employer who has committed intentional discrimination unless it is under conditions of a constructive discharge, the court affirmed the back pay award. All that was required for back pay according to the court was reasonable mitigation.

> Dennis reasonably mitigated Colleton's damages even though she left its employ. Because she was at a low paying job, she could be reasonably certain of finding equivalent pay elsewhere. After leaving Colleton, Dennis actively applied for other work and quickly did find comparable alternative employment in a doctors office, and later as an emergency medical technician. Dennis' expert testified that

she made substantially more money over the three year period between leaving Colleton and trial than she would have made had she stayed at the hospital after being denied promotion.

290 F.3d at 651. Presumably Dennis' back pay award was based on a comparison between what she would have earned had she received the promotion and her actual interim earnings after leaving Colleton. Under these circumstances would not denial of back pay be contrary to the make whole doctrine articulated in *Albemarle Paper Co.?*

5. In *Burlington Industries* and *Faragher*, discussed *supra*, at Chapter 2, Section B.4, the Supreme Court addressed the scope of an employer's vicarious liability for workplace harassment by a supervisor. The Court held that where a supervisor's acts of harassment do not result in a "tangible employment action", the employer can escape liability by establishing, as an affirmative defense, that (1) it exercised reasonable care to prevent and correct any harassing behavior, and (2) the plaintiff unreasonably failed to take advantage of the preventive or corrective opportunities provided by the employer. If, however, the supervisor's conduct results in a "tangible employment action," the employer is absolutely liable and cannot invoke this affirmative defense. The Court stated that a "tangible employment action constitutes a significant change in employment status, such as hiring, firing, failing to promote, reassignment with significantly different responsibilities, or a decision causing a significant change in benefits." But it did not provide a definitive list of such actions. This forced the circuit courts to examine whether any particular employer response fir within the "tangible employment action" denomination. Among the most difficult to characterize was the constructive discharge.

A constructive discharge, like a termination, ends employment. Consequently, *for remedial purposes*, it traditionally has been treated like a discharge, not a resignation. But unlike a formal discharge, a constructive discharge does not usually result from the employer's decision to rid itself of the employee. A constructive discharge could, for example, result from co-worker harassment in which management was not involved or from the unwelcome attentions of a supervisor who had no desire to terminate the employee. For several years, the circuit courts divided over whether a constructive discharge constituted a "tangible employment action" thus depriving the employer of the affirmative defense provided by *Ellerth* and *Faragher*. The conflict finally was resolved by the Supreme Court in PENNSYLVANIA STATE POLICE v. SUDERS, 542 U.S. 129, 124 S.Ct. 2342, 159 L.Ed.2d 204 (2004). There, the plaintiff alleged that she had suffered severe sexual harassment by her three supervisors. She consulted with the employer's Equal Employment Opportunity Officer, but did not file any formal charge and was immediately subjected to further harassment and resigned before there was any internal investigation of her grievances. Relying on *Burlington,* the district court granted the employer's motion for summary judgment because the plaintiff had unreasonably failed to avail herself of the internal procedures for reporting harassment. The Third Circuit held that, if plaintiff was constructively discharged, the employer was not entitled to the *Burlington* affirmative defense. Because there were material fact issues regarding whether plaintiff was in fact constructively discharged the summary judgment was reversed and the case remanded for trial.

Justice Ginsburg, writing for eight members of the Court, reasoned that while a constructive discharge terminates employment, under *Burlington* the employer should only be deprived of the affirmative defense where an "official act" of the employer has resulted in the constructive discharge.

> Unlike an actual termination, which is *always* effected through an official act of the company, a constructive discharge need not be. A constructive discharge involves both an employee's decision to leave and precipitating conduct: The former involves no official action; the latter, like a harassment claim without any constructive discharge assertion, may or may not involve official action. * * * To be sure, a constructive discharge is functionally the same as an actual termination in damages-enhancing respects. * * * But when an official act does not underlie the constructive discharge, the [*Burlington*] analysis, we here hold, calls for extension of the affirmative defense to the employer. As those leading cases indicate, official directions and declarations are the acts most likely to be brought home to the employer, the measures over which the employer can exercise greatest control. Absent "an official act of the enterprise," as the last straw, the employer ordinarily would have no particular reason to suspect that a resignation is not the typical kind daily occurring in the work force. And as *Burlington* and *Faragher* further point out, an official act reflected in the company records — a demotion or a reduction in compensation, for example — shows "beyond question" that the supervisor has used his managerial or controlling position to the employee's disadvantage. Absent such an official act, the extent to which the supervisor's misconduct has been aided by the agency relation, as we earlier recounted, is less certain. That uncertainty, our precedent establishes, justifies affording the employer the chance to establish, through the [*Burlington*] affirmative defense, that it should be held vicariously liable.

124 S.Ct. at 2355. Accordingly, the Third Circuit had erred in holding that the affirmative defense was never available in constructive discharge cases. The Supreme Court agreed, however, with the court of appeals that there were genuine issues of material fact concerning plaintiff's hostile work environment and constructive discharge claims that precluded summary judgment. The case was remanded for determination of whether or not the constructive discharge had been the product of some other tangible employment action.

3. PROSPECTIVE INJUNCTIONS

Sometimes a court is asked not only to make the victim of discrimination whole through reinstatement and monetary relief, but also to issue an injunction to insure that the employer will not continue to engage in discriminatory conduct. Such prospective relief is relatively common in class actions where the class is composed of persons who will be subject in the future to the same procedures and practices that have been exercised in a discriminatory fashion in the past by the employer.

Courts exercising equitable powers, however, are reluctant to grant injunctive relief beyond that necessary to cure the proven violation of law. Consequently, in an individual disparate treatment case, rightful place relief may be all the equity to which the victim of discrimination is entitled. In BROWN v. TRUSTEES OF BOSTON UNIV., 891 F.2d 337 (1st Cir. 1989), cert. denied, 496 U.S. 937, 110 S.Ct. 3217, 110

L.Ed.2d 664 (1990), for example, the district court, in addition to reinstating the plaintiff to a faculty position with tenure, enjoined the university from discriminating against her in the future and from discriminating on the basis of sex in the appointment, promotion, and tenure of other faculty members. But while affirming all of the individual relief awarded the plaintiff, the Court of Appeals vacated the injunction to the extent that it prohibited discrimination against persons other than the plaintiff as "overbroad." A decree barring further discrimination against the plaintiff, the court explained, was "the outer limit of the relief to which she is entitled." *See also* Spencer v. Gen. Elec. Co., 894 F.2d 651, 660 (4th Cir. 1990) (in a sexual harassment case, the trial judge's refusal to issue a prospective injunction was not error where the employer had responded promptly to the employee's complaint and there was no proof of systemic discrimination but only "an isolated incident of one supervisor run amok."). Nevertheless, on occasion, the courts find that broad prospective is appropriate in individual disparate treatment cases. In BRISCOE v. FRED'S DOLLAR STORE, INC., 24 F.3d 1026 (8th Cir. 1994), for example, the Eighth Circuit upheld the district court's issuance of an injunction barring the defendant from discriminating against all of its African-American employees. The court concluded that the trial court's exercise of discretion was justified on the basis of its determination that the employer had engaged in a "consistent practice" of discrimianting against its African-American employees. The main benefit to be derived from such an "obey-the-law" injunction is that the jurisdiction of the court will be continuing, and future unlawful acts can be prosecuted under the contempt sanctions rather than through independent suits.

Because of the EEOC's special role in enforcing Title VII, some courts have held that the agency has standing to seek permanent injunctions against future discrimination even in cases where such relief might not be appropriate under traditional equitable principles. In EEOC v. FRANK'S NURSERY & CRAFTS, INC., 177 F.3d 448 (6th Cir. 1999), the Sixth Circuit held that the agency may seek equitable relief for the class "upon proof even of just one instance of discrimination that violates Title VII" without identifying a class of victims or a pattern or practice of discrimination. *See also* EEOC v. FLC & Brothers Rebel, Inc., 663 F.Supp. 864 (W.D. Va. 1987), affirmed per curiam, 846 F.2d 70 (4th Cir. 1988) (in a sexual harassment case, the fact that the EEOC did not allege a pattern of discrimination does not prevent issuance of an injunction where the evidence showed that there were other employees who were subject to unwelcome sexual advances by the manager but who did not report harassment out of fear of retaliation).

Are there any circumstances that would justify the award of prospective relief to a plaintiff who has not been the victim of discrimination? In THOMAS v. WASH. COUNTY SCH. BD., 915 F.2d 922 (4th Cir. 1990), the court found that the employer's failure to consider hiring the plaintiff was a mistake rather than an act of intentional discrimination and denied her relief of any kind. The court also concluded that the school board's hiring policies constituted arbitrary and unnecessary barriers to minority applicants under *Griggs*. Even though the plaintiff had not filed a class action and had not shown that the discriminatory practices had affected her application, the Fourth Circuit held that she was entitled to an injunction prohibiting continuation of the challenged policies. The court based its decision partly on the fact that the plaintiff remained a "prospective applicant" and was entitled to lawful hiring practices if she renewed her application, and partly on prior Fourth Circuit authority that a Title VII action is of "a public character in which remedies are devised to vindicate the policies of the Act, not merely to afford private relief to the employee."

In a mixed-motive case where the employer has demonstrated that it would have taken the same action in the absence of an unlawful motive, §706(g), as amended by the 1991 Act, authorizes the court to grant declaratory and injunctive relief (not including reinstatement or back pay). Does this provision provide further support for the kind of prospective relief awarded in *Thomas*? Cf. Tyler v. Bethlehem Steel Corp., 958 F.2d 1176, 1182 (2d Cir.), cert. denied, 506 U.S. 826, 113 S.Ct. 82, 121 L.Ed.2d 46 (1992) (questioning in dictum whether "there may be case-and-controversy difficulties with the remedial portion [of the 1991 Act,] which allows a plaintiff without a personal stake in the litigation to act as a private attorney general for purposes of obtaining declaratory or injunctive relief.")

4. THE IMPACT OF INJUNCTIVE RELIEF ON THIRD PARTIES

In most cases, the grant of injunctive relief to an employee or applicant will affect the future progress of other employees or applicants in some way. For example, even an order, as in *Locke*, directing that a single employee be reinstated in his rightful place or placed in the next such vacant position, as a practical matter will deny that position to all other eligible persons. Where injunctive relief is granted to a whole class of persons, as in *Franks*, the relief may disadvantage virtually all employees who are not in the plaintiff's class. Such affected employees normally will not be joined as parties in the action in which the injunctive relief is sought, and may not even be aware of the litigation until the court's order is implemented. This will be the case particularly where the litigation between the plaintiffs and the employer is settled and the injunctive relief is incorporated in a consent decree. One of the most troubling issues in modern institutional reform litigation concerns the accommodation of the interests of those whose legal rights have been violated by government or private institutions and the interests of other persons whose lives and livelihoods are controlled by those same institutions and who will necessarily be affected by injunctive relief intended to correct past wrongs done to others. See generally Abram Chayes, *The Role of the Judge in Public Law Litigation*, 89 HARV. L. REV. 1281, 1289-94 (1976).

May employees who are not in the plaintiffs' class, and whose job opportunities will be impaired by relief granted to the plaintiffs' class, block implementation of such decrees on the ground that as non-parties to the litigation they cannot be "bound" by the results of the suit? May such employees litigate their own independent actions claiming that they are the victims of discrimination? In the past, the answer to these questions typically was "no." Prior to 1989, most circuits followed the "impermissible collateral attack" doctrine under which the failure to intervene seasonably in an action that could affect one's interests barred not only subsequent collateral attacks on the decree entered in the original litigation, but also all challenges to actions taken pursuant to such a decree. *See e.g.*, Thaggard v. City of Jackson, 687 F.2d 66 (5th Cir. 1982), cert. denied, 464 U.S. 900, 104 S.Ct. 255, 78 L.Ed.2d 241 (1983); Douglas Laycock, *Consent Decrees Without Consent: The Rights of Nonconsenting Third Parties*, 1987 U. CHI. LEGAL F. 103, 108-14.

This "impermissible collateral attack" doctrine, however, was rejected by the Supreme Court in MARTIN v. WILKS, 490 U.S. 755, 109 S.Ct. 2180, 104 L.Ed.2d 835 (1989). *Martin* arose from several Title VII class actions filed by African-Americans and women who were either employees or rejected applicants for employment with the city of Birmingham, Alabama. The plaintiffs in those suits alleged discrimination in the hiring and promotion practices of various city agencies, including the police and fire departments. After seven years of litigation and two trials, the parties negotiated a comprehensive settlement which included long-term and interim goals for the hiring and promotion of African-Americans in the police and fire departments. The settlement was incorporated in a consent decree, the immediate effect of which was to reduce substantially the promotional opportunities of incumbent white employees. Before the consent decree was approved by the district court, white firefighters represented by their union filed objections to the proposed decree and moved to intervene in the litigation. The district court overruled all objections to the proposed decree and denied the motions to intervene as untimely. The Eleventh Circuit affirmed.

While appeals from the ruling on intervention were pending, white firefighters filed suit alleging that the implementation of the consent decree and its operation violated their rights under Title VII and the equal protection clause of the Fourteenth Amendment. Specifically, the plaintiffs alleged that they were being denied promotional opportunities solely because of their race in favor of less qualified black firefighters. In their answer, the city defendants, relying on the court-approved consent decree, admitted they had made race-conscious promotions, but denied that they had violated either Title VII or the Constitution in so doing. After a trial of the white firefighters' suit, the district court found that because the consent decree authorized the promotion of minimally qualified African-American candidates over better qualified white candidates to meet the goals contained in the decree, the challenged promotions did not violate the decree and that the decree "immunize[d] the City from liability for actions taken pursuant to it." The decree itself could not be collaterally attacked because the plaintiffs had failed to timely intervene in the original class actions.

The Eleventh Circuit reversed this ruling. IN RE BIRMINGHAM REVERSE DISCRIMINATION EMPLOYMENT LITIGATION, 833 F.2d 1492 (11th Cir. 1987). The court reasoned that since the plaintiffs were neither parties, nor in privity with parties, to the consent decrees, their independent claims of unlawful discrimination could not be precluded without violating their constitutional due process rights. The plaintiffs' claims of unlawful discrimination were remanded and the district court was instructed to treat the consent decree as a voluntary affirmative action plan and to determine the legality of the actions taken pursuant to it under standards established by the Supreme Court for challenges to race-conscious affirmative action plans.

In *Martin*, the Supreme Court affirmed the Eleventh Circuit, but without adopting that court's due process rationale. The Supreme agreed that the impermissible collateral attack doctrine had to be rejected, but not because of constitutional considerations. Rather, the Court relied on the plain language of Rules 19 and 24 of the Federal Rules of Civil Procedure. The Court reasoned that the impermissible collateral attack doctrine operated as a rule of compulsory joinder because its effect was to compel intervention in a case by non-parties. Rule 24, however, casts intervention in permissive terms; although some non-parties may intervene "of right," the rule does not require intervention or forfeiture of rights by any person. Rule 19, on the other hand, the Court explained, requires existing parties to a suit to join non-parties when a judgment rendered in their absence may, as a practical matter, impair the non-parties' interests or leave the parties subject to substantial risk of incurring inconsistent obligations. Based on the text of these rules, the Court concluded that "a party seeking a judgment binding on another cannot obligate that person to intervene; he must be joined" and that "[j]oinder as a party, rather than knowledge of a lawsuit and an opportunity to intervene is the method by which potential parties are subjected to the jurisdiction of the court and bound by a judgment or decree."

The number of white incumbent employees potentially affected by the consent decree at issue in *Martin* was well over 1,100. According to the Court, all these persons should have been joined as necessary party defendants under Rule 19. The petitioners in *Martin* argued that a rule requiring joinder of such large numbers of outsiders would prove too burdensome to plaintiffs and would discourage civil rights class actions. The Court's response to this argument was two-fold. In the first place, the policy argument was misplaced. The Court stated that even if it had been "wholly persuaded by these arguments as a matter of policy, acceptance of them would require a rewriting rather than an interpretation of the relevant rules." In the second place, the practical problem of joinder resulted not from the rules, but from the nature of the relief sought by plaintiffs in such cases. "The breadth of a lawsuit and concomitant relief may be at least partially shaped in advance through Rule 19 to avoid needless clashes with future litigation."

The import of the Court's opinion was clear. A person such as an incumbent employee whose interests, as a practical matter, might be impaired by litigation and who had not voluntarily intervened or been joined as a party may attack a decree (whether by consent or judgment after trial) in the case at any time without regard to his knowledge concerning the original litigation or his actual opportunity to intervene. The Court's message to civil rights plaintiffs was that they could avoid the hardship caused by Rule 19 by limiting the "breadth" of their cases and the nature of relief sought. *See* George M. Strickler, *Martin v. Wilks*, 64 TUL. L. REV. 1557 (1990).

Martin was followed by a spate of "reverse discrimination" suits in which the plaintiffs sought to overturn established consent decrees or court orders.* *See, e.g.,*

---

*On remand from *Martin* a trial was conducted on the plaintiffs' claims. The district court found that the city was justified in entering the consent decree because it had a strong basis in evidence for believing that it had discriminated against minorities in the past. The district further found that the decree was "limited and tailored to the relief necessary to overcome the employment effects of past discrimination," while placing an "acceptable burden" on third parties like the white plaintiffs. Accordingly, the district court denied the plaintiffs' claims. Bennett v. Arrington, 806 F.Supp. 926 (N.D. Ala. 1992). On appeal, the Eleventh Circuit reversed. In Re Birmingham Reverse Discrimination Employment Litigation, 20 F.3d 1525 (11th Cir.1994), cert. denied, 514 U.S. 1065, 115 S.Ct. 1695, 131 L.Ed.2d 558 (1995). The Court of Appeals agreed with the district court that there was a manifest racial imbalance in the employment of fire lieutenants and that the city had a sound basis for entering into an affirmative action plan to remedy the effects of past discrimination in the fire department. The court concluded, however, that there was no legitimate basis for the rigid 50% annual quota adopted for promotion of blacks to fire lieutenant since the figure was completely unrelated to the percentage of blacks in the firefighter ranks from which all promotions were made. To make matters worse, the quota

Mann v. City of Albany, 883 F.2d 999 (11th Cir. 1989) (plaintiffs were entitled under Title VII to collaterally attack a court decree issued in a case in which they were not parties).

In the Civil Rights Act of 1991, Congress attempted to reverse *Martin* by severely restricting the circumstances under which a court decree could be collaterally attacked. Section 108 of the Act amended §703 of Title VII to provide that "an employment practice that implements and is within the scope of a litigated or consent judgment or order that resolves a claim of employment discrimination under the Constitution or Federal civil rights laws may not be challenged" by a person who had "actual notice of the proposed judgment or order sufficient to apprise such person that such judgment or order might adversely affect the interests and legal rights of such person and that an opportunity was available to present objections to such judgment or order." Even without such notice, an outsider is barred from collaterally attacking a decree if his "interests were adequately represented by another person who had previously challenged the judgment or order on the same legal grounds and with a similar factual situation, unless there has been an intervening change in law or fact." The Act explicitly provides that nothing in it affects the rights of existing parties or of those persons who do intervene and that no provision should be construed as "authoriz[ing] or permit[ting] the denial to any person of the due process of law required by the Constitution."

In EDWARDS v. CITY OF HOUSTON, 78 F.3d 983, 998 (5th Cir. 1996) (en banc), a case factually and procedurally similar to *Martin*, the Fifth Circuit ruled that "nonparties seeking to intervene in the proceeding that gives rise to the challenged consent decree are not precluded from doing so because they were afforded notice of their right to object to the decree and the opportunity to do so at a fairness hearing prior to the district court's acceptance of the decree as set forth in [§108]." The court construed §108 of the 1991 Act as affecting only independent reverse discrimination actions filed after the entry of decrees rendered in compliance with the statute. Because unions representing the interests of non-minority employees (police officers) should have been allowed to intervene in the action as a matter of right under Rule 24, even though they first moved to intervene after the consent decree was announced, the court vacated the consent decree and remanded the case for the purpose of allowing the intervenors to take appropriate discovery, and to conduct a new fairness hearing. *See also* United States v. City of Hialeah, 140 F.3d 968 (11th Cir. 1998) (the right to prospective relief which affects the contractual rights of parties must be demonstrated by a trial on the merits and cannot be accomplished by a consent decree absent consent by all parties).

The 1991 Act leaves open at least three questions that must be resolved by the courts. First, does notice of the proposed decree to an incumbent employee and the opportunity to object to the decree satisfy an employee's right to procedural due process? Generally, due process has been construed to require notice and an

---

was permanent and was apparently designed to create a racial balance in the fire lieutenant ranks equivalent to the black/white balance in the civilian labor force. The court held that the plan embodied in the consent decree violated both Title VII and the equal protection clause of the Fourteenth Amendment because it was not narrowly tailored to provide a proper remedy for past discrimination and because it "unnecessarily trammeled" the rights of non-black firefighters. The Supreme Court denied review.

opportunity to appear and to contest a proceeding on the merits before one may be bound by the decree. It is far from clear that an opportunity to object to a proposed judgment without being allowed to litigate the merits of the underlying claim will satisfy due process. In *Edwards*, the court left open the question of "whether a person who is properly denied intervention, or who does not seek it, and who is left only to the procedure afforded under §703(n) has been afforded due process to protect any interests he has that potentially will be affected adversely by the judgment." See Samuel Issacharoff, *When Substance Mandates Procedure: Martin v. Wilks and the Rights of Vested Incumbents in Civil Rights Consent Decrees*, 77 CORN. L. REV. 189, 229-30 (1991) (arguing that permitting incumbent employees to register objections to a consent decree at a fairness hearing would not constitute due process for incumbents absent full evidentiary hearing on any substantive claim). Second, the Act provides that a non-party whose interests have been "adequately represented" may be bound by a judgment or consent decree, but what constitutes "adequate representation"? Without a formal designation of representative status, as in a class action, can a party be said to "represent" a non-party simply because their interests in the litigation coincide? Finally, to what extent will the rationale of *Martin* survive the 1991 Act? The majority in *Martin* strongly implied that the underlying Title VII actions should not have been litigated without joinder of the incumbent employees pursuant to Rule 19. The proper procedure under Rule 19 is for the defendant to move to dismiss for failure of the plaintiff to join indispensable parties. The court must then determine under Rule 19(a) whether the non-parties should be joined. If the answer is in the affirmative and the absent parties can be joined, the court must order the plaintiffs to join them or dismiss the suit. Nothing in the 1991 Act purports to affect Rule 19. The fact that after a judgment or consent decree, absent persons may be barred from challenging the decree does not prevent defendants, at the outset of litigation, from moving pursuant to Rule 19 for joinder of all potentially affected individuals. Such a tactic would, if successful, vastly increase the cost and complexity of class actions seeking institutional relief.

SECTION C. ATTORNEY FEES

1. THE "PREVAILING PARTY"

Hensley v. Eckerhart

United States Supreme Court, 1983.
461 U.S. 424, 103 S.Ct. 1933, 76 L.Ed.2d 40.

JUSTICE POWELL delivered the opinion of the Court.

Title 42 U.S.C. §1988 provides that in federal civil rights actions "the court, in its discretion, may allow the prevailing party, other than the United States, a reasonable attorney's fee as part of the costs." The issue in this case is whether a partially prevailing plaintiff may recover an attorney's fee for legal services on unsuccessful claims.

I

* * *

[The facts and procedural history of the case are omitted. The suit was a class action challenging various conditions in the forensic unit of a state hospital. Some claims in the case were settled before trial, others became moot during the course of the litigation and some were tried. At trial the plaintiff obtained some but not all of the relief requested in the remaining claims.]

B

In February 1980 respondents filed a request for attorney's fees for the period from January 1975 through the end of the litigation. Their four attorneys claimed 2,985 hours worked and sought payment at rates varying from $40 to $65 per hour. This amounted to approximately $150,000. Respondents also requested that the fee be enhanced by 30 to 50 percent, for a total award of somewhere between $195,000 and $225,000. Petitioners opposed the request on numerous grounds, including inclusion of hours spent in pursuit of unsuccessful claims.

The District Court first determined that respondents were prevailing parties under 42 U.S.C. Sec. 1988 even though they had not succeeded on every claim. It then refused to eliminate from the award hours spent on unsuccessful claims:

> "[Petitioners'] suggested method of calculating fees is based strictly on a mathematical approach comparing the total number of issues in the case with those actually prevailed upon. Under this method no consideration is given for the relative importance of various issues, the interrelation of the issues, the difficulty in identifying issues, or the extent to which a party may prevail on various issues."

Finding that respondents "have obtained relief of significant import," the District Court awarded a fee of $133,332.25. This award differed from the fee request in two respects. First, the court reduced the number of hours claimed by one attorney by 30 percent to account for his inexperience and failure to keep contemporaneous records. Second, the court declined to adopt an enhancement factor to increase the award.

The Court of Appeals for the Eighth Circuit affirmed on the basis of the District Court's memorandum opinion and order. We granted certiorari and now vacate and remand for further proceedings.

II

In Alyeska Pipeline Service Co. v. Wilderness Society, 421 U.S. 240, 95 S.Ct. 1612, 44 L.Ed.2d 141 (1975), this Court reaffirmed the "American Rule" that each party in a lawsuit ordinarily shall bear its own attorney's fees unless there is express statutory authorization to the contrary. In response Congress enacted the Civil Rights Attorney's Fees Awards Act of 1976, 42 U.S.C. §1988, authorizing the district courts to award a reasonable attorney's fee to prevailing parties in civil rights litigation. The purpose of §1988 is to ensure "effective access to the judicial process" for persons with civil rights grievances. H.R. Rep. No. 94-1558, p. 1 (1976). Accordingly, a prevailing plaintiff "'should ordinarily recover an attorney's fee unless special circumstances would render such an award unjust.'" S.Rep. No. 94-1011, p. 4 (1976) (quoting Newman v. Piggie Park Enterprises, Inc., 390 U.S. 400, 402, 88 S.Ct. 964, 966, 19 L.Ed.2d 1263 (1968)).[2]

The amount of the fee, of course, must be determined on the facts of each case. On this issue the House Report simply refers to 12 factors set forth in Johnson v. Georgia Highway Express, Inc., 488 F.2d 714 (CA5 1974).[3] The Senate Report cites to *Johnson* as well and also refers to three District Court decisions that "correctly applied" the 12 factors.[4] One of the factors in *Johnson*, "the amount involved and the results obtained," indicates that the level of a plaintiff's success is relevant to the amount of fees to be awarded. The importance of this relationship is confirmed in varying degrees by the other cases cited approvingly in the Senate Report.

* * *

In this case petitioners contend that "an award of attorney's fees must be proportioned to be consistent with the extent to which a plaintiff has prevailed, and only time reasonably expended in support of successful claims should be compensated." Respondents agree that plaintiff's success is relevant, but propose a less stringent standard focusing on "whether the time spent prosecuting [an unsuccessful] claim in any way contributed to the ultimate results achieved." Both parties acknowledge the discretion of the district court in this area. We take this opportunity to clarify the proper relationship of the results obtained to an award of attorney's fees.[6]

---

[2] A prevailing defendant may recover an attorney's fee only where the suit was vexatious, frivolous, or brought to harass or embarrass the defendant. See H.R.Rep. No. 94-1558, p. 7 (1976); Christiansburg Garment Co. v. EEOC, 434 U.S. 412, 421, 98 S.Ct. 694, 700, 54 L.Ed.2d 648 (1978) ("[A] district court may in its discretion award attorney's fees to a prevailing defendant in a Title VII case upon a finding that the plaintiff's action was frivolous, unreasonable, or without foundation, even though not brought in subjective bad faith").

[3] The 12 factors are: (1) the time and labor required; (2) the novelty and difficulty of the questions; (3) the skill requisite to perform the legal service properly; (4) the preclusion of employment by the attorney due to acceptance of the case; (5) the customary fee; (6) whether the fee is fixed or contingent; (7) time limitations imposed by the client or the circumstances; (8) the amount involved and the results obtained; (9) the experience, reputation, and ability of the attorneys; (10) the "undesirability" of the case; (11) the nature and length of the professional relationship with the client; and (12) awards in similar cases. These factors derive directly from the American Bar Association Code of Professional Responsibility, Disciplinary Rule 2-106 (1980).

[4] "It is intended that the amount of fees awarded ... be governed by the same standards which prevail in other types of equally complex Federal litigation, such as antitrust cases[,] and not be reduced because the rights involved may be nonpecuniary in nature. The appropriate standards are correctly applied in such cases as Stanford Daily v. Zurcher, 64 F.R.D. 680 (ND Cal.1974); Davis v. County of Los Angeles, 8 E.P.D. P9444 (CD Cal.1974); and Swann v. Charlotte-Mecklenburg Board of Education, 66 F.R.D. 483 (W.D.N.C.1975). These cases have resulted in fees which are adequate to attract competent counsel, but which do not produce windfalls to attorneys. In computing the fee, counsel for prevailing parties should be paid, as is traditional with attorneys compensated by a fee-paying client, 'for all time reasonably expended on a matter.' Davis, *supra*; Stanford Daily, *supra* at 684." S.Rep. No. 94-1011, p. 6 (1976).

[6] The parties disagree as to the results obtained in this case. Petitioners believe that respondents prevailed only to an extremely limited degree. Respondents contend that they prevailed on practically every claim advanced. As discussed in Part IV, *infra*, we leave this dispute for the District Court on remand.

III

A

A plaintiff must be a "prevailing party" to recover an attorney's fee under §1988.[7] The standard for making this threshold determination has been framed in various ways. A typical formulation is that "plaintiffs may be considered 'prevailing parties' for attorney's fees purposes if they succeed on any significant issue in litigation which achieves some of the benefit the parties sought in bringing suit." Nadeau v. Helgemoe, 581 F.2d 275, 278-279 (CA1 1978). This is a generous formulation that brings the plaintiff only across the statutory threshold. It remains for the district court to determine what fee is "reasonable."

The most useful starting point for determining the amount of a reasonable fee is the number of hours reasonably expended on the litigation multiplied by a reasonable hourly rate. This calculation provides an objective basis on which to make an initial estimate of the value of a lawyer's services. The party seeking an award of fees should submit evidence supporting the hours worked and rates claimed. Where the documentation of hours is inadequate, the district court may reduce the award accordingly.

The district court also should exclude from this initial fee calculation hours that were not "reasonably expended." Cases may be overstaffed, and the skill and experience of lawyers vary widely. Counsel for the prevailing party should make a good-faith effort to exclude from a fee request hours that are excessive, redundant, or otherwise unnecessary, just as a lawyer in private practice ethically is obligated to exclude such hours from his fee submission. "In the private sector, 'billing judgment' is an important component in fee setting. It is no less important here. Hours that are not properly billed to one's *client* also are not properly billed to one's *adversary* pursuant to statutory authority." Copeland v. Marshall, 205 U.S.App.D.C. 390, 401, 641 F.2d 880, 891 (1980) (en banc) (emphasis in original).

B

The product of reasonable hours times a reasonable rate does not end the inquiry. There remain other considerations that may lead the district court to adjust the fee upward or downward, including the important factor of the "results obtained."[9] This factor is particularly crucial where a plaintiff is deemed "prevailing" even though he succeeded on only some of his claims for relief. In this situation two questions must be addressed. First, did the plaintiff fail to prevail on claims that were unrelated to the

---

[7]As we noted in Hanrahan v. Hampton, 446 U.S. 754, 758, n. 4, 100 S.Ct. 1987, 1989, n. 4, 64 L.Ed.2d 670 (1980) (per curiam), "[t]he provision for counsel fees in §1988 was patterned upon the attorney's fees provisions contained in Titles II and VII of the Civil Rights Act of 1964 and Sec. 402 of the Voting Rights Act Amendments of 1975." The legislative history of §1988 indicates that Congress intended that "the standards for awarding fees be generally the same as under the fee provisions of the 1964 Civil Rights Act." S.Rep. No. 94-1011, p. 4 (1976). The standards set forth in this opinion are generally applicable in all cases in which Congress has authorized an award of fees to a "prevailing party."

[9]The district court also may consider other factors identified in Johnson v. Georgia Highway Express, Inc., 488 F.2d 714, 717-719 (CA5 1974), though it should note that many of these factors usually are subsumed within the initial calculation of hours reasonably expended at a reasonable hourly rate.

claims on which he succeeded? Second, did the plaintiff achieve a level of success that makes the hours reasonably expended a satisfactory basis for making a fee award?

In some cases a plaintiff may present in one lawsuit distinctly different claims for relief that are based on different facts and legal theories. In such a suit, even where the claims are brought against the same defendants — often an institution and its officers, as in this case — counsel's work on one claim will be unrelated to his work on another claim. Accordingly, work on an unsuccessful claim cannot be deemed to have been "expended in pursuit of the ultimate result achieved." Davis v. County of Los Angeles, 8 E.P.D., at 5049. The congressional intent to limit awards to prevailing parties requires that these unrelated claims be treated as if they had been raised in separate lawsuits, and therefore no fee may be awarded for services on the unsuccessful claim.

It may well be that cases involving such unrelated claims are unlikely to arise with great frequency. Many civil rights cases will present only a single claim. In other cases the plaintiff's claims for relief will involve a common core of facts or will be based on related legal theories. Much of counsel's time will be devoted generally to the litigation as a whole, making it difficult to divide the hours expended on a claim-by-claim basis. Such a lawsuit cannot be viewed as a series of discrete claims. Instead the district court should focus on the significance of the overall relief obtained by the plaintiff in relation to the hours reasonably expended on the litigation.

Where a plaintiff has obtained excellent results, his attorney should recover a fully compensatory fee. Normally this will encompass all hours reasonably expended on the litigation, and indeed in some cases of exceptional success an enhanced award may be justified. In these circumstances the fee award should not be reduced simply because the plaintiff failed to prevail on every contention raised in the lawsuit. Litigants in good faith may raise alternative legal grounds for a desired outcome, and the court's rejection of or failure to reach certain grounds is not a sufficient reason for reducing a fee. The result is what matters.[11]

If, on the other hand, a plaintiff has achieved only partial or limited success, the product of hours reasonably expended on the litigation as a whole times a reasonable hourly rate may be an excessive amount. This will be true even where the plaintiff's claims were interrelated, nonfrivolous, and raised in good faith. Congress has not authorized an award of fees whenever it was reasonable for a plaintiff to bring a lawsuit or whenever conscientious counsel tried the case with devotion and skill. Again, the most critical factor is the degree of success obtained.

Application of this principle is particularly important in complex civil rights litigation involving numerous challenges to institutional practices or conditions. This type of litigation is lengthy and demands many hours of lawyers' services. Although the plaintiff often may succeed in identifying some unlawful practices or conditions,

---

[11]We agree with the District Court's rejection of "a mathematical approach comparing the total number of issues in the case with those actually prevailed upon." Such a ratio provides little aid in determining what is a reasonable fee in light of all the relevant factors. Nor is it necessarily significant that a prevailing plaintiff did not receive all the relief requested. For example, a plaintiff who failed to recover damages but obtained injunctive relief, or vice versa, may recover a fee award based on all hours reasonably expended if the relief obtained justified that expenditure of attorney time.

the range of possible success is vast. That the plaintiff is a "prevailing party" therefore may say little about whether the expenditure of counsel's time was reasonable in relation to the success achieved. In this case, for example, the District Court's award of fees based on 2,557 hours worked may have been reasonable in light of the substantial relief obtained. But had respondents prevailed on only one of their six general claims, for example the claim that petitioners' visitation, mail, and telephone policies were overly restrictive, a fee award based on the claimed hours clearly would have been excessive.

There is no precise rule or formula for making these determinations. The district court may attempt to identify specific hours that should be eliminated, or it may simply reduce the award to account for the limited success. The court necessarily has discretion in making this equitable judgment. This discretion, however, must be exercised in light of the considerations we have identified.

C

A request for attorney's fees should not result in a second major litigation. Ideally, of course, litigants will settle the amount of a fee. Where settlement is not possible, the fee applicant bears the burden of establishing entitlement to an award and documenting the appropriate hours expended and hourly rates. The applicant should exercise "billing judgment" with respect to hours worked and should maintain billing time records in a manner that will enable a reviewing court to identify distinct claims.[12]

We reemphasize that the district court has discretion in determining the amount of a fee award. This is appropriate in view of the district court's superior understanding of the litigation and the desirability of avoiding frequent appellate review of what essentially are factual matters. It remains important, however, for the district court to provide a concise but clear explanation of its reasons for the fee award. When an adjustment is requested on the basis of either the exceptional or limited nature of the relief obtained by the plaintiff, the district court should make clear that it has considered the relationship between the amount of the fee awarded and the results obtained.

IV

In this case the District Court began by finding that "[t]he relief [respondents] obtained at trial was substantial and certainly entitles them to be considered prevailing . . ., without the need of examining those issues disposed of prior to trial in order to determine which went in [respondents'] favor." It then declined to divide the hours worked between winning and losing claims, stating that this fails to consider "the relative importance of various issues, the interrelation of the issues, the difficulty in identifying issues, or the extent to which a party may prevail on various issues." Finally, the court assessed the "amount involved/results obtained" and declared: "Not

---

[12]We recognize that there is no certain method of determining when claims are "related" or "unrelated." Plaintiff's counsel, of course, is not required to record in great detail how each minute of his time was expended. But at least counsel should identify the general subject matter of his time expenditures. See Nadeau v. Helgemoe, 581 F.2d 275, 279 (CA1 1978) ("As for the future, we would not view with sympathy any claim that a district court abused its discretion in awarding unreasonably low attorney's fees in a suit in which plaintiffs were only partially successful if counsel's records do not provide a proper basis for determining how much time was spent on particular claims").

only should [respondents] be considered prevailing parties, they are parties who have obtained relief of significant import. [Respondents'] relief affects not only them, but also numerous other institutionalized patients similarly situated. The extent of this relief clearly justifies the award of a reasonable attorney's fee."

These findings represent a commendable effort to explain the fee award. Given the interrelated nature of the facts and legal theories in this case, the District Court did not err in refusing to apportion the fee award mechanically on the basis of respondents' success or failure on particular issues.[13] And given the findings with respect to the level of respondents' success, the District Court's award may be consistent with our holding today.

We are unable to affirm the decisions below, however, because the District Court's opinion did not properly consider the relationship between the extent of success and the amount of the fee award. The court's finding that "the [significant] extent of the relief clearly justifies the award of a reasonable attorney's fee" does not answer the question of what is "reasonable" in light of that level of success. We emphasize that the inquiry does not end with a finding that the plaintiff obtained significant relief. A reduced fee award is appropriate if the relief, however significant, is limited in comparison to the scope of the litigation as a whole.

V

We hold that the extent of a plaintiff's success is a crucial factor in determining the proper amount of an award of attorney's fees under 42 U.S.C. §1988. Where the plaintiff has failed to prevail on a claim that is distinct in all respects from his successful claims, the hours spent on the unsuccessful claim should be excluded in considering the amount of a reasonable fee. Where a lawsuit consists of related claims, a plaintiff who has won substantial relief should not have his attorney's fee reduced simply because the district court did not adopt each contention raised. But where the plaintiff achieved only limited success, the district court should award only that amount of fees that is reasonable in relation to the results obtained. On remand the District Court should determine the proper amount of the attorney's fee award in light of these standards.

The judgment of the Court of Appeals is vacated, and the case is remanded for further proceedings consistent with this opinion.

CHIEF JUSTICE BURGER, concurring.

I read the Court's opinion as requiring that when a lawyer seeks to have his adversary pay the fees of the prevailing party, the lawyer must provide detailed records of the time and services for which fees are sought. It would be inconceivable that the prevailing party should not be required to establish at least as much to support a claim under 42 U.S.C. §1988 as a lawyer would be required to show if his own client challenged the fees. A district judge may not, in my view, authorize the payment of attorney's fees unless the attorney involved has established by clear and convincing

---

[13]In addition, the District Court properly considered the reasonableness of the hours expended, and reduced the hours of one attorney by 30 percent to account for his inexperience and failure to keep contemporaneous time records.

evidence the time and effort claimed and shown that the time expended was necessary to achieve the results obtained.

A claim for legal services presented by the prevailing party to the losing party pursuant to §1988 presents quite a different situation from a bill that a lawyer presents to his own client. In the latter case, the attorney and client have presumably built up a relationship of mutual trust and respect; the client has confidence that his lawyer has exercised the appropriate "billing judgment," and unless challenged by the client, the billing does not need the kind of extensive documentation necessary for a payment under §1988. That statute requires the losing party in a civil rights action to bear the cost of his adversary's attorney and there is, of course, no relationship of trust and confidence between the adverse parties. As a result, the party who seeks payment must keep records in sufficient detail that a neutral judge can make a fair evaluation of the time expended, the nature and need for the service, and the reasonable fees to be allowed.

[The separate opinion (concurring in part and dissenting in part) of Justices Brennan, Marshall, Blackmun and Stevens is omitted.]

NOTES AND PROBLEMS FOR DISCUSSION

1. As noted in *Hensley*, the fee shifting provision in §1988 is identical to that contained in §706(k) of Title VII and in most other federal civil rights statutes. By contrast, the remedies section of the Fair Labor Standards Act, 29 U.S.C. §216, which is incorporated in the Equal Pay Act and the Age Discrimination in Employment Act, provides in part that "[t]he court in such action shall, in addition to any judgment awarded to the plaintiff or plaintiffs, allow a reasonable attorney's fee to be paid by the defendant, and costs of the action."

2. The Court in *Hensley* did not provide a specific standard for determining when a party has "prevailed" for purposes of the fee shifting statutes. As applied to plaintiffs, the question of what constitutes "prevailing" has proved troublesome. In TEXAS STATE TEACHERS ASSOCIATION v. GARLAND INDEPENDENT SCHOOL DISTRICT, 489 U.S. 782, 109 S.Ct. 1486, 103 L.Ed.2d 866 (1989), fees were denied by the lower courts because the plaintiffs had not prevailed on the "central issue" in the case. Declaring the "central issue" test "directly contrary to the thrust" of *Hensley*, the Supreme Court reversed.

> The touchstone of the prevailing party inquiry must be the material alteration of the legal relationship of the parties in a manner which Congress sought to promote in the fee statute. Where such a change has occurred, the degree of the plaintiff's overall success goes to the reasonableness of the award under *Hensley*, not to the availability of a fee award *vel non*.

489 U.S. at 792-93. But the Court cautioned that a "technical victory" may be so insignificant as not to support prevailing party status. In HEWITT v. HELMS, 482 U.S. 755, 107 S.Ct. 2672, 96 L.Ed.2d 654 (1987), the Court held that a favorable judicial pronouncement during a case that was of no practical benefit to the plaintiff was not the equivalent of a declaratory judgment and thus did not materially alter the legal relationship of the parties. It found that this plaintiff had obtained nothing from the defendants other than "the moral satisfaction of knowing that a federal court

concluded that his rights had been violated." Such "a favorable judicial statement of law in the course of litigation that results in judgment against the plaintiff", the Court concluded, "does not suffice to render him a prevailing party."

Final relief on the merits of the case, however, may not always be necessary for prevailing party status. In WATSON v. CTY. of RIVERSIDE, 300 F.3d 1092 (9th Cir. 2002), cert. denied, 538 U.S. 923, 123 S.Ct. 1574, 155 L.Ed.2d 313, 155 L.Ed.2d 313 (2003), a deputy sheriff who challenged the constitutionality of his termination obtained a preliminary injunction prohibiting the county from introducing in any proceeding a written statement allegedly obtained from the plaintiff in violation of his due process rights. The district court subsequently granted summary judgment to the defendant on the ground that the plaintiff's due process claims were moot. Nevertheless, the trial judge awarded more than $150,000 in attorneys' fees and costs and this judgment was affirmed by the Ninth Circuit.

> We recognize that there will be occasions when the plaintiff scores an early victory by securing a preliminary injunction, then loses on the merits as the case plays out and judgment is entered against him - a case of winning a battle but loosing the war. The plaintiff would not be a prevailing party in that circumstance. But this case is different because Watson's claim for permanent injunctive relief was not decided on the merits. The preliminary injunction was not dissolved for lack of entitlement. Rather, Watson's claim for permanent injunction was rendered moot when his employment termination hearing was over, but after the preliminary injunction had done its job.

300 F.3d at 1096.

Would nominal relief entitle the plaintiff to a fee? In FARRAR v. HOBBY, 506 U.S. 103, 113 S.Ct. 566, 121 L.Ed.2d 494 (1992), the plaintiff was awarded nominal damages of $1 (and no other relief) in an action alleging a due process violation. Both the trial court and the court of appeals held that the plaintiff had not "prevailed" and thus was not entitled to any attorney fees award. The Supreme Court affirmed, albeit for a different reason. Because the judgment entered on the verdict for nominal damages was actually enforceable, the plaintiff had "prevailed" under the test set forth in *Texas State Teachers*. But the Court also reasoned that the degree of success must govern the amount of fees awarded, and a reasonable fee for one who wins only nominal damages may be no fee at all. That, according to the Court, was what the plaintiff in *Farrar* deserved. Justice O'Connor wrote a concurring opinion in *Farrar* in which she agreed with the majority that "[w]hen the plaintiff's success is purely technical or de minimis, no fee can be awarded." But she went on to say that not all nominal awards are *de minimis* and emphasized that the majority opinion did not hold that recovery of nominal damages could never support an award of attorney fees. In determining whether a nominal damage award could support an attorney fee award, Justice O'Connor identified two factors to be considered: first, "the significance of the legal issue on which the plaintiff claims to have prevailed" and, second, the accomplishment of "some public goal other than occupying the time and energy of counsel, court and client." Justice O'Connor's concurrence has been adopted by a number of courts who have applied these factors in determining whether a plaintiff who has obtained minimal damages is entitled to attorney fees. *See e.g.*, Barber v. T.D. Williamson, Inc., 254 F.3d 1223 (10th Cir. 2001).

Before *Hewitt* and *Farrar*, courts generally held that a plaintiff whose lawsuit was a "catalyst" for a voluntary change in the defendant's conduct was a "prevailing party" under the fee-shifting statutes. *See, e.g.*, Parham v. Southwestern Bell Tel. Co., 433 F.2d 421 (8th Cir. 1970). In neither *Hewitt* nor *Farrar* did the Court reject the catalyst theory, and most circuits, after the decisions in these cases, continued to approve the award of fees to plaintiffs whose suits forced defendants to voluntarily abandon unlawful practices. *See, e.g.*, Morris v. West Palm Beach, 194 F.3d 1203 (11th Cir. 1999) (plaintiff may qualify as a prevailing party it its ends are accomplished as a result of the litigation even without formal judicial recognition). But in BUCKHANNON BOARD AND CARE HOME, INC. v. WEST VIRGINIA DEPT. OF HEALTH and HUMAN RESOURCES, 532 U.S. 598, 121 S.Ct. 1835, 149 L.Ed.2d 855 (2001), a five-member majority concluded that "prevailing party" could only mean a plaintiff who had changed the legal relationship with the defendant by way of a judicial order — either a judgment on the merits or a consent decree.

> A defendant's voluntary change in conduct, although perhaps accomplishing what the plaintiff sought to achieve by the lawsuit, lacks the necessary judicial imprimatur on the change. Our precedents thus counsel against holding that the term "prevailing party" authorizes an award of attorney's fees without a corresponding alteration in the legal relationship of the parties.

Justice Ginsburg, dissenting, took the majority to task for its "anemic construction" of the term "prevailing party" and argued that:

> The decision allows a defendant to escape a statutory obligation to pay a plaintiff's counsel fees, even though the suit's merit led the defendant to abandon the fray, to switch rather than to fight on, to accord plaintiff sooner rather than later the principal redress sought in the complaint. Concomitantly, the Court's constricted definition of "prevailing party," and consequent rejection of the "catalyst theory," impedes access to the court for the less well-heeled, and shrink the incentive Congress created for the enforcement of federal law by private attorneys general.

Will *Buckhannon* drive a plaintiff who otherwise would be prepared to accept adequate relief, though out-of-court and unrecorded, to litigate on and on for a declaratory judgment or some kind of injunctive relief? Could that have been what Congress intended in enacting the fee-shifting statutes? The ruling in *Buckhannon* indicated that a private settlement between the parties, not entailing judicial approval, would not render the plaintiff a "prevailing party" for purposes of a fee-shifting statute. Post-*Buckhannon*, however, the Second Circuit has held that where a district court retains jurisdiction of a case for the purpose of enforcing such a private settlement, the requirements of *Buckhannon* are satisfied and the plaintiff is entitled to recover fees. *See* Roberson v. Giuliani, 346 F.3d 75 (2d Cir. 2003).

Buckhannon applies only to fee applications under federal fee-shifting statutes. State courts may continue to award fees on the "catalyst" theory under state statutory authorization. The California Supreme Court has explicitly rejected *Buckhannon* in actions filed under state antidiscrimination statutes. In TIPTON-WHITTINGHAM v. CITY OF LOS ANGELES, 101 P.3d 174 (Cal. 2004) and GRAHAM v. DAIMLER CHRYSLER CORP., 101 P.3d 140 (Cal. 2004), for example, the court held that under state law a judicially recognized change in the relationship between the parties is not a prerequisite to an award of attorney's fees. To be entitled to an award of attorney fees, the plaintiff must prove (1) a causal connection between the lawsuit and the relief obtained, (2) that the suit was not "frivolous, unreasonable or groundless," and (3) that, prior to filing suit, the plaintiff notified the defendant of its claims and gave the defendant the opportunity to meet its demands within a reasonable time.

3. Section 107 of the Civil Rights Act of 1991 amended Title VII to add §706(g)(2)(B), which delineates one circumstance in which a plaintiff may be entitled to attorney's fees even though he receives no other practical benefit. If a plaintiff demonstrates that unlawful bias was a "motivating factor" behind the challenged employment practice, but the employer establishes that it would have taken the same action in the absence of the unlawful motivation (a mixed motive claim under §703(m)), the court "may grant declaratory, injunctive relief (but not reinstatement) and attorney's fees and costs demonstrated to be directly attributable only to the pursuit of the claim under §703(m)." But *Farrar* holds that a plaintiff who obtains no more than nominal relief may be denied fees altogether. Does §706(g)(2)(B) constitute a statutory exception to *Farrar*? That question has divided the circuit courts. In CANUP v. CHIPMAN-UNION, INC., 123 F.3d 1440 (11th Cir. 1997), the plaintiff convinced a jury that his race was a factor in his discharge but was not awarded any monetary relief because the jury found that he would have been discharged in any event for legitimate reasons. The district court denied attorney fees and the court of appeals affirmed. Emphasizing that the statute distinguishes between attorney fees which "may" be granted in a mixed-motive case and damages or reinstatement which "shall not" be awarded, the court held that the denial of all relief on which attorney fees might be based normally will preclude a fee award. The court reasoned that "[t]he fact that relief is not always available does not justify ignoring this factor in order to make fee awards more prevalent; had Congress wanted to prohibit courts from considering what has historically been a common factor in fee requests in order to make fee awards in same-decision cases more common, it could have drafted a statute that clearly stated this intent."

The Tenth Circuit reached the contrary result in GUDENKAUF v. STAUFFER COMMUNICATIONS, INC., 158 F.3d 1074 (10th Cir. 1998), where a jury concluded that the plaintiff's discharge was motivated in part by her pregnancy but that she would have been terminated in any event for legitimate reasons. The district court denied all relief to the plaintiff, but did make an award of attorney fees reduced by 50% to reflect the degree of plaintiff's overall success on the mixed-motive claim. The Court of Appeals affirmed.

> [W]e conclude that recovery of damages is not a proper factor upon which to assess the propriety of granting a fee award in a mixed motive case. Moreover, we agree with the district court that * * * a plaintiff who prevails under §703(m) should ordinarily be awarded attorney's fees in all but special circumstances.

158 F.3d at 1081.

4. The basic "lodestar" method of calculating fees has been adopted universally in cases where fees are sought under the fee-shifting statutes. Most fee litigation involves disputes over whether the attorney's time and hourly rates are "reasonable."

(a) *Reasonable Hours.* The practical difficulty in applying *Hensley* results from the fact that lawyers' work in litigation seldom can be so compartmentalized that all hours can be attributed to either "winning" or "losing" claims. For example, in depositions of the employer's officials, all the contentions of the plaintiff are likely to be explored. Is such time to be fully compensated so long as some of the discovery was relevant to the winning claim? Who should have the burden of proving that given hours are related to the winning claim? *Compare* Thomlison v. City of Omaha, 63 F.3d 786, 791 (8th Cir. 1995) (a plaintiff who prevailed on only one of three causes of action nevertheless is entitled to full attorney's fee award; because she obtained full relief on the successful claim, "it is difficult to characterize the outcome as providing Thomlison with only limited success."), *with* Schwarz v. Sec. of Health & Human Services, 73 F.3d 895 (9th Cir. 1995) (attorney fees for unsuccessful claims not awarded because they did not arise out of a core of facts common to the successful claims, and because they involved different legal theories, courses of conduct, and claims for relief). *See also* McCombs v. Meijer, Inc., 395 F.3d 346, 361 (6th Cir. 2005) (where a plaintiff prevailed on hostile environment claim but not on retaliation claim, "there is no basis to make the fees proportionate to the successful claim because the quantum of work would be approximately the same."). Plaintiffs can recover attorney fees for work done in state administrative proceedings to which the plaintiff was referred as a prerequisite to the federal action. Carey v. New York Gaslight Club, Inc., 447 U.S. 54, 100 S.Ct. 2024, 64 L.Ed.2d 723 (1980).

Even in a case where the plaintiff has prevailed on all the issues, the district court exercises considerable discretion in deciding whether the claimed hours are "reasonable." In COPELAND v. MARSHALL, 641 F.2d 880, 902 (D.C. Cir. 1980) (en banc), the district judge, while finding that the plaintiffs' counsel had been highly successful, reduced the lodestar by 22% because of his determination that the inexperienced lawyers handling the case had "lacked experienced trial direction." The Court of Appeals affirmed the reduction as within the judge's discretion. *See also* Philipp v. ANR Freight Sys., Inc., 61 F.3d 669 (8th Cir. 1995) (no abuse of discretion to award plaintiff less than half the fees requested since the case was "straight-forward" and there was no need for three attorneys at trial).

Should it be within the trial judge's discretion to reduce a lodestar fee on the ground that limited monetary recovery to the plaintiff made the time spent on the case excessive? In QUARATINO v. TIFFANY & CO., 166 F.3d 422 (2d Cir. 1999), the district court, using "billing judgement," reduced plaintiff counsel's lodestar fee of $124,645 to $79,072 based on the court's view that a "very generous" evaluation of the case would have placed the maximum possible recovery at no more than $200,000 (the jury awarded plaintiff $158,145). Noting that the reason for fee-shifting statutes in civil rights cases is to attract counsel even in cases where the expected monetary recovery is small, the Second Circuit reversed. The appellate court reasoned that the district court's "billing judgement" approach would require plaintiff's counsel to calculate the value of plaintiff's rights solely in monetary terms, undermining the purpose of fee-shifting statutes. The Second Circuit also has held that rejection of settlement offers made during informal negotiations cannot form the basis for reducing plaintiffs' attorney fee awards. NAACP v. Town of East Haven, 259 F.3d 113, 122 (2d Cir. 2001), cert. denied, 534 U.S. 1129, 122 S.Ct. 1068, 151 L.Ed.2d 971 (2002).

When a prevailing plaintiff's requested fees are challenged, should he be entitled to discover from defense counsel the hours charged their client for defense of the case and rates charged by defense counsel? *See* Ruiz v. Estelle, 553 F.Supp. 567, 584 (S.D.

Tex. 1982) ("though an assumption of precise congruity between the amounts of time spent by the two parties would obviously not be warranted, the value of the comparison cannot be assailed.").

Ordinarily, "reasonable hours" will encompass all the time spent on a case, including time necessitated by a retrial. But where the retrial results from the plaintiff's or the plaintiff's counsel's actions, fees may be denied for time spent on the first trial. *See* Shott v. Rush-Presbyterian-St. Luke's Medical Center, 338 F.3d 736, 742 (7th Cir. 2003) (denying attorney's fees for the first trial because of the plaintiff's presentation of evidence "in a way that confused the jury and her opposition to jury instructions that may have alleviated some of the confusion — along with the district court's specific finding that a second trial was necessary because of Shott's unreasonable strategy. We simply do not think it appropriate to award attorney's fees for a trial that was voided by her unreasonable strategy.").

(b) *Reasonable Hourly Rates.* In BLUM v. STENSON, 465 U.S. 886, 104 S.Ct. 1541, 79 L.Ed.2d 891 (1984), the Supreme Court held that the legislative history of the fee-shifting statutes showed that Congress intended for fees to be calculated according to market rates in the relevant community, not according to a cost-plus formula, regardless of whether the prevailing party is represented by private counsel or by a non-profit organization. The fee claimant has the burden of establishing the prevailing rate for attorneys of comparable experience and expertise in the community. In most circuits, the relevant "community" is deemed to be the district where the trial court sits. *See, e.g.,* Polk v. N.Y.; State Dep't of Corr. Services, 722 F. 2d 23 (2d Cir. 1983). The Second Circuit has propounded its own variation on this "forum rule".

Many lawyers whose client base is composed of individuals, non-profit organizations, or unions charge hourly rates substantially below those charged by large law firms that specialize in corporate work (who typically can be found on the other side of the table in employment discrimination cases). To what extent should the successful attorney's private billing rates determine what is reasonable? *See* Save Our Cumberland Mountains, Inc. v. Hodel, 857 F.2d 1516 (D.C. Cir. 1988) (en banc) (market rate method used in awarding fees to traditional for-profit firms and public interest legal service organizations under *Blum* also should apply to attorneys who practice privately, but at reduced rates reflecting non-economic goals). Should a prevailing attorney from outside the community be awarded fees based on the customary rates where she normally practices, or on the prevailing rate in the community where the litigation takes place? In ARBOR HILL CONCERNED CITIZENS NEIGHBORHOOD ASSOCIATION v. COUNTY OF ALBANY, 522 F.3d 182 (2d Cir. 2008), a Voting Rights Act suit in which the prevailing plaintiff sought an attorney fee award pursuant to the terms of the Civil Rights Attorney's Fees Wards Act, the Second Circuit ruled that a trial court can use an out-of-district rate in calculating the lodestar's reasonable hourly rate "if it is clear that a reasonable, paying client would have paid those higher rates." And in making that determination, the Second Circuit announced that it would presume that a reasonable, paying client typically would *not* hire counsel from outside the district, but that this presumption could be rebutted "only in the unusual case" if the party seeking the use of a higher rate demonstrated that retaining an out-of-district attorney was reasonable under the circumstances as they would be assessed by a client paying the bill. *See also* Gates v.

Deukmejian, 987 F.2d 1392 (9th Cir. 1993) (recognizing "narrow exception" to use of local rates where plaintiff proves that counsel in forum location were unavailable).

In PRASEUTH v. RUBBERMAID, INC., 406 F.3d 1245 (10th Cir. 2005), plaintiff's counsel claimed more than $1 million in fees in an ADA case where plaintiff's monetary award was $250,000. The district court awarded $336,025 in fees. Finding the requested fees "unreasonable by any standard" and noting the enormous amounts of time claimed for "relatively straightforward, discrete tasks," the court of appeals affirmed. In doing so, the court commented on the difference between what reasonably may be billed a fee-paying client and what can be claimed from the defendant under a fee-shifting statute.

> The trial judge is not obligated to accept the fee applicant's billing judgment uncritically. Indeed, fee awards under the federal fee-shifting statutes come under close scrutiny. * * * In contrast to a private fee agreement between a party and his attorney in which a party may agree to an aggressive litigation strategy and the inevitably resultant higher fees, a fee-shifting statute is not a voluntary matter. Fee-shifting imposes one party's fee obligations upon the very party who was the subject of that litigation strategy. Thus, awards made under the authority of fee-shifting statutes are not intended to replicate fees which an attorney could earn through a private fee arrangement with a client.

406 F.3d at 1257 (citations omitted).

A major difference between the collection of fees under the fee-shifting statutes and in normal commercial work is that counsel in civil rights cases are not paid as they go and must wait a substantial time to realize their fees for successful cases. In recognition of this delay in payment, most courts have awarded fees based on rates prevailing at the time of judgment rather than at the time the legal work was performed. In MISSOURI v. JENKINS, 491 U.S. 274, 109 S.Ct. 2463, 105 L.Ed.2d 229 (1989), the Supreme Court explained the reason for this rule:

> Clearly, compensation received several years after the services were rendered — as it frequently is in complex civil rights litigation — is not equivalent to the same dollar amount received reasonably promptly as the legal services are performed, as would normally be the case with private billings. We agree, therefore, that an appropriate adjustment for delay in payment — whether by the application of current rather than historic hourly rates or otherwise — is within the contemplation of the statute.

491 U.S. at 283-84, 109 S.Ct. at 2469.

5. Most lawyers who represent plaintiffs in employment discrimination litigation do so on a contingent fee basis; they are not paid unless they are successful. In other kinds of litigation, such as, personal injury suits, contingent fees to the successful plaintiff's lawyer often far exceed what would be justified by the application of reasonable non-contingent hourly rates. Large fees in contingent cases are justified on the ground that the attorney is being compensated for the risk that the suit would be unsuccessful, a risk not taken when the fee is paid on a non-contingent basis. Under the fee-shifting statutes, some courts allowed enhancement of the lodestar fee as compensation for the risk of losing. But in CITY OF BURLINGTON v. DAGUE, 505 U.S. 557, 112 S.Ct. 2638, 120 L.Ed.2d 449 (1992), the Supreme Court put an end to contingency enhancements under federal fee-shifting statutes. The majority reasoned that contingency enhancements are inconsistent with the requirement that only a prevailing party may recover a fee.

> An attorney operating on a contingency fee basis pools the risks presented by his various cases: cases that turn out to be successful pay for the time he gambled on those that did not. To award a contingency enhancement under a fee-shifting statute would in effect pay for the attorney's time (or anticipated time) in cases where his client does not prevail.

505 U.S. at 565. Dissenting Justice Blackmun argued that the very market factors relied upon to determine a "reasonable" fee may require that a lodestar fee be enhanced in order to qualify as a "reasonable fee."

> Two principles, in my view, require the conclusion that the "enhanced" fee awarded to respondents was reasonable. First, this Court consistently has recognized that a "reasonable" fee is to be a "fully compensatory fee," Hensley v. Eckerhart, and is to be "calculated on the basis of rates and practices prevailing in the relevant market." Missouri v. Jenkins. Second, it is a fact of the market that an attorney who is paid only when his client prevails will tend to charge a higher fee than one who is paid regardless of outcome, and relevant professional standards long have recognized that this practice is reasonable.

505 U.S. at 567. Enhanced fees, hoever, may be available on state-law claims. *See* Mangold v. Calif. Public Utilities Comm'n, 67 F.3d 1470, 1478-79 (9th Cir. 1995) (doubling of fee award under California law upheld because the plaintiff had prevailed on both federal and state law claims; "a state right to an attorney's fee reflects a substantial policy of the state.").

Prevailing attorneys sometimes ask the trial court for an enhancement of the lodestar fee based on their exceptional performance and results. In PERDUE v. KENNY, 559 U.S. 542, 130 S.Ct. 1662, 176 L.Ed.2d 494 (2010), the Supreme Court unanimously ruled that superior attorney performance and/or results is presumptively taken into account in making the lodestar calculation and therefore is not properly the basis for any enhancement. However, the Court also noted that it previously had recognized that the strong presumption of the reasonableness of the lodestar fee could be overcome in "rare" and "exceptional" cases where the lodestar fee did not adequately take into account a factor that properly could be considered in determining a reasonable fee. The Court indicated that enhancement might be appropriate, for example, in cases where the attorney had made an extraordinary outlay of expenses in extremely protracted litigation. It even acknowledged that enhancement for superior performance could be possible in a "rare" or "exceptional" case where the prevailing attorney tendered specific evidence that the lodestar fee would not have been "adequate to attract competent counsel." The Court split 5-4, however, in determining how this standard should apply to the instant case. The majority concluded that since the trial court's decision in the instant case to award a 75% enhancement was based on the trial judge's "impressionistic" view of the prevailing attorney's performance and result, the exceptional circumstances standard was not met. Enhancement based on a subjective assessment of performance, the majority explained, did not provide appellate courts with an objective reviewable basis for the fee determination. The four partial dissenters, on the other hand, concluded that the trial court had not abused its discretion in awarding the enhancement.

6. Should the existence of a contingent fee agreement between the plaintiff and her counsel affect either the entitlement to, or the amount of an award of, attorney fees under a fee-shifting statute? In BLANCHARD v. BERGERON, 489 U.S. 87, 109 S.Ct. 939, 103 L.Ed.2d 67 (1989), the Supreme Court held that a contingent fee agreement does not cap the fee that can be awarded under a fee-shifting statute. The court reasoned that fee-shifting statutes contemplated reasonable compensation for the time and effort expended by the prevailing attorney and that, should a fee agreement provide less than a reasonable fee calculated in that manner, the defendant should nevertheless be required to pay the higher amount. In *Bergeron*, application of the contingent fee contract would have reduced the court awarded fees. But in VENEGAS v. MITCHELL, 495 U.S. 82, 110 S.Ct. 1679, 109 L.Ed.2d 74 (1990), a plaintiff who had signed a contingent fee agreement argued that the fee agreement should not be enforced because his counsel had been awarded a reasonable fee to be paid by the defendant and, in the alternative, that the amount of the court-awarded fee should cap the amount owed by the plaintiff under the contingent fee agreement. The Court held that nothing in the fee-shifting statute prevented collection of a contingent fee, even when that fee exceeded the statutory award.

> [S]ection 1988 controls what the losing defendant must pay, not what the prevailing plaintiff must pay his lawyer. What a plaintiff may be bound to pay and what an attorney is free to collect under a fee agreement are not necessarily measured by the "reasonable attorney's fee" that a defendant must pay pursuant to a court order. Section 1988 itself does not interfere with the enforceability of a contingent-fee contract.

495 U.S. at 90. After *Venegas*, the lower courts have split over whether a successful plaintiff's counsel is entitled to receive *both* a contingent fee from the client and a court-awarded fee from the defendant under a fee-shifting statute. In ROSS v. DOUGLAS COUNTY, 244 F.3d 620, 622 (8th Cir. 2001), the court held that "where there exists a contingent fee contract along with a reimbursable attorney fee award * * * claimant's counsel is not entitled to receive both fees. Rather, counsel is limited to the award under the [fee-shifting statute] or the fee under the contract, whichever is greater." The Fifth Circuit has construed *Venegas* to mandate the enforcement of a reasonable contingent fee contract between the client and attorney without regard to the attorney's entitlement to an award from the defendant under a fee-shifting statute. In GOBERT v. WILLIAMS, 323 F.3d 1099 (5th Cir. 2003), the client and attorney entered into a contingent fee contract which guaranteed the attorney 35% of any recovery aside from attorney fees and also specified that all court awarded fees "are and shall remain the property of the attorney." After the plaintiff was awarded back pay for the discriminatory denial of a promotion, she tried to withdraw from the agreement. But the district judge enforced the contingent fee and awarded reasonable fees based on a lodestar calculation. Relying on *Venegas,* the appellate court affirmed. "[T]here is nothing in [§706(k)] to regulate what plaintiffs may or may not promise to pay their attorneys * * * Moreover, because this dispute turns on the enforceability of the retainer agreement rather than the amount of fees shifted to the losing party, our case law regarding the reasonableness of fee awards under §706(k) does not apply."

Christiansburg Garment Co. v. EEOC

Supreme Court of the United States, 1978.
434 U.S. 412, 98 S.Ct. 694, 54 L.Ed.2d 648.

MR. JUSTICE STEWART delivered the opinion of the Court.

* * * The question in this case is under what circumstances an attorney's fee should be allowed when the defendant is the prevailing party in a Title VII action — a question about which the federal courts have expressed divergent views.

I

Two years after Rosa Helm had filed a Title VII charge of racial discrimination against the petitioner Christiansburg Garment Co., the Equal Employment Opportunity Commission notified her that its conciliation efforts had failed and that she had the right to sue the company in federal court. She did not do so. Almost two years later, in 1972, Congress enacted amendments to Title VII. Section 14 of these amendments authorized the Commission to sue in its own name to prosecute "charges pending with the Commission" on the effective date of the amendments. Proceeding under this section, the Commission sued the company, alleging that it had engaged in unlawful employment practices in violation of the amended Act. The company moved for summary judgment on the ground, *inter alia*, that the Rosa Helm charge had not been "pending" before the Commission when the 1972 amendments took effect. The District Court agreed, and granted summary judgment in favor of the company.

The company then petitioned for the allowance of attorney's fees against the Commission pursuant to §706(k) of Title VII. Finding that "the Commission's action in bringing the suit cannot be characterized as unreasonable or meritless," the District Court concluded that "an award of attorney's fees to petitioner is not justified in this case." A divided Court of Appeals affirmed, and we granted certiorari to consider an important question of federal law.

II

It is the general rule in the United States that in the absence of legislation providing otherwise, litigants must pay their own attorney's fees. *Alyeska Pipeline Co. v. Wilderness Society*, 421 U.S. 240, 95 S.Ct. 1612, 44 L.Ed.2d 141. Congress has provided only limited exceptions to this rule "under selected statutes granting or protecting various federal rights." Some of these statutes make fee awards mandatory for prevailing plaintiffs; others make awards permissive but limit them to certain parties, usually prevailing plaintiffs. But many of the statutes are more flexible, authorizing the award of attorney's fees to either plaintiffs or defendants, and entrusting the effectuation of the statutory policy to the discretion of the district courts. Section 706(k) of Title VII of the Civil Rights Act of 1964 falls into this last category, providing as it does that a district court may in its discretion allow an attorney's fee to the prevailing party.

In *Newman v. Piggie Park Enterprises*, 390 U.S. 400, 88 S.Ct. 964, 19 L.Ed.2d 1263, the Court considered a substantially identical statute authorizing the award of attorney's fees under Title II of the Civil Rights Act of 1964. In that case the plaintiffs had prevailed, and the Court of Appeals had held that they should be awarded their attorney's fees "only to the extent that the respondents' defenses had been advanced for purposes of delay and not in good faith." We ruled that this "subjective standard" did not properly effectuate the purposes of the counsel-fee provision of Title II. Relying primarily on the intent of Congress to cast a Title II plaintiff in the role of a "private attorney general vindicating a policy that Congress considered of the highest priority," we held that a prevailing plaintiff under Title II "should ordinarily recover an attorney's fee unless special circumstances would render such an award unjust." We noted in passing that if the objective of Congress had been to permit the award of attorney's fees only against defendants who had acted in bad faith, "no new statutory provision would have been necessary," since even the American common-law rule allows the award of attorney's fees in those exceptional circumstances.

In *Albemarle Paper Co. v. Moody*, the Court made clear that the *Piggie Park* standard of awarding attorney's fees to a successful plaintiff is equally applicable in an action under Title VII. It can thus be taken as established, as the parties in this case both acknowledge, that under §706(k) of Title VII a prevailing plaintiff ordinarily is to be awarded attorney's fees in all but special circumstances.

III

The question in the case before us is what standard should inform a district court's discretion in deciding whether to award attorney's fees to a successful defendant in a Title VII action. Not surprisingly, the parties in addressing the question in their briefs and oral arguments have taken almost diametrically opposite positions.

The company contends that the *Piggie Park* criterion for a successful plaintiff should apply equally as a guide to the award of attorney's fees to a successful defendant. Its submission, in short, is that every prevailing defendant in a Title VII action should receive an allowance of attorney's fees "unless special circumstances would render such an award unjust." The respondent Commission, by contrast, argues that the prevailing defendant should receive an award of attorney's fees only when it is found that the plaintiff's action was brought in bad faith. We have concluded that neither of these positions is correct.

A

Relying on what it terms "the plain meaning of the statute," the company argues that the language of §706(k) admits of only one interpretation: "A prevailing defendant is entitled to an award of attorney's fees on the same basis as a prevailing plaintiff." But the permissive and discretionary language of the statute does not even invite, let alone require, such a mechanical construction. The terms of §706(k) provide no indication whatever of the circumstances under which either a plaintiff or a defendant should be entitled to attorney's fees. And a moment's reflection reveals that there are at least two strong equitable considerations counseling an attorney's fee award to a prevailing Title VII plaintiff that are wholly absent in the case of a prevailing Title VII defendant.

First, as emphasized so forcefully in *Piggie Park*, the plaintiff is the chosen instrument of Congress to vindicate "a policy that Congress considered of the highest priority." Second, when a district court awards counsel fees to a prevailing plaintiff, it is awarding them against a violator of federal law. As the Court of Appeals clearly perceived, "these policy considerations which support the award of fees to a prevailing plaintiff are not present in the case of a prevailing defendant." A successful defendant seeking counsel fees under §706(k) must rely on quite different equitable considerations.

But if the company's position is untenable, the Commission's argument also misses the mark. It seems clear, in short, that in enacting §706(k) Congress did not intend to permit the award of attorney's fees to a prevailing defendant only in a situation where the plaintiff was motivated by bad faith in bringing the action. As pointed out in *Piggie Park*, if that had been the intent of Congress, no statutory provision would have been necessary, for it has long been established that even under the American common-law rule attorney's fees may be awarded against a party who has proceeded in bad faith.

Furthermore, while it was certainly the policy of Congress that Title VII plaintiffs should vindicate "a policy that Congress considered of the highest priority," *Piggie Park*, it is equally certain that Congress entrusted the ultimate effectuation of that policy to the adversary judicial process, *Occidental Life Ins. Co. v. EEOC*, 432 U.S. 355, 97 S.Ct. 2447, 53 L.Ed.2d 402. A fair adversary process presupposes both a vigorous prosecution and a vigorous defense. It cannot be lightly assumed that in enacting §706(k), Congress intended to distort that process by giving the private plaintiff substantial incentives to sue, while foreclosing to the defendant the possibility of recovering his expenses in resisting even a groundless action unless he can show that it was brought in bad faith.

B

The sparse legislative history of §706(k) reveals little more than the barest outlines of a proper accommodation of the competing considerations we have discussed. The only specific reference to §706(k) in the legislative debates indicates that the fee provision was included to "make it easier for a plaintiff of limited means to bring a meritorious suit." During the Senate floor discussions of the almost identical attorney's fee provision of Title II, however, several Senators explained that its allowance of awards to defendants would serve "to deter the bringing of lawsuits without foundation," "to discourage frivolous suits," and "to diminish the likelihood of unjustified suits being brought." If anything can be gleaned from these fragments of legislative history, it is that while Congress wanted to clear the way for suits to be brought under the Act, it also wanted to protect defendants from burdensome litigation having no legal or factual basis. The Court of Appeals for the District of Columbia Circuit seems to have drawn the maximum significance from the Senate debates when it concluded:

> "[From these debates] two purposes for §706(k) emerge. First, Congress desired to 'make it easier for a plaintiff of limited means to bring a meritorious suit' . . . . But second, and equally important, Congress intended to 'deter the bringing of lawsuits without foundation' by providing that the 'prevailing party' — be it plaintiff or defendant — could obtain legal fees." *Grubbs v. Bout*, 79 U.S.App.D.C. 18, 20, 548 F.2d 973, 975.

The first federal appellate court to consider what criteria should govern the award of attorney's fees to a prevailing Title VII defendant was the Court of Appeals for the Third Circuit in United States Steel Corp. v. United States, 519 F.2d 359. There a District Court had denied a fee award to a defendant that had successfully resisted a Commission demand for documents, the court finding that the Commission's action had not been "unfounded, meritless, frivolous or vexatiously brought." The Court of Appeals concluded that the District Court had not abused its discretion in denying the award. A similar standard was adopted by the Court of Appeals for the Second Circuit in Carrion v. Yeshiva University, 535 F.2d 722. In upholding an attorney's fee award to a successful defendant, that court stated that such awards should be permitted "not routinely, not simply because he succeeds, but only where the action brought is found to be unreasonable, frivolous, meritless or vexatious."

To the extent that abstract words can deal with concrete cases, we think that the concept embodied in the language adopted by these two Courts of Appeals is correct. We would qualify their words only by pointing out that the term "meritless" is to be understood as meaning groundless or without foundation, rather than simply that the plaintiff has ultimately lost his case, and that the term "vexatious" in no way implies that the plaintiff's subjective bad faith is a necessary prerequisite to a fee award against him. In sum, a district court may in its discretion award attorney's fees to a prevailing defendant in a Title VII case upon a finding that the plaintiff's action was frivolous, unreasonable, or without foundation, even though not brought in subjective bad faith.

In applying these criteria, it is important that a district court resist the understandable temptation to engage in *post hoc* reasoning by concluding that because a plaintiff did not ultimately prevail, his action must have been unreasonable or without foundation. This kind of hindsight logic could discourage all but the most airtight claims, for seldom can a prospective plaintiff be sure of ultimate success. No matter how honest one's belief that he has been the victim of discrimination, no matter how meritorious one's claim may appear at the outset, the course of litigation is rarely predictable. Decisive facts may not emerge until discovery or trial. The law may change or clarify in the midst of litigation. Even when the law or the facts appear questionable or unfavorable at the outset, a party may have an entirely reasonable ground for bringing suit.

That §706(k) allows fee awards only to prevailing private plaintiffs should assure that this statutory provision will not in itself operate as an incentive to the bringing of claims that have little chance of success. To take the further step of assessing attorney's fees against plaintiffs simply because they do not finally prevail would substantially add to the risks inhering in most litigation and would undercut the efforts of Congress to promote the vigorous enforcement of the provisions of Title VII. Hence, a plaintiff should not be assessed his opponent's attorney's fees unless a court finds that his claim was frivolous, unreasonable, or groundless, or that the plaintiff continued to litigate after it clearly became so. And, needless to say, if a plaintiff is found to have brought or continued such a claim in bad faith, there will be an even stronger basis for charging him with the attorney's fees incurred by the defense.[20]

---

[20]Initially, the Commission argued that the "costs" assessable against the Government under §706(k) did not include attorney's fees. But the Courts of Appeals rejected this position and, during the course of appealing this case, the Commission abandoned its contention that it was legally immune to adverse fee awards under §706(k).

It has been urged that fee awards against the Commission should rest on a standard different from that governing fee awards against private plaintiffs. One amicus stresses that the Commission, unlike private litigants, needs no inducement to enforce Title VII since it is required by statute to do so. But this distinction between the Commission and private plaintiffs

IV

In denying attorney's fees to the company in this case, the District Court focused on the standards we have discussed. The court found that "the Commission's action in bringing the suit cannot be characterized as unreasonable or meritless" because "the basis upon which petitioner prevailed was an issue of first impression requiring judicial resolution" and because the "Commission's statutory interpretation of §14 of the 1972 amendments was not frivolous." The court thus exercised its discretion squarely within the permissible bounds of §706(k). Accordingly, the judgment of the Court of Appeals upholding the decision of the District Court is affirmed.

Mr. Justice Blackmun took no part in the consideration or decision of this case.

NOTES AND PROBLEMS FOR DISCUSSION

1. The determination of when a defendant is eligible for an award of atatutory attorney fees is a two step process. First, §706(k) requires, for all litigants, that the party seeking attorney fees must be a "prevailing party". If that requirement is satisfied by a defendant, we reach the question resolved in *Christiansburg*: the standard that inform a district court's discretion in deciding whether to award attorney's fees to a successful defendant in a Title VII action. But the *Christianburg* Court did not address the initial question of when a *defendant* is deemed to be a "prevailing partry". For several decades, the circuit courts were divided on whether the defendant was required to win a favorable judgment *on the merits* (as opposed to a judgment based on a non-merits ground) to be deemed a prevailing party.

(a) In CRST VAN EXPEDITED, INC. v. EEOC, ___ U.S. ___, 136 S.Ct. 1642, 194 L.Ed.2d 707 (2016), the Court unanimously resolved this conflict, holding that it was *not* required that a defendant succed on the merits on *any* claim in the case in order to be deemed a prevailing party for attorney fee award purposes. In *CRST*, the EEOC had filed suit against the defendant on behalf of a group of female employees who alleged that they had been the victims of sexual harassment. The EEOC suit

---

merely explains why Congress drafted §706(k) to preclude the recovery of attorney's fees by the Commission; it does not support a difference in treatment among private and Government plaintiffs when a prevailing defendant seeks to recover his attorney's fees. Several courts and commentators have also deemed significant the Government's greater ability to pay adverse fee awards compared to a private litigant. See, e.g., United States Steel Corp. v. United States, *supra*, 519 F.2d, at 364 n. 24; Heinsz, Attorney's Fees for Prevailing Title VII Defendants: Toward a Workable Standard, 8 U.Toledo L.Rev. 259, 290 (1977); Comment, Title VII, Civil Rights Act of 1964; Standards for Award of Attorney's Fees to Prevailing Defendants, 1976 Wis.L.Rev. 207, 228. We are informed, however, that such awards must be paid from the Commission's litigation budget, so that every attorney's fee assessment against the Commission will inevitably divert resources from the agency's enforcement of Title VII. See 46 Comp.Gen. 98, 100 (1966); 38 Comp.Gen. 343, 344-345 (1958). The other side of this coin is the fact that many defendants in Title VII claims are small- and moderate-size employers for whom the expense of defending even a frivolous claim may become a strong disincentive to the exercise of their legal rights. In short, there are equitable considerations on both sides of this question. Yet §706(k) explicitly provides that "the Commission and the United States shall be liable for costs the same as a private person." Hence, although a district court may consider distinctions between the Commission and private plaintiffs in determining the reasonableness of the Commission's litigation efforts, we find no grounds for applying a different general standard whenever the Commission is the losing plaintiff.

contained both a pattern and practice allegation as well as individual claims of harassment. The trial court dismissed all claims; most individual claims on the ground that the EEOC had not properly fulfilled its statutory obligation to investigate and attempt conciliation before filing suit against the defendant. It also awarded the defendant over $4 million in attorney fees against the plaintiff EEOC. The Eighth Circuit panel reversed the attorney fee award on the ground that the defendant was not a prevailing party because it had not received a judgment on the merits but had been successful in having the casse dismissed on non-merits grounds.

The Supreme Court unanimously reversed the Eighth Circuit, ruling that a defendant did *not* have to obtain a favorable judgment *on the merits* in order to be deemed a prevailing party under §706(k). Rather, all that is required is that the plaintiff's claim is rebuffed, regardless of the reason. There was no evidence, in the Court's judgment, that Congress intended to distinguish betweenm judgments on the mertis or those on non-merits bases for attorney fee award purposes. Rather, the Court continued, the purpose of the statutory fee award provision was to discourage frivolous litigation, reagdless of whether it was merit-based or non-merit based frivolity. Since the circuit court had not considered the second element of the attorney fee calculation, i.e., whether the plaintiff's suit met the *Christiansburg* "frivolous, unreasonable, or without foundation" standard, the Court remanded the case for resolution of that issue.

(b) With respect to the second part of the attorney fee calculation for victorious defendants, under *Christiansburg Garment*, the employer need not establish that the plaintiff acted in bad faith in order to qualify for a fee award. The *Christianburg* Court did not, however, quantify the proof that the losing plaintiff must produce to escape exposure. To what extent should the plaintiff's good faith in initiation of the litigation preclude an award of fees to the prevailing employer? *See, e.g.,* Mitchell v. Office of L.A. County Superintendent of Sch., 805 F.2d 844 (9th Cir. 1986), cert. denied, 484 U.S. 858, 108 S.Ct. 168, 98 L.Ed.2d 122 (1987) (award of fees to employer reversed on the ground that the plaintiff had received a determination of reasonable cause from the EEOC and was qualified for the position for which he applied); Eichman v. Linden & Sons, Inc., 752 F.2d 1246, 1249 (7th Cir. 1985) (the fact that this employee filed suit in face of EEOC's determination of no probable cause does not necessarily compel conclusion that action was frivolous). Does a defendant "prevail" when the plaintiff voluntarily dismisses her Title VII complaint? *See* Marquart v. Lodge 837, Int'l Ass'n of Machinists & Aerospace Workers, 26 F.3d 842 (8th Cir. 1994) (defendants are to be awarded attorney fees only under "very narrow circumstances"; a prevailing defendant must be able to point to a judicial declaration to its benefit).

2. Where a defendant has established entitlement to fees, should its award be calculated in the same manner as that of a prevailing plaintiff? Most courts that have addressed the issue have ruled that the financial condition of the plaintiff should be taken into account in fixing the fee. *See, e.g.,* Johnson v. New York City Transit Auth., 823 F.2d 31, 33 (2d Cir. 1987) (award of $3,450 in attorney's fees to defendant union was not necessarily excessive, but award vacated and remanded for a determination of whether the amount was more of a sanction than appropriate in light of a discharged transit worker's ability to pay); Durrett v. Jenkins Brickyard, Inc., 678 F.2d 911, 917 (11th Cir. 1982) (in light of plaintiff's ability to pay, reduced fee will fulfill the deterrent purpose of the Act without subjecting plaintiff to financial ruin); Faraci v. Hickey-Freeman Co., 607 F.2d 1025, 1028-29 (2d Cir. 1979) (abuse of discretion for district court not to take into account financial resources of plaintiff: fee of $200 dollars assessed instead of $11,500 awarded in lower court).   Cf. Arnold v. Burger King Corp., 719 F.2d 63, 67-68 (4th Cir. 1983), cert. denied, 469 U.S. 826, 105 S.Ct. 108, 83 L.Ed.2d 51 (1984) (not an abuse of discretion for court to award full lodestar fee to employer given plaintiff's financial ability to pay).

Should the litigation costs ordinarily awarded to a prevailing party under FRCP Rule 54(d)(1) be subject to the *Christianburg Garment* analysis?   In CHERRY v. CHAMPION INT'L CORP., 186 F.3d 442, 447-48 (4th Cir. 1999), the district court granted summary judgment to the defendant on plaintiff's claims of sexual harassment under Title VII, but declined to assess plaintiff with the defendant's costs because the plaintiff had filed the action in good faith and had limited financial resources.   The Fourth Circuit reversed.   Neither the plaintiff's good faith, her modest means, her comparative lack of economic power with her employer, or the public interest served by encouraging Title VII claims justifies the denial of costs to the prevailing party.

3.   The uncertain financial condition of many employment discrimination plaintiffs may frustrate the collection of any kind of an award made to a defendant, and uncollectable awards against plaintiffs do not have the kind of in terrorem effect often sought by prevailing defendants.   These factors have resulted in efforts to assess fees and costs against the unsuccessful plaintiffs' counsel.   In ROADWAY EXPRESS, INC. v. PIPER, 447 U.S. 752, 100 S.Ct. 2455, 65 L.Ed.2d 488 (1980), the defendant argued that an award of fees should be shifted to the plaintiffs' lawyers under Title VII and 28 U.S.C. §1927, which allows the assessment of excess "costs" against attorneys who vexatiously multiply court proceedings.   The Supreme Court construed "costs" under §1927 not to include attorney's fees and held that only a party may be assessed attorney's fees under §706(k) or §1988.   The Court noted, however, that in "narrowly defined circumstances federal courts have inherent power to assess attorney's fees against counsel" for abusive litigation practices.   After the Court issued its ruling in *Piper*, Congress amended §1927 to provide expressly that an attorney who multiplies court proceedings "unreasonably or vexatiously may be required to satisfy personally the excess costs, expenses, and attorney's fees reasonably incurred because of such conduct." *See, e.g.*, Lewis v. Brown & Root, Inc., 711 F.2d 1287 (5th Cir. 1983), cert. denied, 467 U.S. 1231, 104 S.Ct. 2690, 81 L.Ed.2d 884 (1984) (the irresponsible manner in which this litigation was conducted further multiplied needless proceedings and justified an award against counsel).

4.   Although the ruling in *Christianburg Garment* only addressed the standard for awarding attorney fees to prevailing derfendants in Title VII actions, the Court in HUGHES v. ROWE, 449 U.S. 5, 101 S.Ct. 73, 66 L.Ed.2d 163 (1980) extended that standard to attorney fees awards under §1988 (i.e., in cases filed under §§1981, 1983, or 1985).   And the Court subsequently advised the state courts in JAMES v. CITY OF BOISE, ___ U.S. ___, 136 S.Ct. 685, 193 L.Ed.2d 694 (2016) that this ruling binds both state and federal courts when they are awarding attorney fees pursuant to the terms of §1988.

2.   COSTS OF LITIGATION OTHER THAN ATTORNEY'S FEES

Section 706(k) provides for the award of reasonable attorneys fees "as part of the costs of the litigation."   What costs other than attorneys fees may be shifted to a losing party? Federal Rule of Civil Procedure 54(d) and 28 U.S.C. §1920 provide that certain costs, including fees for witnesses, can be taxed against the losing party. 28 U.S.C. §1821 sets the amount of compensation to be paid witnesses at $40 per day. As in other kinds of complex litigation, litigants in employment discrimination cases frequently must resort to expert witnesses for assistance at trial. In class actions where intentional pattern and practice or disproportionate impact is alleged, plaintiffs are unlikely to make out even a prima facie case without the testimony of statisticians. But experts, like lawyers, do not charge for their services at $40 per day. The anomaly of allowing the prevailing party in a civil rights case to recover attorney's fees, but not allowing the recovery of the costs of expert assistance essential to success in the case led some courts to hold that all costs of litigation, including expert witness fees, could be shifted to the losing party under §706(k) or 42 U.S.C. §1988. Congress got into the act when, in §113 of the Civil Rights Act of 1991, it provided courts with express authority under both §706(k) of Title VII and 42 U.S.C. §1988 to award expert fees in addition to attorney fees.

3. PROBLEMS INVOLVING THE SETTLEMENT OF ATTORNEY FEE CLAIMS

Plaintiff's counsel in an employment discrimination case, or other action where a fee-shifting statute is applicable, is in a markedly different position during settlement negotiations than a plaintiff's lawyer who is either paid by his client or who has a standard contingent fee contract which guarantees him a percentage of the recovery. Where the attorney looks to the defendant for his fee and must negotiate for his client and himself at the same time, there is the potential for a conflict of interest.

* * * [T]he spectre persists, absent appropriate judicial inquiry, that plaintiff's attorney may accept an insufficient judgment for the class in trade for immediate and certain compensation for himself in the form of legal fees deducted from the total available funds proffered by defendant. The actual presence and the potential consequences of such a conflict of interest cannot be ignored.

Moreover, it is axiomatic that the overwhelming concern of counsel for the defendant in considering a proposed compromise is the total dollar cost of settlement. The defendant is uninterested in what portion of the total payment will go to the class and what percentage will go to the class attorney.

Foster v. Boise-Cascade, Inc., 420 F.Supp. 674, 686 (S.D. Tex. 1976), affirmed, 577 F.2d 335 (5th Cir. 1978). In recognition of the potential conflict, a number of courts have expressed disapproval of the simultaneous negotiation of the merits of the case and fees. *See* Obin v. Dist. No. 9 of Int'l Ass'n of Machinists & Aerospace Workers, 651 F.2d 574, 582 (8th Cir. 1981) (counsel should not be "placed in the position of negotiating a fee ultimately destined for his pocket at the same time that all thoughts ought to be singlemindedly focused on the client's interests"); Prandini v. Nat'l Tea Co., 557 F.2d 1015, 1021 (3d Cir. 1977) ("Only after court approval of the damage settlement should discussion and negotiation of appropriate compensation for the attorneys begin.").

The Supreme Court, however, has rejected the notion that trial judges can prevent simultaneous negotiations and set aside fee waivers that are coerced by defendants. In

EVANS v. JEFF D., 475 U.S. 717, 106 S.Ct. 1531, 89 L.Ed.2d 747 (1986), the defendants proposed a settlement of a class action attacking institutional conditions and the health care of emotionally handicapped children by the state of Idaho, conditioned on a complete waiver of attorney's fees by class counsel. Counsel agreed to the settlement because he felt no better relief could be obtained through litigation, but then, notwithstanding the settlement, moved the district court to award fees on the ground that the waiver had been coerced. The district court denied the motion, but the Ninth Circuit reversed, holding that district courts in class actions could not approve coerced waiver of fees. The Court of Appeals also stated that ordinarily simultaneous negotiations were improper. The Supreme Court reversed.

With respect to the waiver issue, the Court could find nothing in the language or history of §1988 that mandated payment to successful counsel. On the other hand, a general prohibition against attorney's fee waivers in exchange for settlement would, according to the Court, actually "impede vindication of civil rights, at least in some cases, by reducing the attractiveness of settlement." The Court recognized the difficulty faced by plaintiff's counsel but could perceive no "ethical dilemma" because the lawyer "had no ethical obligation to seek a statutory fee award." The Court even suggested that the attorney would have acted unethically had he turned down the favorable offer because of the demand that fees be waived.

In a dissent, Justice Brennan, joined by Justices Marshall and Blackmun, criticized the majority's opinion as undermining the effectiveness of the fee-shifting statutes in encouraging attorneys to take on civil rights cases.

> The cumulative effect this practice (coerced waivers) will have on the civil rights bar is evident. It does not denigrate the high ideals that motivate many civil rights practitioners to recognize that lawyers are in the business of practicing law, and that, like other business people, they are and must be concerned with earning a living. The conclusion that permitting fee waivers will seriously impair the ability of civil rights plaintiffs to obtain legal assistance is embarrassingly obvious.

475 U.S. at 758. What if a settlement agreement is simply silent on the issue of attorney fees? *See* Torres v. Metro. Life Ins., Co., 189 F.3d 331 (3d Cir. 1999) (a settlement agreement that is silent regarding fees does not constitute a waiver regardless of the course of the parties' negotiations). Can a plaintiff's counsel avoid the impact of *Evans*, or at least shift the burden of the problem, by entering into retainer agreements that hold the client ultimately responsible for fees in the event of a successful resolution of the case where fees are, for any reason, not awarded? *See* Venegas v. Mitchell, 495 U.S. 82, 110 S.Ct. 1679, 109 L.Ed.2d 74 (1990) (counsel and his client can contract for a fee that is greater than what the court would award as a "reasonable fee" under the fee-shifting statute); Peter H. Woodin, Note, *Fee Waivers and Civil Rights Settlement Offers: State Ethics Prohibitions After Evans v. Jeff D.*, 87 COLUM. L. REV. 1214 (1987). Could such a strategy be used in a class action? *See* Charles Silver, *A Restitutions Theory of Attorney's Fees in Class Actions*, 76 CORN. L. REV. 656 (1991).

Plaintiff's counsel in civil rights cases may also face offers of judgment under Federal Rule of Civil Procedure 68, which allows the defendant to serve upon the plaintiff an offer to "allow judgment to be taken against [him] for the money or property or to the effect specified in his offer, with costs then accrued." If the offer is rejected and "the judgment finally obtained by the offeree is not more favorable than the offer, the offeree must pay the costs incurred after the making of the offer." In MAREK v. CHESNY, 473 U.S. 1, 105 S.Ct. 3012, 87 L.Ed.2d 1 (1985), the Court held that the word "costs" in Rule 68 encompasses fees awarded under the fee-shifting statutes. Thus, where the defendant makes an offer to the plaintiff before trial inclusive of fees, and the plaintiff subsequently recovers less than the amount offered, the court may deny all counsel fees incurred after the date of the offer. Should relief obtained by the plaintiff as result of the voluntary action of the employer be considered in determining whether the terms of the employer's offer of judgment were more favorable to the plaintiff than "judgment finally obtained"? *See* Spencer v. Gen. Elec. Co., 894 F.2d 651 (4th Cir. 1990) (distinguishing between judgment and relief; in making the comparison required by Rule 68, a court must compare only the offer of judgment to the "judgment finally obtained"). To be effective, an offer of judgment under Rule 68 must be in an amount that, together with fees and costs then accrued, exceeds the judgment that the plaintiff eventually obtains. *See* Scheeler v. Crane Co., 21 F.3d 791 (8th Cir. 1994).

If the plaintiff ultimately recovers less than a pre-trial offer of judgment, Rule 68 requires that she pay her own costs, including attorney fees, incurred after rejection of the offer as well as the employer's "costs." The issue left undecided after *Marek* was whether the definition of defendant's "costs" under Rule 68 includes the defendant's attorney fees. In other words, can the plaintiff be required under Rule 68 to pay the attorney fees of the defendant whose offer of judgment was rejected? In PAYNE v. MILWAUKEE COUNTY, 288 F.3d 1021 (7th Cir. 2002), the court concluded that such an award would be inconsistent with the fee-shifting statute which provides attorney fees only to a "prevailing party." A defendant who makes an offer of judgment does not thereby become a "prevailing party" and is not entitled to an award of fees. Moreover, under *Christianburg Garment*, a prevailing defendant is entitled to fees from the plaintiff only if the plaintiff's claims were frivolous or vexatious. The court concluded that claims of a plaintiff who has obtained some relief are, by definition, not frivolous or vexatious.

SECTION D. CLASS RELIEF

Employment discrimination class actions typically are litigated in bifurcated proceedings. Liability to the class, whether based upon a disporportionate impact or pattern and practice theory, as well as the claims of the individual class representatives, are tried in the first stage. Neither the class representatives nor individual class members are called upon to prove damages at this stage, and remedy-oriented proof is usually not admitted. If classwide discrimination is found, a second series of proceedings, usually referred to as "Stage II," is conducted for the purpose of determining the relief due the plaintiffs and to individual class members.

A finding that the employer has engaged in a pattern and practice of discrimination does not mean that every class member will be entitled to relief. For example, in a hiring case, although the employer may have discriminated generally against applicants on the basis of race, some class members would not have been hired in the absence of discrimination because either they could not satisfy legitimate requirements of the position or because no vacancies existed at the time of their applications. Thus, in the Stage II proceeding, the court must determine which class members are entitled to relief and the kind and amount of relief to be awarded. Because discrimination against the class has been determined, however, the burden of proof on the issues before the court no longer rests solely with the plaintiffs as it does in the liability phase of the case. In INTERNATIONAL BROTHERHOOD. OF TEAMSTERS v. UNITED STATES, 431 U.S. 324, 97 S.Ct. 1843, 52 L.Ed.2d 396 (1977), the defendants contended that at the remedial stage of class litigation, individual class members should have to establish their entitlement to relief according to the requirements of the *McDonnell Douglas-Burdine* formula. The Supreme Court rejected that argument and stated, in footnote 53 of its opinion, that when class-wide discrimination has been established, the burden "rests on the employer to demonstrate that the individual applicant was denied an employment opportunity for lawful reasons such as his lack of qualifications or the fact that a more qualified applicant would have been chosen for a vacancy." As the three cases in this section demonstrate, however, questions still remain over the exact nature of the employers' burden in Stage II.

The accepted method for determining the amount of back pay and/or retroactive seniority, once entitlement to that remedy has been established, is by the construction of hypothetical work histories, as was done in EEOC v. Ford Motor Co., *supra*, for each class member. The larger the employer and the more complex its organization, the more difficult Stage II will be. Under the best of conditions, this process can be a monumental task, but because of such factors as highly subjective decision-making, lack of records, and fading memories, anything approaching an accurate reconstruction of what an individual employee's work history would have been absent discrimination, often is impossible. In PETTWAY v. AM. CAST IRON PIPE CO., 494 F.2d 211, 260 (5th Cir. 1974) (Pettway III), the Court of Appeals described some of the problems facing courts in typical Stage II litigation:

> There is no way of determining which jobs the class members would have bid on and have obtained if discriminatory testing, seniority, posting and bidding system, and apprentice and on-the-job training programs not been in existence. Class members outnumber promotion vacancies; jobs have become available only over a period of time; the vacancies enjoy different pay rates; and a determination of who was entitled to the vacancy would have to be determined on a judgment of seniority and ability at that time. This process creates a quagmire of hypothetical judgments.

The efforts by the lower courts to solve problems associated with class relief are illustrated in the following cases.

Kyriazi v. Western Electric Co.

United States District Court for New Jersey, 1979.
465 F.Supp. 1141.

STERN, District Judge.

At the conclusion of "Stage I" of this Title VII litigation — the liability phase — this Court found that Western Electric discriminated against its female employees, applicants and former employees in the areas of hiring, promotion, participation in job training programs, layoffs, wages and opportunities for testing. We now enter "Stage II," the damage phase. Stage II requires adjudication of the claims of thousands of class members.[2]

To assist it in this formidable task, the Court has appointed three Special Masters pursuant to Rule 53(a) of the Federal Rules of Civil Procedure. The Court now addresses some of the procedural hurdles which confront it at this stage.

1. Burden of Proof

The Supreme Court has made clear that once there has been a finding of classwide discrimination, the burden then shifts to the employer to prove that a class member was not discriminated against; that is, a finding of discrimination creates a rebuttable presumption in favor of recovery. The Court first addressed this in *Franks v. Bowman*, in which it held that:

> [P]etitioners here have carried their burden of demonstrating the existence of a discriminatory hiring pattern and practice by the respondents and, therefore, the burden will be upon respondents to prove that individuals who reapply were not in fact victims of previous hiring discrimination.

More recently, in *International Brotherhood of Teamsters*, the Court specifically rejected the contention that in the remedial stage of a pattern-or-practice case, the government must prove that the individual was actually the victim of discrimination:

> That basic contention was rejected in the *Franks* case. As was true of the particular facts in *Franks*, and as is typical of Title VII pattern-or-practice suits, the question of individual relief does not arise until it has been proved that the employer has followed an employment policy of unlawful discrimination. The force of that proof does not dissipate at the remedial stage of the trial. The employer cannot, therefore, claim that there is no reason to believe that its individual employment decisions were discriminatorily based; it has already been shown to have maintained a policy of discriminatory decisionmaking.
>
> The proof of the pattern or practice supports an inference that any particular employment decision, during the period in which the discriminatory policy was in force, was made in pursuit of that policy. The Government need only show that an alleged individual discriminatee unsuccessfully applied for a job and therefore was a potential victim of the proved discrimination. As in *Franks*, the burden then rests on the employer to demonstrate that the individual applicant was denied an employment opportunity for lawful reasons.

Accordingly, the sole burden upon class members will be to demonstrate that they are members of the class, that is, that now or at any time since June 9, 1971, they were either employed by Western, applied for employment at Western or were terminated by Western. In practical terms, this will be reflected in the Proof of Claim forms which class members will be required to fill out. Those forms require only that the

---

[2]Western reports that there are approximately 10,000 class members, of which:

—1,131 are retired

—1,887 are active employees

—3,200 were laid off by Western

—3,500 were rejected by Western.

putative class member state the dates of her employment and/or application, the positions she held and/or sought.[3] The Court will not require individual class members to specify the manner in which they were discriminated against. As was held in Stage I, employees remained for the most part ignorant of the fact that they were being passed over for promotion and training programs, and unsuccessful applicants may well be unaware that they were rejected on the basis of their sex. The fact is that employment decisions are rarely put in discriminatory terms, no matter how discriminatorily bottomed. Individual employees should not be put to the almost impossible task of delving into the corporate consciousness to demonstrate how an already proven policy of discrimination exactly impacted each one of them.[4] Thus, once an individual demonstrates that she is a class member, the burden will then shift to Western to demonstrate that the individual class member was not the victim of discrimination.

2. Notice

Pursuant to Rule 23(d)(2), Federal Rules of Civil Procedure, Western is required to give notice to class members in the following manner. All class members whose addresses are known to Western will be sent a notice and Proof of Claim form together with a prepaid envelope. The remaining class members will be notified by publication in six local newspapers for two consecutive weeks in the Sunday editions and three weekday editions.[5] All costs of notification are, of course, to be borne by Western.

The Court has scanned the early returns from the newspaper notices and the mailings and has determined that it would be advisable to supplement the notice to the nearly 1,900 class members who are presently employed by Western by providing an opportunity for class counsel to communicate with them directly at the plant.[6] Accordingly, Western will permit counsel for the class to enter the plant for the purpose of meeting with class members who are presently employed by Western. Western may accomplish this in any manner that will minimize loss of productivity and disruption of its normal activities, provided that the manner selected gives employees advance notice and a reasonable opportunity to meet with counsel. Undoubtedly, mass meetings will be required in order to minimize the number of visits

---

[3]Copies of the notice to the class and the Proof of Claim forms to be distributed to class members are reproduced in the Appendix to this opinion.

[4]Compare Pettway v. American Cast Iron Pipe Co., 494 F.2d 211, 259 (5th Cir.1974), which held that each class member has the "initial burden * * * to bring himself within the class and to describe the harmful effect of the discrimination on his individual employment position." It is noteworthy, however, that *Pettway* was decided before the Supreme Court's decisions in *Franks* and *Teamsters*.

[5]Those newspapers are *The* New York *Times, The* Daily *News, The* Newark *Star Ledger, The* Bergen *Record, The* New York *Post,* and *The* Jersey *Journal.*

A substantial number of class members, approximately 3,500 are women who applied for positions at Western and were rejected. Western reports that it does not have the addresses of these women, only their social security numbers. Counsel for the plaintiff has been directed to prepare a form of notice acceptable to the Social Security Administration to be forwarded to the last known business addresses of these women.

[6]In this Circuit, counsel is permitted to confer with members of the class — indeed, a restriction upon counsel's ability to communicate with class members has been held violative of the First Amendment. Coles v. Marsh, 560 F.2d 186 (3d Cir.), cert. denied, 434 U.S. 985, 98 S.Ct. 611, 54 L.Ed.2d 479 (1977); See also, Developments in the Law — Class Actions, 89 Harv.L.Rev. 1317, 1592-1604 (1976).

which counsel will have to make. These meetings may take place before or after working hours, if Western prefers, but sufficient time must be allocated and a suitable facility must be provided. With these guidelines in mind, counsel are directed to meet and work out a schedule which will commence not later than March 12, 1979 and terminate not later than March 31, 1979, nine days before the April 9, 1979 cutoff date for the filing of claims by class members.

3. Computation of Back Pay Awards

The courts have adopted a number of approaches in connection with the computation of back pay awards.[7] One approach, the "pro rata" formula referred to in Pettway v. American Cast Iron Pipe Co., 494 F.2d 211 (5th Cir.1974), and United States v. United States Steel, 520 F.2d 1043 (5th Cir.1975), looks to the difference between the salary of the class members computed collectively and that received by employees of comparable skills and seniority, not the victims of discrimination. The class member then receives his pro rata share of that collective difference, based upon his salary differential and the number of competitors for the position. Another approach is the "test period" approach, used in Bowe v. Colgate, Palmolive Co., 489 F.2d 896 (7th Cir.1973), in which the court awards class members the difference between the pay they receive after implementation of the Title VII decree and the pay they received while the discriminatory policies were in force. A variation of the "test period" approach was used in Stewart v. General Motors, 542 F.2d 445 (7th Cir.1976), cert. denied, 433 U.S. 919, 97 S.Ct. 2995, 53 L.Ed.2d 1105 (1977), in which the court awarded the class members the difference between the wages of salaried white workers during a test period and that actually received by the class. Yet another approach was used in Stamps v. Detroit Edison Co., 365 F.Supp. 87, 121 (E.D.Mich.1973), rev'd on other grounds sub nom. EEOC v. Detroit Edison Co., 515 F.2d 301 (6th Cir.1975), in which the court awarded class members the difference between their own actual earnings and the earnings of the skilled trade opportunity jobs from the effective date of Title VII.

The Court finds none of these approaches appropriate here. As we found in connection with Stage I, we deal with discrimination which manifests itself in a number of ways. For example, a woman might initially be hired at the lowest grade — 32 — while a comparable male would have been hired at grade 33. During the course of a ten-year period, the woman — perhaps unbeknownst to her — would be passed over for promotion, denied entry into job training programs and, finally, notwithstanding her seniority, would be the first to be laid off because she was in the lowest job category. She may in fact have been laid off and rehired a number of times.[8] By contrast, the male, during the same period and having started at a higher grade, would be promoted several grades — perhaps even trained for a supervisory position — and would thus remain unscathed in times of layoffs. It is, therefore,

---

[7]The back pay period commences two years before the filing of the EEOC charge. §706(g). At Stage I, the Court concluded that the nature of the discrimination alleged and proved brought this case within the "continuing violation" theory of Title VII, therefore, allowing class members to secure relief for acts of discrimination occurring since the effective date of Title VII. While it is clear that the back pay award is statutorily limited, the Court is considering what other forms of relief may be awarded for discrimination which occurred before the two year back pay period.

[8]The preliminary responses already received from class members indicate that this is no rare experience for women at Western.

apparent that a back pay award must take into account the fact that a male and a female entering Western with comparable skills would, over a period of time, take dramatically divergent paths.

While this approach will not yield an exact measure of damages, neither could any other approach. However, the law is clear that where one has been damaged by the wrong of another, the victim is not to be denied any recompense merely because the exact measure of damages is uncertain. The approach we adopt at least gives individual consideration to each claimant and, if not precise, it is no more imprecise than lumping claimants into groups and extracting averages, or otherwise depersonalizing victims of discrimination by running them through a mathematical blender.

Moreover, Western itself objects to any formula type or averaging approach in awarding back pay — that is, to any but an individual approach under which the merits of each woman's claim is separately considered. In the face of Western's objections, it may be that due process considerations require that any award to an individual be on the merits of that individual's case. In any event, it does seem that an individual approach is more fair both to class members and to Western.

In its proposed Order of Reference, Western proposes that:

> 45. If there is more than one eligible claimant for a given designated vacancy, net back pay awards shall be computed for each claimant. One award shall be made in an amount equal to the highest individual net award. Each claimant shall share that award in the proportion that her individual net back pay award bears to her total of all claimants' net back pay awards pursuant to the formula set forth in United States v. United States Steel, 520 F.2d 1043 (5th Cir.1975).

The Court rejects this approach. According to Western, if there were three women who should have been considered for one promotion and none were, and if we cannot now determine which of the three women should have received the promotion, then each one receives one-third of the benefits. As Western notes, this approach does shield Western from having to pay three increases when only one was actually possible, but it also unjustly penalizes the one woman who was entitled to all — not just one-third — of the benefits of that promotion. Under Western's approach, two of the claimants get a windfall while the actual victim receives only one-third of the back pay to which she is statutorily entitled. If we know that all three claimants were discriminated against in that they were not considered for promotion but that only one — which, we do not know — would have actually received the promotion, then all three should get the full benefit of the promotional opportunity. Where it is proved that an employer unlawfully disregarded women for promotion, it is better that it pay a little more than to permit an innocent party to shoulder the burdens of the guilty. Western will be permitted to demonstrate that the promotion would have gone to one class member, rather than the others. However, if Western cannot demonstrate which claimant would have received the promotion, Western cannot divide the benefits of the one job. It is no more unreal to construe three promotions out of one, than to divide the salary increase of one promotion among three prospects. Either smacks of some artificiality but the latter protects the wrongdoer at the expense of the innocent.

The Order of Reference to the Special Masters is reproduced in the Appendix. Among other requirements, in an effort to assure back pay awards on as individualized basis as possible, where appropriate class members will be compared to the male employee with comparable skills upon initial hire and comparable seniority. The class member will then be awarded the difference between her salary and that received by the male counterpart, including bonuses and any other fringe benefits. See *Pettway v. American Cast Iron Pipe Co.*

4. Compensation of Special Masters

The final problem which confronts us at the outset of Stage II is the compensation of the Special Masters.

All parties have recognized that the number of potential claimants virtually mandates the appointment of Special Masters. The parties agree that if any significant portion of the 10,000 potential claimants respond, the existing court mechanism of a district judge and a magistrate is totally inadequate to deal with the issues which will confront the Court. Even 3,000 claimants out of the 10,000 eligible, for example, would exceed the yearly civil filings for this entire district of nine active judges and five magistrates. Moreover, unlike a rough sampling of the typical civil case cross section, many of which will be voluntarily dismissed, others of which will be settled without any judicial supervision, and the overwhelming majority of which will be settled without any judicial factfinding,[9] it appears that each one of the claims of Western's present or former employees will have to be individually considered and adjudicated. Western has objected to any formula approach, and has requested that each claim be considered upon its own merits. The Court agrees that not only is Western entitled to this approach, but that each claimant is also entitled to individual consideration. In many instances this approach requires that efforts be made to project the actual benefits lost by each Western employee who has been found to have been a victim of Western's discrimination. Whole work histories will have to be recast, based on evaluations of the background, education, potential and abilities of each claimant, as compared with the opportunities available to and realized by similarly situated males at Western. In a very real sense, Stage II proceedings under this approach resemble a host of individual cases, sharing many common questions of law and fact, as much as it does the pure class action of more common experience.

Faced with this task, the parties agree not merely to the appointment of a Special Master, but to the appointment of three Special Masters. The parties also agree that these Special Masters should not only be lawyers, but experienced trial lawyers. Western has demanded, and the Court has granted, an opportunity for it to conduct "discovery regarding the . . . claims pursuant to the Federal Rules of Civil Procedure." If the past is any gauge of the future, the Special Masters will be occupied with discovery matters concerning many hundreds of claimants even before they get down to dealing with the merits of each.

* * *

[The Court found that the Special Masters should be compensated "in a manner roughly comparable to that which they receive in the practices from which they are being diverted" — i.e. at hourly rates of $125 and $115. The defendant was ordered to pay all the Masters' fees.]

---

[9] In 1978, approximately 90% of the civil actions filed in this District were terminated sometime prior to trial. *Management Statistics for United States Courts* (1978).

Appendix "A"

TO: Female Applicants, Employees or Former Employees of Western Electric's
        Kearny Plant (including the Clark Shops)

RE: Sex Discrimination Action Against Western

If you are a woman and now or any time since June 9, 1971 you either: (a) applied for employment at Western's Kearny plant and were rejected; or (b) were employed in any position at Western's Kearny plant; or (c) were laid off or discharged from any position at Western's Kearny plant, please read this notice carefully.

On October 30, 1978, in a lawsuit brought by Kyriaki Cleo Kyriazi, a former employee of Western, the United States District Court for the District of New Jersey found that Western has been discriminating against its women employees at its Kearny plant in violation of federal law. It was found that women, as a group, were discriminated against in the following ways:

1) *Hiring* — Women are hired into the lowest grades, while men with equal skills and experience were hired into the higher grades.

2) *Promotion* — Women employees were not given promotional opportunities equal to male employees.

3) *Layoffs* — Women were not treated fairly when employees had to be laid off.

4) *Transfer into Kearny* — Women who transferred into the Kearny plant were placed in lower grades than they were in before they transferred.

5) *Discharge* — More women were fired than men.

6) *Participation in Job Training Programs* — Women were not given the opportunities given to men to participate in job training programs.

7) *Opportunities for Testing* — Women were not given the opportunity to take tests for promotion to better positions.

The Court has completed the first stage of this lawsuit by finding that Western had discriminated against women in its Kearny plant. Copies of the Court's opinion are on file in the United States District Court of the District of New Jersey.

There will be soon be a second stage, "Stage II," at which time the Court will determine the damages and other relief which it will award to individual women. If you are or were at any time since June 9, 1971 an employee of Western, or if you ever applied for a position at Western, you may be entitled to certain benefits, including monetary payments. The "Stage II" proceedings will determine this question. At these "Stage II" proceedings, any eligible woman will be presumed to have been discriminated against. It will be Western's duty to show that it did not deny a woman employment opportunities because of her sex. If Western fails to demonstrate this, that women will be entitled to recovery, which may include back pay and reinstatement.

If you wish to be considered, you must fill out the enclosed form. Your claim will not be considered if you do not do so and return the form by April 2, 1979. If you do fill out the form, you may be required, with no cost to yourself, to participate in court proceedings. You will be furnished an attorney without cost to you. That attorney will be Judith Vladeck, Attorney for plaintiff Kyriazi. If you prefer, you may retain an attorney of your own choosing. If you wish further information, you may contact the attorney for the plaintiff, Judith Vladeck, at (212) 354-8330

    AS PART OF THE COURT'S ORDER, YOUR EMPLOYER MAY NOT PENALIZE YOU IN ANY WAY IF YOU CHOOSE TO FILE A CLAIM AGAINST IT.APPENDIX "B"

Kyriazi v. Western Electric 475-73

_____

NAME

_____

ADDRESS

_____

TELEPHONE NUMBER

Answer each question to the best of your ability.

1) Did you use any other name while employed at Western's Kearny Plant? (Indicate yes or no) _____. If so, please set forth the names you used and the dates you used each name.

NAME	DATES
_____	_____ - _____
_____	_____ - _____

2) What is your social security number? _____

3) Were you rejected for a position at Western's Kearny Plant? (Indicate yes or no) _____. If so, please set forth the date of your application and the position for which you applied._____

_____

4) Are you presently employed at Western's Kearny Plant? _____. If so, when did your employment begin? _____.
Please list all positions you have held at Western, (the grade, if the position was graded), and the dates you held each position.

POSITION	GRADE	DATES
_____	_____	_____ - _____
_____	_____	_____ - _____
_____	_____	_____ - _____

5) Were you laid off or otherwise terminated by Western? _____. If so, when did your employment end? _____. What was the reason given for your termination? _____
_____. Set forth each of the positions you held at Western's Kearny plant and the dates you held each position.

_____   _____ - _____

_____   _____ - _____

_____   _____ - _____

6) Have you been employed since you left Western? _____. If so, please set forth the positions you have held since you left Western and the dates you held each position.

_____   _____ - _____

_____   _____ - _____

_____   _____ - _____

Please send the completed form to:

Angelo Locascio, Clerk

United States District Court

U.S. Post Office and Courthouse

Newark, New Jersey 07101

[Appendix "C" to the opinion, containing detailed guidelines for the Special Masters to follow in resolving the various types of claims to be raised by class members, is omitted.]

Ingram v. Madison Square Garden Center, Inc.

United States Court of Appeals for the Second Circuit, 1983.

709 F.2d 807, cert. denied, 464 U.S. 937, 104 S.Ct. 346, 78 L.Ed.2d 313 (1983).

VAN GRAAFEILAND, Circuit Judge.

Local 3 of the International Brotherhood of Electric Workers appeals from a judgment of the United States District Court for the Southern District of New York which awarded plaintiffs in a class employment discrimination suit retroactive seniority rights with back pay, front pay, and attorneys' fees, the total monetary award, with interest, being substantially in excess of $1 million. * * * Although we find the evidence of discrimination somewhat less persuasive than did the district court, we are not prepared to hold that the district court's findings on this issue were clearly erroneous. See Pullman-Standard v. Swint, 456 U.S. 273, 102 S.Ct. 1781, 72 L.Ed.2d 66 (1982). Accordingly, we affirm the district court's adjudication of liability. However, for reasons hereafter discussed, we find it necessary to modify the relief which the court below granted.

Since 1965, Local 3 of the International Brotherhood, which has more than 4,300 black and Hispanic members, has represented the "maintenance group of utility men" (hereafter "laborers") at Madison Square Garden. These laborers prepare the Garden for its various featured events. The several contracts between the Union and the Garden placed no restrictions on the employer's method of hiring, merely requiring that all laborers become members of the Union within 31 days of their employment. However, in practice, the hirelings, of which there was an average of about 5 per year, were referred to the Garden by the Union representative for the Garden laborers. About 1 in 6 of the hirelings was either black or Hispanic.

Until 1969, the Garden also employed other groups of people as cleaners or porters, bowling alley and lavatory attendants, and elevator operators. In 1969, the Garden subcontracted its cleaning work to Allied Maintenance Corporation, retaining only the elevator operators as its own employees. All of the cleaners are represented by Local 54 of Service Employees International Union, and most of them are either black or Hispanic.

On August 13, 1973, appellees Ingram, Britt, Moody, and Floyd, all of whom were porters working at the Garden, filed charges against the Garden and Allied with the Equal Employment Opportunity Commission, pursuant to Title VII, alleging that these employers had discriminated against them and other black porters by paying them less than the white laborers for doing similar work and by maintaining segregated job classifications. The EEOC concluded that the Garden and Allied were violating Title VII, and, on October 4, 1976, following unsuccessful conciliation efforts, issued right-to-sue letters to the four complainants. On December 30, 1976, the porters filed a proposed class action suit against the Garden and Allied, alleging violations of 42 U.S.C. §§1981 and 1985 as well as Title VII. On June 22, 1977, Local 3 was added to the litigation by means of an amended complaint, which charged that the Union was discouraging competent minority cleaners from seeking and obtaining jobs as laborers and was conspiring with the Garden and Allied towards this end by advising cleaners that the Garden was solely responsible for hiring, that no jobs were available, and that cleaners must do apprenticeships before becoming members of Local 3.

On November 24, 1975, appellees Anderson and Perry, black porters who worked at the Garden, also filed discrimination charges with the EEOC, their charges being directed against the Garden, Allied, and Local 3. On January 16, 1978, a right-to-sue letter issued, and on March 31, 1978, a proposed class action complaint on behalf of the Anderson group was filed.

The district court certified a Title VII class and a §§1981 and 1985 class in both actions. In the *Ingram* action, the Title VII class, whose claims, of necessity, were limited to the Garden and Allied, consisted of all blacks who, after February 14, 1973, had been or would be employed as cleaners at the Garden. The §§1981 and 1985 class consisted of all blacks and Hispanics who, after December 30, 1973, had been or would be employed as cleaners at the Garden. The §§1981 and 1985 class consisted of all blacks and Hispanics who, after December 30, 1973, had been or would be employed as cleaners at the Garden. Certification of both classes in *Ingram* was conditioned on the intervention of lavatory and bowling alley attendants and elevator operators as named plaintiffs. Thereafter, Williams, a black lavatory attendant, Milon, a black bowling alley attendant, Mitchell, a black elevator operator, Bruton, a retired black cleaner, and Garcia, an Hispanic cleaner, intervened. The *Anderson* classes were defined in the same manner as those of *Ingram*, except that the Title VII *Anderson* class limitation was May 28, 1975, and the §§1981 and 1985 *Anderson* class limitation was March 31, 1975, and both classes claimed against the Garden, Allied, and Local 3.

On July 13, 1978, the *Ingram* and *Anderson* actions were consolidated. On July 16, 1979, the district court denied the Union's motion to decertify the classes. Subsequently, the plaintiffs entered into a proposed consent decree with the Garden and Allied, in which the defendants agreed, among other things, to pay $117,500 in settlement of plaintiffs' monetary claims plus $47,500 in attorneys' fees. On October 23, 1979, the settlement was approved by the district court, subject only to the submission of an affidavit in support of counsel fees. In the meantime, the case had proceeded to trial against Local 3, the issue being limited to that of liability.

On October 3, 1979, * * * the district court dismissed plaintiffs' §1985 claims * * * but held the Union liable under both Title VII and §1981.

* * *

[The Court's discussion of the statistical evidence (which showed that African-Americans and Latinos had been referred by the Union in numbers significantly below their percentage in the relevant labor market) and of anecdotal testimony by class members is omitted.]

The Back Pay Award

In fashioning a remedy for employment discrimination, "the court must, as nearly as possible, 'recreate the conditions and relationships that would have been had there been no' unlawful discrimination." *Int'l Bhd. of Teamsters* (quoting *Franks v. Bowman*). We believe that the remedy in the instant case went beyond that.

The district court referred the factual remedial issues to a Magistrate and instructed the Magistrate to award seniority to every class member who desired a laborer's job as of the date of the next laborer hire that followed his application or "qualifying desire," subject to a maximum date of July 2, 1965. The court instructed the Magistrate to make back pay awards on the same basis, subject to the 2-year limitation period of Title VII and the 3-year limitation period applicable in New York to §1981. The computations, made as directed, produced some interesting results. Two class members were awarded retroactive competitive seniority dates to 1970, a year in which 5 laborers were hired, one of whom was Hispanic. If the district court was recreating the conditions that would have existed had there been no discrimination, presumably he intended that three of the five 1970 hirelings should have been either black or Hispanic. In 1974, 6 laborers were hired, one of whom was black. Nevertheless, 4 class members were awarded retroactive competitive seniority to 1974. In recreating the conditions for that year, the district court must have intended that 5 out of the 6 hirelings should have been either black or Hispanic. Although only one laborer, a white man, was hired in 1976, seniority retroactive to 1976 was awarded 4 class members.

According to appellees' own computations, in 1969, the laborer work force at the Garden consisted of 48 whites, 2 blacks and 2 Hispanics. Between 1970 and 1978, the Garden hired 33 laborers referred to it by the Union, of whom 6 were either black or Hispanic. The minority hiring rate during these years was thus 18.2%. The district court held that, for purposes of retroactive competitive seniority, 17 class members should have been hired during this period, for purposes of non-competitive seniority,

10 class members should have been hired, and for purposes of back pay awards, 13 class members should have been hired. Had 17 class members been hired, the racial composition of labor hirings during this period would have been 69% black or Hispanic. Had 13 class members been hired, the composition would have 57% black or Hispanic. Had 10 been hired, 48% of the hirelings would have been black or Hispanic. This is hardly a recreation of the conditions that would have existed had there been no discrimination.

A court that finds unlawful discrimination is not required to grant retroactive relief. *City of Los Angeles v. Manhart*, 435 U.S. 702, 718, 98 S.Ct. 1370, 1380, 55 L.Ed.2d 657 (1978). "To the point of redundancy, the statute stresses that retroactive relief 'may' be awarded if it is 'appropriate.'" *Id.* Moreover, such remedy as is given should not constitute a windfall at the expense of the employer, its union, or its white employees. Title VII imposes no duty to maximize the hiring of minority employees. *Furnco Construction Corp. v. Waters*. Remedial relief should be granted only to those class members who would have filled vacancies had there been no discrimination. The district court's judgment, based on the concept that all class members with unexpressed employment desires should have been hired regardless of the number of vacancies and competing applicants, is based upon a hypothetical hiring practice which the law did not require and which, in actuality, never would have been followed absent any trace of discrimination.

James O'Hara, the Union representative for the Garden laborers and the person who made job referrals, received over 300 requests for jobs during the period at issue, not a single one of which came from a class member. There is nothing in the record to indicate that, discrimination aside, class members would have been given preference over other applicants. Indeed, since the Union counted 4,300 blacks and Hispanics among its own members, it is unlikely that preferred treatment would have been given to members of another union. In view of the limited number of vacancies that occurred, we conclude that, to the extent that back pay was awarded to more than 7 class members, it constituted an unwarranted windfall and did not recreate the conditions that would have existed in the absence of discrimination.

Because of the statistical limitations inherent in the small samples available to plaintiffs' expert witness, her testimony concerning disproportionate hiring did not focus on any particular year. Faced with the same limitations, neither this Court nor the district court can state accurately when the 7 class members should have been hired. Under such circumstances, we think it would be inequitable to award back pay to only the first 7 class members who indicated a "desire" to become laborers. The fairer procedure, we believe, would be to compute a gross award for all the injured class members and divide it among them on a pro rata basis. See Stewart v. General Motors Corp., 542 F.2d 445, 452-53 (7th Cir.1976), cert. denied, 433 U.S. 919, 97 S.Ct. 2995, 53 L.Ed.2d 1105 (1977); Pettway v. American Cast Iron Pipe Co., 494 F.2d 211, 263 n. 154 (5th Cir.1974). In determining the amount of the gross award, however, we think it fair to both the Union and the class members to assume that the Union would have referred the 7 class members who first desired employment, had they applied, and to base the class award on the loss attributable to these 7 men.

The first 7 "applicants," determined by their seniority dates, and the back pay awards made them by the district court, are:

1. Clarence Lamar	$ 55,120
2. Wilfred Boudreaux	$ 51,010
3. William Moody	$ 53,298
4. Herbert Holmes	$ 57,604
5. Henry Ingram	$ 27,202
6. Kenneth Williams	$ 61,494
7. James Britt	$ 39,988
	$345,716

The total award to these men, $345,716, is equal to approximately 52.14% of the total award of $663,085 which the district court made to all 18 back pay recipients. Proration by 52.14% of the 18 individual awards produces the following figures:

1. Shelly Anderson	$ 16,578.43
2. Wilfred Boudreaux	$ 26,596.61
3. James Britt	$ 20,849.74
4. John Carroll	$ 9,630.78
5. Russell Footman	$ 11,123.03
6. Waverly Green	$ 10,675.67
7. Graydon Griffith	$ 18,963.84
8. Lawrence Hawkins	$ 24,746.17
9. Francisco Hernandez	$ 23,836.84
10. Herbert Holmes	$ 30,034.73
11. Henry Ingram	$ 14,183.12
12. Clarence Lamar	$ 28,739.57
13. William Moody	$ 27,789.58
14. James Parrott	$ 19,611.94
15. James Perry	$ 8,775.16
16. James Pettigrew	$ 11,628.78
17. George Sharpe, Sr	$ 9,905.56
18. Kenneth Williams	$ 32,062.97
	$345,732.52

The district court's award of back pay is modified in accordance with the foregoing figures.

Front Pay

Since this action was begun, at least 6 class members to whom the district court made back pay awards have been hired by the Garden, 5 of them on November 5, 1979, and one on December 20, 1980. The district court has indicated that it intends to make front pay awards for future losses to the twelve remaining back pay recipients. For the reasons already expressed, we believe it is completely unrealistic to assume that all 18 back pay beneficiaries would have been hired had there been no discrimination practiced against them. Accordingly, we deem it unfair to the members of the defendant Union, black, Hispanic, and white, to impose a continuing liability upon their association for the loss of future benefits. This unfairness is exacerbated by the fact that the Union has no control over future hirings, which are the sole prerogative of the Garden, and is therefore in no position to bring its liability for front pay to an end. Under these circumstances, we believe that it would be an abuse of discretion for the district court to make front pay awards against the Union to class members not already hired.

Retroactive Seniority

The same factors which dictate the limitation of back pay and front pay awards also militate against the grant of retroactive seniority to future hirelings. In addition, we view pendent grants of retroactive seniority as self-defeating, in that they militate against the likelihood that the beneficiaries of the grants will be employed. Under the consent decree which terminated plaintiffs' action against the Garden, the Garden agreed that every second job opening would be offered to minorities until their representation among the Garden's laborers reached 27%. Because at least 9 minority laborers have been hired since the execution of the consent decree, 6 of whom were class members, it is not at all unlikely that the 27% quota has been reached and the compulsory hiring of class members has come to an end. Relations between the Garden and its presently employed laborers will not be improved by the voluntary hiring of additional class members who will be granted automatic seniority under the terms of the district court's judgment. For all the foregoing reasons, we think that the proper exercise of discretion would limit the grant of retroactive seniority to the 6 or more class members already hired.

* * *

NOTES AND PROBLEMS FOR DISCUSSION

1. How does the district court's treatment of the "limited vacancy" problem in *Kyriazi* differ from the approach taken by the Second Circuit in *Ingram*? Has the Second Circuit in fact put the burden of proof on the employer? Compare the approach taken by the Ninth Circuit in DOMINGO v. NEW ENGLAND FISH Co., 727 F.2d 1429 (9th Cir.), modified, 742 F.2d 520 (9th Cir. 1984), where it stated that:

> [i]n order to be eligible for backpay, claimants need only prove they applied for a position or would have applied if not for Nefco's discriminatory practices. They may be required to show what their qualifications were, but do not have the burden of proving they were qualified for the position sought. Because class-wide discrimination has already been shown, the employer has the burden of proving that the applicant was unqualified or showing some other valid reason why the claimant was not, or would not have been, acceptable. * * * All uncertainties should be resolved against the employer.

727 F.2d at 1445. Which result is fairest for the class member or for the employer?

Where numerous class members are denied the opportunity to compete for a limited number of vacancies and it is impossible to determine after the fact who should have received the position, most courts use a pro rata approach similar to that in *Ingram*. In UNITED STATES v. CITY OF MIAMI, 195 F.3d 1292 (11th Cir. 1999), cert. denied sub nom Fraternal Order of Police v. U.S., 531 U.S. 815, 121 S.Ct. 52, 148

L.Ed.2d 20 (2000), the Court of Appeals held that it was an abuse of discretion for the district court to award full make-whole relief to twenty-three candidates for police lieutenant and twelve candidates for sergeant when the violation of law resulted from the promotion of only one lieutenant and one sergeant. There was no way to determine which of the candidates would have been promoted absent discrimination. The appellate court remanded with directions to the district court to award each candidate a pro rata share of the monetary value of the promotion for which they were eligible.

2. In a subsequent decision in *Kyriazi*, the district court created a hypothetical work history for the named plaintiff, in a manner similar to that employed in EEOC v. Ford Motor Co., *supra*, by modifying the actual work history of a male employee who held the same job as the plaintiff and had similar qualifications. Kyriazi v. Western Elec. Co., 476 F. Supp. 335 (D.N.J. 1979), aff'd , 647 F.2d 388 (3d Cir. 1981). Pursuant to that formula, Ms. Kyriazi was awarded $103,506.75 in back pay and interest and reinstated to the position she would have occupied with all seniority and benefits she would have enjoyed had she been continuously employed by Western Electric. The Stage II proceedings for class members who had filed claim forms proceeded. By June 1980, 108 final judgments had been entered on behalf of class members who were rejected applicants for employment, and back pay awards totalling $234,271.25 had been entered. The claims of sixty rejected applicants had not been adjudicated, and only a few of the claims of the thousands of women actually employed by Western Electric had been heard. At that point the parties settled. Western Electric agreed to pay $7 million to be distributed among class members who had filed claim forms, to give priority consideration for hiring to class members who had been rejected for employment or laid off, and to engage in a four-year affirmative action program. The history of the Kyriazi litigation is recounted in the district court's approval of the settlement. Kyriazi v. Western Elec. Co., 527 F. Supp. 18 (D.N.J. 1981).

Do you agree with the statement of the trial judge in *Kyriazi* that such a marathon proceeding is "fair both to class members and [the employer]?" In KRASZEWSKI v. STATE FARM GENERAL INSURANCE CO., 1986 WL 11746 (N.D. Cal. 1986), the district court directed that the parties begin individual Stage II hearings in a case where there were potentially 50,000 claimants who might make claims based on 1,250 vacancies during the relevant back pay period. The defendant estimated that the process would take nineteen years. The trial judge was more optimistic, estimating that the claim procedure would take between two and three years. The judge based his decision on his finding that "the only way to determine the actual victims is to give each class member the opportunity to demonstrate she was discriminated against with respect to any of the 1250 vacancies filled by men," but cautioned that "if on receipt of the claim forms, it is obvious that many more than one thousand claims establish a prima facie case, this court will be open to a motion from the defendants to reconsider [the procedure for determining class relief on the basis that individual hearings will be unwieldy." After the court's order requiring individual hearings, the parties settled. Kraszewski v. State Farm Gen. Ins. Co., 912 F.2d 1182 (9th Cir. 1990), cert. denied, 499 U.S. 947, 111 S.Ct. 1414, 113 L.Ed.2d 467 (1991). What alternatives are there to individual hearings? See Segar v. Smith, *infra*.

3. After a finding of the existence of a pattern or practice of sexual harassment has been made in a class action, what burden, if any, should shift to the employer in Phase

II regarding liability to individual class members? The lower courts have disagreed on this question. In JENSON v. EVELETH TACONITE CO., 824 F.Supp. 847 (D. Minn. 1993), aff'd on other grounds, 130 F.3d 1287 (8th Cir. 1997), cert. denied, 524 U.S. 953, 118 S.Ct. 2370, 141 L.Ed.2d 738 (1998), the district court held that, because of the nature of a sexual harassment cause of action, which requires the plaintiff to prove that the working environment was hostile or abusive both to her and to a reasonable person, no burden shifting occurs at the relief stage.

> [T]he nature of a hostile environment claim mandates that the nature of the recovery phase differ from traditional pattern or practice cases. Specifically, a determination that the employer engaged in a pattern or practice of discrimination by maintaining a hostile environment does not entitle every member of the plaintiff's class to a presumption that they were sexually harassed — the burden of persuasion does not shift to the employer. Instead, the burden of persuasion remains on the individual class members; each must show by a preponderance of the evidence that she was as affected as the reasonable woman. If this showing is made, the individual member is entitled to all the remedies available under Title VII * * *. In a hostile environment class action, therefore, every member of the class remains a "potential victim" in the true sense of the term.

824 F. Supp. at 875-76.

In EEOC v. MITSUBISHI MOTOR MFG. OF AMERICA, INC., 990 F.Supp. 1059 (C.D. Ill. 1998), on the other hand, the district court criticized the ruling in *Jenson* for "effectively disassociat[ing] the pattern or practice case from the individual cases so that there would be no benefit to the individual class members from a pattern or practice finding." This trial judge reasoned that it was fairer to require the employer to come forward with evidence to show that the individual members of the potential class, either in whole or in part, did not subjectively perceive the environment as hostile. Only if and when the employer satisfied this burden of production wouold the individual class member bear the ultimate burden of persuading the fact finder that she was entitled to relief under the governing legal standard.

> This burden of production allows the [employer] to identify, by its proofs, who belongs in the affected class and who does not. Once the employer comes forward with its individual defenses, those class members who have been challenged with elimination will then carry the ultimate burden of proving and persuading the trier of fact that they were subjectively affected. For the other individuals who have not been challenged, the presumption turns into a finding of individual liability. The parties will then move to * * * the individual damage phase.

990 F. Supp. at 1081-82. Which court's approach is most consistent with the remedial purposes of Title VII?

Implicit in both *Jenson* and *Mitsubishi Motor* is an assumption that legal damages (as opposed to back pay) may be awarded in a class action. That proposition, however, is not universally recognized. The Fourth and Fifth Circuits have held that because of the individualized determinations required for damage computations, class certification under Rule 23 may simply be unavailable where compensatory or punitive damages are sought in an employment discrimination class action. *See* Allison v. Citgo Petroleum Corp., 151 F.3d 402 (5th Cir. 1998); Lowery v. Circuit City Stores,

Inc., 158 F.3d 742 (4th Cir. 1998). The Ninth Circuit has ruled that where nominal damages are awarded, every class member is entitled to receive such relief. Cummings v. Connell, 402 F.3d. 936, 945 (9th Cir. 2005) ("an award of nominal damages to only the named class representatives fails to appreciate the difference between a class action and a conventional lawsuit.").

4. The economic burdens placed on plaintiffs' counsel by protracted class actions like *Kyriazi* and *Kraszewski* are enormous. Recognizing the severe financial problems faced by counsel in such cases, many courts have awarded interim fees after the liability phase of the case. *See, e.g.*, James v. Stockham Valves & Fittings Co., 559 F.2d 310 (5th Cir. 1977), cert. denied, 434 U.S. 1034, 98 S.Ct. 767, 54 L.Ed.2d 781 (1978); Carpenter v. Stephen F. Austin State Univ., 706 F.2d 608, 633 (5th Cir. 1983).

Another area that remains unsettled is how fees of plaintiffs' counsel should be calculated for the remedial stage of a successful class action. If individualized hearings are conducted on class member claims at Stage II, should counsel be compensated for the time spent on unsuccessful claims? In MCKENZIE v. KENNICKELL, 645 F. Supp. 427 (D.C. Cir. 1986), the court reasoned that Stage II hearings are not unrelated claims that should be separated from the class claims for purposes of a fee award, and held that the defendant should pay all fees and costs of individual claimants at the remedial stage, except where the claims are found to be frivolous or vexatious. *But see* Wooldridge v. Marlene Indus. Corp., 898 F.2d 1169 (6th Cir. 1990) (Stage II fees reduced by the percentage of time spent litigating unsuccessful claims); Foster v. Bd. of School Comm'rs of Mobile County, 810 F.2d 1021 (11th Cir.), cert. denied, 484 U.S. 829, 108 S.Ct. 99, 98 L.Ed.2d 60 (1987) (where less than one third of the class members obtained back pay in Stage II proceedings, the trial court did not abuse its discretion by reducing the lodestar for the remedial phase by 12%).

Segar v. Smith

United States Court of Appeals for the District of Columbia Circuit, 1984.

738 F.2d 1249, cert. denied, 471 U.S. 1115, 105 S.Ct. 2357, 86 L.Ed.2d 258 (1985).

J. SKELLY WRIGHT, Circuit Judge.

Title VII of the Civil Rights Act of 1964 proclaims one of this nation's most fundamental, if yet unrealized, principles: a person shall not be denied full equality of employment opportunity on account of race, color, religion, sex, or national origin. Title VII bars both intentional discrimination and artificial, arbitrary, or unnecessary barriers to equal opportunity. In this case we review a decision * * * holding that the federal Drug Enforcement Agency (DEA) had engaged in a pattern or practice of discrimination against its black agents in violation of Title VII. A class comprising black agents initiated this suit in 1977 and the case came to trial in 1979. Finding that DEA had discriminated against black agents in salary, promotions, initial (GS) grade assignments, work assignments, supervisory evaluations, and imposition of discipline, the District Court ordered a comprehensive remedial scheme consisting of a class-wide backpay award, promotion goals and timetables to ensure that qualified black agents received promotions to the upper levels of DEA, and a class-wide frontpay award to compensate such qualified agents while they awaited the promotions they deserved. In the course of the proceedings the court also denied plaintiffs' request for prejudgment interest and issued a preliminary injunction barring transfer or demotion of Carl Jackson (the Jackson injunction), a black agent who was the subject of adverse employment decisions immediately after his testimony for plaintiffs in this lawsuit.

On appeal DEA challenges the liability determination, the remedial scheme, and the Jackson injunction. Plaintiffs cross-appeal the denial of prejudgment interest. As to the liability determination, DEA urges that the trial court erred in finding that plaintiffs had presented sufficient probative evidence to support any inference of discrimination at DEA, and urges that DEA had in any event effectively rebutted plaintiffs' showing. As to the remedial scheme, DEA argues that class-wide relief was inappropriate and that imposition of promotion goals and timetables both exceeded the court's remedial authority under Title VII and violated the equal protection component of the Fifth Amendment Due Process Clause. DEA also argues that Carl Jackson did not make a showing of retaliation sufficient to justify the preliminary injunction.

To resolve this appeal we have had to plumb some of the deepest complexities of Title VII adjudication. After careful review, we affirm the District Court's liability determination in its entirety. We also affirm the trial court's decision to use a class-wide backpay remedy, but we vacate the backpay formula imposed and remand for reformulation of the particular backpay award. We also vacate the part of the District Court's remedy that mandates promotion goals and timetables. We do not hold that such remedies exceed a court's remedial authority under Title VII. Nor do we hold that such remedies violate the Constitution. Nonetheless, we find that the District Court's particular order of goals and timetables was not appropriate on the current factual record. Because the frontpay remedy was specifically linked to the promotion goals and timetables, we vacate that part of the remedial order as well, and remand to the District Court for further consideration of appropriate remedies.[3] We affirm the preliminary injunction against demotion or transfer of Carl Jackson and we expect the District Court to undertake resolution of the status of the Jackson injunction on remand. We affirm the trial court's denial of prejudgment interest.

I

* * *

B. *This Lawsuit*

In January 1977 two black special agents of DEA, and an association representing all black special agents, brought suit alleging that DEA had engaged in a pattern or practice of racial discrimination against black special agents in violation of Title VII of the Civil Rights Act of 1964. These agents alleged discrimination in recruitment, hiring, initial grade assignments, salary, work assignments, evaluations, discipline, and promotions.

On September 9, 1977 the trial court, pursuant to Federal Rule of Civil Procedure 23(b)(2), certified the class of all blacks who then served or had been discharged as special agents at DEA, and who had applied for positions or would in the future apply. Before trial the parties settled the claims involving discriminatory recruitment and

---

[3]We vacate the frontpay remedy only because the trial court specifically linked it to the promotion timetables, and without prejudice to reinstatement of a new frontpay remedy if the trial court finds such a course appropriate on remand.

hiring, but could not come to terms on the other issues. As is common in Title VII class actions, the District Court bifurcated the trial into separate liability and remedial phases. After lengthy discovery, the liability issues came to trial in April 1979. The trial was in large measure a duel of experts armed with sophisticated statistical means of proof.

1. *The plaintiffs' case.* The plaintiffs presented a range of statistical and anecdotal evidence of discrimination. The statistical evidence included several multiple linear regression analyses as well as a number of studies considering the effects of particular employment practices.

Multiple regression is a form of statistical analysis used increasingly in Title VII actions that measures the discrete influence independent variables have on a dependent variable such as salary levels. Typically the independent variables in Title VII cases will be race, age, education level, and experience levels. The first step in a multiple regression analysis is specification of the independent (or explanatory) variables thought likely to affect significantly the dependent variable. The choice of proper explanatory variables determines the validity of the regression analysis. A coherent theory, devised prior to observation of the particular data, must be employed to select the relevant explanatory variables. When the proper variables have been selected, the multiple regression analysis is conducted, generally by a computer. In essence, the regression measures the impact of each potential explanatory variable upon the dependent variable by holding all other explanatory variables constant. The analysis yields figures demonstrating how much of an observed disparity in salaries can be traced to race, as opposed to any of the other potential explanatory variables.

The computer analysis will generally also yield two other measurements that assist in evaluation of the explanatory power of the regression. The first is "T-Ratio." The T-Ratio measures the probability that the result obtained could have occurred by chance.[7] The second is R^2. The R^2 figure measures, to a certain extent, the degree to which a multiple regression analysis taken as a whole explains observed disparities in a dependent variable.

Having observed an average disparity in salary of about $3,000 between white and black special agents at DEA, plaintiffs' experts, Professors Bergmann and Straszheim,[8] formulated a regression analysis to discover whether and to what extent race explained the observed salary disparity. The experts based their analysis on a "human capital model." A widely accepted approach, the model builds on labor economists' findings that the human capital an employee brings to a job — such as education and experience — in large measure determines the employee's success.

Plaintiffs' experts selected education, prior federal experience, prior nonfederal experience, and race as the four independent variables that might explain the salary differential. Information regarding these independent variables came from the computerized JUNIPER personnel information tapes of the Department of Justice. Professors Bergmann and Straszheim then ran the regressions. They first evaluated the

---

[7]The T-Ratio figure for a particular measure of race-related disparity corresponds to the number of standard deviations for that figure. D. Baldus & J. Cole, Statistical Proof of Discrimination 297 n. 14 (1980).

[8]Professors Bergmann and Straszheim both hold Ph.D.'s and teach labor economics at the University of Maryland. Findings ¶ 6, 508 F.Supp. at 695.

causes of salary disparities among all agents as of five dates: the first of January in 1975, 1976, 1977, and 1978 and the first of October in 1978. This study generated the following results:

DATE	RACE COEFFICIENT	T-RATIO
1/1/75	-$1,628	4.65
1/1/76	-$1,744	5.37
1/1/77	-$1,119	5.15
1/1/78	-$1,934	5.15
10/1/78	-$1,877	4.50

The race coefficient measures the salary disparities between white and black agents when education and prior experience are held constant. The T-Ratio figures here correspond to standard deviations of four or five. See D. Baldus & J. Cole, Statistical Proof of Discrimination 297 n. 14 (1980) (hereinafter "D. Baldus & J. Cole"). Since a standard deviation level higher than three indicates that the odds are less than one in a thousand that an observed result could have occurred by chance, these figures indicate that the odds are far less than one in a thousand that the observed disparities for any year could have occurred by chance. A study is generally considered to be statistically significant when the odds that the result occurred by chance are at best one in 20. See D. Baldus & J. Cole, *supra*, at 297.

Professors Bergmann and Straszheim then ran a second regression to measure salary disparities over the same time frame for agents hired after 1972. They intended this study to generate some measure of the effects of race discrimination at DEA after 1972. Title VII applies to DEA in this action only as of that date.[9] Because the first regression measured disparities in the salaries of all black agents, including those hired before 1972, the race coefficient in that study may have reflected disparities resulting from the continuing effects of discrimination that occurred prior to 1972, rather than actionable post-1972 discrimination. This second regression generated the following results:

DATE	RACE COEFFICIENT	T-RATIO
1/1/75	-$378	.84
1/1/76	-$1,864	2.54
1/1/77	-$1,119	3.18
1/1/78	-$866	2.07
10/1/78	-$1,026	2.30

---

[9]Plaintiffs are subject to the statutory limit on the period of actionable discrimination; under Title VII liability may not accrue for a period of more than two years before the date of filing of an administrative complaint with the Equal Employment Opportunity Commission. In this case the actionable period began on July 15, 1972. Although not formally created until 1973, DEA was at its creation a consolidation of other federal agencies engaged in drug enforcement efforts, and agents serving these agencies became DEA agents.

Again a significant salary disparity between agents with comparable education and experience was revealed. The T-Ratios indicate that for every year, save 1975, the possibility that the result could have occurred by chance was at most one in 20. Though these figures are not at as high a level of significance as were those of the first regression, they still meet the generally accepted test for statistical significance. The second regression, moreover, tends to understate the amount of post-1972 discrimination at DEA. Because the post-1972 study measures discrimination among newer agents, the study focuses on the speed with which the new recruits make their way through the lower levels of DEA. Promotions at these levels are relatively automatic, and discrimination thus has less opportunity to work its effects. Discrimination will most adversely affect older agents contending for upper level positions; promotion decisions at these levels incorporate far more discretionary elements and leave more room for bias. The study does not measure any post-1972 discrimination against those hired before 1972. Since these agents would have been the ones contending for the upper level positions during the time frame studied, they would have been the ones on whom discrimination would have been most likely to operate. The problem is particularly severe with respect to the 1975 race coefficient. Almost half of those studied to obtain this figure were hired in 1974. Since they were in their first year at the time of the study, they would not yet have been eligible for a grade promotion.

Having uncovered evidence of significant discrimination in salary levels, plaintiffs' experts undertook a more exacting inquiry into DEA's employment practices to pinpoint where discrimination was taking place. They first examined DEA's initial grade assignment practices. Through regression analyses they determined at a sufficient level of statistical significance that blacks were 16 percent less likely than comparably qualified whites to have been hired at GS-9 rather than GS-7. For those hired after 1972, blacks were 12 percent less likely to be hired at GS-9. The experts then evaluated work assignments, supervisory evaluations, and discipline. In all three categories statistical analysis revealed significant levels of discrimination against black agents. Finally, plaintiffs' experts studied promotions at DEA. Promotions up to the GS-11 level were found to be relatively automatic. The promotion rate from GS-11 to GS-12 was 70 percent for blacks and 82 percent for whites. This differential met generally accepted levels of statistical significance. Differentials in promotion rates for positions above GS-12 were also found, but — largely because of the small sample size — these differentials did not achieve statistical significance at generally accepted levels.

To buttress the statistical proof plaintiffs introduced anecdotal testimony of discrimination. This evidence consisted of accounts by several black agents of perceived discrimination against them in initial grade assignments, work assignments, supervisory evaluations, and discipline. These agents also testified about their general perceptions of racial hostility at DEA.

2. *Defendant DEA's case.* DEA responded to plaintiffs' case in several ways. The rebuttal consisted of expert testimony attacking the methodological integrity and explanatory value of plaintiffs' statistics, alternative statistical analyses tending to show an absence of discrimination, testimonial evidence concerning DEA's equal employment opportunity programs, and cross-examination of plaintiffs' anecdotal accounts of individual discrimination

* * *

Testimonial evidence buttressed DEA's statistical rebuttal. DEA presented extensive general testimony on its efforts to establish equal opportunity programs and implement equal opportunity goals at the agency. Through cross-examination of plaintiffs' witnesses, DEA also sought to rebut every particular anecdotal account of discrimination.

C. *The District Court Decision*

1. *The liability determination.* [The district judge] * * * held that DEA had discriminated against black special agents in violation of Title VII across a range of employment practices. The court found that the salary differentials between white and black agents were a result of race discrimination, and that DEA had discriminated against black agents in grade-at-entry, work assignments, supervisory evaluations, and promotions. The finding of discrimination in promotions extended to promotions above the GS-12 level, even though the court did not credit plaintiffs' statistical evidence of discrimination at that level because the statistics had not achieved acceptable levels of statistical significance. The court based its finding of discrimination at the upper levels on inferences from proven discrimination at the immediately preceding levels and discrimination in the factors that bear most directly on promotions (work assignments, evaluations, and discipline).

To make these determinations the District Court credited the bulk of plaintiffs' statistical evidence[10] and rejected both DEA's critique of this evidence and DEA's alternative statistics. * * *

2. *The remedies determination.* Having found pervasive discrimination at DEA, the District Court — in a separate remedial proceeding — set out to formulate an appropriate remedial plan.[11] The essential elements of the plan were class-wide backpay, promotion goals and timetables, and class-wide frontpay.

Class-wide Backpay. Rather than order individualized relief hearings, see *Int'l Brhd. of Teamsters*, the District Court ordered a class-wide award of backpay for members of the plaintiff class. For successive one-year periods beginning in July 1972, a class-wide backpay pool figure would be calculated. The calculations would derive from plaintiffs' first salary regression study (which measured disparities among all agents including those hired before 1972). For every year for which figures were available — 1975 to 1979 — the class-wide pool figure would be the race coefficient multiplied by the number of black special agents. For the years before 1975 and after 1979 the race coefficient would be derived by extrapolating backward and forward from the available figures, and this extrapolated coefficient would be multiplied by the number of black agents.

The annual backpay pool would be distributed evenly among eligible black agents. Only agents above the GS-9 level during the year in question were made eligible. The court excluded agents at GS-7 and GS-9 because most discrimination

---

[10]The court did, however, refuse to credit most of plaintiffs' anecdotal accounts of specific instances of discrimination.

[11]DEA sought at the remedial hearing to introduce its own regression analyses. These regressions purportedly showed an absence of race-related disparity at DEA. The District Court rejected this proffered evidence of DEA's nonliability as untimely.

was found to occur at the higher levels of DEA. The court did, however, permit individual plaintiffs to come forward and seek backpay for discrimination suffered in initial grade assignment (viz. assignment to GS-7 instead of GS-9). Any such individual awards would be subtracted from the class-wide pool in order to prevent double liability.

Promotion Goals and Timetables. Finding discrimination at the upper levels of DEA, the District Court ordered remedial promotion goals and timetables. Since black agents made up at least 10 percent of agents at every level through GS-12 the court held that a 10 percent goal was appropriate for all levels above GS-12. To meet this goal the court ordered DEA to promote one black agent for every two white agents until 10 percent black representation had been met at GS-13 and above (or until five years had passed).

Class-wide Frontpay. To compensate black agents awaiting promotion under the goals and timetables plan the court established a class-wide frontpay formula. Frontpay pool calculations were also based on extrapolations from the salary regression, but the pool was to be adjusted to reflect progress DEA had made under the promotions goals and timetables. The pool was to be distributed to all black agents at GS-12 for at least two years and all black agents above GS-12.

3. *Other issues.* In the course of the proceeding two other issues arose. Plaintiffs sought and were refused an award of prejudgment interest on the backpay awards. Also, during the time between the liability and remedial determinations the court issued a preliminary injunction barring demotion or transfer of black special agent Carl Jackson. Shortly after Jackson had testified at trial in this case he became the target of harassment and eventually of adverse employment actions including demotion and transfer. The District Court concluded that there was a high likelihood that these actions were in retaliation for Jackson's testimony, and therefore preliminarily enjoined Jackson's demotion or transfer.

* * *

[The Court's analysis of the district court's liability determination is omitted.]

III. THE REMEDIES DETERMINATION

Section 706(g) of Title VII empowers a court that has found illegal discrimination to "order such affirmative action as may be appropriate, which may include, but is not limited to, reinstatement or hiring of employees, with or without back pay * * * or any other equitable relief as the court deems appropriate." * * *

Having found pervasive discrimination at DEA, the District Court fashioned a tripartite remedial scheme: class-wide backpay for those at GS-11 and above,[35] promotion goals and timetables at DEA's upper levels, and class-wide frontpay for those at GS-11 and above. DEA raises three challenges to these remedies. First, the class-wide backpay award impermissibly circumvents the individualized remedial hearings required by Teamsters, supra. Second, the backpay award compensates for

---

[35]Finding most discrimination took place at GS-11 and above, the court did not order classwide relief for discrimination against black agents at GS-7 or GS-9 during any given backpay year. The court did, however, permit these agents to bring individual claims for relief. Any individual awards at these levels are to be deducted from the class-wide backpay pool distributed to agents at GS-11 and above.

nonactionable pre-1972 discrimination. Third, the promotion goals and timetables exceed the court's remedial authority under Section 706(g) and violate the equal protection component of the Fifth Amendment to the Constitution.

A. *Individualized Hearings*

DEA objects to the District Court's decision to forego in this case the individualized relief hearings prescribed in *Teamsters*. The gravamen of DEA's objection is that class-wide relief may benefit some black agents who were not victims of illegal discrimination. The Court in *Teamsters* stated that when plaintiffs seek relief as "victims of the discriminatory practice, a district court must usually conduct additional proceedings after the liability phase of the trial to determine the scope of individual relief." In the wake of *Teamsters* individualized hearings have been common features of Title VII class actions.

Though *Teamsters* certainly raises a presumption in favor of individualized hearings, the case should not be read as an unyielding limit on a court's equitable power to fashion effective relief for proven discrimination.[36] The language of *Teamsters* is not so inflexible; after stating that individual hearings are "usually" required, *Teamsters*, the Court went on to note that "[i]n determining the specific remedies to be afforded, a district court is 'to fashion such relief as the particular circumstances of a case may require to effect restitution.'" (quoting *Franks*). Later courts have often faced situations in which the *Teamsters* hearing preference had to bend to accommodate Title VII's remedial purposes. Primarily, courts have not required hearings when discrimination has so percolated through an employment system that any attempt to reconstruct individual employment histories would drag the court into "a quagmire of hypothetical judgments."

Applying these principles to the present controversy, we note at the outset that the District Court did not rush willy-nilly to impose class-wide relief. The court specifically ordered individual relief hearings where feasible. All claims of backpay for discrimination at levels below GS-11 will be resolved in individualized hearings. At these levels individualized hearings are appropriate because a small number of discernible decisions as to initial grade assignment and promotions will be in issue for each agent. These determinations are akin to those in *Teamsters*, where the required hearings were to involve a single determination as to whether individual plaintiffs had applied and were qualified for particular line driver positions in the trucking industry.

After careful consideration, the District Court here ordered class-wide relief only for discrimination above GS-11. The court had found that discrimination impeded black agents at every turn; blacks faced extra hurdles in DEA's initial grade assignments, work assignments, supervisory evaluations, imposition of discipline, and promotions. At the higher levels the cumulative effect of these pervasive

---

[36]McKenzie v. Sawyer, 684 F.2d 62 (D.C.Cir.1982), does not mandate individual hearings in every case. The panel in *Sawyer* affirmed a District Court's decision to require individual relief hearings. When, in an exercise of its remedial discretion, a trial court orders hearings, an appellate court is properly reluctant to interfere with that judgment. But the appellate panel in *Sawyer* was not faced with a trial court's decision that individual hearings would effectively preclude relief for most members of the plaintiff class. Thus, *Sawyer's* reiteration of the *Teamsters* hearing preference should not be taken as implying that class-wide relief in the present context would be improper.

discriminatory practices became severe, and the increased subjectivity in evaluations gave discrimination more room to work its effects. In such a situation exact reconstruction of each individual claimant's work history, as if discrimination had not occurred, is not only imprecise but impractical. The District Court here specifically found that "[e]ach major criterion in the promotion process at DEA was tainted by discrimination, making discrimination in the promotion process cumulative. Any attempt to recreate the employment histories of individual employees absent discrimination would result in mere guesswork." Our role in reviewing this determination is limited. "The framing of a remedial decree is left largely in the hands of the district judge, whose assessment of the needs of the situation is a factual judgment reviewable only for clear error * * *." *McKenzie v. Sawyer.*

We perceive no error in the District Court's finding that it would be impossible to reconstruct the employment histories of DEA's senior black agents. Examination of discrete promotion decisions, as difficult as even that might be, will not suffice. The decisive criteria for promotions decisions — supervisory evaluations, breadth of experience, and disciplinary history — were themselves found to be tainted with illegal discrimination. The court found that discrimination had skewed evaluations of black agents, but the court could have had no way of knowing how much more favorable a particular agent's evaluation should have been, or how a fair evaluation might have affected the agent's chances for obtaining a particular promotion. Similarly, the court found that discrimination in work assignments — leaving black agents with a disproportionately large share of undercover assignments — had impeded black agents in promotions, but the court could have had no way to divine what other broadening experiences a particular agent might have had, and no way to gauge how this hypothetical additional experience would have affected particular promotion decisions. And though the court found that black agents have been disciplined more frequently and more severely than white agents committing similar infractions, the court could have had no way of knowing exactly what effect the disproportionate disciplinary sanctions had on a particular agent's chances for particular promotions. Finally, because promotions at DEA are cumulative, the effects of discrimination in promotions are also cumulative. Denial of promotion to one grade affects the agent's eligibility for later promotions to higher grades.

To require individualized hearings in these circumstances would be to deny relief to the bulk of DEA's black agents despite a finding of pervasive discrimination against them. In effect, DEA would have us preclude relief unless the remedial order is perfectly tailored to award relief only to those injured and only in the exact amount of their injury. Though §706(g) generally does not allow for backpay to those whom discrimination has not injured, this section should not be read as requiring effective denial of backpay to the large numbers of agents whom DEA's discrimination has injured in order to account for the risk that a small number of undeserving individuals might receive backpay. Such a result cannot be squared with what the Supreme Court has told us about the nature of a court's remedial authority under Title VII. "[T]he scope of a district court's remedial powers under Title VII is determined by the purposes of the Act." A core purpose of Title VII is "to make persons whole for injuries suffered on account of unlawful employment discrimination." *Albemarle Paper Co.* "[F]ederal courts are empowered to fashion such relief as the particular circumstances require to effect restitution, making whole insofar as possible the victims of racial discrimination * * *." *Franks*. The trial court found that the particular circumstances of this case required classwide relief for black agents at GS-11 and above to ensure that they were made whole for the pervasive discrimination they have suffered. If effective relief for the victims of discrimination necessarily entails the risk that a few nonvictims might also benefit from the relief, then the employer, as a proven discriminator, must bear that risk.

B. *The Allegation of Class-Wide Overcompensation*

In calculating the backpay pool the District Court used the race coefficient of the first of plaintiffs' two salary regressions as the measure of average discrimination per agent. The first regression measured discrimination against all black agents, including those hired before 1972. This study may therefore have reflected the continuing effects of some discrimination occurring prior to 1972. Since the actionable period in this case commenced on July 15, 1972, use of the first regression might, according to DEA's argument, amount to compensation for some nonactionable discrimination.[37] Though the remedial order specifically states that backpay begins to accrue only as of July 15, 1972, DEA argues that a portion of the disparities between black and white agents as of that time (and thereafter) was caused by discrimination before 1972, and that DEA is therefore not liable for that portion.

The District Court found in the Liability Determination that "while pre-1972 discrimination may have affected the statistics * * *, post 1972 discrimination largely contributed to those statistics." The court also noted in the Remedial Order that plaintiffs' regressions "provide an accurate measure of the extent to which blacks at DEA were paid less than comparably qualified whites [and] * * * provide an appropriate basis for classwide relief." We are reluctant to disturb the trial court's finding on this factual issue. Nonetheless on the record as it now stands, we cannot affirm the District Court's decision to use the first regression as a basis for calculating the backpay pool.

Although the court properly found that the plaintiff's evidence sufficed to support an inference of actionable discrimination, the court's reliance on the first regression to determine backpay is problematic. The court never found that all of that regression's race coefficient reflected actionable post-1972 discrimination.[38] To do so the court would have had to find either that all discrimination reflected in the salary disparities occurred after 1972 or that the small portion of "continuing effects" of pre-1972 discrimination reflected in the disparities was the result of a "continuing violation."

---

[37]DEA also makes an argument that use of the first salary regression overcompensates plaintiffs based on the R^2 values for this study. DEA argues that, because the R^2 value was roughly .50, only about half of the race coefficient for the years in question actually represents race-related disparity. This argument reveals a basic misunderstanding of the meaning of R^2 figures. An R^2 of .50 does not mean that only half of the race coefficient is attributable to race. Rather, it means that half of the total salary disparity between black and white agents is attributable to the totality of the factors examined in the regression. In any event, R^2 is far from a wholly reliable measure of a study's accuracy. For these reasons, we hold that DEA's objection based on R^2 values is without force.

[38]Of course, the court need not have found that all of the discrimination reflected in the regression occurred after 1972 in order to find the regression sufficient to make out a prima facie case of actionable discrimination. See Valentino v. U.S. Postal Service, 674 F.2d 56, 71 n. 26 (D.C.Cir.1982).

The court made neither finding, and having found in the Liability Determination that pre-1972 discrimination had been "neither admitted nor proven," the court cannot plausibly rely on a continuing violation theory in the Remedial Order as grounds for using the first salary regression as a benchmark for the backpay pool.

It may be that plaintiffs' first regression does reflect only post-1972 discrimination. DEA's complete failure to present evidence showing pre-1972 discrimination in the regression certainly supports this view. It may also be that the portion of the disparity that reflects continuing effects of pre-1972 discrimination might be actionable on a continuing violation theory. Or it may be that the small amount of continuing effects cannot plausibly be factored out of the study; if so, and if no more precise methods of ascertaining the amount of actionable discrimination are reasonably available to the court, the court would be faced with using either a mildly overcompensatory formula based on the first regression or a significantly undercompensatory formula based on the second regression. Use of the first regression under these circumstances might be permissible.

We cannot, however, resolve these matters on the present appeal. * * * [T]his court must scrupulously respect the factfinding prerogative of the District Court. In this case the District Court has not yet determined whether the first regression reflects only post-1972 discrimination, whether a continuing violation occurred that might permit compensation for whatever continuing effects the regression reflects, or whether the small portion of nonactionable continuing effects that might be reflected in the regression cannot be factored out. On remand, if the District Court is unable to find that any of these three factual circumstances exists, the court must devise a new backpay formula.

C. *Promotion Goals and Timetables*

The District Court ordered that one black be promoted for every two whites to positions above GS-12 at DEA until blacks made up 10 percent of all agents at each grade above GS-12 or until five years after the order was entered. DEA objects to this aspect of the remedy for the same reason that it objects to class-wide backpay: some individual agents might receive promotions they do not deserve. DEA argues that promotion goals and timetables exceed a court's remedial power under Title VII unless every person who potentially benefits from the relief has been individually shown to have been discriminatorily denied a specific promotion. According to DEA, §706(g) mandates this result. ("No order of the court shall require the * * * promotion of an individual as an employee, * * * if such individual was refused * * * advancement * * * for any reason other than discrimination * * *."). DEA also argues that such goals and timetables violate the equal protection component of the Fifth Amendment to the Constitution.

Though DEA's claims are not without some superficial appeal, §706(g) must not be read as requiring an exact fit between those whom an employer's discrimination has victimized and those eligible under promotion goals and timetables. The language on which DEA relies was aimed at ensuring that Title VII was not read as giving courts authority to remedy racial imbalance as an evil in itself, i.e., absent any finding that illegal discrimination caused the imbalance. See EEOC v. AT & T, 556 F.2d 167, 175 (3d Cir.1977), cert. denied, 438 U.S. 915, 98 S.Ct. 3145, 57 L.Ed.2d 1161 (1978). The language should not be stretched to support a requirement of absolute precision in fashioning promotion goals and timetables when such a requirement would frustrate effective relief for those who were victimized by discrimination.[39] Every federal Court of Appeals in this nation has approved remedial use of goals and timetables without requiring that each and every potentially eligible person be shown to have been a victim of discrimination. Nor can the imposition of quotas to remedy proven discrimination be said to violate the Constitution's guarantees of equal protection. Whatever the current status of affirmative action absent a finding of discrimination, the Supreme Court has made clear that such relief is not unconstitutional when used to remedy proven discrimination. See Swann v. Charlotte-Mecklenburg School District, 402 U.S. 1, 91 S.Ct. 1267, 28 L.Ed.2d 554 (1971); Bakke v. Board of Regents of the University of California, 438 U.S. 265, 302, 98 S.Ct. 2733, 2754, 57 L.Ed.2d 750 (1978) (Powell, J., concurring); id. at 363-386, 98 S.Ct. at 2785-2797 (Brennan, White, Marshall and Blackmun, JJ, concurring).

Nonetheless promotion goals and timetables — even if as admirably crafted as those at issue here — must be used cautiously. Such relief intrudes into the structure of employment relations and may at times upset the legitimate promotion expectations of individuals in the majority group. We must take a careful look at the District Court's decision to use goals and timetables in this case.

We are persuaded that the District Court's order that one black be promoted for every two whites to positions above GS-12 was not appropriate. Strict goals and timetables should not be imposed when alternative, equally effective methods could supplant resort to a quota. The District Court did not consider whether less severe remedies might prove equally efficacious in this case. We therefore vacate the District Court's imposition of goals and timetables, and remand for additional consideration of the propriety of such remedies in this case.

In determining whether less severe remedies might prove equally effective the court must evaluate the likelihood that the employer will implement the remedy in good faith. One important indicia is the employer's past behavior in implementing equal opportunity programs, either voluntarily or in response to court order. This court has some doubt that DEA's past record on equal employment opportunity warrants application of strict goals and timetables. DEA has not been before this court in the past on identical or related claims of discrimination, and thus has not shown any recalcitrance in remedying discrimination pursuant to court order. Nor does DEA's overall approach to equal employment matters lead us to conclude that DEA will be unlikely to remedy the proven discrimination in promotions once this court orders it to do so. The record contains significant uncontradicted evidence of DEA's institutional

---

[39]DEA has amassed an array of quotes from Title VII's legislative history in support of its contention that promotion goals and timetables are invalid if they benefit any individuals who are not proven victims of discrimination. Many in Congress spoke in 1964, and again in 1972 when Title VII was amended, to assure wavering supporters that Title VII could not be applied to grant preferences for those who were not victims of discrimination. These statements are, however, inapposite to the question before us in this case. Those in Congress who made such statements were not considering the issue whether in affording relief for proven discrimination against a broad class some individual nonvictims might benefit in order to ensure that all actual victims benefitted. Rather, these statements were made with reference to the question whether Title VII could be used as a mandate to correct overall racial imbalance in an employer's workforce when such an imbalance had not been shown to be the result of discrimination.

good faith in implementing equal employment opportunity programs. Of course, the determination of appropriate relief is for the District Court in the first instance. We also vacate the District Court's order of class-wide frontpay because the frontpay order was premised on the existence of promotion goals and timetables. The District Court is free to impose a new frontpay order on remand if it deems one appropriate.

On remand we encourage the District Court to consider other remedial options to ensure that black agents attain their rightful places at the upper levels of DEA. We note in particular that a promotion bottleneck appears to exist at the GS-12 level. While black agents manage to arrive at this level eventually, few progress beyond this point. In remedying promotion discrimination at this point and at all levels, the court is of course free to establish promotion guidelines and to monitor DEA's progress in meeting those guidelines, or to fashion any other appropriate relief.

* * *

[The Court affirmed the district court's grant of a preliminary injunction barring the demotion and transfer of Special Agent Jackson. The Court reasoned that irreparable harm would follow from a refusal to grant such relief because other class members would be deterred from coming forward with claims at the relief stage. The district court's denial of prejudgment interest was also affirmed on the ground that sovereign immunity barred such an award against the federal government.]

[The concurring opinion of Judge Edwards is omitted.]

NOTES AND PROBLEMS FOR DISCUSSION

1. (a) The lower courts consistently have held that difficulty in calculating back pay is not a ground for denying such relief altogether. *See, e.g.*, Pettway v. Am. Cast Iron Pipe Co., 494 F.2d 211 (5th Cir. 1974), cert. denied, 439 U.S. 1115, 99 S.Ct. 1020, 59 L.Ed.2d 74 (1979) (Pettway III). In a much-quoted section of *Pettway III*, the Fifth Circuit declared that "in computing a back pay award two principles are lucid: (1) unrealistic exactitude is not required, and (2) uncertainties in determining what an employee would have earned but for the discrimination, should be resolved against the discriminating employer." But does this reasoning justify the decision in *Segar* not to individualize the relief determinations? Wasn't the DEA entitled to show that particular class members would not have been promoted by introducing objective evidence of their poor job performance? Despite the preference expressed in *Teamsters* for individualized Stage II proceedings, many lower courts, as in *Pettway III*, have adopted class-wide formulas for providing relief. *See, e.g.*, Domingo v. New England Fish Co., 742 F.2d 520 (9th Cir. 1984).

(b) In WAL-MART STORES, INC. v. DUKES, 564 U.S. 338, 131 S.Ct. 2541, 180 L.Ed.2d 374 (2011), the trial court had certified the largest class action in history involving about one and one half million present and former female employees who alleged that Wal-Maart had discriminated against its female employees on the basis of their sex in connection with pay and promotion decisions in all of its stores across the United States. The trial court had certified the class action under Rule 239b)(2), but a split Supreme Court, by a 5-4 vote, ruled that the class could not be certified under (b)(2) because it did not satisfy the commonality requirement. The four dissenting Justices concluded that the majority had misconstrued the commonality requirement applicable to (b)(2) classes and had applied a standard more properly invoked in (b)(3) class certifications. In their view, the plaintiffs satisfied the commonality reuirement for certification under Rule 23(b)(2).

However, all of the Justices agreed that the case had been improperly certified under Rule 23(b)(2). The Justices were unanimous in broadly ruling that a class action could not be certified under Rule 23(b)(2) where the case involved a request for monetary relief, at least where monetary relief was not incidental to the sought-after injunctive or declaratory relief. The Court stated that to be properly certified under Rule 23(b)(2), a single injunction or declaratory judgment would have to provide relief to each and every member's claim. Rule 23(b)(2) class certification, the Court explained, could not be obtained when either each class member was entitled to a different injunction or declaratory judgment or where each individual member was entitled to an *individualized* award of monetary damages. Thus, the Court concluded, Rule 23 did not sanction any combination of individualized and class-wide relief in a (b)(2) class action. Instead, the Court continued, individualized claims for monetary relief were properly within the compass of a (b)(3) class action with its enhanced procedural protections.

On the other hand, the Court noted, in a true (b)(2) class action, i.e., where a single indivisible injunction or declaratory judgment benefits all members at once, the procedural protections attendant to a (b)(3) class action – predominance, superiority, mandatory notice, and the right to opt out – are unnecessary because there is no need to undertake a case-specific inquiry into whether class issues predominate or whether class action is a superior way to adjudicate the dispute.

The unanimous Court also announced that it would not read (b)(2) to allow individualized money claims where monetary relief was only a partial and nonpredominant portion of the sought-after relief. It rejected the argument that the predominance of equitable relief was sufficient to justify (b)(2) class action certification. Individual claimants with individual monetary claims needed the opportunity to choose whether they want to opt in or out of the class, an opportunity that (b)(2) does not ensure.

The Supreme Court also unanimously rejected as irrelevant the argument that back pay claims were appropriate for (b)(2) certification because they were equitable in nature. The Court emphasized that Rule 23(b)(2) refers only to "injunctions" and "declaratory judgments" and not more broadly to "equitable relief". Consequently, the Court reasoned, since back pay is neither an injunction nor a declaratory judgment, a claim for back pay was not properly included within the nature of relief recoverable in a class action certified under Rule 23(b)(2).

Although the language of Justice Scalia's opinion for a unanimous Court is quite broad in terms of removing the possibility of (b)(2) certification for cases involving requests for monetary relief (such as, in the instant case, claims for back pay), he did leave a little wiggle room open for the possibility of some recovery of monetary relief in a (b)(2) class action. His opinion for the unanimous Court expressly reserved judgment on the rule set forth by the Fifth Circuit in *Allison*, which allows certification of a (b)(2) class action where monetary relief is merely "incidental" to the requested injunctive and declaratory relief. The Court noted that the plaintiffs in the instant case had not argued that they met this standard. Nevertheless, adding insult to injury, the

Court also offered its opinion that this standard could not have been met in the case at bar. Consequently, the Court concluded by stating simply that it would not decide whether there was any form of incidental monetary relief cases that could receive (b)(2) certification.

The decision by the Supreme Court rendered moot the trial judge's discussion of whether the relief phase of the litigation would be unmanageable because of the sheer number of potential claimants. The plaintiffs had conceded to the trial judge that any remedy requiring individual *Teamsters* hearings to determine entitlement to back pay (as in *Kyriazi*) would be impracticable. Consequently, for the trial court, class certification depended on whether entitlement to and quantum of back pay could be determined on a formula approach without individualized hearings. In granting (b)(2) certification, the district court agreed with the plaintiffs that a formula for developing a lump sum back liability to the class could be developed for a least some of the promotion claims made by plaintiffs. A split *en banc* Ninth Circuit had upheld the trial judge's certification decision, finding that the trial court had not abused its discretion when it certified the class. But the Supreme Court's ruling excluding the possibility of recovering any form of monetary relief in a (b)(2) class action (with the remote possibility of allowing it where such relief was incidental to the sought-after injunctive or declaratory relief) rendered these rulings moot.

(c)   Courts typically hold that "rough justice" is better than the alternative of no remedy. *See, e.g.*, Stewart v. General Motors Corp., 542 F.2d 445, 453 (7th Cir. 1976) ("Given a choice between no compensation for black employees who have been illegally denied promotions and an approximate measure of damages, we choose the latter."). In *Wal-Mart*, the district court denied class certification for much of the promotion claim for back pay because objective evidence of interest was lacking, a decision rendered moot by the Supreme Court's reversal. But is that any better than a formula that allows all qualified class members to share in a lump sum award perhaps discounted somewhat for the uncertainty of interest? Is the denial of class certification the same thing as denying a remedy for many if not most of the class members?

2.   The "goals and timetables" type of affirmative relief often will have an impact on the employment opportunities of both incumbent employees and non-class applicants for employment. Is that why the injunctive part of the district court's order in *Segar* was vacated? In MCKENZIE v. SAWYER, 684 F.2d 62 (D.C. Cir. 1982), discussed by the court in *Segar*, the court found that the defendant had engaged in a prolonged history of racial discrimination in hiring and promotional decisions. To address the continuing effects of that discrimination, the court imposed upon the defendant goals and timetables for the promotion of members of the plaintiff class similar to those subsequently adopted in *Segar*. In order to insure that the defendant would meet its goals, the court ordered mandatory selection rates for certain positions: 50% to 80% of the vacancies in various positions were to be filled with members of the plaintiff class. Therafter, implementation of that order resulted in the trial judge issuing another order that directed the defendant to promote a class member who was not on the list of those "best qualified" for a position over non-minority employees who were among those "best qualified" for the position. The defendant appealed that subsequent order, and the Court of Appeals reversed.

Title VII remedies are to be designed and enforced with appropriate attention to the interests of nonvictim employees — in the words of this court, "with care to see that they wound as little as possible." (quoting Thompson v. Sawyer, 678 F.2d 257, 293 (D.C. Cir. 1982). The need for flexible enforcement of employment goals is at its maximum when the legitimate interests of third-party employees are at stake. Here when the district court saw that the promotional goals of its final order might not be realized in a timely fashion — for reasons involving no bad faith on the part of the governmental defendant — it was obliged to countenance some delay in their attainment before it could adopt additional remedial measures that would increase the burden borne by other employees whose opportunities for promotion had already been curtailed during the long journey toward nondiscriminatory employment.

McKenzie v. Kennickell, 825 F.2d 429, 436 (D.C. Cir. 1987). Should it matter whether the class member who benefitted from implementation of the order was himself the victim of discrimination? The subject of "bumping" and other effects of injunctive relief on non-party employees is discussed in Section B of this chapter, *supra*. In connection with *Segar* and *McKenzie*, consider the Supreme Court's opinions in *Franks v. Bowman* and *Martin v. Wilks*.

3. The hiring "goals and timetables" ordered by the district court in *Segar* were designed to cure one of the effects of the DEA's discrimination, the absence of black agents above the rank of GS-12. As the Court of Appeals recognized, some of the beneficiaries of this affirmative relief would be agents who had not actually been hurt by discrimination, just as some of the recipients of back pay would not be actual victims of discrimination. The government's objections to non-victim relief were disposed of with the statement that "such relief is not unconstitutional when used to remedy proven discrimination." The justification for and problems surrounding affirmative action plans are explored in Part IV, *infra*.

PART III

OTHER FEDERAL ANTIDISCRIMINATION LEGISLATION

CHAPTER 8

The Reconstruction Civil Rights Acts — 42 U.S.C. §§1981, 1983, 1985(3)

SECTION A. THE CIVIL RIGHTS ACT OF 1866 — 42 U.S.C. §1981

Reiss, Requiem for an "Independent Remedy": The Civil Rights Acts of 1866 and 1871 as Remedies for Employment Discrimination

50 SO.CAL.L.REV. 961, 971-974 (1977).

* * *

In 1865, with the ratification of the thirteenth amendment, Congress obtained authority to pass laws designed to eradicate slavery and its incidents. The Civil Rights Act of 1866[46] was enacted pursuant to that authority. Section 1 furthered two goals:

---

[46]Act of Apr. 9, 1866, ch. 31, §1, 14 Stat. 27. Section 1 of the Civil Rights Act of 1866 provided:

> *That all persons born in the United States* and not subject to any foreign power, excluding Indians not taxed, *are* hereby declared to be *citizens* of the United States; *and such citizens,* of every race and color, without regard to any previous condition of slavery or involuntary servitude, except as a punishment for crime whereof the party shall have been duly convicted, *shall have the same right,* in every State and Territory in the United States, *to*

first, it granted citizenship to all persons born in the United States; and second, it granted those persons the same rights as white citizens. There was some question at the time whether the thirteenth amendment authorized legislation this broad. These doubts, coupled with fears that the Act could easily be repealed in the future, constituted part of the impetus for the subsequent adoption of the fourteenth amendment in 1868. Two years later, Congress reenacted the 1866 Act with only a minor change in wording, removing any doubts concerning its constitutionality. Years later, as part of a general recodification of federal law, the original §1 was split into two separate statutes — §§1981 and 1982. Section 1982 grants all persons the same property rights as white citizens, while §1981 involves other rights, including the right to make and enforce contracts. Courts have held that the right "to make and enforce contracts" on an equal basis, referred to in §1981, includes the right to enter into and enforce employment contracts. Thus, §1981 prohibits discriminatory employment practices in recruitment, hiring, compensation, assignment, promotion, layoff, and discharge of employees.

* * *

* * * Although §1981, by its terms, would seem to prohibit a broad range of private as well as public acts of discrimination, courts have narrowly construed the statute throughout most of its history. In 1883, in the *Civil Rights Cases*, the Supreme Court struck down other civil rights legislation which prohibited discrimination in public accommodations. The Court reasoned that Congress lacked the constitutional authority to reach wholly private conduct. Although the Civil Rights Act of 1866 was not directly involved in that case, the Court indicated that the statute should also be limited to situations involving state action. In 1948 the Court expressly declared that "governmental action" was required in a suit based on the Civil Rights Act of 1866.[54]

More than one hundred years after passage of the statute, the Supreme Court, in JONES v. ALFRED H. MAYER CO.,[55] finally dispensed with the state action requirement and held that the Civil Rights Act of 1866 reached purely private acts of discrimination. While Jones v. Mayer involved the application of §1982, it was immediately apparent that the rationale of the decision applied equally to §1981. Following Jones v. Mayer, §1981 was increasingly used by plaintiffs, in addition to Title VII, to attack discriminatory employment practices in the private sector. In each instance where a court of appeals had the opportunity to rule on the question, the court held that §1981 did provide the basis for an independent federal cause of action against racial discrimination in employment. Finally, in JOHNSON v. RAILWAY EXPRESS AGENCY, INC., the Supreme Court affirmed that view. Courts have held §1981 applicable not only to discrimination by private employers, but also to discrimination

---

§*make and enforce contracts, to sue, be parties, and give evidence,* to inherit, purchase, lease, sell, hold, and convey real and personal property, *and to full and equal benefit of all laws and proceedings for the security of person and property, as is enjoyed by white citizens, and shall be subject to like punishment, pains, and penalties, and to none other,* any law, statute, ordinance, regulation, or custom, to the contrary notwithstanding.

14 Stat. 27 (1866) (emphasis added). The italicized portion is similar to, though not identical with, §1981. The portion dealing with property rights is similar to what is now 42 U.S.C. §1982.

[54]Hurd v. Hodge, 334 U.S. 24, 31, 68 S.Ct. 847, 851, 92 L.Ed. 1187 (1948).
[55]392 U.S. 409, 88 S.Ct. 2186, 20 L.Ed.2d 1189 (1968).

by labor unions. In other contexts, not directly involving employment, courts have held §1981 applicable to contracts involving the purchase of tickets to an amusement park, the admission of patients to a private hospital, membership in private clubs, and, most recently, attendance in private schools. Thus, in the private sector, the coverage of §1981 is at least as broad as the coverage of Title VII. In fact, it is certainly broader.

Title VII has always applied to employers and unions whose "operations affect commerce," if of a minimum size. The original minimum of one hundred members or employees has been reduced to fifteen. Section 1981 contains no statutory minimum, simply providing that "all persons * * * shall have the same right * * * to make and enforce contracts * * * as * * * white citizens." While it is not likely that all enterprises employing fewer than fifteen employees will be covered by §1981, the statute clearly does extend its protection to millions of workers in millions of small business establishments not covered by Title VII.

Read 42 U.S.C. §1981.

As noted in the preceding excerpt, since 1968 (the date of the Supreme Court's decision in *Jones v. Alfred Mayer*), the broad "right to make and enforce contracts" language of §1981 had been interpreted to encompass employment contracts, thereby subjecting a wide range of employment decisions to the requirements of the 1866 Act. In 1989, however, the Supreme Court revisited the fundamental question of the scope of the antidiscrimination principle contained within §1981. In PATTERSON v. MCLEAN CREDIT UNION, 491 U.S. 164, 109 S.Ct. 2363, 105 L.Ed.2d 132 (1989), the Court, while reaffirming its previously stated position that §1981 prohibited discrimination in the making and enforcing of private contracts, dramatically reversed and restricted its decades-old interpretation of the "right to make and enforce contracts" language of §1981. The five member majority, over a stinging dissent, declared that the right to "make" contracts referred only to discriminatory conduct associated with the formation of a contractual relationship. It did not extend, the Court continued, to conduct occurring after the formation of the contractual relation, such as a breach of the terms of the contract or the imposition of discriminatory working conditions. Such postformation conduct involving the performance of contractual obligations did not invoke the right to "make" a contract and, therefore, was not governed by §1981. Rather, the Court announced, these claims were more naturally subject to challenge under state contract law and Title VII. The majority also rejected dissenting Justice Brennan's suggestion that postformation conduct could be so severe or pervasive as to establish that the contract was not entered into in a nondiscriminatory manner. This type of discriminatory postformation conduct, according to the majority, could only be used by the plaintiff as evidence that a divergence in some discrete term of the contract was motivated by racial animus at the time of contract formation. As for the right to "enforce" contracts, the Court ruled that this guarantee embraced only the right of access to the legal process to enforce contractual obligations. Accordingly, this portion of §1981 was construed to proscribe only conduct that impairs an individual's ability to enforce contractual rights through the legal process.

The plaintiff in *Patterson* asserted two claims under §1981. She alleged that she had been the victim of racial harassment and that she had been denied a promotion on the basis of race. Since the alleged harassment involved postformation conduct relating to the terms and conditions of her continued employment, the Court concluded that this claim was not cognizable under §1981. The promotion claim, however, was, in the Court's view "a different matter." A denial of a promotion, the Court reasoned, could constitute a denial of the right to "make" a contract where the promotion would have created a new and distinct relationship between the parties, i.e., where it would have presented the opportunity to enter into a new contractual relationship. Accordingly, while the harassment claim was dismissed, the promotion claim was remanded for further proceedings.

The ruling in *Patterson* generated an avalanche of lower court opinions in which the courts struggled to apply this new construction of the statute to a wide variety of situations. While *Patterson* clearly indicated that certain claims — such as harassment and discharge — did not invoke the right to "make" a contract, many other scenarios arose that presented trial and appellate courts with opportunities to engage their ingenuity and imagination in efforts to avoid what often was perceived as an unduly restrictive interpretation of the statute. For example, could a discharged employee successfully claim that the employer's refusal to rehire him after his discharge constituted a refusal to "make" a contract? What about an employee who claims that he was not recalled from a layoff because of his race? How do you treat employees at will who do not have a contract with the employer? Does §1981 support a claim that the plaintiff was retaliated against because of his protests against the employer's discriminatory refusal to enter into a contractual relationship with a third party? Could retaliation implicate the right to "enforce" the contract? If so, must the retaliation have been undertaken in response to the plaintiff's efforts at enforcing contractual, as opposed to statutory rights? When does the denial of a promotion impair the ability to enter into a new contractual relationship? In making this latter determination, should it matter whether the position also was open to nonemployee applicants (who surely could allege that they were denied the right to "make" a contract) or whether it was restricted to incumbent employees? Does §1981 apply to racially based demotions? And where a company is sold and the successor owner chooses not to retain an employee on the basis of race, has the employee been denied the right to "make" a contract? All of these issues are addressed in the Note material in this section of Chapter 8.

The confusion and uncertainty generated by *Patterson* was matched by the widespread condemnation it received in the academic and legislative communities. Along with several other decisions rendered during its 1989 term, *Patterson* served as a launching pad for the ultimate enactment of the Civil Rights Act of 1991. In §101 of that enactment, Congress emphatically reversed the decision in *Patterson* by amending §1981 to include new subsection "(b)." This provision defines the phrase "make and enforce contracts" to include the making, performance, modification and termination of contracts as well as the enjoyment of all benefits, privileges, terms and conditions of the contractual relationship. The 1991 Act also added subsection 1981(c), which, *inter alia*, codified the *Patterson* Court's ruling that §1981 applies to private acts of discrimination.

Bobo v. ITT, Continental Baking Co.

United States Court of Appeals, Fifth Circuit, 1981.

662 F.2d 340, cert. denied, 456 U.S. 933, 102 S.Ct. 1985, 72 L.Ed.2d 451 (1982).

AINSWORTH, Circuit Judge.

The principal issue raised by this appeal is whether 42 U.S.C. §1981, derived primarily from the Civil Rights Act of 1866, encompasses claims of sex discrimination. The clear answer is that it does not.

Alice Bobo, a black woman, brought this action against her former employer, ITT, Continental Baking Company (ITT). She alleged that ITT discharged her because she had refused to wear a hat that co-employees allegedly were not required to wear. She also averred that prior to her firing, she had been the victim of other discriminatory employment conditions because of her race and sex. Bobo sought relief under Title VII of the Civil Rights Act of 1964 and 42 U.S.C. §1981. Upon motion by ITT, partial summary judgment was entered against Bobo by the district court. The court ruled that Bobo's Title VII claim was barred because of her failure to sue within 90 days of receipt of her right to sue letter from the Equal Employment Opportunity Commission. The court also held that since §1981 did not reach claims of sex discrimination, Bobo was entitled to a trial only on the issue of whether she had been subjected to racial discrimination.

* * *

On appeal, Bobo attacks the district court's * * * determination that sex discrimination is not cognizable under §1981.

Sex Discrimination Under §1981

Section 1981 generally forbids racial discrimination in the making and enforcement of private contracts, including private employment contracts, whether the aggrieved party is black or white. Runyon v. McCrary, 427 U.S. 160, 96 S.Ct. 2586, 49 L.Ed.2d 415 (1976); McDonald v. Santa Fe Trial Transportation Co., 427 U.S. 273, 96 S.Ct. 2574, 49 L.Ed.2d 493 (1976). * * *

Although §1981 strikes at many forms of racial discrimination, no court has held that allegations of gender based discrimination fall within its purview. Courts at every level of the federal judiciary have considered the question and reached the opposite result. The Supreme Court, in framing the question for decision in Runyon, explained that the case did not involve "the right of a private school to limit its student body to boys, to girls, or to adherents of a particular religious faith, since 42 U.S.C. §1981 is in no way addressed to such categories of selectivity." Even if we were to heed Bobo's invitation to regard this statement as dictum and therefore not dispositive of the issue, we could not ignore the Supreme Court's consistent emphasis on the racial character of §1981, as indicated by the law's language and legislative history. The Court has interpreted the phrase "as is enjoyed by white citizens * * *" in §1981 as reflecting its drafters' intention that the statute ban racial discrimination.

The Court's view of the 1866 Act's purpose was expressed in Georgia v. Rachel, 384 U.S. 780, 86 S.Ct. 1783, 16 L.Ed.2d 925 (1966), which construed its removal provisions. In examining the legislative history, the Court noted that the "white citizens" language was not a part of the original Senate bill, but was added later "apparently to emphasize the racial character of the rights being protected." The Court considered the legislative history of the 1866 Act and concluded that it "clearly indicates that Congress intended to protect a limited category of rights, specifically defined in terms of racial equality." Two terms later, while determining the breadth of 42 U.S.C. §1982[4] in *Jones v. Alfred H. Mayer Co.*, the Court repeatedly referred to the 1866 Act's aim of eliminating racial discrimination. The Court observed that unlike the Fair Housing Title (Title VIII) of the Civil Rights Act of 1968, §1982 was addressed only to racial discrimination. Finally, in perhaps its most extensive discussion of the legislative history of the 1866 Act, the Court reaffirmed the limits on §1981 in *McDonald*. Though extending the statute's protection to claims of racial discrimination by whites, the Court ruled that the 1866 Act's goal was to promote equality among the races by precluding discrimination in the making and enforcement of contracts either for or against any particular race.

Bobo nevertheless argues that the term "white citizens" should be deemed synonymous with "most favored group," thereby permitting those who find themselves somehow less favored to advance discrimination charges under §1981. A sweeping interpretation of this sort, however, would thwart the statute's evident meaning and purpose. As the Supreme Court has explained, Congress enacted §1 of the 1866 Act with the ambitious goal of ensuring equal citizenship for the newly freed slaves. Statements in the legislative history, carefully reviewed in *McDonald*, reflect this objective and confirm that the "white citizens" language was added specifically to preclude a construction that might expand the statute's coverage to other groups. Representative Wilson, who proposed amending the original bill to add the "white citizens" language, stated that "the reason for offering [the amendment] was this: it was thought by some persons that unless these qualifying words were incorporated in the bill, those rights might be extended to all citizens, whether male or female, majors or minors." * * *

Bobo further contends that since women obviously lacked equal legal rights during the Reconstruction era, "white citizens" should be read as "white men." But as the legislative history quoted above indicates, Congress meant precisely what it said. The drafters of §1981 had no intention to disturb public or private authority to discriminate against women. Outlawing such discrimination in the United States in 1866 would have signaled an extraordinary social transformation, a result clearly not desired by Congress. Public sensitivity to the ills of gender discrimination is of more recent origin. We cannot ascribe contemporary attitudes to a Congress acting over a century ago when its views to the contrary are so plainly stated.

* * *

Bobo cites *Guerra v. Manchester Terminal Corp.*, 498 F.2d 641 (5th Cir.1974) in support of a broader reading of §1981. In *Guerra* a Mexican citizen lawfully residing in the United States complained that he was the victim of discrimination as a result of a collective bargaining agreement which targeted American citizens for more desirable jobs. The court held that §1981 reached charges of discrimination based on alienage by private employers. In light of *Runyon* and *McDonald*, discussed above, we have previously characterized *Guerra* as a broad construction of §1981 in a case with

---

[4]Section 1982 proscribes discrimination with respect to real or personal property interests. Like §1981, §1982 is principally derived from §1 of the Civil Rights Act of 1866.

"strong racial overtones." Whatever vitality it may retain, *Guerra* did not propose extending §1981 to sex discrimination, and thus lends no support to Bobo's contentions.

In the face of seemingly unambiguous statutory language, emphatic contemporaneous statements by legislators and an unbroken tide of case law rejecting Bobo's arguments, we conclude that the district court properly held that sex discrimination is not cognizable under §1981.

* * *

For the foregoing reasons, the judgment of the district court is affirmed.

NOTES AND PROBLEMS FOR DISCUSSION

1. To what extent should the reasoning in *Bobo* apply to other non-racial classifications? The *Guerra* decision cited by the court in *Bobo* for the proposition that §1981 was applicable to alienage-based discrimination, subsequently was reversed by the Fifth Circuit. In BHANDARI v. FIRST NATIONAL BANK OF COMMERCE, 829 F.2d 1343 (5th Cir. 1987) (en banc), the court held that while it was required to follow the Supreme Court's rulings in *Runyon* and *Jones* that §1981 applied to private acts of racial discrimination, it was not prepared to extend those rulings to include private acts of alienage discrimination within the compass of §1981. (The court did admit, however, that §1981 extended to claims of public sector alienage discrimination.). Although the court, sitting en banc, maintained that the Supreme Court had incorrectly interpreted §1981 to extend to private acts of discrimination, it acknowledged that it was bound to follow the dictates of the High Court on the issue decided in those previous cases — i.e., that §1981 applies to private acts of racial discrimination — even if it was convinced that those cases were wrongly decided. The court emphasized, however, that the Supreme Court had not ruled on whether the statute similarly applied to private acts of alienage discrimination. On this question, the court continued, there was justification in the legislative history to differentiate between racial and non-racial discrimination. It pointed out that §1981 derived both from §1 of the 1866 Act and §16 of the 1870 Act and that it was from the latter enactment that the protection for aliens was derived. Moreover, the court reasoned, while the 1866 Act was concerned primarily with enforcing the 13th Amendment rights of newly freed black slaves, the 1870 enactment was passed as a statutory implementation of the 14th Amendment, and Congress intended for this statute to curtail only state action that discriminated against aliens. The court also suggested that if Congress believed that §1981 already covered private alienage discrimination, there would have been no need for it to enact the antidiscrimination provisions of the 1986 Immigration Reform and Control Act. Finally, while recognizing that construing the same "all persons" language of §1981 to mean something for one class of persons (blacks) and something else for another class (non-citizens) was "awkward and undesirable," the court declared that

> "racial and citizenship distinctions are things of a different kind; * * * the former our polity and increasingly our society as well are resolved * * * to have done [away] with, root and branch as representing an evil, always and everywhere. The latter is not so readily and roundly condemned; when all is said and done, patriotism remains a civic virtue * * *."

829 F.2d at 1352. At the end of its 1989 term, however, the Supreme Court vacated the Fifth Circuit's *en banc* opinion and remanded it for further consideration in light of *Patterson*. On remand, the Fifth Circuit issued a *per curiam* opinion in which the entire circuit court unanimously agreed that the decision in *Patterson* did not affect its earlier ruling. 887 F.2d 609 (5th Cir.1989), cert. denied, 494 U.S. 1061, 110 S.Ct. 1539, 108 L.Ed.2d 778 (1990). The court stated that since the *Patterson* Court had reaffirmed its prior decision in *Runyon*, the precedential landscape had not changed from what existed at the time of the circuit court's original decision in Bhandari. Accordingly, it reinstated its *en banc* opinion.

Two years later, Congress passed the 1991 Civil Rights Act. Among the amendments contained in this enactment was the addition of subsection (c) to §1981, which expressly extended the application of §1981 to private sector defendants. What impact, if any, should this legislative development have on the continued viability of the ruling in *Bhandari*? *See* Anderson v. Conboy, 156 F.3d 167 (2d Cir.1998), cert. dismissed, 527 U.S. 1030, 119 S.Ct. 2418, 144 L.Ed.2d 789 (1999) (since §1981 was always interpreted to cover public sector alienage discrimination and since §1981(c) was enacted to apply coextensively to public and private sector actors, the statute now applies to private sector alienage discrimination; this interpretation of §1981 does not create a conflict with the Immigration Reform and Control Act of 1986 because the prohibition in the IRCA against hiring "illegal" aliens is not inconsistent with §1981's prohibition against alienage discrimination since an employer firing an illegal alien pursuant to the IRCA would be taking that action based on citizenship but on the employee's noncompliance with federal immigration law).

In addition to protecting the right to make and enforce contracts, §1981(a) also guarantees to all persons the same right "to the full and equal benefit of all laws and proceedings for the security of persons and property" that is enjoyed by white citizens. Since §1981(c) states that the "rights" protected by §1981 cannot be impaired by either private or public action, does this mean that a plaintiff can state a claim against a private defendant under both the "make and enforce contracts" and "full and equal benefit" clauses of §1981(a)? For example, can a customer who alleges that she was stopped by a department store's security officer and searched on suspicion of shoplifting because of her race state a §1981 claim against the store? See Chapman v. Higbee Co., 319 F.3d 825 (6th Cir. 2003)(en banc), cert. denied, 542 U.S. 945, 124 S.Ct. 2902, 159 L.Ed.2d 827, (2004) (§1981(c) unambiguously extends the application of the statute to private action; this meaning is not inconsistent with the statute's "equal benefit" clause, and nothing in the legislative history suggests that Congress did not intent for this plain reading to prevail).

2. If the plaintiff in *Bhandari* had been an American citizen of Indian ancestry who claimed that he had been discriminated against on the basis of his national origin, could he state a claim under §1981? Initially, the lower federal courts agreed that although §1981 prohibited discrimination on the basis of race but not national origin, they tended to blur the lines between these classifications and frequently permitted national origin claims to proceed by characterizing them as racial in nature. *See, e.g.,* Gonzalez v. Stanford Applied Engineering, Inc., 597 F.2d 1298 (9th Cir. 1979) (Mexican-American alleging discrimination because of his having brown skin can state a claim under §1981); Budinsky v. Corning Glass Works, 425 F.Supp. 786, 787-788 (W.D.Pa.1977) ("Hispanic persons and Indians, like blacks, have been traditional victims of group discrimination, and, however inaccurately or stupidly, are frequently and even commonly subject to a 'racial' identification as 'non-whites.'").

The Supreme Court confronted the treatment of ethnicity-based claims under §1981 in two companion cases dealing, respectively, with claims of discrimination against Arabs and Jews. In SAINT FRANCIS COLLEGE v. AL-KHAZRAJI, 481 U.S. 604, 107 S.Ct. 2022, 95 L.Ed.2d 582 (1987), an Iranian-born U.S. citizen who had been denied tenure by the defendant college brought, inter alia, a claim of racial discrimination under §1981. The Supreme Court reiterated that §1981 prohibited racial discrimination, notwithstanding the absence of the word "race" from the statutory language. But to ascertain the meaning of "race" (a term not expressly found in the statute), the Court explained that it was essential to uncover the meaning of "race" in the nineteenth century. To that end, the Court turned to nineteenth century dictionaries, which defined "race" as "a family, tribe, people or nation, believed or presumed to belong to the same stock." It was not until the twentieth century, the Court recounted, that dictionaries began referring to the Caucasian, Mongolian and Negro races. The Court also noted that the legislative history of §1981 similarly referred to ethnic groups as races. Accordingly, it concluded that Congress intended to protect individuals who were subjected to intentional discrimination "solely because of their ancestry or ethnic characteristics. Such discrimination is racial discrimination that Congress intended §1981 to forbid, whether or not it would be classified as racial in terms of modern scientific theory." The Court added that a distinctive physiognomy was not essential to qualify for protection under §1981, and that the plaintiff would prevail if, on remand, he could prove that he was subjected to intentional discrimination because he was born an Arab, rather than solely because of the place or nation of his origin, or because of his religion.

In the companion case, SHAARE TEFILA CONGREGATION v. COBB, 481 U.S. 615, 107 S.Ct. 2019, 95 L.Ed.2d 594 (1987), members of a Jewish congregation brought suit under §1982 (the companion provision to §1981 that guarantees to all U.S. citizens the same right to sell, lease, inherit and convey real and personal property that is enjoyed by white citizens) alleging that individuals who, acting out of racial prejudice, had desecrated the outside walls of their synagogue by spraying it with anti-Semitic slogans and symbols had deprived the plaintiffs of their right to hold property because of their race. The lower courts had dismissed the complaint on the ground that Jews did not constitute a distinct racial group. The Supreme Court reversed, applied the reasoning articulated in *St. Francis* and concluded that Jews, as well as Arabs, "were among the peoples [that Congress] then considered to be distinct races and hence within the protection of the statute."

This merger of ethnicity and race claims generated interesting issues concerning the meaning of ethnicity. For example, in SINAI v. NEW ENGLAND TELEPHONE AND TELEGRAPH COMPANY, 3 F.3d 471 (1st Cir. 1993), cert. denied, 513 U.S. 1025, 115 S.Ct. 597, 130 L.Ed.2d 509 (1994), the plaintiff alleged that he was denied employment because he was an Israeli. The jury issued a verdict in favor of the plaintiff, and the defendant appealed on the ground that since it employed several Jewish individuals, the plaintiff's claim involved only discrimination based on his Israeli national origin. The appellate court upheld the verdict, ruling that a jury could find that Israel is one of those countries in which the populace is composed primarily of a particular race and, therefore, that the defendant discriminated against the plaintiff on the basis of his Jewish race by disparaging Israel.

Over the years, the lower courts have construed §1981 to extend to a wide range of ethnicity-based claims. *See, e.g.*, Nieto v. United Auto Workers Local #598, 672 F.Supp. 987 (E.D. Mich. 1987) (§1981 applies to claim based on Mexican ancestry but not fact of plaintiff's birth in Mexico); Quintana v. Byrd, 669 F.Supp. 849 (N.D. Ill. 1987) (discrimination on basis of Hispanic ethnicity, but not country of birth, is proscribed racial discrimination); Cardona v. American Express Travel Related Services Co., 720 F.Supp. 960 (S.D.Fla.1989) (plaintiff with Colombian ancestry or ethnic background can state §1981 claim alleging that he was discriminated against in favor of employees of Cuban ancestry; both groups have distinct ethnic and cultural characteristics despite fact that both are Spanish-speaking peoples); MacDissi v. Valmont Industries, Inc., 856 F.2d 1054 (8th Cir. 1988) (discrimination on basis of Lebanese descent proscribed by §1981). Are these fair readings of the two Supreme Court decisions? *See generally* Lisa Tudiso Evren, Note, *When Is A Race Not A Race?: Contemporary Issues Under The Civil Rights Act of 1866*, 61 N.Y.U.L.REV. 976 (1986).

3. If an employer discriminated against a job applicant on the basis of the mistaken belief that the applicant was a member of a particular racial or ethnic group, would the fact that the plaintiff is not actually a member of the protected group be fatal to her claim? *See* Franceschi v. Hyatt Corp., 782 F. Supp. 712 (D.P.R. 1992) (court "will focus its attention at trial not on physiognomic characteristics but on defendant's perceptions of plaintiff as belonging to a given racial or ethnic group.") (dictum).

4. (a) While most courts now recognize that §1981 applies to national origin claims that involve ethnic or racial characteristics, the courts also have ruled that §1981 does not cover claims of discrimination on the basis of age, Barkley v. Carraux, 533 F. Supp. 242 (S.D. Tex. 1982); religion, Khawaja v. Wyatt, 494 F.Supp. 302 (W.D.N.Y. 1980); or sexual orientation, Grossman v. Bernards Township Board of Education, 11 FEP Cases 1196 (D.N.J. 1975), affirmed, 538 F.2d 319 (3d Cir. 1976), cert. denied, 429 U.S. 897, 97 S.Ct. 261, 50 L.Ed.2d 181 (1976).

(b) Tech Guys, Inc. is a 100% minority-owned technology services contractor certified by the federal Small Business Administration as a firm owned and operated by socially and economically disadvantaged individuals. It alleges that Big Boy Computers, Inc., refused to enter into a contract with it based solely on Tech Guy's status as an African-American owned business. Can the plaintiff state a claim under §1981? In THINKET INK INFORMATION RESOURCES, INC. v. SUN MICROSYSTEMS, Inc., 368 F.3d 1053 (9th Cir.2004), under this set of facts, the Ninth Circuit ruled that the corporation did have standing to assert a §1981 claim of racial discrimination. Noting that standing inquiry involves both constitutional and prudential limitations on the exercise of federal court jurisdiction, the appellate court concluded that this minority-owned business satisfied both requirements. The constitutional standing requirement was met because the corporation had alleged a concrete and particularized harm caused by the defendant. The court also offered two explanations for its ruling that the plaintiff's claim meets the prudential requirements for standing. First, in the face of its 100% minority ownership and certification as a minority-owned business that entitled it to receive certain governmental benefits, the plaintiff corporation had acquired a racial identity and, therefore, could be a direct target of discrimination. Second, because the corporate plaintiff had alleged direct racial discrimination based on its status as an SBA-certified minority-owned business and on the race of its shareholders, the plaintiff's cause of action met the relatively low threshold of falling within the statutory zone of interests protected by §1981.

(c) The flip side of this question confronted the Supreme Court when the sole shareholder and president of a company brought his own individual §1981 claim alleging that another commercial entity had breached a contract with his firm because of racial animus towards him. In DOMINO's PIZZA, INC. v. McDONALD, 546 U.S. 470, 126 S.Ct. 1246, 163 L.Ed.2d 1069 (2006), the Supreme Court ruled that the individual plaintiff did not have standing under §1981 to bring a breach of contract claim. Writing for a unanimous Court (with newly-appointed Justice Alito not participating), Justice Scalia announced that §1981 only protected the right to enter into and enforce proposed or existing contractual relationships in which the plaintiff enjoyed or would enjoy rights. Thus, he reasoned, not even a sole shareholder or chief executive officer could step into the shoes of the corporation and assert its statutory right. Since the individual did not enjoy individual rights under the contract, he could not seek relief under §1981 even when he alleged that he was the actual target of the racial discrimination that prompted the defendant to impair its contractual agreement with the plaintiff's firm. The Court expressly reserved decision on whether a §1981 claim could be asserted by a third party intended beneficiary of a contract.

5. Can §1981 be used to fill in some of the following gaps in Title VII's coverage?

(a) Section 701(b) exempts Native American tribes and governmental entities such as Alaska Native Corporations from the antidiscrimination provisions of Title VII. Can a non-Native American denied employment by a Native American tribe bring a race discrimination action under §1981? *Compare* Wardle v. Ute Indian Tribe, 623 F.2d 670 (10th Cir. 1980) *with* Aleman v. Chugach Support Services, 2007 WL 1289428 (4th Cir. 2007).

(b) Is a race discrimination claim brought by a uniformed member of the armed services cognizable under §1981? *See* Taylor v. Jones, 653 F.2d 1193 (8th Cir. 1981).

(c) Title VII (as well as the Americans with Disabilities Act) applies to claims by *U.S. citizens* employed overseas by American-controlled companies unless compliance would result in a violation of domestic law. The lower courts consistently have ruled that Title VII does not apply to *aliens* employed outside of the U.S. (The ADEA applies to American citizens employed abroad by any American company or its foreign subsidiary except when that would violate local law. The courts construe this amendment to mean that alien employees working for U.S. companies outside of the U.S. are not covered by the ADEA.). On the other hand, §1981 expressly protects only "persons within the jurisdiction of the United States." Does this mean that a U.S. citizen employed abroad cannot state a claim of discrimination under §1981? *See* Ofori-Tenkorang v. American International Group, Inc., 460 F.3d 296 (2d Cir.2006) (the plain text of §1981 manifests Congress's intent to limit protection to individuals within the territorial limits in accordance with legal presumption that Congress intends its statute to have only domestic application; ergo, §1981 does not apply to discriminatory conduct against individuals, aliens or U.S. citizens, that occurs outside the U.S. territorial limits even where the plaintiff's employment contract initially was formed in the U.S. or where the relevant decision maker was located in the U.S.).

(d) Since Title VII only applies to "employers", an independent contractor cannot state a claim under that enactment against the entity with whom it contracted to perform services. But §1981 is worded much more broadly in that it prohibits discrimination in the making and enforcing of any "contracts". This has led several circuit courts to conclude that an independent contractor can state a §1981 claim against the party with whom it contracted for discrimination occurring within the scope of that contractual relationship. *See e.g.*, Brown v. J. Kaz, Inc., 581 F.3d 175 (3d Cir. 2009).

6. Recall that in Chapter 5, in discussing whether the Supreme Court's ruling in *Brown v. G.S.A.* (that Title VII is the exclusive judicial remedy for federal employee discrimination claims) should extend to state and local government employees, we reported the prevailing view that Title VII does not preempt an action brought under §1983 based on a violation of rights that are independent of Title VII. Section 1981(c), added to §1981 as part of the 1991 Civil Rights Act, expressly extends the coverage of §1981 to state and local government employers by prohibiting discrimination "under color of State law." This language, at first blush, suggests that Congress intended to provide state employees with a right of action for racial and alienage discrimination separate and apart from §1983. However, in a pre-1991 Civil Rights Act case, the Supreme Court in JETT v. DALLAS INDEPENDENT SCHOOL DIST., 491 U.S. 701, 109 S.Ct. 2702, 105 L.Ed.2d 598 (1989), had held that §1981 did not provide an independent cause of action for damages against public units, and that the damages action created by §1983 was the exclusive federal damages remedy for violations of the terms of §1981 by state governmental units. Does the language of §1981(c) suggest that in 1991 Congress intended to provide state employees with an independent cause of action under §1981? All circuits, with the exception of the Ninth, that have considered the issue have concluded that the 1991 amendments were not intended by Congress to overrule the Supreme Court's ruling in *Jett* and, therefore, that the statute did not create a private right of action against state and local governmental unit, including municipalities. Silence in the face of Congressional familiarity with existing jurisprudence, the courts reason, does not support an inference that Congress intended to reverse the jurisprudential *status quo*. *See e.g.*, Campbell v. Forest Pres. Dist. Of Cook Cnty, 1924479 (7th Cir. 2014). The Ninth Circuit, however, has taken the position that the enactment of §1981(c) overruled *Jett* to create a cause of action against municipalities and other local governmental units, Federation of African American Contractors v. City of Oakland, 96 F.3d 1204 (9th Cir.1996), but not against "arms of the state" itself, i.e., state actors such as state agencies. Pittman v. Oregon, 509 F.3d 1065 (9th Cir. 2007).

Even if §1981(c) is construed to provide state employees with a right of action for damages against their employer independent from that provided by §1983, there remains the question of whether Congress has constitutionally abrogated the states' Eleventh Amendment right of sovereign immunity from claims for money damages in federal court actions. In a series of cases discussed in detail in Chapter 10, Section A, *infra*, the Supreme Court has held that to resolve whether Congress constitutionally abrogated the states' Eleventh Amendment right of sovereign immunity from damage claims in federal court actions, a court must determine whether the statute in question (1) expressly provided such a remedy; and, if so (2) whether that provision was enacted pursuant to Congress' enforcement authority under §5 of the Fourteenth

Amendment. Whether or not even the first of these requirements is satisfied with respect to §1981(c) is unclear. On the one hand, Congress appears to have intended to provide a damage remedy under §1981 since 42 U.S.C.A. §1981a, the provision authorizing the awarding of compensatory and punitive damages in Title VII cases, limits such awards to cases where the complaining party cannot recover under §1981. On the other hand, however, §1981 does not expressly provide for the recovery of money damages. Moreover, even if this standard is met, one then must determine whether Congress provided this remedy in the exercise of its enforcement authority under the Fourteenth Amendment.

7. Local and municipal governments, on the other hand, cannot claim any Eleventh Amendment immunity from damage actions. Nevertheless, a common law immunity from such suits is generally recognized. In enacting §1981, did Congress intend to override municipal immunity? The Supreme Court has ruled that municipalities do not enjoy a common law immunity from compensatory damage claims in actions brought under §1983 where the challenged conduct is attributable directly to the municipality. Monell v. Department of Social Services of City of New York, 436 U.S. 658, 98 S.Ct. 2018, 56 L.Ed.2d 611 (1978). But the Court also has held that municipalities retain their immunity from punitive damages in §1983 suits. City of Newport v. Fact Concerts, Inc., 453 U.S. 247, 101 S.Ct. 2748, 69 L.Ed.2d 616 (1981). With respect to §1981, the courts are split. *Compare* Sethy v. Alameda County Water District, 545 F.2d 1157 (9th Cir.1976) (§1981 abolishes immunity), *with* Poolaw v. City of Anadarko, 738 F.2d 364 (10th Cir. 1984), cert. denied, 469 U.S. 1108, 105 S.Ct. 784, 83 L.Ed.2d 779 (1985) (municipality is immune from punitive damages under §1981).

8. Can an employee bring a §1981 action against its union? If so, is a federal employee limited by Brown v. G.S.A. to a Title VII action against its union? See Jennings v. American Postal Workers Union, 672 F.2d 712 (8th Cir. 1982).

9. As noted in the introductory material in this Chapter, the Supreme Court's ruling in *Patterson* did not clearly resolve whether claims of retaliation fall within its interpretation of the "make or enforce" language of §1981. Although the definition of the right to "make and enforce contracts" contained in §1981(b) does not explicitly refer to retaliation among the list of proscribed practices, those lower courts agreed that the statute encompassed retaliation claims, but disagreed as to how such claims must be connected to racial discrimination. Some limited the application of §1981 to cases where the plaintiff alleged that the retaliation taken against her was racially motivated. But others construed the statute more broadly to extend to claims that the retaliation was taken in response to the plaintiff's challenge to an act of alleged racial discrimination against others, regardless of whether the plaintiff was targeted because of her race. In CBOCS WEST, INC. v. HUMPHRIES, 553 U.S. 442, 128 S.Ct. 1951, 170 L.Ed.2d 864 (2008), the Supreme Court, by a 7-2 majority, adopted the latter view. Relying on its prior ruling in Jackson v. Birmingham (discussed in Note 4 in Chapter 11, Sec. B, *infra*) which construed the private right of action for claims of intentional sex-based discrimination contained in Title IX of the 1964 Civil Rights Act to encompass retaliation claims, the Court ratified the lower courts' consensus view that the 1991 Act was intended to extend the application of §1981 to retaliation claims notwithstanding the absence of any express reference to "retaliation" in the amended version of §1981, i.e., §1981(b). It further declared that §1981 covered the claim of the instant plaintiff, who had alleged that he had been retaliated against for opposing racial discrimination suffered by others that was prohibited by §1981. The majority rejected the distinction adopted by dissenting Justices Thomas and Scalia that a claim of retaliation for challenging racial discrimination against third parties was not racial discrimination against the plaintiff and, therefore, was not cognizable under §1981.

Now that the Court has resolved that retaliation claims are cognizable under §1981, should the Supreme Court's ruling in *National Railroad v. Morgan* — that acts outside the limitations period can be considered in a Title VII hostile environment claim as long as one of the acts contributing to that environment occurred within the time period — also apply to §1981 hostile environment claims? The four circuits that have considered this question have answered it in the affirmative. *See e.g.,* Fullwiley v. Union Pacific Corp., 273 Fed.Appx. 710 (10th Cir. 2008).

10. More than forty states recognize the existence of an employment-at-will relationship, i.e., one where the employer, in the absence of any specific agreement to the contrary, is permitted to terminate an employee for good cause, bad cause or no cause at all. Can an at-will employee who alleges that she was discharged on the basis of her race state a claim under §1981 or is her status as an at-will employee fatal to her claim that the employment relationship constitutes a "contract" within the meaning of §1981? Every circuit court that has decided this issue has held both (a) that a federal court must look to the state law definition of "contract" in construing §1981; and (b) that under the governing state law an at-will agreement is a "contract" within the meaning of §1981 because it fulfills all the requirements of a valid contract. *See, e.g.,* Skinner v. Maritz Inc., 253 F.3d 337 (8th Cir.2001).

11. In WASHINGTON v. DAVIS, 426 U.S. 229, 96 S.Ct. 2040, 48 L.Ed.2d 597 (1976), the Supreme Court held that plaintiffs alleging violations of the Fourteenth Amendment must prove discriminatory intent as part of their prima facie case. In GENERAL BUILDING CONTRACTORS ASSOCIATION, INC. v. PENNSYLVANIA, 458 U.S. 375, 102 S.Ct. 3141, 73 L.Ed.2d 835 (1982), the Court was asked to determine whether its ruling in *Davis* should extend to §1981 actions in light of the fact that §1981 was enacted, in part, to enforce the provisions of the Fourteenth Amendment. As the Court in *General Building Contractors* explained, the relevant operative language of §1981 originally was enacted shortly after ratification of the Thirteenth Amendment. But it later was reenacted as part of the Enforcement Act of 1870 following the adoption of the Fourteenth Amendment. Moreover, the Court added, the language of §1981 tracked the precise language of the Act of 1870. Accordingly, the Court concluded that §1981 should be construed consistently with the provisions of the Fourteenth Amendment. This meant that a plaintiff under §1981 had to make a showing of discriminatory intent to establish a prima facie case; proof of disproportionate impact would not suffice. This change in the proof standard reduced the attractiveness of §1981 to many plaintiffs. For a suggestion that §1981 should not be limited to claims of intentional discrimination, see Joel Wm. Friedman, *The Burger Court and the Prima Facie Case in Employment Discrimination Litigation: A Critique,* 65 CORN.L.REV. 1, 31-43 (1979). Nevertheless, as the succeeding Note indicates, §1981 remains a viable alternative to Title VII for many plaintiffs because of significant procedure and remedial advantages it offers over Title VII.

If the evidence in a §1981 case suggests the existence of multiple motivations, should the Supreme Court's ruling in *Price Waterhouse* control, or should the parties be bound by the 1991 statutory modification to the *Price Waterhouse* rule, even though the provision containing that change makes no reference to §1981? In MABRA v. UNITED FOOD & COMMERCIAL WORKERS LOCAL UNION #1996, 176 F.3d 1357 (11th Cir.1999), the Eleventh Circuit reasoned that since the mixed motive amendment in the 1991 Act referred solely to Title VII actions, it was not intended to apply to §1981 claims. Consequently, it held, the preexisting *Price Waterhouse* doctrine should govern the resolution of §1981 actions, i.e., that mixed motive operates as a complete defense to liability. But in METOYER v. CHASSMAN, 504 F.3d 919 (9th Cir. 2007), the Ninth Circuit rejected the Eleventh Circuit's analysis in *Mabra* on the ground that it was predicated upon the "faulty premise" that an employer's mixed motive operated as a complete defense to *§1981* claims prior to the passage of the 1991 Act. The majority of a split Ninth Circuit panel explained that prior to the Supreme Court's ruling in *Price Waterhouse*, the Ninth Circuit, and a majority of other circuits, had limited mixed motive in Title VII cases to damages. And although these holdings were reversed by the Supreme Court in *Price Waterhouse*, they subsequently were reinstated by Congress through the 1991 Civil Rights Act. But since the *Price Waterhouse* Court had not ruled on the impact of an employer's mixed motive in §1981 actions, and the prevailing circuit view was that mixed motive should go only to damages and not to liability, "there was no need for Congress to amend §1981 to eliminate a defense never held applicable." Consequently, the Ninth Circuit ruled, an employer's mixed motive operated only to limit damages in a §1981 discrimination claim.

However, the court in *Metoyer* also held that mixed motive operated as a complete defense to liability in a retaliation claim brought under §1981. The Ninth Circuit previously had ruled that because the language of §§703(m) and 706(g)(2)(B) (the mixed motive provisions of the 1991 amendments) refers only to claims asserted under §703, and not under §704, Congress did not intend to terminate the continued application of the *Price Waterhouse* mixed motive defense to retaliation claims brought under §704 of Title VII. And so, the court reasoned, since it already had stated that §1981 claims follow the same principles that govern Title VII cases, the employer's mixed motive similarly should operate as a complete defense to liability in retaliation claims brought under §1981.

12. Plaintiffs who can assert claims under either Title VII or §1981 often look to the latter statute because of certain procedural and remedial advantages that it offers. Perhaps the most significant difference is that the cap on damages applicable to awards in Title VII cases does not apply to actions brought under §1981. In addition, §1981 claimants have immediate access to the courts, since §1981, unlike Title VII, does not require invocation of administrative remedies as a prerequisite to judicial relief. Furthermore, the availability of a longer limitations period and the absence of a minimum employer size continue to make §1981 an attractive alternative cause of action for those plaintiffs who fall within its protection.

Since the text of §1981 is silent on procedural matters, the courts have played a significant role in delineating the procedural relationship between these two related statutes. In JOHNSON v. RAILWAY EXPRESS AGENCY, INC., 421 U.S. 454, 95 S.Ct. 1716, 44 L.Ed.2d 295 (1975), the Supreme Court emphasized that Congress intended for Title VII and §1981 to be separate and independent, rather than mutually exclusive, remedies for employment discrimination. Accordingly, it held that the prosecution of a Title VII suit did not toll the limitations period applicable to an action based on the same facts brought under §1981. The Court recognized that its ruling on the tolling issue would likely encourage a plaintiff interested in retaining its §1981 claim to file a separate action under that statute pending EEOC action on the related Title VII claim, a result inconsistent with Congress' expressed desire (when it enacted Title VII) to encourage administrative resolution of discrimination claims. It suggested, however, with some misgivings, that this undesirable consequence could be moderated if the plaintiff requested the court in the §1981 action to stay that proceeding until the Title VII administrative efforts had been completed. Moreover, the Court concluded, the potential for discouraging reliance on the Title VII administrative machinery was overwhelmed by Congress' clear intent to retain §1981 as an independent remedy for civil rights claimants.

The independent nature of these two remedies has been underscored by rulings that state administrative proceedings undertaken in connection with a Title VII claim do not operate as a bar to the related §1981 action. Where, however, a state court has reviewed a state administrative agency's decision, claim and issue preclusion principles have been applied to preclude relitigation of the same issues in a §1981 action. Is this analysis consistent with the Supreme Court's resolution of the same question with respect to Title VII in *Kremer* or in connection with §1983 in *Elliot*? A ruling on the merits of a §1981 claim has been held to preclude the assertion of an identical Title VII cause of action under the doctrine of collateral estoppel. For more on these issues, see Section E of this Chapter, *infra*

13. In JOHNSON v. RYDER TRUCK LINES, INC., 575 F.2d 471 (4th Cir. 1978), cert. denied, 440 U.S. 979, 99 S.Ct. 1785, 60 L.Ed.2d 239 (1979), the Fourth Circuit ruled that the bona fide seniority system exemption provided by §703(h) of Title VII should be read into §1981 to promote uniformity of result under the two statutes. This interpretation of §1981 subsequently was adopted by nearly all other circuit courts. What effect should the decision in *General Building Contractors Ass'n* have on this issue?

SECTION B. THE CIVIL RIGHTS ACT OF 1871, SECTION ONE — 42 U.S.C. §1983

Personnel Administrator of Massachusetts v. Feeney

Supreme Court of the United States, 1979.
442 U.S. 256, 99 S.Ct. 2282, 60 L.Ed.2d 870.

MR. JUSTICE STEWART delivered the opinion of the Court.

This case presents a challenge to the constitutionality of the Massachusetts Veterans Preference Statute, Mass.Gen.Laws, ch. 31, §23, on the ground that it discriminates against women in violation of the Equal Protection Clause of the Fourteenth Amendment. Under ch. 31, §23,[1] all veterans who qualify for state civil

---

[1]For the text of ch. 31, §23, see n. 10, *infra*.

service positions must be considered for appointment ahead of any qualifying nonveterans. The preference operates overwhelmingly to the advantage of males.

The appellee Helen B. Feeney is not a veteran. She brought this action pursuant to 42 U.S.C. §1983 alleging that the absolute preference formula established in ch. 31, §23 inevitably operates to exclude women from consideration for the best Massachusetts civil service jobs and thus unconstitutionally denies them the equal protection of the laws.[2] The three-judge District Court agreed, one judge dissenting.

The District Court found that the absolute preference afforded by Massachusetts to veterans has a devastating impact upon the employment opportunities of women. Although it found that the goals of the preference were worthy and legitimate and that the legislation had not been enacted for the purpose of discriminating against women, the court reasoned that its exclusionary impact upon women was nonetheless so severe as to require the State to further its goals through a more limited form of preference. Finding that a more modest preference formula would readily accommodate the State's interest in aiding veterans, the court declared ch. 31, §23 unconstitutional and enjoined its operation.

Upon an appeal taken by the Attorney General of Massachusetts,[5] this Court vacated the judgment and remanded the case for further consideration in light of our intervening decision in Washington v. Davis, 426 U.S. 229, 96 S.Ct. 2040, 48 L.Ed.2d 597. The *Davis* case held that a neutral law does not violate the Equal Protection Clause solely because it results in a racially disproportionate impact; instead the disproportionate impact must be traced to a purpose to discriminate on the basis of race.

Upon remand, the District Court, one judge concurring and one judge again dissenting, concluded that a veterans' hiring preference is inherently nonneutral because it favors a class from which women have traditionally been excluded, and that the consequences of the Massachusetts absolute preference formula for the employment opportunities of women were too inevitable to have been "unintended." Accordingly, the court reaffirmed its original judgment. The Attorney General again appealed to this Court pursuant to 28 U.S.C. §1253, and probable jurisdiction of the appeal was noted.

I

A

The Federal Government and virtually all of the States grant some sort of hiring preference to veterans.[6] The Massachusetts preference, which is loosely termed an

---

[2]No statutory claim was brought under Title VII of the Civil Rights Act of 1964. Section 712 of the Act provides that "nothing contained in this subchapter shall be construed to repeal or modify any Federal, State, territorial or local law creating special rights or preference for veterans." The parties have evidently assumed that this provision precludes a Title VII challenge.

[5]The Attorney General appealed the judgment over the objection of other state officers named as defendants. In response to our certification of the question whether Massachusetts law permits this, the Supreme Judicial Court answered in the affirmative. Feeney v. Commonwealth, 373 Mass. 359, 366 N.E.2d 1262 (Mass.1977).

[6]The first comprehensive federal veterans' statute was enacted in 1944. The Federal Government has, however, engaged in preferential hiring of veterans, through official policies and various special laws, since the Civil War. For surveys of state veterans' preference laws,

"absolute lifetime" preference, is among the most generous.[7] It applies to all positions in the State's classified civil service, which constitute approximately 60% of the public jobs in the State. It is available to "any person, male or female, including a nurse," who was honorably discharged from the United States Armed Forces after at least 90 days of active service, at least one day of which was during "wartime."[8] Persons who are deemed veterans and who are otherwise qualified for a particular civil service job may exercise the preference at any time and as many times as they wish.[9]

Civil service positions in Massachusetts fall into two general categories, labor and official. For jobs in the official service, with which the proofs in this action were concerned, the preference mechanics are uncomplicated. All applicants for employment must take competitive examinations. Grades are based on a formula that gives weight both to objective test results and to training and experience. Candidates who pass are then ranked in the order of their respective scores on an "eligible list." Ch. 31, §23 requires, however, that disabled veterans, veterans, and surviving spouses and surviving parents of veterans be ranked — in the order of their respective scores — above all other candidates.[10]

---

many of which also date back to the late 19th century, see State Veterans' Laws, Digest of State Laws Regarding Rights, Benefits and Privileges of Veterans and Their Dependents, House Committee on Veterans' Affairs, 91st Cong., 1st Sess. (1969).

[7]The forms of veterans' hiring preferences vary widely. The Federal Government and approximately 41 States grant veterans a point advantage on civil service examinations, usually 10 points for a disabled veteran and 5 for one who is not disabled. A few offer only tie-breaking preferences. A very few States, like Massachusetts, extend absolute hiring or positional preferences to qualified veterans.

[8]Mass.Gen.Laws Ann., ch. 4, §7, cl. 43 (West 1976), which supplies the general definition of the term "veteran," reads in pertinent part: "Veteran" shall mean any person, male or female, including a nurse, (a) whose last discharge or release from his wartime service, as defined herein, was under honorable conditions and who (b) served in the army, navy, marine corps, coast guard, or air force of the United States for not less than ninety days active service, at least one day of which was for wartime service * * *.

Persons awarded the Purple Heart, or one of a number of specified campaign badges or the Congressional Medal of Honor are also deemed veterans.

"Wartime service" is defined as service performed by a "Spanish War veteran," a "World War I veteran," a "World War II veteran," a "Korean veteran," a "Vietnam veteran," or a member of the "WAAC." Each of these terms is further defined to specify a period of service. The statutory definitions, taken together, cover the entire period from September 16, 1940 to May 7, 1975.

"WAAC" is defined as follows: "any woman who was discharged and so served in any corps or unit of the United States established for the purpose of enabling women to serve with, or as auxiliary to, the armed forces of the United States and such woman shall be deemed to be a veteran.

[9]The Massachusetts preference law formerly imposed a residency requirement, see 1954 Mass.Acts, ch. 627, §3 (eligibility conditioned upon Massachusetts domicile prior to induction or five years residency in State). The distinction was invalidated as violative of the Equal Protection Clause in Stevens v. Campbell, 332 F.Supp. 102, 105 (D.C. Mass.1971). Cf. August v. Bronstein, 369 F.Supp. 190 (S.D.N.Y.1974) (upholding, inter alia, nondurational residency requirement in N.Y. veterans' preference statute), summarily aff'd, 417 U.S. 901, 94 S.Ct. 2596, 41 L.Ed.2d 208.

[10]Chapter 31, §23, provides in full:

"The names of persons who pass examinations for appointment to any position classified under the civil service shall be placed upon the eligible lists in the following order:—

Rank on the eligible list and availability for employment are the sole factors that determine which candidates are considered for appointment to an official civil service position. When a public agency has a vacancy, it requisitions a list of "certified eligibles" from the state personnel division. Under formulas prescribed by civil service rules, a small number of candidates from the top of an appropriate list, three if there is only one vacancy, are certified. The appointing agency is then required to choose from among these candidates.[11] Although the veterans' preference thus does not guarantee that a veteran will be appointed, it is obvious that the preference gives to veterans who achieve passing scores a well-nigh absolute advantage.

B

The appellee has lived in Dracut, Mass., most of her life. She entered the work force in 1948, and for the next 14 years worked at a variety of jobs in the private sector. She first entered the state civil service system in 1963, having competed successfully for a position as Senior Clerk Stenographer in the Massachusetts Civil Defense Agency. There she worked for four years. In 1967, she was promoted to the position of Federal Funds and Personnel Coordinator in the same agency. The agency, and with it her job, was eliminated in 1975.

During her 12-year tenure as a public employee, Ms. Feeney took and passed a number of open competitive civil service examinations. On several she did quite well, receiving in 1971 the second highest score on an examination for a job with the Board of Dental Examiners, and in 1973 the third highest on a test for an Administrative Assistant position with a mental health center. Her high scores, however, did not win her a place on the certified eligible list. Because of the veterans' preference, she was ranked sixth behind five male veterans on the Dental Examiner list. She was not certified, and a lower scoring veteran was eventually appointed. On the 1973 examination, she was placed in a position on the list behind 12 male veterans, 11 of whom had lower scores. Following the other examinations that she took, her name was similarly ranked below those of veterans who had achieved passing grades.

Ms. Feeney's interest in securing a better job in state government did not wane. Having been consistently eclipsed by veterans, however, she eventually concluded that further competition for civil service positions of interest to veterans would be futile. In 1975, shortly after her civil defense job was abolished, she commenced this litigation.

C

The veterans' hiring preference in Massachusetts, as in other jurisdictions, has traditionally been justified as a measure designed to reward veterans for the sacrifice

---

"(1) Disabled veterans . . . in the order of their respective standing; (2) veterans in the order of their respective standing; (3) person described in section twenty-three B[the widow or widowed mother of a veteran killed in action or who died from a service-connected disability incurred in wartime service and who has not remarried] in the order of their respective standing; (4) other applicants in the order of their respective standing. Upon receipt of a requisition, names shall be certified from such lists according to the method of certification prescribed by the civil service rules. A disabled veteran shall be retained in employment in preference to all other persons, including veterans."

A 1977 amendment extended the dependents' preference to "surviving spouses," and "surviving parents." 1977 Mass.Acts, ch. 815.

[11]A 1978 amendment requires the appointing authority to file a written statement of reasons if the person whose name was not highest is selected.

of military service, to ease the transition from military to civilian life, to encourage patriotic service, and to attract loyal and well-disciplined people to civil service occupations.[12] * * *

* * *

D

The first Massachusetts veterans' preference statute defined the term "veterans" in gender-neutral language, and subsequent amendments have followed this pattern. Women who have served in official United States military units during wartime, then, have always been entitled to the benefit of the preference. In addition, Massachusetts, through a 1943 amendment to the definition of "wartime service," extended the preference to women who served in unofficial auxiliary women's units.[17]

When the first general veterans' preference statute was adopted in 1896, there were no women veterans.[18] The statute, however, covered only Civil War veterans. Most of them were beyond middle age, and relatively few were actively competing for public employment.[19] Thus, the impact of the preference upon the employment opportunities of nonveterans as a group and women in particular was slight.[20]

Notwithstanding the apparent attempts by Massachusetts to include as many military women as possible within the scope of the preference, the statute today benefits an overwhelmingly male class. This is attributable in some measure to the variety of federal statutes, regulations, and policies that have restricted the numbers of women who could enlist in the United States Armed Forces,[21] and largely to the simple fact that women have never been subjected to a military draft.

---

[12]Veterans' preference laws have been challenged so often that the rationale in their support has become essentially standardized. See, e.g., Koelfgen v. Jackson, 355 F.Supp. 243 (D.C. Minn.1972), summarily aff'd, 410 U.S. 976, 93 S.Ct. 1502, 36 L.Ed.2d 173.

[17]* * * "Wartime service" is defined as service performed by a . . . member of the "WAAC." A "WAAC" is "any woman who was discharged and so served in any corps or unit of the United States established for the purpose of enabling women to serve with, or as auxiliary to, the armed forces of the United States and such woman shall be deemed to be a veteran."

[18]Small numbers of women served in combat roles in every war before the 20th century in which the United States was involved, but usually unofficially or disguised as men. Among the better-known are Molly Pitcher (Revolutionary War); Deborah Sampson (Revolutionary War), and Lucy Brewer (War of 1812). Passing as one "George Baker," Brewer served for three years as a gunner on the U.S.S. Constitution ("Old Ironsides") and distinguished herself in several major naval battles in the War of 1812. See Laffin, Women in Battle 116-122 (1967).

[19]By 1887, the average age of Civil War veterans in Massachusetts was already over 50. Third Annual Report, Mass. Civil Service Comm'n 22 (Jan. 10, 1887). The tie-breaking preference which had been established under the 1884 statute had apparently been difficult to enforce, since many appointing officers "prefer younger men." Ibid. The 1896 statute which established the first valid absolute preference, again covered only Civil War veterans.

[20]In 1896, for example, 2,804 persons applied for civil service positions: 2,031 were men, of whom only 32 were veterans; 773 were women. Of the 647 persons appointed, 525 were men, of whom only 9 were veterans; 122 were women. Thirteenth Annual Report, Mass. Civil Service Comm'n 5, 6 (Dec. 4, 1896). The average age of the applicants was 38. Ibid.

[21]The Army Nurse Corps, created by Congress in 1901, was the first official military unit for women, but its members were not granted full military rank until 1944. During World War I, a variety of proposals were made to enlist women for work as doctors, telephone operators and clerks, but all were rejected by the War Department. The Navy, however, interpreted its own authority broadly to include a power to enlist women as Yeoman F's and Marine F's. About

When this litigation was commenced, then, over 98% of the veterans in Massachusetts were male; only 1.8% were female. And over one-quarter of the Massachusetts population were veterans. During the decade between 1963 and 1973 when the appellee was actively participating in the State's merit selection system, 47,005 new permanent appointments were made in the classified official service. Forty-three percent of those hired were women, and 57% were men. Of the women appointed, 1.8% were veterans, while 54% of the men had veteran status. A large unspecified percentage of the female appointees were serving in lower paying positions for which males traditionally had not applied. On each of 50 sample eligible lists that are part of the record in this case, one or more women who would have been certified as eligible for appointment on the basis of test results were displaced by veterans whose test scores were lower.

At the outset of this litigation the State conceded that for "many of the permanent positions for which males and females have competed" the veterans' preference has "resulted in a substantially greater proportion of female eligibles than male eligibles" not being certified for consideration. The impact of the veterans' preference law upon the public employment opportunities of women has thus been severe. This impact lies at the heart of the appellee's federal constitutional claim.

II

The sole question for decision on this appeal is whether Massachusetts, in granting an absolute lifetime preference to veterans, has discriminated against women in violation of the Equal Protection Clause of the Fourteenth Amendment.

A

The Equal Protection guarantee of the Fourteenth Amendment does not take from the States all power of classification. Massachusetts Bd. of Retirement v. Murgia, 427 U.S. 307, 314, 96 S.Ct. 2562, 2567, 49 L.Ed.2d 520. Most laws classify, and many affect certain groups unevenly, even though the law itself treats them no differently

---

13,000 women served in this rank, working primarily at clerical jobs. These women were the first in the United States to be admitted to full military rank and status.

Official military corps for women were established in response to the massive personnel needs of the Second World War. The Women's Army Auxiliary Corps (WAAC) — the unofficial predecessor of the Women's Army Corps (WAC) — was created on May 14, 1942, followed two months later by the WAVES (Women Accepted for Voluntary Emergency Service). Not long after, the U.S. Marine Corps Women's Reserve and the Coast Guard Women's Reserve (SPAR) were established. Some 350,000 women served in the four services; some 800 women also served as Women's Airforce Service Pilots (WASPS). Most worked in health care, administration, and communications; they were also employed as airplane mechanics, parachute riggers, gunnery instructors, air traffic controllers, and the like.

The authorizations for the women's units during World War II were temporary. The Women's Armed Services Integration Act of 1948, 62 Stat. 356-375, established the women's services on a permanent basis. Under the Act, women were given regular military status. However, quotas were placed on the numbers who could enlist (no more than 2% of total enlisted strength); eligibility requirements were more stringent than those for men, and career opportunities were limited. During the 1950's and 1960's, enlisted women constituted little more than 1% of the total force. In 1967, the 2% quota was lifted, Act of Nov. 8, 1967, Pub.L. 90-130, §1(b), 81 Stat. 376, and in the 1970's many restrictive policies concerning women's participation in the military have been eliminated or modified. In 1972, women still constituted less than 2% of the enlisted strength. By 1975, when this litigation was commenced, the percentage had risen to 4.0%.

from all other members of the class described by the law.   When the basic classification is rationally based, uneven effects upon particular groups within a class are ordinarily of no constitutional concern.   New York City Transit Authority v. Beazer, 440 U.S. 568, 99 S.Ct. 1355, 59 L.Ed.2d 587.   The calculus of effects, the manner in which a particular law reverberates in a society, is a legislative and not a judicial responsibility.   In assessing an equal protection challenge, a court is called upon only to measure the basic validity of the legislative classification.   When some other independent right is not at stake, and when there is no "reason to infer antipathy," Vance v. Bradley, 440 U.S. 93, 99 S.Ct. 939, 59 L.Ed.2d 171, it is presumed that "even improvident decisions will eventually be rectified by the democratic process . . .." *Ibid.*

Certain classifications, however, in themselves supply a reason to infer antipathy. Race is the paradigm.   A racial classification, regardless of purported motivation, is presumptively invalid and can be upheld only upon an extraordinary justification.   This rule applies as well to a classification that is ostensibly neutral but is an obvious pretext for racial discrimination.   But, as was made clear in Washington v. Davis, 426 U.S. 229, 96 S.Ct. 2040, 48 L.Ed.2d 597 and Village of Arlington Heights v. Metropolitan Housing Development Corp., 429 U.S. 252, 97 S.Ct. 555, 50 L.Ed.2d 450, even if a neutral law has a disproportionately adverse effect upon a racial minority, it is unconstitutional under the Equal Protection Clause only if that impact can be traced to a discriminatory purpose.

Classifications based upon gender, not unlike those based upon race, have traditionally been the touchstone for pervasive and often subtle discrimination.   This Court's recent cases teach that such classifications must bear a "close and substantial relationship to important governmental objectives," and are in many settings unconstitutional.   Although public employment is not a constitutional right, and the States have wide discretion in framing employee qualifications, see, e.g., *Beazer*, these precedents dictate that any state law overtly or covertly designed to prefer males over females in public employment would require an exceedingly persuasive justification to withstand a constitutional challenge under the Equal Protection Clause of the Fourteenth Amendment.

B

The cases of *Davis* and *Arlington Heights* recognize that when a neutral law has a disparate impact upon a group that has historically been the victim of discrimination, an unconstitutional purpose may still be at work.   But those cases signaled no departure from the settled rule that the Fourteenth Amendment guarantees equal laws, not equal results. *Davis* upheld a job-related employment test that white people passed in proportionately greater numbers than Negroes, for there had been no showing that racial discrimination entered into the establishment or formulation of the test. *Arlington Heights* upheld a zoning board decision that tended to perpetuate racially segregated housing patterns, since apart from its effect, the board's decision was shown to be nothing more than an application of constitutionally neutral zoning policy. Those principles apply with equal force to a case involving alleged gender discrimination.

When a statute gender-neutral on its face is challenged on the ground that its effects upon women are disproportionately adverse, a two-fold inquiry is thus appropriate. The first question is whether the statutory classification is indeed neutral in the sense that it is not gender-based. If the classification itself, covert or overt, is not based upon gender, the second question is whether the adverse effect reflects invidious gender-based discrimination. See *Arlington Heights*. In this second inquiry, impact provides an "important starting point," *Arlington Heights*, but purposeful discrimination is "the condition that offends the Constitution." Swann v. Board of Education, 402 U.S. 1, 16, 91 S.Ct. 1267, 1276, 28 L.Ed.2d 554.

It is against this background of precedent that we consider the merits of the case before us.

III

A

The question whether ch. 31, §23 establishes a classification that is overtly or covertly based upon gender must first be considered. The appellee has conceded that ch. 31, §23 is neutral on its face. She has also acknowledged that state hiring preferences for veterans are not *per se* invalid, for she has limited her challenge to the absolute lifetime preference that Massachusetts provides to veterans. The District Court made two central findings that are relevant here: first, that ch. 31, §23 serves legitimate and worthy purposes; second, that the absolute preference was not established for the purpose of discriminating against women. The appellee has thus acknowledged and the District Court has thus found that the distinction between veterans and nonveterans drawn by ch. 31, §23 is not a pretext for gender discrimination. The appellee's concession and the District Court's finding are clearly correct.

If the impact of this statute could not be plausibly explained on a neutral ground, impact itself would signal that the real classification made by the law was in fact not neutral. See *Davis*; *Arlington Heights*. But there can be but one answer to the question whether this veteran preference excludes significant numbers of women from preferred state jobs because they are women or because they are nonveterans. Apart from the fact that the definition of "veterans" in the statute has always been neutral as to gender and that Massachusetts has consistently defined veteran status in a way that has been inclusive of women who have served in the military, this is not a law that can plausibly be explained only as a gender-based classification. Indeed, it is not a law that can rationally be explained on that ground. Veteran status is not uniquely male. Although few women benefit from the preference the nonveteran class is not substantially all-female. To the contrary, significant numbers of nonveterans are men, and all nonveterans — male as well as female — are placed at a disadvantage. Too many men are affected by ch. 31, §23 to permit the inference that the statute is but a pretext for preferring men over women.

Moreover, as the District Court implicitly found, the purposes of the statute provide the surest explanation for its impact. Just as there are cases in which impact alone can unmask an invidious classification, cf. *Yick Wo v. Hopkins*, there are others, in which — notwithstanding impact — the legitimate noninvidious purposes of a law cannot be missed. This is one. The distinction made by ch. 31, §23, is, as it seems to be, quite simply between veterans and nonveterans, not between men and women.

B

The dispositive question, then, is whether the appellee has shown that a gender-based discriminatory purpose has, at least in some measure, shaped the Massachusetts veterans' preference legislation. As did the District Court, she points to two basic factors which in her view distinguish ch. 31, §23 from the neutral rules at issue in the *Davis* and *Arlington Heights* cases. The first is the nature of the preference, which is said to be demonstrably gender-biased in the sense that it favors a status reserved under federal military policy primarily to men. The second concerns the impact of the absolute lifetime preference upon the employment opportunities of women, an impact claimed to be too inevitable to have been unintended. The appellee contends that these factors, coupled with the fact that the preference itself has little if any relevance to actual job performance, more than suffice to prove the discriminatory intent required to establish a constitutional violation.

1

The contention that this veterans' preference is "inherently non-neutral" or "gender-biased" presumes that the State, by favoring veterans, intentionally incorporated into its public employment policies the panoply of sex-based and assertedly discriminatory federal laws that have prevented all but a handful of women from becoming veterans. There are two serious difficulties with this argument. First, it is wholly at odds with the District Court's central finding that Massachusetts has not offered a preference to veterans for the purpose of discriminating against women. Second, it cannot be reconciled with the assumption made by both the appellee and the District Court that a more limiting hiring preference for veterans could be sustained. Taken together, these difficulties are fatal.

To the extent that the status of veteran is one that few women have been enabled to achieve, every hiring preference for veterans, however modest or extreme, is inherently gender-biased. If Massachusetts by offering such a preference can be said intentionally to have incorporated into its state employment policies the historical gender-based federal military personnel practices, the degree of the preference would or should make no constitutional difference. Invidious discrimination does not become less so because the discrimination accomplished is of a lesser magnitude.[23] Discriminatory intent is simply not amenable to calibration. It either is a factor that has influenced the legislative choice or it is not. The District Court's conclusion that the absolute veterans' preference was not originally enacted or subsequently reaffirmed for the purpose of giving an advantage to males as such necessarily compels the conclusion that the State intended nothing more than to prefer "veterans." Given this finding, simple logic suggests that an intent to exclude women from significant public jobs was not at work in this law. To reason that it was, by describing the preference as "inherently non-neutral" or "gender-biased," is merely to restate the fact of impact, not to answer the question of intent.

To be sure, this case is unusual in that it involves a law that by design is not neutral. The law overtly prefers veterans as such. As opposed to the written test at

---

[23]This is not to say that the degree of impact is irrelevant to the question of intent. But it is to say that a more modest preference, while it might well lessen impact and, as the State argues, might lessen the effectiveness of the statute in helping veterans, would not be any more or less "neutral" in the constitutional sense.

issue in *Davis*, it does not purport to define a job related characteristic. To the contrary, it confers upon a specifically described group — perceived to be particularly deserving — a competitive head start. But the District Court found, and the appellee has not disputed, that this legislative choice was legitimate. The basic distinction between veterans and nonveterans, having been found not gender-based, and the goals of the preference having been found worthy, ch. 31 must be analyzed as is any other neutral law that casts a greater burden upon women as a group than upon men as a group. The enlistment policies of the armed services may well have discriminated on the basis of sex. See Frontiero v. Richardson, 411 U.S. 677, 93 S.Ct. 1764, 36 L.Ed.2d 583; cf. Schlesinger v. Ballard, 419 U.S. 498, 95 S.Ct. 572, 42 L.Ed.2d 610. But the history of discrimination against women in the military is not on trial in this case.

2

The appellee's ultimate argument rests upon the presumption, common to the criminal and civil law, that a person intends the natural and foreseeable consequences of his voluntary actions. Her position was well stated in the concurring opinion in the District Court:

> "Conceding . . . that the goal here was to benefit the veteran, there is no reason to absolve the legislature from awareness that the means chosen to achieve this goal would freeze women out of all those state jobs actively sought by men. To be sure, the legislature did not wish to harm women. But the cutting-off of women's opportunities was an inevitable concomitant of the chosen scheme — as inevitable as the proposition that if tails is up, heads must be down. Where a law's consequences are that inevitable, can they meaningfully be described as unintended?"

This rhetorical question implies that a negative answer is obvious, but it is not. The decision to grant a preference to veterans was of course "intentional." So, necessarily, did an adverse impact upon nonveterans follow from that decision. And it cannot seriously be argued that the legislature of Massachusetts could have been unaware that most veterans are men. It would thus be disingenuous to say that the adverse consequences of this legislation for women were unintended, in the sense that they were not volitional or in the sense that they were not foreseeable.

"Discriminatory purpose," however, implies more than intent as volition or intent as awareness of consequences. See United Jewish Organizations v. Carey, 430 U.S. 144, 179, 97 S.Ct. 996, 1016, 51 L.Ed.2d 229 (concurring opinion).[24] It implies that the decisionmaker, in this case a state legislature, selected or reaffirmed a particular course of action at least in part "because of," not merely "in spite of," its adverse effects upon an identifiable group.[25] Yet, nothing in the record demonstrates that this

---

[24]Proof of discriminatory intent must necessarily usually rely on objective factors, several of which were outlined in *Arlington Heights*. The inquiry is practical. What a legislature or any official entity is "up to" may be plain from the results its actions achieve, or the results they avoid. Often it is made clear from what has been called, in a different context, "the give and take of the situation." Cramer v. United States, 325 U.S. 1, 32-33, 65 S.Ct. 918, 934, 89 L.Ed. 1441. (Jackson, J.)

[25]This is not to say that the inevitability or foreseeability of consequences of a neutral rule has no bearing upon the existence of discriminatory intent. Certainly, when the adverse consequences of a law upon an identifiable group are as inevitable as the gender-based consequences of ch. 31, §23, a strong inference that the adverse effects were desired can

preference for veterans was originally devised or subsequently re-enacted because it would accomplish the collateral goal of keeping women in a stereotypic and predefined place in the Massachusetts Civil Service.

To the contrary, the statutory history shows that the benefit of the preference was consistently offered to "any person" who was a veteran. That benefit has been extended to women under a very broad statutory definition of the term veteran.[26] The preference formula itself, which is the focal point of this challenge, was first adopted — so it appears from this record — out of a perceived need to help a small group of older Civil War veterans. It has since been reaffirmed and extended only to cover new veterans.[27] When the totality of legislative actions establishing and extending the Massachusetts veterans' preference are considered, see *Davis*, the law remains what it purports to be: a preference for veterans of either sex over nonveterans of either sex, not for men over women.

IV

Veterans' hiring preferences represent an awkward — and, many argue, unfair — exception to the widely shared view that merit and merit alone should prevail in the employment policies of government. After a war, such laws have been enacted virtually without opposition. During peacetime they inevitably have come to be viewed in many quarters as undemocratic and unwise.[28] Absolute and permanent preferences, as the troubled history of this law demonstrates, have always been subject to the objection that they give the veteran more than a square deal. But the Fourteenth Amendment "cannot be made a refuge from ill-advised . . . laws." District of Columbia v. Brooke, 214 U.S. 138, 150, 29 S.Ct. 560, 563, 53 L.Ed. 941. The substantial edge granted to veterans by ch. 31, §23 may reflect unwise policy. The appellee, however, has simply failed to demonstrate that the law in any way reflects a purpose to discriminate on the basis of sex.

The judgment is reversed, and the case is remanded for further proceedings consistent with this opinion.

---

reasonably be drawn. But in this inquiry — made as it is under the Constitution — an inference is a working tool, not a synonym for proof. When as here, the impact is essentially an unavoidable consequence of a legislative policy that has in itself always been deemed to be legitimate, and when, as here, the statutory history and all of the available evidence affirmatively demonstrate the opposite, the inference simply fails to ripen into proof.

[26]See nn. 8, 17, *supra*.

[27]The appellee has suggested that the former statutory exception for "women's requisitions," supplies evidence that Massachusetts, when it established and subsequently reaffirmed the absolute preference legislation, assumed that women would not or should not compete with men. She has further suggested that the former provision extending the preference to certain female dependents of veterans, see n. 10, *supra*, demonstrates that ch. 31, §23 is laced with "old notions" about the proper roles and needs of the sexes. See Califano v. Goldfarb, 430 U.S. 199, 97 S.Ct. 1021, 51 L.Ed.2d 270; Weinberger v. Wiesenfeld, 420 U.S. 636, 95 S.Ct. 1225, 43 L.Ed.2d 514. But the first suggestion is totally belied by the statutory history, and the second fails to account for the consistent statutory recognition of the contribution of women to this Nation's military efforts.

[28]See generally Veterans' Preference Oversight Hearings before Subcomm. on Civil Service, 95th Cong., 1st Sess. (1977); Report of Comptroller General, Conflicting Congressional Policies: Veterans' Preference and Apportionment vs. Equal Employment Opportunity (Sept. 29, 1977).

MR. JUSTICE STEVENS, with whom MR. JUSTICE WHITE joins, concurring.

While I concur in the Court's opinion, I confess that I am not at all sure that there is any difference between the two questions posed [in this case]. If a classification is not overtly based on gender, I am inclined to believe the question whether it is covertly gender-based is the same as the question whether its adverse effects reflect invidious gender-based discrimination. However the question is phrased, for me the answer is largely provided by the fact that the number of males disadvantaged by Massachusetts' Veterans Preference (1,867,000) is sufficiently large — and sufficiently close to the number of disadvantaged females (2,954,000) — to refute the claim that the rule was intended to benefit males as a class over females as a class.

MR. JUSTICE MARSHALL, with whom MR. JUSTICE BRENNAN joins, dissenting.

Although acknowledging that in some circumstances, discriminatory intent may be inferred from the inevitable or foreseeable impact of a statute, the Court concludes that no such intent has been established here. I cannot agree. In my judgment, Massachusetts' choice of an absolute veterans' preference system evinces purposeful gender-based discrimination. And because the statutory scheme bears no substantial relationship to a legitimate governmental objective, it cannot withstand scrutiny under the Equal Protection Clause.

I

The District Court found that the "prime objective" of the Massachusetts Veterans Preference Statute, was to benefit individuals with prior military service. Under the Court's analysis, this factual determination "necessarily compels the conclusion that the State intended nothing more than to prefer 'veterans.' Given this finding, simple logic suggests than an intent to exclude women from significant public jobs was not at work in this law." I find the Court's logic neither simple nor compelling.

That a legislature seeks to advantage one group does not, as a matter of logic or of common sense, exclude the possibility that it also intends to disadvantage another. Individuals in general and lawmakers in particular frequently act for a variety of reasons. As this Court recognized in *Arlington Heights*, "[r]arely can it be said that a legislature or administrative body operating under a broad mandate made a decision motivated by a single concern." Absent an omniscience not commonly attributed to the judiciary, it will often be impossible to ascertain the sole or even dominant purpose of a given statute. Thus, the critical constitutional inquiry is not whether an illicit consideration was the primary or but-for cause of a decision, but rather whether it had an appreciable role in shaping a given legislative enactment. Where there is "proof that a discriminatory purpose has been a motivating factor in the decision, . . . judicial deference is no longer justified." *Arlington Heights*.

Moreover, since reliable evidence of subjective intentions is seldom obtainable, resort to inference based on objective factors is generally unavoidable. To discern the purposes underlying facially neutral policies, this Court has therefore considered the degree, inevitability, and foreseeability of any disproportionate impact as well as the alternatives reasonably available.

In the instant case, the impact of the Massachusetts statute on women is undisputed. Any veteran with a passing grade on the civil service exam must be placed ahead of a nonveteran, regardless of their respective scores. The District Court found that, as a practical matter, this preference supplants test results as the determinant of upper-level civil service appointments. Because less than 2% of the women in Massachusetts are veterans, the absolute preference formula has rendered desirable state civil service employment an almost exclusively male prerogative.

As the District Court recognized, this consequence followed foreseeably, indeed inexorably, from the long history of policies severely limiting women's participation in the military.[1] Although neutral in form, the statute is anything but neutral in application. It inescapably reserves a major sector of public employment to an already established class which, as a matter of historical fact, is 98% male. Where the foreseeable impact of a facially neutral policy is so disproportionate, the burden should rest on the State to establish that sex-based considerations played no part in the choice of the particular legislative scheme.

Clearly, that burden was not sustained here. The legislative history of the statute reflects the Commonwealth's patent appreciation of the impact the preference system would have on women, and an equally evident desire to mitigate that impact only with respect to certain traditionally female occupations. Until 1971, the statute and implementing civil service regulations exempted from operation of the preference any job requisitions "especially calling for women." In practice, this exemption, coupled with the absolute preference for veterans, has created a gender-based civil service hierarchy, with women occupying low grade clerical and secretarial jobs and men holding more responsible and remunerative positions.

Thus, for over 70 years, the Commonwealth has maintained, as an integral part of its veteran's preference system, an exemption relegating female civil service applicants to occupations traditionally filled by women. Such a statutory scheme both reflects and perpetuates precisely the kind of archaic assumptions about women's roles which we have previously held invalid. Particularly when viewed against the range of less discriminatory alternatives available to assist veterans,[2] Massachusetts' choice of a formula that so severely restricts public employment opportunities for women cannot reasonably be thought gender-neutral. The Court's conclusion to the contrary — that "nothing in the record" evinces a "collateral goal of keeping women in a stereotypic and predefined place in the Massachusetts Civil Service," — displays a singularly myopic view of the facts established below.[3]

---

[1] In addition to the 2% quota on women's participation in the armed forces, enlistment and appointment requirements have been more stringent for females than males with respect to age, mental and physical aptitude, parental consent, and educational attainment. Until the 1970's, the armed forces precluded enlistment and appointment of women, but not men, who were married or had dependent children. Sex-based restrictions on advancement and training opportunities also diminished the incentives for qualified women to enlist.

Thus, unlike the employment examination in *Davis*, which the Court found to be demonstrably job-related, the Massachusetts preference statute incorporates the results of sex-based military policies irrelevant to women's current fitness for civilian public employment.

[2] Only four States afford a preference comparable in scope to that of Massachusetts. Other States and the Federal Government grant point or tie-breaking preferences that do not foreclose opportunities for women.

[3] Although it is relevant that the preference statute also disadvantages a substantial group of men, see *ante* (Stevens, J., concurring), it is equally pertinent that 47% of Massachusetts men over 18 are veterans, as compared to 0.8% of Massachusetts women. Given this disparity, and the indicia of intent noted at p. 2287, supra, the absolute number of men denied preference cannot

II

To survive challenge under the Equal Protection Clause, statutes reflecting gender-based discrimination must be substantially related to the achievement of important governmental objectives. Appellants here advance three interests in support of the absolute preference system: (1) assisting veterans in their readjustment to civilian life; (2) encouraging military enlistment; and (3) rewarding those who have served their country. Although each of those goals is unquestionably legitimate, the "mere recitation of a benign compensatory purpose" cannot of itself insulate legislative classifications from constitutional scrutiny. And in this case, the Commonwealth has failed to establish a sufficient relationship between its objectives and the means chosen to effectuate them.

With respect to the first interest, facilitating veterans' transition to civilian status, the statute is plainly overinclusive. By conferring a permanent preference, the legislation allows veterans to invoke their advantage repeatedly, without regard to their date of discharge. As the record demonstrates, a substantial majority of those currently enjoying the benefits of the system are not recently discharged veterans in need of readjustment assistance.[4]

Nor is the Commonwealth's second asserted interest, encouraging military service, a plausible justification for this legislative scheme. In its original and subsequent re-enactments, the statute extended benefits retroactively to veterans who had served during a prior specified period. If the Commonwealth's "actual purpose" is to induce enlistment, this legislative design is hardly well-suited to that end. For I am unwilling to assume what appellants made no effort to prove, that the possibility of obtaining an *ex post facto* civil service preference significantly influenced the enlistment decisions of Massachusetts residents. Moreover, even if such influence could be presumed, the statute is still grossly overinclusive in that it bestows benefits on men drafted as well as those who volunteered.

Finally, the Commonwealth's third interest, rewarding veterans, does not "adequately justify the salient features" of this preference system. Where a particular statutory scheme visits substantial hardship on a class long subject to discrimination, the legislation cannot be sustained unless "carefully tuned to alternative considerations." Here, there are a wide variety of less discriminatory means by which Massachusetts could effect its compensatory purposes. For example, a point preference system, such as that maintained by many States and the Federal Government, see n. 2, *supra*, or an absolute preference for a limited duration, would reward veterans without excluding all qualified women from upper level civil service positions. Apart from public employment, the Commonwealth, can, and does, afford assistance to veterans in various ways, including tax abatements, educational subsidies, and special programs for needy veterans. Unlike these and similar benefits, the costs of which are distributed across the taxpaying public generally, the Massachusetts statute exacts a substantial price from a discrete group of individuals who have long

---

be dispositive, especially since they have not faced the barriers to achieving veteran status confronted by women. See n. 1, *supra*.

[4] The eligibility lists for the positions Ms. Feeney sought included 95 veterans for whom discharge information was available. Of those 95 males, 64(67%) were discharged prior to 1960.

been subject to employment discrimination,[5] and who, because of circumstances totally beyond their control, have [had] little if any chance of becoming members of the preferred class."   In its present unqualified form, the Veterans Preference Statute precludes all but a small fraction of Massachusetts women from obtaining any civil service position also of interest to men. Given the range of alternatives available, this degree of preference is not constitutionally permissible.

I would affirm the judgment of the court below.

NOTES AND PROBLEMS FOR DISCUSSION

1.   If a private business enacted its own veterans' preference rule, would a suit similar to *Feeney*, but with a cause of action based on Title VII, be likely to produce a different result? Could the plaintiff establish a prima facie case by the introduction of evidence similar to that introduced in *Feeney*? Would the employer's desire to reward veterans for their military service constitute a defense under Title VII? See Chapter 2, Section C, *supra*.

2.   If the evidence in *Feeney* had shown that a bias against women, at least in part, underlay the veteran's preference law, would the plaintiff necessarily have prevailed? As indicated in the majority opinion, in equal protection cases under the Fifth and Fourteenth Amendments, "strict scrutiny" is applied to racial classifications. "Suspect" classifications are allowed to stand only if the state can demonstrate that they serve a "compelling" governmental interest that cannot be achieved by other means. *See* McLaughlin v. Florida, 379 U.S. 184, 85 S.Ct. 283, 13 L.Ed.2d 222 (1964). Despite the similarities between classifications based on sex and those based on race, the Supreme Court has declined to treat sex as a "suspect" classification so as to call for strict-scrutiny, although, at one time, four members of the Court expressed this view. *See* Frontiero v. Richardson, 411 U.S. 677, 93 S.Ct. 1764, 36 L.Ed.2d 583 (1973). Instead, the Court has applied an intermediate standard of review under which sex-based classifications which serve "important" governmental interests and are "substantially related" to the achievement of those objectives are upheld as not violative of equal protection. *See* Craig v. Boren, 429 U.S. 190, 97 S.Ct. 451, 50 L.Ed.2d 397 (1976). What level of scrutiny do Justices Marshall and Brennan feel the veterans' preference should be subjected to?

Can a state employee state an equal protection-founded claim under §1983 alleging that she was treated differently than all other similarly situated employees without asserting that this differential treatment was based on her membership in any particular class? In ENGQUIST v. OREGON DEPARTMENT OF AGRICULTURE, 553 U.S. 591, 128 S.Ct. 2146, 170 L.Ed.2d 975, (2008), the Supreme Court disagreed with the rulings of nine other federal circuits but affirmed the ruling of the Ninth Circuit in rejecting the plaintiff's request to extend the "class-of-one" theory of equal protection to the public employment context. The Court previously had acknowledged

---

[5]See Frontiero v. Richardson, 411 U.S. 677, 689 n. 23, 93 S.Ct. 1764, 1772 n. 23, 36 L.Ed.2d 583 (1973); Kahn v. Shevin, 416 U.S. 351, 353-354, 94 S.Ct. 1734, 1736-1737, 40 L.Ed.2d 189 (1974); United States Bureau of the Census, Current Population Reports, No. 107, Money Income and Poverty Status of Families and Persons in the United States: 1976 (Advance Report) (Table 7) (Sept. 1977).

the availability of a "class-of-one" claim in equal protection challenges to governmental action in non-employment cases. Under this theory, if the plaintiff could establish that she had been treated differently from other similarly situated individuals, the Equal Protection Clause's concern with arbitrary governmental action required the government to establish the existence of a rational basis for the differential treatment. The class-of-one theory, the *Engquist* Court noted, "presupposes that like individuals should be treated alike and that to treat them differently is to classify them in a way that must survive at least rationality review." But, the six member majority continued, this doctrine was inapplicable to situations where the government acted as employer, as opposed to when it exercised its sovereign authority over the citizenry at large. The difference, the majority explained, is that employment decisions involve the application of individualized, subjective factors that do not lend themselves to equal protection analysis unless the differential treatment is alleged to have been based on membership in a particular group or class. Recognition of a class-of-one theory of equal protection in the public employment context, the Court reasoned, not only would require the repudiation of the longstanding and constitutionally permissible employment-at-will doctrine; it also would constitutionalize nearly every adverse employment action taken by a state employer and thereby subject nearly every such claim to judicial constitutional review.

3.   As the Court mentioned in *Feeney*, §1983 is a remedial statute that does not create substantive rights but provides a remedy for the violation of rights created elsewhere. Most §1983 actions, as in *Feeney*, are based on constitutional violations. In MAINE v. THIBOUTOT, 448 U.S. 1, 100 S.Ct. 2502, 65 L.Ed.2d 555 (1980), the Court ruled that §1983 also provides a remedy for actions taken under color of state law which contravene federal substantive statutes. The right to base a §1983 action on a Title VII violation would significantly expand the relief available to plaintiffs with employment discrimination claims against public agencies. For example, a plaintiff who had not filed a timely EEOC charge might still proceed under §1983, since there are no administrative prerequisites to filing suit under §1983. The courts have been unanimous in holding that Title VII provides the exclusive remedy where the only §1983 cause of action is based on an alleged violation of Title VII. *See, e.g.*, Day v. Wayne County Bd. of Auditors, 749 F.2d 1199, 1204 (6th Cir. 1984) ("It would be anomalous to hold that when the only unlawful employment practice consists of the violation of a right created by Title VII, the plaintiff can by-pass all of the administrative processes of Title VII and go directly into court under §1983."). But the courts, as in *Day*, also are careful to distinguish a Title VII-based §1983 claim (not permitted) from an employment discrimination claim filed under §1983 where the plaintiff is asserting that the state agent violated her constitutional rights (permitted).

> Where an employee establishes employer conduct which violates both Title VII and rights derived from another source — the Constitution or a federal statute — which existed at the time of the enactment of Title VII, the claim based on the other source is independent of the Title VII claim, and the plaintiff may seek the remedies provided by §1983 in addition to those created by Title VII.

749 F.2d at 1205. Title VII, therefore, is not the exclusive remedy for employment discrimination by state and local governments. Such individuals possess an alternative cause of action under §1983 where the §1983 claim is based on the Fourteenth Amendment. *See, e.g.*, Beardsley v. Webb, 30 F.3d 524 (4th Cir. 1994). And because

"employer" is defined in §701 of Title VII to include only entities with fifteen or more employees, §1983 will reach some small public employers that are out of Title VII's jurisdictional reach. The Supreme Court also has held, in FITZGERALD v. BARNSTABLE SCHOOL COMMITTEE, 555 U.S. 246, 129 S.Ct. 788, 172 L.Ed.2d 582 (2009), that a plaintiff challenging gender-based discrimination by an educational institution under Title IX of the Education Amendments of 1972, 20 U.S.C. 1681(a) is not precluded from also asserting a §1983 claim alleging gender-based discrimination in violation of the U.S. Constitution.

4. A continuing problem for plaintiffs in §1983 litigation is determining the appropriate party defendant. In MONROE v. PAPE, 365 U.S. 167, 81 S.Ct. 473, 5 L.Ed.2d 492 (1961), the Supreme Court held that because of the explicit language of the Act ("Every person who * * * subjects or causes to be subjected any citizen * * *"), only human beings and not institutions or corporate political bodies were proper party defendants in a §1983 case. *See also* City of Kenosha v. Bruno, 412 U.S. 507, 93 S.Ct. 2222, 37 L.Ed.2d 109 (1973). Thus, for a number of years, §1983 actions typically were filed against the public officials whose actions were being challenged, rather than the agency or political body that they represented. *See* Aldinger v. Howard, 427 U.S. 1, 96 S.Ct. 2413, 49 L.Ed.2d 276 (1976). Note that *Feeney*, filed in 1975, was a suit against the administrator, not his agency.

But in 1977, the Supreme Court, following the lead of a number of circuits, held that a direct action, not dependent on §1983, under the Fourteenth Amendment could be instituted against a public body if jurisdiction was proper under 28 U.S.C. §1331 (general federal question jurisdiction). Mt. Healthy City Sch. Dist. Bd. of Educ. v. Doyle, 429 U.S. 274, 277-278, 97 S.Ct. 568, 571, 50 L.Ed.2d 471 (1977). Eventually, in MONELL v. DEPARTMENT OF SOCIAL SERVICES, 436 U.S. 658, 98 S.Ct. 2018, 56 L.Ed.2d 611 (1978), the Court overruled *Monroe* and held that local governing bodies could be sued as "persons" under 42 U.S.C. §1983 for monetary, declaratory, and injunctive relief where the unlawful action implemented or executed "a policy or custom" of the governing unit. The Court made clear, however, that public agencies would not be liable for all illegal acts of their employees on the theory of respondeat superior. "Instead," it emphasized, "it is when execution of a government's policy or custom, whether made by its lawmakers or by those whose edicts or acts may fairly be said to represent official policy, inflicts the injury that the government as an entity is responsible under §1983." Since individual officials often will be unable to pay damage awards, a critical question in post-*Monell* litigation is whether the actions of the officials in question reflect or establish the "policy" of the public body. *See, e.g.*, Oklahoma City v. Tuttle, 471 U.S. 808, 105 S.Ct. 2427, 85 L.Ed.2d 791 (1985) (the fact that a public official has discretion in the exercise of particular functions does not give rise, without more, to municipal liability based on exercise of that discretion); Pembaur v. Cincinnati, 475 U.S. 469, 106 S.Ct. 1292, 89 L.Ed.2d 452 (1986) (if the decision to adopt a particular course of action is directed by those who establish government policy, the municipality is responsible whether that action is taken only once or repeatedly).

In CITY OF ST. LOUIS v. PRAPROTNIK, 485 U.S. 112, 108 S.Ct. 915, 99 L.Ed.2d 107 (1988), the plaintiff, a city architect, alleged that he had been transferred to a lesser job and then laid off in retaliation for his having successfully appealed earlier disciplinary actions to the city's Civil Service Commission. A jury found the city liable for violations of plaintiff's First Amendment and due process rights. On appeal, the city argued that it could not be held liable for the unlawful and unauthorized acts of Praprotnik's supervisors. The Court of Appeals affirmed on the ground that, under *Monell*, the city was responsible for the actions of those officials whose employment decisions are "final" in the sense that they are not subject to de novo review by higher officials. The Supreme Court reversed. The Court began by holding that the identification of policy-making officials in a government is a matter of state law. "[W]e can be confident that state law (which may include valid local ordinances and regulations) will always direct a court to some official or body that has the responsibility for making law or setting policy in any given area of a local government's business." Consequently, it continued, a federal court has very limited range of movement in assigning "policy maker" status to particular officials.

> [A] federal court would not be justified in assuming that municipal policymaking authority lies somewhere other than where the applicable law purports to put it. And certainly there can be no justification for giving a jury the discretion to determine which officials are high enough in the government that their actions can be said to represent a decision of the government itself.

485 U.S. at 125. The Court determined that the city could not be responsible for damages because the plaintiff had not alleged that the officials with policymaking power (the Mayor, Board of Aldermen, and the Civil Service Commission) had promulgated or directed a policy of retaliating against employees who appealed adverse employment decisions, nor had the plaintiff attempted to prove that such retaliation was ever directed at anyone other than himself. The Court acknowledged that if a city's policymakers could insulate the government from liability by delegating their policymaking authority to others, §1983 could not serve its intended purpose. The opinion leaves unclear, however, under what circumstances the actions of an official, who has received his authority from a policymaker, will constitute official policy. On the one hand, the existence of a widespread practice that is so long standing as to constitute a custom or usage of the municipality must be treated as an official policy. On the other hand, the Court observed, "simply going along with discretionary decisions made by one's subordinates * * * is not a delegation to them of the authority to make policy."

> It would be a different matter if a particular decision by a subordinate was cast in the form of a policy statement and expressly approved by the supervising policymaker. It would be a different matter if a series of decisions by a subordinate official manifested a "custom or usage" of which the supervisor must have been aware. In both those cases, the supervisor could realistically be deemed to have adopted a policy that happened to have been formulated or initiated by a lower-ranking official. But the mere failure to investigate the basis of a subordinate's discretionary decisions does not amount to a delegation of policymaking authority, especially where (as here) the wrongfulness of the subordinate's decision arises from a retaliatory motive or other unstated rationale. In such circumstances, the purposes of 1983 would not be served by treating a subordinate employee's decision as if it were a reflection of municipal policy.

485 U.S. at 130. Does *Praprotnik* mean that in a non-pattern-and-practice case in which the plaintiff alleges race or sex discrimination in employment, no relief, as a practical matter, will be available against the municipal employer? In WILLIAMS v.

BUTLER, 863 F.2d 1398 (8th Cir. 1988) (en banc) cert. denied, 492 U.S. 906, 109 S.Ct. 3215, 106 L.Ed.2d 565 (1989), the Eighth Circuit held that a municipality's complete delegation of authority to an official renders the actions of that official the "policy" of the city.

> A very fine line exists between delegating final policymaking authority to an official, for which a municipality may be held liable, and entrusting discretionary authority to that official, for which no liability attaches. The distinction, we believe, lies in the amount of authority retained by the authorized policymakers. The clear message from *Praprotnik* is that an incomplete delegation of authority will not result in municipal liability whereas an absolute delegation will.

863 F.2d at 1402. In *Williams*, the city had allowed a municipal judge "carte blanche" authority over the employment of court clerks. The Eighth Circuit concluded that by delegating final, unreviewable policy making authority to the judge, the city exposed itself to liability for any unconstitutional action taken by him pursuant to that authority. *Compare* Gray v. County of Dane, 854 F.2d 179 (7th Cir. 1988) (§1983 action against a county properly was dismissed where the plaintiff failed to plead that discrimination against her was attributable to a policy or established practice of the county rather than to the unauthorized conduct of discrete officials). The *Monell-Praprotnik* line of cases applies only to §1983 actions against municipalities and other local governing bodies. Neither the state itself nor a state official acting in his official capacity is a "person" for purposes of §1983. Will v. Mich. Dep't of State Police, 491 U.S. 58, 109 S.Ct. 2304, 105 L.Ed.2d 45 (1989). Suits for injunctive relief and monetary damages against state officials under §1983 must be brought against them as individuals "acting under color of state law."

5. Unlike Title VII, exhaustion of available administrative remedies is not a prerequisite to suit under §1983. In PATSY v. BOARD OF REGENTS OF STATE OF FLORIDA, 457 U.S. 496, 102 S.Ct. 2557, 73 L.Ed.2d 172 (1982), the Court held that neither the language of the statute nor its legislative history indicated a desire by Congress that a claimant aggrieved by the action of a state official be required to resort to grievance mechanisms supplied by the state even if the relief available in such proceedings would fully compensate the claimant. The claimant may, of course, decide to use the internal grievance procedure of the state before filing her federal suit, but it is important to note that resort to such procedure will not necessarily toll the running of the statute of limitations applicable to the §1983 action. Whether the limitation period will be tolled will depend on state law. For more on this, see Section D of this chapter, *infra*. It also is important to remember that resort to state administrative remedies may preclude subsequent federal action under res judicata and collateral estoppel principles. That possibility certainly will exist if the final stage of the state's procedure is judicial review of the claim, and may be the case if, under state law, the findings of the administrative board will be given preclusive effect by the courts of the state. See Univ. of Tenn. v. Elliott, discussed, *infra*, in Section E.

SECTION C. THE CIVIL RIGHTS ACT OF 1871, SECTION TWO — 42 U.S.C. §1985(3)

Section 2 of the Civil Rights Act of 1871,[a] now codified at 42 U.S.C. §1985(3), was enacted primarily to provide protection to southern blacks and Union sympathizers from the violent activities of the Ku Klux Klan, by outlawing conspiracies to deprive persons of "the equal protection of the laws, or of equal privileges and immunities under the law." Since §1985(3) — like its statutory counterpart, §1983 (originally §1 of the 1871 Act) — was enacted pursuant to the Fourteenth Amendment, it was interpreted initially to prohibit only those conspiracies involving state action. In Griffin v. Breckenridge,[b] however, the Supreme Court ruled that black plaintiffs claiming that they were beaten by a group of private white citizens could state a cause of action under §1985(3) without alleging either state action or that the defendants acted under color of state law, since their complaint alleged a "class-based invidiously discriminatory" conspiracy to deprive them of their Thirteenth Amendment right to be free from slavery and their right of interstate travel. Since the ruling in *Griffin*, several questions have arisen in connection with the application of §1985(3) to employment discrimination claims.[c] For example, did the Court intend to preclude the extension of §1985(3) to private conspiracies aimed at depriving persons of other constitutionally or statutorily guaranteed rights? In addition, is the requirement of a "class-based" discriminatory intent restricted to conspiracies motivated by racial animus? Finally, can a plaintiff satisfy the statutory "two or more persons" requirement where the complaint alleges a conspiracy between a corporation and its agents? These questions are addressed in the following materials.

Read 42 U.S.C. §1985(3).

Great American Federal Savings & Loan Association v. Novotny

Supreme Court of the United States, 1979.

442 U.S. 366, 99 S.Ct. 2345, 60 L.Ed.2d 957.

MR. JUSTICE STEWART delivered the opinion of the Court.

* * * In the case now before us, we consider the scope of 42 U.S.C. §1985(3), the surviving version of §2 of the Civil Rights Act of 1871.

I

The respondent, John R. Novotny, began his career with the Great American Federal Savings and Loan Association (hereinafter the Association) in Allegheny County, Pa., in 1950. By 1975, he was secretary of the Association, a member of its

---

[a]Act of April 20, 1871, ch. 22, §2, 17 Stat. 13 (1871).

[b]403 U.S. 88, 91 S.Ct. 1790, 29 L.Ed.2d 338 (1971).

[c]For a provocative critique of the application of §1985(3) to employment discrimination claims, see Mark Fokele, Comment, *A Construction of §1985(3) In Light of Its Original Purpose*, 46 U.CHI.L.REV. 402 (1979).

board of directors, and a loan officer. According to the allegations of the complaint in this case the Association "intentionally and deliberately embarked upon and pursued a course of conduct the effect of which was to deny to female employees equal employment opportunity * * *." When Novotny expressed support for the female employees at a meeting of the board of directors, his connection with the Association abruptly ended. He was not re-elected as secretary; he was not re-elected to the board; and he was fired. His support for the Association's female employees, he alleges, was the cause of the termination of his employment.

Novotny filed a complaint with the Equal Employment Opportunity Commission under Title VII * * *. After receiving a right-to-sue letter, he brought this lawsuit against the Association and its directors in the District Court for the Western District of Pennsylvania. He claimed damages under 42 U.S.C. §1985(3), contending that he had been injured as the result of a conspiracy to deprive him of equal protection of and equal privileges and immunities under the laws.[4] The District Court granted the defendants' motion to dismiss. It held that §1985(3) could not be invoked because the directors of a single corporation could not, as a matter of law and fact, engage in a conspiracy.[5]

Novotny appealed. After oral argument before a three-judge panel, the case was reargued before the en banc Court of Appeals for the Third Circuit, which unanimously reversed the District Court's judgment. The Court of Appeals ruled that Novotny had stated a cause of action under §1985(3). It held that conspiracies motivated by an invidious animus against women fall within §1985(3), and that Novotny, a male allegedly injured as a result of such a conspiracy, had standing to bring suit under that statutory provision. It ruled that Title VII could be the source of a right asserted in an action under §1985(3), and that intracorporate conspiracies come within the intendment of the section. Finally, the court concluded that its construction of §1985(3) did not present any serious constitutional problem.[6]

We granted certiorari to consider the applicability of §1985(3) to the facts alleged in Novotny's complaint.

II

* * *

* * * [I]n Griffin v. Breckenridge, 403 U.S. 88, 91 S.Ct. 1790, 29 L.Ed.2d 338, the Court unanimously concluded that * * * §1985(3) * * * provide[d] a cause of action for damages caused by purely private conspiracies.

---

[4]His complaint also alleged, as a second cause of action, that his discharge was in retaliation for his efforts on behalf of equal employment opportunity, and thus violated §704(a) of Title VII.

[5]As to the Title VII claim, the District Court held that Novotny was not a proper plaintiff under §704(a).

[6]The Court of Appeals ruled that Novotny had also stated a valid cause of action under Title VII. It held that § 704(a) applies to retaliation for both formal and informal actions taken to advance the purposes of the Act. That holding is not now before this Court.

We note the relative narrowness of the specific issue before the Court. It is unnecessary for us to consider whether a plaintiff would have a cause of action under §1985(3) where the defendant was not subject to suit under Title VII or a comparable statute. Nor do we think it necessary to consider whether §1985(3) creates a remedy for statutory rights other than those fundamental rights derived from the Constitution.

The Court's opinion in *Griffin* discerned the following criteria for measuring whether a complaint states a cause of action under §1985(3):

> "To come within the legislation a complaint must allege that the defendants did (1) 'conspire or go in disguise on the highway or on the premises of another' (2) 'for the purpose of depriving, either directly or indirectly, any person or class of persons of the equal protection of the laws, or of equal privileges and immunities under the laws.' It must then assert that one or more of the conspirators (3) did, or caused to be done, 'any act in furtherance of the object of [the] conspiracy,' whereby another was (4a) 'injured in his person of property' or (4b) 'deprived of having and exercising any right or privilege of a citizen of the United States.'"

Section 1985(3) provides no substantive rights itself; it merely provides a remedy for violation of the rights it designates. The primary question in the present case, therefore, is whether a person injured by a conspiracy to violate §704(a) of Title VII * * * is deprived of "the equal protection of the laws, or of equal privileges and immunities under the laws" within the meaning of §1985(3).[11]

Under Title VII, cases of alleged employment discrimination are subject to a detailed administrative and judicial process designed to provide an opportunity for nonjudicial and nonadversary resolution of claims. * * *

* * *

If a violation of Title VII could be asserted through §1985(3), a complainant could avoid most if not all of these detailed and specific provisions of the law. * * * The short and precise time limitations of Title VII would be grossly altered. Perhaps most importantly, the complainant could completely bypass the administrative process, which plays such a crucial role in the scheme established by Congress in Title VII.

The problem in this case is closely akin to that in Brown v. GSA, 425 U.S. 820, 96 S.Ct. 1961, 48 L.Ed.2d 402. There, we held that §717 of Title VII provides the exclusive remedy for employment discrimination claims of those federal employees that it covers. Our conclusion was based on the proposition that

> "[t]he balance, completeness, and structural integrity of §717 are inconsistent with the petitioner's contention that the judicial remedy afforded by §717(c) was designed merely to supplement other putative judicial relief." 425 U.S. at 832.

Here the case is even more compelling. In *Brown*, the Court concluded that §717 displaced other causes of action arguably available to assert substantive rights similar to those granted by §717. Section 1985(3), by contrast, creates no rights. It is a purely remedial statute, providing a civil cause of action when some otherwise defined federal right — to equal protection of the laws or equal privileges and immunities under the laws — is breached by a conspiracy in the manner defined by the section. Thus, we are not faced in this case with a question of implied repeal. The right Novotny claims under §704(a) did not even arguably exist before the passage of Title VII. The only question here, therefore, is whether the rights created by Title VII may be asserted within the remedial framework of §1985(3).

---

[11]For the purposes of this question, we assume but certainly do not decide that the directors of a single corporation can form a conspiracy within the meaning of §1985(3).

This case thus differs markedly from the cases recently decided by this Court that have related the substantive provisions of last century's Civil Rights Acts to contemporary legislation conferring similar substantive rights. In those cases we have held that substantive rights conferred in the 19th century were not withdrawn, sub silentio, by the subsequent passage of the modern statutes. * * *

* * *

This case, by contrast, does not involve two "independent" rights, and for the same basic reasons that underlay the Court's decision in *Brown*, reinforced by the other considerations discussed in this opinion, we conclude that §1985(3) may not be invoked to redress violations of Title VII. It is true that a §1985(3) remedy would not be coextensive with Title VII, since a plaintiff in an action under §1985(3) must prove both a conspiracy and a group animus that Title VII does not require. While this incomplete congruity would limit the damage that would be done to Title VII, it would not eliminate it. Unimpaired effectiveness can be given to the plan put together by Congress in Title VII only by holding that deprivation of a right created by Title VII cannot be the basis for a cause of action under §1985(3).

Accordingly, the judgment of the Court of Appeals is vacated, and the case is remanded to that Court for further proceedings consistent with this opinion.

MR. JUSTICE POWELL, concurring.

* * *

The Court's specific holding is that 42 U.S.C. §1985(3) may not be invoked to redress violations of Title VII. The broader issue argued to us in this case was whether this Civil War era remedial statute, providing no substantive rights itself, was intended to provide a remedy generally for the violation of subsequently created statutory rights. For essentially the reasons suggested by Mr. Justice Stevens, I would hold that §1985(3) should not be so construed, and that its reach is limited to conspiracies to violate those fundamental rights derived from the Constitution.

* * *

MR. JUSTICE STEVENS, concurring.

* * *

Sections 1983 and 1985(3) of Title 42 of the United States Code are the surviving direct descendants of §§1 and 2 of the Civil Rights Act of 1871. Neither of these sections created any substantive rights. Earlier this Term we squarely held that §1983 merely provides a remedy for certain violations of certain federal rights,[1] and today the Court unequivocally holds that §1985(3) "provides no substantive rights itself; it merely provides a remedy for violation of the rights it designates."

* * * The import of the language [of §§1983 and 1985(3)] as well as the relevant legislative history, suggests that the Congress which enacted both provisions was concerned with providing federal remedies for deprivations of rights protected by the Constitution and, in particular, the newly ratified Fourteenth Amendment. If a

---

[1]"Standing alone, § 1983 clearly provides no protection for civil rights since, as we have just concluded, § 1983 does not provide any substantive rights at all." *Chapman v. Houston Welfare Rights Org.,* 441 U.S. 600, 618, 99 S.Ct. 1905, 1916, 60 L.Ed.2d 508.

violation was effected "under color of any law, statute, ordinance, regulation, custom, or usage of any State," §1983 afforded redress; if a violation was caused by private persons who "conspire or go in disguise on the highway," §1985(3) afforded redress. Thus, the former authorized a remedy for state action depriving an individual of his constitutional rights, the latter for private action.

Some privileges and immunities of citizenship, such as the right to engage in interstate travel and the right to be free of the badges of slavery, are protected by the Constitution against interference by private action, as well as impairment by state action. Private conspiracies to deprive individuals of these rights are, as this Court held in *Griffin v. Breckenridge*, actionable under §1985(3) without regard to any state involvement.

Other privileges and immunities of citizenship such as the right to due process of law and the right to the equal protection of the laws are protected by the Constitution only against state action. * * * [I]f private persons take conspiratorial action that prevents or hinders the constituted authorities of any State from giving or securing equal treatment, the private persons would cause those authorities to violate the Fourteenth Amendment; the private persons would then have violated §1985(3).

If, however, private persons engage in purely private acts of discrimination * * * they do not violate the Equal Protection Clause of the Fourteenth Amendment. The rights secured by the Equal Protection and Due Process Clauses of the Fourteenth Amendment are rights to protection against unequal or unfair treatment by the State, not by private parties. Thus, while §1985(3) does not require that a defendant act under color of state law, there still can be no claim for relief based on a violation of the Fourteenth Amendment if there has been no involvement by the State. The requirement of state action, in this context, is no more than a requirement that there be a constitutional violation.

Here, there is no claim of such a violation. Private discrimination on the basis of sex is not prohibited by the Constitution. The right to be free of sex discrimination by other private parties is a statutory right that was created almost a century after §1985(3) was enacted. Because I do not believe that statute was intended to provide a remedy for the violation of statutory rights — let alone rights created by statutes that had not yet been enacted — I agree with the Court's conclusion that it does not provide respondent with redress for injuries caused by private conspiracies to discriminate on the basis of sex.

With this additional explanation of my views, I join the Court's opinion.

MR. JUSTICE WHITE, with whom MR. JUSTICE BRENNAN and MR. JUSTICE MARSHALL join, dissenting.

* * *

I

* * *

* * * [T]he majority holds that the claim under §1985(3) must be dismissed because "deprivation of a right created by Title VII cannot be the basis for a cause of action under §1985(3)."

Unfortunately, the majority does not explain whether the "right created by Title VII" to which it refers is the right guaranteed to women employees under §703(a) or the right guaranteed to respondent under §704(a). Although in stating its view of the issue before the Court, the majority intimates that it is relying on the fact that respondent has a claim directly under §704(a), the reasoning of the majority opinion in no way indicates why the existence of a §704(a) claim should prevent respondent from seeking to vindicate under §1985(3) the entirely separate right provided by §703(a).

Clearly, respondent's right under §704(a) — to be free from retaliation for efforts to aid others asserting Title VII rights — is distinct from the Title VII right implicated in his claim under §1985(3), which is the right of women employees not to be discriminated against on the basis of their sex. Moreover, that respondent in this case is in a position to assert claims under both §1985(3) and §704(a) is due solely to the peculiar facts of this case, rather than to any necessary relationship between the two provisions. First, it is of course possible that a person could be injured in the course of a conspiracy to deny §703(a) rights — as respondent claims under his §1985(3) cause of action — by some means other than retaliatory discrimination prohibited under §704(a). Second, §704(a) itself protects only employees and applicants for employment; others, such as customers or suppliers, retaliated against in the course of a conspiracy to violate §703(a) are not expressly protected under any provision of Title VII. Indeed, if respondent in this case had been only a director, rather than both a director and an employee, of the Great American Federal Savings and Loan Association, he apparently would not be able to assert a claim under §704(a).

Because the existence of a §704(a) claim is due entirely to the peculiar facts of this case, I interpret the majority's broad holding that "deprivation of a right created by Title VII cannot be the basis for a cause of action under §1985(3)" to preclude respondent from suing under §1985(3) not because he coincidentally has a §704(a) claim, but because the purpose of conspiracy alleging resulting in injury to him was to deny §703(a) rights.

II

The pervasive and essential flaw in the majority's approach to reconciliation of §1985(3) and Title VII proceeds from its characterization of the former statute as solely a "remedial" provision. It is true that the words "equal privileges and immunities under the laws" in §1985(3) refer to substantive rights created or guaranteed by other federal law, be it the Constitution or federal statutes other than §1985(3);[5] and in this case it is a conspiracy to deny a substantive right created in

---

[5]The majority opinion does not reach the issue whether §1985(3) encompasses federal statutory rights other than those proceeding in "fundamental" fashion from the Constitution itself. I am not certain in what manner the Court conceives of sex discrimination by private parties to proceed from explicit constitutional guarantees. In any event, I need not pursue this issue because I think it clear that §1985(3) encompasses all rights guaranteed in federal statutes as well as rights guaranteed directly by the Constitution. As originally introduced, §2 of the Civil Rights Act of 1871, encompassed "rights, privileges, or immunities * * * under the Constitution and laws of the United States." The substitution of the terms "the equal protection of the laws" and "equal privileges and immunities under the laws," did not limit the scope of the rights protected but added a requirement of certain "class-based, invidiously discriminatory animus behind the conspirators' action." We have repeatedly held that 18 U.S.C. §241 (derived from §6 of the Civil Rights Act of 1870, 16 Stat. 141), which is the "closest remaining criminal analogue

§703(a) of Title VII[6] that is part of the basis for respondent's suit under §1985(3). However, §1985(3), unlike a remedial statute such as §1983, does not merely provide a cause of action for persons deprived of rights elsewhere guaranteed. Because §1985(3) provides a remedy for any person injured as a result of deprivation of a substantive federal right, it must be seen as itself creating rights in persons other than those to whom the underlying federal right extends.

In this case, for instance, respondent is seeking to redress an injury inflicted upon him, which injury is distinct and separate from the injury inflicted upon the female employees whose §703(a) rights were allegedly denied. * * *

In this circumstance — where the §1985(3) plaintiff is seeking redress for injury caused as a result of the denial of other persons' Title VII rights — it makes no sense to hold that the remedies provided in Title VII are exclusive, for such a §1985(3) plaintiff has no Title VII remedy. It thus can hardly be asserted that allowing this §1985(3) plaintiff to seek redress of his injury would allow such individual to "completely bypass" the administrative and other "detailed and specific" enforcement mechanisms provided in Title VII.

In enacting §1985(3), Congress specifically contemplated that persons injured by private conspiracies to deny the federal rights of others could redress their injuries, quite apart from any redress by those who are the object of the conspiracy. * * *

I I I

I am also convinced that persons whose own Title VII rights have allegedly been violated retain the separate right to seek redress under §1985(3). In seeking to accommodate the civil rights statutes enacted in the decade after the Civil War and the civil rights statutes of the recent era, the Court has recognized that the later statutes cannot be said to have impliedly repealed the earlier unless there is an irreconcilable conflict between them. Of course, the mere fact of overlap in modes of redressing discrimination does not constitute such irreconcilable conflict. * * *

It is clear that such overlap as may exist between Title VII and §1985(3) occurs only because the latter is directed at a discrete and particularly disfavored form of discrimination, and examination of §1985(3) shows that it constitutes a compatible and important supplement to the more general prohibition and remedy provided in Title VII. Thus, while it may be that in many cases persons seeking redress under §1985(3) also have a claim directly under Title VII,[10] this is not sufficient reason to deprive those persons of the right to sue for the compensatory and punitive damages to which they are entitled under the post-Civil War statute.

---

to §1985[c]," *Griffin v. Breckenridge*, encompasses all federal statutory rights. Similarly, we have stated that 42 U.S.C. §1983, derived from §1 of the 1871 Civil Rights Act, encompasses federal statutory as well as constitutional rights.

[6]Although *Griffin v. Breckenridge* did not reach the issue whether discrimination on a basis other than race may be vindicated under §1985(3), the Court correctly assumes that the answer to this question is yes. The statute broadly refers to all privileges and immunities, without any limitation as to the class of persons to whom these rights may be granted. It is clear that sex discrimination may be sufficiently invidious to come within the prohibition of §1985(3).

[10]It is, of course, theoretically possible that an individual could be injured by a conspiracy to violate his Title VII rights even though that conspiracy was never brought to fruition and thus there was no violation of Title VII itself.

As previously indicated, the majority's willingness to infer a silent repeal of §1985(3) is based on its view that the provision only gives a remedy to redress deprivations prohibited by other federal law. But this narrow view of §1985(3) is incorrect even as to §1985(3) plaintiffs themselves denied Title VII rights. Because only conspiracies to deprive persons of federal rights are subject to redress under §1985(3), that statute * * * is itself a prohibition, separate and apart from the prohibitions stated in the underlying provisions of federal law. Moreover, only those deprivations imbued with "invidiously discriminatory motivation" amounting to "class-based * * * animus," are encompassed by §1985(3). Viewed in this manner, the right guaranteed by §1985(3) is the right not to be subjected to an invidious conspiracy to deny other federal rights. This discrete category of deprivations to which §1985(3) is directed stands in sharp contrast to the broad prohibition on discrimination provided in §703(a) of Title VII. If, as the majority suggests, it would not recognize an implied repeal of an earlier statute granting a separate but overlapping right, then it should not do so in this case; for respondent has alleged a violation of §703(a) in a manner independently prohibited by §1985(3), and under the majority's approach should be allowed to redress both deprivations.

* * *

Because respondent exhausted his administrative remedies under Title VII, there is no need in this case to reach the question whether persons whose Title VII rights have been violated may bring suit directly in federal court alleging an invidious conspiracy to deny those Title VII rights. I note, however, that the majority's desire not to undercut the administrative enforcement scheme, including the encouragement of voluntary conciliation, provided by Title VII would be completely fulfilled by insisting that §1985(3) plaintiffs exhaust whatever Title VII remedies they may have. The concerns expressed in the majority opinion do not provide a basis for precluding redress altogether under §1985(3).

NOTES AND PROBLEMS FOR DISCUSSION

1. Should the holding in *Novotny* be extended to cases where the plaintiff alleges a conspiracy to deprive her or someone else of a right guaranteed by some federal statute other than Title VII? While Justices Powell and Stevens would restrict §1985(3) to claimed deprivations of constitutional rights, and Justices White, Brennan and Marshall would not, the four other members of the majority did not address this issue. One year after its decision in *Novotny*, however, in MAINE v. THIBOUTOT, 448 U.S. 1, 100 S.Ct. 2502, 65 L.Ed.2d 555 (1980), the Court interpreted the language in §1983 requiring plaintiffs to allege a deprivation of rights secured by the Constitution "and laws" to embrace claims of statutory as well as constitutional violations. Nevertheless, several lower federal courts have construed *Novotny* to mean that a §1985(3) action cannot be based on a conspiracy to deprive persons of their rights under the Age Discrimination in Employment Act, Sherlock v. Montefiore Med. Ctr., 84 F.3d 522 (2d Cir. 1996); the Equal Pay Act, Lowden v. William M. Mercer, Inc., 903 F.Supp. 212 (D. Mass. 1995); the ADA, Pappas v. Bethesda Hosp. Ass'n, 861 F.Supp. 616 (S.D. Ohio 1994); and the Rehabilitation Act, D'Amato v. Wisconsin Gas Co., 760 F.2d 1474 (7th Cir. 1985). In each of these situations, however, the courts were dealing with a statute that was enacted substantially after §1985(3) and that provided for administrative review of discrimination claims prior to the institution of suit.

(a) What if a §1985(3) complaint alleged a private conspiracy to deprive persons of their rights under a statute — such as §1981 — that was enacted before §1985(3) and that did not require pre-suit exhaustion of administrative remedies? See Spectronics Corp. v. TCI/TKR of Jefferson County, Inc., 17 F.Supp.2d 669 (W.D.Ky.1998) (§1981 is a proper substantive basis for §1985(3) claim since Congress' purpose in enacting the 1871 Act was to enforce the provisions of the pre-existing 1866 Act).

(b) What about an alleged deprivation of a state statutory right? See Life Insurance Co. of North America v. Reichardt, 591 F.2d 499 (9th Cir. 1979).

2. Paul Jones, an African-American male, received a notice from his foreman that because of excessive lateness the foreman was recommending to the plant manager that Jones be discharged. After unsuccessfully requesting his union representative to intervene on his behalf, Jones spoke personally with the plant manager and convinced the manager to reject the foreman's recommendation in light of the company's lenient policy with respect to lateness. Jones subsequently brought a §1985(3) action in federal court against the foreman and union representative charging that they conspired to deprive him of his rights under Title VII by strictly applying the tardiness rule to him because of his race. Jones' complaint alleged that no white employee had been fired because of excessive lateness. How should the court rule on the defendant's motion to dismiss for failure to state a cause of action? Note that in footnote six of *Novotny*, the Court explained that it was not ruling on whether a claim would lie under §1985(3) where the defendant was not subject to suit under Title VII.

The other context in which an individual might allege that he was the victim of a conspiracy, but could not allege a violation of the underlying substantive right, was addressed in Justice White's dissenting opinion — i.e., when the plaintiff is injured as the result of a conspiracy to violate the rights of others. Do you agree with Justice White's conclusion that Congress intended to protect advocates of the victimized class who otherwise would be left remediless?

3. In his concurring opinion in *Novotny*, Justice Powell cited the passage in *Griffin* where a unanimous Court declared that a claim brought under §1985(3) must allege "some racial, or perhaps otherwise class-based, invidiously discriminatory animus behind the conspirators' action." The majority in *Novotny* did not have to decide whether that language could be interpreted to permit a §1985(3) claim challenging discrimination on the basis of a non-racial classification.

In UNITED BROTHERHOOD OF CARPENTERS AND JOINERS OF AMERICA, LOCAL 610 v. SCOTT, 463 U.S. 825, 103 S.Ct. 3352, 77 L.Ed.2d 1049 (1983), two non-union employees were beaten by local residents during a citizen protest against an employer's policy of hiring workers without regard to union membership. The company and these two employees brought suit under §1985(3) against several local unions, a local trades council and various individuals, alleging that these defendants conspired to deprive the plaintiffs of their First Amendment right to associate with their fellow non-union employees. In a 5-4 decision, the majority examined the legislative history of §1985(3) and concluded that as the predominant purpose of the statute was to combat the then prevalent animus against black individuals and their supporters, it could not be construed to protect every political group from any injury perpetrated by a rival organization. While the majority did not hold that all political groups were excluded from the coverage of §1985(3), it ruled that this provision did not reach conspiracies motivated by economic or commercial, as opposed to racial animus. This limited ruling did not address the issue of whether §1985(3) prohibits conspiracies aimed at non-racial groups that are motivated by other than economic animus. The four dissenters, on the other hand, construed §1985(3) to include conspiracies to hinder any group or class of persons in the exercise of their legal rights because of an invidious animus towards members of that class.

The lower federal courts have not taken a consistent position as to the applicability of §1985(3) to all non-racial classes. They have held that §1985(3) does extend to conspiracies to discriminate on the basis of sex, Padway v. Palches, 665 F.2d 965 (9th Cir. 1982); religion, Ward v. Connor, 657 F.2d 45 (4th Cir. 1981), cert. denied, 455 U.S. 907, 102 S.Ct. 1253, 71 L.Ed.2d 445 (1982); national origin, Marlowe v. Fisher Body, 489 F.2d 1057 (6th Cir. 1973); and age, Pavlo v. Stiefel Laboratories, Inc., 22 FEP Cases 489 (S.D.N.Y. 1979). But they have not extended its application to conspiracies to discriminate on the basis of disability, Wilhelm v. Continental Title Co., 720 F.2d 1173 (10th Cir. 1983), cert. denied, 465 U.S. 1103 104 S.Ct. 1601 80 L.E.2d 131 (1984); whistleblowing, Hicks v. Resolution Trust Corp., 970 F.2d 378 (7th Cir. 1992); or sexual orientation, DeSantis v. Pacific Tel. & Tel. Co., Inc., 608 F.2d 327 (9th Cir. 1979).

In an abortion-related controversy, the Supreme Court chose not to take advantage of the opportunity to confront the general question of whether §1985(3) applies to non-race based conspiracies. BRAY v. ALEXANDRIA WOMEN'S HEALTH CLINIC, 506 U.S. 263, 113 S.Ct. 753, 122 L.Ed.2d 34 (1993), was brought by abortion clinics and supporters of legalized abortions against Operation Rescue to enjoin the latter group from continuing its policy of obstructing access to abortion clinics. By a 5-4 vote, the Court concluded that the plaintiffs had established neither the existence of a class-based animus nor any intentional deprivation of protected rights. With respect to the first of these two issues, i.e., the extent, if any, to which non-racial classes are protected by §1985(3), the Court held that opposition to abortion did not qualify alongside race as a class-based discriminatory animus proscribed by the statute. The majority stated that even if the meaning of "class" for §1985(3) purposes extended beyond racial groups, (an issue it expressly did not decide) it did not apply to the subclass of "women seeking abortion." Moreover, the Court also rejected the plaintiffs' contention that the defendant's conduct was directed at the broader class of women in general. Without ruling on whether a sex-based conspiracy would fit within the proscription of §1985(3), the majority offered two reasons why opposition to abortion did not reflect an animus towards the class of women in general. First, it pointed to the absence of any direct evidence that these defendants' demonstrations were motivated by any purpose directed specifically at women. Additionally, the majority was unwilling to presume that the defendants' conduct was intended to disfavor that gender class. It admitted that some activities are such an "irrational object of disfavor" that conduct targeting them can be presumed to arise from an intent to disfavor the class that is the exclusive or predominant participant in such activities. But, the majority quickly added, since there were several "common and respectable" reasons for opposing abortion aside from hatred of or condescension towards women, opposition to abortion did not fall into this category of activities. The Court also rejected the plaintiffs' contention that intention was irrelevant and that a class-based animus could be established by proof of effect; discriminatory purpose implies more than volition or awareness of consequences.

With respect to the absence of any intentional deprivation of a protected right, the Court found that the plaintiffs had failed to prove that the predominant purpose of the alleged conspiracy was to impede or prevent the exercise of the right of interstate travel or to oppress individuals who exercised that right. Once again, the majority reasoned that conduct that produces an effect upon a protected right couldn't be presumed to have been undertaken for the purpose of impairing that right; the impairment must be "a conscious objective of the enterprise." Accordingly, it concluded, the plaintiff needed to prove that the defendant acted because of, and not merely with an awareness of, the adverse effects of its conduct upon a protected group. In the instant case, the Court found, the defendants obstructed access to the clinics because of their opposition to abortion regardless of whether the abortion was performed after interstate travel.

In his dissent, Justice Stevens rejected the majority's limited "irrational object of disfavor" exception and insisted that it was sufficient that the conspiracy be aimed at conduct that only members of a protected class have the capacity to perform. In such a case, he stated, the conspiracy could be presumed to be motivated "at least in part" by its adverse effect upon women. He also criticized the Court's refusal to base a finding of group animus on impact evidence, stating that restrictions imposed on constitutional claims were inapposite to a statutory cause of action. Finally, while the majority declined to rule on the issue, three dissenters expressly stated that women were a protected class under §1985(3).

4. Although the circuit court in *Novotny* ruled that agents of a single corporation could form a conspiracy within the meaning of §1985(3), the Supreme Court reserved decision on this question as well as on whether a conspiracy could occur between the corporation and its agents. Where the employees are found to have acted in the scope of their employment, rather than in pursuit of their personal interests, most courts have refused to recognize intracorporate conspiracies. The majority of courts reason that because a corporation acts through its officers, directors and employees, action taken by a corporation and its agents within the scope of their employ constitutes conduct by only a single entity. Thus, these courts conclude, the statutory requirement of a conspiracy between "two or more persons" is not satisfied — i.e., an entity cannot conspire with itself. *See e.g.*, Herrmann v. Moore, 576 F.2d 453 (2d Cir.), cert. denied, 439 U.S. 1003, 99 S.Ct. 613, 58 L.Ed.2d 679 (1978). On the other hand, where the employees are named as individual defendants, some courts have recognized the existence of an intracorporate conspiracy where the individual employees are found to have acted in concert either (1) outside the scope of their employment and discriminated for personal reasons, Garza v. City of Omaha, 814 F.2d 553 (8th Cir.1987), (2) within the scope of their supervisory authority but in ways which did not further the company's legitimate business concerns, Volk v. Coler, 845 F.2d 1422 (7th Cir.1988), or (3) in connection with multiple acts of discrimination, An-Ti Chai v. Michigan Technological University, 493 F. Supp. 1137 (W.D.Mich.1980).

A union is treated as a single entity for these purposes. Ironically, therefore, where eleven union members joined to subject a supervisor to verbal abuse, the court's determination that this racially-motivated conduct had been discussed and planned at a union meeting and had been executed on behalf of the union immunized the individuals as well as the union from liability under §1985(3). Nieto v. United Auto Workers Local #598, 672 F.Supp. 987 (E.D.Mich.1987). For further discussion of intracorporate conspiracies see Note, *Intracorporate Conspiracies Under 42 U.S.C. §1985(3)*, 13 GA.L.REV. 591 (1979).

5. Must a §1985(3) plaintiff prove discriminatory intent as part of its prima facie case? See Taylor v. St. Louis, 702 F.2d 695 (8th Cir. 1983).

SECTION D. THE APPLICABLE STATUTES OF LIMITATION

Unlike Title VII, the Reconstruction Era Civil Rights Acts discussed in this Chapter do not contain their own statutes of limitation and there is no general, "catch all" federal limitation period. 42 U.S.C. §1988 provides, however, that if in a civil rights case federal law is "deficient," the court should apply the law "of the State wherein the court having jurisdiction of such [claim] is held, so far as the same is not inconsistent with the Constitution and laws of the United States * * *." It is settled that federal courts will look to state law to determine the statutes of limitations for suits filed pursuant to §§1981, 1983, and 1985. *See* Bd. of Regents v. Tomanio, 446 U.S. 478, 100 S.Ct. 1790, 64 L.Ed.2d 440 (1980); Johnson v. Ry. Express Agency, Inc., 421 U.S. 454 95 S.Ct. 1716 44 L.Ed.2d 295 (1975). States typically have different limitation periods for different causes of action (contract, tort, land matters, etc.) and a residual or "catch-all" period for claims not fitting into one of the established causes of action. Because more than one such limitation period could arguably apply to civil rights actions, the decision of which period to adopt has not been without difficulty.

In WILSON v. GARCIA, 471 U.S. 261, 105 S.Ct. 1938, 85 L.Ed.2d 254 (1985), the Court resolved matters, at least for §1983 cases, by adopting a bright-line approach to the problem. The Court held that all §1983 actions should be treated as claims for violation of personal rights and that the state statute governing tort actions for the recovery of damages for personal injuries provided the appropriate limitation period. "[T]his choice," the Court explained, "is supported by the nature of the 1983 remedy, and by the federal interest in insuring that the borrowed period of limitations not discriminate against the federal civil rights remedy." *Wilson* was a police brutality damage action, but the court made clear that its ruling applied to all §1983 actions, including employment discrimination claims, since allowing courts to choose the applicable limitation period based on the facts of each case would lead to "uncertainty and time-consuming litigation that is foreign to the central purpose of §1983." The Court expressly rejected the possibility that states' residuary statutes of limitations be applied in §1983 actions. "The relative scarcity of statutory claims when §1983 was enacted makes it unlikely that Congress would have intended to apply the catchall periods of limitations for statutory claims that were later enacted by many States."

But the ruling in *Wilson* did not end all confusion over the matter, because a number of states provide more than one limitations period for personal injury claims. Some, for example, distinguish between intentional and non-intentional torts. In OWENS v. OKURE, 488 U.S. 235, 109 S.Ct. 573, 102 L.Ed.2d 594 (1989), the Court held that in states having more than one statute of limitation for personal injury actions, courts considering §1983 claims should borrow the general or residual statute for personal injury actions.

In GOODMAN v. LUKENS STEEL CO., 482 U.S. 656, 107 S.Ct. 2617, 96 L.Ed.2d 572 (1987), the Court extended *Wilson* to §1981 cases. The Court noted that although §1981 expressly referred to *contractual* rights, it also referred to such personal rights as the rights to sue, to testify, and to equal rights under the laws. Moreover, the Court added, the statute was part of a federal law barring racial discrimination which, it reasoned, constituted a fundamental injury to a person's individual rights. Consequently, a majority of the Court concluded, Wilson's characterization of §1983 claims was equally applicable to actions brought under §1981.

In 1990, Congress passed a four-year residual statute of limitations for all federal laws enacted after December 1, 1990 — 28 U.S.C. §1658. The circuits were divided over whether the residual statute was applicable to claims filed under §1981, since this statute originally was enacted in 1866, but was substantively amended in 1991. The Supreme Court resolved the conflict in JONES v. R.R. DONNELLEY & SONS CO., 541 U.S. 369, 124 S.Ct. 1836, 158 L.Ed.2d 645 (2004). In *Jones*, the plaintiffs had filed a class action seeking relief under §1981 for a racially hostile work environment, discriminatory job assignments, refusal to transfer, and wrongful termination because of race. The hostile work environment, refusal to transfer, and wrongful termination claims would not have been cognizable under §1981 under the Supreme Court's 1989 decision in *Patterson* (see discussion in Chapter 8, Section A, *supra*), which construed the right "to make and enforce contracts" set forth in §1981 as inapposite to discriminatory conduct occurring after the formation of an employment relationship. But in the Civil Rights Act of 1991, Congress had legislatively overruled *Patterson* by adding a new section to §1981 which provided that the right to make and enforce contracts included "termination of contracts and the enjoyment of all benefits, privileges, terms, and conditions of the contractual relationship." 42 U.S.C. §1981(b). So the plaintiffs' claims in *Jones* were thus viable solely because of the 1991 revisions to §1981. The defendant had sought summary judgment in *Jones* on the ground that the complaint was filed outside of the applicable Illinois two-year limitation period. The plaintiffs had maintained that they were entitled to the four-year limitation period provided by §1658. Thus, whether or not the plaintiffs could take advantage of the four year limitations period provided in §1658 turned completely on whether their claims "arose under" the 1991 Act or under §1981 as originally enacted in 1866. The court of appeals concluded that §1658 "applies only when an act of Congress creates a wholly new cause of action, one that does not depend on the continued existence of a statutory cause of action previously enacted and kept in force by the amendment." Consequently, it ruled that the state limitations period, and not §1658 applied, and therefore directed the trial court to dismiss the case.

The Supreme Court granted review and, in a unanimous opinion, reversed. The Court considered the language of the statute, and its relation to the use of similar "arising under" terminology in other statutes, to be ambiguous and thus not dispositive. But, it concluded, the legislative history of §1658 indicated a congressional intention for the residual limitation period to apply to more, rather than to fewer, of the federal statutes for which state limitation periods were borrowed.

We conclude that a cause of action "arises under an Act of Congress enacted" after December 1, 1990 — and therefore is governed by §1658's 4-year statute of limitations — if the plaintiff's claim against the defendant was made possible by a post-1990 enactment. That construction best serves Congress' interest in alleviating the uncertainty inherent in the practice of borrowing state statutes of limitations while at the same time protecting settled interests. It spares federal judges and litigants the need to identify the approximate state statute of limitations to apply to new claims but leaves in place the "borrowed" limitations periods for existing causes of action, with respect to which the difficult work already has been done.

541 U.S. at 382   Because relief was possible on the plaintiffs' claims solely by virtue of the amendment to §1981 contained in the 1991 Civil Rights Act, the Court ruled that the plaintiffs were entitled to the 4-year limitation period. *Donnelly* means that §1981 claims that continued to be viable after *Patterson*, but prior to the enactment of the 1991 Civil Rights Act, such as a refusal to hire case, will continue to be governed by the applicable state limitation period as determined under *Wilson*. But post-formation claims of intentional race-based discrimination will be subject to the four year limitations period. *See, e.g.*, Johnson v. Crown Enterprises, Inc., 398 F.3d 339 (5th Cir. 2005).

Recall that all but one federal circuit have ruled that in passing the 1991 Act, which extended the application of §1981 to state employers, Congress did *not* intend to overrule the Supreme Court's ruling in Jett v. Dallas Independent School Dist., 491 U.S. 701, 109 S.Ct. 2702, 105 L.Ed.2d 598 (1989) that §1981 did not provide an independent cause of action for damages against public units, and that the damages action created by §1983 was the exclusive federal damages remedy for violations of the terms of §1981 by state governmental units. See Note 6 following *Bobo, supra*. In BAKER v. BIRMINGHAM BOARD OF EDUC., 531 F.3d 1336 (11th Cir. 2008), the first circuit court to rule on the issue held that the Supreme Court's ruling in *Jones* mandated that where a state employee brings a §1981-based claim under §1983, and that claim is of the type that was made viable by the 1991 Civil Rights Act, then it is §1658, and not the state torts limitations statute that otherwise would apply to §1983 claims, that governs.

In Delaware State College v. Ricks, discussed, *supra*, in Chapter 4, the Supreme Court held that the question of when the applicable statute of limitations accrues or begins to run in a suit under the federal civil rights statutes is a matter of federal law. The question of what "tolls" or stops the running of the limitation period is, however, controlled by state law. In BOARD OF REGENTS v. TOMANIO, 446 U.S. 478, 100 S.Ct. 1790, 64 L.Ed.2d 440 (1980), the Court held that when a federal court borrows a state statute of limitations it must also use the state's tolling rules as well, unless to do so would conflict with the federal policies of compensation and deterrence underlying the civil rights acts. State law also controls the effect of tolling, i.e., the amount of time remaining in the period to file suit after the event that tolls the limitation period is over. In CHARDON v. FUMERO SOTO, 462 U.S. 650, 103 S.Ct. 2611, 77 L.Ed.2d 74 (1983), the Court held that Puerto Rican law under which the limitation period starts running anew once tolling has occurred was not inconsistent with the policies behind §1983.

The application of a state tolling doctrine was demonstrated by the Ninth Circuit in DONOGHUE v. COUNTY OF ORANGE, 848 F.2d 926 (9th Cir. 1987). There, the district court dismissed the plaintiff's §§1983, 1985, 1986, and state pendent claims as time barred under the applicable California statute of limitations. Because a timely EEOC charge had been filed, the Title VII cause of action was allowed to proceed to trial. The Court of Appeal reversed and remanded for a determination by the trial court of whether the filing of the EEOC charge tolled the prescriptive period for the other claims under the state's equitable tolling doctrine. The court reasoned that under California law, if the defendant received timely notice of the original claim, was not prejudiced by the delay and the plaintiff acted in good faith, the "[tolling] doctrine suspends the statute of limitations pending exhaustion of administrative remedies, even though no statute makes exhaustion a condition of the right to sue."

SECTION E.   THE ROLE OF RES JUDICATA AND COLLATERAL ESTOPPEL

28 U.S.C. §1738, which requires federal courts to give the same preclusive effect to state court judgments that such judgments would be given in the courts of the state, applies in cases under the Reconstruction Era civil rights statutes as well as in Title VII suits. See Chapter 4, Section A.2, *supra*. Thus, under the doctrine of issue preclusion (also known as collateral estoppel), a factual issue that has been actually litigated in a prior proceeding normally will bar relitigation of the same issue in a subsequent case. Under the doctrine of claim preclusion (also known as *res judicata*), prior litigation may bar litigation of a claim which could have been, but was not, raised in the first proceeding. Whether the second action will be precluded depends on whether it would have been barred had it been filed in state court. *See* Migra v. Warren City Sch. Dist., 465 U.S. 75, 104 S.Ct. 892, 79 L.Ed.2d 56 (1984).

In UNIVERSITY OF TENNESSEE v. ELLIOTT, 478 U.S. 788, 106 S.Ct. 3220, 92 L.Ed.2d 635 (1986), an employment discrimination case filed under Title VII and §1983, the plaintiff contested his discharge before a state administrative law judge prior to filing his federal statutory action. The courts of Tennessee would have given preclusive effect to the administrative ruling even though it was not reviewed by a state court. The Supreme Court concluded that the Title VII claim should be treated differently for preclusion purposes from the §1983 claim. It declared that Congress did not intend for *unreviewed* state *administrative* decisions to have preclusive effect on Title VII claims regardless of the nature of the state procedures or state law. But with respect to the §1983 claim, the Court could "see no reason to suppose that Congress, in enacting the Reconstruction civil rights statutes, wished to foreclose the adaptation of traditional principles of preclusion to such subsequent developments as the burgeoning use of administrative adjudication in the 20th century." Accordingly, the Court held that when a state agency acting in a judicial capacity resolves disputed issues of fact which the parties had an adequate opportunity to litigate, federal courts in suits filed under the Reconstruction Era civil rights statutes must give the agency's fact finding the same preclusive effect to which it would be entitled in the courts of the state.

Under *Elliott*, a state administrative adjudication has preclusive effect in a §1981 or §1983 action *only* if there was "an adequate opportunity to litigate" the claim. In *Elliott*, the plaintiff did not seek judicial review of the administrative ruling, although such review was allowed under state law. Is the availability of judicial review necessary to an "adequate opportunity to litigate"? In WEHRLI v. COUNTY OF ORANGE, 175 F.3d 692 (9th Cir. 1999), cert. denied, 528 U.S. 1004, 120 S.Ct. 498, 145 L.Ed.2d 384 (1999), a court marshal contested his discharge through an administrative process which the parties agreed would be final and binding and in which they explicitly agreed to relinquish all current or future claims to seek or obtain relief in any court. After a hearing, the administrative judge reinstated the marshal but denied any back pay or damages. The plaintiff thereafter filed a §1983 suit seeking damages for his discharge. Citing *Elliott*, the district court granted summary judgment to the county on the ground that the plaintiff was precluded from filing suit by the administrative ruling. The Ninth Circuit held, however, that without an opportunity for judicial review there could be no "adequate opportunity to litigate." It concluded that "a full and fair opportunity to litigate includes the possibility of a chain of appellate review."

SECTION F. REMEDIES

1. DAMAGES

Prior to the passage of the 1991 Civil Rights Act, monetary damages, compensatory or punitive, were not available under Title VII. Plaintiffs who claimed racial discrimination against private employers, any equal protection claim against a public employer, or conspiracy to deprive one of civil rights, had available causes of action under 42 U.S.C. §§1981, 1983, and 1985, each of which allowed for the recovery of compensatory and punitive damages. Where possible, plaintiffs often combined Title VII claims with claims under one of the Reconstruction Era statutes to take advantage of these additional remedies and the opportunity for a jury trial. The 1991 amendments to Title VII eliminated the major distinction between remedies available under Title VII and the earlier statutes with respect to claims of intentional discrimination. Nevertheless, important incentive remained for plaintiffs who could invoke §§1981, 1983, and 1985. Damages under Title VII are subject to statutory limits, the amounts of which depend on the size of the employer, while no such limits attach to recoveries under the Reconstruction Era statutes. The Constitution and federal common law, however, place certain restrictions on the recovery of damages from states and local governments.

The Eleventh Amendment to the Constitution provides in part that "[t]he judicial power of the United States shall not be construed to extend to any suit in law or equity, commenced or prosecuted against one of the United States by Citizens of another State." That language has been construed to bar an award of monetary relief against a state or state agency. Edelman v. Jordan, 415 U.S. 651, 94 S.Ct. 1347, 39 L.Ed.2d 662 (1974). Thus, an award of back pay or damages against a state under §1983 is precluded by the Eleventh Amendment. Quern v. Jordan, 440 U.S. 332, 99 S.Ct. 1139, 59 L.Ed.2d 358 (1979). By contrast, back pay awards and damages against a state under Title VII are not barred by the Eleventh Amendment because Congress exercised its power under the Fourteenth Amendment to abrogate Eleventh Amendment immunity. *See* Varner v. Ill. State Univ., 226 F.3d 927(7th Cir. 2000), cert. denied, 533 U.S. 902, 121 S.Ct. 2241, 150 L.Ed.2d 230 (2001) (Congress properly abrogated states' sovereign immunity with respect to back pay and attorney fees in Title VII actions pursuant to §5 of the Fourteenth Amendment).

The Eleventh Amendment does not apply to suits against political subdivisions of a state such as cities, counties, school districts, and like entities. Moor v. County of Alameda, 411 U.S. 693, 93 S.Ct. 1785, 36 L.Ed.2d 596 (1973). Thus, in employment discrimination actions filed under §1983 against such public employers other than the state, back pay and damages are available to the same extent as in §1981 actions against private employers. Whether a particular public entity is an agency of the state for Eleventh Amendment purposes is a fact question, the answer to which will depend on the significance of state funding for the agency. *See, e.g.*, Keller v. Prince George's County, 923 F.2d 30 (4th Cir. 1991) (the Eleventh Amendment bars suit under §1983 against a county department of social services in view of the fact that the county department was operated by the state department of human resources, that employees were paid by the state, that department operated pursuant to state personnel policies, and only 2% of the department's funding came from the county).

Unlike Title VII actions, which can be filed only against statutory employers, not individual wrongdoers, §1983 actions may be brought against individual public officials who have acted "under color of state law." The Eleventh Amendment does not immunize public officials from personal liability for their illegal acts, though they may benefit from other types of official immunity. *See* Scheuer v. Rhodes, 416 U.S. 232, 94 S.Ct. 1683, 40 L.Ed.2d 90 (1974) (executive immunity); Tenney v. Brandhove, 341 U.S. 367, 71 S.Ct. 783, 95 L.Ed. 1019 (1951). Public officials generally enjoy qualified immunity for "good faith" actions. Wood v. Strickland, 420 U.S. 308, 95 S.Ct. 992, 43 L.Ed.2d 214 (1975). *See* Nicholson v. Ga. Dep't of Human Res., 918 F.2d 145 (11th Cir. 1990) (officials not entitled to qualified immunity for intentional discrimination in connection with transfer and demotion of female employee, since law was quite clear that such conduct violated constitution and such officials either knew or should have known that their actions were unlawful). Will the fact that the state promised to indemnify a public official for damage awards against him in his individual capacity, render him immune from judgment? *See* Beardsley v. Webb, 30 F.3d 524 (4th Cir. 1994) (the fact that the defendant was insured through a state risk management plan does not bar an action against him as an individual).

Punitive damages cannot be recovered against state or local governments. The Supreme Court has held that a public employer has a common law immunity from an award of punitive damages. City of Newport v. Fact Concerts, Inc., 453 U.S. 247, 101 S.Ct. 2748, 69 L.Ed.2d 616 (1981). The damage provisions of the 1991 Civil Rights Act provide for punitive damage awards against employers "other than a government, government agency or political subdivision." A plaintiff may recover punitive damages against individual wrongdoers under §1983. *See* Cornwall v. City of Riverside, 896 F.2d 398 (9th Cir.), cert. denied, 497 U.S. 1026, 110 S.Ct. 3274, 111 L.Ed.2d 784 (1990).

2. INJUNCTIVE RELIEF

Section 1983 provides that persons who, acting under color of state law, violate the constitutional or federal statutory rights of others "shall be liable to the party injured in an action at law, suit in equity, or other proper proceeding for redress." Section 1981 contains no remedial language. But §1988 provides that where the provisions of the civil rights statutes "are not adapted to the object, or are deficient in the provisions necessary to furnish suitable remedies and punish offenses against the law, the common law, as modified and changed by the constitution and statutes of the State * * * so far as not inconsistent with the Constitution and laws of the United States, shall be extended to and govern * * * in the trial and disposition of the cause * * *." Equitable relief, therefore, is available in §1981 and §1983 actions to the same extent that it is available under Title VII. See Chapter 7, Section B, *supra*.

Suits against state entities under §1983 are, however, complicated by the Eleventh Amendment to the United States Constitution. That amendment bars federal actions at law or in equity against states. The effect of the amendment is avoided by naming as the defendant an appropriate state official rather than her agency. In EX PARTE YOUNG, 209 U.S. 123, 28 S.Ct. 441, 52 L.Ed. 714 (1908), the Supreme Court held that the illegal action of a state official is not imputed to the state for Eleventh Amendment purposes (even though it is simultaneously treated as "state action" for Fourteenth Amendment purposes). *Cf.* Pennhurst State Sch. and Hosp. v. Halderman, 465 U.S. 89, 104 S.Ct. 900, 79 L.Ed.2d 67 (1984) (the Eleventh Amendment bars even injunctive relief against state officials if based on state pendent cause of action). Thus, equitable relief is available under §1983 against states and their agencies by way of suits against the responsible state officials. By contrast, equitable relief is directly available against private employers under Title VII, §1981, and other civil rights statutes. It also is available directly against non-state public employers under Title VII and §1983.

3. ATTORNEY'S FEES AND COSTS

Section 1988 provides in part that "[i]n any action or proceeding to enforce a provision of sections 1981, 1982, 1983, 1985 * * *, the court, in its discretion, may allow the prevailing party, other than the United States, a reasonable attorney's fee as part of the costs." That language is identical to the fee-shifting provision in §706(k) of Title VII. The legislative history of §1988 makes it clear that Congress intended that "the standards for awarding fees under [the Act] should be generally the same as under the fee provisions of the 1964 Civil Rights Act." S.Rep. No. 1011, 94th Cong., 2d Sess. 4 (1976). In footnote 7 of its opinion in HENSLEY v. ECKERHART, 461 U.S. 424, 103 S.Ct. 1933, 76 L.Ed.2d 40 (1983), the Supreme Court observed that the standards for award of fees are the same in all cases where Congress has authorized such fees to the "prevailing party." Thus the law regarding entitlement to and calculation of attorney's fees under §1988 is the same as that under Title VII. This includes the heightened standard for awarding attorney fees to prevailing defendants. Hughes v. Rowe, 449 U.S. 5, 101 S.Ct. 173, 66 L.Ed.2d 163 (1980). See Chapter 7, Section C, *supra*.

One factor that formerly distinguished litigation under the Reconstruction Era civil rights statutes from cases filed under Title VII was that monetary relief, including compensatory and punitive damages, was awarded under common law tort principles. See Section F.1, *supra*. In the United States, fees for plaintiffs in personal injury tort cases are generally "contingent" fees and, by agreement of the plaintiff and her attorney, usually are calculated as a percentage of the monetary recovery. After §1988 was amended to include the fee shifting provision, the lower courts initially disagreed on the question of whether a fee award under that section should be influenced by the amount of the monetary recovery for the plaintiff. In CITY OF RIVERSIDE v. RIVERA, 477 U.S. 561, 106 S.Ct. 2686, 91 L.Ed.2d 466 (1986), the Supreme Court considered whether an award of $245,456.25 in attorney's fees pursuant to §1988 could be "reasonable" in light of the fact that a jury had awarded plaintiffs a total of $33,350 in compensatory and punitive damages. The district court made the findings that were required by *Hensley*, and determined that the plaintiffs' counsel were entitled to the full lodestar fee that they had requested. The Court of Appeals affirmed on the basis of the district court's findings. Arguing that in civil rights cases in which only monetary relief is requested, a "reasonable" fee should necessarily be proportionate to the damage award recovered, the City asked the Court to abandon the use of the lodestar method of calculation in such cases and suggested that fee awards in civil rights damage cases should be modeled upon the contingent fee arrangements commonly used in personal injury litigation.

In a plurality opinion, the Court rejected the analogy between civil rights cases seeking monetary relief and garden variety tort litigation on the ground that damage awards do not reflect fully the public benefit advanced by civil rights litigation. The Court also held that limiting attorney fees in civil rights cases to a proportion of the damages awarded would undermine the Congressional purpose behind §1988.

> A rule of proportionality would make it difficult, if not impossible, for individuals with meritorious civil rights claims but relatively small potential damages to obtain redress from the courts. This is totally inconsistent with the Congress' purpose in enacting §1988. Congress recognized that private-sector fee arrangements were inadequate to ensure sufficiently vigorous enforcement of civil rights. In order to ensure that lawyers would be willing to represent persons with legitimate civil rights grievances, Congress determined that it would be necessary to compensate lawyers for all time reasonably expended on a case.

477 U.S. at 575.

In a dissenting opinion, Justice Rehnquist argued that the awarded fees necessarily were unreasonable because "[t]he very 'reasonableness' of the hours expended on a case by a plaintiff's attorney necessarily will depend, to a large extent, on the amount that may reasonably be expected to be recovered if the plaintiff prevails." According to his dissent, a "reasonable" fee under §1988 "means a fee that would have been deemed reasonable if billed to affluent plaintiffs by their own attorneys." Should the overall "reasonableness" of a fee award under the civil rights laws be determined by the same standard applied to fees charged to "affluent" clients motivated solely by the economics of the situation? Is the plurality's or the dissenter's view of "reasonableness" most closely in accord with the purpose of the fee-shifting-statutes?

What should be the effect on a fee award under §1988 of a normal contingent fee agreement between the plaintiff and counsel? Should such an agreement put a ceiling on the fee that the defendant can be required to pay under a fee-shifting statute? That question also had divided the circuits until the Supreme Court resolved the matter in BLANCHARD v. BERGERON, 489 U.S. 87, 109 S.Ct. 939, 103 L.Ed.2d 67 (1989). There, the plaintiff in a §1983 police misconduct case had obtained a $10,000 damage award. The Fifth Circuit ruled that the successful plaintiff's attorney, who had claimed more than $40,000 in fees, was limited to a maximum award of $4,000 because his 40% contingent fee contract with the plaintiff placed a "cap" on the fee that could be shifted to the defendant. The Supreme Court disagreed, holding that the imposition of an automatic ceiling on attorney's fees because of a contingent fee contract would be inconsistent with the policy and the purpose of the fee-shifting statutes. The Court reasoned that the statute contemplated reasonable compensation in light of all the circumstances for the time and effort expended by the prevailing attorney and that, should a fee agreement provide less than a reasonable fee calculated in that manner, the defendant should nevertheless be required to pay the higher amount.

The Court also noted that

> [i]f a contingent fee agreement were to govern as a strict limitation on the award of attorney's fees, an undesirable emphasis might be placed on the importance of the recovery of damages in civil rights litigation. The intention of Congress was to encourage successful civil rights litigation, not to create a special incentive to prove damages and shortchange efforts to seek effective injunctive or declaratory relief.

489 U.S. at 95.

If a contingent fee agreement between a plaintiff and her attorney must be ignored for purposes of setting a fee award under the fee-shifting statutes, can such an agreement that would require a plaintiff to pay more than the statutory "reasonable attorney's fee" be enforced? In VENEGAS v. MITCHELL, 495 U.S. 82, 110 S.Ct. 1679, 109 L.Ed.2d 74 (1990), the plaintiff in a §1983 damage action signed a contingent fee agreement providing that the attorney would receive 40% of any recovery, offset by any fee awarded under §1988. The district court awarded the plaintiff over $2 million in damages and, on the fee application, awarded $75,000 for work done by plaintiff's counsel. The plaintiff attempted to get out of the fee contract by asserting that its enforcement would be inconsistent with the purpose of the fee-shifting statute, which is to relieve successful civil rights plaintiffs of having to pay their attorneys. Both the district court and court of appeal rejected that argument and held that §1988 does not prevent collection of a contingent fee even if it exceeds the statutory award. The Supreme Court affirmed unanimously.

> [S]ection 1988 controls what the losing defendant must pay, not what the prevailing plaintiff must pay his lawyer. What a plaintiff may be bound to pay and what an attorney is free to collect under a fee agreement are not necessarily measured by the "reasonable attorney's fee" that a defendant must pay pursuant to a court order. Section 1988 itself does not interfere with the enforceability of a contingent-fee contract.

495 U.S. at 90. The Court also reasoned that "depriving plaintiffs of the option of promising to pay more than the statutory fee would not further §1988's general

purpose of enabling such plaintiffs in civil rights cases to secure competent counsel." Does the ruling in *Venegas* turn on the fact that the fee agreement offset the statutory fee award against the contingent fee? Does the decision mean that plaintiff's counsel in an employment discrimination case can contract for a percentage of a back pay recovery as a fee and collect such a contingent fee in addition to the court awarded fee? *See* Ross v Douglas County, 244 F.3d 620 (8th Cir. 2001) (where a contingent fee contract exists along with a reimbursable attorney fee award, claimant's counsel is not entitled to receive both fees, but is limited to the higher of the award under the fee-shifting statute or the fee under the contract; if the contingent fee exceeds the court-awarded fee counsel may collect the difference from the claimant).

CHAPTER 9

The Equal Pay Act

In 1963, Congress passed the first modern statute directed at eliminating discrimination in the job market — the Equal Pay Act (EPA).[a] Enacted as an amendment to the Fair Labor Standards Act,[b] the EPA proscribes a limited universe of discriminatory employment practices — sex-based wage differentials between employees performing "equal work." Subject to four statutorily created exceptions, an employer is prohibited from paying an employee of one sex less than an employee of the other sex for "equal work on jobs the performance of which requires equal skill, effort, and responsibility, and which are performed under similar working conditions * * * ." The Act also provides that compliance with its equal pay mandate cannot be achieved by reducing the wages of the higher paid employee.

As it is part of the Fair Labor Standards Act (FLSA), coverage under and enforcement of the Equal Pay Act is tied to the provisions of the FLSA.

Employers can fall within the general jurisdiction of the FLSA under either of two theories. The first ("employee") test focuses on the individual employee and asks whether s/he is "engaged in commerce" or engaged "in the production of goods for commerce." All employees who satisfy this requirement are protected by the FLSA. The use of this criterion, however, can result in one employer having both protected and unprotected employees, depending upon the nature of their particular job duties. To avoid this scenario, the FLSA contains another definition that focuses on the general nature of the employer's business. Under this "enterprise" standard, all the employees of a particular enterprise are covered, regardless of their individual job responsibilities, if the enterprise is (a) engaged in interstate commerce or in the production of goods for interstate commerce, (b) has 2 or more employees so engaged, and (c) except for a few specified industries, makes at least $325,000 in annual gross.

Coverage under the EPA, however, may not be limited to entities meeting either the "employee" or "enterprise" standard. The EPA states that an employer cannot discriminate against "employees subject to any provision of this section" within any "establishment" in which such employees are employed. The absence of any reference in this section to "engaged in commerce," as well as the use of "establishment" instead of "enterprise," has raised the possibility that an employer is covered so long as it has

---

[a]Pub.L. 88-38, 77 Stat. 56, 29 U.S.C. §206(d).
[b]Pub.L. 75-718, 52 Stat. 1060, 29 U.S.C. §§201-209.

at least one male and one female worker engaged in commerce or in the production of goods for commerce.[c]

In 1974, the FLSA was amended to apply to federal, state and local government employees and the constitutionality of the wage and hour provisions of this enactment was affirmed in Garcia v. San Antonio Metropolitan Transit Authority, 469 U.S. 528, 105 S.Ct. 1005, 83 L.Ed.2d 1016 (1985). But since *Garcia* did not involve the equal pay provisions of the FLSA, the constitutionality of the extension of this provision to government workers remained unresolved. In KIMEL v. FLORIDA BD. OF REGENTS, 528 U.S. 62, 120 S.Ct. 631, 145 L.Ed.2d 522 (2000), the Supreme Court announced a two part test to determine whether the creation of a right of action for damages against state governments constitutionally abrogated the States' Eleventh Amendment sovereign immunity. Under this standard, a court must conclude (1) that Congress unequivocally intended to abrogate the States' sovereign immunity; and (2) that the statute was enacted pursuant to a valid exercise of Congress' §5 remedial authority under the Fourteenth Amendment.

The circuit courts have upheld the constitutionality of the provision in the Equal Pay Act that provides a right of action for damages to state government workers. These courts find that this provision, unlike its counterparts in the ADEA and ADA, was an appropriate use of Congressional authority under §5 of the Fourteenth Amendment because it meets the tests of proportionality and congruence articulated in *Kimel*. Gender, unlike disability and age, is reviewed under a stricter standard than the rational basis test applied to age and disability classifications. Since the EPA provides remedies only for intentional gender-based wage disparities, these disparities would not survive constitutional scrutiny under the stricter standard applied to gender classifications. Additionally, the courts reason, since the historical record clearly documents state discrimination on the basis of gender, the absence of specific legislative findings regarding state-sponsored gender discrimination did not preclude upholding the constitutionality of the abrogation of sovereign immunity. *See* Siler-Khodr v. Univ. of Texas Health Science Center, 261 F.3d 542 (5th Cir.2001), cert. denied, 537 U.S. 1087, 123 S.Ct. 694, 154 L.Ed.2d 631 (2002); Hundertmark v. State Of Florida Dep't Of Transportation, 205 F.3d 1272 (11th Cir.2000).

The Equal Pay Act, unlike the other portions of the FLSA, specifically mentions labor organizations, forbidding them from causing or attempting to cause an employer to violate the Act.[d]

Although an aggrieved employee is entitled to file a complaint of an EPA violation with the EEOC, these proceedings need not be invoked prior to filing suit. An employee can bring a private action under the EPA in either federal or state court for amounts withheld in violation of the Act. The EEOC can bring such an action on that employee's behalf, but its exercise of this authority terminates the employee's right to file suit and the EPA, unlike Title VII, does not grant the individual a right to

---

[c]See 1 A. Larson, EMPLOYMENT DISCRIMINATION, §6.41 (1981).
[d]The EPA does not contain a minimum member requirement for labor organizations.

intervene in the EEOC action.ᵉ In addition, the EEOC can seek injunctive relief and liquidated damages as well as backpay. Finally, a two year statute of limitations applies to EPA suits for backpay, except that a case arising out of a willful violation is subject to a three year limitations period.ᵍ

The remaining materials in this Chapter will address the three most frequently litigated issues in cases brought under the EPA: (1) the meaning of the statutory equal work standard, (2) the scope of the statutory exceptions, and (3) the relationship between the EPA and Title VII.

Read 29 U.S.C. §§206(d) and 216.

Brennan v. Prince William Hospital Corp.

United States Court of Appeals, Fourth Circuit, 1974.

503 F.2d 282, cert. denied, 420 U.S. 972, 95 S.Ct. 1392, 43 L.Ed.2d 652 (1975).

BUTZNER, Circuit Judge.

The Secretary of Labor appeals from the dismissal of an action against Prince William Hospital to equalize pay of male hospital orderlies and female nurses' aides in conformity with the Equal Pay Act of 1963. The district court * * * found that although aides and orderlies do the same type of patient care work, the following differences exist between the jobs: the proportions of routine care tasks are not the same; aides do work which orderlies are neither required nor permitted to do; and, most important, orderlies do work, including extra tasks, which aides are neither required nor permitted to do. It concluded, therefore, that the Secretary had failed to establish that the aides and orderlies perform substantially equal work.

We believe that the district court gave undue significance to these differences because it misapprehended the statutory definition of equal work, which embraces the concepts of "skill, effort, and responsibility." Since it applied an improper legal standard to the relevant facts, we reverse and remand for the entry of judgment for the Secretary.

I

In applying the Congressional mandate of equal pay for equal work on jobs which require equal skill, effort, and responsibility, there are two extremes of interpretation that must be avoided. Congress realized that the majority of job differentiations are made for genuine economic reasons unrelated to sex. It did not authorize the Secretary or the courts to engage in wholesale reevaluation of any employer's pay structure in order to enforce their own conceptions of economic worth. But if courts defer to

---

ᵉIntervention may be sought, however, under F.R.Civ.P. 24. In the absence of any express conciliation requirement, the EPA does not require the EEOC to attempt conciliation before instituting suit. EEOC v. Home of Economy, Inc., 712 F.2d 356 (8ᵗʰ Cir.1983).

ᵍTo establish a willful violation, the plaintiff must prove that the defendant knew or should have known that its conduct was governed by the Act. McLaughlin v. Richland Shoe Co., 486 U.S. 128, 108 S.Ct. 1677, 100 L.Ed.2d 115 (1988)(action brought under FLSA but Court states that FLSA provision governs suits under EPA).

overly nice distinctions in job content, employers may evade the Act at will. The response to this dilemma has been to require the Secretary to prove substantial equality of skill, effort, and responsibility as the jobs are actually performed.

One of the most common grounds for justifying different wages is the assertion that male employees perform extra tasks. These may support a wage differential if they create significant variations in skill, effort, and responsibility between otherwise equal jobs. But the semblance of the valid job classification system may not be allowed to mask the existence of wage discrimination based on sex. The Secretary may therefore show that the greater pay received by the male employees is not related to any extra tasks and thus is not justified by them. Higher pay is not related to extra duties when one or more of the following circumstances exists:

Some male employees receive higher pay without doing the extra work.

Female employees also perform extra duties of equal skill, effort, and responsibility.

Qualified female employees are not given the opportunity to do the extra work.

The supposed extra duties do not in fact exist.

The extra task consumes a minimal amount of time and is of peripheral importance.

Third persons who do the extra task as their primary job are paid less than the male employees in question.

In all of these * * * [circumstances] the basic jobs were substantially equal. Despite claims to the contrary, the extra tasks were * * * makeweights. This left sex — which in this context refers to the availability of women at lower wages than men — as the one discernible reason for the wage differential. That, however, is precisely the criterion for setting wages that the Act prohibits.

II

* * * The Act must be applied on a case by case basis to factual situations that are, for practical purposes, unique. It is therefore necessary to examine in some detail the employment practices of Prince William Hospital, even though the material facts are not in dispute.

* * *

Floor orderlies and nurses' aides provide routine patient care under the supervision of nurses. The hospital hires only men as orderlies and only women as aides. * * *

The hospital has maintained a pay differential between the two jobs since 1969. It uses a pay system with thirteen pay grades and five steps within each grade. Grades are assigned to positions and steps within grade show merit or longevity. All nurses' aides are in grade I, in which the hourly pay ranges from $1.98 to $2.31, and all orderlies are in grade II, in which the hourly pay ranges from $2.08 to $2.43, depending on the step in which the employee has been placed.

Before 1969 aides and orderlies had been paid the same wages, but the hospital had difficulty in hiring orderlies. The hospital's administrator believed that a higher wage was needed to attract orderlies because of the limited number of men willing to do housekeeping and personal care work. When the orderlies' wage was raised, they were given the additional duty of catheterizing male patients.

Hiring criteria for aides and orderlies are identical: a tenth grade education, personal cleanliness, and a desire to work with people. Experience, though desirable, is unnecessary. Although the educational level of the aides was somewhat lower, both groups included individuals who had not finished high school. The pay differential follows neither experience nor education. An aide with prior hospital experience starts in grade I step 2 ($2.06), while a completely inexperienced orderly starts in grade II step 1 ($2.08).

Aides and orderlies are the least skilled persons who care for patients. They participate in a common orientation program, but much of their training is acquired on the job. Each is assigned six to eight patients who require routine care. Whenever possible orderlies are assigned to male patients and aides to female, but the shortage of orderlies requires aides to care for males. Most of the time, aides and orderlies are occupied with tasks related to routine patient care that do not require the skills of a trained nurse.

The principal duties of both, which the hospital's director of nursing stated were identical, can be divided into four groups: patient care, which includes oral hygiene, back rubs, baths, bed-making, answering calls, giving bed pans, feeding, transporting the patient, and assistance with ambulation; minor treatment, which includes weighing, taking pulse, temperature, or blood pressure, draping and positioning the patient, administering heat pads and ice packs, assistance with dressing changes, and giving enemas; housekeeping, which includes room cleaning, equipment care and cleaning, work area cleaning, and obtaining supplies; and miscellaneous tasks, including answering the phone, running errands, and transportation to the morgue.

The hospital emphasized statistical evidence which shows that aides and orderlies do not perform all of their routine tasks with equal frequency. One of its exhibits, for example, shows that aides write charts, make beds, give baths, rub backs, and fetch bed pans more often than orderlies. Orderlies, on the other hand, bring supplies, run errands, and assist the nurses with their duties more often than aides. These distinctions, however, do not show any difference in skill, effort, or responsibility. All of the routine tasks are relatively simple. None performed more frequently by the orderlies requires the exertion of significantly more skill, effort, or responsibility than those performed more frequently by the aides. As hired, trained, and employed, the orderlies and aides are practical substitutes for one another in the performance of their basic duties. Disproportionate frequency in the performance of the same routine tasks does not make the job unequal.

III

The district court also found that aides perform certain duties which orderlies do not. Specifically, it found that some of the aides work in the obstetric department and care for infants in the nursery. Orderlies were not assigned to obstetrics, according to the director of nursing, for two reasons: there were no male patients and their lifting ability was unneeded there. Aides assigned to obstetrics performed the same duties as those on the medical and surgical wards.

These facts do not show any differences in skill, effort, or responsibility. Unless there is a difference of working conditions involved, which is not contended here, there is no reason why the performance of the same duties in a different location should be a significant difference in the jobs.

IV

The final — and in some respects the most difficult — aspect of this case pertains to extra duties throughout the hospital that are assigned to the orderlies but not to the aides. These duties are specified in the job description of the orderlies. The district court found that the following extra duties were the most significant: heavy lifting, assisting in the emergency room, performing surgical preps on male patients, providing physical security by dealing with combative or hysterical persons, and catheterization of male patients.

Job descriptions and titles, however, are not decisive. Actual job requirements and performance are controlling. This aspect of the case, therefore, turns primarily on the extent to which the aides and orderlies actually perform the extra duties nominally assigned to the orderlies and on the skill, effort, and responsibility involved in those tasks which the orderlies alone perform.

In addition to caring for assigned patients, orderlies are required to answer calls to different parts of the hospital. On these excursions, called floating, they perform either their basic duties or the extra tasks. Floating itself adds nothing to the level of skill or responsibility, for that depends on the work done in the other locations. It might add to the degree of effort involved if the orderlies, in addition, had to perform their full basic workload. This, however, is not the case. According to the director of nursing, an orderly's routine duties at his assigned station are reassigned to other staff personnel, including the aides, when he is in another part of the hospital.

The job description states that orderlies are expected to perform total lifting of heavy or helpless patients and to set up traction equipment. The district court, however, found that the same tasks are performed by aides when no orderly is available and that aides assist orderlies in these tasks. Due to the small number of orderlies, there are rarely more than two on duty each shift, and from time to time no orderly is available on some of the shifts. It sometimes takes more than one aide, or mechanical assistance, to replace an orderly, but there is no evidence that any heavy lifting cannot be done without male assistance. The performance of tasks involving physical strength, therefore, though necessary to the operation of the hospital, is not a peculiar aspect of the orderlies' job. Strength is not a factor in the hiring of orderlies, except in the very general sense that the hospital assumes that a man is usually stronger than a woman. A large, burly woman would not be hired as an orderly, nor would a small, delicate man be hired as an aide. But the converse is not true. One of the orderlies is 5'2" tall and weighs 125 lbs., while one aide is 6'1" and weighs 225 lbs. The wage differential therefore can not be justified on the grounds that the hospital is maintaining a reserve of strong men for essential tasks.

Heavy lifting does not add significantly to the effort involved in the orderlies' job. In the ten working days covered by the hospital's survey of activities, the orderlies set up traction only once and lifted or assisted patients of unknown weight 54 times. Aides set up traction and lifted or ambulated patients a proportionate number of times. The extra effort, if any, is not substantial.

* * *

All surgical preps during the day shifts are done by the operating room staff. On the evening and night shifts, surgical preps on men are done by orderlies, and on women by aides or nurses. Aides also do surgical preps in the obstetric ward. A person performing a prep explains to the patient what is about to be done, shaves the area where the incision will be made, and washes it with antiseptic soap. The skill, effort, and responsibility involved are identical regardless of the patient's sex.

Physical security, as an extra duty, has two components. Because of his size and sex, the presence of a male orderly is claimed to reassure the other staff and exert a calming and deterrent effect on potentially violent patients or intruders. Because of his superior strength, he is given the primary responsibility for restraining actually violent persons. According to the hospital, he therefore possesses a special skill and is required to exert extra effort.

The hospital's contention, however, is contradicted by the record. Although in theory the orderly deals with disturbances, in practice the nearest staff member is expected to do so until assistance comes. Aides are expected to restrain violent or disoriented patients themselves when possible. They also deal with intruders. The hospital's tabulation of orderly and aide activity shows aides spending a larger proportion of their time than orderlies in applying restraining devices to patients. There is no evidence that orderlies do more actual physical restraint than aides.

No doubt the physical presence of a man in the house does have a comforting effect on the staff. It is doubtful, though, that this is a significant component of the orderly job. Unlike hospitals in which providing physical security has been found significant, Prince William Hospital does not handle psychiatric, alcoholic, criminal, or other potentially dangerous patients. There is no evidence that episodes caused by violent or confused patients are so frequent or dangerous that orderlies are necessary for the safety of the staff. Security guards are called to deal with violent episodes even when orderlies are available. Moreover, the ability to deal with confused or violent patients, according to the director of nursing, is as much a function of attitude and experience as of size and strength. If the orderly's superior strength is an extra skill, it is a peripheral part of his employment.

The hospital places great emphasis on the fact that orderlies insert Foley catheters in male patients. It contends that the task is a highly skilled and responsible procedure, requiring 30 to 45 minutes of an orderly's time.

A Foley catheter is a sterile tube which is inserted in the patient's urethra to drain the bladder. Orderlies catheterize male patients with unobstructed urinary tracts. If any difficulty is foreseen or experienced a physician catheterizes the patient. Nurses catheterize female patients. They are competent to catheterize males, but prefer not to do so for reasons of modesty. Since the hospital has enough nurses to catheterize women, aides are not assigned this duty. The orderly's job therefore does call for the exercise of skill and responsibility which is not required of the aides.

However, no more than one or two routine catheterizations are usually performed each week. When no floor orderly is present, other qualified male personnel are available to do them. The hospital looks for no special skill in this regard from its prospective orderlies but concedes that "any reasonably dextrous person can learn male catheterization on the job." Orderlies were assigned this duty only when the hospital decided that a higher wage rate was needed to attract men for routine care work, and new orderlies who have not yet learned to catheterize are nevertheless paid at the higher rate.

Like any other extra duty, catheterization must be evaluated as part of the entire job.   In Hodgson v. Fairmont Supply Co., 454 F.2d 490, 496 (4th Cir.1972), we pointed out that when jobs were substantially equal, a minimal amount of extra skill, effort, or responsibility cannot justify wage differentials.   Infrequent performance of catheterizations, unaccompanied by other extra skills and responsibilities, has never been held to support a pay differential between aides and orderlies.   * * *   We conclude, therefore, that the orderlies' pay differential cannot be justified on the basis of the occasional extra work involved in catheterizing male patients.

In sum, the work performed by aides and orderlies is not identical.   But, as we have previously held, application of the Equal Pay Act is not restricted to identical work.   The basic routine tasks of the aides and orderlies are equal.   The variations that the district court found, when tested by the Act's standard of "equal skill, effort, and responsibility," do not affect the substantial equality of their overall work.

The judgment of the district court is reversed, and this case is remanded for entry of judgment for the Secretary.

NOTES AND PROBLEMS FOR DISCUSSION

1.   State University operates campuses in three different cities in the State — North, South and West.   Undergraduate instruction is offered at the North and South campuses, while the graduate and professional schools are located on the West campus.   Robert Force, a Professor of English at North with 10 years seniority, receives an annual salary of $25,000.   Ruth Morris, a Professor of English at South with comparable credentials and identical seniority is paid $20,000 per year.   Prof. Morris brings an action under the EPA.

(a)   Should Prof. Morris prevail in her EPA action against the University?   *See* Brennan v. Goose Creek Consolidated Independent School District, 519 F.2d 53 (5th Cir. 1975).

(b)   Could Prof. Morris prevail in an action under Title VII?   *See* Bartelt v. Berlitz School of Languages of America, Inc., 698 F.2d 1003 (9th Cir.), cert. denied, 464 U.S. 915, 104 S.Ct. 277, 78 L.Ed.2d 257 (1983).

(c)   Would your answer to either of the two preceding questions change if Prof. Force had been a Professor of Chemistry at South?   *See* Soble v. University of Maryland, 778 F.2d 164 (4th Cir. 1985).

(d)   Does the statute suggest that a lesser degree of similarity is required with respect to working conditions than with "skill, effort and responsibility"?   *See* Lanegan-Grimm v. Library Ass'n of Portland, 560 F. Supp. 486 (D. Or. 1983).

2.   Federal Airlines pays identical salaries to its male and female flight attendants. During layovers, female flight attendants are required to share double rooms while male attendants are provided with single rooms.   In addition, male attendants are given a monthly uniform cleaning allowance.   No such allowance is provided to female attendants.   Can a female attendant state a claim under the EPA? *Compare* Laffey v. Northwest Airlines, Inc., 642 F.2d 578 (D.C. Cir. 1980), *with* Donovan v. KFC Services, Inc., 547 F. Supp. 503 (E.D.N.Y. 1982).

3. Does the application of the EPA to a religious organization violate the establishment or free exercise clauses of the First Amendment? See Dole v. Shenandoah Baptist Church, 899 F.2d 1389 (4th Cir. 1990), cert. denied, 498 U.S. 846, 111 S.Ct. 131, 112 L.Ed.2d 99 (1990).

Kouba v. Allstate Insurance Co.

United States Court of Appeals, Ninth Circuit, 1982.
691 F.2d 873.

CHOY, Circuit Judge.

This appeal calls into question the scope of the "factor other than sex" exception to the Equal Pay Act of 1963 as incorporated into Title VII * * * by the Bennett Amendment.[2] Because the district court misconstrued the exception, we reverse and remand.

I

Allstate Insurance Co. computes the minimum salary guaranteed to a new sales agent on the basis of ability, education, experience, and prior salary. During an 8-to-13 week training period, the agent receives only the minimum. Afterwards, Allstate pays the greater of the minimum and the commissions earned from sales. A result of this practice is that, on the average, female agents make less than their male counterparts.

Lola Kouba, representing a class of all female agents, argued below that the use of prior salary caused the wage differential and thus constitutes unlawful sex discrimination. Allstate responded that prior salary is a "factor other than sex" within the meaning of the statutory exception. The district court entered summary judgment against Allstate, reasoning that (1) because so many employers paid discriminatory salaries in the past, the court would presume that a female agent's prior salary was based on her gender unless Allstate presented evidence to rebut that presumption, and (2) absent such a showing (which Allstate did not attempt to make), prior salary is not a factor other than sex.

II

The Equal Pay Act prohibits differential payments between male and female employees doing equal work except when made pursuant to any of three specific compensation systems or "any other factor other than sex." These exceptions are affirmative defenses which the employer must plead and prove. Corning Glass Works v. Brennan, 417 U.S. 188, 94 S.Ct. 2223, 41 L.Ed.2d 1 (1974).

---

[2]The Bennett Amendment, which incorporates into Title VII the affirmative defenses fixed in the Equal Pay Act, states:

> It shall not be an unlawful employment practice under [Title VII] for any employer to differentiate upon the basis of sex in determining the amount of the wages or compensation paid or to be paid to employees of such employer if such differentiation is authorized by the provisions of the [Equal Pay Act].

Because Kouba brought her claim under Title VII rather than directly under the Equal Pay Act,[3] Allstate contends that the standard Title VII rules govern the allocation of evidentiary burdens. It cites Texas Department of Community Affairs v. Burdine for the proposition that under Title VII an employee alleging sex discrimination bears the burden of persuasion at all times as to all issues and concludes that Kouba failed to carry the burden of showing that the wage differential did not result from a factor other than sex.[4]

Allstate misallocates the burden. In County of Washington v. Gunther, 452 U.S. 161, 101 S.Ct. 2242, 68 L.Ed.2d 751 (1981), the Supreme Court recognized that very different principles govern the standard structure of Title VII litigation, including burdens of proof, and the structure of Title VII litigation implicating the "factor other than sex" exception to an equal-pay claim (though the Court reserved judgment on specifically how to structure an equal-pay claim under Title VII). Accordingly, we have held that even under Title VII, the employer bears the burden of showing that the wage differential resulted from a factor other than sex. Nothing in *Burdine* converts this affirmative defense, which the employer must plead and prove under *Corning Glass,* into an element of the cause of action, which the employee must show does not exist.

III

In an effort to carry its burden, Allstate asserts that if its use of prior salary caused the wage differential, prior salary constitutes a factor other than sex. An obstacle to evaluating Allstate's contention is the ambiguous statutory language. The parties proffer a variety of possible interpretations of the term "factor other than sex."

A

We can discard at the outset three interpretations manifestly incompatible with the Equal Pay Act. At one extreme are two that would tolerate all but the most blatant discrimination. Kouba asserts that Allstate wrongly reads "factor other than sex" to mean any factor that either does not refer on its face to an employee's gender or does not result in all women having lower salaries than all men. Since an employer could easily manipulate factors having a close correlation to gender as a guise to pay female employees discriminatorily low salaries, it would contravene the Act to allow their use simply because they also are facially neutral or do not produce complete segregation. Not surprisingly, Allstate denies relying on either reading of the exception.

At the other extreme is an interpretation that would deny employers the opportunity to use clearly acceptable factors. Kouba insists that in order to give the Act its full remedial force, employers cannot use any factor that perpetuates historic sex discrimination. The court below adopted a variation of this interpretation: the employer must demonstrate that it made a reasonable attempt to satisfy itself that the factor causing the wage differential was not the product of sex discrimination. But

---

[3]Her apparent reasons for bringing a Title VII action were the uncertainty at that time how the Equal Pay Act affected Title VII and the apparently less-demanding class-consent requirements under Title VII.

[4]Allstate does not dispute that otherwise Kouba established a prima facie case. Thus, * * * we assume that she has.

while Congress fashioned the Equal Pay Act to help cure longstanding societal ills, it also intended to exempt factors such as training and experience that may reflect opportunities denied to women in the past. Neither Kouba's interpretation nor the district court's variation can accommodate practices that Congress and the courts have approved.

B

All three interpretations miss the mark in large part because they do not focus on the reason for the employer's use of the factor. The Equal Pay Act concerns business practices. It would be nonsensical to sanction the use of a factor that rests on some consideration unrelated to business. An employer thus cannot use a factor which causes a wage differential between male and female employees absent an acceptable business reason.[6] Conversely, a factor used to effectuate some business policy is not prohibited simply because a wage differential results.

Even with a business-related requirement, an employer might assert some business reason as a pretext for a discriminatory objective. This possibility is especially great with a factor like prior salary which can easily be used to capitalize on the unfairly low salaries historically paid to women. The ability of courts to protect against such abuse is somewhat limited, however. The Equal Pay Act entrusts employers, not judges, with making the often uncertain decision of how to accomplish business objectives. We have found no authority giving guidance on the proper judicial inquiry absent direct evidence of discriminatory intent. A pragmatic standard, which protects against abuse yet accommodates employer discretion, is that the employer must use the factor reasonably in light of the employer's stated purpose as well as its other practices. The specific relevant considerations will of course vary with the situation. In Part IV of this opinion, we outline how the court below should apply this test to the business reasons given by Allstate for its use of prior salary.

C

Relying on recent Supreme Court precedent, Kouba would limit the category of business reasons acceptable under the exception to those that measure the value of an employee's job performance to his or her employer. In *Gunther*, the Court reported that Congress added the exception "because of a concern that bona fide job evaluation systems used by American businesses would otherwise be disrupted." In *Corning Glass*, the Court explained that these systems "took into consideration four separate factors in determining job value — skill, effort, responsibility and working conditions — and each of these four components was further systematically divided into various subcomponents." Our study of the legislative history of the Equal Pay Act confirms that Congress discussed only factors that reflect job value.

In drafting the Act, however, Congress did not limit the exception to job-evaluation systems. Instead, it excepted "any other factor other than sex" and thus created a "broad general exception." H.R.Rep. No. 309, 88th Cong., 1st Sess. 3.

---

[6]Not every reason making economic sense is acceptable. This appeal does not, however, require us to compile a complete list of unacceptable factors or even formulate a standard to distinguish them from acceptable ones. We leave those tasks for another day.

While a concern about job-evaluation systems served as the impetus for creating the exception, Congress did not limit the exception to that concern.

Other language in the Act supports this conclusion. The statutory definition of equal work incorporates the four factors listed in Corning Glass as the standard components in job-evaluation systems. (The Act refers to "equal work on jobs the performance of which requires equal skill, effort, and responsibility, and which are performed under similar working conditions.") It would render the "factor other than sex" exception surplusage to limit the exception to the same four factors. And while we might be able to distinguish other factors that also reflect job value, the scope of the exception would be exceedingly narrow if limited to other apparently uncommon factors. The broad language of the exception belies such limitation.

Accordingly, no court or other authority has inferred a job-evaluation requirement. We, too, reject that limitation on the "factor other than sex" exception.

IV

Allstate provides two business reasons for its use of prior salary that the district court must evaluate on remand.[7] We will discuss each explanation in turn without attempting to establish a comprehensive framework for its evaluation. The district court should mold its inquiry to the particular facts that unfold at trial.

A

Allstate asserts that it ties the guaranteed monthly minimum to prior salary as part of a sales-incentive program. If the monthly minimum far exceeds the amount that the agent earned previously, the agent might become complacent and not fulfill his or her selling potential. By limiting the monthly minimum according to prior salary, Allstate hopes to motivate the agent to make sales, earn commissions, and thus improve his or her financial position. Presumably, Allstate cannot set a uniform monthly minimum so low that it motivates all sales agents, because then prospective agents with substantially higher prior salaries might not risk taking a job with Allstate.

This reasoning does not explain Allstate's use of prior salary during the initial training period. Because the agents cannot earn commissions at that time, there is no potential reward to motivate them to make sales.

When commissions become available, we wonder whether Allstate adjusts the guaranteed minimum regularly and whether most agents earn commission-based salaries. On remand, the district court should inquire into these and other issues that relate to the reasonableness of the use of prior salary in the incentive program.

---

[7] A third reason given by Allstate is that an individual with a higher prior salary can demand more in the marketplace. Courts disagree whether market demand can ever justify a wage differential. Compare, e.g., Horner v. Mary Institute, 613 F.2d 706, 714 (8th Cir. 1980) (allowing it in limited situations), with Futran v. RING Radio Co., 501 F.Supp. 734, 739 (N.D.Ga. 1980) (disallowing it always). We need not rule whether Congress intended to prohibit the use of market demand. Because Allstate did not present any evidence to support its use of prior salary in response to market demand, the district court properly disposed of that reason on summary judgment.

B

Reasoning that salary corresponds roughly to an employee's ability, Allstate also claims that it uses prior salary to predict a new employee's performance as a sales agent. Relevant considerations in evaluating the reasonableness of this practice include (1) whether the employer also uses other available predictors of the new employee's performance, (2) whether the employer attributes less significance to prior salary once the employee has proven himself or herself on the job, and (3) whether the employer relies more heavily on salary when the prior job resembles the job of sales agent.

V

In conclusion, the Equal Pay Act does not impose a strict prohibition against the use of prior salary. Thus while we share the district court's fear that an employer might manipulate its use of prior salary to underpay female employees the court must find that the business reasons given by Allstate do not reasonably explain its use of that factor before finding a violation of the Act.

Reversed and Remanded.

NOTES AND PROBLEMS FOR DISCUSSION

1. (a) More than a quarter century after the Ninth Circuit's decision in *Kouba*, that court, in an *en banc* opinion, by a 6-5 vote, appeared to have reversed its ruling in *Kouba* in Rizo v. Yovino, 887 F.3d 453 (9th Cir. 2018)(*en banc*). The opinion was written by Judge Steven Reinhardt, who passed away 11 days before that opinion was issued. A footnote in the opinion stated that Reinhardt had "fully participated in this case * * * and voting was completed by the *en banc* court prior to his death." On appeal, the Supreme Court unanimously ruled that since Reinhardt was not alive when the opinion was filed and issued, he no longer was a judge at that moment and, therefore, that the Ninth Circuit erred in counting him as a member of the one-vote majority. Federal judges, the Court declared, "are appointed for life, not for eternity." Accordingly, since his removal left the appellate court deadlocked at 5-5, the Supreme Court vacated the *en banc* judgment. Yovino v. Rizo, 586 U.S. ___, 139 S.Ct. 706, 203 L.Ed.2d 38 (2019).

(b) Would the employer violate the EPA by implementing a policy that based salary of incumbent workers who transfer within the company on their prior salary with that employer? *Compare* Glenn v. General Motors Corp., 841 F.2d 1567 (11th Cir.), cert. denied, 488 U.S. 948, 109 S.Ct. 378, 102 L.Ed.2d 367 (1988), *with* Covington v. S.I.U., 816 F.2d 317 (7th Cir.), cert. denied, 484 U.S. 848, 108 S.Ct. 146, 98 L.Ed.2d 101 (1987).

2. Mel's Clothing Store operates separate departments for men's and women's clothing. The merchandise in the men's department is of better quality and higher price than the women's merchandise and yields a higher profit margin than the women's clothing. Only women are hired for the women's department and only men are permitted to work in the men's department. It is conceded that the sales personnel in both departments perform equal work. Mel's, however, pays all its male sales staff a higher base salary than is paid to its female sales staff. The store maintains that this differential is justified by the greater profitability and dollar volume of gross sales

produced by the salespersons in the men's department. Is Mel's violating the EPA or is this policy more properly challenged under Title VII as a discriminatory job assignment? *See* Hodgson v. Robert Hall Clothes, Inc., 473 F.2d 589 (3d Cir.), cert. denied, 414 U.S. 866, 94 S.Ct. 50, 38 L.Ed.2d 85 (1973); Charles A. Sullivan, *The Equal Pay Act of 1963: Making and Breaking A Prima Facie C*ase, 31 ARK.L.REV. 545 (1978).

3.   Buff Spas Inc. operates a chain of health spas, each of which is divided into a men's and women's division. Men operate the men's division and women operate the women's division. The salary of the manager of each division is based on commissions earned on gross sales of memberships. Male managers are paid 6% of their spa's gross sales of memberships to men; female managers are paid 4% of gross sales of memberships to women. Historically, the gross volume of Buff membership sales to women has been 50% higher than the gross volume of membership sales to men. There is no difference in the job duties of male and female managers and they perform their jobs under similar working conditions. The company says that it pays different commission rates so that men and women will receive substantially equal compensation for equal work performed. Is the company in violation of the Equal Pay Act? *See* Bence v. Detroit Health Corp., 712 F.2d 1024 (6th Cir. 1983), cert. denied, 465 U.S. 1025, 104 S.Ct. 1282, 79 L.Ed.2d 685 (1984).

4.   In connection with the opening of a family planning center, Good Samaritan Hospital sought to hire two additional gynecologists. From a pool of twenty male and two female applicants for the posts, the hospital made offers to Dr. Arlene DeRoy and Dr. Paul Barron. After both joined the Hospital's staff, Dr. Barron discovered that Dr. DeRoy's salary was $10,000 higher than his. Both Drs. Barron and DeRoy were 1975 graduates of the same medical school with comparable prior experience and medical school records. The Hospital contends that because of the great demand and extremely limited supply of female gynecologists, it was compelled to offer Dr. DeRoy a higher salary to lure her away from other offers of employment. Has the Hospital violated the Equal Pay Act? *Compare* Horner v. Mary Institute, 613 F.2d 706 (8th Cir. 1980), *with* Hodgson v. Brookhaven General Hospital, 436 F.2d 719 (5th Cir. 1970).

5.   In CORNING GLASS WORKS v. BRENNAN, 417 U.S. 188, 94 S.Ct. 2223, 41 L.Ed.2d 1 (1974), discussed in the principal case, the employer paid a higher base wage to male night shift inspectors than it paid to female inspectors who performed the same job duties during the day shift. It also paid a separate premium to all workers on the night shift. The defendant argued that since day shift work was not "performed under similar working conditions" as night shift work, the plaintiff Secretary of Labor had failed to prove that Corning was paying unequal pay for equal work. The Secretary contended that day and night shift work were performed under similar working conditions and that while night shift work could constitute a "factor other than sex" defense, Corning had failed to prove that the higher base wage paid to male night shift inspectors was based on a non-sex factor. The Court agreed with the Secretary:

> While a layman might well assume that time of day worked reflects one aspect of a job's "working conditions," the term has a different and much more specific meaning in the language of industrial relations. As Corning's own representative testified at the hearings, the element of working conditions encompasses two subfactors: "surroundings" and "hazards." "Surroundings" measures the elements, such as toxic chemicals or fumes, regularly encountered

by a worker, their intensity, and their frequency. "Hazards" takes into account the physical hazards regularly encountered, their frequency, and the severity of injury they can cause. This definition of "working conditions" is not only manifested in Corning's own job evaluation plans but is also well accepted across a wide range of American industry.

Nowhere in any of these definitions is time of day worked mentioned as a relevant criterion. The fact of the matter is that the concept of "working conditions," as used in the specialized language of job evaluation systems, simply does not encompass shift differentials. Indeed, while Corning now argues that night inspection work is not equal to day inspection work, all of its own job evaluation plans, including the one now in effect, have consistently treated them as equal in all respects, including working conditions. * * * [T]he inspection work at issue in this case, whether performed during the day or night, is "equal work" as that term is defined in the Act.

This does not mean, of course, that there is no room in the Equal Pay Act for nondiscriminatory shift differentials. Work on a steady night shift no doubt has psychological and physiological impacts making it less attractive than work on a day shift. The Act contemplates that a male night worker may receive a higher wage than a female day worker, just as it contemplates that a male employee with 20 years' seniority can receive a higher wage than a woman with two years' seniority. Factors such as these play a role under the Act's four exceptions — the seniority differential under the specific seniority exception, the shift differential under the catch-all exception for differentials "based on any other factor other than sex."

417 U.S. at 202–204.

What is the significance of this ruling?

The Court concluded that Corning had not sustained its burden of proving that the higher base rate paid for night work was based on a factor other than sex, since prior to 1966, Corning allowed only men to work the night shift and the men would not work at the low wage paid to women inspectors. Would the Court have reached a different conclusion if state law had precluded women from working at night? *See* Wirtz v. Rainbo Baking Co. of Lexington, 303 F. Supp. 1049 (E.D. Ky. 1967).

6. The Robin O'Brien Institute determined that the salaries of its female researchers were significantly lower than those of its similarly qualified male researchers. Accordingly, it designed a formula for increasing the salaries of its female researchers to remedy that discrimination. Should a group of male researchers prevail in their claims that the O'Brien Institute violated the EPA by giving raises solely to its female researchers? *See* Ende v. Board of Regents, 757 F.2d 176 (7th Cir. 1985).

7. As noted in the introduction to this Chapter, the Equal Pay Act was enacted as an amendment to the Fair Labor Standards Act (FLSA) and incorporates the remedial provisions of the FLSA. The EPA expressly provides that any amount owing to an employee under the EPA is to be treated just like unpaid minimum wages or unpaid overtime compensation owing under the FLSA. This is important because §16 of the FLSA provides that any employer who violates the provisions of this statute shall be liable to the employee "for the amount of their unpaid minimum wages, or their unpaid overtime compensation, as the case may be, and in an additional equal amount as liquidated damages." Since this provision does not condition the award of punitive damages on a finding of a willful violation, as is the case under the ADEA, it suggests that a successful EPA plaintiff will collect back pay and punitive damages as a matter of course. But the FLSA was amended by the Portal to Portal Act, 29 U.S.C. §260 (1975), to make an award of liquidated damages discretionary where the court finds that the defendant both acted in "good faith" and had "reasonable grounds for believing that [its] act or omission was not a violation" of the FLSA. This language has been interpreted to warrant the awarding of liquidated damages unless the employer comes forward and persuades the court that it has met both the subjective good faith standard and the objective standard of having reasonable grounds to believe its conduct did not violate the Act. *See* Soto v. Adams Elevator Equipment Co., 941 F.2d 543 (7th Cir. 1991). Prejudgment interest on a backpay award will not be granted where liquidated damages are awarded. Moreover, as noted in the introductory paragraph in this Chapter, back pay is limited by the two or three year limitations provision of the FLSA and injunctive relief is unavailable in a private action. Injunctive relief is available, however, if the EEOC files suit under §17 of the FLSA.

8. Attorney fees are treated differently under the FLSA than under either Title VII, the Reconstruction Acts, the ADA or the Rehabilitation Act. First of all, §16 of the FLSA makes the awarding of attorney fees by the court nondiscretionary in those instances where it is available. And second, the FLSA explicitly restricts the availability of attorney fees to prevailing plaintiffs, rather than to prevailing parties.

9. A jury trial is available under the EPA on the issues of liability and back pay. As mentioned in Note 7, *supra*, the FLSA, as amended by the Portal to Portal Act, permits the recovery of liquidated damages unless the defendant demonstrates "to the satisfaction of the court" that it acted in good faith and had reasonable grounds for believing that its conduct did not violate the Act. This language has been interpreted to mean that the issue of good faith is a question for the judge and not the jury. *See* Lorillard v. Pons, 434 U.S. 575, 98 S.Ct. 866, 55 L.Ed.2d 40 (1978). At the same time, the Act also adds a third year to the limitations period for "willful" violations. In light of the allocation of "good faith" determinations (in the liquidated damages context) to the judge, should the issue of "willfulness" (in the limitations period context) similarly be a nonjury question? In FOWLER v. LAND MANAGEMENT GROUP, INC., 978 F.2d 158 (4th Cir. 1992), the court stated that issues of fact bearing on the application of a statute of limitations generally are submitted to the jury. And, the court continued, even if the "good faith" test for assessing liquidated damages is synonymous with the "willfulness" test for extending the limitations period, it did not discern any "negative ramifications" that would result from inconsistent findings on these two issues. Since the consequences of these two determinations were separable, the court reasoned, it was "entirely acceptable" for the jury and judge to render conflicting conclusions. Moreover, the court added, in the absence of explicit statutory language reserving the issue of "good faith" to the court, it would be more appropriate to allow the jury to pass on "willfulness" for limitations purposes and then require the court to be bound by that finding of fact with respect to its determination of "good faith" for damages purposes. Consequently, the court ruled that the issue of willfulness should be submitted to the jury.

County of Washington v. Gunther

Supreme Court of the United States, 1981.
452 U.S. 161, 101 S.Ct. 2242, 68 L.Ed.2d 751.

JUSTICE BRENNAN delivered the opinion of the Court.

The question presented is whether §703(h) of Title VII * * * restricts Title VII's prohibition of sex-based wage discrimination to claims of equal pay for equal work.

I

This case arises over the payment by petitioner * * * of substantially lower wages to female guards in the female section of the county jail than it paid to male guards in the male section of the jail. Respondents are four women who were employed to guard female prisoners and to carry out certain other functions in the jail.[2] In January 1974, the county eliminated the female section of the jail, transferred the female prisoners to the jail of a nearby county, and discharged respondents.

Respondents filed suit against petitioner in Federal District Court under Title VII, seeking backpay and other relief.[3] They alleged that they were paid unequal wages for work substantially equal to that performed by male guards, and in the alternative, that part of the pay differential was attributable to intentional sex discrimination. The latter allegation was based on a claim that, because of intentional discrimination, the county set the pay scale for female guards, but not for male guards, at a level lower than that warranted by its own survey of outside markets and the worth of the jobs.

After trial, the District Court found that the male guards supervised more than 10 times as many prisoners per guard as did the female guards, and that the females devoted much of their time to less-valuable clerical duties. It therefore held that respondents' jobs were not substantially equal to those of the male guards, and that respondents were thus not entitled to equal pay. The Court of Appeals affirmed on that issue, and respondents do not seek review of the ruling.

The District Court also dismissed respondents' claim that the discrepancy in pay between the male and female guards was attributable in part to intentional sex discrimination. It held as a matter of law that a sex-based wage discrimination claim cannot be brought under Title VII unless it would satisfy the equal work standard of the Equal Pay Act. The Court therefore permitted no additional evidence on this claim, and made no findings on whether petitioner's pay scales for female guards resulted from intentional sex discrimination.

The Court of Appeals reversed, holding that persons alleging sex discrimination "are not precluded from suing under Title VII to protest * * * discriminatory compensation practices" merely because their jobs were not equal to higher-paying

---

[2]Oregon requires that female inmates be guarded solely by women and the District Court opinion indicates that women had not been employed to guard male prisoners. For purposes of this litigation, respondents concede that gender is a bona fide occupational qualification for some of the female guard positions.

[3]Respondents could not sue under the Equal Pay Act because the Equal Pay Act did not apply to municipal employees until passage of the Fair Labor Standards Amendments of 1974. Title VII has applied to such employees since passage of the Equal Employment Opportunity Act of 1972.

jobs held by members of the opposite sex. The Court remanded to the District Court with instructions to take evidence on respondents' claim that part of the difference between their rate of pay and that of the male guards is attributable to sex discrimination. We granted certiorari, and now affirm.

We emphasize at the outset the narrowness of the question before us in this case. Respondents' claim is not based on the controversial concept of "comparable worth," under which plaintiffs might claim increased compensation on the basis of a comparison of the intrinsic worth or difficulty of their job with that of other jobs in the same organization or community. Rather, respondents seek to prove, by direct evidence, that their wages were depressed because of intentional sex discrimination, consisting of setting the wage scale for female guards, but not for male guards, at a level lower than its own survey of outside markets and the worth of the jobs warranted. The narrow question in this case is whether such a claim is precluded by the last sentence of §703(h) of Title VII, called the "Bennett Amendment."[8]

II

Title VII makes it an unlawful employment practice for an employer "to discriminate against any individual with respect to his compensation, terms, conditions, or privileges of employment, because of such individual's . . . sex . . . ." The Bennett Amendment to Title VII, however provides:

> "It shall not be an unlawful employment practice under [Title VII] for any employer to differentiate upon the basis of sex in determining the amount of the wages or compensation paid or to be paid to employees of such employer if such differentiation is authorized by the provisions of [the Equal Pay Act]."

To discover what practices are exempted from Title VII's prohibitions by the Bennett Amendment, we must turn to * * * the Equal Pay Act * * *. On its face, the Equal Pay Act contains three restrictions pertinent to this case. First, its coverage is limited to those employers subject to the Fair Labor Standards Act. * * * Second, the Act is restricted to cases involving "equal work on jobs the performance of which requires equal skill, effort, and responsibility, and which are performed under similar working conditions." Third, the Act's four affirmative defenses exempt any wage differentials attributable to seniority, merit, quantity or quality of production, or "any other factor other than sex."

Petitioner argues that the purpose of the Bennett Amendment was to restrict Title VII sex-based wage discrimination claims to those that could also be brought under the Equal Pay Act, and thus that claims not arising from "equal work" are precluded. Respondents, in contrast, argue that the Bennett Amendment was designed merely to incorporate the four affirmative defenses of the Equal Pay Act into Title VII for sex-based wage discrimination claims. Respondents thus contend that claims for sex-based wage discrimination can be brought under Title VII even though no member of the opposite sex holds an equal but higher-paying job, provided that the challenged

---

[8]We are not called upon in this case to decide whether respondents have stated a prima facie case of sex discrimination under Title VII, or to lay down standards for the further conduct of this litigation. The sole issue we decide is whether respondents' failure to satisfy the equal work standard of the Equal Pay Act in itself precludes their proceeding under Title VII.

wage rate is not based on seniority, merit, quantity or quality of production, or "any other factor other than sex." The Court of Appeals found respondents' interpretation the "more persuasive." While recognizing that the language and legislative history of the provision are not unambiguous, we conclude that the Court of Appeals was correct.

A

The language of the Bennett Amendment suggests an intention to incorporate only the affirmative defenses of the Equal Pay Act into Title VII. The Amendment bars sex-based wage discrimination claims under Title VII where the pay differential is "authorized" by the Equal Pay Act. Although the word "authorize" sometimes means simply "to permit," it ordinarily denotes affirmative enabling action. * * * The question, then, is what wage practices have been affirmatively authorized by the Equal Pay Act.

The Equal Pay Act is divided into two parts: a definition of the violation, followed by four affirmative defenses. The first part can hardly be said to "authorize" anything at all: it is purely prohibitory. The second part, however, in essence "authorizes" employers to differentiate in pay on the basis of seniority, merit, quantity or quality of production, or any other factor other than sex, even though such differentiation might otherwise violate the Act. It is to these provisions, therefore, that the Bennett Amendment must refer.

Petitioner argues that this construction of the Bennett Amendment would render it superfluous. Petitioner claims that the first three affirmative defenses are simply redundant of the provisions elsewhere in §703(h) of Title VII that already exempt bona fide seniority and merit systems and systems measuring earnings by quantity or quality of production, and that the fourth defense — "any other factor other than sex" — is implicit in Title VII's general prohibition of sex-based discrimination.

We cannot agree. The Bennett Amendment was offered as a "technical amendment" designed to resolve any potential conflicts between Title VII and the Equal Pay Act. Thus, with respect to the first three defenses, the Bennett Amendment has the effect of guaranteeing that courts and administrative agencies adopt a consistent interpretation of like provisions in both statutes. Otherwise, they might develop inconsistent bodies of case law interpreting two sets of nearly identical language.

More importantly, incorporation of the fourth affirmative defense could have significant consequences for Title VII litigation. Title VII's prohibition of discriminatory employment practices was intended to be broadly inclusive, proscribing "not only overt discrimination but also practices that are fair in form, but discriminatory in operation." *Griggs*. The structure of Title VII litigation, including presumptions, burdens of proof, and defenses, has been designed to reflect this approach. The fourth affirmative defense of the Equal Pay Act, however, was designed differently, to confine the application of the Act to wage differentials attributable to sex discrimination. Equal Pay Act litigation, therefore, has been structured to permit employers to defend against charges of discrimination where their pay differentials are based on a bona fide use of "other factors other than sex." * * * Although we do not decide in this case how sex-based wage discrimination litigation under Title VII should be structured to accommodate the fourth affirmative defense of the Equal Pay Act, we consider it clear that the Bennett Amendment, under this interpretation, is not rendered superfluous.

We therefore conclude that only differentials attributable to the four affirmative defenses of the Equal Pay Act are "authorized" by that Act within the meaning of §703(h) of Title VII.[14]

* * *

D

Our interpretation of the Bennett Amendment draws additional support from the remedial purposes of Title VII and the Equal Pay Act. * * * As Congress itself has indicated, a "broad approach" to the definition of equal employment opportunity is essential to overcoming and undoing the effect of discrimination. S.Rep.No. 867, 88th Cong., 2d Sess., 12 (1964). We must therefore avoid interpretations of Title VII that deprive victims of discrimination of a remedy, without clear congressional mandate.

Under petitioner's reading of the Bennett Amendment, only those sex-based wage discrimination claims that satisfy the "equal work" standard of the Equal Pay Act could be brought under Title VII. In practical terms, this means that a woman who is discriminatorily underpaid could obtain no relief — no matter how egregious the discrimination might be — unless her employer also employed a man in an equal job in the same establishment, at a higher rate of pay. Thus, if an employer hired a woman for a unique position in the company and then admitted that her salary would have been higher had she been male, the woman would be unable to obtain legal redress under petitioner's interpretation. Similarly, if an employer used a transparently sex-biased system for wage determination, women holding jobs not equal to those held by men would be denied the right to prove that the system is a pretext for discrimination. * * * Congress surely did not intend the Bennett Amendment to insulate such blatantly discriminatory practices from judicial redress under Title VII.[19]

Moreover, petitioner's interpretation would have other far-reaching consequences. Since it rests on the proposition that any wage differentials not prohibited by the Equal Pay Act are "authorized" by it, petitioner's interpretation would lead to the conclusion that discriminatory compensation by employers not covered by the Fair Labor Standards Act is "authorized" — since not prohibited — by the Equal Pay Act. Thus it would deny Title VII protection against sex-based wage discrimination by those employers not subject to the Fair Labor Standards Act but covered by Title VII. There is no persuasive evidence that Congress intended such a result, and the EEOC has

---

[14]The argument in the dissent that under our interpretation, the Equal Pay Act would be impliedly repealed and rendered a nullity is mistaken. Not only might the substantive provisions of the Equal Pay Act's affirmative defenses affect the outcome of some Title VII sex-based wage discrimination cases, but the procedural characteristics of the Equal Pay Act also remain significant. For example, the statute of limitations for backpay relief is more generous under the Equal Pay Act than under Title VII, and the Equal Pay Act, unlike Title VII, has no requirement of filing administrative complaints and awaiting administrative conciliation efforts. Given these advantages, many plaintiffs will prefer to sue under the Equal Pay Act rather than Title VII.

[19]The dissent attempts to minimize the significance of the Title VII remedy in these cases on the ground that the Equal Pay Act already provides an action for sex-biased wage discrimination by women who hold jobs not *currently* held by men. But the dissent's position would still leave remediless all victims of discrimination who hold jobs *never* held by men.

rejected it since at least 1965. Indeed, petitioner itself apparently acknowledges that Congress intended Title VII's broader coverage to apply to equal pay claims under Title VII, thus impliedly admitting the fallacy in its own argument.

* * *

III

Petitioner argues strenuously that the approach of the Court of Appeals * * * raise[s] the spectre that "Title VII plaintiffs could draw any type of comparison imaginable concerning job duties and pay between any job predominantly performed by women and any job predominantly performed by men." But whatever the merit of petitioner's arguments in other contexts, they are inapplicable here, for claims based on the type of job comparisons petitioner describes are manifestly different from respondents' claim. Respondents contend that the County of Washington evaluated the worth of their jobs; that the county determined that they should be paid approximately 95% as much as the male correctional officers; that it paid them only about 70% as much, while paying the male officers the full evaluated worth of their jobs; and that the failure of the county to pay respondents the full evaluated worth of their jobs can be proven to be attributable to intentional sex discrimination. Thus, respondents' suit does not require a court to make its own subjective assessment of the value of the male and female guard jobs, or to attempt by statistical technique or other method to quantify the effect of sex discrimination on the wage rates.

We do not decide in this case the precise contours of lawsuits challenging sex discrimination in compensation under Title VII. It is sufficient to note that respondents' claims of discriminatory undercompensation are not barred by §703(h) of Title VII merely because respondents do not perform work equal to that of male jail guards. The judgment of the Court of Appeals is therefore

Affirmed.

JUSTICE REHNQUIST, with whom THE CHIEF JUSTICE, JUSTICE STEWART, and JUSTICE POWELL join, dissenting.

* * * Because I believe that the legislative history of both the Equal Pay Act and Title VII clearly establishes that there can be no Title VII claim of sex-based wage discrimination without proof of "equal work," I dissent.

I

* * *

* * * [T]he Court ignores traditional canons of statutory construction and relevant legislative history. * * * It insists that there simply must be a remedy for wage discrimination beyond that provided in the Equal Pay Act. The Court does not explain why that must be so, nor does it explain what that remedy might be. And, of course, the Court cannot explain why it and not Congress is charged with determining what is and what is not sound public policy.

The closest the Court can come in giving a reason for its decision is its belief that interpretations of Title VII which "deprive victims of discrimination of a remedy, without clear congressional mandate" must be avoided. But that analysis turns traditional canons of statutory construction on their head. It has long been the rule that when a legislature enacts a statute to protect a class of persons, the burden is on the plaintiff to show statutory coverage, not on the defendant to show that there is a "clear congressional mandate" for excluding the plaintiff from coverage. Such a departure from traditional rules is particularly unwarranted in this case, where the doctrine of in pari materia suggests that all claims of sex-based wage discrimination are governed by the substantive standards of the previously enacted and more specific legislation, the Equal Pay Act.

Because the decision does not rest on any reasoned statement of logic or principle, it provides little guidance to employers or lower courts as to what types of compensation practices might now violate Title VII. * * * All we know is that Title VII provides a remedy when, as here, plaintiffs seek to show by direct evidence that their employer intentionally depressed their wages. And, for reasons that go largely unexplained, we also know that a Title VII remedy may not be available to plaintiffs who allege theories different than that alleged here, such as the so-called "comparable worth" theory. One has the sense that the decision today will be treated like a restricted railroad ticket, "good for this day and train only."

* * *

II

The Equal Pay Act

* * * In adopting the "equal pay for equal work" formula, Congress carefully considered and ultimately rejected the "equal pay for comparable worth" standard * * *. As the legislative history of the Equal Pay Act amply demonstrates, Congress realized that the adoption of the comparable worth doctrine would ignore the economic realities of supply and demand and would involve both governmental agencies and courts in the impossible task of ascertaining the worth of comparable work, an area in which they have little expertise.

* * *

* * * Instead, Congress concluded that governmental intervention to equalize wage differentials was to be undertaken only within one circumstance: when men's and women's jobs were identical or nearly so, hence unarguably of equal worth. It defies common sense to believe that the same Congress — which, after 18 months of hearings and debates, had decided in 1963 upon the extent of federal involvement it desired in the area of wage rate claims — intended sub silentio to reject all of this work and to abandon the limitations of the equal work approach just one year later, when it enacted Title VII.

Title VII

* * * The question is whether Congress intended to completely turn its back on the "equal work" standard enacted in the Equal Pay Act of 1963 when it adopted Title VII only one year later.

The Court answers that question in the affirmative, concluding that Title VII must be read more broadly than the Equal Pay Act. In so holding, the majority wholly ignores this Court's repeated adherence to the doctrine of *in pari materia*, namely, that "where there is no clear intention otherwise, a specific statute will not be controlled or nullified by a general one, regardless of the priority of enactment." * * *

When those principles are applied to this case, there can be no doubt that the Equal Pay Act and Title VII should be construed *in pari materia*. The Equal Pay Act is the more specific piece of legislation, dealing solely with sex-based wage discrimination, and was the product of exhaustive congressional study. Title VII, by contrast, is a general antidiscrimination provision, passed with virtually no consideration of the specific problem of sex-based wage discrimination. Most significantly, there is absolutely nothing in the legislative history of Title VII which reveals an intent by Congress to repeal by implication the provisions of the Equal Pay Act. Quite the contrary, what little legislative history there is on the subject * * * indicates that Congress intended to incorporate the substantive standards of the Equal Pay Act into Title VII so that sex-based wage discrimination claims would be governed by the equal work standard of the Equal Pay Act and by that standard alone.

* * *

* * * In response to questions by Senator Dirksen, Senator Clark, the floor manager for the bill, prepared a memorandum in which he attempted to put to rest certain objections which he believed to be unfounded. Senator Clark's answer to Senator Dirksen reveals that Senator Clark believed that all cases of wage discrimination under Title VII would be treated under the standards of the Equal Pay Act:

> * * * The Equal Pay Act is a part of the Wage Hour Law, with different coverage and with numerous exemptions unlike Title VII. * * * *The standards in the Equal Pay Act for determining discrimination as to wages, of course, are applicable to the comparable situation under Title VII.*" 110 Cong. Rec. 7217 (1964) (emphasis added).

* * *

Notwithstanding Senator Clark's explanation, Senator Bennett remained concerned that, absent an explicit cross reference to the Equal Pay Act, the "wholesale assertion" of the word "sex" in Title VII could nullify the carefully conceived Equal Pay Act standard. 110 Cong.Rec. 13647 (1964). Accordingly, he offered, and the Senate accepted, the * * * amendment to Title VII * * *.

Although the language of the Bennett Amendment is ambiguous, the most plausible interpretation of the Amendment is that it incorporates the substantive standard of the Equal Pay Act — the equal pay for equal work standard — into Title VII. A number of considerations support that view. In the first place, that interpretation is wholly consistent with, and in fact confirms, Senator Clark's earlier explanation of Title VII. Second, in the limited time available to Senator Bennett when he offered his amendment — the time for debate having been limited by cloture — he explained the Amendment's purpose.

* * *

> * * * *The purpose of my amendment is to provide that in the event of conflicts, the provisions of the Equal Pay Act shall not be nullified.*" 110 Cong.Rec. 13647 (1964) (emphasis supplied).

It is obvious that the principal way in which the Equal Pay Act could be "nullified" would be to allow plaintiffs unable to meet the "equal pay for equal work" standard to proceed under Title VII asserting some other theory of wage discrimination, such as "comparable worth." If plaintiffs can proceed under Title VII without showing that they satisfy the "equal work" criterion of the Equal Pay Act, one would expect all plaintiffs to file suit under the "broader" Title VII standard. Such a result would, for all practical purposes, constitute an implied repeal of the equal work standard of the Equal Pay Act and render that Act a nullity. This was precisely the result Congress sought to avert when it adopted the Bennett Amendment, and the result the Court today embraces.

* * *

The Court blithely ignores all of his legislative history and chooses to interpret the Bennett Amendment as incorporating only the Equal Pay Act's four affirmative defenses, and not the equal work requirement.[10] That argument does not survive scrutiny. In the first place, the language of the amendment draws no distinction between the Equal Pay Act's standard for liability — equal pay for equal work — and the Act's defenses. * * * In this case, it stands Congress' concern on its head to suppose that Congress sought to incorporate the affirmative defenses, but not the equal work standard. It would be surprising if Congress in 1964 sought to reverse its decision in 1963 to require a showing of "equal work" as a predicate to an equal pay claim and at the same time carefully preserve the four affirmative defenses.

Moreover, even on its own terms the Court's argument is unpersuasive. * * * The flaw in interpreting the Bennett Amendment as incorporating only the four defenses of the Equal Pay Act into Title VII is that Title VII, even without the Bennett Amendment, contains those very same defenses. The opening sentence of §703(h) protects differentials and compensation based on seniority, merit, or quantity or quality of production. These are three of the four EPA defenses. The fourth EPA defense, "a factor other than sex," is already implicit in Title VII because the statute's prohibition of sex discrimination applies only if there is discrimination on the basis of sex. Under the Court's interpretation, the Bennett Amendment, the second sentence of §703(h), is mere surplusage. The Court's answer to this argument is curious. It suggests that repetition ensures that the provisions would be consistently interpreted by the courts. But that answer only speaks to the purpose for incorporating the defenses in each statute, not for stating the defenses twice in the same statute. Courts are not quite as dense as the majority assumes.

* * *

III

Perhaps recognizing that there is virtually no support for its position in the legislative history, the Court rests its holding on its belief that any other holding would be unacceptable public policy. It argues that there must be remedy for wage discrimination beyond that provided for in the Equal Pay Act. Quite apart from the

---

[10]In reaching this conclusion, the Court relies far too heavily on a definition of the word "authorize." Rather than "make a fortress out of the dictionary," the Court should instead attempt to implement the legislative intent of Congress. Even if dictionary definitions were to be our guide, the word "authorized" has been defined to mean exactly what petitioners contend. Black's Law Dictionary defines "authorized" to mean "to permit a thing to be done in the future." Accordingly, the language of the Bennett Amendment suggests that those differentiations which are authorized under the Equal Pay Act — and thus Title VII — are those based on "skill, effort, responsibility and working conditions" and those related to the four affirmative defenses. * * *

fact that that is an issue properly left to Congress and not the Court, the Court is wrong even as a policy matter. The Court's parade of horribles that would occur absent a distinct Title VII remedy simply do not support the result it reaches.

First, the Court contends that a separate Title VII remedy is necessary to remedy the situation where an employer admits to a female worker, hired for a unique position, that her compensation would have been higher had she been male. Stated differently, the Court insists that an employer could isolate a predominantly female job category and arbitrarily cut its wages because no men currently perform equal or substantially equal work. But a Title VII remedy is unnecessary in these cases because an Equal Pay Act remedy is available. Under the Equal Pay Act, it is not necessary that every Equal Pay Act violation be established through proof that members of the opposite sex are currently performing equal work for greater pay. However, unlikely such an admission might be in the bullpen of litigation, an employer's statement that "if my female employees performing a particular job were males, I would pay them more simply because they are males" would be admissible in a suit under that Act. Overt discrimination does not go unremedied by the Equal Pay Act. In addition, insofar as hiring or placement discrimination caused the isolated job category, Title VII already provides numerous remedies * * * without resort to job comparisons. In short, if women are limited to low paying jobs against their will, they have adequate remedies under Title VII for denial of job opportunities even under what I believe is the correct construction of the Bennett Amendment.

* * *

There is of course a situation in which petitioners' position would deny women a remedy for claims of sex-based wage discrimination. A remedy would not be available where a lower paying job held primarily by women is "comparable," but not substantially equal to, a higher paying job performed by men. That is, plaintiffs would be foreclosed from showing that they received unequal pay for work of "comparable worth" or that dissimilar jobs are of "equal worth." The short, and best, answer to that contention is that Congress in 1963 explicitly chose not to provide a remedy in such cases. And contrary to the suggestion of the Court, it is by no means clear that Title VII was enacted to remedy all forms of alleged discrimination. * * * Congress balanced the need for a remedy for wage discrimination against its desire to avoid the burdens associated with governmental intervention into wage structures. The Equal Pay Act's "equal pay for equal work" formula reflects the outcome of this legislative balancing. In construing Title VII, therefore, the courts cannot be indifferent to this sort of political compromise.

IV

* * *

Because there are no logical underpinnings to the Court's opinion, all we may conclude is that even absent a showing of equal work there is a cause of action under Title VII where there is direct evidence that an employer has intentionally depressed a woman's salary because she is a woman. The decision today does not approve a cause of action based on a comparison of the wage rates of dissimilar jobs.

For the foregoing reasons, however, I believe that even that narrow holding cannot be supported by the legislative history of the Equal Pay Act and Title VII. This is simply a case where the Court has superimposed upon Title VII a "gloss of its own choosing."

NOTES AND PROBLEMS FOR DISCUSSION

1. As the minority pounded home in its dissenting opinion, the majority in *Gunther* left the difficult task of formulating the proof standards to be applied to plaintiffs in Title VII-based claims of intentional wage discrimination to the lower courts. In WILKINS v. UNIVERSITY OF HOUSTON, 654 F.2d 388 (5th Cir. 1981), vacated and remanded, 459 U.S. 809, 103 S.Ct. 34, 74 L.Ed.2d 47 (1982), affirmed on remand, 695 F.2d 134 (5th Cir. 1983), a post-*Gunther* case, the plaintiffs' Title VII complaint alleged that the defendant University had evaluated all of the jobs held by its professional and administrative staff employees and had classified each of them into one of nine levels. Although they did not offer evidence that women were paid less than men for equal work, the plaintiffs did show that in the University's academic division, a disproportionate number of those employees paid less than the minimum salary established for the level of their jobs were women and that all of the employees who received a salary in excess of the maximum assigned to their job levels were men. This statistical evidence of disparate wage treatment effected through the discriminatory application of a job classification system, the court held, established a prima facie Title VII violation.

2. The *Gunther* Court emphasized that the plaintiffs did not assert a "comparable worth" claim and thus it specifically reserved decision on whether such a claim was cognizable under Title VII. Under this theory, employees are entitled to equal pay for jobs that are not substantially equal but that are comparable in their value to the employer. This, its proponents contend, would respond to the general undervaluation of jobs traditionally dominated by women, which goes unremedied under traditional Equal Pay doctrine because of the absence of male workers in those positions. Its opponents argue that such a theory would result in an unacceptable intrusion into the labor market and require courts to engage in a comparative appraisal of the value of unrelated jobs, an area in which they have little institutional expertise. Nevertheless, the lower courts typically dismiss comparable worth claims absent evidence that the plaintiffs' wages are lower solely because they are women, either because they are convinced that Congress did not intend to recognize such comparable worth claims or because they are disinclined to evaluate the worth of different jobs and rank them according to their relative values. *See* Plemer v. Parsons-Gilbane, 713 F.2d 1127 (5th Cir. 1983). *But see* Cox v. American Cast Iron Pipe Co., 784 F.2d 1546 (11th Cir. 1986), cert. denied, 479 U.S. 883, 107 S.Ct. 274, 93 L.Ed.2d 250 (1986) (plaintiff can state a Title VII claim when alleging that traditionally male jobs are compensated "objectively" based on a system of detailed job descriptions, standardized evaluations, job classifications, pay scales, and review provisions, while compensation for women's jobs is subjectively determined).

In AFSCME v. STATE OF WASHINGTON, 770 F.2d 1401 (9th Cir. 1985), however, after commissioning an independent study of civil service positions that concluded that clear indications of pay differences existed between job groups predominantly held by men and those predominantly held by women and that the jobs were of comparable worth, the State chose not to implement the report's recommendations for eliminating these disparities. The Ninth Circuit reversed the trial court's holding that the State's failure to eliminate an admittedly discriminatory compensation system constituted an intentional violation of Title VII since the State had not presented convincing evidence of a good faith reason for its failure to pay women their evaluated worth. The appellate court on the other hand, declared that employers should be commended rather than penalized for undertaking job evaluation studies. Consequently, it ruled that the State's failure to adopt the recommendations of a study that it had commissioned did not establish the discriminatory motive required in a disparate treatment claim. To do otherwise, the court reasoned, would create a disincentive to employers to conduct job evaluation studies.

The Seventh Circuit has suggested that if the plaintiff in a situation like this could establish that the employer's decision not to implement the results of its own job evaluation study was because it believed that women should be paid less than men for equal work, she could state a claim under Title VII. American Nurses Ass'n v. State Of Illinois, 783 F.2d 716 (7th Cir.1986). Despite the judiciary's disinclination to recognize comparable worth claims, several states have passed statutes requiring employers to provide equal pay for comparable work.

If the plaintiff convinces the trial court that the employer has violated Title VII by intentionally depressing the wages in those job classifications in which women predominate, the prevailing view is that such an action cannot be brought by a male employee on the ground that he lacks standing to sue because he is not a "person aggrieved" from discrimination "on the basis of sex." See Patee v. Pacific Northwest Bell Tel. Co., 803 F.2d 476 (9th Cir. 1986).

For more on the viability of comparable worth claims, see Winn Newman & Jeanne M. Vonhof, *Separate But Equal — Job Segregation and Pay Equity in the Wake of Gunther*, 1981 U.ILL.L.REV. 269 (1981); Deborah L. Rhode, Occupational Inequality, 1988 Duke L.J. 1207 (1988); Daniel R. Fischel & Edward P. Lazear, *Comparable Worth and Discrimination in Labor Markets,* 53 U.CHI.L.REV. 891 (1986); James D. Holzhauer, *The Economic Possibilities of Comparable Worth*, 53 U.CHI.L.REV. 919 (1986); Mary E. Becker, *Barriers Facing Women in the Wage Labor Market and the Need for Additional Remedies: A Reply to Fischel and Lazear*, 53 U.CHI.L.REV. 934 (1986); Daniel R. Fischel & Edward P. Lazear, *Comparable Worth: A Rejo*inder, 53 U.CHI.L.REV. 950 (1986).

4. (a) Where a plaintiff establishes a prima facie case of wage discrimination under Title VII, does the Court's treatment of the Bennett Amendment in *Gunther* suggest that the defendant in a Title VII case alleging sex-based wage discrimination must shoulder a heavier burden of proof than it would confront in a non-wage Title VII claim?

(b) Did the *Gunther* Court imply that defendants in Title VII wage discrimination cases are limited to the four EPA defenses? *Compare* Fallon v. Illinois, 882 F.2d 1206 (7th Cir.1989), *with* Kouba v. Allstate Insurance Co., 691 F.2d 873 (9th Cir. 1982).

5. To the extent that a federal employee's wage discrimination claim falls within the jurisdiction of Title VII as well as the Equal Pay Act, does the exclusivity rule announced by the Supreme Court in *Brown* preclude that individual from bringing an action under the EPA? See Epstein v. Secretary, U.S. Dep't of Treasury, 552 F.Supp. 436 (N.D. Ill. 1982).

CHAPTER 10

The Age Discrimination in Employment Act

SECTION A. OVERVIEW OF STATUTORY PROVISIONS

The Age Discrimination in Employment Act of 1967 (ADEA)[a] as amended in 1974,[b] 1978,[c] 1986[d] and 1990[e] is the exclusive federal statutory remedy for age discrimination in employment. Before the enactment of the ADEA, federal protection against age discrimination was limited to government workers (through the equal protection and due process clauses of the Constitution) and employees of federal contractors and subcontractors (through Executive Order 11141[f]).[g] The ADEA, like Title VII, applies to employers, labor organizations and employment agencies. It defines employers as private business organizations that are engaged in commerce and have at least twenty employees,[h] their agents, and state and local government[i] entities.[j]

---

[a]Pub.L. 90-202, 81 Stat. 602, 29 U.S.C. §§621-634 (1976).

[b]Pub.L. 93-259, 88 Stat. 74, 29 U.S.C. §§630(b), (c), (f), 633a, 634 (1976).

[c]Pub.L. 95-256, 92 Stat. 189, 29 U.S.C. §§623, (f)(2), 624, 626(c), (d), (e), 631, 633a(a), (f), (g), 634 (1981).

[d]Pub.L. 99-592, 100 Stat. 3342, 29 U.S.C. §623 (1986).

[e]Pub.L. 101-433, 104 Stat. 978, 29 U.S.C. §621 et seq. (1990).

[f]3 C.F.R. §179 (1964), 29 Fed.Reg. 2477 (1964). This Order, promulgated by President Johnson, provides that federal contractors and subcontractors shall not discriminate on the basis of age except upon the basis of a bona fide occupational qualification, retirement plan or statutory requirement.

[g]A few states, such as Arizona, Hawaii, Idaho, Kentucky, Texas and Utah, had enacted state laws prohibiting age discrimination in employment before the passage of the ADEA.

[h]As the result of a 1984 amendment to the ADEA, the statute expressly applies to U.S. citizens employed abroad by American corporations or their subsidiaries except in cases where application of the ADEA would violate the law of the nation in which the U.S. citizen is employed. In determining whether compliance with the ADEA would cause an employer to violate "the laws" of the host country, is it sufficient for the defendant to establish that ADEA compliance would violate well established and customary practices and policies or must the plaintiff demonstrate that compliance would violate domestic positive law? *See* Mahoney v. Rfe/Rl Inc., 47 F.3d 447 (D.C.Cir.1995), cert. denied, 516 U.S. 866, 116 S.Ct. 181, 133 L.Ed.2d 120 (1995) (contractual provisions, practices and policies fall within the meaning of "laws" even though they are the product of private arrangements because they are legally enforceable).

[i]The constitutionality of the 1974 amendment to the ADEA that extended its coverage to state and local government employees was initially upheld by the Supreme Court in EEOC v. WYOMING, 460 U.S. 226, 103 S.Ct. 1054, 75 L.Ed.2d 18 (1983). The Court rejected the

contention that the statutory amendment violated the Tenth Amendment on the ground that the Tenth Amendment prohibits federal interference in certain core state functions and requiring state and local governments to comply with the ADEA did not directly impair a state's ability to structure integral operations in areas of traditional governmental functions. The Court ruled that the degree of federal intrusion occasioned by application of the ADEA to a Wyoming statute requiring employer approval of the employment of game wardens who reach age 55 was not significant enough to override Congress' choice to extend its anti-age bias policy to the states. The Court did not, however, determine the precise constitutional parentage of the legislative extension of the ADEA to state employees. This issue is also relevant in determining whether the statute's provision of a private cause of action for damages against a state employer operated as a constitutional abrogation of the states' Eleventh Amendment right of sovereign immunity from damage claims in federal court. In SEMINOLE TRIBE OF FLORIDA v. FLORIDA, 517 U.S. 44, 116 S.Ct. 1114, 134 L.Ed.2d 252 (1996), the Court ruled that in order for a federal statute to constitutionally abrogate an unconsenting states' Eleventh Amendment right to sovereign immunity, the statute (1) must reflect Congress' clear intent to create a private cause of action for damages; and (2) must have been enacted pursuant only to Congress enforcement authority under §5 of the Fourteenth Amendment. In doing so, the Court reversed its earlier jurisprudence that the Commerce Clause could also serve as constitutional authority for federal statutory abrogation of sovereign immunity. As a result of this ruling, courts examining the constitutionality of federal statutes regulating the employment practices of state governments (such as the ADEA, the ADA, and the EPA) had to determine whether Congress intended to remove the states' right of sovereign immunity and whether that provision was enacted pursuant to the Fourteenth Amendment.

The Court applied this bipartite test to the ADEA in KIMEL v. FLORIDA BOARD OF REGENTS, 528 U.S. 62, 120 S.Ct. 631, 145 L.Ed.2d 522 (2000). There, the Court ruled that the 1974 amendment to the ADEA did not constitutionally abrogate the State's Eleventh Amendment immunity from private suits for monetary damages in federal court. Seven Members of the Court agreed that the language of the 1974 amendment clearly and unmistakably provided for suits by individual employees against States for money damages. (Interestingly, this group of seven consisted of only three Justices who signed onto the opinion of the Court and all four signees of a separate concurring and dissenting opinion. The other two members who joined in the opinion of the Court dissented from this particular portion of that opinion.) However, all five Justices who signed on to the opinion of the Court agreed that the amendment to the ADEA could not be justified as an exercise of Congress' enforcement authority under §5 of the Fourteenth Amendment. This latter conclusion was made pursuant to the language in *Seminole Tribe*, i.e., whether there was a "congruence and proportionality between the injury to be prevented or remedied and the means adopted to that end." The majority reasoned that since age classifications are subject to minimal equal protection scrutiny and, therefore, can survive constitutional challenge by the mere showing of a rational relation to a legitimate state interest, age-based classifications undertaken by public actors can be based on broad generalizations that are not universally (or even generally) accurate without running afoul of constitutional restrictions on the exercise of state power. In comparison, however, the majority continued, the proscriptions against age discrimination contained in the ADEA far exceeded the range of age-based conduct that would be unconstitutional since under the statute, any age-based classification was presumptively unlawful, subject to the defendant's establishment of an affirmative defense. This fact, coupled with the lack of a legislative record identifying a pattern of age discrimination by the States, convinced the majority that Congress had "no reason" to believe that broad prophylactic legislation was necessary in this field and, therefore, that the 1974 amendment was not a valid exercise of Congress' power under §5 of the Fourteenth Amendment. Finally, as almost an afterthought, the Court mentioned that its ruling did not leave state employees defenseless against age discrimination since age discrimination legislation existed in nearly every state that provided state employees with a right to recover money damages from their employers.

In the final paragraph of its opinion, the majority declared that "we hold only that, in the

ADEA, Congress did not validly abrogate the States' sovereign immunity to suits by private individuals." Does this mean that the Court was not reversing its decision in *Wyoming* in which it upheld the constitutionality of the extension of the *substantive* provisions of the ADEA to state and local employees? In other words, was the Court only striking down the right of a state employee to bring a private action for money damages, but leaving intact that individual's opportunity to bring an action for equitable relief against the appropriate governmental official? In KATZ v. REGENTS OF UNIV. OF CAL., 229 F.3d 831 (9th Cir.2000), a post-*Kimel* case, the court asserted that not only did *Kimel* not strike down the substantive provisions of the ADEA as applied to state government employees, but that *Kimel* also did not preclude the possibility of state employees receiving monetary awards in ADEA claims against their state employers. The appellate panel noted that any State could affirmatively waive its sovereign immunity on a case-by-case basis. The court also stated that sovereign immunity is a defense that could be waived by failure to assert it. But since there was evidence in the instant case that the state had expressly disavowed its Eleventh Amendment immunity as a defense, the court did not rely on the waiver-by-failure-to-assert doctrine. Alternatively, does this "private individuals" language of the sentence suggest that the States could not successfully assert a sovereign immunity defense against and ADEA action brought against them by the EEOC? The Supreme Court consistently has recognized an exception to sovereign immunity doctrine with respect to suits brought against states by the federal government. *See e.g.*, Alden v. Maine, 527 U.S. 706, 119 S.Ct. 2240, 144 L.Ed.2d 636 (1999). Moreover, when the Supreme Court applied the teachings of *Kimel* to strike down those provisions of the ADA providing state employees with a private cause of action for damages against States, Bd. Of Trustees of Univ. of Alabama v. Garrett, 531 U.S. 356, 121 S.Ct. 955, 148 L.Ed.2d 866 (2001), it noted that such suits could lawfully be brought against the states under the ADA by the federal government. Consequently, the courts have permitted EEOC suits for money damages (including make-whole relief for the aggrieved individual) against States under the ADEA. *See e.g.*, EEOC v. Bd. Of Supervisors for the Univ. of La. Sys., 559 F.3d 270 (5th Cir. 2009).

Years before its rulings in *Seminole Tribe* and *Kimel*, the Supreme Court, in Fitzpatrick v. Bitzer, 427 U.S. 445, 96 S.Ct. 2666, 49 L.Ed.2d (614) (1976) held that the 1972 amendments to Title VII that extended this statute's substantive provisions to state governments and authorized federal courts to award monetary damages against state governments was enacted pursuant to Congress' authority under §5 of the Fourteenth Amendment. Many circuit courts have taken *Fitzpatrick* to resolve all Eleventh Amendment challenges to Title VII. Others have expressly ruled, post-*Kimel*, that, at least with respect to the disparate treatment prohibition of Title VII, Congress validly abrogated the States' Eleventh Amendment immunity in passing the 1972 amendment. See Nanda v. Board of Trustees of University of Illinois, 303 F.3d 817 (7th Cir.2002, cert. denied, 539 U.S. 902, 123 S.Ct. 2246, 156 L.Ed.2d 110 (2003).

Minnesota became the first State to respond to *Kimel* when its legislature passed a statute on May 21, 2001, waiving its immunity from suit for money damages in federal court under the ADEA, ADA, FLSA (Equal Pay Act) and FMLA.

The ruling in *Kimel*, of course, does not affect the ability of state employees to seek protection under state disability discrimination laws. Two states, however, Alabama and Maryland, do not provide a private right of action to individuals with disability claims and seven States do not permit the recovery of compensatory damages.

Section 11 of the ADEA defines covered "employers" in two sentences. The first contains a twenty employee numerosity requirement for an organization "engaged in an industry affecting commerce." The second sentence provides that "employer" "also means" a State or political subdivision of a State. This created a circuit conflict as to whether the numerosity requirement applied to state and local governments. In MOUNT LEMMON FIRE DISTRICT v. GUIDO, 586 U.S. ___, 139 S.Ct. 22, 202 L.Ed.2d 262 (2018), the Court unanimously resolved this conflict by ruling that the "also means" language of that second sentence was intended to create two categories of covered employees: private sector companies with twenty or more employees and States or political subdivisions with no attendant numerosity limitation. The Court also noted that while this ruling meant that the ADEA would have a wider scope of

A separate provision, patterned exactly after §717 of Title VII, extends the coverage of the Act to federal employees.[k] Similarly, the ADEA's definition of labor organizations and employment agencies, with one minor exception, duplicates the language of the corresponding Title VII provisions.[l]

The substantive portions of the ADEA, including the prohibitions against retaliation and discriminatory advertising, are also virtually identical to the antidiscrimination provisions of Title VII. The major difference, of course, is that the ADEA only prohibits discrimination on the basis of age and only as to persons 40 years of age or older. Finally, an aggrieved can bring a private cause of action under the ADEA, but only, as with Title VII claims, after he or she has pursued certain administrative remedies. The materials in this chapter are designed to offer a more detailed examination of the substantive and procedural components of the ADEA.

---

application in the nonfederal public sector than Title VII (which does contain a numerosity requirement for state and local government employers), this nonparallelism was justified by the disparate language of the two statutes.

[j]As the result of amendments to the ADEA contained within the 1991 Civil Rights Act, elected officials are exempted from the statutory definition of "employee." Section 630(b) of the ADEA defines "employer" to include (1) agents of "persons" and (2) states and their political subdivisions. Section 630(a) defines "person" to include all forms of business associations, but does not explicitly include state and local governments. Does this failure to include state and local governments within the "person" or "agent" definitions suggest that agents of a state's instrumentalities are not "employers" within the meaning of the Act and therefore cannot be sued individually? See Price v. Erie County, 654 F.Supp. 1206 (W.D.N.Y.1987) ("agents" language does not apply to state employers; although Congress intended to provide government employees with the same protection previously enjoyed by private sector workers, the denial of a remedy against agents of states only "marginally" distinguished the protections afforded public and private sector employees). By contrast, the court noted, when Congress amended Title VII to include public sector workers, it explicitly added state and local governments to the definition of both "person" and "employer."

[k] This provision, in language identical to that found in §717 of Title VII, extends the application of the Act to employees or applicants for employment in the "military departments." Nevertheless, relying on a series of lower court cases arising under Title VII, the courts have held that Congress did not intend for this provision to extend the protections of the Act to uniformed personnel. See Kawitt v. United States, 842 F.2d 951 (7th Cir.1988). And though the definition of "employer" in this provision does not contain any express minimum employee requirement for public sector employers, one court has reasoned that since the statutory history indicates that Congress intended the law to extend the same coverage to private and public employees, "common sense" dictated that the minimum employee size be equally applicable to public employers. See EEOC v. Monclova Township, 920 F.2d 360 (6th Cir.1990).

[l] The ADEA requires statutory labor organizations that do not operate a hiring hall to have twenty-five members, whereas only fifteen members are required by Title VII. The ADEA, like the Equal Pay Act, incorporates the remedial scheme of the FLSA. The FLSA authorizes an employee to bring an action for damages against an "employer" and expressly excludes labor organizations from the definition of "employer." Accordingly, an employee cannot recover damages against a union under the ADEA.

SECTION B. SUBSTANTIVE PROVISIONS

Read §4 of the ADEA.

1. THE MEANING OF "AGE"

General Dynamics Land Systems, Inc v. Cline

Supreme Court of the United States, 2004.

540 U.S. 581, 124 S.Ct. 1236, 157 L.Ed.2d 1094.

JUSTICE SOUTER delivered the opinion of the Court.

The Age Discrimination in Employment Act of 1967 (ADEA or Act), forbids discriminatory preference for the young over the old. The question in this case is whether it also prohibits favoring the old over the young. We hold it does not.

I

In 1997, a collective-bargaining agreement between petitioner General Dynamics and the United Auto Workers eliminated the company's obligation to provide health benefits to subsequently retired employees, except as to then-current workers at least 50 years old. Respondents (collectively, Cline) were then at least 40 and thus protected by the Act, but under 50 and so without promise of the benefits. All of them objected to the new terms, although some had retired before the change in order to get the prior advantage, some retired afterwards with no benefit, and some worked on, knowing the new contract would give them no health coverage when they were through.

Before the Equal Employment Opportunity Commission (EEOC or Commission) they claimed that the agreement violated the ADEA, because it discriminated against them with respect to terms, conditions, or privileges of employment because of their age. The EEOC agreed and invited General Dynamics and the union to settle informally with Cline.

When they failed, Cline brought this action against General Dynamics, combining claims under the ADEA and state law. The District Court called the federal claim one of "reverse age discrimination," upon which, it observed, no court had ever granted relief under the ADEA. It dismissed in reliance on the Seventh Circuit's opinion in Hamilton v. Caterpillar Inc., 966 F.2d 1226 (1992), that "the ADEA 'does not protect ... the younger against the older'."

A divided panel of the Sixth Circuit reversed, with the majority reasoning that the prohibition of §4(a)(1), covering discrimination against "any individual ... because of such individual's age," is so clear on its face that if Congress had meant to limit its coverage to protect only the older worker against the younger, it would have said so. The court acknowledged the conflict of its ruling with earlier cases, including Hamilton, but it criticized the cases going the other way for paying too much attention to the "hortatory, generalized language" of the congressional findings incorporated in the ADEA. The Sixth Circuit drew support for its view from the position taken by the EEOC in an interpretive regulation.[1]

* * *

We granted certiorari to resolve the conflict among the Circuits, and now reverse.

II

The common ground in this case is the generalization that the ADEA's prohibition covers "discriminat[ion] ... because of [an] individual's age," §4(a)(1), that helps the younger by hurting the older. In the abstract, the phrase is open to an argument for a broader construction, since reference to "age" carries no express modifier and the word could be read to look two ways. This more expansive possible understanding does not, however, square with the natural reading of the whole provision prohibiting discrimination, and in fact Congress's interpretive clues speak almost unanimously to an understanding of discrimination as directed against workers who are older than the ones getting treated better.

Congress chose not to include age within discrimination forbidden by Title VII of the Civil Rights Act of 1964, being aware that there were legitimate reasons as well as invidious ones for making employment decisions on age. Instead it called for a study of the issue by the Secretary of Labor, who concluded that age discrimination was a serious problem, but one different in kind from discrimination on account of race.[2] The Secretary spoke of disadvantage to older individuals from arbitrary and stereotypical employment distinctions (including then-common policies of age ceilings on hiring), but he examined the problem in light of rational considerations of increased pension cost and, in some cases, legitimate concerns about an older person's ability to do the job. When the Secretary ultimately took the position that arbitrary discrimination against older workers was widespread and persistent enough to call for a federal legislative remedy, he placed his recommendation against the background of common experience that the potential cost of employing someone rises with age, so that the older an employee is, the greater the inducement to prefer a younger substitute. The report contains no suggestion that reactions to age level off at some point, and it was devoid of any indication that the Secretary had noticed unfair advantages accruing to older employees at the expense of their juniors.

Congress then asked for a specific proposal. Extensive House and Senate hearings ensued.

---

[1] 29 CFR §1625.2(a)(2003) ("[I]f two people apply for the same position, and one is 42 and the other 52, the employer may not lawfully turn down either one on the basis of age, but must make such decision on the basis of some other factor").

[2] That report found that "[e]mployment discrimination because of race is identified ... with ... feelings about people entirely unrelated to their ability to do the job. There is *no* significant discrimination of this kind so far as older workers are concerned. The most closely related kind of discrimination in the non-employment of older workers involves their rejection because of assumptions about the effect of age on their ability to do a job *when there is in fact no basis for these assumptions*." Report of the Secretary of Labor, The Older American Worker: Age Discrimination in Employment 2 (1965) (hereinafter Wirtz Report) (emphasis in original).

The testimony at both hearings dwelled on unjustified assumptions about the effect of age on ability to work. The hearings specifically addressed higher pension and benefit costs as heavier drags on hiring workers the older they got. The record thus reflects the common facts that an individual's chances to find and keep a job get worse over time; as between any two people, the younger is in the stronger position, the older more apt to be tagged with demeaning stereotype. Not surprisingly, from the voluminous records of the hearings, we have found (and Cline has cited) nothing suggesting that any workers were registering complaints about discrimination in favor of their seniors.

Nor is there any such suggestion in the introductory provisions of the ADEA, which begins with statements of purpose and findings that mirror the Wirtz Report and the committee transcripts. The findings stress the impediments suffered by "older workers ... in their efforts to retain ... and especially to regain employment,"; "the [burdens] of arbitrary age limits regardless of potential for job performance,"; the costs of "otherwise desirable practices [that] may work to the disadvantage of older persons,"; and "the incidence of unemployment, especially long-term unemployment [, which] is, relative to the younger ages, high among older workers." The statutory objects were "to promote employment of older persons based on their ability rather than age; to prohibit arbitrary age discrimination in employment; [and] to help employers and workers find ways of meeting problems arising from the impact of age on employment."

In sum, except on one point, all the findings and statements of objectives are either cast in terms of the effects of age as intensifying over time, or are couched in terms that refer to "older" workers, explicitly or implicitly relative to "younger" ones. The single subject on which the statute speaks less specifically is that of "arbitrary limits" or "arbitrary age discrimination." But these are unmistakable references to the Wirtz Report's finding that "[a]lmost three out of every five employers covered by [a] 1965 survey have in effect age limitations (most frequently between 45 and 55) on new hires which they apply without consideration of an applicant's other qualifications." The ADEA's ban on "arbitrary limits" thus applies to age caps that exclude older applicants, necessarily to the advantage of younger ones.

Such is the setting of the ADEA's core substantive provision, §4, prohibiting employers and certain others from discrimination because of an individual's age * * *. The prefatory provisions and their legislative history make a case that we think is beyond reasonable doubt, that the ADEA was concerned to protect a relatively old worker from discrimination that works to the advantage of the relatively young.

Nor is it remarkable that the record is devoid of any evidence that younger workers were suffering at the expense of their elders, let alone that a social problem required a federal statute to place a younger worker in parity with an older one. Common experience is to the contrary, and the testimony, reports, and congressional findings simply confirm that Congress used the phrase "discriminat[ion] ... because of [an] individual's age" the same way that ordinary people in common usage might speak of age discrimination any day of the week. One commonplace conception of American society in recent decades is its character as a "youth culture," and in a world where younger is better, talk about discrimination because of age is naturally understood to refer to discrimination against the older.

This same, idiomatic sense of the statutory phrase is confirmed by the statute's restriction of the protected class to those 40 and above. If Congress had been worrying about protecting the younger against the older, it would not likely have ignored everyone under 40. The youthful deficiencies of inexperience and unsteadiness invite stereotypical and discriminatory thinking about those a lot younger than 40, and prejudice suffered by a 40-year-old is not typically owing to youth, as 40-year-olds sadly tend to find out. The enemy of 40 is 30, not 50. Thus, the 40-year threshold makes sense as identifying a class requiring protection against preference for their juniors, not as defining a class that might be threatened by favoritism toward seniors.[5]

The federal reports are as replete with cases taking this position as they are nearly devoid of decisions like the one reviewed here. To start closest to home, the best example is Hazen Paper Co. v. Biggins, 507 U.S. 604, 113 S.Ct. 1701, 123 L.Ed.2d 338 (1993), in which we held there is no violation of the ADEA in firing an employee because his pension is about to vest, a basis for action that we took to be analytically distinct from age, even though it would never occur without advanced years. We said that "the very essence of age discrimination [is] for an older employee to be fired because the employer believes that productivity and competence decline with old age," whereas discrimination on the basis of pension status "would not constitute discriminatory treatment on the basis of age [because t]he prohibited stereotype [of the faltering worker] would not have figured in this decision, and the attendant stigma would not ensue." And we have relied on this same reading of the statute in other cases. See, e.g., O'Connor v. Consolidated Coin Caterers Corp., 517 U.S. 308, 313, 116 S.Ct 1307, 145 L.Ed.2d 433 (1996) ("Because the ADEA prohibits discrimination on the basis of age ... the fact that a replacement is substantially younger than the plaintiff is a ... reliable indicator of age discrimination"); Western Air Lines, Inc. v. Criswell, 472 U.S. 400, 409, 105 S.Ct. 2743, 86 L.Ed.2d 321 (1985) ("[T]he legislative history of the ADEA ... repeatedly emphasize[s that] the process of psychological and physiological degeneration caused by aging varies with each individual"). While none of these cases directly addresses the question presented here, all of them show our consistent understanding that the text, structure, and history point to the ADEA as a remedy for unfair preference based on relative youth, leaving complaints of the

---

[5]JUSTICE THOMAS charges our holding with unnaturally limiting a comprehensive prohibition of age discrimination to "the principal evil that Congress targeted," which he calls inconsistent with the method of *McDonald v. Santa Fe Trail Transp. Co.,* 427 U.S. 273, 96 S.Ct. 2574, 49 L.Ed.2d 493 (1976) (the Title VII prohibition of discrimination because of race protects whites), and *Oncale v. Sundowner Offshore Services, Inc.,* 523 U.S. 75, 118 S.Ct. 998, 140 L.Ed.2d 201 (1998) (the Title VII prohibition of discrimination because of sex protects men from sexual harassment by other men). His objection is aimed at the wrong place. As we discuss at greater length *infra,* we are not dealing here with a prohibition expressed by the unqualified use of a term without any conventionally narrow sense (as "race" or "sex" are used in Title VII), and are not narrowing such a prohibition so that it covers only instances of the particular practice that induced Congress to enact the general prohibition. We hold that Congress expressed a prohibition by using a term in a commonly understood, narrow sense ("age" as "relatively old age"). Justice THOMAS may think we are mistaken, when we infer that Congress used "age" as meaning the antithesis of youth rather than meaning any age, but we are not making the particular mistake of confining the application of terms used in a broad sense to the relatively narrow class of cases that prompted Congress to address their subject matter.

relatively young outside the statutory concern.

The Courts of Appeals and the District Courts have read the law the same way, and prior to this case have enjoyed virtually unanimous accord in understanding the ADEA to forbid only discrimination preferring young to old. So the Seventh Circuit held in *Hamilton* * * * and so the District Courts have ruled in cases too numerous for citation here in the text.[6] The very strength of this consensus is enough to rule out any serious claim of ambiguity, and congressional silence after years of judicial interpretation supports adherence to the traditional view.[7]

III

Cline and *amicus* EEOC proffer three rejoinders in favor of their competing view that the prohibition works both ways. First, they say (as does Justice Thomas), that the statute's meaning is plain when the word "age" receives its natural and ordinary meaning and the statute is read as a whole giving "age" the same meaning throughout. And even if the text does not plainly mean what they say it means, they argue that the soundness of their version is shown by a colloquy on the floor of the Senate involving Senator Yarborough, a sponsor of the bill that became the ADEA. Finally, they fall back to the position (fortified by Justice Scalia's dissent) that we should defer to the EEOC's reading of the statute. On each point, however, we think the argument falls short of unsettling our view of the natural meaning of the phrase speaking of discrimination, read in light of the statute's manifest purpose.

A

The first response to our reading is the dictionary argument that "age" means the length of a person's life, with the phrase "because of such individual's age" stating a simple test of causation: discrimination because of an individual's age is treatment that would not have occurred if the individual's span of years had been longer or shorter. The case for this reading calls attention to the other instances of "age" in the ADEA that are not limited to old age, such as §4(f), which gives an employer a defense to charges of age discrimination when "age is a bona fide occupational qualification." Cline and the EEOC argue that if "age" meant old age, §4(f) would then provide a defense (old age is a bona fide qualification) only for an employer's action that on our reading would never clash with the statute (because preferring the older is not forbidden).

The argument rests on two mistakes. First, it assumes that the word "age" has the

---

[6] * * *. The only case we have found arguably to the contrary is *Mississippi Power & Light Co. v. Local Union Nos. 605 & 985, IBEW*, 945 F.Supp. 980, 985 (S.D.Miss.1996), which allowed a claim objecting to a benefit given to individuals between 60 and 65 and denied to those outside that range, without discussing *Hamilton* or any of the other authority holding that the plaintiffs under 60 would lack a cause of action.

[7] Congress has not been shy in revising other judicial constructions of the ADEA. See Public Employees Retirement System of Ohio v. Betts, 492 U.S. 158, 167-168, 109 S.Ct. 854, 106 L.Ed.2d 134 (1989) (observing that the 1978 amendment to the ADEA "changed the specific result" of this Court's earlier case of United Air Lines, Inc. v. McMann, 434 U.S. 192, 98 S.Ct. 444, 54 L.Ed.2d 402 (1977)); H.R.Rep. No. 101-664, pp. 10-11, 34 (1990) (stating that Congress in 1978 had also disapproved *McMann's* reasoning, and that with the 1990 amendments it meant to overrule *Betts* as well).

same meaning wherever the ADEA uses it. But this is not so, and Cline simply misemploys the "presumption that identical words used in different parts of the same act are intended to have the same meaning." Atlantic Cleaners & Dyers, Inc. v. United States, 286 U.S. 427, 433, 52 S.Ct. 607, 76 L.Ed. 1204 (1932). Cline forgets that "the presumption is not rigid and readily yields whenever there is such variation in the connection in which the words are used as reasonably to warrant the conclusion that they were employed in different parts of the act with different intent." *Ibid.*; see also Robinson v. Shell Oil Co., 519 U.S. 337, 343-344, 117 S.Ct. 843, 136 L.Ed.2d 808 (1997) (term "employee" has different meanings in different parts of Title VII). The presumption of uniform usage thus relents when a word used has several commonly understood meanings among which a speaker can alternate in the course of an ordinary conversation, without being confused or getting confusing.

"Age" is that kind of word. As Justice Thomas agrees, the word "age" standing alone can be readily understood either as pointing to any number of years lived, or as common shorthand for the longer span and concurrent aches that make youth look good. Which alternative was probably intended is a matter of context; we understand the different choices of meaning that lie behind a sentence like "Age can be shown by a driver's license," and the statement, "Age has left him a shut-in." So it is easy to understand that Congress chose different meanings at different places in the ADEA, as the different settings readily show. Hence the second flaw in Cline's argument for uniform usage: it ignores the cardinal rule that "[s]tatutory language must be read in context [since] a phrase 'gathers meaning from the words around it.'" Jones v. United States, 527 U.S. 373, 389, 119 S.Ct. 2090, 144 L.Ed.2d 370 (1999). The point here is that we are not asking an abstract question about the meaning of "age"; we are seeking the meaning of the whole phrase "discriminate ... because of such individual's age," where it occurs in the ADEA. As we have said, social history emphatically reveals an understanding of age discrimination as aimed against the old, and the statutory reference to age discrimination in this idiomatic sense is confirmed by legislative history. For the very reason that reference to context shows that "age" means "old age" when teamed with "discrimination," the provision of an affirmative defense when age is a bona fide occupational qualification readily shows that "age" as a qualification means comparative youth. As context tells us that "age" means one thing in §4(a)(1) and another in §4(f),[9] so it also tells us that the presumption of uniformity cannot

---

[9]An even wider contextual enquiry supports our conclusion, for the uniformity Cline and the EEOC claim for the uses of "age" within the ADEA itself would introduce unwelcome discord among the federal statutes on employee benefit plans. For example, the Tax Code requires an employer to allow certain employees who reach age 55 to diversify their stock ownership plans in part, 26 U.S.C. §401(a)(28)(B); removes a penalty on early distributions from retirement plans at age 59 1/2, §72(t)(2)(A)(i); requires an employer to allow many employees to receive benefits immediately upon retiring at age 65, §401(a)(14); and requires an employer to adjust upward an employee's pension benefits if that employee continues to work past age 70 ½, §401(a)(9)(C)(iii). The Employee Retirement Income Security Act of 1974 makes similar provisions. *See, e.g.,* 29 U.S.C. §1002(24) ("normal retirement age" may come at age 65, although the plan specifies later); §1053(a) (a plan must pay full benefits to employees who retire at normal retirement age). Taken one at a time any of these statutory directives might be viewed as an exception Congress carved out of a generally recognized principle that employers may not give benefits to older employees that they withhold from younger ones. Viewed as a

sensibly operate here.

The comparisons Justice Thomas urges, to McDonald v. Santa Fe Trail Transp. Co., and Oncale v. Sundowner Offshore Services, Inc., serve to clarify our position. Both cases involved Title VII of the Civil Rights Act of 1964 and its prohibition on employment discrimination "because of [an] individual's race ... [or] sex." The term "age" employed by the ADEA is not, however, comparable to the terms "race" or "sex" employed by Title VII. "Race" and "sex" are general terms that in every day usage require modifiers to indicate any relatively narrow application. We do not commonly understand "race" to refer only to the black race, or "sex" to refer only to the female. But the prohibition of age discrimination is readily read more narrowly than analogous provisions dealing with race and sex. That narrower reading is the more natural one in the textual setting, and it makes perfect sense because of Congress's demonstrated concern with distinctions that hurt older people.

B

The second objection has more substance than the first, but still not enough. The record of congressional action reports a colloquy on the Senate floor between two of the legislators most active in pushing for the ADEA, Senators Javits and Yarborough. Senator Javits began the exchange by raising a concern mentioned by Senator Dominick, that "the bill might not forbid discrimination between two persons each of whom would be between the ages of 40 and 65." 113 Cong. Rec. 31255 (1967). Senator Javits then gave his own view that, "if two individuals ages 52 and 42 apply for the same job, and the employer selected the man aged 42 solely ... because he is younger than the man 52, then he will have violated the act," and asked Senator Yarborough for his opinion. Senator Yarborough answered that "[t]he law prohibits age being a factor in the decision to hire, as to one age over the other, whichever way [the] decision went."

Although in the past we have given weight to Senator Yarborough's views on the construction of the ADEA because he was a sponsor, see, e.g., Public Employees Retirement System of Ohio v. Betts, 492 U.S. 158, 179, 109 S.Ct. 2854, 106 L.Ed.2d 134 (1989), his side of this exchange is not enough to unsettle our reading of the statute. It is not merely that the discussion was prompted by the question mentioned in O'Connor v. Consolidated Coin Caterers Corp., the possibility of a 52-year-old suing over a preference for someone younger but in the over-40 protected class. What matters is that the Senator's remark, "whichever way [the] decision went," is the only item in all the 1967 hearings, reports, and debates going against the grain of the common understanding of age discrimination. Even from a sponsor, a single outlying statement cannot stand against a tide of context and history, not to mention 30 years of judicial interpretation producing no apparent legislative qualms.

C

The third objection relies on a reading * * * adopted by the agency now charged with enforcing the statute. When the EEOC adopted §1625.2(a) in 1981, shortly after assuming administrative responsibility for the ADEA, it gave no reasons for the view

---

whole, however, they are incoherent with the alleged congressional belief that such a background principle existed.

expressed, beyond noting that the provision was carried forward from an earlier Department of Labor regulation; that earlier regulation itself gave no reasons.

The parties contest the degree of weight owed to the EEOC's reading, with General Dynamics urging us that Skidmore v. Swift & Co., 323 U.S. 134, 65 S.Ct. 161, 89 L.Ed. 124 (1944), sets the limit, while Cline and the EEOC say that §1625.2(a) deserves greater deference under Chevron U.S.A. Inc. v. Natural Resources Defense Council, Inc., 467 U.S. 837, 104 S.Ct. 2778, 81 L.Ed.2d 694 (1984). Although we have devoted a fair amount of attention lately to the varying degrees of deference deserved by agency pronouncements of different sorts, the recent cases are not on point here. In Edelman v. Lynchburg College, 535 U.S. 106, 114, 122 S.Ct. 1145, 152 L.Ed.2d 188 (2002), we found no need to choose between *Skidmore* and *Chevron*, or even to defer, because the EEOC was clearly right; today, we neither defer nor settle on any degree of deference because the Commission is clearly wrong.

Even for an agency able to claim all the authority possible under Chevron, deference to its statutory interpretation is called for only when the devices of judicial construction have been tried and found to yield no clear sense of congressional intent. Here, regular interpretive method leaves no serious question, not even about purely textual ambiguity in the ADEA. The word "age" takes on a definite meaning from being in the phrase "discriminat[ion] ... because of such individual's age," occurring as that phrase does in a statute structured and manifestly intended to protect the older from arbitrary favor for the younger.

IV

We see the text, structure, purpose, and history of the ADEA, along with its relationship to other federal statutes, as showing that the statute does not mean to stop an employer from favoring an older employee over a younger one. The judgment of the Court of Appeals is

Reversed.

Justice Scalia, dissenting.

* * * The question in this case is whether, in the absence of an affirmative defense, the ADEA prohibits an employer from favoring older over younger workers when both are protected by the Act, i.e., are 40 years of age or older.

The Equal Employment Opportunity Commission (EEOC) has answered this question in the affirmative. * * *

The Court brushes aside the EEOC's interpretation as "clearly wrong." I cannot agree with the contention upon which that rejection rests: that "regular interpretive method leaves no serious question, not even about purely textual ambiguity in the ADEA." It is evident, for the reasons given in Part II of Justice Thomas's dissenting opinion, that the Court's interpretive method is anything but "regular." And for the reasons given in Part I of that opinion, the EEOC's interpretation is neither foreclosed by the statute nor unreasonable.

Because §4(a) does not unambiguously require a different interpretation, and the EEOC's regulation is an entirely reasonable interpretation of the text, I would defer to the agency's authoritative conclusion. I respectfully dissent.

JUSTICE THOMAS, with whom JUSTICE KENNEDY joins, dissenting.

This should have been an easy case. The plain language of §4(a)(1) mandates a particular outcome: that the respondents are able to sue for discrimination against them in favor of older workers. The agency charged with enforcing the statute has adopted a regulation and issued an opinion as an adjudicator, both of which adopt this natural interpretation of the provision. And the only portion of legislative history relevant to the question before us is consistent with this outcome. Despite the fact that these traditional tools of statutory interpretation lead inexorably to the conclusion that respondents can state a claim for discrimination against the relatively young, the Court, apparently disappointed by this result, today adopts a different interpretation. In doing so, the Court, of necessity, creates a new tool of statutory interpretation, and then proceeds to give this newly created "social history" analysis dispositive weight. Because I cannot agree with the Court's new approach to interpreting anti-discrimination statutes, I respectfully dissent.

I

"The starting point for [the] interpretation of a statute is always its language," Community for Creative Non-Violence v. Reid, 490 U.S. 730, 739, 109 S.Ct. 2166, 104 L.Ed.2d 811 (1989), and "courts must presume that a legislature says in a statute what it means and means in a statute what it says there," Connecticut Nat. Bank v. Germain, 503 U.S. 249, 253-254, 112 S.Ct. 1146, 117 L.Ed.2d 391 (1992). Thus, rather than looking through the historical background of the Age Discrimination in Employment Act of 1967, I would instead start with the text of §4(a)(1) itself, and if the words of the statute are unambiguous, my judicial inquiry would be complete.

The plain language of the ADEA clearly allows for suits brought by the relatively young when discriminated against in favor of the relatively old. The phrase "discriminate ... because of such individual's age" is not restricted to discrimination because of relatively older age. If an employer fired a worker for the sole reason that the worker was under 45, it would be entirely natural to say that the worker had been discriminated against because of his age. I struggle to think of what other phrase I would use to describe such behavior. I wonder how the Court would describe such incidents, because the Court apparently considers such usage to be unusual, atypical, or aberrant.

The parties do identify a possible ambiguity, centering on the multiple meanings of the word "age." As the parties note, "age," does have an alternative meaning, namely "[t]he state of being old; old age." American Heritage Dictionary 33 (3d ed.1992). First, this secondary meaning is, of course, less commonly used than the primary meaning, and appears restricted to those few instances where it is clear in the immediate context of the phrase that it could have no other meaning. The phrases "hair white with age," or "eyes dim with age," cannot possibly be using "age" to include "young age," unlike a phrase such as "he fired her because of her age." Second, the use of the word "age" in other portions of the statute effectively destroys any doubt. The ADEA's advertising prohibition, §4(e), and the bona fide occupational qualification defense, §4(f)(1), would both be rendered incoherent if the term "age" in those provisions were read to mean only "older age."[1] Although it is true that the presumption that identical words used in different parts of the same act are intended to have the same meaning is not rigid and can be overcome when the context is clear, the presumption is not rebutted here. As noted, the plain and common reading of the phrase "such individual's age" refers to the individual's chronological age. At the very least, it is manifestly unclear that it bars only discrimination against the relatively older. Only by incorrectly concluding that § 4(a)(1) clearly and unequivocally bars only discrimination as "against the older," can the Court then conclude that the "context" of §§4(f)(1) and 4(e) allows for an alternative meaning of the term "age."

The one structural argument raised by the Court in defense of its interpretation of "discriminates ... because of such individual's age" is the provision limiting the ADEA's protections to those over 40 years of age. At first glance, this might look odd when paired with the conclusion that §4(a)(1) bars discrimination against the relatively young as well as the relatively old, but there is a perfectly rational explanation. Congress could easily conclude that age discrimination directed against those under 40 is not as damaging, since a young worker unjustly fired is likely to find a new job or otherwise recover from the discrimination. A person over 40 fired due to irrational age discrimination (whether because the worker is too young or too old) might have a more difficult time recovering from the discharge and finding new employment. Such an interpretation also comports with the many findings of the Wirtz report and the parallel findings in the ADEA itself.

This plain reading of the ADEA is bolstered by the interpretation of the agency charged with administering the statute. * * * I agree with the Court that we need not address whether deference under Chevron would apply to the EEOC's regulation in this case. Of course, I so conclude because the EEOC's interpretation is consistent with the best reading of the statute. The Court's position, on the other hand, is untenable. Even if the Court disagrees with my interpretation of the language of the statute, it strains credulity to argue that such a reading is so unreasonable that an agency could not adopt it. To suggest that, in the instant case, the "regular interpretive method leaves no serious question, not even about purely textual ambiguity in the ADEA," is to ignore the entirely reasonable (and, incidentally, correct) contrary interpretation of the ADEA that the EEOC and I advocate.

Finally, the only relevant piece of legislative history addressing the question before the Court — whether it would be possible for a younger individual to sue based on discrimination against him in favor of an older individual — comports with the plain reading of the text. Senator Yarborough, in the only exchange that the parties

---

[1]Section 4(f)(1) provides a defense where "age is a bona fide occupational qualification." If "age" were limited to "older age," then §4(f)(1) would provide a defense only where a defense is not needed, since under the Court's reading, discrimination against the relatively young is always legal under the ADEA. Section 4(e) bans the "print[ing] ... [of] any notice or advertisement relating to ... indicating any preference, limitation, specification, or discrimination ... based on age." Again, if "age" were read to mean only "older age," an employer could print advertisements asking only for young applicants for a new job (where hiring or considering only young applicants is banned by the ADEA), but could not print advertisements requesting only older applicants (where hiring only older applicants would be legal under the Court's reading of the ADEA).

identified from the legislative history discussing this particular question, confirmed that the text really meant what it said. Although the statute is clear, and hence there is no need to delve into the legislative history, this history merely confirms that the plain reading of the text is correct.

II

Strangely, the Court does not explain why it departs from accepted methods of interpreting statutes. It does, however, clearly set forth its principal reason for adopting its particular reading of the phrase "discriminate ... based on [an] individual's age" in Part III-A of its opinion. "The point here," the Court states, "is that we are not asking in the abstract how the ADEA uses the word 'age,' but seeking the meaning of the whole phrase 'discriminate ... because of [an] individual's age.' . . . As we have said, *social history* emphatically points to the sense of age discrimination as aimed against the old, and this idiomatic understanding is confirmed by legislative history." (emphasis added). The Court does not define "social history," although it is apparently something different from legislative history, because the Court refers to legislative history as a separate interpretive tool in the very same sentence. Indeed, the Court has never defined "social history" in any previous opinion, probably because it has never sanctioned looking to "social history" as a method of statutory interpretation. Today, the Court takes this unprecedented step, and then places dispositive weight on the new concept.

It appears that the Court considers the "social history" of the phrase "discriminate ... because of [an] individual's age" to be the principal evil that Congress targeted when it passed the ADEA. In each section of its analysis, the Court pointedly notes that there was no evidence of widespread problems of antiyouth discrimination, and that the primary concerns of Executive Branch officials and Members of Congress pertained to problems that workers generally faced as they increased in age. The Court reaches its final, legal conclusion as to the meaning of the phrase (that "ordinary people employing the common usage of language" would "talk about discrimination because of age [as] naturally [referring to] discrimination against the older,") only after concluding both that "the ADEA was concerned to protect a relatively old worker from discrimination that works to the advantage of the relatively young" and that "[t]here is ... no record indication that younger workers were suffering at the expense of their elders, let alone that a social problem required a federal statute to place a younger worker in parity with an older one." Hence, the Court apparently concludes that if Congress has in mind a particular, principal, or primary form of discrimination when it passes an antidiscrimination provision prohibiting persons from "discriminating because of [some personal quality]," then the phrase "discriminate because of [some personal quality]" only covers the principal or most common form of discrimination relating to this personal quality.

The Court, however, has not typically interpreted nondiscrimination statutes in this odd manner. "[S]tatutory prohibitions often go beyond the principal evil to cover reasonably comparable evils, and it is ultimately the provisions of our laws rather than the principal concerns of our legislators by which we are governed." Oncale v. Sundowner Offshore Services, Inc., 523 U.S. at 79, 118 S.Ct. 998, 140 L.Ed.2d 201 (1998). The oddity of the Court's new technique of statutory interpretation is highlighted by this Court's contrary approach to the racial-discrimination prohibition of Title VII of the Civil Rights Act of 1964.

There is little doubt that the motivation behind the enactment of the Civil Rights Act of 1964 was to prevent invidious discrimination against racial minorities, especially blacks. President Kennedy, in announcing his Civil Rights proposal, identified several social problems, such as how a "Negro baby born in America today ... has about one-half as much chance of completing a high school as a white baby ... one-third as much chance of becoming a professional man, twice as much chance of becoming unemployed, ... and the prospects of earning only half as much." Radio and Television Report to the American People on Civil Rights, Public Papers of the Presidents, John F. Kennedy, No. 237, June, 11, 1963, pp. 68-469 (1964). He gave no examples, and cited no occurrences, of discrimination against whites or indicated that such discrimination motivated him (even in part) to introduce the bill. Considered by some to be the impetus for the submission of a Civil Rights bill to Congress, the 1961 Civil Rights Commission Report focused its employment section solely on discrimination against racial minorities. It also discussed and analyzed the more severe unemployment statistics of black workers compared to white workers. The report presented no evidence of any problems (or even any incidents) of discrimination against whites.

The congressional debates and hearings, although filled with statements decrying discrimination against racial minorities and setting forth the disadvantages those minorities suffered, contain no references that I could find to any problem of discrimination against whites. I find no evidence that even a single legislator appeared concerned about whether there were incidents of discrimination against whites, and I find no citation to any such incidents.

In sum, there is no record evidence that white workers were suffering at the expense of racial minorities and in 1964, discrimination against whites in favor of racial minorities was hardly a social problem requiring a federal statute to place a white worker in parity with racial minorities. * * * In light of the Court's opinion today, it appears that this Court has been treading down the wrong path with respect to Title VII since at least 1976. See McDonald v. Santa Fe Trail Transp. Co., 427 U.S. 273, 96 S.Ct. 2574, 49 L.Ed.2d 493 (1976) (holding that Title VII protected whites discriminated against in favor of racial minorities).

In *McDonald*, the Court relied on the fact that the terms of Title VII, prohibiting the discharge of "any individual" because of "such individual's race" are not limited to discrimination against members of any particular race. Admittedly, the Court there also relied on the EEOC's interpretation of Title VII * * * and also on statements from the legislative history of the enactment of Title VII. But, in the instant case, as I have already noted above, the EEOC has issued a regulation and a binding EEOC decision adopting the view contrary to the Court's and in line with the interpretation of Title VII. And, again as already noted, the only relevant piece of legislative history with respect to the question before the Court is in the same posture as the legislative history behind Title VII: namely, a statement that age discrimination cuts both ways and a relatively younger individual could sue when discriminated against.

It is abundantly clear, then, that the Court's new approach to antidiscrimination statutes would lead us far astray from well-settled principles of statutory interpretation.

The Court's examination of "social history" is in serious tension (if not outright conflict) with our prior cases in such matters. Under the Court's current approach, for instance, *McDonald* and *Oncale*[6] are wrongly decided. One can only hope that this new technique of statutory interpretation does not catch on, and that its errors are limited to only this case.

Responding to this dissent, the Court insists that it is not making this "particular mistake," namely "confining the application of terms used in a broad sense to the relatively narrow class of cases that prompted Congress to address their subject matter." It notes that, in contrast to the term "age," the terms "race" and "sex" are "general terms that in every day usage require modifiers to indicate any relatively narrow application." The Court, thus, seems to claim that it is merely trying to identify whether "the narrower reading" of the term "age" is "the more natural one in the textual setting."[7] But the Court does not seriously attempt to analyze whether the term "age" is more naturally read narrowly in the context of §4(a)(1). Instead, the Court jumps immediately to, and rests its entire "common usage" analysis, on, the "social history" of the whole phrase "discriminate ... because of such individual's age." In other words, the Court concludes that the "common usage" of "age discrimination" refers exclusively to discrimination against the relatively old only because the "social history" of the phrase as a whole mandates such a reading. As I have explained here, the "social history" of the whole phrase "discriminate ... because of such individual's age," found in §4(a)(1) is no different than the "social history" of the whole phrase "discriminate ... because of such individual's race."

As the ADEA clearly prohibits discrimination because of an individual's age, whether the individual is too old or too young, I would affirm the Court of Appeals. Because the Court resorts to interpretive sleight of hand to avoid addressing the plain language of the ADEA, I respectfully dissent.

NOTES AND PROBLEMS FOR DISCUSSION

1. Who has the better of the statutory interpretation argument; Justice Souter speaking for the majority, who relies heavily on the Act's "social history"; Justice Scalia, who would simply defer to the EEOC's interpretation; or Justice Thomas, who offered a strictly textualist approach? How does this compare with the method of statutory interpretation used by the Court in *Desert Palace* (discussed in Chapter 2, Section B.2, *supra*) with respect to whether mixed motive analysis could be invoked in cases involving circumstantial as well as direct evidence of discrimination?

---

[6] "[M]ale-on-male sexual harassment in the workplace was assuredly not the principal evil Congress was concerned with when it enacted Title VII." *Oncale*. I wonder if there is even a single reference in all the committee reports and congressional debates on Title VII's prohibition of sex discrimination to any "social problem" * * * arising out of excessive male-on-male sexual harassment.

[7] The Court phrases this differently: it states that the "prohibition of age *discrimination* is readily read more narrowly than analogous provisions dealing with race and sex." (emphasis added). But this can only be true if the Court believes that the term "age" is more appropriately read in the narrower sense

2. In response to the ruling in *General Dynamics*, the EEOC revised its regulations to provide that the ADA permits, but does not require, employers to favor older workers over younger ones, including when the younger workers are within the statutorily protected class, i.e., over age 40. 29 C.F.R. §1625.2 (2007).

3. The Court revisited the meaning of age-based discrimination, this time in the retirement pension plan context, in KENTUCKY RETIREMENT SYSTEMS v. E.E.O.C., 554 U.S. 135, 128 S.Ct. 2361, 171 L.Ed.2d 322 (2008). The Commonwealth of Kentucky had created a two track retirement system for fire fighters, police officers, and other "hazardous position" workers. These workers became eligible for retirement under the normal retirement plan when they either completed twenty years of service or completed five years of service and had attained the age of 55. But the Commonwealth also provided disability-based retirement benefits to such workers who became disabled before eligibility under either of these two formulae. Furthermore, the benefits paid to workers under the normal retirement plan were calculated on the basis of the number of actual years served. But benefits paid to workers who retired because of disability had their benefits calculated on the basis of actual years of servicer plus the number of years they would have had to continue to work to meet normal retirement eligibility. The plaintiff was a hazardous position worker who became eligible for retirement at age 55 but chose to continue to work. He later became disabled and then retired. Pursuant to the normal retirement plan, he received benefits based on his actual years of service. He did not receive the additional years that he could have received had he become disabled prior to reaching normal retirement eligibility. He brought an ADEA action, alleging that since he did not receive the additional years for benefit calculation purposes solely because he had become disabled *after* reaching age 55 (and thereby qualifying for normal retirement), he had been discriminated against on the basis of his age. The Court, by a 5-4 margin, rejected his claim and held that this did not amount to age-based discrimination. The core of the Court's reasoning was that a plaintiff who asserted a disparate treatment claim of age discrimination had to offer evidence proving that his age "actually motivated" the employer's decision. The defendant's two-tiered retirement plan, the majority explained, treated people differently based on their eligibility for a retirement pension. And differentiation on the basis of pension eligibility, even when pension eligibility itself was based, in part, on an employee's age, did not render the retirement plan age-based on its face. Instead, the plaintiff would have to offer evidence that the employer's retirement plan was motivated by a desire to discriminate against older workers in favor of younger workers. In the instant case, the Court continued, the whole purpose of the disability scheme was to treat a disabled worker as though she had become disabled after, rather than before, she had become eligible for normal retirement benefits. That is why the extra years were added to the calculation for retirement-ineligible disabled workers. And though age obviously was a factor in determining whether a worker was retirement-eligible, that was not the reason that the company provided this extra benefit to non-retirement eligible disabled workers. "The disparity turns upon pension eligibility," the Court concluded, "and nothing more." Moreover, even if the system relied in part upon the employee's age, the bonus system was not based on the sort of stereotypical assumptions about the relative capacity of older vs. younger workers that the ADEA was designed to eradicate. Thus, the Court ruled, where an employer adopts a pension plan that treats employees differently based on pension status which, in turn, is based on part on age, the plaintiff must tender independent evidence to show that this differential treatment was actually motivated by age and not merely pension status. The Court will not treat the system as age-based on its face. The four dissenters, on the other hand, came to the precisely opposite conclusion. Since age was a factor in determining pension eligibility and pension eligibility was the determinant for access to the extra bonus years, the use of age as a factor in this calculation meant that the system was age-based on its face and the plaintiff had established a prima facie violation without need for independent evidence of the employer's motivation. Therefore, absent the availability of some exemption or defense, such a plan violated the ADEA.

4. Suppose an employer's use of a physical endurance examination excluded almost all candidates over the age of fifty even though two thirds of its incumbent employees were over age forty. Can the plaintiff, a fifty-five-year-old individual who was rejected for failure to pass the physical examination, state a prima facie case of disproportionate impact under the ADEA? In HAZEN PAPER CO. v. BIGGINS, 507 U.S. 604, 113 S.Ct. 1701, 123 L.Ed.2d 338 (1993), the Supreme Court cast some doubt on whether disproportionate impact analysis should be available in ADEA cases. In *Hazen*, the jury believed the plaintiff's claim that he had been discharged just weeks before he would have accumulated enough years of service for his pension to vest. Speaking for a unanimous court, Justice O'Connor noted that the Supreme Court had never decided whether ADEA liability could be based on a showing of disproportionate impact and stated that since the plaintiff had only alleged disparate treatment discrimination, the Court did not have to decide that question in this case. But Justice Kennedy, joined by Chief Justice Rehnquist and Justice Thomas, issued a concurring opinion for the sole purpose of emphasizing that the Court's opinion should not be read as incorporating disproportionate impact theory into the ADEA context and suggesting that "there are substantial arguments that it is improper to carry over * * * impact analysis from Title VII to the ADEA." The Supreme Court agreed to resolve the post-*Hazen* circuit split over whether disparate impact analysis applies in ADEA cases, but at the last minute changed its mind. In ADAMS v. FLORIDA POWER CORP., 255 F.3d 1322 (11th Cir.), cert. granted, 534 U.S. 1054, 122 S.Ct. 643, 151 L.Ed.2d 561 (2001) the Eleventh Circuit joined five other circuits in holding that an ADEA violation could not be proved via the disproportionate impact theory. The Supreme Court granted review in *Adams* but, after oral argument, dismissed certiorari as improvidently granted. 535 U.S. 228, 122 S.Ct. 1290, 152 L.Ed.2d 345 (2002). Is it significant, in this regard, that §105, the provision of the 1991 Civil Rights Act that lists those types of cases in which impact analysis is permitted, does not refer to age claims? The Supreme Court finally resolved this important issue in the following case.

2. Proving and Defending Age Discrimination Claims

Smith v. City of Jackson

Supreme Court of the United States, 2005.
544 U.S. 228, 125 S.Ct. 1536, 161 L.Ed.2d 410.

Justice Stevens announced the judgment of the Court and delivered the opinion of the Court with respect to Parts I, II, and IV, and an opinion with respect to Part III, in which Justice Souter, Justice Ginsburg, and Justice Breyer join.

Petitioners, police and public safety officers employed by the city of Jackson, Mississippi (hereinafter City), contend that salary increases received in 1999 violated the Age Discrimination in Employment Act of 1967 (ADEA) because they were less generous to officers over the age of 40 than to younger officers. Their suit raises the question whether the "disparate-impact" theory of recovery announced in Griggs v. Duke Power Co., 401 U.S. 424 (1971), for cases brought under Title VII of the Civil Rights Act of 1964, is cognizable under the ADEA. Despite the age of the ADEA, it is a question that we have not yet addressed. See Hazen Paper Co. v. Biggins, 507 U.S. 604 (1993).

I

On October 1, 1998, the City adopted a pay plan granting raises to all City employees. The stated purpose of the plan was to "attract and retain qualified people, provide incentive for performance, maintain competitiveness with other public sector agencies and ensure equitable compensation to all employees regardless of age, sex, race and/or disability." On May 1, 1999, a revision of the plan, which was motivated, at least in part, by the City's desire to bring the starting salaries of police officers up to the regional average, granted raises to all police officers and police dispatchers. Those who had less than five years of tenure received proportionately greater raises when compared to their former pay than those with more seniority. Although some officers over the age of 40 had less than five years of service, most of the older officers had more.

Petitioners are a group of older officers who filed suit under the ADEA claiming both that the City deliberately discriminated against them because of their age (the "disparate-treatment" claim) and that they were "adversely affected" by the plan because of their age (the "disparate-impact" claim). The District Court granted summary judgment to the City on both claims. The Court of Appeals held that the ruling on the former claim was premature because petitioners were entitled to further discovery on the issue of intent, but it affirmed the dismissal of the disparate-impact claim. Over one judge's dissent, the majority concluded that disparate-impact claims are categorically unavailable under the ADEA. Both the majority and the dissent assumed that the facts alleged by petitioners would entitle them to relief under the reasoning of *Griggs*.

We granted the officers' petition for certiorari and now hold that the ADEA does authorize recovery in "disparate-impact" cases comparable to *Griggs*. Because, however, we conclude that petitioners have not set forth a valid disparate-impact claim, we affirm.

II

During the deliberations that preceded the enactment of the Civil Rights Act of 1964, Congress considered and rejected proposed amendments that would have included older workers among the classes protected from employment discrimination. Congress did, however, request the Secretary of Labor to "make a full and complete study of the factors which might tend to result in discrimination in employment because of age and of the consequences of such discrimination on the economy and individuals affected." The Secretary's report, submitted in response to Congress' request, noted that there was little discrimination arising from dislike or intolerance of older people, but that "arbitrary" discrimination did result from certain age limits. (hereinafter Wirtz Report) Moreover, the report observed that discriminatory effects resulted from "[i]nstitutional arrangements that indirectly restrict the employment of older workers."

In response to that report Congress directed the Secretary to propose remedial legislation and then acted favorably on his proposal. As enacted in 1967, §4(a)(2) of the ADEA provided that it shall be unlawful for an employer "to limit, segregate, or classify his employees in any way which would deprive or tend to deprive any individual of employment opportunities or otherwise adversely affect his status as an employee, because of such individual's age ...." Except for substitution of the word "age" for the words "race, color, religion, sex, or national origin," the language of that provision in the ADEA is identical to that found in §703(a)(2) of Title VII. Other provisions of the ADEA also parallel the earlier statute. Unlike Title VII, however, §4(f)(1) of the ADEA contains language that significantly narrows its coverage by permitting any "otherwise prohibited" action "where the differentiation is based on reasonable factors other than age" (hereinafter RFOA provision).

III

In determining whether the ADEA authorizes disparate-impact claims, we begin with the premise that when Congress uses the same language in two statutes having similar purposes, particularly when one is enacted shortly after the other, it is appropriate to presume that Congress intended that text to have the same meaning in both statutes. We have consistently applied that presumption to language in the ADEA that was "derived *in haec verba* from Title VII." Lorillard v. Pons, 434 U.S. 575 (1978).[4] Our unanimous interpretation of §703(a)(2) of the Title VII in *Griggs* is therefore a precedent of compelling importance.

In *Griggs*, a case decided four years after the enactment of the ADEA, we considered whether §703 of Title VII prohibited an employer "from requiring a high school education or passing of a standardized general intelligence test as a condition of employment in or transfer to jobs when (a) neither standard is shown to be significantly related to successful job performance, (b) both requirements operate to disqualify Negroes at a substantially higher rate than white applicants, and (c) the jobs

---

[4]*Oscar Mayer & Co. v. Evans,* 441 U.S. 750 (1979) (interpreting §14(b) of the ADEA in light of §706(c) of Title VII); *Western Air Lines, Inc. v. Criswell,* 472 U.S. 400 (1985) (interpreting ADEA's bona fide occupational qualification exception in light of Title VII's BFOQ exception); *Trans World Airlines, Inc. v. Thurston,* 469 U.S. 111 (1985) (interpreting the ADEA to apply to denial of privileges cases in a similar manner as under Title VII).

in question formerly had been filled only by white employees as part of a longstanding practice of giving preference to whites." Accepting the Court of Appeals' conclusion that the employer had adopted the diploma and test requirements without any intent to discriminate, we held that good faith "does not redeem employment procedures or testing mechanisms that operate as 'built-in headwinds' for minority groups and are unrelated to measuring job capability."

We explained that Congress had "directed the thrust of the Act to the consequences of employment practices, not simply the motivation." We relied on the fact that history is "filled with examples of men and women who rendered highly effective performance without the conventional badges of accomplishment in terms of certificates, diplomas, or degrees. Diplomas and tests are useful servants, but Congress has mandated the commonsense proposition that they are not to become masters of reality." And we noted that the Equal Employment Opportunity Commission (EEOC), which had enforcement responsibility, had issued guidelines that accorded with our view. We thus squarely held that §703(a)(2) of Title VII did not require a showing of discriminatory intent.[5]

While our opinion in *Griggs* relied primarily on the purposes of the Act, buttressed by the fact that the EEOC had endorsed the same view, we have subsequently noted that our holding represented the better reading of the statutory text as well. See Watson v. Fort Worth Bank & Trust. Neither §703(a)(2) nor the comparable language in the ADEA simply prohibits actions that "limit, segregate, or classify" persons; rather the language prohibits such actions that "deprive any individual of employment opportunities or otherwise adversely affect his status as an employee, because of such individual's" race or age. Thus the text focuses on the effects of the action on the employee rather than the motivation for the action of the employer.[6]

---

[5]The congressional purposes on which we relied in *Griggs* have a striking parallel to two important points made in the Wirtz Report. Just as the *Griggs* opinion ruled out discrimination based on racial animus as a problem in that case, the Wirtz Report concluded that there was no significant discrimination of that kind so far as older workers are concerned. And just as *Griggs* recognized that the high school diploma requirement, which was unrelated to job performance, had an unfair impact on African-Americans who had received inferior educational opportunities in segregated schools, the Wirtz Report identified the identical obstacle to the employment of older workers. "Any formal employment standard which requires, for example, a high school diploma will obviously work against the employment of many older workers--unfairly if, despite his limited schooling, an older worker's years of experience have given him the relevant equivalent of a high school education." Wirtz Report 21. Thus, just as the statutory text is identical, there is a remarkable similarity between the congressional goals we cited in *Griggs* and those present in the Wirtz Report.

[6]In reaching a contrary conclusion, Justice O'CONNOR ignores key textual differences between §4(a)(1), which does not encompass disparate-impact liability, and §4(a)(2). Section (a)(1) makes it unlawful for an employer "to fail or refuse to hire ... any individual ... because of *such individual*'s age." (Emphasis added.) The focus of the section is on the employer's actions with respect to the targeted individual. Paragraph (a)(2), however, makes it unlawful for an employer "to limit ... his *employees* in any way that would deprive or tend to deprive *any individual* of employment opportunities or otherwise adversely affect his status as an employee, because of *such individual*'s age." (Emphasis added.) Unlike in paragraph (a)(2), there is thus an incongruity between the employer's actions — which are focused on his employees generally —

Griggs, which interpreted the identical text at issue here, thus strongly suggests that a disparate-impact theory should be cognizable under the ADEA.[7]   Indeed, for over two decades after our decision in *Griggs*, the Courts of Appeal uniformly interpreted the ADEA as authorizing recovery on a "disparate-impact" theory in appropriate cases. It was only after our decision in Hazen Paper Co. v. Biggins, that some of those courts concluded that the ADEA did not authorize a disparate-impact theory of liability. Our opinion in *Hazen Paper*, however, did not address or comment on the issue we decide today. In that case, we held that an employee's allegation that he was discharged shortly before his pension would have vested did not state a cause of action under a disparate-treatment theory. The motivating factor was not, we held, the employee's age, but rather his years of service, a factor that the ADEA did not prohibit an employer from considering when terminating an employee. While we noted that disparate-treatment "captures the essence of what Congress sought to prohibit in the ADEA," we were careful to explain that we were not deciding "whether a disparate impact theory of liability is available under the ADEA." In sum, there is nothing in our opinion in *Hazen Paper* that precludes an interpretation of the ADEA that parallels our holding in *Griggs*.

The Court of Appeals' categorical rejection of disparate-impact liability, like Justice O'CONNOR's, rested primarily on the RFOA provision and the majority's analysis of legislative history. As we have already explained, we think the history of the enactment of the ADEA, with particular reference to the Wirtz Report, supports the pre-*Hazen Paper* consensus concerning disparate-impact liability. And *Hazen Paper* itself contains the response to the concern over the RFOA provision.

The RFOA provision provides that it shall not be unlawful for an employer "to take any action otherwise prohibited under subsectio[n] (a) ... where the differentiation is based on reasonable factors other than age discrimination ...." In most disparate-treatment cases, if an employer in fact acted on a factor other than age, the action would not be prohibited under subsection (a) in the first place. See *Hazen Paper* ("[T]here is no disparate treatment under the ADEA when the factor motivating the employer is some feature other than the employee's age."). In those disparate-

---

and the individual employee who adversely suffers because of those actions. Thus, an employer who classifies his employees without respect to age may still be liable under the terms of this paragraph if such classification adversely affects the employee because of that employee's age — the very definition of disparate impact. Justice O'CONNOR is therefore quite wrong to suggest that the textual differences between the two paragraphs are unimportant.

[7]Justice O'CONNOR reaches a contrary conclusion based on the text of the statute, the legislative history, and the structure of the statute. As we explain above, n. 6, *supra,* her textual reasoning is not persuasive. Further, while Congress may have intended to remedy disparate-impact type situations through "noncoercive measures" in part, there is nothing to suggest that it intended such measures to be the sole method of achieving the desired result of remedying practices that had an adverse effect on older workers. Finally, we agree that the differences between age and the classes protected in Title VII are relevant, and that Congress might well have intended to treat the two differently. However, Congress obviously considered those classes of individuals to be sufficiently similar to warrant enacting identical legislation, at least with respect to employment practices it sought to prohibit. While those differences, *coupled with a difference in the text of the statute* such as the RFOA provision, may warrant addressing disparate-impact claims in the two statutes differently, it does not justify departing from the plain text and our settled interpretation of that text.

treatment cases, such as in *Hazen Paper* itself, the RFOA provision is simply unnecessary to avoid liability under the ADEA, since there was no prohibited action in the first place. The RFOA provision is not, as Justice O'CONNOR suggests, a "safe harbor from liability" since there would be no liability under §4(a). See *Texas Dept. of Community Affairs v. Burdine* (noting, in a Title VII case, that an employer can defeat liability by showing that the employee was rejected for "a legitimate, nondiscriminatory reason" without reference to an RFOA provision).

In disparate-impact cases, however, the allegedly "otherwise prohibited" activity is not based on age. "Claims that stress 'disparate impact' [by contrast] involve employment practices that are facially neutral in their treatment of different groups but that in fact fall more harshly on one group than another ..." Teamsters v. United States, 431 U.S. 324, 335-336, n.15 (1977). It is, accordingly, in cases involving disparate-impact claims that the RFOA provision plays its principal role by precluding liability if the adverse impact was attributable to a nonage factor that was "reasonable." Rather than support an argument that disparate impact is unavailable under the ADEA, the RFOA provision actually supports the contrary conclusion.[11]

Finally, we note that both the Department of Labor, which initially drafted the legislation, and the EEOC, which is the agency charged by Congress with responsibility for implementing the statute, have consistently interpreted the ADEA to authorize relief on a disparate-impact theory. The initial regulations, while not mentioning disparate impact by name, nevertheless permitted such claims if the employer relied on a factor that was not related to age. 29 CFR §860.103(f)(1)(i) (1970) (barring physical fitness requirements that were not "reasonably necessary for the specific work to be performed"). See also §1625.7 (2004) (setting forth the standards for a disparate-impact claim).

The text of the statute, as interpreted in *Griggs*, the RFOA provision, and the EEOC regulations all support petitioners' view. We therefore conclude that it was error for the Court of Appeals to hold that the disparate-impact theory of liability is categorically unavailable under the ADEA.

IV

Two textual differences between the ADEA and Title VII make it clear that even though both statutes authorize recovery on a disparate-impact theory, the scope of disparate-impact liability under ADEA is narrower than under Title VII. The first is the RFOA provision, which we have already identified. The second is the amendment to Title VII contained in the Civil Rights Act of 1991. One of the purposes of that amendment was to modify the Court's holding in *Wards Cove Packing Co. v. Atonio*, a case in which we narrowly construed the employer's exposure to liability on a disparate-impact theory. While the relevant 1991 amendments expanded the coverage of Title VII, they did not amend the ADEA or speak to the subject of age

---

[11]We note that if Congress intended to prohibit all disparate-impact claims, it certainly could have done so. For instance, in the Equal Pay Act of 1963, Congress barred recovery if a pay differential was based "on any other factor" — reasonable or unreasonable — "other than sex." The fact that Congress provided that employees could use only *reasonable* factors in defending a suit under the ADEA is therefore instructive.

discrimination. Hence, *Wards Cove*'s pre-1991 interpretation of Title VII's identical language remains applicable to the ADEA.

Congress' decision to limit the coverage of the ADEA by including the RFOA provision is consistent with the fact that age, unlike race or other classifications protected by Title VII, not uncommonly has relevance to an individual's capacity to engage in certain types of employment. To be sure, Congress recognized that this is not always the case, and that society may perceive those differences to be larger or more consequential than they are in fact. However, as Secretary Wirtz noted in his report, "certain circumstances ... unquestionably affect older workers more strongly, as a group, than they do younger workers." Thus, it is not surprising that certain employment criteria that are routinely used may be reasonable despite their adverse impact on older workers as a group. Moreover, intentional discrimination on the basis of age has not occurred at the same levels as discrimination against those protected by Title VII. While the ADEA reflects Congress' intent to give older workers employment opportunities whenever possible, the RFOA provision reflects this historical difference.

Turning to the case before us, we initially note that petitioners have done little more than point out that the pay plan at issue is relatively less generous to older workers than to younger workers. They have not identified any specific test, requirement, or practice within the pay plan that has an adverse impact on older workers. As we held in *Wards Cove*, it is not enough to simply allege that there is a disparate impact on workers, or point to a generalized policy that leads to such an impact. Rather, the employee is "responsible for isolating and identifying the *specific* employment practices that are allegedly responsible for any observed statistical disparities." [citing *Wards Cove*] (emphasis added). Petitioners have failed to do so. Their failure to identify the specific practice being challenged is the sort of omission that could "result in employers being potentially liable for the myriad of innocent causes that may lead to statistical imbalances ...." [citing *Wards Cove*]. In this case not only did petitioners thus err by failing to identify the relevant practice, but it is also clear from the record that the City's plan was based on reasonable factors other than age.

The plan divided each of five basic positions — police officer, master police officer, police sergeant, police lieutenant, and deputy police chief — into a series of steps and half-steps. The wage for each range was based on a survey of comparable communities in the Southeast. Employees were then assigned a step (or half-step) within their position that corresponded to the lowest step that would still give the individual a 2% raise. Most of the officers were in the three lowest ranks; in each of those ranks there were officers under age 40 and officers over 40. In none did their age affect their compensation. The few officers in the two highest ranks are all over 40. Their raises, though higher in dollar amount than the raises given to junior officers, represented a smaller percentage of their salaries, which of course are higher than the salaries paid to their juniors. They are members of the class complaining of the "disparate impact" of the award.

Petitioners' evidence established two principal facts: First, almost two-thirds (66.2%) of the officers under 40 received raises of more than 10% while less than half (45.3%) of those over 40 did. Second, the average percentage increase for the entire class of officers with less than five years of tenure was somewhat higher than the percentage for those with more seniority. Because older officers tended to occupy more senior positions, on average they received smaller increases when measured as a percentage of their salary. The basic explanation for the differential was the City's perceived need to raise the salaries of junior officers to make them competitive with comparable positions in the market.

Thus, the disparate impact is attributable to the City's decision to give raises based on seniority and position. Reliance on seniority and rank is unquestionably reasonable given the City's goal of raising employees' salaries to match those in surrounding communities. In sum, we hold that the City's decision to grant a larger raise to lower echelon employees for the purpose of bringing salaries in line with that of surrounding police forces was a decision based on a "reasonable factor other than age" that responded to the City's legitimate goal of retaining police officers.

While there may have been other reasonable ways for the City to achieve its goals, the one selected was not unreasonable. Unlike the business necessity test, which asks whether there are other ways for the employer to achieve its goals that do not result in a disparate impact on a protected class, the reasonableness inquiry includes no such requirement.

Accordingly, while we do not agree with the Court of Appeals' holding that the disparate-impact theory of recovery is never available under the ADEA, we affirm its judgment.

THE CHIEF JUSTICE took no part in the decision of this case.

JUSTICE SCALIA, concurring in part and concurring in the judgment.

I concur in the judgment of the Court, and join all except Part III of its opinion. As to that Part, I agree with all of the Court's reasoning, but would find it a basis, not for independent determination of the disparate-impact question, but for deferral to the reasonable views of the Equal Employment Opportunity Commission pursuant to Chevron U.S.A. Inc. v. Natural Resources Defense Council, Inc., 467 U.S. 837 (1984). See General Dynamics Land Systems, Inc. v. Cline, 540 U.S. 581, 601-602 (2004) (Scalia, J., dissenting).

This is an absolutely classic case for deference to agency interpretation. The Age Discrimination in Employment Act of 1967 (ADEA) confers upon the EEOC authority to issue "such rules and regulations as it may consider necessary or appropriate for carrying out the" ADEA. Pursuant to this authority, the EEOC promulgated, after notice-and-comment rulemaking, a regulation that reads as follows:

> "When an employment practice, including a test, is claimed as a basis for different treatment of employees or applicants for employment on the grounds that it is a 'factor other than' age, and such a practice has an adverse impact on individuals within the protected age group, it can only be justified as a business necessity." 29 CFR § 1625.7(d) (2004).

The statement of the EEOC which accompanied publication of the agency's final interpretation of the ADEA said the following regarding this regulation: "Paragraph (d) of §1625.7 has been rewritten to make it clear that employment criteria that are age-neutral on their face but which nevertheless have a disparate impact on members of the protected age group must be justified as a business necessity." The regulation affirmed, moreover, what had been the longstanding position of the Department of Labor, the agency that previously administered the ADEA. And finally, the Commission has appeared in numerous cases in the lower courts, both as a party and as amicus curiae, to defend the position that the ADEA authorizes disparate-impact claims. Even under the unduly constrained standards of agency deference recited in United States v. Mead Corp., 533 U.S. 218 (2001), the EEOC's reasonable view that the ADEA authorizes disparate-impact claims is deserving of deference. *A fortiori*, it is entitled to deference under the pre-*Mead* formulation of *Chevron*, to which I continue to adhere.

Justice O'CONNOR both denies that the EEOC has taken a position on the existence of disparate-impact claims and asserts that, even if it has, its position does not deserve deference. The first claim cannot be squared with the text of the EEOC's regulation, quoted above. This cannot possibly be read as agnostic on the question whether the ADEA prohibits employer practices that have a disparate impact on the aged. It provides that such practices "can only be justified as a business necessity," compelling the conclusion that, absent a "business necessity," such practices are prohibited.[2]

Justice O'CONNOR would not defer to the EEOC regulation, even if it read as it does, because, she says, the regulation "does not purport to interpret the language of §4(a) at all," but is rather limited to an interpretation of the "reasonable factors other than age" (RFOA) clause of §4(f)(1) of the ADEA, which she says is not at issue. This argument assumes, however, that the RFOA clause operates independently of the remainder of the ADEA. It does not. Section 4(f)(1) provides, in relevant part:

> "It shall not be unlawful for an employer, employment agency, or labor organization ... to take any action *otherwise prohibited* under subsections (a), (b), (c), or (e) of this section ... where the differentiation is based on reasonable factors other than age ...." (emphasis added).

As this text makes clear, the RFOA defense is relevant only as a response to employer actions "otherwise prohibited" by the ADEA. Hence, the unavoidable meaning of the regulation at issue is that the ADEA prohibits employer actions that have an "adverse impact on individuals within the protected age group." 29 CFR §1625.7(d) (2004). And, of course, the only provision of the ADEA that could conceivably be interpreted to effect such a prohibition is §4(a)(2) — the provision that Justice O'CONNOR maintains the EEOC "does not purport to interpret ... at all."[3]

---

[2]Perhaps Justice O'CONNOR adopts the narrower position that, while the EEOC has taken the view that the ADEA prohibits actions that have a disparate impact, it has stopped short of recognizing disparate impact claims. If so, this position is equally misguided. The EEOC need not take the extra step of recognizing that individuals harmed by prohibited actions have a right to sue; the ADEA itself makes that automatic. 29 U.S.C. §626(c) ("Any person aggrieved may bring a civil action in any court of competent jurisdiction for such legal or equitable relief as will effectuate the purposes of this chapter ...").

[3]Justice O'CONNOR argues that the regulation does not necessarily construe subsection (4)(a)(2) to prohibit disparate impact, because disparate treatment *also* can have the effect which the regulation addresses — viz., "an adverse impact on individuals within the protected age group." That is true enough. But the question here is not whether disparate treatment claims (when they have a disparate impact) are *also* covered by the regulation; it is whether disparate

Lastly, Justice O'CONNOR argues that the EEOC's interpretation of what is "otherwise prohibited" by the ADEA is not entitled to deference because the Court concludes that the same regulation's interpretation of another term — the term "reasonable factors other than age," which the regulation takes to include only "business necessity" — is unreasonable. Her logic seems to be that, because the two interpretations appear in the same paragraph, they should stand or fall together. She cites no case for this proposition, and it makes little sense. If the two simultaneously adopted interpretations were contained in distinct paragraphs, the invalidation of one would not, of course, render the other infirm. (Justice O'CONNOR does not mean to imply, I assume, that our rejection of the EEOC's application of the phrase "reasonable factors other than age" to disparate impact claims in paragraph (d) of §1625.7 relieves the lower courts of the obligation to defer to the EEOC's other applications of the same phrase in paragraph (c) or (e)). I can conceive no basis for a different rule simply because the two simultaneously adopted interpretations appear in the same paragraph.

The EEOC has express authority to promulgate rules and regulations interpreting the ADEA. It has exercised that authority to recognize disparate-impact claims. And, for the reasons given by the plurality opinion, its position is eminently reasonable. In my view, that is sufficient to resolve this case.

JUSTICE O'CONNOR with whom JUSTICE KENNEDY and JUSTICE THOMAS join, concurring in the judgment.

"Disparate treatment ... captures the essence of what Congress sought to prohibit in the Age Discrimination in Employment Act of 1967. It is the very essence of age discrimination for an older employee to be fired because the employer believes that productivity and competence decline with old age." Hazen Paper Co. v. Biggins. In the nearly four decades since the ADEA's enactment, however, we have never read the statute to impose liability upon an employer without proof of discriminatory intent. I decline to join the Court in doing so today.

I would instead affirm the judgment below on the ground that disparate impact claims are not cognizable under the ADEA. The ADEA's text, legislative history, and purposes together make clear that Congress did not intend the statute to authorize such claims. Moreover, the significant differences between the ADEA and Title VII of the Civil Rights Act of 1964 counsel against transposing to the former our construction of the latter in Griggs v. Duke Power Co. Finally, the agencies charged with

---

impact claims of *all* sorts *are* covered; and there is no way to avoid the conclusion (consistently reaffirmed by the agency's actions over the years) that they are. That is also a complete response to Justice O'CONNOR's point that the regulation could not refer to §4(a)(2) because it includes "applicants for employment," who are protected only under §4(a)(1). Perhaps applicants for employment are covered only when (as Justice O'CONNOR posits) disparate treatment results in disparate impact; or perhaps the agency's attempt to sweep employment applications into the disparate impact prohibition is mistaken. But whatever *in addition* it may cover, or may erroneously seek to cover, it is impossible to contend that the regulation does *not* cover actions that "limit, segregate or classify" employees in a way that produces a disparate impact on those within the protected age group; and the only basis for its interpretation that those actions are prohibited is §(4)(a)(2).

administering the ADEA have never authoritatively construed the statute's prohibitory language to impose disparate impact liability. Thus, on the precise question of statutory interpretation now before us, there is no reasoned agency reading of the text to which we might defer.

I

A

Our starting point is the statute's text. Section 4(a) of the ADEA makes it unlawful for an employer:

"(1) to fail or refuse to hire or to discharge any individual or otherwise discriminate against any individual with respect to his compensation, terms, conditions, or privileges of employment, because of such individual's age; [or]

"(2) to limit, segregate, or classify his employees in any way which would deprive or tend to deprive any individual of employment opportunities or otherwise adversely affect his status as an employee, because of such individual's age ...."

Neither petitioners nor the plurality contend that the first paragraph, §4(a)(1), authorizes disparate impact claims, and I think it obvious that it does not. That provision plainly requires discriminatory intent, for to take an action against an individual "because of such individual's age" is to do so "by reason of" or "on account of" her age. See Webster's Third New International Dictionary 194 (1961).

Petitioners look instead to the second paragraph, §4(a)(2), as the basis for their disparate impact claim. But petitioners' argument founders on the plain language of the statute, the natural reading of which requires proof of discriminatory intent. Section 4(a)(2) uses the phrase "because of ... age" in precisely the same manner as does the preceding paragraph — to make plain that an employer is liable only if its adverse action against an individual is motivated by the individual's age.

Paragraphs (a)(1) and (a)(2) do differ in one informative respect. The employer actions targeted by paragraph (a)(1) — i.e., refusing to hire, discharging, or discriminating against — are inherently harmful to the targeted individual. The actions referred to in paragraph (a)(2), on the other hand — i.e., limiting, segregating, or classifying — are facially neutral. Accordingly, paragraph (a)(2) includes additional language which clarifies that, to give rise to liability, the employer's action must actually injure someone: The decision to limit, segregate, or classify employees must "deprive or tend to deprive [an] individual of employment opportunities or otherwise adversely affect his status as an employee." That distinction aside, the structures of paragraphs (a)(1) and (a)(2) are otherwise identical. Each paragraph prohibits an employer from taking specified adverse actions against an individual "because of such individual's age."

The plurality instead reads paragraph (a)(2) to prohibit employer actions that "adversely affect [an individual's] status as an employe[e] because of such individual's age." Under this reading, "because of ... age" refers to the cause of the adverse effect rather than the motive for the employer's action. This reading is unpersuasive for two reasons. First, it ignores the obvious parallel between paragraphs (a)(1) and (a)(2) by giving the phrase "because of such individual's age" a different meaning in each of the two paragraphs. And second, it ignores the drafters' use of a comma separating the "because of ... age" clause from the preceding language. That comma makes plain that the "because of ... age" clause should not be read, as the plurality would have it, to modify only the "adversely affect" phrase. See B. Garner, A Dictionary of Modern Legal Usage 101 (2d ed. 1995) ("Generally, the word because should not follow a comma"). Rather, the "because of ... age" clause is set aside to make clear that it modifies the entirety of the preceding paragraph: An employer may not, because of an individual's age, limit, segregate, or classify his employees in a way that harms that individual.

The plurality also argues that its reading is supported by the supposed "incongruity" between paragraph (a)(2)'s use of the plural in referring to the employer's actions ("limit, segregate, or classify his employees ") and its use of the singular in the "because of such individual's age" clause. (Emphases added.) Not so. For the reasons just stated, the "because of ... age" clause modifies all of the preceding language of paragraph (a)(2). That preceding language is phrased in both the plural (insofar as it refers to the employer's actions relating to employees) and the singular (insofar as it requires that such action actually harm an individual). The use of the singular in the "because of ... age" clause simply makes clear that paragraph (a)(2) forbids an employer to limit, segregate, or classify his employees if that decision is taken because of even one employee's age and that individual (alone or together with others) is harmed.

B

* * * [The] "reasonable factors other than age" (RFOA) provision "insure[s] that employers [are] permitted to use neutral criteria" other than age, EEOC v. Wyoming, 460 U.S. 226, 232-233 (1983), even if this results in a disparate adverse impact on older workers. The provision therefore expresses Congress' clear intention that employers not be subject to liability absent proof of intentional age-based discrimination. That policy, in my view, cannot easily be reconciled with the plurality's expansive reading of §4(a)(2).

The plurality however, reasons that the RFOA provision's language instead confirms that §4(a) authorizes disparate impact claims. If §4(a) prohibited only intentional discrimination, the argument goes, then the RFOA provision would have no effect because any action based on a factor other than age would not be "otherwise prohibited" under §4(a). Moreover, the plurality says, the RFOA provision applies only to employer actions based on reasonable factors other than age — so employers may still be held liable for actions based on unreasonable nonage factors.

This argument misconstrues the purpose and effect of the RFOA provision. Discriminatory intent is required under §4(a), for the reasons discussed above. The role of the RFOA provision is to afford employers an independent safe harbor from liability. It provides that, where a plaintiff has made out a prima facie case of intentional age discrimination under §4(a) — thus "creat[ing] a presumption that the employer unlawfully discriminated against the employee," *Texas Dept. of Community Affairs v. Burdine* — the employer can rebut this case by producing evidence that its action was based on a reasonable nonage factor. Thus, the RFOA provision codifies a safe harbor analogous to the "legitimate, nondiscriminatory reason" (LNR) justification later recognized in Title VII suits.

Assuming the *McDonnell Douglas* framework applies to ADEA suits, this "rebuttal" function of the RFOA provision is arguably redundant with the judicially established LNR justification.   But, at most, that merely demonstrates Congress' abundance of caution in codifying an express statutory exemption from liability in the absence of discriminatory intent.   It is noteworthy that even after *McDonnell Douglas* was decided, lower courts continued to rely on the RFOA exemption, in lieu of the LNR justification, as the basis for rebutting a prima facie case of age discrimination.

In any event, the RFOA provision also plays a distinct (and clearly nonredundant) role in "mixed-motive" cases.   In such cases, an adverse action taken in substantial part because of an employee's age may be "otherwise prohibited" by §4(a).   The RFOA exemption makes clear that such conduct is nevertheless lawful so long as it is "based on" a reasonable factor other than age.

Finally, the RFOA provision's reference to "reasonable" factors serves only to prevent the employer from gaining the benefit of the statutory safe harbor by offering an irrational justification.   Reliance on an unreasonable nonage factor would indicate that the employer's explanation is, in fact, no more than a pretext for intentional discrimination.

II

The legislative history of the ADEA confirms what its text plainly indicates — that Congress never intended the statute to authorize disparate impact claims.   The drafters of the ADEA and the Congress that enacted it understood that age discrimination was qualitatively different from the kinds of discrimination addressed by Title VII, and that many legitimate employment practices would have a disparate impact on older workers.   Accordingly, Congress determined that the disparate impact problem would best be addressed through noncoercive measures, and that the ADEA's prohibitory provisions should be reserved for combating intentional age-based discrimination.

A

* * * Because the ADEA was modeled on the Wirtz Report's findings and recommendations, the Report provides critical insights into the statute's meaning.

The Wirtz Report reached two conclusions of central relevance to the question presented by this case.   First, the Report emphasized that age discrimination is qualitatively different from the types of discrimination prohibited by Title VII of the Civil Rights Act of 1964 (i.e., race, color, religion, sex, and national origin discrimination).   Most importantly — in stark contrast to the types of discrimination addressed by Title VII — the Report found no evidence that age discrimination resulted from intolerance or animus towards older workers. Rather, age discrimination was based primarily upon unfounded assumptions about the relationship between an individual's age and her ability to perform a job.   In addition, whereas ability is nearly always completely unrelated to the characteristics protected by Title VII, the Report found that, in some cases, "there is in fact a relationship between [an individual's] age and his ability to perform the job."

Second, the Wirtz Report drew a sharp distinction between "arbitrary discrimination" (which the Report clearly equates with disparate treatment) and circumstances or practices having a disparate impact on older workers.   The Report defined "arbitrary" discrimination as adverse treatment of older workers "because of assumptions about the effect of age on their ability to do a job when there is in fact no basis for these assumptions."   While the "most obvious kind" of arbitrary discrimination is the setting of unjustified maximum age limits for employment, naturally the Report's definition encompasses a broad range of disparate treatment.

The Report distinguished such "arbitrary" (i.e., intentional and unfounded) discrimination from two other phenomena. One involves differentiation of employees based on a genuine relationship between age and ability to perform a job. In this connection, the Report examined "circumstances which unquestionably affect older workers more strongly, as a group, than they do younger workers," including questions of health, educational attainment, and technological change.[1] In addition, the Report assessed "institutional arrangements" — such as seniority rules, workers' compensation laws, and pension plans — which, though intended to benefit older workers, might actually make employers less likely to hire or retain them.

The Report specifically recommended legislative action to prohibit "arbitrary discrimination," i.e., disparate treatment. In sharp contrast, it recommended that the other two types of "discrimination" — both involving factors or practices having a disparate impact on older workers — be addressed through noncoercive measures: programs to increase the availability of employment; continuing education; and adjustment of pension systems, workers' compensation, and other institutional arrangements. These recommendations found direct expression in the ADEA * * *.

B

The ADEA's structure confirms Congress' determination to prohibit only "arbitrary" discrimination (i.e., disparate treatment based on unfounded assumptions), while addressing practices with a disparate adverse impact on older workers through noncoercive measures. Section 2 — which sets forth the findings and purposes of the statute — draws a clear distinction between "the setting of arbitrary age limits regardless of potential for job performance" and "certain otherwise desirable practices [that] may work to the disadvantage of older persons." In response to these problems, §2 identifies three purposes of the ADEA: "[1] to promote employment of older persons based on their ability rather than age; [2] to prohibit arbitrary age discrimination in employment; [and 3] to help employers and workers find ways of meeting problems arising from the impact of age on employment."

Each of these three purposes corresponds to one of the three substantive statutory sections that follow. Section 3 seeks to "promote employment of older persons" by directing the Secretary of Labor to undertake a program of research and education

---

[1] It is in this connection that the Report refers to formal employment standards requiring a high school diploma. The Wirtz Report did say that such a requirement would be "unfair" if an older worker's years of experience had given him an equivalent education. But the plurality is mistaken to find in this statement a congressional "goal" of eliminating job requirements with a disparate impact on older workers. See *ante,* at n. 5. Rather, the Wirtz Report discussed the diploma requirement in the context of a broader discussion of the effects of "wholly impersonal forces — most of them part of what is properly, if sometimes too casually, called 'progress.'" These forces included "the pace of changing technology, changing jobs, *changing educational* requirements, and changing personnel practices," which "increase[d] the need for special efforts if older workers' employment prospects are to improve significantly." The Report recommended that such forces be addressed through noncoercive instead of prohibitory measures, and it specifically focused on the need for educational opportunities for older workers.

related to "the needs and abilities of older workers, and their potentials for continued employment and contribution to the economy." Section 4, which contains the ADEA's core prohibitions, corresponds to the second purpose: to "prohibit arbitrary age discrimination in employment." Finally, §5 addresses the third statutory purpose by requiring the Secretary of Labor to undertake a study of "institutional and other arrangements giving rise to involuntary retirement" and to submit any resulting findings and legislative recommendations to Congress.

Section 4 — including §4(a)(2) — must be read in light of the express statutory purpose the provision was intended to effect: the prohibition of "arbitrary age discrimination in employment." As the legislative history makes plain, "arbitrary" age discrimination had a very specific meaning for the ADEA's drafters. It meant disparate treatment of older workers, predominantly because of unfounded assumptions about the relationship between age and ability. Again, such intentional discrimination was clearly distinguished from circumstances and practices merely having a disparate impact on older workers, which — as ADEA §§2, 3, and 5 make clear — Congress intended to address through research, education, and possible future legislative action.

C

In addition to this affirmative evidence of congressional intent, I find it telling that the legislative history is devoid of any discussion of disparate impact claims or of the complicated issues such claims raise in the ADEA context. At the time the ADEA was enacted, the predominant focus of antidiscrimination law was on intentional discrimination; the concept of disparate impact liability, by contrast, was quite novel. Had Congress intended to inaugurate disparate impact liability in the ADEA, one would expect to find some indication of that intent in the text and the legislative history. There is none.

D

Congress' decision not to authorize disparate impact claims is understandable in light of the questionable utility of such claims in the age-discrimination context. No one would argue that older workers have suffered disadvantages as a result of entrenched historical patterns of discrimination, like racial minorities have. Accordingly, disparate impact liability under the ADEA cannot be justified, and is not necessary, as a means of redressing the cumulative results of past discrimination.

Moreover, the Wirtz Report correctly concluded that — unlike the classifications protected by Title VII — there often is a correlation between an individual's age and her ability to perform a job. That is to be expected, for physical ability generally declines with age, and in some cases, so does mental capacity. Perhaps more importantly, advances in technology and increasing access to formal education often leave older workers at a competitive disadvantage vis-a-vis younger workers. Beyond these performance-affecting factors, there is also the fact that many employment benefits, such as salary, vacation time, and so forth, increase as an employee gains experience and seniority. Accordingly, many employer decisions that are intended to cut costs or respond to market forces will likely have a disproportionate effect on older workers. Given the myriad ways in which legitimate business practices can have a disparate impact on older workers, it is hardly surprising that Congress declined to subject employers to civil liability based solely on such effects.

III

The plurality and Justice SCALIA offer two principal arguments in favor of their reading of the statute: that the relevant provision of the ADEA should be read in pari materia with the parallel provision of Title VII, and that we should give interpretive weight or deference to agency statements relating to disparate impact liability. I find neither argument persuasive.

A

The language of the ADEA's prohibitory provisions was modeled on, and is nearly identical to, parallel provisions in Title VII. Because *Griggs* held that Title VII's §703(a)(2) permits disparate impact claims, the plurality concludes that we should read §4(a)(2) of the ADEA similarly.

Obviously, this argument would be a great deal more convincing had *Griggs* been decided before the ADEA was enacted. In that case, we could safely assume that Congress had notice (and therefore intended) that the language at issue here would be read to authorize disparate impact claims. But *Griggs* was decided four years after the ADEA's enactment, and there is no reason to suppose that Congress in 1967 could have foreseen the interpretation of Title VII that was to come.

To be sure, where two statutes use similar language we generally take this as a strong indication that they should be interpreted *pari passu*. But this is not a rigid or absolute rule, and it readily yields to other indicia of congressional intent. Accordingly, we have not hesitated to give a different reading to the same language — whether appearing in separate statutes or in separate provisions of the same statute — if there is strong evidence that Congress did not intend the language to be used uniformly. See, e.g., General Dynamics ("age" has different meaning where used in different parts of the ADEA); Robinson v. Shell Oil Co., 519 U.S. 337, 343-344 (1997) ("employee" has different meanings in different parts of Title VII). Such is the case here.

First, there are significant textual differences between Title VII and the ADEA that indicate differences in congressional intent. Most importantly, whereas the ADEA's RFOA provision protects employers from liability for any actions not motivated by age, Title VII lacks any similar provision. In addition, the ADEA's structure demonstrates Congress' intent to combat intentional discrimination through §4's prohibitions while addressing employment practices having a disparate impact on older workers through independent noncoercive mechanisms. There is no analogy in the structure of Title VII. Furthermore, as the Congresses that adopted both Title VII and the ADEA clearly recognized, the two statutes were intended to address qualitatively different kinds of discrimination. Disparate impact liability may have a legitimate role in combating the types of discrimination addressed by Title VII, but the nature of aging and of age discrimination makes such liability inappropriate for the ADEA.

Finally, nothing in the Court's decision in *Griggs* itself provides any reason to extend its holding to the ADEA. As the plurality tacitly acknowledges, the decision in *Griggs* was not based on any analysis of Title VII's actual language. Rather, the *ratio decidendi* was the statute's perceived purpose * * *.

* * * [T]he Court in *Griggs* reasoned that disparate impact liability was necessary to achieve Title VII's ostensible goal of eliminating the cumulative effects of historical

racial discrimination. However, that rationale finds no parallel in the ADEA context and it therefore should not control our decision here.

Even venerable canons of construction must bow, in an appropriate case, to compelling evidence of congressional intent. In my judgment, the significant differences between Title VII and the ADEA are more than sufficient to overcome the default presumption that similar language is to be read similarly.

B

The plurality asserts that the agencies charged with the ADEA's administration "have consistently interpreted the [statute] to authorize relief on a disparate-impact theory." In support of this claim, the plurality describes a 1968 interpretive bulletin issued by the Department of Labor as "permitt[ing]" disparate impact claims. And the plurality cites, without comment, an Equal Employment Opportunities Commission (EEOC) policy statement construing the RFOA provision. It is unclear what interpretive value the plurality means to assign to these agency statements. But Justice SCALIA, at least, thinks that the EEOC statement is entitled to deference under Chevron and that "that is sufficient to resolve this case." I disagree and, for the reasons that follow, would give no weight to the statements in question.

The 1968 Labor Department bulletin to which the plurality alludes was intended to "provide a practical guide to employers and employees as to how the office representing the public interest in its enforcement will seek to apply it." 29 CFR §860.1 (1970). In discussing the RFOA provision, the bulletin states that "physical fitness requirements" and "[e]valuation factors such as quantity or quality of production, or educational level" can qualify as reasonable nonage factors, so long as they have a valid relationship to job qualifications and are uniformly applied. But the bulletin does not construe the ADEA's prohibitory provisions, nor does it state or imply that §4(a) authorizes disparate impact claims. Rather, it establishes "a nonexclusive objective test for employers to use in determining whether they could be certain of qualifying for the" RFOA exemption. Public Employees Retirement System of Ohio v. Betts, 492 U.S. 158, 172 (1989) (discussing 1968 bulletin's interpretation of the §4(f)(2) exemption). Moreover, the very same bulletin states unequivocally that "[t]he clear purpose [of the ADEA] is to insure that age, within the limits prescribed by the Act, is not a determining factor in making any decision regarding the hiring, dismissal, promotion or any other term condition or privilege of employment of an individual." That language is all about discriminatory intent.

The EEOC statement cited by the plurality and relied upon by Justice SCALIA is equally unhelpful. This "interpretative rule or policy statement," promulgated in 1981, superseded the 1968 Labor Department bulletin after responsibility for enforcing the ADEA was transferred from Labor to the EEOC. It states, in relevant part:

> "[W]hen an employment practice, including a test, is claimed as a basis for different treatment of employees or applicants for employment on the grounds that it is a 'factor other than' age, and such a practice has an adverse impact on individuals within the protected age group, it can only be justified as a business necessity." 29 C.F.R. §1625.7(d) (2004).

Like the 1968 bulletin it replaces, this statement merely spells out the agency's view, for purposes of its enforcement policy, of what an employer must do to be certain of gaining the safety of the RFOA haven. It says nothing about whether disparate impact claims are authorized by the ADEA.

For Justice SCALIA, "[t]his is an absolutely classic case for deference to agency interpretation." I disagree. Under *Chevron*, we will defer to a reasonable agency interpretation of ambiguous statutory language provided that the interpretation has the requisite "force of law," Christensen v. Harris County, 529 U.S. 576, 587 (2000). The rationale for such deference is that Congress has explicitly or implicitly delegated to the agency responsible for administering a statute the authority to choose among permissible constructions of ambiguous statutory text. The question now before us is not what it takes to qualify for the RFOA exemption, but rather whether §4(a)(2) of the ADEA authorizes disparate impact claims. But the EEOC statement does not purport to interpret the language of §4(a) at all. Quite simply, the agency has not actually exercised its delegated authority to resolve any ambiguity in the relevant provision's text, much less done so in a reasonable or persuasive manner. As to the specific question presented, therefore, the regulation is not entitled to any deference.

Justice SCALIA's attempt to link the EEOC's RFOA regulation to §4(a)(2) is premised on a dubious chain of inferences that, in my view, highlights the hazards of his approach. Because the RFOA provision is "relevant only as a response to employer actions 'otherwise prohibited' by the ADEA," he reasons, the "unavoidable meaning" of the EEOC statement is that the agency "interprets the ADEA to prohibit employer actions that have an 'adverse impact on individuals within the protected age group.'" But, of course, disparate treatment clearly has an "adverse impact on individuals within the protected age group," and Justice SCALIA's reading of the EEOC's rule is hardly "unavoidable." The regulation says only that if an employer wants to rely on a practice — say, a physical fitness test — as the basis for an exemption from liability, and that test adversely affects older workers, the employer can be sure of qualifying for the exemption only if the test is sufficiently job related. Such a limitation makes sense in disparate treatment cases. A test that harms older workers and is unrelated to the job may be a pretext for — or even a means of effectuating — intentional discrimination. Justice SCALIA completes his analytical chain by inferring that the EEOC regulation must be read to interpret §4(a)(2) to allow disparate impact claims because that is the only provision of the ADEA that could "conceivably" be so interpreted. But the support for that inference is doubtful, to say the least. The regulation specifically refers to employment practices claimed as a basis for "different treatment of employees or applicants for employment." Section 4(a)(2), of course, does not apply to "applicants for employment" at all — it is only §4(a)(1) that protects this group. That suggests that the EEOC must have read the RFOA to provide a defense against claims under §4(a)(1) — which unquestionably permits only disparate treatment claims.

This discussion serves to illustrate why it makes little sense to attribute to the agency a construction of the relevant statutory text that the agency itself has not actually articulated so that we can then "defer" to that reading. Such an approach is particularly troubling where applied to a question as weighty as whether a statute does or does not subject employers to liability absent discriminatory intent. This is not, in my view, what *Chevron* contemplated.

As an interpretation of the RFOA provision, moreover, the EEOC regulation is both unreasonable on its face and directly at odds with the Court's holding in today's case. It says that the RFOA exemption is available only if the employer's practice is justified by a "business necessity." But the Court has rejected that reading of the RFOA provision, and rightly so: There may be many "reasonable" means by which an employer can advance its goals, and a given nonage factor can certainly be "reasonable" without being necessary. Of course, it is elementary that no deference is due to agency interpretations at odds with the plain language of the statute itself. The agency clearly misread the RFOA provision it was attempting to construe. That error is not necessarily dispositive of the disparate impact question. But I think it highlights the improvidence of giving weight (let alone deferring) to the regulation's purported assumption that an entirely different provision of the statute, which is not even the subject of the regulation, authorizes disparate impact claims. In my view, we should simply acknowledge that this regulation is of no help in answering the question presented.

IV

Although I would not read the ADEA to authorize disparate impact claims, I agree with the Court that, if such claims are allowed, they are strictly circumscribed by the RFOA exemption. That exemption requires only that the challenged employment practice be based on a "reasonable" nonage factor — that is, one that is rationally related to some legitimate business objective. I also agree with the Court that, if disparate impact claims are to be permitted under the ADEA, they are governed by the standards set forth in our decision in *Wards Cove*. That means, as the Court holds, that "a plaintiff must demonstrate that it is the application of a specific or particular employment practice that has created the disparate impact under attack." *Wards Cove*. It also means that once the employer has produced evidence that its action was based on a reasonable nonage factor, the plaintiff bears the burden of disproving this assertion. Even if petitioners' disparate impact claim were cognizable under the ADEA, that claim clearly would fail in light of these requirements.

NOTES AND PROBLEMS FOR DISCUSSION

1. Although the five-member majority's ruling that impact-based claims are cognizable under the ADEA was received with resounding approval by the plaintiff's bar, was the decision a full-throated victory for plaintiffs? After all, all eight Justices concurred in the affirmance of the lower courts' grant of summary judgment in favor of the defendant. The plurality of four, plus Justice Scalia, concluded that where an ADEA plaintiff states an impact-based claim, the defendant can avoid liability pursuant to the "reasonable factor of than age" clause in §4(f)(1). Although they do not expressly address the burden of proof issue, the plurality opinion suggests that the RFOA provision should be treated as an affirmative defense to an impact claim. Note however, that although Justice O'Connor (joined by Justices Kennedy and Thomas) agreed with the five others that the RFOA exemption "circumscribes" impact claims, she stated that, per *Wards Cove* (still in play because the 1991 Act which overruled *Wards Cove* did not expressly mention the ADEA) the defendant need only *come forward* with evidence of a reasonable non-age factor, and that the plaintiff ultimately bears the burden of persuasion on this issue.

Post-*City of Jackson*, the circuit courts disagreed on whether the defendant bore only the burden of producing evidence relative to RFOA or also bore the burden of persuasion as an affirmative defense. The Supreme Court resolved the conflict in MEACHAM v. KNOLLS ATOMIC POWER LABORATORY, 554 U.S. 84, 128 S.Ct. 2395, 171 L.Ed.2d 183 (2008). The 7 member majority, in an opinion authored by Justice Souter, held that the RFOA was an affirmative defense to impact claims brought under the ADEA as to which the defendant bore the burden of persuasion. The Court reasoned that both the text of the RFOA exemption (it exempts practices that are "otherwise prohibited" if based on a reasonable factor other than age) and its placement alongside the BFOQ exemption in §623(f) of the ADEA underscored Congress' understanding that this was to be construed as an affirmative defense as to which the proponent bore the burden of persuasion. Reiterating the analysis upon which it based its ruling in *City of Jackson*, the Court stated that the only relevance of the RFOA provision was to legitimate the use of a facially neutral, non age-based criterion that produced a disproportionate disadvantageous impact on the statutorily protected age group. Consequently, it operated as a justification or affirmative defense rather than as a denial of the plaintiff's impact claim. The Court also reemphasized its statement in *City of Jackson* that the business necessity defense played no role in age-based *impact* claims. Consequently, since the Second Circuit had ruled in favor of the defendant on the ground that the plaintiff had not carried the burden of persuasion as to the reasonableness of the challenged factor, the Court vacated that judgment and remanded for a determination of whether the outcome should be different when the burden was properly placed on the employer. Consistently with his opinion in *City of Jackson*, Justice Scalia wrote separately to state that he based his conclusions (agreeing with the majority that RFOA was an affirmative defense as to which the defendant bore the burden of persuasion, and that it replaced the business necessity defense in age-based impact cases) exclusively on the ground of deferring to the position taken by the EEOC on these issues. Justice Thomas wrote separately, concurring and dissenting in part. While agreeing with the Court that the RFOA was an affirmative defense, he continued to insist, as he had in *City of Jackson*, that impact claims were not cognizable under the ADEA. Consequently, he concluded the RFOA defense was only available in disparate treatment cases. Justice Breyer did not participate in the consideration or decision of the case.

2. Note that the plaintiffs in *City of Jackson* were all incumbent employees. Suppose an employer limited employment to applicants who had graduated from college within the past ten years. Could a group of older job applicants challenge this job requirement by alleging that it was a facially neutral criterion that produced a disproportionately adverse effect on older workers? The main substantive provision of the ADEA, §4, is, like §703 of Title VII, divided into two subparts. Section 4(a)(1) prohibits discrimination against any "individual" "because of" that individual's age. The courts agree that this provision, like §703(a)(1) of Title VII – after which it was modeled – is the statutory basis for claims of intentional (disparate treatment) discrimination. Section 4(f)(2), however, states that it is unlawful to limit or classify "employees" in a way that would deprive or tend to deprive "any individual" of employment opportunities. If this provision is a statutory justification for the assertion of an impact claim under the ADEA, aside from what the Court said in *City of Jackson*, does the reference to "employees" – a term that is not contained in (a)(1) – suggest that impact claims cannot be brought by job applicants under the ADEA? But what about the reference, in that same section to "individual"? The circuit courts are not in agreement on this issue. Compare Villarreal v. R.J. Reynolds Tobacco Co., 806 F.3d 1299 (11th Cir. 2015) (impact claims can be filed by job applicants under the ADEA) with Smith v. City of Des Moines, 99 F.3d 1466 (8th Cir. 1996)(impact claims under §4(a)(2) of the ADEA are limited to claims by incumbent employees).

3. The availability of disparate impact analysis is one, but not the only, issue that was addressed by the 1991 Civil Rights Act through amending Title VII but not the ADEA. In light of the Court's ruling in *Smith v. City of Jackson*, what is the significance of the fact that §107 of the 1991 Civil Rights Act — the provision that codified an amended version of the *Price Waterhouse* evidentiary formula for mixed motive cases — expressly applied only to Title VII and not to the ADEA? Does this mean, for example, that this legislative modification of the *Price Waterhouse* mixed motive doctrine should not apply to age-based mixed motive cases and, therefore, that mixed motive analysis in age discrimination cases should be governed by the pre-existing *Price Waterhouse* rule that the same decision defense constitutes an absolute defense to liability? Or does it go so far as to mean that Congress did not intend for mixed motive analysis to be applied at all in age discrimination cases? Finally, if mixed motive claims are cognizable under the ADEA, are they available only when the plaintiff's prima facie case is established through direct evidence or, as the Court ruled in *Desert Palace* in the Title VII context, regardless of whether the plaintiff has relied on direct or circumstantial evidence? All of these questions confronted the Supreme Court in the following case.

Gross v. FBL Financial Services, Inc.

Supreme Court of the United States, 2009.
557 U.S. 167, 129 S.Ct. 2343, 174 L.Ed.2d 119.

JUSTICE THOMAS delivered the opinion of the Court.

The question presented by the petitioner in this case is whether a plaintiff must present direct evidence of age discrimination in order to obtain a mixed-motives jury instruction in a suit brought under the Age Discrimination in Employment Act of 1967. Because we hold that such a jury instruction is never proper in an ADEA case, we vacate the decision below.

I

Petitioner Jack Gross began working for respondent FBL Financial Group, Inc. (FBL), in 1971. As of 2001, Gross held the position of claims administration director. But in 2003, when he was 54 years old, Gross was reassigned to the position of claims project coordinator. At that same time, FBL transferred many of Gross' job responsibilities to a newly created position-claims administration manager. That position was given to Lisa Kneeskern, who had previously been supervised by Gross and who was then in her early forties. Although Gross (in his new position) and Kneeskern received the same compensation, Gross considered the reassignment a demotion because of FBL's reallocation of his former job responsibilities to Kneeskern.

In April 2004, Gross filed suit in District Court, alleging that his reassignment to the position of claims project coordinator violated the ADEA * * *. The case proceeded to trial, where Gross introduced evidence suggesting that his reassignment was based at least in part on his age. FBL defended its decision on the grounds that Gross' reassignment was part of a corporate restructuring and that Gross' new position was better suited to his skills.

At the close of trial, and over FBL's objections, the District Court instructed the jury that it must return a verdict for Gross if he proved, by a preponderance of the evidence, that FBL "demoted [him] to claims projec[t] coordinator" and that his "age was a motivating factor" in FBL's decision to demote him. The jury was further instructed that Gross' age would qualify as a " 'motivating factor,' if [it] played a part or a role in [FBL]'s decision to demote [him]." The jury was also instructed regarding FBL's burden of proof. According to the District Court, the "verdict must be for [FBL] ... if it has been proved by the preponderance of the evidence that [FBL] would have demoted [Gross] regardless of his age." The jury returned a verdict for Gross, awarding him $46,945 in lost compensation.

FBL challenged the jury instructions on appeal. The United States Court of Appeals for the Eighth Circuit reversed and remanded for a new trial, holding that the jury had been incorrectly instructed under the standard established in *Price Waterhouse v. Hopkins.* In *Price Waterhouse,* this Court addressed the proper allocation of the burden of persuasion in cases brought under Title VII of the Civil Rights Act of 1964 when an employee alleges that he suffered an adverse employment action because of both permissible and impermissible considerations — *i.e.,* a "mixed-motives" case. The *Price Waterhouse* decision was splintered. Four Justices joined a plurality opinion. Justices White and O'Connor separately concurred in the judgment and three Justices dissented. Six Justices ultimately agreed that if a Title VII plaintiff shows that discrimination was a "motivating" or a "substantial" factor in the employer's action, the burden of persuasion should shift to the employer to show that it would have taken the same action regardless of that impermissible consideration. Justice O'Connor further found that to shift the burden of persuasion to the employer, the employee must present "direct evidence that an illegitimate criterion was a substantial factor in the [employment] decision."

In accordance with Circuit precedent, the Court of Appeals identified Justice O'Connor's opinion as controlling. Applying that standard, the Court of Appeals found that Gross needed to present "[d]irect evidence ... sufficient to support a finding by a reasonable fact finder that an illegitimate criterion actually motivated the adverse employment action." * * * Only upon a presentation of such evidence, the Court of Appeals held, should the burden shift to the employer " 'to convince the trier of fact that it is more likely than not that the decision would have been the same absent consideration of the illegitimate factor.' " (quoting *Price Waterhouse* (opinion of O'Connor, J.)).

The Court of Appeals thus concluded that the District Court's jury instructions were flawed because they allowed the burden to shift to FBL upon a presentation of a preponderance of *any* category of evidence showing that age was a motivating factor-not just "direct evidence" related to FBL's alleged consideration of age. Because Gross conceded that he had not presented direct evidence of discrimination, the Court of Appeals held that the District Court should not have given the mixed-motives instruction. Rather, Gross should have been held to the burden of persuasion applicable to typical, non-mixed-motives claims; the jury thus should have been instructed only to determine whether Gross had carried his burden of proving that age was the determining factor in FBL's employment action.

We granted certiorari and now vacate the decision of the Court of Appeals.

II

The parties have asked us to decide whether a plaintiff must "present direct evidence of discrimination in order to obtain a mixed-motive instruction in a non-Title VII discrimination case." Pet. for Cert. i. Before reaching this question, however, we must first determine whether the burden of persuasion ever shifts to the party defending an alleged mixed-motives discrimination claim brought under the ADEA.[3] We hold that it does not.

A

Petitioner relies on this Court's decisions construing Title VII for his interpretation of the ADEA. Because Title VII is materially different with respect to the relevant burden of persuasion, however, these decisions do not control our construction of the ADEA.

In *Price Waterhouse,* a plurality of the Court and two Justices concurring in the judgment determined that once a "plaintiff in a Title VII case proves that [the plaintiff's membership in a protected class] played a motivating part in an employment decision, the defendant may avoid a finding of liability only by proving by a preponderance of the evidence that it would have made the same decision even if it had not taken [that factor] into account." But as we explained in *Desert Palace, Inc. v. Costa,* Congress has since amended Title VII by explicitly authorizing discrimination claims in which an improper consideration was "a motivating factor" for an adverse employment decision

This Court has never held that this burden-shifting framework applies to ADEA claims. And, we decline to do so now. When conducting statutory interpretation, we "must be careful not to apply rules applicable under one statute to a different statute without careful and critical examination." *Federal Express Corp. v. Holowecki,* 128 S.Ct. 1147, 1153 (2008). Unlike Title VII, the ADEA's text does not provide that a plaintiff may establish discrimination by showing that age was simply a motivating factor. Moreover, Congress neglected to add such a provision to the ADEA when it amended Title VII to add §§703(m) and 706(g)(2)(B), even though it contemporaneously amended the ADEA in several ways.

We cannot ignore Congress' decision to amend Title VII's relevant provisions but

---

[3]Although the parties did not specifically frame the question to include this threshold inquiry, "[t]he statement of any question presented is deemed to comprise every subsidiary question fairly included therein." This Court's Rule 14.1; see also *City of Sherrill v. Oneida Indian Nation of N. Y.,*544 U.S. 197, 214, n. 8, 125 S.Ct. 1478, 161 L.Ed.2d 386 (2005) (" 'Questions not explicitly mentioned but essential to the analysis of the decisions below or to the correct disposition of the other issues have been treated as subsidiary issues fairly comprised by the question presented' " (quoting R. Stern, E. Gressman, S. Shapiro, & K. Geller, Supreme Court Practice 414 (8th ed.2002))); *Ballard v. Commissioner,* 544 U.S. 40, 46-47, and n. 2, 125 S.Ct. 1270, 161 L.Ed.2d 227 (2005) (evaluating "a question anterior" to the "questions the parties raised").

not make similar changes to the ADEA. When Congress amends one statutory provision but not another, it is presumed to have acted intentionally. See *EEOC v. Arabian American Oil Co.,* 499 U.S. 244, 256 (1991). Furthermore, as the Court has explained, "negative implications raised by disparate provisions are strongest" when the provisions were "considered simultaneously when the language raising the implication was inserted." *Lindh v. Murphy,* 521 U.S. 320, 330 (1997). As a result, the Court's interpretation of the ADEA is not governed by Title VII decisions such as *Desert Palace* and *Price Waterhouse*.[2]

B

Our inquiry therefore must focus on the text of the ADEA to decide whether it authorizes a mixed-motives age discrimination claim. It does not. "Statutory construction must begin with the language employed by Congress and the assumption that the ordinary meaning of that language accurately expresses the legislative purpose." *Engine Mfrs. Assn. v. South Coast Air Quality Management Dist.,* 541 U.S. 46, 252 (2004). The ADEA provides, in relevant part, that "[i]t shall be unlawful for an employer ... to fail or refuse to hire or to discharge any individual or otherwise discriminate against any individual with respect to his compensation, terms, conditions, or privileges of employment, *because of* such individual's age." (emphasis added).

The words "because of" mean "by reason of: on account of." 1 Webster's Third New International Dictionary 194 (1966); see also 1 Oxford English Dictionary 746 (1933) (defining "because of" to mean "By reason *of,* on account *of* " (italics in original)); The Random House Dictionary of the English Language 132 (1966) (defining "because" to mean "by reason; on account"). Thus, the ordinary meaning of the ADEA's requirement that an employer took adverse action "because of" age is that age was the "reason" that the employer decided to act. See *Hazen Paper Co. v. Biggins,* 507 U.S. 604, 610 (1993) (explaining that the claim "cannot succeed unless the employee's protected trait actually played a role in [the employer's decisionmaking] process *and had a determinative influence on the outcome* " (emphasis added)). To establish a disparate-treatment claim under the plain language of the ADEA, therefore, a plaintiff must prove that age was the "but-for" cause of the employer's adverse decision. See *Bridge v. Phoenix Bond & Indemnity Co.,* 128 S.Ct. 2131, 2141-2142 (2008) (recognizing that the phrase, "by reason of," requires at least

---

[2]JUSTICE STEVENS argues that the Court must incorporate its past interpretations of Title VII into the ADEA because "the substantive provisions of the ADEA were derived *in haec verba* from Title VII," and because the Court has frequently applied its interpretations of Title VII to the ADEA. But the Court's approach to interpreting the ADEA in light of Title VII has not been uniform. In *General Dynamics Land Systems, Inc. v. Cline,* for example, the Court declined to interpret the phrase "because of ... age" in [the ADEA] to bar discrimination against people of all ages, even though the Court had previously interpreted "because of ... race [or] sex" in Title VII to bar discrimination against people of all races and both sexes. And the Court has not definitively decided whether the evidentiary framework of *McDonnell Douglas Corp. v. Green* utilized in Title VII cases is appropriate in the ADEA context. See *Reeves v. Sanderson Plumbing Products, Inc.; O'Connor v. Consolidated Coin Caterers Corp.* In this instance, it is the textual differences between Title VII and the ADEA that prevent us from applying *Price Waterhouse* and *Desert Palace* to federal age discrimination claims.

a showing of "but for" causation (internal quotation marks omitted)); cf. W. Keeton, D. Dobbs, R. Keeton, & D. Owen, Prosser and Keeton on Law of Torts 265 (5th ed. 1984) ("An act or omission is not regarded as a cause of an event if the particular event would have occurred without it").[3]

It follows, then, that under §623(a)(1), the plaintiff retains the burden of persuasion to establish that age was the "but-for" cause of the employer's adverse action. Indeed, we have previously held that the burden is allocated in this manner in ADEA cases. See *Kentucky Retirement Systems v. EEOC,* 128 S.Ct. 2361, 2363-2366 (2008); *Reeves v. Sanderson Plumbing Products, Inc.* And nothing in the statute's text indicates that Congress has carved out an exception to that rule for a subset of ADEA cases. Where the statutory text is "silent on the allocation of the burden of persuasion," we "begin with the ordinary default rule that plaintiffs bear the risk of failing to prove their claims." *Schaffer v. Weast,* 546 U.S. 49, 56 (2005); see also *Meacham v. Knolls Atomic Power Laboratory,* 128 S.Ct. 2395, 2400-2401 (2008) ("Absent some reason to believe that Congress intended otherwise, ... we will conclude that the burden of persuasion lies where it usually falls, upon the party seeking relief"). We have no warrant to depart from the general rule in this setting.

Hence, the burden of persuasion necessary to establish employer liability is the same in alleged mixed-motives cases as in any other ADEA disparate-treatment action. A plaintiff must prove by a preponderance of the evidence (which may be direct or circumstantial), that age was the "but-for" cause of the challenged employer decision. See *Reeves.*[4]

III

Finally, we reject petitioner's contention that our interpretation of the ADEA is controlled by *Price Waterhouse,* which initially established that the burden of persuasion shifted in alleged mixed-motives Title VII claims.[5] In any event, it is far

---

[3]JUSTICE BREYER contends that there is "nothing unfair or impractical" about hinging liability on whether "forbidden motive ... play [ed] a role in the employer's decision." But that is a decision for Congress to make. Congress amended Title VII to allow for employer liability when discrimination "was *a motivating factor* for any employment practice, even though other factors also motivated the practice," 42 U.S.C. §703(m) (emphasis added), but did not similarly amend the ADEA. We must give effect to Congress' choice. See *14 Penn Plaza LLC v. Pyett,* 129 S.Ct. 1456, 1472 (2009).

[4]Because we hold that ADEA plaintiffs retain the burden of persuasion to prove all disparate-treatment claims, we do not need to address whether plaintiffs must present direct, rather than circumstantial, evidence to obtain a burden-shifting instruction. There is no heightened evidentiary requirement for ADEA plaintiffs to satisfy their burden of persuasion that age was the "but-for" cause of their employer's adverse action, and we will imply none. "Congress has been unequivocal when imposing heightened proof requirements" in other statutory contexts, including in other subsections within Title 29, when it has seen fit. See *Desert Palace, Inc. v. Costa,* 539 U.S. 90, 99 (2003); see also, *e.g.,* 25 U.S.C. §2504(b)(2)(B) (imposing "clear and convincing evidence" standard).

[5]JUSTICE STEVENS also contends that we must apply *Price Waterhouse* under the reasoning of *Smith v. City of Jackson,* 544 U.S. 228 (2005). In *Smith,* the Court applied to the ADEA its pre-1991 interpretation of Title VII with respect to disparate-impact claims despite Congress' 1991

from clear that the Court would have the same approach were it to consider the question today in the first instance. Cf. *14 Penn Plaza LLC v. Pyett,* 129 S.Ct. 1456, 1472 (2009) (declining to "introduc[e] a qualification into the ADEA that is not found in its text"); Meacham, 128 S.Ct. at 2406 (explaining that the ADEA must be "read ... the way Congress wrote it").

Whatever the deficiencies of *Price Waterhouse* in retrospect, it has become evident in the years since that case was decided that its burden-shifting framework is difficult to apply. For example, in cases tried to a jury, courts have found it particularly difficult to craft an instruction to explain its burden-shifting framework. See, *e.g., Tyler v. Bethlehem Steel Corp.,* 958 F.2d 1176, 1179 (C.A.2 1992) (referring to "the murky water of shifting burdens in discrimination cases"). Thus, even if *Price Waterhouse* was doctrinally sound, the problems associated with its application have eliminated any perceivable benefit to extending its framework to ADEA claims. Cf. *Continental T. V., Inc. v. GTE Sylvania Inc.,* 433 U.S. 36, 47 (1977) (reevaluating precedent that was subject to criticism and "continuing controversy and confusion").[6]

IV

We hold that a plaintiff bringing a disparate-treatment claim pursuant to the ADEA must prove, by a preponderance of the evidence, that age was the "but-for" cause of the challenged adverse employment action. The burden of persuasion does not shift to the employer to show that it would have taken the action regardless of age, even when a plaintiff has produced some evidence that age was one motivating factor in that decision. Accordingly, we vacate the judgment of the Court of Appeals and remand the case for further proceedings consistent with this opinion.

It is so ordered.

Justice Stevens, with whom Justice Souter, Justice Ginsburg, and Justice Breyer join, dissenting.

---

amendment adding disparate-impact claims to Title VII but not the ADEA. But the amendments made by Congress in this same legislation, which added the "motivating factor" language to Title VII, undermine Justice Stevens' argument. Congress not only explicitly added "motivating factor" liability to Title VII, but it also partially abrogated *Price Waterhouse* 's holding by eliminating an employer's complete affirmative defense to "motivating factor" claims. If such "motivating factor" claims were already part of Title VII, the addition of §706(g)(2)(B) alone would have been sufficient. Congress' careful tailoring of the "motivating factor" claim in Title VII, as well as the absence of a provision parallel to §703(m) in the ADEA, confirms that we cannot transfer the *Price Waterhouse* burden-shifting framework into the ADEA.

[6]Gross points out that the Court has also applied a burden-shifting framework to certain claims brought in contexts other than pursuant to Title VII. See Brief for Petitioner 54-55 (citing, *inter alia, NLRB v. Transportation Management Corp.,* 462 U.S. 393 (1983) (claims brought under the National Labor Relations Act (NLRA)); *Mt. Healthy City Bd. of Ed. v. Doyle,* 429 U.S. 274 (1977) (constitutional claims)). These cases, however, do not require the Court to adopt his contra statutory position. The case involving the NLRA did not require the Court to decide in the first instance whether burden shifting should apply as the Court instead deferred to the National Labor Relation Board's determination that such a framework was appropriate. And the constitutional cases such as *Mt. Healthy* have no bearing on the correct interpretation of ADEA claims, which are governed by statutory text.

The Age Discrimination in Employment Act of 1967 makes it unlawful for an employer to discriminate against any employee "because of" that individual's age. The most natural reading of this statutory text prohibits adverse employment actions motivated in whole or in part by the age of the employee. The "but-for" causation standard endorsed by the Court today was advanced in JUSTICE KENNEDY's dissenting opinion in *Price Waterhouse*, a case construing identical language in Title VII of the Civil Rights Act of 1964. Not only did the Court reject the but-for standard in that case, but so too did Congress when it amended Title VII in 1991. Given this unambiguous history, it is particularly inappropriate for the Court, on its own initiative, to adopt an interpretation of the causation requirement in the ADEA that differs from the established reading of Title VII. I disagree not only with the Court's interpretation of the statute, but also with its decision to engage in unnecessary lawmaking. I would simply answer the question presented by the certiorari petition and hold that a plaintiff need not present direct evidence of age discrimination to obtain a mixed-motives instruction.

I

The Court asks whether a mixed-motives instruction is ever appropriate in an ADEA case. As it acknowledges, this was not the question we granted certiorari to decide.[1] Instead, the question arose for the first time in respondent's brief, which asked us to overrule *Price Waterhouse* with respect to its application to the ADEA. In the usual course, this Court would not entertain such a request raised only in a merits brief: "We would normally expect notice of an intent to make so far-reaching an argument in the respondent's opposition to a petition for certiorari, cf. this Court's Rule 15.2, thereby assuring adequate preparation time for those likely affected and wishing to participate." *Alabama v. Shelton,* 535 U.S. 654, 660, n. 3 (2002). Yet the Court is unconcerned that the question it chooses to answer has not been briefed by the parties or interested *amici curiae*. Its failure to consider the views of the United States, which represents the agency charged with administering the ADEA, is especially irresponsible.[2]

Unfortunately, the majority's inattention to prudential Court practices is matched by its utter disregard of our precedent and Congress' intent. The ADEA provides that "[i]t shall be unlawful for an employer ... to fail or refuse to hire or to discharge any individual or otherwise discriminate against any individual with respect to his compensation, terms, conditions, or privileges of employment, *because of* such individual's age." (emphasis added). As we recognized in *Price Waterhouse* when we construed the identical "because of" language of Title VII (§703a)(1)) making it unlawful for an employer "to fail or refuse to hire or to discharge any individual ... with respect to his compensation, terms, conditions, or privileges of employment, *because of* such individual's race, color, religion, sex, or national origin" (emphasis

---

[1]"The question presented by the petitioner in this case is whether a plaintiff must present direct evidence of age discrimination in order to obtain a mixed-motives jury instruction in a suit brought under the [ADEA]." *Ante,* 129 S.Ct. at 2346

[2]The United States filed an *amicus curiae* brief supporting petitioner on the question presented. At oral argument, the Government urged that the Court should not reach the issue it takes up today.

added)), the most natural reading of the text proscribes adverse employment actions motivated in whole or in part by the age of the employee.

In *Price Waterhouse,* we concluded that the words "because of" such individual's sex mean that gender must be irrelevant to employment decisions. To establish a violation of Title VII, we therefore held, a plaintiff had to prove that her sex was a motivating factor in an adverse employment decision.[3] We recognized that the employer had an affirmative defense: It could avoid a finding of liability by proving that it would have made the same decision even if it had not taken the plaintiff's sex into account. But this affirmative defense did not alter the meaning of "because of." As we made clear, when "an employer considers both gender and legitimate factors at the time of making a decision, that decision was 'because of' sex." We readily rejected the dissent's contrary assertion. "To construe the words 'because of' as colloquial shorthand for 'but-for' causation," we said, "is to misunderstand them." 490 U.S. at 240 (plurality opinion).[4]

Today, however, the Court interprets the words "because of" in the ADEA "as colloquial shorthand for 'but-for' causation." That the Court is construing the ADEA rather than Title VII does not justify this departure from precedent. The relevant language in the two statutes is identical, and we have long recognized that our interpretations of Title VII's language apply "with equal force in the context of age discrimination, for the substantive provisions of the ADEA 'were derived *in haec verba* from Title VII." *Trans World Airlines, Inc. v. Thurston,* 469 U.S. 111, 121 (1985). For this reason, JUSTICE KENNEDY's dissent in *Price Waterhouse* assumed the plurality's mixed-motives framework extended to the ADEA and the Courts of Appeals to have considered the issue unanimously have applied *Price Waterhouse* to ADEA claims.

The Court nonetheless suggests that applying *Price Waterhouse* would be inconsistent with our ADEA precedents. In particular, the Court relies on our statement in *Hazen Paper Co. v. Biggins* that "[a disparate-treatment] claim 'cannot succeed unless the employee's protected trait actually played a role in [the employer's decisionmaking] process *and had a determinative influence on the outcome.*' " The italicized phrase is at best inconclusive as to the meaning of the ADEA's "because of" language, however, as other passages in *Hazen Paper Co.* demonstrate. We also stated, for instance, that the ADEA "requires the employer to *ignore* an employee's

---

[3]Although JUSTICE WHITE stated that the plaintiff had to show that her sex was a "substantial" factor, while the plurality used the term "motivating" factor, these standards are interchangeable, as evidenced by JUSTICE WHITE's quotation of *Mt. Healthy*: "[T]he burden was properly placed upon [the plaintiff to show that the illegitimate criterion] was a 'substantial factor' — or, *to put it in other words,* that it was a 'motivating factor' in the adverse decision" in *Price Waterhouse* (emphasis added); see also 490 U.S. at 249 (plurality opinion) (using "substantial" and "motivating" interchangeably).

[4]We were no doubt aware that dictionaries define "because of" as "by reason of" or "on account of." Contrary to the majority's bald assertion, however, this does not establish that the term denotes but-for causation. The dictionaries the Court cites do not, for instance, define "because of" as "*solely* by reason of" or "*exclusively* on account of." In *Price Waterhouse,* we recognized that the words "because of" do not mean "*solely* because of," and we held that the inquiry "commanded by the words" of the statute was whether gender was a motivating factor in the employment decision.

age," (emphasis added), and noted that "[w]hen the employer's decision is *wholly motivated* by factors other than age," there is no violation (emphasis altered). So too, we indicated the possibility of dual liability under ERISA and the ADEA where the decision to fire the employee was motivated both by the employee's age and by his pension status — a classic mixed-motives scenario.

Moreover, both *Hazen Paper Co.* and *Reeves*, on which the majority also relies, support the conclusion that the ADEA should be interpreted consistently with Title VII. In those non-mixed-motives ADEA cases, the Court followed the standards set forth in non-mixed-motives Title VII cases including *McDonnell Douglas* and *Burdine*. This by no means indicates, as the majority reasons, that *mixed-motives* ADEA cases should follow those standards. Rather, it underscores that ADEA standards are generally understood to conform to Title VII standards.

II

The conclusion that "because of" an individual's age means that age was a motivating factor in an employment decision is bolstered by Congress' reaction to *Price Waterhouse* in the 1991 Civil Rights Act. As part of its response to a number of recent decisions by the United States Supreme Court that sharply cut back on the scope and effectiveness of civil rights laws, Congress eliminated the affirmative defense to liability that *Price Waterhouse* had furnished employers and provided instead that an employer's same-decision showing would limit only a plaintiff's remedies. Importantly, however, Congress ratified *Price Waterhouse*'s interpretation of the plaintiff's burden of proof, rejecting the dissent's suggestion in that case that but-for causation was the proper standard. See §703(m).

Because the 1991 Act amended only Title VII and not the ADEA with respect to mixed-motives claims, the Court reasonably declines to apply the amended provisions to the ADEA.[6] But it proceeds to ignore the conclusion compelled by this interpretation of the Act: *Price Waterhouse*'s construction of "because of" remains the governing law for ADEA claims.

Our recent decision in *Smith v. City of Jackson* is precisely on point, as we considered in that case the effect of Congress' failure to amend the disparate-impact provisions of the ADEA when it amended the corresponding Title VII provisions in the 1991 Act. Noting that "the relevant 1991 amendments expanded the coverage of Title VII [but] did not amend the ADEA or speak to the subject of age discrimination," we held that "*Wards Cove*'s pre-1991 interpretation of Title VII's identical language remains applicable to the ADEA." If the *Wards Cove* disparate-impact framework that Congress flatly repudiated in the Title VII context continues to apply to ADEA claims, the mixed-motives framework that Congress substantially endorsed surely applies.

Curiously, the Court reaches the opposite conclusion, relying on Congress' partial ratification of *Price Waterhouse* to argue against that case's precedential value. It

---

[6]There is, however, some evidence that Congress intended the 1991 mixed-motives amendments to apply to the ADEA as well. See H.R. Rep., pt. 2, at 4 (noting that a "number of other laws banning discrimination, including ... the ADEA are modeled after and have been interpreted in a manner consistent with Title VII," and that "these other laws modeled after Title VII [should] be interpreted consistently in a manner consistent with Title VII as amended by this Act," including the mixed-motives provisions).

reasons that if the 1991 amendments do not apply to the ADEA, *Price Waterhouse* likewise must not apply because Congress effectively codified *Price Waterhouse's* holding in the amendments. This does not follow. To the contrary, the fact that Congress endorsed this Court's interpretation of the "because of" language in *Price Waterhouse* (even as it rejected the employer's affirmative defense to liability) provides all the more reason to adhere to that decision's motivating-factor test. Indeed, Congress emphasized in passing the 1991 Act that the motivating-factor test was consistent with its original intent in enacting Title VII. See, *e.g.,* H.R. Rep., pt. 2, at 17 ("When enacting the Civil Rights Act of 1964, Congress made clear that it intended to prohibit all invidious consideration of sex, race, color, religion, or national origin in employment decisions"); *id.,* at 2 (stating that the Act "reaffirm[ed] that any reliance on prejudice in making employment decisions is illegal").

The 1991 amendments to Title VII also provide the answer to the majority's argument that the mixed-motives approach has proved unworkable. Because Congress has codified a mixed-motives framework for Title VII cases — the vast majority of antidiscrimination lawsuits — the Court's concerns about that framework are of no moment. Were the Court truly worried about difficulties faced by trial courts and juries, moreover, it would not reach today's decision, which will further complicate every case in which a plaintiff raises both ADEA and Title VII claims.

The Court's resurrection of the but-for causation standard is unwarranted. *Price Waterhouse* repudiated that standard 20 years ago, and Congress' response to our decision further militates against the crabbed interpretation the Court adopts today. The answer to the question the Court has elected to take up-whether a mixed-motives jury instruction is ever proper in an ADEA case-is plainly yes.

III

Although the Court declines to address the question we granted certiorari to decide, I would answer that question by following our unanimous opinion in *Desert Palace, Inc. v. Costa.* I would accordingly hold that a plaintiff need not present direct evidence of age discrimination to obtain a mixed-motives instruction.

The source of the direct-evidence debate is Justice O'Connor's opinion concurring in the judgment in *Price Waterhouse.* Writing only for herself, Justice O'Connor argued that a plaintiff should be required to introduce "direct evidence" that her sex motivated the decision before the plurality's mixed-motives framework would apply.[7] Many courts have treated Justice O'Connor's opinion in *Price Waterhouse* as controlling for both Title VII and ADEA mixed-motives cases in light of our statement in *Marks v. United States,* 430 U.S. 188, 193 (1977), that "when a fragmented Court decides a case and no single rationale explaining the result enjoys the assent of five Justices, the holding of the Court may be viewed as that position taken by those Members who concurred in the judgments on the narrowest grounds." Unlike the cases *Marks* addressed, however, *Price Waterhouse* garnered five votes for a single

---

[7] While Justice O'Connor did not define precisely what she meant by "direct evidence," we contrasted such evidence with circumstantial evidence in *Desert Palace.* That Justice O'Connor might have intended a different definition does not affect my conclusion, as I do not believe a plaintiff is required to introduce any special type of evidence to obtain a mixed-motives instruction.

rationale: Justice White agreed with the plurality as to the motivating-factor test; he disagreed only as to the type of evidence an employer was required to submit to prove that the same result would have occurred absent the unlawful motivation. Taking the plurality to demand objective evidence, he wrote separately to express his view that an employer's credible testimony could suffice. Because Justice White provided a fifth vote for the "rationale explaining the result" of the *Price Waterhouse* decision, his concurrence is properly understood as controlling, and he, like the plurality, did not require the introduction of direct evidence.

Any questions raised by *Price Waterhouse* as to a direct evidence requirement were settled by this Court's unanimous decision in *Desert Palace,* in which we held that a plaintiff need not introduce direct evidence to meet her burden in a mixed-motives case under Title VII, as amended by the Civil Rights Act of 1991. In construing the language of §703(m), we reasoned that the statute did not mention, much less require, a heightened showing through direct evidence and that "Congress has been unequivocal when imposing heightened proof requirements." The statute's silence with respect to direct evidence, we held, meant that "we should not depart from the conventional rule of civil litigation that requires a plaintiff to prove his case by a preponderance of the evidence using direct or circumstantial evidence." We also recognized the Court's consistent acknowledgment of the utility of circumstantial evidence in discrimination cases.

Our analysis in *Desert Palace* applies with equal force to the ADEA. As with the 1991 amendments to Title VII, no language in the ADEA imposes a heightened direct evidence requirement, and we have specifically recognized the utility of circumstantial evidence in ADEA cases. See *Reeves.* Moreover, in *Hazen Paper Co.,* we held that an award of liquidated damages for a "willful" violation of the ADEA did not require proof of the employer's motivation through direct evidence, and we have similarly rejected the imposition of special evidentiary rules in other ADEA cases. See, *e.g., Swierkiewicz v. Sorema N. A.*; *O'Connor v. Consolidated Coin Caterers Corp. Desert Palace* thus confirms the answer provided by the plurality and Justice White in *Price Waterhouse:* An ADEA plaintiff need not present direct evidence of discrimination to obtain a mixed-motives instruction.

IV

The Court's endorsement of a different construction of the same critical language in the ADEA and Title VII is both unwise and inconsistent with settled law. The but-for standard the Court adopts was rejected by this Court in *Price Waterhouse* and by Congress in the Civil Rights Act of 1991. Yet today the Court resurrects the standard in an unabashed display of judicial lawmaking. I respectfully dissent.

JUSTICE BREYER, with whom JUSTICE SOUTER and JUSTICE GINSBURG join, dissenting.

I agree with JUSTICE STEVENS that mixed-motive instructions are appropriate in the Age Discrimination in Employment Act context. And I join his opinion. The Court rejects this conclusion on the ground that the words "because of" require a plaintiff to prove that age was the "but-for" cause of his employer's adverse employment action. But the majority does not explain why this is so. The words "because of" do not inherently require a showing of "but-for" causation, and I see no reason to read them to require such a showing.

It is one thing to require a typical tort plaintiff to show "but-for" causation. In that context, reasonably objective scientific or commonsense theories of physical causation make the concept of "but-for" causation comparatively easy to understand and relatively easy to apply. But it is an entirely different matter to determine a "but-for" relation when we consider, not physical forces, but the mind-related characterizations that constitute motive. Sometimes we speak of *determining* or *discovering* motives, but more often we *ascribe* motives, after an event, to an individual in light of the individual's thoughts and other circumstances present at the time of decision. In a case where we characterize an employer's actions as having been taken out of multiple motives, say, both because the employee was old and because he wore loud clothing, to apply "but-for" causation is to engage in a hypothetical inquiry about what would have happened if the employer's thoughts and other circumstances had been different. The answer to this hypothetical inquiry will often be far from obvious, and, since the employee likely knows less than does the employer about what the employer was thinking at the time, the employer will often be in a stronger position than the employee to provide the answer.

All that a plaintiff can know for certain in such a context is that the forbidden motive did play a role in the employer's decision. And the fact that a jury has found that age did play a role in the decision justifies the use of the word "because," *i.e.*, the employer dismissed the employee because of his age (and other things). See *Price Waterhouse* (plurality opinion). I therefore would see nothing wrong in concluding that the plaintiff has established a violation of the statute.

But the law need not automatically assess liability in these circumstances. In *Price Waterhouse,* the plurality recognized an affirmative defense where the defendant could show that the employee would have been dismissed regardless. The law permits the employer this defense, not because the forbidden motive, age, had no role in the *actual* decision, but because the employer can show that he would have dismissed the employee anyway in the *hypothetical* circumstance in which his age-related motive was absent. And it makes sense that this would be an affirmative defense, rather than part of the showing of a violation, precisely because the defendant is in a better position than the plaintiff to establish how he would have acted in this hypothetical situation. I can see nothing unfair or impractical about allocating the burdens of proof in this way.

The instruction that the District Court gave seems appropriate and lawful. * * *

For these reasons as well as for those set forth by Justice Stevens, I respectfully dissent.

NOTES AND PROBLEMS FOR DISCUSSION

1. How does the Court's ruling in *Gross* comport with its prior decision in *Smith v. City of Jackson*? Did either the majority or the dissenters' discussion of this issue persuade you?

2. Should the Supreme Court's recognition of hostile environment-based sexual harassment claims under Title VII be extended to claims of age-based hostile environment harassment under the ADEA? *See* Crawford v. Medina General Hospital,

96 F.3d 830, 834 (6th Cir. 1996) (since the ADEA, like Title VII, prohibits discrimination in terms and conditions of employment, "we have no doubt that a hostile work environment claim may be stated."). *Accord,* Dediol v. Best Chevrolet, Inc., 655 F.3d 435 (5th Cir. 2011) (adopting reasoning in *Crawford*).

3.   (a) Does the Court's decision in *Gross* not to extend mixed motive analysis to ADEA cases cast doubt on the continued viability of the *McDonnell Douglas/Burdine* proof scheme for single-motive claims of intentional discrimination? The First, Second, Third, Fifth, Sixth, and Ninth Circuits have concluded that it does not. In SMITH v. CITY OF ALLENTOWN, 589 F.3d 684 (3d Cir. 2009), for example, the Third Circuit concluded that *Gross* did not disturb the continued applicability of the *McDonnell Douglas* formulation to age discrimination claims. It read *Gross* as rejecting mixed motive analysis because that formulation shifted the burden of persuasion to the defendant (on causation) and that since *McDonnell Douglas* never shifted the burden of *persuasion* to the defendant, it would continue to govern the analysis of single motive claims of intentional age-based discrimination.

Should the *Gross* Court's rejection of the applicability of mixed motive analysis to an ADEA action brought by a private sector employee also apply to ADEA claims by federal employees? Section 15 of the ADEA mandates that all covered employment decisions concerning federal employees "be made free from any discrimination based on age", while §4(a) prohibits a nonfederal employer from discriminating against any individual "because of such individual's age". Does this textual difference suggest that *Gross* should not be extended to federal employee ADEA claims? *See* Ford v. Mabus, 629 F.3d 198 (D.C.Cir. 2010) (refusing to extend *Gross* to federal employee ADEA claim because this textual difference reflected Congressional intent to provide "more sweeping" protection to federal employees).

What impact, if any, should the ruling in *Gross* have on "cat's paw"-based claims, i.e., where the plaintiff alleges that the discriminatory decision was a product of discriminatory bias by someone other than the ultimate decision-maker? Recall that in *Staub,* the Supreme Court endorsed the theory of subordinate liability in a case brought under the Uniformed Services Employment and Reemployment Rights Act (USERRA), holding that it was sufficient for the plaintiff to prove that the supervisor's discriminatorily motivated conduct was *a* cause of the ultimate employment action. In SIMMONS v. SYKES ENTERPRISES, INC. 647 F.3d 943 (10th Cir. 2011), the Court, relying on *Gross*, held that since causation under the ADEA, unlike Title VII or the USERRA, was not subject to mixed motive theory, "the relationship between a subordinate's animus and the ultimate employment decision must be more closely linked." Specifically, the court held, the plaintiff must establish that the subordinate's animus was a "but-for" cause of the adverse action, and not simply a contributing cause. Similarly, in SIMS v. MVM, INC., 704 F.3d 1327 (11th Cir. 2013), the Eleventh Circuit held that because ADEA actions were subject to a "but-for" causation standard, in a cat's paw case under the ADEA, the plaintiff must prove that the proscribed animus was a but-for cause of, or had a "determinative influence" on, the challenged employment decision rather than meet only the "proximate cause" standard applied by the Supreme Court in *Staub* in a cat's paw case arising under USERRA.

(b) If a plaintiff is replaced by a younger employee who, nevertheless, is over the age of forty and, therefore, is also a member of the statutorily protected group, can he still state a claim under the ADEA or would the application of *Burdine* analysis suggest that he must establish that he was replaced by someone outside the statutorily protected age class to make out a prima facie case of age discrimination? Age differs from the categories protected under Title VII in that it is not a discrete characteristic separating members from nonmembers of the protected group. Rather, age is a continuum along which relative distinctions can be made. A terminated sixty-year-old worker is not always replaced by a twenty-five year old. And when she is not, can she still claim that she was terminated because of her age? In O'CONNOR v. CONSOLIDATED COIN CATERERS CORPORATION, 517 U.S. 308, 116 S.Ct. 1307, 134 L.Ed.2d 433 (1996), a unanimous Court held that the fact that a statutorily protected individual was replaced by someone within the protected class "lacks probative value" and is "utterly irrelevant." The relevant issue, the Court declared, was whether the decision was based on the plaintiff's age, not whether or not the replacement was a member of the protected class. The requisite inference of age-based decision making could not be drawn when one worker is replaced by another "insignificantly younger" individual, as, for example, when a (statutorily protected) 40 year old plaintiff is replaced by an (unprotected) 39 year old worker. However, the Court explained, "the fact that a replacement is substantially younger than the plaintiff is a far more reliable indicator of age discrimination than is the fact that the plaintiff was replaced by someone outside the protected class." The Court also noted that although it had never previously ruled on whether Title VII pleading rules should be transplanted to ADEA cases, it was assuming that Title VII standards applied here since the parties had not raised this issue.

Recall, however, how the Supreme Court distinguished the result in *O'Connor* from its treatment in *General Dynamics* of precisely the opposite situation, i.e., discrimination against one (the relatively younger) segment of the protected class in favor of another (the relatively older) segment of the protected class in *General Dynamics*.

4. After terminating Lori Charter solely on the basis of her age, Grotto Co. discovered that she had embezzled funds from the company's bank account. When Lori brings an ADEA suit against Grotto, can the company introduce evidence of this embezzlement for the purpose of absolving itself from liability? In McKENNON v. NASHVILLE BANNER PUBLISHING CO., 513 U.S. 352, 110 S.Ct. 879, 130 L.Ed.2d 852 (1995), the Court announced what is now known as the "after-acquired evidence" rule. In this case, the defendant sought to avoid liability for discharging an employee on the basis of her age by establishing that it discovered that she had engaged in misconduct (embezzlement) so grave that it warranted termination. The appellate court accepted this argument and affirmed the trial court's grant of summary judgment for the defense. The Supreme Court emphasized that the remedial provisions of the ADEA, like those of Title VII, were enacted with three objectives in mind: (1) to deter future violations; (2) to compensate victims of discrimination; and (3) to encourage employers to examine and evaluate their own employment policies and to try to eliminate the vestiges of prior discrimination. Relieving the employer of all liability on the basis of its post-discharge acquisition of evidence of employee wrongdoing, it reasoned, would not further these objectives. Under these presumed circumstances, the employer clearly acted unlawfully at the moment it made the discharge decision. Thus, the Court reasoned, imposing liability promoted the statutory policies of deterrence and promotion of employer self-evaluation. On the other hand, the Court admitted, it made little sense to order the reinstatement of, or to award front pay to, an employee that the employer would and could summarily fire for engaging in the presumed misconduct. Consequently, the Court announced, the evidence of employee misconduct, while not relevant on the issue of liability, was admissible to limit the plaintiff's recovery. As a general rule in cases of this type, the Court stated, reinstatement or front pay is not an appropriate remedy, but a plaintiff should be entitled to compensation for the loss of income from, at least, the date of her discharge until the date of discovery of her misconduct. Why didn't the *McKennon* Court analyze that claim as a mixed motive case?

5.   The ADEA, like Title VII, contains a BFOQ affirmative defense. The circuit courts have tended to agree that where the employer asserts safety as a consideration for its challenged decision, a lesser showing is required than in cases where safety is not a concern. *See* Tuohy v. Ford Motor Co., 675 F.2d 842, 845 (6th Cir. 1982) ("The presence of an overriding safety factor might well lead a court to conclude as a matter of policy that the level of proof required to establish the reasonable necessity of a BFOQ is relatively low."). Otherwise, the rules governing the BFOQ defense in Title VII cases have been transplanted to the ADEA context. In WESTERN AIR LINES, INC. v. CRISWELL, 472 U.S. 400, 105 S.Ct. 2743, 86 L.Ed.2d 321 (1985), the Court rejected the employer's contention that the ADEA required only that an employer establish a "rational basis in fact" for believing that identification of those individuals lacking suitable qualifications could not occur on an individualized basis. Rather, the Court held, to establish a BFOQ defense, an employer must first demonstrate that the qualification used to justify the age requirement is reasonably necessary to the essence of its business and then prove that it was compelled to rely on age as a proxy for this qualification by establishing either that all or substantially all individuals over a particular age lack the qualification or that it is impracticable or impossible to treat persons over this age on an individualized basis.

Moreover, in JOHNSON v. MAYOR AND CITY COUNCIL OF BALTIMORE, 472 U.S. 353, 105 S.Ct. 2717, 86 L.Ed.2d 286 (1985), decided the same day as *Western Air Lines*, the Court stated that the existence of a federal statute establishing a mandatory retirement policy for a class of federal firefighters did not automatically establish a BFOQ defense to a state or local government rule imposing an identical mandatory retirement age on analogous state and local government workers. It concluded that the federal statute relied on by the defendants in this case was not intended by Congress to apply to nonfederal employees. The Court also concluded that the federal decision to implement a mandatory retirement policy was not based on a congressional determination that age was a bona fide occupational qualification for the subject class (federal firefighters), but, rather, on the idiosyncratic problems of federal civil servants and Congress' desire to create an image of a "young man's service." Accordingly, the Court stated that the federal statute authorizing mandatory retirement was not relevant to the question of whether age was a BFOQ for firefighters.

6.   Luther Clark, a 45-year-old former Air Force pilot, applied for a pilot position with Ace Airlines, Inc. The company rejected his application in a letter stating that while Clark was otherwise qualified for the job, airline policy precluded hiring pilots over the age of 35. Ace maintains a pilot training and progression system under which all pilot applicants are hired as Second Officers, are promoted to First Officers after 8

to 10 years of service with Ace and are advanced to Captain after an additional 6 to 8 years. The company contends that substantial costs are involved in operating its pilot training and progression system and, when coupled with an F.A.A. requirement that all pilots retire at 60, a maximum age of 35 at initial hire is necessary to achieve peak pilot productivity. Has Ace violated the ADEA? *Compare* Smallwood v. United Air Lines, Inc., 661 F.2d 303 (4th Cir. 1981), cert. denied, 456 U.S. 1007, 102 S.Ct. 2299, 73 L.Ed.2d 1302 (1982), *with* Murnane v. American Airlines, Inc., 667 F.2d 98 (D.C.Cir.1981), cert. denied, 456 U.S. 915, 102 S.Ct. 1770, 72 L.Ed.2d 174 (1982).

7. Kevin Conroy was discharged as Manager of the men's clothing department of Watson's Department Store one month after his 55th birthday. At the time of his discharge, Conroy had worked at Watson's for 25 years and was earning $47,000. The store contends that a sharp decrease in revenues forced it to adopt several cost-cutting techniques. Watson's had offered to retain Conroy at the $21,000 salary it is prepared to offer Lou Dix, a 25-year-old recent college graduate with no experience. Would making that offer violate §4(a)(3) of the ADEA, which makes it unlawful for an employer "to reduce the wage rate of any employee in order to comply with the Act"? See generally, Terrence P. Collingsworth, Note, *The Cost Defense Under the ADEA*, 1982 Duke L.J. 580 (1982).

8. In EMPLOYMENT DIVISION v. SMITH, 494 U.S. 872, 110 S.Ct. 1595, 108 L.Ed.2d 876 (1990), the Supreme Court ruled that the Free Exercise Clause of the First Amendment did not justify an individual from failing to comply with the requirements of a facially neutral law of general applicability when compliance would contravene that individual's religious beliefs or practices. The *Smith* Court also, however, invited legislative enactment of religious exceptions to neutral laws. In 1993, Congress passed the Religious Freedom Restoration Act (RFRA), 42 U.S.C. §2000bb et seq., in response to that ruling. The RFRA prohibits the government from substantially burdening a person's exercise of religion, including when that burden is the result of the enforcement of a facially neutral statute of general applicability, except where the government proves that the source of that burden furthers a compelling governmental interest and represents the least restrictive means of furthering that compelling state interest.

In HANKINS v. LYGHT, 441 F.3d 96 (2d Cir.2006), an ordained minister brought an ADEA challenge to his church's age-based mandatory retirement policy. The church invoked the terms of the RFRA as a complete defense to the plaintiff's claim, arguing that application of the ADEA would substantially burden the exercise of its religion in the absence of a compelling state interest. The trial court dismissed the case by transplanting the "ministerial exception" formulated in Title VII cases to this ADEA claim. With respect to whether the ministerial exception could be extended to ADEA cases, the Second Circuit declared that "[w]hatever the merits of that exception as statutory interpretation or policy, it has no basis in statutory text, whereas the RFRA, if applicable, is explicit legislation that could not be more on point." Consequently, the court ruled that in the absence of express codification of the ministerial exception, "the RFRA must be deemed the full expression of Congress' intent with regard to the religion-related issues before us and displace earlier judge-made doctrines that might have been used to ameliorate the ADEA's impact on religious organizations and activities." The Court then explained that since the defendant had alleged that application of the ADEA (a facially neutral law of general applicability) substantially burdened its exercise of religion, the RFRA operated as a complete defense if the government could not meet the statutory compelling state interest and least restrictive means tests. And after noting that the RFRA defense could be asserted against both a private and governmental party, the court ruled that the RFRA was constitutional when invoked as a defense to a claim under federal law and remanded the case for consideration on the merits of the RFRA defense. On remand, the trial court ruled that RFRA had displaced the ministerial exception. But then, on appeal, the Second Circuit panel declared that the RFRA must yield to a constitutionally mandated rule of law. This, in turn, led it to conclude that the constitutionally–based ministerial exception applied to the case and required the dismissal of the suit. Hankins v. New York Annual Conference of the United Methodist Church, 2009 WL 3259425 (2d Cir. 2009) (unpublished opinion). *See also* Tomic v. Catholic Diocese of Peoria, 442 F.3d 1036 (7th Cir.2006), cert. denied, 549 U.S. 881, 127 S.Ct. 190, 166 L.Ed.2d 142 (2006) (applying ministerial exception to ADEA suit challenging the termination of a Catholic diocese's music director and organist).

9. Does the ADEA's prohibition of mandatory retirement (albeit subject to the statutory BFOQ exception) preclude the use of voluntary retirement plans? *See* Henn v. National Geographic Society, 819 F.2d 824 (7th Cir.), cert. denied, 484 U.S. 964, 108 S.Ct. 454, 98 L.Ed.2d 394 (1987) (no ADEA violation when an employer offers employees over a prescribed age the option of retaining their jobs or taking early retirement). Pursuant to amendments to the ADEA contained in the 1990 Older Workers Benefit Protection Act (OWBPA), voluntary early retirement incentive plans are lawful as long as the employer can demonstrate that the plan is consistent with promoting the employment of older workers based on ability rather than age, prohibiting arbitrary age-based discrimination in employment, and assisting employers and employees in addressing problems associated with the impact of age on employment.

10. (a) A question frequently associated with early retirement plans arises when the employer offers enhanced benefits in exchange for the employees' waiver of statutory rights. Under the OWBPA, a waiver of rights under the ADEA, including those sought as a condition for receipt of early retirement or severance pay, is permissible where the waiver is "knowing and voluntary." The statute sets forth a list of threshold requirements for courts to consider in determining whether the waiver was "knowing and voluntary." Among these are that the waiver must (a) be written in a manner calculated to be understood by the average worker; (b) specifically refer to rights or claims arising under the ADEA; (c) not include a waiver of rights or claims that may arise after the date of execution of the waiver; (d) be made in exchange for consideration beyond anything to which the individual already was entitled; (e) contain a written statement advising the individual to consult with an attorney prior to executing the agreement; and (f) provide the individual with at least 21 days within which to consider the agreement (or 45 days where the waiver is part of an exit incentive or other employment termination program offered to a group of employees) and with another seven days after the execution of the agreement to revoke the agreement. In addition, the waiver agreement will not become enforceable until the expiration of the revocation period and the burden of proving that the waiver was knowing and voluntary is on the party asserting the validity of the waiver. Note, in this regard, that the statute requires the employer to prove that the waiver was written in a manner calculated to be understood by the average worker. This suggests that an individual employee may not be bound to a waiver when the employer only demonstrates that she personally understood the meaning of the waiver. Rather, it suggests that the employer must prove that the average worker subject to the waiver would understand it.

An individual waiver also does not bar the EEOC from taking action to enforce the Act, such as processing a charge filed by the individual employee or bringing suit in the individual's name. This means that, under the OWBPA, a waiver of the individual's right to file an age discrimination charge with the EEOC, as opposed to an ADEA cause of action in court, cannot be enforced. And the inclusion of an unenforceable prohibition on filing an EEOC charge in an otherwise enforceable waiver agreement does not invalidate that agreement's waiver of the individual's right to bring a lawsuit. Moreover, if a waiver is sought in settlement of a pending EEOC charge or judicial proceeding, the waiver must comply with all of the aforesaid requirements, except for the mandatory consideration and revocation periods. Rather, the statute provides only that the individual must be given "a reasonable period of time within which to consider the settlement agreement" when it relates to a pending administrative or judicial proceeding.

(b) Suppose that after signing a general release and waiver, a terminated employee filed an age discrimination claim in which she alleged that the release did not satisfy the requirements of the OWBPA and that she was discharged on the basis of her age. If this employee already had accepted and retained severance benefits paid following execution of that release, does this conduct ratify the release and bar her from pursuing her statutory claim? In OUBRE v. ENTERGY OPERATIONS, INC., 522 U.S. 422, 118 S.Ct. 838, 139 L.Ed.2d 849 (1998), the Court held that irrespective of whether a party's retention of benefits could effect a ratification of an otherwise voidable contract under general common law principles, the circumstances that would render a release of ADEA-protected rights enforceable were limited solely to those expressly contained within the OWBPA's statutory stricture on waivers. Therefore, the Court reasoned, since the OWBPA permits waivers of ADEA rights only when a release satisfies the OWBPA's criteria for a knowing and voluntary waiver, a release that does not comport with these statutory requirements cannot be enforced, regardless of whatever other conduct (including retention of benefits) is engaged in by either of the parties. To subject the statutory rule on waivers to this common law doctrine, the Court continued, would frustrate the statutory policy of protecting the rights of older workers because many discharged employees will have spent the money received and be unable to return the funds prior to instituting litigation. This factor, the Court reasoned, might tempt employers to risk noncompliance with the OWBPA waiver requirements on the assumption that most of their former employees will be unable to repay the monies and thus be subject to this ratification defense. Yet while the Court ruled that the plaintiff's failure to return the severance payments did not bar her suit, it expressly left the door open for the employer to attempt to recover those funds through a claim for restitution, recoupment or setoff against whatever award the plaintiff might receive on her underlying claim.

(c) Where an employee alleges that he did not determine that he had been discharged on the basis of age until after signing the release, can he successfully claim that the waiver is unenforceable under the OWBPA because his claim is one that "arose" after the date of the execution of the waiver? *See* Wastak v. Lehigh Valley Health Network, 342 F.3d 281 (3d Cir. 2003) (the discovery of the legal wrong, though relevant to the possible tolling of the statute of limitations, is inapplicable to the issue of the validity of a waiver; the claim accrues for waiver purposes upon awareness of the adverse action (the discharge) and not upon awareness of the reason for the adverse action).

11. Although involuntary retirement plans are expressly removed from the coverage of the bona fide employee benefit and seniority plan defense of §4(f)(2), this defense does apply to all other age-based decisions. Suppose the employees of Dimitri Enterprises are covered by an employer-funded disability, life and health insurance benefits plan. Since the cost of premiums for employees over the age of 60 is substantially higher than the cost of such premiums for those under age 60, Dimitri's employee benefits plan terminates disability, life and health insurance benefits to all employees at age 60. The ADEA requires employers to continue to provide group health care insurance coverage to all employees over age 40, irrespective of age. Does this mean that the Dimitri policy is unlawful and that the company must either absorb the extra cost of these higher premiums or, at least, make equal premium contributions for all employees and simply provide reduced coverage or require the older employees to fund the difference? See §4(f)(2)(B)(i).

In 2003, the EEOC published a notice of proposed rulemaking to exempt from the prohibitions of the ADEA "the practice of altering, reducing or eliminating employer-sponsored retiree health benefits when retirees become eligible for Medicare or a State-sponsored retiree health benefit program." The AARP challenged this regulation as violative of, *inter alia*, the ADEA. The trial court ruled in favor of the EEOC, but enjoined implementation of the regulation pending appeal to the Third Circuit. The issue under the ADEA was whether the EEOC possessed the authority to issue a regulation that created this exemption from the prohibitions of the ADEA. Section 9 of the ADEA authorizes the EEOC to establish "such reasonable exemptions" to the Act as it finds "necessary and proper in the public interest". The Third Circuit ruled that §9 demonstrated Congress' unambiguous intention to grant to the EEOC the authority to allow limited practices that otherwise would violate the nondiscrimination mandate of the ADEA. Thus, the only question before the court was whether the exemption in question was reasonable, necessary, and proper. The court found that the EEOC had issued the regulation in response to its finding that employer-sponsored retiree health benefits were decreasing. And since employers had no statutory duty to provide any health benefits to retirees, the EEOC decided to issue the proposed regulation to encourage employers to continue to offer health benefits to all retirees, regardless of age, despite the rising cost of health care. Consequently, even though the court acknowledged that the regulation would permit employers to reduce health benefits to Medicare eligible retirees, i.e., those over the age of sixty-five, while maintaining greater benefits for younger retirees, it nevertheless concluded that the EEOC had established that this was a narrow exemption that was reasonable, necessary and proper. AARP v. EEOC, 489 F.3d 558 (3rd Cir. 2007), cert. denied, 552 U.S. 1279, 128 S.Ct. 1733, 170 L.Ed.2d 512 (2008).

12. Can a defendant claim that its reliance upon a state statute that conflicts with the provisions of the ADEA constitutes a "differentiation based on factors other than age?" *See* EEOC v. County of Allegheny, 705 F.2d 679 (3d Cir. 1983) (*rejecting this argument*).

13. Section 7(b) of the ADEA provides for the award of liquidated damages in case of willful violations. Does this mean that liquidated damages are also recoverable against a municipality in cases involving willful violations? In POTENCE v. HAZLETON AREA SCHOOL DISTRICT, 357 F.3d 366 (3d Cir.2004), the Third Circuit acknowledged that although liquidated damages were intended by the legislature to be punitive in nature, a municipality's common law immunity against punitive damages does not apply when such damages are expressly authorized by statute. Turning to the language of the ADEA, the court concluded that since (a) the ADEA provides for liquidated damages against an "employer" who engages in a willful violation, and (b) municipalities are included under that statute's definition of "employer", the plain language of the ADEA made clear that Congress intended to subject municipalities to its liquidated damages provision.

14. Public sector age classifications also are subject to constitutional scrutiny under the equal protection and due process guarantees of the Fifth and Fourteenth Amendments of the U.S. Constitution. In MASSACHUSETTS BOARD OF RETIREMENT v. MURGIA, 427 U.S. 307, 96 S.Ct. 2562, 49 L.Ed.2d 520 (1976), involving a Massachusetts statute requiring uniformed state police officers to retire at age fifty, the Supreme Court stated that an age classification need only pass the rationality, rather than strict scrutiny standard. It then found that mandatory retirement at age 50 rationally furthered Massachusetts' interest in protecting the public by assuring the physical preparedness of the uniformed police. Similarly, in VANCE v. BRADLEY, 440 U.S. 93, 99 S.Ct. 939, 59 L.Ed.2d 171 (1979), a federal statute mandating retirement at age 60 of Foreign Service personnel was upheld in the face of an equal protection challenge. The Supreme Court held that the retirement provision rationally furthered Congress' legitimate objective of maintaining a competent Foreign Service. For a comprehensive assessment of the impact of the Court's ruling in *Murgia* on the elimination of ageist policies and, in particularly, on the implementation of mandatory retirement policies, see Howard Eglit, *The Story of Mandatory Retirement, Massachusetts Board of Retirement v. Murgia and Ageism*, EMPLOYMENT DISCRIMINATION STORIES 259 (Friedman, ed. 2006).

15. Since the ADEA, unlike Title VII, does not contain an express exemption for religious institutions or Native American tribal employers, consider the following:

(a) Does the application of the ADEA to decisions affecting lay employees of religious institutions create a conflict with either of the religion clauses of the First Amendment? *Compare* DeMarco v. Holy Cross High School, 4 F.3d 166 (2d Cir. 1993) (application of ADEA to lay teacher does not create a serious risk of a constitutional violation as long as the plaintiff may not challenge the plausibility of the religious institution's asserted religious motive for its challenged action), *with* Cochran v. St. Louis Preparatory Seminary, 717 F.Supp. 1413 (E.D. Mo. 1989) (ADEA is not applicable to church-operated schools because application of this statute to the employment practices of a religious seminary would raise serious problems under the First Amendment religion clauses as it could cause the seminary to steer wide of the zone of prohibited conduct, thereby chilling its performance of its religious mission, and Congressional silence on inclusion of religious institutions within class of covered employers indicates that Congress did not contemplate that the Act would apply to such institutions).

(b) Can the ADEA constitutionally regulate employment matters affecting clergy? *See* Scharon v. St. Luke's Episcopal Presbyterian Hospitals, 929 F.2d 360 (8th Cir. 1991)(application of the ADEA to the employment relationship between a religious institution and an ordained priest who performed religious and secular duties would violate the First Amendment free exercise and establishment clauses).

(c) Traditional federal common law principles provide Native American tribes with the rights of self-government and sovereign immunity. In addition, special canons of statutory construction relevant to Native American tribes provide that when a federal statute of federal applicability is silent on the issue of its applicability to Native American tribes, the statute will be construed not to apply to tribes if either (a) the law touches exclusive rights of self-governance in purely intramural matters; (b) applying the law would abrogate rights guaranteed by Indian treaties; or (c) there is evidence that Congress intended the statute not to apply to Native Americans on their reservations. Where any one of these three conditions is met, Congress must expressly extend the statute to Native Americans in order for it to apply to them. Do the antidiscrimination provisions of the ADEA apply to tribal employers? Is it relevant that the ADEA (unlike Title VII) does not contain an exemption for tribal employers? Circuit courts have concluded that the ADEA is inapplicable to Native Indian tribes on the basis of the first two of these three criteria in EEOC v. Karuk Tribe Housing Authority, 260 F.3d 1071 (9th Cir.2001); EEOC v. Fond du Lac Heavy Equip. & Constr. Co., Inc., 986 F.2d 246 (8th Cir.1993); and EEOC v. Cherokee Nation, 871 F.2d 937 (10th Cir. 1989). For a thorough discussion of these and other cases examining the issue of the applicability of the ADEA and §1981 to Indian tribal employers, see Vicki J. Limas, *Application of Federal Labor and Employment Statutes to Native American Tribes: Respecting Sovereignty and Achieving Consistency*, 26 ARIZ.ST.L.J. 681 (1994).

16. Recall the discussion concerning the availability of a "market defense" in the context of the Equal Pay Act. Suppose an employer states that it will pay the market rate for all new employees but will not adjust the salaries of incumbent workers to meet the market rate. Does such a practice violate the Act by creating a disproportionate impact on older workers or is it justified by the "factor other than age" or alternative defense? *Compare* MacPherson v. University of Montevallo, 922 F.2d 766 (11th Cir. 1991) (the practice of paying market rates to newly-hired faculty members but not to others has a disproportionate impact on older professors, but is supported by the defendant's "legitimate business interest" in attracting and hiring good new faculty members), *with* Davidson v. Board of Governors of State Colleges & Universities, 920 F.2d 441, 446 (7th Cir. 1990) (the "limited" disproportionate impact created by the defendant's policy of paying market rate "does not come close to demonstrating a taint of age discrimination.").

17. Section 4(h)(1) provides that foreign employers that are controlled by an American company are subject to the substantive requirements of the ADEA, and 4(h)(2) states that foreign employers that are not controlled by an American company are not subject to the terms of the statute. At the same time, under §11(f), the statute also applies to U.S. (but not foreign) citizens working for an American company located in a foreign country. Does this mean that a foreign-owned company that is not controlled by an American employer, but which operates within the U.S. is exempted from the requirements of the ADEA as to both its foreign and American workers? See Morelli v. Cedel, 141 F.3d 39 (2d Cir. 1998) (the two provisions need to be read in tandem and the natural implication of the combined provisions is that Congress intended to exempt only the foreign operations of foreign employers from the application of the ADEA; the American branch of a foreign-controlled employer is subject to the provisions of the ADEA absent treaty protection to the contrary).

As mentioned in footnote "h" at the beginning of this Chapter, the ADEA was amended in 1984 to expressly extend its application to American citizens employed abroad by an American company or its foreign subsidiary except when that would violate local law. The circuit courts have construed this amendment to restrict the extraterritorial application of the ADEA to U.S. citizens, which means that alien employees working for U.S. companies outside of the U.S. are not covered by the ADEA. Nevertheless, the statute clearly applies to foreign nationals who are legally employed within the United States. But what about an alien who applies in his home country for a position with an American company that is located in the U.S.? See Reyes-Gaona v. North Carolina Growers Ass'n, 250 F.3d 861 (4th Cir.2001), cert. denied, 534 U.S. 995, 122 S.Ct. 463, 151 L.Ed.2d 380 (2001) (rejecting the Mexican national plaintiff's claim that since he worked in the U.S., no issue of extraterritoriality was raised; expanding coverage of statute to millions of foreign nationals who file overseas applications for U.S. employment could exponentially increase number of suits filed and such step must be taken by clear and unambiguous congressional action rather than by judicial fiat).

SECTION C. PROCEDURAL REQUIREMENTS

Read §§7, 14 and 15 of the ADEA.

Litigants proceeding under the ADEA are subject to most of the same procedural requirements placed before Title VII claimants. For example, pursuant to §7(d), a grievant (other than a federal employee) intent on filing a civil action under the ADEA must first file a charge with the EEOC within 180 days after the alleged unlawful practice,[a] or within 300 days of the alleged unlawful practice where a recognized state agency exists, or within 30 days after receipt of notice of termination of proceedings under State law, whichever comes first.[b] But, unlike a Title VII plaintiff, an age

---

[a]Most circuit courts have rejected the plaintiffs' suggestions that they engraft a "discovery rule" onto the ADEA limitations period and, instead, have held that the language of §7(d) clearly indicates that the limitations period begins to run from the date of the alleged event and not from the time the claimant discovered its discriminatory nature. See, e.g., Hamilton v. 1st Source Bank, 928 F.2d 86 (4th Cir.1990) (en banc) (where Congress has intended a discovery rule, it has explicitly provided for it).

[b]There is an important exception to this rule. It is not always necessary for an EEOC charge to be filed by the individual bringing suit under the ADEA. The lower courts have regularly held that the timely filing of an administrative charge by a named plaintiff in a class action is sufficient to satisfy the charge filing obligations of all other members of the class. This "single filing rule" has been applied in both Title VII and ADEA actions. Moreover, the courts have

discrimination claimant is not required to wait for receipt of a right-to-sue letter before filing a civil action. Section 7(d) of the ADEA permits an ADEA claimant to file suit as early as sixty days after he or she files an age charge with the EEOC. No analogous provision exists in Title VII.

With respect to the latest date for filing an age discrimination action, however, the age plaintiff is in the same situation as a Title VII claimant. Pursuant to an amendment contained in the 1991 Civil Rights Act, §7(e) of the ADEA provides that ADEA plaintiffs, like those proceeding under Title VII, must file suit no later than 90 days after receiving notice from the EEOC that it has concluded or terminated its proceedings. This provision also requires the EEOC to provide such notification to the aggrieved.

---

extended the "single filing rule" to non-class actions involving multiple individual plaintiffs. Under certain conditions, the courts will permit an individual who has not filed a timely administrative charge to join the lawsuit by "piggybacking" his or her charge to the timely administrative charge of the named plaintiff. A variety of tests have been employed by the circuit courts in determining when to allow such "piggybacking." The broadest test requires only that the claims of the administrative claimant and the subsequent plaintiffs arise out of the same circumstances and occur within the same general time period. *See, e.g.*, Grayson v. K Mart Corp., 79 F.3d 1086 (11th Cir.), cert. denied, 519 U.S. 987, 117 S.Ct. 447, 136 L.Ed.2d 342 (1996). Other circuits have adopted a somewhat more narrow standard under which piggybacking will be permitted only when the employer was given notice that the alleged discrimination is classwide, i.e., that the administrative charge alleged discrimination against a class of which the subsequent plaintiff is a member. *See, e.g.*, Kloos v. Carter-Day Co., 799 F.2d 397 (8th Cir.1986). A third, and even narrower, approach also has been utilized. Under this standard, the administrative charge must have alleged not only classwide discrimination but also that the administrative claimant purports to represent the class or other similarly situated individuals. *See, e.g.*, Naton v. Bank of California, 649 F.2d 691 (9th Cir.1981). In HOWLETT v. HOLIDAY INNS, 49 F.3d 189 (6th Cir.), cert. denied, 516 U.S. 943, 116 S.Ct. 379, 133 L.Ed.2d 302 (1995), the Sixth Circuit offered its own variation on this theme. The court reasoned that its choice between these three standards should be based on the purpose served by the administrative charge requirement, i.e., to provide enough information for the EEOC to notify prospective defendants of their potential liability and to attempt informal conciliation of the claims before a suit is filed. Whether an administrative charge will provide this information, the court continued, would depend upon the type of work unit involved in the case. Where the complaints arise in a modestly sized work unit, the mere similarity of the grievances within the same time period would be sufficient to permit the use of the single filing rule. But where the charges arise throughout a large work group, there must be some indication in the charge that the grievance affects a group of individuals that would include the additional plaintiffs who seek to piggyback on that charge, although it need not go so far as to specify that the administrative claimant purports to represent a class or others similarly situated. Such a claim alerts the EEOC that more than an isolated act of discrimination is involved and this provides the company with sufficient notice to explore conciliation with the affected group.

In BETTCHER v. THE BROWN SCHOOLS INC., 262 F.3d 492 (5th Cir.2001), the Fifth Circuit stated that since the essence of the "single filing rule" rule was that the "piggyback" plaintiff was being allowed to join an extant lawsuit filed by a grievant who *had* filed an administrative charge, the rule was not intended to permit a *non-charging* grievant to institute a *separate* lawsuit predicated on the charge of an individual who had not filed suit.

Oscar Mayer & Co. v. Evans

Supreme Court of the United States, 1979.

441 U.S. 750, 99 S.Ct. 2066, 60 L.Ed.2d 609.

MR. JUSTICE BRENNAN delivered the opinion of the Court.

* * *

This case presents three questions * * *. First, whether §14(b) requires an aggrieved person to resort to appropriate state remedies before bringing suit under §7(c) of the ADEA. Second, if so, whether the state proceedings must be commenced within time limits specified by state law in order to preserve the federal right of action. Third, if so, whether any circumstances may excuse the failure to commence timely state proceedings.

We hold that §14(b) mandates that a grievant not bring suit in federal court under §7(c) * * * until he has first resorted to appropriate state administrative proceedings. We also hold, however, that the grievant is not required by §14(b) to commence the state proceedings within time limits specified by state law. In light of these holdings, it is not necessary to address the question of the circumstances, if any, in which failure to comply with §14(b) may be excused.

I

Respondent Joseph Evans was employed by petitioner * * * for 23 years until his involuntary retirement in January 1976. On March 10, 1976, respondent filed with the United States Department of Labor a notice of intent to sue the company under the ADEA. Respondent charged that he had been forced to retire because of his age in violation of the Act. At approximately this time respondent inquired of the Department whether he was obliged to file a state complaint in order to preserve his federal rights. The Department informed respondent that the ADEA contained no such requirement. Relying on this official advice, respondent refrained from resorting to state proceedings. On March 7, 1977, after federal conciliation efforts had failed, respondent brought suit against petitioner * * * in the United States District Court for the Southern District of Iowa.

Petitioners moved to dismiss the complaint on the grounds that the Iowa State Civil Rights Commission was empowered to remedy age discrimination in employment and that §14(b) required resort to this state remedy prior to the commencement of the federal suit. The District Court denied the motion, and the Court of Appeals for the Eighth Circuit affirmed. * * * We reverse.

II

Petitioners argue that §14(b) mandates that in States with agencies empowered to remedy age discrimination in employment (deferral States) a grievant may not bring suit under the ADEA unless he has first commenced a proceeding with the appropriate state agency. Respondent, on the other hand, argues that the grievant has the option of whether to resort to state proceedings, and that §14(b) requires only that grievants choosing to resort to state remedies wait 60 days before bringing suit in federal court. The question of construction is close, but we conclude that petitioners are correct.

Section 14(b) of the ADEA was patterned after and is virtually *in haec verba* with §706(c) of Title VII of the Civil Rights Act of 1964 * * *.

* * *

Since the ADEA and Title VII share a common purpose, the elimination of discrimination in the workplace, since the language of §14(b) is almost *in haec verba* with §706(c), and since the legislative history of §14(b) indicates that its source was §706(c), we may properly conclude that Congress intended that the construction of §14(b) should follow that of §706(c). We therefore conclude that §14(b), like §706(c), is intended to screen from the federal courts those discrimination complaints that might be settled to the satisfaction of the grievant in state proceedings. We further conclude that prior resort to appropriate state proceedings is required under §14(b), just as under §706(c).

The contrary arguments advanced by respondent in support of construing §14(b) as merely optional are not persuasive. Respondent notes first that under Title VII persons aggrieved must file with a state antidiscrimination agency before filing with the Equal Employment Opportunity Commission (EEOC). Under the ADEA, by contrast, grievants may file with state and federal agencies simultaneously.[4] From this respondent concludes that the ADEA pays less deference to state agencies and that, as a consequence, ADEA claimants have the option to ignore state remedies.

We disagree. The ADEA permits concurrent rather than sequential state and federal administrative jurisdiction in order to expedite the processing of age-discrimination claims. The premise for this difference is that the delay inherent in sequential jurisdiction is particularly prejudicial to the rights of "older citizens to whom, by definition, relatively few productive years are left."

The purpose of expeditious disposition would not be frustrated were ADEA claimants required to pursue state and federal administrative remedies simultaneously. Indeed, simultaneous state and federal conciliation efforts may well facilitate rapid settlements. There is no reason to conclude, therefore, that the possibility of concurrent state and federal cognizance supports the construction of §14(b) that ADEA grievants may ignore state remedies altogether.

Respondent notes a second difference between the ADEA and Title VII. Section 14(a) of the ADEA, for which Title VII has no counterpart, provides that upon commencement of an action under ADEA, all state proceedings are superseded. From this, respondent concludes that it would be an exercise in futility to require aggrieved persons to file state complaints since those persons may, after only 60 days, abort their involuntary state proceeding by filing a federal suit.

We find no merit in the argument. Unless §14(b) is to be stripped of all meaning, state agencies must be given at least some opportunity to solve problems of discrimination. While 60 days provides a limited time for the state agency to act, that was a decision for Congress to make and Congress apparently thought it sufficient.
* * *

---

[4]ADEA grievants may file with the State before or after they file with the Secretary of Labor.

* * *

III

We consider now the consequences of respondent's failure to file a complaint with the Iowa State Civil Rights Commission. Petitioners argue that since Iowa's 120-day age-discrimination statute of limitations has run, it is now too late for respondent to remedy his procedural omission and that respondent's federal action is therefore jurisdictionally barred. Respondent pleads that since his failure to file was due to incorrect advice by the Department of Labor, his tardiness should be excused.

Both arguments miss the mark. Neither questions of jurisdiction nor questions of excuse arise unless Congress mandated that resort to state proceedings must be within time limits specified by the State. We do not construe §14(b) to make that requirement. Section 14(b) requires only that the grievant commence state proceedings. Nothing whatever in the section requires the respondent here to commence those proceedings within the 120 days allotted by Iowa law in order to preserve a right of action under §7(c).

* * * By its terms, * * * the section requires only that state proceedings be commenced 60 days before federal litigation is instituted; besides commencement no other obligation is placed upon the ADEA grievant. In particular, there is no requirement that, in order to commence state proceedings and thereby preserve federal rights, the grievant must file with the State within whatever time limits are specified by state law. * * *

This implication is made express by the last sentence of §14(b), which specifically provides:

> "If any requirement for the commencement of such proceedings is imposed by a State authority other than a requirement of the filing of a written and signed statement of the facts upon which the proceeding is based, the proceeding shall be deemed to have been commenced for the purposes of this subsection at the time such statement is sent by registered mail to the appropriate State authority."

State limitations periods are, of course, requirements "other than a requirement of the filing of a written and signed statement of the facts upon which the proceeding is based." Therefore, even if a State were to make timeliness a precondition for commencement, rather than follow the more typical pattern of making untimeliness an affirmative defense, a state proceeding will be deemed commenced for purposes of §14(b) as soon as the complaint is filed.

* * *

This construction of the statute is fully consistent with * * * the purposes of §14(b). Section 14(b) does not stipulate an exhaustion requirement. The section is intended only to give state agencies a limited opportunity to settle the grievances of ADEA claimants in a voluntary and localized manner so that the grievants thereafter have no need or desire for independent federal relief. Individuals should not be penalized if States decline, for whatever reason, to take advantage of these opportunities. Congress did not intend to foreclose federal relief simply because state relief was also foreclosed.

The structure of the ADEA reinforces the conclusion that state procedural defaults cannot foreclose federal relief and that state limitations periods cannot govern the efficacy of the federal remedy. * * * Congress could not have intended to consign federal lawsuits to the vagaries of diverse state limitations statutes, particularly since, in many States, including Iowa, the limitations periods are considerably shorter than the 180-day period allowed grievants in nondeferral States * * *.

That Congress regarded incorporation as inconsistent with the federal scheme is made clear by the legislative history of §706(c)'s definition of commencement — the same definition later used in §14(b). Proponents of Title VII were concerned that localities hostile to civil rights might enact sham discrimination ordinances for the purpose of frustrating the vindication of federal rights. The statutory definition of commencement as requiring the filing of a state complaint and nothing more was intended to meet this concern while at the same time avoiding burdensome case-by-case inquiry into the reasonableness of various state procedural requirements. * * *

* * *

We therefore hold that respondent may yet comply with the requirements of §14(b) by simply filing a signed complaint with the Iowa State Civil Rights Commission. That Commission must be given an opportunity to entertain respondent's grievance before his federal litigation can continue. Meanwhile, the federal suit should be held in abeyance. If, as respondent fears, his state complaint is subsequently dismissed as untimely, respondent may then return to federal court. But until that happens, or until 60 days have passed without a settlement, respondent must pursue his state remedy.

Accordingly, the judgment of the Court of Appeals is reversed, and the case is remanded to that court with instructions to enter an order directing the District Court to hold respondent's suit in abeyance until respondent has complied with the mandate of §14(b).

[The concurring opinion of Mr. Justice Blackmun is omitted.]

MR. JUSTICE STEVENS, with whom THE CHIEF JUSTICE, MR. JUSTICE POWELL, and MR. JUSTICE REHNQUIST join, concurring in part and dissenting in part.

Section 14(b) explicitly states that "no suit may be brought" under the Act until the individual has first resorted to appropriate state remedies. Respondent has concededly never resorted to state remedies. In my judgment, this means that his suit should not have been brought and should now be dismissed.

* * *

* * * If respondent should decide at this point to resort to state remedies, and if his complaint there is found to be time barred, and if he should then seek relief in federal court, the question addressed in * * * the Court's opinion — whether §14(b) requires resort to state remedies "within time limits specified by the State" — would then be presented. But that question is not presented now, and I decline to join or to render

any advisory opinion on its merits. I would simply order that this suit be dismissed in accordance with the mandate of §14(b).

NOTES AND PROBLEMS FOR DISCUSSION

1. Among the technical issues created by the ruling in *Oscar Mayer* that an age claimant does not have to file a state administrative charge within the state limitations period in order to preserve her federal remedy are the following:

(a) Is a claimant who files an untimely state charge still entitled to the extended 300 day period for filing an age charge with the EEOC in deferral states? *See* Aronsen v. Crown Zellerbach, 662 F.2d 584 (9th Cir. 1981), cert. denied, 459 U.S. 1200, 103 S.Ct. 1183, 75 L.Ed.2d 431 (1983).

(b) Is there any time limit within which an ADEA claimant must file a state charge to preserve her federal claim? Consider, in answering this question, the provision in §14(b) requiring plaintiffs to wait for sixty days after the state filing a federal cause of action. *See* Fugate v. Allied Corp., 582 F.Supp. 780 (N.D. Ill. 1984).

2. After the Court rendered its decision in the principal case, pursuant to President Carter's Reorganization Plan, the EEOC was substituted for the Secretary of Labor as the federal agency authorized under §7(b) to sue on behalf of the aggrieved.

(a) Should the invocation of state remedies requirement announced in *Oscar Mayer* be extended to ADEA actions brought by the EEOC? *See* Marshall v. Chamberlain Manufacturing Corp., 601 F.2d 100 (3d Cir.1979).

(b) What is the extent of the EEOC's statutory duty to attempt to achieve conciliation prior to instituting suit? Should the trial court dismiss or stay an EEOC age suit where it finds the EEOC has not fulfilled this statutory obligation? *Compare* Marshall v. Sun Oil Co., 592 F.2d 563 (10th Cir.), cert. denied, 444 U.S. 826, 100 S.Ct. 49, 62 L.Ed.2d 33 (1979), *with* Brennan v. Ace Hardware Corp., 495 F.2d 368 (8th Cir. 1974).

(c) The EEOC has no duty to invoke its own administrative remedies prior to bringing suit. But if the EEOC chooses to invoke its statutory authority to bring suit seeking relief on behalf of individual victims of alleged age discrimination, is such an action barred by the individuals' failure to timely file a charge of discrimination with the agency? In EEOC v. SIDLEY AUSTIN LLP, 437 F.3d 695 (7th Cir.2006), cert. denied, 549 U.S. 815, 127 S.Ct. 76, 166 L.Ed.2d 27 (2006), the court construed the Supreme Court's ruling in EEOC v. WAFFLE HOUSE, 534 U.S. 279, 122 S.Ct. 754, 151 L.Ed.2d 755 (2002) that an EEOC claim for monetary relief for a victim of an alleged violation of the ADA was not barred by the individual's promise to arbitrate any and all employment-related disputes to mean that the agency's enforcement authority was not derivative of the legal rights of the individuals for whom it sought relief. Consequently, the Seventh Circuit ruled, the agency was not precluded from bringing suit by the individual' failure to timely file an administrative challenge to their involuntary retirement. And since the EEOC has no independent requirement to invoke its administrative remedies before filing suit, the court concluded that there was no duty to exhaust in the instant case.

(d) Section 7(d) of the ADEA states that an aggrieved cannot file a civil action until sixty days after a "charge" alleging unlawful discrimination has been filed with the EEOC. But the term "charge" is nowhere defined in the statute. In FEDERAL EXPRESS CORP. v. HOLOWECKI, 552 U.S. 389, 128 S.Ct. 1147, 170 L.Ed.2d 10 (2008), the Supreme Court sought to resolve a circuit conflict concerning the meaning of the word "charge" in the context of an ADEA suit that had been preceded by the plaintiff's filing only an intake questionnaire accompanied by a signed affidavit describing the alleged discriminatory practices in greater detail. The Court, in a 7-2 opinion, concluded that the EEOC's guidelines, as well as the agency's interpretations of those guidelines and of the relevant provisions of the ADEA were reasonable and entitled to deference. Accordingly, the Court adopted the EEOC's position that a filing is deemed a charge where — in addition to an allegation of age discrimination and the name of the charged party — "the document reasonably can be construed to request agency action and appropriate relief on the employee's part."

Is an ADEA plaintiff's failure to file a charge with the EEOC prior to instituting suit a jurisdictional or nonjurisdictional prerequisite to suit? Recall that in ARBAUGH v. Y&H CORP., 546 U.S. 500, 126 S.Ct. 1235, 163 L.Ed.2d 1097 (2006), discussed at Note 1(c) following *Rinella & Rinella* in Chapter 1A, *supra*, the Court established a "clear statement" rule that presumes that statutory prerequisites to suit are presumed *non*-jurisdictional absent a clear statement to the contrary in the relevant statutory text. Applying that doctrine to this context, one circuit court has concluded that the requirement of filing an EEOC charge is a nonjurisdictional, and therefore waiveable, prerequisite to filing suit under the ADEA. See Allen v. Highlands Hospital Corp., 545 F.3d 387 (6th Cir.1008) (noting that §7(d) contains no reference to "jurisdiction" while §7(c) contains "jurisdiction" in both its title and text).

3. Prior to the enactment of the 1991 Civil Rights Act, the ADEA expressly incorporated the statute of limitations contained in the Portal-to-Portal Act. Thus, as in actions brought under the Equal Pay Act, an ADEA claimant had to file suit no later than two years after the alleged discriminatory act, or within three years in cases arising out of a willful violation. But §115 of the 1991 Act eliminated this limitations period and amended §7(e) of the ADEA to require that, as in Title VII actions, suit be filed within ninety days after a private individual received a notice from the EEOC that it had dismissed or otherwise terminated its proceedings. Thus, depending upon when the individual files the EEOC claim and when it transmits this notice, the ninety-day period could extend beyond the superseded two or three year limitations period.

4. Section 7(c)(1) provides that suit by the EEOC terminates the individual's right to bring a separate action under the ADEA.

(a) Does the EEOC's filing of an action similarly preclude the aggrieved from pursuing his or her state law remedies? *See* Dunlop v. Pan American World Airways, Inc., 672 F.2d 1044 (2d Cir. 1982).

(b) Must a trial court dismiss a pending private ADEA action when the EEOC subsequently decides to file suit? *See* Burns v. Equitable Life Assurance Society, 696 F.2d 21 (2d Cir. 1982), cert. denied, 464 U.S. 933, 104 S.Ct. 336, 78 L.Ed.2d 306 (1983).

(c) Does the filing of an action by the individual aggrieved preclude the EEOC from bringing its own action on behalf of that individual? *See* EEOC v. Wackenhut Corp., 939 F.2d 241 (5th Cir. 1991).

5. Section 15 of the ADEA provides federal employees (including applicants for federal employment) with a different remedial scheme than is prescribed for non-federal employees. Specifically, federal employees are not required to invoke any state or federal administrative remedy prior to instituting suit. Rather, a federal employee can either seek administrative resolution of a claim by the employing agency (with an appeal to the EEOC from a final agency decision) before filing suit, or bypass the administrative mechanism entirely and directly file suit in federal district court. However, if the second option is chosen, the federal employee, like all other claimants, must file a notice of intent to sue with the EEOC at least thirty days prior to instituting suit. Additionally, as the Supreme Court held in STEVENS v. DEPARTMENT OF TREASURY, 500 U.S. 1, 111 S.Ct. 1562, 114 L.Ed.2d 1 (1991), Section 15(d) requires the claimant to file this notice with the EEOC within 180 days of the alleged discriminatory occurrence and then to wait at least 30 days from said filing before bringing a federal civil action.

(a) Is a federal employee who chooses to invoke the EEOC machinery (rather than simply filing a notice of intention to sue and waiting for thirty days) required to exhaust that administrative mechanism before bringing suit? The overwhelming majority of the circuit courts have concluded that a federal ADEA complainant must completely exhaust the administrative process prior to filing suit. *See e.g.*, Wrenn v. Secretary, Dep't of Veterans Affairs, 918 F.2d 1073 (2d Cir. 1990), cert. denied, 499 U.S. 977, 111 S.Ct. 1625, 113 L.Ed.2d 721 (1991) (requiring exhaustion because permitting the plaintiff to abandon the administrative remedies he has initiated would tend to frustrate the ability of that agency to deal with complaints).

(b) As the Supreme Court noted in *Stevens*, the ADEA does not contain an express limitations period applicable to civil actions filed by federal employees (including applicants for federal employment). The *Stevens* Court added, therefore, that it would "assume that Congress intended to impose an appropriate period borrowed either from a state statute or from an analogous federal one." But since the plaintiff in *Stevens* had filed suit within one year and six days after the allegedly discriminatory event, the Court concluded that the action had been filed "well within whatever statute of limitations might apply" and, therefore, did not rule on which limitations period was applicable to this action. In light of the ruling in *Stevens*, which statutory limitations period should apply to ADEA actions by federal employees and should the answer depend upon whether or not the federal employee utilized or bypassed the administrative process?

Most of the circuit courts that have considered the question have concluded that where a federal employee utilizes the administrative process prior to filing suit under the ADEA, the appropriate limitations period to borrow in is the one contained in Title VII, i.e., 90 days from the termination of the administrative process. *See, e.g.*, Burzynski v. Cohen, 264 F.3d 611 (6th Cir.2001).

There is a split among the circuits, however, with respect to federal employees who have elected to bypass the administrative process and to proceed directly with filing an ADEA suit in court. In ROSSITER v. POTTER, 357 F.3d 26 (1st Cir.2004), the First Circuit elected to apply the Fair Labor Standards Act limitations period rather than the timing requirements contained in Title VII. The court reasoned that since Title VII's ninety-day limitations period for filing suit was triggered by the end of the administrative process, it would be anomalous to apply that scheme to the case of a federal employee who has bypassed the administrative process. On the other hand, the court explained, since FLSA claimants are not required to invoke administrative remedies as a precondition to filing suit, that statute's enforcement mechanism was closely parallel to the one governing federal employee ADEA bypass actions. The court also concluded that the interest in providing federal employees with a uniform limitations period argued strongly in favor of incorporating the limitations period from federal, rather than state law. Finally, the court offered two explanations for its conclusion that the ruling in *Stevens* precluded the application of the Title VII period for ADEA bypass actions. First, the focus of the Supreme Court's inquiry in *Stevens* was on the date of discrimination as the accrual date for limitations purposes and Title VII's ninety-day period relates to final administrative action or expiration of the thirty-day notice period. Second, it noted that if Title VII's limitations period were to be applied to bypass actions, the plaintiff's claim in *Stevens* would have been time-barred since the suit in that case was brought more than 120 days after he had filed his notice of intent to sue (i.e., more than ninety days after expiration of the earliest date on which suit can be brought — thirty days following the filing of a notice of intent to sue).

On the other hand, in EDWARDS v. SHALALA, 64 F.3d 601 (11th Cir.1995), the Eleventh Circuit concluded that Title VII was the most closely analogous statute to the ADEA and, therefore, the most appropriate statute from which to borrow an applicable limitations period. It noted that Title VII and the ADEA shared a common purpose — the elimination of discrimination — and that much of the language of the ADEA was patterned after analogous provisions in Title VII.

(c) Section 15(c) provides that a federal employee may bring an age-based claim for "such legal or equitable relief as will effectuate the purposes of this chapter." Does this constitute an express Congressional waiver of federal sovereign immunity? In VILLESCAS v. ABRAHAM, 311 F.3d 1253 (10th Cir.2002), a federal employee alleging retaliation for engaging in protected conduct asserted a claim for compensatory damages for emotional distress. The Tenth Circuit reasoned that since it and most other circuits previously had ruled that emotional distress damages were not recoverable under an identical "legal or equitable relief" clause governing private sector ADEA claims, and since, in its view, Congress did not intend to provide broader relief to federal employees, such damages were similarly nonrecoverable by federal employees. It also rejected the plaintiff's request to recognize an exception to the general ban on recovery of distress damages in retaliation cases. It noted that although the FLSA had been amended in 1977 to provide a separate remedial provision for retaliation claims, §15(f) of the ADEA (enacted in 1978) not only expressly barred the importation of FLSA remedies to federal employee claims but also failed to contain any comparable remedial provision for federal employee retaliation cases.

(d) Section 15(a), the general prohibition against age-based discrimination by federal employers, does not contain any express reference to retaliation. On the other hand, §4(d) expressly prohibits acts of retaliation by private employers. Does this mean that a federal employee cannot state a retaliation claim under the ADEA? In GOMEZ-PEREZ v. POTTER, 553 U.S. 474, 128 S.Ct. 1931, 170 L.Ed.2d 887 (2008), the Supreme Court resolved a circuit conflict and held that the absence of such explicit terminology did not preclude a determination that federal employees can assert retaliation claims under the ADEA. By a 6-3 margin, the majority ruled that the statutory prohibition on discrimination based on age includes retaliation based on the filing of an age discrimination charge. As it did in the §1981 context in CBOCS West, Inc. v. Humphries, a case decided on the same day as *Gomez-Perez* (discussed in Note 9 following *Bobo* in Chapter 8, *supra*), the majority relied on the Court's prior ruling in Jackson v. Birmingham (discussed in Note 4 of Chapter 11, Sec. B, *infra*) which had construed the private right of action for claims of intentional sex-based discrimination contained in Title IX of the 1964 Civil Rights Act to encompass retaliation claims. The Court reasoned that retaliating against a person for complaining of age discrimination is another form of intentional age-based discrimination just as, as in *Jackson*, retaliating against someone for complaining about sex discrimination is a form of intentional sex discrimination. The majority rejected the argument (adopted by the dissenting Justices) that the absence of an express prohibition against retaliation in the federal employee provision in the face of an express anti-retaliation provision in the section dealing with private sector employees should be construed as evidence of Congress' intention not to extend anti-retaliation protection to federal employees. The majority opinion stated that negative implications raised by textual differences are strongest when the provisions in question were considered simultaneously. Here, however, the prohibition on private sector retaliation was enacted in 1967, whereas the federal sector provision was not added to the ADEA until 1974. The Court also noted that the private sector anti-discrimination provision contained a specific list of forbidden employment practices, while the federal employee provision contained merely a broad prohibition of "discrimination" rather than a list of specific prohibited practices. Thus, while Congress might have concluded that it was necessary to include a reference to retaliation in the list of proscribed private sector practices, such detail was unnecessary with respect to federal employees. Having concluded that the text of the ADEA's federal employee provision encompassed retaliation claims, the Court also ruled that this provision waived the federal government's sovereign immunity against age-based retaliation claims. On remand, the trial court granted summary judgment to the defendant on the ground that the plaintiff had not established the existence of a materially adverse action. The ruling was affirmed by the First Circuit in an unpublished opinion. 452 Fed.Appx. 3 (1st Cir. 2011).

6. (a) Is the ADEA, like Title VII, the exclusive remedy for a federal employee? *See* Chennareddy v. Bowsher, 935 F.2d 315 (D.C. Cir. 1991) (the ADEA provides the exclusive remedy for a federal employee claiming age discrimination).

(b) Should a state government worker be permitted to eschew the procedural prerequisites to filing an action under the ADEA by bringing an age discrimination charge directly under §1983? The circuits are split on this question. In LEVIN v. MADIGAN, 692 F.3d 607 (7th Cir. 2012), the Seventh Circuit, rejecting the otherwise prevailing view, held that the ADEA did not preclude a §1983 claim of age-based discrimination in violation of the U.S. Constitution. While acknowledging that ADEA claimants face a series of pre-litigation administrative requirements that do not apply to §1983 claimants, the panel concluded that Congress intended that enforcement scheme to be limited to *statutorily*-based claims and *not* to claims alleging violations of the U.S. Constitution. The panel rejected the notion that Congress, in passing the ADEA, intended to foreclose preexisting constitutional claims. Thus, it concluded where a §1983 plaintiff alleges age discrimination in violation of the equal protection clause and not in violation of the ADEA, such a claim is not precluded by the ADEA. All circuits other than the Seventh have concluded that the ADEA is the exclusive remedy for age-based discrimination claims on the ground that allowing a plaintiff to seek recovery for age discrimination through a §1983-based equal protection claim would undermine the comprehensive remedial scheme set forth in the ADEA. See e.g., Zombro v. Baltimore City Police Department, 868 F.2d 1364 (4th Cir. 1989). Although the Supreme Court initially was poised to resolve this conflict when it granted a writ of *certiorari* in *Levin*, it subsequently dismissed the writ as improvidently granted, 134 S.Ct. 2, 187 L.Ed.2d 1 (2013).

7. Does an unreviewed state agency finding of fact have preclusive effect in a subsequent ADEA action in federal court? In ASTORIA FEDERAL SAVINGS & LOAN ASS'N v. SOLIMINO, 501 U.S. 104, 111 S.Ct. 2166, 115 L.Ed.2d 96 (1991), a unanimous Supreme Court ruled that judicially unreviewed state administrative agency findings have no preclusive effect on ADEA claims filed in federal court. The Court noted its longstanding support of the common law doctrines of preclusion as applied to final administrative determinations where the federal or state agency acted in a judicial capacity and the parties had an adequate opportunity to litigate before the administrative body. But when the Court examined the text of the ADEA, it found that although there was no express provision addressing the deference to be accorded administrative determinations, several provisions carried an implication that Congress did not intend for federal courts to be precluded by state administrative findings. For example, it pointed to the language in §14(b) referring to the termination of proceedings under State law as one of the alternative prerequisites to filing an action under the federal statute in federal court. Similarly, it noted that the statute lists the termination of state proceedings as one of the reference points for the commencement of the period within which a charge must be filed with the EEOC. This language, in the Court's judgment, reflected Congress' assumption that federal consideration could occur after the termination of state agency proceedings. And invoking preclusion would render the invocation of federal proceedings under these circumstances, the Court reasoned, "strictly pro forma." Moreover, the Court urged, granting administrative preclusion would simply encourage claimants committed to preserving their federal claim to perfunctorily file their state claim, wait the minimum sixty day period and then initiate their federal suit, thereby defeating the main purpose of state law deferral — to resolve complaints outside the federal system.

The Court also maintained that denying administrative preclusion would avoid future litigation over whether the instant agency had acted in a judicial capacity and whether the parties had been afforded an adequate opportunity to litigate. Additionally, since this ruling was limited to judicially unreviewed agency findings, the Court emphasized that it was only providing claimants with "no more than a second chance to prove the claim" and that the state administrative findings could always be considered by the federal court in an attempt to minimize any duplication of effort.

8. The provisions of the 1991 Civil Rights Act giving Title VII, ADA and Rehabilitation Act plaintiffs the right to seek compensatory and punitive damages do not contain any express reference to actions brought under the ADEA. Does this, coupled with the fact that other portions of the 1991 Act do refer to the ADEA, suggest that this is one instance in which Title VII rules should not extend to age claims? *See* Collazo v. Nicholson, 535 F.3d 41 (1ˢᵗ Cir. 2008) ("it is well established that the [ADEA] does not allow compensatory damages for pain and suffering").

9. In contrast to the treatment of back pay claims under Title VII as "equitable relief," private actions by employees for back pay under the FLSA (and, therefore, under the EPA and ADEA) consistently have been held to include a right to trial by jury. *See* Lorillard v. Pons, 434 U.S. 575, 98 S.Ct. 866, 55 L.Ed.2d 40 (1978). In 1978, the ADEA was amended to specifically authorize trial by jury "of any issue of fact in any * * * action for recovery of amounts owing as a result of a violation of this chapter." Thus, under the ADEA, all claims for monetary relief, whether back wages or liquidated damages, may be tried to a jury. A jury trial, however, is not available in an age claim against the federal government. Lehman v. Nakshian, 453 U.S. 156, 101 S.Ct. 2698, 69 L.Ed.2d 548 (1981) (a jury trial is available against the federal government only where Congress expressly authorizes it and §15 of ADEA only mentions a right to jury trial in actions against private employers). Nor does this right attach when a private plaintiff seeks only equitable relief. When the plaintiff seeks both equitable and legal relief, the jury rules on the legal claims while the equitable claims go to the court. In such a case, factual issues common to both claims are submitted initially to the jury for determination of the legal claims. These findings are then binding on the court in order to prevent inconsistent findings by the court with respect to the request for equitable relief and thereby preserve the right to jury trial. *See* Cancellier v. Federated Department Stores, 672 F.2d 1312 (9th Cir.), cert. denied, 459 U.S. 859, 103 S.Ct. 131, 74 L.Ed.2d 113 (1982). Occasionally a dispute arises as to whether a given claim is legal or equitable in nature. For example, while attorney fees and costs are consistently viewed as equitable in nature, the courts are divided on the question of whether a request for front pay or pension benefits is legal or equitable.

The Back Pay Act, 5 U.S.C. §§5596(b)(1) (1966), waives the federal government's sovereign immunity from liability for interest on back pay awarded to a federal employee who is found to have been affected "by an unjustified or unwarranted personnel action * * *." The overwhelming majority of circuit courts that have considered the question have held that although this statute does not expressly refer to employees terminated in violation of federal antidiscrimination statutes, it applies to interest on back pay awards against the federal government for terminating an employee in violation of substantive anti-discrimination statutes. *See e.g.*, Adam v. Norton, 636 F.3d 1190 (9th Cir. 2011) (Back Pay Act waives federal sovereign immunity from interest on back pay award issued to employee terminated in violation of the ADEA).

10. The ADEA, like the EPA, incorporates the FLSA provisions concerning attorney fees. This means that a grant of attorney fees is mandatory when the plaintiff prevails and is unavailable to prevailing defendants. But since these FLSA provisions do not expressly authorize the recovery of expert witness fees, and since the section of the 1991 Civil Rights Act authorizing the recovery of such fees does not expressly mention the ADEA, it is likely that such fees are not recoverable in age actions. *See* James v. Sears, Roebuck & Co., Inc., 21 F.3d 989 (10th Cir. 1994).

11. Section 104(a)(2) of the Internal Revenue Code provides that "gross income does not include * * * (2) the amount of any damages received (whether by suit or agreement and whether in lump sums or periodic payments) on account of personal injuries or sickness." In COMMISSIONER OF IRS v. SCHLEIER, 515 U.S. 323 115 S.Ct. 2159, 132 L.Ed.2d 294 (1995), the Court held that liquidated damages obtained in an ADEA case are not excludable from taxable income because they are not received "on account of personal injury." Since Congress intended the ADEA's liquidated damages to be punitive in nature, the Court reasoned, such damages serve no compensatory function and in the absence of a compensatory function, liquidated damages could not be described as "on account of personal injuries or sickness" within the meaning of the Internal Revenue Code.

12. It is becoming increasingly common for employers to require employees to agree to resolve both contractual and statutory discrimination claims exclusively through arbitration. For a thorough discussion of whether such clauses will be enforced and, thereby, effect a waiver of a judicial tribunal for the enforcement of rights under the ADEA, see Chapter 4, Section 5, *supra*.

CHAPTER 11

The Statutory Response to Disability-Based Discrimination

SECTION A. THE AMERICANS WITH DISABILITIES ACT

1. GENERAL OVERVIEW

In 1990, Congress passed the Americans with Disabilities Act (ADA)[a] in an effort to expand the protections against job discrimination offered to persons with disabilities. This statute, like the Civil Rights Act of 1964, is a comprehensive package of protections intended to address (as stated in §2(b)'s declaration of legislative purpose) the "major areas" of discrimination against individuals with disabilities. Its various Titles prohibit discrimination in public services, public accommodations and telecommunications services, as well as employment. Title I, however, is the portion of the ADA that contains most of the rules concerning discrimination in employment. (A few other relevant provisions are found in Title V.)

Prior to the enactment of the ADA, the major piece of federal legislation prohibiting employment discrimination on the basis of mental and physical disability was the Federal Rehabilitation Act of 1973. (Disabled employees of state and local governments could assert claims under the equal protection clause of the fourteenth amendment and most states provided some measure of protection against public and, sometimes, private sector disability-based discrimination under state law.) This statute, however, is of limited usefulness because it applies only to the federal government, the U.S. Postal Service, federal contractors and entities receiving federal funds. Consequently, it left employees of a large portion of the private sector without any federal statutory protection against disability-based employment bias. The ADA was enacted to close this gap and to provide disabled individuals with more expansive protection against discrimination in the workplace. (Section 501(a) expressly states that except as otherwise provided in the Act, nothing in the ADA shall be construed to apply a lesser standard than is applied under the Rehabilitation Act.)

To accomplish these objectives, the ADA incorporates the substantive jurisprudence developed under the Rehabilitation Act and the proof standards

---

[a]Pub.L. 101–336; 104 Stat. 327; 42 U.S.C. §12101 (1990).

developed under Title VII, and applies these rules to the broad class of individuals, employers and unions covered by Title VII.[b]

The fact that much of the proscriptive language of the ADA is derived directly from the Rehabilitation Act indicates that Congress did not intend for the body of Rehabilitation Act caselaw to be ignored by courts deciding cases under the newer statute. Consequently, the caselaw interpreting the substantive terms of the Rehabilitation Act continues to play an important role in the resolution of interpretive questions arising under the ADA. And, naturally, it remains vitally important to litigants who choose to proceed under the Rehabilitation Act.

Boiled down to its essence, the ADA prohibits covered entities from

     (1) discriminating against

     (2) a disabled individual

     (3) who is otherwise qualified for the position in question

     (4) because of that individual's disability.

The first three of these elements must, in turn, be further divided into subcomponents:

1. Beyond encompassing the obligation not to take adverse action on the basis of one's disability, the statutory command not to discriminate also requires a covered entity to make

     (1) a reasonable accommodation to the individual's disability

     (2) that does not impose an undue hardship upon the employer.

2. An individual is defined as disabled under the ADA only if s/he

     (1) has, had, or is regarded as having

     (2) a physical or mental impairment

     (3) that substantially limits

     (4) a major life activity.

3. A disabled individual is "otherwise qualified" for a position if s/he

     (1) can perform the essential job functions

---

[b]Like Title VII, the ADA applies to private employers with fifteen or more employees, state and local government employers, labor organizations and employment agencies, and is inapplicable to Indian tribes and bona fide private membership clubs. Similarly, under both statutes, American employees of U.S. companies, or foreign companies controlled by U.S. companies, are covered when working outside the territorial limits of the U.S., except where compliance with the requirements of the ADA would compel the defendant to violate foreign domestic law. And the "ministerial exception" read into Title VII in order to comply with the requirements of the First Amendment has been incorporated into ADA caselaw. *See e.g.*, Starkman v. Evans, 198 F.3d 173 (5th Cir.1999), cert. denied, 531 U.S. 814, 121 S.Ct. 49, 148 L.Ed.2d 18 (2000). The statutory definition of "covered entity" in the ADA, like the definition of "employer" in Title VII, has been construed to preclude suit against an individual employee or supervisor. *See* Albra v. Advan Inc., 490 F.3d 826 (11th Cir. 2007). The major difference in coverage between the two Acts is that the ADA does not apply to federal employees, other than those employed by the U.S. Senate, the House of Representatives and Congressional instrumentalities (such as the General Accounting Office, Library of Congress, Congressional Budget Office and Government Printing Office).

(2) with or without the assistance of a reasonable accommodation

(3) and does not pose a direct threat to the health and safety of others in the workplace.

As this parsing of the statute's nondiscrimination mandate demonstrates, the analysis of disability claims is an unusually complex, multi-faceted, and heavily fact-dependent undertaking. In this chapter, we shall examine each of these variables as well as many of the interpretive issues associated with them.

2. THE MEANING OF "DISABILITY"

Bragdon v. Abbott

Supreme Court of the United States, 1998.
524 U.S. 624, 118 S.Ct. 2196, 141 L.Ed.2d 540.

KENNEDY, J., delivered the opinion of the Court, in which STEVENS, SOUTER, GINSBURG, and BREYER, JJ., joined. STEVENS, J., filed a concurring opinion, in which BREYER, J., joined. GINSBURG, J., filed a concurring opinion. RHENQUIST, C. J., filed an opinion concurring in the judgment in part and dissenting in part, in which SCALIA and THOMAS, JJ., joined, and in Part II of which O'CONNOR, J., joined. O'CONNOR, J., filed an opinion concurring in the judgment in part and dissenting in part.

MR. JUSTICE KENNEDY delivered the opinion of the Court.

We address in this case the application of the Americans with Disabilities Act of 1990(ADA), to persons infected with the human immunodeficiency virus (HIV). We granted certiorari to review * * * whether HIV infection is a disability under the ADA when the infection has not yet progressed to the so-called symptomatic phase * * *.

I

Respondent Sidney Abbott has been infected with HIV since 1986. When the incidents we recite occurred, her infection had not manifested its most serious symptoms. On September 16, 1994, she went to the office of petitioner * * * for a dental appointment. She disclosed her HIV infection on the patient registration form. Petitioner completed a dental examination, discovered a cavity, and informed respondent of his policy against filling cavities of HIV-infected patients. He offered to perform the work at a hospital with no added fee for his services, though respondent would be responsible for the cost of using the hospital's facilities. Respondent declined.

* * *

* * * [T]he parties filed cross-motions for summary judgment. The District Court ruled in favor of the plaintiffs, holding that respondent's HIV infection satisfied the ADA's definition of disability. * * *

The Court of Appeals affirmed. It held respondent's HIV infection was a disability under the ADA, even though her infection had not yet progressed to the symptomatic stage. * * *

II

* * * The statute defines disability as:

"(A) a physical or mental impairment that substantially limits one or more of the major life activities of such individual;

(B) a record of such an impairment; or

(C) being regarded as having such impairment."

We hold respondent's HIV infection was a disability under subsection (A) of the definitional section of the statute. In light of this conclusion, we need not consider the applicability of subsections (B) or (C).

Our consideration of subsection (A) of the definition proceeds in three steps. First, we consider whether respondent's HIV infection was a physical impairment. Second, we identify the life activity upon which respondent relies (reproduction and child bearing) and determine whether it constitutes a major life activity under the ADA. Third, tying the two statutory phrases together, we ask whether the impairment substantially limited the major life activity. In construing the statute, we are informed by interpretations of parallel definitions in previous statutes and the views of various administrative agencies which have faced this interpretive question.

A

The ADA's definition of disability is drawn almost verbatim from the definition of "handicapped individual" included in the Rehabilitation Act of 1973, and the definition of "handicap" contained in the Fair Housing Amendments Act of 1988. Congress' repetition of a well-established term carries the implication that Congress intended the term to be construed in accordance with pre-existing regulatory interpretations. In this case, Congress did more than suggest this construction; it adopted a specific statutory provision in the ADA directing as follows:

"Except as otherwise provided in this chapter, nothing in this chapter shall be construed to apply a lesser standard than the standards applied under title V of the Rehabilitation Act of 1973 or the regulations issued by Federal agencies pursuant to such title."

The directive requires us to construe the ADA to grant at least as much protection as provided by the regulations implementing the Rehabilitation Act.

1.

The first step in the inquiry under subsection (A) requires us to determine whether respondent's condition constituted a physical impairment. The Department of Health, Education and Welfare (HEW) issued the first regulations interpreting the Rehabilitation Act in 1977. The regulations are of particular significance because, at the time, HEW was the agency responsible for coordinating the implementation and enforcement of § 504. The HEW regulations, which appear without change in the current regulations issued by the Department of Health and Human Services, define "physical or mental impairment" to mean:

"(A) any physiological disorder or condition, cosmetic disfigurement, or anatomical loss affecting one or more of the following body systems: neurological; musculoskeletal; special sense organs; respiratory, including speech organs; cardiovascular; reproductive, digestive, genito-urinary; hemic and lymphatic; skin; and endocrine; or

(B) any mental or psychological disorder, such as mental retardation, organic brain syndrome, emotional or mental illness, and specific learning disabilities." 45 C.F.R. §84.3(j)(2)(i) (1997).

In issuing these regulations, HEW decided against including a list of disorders constituting physical or mental impairments, out of concern that any specific enumeration might not be comprehensive. The commentary accompanying the regulations, however, contains a representative list of disorders and conditions constituting physical impairments, including "such diseases and conditions as orthopedic, visual, speech, and hearing impairments, cerebral palsy, epilepsy, muscular dystrophy, multiple sclerosis, cancer, heart disease, diabetes, mental retardation, emotional illness, and ... drug addiction and alcoholism."

In 1980, the President transferred responsibility for the implementation and enforcement of § 504 to the Attorney General. The regulations issued by the Justice Department, which remain in force to this day, adopted verbatim the HEW definition of physical impairment quoted above. In addition, the representative list of diseases and conditions originally relegated to the commentary accompanying the HEW regulations were incorporated into the text of the regulations.

HIV infection is not included in the list of specific disorders constituting physical impairments, in part because HIV was not identified as the cause of AIDS until 1983. HIV infection does fall well within the general definition set forth by the regulations, however.

* * *

The initial stage of HIV infection is known as acute or primary HIV infection. In a typical case, this stage lasts three months. The virus concentrates in the blood. The assault on the immune system is immediate. The victim suffers from a sudden and serious decline in the number of white blood cells. There is no latency period. Mononucleosis-like symptoms often emerge between six days and six weeks after infection, at times accompanied by fever, headache, enlargement of the lymph nodes (lymphadenopathy), muscle pain (myalgia), rash, lethargy, gastrointestinal disorders, and neurological disorders. Usually these symptoms abate within 14 to 21 days. HIV antibodies appear in the bloodstream within 3 weeks; circulating HIV can be detected within 10 weeks.

After the symptoms associated with the initial stage subside, the disease enters what is referred to sometimes as its asymptomatic phase. The term is a misnomer, in some respects, for clinical features persist throughout, including lymphadenopathy, dermatological disorders, oral lesions, and bacterial infections. Although it varies with each individual, in most instances this stage lasts from 7 to 11 years. The virus now tends to concentrate in the lymph nodes, though low levels of the virus continue to appear in the blood. It was once thought the virus became inactive during this period, but it is now known that the relative lack of symptoms is attributable to the virus' migration from the circulatory system into the lymph nodes. The migration reduces the viral presence in other parts of the body, with a corresponding diminution in physical manifestations of the disease. The virus, however, thrives in the lymph nodes, which, as a vital point of the body's immune response system, represents an ideal environment for the infection of other CD4+ cells.

A person is regarded as having AIDS when his or her CD4+ count drops below 200 cells/mm3of blood or when CD4+ cells comprise less than 14% of his or her total lymphocytes. During this stage, the clinical conditions most often associated with HIV, such as pneumocystis carninii pneumonia, Kaposi's sarcoma, and non-Hodgkins lymphoma, tend to appear. In addition, the general systemic disorders present during all stages of the disease, such as fever, weight loss, fatigue, lesions, nausea, and diarrhea, tend to worsen. In most cases, once the patient's CD4+ count drops below 10 cells/mm3, death soon follows.

In light of the immediacy with which the virus begins to damage the infected person's white blood cells and the severity of the disease, we hold it is an impairment from the moment of infection. As noted earlier, infection with HIV causes immediate abnormalities in a person's blood, and the infected person's white cell count continues to drop throughout the course of the disease, even when the attack is concentrated in the lymph nodes. In light of these facts, HIV infection must be regarded as a physiological disorder with a constant and detrimental effect on the infected person's hemic and lymphatic systems from the moment of infection. HIV infection satisfies the statutory and regulatory definition of a physical impairment during every stage of the disease.

2.

The statute is not operative, and the definition not satisfied, unless the impairment affects a major life activity. Respondent's claim throughout this case has been that the HIV infection placed a substantial limitation on her ability to reproduce and to bear children. Given the pervasive, and invariably fatal, course of the disease, its effect on major life activities of many sorts might have been relevant to our inquiry. Respondent and a number of *amici* make arguments about HIV's profound impact on almost every phase of the infected person's life. In light of these submissions, it may seem legalistic to circumscribe our discussion to the activity of reproduction. We have little doubt that had different parties brought the suit they would have maintained that an HIV infection imposes substantial limitations on other major life activities.

From the outset, however, the case has been treated as one in which reproduction was the major life activity limited by the impairment. It is our practice to decide cases on the grounds raised and considered in the Court of Appeals and included in the question on which we granted certiorari. We ask, then, whether reproduction is a major life activity.

We have little difficulty concluding that it is. As the Court of Appeals held, "[t]he plain meaning of the word 'major' denotes comparative importance" and "suggest[s] that the touchstone for determining an activity's inclusion under the statutory rubric is its significance." Reproduction falls well within the phrase "major life activity." Reproduction and the sexual dynamics surrounding it are central to the life process itself.

While petitioner concedes the importance of reproduction, he claims that Congress intended the ADA only to cover those aspects of a person's life which have a public, economic, or daily character. The argument founders on the statutory language. Nothing in the definition suggests that activities without a public, economic, or daily dimension may somehow be regarded as so unimportant or insignificant as to fall outside the meaning of the word "major." The breadth of the term confounds the attempt to limit its construction in this manner.

As we have noted, the ADA must be construed to be consistent with regulations issued to implement the Rehabilitation Act. Rather than enunciating a general principle for determining what is and is not a major life activity, the Rehabilitation Act regulations instead provide a representative list, defining term to include "functions such as caring for one's self, performing manual tasks, walking, seeing, hearing, speaking, breathing, learning, and working." As the use of the term "such as" confirms, the list is illustrative, not exhaustive.

These regulations are contrary to petitioner's attempt to limit the meaning of the term "major" to public activities. The inclusion of activities such as caring for one's self and performing manual tasks belies the suggestion that a task must have a public or economic character in order to be a major life activity for purposes of the ADA. On the contrary, the Rehabilitation Act regulations support the inclusion of reproduction as a major life activity, since reproduction could not be regarded as any less important than working and learning. Petitioner advances no credible basis for confining major life activities to those with a public, economic, or daily aspect. In the absence of any reason to reach a contrary conclusion, we agree with the Court of Appeals' determination that reproduction is a major life activity for the purposes of the ADA.

3.

The final element of the disability definition in subsection (A) is whether respondent's physical impairment was a substantial limit on the major life activity she asserts. The Rehabilitation Act regulations provide no additional guidance.

Our evaluation of the medical evidence leads us to conclude that respondent's infection substantially limited her ability to reproduce in two independent ways. First, a woman infected with HIV who tries to conceive a child imposes on the man a significant risk of becoming infected. * * *

Second, an infected woman risks infecting her child during gestation and childbirth, i.e., perinatal transmission. Petitioner concedes that women infected with HIV face about a 25% risk of transmitting the virus to their children. * * *

* * *

The Act addresses substantial limitations on major life activities, not utter inabilities. Conception and childbirth are not impossible for an HIV victim but, without doubt, are dangerous to the public health. This meets the definition of a substantial limitation. The decision to reproduce carries economic and legal consequences as well. There are added costs for antiretroviral therapy, supplemental insurance, and long-term health care for the child who must be examined and, tragic to think, treated for the infection. The laws of some States, moreover, forbid persons infected with HIV from having sex with others, regardless of consent.

In the end, the disability definition does not turn on personal choice. When significant limitations result from the impairment, the definition is met even if the difficulties are not insurmountable. For the statistical and other reasons we have cited, of course, the limitations on reproduction may be insurmountable here. Testimony from the respondent that her HIV infection controlled her decision not to have a child is unchallenged. In the context of reviewing summary judgment, we must take it to be true. We agree with the District Court and the Court of Appeals that no triable issue of fact impedes a ruling on the question of statutory coverage. Respondent's HIV infection is a physical impairment which substantially limits a major life activity, as the ADA defines it. In view of our holding, we need not address the second question presented, i.e., whether HIV infection is a *per se* disability under the ADA.

* * *

[The Court then examined whether or not the plaintiff's disability created a direct threat to the safety and health of others. This section of the opinion is reprinted, *infra*, at Section 3.]

III

* * *

The determination of the Court of Appeals that respondent's HIV infection was a disability under the ADA is affirmed. The judgment is vacated, and the case is remanded for further proceedings consistent with this opinion.

[The concurring opinions of Justices Stevens and Ginsburg are omitted.]

CHIEF JUSTICE REHNQUIST, with whom JUSTICE SCALIA and JUSTICE THOMAS join, and with whom JUSTICE O'CONNOR joins as to Part II, concurring in the judgment in part and dissenting in part.

I

* * * It is important to note that whether respondent has a disability covered by the ADA is an individualized inquiry. The Act could not be clearer on this point: Section 12102(2) states explicitly that the disability determination must be made "with respect to an individual." Were this not sufficiently clear, the Act goes on to provide that the "major life activities" allegedly limited by an impairment must be those "of such individual."

The individualized nature of the inquiry is particularly important in this case because the District Court disposed of it on summary judgment. Thus all disputed issues of material fact must be resolved against respondent. She contends that her asymptomatic HIV status brings her within the first definition of a "disability."[1] She must therefore demonstrate, *inter alia*, that she was (1) physically or mentally impaired and that such impairment (2) substantially limited (3) one or more of her major life activities.

Petitioner does not dispute that asymptomatic HIV-positive status is a physical impairment. I therefore assume this to be the case, and proceed to the second and third statutory requirements for "disability."

---

[1]Respondent alternatively urges us to find that she is disabled in that she is "regarded as" such. We did not, however, grant certiorari on that question. In any event, the "regarded as" prong requires a plaintiff to demonstrate that the defendant regarded him as having "such an impairment" (i.e., one that substantially limits a major life activity). Respondent has offered no evidence to support the assertion that petitioner regarded her as having an impairment that substantially limited her ability to reproduce, as opposed to viewing her as simply impaired.

According to the Court, the next question is "whether reproduction is a major life activity." That, however, is only half of the relevant question. As mentioned above, the ADA's definition of a "disability" requires that the major life activity at issue be one "of such individual." The Court truncates the question, perhaps because there is not a shred of record evidence indicating that, prior to becoming infected with HIV, respondent's major life activities included reproduction (assuming for the moment that reproduction is a major life activity at all). At most, the record indicates that after learning of her HIV status, respondent, whatever her previous inclination, conclusively decided that she would not have children. There is absolutely no evidence that, absent the HIV, respondent would have had or was even considering having children. Indeed, when asked during her deposition whether her HIV infection had in any way impaired her ability to carry out any of her life functions, respondent answered "No." It is further telling that in the course of her entire brief to this Court, respondent studiously avoids asserting even once that reproduction is a major life activity to her. To the contrary, she argues that the "major life activity" inquiry should not turn on a particularized assessment of the circumstances of this or any other case.

But even aside from the facts of this particular case, the Court is simply wrong in concluding as a general matter that reproduction is a "major life activity." Unfortunately, the ADA does not define the phrase "major life activities." But the Act does incorporate by reference a list of such activities contained in regulations issued under the Rehabilitation Act. The Court correctly recognizes that this list of major life activities "is illustrative, not exhaustive," but then makes no attempt to demonstrate that reproduction is a major life activity in the same sense that "caring for one's self, performing manual tasks, walking, seeing, hearing, speaking, breathing, learning, and working" are.

Instead, the Court argues that reproduction is a "major" life activity in that it is "central to the life process itself." In support of this reading, the Court focuses on the fact that "major" indicates "comparative importance", ignoring the alternative definition of "major" as "greater in quantity, number, or extent." It is the latter definition that is most consistent with the ADA's illustrative list of major life activities.

No one can deny that reproductive decisions are important in a person's life. But so are decisions as to who to marry, where to live, and how to earn one's living. Fundamental importance of this sort is not the common thread linking the statute's listed activities. The common thread is rather that the activities are repetitively performed and essential in the day-to-day existence of a normally functioning individual. They are thus quite different from the series of activities leading to the birth of a child.

* * *

But even if I were to assume that reproduction is a major life activity of respondent, I do not agree that an asymptomatic HIV infection "substantially limits" that activity. The record before us leaves no doubt that those so infected are still entirely able to engage in sexual intercourse, give birth to a child if they become pregnant, and perform the manual tasks necessary to rear a child to maturity. While individuals infected with HIV may choose not to engage in these activities, there is no support in language, logic, or our case law for the proposition that such voluntary choices constitute a "limit" on one's own life activities.

The Court responds that the ADA "addresses substantial limitations on major life activities, not utter inabilities." I agree, but fail to see how this assists the Court's cause. Apart from being unable to demonstrate that she is utterly unable to engage in the various activities that comprise the reproductive process, respondent has not even explained how she is less able to engage in those activities.

Respondent contends that her ability to reproduce is limited because the fatal nature of HIV infection means that a parent is unlikely to live long enough to raise and nurture the child to adulthood. But the ADA's definition of a disability is met only if the alleged impairment substantially "limits" (present tense) a major life activity. Asymptomatic HIV does not presently limit respondent's ability to perform any of the tasks necessary to bear or raise a child. Respondent's argument, taken to its logical extreme, would render every individual with a genetic marker for some debilitating disease "disabled" here and now because of some possible future effects.

In my view, therefore, respondent has failed to demonstrate that any of her major life activities were substantially limited by her HIV infection.

* * *

JUSTICE O'CONNOR, concurring in the judgment in part and dissenting in part.

I agree with The Chief Justice that respondent's claim of disability should be evaluated on an individualized basis and that she has not proven that her asymptomatic HIV status substantially limited one or more of her major life activities. In my view, the act of giving birth to a child, while a very important part of the lives of many women, is not generally the same as the representative major life activities of all persons — "caring for one's self, performing manual tasks, walking, seeing, hearing, speaking, breathing, learning, and working" — listed in regulations relevant to the Americans with Disabilities Act of 1990. Based on that conclusion, there is no need to address whether other aspects of intimate or family relationships not raised in this case could constitute major life activities; nor is there reason to consider whether HIV status would impose a substantial limitation on one's ability to reproduce if reproduction were a major life activity.

* * *

NOTES AND PROBLEMS FOR DISCUSSION

1. As noted at the outset of this Chapter and by the Supreme Court in *Bragdon*, the proper framework for resolving whether a plaintiff is "disabled" as that term is defined in §3(2) of the ADA, is to determine whether that person (a) has or had or is regarded as having (b) a physical or mental impairment (c) that substantially limits (d) a major life activity. Reserving the first of these factors for discussion in the following Note, we will now examine each of the other three criteria in turn:

(a) *Physical or Mental Impairment*

Since the ADA does not contain either an exhaustive or illustrative list of covered impairments, pursuant to the Supreme Court's lead in *Bragdon*, the courts undertake an individualized evaluation of each condition before them, guided in large part by interpretive regulations issued by a variety of federal agencies delegated the task of administering and enforcing the various provisions of the ADA and the Rehabilitation Act. The EEOC has issued regulations interpreting the meaning of "disability." These regulations provide that a "physical impairment" includes "any physiological disorder, or condition, cosmetic disfigurement, or anatomical loss affecting one or more of the following body systems: neurological, musculoskeletal, special sense organs, respiratory (including speech organs), cardiovascular, reproductive, digestive, genitourinary, hemic and lymphatic, skin, and endocrine." 29 CFR §1630.2(h)(1) (1998).

Sections 510 and 511 of the ADA, however, explicitly exclude several conditions from statutory protection: homosexuality, bisexuality, transvestism, current illegal drug use, transsexualism, pedophilia, exhibitionism, voyeurism, gender identity disorders not resulting from physical impairments or other sexual behavior disorders, compulsive gambling, kleptomania, pyromania, and psychoactive substance use disorders resulting from current illegal use of drugs.

Although current use of illegal drugs is not a protected impairment, §104(b) of the ADA provides that an individual who has either successfully completed, or is presently participating in, a supervised drug rehabilitation program and is not currently using illegal drugs, as well as someone who is erroneously regarded as engaging in such use, is deemed to have a covered impairment.

Since an employee, therefore, can lawfully be disciplined solely on the basis of being a "current" user of illegal drugs, it is often crucial to determine whether the plaintiff is or is not "currently" using illegal drugs at the relevant period, i.e., the time of the defendant's challenged employment action. Suppose that a chemically dependent employee joins a supervised rehabilitation program and immediately stops taking all illegal drugs. Three weeks later, while still in the program and drug-free, the employee is fired on the basis of his prior use of illegal drugs on the job. Is the employee covered by §104(b)? *See* Mauerhan v. Wagner Corp., 649 F.3d 1180 (10th Cir. 2011) (eschewing a bright-line rule; eligibility for the "no longer currently using" component of the two-factored safe harbor must be determined on a case-by-case basis, examining whether the circumstances of the plaintiff's drug use and recovery justify an employer's reasonable belief that the plaintiff's prior drug use is no longer a problem. Courts should focus not only on length of abstinence but other factors from which employer could reasonably conclude that the plaintiff's drug use is no longer a problem such as the severity of the prior addiction, relapse rates for the drugs that the plaintiff had used, the level of job responsibility, and the employer's performance requirements); McDaniel v. Mississippi Baptist Medical Center, 877 F.Supp. 321 (S.D.Miss.1995), aff'd, 74 F.3d 1238 (5th Cir. 1995) (the legislative history of §104(b) reveals that Congress meant for "no longer engaging in such use" language of §104(b)(2) to apply to a drug free period of considerable length, not an immediate abstinence from drug use).

Assume that a nurse is accidentally scratched with a needle that had just been used on a surgery patient who was HIV-positive. Assume further that another member of the surgical team saw the nurse get scratched by that needle. If either of these individuals now harbors a fear of contracting AIDS that has rendered her incapable of performing her job, does her fear constitute a mental impairment that renders her disabled within the meaning of the ADA? *See* Doe v. Aliquippa Hospital Ass'n, 1994 WL 579843 (W.D.Pa.1994) (this fear does not represent the type of mental disorder contemplated by the Rehabilitation Act, which uses the identical mental impairment language found in the ADA).

Suppose an employer rejects an applicant for employment because that individual is morbidly obese and the employer is concerned that this individual's obesity rendered him a health and safety risk. Can the worker state a claim under the ADA? Is he disabled? Although the Supreme Court has not ruled on whether obesity constitutes a physical impairment for disability definition purposes, there have been several circuits that have agreed that obesity is only a physical impairment if it is the result of a physiological disorder. These courts, therefore, require the plaintiff to establish that his or her obesity is caused by a physiological disorder. But in one of these cases, MORRISS v. BNSF RAILWAY CO., 817 F.3d 1104 (8th Cir. 2016), cert. denied, 137 S.Ct. 256, 196 L.Ed.2d 136 (2016), the Court also addressed the issue of whether a morbidly obese plaintiff whose obesity was *not* the result of a physiological disorder could meet the "regarded as" component of the definition of disability. In *Morris*, the court noted that even after the passage of the ADA Amendments Act of 2008, the ADA still defined disability to include someone who was regarded as having "such an impairment"; i.e., a physical or mental impairment. Furthermore, the court noted that although the meaning of "regarded as" was changed under the ADAAA, that amendment did not change the meaning of "impairment"; the statute still requires the plaintiff to have been regarded as having a physical or mental impairment. Rather, the court explained, the amendment only removed the requirement of proving that a perceived or actual impairment substantially limited a major life activity. Accordingly, the Eighth Circuit reasoned, since Congress did not intend for the ADAAA to change the extant meaning of physical impairment, a post-ADAAA plaintiff alleging that the employer regarded him as being disabled would still have to prove that the employer correctly or incorrectly perceived him to be obese as the result of a physiological disorder.

(b) *Substantially Limits*

1. The General Standard

Assuming a plaintiff has cleared the hurdle of establishing a physical or mental impairment, it also must prove that this impairment "substantially limits" a major life activity. To sustain this burden, is the plaintiff required to prove that he is completely or nearly totally incapable of performing that major life activity? And where, or example, he claims work as the limited life activity, must he demonstrate that he is unable to work at his current job or any job or a a job that best utilizes his talents and/or skills? The EEOC regulations construe "substantially limits" to include both the inability to perform a major life function that the average person in the general population can perform, and a significant restriction as to the condition, manner or duration under which an individual performs a particular activity as compared to an average person in the general population. 29 CFR §§1630.2(j)(1)(i) and (ii)(1998).

In a trio of cases decided on the same day, the Supreme Court stated that where an ADA plaintiff alleges substantial impairment in the major life activity of working, and *assuming* that working is a "major life activity", the grievant must allege, at a minimum, that she is unable to work in a "broad" or "substantial" class of jobs. In SUTTON v. UNITED AIR LINES, INC., 527 U.S. 471, 119 S.Ct. 2139, 144 L.Ed.2d 450 (1999), severely myopic twin sisters who were rejected by the defendant airline for employment as commercial pilots because they did not satisfy its visual acuity requirements file suit under the ADA. Rejecting the plaintiffs' claim that their myopia constituted a physical impairment that substantially limited their major life activity of working, and affirming the trial court's dismissal of the complaint for failure to state a claim, the Court offered this analysis of the "substantially limits" component of "disabled" status:

> * * * The ADA does not define "substantially limits," but "substantially" suggests "considerable" or "specified to a large degree." See Webster's Third New International Dictionary 2280 (1976) (defining "substantially" as "in a substantial manner" and "substantial" as "considerable in amount, value, or worth" and "being that specified to a large degree or in the main"); see also 17 Oxford English Dictionary 66-67 (2d ed.1989) ("substantial": "[r]elating to or proceeding from the essence of a thing; essential"; "of ample or considerable amount, quantity or dimensions"). * * *

> When the major life activity under consideration is that of working, [all parties conceded that working constituted a "major life activity"], the statutory phrase "substantially limits" requires, at a minimum, that plaintiffs allege they are unable to work in a broad class of jobs. Reflecting this requirement, the EEOC uses a specialized definition of the term "substantially limits" when referring to the major life activity of working:

>> "significantly restricted in the ability to perform either a class of jobs or a broad range of jobs in various classes as compared to the average person having comparable training, skills and abilities. The inability to perform a single, particular job does not constitute a substantial limitation in the major life activity of working." §1630.2(j)(3)(i).

> The EEOC further identifies several factors that courts should consider when determining whether an individual is substantially limited in the major life activity of working, including the geographical area to which the individual has reasonable access, and "the number and types of jobs utilizing similar training, knowledge, skills or abilities, within the geographical area, from which the individual is also disqualified." §§1630.2(j)(3)(ii)(A), (B). To be substantially limited in the major life activity of working, then, one must be precluded from more than one type of job, a specialized job, or a particular job of choice. If jobs utilizing an individual's skills (but perhaps not his or her unique talents) are available, one is not precluded from a substantial class of jobs. Similarly, if a host of different types of jobs are available, one is not precluded from a broad range of jobs.

527 U.S. at 491-92.

The *Sutton* Court then concluded that since the plaintiffs had alleged only that their eyesight precluded them from working as global airline pilots, they did not meet this definition of "substantially limits", since the position of global airline pilot was but a single job and there were many other positions utilizing the plaintiffs' skills, such as regional pilot and pilot instructor, that remained available to them. Moreover, the Court added, the fact that most other airline carriers imposed similar vision requirements would not, even if proved, change the result because it still would reflect only the plaintiffs' inability to pursue one specific position. The behind-the-scenes story of the Court's ruling in *Sutton* is set forth in fascinating detail in Stephen F.

Befort, *The Story of Sutton v. United Air Lines, Inc: Narrowing the Reach of the Americans with Disabilities Act*, EMPLOYMENT DISCRIMINATION STORIES 329 (Friedman, ed. 2006).

Similarly, in MURPHY v. UNITED PARCEL SERVICE, INC., 527 U.S. 516, 119 S.Ct. 2133, 144 L.Ed.2d 484 (1999), where the evidence demonstrated that a plaintiff with allegedly high blood pressure was regarded as unable to perform the single job of UPS mechanic (a position that required him to drive commercial vehicles) the Court upheld the lower courts' grant of summary judgment for the defendant on the ground that the plaintiff's allegation was insufficient, as a matter of law, to prove that he was regarded as substantially limited in the major life activity of working. And in ALBERTSONS, INC. v. KIRKINGBURG, 527 U.S. 555, 119 S.Ct. 2162, 144 L.Ed.2d 518 (1999), the Court rejected the Ninth Circuit's decision that a plaintiff with monocular vision had a physical impairment that substantially limited the major life activity of seeing. The Ninth Circuit had determined that since the manner in individuals with monocular vision (the inability to see out of one eye) saw differed significantly from the manner in which most people see, their vision was substantially limited. The Supreme Court reversed this ruling, finding that the appellate court had lowered the bar established by the statutory "significantly limits" requirement. It did not think that "difference" was equivalent to "substantial restriction" as a matter of law and thus the circuit court erred in not making an individualized determination of whether the impact of monocular vision on this plaintiff was substantial. However, the Court acknowledged that, given the proper evidentiary foundation, a monocular individual might very well be able to sustain the burden of establishing the presence of a substantial limitation on the major life activity of seeing.

What do you make of the *Bragdon* Court's statement that in view of its holding that there was no triable issue of fact on whether or not the plaintiff's HIV infection substantially limited her major life activity of procreation, it was unnecessary to address the issue of whether HIV infection is a *per se* disability under the ADA? Although the Court framed the issue before it as whether the HIV infection substantially limited *this plaintiff's* major life activity of procreation, it initially answered this query in objective terms by referring to any woman's risk of transmitting the infection to her male partner or child. (And, in fact, the dissenters chide the majority for not making an individualized determination of whether the physical impairment substantially limited one or more of the plaintiff's major life activities.). On the other hand, this objective analysis immediately was followed by the statement that since the plaintiff's testimony that her infection controlled her decision not to have a child was uncontradicted, the court was prepared to affirm the lower courts' rulings in favor of her coverage under the ADA as a matter of law. Presumably, the Court's intention was not to issue a general proclamation that HIV infection always results in a substantial limitation on the ability to engage in, at least, the major life activity of reproduction. *See e.g.*, EEOC v. Lee's Log Cabin, Inc., 546 F.3d 438 (7th Cir. 2008) (declining to read *Bragdon* as holding that HIV infection is a *per se* disability; reading it as relying upon uncontroverted evidence of the infection's impact on that plaintiff's decision to procreate); Blanks v. Southwestern Bell Communications, Inc., 310 F.3d 398 (5th Cir.2002)(construing *Bragdon* to say that HIV substantially limits the major life activity of reproduction but that each HIV-positive plaintiff must show that she/he is substantially limited in that regard).

2. The Impact of "Mitigating Factors"

After the passage of the ADA, the federal circuit courts were deeply divided on whether the impact of a physical or mental impairment on an individual's ability to engage in a major life activity should be measured by evaluating that condition in its natural state or as affected by the use of corrective or mitigative measures, such as glasses, medication, or prosthetic devices. The courts struggled, for example, with whether a diabetic whose impairment could be controlled by the injection of insulin, or an extremely myopic individual whose vision was completely corrected by the use of glasses was "disabled" and therefore entitled to coverage under the ADA. The Supreme Court resolved this conflict in SUTTON v. UNITED AIR LINES, INC., 527 U.S. 471, 119 S.Ct. 2139, 144 L.Ed.2d 450 (1999). By a 7-2 margin, the majority voted to reject the approach codified in interpretive guidelines issued by both the EEOC and the Justice Department that provided that a determination of disability should be made without reference to mitigating or corrective measures:

We conclude that respondent is correct that the approach adopted by the agency guidelines — that persons are to be evaluated in their hypothetical uncorrected state — is an impermissible interpretation of the ADA. Looking at the Act as a whole, it is apparent that if a person is taking measures to correct for, or mitigate, a physical or mental impairment, the effects of those measures — both positive and negative — must be taken into account when judging whether that person is "substantially limited" in a major life activity and thus "disabled" under the Act. The dissent relies on the legislative history of the ADA for the contrary proposition that individuals should be examined in their uncorrected state. Because we decide that, by its terms, the ADA cannot be read in this manner, we have no reason to consider the ADA's legislative history.

Three separate provisions of the ADA, read in concert, lead us to this conclusion. The Act defines a "disability" as "a physical or mental impairment that *substantially limits* one or more of the major life activities" of an individual. (emphasis added). Because the phrase "substantially limits" appears in the Act in the present indicative verb form, we think the language is properly read as requiring that a person be presently — not potentially or hypothetically — substantially limited in order to demonstrate a disability. A "disability" exists only where an impairment "substantially limits" a major life activity, not where it "might," "could," or "would" be substantially limiting if mitigating measures were not taken. A person whose physical or mental impairment is corrected by medication or other measures does not have an impairment that presently "substantially limits" a major life activity. To be sure, a person whose physical or mental impairment is corrected by mitigating measures still has an impairment, but if the impairment is corrected it does not "substantially limit" a major life activity.

The definition of disability also requires that disabilities be evaluated "with respect to an individual" and be determined based on whether an impairment substantially limits the "major life activities of such individual." Thus, whether a person has a disability under the ADA is an individualized inquiry. See Bragdon v. Abbott, 524 U.S. 624, 118 S.Ct. 2196, 141 L.Ed.2d 540 (1998) (declining to consider whether HIV infection is a *per se* disability under the ADA).

The agency guidelines' directive that persons be judged in their uncorrected or unmitigated state runs directly counter to the individualized inquiry mandated by the ADA. The agency approach would often require courts and employers to speculate about a person's condition and would, in many cases, force them to make a disability determination based on general information about how an uncorrected impairment usually affects individuals, rather than on the individual's actual condition. For instance, under this view, courts would almost certainly find all diabetics to be disabled, because if they failed to monitor their blood sugar levels and administer insulin, they would almost certainly be substantially limited in one or more major life activities. A diabetic whose illness does not impair his or her daily activities would therefore be considered disabled simply because he or she has diabetes. Thus, the guidelines approach would create a system in which persons often must be treated as members of a group of people with similar impairments, rather than as individuals. This is contrary to both the letter and the spirit of the ADA.

The guidelines approach could also lead to the anomalous result that in determining whether an individual is disabled, courts and employers could not consider any negative side effects suffered by an individual resulting from the use of mitigating measures, even when those side effects are very severe. This result is also inconsistent with the individualized approach of the ADA.

Finally, and critically, findings enacted as part of the ADA require the conclusion that Congress did not intend to bring under the statute's protection all those whose uncorrected conditions amount to disabilities. Congress found that "some 43,000,000 Americans have one or more physical or mental disabilities, and this number is increasing as the population as a whole is growing older." This figure is inconsistent with the definition of disability pressed by petitioners.

Although the exact source of the 43 million figure is not clear, the corresponding finding in the 1988 precursor to the ADA was drawn directly from a report prepared by the National Council on Disability. That report * * * explained that the estimates of the number of disabled Americans ranged from an overinclusive 160 million under a "health conditions approach," which looks at all conditions that impair the health or normal functional abilities of an individual, to an underinclusive 22.7 million under a "work disability approach," which focuses on individuals' reported ability to work. * * *

* * *

Because it is included in the ADA's text, the finding that 43 million individuals are disabled gives content to the ADA's terms, specifically the term "disability." Had Congress intended to include all persons with corrected physical limitations among those covered by the Act, it undoubtedly would have cited a much higher number of disabled persons in the findings. That it did not is evidence that the ADA's coverage is restricted to only those whose impairments are not mitigated by corrective measures.

527 U.S. at 482-87.

In ALBERTSONS, INC. v. KIRKINGBURG, 527 U.S. 555, 119 S.Ct. 2162, 144 L.Ed.2d 518 (1999), the Court extended this rule concerning mitigating to cases where the mitigation was undertaken, whether consciously or not, with the body's own system as well as with artificial aids or medications. In that case, the Supreme Court criticized the Ninth Circuit for disregarding the fact that the plaintiff had learned to compensate for his disability by making subconscious adjustments to the manner in which he sensed depth and perceived peripheral objects.

In 2008, Congress responded to the ruling in *Sutton* and other Supreme Court cases construing various provisions of the ADA by passing the ADA Amendments Act of 2008, P.L. 110-325, 122 Stat. 3553, 42 U.S.C. §12101. Among the foci of this statutory attention was the *Sutton* Court's ruling on the mitigating measures issue. The 2008 Act overturned the Court's interpretation, declaring in its Findings and Purposes section that the ruling in *Sutton* had "narrowed the broad scope of protection intended to be afforded by the ADA" and that one of the purposes of the Act was "to reject the requirement enunciated by the Supreme Court in *Sutton* and its companion cases that whether an impairment substantially limits a major life activity is to be determined with reference to the ameliorative effects of mitigating measures." To that end, it added a section setting forth Rules of Construction providing, *inter alia*, that "the determination of whether an impairment substantially limits a major life activity shall be made without regard to the ameliorative effects of mitigating measures" and also including a non-exclusive list of such measures. However, the Act also expressly creates an exception to this general rule for two mitigating measures — "ordinary eyeglasses" and contact lenses. The ameliorative impact of these two items "must" be considered in making the "substantially limits" assessment. But the Act also provides that if an employer utilizes an employment criterion based on an individual's uncorrected vision, the employer must prove that this criterion is job-related and consistent with business necessity.

If a cancer patient undergoes aggressive chemotherapy that leaves her incapacitated and her employer discharges her, can she state a claim under the ADA even though her cancer, prior to the treatment, did not substantially impair her ability to work? Can the court consider any negative side effects produced by mitigating measures in determining whether the individual was disabled? Is that relevant in this context? In CHRISTIAN v. ST. ANTHONY MEDICAL CENTER, INC., 117 F.3d 1051 (7th Cir.1997), cert. denied, 523 U.S. 1022, 118 S.Ct. 1304, 140 L.Ed.2d 469 (1998), the appellate court ruled that treatment of a condition that is not itself disabling could constitute a disability where the treatment rendered the victim disabled, if, but only if, that particular treatment was medically necessary and not "merely an attractive option." In the instant case, the plaintiff suffered from hypercholesterolemia (an excessive amount of cholesterol in the blood) and claimed that she was fired because she planned to undergo pheresis, a treatment in which in the blood is drained from the patient's body, the cholesterol is removed, and the blood is then returned to the body. This treatment would have rendered the plaintiff completely unable to work for a day or two per month for the rest of her life. The court stated, however, that pheresis was not the indicated treatment for high cholesterol and, therefore, ruled that she was not disabled. *See also* Rohr v. Salt River Project, 555 F.3d 850 (9th Cir. 2009) (where plaintiff alleges that his diabetes substantially limits major life activity of eating, court most not only determine impact of diabetes on eating but whether efforts to mitigate the diabetes, such as dietary restrictions, eating many small meals, arranging schedule around diet, also substantially limit eating). For a suggestion that some diseases and other disorders, such as cancer, are so obviously within the class of disabilities that

Congress intended to cover under the ADA that they should be viewed as inherently substantially limiting impairments as a matter of law, thereby obviating the necessity for an ad hoc evaluation of whether the disease or other disorder substantially impairs a major life activity, see Catherine J. Lanctot, *Ad Hoc Decision Making and Per Se Prejudice: How Individualizing The Determination Of "Disability" Undermines the ADA*, 42 VILL. L.REV. 327 (1997).

(c) *Major Life Activities*

As originally enacted, the ADA did not define "major life activity". The ADA Amendments Act of 2008, however, filled this gap by creating two categories of covered activities: (1) an expressly non-exclusive ("but not limited to") list of general activities and similarly non-exclusive list of major bodily functions. But since Congress stated that these lists were merely illustrative rather than exclusive, interpretive issues still arise post-amendment. For example, while "reproductive functions" are now expressly contained within the definition (consistent with the Court's interpretation of the general term in *Bragdon*), would engaging in sexual relations for *nonprocreative* purposes is a major life activity? See McAlindin v. County of San Diego, 192 F.3d 1226, 1234 (9th Cir.1999), cert. denied, 530 U.S. 1243, 120 S.Ct. 2689, 147 L.Ed.2d 961 (2000) (engaging in sexual relations is a major life activity because procreation has been held to be a major life activity and "the number of people who engage in sexual relations is plainly larger than the number who choose to have children. Moreover *** sexuality is important in how we define ourselves and how we are perceived by others and is a fundamental part of how we bond in intimate relations."); Jacques v. Dimarzio, Inc., 386 F.3d 192 (2d Cir.2004) ("interacting", but not "getting along" with others is a major life activity as the former deals with the ability to communicate on the most basic level with others while the latter is a subjective evaluation of the success or efficacy of those communications.).

In WEAVING v. CITY OF HILLSBORO, 763 F.3d 1106 (9th Cir. 2013), a Ninth Circuit panel reaffirmed its ruling in *McAlindin* that interacting with others is a major life activity. The panel also addressed the slippery slope problems associated with assessing the existence *vel non* of a substantial limitation of that major life activity. To that end, the court invoked language from another of its earlier cases in which it had stated that by recognizing interacting with others as a major life activity, the court did not mean to conclude "that any cantankerous person will be deemed substantially limited * * *. Mere trouble getting along with coworkers is not sufficient to show a substantial limitation * * *. [A] plaintiff must show that his relations with others were characterized on a regular basis by severe problems, for example, consistently high levels of hostility, social withdrawal, or failure to communicate when necessary." Applying this standard to the instant facts, the court ruled that since the plaintiff had little difficulty comporting himself appropriately with his supervisors, the fact that he had problems interacting with his peers and subordinates did not satisfy the statutory substantially limiting standard. It added that "[o]ne who is able to communicate with others, though his communications may at times be offensive, inappropriate, ineffective, or unsuccessful, is not substantially limited in his ability to interact with others within the meaning of the ADA."

If a plaintiff alleges that her disability substantially limits her ability to work (a covered major life activity) is it sufficient to show the limiting impact it has on her job performance? The next case was a major impetus for passage of the 2008 Act.

Toyota Motor Manufacturing, Kentucky, Inc. v. Williams

Supreme Court of the United States, 2002.

534 U.S. 184, 122 S.Ct. 681, 151 L.Ed. 2d 615 (2002).

O'CONNOR, J., delivered the opinion for a unanimous Court.

Under the Americans with Disabilities Act of 1990 (ADA or Act), a physical impairment that "substantially limits one or more ... major life activities" is a "disability". Respondent, claiming to be disabled because of her carpal tunnel syndrome and other related impairments, sued petitioner, her former employer, for failing to provide her with a reasonable accommodation as required by the ADA. The District Court granted summary judgment to petitioner, finding that respondent's impairments did not substantially limit any of her major life activities. The Court of Appeals for the Sixth Circuit reversed, finding that the impairments substantially limited respondent in the major life activity of performing manual tasks, and therefore granting partial summary judgment to respondent on the issue of whether she was disabled under the ADA. We conclude that the Court of Appeals did not apply the proper standard in making this determination because it analyzed only a limited class of manual tasks and failed to ask whether respondent's impairments prevented or restricted her from performing tasks that are of central importance to most people's daily lives.

I

Respondent began working at petitioner's automobile manufacturing plant in Georgetown, Kentucky, in August 1990. She was soon placed on an engine fabrication assembly line, where her duties included work with pneumatic tools. Use of these tools eventually caused pain in respondent's hands, wrists, and arms. She sought treatment at petitioner's in-house medical service, where she was diagnosed with bilateral carpal tunnel syndrome and bilateral tendinitis. Respondent consulted a personal physician who placed her on permanent work restrictions that precluded her from lifting more than 20 pounds or from frequently lifting or carrying of objects weighing up to 10 pounds, engaging in constant repetitive flexion or extension of her wrists or elbows, performing overhead work, or using vibratory or pneumatic tools.

In light of these restrictions, for the next two years petitioner assigned respondent to various modified duty jobs. Nonetheless, respondent missed some work for medical leave, and eventually filed a claim under the Kentucky Workers' Compensation Act. The parties settled this claim, and respondent returned to work. She was unsatisfied by petitioner's efforts to accommodate her work restrictions, however, and responded by bringing an action in the United States District Court for the Eastern District of Kentucky alleging that petitioner had violated the ADA by refusing to accommodate her disability. That suit was also settled, and as part of the settlement, respondent returned to work in December 1993.

Upon her return, petitioner placed respondent on a team in Quality Control Inspection Operations (QCIO). QCIO is responsible for four tasks: (1) "assembly paint"; (2) "paint second inspection"; (3) "shell body audit"; and (4) "ED surface repair." Respondent was initially placed on a team that performed only the first two of these tasks, and for a couple of years, she rotated on a weekly basis between them. In assembly paint, respondent visually inspected painted cars moving slowly down a conveyor. She scanned for scratches, dents, chips, or any other flaws that may have occurred during the assembly or painting process, at a rate of one car every 54 seconds. When respondent began working in assembly paint, inspection team members were required to open and shut the doors, trunk, and/or hood of each passing car. Sometime during respondent's tenure, however, the position was modified to include only visual inspection with few or no manual tasks. Paint second inspection required team members to use their hands to wipe each painted car with a glove as it moved along a conveyor. The parties agree that respondent was physically capable of performing both of these jobs and that her performance was satisfactory.

During the fall of 1996, petitioner announced that it wanted QCIO employees to be able to rotate through all four of the QCIO processes. Respondent therefore received training for the shell body audit job, in which team members apply a highlight oil to the hood, fender, doors, rear quarter panel, and trunk of passing cars at a rate of approximately one car per minute. The highlight oil has the viscosity of salad oil, and employees spread it on cars with a sponge attached to a block of wood. After they wipe each car with the oil, the employees visually inspect it for flaws. Wiping the cars required respondent to hold her hands and arms up around shoulder height for several hours at a time.

A short while after the shell body audit job was added to respondent's rotations, she began to experience pain in her neck and shoulders. Respondent again sought care at petitioner's in-house medical service, where she was diagnosed with myotendinitis bilateral periscapular, an inflammation of the muscles and tendons around both of her shoulder blades; myotendinitis and myositis bilateral forearms with nerve compression causing median nerve irritation; and thoracic outlet compression, a condition that causes pain in the nerves that lead to the upper extremities. Respondent requested that petitioner accommodate her medical conditions by allowing her to return to doing only her original two jobs in QCIO, which respondent claimed she could still perform without difficulty.

The parties disagree about what happened next. According to respondent, petitioner refused her request and forced her to continue working in the shell body audit job, which caused her even greater physical injury. According to petitioner, respondent simply began missing work on a regular basis. Regardless, it is clear that on December 6, 1996, the last day respondent worked at petitioner's plant, she was placed under a no-work-of-any-kind restriction by her treating physicians. On January 27, 1997, respondent received a letter from petitioner that terminated her employment, citing her poor attendance record.

Respondent filed a charge of disability discrimination with the Equal Employment Opportunity Commission (EEOC). After receiving a right to sue letter, respondent filed suit against petitioner in the United States District Court for the Eastern District of Kentucky. Her complaint alleged that petitioner had violated the ADA * * * by failing to reasonably accommodate her disability and by terminating her employment. * * *

Respondent based her claim that she was "disabled" under the ADA on the ground that her physical impairments substantially limited her in (1) manual tasks; (2) housework; (3) gardening; (4) playing with her children; (5) lifting; and (6) working, all of which, she argued, constituted major life activities under the Act. * * *.

After petitioner filed a motion for summary judgment and respondent filed a motion for partial summary judgment on her disability claims, the District Court granted summary judgment to petitioner. The court found that respondent had not been disabled * * * at the time of petitioner's alleged refusal to accommodate her, and that she had therefore not been covered by the Act's protections * * *. The District Court held that respondent had suffered from a physical impairment, but that the impairment did not qualify as a disability because it had not substantially limited any major life activity. The court rejected respondent's arguments that gardening, doing housework, and playing with children are major life activities. Although the court agreed that performing manual tasks, lifting, and working are major life activities, it found the evidence insufficient to demonstrate that respondent had been substantially limited in lifting or working. The court found respondent's claim that she was substantially limited in performing manual tasks to be irretrievably contradicted by respondent's continual insistence that she could perform the tasks in assembly paint and paint second inspection without difficulty. * * *

* * *

Respondent appealed all but the gardening, housework, and playing-with- children rulings. The Court of Appeals for the Sixth Circuit reversed the District Court's ruling on whether respondent was disabled at the time she sought an accommodation * * *. The Court of Appeals held that in order for respondent to demonstrate that she was disabled due to a substantial limitation in the ability to perform manual tasks at the time of her accommodation request, she had to show that her manual disability involved a "class" of manual activities affecting the ability to perform tasks at work. Respondent satisfied this test, according to the Court of Appeals, because her ailments "prevent[ed] her from doing the tasks associated with certain types of manual assembly line jobs, manual product handling jobs and manual building trade jobs (painting, plumbing, roofing, etc.) that require the gripping of tools and repetitive work with hands and arms extended at or above shoulder levels for extended periods of time." In reaching this conclusion, the court disregarded evidence that respondent could "ten[d] to her personal hygiene [and] carr[y] out personal or household chores," finding that such evidence "does not affect a determination that her impairment substantially limit[ed] her ability to perform the range of manual tasks associated with an assembly line job." Because the Court of Appeals concluded that respondent had been substantially limited in performing manual tasks and, for that reason, was entitled to partial summary judgment on the issue of whether she was disabled under the Act, it found that it did not need to determine whether respondent had been substantially limited in the major life activities of lifting or working * * *.

We granted certiorari to consider the proper standard for assessing whether an individual is substantially limited in performing manual tasks. We now reverse the Court of Appeals' decision to grant partial summary judgment to respondent on the issue whether she was substantially limited in performing manual tasks at the time she sought an accommodation. We express no opinion on the working, lifting, or other arguments for disability status that were preserved below but which were not ruled upon by the Court of Appeals.

II

The ADA * * * defines a "qualified individual with a disability" as "an individual with a disability who, with or without reasonable accommodation, can perform the essential functions of the employment position that such individual holds or desires." In turn, a "disability" is:

"(A) a physical or mental impairment that substantially limits one or more of the major life activities of such individual;

"(B) a record of such an impairment; or

"(C) being regarded as having such an impairment."

There are two potential sources of guidance for interpreting the terms of this definition — the regulations interpreting the Rehabilitation Act of 1973 and the EEOC regulations interpreting the ADA. Congress drew the ADA's definition of disability almost verbatim from the definition of "handicapped individual" in the Rehabilitation Act, and Congress' repetition of a well-established term generally implies that Congress intended the term to be construed in accordance with pre-existing regulatory interpretations. As we explained in Bragdon v. Abbott, 524 U.S. 624,631, 118 S.Ct. 2196, 141 L.Ed.2d 540 (1998), Congress did more in the ADA than suggest this construction; it adopted a specific statutory provision directing as follows:

"Except as otherwise provided in this chapter, nothing in this chapter shall be construed to apply a lesser standard than the standards applied under title V of the Rehabilitation Act of 1973 or the regulations issued by Federal agencies pursuant to such title."

The persuasive authority of the EEOC regulations is less clear. As we have previously noted, see Sutton v. United Air Lines, Inc., 527 U.S. 471,479, 119 S.Ct. 2139, 144 L.Ed.2d 450 (1999), no agency has been given authority to issue regulations interpreting the term "disability" in the ADA. Nonetheless, the EEOC has done so. Because both parties accept the EEOC regulations as reasonable, we assume without deciding that they are, and we have no occasion to decide what level of deference, if any, they are due.

To qualify as disabled under subsection (A) of the ADA's definition of disability, a claimant must initially prove that he or she has a physical or mental impairment * * * that * * * limits a major life activity. The HEW Rehabilitation Act regulations provide a list of examples of "major life activities," that includes "walking, seeing, hearing," and, as relevant here, "performing manual tasks."

To qualify as disabled, a claimant must further show that the limitation on the major life activity is "substantia[l]." Unlike "physical impairment" and "major life activities," the HEW regulations do not define the term "substantially limits." The EEOC, therefore, has created its own definition for purposes of the ADA. According to the EEOC regulations, "substantially limit[ed]" means "[u]nable to perform a major life activity that the average person in the general population can perform"; or "[s]ignificantly restricted as to the condition, manner or duration under which an individual can perform a particular major life activity as compared to the condition, manner, or duration under which the average person in the general population can perform that same major life activity." 29 CFR §1630.2(j) (2001). In determining whether an individual is substantially limited in a major life activity, the regulations instruct that the following factors should be considered: "[t]he nature and severity of the impairment; [t]he duration or expected duration of the impairment; and [t]he permanent or long-term impact, or the expected permanent or long-term impact of or resulting from the impairment." §§1630.2(j)(2)(i)-(iii).

III

The question presented by this case is whether the Sixth Circuit properly determined that respondent was disabled under subsection (A) of the ADA's disability definition at the time that she sought an accommodation from petitioner. The parties do not dispute that respondent's medical conditions * * * amount to physical impairments. The relevant question, therefore, is whether the Sixth Circuit correctly analyzed whether these impairments substantially limited respondent in the major life activity of performing manual tasks. Answering this requires us to address an issue about which the EEOC regulations are silent: what a plaintiff must demonstrate to establish a substantial limitation in the specific major life activity of performing manual tasks.

Our consideration of this issue is guided first and foremost by the words of the disability definition itself. "[S]ubstantially" in the phrase "substantially limits" suggests "considerable" or "to a large degree." See Webster's Third New International Dictionary 2280 (1976) (defining "substantially" as "in a substantial manner" and "substantial" as "considerable in amount, value, or worth" and "being that specified to a large degree or in the main"); see also 17 Oxford English Dictionary 66-67 (2d ed.1989) ("substantial": "[r]elating to or proceeding from the essence of a thing; essential"; "[o]f ample or considerable amount, quantity, or dimensions"). The word "substantial" thus clearly precludes impairments that interfere in only a minor way with the performance of manual tasks from qualifying as disabilities.

"Major" in the phrase "major life activities" means important. See Webster's, supra, at 1363 (defining "major" as "greater in dignity, rank, importance, or interest"). "Major life activities" thus refers to those activities that are of central importance to daily life. In order for performing manual tasks to fit into this category — a category that includes such basic abilities as walking, seeing, and hearing — the manual tasks in question must be central to daily life. If each of the tasks included in the major life activity of performing manual tasks does not independently qualify as a major life activity, then together they must do so.

That these terms need to be interpreted strictly to create a demanding standard for qualifying as disabled is confirmed by the first section of the ADA, which lays out the legislative findings and purposes that motivate the Act. When it enacted the ADA in 1990, Congress found that "some 43,000,000 Americans have one or more physical or mental disabilities." If Congress intended everyone with a physical impairment that precluded the performance of some isolated, unimportant, or particularly difficult manual task to qualify as disabled, the number of disabled Americans would surely have been much higher. Cf. *Sutton* (finding that because more than 100 million people need corrective lenses to see properly, "[h]ad Congress intended to include all persons with corrected physical limitations among those covered by the Act, it undoubtedly would have cited a much higher number than 43 million disabled persons in the findings").

We therefore hold that to be substantially limited in performing manual tasks, an individual must have an impairment that prevents or severely restricts the individual from doing activities that are of central importance to most people's daily lives. The impairment's impact must also be permanent or long-term.   See 29 CFR §§630.2(j)(2)(ii)-(iii) (2001).

It is insufficient for individuals attempting to prove disability status under this test to merely submit evidence of a medical diagnosis of an impairment. Instead, the ADA requires those "claiming the Act's protection ... to prove a disability by offering evidence that the extent of the limitation [caused by their impairment] in terms of their own experience ... is substantial." Albertson's, Inc. v. Kirkingburg, 527 U.S. 555,567, 119 S.Ct. 2162, 144 L.Ed.2d 518 (1999) (holding that monocular vision is not invariably a disability, but must be analyzed on an individual basis, taking into account the individual's ability to compensate for the impairment). That the Act defines "disability" "with respect to an individual," makes clear that Congress intended the existence of a disability to be determined in such a case-by-case manner.

An individualized assessment of the effect of an impairment is particularly necessary when the impairment is one whose symptoms vary widely from person to person. Carpal tunnel syndrome, one of respondent's impairments, is just such a condition. While cases of severe carpal tunnel syndrome are characterized by muscle atrophy and extreme sensory deficits, mild cases generally do not have either of these effects and create only intermittent symptoms of numbness and tingling. Studies have further shown that, even without surgical treatment, one quarter of carpal tunnel cases resolve in one month, but that in 22 percent of cases, symptoms last for eight years or longer. When pregnancy is the cause of carpal tunnel syndrome, in contrast, the symptoms normally resolve within two weeks of delivery. Given these large potential differences in the severity and duration of the effects of carpal tunnel syndrome, an individual's carpal tunnel syndrome diagnosis, on its own, does not indicate whether the individual has a disability within the meaning of the ADA.

IV

The Court of Appeals' analysis of respondent's claimed disability suggested that in order to prove a substantial limitation in the major life activity of performing manual tasks, a "plaintiff must show that her manual disability involves a 'class' of manual activities," and that those activities "affec[t] the ability to perform tasks at work." Both of these ideas lack support.

The Court of Appeals relied on our opinion in *Sutton* for the idea that a "class" of manual activities must be implicated for an impairment to substantially limit the major life activity of performing manual tasks. But *Sutton* said only that "[w]hen the major life activity under consideration is that of working, the statutory phrase 'substantially limits' requires ... that plaintiffs allege that they are unable to work in a broad class of jobs." Because of the conceptual difficulties inherent in the argument that working could be a major life activity, we have been hesitant to hold as much, and we need not decide this difficult question today. In *Sutton* we noted that even assuming that working is a major life activity, a claimant would be required to show an inability to work in a "broad range of jobs," rather than a specific job. But *Sutton* did not suggest that a class-based analysis should be applied to any major life activity other than working. Nor do the EEOC regulations. In defining "substantially limits," the EEOC regulations only mention the "class" concept in the context of the major life activity of working. 29 CFR §1630.2(j)(3) (2001)("With respect to the major life activity of working [,][t]he term substantially limits means significantly restricted in the ability to perform either a class of jobs or a broad range of jobs in various classes as compared to the average person having comparable training, skills and abilities"). Nothing in the text of the Act, our previous opinions, or the regulations suggests that a class-based framework should apply outside the context of the major life activity of working.

While the Court of Appeals in this case addressed the different major life activity of performing manual tasks, its analysis circumvented *Sutton* by focusing on respondent's inability to perform manual tasks associated only with her job. This was error. When addressing the major life activity of performing manual tasks, the central inquiry must be whether the claimant is unable to perform the variety of tasks central to most people's daily lives, not whether the claimant is unable to perform the tasks associated with her specific job. Otherwise, *Sutton*'s restriction on claims of disability based on a substantial limitation in working will be rendered meaningless because an inability to perform a specific job always can be recast as an inability to perform a "class" of tasks associated with that specific job.

There is also no support in the Act, our previous opinions, or the regulations for the Court of Appeals' idea that the question of whether an impairment constitutes a disability is to be answered only by analyzing the effect of the impairment in the workplace. Indeed, the fact that the Act's definition of "disability" applies not only to Title I of the Act, which deals with employment, but also to the other portions of the Act, which deal with subjects such as public transportation and privately provided public accommodations, demonstrates that the definition is intended to cover individuals with disabling impairments regardless of whether the individuals have any connection to a workplace.

Even more critically, the manual tasks unique to any particular job are not necessarily important parts of most people's lives. As a result, occupation-specific tasks may have only limited relevance to the manual task inquiry. In this case, repetitive work with hands and arms extended at or above shoulder levels for extended periods of time, the manual task on which the Court of Appeals relied, is not an important part of most people's daily lives. The court, therefore, should not have considered respondent's inability to do such manual work in her specialized assembly line job as sufficient proof that she was substantially limited in performing manual tasks.

At the same time, the Court of Appeals appears to have disregarded the very type of evidence that it should have focused upon. It treated as irrelevant the fact that respondent can tend to her personal hygiene and carry out personal or household chores. Yet household chores, bathing, and brushing one's teeth are among the types of manual tasks of central importance to people's daily lives, and should have been part of the assessment of whether respondent was substantially limited in performing manual tasks.

The District Court noted that at the time respondent sought an accommodation from petitioner, she admitted that she was able to do the manual tasks required by her original two jobs in QCIO. In addition, according to respondent's deposition testimony, even after her condition worsened, she could still brush her teeth, wash her face, bathe, tend her flower garden, fix breakfast, do laundry, and pick up around the house. The record also indicates that her medical conditions caused her to avoid sweeping, to quit dancing, to occasionally seek help dressing, and to reduce how often she plays with her children, gardens, and drives long distances. But these changes in her life did not amount to such severe restrictions in the activities that are of central importance to most people's daily lives that they establish a manual-task disability as a matter of law. On this record, it was therefore inappropriate for the Court of Appeals to grant partial summary judgment to respondent on the issue whether she was substantially limited in performing manual tasks, and its decision to do so must be reversed.

In its brief on the merits, petitioner asks us to reinstate the District Court's grant of summary judgment to petitioner on the manual task issue. In its petition for certiorari, however, petitioner did not seek summary judgment; it argued only that the Court of Appeals' reasons for granting partial summary judgment to respondent were unsound. This Court's Rule 14(1)(a) provides: "Only the questions set out in the petition, or fairly included therein, will be considered by the Court." The question whether petitioner was entitled to summary judgment on the manual task issue is therefore not properly before us.

Accordingly, we reverse the Court of Appeals' judgment granting partial summary judgment to respondent and remand the case for further proceedings consistent with this opinion.

NOTES AND PROBLEMS FOR DISCUSSION

1.   How did the *Toyota* Court define "substantially limits" and "major life activity"? The unanimous decision reached in *Toyota* was viewed by many observers as significantly cutting back on the scope of protection offered by the ADA. Specifically, the Court announced that these terms "need to be interpreted strictly to create a demanding standard for qualifying as disabled" and that this interpretation was supported by the introductory provision of the ADA setting forth the legislative findings and purposes that motivate the Act. Accordingly, the Court chided the circuit court for focusing solely on the impact of the plaintiff's medical condition on her ability to perform job tasks. But in light of the specific issue on which the Court granted certiorari, is it fair to interpret *Toyota* as requiring all ADA plaintiffs to demonstrate that their impairments limit them in ways beyond their ability to perform the functions of either their specific job or a broad class of jobs? The circuit courts have transplanted the ruling in *Toyota* on this point to cases involving other major life activities. *See e.g.*, Mack v. Great Dane Trailers, 308 F.3d 776 (7th Cir.2002) (applying *Toyota* to a claim alleging impairment of the major life activity of lifting); EEOC v. United Parcel Service, Inc., 306 F.3d 794 (9th Cir.2002) (extending *Toyota* to case involving the major life activity of seeing).

In 2008, Congress passed the ADA Amendments Act of 2008 (ADAA), a statute designed to respond to several Supreme Court cases interpreting a variety of sections of the ADA. The Findings and Purposes section of the ADAA expressly finds that the *Toyota* Court "interpreted the term 'substantially limits' to require a greater degree of limitation than was intended by Congress" and, therefore, that among the purposes of the Amendments is to "reject the standards enunciated by the Supreme Court in *Toyota* * * * that the terms 'substantially' and 'major' in the definition of disability * * * 'need to be interpreted strictly to create a demanding standard for qualifying as disabled'". Additionally, this Act contains a section of "Rules of Construction" providing, *inter alia*, that "the definition of disability * * * shall be construed in favor of broad coverage of individuals * * * to the maximum extent permitted by the terms of this Act" and that the definition of "substantially limits" "shall be interpreted consistently with the findings and purposes of the ADA Amendments Act."

Citing the EEOC regulations, the *Toyota* Court also stated that in order to establish that an impairment substantially limits a major life activity, an ADA plaintiff must establish that the impairment "prevents or severely restricts" the performance of a major life activity. The Findings and Purposes section of the ADAA also address this aspect of the Court's construction of "substantially limits" by declaring that "the current EEOC ADA regulations defining the term 'substantially limits' as 'significantly restricted' are inconsistent with congressional intent, by expressing too high a standard" and "rejects" the "prevents or severely restricts" standard set forth in *Toyota* as creating an "inappropriately high level of limitation necessary to obtain coverage under the ADA." Moreover, this section of the ADAA expresses "Congress' expectation that the EEOC will revise that portion of its current regulations" consistently with the terms of these amendments.

The *Toyota* Court further defined "substantially limits" to mean that the impact of the plaintiff's impairment must be "permanent or long-term." The ADAA expanded the protections afforded to plaintiffs by providing that an impairment that is "episodic or in remission" fits within the definition of "disability" if it "would substantially limit a major life activity when active." Now, therefore, courts must attempt to divine the impact of an episodic condition were it to be active when the plaintiff is not presently suffering from its ill effects.

In addition, the revised definition of the "regarded as" prong of the category of disabled individuals states that *it* shall not apply to impairments that are "transitory and minor". It further defines a transitory impairment as one with "an actual or expected duration of six months or less." This provision has led the Seventh Circuit to conclude that Congress intended for impairments of a "transitory and minor" duration *to be included* within the definition of impairment for non-"regarded as" plaintiffs, i.e., those who allege that they either have or had a physical or mental impairment. Gogos v. AMS Mechanical Systems, Inc., 737 F.3d 1170 (7th Circuit 2013). On the other hand, the Fourth Circuit has ruled that this six-month provision was intended by Congress to apply *only* to claims of "regarded as"-based disability and not to claims alleging an "actual" disability. Summers v. Altarum Institute Corp., 740 F.3d 325 (4th Cir. 2013). Further, as mentioned *supra*, Congress, in the ADAA, expressly directed the EEOC to promulgate regulations enunciating a construction of "substantially limits" consistent with the broadened scope of the statute. Pursuant to that authorization, the EEOC promulgated a regulation stating that the effects of an impairment lasting or expected to last fewer than six months *can* be substantially limiting. And the appendix to the EEOC regulations states that the duration of any impairment is but one factor to be considered in determining whether the impairment in question substantially limits a major life activity. It goes on to state that although short-term impairments typically shall not be viewed as substantially limiting, they can meet the statutory standard if they are "sufficiently severe". Thus, in a case of first impression, the Fourth Circuit ruled that the EEOC's regulation constituted a reasonable interpretation of the ADAA and, therefore, held that a short-term impairment can qualify as a disability if it is sufficiently severe. Summers v. Altarum Institute Corp., 740 F.3d 325 (4th Cir. 2013).

In FRASER v. GOODALE, 342 F.3d 1032 (9th Cir.2003), cert. denied, 541 U.S. 937, 124 S.Ct. 1663, 158 L.Ed.2d 358 (2004), the Ninth Circuit joined several other circuits in ruling that eating is a major life activity. However, concerned about the possibility that this might open the floodgates to disability claims by ordinary dieters, the court added that it would carefully scrutinize whether a plaintiff's particular impairment substantially limited the ability to eat. The fact, for example, that a plaintiff's impairment caused her to suffer some limit in what she could eat was patently insufficient to meet the substantial impairment test. In the instant case, however, the plaintiff's life-threatening form of diabetes not only severely restricted the categories of food that she could eat but also imposed a highly demanding regimen of testing and medication. Accordingly, the court found that she had established a genuine issue of material fact with respect to whether her physical impairment substantially limited this major life activity to justify reversing the trial court's grant of summary judgment in favor of the defendant.

2.   (a) What do you make of the Court's skeptical reference to the enforceability of the EEOC regulations concerning the meaning of "major life activity" and "substantially limiting"? Congress responded to this in §6(a)(2) of the ADA Amendments Act of 2008, by providing that the EEOC's authority to issue regulations under the ADA "includes the authority to issue regulations implementing the definitions of disability * * * consistent with" this Act. Moreover, it added a new subsection to the definition of disability, §3(2), which defines major life activity by reference to a nonexclusive list of major life activities, including working, reading, and communicating, as well as a nonexclusive list of major bodily functions. Cases arising before the applicability of the 2008 amendments held that driving is not a major life activity because (1) it is a privilege revocable by the state for various reasons; and (2) it is not deemed crucial to the lifestyle of many Americans in certain (typically urban) arts of the country. *See e.g.,* Winsley v. Cook County, 563 F.3d 598 (7th Cir. 2009). Additionally, in §3(4)'s "Rules of Construction", Congress codified the general understanding that a plaintiff need only show that an impairment substantially limits only one major life activity. This list also includes learning, reading, concentrating, thinking, and communicating.

3.   The ADA, like the Rehabilitation Act, applies to individuals who are "regarded as" disabled, as well as those who presently have or previously had a physical or mental impairment. Since this is a category that is unknown to all other antidiscrimination statutes, the lower courts had a difficult time defining the contours of this concept. In SUTTON v. UNITED AIR LINES, 527 U.S. 471, 119 S.Ct. 2139, 144 L.Ed.2d 450 (1999), however, the Supreme Court offered this guidance on the scope of the "regarded as" form of disability:

> There are two apparent ways in which individuals may fall within this statutory definition: (1) a covered entity mistakenly believes that a person has a physical impairment that substantially limits one or more major life activities, or (2) a covered entity mistakenly believes that an actual, nonlimiting impairment substantially limits one or more major life activities. In both cases, it is necessary that a covered entity entertain misperceptions about the individual — it must believe either than one has a substantially limiting impairment that one does not

have or that one has a substantially limiting impairment when, in fact, the impairment is not so limiting.

527 U.S. at 489.

As previously mentioned, the ADA Amendments Act of 2008 was enacted primarily, though not exclusively, to reverse several aspects of the Supreme Court's rulings in *Sutton* and *Toyota*. With respect to that portion of *Sutton* addressing the "regarded as" prong of the definition of "disability", the 2008 Act's Findings and Purposes section states that among the statutory purposes is "to reject the Supreme Court's reasoning in *Sutton* with regard to coverage under the ["regarded as"] definition of disability and to * * * set forth a broad view" of that term. To that end, the Act adds a section to the definition of "disability" providing that a plaintiff can establish that she is "regarded as" being impaired simply by proving that the defendant's challenged conduct was motivated by the plaintiff's actual or perceived (by the employer) impairment, irrespective of the impairment's actual or perceived limiting impact upon a major life activity. Thus, a "regarded as" plaintiff no longer needs to establish that the defendant believed, correctly or not, that the impairment had a substantially limiting impact upon a major life activity. The plaintiff only has to establish a causal link between the adverse action and an actual or perceived impairment. See e.g., Adair v. City of Muskogee, 823 F.3d 1297 (10th Cir. 2016); Burton v. Freescale Semiconductors, Inc., 798 F.3d 222 (5th Cir. 2015). This suggests that it will be easier for a plaintiff to establish that she is disabled under the "regarded as" definition of that term since, unlike a plaintiff who alleges that she has or previously had a physical or mental impairment, the regarded as plaintiff does not have to establish that she actually was or was incorrectly perceived as being substantially limited in the performance of one or more major life activities. Note also, however, on the downside from the "regarded as" plaintiff's point of view, the 2008 Act also provides that "regarded as" status will not attach when the impairment is merely "transitory or minor"; with transitory being defined as "an actual or expected duration of six months or less." And, as part of the compromise that led Congress to expand the definition of "regarded as" disabled, it states that a defendant is under no obligation to make a reasonable accommodation to a "regarded as" plaintiff.

Additionally, as mentioned in Note 1, *supra*, the revised definition of the "regarded as" form of disability states that *it* shall not apply to impairments that are "transitory and minor". This has led at least one circuit court to conclude that in a "regarded as" claim, it is the *defendant's* burden to persuade the factfinder that the alleged impairment was both transitory and minor. Moreover, the court added, it is insufficient for the defendant to establish that it subjectively believed the impairment met those standards; the standard is "an objective one." Silk v. Board of Trustees, Moraine Valley Community College, 795 F.3d 698, 706 (7th Cir. 2015).

(a) If an individual can qualify as being "regarded as" disabled on the basis of a showing that the employer's mistaken belief that she has an impairment led to the adverse action, must that mistake rise to the level of negligence or malice, or is an "innocent" mistake a sufficient basis for liability under the ADA? In TAYLOR v. PATHMARK STORES, INC., 177 F.3d 180 (3d Cir.1999), the court held that an employer's mistaken perception, however reasonable, that an employee is "disabled" is a sufficient basis for finding that the employee was "regarded as" having a disability unless the employer can establish (a) that it did not rely on stereotyped views of the plaintiff's condition; and (b) that the plaintiff or the plaintiff's agent is responsible for the employer's mistaken judgment. So, the court suggested, if the employer receives generalized medical information about an employee's status and then takes adverse action pursuant to its belief that this status inherently precludes successful performance of essential job functions, there is no defense. But if the defendant makes an individualized determination of the particular individual's abilities and that determination is faulty, then the employer will have a defense if the employee failed to reasonably inform the employer of his actual physical condition.

(b) If a plaintiff establishes that he is "regarded" as being disabled by his employer, is the employer obligated to make a reasonable accommodation to this perceived, but nonexistent disability? How can an employer make an accommodation to a disability that does not exist, other than in its own mind? Although the circuit courts initially split on whether or not a "regarded as" plaintiff is not entitled to a reasonable accommodation under the ADA, Congress resolved the matter in §6(a)(1) of the ADA Amendments Act of 2008 by providing that ADA-covered entities need not make a reasonable accommodation to an individual who is "regarded as" being disabled.

(c) Suppose an employer refuses to hire a job applicant because she reveals that although she is asymptomatic, she has undergone genetic testing that indicates a predisposition towards a disabling disease. Is she "regarded as" having a physical or mental impairment that substantially limits a major life activity? Although not referring specifically to genetic testing, ADA regulations promulgated by the EEOC state that a "characteristic predisposition to illness or disease" does not constitute an impairment and, therefore, cannot be the basis for being considered a disability under the statute. 29 C.F.R. §1630 app. 11 (1997). For a discussion of the genetic testing aspect of this issue, see Mark S. Dichter & Sarah E. Sutor, *The New Genetic Age: Do Our Genes Make Us Disabled Individuals Under the ADA*, 42 VILL. L.REV. 613 (1997).

On February 8, 2000, President Clinton issued Executive Order 13145: To Prohibit Discrimination in Federal Employment Based on Genetic Information. Under this Order, every federal department or agency subject to the terms of Title VII is precluded from discriminating with respect to any term, condition, or privilege of employment on the basis of genetic information or because of information it has received concerning a request for or the receipt of genetic services by a present, prospective or former employee. Federal employers also are forbidden from making any employment decision on the basis of an individual's genetic predisposition for illnesses. The Order further prohibits requiring any incumbent, prospective or former employee (other than military employees at the Department of Defense) to undergo a genetic test as a precondition for obtaining employment or receiving employment benefits. In addition to the ban on obtaining genetic information, federal employees are similarly banned from disclosing such information about incumbent or prospective employees except (1) to the employee upon his or her request; (2) to a research organization for the purposes of authorized research; or (3) pursuant to a lawful court order or congressional subpoena after providing the individual with notice to challenge the subpoena or court order. A federal employer, however, may require or request genetic information from an applicant who has been given a conditional offer of employment if that information is used solely to assess whether further medical evaluation is needed to diagnose a current condition that could prevent the applicant or employee from performing essential job functions and the information is not disclosed to other than medical personnel responsible for assessing whether such further medical evaluation is needed. This Order, however, does not prevent a federal employer from making an employment decision on the basis of an existing medical condition that prevents the victim from performing the essential functions of the job. Rather, it prohibits that same decision from being made on the basis of an individual's genetic predisposition for a disease or other condition.

On May 21, 2008, President Bush signed The Genetic Information Nondiscrimination Act of 2008, PL 110-233, 122 Stat 881 (2008) (GINA) into law. This statute extends the types of protections contained in Executive Order 13145 to employees and applicants for employment with all entities (employers, employment agencies, and unions) covered by Title VII by prohibiting the use of genetic information (other than information about the sex or age of any individual) of employees and job applicants (or their family members) in connection with decisions concerning any term or condition of employment. The statute also prohibits group health plans and health insurers from denying coverage or charging more to individuals solely because of their genetic predisposition to a disease. Like Title VII, it provides plaintiffs with a private cause of action with a jury trial as well as compensatory and punitive damages, subject to the caps established in the 1991 Civil Rights Act. The statute also requires plaintiffs to invoke the EEOC enforcement machinery prior to filing suit. Distinct from Title VII in one important way, the GINA expressly provides that disproportionate impact claims are *not* cognizable in claims brought under its provisions. But it also instructs Congress to create a commission to revisit the question of the availability of impact claims for genetic bias claims six years after the statute's enactment. More than thirty states have enacted laws that prohibit discrimination based on genetic data.

(d) If an employee is discharged because of a condition that does not qualify as a disability under the ADA, can the mere fact of this adverse action *ipso facto* establish or at least suggest that the individual was "regarded as" disabled by his employer?

3. THE MEANING OF "QUALIFIED INDIVIDUAL"

Section 102 of the ADA prohibits discrimination against any "qualified individual with a disability." This latter term is defined in §101(8) to include any individual with a "disability" who, with or without reasonable accommodation, can perform the "essential functions" of the job held or sought by that individual. It further provides that in determining what constitutes an "essential function," the employer's judgment on this matter, including any written job description prepared before advertising or interviewing applicants for the particular job, must be considered.

NOTES AND PROBLEMS FOR DISCUSSION

1. The ADA defines a "qualified" individual with a disability as someone who, notwithstanding his impairment, (a) can perform (b) the essential functions of the relevant position (c) with or without a reasonable accommodation. However, the courts have not agreed on the related evidentiary question of which party bears the

burden of persuasion on any or all of these issues. Although most circuit courts concur that this "otherwise qualified" variable is an essential element of the plaintiff's prima facie case, a few circuits separate out some of these components and treat them as part of the defense case for evidentiary purposes. The prevailing trend requires the plaintiff to demonstrate that she can, in fact, perform the essential functions of the job with or without a reasonable accommodation. *See e.g.*, Laurin v. Providence Hosp., 150 F.3d 52 (1st Cir. 1998). But when the issues of what is an essential function of the job, or what constitutes a reasonable accommodation are raised, some circuits view these questions as part of the defense case. With respect to the "essential functions" requirement, for example, these courts treat this as an affirmative defense and require the defendant to shoulder the burden of convincing the fact finder that the functions that the plaintiff is unable to perform are essential. *See, e.g.*, Hamlin v. Charter Township of Flint, 165 F.3d 426 (6th Cir.1999). For a detailed discussion of the evidentiary burdens concerning the duty to make a reasonable accommodation, see Section 4(b) of this Chapter, *infra*.

2. After suffering a stroke, Emily Jones applied for and received disability benefits from the Social Security Administration (SSA). In her application, Jones claimed that she was rendered totally unable to work by this disability. While her application was pending before the SSA, Jones was discharged and sued her employer, Gordon Domes, Inc., claiming that she had been discharged on account of her disability in violation of the ADA. Gordon Domes filed a motion to dismiss her complaint on the ground that Jones' application for, and subsequent receipt of, disability benefits from the SSA estopped her from claiming that she was capable of performing the essential functions of her job and, therefore, that she was not a "qualified person with a disability" under the ADA. How should the court rule on this motion?

In CLEVELAND v. POLICY MANAGEMENT SYSTEMS CORP., 526 U.S. 795, 119 S.Ct. 1597, 143 L.Ed.2d 966 (S.Ct. 1999), the Supreme Court unanimously ruled that the ADA and the Social Security Disability Insurance (SSDI) program contained enough differences to make it inappropriate to utilize the doctrine of judicial estoppel against an ADA claimant who previously had filed for SSDI benefits. For example, the Court noted, the SSI definition of disability does not include the applicant's ability to perform job functions with the help of a reasonable accommodation. The Court mentioned that for purposes of administrative convenience, the SSA determines disability on the basis of presumptions that preclude assessments of individual circumstances, whereas the ADA mandates individualized determinations of disability. Nevertheless, the Court warned, a plaintiff cannot ignore the impact of statements made in the context of an application for SSDI benefits. Accordingly, it ruled that to defeat a defense motion for summary judgment, a plaintiff must explain or attempt to resolve the disparity between the previous sworn statements and the allegations in the subsequent ADA action. This explanation must be "sufficient to warrant a reasonable juror's concluding that, assuming the truth of * * * the earlier statement, the plaintiff could nonetheless perform the essential functions of her job with or without reasonable accommodation." Merely filing a subsequent affidavit that contradicted the prior statements, the Court added, would not be enough to create a genuine issue of fact to survive summary judgment. The Court then reported that in her brief before it, the plaintiff explained the discrepancy by stating that the statements to the SSA did not consider the effect that a reasonable accommodation would have on her ability to perform essential job functions and that these statements were accurate at the time they were made. The Court remanded the case to the trial court for a determination of whether or not this explanation satisfied the newly articulated standard for defeating the defendant's motion for summary judgment.

In MOTLEY v. NEW JERSEY STATE POLICE, 196 F.3d 160 (3d Cir. 1999), cert. denied, 529 U.S. 1087, 120 S.Ct. 1719, 146 L.Ed.2d 641 (2000), the Third Circuit took this next step and upheld the trial court's grant of summary judgment dismissing the ADA claim of a police officer that had applied for and received disability benefits. The court emphasized that simply averring that the statutory schemes differ is not sufficient to meet the *Cleveland* standard for defeating a motion for summary judgment. Otherwise, the court reasoned, summary judgment never would be granted. Rather, the court continued, the plaintiff was obliged to provide some additional rationale to explain the apparent about-face between the statements in the disability application and the claim that he was "otherwise qualified" under the ADA. The court suggested that the plaintiff in *Cleveland* had met this standard by indicating that the statements made at the time of the disability application were correct then, but that her physical situation had changed by the time of the filing of the ADA action. Thus, it explained, not only had that plaintiff noted that the statutory standards were different, but she also had made a fact-based argument that her condition had changed during the applicable time periods and that this amounted to a sufficient explanation. In the instant case, however, the plaintiff did nothing more than assert the different statutory standards. His prior statement of complete and permanent disability was not a mere blanket statement checked on a box to obtain pension benefits; he had provided detailed descriptions of his injuries and their impact on his continued ability to work. Additionally his employer's medical board had examined him and concurred in his statement of permanent incapacity. Under these circumstances, the court concluded, the plaintiff had not sufficiently explained the contradiction and the trial court's grant of summary judgment against him on the ADA claim was upheld.

Should the Court's analysis in *Cleveland* also apply to an individual who after applying for disability benefits with the SSA subsequently challenges his termination under a statute other than the ADA, like, for example, the ADEA? See Detz v. Greiner Industries, Inc., 346 F.3d 109 (3d Cir.2003) (extending *Cleveland* judicial estoppel doctrine to terminated employee who sought and was awarded post-termination Social Security disability benefits on the basis of a claim of total disability-based inability to work and subsequently challenged his discharge under the ADEA).

The Seventh Circuit has applied the doctrine of estoppel (as opposed to judicial estoppel) to preclude an employee from seeking relief under the ADA on the basis of a position that was inconsistent with prior representations made to his employer (rather than to a court) in order to obtain benefits from that employer. *See* DeVito v. Chicago Park District, 270 F.3d 532 (7th Cir.2001).

3. Mendes Construction Co. permits all workers to retire at full pay after twenty years of service. Emily Lace chose to retire after working at Mendes for twenty-three years. One week after she retired, Emily was in an automobile accident that left her permanently disabled. A few months later, she received a letter from Mendes indicating that she would no longer receive her pension since she had become eligible for disability benefits from the SSA. In its motion to dismiss Lace's ADA complaint,

Mendes maintained that she was not a "qualified individual with a disability" and thus was not entitled to protection under the ADA, because she (1) was not an employee, and (2) no longer was qualified to perform the essential functions of her job. How should the court rule on this motion?

The circuits have divided on the question of whether a disabled *former* employee has standing to bring a Title I ADA claim. One group has concluded that a former employee who no longer can perform the essential functions of the former job does not meet the statutory "otherwise qualified" requirement. *See e.g.*, McKnight v. General Motors Corp., 550 F.3d 519 (6th Cir. 2008); and Weyer v. Twentieth Century Fox Films Corp., 198 F.3d 1104 (9th Cir. 2000). In *McKnight*, the court emphasized that the statute defines a qualified individual as one who "can perform" essential job functions and that this use of the present tense reflects Congress' intent to limit the application of the statute to individuals who were able to perform the job functions at the time of the alleged discrimination as well to situations where the plaintiff can establish that her disability was the motivation for the alleged discriminatory act. However, in CASTELLANO v. CITY OF NEW YORK, 142 F.3d 58 (2d Cir.), cert. denied, 525 U.S. 820, 119 S.Ct. 60, 142 L.Ed.2d 47 (1998), concluded that a disabled former employee could fall within the protections of the ADA. The court concluded that the "qualified individual with a disability" requirement was satisfied if the disabled former employee established that she had been able to perform the essential functions of the job while employed and, on that basis, had earned the post-employment fringe benefit. Since the fringe benefit was earned for actual service, whether a former employee could still perform the essential functions of the former job after termination of employment was irrelevant. To rule otherwise, the court explained, would permit an employer to engage in wholesale discrimination against disabled retirees the moment either they retired or no longer could perform the essential functions of their former jobs, a result that would conflict with the legislative purpose to provide comprehensive protection from disability-based discrimination in the provision of fringe benefits.

4.   Lauren Picot contracted an extremely rare, but fatal disease while on vacation in the jungles of South America. When she returned to work, she informed her supervisor of her situation, but also provided a letter from her physician stating that Lauren remained fully capable of performing all of her job functions and that the risk of transmitting this disease to others was "remote, though not nonexistent." The supervisor informed the company president, who discharged Picot because of the risk she posed to everyone else in the company. Picot then brought suit under the ADA. The defendant filed a motion to dismiss the case on the ground that since Picot posed a direct threat to the safety and health of others in the workplace, she was not a "qualified individual with a disability" and therefore is not protected by the ADA.

(a)   Which party bears the burden of establishing that Lauren constitutes a direct threat to the safety and health of others? Is this part of the plaintiff's prima facie case of proving that she is a "qualified person with a disability" or is it an affirmative defense as to which the defendant bears the burden of persuasion? In answering this question, consider the fact that the sole reference to "direct threat" in the ADA (other than in §101(3), where it is defined) is found in §103(b) — entitled "Defenses" — which permits an employer to require, as a qualification for employment, that an individual not pose a direct threat to the health or safety of others.

Most, though not all, federal appellate courts have treated the existence of a "direct threat" as an affirmative defense, predominantly because its codification in a provision located under the heading of "Defenses". *Compare* Branham v. Show, 392 F.3d 896 (7ᵗʰ Cir. 2005) (direct threat is an affirmative defense as to which the defendant bears the evidentiary burden); *and* Rizzo v. Children's World Learning Centers, Inc., 213 F.3d 209 (5th Cir.) (*en banc*), cert. denied, 531 U.S. 958, 121 S.Ct. 382, 148 L.Ed.2d 294 (2000) (Id.) *with* EEOC v. Amego, Inc., 110 F.3d 135 (1st Cir.1997) (an individual who poses a direct threat is not "qualified" for the job and, therefore, this is an essential element of the plaintiff's prima facie case).

There is yet a further split among those courts that characterize this an affirmative defense. Although most of these courts place the burden of persuasion on the defendant as to the existence of a direct threat regardless of the circumstances, see e.g., Moses v. American Nonwovens, Inc., 97 F.3d 446 (11th Cir.1996), cert. denied, 519 U.S. 1118, 117 S.Ct. 964, 136 L.Ed.2d 849 (1997), a few circuits have ruled that the burden of persuasion should fall on the plaintiff when the essential job duties of her position necessarily implicate the safety of others. In McKENZIE v. BENTON, 388 F.3d 1342 (10th Cir.2004), cert. denied, 544 U.S. 1048, 125 S.Ct. 2294, 161 L.Ed.2d 1088 (2005), for example, the plaintiff was a deputy sheriff who suffered from a variety of psychological disorders, including post-traumatic stress disorder related to childhood sexual abuse by her father. One day after the plaintiff fired six rounds from her off-duty revolver into the ground at her father's grave, she was placed on leave. She subsequently suffered serious self-inflicted wounds and drug overdoses requiring hospitalization. She resigned to seek psychological care, but when she later applied for reinstatement, the Sheriff denied her request and she filed a claim under the ADA. After the trial judge's grant of summary judgment in favor of the defendant was reversed on appeal, the jury found that although the plaintiff had been discriminated against because of her disability, she also posed a direct threat to herself or others and was therefore not qualified to be a police officer. On appeal, the plaintiff maintained that the trial court had erred in instructing the jury that she, rather than her employer, bore the burden of proving that she did not pose a direct threat to herself or others. The Tenth Circuit affirmed the jury verdict and upheld the trial court's instruction. It reasoned that in light of the plaintiff's history of erratic behavior, she posed a special risk to co-workers and to the members of the public who were exposed to the danger of a firearm in her control. And since the job qualifications of a police officer included the essential function of performing duties without endangering co-workers or members of the public with whom the officer came into contact, it was proper for the trial court to require the plaintiff to prove that she was not a direct threat in order to establish her claim of disability-based discrimination.

(b) How should the court rule on the merits of the motion to dismiss Lauren's claim? The issue of whether an individual poses a direct threat to the health and safety of others is particularly thorny when the communicability of a disease is either unknown or uncertain. For many years, this issue dogged the courts in the context of the treatment of HIV-infected individuals. In Section A of this Chapter, we reproduced that portion of the Supreme Court's ruling in *Bragdon* dealing with whether an HIV-infected individual is "disabled" within the meaning of the ADA. But the defendant dentist in that case also justified his refusal to treat the plaintiff in his office on the ground that she posed a direct threat to his health and safety. Here is the other portion of the Court's opinion that instructs the lower courts on how to evaluate the level of risk associated with a plaintiff's disability.

Bragdon v. Abbott

Supreme Court of the United States, 1998.
524 U.S. 624, 118 S.Ct. 2196, 141 L.Ed.2d 540.

KENNEDY, J., delivered the opinion of the Court, in which STEVENS, SOUTER, GINSBURG, and BREYER, JJ., joined. STEVENS, J., filed a concurring opinion, in which BREYER, J., joined. GINSBURG, J., filed a concurring opinion. REHNQUIST, C. J., filed an opinion concurring in the judgment in part and dissenting in part, in which SCALIA and THOMAS, JJ., joined, and in Part II of which O'CONNOR, J., joined. O'CONNOR, J., filed an opinion concurring in the judgment in part and dissenting in part.

MR. JUSTICE KENNEDY delivered the opinion of the Court.

We address * * * whether the Court of Appeals, in affirming a grant of summary judgment, cited sufficient material in the record to determine, as a matter of law, that respondent's infection with HIV posed no direct threat to the health and safety of her treating dentist.

I

* * *

* * * The District Court ruled in favor of the plaintiffs, holding that respondent's HIV infection satisfied the ADA's definition of disability. The court held further that petitioner raised no genuine issue of material fact as to whether respondent's HIV infection would have posed a direct threat to the health or safety of others during the course of a dental treatment. The court relied on affidavits submitted by Dr. Donald Wayne Marianos, Director of the Division of Oral Health of the Centers for Disease Control and Prevention (CDC). The Marianos affidavits asserted it is safe for dentists to treat patients infected with HIV in dental offices if the dentist follows the so-called universal precautions described in the Recommended Infection-Control Practices for Dentistry issued by CDC in 1993 (1993 CDC Dentistry Guidelines).

The Court of Appeals affirmed. It held respondent's HIV infection was a disability under the ADA, even though her infection had not yet progressed to the symptomatic stage. 107 F.3d 934, 939-943 (C.A.1 1997). The Court of Appeals also agreed that treating the respondent in petitioner's office would not have posed a direct threat to the health and safety of others. Unlike the District Court, however, the Court of Appeals declined to rely on the Marianos affidavits. Instead the court relied on the 1993 CDC Dentistry Guidelines, as well as the Policy on AIDS, HIV Infection and the Practice of Dentistry, promulgated by the American Dental Association in 1991 (1991 American Dental Association Policy on HIV).

* * *

III

The petition for certiorari presented three other questions for review. The questions stated:

"3. When deciding under title III of the ADA whether a private health care provider must perform invasive procedures on an infectious patient in his office, should courts defer to the health care provider's professional judgment, as long as it is reasonable in light of then-current medical knowledge?

"4. What is the proper standard of judicial review under Title III of the ADA of a private health care provider's judgment that the performance of certain invasive procedures in his office would pose a direct threat to the health or safety of others?

"5. Did petitioner, Randon Bragdon, D.M.D., raise a genuine issue of fact for trial as to whether he was warranted in his judgment that the performance of certain invasive procedures on a patient in his office would have posed a direct threat to the health or safety of others?"

Of these, we granted certiorari only on question three. The question is phrased in an awkward way, for it conflates two separate inquiries. In asking whether it is appropriate to defer to petitioner's judgment, it assumes that petitioner's assessment of the objective facts was reasonable. The central premise of the question and the assumption on which it is based merit separate consideration.

Again, we begin with the statute. Notwithstanding the protection given respondent by the ADA's definition of disability, petitioner could have refused to treat her if her infectious condition "pose[d] a direct threat to the health or safety of others." The ADA defines a direct threat to be "a significant risk to the health or safety of others that cannot be eliminated by a modification of policies, practices, or procedures or by the provision of auxiliary aids or services." * * *

The ADA's direct threat provision stems from the recognition in School Bd. of Nassau Cty. v. Arline, 480 U.S. 273, 107 S.Ct. 1123, 94 L.Ed.2d 307 (1987), of the importance of prohibiting discrimination against individuals with disabilities while protecting others from significant health and safety risks, resulting, for instance, from a contagious disease. In Arline, the Court reconciled these objectives by construing the Rehabilitation Act not to require the hiring of a person who posed "a significant risk of communicating an infectious disease to others." Congress amended the Rehabilitation Act and the Fair Housing Act to incorporate the language. It later relied on the same language in enacting the ADA. Because few, if any, activities in life are risk free, Arline and the ADA do not ask whether a risk exists, but whether it is significant.

The existence, or nonexistence, of a significant risk must be determined from the standpoint of the person who refuses the treatment or accommodation, and the risk assessment must be based on medical or other objective evidence. As a health care professional, petitioner had the duty to assess the risk of infection based on the objective, scientific information available to him and others in his profession. His belief that a significant risk existed, even if maintained in good faith, would not relieve him from liability. To use the words of the question presented, petitioner receives no special deference simply because he is a health care professional. It is true that Arline reserved "the question whether courts should also defer to the reasonable medical judgments of private physicians on which an employer has relied." At most, this statement reserved the possibility that employers could consult with individual physicians as objective third-party experts. It did not suggest that an individual physician's state of mind could excuse discrimination without regard to the objective reasonableness of his actions.

Our conclusion that courts should assess the objective reasonableness of the views of health care professionals without deferring to their individual judgments does not answer the implicit assumption in the question presented, whether petitioner's actions were reasonable in light of the available medical evidence. In assessing the reasonableness of petitioner's actions, the views of public health authorities, such as the U.S. Public Health Service, CDC, and the National Institutes of Health, are of special weight and authority. The views of these organizations are not conclusive, however. A health care professional who disagrees with the prevailing medical consensus may refute it by citing a credible scientific basis for deviating from the accepted norm.

We have reviewed so much of the record as necessary to illustrate the application of the rule to the facts of this case. For the most part, the Court of Appeals followed the proper standard in evaluating the petitioner's position and conducted a thorough review of the evidence. Its rejection of the District Court's reliance on the Marianos affidavits was a correct application of the principle that petitioner's actions must be evaluated in light of the available, objective evidence. The record did not show that CDC had published the conclusion set out in the affidavits at the time petitioner refused to treat respondent.

A further illustration of a correct application of the objective standard is the Court of Appeals' refusal to give weight to the petitioner's offer to treat respondent in a hospital. Petitioner testified that he believed hospitals had safety measures, such as air filtration, ultraviolet lights, and respirators, which would reduce the risk of HIV transmission. Petitioner made no showing, however, that any area hospital had these safeguards or even that he had hospital privileges. His expert also admitted the lack of any scientific basis for the conclusion that these measures would lower the risk of transmission. Petitioner failed to present any objective, medical evidence showing that treating respondent in a hospital would be safer or more efficient in preventing HIV transmission than treatment in a well-equipped dental office.

We are concerned, however, that the Court of Appeals might have placed mistaken reliance upon two other sources. In ruling no triable issue of fact existed on this point, the Court of Appeals relied on the 1993 CDC Dentistry Guidelines and the 1991 American Dental Association Policy on HIV. This evidence is not definitive. As noted earlier, the CDC Guidelines recommended certain universal precautions which, in CDC's view, "should reduce the risk of disease transmission in the dental environment." The Court of Appeals determined that, "[w]hile the guidelines do not state explicitly that no further risk-reduction measures are desirable or that routine dental care for HIV-positive individuals is safe, those two conclusions seem to be implicit in the guidelines' detailed delineation of procedures for office treatment of HIV- positive patients." In our view, the Guidelines do not necessarily contain implicit assumptions conclusive of the point to be decided. The Guidelines set out CDC's recommendation that the universal precautions are the best way to combat the risk of HIV transmission. They do not assess the level of risk.

Nor can we be certain, on this record, whether the 1991 American Dental Association Policy on HIV carries the weight the Court of Appeals attributed to it.

The Policy does provide some evidence of the medical community's objective assessment of the risks posed by treating people infected with HIV in dental offices. It indicates:

> "Current scientific and epidemiologic evidence indicates that there is little risk of transmission of infectious diseases through dental treatment if recommended infection control procedures are routinely followed. Patients with HIV infection may be safely treated in private dental offices when appropriate infection control procedures are employed. Such infection control procedures provide protection both for patients and dental personnel."

We note, however, that the Association is a professional organization, which, although a respected source of information on the dental profession, is not a public health authority. It is not clear the extent to which the Policy was based on the Association's assessment of dentists' ethical and professional duties in addition to its scientific assessment of the risk to which the ADA refers. Efforts to clarify dentists' ethical obligations and to encourage dentists to treat patients with HIV infection with compassion may be commendable, but the question under the statute is one of statistical likelihood, not professional responsibility. Without more information on the manner in which the American Dental Association formulated this Policy, we are unable to determine the Policy's value in evaluating whether petitioner's assessment of the risks was reasonable as a matter of law.

The court considered materials submitted by both parties on the cross motions for summary judgment. The petitioner was required to establish that there existed a genuine issue of material fact. Evidence which was merely colorable or not significantly probative would not have been sufficient.

We acknowledge the presence of other evidence in the record before the Court of Appeals which, subject to further arguments and examination, might support affirmance of the trial court's ruling. For instance, the record contains substantial testimony from numerous health experts indicating that it is safe to treat patients infected with HIV in dental offices. We are unable to determine the import of this evidence, however. The record does not disclose whether the expert testimony submitted by respondent turned on evidence available in September 1994.

There are reasons to doubt whether petitioner advanced evidence sufficient to raise a triable issue of fact on the significance of the risk. Petitioner relied on two principal points: First, he asserted that the use of high-speed drills and surface cooling with water created a risk of airborne HIV transmission. The study on which petitioner relied was inconclusive, however, determining only that "[f]urther work is required to determine whether such a risk exists." Petitioner's expert witness conceded, moreover, that no evidence suggested the spray could transmit HIV. His opinion on airborne risk was based on the absence of contrary evidence, not on positive data. Scientific evidence and expert testimony must have a traceable, analytical basis in objective fact before it may be considered on summary judgment.

Second, petitioner argues that, as of September 1994, CDC had identified seven dental workers with possible occupational transmission of HIV. These dental workers were exposed to HIV in the course of their employment, but CDC could not determine whether HIV infection had resulted. It is now known that CDC could not ascertain whether the seven dental workers contracted the disease because they did not present themselves for HIV testing at an appropriate time after their initial exposure. It is not clear on this record, however, whether this information was available to petitioner in September 1994. If not, the seven cases might have provided some, albeit not necessarily sufficient, support for petitioner's position. Standing alone, we doubt it would meet the objective, scientific basis for finding a significant risk to the petitioner.

Our evaluation of the evidence is constrained by the fact that on these and other points we have not had briefs and arguments directed to the entire record. In accepting the case for review, we declined to grant certiorari on question five, which asked whether petitioner raised a genuine issue of fact for trial. As a result, the briefs and arguments presented to us did not concentrate on the question of sufficiency in light all of the submissions in the summary judgment proceeding. * * * Resolution of the issue will be of importance to health care workers not just for the result but also for the precision and comprehensiveness of the reasons given for the decision.

We conclude the proper course is to give the Court of Appeals the opportunity to determine whether our analysis of some of the studies cited by the parties would change its conclusion that petitioner presented neither objective evidence nor a triable issue of fact on the question of risk. In remanding the case, we do not foreclose the possibility that the Court of Appeals may reach the same conclusion it did earlier. A remand will permit a full exploration of the issue through the adversary process.

* * * The judgment is vacated, and the case is remanded for further proceedings consistent with this opinion.

NOTES AND PROBLEMS FOR DISCUSSION

1. On remand, the First Circuit reaffirmed its prior decision upholding the trial court's rejection of the defendant's "direct threat" defense on the ground that he had not raised a genuine issue of fact on this issue and, therefore, that the plaintiff remained entitled to judgment as a matter of law. Abbott v. Bragdon, 163 F.3d 87 (1st Cir.1998), cert. denied, 526 U.S. 1131, 119 S.Ct. 1805, 143 L.Ed.2d 1009 (1999).

2. Is the "direct threat" defense limited to threats posed by the plaintiff to others in the workplace? For example:

(a) Can an employer refuse to hire a disabled individual because the employer reasonably concludes that employment will constitute a direct threat to that applicant's own health? The EEOC regulations state that "direct threat" encompasses a direct threat to the health or safety of "the individual or others" in the workplace. 29 CFR §1630.15(b)(2) (1999). Does this regulation fairly interpret the statutory language?

In CHEVRON v. ECHAZABAL, 536 U.S. 73, 122 S.Ct. 2045, 153 L.Ed.2d 82 (2002), the Supreme Court resolved a conflict between the circuits on this precise question. In *Echazabal*, the Ninth Circuit, relying on the interpretative canon *expressio unius exclusio alterius* (expressing one item of an associated group or series excludes another left unmentioned), reversed the trial court's grant of summary judgment to the employer. The court of appeals held that the express limitation in the "direct threat" defense to threats to others rendered that defense unavailable to employment decisions based on a perceived threat to the disabled employee himself and, therefore, that the EEOC regulation could not be enforced. The Supreme Court unanimously reversed, holding that the EEOC regulation constituted a reasonable (and, therefore, permissible) interpretation of the statutory language and that the *expressio unius* canon was inapplicable in this instance for three reasons.

First, the Court explained, interpreting the reference to harm to others to exclude decisions based on harm to the disabled individual was inconsistent with the statutory text. Although §103(a) provides defendants with an affirmative defense when a "qualification standard" that excludes a disabled individual can be shown to be job–related and consistent with business necessity, §103(b) expands upon that defense by stating that such a qualification standard "may" include a requirement that an individual not pose a direct threat of harm to others. Congress' use of "may" in this context, the Court reasoned, indicated that harm to others was intended to be an illustrative, but non-exclusive example of a standard that could meet the job-related/business necessity defense.

Second, the Court pointed to the fact that the Rehabilitation Act, like the subsequently enacted ADA, similarly referred to direct threats to others without saying anything about threats to self. And the EEOC guidelines interpreting the Rehabilitation Act, like those interpreting the ADA, construed that language to extend to harm to self. Although the plaintiff argued that Congress' decision to exclude a direct reference to threat to self in the ADA suggested its rejection of the EEOC's construction of the Rehabilitation Act, the Court found the opposite inference equally plausible — i.e., that Congress assumed that "the agency was free to do under the ADA what it had already done under the earlier Act's identical language." Consequently, it was not prepared to draw the negative inference mandated by the *expressio unius* canon.

The third strike against invoking the negative inference to limit the defense to avoiding harm to others in the workplace, the Court reasoned, was that it was inconsistent with a common sense reading of the statute, since, for example, it would necessarily preclude an employer from excluding disabled individuals whose disability threatened others outside the workplace. And this, the Court insisted, was a result that the Congress could not possibly have intended.

Finally, the Court rejected the Ninth Circuit's notion that extending the defense to harm to self would constitute the type of paternalistic attitude towards disabled individuals that the statute was designed to preclude. Acknowledging that Congress clearly had workplace paternalism in its sights when it passed the ADA, the Court nevertheless concluded that the legislature did not intend to limit an employer's refusal to subject disabled individuals to specifically demonstrated risks. Rather, it reasoned, the statute was intended to prevent employers from relying on untested and pretextual stereotypes. But since the direct threat defense must be based on reasonable medical judgments and an individualized assessment of the individual's present ability to safely perform the essential functions of the jobs, extending that defense to harm to self would not sanction the evil that Congress intended to eliminate. The case was remanded for determination of whether the defendant met the requirements for assertion of the "direct threat" defense.

On remand, the Ninth Circuit reversed the trial court's grant of summary judgment to the defendant. Echazabal v. Chevron, USA, Inc., 336 F.3d 1023 (9th Cir. 2003). The appellate court ruled that a genuine issue of fact remained as to whether or not the company's assessment of the threat to the plaintiff's own health and safety was based on a reasonable medical judgment that relied on the most current medical knowledge and/or the best available objective evidence since (1) the company relied solely on physicians who did not possess expertise in liver disease (the plaintiff suffered from chronic hepatitis C); and (2) the plaintiff had offered testimony from liver specialists indicating that the job posed only a minimal risk to him.

(b) Suppose that a non-disabled employee is discharged because he brings his disabled son onto company property and the son's mental disability poses a threat to the security of others in the workplace. Has the employer violated the ADA, or would it have to establish that the employee himself created a direct threat to the safety of others in the workplace? Is it significant, in this regard, that the statutory reference to "direct threat" does not explicitly refer to direct threats caused by the disabled relatives or associates of non-disabled employees? *See* Den Hartog v. Wasatch Academy, 129 F.3d 1076 (10th Cir. 1997) ("direct threat" defense is applicable to disabled relative or associate of non-disabled employee).

3. The definition of "direct threat" in §101(3) is expressly limited to risks "that cannot be eliminated by reasonable accommodation." Consequently, it is not enough merely to determine whether the plaintiff creates a risk in the abstract. The court must evaluate whether that risk can be "eliminated" by a "reasonable" accommodation. In DOE v. UNIVERSITY OF MARYLAND MEDICAL SYSTEM CORPORATION, 50 F.3d 1261 (4th Cir. 1995), the appellate court upheld the defendant's decision to terminate the plaintiff's neurosurgical residency after he became infected with HIV while treating an infected patient. The defendant Medical Center initially asked a panel of experts on blood-borne pathogens to evaluate the plaintiff's condition and the panel had recommended that Dr. Doe be allowed to return to surgical practice with the exception of certain specific procedures involving the use of exposed wire. After considering its panel's recommendation, however, the defendant permanently suspended Dr. Doe from surgical practice and offered him alternative residencies in non-surgical fields. He refused the alternatives and filed suit under, *inter alia*, the ADA. The only issue before the court was whether the plaintiff created a serious risk to others and, therefore, was not an "otherwise qualified" individual with a disability. The court reasoned that although there was no presently documented case of surgeon-to-patient transmission, such transmission was possible and could not be eliminated through reasonable accommodation. Thus, even though the possibility of transmission was remote, the potential consequences were so devastating that the plaintiff did pose a significant risk to the health or safety of his patients that could not be eliminated by reasonable accommodation. The court noted that the Recommendations of the Center for Disease Control provided that hospitals should be permitted to bar HIV-positive surgeons from performing procedures identified by the hospital as "exposure prone." Since the defendant Medical Center reasonably had concluded that all neurosurgical procedures were within the category of such exposure-prone procedures, the court determined that its decision to terminate this HIV-positive neurosurgical resident based upon the risk of transmission of the disease during the performance of exposure-prone procedures did not violate either the Rehabilitation Act or the ADA.

4. As one of several manifestations of his severe depressive disorder, Simon Templar issued a threat to the physical well-being of one of his co-workers in a conversation with another co-worker that was overheard by the intended target of the threat. Upon hearing of the threat, Templar's supervisor terminated Templar's employment. In response to Templar's subsequent ADA action, the defendant moved for summary judgment on the alternative grounds that the existence of this inappropriate conduct either rendered Templar a direct threat to the health or safety of others as a matter of law (and therefore not "otherwise qualified" to continue his employment), or constituted a legitimate nondiscriminatory explanation for its decision. How should the court rule? In SISTA v. CDC IXIS NORTH AMERICA, INC., 445 F.3d 161 (2d Cir. 2006), the trial court had granted summary judgment to the defendant on both of these grounds. The Second Circuit ruled that the trial court erred in holding that the plaintiff was not otherwise qualified because he posed a direct threat to his co-workers. It declared that the trial court should have distinguished between "posing" a threat and "making" a threat. Here, the plaintiff made a threat and that conduct constituted a legitimate, nondiscriminatory explanation for the employer's decision. And though, at this stage of the proceedings, it was not possible to determine with certainty whether the plaintiff could establish a prima facie showing of discrimination, since the actual threat constituted a nondiscriminatory explanation as a matter of law and the plaintiff had offered no evidence from which a reasonable jury could conclude that he had been fired because of his mental illness rather than as a consequence of his behavior, the Second Circuit nonetheless upheld the trial court's granting of summary judgment.

4. THE DUAL DUTY OF NONDISCRIMINATION

Section 102(a) sets forth the basic nondiscrimination commandment of the ADA in language strikingly parallel to that found in Title VII. It provides that a covered entity shall not discriminate against a qualified individual with a disability with respect to all terms and conditions of employment. And in §102(b), in terminology that also tracks the text of Title VII, it describes a range of employment practices and policies that could result in forbidden discrimination. The plain language of this provision, coupled with its incorporation of Title VII terminology, reflects Congress' intention that ADA plaintiffs be armed with both disparate treatment and disproportionate impact-based causes of action. Not surprisingly, the courts in ADA cases lean heavily on Title VII jurisprudence in analyzing such claims.

Sometimes, however, the line of demarcation between claims of intentional and impact-based discrimination are blurred. In RAYTHEON CO. v. HERNANDEZ, 540 U.S. 44, 124 S.Ct. 513, 157 L.Ed.2d 357 (2003), an employee with 25 years seniority was fired for violating company rules when he tested positive for cocaine. Two years later, after regularly attending Alcoholics Anonymous meetings, he applied to be rehired. The company had a blanket policy of refusing to rehire any former employee who had previously been discharged for violating a company rule. Pursuant to that policy, the man was not rehired. He brought an ADA claim alleging only that he had been denied reemployment because of his record of past drug use. The trial court granted the defense motion for summary judgment on the plaintiff's disparate treatment claim. Although the plaintiff asserted, in response to the summary judgment motion, that the defendant's reliance on its no-rehire policy would disproportionately impact rehabilitated individuals whose discharge was based on drug use, the trial court refused to consider the disproportionate impact argument because the plaintiff had failed to plead or raise it in a timely manner.

The Ninth Circuit agreed with the trial court that the plaintiff had failed to timely raise his disproportionate impact claim. Nevertheless, it reversed the summary judgment on the ground that the defendant's proffered explanation (reliance on its neutral no-rehire rule), as a matter of law, did not constitute a nondiscriminatory explanation as applied to former drug addicts. In the appellate court's opinion, the application of this policy to reformed addicts who had been previously discharged because of their drug use would have a disproportionate impact on recovering drug users.

By a 7-0 vote (Justices Breyer and Souter did not participate in the case), the Supreme Court unanimously reversed the Ninth Circuit. The Court, in an opinion authored by Justice Thomas, ruled that after acknowledging that the plaintiff had waived his right to bring a disproportionate impact claim, the Ninth Circuit nevertheless let impact analysis in through the back door by incorporating impact analysis into its treatment of the defendant's legitimate, nondiscriminatory response defense to the plaintiff's disparate treatment claim of disability-based discrimination. The proper approach, the Supreme Court explained, would have been to hold that this no-rehire policy constituted a legitimate, nondiscriminatory explanation, and then to focus on whether or not the defendant actually relied on this or whether this was merely a pretext for discrimination. The Court remanded the case for further proceedings consistent with that ruling. On remand, the Ninth Circuit reversed the trial court's grant of summary judgment to the defendant on the ground that the plaintiff had raised a genuine issue of fact as to whether his termination had been based on the employer's application of the no-rehire rule. Hernandez v. Hughes Missile Systems Co., 362 F.3d 564 (9th Cir. 2004). Subsequently, in an entirely separate case, the Ninth Circuit ruled on the merits of such an intentional discrimination claim. In LOPEZ v. PACIFIC MARITIME ASS'N, 657 F.3d 762 (9th Cir. 2011), the appellate panel ruled that an employer's "one-strike rule", which *permanently* eliminated from employment any applicant who had a single positive result on a test for drug or alcohol use during the pre-employment screening process did not discriminate against recovering or recovered drug addicts. The court explained that this rule eliminated all candidates who tested positive, regardless of whether the cause of the positive test was addiction or a decision to try drugs for the first time the day before the test. The court similarly rejected the plaintiff's claim that the one-strike rule produced a disparate impact on recovering drug addicts. As to this claim, the court found that the plaintiff had not proffered evidence establishing that the one-strike rule resulted in a smaller proportion of recovered drug addicts being employed as compared to the proportion of qualified recovered drug addicts in the relevant labor market.

Section 102(b)(5) also includes the failure to make a reasonable accommodation among its list of forbidden practices. So, much (but not precisely, as we shall see) like the treatment of religious discrimination under Title VII, the duty not to discriminate against the disabled imposes a dual obligation on covered entitles. On the one hand, they are obliged not to take adverse action against disabled individuals on the basis of their disabilities. But, simultaneously, they also have an affirmative obligation to make "reasonable" accommodations to the disability of disabled individuals where this will allow the disabled individuals to perform the essential functions of their job while not imposing an undue hardship on the employer.

(a) The Antidiscrimination Mandate

Many of the issues raised in connection with allegations of intentional and impact-based discrimination on the basis of disability are analogous to those previously discussed in connection with Title VII and the ADEA and, therefore, will not be repeated here. However, there is one in which the ADA is unlike all other antidiscrimination statutes. A totally unique feature of the ADA is its prohibition against "associational discrimination." In the following Notes, we will examine the nature of associational discrimination. These materials also will focus on two elements of a plaintiff's prima facie showing in intentional discrimination cases that create unusual analytical problems in the disability context — the requirement that she establish (1) that the defendant took some form of adverse action against her; and (2) that this adverse action was causally linked to her disability.

NOTES AND PROBLEMS FOR DISCUSSION

1. Section 102(b)(4) prohibits discrimination against any individual because of that person's relationship to or association with someone with a known disability. Although neither the statute nor the EEOC's interpretive guidelines define the nature of a qualifying "association," they do state that the purpose of this provision is to prevent conduct predicated upon unfounded stereotypes about persons who associate with disabled individuals. Moreover, the guidelines include a collection of examples of proscribed associational discrimination, not all of which are limited to familial relationships. Most associational discrimination claims fall into one or more of these three categories: (1) expense claims — where the employer is alleged to have discriminated against an employee because that employee's association (typically familial) with a disabled individual imposed significant costs (usually in connection with an employer's health or disability plan) on the employer; (2) distraction claims — where the employer is alleged to have discriminated against an employee out of concern that the employee would be distracted from work by obligations (such as caring for) to a disabled person with whom the employee is associated; or (3) disability by association claims — where the employer is alleged to have discriminated against an employee because the employer is concerned that the employee would develop a disabling condition (such as an infection or disease) because of the employee's relationship to a disabled individual. But regardless of the nature of the associational discrimination claim, the plaintiff must establish causation, i.e., that she was disadvantaged because of her association with a disabled person. In DEWITT v. PROCTOR HOSPITAL, 517 F.3d 944 (7th Cir. 2008), the plaintiff alleged that she had been fired because the employer wanted to be relieved of the obligation under its self-insured health insurance plan to pay for the medical costs incurred by her cancer-infected husband. The Seventh Circuit panel reversed the trial judge's issuance of summary judgment in favor of the defendant. The court concluded that the plaintiff had offered sufficient evidence to permit a reasonable jury to infer that the discharge decision was motivated by a desire to avoid having to continue to pay for medical costs incurred by the plaintiff's husband. In a concurring opinion, Judge Posner agreed that the trial court had erred in not letting a jury consider the claim. But he also stated that in an "expense" form of associational discrimination claim such as the case at bar, if the employer would have taken adverse action against an employee simply to avoid paying the medical costs incurred by that employee's *nondisabled* dependent, that would not be constitute disability-based discrimination. And though the instant case seemed to fall into that category, Posner concluded that since this defendant never raised that argument, reversal was proper. He also noted, however, that the defendant should feel free to assert that defense at trial on remand.

The circuit courts agree that under the limited language of §102(b)(4), although a non-disabled individual enjoys a right to be free from discrimination in the form of an adverse action taken because of that person's relationship to or association with someone with a known disability, that non-disabled individual does *not* enjoy a statutory right to an accommodation. *See* Erdman v. Nationwide Insurance Co., 582 F.3d 500 (3d Cir. 2009) (employee with disabled family member is not entitled to accommodation to deal with relative's disability, but only to freedom from discrimination because of association with a disabled person; decision to terminate employee who requests time off to deal with needs of disabled child does not constitute protected "associational" discrimination unless plaintiff can show that employer would not have fired an employee who requested time off for some other purpose).

Suppose an employee was discharged for engaging in public advocacy on behalf of individuals with AIDS. Could that person state an association-based claim under the ADA? *See* Oliveras-Sifre v. Puerto Rico Health Dep't, 214 F.3d 23 (1st Cir. 2000) (advocacy does not constitute a covered form of "association"; rather, the statute requires the plaintiff to allege some specific relationship with a particular a disabled individual).

2. In DOE v. DEKALB COUNTY SCHOOL DIST., 145 F.3d 1441 (11th Cir. 1998), the school district transferred the plaintiff, who was infected with HIV, from a classroom of children with severe behavior disorders to a classroom of children with mild disorders at a different school. The school's explanation was that it feared that the plaintiff might have blood-to-blood contact with one of the sometimes-violent students. It also argued that the transfer did not constitute an "adverse employment action" and, therefore, that the plaintiff could not state a prima facie claim under the ADA. The court noted that no panel in its circuit had previously examined whether a court should view an employment action from the subjective perspective of the plaintiff or the objective perspective of a reasonable person. The panel in this case instructed the trial judge to apply the objective standard, i.e., to determine whether a reasonable person in the plaintiff's position would view the employment action in question as adverse. This choice, the panel reasoned, was consistent with the use of an objective standard in related employment issues, such as the doctrine of constructive discharge and reasonable accommodation. It then remanded the case to the trial court for a determination of whether the plaintiff's lateral transfer constituted an adverse action.

3. Can a plaintiff state an ADA claim of disability-based harassment creating a hostile environment? *See, e.g.*, Shaver v. Independent Stave Co., 350 F.3d 716 (8th Cir. 2003) (recognizing a hostile work environment claim under the ADA and incorporating Title VII jurisprudence).

4. Section 102 of the ADA states that the plaintiff must establish that the defendant discriminated against her "because of" her disability. Section 504(a) of the

Rehabilitation Act, on the other hand, states that a qualified individual with a disability shall not be discriminated against "solely by reason of" her disability.

(a) In light of the language in §501(a) of the ADA providing that "nothing in this chapter shall be construed to apply a lesser standard than the standards applied under Title V of the Rehabilitation Act," should an ADA plaintiff, like a §504 Rehabilitation Act claimant, have to prove that the employer acted solely because of her disability, or should the mixed motive analysis employed in Title VII cases be extended to ADA claims? The prevailing view, adopted in nearly all of the federal circuits, is reflected in PARKER v. COLUMBIA PICTURES INDUSTRIES, 204 F.3d 326 (2d Cir. 2000). There, the Second Circuit concluded that the absence of the word "solely" in the ADA trumped the ADA provision linking its interpretation to that of the Rehabilitation Act and, the court reasoned, suggested "forcefully" that Congress intended the statute to cover situations in which discrimination on the basis of disability is one, but not the only factor motivating an adverse employment action. *But see* Lewis v. Humboldt Acquisition Corp. Inc., 634 F.3d 879 (6th Cir. 2011) recognizing that a "super-majority" of circuits reject "sole reason" standard but adhering to circuit precedent that ADA claims should be analyzed consistently with claims brought under Rehabilitation Act).

This, however, does not necessarily resolve the issue of the availability of mixed motive analysis in ADA cases. Section 107, the enforcement provision of the ADA, provides that the "remedies and procedures" set forth in §§705-709 of Title VII shall govern cases filed under Title I of the ADA. Does this incorporation of Title VII remedies incorporate the mixed-motive language that was added to Title VII, but not to the ADA, by the 1991 Civil Rights Act? Moreover, do the Supreme Court's rulings in *Gross* and *Nassar* that mixed motive analysis is inapplicable to claims brought under the ADEA and the anti-retaliation provision(§704(a)) of Title VII shed any light on this question? In SERWATKA v. ROCKWELL AUTOMATION, INC., 591 F.3d 957 (7th Cir. 2010), the Seventh Circuit read *Gross* to mean that with respect to claims brought under any employment statute that was not expressly amended to codify mixed motive analysis, a mixed motive claim is not viable and the plaintiff must establish but-for causation. And as to the language in §107 of the ADA linking it to the enforcement provisions of Title VII, the court emphasized that the pertinent language of §107 referred only to the "remedies" available under §706 and not to liability established under §703. Consequently, it held, this linkage provision did not incorporate the codification of mixed motive analysis found in §703(m) of Title VII as amended by the 1991 Civil Rights Act. Accordingly, it ruled that mixed motive claims were not cognizable under the ADA and vacated a mixed motive judgment that the trial court had entered in favor of the plaintiff based on the jury's answers to a special verdict form and directed the court to enter judgment in favor of the defendant.

(b) But if mixed motive analysis is available in ADA cases, should the content of that doctrine be drawn from the Supreme Court's ruling in *Price Waterhouse*, or the revised standard codified by the 1991 Civil Rights Act? Section 107(a) of the 1991 Act amendment, which partially reversed *Price Waterhouse*, does not refer to actions brought under the ADA. *See* Watson v. Southeastern Pennsylvania Transp. Authority, 207 F.3d 207 (3d Cir. 2000), cert. denied, 531 U.S. 1147, 121 S.Ct. 1086, 148 L.Ed.2d 961(2001) (applying §107(a) to a mixed motive claim in an ADA action).

5. Suppose that in response to a plaintiff's claim that she was discharged on the basis of her disability, the employer states that the supervisor who discharged the plaintiff was the same individual that had hired her and that this supervisor was aware of the plaintiff's disability when she was hired. To what extent does, or should this evidence support the defendant's claim that discrimination did not motivate the discharge? *See* Susie v. Apple Tree Preschool, 866 F. Supp. 390 (N.D. Iowa 1994) (because the scope and nature of an employee's disability may worsen over time, the scope and nature of the employer's duty to make a reasonable accommodation may also vary over time; accordingly, one may not want to infer a nondiscriminatory motive from the fact that the person hiring and firing are the same individual).

6. State University discharged one of its assistant football coaches after he was arrested for and charged with driving an automobile while under the influence of alcohol. The coach brought an action under the ADA, alleging that he was an alcoholic and that driving under the influence of alcohol was a manifestation of his statutorily protected disability of alcoholism. Should the court recognize this claim or should it dismiss the complaint on the ground that the plaintiff was not discharged *because of* his disability? The courts have not agreed on whether it is appropriate to separate an individual's disability from its consequences in determining whether that individual was discriminated against by reason of his or her disability. *Compare* Maddox v. University Of Tennessee, 62 F.3d 843 (6th Cir. 1995) (it is appropriate to distinguish between a disability and its consequences or otherwise an employer could be forced to accommodate otherwise criminal behavior related to alcoholism that it would not have to tolerate from a non-alcoholic; though the plaintiff's alcoholism may have compelled him to drink, it did not compel him to operate a motor vehicle while intoxicated), *and* Newland v. Dalton, 81 F.3d 904 (9th Cir. 1996) (a civilian Naval employee who was discharged for firing an assault rifle in a bar and who claimed that his conduct was a "drunken rampage" brought on by his alcoholism cannot state a claim because the discharge was based on misconduct and was not retribution for his alcoholism), *with* Den Hartog v. Wasatch Academy, 129 F.3d 1076 (10th Cir. 1997) (limiting the consequences/disability distinction to cases involving the consequences of alcoholism or illegal drug use; in cases involving the mental disability of bipolar disorder, the plaintiff should be viewed as a member of the protected class, subject to the defense that either the objectionable conduct prevents the plaintiff from performing the essential functions of the job with a reasonable accommodation, or that the continued presence of the individual at the workplace creates a direct threat to the health or safety of others).

7. Suppose an employer provides retirement benefits to those employees who retire after twenty years of service. A group of disabled employees, who were required to retire because of their disability, are denied pension benefits because they retired before they had met the twenty years of service requirement. Can they state a claim under the ADA? Were they denied a pension "because of" their disability? *See* Castellano v. New York, 142 F.3d 58 (2d Cir.), cert. denied, 525 U.S. 820, 119 S.Ct. 60, 142 L.Ed.2d 47 (1998) (the service-based requirement does not discriminate on the basis of disability since it excludes both disabled and nondisabled individuals who retire with less than twenty years of service).

8. Posin Labs, Inc. requires random drug testing of all employees. The company compels former drug addicts to be tested once every month while all other employees are subject to a random test approximately once every year. Dena Green, an employee who is a rehabilitated former addict, suffers from a medical condition that prevents her from urinating on demand. When asked to provide a urine sample for a random drug test, Dena could not provide the sample within the requisite time period. Consequently, she was fired for failing to provide the urine sample in a timely fashion. Assuming that it is not unlawful for an employer to require random drug tests of employees or to require more extensive testing of former addicts, has the employer nevertheless violated the ADA? *See* Buckley v. Consolidated Edison, 155 F.3d 150 (2d Cir. 1998) (*en banc*).

9. To some extent, disability claims are more like age-based claims than other forms of discrimination. Both of these classifications categorize individuals on a continuum in the sense that persons protected by the ADA can be more or less disabled just as the ADEA protects individuals of a range of ages. Suppose, for example, that a disabled individual is passed over for a promotion in favor of either a less disabled person, or someone whose disability required a less expensive method of accommodation. Could the person denied the promotion establish that the employer's decision was made "because of" her disability even though she was rejected in favor of another disabled individual? *See* Monette v. Electronic Data Systems Corp., 90 F.3d 1173 (6th Cir. 1996) (a plaintiff need not establish that he was replaced with a nondisabled individual; replacement of one disabled individual with someone with a different type or level of disability does not necessarily weaken the inference of discrimination on the basis of disability).

10. Section 503 of Title V of the ADA contains two anti-retaliation provisions. The first, codified at §503(a), mirrors the provisions of §704 of Title VII. The other, found at §503(b), prohibits conduct that coerces, intimidates, threatens, or interferes with any individual's exercise of rights provided under the ADA. Suppose that Jane Fuller sues her employer under the ADA claiming that she was discharged because of her disability. Shortly after receiving a copy of the complaint, her employer also fires Jane's son. Can he state a claim under the ADA? In FOGLEMAN v. MERCY HOSPITAL, INC., 283 F.3d 561 (3d Cir.2002), cert. denied, 537 U.S. 824, 123 S.Ct. 112, 154 L.Ed.2d 35 (2002), the Third Circuit held that §503*(a)* claims should be limited to individuals who personally participated in protective activity. The plain meaning of the text, the court reasoned, indicated that Congress intended to exclude third-party retaliation claims. However, the court added, since the text of §503*(b)* was more akin to §8(a)(1) of the National Labor Relations Act, it should be construed consistently with the NLRA, i.e., to permit a third party claim. Additionally, the court held that the son could state a retaliation claim under §503(a) by alleging that he was discharged because the defendant (wrongfully) perceived him to be engaged in protected activity. Consequently, it reversed the trial court's decision to dismiss that "perception theory" claim as a matter of law and remanded for further fact finding. Should this ruling survive the Court's 2011 decision in *Thompson v. North American Stainless*, where it held that third party harassment claims are cognizable under §704(a) of Title VII, depending upon the closeness of the relationship and the severity of the adverse reaction by the employer?

Suppose an employee's request for an accommodation is denied. Suppose further that the employee does not challenge that decision, but is subsequently terminated. Can the worker state a retaliation claim under the ADA, i.e., is requesting an accommodation, in the absence of the filing of any formal charge, protected activity? *See* Carreras v. Sajo, Garcia & Partners, 596 F.3d 25 (1st Cir. 2010) ("requesting an accommodation, without filing a formal charge or engaging in other * * * behaviors * * * is nonetheless behavior protected from an employer's retaliation").

Does a plaintiff asserting a retaliation claim under the ADA have to prove that he or she is disabled within the meaning of the statute? See Foster v. Mountain Coal Co., LLC, 830 F.3d 1178 (10th Cir. 2016)("in distinction from a claim of discrimination, a plaintiff asserting a claim of retaliation under the ADA "need not show that he suffers from an actual disability * * * [he] need only show that he had a reasonable, good faith belief that he was disabled.").

(b) The Duty to Accommodate

The ADA requires a covered entity to make a "reasonable accommodation" up to the point of "undue hardship." Although the ADA incorporates the general "reasonable accommodation" and "undue hardship" concepts found in §701(j) of Title VII relating to religious discrimination, these two terms are explicitly defined in the ADA, which is not the case in Title VII. Section 101(9) defines "reasonable accommodation" by setting forth a non-exclusive list of responses including (a) redesigning physical facilities to make them accessible to and usable by individuals with disabilities; (b) restructuring such aspects of the work environment as job requirements and assignments, work schedules, working equipment and devices, examinations and training materials; and (c) providing qualified readers or interpreters. And in language clearly more expansive than the standard imposed under Title VII by the Supreme Court in *Hardison*, §101(10)(A) defines "undue hardship" to mean a response that requires "significant difficulty or expense" when considered in light of the, apparently non-exclusive, list of factors set forth in §101(10)(B). Notice, by the way, that these factors refer not only to the nature and cost of the requisite accommodation, but also to the financial resources of the particular facility at which the accommodation is sought as well as to the resources, size, and structure of the defendant's overall business. Does this language suggest that Congress intended to mandate a fact-specific, case-by-case approach to determining the reasonableness of accommodations? In the following Note material, we address this and many other important issues relating to the statutory duty to make a reasonable accommodation. For example, recall that in the Title VII accommodation-to-religious beliefs and practices context, the Court in *Hardison* held that an accommodation that would require an employer to violate the terms of a collectively bargaining seniority system would constitute an undue hardship as a matter of law. Should that ruling extend to the disability context? Would it make a difference if the seniority system was unilaterally imposed by the employer rather than being the result of a collectively bargained agreement? Consider the following:

US Airways, Inc. v. Barnett

Supreme Court of the United States, 2002.
535 U.S. 391, 122 S.Ct. 1516, 152 L.Ed.2d 257.

BREYER, J., delivered the opinion of the Court, in which REHNQUIST, C.J., and STEVENS, O'CONNOR, and KENNEDY, JJ., joined. STEVENS, J., and O'CONNOR, J., filed concurring opinions. SCALIA, J., filed a dissenting opinion, in which THOMAS, J., joined. SOUTER, J., filed a dissenting opinion, in which GINSBURG, J., joined.

JUSTICE BREYER delivered the opinion of the Court.

The Americans with Disabilities Act of 1990 (ADA or Act) prohibits an employer from discriminating against an "individual with a disability" who, with "reasonable accommodation," can perform the essential functions of the job. This case, arising in the context of summary judgment, asks us how the Act resolves a potential conflict between: (1) the interests of a disabled worker who seeks assignment to a particular position as a "reasonable accommodation," and (2) the interests of other workers with superior rights to bid for the job under an employer's seniority system. In such a case, does the accommodation demand trump the seniority system?

In our view, the seniority system will prevail in the run of cases. As we interpret the statute, to show that a requested accommodation conflicts with the rules of a seniority system is ordinarily to show that the accommodation is not "reasonable." Hence such a showing will entitle an employer/defendant to summary judgment on the question — unless there is more. The plaintiff remains free to present evidence of special circumstances that make "reasonable" a seniority rule exception in the particular case. And such a showing will defeat the employer's demand for summary judgment.

I

In 1990, Robert Barnett, the plaintiff and respondent here, injured his back while working in a cargo-handling position at petitioner U.S Airways, Inc. He invoked seniority rights and transferred to a less physically demanding mailroom position. Under U.S. Airways' seniority system, that position, like others, periodically became open to seniority-based employee bidding. In 1992, Barnett learned that at least two employees senior to him intended to bid for the mailroom job. He asked U.S. Airways to accommodate his disability-imposed limitations by making an exception that would allow him to remain in the mailroom. After permitting Barnett to continue his mailroom work for five months while it considered the matter, U.S. Airways eventually decided not to make an exception. And Barnett lost his job.

Barnett then brought this ADA suit claiming, among other things, that he was an "individual with a disability" capable of performing the essential functions of the mailroom job, that the mailroom job amounted to a "reasonable accommodation" of his disability, and that U.S. Airways, in refusing to assign him the job, unlawfully discriminated against him. US Airways moved for summary judgment. * * *

The District Court found that the undisputed facts about seniority warranted summary judgment in U.S. Airways' favor. The Act says that an employer who fails to make "reasonable accommodations to the known physical or mental limitations of an [employee] with a disability" discriminates "*unless*" the employer "can demonstrate that the accommodation would impose an *undue hardship* on the operation of [its] business." (emphasis added)   The court said:

> "[T]he uncontroverted evidence shows that the USAir seniority system has been in place for 'decades' and governs over 14,000 USAir Agents.   Moreover, seniority policies such as the one at issue in this case are common to the airline industry.   Given this context, it seems clear that the USAir employees were justified in relying upon the policy.   As such, any significant alteration of that policy would result in undue hardship to both the company and its non- disabled employees."

An *en banc* panel of the United States Court of Appeals for the Ninth Circuit reversed.   It said that the presence of a seniority system is merely "a factor in the undue hardship analysis."   228 F.3d 1105, 1120 (C.A.9 2000).   And it held that "[a] case-by-case fact intensive analysis is required to determine whether any particular reassignment would constitute an undue hardship to the employer."

US Airways petitioned for certiorari, asking us to decide whether

> "the [ADA] requires an employer to reassign a disabled employee to a position as a 'reasonable accommodation' even though another employee is entitled to hold the position under the employer's bona fide and established seniority system."

The Circuits have reached different conclusions about the legal significance of a seniority system.   We agreed to answer U.S. Airways' question.

II

In answering the question presented, we must consider the following statutory provisions.   First, the ADA says that an employer may not "discriminate against a qualified individual with a disability."   Second, the ADA says that a "qualified" individual includes "an individual with a disability who, *with* or without *reasonable accommodation*, can perform the essential functions of" the relevant "employment position." (emphasis added).   Third, the ADA says that "discrimination" includes an employer's "*not making reasonable accommodations* to the known physical or mental limitations of an otherwise qualified . . . employee, *unless* [the employer] can demonstrate that the accommodation would impose an *undue hardship* on the operation of [its] business." (emphasis added).   Fourth, the ADA says that the term " 'reasonable accommodation' may include . . . reassignment to a vacant position."

The parties interpret this statutory language as applied to seniority systems in radically different ways.   In U.S. Airways' view, the fact that an accommodation would violate the rules of a seniority system always shows that the accommodation is not a "reasonable" one.   In Barnett's polar opposite view, a seniority system violation never shows that an accommodation sought is not a "reasonable" one.   Barnett concedes that a violation of seniority rules might help to show that the accommodation will work "undue" employer "hardship," but that is a matter for an employer to demonstrate case by case.   We shall initially consider the parties' main legal arguments in support of these conflicting positions.

A

US Airways' claim that a seniority system virtually always trumps a conflicting accommodation demand rests primarily upon its view of how the Act treats workplace "preferences." Insofar as a requested accommodation violates a disability-neutral workplace rule, such as a seniority rule, it grants the employee with a disability treatment that other workers could not receive. Yet the Act, U.S. Airways says, seeks only "equal" treatment for those with disabilities. It does not, it contends, require an employer to grant preferential treatment. Hence it does not require the employer to grant a request that, in violating a disability-neutral rule, would provide a preference.

While linguistically logical, this argument fails to recognize what the Act specifies, namely, that preferences will sometimes prove necessary to achieve the Act's basic equal opportunity goal. The Act requires preferences in the form of "reasonable accommodations" that are needed for those with disabilities to obtain the same workplace opportunities that those without disabilities automatically enjoy. By definition any special "accommodation" requires the employer to treat an employee with a disability differently, i.e., preferentially. And the fact that the difference in treatment violates an employer's disability-neutral rule cannot by itself place the accommodation beyond the Act's potential reach.

Were that not so, the "reasonable accommodation" provision could not accomplish its intended objective. Neutral office assignment rules would automatically prevent the accommodation of an employee whose disability-imposed limitations require him to work on the ground floor. Neutral "break-from-work" rules would automatically prevent the accommodation of an individual who needs additional breaks from work, perhaps to permit medical visits. Neutral furniture budget rules would automatically prevent the accommodation of an individual who needs a different kind of chair or desk. Many employers will have neutral rules governing the kinds of actions most needed to reasonably accommodate a worker with a disability. See 42 U.S.C. § 12111(9)(b) (setting forth examples such as "job restructuring," "part-time or modified work schedules," "acquisition or modification of equipment or devices," "and other similar accommodations"). Yet Congress, while providing such examples, said nothing suggesting that the presence of such neutral rules would create an automatic exemption. Nor have the lower courts made any such suggestion.

In sum, the nature of the "reasonable accommodation" requirement, the statutory examples, and the Act's silence about the exempting effect of neutral rules together convince us that the Act does not create any such automatic exemption. The simple fact that an accommodation would provide a "preference" — in the sense that it would permit the worker with a disability to violate a rule that others must obey — cannot, in and of itself, automatically show that the accommodation is not "reasonable." As a result, we reject the position taken by U.S. Airways and Justice Scalia to the contrary.

US Airways also points to the ADA provisions stating that a " 'reasonable accommodation' may include ... reassignment to a *vacant* position." (emphasis added). And it claims that the fact that an established seniority system would assign that position to another worker automatically and always means that the position is not a "vacant" one. Nothing in the Act, however, suggests that Congress intended the word "vacant" to have a specialized meaning. And in ordinary English, a seniority system can give employees seniority rights allowing them to bid for a "vacant" position. The position in this case was held, at the time of suit, by Barnett, not by some other worker; and that position, under the U.S. Airways seniority system, became an "open" one. Moreover, U.S. Airways has said that it reserves the right to change any and all portions of the seniority system at will. Consequently, we cannot agree with U.S.

Airways about the position's vacancy; nor do we agree that the Act would automatically deny Barnett's accommodation request for that reason.

B

Barnett argues that the statutory words "reasonable accommodation" mean only "effective accommodation," authorizing a court to consider the requested accommodation's ability to meet an individual's disability-related needs, and nothing more. On this view, a seniority rule violation, having nothing to do with the accommodation's effectiveness, has nothing to do with its "reasonableness." It might, at most, help to prove an "undue hardship on the operation of the business." But, he adds, that is a matter that the statute requires the employer to demonstrate, case by case.

In support of this interpretation Barnett points to Equal Employment Opportunity Commission (EEOC) regulations stating that "reasonable accommodation means . . . [m]odifications or adjustments . . . that *enable* a qualified individual with a disability to perform the essential functions of [a] position." 29 CFR §1630(o)(ii) (2001) (emphasis added). Barnett adds that any other view would make the words "reasonable accommodation" and "undue hardship" virtual mirror images — creating redundancy in the statute. And he says that any such other view would create a practical burden of proof dilemma.

The practical burden of proof dilemma arises, Barnett argues, because the statute imposes the burden of demonstrating an "undue hardship" upon the employer, while the burden of proving "reasonable accommodation" remains with the plaintiff, here the employee. This allocation seems sensible in that an employer can more frequently and easily prove the presence of business hardship than an employee can prove its absence. But suppose that an employee must counter a claim of "seniority rule violation" in order to prove that an "accommodation" request is "reasonable." Would that not force the employee to prove what is in effect an absence, i.e., an absence of hardship, despite the statute's insistence that the employer "demonstrate" hardship's presence?

These arguments do not persuade us that Barnett's legal interpretation of "reasonable" is correct. For one thing, in ordinary English the word "reasonable" does not mean "effective." It is the word "accommodation," not the word "reasonable," that conveys the need for effectiveness. An ineffective "modification" or "adjustment" will not accommodate a disabled individual's limitations. Nor does an ordinary English meaning of the term "reasonable accommodation" make of it a simple, redundant mirror image of the term "undue hardship." The statute refers to an "undue hardship on the operation of the business." Yet a demand for an effective accommodation could prove unreasonable because of its impact, not on business operations, but on fellow employees — say because it will lead to dismissals, relocations, or modification of employee benefits to which an employer, looking at the matter from the perspective of the business itself, may be relatively indifferent.

Neither does the statute's primary purpose require Barnett's special reading. The statute seeks to diminish or to eliminate the stereotypical thought processes, the thoughtless actions, and the hostile reactions that far too often bar those with disabilities from participating fully in the Nation's life, including the workplace. These objectives demand unprejudiced thought and reasonable responsive reaction on the part of employers and fellow workers alike. They will sometimes require affirmative conduct to promote entry of disabled people into the workforce. They do not, however, demand action beyond the realm of the reasonable.

Neither has Congress indicated in the statute, or elsewhere, that the word "reasonable" means no more than "effective." The EEOC regulations do say that reasonable accommodations "enable" a person with a disability to perform the essential functions of a task. But that phrasing simply emphasizes the statutory provision's basic objective. The regulations do not say that "enable" and "reasonable" mean the same thing. And as discussed below, no circuit court has so read them.

Finally, an ordinary language interpretation of the word "reasonable" does not create the "burden of proof" dilemma to which Barnett points. Many of the lower courts, while rejecting both U.S. Airways' and Barnett's more absolute views, have reconciled the phrases "reasonable accommodation" and "undue hardship" in a practical way.

They have held that a plaintiff/employee (to defeat a defendant/employer's motion for summary judgment) need only show that an "accommodation" seems reasonable on its face, i.e., ordinarily or in the run of cases. See, e.g., Borkowski v. Valley Central School Dist., 63 F.3d 131, 138 (C.A.2 1995) (plaintiff satisfies "burden of production" by showing "plausible accommodation").

Once the plaintiff has made this showing, the defendant/employer then must show special (typically case-specific) circumstances that demonstrate undue hardship in the particular circumstances.

Not every court has used the same language, but their results are functionally similar. In our opinion, that practical view of the statute, applied consistently with ordinary summary judgment principles, avoids Barnett's burden of proof dilemma, while reconciling the two statutory phrases ("reasonable accommodation" and "undue hardship").

III

The question in the present case focuses on the relationship between seniority systems and the plaintiff's need to show that an "accommodation" seems reasonable on its face, i.e., ordinarily or in the run of cases. We must assume that the plaintiff, an employee, is an "individual with a disability." He has requested assignment to a mailroom position as a "reasonable accommodation." We also assume that normally such a request would be reasonable within the meaning of the statute, were it not for one circumstance, namely, that the assignment would violate the rules of a seniority system. Does that circumstance mean that the proposed accommodation is not a "reasonable" one?

In our view, the answer to this question ordinarily is "yes." The statute does not require proof on a case-by-case basis that a seniority system should prevail. That is because it would not be reasonable in the run of cases that the assignment in question trump the rules of a seniority system. To the contrary, it will ordinarily be unreasonable for the assignment to prevail.

A

Several factors support our conclusion that a proposed accommodation will not be reasonable in the run of cases. Analogous case law supports this conclusion, for it has recognized the importance of seniority to employee-management relations. This Court has held that, in the context of a Title VII religious discrimination case, an employer need not adapt to an employee's special worship schedule as a "reasonable accommodation" where doing so would conflict with the seniority rights of other employees. *Hardison.* The lower courts have unanimously found that collectively bargained seniority trumps the need for reasonable accommodation in the context of the linguistically similar Rehabilitation Act. And several Circuits, though differing in their reasoning, have reached a similar conclusion in the context of seniority and the ADA. All these cases discuss collectively bargained seniority systems, not systems (like the present system) which are unilaterally imposed by management. But the relevant seniority system advantages, and related difficulties that result from violations of seniority rules, are not limited to collectively bargained systems.

For one thing, the typical seniority system provides important employee benefits by creating, and fulfilling, employee expectations of fair, uniform treatment. These benefits include job security and an opportunity for steady and predictable advancement based on objective standards. They include an element of due process limiting unfairness in personnel decisions. And they consequently encourage employees to invest in the employing company, accepting less than their value to the firm early in their careers in return for greater benefits in later years.

Most important for present purposes, to require the typical employer to show more than the existence of a seniority system might well undermine the employees' expectations of consistent, uniform treatment — expectations upon which the seniority system's benefits depend. That is because such a rule would substitute a complex case-specific "accommodation" decision made by management for the more uniform, impersonal operation of seniority rules. Such management decisionmaking, with its inevitable discretionary elements, would involve a matter of the greatest importance to employees, namely, layoffs; it would take place outside, as well as inside, the confines of a court case; and it might well take place fairly often. We can find nothing in the statute that suggests Congress intended to undermine seniority systems in this way. And we consequently conclude that the employer's showing of violation of the rules of a seniority system is by itself ordinarily sufficient.

B

The plaintiff (here the employee) nonetheless remains free to show that special circumstances warrant a finding that, despite the presence of a seniority system (which the ADA may not trump in the run of cases), the requested "accommodation" is "reasonable" on the particular facts. That is because special circumstances might alter the important expectations described above. The plaintiff might show, for example, that the employer, having retained the right to change the seniority system unilaterally, exercises that right fairly frequently, reducing employee expectations that the system will be followed — to the point where one more departure, needed to accommodate an individual with a disability, will not likely make a difference. The plaintiff might show that the system already contains exceptions such that, in the circumstances, one further exception is unlikely to matter. We do not mean these examples to exhaust the kinds of showings that a plaintiff might make. But we do mean to say that the plaintiff must bear the burden of showing special circumstances that make an exception from the seniority system reasonable in the particular case. And to do so, the plaintiff must explain why, in the particular case, an exception to the employer's seniority policy can constitute a "reasonable accommodation" even though in the ordinary case it cannot.

IV

In its question presented, U.S. Airways asked us whether the ADA requires an employer to assign a disabled employee to a particular position even though another employee is entitled to that position under the employer's "established seniority system." We answer that ordinarily the ADA does not require that assignment. Hence, a showing that the assignment would violate the rules of a seniority system warrants summary judgment for the employer — unless there is more. The plaintiff must present evidence of that "more," namely, special circumstances surrounding the particular case that demonstrate the assignment is nonetheless reasonable.

Because the lower courts took a different view of the matter, and because neither party has had an opportunity to seek summary judgment in accordance with the principles we set forth here, we vacate the Court of Appeals' judgment and remand the case for further proceedings consistent with this opinion.

[The concurring opinion of Justice Stevens is omitted.]

JUSTICE O'CONNOR, concurring.

I agree with portions of the opinion of the Court, but I find problematic the Court's test for determining whether the fact that a job reassignment violates a seniority system makes the reassignment an unreasonable accommodation under the Americans with Disabilities Act of 1990 (ADA or Act). Although a seniority system plays an important role in the workplace, for the reasons I explain below, I would prefer to say that the effect of a seniority system on the reasonableness of a reassignment as an accommodation for purposes of the ADA depends on whether the seniority system is legally enforceable. "Were it possible for me to adhere to [this belief] in my vote, and for the Court at the same time to [adopt a majority rule]," I would do so. Screws v. United States, 325 U.S. 91, 134, 65 S.Ct. 1031, 89 L.Ed. 1495 (1945) (Rutledge, J., concurring in result). "The Court, however, is divided in opinion," and if each member voted consistently with his or her beliefs, we would not agree on a resolution of the question presented in this case. Yet "[s]talemate should not prevail," *ibid.*, particularly in a case in which we are merely interpreting a statute. Accordingly, in order that the Court may adopt a rule, and because I believe the Court's rule will often lead to the same outcome as the one I would have adopted, I join the Court's opinion despite my concerns.

The ADA specifically lists "reassignment to a vacant position" as one example of a "reasonable accommodation." In deciding whether an otherwise reasonable accommodation involving a reassignment is unreasonable because it would require an exception to a seniority system, I think the relevant issue is whether the seniority system prevents the position in question from being vacant. The word "vacant" means "not filled or occupied by an incumbent [or] possessor." Webster's Third New International Dictionary 2527 (1976). In the context of a workplace, a vacant position is a position in which no employee currently works and to which no individual has a legal entitlement. For example, in a workplace without a seniority system, when an employee ceases working for the employer, the employee's former position is vacant until a replacement is hired. Even if the replacement does not start work immediately, once the replacement enters into a contractual agreement with the employer, the position is no longer vacant because it has a "possessor." In contrast, when an employee ceases working in a workplace with a legally enforceable seniority system, the employee's former position does not become vacant if the seniority system entitles another employee to it. Instead, the employee entitled to the position under the seniority system immediately becomes the new "possessor" of that position. In a workplace with an unenforceable seniority policy, however, an employee expecting assignment to a position under the seniority policy would not have any type of contractual right to the position and so could not be said to be its "possessor." The position therefore would become vacant.

Given this understanding of when a position can properly be considered vacant, if a seniority system, in the absence of the ADA, would give someone other than the individual seeking the accommodation a legal entitlement or contractual right to the position to which reassignment is sought, the seniority system prevents the position from being vacant. If a position is not vacant, then reassignment to it is not a reasonable accommodation. The Act specifically says that "reassignment to a *vacant* position" is a type of "reasonable accommodation." (emphasis added). Indeed, the legislative history of the Act confirms that Congress did not intend reasonable accommodation to require bumping other employees.

Petitioner's Personnel Policy Guide for Agents, which contains its seniority policy, specifically states that it is "*not* intended to be a contract (express or implied) or otherwise to create legally enforceable obligations," and that petitioner "reserves the right to change any and all of the stated policies and procedures in [the] Guide at any time, without advanc[e] notice." (emphasis in original). Petitioner conceded at oral argument that its seniority policy does not give employees any legally enforceable rights. Because the policy did not give any other employee a right to the position respondent sought, the position could be said to have been vacant when it became open for bidding, making the requested accommodation reasonable.

In Part II of its opinion, the Court correctly explains that "a plaintiff/employee (to defeat a defendant/employer's motion for summary judgment) need only show that an 'accommodation' seems reasonable on its face, *i.e.*, ordinarily or in the run of cases." In other words, the plaintiff must show that the method of accommodation the employee seeks is reasonable in the run of cases. As the Court also correctly explains, "[o]nce the plaintiff has made this showing, the defendant/employer then must show special . . . circumstances that demonstrate undue hardship" in the context of the particular employer's operations. These interpretations give appropriate meaning to both the term "reasonable," and the term "undue hardship," preventing the concepts from overlapping by making reasonableness a general inquiry and undue hardship a specific inquiry. When the Court turns to applying its interpretation of the Act to seniority systems, however, it seems to blend the two inquiries by suggesting that the plaintiff should have the opportunity to prove that there are special circumstances in the context of that particular seniority system that would cause an exception to the system to be reasonable despite the fact that such exceptions are unreasonable in the run of cases.

Although I am troubled by the Court's reasoning, I believe the Court's approach for evaluating seniority systems will often lead to the same outcome as the test I would have adopted. Unenforceable seniority systems are likely to involve policies in which employers "retai[n] the right to change the system," and will often "permi[t] exceptions". They will also often contain disclaimers that "reduc[e] employee expectations that the system will be followed." Thus, under the Court's test, disabled employees seeking accommodations that would require exceptions to unenforceable seniority systems may be able to show circumstances that make the accommodation "reasonable in the[ir] particular case." Because I think the Court's test will often lead to the correct outcome, and because I think it important that a majority of the Court agree on a rule when interpreting statutes, I join the Court's opinion.

JUSTICE SCALIA, with whom JUSTICE THOMAS joins, dissenting.

The question presented asks whether the "reasonable accommodation" mandate of the Americans with Disabilities Act of 1990 (ADA or Act) requires reassignment of a disabled employee to a position that "another employee is entitled to hold . . . under the employer's bona fide and established seniority system." Indulging its penchant for eschewing clear rules that might avoid litigation, the Court answers "maybe." It creates a presumption that an exception to a seniority rule is an "unreasonable" accommodation, but allows that presumption to be rebutted by showing that the exception "will not likely make a difference."

The principal defect of today's opinion, however, goes well beyond the uncertainty it produces regarding the relationship between the ADA and the infinite variety of seniority systems. The conclusion that any seniority system can ever be overridden is merely one consequence of a mistaken interpretation of the ADA that makes all employment rules and practices — even those which (like a seniority system) pose no distinctive obstacle to the disabled — subject to suspension when that is (in a court's view) a "reasonable" means of enabling a disabled employee to keep his job. That is a far cry from what I believe the accommodation provision of the ADA requires: the suspension (within reason) of those employment rules and practices *that the employee's disability prevents him from observing*.

I

* * *

* * * [T]he ADA eliminates workplace barriers only if a disability prevents an employee from overcoming them — those barriers that would not be barriers but for the employee's disability. These include, for example, work stations that cannot accept the employee's wheelchair, or an assembly-line practice that requires long periods of standing. But they do not include rules and practices that bear no more heavily upon the disabled employee than upon others — even though an exemption from such a rule or practice might in a sense "make up for" the employee's disability. It is not a required accommodation, for example, to pay a disabled employee more than others at his grade level — even if that increment is earmarked for massage or physical therapy that would enable the employee to work with as little physical discomfort as his co- workers. That would be "accommodating" the disabled employee, but it would not be making accommodation to the known physical or

mental limitations of the employee because it would not eliminate any workplace practice that constitutes an obstacle because of his disability.

So also with exemption from a seniority system, which burdens the disabled and nondisabled alike. In particular cases, seniority rules may have a harsher effect upon the disabled employee than upon his co-workers. If the disabled employee is physically capable of performing only one task in the workplace, seniority rules may be, for him, the difference between employment and unemployment. But that does not make the seniority system a disability-related obstacle, any more than harsher impact upon the more needy disabled employee renders the salary system a disability-related obstacle. When one departs from this understanding, the ADA's accommodation provision becomes a standardless grab bag — leaving it to the courts to decide which workplace preferences (higher salary, longer vacations, reassignment to positions to which others are entitled) can be deemed "reasonable" to "make up for" the particular employee's disability.

Some courts, including the Ninth Circuit in the present case, have accepted respondent's contention that the ADA demands accommodation even with respect to those obstacles that have nothing to do with the disability. Their principal basis for this position is that the definition of "reasonable accommodation" includes "reassignment to a vacant position." This accommodation would be meaningless, they contend, if it required only that the disabled employee be *considered* for a vacant position. The ADA already prohibits employers from discriminating against the disabled with respect to hiring, advancement, or discharge and other terms, conditions, and privileges of employment. Surely, the argument goes, a disabled employee must be given preference over a nondisabled employee when a vacant position appears.

This argument seems to me quite mistaken. The right to be given a vacant position so long as there are no obstacles to that appointment (including another candidate who is better qualified, if "best qualified" is the workplace rule) is of considerable value. If an employee is hired to fill a position but fails miserably, he will typically be fired. Few employers will search their organization charts for vacancies to which the low-performing employee might be suited. The ADA, however, prohibits an employer from firing a person whose disability is the cause of his poor performance without first seeking to place him in a vacant job where the disability will not affect performance. Such reassignment is an accommodation *to the disability* because it removes an obstacle (the inability to perform the functions of the assigned job) arising solely from the disability.

The phrase "reassignment to a vacant position" appears in a subsection describing a variety of potential "reasonable accommodation[s]":

"(A) making existing facilities used by employees readily accessible to and usable by individuals with disabilities; and

"(B) job restructuring, part-time or modified work schedules, *reassignment to a vacant position*, acquisition or modification of equipment or devices, appropriate adjustment or modifications of examinations, training materials or policies, the provision of qualified readers or interpreters, and other similar accommodations for individuals with disabilities." (emphasis added).

Subsection (A) clearly addresses features of the workplace that burden the disabled *because of* their disabilities. Subsection (B) is broader in scope but equally targeted at disability-related obstacles. Thus it encompasses "modified work schedules" (which may accommodate inability to work for protracted periods), "modification of equipment and devices," and "provision of qualified readers or interpreters." There is no reason why the phrase "reassignment to a vacant position" should be thought to have a uniquely different focus. It envisions elimination of the obstacle of the *current position* (which requires activity that the disabled employee cannot tolerate) when there is an alternate position freely available. If he is qualified for that position, and no one else is seeking it, or no one else who seeks it is better qualified, he *must* be given the position. But "reassignment to a vacant position" does *not* envision the elimination of obstacles to the employee's service in the new position that have nothing to do with his disability — for example, another employee's claim to that position under a seniority system, or another employee's superior qualifications.

Unsurprisingly, most Courts of Appeals addressing the issue have held or assumed that the ADA does not mandate exceptions to a "legitimate, nondiscriminatory policy" such as a seniority system or a consistent policy of assigning the most qualified person to a vacant position.

* * *

Sadly, this analysis is lost on the Court, which mistakenly and inexplicably concludes that my position here is the same as that attributed to U.S. Airways. In rejecting the argument that the ADA creates no "automatic exemption" for neutral workplace rules such as "break-from-work" and furniture budget rules, the Court rejects an argument I have not made.

II

Although, as I have said, the uncertainty cast upon bona fide seniority systems is the least of the ill consequences produced by today's decision, a few words on that subject are nonetheless in order. Since, under the Court's interpretation of the ADA, *all* workplace rules are eligible to be used as vehicles of accommodation, the one means of saving seniority systems is a judicial finding that accommodation through the suspension of *those* workplace rules would be unreasonable. The Court is unwilling, however, to make that finding categorically, with respect to all seniority systems. Instead, it creates (and "creates" is the appropriate word) a *rebuttable presumption* that exceptions to seniority rules are not "reasonable" under the ADA, but leaves it free for the disabled employee to show that *under the "special circumstances" of his case*, an exception would be "reasonable." The employee would be entitled to an exception, for example, if he showed that "one more departure" from the seniority rules "will not likely make a difference."

I have no idea what this means. When is it possible for a departure from seniority rules to "not likely make a difference"? Even when a bona fide seniority system has multiple exceptions, employees expect that these are the *only* exceptions. One more unannounced exception will invariably undermine the values ("fair, uniform treatment," "job security," "predictable advancement," etc.) that the Court cites as its reasons for believing seniority systems so important that they merit a presumption of exemption

One is tempted to impart some rationality to the scheme by speculating that the Court's burden-shifting rule is merely intended to give the disabled employee an opportunity to show that the employer's seniority system is in fact a sham — a system so full of exceptions that it creates no meaningful employee expectations. The rule applies, however, even if the seniority system is bona fide and established. And the Court says that "to require the typical employer to show more than the existence of a seniority system might well undermine the employees' expectations of consistent, uniform treatment ...." How could deviations from a sham seniority system "undermine the employees' expectations"?

I must conclude, then, that the Court's rebuttable presumption does not merely give disabled employees the opportunity to unmask sham seniority systems; it gives them a vague and unspecified power (whenever they can show "special circumstances") to undercut *bona fide* systems. The Court claims that its new test will not require exceptions to seniority systems "in the run of cases," but that is belied by the disposition of this case. The Court remands to give respondent an opportunity to show that an exception to petitioner's seniority system "will not likely make a difference" to employee expectations, despite the following finding by the District Court:

> "[T]he uncontroverted evidence shows that [petitioner's] seniority system has been in place for 'decades' and governs over 14,000 ... Agents. Moreover, seniority policies such as the one at issue in this case are common to the airline industry. Given this context, it seems clear that [petitioner's] employees were justified in relying upon the policy. As such, any significant alteration of that policy would result in undue hardship to both the company and its non-disabled employees."

Because the Court's opinion leaves the question whether a seniority system must be disregarded in order to accommodate a disabled employee in a state of uncertainty that can be resolved only by constant litigation; and because it adopts an interpretation of the ADA that incorrectly subjects all employer rules and practices to the requirement of reasonable accommodation; I respectfully dissent.

JUSTICE SOUTER, whom Justice GINSBURG joins, dissenting.

* * * The Court today holds that a request for reassignment will nonetheless most likely be unreasonable when it would violate the terms of a seniority system imposed by an employer. Although I concur in the Court's appreciation of the value and importance of seniority systems, I do not believe my hand is free to accept the majority's result and therefore respectfully dissent.

Nothing in the ADA insulates seniority rules from the "reasonable accommodation" requirement, in marked contrast to Title VII of the Civil Rights Act of 1964 and the Age Discrimination in Employment Act of 1967, each of which has an explicit protection for seniority. Because Congress modeled several of the ADA's provisions on Title VII, its failure to replicate Title VII's exemption for seniority systems leaves the statute ambiguous, albeit with more than a hint that seniority rules do not inevitably carry the day.

In any event, the statute's legislative history resolves the ambiguity. The Committee Reports from both the House of Representatives and the Senate explain that seniority protections contained in a collective-bargaining agreement should not amount to more than "a factor" when it comes to deciding whether some accommodation at odds with the seniority rules is "reasonable" nevertheless.

H.R.Rep. No. 101-485, pt. 2, p. 63 (1990), U.S.Code Cong. & Admin.News 1990, pp.303, 345, (existence of collectively bargained protections for seniority "would not be determinative" on the issue whether an accommodation was reasonable); S.Rep. No. 101-116, p.32 (1989) (a collective-bargaining agreement assigning jobs based on seniority "may be considered as a factor in determining" whether an accommodation is reasonable). Here, of course, it does not matter whether the congressional committees were right or wrong in thinking that views of sound ADA application could reduce a collectively bargained seniority policy to the level of "a factor," in the absence of a specific statutory provision to that effect. In fact, I doubt that any interpretive clue in legislative history could trump settled law specifically making collective bargaining agreements enforceable. The point in this case, however, is simply to recognize that if Congress considered that sort of agreement no more than a factor in the analysis, surely no greater weight was meant for a seniority scheme like the one before us, unilaterally imposed by the employer, and, unlike collective bargaining agreements, not singled out for protection by any positive federal statute.

This legislative history also specifically rules out the majority's reliance on *Hardison*, a case involving a request for a religious accommodation under Title VII that would have broken the seniority rules of a collective-bargaining agreement. We held that such an accommodation would not be "reasonable," and said that our conclusion was "supported" by Title VII's explicit exemption for seniority systems. The committees of both Houses of Congress dealing with the ADA were aware of this case and expressed a choice against treating it as authority under the ADA, with its lack of any provision for maintaining seniority rules. E.g., H.R.Rep. No. 101-485, pt. 2, at 68, U.S.Code Cong. & Admin.News 1990, pp.303, 350 ("The Committee wishes to make it clear that the principles enunciated by the Supreme Court in TWA v. Hardison ... are not applicable to this legislation.").

Because a unilaterally-imposed seniority system enjoys no special protection under the ADA, a consideration of facts peculiar to this very case is needed to gauge whether Barnett has carried the burden of showing his proposed accommodation to be a "reasonable" one despite the policy in force at U.S. Airways. The majority describes this as a burden to show the accommodation is "plausible" or "feasible," and I believe Barnett has met it.

He held the mailroom job for two years before learning that employees with greater seniority planned to bid for the position, given U.S. Airways's decision to declare the job "vacant." Thus, perhaps unlike ADA claimants who request accommodation through reassignment, Barnett was seeking not a change but a continuation of the status quo. All he asked was that U.S. Airways refrain from declaring the position "vacant"; he did not ask to bump any other employee and no one would have lost a job on his account. There was no evidence in the District Court of any unmanageable ripple effects from Barnett's request, or showing that he would have overstepped an inordinate number of seniority levels by remaining where he was.

In fact, it is hard to see the seniority scheme here as any match for Barnett's ADA requests, since U.S. Airways apparently took pains to ensure that its seniority rules raised no great expectations. In its policy statement, U.S. Airways said that "[t]he Agent Personnel Policy Guide is not intended to be a contract" and that "USAir reserves the right to change any and all of the stated policies and procedures in this Guide at any time, without advanced notice." While I will skip any state-by-state analysis of the legal treatment of employee handbooks (a source of many lawyers' fees) it is safe to say that the contract law of a number of jurisdictions would treat this disclaimer as fatal to any claim an employee might make to enforce the seniority policy over an employer's contrary decision.

With U.S. Airways itself insisting that its seniority system was noncontractual and modifiable at will, there is no reason to think that Barnett's accommodation would have resulted in anything more than minimal disruption to U.S. Airways's operations, if that. Barnett has shown his requested accommodation to be "reasonable," and the burden ought to shift to U.S. Airways if it wishes to claim that, in spite of surface appearances, violation of the seniority scheme would have worked an undue hardship. I would therefore affirm the Ninth Circuit.

NOTES AND PROBLEMS FOR DISCUSSION

1.　The majority opinion in *Barnett* adopted the view of the preponderance of the circuit courts that accorded a separate and independent meaning to "reasonable accommodation" and "undue hardship". Specifically, these courts had coalesced around the view that "reasonable accommodation" is an essentially objectively determined standard. It is viewed as comprising something less than the maximum effort it would take to permit a disabled individual to work, while requiring the implementation of an effective alteration of the workplace based on either a survey of accommodations made by other employers, or by a calculation of whether the costs incurred in providing the accommodation are proportionate to the benefit obtained by the disabled employee. "Undue hardship," on the other view, is viewed as an economic safe harbor for the particular employer, i.e., it requires an evaluation of the specific defendant's ability to sustain the cost of an otherwise reasonable accommodation, regardless of whether a different employer might be required to adopt that same proposed accommodation.

The *Barnett* Court also, however, added an additional twist to this calculation, at least with respect to proposed accommodations that would violate the terms of either a unilaterally implemented or collectively bargained seniority system. The employer is entitled to the benefit of a rebuttable presumption that any accommodation that requires it to violate the terms of its seniority system is unreasonable in the general run of cases. But the plaintiff has the opportunity to demonstrate that "special circumstances" warrant a finding that, notwithstanding the existence of a seniority system, the requested "accommodation" is "reasonable" under the circumstances of the particular case. And the Court offered a nonexhaustive list of two situations where the presumption of unreasonableness could be rebutted: (1) where the employer's retention and "fairly frequent" exercise of the right to make unilateral changes to its seniority system suggested that one more departure, designed to accommodate a disabled individual, would not likely make a difference; and (2) where the seniority system already contained exceptions such that, in the circumstances, one further exception was unlikely to matter.

Note that if the defendant fails to meet its statutory duty to make a reasonable accommodation, a violation will be found regardless of the employer's motivation. No requirement of discriminatory intent, in other words, is necessary when the alleged violation is failure to accommodate, as opposed to when the defendant is alleged to have engaged in differential treatment because of the plaintiff's disability. *See e.g.*, Nadler v. Harvey, 2007 WL 2404705 (11th Cir. 2007) (unpublished).

2. The duty to accommodate, of course, is not only subject to these "reasonable" and "undue hardship" limitations. The ADA requires an employer to accommodate only if the accommodation will result in the disabled individual's being able perform the essential functions of the job. It does not require the employer to accommodate by modifying or eliminating an essential job function. So, for example, if an employee with chronic psoriasis requests a leave of absence during one of the disease's intermittent flare-ups, is granting that leave objectively reasonable, or is uninterrupted attendance an essential job requirement so that granting a leave of absence is objectively unreasonable as a matter of law? *See* Cehrs v. Northeast Ohio Alzheimer's, 155 F.3d 775 (6th Cir. 1998) (any presumption that uninterrupted attendance is an essential job requirement is inappropriate as it would always relieve employer of obligation of proving that granting leave of absence would impose an undue hardship on it; a medical leave of absence can constitute a reasonable accommodation under appropriate circumstances).

Additionally, the accommodation must be related to the nature of the plaintiff's disability. Put another way, a reasonable accommodation must respond to the limitations on a major life activity that were the result of the worker's physical or mental impairment. See, e.g., Hustvet v. Allina Health System, 910 F.3d 399 (8th Cir. 2018).

3. Although the majority in *Barnett* addressed one of the crucial evidentiary issues that arise in disability cases involving the duty to accommodate, i.e., the parties' respective burdens with respect to the "reasonable accommodation" and "undue hardship" components of ADA analysis, other questions were left unresolved. For example:

(a) How and when is an employer expected to determine the extent, if any, of its duty to accommodate the needs of a particular disabled employee or job applicant? The ADA's implementing regulations state that "[t]o determine the appropriate reasonable accommodation it may be necessary for the covered entity to initiate an informal, interactive process with the qualified individual with a disability in need of the accommodation. This process should identify the precise limitations resulting from the disability and potential reasonable accommodations that could overcome those limitations." 29 C.F.R. §1630.2(o)(3). In addition, the EEOC Interpretive Guidelines declare that "[o]nce a qualified individual with a disability has requested * * * a reasonable accommodation, the employer must make a reasonable effort to determine the appropriate accommodation. The appropriate reasonable accommodation is best determined through a flexible, interactive process that involves both the employer and the qualified individual with a disability." 29 C.F.R. §1630, App. §1630.9.

In light of this language, what are the precise roles played by the employer and employee in this interactive process and does a total failure or refusal to engage in this process constitute a per se violation of the duty to accommodate?

In FJELLESTAD v. PIZZA HUT of AMERICA, INC., 188 F.3d 944 (8th Cir. 1999), the court stated the prevailing rule that the plaintiff bears the initial burden of informing her employer that she is disabled and requesting an accommodation that will render her "otherwise qualified" for employment. At that point, the employer must initiate an "informal interactive process" with the employee to determine whether an appropriate reasonable accommodation exists. If the employer fails to make a good faith effort to engage in this interactive process, it will be found to have violated the Act unless it can prove that no reasonable accommodation was possible, or it ultimately makes what is deemed to be a reasonable accommodation. But if the employer does not persuade the fact finder that no reasonable accommodation was possible, or that its proposed accommodation (made without consultation) was not reasonable, its failure to commence the interactive process will result in *per se* liability under the ADA. But see Snapp v. United Transportation Union, 889 F.3d 1088 (9th Cir. 2018)(while *employer* bears burden of proving that a reasonable accommodation would *not* have been possible in connection with a plaintiff's *motion for summary judgment* on a failure-to engage-in-interactive-process claim, this shifting of the burden of persuasion to the defense should not be extended to *trial* where the plaintiff retains the burden of showing the existence of a reasonable accommodation). Moreover, the court concluded, in attempting to establish that no reasonable accommodation was possible, it is not sufficient for the employer to assert that the employee did not come forward with a proposal that constituted a reasonable accommodation. Conversely, if an employee rejects a reasonable accommodation, that individual no longer will be considered to be a qualified individual with a disability and, therefore, will fall outside the protection of the statute.

A minority of the circuits, however, are of the view that an employer's refusal to participate in the interactive process constitutes only evidence of a statutory violation and not a *per se* violation. *See e.g.*, Calero-Cerezo v. U.S. Dep't of Justice, 355 F.3d 6 (1st Cir. 2004).

Though most circuits have held that the employer's statutory duty to provide a reasonable accommodation is not triggered unless the disabled individual makes a specific demand for an accommodation, see, e.g., Gaston v. Bellingrath Gardens & Home, 167 F.3d 1361 (11th Cir. 1999), the Ninth Circuit has adopted a more relaxed standard. In the principal case, for example, the Ninth Circuit had ruled that the interactive process is triggered either by a request for accommodation by a disabled employee or by the employer's recognition of the need for such an accommodation. The latter standard would be invoked, the court explained, where the employer knows or has reason to know (1) that the employee has a disability; (2) that the employee is experiencing workplace problems caused by the disability; and (3) that the employee's disability prevents her from requesting a reasonable accommodation. Thus, the appellate court reasoned, where all three of these facts are established, the employee is not required to request an accommodation in order to generate the employer's duty to initiate the interactive process. The court also rejected the notion that the employee must suggest any particular accommodation. Since, in the court's view, the employer, rather than the employee, possesses superior knowledge of possible alternative employment positions or accommodations, it is inappropriate the place the entire burden on the employee to identify a reasonable accommodation. At the same time, the court recognized, the employee has an obligation to assist the employer in this interactive process by providing the information that is most likely within its possession, i.e., information concerning the employee's capacities and limitations. Nevertheless, the issue of when the duty to invoke the interactive process is triggered was not included in the company's petition for certiorari. Consequently, the Supreme Court opinion did not address it. *Accord*, Brady v. Wal-Mart Stores, Inc., 531 F.3d 127 (2d Cir. 2008) (an employer has a duty to invoke the interactive process if the disability is obvious — i.e., where the employer knew or reasonably should have known of the disability — even if the worker never requested an accommodation and testified that he did not think he needed one).

In TAYLOR v. PRINCIPAL FINANCIAL GROUP, INC., 93 F.3d 155 (5th Cir.), cert. denied, 519 U.S. 1029, 117 S.Ct. 586, 136 L.Ed.2d 515 (1996), the plaintiff employee had informed his supervisor that he had been diagnosed with bipolar disorder and that he wanted the supervisor to "investigate" the condition. When no effort at accommodation was made, the plaintiff filed a failure to accommodate claim under the ADA. The Fifth Circuit upheld the trial court's grant of summary judgment in favor of the defendant. Both courts rejected the plaintiff's argument that once he had revealed his disability to his supervisor, the company had an affirmative obligation to make a reasonable accommodation. The circuit court emphasized that the plaintiff had never informed his supervisor of any limitation or restriction imposed by his bipolar disorder. To prove a case under the ADA, the appellate court declared, it is important to distinguish between an employer's knowledge of an employee's disability and an employer's knowledge of limitations experienced by the employee as a result of that disability. The statutory duty to accommodate, the court ruled, does not require an employer to assume that an employee with a disability suffers from a limitation. To the contrary, it added, the statute embodied the opposite presumption and prohibits employers from evaluating the capabilities of disabled individuals on the basis of stereotypes and myths. Accordingly, the court concluded, since the plaintiff had not sustained his burden of informing the employer that an accommodation was needed, the employer was under no obligation to participate in the interactive process of determining one. However, the court did note that that the duty to accommodate will exist even where the plaintiff fails to request an accommodation *if* the plaintiff establishes that the disability, the resulting limitation, and necessary reasonable accommodation were open, obvious and apparent.

(b) Suppose the employee agrees to the employer's proposed accommodation but, over time, it is discovered that the accommodation is not effective in meeting the employee's needs. In other words, does the employer have a continuing obligation to propose accommodations or is the duty satisfied once the employer has made one good faith effort at accommodation? In HUMPHREY v. MEMORIAL HOSPITALS ASS'N, 239 F.3d 1128 (9th Cir. 2001), cert. denied, 535 U.S. 1011, 122 S.Ct. 1592, 152 L.Ed.2d 509 (2002), the plaintiff, a medical transcriptionist whose obsessive compulsive disorder (OCD) resulted in excessive tardiness and absence, which were the subject of several disciplinary warnings, rejected the defendant's offer of a leave of absence but accepted its offer of a flexible starting time schedule to accommodate her disability. When the flexible starting time schedule did not eliminate her absences, the defendant rejected the plaintiff's request for an alternative accommodation — the opportunity to work at home — pursuant to its departmental policy to deny requests for work-at-home accommodations to those employees who previously had been involved in disciplinary actions. When the plaintiff continued to be absent, she was discharged. The defendant conceded that it would have granted a request for a leave of absence if one had been requested prior to her termination. The trial court granted the hospital's motion for summary judgment on the ground that it had satisfied its duty to make a reasonable accommodation by initially offering a leave of absence, which the plaintiff had rejected.

The Ninth Circuit reversed on several grounds. First, it noted that in order to establish that a leave of absence is a reasonable accommodation, a plaintiff does not have to prove that it is certain or even likely to be successful. Rather, the plaintiff need only show that the leave "could plausibly have enabled" the plaintiff adequately to perform her job. It also stated that it was inconsistent with the purposes of the ADA to permit an employer to deny an otherwise reasonable accommodation (here, the opportunity to work at home) solely because of past disciplinary action taken as a result of conduct caused by the employee's disability. Having determined that both working at home and a leave of absence were reasonable accommodations that would have rendered the plaintiff otherwise qualified for her job, the court found that the defendant was not entitled to summary judgment on the issue of whether the plaintiff was a "qualified individual with a disability" within the meaning of the ADA.

Second, with respect to the issue of the extent of the employer's duty to accommodate, the court ruled that an employer is under a continuing duty to explore further methods of accommodation, which includes offering a reasonable accommodation, when it discovers that an initial attempt at accommodation has proven to be ineffective, even when the employee has not tendered an alternative suggestion. An employer's participation in the statutorily mandated interactive process, it declared, "extends beyond the first attempt at accommodation and continues when the employee asks for a different accommodation or where the employer is aware that the initial accommodation is failing and further accommodation is needed." It reasoned that a plaintiff's attempt to perform her job via a less drastic accommodation does not forfeit her right to a more substantial accommodation upon the failure of the initial effort.

(c) Which party must establish whether or not the plaintiff is qualified for the position with the aid of a reasonable accommodation? In BENSON v. NORTHWEST AIRLINES, INC., 62 F.3d 1108 (8th Cir. 1995), the Eighth Circuit declared that once the plaintiff sustained its burden of producing evidence that a reasonable accommodation exists, the defendant bore the burden of establishing that the employee could not perform the essential functions of the job even with the proposed reasonable accommodation. This analysis was rejected by the Sixth Circuit in MONETTE v. EDS CORP., 90 F.3d 1173 (6th Cir. 1996), where the court stated that although the defendant must establish that the proposed accommodation would impose an undue hardship upon it, it was the plaintiff's responsibility to prove that he or she could perform essential job functions with the assistance of the proposed accommodation.

4. Has the employer fully complied with its accommodation obligation when it offers an accommodation that is contained within the statutory list of reasonable accommodations? In TERRELL v. USAIR, 132 F.3d 621 (11th Cir. 1998), a reservations sales agent with the defendant airline alleged that she had developed carpal tunnel syndrome as a result of her job. While on medical leave of absence for surgery for her condition, the plaintiff requested that she be provided with a part-time position upon her return. The defendant refused this and other proposed accommodations. She brought suit under the ADA and the trial court granted summary judgment for the defendant on the ground that it had fulfilled its statutory duty to accommodate. The Eleventh Circuit affirmed, ruling that even though

providing part-time work was contained in the statutory list of accommodations, the plaintiff still had the burden of proving that the listed accommodation was reasonable under the circumstances of this case. Since this defendant had terminated all part-time positions prior to the plaintiff's request, the court ruled that the statutory duty of accommodation did not require the airline to create a part-time position for the plaintiff where all part-time positions had been eliminated.

5. Jennifer Michaels admitted to her employer that her newly sustained disability prevented her from continuing to fulfill the essential functions of her job under any circumstances. She also reported, however, that she could meet the requirements of a different, vacant job and asked for a reassignment. The employer refused this request. Has the employer failed to meet its statutory duty to make a reasonable accommodation to Jennifer's disability, or is she not entitled to any accommodation because her inability to perform the functions of her existing job, with or without an accommodation, placed her outside the protection of the ADA? There is an evolving consensus among the circuit courts that since the statutory definition of "otherwise qualified" includes ability to perform the essential functions of a job that the plaintiff holds "or desires," this language should be read to mean that a disabled employee is covered under the statute if she is able to perform the essential functions of a reasonably available alternative position (with or without a reasonable accommodation), even if she is no longer able to fulfill the essential functions of her present position (with or without a reasonable accommodation). *See, e.g.*, Smith v. Midland Brake, Inc., 180 F.3d 1154 (10th Cir. 1999) (*en banc*).

6. As the majority noted in *Barnett*, §101(9)(B) of the ADA expressly recognizes "reassignment to a vacant position" as a form of reasonable accommodation.

(a) Does the employer's duty to make a reasonable accommodation require it to *consider* the disabled individual for a reassignment along with all other individuals interested in that position or does the disabled employee enjoy an *automatic* right to that reassignment? In SMITH v. MIDLAND BRAKE INC., 180 F.3d 1154 (10th Cir. 1999) (*en banc*), the Tenth Circuit reasoned that to construe the duty to accommodate to require no more than to consider the disabled employee on an equal basis with other candidates would render it redundant as it would add nothing to the obligation not to discriminate. The court also noted that the statutory list of reasonable accommodations included "reassignment" and not "consideration of a reassignment." Accordingly, it held, once an employer determined that no reasonable accommodation could be made to keep the disabled employee in her current position, the employer was obliged to award the reassignment to a disabled individual who was qualified for that position and not require it to be the best qualified applicant. But in HUBER v. WAL-MART STORES, INC., 486 F.3d 480 (8th Cir.2007), the Eight Circuit rejected the Tenth Circuit's analysis, concluding that the ADA "is not an affirmative action statute" and does not require an employer to reassign a qualified disabled employee to a vacant position in the face of its nondiscriminatory policy of hiring the most qualified candidate. In refusing to reassign the plaintiff to her requested position in favor of a more qualified candidate, the defendant had treated the plaintiff exactly like all other candidates and, therefore, had not discriminated against her on the basis of her disability. Thereafter, the Seventh Circuit rejected the *Huber* analysis and endorsed the position taken by the Tenth Circuit in *Smith*. In E.E.O.C. v. UNITED AIRLINES, INC., 693 F.3d 760 (7th Cir. 2012), the defendant's accommodation policy provided that where a disabled employee sought accommodation in the form of reassignment to a vacant position for which that employee was otherwise qualified, that person would be guaranteed an interview and would receive the transfer if the competing candidates were equally qualified. However, the company retained the right to award the vacant position to a non-disabled candidate who was deemed better qualified than the disabled candidate seeking an accommodation. The Seventh Circuit read the Supreme Court's ruling in *Barnett* as holding that reassignment to a vacant position for which the disabled employee is qualified was reasonable in the run of cases unless reassignment would require the employer to violate the terms of a seniority system. It rejected the notion that a "best-qualified" selection policy, like a seniority system, rendered reassignment not reasonable in the run of cases. Accordingly, the court declined to adopt a *per se* approach to whether mandatory reassignment was or was not required by the ADA. Instead, it remanded the case to the trial judge to decide, pursuant to the two-step analysis enunciated in *Barnett*, (1) if a mandatory reassignment policy was a reasonable accommodation in the run of cases; and, if so, (2) whether there were facts specific to United's employment system that would create an undue hardship if a mandatory reassignment policy was imposed. On the other hand, rejecting the Seventh Circuit's analysis, the Eleventh Circuit, in E.E.O.C. v. ST. JOSEPH'S HOSPITAL, INC., 842 F.3d 1333 (11th Cir. 2016), declared that "[r]equiring reassignment in violation of an employer's best-qualified hiring or transfer policy is not reasonable in the run of cases." Rather, it held, the ADA only requires an employer to permit a disabled individual to compete with the rest of the world for a vacant position.

(b) When an employee seeks reassignment, in order to establish that he or she is a "qualified individual" so as to qualify for protection under the ADA, must that individual establish that he or she is able to perform, with or without a reasonable accommodation, the essential function of the current job or the prospective job for which he or she has applied? *See* E.E.O.C. v. ST. JOSEPH'S HOSPITAL, INC., 842 F.3d 1333 (11th Cir. 2016) (the prospective job). If the only available reassignment is to a position for which the disabled employee is unqualified, does the duty to accommodate require the employer to provide special training to that disabled individual so that she can meet the qualifications for the available position? *See* Williams v. United Insurance Co. of America, 253 F.3d 280 (7th Cir.), cert. denied, 534 U.S. 1025, 122 S.Ct. 556, 151 L.Ed.2d 431 (2001) (the duty to accommodate does not require an employer to provide training that is not offered to nondisabled employees in order to enable a disabled employee to qualify for a promotion or reassignment; that type of affirmative action would constitute forbidden discrimination on the basis of disability).

Where the employer offers reassignment as an accommodation, does the proposed new position have to be comparable to the plaintiff's existing position, e.g., in terms of salary, responsibility, etc.? See Gardea v. JBS USA, LLC, 915 F.3d 537 (8th Cir. 2019) ("If an employer has offered reassignment as a reasonable accommodation, then the [plaintiff] must offer evidence showing both that the position offered was inferior to the employee's former job and that a comparable position for which the employee was qualified was open.).

7. As the result of an automobile accident, Bob Stone was rendered paralyzed from the hip down and began to suffer intermittent bouts of severe upper body pain.

Although these disabilities prevented him from fulfilling his job duties at the office, Bob's doctors reported to his employer that Bob could perform all of his essential job functions if he were permitted to work at home.

(a) If the employer refuses the employee's proposed work-at-home accommodation, has it failed to make a reasonable accommodation to his disability? *Compare* Humphrey v. Memorial Hospitals Association, 239 F.3d 1128 (9th Cir.2001), cert. denied, 535 U.S. 1011, 122 S.Ct. 1592, 152 L.Ed.2d 509 (2002) (working at home is a reasonable accommodation when the essential functions of the job can be performed at home and such an arrangement would not pose an undue hardship upon the employer), *with* Vande Zande v. State of Wis. Dep't of Admin., 44 F.3d 538, 545 (7th Cir. 1995) ("An employer is not required to allow disabled workers to work at home, where their productivity inevitably would be greatly reduced. No doubt * * * there are exceptions, but it would take a very extraordinary case for the employee to be able to create a triable issue of the employer's failure to allow the employee to work at home.").

(b) Alternatively, suppose the plaintiff can return to work, but that her paralysis makes it impossible for her to get to work by public transportation. She is able to drive a car, but is unable to afford the cost of a parking space close enough to her office. Is it a violation of the ADA if the employer denies her request for a paid parking spot near the office? In LYONS v. LEGAL AID SOCIETY, 68 F.3d 1512 (2d Cir. 1995), the Second Circuit ruled that the trial court had erred in granting the defendant's motion to dismiss for failure to state a claim. The appellate court noted that it is an essential part of many jobs to appear at work regularly and on time. In its judgment, there was no suggestion in the plaintiff's complaint that she was asking for a "personal amenity," i.e., that the requested parking space was sought for reasons of personal convenience. To the contrary, the complaint alleged that the request was made solely to enable the plaintiff to reach and perform her job. Accordingly, the court remanded the case for trial on the issue of whether this accommodation was reasonable based on an analysis of the cost and benefits of this proposed accommodation to both parties.

8.   In a case alleging "associational" discrimination, is the employer required to make a reasonable accommodation to the known disability of the relative or associate of the non-disabled employee? *See* Den Hartog v. Wasatch Academy, 129 F.3d 1076 (10th Cir. 1997) (nothing in language or legislative history of ADA suggests that Congress intended to impose this duty upon employers).

9.   Suppose that a disabled individual is able to perform all the essential functions of her job without any accommodation, but that she requests her employer make an accommodation to enhance her ability to gain access to treatment for her disability. Does this request fall within the statutory duty to accommodate? In BUCKINGHAM v. U.S., 998 F.2d 735 (9th Cir. 1993), an action brought under the Rehabilitation Act, an HIV-infected individual was hired by the postal service at a time when he was not experiencing the symptoms of AIDS. After successfully completing his probationary period, the plaintiff began to experience these symptoms. He informed his Postmaster in Columbus, Ohio, that he wished to be transferred to a post office in Los Angeles to obtain better medical treatment for his condition. After the request was forwarded to Los Angeles, the plaintiff took a leave of absence, moved to Los Angeles, and pursued his request with the Los Angeles Postmaster. The Los Angeles Post Office denied the transfer request on the ground, *inter alia*, that an employer was relieved of its duty to accommodate when the subject employee was already able to perform the essential functions of the job. The Ninth Circuit rejected this contention, declaring that a qualified, disabled individual who can perform the essential job functions is entitled to a reasonable accommodation to allow him to pursue therapy or treatment for his disability. The duty to accommodate, the court reasoned,

> is not limited to an employee's ability to function on the job. This reading of the Act is consistent with Congress' express purpose of promoting and expanding employment opportunities in the public and private sectors for handicapped individuals. Furthermore, we have found nothing in the Act or its legislative history to indicate that Congress intended to limit the employer's duty of reasonable accommodation to the facilitation of employment tasks.

998 F.2d at 741.

In the court's view, the statute was designed to promote the ability of disabled individuals to lead normal lives in aspects of their existence outside of the workplace and that this meant that employers were obliged to promote this objective. If you do not agree that the legislature intended to put such a wide-ranging obligation upon employers, what about the argument that improving the employee's access to treatment or therapy is linked to the employee's future ability to perform the essential functions of her job?

10. Suppose a worker's disability prevents her from performing the essential functions of her job, but does not disqualify her from a sufficiently wide range of jobs for her to be deemed substantially limited in the major life activity of working. But also assume that the condition does substantially limit her ability to engage in the major life activity of procreation. Is she, therefore, entitled to a reasonable accommodation from her employer? *See* Wood v. Redi-Mix, Inc., 339 F.3d 682 (8th Cir.2003) (the reasonable accommodation must be related to the limitation on the plaintiff's major life activity and this plaintiff's requested accommodation was related to insubstantial limitations on other major life activities and unrelated to the substantial limitation on his ability to procreate). For a thoughtful and thought-provoking economic analysis of the duty to accommodate under the ADA as framed in *Barnett*, see Seth D. Harris, *Re-Thinking the Economics of Discrimination: U.S. Airways v. Barnett, the ADA, and the Application of Internal Labor Market Theory*, 89 IOWA L.REV. 123 (2003).

5. DEFENSES

We already have examined a few matters that the courts have construed to fall within the realm of affirmative defenses, including the direct threat standard and the undue hardship response to a failure to accommodate claim. In the context of our discussion o n f the "direct threat" defense, we noted that §103 expressly provides covered entities with several "defenses". In addition to an exemption accorded religious institutions and an exception for food handlers with infections or communicable diseases that are transmitted through the handling of food, §103 provides that when a plaintiff asserts that qualification standards, tests or other selection criteria create a disproportionate exclusionary impact on disabled individuals that cannot be cured by a reasonable accommodation, the defendant is relieved of liability if it can prove that the challenged policy is job-related and consistent with business necessity.

(a) Job-Relatedness and Business Necessity

In EEOC v. EXXON CORP., 203 F.3d 871 (5th Cir.2000), the defendant had a substance abuse policy that mandated the automatic termination of any employee in a safety-sensitive, unsupervised position who had undergone treatment for substance abuse. This policy grew out of the 1989 Exxon Valdez incident in which one of defendant's tankers ran aground, causing substantial environmental damage and subjecting Exxon to massive liability. In response to a concern that the accident might have been caused by the tanker's chief officer's previously treated alcoholism, Exxon implemented this policy to avoid the possibility that one of these largely unsupervised employees would relapse into substance abuse and cause another such catastrophe for the environment and for Exxon. The defendant acknowledged that this employment qualification screened out disabled individuals (such as recovering alcoholics who otherwise were qualified to perform the essential functions of the job), but it sought to justify this safety-based qualification standard under the business necessity defense. The EEOC brought suit on behalf of a group of Exxon employees and maintained that the defendant had to demonstrate that its policy satisfied the "direct threat" standard in order to show that it was job related and consistent with business necessity.

The Fifth Circuit rejected this argument, concluding that these two affirmative defenses were separable and applicable in two distinct contexts. The court noted that the business necessity defense of §103(a) was linked to cases in which the defendant was alleged to have relied on an employment qualification standard that disproportionately excluded disabled individuals. Thus, it reasoned, this defense was intended to be relevant to facially neutral standards of general applicability. On the other hand, the court continued, the "direct threat" defense codified in §103(b) was explicitly linked to an employment requirement applied to an "individual." Consequently, the court concluded that this defense was to be used in cases where an employer responded to a particular employee's supposed risk, and not when the employer applied a pre-existing, across-the-board policy to an individual or group. Having said that, however, the court admitted that neither of these two defenses "presents hurdles that comparatively are inevitably higher or lower." Rather, each requires a different type of proof. The "direct threat" defense requires evidence that focuses on the specific risks posed by the subject individual's disability, whereas the business necessity defense examines whether the challenged employment qualification is justified as a policy of general applicability. The court acknowledged, however, that in making this latter determination, a court should examine the magnitude, as well as the probability, of the risks addressed by the challenged policy. It then remanded the case to the trial court for a determination pursuant to this articulation of the business necessity defense.

The Ninth Circuit, on the other hand, has applied the business necessity defense to a challenge to a facially discriminatory employment standard. In BATES v. UNITED PARCEL SERVICE, INC., 511 F.3d 974 (9th Cir. 2007), the defendant required drivers on all its package cars to meet U.S. Department of Transportation (DOT) hearing standards. In an *en banc* ruling, the Ninth Circuit held that the defendant could assert the business necessity defense to the claim that application of this facially discriminatory standard violated the ADA. It also ruled that the trial court had erred in incorporating into the business necessity defense the concepts traditionally associated with the Title VII bona fide occupational qualification (BFOQ) defense. The *en banc* court stated that the ADA business necessity defense required an employer to prove only that its standard was (1) job-related; (2) consistent with business necessity; and (3) that performance could not be accomplished by a reasonable accommodation. In ruling that the defendant had failed to demonstrate that all or substantially all deaf drivers posed a higher risk of traffic accidents than non-deaf drivers, the trial court, according to the Ninth Circuit, improperly incorporated the elements of the BFOQ defense into the business necessity defense.

(b) Bona Fide Insurance Plans

Although each of the previously mentioned defenses is contained in Title I (the provision relating directly to discrimination in employment) of the ADA, there is an important defense provided in Title V (the section composed of miscellaneous provisions) that raises a particularly sensitive and complex issue concerning the interplay between the statute's nondiscrimination provisions and the existence of employer-sponsored health insurance plans. Section 501(c) contains a safe harbor covering the insurance industry as well as those employers that provide insurance coverage for their employees with respect to any insurance policy containing a disability-based distinction. Section 501(c)(1) permits employers, insurers, and plan administrators to establish and implement the terms of an "insured" health insurance plan (i.e., one that is purchased from either an insurance company or some other entity such as a health maintenance organization, as opposed to a self-insured plan where the employer assumes the liability of an insurer) based on underwriting, classifying, or administering risks that are neither inconsistent with State law nor used as a subterfuge to evade the purposes of the Act. Additionally, §501(c)(2) permits employers to create, or observe the terms of, a bona fide self-insured health insurance plan that is not used as a subterfuge to evade the purposes of the Act. Thus, where a plaintiff alleges that an employer's health insurance plan contains a disability-based distinction, in order to fall within the protection of §501(c), the employer must establish that this provision is part of either a bona fide insured plan that is not inconsistent with State law or a bona fide self-insured plan and, in either case, that the plan is not being used as a subterfuge to evade the purposes of the ADA.

NOTES AND PROBLEMS FOR DISCUSSION

1.   The ADA does not contain any definition for "subterfuge to evade the purposes of" that Act. This same undefined "subterfuge" terminology also was contained in the original edition of the ADEA. In PUBLIC EMPLOYEES RETIREMENT SYSTEM OF OHIO v. BETTS, 492 U.S. 158, 109 S.Ct. 2854, 106 L.Ed.2d 134 (1989), the Supreme Court interpreted the "subterfuge to evade the purposes of the Act" language in the ADEA to mean that age-based distinctions in a fringe benefit plan would not constitute a subterfuge to evade the purposes of the Act unless they were shown to have been implemented for the purpose of discriminating with respect to some other aspect of the employment relationship. However, Congress subsequently passed the

Older Workers Benefit Act (OWBPA), which amended the ADEA for the express purpose of overruling that portion of *Betts*. This amendment deleted the "subterfuge" terminology from the ADEA and replaced it with language permitting an employer to invoke cost-based differentials in benefit coverage. The OWBPA, however, did not amend the ADA and, consequently, the "subterfuge" language remains in that statute, albeit undefined. Does this suggest that the meaning ascribed to "subterfuge" in *Betts* for ADEA purposes, should apply in the ADA context? In Krauel v. Iowa Methodist Medical Center, 95 F.3d 674 (9th Cir. 1996), the court reasoned that since Congress presumably knew about the Supreme Court's interpretation of "subterfuge" in *Betts* when it included that phrase in the ADA, it is logical to assume that Congress intended to incorporate the *Betts* interpretation of "subterfuge" into the ADA. The court also noted that had Congress intended to eliminate that phrase from the ADA as well as from the ADEA when it enacted the OWBPA, it could have done so.

2. Enforcement guidelines issued by the EEOC instruct its investigators on how to determine whether any provision in a health insurance plan constitutes a distinction on the basis of disability and, if so, whether it violates the statutory nondiscrimination requirements. For example, the guidelines reveal that any insurance policy that excludes "AZT," a drug used primarily to treat AIDS, will be treated as suspect. They also offer some general direction on how an investigator is to determine whether a disability-based provision is being used as a subterfuge to evade the purposes of the Act. While no bright line definition is proffered, investigators are provided with a nonexhaustive list of permissible justifications for disability-based distinctions. The list includes reliance on actuarial data, identical treatment of all similarly catastrophic conditions, maintenance of the fiscal soundness of the plan and the absence of a financially feasible alternative solution, and a determination, based on expert medical or health professional testimony, that disability-specific treatment has absolutely no medical value.

In ANDERSON v. GUS MAYER BOSTON, 924 F. Supp. 763 (E.D. Tex. 1996), the employer provided its employees with the opportunity to subscribe to a group health policy, with the premiums split evenly between the employer and each subscribing employee. When some employees complained to the owner of their company that they would withdraw from the group if premiums were not reduced, the employer contracted with a new carrier that had the flexibility to deny coverage to some members of the group. At the time the employer made this change, it was aware that one of its employees, the plaintiff, had AIDS. It was also aware that its newly chosen carrier could and would reject the plaintiff on the basis of his disability. When the carrier rejected the plaintiff, he brought suit against his employer under the ADA, claiming that he had been denied equal access to a covered fringe benefit (health insurance) on the basis of his disability. The court agreed with the plaintiff, ruling that when an employer changes group health providers to an insurer that would never consider covering one of the employees in the group because of that employee's disability, the employer violates the ADA unless the employer makes provisions for the excluded employee to receive comparable health insurance in some other way. Having found a disability-based distinction, the court then rejected the defendant's claim that its decision was protected by §501(c). The court concluded that this exception was inapplicable to a case where an individual with a disability has been totally denied coverage of any kind. The case was then remanded for trial on the sole factual question of whether the expense of providing coverage to the plaintiff was of such an enormity that it would cause the employer's plan to become financially insolvent and, therefore, constitute an undue hardship.

3. Can an employer's disability plan place a limit on benefits for mental disabilities that does not apply to recovery for physical disabilities, or does this constitute "discrimination" within the meaning of the ADA? Does the plaintiff have standing under Title I as a "qualified individual with a disability?" If not, could she bring a claim against the employer's insurance company under Title III of the ADA? Has she been subjected to discrimination on the basis of her disability in the provision of "goods or services?" See PARKER v. METROPOLITAN LIFE INS. CO., 121 F.3d 1006 (6th Cir. 1997) (*en banc*), cert. denied, 522 U.S. 1084, 118 S.Ct. 871, 139 L.Ed.2d 768 (1998) (the ADA does not mandate equality between individuals with different disabilities, only between the disabled and the non-disabled).

The MENTAL HEALTH PARITY ACT OF 1996, 42 USC §300gg-5 (1996), however, requires employers who offer mental health benefits in a health insurance plan to provide the same level of coverage for mental health care as is provided for physical illnesses. The Act prohibits any group health plan or health insurance company from establishing a lesser annual or lifetime limit for mental health care than it does for any other condition. There are, however, major exceptions contained in the law which will limit its impact on most employer-sponsored health plans. For example, the statute does not require parity with respect to number of inpatient or outpatient care days, it expressly excludes employers with less than fifty (50) employees, and health plans and health insurance companies are permitted to provide different annual and lifetime caps for mental health care than for other covered services. Most importantly, perhaps, the Act exempts "disability income insurance" from its coverage, thereby not requiring parity for mental and physical disabilities in employer-provided disability (as opposed to health insurance) plans. Additionally, group health plans may also be exempted from this Act if the application of the "leveling-up" provision results in a cost increase to the plan of at least one (1) percent. For a discussion of the analytical models used by the courts to determine whether a particular illness should be categorized as mental or physical for these purposes, see Jane Byeff Korn, *Crazy (Mental Illness Under the ADA)*, 36 J. L. REF. 585 (2003).

4. As previously mentioned, among the defenses contained in §103 of the ADA are two defenses accorded religious institutions. Section 103(c)(1) states that religious institutions do not violate the ADA by giving a preference to individuals of a particular religion with respect to any position, regardless of whether or not it is associated the institution's religious activities. Section 103(c)(2) states that a religious organization can require all applicants and employees to conform to its religious tents. And as discussed at Chapter 1, Sec. D., *supra*, in *Hosanna-Tabor Lutheran Church & School v. E.E.O.C.*, the Supreme Court expressly recognized the existence of a constitutionally-premised "ministerial exception" in a retaliation suit brought under the ADA. Under this doctrine, in order to avoid constitutionally impermissible governmental interference with the relationship between a religious organizations and its clergy, the Free Exercise and Establishment Clauses of the First Amendment Clauses were construed to require that religious institutions have unfettered freedom in the choice and employment of their clergy. Consequently, regardless of the motivation, any decision involving the employment relationship between a religious

entity and its ministers is exempt from governmental interference. However, in *Hosanna-Tabor*, the Supreme Court noted that the dual §103(c) defenses to claims of discrimination do *not* apply to retaliation claims since these defenses refer to "this subchapter" and the anti-retaliation provision appears in a different subchapter than the general prohibition against disability-based discrimination.

6. SPECIAL PROVISIONS CONCERNING DRUG TESTING AND OTHER MEDICAL EXAMINATIONS

Section 104(b)(3) of the ADA permits covered entities to use "reasonable policies or procedures," including drug testing, to ensure that a rehabilitated or rehabilitating individual is not currently using illegal drugs. The right to require employees and/or applicants to undergo drug tests also includes the right to ask follow-up questions in response to a positive drug test. But these questions must be limited to information relevant to validating the test (e.g., whether the drug was taken pursuant to a lawful prescription); they cannot require the individual to reveal the nature of a medical condition that would transform the question into an unlawful disability-related inquiry. Employers and other covered entities also are permitted, under §104(c), to prohibit illegal drug use and alcohol use at the workplace and to enforce policies requiring that employees not be under the influence of alcohol or be engaged in using illegal drugs at the workplace. However, since alcoholism is uniformly viewed by the courts to constitute a covered disability, alcoholics are entitled to a reasonable accommodation that would render them otherwise qualified to perform their job. Is there an inherent contradiction between these two principles? In FLYNN v. RAYTHEON CO., 868 F.Supp. 383 (D.Mass.1994), the court ruled that the right to prohibit alcohol or drug use on the job is not incompatible with the requirement to make a reasonable accommodation to the known physical limitations of an otherwise qualified disabled worker. The court reasoned that Congress did not intend to require an employer to accommodate an alcoholic employee's appearance at the workplace in an inebriated condition. As long as the employer applies the anti-drug or alcohol policy to all employees in a nondiscriminatory manner, the court concluded, it can discipline an alcoholic for working under the influence of alcohol or for drinking on the job.

Section 102(d) of the ADA prohibits the use of medical examinations and inquiries designed to ascertain the existence, nature and severity of a disability. (Recall, however, that §104(d) provides that tests to determine the illegal use of drugs are not considered medical examinations for the purposes of §102(d)). The statute distinguishes between three types of medical exams, i.e., those given (1) to applicants for employment (referred to as preemployment examinations); (2) to individuals who have been offered a job but whose offer is conditioned upon the results of the examination (referred to as employment entrance examinations); and (3) to incumbent employees. The rules concerning the manner in which such examinations and inquiries can be required differ according to the class of individuals tested. With respect to preemployment exams, the provision prohibits employers from requiring job applicants to undergo medical examinations or inquiries (other than tests for the presence of illegal drugs) for the purpose of determining the presence, nature, or severity of a disability, except that the employer can inquire about the applicant's ability to perform relevant job functions.

Similarly, incumbent employees cannot be subjected to medical exams for the purpose of determining the presence, nature, or severity of a disability, except that the employer can conduct such an examination or inquiry if it is shown to be job-related and consistent with business necessity. For example, in YIN v. STATE OF CALIFORNIA, 95 F.3d 864 (9th Cir.1996), cert. denied, 519 U.S. 1114, 117 S.Ct. 955, 136 L.Ed.2d 842 (1997), the plaintiff tax auditor's excessive absences significantly impaired her productivity. After returning from one of her absences, her supervisor requested that the plaintiff provide a copy of her medical records. After the plaintiff refused, and after several additional absences, she was asked by her supervisor to submit to an independent medical examination by a doctor selected by the State. The employee again refused and brought suit to enjoin the State from requiring her to release her medical records and submit to an examination, or to discipline her for refusing to do so. The appellate court affirmed the trial court's grant of summary judgment in favor of the defendant, ruling that even if the medical examination had been requested for the purpose of determining whether or not the plaintiff was disabled, it was job-related and consistent with business necessity. Since the plaintiff's excessive absenteeism had taken a serious toll on her productivity and overall job performance, and there was no evidence that the supervisors were merely trying to discover whether or not she suffered from a particular disability or that they harbored any bias against disabled individuals, the court concluded that the purpose for the examination request was to determine whether the plaintiff was still capable of doing her job. "When health problems have had a substantial and injurious impact on an employee's job performance," the court concluded, "the employer can require the employee to undergo a physical examination designed to determine his or her ability to work." *See also* EEOC v. Prevo's Family Market, Inc., 135 F.3d 1089 (6th Cir.1998) (a produce clerk who use knives and frequently receive cuts and nicks in preparing produce for presentation can be required by the employer to undergo medical testing for HIV, hepatitis, and related conditions after he informs them that he had tested positive for the HIV; such a test under these unique circumstances is job-related and consistent with a business necessity to protect the health of the plaintiff, the defendant's other employees and the general public from HIV infection).

In CONROY v. NEW YORK STATE DEP'T OF CORRECTIONAL SERVICES, 333 F.3d 88 (2d Cir. 2003), the defendant's sick leave policy required employees to submit "general diagnoses" as part of its medical certification procedure following certain absences. One of the issues in the case was whether the requirement of a general diagnosis constituted a medical inquiry of an incumbent employee forbidden by §102(d). The Second Circuit agreed with the trial court that requiring medical certification was an "inquiry" within the meaning of the statute because the information contained in even a general diagnosis might tend to reveal the existence of a disability or give rise to the perception of a disability. Secondly, noting that §102(d) contains an exception for inquiries supported by business necessity, the Second Circuit ruled that to fall within this affirmative defense, the employer bears the burden of proving (1) that the inquiry serves a vital business interest; and (2) that the request is not broader or more intrusive than necessary, i.e., that it is a reasonably effective method of achieving the employer's stated goal without being the only way of achieving the stated vital interest. The court also offered two illustrative examples of vital business interests that would support a business necessity defense: (1) where an inquiry is necessary to determine whether the employee can perform job-related tasks and the employer has a nondiscriminatory reason to doubt the employee's capacity to perform such as a history of frequent absences; and (2) where the inquiry is necessary to determine whether the employee's absence or request for absence is due to legitimate medical reasons and the employer has reason to suspect abuse of its attendance policy.

The Seventh Circuit has rejected the suggestion that a psychological test given to an incumbent employee constitutes a "search" within the meaning of the Fourth Amendment. In GREENAWALT v. INDANA DEPARTMENT OF CORRECTIONS, 397 F.3d 587 (7th Cir. 2005), the plaintiff was required to submit to a psychological examination in order to retain her job as a research analyst with the state department of corrections. She claimed that the test, which took about two hours and included questions probing the details of her personal life, constituted an unreasonable search in violation of her Fourth Amendment rights. The court concluded that the Fourth Amendment should not reach a test that did not involve a physical touching even when the inquiries were designed to elicit information of a highly personal nature. To rule otherwise, it reasoned, would create the possibility of requiring a search warrant or waiver every time an employer conducted a background investigation, a credit check, or any other employment-related inquiry. The court added, however, that the fact that the objective of the inquiry by this public employer was to obtain testimonial evidence might bring the Fifth Amendment into play. But since the plaintiff did not raise this argument, the court went no further than to mention its possible applicability to a situation like this. It simply ruled that the Fourth Amendment did not provide a remedy for the unpleasantness of being subjected to this psychological test. Finally, the court acknowledged that its ruling did not leave the plaintiff remediless since she remained able to press her state law damage claims alleging invasion of privacy and intentional infliction of emotional distress.

Employment entrance examinations, however, are subject to a different set of rules. The statute permits the employer to require a medical examination after the offer has been made but before commencement of employment, and to condition the offer on the results of that examination so long as three requirements are satisfied: (1) all new employees are subjected to such an examination; (2) information regarding the applicant's medical condition or history is treated confidentially and kept apart from other employment files and records; and (3) the results of the examination are used in accordance with the statute. Unlike the situation with preemployment exams or exams of incumbent employees, the statute does not place any restriction on the scope of employment entrance exams, i.e., it does not require that these medical examinations be concerned solely with the individual's ability to perform job-related functions or be job-related and consistent with business necessity. The only restrictions placed on such exams by the statute is the use to which the employer can put the information and the confidentiality of the way in which the information is gathered. See Norman-Bloodsaw v. Lawrence Berkeley Laboratory, 135 F.3d 1260 (9th Cir. 1998) (an employer can use blood and urine samples collected during an employment entrance examination to test for highly private and sensitive medical and genetic information such as syphilis, sickle cell trait, and pregnancy without the employee's knowledge or consent; but plaintiffs can state a claim of racial and gender discrimination under Title

VII if sickle cell trait and pregnancy tests are given only to African-Americans and women, respectively).

With respect to employment entrance examinations, the ADA does not define the nature of a conditional offer. But the EEOC has taken the position that medical exams can only be given after the employer has made a "real" offer, i.e., after the employer has completed all non-medical components of the application process. This means, according to the EEOC, that an employer must undertake a two-step investigation prior to finalizing the offer. It must first determine that the individual has met all non-medical job requirements, such as a background investigation, polygraph test, personal interview, etc. Only after those steps are concluded, the EEOC requires, can the employer undertake the medical examination. Equal Employment Opportunity Commission, ADA ENFORCEMENT GUIDANCE: PREEMPLOYMENT DISABILITY–RELATED QUESTIONS AND MEDICAL EXAMINATIONS, 17 (1995).

The dual purpose of this two-step sequence is to enable applicants to determine whether they were rejected for medical or non-medical reasons and to withhold decision on whether or not to reveal certain medical information until the last stage of the hiring process. By isolating the medical considerations, the candidate is in a position to know that he or she will get the job as long as they meet job-related medical standards. The circuit courts have largely adopted the EEOC's proposed sequencing procedure. Thus, for example, in LEONEL v. AMERICAN AIRLINES, INC., 400 F.3d 702 (9th Cir. 2005), the employer was found to have violated the ADA by revoking its conditional offer of employment on the ground that the three plaintiff candidates had failed to disclose their HIV status during a series of medical examinations. The airline had sent the plaintiffs to its on-site medical department for medical exams, to fill out medical history questionnaires, and to give blood and urine samples immediately after issuing the conditional offers of employment. Only later did the airline conduct the background checks. The Ninth Circuit held that the ADA prohibited all medical examinations and inquiries until after the employer had completed all non-medical phases of the selection process, unless the employer could establish that it could not reasonably have completed the non-medical components before conducting the medical inquiries. Reversing the trial court's grant of summary judgment in favor of the defendant, the court found that the airline had not established as a matter of law that it could not reasonably have completed the background checks before subjecting the plaintiffs to the medical examinations and questioning.

The Ninth Circuit also rejected the defense claim that although it had collected the medical information before the non-medical information, it had not evaluated the medical information until after it had evaluated the non-medical information from the background check. In its view, the ADA regulated the sequence in which employers collect, rather than evaluate, information. Otherwise, applicants will not be in a position to shield their private medical information until they know that they will be hired absent their ability to meet the job's bona fide medical requirements.

Similarly, in BUCHANAN v. CITY OF SAN ANTONIO, 85 F.3d 196 (5th Cir.1996), the defendant required the plaintiff to undertake a medical examination after the plaintiff had signed an acknowledgment that his offer was conditioned on successful completion "of the entire screening process," which included psychological exams, a polygraph examination, an assessment board, and an extensive background investigation. Under these circumstances, the court determined that this was not a "real" offer that permitted the employer to require a medical examination.

An employer's obligation to treat medical information confidentially only arises when the employer obtains that information as a result of "medical examinations and inquiries". This issue typically arises in cases where a former employer unilaterally provides medical information about a former employee to that individual's prospective new employer. For example, in EEOC v. THRIVENT FINANCIAL FOR LUTHERANS, 700 F.3d 1044 (7th Cir. 2012), when an employee failed to report to work, the supervisor sent him an email asking to explain his absence. In response, the worker sent an email stating that he was in bed with a severe migraine and that he had suffered from migraines for over twenty-five years as the result of a head trauma he had sustained in a major car accident. He also stated that his medication did not help when he had the type of severe migraine that prevented him from working on that day. The worker subsequently quit that job but had trouble finding new employment after potential employers conducted reference checks. So he hired an online reference checking agency to pretend to be a prospective employer in order to determine what his former employer was saying about him. In that conversation, the former employer indicated that the plaintiff "has medical conditions where he gets migraines." Based on this information, the worker filed an EEOC charge and the EEOC ultimately filed suit against the company under the ADA alleging that the company had violated the confidentiality provision of §§102(d)(3)(A) and (4)(C) which require employers to keep information regarding an employees' medical condition in separate medical files and to treat them as confidential. The trial judge granted summary judgment to the defense, finding that the information that had been disclosed had *not* been obtained as the result of any medical examination or inquiry made by the company. The Seventh Circuit affirmed. First, it ruled that both the examination and inquiry contemplated by the statute had to be medical in nature because of the use of the inclusive conjunction "and" between "examination" and "inquiry" in "medical examinations and inquiries". Thus, since "inquiries" referred to medical, and not generalized inquiries, the court reasoned, since the information had been obtained in response to a general email inquiring as to why the employee had not reported to work, this information was not subject to the statutory command of confidentiality. In doing so, the Seventh Circuit rejected the EEOC's claim that the duty of confidentiality extended to information obtained through all interactions between the employer and employee that were employer-initiated, and which resulted in the employer revealing medical information. It distinguished cases from other circuits where the employer had knowledge that the plaintiff was ill or otherwise physically incapacitated prior to initiating the conversation that resulted in a medical disclosure. Thus, since the defendant employer had no prior knowledge of the worker's medical problems and therefore had no reason to believe that the worker's absence was due to a medical condition, the email it sent to the worker could not be an "inquiry" for ADA purposes.

Does the ADA provide a private cause of action for an otherwise prohibited medial inquiry and, if so, is that true regardless of whether or not the plaintiff is "disabled" within the meaning of the statute? Relying principally on the fact that §102(d)(2) prohibits preemployment medical inquiries of a "job applicant" whereas the general proscription against discrimination contained in §102(a) refers repeatedly to a "qualified individual with a disability", the majority of circuits recognize a private cause of action alleging an unlawful medical inquiry by any job applicant, regardless of the plaintiff's disability status. However, the courts also require that a non-disabled plaintiff challenging a medical inquiry must establish some form of emotional, pecuniary, or other damage. *See, e.g.*, Harrison v. Benchmark Electronics Huntsville, 593 F.3d 1206 (11th Cir. 2010). For example, suppose an employer makes unlawful preemployment inquiries, but it can demonstrate that the decision not to hire the applicant was not based on the applicant's answers to those impermissible questions. Can the plaintiff recover compensatory or nominal damages? *See* Griffin v. Steeltek, Inc., 261 F.3d 1026 (10th Cir.2001) (where the jury found that the defendant did not base its hiring decision on the plaintiff's answer to impermissible questions and that the plaintiff did not suffer any emotional distress from being asked impermissible questions about his medical condition, the plaintiff cannot recover either compensatory or nominal damages for this technical violation).

7. PROCEDURAL AND REMEDIAL ISSUES

Since §107(a) of the ADA incorporates by reference the enforcement mechanism of Title VII, most of the rules and issues concerning both the procedure for asserting claims of employment-related disability claims under Title I of the ADA and the remedies available in such actions are identical to those governing Title VII actions. For a thorough discussion of those matters, see Chapters 4 and 7, *supra*.

However, certain procedural and remedial issues are unique to the ADA context. For example, although Title I incorporates the remedial and procedural scheme of Title VII, Title II of the ADA adopts the remedies and procedures of §504 of the Rehabilitation Act. Title II, the "Public Services" title of the ADA, prohibits otherwise qualified persons with disabilities from (1) being excluded from participating in, or being denied the benefits of, programs and services offered by public entities; or (2) being subjected to discrimination by any such agency. Consequently, private and nonfederal public employees seeking relief under Title I of the ADA (recall that nearly all federal employers are not subject to Title I), pursuant to the Title VII enforcement mechanism, must file an administrative charge with the EEOC prior to instituting suit. However, claimants alleging discrimination by a public agency under Title II of the ADA, pursuant to the Rehabilitation Act enforcement scheme, are not required to invoke this administrative remedy prior to filing suit. Does this mean that when a state or local government employee alleging disability-based discrimination in employment forgets or otherwise fails to file a timely EEOC charge, she can still file an action under Title II?

Although Title II does not expressly refer to employment, the Justice Department has issued regulations extending this section's prohibition against discrimination to employment-related decisions. *See* 28 CFR §35.140 ("no qualified individual with a disability shall *** be subjected to discrimination in employment under any service, program or activity conducted by a public entity."). Moreover, another portion of this Justice Department regulation provides that the "requirements" of Title I, as established by EEOC regulations, apply to employment in any activity conducted by a public entity covered by Title I. 28 C.F.R. §35.140(b)(1). The immediately succeeding subsection, however, adds that if the public entity is not subject to the jurisdiction of Title I, the requirements of §504 shall apply. 28 C.F.R. §35.140(b)(2).

The Eleventh Circuit has relied on the Justice Department regulations, and the extensive legislative history concerning the ADA, to conclude that Title II does provide for a cause of action for employment discrimination by a nonfederal public employee. *See* Bledsoe v. Palm Beach County Soil and Water Conservation District, 133 F.3d 816 (11th Cir.), cert. denied, 525 U.S. 826, 119 S.Ct. 72, 142 L.Ed.2d 57 (1998). On the other hand, the Ninth Circuit has rejected that analysis and concluded that since the language of Title II reflects Congress' unambiguous intent for this section of the statute not to apply to claims of employment discrimination, under traditional tools of statutory construction, it was unnecessary to accord any weight to the Attorney General's regulation. *See* Zimmerman v. Oregon Dep't of Justice, 170 F.3d 1169 (9th Cir.1999), cert. denied, 121 S.Ct. 1186, 149 L.Ed.2d 103 (2001).

Section 107(a) of Title I of the ADA also incorporates the remedial provisions of Title VII. As you know, prior to the enactment of the 1991 Civil Rights Act, recovery under Title VII was limited to equitable relief. But the 1991 Act authorized the recovery of compensatory and punitive damages in those Title VII cases alleging intentional discrimination. Moreover, §102(a)(2) of the 1991 Civil Rights Act expressly amended Title I of the ADA to provide for the recovery of compensatory and punitive damages in cases brought under §§ 102 (prohibiting disability-based discrimination) and 102(b)(5) (prohibiting the failure to make a reasonable accommodation to a known disability) of the ADA. This recovery is subject to the same rules that apply to Title VII cases, except that such relief is unavailable under the ADA where the defendant establishes that it made a good faith effort, after consulting with the plaintiff, to make a reasonable accommodation.

It is, however, §103 of the ADA, in language comparable to that found in §704 of Title VII, that prohibits disability-based retaliation. In light of this statutory scheme, can a retaliation claimant state a claim for compensatory and punitive damages under the ADA? The Seventh Circuit, in KRAMER v. BANC OF AMERICA SECURITIES, LLC., 355 F.3d 961 (7th Cir.), cert. denied, 542 U.S. 932, 124 S.Ct. 2876, 159 L.Ed.2d 798 (2004), said no. It ruled that when Congress expanded the remedies available under the ADA through its enactment of the 1991 Civil Rights Act, it intended only to provide these additional remedies only for those claims listed therein, i.e., claims brought under §102 and 102(b)(5). Thus, the court reasoned, since §103 claims were not listed, the clear language of the statute established that Congress did not intend to expand the remedies available to a party bringing an ADA retaliation claim. Since the statute was specific on this point, the court concluded that it did not need to consider a legislative committee report's summary of legislative intent suggesting a contrary result. Having found that the plaintiff was not entitled to recover compensatory or punitive damages, the court also ruled that she had no statutory or constitutional right to a jury trial. The Ninth Circuit agreed, noting also, in ALVARADO v. CAJUN OPERATING CO., 588 F.3d 1261 (2009), that Congress could well have intended to have a more limited remedy available for ADA retaliation claims since such claims, unlike discrimination claims, do not require the plaintiff to establish that she was disabled or that she was discriminated against because of her disability; only that she was retaliated for engaging in protected participation or opposition conduct. A few district courts, however, have come to the contrary conclusion, based on the rationale that in the absence of any remedial language in the anti-retaliation provision of the ADA, retaliation claims should be amenable to the same remedial options available for all other Title I claims.

On the other hand, as previously mentioned, Title II of the ADA (the provision regulating recipients of federal funding) is subject to the remedial scheme governing suits filed under §504 of the Rehabilitation Act and §504 actions, in turn, are subject to the remedies available under Title VI of the 1964 Civil Rights Act. In BARNES v. GORMAN, 536 U.S. 181, 122 S.Ct. 2097, 153 L.Ed.2d 230 (2002), the Supreme Court unanimously held that punitive damages are not recoverable under private actions brought under Title VI. Barnes was a non-employment related claim brought by a disabled individual against the Kansas City police department under Title II of the ADA challenging the department's failure to provide appropriate facilities for the transportation of persons with spinal cord injuries in police vehicles. The Court held that since Title VI invoked Congress' power under the Spending Clause to place conditions on the grant of federal funds, it was appropriate to apply contract law rules to Spending Clause legislation. Moreover, the Court continued, though it previously had ruled, in Franklin v. Gwinnet County Public Schools, that absent clear direction to the contrary by Congress, federal courts were authorized to award "appropriate relief" in a cognizable claim brought under a federal statute, a particular remedy was "appropriate relief" in Spending Clause legislation cases only if the funding recipient was on notice that its acceptance of public funding left it exposed to liability of that nature. Funding recipients, the Court explained, are presumed to be on notice only of those remedies either explicitly provided in the relevant legislation or those traditionally available in breach of contract actions. And punitive damages, unlike compensatory damages, are generally not available for a breach of contract.

The Court also found no basis for implying a punitive damages provision in Title VI. Since an indeterminate amount of punitive damages could well exceed a recipient's level of funding, such an award could be "disastrous" and, therefore, the Court found it doubtful that any recipient would have agreed to exposure to such indeterminate liability in order to receive federal funding or to even have accepting such funding if punitive damages liability was a required condition. Consequently, the Court rejected the conclusion that a Title VI funding recipient had, by accepting funds, implicitly consented to punitive damages liability. Thus, since punitive damages were not awardable under Title VI, the Court ruled, they were similarly unavailable in actions brought under §504 of the Rehabilitation Act. This, in turn, means that punitive damages are unavailable under §202 of Title II of the ADA.

NOTES AND PROBLEMS FOR DISCUSSION

1. As is true in Title VII cases, the cap on the recovery of compensatory and punitive damages enacted as part of the 1991 Civil Rights Act applies to ADA actions. When a jury's award exceeds the statutory cap (and this can easily happen since the statute prohibits advising the jury of the limitations on damages), how is the jury's award modified in order to comply with the statutory limit? In EEOC v. AIC SECURITY INVESTIGATIONS, LTD., 823 F.Supp. 571 (N.D. Ill. 1993), the jury found that the plaintiff had been unlawfully discharged on the basis of a disability and awarded $50,000 in compensatory damages and $250,000 in punitive damages, the sum of which exceeded the $200,000 cap on damage recoveries applicable to companies of

this size. Although, as the trial court acknowledged, it would have been ideal to ask the jury to recalculate its award, since the statute prohibited advising the jury of the limitations on damages, the trial judge was required to reassess the damages. The court then had to decide where to allocate the reduction. Since the statute was silent on how reduced awards should be apportioned between compensatory and punitive damages, the trial judge agreed with the plaintiff that the entire reduction should come out of the punitive damage award. This portion of the court's opinion was affirmed on appeal. 55 F.3d 1276 (7th Cir. 1995).

Suppose an ADA claimant dies prior to the adjudication of his or her lawsuit. Can a claim for compensatory damages under the ADA survive the claimant's death? In a case of first impression, the Eighth Circuit reversed the trial court's ruling that this issue, as to which the text of the ADA is silent, should be governed by state law. In GUENTHER v. GRIFFIN CONSTRUCTION CO., 846 F.3d 979 (8th Cir. 2017), the appellate court reasoned that since (1) the ADA was silent on the matter, (2) there was no general federal survival statute for federal question cases, and (3) 42 U.S.C. §1988(a) – which directs federal courts to fill gaps in certain federal actions with state law when state law is not inconsistent with federal law – did not apply to the ADA, the question of survival was governed by federal common law absent an expression of contrary intent from Congress. Then, in confecting the content of the federal common law, the Eighth Circuit concluded that the interests in providing a uniform federal rule weighed in favor of not incorporating state law. Finally, because, the court reasoned, the very nature of ADA claims made it more likely that the aggrieved could die before the case was completed, a rule allowing claims for compensatory damages under the ADA to abate when the aggrieved party died would impede the broad remedial purposes of this statute. Accordingly, it held that a claim for compensatory damages under the ADA survives the death of the aggrieved party. However, the panel expressly reserved judgment on whether a claim of punitive damages similarly would survive, particularly in light of the traditional federal common law rule that claims for punitive damages abate on death.

2. Section 502 of the ADA explicitly removes a State's Eleventh Amendment immunity from suit under Title I by providing state employees with the same right to sue their employer for equitable and legal damages that is available to employees of private and non-State public entities. You will recall from our discussion of the ADEA, that in KIMEL v. FLORIDA BD. OF REGENTS, 528 U.S. 62, 120 S.Ct. 631, 145 L.Ed.2d 522 (2000), the Supreme Court held that Congress did not constitutionally abrogate the States' right of sovereign immunity when it enacted an amendment to the ADEA creating a right of action for damages against state governments. The Court, applying a standard it had previously articulated in *Seminole Tribe*, found that this statutory provision was not enacted pursuant Congress' §5 remedial authority under the Fourteenth Amendment. See Chapter 10, Section A, *supra*.

(a) In light of the Court's ruling in *Kimel*, what is the constitutional viability of §502 of the ADA?

In BD. OF TRUSTEES OF UNIV. OF ALABAMA v. GARRETT, 531 U.S. 356, 121 S.Ct. 955, 148 L.Ed. 2d 866 (2001), the Court, by another 5-4 vote, continued down the road it had traveled in *Kimel* by striking down the private right of action for damages in federal court provided to state employees by §502. The Court concluded that although Congress clearly intended to waive the States' sovereign immunity against damage actions brought under Title I of the ADA, this provision did not meet constitutional muster because it could not be deemed to have been enacted pursuant to Congress' authority under §5 of the Fourteenth Amendment. The majority reached this conclusion based on its determination that the legislative record of the ADA did not sufficiently identify a history and pattern of unconstitutional (i.e., irrational discrimination since disability classifications are subject only to rational basis scrutiny) employment discrimination by the States against individuals on the basis of their disability. The Court added that the evidence relevant to this inquiry is limited to conduct undertaken by the States themselves and not by units of local governments such as cities and counties.

The Court also declared that even if the legislative record were found to have demonstrated a sufficient pattern of unconstitutional conduct against disabled individuals by the States, the statutory response to such unconstitutional conduct was not congruent and proportional to the injury in at least three respects. First, the statute imposed a duty of accommodation that "far exceeds what is constitutionally required in that it makes unlawful a range of alternate responses that would be reasonable but would fall short of imposing an 'undue burden' upon the employer." Second, the statute required the employer to prove that it would suffer an undue burden instead of requiring, as the Constitution would, that the plaintiff bear the burden of negating all reasonable bases for the employer's decision. Finally, the ADA prohibited the use of standards that disproportionately disadvantage disabled individuals, while the Constitution requires more than mere evidence of disproportionate impact to establish intentional discrimination.

The Court in *Garrett*, however, expressly limited its decision to the provision of a damages remedy against a State in Title I of the ADA, reserving decision on the constitutionality of similar provisions in Titles II (prohibiting disability-based discrimination in access to public services and programs) and III (prohibiting disability-based discrimination in public accommodations). Three years later, the Supreme Court partially filled this void with respect to damage claims against States alleging violations of Title II. In TENNESSEE v. LANE, 541 U.S. 509, 124 S.Ct. 1978, 158 L.Ed.21d 820 (2004), once again by a 5-4 margin, the Court rejected the defendant State's Eleventh Amendment immunity defense and held that Congress had validly abrogated the State's Eleventh Amendment right of sovereign immunity with respect to that portion of Title II that provided a cause of action for damages to disabled plaintiff alleging that a State had denied them physical access to its courts. The Court distinguished its prior ruling in *Garrett* on two grounds.

First, it declared that unlike the situation with respect to Title I, Congress had produced and relied upon extensive documentation of a history and pattern of unconstitutional discrimination by the States in the provision of physical access to courthouses. Second, the injury inflicted upon disabled individuals in this instance was the denial of access to the courts, a fundamental right protected by the Due Process Clause of the Fourteenth Amendment. Interference with this fundamental right was subject to a higher level of scrutiny than the rational basis scrutiny applied to employment discrimination against the non-suspect class of disabled workers. Accordingly, the majority reasoned, this finding, together with the extensive record of disability discrimination made it "clear beyond peradventure" that inadequate provision access to the courts was an appropriate subject for legislation under §5 of the Fourteenth Amendment.

The Court also concluded that the obligations imposed on States under Title II constituted both a congruent and proportional response to the history and pattern of unequal treatment in access to the courts. Since the statute, the Court explained, required the State only to take reasonable measures to remove architectural and other barriers to accessibility, this constituted as reasonable prophylactic measure targeted to a legitimate objective.

The Court revisited the question of the constitutionality of Congress' abrogation of state sovereign immunity from damage actions brought under Title II in U.S. v. GEORGIA, 546 U.S. 151, 126 S.Ct. 877, 163 L.Ed.2d 650 (2006). But the procedural posture of the case left the Court with only a very limited issue before it. A disabled inmate in a state prison had filed a *pro se* complaint in federal court against the State of Georgia, the Georgia Department of Corrections, and individual prison officials challenging the conditions of his confinement and seeking injunctive relief and money damages under Title II and 42 U.S.C. §1983. The trial court had dismissed the §1983 claims against all defendants without leave to amend on the ground that the allegations in the complaint were too vaguely stated. The court also had dismissed the Title II claims against the individual defendants. Finally, the trial judge also had granted the State defendants summary judgment on the plaintiff's Title II claims on the ground that those claims were barred by state sovereign immunity. On appeal, the Eleventh Circuit reversed the dismissal of the §1983 claims, ruling that the trial court should have granted the plaintiff leave to amend his complaint. As to the Title II claims, the Eleventh Circuit affirmed the trial judge's ruling that the claims against the State defendants were barred by sovereign immunity.

The Supreme Court granted certiorari only on the question of whether Title II validly abrogated state sovereign immunity with respect to the claims asserted in the instant case. This was a critical factor, since the Eleventh Circuit, in reversing the dismissal of the plaintiff's §1983 claims, had ruled that some of the allegations in the plaintiff's complaint constituted violations of the Eighth Amendment ban on cruel and unusual punishment, a constitutional guarantee that applied to the States through the Due Process Clause of the Fourteenth Amendment. Moreover, the State defendants did not contest that holding. Neither did the State dispute the plaintiff's claim that the same conduct that violated the Eighth Amendment also violated Title II. Consequently, this left the Court only with the question of whether the damage remedy in Title II constitutionally abrogated state sovereign immunity when applied to a case in which the challenged conduct violated the Fourteenth Amendment as well as the statute. Not surprisingly, the Court was of a single mind on that circumscribed issue. Writing for a unanimous Court, Justice Scalia announced that §5 of the Fourteenth Amendment authorized Congress to provide a private remedy for monetary damages against a State for conduct that "actually" violates the Fourteenth Amendment. But the Court expressly left open the question of whether the Constitutional sanctioned Congress' purported abrogation of state sovereign immunity in cases involving misconduct that violated Title II but did not also violate the Fourteenth Amendment. In a brief concurring opinion, Justice Stevens, joined by Justice Ginsburg, suggested that the Court's ruling should not be limited to cases involving actual violations of the Eighth Amendment. He pointed out that the history of inmate mistreatment was not limited to violations of the constitutional right to be free from cruel and unusual punishment.

Since the ADA adopts the remedial procedures set forth in Title VII, pursuant to §706(f)(1) of the 1964 Act, the federal government is authorized to bring suit on behalf of an aggrieved disabled individual and to seek damages for the benefit of that individual. In light of the Supreme Court's ruling in *Garrett*, can a State successfully argue that it retains sovereign immunity from suit brought in a federal court by the federal government under the ADA seeking damages for the benefit of a specifically identified individual? The Supreme Court consistently has held that the Eleventh Amendment does not apply to suits filed by the federal government. *See, e.g.*, Alden v. Maine, 527 U.S. 706, 119 S.Ct. 2240, 144 L.Ed.2d 636 (1999); West Virginia v. U.S., 479 U.S. 305, 107 S.Ct. 702, 93 L.Ed.2d 639 (1987). On the other hand, where the federal government brings an action to remedy an individual instance of discrimination, rather than to remedy a pattern of intentional discrimination against a class of individuals, can the federal government be viewed as a proxy for the individual? If so, since, per *Garrett*, the Eleventh Amendment shields the State from a suit for damages in federal court by the individual, should the same result not apply when the federal government is standing in that individual's shoes? *See* U.S. v. Mississippi Dep't of Public Safety, 321 F.3d 495 (5th Cir.2003) (a state does not enjoy sovereign immunity from suit brought by the federal government even when the U.S. is seeking to recovery a benefit solely for the private individual; the federal government is not a mere proxy for the individual because it retains control of the case and acts in furtherance of a substantial federal interest in securing the State's compliance with federal law).

(b) How are the Court's rulings in *Kimel* and *Garrett* likely to affect the continued viability of claims for money damages by public employees under the other antidiscrimination statutes? *Compare* Wilson-Jones v. Caviness, 99 F.3d 203 (6th Cir. 1996) (since the amendment to the FLSA extending a private right action for damages for a violation of the minimum wage and overtime provisions to State employees was designed to provide public sector workers with the same level of protection previously accorded to private sector employees, this amendment could not be regarded as an enactment to enforce the Fourteenth Amendment), *with* Siler-Khodr v. University of Texas Health Science Ctr. at San Antonio, 261 F.3d 542 (5th Cir.2001), cert. denied, 537 U.S. 1087, 123 S.Ct. 694, 154 L.Ed.2d 631 (2002) (the extension of a private cause of action for damages for violations of Equal Pact Act provisions of FLSA to State employees was enacted pursuant to Congress' authority under §5 of the Fourteenth Amendment).

3. There is no provision in the ADA comparable to that present in the OWBPA amendments to the ADEA restricting the way in which employers obtain releases or other waivers of statutory rights from their employees. What, if anything, does this suggest about the enforceability of waivers and releases of ADA rights in light of the fact that the ADA does explicitly encourage private resolution of disability-based employment disputes? *See* Rivera-Flores v. Bristol-Myers Squibb Caribbean, 112 F.3d 9 (1st Cir. 1997) (ADA waivers and releases are enforceable where the defendant employer sustains the burden of proving that they are knowing and voluntary because (1) the ADA encourages private resolution of disability disputes; (2) ADA claims are subject to Title VII enforcement mechanism and releases have been traditionally

accepted in that context; and (3) prohibiting waivers would display stereotyped and patronizing attitudes towards the disabled that the statute was designed to prevent.).

SECTION B.   THE REHABILITATION ACT OF 1973

Read §§7(8), 501 and 503–505 of the Rehabilitation Act.

As noted at the outset of this Chapter, the substantive obligations contained in the ADA were patterned after the preexisting terms of the Rehabilitation Act. Consequently, the courts typically apply the same legal analysis to claims made under both statutes including, for example, issues such as whether a plaintiff is "disabled". *See, e.g.*, Mahon v. Crowell, 295 F.3d 585 (6th Cir.2002) (extending the Supreme Court's holding in *Toyota* to a §501 claim under the Rehabilitation Act). At the same time, however, the Rehabilitation Act is significantly less comprehensive in its coverage than the ADA. Specifically, it applies only to the federal government, the U.S. Postal Service, federal contractors, and entities receiving federal funds. Nevertheless, because of some procedural and remedial advantages that the Rehabilitation Act enjoys over the ADA, and the fact that it applies to federal employees who remain unprotected by the ADA, it is still a useful litigative tool for those employees that are subject to its provisions.

The Act contains three substantive provisions — §§501, 503 and 504. Section 501 requires federal agencies and departments to create affirmative action programs for their employment of disabled individuals. Section 503 imposes a similar affirmative action obligation on parties to a contract in excess of $2500 with a federal agency or department. Neither of these two provisions contains an express prohibition against discriminating on the basis of disability. Section 504, on the other hand, prohibits entities receiving federal financial assistance, the U.S. Postal Service, and the federal government from discriminating against disabled individuals. Thus, since §504 provides federal employees with the right to be free from disability-based discrimination that is absent from §501, the only category of covered employees without an express right to be free from disability-based discrimination under the Rehabilitation Act are employees of federal contractors.

The procedural and remedial terms of the Rehabilitation Act are contained in §505. Section 505(a) subjects complaints brought under §501 to the "remedies, procedures, and rights" provided to federal employees by §717 of Title VII, while §505(b) subjects employees of federal funding recipients who allege a violation of §504 to the remedial and procedural provisions of Title VI. As a result of these provisions, §501 and 504 claimants can assert a private cause of action to enforce their substantive right to be free from disability-based discrimination in employment by the federal government, the U.S. Postal Service, and federal grantees. The circuit courts have construed the terms of §505 to mean that federal employees can assert claims under either §501 or §504.

NOTES AND PROBLEMS FOR DISCUSSION

1. Since §505(a)(2) links the enforcement of §504 rights to the rules governing claims under Title VI of the 1964 Civil Rights Act, what proof standards should apply to §504 claims? For example, should a plaintiff be able to assert an impact-based claim or is she limited to charges of intentional discrimination? Despite several opportunities, the Supreme Court has chosen not to rule definitively on whether a §504 plaintiff can assert an impact-based claim of discrimination. In GUARDIANS ASS'N v. CIVIL SERVICE COMM'N, 463 U.S. 582, 103 S.Ct. 3221, 77 L.Ed.2d 866 (1983), a case composed of several separate opinions, no one of which commanded the support of a majority of the Court, seven Justices agreed that proof of discriminatory intent was necessary to establish a statutory violation. At the same time, however, a majority of five also concluded that a Griggs-type showing of disproportionate impact would suffice in a suit brought to enforce the provisions of administrative regulations issued pursuant to this statute. This left many lower courts with the impression (or hope?) that the Court had not definitively ruled on the availability of impact-based claims of violations of §504.

The Court only further muddied these interpretive waters in ALEXANDER v. CHOATE, 469 U.S. 287, 105 S.Ct. 712, 83 L.Ed.2d 661 (1985). There, the director of the Tennessee Medicaid program decided to institute a variety of cost-cutting measures to respond to projected Medicaid costs in excess of the State's Medicaid budget. One of the proposed changes was to reduce from twenty to fourteen the number of annual inpatient hospital days that Tennessee Medicaid would pay to hospitals on behalf of Medicaid patients. A class of Tennessee Medicaid recipients brought an action under §504 to enjoin this proposed change on the ground that the reduced limitation on inpatient coverage would have a disproportionately disadvantageous impact on the disabled. The Supreme Court refused to rule explicitly on whether an impact-based claim was cognizable under either §504 or its implementing regulations. The Court announced that its opinion in *Guardians Ass'n* was not dispositive of either question. The ruling in *Guardians Ass'n* that a Title VI violation requires proof of discriminatory intent, the *Alexander* Court explained, was solely a function of the stare decisis effect of the Court's prior interpretation of Title VI in *Bakke*. But since *Bakke* did not purport to construe §504, it was inapplicable to the §504 proof issue. But after noting that the legislative history of §504 reflected Congress' recognition that most discrimination against the disabled was the product of indifference rather than animus as well as its intention to proscribe this manifestation of bias, the Court expressed its concern that the recognition of impact claims under §504 would create a potentially unwieldy administrative and adjudicative burden. Ultimately, however, the Court ducked the issue be assuming that §504 reached nonintentional discrimination and then finding that the defendant's conduct did create a disproportionate impact on disabled individuals.

2. Since, under §505, claims brought under §501 are governed by the Title VII enforcement mechanism, whereas §504 plaintiffs are subject to the remedial and procedural provisions of Title VI, what procedural rules govern claims brought by federal employees, who can assert a cause of action under either §501 or §504? To promote uniform treatment of federal employee disability claims, the circuits agree that disability claims by federal employees, whether brought under §§501 or 504, are subject to the procedural constraints imposed upon federal employees by §717 of Title VII. This means that all such claims are subject to the limitations period applied to federal employee Title VII claims and that these plaintiffs are required to invoke administrative remedies prior to filing suit. But the lower courts do not agree on whether the method of proving causation should be identical in §501 and §504 claims. *Compare* Joachim v. Babbit, 60 F.Supp. 2d 581 (M.D.La. 1999) (applying §504's sole cause standard to §501 cases without comment) with Pinkerton v. U.S. Dep't of Education, 518 F.3d 278 (5th Cir. 2007) (language in §501(g) incorporating the use of ADA proof standards for §501 claims means that ADA causation standard — permitting use of mixed motive theory and not requiring the plaintiff to establish that disability was the sole cause of the challenged decision — governs claims brought under §501; applying different causation standards to claims brought under §§501 and 504 — which requires showing of sole causation — is consistent with Supreme Court cases distinguishing between these two provisions with respect to remedies).

The provision in the 1991 Civil Rights Act that provides plaintiffs in Title VII actions alleging intentional discrimination the right to recover compensatory and punitive damages also expressly makes these same remedies available to federal employees in actions alleging intentional discrimination under §501 of the Rehabilitation Act. But since federal employees also can rely on §504 as a statutory predicate for those same claims, should these damage remedies be similarly available under §504? Since §504 does not expressly provide such a remedy, a question is raised as to whether the judicial recognition of such a remedy constitutes a valid abrogation of the federal government's right to sovereign immunity. In LANE v. PENA, 518 U.S. 187, 116 S.Ct. 2092, 135 L.2d. 486 (1996), the Supreme Court concluded that Congress had not waived the federal government's immunity against monetary damages awards in §504(a) violations. It stated that the fact that Congress subjected the federal government to some liability under §504(a) did not mean that it intended to waive its immunity from monetary damage awards.

As previously discussed in Section A of this Chapter, *supra*, the Supreme Court unanimously held in BARNES v. GORMAN, 536 U.S. 181, 122 S.Ct. 2097, 153 L.Ed.2d 230 (2002) that punitive damages are not recoverable under private actions brought under Title VI. The *Barnes* Court held that since Title VI invoked Congress' power under the Spending Clause to place conditions on the grant of federal funds, it was appropriate to apply contract law rules to Spending Clause legislation. Moreover, although in *Franklin*, see Note 4(b), *infra*, the Court held that absent clear direction to the contrary by Congress, federal courts were authorized to award "appropriate relief" in a cognizable claim brought under a federal statute, a particular remedy was "appropriate relief" in Spending Clause legislation cases only if the funding recipient was on notice that its acceptance of public funding left it exposed to liability of that nature. Funding recipients, the Court explained in *Barnes*, are presumed to be on notice only of those remedies either explicitly provided in the relevant legislation or those traditionally available in breach of contract actions. And punitive damages, unlike compensatory damages, are generally not available for a breach of contract.

3. Under the guidelines set forth by the Supreme Court in *Kimel*, do the states retain an Eleventh Amendment right of sovereign immunity against damage awards in actions brought under §504? The Civil Rights Remedies Equalization Act, 42 U.S.C. §2000d–7 (1986), enacted as part of the Rehabilitation Act Amendments of 1986, explicitly removed a State's Eleventh Amendment immunity from damage suits in actions brought under §504, Title IX, Title VI, the ADEA, and any other federal statute prohibiting discrimination by recipients of federal financial assistance. It specifically provided that legal and equitable remedies in suits against a State are available to the same extent that they are available in actions against non-State defendants. In *Lane*, the Supreme Court acknowledged that this amendment to §504 constituted an "unambiguous waiver of the State's Eleventh Amendment immunity."

Although the circuit courts are split on whether, under the Fourteenth Amendment "congruence and proportionality" standard set forth in *Kimel* and *Garrett*, Congress validly abrogated the states' immunity in the 1986 Rehabilitation Act Amendments, they generally have agreed that, in light of *Lane*, the amendment unambiguously informs states that their acceptance of federal funding constitutes a waiver of their Eleventh Amendment immunity to Rehabilitation Act claims asserted against the specific department or agency within the state that receives that funding. *See, e.g.,* Koslow v. Comm. Of Pa., 302 F.3d 161 (3d Cir.2002), cert. denied, 537 U.S. 1232, 123 S.Ct. 1353, 155 L.Ed.2d 196 (2003).

4. Linking the procedural and remedial provisions of §504 to Title VI has raised a series of issues. For example:

(a) Most, if not all federal funding agencies have their own administrative rules for investigating and adjudicating claims of disability discrimination brought against their recipient institutions. Does Title VI require the aggrieved to invoke these administrative remedies prior to instituting suit under §504? In CANNON v. UNIVERSITY OF CHICAGO, 441 U.S. 677, 99 S.Ct. 1946, 60 L.Ed.2d 560 (1979), the Supreme Court held that a Title IX plaintiff was not required to pursue administrative remedies prior to filing suit. Because of the similarity between the enforcement schemes provided in Titles VI and IX, and in light of the fact that the available administrative remedy — termination of funding — does not compensate the individual victim of discrimination, the lower federal courts have extended the ruling in Cannon to claims brought under Title VI. And since Title VI does not impose an exhaustion of administrative remedies requirement, §504 claimants are similarly free to go directly to court with their cause of action. *See* Camenisch v. University of Texas, 616 F.2d 127 (5th Cir. 1980), vacated and remanded for mootness, 451 U.S. 390, 101 S.Ct. 1830, 68 L.Ed.2d 175 (1981). In comparison, since §107(a) of the ADA incorporates the remedial and enforcement mechanism of Title VII with respect to claims filed under Title I, private sector and federal employee plaintiffs with ADA claims are required to invoke the EEOC administrative machinery prior to filing suit.

(b) Title VI, in language nearly identical to that later used in §504, prohibits discrimination on the basis of race, color, and national origin in federally funded programs. But since it does not contain any express remedial provision, what forms of relief are available to a §504 claimant? In *Guardians Ass'n*, a majority of the Court agreed that back pay is recoverable in Title VI actions, at least with respect to claims of intentional discrimination. This ruling was extended to §504 claims in Consolidated Rail Corp. v. Darrone, 465 U.S. 624, 104 S.Ct. 1248, 79 L.Ed.2d 568 (1984). In neither case, however, did the Court discuss whether either compensatory or punitive damages are recoverable under either of these two statutes.

The Supreme Court offered some limited guidance on this issue in FRANKLIN v. GWINNETT COUNTY PUBLIC SCHOOLS, 503 U.S. 60, 112 S.Ct. 1028, 117 L.Ed.2d 208 (1992). This case was brought under Title IX, a provision that mirrors Title VI except that it prohibits discrimination on the basis of gender rather than race. The plaintiff, a female high school student, brought an action for damages against the defendant school district alleging that she had been sexually harassed and abused by a teacher in her school. Although the Supreme Court unanimously held that money damages were recoverable in Title IX cases, it expressly limited this ruling to cases allegations intentional discrimination. And the first circuit court to rule on the issue has held that non-economic (i.e., emotional distress) compensatory damages are recoverable under Title VI, and thus under §504, in cases of intentional discrimination. In SHEELY v. MRI RADIOLOGY NETWORK, P.A., 505 F.3d 1173 (11th Cir. 2007), the Eleventh Circuit, invoking the contract law metaphor employed by the Supreme Court in *Barnes* (see Note 2, *supra*), held that since emotional distress is a predictable, and therefore foreseeable, consequence of a funding recipient's breach of its promise not to discriminate, funding recipients are under fair notice that, in breaching, they may be subject to liability for emotional damages. Consequently, it ruled, emotional distress damages are recoverable for intentional violations of §504, particularly where, as in the instant case, emotional distress was the only alleged damage to the victim and thus the only available remedy "to make good the wrong done".

After the Court's ruling in *Franklin*, the circuit courts split on whether Title IX covered retaliation claims. Unlike Title VII, Title IX doesn't contain an independent anti-retaliation provision. The conflict was resolved in JACKSON v. BIRMINGHAM BOARD OF EDUCATION, 544 U.S. 167, 125 S.Ct. 149, 161L.Ed.2d 361 (2005), a case involving the coach of a girl's high school basketball team who was removed as coach after complaining to school authorities, without success, that his team was not receiving equal funding and equal access to athletic equipment and facilities. The Court, by a 5-4 margin, held that Title IX's private right of action for claims of intentional discrimination on the basis of sex extends to complaints of retaliation taken because the victim complained of sex discrimination. The fact that Title IX did not contain an express prohibition against retaliation, the majority reasoned, "ignores the import of our repeated holdings construing 'discrimination' under Title IX broadly." Unlike Title VII, which spelled out in great detail the conduct that constitutes discrimination, Title IX, the majority explained, was a broadly written general prohibition on discrimination. Congress chose not to list any specific discriminatory practice in Title IX, and so its failure to mention any particular one, such as retaliation, did not say anything about whether it intended for that practice to be covered by the general antidiscrimination command. Retaliating against someone because that person has complained of sex discrimination, the Court ruled, was a form of intentional sex discrimination encompassed by Title IX's private cause of action.

5. (a) Louise Ross, an associate professor of physics, was dismissed shortly after she was involved in an automobile accident that left her blind and paralyzed from the waist down. The University maintained that her disability made it impossible for Professor Ross to engage in the type of research activity expected of a teacher in her chosen field. In addition, the University indicated that while it received a substantial amount of federal funding, all of those monies were used to finance scholarships for minority students in the foreign language department, with none going to the physics department. Based on these contentions, the University filed a motion to dismiss for failure to state a cause of action? Does the language in §504 prohibiting discrimination in "any program or activity receiving Federal financial assistance" limit §504 plaintiffs to challenging discrimination only in the program that receives federal funding? In the Civil Rights Restoration Act, 20 U.S.C. §§1687, 1688 (1987),

Congress explicitly amended the "program or activity" language found, *inter alia*, in Title VI and §504 of the Rehabilitation Act. The amendment redefines "program or activity" to encompass all the operations of any governmental entity or educational institution where any part of that entity or institution receives federal financial assistance.

(b) Title I of the ADA has been construed by the circuit courts to apply only to the employer-employee relationship; so it does not encompass a claim by an independent contractor. Section 504(d) states that "[t]he standards used to determine whether this section has been violated in a *complaint alleging employment discrimination* under this section shall be the standards applied under Title I of the ADA". (emphasis added). Does this incorporation of Title I standards mean that §504, like Title I, only applies to employees and applicants for employment and not, for example, to independent contractors? The courts are split on this question. Some employ a purely textualist approach to conclude that the Title I limitations are incorporated into §504. *See e.g.*, Wojewski v. Rapid City Regional Hospital, 450 F.3d 338 (8th Cir. 2006). Others, however, construe this portion of §504(d) to incorporate only the Title I substantive standard of actionable discrimination, i.e., what conduct violates the statute, but not who is covered by the statute. They rely primarily on the fact that the scope of §504 is broader than that of Title I since it covers all operations, not only employment decisions, of programs receiving federal funds, whereas Title I is restricted to aspects of the employment relationship, leaving other relationships to be addressed by other Titles of the ADA, to conclude that an independent contractor can state a claim under §504. *See e.g.*, Fleming v. Yuma Regional Medical Center, 587 F.3d 938 (9th Cir. 2009), cert. denied, 561 U.S. 1006, 130 S.Ct. 3468, 177 L.Ed.2d. 1076 (2010).

6. Although the Rehabilitation Act and the ADA are the primary federal *statutory* sources of protection for disabled individuals, state and local government employees also can look to the Fourteenth Amendment for redress. Since the Supreme Court no longer favors the argument that absolute rules precluding all employment on the basis of specified disabilities enforce irrebutable presumptions in violation of the Due Process Clause, constitutional challenges to disability discrimination by state and local government workers primarily focus on the Equal Protection Clause. Such was the case, for example, in NEW YORK CITY TRANSIT AUTHORITY v. BEAZER, 440 U.S. 568, 99 S.Ct. 1355, 59 L.Ed.2d 587 (1979). The trial court had ruled that the defendant's blanket exclusion of methadone users from all positions violated the Due Process Clause because it created an irrebutable presumption of unemployability as to all methadone users. The Supreme Court noted that the respondent employees no longer asserted that argument and, moreover, that it was without merit. The Court then turned to the respondent's equal protection claim and found that it survived scrutiny under the rationality standard.

7. Can a federal employee state a constitutional cause of action for disability discrimination or does §505 of the Rehabilitation Act suggest that the Supreme Court's ruling in *Brown* should be extended to make the Rehabilitation Act the exclusive remedy for such federal employee claims? *See* McGuinness v. U.S. Postal Service, 744 F.2d 1318 (7th Cir. 1984).

8. Section 102 of the ADA states that the plaintiff must establish that the defendant discriminated against her "because of" her disability, while §504(a) of the

Rehabilitation Act states that a qualified individual with a disability shall not be discriminated against "solely by reason of" her disability. However, in 1992, Congress amended the Rehabilitation Act by including a new section 504(d) that explicitly incorporates the ADA standards governing the existence of a violation of the ADA's employment provisions for employment claims brought under the Rehabilitation Act. Does this amendment mean that the ADA causation standard should also apply in Rehabilitation Act cases? In SOLEDAD v. U.S.DEP'T OF TREASURY, 304 F.3d 500 (5th Cir.2002), the Fifth Circuit ruled that Congress didn't intend to adopt the ADA causation standard when it amended the Rehabilitation Act in 1992. The court based its conclusion on the fact that Congress chose not to repeal the "solely because of" language in §504(a) when it amended the Rehabilitation Act in 1992. In effect, the court said, the specific language in §504(a) trumped the more generally worded text of §504(d).

PART IV

AFFIRMATIVE ACTION

Read §§703(j) and 706(g) of Title VII.

Section 706(g) of Title VII provides that if a defendant is found to have intentionally engaged in or be intentionally engaging in an unlawful employment practice, the court may "order such affirmative action as may be appropriate, which may include, but is not limited to, reinstatement or hiring of employees * * * or any other equitable relief as the court deems appropriate." This remedial provision has generated several of the most complex and controversial issues in the entire field of employment discrimination law. The questions raised by the use of affirmative action fall into two broad categories. First, to what extent, if any, will a court's exercise of this statutory remedial authority conflict with the antidiscrimination provisions of §703, the anti-preferential treatment mandate of §703(j), the protection afforded seniority systems by §703(h), or the equal protection guarantees of the Fifth or Fourteenth Amendments? Second, will any of these statutory or constitutional provisions be violated if an employer or union undertakes an affirmative action program on a voluntary basis?

Local 28 of Sheet Metal Workers Intern. Ass'n v. EEOC

Supreme Court of the United States, 1986.
478 U.S. 421, 106 S.Ct. 3019, 92 L.Ed.2d 344.

JUSTICE BRENNAN announced the judgment of the Court and delivered the opinion of the Court with respect to Parts I, II, III, and VI, and an opinion with respect to Parts IV, V, and VII in which JUSTICE MARSHALL, JUSTICE BLACKMUN, and JUSTICE STEVENS join.

In 1975, petitioners were found guilty of engaging in a pattern and practice of discrimination against black and Hispanic individuals (nonwhites) in violation of Title VII and ordered to end their discriminatory practices, and to admit a certain percentage of nonwhites to union membership by July 1982. In 1982 and again in 1983, petitioners were found guilty of civil contempt for disobeying the District Court's earlier orders. They now challenge the District Court's contempt finding, and also the remedies the court ordered both for the Title VII violation and for contempt. Principally, the issue presented is whether the remedial provision of Title VII, §706(g), empowers a district court to order race-conscious relief that may benefit individuals who are not identified victims of unlawful discrimination.

I

Petitioner Local 28 of the Sheet Metal Workers' International Association (Local 28) represents sheet metal workers employed by contractors in the New York City metropolitan area. Petitioner Local 28 Joint Apprenticeship Committee (JAC) is a management-labor committee which operates a 4-year apprenticeship training program designed to teach sheet metal skills. Apprentices enrolled in the program receive training both from classes and from on the job work experience. Upon completing the program, apprentices become journeyman members of Local 28. Successful completion of the program is the principal means of attaining union membership.[1]

In 1964, the New York State Commission for Human Rights determined that petitioners had excluded blacks from the union and the apprenticeship program in violation of state law. The State Commission found, among other things, that Local 28 had never had any black members or apprentices, and that "admission to apprenticeship is conducted largely on a nepot[is]tic basis involving sponsorship by incumbent union members," creating an impenetrable barrier for nonwhite applicants.[2] Petitioners were ordered to "cease and desist" their racially discriminatory practices. The New York State Supreme Court affirmed the State Commission's findings, and directed petitioners to implement objective standards for selecting apprentices.

When the court's orders proved ineffective, the State commission commenced other state-court proceedings in an effort to end petitioners' discriminatory practices. Petitioners had originally agreed to indenture two successive classes of apprentices using nondiscriminatory selection procedures, but stopped processing applications for the second apprentice class, thus requiring that the State Commission seek a court order requiring petitioners to indenture the apprentices. The court subsequently denied the union's request to reduce the size of the second apprentice class, and chastized the union for refusing "except for token gestures, to further the integration process." Petitioners proceeded to disregard the results of the selection test for a third apprentice class on the ground that nonwhites had received "unfair tutoring" and had passed in unreasonably high numbers. The state court ordered petitioners to indenture the apprentices based on the examination results.

In 1971, the United States initiated this action under Title VII and Executive Order 11246 to enjoin petitioners from engaging in a pattern and practice of discrimination against black and Hispanic individuals (nonwhites).[3] The New York

---

[1] In addition to completing the apprenticeship program, an individual can gain membership in Local 28 by (1) transferring directly from a "sister" union; (2) passing a battery of journeyman level tests administered by the union; and (3) gaining admission at the time a nonunion sheet metal shop is organized by Local 28. In addition, during periods of full employment, Local 28 issues temporary work permits which allow nonmembers to work within its jurisdiction.

[2] The Sheet Metal Workers' International Union was formed in 1888, under a Constitution which provided for the establishment of "white local unions" and relegated blacks to membership in subordinate locals. Local 28 was established in 1913 as a "white local union." Although racial restrictions were formally deleted from the International Constitution in 1946, Local 28 refused to admit blacks until 1969.

[3] The Equal Employment Opportunity Commission was substituted as named plaintiff in this case. The Sheet Metal and Air Conditioning Contractors' Association of New York City (Contractor's Association) was also named as a defendant. The New York State Division of Human Rights (State), although joined as a third and fourth-party defendant in this action, realigned itself as a plaintiff.

City Commission on Human Rights (City) intervened as plaintiff to press claims that petitioners had violated municipal fair employment laws, and had frustrated the City's efforts to increase job opportunities for minorities in the construction industry. In 1970, the City had adopted a plan requiring contractors on its projects to employ one minority trainee for every four journeyman union members. Local 28 was the only construction local which refused to comply voluntarily with the plan. In early 1974, the City attempted to assign six minority trainees to sheet metal contractors working on municipal construction projects. After Local 28 members stopped work on the projects, the District Court directed the JAC to admit the six trainees into the apprenticeship program, and enjoined Local 28 from causing any work stoppage at the affected job sites. The parties subsequently agreed to a consent order that required the JAC to admit up to 40 minorities into the apprenticeship program by September 1974. The JAC stalled compliance with the consent order, and only completed the indenture process under threat of contempt.

Following a trial in 1975, the District Court concluded that petitioners had violated both Title VII and New York law by discriminating against nonwhite workers in recruitment, selection, training, and admission to the union. Noting that as of July 1, 1974, only 3.19% of the union's total membership, including apprentices and journeymen, was nonwhite, the court found that petitioners had denied qualified nonwhites access to union membership through a variety of discriminatory practices. First, the court found that petitioners had adopted discriminatory procedures and standards for admission into the apprenticeship program. The court examined some of the factors used to select apprentices, including the entrance examination and high-school diploma requirement, and determined that these criteria had an adverse discriminatory impact on nonwhites, and were not related to job performance. The court also observed that petitioners had used union funds to subsidize special training sessions for friends and relatives of union members taking the apprenticeship examination.[4]

Second, the court determined that Local 28 had restricted the size of its membership in order to deny access to nonwhites. The court found that Local 28 had refused to administer yearly journeymen's examinations despite a growing demand for members' services.[5] Rather, to meet this increase in demand, Local 28 recalled pensioners who obtained doctors' certificates that they were able to work, and issued hundreds of temporary work permits to nonmembers; only one of these permits was issued to a nonwhite. Moreover, the court found that "despite the fact that Local 28 saw fit to request [temporary workers] from sister locals all across the country, as well

---

[4]The court also noted that petitioners' failure to comply with EEOC regulations requiring them to keep records of each applicant's race had made it difficult for the court to evaluate the discriminatory impact of petitioners' selection procedures.

[5]The Court noted that Local 28 had offered journeymen's examinations in 1968 and 1969 as a result of arbitration proceedings initiated by the Contractors' Association to force Local 28 to increase its manpower. Only 24 of 330 individuals, all of them white, passed the first examination and were admitted to the union. The court found that this examination had an adverse impact on nonwhites and had not been validated in accordance with EEOC guidelines, and was therefore violative of Title VII. Some nonwhites did pass the second examination, and the court concluded that Local 28's failure to keep records of the number of white and nonwhites tested made it impossible to determine whether that test had also had an adverse impact on nonwhites.

as from allied New York construction unions such as plumbers, carpenters, and iron workers, it never once sought them from Sheet Metal Local 400," a New York City union comprised almost entirely of nonwhites. The court concluded that by using the temporary permit system rather than continuing to administer journeymen's tests, Local 28 successfully restricted the size of its membership with the "illegal effect, if not the intention, of denying non-whites access to employment opportunities in the industry.".

Third, the District Court determined that Local 28 had selectively organized nonunion sheet metal shops with few, if any, minority employees, and admitted to membership only white employees from those shops. The court found that "[p]rior to 1973 no non-white ever became a member of Local 28 through the organization of a non-union shop." The court also found that, despite insistent pressure from both the International Union and local contractors, Local 28 had stubbornly refused to organize sheet metal workers in the local blowpipe industry because a large percentage of such workers were nonwhite.

Finally, the court found that Local 28 had discriminated in favor of white applicants seeking to transfer from sister locals. The court noted that from 1967 through 1972, Local 28 had accepted 57 transfers from sister locals, all of them white, and that it was only after this litigation had commenced that Local 28 accepted its first nonwhite transfers, two journeymen from Local 400. The court also found that on one occasion, the union's president had incorrectly told nonwhite Local 400 members that they were not eligible for transfer.

The District Court entered an order and judgment (O & J) enjoining petitioners from discriminating against nonwhites, and enjoining the specific practices the court had found to be discriminatory. Recognizing that "the record in both state and federal court against these defendants is replete with instances of * * * bad faith attempts to prevent or delay affirmative action,"[6] the court concluded that "the imposition of a remedial racial goal in conjunction with an admission preference in favor of non-whites is essential to place the defendants in a position of compliance with [Title VII]." The court established a 29% nonwhite membership goal, based on the percentage of nonwhites in the relevant labor pool in New York City, for the union to achieve by July 1, 1981. The parties were ordered to devise and to implement recruitment and admission procedures designed to achieve this goal under the supervision of a court-appointed administrator.[7]

---

[6]The court remarked:

"After [state] Justice Markowitz [in the 1964 state-court proceeding] ordered implementation of [a plan intended to] create a 'truly nondiscriminatory union[,]' Local 28 flouted the court's mandate by expending union funds to subsidize special training sessions designed to give union members' friends and relatives a competitive edge in taking the [apprenticeship examination]. JAC obtained an exemption from state affirmative action regulations directed towards the administration of apprentice programs on the ground that its program was operating pursuant to court order; yet Justice Markowitz had specifically provided that all such subsequent regulations, to the extent not inconsistent with his order, were to be incorporated therein and applied to JAC's program. More recently, the defendants unilaterally suspended court-ordered time tables for admission of forty non-whites to the apprentice program pending trial of this action, only completing the admission process under threat of contempt citations."

[7]The O & J also awarded backpay to those nonwhites who could demonstrate that they were discriminatorily excluded from union membership.

The administrator proposed, and the court adopted, an Affirmative Action Program which, among other things, required petitioners to offer annual, nondiscriminatory journeyman and apprentice examinations, select members according to a white-nonwhite ratio to be negotiated by the parties, conduct extensive recruitment and publicity campaigns aimed at minorities,[8] secure the administrator's consent before issuing temporary work permits, and maintain detailed membership records, including separate records for whites and nonwhites. Local 28 was permitted to extend any of the benefits of the program to whites and other minorities, provided that this did not interfere with the program's operation.

The Court of Appeals for the Second Circuit affirmed the District Court's determination of liability, finding that petitioners had "consistently and egregiously violated Title VII." The court upheld the 29% nonwhite membership goal as a temporary remedy, justified by a "long and persistent pattern of discrimination," and concluded that the appointment of an administrator with broad powers was clearly appropriate, given petitioners' refusal to change their membership practices in the face of prior state and federal court orders. However, the court modified the District Court's order to permit the use of a white-nonwhite ratio for the apprenticeship program only pending implementation of valid, job-related entrance tests. Local 28 did not seek certiorari in this Court to review the Court of Appeals' judgment.

On remand, the District Court adopted a Revised Affirmative Action Program and Order (RAAPO) to incorporate the Court of Appeals' mandate. RAAPO also modified the original Affirmative Action Program to accommodate petitioners' claim that economic problems facing the construction industry had made it difficult for them to comply with the court's orders. Petitioners were given an additional year to meet the 29% membership goal. RAAPO also established interim membership goals designed to "afford the parties and the Administrator with some device to measure progress so that, if warranted, other provisions of the program could be modified to reflect change (sic) circumstances." The JAC was directed to indenture at least 36 apprentices by February 1977, and to determine the size of future apprenticeship classes subject to review by the administrator.[9] A divided panel of the Court of Appeals affirmed RAAPO in its entirety, including the 29% nonwhite membership goal. Petitioners again chose not to seek certiorari from this Court to review the Court of Appeals' judgment.

In April 1982, the City and State moved in the District Court for an order holding petitioners in contempt.[10] They alleged that petitioners had not achieved RAAPO's

---

[8]The District Court had concluded that petitioners had earned a well-deserved reputation for discriminating against nonwhites, and that this reputation "operated and still operates to discourage non-whites seeking membership in the local union or its apprenticeship program." The publicity campaign was consequently designed to dispel this reputation, and to encourage nonwhites to take advantage of opportunities for union membership.

[9]The Affirmative Action Program originally had required the JAC to indenture at least 300 apprentices by July 1, 1976, and at least 200 apprentices in each year thereafter, up to and including 1981. These figures were adjusted downward after petitioners complained that economic conditions made it impossible for them to indenture this number of apprentices. The District Court also permitted petitioners to defer administration of the journeyman's examination for the same reason.

[10]The Contractor's Association and individual Local 28 contractors were also named as respondents to the contempt proceeding.

29% nonwhite membership goal, and that this failure was due to petitioners' numerous violations of the O & J, RAAPO, and orders of the administrator. The District Court, after receiving detailed evidence of how the O & J and RAAPO had operated over the previous six years, held petitioners in civil contempt. The court did not rest its contempt finding on petitioners' failure to meet the 29% membership goal, although nonwhite membership in Local 28 was only 10.8% at the time of the hearing. Instead, the court found that petitioners had "failed to comply with RAAPO * * * almost from its date of entry," identifying six "separate actions or omissions on the part of the defendants [that] have impeded the entry of non-whites into Local 28 in contravention of the prior orders of this court." Specifically, the court determined that petitioners had (1) adopted a policy of underutilizing the apprenticeship program in order to limit nonwhite membership and employment opportunities;[11] (2) refused to conduct the general publicity campaign required by the O & J and RAAPO to inform nonwhites of membership opportunities; (3) added a job protection provision to the union's collective-bargaining agreement that favored older workers and discriminated against nonwhites (older workers provision); (4) issued unauthorized work permits to white workers from sister locals; and (5) failed to maintain and submit records and reports required by RAAPO, the O & J, and the administrator, thus making it difficult to monitor petitioners' compliance with the court's orders.

To remedy petitioners' contempt, the court imposed a $150,000 fine to be placed in a fund designed to increase nonwhite membership in the apprenticeship program and the union. The administrator was directed to propose a plan for utilizing the fund. The court deferred imposition of further coercive fines pending receipt of the administrator's recommendations for modifications to RAAPO.[12]

In 1983, the City brought a second contempt proceeding before the administrator, charging petitioners with additional violations of the O & J, RAAPO, and various administrative orders. The administrator found that the JAC had violated RAAPO by failing to submit accurate reports of hours worked by apprentices, thus preventing the court from evaluating whether non-white apprentices had shared in available employment opportunities, and that Local 28 had: (1) failed, in a timely manner, to provide the racial and ethnic data required by the O & J and RAAPO with respect to new members entering the union as a result of its merger with five predominately white sheet metal locals, (2) failed to serve copies of the O & J and RAAPO on

---

[11]The court explained that the "journeymen benefiting from this policy of underutilizing the apprenticeship program comprise Local 28's white incumbent membership." The court rejected Local 28's contention that any underutilization of the apprenticeship program could be blamed on difficult economic circumstances, emphasizing that the court had "not overlooked the obstacles or problems with which [petitioners] have had to contend," and that it had "given much consideration to the economic condition of the sheet metal trade in particular and the construction industry in general over the past six years."

[12]The District Court found it necessary to modify RAAPO in light of the fact that the 29% nonwhite membership goal was no longer viable on the present timetable, and also because five other locals with predominantly white memberships had recently merged with Local 28. The court denied petitioners cross-motion for an order terminating both the O & J and RAAPO, finding that these orders had not caused petitioners unexpected or undue hardship.

contractors employing Local 28 members, as ordered by the administrator, and (3) submitted inaccurate racial membership records.[13]

The District Court adopted the administrator's findings and once again adjudicated petitioners guilty of civil contempt. The court ordered petitioners to pay for a computerized recordkeeping system to be maintained by outside consultants, but deferred ruling on additional contempt fines pending submission of the administrator's fund proposal. The court subsequently adopted the administrator's proposed Employment, Training, Education, and Recruitment Fund (Fund) to "be used for the purpose of remedying discrimination." The Fund was used for a variety of purposes. In order to increase the pool of qualified nonwhite applicants for the apprenticeship program, the Fund paid for nonwhite union members to serve as liaisons to vocational and technical schools with sheet metal programs, created part-time and summer sheet metal jobs for qualified nonwhite youths, and extended financial assistance to needy apprentices. The Fund also extended counseling and tutorial services to nonwhite apprentices, giving them the benefits that had traditionally been available to white apprentices from family and friends. Finally, in an effort to maximize employment opportunities for all apprentices, the Fund provided financial support to employers otherwise unable to hire a sufficient number of apprentices, as well as matching funds to attract additional funding for job training programs.[14]

The District Court also entered an Amended Affirmative Action Plan and Order (AAAPO) which modified RAAPO in several respects. AAAPO established a 29.23% minority membership goal to be met by August 31, 1987. The new goal was based on the labor pool in the area covered by the newly expanded union. The court abolished the apprenticeship examination, concluding that "the violations that have occurred in the past have been so egregious that a new approach must be taken to solve the apprentice selection problem." Apprentices were to be selected by a three-member Board, which would select one minority apprentice for each white apprentice indentured. Finally, to prevent petitioners from underutilizing the apprenticeship program, the JAC was required to assign to Local 28 contractors one apprentice for every four journeymen, unless the contractor obtained a written waiver from respondents.

Petitioners appealed the District Court's contempt orders, the Fund order, and the order adopting AAAPO.[15] A divided panel of the Court of Appeals affirmed the

---

[13]The administrator's comments revealed that he was more concerned with Local 28's "inability to provide accurate data" than with the specific errors he had discovered. He emphasized that Local 28 had "no formal system to verify the racial and ethnic composition of [its] membership," and that "[s]uch verification that was done, was done on a totally haphazard basis." He concluded that "[t]he lack of any proper verification controls confirms * * * that Local 28 has not acted in the affirmative manner contemplated by the court." More generally, he observed that "[t]he violations found herein cannot be viewed in isolation, rather they must be seen as part of a pattern of disregard for state and federal court orders and as a continuation of conduct which led the court to find defendants in contempt."

[14]The Fund was to be financed by the $150,000 fine from the first contempt proceeding, plus an additional payment of $.02 per hour for each hour worked by a journeyman or apprentice. The Fund would remain in existence until the union achieved its nonwhite membership goal, and the District Court determined that the Fund was no longer necessary.

[15]Petitioners did not appeal the denial of their cross-motion to terminate the O & J and RAAPO. The city cross-appealed from that part of AAAPO establishing a temporary 29.23% nonwhite

District Court's contempt findings,[16] except the finding based on adoption of the older workers' provision.[17]   The court concluded that "[p]articularly in light of the determined resistance by Local 28 to all efforts to integrate its membership, * * * the combination of violations found by [the District Court] amply demonstrates the union's foot-dragging egregious noncompliance * * * and adequately supports [its] findings of civil contempt against both Local 28 and the JAC." The court also affirmed the District Court's contempt remedies, including the Fund order, and affirmed AAAPO with two modifications: it set aside the requirement that one minority apprentice be indentured for every white apprentice,[18] and clarified the Disrict Court's orders to allow petitioners to implement objective, nondiscriminatory apprentice selection procedures.[19] The court found the 29.23% nonwhite membership goal to be proper in light of Local 28's "long continued and egregious racial discrimination," and because it "will not unnecessarily trammel the rights of any readily ascertainable group of nonminority individuals."   The court rejected petitioners' argument that the goal violated Title VII or the Constitution. The court also distinguished AAAPO from the race-conscious order invalidated by this Court in Firefighters v. Stotts, 467 U.S. 561, 104 S.Ct. 2576, 81 L.Ed.2d 483 (1984), on three grounds: (1) unlike the order in Stotts, AAAPO did not conflict with a bona fide seniority plan; (2) the Stotts discussion of §706(g) of Title VII, applied only to "make whole" relief and did not address the prospective relief contained in AAAPO and the Fund order; and (3) this case, unlike Stotts, involved intentional discrimination.

Local 28 and the JAC filed a petition for a writ of certiorari. They present several claims for review: (1) that the District Court relied on incorrect statistical data; (2) that

---

membership goal, claiming that the percentage should be higher. The Court of Appeals denied the cross-motion.

[16]With respect to the finding of underutilization of the apprenticeship program, the court noted that the District Court had mistakenly compared the total number of apprentices enrolled during the period before the O & J was entered against the number of new enrollees admitted during the period after entry of the O & J. However, the court found this error inconsequential, since the statistical comparison was "only a small part of the overall evidence showing underutilization of the apprenticeship program."   The court determined that the District Court's finding of underutilization was supported by strong evidence that despite a need for more apprentices, petitioners refused to advertise the apprenticeship program and thereby help fill the need. See n. 22, *infra*. The court also noted that "[m]any of the uncertainties about underutilization that are urged by defendants are due in large part to the union's noncompliance with the reporting provisions of RAAPO."

[17]The court held that plaintiffs had failed to prove that the older workers' provision had either a discriminatory purpose or effect, because although negotiated, it was never actually implemented.   The court instructed the District Court on remand to determine the status and effect of the provision. Because adoption of this provision was the only contemptuous conduct that the Contractors' Association had been charged with, the Court of Appeals vacated all contempt relief against the Association.

[18]The court recognized that "temporary hiring rations may be necessary in order to achieve integration of a work force from which minorities have been unlawfully barred," but cautioned that "such race-conscious ratios are extreme remedies that must be used sparingly and 'carefully tailored to fit the violations found.' " Noting that petitioners had voluntarily indentured 45% nonwhites since January of 1981, the court concluded that a strict one-to-one hiring requirement was not needed to insure that a sufficient number of nonwhites were selected for the apprenticeship program.

[19]The EEOC had argued that AAAPO prohibited the use of any new selection procedures until the 29.23% membership goal was reached.

the contempt remedies ordered by the District Court were criminal in nature and were imposed without due process; (3) that the appointment of an administrator to supervise membership practices interferes with their right to self-governance; and (4) that the membership goal and Fund are unconstitutional. Principally, however, petitioners, supported by the Solicitor General, maintain that the membership goal and Fund exceed the scope of remedies available under Title VII because they extend race-conscious preferences to individuals who are not the identified victims of petitioners' unlawful discrimination. We granted the petition, and now affirm the Court of Appeals.

II

Petitioners argue that the District Court relied on incorrect statistical evidence in violation of Title VII and of petitioners' right to due process.

A

Under the O & J and RAAPO, petitioners were directed to attain a 29% nonwhite membership goal by July of 1981. This goal was based on the percentage of minorities in the relevant labor pool within New York City. Petitioners argue that because members and applicants for Local 28 membership have always been drawn from areas outside of New York City, the nonwhite membership goal should have accounted for the percentage of minorities in the relevant labor pool in these areas. Although they concede that there is no evidence in the record from which the correct percentage could be derived, they insist that the District Court's figure is erroneous, and that this error was "significant."[20]

The 29% nonwhite membership goal was established more than a decade ago and was twice affirmed by the Court of Appeals. Petitioners did not seek certiorari from this Court to review either of the Court of Appeals' judgments. Consequently, we do not have before us any issue as to the correctness of the 29% figure. Under AAAPO, petitioners are now obligated to attain a 29.23% nonwhite-membership goal by August 1987. AAAPO adjusted the original 29% membership goal to account for the fact that Local 28's members were now drawn from areas outside of New York City. Thus, even assuming that the original 29% membership goal was erroneous, it would not affect petitioners' existing obligations under AAAPO, or any other issue now before us.[21]

---

[20]In their brief, petitioners also suggest that the District Court's 29% membership goal was used to confirm its original finding of discrimination, and was therefore invalid under Hazelwood School District v. United States, 433 U.S. 299, 97 S.Ct. 2736, 53 L.Ed.2d 768 (1977) (proof of a pattern of discrimination by statistical evidence must be drawn from relevant geographical locations). However, the Court of Appeals recognized that the District Court's finding of liability "did not rely on inferences from racial ratios of population and employment in the area," but rather "was based on direct and overwhelming evidence of purposeful racial discrimination over a period of many years." In any event, petitioners conceded at oral argument that they do not "challeng[e] any finding that there was deliberate discrimination."

[21]Petitioners contend that "[i]nasmuch as [they] have now been held in contempt for not achieving the [29% membership] quota, the propriety of the evidence upon which it was derived is relevant." In the first place, the District Court expressly stated that petitioners were not held in contempt for failing to attain the 29% membership goal. In any event, a "contempt proceeding does not open to reconsideration the legal or factual basis of the order alleged to

B

Petitioners argue that the District Court also relied on incorrect data in finding that they had underutilized the apprenticeship program. The Court of Appeals recognized this error, see n. 20, supra, but affirmed the finding based on other evidence presented to the District Court.[22] Petitioners do not explain whether, and if so, why, the Court of Appeals' evaluation of the evidence was incorrect. Based on our own review of the record, we cannot say that the District Court's resolution of the evidence presented on this issue was clearly erroneous. Moreover, because petitioners do not challenge three of the findings on which the first contempt order was based, any alleged use of incorrect statistical evidence by the District Court provides no basis for disturbing the contempt citation. As the Court of Appeals observed, petitioners' "failure to have the apprentices employed is both an independent ground for contempt and a symptom of the effects of defendants' other kinds of contemptuous conduct."

* * *

IV

Petitioners, joined by the Solicitor General, argue that the membership goal, the Fund order, and other orders which require petitioners to grant membership preferences to nonwhites are expressly prohibited by §706(g), which defines the remedies available under Title VII. Petitioners and the Solicitor General maintain that §706(g) authorizes a district court to award preferential relief only to the actual victims of unlawful discrimination.[23] They maintain that the membership goal and the Fund violate this provision, since they require petitioners to admit to membership, and otherwise to extend benefits to black and Hispanic individuals who are not the

---

have been disobeyed and thus become a retrial of the original controversy." Maggio v. Zeitz, 333 U.S. 56, 69, 68 S.Ct. 401, 408, 92 L.Ed. 476 (1948).

[22]The court pointed to evidence before the District Court showing that after the O & J was entered: (1) there was a "sharp increase" in the ratio of journeymen to apprentices employed by contractors; (2) the average number of hours worked annually by journeymen "increased dramatically"; (3) the percentage of unemployed apprentices decreased; and (4) the union issued hundreds of temporary work permits, mostly to white journeymen. Based on this evidence, the Court of Appeals concluded that despite the need for more apprentices, Local 28 had deliberately shifted employment opportunities from apprentices to predominately white journeymen, and had refused to conduct the general publicity campaign required by RAAPO to attract nonwhites to the apprenticeship program.

[23]Both petitioners and the Solicitor General present this challenge from a rather curious position. Petitioners did not seek review in this Court of the 29% membership goal twice approved by the Court of Appeals, even though that goal was similar to the 29.23% goal they now challenge. However, we reject the State's contention that either res judicata or the law of the case prohibits us from now addressing the legality of the membership goal.

The Solicitor General challenges the membership goal and Fund order even though the EEOC has, throughout this litigation, joined the other plaintiffs in asking the courts to order numerical goals, implementing ratios, and timetables. In the complaint, the Government sought the "selection of sufficient apprentices from among qualified non-white applicants to overcome the effects of past discrimination." In its post-trial memorandum, the Government urged the court to "establish a goal of no less than 30 per cent non white membership in Local 28." To achieve this goal, the Government asked the court to order petitioners to select apprentices based on a one-to-one white to nonwhite ratio, and argued that "a reasonable preference in favor of minority persons to remedy past discriminatory injustices is permissable [*sic*]." Ibid.

identified victims of unlawful discrimination.[25] We reject this argument, and hold that §706(g) does not prohibit a court from ordering, in appropriate circumstances, affirmative race-conscious relief as a remedy for past discrimination. Specifically, we hold that such relief may be appropriate where an employer or a labor union has engaged in persistent or egregious discrimination, or where necessary to dissipate the lingering effects of pervasive discrimination.

A

* * * The language of §706(g) plainly expresses Congress's intent to vest district courts with broad discretion to award "appropriate" equitable relief to remedy unlawful discrimination. *Teamsters*; *Franks*; *Albermarle*.[26] Nevertheless, petitioners and the Solicitor General argue that the last sentence of §706(g) prohibits a court from ordering an employer or labor union to take affirmative steps to eliminate discrimination which might incidentally benefit individuals who are not the actual victims of discrimination. This reading twists the plain language of the statute.

The last sentence of §706(g) prohibits a court from ordering a union to admit an individual who was "refused admission * * * for any reason other than discrimination." It does not, as petitioners and the Solicitor General suggest, say that a court may order relief only for the actual victims of past discrimination. The sentence on its face addresses only the situation where a plaintiff demonstrates that a union (or

---

[25]The last sentence of §706(g) addresses only court orders requiring the "admission or reinstatement of an individual as a member of a union." Thus, even under petitioners' reading of §706(g), that provision would not apply to several of the benefits conferred by the Fund, to wit the tutorial, liaison, counseling, stipend, and loan programs extended to nonwhites. Moreover, the District Court established the Fund in the exercise of its contempt powers. Thus, even assuming that petitioners correctly read §706(g) to limit the remedies a court may impose *for a violation of Title VII,* that provision would not necessarily limit the District Court's authority to order petitioners to implement the Fund. The Solicitor General, without citing any authority, maintains that "contempt sanctions imposed to enforce Title VII must not themselves violate the statute's policy of providing relief only to the actual victims of discrimination." We need not decide whether §706(g) restricts a court's contempt powers, since we reject the proposition that §706(g) always prohibits a court from ordering affirmative race-conscious relief which might incidentally benefit individuals who were not the actual victims of discrimination.

[24]Section 706(g) was modeled after §10(c) of the National Labor Relations Act, 29 U.S.C. §160(c). Principles developed under the National Labor Relations Act "guide, but do not bind, courts tailoring remedies under Title VII." Ford Motor Co. v. EEOC, 458 U.S. 219, 226, n. 8, 102 S.Ct. 3057, 3062-3063, n. 8, 73 L.Ed.2d 721 (1982). Section 10(c) as we have noted, was intended to give the National Labor Relations Board broad authority to formulate appropriate remedies: "[I]n the nature of things Congress could not catalogue all the devices and strategems for circumventing the policies of the Act. Nor could it define the whole gamut of remedies to effectuate these policies in an infinite variety of specific situations. Congress met these difficulties by leaving the adaption of means to end to the empiric process of administration." Phelps Dodge Corp. v. NLRB, 313 U.S. 177, 194, 61 S.Ct. 845, 852, 85 L.Ed. 1271 (1941).

[26]We have steadfastly recognized that affirmative race-conscious relief may provide an effective means of remedying the effects of past discrimination. See Wygant v. Jackson Board of Education, 476 U.S. 267, 106 S.Ct. 1842, 90 L.Ed.2d 260 (1986) (opinion of Powell, J.) ("to eliminate every vestige of racial segregation and discrimination * * * race-conscious remedial action may be necessary"); *id.,* at 301, 106 S.Ct., at 1861 (Marshall, J., dissenting) ("racial distinctions * * * are highly relevant to the one legitimate state objective of eliminating the pernicious vestiges of past discrimination"); Fullilove v. Klutznick, 448 U.S. 448, 100 S.Ct. 2758, 65 L.Ed.2d 902 (1980) (upholding 10% set aside of federal contract funds for minority businesses).

an employer) has engaged in unlawful discrimination, but the union can show that a particular individual would have been refused admission even in the absence of discrimination, for example because that individual was unqualified. In these circumstances §706(g) confirms that a court could not order the union to admit the unqualified individual. In this case, neither the membership goal nor the Fund order required petitioners to admit to membership individuals who had been refused admission for reasons unrelated to discrimination. Thus, we do not read §706(g) to prohibit a court from ordering the kind of affirmative relief the District Court awarded in this case.

B

The availability of race-conscious affirmative relief under §706(g) as a remedy for a violation of Title VII also furthers the broad purposes underlying the statute. Congress enacted Title VII based on its determination that racial minorities were subject to pervasive and systematic discrimination in employment. "[I]t was clear to Congress that '[t]he crux of the problem [was] to open employment opportunities for Negroes in occupations which have been traditionally closed to them,' * * * and it was to this problem that Title VII's prohibition against racial discrimination in employment was primarily addressed." Steelworkers v. Weber, 443 U.S. 193, 203, 99 S.Ct. 2721, 2727, 61 L.Ed.2d 480 (1979) (quoting 110 Cong.Rec. 6548 (1964) (remarks of Sen. Humphrey)). Title VII was designed "to achieve equality of employment opportunities and remove barriers that have operated in the past to favor an identifiable group of white employees over other employees." *Griggs.* In order to foster equal employment opportunities, Congress gave the lower courts broad power under §706(g) to fashion "the most complete relief possible" to remedy past discrimination. *Franks..*

In most cases, the court need only order the employer or union to cease engaging in discriminatory practices, and award make-whole relief to the individuals victimized by those practices. In some instances, however, it may be necessary to require the employer or union to take affirmative steps to end discrimination effectively to enforce Title VII. Where an employer or union has engaged in particularly longstanding or egregious discrimination, an injunction simply reiterating Title VII's prohibition against discrimination will often prove useless and will only result in endless enforcement litigation. In such cases, requiring recalcitrant employers or unions to hire and to admit qualified minorities roughly in proportion to the number of qualified minorities in the work force may be the only effective way to ensure the full enjoyment of the rights protected by Title VII.

Further, even where the employer or union formally ceases to engage in discrimination, informal mechanisms may obstruct equal employment opportunities. An employer's reputation for discrimination may discourage minorities from seeking available employment. In these circumstances, affirmative race-conscious relief may be the only means available "to assure equality of employment opportunities and to eliminate those discriminatory practices and devices which have fostered racially stratified job environments to the disadvantage of minority citizens." *McDonnell Douglas.*[27] Affirmative action "promptly operates to change the outward and visible

---

[27]We have steadfastly recognized that affirmative race-conscious relief may provide an effective means of remedying the effects of past discrimination. See Wygant v. Jackson Board of Education, 476 U.S. 267, 106 S.Ct. 1842, 90 L.Ed.2d 260 (1986) (opinion of Powell, J.) ("to

signs of yesterday's racial distinctions and thus, to provide an impetus to the process of dismantling the barriers, psychological or otherwise, erected by past practices." NAACP v. Allen, 493 F.2d 614, 621 (CA5 1974).

Finally, a district court may find it necessary to order interim hiring or promotional goals pending the development of nondiscriminatory hiring or promotion procedures. In these cases, the use of numerical goals provides a compromise between two unacceptable alternatives: an outright ban on hiring or promotions, or continued use of a discriminatory selection procedure.

We have previously suggested that courts may utilize certain kinds of racial preferences to remedy past discrimination under Title VII. See Fullilove v. Klutznick, 448 U.S. 448, 483, 100 S.Ct. 2758, 2777, 65 L.Ed.2d 902 (1980) (opinion of Burger, C.J.) ("Where federal antidiscrimination laws have been violated, an equitable remedy may in the appropriate case include a racial or ethnic factor"); id., at 513, 100 S.Ct., at 2792-2793 (Powell, J., concurring) ("The Courts of Appeals have approved temporary hiring remedies insuring that the percentage of minority group workers in a business or governmental agency will be reasonably related to the percentage of minority group members in the relevant population"); University of California Regents v. Bakke, 438 U.S. 265, 353, 98 S.Ct. 2733, 2780, 57 L.Ed.2d 750 (1978) (opinion of Brennan, White, Marshall, and Blackmun, JJ.) ("the Court has required that preferences be given by employers to members of racial minorities as a remedy for past violations of Title VII"). The Courts of Appeals have unanimously agreed that racial preferences may be used, in appropriate cases, to remedy past discrimination under Title VII.

C

Despite the fact that the plain language of §706(g) and the purposes of Title VII suggest the opposite, petitioners and the Solicitor General maintain that the legislative history indicates that Congress intended that affirmative relief under §706(g) benefit only the identified victims of past discrimination. To support this contention, petitioners and the Solicitor General rely principally on statements made throughout the House and Senate debates to the effect that Title VII would not require employers or labor unions to adopt quotas or preferences that would benefit racial minorities.

Our examination of the legislative history of Title VII convinces us that, when examined in context, the statements relied upon by petitioners and the Solicitor General do not indicate that Congress intended to limit relief under §706(g) to that which benefits only the actual victims of unlawful discrimination. Rather, these statements were intended largely to reassure opponents of the bill that it would not require employers or labor unions to use racial quotas or to grant preferential treatment to racial minorities in order to avoid being charged with unlawful discrimination. See United Steelworkers of America, AFL CIO CLC v. Weber, (1979), 443 U.S. 193, at 205, 99 S.Ct. 2721, 2728, 61 L.Ed.2d 480. The bill's supporters insisted that this would not be the intent and effect of the legislation, and eventually agreed to state this

---

eliminate every vestige of racial segregation and discrimination * * * race-conscious remedial action may be necessary"); id., at 301, 106 S.Ct., at 1861 (Marshall, J., dissenting) ("racial distinctions * * * are highly relevant to the one legitimate state objective of eliminating the pernicious vestiges of past discrimination"); Fullilove v. Klutznick, 448 U.S. 448, 100 S.Ct. 2758, 65 L.Ed.2d 902 (1980) (upholding 10% set aside of federal contract funds for minority businesses).

expressly in §703(j). Contrary to the arguments made by petitioners and the Solicitor General, these statements do not suggest that a court may not order preferential relief under §706(g) when appropriate to remedy past discrimination. Rather, it is clear that the bill's supporters only wished to emphasize that an employer would not violate the statute merely by having a racially imbalanced work force, and, consequently, that a court could not order an employer to adopt racial preferences merely to correct such an imbalance.

1

H.R. 7152, the bill that ultimately became the Civil Rights Act of 1964, was introduced in the House by Representatives on June 20, 1963, and referred to the Committee on the Judiciary. The bill contained no provisions addressed to discrimination in employment, but the Judiciary Committee amended it by adding Title VII. Title VII as reported by the Judiciary Committee included a version of §706(g), which read, in relevant part: "No order of the court shall require the admission or reinstatement of an individual as a member of a union * * * if such individual was refused admission, suspended, or expelled * * * for cause." The word "cause" was deleted from the bill on the House floor and replaced by the language "any reason other than discrimination on account of race, color, religion, or national origin." Representative Celler, the Chairman of the House Judiciary Committee and the sponsor of this amendment, explained:

> "[T]he purpose of the amendment is to specify cause. Here the court, for example, cannot find any violation of the act which is based on facts other—and I emphasize 'other'—than discrimination on the grounds of race, color, religion, or national origin. The discharge might be based, for example, on incompetence or a morals charge or theft, but the court can only consider charges based on race, color, religion, or national origin. That is the purpose of this amendment."

2

Even before the Judiciary Committee's bill reached the House floor, opponents charged that Title VII would require that an employer maintain a racially balanced work force. The Minority Report of the Judiciary Committee observed that "the word discrimination is nowhere defined in the bill," and charged that "the administration intends to rely upon its own construction of 'discrimination' as including the lack of racial balance." To demonstrate how the bill would operate in practice, the Report posited a number of hypothetical employment situations, concluding each time that Title VII would compel employers "to 'racially balance' those who work for him in every job classification or be in violation of Federal law."[30] In response, Republican

---

[30]For illustrative purposes, we include two of these "examples":

"Under the power granted in this bill, if a carpenters' hiring hall, say, had 20 men awaiting call, the first 10 in seniority being white carpenters, the union could be forced to pass them over in favor of carpenters beneath them in seniority, but of the stipulated race. And if the union roster did not contain the names of the carpenters of the race needed to 'racially balance' the job, the union agent must, then, go into the street and recruit members of the stipulated race in sufficient number * * * else his local could be held in violation of Federal law."

"Assume two women of separate races apply to [a] firm for the position of stenographer; further assume that the employer for some indefinable reason, prefers one above the other, whether because of personality, superior alertness, intelligence, work history, or general neatness. Assume the employer has learned good things about the character of one and

proponents of the bill issued a statement emphasizing that the EEOC could not enforce the statute merely to achieve racial balance:

> "[T]he Commission must confine its activities to correcting abuse, not promoting equality with mathematical certainty. In this regard, nothing in the title permits a person to demand employment. Of greater importance, the Commission will only jeopardize its continued existence if it seeks to impose forced racial balance upon employers or labor unions."

When H.R. 7152 actually reached the House floor, Representative Celler attempted to respond to charges that the existence of racial imbalance would constitute "discrimination" under Title VII, or that the EEOC would be authorized to "order the hiring and promotion only of employees of certain races or religious groups."[31] Nevertheless, accusations similar to those made in the Judiciary Committee's Minority Report were repeatedly raised on the House floor. For example, Representative Alger charged that Title VII would "demand by law, special privileges for Negroes":

> "The Negro represents about 10 percent of the population of the United States and it cannot be said he is being kept from opportunity if he is represented in 10 percent of the working force. Now we are asked to ignore population ratios and force the hiring of Negroes even when it will mean, as in Government, that they are given preferential hiring far beyond the 10 percent of the population they represent."

Representative Abernathy raised the scenario of a "union [having] to send out a 'racially' balanced staff of organizers to sign up a crew of 'racially balanced' carpenters, a crew of 'racially balanced' laborers, 'racially balanced' plumbers, electricians, plasterers, roofers, and so forth, before a construction job could begin. Supporters of the bill stridently denied any intent to require "racial balancing."[32] Thus, in response to charges that an employer or labor union would be guilty of "discrimination" under Title VII simply because of a racial imbalance in its work force or membership roster, supporters of the bill insisted repeatedly that Title VII would not

---

derogatory things about the character of the other which are not subject to proof. If his firm is not 'racially balanced,' [the employer] has no choice, he must employ the person of that race which, by ratio, is next up, even though he is certain in his own mind that the woman he is not allowed to employ would be a superior employee."

[31]Representative Celler explained that the Commission would have no power "to rectify existing 'racial or religious imbalance' in employment by requiring the hiring of certain people * * * simply because they are of a given race or religion." He emphasized that "[n]o order could be entered against an employer except by a court," and that "[e]ven then, the court could not order that any preference be given to any particular race, religion or other group, but would be limited to ordering an end to discrimination."

[32]See 110 Cong.Rec. 1540 (1964) (remarks of Rep. Lindsay) (The bill "does not impose quotas or any special privileges of seniority or acceptance. There is nothing whatever in this bill about racial balance as appears so frequently in the minority report of the committee"); id., at 1600 (remarks of Rep. Minish) ("[U]nder title VII. * * * no quota system will be set up, no one will be forced to hire incompetent help because of race or religion, and no one will be given a vested right to demand employment for a certain job"); id., at 1994 (remarks of Rep. Healy) ("Opponents of the bill say that it sets up racial quotas for job[s] * * *. The bill does not do that"); id., at 2558 (remarks of Rep. Goodell) ("There is nothing here as a matter of legislative history that would require racial balancing * * *. We are not talking about a union having to balance its membership or an employer having to balance the number of employees. There is no quota involved").

require employers or unions to implement hiring or promotional quotas in order to achieve racial balance. The question whether there should be any comparable restrictions with respect to a court's use of racial preferences as an appropriate remedy for past discrimination under §706(g) simply did not arise during the House debates.

3

After passing the House by a vote of 290-130, the bill ran into equally strong opposition in the Senate. Opponents initially sought to have it sent to the Senate Judiciary Committee, which was hostile to civil rights legislation. The debate on this motion focused on the merits of the bill; many Senators again raised the specter of "racial balancing." Senator Ervin charged that under the substantive provisions of Title VII, "the Commission could * * * tell an employer that he had too few employees * * * and enter an order * * * requiring him to hire more persons, not because the employer thought he needed more persons, but because the Commission wanted to compel him to employ persons of a particular race." Similarly, Senator Robertson stated:

> "This title suggests that hiring should be done on some percentage basis in order that racial imbalance will be overcome. It is contemplated by this title that the percentage of colored and white population in a community shall be in similar percentages in every business establishment that employs over 25 persons. Thus, if there were 10,000 colored persons in a city and 15,000 whites, an employer with 25 employees would, in order to overcome racial imbalance, be required to have 10 colored personnel and 15 white. And, if by chance that employer had 20 colored employees he would have to fire 10 of them in order to rectify the situation."

Senator Humphrey, one of the most vocal proponents of H.R. 7152, rose to the bill's defense. He introduced a newspaper article quoting the answers of a Justice Department expert to common objections to Title VII. In response to the "objection" that "[w]hite people would be fired, to make room for Negroes," the article stated that "[t]he bill would not authorize anyone to order hiring or firing to achieve racial or religious balance." Later, responding to a political advertisement suggesting that federal agencies would interpret "discrimination" under Title VII as synonymous with racial imbalance, Senator Humphrey stressed that Title VII "does [not] in any way authorize the Federal Government to prescribe, as the advertisement charges, a 'racial balance' of job classifications or office staffs or 'preferential treatment of minorities' to achieve such a balance." After 17 days of debate, the Senate voted to take up the bill directly without referring it to a committee.

Senators Humphrey and Kuchel, who served as bipartisan floor managers for H.R. 7152, opened formal debate on the merits of the bill and addressed opponent's charges that Title VII would require employers to implement quotas to achieve a certain racial balance. Senator Humphrey stressed that "[c]ontrary to the allegations of some opponents of this title, there is nothing in it that will give any power to the Commission or to any court to require hiring, firing, or promotion of employees in order to meet a racial 'quota' or to achieve a certain racial balance." Senator Kuchel elaborated:

> "[Title VII] is pictured by its opponents and detractors as an intrusion of numerous Federal inspectors into our economic life. These inspectors would

presumably dictate to labor unions and their members with regard to * * * racial balance in job classifications, racial balance in membership, and preferential advancement for members of so called minority groups. Nothing could be further from the truth * * *. [T]he important point * * * is that the court cannot order preferential hiring or promotion consideration for any particular race, religion, or other group."

These sentiments were echoed by Senators Case and Clark, who spoke as bipartisan team "captains" in support of Title VII. The Senators submitted an interpretative memorandum which explained that "[t]here is no requirement in title VII that an employer maintain a racial balance in his work force." Senator Clark also introduced a Justice Department memorandum which repeated what supporters of the bill had tried to make clear:

> "There is no provision, either in title VII or in any other part of this bill, that requires or authorizes any Federal agency or Federal court to require preferential treatment for any individual or any group for the purpose of achieving racial balance. No employer is required to hire an individual because that individual is a Negro. No employer is required to maintain any ratio of Negroes to whites, Jews to gentiles, Italians to English, or women to men."

Opponents of the bill invoked a 2-month filibuster, again raising the charge that "discrimination" would be defined to include racial imbalance. Senator Robertson remarked: "What does discrimination mean? If it means what I think it does, and which it could mean, it means that a man could be required to have a quota or he would be discriminating." Senators Smathers and Sparkman conceded that Title VII did not in so many words require the use of quotas, but feared that employers would adopt racial quotas or preferences to avoid being charged with discrimination. Even outsiders joined in the debate, Senator Javits referred to charges raised by Governor Wallace of Alabama that the bill "vested power in a federal inspector who, under an allegation of racial imbalance * * * can establish a quota system whereby a certain percentage of a certain ethnic group must be employed." The bill's supporters insisted that employers would not be required to implement racial quotas to avoid being charged with liability.[33] Nonetheless, opponents remained skeptical.

Recognizing that their own verbal assurances would not end the dispute over "racial balancing," supporters of the bill eventually agreed to insert an explicit disclaimer into the language of the bill to assuage opponents' fears. Senator Dirksen introduced the comprehensive "Dirksen-Mansfield" amendment as a substitute for the entire bill, which added several provisions defining and clarifying the scope of Title VII's substantive provisions. One of those provisions, §703(j), specifically addressed the charges of "racial balancing":

---

[33]See id., at 7420 (remarks of Sen. Humphrey) ("if [Senator Robertson] can find in title VII * * * any language which provides that an employer will have to hire on the basis of percentage or quota related to color, race * * * I will start eating the pages"); id., at 8500-8501 (remarks of Sen. Allott) ("if anyone sees in the bill quotas or percentages, he must read that language into it. It is not in the bill"); id., at 8921 (remarks of Sen. Williams) ("there is nothing whatever in the bill which provides for racial balance or quotas in employment"); id., at 11471 (remarks of Sen. Javits) (the bill "in no respect imposes a quota system or racial imbalance standard"); id., at 11848 (remarks of Sen. Humphrey) (the title "does not provide that any quota systems may be established to maintain racial balance in employment").

"Nothing contained in this subchapter shall be interpreted to require any * * * labor organization, or joint labor-management committee * * * to grant preferential treatment to any individual or to any group because of the race * * * of such individual or group on account of an imbalance which may exist with respect to the total number or percentage of persons of any race [admitted to the labor organization, or to any apprenticeship program] in comparison with the total number or percentage of persons of such race * * * in any community, State, section, or other area, or in the available work force in any community, State, section, or other area."

As Senator Humphrey explained:

"A new subsection 703(j) is added to deal with the problem of racial balance among employees. The proponents of this bill have carefully stated on numerous occasions that title VII does not require an employer to achieve any sort of racial balance in his work force by giving preferential treatment to any individual or group. Since doubts have persisted, subsection (j) is added to state this point expressly. This subsection does not represent any change in the substance of the title. It does state clearly and accurately what we have maintained all along about the bill's intent and meaning."

* * * Section 703(j) apparently calmed the fears of most opponents, for complaints of "racial balance" and "quotas" died down considerably after its adoption.

In contrast to the heated debate over the substantive provisions of §703, the Senate paid scant attention to the remedial provisions of §706(g). Several Senators did emphasize, in reference to the last sentence of section 706(g), that "[t]he title does not provide for the reinstatement or employment of a person * * * if he was fired or refused employment or promotion for any reason other than discrimination prohibited by the Title." 110 Cong.Rec., at 11848 (remarks of Sen. Humphrey).[35] While both petitioners and the Solicitor General liberally quote from these excerpts, we do not read these statements as supporting their argument that a district court may not order affirmative race-conscious relief which may incidentally benefit individuals who are not identified victims of unlawful discrimination. To the contrary, these statements confirm our reading of the last sentence of §706(g): that a court has no power to award relief to an individual who was denied an employment opportunity for reasons other than discrimination.

After 83 days of debate, the Senate adopted Title VII by a vote of 73 to 27. Rather than setting up a Conference Committee, the House voted directly upon, and passed, the Senate version of the bill. The bill's sponsors repeated, for the last time, that Title VII "[did] not require quotas, racial balance, or any of the other things that the opponents have been saying about it."

---

[35] See id., at 6549 (remarks of Sen. Humphrey) ("No court order can require hiring, reinstatement, admission to membership, or payment of back pay for anyone who was not fired, refused employment or advancement or admission to a union by an act of discrimination forbidden by this title. This is stated expressly in the last sentence of [§706(g)], which makes clear what is implicit throughout the whole title; namely, that employers may hire and fire, promote and refuse to promote for any reason, good or bad, provided only that individuals may not be discriminated against because of race, religion, sex, or national origin").

To summarize, many opponents of Title VII argued that an employer could be found guilty of discrimination under the statute simply because of a racial imbalance in his work force, and would be compelled to implement racial "quotas" to avoid being charged with liability. At the same time, supporters of the bill insisted that employers would not violate Title VII simply because of racial imbalance, and emphasized that neither the Commission nor the courts could compel employers to adopt quotas solely to facilitate racial balancing. The debate concerning what Title VII did and did not require culminated in the adoption of §703(j), which stated expressly that the statute did not require an employer or labor union to adopt quotas or preferences simply because of a racial imbalance. However, while Congress strongly opposed the use of quotas or preferences merely to maintain racial balance, it gave no intimation as to whether such measures would be acceptable as remedies for Title VII violations.[36]

Congress' failure to consider this issue is not surprising, since there was relatively little civil rights litigation prior to the adoption of the 1964 Civil Rights Act. More importantly, the cases that had been litigated had not resulted in the sort of affirmative-action remedies that, as later became apparent, would sometimes be necessary to eliminate effectively the effects of past discrimination. Thus, the use of racial preferences as a remedy for past discrimination simply was not an issue at the time Title VII was being considered. Our task then, is to determine whether Congress intended to preclude a district court from ordering affirmative action in appropriate circumstances as a remedy for past discrimination. Our examination of the legislative policy behind Title VII leads us to conclude that Congress did not intend to prohibit a court from exercising its remedial authority in that way.[37] Congress deliberately gave the district courts broad authority under Title VII to fashion the most complete relief possible to eliminate "the last vestiges of an unfortunate and ignominious page in this country's history," Albemarle Paper, 422 U.S., at 418, 95 S.Ct., at 2372. As we noted above, affirmative race-conscious relief may in some instances be necessary to accomplish this task. In the absence of any indication that Congress intended to limit a district court's remedial authority in a way which would frustrate the court's ability to enforce Title VII's mandate, we decline to fashion such a limitation ourselves.

4

---

[36]Cf. *Bakke,* 438 U.S., at 342, n. 17, 98 S.Ct., at 2774-2775, n. 17 (opinion of Brennan, White, Marshall, and Blackmun, JJ.) ("Even assuming that Title VII prohibits employers from deliberately maintaining a particular racial composition in their work force as an end in itself, this does not imply, in the absence of any consideration of the question, that Congress intended to ban the use of racial preferences as a tool for achieving the objective of remedying past discrimination or other compelling ends").

[37]We also reject petitioners' argument that the District Court's remedies contravened §703(j), since they require petitioners to grant preferential treatment to blacks and Hispanics based on race. Our examination of the legislative history convinces us that §703(j) was added to Title VII to make clear that an employer or labor union does not engage in "discrimination" simply because of a racial imbalance in its workforce or membership, and would not be required to institute preferential quotas to avoid Title VII liability. See *Weber* ("§703(j) speaks to substantive liability under Title VII"); *Teamsters* ("§703(j) makes clear that Title VII imposes no requirement that a work force mirror the general population"); *Franks* ("the * * * provisions of §703 * * * delineat[e] which employment practices are illegal and thereby prohibited and which are not"). We reject the notion that §703(j) somehow qualifies or proscribes a court's authority to order relief otherwise appropriate under §706(g) in circumstances where an illegal discriminatory act or practice is established.

Our reading of the scope of the district court's remedial powers under §706(g) is confirmed by the contemporaneous interpretations of the EEOC and the Justice Department.[38] Following the enactment of the Civil Rights Act of 1964, both the Justice Department and the EEOC, the two federal agencies charged with enforcing Title VII, steadfastly maintained that race-conscious remedies for unlawful discrimination are available under the statute. Both agencies have, in appropriate cases, sought court orders and consent decrees containing such provisions. See, e.g., United States v. City of Alexandria, 614 F.2d 1358 (CA5 1980). The agencies' contemporaneous reading of the statute lends strong support for our interpretation.

5

Finally, our interpretation of §706(g) is confirmed by the legislative history of the Equal Employment Opportunity Act of 1972, which amended Title VII in several respects. One such change modified the language of §706(g) to empower a court to order "such affirmative action as may be appropriate, which may include, but is not limited to reinstatement or hiring of employees * * *or any other equitable relief as the court deems appropriate." (emphasized language added in 1972). This language was intended "to give the courts wide discretion exercising their equitable powers to fashion the most complete relief possible." While the section-by-section analysis undertaken in the Conference Committee Report stressed the need for "make-whole" relief for the "victims of unlawful discrimination," nowhere did Congress suggest that a court lacked the power to award preferential remedies that might benefit nonvictims. Indeed, the Senate's rejection of two other amendments supports a contrary conclusion.

During the 1972 debates, Senator Ervin introduced an amendment to counteract the effects of the Department of Labor's so-called Philadelphia Plan. The Philadelphia Plan was established pursuant to Executive Order No. 11246 and required prospective federal contractors to submit affirmative-action programs including "specific goals of minority manpower utilization." Attacking the Plan as "[t]he most notorious example of discrimination in reverse," Senator Ervin proposed an amendment to Title VII that read, in relevant part: "No department, agency, or officer of the United States shall require an employer to practice discrimination in reverse by employing persons of a particular race * * * in either fixed or variable numbers, proportions, percentages, quotas, goals, or ranges." Senator Ervin complained that the amendment was needed

---

[38]Although the Solicitor General now makes a contrary argument, we note that the brief for the EEOC submitted by the Solicitor General in *Weber* described the 1964 legislative history as follows:

"To be sure, there was considerable concern that the Act would be construed to require the use of quota systems to establish and maintain racial balance in employers' work forces. [citations omitted]. The sponsors of the bill repeatedly assured its opponents that this was not the intent and would not be the effect of the statute. [citations omitted]. But these assurances did not suggest restrictions on remedies that could be ordered after a finding of discrimination. Instead, they made it clear that the statute would not impose a duty on employers to establish racially balanced work forces and that it would not require or even permit employers to establish racial quotas for employment in the absence of discrimination of the kind prohibited by the Act. [citations omitted]."

The brief concludes that "the last sentence of Section 706(g) simply state[s] that a court could not order relief under the authority of the Act if employers took action against employees or applicants on grounds other than those prohibited by the Act."

because both the Department of Labor and the EEOC were ignoring §703(j)'s prohibition against requiring employers to engage in preferential hiring for racial minorities.

Senator Javits vigorously opposed Senator Ervin's proposal. First, he recognized that the amendment, while targeted at the Philadelphia Plan, would also jettison "the whole concept of 'affirmative action' as it has been developed under Executive Order 11246 and as a remedial concept under Title VII." (emphasis added). He explained that the amendment would "deprive the courts of the opportunity to order affirmative action under title VII of the type which they have sustained in order to correct a history of unjust and illegal discrimination in employment." * * * The Ervin amendment was defeated by a margin of 2 to 1.

Senator Ervin proposed a second amendment that would have extended §703(j)'s prohibition against racial preferences to "Executive Order Numbered 11246, or any other law or Executive Order," this amendment was also defeated resoundingly. Thus, the legislative history of the 1972 amendments to Title VII confirms the availability of race-conscious affirmative action as a remedy under the statute. Congress was aware that both the Executive and Judicial Branches had used such measures to remedy past discrimination,[41] and rejected amendments that would have barred such remedies. Instead, Congress reaffirmed the breadth of the court's remedial powers under §706(g) by adding language authorizing courts to order "any other equitable relief as the court deems appropriate." The section-by-section analysis undertaken by the Conference Committee Report confirms Congress' resolve to accept prevailing judicial interpretations regarding the scope of Title VII: "[I]n any area where the new law does not address itself, or in any area where a specific contrary intention is not indicated, it was assumed that the present case law as developed by the courts would continue to govern the applicability and construction of Title VII." 118 Cong.Rec., at 7166, 7564. Thus, "[e]xecutive, judicial, and congressional action subsequent to the passage of Title VII conclusively established that the Title did not bar the remedial use of race." *Bakke*.[42]

---

[41]In addition, * * * other federal courts had, prior to the passage of the 1972 amendments, approved of the use of racial preferences to remedy the effects of illegal employment discrimination. See e.g., Carter v. Gallagher, 452 F.2d 315, 330 (CA8 1971) (*en banc*), cert. denied, 406 U.S. 950, 92 S.Ct. 2045, 32 L.Ed.2d 338 (1972); Local 53, Heat & Frost Insulators v. Volger, 407 F.2d 1047, 1055 (CA5 1969); United States v. Central Motor Lines, Inc., 338 F.Supp. 532, 560-562 (WDNC 1971); United States v. Sheet Metal Workers International Association, Local 10, 3 Empl.Prac.Dec. ¶ 8068 (D NJ 1970).

[42]Again, we note that the brief submitted by the Solicitor General in *Weber* urged this reading of the 1972 legislative history. The Solicitor General argued that "[a]ny doubts that Title VII authorized the use of race-conscious remedies were put to rest with the enactment of the Equal Employment Opportunity Act of 1972." Referring specifically to the amendment to the language of §706(g), the Government argued:
"In light of Congress's keen awareness of the kinds of remedies courts had been granting in Title VII cases, and in light of the protests from Senator Ervin and others over the use of race-conscious remedies, this amendment to Section 706(g) provides substantial support for the proposition that Congress intended that numerical, race-conscious relief is available under Title VII to remedy employment discrimination."

D

Finally, petitioners and the Solicitor General find support for their reading of §706(g) in several of our decisions applying that provision. Petitioners refer to several cases for the proposition that court-ordered remedies under §706(g) are limited to make-whole relief benefiting actual victims of past discrimination. See Ford Motor Co. v. EEOC, 458 U.S. 219, 102 S.Ct. 3057, 73 L.Ed.2d 721 (1982); Connecticut v. Teal, 457 U.S. 440, 102 S.Ct. 2525, 73 L.Ed.2d 130 (1982); *Teamsters*; *Franks*; *Albemarle*. This reliance is misguided. The cases cited hold only that a court may order relief designed to make individual victims of racial discrimination whole. See *Teamsters* (competitive seniority); *Franks* (competitive seniority); *Albemarle*, (backpay). None of these decisions suggested that individual "make-whole" relief was the only kind of remedy available under the statute, on the contrary, several cases emphasized that the district court's remedial powers should be exercised both to eradicate the effects of unlawful discrimination as well as to make the victims of past discrimination whole. Neither do these cases suggest that §706(g) prohibits a court from ordering relief which might benefit nonvictims; indeed several cases acknowledged that the district court has broad authority to "devise prospective relief designed to assure that employers found to be in violation of [Title VII] eliminate their discriminatory practices and the effects therefrom." *Teamsters*.

Petitioners claim to find their strongest support in Firefighters v. Stotts, 467 U.S. 561, 104 S.Ct. 2576, 81 L.Ed.2d 483 (1984). * * *

First, we rejected the claim that the District Court was merely enforcing the terms of the consent decree since the parties had expressed no intention to depart from the existing seniority system in the event of layoffs. Second, we concluded that the District Court's order conflicted with §703(h) of Title VII, which "permits the routine application of a seniority system absent proof of an intention to discriminate." Since the District Court had found that the proposed layoffs were not motivated by a discriminatory purpose, we held that the court erred in enjoining the city from applying its seniority system in making the layoffs.

We also rejected the Court of Appeals' suggestion that the District Court's order was justified by the fact that, had plaintiffs prevailed at trial, the court could have entered an order overriding the city's seniority system. Relying on *Teamsters*, we observed that a court may abridge a bona fide seniority system in fashioning a Title VII remedy only to make victims of intentional discrimination whole, that is, a court may award competitive seniority to individuals who show that they had been discriminated against. However, because none of the firefighters protected by the court's order was a proven victim of illegal discrimination, we reasoned that at trial the District Court would have been without authority to override the city's seniority system, and therefore the court could not enter such an order merely to effectuate the purposes of the consent decree.

While not strictly necessary to the result, we went on to comment that "[o]ur ruling in *Teamsters* that a court can award competitive seniority only when the beneficiary of the award has actually been a victim of illegal discrimination is consistent with the policy behind §706(g)" which, we noted, "is to provide 'make-whole' relief only to those who have been actual victims of illegal discrimination." Relying on this language, petitioners, joined by the Solicitor General, argue that both the membership goal and the Fund order contravene the policy behind §706(g) since they extend preferential relief to individuals who were not the actual victims of illegal discrimination. We think this argument both reads *Stotts* too broadly and ignores the important differences between *Stotts* and this case.

Stotts discussed the "policy" behind §706(g) in order to supplement the holding that the District Court could not have interfered with the city's seniority system in fashioning a Title VII remedy. This "policy" was read to prohibit a court from awarding make-whole relief, such as competitive seniority, backpay, or promotion, to individuals who were denied employment opportunities for reasons unrelated to discrimination. The District Court's injunction was considered to be inconsistent with this "policy" because it was tantamount to an award of make-whole relief (in the form of competitive seniority) to individual black firefighters who had not shown that the proposed layoffs were motivated by racial discrimination.[44] However, this limitation on individual make-whole relief does not affect a court's authority to order race-conscious affirmative action. The purpose of affirmative action is not to make identified victims whole, but rather to dismantle prior patterns of employment discrimination and to prevent discrimination in the future. Such relief is provided to the class as a whole rather than to individual members; no individual is entitled to relief, and beneficiaries need not show that they were themselves victims of, discrimination.[45] In this case, neither the membership goal nor the Fund order required the petitioners to indenture or train particular individuals, and neither required them to admit to membership individuals who were refused admission for reasons unrelated to discrimination. We decline petitioners' invitation to read *Stotts* to prohibit a court from ordering any kind of race-conscious affirmative relief that might benefit nonvictims.[46] This reading would distort the language of §706(g), and would deprive

---

[44]We note that, consistent with *Stotts,* the District Court in this case properly limited make-whole relief to the actual victims of discrimination. The court awarded back pay, for example, only to those class members who could establish that they were discriminated against.

[45]Even where the district court orders such relief, we note that §706(g) protects the right of the employer or the union to exclude a particular individual from its workforce or membership for reasons unrelated to discrimination.

[46]The Government urged a different interpretation of *Stotts* earlier in this lawsuit. In July 1984, petitioners' counsel, in a letter to the Court of Appeals, argued that *Stotts* "affects the propriety [of the remedies ordered] by the district court." In response, counsel for the EEOC submitted that "the decision in *Stotts* does not affect the disposition of the issues in this appeal." Counsel explained that "the court's discussion [in *Stotts*] of §706(g) is not relevant to the relief challenged by the appellants since it relates only to the award of retroactive or 'make whole' relief and not to the use of prospective remedies," like those ordered by the District Court. With respect to the last sentence of §706(g), counsel stated:

> "The last sentence of §706(g) * * * deals with 'make whole' relief and does not even address prospective relief, let alone state that all prospective remedial orders must be limited so that they only benefit the specific victims of the employer's or union's past discriminatory acts. Moreover, the language and the legislative history of §706(g) support the Commission's position that carefully tailored prospective race-conscious measures are permissible Title VII remedies. * * * [T]he fact that this interpretation was consistently followed by the Commission and the Department of Justice, during the years immediately following enactment of Title VII entitles the interpretation to great deference."

the courts of an important means of enforcing Title VII's guarantee of equal employment opportunity.[47]

E

Although we conclude that §706(g) does not foreclose a district court from instituting some sorts of racial preferences where necessary to remedy past discrimination, we do not mean to suggest that such relief is always proper. While the fashioning of "appropriate" remedies for a particular Title VII violation invokes the "equitable discretion of the district courts," *Franks*, we emphasize that a court's judgment should be guided by sound legal principles. In particular, the court should exercise its discretion with an eye towards Congress' concern that race-conscious affirmative measures not be invoked simply to create a racially balanced work force. In the majority of Title VII cases, the court will not have to impose affirmative action as a remedy for past discrimination, but need only order the employer or union to cease engaging in discriminatory practices and award make-whole relief to the individuals victimized by those practices. However, in some cases, affirmative action may be necessary in order effectively to enforce Title VII. As we noted before, a court may have to resort to race-conscious affirmative action when confronted with an employer or labor union that has engaged in persistent or egregious discrimination. Or, such relief may be necessary to dissipate the lingering effects of pervasive discrimination. Whether there might be other circumstances that justify the use of court-ordered affirmative action is a matter that we need not decide here. We note only that a court should consider whether affirmative action is necessary to remedy past discrimination in a particular case before imposing such measures, and that the court should also take care to tailor its orders to fit the nature of the violation it seeks to correct.[48] In this case, several factors lead us to conclude that the relief ordered by the District Court was proper.

First, both the District Court and the Court of Appeals agreed that the membership goal and Fund order were necessary to remedy petitioners' pervasive and egregious discrimination. The District Court set the original 29% membership goal upon observing that "[t]he record in both state and federal courts against [petitioners] is replete with instances of their bad faith attempts to prevent or delay affirmative action." The court extended the goal after finding petitioners in contempt for refusing to end their discriminatory practices and failing to comply with various provisions of RAAPO. In affirming the revised membership goal, the Court of Appeals observed that "[t]his court has twice recognized Local 28's long continued and egregious racial discrimination * * * and Local 28 has presented no facts to indicate that our earlier observations are no longer apposite." In light of petitioners' long history of "foot-dragging resistance" to court orders, simply enjoining them from once again engaging in discriminatory practices would clearly have been futile. Rather, the District Court properly determined that affirmative race-conscious measures were necessary to put an end to petitioners' discriminatory ways.

---

[47]The federal courts have declined to read *Stotts* broadly, and have instead limited the decision to its facts.

[48]This cautious approach to the use of racial preferences has been followed by the Courts of Appeals.

Both the membership goal and Fund order were similarly necessary to combat the lingering effects of past discrimination. In light of the District Court's determination that the union's reputation for discrimination operated to discourage nonwhites from even applying for membership, it is unlikely that an injunction would have been sufficient to extend to nonwhites equal opportunities for employment. Rather, because access to admission, membership, training, and employment in the industry had traditionally been obtained through informal contacts with union members, it was necessary for a substantial number of nonwhite workers to become members of the union in order for the effects of discrimination to cease. The Fund, in particular, was designed to insure that nonwhites would receive the kind of assistance that white apprentices and applicants had traditionally received through informal sources. On the facts of this case, the District Court properly determined that affirmative, race-conscious measures were necessary to assure the equal employment opportunities guaranteed by Title VII.

Second, the District Court's flexible application of the membership goal gives strong indication that it is not being used simply to achieve and maintain racial balance, but rather as a benchmark against which the court could gauge petitioners' efforts to remedy past discrimination. The court has twice adjusted the deadline for achieving the goal, and has continually approved of changes in the size of the apprenticeship classes to account for the fact that economic conditions prevented petitioners from meeting their membership targets; there is every reason to believe that both the court and the administrator will continue to accommodate legitimate explanations for the petitioners' failure to comply with the court's orders. Moreover, the District Court expressly disavowed any reliance on petitioners' failure to meet the goal as a basis for the contempt finding, but instead viewed this failure as symptomatic of petitioners' refusal to comply with various subsidiary provisions of RAAPO. In sum, the District Court has implemented the membership goal as a means by which it can measure petitioners' compliance with its orders, rather than as a strict racial quota.[49]

Third, both the membership goal and the Fund order are temporary measures. Under AAAPO "[p]referential selection of union members [w]ill end as soon as the

---

[49]Other factors support the finding that the membership goal has not been applied as a strict racial quota. For example, the Court of Appeals has twice struck down provisions requiring petitioners to indenture one nonwhite apprentice for each white apprentice indentured. Petitioners, however, characterize the following comments by the District Court as evidence that the 29.23% membership goal is in reality an inflexible quota:

"Although defendants were given seven years to attain [the 29% membership] goal * * * they have not. Indeed, they have a long way to go. In addition, they consistently have violated numerous court orders that were designed to assist in the achievement of that goal. The court therefore sees no reason to be lenient with defendants, for whatever reason, and orders that the * * * merged locals must reach a nonwhite membership of 29.23% by August 31, 1987. If the goal is not attained by that date, defendants will face fines that will threaten their very existence."

The District Court's comments express the understandable frustration of a court faced with 15 years of petitioners' deliberate resistance to ending discrimination. We do not view these statements as evidence that the court intends to apply the nonwhite membership goal as an inflexible quota. The record shows that the District Court has been willing to accommodate *legitimate* reasons for petitioners' failure to comply with court orders, and we have no reason to expect that this will change in the future.

percentage of [minority union members] approximates the percentage of [minorities] in the local labor force." *Weber*. Similarly, the Fund is scheduled to terminate when petitioners achieve the membership goal, and the court determines that it is no longer needed to remedy past discrimination. The District Court's orders thus operate "as a temporary tool for remedying past discrimination without attempting to 'maintain' a previously achieved balance." *Weber*.

Finally, we think it significant that neither the membership goal nor the Fund order "unnecessarily trammel the interests of white employees." Petitioners concede that the District Court's orders did not require any member of the union to be laid off, and did not discriminate against existing union members. While whites seeking admission into the union may be denied benefits extended to their nonwhite counterparts, the court's orders do not stand as an absolute bar to such individuals; indeed, a majority of new union members have been white. Many provisions of the court's orders are race-neutral (for example, the requirement that the JAC assign one apprentice for every four journeymen workers), and petitioners remain free to adopt the provisions of AAAPO and the Fund Order for the benefit of white members and applicants.

V

Petitioners also allege that the membership goal and Fund order contravene the equal protection component of the Due Process Clause of the Fifth Amendment because they deny benefits to white individuals based on race. We have consistently recognized that government bodies constitutionally may adopt racial classifications as a remedy for past discrimination. See Wygant v. Jackson Board of Education, 476 U.S. 267, 106 S.Ct. 1842, 90 L.Ed.2d 260 (1986); Fullilove v. Klutznick, 448 U.S. 448, 100 S.Ct. 2758, 65 L.Ed.2d 902 (1980); University of California Regents v. Bakke, 438 U.S. 265, 98 S.Ct. 2733, 57 L.Ed.2d 750 (1978); Swann v. Charlotte-Mecklenburg Board of Education, 402 U.S. 1, 91 S.Ct. 1267, 28 L.Ed.2d 554 (1971). We have not agreed however, on the proper test to be applied in analyzing the constitutionality of race-conscious remedial measures. We need not resolve this dispute here, since we conclude that the relief ordered in this case passes even the most rigorous test — it is narrowly tailored to further the Government's compelling interest in remedying past discrimination.

In this case, there is no problem, as there was in *Wygant*, with a proper showing of prior discrimination that would justify the use of remedial racial classifications. Both the District Court and Court of Appeals have repeatedly found petitioners guilty of egregious violations of Title VII, and have determined that affirmative measures were necessary to remedy their racially discriminatory practices. More importantly, the District Court's orders were properly tailored to accomplish this objective. First, the District Court considered the efficacy of alternative remedies, and concluded that, in light of petitioners' long record of resistance to official efforts to end their discriminatory practices, stronger measures were necessary. The court devised the temporary membership goal and the Fund as tools for remedying past discrimination. More importantly, the District Court's orders will have only a marginal impact on the interests of white workers. Again, petitioners concede that the District Court's orders did not disadvantage existing union members. While white applicants for union membership may be denied certain benefits available to their nonwhite counterparts, the court's orders do not stand as an absolute bar to the admission of such individuals;

again, a majority of those entering the union after entry of the court's orders have been white. We therefore conclude that the District Court's orders do not violate the equal protection safeguards of the Constitution.[50]

* * *

To summarize our holding today, six members of the Court agree that a district court may, in appropriate circumstances, order preferential relief benefitting individuals who are not the actual victims of discrimination as a remedy for violations of Title VII, [and] that the District Court did not use incorrect statistical evidence in establishing petitioners' nonwhite membership goal * * *. Five members of the Court agree that in this case, the District Court did not err in evaluating petitioners' utilization of the apprenticeship program, and that the membership goal and the Fund order are not violative of either Title VII or the Constitution. The judgment of the Court of Appeals is hereby

Affirmed.

JUSTICE POWELL, concurring in part and concurring in the judgment.

I join Parts I, II, III, and VI of Justice Brennan's opinion. I further agree that §706(g) does not limit a court in all cases to granting relief only to actual victims of discrimination. I write separately * * * to explain why I think the remedy ordered under the circumstances of this case [did not violate] the Constitution.

I

* * * I have recently reiterated what I believe to be the standard for assessing a constitutional challenge to a racial classification:

> "Any preference based on racial or ethnic criteria must necessarily receive a most searching examination to make sure that it does not conflict with constitutional guarantees. There are two prongs to this examination. First, any racial classification must be justified by a compelling governmental interest. Second, the means chosen by the State to effectuate its purpose must be narrowly tailored to the achievement of that goal."

The finding by the District Court and the Court of Appeals that petitioners have engaged in egregious violations of Title VII establishes, without doubt, a compelling governmental interest sufficient to justify the imposition of a racially classified remedy. It would be difficult to find defendants more determined to discriminate against minorities. My inquiry, therefore, focuses on whether the District Court's remedy is "narrowly tailored," to the goal of eradicating the discrimination engaged in by petitioners. I believe it is.

The Fund order is supported not only by the governmental interest in eradicating petitioners' discriminatory practices, it also is supported by the societal interest in compliance with the judgments of federal courts. The Fund order was not imposed until after petitioners were held in contempt. In requiring the Union to create the Fund, the District Court expressly considered the consequent seriousness of the burden

---

[50]Petitioners also argue that "the construction of Title VII adopted by the Court of Appeals has the effect of making the Civil Rights Act an unconstitutional bill of attainder, visiting upon white persons the sins of past discrimination by others." We reject this contention as without merit.

to the defendants. Moreover, the focus of the Fund order was to give minorities opportunities that for years had been available informally only to nonminorities. The burden this imposes on nonminorities is slight. Under these circumstances, I have little difficulty concluding that the Fund order was carefully structured to vindicate the compelling governmental interests present in this case.

The percentage goal raises a different question. In Fullilove v. Klutznick, 448 U.S. 448, 100 S.Ct. 2758, 65 L.Ed.2d 902 (1980), this Court upheld the constitutionality of the "minority business enterprise" provision of the Public Works Employment Act of 1977, which required, absent administrative waiver, that at least 10% of federal funds granted for local public works projects be used by grantees to procure services or supplies from businesses owned by minority group members. In my concurring opinion, I relied on four factors that had been applied by courts of appeals when considering the proper scope of race-conscious hiring remedies. Those factors were: (i) the efficacy of alternative remedies; (ii) the planned duration of the remedy; (iii) the relationship between the percentage of minority workers to be employed and the percentage of minority group members in the relevant population or work force; and (iv) the availability of waiver provisions if the hiring plan could not be met. A final factor of primary importance that I considered in Fullilove, as well as in Wygant, was "the effect of the [remedy] upon innocent third-parties." Application of those factors demonstrates that the goal in this case comports with constitutional requirements.

First, it is doubtful, given petitioners' history in this litigation, that the District Court had available to it any other effective remedy. That court, having had the parties before it over a period of time, was in the best position to judge whether an alternative remedy, such as a simple injunction, would have been effective in ending petitioners' discriminatory practices. Here, the court imposed the 29% goal in 1975 only after declaring that "[i]n light of Local 28's and JAC's failure to 'clean house' this court concludes that the imposition of a remedial racial goal * * * is essential to place the defendants in a position of compliance with the 1964 Civil Rights Act." On these facts, it is fair to conclude that absent authority to set a goal as a benchmark against which it could measure progress in eliminating discriminatory practices, the District Court may have been powerless to provide an effective remedy. Second, the goal was not imposed as a permanent requirement, but is of limited duration. Third, the goal is directly related to the percentage of nonwhites in the relevant workforce.

As a fourth factor, my concurring opinion in Fullilove considered whether waiver provisions were available in the event that the hiring goal could not be met. The requirement of a waiver provision or, more generally, of flexibility with respect to the imposition of a numerical goal reflects a recognition that neither the Constitution nor Title VII requires a particular racial balance in the workplace. Indeed, the Constitution forbids such a requirement if imposed for its own sake. *Fullilove.* "We have recognized, however, that in order to remedy the effects of prior discrimination, it may be necessary to take race into account." *Wygant.* Thus, a court may not choose a remedy for the purpose of attaining a particular racial balance; rather, remedies properly are confined to the elimination of proven discrimination. A goal is a means, useful in limited circumstances, to assist a court in determining whether discrimination has been eradicated.

The flexible application of the goal requirement in this case demonstrates that it is not a means to achieve racial balance. The contempt order was not imposed for the Union's failure to achieve the goal, but for its failure to take the prescribed steps that would facilitate achieving the goal. Additional flexibility is evidenced by the fact that this goal, originally set to be achieved by 1981, has been twice delayed and is now set for 1987.

It is also important to emphasize that on the record before us, it does not appear that nonminorities will be burdened directly, if at all. Petitioners' counsel conceded at oral argument that imposition of the goal would not require the layoff of nonminority union workers, and that therefore the District Court's order did not disadvantage existing union members. This case is thus distinguishable from Wygant where the plurality opinion noted that "layoffs impose the entire burden of achieving racial equality on particular individuals, often resulting in serious disruption of their lives." In contrast to the layoff provision in Wygant, the goal at issue here is akin to a hiring goal. In Wygant the plurality observed:

> "In cases involving valid hiring goals, the burden to be borne by individuals is diffused to a considerable extent among society generally. Though hiring goals may burden some innocent individuals, they simply do not impose the same kind of injury that layoffs impose."[3]

My view that the imposition of flexible goals as a remedy for past discrimination may be permissible under the Constitution is not an endorsement of their indiscriminate use. Nor do I imply that the adoption of such a goal will always pass constitutional muster.[4]

JUSTICE O'CONNOR, concurring in part and dissenting in part.

I join Parts II-A, III, and VI of the Court's opinion. I would reverse the judgment of the Court of Appeals on statutory grounds insofar as the membership "goal" and the Fund order are concerned, and I would not reach petitioners' constitutional claims. I agree with Justice White, however, that the membership "goal" in this case operates as a rigid racial quota that cannot feasibly be met through good-faith efforts by Local 28. In my view, §703(j), and §706(g), read together, preclude courts from ordering racial quotas such as this. I therefore dissent from the Court's judgment insofar as it affirms the use of these mandatory quotas.

---

[3]Of course, it is too simplistic to conclude from the combined holdings in *Wygant* and this case that hiring goals withstand constitutional muster whereas layoff goals and fixed quotas do not. There may be cases, for example, where a hiring goal in a particularly specialized area of employment would have the same pernicious effect as the layoff goal in *Wygant*. The proper constitutional inquiry focuses on the effect, if any, and the diffuseness of the burden imposed on innocent nonminorities, not on the label applied to the particular employment plan at issue.

[4]If the record now before us supported the position taken by Justice O'Connor, I might well view this case differently. Justice O'Connor apparently assumes that the goal can be achieved by August 31, 1987, only if the District Court requires "the replacement of journeymen by apprentices on a strictly racial basis." If and when that happens, petitioners will be free to argue that an impermissible quota has been imposed on the union and the JAC. An examination of what *has occurred* in this litigation over the years makes plain that the District Court has not enforced the goal in the rigid manner that concerns Justice O'Connor. Based on the record actually before us, I am satisfied that the goal imposed by the District Court is a flexible one.

In *Stotts*, the Court interpreted §706(g) as embodying a policy against court-ordered remedies under Title VII that award racial preferences in employment to individuals who have not been subjected to unlawful discrimination. The dissenting opinion in Stotts urged precisely the position advanced by Justice Brennan's plurality opinion today — that any such policy extends only to awarding make-whole relief to particular non-victims of discrimination, and does not bar class-wide racial preferences in certain cases. The Court unquestionably rejected that view in Stotts. Although technically dicta, the discussion of §706(g) in Stotts was an important part of the Court's rationale for the result it reached, and accordingly is entitled to greater weight than the Court gives it today.

It is now clear, however, that a majority of the Court believes that the last sentence of §706(g) does not in all circumstances prohibit a court in a Title VII employment discrimination case from ordering relief that may confer some racial preferences with regard to employment in favor of non-victims of discrimination. Even assuming that some forms of race-conscious affirmative relief, such as racial hiring goals, are permissible as remedies for egregious and pervasive violations of Title VII, in my view the membership "goal" and fund order in this case were impermissible because they operate not as goals but as racial quotas. Such quotas run counter to §703(j) of Title VII, and are thus impermissible under §706(g) when that section is read in light of §703(j), as I believe it should be.

The plurality asserts that §703(j) in no way "qualifies or proscribes a court's authority to order relief otherwise appropriate under §706(g) in circumstances where an illegal discriminatory act or practice is established." According to the plurality, §703(j) merely provides that an employer or union does not engage in unlawful discrimination simply on account of a racial imbalance in its workforce or membership, and thus is not required to institute preferential quotas to avoid Title VII liability. Thus, the plurality concedes that §703(j) is aimed at racial quotas, but interprets it as limiting only the substantive liability of employers and unions, not the remedial powers of courts.

This interpretation of §703(j) is unduly narrow. * * *

In *Weber*, the Court stated that "Section 703(j) speaks to substantive liability under Title VII." While this is one purpose of §703(j), the Court in *Weber* had no occasion to consider whether it was the exclusive purpose. In my view, the words "Nothing contained in this title shall be interpreted to require" plainly make §703(j) applicable to the interpretation of any provision of Title VII, including §706(g). Therefore, when a court interprets §706(g) as authorizing it to require an employer to adopt a racial quota, that court contravenes §703(j) to the extent that the relief imposed as a purported remedy for a violation of Title VII's substantive provisions in fact operates to require racial preferences "on account of [a racial] imbalance." In addition, since §703(j) by its terms limits the circumstances in which an employer or union may be required to extend "preferential treatment to any individual or to any group because of * * * race," the plurality's distinction between make-whole and class-wide relief is plainly ruled out insofar as §703(j) is concerned.

The plurality's restrictive reading of §703(j) rests largely on its view of the legislative history, which the plurality claims establishes that Congress simply did not consider the use of racial preferences to remedy past discrimination when it enacted

Title VII. According to the plurality, the sole focus of concern over racial quotas involved the scope of substantive liability under Title VII: the fear was that employers or unions would be found liable for violating Title VII merely on account of a racial imbalance. This reading of the legislative history ignores authoritative statements — relied on by the Court in *Stotts* — addressing the relief courts could order, and making plain that racial quotas, at least, were not among the permissible remedies for past discrimination. See, e.g., 110 Cong.Rec. 6549 (1964) ("Contrary to the allegations of some opponents of this title, there is nothing in it that will give any power to the Commission or to any court to require hiring, firing, or promotion of employees in order to meet a racial 'quota' or to achieve a certain racial balance") (Sen. Humphrey); id., at 6566 ("[T]itle VII does not permit the ordering of racial quotas in businesses or unions * * *.") (memorandum of Republican House sponsors); id., at 14665 ("under title VII, not even a court, much less the Commission, could order racial quotas or the hiring, reinstatement, admission to membership or payment of back pay for anyone who is not discriminated against in violation of this title") (statement of Senate sponsors in a bipartisan newsletter delivered to Senators supporting the bill during an attempted filibuster).

The plurality's reading of the legislative history also defies common sense. Legislators who objected to racial quotas obviously did so because of the harm that such quotas would impose on innocent nonminority workers as well as because of the restriction on employer freedom that would follow from an across-the-board requirement of racial balance in every workplace. Racial quotas would inflict such harms on nonminority workers whether such quotas were imposed directly by federal law in the form of a requirement that every workforce be racially balanced, or imposed as part of a court-ordered remedy for an employer's violations of Title VII. The legislative history, fairly read, indicates that such racial quotas are impermissible as a means of enforcing Title VII, and that even racial preferences short of quotas should be used only where clearly necessary if these preferences would benefit nonvictims at the expense of innocent nonminority workers.

At bottom, the plurality recognizes that this is so, although it prefers to cut the congressional rejection of racial quotas loose from any statutory moorings and make this policy simply another factor that should inform the remedial discretion of district courts. Indeed, notwithstanding its claim that §703(j) is irrelevant to interpretation of §706(g), the plurality tacitly concedes that racial quotas are improper, and that they are improper by virtue of §703(j). The plurality says that in considering whether to grant race-conscious affirmative relief "the court should exercise its discretion with an eye towards Congress' concern that race-conscious affirmative measures not be invoked simply to create a racially balanced work force." Since this is precisely the congressional concern that the plurality locates in §703(j), the plurality appears to recognize that §703(j) is relevant, after all, to the choice of remedies under §706(g). Moreover, the plurality indicates that a hiring or membership goal must be applied flexibly in order that the goal not be "used simply to achieve and maintain racial balance, but rather as a benchmark against which the court [can] gauge [an employer's or union's] efforts to remedy past discrimination." It is fair to infer that the plurality approves the use of the membership goal in this case only because, in its view, that goal can be characterized as "a means by which [the court] can measure petitioners' compliance with its orders, rather than as a strict racial quota."

The plurality correctly indicates that, as to any racial goal ordered by a court as a remedy for past discrimination, the employer always has a potential defense by virtue of §706(g) against a claim that it was required to hire a particular employee, to wit, that the employee was not hired for "reasons unrelated to discrimination." Although the plurality gives no clues as to the scope of this defense, it is clear that an employer would remain free to refuse to hire unqualified minority applicants, even if as a result the employer failed to meet a racial hiring goal. Thus, an employer's undoubted freedom to refuse to hire unqualified minority applicants, even in the face of a court-ordered racial hiring goal, operates as one important limitation on the extent of any racially preferential treatment that can result from such a goal.

The plurality offers little guidance as to what separates an impermissible quota from a permissible goal. Reference to benchmarks such as the percentage of minority workers in the relevant labor pool will often be entirely proper in order to estimate how an employer's workforce would be composed absent past discrimination. But it is completely unrealistic to assume that individuals of each race will gravitate with mathematical exactitude to each employer or union absent unlawful discrimination. That, of course, is why there must be a substantial statistical disparity between the composition of an employer's workforce and the relevant labor pool, or the general population, before an intent to discriminate may be inferred from such a disparity. *Teamsters*. Thus, the use of a rigid quota turns a sensible rule of thumb into an unjustified conclusion about the precise extent to which past discrimination has lingering effects, or into an unjustified prediction about what would happen in the future in the absence of continuing discrimination. The imposition of a quota is therefore not truly remedial, but rather amounts to a requirement of racial balance, in contravention of §703(j)'s clear policy against such requirements.

To be consistent with §703(j), a racial hiring or membership goal must be intended to serve merely as a benchmark for measuring compliance with Title VII and eliminating the lingering effects of past discrimination, rather than as a rigid numerical requirement that must unconditionally be met on pain of sanctions. To hold an employer or union to achievement of a particular percentage of minority employment or membership, and to do so regardless of circumstances such as economic conditions or the number of available qualified minority applicants, is to impose an impermissible quota. By contrast, a permissible goal should require only a good faith effort on the employer's or union's part to come within a range demarcated by the goal itself.

This understanding of the difference between goals and quotas essentially comports with the definitions jointly adopted by the EEOC and the Departments of Justice and Labor in a 1973 memorandum, and reaffirmed on several occasions since then by the EEOC and the Department of Labor. In the view of these federal agencies, which are charged with responsibility for enforcing equal employment opportunity laws, a quota "would impose a fixed number or percentage which must be attained, or which cannot be exceeded," and would do so "regardless of the number of potential applicants who meet necessary qualifications." By contrast, a goal is "a numerical objective, fixed realistically in terms of the number of vacancies expected, and the number of qualified applicants available in the relevant job market." An employer's failure to meet a goal despite good faith efforts "is not subject to sanction, because [the employer] is not expected to displace existing employees or to hire unneeded employees to meet [the] goal." This understanding of the difference between goals and quotas seems to me workable and far more consistent with the policy underlying §703(j) and §706(g) than the plurality's forced distinction between make-whole relief and class-wide relief. If, then, some racial preferences may be ordered by a court as a remedy for past discrimination even though the beneficiaries may be nonvictims, I would employ a distinction such as this between quotas and goals in setting standards to inform use by district courts of their remedial powers under §706(g) to fashion such relief.

If, as the Court holds, Title VII sometimes allows district courts to employ race-conscious remedies that may result in racially preferential treatment for non-victims, it does so only where such remedies are truly necessary. In fashioning any such remedy, including racial hiring goals, the court should exercise caution and "take care to tailor its orders to fit the nature of the violation it seeks to correct." As the plurality suggests, goals should generally be temporary measures rather than efforts to maintain a previously achieved racial balance, and should not unnecessarily trammel the interests of nonminority employees. Furthermore, the use of goals is least likely to be consistent with §703(j) where the adverse effects of any racially preferential treatment attributable to the goals will be "concentrated upon a relatively small, ascertainable group of non-minority persons." In sum, the creation of racial preferences by courts, even in the more limited form of goals rather than quotas, must be done sparingly and only where manifestly necessary to remedy violations of Title VII if the policy underlying §703(j) and §706(g) is to be honored.

In this case, I agree with Justice White that the membership "goal" established by the District Court's successive orders in this case has been administered and will continue to operate "not just [as] a minority membership goal but also [as] a strict racial quota that the union was required to attain." It is important to realize that the membership "goal" ordered by the District Court goes well beyond a requirement, such as the ones the plurality discusses approvingly, that a union "admit qualified minorities roughly in proportion to the number of qualified minorities in the work force." The "goal" here requires that the racial composition of Local 28's entire membership mirror that of the relevant labor pool by August 31, 1987, without regard to variables such as the number of qualified minority applicants available or the number of new apprentices needed. The District Court plainly stated that "[i]f the goal is not attained by that date, defendants will face fines that will threaten their very existence."

I see no reason not to take the District Court's mandatory language at face value, and certainly none is supplied by the plurality's conclusory assertion that "the District Court has been willing to accommodate legitimate reasons for petitioners' failure to comply with court orders." As Judge Winter persuasively argued in dissent below, the District Court was clearly not willing to take due account of the economic conditions that led to a sharp decline in the demand for the union skills involved in this case. Indeed, notwithstanding that petitioners have "voluntarily indentured 45% nonwhites in the apprenticeship classes since January 1981," the District Court ordered the JAC to indenture one nonwhite apprentice for every white apprentice. The Court of Appeals set this portion of the District Court's order aside as an abuse of discretion, but the District Court's willingness to impose such a rigid hiring quota certainly suggests that the District Court intended the membership "goal" to be equally absolute.

It is no answer to these observations that the District Court on two previous occasions postponed the final date for full compliance with the membership goal. At the time of the Court of Appeals' decision, Local 28's membership was approximately 10.8% nonwhite, and at oral argument counsel for petitioners represented that Local 28's membership of about 3,100 workers is now approximately 15.5% nonwhite. Absent an enormous expansion in the size of the apprentice program — which would be feasible only if the demand for the services of Local 28's members were dramatically to increase — it is beyond cavil that neither the "voluntary" 45% minority ratio now employed for apprenticeship classes nor the District Court's one-to-one order could achieve the 29.23% membership goal by Aug. 31, 1987. Indeed, at oral argument counsel for respondent conceded as much.

I do not question that petitioners' past violations of Title VII were egregious, or that in some respects they exhibited inexcusable recalcitrance in the face of the District Court's earlier remedial orders. But the timetable with which petitioners were ordered to comply was quite unrealistic and clearly could not be met by good-faith efforts on petitioners' part. In sum, the membership goal operates as a rigid membership quota, which will in turn spawn a sharp curtailment in the opportunities of nonminorities to be admitted to the apprenticeship program. * * *

Whether the unequivocal rejection of racial quotas by the Congress that enacted Title VII is said to be expressed in §706(g), in §703(j), or in both, a "remedy" such as this membership quota cannot stand. For similar reasons, I believe that the Fund order, which created benefits for minority apprentices that nonminority apprentices were precluded from enjoying, operated as a form of racial quota. Accordingly, I would reverse the judgment of the Court of Appeals on statutory grounds insofar as the membership "goal" and Fund order are concerned, without reaching petitioners' constitutional claims.

JUSTICE WHITE, dissenting.

As the Court observes, the general policy under Title VII is to limit relief for racial discrimination in employment practices to actual victims of the discrimination. But I agree that §706(g) does not bar relief for nonvictims in all circumstances. Hence, I generally agree with Parts I through IV-D of the Court's opinion. It may also be that this is one of those unusual cases where nonvictims of discrimination were entitled to a measure of the relief ordered by the District Court and affirmed by the Court of Appeals. But Judge Winter, in dissent below, was correct in concluding that critical parts of the remedy ordered in this case were excessive under §706(g), absent findings that those benefiting from the relief had been victims of discriminatory practices by the union. As Judge Winter explained and contrary to the Court's views, the cumulative effect of the revised affirmative action plan and the contempt judgments against the union established not just a minority membership goal but also a strict racial quota that the union was required to attain. We have not heretofore approved this kind of racially discriminatory hiring practice, and I would not do so now. Beyond this, I am convinced, as Judge Winter was, that holding the union in contempt for failing to attain the membership quota during a time of economic doldrums in the construction industry and a declining demand for the union skills involved in this case was for all practical purposes equivalent to a judicial insistence that the union comply even if it required the displacement of nonminority workers by members of the plaintiff class. The remedy is inequitable in my view, and for this reason I dissent from the judgment affirming the Court of Appeals.

JUSTICE REHNQUIST, with whom THE CHIEF JUSTICE joins, dissenting.

* * * I express my belief that §706(g) forbids a court from ordering racial preferences that effectively displace non-minorities except to minority individuals who have been the actual victims of a particular employer's racial discrimination. Although the pervasiveness of the racial discrimination practiced by a particular union or employer is likely to increase the number of victims who are entitled to a remedy under the Act, §706(g) does not allow us to go further than that and sanction the granting of relief to those who were not victims at the expense of innocent non-minority workers injured by racial preferences. * * * [B]oth the language and the legislative history of §706(g) clearly support this reading of §706(g), and that this Court stated as much just two Terms ago in *Stotts*. Because of this, I would not reach the equal protection question, but would rely solely on §706(g) to reverse the Court of Appeals' judgment approving the order of class-based relief for petitioners' past discrimination.

NOTES AND PROBLEMS FOR DISCUSSION

1. The opinions written by Justices Brennan and Powell state that an employer cannot be found in violation of Title VII "simply" because of a racial imbalance in its workforce and, therefore, that racial preferences cannot be imposed solely for the purpose of attaining or maintaining racial balance. Nevertheless, the opinions continue, racial preferences can be ordered by the courts as remedies for Title VII violations. But if racial imbalance is not *per se* violative of Title VII, i.e., if discrimination means something more than the mere fact of imbalance, should racial balance be an objective of a remedy for discrimination? Is that the effect of including a specific numerical hiring or promotion goal in a court ordered affirmative action plan? Or is the Court using a numerical goal merely as a gauge by which it can measure the nondiscriminatory effect of the defendant's future personnel policy? Yet, if discrimination is not to be measured solely by the level of racial representation, should the effectiveness of efforts to remedy discrimination be gauged by racial proportionality?

Of course, the parties frequently contest the issue of whether the employer has employed a race or sex-based preference. For example, suppose an employer enters into a consent decree in which it agrees to promote all of the top 59 finishers on a promotion examination (composed of white and black applicants) even though this means that it will overfill at this position and, therefore, that it will promote fewer individuals from the next group of examinees. Has the employer utilized a racial preference that must be supported by evidence of prior discrimination? In UNITED BLACK FIREFIGHTERS ASS'N v. CITY OF AKRON, 976 F.2d 999 (6th Cir. 1992), the court held that while a cut-off point on the promotion list had to be utilized, if the choice of the cut-off point was shown to be racially motivated, the plaintiff would establish the use of a racial preference. It then noted that in the instant case, the 59th position on the promotion list was held by a black candidate, while a white applicant occupied the 60th position on the list. This fact led the court to reject the defendant's claim that the consent decree did not institute a racial preference but simply expedited the promotions process. It concluded, rather, that the decision to promote 59 employees and no more was based on the fact that the 60th candidate was white and, therefore, that the employer had used a racial preference. It added, moreover, that other evidence (unmentioned) established that the employer's clear purpose for overfilling was the attainment of a higher percentage of blacks at the promoted position.

2. In *Local 28*, the Court interpreted the last sentence of §706(g) as permitting the awarding of race-conscious affirmative relief that might benefit non-victims as long as that relief was designed to remedy prior discrimination. Yet in footnote 45, the Court added that specific individuals could be precluded from such relief where they are proven non-victims, i.e., where action taken against them was proven to be unrelated to discrimination. But if, as the Court also indicated, affirmative action is designed "to dismantle prior patterns of employment discrimination and to prevent discrimination in the future" and "is provided to the class as a whole rather than to individual members," is there a justification for distinguishing between proven and unproven non-victims? Does Justice O'Connor's opinion shed light on this question?

Note that on this critical question of whether a court can order race-conscious relief that might benefit non-victims, six members (Brennan, Marshall, Blackmun, Stevens, Powell and White) agreed that "in appropriate circumstances," Title VII would not preclude such relief. Only Justice Rehnquist and Chief Justice Burger agreed with the Solicitor General's contention that Title VII relief must be limited to proven victims of discrimination. Note that while Justice O'Connor concluded that the goal and Fund in this case exceeded the statutory limits on the court's remedial authority, she carefully avoided ruling on whether a Title VII remedy could ever provide relief to non-victims.

3. Justice Powell upheld the trial court's order, at least in part, because he concluded that incumbent nonminority workers would not be burdened directly, if at all, by the race-based hiring goal. Justices O'Connor and White, on the other hand, maintained that the plan would result in a "sharp curtailment in the opportunities of nonminorities to be admitted to the apprenticeship program." Justice Brennan, writing for the Court, concluded that while incumbents would not suffer any disadvantage under the challenged plan, whites seeking admission into the union might be temporarily disadvantaged in favor of minority candidates. What is the significance of this difference of opinion?

4. Do the opinions in *Local 28* reflect a consensus on the issue of whether court ordered affirmative action can respond to societal discrimination? The plurality opinion states that race-conscious relief "may be appropriate where an employer or a labor union has engaged in persistent or egregious discrimination, or where necessary to dissipate the lingering effects of pervasive discrimination." Justice Powell, whose critical swing vote produced a majority in favor of upholding the judgments below, while concentrating on the constitutional question, said only that such relief was permitted under Title VII "in cases involving particularly egregious conduct." Justice O'Connor declared that "assuming that some forms of race-conscious affirmative relief, such as racial hiring goals, are permissible as remedies for egregious and pervasive violations," such relief must be intended to serve as a benchmark for "eliminating the lingering effects of past discrimination." Justice White "agreed generally" with the plurality's statement on the issue. Justice Rehnquist and the Chief Justice dissented on the ground that affirmative relief that effectively displaced nonminority individuals could be awarded only to "actual victims of a particular employer's racial discrimination." The Court did address the issue of the propriety of voluntarily adopted affirmative responses to societal discrimination in *Weber*, *infra*.

5.   The legislative debates surrounding the passage by Congress of the 1990 and 1991 Civil Rights Acts, as well as the statements issued by the White House in connection with President Bush's veto of the 1990 Act and endorsement of the 1991 statute, are replete with references to the authors' perceptions of the intended and/or desired impact of the new legislation on affirmative action jurisprudence. The result of the intensive and extensive negotiations that surrounded the ultimate passage and signing of the 1991 Act is codified in the one sentence designated as §116. It states that the new statute shall not be construed to affect court-ordered remedies, conciliation agreements, or voluntary affirmative action that are "in accordance with the law." At first blush, this appears to mean that Congress decided to leave the extant jurisprudence intact. But when Congress states that the Act does not affect affirmative action that is in accord with "the law," does "the law" include relevant provisions of the 1991 statute or does it refer only to pre-Act jurisprudence? The ramifications of these alternative interpretations are particularly meaningful in the context of voluntary affirmative action, a matter that is addressed in more detail in Note 10 following *Weber*, *infra*. Nevertheless, this language could also affect court ordered remedies. For example, if §116 encompasses the other provisions of the 1991 Act, this would suggest that a court could not order an employer to engage in "race-norming" (i.e., the use of adjusted scores, different cutoff scores, or other alterations of the results of employment related tests on the basis of race or any other proscribed classification in connection with the selection or referral of applicants) since this practice is expressly prohibited by §106 of the 1991 Act.

6.   Frequently, the parties to litigation choose to settle their case in order to save the time, expense and risks associated with litigation. Where the parties in a class action choose to do so through the execution of a consent decree, their settlement must be approved by the trial judge. As part of the approval process, the court will hold a hearing in which interested third parties can assert objections to the terms of the proposed consent decree. In LOCAL NUMBER 93, INTERNATIONAL ASSOCI-ATION OF FIREFIGHTERS v. CLEVELAND, 478 U.S. 501, 106 S.Ct. 3063, 92 L.Ed.2d 405 (1986), a union representing a majority of the firefighters of the City of Cleveland objected to the terms of a proposed consent decree between the City of Cleveland and an organization of African-American and Hispanic firefighters in Cleveland. This union claimed that the consent decree violated the terms of Title VII and the Fourteenth Amendment Equal Protection Clause by giving a race-based preference in promotion to minority firefighters who had not been found to be victims of discrimination. These objections were overruled by the trial judge, who adopted the consent decree. The union then appealed the trial court's ruling to the Seventh Circuit, which affirmed the trial court. The Supreme Court was then asked to rule on the limited question of whether the limits on judicially ordered relief contained in §706(g) applied to consent decrees. (Recall that in *Local 28*, decided the same day as *Local 93*, a majority agreed that §706(g) did not preclude a trial court from granting relief after trial, in exceptional cases, to a group that included non-victims of discrimination.) The

Court concluded that §706(g) was inapplicable to consent decrees and, therefore, that the terms of this decree were subject only to the limitations imposed by §703(a) of Title VII and the Fourteenth Amendment. The Court reasoned that while a consent decree bears some of the earmarks of judgments after litigation, it also enjoys many of the characteristics of a private contract. Moreover, the Court added, since the language of §706(g) did not clearly include consent decrees, it was appropriate to consider the legislative history of Title VII which reflected Congress' desire not to preclude all voluntary race-conscious affirmative action. Accordingly, it held that a consent decree should not be viewed as an "order" within the meaning of §706(g).

The Court in *Local 93* also noted that judicial approval of a consent decree did not and could not dispose of the claims of nonconsenting intervenors; which, if properly raised, remained subject to separate litigation efforts by the intervenor. This left open the question of the extent to which third parties are free to bring their own legal challenge to the terms of a consent decree. Suppose Local 93 had neither participated in the hearings concerning the proposed consent decree, nor objected to the terms of the proposed consent decree, nor appealed the trial court's approval of the consent decree. Assume, rather, that after the consent decree was approved between the employer and the Vanguards, a group of nonminority individuals filed a separate action under Title VII alleging that hiring and promotion decisions were made on the basis of race pursuant to the terms of the consent decree and that those decisions constituted prohibited racial discrimination. Further assume that in response to this complaint, the defendant employer filed a motion to dismiss on the ground that the plaintiffs' failure to intervene in the original action prohibited them from making this collateral challenge to the terms of the consent decree. How should the court rule on this motion?

As discussed in Chapter 7, Section B, *supra*, this issue was addressed by the Supreme Court in MARTIN v. WILKS, 490 U.S. 755, 109 S.Ct. 2180, 104 L.Ed.2d 835 (1989). There, the City of Birmingham and the County Personnel Board had been sued by the NAACP and seven black individuals in separate actions alleging that these governmental entities engaged in racially discriminatory hiring and promotion practices in violation of Title VII. After a bench trial, but before judgment, the black individuals entered into one consent decree with the City and another with the County, each of which contained, inter alia, long-term and interim annual goals for the hiring and promotion of black firefighters. Notice of the final fairness hearings, along with a general description of the proposed decrees, was published in two local newspapers. A group representing some white firefighters, as well as two of its members, appeared and filed objections at the hearing. Additionally, after the hearing, but before final approval of the decrees, this association and these two members moved to intervene. The trial court denied the motions to intervene as untimely. Seven other members of the group then filed a separate complaint against the City and the Personnel Board seeking injunctive relief against enforcement of the decrees. The trial court also denied their request for relief. The appeal of the denial of intervention was consolidated with the appeal from the denial of injunctive relief and the Eleventh Circuit ruled that the trial court had not abused its discretion in connection with either decision. With respect to the denial of intervention, the appellate court rested its decision, in part, on the ground that these firefighters could safeguard their interests by instituting an independent Title VII action. Similarly, as to the request for injunctive relief, the availability of a separate forum led the appellate court to conclude that the plaintiffs had not demonstrated that operation of the challenged decrees would cause them irreparable injury.

Subsequently, a different group of white firefighters in Birmingham filed the instant suit against the City and the Personnel Board, alleging that they were denied promotions on the basis of their race in violation of the Constitution and Title VII. They, of course, had not participated in any of the prior proceedings concerning the consent decrees. The defendants admitted that the challenged promotion decisions were made on the basis of race, but maintained that these decisions were immunized from statutory challenge because they were undertaken pursuant to the terms of the consent decrees. Moreover, they filed a motion to dismiss the complaint as an impermissible collateral attack on the consent decree. The trial court denied the motion to dismiss. However, it also ruled that the decrees provided a defense to the merits of the claim of discrimination with respect to those promotion decisions mandated by the decrees. Consequently, after trial, the trial court dismissed the complaint upon finding that the promotion decisions were required by the consent decree. The Eleventh Circuit reversed, rejecting the doctrine of impermissible collateral attack and holding that nonparties to the consent decrees could not be precluded from bringing an independent challenge to the terms of the decree. It also remanded the case for trial on the discrimination claims and suggested that the legality of the terms of the consent decree should be determined by reference to the substantive law applicable to voluntary affirmative action plans.

The Supreme Court, by a vote of five to four, affirmed the Eleventh Circuit. In an opinion authored by Chief Justice Rehnquist and joined in by Justices White, O'Connor, Scalia and Kennedy, the majority noted that a "great majority" of the federal circuit courts had adopted the "impermissible collateral attack" doctrine to preclude those individuals who chose not to intervene from later litigating the issues in an independent action. Nevertheless, the Court agreed with the Eleventh Circuit's view that "[t]he linchpin of the 'impermissible collateral attack' doctrine — the attribution of preclusive effect to a failure to intervene — is * * * quite inconsistent with [Federal] Rule [of Civil Procedure] 19 and Rule 24." The majority emphasized that the language of Rule 24 (intervention) and Rule 19 (mandatory joinder) incorporated the "principle of general application in Anglo-American jurisprudence that one is not bound by a judgment in personam in a litigation in which he is not designated as a party or to which he has not been made a party by service of process." Moreover, the majority continued, this same principle mandated that "a party seeking a judgment binding on another cannot obligate that person to intervene; he must be joined." Thus, the majority concluded, joinder as a party, and not mere knowledge of the lawsuit and an opportunity to intervene, was a prerequisite to binding someone to the terms of a judgment or consent decree. Preclusive effect could not be predicated upon a failure to intervene. Putting the burden of fulfilling the requirements for preclusive effect on the named parties, rather than on the potential intervenor, the Court reasoned, was appropriate since the parties are in the best position to know the nature and scope of the relief sought and, therefore, at whose expense such relief might be awarded. The majority discounted the contention that such a ruling would be unduly burdensome and discouraging to civil rights litigants since potential adverse claimants might be numerous and/or difficult to identify and that failure to join all such claimants raised the spectre of repetitive litigation and potentially inconsistent judgments. It suggested, in response, that these difficulties were not a function of the choice between mandatory intervention and joinder, but, rather, of the nature and scope of the relief sought by the plaintiff. The Court indicated that the rules for joinder were adequate to the task and that, in its opinion, a mandatory intervention rule would not be "less awkward" since it would not prevent relitigation by individuals without knowledge of the initial action and would generate additional litigation over such issues as the timeliness and adequacy of the intervenors' notice of the lawsuit. In the end, the question, in the majority's view, was simply who should bear the burden of overcoming these difficulties and it concluded that the parties, rather than any potential intervenors, were best able to do so. Accordingly, in affirming the decision of the Eleventh Circuit, the Court remanded the case for trial of the respondents' "reverse discrimination" claims, thereby rejecting the trial court's ruling that the existence of the consent decree acted as a defense to promotion decisions made pursuant to that decree. Instead, the clear and intended result of the Court's decision was to permit the non-intervenors to bring their own substantive challenge to the terms of the consent decree.

The Court's ruling in *Wilks* was another one of the direct targets of Congress' efforts in 1990 and 1991 to enact a new civil rights bill. Section 108 of the 1991 Act substantially limits this ruling by severely restricting the opportunities for collateral challenges to litigated or consent judgments. It adds a new subsection to §703 of Title VII that precludes challenges (under the Constitution or federal civil rights laws) to any employment practice that "implements or is within the scope of" a litigated or consent judgment by nonparties, nonintervenors or non-class members who received actual notice of their opportunity to present objections to the judgment. Moreover, the provision precludes such a collateral challenge by anyone whose interests were adequately represented by someone else who had challenged the judgment on the same legal grounds and with a similar fact situation, unless there is an intervening change in the law or facts. The statute also contains the traditional exceptions permitting collateral challenges on the ground that the judgment (1) was obtained through collusion or fraud, (2) is transparently invalid, or (3) was entered by a court lacking subject matter jurisdiction. Finally, §108 adds that where collateral challenges are available, they shall be filed in the same court and, if possible, in front of the same judge, that issued the original judgment. Keep in mind, however, that this provision only applies to collateral challenges and does not alter the extant rules governing when parties represented in the original action may reopen a decree.

The detailed language of §108 raises interpretive problems that did not exist under the *Wilks* rule. For example, does this provision restrict collateral challenges only to express terms of the judgment, or does it also limit collateral attacks on subsequent implementation of the judgment by either the issuing court or the parties? The exception permitting collateral challenges in the face of intervening changes in the law or facts is contained only in amended §703(n)(1)(B)(ii) — the subsection that otherwise bars collateral challenges by individuals whose interests were adequately represented by another party. Does this mean that individuals who received adequate notice of their opportunity to object would continue to be barred in the face of an intervening change in the law or facts? Could such an individual contend that the intervening change vitiated the adequacy of the notice that his interests might be adversely affected by the challenged judgment?

7. In the last section of its opinion in *Local 28*, the Court briefly addressed the petitioners' constitutional equal protection challenge to portions of the trial court's order. As the Court readily admitted, the Justices were (and for some time had been) unable to agree on the appropriate level of scrutiny to be applied to race-conscious remedies. But since a majority agreed that the order satisfied even the rigorous scrutiny associated with suspect classification analysis, they did not discuss this issue in depth.

During its next term, the Court had another opportunity to examine this issue; this time in the context of a constitutional challenge to a court ordered race-conscious promotion plan. In UNITED STATES v. PARADISE, 480 U.S. 149, 107 S.Ct. 1053, 94 L.Ed.2d 203 (1987), the trial court had found that the Alabama Public Safety Department had committed an egregious violation of the Fourteenth Amendment by systematically excluding blacks from trooper positions over a period of four decades. As a result of this finding, the trial court issued an order requiring the Department to hire one black trooper for each white trooper hired until blacks constituted approximately 25% of the state trooper force. Several years later, the parties entered into a consent decree wherein the Department agreed to develop a promotion procedure within one year that would not have an adverse impact on black applicants. The decree also provided for judicial enforcement of its terms. Two years later, the Department proposed a promotion procedure which the plaintiff class objected to on the ground that it had not been validated. This dispute was resolved when the Department agreed to execute a second consent decree in which it reaffirmed its commitment to developing a nondiscriminatory promotion policy and in which the parties agreed to implementation of the Department's proposed policy, subject to review of its impact. The decree also provided that if the parties could not agree on the validity of the promotion policy, the issue would be resolved by the trial court. In April, 1983, the Department announced that there was an immediate need to make eight to ten promotions to the rank of corporal and proposed to make these promotions pursuant to their disputed promotion procedure.

The plaintiffs asked the trial court to enforce the consent decrees by requiring the Department to promote one black trooper for each white trooper promoted to corporal until the Department implemented a nondiscriminatory promotion procedure. The trial court ruled that the Department's promotion policy had an adverse impact on blacks and ordered the Department to produce a nondiscriminatory procedure within about two weeks. In response, the Department offered a plan to promote fifteen troopers to corporal, including four black troopers, and asked for more time to develop a nondiscriminatory procedure. The plaintiff class opposed this proposal and the trial court granted the class' motion to enforce the consent decrees. Pursuant to the language in the second decree granting the trial court authority to resolve any dispute over the validity of proposed promotion policies, the trial court fashioned the relief at issue before the Supreme Court. It ordered that 50% of the promotions to corporal be awarded to qualified black troopers until either blacks occupied 25% of the corporal positions or until the Department implemented a promotion policy that did not have an adverse impact on black troopers. The Department, pursuant to this order, promoted eight black and eight white troopers to corporal. When the Department subsequently submitted a new set of promotion procedures, the trial court accepted them and suspended application of the one-for-one promotion requirement. The Eleventh Circuit affirmed the district court order.

The Supreme Court, by a vote of five to four, also affirmed the order. Four Justices (Brennan, Marshall, Blackmun and Powell) joined in the opinion of the Court. Once again, however, after noting that the Court had been unable to reach consensus on the appropriate level of scrutiny for such race-conscious remedies, they stated that the relief ordered in the instant case survived even a strict scrutiny standard. Thus, even though three of these Justices, Brennan, Marshall and Blackmun, had acknowledged the propriety of a less-than-strict standard in *Local 28*, they were not compelled to reiterate this position in *Paradise*. The plurality reasoned that the one-for-one promotion order withstood strict scrutiny since it was narrowly tailored to serve the compelling governmental purpose of remedying the defendant's unconstitutionally "pervasive, systematic and obstinate" discriminatory conduct. They rejected the claim that promotion-based relief could not be awarded in the context of a finding of discrimination in hiring, reasoning that this relief was necessary to remedy the discrimination that permeated the defendant's hiring and promotion policies. With respect to whether the remedy was sufficiently "narrowly tailored" to serve that compelling interest, the plurality declared that it would look to five factors: (1) the necessity of such relief; (2) the efficacy of alternative remedies; (3) the flexibility and duration of the remedy (including the availability of waiver provisions); (4) the relationship of the numerical goals to the labor market; and (5) the extent of the impact of the relief on the rights of third parties. They then concluded that in light of the Department's historically inadequate efforts at eliminating discrimination in hiring and promotions, the trial court's remedy was necessary to serve the compelling federal interest in remedying that discrimination. The plurality also noted that race-neutral alternatives, such as fines, awards of attorney fees and additional time to develop nondiscriminatory policies would not serve either the interest of preventing further foot-dragging or compensating the plaintiffs for the delays in implementing acceptable promotion policies.

The remedial plan also was determined to be sufficiently flexible since it was designed to terminate either when the defendant implemented a nondiscriminatory procedure or when blacks obtained 25% of the upper level positions. This 25% figure, moreover, was found to reflect the percentage of blacks in the relevant labor market. And although 50% of the promotions in the short run were reserved for black troopers, this figure was chosen simply to hasten the attainment of the ultimate 25% goal. The plurality also mentioned the fact that the racial preference was limited solely to qualified blacks.

Finally, the use of race as a factor in promotions did not impose burdens on innocent nonminority third parties since it did not involve the layoff or discharge of white workers and was limited to qualified black troopers. Justice Powell also issued a separate opinion in which he explicitly reiterated his reliance on the five factors he had set forth in his separate opinion in *Local 28*. The fifth vote in support of the race-based remedy came from Justice Stevens, who declared that, as a proven discriminator, the defendant Department bore the burden of persuasion as to the unconstitutionality of the remedial order, i.e., that the relief exceeded "the bounds of reasonableness." He then concluded that this burden had not been met. In dissent, Justice O'Connor, Chief

Justice Rehnquist, Justice Scalia and Justice White found the remedy not "sufficiently tailored" because (1)the 50% promotion quota was substantially in excess of the percentage of blacks in the relevant labor market, (2)the trial court had not expressly evaluated available alternative remedies, and (3)these alternatives would have fulfilled the stated purpose of compelling the Department to comply with the consent decree.

The Supreme Court's constitutional jurisprudence makes manifest that the Court's choice of which level of scrutiny is to be applied to a particular classification is highly significant to, if not often determinative of the results. For many years, a majority of the Court could not coalesce around any single formulation of the constitutional standard for race-based preferences. A consensus finally was reached in the following case.

City of Richmond v. J.A. Croson Co.

Supreme Court of the United States, 1989.
488 U.S. 469, 109 S.Ct. 706, 102 L.Ed.2d 854.

JUSTICE O'CONNOR announced the judgment of the Court and delivered the opinion of the Court with respect to Parts I, III-B, and IV, an opinion with respect to Part II, in which THE CHIEF JUSTICE and JUSTICE WHITE join, and an opinion with respect to Parts III-A and V, in which THE CHIEF JUSTICE, JUSTICE WHITE and JUSTICE KENNEDY join.

In this case, we confront once again the tension between the Fourteenth Amendment's guarantee of equal treatment to all citizens, and the use of race-based measures to ameliorate the effects of past discrimination on the opportunities enjoyed by members of minority groups in our society. In Fullilove v. Klutznick, 448 U.S. 448, 100 S.Ct. 2758, 65 L.Ed.2d 902 (1980), we held that a congressional program requiring that 10% of certain federal construction grants be awarded to minority contractors did not violate the equal protection principles embodied in the Due Process Clause of the Fifth Amendment. Relying largely on our decision in *Fullilove*, some lower federal courts have applied a similar standard of review in assessing the constitutionality of state and local minority set-aside provisions under the Equal Protection Clause of the Fourteenth Amendment. Since our decision two Terms ago in Wygant v. Jackson Board of Education, 476 U.S. 267, 106 S.Ct. 1842, 90 L.Ed.2d 260 (1986), the lower federal courts have attempted to apply its standards in evaluating the constitutionality of state and local programs which allocate a portion of public contracting opportunities exclusively to minority-owned businesses. We noted probable jurisdiction in this case to consider the applicability of our decision in *Wygant* to a minority set-aside program adopted by the city of Richmond, Virginia.

I

On April 11, 1983, the Richmond City Council adopted the Minority Business Utilization Plan (the Plan). The Plan required prime contractors to whom the city awarded construction contracts to subcontract at least 30% of the dollar amount of the contract to one or more Minority Business Enterprises (MBEs). The 30% set-aside did not apply to city contracts awarded to minority-owned prime contractors.

The Plan defined an MBE as "[a] business at least fifty-one (51) percent of which is owned and controlled * * * by minority group members." "Minority group members" were defined as "[c]itizens of the United States who are Blacks, Spanish-speaking, Orientals, Indians, Eskimos, or Aleuts." There was no geographic limit to the Plan; an otherwise qualified MBE from anywhere in the United States could avail itself of the 30% set-aside. The Plan declared that it was "remedial" in nature, and enacted "for the purpose of promoting wider participation by minority business enterprises in the construction of public projects." The Plan expired on June 30, 1988, and was in effect for approximately five years.[1]

The Plan authorized the Director of the Department of General Services to promulgate rules which "shall allow waivers in those individual situations where a contractor can prove to the satisfaction of the director that the requirements herein cannot be achieved." To this end, the Director promulgated Contract Clauses, Minority Business Utilization Plan (Contract Clauses). Section D of these rules provided:

> "No partial or complete waiver of the foregoing [30% set-aside] requirement shall be granted by the city other than in exceptional circumstances. To justify a waiver, it must be shown that every feasible attempt has been made to comply, and it must be demonstrated that sufficient, relevant, qualified Minority Business Enterprises * * * are unavailable or unwilling to participate in the contract to enable meeting the 30% MBE goal."

The Director also promulgated "purchasing procedures" to be followed in the letting of city contracts in accordance with the Plan. Bidders on city construction contracts were provided with a "Minority Business Utilization Plan Commitment Form." Within 10 days of the opening of the bids, the lowest otherwise responsive bidder was required to submit a commitment form naming the MBEs to be used on the contract and the percentage of the total contract price awarded to the minority firm or firms. The prime contractor's commitment form or request for a waiver of the 30% set-aside was then referred to the city Human Relations Commission (HRC). The HRC verified that the MBEs named in the commitment form were in fact minority owned, and then either approved the commitment form or made a recommendation regarding the prime contractor's request for a partial or complete waiver of the 30% set-aside. The Director of General Services made the final determination on compliance with the set-aside provisions or the propriety of granting a waiver. His discretion in this regard appears to have been plenary. There was no direct administrative appeal from the Director's denial of a waiver. Once a contract had been awarded to another firm a bidder denied an award for failure to comply with the MBE requirements had a general right of protest under Richmond procurement policies.

The Plan was adopted by the Richmond City Council after a public hearing. Seven members of the public spoke to the merits of the ordinance: five were in opposition, two in favor. Proponents of the set-aside provision relied on a study which indicated that, while the general population of Richmond was 50% black, only .67% of

---

[1]The expiration of the ordinance has not rendered the controversy between the city and Croson moot. There remains a live controversy between the parties over whether Richmond's refusal to award Croson a contract pursuant to the ordinance was unlawful and thus entitles Croson to damages.

the city's prime construction contracts had been awarded to minority businesses in the 5-year period from 1978 to 1983. It was also established that a variety of contractors' associations, whose representatives appeared in opposition to the ordinance, had virtually no minority businesses within their membership. The city's legal counsel indicated his view that the ordinance was constitutional under this Court's decision in Fullilove. Councilperson Marsh, a proponent of the ordinance, made the following statement:

> "There is some information, however, that I want to make sure that we put in the record. I have been practicing law in this community since 1961, and I am familiar with the practices in the construction industry in this area, in the State, and around the nation. And I can say without equivocation, that the general conduct of the construction industry in this area, and the State, and around the nation, is one in which race discrimination and exclusion on the basis of race is widespread."

There was no direct evidence of race discrimination on the part of the city in letting contracts or any evidence that the city's prime contractors had discriminated against minority-owned subcontractors.

Opponents of the ordinance questioned both its wisdom and its legality. They argued that a disparity between minorities in the population of Richmond and the number of prime contracts awarded to MBEs had little probative value in establishing discrimination in the construction industry. Representatives of various contractors' associations questioned whether there were enough MBEs in the Richmond area to satisfy the 30% set-aside requirement. Mr. Murphy noted that only 4.7% of all construction firms in the United States were minority owned and that 41% of these were located in California, New York, Illinois, Florida, and Hawaii. He predicted that the ordinance would thus lead to a windfall for the few minority firms in Richmond. Councilperson Gillespie indicated his concern that many local labor jobs, held by both blacks and whites, would be lost because the ordinance put no geographic limit on the MBEs eligible for the 30% set-aside. Some of the representatives of the local contractors organizations indicated that they did not discriminate on the basis of race and were in fact actively seeking out minority members. Councilperson Gillespie expressed his concern about the legality of the Plan, and asked that a vote be delayed pending consultation with outside counsel. His suggestion was rejected, and the ordinance was enacted by a vote of six to two, with councilmember Gillespie abstaining.

On September 6, 1983, the city of Richmond issued an invitation to bid on a project for the provision and installation of certain plumbing fixtures at the city jail. On September 30, 1983, Eugene Bonn, the regional manager of J.A. Croson Company (Croson), a mechanical plumbing and heating contractor, received the bid forms. The project involved the installation of stainless steel urinals and water closets in the city jail. Products of either of two manufacturers were specified, Acorn Engineering Company (Acorn) or Bradley Manufacturing Company (Bradley). Bonn determined that to meet the 30% set-aside requirement, a minority contractor would have to supply the fixtures. The provision of the fixtures amounted to 75% of the total contract price.

On September 30, Bonn contacted five or six MBEs that were potential suppliers of the fixtures, after contacting three local and state agencies that maintained lists of

MBEs. No MBE expressed interest in the project or tendered a quote. On October 12, 1983, the day the bids were due, Bonn again telephoned a group of MBEs. This time, Melvin Brown, president of Continental Metal Hose (Continental), a local MBE, indicated that he wished to participate in the project. Brown subsequently contacted two sources of the specified fixtures in order to obtain a price quotation. One supplier, Ferguson Plumbing Supply, which is not an MBE, had already made a quotation directly to Croson, and refused to quote the same fixtures to Continental. Brown also contacted an agent of Bradley, one of the two manufacturers of the specified fixtures. The agent was not familiar with Brown or Continental, and indicated that a credit check was required which would take at least 30 days to complete.

On October 13, 1983, the sealed bids were opened. Croson turned out to be the only bidder, with a bid of $126,530. Brown and Bonn met personally at the bid opening, and Brown informed Bonn that his difficulty in obtaining credit approval had hindered his submission of a bid.

By October 19, 1983, Croson had still not received a bid from Continental. On that date it submitted a request for a waiver of the 30% set-aside. Croson's waiver request indicated that Continental was "unqualified" and that the other MBEs contacted had been unresponsive or unable to quote. Upon learning of Croson's waiver request, Brown contacted an agent of Acorn, the other fixture manufacturer specified by the city. Based upon his discussions with Acorn, Brown subsequently submitted a bid on the fixtures to Croson. Continental's bid was $6,183.29 higher than the price Croson had included for the fixtures in its bid to the city. This constituted a 7% increase over the market price for the fixtures. With added bonding and insurance, using Continental would have raised the cost of the project by $7,663.16. On the same day that Brown contacted Acorn, he also called city procurement officials and told them that Continental, an MBE, could supply the fixtures specified in the city jail contract. On November 2, 1983, the city denied Croson's waiver request, indicating that Croson had 10 days to submit an MBE Utilization Commitment Form, and warned that failure to do so could result in its bid being considered unresponsive.

Croson wrote the city on November 8, 1983. In the letter, Bonn indicated that Continental was not an authorized supplier for either Acorn or Bradley fixtures. He also noted that Acorn's quotation to Brown was subject to credit approval and in any case was substantially higher than any other quotation Croson had received. Finally, Bonn noted that Continental's bid had been submitted some 21 days after the prime bids were due. In a second letter, Croson laid out the additional costs that using Continental to supply the fixtures would entail, and asked that it be allowed to raise the overall contract price accordingly. The city denied both Croson's request for a waiver and its suggestion that the contract price be raised. The city informed Croson that it had decided to rebid the project. On December 9, 1983, counsel for Croson wrote the city asking for a review of the waiver denial. The city's attorney responded that the city had elected to rebid the project, and that there is no appeal of such a decision. Shortly thereafter Croson brought this action under 42 U.S.C. §1983 in the Federal District Court for the Eastern District of Virginia, arguing that the Richmond ordinance was unconstitutional on its face and as applied in this case.

The District Court upheld the Plan in all respects. In its original opinion, a divided panel of the Fourth Circuit Court of Appeals affirmed. Both courts applied a test derived from "the common concerns articulated by the various Supreme Court opinions" in *Fullilove* and University of California Regents v. Bakke, 438 U.S. 265, 98 S.Ct. 2733, 57 L.Ed.2d 750 (1978). Relying on the great deference which this Court accorded Congress' findings of past discrimination in *Fullilove*, the panel majority indicated its view that the same standard should be applied to the Richmond City Council, stating:

> "Unlike the review we make of a lower court decision, our task is not to determine if there was sufficient evidence to sustain the council majority's position in any traditional sense of weighing the evidence. Rather, it is to determine whether the legislative history demonstrates that the council reasonably concluded that private and governmental discrimination had contributed to the negligible percentage of public contracts awarded minority contractors."

The majority found that national findings of discrimination in the construction industry, when considered in conjunction with the statistical study concerning the awarding of prime contracts in Richmond, rendered the city council's conclusion that low minority participation in city contracts was due to past discrimination "reasonable." The panel opinion then turned to the second part of its "synthesized *Fullilove*" test, examining whether the racial quota was "narrowly tailored to the legislative goals of the Plan." First, the court upheld the 30% set-aside figure, by comparing it not to the number of MBEs in Richmond, but rather to the percentage of minority persons in the city's population. The panel held that to remedy the effects of past discrimination, "a set-aside program for a period of five years obviously must require more than a 0.67% set-aside to encourage minorities to enter the contracting industry and to allow existing minority contractors to grow." Thus, in the court's view the 30% figure was "reasonable in light of the undisputed fact that minorities constitute 50% of the population of Richmond."

Croson sought certiorari from this Court. We granted the writ, vacated the opinion of the Court of Appeals, and remanded the case for further consideration in light of our intervening decision in *Wygant*.

On remand, a divided panel of the Court of Appeals struck down the Richmond set-aside program as violating both prongs of strict scrutiny under the Equal Protection Clause of the Fourteenth Amendment. The majority found that the "core" of this Court's holding in Wygant was that, "[t]o show that a plan is justified by a compelling governmental interest, a municipality that wishes to employ a racial preference cannot rest on broad-brush assumptions of historical discrimination." As the court read this requirement, "[f]indings of societal discrimination will not suffice; the findings must concern prior discrimination by the government unit involved."

In this case, the debate at the city council meeting revealed no record of prior discrimination by the city in awarding public contracts * * *. Moreover, the statistics comparing the minority population of Richmond to the percentage of prime contracts awarded to minority firms had little or no probative value in establishing prior discrimination in the relevant market, and actually suggested "more of a political than a remedial basis for the racial preference." The court concluded that, "[i]f this plan is supported by a compelling governmental interest, so is every other plan that has been enacted in the past or that will be enacted in the future."

The Court of Appeals went on to hold that even if the city had demonstrated a compelling interest in the use of a race-based quota, the 30% set-aside was not narrowly tailored to accomplish a remedial purpose. The court found that the 30% figure was "chosen arbitrarily" and was not tied to the number of minority subcontractors in Richmond or to any other relevant number. * * * We * * * now affirm the judgment.

II

The parties and their supporting *amici* fight an initial battle over the scope of the city's power to adopt legislation designed to address the effects of past discrimination. Relying on our decision in *Wygant*, appellee argues that the city must limit any race-based remedial efforts to eradicating the effects of its own prior discrimination. This is essentially the position taken by the Court of Appeals below. Appellant argues that our decision in *Fullilove* is controlling, and that as a result the city of Richmond enjoys sweeping legislative power to define and attack the effects of prior discrimination in its local construction industry. We find that neither of these two rather stark alternatives can withstand analysis.

In *Fullilove*, we upheld the minority set-aside contained in §103(f)(2) of the Public Works Employment Act of 1977 (the Act) against a challenge based on the equal protection component of the Due Process Clause. The Act authorized a four billion dollar appropriation for federal grants to state and local governments for use in public works projects. The primary purpose of the Act was to give the national economy a quick boost in a recessionary period; funds had to be committed to state or local grantees by September 30, 1977. The Act also contained the following requirement: "Except to the extent the Secretary determines otherwise, no grant shall be made under this Act * * * unless the applicant gives satisfactory assurance to the Secretary that at least 10 per centum of the amount of each grant shall be expended for minority business enterprises." MBEs were defined as businesses effectively controlled by "citizens of the United States who are Negroes, Spanish-speaking, Orientals, Indians, Eskimos, and Aleuts."

The principal opinion in *Fullilove*, written by Chief Justice Burger, did not employ "strict scrutiny" or any other traditional standard of equal protection review. The Chief Justice noted at the outset that although racial classifications call for close examination, the Court was at the same time, "bound to approach [its] task with appropriate deference to the Congress, a co-equal branch charged by the Constitution with the power to 'provide for the * * * general Welfare of the United States' and 'to enforce by appropriate legislation,' the equal protection guarantees of the Fourteenth Amendment." The principal opinion asked two questions: first, were the objectives of the legislation within the power of Congress? Second, was the limited use of racial and ethnic criteria a permissible means for Congress to carry out its objectives within the constraints of the Due Process Clause?

On the issue of congressional power, the Chief Justice found that Congress' commerce power was sufficiently broad to allow it to reach the practices of prime contractors on federally funded local construction projects. Congress could mandate state and local government compliance with the set-aside program under its §5 power to enforce the Fourteenth Amendment.

The Chief Justice next turned to the constraints on Congress' power to employ race-conscious remedial relief. His opinion stressed two factors in upholding the MBE set-aside. First was the unique remedial powers of Congress under §5 of the Fourteenth Amendment:

> "Here we deal * * * not with the limited remedial powers of a federal court, for example, but with the broad remedial powers of Congress. It is fundamental that *in no organ of government, state or federal, does there repose a more comprehensive remedial power than in the Congress*, expressly charged by the Constitution with competence and authority to enforce equal protection guarantees." (emphasis added).

Because of these unique powers, the Chief Justice concluded that "Congress not only may induce voluntary action to assure compliance with existing federal statutory or constitutional antidiscrimination provisions, but also, where Congress has authority *to declare certain conduct unlawful*, it may, as here, authorize and induce state action to avoid such conduct." (emphasis added).

In reviewing the legislative history behind the Act, the principal opinion focused on the evidence before Congress that a nationwide history of past discrimination had reduced minority participation in federal construction grants. The Chief Justice also noted that Congress drew on its experience under §8(a) of the Small Business Act of 1953, which had extended aid to minority businesses. The Chief Justice concluded that "Congress had abundant historical basis from which it could conclude that traditional procurement practices, when applied to minority businesses, could perpetuate the effects of prior discrimination."

The second factor emphasized by the principal opinion in *Fullilove* was the flexible nature of the 10% set-aside. Two "congressional assumptions" underlay the MBE program: first, that the effects of past discrimination had impaired the competitive position of minority businesses, and second, that "adjustment for the effects of past discrimination" would assure that at least 10% of the funds from the federal grant program would flow to minority businesses. The Chief Justice noted that both of these "assumptions" could be "rebutted" by a grantee seeking a waiver of the 10% requirement. Thus a waiver could be sought where minority businesses were not available to fill the 10% requirement or, more importantly, where an MBE attempted "to exploit the remedial aspects of the program by charging an unreasonable price, *i.e.*, a price not attributable to the present effects of prior discrimination." The Chief Justice indicated that without this fine tuning to remedial purpose, the statute would not have "pass[ed] muster."

In his concurring opinion, Justice Powell relied on the legislative history adduced by the principal opinion in finding that "Congress reasonably concluded that private and governmental discrimination had contributed to the negligible percentage of public contracts awarded minority contractors." Justice Powell also found that the means chosen by Congress, particularly in light of the flexible waiver provisions, were "reasonably necessary" to address the problem identified. Justice Powell made it clear that other governmental entities might have to show more than Congress before undertaking race-conscious measures: "The degree of specificity required in the findings of discrimination and the breadth of discretion in the choice of remedies may vary with the nature and authority of the governmental body."

Appellant and its supporting *amici* rely heavily on *Fullilove* for the proposition that a city council, like Congress, need not make specific findings of discrimination to engage in race-conscious relief. Thus, appellant argues "[i]t would be a perversion of federalism to hold that the federal government has a compelling interest in remedying the effects of racial discrimination in its own public works program, but a city government does not."

What appellant ignores is that Congress, unlike any State or political subdivision, has a specific constitutional mandate to enforce the dictates of the Fourteenth Amendment. The power to "enforce" may at times also include the power to define situations which Congress determines threaten principles of equality and to adopt prophylactic rules to deal with those situations. See Katzenbach v. Morgan, supra, 384 U.S., at 651, 86 S.Ct., at 1723 ("Correctly viewed, §5 is a positive grant of legislative power authorizing Congress to exercise its discretion in determining whether and what legislation is needed to secure the guarantees of the Fourteenth Amendment"). See also South Carolina v. Katzenbach, 383 U.S. 301, 326, 86 S.Ct. 803, 817, 15 L.Ed.2d 769 (1966) (similar interpretation of congressional power under §2 of the Fifteenth Amendment). The Civil War Amendments themselves worked a dramatic change in the balance between congressional and state power over matters of race. Speaking of the Thirteenth and Fourteenth Amendments in Ex parte Virginia, 100 U.S. 339, 345, 25 L.Ed. 676 (1880), the Court stated: "They were intended to be, what they really are, limitations of the powers of the States and enlargements of the power of Congress."

That Congress may identify and redress the effects of society-wide discrimination does not mean that, *a fortiori*, the States and their political subdivisions are free to decide that such remedies are appropriate. Section 1 of the Fourteenth Amendment is an explicit constraint on state power, and the States must undertake any remedial efforts in accordance with that provision. To hold otherwise would be to cede control over the content of the Equal Protection Clause to the 50 state legislatures and their myriad political subdivisions. The mere recitation of a benign or compensatory purpose for the use of a racial classification would essentially entitle the States to exercise the full power of Congress under §5 of the Fourteenth Amendment and insulate any racial classification from judicial scrutiny under §1. We believe that such a result would be contrary to the intentions of the Framers of the Fourteenth Amendment, who desired to place clear limits on the States' use of race as a criterion for legislative action, and to have the federal courts enforce those limitations.

We do not, as Justice Marshall's dissent suggests, find in §5 of the Fourteenth Amendment some form of federal pre-emption in matters of race. We simply note what should be apparent to all — §1 of the Fourteenth Amendment stemmed from a distrust of state legislative enactments based on race; §5 is, as the dissent notes, "'a positive grant of legislative power'" to Congress. Thus, our treatment of an exercise of congressional power in *Fullilove* cannot be dispositive here. In the *Slaughter-House Cases*, 16 Wall. 36, 21 L.Ed. 394 (1873), cited by the dissent, the Court noted that the Civil War Amendments granted "additional powers to the Federal government," and laid "additional restraints upon those of the States."

It would seem equally clear, however, that a state or local subdivision (if delegated the authority from the State) has the authority to eradicate the effects of private discrimination within its own legislative jurisdiction.[2] This authority must, of course, be exercised within the constraints of §1 of the Fourteenth Amendment. Our decision in *Wygant* is not to the contrary. *Wygant* addressed the constitutionality of the use of racial quotas by local school authorities pursuant to an agreement reached with the local teachers' union. It was in the context of addressing the school board's power to adopt a race-based layoff program affecting its own work force that the *Wygant* plurality indicated that the Equal Protection Clause required "some showing of prior discrimination by the governmental unit involved." As a matter of state law, the city of Richmond has legislative authority over its procurement policies, and can use its spending powers to remedy private discrimination, if it identifies that discrimination with the particularity required by the Fourteenth Amendment. To this extent, on the question of the city's competence, the Court of Appeals erred in following *Wygant* by rote in a case involving a state entity which has state-law authority to address discriminatory practices within local commerce under its jurisdiction.

Thus, if the city could show that it had essentially become a "passive participant" in a system of racial exclusion practiced by elements of the local construction industry, we think it clear that the city could take affirmative steps to dismantle such a system. It is beyond dispute that any public entity, state or federal, has a compelling interest in assuring that public dollars, drawn from the tax contributions of all citizens, do not serve to finance the evil of private prejudice.

III

A

The Equal Protection Clause of the Fourteenth Amendment provides that "[N]o State shall * * * deny to *any person* within its jurisdiction the equal protection of the laws" (emphasis added). As this Court has noted in the past, the "rights created by the first section of the Fourteenth Amendment are, by its terms, guaranteed to the individual. The rights established are personal rights." Shelly v. Kraemer, 334 U.S. 1, 22, 68 S.Ct. 836, 846, 92 L.Ed. 1161 (1948). The Richmond Plan denies certain citizens the opportunity to compete for a fixed percentage of public contracts based solely upon their race. To whatever racial group these citizens belong, their "personal rights" to be treated with equal dignity and respect are implicated by a rigid rule erecting race as the sole criterion in an aspect of public decisionmaking.

Absent searching judicial inquiry into the justification for such race-based measures, there is simply no way of determining what classifications are "benign" or "remedial" and what classifications are in fact motivated by illegitimate notions of racial inferiority or simple racial politics. Indeed, the purpose of strict scrutiny is to "smoke out" illegitimate uses of race by assuring that the legislative body is pursuing a goal important enough to warrant use of a highly suspect tool. The test also ensures that the means chosen "fit" this compelling goal so closely that there is little or no

---

[2]In its original panel opinion, the Court of Appeals held that under Virginia law the city had the legal authority to enact the set-aside program. That determination was not disturbed by the court's subsequent holding that the Plan violated the Equal Protection Clause.

possibility that the motive for the classification was illegitimate racial prejudice or stereotype.

Classifications based on race carry a danger of stigmatic harm. Unless they are strictly reserved for remedial settings, they may in fact promote notions of racial inferiority and lead to a politics of racial hostility. See University of California Regents v. Bakke, 438 U.S. at 298, 98 S.Ct., at 2752 (opinion of Powell, J.) ("[P]referential programs may only reinforce common sterotypes holding that certain groups are unable to achieve success without special protection based on a factor having no relation to individual worth"). We thus reaffirm the view expressed by the plurality in *Wygant* that the standard of review under the Equal Protection Clause is not dependent on the race of those burdened or benefited by a particular classification.

Our continued adherence to the standard of review employed in *Wygant*, does not, as Justice Marshall's dissent suggests, indicate that we view "racial discrimination as largely a phenomenon of the past" or that "government bodies need no longer preoccupy themselves with rectifying racial injustice." As we indicate below, States and their local subdivisions have many legislative weapons at their disposal both to punish and prevent present discrimination and to remove arbitrary barriers to minority advancement. Rather, our interpretation of §1 stems from our agreement with the view expressed by Justice Powell in *Bakke*, that "[t]he guarantee of equal protection cannot mean one thing when applied to one individual and something else when applied to a person of another color."

Under the standard proposed by Justice Marshall's dissent, "[r]ace-conscious classifications designed to further remedial goals," are forthwith subject to a relaxed standard of review. How the dissent arrives at the legal conclusion that a racial classification is "designed to further remedial goals," without first engaging in an examination of the factual basis for its enactment and the nexus between its scope and that factual basis we are not told. However, once the "remedial" conclusion is reached, the dissent's standard is singularly deferential, and bears little resemblance to the close examination of legislative purpose we have engaged in when reviewing classifications based either on race or gender. See Weinberger v. Wiesenfeld, 420 U.S. 636, 648, 95 S.Ct. 1225, 1233, 43 L.Ed.2d 514 (1975) ("[T]he mere recitation of a benign, compensatory purpose is not an automatic shield which protects against any inquiry into the actual purposes underlying a statutory scheme"). The dissent's watered-down version of equal protection review effectively assures that race will always be relevant in American life, and that the "ultimate goal" of eliminating entirely from governmental decisionmaking such irrelevant factors as a human being's race will never be achieved.

Even were we to accept a reading of the guarantee of equal protection under which the level of scrutiny varies according to the ability of different groups to defend their interests in the representative process, heightened scrutiny would still be appropriate in the circumstances of this case. One of the central arguments for applying a less exacting standard to "benign" racial classifications is that such measures essentially involve a choice made by dominant racial groups to disadvantage themselves. If one aspect of the judiciary's role under the Equal Protection Clause is to protect "discrete and insular minorities" from majoritarian prejudice or indifference, see United States v. Carolene Products Co., 304 U.S. 144, 153, n. 4, 58 S.Ct. 778, 784,

n. 4, 82 L.Ed. 1234 (1938), some maintain that these concerns are not implicated when the "white majority" places burdens upon itself.

In this case, blacks comprise approximately 50% of the population of the city of Richmond. Five of the nine seats on the City Council are held by blacks. The concern that a political majority will more easily act to the disadvantage of a minority based on unwarranted assumptions or incomplete facts would seem to militate for, not against, the application of heightened judicial scrutiny in this case.

In *Bakke*, the Court confronted a racial quota employed by the University of California at Davis Medical School. Under the plan, 16 out of 100 seats in each entering class at the school were reserved exclusively for certain minority groups. Among the justifications offered in support of the plan were the desire to "reduc[e] the historic deficit of traditionally disfavored minorities in medical school and the medical profession" and the need to "counte[r] the effects of societal discrimination." Five Members of the Court determined that none of these interests could justify a plan that completely eliminated nonminorities from consideration for a specified percentage of opportunities.

Justice Powell's opinion applied heightened scrutiny under the Equal Protection Clause to the racial classification at issue. His opinion decisively rejected the first justification for the racially segregated admissions plan. The desire to have more black medical students or doctors, standing alone, was not merely insufficiently compelling to justify a racial classification, it was "discrimination for its own sake," forbidden by the Constitution. Nor could the second concern, the history of discrimination in society at large, justify a racial quota in medical school admissions. Justice Powell contrasted the "focused" goal of remedying "wrongs worked by specific instances of racial discrimination" with "the remedying of the effects of 'societal discrimination,' an amorphous concept of injury that may be ageless in its reach into the past." He indicated that for the governmental interest in remedying past discrimination to be triggered "judicial, legislative, or administrative findings of constitutional or statutory violations" must be made. Only then does the Government have a compelling interest in favoring one race over another.

In *Wygant*, four Members of the Court applied heightened scrutiny to a race-based system of employee layoffs. Justice Powell, writing for the plurality, again drew the distinction between "societal discrimination" which is an inadequate basis for race-conscious classifications, and the type of identified discrimination that can support and define the scope of race-based relief. The challenged classification in that case tied the layoff of minority teachers to the percentage of minority students enrolled in the school district. The lower courts had upheld the scheme, based on the theory that minority students were in need of "role models" to alleviate the effects of prior discrimination in society. This Court reversed, with a plurality of four Justices reiterating the view expressed by Justice Powell in *Bakke* that "[s]ocietal discrimination, without more, is too amorphous a basis for imposing a racially classified remedy."

The role model theory employed by the lower courts failed for two reasons. First, the statistical disparity between students and teachers had no probative value in demonstrating the kind of prior discrimination in hiring or promotion that would justify race-based relief. Second, because the role model theory had no relation to some basis for believing a constitutional or statutory violation had occurred, it could be used to "justify" race-based decisionmaking essentially limitless in scope and duration.

III

B

We think it clear that the factual predicate offered in support of the Richmond Plan suffers from the same two defects identified as fatal in *Wygant*. The District Court found the city council's "findings sufficient to ensure that, in adopting the Plan, it was remedying the present effects of past discrimination in the *construction industry*." (emphasis added). Like the "role model" theory employed in *Wygant*, a generalized assertion that there has been past discrimination in an entire industry provides no guidance for a legislative body to determine the precise scope of the injury it seeks to remedy. It "has no logical stopping point." *Wygant*. "Relief" for such an ill-defined wrong could extend until the percentage of public contracts awarded to MBEs in Richmond mirrored the percentage of minorities in the population as a whole.

Appellant argues that it is attempting to remedy various forms of past discrimination that are alleged to be responsible for the small number of minority businesses in the local contracting industry. Among these the city cites the exclusion of blacks from skilled construction trade unions and training programs. This past discrimination has prevented them from following the traditional path from laborer to entrepreneur. The city also lists a host of nonracial factors which would seem to face a member of any racial group attempting to establish a new business enterprise, such as deficiencies in working capital, inability to meet bonding requirements, unfamiliarity with bidding procedures, and disability caused by an inadequate track record.

While there is no doubt that the sorry history of both private and public discrimination in this country has contributed to a lack of opportunities for black entrepreneurs, this observation, standing alone, cannot justify a rigid racial quota in the awarding of public contracts in Richmond, Virginia. Like the claim that discrimination in primary and secondary schooling justifies a rigid racial preference in medical school admissions, an amorphous claim that there has been past discrimination in a particular industry cannot justify the use of an unyielding racial quota.

It is sheer speculation how many minority firms there would be in Richmond absent past societal discrimination, just as it was sheer speculation how many minority medical students would have been admitted to the medical school at Davis absent past discrimination in educational opportunities. Defining these sorts of injuries as "identified discrimination" would give local governments license to create a patchwork of racial preferences based on statistical generalizations about any particular field of endeavor.

These defects are readily apparent in this case. The 30% quota cannot in any realistic sense be tied to any injury suffered by anyone. The District Court relied upon five predicate "facts" in reaching its conclusion that there was an adequate basis for the 30% quota: (1) the ordinance declares itself to be remedial; (2) several proponents of the measure stated their views that there had been past discrimination in the construction industry; (3) minority businesses received .67% of prime contracts from the city while minorities constituted 50% of the city's population; (4) there were very few minority contractors in local and state contractors' associations; and (5) in 1977, Congress made a determination that the effects of past discrimination had stifled minority participation in the construction industry nationally.

None of these "findings," singly or together, provide the city of Richmond with a "strong basis in evidence for its conclusion that remedial action was necessary." *Wygant.* There is nothing approaching a prima facie case of a constitutional or statutory violation by anyone in the Richmond construction industry.

The District Court accorded great weight to the fact that the city council designated the Plan as "remedial." But the mere recitation of a "benign" or legitimate purpose for a racial classification, is entitled to little or no weight. See Weinberger v. Wiesenfeld, 420 U.S., at 648, n. 16, 95 S.Ct., at 1233, n. 16 ("This Court need not in equal protection cases accept at face value assertions of legislative purposes, when an examination of the legislative scheme and its history demonstrates that the asserted purpose could not have been a goal of the legislation"). Racial classifications are suspect, and that means that simple legislative assurances of good intention cannot suffice.

The District Court also relied on the highly conclusionary statement of a proponent of the Plan that there was racial discrimination in the construction industry "in this area, and the State, and around the nation." It also noted that the city manager had related his view that racial discrimination still plagued the construction industry in his home city of Pittsburg. These statements are of little probative value in establishing identified discrimination in the Richmond construction industry. The fact finding process of legislative bodies is generally entitled to a presumption of regularity and deferential review by the judiciary. See Williamson v. Lee Optical of Oklahoma, Inc., 348 U.S. 483, 488-489, 75 S.Ct. 461, 464-465, 99 L.Ed. 563 (1955). But when a legislative body chooses to employ a suspect classification, it cannot rest upon a generalized assertion as to the classification's relevance to its goals. See McLaughlin v. Florida, 379 U.S. 184, 190-192, 85 S.Ct. 283, 287-289, 13 L.Ed.2d 222 (1964). A governmental actor cannot render race a legitimate proxy for a particular condition merely by declaring that the condition exists. The history of racial classifications in this country suggests that blind judicial deference to legislative or executive pronouncements of necessity has no place in equal protection analysis. See Korematsu v. United States, 323 U.S. 214, 235-240, 65 S.Ct. 193, 202-205, 89 L.Ed. 194 (1944) (Murphy, J., dissenting).

Reliance on the disparity between the number of prime contracts awarded to minority firms and the minority population of the city of Richmond is similarly misplaced. There is no doubt that "[w]here gross statistical disparities can be shown, they alone in a proper case may constitute prima facie proof of a pattern or practice of discrimination" under Title VII. Hazelwood School Dist. v. United States, 433 U.S. 299, 307-308, 97 S.Ct. 2736, 2741, 53 L.Ed.2d 768 (1977). But it is equally clear that "[w]hen special qualifications are required to fill particular jobs, comparisons to the general population (rather than to the smaller group of individuals who possess the necessary qualifications) may have little probative value." *Id.*

In the employment context, we have recognized that for certain entry level positions or positions requiring minimal training, statistical comparisons of the racial composition of an employer's workforce to the racial composition of the relevant population may be probative of a pattern of discrimination. See *Teamsters* (statistical comparison between minority truck drivers and relevant population probative of discriminatory exclusion). But where special qualifications are necessary, the relevant statistical pool for purposes of demonstrating discriminatory exclusion must be the number of minorities qualified to undertake the particular task. See *Hazelwood*.

In this case, the city does not even know how many MBEs in the relevant market are qualified to undertake prime or subcontracting work in public construction projects. Nor does the city know what percentage of total city construction dollars minority firms now receive as subcontractors on prime contracts let by the city.

To a large extent, the set-aside of subcontracting dollars seems to rest on the unsupported assumption that white prime contractors simply will not hire minority firms.[3] Indeed, there is evidence in this record that overall minority participation in city contracts in Richmond is seven to eight percent, and that minority contractor participation in Community Block Development Grant construction projects is 17% to 22%. Without any information on minority participation in subcontracting, it is quite simply impossible to evaluate overall minority representation in the city's construction expenditures.

The city and the District Court also relied on evidence that MBE membership in local contractors' associations was extremely low. Again, standing alone this evidence is not probative of any discrimination in the local construction industry. There are numerous explanations for this dearth of minority participation, including past societal discrimination in education and economic opportunities as well as both black and white career and entrepreneurial choices. Blacks may be disproportionately attracted to industries other than construction. The mere fact that black membership in these trade organizations is low, standing alone, cannot establish a prima facie case of discrimination.

For low minority membership in these associations to be relevant, the city would have to link it to the number of local MBEs eligible for membership. If the statistical disparity between eligible MBEs and MBE membership were great enough, an inference of discriminatory exclusion could arise. In such a case, the city would have a compelling interest in preventing its tax dollars from assisting these organizations in maintaining a racially segregated construction market.

Finally, the city and the District Court relied on Congress' finding in connection with the set-aside approved in *Fullilove* that there had been nationwide discrimination in the construction industry. The probative value of these findings for demonstrating the existence of discrimination in Richmond is extremely limited. By its inclusion of a waiver procedure in the national program addressed in *Fullilove*, Congress explicitly recognized that the scope of the problem would vary from market area to market area.

---

[3]Since 1975 the city of Richmond has had an ordinance on the books prohibiting both discrimination in the award of public contracts and employment discrimination by public contractors. The city points to no evidence that its prime contractors have been violating the ordinance in either their employment or subcontracting practices. The complete silence of the record concerning enforcement of the city's own anti-discrimination ordinance flies in the face of the dissent's vision of a "tight-knit industry" which has prevented blacks from obtaining the experience necessary to participate in construction contracting.

Moreover, as noted above, Congress was exercising its powers under §5 of the Fourteenth Amendment in making a finding that past discrimination would cause federal funds to be distributed in a manner which reinforced prior patterns of discrimination. While the States and their subdivisions may take remedial action when they possess evidence that their own spending practices are exacerbating a pattern of prior discrimination, they must identify that discrimination, public or private, with some specificity before they may use race-conscious relief. Congress has made national findings that there has been societal discrimination in a host of fields. If all a state or local government need do is find a congressional report on the subject to enact a set-aside program, the constraints of the Equal Protection Clause will, in effect, have been rendered a nullity.

Justice Marshall apparently views the requirement that Richmond identify the discrimination it seeks to remedy in its own jurisdiction as a mere administrative headache, an "onerous documentary obligatio[n]." We cannot agree. In this regard, we are in accord with Justice Stevens' observation in *Fullilove*, that "[b]ecause racial characteristics so seldom provide a relevant basis for disparate treatment, and because classifications based on race are potentially so harmful to the entire body politic, it is especially important that the reasons for any such classification be clearly identified and unquestionably legitimate." The "evidence" relied upon by the dissent, the history of school desegregation in Richmond and numerous congressional reports, does little to define the scope of any injury to minority contractors in Richmond or the necessary remedy. The factors relied upon by the dissent could justify a preference of any size or duration.

Moreover, Justice Marshall's suggestion that findings of discrimination may be "shared" from jurisdiction to jurisdiction in the same manner as information concerning zoning and property values is unprecedented. We have never approved the extrapolation of discrimination in one jurisdiction from the experience of another. See Milliken v. Bradley, 418 U.S. 717, 746, 94 S.Ct. 3112, 3128, 41 L.Ed.2d 1069 (1974) ("Disparate treatment of white and Negro students occurred within the Detroit school system, and not elsewhere, and on this record the remedy must be limited to that system").

In sum, none of the evidence presented by the city points to any identified discrimination in the Richmond construction industry. We, therefore, hold that the city has failed to demonstrate a compelling interest in apportioning public contracting opportunities on the basis of race. To accept Richmond's claim that past societal discrimination alone can serve as the basis for rigid racial preferences would be to open the door to competing claims for "remedial relief" for every disadvantaged group. The dream of a Nation of equal citizens in a society where race is irrelevant to personal opportunity and achievement would be lost in a mosaic of shifting preferences based on inherently unmeasurable claims of past wrongs. "Courts would be asked to evaluate the extent of the prejudice and consequent harm suffered by various minority groups. Those whose societal injury is thought to exceed some arbitrary level of tolerability then would be entitled to preferential classifications * * *." *Bakke* (Powell, J.). We think such a result would be contrary to both the letter and spirit of a constitutional provision whose central command is equality.

The foregoing analysis applies only to the inclusion of blacks within the Richmond set-aside program. There is absolutely no evidence of past discrimination against Spanish-speaking, Oriental, Indian, Eskimo, or Aleut persons in any aspect of the Richmond construction industry. The District Court took judicial notice of the fact that the vast majority of "minority" persons in Richmond were black. It may well be that Richmond has never had an Aleut or Eskimo citizen. The random inclusion of racial groups that, as a practical matter, may never have suffered from discrimination in the construction industry in Richmond, suggests that perhaps the city's purpose was not in fact to remedy past discrimination.

If a 30% set-aside was "narrowly tailored" to compensate black contractors for past discrimination, one may legitimately ask why they are forced to share this "remedial relief" with an Aleut citizen who moves to Richmond tomorrow? The gross overinclusiveness of Richmond's racial preference strongly impugns the city's claim of remedial motivation.

IV

As noted by the court below, it is almost impossible to assess whether the Richmond Plan is narrowly tailored to remedy prior discrimination since it is not linked to identified discrimination in any way. We limit ourselves to two observations in this regard.

First, there does not appear to have been any consideration of the use of race-neutral means to increase minority business participation in city contracting. See United States v. Paradise, 480 U.S. 149, 171, 107 S.Ct. 1053, 1067, 94 L.Ed.2d 203 (1987) ("In determining whether race-conscious remedies are appropriate, we look to several factors, including the efficacy of alternative remedies"). Many of the barriers to minority participation in the construction industry relied upon by the city to justify a racial classification appear to be race neutral. If MBEs disproportionately lack capital or cannot meet bonding requirements, a race-neutral program of city financing for small firms would, a fortiori, lead to greater minority participation. The principal opinion in *Fullilove* found that Congress had carefully examined and rejected race-neutral alternatives before enacting the MBE set-aside. There is no evidence in this record that the Richmond City Council has considered any alternatives to a race-based quota.

Second, the 30% quota cannot be said to be narrowly tailored to any goal, except perhaps outright racial balancing. It rests upon the "completely unrealistic" assumption that minorities will choose a particular trade in lockstep proportion to their representation in the local population. See Sheet Metal Workers v. EEOC, 478 U.S. 421, 494, 106 S.Ct. 3019, 3060, 92 L.Ed.2d 344 (1986) (O'Connor, J., concurring in part and dissenting in part) ("[I]t is completely unrealistic to assume that individuals of one race will gravitate with mathematical exactitude to each employer or union absent unlawful discrimination").

Since the city must already consider bids and waivers on a case-by-case basis, it is difficult to see the need for a rigid numerical quota. As noted above, the congressional scheme upheld in *Fullilove* allowed for a waiver of the set-aside provision where an MBE's higher price was not attributable to the effects of past discrimination. Based upon proper findings, such programs are less problematic from an equal protection standpoint because they treat all candidates individually, rather than making the color of an applicant's skin the sole relevant consideration. Unlike the program upheld in *Fullilove*, the Richmond Plan's waiver system focuses solely on the availability of

MBEs; there is no inquiry into whether or not the particular MBE seeking a racial preference has suffered from the effects of past discrimination by the city or prime contractors.

Given the existence of an individualized procedure, the city's only interest in maintaining a quota system rather than investigating the need for remedial action in particular cases would seem to be simple administrative convenience. But the interest in avoiding the bureaucratic effort necessary to tailor remedial relief to those who truly have suffered the effects of prior discrimination cannot justify a rigid line drawn on the basis of a suspect classification. See Frontiero v. Richardson, 411 U.S. 677, 690, 93 S.Ct. 1764, 1772, 36 L.Ed.2d 583 (1973) (plurality opinion) ("[W]hen we enter the realm of 'strict judicial scrutiny,' there can be no doubt that 'administrative convenience' is not a shibboleth, the mere recitation of which dictates constitutionality"). Under Richmond's scheme, a successful black, Hispanic, or Oriental entrepreneur from anywhere in the country enjoys an absolute preference over other citizens based solely on their race. We think it obvious that such a program is not narrowly tailored to remedy the effects of prior discrimination.

V

Nothing we say today precludes a state or local entity from taking action to rectify the effects of identified discrimination within its jurisdiction. If the city of Richmond had evidence before it that non-minority contractors were systematically excluding minority businesses from subcontracting opportunities it could take action to end the discriminatory exclusion. Where there is a significant statistical disparity between the number of qualified minority contractors willing and able to perform a particular service and the number of such contractors actually engaged by the locality or the locality's prime contractors, an inference of discriminatory exclusion could arise. Under such circumstances, the city could act to dismantle the closed business system by taking appropriate measures against those who discriminate on the basis of race or other illegitimate criteria. See, e.g., New York State Club Assn. v. New York City, 487 U.S. 1, 108 S.Ct. 2225, 101 L.Ed.2d 1 (1988). In the extreme case, some form of narrowly tailored racial preference might be necessary to break down patterns of deliberate exclusion.

Nor is local government powerless to deal with individual instances of racially motivated refusals to employ minority contractors. Where such discrimination occurs, a city would be justified in penalizing the discriminator and providing appropriate relief to the victim of such discrimination. See generally *McDonnell Douglas*. Moreover, evidence of a pattern of individual discriminatory acts can, if supported by appropriate statistical proof, lend support to a local government's determination that broader remedial relief is justified.

Even in the absence of evidence of discrimination, the city has at its disposal a whole array of race-neutral devices to increase the accessibility of city contracting opportunities to small entrepreneurs of all races. Simplification of bidding procedures, relaxation of bonding requirements, and training and financial aid for disadvantaged entrepreneurs of all races would open the public contracting market to all those who have suffered the effects of past societal discrimination or neglect. Many of the formal barriers to new entrants may be the product of bureaucratic inertia more than actual necessity, and may have a disproportionate effect on the opportunities open to new minority firms. Their elimination or modification would have little detrimental effect on the city's interests and would serve to increase the opportunities available to minority business without classifying individuals on the basis of race. The city may also act to prohibit discrimination in the provision of credit or bonding by local suppliers and banks. Business as usual should not mean business pursuant to the unthinking exclusion of certain members of our society from its rewards.

In the case at hand, the city has not ascertained how many minority enterprises are present in the local construction market nor the level of their participation in city construction projects. The city points to no evidence that qualified minority contractors have been passed over for city contracts or subcontracts, either as a group or in any individual case. Under such circumstances, it is simply impossible to say that the city has demonstrated "a strong basis in evidence for its conclusion that remedial action was necessary." *Wygant.*

Proper findings in this regard are necessary to define both the scope of the injury and the extent of the remedy necessary to cure its effects. Such findings also serve to assure all citizens that the deviation from the norm of equal treatment of all racial and ethnic groups is a temporary matter, a measure taken in the service of the goal of equality itself. Absent such findings, there is a danger that a racial classification is merely the product of unthinking stereotypes or a form of racial politics. "[I]f there is no duty to attempt either to measure the recovery by the wrong or to distribute that recovery within the injured class in an evenhanded way, our history will adequately support a legislative preference for almost any ethnic, religious, or racial group with the political strength to negotiate 'a piece of the action' for its members." *Fullilove* (Stevens, J., dissenting). Because the city of Richmond has failed to identify the need for remedial action in the awarding of its public construction contracts, its treatment of its citizens on a racial basis violates the dictates of the Equal Protection Clause. Accordingly, the judgment of the Court of Appeals for the Fourth Circuit is

Affirmed.

JUSTICE STEVENS, concurring in part and concurring in the judgment.

A central purpose of the Fourteenth Amendment is to further the national goal of equal opportunity for all our citizens. In order to achieve that goal we must learn from our past mistakes, but I believe the Constitution requires us to evaluate our policy decisions — including those that govern the relationships among different racial and ethnic groups — primarily by studying their probable impact on the future. I therefore do not agree with the premise that seems to underlie today's decision, as well as the decision in *Wygant,* that a governmental decision that rests on a racial classification is never permissible except as a remedy for a past wrong.[1] I do, however, agree with the

---

[1] In my view the Court's approach to this case gives unwarranted deference to race-based legislative action that purports to serve a purely remedial goal, and overlooks the potential value of race-based determinations that may serve other valid purposes. With regard to the former point — as I explained at some length in *Fullilove* — I am not prepared to assume that even a more narrowly tailored set-aside program supported by stronger findings would be constitutionally justified. Unless the legislature can identify both the particular victims and the particular perpetrators of past discrimination, which is precisely what a court does when it makes findings of fact and conclusions of law, a *remedial* justification for race-based legislation will almost certainly sweep too broadly. With regard to the latter point: I think it unfortunate

Court's explanation of why the Richmond ordinance cannot be justified as a remedy for past discrimination, and therefore join Parts I, III-B, and IV of its opinion. I write separately to emphasize three aspects of the case that are of special importance to me.

First, the city makes no claim that the public interest in the efficient performance of its construction contracts will be served by granting a preference to minority-business enterprises. This case is therefore completely unlike *Wygant*, in which I thought it quite obvious that the School Board had reasonably concluded that an integrated faculty could provide educational benefits to the entire student body that could not be provided by an all-white, or nearly all-white faculty. As I pointed out in my dissent in that case, even if we completely disregard our history of racial injustice, race is not always irrelevant to sound governmental decisionmaking. In the case of public contracting, however, if we disregard the past, there is not even an arguable basis for suggesting that the race of a subcontractor or general contractor should have any relevance to his or her access to the market.

Second, this litigation involves an attempt by a legislative body, rather than a court, to fashion a remedy for a past wrong. Legislatures are primarily policymaking bodies that promulgate rules to govern future conduct. The constitutional prohibitions against the enactment of *ex post facto* laws and bills of attainder reflect a valid concern about the use of the political process to punish or characterize past conduct of private citizens.[3] It is the judicial system, rather than the legislative process, that is best equipped to identify past wrongdoers and to fashion remedies that will create the conditions that presumably would have existed had no wrong been committed. Thus, in cases involving the review of judicial remedies imposed against persons who have been proved guilty of violations of law, I would allow the courts in racial discrimination cases the same broad discretion that chancellors enjoy in other areas of the law.

Third, instead of engaging in a debate over the proper standard of review to apply in affirmative-action litigation, I believe it is more constructive to try to identify the characteristics of the advantaged and disadvantaged classes that may justify their disparate treatment. See Cleburne v. Cleburne Living Center, Inc., 473 U.S. 432, 452-453, 105 S.Ct. 3249, 3261, 87 L.Ed.2d 313 (1985) (Stevens, J., concurring). In this case that approach convinces me that, instead of carefully identifying the characteristics of the two classes of contractors that are respectively favored and disfavored by its ordinance, the Richmond City Council has merely engaged in the type of stereotypical analysis that is a hallmark of violations of the Equal Protection

---

that the Court in neither *Wygant* nor this case seems prepared to acknowledge that some race-based policy decisions may serve a legitimate public purpose. I agree, of course, that race is so seldom relevant to legislative decisions on how best to foster the public good that legitimate justifications for race-based legislation will usually not be available. But unlike the Court, I would not totally discount the legitimacy of race-based decisions that may produce tangible and fully justified future benefits.

[3]Of course, legislatures frequently appropriate funds to compensate victims of past governmental misconduct for which there is no judicial remedy. See, e.g., Pub.L. 100-383, 102 Stat. 903 (provision of restitution to interned Japanese-Americans during World War II). Thus, it would have been consistent with normal practice for the city of Richmond to provide direct monetary compensation to any minority-business enterprise that the city might have injured in the past. Such a voluntary decision by a public body is, however, quite different from a decision to require one private party to compensate another for an unproven injury.

Clause. Whether we look at the class of persons benefited by the ordinance or at the disadvantaged class, the same conclusion emerges.

The justification for the ordinance is the fact that in the past white contractors — and presumably other white citizens in Richmond — have discriminated against black contractors. The class of persons benefited by the ordinance is not, however, limited to victims of such discrimination — it encompasses persons who have never been in business in Richmond as well as minority contractors who may have been guilty of discriminating against members of other minority groups. Indeed, for all the record shows, all of the minority-business enterprises that have benefited from the ordinance may be firms that have prospered notwithstanding the discriminatory conduct that may have harmed other minority firms years ago. Ironically, minority firms that have survived in the competitive struggle, rather than those that have perished, are most likely to benefit from an ordinance of this kind.

The ordinance is equally vulnerable because of its failure to identify the characteristics of the disadvantaged class of white contractors that justify the disparate treatment. That class unquestionably includes some white contractors who are guilty of past discrimination against blacks, but it is only habit, rather than evidence or analysis, that makes it seem acceptable to assume that every white contractor covered by the ordinance shares in that guilt. Indeed, even among those who have discriminated in the past, it must be assumed that at least some of them have complied with the city ordinance that has made such discrimination unlawful since 1975. Thus, the composition of the disadvantaged class of white contractors presumably includes some who have been guilty of unlawful discrimination, some who practiced discrimination before it was forbidden by law,[8] and some who have never discriminated against anyone on the basis of race. Imposing a common burden on such a disparate class merely because each member of the class is of the same race stems from reliance on a stereotype rather than fact or reason.[9]

There is a special irony in the stereotypical thinking that prompts legislation of this kind. Although it stigmatizes the disadvantaged class with the unproven charge of past racial discrimination, it actually imposes a greater stigma on its supposed beneficiaries. For, as I explained in my *Fullilove* opinion:

"[E]ven though it is not the actual predicate for this legislation, a statute of this kind inevitably is perceived by many as resting on an assumption that those who are granted this special preference are less qualified in some respect that is identified purely by their race." * * *

Accordingly, I concur in parts I, III-B, and IV of the Court's opinion, and in the judgment.

---

[8]There is surely some question about the power of a legislature to impose a statutory burden on private citizens for engaging in discriminatory practices at a time when such practices were not unlawful.

[9]There is, of course, another possibility that should not be overlooked. The ordinance might be nothing more than a form of patronage. But racial patronage, like a racial gerrymander, is no more defensible than political patronage or a political gerrymander. A southern State with a long history of discrimination against Republicans in the awarding of public contracts could not rely on such past discrimination as a basis for granting a legislative preference to Republican contractors in the future.

JUSTICE KENNEDY, concurring in part and concurring in the judgment.

I join all but Part II of Justice O'Connor's opinion and give this further explanation.

Part II examines our caselaw upholding Congressional power to grant preferences based on overt and explicit classification by race. With the acknowledgement that the summary in Part II is both precise and fair, I must decline to join it. The process by which a law that is an equal protection violation when enacted by a State becomes transformed to an equal protection guarantee when enacted by Congress poses a difficult proposition for me; but as it is not before us, any reconsideration of that issue must await some further case. For purposes of the ordinance challenged here, it suffices to say that the State has the power to eradicate racial discrimination and its effects in both the public and private sectors, and the absolute duty to do so where those wrongs were caused intentionally by the State itself. The Fourteenth Amendment ought not to be interpreted to reduce a State's authority in this regard, unless, of course, there is a conflict with federal law or a state remedy is itself a violation of equal protection. The latter is the case presented here.

The moral imperative of racial neutrality is the driving force of the Equal Protection Clause. Justice Scalia's opinion underscores that proposition, quite properly in my view. The rule suggested in his opinion, which would strike down all preferences which are not necessary remedies to victims of unlawful discrimination, would serve important structural goals, as it would eliminate the necessity for courts to pass upon each racial preference that is enacted. Structural protections may be necessities if moral imperatives are to be obeyed. His opinion would make it crystal clear to the political branches, at least those of the States, that legislation must be based on criteria other than race.

Nevertheless, given that a rule of automatic invalidity for racial preferences in almost every case would be a significant break with our precedents that require a case-by-case test, I am not convinced we need adopt it at this point. On the assumption that it will vindicate the principle of race neutrality found in the Equal Protection Clause, I accept the less absolute rule contained in Justice O'Connor's opinion, a rule based on the proposition that any racial preference must face the most rigorous scrutiny by the courts. My reasons for doing so are as follows. First, I am confident that, in application, the strict scrutiny standard will operate in a manner generally consistent with the imperative of race neutrality, because it forbids the use even of narrowly drawn racial classifications except as a last resort. Second, the rule against race-conscious remedies is already less than an absolute one, for that relief may be the only adequate remedy after a judicial determination that a State or its instrumentality has violated the Equal Protection Clause. I note, in this connection, that evidence which would support a judicial finding of intentional discrimination may suffice also to justify remedial legislative action, for it diminishes the constitutional responsibilities of the political branches to say they must wait to act until ordered to do so by a court. Third, the strict scrutiny rule is consistent with our precedents, as Justice O'Connor's opinion demonstrates.

The ordinance before us falls far short of the standard we adopt. The nature and scope of the injury that existed; its historical or antecedent causes; the extent to which the City contributed to it, either by intentional acts or by passive complicity in acts of discrimination by the private sector; the necessity for the response adopted, its duration in relation to the wrong, and the precision with which it otherwise bore on whatever injury in fact was addressed, were all matters unmeasured, unexplored, or unexplained by the City Council. We are left with an ordinance and a legislative record open to the fair charge that it is not a remedy but is itself a preference which will cause the same corrosive animosities that the Constitution forbids in the whole sphere of government and that our national policy condemns in the rest of society as well. This ordinance is invalid under the Fourteenth Amendment.

JUSTICE SCALIA, concurring in the judgment.

I agree with much of the Court's opinion, and, in particular, with its conclusion that strict scrutiny must be applied to all governmental classification by race, whether or not its asserted purpose is "remedial" or "benign." I do not agree, however, with the Justice O'Connor's dictum suggesting that, despite the Fourteenth Amendment, state and local governments may in some circumstances discriminate on the basis of race in order (in a broad sense) "to ameliorate the effects of past discrimination." The benign purpose of compensating for social disadvantages, whether they have been acquired by reason of prior discrimination or otherwise, can no more be pursued by the illegitimate means of racial discrimination than can other assertedly benign purposes we have repeatedly rejected. The difficulty of overcoming the effects of past discrimination is as nothing compared with the difficulty of eradicating from our society the source of those effects, which is the tendency — fatal to a nation such as ours — to classify and judge men and women on the basis of their country of origin or the color of their skin. A solution to the first problem that aggravates the second is no solution at all. I share the view expressed by Alexander Bickel that "[t]he lesson of the great decisions of the Supreme Court and the lesson of contemporary history have been the same for at least a generation: discrimination on the basis of race is illegal, immoral, unconstitutional, inherently wrong, and destructive of democratic society." A. Bickel, The Morality of Consent 133 (1975). At least where state or local action is at issue, only a social emergency rising to the level of imminent danger to life and limb — for example, a prison race riot, requiring temporary segregation of inmates, cf. Lee v. Washington, supra — can justify an exception to the principle embodied in the Fourteenth Amendment that "[o]ur Constitution is color-blind, and neither knows nor tolerates classes among citizens," Plessy v. Ferguson, 163 U.S. 537, 559, 16 S.Ct. 1138, 1146, 41 L.Ed. 256 (1896) (Harlan, J., dissenting).

We have in some contexts approved the use of racial classifications by the Federal Government to remedy the effects of past discrimination. I do not believe that we must or should extend those holdings to the States. In *Fullilove*, we upheld legislative action by Congress similar in its asserted purpose to that at issue here. And we have permitted federal courts to prescribe quite severe race-conscious remedies when confronted with egregious and persistent unlawful discrimination, see, e.g., United States v. Paradise, 480 U.S. 149, 107 S.Ct. 1053, 94 L.Ed.2d 203 (1987); Sheet Metal Workers v. EEOC, 478 U.S. 421, 106 S.Ct. 3019, 92 L.Ed.2d 344 (1986). As the Court acknowledges, however, it is one thing to permit racially based conduct by the Federal Government — whose legislative powers concerning matters of race were explicitly enhanced by the Fourteenth Amendment, see U.S. Const., Amdt. 14, §5 — and quite another to permit it by the precise entities against whose conduct in matters of race that Amendment was specifically directed, see Amdt. 14, §1. As we said in *Ex parte Virginia*, the Civil War Amendments were designed to "take away all possibility of oppression by law because of race or color" and "to be * * * limitations on the power of the States and enlargements of the power of Congress." Thus, without revisiting what we held in *Fullilove* or trying to derive a rationale from the three separate opinions supporting the judgment, none of which commanded more than three votes, I do not believe our decision in that case controls the one before us here.

A sound distinction between federal and state (or local) action based on race rests not only upon the substance of the Civil War Amendments, but upon social reality and governmental theory. It is a simple fact that what Justice Stewart described in *Fullilove* as "the dispassionate objectivity [and] the flexibility that are needed to mold a race-conscious remedy around the single objective of eliminating the effects of past or present discrimination" — political qualities already to be doubted in a national legislature — are substantially less likely to exist at the state or local level. The struggle for racial justice has historically been a struggle by the national society against oppression in the individual States. See, e.g., Ex parte Virginia, supra (denying writ of habeas corpus to a state judge in custody under federal indictment for excluding jurors on the basis of race). And the struggle retains that character in modern times. See, e.g., Brown v. Board of Education, 349 U.S. 294, 75 S.Ct. 753, 99 L.Ed. 1083 (1955) (Brown II). Not all of that struggle has involved discrimination against blacks, see, e.g., Yick Wo v. Hopkins, 118 U.S. 356, 6 S.Ct. 1064, 30 L.Ed. 220 (1886) (Chinese); Hernandez v. Texas, 347 U.S. 475, 74 S.Ct. 667, 98 L.Ed. 866 (1954) (Hispanics), and not all of it has been in the Old South, see, e.g., Columbus Board of Education v. Penick, 443 U.S. 449, 99 S.Ct. 2941, 61 L.Ed.2d 666 (1979); Keyes v. School District No. 1, Denver, Colorado, 413 U.S. 189, 93 S.Ct. 2686, 37 L.Ed.2d 548 (1973). What the record shows, in other words, is that racial discrimination against any group finds a more ready expression at the state and local than at the federal level. To the children of the Founding Fathers, this should come as no surprise. An acute awareness of the heightened danger of oppression from political factions in small, rather than large, political units dates to the very beginning of our national history. As James Madison observed in support of the proposed Constitution's enhancement of national powers:

> "The smaller the society, the fewer probably will be the distinct parties and interests composing it; the fewer the distinct parties and interests, the more frequently will a majority be found of the same party; and the smaller the number of individuals composing a majority, and the smaller the compass within which they are placed, the more easily will they concert and execute their plan of oppression. Extend the sphere and you take in a greater variety of parties and interests; you make it less probable that a majority of the whole will have a common motive to invade the rights of other citizens; or if such a common motive exists, it will be more difficult for all who feel it to discover their own strength and to act in unison with each other." The Federalist No. 10, pp. 82-84.

The prophecy of these words came to fruition in Richmond in the enactment of a set-aside clearly and directly beneficial to the dominant political group, which happens also to be the dominant racial group. The same thing has no doubt happened before in other cities (though the racial basis of the preference has rarely been made textually explicit) — and blacks have often been on the receiving end of the injustice. Where injustice is the game, however, turn-about is not fair play.

In my view there is only one circumstance in which the States may act by race to "undo the effects of past discrimination": where that is necessary to eliminate their own maintenance of a system of unlawful racial classification. If, for example, a state agency has a discriminatory pay scale compensating black employees in all positions at 20% less than their nonblack counterparts, it may assuredly promulgate an order raising the salaries of "all black employees" by 20%. Cf. Bazemore v. Friday, 478 U.S. 385, 395-396, 106 S.Ct. 3000, 3006-3007, 92 L.Ed.2d 315 (1986). This distinction explains our school desegregation cases, in which we have made plain that States and localities sometimes have an obligation to adopt race-conscious remedies. While there is no doubt that those cases have taken into account the continuing "effects" of previously mandated racial school assignment, we have held those effects to justify a race-conscious remedy only because we have concluded, in that context, that they perpetuate a "dual school system." We have stressed each school district's constitutional "duty to *dismantle* its dual system," and have found that "[e]ach instance of a failure or refusal to fulfill this affirmative duty *continues the violation* of the Fourteenth Amendment." Columbus Board of Education v. Penick (emphasis added). Concluding in this context that race-neutral efforts at "dismantling the state-imposed dual system" were so ineffective that they might "indicate a lack of good faith," Green v. County School Board, 391 U.S. 430, 439, 88 S.Ct. 1689, 1695, 20 L.Ed.2d 716 (1968), we have permitted, as part of the local authorities' "affirmative duty to disestablish the dual school system[s]," such voluntary (that is, noncourt-ordered) measures as attendance zones drawn to achieve greater racial balance, and out-of-zone assignment by race for the same purpose. McDaniel v. Barresi, 402 U.S. 39, 40-41, 91 S.Ct. 1287, 1288, 28 L.Ed.2d 582 (1971). While thus permitting the use of race to *de* classify racially classified students, teachers, and educational resources, however, we have also made it clear that the remedial power extends no further than the scope of the continuing constitutional violation. See e.g., Columbus Board of Education v. Penick; Dayton Board of Education v. Brinkman, 433 U.S. 406, 420, 97 S.Ct. 2766, 2775, 53 L.Ed.2d 851 (1977); Milliken v. Bradley, 418 U.S. 717, 744, 94 S.Ct. 3112, 3127, 41 L.Ed.2d 1069 (1974); Keyes v. School District No. 1, Denver, Colorado, 413 U.S., at 213, 93 S.Ct., at 2699. And it is implicit in our cases that after the dual school system has been completely disestablished, the States may no longer assign students by race. Cf. Pasadena City Board of Education v. Spangler, 427 U.S. 424, 96 S.Ct. 2697, 49 L.Ed.2d 599 (1976) (federal court may not require racial assignment in such circumstances).

Our analysis in *Bazemore* reflected our unwillingness to conclude, outside the context of school assignment, that the continuing effects of prior discrimination can be equated with state maintenance of a discriminatory system. There we found both that the government's adoption of "wholly neutral admissions" policies for 4-H and Homemaker clubs sufficed to remedy its prior constitutional violation of maintaining segregated admissions, and that there was no further obligation to use racial reassignments to eliminate continuing effects—that is, any remaining all-black and all-white clubs. "[H]owever sound Green [v. County School Board, supra] may have been in the context of the public schools," we said, "it has no application to this wholly different milieu." The same is so here.

A State can, of course, act "to undo the effects of past discrimination" in many permissible ways that do not involve classification by race. In the particular field of state contracting, for example, it may adopt a preference for small businesses, or even for new businesses — which would make it easier for those previously excluded by discrimination to enter the field. Such programs may well have racially disproportionate impact, but they are not based on race. And, of course, a State may "undo the effects of past discrimination" in the sense of giving the identified victim of state discrimination that which it wrongfully denied him — for example, giving to a previously rejected black applicant the job that, by reason of discrimination, had been awarded to a white applicant, even if this means terminating the latter's employment. In such a context, the white job-holder is not being selected for disadvantageous treatment because of his race, but because he was wrongfully awarded a job to which another is entitled. That is worlds apart from the system here, in which those to be disadvantaged are identified solely by race.

I agree with the Court's dictum that a fundamental distinction must be drawn between the effects of "societal" discrimination and the effects of "identified" discrimination, and that the situation would be different if Richmond's plan were "tailored" to identify those particular bidders who "suffered from the effects of past discrimination by the city or prime contractors." In my view, however, the reason that would make a difference is not, as the Court states, that it would justify race-conscious action — but rather that it would enable race-neutral remediation. Nothing prevents Richmond from according a contracting preference to identified victims of discrimination. While most of the beneficiaries might be black, neither the beneficiaries nor those disadvantaged by the preference would be identified *on the basis of their race*. In other words, far from justifying racial classification, identification of actual victims of discrimination makes it less supportable than ever, because more obviously unneeded. * * * Apart from their societal effects, however, * * * it is important not to lose sight of the fact that even "benign" racial quotas have individual victims, whose very real injustice we ignore whenever we deny them enforcement of their right not to be disadvantaged on the basis of race. Johnson v. Transportation Agency, Santa Clara County, Cal., 480 U.S. 616, 677, 107 S.Ct. 1442, 1476, 94 L.Ed.2d 615 (1987) (SCALIA, J., dissenting). As Justice Douglas observed: "A. DeFunis who is white is entitled to no advantage by virtue of that fact; nor is he subject to any disability, no matter what his race or color. Whatever his race, he had a constitutional right to have his application considered on its individual merits in a racially neutral manner." DeFunis v. Odegaard, 416 U.S. 312, 337, 94 S.Ct. 1704, 1716, 40 L.Ed.2d 164 (1974) (Douglas, J., dissenting). When we depart from this American principle we play with fire, and much more than an occasional DeFunis, Johnson, or Croson burns.

It is plainly true that in our society blacks have suffered discrimination immeasurably greater than any directed at other racial groups. But those who believe that racial preferences can help to "even the score" display, and reinforce, a manner of thinking by race that was the source of the injustice and that will, if it endures within our society, be the source of more injustice still. The relevant proposition is not that it was blacks, or Jews, or Irish who were discriminated against, but that it was individual men and women, "created equal," who were discriminated against. And the relevant resolve is that that should never happen again. Racial preferences appear to "even the score" (in some small degree) only if one embraces the proposition that our society is appropriately viewed as divided into races, making it right that an injustice rendered in the past to a black man should be compensated for by discriminating against a white. Nothing is worth that embrace. Since blacks have been disproportionately disadvantaged by racial discrimination, any race-neutral remedial program aimed at the disadvantaged *as such* will have a disproportionately beneficial impact on blacks. Only such a program, and not one that operates on the basis of race, is in accord with the letter and the spirit of our Constitution.

Since I believe that the appellee here had a constitutional right to have its bid succeed or fail under a decisionmaking process uninfected with racial bias, I concur in the judgment of the Court.

JUSTICE MARSHALL, with whom JUSTICE BRENNAN and JUSTICE BLACKMUN join, dissenting.

It is a welcome symbol of racial progress when the former capital of the Confederacy acts forthrightly to confront the effects of racial discrimination in its midst. In my view, nothing in the Constitution can be construed to prevent Richmond, Virginia, from allocating a portion of its contracting dollars for businesses owned or controlled by members of minority groups. Indeed, Richmond's set-aside program is indistinguishable in all meaningful respects from — and in fact was patterned upon — the federal set-aside plan which this Court upheld in *Fullilove*.

A majority of this Court holds today, however, that the Equal Protection Clause of the Fourteenth Amendment blocks Richmond's initiative. The essence of the majority's position[1] is that Richmond has failed to catalogue adequate findings to prove that past discrimination has impeded minorities from joining or participating fully in Richmond's construction contracting industry. I find deep irony in second-guessing Richmond's judgment on this point. As much as any municipality in the United States, Richmond knows what racial discrimination is; a century of decisions by this and other federal courts has richly documented the city's disgraceful history of public and private racial discrimination. In any event, the Richmond City Council has supported its determination that minorities have been wrongly excluded from local construction contracting. Its proof includes statistics showing that minority-owned businesses have received virtually no city contracting dollars and rarely if ever belonged to area trade associations; testimony by municipal officials that discrimination has been widespread in the local construction industry; and the same exhaustive and widely publicized federal studies relied on in *Fullilove*, studies which showed that pervasive discrimination in the Nation's tight-knit construction industry had operated to exclude minorities from public contracting. These are precisely the types of statistical and testimonial evidence which, until today, this Court had credited in cases approving of race-conscious measures designed to remedy past discrimination.

More fundamentally, today's decision marks a deliberate and giant step backward in this Court's affirmative action jurisprudence. Cynical of one municipality's attempt to redress the effects of past racial discrimination in a particular industry, the majority

---

[1] In the interest of convenience, I refer to the opinion in this case authored by Justice O'Connor as "the majority," recognizing that certain portions of that opinion have been joined by only a plurality of the Court.

launches a grapeshot attack on race-conscious remedies in general. The majority's unnecessary pronouncements will inevitably discourage or prevent governmental entities, particularly States and localities, from acting to rectify the scourge of past discrimination. This is the harsh reality of the majority's decision, but it is not the Constitution's command.

I

As an initial matter, the majority takes an exceedingly myopic view of the factual predicate on which the Richmond City Council relied when it passed the Minority Business Utilization Plan. The majority analyzes Richmond's initiative as if it were based solely upon the facts about local construction and contracting practices adduced during the City Council session at which the measure was enacted. In so doing, the majority down-plays the fact that the City Council had before it a rich trove of evidence that discrimination in the Nation's construction industry had seriously impaired the competitive position of businesses owned or controlled by members of minority groups. It is only against this backdrop of documented national discrimination, however, that the local evidence adduced by Richmond can be properly understood. The majority's refusal to recognize that Richmond has proven itself no exception to the dismaying pattern of national exclusion which Congress so painstakingly identified infects its entire analysis of this case.

Six years before Richmond acted, Congress passed, and the President signed, the Public Works Employment Act of 1977, a measure which appropriated $4 billion in federal grants to state and local governments for use in public works projects. Section 103(f)(2) of the Act was a minority business set-aside provision. It required state or local grantees to use 10% of their federal grants to procure services or supplies from businesses owned or controlled by members of statutorily identified minority groups, absent an administrative waiver. In 1980, in *Fullilove*, this Court upheld the validity of this federal set-aside. Chief Justice Burger's opinion noted the importance of overcoming those "criteria, methods, or practices thought by Congress to have the effect of defeating, or substantially impairing, access by the minority business community to public funds made available by congressional appropriations." Finding the set-aside provision properly tailored to this goal, the plurality concluded that the program was valid under either strict or intermediate scrutiny.

The congressional program upheld in *Fullilove* was based upon an array of congressional and agency studies which documented the powerful influence of racially exclusionary practices in the business world. * * *

Congress further found that minorities seeking initial public contracting assignments often faced immense entry barriers which did not confront experienced nonminority contractors. A report submitted to Congress in 1975 by the United States Commission on Civil Rights, for example, described the way in which fledgling minority-owned businesses were hampered by "deficiencies in working capital, inability to meet bonding requirements, disabilities caused by an inadequate 'track record,' lack of awareness of bidding opportunities, unfamiliarity with bidding procedures, preselection before the formal advertising process, and the exercise of discretion by government procurement officers to disfavor minority businesses."

Thus, as of 1977, there was "abundant evidence" in the public domain "that minority businesses ha[d] been denied effective participation in public contracting opportunities by procurement practices that perpetuated the effects of prior discrimination." *Fullilove*.[2] Significantly, this evidence demonstrated that discrimination had prevented existing or nascent minority-owned businesses from obtaining not only federal contracting assignments, but state and local ones as well. See Fullilove.[3]

The members of the Richmond City Council were well aware of these exhaustive congressional findings, a point the majority, tellingly, elides. The transcript of the session at which the Council enacted the local set-aside initiative contains numerous references to the 6-year-old congressional set-aside program, to the evidence of nationwide discrimination barriers described above, and to the Fullilove decision itself.

The City Council's members also heard testimony that, although minority groups made up half of the city's population, only .67% of the $24.6 million which Richmond had dispensed in construction contracts during the five years ending in March 1983 had gone to minority-owned prime contractors. They heard testimony that the major Richmond area construction trade associations had virtually no minorities among their hundreds of members.[4] Finally, they heard testimony from city officials as to the exclusionary history of the local construction industry.[5] As the District Court noted, not a single person who testified before the City Council denied that discrimination in

---

[2]Other reports indicating the dearth of minority-owned businesses include H.R.Rep. No. 92-1615, p. 3 (1972) (Report of the Subcommittee on Minority Small Business Enterprise, finding that the "long history of racial bias" has created "major problems" for minority businessmen); H.R.Doc. No. 92-194, p. 1 (1972) (text of message from President Nixon to Congress, describing federal efforts "to press open new doors of opportunity for millions of Americans to whom those doors had previously been barred, or only half-open"); H.R.Doc. No. 92-169, p. 1 (1971) (text of message from President Nixon to Congress, describing paucity of minority business ownership and federal efforts to give "every man an equal chance at the starting line").

[3]Numerous congressional studies undertaken after 1977 and issued before the Richmond City Council convened in April 1983 found that the exclusion of minorities had continued virtually unabated — and that, because of this legacy of discrimination, minority businesses across the nation had still failed, as of 1983, to gain a real toehold in the business world. See, e.g., H.R.Rep. No. 95-949, pp. 2, 8 (1978) (Report of House Committee on Small Business, finding that minority businesses "are severely undercapitalized" and that many minorities are disadvantaged "because they are identified as members of certain racial categories").

[4]According to testimony by trade association representatives, the Associated General Contractors of Virginia had no blacks among its 130 Richmond-area members; the American Subcontractors Association had no blacks among its 80 Richmond members, id., at 36 (remarks of Patrick Murphy); the Professional Contractors Estimators Association had one black member among its 60 Richmond members; the Central Virginia Electrical Contractors Association had one black member among its 45 members; and the National Electrical Contractors Association had two black members among its 81 Virginia members.

[5]Among those testifying to the discriminatory practices of Richmond's construction industry was councilmember Henry Marsh, who had served as Mayor of Richmond from 1977 to 1982. Marsh stated:

"I have been practicing law in this community since 1961, and I am familiar with the practices in the construction industry in this area, in the State, and around the nation. And I can say without equivocation, that the general conduct in the construction industry in this area, and the State and around the nation, is one in which race discrimination and exclusion on the basis of race is widespread.

"I think the situation involved in the City of Richmond is the same * * *. I think the question of whether or not remedial action is required is not open to question." Manuel Deese, who in his capacity as City Manager had oversight responsibility for city procurement matters, stated that he fully agreed with Marsh's analysis.

Richmond's construction industry had been widespread.[6] So long as one views Richmond's local evidence of discrimination against the back-drop of systematic nationwide racial discrimination which Congress had so painstakingly identified in this very industry, this case is readily resolved.

II

* * * My view has long been that race-conscious classifications designed to further remedial goals "must serve important governmental objectives and must be substantially related to achievement of those objectives" in order to withstand constitutional scrutiny. Analyzed in terms of this two-prong standard, Richmond's set-aside, like the federal program on which it was modeled, is plainly constitutional.

A

1

Turning first to the governmental interest inquiry, Richmond has two powerful interests in setting aside a portion of public contracting funds for minority-owned enterprises. The first is the city's interest in eradicating the effects of past racial discrimination. It is far too late in the day to doubt that remedying such discrimination is a compelling, let alone an important, interest. In *Fullilove*, six members of this Court deemed this interest sufficient to support a race-conscious set-aside program governing federal contract procurement. The decision, in holding that the federal set-aside provision satisfied the Equal Protection Clause under any level of scrutiny, recognized that the measure sought to remove "barriers to competitive access which had their roots in racial and ethnic discrimination, and which continue today, even absent any intentional discrimination or unlawful conduct." Indeed, we have repeatedly reaffirmed the government's interest in breaking down barriers erected by past racial discrimination, in cases involving access to public education, McDaniel v. Barresi, 402 U.S. 39, 41, 91 S.Ct. 1287, 1288, 28 L.Ed.2d 582 (1971); *Bakke*, employment, United States v. Paradise, 480 U.S. 149, 167, 107 S.Ct. 1053, 1064, 94 L.Ed.2d 203 (1987) (plurality opinion); and valuable government contracts. *Fullilove*.

Richmond has a second compelling interest in setting aside, where possible, a portion of its contracting dollars. That interest is the prospective one of preventing the city's own spending decisions from reinforcing and perpetuating the exclusionary effects of past discrimination. See *Fullilove*.

The majority pays only lip service to this additional governmental interest. But our decisions have often emphasized the danger of the government tacitly adopting, encouraging, or furthering racial discrimination even by its own routine operations. In Shelley v. Kraemer, 334 U.S. 1, 68 S.Ct. 836, 92 L.Ed. 1161 (1948), this Court recognized this interest as a constitutional command, holding unanimously that the Equal Protection Clause forbids courts to enforce racially restrictive covenants even where such covenants satisfied all requirements of state law and where the State harbored no discriminatory intent. Similarly, in Norwood v. Harrison, 413 U.S. 455, 93 S.Ct. 2804, 37 L.Ed.2d 723 (1973), we invalidated a program in which a State purchased textbooks and loaned them to students in public and private schools, including private schools with racially discriminatory policies. We stated that the

---

[6]The representatives of several trade associations did, however, deny that their particular organizations engaged in discrimination.

Constitution requires a State "to steer clear, not only of operating the old dual system of racially segregated schools, but also of giving significant aid to institutions that practice racial or other invidious discrimination."

The majority is wrong to trivialize the continuing impact of government acceptance or use of private institutions or structures once wrought by discrimination. When government channels all its contracting funds to a white-dominated community of established contractors whose racial homogeneity is the product of private discrimination, it does more than place its imprimatur on the practices which forged and which continue to define that community. It also provides a measurable boost to those economic entities that have thrived within it, while denying important economic benefits to those entities which, but for prior discrimination, might well be better qualified to receive valuable government contracts. In my view, the interest in ensuring that the government does not reflect and reinforce prior private discrimination in dispensing public contracts is every bit as strong as the interest in eliminating private discrimination — an interest which this Court has repeatedly deemed compelling. See, e.g., New York State Club Assn. v. New York City, 487 U.S. 1 n. 5; Board of Directors v. Rotary Club, 481 U.S. 537, 549 (1987); Roberts v. United States Jaycees, 468 U.S. 609, 623 (1984); Bob Jones University v. United States, 461 U.S. 574, 604 (1983); Runyon v. McCrary, 427 U.S. 160, 179 (1976). The more government bestows its rewards on those persons or businesses that were positioned to thrive during a period of private racial discrimination, the tighter the dead-hand grip of prior discrimination becomes on the present and future. Cities like Richmond may not be constitutionally required to adopt set-aside plans. But there can be no doubt that when Richmond acted affirmatively to stem the perpetuation of patterns of discrimination through its own decision-making, it served an interest of the highest order.

2

The remaining question with respect to the "governmental interest" prong of equal protection analysis is whether Richmond has proffered satisfactory proof of past racial discrimination to support its twin interests in remediation and in governmental nonperpetuation. Although the Members of this Court have differed on the appropriate standard of review for race-conscious remedial measures, we have always regarded this factual inquiry as a practical one. Thus, the Court has eschewed rigid tests which require the provision of particular species of evidence, statistical or otherwise. At the same time we have required that government adduce evidence that, taken as a whole, is sufficient to support its claimed interest and to dispel the natural concern that it acted out of mere "paternalistic stereotyping, not on a careful consideration of modern social conditions." *Fullilove* (Marshall, J., concurring in judgment).

The separate opinions issued in *Wygant* * * *, reflect this shared understanding. Justice Powell's opinion for a plurality of four Justices stated that "the trial court must make a factual determination that the employer had a strong basis in evidence for its conclusion that remedial action was necessary." Justice O'Connor's separate concurrence required "a firm basis for concluding that remedial action was appropriate." The dissenting opinion I authored, joined by Justices Brennan and Blackmun, required a government body to present a "legitimate factual predicate" and a reviewing court to "genuinely consider the circumstances of the provision at issue." Finally, Justice Stevens' separate dissent sought and found "a rational and unquestionably legitimate basis" for the school board's action. Our unwillingness to go beyond these generalized standards to require specific types of proof in all circumstances reflects, in my view, an understanding that discrimination takes a myriad of "ingenious and pervasive forms." *Bakke* (separate opinion of Marshall, J.).

The varied body of evidence on which Richmond relied provides a "strong," "firm," and "unquestionably legitimate" basis upon which the City Council could determine that the effects of past racial discrimination warranted a remedial and prophylactic governmental response. As I have noted, supra, Richmond acted against a backdrop of congressional and Executive Branch studies which demonstrated with such force the nationwide pervasiveness of prior discrimination that Congress presumed that present economic inequities in construction contracting resulted from past discriminatory systems. The city's local evidence confirmed that Richmond's construction industry did not deviate from this pernicious national pattern. The fact that just .67% of public construction expenditures over the previous five years had gone to minority-owned prime contractors, despite the city's racially mixed population, strongly suggests that construction contracting in the area was rife with "present economic inequities." To the extent this enormous disparity did not itself demonstrate that discrimination had occurred, the descriptive testimony of Richmond's elected and appointed leaders drew the necessary link between the pitifully small presence of minorities in construction contracting and past exclusionary practices. That no one who testified challenged this depiction of widespread racial discrimination in area construction contracting lent significant weight to these accounts. The fact that area trade associations had virtually no minority members dramatized the extent of present inequities and suggested the lasting power of past discriminatory systems. In sum, to suggest that the facts on which Richmond has relied do not provide a sound basis for its finding of past racial discrimination simply blinks credibility.

Richmond's reliance on localized, industry-specific findings is a far cry from the reliance on generalized "societal discrimination" which the majority describes as a basis for remedial action. But characterizing the plight of Richmond's minority contractors as mere "societal discrimination" is not the only respect in which the majority's critique shows an unwillingness to come to grips with why construction-contracting in Richmond is essentially a whites-only enterprise. The majority also takes the disingenuous approach of disaggregating Richmond's local evidence, attacking it piecemeal, and thereby concluding that no single piece of evidence adduced by the city, "standing alone," suffices to prove past discrimination. But items of evidence do not, of course, "stan[d] alone" or exist in alien juxtaposition; they necessarily work together, reinforcing or contradicting each other.

In any event, the majority's criticisms of individual items of Richmond's evidence rest on flimsy foundations. The majority states, for example, that reliance on the disparity between the share of city contracts awarded to minority firms (.67%) and the minority population of Richmond (approximately 50%) is "misplaced." It is true that, when the factual predicate needed to be proved is one of present discrimination, we have generally credited statistical contrasts between the racial composition of a work force and the general population as proving discrimination only where this contrast revealed "gross statistical disparities." *Hazelwood.* But this principle does not impugn Richmond's statistical contrast, for two reasons. First, considering how miniscule the share of Richmond public construction contracting dollars received by minority-owned businesses is, it is hardly unreasonable to conclude that this case involves a "gross statistical disparit[y]." There are roughly equal numbers of minorities and nonminorities in Richmond — yet minority-owned businesses receive one-seventy-fifth the public contracting funds that other businesses receive.

Second, and more fundamentally, where the issue is not present discrimination but rather whether past discrimination has resulted in the continuing exclusion of minorities from an historically tight-knit industry, a contrast between population and work force is entirely appropriate to help gauge the degree of the exclusion. In *Johnson v. Transportation Agency*, Justice O'Connor specifically observed that, when it is alleged that discrimination has prevented blacks from "obtaining th[e] experience" needed to qualify for a position, the "relevant comparison" is not to the percentage of blacks in the pool of qualified candidates, but to "the total percentage of blacks in the labor force." This contrast is especially illuminating in cases like this, where a main avenue of introduction into the work force — here, membership in the trade associations whose members presumably train apprentices and help them procure subcontracting assignments — is itself grossly dominated by nonminorities. The majority's assertion that the city "does not even know how many MBE's in the relevant market are qualified," is thus entirely beside the point. If Richmond indeed has a monochromatic contracting community — a conclusion reached by the District Court, — this most likely reflects the lingering power of past exclusionary practices. Certainly this is the explanation Congress has found persuasive at the national level. See *Fullilove*. The city's requirement that prime public contractors set aside 30% of their subcontracting assignments for minority-owned enterprises, subject to the ordinance's provision for waivers where minority-owned enterprises are unavailable or unwilling to participate, is designed precisely to ease minority contractors into the industry.

The majority's perfunctory dismissal of the testimony of Richmond's appointed and elected leaders is also deeply disturbing. These officials — including councilmembers, a former mayor, and the present city manager — asserted that race discrimination in area contracting had been widespread, and that the set-aside ordinance was a sincere and necessary attempt to eradicate the effects of this discrimination. The majority, however, states that where racial classifications are concerned, "simple legislative assurances of good intention cannot suffice." It similarly discounts as minimally probative the City Council's designation of its set-aside plan as remedial. "[B]lind judicial deference to legislative or executive pronouncements," the majority explains, "has no place in equal protection analysis."

No one, of course, advocates "blind judicial deference" to the findings of the City Council or the testimony of city leaders. The majority's suggestion that wholesale deference is what Richmond seeks is a classic straw-man argument. But the majority's trivialization of the testimony of Richmond's leaders is dismaying in a far more serious respect. By disregarding the testimony of local leaders and the judgment of local government, the majority does violence to the very principles of comity within our federal system which this Court has long championed. Local officials, by virtue of their proximity to, and their expertise with, local affairs, are exceptionally well-qualified to make determinations of public good "within their respective spheres of authority." Hawaii Housing Authority v. Midkiff, 467 U.S. 229, 244, 104 S.Ct. 2321,

2331, 81 L.Ed.2d 186 (1984). The majority, however, leaves any traces of comity behind in its headlong rush to strike down Richmond's race-conscious measure.

Had the majority paused for a moment on the facts of the Richmond experience, it would have discovered that the city's leadership is deeply familiar with what racial discrimination is. The members of the Richmond City Council have spent long years witnessing multifarious acts of discrimination, including, but not limited to, the deliberate diminution of black residents' voting rights, resistance to school desegregation, and publicly sanctioned housing discrimination. Numerous decisions of federal courts chronicle this disgraceful recent history. In Richmond v. United States, 422 U.S. 358, 95 S.Ct. 2296, 45 L.Ed.2d 245 (1975), for example, this Court denounced Richmond's decision to annex part of an adjacent county at a time when the city's black population was nearing 50% because it was "infected by the impermissible purpose of denying the right to vote based on race through perpetuating white majority power to exclude Negroes from office." (Brennan, J., dissenting) (describing Richmond's "flagrantly discriminatory purpose * * *. to avert a transfer of political control to what was fast becoming a black-population majority").

In Bradley v. School Board of City of Richmond, Virginia, 462 F.2d 1058, 1060, n. 1 (CA4 1972), aff'd by an equally divided Court, 412 U.S. 92, 93 S.Ct. 1952, 36 L.Ed.2d 771 (1973), the Court of Appeals for the Fourth Circuit, sitting en banc, reviewed in the context of a school desegregation case Richmond's long history of inadequate compliance with Brown v. Board of Education, 347 U.S. 483, 74 S.Ct. 686, 98 L.Ed. 873 (1954), and the cases implementing its holding. * * * The Court of Appeals majority in Bradley used * * * pungent words in describing public and private housing discrimination in Richmond. Though rejecting the black plaintiffs' request that it consolidate Richmond's school district with those of two neighboring counties, the majority nonetheless agreed with the plaintiffs' assertion that "within the City of Richmond there has been state (also federal) action tending to perpetuate apartheid of the races in ghetto patterns throughout the city."

When the legislatures and leaders of cities with histories of pervasive discrimination testify that past discrimination has infected one of their industries, armchair cynicism like that exercised by the majority has no place. It may well be that "the autonomy of a state is an essential component of federalism," Garcia v. San Antonio Metropolitan Transit Authority, 469 U.S. 528, 588, 105 S.Ct. 1005, 1037, 83 L.Ed.2d 1016 (1985) (O'Connor, J., dissenting), and that "each State is sovereign within its own domain, governing its citizens and providing for their general welfare," FERC v. Mississippi, 456 U.S., at 777, 102 S.Ct., at 2147 (O'Connor, J., dissenting), but apparently this is not the case when federal judges, with nothing but their impressions to go on, choose to disbelieve the explanations of these local governments and officials. Disbelief is particularly inappropriate here in light of the fact that appellee Croson, which had the burden of proving unconstitutionality at trial, Wygant (plurality opinion), has at no point come forward with any direct evidence that the City Council's motives were anything other than sincere.[9]

Finally, I vehemently disagree with the majority's dismissal of the congressional and Executive Branch findings noted in Fullilove as having "extremely limited"

---

[9]Compare Fullilove (Stevens, J., dissenting) (noting statements of sponsors of federal set-aside that measure was designed to give their constituents "a piece of the action").

probative value in this case. The majority concedes that Congress established nothing less than a "presumption" that minority contracting firms have been disadvantaged by prior discrimination. The majority, inexplicably, would forbid Richmond to "share" in this information, and permit only Congress to take note of these ample findings. In thus requiring that Richmond's local evidence be severed from the context in which it was prepared, the majority would require cities seeking to eradicate the effects of past discrimination within their borders to reinvent the evidentiary wheel and engage in unnecessarily duplicative, costly, and time-consuming factfinding.

No principle of federalism or of federal power, however, forbids a state or local government from drawing upon a nationally relevant historical record prepared by the Federal Government.[10] Of course, Richmond could have built an even more compendious record of past discrimination, one including additional stark statistics and additional individual accounts of past discrimination. But nothing in the Fourteenth Amendment imposes such onerous documentary obligations upon States and localities once the reality of past discrimination is apparent.

B

In my judgment, Richmond's set-aside plan also comports with the second prong of the equal protection inquiry, for it is substantially related to the interests it seeks to serve in remedying past discrimination and in ensuring that municipal contract procurement does not perpetuate that discrimination. The most striking aspect of the city's ordinance is the similarity it bears to the "appropriately limited" federal set-aside provision upheld in *Fullilove*. Like the federal provision, Richmond's is limited to five years in duration, and was not renewed when it came up for reconsideration in 1988. Like the federal provision, Richmond's contains a waiver provision freeing from its subcontracting requirements those nonminority firms that demonstrate that they cannot comply with its provisions. Like the federal provision, Richmond's has a minimal impact on innocent third parties. While the measure affects 30% of public contracting dollars, that translates to only 3% of overall Richmond area contracting.

Finally, like the federal provision, Richmond's does not interfere with any vested right of a contractor to a particular contract; instead it operates entirely prospectively. Richmond's initiative affects only future economic arrangements and imposes only a diffuse burden on nonminority competitors — here, businesses owned or controlled by nonminorities which seek subcontracting work on public construction projects. The plurality in Wygant emphasized the importance of this not disrupting the settled and legitimate expectations of innocent parties. "While hiring goals impose a diffuse burden, often foreclosing only one of several opportunities, layoffs impose the entire burden of achieving racial equality on particular individuals, often resulting in serious disruption of their lives. That burden is too intrusive." *Wygant*.

These factors, far from "justify[ing] a preference of any size or duration," are precisely the factors to which this Court looked in Fullilove. The majority takes issue,

---

[10]Although the majority sharply criticizes Richmond for using data which it did not itself develop, it is noteworthy that the federal set-aside program upheld in *Fullilove* was adopted as a floor amendment "without any congressional hearings or investigation whatsoever." L. Tribe, American Constitutional Law 345 (2d ed. 1988). The principal opinion in *Fullilove* justified the set-aside by relying heavily on the aforementioned studies by agencies like the Small Business Administration and on legislative reports prepared in connection with prior, failed legislation.

however, with two aspects of Richmond's tailoring: the city's refusal to explore the use of race-neutral measures to increase minority business participation in contracting, and the selection of a 30% set-aside figure. The majority's first criticism is flawed in two respects. First, the majority overlooks the fact that since 1975, Richmond has barred both discrimination by the city in awarding public contracts and discrimination by public contractors. See Richmond, Va., City Code, §17.1 et seq. (1985). The virtual absence of minority businesses from the city's contracting rolls, indicated by the fact that such businesses have received less than 1% of public contracting dollars, strongly suggests that this ban has not succeeded in redressing the impact of past discrimination or in preventing city contract procurement from reinforcing racial homogeneity. Second, the majority's suggestion that Richmond should have first undertaken such race-neutral measures as a program of city financing for small firms, ignores the fact that such measures, while theoretically appealing, have been discredited by Congress as ineffectual in eradicating the effects of past discrimination in this very industry. For this reason, this Court in *Fullilove* refused to fault Congress for not undertaking race-neutral measures as precursors to its race-conscious set-aside. The Equal Protection Clause does not require Richmond to retrace Congress' steps when Congress has found that those steps lead nowhere. Given the well-exposed limitations of race-neutral measures, it was thus appropriate for a municipality like Richmond to conclude that, in the words of Justice Blackmun, "[i]n order to get beyond racism, we must first take account of race. There is no other way." *Bakke*.[25]

As for Richmond's 30% target, the majority states that this figure "cannot be said to be narrowly tailored to any goal, except perhaps outright racial balancing." The majority ignores two important facts. First, the set-aside measure affects only 3% of overall city contracting; thus, any imprecision in tailoring has far less impact than the majority suggests. But more important, the majority ignores the fact that Richmond's 30% figure was patterned directly on the Fullilove precedent. Congress' 10% figure fell "roughly halfway between the present percentage of minority contractors and the percentage of minority group members in the Nation." *Fullilove*. The Richmond City Council's 30% figure similarly falls roughly halfway between the present percentage of Richmond-based minority contractors (almost zero) and the percentage of minorities in Richmond (50%). In faulting Richmond for not presenting a different explanation for its choice of a set-aside figure, the majority honors *Fullilove* only in the breach.

III

I would ordinarily end my analysis at this point and conclude that Richmond's ordinance satisfies both the governmental interest and substantial relationship prongs of our Equal Protection Clause analysis. However, I am compelled to add more, for the majority has gone beyond the facts of this case to announce a set of principles

---

[25]The majority also faults Richmond's ordinance for including within its definition of "minority group members" not only black citizens, but also citizens who are "Spanish-speaking, Oriental, Indian, Eskimo, or Aleut persons." This is, of course, precisely the same definition Congress adopted in its set-aside legislation. *Fullilove*. Even accepting the majority's view that Richmond's ordinance is overbroad because it includes groups, such as Eskimos or Aleuts, about whom no evidence of local discrimination has been proffered, it does not necessarily follow that the balance of Richmond's ordinance should be invalidated.

which unnecessarily restrict the power of governmental entities to take race-conscious measures to redress the effects of prior discrimination.

A

Today, for the first time, a majority of this Court has adopted strict scrutiny as its standard of Equal Protection Clause review of race-conscious remedial measures. This is an unwelcome development. A profound difference separates governmental actions that themselves are racist, and governmental actions that seek to remedy the effects of prior racism or to prevent neutral governmental activity from perpetuating the effects of such racism.

Racial classifications "drawn on the presumption that one race is inferior to another or because they put the weight of government behind racial hatred and separatism" warrant the strictest judicial scrutiny because of the very irrelevance of these rationales. By contrast, racial classifications drawn for the purpose of remedying the effects of discrimination that itself was race-based have a highly pertinent basis: the tragic and indelible fact that discrimination against blacks and other racial minorities in this Nation has pervaded our Nation's history and continues to scar our society. As I stated in *Fullilove*: "Because the consideration of race is relevant to remedying the continuing effects of past racial discrimination, and because governmental programs employing racial classifications for remedial purposes can be crafted to avoid stigmatization, * * * such programs should not be subjected to conventional 'strict scrutiny' — scrutiny that is strict in theory, but fatal in fact." *Fullilove*.

In concluding that remedial classifications warrant no different standard of review under the Constitution than the most brute and repugnant forms of state-sponsored racism, a majority of this Court signals that it regards racial discrimination as largely a phenomenon of the past, and that government bodies need no longer preoccupy themselves with rectifying racial injustice. I, however, do not believe this Nation is anywhere close to eradicating racial discrimination or its vestiges. In constitutionalizing its wishful thinking, the majority today does a grave disservice not only to those victims of past and present racial discrimination in this Nation whom government has sought to assist, but also to this Court's long tradition of approaching issues of race with the utmost sensitivity.

B

I am also troubled by the majority's assertion that, even if it did not believe generally in strict scrutiny of race-based remedial measures, "the circumstances of this case" require this Court to look upon the Richmond City Council's measure with the strictest scrutiny. The sole such circumstance which the majority cites, however, is the fact that blacks in Richmond are a "dominant racial grou[p]" in the city. In support of this characterization of dominance, the majority observes that "blacks comprise approximately 50% of the population of the city of Richmond" and that "[f]ive of the nine seats on the City Council are held by blacks."

While I agree that the numerical and political supremacy of a given racial group is a factor bearing upon the level of scrutiny to be applied, this Court has never held that numerical inferiority, standing alone, makes a racial group "suspect" and thus entitled to strict scrutiny review. Rather, we have identified other "traditional indicia of suspectness": whether a group has been "saddled with such disabilities, or subjected to such a history of purposeful unequal treatment, or relegated to such a position of political powerlessness as to command extraordinary protection from the majoritarian political process." San Antonio Independent School District v. Rodriguez, 411 U.S. 1, 28, 93 S.Ct. 1278, 1294, 36 L.Ed.2d 16 (1973).

It cannot seriously be suggested that nonminorities in Richmond have any "history of purposeful unequal treatment." Nor is there any indication that they have any of the disabilities that have characteristically afflicted those groups this Court has deemed suspect. Indeed, the numerical and political dominance of nonminorities within the State of Virginia and the Nation as a whole provide an enormous political check against the "simple racial politics" at the municipal level which the majority fears. If the majority really believes that groups like Richmond's non-minorities, which comprise approximately half the population but which are outnumbered even marginally in political fora, are deserving of suspect class status for these reasons alone, this Court's decisions denying suspect status to women, see Craig v. Boren, 429 U.S. 190, 197, 97 S.Ct. 451, 456, 50 L.Ed.2d 397 (1976), and to persons with below-average incomes, see *San Antonio Independent School Dist.*, stand on extremely shaky ground.

In my view, the "circumstances of this case," underscore the importance of not subjecting to a strict scrutiny straitjacket the increasing number of cities which have recently come under minority leadership and are eager to rectify, or at least prevent the perpetuation of, past racial discrimination. In many cases, these cities will be the ones with the most in the way of prior discrimination to rectify. Richmond's leaders had just witnessed decades of publicly sanctioned racial discrimination in virtually all walks of life — discrimination amply documented in the decisions of the federal judiciary. This history of "purposefully unequal treatment" forced upon minorities, not imposed by them, should raise an inference that minorities in Richmond had much to remedy — and that the 1983 set-aside was undertaken with sincere remedial goals in mind, not "simple racial politics."

Richmond's own recent political history underscores the facile nature of the majority's assumption that elected officials' voting decisions are based on the color of their skins. In recent years, white and black councilmembers in Richmond have increasingly joined hands on controversial matters. When the Richmond City Council elected a black man Mayor in 1982, for example, his victory was won with the support of the City Council's four white members. The vote on the set-aside plan a year later also was not purely along racial lines. Of the four white councilmembers, one voted for the measure and another abstained. The majority's view that remedial measures undertaken by municipalities with black leadership must face a stiffer test of Equal Protection Clause scrutiny than remedial measures undertaken by municipalities with white leadership implies a lack of political maturity on the part of this Nation's elected minority officials that is totally unwarranted. Such insulting judgments have no place in constitutional jurisprudence.

C

Today's decision, finally, is particularly noteworthy for the daunting standard it imposes upon States and localities contemplating the use of race-conscious measures to eradicate the present effects of prior discrimination and prevent its perpetuation. The majority restricts the use of such measures to situations in which a State or locality can put forth "a prima facie case of a constitutional or statutory violation." In so doing, the majority calls into question the validity of the business set-asides which dozens of municipalities across this Nation have adopted on the authority of *Fullilove.*

Nothing in the Constitution or in the prior decisions of this Court supports limiting state authority to confront the effects of past discrimination to those situations in which a prima facie case of a constitutional or statutory violation can be made out. By its very terms, the majority's standard effectively cedes control of a large component of the content of that constitutional provision to Congress and to state legislatures. If an antecedent Virginia or Richmond law had defined as unlawful the award to nonminorities of an overwhelming share of a city's contracting dollars, for example, Richmond's subsequent set-aside initiative would then satisfy the majority's standard. But without such a law, the initiative might not withstand constitutional scrutiny. The meaning of "equal protection of the laws" thus turns on the happenstance of whether a State or local body has previously defined illegal discrimination. Indeed, given that racially discriminatory cities may be the ones least likely to have tough antidiscrimination laws on their books, the majority's constitutional incorporation of state and local statutes has the perverse effect of inhibiting those States or localities with the worst records of official racism from taking remedial action.

Similar flaws would inhere in the majority's standard even if it incorporated only federal anti-discrimination statutes. If Congress tomorrow dramatically expanded Title VII of the Civil Rights Act of 1964, — or alternatively, if it repealed that legislation altogether — the meaning of equal protection would change precipitously along with it. Whatever the Framers of the Fourteenth Amendment had in mind in 1868, it certainly was not that the content of their Amendment would turn on the amendments to or the evolving interpretations of a federal statute passed nearly a century later.[26]

---

[26]Although the majority purports to "adher[e] to the standard of review employed in *Wygant,*" the "prima facie case" standard it adopts marks an implicit rejection of the more generally framed "strong basis in evidence" test endorsed by the *Wygant* plurality, and the similar "firm basis" test endorsed by Justice O'Connor in her separate concurrence in that case. Under those tests, proving a prima facie violation of Title VII would appear to have been but one means of adducing sufficient proof to satisfy Equal Protection Clause analysis. See Johnson v. Transportation Agency, 480 U.S. 616, 632, 107 S.Ct. 1442, 1452, 94 L.Ed.2d 615 (1987) (plurality opinion) (criticizing suggestion that race-conscious relief be conditioned on showing of a prima facie Title VII violation).

The rhetoric of today's majority opinion departs from *Wygant* in another significant respect. In *Wygant,* a majority of this Court rejected as unduly inhibiting and constitutionally unsupported a requirement that a municipality demonstrate that its remedial plan is designed only to benefit specific victims of discrimination. Justice O'Connor noted that the Court's general agreement that a "remedial purpose need not be accompanied by contemporaneous findings of actual discrimination to be accepted as legitimate as long as the public actor has a firm basis for believing that remedial action is required * * *. [A] plan need not be limited to the remedying of specific instances of identified discrimination for it to be deemed sufficiently narrowly tailored, or substantially related, to the correction of prior discrimination by the state actor." The majority's opinion today, however, hints that a "specific victims" proof requirement might be appropriate in equal protection cases. Given that just three Terms ago this Court rejected the "specific victims" idea as untenable, I believe these references — and the majority's cryptic "identified discrimination" requirement — cannot be read to require States and localities to make such highly particularized showings. Rather, I take the majority's standard of

To the degree that this parsimonious standard is grounded on a view that either §1 or §5 of the Fourteenth Amendment substantially disempowered States and localities from remedying past racial discrimination, the majority is seriously mistaken. With respect, first, to §5, our precedents have never suggested that this provision — or, for that matter, its companion federal-empowerment provisions in the Thirteenth and Fifteenth Amendments — was meant to pre-empt or limit state police power to undertake race-conscious remedial measures. To the contrary, in Katzenbach v. Morgan, 384 U.S. 641, 86 S.Ct. 1717, 16 L.Ed.2d 828 (1966), we held that §5 "is a positive grant of legislative power authorizing Congress to exercise its discretion in determining whether and what legislation is needed to secure the guarantees of the Fourteenth Amendment." Indeed, we have held that Congress has this authority even where no constitutional violation has been found. See *Katzenbach* (upholding Voting Rights Act provision nullifying state English literacy requirement we had previously upheld against Equal Protection Clause challenge). Certainly *Fullilove* did not view §5 either as limiting the traditionally broad police powers of the States to fight discrimination, or as mandating a zero-sum game in which state power wanes as federal power waxes. On the contrary, the *Fullilove* plurality invoked §5 only because it provided specific and certain authorization for the Federal Government's attempt to impose a race-conscious condition on the dispensation of federal funds by state and local grantees.

As for §1, it is too late in the day to assert seriously that the Equal Protection Clause prohibits States — or for that matter, the Federal Government, to whom the equal protection guarantee has largely been applied, see Bolling v. Sharpe, 347 U.S. 497, 74 S.Ct. 693, 98 L.Ed. 884 (1954) — from enacting race-conscious remedies. Our cases in the areas of school desegregation, voting rights, and affirmative action have demonstrated time and again that race is constitutionally germane, precisely because race remains dismayingly relevant in American life.

In adopting its prima facie standard for States and localities, the majority closes its eyes to this constitutional history and social reality. So, too, does Justice Scalia. He would further limit consideration of race to those cases in which States find it "necessary to eliminate their own maintenance of a system of unlawful racial classification" — a "distinction" which, he states, "explains our school desegregation cases." But this Court's remedy-stage school desegregation decisions cannot so conveniently be cordoned off. These decisions (like those involving voting rights and affirmative action) stand for the same broad principles of equal protection which Richmond seeks to vindicate in this case: all persons have equal worth, and it is permissible, given a sufficient factual predicate and appropriate tailoring, for government to take account of race to eradicate the present effects of race-based subjugation denying that basic equality. Justice Scalia's artful distinction allows him to avoid having to repudiate "our school desegregation cases," but, like the arbitrary limitation on race-conscious relief adopted by the majority, his approach would freeze the status quo that is the very target of the remedial actions of States and localities.

The fact is that Congress' concern in passing the Reconstruction Amendments, and particularly their congressional authorization provisions, was that States would not

---

"identified discrimination" merely to require some quantum of proof of discrimination within a given jurisdiction that exceeds the proof which Richmond has put forth here.

adequately respond to racial violence or discrimination against newly freed slaves. To interpret any aspect of these Amendments as proscribing state remedial responses to these very problems turns the Amendments on their heads. As four Justices, of whom I was one, stated in *Bakke*:

> "[There is] no reason to conclude that the States cannot voluntarily accomplish under §1 of the Fourteenth Amendment what Congress under §5 of the Fourteenth Amendment validly may authorize or compel either the States or private persons to do. A contrary position would conflict with the traditional understanding recognizing the competence of the States to initiate measures consistent with federal policy in the absence of congressional pre-emption of the subject matter. *Nothing whatever in the legislative history of either the Fourteenth Amendment or the Civil Rights Acts even remotely suggests that the States are foreclosed from furthering the fundamental purpose of equal opportunity to which the Amendment and those Acts are addressed.* Indeed, voluntary initiatives by the States to achieve the national goal of equal opportunity have been recognized to be essential to its attainment. 'To use the Fourteenth Amendment as a sword against such State power would stultify that Amendment.' Railway Mail Assn. v. Corsi, 326 U.S. 88, 98, 65 S.Ct. 1483, 1489, 89 L.Ed. 2072 (Frankfurter, J., concurring)." 438 U.S., at 368, 98 S.Ct., at 2788 (1978) (footnote omitted) (emphasis added).

In short, there is simply no credible evidence that the Framers of the Fourteenth Amendment sought "to transfer the security and protection of all the civil rights * * * from the States to the Federal government." The *Slaughter-House Cases*.[27] The three Reconstruction Amendments undeniably "worked a dramatic change in the balance between congressional and state power," they forbade state-sanctioned slavery, forbade the state-sanctioned denial of the right to vote, and (until the content of the Equal Protection Clause was substantially applied to the Federal Government through the Due Process Clause of the Fifth Amendment) uniquely forbade States from denying equal protection. The Amendments also specifically empowered the Federal Government to combat discrimination at a time when the breadth of federal power under the Constitution was less apparent than it is today. But nothing in the Amendments themselves, or in our long history of interpreting or applying those momentous charters, suggests that States, exercising their police power, are in any way constitutionally inhibited from working alongside the Federal Government in the fight against discrimination and its effects.

IV

The majority today sounds a full-scale retreat from the Court's longstanding solicitude to race-conscious remedial efforts "directed toward deliverance of the century-old promise of equality of economic opportunity." *Fullilove.* The new and restrictive tests it applies scuttle one city's effort to surmount its discriminatory past, and imperil those of dozens more localities. I, however, profoundly disagree with the

---

[27]Tellingly, the sole support the majority offers for its view that the Framers of the Fourteenth Amendment intended such a result are two law review articles analyzing this Court's recent affirmative action decisions, and a court of appeals decision which relies upon statements by James Madison. Madison, of course, had been dead for 32 years when the Fourteenth Amendment was enacted.

cramped vision of the Equal Protection Clause which the majority offers today and with its application of that vision to Richmond, Virginia's, laudable set-aside plan. The battle against pernicious racial discrimination or its effects is nowhere near won. I must dissent.

JUSTICE BLACKMUN, with whom JUSTICE BRENNAN joins, dissenting.

I join Justice Marshall's perceptive and incisive opinion revealing great sensitivity toward those who have suffered the pains of economic discrimination in the construction trades for so long.

I never thought that I would live to see the day when the city of Richmond, Virginia, the cradle of the Old Confederacy, sought on its own, within a narrow confine, to lessen the stark impact of persistent discrimination. But Richmond, to its great credit, acted. Yet this Court, the supposed bastion of equality, strikes down Richmond's efforts as though discrimination had never existed or was not demonstrated in this particular litigation. Justice Marshall convincingly discloses the fallacy and the shallowness of that approach. History is irrefutable, even though one might sympathize with those who — though possibly innocent in themselves — benefit from the wrongs of past decades.

So the Court today regresses. I am confident, however, that, given time, it one day again will do its best to fulfill the great promises of the Constitution's Preamble and of the guarantees embodied in the Bill of Rights — a fulfillment that would make this Nation very special.

NOTES AND PROBLEMS FOR DISCUSSION

1. The decision in *Croson* dramatically altered the legal landscape and had a significant impact on the subsequent adoption and continuation of affirmative action plans. Most significantly, of course, a majority of the Court, for the first time, agreed on the level of scrutiny to be applied to race-based preferences. Perhaps equally important, however, was the analysis employed by the Court with respect to the evidentiary showing that now would be required to sustain this heightened level of scrutiny. Not surprisingly, this ruling led to the invalidation of several such plans. For example, In MICHIGAN ROAD BUILDERS ASS'N, INC. v. MILLIKEN, 834 F.2d 583 (6th Cir. 1987), affirmed without opinion, 489 U.S. 1061, 109 S.Ct. 1333, 103 L.Ed.2d 804 (1989), the Michigan legislature had enacted a "set-aside" statute that required each state department to award not less than 7% of its expenditures for construction, goods and services to MBEs ("black, hispanic, oriental, eskimo or American Indian" fell within definition of "minority") and not less than 5% to WBEs (woman owned businesses). The circuit court applied strict scrutiny to the racial classification and upheld the trial court's grant of summary judgment in favor of the plaintiff, ruling that the statute was unconstitutional under the equal protection clause of the Fourteenth Amendment. In reviewing the record, the Sixth Circuit indicated that the Michigan legislature had relied on information collected with respect to prior, unrelated legislation dealing with the inability of small businesses, rather than MBEs, to break into the market and that the legislative history of the set-aside statute attributed the scarcity of MBE contracts with the state to the effects of societal discrimination. Accordingly, the court concluded that the State had not demonstrated a compelling interest in remedying past discrimination since the legislature did not have sufficient evidence to warrant a finding that the State itself had discriminated against MBEs in awarding state contracts for the purchase of goods and services. The Sixth Circuit interpreted the Supreme Court's ruling in *Wygant* as requiring the State to demonstrate that it had engaged in racial discrimination in order to justify a race-based set-aside program designed to remedy the effects of prior discrimination. With respect to the sex-based set aside, the court stated that intermediate scrutiny was appropriate, but that the statute even failed to meet that lesser burden since the legislature had offered absolutely no evidence of its past discrimination against women owned businesses. The Supreme Court affirmed these rulings, but did not issue a written opinion. *See also* O'Donnell Construction Co. v. District of Columbia, 963 F.2d 420 (D.C. Cir. 1992) (reversing trial court's denial of preliminary injunction against enforcement of D.C. statute requiring 35% of dollar volume of all construction contracts awarded by District to be reserved for local minority owned businesses; District failed to present sufficient evidence of past discrimination beyond unsupported statement in statutory "Findings" section and unexplained statistic relating to number and value of contracts awarded to MBE's).

On the other hand, some municipalities have been able to conform to the standards articulated in *Croson*. For example, in CONE CORP. v. HILLSBOROUGH COUNTY, 908 F.2d 908 (11th Cir. 1990), cert. denied, 498 U.S. 983, 111 S.Ct. 516, 112 L.Ed.2d 528 (1990), an ordinance establishing an annual goal of twenty-five percent total MBE participation in County construction was upheld. This statute set an MBE participation goal for each project. In the fiscal year following the implementation of the ordinance, MBE participation in those projects in which goals were set totaled almost 20%, that is, less than the 25% goal, but higher than the percentage of minority contractors in the County. The court concluded that this statute was materially different from the Richmond ordinance struck down in *Croson*. It noted that the statute was enacted after the County had undertaken a statistical survey of minority business participation in contracts awarded by the County which indicated that minorities were significantly underrepresented in such awards in comparison to the percentage of MBE contractors in the local community. Thus, the court concluded, the legislature had relied on statistics which indicated that there was discrimination specifically in the construction business commissioned by the County, not just in the construction industry in general. The legislature also had evidence before it of numerous complaints made by MBE contractors to the County regarding discrimination by prime contractors. On the basis of all of this information, the court stated, the legislature had more than enough evidence on the question of prior discrimination and the need for racial classification to remedy the situation. With respect to whether the use of a racial classification was narrowly tailored, the court added that the County had tried a race-neutral program for six years prior to adopting the set-aside program. In addition, the MBE law included all of the race-neutral measures suggested by the Court in *Croson*. Moreover, the goal was flexible and did not apply to every individual project. Rather, it applied only to projects based on the number of qualified MBE subcontractors available for each subcontractable area. Under the plan, no goal would be set if there were not at least three qualified MBE subcontractors available for the subcontractable area. Finally, this statute, unlike the Richmond plan, did not apply the 25% participation goal to all covered minority groups. Accordingly, the court held, the plan passed constitutional muster. *See also* Stuart v. Roache, 951 F.2d 446 (1st Cir. 1991), cert. denied, 504 U.S. 913, 112 S.Ct. 1948, 118 L.Ed.2d 553 (1992) (consent decree entered into by Boston Police Department containing goal for promotion of black police sergeants survives strict scrutiny; since decree compared percentage of black sergeants with percentage of black police officers possessing minimal qualifications needed for promotion to sergeant and in light of defendant's adjudicated past history of entry-level racial discrimination, there was sufficient evidence of prior discrimination by defendant to support determination that racially-based preference was designed to remedy prior discrimination. Court also finds plan to be narrowly tailored.).

In CORAL CONSTRUCTION CO. v. KING COUNTY, 941 F.2d 910 (9th Cir. 1991), cert. denied, 502 U.S. 1033, 112 S.Ct. 875, 116 L.Ed.2d 780 (1992), however, the Ninth Circuit appears to have relaxed, to some degree, the evidentiary requirements discussed in *Croson*. Specifically, it addressed the language in *Croson* that requires a municipality to demonstrate that it relied on evidence of discrimination within the industry affected by the affirmative action plan in order to establish the remedial nature of the plan. This case involved a program implemented by Kings County (which encompasses the city of Seattle) that established a preference for the use of minority-owned and women-owned businesses in letting county contracts or subcontracts. The appellate court ruled that *Croson* did not require the County to compile a factual record on its own. Rather, the court declared, it was permissible for the County to demonstrate that it had relied on data compiled by the City of Seattle, a city agency, and another municipality contained within the territorial limits of the County. Data sharing under these limited circumstances, the court reasoned, was not inconsistent with the underlying concern in *Croson* that an MBE program not be based on extraterritorial data. Extraterritorial data was precluded by *Croson*, the court continued, because it constituted evidence of "societal discrimination," a situation that was beyond the remedial authority of local jurisdictions. Here, the evidence related directly to discrimination within the County limits.

The court then addressed the question of the kind of evidence that could be relied upon to prove the existence of a systemic pattern of discrimination necessary for the adoption of an affirmative action plan. In this case, the factual record contained an extensive amount of anecdotal evidence from individual contractors with respect to specific incidents of discrimination, but was devoid of statistical evidence. The court ruled that while anecdotal evidence suggested the existence of a systemic pattern, it was not enough, in the absence of statistical evidence, to prove such a pattern and, therefore, did not meet the County's burden of proving that its program was justified by the compelling interest of remedying prior county-wide discrimination. Nevertheless, the court added, this defect was cured by the fact that the trial court had been presented by the County with such statistical evidence contained in studies undertaken after the adoption of the MBE program. The court reasoned that although the County was required to have some concrete evidence of discrimination within the construction industry before it adopted a remedial program, the ultimate determination of whether the plan complied with the stringent requirements of the constitutional strict scrutiny standard should be made by a court on the basis of all evidence presented to it, regardless of when it was adduced. Otherwise, in the Ninth Circuit's judgment, a municipality would face the dilemma of deciding whether (1) to wait for further development of the record before acting and thereby risk potential constitutional liability for failing to eradicate extant discrimination, or (2) to act and risk liability for acting prematurely. Thus, it concluded, it would not invalidate an MBE program solely because the record at the time of adoption did not measure up to constitutional standards, as long as an adequate factual record was subsequently provided. Accordingly, it remanded the case to the trial court for a determination of whether the statistical studies compiled after the adoption of the plan provided an adequate factual justification for the implementation of this MBE program. The ruling in *Croson* also has been extended to racial preferences contained in consent decrees. *See* United Black Firefighters Ass'n v. City of Akron, 976 F.2d 999 (6th Cir. 1992).

2. A majority of the Supreme Court took great pains to distinguish *Croson* from *Fullilove* with respect to the method of proving that a racial classification was adopted for the purpose of remedying prior discrimination. What impact, if any, will this aspect of the Court's analysis have on future equal protection scrutiny of affirmative action preferences that are either judicially imposed or are voluntarily undertaken by non-legislative public institutions? For example, suppose a city police department transferred white police officers out of a special investigatory unit because it desired to correct what it perceived to be a racial imbalance within that investigatory unit? Could the department overcome an equal protection challenge to this race-based decision on the ground that it was undertaking voluntary affirmative action to remedy this racial imbalance? In CYGNAR v. CITY OF CHICAGO, 865 F.2d 827 (7th Cir. 1989), the Seventh Circuit held that the defendants could not justify such a race-based transfer of white police officers out of a special investigatory unit on the ground that it was attempting to correct what it perceived to be a previously existing racial imbalance within that investigatory unit. The court ruled that this "affirmative action defense" could not withstand equal protection scrutiny (even though the jury had found that the defendants' decision was motivated by a desire to correct the perceived racial imbalance) because the defendants had not offered any evidence as to which population groups, if any, they had compared with the percentage of minority employees in the investigatory unit in concluding that an imbalance existed. In fact, the court continued, the defendants even failed to convince it that they had attempted to make any comparison whatsoever. Is this result mandated by *Croson*? Should a police department be subjected to the same standard of fact finding that is demanded of a state or local legislature?

Alternatively, what if the police department decided to transfer some African-American officers to another precinct in response to the brutal torture of an African-American prisoner by white officers of that precinct? Would the City's argument that the admittedly race-based decision was necessary to maintain public order and promote effective police enforcement constitute a compelling state interest? In PATROLMEN'S BENEVOLENT ASS'N v. CITY OF NEW YORK, 310 F.3d 43 (2d Cir.2002), cert. denied, 538 U.S. 1032, 123 S.Ct. 2076, 155 L.Ed.2d 1061 (2003), the defendant had transferred several police officers, admittedly on basis of race, to a precinct where white police officers had previously tortured and beaten Haitian immigrant Abner Louima. The City justified its action on the ground that this response was necessary to avoid the imminent potential for violence in the community after the Louima incident and to promote effective law enforcement in a hostile environment. The plaintiffs asserted both Title VII and §1983 claims, with the §1983 claim based on a violation of the Equal Protection Clause of the 14th Amendment. With respect to the constitutional question, the court ruled that a police department's ability to effectively carry out its mission with a workforce that is perceived to be unbiased and which can communicate with and be respected by the public could constitute a compelling state interest for strict scrutiny purposes despite the fact that the remediation of past discrimination was the only compelling state interest explicitly recognized as such by the Supreme Court. But to establish the compelling nature of that state interest, the court continued, the government actor must demonstrate, through the introduction of objective evidence and not mere speculation or conjecture, that it was motivated by a truly powerful and worthy concern and that the race-based remedy was narrowly tailored to serve that identified interest. Applying that standard, the appellate court found that the jury, which had issued a verdict in favor of the plaintiffs on the constitutional claim, could reasonably have concluded on the basis of the evidence presented by the plaintiffs that the defendant had not demonstrated that the transfers were narrowly tailored to meet a compelling state interest. The City's reliance on "common knowledge" regarding the "historical reality" of race relations in police work, the court reasoned, did not suffice to meet that evidentiary standard.

3. Did the *Croson* Court mean to imply that remedying prior discrimination is the only compelling interest that would justify the use of a race-based preference? And, if so, what precisely did the Court intend when it said that this involves "some showing of prior discrimination by the governmental unit involved?" Does this mean, for example, that another interest, such as promoting diversity, is not constitutionally acceptable? In a highly anticipated decision in a pair of companion cases involving constitutional challenges to the admissions policies of the University of Michigan's undergraduate college and law school, the Supreme Court addressed a conflict that had existed between the circuit courts on this vexing question.

In GRUTTER v. BOLLINGER, 539 U.S. 306, 123 S.Ct. 2325, 156 L.Ed.2d 304 (2003), the plaintiff alleged that the University of Michigan Law School's admissions policy violated the Equal Protection Clause of the Fourteenth Amendment because it permitted the consideration of a candidate's race or ethnicity in the admissions decision process. Law School personnel testified at trial that this policy reflected a longstanding commitment to racial and ethnic diversity with special reference to the inclusion of students from groups that had been historically discriminated against. The stated goal of this policy was not to remedy past discrimination but, rather, to obtain the educational benefits that flow from a diverse student body. To that end, the policy was designed to enroll a "critical mass" of underrepresented minority students to bring a different perspective to the Law School from that of members of nondisadvantaged groups and of disadvantaged groups who already were being admitted to the Law School in significant numbers. The law school officials also testified that they did not attach any specific number or percentage to the meaning of "critical mass" and, therefore, that the school did not seek to admit any particular number or percentage of underrepresented minority students.

In a 5-4 decision authored by Justice O'Connor, a majority of the Court, for the first time, endorsed the view, initially articulated in Justice Powell's opinion for the Court in *Bakke*, that student body racial diversity is a compelling state interest that could justify the use of race in public university admissions. Applying the *Croson* doctrine that all state-imposed racial classifications must be subjected to strict scrutiny under the Fourteenth Amendment, the Court then set out to evaluate whether the use of race by the University of Michigan Law School was narrowly tailored to further a compelling state interest.

The Court began its analysis of the compelling state interest half of this constitutional equation by expressly rejecting the notion that its decisions in *Croson* and other affirmative action cases suggested that remedying past discrimination was the only permissible justification for race-based governmental action. While acknowledging that language in some of those cases (particularly the plurality opinion in *Croson*) could lend itself to that interpretation, the majority insisted that it had never "held" that remedying past discrimination was the only compelling state interest that could justify governmental use of race. "Today", the Court declared, "we hold that the Law School has a compelling interest in attaining a diverse student body." It reached this conclusion the basis of the following three factors: (1) its deference to the Law School's educational judgment that such diversity was essential to its educational mission; (2) its adoption of the justifications offered by Justice Powell in *Bakke* for acknowledging the importance of student body diversity in public higher education; and (3) its adherence to the contention asserted by several major American businesses, military leaders, and other amici curiae that student body diversity promotes learning outcomes, better prepares students for an increasingly diverse workforce, society, and global marketplace, and is necessary to the creation of a racially diverse officer corps which, in turn, is essential to the military's ability to fulfill its national security mission.

With respect to its means inquiry, the Court declared that although a race-conscious admissions program could not use a quota system that reserved a fixed number or proportion of opportunities exclusively for minority group members, or put minority group members on separate admissions tracks, it could consider race or ethnicity in a "flexible, nonmechanical way", i.e., by using race or ethnicity as a "plus" factor in the context of individualized consideration of each applicant.

It then found that the Law School's goal of attaining a critical mass of underrepresented minority students, like the Harvard program described in Justice Powell's *Bakke* opinion, met this definition of a narrowly tailored plan. The Court acknowledged that some attention to numbers, such as consultation of reports that keep track of the racial and ethnic composition of the class, did not necessarily transform a flexible system into a forbidden quota. The fact that the percentage of minority students in each class at the Law School varied from 13 to 20%, the Court determined, was inconsistent with the conclusion that the school had adopted a rigid quota. Additionally, the Court found that through its highly individualized, holistic review of the file of applicants of all races that gave substantial weight to other, nonracial diversity factors such as multilingualism, prior career performance, family background, and community service, the Law School policy, unlike the policy governing undergraduate admissions that was addressed and struck down in *Gratz*, *infra*, avoided the pitfall of awarding a mechanical, predetermined diversity "bonus" based solely on race or ethnicity.

The Court also rejected the plaintiff's contention that the defendant's plan was not narrowly tailored because race-neutral means existed to obtain the educational benefits of student body diversity sought by the Law School. Narrow tailoring, the Court announced, required neither the exhaustion of every conceivable race-neutral alternative nor the abandonment of a highly selective admissions process. Rather, it declared, narrow tailoring required serious, good faith consideration of workable race-neutral alternatives that would achieve the sought-after diversity. And, the majority concluded, the Law School had met its burden of considering workable race-neutral alternatives. The Law School's failure to adopt either a lottery system of admissions or a system that placed diminished reliance on grades and LSAT scores was not inconsistent with this determination, the Court explained, because these alternatives would require a dramatic sacrifice of either diversity or the academic quality of admitted students, or both. And the type of "percentage plans" used in California and Texas that guarantee admission to all students above a certain class rank in every high school in the State were not only unworkable for graduate and professional schools, but also might operate to preclude the university from conducting the individualized assessment necessary to assemble a student body diverse along all the qualities valued by the university. Consequently, the Court concluded, the Law School adequately had considered race-neutral alternatives currently capable of producing a critical mass without forcing it to rely on stratagems that would sacrifice the academic selectivity that is the cornerstone of its educational mission.

In keeping with its earlier decisions, the Court added that to be narrowly tailored, a race-conscious program must not unduly burden individuals who are not members of the preferred racial or ethnic groups and must be limited in duration. Since the Law School had considered nonracial elements of diversity, and only had considered race as a plus factor in the context of individualized consideration, its program did not unduly harm nonminority applicants. In the context of higher education, the Court stated, the durational requirement can be met by sunset provisions and periodic reviews to determine whether racial preferences remain necessary to achieve student body diversity. The requirement that all race-conscious admissions programs have a termination point was met in the instant case because the majority took the Law School at its word that it would terminate its race-conscious program as soon as practicable.

Finally, consistent with the language in Justice Powell's opinion in *Bakke* that the prohibitions against racial discrimination in Title VI of the 1964 Civil Rights Act and 42 U.S.C. §1981 were coextensive with the Equal Protection Clause, the Court dismissed the plaintiff's claims under those statutes.

In his dissenting opinion, Chief Justice Rehnquist, joined by Justices Scalia, Kennedy, and Thomas, insisted that the Law School's admission program was not narrowly tailored to its asserted goal of obtaining the educational benefits that flow from a diverse student body by achieving a critical mass of underrepresented minority students. Instead, he characterized it as "a naked effort to achieve racial balancing." Pointing to the fact that the Law School had admitted between 91 and 108 African-Americans between 1995 and 2000, but only between 13 and 19 Native Americans and between 47 and 56 Hispanics during that same period, the Chief Justice maintained that the Law School's failure to offer any race-specific reason for why significantly more individuals from one underrepresented minority group were needed to achieve critical mass demonstrated that its alleged goal of critical mass "is simply a sham." The Chief Justice also based this conclusion on his analysis of the Law School's admission data, which, he reported, demonstrated that the percentage of admitted applicants who were members of each of these three minority groups closely tracked the percentage of members of those same three groups in the school's applicant pool. The tight correlation between the percentage of applicants and admittees of a given race, he surmised, suggested that the Law School was motivated by a plan to ensure that the proportion of each group admitted should be the same as the proportion of that group in the school's applicant pool. And such racial balancing, he concluded, was patently unconstitutional. Finally, Chief Justice Rehnquist criticized the program for its failure to include any reasonably precise time limit, characterizing the school's pledge as "the vaguest of assurances."

Justice Kennedy's separate dissent chastised the majority for according a level of deference to the law school's protestations of lawful purpose and objective that was inconsistent with the strict scrutiny that must be accorded any governmental use of a racial classification. The rest of his opinion focused on the failure of the school's program to meet the means-analysis component of strict scrutiny. In addition to endorsing wholesale the points made by the Chief Justice, Justice Kennedy emphasized the fact that the admissions office's daily consultation of racial breakdown meant that during the last stages of the admissions process, the need to achieve a critical mass of minority students meant the end of individual review of all candidates and the emergence of race/ethnicity as the outcome determinative factor.

Justice Scalia, in an opinion concurring in part and dissenting in part, expressed his concern that the split decision in *Grutter* and *Gratz* meant that the country could look forward to interminable litigation on issues such as whether the admissions scheme in question contained sufficient individualized evaluation of each applicant and avoided separate admissions tracks to fall under *Grutter* rather than *Gratz*.

Like Justice Kennedy, Justice Thomas, in an opinion concurring in part and dissenting in part, criticized the "unprecedented deference" the majority had accorded the Law School as inconsistent with the concept of strict scrutiny. He also maintained that by upholding the use of racial preferences to maintain a diverse student body, rather than acknowledging that the Law School could achieve its vision of a racially diverse student body by such race-neutral policies as accepting all students who met minimum qualifications, the Court was really advancing the Law School's primary interest — that of maintaining its elite, selective status, a concern that did not rise to the level of a compelling state interest. He also pointed to the fact that elite public law schools in Virginia and California had achieved a diverse student body and maintained their elite status without the use of racial preferences.

GRATZ v. BOLLINGER, 539 U.S. 244, 123 S.Ct. 2411, 156 L.Ed.2d 257 (2003), is the undergraduate companion case to *Grutter*. The University of Michigan's Office of Undergraduate Admissions had relied on written guidelines to govern admissions decisions. These guidelines mandated the consideration of a number of factors, including high school grades, standardized test scores, geography, alumni relationships, and race. Applicants received points based on each of these factors, including an automatic 20 points based on membership in an underrepresented racial or ethnic minority group. And though the guidelines did assign twenty points to some other, nonracial variables, the points available for other diversity contributions, such as geographical diversity, leadership, or personal achievement, were capped at much lower levels.

Six members of the Court voted to declare the undergraduate admissions program unconstitutional. The majority opinion, authored by Chief Justice Rehnquist and joined by Justices O'Connor, Scalia, Kennedy and Thomas, relied on the reasoning set forth in *Grutter* to reject the plaintiffs' claim that student body diversity in public higher education was not a compelling state interest that could justify the use of race in student admission decisions. But unlike its ruling in *Grutter*, the majority in *Gratz* concluded that the use of race in the undergraduate admissions policy was not narrowly tailored to accomplish the compelling state interest. It found that a policy that automatically assigned twenty points, i.e., one-fifth of the points needed to guarantee admission, to every member of an underrepresented minority group solely because of race, was not narrowly tailored to achieve the interest in educational diversity. This policy did not provide the individualized consideration mandated in *Grutter* and contemplated by Justice Powell in *Bakke* and had the effect of making the factor of race decisive for virtually every minimally qualified underrepresented minority applicant.

The majority also declined to accept the defendant's contention that the volume of applications at the undergraduate level made it impractical to use the individualized admission system upheld in *Grutter*. The fact that implementation of a program capable of providing individualized consideration might present administrative challenges to the university was not a sufficient justification for failing to meet the Grutter standard of a narrowly tailored use of race in student admissions. Having found, therefore, that the University of Michigan's use of race in its undergraduate admissions policy violated the Equal Protection Clause of the Fourteenth Amendment, the Court also found the policy violative of both Title VI of the 1964 Civil Rights Act and 42 U.S.C. §1981.

Justice Breyer wrote a brief separate opinion concurring in the judgment of the Court but not joining in its opinion. Justices Stevens, Souter and Ginsburg dissented. Justice Stevens did not address the merits, concluding instead that the case should be dismissed for lack of standing. Since both of the plaintiffs had enrolled at other schools before filing this class action complaint for prospective relief and neither had reapplied for admission to the University of Michigan at the time the suit was filed or thereafter, Justice Stevens concluded that neither plaintiff had a personal stake in the outcome of the case and neither had standing to seek prospective relief on behalf of unidentified class members who might or might not have standing to litigate on their own behalf.

Justices Souter and Ginsburg agreed with Stevens on the standing question but added that even if the merits were reachable, they would dissent from the majority's decision. Justice Souter characterized the undergraduate admissions guidelines as closer to what *Grutter* approved than to what *Bakke* condemned. In contrast to the outlawed plan in *Bakke* that focused solely on ethnic diversity, the instant plan considered both racial and nonracial factors related to diversity, even if they were not all accorded the same weight.

Justice Ginsburg restated her call for an intermediate level of constitutional scrutiny for "benign" racial classifications designed to ameliorate the effects of entrenched discrimination. Applying this less-than-strict scrutiny standard, Justice Ginsburg concluded that the university's undergraduate admissions guidelines passed constitutional muster.

With its repeated references to the end of achieving student body diversity, to what extent will or should the ruling in *Grutter* extend to the employment sphere? After all, is the Court's ruling that racial and ethnic diversity in a public university's student body is a compelling state interest necessarily transferable to the employment arena, whether in public higher education or other public sector jobs? In PETIT v. CITY OF CHICAGO, 352 F.3d 1111 (7th Cir.2003), cert. denied, 541 U.S. 1074, 124 S.Ct. 2426, 158 L.Ed.2d 984 (2004), the Seventh Circuit transplanted the Supreme Court's analysis to a case involving an equal protection challenge to a city police department's use of affirmative action in promotion decisions. Noting that the *Grutter* Court had determined that achieving diversity (as opposed to remedying prior acts of discrimination) was a compelling state interest in the University admissions context, the Seventh Circuit concluded that there was "an even more compelling need for diversity in a large metropolitan force charged with protecting a racially and ethnically divided major American city like Chicago." Similarly, just as the Court had deferred to the University of Michigan's judgment that diversity was essential to its educational mission, the Seventh Circuit ruled that it was proper to defer to the view of experts and police department executives that the city's operational need for a diverse police department met the compelling state interest test. Specifically, it held, the city had a compelling interest in a diverse pool of sergeants to both set a proper tone within the department and to earn the trust of the external community.

Finally, with respect to the means-oriented, second phase of strict scrutiny, i.e., whether the use of race-based affirmative action was sufficiently narrowly tailored to satisfy the identified compelling state interest, the court similarly looked to the teachings of both *Grutter* and *Gratz*. The City's promotion exam had a demonstrated adverse impact on African-American and Hispanic candidates and it already was under a federal court order not to promote officers on unvalidated rank-order exams. Since the City was unable to validate the promotion exam in question, it chose to standardize the scores based on race to produce results that reflected the scores a candidate would have received if the test had not had an adverse racial impact. All of the African-American and Hispanic patrol officers who received promotions pursuant to their rank order after standardization had obtained an unstandardized score above the passing level. Accordingly, the court held, standardization did not operate as a deciding factor for only minimally qualified minority applicants, the defect that rendered the affirmative action plan in *Gratz* unconstitutional. Rather, it concluded, standardizing the test results merely eliminated an advantage the white officers had on the test. The court also found that the race-conscious promotions met the other *Grutter* standards because the system employed by the city minimized harm to members of the nonpreferred group and was limited in duration. Consequently, it upheld the constitutionality of the city's affirmative action.

The Court revisited the issue of the extent to which promoting diversity in education can constitute a compelling interest at the end of its 2007-2007 term. In PARENTS INVOLVED IN COMMUNITY SCHOOLS v. SEATTLE SCHOOL DISTRICT NO.1, 551 U.S. 701, 127 S.Ct. 2738, 168 L.Ed.2d 508 (2007), a 5-4 majority overturned the voluntary decision by two school districts to use race to assign certain students to public elementary and secondary schools to promote the racial diversity of their student bodies. One of these school districts had never operated legally segregated schools and the other had been declared unitary by a federal court prior to implementing this race-based assignment policy. The majority distinguished the instant cases from *Grutter* on the ground that in *Grutter* race was but one of several factors going into the diversity assessment; whereas race was, for some students in the instant case, determinative of the diversity calculation. The majority also noted that the instant case involved elementary and secondary schools, whereas the decision in *Grutter* relied upon considerations "unique to institutions of higher education." And though the majority noted that some circuit courts had extended the ruling in *Grutter* to race-based assignment plans in primary and secondary schools, it nevertheless declared that the instant cases "are not governed by *Grutter*." The opinion, written by Chief Justice Roberts, then turned to an analysis of whether the plan was justified by a compelling state interest and whether, if so, it was narrowly tailored. But Justice Kennedy declined to join those parts of the opinion, thereby rendering it the opinion of a four member plurality.

The plurality determined that the numerical benchmarks for achieving diversity in both student assignment plans were tied exclusively to the racial demographics of the districts's respective locations, rather than to the degree of diversity that would achieve those educational and social benefits flowing from diversity. Accordingly, the districts's reliance on race was an (unconstitutional) attempt at racial balancing that was not narrowly tailored to achieving the asserted compelling interest of attaining the educational benefits of a diverse (broadly defined to encompass race and other characteristics) student body. The plurality also declared that the districts had failed to establish that they had considered methods other than "explicit" racial classifications to achieve the stated goals. Justice Kennedy, on the other hand, concluded that achieving a racially diverse student body and overcoming racial isolation in public schools did constitute compelling interests. He concurred in the judgment, however, because he agreed with the plurality that the districts had not convinced him that their use of race was narrowly tailored to accomplish that objective. He concurred in the plurality's determination that the small number of student assignments actually affected by the use of race suggested that the schools could have achieved their desired result through the use of non-racial criteria. In his view, before the state could rely on race as one criterion to accomplish these compelling interests, other non-racial factors "must be exhausted."

Justice Kennedy did join, however, in that part of the Chief Justice's opinion for the Court that characterized the Court's prior rulings as recognizing that remedying the effects of past intentional discrimination qualified as a compelling state interest that would justify the use of a narrowly tailored racial classification. Does this suggest that *Croson* should now be construed to sanction the use of race to remedy the present effects of past discrimination only when that discrimination took the form of intentional bias and not when the defendant was shown to have relied upon a facially neutral criterion that produced a disproportionate exclusionary impact on a particular racial group? Post-*Croson*, but pre-*Seattle School District*, the circuit courts had split on this question. *Compare* Stuart v. Roache, 951 F.2d 446 (1st Cir. 1991), cert. denied, 504 U.S. 913, 112 S.Ct. 1948, 118 L.Ed.2d 553 (1992) (*Croson* permits the use of race to respond to impact discrimination) *with* Biondo v. Chicago, 382 F.3d 680 (7th Cir. 2004) (*Croson* authorizes using race to remedy only intentional discrimination; responding to disproportionate impact is not a compelling state interest).

Recall that in *Grutter* and *Gratz* the Court deferred to the defendant state university's determination that the objective of attaining of a diverse student body constituted a compelling state interest for Equal Protection Purposes. Subsequently, in FISHER v. UNIVERSITY OF TEXAS AT AUSTIN, 570 U.S. 297, 133 S.Ct. 2411, 186 L.Ed.2d 474 (2013), by a 7-1 vote (Justice Kagan did not participate), the Court added that such deference was not appropriate to the second half of the strict scrutiny standard applied to all governmental uses of race or ethnicity-based criteria. In determining whether the use of race was narrowly tailored to achieve the compelling state interest of attaining a diverse student body, the Court declared, it was the judiciary's obligation to undertake "careful judicial scrutiny into whether a university could achieve sufficient diversity without using racial classifications." The majority quickly noted that such scrutiny does not require the University to establish that it exhausted every conceivable race-neutral alternative before explicitly relying on a racial classification. Rather, the Court continued, it was the judiciary's task to examine "with care, and not defer to" a university's "serious, good faith consideration of workable race-neutral alternatives." To meet the strict scrutiny standard, the university must convince the court that "no workable race-neutral alternatives would produce the educational benefits of diversity." If a race-neutral strategy could promote the diversity objective "about as well and at tolerable administrative expense", the Court continued, then the university's reliance on race would contravene the dictates of the Equal Protection Clause of the Fourteenth Amendment. The Court of Appeals in this case had limited its consideration to determining whether the university's use of race had been in "good faith" and, moreover, had presumed that the University acted in good faith and therefore required the plaintiff to rebut that presumption. This, the Court held, was inconsistent with its formulation of the "narrowly tailored" portion of the strict scrutiny standard applicable to all governmental uses of racial classifications. Accordingly, it vacated the lower court's grant of summary judgment in favor of the defendant and remanded for reconsideration by that court under the Court's articulated standard.

On remand, the Fifth Circuit ruled that it was unnecessary for it to remand the case to the trial court since, in the appellate court's opinion, there were no new issues of fact to be resolved, nor was there any need for additional discovery. Thus, turning to the merits, the panel explained that its "narrowly tailored" inquiry did not require the defendant to exhaust every racial neutral alternative, but, rather, to establish that it undertook "serious, good faith consideration of workable race-neutral alternatives". It then found that the original state statutory, race-neutral "Top Ten Percent" Law had not produced a sufficient number of minority students (the "critical mass") requisite to diversity until race and ethnicity were added to this "holistic" review process. The University's limited use of race and ethnicity in this holistic review, the panel concluded, was "nearly indistinguishable" from the policy of the University of Michigan Law School that the Supreme Court had upheld in *Grutter*. Consequently, the court held, this policy was sufficiently narrowly tailored to pass equal protection scrutiny. 758 F.3d 633 (5th Cir. 2014). This time, on appeal, the Supreme Court affirmed the circuit court by a 4-3 vote (Justice Kagan again recused herself and the case was decided after the death of Justice Scalia and before any new appointment was made). Fisher v. University of Texas at Austin (*Fisher II*), 579 U.S. ___, 136 S.Ct. 2198, 195 L.Ed.2d 511 (2016).

The majority in *Fisher II* derived three governing principles from its earlier ruling in *Fisher I*. First, that the strict scrutiny that must be applied to this governmental use of race requires a two step judicial analysis: (1) assessment of whether the objective of the race-as-a-factor program is constitutionally substantial; and (2) a determination of whether the use of race is necessary to accomplish that objective. Second, with respect to the first of these two components of strict scrutiny, "some, but not complete" deference must be given to a public university's determination that a diverse student body serves its educational goals once the university has offered a principled explanation for that decision. And third, that in applying the second prong of strict scrutiny – whether the use of race is narrowly tailored to attaining the permissible goals – no judicial deference is owed to the defendant's judgment. Rather, the defendant bears the burden of persuading the court that a nonracial approach would not promote its interest "about as well [as a race-based approach] and at tolerable administrative expense." Reciting language from *Grutter*, the majority in *Fisher II* reiterated that to meet that burden, the university was not required to establish that it had exhausted every conceivable race-neutral approach or choose between maintaining a reputation for excellence and providing educational opportunities to members of all racial groups. Rather, the university had to establish that available and workable race-neutral alternatives did not suffice to meet its diversity-based objectives.

Applying these standards to the instant facts, the Court concluded that the university had sufficiently documented the bases for determining that educational benefits flowed from a diverse student body and had offered a principled explanation for its decision to pursue those educational objectives. The majority also concluded that the University had established that the use of race-neutral policies and programs had not been successful in accomplishing those permissible objectives; that its race-as-a-factor policy did have a meaningful "if still limited" impact on the diversity of the its student body; and that none of the plaintiff's proposed race-neutral alternatives (including a proposal to lift the 75% cap on the race-neutral Top Ten Percent Plan) was a workable means to attain the benefits that it sought to derive from student body diversity. Finally, while upholding the admissions policy's limited use of race as a factor in filling those 25% of the student body slots that were not reserved to the Top Ten Percent Plan, the Court advised the University to continue to monitor its student data to systematically and periodically review whether continuation of the race-conscious policy is necessary to achieve its educational objectives.

As a result of the Supreme Court's ruling in *Gratz*, the University of Michigan revised its undergraduate admissions program, although the revised version continued to contain a modified form of race-based preference. In response to that decision, Michigan voters approved a constitutional amendment banning all state universities from granting preferences, including race-based preferences, in admissions and other decisions. Ironically, the moving force behind this amendment was Jennifer Gratz, the plaintiff who had won a personal victory in *Gratz v. Bollinger*, but who had had lost on the larger question when the Court in *Grutter v. Bollinger* generally upheld the University's consideration of race as a factor in admissions. The Sixth Circuit, sitting *en banc*, affirmed the appellate panel decision which had upheld the constitutional amendment.   In SCHUETTE v. COALITION TO DEFEND AFFIRMATIVE ACTION, 572 U.S. 291, 134 S.Ct. 1623, 188 L.Ed.2d 613 (2014), a six member majority (a plurality of three signed onto the opinion of the Court with a concurring opinion joined in by Justices Scalia and Thomas and another concurrence written by Justice Breyer) of the Court (Justice Kagan recused herself) reversed the Sixth Circuit, expressly rejecting that court's reliance on the "political process doctrine" that the circuit court had read as emanating from three prior Supreme Court rulings. The Sixth Circuit interpreted these three prior opinions to mean that a State could not change the governmental decision-making process by removing authority from political officials to address racial issues in a way that burden the interest of minority groups. Such a broad statement of law, the opinion of the Court announced, went beyond the necessary holding of those cases and also created its own constitutional problems by, *inter alia*, removing from the people their fundamental right of self-governance. To say that the question of how to resolve racial issues was beyond the capacity of voters was, the plurality declared, demeaning to the democratic process. Consequently, the Court emphasized, its ruling did not touch on the constitutionality of governmental use of race-based preferences, but, rather, only on the question of whether voters could be restricted in their ability to prohibit governmental use of racial preferences. The issue was not how the debate over racial preferences was to be resolved, but about who can resolve it. "There is no authority in the Constitution of the United States or in this Court's precedents," the Court concluded, "for the judiciary to set aside * * * laws that commit this policy determination to the voters." Justices Scalia and Thomas agreed with the plurality's rejection of the political process doctrine. Justice Breyer voted to uphold the Michigan amendment solely on the limited basis that the U.S. Constitution did not prohibit a state from moving decision-making from an unelected administrative body (the State University trustees and administrators) to a politically responsive one (the voters) with respect to a race-conscious admissions program that considered race solely in order to obtain the educational benefits derived from a diverse student body.

4. Would the result in *Croson* have changed if Croson had filed a timely bid with the appropriate level of minority subcontracting, but had lost out on the contract because his total bid was not the lowest bid received by the city? In other words, would this have affected Croson's standing to bring this action? In NORTHEASTERN FLORIDA CHAPTER OF THE ASSOCIATED GENERAL CONTRACTORS OF AMERICA v. CITY OF JACKSONVILLE, 508 U.S. 656, 113 S.Ct. 2297, 124 L.Ed.2d 586 (1993), the Supreme Court examined the application of its traditional three part standing requirement to equal protection challenges to municipal "set-aside" ordinances. In *Northeastern*, the defendant City had passed an ordinance requiring that 10% of the total amount spent annually on city contracts be set aside for MBE's. Once projects were earmarked for MBE bidding, they were deemed reserved solely for MBE's. The plaintiff association was composed of construction firms, most of which did not qualify as MBE's under the city ordinance. The trial court had granted summary judgment in favor of the plaintiffs on the ground that the plan violated the equal protection guarantees of the Fourteenth Amendment. The Eleventh Circuit panel reversed, but instead of addressing the merits of the constitutional claim, ordered the trial court to dismiss the complaint on the ground that the plaintiff association lacked standing since it had not alleged that any one of its members would have successfully bid for any contract in the absence of the set-aside ordinance. In opposing the plaintiff's motion for summary judgment and in its cross-motion for summary judgment, the City had never challenged the plaintiff's standing. The Supreme Court (by a 7-2 vote with the two dissenters not addressing the standing question) reversed the Eleventh Circuit and found that the association had standing to bring this action. In his opinion for the Court, Justice Thomas stated that the "injury in fact" element of the Court's well established tripartite standard for standing only required that the plaintiff allege that it had wished to be considered for the benefit that was subject to the challenged governmental requirement. Relying on, *inter alia*, its ruling in *Bakke*, Justice Thomas noted that the Court had never required the plaintiff to establish that it would have received the benefit in the absence of the challenged preference. Rather, Justice Thomas declared,

> these cases stand for the following proposition: When the government erects a barrier that makes it more difficult for members of one group to obtain a benefit than it is for members of another group, a member of the former group seeking to challenge the barrier need not allege that he would have obtained the benefit but for the barrier in order to establish standing. The "injury in fact" in an equal protection case of this variety is the denial of equal treatment resulting from the imposition of the barrier, not the ultimate inability to obtain the benefit.

5. As the material in Notes 1 and 2 indicates, the Court, in *Croson*, finally achieved majority agreement on the level of scrutiny to be applied in an equal protection challenge to a remedial affirmative action plan. The Note materials also indicate, however, that the *Croson* Court clearly sought to distinguish its constitutional analysis from the approach it had taken in *Fullilove* on the ground that *Croson* involved an equal protection challenge to a racially-based set-aside enacted by a local legislature, rather than by Congress. The relatively broad language in Croson, however, suggested that the Court might subsequently extend strict scrutiny analysis to a federally promulgated affirmative action plan.

The Court explicitly rejected such an extension of strict scrutiny, however, by a vote of 5-4 in METRO BROADCASTING, INC. v. FEDERAL COMMUNICATIONS COMMISSION, 497 U.S. 547, 110 S.Ct. 2997, 111 L.Ed.2d 445 (1990). In *Metro Broadcasting*, the Court was asked to rule on an equal protection challenge to two minority preference policies that had been adopted by the Federal Communications Commission. The FCC was granted exclusive authority to grant broadcast licenses based on the public interest by the terms of the Communications Act of 1934. Pursuant to this authority, and after holding hearings and conferences on minority ownership policies, the FCC adopted a Statement of Policy on Minority Ownership of Broadcasting Facilities which included two provisions intended to improve the opportunity for minority businesses to obtain broadcast licenses. The first provision stated that in comparative proceedings for new licenses it would consider minority ownership and participation in management as a plus factor to be weighed with all other relevant factors. Second, the Commission announced a plan to increase minority opportunities to receive reassigned and transferred licenses by creating an exception to its general rule forbidding the transfer of a license by a licensee whose qualifications to maintain its license had come under question. Under this provision, a licensee who was willing to sell the license at a "distress sale" could assign the license, but only to an FCC-approved minority enterprise. Each of these preferences was challenged as violative of the Fifth Amendment guarantee of equal protection.

The Court began its analysis by emphasizing that this FCC policy encouraging minority ownership was specifically approved and, in fact, mandated by Congress. (Congress had enacted and the President had signed FCC appropriations bills for fiscal years 1988 and 1989 that prohibited the Commission from spending any appropriated funds to examine or change its minority ownership policies.) Thus, the five member majority (Brennan, Marshall, Blackmun, White and Stevens) reasoned, this case was closer to *Fullilove* than it was to *Croson*. The majority then stated that strict scrutiny had not been applied by a majority in *Fullilove* because the racial classification in that case had been adopted by Congress and that *Croson* did not prescribe the level of scrutiny to be applied to a benign racial classification employed by Congress. In the critical sentence of the opinion, the majority then stated that "benign race-conscious measures mandated by Congress — even if those measures are not 'remedial' in the sense of being designed to compensate victims of past governmental or societal discrimination — are constitutionally permissible to the extent that they serve important governmental objectives within the power of Congress and are substantially related to achievement of those objectives."

In her dissenting opinion, Justice O'Connor (joined by Justices Scalia, Kennedy and the Chief Justice) lamented that the majority's analysis "marks a renewed toleration of racial classifications" and that the application of a lessened equal protection standard to congressional actions "finds no support in our cases or in the Constitution." She maintained that the equal protection guarantee in the Fifth Amendment compelled application of the same level of scrutiny to racial classifications employed by Congressional enactments as the Fourteenth Amendment required with respect to racial preferences adopted by state and local governments. Moreover, she emphasized, a lessened standard of scrutiny was applied in *Fullilove* because the racial classification was adopted pursuant to Congress' exercise of its powers under §5 of the Fourteenth Amendment and because the classification was used to remedy identified past discrimination, neither of which factor existed in the instant case. She also expressed her dissatisfaction with the majority's characterization of the racial preference as "benign," a term she found to be indeterminate, at best.

The FCC policy upheld in *Metro Broadcasting* also contained a gender preference in its comparative licensing program. This preference, which made female ownership and participation a "plus factor" in comparative hearings, was not before the Court in *Metro*. It was, however, addressed and struck down as violative of the Equal Protection Clause of the Fifth Amendment by the D.C. Circuit (in an opinion written by then-Judge Thomas). In LAMPRECHT v. FCC, 958 F.2d 382 (D.C. Cir.1992), the appellate court applied the intermediate scrutiny standard employed in *Metro Broadcasting* and found that there was insufficient evidence to establish that granting preferences to women would increase programming diversity. Accordingly, the majority concluded, the gender preference was not "substantially related to achieving" the government's legitimate interest in achieving diversity of viewpoints. The court distinguished this case from *Metro Broadcasting* on the ground that although there was a "host of empirical evidence" supporting the judgment linking minority ownership of stations with the stations' programming practices, there was no "statistically meaningful" proof supporting the Commission's judgment that women owners would broadcast women's or minority or any other underrepresented type of programming at any different rate than male owners. With the elevation of Justice Thomas to the Supreme Court, the four dissenters in *Metro Broadcasting*, now commanded a majority of votes on the Court. In ADARAND CONSTRUCTORS, INC. v. PENA,

512 U.S. 1288, 115 S.Ct. 2097, 132 L.Ed.2d 158 (1995), the Court's newly constituted majority reversed *Metro Broadcasting*. In an opinion authored by Justice O'Connor, the Court repudiated *Metro Broadcasting* for "turning its back on *Croson's* explanation of why strict scrutiny of all governmental racial classifications is essential," and as a departure from the Court's prior adherence to the principles of "congruence between the standards applicable to federal and state racial classifications," of "skepticism of all racial classifications," and "consistency of treatment irrespective of the race of the burdened or benefited group." Accordingly, over the dissent joined in by Justices Stevens, Souter, Ginsburg, and Breyer, the majority ruled that "all racial classifications, imposed by whatever federal, state or local governmental actor, must be analyzed by a reviewing court under strict scrutiny."

Although the majority in *Adarand* reversed that part of the ruling in *Metro Broadcasting* in which the Court had ruled that intermediate scrutiny could apply to a federally-imposed "benign" racial preference, it did not expressly rule on the *Metro Broadcasting* Court's determination that the FCC interest in promoting diversity justified its use of a racial preference. Presumably, the Court's acceptance of the diversity justification in *Metro Broadcasting* was influenced by the fact that it did not apply strict scrutiny and, therefore, did not have the find the government's interest to be "compelling."

In response to the Court's ruling in *Adarand*, the U.S. Justice Department issued regulations on March 1, 1996, intended to provide guidance to federal agencies on their use of affirmative action. In light of the language in *Adarand* that requires race-based decision-making to be subjected to strict scrutiny, the guidelines provide that the goal of affirmative action "cannot be diversity for diversity's sake." Rather, diversity must be "rooted in an identifiable and articulated operational need for diversity of opinion in the agency's workforce." Where an agency has a basis for believing that greater workforce diversity will enhance its performance, race and ethnicity can be considered in promoting diversity of perspectives. However, the agencies are directed not to rely solely on racial or ethnic stereotypes to obtain diversity. The Justice Department suggests that factors other than race and ethnicity, such as geography, education and work experience, be considered.

Could it be argued, however, that since the FCC policy does not require racially-based hiring but, rather, merely requires stations to use recruiting sources that provide minority candidates, to produce evaluations of the availability of minorities and women in its recruiting areas and to provide a written analysis of its efforts to recruit, hire and promote minorities and women, that these limited racially-based actions do not constitute race-conscious "hiring decisions," and, as such, need not be subjected to strict scrutiny under Adarand? This argument confronted the D.C. Circuit Court of Appeals in LUTHERAN CHURCH-MISSOURI SYNOD v. FEDERAL COMMUNI-CATIONS COMMISSION, 141 F.3d 344 (D.C. Cir. 1998). The court cautiously sidestepped the issue by ruling that this policy effectively extended beyond outreach efforts to influence ultimate hiring decisions since the entire reporting scheme was predicated on the notion that stations should aspire to a workforce that at least approaches proportional representation and pressured stations to achieve a workforce that mirrored the racial composition of its recruiting area. Then, the court added, "we do not think it matters whether a government hiring program imposes hard quotas, soft quotas, or goals. Any one of these techniques induces an employer to hire with an eye toward meeting the numerical target. As such, they can and surely will result in individuals being granted a preference because of their race." The court read *Adarand* to require the invocation of strict scrutiny for all governmental action based on race. In a supplemental opinion denying the defendant's petition for rehearing, the panel reemphasized that it had not addressed the issue of whether an outreach program targeted on minorities that does not involve any degree of government pressure to grant a racial preference in hiring would be subject to strict scrutiny. 154 F.3d 487 (D.C. Cir. 1998).

6. Although some state and local jurisdictions sought to implement racial preferences consistent with the constitutional limits set forth in *Croson* and *Adarand*, others responded by seeking to ban the use of gender and/or race-based preferences in public programs such as employment, education and contracting. Would a state statute or constitutional provision precluding the use of race or gender-based preferences in all governmental decisionmaking withstand constitutional scrutiny? Does the fact that the Constitution permits the use of race-based remedies to respond to prior acts of discrimination mean that a state cannot preclude the use of such remedies in response to prior discrimination? In COALITION FOR ECONOMIC EQUITY v. WILSON, 122 F.3d 692 (9th Cir.), cert. denied, 522 U.S. 963, 118 S.Ct. 397, 139 L.Ed.2d 310 (1997), the appellate court vacated the preliminary injunction issued by the trial court against the enforcement of a state constitutional amendment which prohibited the state from granting preferential treatment to any individual or group on the basis of race, sex, color, ethnicity or national origin. The appellate court held that the trial judge had erred in determining that the plaintiffs had demonstrated a likelihood of success on their two claims. The district judge had ruled that the state constitutional amendment (1) violated the fourteenth amendment equal protection clause, and (2) was invalid under the Supremacy Clause because it violated the terms of Title VII. With respect to the constitutional question, the appellate panel reasoned that the amendment prohibited the State from classifying individuals by race or gender, *a fortiori* it did not classify individuals on that basis and, therefore, could not, as a matter of law, violate the Equal Protection Clause of the Fourteenth Amendment "in any conventional sense." The court also rejected the plaintiffs' argument that because this amendment burdened members of insular minorities who otherwise would seek "preferential treatment", it deprived them of their right to equal protection under the laws. In the court's judgment, when a state prohibits all its instrumentalities from discriminating against or granting preferential treatment to anyone on the basis of race or gender, it has operated in a race and gender-neutral fashion that does not violate the equal protection clause. Finally, the court held that the amendment was not preempted by Title VII because it did not require the commission of any act that was prohibited by Title VII.

The Supreme Court addressed the interplay between Title VII and voluntary private-sector affirmative action in the following landmark case:

United Steelworkers of America v. Weber

Supreme Court of the United States, 1979.
443 U.S. 193, 99 S.Ct. 2721, 61 L.Ed.2d 480.

MR. JUSTICE BRENNAN delivered the opinion of the Court.

Challenged here is the legality of an affirmative action plan — collectively bargained by an employer and a union — that reserves for black employees 50% of the openings in an in-plant craft-training program until the percentage of black craftworkers in the plant is commensurate with the percentage of blacks in the local labor force. The question for decision is whether Congress, in Title VII of the Civil Rights Act of 1964, left employers and unions in the private sector free to take such race-conscious steps to eliminate manifest racial imbalances in traditionally segregated job categories. We hold that Title VII does not prohibit such race-conscious affirmative action plans.

I

In 1974, petitioner United Steelworkers of America (USWA) and petitioner Kaiser Aluminum & Chemical Corp. (Kaiser) entered into a master collective-bargaining agreement covering terms and conditions of employment at 15 Kaiser plants. The agreement contained, inter alia, an affirmative action plan designed to eliminate conspicuous racial imbalances in Kaiser's then almost exclusively white craftwork forces. Black craft-hiring goals were set for each Kaiser plant equal to the percentage of blacks in the respective local labor forces. To enable plants to meet these goals, on-the-job training programs were established to teach unskilled production workers — black and white — the skills necessary to become craftworkers. The plan reserved for black employees 50% of the openings in these newly created in-plant training programs.

This case arose from the operation of the plan at Kaiser's plant in Gramercy, La. Until 1974, Kaiser hired as craftworkers for that plant only persons who had had prior craft experience. Because blacks had long been excluded from craft unions,[1] few were able to present such credentials. As a consequence, prior to 1974 only 1.83% (5 out of 273) of the skilled craftworkers at the Gramercy plant were black, even though the work force in the Gramercy area was approximately 39% black.

Pursuant to the national agreement Kaiser altered its craft-hiring practice in the Gramercy plant. Rather than hiring already trained outsiders, Kaiser established a training program to train its production workers to fill craft openings. Selection of craft trainees was made on the basis of seniority, with the proviso that at least 50% of the new trainees were to be black until the percentage of black skilled craftworkers in the Gramercy plant approximated the percentage of blacks in the local labor force.

During 1974, the first year of the operation of the Kaiser-USWA affirmative action plan, 13 craft trainees were selected from Gramercy's production work force. Of these, seven were black and six white. The most senior black selected into the program had less seniority than several white production workers whose bids for

---

[1] Judicial findings of exclusion from crafts on racial grounds are so numerous as to make such exclusion a proper subject for judicial notice.

admission were rejected. Thereafter one of those white production workers, respondent Brian Weber (hereafter respondent), instituted this class action in the United States District Court for the Eastern District of Louisiana.

The complaint alleged that the filling of craft trainee positions at the Gramercy plant pursuant to the affirmative action program had resulted in junior black employees' receiving training in preference to senior white employees, thus discriminating against respondent and other similarly situated white employees in violation of §§703(a) and (d) of Title VII. The District Court held that the plan violated Title VII, entered a judgment in favor of the plaintiff class, and granted a permanent injunction prohibiting Kaiser and the USWA "from denying plaintiffs, Brian F. Weber and all other members of the class, access to on-the-job training programs on the basis of race." A divided panel of the Court of Appeals for the Fifth Circuit affirmed, holding that all employment preferences based upon race, including those preferences incidental to bona fide affirmative action plans, violated Title VII's prohibition against racial discrimination in employment. * * * We reverse.

II

We emphasize at the outset the narrowness of our inquiry. Since the Kaiser-USWA plan does not involve state action, this case does not present an alleged violation of the Equal Protection Clause of the Fourteenth Amendment. Further, since the Kaiser-USWA plan was adopted voluntarily, we are not concerned with what Title VII requires or with what a court might order to remedy a past proved violation of the Act. The only question before us is the narrow statutory issue of whether Title VII forbids private employers and unions from voluntarily agreeing upon bona fide affirmative action plans that accord racial preferences in the manner and for the purpose provided in the Kaiser-USWA plan. That question was expressly left open in McDonald v. Santa Fe Trail Transp. Co., 427 U.S. 273, 281 n. 8, 96 S.Ct. 2574, 2579, 49 L.Ed.2d 493 (1976), which held, in a case not involving affirmative action, that Title VII protects whites as well as blacks from certain forms of racial discrimination.

Respondent argues that Congress intended in Title VII to prohibit all race-conscious affirmative action plans. Respondent's argument rests upon a literal interpretation of §§703(a) and (d) of the Act. Those sections make it unlawful to "discriminate * * * because of * * * race" in hiring and in the selection of apprentices for training programs. Since, the argument runs, McDonald settled that Title VII forbids discrimination against whites as well as blacks, and since the Kaiser-USWA affirmative action plan operates to discriminate against white employees solely because they are white, it follows that the Kaiser-USWA plan violates Title VII.

Respondent's argument is not without force. But it overlooks the significance of the fact that the Kaiser-USWA plan is an affirmative action plan voluntarily adopted by private parties to eliminate traditional patterns of racial segregation. In this context respondent's reliance upon a literal construction of §§703(a) and (d) and upon McDonald is misplaced. It is a "familiar rule, that a thing may be within the letter of the statute and yet not within the statute, because not within its spirit, nor within the intention of its makers." Holy Trinity Church v. United States, 143 U.S. 457, 459, 12 S.Ct. 511, 512, 36 L.Ed. 226 (1892). The prohibition against racial discrimination in §§703(a) and (d) of Title VII must therefore be read against the background of the legislative history of Title VII and the historical context from which the Act arose.

Examination of those sources makes clear that an interpretation of the sections that forbade all race-conscious affirmative action would "bring about an end completely at variance with the purpose of the statute" and must be rejected.

Congress' primary concern in enacting the prohibition against racial discrimination in Title VII of the Civil Rights Act of 1964 was with "the plight of the Negro in our economy." 110 Cong. Rec. 6548 (1964) (remarks of Sen. Humphrey). Before 1964, blacks were largely relegated to "unskilled and semi-skilled jobs." Because of automation the number of such jobs was rapidly decreasing. As a consequence, "the relative position of the Negro worker [was] steadily worsening. * * *." *Id.,* at 6547.

Congress feared that the goals of the Civil Rights Act — the integration of blacks into the mainstream of American society — could not be achieved unless this trend were reversed. And Congress recognized that that would not be possible unless blacks were able to secure jobs "which have a future." *Id.,* at 7204 (remarks of Sen. Clark). * * * Accordingly, it was clear to Congress that "[t]he crux of the problem [was] to open employment opportunities for Negroes in occupations which have been traditionally closed to them," *Id.,* at 6548 (remarks of Sen. Humphrey) and it was to this problem that Title VII's prohibition against racial discrimination in employment was primarily addressed.

It plainly appears from the House Report accompanying the Civil Rights Act that Congress did not intend wholly to prohibit private and voluntary affirmative action efforts as one method of solving this problem. The Report provides:

> "No bill can or should lay claim to eliminating all of the causes and consequences of racial and other types of discrimination against minorities. There is reason to believe, however, that national leadership provided by the enactment of Federal legislation dealing with the most troublesome problems will create an atmosphere conducive to voluntary or local resolution of other forms of discrimination."

Given this legislative history, we cannot agree with respondent that Congress intended to prohibit the private sector from taking effective steps to accomplish the goal that Congress designed Title VII to achieve. The very statutory words intended as a spur or catalyst to cause "employers and unions to self-examine and to self-evaluate their employment practices and to endeavor to eliminate, so far as possible, the last vestiges of an unfortunate and ignominious page in this country's history," Albemarle Paper Co. v. Moody, 422 U.S. 405, 418, 95 S.Ct. 2362, 2372, 45 L.Ed.2d 280 (1975), cannot be interpreted as an absolute prohibition against all private, voluntary, race-conscious affirmative action efforts to hasten the elimination of such vestiges. It would be ironic indeed if a law triggered by a Nation's concern over centuries of racial injustice and intended to improve the lot of those who had "been excluded from the American dream for so long," constituted the first legislative prohibition of all voluntary, private, race-conscious efforts to abolish traditional patterns of racial segregation and hierarchy.

Our conclusion is further reinforced by examination of the language and legislative history of §703(j) of Title VII. Opponents of Title VII raised two related arguments against the bill. First, they argued that the Act would be interpreted to require employers with racially imbalanced work forces to grant preferential treatment to racial minorities in order to integrate. Second, they argued that employers with racially imbalanced work forces would grant preferential treatment to racial minorities, even if not required to do so by the Act. Had Congress meant to prohibit all race-conscious affirmative action, as respondent urges, it easily could have answered both objections by providing that Title VII would not require or permit racially preferential integration efforts. But Congress did not choose such a course. Rather Congress added §703(j) which addresses only the first objection. The section provides that nothing contained in Title VII "shall be interpreted to require any employer * * * to grant preferential treatment * * * to any group because of the race * * * of such * * * group on account of" a de facto racial imbalance in the employer's work force. The section does *not* state that "nothing in Title VII shall be interpreted to *permit*" voluntary affirmative efforts to correct racial imbalances. The natural inference is that Congress chose not to forbid all voluntary race-conscious affirmative action.

The reasons for this choice are evident from the legislative record. Title VII could not have been enacted into law without substantial support from legislators in both Houses who traditionally resisted federal regulation of private business. Those legislators demanded as a price for their support that "management prerogatives, and union freedoms * * * be left undisturbed to the greatest extent possible." H. R. Rep. No. 914, 88th Cong., 1st Sess., pt. 2, p. 29 (1963). Section 703(j) was proposed by Senator Dirksen to allay any fears that the Act might be interpreted in such a way as to upset this compromise. The section was designed to prevent §703 of Title VII from being interpreted in such a way as to lead to undue "Federal Government interference with private businesses because of some Federal employee's ideas about racial balance or racial imbalance." Clearly, a prohibition against all voluntary, race-conscious, affirmative action efforts would disserve these ends. Such a prohibition would augment the powers of the Federal Government and diminish traditional management prerogatives while at the same time impeding attainment of the ultimate statutory goals. In view of this legislative history and in view of Congress' desire to avoid undue federal regulation of private businesses, use of the word "require" rather than the phrase "require or permit" in §703(j) fortifies the conclusion that Congress did not intend to limit traditional business freedom to such a degree as to prohibit all voluntary, race-conscious affirmative action.

We therefore hold that Title VII's prohibition in §§703(a) and (d) against racial discrimination does not condemn all private, voluntary, race-conscious affirmative action plans.

III

We need not today define in detail the line of demarcation between permissible and impermissible affirmative action plans. It suffices to hold that the challenged Kaiser-USWA affirmative action plan falls on the permissible side of the line. The purposes of the plan mirror those of the statute. Both were designed to break down old patterns of racial segregation and hierarchy. Both were structured to "open employment opportunities for Negroes in occupations which have been traditionally closed to them."[8]

---

[8]See n. 1, *supra*. This is not to suggest that the freedom of an employer to undertake race-conscious affirmative action efforts depends on whether or not his effort is motivated by fear of liability under Title VII.

At the same time, the plan does not unnecessarily trammel the interests of the white employees. The plan does not require the discharge of white workers and their replacement with new black hires. Nor does the plan create an absolute bar to the advancement of white employees; half of those trained in the program will be white. Moreover, the plan is a temporary measure; it is not intended to maintain racial balance, but simply to eliminate a manifest racial imbalance. Preferential selection of craft trainees at the Gramercy plant will end as soon as the percentage of black skilled craftworkers in the Gramercy plant approximates the percentage of blacks in the local labor force.

We conclude, therefore, that the adoption of the Kaiser-USWA plan for the Gramercy plant falls within the area of discretion left by Title VII to the private sector voluntarily to adopt affirmative action plans designed to eliminate conspicuous racial imbalance in traditionally segregated job categories.[9] Accordingly, the judgment of the Court of Appeals for the Fifth Circuit is

Reversed.

MR. JUSTICE POWELL and MR. JUSTICE STEVENS took no part in the consideration or decision of these cases.

MR. JUSTICE BLACKMUN, concurring.

* * *

I

In his dissent from the decision of the United States Court of Appeals for the Fifth Circuit, Judge Wisdom pointed out that this case arises from a practical problem in the administration of Title VII. The broad prohibition against discrimination places the employer and the union on what he accurately described as a "high tightrope without a net beneath them." If Title VII is read literally, on the one hand they face liability for past discrimination against blacks, and on the other they face liability to whites for any voluntary preferences adopted to mitigate the effects of prior discrimination against blacks.

In this litigation, Kaiser denies prior discrimination but concedes that its past hiring practices may be subject to question. Although the labor force in the Gramercy area was approximately 39% black, Kaiser's work force was less than 15% black, and its craftwork force was less than 2% black. Kaiser had made some effort to recruit black painters, carpenters, insulators, and other craftsmen, but it continued to insist that those hired have five years prior industrial experience, a requirement that arguably was not sufficiently job related to justify under Title VII any discriminatory impact it may have had. The parties dispute the extent to which black craftsmen were available in the local labor market. They agree, however, that after critical reviews from the Office of Federal Contract Compliance, Kaiser and the Steelworkers established the training program in question here and modeled it along the lines of a Title VII consent

---

[9]Our disposition makes unnecessary consideration of petitioners' argument that their plan was justified because they feared that black employees would bring suit under Title VII if they did not adopt an affirmative action plan. Nor need we consider petitioners' contention that their affirmative action plan represented an attempt to comply with Exec. Order No. 11246.

decree later entered for the steel industry. Yet when they did this, respondent Weber sued, alleging that Title VII prohibited the program because it discriminated against him as a white person and it was not supported by a prior judicial finding of discrimination against blacks.

Respondent Weber's reading of Title VII, endorsed by the Court of Appeals, places voluntary compliance with Title VII in profound jeopardy. The only way for the employer and the union to keep their footing on the "tightrope" it creates would be to eschew all forms of voluntary affirmative action. Even a whisper of emphasis on minority recruiting would be forbidden. Because Congress intended to encourage private efforts to come into compliance with Title VII, Judge Wisdom concluded that employers and unions who had committed "arguable violations" of Title VII should be free to make reasonable responses without fear of liability to whites. Preferential hiring along the lines of the Kaiser program is a reasonable response for the employer, whether or not a court, on these facts, could order the same step as a remedy. The company is able to avoid identifying victims of past discrimination, and so avoids claims for backpay that would inevitably follow a response limited to such victims. If past victims should be benefited by the program, however, the company mitigates its liability to those persons. Also, to the extent that Title VII liability is predicated on the "disparate effect" of an employer's past hiring practices, the program makes it less likely that such an effect could be demonstrated. And the Court has recently held that work-force statistics resulting from private affirmative action were probative of benign intent in a "disparate treatment" case. Furnco Construction Corp. v. Waters, 438 U.S. 567, 579-580, 98 S.Ct. 2943, 2950-951, 57 L.Ed.2d 957 (1978).

The "arguable violation" theory has a number of advantages. It responds to a practical problem in the administration of Title VII not anticipated by Congress. It draws predictability from the outline of present law and closely effectuates the purpose of the Act. Both Kaiser and the United States urge its adoption here. Because I agree that it is the soundest way to approach this case, my preference would be to resolve this litigation by applying it and holding that Kaiser's craft training program meets the requirement that voluntary affirmative action be a reasonable response to an "arguable violation" of Title VII.

II

The Court, however, declines to consider the narrow "arguable violation" approach and adheres instead to an interpretation of Title VII that permits affirmative action by an employer whenever the job category in question is "traditionally segregated." The sources cited suggest that the Court considers a job category to be "traditionally segregated" when there has been a societal history of purposeful exclusion of blacks from the job category, resulting in a persistent disparity between the proportion of blacks in the labor force and the proportion of blacks among those who hold jobs within the category.

"Traditionally segregated job categories," where they exist, sweep far more broadly than the class of "arguable violations" of Title VII. The Court's expansive approach is somewhat disturbing for me because, as Mr. Justice Rehnquist points out, the Congress that passed Title VII probably thought it was adopting a principle of nondiscrimination that would apply to blacks and whites alike. While setting aside that principle can be justified where necessary to advance statutory policy by encouraging reasonable responses as a form of voluntary compliance that mitigates "arguable violations," discarding the principle of nondiscrimination where no countervailing statutory policy exists appears to be at odds with the bargain struck when Title VII was enacted.

A closer look at the problem, however, reveals that in each of the principal ways in which the Court's "traditionally segregated job categories" approach expands on the "arguable violations" theory, still other considerations point in favor of the broad standard adopted by the Court, and make it possible for me to conclude that the Court's reading of the statute is an acceptable one.

A. The first point at which the Court departs from the "arguable violations" approach is that it measures an individual employer's capacity for affirmative action solely in terms of a statistical disparity. The individual employer need not have engaged in discriminatory practices in the past. While, under Title VII, a mere disparity may provide the basis for a prima facie case against an employer, Dothard v. Rawlinson, 433 U.S. 321, 329-331, 97 S.Ct. 2720, 2726-2727, 53 L.Ed.2d 786 (1977), it would not conclusively prove a violation of the Act. Teamsters v. United States, 431 U.S. 324, 339-340, n. 20, 97 S.Ct. 1843, 1856, 52 L.Ed.2d 396 (1977). As a practical matter, however, this difference may not be that great. While the "arguable violation" standard is conceptually satisfying, in practice the emphasis would be on "arguable" rather than on "violation." The great difficulty in the District Court was that no one had any incentive to prove that Kaiser had violated the Act. Neither Kaiser nor the Steelworkers wanted to establish a past violation, nor did Weber. The blacks harmed had never sued and so had no established representative. The Equal Employment Opportunity Commission declined to intervene, and cannot be expected to intervene in every case of this nature. To make the "arguable violation" standard work, it would have to be set low enough to permit the employer to prove it without obligating himself to pay a damages award. The inevitable tendency would be to avoid hairsplitting litigation by simply concluding that a mere disparity between the racial composition of the employer's work force and the composition of the qualified local labor force would be an "arguable violation," even though actual liability could not be established on that basis alone.

B. The Court also departs from the "arguable violation" approach by permitting an employer to redress discrimination that lies wholly outside the bounds of Title VII. For example, Title VII provides no remedy for pre-Act discrimination, yet the purposeful discrimination that creates a "traditionally segregated job category" may have entirely predated the Act. More subtly, in assessing a prima facie case of Title VII liability, the composition of the employer's work force is compared to the composition of the pool of workers who meet valid job qualifications. When a "job category" is traditionally segregated, however, that pool will reflect the effects of segregation, and the Court's approach goes further and permits a comparison with the composition of the labor force as a whole, in which minorities are more heavily represented.

Strong considerations of equity support an interpretation of Title VII that would permit private affirmative action to reach where Title VII itself does not. The bargain struck in 1964 with the passage of Title VII guaranteed equal opportunity for white and black alike, but where Title VII provides no remedy for blacks, it should not be construed to foreclose private affirmative action from supplying relief. It seems unfair for respondent Weber to argue, as he does, that the asserted scarcity of black craftsmen in Louisiana, the product of historic discrimination, makes Kaiser's training program illegal because it ostensibly absolves Kaiser of all Title VII liability. Absent compelling evidence of legislative intent, I would not interpret Title VII itself as a means of "locking in" the effects of segregation for which Title VII provides no remedy. Such a construction, as the Court points out, would be "ironic," given the broad remedial purposes of Title VII.

Mr. Justice Rehnquist's dissent, while it focuses more on what Title VII does not require than on what Title VII forbids, cites several passages that appear to express an intent to "lock in" minorities. In mining the legislative history anew, however, the dissent, in my view, fails to take proper account of our prior cases that have given that history a much more limited reading than that adopted by the dissent. For example, in Griggs v. Duke Power Co., 401 U.S. 424, 434-436, and n. 11, 91 S.Ct. 849, 855-856, 28 L.Ed.2d 158 (1971), the Court refused to give controlling weight to the memorandum of Senators Clark and Case which the dissent now finds so persuasive. And in quoting a statement from that memorandum that an employer would not be "permitted * * * to prefer Negroes for future vacancies," the dissent does not point out that the Court's opinion in *Teamsters* implies that that language is limited to the protection of established seniority systems. Here, seniority is not in issue because the craft training program is new and does not involve an abrogation of pre-existing seniority rights. In short, the passages marshaled by the dissent are not so compelling as to merit the whip hand over the obvious equity of permitting employers to ameliorate the effects of past discrimination for which Title VII provides no direct relief.

* * *

MR. CHIEF JUSTICE BURGER, dissenting.

The Court reaches a result I would be inclined to vote for were I a Member of Congress considering a proposed amendment of Title VII. I cannot join the Court's judgment, however, because it is contrary to the explicit language of the statute and arrived at by means wholly incompatible with long-established principles of separation of powers. Under the guise of statutory "construction," the Court effectively rewrites Title VII to achieve what it regards as a desirable result. It "amends" the statute to do precisely what both its sponsors and its opponents agreed the statute was not intended to do.

When Congress enacted Title VII after long study and searching debate, it produced a statute of extraordinary clarity, which speaks directly to the issue we consider in this case.

Often we have difficulty interpreting statutes either because of imprecise drafting or because legislative compromises have produced genuine ambiguities. But here there is no lack of clarity, no ambiguity. The quota embodied in the collective-bargaining agreement between Kaiser and the Steelworkers unquestionably discriminates on the basis of race against individual employees seeking admission to on-the-job training programs. And, under the plain language of §703(d), that is "an unlawful employment practice."

Oddly, the Court seizes upon the very clarity of the statute almost as a justification for evading the unavoidable impact of its language. The Court blandly tells us that

Congress could not really have meant what it said, for a "literal construction" would defeat the "purpose" of the statute — at least the congressional "purpose" as five Justices divine it today. But how are judges supposed to ascertain the purpose of a statute except through the words Congress used and the legislative history of the statute's evolution? One need not even resort to the legislative history to recognize what is apparent from the face of Title VII — that it is specious to suggest that §703(j) contains a negative pregnant that permits employers to do what §§703(a) and (d) unambiguously and unequivocally forbid employers from doing. Moreover, as Mr. Justice Rehnquist's opinion — which I join — conclusively demonstrates, the legislative history makes equally clear that the supporters and opponents of Title VII reached an agreement about the statute's intended effect. That agreement, expressed so clearly in the language of the statute that no one should doubt its meaning, forecloses the reading which the Court gives the statute today.

* * *

MR. JUSTICE REHNQUIST, with whom THE CHIEF JUSTICE joins, dissenting.

* * *

* * * It may be that one or more of the principal sponsors of Title VII would have preferred to see a provision allowing preferential treatment of minorities written into the bill. Such a provision, however, would have to have been expressly or impliedly excepted from Title VII's explicit prohibition on all racial discrimination in employment. There is no such exception in the Act. And a reading of the legislative debates concerning Title VII, in which proponents and opponents alike uniformly denounced discrimination in favor of, as well as discrimination against, Negroes, demonstrates clearly that any legislator harboring an unspoken desire for such a provision could not possibly have succeeded in enacting it into law.

I

* * *

* * * In February 1974, under pressure from the Office of Federal Contract Compliance to increase minority representation in craft positions at its various plants,[2] and hoping to deter the filing of employment discrimination claims by minorities,

---

[2]The Office of Federal Contract Compliance (OFCC), subsequently renamed the Office of Federal Contract Compliance Programs (OFCCP), is an arm of the Department of Labor responsible for ensuring compliance by Government contractors with the equal employment opportunity requirements established by Exec. Order No. 11246.

Executive Order 11246, as amended, requires all applicants for federal contracts to refrain from employment discrimination and to "take affirmative action to ensure that applicants are employed, and that employees are treated during employment, without regard to their race, color, religion, sex or national origin." The Executive Order empowers the Secretary of Labor to issue rules and regulations necessary and appropriate to achieve its purpose. He, in turn, has delegated most enforcement duties to the OFCC.

The affirmative action program mandated * * * for nonconstruction contractors requires a "utilization" study to determine minority representation in the work force. Goals for hiring and promotion must be set to overcome any "underutilization" found to exist.

The OFCC employs the "power of the purse" to coerce acceptance of its affirmative action plans. Indeed, in this case, the district court found that the 1974 collective bargaining agreement reflected less of a desire on Kaiser's part to train black craft workers than a self-interest in satisfying the OFCC in order to retain lucrative government contracts.

Kaiser entered into a collective-bargaining agreement with the United Steelworkers of America (Steelworkers) which * * * required that no less than one minority applicant be admitted to the training program for every nonminority applicant until the percentage of blacks in craft positions equaled the percentage of blacks in the local work force. * * *

* * *

II

* * *

* * * To be sure, the reality of employment discrimination against Negroes provided the primary impetus for passage of Title VII. But this fact by no means supports the proposition that Congress intended to leave employers free to discriminate against white persons.[11] In most cases, "[l]egislative history * * * is more vague than

---

[11]The only shred of legislative history cited by the Court in support of the proposition that "Congress did not intend wholly to prohibit private and voluntary affirmative action efforts," ante, at 203, is the following excerpt from the Judiciary Committee Report accompanying the civil rights bill reported to the House:

"No bill can or should lay claim to eliminating all of the causes and consequences of racial and other types of discrimination against minorities. There is reason to believe, however, that national leadership provided by the enactment of Federal legislation dealing with the most troublesome problems *will create an atmosphere conducive to voluntary or local resolution of other forms of discrimination.*" H.R.Rep.No. 914, 88th Cong., 1st Sess., pt. 1, p. 18 (1963) (hereinafter H.R.Rep.).

The Court seizes on the italicized language to support its conclusion that Congress did not intend to prohibit voluntary imposition of racially discriminatory employment quotas. The Court, however, stops too short in its reading of the House Report. The words immediately following the material excerpted by the Court are as follows:

"It is, however, possible and necessary for the Congress to enact legislation which prohibits and provides the means of terminating *the most serious types of discrimination.* This H.R. 7152, as amended, would achieve in a number of related areas. It would reduce discriminatory obstacles to the exercise of the right to vote and provide means of expediting the vindication of that right. It would make it possible to remove the daily affront and humiliation involved in discriminatory denials of access to facilities ostensibly open to the general public. It would guarantee that there will be no discrimination upon recipients of Federal financial assistance. It would prohibit discrimination in employment, and provide means to expedite termination of discrimination in public education. It would open additional avenues to deal with redress of denials of equal protection of the laws on account of race, color, religion, or national origin by State or local authorities." H.R.Rep., pt. 1, p. 18 (emphasis added).

When thus read in context, the meaning of the italicized language in the Court's excerpt of the House Report becomes clear. By dealing with "the most serious types of discrimination," such as discrimination in voting, public accommodations, employment, etc., H.R. 7152 would hopefully inspire "voluntary or local resolution of other forms of discrimination," that is, forms other than discrimination in voting, public accommodations, employment, etc.

One can also infer from the House Report that the Judiciary Committee hoped that federal legislation would inspire voluntary elimination of discrimination against minority groups other than those protected under the bill, perhaps the aged and handicapped to name just two. In any event, the House Report does not support the Court's proposition that Congress, by banning racial discrimination in employment, intended to permit racial discrimination in employment.

Thus, examination of the House Judiciary Committee's report reveals that the Court's interpretation of Title VII, far from being compelled by the Act's legislative history, is utterly without support in that legislative history. Indeed, as demonstrated in Part III, *infra*, the Court's interpretation of Title VII is totally refuted by the Act's legislative history.

the statute we are called upon to interpret." Here, however, the legislative history of Title VII is as clear as the language of §§703(a) and (d), and it irrefutably demonstrates that Congress meant precisely what it said in §§703(a) and (d)—that no racial discrimination in employment is permissible under Title VII, not even preferential treatment of minorities to correct racial imbalance.

III

* * *

B

* * *

2

* * *

In the opening speech of the formal Senate debate on the bill, Senator Humphrey addressed the main concern of Title VII's opponents, advising that not only does Title VII not require use of racial quotas, *it does not permit* their use. "The truth," stated the floor leader of the bill, "is that this title forbids discriminating against anyone on account of race. This is the simple and complete truth about Title VII." * * * At the close of his speech, Senator Humphrey returned briefly to the subject of employment quotas: "It is claimed that the bill would require racial quotas for all hiring, when in fact it provides that race shall not be a basis for making personnel decisions."

* * *

A few days later the Senate's attention focused exclusively on Title VII, as Senators Clark and Case rose to discuss the title of H.R. 7152 on which they shared floor "captain" responsibilities. In an interpretative memorandum submitted jointly to the Senate, Senators Clark and Case took pains to refute the opposition's charge that Title VII would result in preferential treatment of minorities. Their words were clear and unequivocal:

> "There is no requirement in Title VII that an employer maintain a racial balance in his work force. On the contrary, any deliberate attempt to maintain a racial balance, whatever such a balance may be, would involve a violation of Title VII because maintaining such a balance would require an employer to hire or to refuse to hire on the basis of race. It must be emphasized that discrimination is prohibited as to any individual." Id., at 7213.

Of particular relevance to the instant case were their observations regarding seniority rights. As if directing their comments at Brian Weber, the Senators said:

> "Title VII would have no effect on established seniority rights. Its effect is prospective and not retrospective. Thus, for example, if a business has been discriminating in the past and as a result has an all-white working force, when the title comes into effect the employer's obligation would be simply to fill future vacancies on a nondiscriminatory basis. He would not be obliged — *or indeed permitted* — to fire whites in order to hire Negroes, *or to prefer Negroes for future vacancies, or, once Negroes are hired, to give them*

special seniority rights at the expense of the white workers hired earlier." Ibid. (emphasis added).[19]

Thus, with virtual clairvoyance the Senate's leading supporters of Title VII anticipated precisely the circumstances of this case and advised their colleagues that the type of minority preference employed by Kaiser would violate Title VII's ban on racial discrimination. To further accentuate the point, Senator Clark introduced another memorandum dealing with common criticisms of the bill, including the charge that racial quotas would be imposed under Title VII. The answer was simple and to the point: "Quotas are themselves discriminatory."

* * * Senators Smathers and Sparkman, while conceding that Title VII does not in so many words require the use of hiring quotas, repeated the opposition's view that employers would be coerced to grant preferential hiring treatment to minorities by agencies of the Federal Government. Senator Williams was quick to respond:

"Those opposed to H.R. 7152 should realize that to hire a Negro solely because he is a Negro is racial discrimination, just as much as a 'white only' employment policy. Both forms of discrimination are prohibited by Title VII of this bill. The language of that title simply states that race is not a qualification for employment.

---

[19]A Justice Department memorandum earlier introduced by Senator Clark, see n. 18, *supra*, expressed the same view regarding Title VII's impact on seniority rights of employees:
"Title VII would have no effect on seniority rights existing at the time it takes effect. * * * This would be true even in the case where owing to discrimination prior to the effective date of the title, white workers had more seniority than Negroes. * * * [A]ssuming that seniority rights were built up over a period of time during which Negroes were not hired, these rights would not be set aside by the taking effect of Title VII. Employers and labor organizations would simply be under a duty not to discriminate against Negroes because of their race." 110 Cong.Rec. 7207 (1964).

The interpretation of Title VII contained in the memoranda introduced by Senator Clark totally refutes the Court's implied suggestion that Title VII would prohibit an employer from discriminating on the basis of race in order to *maintain* a racial balance in his work force, but would permit him to do so in order to *achieve* racial balance.

The maintain-achieve distinction is analytically indefensible in any event. Apparently, the Court is saying that an employer is free to *achieve* a racially balanced work force by discriminating against whites, but that once he has reached his goal, he is no longer free to discriminate in order to maintain that racial balance. In other words, once Kaiser reaches its goal of 39% minority representation in craft positions at the Gramercy plant, it can no longer consider race in admitting employees into its on-the-job training programs, even if the programs become as "all-white" as they were in April 1974.

Obviously, the Court is driven to this illogical position by the glaring statement, quoted in text, of Senators Clark and Case that "any deliberate attempt to *maintain* a racial balance * * * would involve a violation of Title VII because *maintaining* such a balance would require an employer to hire or to refuse to hire on the basis of race." Achieving a certain racial balance, however, no less than maintaining such a balance, would require an employer to hire or to refuse to hire on the basis of race. Further, the Court's own conclusion that Title VII's legislative history, coupled with the wording of §703(j), evinces a congressional intent to leave employers free to employ "private, voluntary, race-conscious affirmative action plans," is inconsistent with its maintain-achieve distinction. If Congress' primary purpose in enacting Title VII was to open employment opportunities previously closed to Negroes, it would seem to make little difference whether the employer opening those opportunities was achieving or maintaining a certain racial balance in his work force. Likewise, if §703(j) evinces Congress' intent to permit imposition of race-conscious affirmative action plans, it would seem to make little difference whether the plan was adopted to achieve or maintain the desired racial balance.

* * * Some people charge that H.R. 7152 favors the Negro, at the expense of the white majority. But how can the language of equality favor one race or one religion over another? Equality can have only one meaning, and that meaning is self-evident to reasonable men. Those who say that equality means favoritism do violence to common sense."

* * *

While the debate in the Senate raged, a bipartisan coalition under the leadership of Senators Dirksen, Mansfield, Humphrey, and Kuchel was working with House leaders and representatives of the Johnson administration on a number of amendments to H.R. 7152 designed to enhance its prospects of passage. The so-called "Dirksen-Mansfield" amendment was introduced on May 26 by Senator Dirksen as a substitute for the entire House-passed bill. The substitute bill, which ultimately became law, left unchanged the basic prohibitory language of §§703(a) and (d), as well as the remedial provisions in §706(g). It added, however, several provisions defining and clarifying the scope of Title VII's substantive prohibitions. One of those clarifying amendments, §703(j), was specifically directed at the opposition's concerns regarding racial balancing and preferential treatment of minorities * * *.

* * *

Contrary to the Court's analysis, the language of §703(j) is precisely tailored to the objection voiced time and again by Title VII's opponents. Not once during the 83 days of debate in the Senate did a speaker, proponent or opponent, suggest that the bill would allow employers voluntarily to prefer racial minorities over white persons. In light of Title VII's flat prohibition on discrimination "against any individual * * * because of such individual's race," §703(a), such a contention would have been, in any event, too preposterous to warrant response. Indeed, speakers on both sides of the issue, as the legislative history makes clear, recognized that Title VII would tolerate no voluntary racial preference, whether in favor of blacks or whites. The complaint consistently voiced by the opponents was that Title VII, particularly the word "discrimination," would be interpreted by federal agencies such as the EEOC to require the correction of racial imbalance through the granting of preferential treatment to minorities. Verbal assurances that Title VII would not require — indeed, would not permit — preferential treatment of blacks having failed, supporters of H.R. 7152 responded by proposing an amendment carefully worded to meet, and put to rest, the opposition's charge. Indeed, unlike §§703(a) and (d), which are by their terms directed at entities — e.g., employers, labor unions — whose actions are restricted by Title VII's prohibitions, the language of §703(j) is specifically directed at entities — federal agencies and courts — charged with the responsibility of interpreting Title VII's provisions.

In light of the background and purpose of §703(j), the irony of invoking the section to justify the result in this case is obvious. The Court's frequent references to the "voluntary" nature of Kaiser's racially discriminatory admission quota bear no relationship to the facts of this case. Kaiser and the Steelworkers acted under pressure from an agency of the Federal Government, the Office of Federal Contract Compliance, which found that minorities were being "underutilized" at Kaiser's plants. See n. 2, *supra*. That is, Kaiser's work force was racially imbalanced. Bowing to that pressure, Kaiser instituted an admissions quota preferring blacks over whites, thus confirming that the fears of Title VII's opponents were well founded. Today, §703(j), adopted to allay those fears, is invoked by the Court to uphold imposition of a racial quota under the very circumstances that the section was intended to prevent.

* * *

IV

Reading the language of Title VII, as the Court purports to do, "against the background of [its] legislative history * * * and the historical context from which the Act arose," ante, at 201, one is led inescapably to the conclusion that Congress fully understood what it was saying and meant precisely what it said. Opponents of the civil rights bill did not argue that employers would be permitted under Title VII voluntarily to grant preferential treatment to minorities to correct racial imbalance. The plain language of the statute too clearly prohibited such racial discrimination to admit of any doubt. They argued, tirelessly, that Title VII would be interpreted by federal agencies and their agents to require unwilling employers to racially balance their work forces by granting preferential treatment to minorities. Supporters of H.R. 7152 responded, equally tirelessly, that the Act would not be so interpreted because not only does it not require preferential treatment of minorities, it does not permit preferential treatment of any race for any reason. * * *

To put an end to the dispute, supporters of the civil rights bill drafted and introduced §703(j). Specifically addressed to the opposition's charge, §703(j) simply enjoins federal agencies and courts from interpreting Title VII to require an employer to prefer certain racial groups to correct imbalances in his work force. The section says nothing about voluntary preferential treatment of minorities because such racial discrimination is plainly proscribed by §§703(a) and (d). Indeed, had Congress intended to except voluntary, race-conscious preferential treatment from the blanket prohibition of racial discrimination in §§703(a) and (d), it surely could have drafted language better suited to the task than §703(j). It knew how. Section 703(i) provides:

> "Nothing contained in [Title VII] shall apply to any business or enterprise on or near an Indian reservation with respect to any publicly announced employment practice of such business or enterprise under which a preferential treatment is given to any individual because he is an Indian living on or near a reservation."

* * *

Weber v. Kaiser Aluminum & Chemical Corp.

United States Court of Appeals, Fifth Circuit, 1980.

611 F.2d 132, on remand from the Supreme Court of the United States, 443 U.S. 193, 99 S.Ct. 2721, 61 L.Ed.2d 480 (1979).

GEE, Circuit Judge.

* * *

II

For myself only, and with all respect and deference, I here note my personal conviction that the decision of the Supreme Court in this case is profoundly wrong.

That it is wrong as a matter of statutory construction seems to me sufficiently demonstrated by the dissenting opinions of the Chief Justice and of Mr. Justice Rehnquist. To these I can add nothing. They make plain beyond peradventure that the Civil Rights Act of 1964 passed the Congress on the express representation of its sponsors that it would not and could not be construed as the Court has now construed it. What could be plainer than the words of the late Senator Humphrey—defending the bill against the charge that it adumbrated quotas and preferential treatment—that "the title would prohibit preferential treatment for any particular group * * * "? The Court now tells us that this is not so. That it feels it may properly do so seems to me a grievous thing.

But sadder still — tragic, in my own view—is the Court's departure from the long road that we have travelled from Plessy v. Ferguson, 163 U.S. 537, 16 S.Ct. 1138, 41 L.Ed. 256 (1896), toward making good Mr. Justice Harlan's anguished cry in dissent that "[o]ur Constitution is color-blind, and neither knows nor tolerates classes among citizens." I voice my profound belief that this present action, like *Plessy*, is a wrong and dangerous turning, and my confident hope that we will soon return to the high, bright road on which we disdain to classify a citizen, any citizen, to any degree or for any purpose by the color of his skin.

Though for the above reasons I think it gravely mistaken, I do not say that the Court's decision is immoral or unjust—indeed, in some basic sense it may well represent true justice. But there are many actions roughly just that our laws do not authorize and our Constitution forbids, actions such as preventing a Nazi Party march through a town where reside former inmates of concentration camps or inflicting summary punishment on one caught redhanded in a crime.

Subordinate magistrates such as I must either obey the orders of higher authority or yield up their posts to those who will. I obey, since in my view the action required of me by the Court's mandate is only to follow a mistaken course and not an evil one.

VACATED and REMANDED.

WISDOM, Circuit Judge, specially concurring:

With deference to the views expressed by the majority of this Court, I express the view that the decision of the Supreme Court in this case is profoundly right for the reasons stated in my dissenting opinion. Weber v. Kaiser Aluminum & Chemical Corporation and United Steelworkers of America, 563 F.2d 216, 227 (5th Cir. 1977).

NOTES AND PROBLEMS FOR DISCUSSION

1. Was the result in *Weber* a necessary consequence of the Court's prior rulings in *Griggs* and *Albemarle*? Can it be explained as a response to the dilemma (alluded to in Justice Blackmun's concurring opinion) that confronts employers who artificially increase their proportion of black employees in order to either avoid liability under a disproportionate impact discrimination claim predicated on a showing of racial imbalance in the employers' workforce, or to eschew the burden of validating the job relatedness of their employment criteria? If so, how does the Court's opinion in *Teal* fit into this calculation? See Alfred Blumrosen, *The "Bottom Line" After Connecticut v. Teal*, 8 EMP.REL.L.J. 572 (1983). For a revealing account of the story behind the

Court's ruling in *Weber*, see Deborah Malamud, *The Story of United Steelworkers of America v. Weber*, EMPLOYMENT DISCRIMINATION STORIES 173 (Friedman, ed. 2006).

Another potential version of this dilemma confronted the Supreme Court when the City of New Haven chose to discard the results of examinations that were devised as part of the process for choosing candidates for promotion to lieutenant and captain positions with the fire department. When the examination results revealed that white candidates had outperformed minority candidates, the City discarded the test results and declined to make promotion decisions based on those results. Several white and Hispanic firefighters who likely would have received promotions based on their test results sued the City and several of its officials, alleging that the decision to discard the results because of their disproportionate exclusionary impact upon minority candidates constituted intentional discrimination on the basis of race in violation of Title VII. They also included claims under 42 U.S.C. §§1983 and 1985, alleging that by engaging in that conduct, the defendants had violated and conspired to violate the Equal Protection Clause of the Fourteenth Amendment. The trial court granted summary judgment to the City, ruling that the City was not required to certify test results just because it could not pinpoint the cause of the disproportionate impact and that the intention to avoid making promotions based on a test with a racially disproportionate impact did not, as a matter of law, constitute intentional discrimination under Title VII. The Second Circuit issued a one-paragraph *per curiam* affirmance, adopting the trial court's reasoning. In RICCI v. DESTEFANO, 557 U.S. 557, 129 S.Ct. 2658, 174 L.Ed.2d 490 (2009), the Court, by a 5-4 vote, reversed both lower court rulings.

Rejecting the trial court's analysis, the majority declared that choosing not to certify test results (i.e., a change to an existing employment practice) because of their statistical disparity based on race did constitute intentional race-based discrimination violative of Title VII. However, the majority also concluded that the City could avoid liability if its decision was justified by a valid defense:

> Whatever the City's ultimate aim — however well intentioned or benevolent it might have seemed — the City made its employment decision because of race. The City rejected the test results solely because the higher scoring candidates were white. The question is not whether that conduct was discriminatory but whether the City had a lawful justification for its race-based action.

To provide guidance to employers and courts dealing with the apparent conflict between the disproportionate impact and disparate treatment provisions of Title VII, the Court then turned its attention to the question of whether a purpose of avoiding disproportionate impact liability was a valid excuse for engaging in what the majority declared to be disparate treatment discrimination. The Court rejected the plaintiffs' argument that the employer must in fact be in violation of the disproportionate impact provision before it could assert avoidance of disproportionate impact liability as a defense to a disparate treatment claim as inconsistent with Congress' intent to encourage voluntary compliance as the preferred means of promoting the statutory objectives:

> Forbidding employers to act unless they know, with certainty, that a practice violates the disparate-impact provision would bring compliance efforts to a near standstill. Even in the limited situations when this restricted standard could be

met, employers likely would hesitate before taking voluntary action for fear of later being proven wrong in the course of litigation and then held to account for disparate treatment.

But the majority also declined to accept the defense position that an employer's good faith belief that its actions were necessary to avoid impact liability sufficed to justify race-conscious conduct. It noted that the §703(k), the provision codifying impact-based liability, did not contain an exception for actions based on a good faith effort to avoid impact-based discrimination:

> Allowing employers to violate the disparate-treatment prohibition based on a mere good-faith fear of disparate-impact liability would encourage race-based action at the slightest hint of disparate impact. A minimal standard could cause employers to discard the results of lawful and beneficial promotional examinations even where there is little if any evidence of disparate-impact discrimination. * * * Even worse, an employer could discard test results (or other employment practices) with the intent of obtaining the employer's preferred racial balance. That operational principle could not be justified, for Title VII is express in disclaiming any interpretation of its requirements as calling for outright racial balancing. §703(j).

Accordingly, the majority transplanted a standard "that strikes a more appropriate balance" from its Equal Protection Clause jurisprudence dealing with the constitutionality of the remedial use of race-based classifications. In *Croson* and *Wygant*, the Court had held that governmental remedial use of race passed constitutional muster only where there was a "strong basis in evidence" that remedial action was necessary. While expressly not ruling on whether the statutory restraints under Title VII *always* must parallel the constitutional limitations on the use of race, the majority concluded that in this statutory context the constitutional standard provided "helpful guidance". Using this standard, the majority reasoned, best accommodated both the disparate treatment and disproportionate impact provisions of Title VII by "allowing violations of one in the name of compliance with the other only in certain, narrow circumstances." It promoted voluntary compliance by giving employers a reasonable amount of leeway in that it limited their discretion to make race-based decisions to instances where there is a strong basis in evidence of impact-based liability while not restricting them to situations where there is a provable violation. The majority also stated that this compromise best promoted the objectives of §703(l)'s prohibition against adjusting employment-related scores on the basis of race. If an employer cannot rescore test results based on a candidate's race, the majority reasoned, then it surely could not take the more aggressive step of discarding the test altogether to achieve a more proportionate botton line result — unless there was a demonstration of a strong basis in evidence that the test was deficient and discarding it was necessary to avoid impact-based liability. Similarly, the majority explained, the standard was in keeping with §703(h)'s protection of bona fide promotional examinations.

The majority then found that the record clearly demonstrated that the City did not establish its statutory defense, i.e., it did not have a strong basis in evidence to find the tests inadequate in a way that would result in impact-based liability. Although the Court found that the racial adverse impact of the test was significant and that the City did face a prima facie case of disproportionate impact liability, this did not suffice to meet the strong-basis-in-evidence standard. Even in the face of a prima facie showing of impact, the Court reasoned, the City could be liable for impact-based discrimination only if its examination was not job related and consistent with business necessity or if it refused to adopt an equally valid, less discriminatory alternative. But the Court found that there was no genuine dispute that the City lacked a strong basis in evidence to establish the inadequacy of the examination under either of those propositions. Therefore, the Court ruled, the City's decision to discard the test results constituted unlawful intentional discrimination under Title VII and the plaintiffs were entitled to summary judgment. Accordingly, the Court did not address the plaintiffs' constitutional claims, including the question of whether the strong-basis-in-evidence test would be applied to a constitutional challenge to such action.

The case produced several separate opinions. Justice Scalia wrote a concurring opinion solely to raise, without answering, the question of whether the disproportionate impact provision of Title VII would pass constitutional muster since per the majority's ruling, Title VII would permit and even require remedial race-based action when impact violation would otherwise result. Justice Alito also wrote a concurring opinion outlining both his disagreement with the dissent's adoption of a "good cause" standard and their application of that standard to the instant facts. He also concluded that the City's explanation for discarding the test — avoiding impact-based liability — was a pretext for the real reason — the desire to placate a politically important racial constituency. In dissent, Justice Ginsburg, joined by Justices Stevens, Souter and Breyer, charged the majority with creating a false conflict between §§703(a) and (k), rejecting the majority's fundamental premise that an employer's change in an employment practice to comply with the impact provision constitutes intentional race-based action. The proper accommodation, the dissenters maintained, was to permit employers to discard criteria in the face of "reasonable doubts" about their reliability. Such action, they insisted, did not constitute intentional race-based discrimination. Rather, such conduct was warranted as long as the employer had "good cause" to believe the device would not withstand examination for business necessity. The majority's strong-basis-in-evidence standard was "particularly inapt", in the dissenters' view, because it concerned the constitutionality of absolute racial preferences. Discarding the test results, on the other hand, was race-neutral since all firefighters were subjected to the same decision — all of their test results were discarded and all were required to participate in some other selection process to be considered for promotion. Finally, the dissenters found that the City had ample cause to fear impact-based liability based on a good cause belief that its selection processes were flawed and not justified by business necessity.

Based on its statutory ruling, the majority ordered the City to certify the test results and to make promotion decisions based on those results. But it also advised the City that:

> [i]f, after it certifies the test results, the City faces a disparate-impact suit, then in light of our holding today it should be clear that the City would avoid disparate-impact liability based on the strong basis in evidence that, had it not certified the results, it would have been subject to disparate-treatment liability.

Not surprisingly, after the City certified the test results and promoted some of the *Ricci* plaintiffs based on those results, an African-American firefighter who had not been a party to the *Ricci* litigation and who had not been promoted, brought a Title VII action against the City alleging that its promotion exams produced a racially disparate impact. The trial judge dismissed the complaint on the ground that it was precluded by the Supreme Court's judgment in *Ricci*. In BRISCOE v. CITY OF NEW HAVEN, 654 F.3d 200 (2d Cir. 2011), cert. denied, 567 U.S. 913, 132 S.Ct. 2741, 183 L.Ed.2d 630 (2012), a Second Circuit panel vacated that decision and held that Briscoe, a non-party to the *Ricci* litigation, was not precluded from filing the instant suit by that prior judgment. The circuit court invoked doctrine that a judgment does not preclude non-parties except in a limited set of circumstances that did not apply to this plaintiff. More importantly, however, the court also rejected the City's argument that the *Ricci* "strong basis in evidence" standard should also apply to the plaintiff's disparate *impact* claim, i.e., that it could defeat the plaintiff's disparate *impact* claim if it had a strong basis in evidence that it would have been subject to disparate *treatment* liability if it had ignored the test results. The Second Circuit rejected this attempt to extend the *Ricci* Court's statement about avoiding disparate *treatment* liability to an effort to avoid disparate *impact* liability. This sort of symmetrical formulation, the court concluded was neither mandated nor contemplated by the *Ricci* Court. For one thing, the court explained, the "strong basis in evidence" test is much more difficult to apply in the disparate *treatment* (i.e., intentional discrimination) than the disparate impact context. It is easier to assess whether there is a strong basis for believing that taking certain action will subsequently result in impact liability because the impact calculation involves quantitative metrics. But determining whether action will subsequently engender intentional discrimination-based liability is more challenging precisely because intent is a subjective concept for which consistent standards are impractical. Consequently, the court ruled that the plaintiff's claim could proceed. It also noted that the victorious plaintiffs in *Ricci* remained entitled to the promotions they had received as a result of the Supreme Court's order to certify and apply the promotion test results.

2. Is the "traditional pattern of segregation" standard more or less satisfactory than Judge Wisdom's "arguable violation" theory? Is an individual employer competent to make a determination as to the existence of either of these two criteria? What about Justice Blackmun's concern that the "traditional pattern" standard can, and likely will, include consideration of lawful pre-Act discrimination? On the other hand, is the majority saying that affirmative action is permissible where current employment practices perpetuate the discriminatory effects of a lawful pre-Act tradition of racial bias? Does the "traditional pattern" criterion permit the use of affirmative action in a historically segregated industry by a nondiscriminating employer that played no part in creating or maintaining that tradition? Would this issue arise under the "arguable violation" standard? *See* Cohen v. Community College of Philadelphia, 484 F. Supp. 411, 434 (E.D. Pa. 1980) ("* * * I do not read *Weber* as requiring an employer to establish a history of actual discrimination on his own part before he is permitted to adopt an affirmative action plan designed to eliminate that discrimination. Rather, I hold that under *Weber*, an employer's affirmative action plan can be justified by the existence of a history of racial discrimination in the relevant occupation or profession at large.").

3. Are you convinced by either the majority's or Justice Rehnquist's opinion as to whether Congress seriously considered the issue of voluntary affirmative action during its deliberations over Title VII? If not, what impact should an inconclusive legislative history have on the construction of a statute?

4. The majority opinion notes that Kaiser's craft training program was established as part of an affirmative action plan designed specifically to increase the number of black craft workers. Prior to the creation of this training program, Kaiser hired only craftworkers with craft experience. The plaintiff sought admission to the training program because he couldn't satisfy the experience requirement for a craft job. Thus, he sought and was denied a benefit — training — that was created for the sole purpose of helping train black workers. Clearly, Weber would not have benefited from the termination of the affirmative action plan since this would have eliminated any opportunity for him to obtain a craft job with Kaiser. Does this diminish the extent of the injury Weber suffered from being denied admission to the program to the preference of a less senior black employee?

5. Was Kaiser's plan limited to providing training to identifiable victims of discrimination? If not, what was the purpose of the plan? Does this suggest anything about Kaiser's, and perhaps the Court's, view of equality?

6. The majority in *Weber* concluded that Kaiser's plan constituted a permissible form of affirmative action because, in part, it was a temporary measure — lasting until the percentage of black craftworkers in the plant approximated the percentage of blacks in the local labor force. The significance attached to the temporary nature of the preference indicates that the Court believed that racial preferences could be used to attain, but not maintain racial balance in traditionally segregated job classifications. Is this distinction justifiable or is it merely an attempt to effect a compromise of an extremely sensitive issue? Is Justice Rehnquist right in suggesting that this distinction is at variance with other portions of the majority's opinion?

7. In determining whether a "traditional pattern" of discrimination exists, must a court compare the minority composition of the defendant's or industry's workforce with that minority's representation in the local area population? *See* Minnick v. California Department of Corrections, 95 Cal.App.3d 506, 157 Cal.Rptr. 260 (1979), cert. dismissed for want of finality, 452 U.S. 105, 101 S.Ct. 2211, 68 L.Ed.2d 706 (1981) (neither Title VII nor U.S. Constitution is violated by a voluntarily adopted affirmative action hiring plan that is designed to have the percentage of minority prison employees approximate the proportion of minority persons in the State prison inmate population).

8. In light of the extensive factual inquiry associated with judicial review of affirmative action plans, is the issue of the validity of such a plan a question of law or of fact? Where the defendant is a public entity, is the validity of the plan a question of law to be determined by a court or is the plaintiff entitled under the Seventh Amendment to a jury determination on this issue? *See* Bratton v. Detroit, 704 F.2d 878 (6th Cir. 1983), modified, 712 F.2d 222 (6th Cir.1983), cert. denied, 464 U.S. 1040, 104 S.Ct. 703, 79 L.Ed.2d 168 (1984). Additionally, is the determination of the validity of a plan or hiring order subject to the "clearly erroneous" standard of review on appeal?

9. In JOHNSON v. TRANSPORTATION AGENCY, 480 U.S. 616, 107 S.Ct. 1442, 94 L.Ed.2d 615 (1987), a 6-3 majority extended the ruling in *Weber* to a challenge to a sex-based affirmative action program. Since the defendant in Johnson was an agency of Santa Clara County, the Court also had to determine whether *Weber* should also apply to a plan implemented by a public employer. The plaintiffs argued that the government should be subjected to a unitary standard of review when it engaged in affirmative action — and that it should be the constitutional standard. The majority rejected this claim, stating that when Congress amended Title VII in 1972 to extend to the public sector, it did not intend for the government's statutory obligations to be co-extensive with its constitutional duties. For a contrary view, see George Rutherglen and Daniel R. Ortiz, *Affirmative Action Under the Constitution And Title VII: From Confusion to Convergence*, 35 UCLA L.REV. 467 (1988).

The majority in *Johnson* also stated that where the plaintiff challenges an affirmative action plan, the defendant can satisfy its burden of coming forward with a legitimate, nondiscriminatory explanation by demonstrating the existence of an affirmative action plan. Did the Court mean that the defendant only needs to offer evidence that it had such a plan, or that it must provide testimony that the challenged employment decision was actually made in reliance upon the terms of the plan? In GILLIGAN v. DEPARTMENT OF LABOR, 81 F.3d 835 (9th Cir. 1996), one of the defendant's hiring officers testified that gender had played no role in the denial of the plaintiff's application for a promotion. The trial court, however, believed the plaintiff's testimony that gender had played a role. The court also found that although the employer had a well-established affirmative action plan, the hiring officials had not relied upon that plan in rejecting the male plaintiff. However, the trial judge also found that the employment decision was "consistent with" the terms of the plan and entered a judgment in favor of the defendant. On appeal, the plaintiff claimed that the trial court had erred in ruling that acting consistently with an extant affirmative action plan was a defense to his claim of gender discrimination. The Ninth Circuit affirmed the lower court's ruling, stating that "in an institutional setting, it is not necessarily determinative whether the hiring officials actually relied upon the plan as long as they acted consistently with it." In the appellate court's view, although the mere existence of a plan was not a sufficient defense, it was enough to establish that the company acted consistently with such a plan. In the court's opinion, "a hiring official who acts consistently with a plan is indistinguishable from one who actually relied upon the plan," particularly since the impact on the nonfavored individual is the same in either case. Finally, the court rejected the plaintiff's contention that it should subject the case to mixed-motive analysis and require the defendant to establish that it would have reached the same decision in the absence of any consideration of his gender. The court reasoned that mixed motive analysis is only appropriate when the defendant relies on lawful and unlawful factors. Here, the court continued, the defendant's consideration of gender was lawful (consistent with an existing, lawful affirmative action plan) and, therefore, mixed motive analysis was inapposite.

For nearly a quarter of a century, the Court's rulings in *Weber* and *Johnson* served as the analytic touchstone for all Title VII challenges to voluntary race-conscious decisions by employers. However, in *Ricci*, discussed in Note 1, *supra*, a case involving a Title VII challenge to a City's voluntary decision to disregard the results of an employment test because of its racially disparate results and fear of a disparate-impact-based lawsuit by minority firefighters, the Supreme Court never cited either of these opinions. Does this suggest that this, and perhaps other, forms of race or sex-based voluntary action by an employer are now subject to the *Ricci* "strong basis in evidence" standard rather than the *Weber/Johnson* "manifest imbalance" and "no unnecessarily trammeling" criteria?

In U.S. v. BRENNAN, 650 F.3d 65 (2d Cir. 2011), the Second Circuit examined this question in the context of a Title VII and Equal Protection Clause challenge to some terms of a settlement agreement entered into between the New York City Board of Education and the U.S. The federal government had sued the City claiming, *inter alia*, that the City's civil service examinations results produced a disparate impact on the bases of race and sex. The settlement agreement provided permanent appointments and retroactive competitive seniority to a group of minority and female individuals. A group of incumbent employees brought a "reverse discrimination" suit against the City under Title VII. The trial judge, relying on *Weber* and *Johnson*, ruled that some of the retroactive seniority provisions violated Title VII and that many did not. The Second Circuit, in a lengthy opinion by Judge Calabresi, ruled that the decision in *Ricci* "makes clear that at least some race- or sex-conscious voluntary employer actions are not subject to the 'affirmative action' analysis of *Weber* and *Johnson*." 650 F.3d at 98. The appellate panel concluded that *Weber* and *Johnson* involved challenges to employer action taken pursuant to an affirmative action plan and that the City's decision in the case at bar did not constitute affirmative action. Accordingly, it ruled, the defendant's action was "not subject to the more employer-favorable test of *Johnson* and *Weber*", Id., at n.40, but, instead, was subject to review under *Ricci*'s "strong basis in evidence" standard. In order to qualify as action taken pursuant to an affirmative action plan, the court explained, the employer must provide *ex ante* sex- or race-conscious benefits to *all* members of a protected class. But "where an employer, already having established its procedures in a certain way – such as through a seniority system – throws out the results of those procedures *ex post* because of the racial or gender composition of those results, that constitutes an individualized grant of employment benefits which must be individually justified, and not affirmative action." 650 F.3d at 102. So whereas the defendant in *Weber* had chosen to benefit "all members of the racially defined class in a forward-looking manner," the City had offered make-whole relief, in the form of retroactive seniority, to a discrete group of individuals that it believed had been disadvantaged by its impact-generating selection procedure. Accordingly, the court concluded, since the City had not implemented an affirmative action plan, it had to show a strong basis in evidence that it was faced with disparate impact liability at the time it decided to take race- or sex-conscious action (by showing (1) a strong basis in evidence of a prima facie case of impact discrimination, and (2) of either (a) that its allegedly impact-creating selection device was neither job-related nor consistent with business necessity, or (b) that there was a less discriminatory alternative procedure that it refused to adopt that would have met its needs), and that such action was necessary to avoid or remedy that liability. Moreover, the court rejected the argument that the ruling in *Ricci* was limited to cases where the employer sought to avoid a current violation. Instead, it relied on language in *Ricci* stating that its core holding applies "whenever an employer takes race-conscious action for the asserted purpose of avoiding *or remedying* an unintentional disparate impact." However, the court also emphasized that it was not ruling on whether *Ricci* had overruled *Johnson* and *Weber* in *all* cases involving race- or sex-conscious decisionmaking, i.e., it was *not* deciding that the strong basis in evidence" standard also applied in instances where an employer took voluntary action pursuant to an affirmative action plan. But since the trial judge had decided the case under *Weber/Johnson* analysis, the court vacated the judgment and remanded for reconsideration under the *Ricci* "strong basis in evidence" standard.

10. As mentioned in Note 5 after *Local 28, supra*, it is unclear whether Congress intended the 1991 Civil Rights Act to alter the manner in which the Supreme Court has construed Title VII to apply to voluntary affirmative action. Section 107 of the 1991 law partially reversed the Court's ruling in *Price Waterhouse*, providing that if any proscribed classification is shown to have been a motivating factor in the decisionmaking process, the defendant will be found to have violated the Act. Voluntarily adopted affirmative action plans, by definition, take race or sex into account. Thus, since §116 of the 1991 statute preserves affirmative action plans that are in accord with "the law," if "the law" includes §107 of that same statute, this enactment would have a devastating effect on the continued viability of voluntary affirmative action plans under Title VII. In UNITED BLACK OFFICERS FOR JUSTICE v. SAN FRANCISCO POLICE OFFICERS ASS'N, 979 F.2d 721 (9th Cir. 1992), cert. denied, 507 U.S. 1004, 113 S.Ct. 1645, 123 L.Ed.2d 267 (1993), the Ninth Circuit rejected this interpretation of §116 on the ground that Congress had not evinced any intention to overturn affirmative action. In the court's opinion, "a more natural reading of the phrase 'in accordance with law' is that affirmative action programs that were in accordance with law prior to passage of the 1991 Act are unaffected by the amendments."

11. How should a court analyze the legality of a private employer's voluntarily adopted race-based affirmative action plan under §1981? Recall that although §1981 applies to private acts of racial discrimination, the Supreme Court in *General Building Contractors Ass'n* ruled that this statute only prohibits intentional acts of discrimination. In light this latter ruling, should the court apply the strict scrutiny standard of equal protection or Title VII standards? *See* Doe v. Kamehameha Schools, 470 F.3d 827 (9th Cir.2006) (en banc) (applying Title VII analysis to a race-based affirmative action plan adopted by a private school to govern student admissions).

APPENDIX

Title VII of Civil Rights Act of 1964, as Amended by the Civil Rights Act of 1991 and the Lilly Ledbetter Fair Pay Act of 2009, 42 U.S.C.A. §2000e et seq.

§701. Definitions

For the purposes of this Title—

(a) The term "person" includes one or more individuals, governments, governmental agencies, political subdivisions, labor unions, partnerships, associations, corporations, legal representatives, mutual companies, joint-stock companies, trusts, unincorporated organizations, trustees, trustees in cases under Title 11, or receivers.

(b) The term "employer" means a person engaged in an industry affecting commerce who has fifteen or more employees for each working day in each of twenty or more calendar weeks in the current or preceding calendar year, and any agent of such a person, but such term does not include (1) the United States, a corporation wholly owned by the Government of the United States, an Indian tribe, or any department or agency of the District of Columbia subject by statute to procedures of the competitive service (as defined in section 2102 of Title 5), or (2) a bona fide private membership club (other than a labor organization) which is exempt from taxation under section 501(c) of Title 26, except that during the first year after March 24, 1972, persons having fewer than twenty-five employees (and their agents) shall not be considered employers.

(c) The term "employment agency" means any person regularly undertaking with or without compensation to procure employees for an employer or to procure for employees opportunities to work for an employer and includes an agent of such a person.

(d) The term "labor organization" means a labor organization engaged in an industry affecting commerce, and any agent of such an organization, and includes any organization of any kind, any agency, or employee representation committee, group, association, or plan so engaged in which employees participate and which exists for the purpose, in whole or in part, of dealing with employers concerning grievances, labor disputes, wages, rates of pay, hours, or other terms or conditions of employment, and any conference, general committee, joint or system board, or joint council so engaged which is subordinate to a national or international labor organization.

(e) A labor organization shall be deemed to be engaged in an industry affecting commerce if (1) it maintains or operates a hiring hall or hiring office which procures employees for an employer or procures for employees opportunities to work for an employer, or (2) the number of its members (or, where it is a labor organization composed of other labor organizations or their representatives, if the aggregate number of the members of such other labor organization) is (A) twenty-five or more during the first year after March 24, 1972, or (B) fifteen or more thereafter, and such labor organization—

(1) is the certified representative of employees under the provisions of the National Labor Relations Act, as amended, or the Railway Labor Act, as amended;

(2) although not certified, is a national or international labor organization or a local labor organization recognized or acting as the representative of employees of an employer or employers engaged in an industry affecting commerce; or

(3) has chartered a local labor organization or subsidiary body which is representing or actively seeking to represent employees of employers within the meaning of paragraph (1) or (2); or

(4) has been chartered by a labor organization representing or actively seeking to represent employees within the meaning of paragraph (1) or (2) as the local or subordinate body through which such employees may enjoy membership or become affiliated with such labor organization; or

(5) is a conference, general committee, joint or system board, or joint council subordinate to a national or international labor organization, which includes a labor organization engaged in an industry affecting commerce within the meaning of any of the preceding paragraphs of this subsection.

(f) The term "employee" means an individual employed by an employer, except that the term "employee" shall not include any person elected to public office in any State or political subdivision of any State by the qualified voters thereof, or any person chosen by such officer to be on such officer's personal staff, or an appointee on the policy making level or an immediate adviser with respect to the exercise of the constitutional or legal powers of the office. The exemption set forth in the preceding sentence shall not include employees subject to the civil service laws of a State government, governmental agency or political subdivision. With respect to employment in a foreign country, such term includes an individual who is a citizen of the United States.

(g) The term "commerce" means trade, traffic, commerce, transportation, transmission, or communication among the several States; or between a State and any place outside thereof; or within the District of Columbia, or a possession of the United States; or between points in the same State but through a point outside thereof.

(h) The term "industry affecting commerce" means any activity, business, or industry in commerce or in which a labor dispute would hinder or obstruct commerce or the free flow of commerce and includes any activity or industry "affecting commerce" within the meaning of the Labor–Management Reporting and Disclosure Act of 1959, and further includes any governmental industry, business, or activity.

(i) The term "State" includes a State of the United States, the District of Columbia, Puerto Rico, the Virgin Islands, American Samoa, Guam, Wake Island, the Canal Zone, and Outer Continental Shelf lands defined in the Outer Continental Shelf Lands Act.

(j) The term "religion" includes all aspects of religious observance and practice, as well as belief, unless an employer demonstrates that he is unable to reasonably accommodate to an employee's or prospective employee's religious observance or practice without undue hardship on the conduct of the employer's business.

(k) The terms "because of sex" or "on the basis of sex" include, but are not limited to, because of or on the basis of pregnancy, childbirth, or related medical conditions; and women affected by pregnancy, childbirth, or related medical conditions shall be treated the same for all employment-related purposes, including receipt of benefits under fringe benefit programs, as other persons not so affected but similar in their ability or inability to work, and nothing in section 703(h) of this Act shall be interpreted to permit otherwise. This subsection shall not require an employer to pay for health insurance benefits for abortion, except where the life of the mother would be endangered if the fetus were carried to term, or except where medical complications have arisen from an abortion: Provided, That nothing herein shall preclude an employer from providing abortion benefits or otherwise affect bargaining agreements in regard to abortion.

(l) The term "complaining party" means the Commission, the Attorney General, or a person who may bring an action or proceeding under this title.

(m) The term "demonstrates" means meets the burdens of production and persuasion.

(n) The term "respondent" means an employer, employment agency, labor organization, joint labor-management committee controlling apprenticeship or other training or retraining program, including an on-the-job training program, or Federal entity subject to section 717.

§702.   Exemptions

(a) This Title shall not apply to an employer with respect to the employment of aliens outside any State, or to a religious corporation, association, educational institution, or society with respect to the employment of individuals of a particular religion to perform work connected with the carrying on by such corporation, association, educational institution, or society of its activities.

(b) It shall not be unlawful under section 703 or 704 for an employer (or a corporation controlled by an employer), labor organization, employment agency, or joint labor-management committee controlling apprenticeship or other training or retraining (including on-the-job training programs) to take any action otherwise prohibited by such section, with respect to an employee in a workplace in a foreign country if compliance with such section would cause such employer (or such corporation), such organization, such agency, or such committee to violate the law of the foreign country in which such workplace is located.

(c) (1) If an employer controls a corporation whose place of incorporation is a foreign country, any practice prohibited by section 703 or 704 engaged in by such corporation shall be presumed to be engaged in by such employer.

(2) Sections 703 and 704 shall not apply with respect to the foreign operations of an employer that is a foreign person not controlled by an American employer.

(3) For purposes of this subsection, the determination of whether an employer controls a corporation shall be based on—

(A) the interrelation of operations;

(B) the common management;

(C) the centralized control of labor relations; and

(D) the common ownership or financial control, of the employer and the corporation.

§703. Unlawful Employment Practices

(a) It shall be an unlawful employment practice for an employer—

(1) to fail or refuse to hire or to discharge any individual, or otherwise to discriminate against any individual with respect to his compensation, terms, conditions, or privileges of employment, because of such individual's race, color, religion, sex, or national origin; or

(2) to limit, segregate, or classify his employees or applicants for employment in any way which would deprive or tend to deprive any individual of employment opportunities or otherwise adversely affect his status as an employee, because of such individual's race, color, religion, sex, or national origin.

(b) It shall be an unlawful employment practice for an employment agency to fail or refuse to refer for employment, or otherwise to discriminate against, any individual because of his race, color, religion, sex, or national origin, or to classify or refer for employment any individual on the basis of his race, color, religion, sex, or national origin.

(c) It shall be an unlawful employment practice for a labor organization—

(1) to exclude or to expel from its membership, or otherwise to discriminate against, any individual because of his race, color, religion, sex, or national origin;

(2) to limit, segregate, or classify its membership or applicants for membership, or to classify or fail or refuse to refer for employment any individual, in any way which would deprive or tend to deprive any individual of employment opportunities, or would limit such employment opportunities or otherwise adversely affect his status as an employee or as an applicant for employment, because of such individual's race, color, religion, sex, or national origin; or

(3) to cause or attempt to cause an employer to discriminate against an individual in violation of this section.

(d) It shall be an unlawful employment practice for any employer, labor organization, or joint labor-management committee controlling apprenticeship or other training or retraining, including on-the-job training programs to discriminate against any individual because of his race, color, religion, sex, or national origin in admission to, or employment in, any program established to provide apprenticeship or other training.

(e) Notwithstanding any other provision of this Title, (1) it shall not be an unlawful employment practice for an employer to hire and employ employees, for an employment agency to classify, or refer for employment any individual, for a labor organization to classify its membership or to classify or refer for employment any individual, or for an employer, labor organization, or joint labor-management committee controlling apprenticeship or other training or retraining programs to admit or employ any individual in any such program, on the basis of his religion, sex, or national origin in those certain instances where religion, sex, or national origin is a bona fide occupational qualification reasonably necessary to the normal operation of that particular business or enterprise, and (2) it shall not be an unlawful employment practice for a school, college, university, or other educational institution or institution of learning to hire and employ employees of a particular religion if such school, college, university, or other educational institution or institution of learning is, in whole or in substantial part, owned, supported, controlled, or managed by a particular religion or by a particular religious corporation, association, or society, or if the curriculum of such school, college, university, or other educational institution or institution of learning is directed toward the propagation of a particular religion.

(f) As used in this Title, the phrase "unlawful employment practice" shall not be deemed to include any action or measure taken by an employer, labor organization, joint labor-management committee, or employment agency with respect to an individual who is a member of the Communist Party of the United States or of any other organization required to register as a Communist-action or Communist-front organization by final order of the Subversive Activities Control Board pursuant to the Subversive Activities Control Act of 1950.

(g) Notwithstanding any other provision of this Title, it shall not be an unlawful employment practice for an employer to fail or refuse to hire and employ any individual for any position, for an employer to discharge any individual from any position, or for an employment agency to fail or refuse to refer any individual for employment in any position, or for a labor organization to fail or refuse to refer any individual for employment in any position, if—

(1) the occupancy of such position, or access to the premises in or upon which any part of the duties of such position is performed or is to be performed, is subject to any requirement imposed in the interest of the national security of the United States under any security program in effect pursuant to or administered under any statute of the United States or any Executive order of the President; and

(2) such individual has not fulfilled or has ceased to fulfill that requirement.

(h) Notwithstanding any other provision of this Title, it shall not be an unlawful employment practice for an employer to apply different standards of compensation, or different terms, conditions, or privileges of employment pursuant to a bona fide seniority or merit system, or a system which measures earnings by quantity or quality of production or to employees who work in different locations, provided that such differences are not the result of an intention to discriminate because of race, color, religion, sex, or national origin, nor shall it be an unlawful employment practice for an employer to give and to act upon the results of any professionally developed ability test provided that such test, its administration or action upon the results is not designed, intended or used to discriminate because of race, color, religion, sex or national origin. It shall not be an unlawful employment practice under this Title for any employer to differentiate upon the basis of sex in determining the amount of the wages or compensation paid or to be paid to employees of such employer if such differentiation is authorized by the provisions of the Equal Pay Act.

(i) Nothing contained in this Title shall apply to any business or enterprise on or near an Indian reservation with respect to any publicly announced employment practice of such business or enterprise under which a preferential treatment is given to any individual because he is an Indian living on or near a reservation.

(j) Nothing contained in this Title shall be interpreted to require any employer, employment agency, labor organization, or joint labor-management committee subject to this subchapter to grant preferential treatment to any individual or to any group because of the race, color, religion, sex, or national origin of such individual or group on account of an imbalance which may exist with respect to the total number or percentage of persons of any race, color, religion, sex, or national origin employed by any employer, referred or classified for employment by any employment agency or labor organization, admitted to membership or classified by any labor organization, or admitted to, or employed in, any apprenticeship or other training program, in comparison with the total number or percentage of persons of such race, color, religion, sex, or national origin in any community, State, section, or other area, or in the available work force in any community, State, section, or other area.

(k)(1)(A)An unlawful employment practice based on disparate impact is established under this Title only if—

(i) a complaining party demonstrates that a respondent uses a particular employment practice that causes a disparate impact on the basis of race, color, religion, sex, or national origin and the respondent fails to demonstrate that the challenged practice is job related for the position in question and consistent with business necessity; or

(ii) the complaining party makes the demonstration described in subparagraph (C) with respect to an alternative employment practice and the respondent refuses to adopt such alternative employment practice.

(B) (i) With respect to demonstrating that a particular employment practice causes a disparate impact as described in subparagraph (A)(i), the complaining party shall demonstrate that each particular challenged employment practice causes a disparate impact, except that if the complaining party can demonstrate to the court that the elements of a respondent's decisionmaking process are not capable of separation for analysis, the decisionmaking process may be analyzed as one employment practice.

(ii) If the respondent demonstrates that a specific employment practice does not cause the disparate impact, the respondent shall not be required to demonstrate that such practice is required by business necessity.

(C) The demonstration referred to by subparagraph (A)(ii) shall be in accordance with the law as it existed on June 4, 1989, with respect to the concept of "alternative employment practice."

(2) A demonstration that an employment practice is required by business necessity may not be used as a defense against a claim of intentional discrimination under this title.

(3) Notwithstanding any other provision of this Title, a rule barring the employment of an individual who currently and knowingly uses or possesses a controlled substance, as defined in schedules I and II of section 102(6) of the Controlled Substances Act, other than the use or possession of a drug taken under the supervision of a licensed health care professional, or any other use or possession authorized by the Controlled Substances Act or any other provision of Federal law, shall be considered an unlawful employment practice under this title only if such rule is adopted or applied with an intent to discriminate because of race, color, religion, sex, or national origin.

[§105(b) of the Civil Rights Act of 1991
provides as follows:

No statements other than the interpretive memorandum appearing at Vol. 137 Congressional Record S 15276 (daily ed. Oct. 25, 1991) shall be considered legislative history of, or relied upon in any way as legislative history in construing or applying, any provision of this Act that relates to Wards Cove — Business necessity/cumulation /alternative business practice. For reproduction of relevant portion of Congressional Record, see §105(b) of 1991 Civil Rights Act, *infra*, at 1126]

(l) It shall be an unlawful employment practice for a respondent, in connection with the selection or referral of applicants or candidates for employment or promotion, to adjust the scores of, use different cutoff scores for, or otherwise alter the results of, employment related tests on the basis of race, color, religion, sex, or national origin.

(m) Except as otherwise provided in this Title, an unlawful employment practice is established when the complaining party demonstrates that race, color, religion, sex, or national origin was a motivating factor for any employment practice, even though other factors also motivated the practice.

(n)(1)(A)Notwithstanding any other provision of law, and except as provided in paragraph (2), an employment practice that implements and is within the scope of a litigated or consent judgment or order that resolves a claim of employment discrimination under the Constitution or Federal civil rights laws may not be challenged under the circumstances described in subparagraph (B).

(B) A practice described in subparagraph (A) may not be challenged in a claim under the Constitution or Federal civil rights laws—

(i) by a person who, prior to the entry of the judgment or order described in subparagraph (A), had—

(I) actual notice of the proposed judgment or order sufficient to apprise such person that such judgment or order might adversely affect the interests and legal rights of such person and that an opportunity was available to present objections to such judgment or order by a future date certain; and

(II) a reasonable opportunity to present objections to such judgment or order; or

(ii) by a person whose interests were adequately represented by another person who had previously challenged the judgment or order on the same legal grounds and with a similar factual situation, unless there has been an intervening change in law or fact.

(2) Nothing in this subsection shall be construed to—

(A) alter the standards for intervention under rule 24 of the Federal Rules of Civil Procedure or apply to the rights of parties who have successfully intervened pursuant to such rule in the proceeding in which the parties intervened;

(B) apply to the rights of parties to the action in which a litigated or consent judgment or order was entered, or of members of a class represented or sought to be represented in such action, or of members of a group on whose behalf relief was sought in such action by the Federal Government;

(C) prevent challenges to a litigated or consent judgment or order on the ground that such judgment or order was obtained through collusion or fraud, or is transparently invalid or was entered by a court lacking subject matter jurisdiction; or

(D) authorize or permit the denial to any person of the due process of law required by the Constitution.

(3) Any action not precluded under this subsection that challenges an employment consent judgment or order described in paragraph (1) shall be brought in the court, and if possible before the judge, that entered such judgment or order. Nothing in this subsection shall preclude a transfer of such action pursuant to 28 U.S.C. §1404 [the change of venue statute].

§704.   Other Unlawful Employment Practices

(a) It shall be an unlawful employment practice for an employer to discriminate against any of his employees or applicants for employment, for an employment agency, or joint labor-management committee controlling apprenticeship or other training or retraining, including on-the-job training programs, to discriminate against any individual, or for a labor organization to discriminate against any member thereof or applicant for membership, because he has opposed any practice made an unlawful employment practice by this Title, or because he has made a charge, testified, assisted, or participated in any manner in an investigation, proceeding, or hearing under this Title.

(b) It shall be an unlawful employment practice for an employer, labor organization, employment agency, or joint labor-management committee controlling apprenticeship or other training or retraining, including on-the-job training programs, to print or publish or cause to be printed or published any notice or advertisement relating to employment by such an employer or membership in or any classification or referral for employment by such a labor organization, or relating to any classification or referral for employment by such an employment agency, or relating to admission to, or employment in, any program established to provide apprenticeship or other training by such a joint labor-management committee, indicating any preference, limitation, specification, or discrimination, based on race, color, religion, sex, or national origin, except that such a notice or advertisement may indicate a preference, limitation, specification, or discrimination based on religion, sex, or national origin when religion, sex, or national origin is a bona fide occupational qualification for employment.

§705. Equal Employment Opportunity Commission

(a) There is hereby created a Commission to be known as the Equal Employment Opportunity Commission, which shall be composed of five members, not more than three of whom shall be members of the same political party. Members of the Commission shall be appointed by the President by and with the advice and consent of the Senate for a term of five years. Any individual chosen to fill a vacancy shall be appointed only for the unexpired term of the member whom he shall succeed, and all members of the Commission shall continue to serve until their successors are appointed and qualified, except that no such member of the Commission shall continue to serve (1) for more than sixty days when the Congress is in session unless a nomination to fill such vacancy shall have been submitted to the Senate, or (2) after the adjournment sine die of the session of the Senate in which such nomination was submitted. The President shall designate one member to serve as Chairman of the Commission, and one member to serve as Vice Chairman. The Chairman shall be responsible on behalf of the Commission for the administrative operations of the Commission, and, except as provided in subsection (b) of this section, shall appoint, in accordance with the provisions of Title 5 governing appointments in the competitive service, such officers, agents, attorneys, administrative law judges, and employees as he deems necessary to assist it in the performance of its functions and to fix their compensation in accordance with the provisions of chapter 51 and subchapter III of chapter 53 of Title 5, relating to classification and General Schedule pay rates: Provided, That assignment, removal, and compensation of administrative law judges shall be in accordance with sections 3105, 3344, 5372, and 7521 of Title 5.

(b)(1) There shall be a General Counsel of the Commission appointed by the President, by and with the advice and consent of the Senate, for a term of four years.

The General Counsel shall have responsibility for the conduct of litigation as provided in sections 706 and 707 of this Act. The General Counsel shall have such other duties as the Commission may prescribe or as may be provided by law and shall concur with the Chairman of the Commission on the appointment and supervision of regional attorneys. The General Counsel of the Commission on the effective date of this Act shall continue in such position and perform the functions specified in this subsection until a successor is appointed and qualified.

(2) Attorneys appointed under this section may, at the direction of the Commission, appear for and represent the Commission in any case in court, provided that the Attorney General shall conduct all litigation to which the Commission is a party in the Supreme Court pursuant to this Title.

(c) A vacancy in the Commission shall not impair the right of the remaining members to exercise all the powers of the Commission and three members thereof shall constitute a quorum.

(d) The Commission shall have an official seal which shall be judicially noticed.

(e) The Commission shall at the close of each fiscal year report to the Congress and to the President concerning the action it has taken and the moneys it has disbursed. It shall make such further reports on the cause of and means of eliminating discrimination and such recommendations for further legislation as may appear desirable.

(f) The principal office of the Commission shall be in or near the District of Columbia, but it may meet or exercise any or all its powers at any other place. The Commission may establish such regional or State offices as it deems necessary to accomplish the purpose of this Title.

(g) The Commission shall have power—

(1) to cooperate with and, with their consent, utilize regional, State, local, and other agencies, both public and private, and individuals;

(2) to pay to witnesses whose depositions are taken or who are summoned before the Commission or any of its agents the same witness and mileage fees as are paid to witnesses in the courts of the United States;

(3) to furnish to persons subject to this subchapter such technical assistance as they may request to further their compliance with this Title or an order issued thereunder;

(4) upon the request of (i) any employer, whose employees or some of them, or (ii) any labor organization, whose members or some of them, refuse or threaten to refuse to cooperate in effectuating the provisions of this Title, to assist in such effectuation by conciliation or such other remedial action as is provided by this Title;

(5) to make such technical studies as are appropriate to effectuate the purposes and policies of this Title and to make the results of such studies available to the public;

(6) to intervene in a civil action brought under section 706 of this Act by an aggrieved party against a respondent other than a government, governmental agency or political subdivision.

(h) (1) The Commission shall, in any of its educational or promotional activities, cooperate with other departments and agencies in the performance of such educational and promotional activities.

(2) In exercising its powers under this title, the Commission shall carry out educational and outreach activities (including dissemination of information in languages other than English) targeted to—

(A) individuals who historically have been victims of employment discrimination and have not been equitably served by the Commission; and

(B) individuals on whose behalf the Commission has authority to enforce any other law prohibiting employment discrimination, concerning rights and obligations under this title or such law, as the case may be.

(i) All officers, agents, attorneys, and employees of the Commission shall be subject to the provisions of section 7324 of Title 5, notwithstanding any exemption contained in such section.

(j) (1) The Commission shall establish a Technical Assistance Training Institute, through which the Commission shall provide technical assistance and training regarding the laws and regulations enforced by the Commission.

(2) An employer or other entity covered under this title shall not be excused from compliance with the requirements of this title because of any failure to receive technical assistance under this subsection.

(3) There are authorized to be appropriated to carry out this subsection such sums as may be necessary for fiscal year 1992.

§706.   Enforcement Provisions

(a) The Commission is empowered, as hereinafter provided, to prevent any person from engaging in any unlawful employment practice as set forth in section 703 or 704 of this Act.

(b) Whenever a charge is filed by or on behalf of a person claiming to be aggrieved, or by a member of the Commission, alleging that an employer, employment agency, labor organization, or joint labor-management committee controlling apprenticeship or other training or retraining, including on-the-job training programs, has engaged in an unlawful employment practice, the Commission shall serve a notice of the charge (including the date, place and circumstances of the alleged unlawful employment practice) on such employer, employment agency, labor organization, or joint labor-management committee (hereinafter referred to as the "respondent") within ten days, and shall make an investigation thereof. Charges shall be in writing under oath or affirmation and shall contain such information and be in such form as the Commission requires. Charges shall not be made public by the Commission. If the Commission determines after such investigation that there is not reasonable cause to believe that the charge is true, it shall dismiss the charge and promptly notify the person claiming to be aggrieved and the respondent of its action. In determining whether reasonable cause exists, the Commission shall accord substantial weight to final findings and orders made by State or local authorities in proceedings commenced under State or local law pursuant to the requirements of subsections (c) and (d) of this section. If the Commission determines after such investigation that there is reasonable cause to believe that the charge is true, the Commission shall endeavor to eliminate any such alleged unlawful employment practice by informal methods of conference, conciliation, and persuasion. Nothing said or done during and as a part of such informal endeavors may be made public by the Commission, its officers or employees, or used as evidence in a subsequent proceeding without the written consent of the persons concerned. Any person who makes public information in violation of this subsection shall be fined not more than $1,000 or imprisoned for not more than one year, or both. The Commission shall make its determination on reasonable cause as promptly as possible and, so far as practicable, not later than one hundred and twenty days from the filing of the charge or, where applicable under subsection (c) or (d) of this section, from the date upon which the Commission is authorized to take action with respect to the charge.

(c) In the case of an alleged unlawful employment practice occurring in a State, or political subdivision of a State, which has a State or local law prohibiting the unlawful employment practice alleged and establishing or authorizing a State or local authority to grant or seek relief from such practice or to institute criminal proceedings with respect thereto upon receiving notice thereof, no charge may be filed under subsection (b) of this section by the person aggrieved before the expiration of sixty days after proceedings have been commenced under the State or local law, unless such proceedings have been earlier terminated, provided that such sixty-day period shall be extended to one hundred and twenty days during the first year after the effective date of such State or local law. If any requirement for the commencement of such proceedings is imposed by a State or local authority other than a requirement of the filing of a written and signed statement of the facts upon which the proceeding is based, the proceeding shall be deemed to have been commenced for the purposes of this subsection at the time such statement is sent by registered mail to the appropriate State or local authority.

(d) In the case of any charge filed by a member of the Commission alleging an unlawful employment practice occurring in a State or political subdivision of a State which has a State or local law prohibiting the practice alleged and establishing or authorizing a State or local authority to grant or seek relief from such practice or to institute criminal proceedings with respect thereto upon receiving notice thereof, the Commission shall, before taking any action with respect to such charge, notify the appropriate State or local officials and, upon request, afford them a reasonable time, but not less than sixty days (provided that such sixty-day period shall be extended to one hundred and twenty days during the first year after the effective day of such State or local law), unless a shorter period is requested, to act under such State or local law to remedy the practice alleged.

(e) (1) A charge under this section shall be filed within one hundred and eighty days after the alleged unlawful employment practice occurred and notice of the charge (including the date, place and circumstances of the alleged unlawful employment practice) shall be served upon the person against whom such charge is made within ten days thereafter, except that in a case of an unlawful employment practice with respect to which the person aggrieved has initially instituted proceedings with a State or local agency with authority to grant or seek relief from such practice or to institute criminal proceedings with respect thereto upon receiving notice thereof, such charge shall be filed by or on behalf of the person aggrieved within three hundred days after the alleged unlawful employment practice occurred, or within thirty days after receiving notice that the State or local agency has terminated the proceedings under the State or local law, whichever is earlier, and a copy of such charge shall be filed by the Commission with the State or local agency.

(2) For purposes of this section, an unlawful employment practice occurs, with respect to a seniority system that has been adopted for an intentionally discriminatory purpose in violation of this title (whether or not that discriminatory purpose is apparent on the face of the seniority provision), when the seniority system is adopted, when an individual becomes subject to the seniority system, or when a person aggrieved is injured by the application of the seniority system or provision of the system.

(3)(A) For purposes of this section, an unlawful employment practice occurs, with respect to discrimination in compensation in violation of this title, when a discriminatory compensation decision or other practice is adopted, when an individual becomes subject to a discriminatory compensation decision or other practice, or when an individual is affected by application of a discriminatory compensation decision or other practice, including each time wages, benefits, or other compensation is paid, resulting in whole or in part from such a decision or other practice.

(B) In addition to any relief authorized by section 1977A of the Revised Statutes (42 U.S.C. 1981a), liability may accrue and an aggrieved person may obtain relief as provided in subsection (g)(1), including recovery of back pay for up to two years preceding the filing of the charge, where the unlawful employment practices that have occurred during the charge filing period are similar or related to unlawful employment practices with regard to discrimination in compensation that occurred outside the time for filing a charge.

(f) (1) If within thirty days after a charge is filed with the Commission or within thirty days after expiration of any period of reference under subsection (c) or (d) of this section, the Commission has been unable to secure from the respondent a conciliation agreement acceptable to the Commission, the Commission may bring a civil action against any respondent not a government, governmental agency, or political subdivision named in the charge. In the case of a respondent which is a government, governmental agency, or political subdivision, if the Commission has been unable to secure from the respondent a conciliation agreement acceptable to the Commission, the Commission shall take no further action and shall refer the case to the Attorney General who may bring a civil action against such respondent in the appropriate United States district court. The person or persons aggrieved shall have the right to intervene in a civil action brought by the Commission or the Attorney General in a case involving a government, governmental agency, or political subdivision. If a charge filed with the Commission pursuant to subsection (b) of this section is dismissed by the Commission, or if within one hundred and eighty days from the filing of such charge or the expiration of any period of reference under subsection (c) or (d) of this section, whichever is later, the Commission has not filed a civil action under this section or the Attorney General has not filed a civil action in a case involving a government, governmental agency, or political subdivision, or the Commission has not entered into a conciliation agreement to which the person aggrieved is a party, the Commission, or the Attorney General in a case involving a government, governmental agency, or political subdivision, shall so notify the person aggrieved and within ninety days after the giving of such notice a civil action may be brought against the respondent named in the charge (A) by the person claiming to be aggrieved or (B) if such charge was filed by a member of the Commission, by any person whom the charge alleges was aggrieved by the alleged unlawful employment practice. Upon application by the complainant and in such circumstances as the court may deem just, the court may appoint an attorney for such complainant and may authorize the commencement of the action without the payment of fees, costs, or security. Upon timely application, the court may, in its discretion, permit the Commission, or the Attorney General in a case involving a government, governmental agency, or political subdivision, to intervene in such civil action upon certification that the case is of general public importance. Upon request, the court may, in its discretion, stay further proceedings for not more than sixty days pending the termination of State or local proceedings described in subsection (c) or (d) of this section or further efforts of the Commission to obtain voluntary compliance.

(2) Whenever a charge is filed with the Commission and the Commission concludes on the basis of a preliminary investigation that prompt judicial action is necessary to carry out the purposes of this Act, the Commission, or the Attorney General in a case involving a government, governmental agency, or political subdivision, may bring an action for appropriate temporary or preliminary relief pending final disposition of such charge. Any temporary restraining order or other order granting preliminary or temporary relief shall be issued in accordance with rule 65 of the Federal Rules of Civil Procedure. It shall be the duty of a court having jurisdiction over proceedings under this section to assign cases for hearing at the earliest practicable date and to cause such cases to be in every way expedited.

(3) Each United States district court and each United States court of a place subject to the jurisdiction of the United States shall have jurisdiction of actions brought under this Title. Such an action may be brought in any judicial district in the State in which the unlawful employment practice is alleged to have been committed, in the judicial district in which the employment records relevant to such practice are maintained and administered, or in the judicial district in which the aggrieved person would have worked but for the alleged unlawful employment practice, but if the respondent is not found within any such district, such an action may be brought within the judicial district in which the respondent has his principal office. For purposes of sections 1404 and 1406 of Title 28, the judicial district in which the respondent has his principal office shall in all cases be considered a district in which the action might have been brought.

(4) It shall be the duty of the chief judge of the district (or in his absence, the acting chief judge) in which the case is pending immediately to designate a judge in such district to hear and determine the case. In the event that no judge in the district is available to hear and determine the case, the chief judge of the district, or the acting chief judge, as the case may be, shall certify this fact to the chief judge of the circuit (or in his absence, the acting chief judge) who shall then designate a district or circuit judge of the circuit to hear and determine the case.

(5) It shall be the duty of the judge designated pursuant to this subsection to assign the case for hearing at the earliest practicable date and to cause the case to

be in every way expedited. If such judge has not scheduled the case for trial within one hundred and twenty days after issue has been joined, that judge may appoint a master pursuant to rule 53 of the Federal Rules of Civil Procedure.

(g) (1) If the court finds that the respondent has intentionally engaged in or is intentionally engaging in an unlawful employment practice charged in the complaint, the court may enjoin the respondent from engaging in such unlawful employment practice, and order such affirmative action as may be appropriate, which may include, but is not limited to, reinstatement or hiring of employees, with or without back pay (payable by the employer, employment agency, or labor organization, as the case may be, responsible for the unlawful employment practice), or any other equitable relief as the court deems appropriate. Back pay liability shall not accrue from a date more than two years prior to the filing of a charge with the Commission. Interim earnings or amounts earnable with reasonable diligence by the person or persons discriminated against shall operate to reduce the back pay otherwise allowable.

(2)(A) No order of the court shall require the admission or reinstatement of an individual as a member of a union, or the hiring, reinstatement, or promotion of an individual as an employee, or the payment to him of any back pay, if such individual was refused admission, suspended, or expelled, or was refused employment or advancement or was suspended or discharged for any reason other than discrimination on account of race, color, religion, sex, or national origin or in violation of section 704 of this Act.

(B) On a claim in which an individual proves a violation under section 703(m) and a respondent demonstrates that the respondent would have taken the same action in the absence of the impermissible motivating factor, the court—

(i) may grant declaratory relief, injunctive relief (except as provided in clause (ii)), and attorney's fees and costs demonstrated to be directly attributable only to the pursuit of a claim under section 703(m); and

(ii) shall not award damages or issue an order requiring any admission, reinstatement, hiring, promotion, or payment, described in subparagraph (A).

(h) The provisions of sections 101 to 115 of Title 29 shall not apply with respect to civil actions brought under this section.

(i) In any case in which an employer, employment agency, or labor organization fails to comply with an order of a court issued in a civil action brought under this section, the Commission may commence proceedings to compel compliance with such order.

(j) Any civil action brought under this section and any proceedings brought under subsection (i) of this section shall be subject to appeal as provided in sections 1291 and 1292, Title 28.

(k) In any action or proceeding under this Title the court, in its discretion, may allow the prevailing party, other than the Commission or the United States, a reasonable attorney's fee (including expert fees) as part of the costs, and the Commission and the United States shall be liable for costs the same as a private person.

§707.   Civil Actions by Attorney General

(a) Whenever the Attorney General has reasonable cause to believe that any person or group of persons is engaged in a pattern or practice of resistance to the full enjoyment of any of the rights secured by this Title, and that the pattern or practice is of such a nature and is intended to deny the full exercise of the rights herein described, the Attorney General may bring a civil action in the appropriate district court of the United States by filing with it a complaint (1) signed by him (or in his absence the Acting Attorney General), (2) setting forth facts pertaining to such pattern or practice, and (3) requesting such relief, including an application for a permanent or temporary injunction, restraining order or other order against the person or persons responsible for such pattern or practice, as he deems necessary to insure the full enjoyment of the rights herein described.

(b) The district courts of the United States shall have and shall exercise jurisdiction of proceedings instituted pursuant to this section, and in any such proceeding the Attorney General may file with the clerk of such court a request that a court of three judges be convened to hear and determine the case. Such request by the Attorney General shall be accompanied by a certificate that, in his opinion, the case is of general public importance. A copy of the certificate and request for a three-judge court shall be immediately furnished by such clerk to the chief judge of the circuit (or in his absence, the presiding circuit judge of the circuit) in which the case is pending. Upon receipt of such request it shall be the duty of the chief judge of the circuit or the presiding circuit judge, as the case may be, to designate immediately three judges in such circuit, of whom at least one shall be a circuit judge and another of whom shall be a district judge of the court in which the proceeding was instituted, to hear and determine such case, and it shall be the duty of the judges so designated to assign the case for hearing at the earliest practicable date, to participate in the hearing and determination thereof, and to cause the case to be in every way expedited. An appeal from the final judgment of such court will lie to the Supreme Court.

In the event the Attorney General fails to file such a request in any such proceeding, it shall be the duty of the chief judge of the district (or in his absence, the acting chief judge) in which the case is pending immediately to designate a judge in such district to hear and determine the case. In the event that no judge in the district is available to hear and determine the case, the chief judge of the district, or the acting chief judge, as the case may be, shall certify this fact to the chief judge of the circuit (or in his absence, the acting chief judge) who shall then designate a district or circuit judge of the circuit to hear and determine the case.

It shall be the duty of the judge designated pursuant to this section to assign the case for hearing at the earliest practicable date and to cause the case to be in every way expedited.

(c) Effective two years after March 24, 1972, the functions of the Attorney General under this section shall be transferred to the Commission, together with such personnel, property, records, and unexpended balances of appropriations, allocations, and other funds employed, used, held, available, or to be made available in connection with such functions unless the President submits, and neither House of Congress vetoes, a reorganization plan pursuant to chapter 9 of Title 5, inconsistent with the provisions of this subsection. The Commission shall carry out such functions in accordance with subsections (d) and (e) of this section.

(d) Upon the transfer of functions provided for in subsection (c) of this section, in all suits commenced pursuant to this section prior to the date of such transfer, proceedings shall continue without abatement, all court orders and decrees shall remain in effect, and the Commission shall be substituted as a party for the United States of America, the Attorney General, or the Acting Attorney General, as appropriate.

(e) Subsequent to March 24, 1972, the Commission shall have authority to investigate and act on a charge of a pattern or practice of discrimination, whether filed by or on behalf of a person claiming to be aggrieved or by a member of the Commission. All such actions shall be conducted in accordance with the procedures set forth in section 706 of this Act.

§708. Effect on State Laws

Nothing in this Title shall be deemed to exempt or relieve any person from any liability, duty, penalty, or punishment provided by any present or future law of any State or political subdivision of a State, other than any such law which purports to require or permit the doing of any act which would be an unlawful employment practice under this Title.

§709. Investigations

(a) In connection with any investigation of a charge filed under section 706 of this Act, the Commission or its designated representative shall at all reasonable times have access to, for the purposes of examination, and the right to copy any evidence of any person being investigated or proceeded against that relates to unlawful employment practices covered by this Title and is relevant to the charge under investigation.

(b) The Commission may cooperate with State and local agencies charged with the administration of State fair employment practices laws and, with the consent of such agencies, may, for the purpose of carrying out its functions and duties under this Title and within the limitation of funds appropriated specifically for such purpose, engage in and contribute to the cost of research and other projects of mutual interest undertaken by such agencies, and utilize the services of such agencies and their employees, and, notwithstanding any other provision of law, pay by advance or reimbursement such agencies and their employees for services rendered to assist the Commission in carrying out this Title. In furtherance of such cooperative efforts, the Commission may enter into written agreements with such State or local agencies and such agreements may include provisions under which the Commission shall refrain from processing a charge in any cases or class of cases specified in such agreements or under which the Commission shall relieve any person or class of persons in such State or locality from requirements imposed under this section. The Commission shall rescind any such agreement whenever it determines that the agreement no longer serves the interest of effective enforcement of this Title.

(c) Every employer, employment agency, and labor organization subject to this Title shall (1) make and keep such records relevant to the determinations of whether unlawful employment practices have been or are being committed, (2) preserve such records for such periods, and (3) make such reports therefrom as the Commission shall prescribe by regulation or order, after public hearing, as reasonable, necessary, or appropriate for the enforcement of this Title or the regulations or orders thereunder. The Commission shall, by regulation, require each employer, labor organization, and joint labor-management committee subject to this Title which controls an apprenticeship or other training program to maintain such records as are reasonably necessary to carry out the purposes of this Title, including, but not limited to, a list of applicants who wish to participate in such program, including the chronological order in which applications were received, and to furnish to the Commission upon request, a detailed description of the manner in which persons are selected to participate in the apprenticeship or other training program. Any employer, employment agency, labor organization, or joint labor-management committee which believes that the application to it of any regulation or order issued under this section would result in undue hardship may apply to the Commission for an exemption from the application of such regulation or order, and, if such application for an exemption is denied, bring a civil action in the United States district court for the district where such records are kept. If the Commission or the court, as the case may be, finds that the application of the regulation or order to the employer, employment agency, or labor organization in question would impose an undue hardship, the Commission or the court, as the case may be, may grant appropriate relief. If any person required to comply with the provisions of this subsection fails or refuses to do so, the United States district court for the district in which such person is found, resides, or transacts business, shall, upon application of the Commission, or the Attorney General in a case involving a government, governmental agency or political subdivision, have jurisdiction to issue to such person an order requiring him to comply.

(d) In prescribing requirements pursuant to subsection (c) of this section, the Commission shall consult with other interested State and Federal agencies and shall endeavor to coordinate its requirements with those adopted by such agencies. The Commission shall furnish upon request and without cost to any State or local agency charged with the administration of a fair employment practice law information obtained pursuant to subsection (c) of this section from any employer, employment agency, labor organization, or joint labor-management committee subject to the jurisdiction of such agency. Such information shall be furnished on condition that it not be made public by the recipient agency prior to the institution of a proceeding under State or local law involving such information. If this condition is violated by a recipient agency, the Commission may decline to honor subsequent requests pursuant to this subsection.

(e) It shall be unlawful for any officer or employee of the Commission to make public in any manner whatever any information obtained by the Commission pursuant to its authority under this section prior to the institution of any proceeding under this Title involving such information. Any officer or employee of the Commission who shall make public in any manner whatever any information in violation of this subsection shall be guilty of a misdemeanor and upon conviction thereof, shall be fined not more than $1,000, or imprisoned not more than one year.

§710. Conduct of Hearings and Investigations

For the purpose of all hearings and investigations conducted by the Commission or its duly authorized agents or agencies, section 161 of Title 29 shall apply.

§711.　Posting of Notices; Penalties

(a) Every employer, employment agency, and labor organization, as the case may be, shall post and keep posted in conspicuous places upon its premises where notices to employees, applicants for employment, and members are customarily posted a notice to be prepared or approved by the Commission setting forth excerpts from or, summaries of, the pertinent provisions of this Title and information pertinent to the filing of a complaint.

(b) A willful violation of this section shall be punishable by a fine of not more than $100 for each separate offense.

§712.　Veterans' Special Rights or Preference

Nothing contained in this Title shall be construed to repeal or modify any Federal, State, territorial, or local law creating special rights or preference for veterans.

§713.　Regulations and Reliance on Interpretations and Instructions of Commission

(a) The Commission shall have authority from time to time to issue, amend, or rescind suitable procedural regulations to carry out the provisions of this Title. Regulations issued under this section shall be in conformity with the standards and limitations of subchapter II of chapter 5 of Title 5.

(b) In any action or proceeding based on any alleged unlawful employment practice, no person shall be subject to any liability or punishment for or on account of (1) the commission by such person of an unlawful employment practice if he pleads and proves that the act or omission complained of was in good faith, in conformity with, and in reliance on any written interpretation or opinion of the Commission, or (2) the failure of such person to publish and file any information required by any provision of this Title if he pleads and proves that he failed to publish and file such information in good faith, in conformity with the instructions of the Commission issued under this Title regarding the filing of such information. Such a defense, if established, shall be a bar to the action or proceeding, notwithstanding that (A) after such act or omission, such interpretation or opinion is modified or rescinded or is determined by judicial authority to be invalid or of no legal effect, or (B) after publishing or filing the description and annual reports, such publication or filing is determined by judicial authority not to be in conformity with the requirements of this Title.

* * *

§715.　Coordination of Efforts and Elimination of Competition Among Federal Departments, Agencies, etc. in Implementation and Enforcement of Equal Employment Opportunity Legislation, Orders, and Policies; Report to President and Congress

The Equal Employment Opportunity Commission shall have the responsibility for developing and implementing agreements, policies and practices designed to maximize effort, promote efficiency, and eliminate conflict, competition, duplication and inconsistency among the operations, functions and jurisdictions of the various departments, agencies and branches of the Federal Government responsible for the implementation and enforcement of equal employment opportunity legislation, orders, and policies. On or before October 1 of each year, the Equal Employment Opportunity Commission shall transmit to the President and to the Congress a report of its activities, together with such recommendations for legislative or administrative changes as it concludes are desirable to further promote the purposes of this section.

* * *

§717.   Employment by Federal Government

(a) All personnel actions affecting employees or applicants for employment (except with regard to aliens employed outside the limits of the United States) in military departments as defined in section 102 of Title 5, in executive agencies as defined in section 105 of Title 5 (including employees and applicants for employment who are paid from nonappropriated funds), in the United States Postal Service and the Postal Rate Commission, in those units of the Government of the District of Columbia having positions in the competitive service, and in those units of the legislative and judicial branches of the Federal Government having positions in the competitive service, and in the Library of Congress shall be made free from any discrimination based on race, color, religion, sex, or national origin.

(b) Except as otherwise provided in this subsection, the Equal Employment Opportunity Commission shall have authority to enforce the provisions of subsection (a) of this section through appropriate remedies, including reinstatement or hiring of employees with or without back pay, as will effectuate the policies of this section, and shall issue such rules, regulations, orders and instructions as it deems necessary and appropriate to carry out its responsibilities under this section. The Equal Employment Opportunity Commission shall—

(1) be responsible for the annual review and approval of a national and regional equal employment opportunity plan which each department and agency and each appropriate unit referred to in subsection (a) of this section shall submit in order to maintain an affirmative program of equal employment opportunity for all such employees and applicants for employment;

(2) be responsible for the review and evaluation of the operation of all agency equal employment opportunity programs, periodically obtaining and publishing (on at least a semiannual basis) progress reports from each such department, agency, or unit; and

(3) consult with and solicit the recommendations of interested individuals, groups, and organizations relating to equal employment opportunity.

The head of each such department, agency, or unit shall comply with such rules, regulations, orders, and instructions which shall include a provision that an employee or applicant for employment shall be notified of any final action taken on any complaint of discrimination filed by him thereunder. The plan submitted by each department, agency, and unit shall include, but not be limited to—

(1) provision for the establishment of training and education programs designed to provide a maximum opportunity for employees to advance so as to perform at their highest potential; and

(2) a description of the qualifications in terms of training and experience relating to equal employment opportunity for the principal and operating officials of each such department, agency, or unit responsible for carrying out the equal employment opportunity program and of the allocation of personnel and resources proposed by such department, agency, or unit to carry out its equal employment opportunity program.

With respect to employment in the Library of Congress, authorities granted in this subsection to the Equal Employment Opportunity Commission shall be exercised by the Librarian of Congress.

(c) Within ninety (90) days of receipt of notice of final action taken by a department, agency, or unit referred to in subsection (a) of this section, or by the Equal Employment Opportunity Commission upon an appeal from a decision or order of such department, agency, or unit on a complaint of discrimination based on race, color, religion, sex or national origin, brought pursuant to subsection (a) of this section, Executive Order 11478 or any succeeding Executive orders, or after one hundred and eighty days from the filing of the initial charge with the department, agency, or unit or with the Equal Employment Opportunity Commission on appeal from a decision or order of such department, agency, or unit until such time as final action may be taken by a department, agency, or unit, an employee or applicant for employment, if aggrieved by the final disposition of his complaint, or by the failure to take final action on his complaint, may file a civil action as provided in section 706 of this Act, in which civil action the head of the department, agency, or unit, as appropriate, shall be the defendant.

(d) The provisions of section 706(f) through (k) of this Act, as applicable, shall govern civil actions brought hereunder, and the same interest to compensate for delay in payment shall be available as in cases involving nonpublic parties.

(e) Nothing contained in this Act shall relieve any Government agency or official of its or his primary responsibility to assure nondiscrimination in employment as required by the Constitution and statutes or of its or his responsibilities under Executive Order 11478 relating to equal employment opportunity in the Federal Government.

(f) Section 706(e)(3) shall apply to complaints of discrimination in compensation under this section.

§718. Procedure for Denial, Withholding, Termination, or Suspension of Government Contract

No Government contract, or portion thereof, with any employer, shall be denied, withheld, terminated, or suspended, by any agency or officer of the United States under any equal employment opportunity law or order, where such employer has an affirmative action plan which has previously been accepted by the Government for the same facility within the past twelve months without first according such employer full hearing and adjudication under the provisions of section 554 of Title 5, and the following pertinent sections: Provided, That if such employer has deviated substantially from such previously agreed to affirmative action plan, this section shall not apply: Provided further, That for the purposes of this section an affirmative action plan shall be deemed to have been accepted by the Government at the time the appropriate compliance agency has accepted such plan unless within forty-five days thereafter the Office of Federal Contract Compliance has disapproved such plan.

Civil Rights Act of 1991
P.L. 102–166; 105 Stat. 1071.

An Act to amend the Civil Rights Act of 1964 to strengthen and improve Federal civil rights laws, to provide for damages in cases of intentional employment discrimination, to clarify provisions regarding disparate impact actions, and for other purposes.

Be it enacted by the Senate and House of Representatives of the United States of America in Congress assembled,

§1. Short Title

This Act may be cited as the "Civil Rights Act of 1991."

§2. Findings

The Congress finds that—

(1) additional remedies under Federal law are needed to deter unlawful harassment and intentional discrimination in the workplace;

(2) the decision of the Supreme Court in Wards Cove Packing Co. v. Atonio, 490 U.S. 642 (1989) has weakened the scope and effectiveness of Federal civil rights protections; and

(3) legislation is necessary to provide additional protections against unlawful discrimination in employment.

§3. Purposes

The purposes of this Act are—

(1) to provide appropriate remedies for intentional discrimination and unlawful harassment in the workplace;

(2) to codify the concepts of "business necessity" and "job related" enunciated by the Supreme Court in Griggs v. Duke Power Co., 401 U.S. 424 (1971), and in the other Supreme Court decisions prior to Wards Cove Packing Co. v. Atonio, 490 U.S. 642 (1989);

(3) to confirm statutory authority and provide statutory guidelines for the adjudication of disparate impact suits under Title VII of the Civil Rights Act of 1964; and

(4) to respond to recent decisions of the Supreme Court by expanding the scope of relevant civil rights statutes in order to provide adequate protection to victims of discrimination.

TITLE I—FEDERAL CIVIL RIGHTS REMEDIES

* * *

§102. Damages in Cases of Intentional Discrimination

The Revised Statutes are amended by inserting after 42 U.S.C. §1981 the following new section, 42 U.S.C. §1981A. [Text of this provision can be found *infra*, at 1262–1263.]

* * *

§105. Burden of Proof in Disparate Impact Cases

* * *

(b) No statements other than the interpretive memorandum appearing at Vol. 137 Congressional Record S 15276 (daily ed. Oct. 25, 1991) shall be considered legislative history of, or relied upon in any way as legislative history in construing or applying, any provision of this Act that relates to Wards Cove—Business necessity/cumulation/alternative business practice.

[The portion of the Congressional Record cited in §105(b) provides as follows:

Mr. Danforth.

Mr. President, I ask unanimous consent that the attached interpretive memorandum be printed in the RECORD.

There being no objection, the memorandum was ordered to be printed in the RECORD, as follows:

Interpretive Memorandum

The final compromise on S. 1745 agreed to by several Senate sponsors, including Senators Danforth, Kennedy, and Dole, and the Administration states that with respect to Wards Cove–Business necessity/cumulation/alternative business practice-the exclusive legislative history is as follows:

The terms "business necessity" and "job related" are intended to reflect the concepts enunciated by the Supreme Court in Griggs v. Duke Power Co., 401 U.S. 424 (1971), and in the other Supreme Court decisions prior to Wards Cove Packing Co. v. Atonio, 490 U.S. 642 (1989).

When a decision-making process includes particular, functionally-integrated practices which are components of the same criterion, standard, method of administration, or test, such as the height and weight requirements designed to measure strength in Dothard v. Rawlinson, 433 U.S. 321 (1977), the particular, functionally-integrated practices may be analyzed as one employment practice.]

* * *

§116. Lawful Court-Ordered Remedies, Affirmative Action, and Conciliation Agreements Not Affected

Nothing in the amendments made by this title shall be construed to affect court-ordered remedies, affirmative action, or conciliation agreements, that are in accordance with the law.

§117. Coverage of House of Representatives and the Agencies of the Legislative Branch

(a) Coverage of the House of Representatives—

(1) In General—Notwithstanding any provision of Title VII of the Civil Rights Act of 1964 or of other law, the purposes of such title shall, subject to paragraph (2), apply in their entirety to the House of Representatives.

(2) Employment in the House—

(A) Application—The rights and protections under Title VII of the Civil Rights Act of 1964 shall, subject to subparagraph (B), apply with respect to any employee in an employment position in the House of Representatives and any employing authority of the House of Representatives.

(B) Administration—

(i) In General—In the administration of this paragraph, the remedies and procedures made applicable pursuant to the resolution described in clause (ii) shall apply exclusively.

(ii) Resolution—The resolution referred to in clause (i) is the Fair Employment Practices Resolution (House Resolution 558 of the One Hundredth Congress, as agreed to October 4, 1988), as incorporated into the Rules of the House of Representatives of the One Hundred Second Congress as Rule LI, or any other provision that continues in effect the provisions of such resolution.

(C) Exercise of Rulemaking Power—The provisions of subparagraph (B) are enacted by the House of Representatives as an exercise of the rulemaking power of the House of Representatives, with full recognition of the right of the House to change its rules, in the same manner, and to the same extent as in the case of any other rule of the House.

(b) Instrumentalities of Congress—

(1) In General—The rights and protections under this title and Title VII of the Civil Rights Act of 1964 shall, subject to paragraph (2), apply with respect to the conduct of each instrumentality of the Congress.

(2) Establishment of Remedies and Procedures by Instrumentalities—The chief official of each instrumentality of the Congress shall establish remedies and procedures to be utilized with respect to the rights and protections provided pursuant to paragraph (1). Such remedies and procedures shall apply exclusively, except for the employees who are defined as Senate employees, in section 301(c)(1).

(3) Report to Congress—The chief official of each instrumentality of the Congress shall, after establishing remedies and procedures for purposes of paragraph (2), submit to the Congress a report describing the remedies and procedures.

(4) Definition of Instrumentalities—For purposes of this section, instrumentalities of the Congress include the following: the Architect of the Capitol, the Congressional Budget Office, the General Accounting Office, the Government Printing Office, the Office of Technology Assessment, and the United States Botanic Garden.

(5) Construction—Nothing in this section shall alter the enforcement procedures for individuals protected under section 717 of Title VII for the Civil Rights Act of 1964.

§118. Alternative Means of Dispute Resolution

Where appropriate and to the extent authorized by law, the use of alternative means of dispute resolution, including settlement negotiations, conciliation, facilitation, mediation, factfinding, minitrials, and arbitration, is encouraged to resolve disputes arising under the Acts or provisions of Federal law amended by this Act.

* * *

TITLE IV—GENERAL PROVISIONS

§402. Effective Date

(a) In General—Except as otherwise specifically provided, this Act and the amendments made by this Act shall take effect upon enactment.

(b) Certain Disparate Impact Cases—Notwithstanding any other provision of this Act, nothing in this Act shall apply to any disparate impact case for which a complaint was filed before March 1, 1975, and for which an initial decision was rendered after October 30, 1983.

Selected Constitutional Amendments

Amendment V

No person shall * * * be deprived of life, liberty, or property, without due process of law; nor shall private property be taken for public use, without just compensation.

Amendment XIII [1865]

Section 1. Neither slavery nor involuntary servitude, except as a punishment for crime whereof the party shall have been duly convicted, shall exist within the United States, or any place subject to their jurisdiction.

Section 2. Congress shall have power to enforce this article by appropriate legislation.

Amendment XIV [1868]

Section 1. All persons born or naturalized in the United States, and subject to the jurisdiction thereof, are citizens of the United States and of the State wherein they reside. No State shall make or enforce any law which shall abridge the privileges or immunities of citizens of the United States; nor shall any State deprive any person of life, liberty, or property, without due process of law; nor deny to any person within its jurisdiction the equal protection of the laws.

* * *

Section 5. The Congress shall have power to enforce, by appropriate legislation, the provisions of this article.

Reconstruction Civil Rights Acts, as Amended by the Civil Rights Act of 1991

42 U.S.C.A. §1981

EQUAL RIGHTS UNDER THE LAW

(a) All persons within the jurisdiction of the United States shall have the same right in every State and Territory to make and enforce contracts, to sue, be parties, give evidence, and to the full and equal benefit of all laws and proceedings for the security of persons and property as is enjoyed by white citizens, and shall be subject to like punishment, pains, penalties, taxes, licenses, and exactions of every kind, and to no other.

(b) For purposes of this section, the term "make and enforce contracts" includes the making, performance, modification, and termination of contracts, and the enjoyment of all benefits, privileges, terms, and conditions of the contractual relationship.

(c) The rights protected by this section are protected against impairment by nongovernmental discrimination and impairment under color of State law.

42 U.S.C.A. §1981A

DAMAGES IN CASES OF INTENTIONAL DISCRIMINATION IN EMPLOYMENT

(a) Right of Recovery—

(1) Civil Rights—In an action brought by a complaining party under section 706 or 717 of the Civil Rights Act of 1964 against a respondent who engaged in unlawful intentional discrimination (not an employment practice that is unlawful because of its disparate impact) prohibited under section 703, 704, or 717 of the Act, and provided that the complaining party cannot recover under 42 U.S.C. §1981, the complaining party may recover compensatory and punitive damages as allowed in subsection (b), in addition to any relief authorized by section 706(g) of the Civil Rights Act of 1964, from the respondent.

(2) Disability—In an action brought by a complaining party under the powers, remedies, and procedures set forth in section 706 or 717 of the Civil Rights Act of 1964 (as provided in section 107(a) of the Americans with Disabilities Act of 1990, and section 505(a)(1) of the Rehabilitation Act of 1973, respectively) against a respondent who engaged in unlawful intentional discrimination (not an employment practice that is unlawful because of its disparate impact) under section 501 of the Rehabilitation Act of 1973 and the regulations implementing section 501, or who violated the requirements of section 501 of the Act or the regulations implementing section 501 concerning the provision of a reasonable accommodation, or section 102 of the Americans with Disabilities Act of 1990, or committed a violation of section 102(b)(5) of the Act, against an individual, the complaining party may recover compensatory and punitive damages as allowed in subsection (b), in addition to any relief authorized by section 706(g) of the Civil Rights Act of 1964, from the respondent.

(3) Reasonable Accommodation and Good Faith Effort—In cases where a discriminatory practice involves the provision of a reasonable accommodation pursuant to section 102(b)(5) of the Americans with Disabilities Act of 1990 or regulations implementing section 501 of the Rehabilitation Act of 1973, damages may not be awarded under this section where the covered entity demonstrates good faith efforts, in consultation with the person with the disability who has informed the covered entity that accommodation is needed, to identify and make a reasonable accommodation that would provide such individual with an equally effective opportunity and would not cause an undue hardship on the operation of the business.

(b) Compensatory and Punitive Damages—

(1) Determination of Punitive Damages—A complaining party may recover punitive damages under this section against a respondent (other than a government, government agency or political subdivision) if the complaining party demonstrates that the respondent engaged in a discriminatory practice or discriminatory practices with malice or with reckless indifference to the federally protected rights of an aggrieved individual.

(2) Exclusions from Compensatory Damages—Compensatory damages awarded under this section shall not include backpay, interest on backpay, or any other type of relief authorized under section 706(g) of the Civil Rights Act of 1964.

(3) Limitations—The sum of the amount of compensatory damages awarded under this section for future pecuniary losses, emotional pain, suffering,

inconvenience, mental anguish, loss of enjoyment of life, and other nonpecuniary losses, and the amount of punitive damages awarded under this section, shall not exceed, for each complaining party—

(A) in the case of a respondent who has more than 14 and fewer than 101 employees in each of 20 or more calendar weeks in the current or preceding calendar year, $50,000;

(B) in the case of a respondent who has more than 100 and fewer than 201 employees in each of 20 or more calendar weeks in the current or preceding calendar year, $100,000; and

(C) in the case of a respondent who has more than 200 and fewer than 501 employees in each of 20 or more calendar weeks in the current or preceding calendar year, $200,000; and

(D) in the case of a respondent who has more than 500 employees in each of 20 or more calendar weeks in the current or preceding calendar year, $300,000.

(4) Construction—Nothing in this section shall be construed to limit the scope of, or the relief available under 42 U.S.C. §1981.

(c) Jury Trial—If a complaining party seeks compensatory or punitive damages under this section—

(1) any party may demand a trial by jury; and

(2) the court shall not inform the jury of the limitations described in subsection (b)(3).

(d) Definitions—As used in this section:

(1) Complaining Party—The term "complaining party" means—

(A) in the case of a person seeking to bring an action under subsection (a)(1), the Equal Employment Opportunity Commission, the Attorney General, or a person who may bring an action or proceeding under Title VII of the Civil Rights Act of 1964; or

(B) in the case of a person seeking to bring an action under subsection (a)(2), the Equal Employment Opportunity Commission, the Attorney General, a person who may bring an action or proceeding under section 505(a)(1) of the Rehabilitation Act of 1973, or a person who may bring an action or proceeding under Title I of the Americans with Disabilities Act of 1990.

(2) Discriminatory Practice—The term "discriminatory practice" means the discrimination described in paragraph (1), or the discrimination or the violation described in paragraph (2), of subsection (a).

42 U.S.C.A. §1983

CIVIL ACTION FOR DEPRIVATION OF RIGHTS

Every person who, under color of any statute, ordinance, regulation, custom, or usage, of any State or Territory or the District of Columbia, subjects, or causes to be subjected, any citizen of the United States or other person within the jurisdiction thereof to the deprivation of any rights, privileges, or immunities secured by the Constitution and laws, shall be liable to the party injured in an action at law, suit in equity, or other proper proceeding for redress. For the purposes of this section, any Act of Congress applicable exclusively to the District of Columbia shall be considered to be a statute of the District of Columbia.

42 U.S.C.A. §1985(3)

CONSPIRACY TO INTERFERE WITH CIVIL RIGHTS

If two or more persons in any State or Territory conspire or go in disguise on the highway or on the premises of another, for the purpose of depriving, either directly or indirectly, any person or class of persons of the equal protection of the laws, or of equal privileges and immunities under the laws; or for the purpose of preventing or hindering the constituted authorities of any State or Territory from giving or securing to all persons within such State or Territory the equal protection of the laws; or if two or more persons conspire to prevent by force, intimidation, or threat, any citizen who is lawfully entitled to vote, from giving his support or advocacy in a legal manner, toward or in favor of the election of any lawfully qualified person as an elector for President or Vice President, or as a Member of Congress of the United States; or to injure any citizen in person or property on account of such support or advocacy; in any case of conspiracy set forth in this section, if one or more persons engaged therein do, or cause to be done, any act in furtherance of the object of such conspiracy, whereby another is injured in his person or property, or deprived of having and exercising any right or privilege of a citizen of the United States, the party so injured or deprived may have an action for the recovery of damages occasioned by such injury or deprivation, against anyone or more of the conspirators.

42 U.S.C.A. §1988

PROCEEDINGS IN VINDICATION OF CIVIL RIGHTS, ATTORNEY'S FEES, AS AMENDED

* * *

(b) In any action or proceeding to enforce a provision of sections 1981, 1981A, 1982, 1983, 1985, and 1986 of this title, title IX of Public Law 92–318, or title VI of the Civil Rights Act of 1964, the court, in its discretion, may allow the prevailing party, other than the United States, a reasonable attorney's fee as part of the costs.

(c) In awarding an attorney's fee under subsection (b) in any action or proceeding to enforce a provision of 42 U.S.C. §§1981 or 1981A, the court, in its discretion, may include expert fees as part of the attorney's fee.

Equal Pay Act
29 U.S.C.A. §206(D)

§206(d).   Prohibition of Sex Discrimination

(1) No employer having employees subject to any provisions of this section shall discriminate, within any establishment in which such employees are employed, between employees on the basis of sex by paying wages to employees in such establishment at a rate less than the rate at which he pays wages to employees of the opposite sex in such establishment for equal work on jobs the performance of which requires equal skill, effort, and responsibility, and which are performed under similar working conditions, except where such payment is made pursuant to (i) a seniority system; (ii) a merit system; (iii) a system which measures earnings by quantity or quality of production; or (iv) a differential based on any other factor other than sex: Provided, That an employer who is paying a wage rate differential in violation of this subsection shall not, in order to comply with the provisions of this subsection, reduce the wage rate of any employee.

(2) No labor organization, or its agents, representing employees of an employer having employees subject to any provisions of this section shall cause or attempt to cause such an employer to discriminate against an employee in violation of paragraph (1) of this subsection.

(3) For purposes of administration and enforcement, any amounts owing to any employee which have been withheld in violation of this subsection shall be deemed to be unpaid minimum wages or unpaid overtime compensation under this Act.

(4) As used in this subsection, the term "labor organization" means any organization of any kind, or any agency or employee representation committee or plan, in which employees participate and which exists for the purpose, in whole or in part, of dealing with employers concerning grievances, labor disputes, wages, rates of pay, hours of employment, or conditions of work.

29 U.S.C. §216. Remedies [§16(b) of Fair Labor Standards Act of 1938, as amended]

(b) Any employer who violates the provisions of section 206 or section 207 of this title shall be liable to the employee or employees affected in the amount of their unpaid minimum wages, or their unpaid overtime compensation, as the case may be, and in an additional equal amount as liquidated damages. Any employer who violates the provisions of section 215(a)(3) of this title shall be liable for such legal or equitable relief as may be appropriate to effectuate the purposes of section

215(a)(3) of this title, including without limitation employment, reinstatement, promotion, and the payment of wages lost and an additional equal amount as liquidated damages.   An action to recover the liability prescribed in either of the preceding sentences may be maintained against any employer (including a public agency) in any Federal or State court of competent jurisdiction by any one or more employees for and in behalf of himself or themselves and other employees similarly situated.   No employee shall be a party plaintiff to any such action unless he gives his consent in writing to become such a party and such consent is filed in the court in which such action is brought.   The court in such action shall, in addition to any judgment awarded to the plaintiff or plaintiffs, allow a reasonable attorney's fee to be paid by the defendant, and costs of the action.   The right provided by this subsection to bring an action by or on behalf of any employee, and the right of any employee to become a party plaintiff to any such action, shall terminate upon the filing of a complaint by the Secretary of Labor in an action under section 217 of this title in which (1) restraint is sought of any further delay in the payment of unpaid minimum wages, or the amount of unpaid overtime compensation, as the case may be, owing to such employee under section 206 or section 207 of this title by an employer liable therefor under the provisions of this subsection or (2) legal or equitable relief is sought as a result of alleged violations of section 215(a)(3) of this title.

Age Discrimination in Employment Act, as amended by The Lilly Ledbetter Fair Pay Act of 2009, 29 U.S.C.A. §621 et seq.

§2. Congressional Statement of Findings and Purpose

(a) The Congress hereby finds and declares that—

(1) in the face of rising productivity and affluence, older workers find themselves disadvantaged in their efforts to retain employment, and especially to regain employment when displaced from jobs;

(2) the setting of arbitrary age limits regardless of potential for job performance has become a common practice, and certain otherwise desirable practices may work to the disadvantage of older persons;

(3) the incidence of unemployment, especially long-term unemployment with resultant deterioration of skill, morale, and employer acceptability is, relative to the younger ages, high among older workers; their numbers are great and growing; and their employment problems grave;

(4) the existence in industries affecting commerce, of arbitrary discrimination in employment because of age, burdens commerce and the free flow of goods in commerce.

(b) It is therefore the purpose of this chapter to promote employment of older persons based on their ability rather than age; to prohibit arbitrary age discrimination in employment; to help employers and workers find ways of meeting problems arising from the impact of age on employment.

* * *

§4. Prohibition of Age Discrimination

(a) Employer practices

It shall be unlawful for an employer—

(1) to fail or refuse to hire or to discharge any individual or otherwise discriminate against any individual with respect to his compensation, terms, conditions, or privileges of employment, because of such individual's age;

(2) to limit, segregate, or classify his employees in any way which would deprive or tend to deprive any individual of employment opportunities or otherwise adversely affect his status as an employee, because of such individual's age; or

(3) to reduce the wage rate of any employee in order to comply with this Act.

(b) Employment agency practices

It shall be unlawful for an employment agency to fail or refuse to refer for employment, or otherwise to discriminate against, any individual because of such individual's age, or to classify or refer for employment any individual on the basis of such individual's age.

(c) Labor organization practices

It shall be unlawful for a labor organization—

(1) to exclude or to expel from its membership, or otherwise to discriminate against, any individual because of his age;

(2) to limit, segregate, or classify its membership, or to classify or fail or refuse to refer for employment any individual, in any way which would deprive or tend to deprive any individual of employment opportunities, or would limit such employment opportunities or otherwise adversely affect his status as an employee or as an applicant for employment, because of such individual's age;

(3) to cause or attempt to cause an employer to discriminate against an individual in violation of this section.

(d) Opposition to unlawful practices; participation in investigations, proceedings, or litigation

It shall be unlawful for an employer to discriminate against any of his employees or applicants for employment, for an employment agency to discriminate against any individual, or for a labor organization to discriminate against any member thereof or applicant for membership, because such individual, member or applicant for membership has opposed any practice made unlawful by this section, or because such individual, member or applicant for membership has made a charge, testified, assisted, or participated in any manner in an investigation, proceeding, or litigation under this Act.

(e) Printing or publication of notice or advertisement indicating preference, limitation, etc.

It shall be unlawful for an employer, labor organization, or employment agency to print or publish, or cause to be printed or published, any notice or advertisement relating to employment by such an employer or membership in or any classification or referral for employment by such a labor organization, or relating to any classification or referral for employment by such an employment agency, indicating any preference, limitation, specification, or discrimination, based on age.

(f) Lawful practices; age an occupational qualification; other reasonable factors; laws of foreign workplace; seniority system; employee benefit plans; discharge or discipline for good cause

It shall not be unlawful for an employer, employment agency, or labor organization—

(1) to take any action otherwise prohibited under subsections (a), (b), (c), or (e) of this section where age is a bona fide occupational qualification reasonably necessary to the normal operation of the particular business, or where

the differentiation is based on reasonable factors other than age, or where such practices involve an employee in a workplace in a foreign country, and compliance with such subsections would cause such employer, or a corporation controlled by such employer, to violate the laws of the country in which such workplace is located;

(2) to take any action otherwise prohibited under subsection (a), (b), (c), or (e) of this section—

(A) to observe the terms of a bona fide seniority system that is not intended to evade the purposes of this Act, except that no such seniority system shall require or permit the involuntary retirement of any individual specified by section 12(a) of this Act because of the age of such individual; or

(B) to observe the terms of a bona fide employee benefit plan—

(i) where, for each benefit or benefit package, the actual amount of payment made or cost incurred on behalf of an older worker is no less than that made or incurred on behalf of a younger worker, as permissible under section 1625.10, Title 29, Code of Federal Regulations (as in effect on June 22, 1989); or

(ii) that is a voluntary early retirement incentive plan consistent with the relevant purpose or purposes of this Act.

Notwithstanding clause (i) or (ii) of subparagraph (B), no such employee benefit plan or voluntary early retirement incentive plan shall excuse the failure to hire any individual, and no such employee benefit plan shall require or permit the involuntary retirement of any individual specified by section 12(a) of this Act, because of the age of such individual. An employer, employment agency, or labor organization acting under subparagraph (A), or under clause (i) or (ii) of subparagraph (B), shall have the burden of proving that such actions are lawful in any civil enforcement proceeding brought under this chapter; or

(3) to discharge or otherwise discipline an individual for good cause.

[(g) Repealed.]

(h) Practices of foreign corporations controlled by American employers; foreign persons not controlled by American employers; factors determining control

(1) If an employer controls a corporation whose place of incorporation is in a foreign country, any practice by such corporation prohibited under this section shall be presumed to be such practice by such employer.

(2) The prohibitions of this section shall not apply where the employer is a foreign person not controlled by an American employer.

(3) For the purpose of this subsection the determination of whether an employer controls a corporation shall be based upon the—

(A) interrelation of operations,

(B) common management,

(C) centralized control of labor relations, and

(D) common ownership or financial control, of the employer and the corporation.

(i) Firefighters and law enforcement officers attaining hiring or retiring age under State or local law on March 3, 1983

It shall not be unlawful for an employer which is a State, a political subdivision of a State, an agency or instrumentality of a State or a political subdivision of a State, or an interstate agency to fail or refuse to hire or to discharge any individual because of such individual's age if such action is taken—

(1) with respect to the employment of an individual as a firefighter or as a law enforcement officer and the individual has attained the age of hiring or retirement in effect under applicable State or local law on March 3, 1983, and

(2) pursuant to a bona fide hiring or retirement plan that is not a subterfuge to evade the purposes of this chapter.

(j) Employee pension benefit plans; cessation or reduction of benefit accrual or of allocation to employee account; distribution of benefits after attainment of normal retirement age; compliance; highly compensated employees

(1) Except as otherwise provided in this subsection, it shall be unlawful for an employer, an employment agency, a labor organization, or any combination thereof to establish or maintain an employee pension benefit plan which requires or permits—

(A) in the case of a defined benefit plan, the cessation of an employee's benefit accrual, or the reduction of the rate of an employee's benefit accrual, because of age, or

(B) in the case of a defined contribution plan, the cessation of allocations to an employee's account, or the reduction of the rate at which amounts are allocated to an employee's account, because of age.

(2) Nothing in this section shall be construed to prohibit an employer, employment agency, or labor organization from observing any provision of an employee pension benefit plan to the extent that such provision imposes (without regard to age) a limitation on the amount of benefits that the plan provides or a limitation on the number of years of service or years of participation which are taken into account for purposes of determining benefit accrual under the plan.

(3) In the case of any employee who, as of the end of any plan year under a defined benefit plan, has attained normal retirement age under such plan—

(A) if distribution of benefits under such plan with respect to such employee has commenced as of the end of such plan year, then any requirement of this subsection for continued accrual of benefits under such plan with respect to such employee during such plan year shall be treated as satisfied to the extent of the actuarial equivalent of in-service distribution of benefits, and

(B) if distribution of benefits under such plan with respect to such employee has not commenced as of the end of such year in accordance with section 206(a)(3) of the Employee Retirement Income Security Act of 1974 and section 401(a)(14)(C) of the Internal Revenue Code of 1986, and the payment of benefits under such plan with respect to such employee is not suspended during such plan year pursuant to section 203(a)(3)(B) of the Employee Retirement Income Security Act of 1974 or section 411(a)(3)(B) of the Internal Revenue Code of 1986 then any requirement of this subsection for continued accrual of benefits under such plan with respect to such employee during such plan year shall be treated as satisfied to the extent of any adjustment in the benefit payable under the plan during such plan year attributable to the delay in the distribution of benefits after the attainment of normal retirement age.

The provisions of this paragraph shall apply in accordance with regulations of the Secretary of the Treasury. Such regulations shall provide for the application of the preceding provisions of this paragraph to all employee pension benefit plans subject to this subsection and may provide for the application of such provisions, in the case of any such employee, with respect to any period of time within a plan year.

(4) Compliance with the requirements of this subsection with respect to an employee pension benefit plan shall constitute compliance with the requirements of this section relating to benefit accrual under such plan.

(5) Paragraph (1) shall not apply with respect to any employee who is a highly compensated employee (within the meaning of section 414(q) of the Internal Revenue Code of 1986) to the extent provided in regulations prescribed by the Secretary of the Treasury for purposes of precluding discrimination in favor of highly compensated employees within the meaning of sections 401–425 of the Internal Revenue Code of 1986.

(6) A plan shall not be treated as failing to meet the requirements of paragraph (1) solely because the subsidized portion of any early retirement benefit is disregarded in determining benefit accruals.

(7) Any regulations prescribed by the Secretary of the Treasury pursuant to clause (v) of section 411(b)(1)(H) of the Internal Revenue Code and subparagraphs (C) and (D) of section 411(b)(2) of the Internal Revenue Code shall apply with respect to the requirements of this subsection in the same manner and to the same extent as such regulations apply with respect to the requirements of such sections 411(b)(1)(H) and 411(b)(2) of the Internal Revenue Code.

(8) A plan shall not be treated as failing to meet the requirements of this section solely because such plan provides a normal retirement age described in section 3(24)(B) of the Employee Retirement Income Security Act and section 411(a)(8)(B) of the Internal Revenue Code.

(9) For purposes of this subsection—

(A) The terms "employee pension benefit plan," "defined benefit plan," "defined contribution plan," and "normal retirement age" have the meanings provided such terms in section 3 of the Employment Retirement Income Security Act.

(B) The term "compensation" has the meaning provided by section 414(s) of the Internal Revenue Code.

(k) Date of adoption of system or plan

A seniority system or employee benefit plan shall comply with this chapter regardless of the date of adoption of such system or plan.

(l) Minimum age requirements; early retirement benefits

Notwithstanding clause (i) or (ii) of subsection (f)(2)(B) of this section—

(1) It shall not be a violation of subsection (a), (b), (c), or (e) of this section solely because—

(A) an employee pension benefit plan (as defined in section 1002(2) of this title) provides for the attainment of a minimum age as a condition of eligibility for normal or early retirement benefits; or

(B) a defined benefit plan (as defined in section 3(35) of the Employment Retirement Income Security Act) provides for—

(i) payments that constitute the subsidized portion of an early retirement benefit; or

(ii) social security supplements for plan participants that commence before the age and terminate at the age (specified by the plan) when participants are eligible to receive reduced or unreduced old-age insurance benefits under title II of the Social Security Act (42 U.S.C. 401 et seq.), and that do not exceed such old-age insurance benefits.

(2) (A) It shall not be a violation of subsection (a), (b), (c), or (e) of this section solely because following a contingent event unrelated to age—

(i) the value of any retiree health benefits received by an individual eligible for an immediate pension;

(ii) the value of any additional pension benefits that are made available solely as a result of the contingent event unrelated to age and following which the individual is eligible for not less than an immediate and unreduced pension; or

(iii) the values described in both clauses (i) and (ii); are deducted from severance pay made available as a result of the contingent event unrelated to age.

(B) For an individual who receives immediate pension benefits that are actuarially reduced under subparagraph (A)(i), the amount of the deduction available pursuant to subparagraph (A)(i) shall be reduced by the same percentage as the reduction in the pension benefits.

(C) For purposes of this paragraph, severance pay shall include that portion of supplemental unemployment compensation benefits (as described in section 501(c)(17) of the Internal Revenue Code) that—

(i) constitutes additional benefits of up to 52 weeks;

(ii) has the primary purpose and effect of continuing benefits until an individual becomes eligible for an immediate and unreduced pension; and

(iii) is discontinued once the individual becomes eligible for an immediate and unreduced pension.

(D) For purposes of this paragraph and solely in order to make the deduction authorized under this paragraph, the term "retiree health benefits" means benefits provided pursuant to a group health plan covering retirees, for which (determined as of the contingent event unrelated to age)—

(i) the package of benefits provided by the employer for the retirees who are below age 65 is at least comparable to benefits provided under Title XVIII of the Social Security Act (42 U.S.C. 1395 et seq.);

(ii) the package of benefits provided by the employer for the retirees who are age 65 and above is at least comparable to that offered under a plan that provides a benefit package with one-fourth the value of benefits provided under Title XVIII of such Act; or

(iii) the package of benefits provided by the employer is as described in clauses (i) and (ii).

(E) (i) If the obligation of the employer to provide retiree health benefits is of limited duration, the value for each individual shall be calculated at a rate of $3,000 per year for benefit years before age 65, and $750 per year for benefit years beginning at age 65 and above.

(ii) If the obligation of the employer to provide retiree health benefits is of unlimited duration, the value for each individual shall be calculated at a rate of $48,000 for individuals below age 65, and $24,000 for individuals age 65 and above.

(iii) The values described in clauses (i) and (ii) shall be calculated based on the age of the individual as of the date of the contingent event unrelated to age. The values are effective on October 16, 1990, and shall be adjusted on an annual basis, with respect to a contingent event that occurs subsequent to the first year after October 16, 1990, based on the medical component of the Consumer Price Index for all-urban consumers published by the Department of Labor.

(iv) If an individual is required to pay a premium for retiree health benefits, the value calculated pursuant to this subparagraph shall be reduced by whatever percentage of the overall premium the individual is required to pay.

(F) If an employer that has implemented a deduction pursuant to subparagraph (A) fails to fulfill the obligation described in subparagraph (E), any aggrieved individual may bring an action for specific performance of the obligation described in subparagraph (E). The relief shall be in addition to any other remedies provided under Federal or State law.

(3) It shall not be a violation of subsection (a), (b), (c), or (e) of this section solely because an employer provides a bona fide employee benefit plan or plans under which long-term disability benefits received by an individual are reduced by any pension benefits (other than those attributable to employee contributions)—

(A) paid to the individual that the individual voluntarily elects to receive; or

(B) for which an individual who has attained the later of age 62 or normal retirement age is eligible.

* * *

§7. Recordkeeping, Investigation, and Enforcement

(a) Attendance of witnesses; investigations, inspections, records, and homework regulations

The Equal Employment Opportunity Commission shall have the power to make investigations and require the keeping of records necessary or appropriate for the administration of this chapter in accordance with the powers and procedures provided in sections 9 and 11 of the Fair Labor Standards Act of 1938, as amended.

(b) Enforcement; prohibition of age discrimination under fair labor standards; unpaid minimum wages and unpaid overtime compensation; liquidated damages; judicial relief; conciliation, conference, and persuasion

The provisions of this chapter shall be enforced in accordance with the powers, remedies, and procedures provided in sections 11(b), 16 (except for subsection (a) thereof), and 17 of the Fair Labor Standards Act of 1938, as amended, and subsection (c) of this section. Any act prohibited under section 4 of this Act shall be deemed to be a prohibited act under section 15 of the Fair Labor Standards Act of 1938, as amended. Amounts owing to a person as a result of a violation of this Act shall be deemed to be unpaid minimum wages or unpaid overtime compensation for purposes of sections 16 and 17 of the Fair Labor Standards Act of 1938, as amended: Provided, That liquidated damages shall be payable only in cases of willful violations of this Act. In any action brought to enforce this chapter the court shall have jurisdiction to grant such legal or equitable relief as may be appropriate to effectuate the purposes of this Act, including without limitation judgments compelling employment, reinstatement or promotion, or enforcing the liability for amounts deemed to be unpaid minimum wages or unpaid overtime compensation under this section. Before instituting any action under this section, the Equal Employment Opportunity Commission shall attempt to eliminate the discriminatory practice or practices alleged, and to effect voluntary compliance with the requirements of this chapter through informal methods of conciliation, conference, and persuasion.

(c) Civil actions; persons aggrieved; jurisdiction; judicial relief; termination of individual action upon commencement of action by Commission; jury trial

(1) Any person aggrieved may bring a civil action in any court of competent jurisdiction for such legal or equitable relief as will effectuate the purposes of this chapter: Provided, That the right of any person to bring such action shall terminate upon the commencement of an action by the Equal Employment Opportunity Commission to enforce the right of such employee under this Act.

(2) In an action brought under paragraph (1), a person shall be entitled to a trial by jury of any issue of fact in any such action for recovery of amounts owing as a result of a violation of this Act, regardless of whether equitable relief is sought by any party in such action.

(d) Filing of charge with Commission; timeliness; conciliation, conference, and persuasion

(1) No civil action may be commenced by an individual under this section until 60 days after a charge alleging unlawful discrimination has been filed with the Equal Employment Opportunity Commission. Such a charge shall be filed—

(A) within 180 days after the alleged unlawful practice occurred; or

(B) in a case to which section 14(b) of this Act applies, within 300 days after the alleged unlawful practice occurred, or within 30 days after receipt by the individual of notice of termination of proceedings under State law, whichever is earlier.

(2) Upon receiving such a charge, the Commission shall promptly notify all persons named in such charge as prospective defendants in the action and shall promptly seek to eliminate any alleged unlawful practice by informal methods of conciliation, conference, and persuasion.

(3) For purposes of this section, an unlawful practice occurs, with respect to discrimination in compensation in violation of this Act, when a discriminatory compensation decision or other practice is adopted, when a person becomes subject to a discriminatory compensation decision or other practice, or when a person is affected by application of a discriminatory compensation decision or other practice, including each time wages, benefits, or other compensation is paid, resulting in whole or in part from such a decision or other practice.

(e) Statute of limitations; reliance in future on administrative ruling, etc.; tolling

Section 59 of the Fair Labor Standards Act of 1938, as amended, shall apply to actions under this Act. If a charge filed with the Commission under this Act is dismissed or the proceedings of the Commission are otherwise terminated by the Commission, the Commission shall notify the person aggrieved. A civil action may be brought under this section by a person defined in section 11(a) against the respondent named in the charge within 90 days after the date of the receipt of such notice.

(f) Waiver

(1) An individual may not waive any right or claim under this Act unless the waiver is knowing and voluntary. Except as provided in paragraph (2), a waiver may not be considered knowing and voluntary unless at a minimum—

(A) the waiver is part of an agreement between the individual and the employer that is written in a manner calculated to be understood by such individual, or by the average individual eligible to participate;

(B) the waiver specifically refers to rights or claims arising under this chapter;

(C) the individual does not waive rights or claims that may arise after the date the waiver is executed;

(D) the individual waives rights or claims only in exchange for consideration in addition to anything of value to which the individual already is entitled;

(E) the individual is advised in writing to consult with an attorney prior to executing the agreement;

(F) (i) the individual is given a period of at least 21 days within which to consider the agreement; or

(ii) if a waiver is requested in connection with an exit incentive or other employment termination program offered to a group or class of employees, the individual is given a period of at least 45 days within which to consider the agreement;

(G) the agreement provides that for a period of at least 7 days following the execution of such agreement, the individual may revoke the agreement, and the agreement shall not become effective or enforceable until the revocation period has expired;

(H) if a waiver is requested in connection with an exit incentive or other employment termination program offered to a group or class of employees, the employer (at the commencement of the period specified in subparagraph (F)) informs the individual in writing in a manner calculated to be understood by the average individual eligible to participate, as to—

(i) any class, unit, or group of individuals covered by such program, any eligibility factors for such program, and any time limits applicable to such program; and

(ii) the job titles and ages of all individuals eligible or selected for the program, and the ages of all individuals in the same job classification or organizational unit who are not eligible or selected for the program.

(2) A waiver in settlement of a charge filed with the Equal Employment Opportunity Commission, or an action filed in court by the individual or the individual's representative, alleging age discrimination of a kind prohibited under section 4 or 15 of this Act may not be considered knowing and voluntary unless at a minimum—

(A) subparagraphs (A) through (E) of paragraph (1) have been met; and

(B) the individual is given a reasonable period of time within which to consider the settlement agreement.

(3) In any dispute that may arise over whether any of the requirements, conditions, and circumstances set forth in subparagraph (A), (B), (C), (D), (E), (F), (G), or (H) of paragraph (1), or subparagraph (A) or (B) of paragraph (2), have been met, the party asserting the validity of a waiver shall have the burden of proving in a court of competent jurisdiction that a waiver was knowing and voluntary pursuant to paragraph (1) or (2).

(4) No waiver agreement may affect the Commission's rights and responsibilities to enforce this Act. No waiver may be used to justify interfering with the protected right of an employee to file a charge or participate in an investigation or proceeding conducted by the Commission.

§8. Notices to Be Posted

Every employer, employment agency, and labor organization shall post and keep posted in conspicuous places upon its premises a notice to be prepared or approved by the Equal Employment Opportunity Commission setting forth information as the Commission deems appropriate to effectuate the purposes of this Act.

§9. Rules and Regulations; Exemptions

In accordance with the provisions of the Administrative Procedure Act, the Equal Employment Opportunity Commission may issue such rules and regulations as it may consider necessary or appropriate for carrying out this chapter, and may establish such reasonable exemptions to and from any or all provisions of this chapter as it may find necessary and proper in the public interest.

* * *

§11. Definitions

For the purposes of this Act—

(a) The term "person" means one or more individuals, partnerships, associations, labor organizations, corporations, business trusts, legal representatives, or any organized groups of persons.

(b) The term "employer" means a person engaged in an industry affecting commerce who has twenty or more employees for each working day in each of twenty or more calendar weeks in the current or preceding calendar year: Provided, That prior to June 30, 1968, employers having fewer than fifty employees shall not be considered employers. The term also means (1) any agent of such a person, and (2) a State or political subdivision of a State and any agency or instrumentality of a State or a political subdivision of a State, and any interstate agency, but such term does not include the United States, or a corporation wholly owned by the Government of the United States.

(c) The term "employment agency" means any person regularly undertaking with or without compensation to procure employees for an employer and includes an agent of such a person; but shall not include an agency of the United States.

(d) The term "labor organization" means a labor organization engaged in an industry affecting commerce, and any agent of such an organization, and includes any organization of any kind, any agency, or employee representation committee, group, association, or plan so engaged in which employees participate and which exists for the purpose, in whole or in part, of dealing with employers concerning grievances, labor disputes, wages, rates of pay, hours, or other terms or conditions of employment, and any conference, general committee, joint or system board, or joint council so engaged which is subordinate to a national or international labor organization.

(e) A labor organization shall be deemed to be engaged in an industry affecting commerce if (1) it maintains or operates a hiring hall or hiring office which procures employees for an employer or procures for employees opportunities to work for an employer, or (2) the number of its members (or, where it is a labor organization composed of other labor organizations or their representatives, if the aggregate number of the members of such other labor organization) is fifty or more prior to

July 1, 1968, or twenty-five or more on or after July 1, 1968, and such labor organization—

(1) is the certified representative of employees under the provisions of the National Labor Relations Act, as amended, or the Railway Labor Act, as amended; or

(2) although not certified, is a national or international labor organization or a local labor organization recognized or acting as the representative of employees of an employer or employers engaged in an industry affecting commerce; or

(3) has chartered a local labor organization or subsidiary body which is representing or actively seeking to represent employees of employers within the meaning of paragraph (1) or (2); or

(4) has been chartered by a labor organization representing or actively seeking to represent employees within the meaning of paragraph (1) or (2) as the local or subordinate body through which such employees may enjoy membership or become affiliated with such labor organization; or

(5) is a conference, general committee, joint or system board, or joint council subordinate to a national or international labor organization, which includes a labor organization engaged in an industry affecting commerce within the meaning of any of the preceding paragraphs of this subsection.

(f) The term "employee" means an individual employed by any employer except that the term "employee" shall not include any person elected to public office in any State or political subdivision of any State by the qualified voters thereof, or any person chosen by such officer to be on such officer's personal staff, or an appointee on the policymaking level or an immediate adviser with respect to the exercise of the constitutional or legal powers of the office.

The exemption set forth in the preceding sentence shall not include employees subject to the civil service laws of a State government, governmental agency, or political subdivision. The term "employee" includes any individual who is a citizen of the United States employed by an employer in a workplace in a foreign country.

(g) The term "commerce" means trade, traffic, commerce, transportation, transmission, or communication among the several States; or between a State and any place outside thereof; or within the District of Columbia, or a possession of the United States; or between points in the same State but through a point outside thereof.

(h) The term "industry affecting commerce" means any activity, business, or industry in commerce or in which a labor dispute would hinder or obstruct commerce or the free flow of commerce and includes any activity or industry "affecting commerce" within the meaning of the Labor–Management Reporting and Disclosure Act of 1959.

(i) The term "State" includes a State of the United States, the District of Columbia, Puerto Rico, the Virgin Islands, American Samoa, Guam, Wake Island, the Canal Zone, and Outer Continental Shelf lands defined in the Outer Continental Shelf Lands Act.

(j) The term "firefighter" means an employee, the duties of whose position are primarily to perform work directly connected with the control and extinguishment of fires or the maintenance and use of firefighting apparatus and equipment, including an employee engaged in this activity who is transferred to a supervisory or administrative position.

(k) The term "law enforcement officer" means an employee, the duties of whose position are primarily the investigation, apprehension, or detention of individuals suspected or convicted of offenses against the criminal laws of a State, including an employee engaged in this activity who is transferred to a supervisory or administrative position. For the purpose of this subsection, "detention" includes the duties of employees assigned to guard individuals incarcerated in any penal institution.

(l) The term "compensation, terms, conditions, or privileges of employment" encompasses all employee benefits, including such benefits provided pursuant to a bona fide employee benefit plan.

§12. Age Limits

(a) Individuals at least 40 years of age

The prohibitions in this chapter shall be limited to individuals who are at least 40 years of age.

(b) Employees or applicants for employment in Federal Government

In the case of any personnel action affecting employees or applicants for employment which is subject to the provisions of section 15 of this Act, the prohibitions established in section 15 of this Act shall be limited to individuals who are at least 40 years of age.

(c) Bona fide executives or high policymakers

(1) Nothing in this chapter shall be construed to prohibit compulsory retirement of any employee who has attained 65 years of age and who, for the 2–year period immediately before retirement, is employed in a bona fide executive or a high policymaking position, if such employee is entitled to an immediate nonforfeitable annual retirement benefit from a pension, profit-sharing, savings, or deferred compensation plan, or any combination of such plans, of the employer of such employee, which equals, in the aggregate, at least $44,000.

(2) In applying the retirement benefit test of paragraph (1) of this subsection, if any such retirement benefit is in a form other than a straight life annuity (with no ancillary benefits), or if employees contribute to any such plan or make rollover contributions, such benefit shall be adjusted in accordance with regulations prescribed by the Equal Employment Opportunity Commission, after consultation with the Secretary of the Treasury, so that the benefit is the equivalent of a straight life annuity (with no ancillary benefits) under a plan to which employees do not contribute and under which no rollover contributions are made.

(d) Tenured employee at institution of higher education

Nothing in this chapter shall be construed to prohibit compulsory retirement of any employee who has attained 70 years of age, and who is serving under a contract of unlimited tenure (or similar arrangement providing for unlimited tenure) at an institution of higher education (as defined by section 1201(a) of the Higher Education Act of 1965).

§13. Annual Report to Congress

The Equal Employment Opportunity Commission shall submit annually in January a report to the Congress covering its activities for the preceding year and including such information, data, and recommendations for further legislation in connection with the matters covered by this chapter as it may find advisable. Such report shall contain an evaluation and appraisal by the Commission of the effect of the minimum and maximum ages established by this chapter, together with its recommendations to the Congress. In making such evaluation and appraisal, the Commission shall take into consideration any changes which may have occurred in the general age level of the population, the effect of the chapter upon workers not covered by its provisions, and such other factors as it may deem pertinent.

§14. Federal–State Relationship

(a) Federal action superseding State action

Nothing in this Act shall affect the jurisdiction of any agency of any State performing like functions with regard to discriminatory employment practices on account of age except that upon commencement of action under this Act such action shall supersede any State action.

(b) Limitation of Federal action upon commencement of State proceedings

In the case of an alleged unlawful practice occurring in a State which has a law prohibiting discrimination in employment because of age and establishing or authorizing a State authority to grant or seek relief from such discriminatory practice, no suit may be brought under section 7 of this Act before the expiration of sixty days after proceedings have been commenced under the State law, unless such proceedings have been earlier terminated: Provided, That such sixty-day period shall be extended to one hundred and twenty days during the first year after the effective date of such State law. If any requirement for the commencement of such proceedings is imposed by a State authority other than a requirement of the filing of a written and signed statement of the facts upon which the proceeding is based, the proceeding shall be deemed to have been commenced for the purposes of this subsection at the time such statement is sent by registered mail to the appropriate State authority.

§15. Nondiscrimination on Account of Age in Federal Government Employment

(a) Federal agencies affected

All personnel actions affecting employees or applicants for employment who are at least 40 years of age (except personnel actions with regard to aliens employed outside the limits of the United States) in military departments as defined in section 102 of Title 5, in executive agencies as defined in section 105 of Title 5 (including employees and applicants for employment who are paid from nonappropriated funds), in the United States Postal Service and the Postal Rate Commission, in those units in the government of the District of Columbia having positions in the competitive service, and in those units of the legislative and judicial branches of the

Federal Government having positions in the competitive service, and in the Library of Congress shall be made free from any discrimination based on age.

(b) Enforcement by Equal Employment Opportunity Commission and by Librarian of Congress in Library of Congress; remedies; rules, regulations, orders, and instructions of Commission: compliance by Federal agencies; powers and duties of Commission; notification of final action on complaint of discrimination; exemptions: bona fide occupational qualification

Except as otherwise provided in this subsection, the Equal Employment Opportunity Commission is authorized to enforce the provisions of subsection (a) of this section through appropriate remedies, including reinstatement or hiring of employees with or without backpay, as will effectuate the policies of this section. The Equal Employment Opportunity Commission shall issue such rules, regulations, orders, and instructions as it deems necessary and appropriate to carry out its responsibilities under this section. The Equal Employment Opportunity Commission shall—

(1) be responsible for the review and evaluation of the operation of all agency programs designed to carry out the policy of this section, periodically obtaining and publishing (on at least a semiannual basis) progress reports from each department, agency, or unit referred to in subsection (a) of this section;

(2) consult with and solicit the recommendations of interested individuals, groups, and organizations relating to nondiscrimination in employment on account of age; and

(3) provide for the acceptance and processing of complaints of discrimination in Federal employment on account of age.

The head of each such department, agency, or unit shall comply with such rules, regulations, orders, and instructions of the Equal Employment Opportunity Commission which shall include a provision that an employee or applicant for employment shall be notified of any final action taken on any complaint of discrimination filed by him thereunder. Reasonable exemptions to the provisions of this section may be established by the Commission but only when the Commission has established a maximum age requirement on the basis of a determination that age is a bona fide occupational qualification necessary to the performance of the duties of the position. With respect to employment in the Library of Congress, authorities granted in this subsection to the Equal Employment Opportunity Commission shall be exercised by the Librarian of Congress.

(c) Civil actions; jurisdiction; relief

Any person aggrieved may bring a civil action in any Federal district court of competent jurisdiction for such legal or equitable relief as will effectuate the purposes of this Act.

(d) Notice to Commission; time of notice; Commission notification of prospective defendants; Commission elimination of unlawful practices

When the individual has not filed a complaint concerning age discrimination with the Commission, no civil action may be commenced by any individual under this section until the individual has given the Commission not less than thirty days' notice of an intent to file such action. Such notice shall be filed within one hundred and eighty days after the alleged unlawful practice occurred. Upon receiving a notice of intent to sue, the Commission shall promptly notify all persons named therein as prospective defendants in the action and take any appropriate action to assure the elimination of any unlawful practice.

(e) Duty of Government agency or official

Nothing contained in this section shall relieve any Government agency or official of the responsibility to assure nondiscrimination on account of age in employment as required under any provision of Federal law.

(f) Applicability of statutory provisions to personnel action of Federal departments, etc.

Any personnel action of any department, agency, or other entity referred to in subsection (a) of this section shall not be subject to, or affected by, any provision of this Act, other than the provisions of sections 7(d)(3) and 12(b) of this Act and the provisions of this section.

* * *

[See also §16(b) of the Fair Labor Standards Act of 1938, as amended, reprinted in this Appendix as part of the Equal Pay Act]

The Rehabilitation Act, as Amended By the Americans with Disabilities Act, the 1991 Civil Rights Act, and the Lilly Ledbetter Fair Pact Act of 2009, 29 U.S.C.A. §§705(20), 791, 793, 794, 794a.

§7. Definitions

(8) (A) Except as otherwise provided in subparagraph (B), the term "an individual with a disability" means any individual who (i) has a physical or mental disability which for such individual constitutes or results in a substantial handicap to employment and (ii) can reasonably be expected to benefit in terms of employability from vocational rehabilitation services provided pursuant to Titles I and III of this Act.

(B) Subject to subparagraphs (C) and (D), the term "an individual with a disability" means, for purposes of this Act, any person who (i) has a physical or mental impairment which substantially limits one or more of such person's major life activities, (ii) has a record of such an impairment, or (iii) is regarded as having such an impairment. For purposes of sections 503 and 504 as such sections relate to employment, such term does not include any individual who is an alcoholic or drug abuser whose current use of alcohol or drugs prevents such individual from performing the duties of the job in question or whose employment, by reason of such current alcohol or drug abuse, would constitute a direct threat to property or the safety of others.

(C) (i) For purposes of this statute, the term "individual with a disability" does not include an individual who is currently engaging in the illegal use of drugs, when a covered entity acts on the basis of such use.

(ii) Nothing in clause (i) shall be construed to exclude as an individual with a disability an individual who—

(I) has successfully completed a supervised drug rehabilitation program and is no longer engaging in the illegal use of drugs, or has otherwise been rehabilitated successfully and is no longer engaging in such use;

(II) is participating in a supervised rehabilitation program and is no longer engaging in such use; or

(III) is erroneously regarded as engaging in such use, but is not engaging in such use; except that it shall not be a violation of this statute for a covered entity to adopt or administer reasonable policies or procedures, including but not limited to drug testing, designed to ensure that an individual described in subclause (I) or (II) is no longer engaging in the illegal use of drugs.

* * *

(v) For purposes of sections 503 and 504 of this statute as such sections relate to employment, the term "individual with a disability" does not include any individual who is an alcoholic whose current use of alcohol prevents such individual from performing the duties of the job in question or whose employment, by reason of such current alcohol abuse, would constitute a direct threat to property or the safety of others.

(D) For the purpose of sections 503 and 504 of this statute, as such sections relate to employment, such term does not include an individual who has a currently contagious disease or infection and who, by reason of such disease or infection, would constitute a direct threat to the health or safety of other individuals or who, by reason of the currently contagious disease or infection, is unable to perform the duties of the job.

* * *

§501. Employment of Handicapped Individuals

(a) There is established within the Federal Government an Interagency Committee on Employees who are Individuals with Disabilities (hereinafter in this section referred to as the "Committee"), comprised of such members as the President may select, including the following (or their designees whose positions are Executive Level IV or higher): the Chairman of the Civil Service Commission, the Administrator of Veterans' Affairs, and the Secretaries of Labor and Health, Education, and Welfare. The Secretary of Health, Education, and Welfare and the Chairman of the Civil Service Commission shall serve as co-chairmen of the

Committee. The resources of the President's Committees on Employment of People with Disabilities and on Mental Retardation shall be made fully available to the Committee. It shall be the purpose and function of the Committee (1) to provide a focus for Federal and other employment of individuals with a disability, and to review, on a periodic basis, in cooperation with the Civil Service Commission, the adequacy of hiring, placement, and advancement practices with respect to individuals with disabilities, by each department, agency, and instrumentality in the executive branch of Government, and to insure that the special needs of such individuals are being met; and (2) to consult with the Civil Service Commission to assist the Commission to carry out its responsibilities under subsections (b), (c), and (d) of this section. On the basis of such review and consultation, the Committee shall periodically make to the Civil Service Commission such recommendations for legislative and administrative changes as it deems necessary or desirable. The Civil Service Commission shall timely transmit to the appropriate committees of Congress any such recommendations.

(b) Each department, agency, and instrumentality (including the United States Postal Service and the Postal Rate Commission) in the executive branch shall, within one hundred and eighty days after September 26, 1973, submit to the Civil Service Commission and to the Committee an affirmative action program plan for the hiring, placement, and advancement of individuals with disabilities in such department, agency, or instrumentality. Such plan shall include a description of the extent to which and methods whereby the special needs of employees who are individuals with disabilities are being met. Such plan shall be updated annually, and shall be reviewed annually and approved by the Commission, if the Commission determines, after consultation with the Committee, that such plan provides sufficient assurances, procedures and commitments to provide adequate hiring, placement, and advancement opportunities for individuals with disabilities.

(c) The Civil Service Commission, after consultation with the Committee, shall develop and recommend to the Secretary for referral to the appropriate State agencies, policies and procedures which will facilitate the hiring, placement, and advancement in employment of individuals who have received rehabilitation services under State vocational rehabilitation programs, veterans' programs, or any other program for individuals with disabilities, including the promotion of job opportunities for such individuals. The Secretary shall encourage such State agencies to adopt and implement such policies and procedures.

(d) The Civil Service Commission, after consultation with the Committee, shall, on June 30, 1974, and at the end of each subsequent fiscal year, make a complete report to the appropriate committees of the Congress with respect to the practices of and achievements in hiring, placement, and advancement of individuals with disabilities by each department, agency, and instrumentality and the effectiveness of the affirmative action programs required by subsection (b) of this section, together with recommendations as to legislation which have been submitted to the Civil Service Commission under subsection (a) of this section, or other appropriate action to insure the adequacy of such practices. Such report shall also include an evaluation by the Committee of the effectiveness of the Civil Service Commission's activities under subsections (b) and (c) of this section.

* * *

§503.   Employment Under Federal Contracts

(a) Any contract in excess of $10,000 entered into by any Federal department or agency for the procurement of personal property and nonpersonal services (including construction) for the United States shall contain a provision requiring that, in employing persons to carry out such contract, the party contracting with the United States shall take affirmative action to employ and advance in employment qualified individuals with disabilities as defined in section 7(8). The provisions of this section shall apply to any subcontract in excess of $10,000 entered into by a prime contractor in carrying out any contract for the procurement of personal property and nonpersonal services (including construction) for the United States. The President shall implement the provisions of this section by promulgating regulations within ninety days after September 26, 1973.

(b) If any individual with a disability believes any contractor has failed or refused to comply with the provisions of a contract with the United States, relating to employment of individuals with a disability, such individual may file a complaint with the Department of Labor. The Department shall promptly investigate such complaint and shall take such action thereon as the facts and circumstances warrant, consistent with the terms of such contract and the laws and regulations applicable thereto.

(c) The requirements of this section may be waived, in whole or in part, by the President with respect to a particular contract or subcontract, in accordance with guidelines set forth in regulations which he shall prescribe, when he determines that special circumstances in the national interest so require and states in writing his reasons for such determination.

§504.   Nondiscrimination Under Federal Grants and Programs

(a) No otherwise qualified individual with a disability in the United States, as defined in section 7(8) shall, solely by reason of her or his disability, be excluded from the participation in, be denied the benefits of, or be subjected to discrimination under any program or activity receiving Federal financial assistance or under any program or activity conducted by any Executive agency or by the United States Postal Service. The head of each such agency shall promulgate such regulations as may be necessary to carry out the amendments to this section made by the Rehabilitation, Comprehensive Services, and Developmental Disabilities Act of 1978. Copies of any proposed regulation shall be submitted to appropriate authorizing committees of the Congress, and such regulation may take effect no earlier than the thirtieth day after the date on which such regulation is so submitted to such committees.

(b) For the purposes of this section, the term "program or activity" means all of the operations of—

(1) (A) a department, agency, special purpose district, or other instrumentality of a State or of a local government; or

(B) the entity of such State or local government that distributes such assistance and each such department or agency (and each other State or local government entity) to which the assistance is extended, in the case of assistance to a State or local government;

(2) (A) a college, university, or other postsecondary institution, or a public system of higher education; or

(B) a local educational agency (as defined in section 198(a)(10) of the Elementary and Secondary Education Act of 1965), system of vocational education, or other school system;

(3) (A) an entire corporation, partnership, or other private organization, or an entire sole proprietorship—

(i) if assistance is extended to such corporation, partnership, private organization, or sole proprietorship as a whole; or

(ii) which is principally engaged in the business of providing education, health care, housing, social services, or parks and recreation; or

(B) the entire plant or other comparable, geographically separate facility to which Federal financial assistance is extended, in the case of any other corporation, partnership, private organization, or sole proprietorship; or

(4) any other entity which is established by two or more of the entities described in paragraph (1), (2), or (3);

any part of which is extended Federal financial assistance.

(c) Small providers are not required by subsection (a) to make significant structural alterations to their existing facilities for the purpose of assuring program accessibility, if alternative means of providing the services are available. The terms used in this subsection shall be construed with reference to the regulations existing on March 22, 1988.

(d) The standards used to determine whether this section has been violated in a complaint alleging employment discrimination under this section shall be the standards applied under Title I of the Americans with Disabilities Act of 1990 and the provisions of sections 501 through 504, and 510, of the Americans with Disabilities Act of 1990, as such sections relate to employment.

§505. Remedies and Attorney Fees

(a) (1) The remedies, procedures, and rights set forth in section 717 of the Civil Rights Act of 1964, including the application of sections 706(f) through 706(k), and the application of §706(e)(3) to claims of discrimination in compensation, shall be available, with respect to any complaint under section 501 of this Act, to any employee or applicant for employment aggrieved by the final disposition of such complaint, or by the failure to take final action on such complaint. In fashioning an equitable or affirmative action remedy under such section, a court may take into account the reasonableness of the cost of any necessary work place accommodation, and the availability of alternatives therefor or other appropriate relief in order to achieve an equitable and appropriate remedy.

(2) The remedies, procedures, and rights set forth in Title VI of the Civil Rights Act of 1964 and in §706(e)(3) of Title VII of the Civil Rights Act of 1964, applied to claims of discrimination in compensation shall be available to any person aggrieved by any act or failure to act by any recipient of Federal assistance or Federal provider of such assistance under section 504 of this Act.

(b)   In any action or proceeding to enforce or charge a violation of a provision of this Act, the court, in its discretion, may allow the prevailing party, other than the United States, a reasonable attorney's fee as part of the costs.

Americans with Disabilities Act of 1990, as Amended by the Civil Rights Act of 1991, the ADA Amendments Act of 2008, and the Lilly Ledbetter Fair Play Act of 2009, 42 U.S.C. §12101 et seq.

§2.   Findings and Purposes

(a)   Findings

The Congress finds that—

(1)   physical or mental disabilities in no way diminish a person's right to fully participate in all aspects of society, yet many people with physical or mental disabilities have been precluded from doing so because of discrimination; others who have a record of a disability or are regarded as having a disability also have been subjected to discrimination;

(2)   historically, society has tended to isolate and segregate individuals with disabilities, and, despite some improvements, such forms of discrimination against individuals with disabilities continue to be a serious and pervasive social problem;

(3)   discrimination against individuals with disabilities persists in such critical areas as employment, housing, public accommodations, education, transportation, communication, recreation, institutionalization, health services, voting, and access to public services;

(4)   unlike individuals who have experienced discrimination on the basis of race, color, sex, national origin, religion, or age, individuals who have experienced discrimination on the basis of disability have often had no legal recourse to redress such discrimination;

(5)   individuals with disabilities continually encounter various forms of discrimination, including outright intentional exclusion, the discriminatory effects of architectural, transportation, and communication barriers, overprotective rules and policies, failure to make modifications to existing facilities and practices, exclusionary qualification standards and criteria,

segregation, and relegation to lesser services, programs, activities, benefits, jobs, or other opportunities;

(6) census data, national polls, and other studies have documented that people with disabilities, as a group, occupy an inferior status in our society, and are severely disadvantaged socially, vocationally, economically, and educationally;

(7) the Nation's proper goals regarding individuals with disabilities are to assure equality of opportunity, full participation, independent living, and economic self-sufficiency for such individuals; and

(8) the continuing existence of unfair and unnecessary discrimination and prejudice denies people with disabilities the opportunity to compete on an equal basis and to pursue those opportunities for which our free society is justifiably famous, and costs the United States billions of dollars in unnecessary expenses resulting from dependency and nonproductivity.

(b) Purpose

It is the purpose of this Act—

(1) to provide a clear and comprehensive national mandate for the elimination of discrimination against individuals with disabilities;

(2) to provide clear, strong, consistent, enforceable standards addressing discrimination against individuals with disabilities;

(3) to ensure that the Federal Government plays a central role in enforcing the standards established in this Act on behalf of individuals with disabilities; and

(4) to invoke the sweep of congressional authority, including the power to enforce the fourteenth amendment and to regulate commerce, in order to address the major areas of discrimination faced day-to-day by people with disabilities.

§3. Definition of Disability

As used in this Act:

(1) Disability — The term "disability" means, with respect to an individual —

(A) a physical or mental impairment that substantially limits one or more major life activities of such individual;

(B) a record of such an impairment; or

(C) being regarded as having such an impairment (as described in paragraph (3)).

(2) Major Life Activities —

(A) In General — For purposes of paragraph (1), major life activities include, but are not limited to, caring for oneself, performing manual tasks, seeing, hearing, eating, sleeping, walking, standing, lifting, bending, speaking, breathing, learning, reading, concentrating, thinking, communicating, and working.

(B) Major Bodily Functions — For purposes of paragraph (1), a major life activity also includes the operation of a major bodily function, including but not limited to, functions of the immune system, normal cell growth, digestive, bowel, bladder, neurological, brain, respiratory, circulatory, endocrine, and reproductive functions.

(3) Regarded As Having Such An Impairment — For purposes of paragraph (1)(C):

(A) An individual meets the requirement of "being regarded as having such an impairment" if the individual establishes that he or she has been subjected to an action prohibited under this Act because of an actual or perceived physical or mental impairment whether or not the impairment limits or is perceived to limit a major life activity.

(B) Paragraph (1)(C) shall not apply to impairments that are transitory and minor. A transitory impairment is an impairment with an actual or expected duration of 6 months or less.

(4) Rules Of Construction Regarding The Definition Of Disability — The definition of "disability" in paragraph (1) shall be construed in accordance with the following:

(A) The definition of disability in this Act shall be construed in favor of broad coverage of individuals under this Act, to the maximum extent permitted by the terms of this Act.

(B) The term "substantially limits" shall be interpreted consistently with the findings and purposes of the ADA Amendments Act of 2008.

(C) An impairment that substantially limits one major life activity need not limit other major life activities in order to be considered a disability.

(D) An impairment that is episodic or in remission is a disability if it would substantially limit a major life activity when active.

(E)(i) The determination of whether an impairment substantially limits a major life activity shall be made without regard to the ameliorative effects of mitigating measures such as--

(I) medication, medical supplies, equipment, or appliances, low-vision devices (which do not include ordinary eyeglasses or contact lenses), prosthetics including limbs and devices, hearing aids and cochlear implants or other implantable hearing devices, mobility devices, or oxygen therapy equipment and supplies;

(II) use of assistive technology;

(III) reasonable accommodations or auxiliary aids or services; or

(IV) learned behavioral or adaptive neurological modifications.

(ii) The ameliorative effects of the mitigating measures of ordinary eyeglasses or contact lenses shall be considered in determining whether an impairment substantially limits a major life activity.

(iii) As used in this subparagraph —

(I) the term "ordinary eyeglasses or contact lenses" means lenses that are intended to fully correct visual acuity or eliminate refractive error; and

(II) the term "low-vision devices" means devices that magnify, enhance, or otherwise augment a visual image.

§4. Additional Definitions

As used in this Act:

(1) Auxiliary Aids and Services — The term "auxiliary aids and services" includes —

(A) qualified interpreters or other effective methods of making aurally delivered materials available to individuals with hearing impairments;

(B) qualified readers, taped texts, or other effective methods of making visually delivered materials available to individuals with visual impairments;

(C) acquisition or modification of equipment or devices; and

D) other similar services and actions.

(2) State — The term 'State' means each of the several States, the District of Columbia, the Commonwealth of Puerto Rico, Guam, American Samoa, the Virgin Islands of the United States, the Trust Territory of the Pacific Islands, and the Commonwealth of the Northern Mariana Islands.

TITLE I—EMPLOYMENT

§101. Definitions

As used in this Title:

(1) Commission

The term "Commission" means the Equal Employment Opportunity Commission established by §705 of [Title VII of] the Civil Rights Act of 1964.

(2) Covered entity

The term "covered entity" means an employer, employment agency, labor organization, or joint labor-management committee.

(3) Direct threat

The term "direct threat" means a significant risk to the health or safety of others that cannot be eliminated by reasonable accommodation.

(4) Employee

The term "employee" means an individual employed by an employer. With respect to employment in a foreign country, such term includes an individual who is a citizen of the United States.

(5) Employer

(A) In general

The term "employer" means a person engaged in an industry affecting commerce who has 15 or more employees for each working day in each of 20 or more calendar weeks in the current or preceding calendar year, and any agent of such person, except that, for two years following the effective date of this Title, an employer means a person engaged in an industry affecting commerce who has 25 or more employees for each working day in each of 20 or more calendar weeks in the current or preceding year, and any agent of such person.

(B) Exceptions

The term "employer" does not include—

(i) the United States, a corporation wholly owned by the government of the United States, or an Indian tribe; or

(ii) a bona fide private membership club (other than a labor organization) that is exempt from taxation under section 501(c) of the Internal Revenue Code of 1986.

(6) Illegal use of drugs

(A) In general

The term "illegal use of drugs" means the use of drugs, the possession or distribution of which is unlawful under the Controlled Substances Act (21 U.S.C. 812). Such term does not include the use of a drug taken under supervision by a licensed health care professional, or other uses authorized by the Controlled Substances Act or other provisions of Federal law.

(B) Drugs

The term "drug" means a controlled substance, as defined in schedules I through V of section 202 of the Controlled Substances Act.

(7) Person, etc.

The terms "person," "labor organization," "employment agency," "commerce," and "industry affecting commerce," shall have the same meaning given such terms in §701 of [Title VII of] the Civil Rights Act of 1964.

(8) Qualified individual

The term "qualified individual" means an individual who, with or without reasonable accommodation, can perform the essential functions of the employment position that such individual holds or desires. For the purposes of this Title, consideration shall be given to the employer's judgment as to what functions of a job are essential, and if an employer has prepared a written description before advertising or interviewing applicants for the job, this description shall be considered evidence of the essential functions of the job.

(9) Reasonable accommodation

The term "reasonable accommodation" may include—

(A) making existing facilities used by employees readily accessible to and usable by individuals with disabilities; and

(B) job restructuring, part-time or modified work schedules, reassignment to a vacant position, acquisition or modification of equipment or devices, appropriate adjustment or modifications of examinations, training materials or policies, the provision of qualified readers or interpreters, and other similar accommodations for individuals with disabilities.

(10) Undue hardship

(A) In general

The term "undue hardship" means an action requiring significant difficulty or expense, when considered in light of the factors set forth in subparagraph (B).

(B) Factors to be considered

In determining whether an accommodation would impose an undue hardship on a covered entity, factors to be considered include—

(i) the nature and cost of the accommodation needed under this Act;

(ii) the overall financial resources of the facility or facilities involved in the provision of the reasonable accommodation; the number of persons employed at such facility; the effect on expenses and resources, or the impact otherwise of such accommodation upon the operation of the facility;

(iii) the overall financial resources of the covered entity; the overall size of the business of a covered entity with respect to the number of its employees; the number, type, and location of its facilities; and

(iv) the type of operation or operations of the covered entity, including the composition, structure, and functions of the workforce of such entity; the geographic separateness, administrative, or fiscal relationship of the facility or facilities in question to the covered entity.

§102. Discrimination

(a) General rule

No covered entity shall discriminate against a qualified individual on the basis of disability in regard to job application procedures, the hiring, advancement, or discharge of employees, employee compensation, job training, and other terms, conditions, and privileges of employment.

(b) Construction

As used in subsection (a) of this section, the term "discriminate against a qualified individual on the basis of disability" includes—

(1) limiting, segregating, or classifying a job applicant or employee in a way that adversely affects the opportunities or status of such applicant or employee because of the disability of such applicant or employee;

(2) participating in a contractual or other arrangement or relationship that has the effect of subjecting a covered entity's qualified applicant or employee with a disability to the discrimination prohibited by this Title (such relationship includes a relationship with an employment or referral agency, labor union, an organization providing fringe benefits to an employee of the covered entity, or an organization providing training and apprenticeship programs);

(3) utilizing standards, criteria, or methods of administration—

> (A) that have the effect of discrimination on the basis of disability; or

> (B) that perpetuate the discrimination of others who are subject to common administrative control;

(4) excluding or otherwise denying equal jobs or benefits to a qualified individual because of the known disability of an individual with whom the qualified individual is known to have a relationship or association;

(5) (A) not making reasonable accommodations to the known physical or mental limitations of an otherwise qualified individual with a disability who is an applicant or employee, unless such covered entity can demonstrate that the accommodation would impose an undue hardship on the operation of the business of such covered entity; or

> (B) denying employment opportunities to a job applicant or employee who is an otherwise qualified individual with a disability, if such denial is based on the need of such covered entity to make reasonable accommodation to the physical or mental impairments of the employee or applicant;

(6) using qualification standards, employment tests or other selection criteria that screen out or tend to screen out an individual with a disability or a class of individuals with disabilities unless the standard, test or other selection criteria, as used by the covered entity, is shown to be job-related for the position in question and is consistent with business necessity; and

(7) failing to select and administer tests concerning employment in the most effective manner to ensure that, when such test is administered to a job applicant or employee who has a disability that impairs sensory, manual, or speaking skills, such test results accurately reflect the skills, aptitude, or whatever other factor of such applicant or employee that such test purports to measure, rather than reflecting the impaired sensory, manual, or speaking skills of such employee or applicant (except where such skills are the factors that the test purports to measure).

(c) Covered entities in foreign countries

(1) In general

It shall not be unlawful under this section for a covered entity to take any action that constitutes discrimination under this section with respect to an employee in a workplace in a foreign country if compliance with this section would cause such covered entity to violate the law of the foreign country in which such workplace is located.

(2) Control of corporation

(A) Presumption

If an employer controls a corporation whose place of incorporation is a foreign country, any practice that constitutes discrimination under this section and is engaged in by such corporation shall be presumed to be engaged in by such employer.

(B) Exception

This section shall not apply with respect to the foreign operations of an employer that is a foreign person not controlled by an American employer.

(C) Determination

For purposes of this paragraph, the determination of whether an employer controls a corporation shall be based on—

   (i)   the interrelation of operations;

   (ii) the common management;

   (iii) the centralized control of labor relations; and

   (iv) the common ownership or financial control, of the employer and the corporation.

(d)   Medical examinations and inquiries

(1)   In general

The prohibition against discrimination as referred to in subsection (a) of this section shall include medical examinations and inquiries.

(2)   Preemployment

(A)   Prohibited examination or inquiry

Except as provided in paragraph (3), a covered entity shall not conduct a medical examination or make inquiries of a job applicant as to whether such applicant is an individual with a disability or as to the nature or severity of such disability.

(B)   Acceptable inquiry

A covered entity may make preemployment inquiries into the ability of an applicant to perform job-related functions.

(3)   Employment entrance examination

A covered entity may require a medical examination after an offer of employment has been made to a job applicant and prior to the commencement of the employment duties of such applicant, and may condition an offer of employment on the results of such examination, if—

(A)   all entering employees are subjected to such an examination regardless of disability;

(B)   information obtained regarding the medical condition or history of the applicant is collected and maintained on separate forms and in separate medical files and is treated as a confidential medical record, except that—

   (i)   supervisors and managers may be informed regarding necessary restrictions on the work or duties of the employee and necessary accommodations;

   (ii) first aid and safety personnel may be informed, when appropriate, if the disability might require emergency treatment; and

(iii) government officials investigating compliance with this Act shall be provided relevant information on request; and

(C) the results of such examination are used only in accordance with this Title.

(4) Examination and inquiry

(A) Prohibited examinations and inquiries

A covered entity shall not require a medical examination and shall not make inquiries of an employee as to whether such employee is an individual with a disability or as to the nature or severity of the disability, unless such examination or inquiry is shown to be job-related and consistent with business necessity.

(B) Acceptable examinations and inquiries

A covered entity may conduct voluntary medical examinations, including voluntary medical histories, which are part of an employee health program available to employees at that work site. A covered entity may make inquiries into the ability of an employee to perform job-related functions.

(C) Requirement

Information obtained under subparagraph (B) regarding the medical condition or history of any employee are subject to the requirements of subparagraphs (B) and (C) of paragraph (3).

§103.   Defenses

(a) In general

It may be a defense to a charge of discrimination under this Act that an alleged application of qualification standards, tests, or selection criteria that screen out or tend to screen out or otherwise deny a job or benefit to an individual with a disability has been shown to be job-related and consistent with business necessity, and such performance cannot be accomplished by reasonable accommodation, as required under this Title.

(b) Qualification standards

The term "qualification standards" may include a requirement that an individual shall not pose a direct threat to the health or safety of other individuals in the workplace.

(c) Qualification standards and tests related to uncorrected vision

 Notwithstanding section 3(4)(E)(ii), a covered entity shall not use qualification standards, employment tests, or other selection criteria based on an individual's uncorrected vision unless the standard, test, or other selection criteria, as used by the covered entity, is shown to be job-related for the position in question and consistent with business necessity.

(d) Religious entities

(1) In general

This Title shall not prohibit a religious corporation, association, educational institution, or society from giving preference in employment to individuals of a particular religion to perform work connected with the carrying on by such corporation, association, educational institution, or society of its activities.

(2) Religious tenets requirement

Under this Title, a religious organization may require that all applicants and employees conform to the religious tenets of such organization.

(e) List of infectious and communicable diseases

(1) In general

The Secretary of Health and Human Services, not later than 6 months after July 26, 1990, shall—

(A) review all infectious and communicable diseases which may be transmitted through handling the food supply;

(B) publish a list of infectious and communicable diseases which are transmitted through handling the food supply;

(C) publish the methods by which such diseases are transmitted; and

(D) widely disseminate such information regarding the list of diseases and their modes of transmissibility to the general public.

Such list shall be updated annually.

(2) Applications

In any case in which an individual has an infectious or communicable disease that is transmitted to others through the handling of food, that is included on the list developed by the Secretary of Health and Human Services under paragraph (1), and which cannot be eliminated by reasonable accommodation, a covered entity may refuse to assign or continue to assign such individual to a job involving food handling.

(3) Construction

Nothing in this Act shall be construed to preempt, modify, or amend any State, county, or local law, ordinance, or regulation applicable to food handling which is designed to protect the public health from individuals who pose a significant risk to the health or safety of others, which cannot be eliminated by reasonable accommodation, pursuant to the list of infectious or communicable diseases and the modes of transmissibility published by the Secretary of Health and Human Services.

§104. Illegal Use of Drugs and Alcohol

(a) Qualified individual with a disability

For purposes of this Title, "a qualified individual with a disability" shall not include any employee or applicant who is currently engaging in the illegal use of drugs, when the covered entity acts on the basis of such use.

(b) Rules of construction

Nothing in subsection (a) of this section shall be construed to exclude as a qualified individual with a disability an individual who—

(1) has successfully completed a supervised drug rehabilitation program and is no longer engaging in the illegal use of drugs, or has otherwise been rehabilitated successfully and is no longer engaging in such use;

(2) is participating in a supervised rehabilitation program and is no longer engaging in such use; or

(3) is erroneously regarded as engaging in such use, but is not engaging in such use; except that it shall not be a violation of this Act for a covered entity to adopt or administer reasonable policies or procedures, including but not limited to drug testing, designed to ensure that an individual described in paragraph (1) or (2) is no longer engaging in the illegal use of drugs.

(c) Authority of covered entity

A covered entity—

(1) may prohibit the illegal use of drugs and the use of alcohol at the workplace by all employees;

(2) may require that employees shall not be under the influence of alcohol or be engaging in the illegal use of drugs at the workplace;

(3) may require that employees behave in conformance with the requirements established under the Drug–Free Workplace Act of 1988 (41 U.S.C. 701 et seq.);

(4) may hold an employee who engages in the illegal use of drugs or who is an alcoholic to the same qualification standards for employment or job performance and behavior that such entity holds other employees, even if any unsatisfactory performance or behavior is related to the drug use or alcoholism of such employee; and

(5) may, with respect to Federal regulations regarding alcohol and the illegal use of drugs, require that—

(A) employees comply with the standards established in such regulations of the Department of Defense, if the employees of the covered entity are employed in an industry subject to such regulations, including complying with regulations (if any) that apply to employment in sensitive positions in such an industry, in the case of employees of the covered entity who are employed in such positions (as defined in the regulations of the Department of Defense);

(B) employees comply with the standards established in such regulations of the Nuclear Regulatory Commission, if the employees of the covered entity are employed in an industry subject to such regulations, including complying with regulations (if any) that apply to employment in sensitive positions in such an industry, in the case of employees of the covered entity who are employed in such positions (as defined in the regulations of the Nuclear Regulatory Commission); and

(C) employees comply with the standards established in such regulations of the Department of Transportation, if the employees of the covered entity are employed in a transportation industry subject to such regulations, including complying with such regulations (if any)

that apply to employment in sensitive positions in such an industry, in the case of employees of the covered entity who are employed in such positions (as defined in the regulations of the Department of Transportation).

(d) Drug testing

(1) In general

For purposes of this Title, a test to determine the illegal use of drugs shall not be considered a medical examination.

(2) Construction

Nothing in this Title shall be construed to encourage, prohibit, or authorize the conducting of drug testing for the illegal use of drugs by job applicants or employees or making employment decisions based on such test results.

(e) Transportation employees

Nothing in this Title shall be construed to encourage, prohibit, restrict, or authorize the otherwise lawful exercise by entities subject to the jurisdiction of the Department of Transportation of authority to—

(1) test employees of such entities in, and applicants for, positions involving safety-sensitive duties for the illegal use of drugs and for on-duty impairment by alcohol; and

(2) remove such persons who test positive for illegal use of drugs and on-duty impairment by alcohol pursuant to paragraph (1) from safety-sensitive duties in implementing subsection (c) of this section.

§105. Posting Notices

Every employer, employment agency, labor organization, or joint labor-management committee covered under this Title shall post notices in an accessible format to applicants, employees, and members describing the applicable provisions of this Act, in the manner prescribed by §711 of [Title VII of] the Civil Rights Act of 1964.

§106. Regulations

Not later than 1 year after July 26, 1990, the Commission shall issue regulations in an accessible format to carry out this Title in accordance with the provisions of the Administrative Procedure Act.

§107. Enforcement

(a) Powers, remedies, and procedures

The powers, remedies, and procedures set forth in §§705, 706, 707, 708, 709 and 710 of [Title VII of] the Civil Rights Act of 1964 shall be the powers, remedies, and procedures this Title provides to the Commission, to the Attorney General, or to any person alleging discrimination on the basis of disability in violation of any provision of this Act, or regulations promulgated under §106, concerning employment.

(b) Coordination

The agencies with enforcement authority for actions which allege employment discrimination under this Title and under the Rehabilitation Act of 1973 shall develop procedures to ensure that administrative complaints filed under this Title and under the Rehabilitation Act of 1973 are dealt with in a manner that avoids duplication of effort and prevents imposition of inconsistent or conflicting standards for the same requirements under this Title and the Rehabilitation Act of 1973. The Commission, the Attorney General, and the Office of Federal Contract Compliance Programs shall establish such coordinating mechanisms (similar to provisions contained in the joint regulations promulgated by the Commission and the Attorney General at part 42 of Title 28 and part 1691 of Title 29, Code of Federal Regulations, and the Memorandum of Understanding between the Commission and the Office of Federal Contract Compliance Programs dated January 16, 1981 (46 Fed.Reg. 7435, January 23, 1981)) in regulations implementing this Title and Rehabilitation Act of 1973 not later than 18 months after July 26, 1990.

TITLE V—MISCELLANEOUS PROVISIONS

§501.   Construction

(a) In general

Except as otherwise provided in this Act, nothing in this Act shall be construed to apply a lesser standard than the standards applied under Title V of the Rehabilitation Act of 1973 (29 U.S.C. 790 et seq.) or the regulations issued by Federal agencies pursuant to such Title.

(b) Relationship to other laws

Nothing in this Act shall be construed to invalidate or limit the remedies, rights, and procedures of any Federal law or law of any State or political subdivision of any State or jurisdiction that provides greater or equal protection for the rights of individuals with disabilities than are afforded by this Act. Nothing in this Act shall be construed to preclude the prohibition of, or the imposition of restrictions on, smoking in places of employment covered by Title I of this Act * * *.

(c) Insurance

Title I * * * of this Act shall not be construed to prohibit or restrict—

(1) an insurer, hospital or medical service company, health maintenance organization, or any agent, or entity that administers benefit plans, or similar organizations from underwriting risks, classifying risks, or administering such risks that are based on or not inconsistent with State law; or

(2) a person or organization covered by this Act from establishing, sponsoring, observing or administering the terms of a bona fide benefit plan that are based on underwriting risks, classifying risks, or administering such risks that are based on or not inconsistent with State law; or

(3) a person or organization covered by this Act from establishing, sponsoring, observing or administering the terms of a bona fide benefit plan that is not subject to State laws that regulate insurance.

Paragraphs (1), (2), and (3) shall not be used as a subterfuge to evade the purposes of Title I.

(d) Accommodations and services

Nothing in this Act shall be construed to require an individual with a disability to accept an accommodation, aid, service, opportunity, or benefit which such individual chooses not to accept.

(e) Benefits under state worker's compensation laws

Nothing in this Act alters the standards for determining eligibility for benefits under State worker's compensation laws or under State and Federal disability benefit programs.

(f) Fundamental alteration

Nothing in this Act alters the provision of section 302(b)(2)(A)(ii), specifying that reasonable modifications in policies, practices, or procedures shall be required, unless an entity can demonstrate that making such modifications in policies, practices, or procedures, including academic requirements in postsecondary education, would fundamentally alter the nature of the goods, services, facilities, privileges, advantages, or accommodations involved.

(g) Claims of no disability

Nothing in this Act shall provide the basis for a claim by an individual without a disability that the individual was subject to discrimination because of the individual's lack of disability.

(h) Reasonable accommodations and modifications

A covered entity under title I, a public entity under title II, and any person who owns, leases (or leases to), or operates a place of public accommodation under title III, need not provide a reasonable accommodation or a reasonable modification to policies, practices, or procedures to an individual who meets the definition of disability in section 3(1) solely under subparagraph (C) of such section.

§502. State Immunity

A State shall not be immune under the eleventh amendment to the Constitution of the United States from an action in Federal or State court of competent jurisdiction for a violation of this Act. In any action against a State for a violation of the requirements of this Act, remedies (including remedies both at law and in equity) are available for such a violation to the same extent as such remedies are available for such a violation in an action against any public or private entity other than a State.

§503. Prohibition Against Retaliation and Coercion

(a) Retaliation

No person shall discriminate against any individual because such individual has opposed any act or practice made unlawful by this Act or because such individual made a charge, testified, assisted, or participated in any manner in an investigation, proceeding, or hearing under this Act.

(b) Interference, coercion, or intimidation

It shall be unlawful to coerce, intimidate, threaten, or interfere with any individual in the exercise or enjoyment of, or on account of his or her having exercised or enjoyed, or on account of his or her having aided or encouraged any other individual in the exercise or enjoyment of, any right granted or protected by this Act.

(c) Remedies and procedures

The remedies and procedures available under §107 * * * of this Act shall be available to aggrieved persons for violations of subsections (a) and (b) of this section, with respect to Title I * * * of this Act.

* * *

§505. Attorney's fees

In any action or administrative proceeding commenced pursuant to this Act, the court or agency, in its discretion, may allow the prevailing party, other than the United States, a reasonable attorney's fee, including litigation expenses, and costs, and the United States shall be liable for the foregoing the same as a private individual.

§506 Rule of construction regarding regulatory authority

The authority to issue regulations granted to the Equal Employment Opportunity Commission, the Attorney General, and the Secretary of Transportation under this Act includes the authority to issue regulations implementing the definitions of disability in section 3 (including rules of construction) and the definitions in section 4, consistent with the ADA Amendments Act of 2008.

* * *

§509. Transvestites

For the purposes of this Act, the term "disabled" or "disability" shall not apply to an individual solely because that individual is a transvestite.

* * *

§511. Illegal Use of Drugs

(a) In general

For purposes of this Act, the term "individual with a disability" does not include an individual who is currently engaging in the illegal use of drugs, when the covered entity acts on the basis of such use.

(b) Rules of construction

Nothing in subsection (a) of this section shall be construed to exclude as an individual with a disability an individual who—

(1) has successfully completed a supervised drug rehabilitation program and is no longer engaging in the illegal use of drugs, or has otherwise been rehabilitated successfully and is no longer engaging in such use;

(2) is participating in a supervised rehabilitation program and is no longer engaging in such use; or

(3) is erroneously regarded as engaging in such use, but is not engaging in such use; except that it shall not be a violation of this Act for a covered entity to adopt or administer reasonable policies or procedures, including but not limited to drug testing, designed to ensure that an individual described in paragraph (1) or (2) is no longer engaging in the illegal use of drugs; however, nothing in this section shall be construed to encourage, prohibit, restrict, or authorize the conducting of testing for the illegal use of drugs.

(c) Health and other services

Notwithstanding subsection (a) of this section and §512(b)(3), an individual shall not be denied health services, or services provided in connection with drug rehabilitation, on the basis of the current illegal use of drugs if the individual is otherwise entitled to such services.

(d) Definition of illegal use of drugs

(1) In general

The term "illegal use of drugs" means the use of drugs, the possession or distribution of which is unlawful under the Controlled Substances Act (21 U.S.C. 812). Such term does not include the use of a drug taken under supervision by a licensed health care professional, or other uses authorized by the Controlled Substances Act or other provisions of Federal law.

(2) Drugs

The term "drug" means a controlled substance, as defined in schedules I through V of section 202 of the Controlled Substances Act.

§512. Definitions

(a) Homosexuality and bisexuality

For purposes of the definition of "disability" in §3(2), homosexuality and bisexuality are not impairments and as such are not disabilities under this Act.

(b) Certain conditions

Under this Act, the term "disability" shall not include—

(1) transvestism, transsexualism, pedophilia, exhibitionism, voyeurism, gender identity disorders not resulting from physical impairments, or other sexual behavior disorders;

(2) compulsive gambling, kleptomania, or pyromania; or

(3) psychoactive substance use disorders resulting from current illegal use of drugs.

* * *

ADA Amendments Act of 2008, 42 U.S.C. §12101 et seq.

An Act To restore the intent and protections of the Americans with Disabilities Act of 1990.

§1. Short Title.

This Act may be cited as the "ADA Amendments Act of 2008".

§2. Findings And Purposes

(a) Findings

Congress finds that —

(1) in enacting the Americans with Disabilities Act of 1990 (ADA), Congress intended that the Act "provide a clear and comprehensive national mandate for the elimination of discrimination against individuals with disabilities" and provide broad coverage;

(2) in enacting the ADA, Congress recognized that physical and mental disabilities in no way diminish a person's right to fully participate in all aspects of society, but that people with physical or mental disabilities are frequently precluded from doing so because of prejudice, antiquated attitudes, or the failure to remove societal and institutional barriers;

(3) while Congress expected that the definition of disability under the ADA would be interpreted consistently with how courts had applied the definition of a handicapped individual under the Rehabilitation Act of 1973, that expectation has not been fulfilled;

(4) the holdings of the Supreme Court in Sutton v. United Air Lines, Inc., 527 U.S. 471 (1999) and its companion cases have narrowed the broad scope of protection intended to be afforded by the ADA, thus eliminating protection for many individuals whom Congress intended to protect;

(5) the holding of the Supreme Court in Toyota Motor Manufacturing, Kentucky, Inc. v. Williams, 534 U.S. 184 (2002) further narrowed the broad scope of protection intended to be afforded by the ADA;

(6) as a result of these Supreme Court cases, lower courts have incorrectly found in individual cases that people with a range of substantially limiting impairments are not people with disabilities;

(7) in particular, the Supreme Court, in the case of Toyota Motor Manufacturing, Kentucky, Inc. v. Williams, 534 U.S. 184 (2002), interpreted the term "substantially limits" to require a greater degree of limitation than was intended by Congress; and

(8) Congress finds that the current Equal Employment Opportunity Commission ADA regulations defining the term "substantially limits" as "significantly restricted" are inconsistent with congressional intent, by expressing too high a standard.

(b) Purposes

The purposes of this Act are —

(1) to carry out the ADA's objectives of providing "a clear and comprehensive national mandate for the elimination of discrimination" and "clear, strong, consistent, enforceable standards addressing discrimination" by reinstating a broad scope of protection to be available under the ADA;

(2) to reject the requirement enunciated by the Supreme Court in Sutton v. United Air Lines, Inc., 527 U.S. 471 (1999) and its companion cases that whether an impairment substantially limits a major life activity is to be determined with reference to the ameliorative effects of mitigating measures;

(3) to reject the Supreme Court's reasoning in Sutton v. United Air Lines, Inc., 527 U.S. 471 (1999) with regard to coverage under the third prong of the definition of disability and to reinstate the reasoning of the Supreme Court in School Board of Nassau County v. Arline, 480 U.S. 273 (1987) which set forth a broad view of the third prong of the definition of handicap under the Rehabilitation Act of 1973;

(4) to reject the standards enunciated by the Supreme Court in Toyota Motor Manufacturing, Kentucky, Inc. v. Williams, 534 U.S. 184 (2002), that the terms "substantially" and "major" in the definition of disability under the ADA "need to be interpreted strictly to create a demanding standard for qualifying as disabled," and that to be substantially limited in performing a major life activity under the ADA "an individual must have an impairment that prevents or severely restricts the individual from doing activities that are of central importance to most people's daily lives";

(5) to convey congressional intent that the standard created by the Supreme Court in the case of Toyota Motor Manufacturing, Kentucky, Inc. v. Williams, 534 U.S. 184 (2002) for "substantially limits", and applied by lower courts in numerous decisions, has created an inappropriately high level of limitation necessary to obtain coverage under the ADA, to convey that it is the intent of Congress that the primary object of attention in cases brought under the ADA should be whether entities covered under the ADA have complied with their obligations, and to convey that the question of whether an individual's impairment is a disability under the ADA should not demand extensive analysis; and

(6) to express Congress' expectation that the Equal Employment Opportunity Commission will revise that portion of its current regulations that defines the term "substantially limits" as "significantly restricted" to be consistent with this Act, including the amendments made by this Act.

CIVIL RIGHTS RESTORATION ACT OF 1987, 20 U.S.C. §1687 ET SEQ.

An act to restore the broad scope of coverage and to clarify the application of Title IX of the Education Amendments of 1972 * * * and Title VI of the Civil Rights Act of 1964.

Be it enacted by the Senate and House of Representatives of the United States of America in Congress assembled,

Short Title

Sec. 1. This Act may be cited as the "Civil Rights Restoration Act of 1987."

Findings of Congress

Sec. 2. The Congress finds that—

(1) certain aspects of recent decisions and opinions of the Supreme Court have unduly narrowed or cast doubt upon the broad application of Title IX of the Education Amendments of 1972, section 504 of the Rehabilitation Act of 1973, the Age Discrimination Act of 1975, and Title VI of the Civil Rights Act of 1964; and

(2) legislative action is necessary to restore the prior consistent and long-standing executive branch interpretation and broad, institution-wide application of those laws as previously administered.

Education Amendments Amendment

Sec. 3.   (a) Title IX of the Education Amendments of 1972 is amended by adding at the end the following new sections:

"Interpretation of 'Program or Activity'"

"Sec. 908.   For the purposes of this Title, the term 'program or activity' and 'program' mean all of the operations of—

"(1) (A) a department, agency, special purpose district, or other instrumentality of a State or of a local government; or

"(B) the entity of such State or local government that distributes such assistance and each such department or agency (and each other State or local government entity) to which the assistance is extended, in the case of assistance to a State or local government;

"(2) (A) a college, university, or other postsecondary institution, or a public system of higher education; or

"(B) a local educational agency (as defined in section 198(a)(10) of the Elementary and Secondary Education Act of 1965), system of vocational education, or other school system;

"(3) (A) an entire corporation, partnership, or other private organization, or an entire sole proprietorship—

"(i) if assistance is extended to such corporation, partnership, private organization, or sole proprietorship as a whole; or

"(ii) which is principally engaged in the business of providing education, health care, housing, social services, or parks and recreation; or

"(B) the entire plant or other comparable, geographically separate facility to which Federal financial assistance is extended, in the case of any other corporation, partnership, private organization, or sole proprietorship; or

"(4) any other entity which is established by two or more of the entities described in paragraph (1), (2), or (3); any part of which is extended Federal financial assistance, except that such term does not include any operation of an entity which is controlled by a religious organization if the application of section 901 to such operation would not be consistent with the religious tenets of such organization."

(b) Notwithstanding any provision of this Act or any amendment adopted thereto.

"Neutrality with Respect to Abortion"

"Sec. 909.   Nothing in this Title shall be construed to require or prohibit any person, or public or private entity, to provide or pay for any benefit or service, including the use of facilities, related to an abortion.   Nothing in this section shall be construed to permit a penalty to be imposed on any person or individual because such person or individual is seeking or has received any benefit or service related to a legal abortion."

* * *

Civil Rights Act Amendment

Sec. 6. Title VI of the Civil Rights Act of 1964 is amended by adding at the end the following new section:

"Sec. 606. For the purposes of this Title, the term 'program or activity' and the term 'program' mean all of the operations of—

"(1) (A) a department, agency, special purpose district, or other instrumentality of a State or of a local government; or

"(B) the entity of such State or local government that distributes such assistance and each such department or agency (and each other State or local government entity) to which the assistance is extended, in the case of assistance to a State or local government;

"(2) (A) a college, university, or other postsecondary institution, or a public system of higher education; or

"(B) a local educational agency (as defined in section 198(a)(10) of the Elementary and Secondary Education Act of 1965), system of vocational education, or other school system;

"(3) (A) an entire corporation, partnership, or other private organization, or an entire sole proprietorship—

"(i) if assistance is extended to such corporation, partnership, private organization, or sole proprietorship as a whole; or

"(ii) which is principally engaged in the business of providing education, health care, housing, social services, or parks and recreation; or

"(B) the entire plant or other comparable, geographically separate facility to which Federal financial assistance is extended, in the case of any other corporation, partnership, private organization, or sole proprietorship; or

"(4) any other entity which is established by two or more of the entities described in paragraph (1), (2), or (3); any part of which is extended Federal financial assistance."

Rule of Construction

Sec. 7. Nothing in the amendments made by this Act shall be construed to extend the application of the Acts so amended to ultimate beneficiaries of Federal financial assistance excluded from coverage before the enactment of this Act.

Abortion Neutrality

Sec. 8. No provision of this Act or any amendment made by this Act shall be construed to force or require any individual or hospital or any other institution, program, or activity receiving Federal Funds to perform or pay for an abortion.

* * *

Congressional Accountability Act of 1995, P.L. 104-1 (S 2), 109 Stat. 3

January 23, 1995

An Act to make certain laws applicable to the legislative branch of the Federal Government.

* * *

§1. Short Title and Table of Contents

(a) Short title.—This Act may be cited as the "Congressional Accountability Act of 1995."

* * *

TITLE I—GENERAL

§101.   Definitions.

Except as otherwise specifically provided in this Act, as used in this Act:

(1) Board.—The term "Board" means the Board of Directors of the Office of Compliance.

(2) Chair.—The term "Chair" means the Chair of the Board of Directors of the Office of Compliance.

(3) Covered employee.—The term "covered employee" means any employee of—

(A) the House of Representatives;

(B) the Senate;

(C) the Capitol Guide Service;

(D) the Capitol Police;

(E) the Congressional Budget Office;

(F) the Office of the Architect of the Capitol;

(G) the Office of the Attending Physician;

(H) the Office of Compliance; or

(I) the Office of Technology Assessment.

(4) Employee.—The term "employee" includes an applicant for employment and a former employee.

(5) Employee of the office of the Architect of the Capitol.—The term "employee of the Office of the Architect of the Capitol" includes any employee of

the Office of the Architect of the Capitol, the Botanic Garden, or the Senate Restaurants.

(6) Employee of the Capitol Police.—The term "employee of the Capitol Police" includes any member or officer of the Capitol Police.

(7) Employee of the House of Representatives.—The term "employee of the House of Representatives" includes an individual occupying a position the pay for which is disbursed by the Clerk of the House of Representatives, or another official designated by the House of Representatives, or any employment position in an entity that is paid with funds derived from the clerk-hire allowance of the House of Representatives but not any such individual employed by any entity listed in subparagraphs (C) through (I) of paragraph (3).

(8) Employee of the Senate.—The term "employee of the Senate" includes any employee whose pay is disbursed by the Secretary of the Senate, but not any such individual employed by any entity listed in subparagraphs (C) through (I) of paragraph (3).

(9) Employing office.—The term "employing office" means—

(A) the personal office of a Member of the House of Representatives or of a Senator;

(B) a committee of the House of Representatives or the Senate or a joint committee;

(C) any other office headed by a person with the final authority to appoint, hire, discharge, and set the terms, conditions, or privileges of the employment of an employee of the House of Representatives or the Senate; or

(D) the Capitol Guide Board, the Capitol Police Board, the Congressional Budget Office, the Office of the Architect of the Capitol, the Office of the Attending Physician, the Office of Compliance, and the Office of Technology Assessment.

(10) Executive Director.—The term "Executive Director" means the Executive Director of the Office of Compliance.

(11) General Counsel.—The term "General Counsel" means the General Counsel of the Office of Compliance.

(12) Office.—The term "Office" means the Office of Compliance.

§102.   Application of Laws

(a) Laws made applicable.—The following laws shall apply, as prescribed by this Act, to the legislative branch of the Federal Government:

(1) The Fair Labor Standards Act of 1938.

(2) Title VII of the Civil Rights Act of 1964.

(3) The Americans with Disabilities Act of 1990.

(4) The Age Discrimination in Employment Act of 1967.

(5) The Family and Medical Leave Act of 1993.

(6) The Occupational Safety and Health Act of 1970.

(7) Chapter 71 (relating to Federal service labor-management relations) of title 5, United States Code.

(8) The Employee Polygraph Protection Act of 1988.

(9) The Worker Adjustment and Retraining Notification Act.

(10) The Rehabilitation Act of 1973.

(11) Chapter 43 (relating to veterans' employment and reemployment) of title 38, United States Code.

(b) Laws which may be made applicable.—

(1) In general.—The Board shall review provisions of Federal law (including regulations) relating to (A) the terms and conditions of employment (including hiring, promotion, demotion, termination, salary, wages, overtime compensation, benefits, work assignments or reassignments, grievance and disciplinary procedures, protection from discrimination in personnel actions, occupational health and safety, and family and medical and other leave) of employees, and (B) access to public services and accommodations.

(2) Board report.—Beginning on December 31, 1996, and every 2 years thereafter, the Board shall report on (A) whether or to what degree the provisions described in paragraph (1) are applicable or inapplicable to the legislative branch, and (B) with respect to provisions inapplicable to the legislative branch, whether such provisions should be made applicable to the legislative branch. The presiding officers of the House of Representatives and the Senate shall cause each such report to be printed in the Congressional Record and each such report shall be referred to the committees of the House of Representatives and the Senate with jurisdiction.

(3) Reports of congressional committees.—Each report accompanying any bill or joint resolution relating to terms and conditions of employment or access to public services or accommodations reported by a committee of the House of Representatives or the Senate shall—

(A) describe the manner in which the provisions of the bill or joint resolution apply to the legislative branch; or

(B) in the case of a provision not applicable to the legislative branch, include a statement of the reasons the provision does not apply.

On the objection of any Member, it shall not be in order for the Senate or the House of Representatives to consider any such bill or joint resolution if the report of the committee on such bill or joint resolution does not comply with the provisions of this paragraph. This paragraph may be waived in either House by majority vote of that House.

TITLE II—EXTENSION OF RIGHTS AND PROTECTIONS

Part A—Employment Discrimination, Family and Medical Leave, Fair Labor Standards, Employee Polygraph Protection, Worker Adjustment and Retraining, Employment and Reemployment of Veterans, and Intimidation

§ 201. **Rights and Protections Under Title VII of the Civil Rights Act of 1964, the Age Discrimination in Employment Act of 1967, the Rehabilitation Act of 1973, and Title I of the Americans With Disabilities Act of 1990**

(a) Discriminatory practices prohibited.—All personnel actions affecting covered employees shall be made free from any discrimination based on—

(1) race, color, religion, sex, or national origin, within the meaning of section 703 of the Civil Rights Act of 1964;

(2) age, within the meaning of section 15 of the Age Discrimination in Employment Act of 1967; or

(3) disability, within the meaning of section 501 of the Rehabilitation Act of 1973 and sections 102 through 104 of the Americans with Disabilities Act of 1990.

(b) Remedy.—

(1) Civil rights.—The remedy for a violation of subsection (a)(1) shall be—

(A) such remedy as would be appropriate if awarded under section 706(g) of the Civil Rights Act of 1964; and

(B) such compensatory damages as would be appropriate if awarded under section 1977 of the Revised Statutes, or as would be appropriate if awarded under sections 1977A(a)(1), 1977A(b)(2), and, irrespective of the size of the employing office, 1977A(b)(3)(D) of the 42 U.S.C. §§1981a(a)(1), 1981a(b)(2), and 1981a(b(3)(D)).

(2) Age discrimination.—The remedy for a violation of subsection (a)(2) shall be—

(A) such remedy as would be appropriate if awarded under section 15(c) of the Age Discrimination in Employment Act of 1967; and

(B) such liquidated damages as would be appropriate if awarded under section 7(b) of such Act.

In addition, the waiver provisions of section 7(f) of such Act shall apply to covered employees.

(3) Disabilities discrimination.—The remedy for a violation of subsection (a)(3) shall be—

(A) such remedy as would be appropriate if awarded under section 505(a)(1) of the Rehabilitation Act of 1973 or section 107(a) of the Americans with Disabilities Act of 1990; and

(B) such compensatory damages as would be appropriate if awarded under sections 1977A(a)(2), 1977A(a)(3), 1977A(b)(2), and, irrespective of the size of the employing office, 1977A(b)(3)(D) of the

Revised Statutes (42 U.S.C. 1981a(a)(2), 1981a(a)(3), 1981a(b)(2), and 1981a(b)(3)(D)).

(c) Application to General Accounting Office, Government Printing Office, and Library of Congress.—

(1) Section 717 of the Civil Rights Act of 1964.—Section 717(a) of the Civil Rights Act of 1964 is amended by—

(A) striking "legislative and";

(B) striking "branches" and inserting "branch"; and

(C) inserting "Government Printing Office, the General Accounting Office, and the" after "and in the."

(2) Section 15 of the Age Discrimination In Employment Act of 1967.— Section 15(a) of the Age Discrimination in Employment Act of 1967 is amended by—

(A) striking "legislative and";

(B) striking "branches" and inserting "branch"; and

(C) inserting "Government Printing Office, the General Accounting Office, and the" after "and in the."

(3) Section 509 of the Americans With Disabilities Act of 1990.—Section 509 of the Americans with Disabilities Act of 1990 is amended—

(A) by striking subsections (a) and (b) of section 509;

(B) in subsection (c), by striking "(c) Instrumentalities Of Congress.—" and inserting "The General Accounting Office, the Government Printing Office, and the Library of Congress shall be covered as follows:";

(C) by striking the second sentence of paragraph (2);

(D) in paragraph (4), by striking "the instrumentalities of the Congress include" and inserting "the term 'instrumentality of the Congress' means," by striking "the Architect of the Capitol, the Congressional Budget Office," by inserting "and" before "the Library," and by striking "the Office of Technology Assessment, and the United States Botanic Garden";

(E) by redesignating paragraph (5) as paragraph (7) and by inserting after paragraph (4) the following new paragraph:

"(5) Enforcement Of Employment Rights.—The remedies and procedures set forth in section 717 of the Civil Rights Act of 1964 shall be available to any employee of an instrumentality of the Congress who alleges a violation of the rights and protections under sections 102 through 104 of this Act that are made applicable by this section, except that the authorities of the Equal Employment Opportunity Commission shall be exercised by the chief official of the instrumentality of the Congress."; and

(F) by amending the title of the section to read "Instrumentalities of the congress."

(d) Effective date.—This section shall take effect 1 year after the date of the enactment of this Act.

§202. **Rights and Protections Under the Family and Medical Leave Act of 1993**

(a) Family and medical leave rights and protections provided.—

(1) In general.—The rights and protections established by sections 101 through 105 of the Family and Medical Leave Act of 1993 shall apply to covered employees.

(2) Definition.—For purposes of the application described in paragraph (1)—

(A) the term "employer" as used in the Family and Medical Leave Act of 1993 means any employing office, and

(B) the term "eligible employee" as used in the Family and Medical Leave Act of 1993 means a covered employee who has been employed in any employing office for 12 months and for at least 1,250 hours of employment during the previous 12 months.

(b) Remedy.—The remedy for a violation of subsection (a) shall be such remedy, including liquidated damages, as would be appropriate if awarded under paragraph (1) of section 107(a) of the Family and Medical Leave Act of 1993.

(c) Application to General Accounting Office and Library Of Congress.—

(1) Amendments to the Family and Medical Leave Act of 1993.—

(A) Coverage.—Section 101(4)(A) of the Family and Medical Leave Act of 1993 is amended by striking "and" at the end of clause (ii), by striking the period at the end of clause (iii) and inserting "; and," and by adding after clause (iii) the following:

"(iv)   includes the General Accounting Office and the Library of Congress.."

(B) Enforcement.—Section 107 of the Family and Medical Leave Act of 1993 is amended by adding at the end the following:

"(f) GENERAL ACCOUNTING OFFICE AND LIBRARY OF CONGRESS.—In the case of the General Accounting Office and the Library of Congress, the authority of the Secretary of Labor under this title shall be exercised respectively by the Comptroller General of the United States and the Librarian of Congress.."

(2) Conforming amendment to Title 5, United States Code.—Section 6381(1)(A) of title 5, United States Code, is amended by striking "and" after "District of Columbia" and inserting before the semicolon the following: "and any employee of the General Accounting Office or the Library of Congress."

(d) Regulations.—

(1) In general.—The Board shall, pursuant to section 304, issue regulations to implement the rights and protections under this section.

(2) Agency regulations.—The regulations issued under paragraph (1) shall be the same as substantive regulations promulgated by the Secretary of Labor to

implement the statutory provisions referred to in subsection (a) except insofar as the Board may determine, for good cause shown and stated together with the regulation, that a modification of such regulations would be more effective for the implementation of the rights and protections under this section.

(e) Effective date.—

(1) In general.—Subsections (a) and (b) shall be effective 1 year after the date of the enactment of this Act.

(2) General Accounting Office and Library of Congress.—Subsection (c) shall be effective 1 year after transmission to the Congress of the study under section 230.

* * *

§207. Prohibition of Intimidation or Reprisal

(a) In general.—It shall be unlawful for an employing office to intimidate, take reprisal against, or otherwise discriminate against, any covered employee because the covered employee has opposed any practice made unlawful by this Act, or because the covered employee has initiated proceedings, made a charge, or testified, assisted, or participated in any manner in a hearing or other proceeding under this Act.

(b) Remedy.—The remedy available for a violation of subsection (a) shall be such legal or equitable remedy as may be appropriate to redress a violation of subsection (a).

* * *

PART E—GENERAL

§225. Generally Applicable Remedies and Limitations

(a) Attorney's fees.—If a covered employee, with respect to any claim under this Act, or a qualified person with a disability, with respect to any claim under section 210, is a prevailing party in any proceeding under section 405, 406, 407, or 408, the hearing officer, Board, or court, as the case may be, may award attorney's fees, expert fees, and any other costs as would be appropriate if awarded under section 706(k) of the Civil Rights Act of 1964.

(b) Interest.—In any proceeding under section 405, 406, 407, or 408, the same interest to compensate for delay in payment shall be made available as would be appropriate if awarded under section 717(d) of the Civil Rights Act of 1964.

(c) Civil penalties and punitive damages.—No civil penalty or punitive damages may be awarded with respect to any claim under this Act.

(d) Exclusive procedure.—

(1) In general.—Except as provided in paragraph (2), no person may commence an administrative or judicial proceeding to seek a remedy for the rights and protections afforded by this Act except as provided in this Act.

(2) Veterans.—A covered employee under section 206 may also utilize any provisions of chapter 43 of title 38, United States Code, that are applicable to that employee.

(e) Scope of remedy.—Only a covered employee who has undertaken and completed the procedures described in sections 402 and 403 may be granted a remedy under part A of this title.

(f) Construction.—

(1) Definitions and exemptions.—Except where inconsistent with definitions and exemptions provided in this Act, the definitions and exemptions in the laws made applicable by this Act shall apply under this Act.

(2) Size limitations.—Notwithstanding paragraph (1), provisions in the laws made applicable under this Act (other than the Worker Adjustment and Retraining Notification Act) determining coverage based on size, whether expressed in terms of numbers of employees, amount of business transacted, or other measure, shall not apply in determining coverage under this Act.]

(3) Executive branch enforcement.—This Act shall not be construed to authorize enforcement by the executive branch of this Act.

* * *

TITLE III—OFFICE OF COMPLIANCE

§301. Establishment of Office of Compliance

(a) Establishment.—There is established, as an independent office within the legislative branch of the Federal Government, the Office of Compliance.

(b) Board of directors.—The Office shall have a Board of Directors. The Board shall consist of 5 individuals appointed jointly by the Speaker of the House of Representatives, the Majority Leader of the Senate, and the Minority Leaders of the House of Representatives and the Senate. Appointments of the first 5 members of the Board shall be completed not later than 90 days after the date of the enactment of this Act.

* * *

§304. Substantive regulations.

(a) Regulations.—

(1) In general.—The procedures applicable to the regulations of the Board issued for the implementation of this Act, which shall include regulations the Board is required to issue under title II (including regulations on the appropriate application of exemptions under the laws made applicable in title II) are as prescribed in this section.

(2) Rulemaking procedure.—Such regulations of the Board—

(A) shall be adopted, approved, and issued in accordance with subsection (b); and

(B) shall consist of 3 separate bodies of regulations, which shall apply, respectively, to—

(i) the Senate and employees of the Senate;

(ii) the House of Representatives and employees of the House of Representatives; and

(iii) all other covered employees and employing offices.

(b) Adoption by the Board.—The Board shall adopt the regulations referred to in subsection (a)(1) in accordance with the principles and procedures set forth in section 553 of title 5, United States Code, and as provided in the following provisions of this subsection:

(1) Proposal.—The Board shall publish a general notice of proposed rulemaking under section 553(b) of title 5, United States Code, but, instead of publication of a general notice of proposed rulemaking in the Federal Register, the Board shall transmit such notice to the Speaker of the House of Representatives and the President pro tempore of the Senate for publication in the Congressional Record on the first day on which both Houses are in session following such transmittal. Such notice shall set forth the recommendations of the Deputy Director for the Senate in regard to regulations under subsection (a)(2)(B)(i), the recommendations of the Deputy Director for the House of Representatives in regard to regulations under subsection (a)(2)(B)(ii), and the recommendations of the Executive Director for regulations under subsection (a)(2)(B)(iii).

(2) Comment.—Before adopting regulations, the Board shall provide a comment period of at least 30 days after publication of a general notice of proposed rulemaking.

(3) Adoption.—After considering comments, the Board shall adopt regulations and shall transmit notice of such action together with a copy of such regulations to the Speaker of the House of Representatives and the President pro tempore of the Senate for publication in the Congressional Record on the first day on which both Houses are in session following such transmittal.

(4) Recommendation as to method of approval.—The Board shall include a recommendation in the general notice of proposed rulemaking and in the regulations as to whether the regulations should be approved by resolution of the Senate, by resolution of the House of Representatives, by concurrent resolution, or by joint resolution.

(c) Approval of regulations.—

(1) In general.—Regulations referred to in paragraph (2)(B)(i) of subsection (a) may be approved by the Senate by resolution or by the Congress by concurrent resolution or by joint resolution. Regulations referred to in paragraph (2)(B)(ii) of subsection (a) may be approved by the House of Representatives by resolution or by the Congress by concurrent resolution or by joint resolution. Regulations referred to in paragraph (2)(B)(iii) may be approved by Congress by concurrent resolution or by joint resolution.

(2) Referral.—Upon receipt of a notice of adoption of regulations under subsection (b)(3), the presiding officers of the House of Representatives and the Senate shall refer such notice, together with a copy of such regulations, to the appropriate committee or committees of the House of Representatives and of the Senate. The purpose of the referral shall be to consider whether such regulations should be approved, and, if so, whether such approval should be by resolution of the House of Representatives or of the Senate, by concurrent resolution or by joint resolution.

(3) Joint referral and discharge in the Senate.—The presiding officer of the Senate may refer the notice of issuance of regulations, or any resolution of approval of regulations, to one committee or jointly to more than one committee. If a committee of the Senate acts to report a jointly referred measure, any other committee of the Senate must act within 30 calendar days of continuous session, or be automatically discharged.

(4) One-house resolution or concurrent resolution.—In the case of a resolution of the House of Representatives or the Senate or a concurrent resolution referred to in paragraph (1), the matter after the resolving clause shall be the following: "The following regulations issued by the Office of Compliance on ___ are hereby approved:" (the blank space being appropriately filled in, and the text of the regulations being set forth).

(5) Joint resolution.—In the case of a joint resolution referred to in paragraph (1), the matter after the resolving clause shall be the following: "The following regulations issued by the Office of Compliance on ___ are hereby approved and shall have the force and effect of law:" (the blank space being appropriately filled in, and the text of the regulations being set forth).

(d) Issuance and effective date.—

(1) Publication.—After approval of regulations under subsection (c), the Board shall submit the regulations to the Speaker of the House of Representatives and the President pro tempore of the Senate for publication in the Congressional Record on the first day on which both Houses are in session following such transmittal.

(2) Date of issuance.—The date of issuance of regulations shall be the date on which they are published in the Congressional Record under paragraph (1).

(3) Effective date.—Regulations shall become effective not less than 60 days after the regulations are issued, except that the Board may provide for an earlier effective date for good cause found (within the meaning of 5 U.S.C. §553(d)(3) and published with the regulation.

(e) Amendment of regulations.—Regulations may be amended in the same manner as is described in this section for the adoption, approval, and issuance of regulations, except that the Board may, in its discretion, dispense with publication of a general notice of proposed rulemaking of minor, technical, or urgent amendments that satisfy the criteria for dispensing with publication of such notice pursuant to 5 U.S.C. §553(b)(B).

(f) Right to petition for rulemaking.—Any interested party may petition to the Board for the issuance, amendment, or repeal of a regulation.

* * *

TITLE IV—ADMINISTRATIVE AND JUDICIAL DISPUTE-RESOLUTION PROCEDURES

§401. Procedure for Consideration of Alleged Violations

Except as otherwise provided, the procedure for consideration of alleged violations of part A of Title II consists of—

(1)   counseling as provided in section 402;

(2)   mediation as provided in section 403; and

(3)   election, as provided in section 404, of either—

(A) a formal complaint and hearing as provided in section 405, subject to Board review as provided in section 406, and judicial review in the United States Court of Appeals for the Federal Circuit as provided in section 407, or

(B) a civil action in a district court of the United States as provided in section 408.

In the case of an employee of the Office of the Architect of the Capitol or of the Capitol Police, the Executive Director, after receiving a request for counseling under section 402, may recommend that the employee use the grievance procedures of the Architect of the Capitol or the Capitol Police for resolution of the employee's grievance for a specific period of time, which shall not count against the time available for counseling or mediation.

§402.   Counseling

(a)   In general.—To commence a proceeding, a covered employee alleging a violation of a law made applicable under part A of title II shall request counseling by the Office. The Office shall provide the employee with all relevant information with respect to the rights of the employee. A request for counseling shall be made not later than 180 days after the date of the alleged violation.

(b)   Period of counseling.—The period for counseling shall be 30 days unless the employee and the Office agree to reduce the period. The period shall begin on the date the request for counseling is received.

(c)   Notification of end of counseling period.—The Office shall notify the employee in writing when the counseling period has ended.

§403.   Mediation

(a)   Initiation.—Not later than 15 days after receipt by the employee of notice of the end of the counseling period under section 402, but prior to and as a condition of making an election under section 404, the covered employee who alleged a violation of a law shall file a request for mediation with the Office.

(b)   Process.—Mediation under this section

(1)   may include the Office, the covered employee, the employing office, and one or more individuals appointed by the Executive Director after considering recommendations by organizations composed primarily of individuals experienced in adjudicating or arbitrating personnel matters, and

(2)   shall involve meetings with the parties separately or jointly for the purpose of resolving the dispute between the covered employee and the employing office.

(c)   Mediation period.—The mediation period shall be 30 days beginning on the date the request for mediation is received. The mediation period may be extended for additional periods at the joint request of the covered employee and the employing office. The Office shall notify in writing the covered employee and the employing office when the mediation period has ended.

(d) Independence of mediation process.—No individual, who is appointed by the Executive Director to mediate, may conduct or aid in a hearing conducted under section 405 with respect to the same matter or shall be subject to subpoena or any other compulsory process with respect to the same matter.

§404. Election of Proceeding

Not later than 90 days after a covered employee receives notice of the end of the period of mediation, but no sooner than 30 days after receipt of such notification, such covered employee may either—

(1) file a complaint with the Office in accordance with section 405, or

(2) file a civil action in accordance with section 408 in the United States district court for the district in which the employee is employed or for the District of Columbia.

§405. Complaint and Hearing

(a) In general.—A covered employee may, upon the completion of mediation under section 403, file a complaint with the Office. The respondent to the complaint shall be the employing office—

(1) involved in the violation, or

(2) in which the violation is alleged to have occurred, and about which mediation was conducted.

(b) Dismissal.—A hearing officer may dismiss any claim that the hearing officer finds to be frivolous or that fails to state a claim upon which relief may be granted.

(c) Hearing officer.—

(1) Appointment.—Upon the filing of a complaint, the Executive Director shall appoint an independent hearing officer to consider the complaint and render a decision. No Member of the House of Representatives, Senator, officer of either the House of Representatives or the Senate, head of an employing office, member of the Board, or covered employee may be appointed to be a hearing officer. The Executive Director shall select hearing officers on a rotational or random basis from the lists developed under paragraph (2). Nothing in this section shall prevent the appointment of hearing officers as full-time employees of the Office or the selection of hearing officers on the basis of specialized expertise needed for particular matters.

(2) Lists.—The Executive Director shall develop master lists, composed of—

(A) members of the bar of a State or the District of Columbia and retired judges of the United States courts who are experienced in adjudicating or arbitrating the kinds of personnel and other matters for which hearings may be held under this Act, and

(B) individuals expert in technical matters relating to accessibility and usability by persons with disabilities or technical matters relating to occupational safety and health.

In developing lists, the Executive Director shall consider candidates recommended by the Federal Mediation and Conciliation Service or the Administrative Conference of the United States.

(d) Hearing.—Unless a complaint is dismissed before a hearing, a hearing shall be—

(1) conducted in closed session on the record by the hearing officer;

(2) commenced no later than 60 days after filing of the complaint under subsection (a), except that the Office may, for good cause, extend up to an additional 30 days the time for commencing a hearing; and

(3) conducted, except as specifically provided in this Act and to the greatest extent practicable, in accordance with the principles and procedures set forth in sections 554 through 557 of Title 5, United States Code.

(e) Discovery.—Reasonable prehearing discovery may be permitted at the discretion of the hearing officer.

(f) Subpoenas.—

(1) In general.—At the request of a party, a hearing officer may issue subpoenas for the attendance of witnesses and for the production of correspondence, books, papers, documents, and other records. The attendance of witnesses and the production of records may be required from any place within the United States. Subpoenas shall be served in the manner provided under rule 45(b) of the Federal Rules of Civil Procedure.

(2) Objections.—If a person refuses, on the basis of relevance, privilege, or other objection, to testify in response to a question or to produce records in connection with a proceeding before a hearing officer, the hearing officer shall rule on the objection. At the request of the witness or any party, the hearing officer shall (or on the hearing officer's own initiative, the hearing officer may) refer the ruling to the Board for review.

(3) Enforcement.—

(A) In general.—If a person fails to comply with a subpoena, the Board may authorize the General Counsel to apply, in the name of the Office, to an appropriate United States district court for an order requiring that person to appear before the hearing officer to give testimony or produce records. The application may be made within the judicial district where the hearing is conducted or where that person is found, resides, or transacts business. Any failure to obey a lawful order of the district court issued pursuant to this section may be held by such court to be a civil contempt thereof.

(B) Service of process.—Process in an action or contempt proceeding pursuant to subparagraph (A) may be served in any judicial district in which the person refusing or failing to comply, or threatening to refuse or not to comply, resides, transacts business, or may be found, and subpoenas for witnesses who are required to attend such proceedings may run into any other district.

(g) Decision.—The hearing officer shall issue a written decision as expeditiously as possible, but in no case more than 90 days after the conclusion of the hearing. The written decision shall be transmitted by the Office to the parties. The decision shall state the issues raised in the complaint, describe the evidence in the record, contain findings of fact and conclusions of law, contain a determination of whether a violation has occurred, and order such remedies as are appropriate pursuant to title II. The decision shall be entered in the records of the Office. If a decision is not appealed under section 406 to the Board, the decision shall be considered the final decision of the Office.

(h) Precedents.—A hearing officer who conducts a hearing under this section shall be guided by judicial decisions under the laws made applicable by section 102 and by Board decisions under this Act.

§406.   Appeal to the Board

(a) In general.—Any party aggrieved by the decision of a hearing officer under section 405(g) may file a petition for review by the Board not later than 30 days after entry of the decision in the records of the Office.

(b) Parties' opportunity to submit argument.—The parties to the hearing upon which the decision of the hearing officer was made shall have a reasonable opportunity to be heard, through written submission and, in the discretion of the Board, through oral argument.

(c) Standard of review.—The Board shall set aside a decision of a hearing officer if the Board determines that the decision was—

(1) arbitrary, capricious, an abuse of discretion, or otherwise not consistent with law;

(2) not made consistent with required procedures; or

(3) unsupported by substantial evidence.

(d) Record.—In making determinations under subsection (c), the Board shall review the whole record, or those parts of it cited by a party, and due account shall be taken of the rule of prejudicial error.

(e) Decision.—The Board shall issue a written decision setting forth the reasons for its decision. The decision may affirm, reverse, or remand to the hearing officer for further proceedings. A decision that does not require further proceedings before a hearing officer shall be entered in the records of the Office as a final decision.

§407.   Judicial Review of Board Decisions and Enforcement

(a) Jurisdiction.—

(1) Judicial review.—The United States Court of Appeals for the Federal Circuit shall have jurisdiction over any proceeding commenced by a petition of—

(A) a party aggrieved by a final decision of the Board under section 406(e) in cases arising under part A of Title II,

(B) a charging individual or a respondent before the Board who files a petition under section 210(d)(4),

(C) the General Counsel or a respondent before the Board who files a petition under section 215(c)(5), or

(D) the General Counsel or a respondent before the Board who files a petition under section 220(c)(3).

The court of appeals shall have exclusive jurisdiction to set aside, suspend (in whole or in part), to determine the validity of, or otherwise review the decision of the Board.

(2) Enforcement.—The United States Court of Appeals for the Federal Circuit shall have jurisdiction over any petition of the General Counsel, filed in the name of the Office and at the direction of the Board, to enforce a final decision under section 405(g) or 406(e) with respect to a violation of part A, B, C, or D of title II.

(b) Procedures.—

(1) Respondents.—

(A) In any proceeding commenced by a petition filed under subsection (a)(1) (A) or (B), or filed by a party other than the General Counsel under subsection (a)(1) (C) or (D), the Office shall be named respondent and any party before the Board may be named respondent by filing a notice of election with the court within 30 days after service of the petition.

(B) In any proceeding commenced by a petition filed by the General Counsel under subsection (a)(1) (C) or (D), the prevailing party in the final decision entered under section 406(e) shall be named respondent, and any other party before the Board may be named respondent by filing a notice of election with the court within 30 days after service of the petition.

(C) In any proceeding commenced by a petition filed under subsection (a)(2), the party under section 405 or 406 that the General Counsel determines has failed to comply with a final decision under section 405(g) or 406(e) shall be named respondent.

(2) Intervention.—Any party that participated in the proceedings before the Board under section 406 and that was not made respondent under paragraph (1) may intervene as of right.

(c) Law applicable.—Chapter 158 of title 28, United States Code, shall apply to judicial review under paragraph (1) of subsection (a), except that—

(1) with respect to section 2344 of title 28, United States Code, service of a petition in any proceeding in which the Office is a respondent shall be on the General Counsel rather than on the Attorney General;

(2) the provisions of section 2348 of title 28, United States Code, on the authority of the Attorney General, shall not apply;

(3) the petition for review shall be filed not later than 90 days after the entry in the Office of a final decision under section 406(e); and

(4) the Office shall be an "agency" as that term is used in chapter 158 of title 28, United States Code.

(d) Standard of review.—To the extent necessary for decision in a proceeding commenced under subsection (a)(1) and when presented, the court shall decide all relevant questions of law and interpret constitutional and statutory provisions. The court shall set aside a final decision of the Board if it is determined that the decision was—

(1) arbitrary, capricious, an abuse of discretion, or otherwise not consistent with law;

(2) not made consistent with required procedures; or

(3) unsupported by substantial evidence.

(e) Record.—In making determinations under subsection (d), the court shall review the whole record, or those parts of it cited by a party, and due account shall be taken of the rule of prejudicial error.

§408. Civil Action

(a) Jurisdiction.—The district courts of the United States shall have jurisdiction over any civil action commenced under section 404 and this section by a covered employee who has completed counseling under section 402 and mediation under section 403. A civil action may be commenced by a covered employee only to seek redress for a violation for which the employee has completed counseling and mediation.

(b) Parties.—The defendant shall be the employing office alleged to have committed the violation, or in which the violation is alleged to have occurred.

(c) Jury trial.—Any party may demand a jury trial where a jury trial would be available in an action against a private defendant under the relevant law made applicable by this Act. In any case in which a violation of section 201 is alleged, the court shall not inform the jury of the maximum amount of compensatory damages available under section 201(b)(1) or 201(b)(3).

§409. Judicial Review of Regulations

In any proceeding brought under section 407 or 408 in which the application of a regulation issued under this Act is at issue, the court may review the validity of the regulation in accordance with the provisions of subparagraphs (A) through (D) of 5 U.S.C. §706(2), except that with respect to regulations approved by a joint resolution under section 304(c), only the provisions of section 5 U.S.C. §706(2)(B) shall apply. If the court determines that the regulation is invalid, the court shall apply, to the extent necessary and appropriate, the most relevant substantive executive agency regulation promulgated to implement the statutory provisions with respect to which the invalid regulation was issued. Except as provided in this section, the validity of regulations issued under this Act is not subject to judicial review.

§410. Other Judicial Review Prohibited

Except as expressly authorized by sections 407, 408, and 409, the compliance or noncompliance with the provisions of this Act and any action taken pursuant to this Act shall not be subject to judicial review.

§411. Effect of Failure to Issue Regulations

In any proceeding under section 405, 406, 407, or 408, except a proceeding to enforce section 220 with respect to offices listed under section 220(e)(2), if the Board has not issued a regulation on a matter for which this Act requires a regulation to be issued, the hearing officer, Board, or court, as the case may be, shall apply, to the extent necessary and appropriate, the most relevant substantive executive agency regulation promulgated to implement the statutory provision at issue in the proceeding.

§412. Expedited Review of Certain Appeals

(a) In general.—An appeal may be taken directly to the Supreme Court of the United States from any interlocutory or final judgment, decree, or order of a court upon the constitutionality of any provision of this Act.

(b) Jurisdiction.—The Supreme Court shall, if it has not previously ruled on the question, accept jurisdiction over the appeal referred to in subsection (a), advance the appeal on the docket, and expedite the appeal to the greatest extent possible.

§413. Privileges and Immunities

The authorization to bring judicial proceedings under sections 405(f)(3), 407, and 408 shall not constitute a waiver of sovereign immunity for any other purpose, or of the privileges of any Senator or Member of the House of Representatives under article I, section 6, clause 1, of the Constitution, or a waiver of any power of either the Senate or the House of Representatives under the Constitution, including under article I, section 5, clause 3, or under the rules of either House relating to records and information within its jurisdiction.

§414. Settlement of Complaints

Any settlement entered into by the parties to a process described in section 210, 215, 220, or 401 shall be in writing and not become effective unless it is approved by the Executive Director. Nothing in this Act shall affect the power of the Senate and the House of Representatives, respectively, to establish rules governing the process by which a settlement may be entered into by such House or by any employing office of such House.

§415. Payments

(a) Awards and settlements.—Except as provided in subsection (c), only funds which are appropriated to an account of the Office in the Treasury of the United States for the payment of awards and settlements may be used for the payment of awards and settlements under this Act. There are authorized to be appropriated for such account such sums as may be necessary to pay such awards and settlements. Funds in the account are not available for awards and settlements involving the General Accounting Office, the Government Printing Office, or the Library of Congress.

(b) Compliance.—Except as provided in subsection (c), there are authorized to be appropriated such sums as may be necessary for administrative, personnel, and similar expenses of employing offices which are needed to comply with this Act.

(c) OSHA, accommodation, and access requirements.—Funds to correct violations of section 201(a)(3) * * * of this Act may be paid only from funds appropriated to the employing office or entity responsible for correcting such violations. There are authorized to be appropriated such sums as may be necessary for such funds.

§416. Confidentiality

(a) Counseling.—All counseling shall be strictly confidential, except that the Office and a covered employee may agree to notify the employing office of the allegations.

(b) Mediation.—All mediation shall be strictly confidential.

(c) Hearings and deliberations.—Except as provided in subsections (d), (e), and (f), all proceedings and deliberations of hearing officers and the Board, including any related records, shall be confidential. This subsection shall not apply to proceedings under section 215, but shall apply to the deliberations of hearing officers and the Board under that section.

(d) Release of records for judicial action.—The records of hearing officers and the Board may be made public if required for the purpose of judicial review under section 407.

(e) Access by Committees of Congress.—At the discretion of the Executive Director, the Executive Director may provide to the Committee on Standards of Official Conduct of the House of Representatives and the Select Committee on Ethics of the Senate access to the records of the hearings and decisions of the hearing officers and the Board, including all written and oral testimony in the possession of the Office. The Executive Director shall not provide such access until the Executive Director has consulted with the individual filing the complaint at issue, and until a final decision has been entered under section 405(g) or 406(e).

(f) Final decisions.—A final decision entered under section 405(g) or 406(e) shall be made public if it is in favor of the complaining covered employee, or in favor of the charging party under section 210, or if the decision reverses a decision of a hearing officer which had been in favor of the covered employee or charging party. The Board may make public any other decision at its discretion.

Title V—Miscellaneous Provisions

* * *

§502. Political Affiliation and Place of Residence

(a) In general.—It shall not be a violation of any provision of section 201 to consider the—

(1) party affiliation;

(2) domicile; or

(3) political compatibility with the employing office; of an employee referred to in subsection (b) with respect to employment decisions.

(b) Definition.—For purposes of subsection (a), the term "employee" means—

(1) an employee on the staff of the leadership of the House of Representatives or the leadership of the Senate;

(2) an employee on the staff of a committee or subcommittee of—

(A) the House of Representatives;

(B) the Senate; or

(C) a joint committee of the Congress;

(3) an employee on the staff of a Member of the House of Representatives or on the staff of a Senator;

(4) an officer of the House of Representatives or the Senate or a congressional employee who is elected by the House of Representatives or Senate or is appointed by a Member of the House of Representatives or by a Senator (in addition an employee described in paragraph (1), (2), or (3)); or

(5) an applicant for a position that is to be occupied by an individual described in any of paragraphs (1) through (4).

§503. Nondiscrimination Rules of the House and Senate

The Select Committee on Ethics of the Senate and the Committee on Standards of Official Conduct of the House of Representatives retain full power, in accordance with the authority provided to them by the Senate and the House, with respect to the discipline of Members, officers, and employees for violating rules of the Senate and the House on nondiscrimination in employment.

§504. Technical and Conforming Amendments.

(a) Civil rights remedies.—

(1) Sections 301 and 302 of the Government Employee Rights Act of 1991 (2 U.S.C. 1201 and 1202) are amended to read as follows:

"§301. Government Employee Rights Act of 1991.

"(a) Short title.—This title may be cited as the 'Government Employee Rights Act of 1991'.

"(b) Purpose.—The purpose of this title is to provide procedures to protect the rights of certain government employees, with respect to their public employment, to be free of discrimination on the basis of race, color, religion, sex, national origin, age, or disability.

"(c) Definition.—For purposes of this title, the term 'violation' means a practice that violates section 302(a) of this title.

§302. Discriminatory practices prohibited.

"(a) Practices.—All personnel actions affecting the Presidential appointees described in section 303 or the State employees described in section 304 shall be made free from any discrimination based on—

"(1) race, color, religion, sex, or national origin, within the meaning of section 717 of the Civil Rights Act of 1964;

"(2) age, within the meaning of section 15 of the Age Discrimination in Employment Act of 1967; or

"(3) disability, within the meaning of section 501 of the Rehabilitation Act of 1973 and sections 102 through 104 of the Americans with Disabilities Act of 1990.

"(b) Remedies.—The remedies referred to in sections 303(a)(1) and 304(a)—

"(1) may include, in the case of a determination that a violation of subsection (a)(1) or (a)(3) has occurred, such remedies as would be appropriate if awarded under sections 706(g), 706(k), and 717(d) of the Civil Rights Act of 1964, and such compensatory damages as would be appropriate if awarded under section 1977 or sections 1977A(a) and 1977A(b)(2) of the Revised Statutes (42 U.S.C. 1981 and 1981a (a) and (b)(2));

"(2) may include, in the case of a determination that a violation of subsection (a)(2) has occurred, such remedies as would be appropriate if awarded under section 15(c) of the Age Discrimination in Employment Act of 1967; and

"(3) may not include punitive damages.."

(2) Sections 303 through 319, and sections 322, 324, and 325 of the Government Employee Rights Act of 1991 are repealed, except as provided in section 506 of this Act.

(3) Sections 320 and 321 of the Government Employee Rights Act of 1991 are redesignated as sections 303 and 304, respectively.

(4) Sections 303 and 304 of the Government Employee Rights Act of 1991, as so redesignated, are each amended by striking "and 307(h) of this title."

(5) Section 1205 of the Supplemental Appropriations Act of 1993 (2 U.S.C. 1207a) is repealed, except as provided in section 506 of this Act.

(b) Family And Medical Leave Act of 1993.—Title V of the Family and Medical Leave Act of 1993 is repealed, except as provided in section 506 of this Act.

* * *

§506.   Savings Provisions

(a) Transition provisions for employees of the house of representatives and of the senate.—

(1) Claims arising before effective date.—If, as of the date on which section 201 takes effect, an employee of the Senate or the House of Representatives has or could have requested counseling under section 305 of the Government Employees Rights Act of 1991 or Rule LI of the House of Representatives, including counseling for alleged violations of family and medical leave rights under title V of the Family and Medical Leave Act of 1993, the employee may complete, or initiate and complete, all procedures under the Government Employees Rights Act of 1991 and Rule LI, and the provisions of that Act and Rule shall remain in effect with respect to, and provide the exclusive procedures for, those claims until the completion of all such procedures.

(2) Claims arising between effective date and opening of office.—If a claim by an employee of the Senate or House of Representatives arises under

section 201 or 202 after the effective date of such sections, but before the opening of the Office for receipt of requests for counseling or mediation under sections 402 and 403, the provisions of the Government Employees Rights Act of 1991 and Rule LI of the House of Representatives relating to counseling and mediation shall remain in effect, and the employee may complete under that Act or Rule the requirements for counseling and mediation under sections 402 and 403. If, after counseling and mediation is completed, the Office has not yet opened for the filing of a timely complaint under section 405, the employee may elect—

(A) to file a complaint under section 307 of the Government Employees Rights Act of 1991 or Rule LI of the House of Representatives, and thereafter proceed exclusively under that Act or Rule, the provisions of which shall remain in effect until the completion of all proceedings in relation to the complaint, or

(B) to commence a civil action under section 408.

(3) §1205 of the supplemental appropriations act of 1993.—With respect to payments of awards and settlements relating to Senate employees under paragraph (1) of this subsection, section 1205 of the Supplemental Appropriations Act of 1993 remains in effect.

* * *

§509. Severability

If any provision of this Act or the application of such provision to any person or circumstance is held to be invalid, the remainder of this Act and the application of the provisions of the remainder to any person or circumstance shall not be affected thereby.

INDEX

References are to Pages